SURVEY OF ENGLISH DIALECTS:
THE DICTIONARY AND GRAMMAR

TITLES OF RELATED INTEREST

The Linguistic Atlas of England
Edited by Harold Orton, Stewart Sanderson and John Widdowson
ISBN 0856642940

A Structural Atlas of the English Dialects
Peter Anderson
ISBN 0709951167

Studies in Linguistic Geography
John M. Kirk, Stewart Sanderson and John Widdowson
ISBN 0709915020

SURVEY OF ENGLISH DIALECTS: THE DICTIONARY AND GRAMMAR

Clive Upton, David Parry, J.D.A. Widdowson

London and New York

First published 1994
by Routledge
11 New Fetter Lane, London EC4P 4EE

Simultaneously published in the USA and Canada
by Routledge
a division of Routledge, Chapman and Hall, Inc.
29 West 35th Street, New York, NY10001

© 1994 Routledge

Typeset in 9/10$\frac{1}{2}$ pt Times by Quorum Technical Services Ltd, Cheltenham
Printed in Great Britain by T J Press (Padstow) Ltd, Cornwall
Printed on acid-free paper.

British Library Cataloguing-in-Publication Data
A catalogue record for this book is available from the British Library

Library of Congress Cataloguing-in-Publication Data
A catalog record for this book is available on request.

ISBN 0-415-02029-8

PREFACE

This volume marks a further stage in the publication of the data collected in the Survey of English Dialects (SED). The Survey generated a database of more than 404,000 items of information during fieldwork in 313 localities between 1950 and 1961. The *Introduction* and *Basic Material* of the Survey were published between 1962 and 1971 (by E.J. Arnold), and these were followed by two atlases, *The Linguistic Atlas of England* (Croom Helm, 1978) and *Word Maps* (Croom Helm, 1987).

In our new analysis of the Basic Material for this work we have addressed the variations in approach and interpretation which are an inevitable feature of the original twelve books of data, seeking to create both a synthesis and an interpretation of those books whilst allowing them, as detailed records, to speak for themselves on many matters. Presentation here in dictionary format allows easy access to the data, and reveals the extraordinary richness of the regional dialects of England at a crucial stage in their history. In the absence of a general dictionary of English dialects since Joseph Wright's *English Dialect Dictionary* (1898–1905), this book brings together for the first time an alphabetical listing of the wealth of regional vocabulary in use during the decades following the Second World War, a vocabulary which has suffered substantial erosion in recent years.

In presenting a Grammar of the dialects as a companion to the Dictionary we are following the example of Joseph Wright, who provided *The English Dialect Grammar* as an essential companion to his *Dictionary*. Much of the grammatical material of the SED does not allow of presentation in dictionary format, and yet we consider it to be essential to a proper understanding of the functioning of the lexis.

This Dictionary and Grammar therefore provide a new and accessible overview of the variety, pronunciation, distribution and functioning of regional lexis throughout the country before the advent of social and technological developments which continue to create major changes in all aspects of English usage, and especially in the dialects.

Our work is ultimately the product of discussions which took place at the former Institute of Dialect and Folk Life Studies at the University of Leeds some ten years ago. The Director of the Institute, Mr Stewart Sanderson, who for many years spearheaded work based on data from the Survey of English Dialects, invited a number of colleagues to discuss the feasibility of such a project. We acknowledge with gratitude the advice and assistance of Dr Gunnel Melchers and the late Dr Bertil Hedevind at the initial planning stage, and also the interest and support of Professor Aarne Zettersten. Essential preliminary work on the data was carried out by our colleague Dr Robert Penhallurick of University College Swansea, who identified numerous problems in the analysis of the material and suggested solutions to many of them.

Stewart Sanderson initiated negotiations with Croom Helm, publishers of the two atlases based on the SED data. The project received their wholehearted support, and especially that of Christopher Helm. Croom Helm undertook to fund analysis and inputting of data over a six-year period from 1986, and provided the hardware and software for the project, a commitment which was maintained when Croom Helm became part of Routledge in 1988. Particularly at the outset of the project we were also most fortunate to receive expert guidance from Dr David Jackson of Vuman Computer Systems, designers of our phonetics-handling system.

The Institute of Dialect and Folk Life Studies closed and Stewart Sanderson retired in 1982, while plans for the present work were still being laid. The project then moved to the Centre for English Cultural Tradition and Language at the University of Sheffield. In paying tribute to the seminal role of Stewart Sanderson in the conception of the present work, we also acknowledge the action of the successive Heads of the School of English at the University of Leeds, and especially that of Professor T.A. Shippey, in allowing us continued access to the

School's archives.

Our greatest debt of gratitude is to all those directly involved in the SED: to almost a thousand individuals who answered the questionnaire, to the fieldworkers and editors who collected and ordered the responses, and above all to the Survey's architects, Professors Eugen Dieth and Harold Orton. They planned the Survey jointly with vision and foresight and in a spirit of friendship and co-operation, and after Eugen Dieth's untimely death Harold Orton carried the work through to its conclusion with remarkable singlemindedness and tenacity. The Survey stands as a lasting monument to their scholarly achievements.

Clive Upton
David Parry
J.D.A. Widdowson

The Centre for English Cultural Tradition and Language
University of Sheffield

June 1992

ABBREVIATIONS AND SYMBOLS

Abbreviations and symbols used in the Dictionary and Grammar:

adj	adjective	L	Lincolnshire
aux	auxiliary	La	Lancashire
		Lei	Leicestershire
Bd	Bedfordshire		
Bk	Buckinghamshire	Man	(Isle of) Man
BM	(SED) Basic Material	mod	modal
Brk	Berkshire	Mon	Monmouthshire
		MxL	Middlesex and London
C	Cambridgeshire		
Ch	Cheshire	n	noun
Co	Cornwall	N	Northern
comp	comparative	Nb	Northumberland
conj	conjunction	Nf	Norfolk
cp	compare	n.r.	not recorded
Cu	Cumberland	Nt	Nottinghamshire
		Nth	Northamptonshire
D	Devon		
Db	Derbyshire	O	Oxfordshire
demonstr	demonstrative	obj	object
det	determiner		
Do	Dorset	p	response pressed for by SED
Du	Durham		fieldworker
		pass	passive
-ed	verbal 'ed'-form	perf	perfect
Edd	(SED Basic Material) editors	phr	phrasal, phrase
EM	East Midland	pl	plural
Eng	England	poss	possessive
Ess	Essex	ppl	participle
exc.	except	pr	present (tense)
		pred	predicative
fw(s)	fieldwork, fieldworker(s)	predet	predeterminer
		prep	preposition
Gl	Gloucestershire	prog	progressive
		pron	pronoun
Ha	Hampshire	pt	past (tense)
He	Herefordshire		
Hrt	Hertfordshire	q	question
Hu	Huntingdonshire		
		R	Rutland
i(i).	informant(s)	refl	reflexive
IM	(SED) Incidental Material	rel	relative
imp	imperative	Rev.	reverse (definition-seeking)
inf	infinitive		question in SED questionnaire
-ing	verbal 'ing'-form	r(r).	response(s)
i.r(r).	irrelevant response(s)		
		S	Southern
K	Kent		

vii

Sa	Shropshire	vt	transitive verb
SED	Survey of English Dialects	W	Wiltshire
Sf	Suffolk	Wa	Warwickshire
sg	singular	wc	wordclass
So	Somerset	We	Westmorland
Sr	Surrey	WM	West Midland
St	Staffordshire	Wo	Worcestershire
sup	superlative		
s.w.	word suggested to informant by SED fieldworker	Y	Yorkshire
Sx	Sussex	⇒	see
		⇐	from
u.r(r).	unwanted response(s)	*	dictionary headword or sense not a headword in SED BM
v	verb		
vbln	verbal noun	~	varying with
vi	intransitive verb		

THE DICTIONARY

INTRODUCTION

Basic Design: Core and Ordinary Entries

The raw material for this dictionary is unlike that from which conventional dictionaries are derived. It is usual for dictionaries to be built around a fixed headword list of predetermined length, and for each headword to have a unique definition. At the start of compilation, however, the essentially fixed element of this dictionary was the set of semantic notions to be covered, whilst the list of lexical items with which those notions is realized was a somewhat uncertain quantity.

The circumscribed set of notions treated here is that covered by the SED Questionnaire. Additional lexical items appear which are not direct responses to questions asked during the SED fieldwork. These are 'Incidental Material' responses which are printed in the volumes of SED findings (Basic Material) from which the dictionary is compiled. The SED Questionnaire covers some 1,300 notions, the precise number varying slightly depending on the version of the questionnaire in use at various periods of the fieldwork programme. It was therefore not feasible to adopt a conventional lexicographic approach to the data, since a conventional dictionary would contain only a small set of definitions, which would have to be repeated many times whenever a notion was realized by a wide variety of lexical items countrywide.

To this most basic difficulty of attempting a standard lexicographic approach others can be added. The SED notions are essentially everyday ones. Although some, especially those concerned with bygone farming practices, are of a technical or subtechnical nature and are therefore beyond the knowledge of the average native speaker, the majority treat of activities, attributes, and artifacts with which English speakers of all ages and backgrounds are generally very familiar. Closely to define **kitten** or **happy** or **to cut** in a dictionary whose focus is the variety, distribution, and pronunciation of the dialect words with which such concepts are realized would be unnecessary, if not otiose; frequently to repeat such definitions, in the not unusual case of such a notion as **weakling** ('the smallest and weakest pig of the litter') upwards of seventy times, would be out of the question.

The fact that many dialectal forms exist to render one semantic notion necessitates the introduction of a thesaurus element into the dictionary, if these forms are all to be linked to each other as well as, by definition, to the notion. However, such linking needs to be economical: to cross-refer each of seventy items to some seventy others, and to undertake a similar exercise for many notions, would be to overburden the text with repetitive lists to no good effect.

It is for these reasons that the concept of the CORE ENTRY has been devised, to carry the burdens of notion definition and cross-referencing. The dictionary is constructed around a set of such entries, typically one for each notion yielding dictionary material. The user has only to master the operation of core entries and of the linking of the ordinary entries to them in order to be able to make full use of the data that the dictionary contains.

Except for the fact that core entries uniquely hold all cross-referencing information, the two kinds of entry, core and ordinary, are in essence the same, performing the functions of displaying wordclass, meaning, pronunciation and distribution for their headword items. As will be seen below, however, they perform some of these functions in slightly different ways.

Headwords and Numbering

All dictionary entries begin with alphabetically-ordered headwords in bold type. Headwords may relate to one or more meanings. Alphabetical ordering has been very strictly adhered to in order to present an unconventional lexis in as logical a way as possible. Thus, for example, the adverbial or prepositional element of a phrasal verb is counted as significant for its ordering [e.g. **beal out** follows **bealing**], and those headwords which carry a final **(s)**, indicating that under them are treated responses both with and without **-s**, have this **s** taken as significant when their placing is determined [e.g. **fallow(s)** is placed after such forms as **fallow-ground**].

The headword-form for an ordinary entry is normally the orthographic representation of the item used in the Basic Material. Occasionally a decision has been taken to use a spelling different from that used in SED, especially where it is felt that the SED headword is misleading [e.g. **boar-thistle**]: in such unusual cases the original SED headword is included in the cross-referencing list at the core entry with an indication as to the dictionary headword under which it is treated. (See below for the way in which this cross-referral is effected.)

Some extended response-forms are represented only in part in the headword run, the full forms appearing later in an entry [e.g. **breathing hard** and **breathing heavy** are located at headword **breathing** instead of being given separate headwords]. Such full forms are usually listed immediately after the wordclass notation and are then repeated individually to introduce relevant phonetic transcriptions. Exceptions to this procedure typically occur when the headword-form that introduces extended forms is itself a response, upon which occasions the extended forms may follow transcriptions of the headword-form without receiving prior listing [e.g. **ague**].

The core entry headword is typically that 'notion word' which is given in the SED Questionnaire as a guide to the fieldworker as to the concept for which an expression is being sought from the informant, and which is used also as a title to the response-form listings in the SED Basic Material itself. In the large majority of cases the notion word is well known and from Standard English. However, in a few instances the Questionnaire/Basic Material notion word may now be judged to be dated or regional, and substitutable by a more familiar standard word [e.g. original SED notion word **whelps** is replaced by core entry headword **pups**].

Some headwords or headword subdivision numbers carry an asterisk, indicating that they are not listed in the Basic Material for the meaning under consideration. This may be for one of four reasons. First, as explained above, a decision may have been taken to use a more familiar standard word than that used in the original work as a notion word. Second, an original SED orthographic representation may have been changed for the dictionary, the original being deemed to be erroneous or otherwise unsatisfactory [e.g. West Midland EARTH-CLOSET form **mixen** in the Basic Material yields both **mixen** and a further headword, **mizzen***, for the dictionary]. Third, in a few cases a form found in the phonetic listings was erroneously given no headword at all in the Basic Material, whilst it of course merits one here. Fourth, some headwords relate to items found only in the Incidental Material which, for various reasons, were included in the Basic Material: such items were regarded by the editors of the Basic Material as supplementary to the main responses and are therefore not shown in the headword lists in the Basic Material.

The essential principle for ordering the various meanings under a two- or multi-meaning headword has been to follow the SED reference-number order [e.g. **abide**]. However, this basic principle has been departed from in particular circumstances. When certain meanings have been seen to be closely linked semantically, it has often been judged prudent to present them together regardless of their SED reference numbers [e.g. **band**]. Also, sense-divisions that constitute core entries are usually placed before those that are ordinary entries [e.g. **about**]. An exception to this is made when a headword contains more than one core entry and it has been deemed sensible to follow an early core entry with ordinary entries of related meaning before proceeding to the next (unrelated) core entry [e.g. **dry**].

Whenever a headword has more than one meaning, italic numbers immediately preceding the wordclass notation are used to indicate the divisions of the entry. Similarly, when an ordinary-entry headword holds transitive and intransitive or indeterminate forms of the same verb, numbering is used to separate them: when the related verbal meanings are the only ones pertaining to that headword, these are simply marked *1* and *2* [e.g. **balk**]; when the headword has other senses besides the transitive/intransitive(/or indeterminate) split, the verb is given the same sense-number with further numbers to indicate status [e.g. **bait** *1.1, 1.2*; **bag** *5.1, 5.2*]. (Because of the special defining procedure adopted for core entries, using the SED question as explained below, it has been decided that the usual numbering of a transitive/intransitive/indeterminate split should not be used in such entries. When such a split does occur in a core entry, the wordclass notations only are used, since the question-style 'definition' applies equally to both parts of the entry [e.g. **clear**].)

Very occasionally subdivision of an entry occurs according to the material an artifact is made of, or its use, when the artifact remains essentially the same [e.g. **besom**]: in such cases letters (*a*, *b*, etc.) are used, indicating semantic separation at a level lower than that implied by *1, 2*, etc.

Wordclasses

Each headword is followed by a wordclass label: for the abbreviations used see pp. vii–viii. The label relates to the wordclass of the headword. Notation is at the same time both necessarily broad and cautious, having to be able to cover very diverse material and to describe forms often recorded as responses to questions whose focus was not grammatical. Consequently, for example, some noun headwords are (unusually for a dictionary) plural forms, since the question asked by fieldworkers deliberately elicited plural responses and, for nonstandard dialects, singular forms cannot be inferred from given plurals. Such headwords are therefore designated *npl*. However, if a noun is recorded as carrying a final **-s** and no evidence is available to suggest that it is a plural form, notation is simply *n*. Similarly, for verbs, although the questions prompting forms ending in **-ing** generally envisage quite clearly a response that is sometimes a verbal noun [e.g. VIII.6.6 'If, as a boy, you wrote badly, you could say: I used to be bad at ... **writing**'] and sometimes a present participle [e.g. IX.5.3 'You see a child very busy with something out there; so you ask: What's that child ... **doing** there?'], there are many cases in which the response recorded cannot with certainty be categorized as the one or the other. It has therefore seemed advisable to include all such forms under the designation *v-ing*. Where, in this latter case, fieldworkers state categorically that the forms are participial or nominal, the labels *prppl* and *vbln* are of course used.

Definitions

Definitions for ordinary entries are immediately recognizable as such even though, as explained above, they are designed to avoid repetition of the obvious. The simplest form of definition gives only the notion word of which the lexical item is a dialect synonym, and the Questionnaire/Basic Material reference number for that notion. The notion-word is given in upper-case lettering, and indicates the core entry headword under which the relevant question in the Questionnaire and related dialect forms can be found. Thus **face-ache** is defined as 'TOOTHACHE IV.5.8': this indicates that it is synonymous with standard **toothache**, that it was recorded as a response to question 8 of Section 5 of Book IV of the SED Questionnaire, and that the question used to elicit the form, and other related dialect words, can be seen by referring to the headword **toothache**. The question reference number is to be considered as an integral part of any definition, since the question represents the precise context in which each lexical item was recorded and therefore within which the item is known to operate. If an entry under a headword with two or more divisions has no question reference number, it can be assumed that its number is the same as that of the last entry preceding it for which a reference number is given.

When, as in **brimming over**, part of the upper-case definition is italicized [e.g. '*IN* FLOOD'], the interpretation should be that the full wording (IN FLOOD) provides the definition but that the core entry is to be located in the dictionary at the non-italicized element (FLOOD). Also, a few upper-case defining-words have lower-case letters added: here the complete word provides the definition, with the upper-case element providing the core-entry reference [e.g. **elves** defined as 'BOGEYs VIII.8.1'].

At times words other than the notion-word(s) are introduced into ordinary-entry definitions. These words either amplify the upper-case defining words or provide a context in which those words were set in the Survey. Thus an indefinite article may simply be provided [e.g. **rub** defined as 'a GRINDSTONE IV.2.7'], a longer definition supplied [e.g. **dog-jumps** defined as 'HIPS of the wild rose

IV.11.7'], or the context of an utterance added to the headword [e.g. 'we CRUNCH apples or biscuits VI.5.12'; 'PUTTING your tongue OUT VI.5.4']. Where it is thought that ambiguity might arise as to the precise referent owing to this practice, parentheses are used to indicate contextual wording [e.g. **dibble** defined as 'a DRINK (of milk) given to a kitten', since the full response-form was **dibble of milk** and DRINK therefore strictly defines only **dibble**].

In core entries it is the question asked by fieldworkers to elicit the responses which forms the 'definition'. By showing the way in which responses were obtained, it is the intention at this point to provide the user with the means fully to interpret them. The question, together with any instructions given to the fieldworker for its delivery, is printed in italics, italicization of the definition being the first graphical indication to the dictionary user that an entry is a core entry. As with ordinary entries, the core entry contains an essential question reference number. In cases where different versions of the Questionnaire were used at various stages of SED fieldwork, it is the final version which furnishes the main core-entry definition; earlier versions of the question are given parenthetically for information.

Pronunciations and Distributions

Information concerning the pronunciations given to the headword item normally follows definitions, each pronunciation being accompanied by abbreviated names of counties in which it was recorded: for these abbreviations, see pp. vii–viii. The pre-1974 counties are used to indicate distributions, these being used in other records of SED.

The narrow transcriptions to be found in the SED Basic Material have been broadened for this dictionary, permitting the combining of forms which, if held separately, would overwhelm the text by their length and complexity. Also, distributions are by county only. Full pronunciation and locality details are available in the Basic Material for those who require them.

Presentation of the phonological material is generally determined by the initial point of vowel articulation in the stressed or first primary-stressed syllable of the headword form: progression is made from the high front position in an anticlockwise direction around the vowel quadrilateral, ending with the central vowels. This system is operated to impose some regularity in the ordering of diverse material, but it is at times varied to permit other ordering, for example when it has been considered sensible to juxtapose forms which would be separated if the rule were to be applied rigidly.

County abbreviations are sometimes accompanied by italicized, square-bracketed notes.

These present, or at times interpret, comments given by informants on the responses they made during interviews. Where several informants in the same county gave the same response but not all made the same comment regarding it, this is indicated by the use of the multiplication sign and the number of informants commenting [e.g. *[old x1]* indicates that one of the two or more informants responding with the form in question regarded their response as being an old form].

An exception to the normal presentation of phonological realizations and geographical distributions occurs when an item has all-county or extremely widespread English coverage. In such cases details of phonology are omitted and the indication of distribution is replaced by the abbreviation 'Eng' (i.e. 'England') for total coverage, or 'Eng exc.' (i.e. 'England except') followed by abbreviated forms of counties not exhibiting the form, to indicate almost total coverage. Thus we, like Wright in *The English Dialect Dictionary*, acknowledge that an item may be nonstandard dialectal but that it is in 'general dialectal use'; we accord it a place in the headword list whilst avoiding what would be a very lengthy entry if it were to be given full conventional treatment. In any such case the user who requires the full fieldwork information should refer to the SED Basic Material.

Cross-referencing

Ordinary dictionary entries usually end with the presentation of phonology and distributions. From this point core entries proceed to the linking of all those recorded items that are related to the notion of which the core entry headword is the notion word.

Cross-referencing is introduced by the right-pointing arrow (⇒), and takes the form of an alphabetically-ordered list of bold-faced items that are separated by commas. Each item represents a response-type recorded for the notion: those in ordinary script are dictionary headwords; items in italic script are responses or parts of responses which have not been used as headwords; sometimes an italicized item is followed by an arrow ($\Rightarrow$) and an unitalicized item, indicating the headword at which the italicized form is treated.

This part of a core entry, therefore, presents an inventory of the responses generated by the SED question under consideration. It also indicates the dictionary status of the responses as follows: responses providing dictionary headwords (ordinary font); responses containing some items which are headwords (mixed ordinary and italicized fonts, ordinary font indicating the dictionary headword); responses consisting of items treated under other headwords (italicized form with arrow to ordinary-font headword); or items omitted from the dictionary (italicized only).

When a core entry has more than one related meaning and therefore contains two or more numbered parts, the cross-referencing list is placed at the point at which it is judged to be most appropriate. This is usually at the end of any entries specifically generated by the core-entry question [e.g. **fallow-land**].

The main cross-referencing list is sometimes followed by a secondary list, introduced by '$\Rightarrow$ also' and separated from the main list by a semicolon. This group contains those forms in the dictionary that are not precise or close synonyms of those in the main list, but that were nevertheless recorded as incidental responses at the question concerned.

Additional Notes

Occasionally, entries conclude with italicized notes held within square brackets. These notes contain any information, such as an indication of editorial policy in the Basic Material, that does not fit into the standard form for ordinary or core entries but is judged to be of potential value to the dictionary user.

A

abate *vi* to WANE, referring to the moon VII.6.5(b). *vbln* beːtɪn Co, *prppl* beːtən Co, *-ing* beːtən Co, *vbln* beːdən Co

abear *vt-2prsg* you BEAR pain VI.5.9. əbɛːɹ (+V) Mon, əbɛəɹ (+V) Mon, əbɛəᵗɹ (+V) Mon

a-beasty *adj* ON HEAT, describing a cow III.1.6. əbiːstɪ Wo, əbɪəᵗʂtɪ Sa

abide *1. vt-2prsg* you BEAR pain VI.5.9. əbaːd La, əbaɪd Db, əbɑːd La Y, əbɑɪd La Y Db, əbɒɪd St
2. v to AGREE with somebody VIII.8.12. əbɒɪd W

abide with *vtphr-2prsg* you BEAR pain VI.5.9. əbaɪd wɪð Db, əbaːd wɪð Y, əbɑɪd wɪð Ch

abort *1. vi* to slip a calf, ⇐ SLIPS *THE CALF* III.1.11. *3ptsg* əbɔːtɪd St
2. vi to SLIP *A FOAL* III.4.6. *ptppl* əbɔʊtɪd St

about *1. adv* And what time, roughly, does he [i.e. the postman] come? ... ten. VII.2.8. Eng. ⇒ **near about**
2. adv ALMOST VII.7.9. əbaːt Db
*3. *adv* WITHOUT V.8.10(a). əbaʊt Y

abrim *n* on abrim ON HEAT, describing a sow III.8.9. ɒn əbɹɪm Gl

abrimming *n* on abrimming ON HEAT, describing a sow III.8.9. ɒn əbɹɪmɪn Wo, ɔn əbɹɪmɪn Wo

abroad *adj* half abroad AJAR IX.2.7. aːf əbɹɔːd Co

abusing *v-ing* SWEARING VIII.8.9(b). bjuːzɪn So

ache *vi* [Supposing you have a bandage taken off a wound and it is not done gently, you would probably cry: Stop, it ...!] But what would you say your belly does? VI.13.3(b). Eng. ⇒ **belly-ache**, **gnaw**, **gripe**, **guts-ache**, **hurt**, **pain**, **warch**, **wark**, **yuck**

acorn *n* What do you call the seed of this tree [the oak]? IV.10.3. Eng. ⇒ **atchorn**, **bob**, **mass**, **oak-cratching**, **oak-fillip**, **pig's-nut**, *pigs'-nut* ⇒ **pig's-nut**, **yakker**

across *1. adj* ASKEW, describing a picture that is not hanging straight IX.1.3. əkɹɔːs W
2. adv DIAGONALLY, referring to harrowing a field IX.1.8. əkɹɑːs Wo, əkɹɒs Du La Y Brk, əkɹɔːs La Sa He, əkrɔːs Ha, əkɹɒᵗːʂ Sa; **across the corner** əkɹɒs t kɔːnə Db

across-eyed *adj* CROSS-EYED VI.3.6. əkɹɔːsəɪd Sx

active *adj* A strong and healthy child who is never content to be still, but must always be doing something, you say is very .... VIII.9.1. Eng exc. Du We Man Brk. ⇒ *always* **a-going**, *always on the* **fidgets**, *always on the* **go**, *always on the* **move**, *always on the* **rouk**, *always on the* **wriggle**, *always*

riving about, *a* **raddle-head**, *a* **rake**, *a riving little lubber*, *a* **rummager**, *a* **tear-down**, **boisterous**, **bothersome**, **brave**, *breviting about*, **busy**, **energetic**, **fidgety**, **fresh**, **frim**, **frisky**, *full of* **beans**, *full of* energy, *full of* **ganning-on**, *full of* go, *full of* life, *full of* vim, **hardy**, **healthy**, *here there and everywhere*, **highly strung**, **industrious**, **irritable**, **lish**, **lissom**, **litty**, **lively**, **mischiefful**, **mischievous**, **nervous**, *never at rest* ⇒ **restless**, *never easy* ⇒ **uneasy**, **nimble**, *on the* **fidget**, *on the* **go**, *on the* **move**, *on the* **wander**, **pert**, **quick**, **raddle-head**, **restless**, **riving about**, **sharp**, **sprack**, **sprightly**, **spry**, **uneasy**, **upstrigolous**, **waken**, **wick**, **wiggy-arsed**, **wiry**

adder *n* What do you call the small poisonous snake we sometimes find in the country? IV.9.4. Eng exc. C. ⇒ **asp**, **grass-snake**, **grass-worm**, **hag-worm**, **nadder**, **snake**, **viper**

addle *adj* BAD, describing an egg V.7.11. ædl He, ædɫ So, adl St

addled *1. adj* BAD, describing an egg V.7.11. ɛdɫd K[old], ɛdʊɫd Sx, ædɫd So K Ha, ædʊɫd Brk, adəld Y St, adld Ch, adɫd Wo So
2. adj SILLY VIII.9.3. ædʊɫd Sx [not a SBM headword]
3. vt-3sgperf EARNED VIII.1.26. ɛdld Db, adlt Cu, adld Nb Du We La Y St Nt L, ?inf/pt adl L[old x1]

addle-headed *1. adj* STUPID VI.1.5. ædʊɫjɛdɪd Brk
2. adj SILLY VIII.9.3. ædɫhɛdɪd W, æɫdjɛdɪd Brk[old], ædʊɫɛdɪd W Brk Ha, ædʊɫjɛdɪd Brk

adjuster *n* the T-SHAPED PLOUGH-BEAM END of a horse-drawn plough I.8.5. ədʒʊstə St

advantage bodkin *n* an EVENER, the main adjustable swingle-tree of a horse-drawn plough harness I.8.4. ədvaːntɪdʒ bɒdkɪn Gl

afeared *adj* AFRAID VIII.8.2. əfɪəᵗd Ha, əfɪəᵗːd So, əvɪəᵗːd So W D Do

aflood *adj* IN FLOOD, describing a river IV.1.4. əflœːd Gl, əfluːd Wo

afore *1. prep* TILL IX.2.2. əvɔᵗː D
2. prep IN FRONT OF a door IX.2.6. əfɔᵗː So, əvɔᵗː So, əfʊəɹ (+V) Cu; **afore on** əfɔˑɹ ɒn Nf

afore dinner *n* THIS FORENOON VII.3.15. əfʊə dɪnə Y Ch, fʊə dɪnə Y; **afore the dinner** əfʊə tʔ dɪnə Y [marked u.r. NBM]

afore noon *n* THIS FORENOON VII.3.15. əfʊəᴵ nuːn La [marked u.r. NBM]

afraid *adj Nowadays, of course, that trick [i.e. frightening a child with the bogey-man] doesn't work, for some children are not ....* VIII.8.2. əfrˡid Man, əf.ɪɪˈəd L, əf.ɪeːd Sa Mon Sf W Brk, əf.reːd O Ha, əv.ɹeːd W, əv.ɹeːd D Do Ha, əf.ɹeɪd Man Nf, əf.ɹeɪd So, əv.ɹeɪd Ha, əf.ɹeːd W, əf.ɹɪeɪd St Gl L Nth Nf Ess Brk Sr K Sx, əf.ɹeɪd W Co, əv.ɹɛɪd Co D, əf.ɹeˈəd L, əf.ɹaɪd So, əv.ɹaɪd W Do Ha, əf.ɹæɪd Nf Hrt Ess K, əv.ɹæɪd So, əf.ɹʌɪd Brk. ⇒ **afeared, afraint, duberous, feared, flayed, fraid, freckened, freet, freetened, fright, frightened, frit, fritened, fritted, fritten, gallied, gliffed, scared**

afraint *adj* AFRAID VIII.8.2. əf.ɪɛɪnt W

afront on *prep* IN FRONT OF a door IX.2.6. əf.ɹʊnt ɒn Ch

aft *adv* BACKWARDS IX.1.7(a). æːf Co

after *prep* Half PAST seven VII.5.4. eːdəˡ: Do, ɛftə Y, ædəˡ Ha, æːdəˡ: So W, æːʔəˡ: W, aːtə Nf Sf Hrt Ess, aːtəˡ: W, aːtʔə Sf, aːʔə Sf, aːdə Ess, aːdəˡ: Ha, aˡːtəˡ O, aˡːʔəˡ Bk, aː Hrt, aːtə Nf, aːʔə Nf

afterbirth *n What do you call the stuff that comes out after the calf [when it has just been born]?* III.1.13. æˈftəbɜːθ Man, æftəˡbˡəˡːθ Wo, æːftəˡːbəˡːθ Co, aftəbəθ Y, aftəbəːθ L, aftəbəɾθ Nf, aːftəbəːθ Ess, aːftəˡbəˡθ Ha, aːftəbəɾːθ Ess, aːftəbəˡːθ Nf Ess, aːftəbəˡːθ Ess, aːftəˡbəːθ K, aːftəˡbəˡːθ Brk K, aːftəbəːf Sr. ⇒ **back-water(s), bed, bedding, calf's-bed, clame, clean(s), cleaning(s), cleanse, cleansing(s), clearance, clearing(s), healing, slinkings, wound**

after-grass *n* AFTERMATH, a second crop of grass II.9.17. æːftəˡ:gɹæːs So Co, æːʔəˡ:gɹæːs W, aftəgɹes La, aftəgɹas La, aːftəˡ:gɹaːs So Co D, aˡːtəˡː:gɹaːs So, aˡːdəˡ:gɹæːs D, aˡːdəˡː:gɹaːs So D, aˡːdəˡ:gɹaːs Co

afterings *1. n* STRIPPINGS, the last drops at milking III.3.4. aft.ɪɪnz Db St, aftə.ɪɪnz La Y

2. n BEESTINGS V.5.10. aːftəˡ:ɾɳz Sx[*i. unsure*]

aftermath *1. n When you let the grass grow again [after haymaking] in order to cut it again, you call it...?* [before April 1957: *for a second crop* instead of *in order to cut it again*] II.9.17. æˈəftəmɪθ Man, æˈəfəmɪθ Man, æˈftəˡmæθ Ha, æftəˡmæθ Sa He, æftəˡməθ He, æːftəˡmæθ Sa, æːftəˡmæːθ Gl, æːftəˡːmæːθ So, aftəməθ Y St, atəməθ St, aftəmaːθ Ess, aftəmɒθ Lei, aftəmʊθ Lei, aftəməθ St, aːftəˡmæθ Wo, aˈftəˡmaθ Sa, aːftəˡː:maθ W, aːftəmaːθ Gl Nth Bk Bd Ess, aːftəˡma:θ Sa Wo, aːftəˡ:ma:θ W Ha, aːftəˡməθ Sa, aːθəˡmas Gl, aːθəˡmas Gl, aːftəˡmɛθ K. ⇒ **after-grass, after-shear, eddidge, eddish, entilage, ettidge, fog, hay-math, head-grow, latter-cut, latter-math, oldfield, re-lay, rowen(s), second-crop, second-cut, second cutting, second-grass, second-growth, second-hay, stubber, under-math, year-grass**

2. n grass that is left to stand after mowing. æːftəmæˈθ Man

afternoon *n [You will see him again, not this morning, but] Today, between 2 and 4 p.m., so [this] ....* VII.3.14. Eng. ⇒ **evening**

afternoon-apron *n* a decorative APRON V.11.2(b). æˈftəˡnəuːnɛɪp.ɹɒn Brk, æˈfɹuːnɛɪpəˡˈn Brk[*lace-trimmed*], aftənuːnɛɪp.ɹən St, aːfnʊuːnɛɪp.ɹən Sx, aːftəˡnʊuːnɛɪp.ɪɲ Sr, aːftəˡnuːnɛɪp.ɹɲ Sr, aːftəˡnuːnɛɪpəˡ:ɾɳ Sx, ɛftənuːn ɛˈəp.ɪɛd L, *pl* aftənuːnap.ɹənz Y

after-season *n* AUTUMN VII.3.7. æːftəˡ:şiːzn Co

after-shear *n* AFTERMATH, a second crop of grass II.9.17. aːftəˡ:ʃəˡ: Do

again *1. prep* BESIDE a door IX.2.5. əgɪn Ess Sx, əgɪən Y L, əgeːn We Y, əgeən Du Y, əgɛn We Y Ch St Wo, əgɛˈən Y

2. prep NEAR IX.2.10. əgeən Y, əgɛn Y

against *prep* BESIDE a door IX.2.5. əgjʊnst Wo, əgɪnst Nf, əgɪˈəns L, əgɛnst St Wo L Lei, əgɛns W, əgeɪnst Ess, əgæɪnst Ess

agate *adj* AJAR IX.2.7. əgeːt Y

aghast *adj* **looking aghast** gaping, ⇐ GAPES VI.3.7. lʊkɪn əgæːst So

aglee *adj* ASKEW, describing a picture that is not hanging straight IX.1.3. aˈgli Nb, əgli Nb

aglons *npl* HAWS IV.11.6. agłnz Co

ago *adv If you wanted to tell me that something happened seven days back from now, you'd say: It happened [a week] ....* VII.3.1. Eng exc. Nb Cu We. ⇒ *ago today*, **agone, back, past, sin, sine, since,** *the day*, *today*

a-going *adj* ACTIVE, describing a child VIII.9.1. əgʊɪn Y

agone *adv* AGO VII.3.1. əgɔːn So Co D

agree *v When your friend is of the same opinion as yourself and will support what you say, you can say: I can always count on him to ... with me.* VIII.8.12. ɪgri Cu, əgri Man, əgʁi Nb, əg.ɪi Nb La Y Db Sa St Wo Wa Mon Gl L Lei R Bk Hrt Ess W Brk Sr K Ha Sx, g.ɪi O Sx, əgɾi O So W Co D Do Ha, gɾi Co Do, əg.ɪe Ch, əgɾeː Ha, əg.ɪɛɪ Ch St, əgɾɛɪ Ha, əgɾaɪ Ha, əg.ɪəɪ Y. ⇒ **abide, agree** *by*, **back out, back up, bear out, bear up,** *be on my side*, *be the same mind*, **hang** *in*, **help, help out, hold, hold in, side, stand by, stick up for, support,** *take my part*, *talk alike*, **uphold**

agricultural labourer *n* a FARM-LABOURER I.2.4. ag.ɹəkʊltʃəɹəl lɛˈəb.ɪə L

agrist *v* to HIRE *PASTURAGE* III.3.8. -*ing* əg.ɹɪstɪn Bk

ague *n* TREMORS suffered by a person who cannot keep still VI.1.4. eːguː Ha, eɪgjuː K, eɪguː:

K, eɪɪg So, ɛgjuː So, ɛguː K*[old]*, ɛɪgjuː Ess, ɛɪguː Sx; **the ague** ð eɪg Co; **the agues** ðə eːgoːz Wo

ah *adv* YES VIII.8.13(a). æː Y He, aː La Y Ch Db St He Wa Gl Lei Nth Sf Bk Bd Hrt Ess So Ha, aˡː O, aˤː Sa He Wa O Bk Bd, ɑː Y St Wo Wa Gl O Nf Bd Ess MxL Sr Ha Sx, aˡː Brk, aˤː He Wo Gl W Sr; **oh ah** oː æː He, oː aː Ha, oʊ aː Nth, ʌʊ aːɹ Hrt, oː ɑː Nf, ɒʊ aˤːɪ̯ Sx; **oh ah yes** oː ɑː jɪs Nf

ahuh *adj* ASKEW, describing a picture that is not hanging straight IX.1.3. əhə Brk

ahzygahzies *npl* HAWS IV.11.6. ɑːzɪgɑːzɪz K *[queried SBM]*

ailing 1. *adj* ILL, describing a person who is unwell VI.13.1(b). eːlɪn Sa
2. *adj* SICK, describing an animal that is unwell VI.13.1(c). eːlɪn La, eɪɬɪn O, ɛɪlɪn St, ɛɪlɪŋg St

ail(s) *n* barley AWNS II.5.3. *no -s:* eːɪᵊɬ Gl, haːɬ Sf *-s:* eːɬz Wo Mon Gl, eɪᵊɬz Bd Hrt, ɛɪɬz Gl Ess Sx, hɛɪɬz Ess, ɛɪᵊɬz Wo Wa Gl Nth Hrt Ess, *sg* ɛɪᵊɬ W, ɛɪəɬts Gl, ɛɪʊɬz W Brk Ha, hɛɪʊz Ess, æɪɬz He Mon O Ess, æɪᵊɬz He Wa Ess So, æɪʊz Ess, aɪɬz W Co D, haɪɬz Do, aɪᵊɬz So Do, haɪᵊɬz Do, aɪʊz K, ɑɪɬz Sf, ɑɪᵊɬz C Bk, ɒɪɬz So Brk Sr K Co Ha Sx, ɒɪɬz K, ɒɪʊz Sx, ɔːɬz Ha, ɔɪɬz O Bk K Sx, ɔɪʊz K, ʌɪɬz Sr, əɪɬz Mon Brk

aiming *v-ing* THROWING a stone VIII.7.7. eːmən Do *[marked u.r. SBM]*

ains *n* barley AWNS II.5.3. eːnz Nt

aitch-bone *n* the HIP-BONE of a cow III.2.1. ɪtʃbuːn St

ajar *adj* A door left like this *[i.e. partly open]*, you say is .... IX.2.7. Eng exc. Do. ⇒ *a bit of way* open, *a bit ope*, *a bit* open, *agate*, *agee*, *ajar a bit*, *a-jarred*, *a little ajar*, *a little bit* open, *a little* jar, *a piece of way* open, *a-sam*, *a shade* open, *askew*, *half* abroad, *half ajar*, *half* ope, *half* open, *half* shut, *half-way* ope, *half-way* open, *half-ways* open, *jar*, *just off the sneck*, *not* snecked, *off the* sneck, *on a* jar, *on* jar, *on the* alert, *on the* jag, *on the* jar, open, open *a bit*, *partly* open, *part* open, *part-way* broad, *part-way* open, *piece of the way* open, *slotten*, *standing ajar*, *undone*, *unlatched*, *wee bit* open

a-jarred *adj* AJAR IX.2.7. ədʒaˤːd̞ So

albert *n* a watch-CHAIN VI.14.12. ɛɬbət Ess

alder *n* the bush ELDER IV.10.6. haldə Du, aldɻ O, ɒldə Y, ɔldə O

alder-berry *n* the bush ELDER IV.10.6. ɒldəbɹɹɪ Y

aldern *n* the bush ELDER IV.10.6. aɬdən Bd

aldern-berry *n* the bush ELDER IV.10.6. aɬdənbɛɹɪ Bd

aldern-tree *n* the bush ELDER IV.10.6. aɬdəˤ·n̩ tɹiː Bk

alder-tree* *n* the bush ELDER IV.10.6. ɒldətɹiː Y

alegar *n* VINEGAR V.7.19. ɛlɪkə Y*[older than* vinegar *x1]*, ælɪkə Y*[old name]*, alɪkə La Y, alɪkəɹ La, alɪgəˡ Db, alɪkəˡ La*[older than* vinegar *x1]* Y

alert *n* **on the alert** AJAR IX.2.7. ɔːn ð ələˤːɾt̩ Sx

alive *adj* HEAVING *WITH MAGGOTS* IV.8.6. əlɛɪv Nb Sa, əlæːv D, əlaːv D, əlaɪv Nb Cu Du La Y St L, əlaːv Ch, əlaɪv Y Ch Db Wa Nt L Nth Hu C Bk Bd Hrt Ess MxL K, əlɒɪv Wa Nf So, əlɒɪv Ha, ɔlɒɪv Sf, əlɒɪv Wa Gl O Nth Sf Bk Ess, əlɒɪv O, əlʌɪv Gl Nf Sf Bk, əlʌʏv O, əlɛɪv Wo Mon Gl So, əɬəɪv Mon W Do

all but *adv* ALMOST VII.7.9. ɔːɬ bʌt So Co, ɔːɬ bʌʔ Bd, ɔːl bʊt La St, ɔː bət La Y, ɔˑəl bʊt L

alley 1. *n* the GANGWAY in a cow-house I.3.7. æɬi Co, æli K, ælə Co, *pl* æɬəs Co, ali W, aɬi W, ali Cu
2. *n* a DRAIN in a cow-house I.3.8. alɪ Sa

alleyway *n* the GANGWAY in a cow-house I.3.7. aliweː Nb, aliweə Nb, aliweː Cu, aliwæɪ K

all-rounder *n* a FARM-LABOURER I.2.4. ɔːlɹæundə K

all-round farm-hand *n* a FARM-LABOURER I.2.4. ɔːlɹɛwn faːmænd Sf

all-round labourer *n* a FARM-LABOURER I.2.4. ɔːlɹæund lɛɪbɹɹə Nth

all-round man *n* a FARM-LABOURER I.2.4. ɔlɹæunmæn Ess, ɔːɬɹɛʊnmæn Sf, ɔːɬɹæundman Nth, ɔːlɹɛʊn man O, ɔːɬɹɛʊnman Nth Bk Bd, ɔːlɹæundmæn L, ɔːlɹæunmæn K, ɔːɬɹæund man Wa, ɔːɬɹæundman R, ɔːɹaːndmɒn La, ɔːɹaundman La, ɔːlɹaʊnman Nt L, aːlɹɪᵊuːndman Du, ɔːɹuːndman Cu

all-works *n* a FARM-LABOURER I.2.4. ɔːlwəˤːks K

almost *adv* I paid 19/- *[i.e. 19 shillings]*, that is, not quite a pound, but ... a pound. VII.7.9. aːlməs W, aːlmoʊst Wo, aːlməst He Mon, aːmoːst Gl, aːmoʊst Wo, aːmʊs Wo, aːməst Mon Gl, ɒmʊst He Wo Gl, ɒmʊs He, ɒməst Y*[old x1]* Ch Db Sa He Wo Nt L R, ɒməs He L, ɒməˤɪ̯st Sa He, ɒməˤːɪ̯st Sa, ɔlmɒuˢt K, ɔlmost Nf, ɔɬmʌʊst Ess, ɔməst Y Nt L Hrt Ess, ɔːlmɒust K, ɔːlmoʊst L, ɔːlmɒus Brk, ɔːlmost Nf, ɔːlmoːst Mon So, ɔːlmoʊst St Wa, ɔːlmoːʊs So, ɔːlməst Du Lei, ɔːlməs Man Brk, ɔːɬmɒus Brk, ɔːɬmoːst So, ɔːɬmʌust Brk K, ɔːɬmʌust Bd, ɔːɬmoːst W Do, ɔːɬmoːs W Co D Do, ɔːɬmoust Brk, ɔːɬməst Lei Ess, ɔːɬməs Do, ɔːmʏːst Ch, ɔːmɒust Sr, ɔːməst Y Ch Lei R, oʊɬmoust Ha, əmus Wo; **e'en almost** ɪn əmɒust Brk*[old]*. ⇒ *about*, *all but*, *almost*, *a pound all but a shilling*, *a shilling off*, *close on*, *close on to*, *close to*, *damn near*, *e'en almost*, *e'en most*, *gain enough*, *gayly near*, *gay near*, *getting on for*, *just about*, *just on*, *just short of*, *just under*, *most*, *near*, *near about*, *near as could be*, *near enough*, *nearhand*, *nearish*, *nearly*, *nigh*, *nigh enough*, *nigh on*, *none so far off*, *not far off*, *pretty near*, *pretty nearhand*, *pretty nigh*, *pretty well*, *pushing*, *tight on*, *very* close to, *very* near, *very* nearhand, *very* nearly, *very* nigh, welly, *welly* near, *wholly* near

alongside *prep* BESIDE a door IX.2.5. əlɒŋsaɪd St, ɫɒŋzɒɪd Ha, ɫɒŋzɒɪd Ha, lɒŋsɔɪd Ess, lɒŋzəɪd W, lɔˈŋzaɪd So, lɒŋzɒɪd So; **alongside of** əlaŋsɛɪd ə Nb, lɒŋzæɪd ou So, lɒŋsɒɪd əv So, lɒŋsʌɪd ə Nf, lɔˈŋzɒɪd ou So; **alongside on** əlaŋsɛɪd ɒn Nb, ɫɒŋzɒɪd ɒn W; **down alongside of** dæun ɫɔːŋzɒɪd ou Do

altch *vi* to RETCH VI.13.15. *prppl* altʃɪn Db, -*ing* altʃɪn Db *[queried WMBM]*

always *adv* A man who is never idle is a man that's busy, not just now and again, but .... VII.3.17. Eng. ⇒ **all the time**, regular

amazed *adj* **looks amazed** he GAPES VI.3.7. *3prsg* lʊk əmeɪzd Ess *[marked u.r. EMBM]*

American-tine fork *n* a MUCK-FORK I.3.13. mɛɹɪkntɔɪn fɔːk Ess

amiss *1. adj ON* HEAT, describing a cow III.1.6. əmɪs Y

2. adj ON HEAT, describing a sow III.8.9. əmɪs Y L

among *prep* Where did you say that rabbit was in the garden? Well, do you see those potatoes? I think it's somewhere ... them. IX.2.12. Eng. ⇒ **amongst, between, *down among*, in, *in among*, in amongst, *in* between, *in betwixt, in round they, in the* middle, *in the* midst *of*, *in the potato-bind*, *in the potatoes*, *in the* spuds, mong, mongst, *nigh*, *round there*, *under cover of***

amongst *prep* AMONG IX.2.12. əmaŋst Y, əmɒŋst Sa He Hu So K Ha Sx, əmɒŋs Ha, əmɔːŋs So, əmʌŋst Sa He Nth Nf Bk Bd Ess MxL Brk Sr K, əmʌŋkst Hrt, əmʌŋs So Brk Co D Do Ha, əmʏŋst Nf, ʊmʊŋst Wo, əmʊŋst Sa St He Wo Wa Gl O L Lei Bk, əmʊŋs He; **in amongst** ɪn əmɒŋs W, ɪn əmɔːŋs Do, ɪn əmʌŋst Mon Do, ɪn əmʌŋs Co D Ha, ɪn ʊmʊŋst Wo, ɪn əmʊŋst St*[old xl]* Mon

anenst *prep* BESIDE a door IX.2.5. ənɛnst Y*[very rare]*

anent *1. prep* IN FRONT OF a door IX.2.6. ənɛnt Y *2. prep* NEAR IX.2.10. ənɛnt Y

anger-nail *n* a LOOSE *PIECE OF* SKIN at the bottom of a finger-nail VI.7.11. æŋənæɪᵊɫ Sf, *pl* aŋɔᵏneːlz Nb, *pl* aŋgɔᵏneːlz Nb, aŋəneːl Nb, aŋəɹneːl Cu, aŋəneːl We, *pl* aŋgənɛːlz Cu *[not an EMBM headword]*

angle *n* **out of angle** ASKEW, describing a picture that is not hanging straight IX.1.3. ɛət əv æŋgʊ K

angle-board *n* a DIAGONAL BAR of a gate IV.3.7. æŋglbоᵊd Man

angle-dogs *npl* long WORMS IV.9.1. æŋɫdɒgz Do

angle-end *n* the GABLE-END of a house V.1.5. æŋgɫɛnd D

angle-iron *n* a sliding RING to which a tether is attached in a cow-house I.3.5. aŋglaɪən Y

angle-twitches *npl* WORMS IV.9.1. *sg* aŋgɫtwɪtʃ Co*[long]*, æŋgɫdʌtʃɪz Co*[large] [but on Gower* **angletouch***]*

angly *adj* TANGLED, describing hair VI.2.5. æˈŋglɪ K *[queried fw's error for* **tangly** *SBM]*

angry-nail *n* a LOOSE *PIECE OF* SKIN at the bottom of a finger-nail VI.7.11. *pl* aŋəɹɪneːlz Cu

angry wheal *n* a LOOSE *PIECE OF* SKIN at the bottom of a finger-nail VI.7.11. haŋəɹɪ wɪl Y

ankle *n* What do you call this [indicate the ankle]? VI.10.7. Eng. ⇒ **ankle-bone, anklet, shackle, wrist, wrist *of your foot*;** ⇒ also **wrist *of my foot***

ankle-bone *n* an ANKLE VI.10.7. æŋklboun Nf

anklet *n* an ANKLE VI.10.7. aŋklət Nb

ant-banks *npl* ANT-HILLS IV.8.13. antbæŋks Wa, antbaŋks Wa Nth, anʔbaŋks Bd, aːnʔbaŋks Bk*[modern]*, *sg* ɑːnʔbaŋk Bk

ant-heaps *npl* ANT-HILLS IV.8.13. *sg* ænthiˈp Nf, ænthiːps Sf Ess, æntiːps He, æntjʌps Gl, *sg* æntjʌp He, *sg* æntjʊp He, æntheˈps Nf, æˈntheɪps Nf, *sg* æːntᵊiːp Hrt, anthiːps Nb*[large xl]* We, antiːps La St Nt L Lei R Bd, antɪəps Y, *sg* antɪəp La, *sg* antɛːᵊp Ch, antɛɪps Lei, aːntiːps Wa, *sg* aːntjʊp Gl

ant-heavals *npl* ANT-HILLS IV.8.13. ænthiːvəɫz Sf *[queried EMBM]*

ant-hillocks *npl* ANT-HILLS IV.8.13. antɪlʊks Ch, *sg* antɪlʊk Sa, antɪləks Db, antʊləks Sa St, aːntɪlʊks Wa, ɑːntɪlʊks Wo

ant-hills *npl* What do you call the heaps where they [i.e. ants] live? IV.8.13. ɛnthɪlz Nf, *sg* ɛntɪʊ Sr, *sg* ɛnʔɪʊ Ess, ænthɪlz Nf, æntɪls Man, æntɪlz Y He, *sg* æntɪl Y*[modern]* Man, ænthɪɫz Ess, *sg* ænthɪɫ Ess, æntɪɫz Hu So, *sg* æntɪɫ Mon, æntɪʊz MxL Sr K, æːntɪɫz Hrt, anthɪlz Nb Du We C, *sg* anthɪl Nb*[of big black ant]*, antɪlz Cu Du La Y Db St He L, hantɪlz Wa, antɪɫz Lei Nth Nf, anʔɪɫz Hu Bd, antɪᵊɫz O, aˈntəɫz Wo, aːnthɪlz Sf, aːnthɪɫz Ess, aːntɪɫz Wa Ess, *sg* aːnthɪᵊɫ Sf, aᵗːn̩tɪɫz Wa, ɑˈnthɪlˑz Nf, ɑːntɪɫz Wo Ess, ɔntɪlz L. ⇒ **ant-banks, ant-heaps, ant-heavals, ant-hillocks, ant-moulds, ant-mounds, ant-nests, ants'-heaps, *ants'-hill* ⇒ ants'-hills, ants'-hills, ants'-nests, ant-tumps, anty-heaps, anty-tumps, emmet-banks, emmet-batches, emmet-butts, *emmet-cast* ⇒ emmet-casts, emmet-casts, emmet-heaps, emmet-heaves, emmet-hills, *emmet-hump* ⇒ emmet-humps, emmet-humps, *emmet-knoll* ⇒ emmet-knolls, emmet-knolls, emmet-moulds, emmet-mounds, emmets'-batches, emmets'-butts, emmets'-casts, emmets'-heaps, *emmets'-heave* ⇒ emmets'-heaves, emmets'-heaves, emmets'-hills, emmets'-nests, emmets'-patches, emmet-tumps, heaps, moulds, mounds, *muryan-bank* ⇒ muryan-banks, muryan-banks, *nest of***

pissymires ⇒ nests of pissymires, nests of pissymires, piss-annats'-nests, piss-ants'-nests, piss-emmet-banks, *piss-emmet-heap* ⇒ piss-emmet-heaps, piss-emmet-heaps, piss-emmet-mounds, piss-hills, pissmice-nests, pissmire-heaps, pissmire-hills, pissmower-nests, pissymare-nests, pissymer-heaps, pissymer-hills, pissymer-nests, pissymire- heaps, pissymire-hills, pissymire-nests, pissymoo-nests, pissymoor-heaps, pissymoor-hills, pissymoor-nests, pissymoors'-hills, *pissy-mote-mounds* ⇒ piss-emmet-mounds, pissymote-rucks, pissymother-hills, pissymothers'-nests, pissymower-hillocks, *pissymower-nests* **pissmower-nests,** *pissymower-*hills

anthony *n* a WEAKLING piglet III.8.4. ɛnʔnɪ K, æˑntnɪ K, æːʔnɪ K, æmpnɪ Sf

ant-moulds *npl* ANT-HILLS IV.8.13. æntmoːɫz He, æntmouls Man*[old]*, antmøːlz Nb, antmʌuɫz Hrt, antmoːlz Sa, antmouɫz Mon

ant-mounds *npl* ANT-HILLS IV.8.13. æntmɛundz Sx, antmæunz Ha

ant-nests *npl* ANT-HILLS IV.8.13. æˑntnɛsts MxL, *sg* antnɛst Ch

ants *npl* What do you call those fussy little insects that crawl about quickly all over the place and seem to be working hard? IV.8.12. Eng exc. C Bk Bd W Brk Co D. ⇒ **emmets, horse-ants, muryans, nants, pee-ants,** *pismires* ⇒ **piss-mires, piss-annats, piss-ants, piss-emmets, piss-mice, piss-mires, piss-mowers, pissy-ants, pissy-beds, pissy-mares, pissy-mers, pissy-mice(s), pissy-mires, pissy-moors, pissy-moos, pissy-motes, pissy-mothers, pissy-mowers**

ants'-heaps *npl* ANT-HILLS IV.8.13. æntsiːps Wa, antsᵊiːps Hrt

ants'-hills* *npl* ANT-HILLS IV.8.13. *sg* æntsɪʊ Sr

ants'-nests *npl* ANT-HILLS IV.8.13. *sg* ɛːntsnɛst Nf, æntsnɛsts Sf, antsnɛsts Sa, *sg* antsnɛst Nb Ch St, aːntsnɛsts Ess

ant-tumps *npl* ANT-HILLS IV.8.13. ænttʌmps Sa, æntʊmps Wo, æːntʊmps Gl, *sg* æːntʊmp Wo, *sg* aːntʊmp Wo, ɒntʊmps He *[some forms may be -humps]*

anty-heaps *npl* ANT-HILLS IV.8.13. antɪ-iːps Wo

anty-tumps *npl* ANT-HILLS IV.8.13. æntɪtʌmps Mon, antɪtʌmps Sa Mon, antɪtʊmps Wo, ɒntɪtʊmps He

anunst *prep* BESIDE a door IX.2.5. ənʌnst Sa He, ənʊnst Sa

anunt *prep* BESIDE a door IX.2.5. ənʌnt He Mon, ənʊnt He Gl

anvil *n* By the way, we haven't mentioned the blacksmith, but what does he hammer things on? VIII.4.10. Eng. ⇒ **stithy**

any *pron* ANYTHING V.8.16. ɛni Mon So, ɛnɪ St Wo Wa Gl O Nth Hu C Nf Sf Bk Bd Hrt Ess So Sr Do Sx, ɒnɪ St *[taken as u.r. WMBM]*

any amount *n* A LOT (of money) VII.8.7. ɛnɪ əmuːnt Nb

anything *pron* If you come in very late for a meal and are wondering whether the food is all eaten up, you'd ask: Is there ... left? V.8.16. Eng exc. Cu We La Db Nt C Hrt. ⇒ **any,** *any food, any grub, any layings, any more, any victuals, a thumb bit, nothing*

any time *n* If you don't mind when you see him, you say, not come some time, but come .... VII.3.16. Eng. ⇒ *any old time, any* **season,** *any time when you like,* **anywhen**

anywhen *n* ANY TIME VII.3.16. ɪnɪwɛn Sx, ɛnɪwɪn Sr, ɛnɪwɛn W Brk Sr*[old x1]* Do Ha Sx*[old x1]*

apart *adv* ASTRIDE VI.9.8. əpaːt Y St, əpaˤːt Nth; **feet apart** fiːt əpæˡːt La, fiːt əpaːt Nth; **legs apart** lɛgz əpaːt We, lɛgz əpɜˡːɪt La, lɛgz əpɑːt Nf; **legs wide apart** lɛgz waɪd əpɑːˤt K

apigging *adj* ON HEAT, describing a sow III.8.9. əpɪgɪn We

appetite *n* (off her) FOOD V.8.2. æpətɔɪt Ess, apɪtæːt D, apɪtaɪt Co, apətɔɪt Wo *[marked u.r. WMBM]*

apple *npl* APPLES IV.11.8(a). æːpł Ess, *mass n* ɑːpł Wo, ɒpł He

apple-bees *npl* WASPS IV.8.7. æpłbiːz Co, apłbiːz Co

apple-dranes *npl* WASPS IV.8.7. apłd̮ɾeːənz D, apłd̮ɾɛɪnz D, *sg* abłd̮ɾɛɪn D, abłd̮ɾɛːənz D

apple-drones *npl* WASPS IV.8.7. apłd̮ɾoːnz Co, *sg* apłd̮ɾoːn D

apples *npl* What common fruits do you grow round here? IV.11.8(a). Eng. ⇒ **apple**

apron 1. *n* What do you call the thing that women put on in front to keep their dresses clean? V.11.2(a). Eng. ⇒ **bag-apron, barras-apron, brat, coarse-apron, coarse-brat,** *dustcoat*, **harden-apron, hessian-apron, holland-apron, mantle, napron, pinafore, pinner, pinny, rough-apron, rough-brat, sack-apron, sacking-apron, sacking-mantle, scuffling-apron, spread-apron, touser, touser-apron, tuck-apron, wrapper, wrapper-brat;** ⇒ also **fettling-apron** 2. *n* a decorative APRON V.11.2(b). eːpɹʊn La, eːpɾən Cu, eːpɹən La Ch Db, eːpən Ch, eːpəˤn Gl, eːpəˤːn Sa Co Ha, eɪpɹʊn Wo, eɪpɾən Man, eɪpɹən Db Nf Hrt Ha, eɪpəˤːn So W, e·əpɾən Cu, *pl* ɛpənz Sr, ɛːpɹən Cu, ɛːpɹn Nf, ɛːpəˤːn So, ɛɪpɹən St Nf Ess MxL Sx, *pl* ɛɪpɹənz L, ɛɪpɹəˤːɾn Sx, ɛɪpɹn Lei R Ess, ɛɪpəˤːɾn Sx, ɛ·əpɾən L, æpəˤːn Brk, jæpəˤːn So, æɪpɹən Nf Ess MxL Sr, apɾən Y, apɹən We Y Ch, apɹ̩ən Y, apən Db St, apəˤːn D

Do, japə^ˈ:ɳ D, aɪpə^ˈ:ɳ Ha. ⇒ **afternoon-apron, best apron, bib, bib-apron, brat, cotton-apron, dress-apron, dress-pinny, dutch-apron, evening-apron, fancy-apron, fancy-pinner, fingerin, muslin apron, napron, pinafore, pinner, pinnerette, pinny, slip, sunday-apron, tea-apron, tidy, touser, white-apron**; ⇒ also **lace-apron**

3. n the FAT round the kidneys of a pig III.12.7. eːprən Co, eːpə^ˈ:ɳ Co, ɛːpə^ˈ:ɳ Co

apses *npl* BOILS VI.11.6. æpsɪz Brk*[old]*, *sg* æps So, æspsɪs Brk, *sg* aps D

arain *n* a SPIDER IV.8.9. aɹɪn Y, aɹen Y

arm *n* a BRANCH of a tree IV.12.3. ɑːm Nf

arm-chair *n* a CHAIR V.2.9. ɛːmtʃɛə Y, ɛəmtʃɪə^ˈ La, ɛəmtʃɛə Y, ɛəmtʃɛə^ˈ Y, aːmtʃɪə St, aːmtʃɛː Mon, aːmtʃɛˑə Nf, aɽmtʃɛəɽ O, ɑːmtʃɪə Nf, ɑːmtʃɛə Wo Nf MxL

armflop *n* an ARMPIT VI.6.7. ɑ^ˈ:mflɒp D

armful *n* What do you call this [indicate an armful]? VII.8.10(c). Eng. ⇒ **armsful, armtleful, bolting, lock, yafful**

armhole *n* an ARMPIT VI.6.7. ɛˑəmɒɪl Y, ɛəmɔɪl La Y, ɛˑəmʊəl L*[old x2]*, æːmoʊł C, æ^ˈ:moːl La, æːɹmʊəl La, aːmɒɪl Y, aːmɔːl Cu, aːmɔɪl L, aːmoʊł Lei R Hu, aːmʌʊł C Bk Bd Hrt*[old]* Ess, aːmoːl Ch, aːmoʊl Db St Wo Wa Mon, aːmoʊł Wa Lei, aːmʊːł St, aːmʊəl Y Nt L, aˈːɹmɒɪl La, aˈːmoːl Db, aˈːmʊəl La Y, aˈ^ˈ:moːl Sa, a^ˈ:moːł Bk, a^ˈ:moʊł Wa, ɑːmhoʊl Nf, ɑːmoʊl Nf, ɜˈ^ˈ:ɹmoːl La, ɜˈ^ˈ:mʊəl La

armpit *n* What do you call this [indicate the armpit]? VI.6.7. Eng exc. Nb R C. ⇒ **armflop, armhole, oxter, pit of my arm, pit of your arm, under-arm, under my arm, underneath your arm, under the arm, under your arm**

arms *1. npl* the SPOKES of a cart-wheel I.9.6. ɛəmz Y, a^ˈ:mz He

2. npl BOUGHS of a tree IV.12.2. aːmz Db L Hu Bd Ess*[rare x1]*, ɑːmz Nf Hrt Ess

armsful *n* an ARMFUL VII.8.10(c). jɑ^ˈ:ɽmzfʊʊ Brk *[queried pl SBM]*

armtleful *n* an ARMFUL VII.8.10(c). aːmtlfʊl Ch

arm-wrist *n* a WRIST VI.6.9. ɛˑəmɹɪst L

arrish *n* STUBBLE remaining in a cornfield after harvesting II.1.2. ɛɽɪʃ Co D, æɽɪʃ Co, aɽɪʃ Co D, əɽɪʃ So

arse *1. n* What do you call this, that you sit on? VI.9.2. Eng. ⇒ **backside, behind, bottle and glass, bottom, bum, fart, hinder-end, rump, seat, stern**; ⇒ also **arse-wiper, yellow-arse**

2. n the BUTT of a sheaf of corn II.6.4. eːs La, æːs La Y, æ^ˈ:s La, aːs Cu Du We Y Ch Nt L Hu C Sf Ess, a^ʁ:s Nb, aˈ:s La, ɑːs L Ess

arse-afore *adv* BACKWARDS IX.1.7(a). aˈ:səfʊə^ˈ La

arse backwards *adv* HEAD OVER HEELS IX.1.10. æs bækə^ˈ:dʑ So

arse-band *n* the BREECH-BAND of the harness of a cart-horse I.5.10. a^ʁ:sband Du

arse-board *n* the TAILBOARD of a cart I.10.2. eːsbʊəd La, æːsboˑəɪd La, æ^ˈ:sbyˑəd La, asbɔ^ˈ:d W, aːsbɛʊəd Ch, aːsbɔːəd St, aːsboˑəd Nb Ch Db, aːsbɒʊəd St, aːsbʊəd La Y Ch St, a^ʁ:sbɔ^ʁ:d Nb, ɑːsbʊəd Ch, ɑ^ˈ:ɽsbɔːə^ˈɽd Sx

arse-end *1. n* the BUTT of a sheaf of corn II.6.4. æsɪnd Nf, æːsɛnd Du Nf, hæːsɛnd Du, æ^ˈ:siːnd La, aːsɪnd Sf Ess, aːsɛn Ch, aːsɛnd Y Ch St L Lei Nth Hu Nf Sf Hrt Ess, aˈ:siːnd Db, aˈ:sɛnd La, ɑːsɪnd Nf Ess, ɑːsɛnd Nf Ess

2. n a tree STUMP IV.12.4. aːsɛnd Ess, ɑːsɪnd Ess

arse-end-post *n* the HANGING-POST of a gate IV.3.3. aːsɛndpɒst Y

arse-first *1. adv* BACKWARDS IX.1.7(a). aːsfɒst Y, aːsfɔːˀst Nb, aːsfəst Y

2. adv HEAD OVER HEELS IX.1.10. aːsfəst Y

arse over appetite *adv* HEAD OVER HEELS IX.1.10. aːs oːvə^ˈ:ɽ apɪtaɪt Co

arse over backwards *adv* HEAD OVER HEELS IX.1.10. aːs ouvə bækədz Nf

arse over end *adv* HEAD OVER HEELS IX.1.10. aːs ɑʊəɹ ɛnd Y, aːs ɔʊəɹ ɛnd L

arse over head *1. adv* overturned, referring to a cart, ⇐ to OVERTURN I.11.5. aːsɔʊvəhɪd Ess, aːsɔʊvəɹɪɪd Ess, aːəˈs ɒʊvəˈɹ ɪd Sr, æs ɒvə^ˈ ɛd Brk, aːsʌʊvəhɛd Ess, aːs ɔːvə^ˈ:ɽ ɛd Ha, aːs oːvə^ˈ:ɽ ɛd Ha, aːs ɒʊvəɹ ɛd K, aˈ^ˈ:ɽṣ ɒʊvəɹ ɛd Sr Sx, aˈ^ˈ:ɽṣ ovə^ˈ ɛd Brk, aˈ:s ɒʊvəɹ ɛˑd K, aˈ:əs ɔʊvə^ˈ ɛˑd Brk, aˈ:s ʊvəɹ ɛˑd K

2. v to turn over. aːsʌʊvəhɛd Ess

3. adv HEAD OVER HEELS IX.1.10. æːs ɔːvə^ˈ: hiːd So, aːs ɔːvə^ˈ:ɽ iːd So D Do, aːs oːvə^ˈ:ɽ iːd So, æs ʌʊvə hɪd Sf, æːs ouvə hɪd Nf, aːs ɔːvə^ˈ:ɽ ɪd D Do, aːs ʌʊvə hɪˀd Sf, aːs ɑʊvəɹ ɪd Ess, aːs ɔʊvə hɪd Ess, aːs ouvə hɪd Nf, a^ˈ:ṣ ɒʊvəˈɹ ɪd Sr*[old]* Sx, a^ˈ:ɽṣ ɒʊvə^ˈ ɪd Sx, aːs ɒʊəɹ ɪəd Y, æs ɔːvə^ˈ: hɛd So, æs ɔːvə^ˈ:ɽ ɛd W, æs ɒʊvə^ˈ:ɽ ɛd So, æːs ɔːvə^ˈ:ɽ ɛd W, æːs ʌʊvə hɛd Sf, as ɔːvə^ˈ:ɽ ɛd W Do, aːs ɔːvə^ˈ: hɛd W, aːs ɔːvə^ˈ:ɽ hɛd W, aːs ɔːvə^ˈ:ɽ ɛd W Ha, aːs ʌʊvə hɛd Sf Ess, aːs ouvə hɛd Nf, aːs ʌʊvə hɛd Ess, aːs ʌʊvəɹ ɛd Hrt Ess, aːs ʌʊvəɹ ɛd Sf, aːs oˑvəɹ ɛd O, aːs ɔːvəˈɹ ɛd Mon, aːs ɔːvə^ˈ: hɛːd Do, aːs ɔːvə^ˈ:ɽ ɛd Ha, aːs ɒʊvəɹ ɛd Nth, a^ˈ:ṣ ʌʊvəɹ ɛd Bk, a^ˈ:ṣ oːvəˈɹ ɛd Mon, a^ˈ:ṣ ɒʊvəɹ ɛd Bk, a^ˈ:ṣ ɒʊvə^ˈɽ ɛd O, aːs ɒʊvəɹ ɛˀd K, aːs ɔʊvəɹ ɛd Ess Brk, aːs ʌʊvəɹ ɛd Sr, aˈ:s ɒʊvəɹ ɛd K, aˈ:s ɔʊvəɹ ɛˑd K, aˈ:s ɔʊvə^ˈɹ ɛˑd Brk, a^ˈ:ɽṣ ɔʊvə^ˈɹ ɛd Ha, a^ˈ:ɽṣ ɔʊvə^ˈ ɛd Sx, aːəˈs ɒʊvə^ˈɹ ɛd Sr, a:ə^ˈṣ ɒʊvə^ˈɹ ɛd Sr*[old]*, aːs ɒvə jɛd Gl, aᵗːʂ oːvəᵗː jɛd Sa, aᵗːʂ ouvəᵗ jɛd Wa, aːs ɔːvəᵗːɪ eːd Do, aːs oːvəᵗ jʌd He, æs oːvəᵗ jʊd He, aːs oːvəᵗ jʊd He, aᵗːʂ ɒvəɪ jʊd Gl, aᵗːʂ oːvəᵗ jʊd Wo, aᵗːʂ ouvəᵗ jʊd Wo, aᵗːʂ oːvə jəd Gl; **arse over head backwards** aːs ʌuvə hɛd bækwədz Ess

arse over heels *adv* HEAD OVER HEELS IX.1.10. aːs ɒvə ⁱiːlz Nt, aːs ɔwəɪ iːlz L, aːs ɔːvəᵗ hiːłz So, aːs ɔːvəᵗːɪ iːłz Co D, aːs ouvəɪ iːᵊłz Bk

arse over hips *adv* HEAD OVER HEELS IX.1.10. æːs oːvəᵗːɪ iːps Co

arse over shit *adv* HEAD OVER HEELS IX.1.10. æˑs ouvə ʃɪt Nf, aːs ɑuə ʃɪt Y, aːs oˑə ʃɪt Y, aᴵːs uəᴵ ʃɪt La

arse over tip *adv* HEAD OVER HEELS IX.1.10. æs ouvəᵗˑ tɪp So, æːs ɔːvəᵗː tɪp Co, æᴵːs ɒəɪ tɪp La, as oːvəᵗː tɪp W, aːs ɔːvəᵗː tɪp D, aːs oːvəᵗː tɪp Co, as ouvə tɪp Wa*[old]*, aːs ouvə tɪp Wa, aːs oːvəᵗ tɪp Sa aːs oːuvəᵗ tɪp Gl, aːs ʌuvə tɪp Bd, aᵗːʂ ʌuvə tɪp Bk

arse-smart *n* BINDWEED II.2.4. asmaᵗːt Co, asmaᵗːt D

arsewards *adv* HEAD OVER HEELS IX.1.10. æsədz Mon

arse-wiper *n* a ne'er-do-well, ⇐ ARSE VI.9.2. æːswʌɪpə Nf

art *n* the DIRECTION from which the wind blows VII.6.26. ɛɔᴿt Nb, eˑəᴿt Nb, ɛɔᴿt Nb, ɛɑt Nb, ɛɑrt Cu, ɛɔᴿt Du, aːt Du, aᴿːt Nb, ɑːt Man

as *prep* THAN VI.12.4. əz Y

a-sam *adj* AJAR IX.2.7. əzam D

ash 1. *n What do you call this greyish white stuff that falls through the grate [when the fire is burning]?* V.4.4. Eng. ⇒ **ash-dust, ashes, cinder-dirt, cinder-muck, dust, white ash(es), wood-ash(es)**
2. *n* ASHES from a cold fire V.4.5. ɛs La Ch Db Sa St, æʃ Bk, aʃ Nb Du St Nt, as Cu We La Y, aɪʃ Co

ash-bin 1. *n* a container for ash, ⇐ CORN-BIN I.7.4. ɛsbɪn La, asbɪn Y
2. *n* an ASH-MIDDEN V.1.14. ɛʃbɪn K*[old x1, of brick x1]*, æʃbɪn MxL, aʃbɪn L

ash-bing *n* an ASH-MIDDEN V.1.14. æʃbɪŋ Nf, aʃbɪŋ Y L Nth

ash-box *n* the ASH-HOLE or other place beneath a domestic fire in which the ashes are collected V.3.3. aᴵʃbɒks So

ash-drawer *n* the place in which the ashes are collected beneath a domestic fire, ⇐ ASH-HOLE V.3.3. aɪʃdɹɔːəᵗː Co

ash-dump *n* an ASH-MIDDEN V.1.14. aʃdʊmp Sa

ash-dust *n* ASH in a burning fire V.4.4. aʃdʊst Y, asdʊst Y *[marked u.r. NBM]*

ashen-faggot night *n* CHRISTMAS EVE VII.4.8. æɪʃənfakət næɪt So

ashes 1. *n [What do you call this greyish white stuff that falls through the grate (when the fire is burning)?] And when you clean up in the morning, what do you take out from underneath the grate?*

V.4.5. Eng. ⇒ **ash, ash-muck, cinder-ashes, cinder-dirt, cinder-muck, cinders, dirt, money-dust, waste, wood-ashes**
2. *n* ASH in a burning fire V.4.4. eːʃəz Do, ɛʃɪz Y Ess MxL, ɛsəz Db, ɛɪʃəz Db, æʃɪs Nf, æʃɪz Hu C Nf Sf Ess K, æʃəz Sf Ess, aʃɪs Nb Nf, aʃɪz Nb Cu We Y St Wa Mon Gl O Nt L Nth Bk Bd Hrt Ha, aʃəz Nb Y Db, aːʃəz Do, aᵗːʃəz So, aɪʃəz So Co

ashes-heap *n* an ASH-MIDDEN V.1.14. aɪʃəziːp Co

ash-heap *n* an ASH-MIDDEN V.1.14. eɪʃiːp D, ɛʃiːp O, ɛsɪəp La, æʃiːp Mon Hu So Co, æʃhiːp Ess, æʃiːp W, æʃjʌp Gl, æʃjʊp Wo Gl, æᴵʃhiːp So, æɪʃiːp So, aʃhiːp Du, aʃiːp We Db St Gl Nt L Lei Nth Hrt W Ha, aʃɪp Sa Gl, aʃɪəp L Bk, aɪʃhiːp So, aɪʃiːp So W Co D Do Ha, aᴵʃhaɪp Do

ash-hill *n* an ASH-MIDDEN V.1.14. asɪl La

ash-hole 1. *n What do you call this, where the cinders drop [indicate under the fire]?* V.3.3. Eng exc. He Mon Hrt MxL Sx. ⇒ **ash-box, ash-drawer,** *ashes-hole,* **ash-nook, ash-pan, ash-pit, ash-plate, ash-tin, ash-tray,** *below the bars,* **cinder-hole, cinder-pit, cubby-hole, fire-hole, flag, grate, grate-hole, grid-hole, grit-hole, hearth, hearth-pan, hod,** *hole,* **muck-hole, muck-pit, pick-grate, pit, pit-grate,** *privy-hole,* **purgat, purgat-hole, purgatory, purgy-hole, under-grate,** *under the bars,* **well, well-grate**
2. *n* an ASH-MIDDEN V.1.14. ɛʃɒuł Sx, ɛʃoːᵁl Db, æʃɒuł Sr Sx, æˑʃhɔuł Ha, æʃoːł Wo, aʃɒɪl Db, asɔɪl Y, *pl* aʃɒułz St, aʃʌuł Bd, aʃoːl Gl, aʃoˑʊl Db, aʃouł Lei, aʃʊəl L, asʊəl Db, aɪʃoːł Ha

ash-house *n* an ASH-MIDDEN V.1.14. aᵗːʃæys So, aɪʃæyz D

ash-lum *n* an ASH-MIDDEN V.1.14. æˑʃlʌm K

ash-lump *n* an ASH-MIDDEN V.1.14. aʃlʌmp C

ash-midden *n What do you call the place outside where you put your cinders and other stuff you throw away?* V.1.14. ɛsmɪdɪn Db, ɛɪʃmɪdɪn Db, aʃmɪdɪn Cu We Y St Nt, asmɪdɪn Cu We Y, aʃmɪdn Nb Y Nt. ⇒ **ash-bin, ash-bing, ash-dump, ashes-heap, ash-heap, ash-hill, ash-hole, ash-house, ash-lum, ash-lump, ash-mixen, ash-pile, ash-pit, ash-ruck, ash-tip, bin, bing,** *buckets,* **bumble-hole, bumby, bumby-hole, cess-pool, cinder-bing, cinder-heap, cinder-midden, cinder-ruck, cistern, closet-pit, dirt-bing, dump, dung-hill, dung-pit, dust-heap, dust-hole, dust-pit, gather, gutter, gutter-dike, gutter-hole, guzzle, guzzle-hole, heap, hole, midden, midden-hole, mixen, mixen-hole, muck-bin, muck-bing, muck-heap,** *muck-hill* ⇒ **muck-hole/muckle, muck-hole, muckle, muck-ruck, nessy, pit, pouk, privy-midden, rubbish-bin, rubbish-dump, rubbish-heap,**

rubbish-hole, ruck, rummage-heap, rummage-shed, shed, sink-hole, slut's-hole, tump, vault, waste-dump, waste-heap

ash-mixen *n* an ASH-MIDDEN V.1.14. ɛsmɪksən Sa

ash-muck *n* ASHES from a cold fire V.4.5. æʃmʌk Nf, aʃmʊk Y *[marked u.r. NBM]*

ash-nook *n* the ASH-HOLE beneath a domestic fire V.3.3. aʃnᵁuːk Y, asnʊuk Y

ash-pan *n* the container or place in which the ashes are collected beneath a domestic fire, ⇐ ASH-HOLE V.3.3. ɛʃpɛn Ess MxL, ɛʃpɛən Ess, ɛʃpæn Nf K Sx, æʃpɛn Ess, æʃpæn He*[modern]* Nf Hrt Ess Brk Sr K Ha, æʃpan Nf, aʃpan Wo*[modern]* Mon O L Bk Hrt, aspan Ha, aɪʃpan Co D Do

ash-pile *n* an ASH-MIDDEN V.1.14. æʃpaɪl Sa, æʃpaɪɫ Co

ash-pit *1. n* an ASH-MIDDEN V.1.14. eɪʃpɪt D, ɛʃpɪt Sr K, ɛspɪt He, ɛɪʃpɪt La D, æʃpɪt Sa He Wo C Ess Sr, æːʃpɪt Man So, æɪʃpɪt So, aʃpɪt Nb Cu La*[modern x1]* Y Ch Db Sa St Wo Wa Nt L Lei R Nth Hu Db Hrt MxL So, aspɪt Y, aᵗːʃpɪt So, aɪʃpɪt So D Ha

2. n the ASH-HOLE beneath a domestic fire V.3.3. eɪʃpɪt D, ɛspɪt Sa, æʃpɪt Man He Wo Mon Gl So Brk*[old x1]*, aʃpɪt Cu La Y Ch Db St He Wo Wa Gl O Lei R Nth Bd, aʃpɪʔ Bk, aspɪt Cu We Y, aɪʃpɪt D Ha

3. n the place in which ashes are collected. ɛʃpɪt Sr, æʃpɪt Nf*[a pan x1]* Sf Ess Brk K Co Sx, æᵁʃpɪt Nf, aʃpɪt So, aᵗːʃpət So*[iron box]*, aɪʃpɪt So*[metal tray x1]*

ash-plate *n* the container or place beneath a domestic fire in which the ashes are collected, ⇐ ASH-HOLE V.3.3. æʃpleɪt Nf

ash-rake *n* a RAKE used in a domestic fire V.3.8(a). aʃɹeɪk Wo

ash-ruck *n* an ASH-MIDDEN V.1.14. ɛsɹʊk Ch Sa St, ɛsɹᵁuːk La*[old]*, aʃɹʊk Wo

ash-tin *n* the container or place beneath a domestic fire in which the ashes are collected, ⇐ ASH-HOLE V.3.3. æʃtɪn Sf, aɪʃtɪn W

ash-tip *n* an ASH-MIDDEN V.1.14. ɛstɪp Sa, aʃtɪp He

ash-tray *n* the container or place beneath a domestic fire in which the ashes are collected, ⇐ ASH-HOLE V.3.3. æʃtɹeɪ MxL*[modern]*, æʃtɹæɪ Nf Ess, æːʃtɹeɪ Sx, aɪʃtɹeɪ D, aɪʃtɹeɪ D

aside *prep* BESIDE a door IX.2.5. əsɛɪd Nb Cu Du, əsaɪd Cu We La Sa He, əsaɪd La Hu C Bd Hrt, əsɒɪd Nf, əsɔɪd Sf Ess; **aside of** ə saːɪd ə Y, əsaɪd ə Ch, ə saɪd ə Y, əsaɪd ɒv Wa, əsaɪd əv Bk Bd Hrt, əsaɪd ə Bd MxL, ə saɪd ə La, əsɔɪd əv Sf, əsɔɪd ə Ess, əsʌɪd ə Nf Brk; **aside on** əsɛɪd ɒn Nb, əsaɪd ɒn Cu La Nt, əsaɪd ɒn L, əsaːɪd ɒn Db, əsaɪd ɑn C, əsaɪd ɒn La Ch Nt Hu Nf, əsaɪd ɔn Ess, əsɒːɪd ɒn St, bɪəsɛ an Bk, əsɔɪd ɑn Nth Bk, əsɔɪd ɒn Ess, əsɔɪcɛ ɔn Sf, əsʌɪd ɒn Nf *[ambiguity over **aside** and **at side** in NBM: forms lacking first consonant ([t]) placed here, but fws' graphical separations retained]*

ask *1. v* If you've lost your way and someone comes along, you'd go up to him and ... HIM. IX.2.4. Eng. ⇒ **speer**

2. n a NEWT IV.9.8. æsk Y, ask Nb Cu Du We La Y

asker *n* a NEWT IV.9.8. ɛəskə Y, æskəᵗ Sa He, askə La Y Ch Sa St, askəɹ La, askəᴶ St, askəᵗ Sa He

askert *n* a NEWT IV.9.8. ɛəskəd Y, askət Nb La, askəd Y

askew *1. adj A picture not hanging straight, is hanging [indicate] ....* IX.1.3. əskɪaʊ Sa, əskɪʊ Y, əskju: Y Sa He Wa Gl O L W Brk K Ha, əskɪuː Du Wo Wa, əskʏ: D, əskəu Man, əskwəɪ W. ⇒ *a bit crooked, a bit* **screw-ways,** *across, aglee, all* **ahuh,** *all* **askew,** *all* **askew-whiffed,** *all* **aslant,** *all* **awry,** *all of a oner,* *all of a* **screw,** *all of a* **slant,** *all on a* **skew,** *all* **one-haw,** *all* **one huh,** *all on* **one huh,** *all on* one side, *all on the one* huh, *all* **skew-whiff,** *all* **slant,** *all to a* **skew-ways,** *a***skew-whiffed,** *aslant, aslew, aswint, athwart, atwist, awry, bit* one side, *cater-cornered, cob-wobbly, cock-eyed, cocks-eyed, crook, crooked, crookled, cross-ways, gawbosh, gawison, gee-waw, gee-wom, gee-y, jye, lop-ended, lopsided, off-side, on a* **skew,** *on a* **slant,** *on a* slew ⇒ slewed, *on a* **squint,** *on a* **twist** ⇒ twisted, one side, *on the* cross, *on the* huh, *on the* screw, *on the* skew, *on the* skew-ways, *on the* **skew-wiffed** ⇒ skew-whiffed, *on the* skewy side, *on the* slant, *on the* slope, *on the* sosh, *on the* squint, *on the* swin, *on the* tilt, *on the* wry, *out-inner,* *out of* angle, *out of* line, *out of* true, *screw-jye, screw-ways, screw-whiff, screwy, sideways, skew, skewdy-whiff, skew-way(s), skew-whiff, skew-whiffed, skew-whifted, skew-whish, skew-wiff* ⇒ skew-whiff, *skew-wiffed* ⇒ *skew-whiffed, skew-wifted* ⇒ **skew-whifted,** *skewy, skumjot, skwift, sky-bald, sky-wannock, sky-wobbled, slant, slanting, slanty, slewed, sosh-way, squint, squinty, swint-way, swish, swush-way, to* one side, *twisted, unlevel, **walted, wee-wub***

2. adv DIAGONALLY, referring to harrowing a field IX.1.8. əskju: He Wa Mon Gl O, əskɪu: Wa Ess

3. adj AJAR IX.2.7. əskɪu La

askgel *n* a NEWT IV.9.8. æskəⁱ He, æzgəⁱ He*[modern x1]*, æzgʊɫ He Wo, æːskl Sa, askl Sa, askəl Sa, *pl* askəlz He

aslant* *adj* ASKEW, describing a picture that is not hanging straight IX.1.3. əslant Nb Y

aslew* *adj* ASKEW, describing a picture that is not hanging straight IX.1.3. əslıʊ Y, əslʌʊ Y, əslu: Y

asp *n* an ADDER IV.9.4. asp Du*[old]*

ass *n* a DONKEY III.13.16. æs C Nf Ess So Sx, as Nb Y*[half-bred]* St O L Nth, aːs Nf Sf Bk

aster *n* a NEWT IV.9.8. æstəᵗ He

astraddle *adv* ASTRIDE VI.9.8. əstɹædɫ Ess Brk, əstɹadɫ Lei, əʂtɹadɫ W D Do Ha

astraddled *adv* ASTRIDE VI.9.8. əʂtɹadɫd W

astraddling *adv* ASTRIDE VI.9.8. əstɹædlın Brk, əstɹæᵊdlən Sf, əstɹadlın Wa

astriddlings *adv* ASTRIDE VI.9.8. əstɹıdlınz Cu

astride *adv* *What is your word for standing like this [indicate standing astride]?* VI.9.8. əʂtɹæːd D, əstɹæıd Man, əʂtɹæıd So, əstɹaıd La Y Ch Sa He Nt L Lei, əʂtɹaıd Co, əstɹaıd La Ch Db L Lei R Nth Hu Bk Sr, əstɹɒıd St Lei R K, əʂtɹɒıd So Co Do Ha, əstɹɔıd St Wa O Sf Ess Sx, əstɹʌʏd O, əstɹəıd Mon Gl, əʂtɹəıd So. ⇒ **apart, astraddle, astraddled, astraddling, astriddlings, astroddle, astroddled, astroddle-legged, astroddling, astrut, athwart, broad-legged,** *feet* **apart,** *legs* **apart,** *legs* **striddled out,** *legs* **wide apart, open, opened out, open-legged, open-legs, propping, scrod out, splar-footed, splaudered, splauder-legged, splauder-legs, splaw, sprad-legged, sprawed-footed, sprawled, sprawled out, spraw-legged, sprawling, sprawling out, spray-legged, spread, spread-addled, staddled, straddle, straddled, straddled out, straddle-leg, straddle-legged, straddle-legs, straddling, straddly, striddled, striddled out, striddle-legged, striddle-legs, striddling, striddlings, stride, stride-legged, striding, strid-legged, stroddle, stroddled, stroddle-legged, stroddling, stroddling out, strog-legged, struddle, wide, wide-legged,** *wide* **open,** *with his feet wide* **open,** *with his legs* **apart,** *with his legs gaping* **open,** *with his legs* **out,** *with his legs wide* **open,** *with legs* **open,** *with my legs* **open,** *with your feet* **apart,** *with your legs* **apart,** *with your legs* **open,** *with your legs wide* **open**

astroddle *adv* ASTRIDE VI.9.8. əʂtɹɒdɫ Mon, əʂtɹɒdɫ So W D Do

astroddled *adv* ASTRIDE VI.9.8. əʂtɹɒdɫd D

astroddle-legged *adv* ASTRIDE VI.9.8. əʂtɹɒdɫlagıd Do

astroddling *adv* ASTRIDE VI.9.8. əstɹɒdlın Wo

astrut *adv* ASTRIDE VI.9.8. əstɹʊt Y

aswint* *adj* ASKEW, describing a picture that is not hanging straight IX.1.3. əswınt La

at *adj* NEAR IX.2.10. at Y

atchorn *n* an ACORN IV.10.3. atʃın Ch, atʃən Sa St

at front of *prep* IN FRONT OF a door IX.2.6. ət fʀʊnt əv Nb, ət fɹʊnt ə La Y; **at the front of** ət ðə fʀʊnt ə Du

at front on *prep* IN FRONT OF a door IX.2.6. ət fɹʌnt œn Nb, ə fʀʊnt œn Nb, ə fʀʊnt ɒn Du, ʊt fɹʊnt ɒn La, ət fɹʊnt ɒn Nb Du We La Y Nt, ə fɹʊnt ɒn La Cu Du We La Y, ət fɹʊnt ɔn Y L, ə fɹʊnt ɔn La; **at the front on** ət ðə fɹənt ɑn Gl

athisen(s) *adv* IN THIS WAY IX.10.7. *no -s:* əðısn La Ch *-s:* əðısns Sa

athwart 1. *adv* ASTRIDE VI.9.8. əθəːɹt Brk

2. *adj* ASKEW, describing a picture that is not hanging straight IX.1.3. əðəᵗːt So

3. *adv* DIAGONALLY, referring to harrowing a field IX.1.8. əðəᵗːt D, əðət Brk, əθəᵗːt Gl So, əðəᵗːt So W Co D Do Ha, əðəᵗːʔ Bk, əðəᵗːɹt Brk

athwart-ways *adv* DIAGONALLY, referring to harrowing a field IX.1.8. əðəᵗːɹtweız Ha

atilt over *viphr* to OVERTURN, referring to a cart I.11.5. ətıɫt ʊvəᵗ Sx

at side *prep* BESIDE a door IX.2.5. ət saıd Y, ət saıd La; **at side of** ət saːd ə Y, ət saıd əv L, ət saıd ə La, əʔ saıd ə La, ət saːd ə Y, ət saıd ə Y; **at side on** ət saːd ɒn Y, ʊt saıd ɒn La, ət saıd ɒn We La Y, ət saıd ɒn L, ət saːd ɒn Y, ət saıd ɒn La Y Nt, ət saˑıd ɒn L; **at the side** ət ðə saıd MxL, ə θ sɒıd St; **at the side of** ət ðə sɛıd ə Du, ət ðə saˑıd əv L, ət ðə sɔıd əv Ha, ət ðə zʌıd ə Gl, ət ðə səıd ə Sx; **at the side on** ət ðə sɛıd œn Nb, ət ðə sɛıd ɒn Cu, ə t saıd ɒn Db, ə t saːd ɒn Db, ət ðə saıd ɒn Nth, ə ðə saıd ɒn Nth, ət ðə saˑıd ɔn L, ə t saıd ɒn Ch Db, ə t sɒıd ɒn St, ət ðə sɔıd ɒn Wa, ə ðə sɔıd ɒn Gl, ə t sʌʏd ɒn O *[at side marked u.r. NBM]*

atter *n* PUS VI.11.9. ætʔə Nf, atʔə C

attercrop *n* a SPIDER IV.8.9. ɛðəkɹɒp La*[old]*, atəkɹɒp La, atəɹkɹɒp La, *pl* atəkɹɒps La

attractive *adj* PRETTY, describing a girl VI.5.18. tɹɛktıv Sr

atween *prep* BETWEEN IX.2.11. ətwiːn Nb Cu Du We La Y Sa He Wo*[old]* Lei C Nf Bd, ətweın Du, ətwɛın Y, ətwəın Y

atwist *adj* ASKEW, describing a picture that is not hanging straight IX.1.3. ətwıst Y

atwixt *prep* BETWEEN IX.2.11. ətwıkst Y Brk; **atwixt of** ətwıkst ə Y

aught *pron* ANYTHING V.8.16. ɛʊt La Ch*[old xl]* Db St Nt, æʊt Du Ch St L Lei, aʊt Cu Du We La Y St So, aʊt Nb Y, ɒʊt Nb Cu Du We La Y Db Nt L Lei, ɔːt Y D, ɔᵗːt So Co D, ɔʊt Nb La Y L Lei R, ɔʊʔ L, ɔˑət Y, oʊt St Lei, ʊːt Lei

aunt *n* *[Show a picture of a family.] And if he [i.e. the children's father] had a sister she'd be their [i.e. the children's]* .... VIII.1.12(b). Eng. ⇒ **auntie, naunt**

auntie 1. *n* a HARE IV.5.10. ɑːntı O *[queried WMBM]*

2. *n* an AUNT VIII.1.12(b). ænti So Co, æntiː He, æːntı Wo Ha, anti Co D, antı Nb We, antᵉı

Wa*[old]*, aːnti So W Do, aːntɪ St Wa Do, aːnti: He, ɑːntɪ Hrt Sx

aunt sally *n* a HARE IV.5.10. ɑˑnt sælɪ Nf, aːnʔ salɪ Bk

autumn *n [If you wanted to tell me that something happened seven days back from now, you'd say: It happened ....] If in the season after summer?* VII.3.7. Eng. ⇒ after-season, back-end, back-end *of the* year, back-end *of year*, fall, fall *of the leaf*, fall *of the leaves*, fall *of the year*, harvest-time, latter end

aw *adv* YES VIII.8.13(a). ɔː Sa Wa, ɔˡ: Sa He

award *adj* OVERTURNED, describing a sheep on its back unable to get up III.7.4. ɒʊɔᵏt Nb

away *imp* **away with you** GO AWAY! VIII.7.9(a). əwɛˑə wɪ ðɪ Y

aweld *adj* OVERTURNED, describing a sheep on its back unable to get up III.7.4. aʊld Nb, aʊəld Nb, ɔʊld Nb

awful *adv* VERY VIII.3.2. æˑfə Nb, aːfl Nb, aːfə Cu, ɔːfʊl St, ɔːfəl Y

awkward 1. *adj* RESTIVE, describing a horse III.5.6. akwɔᵏd Nb, ɒkəˡd O, ɒkəˡːd Co, ɔːkəd Y Nf, ɔːkwəˡːd Co *[marked u.r. WMBM]*

2. *adj* OVERTURNED, describing a sheep on its back unable to get up III.7.4. akwɔᵏd Nb

3. *adj* STUPID VI.1.5. akwəd We, aːkwəd Nb, aˡːkəˡt He, aˡːkəˡːd O, ɒkəd Ch Mon Nt Bd, ɒkəˡd Brk, ɒkəˡd Wo Wa O Nth Bk, ɒkwəˡːd W Co, ɒkəˡːt Sa, ɒkəˡːd Sa Bk W D Ha, ɔːkʊd La, ɔːkwəd Sa Hu Ess, ɔːkʔwəd Sf, ɔːkət Db Sf, ɔːkəd Nth Hu C Nf Bd Hrt Ess*[old x1]*, ɔːkʔəd Nf Sf, ɔːkəˡd Nf, ɔːkəˡd Nth, ɔːkwəˡːd W D Do, ɔːkəˡːd Ha, ɔˡːkəˡt He

4. *adj* CLUMSY, describing a person VI.7.14. ækəˡːd So Brk, aˑkwɔᵏˑd Nb, akwəd Nb, aːkwəd Du, aːkwəˡd Mon, aːkəˡd Gl, aːkəˡd Ha, aˡːkəˡt He, ɒkʊd Gl, ɒkət Wo, ɒkwəd K, ɒkəd Ch*[old x1]* Sa K*[old x1]*, ɒkəˡːd Brk, ɒkəˡːt Sa, ɒkwəˡd He, ɒkəˡd Wo Mon Gl Nth Bk, ɒkwəˡːd Co, ɒkəˡːd Sa Wa O W, ɔːkəˡd O, ɔːkwəd Ess MxL K, ɔːkʔwəd Ess, ɔːkəd Cu We Y Ch Db St Wa Nth C Nf Sf Hrt Ess, ɔːkʔəd Nf Sf, ɔːkwəd He, ɔːkəɹd La, ɔːkəˡˑt Sa, ɔːkəˡd He, ɔːkwəˡːd So Co D, ɔːkəˡːd So D

5. *adj* SILLY VIII.9.3. ɔːkwəd Ess, ɔːkət Nf

awns *n* **awns, barley-awns** *What do you call the bristles of barley?* II.5.3. **awns** eːnz La Y Nt, eːnts La, æˀnz Nb, æːˀnz Nb, aːns Nb Cu, aːnz Nb La, *sg* aːn Cu, aʊnz Sa, ɑːnz Y, ɔːnz Y Ch Db St Wa Nt L R Hu C Bd K, jɔːnz Lei R, ɔːrnz Cu, ɔːənz Du Y L Nth, ɔˡːˀəˡnz L, ʊənz Y L; **barley-awns** baːlɪ-eːnz Y, *sg* baːlɪ-an Y, baːlɪ-ɔːnz Y L, bɑːlɪ-ɔːnz Y, baːlɪ-ɔˑənz Y, baːlɪ-ʊənz Y. ⇒ ail(s), ains, barley-ails, *barley-*awns, barley-beards, barley-bristles, barley-elves, barley-hangs, barley-haulms, barley-havels, barley-horns, barley-hucks, barley-husks, barley-pails, barley-piles, barley-whiskers, barley-zears, beard(s), bristles, colg, *comes* ⇒ cooms, ears, fins,

hangs, haulm(s), havels, horns, hucks, hulkings, hulls, olves, pails, piles, prickles, sharps, spears, spikes, tails, whiskers, yokes, zears

awry *adj* ASKEW, describing a picture that is not hanging straight IX.1.3. əɹɔɪ Ess, əɹəɪ Brk

ax *n* the AXLE of a horse-drawn farmcart I.9.11. ɪks Sx, aks W

axle *n [Show a picture of a farmcart.] What do you call this, the beam or rod connecting the two wheels?* I.9.11. ɛksl Nb Db Nf, ɛksɫ Gl O C Bk Ess K D, ɛksɪɫ W, ɛksʊɫ Brk Sr Ha, ɛksʊ Ess Sr K Ha Sx, ɛksəɫ Bk, ɛɪkəsl Nf, ɛkstl Gl, ɛʃəl Nf, æksl La Sa He Wo L Nf Co, æksɫ Man He O Hu Nf Sf Hrt Ess MxL So W K Co, æksʊl Gl, æksʊɫ Gl Brk, æksʊ So Brk Sr K Sx, æksəl Gl Nf, æksəɫ He Mon Gl Bk, ækstɫ Ess, aksl Nb Cu Du We La Y Ch Db Sa St Wo Wa Nt L, haksl Du, aksɫ Wa Mon Gl O Lei R Nth Bk Hrt So W Co D Do Ha, aksɪl Y Ch Db, aksʊɫ Wa O, aksəl Du La Y, aksəɫ Bk Bd Hrt, askl He, asl La Y, ɑːksʊ Sx. ⇒ ax, axle-tree, ax-tree, cart-arm, cart-axle, *extra* ⇒ ax-tree

axle-box 1. *n* the HUB of a cart-wheel I.9.7. aksɫbɒks D

2. *n* the metal BUSH at the centre of a cart-wheel I.9.8. æksɫbɒks So, aksɫbɒks So D Do

axle-case *n* the metal BUSH at the centre of a cart-wheel I.9.8. ɛksɫkeːs D, aksɫkeːs D

axle-pin 1. *n* a LINCH-PIN holding a wheel on a cart I.9.12. æksʊpɪn Brk, akslpɪn Nb Y L, asəlpɪn Y, aslpɪn La

2. *n* a metal linch-pin. æksɫpɪn Wo, akslpɪn La

axles *npl* MOLARS VI.5.7. aʃlz Y

axle-teeth *npl* MOLARS VI.5.7. eːzltiːθ Cu, ɛsəltiːθ Y, aksɪltiːθ Y, akslti:θ Du La Y, aksəltiːθ La Y, asltiːθ Nb Cu Du We, haslt⁹iːθ Du, azltiːθ Cu, asltɪəθ Cu, asltᵉiθ Du, asəltɛɪθ Y, asltəɪθ Y, aʃltəɪθ Y, asəltəɪθ Y

axle-tree *n* the AXLE of a horse-drawn farmcart I.9.11. ɛˑksltɹɪ K, ɛksɫtɹɪ Ess, ɛklstɹɪ Nf, ɛklstə Nf, æksltɹɪ Man, æksɫtɹɪ He Wo, æksʊɫtrɪ Gl, æksəɫtɹɪ He Mon, æksɫtɹɪ Sf, æklstɹə Nf, ækʔəlstə Nf, æːksltɹɪ Sa, aksltɹɪ La Y Sa Wo L, aksɫtɹɪ Wo Mon Nth, aksltrɪ Cu We, aksəltɹɪ Y, aksltrəɪ Y, asltɹɪ Cu Du We Y, asltri Cu We, asəltɹɪ Y, asəltɹɛɪ Y, asltrəɪ Y

ax-tree *n* the AXLE of a horse-drawn farmcart I.9.11. ɛkstʁɪ Nb, ɛkstɹə Sf, ækstɹɪ He Mon, akstɹɪ Gl, akstrɪ Cu, akstɹɪ Sa

aye *adv* YES VIII.8.13(a). ɛɪ L W, æɪ Y He Mon, aɪ Nb Cu Du We La Y Ch Db Sa Wo Nt L Lei So*[old]* W Ha, aːɪ Sa He, ɑɪ La Db He Nt, ɑːɪ He Wo Gl, ɒɪ Sa Wo Gl

ayer *n* FATHER VIII.1.1(a). eɪə Man*[informal]*

B

baa *1. vi-3prpl* bulls BELLOW III.10.2. baˠ: W [*queried BM*]

2. *vi-3prpl* sheep BLEAT III.10.5. be: Y Gl O, bɛː Db St Mon Gl Nf Sf So W D Do Ha, bɛə Lei R Ess, bɛəˠ Sx, bæː Lei R C Nf Ess Sx, bæːz Gl, bæː-æ Nf, baː La Y Sa He Wa O L Nf Sf Bk Hrt Ess So W Co D Do, baːz Gl Ha, baːʔ Bk, baˠ: Gl, bɑ: Y St Nf Brk Sr K Ha Sx, bɑːz MxL, bɑˑ˩: K, bɑˠ: K, bəˠ: Ess

baa out *viphr-3prpl* bulls BELLOW III.10.2. baˠ:ɽ əʊt W [*queried SBM*]

baba *n* GRANNY VIII.1.8(b). bæbæ Brk

bache *n* a SLOPE IV.1.10. bætʃ So

bachy* *adj* sloping, ⇐ SLOPE IV.1.10. bætʃi So

back *1. n* the RIDGE of a stack of corn II.7.2. bak Co

2. *n* the SCRUFF (of the neck) VI.6.2. bæk Hu Nf Sf Ess MxL K, bak Y Ch O L Bd

3. *n* **back of your leg** the CALF of the leg VI.9.7. bak ə jə lɛg Cu

4. *adv* AGO VII.3.1. bæk Hu, bak Y L Nth Bd

5. *n* **on her back** waning, referring to the moon, ⇐ to WANE VII.6.5(b). ɒn ə bak Y

6. *adv* BACKWARDS IX.1.7(a). bak We

back-biter *n* a LOOSE *PIECE OF* SKIN at the bottom of a finger-nail VI.7.11. bækbæɪtəˠ He, bækbʌɪtəˠ He, *pl* bækbəɪtəˠz He, *pl* bakbaɪtəz Db, bakbɑɪtə Db, *pl* bakbɑˑɪtəz Lei, *pl* bakbɒɪtəz St

back-biting *v-ing* GOSSIPING VIII.3.5(a). bakbaɪtɪn Y, bakbəɪtʔən Do

back-board *1. n* the TAILBOARD of a cart I.10.2. bækbɔːd Ess, bækboˑəd Sf, bakbɔːd St Wo Wa Lei R, bakbɔˠːd̥ Sa, bakbɔːəd St, bakbɔːd Mon, bakboˑəd Ch Wa Nth, bakbuəd St Lei

2. *n* an END-BOARD of a cart I.10.4. bækbɔːᵊd Sf, bakbɛʊəd Ch, bakbœːd Du, bakbɔːd Wo Lei, bakbɔˠːd̥ Sa W, bakbɔəd Wa O L, bakbɔːəd St, bakbɔəɽd O, bakboˑəd Ch Db Nt Nth, bakboəˠd̥ Gl, bakbuəd We Y Db, bakbuˑəˠd̥ Bk, bakbuːɽd̥ D

back bodkin *n* an EVENER, the main swingle-tree of a horse-drawn plough harness I.8.4. bak bɒdkɪn W

back-cage *n* an END-BOARD of a cart I.10.4. bakkeədʒ La

back-court *n* a FARMYARD I.1.3. bakkɔˠ:ʈ W

back-crook *1. n* a CRANE on which a kettle is hung over a domestic fire V.3.4. bakkɽʊk Do

2. *n* the vertical BAR or CHAIN of a crane over a domestic fire V.3.5(b). bakkɽʏk D

3. *n* the vertical part of a crane over a domestic fire, consisting of a *BAR* or *CHAIN* and a HOOK(/*CROOK*) V.3.5b+c. *pl* bakkɽuks So

back-cut *v* to CLEAR grass at the edges of a field II.9.5. *-ing* bakkʊtɪn Lei; **have a backcut** ɛv ə bɛkkʌt K

back-door *n* the TAILBOARD of a cart I.10.2. bakduə Y Nt

back-end *n* AUTUMN VII.3.7. 'bæk'ɛnd Sa He, bæke³n Man[*old*], 'bak'ɛnd Ch Sa St, 'bakɛnd Sa St[*old x1*] He[*late autumn*], bak'ɛnd Nb Cu Ch Db, bakɛnd Nb Du We La[*old x1*] Y[*old and more usual x1*] Ch Db St[*old*] Wo[*late autumn*] Wa[*rare x1*] Nt L Lei R Nth, 'bakɛn Sa, bak'ɛn Cu; **back-end of the year** bakɛnd ə ðə jɪə Nt L R Nth C, bakɛnd ə ð jɪə Nt, bakɛnd ə t jɪə Y, bakɛnd ə tð ɪə Ch, bakɛnd ə d ɪə Y, bɑkɛnd ə t jɪə Y; **back-end of year** bakɛnd ə jɪə Lei

back-end-board *n* an END-BOARD of a cart I.10.4. bakɛndbuəd Y

back-fiend *n* a LOOSE *PIECE OF* SKIN at the bottom of a finger-nail VI.7.11. bakfiːn Wa, *pl* bakfɛnz Ch

back-flake *n* a rear cart-ladder, ⇐ CART-LADDERS I.10.5. bakflɛɪk Y

back-flea *n* a LOOSE *PIECE OF* SKIN at the bottom of a finger-nail VI.7.11. bækfliː Sa [*queried WMBM*]

back-friend *n* a LOOSE *PIECE OF* SKIN at the bottom of a finger-nail VI.7.11. bækfɪɛn Sa Wo Gl, bakfɪɛnd Sa, bakfɪɛn Sa Wo, *pl* bakfɪɛnz Ch Db Wa Gl Lei, *pl* bakfɽɛnz W, bakfɪan Sa, *pl* bakfɪənz We

back-fringe *n* a LOOSE *PIECE OF* SKIN at the bottom of a finger-nail VI.7.11. *pl* bakfɪɪnʒɪz Ch, *pl* bakfɪɪndʒəz Ch, bakfɪɛnʒ Gl

back-hack *v* to CLEAR grass at the edges of a field II.9.5. bakak St

back-handed *1. adj* LEFT-HANDED VI.7.13(a). bækændɪd He Ha, bakhandɪd Cu, bakandɪd La, bakandəd Do

2. *adj* CLUMSY, describing a person VI.7.14. bakandɪd Y, bakandəd C

back-hander *n* a LEFT-HANDED person VI.7.13(a). bækændəˡ Ha

back-heck *n* an END-BOARD of a cart I.10.4. bakɛk Y

back-hole* *n* the scullery of a house, ⇐ LIVING-ROOM V.2.1. bakɔɪl Y

back-house *1. n* the LIVING-ROOM of a house V.2.1. bækhɛʊs Nf, bækəs Sf, bæˑkʔəs Sf, bakɛʊs Bk

2. *n* a scullery. bækəs Nf, bæk?əs Nf, bakɛus Bk

3. *n* a PANTRY V.2.6. bakhuːs Nb*[rare]*

backing *n* COAL-DUST V.4.1. bækɪn Man, bakɪn Db L Lei

backing-arse *adv* BACKWARDS IX.1.7(a). bakənaːs Y

back-kitchen *1. n* the LIVING-ROOM of a house V.2.1. bæˈkɪtʃɪn Wo, bækkɪtʃɪn Nf, bæk?kɪtʃɪn Nf

2. *n* a scullery. bækˈkɪtʃɪn Sa, bakkɪtʃɪn Ch Wo Wa L Lei Y, bakɪtʃɪn Cu La Y, bakɪtʃn Du, bɑkkɪtʃɪn Y

back-ladder *n* a rear cart-ladder, ⇐ CART-LADDERS I.10.5. *pl* bakladəᵗz Bk

back lantree *n* an EVENER, the main swingle-tree of a horse-drawn plough harness I.8.4. bak lantɹiː He

back-meadow *n* a PADDOCK I.1.10. bækmɛdə Ess

back out *vtphr* to AGREE *WITH* somebody VIII.8.12. bak ... aut La, bak ... uːt Du Y

back over *adv* HEAD OVER HEELS IX.1.10. bak auə Du, bak ɒuə Du, bak ɒuʷəᴿ Du, bakɔuəᴿ Nb

back part *n* a DRAIN in a cow-house I.3.8. bak pəᵗːt Gl

back-place *n* the LIVING-ROOM of a house V.2.1. bakpleːs Gl

back-post *n* the SHUTTING-POST of a gate IV.3.4. bɛkpɔust Ess

back-rail *n* a rear cart-ladder, ⇐ CART-LADDERS I.10.5. bakɹɛˑəl L

back-rest *n* a STICK used to support the shaft of a cart I.11.1. bakɹɪst Nb

back-room *n* the LIVING-ROOM of a house V.2.1. bækɹum Ess, bækɹuːm Ess

backs *npl* the RIDGES between furrows in a ploughed field II.3.2. *sg* bæk K

back-shelving *n* an END-BOARD of a cart I.10.4. bakʃɛlvɪn Cu

backside *1. n* the BUTT of a sheaf of corn II.6.4. baksaid Sa

2. *n* the ARSE VI.9.2. bɛksaɪd K, bɛksʌɪd Sr, bæksaɪd Nf, bæksɔɪd Ess, bæksʌɪd Sr, bæksəɪd Brk, baksaɪd Du

back-side-board *n* an END-BOARD of a cart I.10.4. bæksɔɪdbɔːd Sr

back-skirt* *n* a wrapper worn over a DIAPER V.11.3. bæk?skəːt Nf

back-slasher *n* a HEDGING-BILL IV.2.5. bakslaʃəᵗ O

back-stay *n* an END-BOARD of a cart I.10.4. bakstɛɪ St

backstone *n* a GIRDLE for baking cakes V.7.4(b). bækstoːn He Mon, bækstoːun Mon Gl, bækstun Gl, bækstən So, bakstɪn Y*[for oat-cakes x1]*, bakstoːn Sa, bakstuən La*[for oat-cakes]*, bakstən La*[for oat-cakes]* Y*[for oat-cakes x1, old x1]* Ch*[old x1]* Db St*[old x1]*

back-strap *1. n* the BELLY-BAND of the harness of a cart-horse I.5.7. bækstɹæp So

2. *n* the GIRTH of the harness of a cart-horse

I.5.8. bækstɹæp Nf

back-swath *1. v* to CLEAR grass at the edges of a field II.9.5. bakswaθ Db St

2. *n* grass at the edges of a field, uncut by the first cutting of the mowing machine. bækswæθ He, bækswaːθ Mon, bækswaːð Gl, bækswɒθ Mon, bakswaθ Sa He Lei, bakswɒθ Mon, bakswɔːθ O, bakswɔːv W, *-s* bakswɔːz Ha

backsyfore *1. adv* BACKWARDS IX.1.7(a). baksɪvɔᵗː Co

2. *adv/adj* back to front, reversed. baksivɔᵗː D

back-teeth *npl* MOLARS VI.5.7. bɛktiːθ Nf K, bæktɪθ He, bæktiːθ Ess MxL Brk, baktiːθ Y Wa O Lei R So K, bɑktiːθ O

back-tie-strap *n* the CRUPPER of the harness of a cart-horse I.5.9. baktɪstɹap O

back up *vtphr* to AGREE *WITH* somebody VIII.8.12. Eng exc. Man R Brk Co D Do

backward *adv* BACKWARDS IX.1.7(a). bɛkəd K, bækwəd Nf Brk Sr Sx, bækəd Ess K, bækwəᵗd̩ Mon, bækwəᵗːd̩ So, bækəᵗːd̩ So*[old]*, bækəᵗːɾd̩ Sx, bakwɒɹd Y, bakwɔᴿd Nb, bakwɜᴵːd La, bakwəd Nb Cu Du We Y Db Wa, bakət Ch Db, bakəd Du*[rare]* Y L Nth, bakəᴵt La, bakəᴵd La, bakəᵗd̩ Wa Ha, bakwəᵗːd̩ So Co D Do, bakəᵗːd̩ Gl So W Co D Do

backwards *adv Here are two ways of walking. This way, I'm walking .... [And this way, ...]* IX.1.7(a). Eng. ⇒ **aft, arse-afore, arse-first, back, backing-arse, backward, backwards-road, backwards-way, backways, backsyfore, heelway**

backward(s) over *adv* HEAD OVER HEELS IX.1.10.

no -s: bakwəd ɒuə Cu

-s: bakwədz auə Y, bakwədz ɑuə Y, bakədz auə Y, bakwədz ɒuə Nb Cu We

backwards-road *1. adv* BACKWARDS IX.1.7(a). bakədzɹuəd Y, bakəsɹuəd La

2. *adv* HEAD OVER HEELS IX.1.10. bakədzɹuəd Y, bakəɹtsɹuəd La, bakəsɹuəd La

backwards-road over *adv* HEAD OVER HEELS IX.1.10. bakəᴵtsɹuəd ɔɹə La

backwards-way *adv* BACKWARDS IX.1.7(a). bækwədswɛɪ Man

backwards-way first *adv* HEAD OVER HEELS IX.1.10. bakədzwɛə fɒst Y

backwards-way over *adv* HEAD OVER HEELS IX.1.10. bakwədzweː ɒuə Y, bakətsweː ɔɹə La, bakəstwɛˑə ɑuə Y

back-water(s) *n* the AFTERBIRTH that comes from a cow's uterus after a calf is born III.1.13.

no -s: bækwæˑtəᴵ Man

-s: bækwæˑtəs Man

backways *adv* BACKWARDS IX.1.7(a). bækweɪs Man, bækwəs Man

back whipper *n* an EVENER, the main swingle-tree of a horse-drawn plough harness I.8.4. bɑk wɪpəɾ O

back-wire *n* the GRASS-NAIL of a scythe II.9.9. bakwaɪəᵗ: D

backy *n* COLT'S-FOOT II.2.7. baki So

back-yard *n* a FARMYARD I.1.3. bakjaːd Cu, bakjaᵗːd̩ Gl Co

bacon-bing *n* a container for bacon, ⇐ CORN-BIN I.7.4. beˈəknbɪŋ L

bacon-dip *n* BACON-FAT V.7.5(b). biːkndɪp Ch, beːkndɪp Y Db, beːkəndɪp Y, beəkndɪp Y

bacon-dripping *n* BACON-FAT V.7.5(b). beːkndɹɪpɪn Ch, beɪkndɹɪpɪn He, beˈəkndɹɪpɪn Bk, beɪkəndɹɪpɪn Ess, beɪknbɹɪpm Ess, beəkndɹɪpɪn Y, bæɪkndɹɪpɪn K

bacon-fat *n* [*What do you call the fat from roasting meat?] And from bacon?* V.7.5(b). Eng exc. Man. ⇒ **bacon-dip, bacon-dripping, bacon-gravy, bacon-grease, bacon-liquor, collop-fat, dip, dipping, dippo, drip, dripping, fat, grease, lard, liquor, pork-fat, rasher-fat, skimmings;** ⇒ also **dipping-bread, pot-skimmings**

bacon-gravy *n* BACON-FAT V.7.5(b). beːɪkngɹeːɪvɪ Mon Gl, bjʊkngɹevɪ He

bacon-grease *n* BACON-FAT V.7.5(b). beːkngʁiːs Nb, beːkəngʁiːz Nb, beːkŋgɹaɪs Ha, beɪkngɹɪiːs Y

bacon-hog *n* a male HOG III.8.8. beːkŋɒg O

bacon-liquor *n* BACON-FAT V.7.5(b). beːknlɪkəᵗ Sa He, beːkənlɪkəᵗ Sa, beːɪknlɪkəᵗ He Wo, beɪknlɪkə St Wo, beɪknlɪkəᴵ St

bacon-pig *n* a male or female HOG III.8.8. beːknpɪg Gl

bad *1. adj* A husband asks his wife: *Why didn't you fry all three eggs? She answers: Because one was a ... ONE.* V.7.11. Eng. ⇒ **addle, addled** *one, bad egg, bad one, rotten one,* settly, setty, stale *one*
2. adj **bad for calving** *IN* CALF III.1.10. *3prsg* bad vəᵗ: kaːvən D
3. adj **go bad** to CURDLE, referring to milk V.5.9. gʊ bæˈᴵd Ess, goː baˈd So, guː bad So
4. adj RANCID, describing bacon V.7.9. bɛd Ess, bæd Sx, bæːd Nf *[considered u.r. EMBM]*
5. adj **go bad, turn bad** to SPOIL, referring to meat or fish V.7.10. **go bad** gɒʊ bɛd Sx, gɔʊ bɛd Sx, gʊuː beəd Ess, gɒʊ bæd Sx, gɔʊ bæˈd Brk, goː bæd So Brk, gʊ bæd Y He Gl Ess, guː bæd Sr D, gʌʊ bæːd Ess K, gou bæˈd Nf, gəʊ bæːd Hrt, gou bæəd Man, gan bæːəd Nb, gan bad Nb Cu Du Y, ga bad Cu La Y, gʊ bad La Y, gɔː bad Y, gɔʊ bad Lei, goː bad Sa So W Do, gou baˈd O Ha, gʊ bad Wo Gl L, guː bad Y Ch So Do, gʊə bad La L, gə bad Lei R; **turn bad** təᵗːŋ bæd So, tʌn bæˈᴵd Ess
6. adj ILL, describing a person who is unwell VI.13.1(b). beːd So, bæd Nb Ess So, bæˈəd Nb, bæːᴵd So, bad Nb Cu Du La Y Ch Db St Wa Gl O Nt L Lei

R Nth Hu C Bk Bd Hrt Ess Co Do Ha; **right bad** ɹʌɪt bæd Nf
7. adj SICK, describing an animal that is unwell VI.13.1(c). bɛd Sr, bæd He Mon Nf Sf Ess So Brk Sx, bæːd Sa He Wo Gl Ess, bæˈəd Nb Sf, bæːᴵd So, bad Nb Cu Du We La Y Ch Db Sa St Wo Wa Gl O Nt L Lei R Nth Hu Bk Hrt W Co D Do Ha, badn La, baːd Sa He Wo Mon Gl O Ess, bɑːd Wo

bad-collared *adj* RESTIVE, describing a horse III.5.6. badkɔləd L

badge *v* to CLEAR grass at the edges of a field II.9.5. badʒ La*[with scythe]* Ch Db St

badge out *vtphr* to CLEAR grass at the edges of a field II.9.5. badʒ ... aːᵊt Lei, badʒ ... aʊt St*[with scythe]*

badger *n What do you call that grey animal that lives in burrows; it fights fiercely when drawn out by dogs?* IV.5.9. Eng. ⇒ **brock, pate**

badging-hook *1. n* a BILLHOOK IV.2.6. badʒɪnyːk Ch, badʒənyːk Ch, badʒɪnuːk St
2. n an implement larger than a billhook, used for cutting corn. badʒɪnuːk Ch

bad head *n* a HEADACHE VI.1.6. bæˈd hiːd Nb, bad hiːd Nb Cu Du, bad iːd Cu, bad jɛd Ch *[marked u.r. WMBM]*

badly *1. adj* ILL, describing a person who is unwell VI.13.1(b). bædlɪ Hu, badlɪ Cu Du We La Y Db Nt L Nth Bk, badlɛ Y
2. adj SICK, describing an animal that is unwell VI.13.1(c). bædlɪ Hu, badlɪ Nb Cu Du We La Y Db Nt L Nth, badɬɪ Lei, badlə Y

bad pap *n* a BLIND TEAT III.2.7. bad pap Nth

bad quarter *n* a BLIND TEAT III.2.7. bæd kwɔːᵊtə Ess, bæd kwɔˈtəɹ Brk, bæd kwɔːdə Ess, bæd kwɔːdəᵗ: So, bæd kwɔːʔə Ess, bæd kwɔːʔəᴵ Sr, bæd kwɔᵗːtəᵗ: So, bæd kwɔᵗːd̩əᵗ: Do, bad kwɔːtə L Hu

bad teat *n* a BLIND TEAT III.2.7. bæd tɪt Sf, bad tɪt O, bad tɪʔ O, bad tɛt Bd

baffs *npl* BOOTS VI.14.23. bafs Nth

bag *1. n* [*If you wished to please a child, you might say: Here's 3d, go and buy yourself (some sweets).] And the child would take them away in a ....* V.8.5. Eng exc. Bk. ⇒ **bit of** *paper*, **cornet bag, goody-packet, packet,** *paper, paper bag,* **paper funnel, paper-packet, paper-parcel,** *piece of paper,* **satchel, screw of** *paper,* **some** *paper,* **square bag**
2. n a SACK in which grain is weighed I.7.2. bɛg D, bæg Nb Sa He Wo C Sf Ess Co, bag Cu Du We Y Ch Db Sa St Wa O L R C Bk Bd, *pl* bagz La, baːg Sa, bɑg Y
3. n the UTERUS of a cow III.2.4. bɛg K Sx, beəg Ess, bæg So Brk Co, bag So, baɪg Ha
4. n the UDDER of a cow III.2.5. bɛg Ess Sr K, beəg Ess, bæg He O L Hu Nf Sf Bk Ess So Brk

Sr, bæːg Ha, bæːg Wo Gl Ess MxL Sr, bæˡg Nf Sf
Ess, bæ·ᵊg Nb, bag Nb Cu Du We La Y Ch Db Sa St
Wa Gl O Nt L Lei R Nth Hu C Bk Bd Hrt K, baːg Wo
Mon Gl, bɑg Y O

5.1. *vt* to STOCK a cow III.3.6. *pt* bæ·gd MxL

5.2. *v* to stock. bag Nth, *-ing* bagɪn Db

6. *n* the scrotum of a horse, ⇐ SHEATH III.4.9.
bæ·g Ess, bæːg Wo

7. *n* a container for carrying horse-feed, ⇐
BASKET III.5.4. bɛg D, bag Ch*[for journey]* Co
[marked u.r. WMBM]

bag-apron *n* a working APRON made of sacking
V.11.2(a). bagapən St

bagging 1. *n* STRING used to tie up a grain-sack
I.7.3. bagɪn Bk

2. *v-ing* BAITING a horse when resting from work
III.5.2. bagɪn St, *v* bag La

3. *n* horse-feed. bagɪn La

4. *n* MEAL OUT VII.5.12. bagɪn La Sa St

bagging-hook *n* a BILLHOOK IV.2.6. bæginʊk Wo
Ess, bɛginʊk K

bagging(s) *n* a SNACK VII.5.11.
no -s: bagɪn La Ch Db St
-s: bagɪnz La Ch

bagging-string *n* STRING used to tie up a grain-sack
I.7.3. bagɪnstɹɪŋ Sa

bagies *n* TURNIPS II.4.1(b). *sg* beːgɪ Nb

bag-needle* *n* a NEEDLE for mending sacks
V.10.2(a). bagniːdl Wa

bags *n* A LOT (of money) VII.8.7. bagz Y

bag-skin *n* RENNET V.5.6. bagskɪn Ch, badʒskɪn
Ch

bag-tie *n* STRING used to tie up a grain-sack I.7.3.
bagtɔɪ Gl

bag up 1. *viphr* to show signs of calving, referring to
a cow with a swelling udder, ⇐ SHOWS SIGNS OF
CALVING III.1.12(a). *-ed* bɛgd ʌp Sr, *3prprogsg*
bɛgɪn ʌp Sr, *-ing* bɛgɪn ʌp Ess K Sx, *-ing* bɛgɪn ʊp
K, *-ed* bægd ɤp Nf, *prppl* bægɪn ʌp Sx, *-ing* bægɪn
ʌp Nf Ess Brk K Sx, *-ing* bægən ʌp Ess, *-ing* bægɪn
ʊp Ess, bag ʌp Bd, *-ing* bagɪn ʌp Bd Hrt, *-ing* bagɪn
ʊp La Ch Db Wa Nth, *3prprogsg* bagən ʊp Cu We,
-ing bagən ʊp C

2.1. *vtphr* to STOCK a cow III.3.6. *-ing* bɛgɪn ... ʌp
Sr, *-ed* bæ·g ... ʌp Sf, *-ing* bægɪn ... ʊp Brk, *-ing* bagɪn
... ʌp Ha, bag ... ʊp Du La Y St Wa L Lei, *-ing* bagɪn
... ʊp Ch R, *-ing* bagən ... ʊp Cu, bɑg ... ʊp Wo

2.2. *vphr* to stock. bɛg ʊp Db, *-ed* bɛgd ʌp Sx, bæg
ʌp Hu Bk, *-ing* bægɪn ʌp Sr K, bag ʌp O C Bk Bd
Hrt, bag ʊp Cu Du La Y Ch Db Nt L Nth, *-ing* bagɪn
ʊp St Lei; **letting them bag up** lɛʔɪn ðəm bɛg ʌp Ess

baikie-band *n* a rope TETHER for a cow I.3.4.
bɪəkɪband Nb

bail 1. *n* a rail separating stalls in a cow-house, ⇐
PARTITION I.3.2. beːɬ Ha *[marked u.r. SBM]*

2. *n* the GRASS-NAIL of a scythe II.9.9. beɪᵊɬ
Sf

3. *n* the YIELD of milk from a cow III.3.5. beɪᵊɬ
Nth

bailiff *n* a CARTMAN on a farm I.2.2. beɪləf Sf

bairn 1. *n* a CHILD VIII.1.2(b). beːʁən Nb,
beɔʁn Nb, beɔʁʁn Nb, bean NbL, beaʁn Nb, beːn
Y St, beːᵊn Cu Du Y, beːrn Cu, beːʁan Nb, beɔʁn
Nb, bean Du Y Nt L, bɛarn Cu, beaʁn Nb Du,
beaˡn L, be·əɹn Y, bæːn Du, bæˡɪn La, baɹn Y,
baːn Cu Du We Y*[old x1]*, baˡɪn La Y, bɑɹn Y

2. *n* a new-born girl, ⇐ GIRLS VIII.1.3(b).
bɛarn Cu

bairns *npl* CHILDREN VIII.1.2(a). beːʁənz Nb,
beɔʁnz Nb, beɔʁnz Nb, beɔʁʁnz Nb, beanz NbL,
beaʁnz Nb, beːnz Cu We St, beːᵊnz Du We,
beːrnz Cu, beənz Du We*[rare]* Y Nt L, beaʁnz
Du, bearnz Cu, beaʁnz Nb, beəɹnz Du, be·əˡnz
L, bæːnz Du, bæˡːnz La, baːnz Cu Du We
Y*[modern x1, old x1]*, baˡːnz La Y, bɑɹnz Y

baiseler *n* a COWMAN on a farm I.2.3. beːslɔʁ
Nb

bait 1.1. *vt* to FEED cattle III.3.1. bæɪt Sf

1.2. *v* to feed cattle. *-ing* beɪtɪn Brk

2. *n* an allowance of food given to a horse when
resting from work, ⇐ BAITING III.5.2. beːt Y Ch
Sa*[midday]*, beɪt Wa Hrt, beɪt Nb L Sr K Sx, beət
Y L, bæɪt Sf Ess MxL, baɪt Nf W

3. *n* a short meal given to a horse. beət Y

4. *n* CHAFF fed to horses III.5.3. beɪt O, bæɪt
Nth Ess

5. *n* FOOD V.8.2. bɪət Nb Du, be·ət Nb

6. *n* a SNACK VII.5.11. bɪət Du, beːt Nb*[old x1]*
Du La Y Sa Mon, beɪt He Wo, beːɪt He Wo, beat
La, beət Du*[old]* Y, beːt Cu We, beɪt Nb Wo Gl
K, bæɪt He Mon Gl Sx, baɪt Wo; **bit bait** bɪt bɪət
Du; **bit of bait** bɪt ə beət Sx

7. *n* MEAL OUT VII.5.12. bɪət Nb Du, beːt Nb
Cu Du La Y*[miner's word x1]* Sa Mon, beət Nb
Du Y, beːt Cu, beət Y, bæɪt Ess

baiting 1. *v-ing* *What is your word for giving*
horses their food while resting from work in the
field? III.5.2.

v-ing biːtɪn Ch St, *v* biːt Db, beːtɪn La Y Ch Sa
Wo Nt, beːtn Du, *v* beːt Cu We Db, *prppl* beɪtɪn
He Bk, beɪtn Nf, *v* beɪt Db Hrt, *v* be·at La, beətɪn
Y, *v* beət Nb La, beːtɪn We, *v* beːt Cu, beɪtɪn St
He Wo L Lei R Nth Bd Hrt Brk K Sx, *v* beɪt Du
Wa O, beɪʔɪn Sr, beɪtɪn Sf Ess, beɪʔn Ess, beətɪn
Y L, bæɪtɪn Y He Gl K, bæɪtn Sf Ess, bæɪtʔn Ess,
v bæɪt MxL, baɪtɪn Sa Wo Gl W, baɪʔɪn W, baɪtən
Do, *v* baɪt Ess

vt-ing beːtɪn Ha, bɛɪtɪn Bk Sx, bɛɪtn L, bæɪtn Nf,
baɪtɪn W Ha, baɪtn Nf, baɪtən Do Ha, bɒɪtən Do

2. *n* an allowance of food given to a horse when
resting from work. be·ɪtn Nf

⇒ **bagging, bait,** *dinner-time,* **docky, docky-bag, doddy-bag, feeding, foddering, fodder out, foddering up,** *give a bag of hay, give a* **bait,** *give a bit feed, give a bit of a feed, give a* **mouth-poke,** *give a nosebag, give a* **nose-bait,** *give a snack, give a snack of grub, give* **bait,** *give his* **docky,** *give his nosebag, give some nosebag, give the* **bever,** *give their* **bait,** *give their* **crib,** *give their feed, give their nosebag(s), give them the* **bait,** *give them the nosebag, give the nosebag, give the old horse a* **baiting** *in a nosebag, giving them a nosebag,* **grub,** *have a* **bait,** *have a feed,* **heck,** *hitch up their nosebags,* **nosebag, nosebag time, provand,** *put a nosebag on, put her nosebag on, put him in his nosebag, put his nosebag on, put on the nosebag, put the bags on, put their nosebags on, put the* **mouth-bag** *on, put the nosebag(s) on, put the old horse's nosebag on, put those nosebags on, putting the nosebags on them, put up their nosebag*

3.1. v-ing FEEDING horses in the stable III.5.1. beːtɪn La Mon Nt, beːʔɪn O, *v* beɪt Hrt, beɪtɪn Bk, beɪtn Nf, beːɪtɪn He Wo, bɛɪtɪn He Wo Wa L Lei R Nth Bd Hrt Brk K Sx, bɛɪʔɪn Sr, bɛɪtn Sf Ess, bɛɪʔn Ess, *v* bɛɪt O, bɛˑətɪn L, bæɪtɪn He Mon K, bæɪtn Sf Ess, bæɪtʔn Ess, *v* bæɪt O MxL, baɪtɪn W, baɪtən Do, *v* baɪt Ess

3.2. vt-ing feeding horses. beːtɪn Ha, bɛɪtɪn Bk Sx, bɛɪtn L, *vt* bɛˑət L, bæɪtn Nf, baɪtɪn W, əbaɪtɪn Wo, baɪʔɪn W, baɪtn Nf, baɪtən Do Ha, bɒɪtən Do

4. n a feed given to horses. bɛˑɪtn Nf

baiting-sieve *n* a BASKET for carrying horse-feed III.5.4. beːtɪn sɪv Brk*[round, wicker bottom],* bɛɪtɪnsɪv O*[wicker, no handle],* bɛɪʔn sɪv K, bæɪtɪnsɪv O, bæɪtnsɪv Ess

baiting up *vtphr-ing* FEEDING horses in the stable III.5.1. bɛɪʔɪn ... ʌp Ess

bait sieve *n* a wooden BASKET, 3 feet in diameter, with a cane bottom and no handles, for carrying horse-feed III.5.4. bɛɪt sɪv K

bake-board *n* a PASTE-BOARD V.6.5. bjɛkbɔːd Nb*[old],* bjɛkbɔ^ʁːd Du, bɪakbɒ^ʁd Nb, bɪakbøːd Nb, bɪakbøəd Nb, bɪakbuəd Du, bɪakboəd Nb, bekbɔːˀrd Cu, beːkbɔːd Nb, beəkbɔ^ʁːd Nb, bɛkbɔ^ʁːd Nb, bɛːkbɔːd Cu, bakbɔːd Cu, bakbuəd Y, bakbuəᵈd La

baked *adj* TANGLED, describing hair VI.2.5. bɪɛkt Du *[queried NBM]*

baker *n* a GIRDLE for baking cakes V.7.4(b). beːkəˤː Co

bakestone *n* a GIRDLE for baking cakes V.7.4(b). beːkstoːn Sa He Mon Gl, beːkstwun Gl, beːɪkstoːn He

baking-board *n* a PASTE-BOARD V.6.5. bɪakɪnbɔːd We Y, bɪakənbɔːd Cu, bɪakɪnbɔˑəd Y, bɪakɪnbuəd Y, bɪəkɪnbuəd Nb Cu Y, beːkɪnbɔˤːd̩ Sa, beːkɪnboːəˤd̩ Sa, beːɪkɪnboːəˤd̩ He, beːkɪnbuəd Y, beːkɪnbuəɹd La, beːkɪnbuəᵈd La Ch, beɪkɪnboˑəᵈd Man, beɪəknboᵊd Man, beakɪnbɔːd

Du, beakɪnbuəd We La, beəkɪnbuəd La Y, bɛːkɪnbuəd Y, bɛɪkɪnbɔːd MxL, bɛɪknbɔːd Nf, bakɪnbuəd Y

baking-iron *n* a GIRDLE for baking cakes V.7.4(b). beːkɪnaɪəˤː Co, beːkŋaɪəˤː Co, beːkənaɪəˤː D, beːkɪnɒɪəˤːn̩ D

baking-tin *n* a GIRDLE for baking cakes V.7.4(b). beːkɪntɪn Wo

balancer *1. n* an EVENER on a horse-drawn plough I.8.4. baлənsə St

2. n a STICK used to support the shaft of a cart I.11.1. baлənsə Nf

balch *adj* BALD VI.2.3. bɒɫtʃ Wa

balch bird *n* a NESTLING IV.7.1. bɒɫtʃ bəˤːd̩ Wa

balcher *n* a NESTLING IV.7.1. bɒɫtʃəˤ Nth, bɔʊɫtʃəˡ O, boɫʃə Nth

balch-headed *adj* BALD VI.2.3. bɒɫtʃjɛdɪd Wa

balchin *n* a NESTLING IV.7.1. bɒɫtʃɪn St Lei, bɒɫtʃɪn Nth, bɒɫʃɪn Lei R, bɒɫʃɪn Lei Nth, bɒɫʃən Wa, *pl* bɒɫʃɪnz Wa, bɔːɫtʃɪn St, *pl* bɔːɫʃɪnz Wo

balch over *viphr* to OVERTURN, referring to a cart I.11.5. *-ed* bɒɫtʃt ɔʊvəˡ O

bald *adj* A man who has lost his hair you say is .... VI.2.3. Eng. ⇒ **balch, balch-headed, bald-head,** *bald-headed,* **bald-pate, bald-pated, bald-polled, baldy, baldy-headed, bare, slape**

bald-arse *n* a NESTLING IV.7.1. *pl* bɔːldaˤːʂɪz Bk*[perhaps facetious]*

bald-head *adj* BALD VI.2.3. bæˀldhiːd Nb, bɔːlɪəd La

bald one *n* a NESTLING IV.7.1. *pl* bɔːˀd ənz Bk

bald-pate *adj* BALD VI.2.3. bɔːpeːt Ch

bald-pated *adj* BALD VI.2.3. baːɫdpeːtəd D

bald-polled *adj* BALD VI.2.3. baːɫpɔːɫd D, bɔːɫpoːɫd D

baldy *1. n* a NESTLING IV.7.1. bɒldɪ Sa, *pl* bɔːldɪz Sa

2. adj BALD VI.2.3. bæˀᵊldɪ Nb, baːldɪ Du

baldy-headed *adj* BALD VI.2.3. bæˀəlɪhiːdəd Nb, baːlɪhiːdəd Du, baːlɪ-eɪdɪd Du, baːlɪheɪdɪd Du, bɔːldɪiːdɪd Y, bɔːl^ɪiːdɪd We, bɔːlɪ-ɛdɪd MxL

baler *n* a SCOOP used to take water out of a boiler V.9.9. beələ^ʁ Nb, bɛɪɫəˤ Sr

balk *1. vt* to guzzle a drink, ⇐ GUZZLES VI.5.13(a). *-ing* boːkɪn D

2. vi to WARP, referring to wood IX.2.9. bɔːk Sf

balker *1. n* a WHETSTONE made of stone II.9.10. balkəˤː Co, baˤːkəˤː Co D, bɑˤːkəˤː D, baˤːgəˤː D, bɔːɫkəˤː So D, bɔˤːkəˤː So, bɔˤːkəˤː So

2. n a whetstone made of unspecified material. baˤːkəˤː D

ball *1. n* the CLOG on a horse's tether I.4.3. bɔːɫ So Do

2. n the PALM of the hand VI.7.5. bɔːl Sa; **ball**

of my/the/thy*/your hand bɔːl ə t and Y, bɔːl ə ðɪ
and Y, bɔːl əv jəɹ and L, bɔːl ə jəɹ and Ch Db St L,
bɔː ə mɪ and La, bɔː ə jəɹ and Db /[ðɪ] *taken as your
BM]*

3. n **ball of my/the/your leg** the CALF of the leg
VI.9.7. **ball of my leg** baː ə mɪ lɛg Cu; **ball of the leg**
baˑl ə ðə lɛˑg Nb; **ball of your leg** bæˀl ə jə leˀg Nb

4. n a HALO round the moon VII.6.4. bɔːɫ D

ball-bag *n* the scrotum of a horse, ⇐ SHEATH
III.4.9. bɔːˀɫbag Hrt

ballock-handed *adj* LEFT-HANDED VI.7.13(a).
baləkandɪd Y, baləkandəd Nt

ball-string *n* STRING used to tie up a grain-sack
I.7.3. bɔːɫstɹɪŋ Hrt

balmed up *adj* STICKY, describing a child's hands
VIII.8.14. baːmd ʌp Sf, bɔːmd ʊp St*[old x1]*, boʊmd
ʊp St

balm up *vtphr* to DIRTY a floor V.2.8. baːm ... ʌp
Ess

balmy *adj* STICKY, describing a child's hands
VIII.8.14. baːmɪ Ess

balsers *n* SWEETS V.8.4. bɔːsəˤːẓ Ha *[queried
SBM]*

bams *npl* LEGGINGS VI.14.18. bamz W

band *1. n* a TETHER for a cow, made of iron or rope
I.3.4. band Nb

2. n a chain tether. band Cu

3. n STRING used to tie up a grain-sack I.7.3. bænd
Y So, band Du La Y Db Nt L, bant La Db St, bɑnt Ch,
bɒnd Sa, bɒnt Db, bʊn Sa

4. n TWINE used to fasten thatch on a stack
II.7.7(b1). bæˑnd MxL, band Du Y Db Sa L, ban Lei

5. n KNEE-STRAPS used to lift the legs of working
trousers VI.14.17. bant Db; **bit of band** bɪt ə bænd Y,
bɪt ə band Y

6. n the iron TIRE round a cart-wheel I.9.10. bænd
Sa He Mon Gl, band Sa Wo Mon O

band-hook *n* a ROPE-TWISTER II.7.8. bandʏːk
Sa

band-maker *n* a ROPE-TWISTER II.7.8.
bæˑnmæɪkə MxL, bandmɛkə Db

bands *1. npl* two iron strips forming the TIRE round
a cart-wheel I.9.10. banz Gl, bandz Gl

2. n ROPES used to fasten thatch on a stack
II.7.7(b2). banz Y, bɒnz Wo*[straw or twine]*

3. npl the HINGES of a door V.1.11a. bæˀndz Nb,
bæˀnz Nb, bandz Nb*[old]* Du

band-twirler *n* a ROPE-TWISTER II.7.8.
bandtwaˡːɹləɹ La

band-twister *n* a ROPE-TWISTER II.7.8. bɛntwɪstə
Hrt Ess, bændtwɪstə L, bæntwɪstə Ess, bæntwɪstəˤ
Mon, bandtwɪstə Nb Y L, bandtwɪstəɹ Y, bandtwɪstəɹ
O, banttwɪstə La Lei, bantwɪstə La Nt Lei R C Bd

band-winder *n* a ROPE-TWISTER II.7.8.
bændwəɪndə Mon

bandy *adj* BOW-LEGGED VI.9.6. bændɪ Man
Ess MxL Brk, bandɪ Wa

bandy-kneed *adj* BOW-LEGGED VI.9.6.
bandɪnˡiːd Sa

bandy-legged *1. adj* KNOCK-KNEED VI.9.5.
bændɪlɛgd Ess, bandɪlɛgd La Y O

2. adj BOW-LEGGED VI.9.6. bɛndɪlɪgd Ess,
bɛndɪlɛgd K, bɛndɪlɛgɪd K, bɛndɪlɛgəd Sr,
bɛəndɪlɪgd Ess, bændɪlɛgd He Nf Sf Ess Sr K Sx,
bændɪlɛgɪd He Wo Mon Gl So Brk K, bantɪlɛgd
Y Ch, bandɪlɛgt Nth, bandɪlɛgd We La Y Ch Db
Sa Wo Nt Hrt, bandilɛgd D, bandɪlɛgɪd Gl,
bandɪɫɛgɪd W D Ha

bang-down *n* the FLAP at the front of old-
fashioned trousers VI.14.16. baŋdaʊn La

bang-hand *adj* LEFT-HANDED VI.7.13(a).
baŋant La

bang-handed *adj* LEFT-HANDED VI.7.13(a).
bɛŋgandəd Db, baŋandɪd We Y, baŋgandɪd Ch

bank *1. n* a CLAMP in which potatoes are stored
out of doors II.4.6. bæŋk Nf

2. n a CUTTING of hay II.9.15. baŋk Y

3. n a SLOPE IV.1.10. bæŋk Wo, baŋk We Y Sa
St He Wo Wa Gl Bk, bɒŋk Ch Sa St He

4. n a hill. bæŋk He, baŋk Du*[steep x1]*, bɒŋk St,
pl bɒŋks Sa

5. n a hillside. baŋk Gl

bank-high *adj* IN FLOOD, describing a river
IV.1.4. bæŋkəɪ Brk

bank-hole *n* a man-made hole in a wall through
which rabbits and hares can pass, ⇐
SHEEP-HOLE IV.2.8. *-s* bʌŋkoːlz Gl

bank-hook *n* a BILLHOOK IV.2.6. bæŋkʌk He,
bɒŋkɛʊk St

banky *adj* STEEP, describing a hill IV.1.11.
bæŋkɪ He Gl, baŋkɪ We, bɒŋkɪ Ch

bannicking *vbln* **give him a good bannicking** to
BEAT a boy on the buttocks VIII.8.10. gɪv ɪm ə
gʊd bænɪkɪn Sr

bannister-brush* *n* a short, stiff-haired hand-
BRUSH V.9.11. bænɪstəˡbɹʌʃ Brk

ban-stickles *npl* MINNOWS IV.9.9. banstɪkɫz
Bk *[marked u.r. and interpreted as 'stickleback'
EMBM]*

bantams *npl* MINNOWS IV.9.9. bantəmz Gl

banty-tickles *npl* MINNOWS IV.9.9. baːntɪtɪkɫz
Gl

bar *1. n [What do you call that old-fashioned
arrangement for hanging a kettle on to heat it over
the fire?] What do you call its parts [a. ref the
HORIZONTAL BAR in or beside the chimney]?*
V.3.5(a). Eng exc. We Man Wa Sf MxL. ⇒
**bar-iron, bar-rig, beam, chimney-bar, crane,
cross-bar, cross-beam, crow-bar, galloper,
gally-balk, gally-bar,** *gally-baulk* ⇒ **gally-balk,
hake-bar, hook, iron bar, iron beam, long-bar,**

pole, rack, rack-iron, randle-balk, randle-tree, reckan-bar, reckan-hook-bar, reckan(s), reddy-pole, rest-bar, roasting-bar, rod, slot-bar, staple, swabble, sway, sway-bar, sway-pole, sweak, swing-bar, swivel, tripod, wooden bar

2. *n [What do you call that old-fashioned arrangement for hanging a kettle on to heat it over the fire?] What do you call its parts [b. ref the vertical BAR or CHAIN in or beside the chimney]?* V.3.5(b). baː Du O Lei, baː Lei R, baˑɹ (+V) Nf, baˑᴶ: K. ⇒ **back-crook, chain, crook, cutterlug, eye-hook, hake, handle, hanger, hangle, hangle-iron, iron bar, jack, jib-hook, notches, pot-bed, pot-hanger, ratchet, reckan, recknan, rod, sneck, snotches, sway**

3. *n* a CRANE on which a kettle is hung over a domestic fire V.3.4. baˑᴶ: K

4. *n* a TETHERING-STAKE in a cow-house I.3.3. baː Wa, baˤ: O So, baˤˑ Ha

5. *n* a RUNG of a ladder I.7.15. *pl* baɹz Y, baˤ: Co, *pl* baˤːz D, baː Wo

6. *n* the T-SHAPED PLOUGH-BEAM END of a horse-drawn plough I.8.5. baˤ: So

7. *n* a BUMPER of a cart I.10.1(a). baˤ: D

8. *n* a movable horizontal rod stretching between the shafts of a cart, fixing them to the cart-body and stopping the cart from tipping, ⇐ ROD/PIN I.10.3. baː Nth, baˤ: Wa Nth Bk So, baː Nf

9. *n* a DIAGONAL BAR of a gate IV.3.7. baː L, *pl* baːz Y Ch

10. *n* **piece of bar** a PIECE *OF BREAD AND BUTTER* V.6.11(a). piːs ə baː Co *[queried SBM]*

11. *n* a HALO round the moon VII.6.4. baː Sf, baː Ess *[old]*, baˑᴶ: La *[not a NBM headword]*

bare *adj* BALD VI.2.3. baːɪ Y

bare-arse *n* a NESTLING IV.7.1. *pl* bɛəɹaːsɪz Y

bare-balchin *n* a NESTLING IV.7.1. bɛəbɒlʃɪn Lei, bɛəbolʃɪn Lei

bare-bubb *n* a NESTLING IV.7.1. bɛəbʊb Nt

bare-bubbling *n* a   NESTLING   IV.7.1.   *pl* bɪˑəbʊblənz L, baːbʊblɪn L

bare-fallow(s) *n* FALLOW-LAND II.1.1.
no -s: bɛəfalə Y Nt, bɛˑəfalɹ L, bɛˑəˤ fɒlə Wa, bæː falə Ch
-s: bɛˑəfaləz L

bare-faugh *n* FALLOW-LAND II.1.1. bɛəfɔˑəf Y

bare-feet *adj* BARE-FOOT VI.10.2. beˑəfɪʔ Bk, bɛˤːvɪt W, bɛɪəᴶfɪit Brk, bɛəfiːt Y, bɛəfɪt Ess, baːfiːt Nb, bəˑᴶfᴵit K

bare-feeted *adj* BARE-FOOT VI.10.2. bɛˤːviːtəd W

bare-foot *adj When someone has no shoes or socks on, you say he is ....* VI.10.2. beɪəfʊt Man, beˑɔᴿfʊt Nb, bɛəᴿfʊt Nb, beːəˤfʌt Sa, bɛːfʊt We Db Wa, bɛːɹfɪt Cu, bɛɔᴿfʏt Nb, bɛəfɪət Y, bɛəfʊt Du Y Db Sa Wa Nt L Lei Nf Sf K, bɛəfʊɪt Y, bɛəfuːt Y, bɛˑəɹfʊt L, bɛəˤfʌt Sa, bɛəˤfʊt Sa Wo Brk, bɛəˤvʊt

W, bæːfət La, bæˑᴶːfʊt La, bæəfʏt Nf, bæəfʊt Nf, baɹfɪʊt Y, baːfɪət We Y, baːfʏt Nb, baːfʊt Y Ch Db St, baːfət Nb We Ch Db St, baːfəd Y, baᴿːfət Nb, baˑᴶːɹfʊt La, baˑᴶːɹfuːt La, baˑᴶːfət We La Y, baˤːfʊt Sa O, baˤːfət Db, baːfʊt St Nf, bɜˑᴶːɹfʊt La, bɜˑᴶːɹfuːt La, bəˤːfʌt Sa. ⇒ **bare-feet, bare-feeted, bare-foot foot, bare-footed, naked-feet, naked-foot, shoeless**

bare-footed *adj* BARE-FOOT VI.10.2. Eng exc. We Db Nt

bare-foot foot *adj* BARE-FOOT VI.10.2. baːfət fuːt Ch

bare-golling *n* a NESTLING IV.7.1. bɛːgaʊlɪn Cu, bɛːgɒʊlɪn Cu, bɛəgɒlɪn Y

bare-golly *n* a NESTLING IV.7.1. bɛəgɒlɪ Y, baːgɒlɪ Y, bɛəgɔlɪ Y

bare pasture *n* PASTURE II.1.3. bɛː paːstjə Mon

barge 1. *v* to TRIM hedges IV.2.3. *-ing* baˤːdʒɪn W

2. *v* to trim the sides of a hedge. baˤːdʒ W

3. *v* to DITCH IV.2.11. baˤːdʒ So

4. *v* to cut grass from banks before cleaning out ditches. *-ing* baˤːdʒɪn W

5. *n* the RIDGE of a house roof V.1.2(a). baːdʒ Man

barge down *vtphr* to TRIM a hedge IV.2.3. baˤːdʒ ... dəʊn W

barged-up rick *n* a long stack with square ends, ⇐ STACKS II.7.1. baˤːdʒdʊp ɹɪk Bk

barge-end *n* the BUTT of a sheaf of corn II.6.4. baːdʒɛnd Hrt

barge out *vtphr* to TRIM a hedge IV.2.3. baˤːdʒ ... əʊt W

bargham *n* the COLLAR of the harness of a cart-horse I.5.3. baːfɪn Y, baːfən Y, baːfəm Y, baːfm We, baːkəm Y, baˑᴶːkəm Y, baɹɪəm Cu We La, baːfɪn Y, baːfən Y, baːfəm Y, baːkəm Y, bəfɪn Y, bʁɛɪm Nb, bʁɛɪəm Nb, bʁɛhəm Nb, bɹɛhəm Cu, bʁɛfən Nb, bɹɛθəm Nb, bʁaɪm Nb, bɹafɪn Cu We Y, bʁafn Nb Du, bɹafən Du, bɹafn Du We La Y, bɹafm Cu Y; **pair of barghams** pɛəɹ ə baɹfənz Y

barging *v-ing* BELCHING VI.13.13. baːdʒɪn Gl

barging-hook *n* a   HEDGING-BILL   IV.2.5. baˤːdʒɪnʊk W

bar-hurdles *npl* HURDLES used to pen sheep in part of a field III.7.11. baːhəːdɫz Sr *[like gates]*

bar-iron *n* the *HORIZONTAL* BAR of a crane over a domestic fire V.3.5(a). baˤːɾɪn D

bark 1.1. *v* to WHITTLE a stick I.7.19. *-ing* baːkɪn Ess *[marked u.r EMBM]*

1.2. *vt* to whittle. baːk Wo

2. *vt* to cut small branches from a tree, ⇐ to LOP IV.12.5. *-ing* baˤːkɪn W

barken *v* to LOP a tree IV.12.5. *vbln* bəˈɹːknɪn L, bəˈɹːʔn L

barking *v-ing* COUGHING VI.8.2. baᶜːkɪn So, baᶜːkən Co, bəᶜːkɪn So

barking about *vphr-ing* COUGHING VI.8.2. baˈɹːkɪn əbɐʊt Brk*[old]*

barley-ails *n* barley AWNS II.5.3. baˈɽɬɪ-eˑʊɬz O, baᶜɬɪ-eɪʊɬz Ha*[while growing]*, baᶜːɬɪ-ɛɪɬz Ha, baᶜːɬɪ-ɛɪᵊɬz W, baᶜːɬɪ-ɛɪᵁɬz W, baᶜːɬɪ-æɪɬz He, baᶜːɬɪ-aɪɬz Ha, baᶜːɬɪ-aɪɬz D Ha, baːlɪ-aɪɬz Ess, baᶜːɬɪ-aɪᵊɬz So W, baᶜːɬɪ-aɪᵊɬz W, baᶜːɬɪhaɪᵊɬz So, bəᶜːɬɪ-aɪɬz Wo*[old]*, baːlɪ-ɑɪɬz Sr, baᶜːɬɪ-ɒɪɬz D, baᶜɬɪ-ɔːɬz Ha*[after threshing]*, baᶜːɬɪ-ɔːɬz Co, baᶜːɬɪ-ɔɪlz O

barley-beards *n* barley AWNS II.5.3. baᶜːɬɪbɪɵᶜːdẓ Co

barley-bristles *n* barley AWNS II.5.3. baːlɪbɹɪslz Y

barleycart *vbln* CARTING barley from the field II.6.6. baᶜːɬɪkaᶜːt̩ W

barley-elves* *n* barley AWNS II.5.3. baᶜːɬɪ-ɛɬvz W

barley-hangs* *n* barley AWNS II.5.3. baːlɪ-aŋz La, baˈːlɪ-aŋz La

barley-haulms *n* barley AWNS II.5.3. baːlɪhæːmz Nf

barley-havels *n* barley AWNS II.5.3. baːlɪ-ɛɪvɬz Ess

barley-horns *n* barley AWNS II.5.3. baˈːlɪhaːnz Nf, baːlɪhaːnz Nf, baˈlihɔːnz Nf

barley-hucks *n* barley AWNS II.5.3. baːlɪ-ʌks MxL

barley-husks *n* barley AWNS II.5.3. baːlɪ-ʊsks Y

barley-meal *n* MEAL V.6.1(b). baːlɪmɪəɬ Ess

barley-pails *n* barley AWNS II.5.3. baᶜːɬɪpeːlz Sa

barley-piles *n* barley AWNS II.5.3. baɹlɪpaɪlz He, baːlɪpaːɪlz St, baːlɪpɒɪlz St, bəᶜːɬɪpɒɪɬz Wo, baːlɪpɔɪlz Wa

barley-whiskers *n* barley AWNS II.5.3. baᶜːɽlɪwɪskəᶜːɽẓ Sx

barley-zears *n* barley AWNS II.5.3. baᶜːɬɪzɪɪɵᶜːẓ Co

barm *1. n* YEAST V.6.2. bɛəm Y, bæˈːm La, bæˈːɹm La, bæᶜːm O, baɬm O*[old]*, baɹm*[old]*, baːm Y Ch*[old x1]* Db St*[old x2]* Wa L Lei, baˈːm La Ch O*[old]*, baˈːɹm La Y*[old]*, baᶜːm Sa He*[old]* Wo Wa Gl O Nth So*[old x1, from malt x1]* W*[old x1]* Co D Do Ha, baːm Ch St*[old]* Wo*[old x1]* Wa Lei Nf*[old]*, baːɽm Brk, bɔːm St*[old]*, baᶜːɽm Brk Ha*[old]*, bɜˈːɹm La

2. n brewer's yeast, usually soft or wet. bæᵊm Nb*[old]*, baːm Y Nt Nth Hu C, baᶜːm Gl Bk*[old]*, baᶜːm D*[old]*

barmy *1. adj* STUPID VI.1.5. baːmɪ L, baᶜːmɪ Mon, baːmɪ Sr

2. adj SILLY VIII.9.3. baːmɪ Nb La Y Ch St O L Ess, blaːmɪ L, baᶜːmɪ Sa O Ha, baːme Y, baːmɪ O L Nf MxL K *[[blaːmɪ] form at L queried as error EMBM]*

barn *1. n* What's the **barn** for and where is it? I.1.11. Eng

use:

a. for storing corn: Eng exc. MxL

b. for storing straw: Nb La Y Db St Mon Gl L Nf Bk Bd So W Sr K D

c. for storing hay: Nb Cu Du We La Y Db St He Mon Gl L Nf Bk MxL So W Brk Sr K Co D Ha

d. for storing root crops: He K

e. for storing meal: Lei Ess

f. for storing other cattle fodder: Ch W Sr

g. for storing tools and/or implements: Cu La Y Db He Wo Wa O Nt L Nf Hrt Ess Sr Do Ha

h. for housing cows: We La Y

i. for threshing in: Nb La Y Ch Db Sa St He Wo Wa Mon Gl O Nt L Lei R Nth Bk Ess So W Co D Do Ha Sx

j. for shearing sheep or stacking wool: Nf W Sx

location:

a. part of farm buildings, near farmhouse: Cu Du We La Y Db St He Wo Wa Nt Lei R Nth C Nf Sf Bk Ess So W Brk Sr K D Do Ha Sx

b. above cow-house or stable: Nb Du Man So

c. near cow-house: We La

d. in field or away from other farm buildings: Db Sa Mon

⇒ **hay-barn**, **lathe**; ⇒ also **dighting-barn** *[main uses only given, locations generalized]*

2. n the place where hay is stored on a farm, ⇐ HAY-LOFT I.3.18. bæːn La, baːn Cu We Y St Wa Hu Nf Bk Hrt Ess, baˈːn La Y Db, baᶜːn̩ Wa O So, baᶜn̩ Wo O Ha, baːn St Nf Ess, baᶜːn̩ D; **hay-barn** iːbaːn St, heːbaᴮːn Nb, eɪbaɹn He, heːɪbaᶜːn̩ So, ɛɪbaːn St, *pl* ɛəbaːnz Y, ɛˈˑəbaˈːn L, hæɪbaːn Ess

3. n a CART-SHED I.11.7. bɜˈːɹn La

barnaby *n* a local FESTIVAL or holiday on the feast of St Barnabas, 11 June VII.4.11. bəːnəbɪ Ch

barn-door *n* the FLAP at the front of old-fashioned trousers VI.14.16. *pl* baːndʊəz La, *pl* baˈːndʊəˈz La*[old]*, *pl* baᶜːn̩dɔːɵᶜz He, baᶜːn̩dʊəᶜː W, *pl* baᶜːɽn̩dɔːɵᶜɽẓ Sx

barn-owl *n* an OWL IV.7.6. baːnuːl Y *[presumably special, but not noted as such in NBM]*

barn's-door *n* the FLAP at the front of old-fashioned trousers VI.14.16. *pl* baᶜːn̩ẓdɔːɵᶜːẓ Do, baᶜːn̩ẓduəᶜː W Ha

barn stacks *npl* long STACKS with square ends, for hay II.7.1. baːn stæks Sf

barraquail *n* a SWINGLE-TREE of a horse-drawn plough harness I.8.3. baɽəkweɪɬ D, *pl* baɽəkɬz D

barras-apron* *n* a working APRON made of coarse sacking V.11.2(a). baɽəseːpəᶜːn̩ D

barrel *1. n* What is beer carried in, from the brewery? VI.13.12. Eng. ⇒ **beer-tub**, **cask**,

firkin, tub, vessel
2. *n* a CORN-BIN I.7.4. baɹɬ We

barren *1. adj* barren, is a barren, is barren HAS
NOT HELD, describing a cow that has not conceived
III.1.7. bæɹɪn Sa Wo, baɹɪn Sa Lei R, baɹən Sa St Lei
2. *n* a cow that has not conceived. baɹɪn Sa
3. *adj NOT IN* CALF III.1.8. beɹən Ess, bæɹʊn Wo,
bæɹən MxL Sx, bæʈən K, baɹɪn Db St Bk, baʈɪn So,
baʁən Nb, baɹən La Y St He Wa Gl Nt L, baʈən O
4. *adj* not in calf but able to conceive. bæɹɪn Sa He
Wo K, bæʈɪn So, bæɹœn Gl, bæɹʊn He Wo Gl, bæɹən
Man, bæɹən He Mon Sf Bk Ess, bæʈən So Sr, baɹɪn
Ch Db Sa St Bk, baʈɪn W Do, baɹʊn Wa Gl Nth, baɹən
La Y Db Sa St Wo Wa Mon O Nt Nth Bk Bd Hrt,
baʈən So W Co Do
5. *adj* unlikely to conceive. beɹɪn Sr, bæɹɪn K
6. *adj* unable to conceive, describing a cow. beəɹŋ
Ess, bæɹɪn K Sx, bæɹʊn Gl, bæɹŋ Sr K, bæɹən He
Mon Hrt Brk Sr Sx, baɹɪn Wo, baɹən Y Wa O Hu C
Bk, baʈən Do
7. *n* a cow that is not in calf but that can conceive.
bæɹən Mon, baɹɪn Sa
8. *n* a cow that cannot conceive. bæɹən He Sx
9. *adj* DRY, describing a cow with no milk III.1.9.
baɹən La Wo, baʈən W
10. *n* the VULVA of a cow III.2.3. bɪəʁən Nb,
bɪəɹən L Nth, beːʈən Do, beːɹən Ha, beˈɹɪn Nf, beːʈɪn
So W Ha, beːʈən W D Ha, beˈ ːʈʊn W Co D Ha,
beˈˡːʈən Co, beːəˡɹɪn Nf, beəɹɪn O Nf, beəˡɹɪn Brk Sr,
beˀʁən Nb, beəˡɹən Sr, bæɹŋ Du, bæɹən Sx, baɹɪn
O, baɹŋ Cu Du We Y, baɹən Du We La Y Nt L Lei,
baʈən La , bəɹən La, bəʈːɹɪn W
11. *n* the UTERUS of a cow III.2.4. beəˡɹɪn Brk,
beəˡɹən Sx, beəɹɪn Brk K, baɹən Nt

barren-bag *n* the UTERUS of a cow III.2.4.
beːʈɪnbag So

barrener *1. n* a cow that has not conceived, ⇐ HAS
NOT HELD III.1.7. baɹənə R
2. *n* a cow that is *NOT IN* CALF III.1.8. bæɹəˡnəˡ
Brk, bæɹənəˡ Brk, bæʈənə K, baɹɪnəˡ Bk, baʈɪnəˡ O,
pl baʈɪnəˡːz Do, baʈənə K
3. *n* a cow that is not in calf but that can conceive.
bæɹənəˡ Sr
4. *n* a cow that is unlikely to conceive. bæɹɪnəˡ Brk,
bæɹənəˡ Sx
5. *n* a cow that cannot conceive. beɹənə Ess, bæɹənə
MxL, bæɹənəˡ Ha, bæɹənəˡ Sx, baʈɪnəʈ O, baʈɪnəʈː
Ha, baʈənəˡ Ha, baʈːɹɪnəʈː W
*6. *n* a DRY cow III.1.9. baʈːɹɪnəʈː D [*also at So,
but unclear whether adjcomp or n*]
7. *n* a BLIND TEAT III.2.7. bæɹənə Brk [*queried
ir.r. SBM*]
8. *n* a HOG III.8.8. bæɹɪnəʈ Brk

barren-field *n* FALLOW-LAND II.1.1. bæɹənfiːˀɬd
Ess

barren-ground *n* FALLOW-LAND   II.1.1.
bæɹəngɹɛʊnd Nf

barren-land *n* FALLOW-LAND   II.1.1.
baɹənland La Y

barren teat *n* a BLIND TEAT III.2.7. baʈən tɛt
W

bar-rig *n* the *HORIZONTAL* BAR of a crane over
a domestic fire V.3.5(a). baʈːɹɪg So, baʈːɹɛˡg So

barrow *1. n* a male HOG III.8.8. baʈə Co D
2. *n* a hog. baʈə O So D
3. *n* a DIAPER V.11.3. baɹə L
4. *n* a wrapper worn over a diaper. baɹə Nt

barrow-hog *1. n* a male or female HOG III.8.8.
bʌɹəhɒg Ess[*when animal gets fat*]
2. *n* a hog. bæɹə-ɒg K, bæʈːɹɒg Sx, baʈːɹɒg Sx

barrow-pig *1. n* a male or female HOG III.8.8.
baɹəpɪg Hrt, baʈəpɪg So, baʈːpɪg So
2. *n* a male hog. bæɹəpɪg O Sf, baʈoupɪg Ha,
baɹəpɪg Bk, baʈəpɪg So D Ha, baʈːʈəpɪg W Ha,
baʈːpɪg Do, bɒʈəpɪg D, bʌɹəpɪg Ess
3. *n* a hog. bæɹʌupɪg Sr, bæɹəpɪg Brk, baɹəpɪg
O, baʈəpɪg So W D Ha, baʈːʈəpɪg So, baʈːpɪg So
Do, baˡːɹəˡpɪg Brk, baːpɪg Ess, baʈːpɪg K,
bʌɹəpɪg Ess

bars *1. npl What do you call these horizontals [of
a gate]?* IV.3.6. Eng exc. Hu Brk Sx; **gate-bars**
jətbæˡːz La. ⇒ **cross-pieces, frames, gate-back,**
gate-bars, gate-lackses, gate-laths, gate-ledges,
gate-rails, gate-shivers, gate-shuttles, gate-
slices, gate-spells, lacings, lackses, larras, laths,
lats, ledges, little-bars, rails, sheaths, shittles,
shivers, shots, shuttles, slads, slats, slices, slits,
spars, speans, spells, spleats, staves
2. *npl* HURDLES used to pen sheep in part of a
field III.7.11. baːz Y
3. *n* a GRIDIRON V.7.4(a). baʈːz̩ Sa

barton *1. n* a FARMYARD I.1.3. baʈːtn̩ So,
baʈːkŋ Do
2. *n* the yard outside the back door of a
farmhouse. baʈːʔn So
3. *n* the STACKYARD of a farm I.1.4. baʈːtɪn
So, baʈːtn̩ So
4. *n* the STRAW-YARD of a farm I.1.9. baʈːtɪn
So, baʈːtn̩ Gl, baʈːkn Gl

barton-yard *n* the STACKYARD of a farm I.1.4.
baʈːʈʔnjaʈːd̩ So

bar up *vtphr* to PEN or FOLD sheep in part of a
field III.7.10. baː ... ʊp Du

base *1. n* [*Show a picture of some stacks.*] *What
do you call this [indicate the base of a stack]?*
II.7.4. beɪəs Man, bɛɪs Brk. ⇒ **bed, bedding,**
body, bottom, brandreth, brandrick, foot,
footing, foundation, frame, helm-stones,
hemmel(s), iron standards, iron stands, leg,
mow-bed, mow-stage, mow-stead, rick, rick-
bed, rick-bottom, rick-saddle, rick-staddle,

rick-stones, rick-stool, saddle, stack-bed, stack-bottom, *stack-brandreth* ⇒ stack-brandrick, stack-frame, stack-staddle, staddle(s), staddle-bottom, staddling, stavel, stead, stedding, stem, stilts, stool, straddle, *straw* bottom, stud, trestle-bottom, walls; ⇒ also browse, staddle-stones

2. *n* a wooden curb in a cow-house, ⇐ CURB-STONE I.3.9. bɪəs Du

3. *n* the BUTT of a sheaf of corn II.6.4. bəɪəs Gl

bash *1. vt* to BEAT a boy on the buttocks VIII.8.10. bæɪʃ W

2. *adj* SHY VIII.9.2. baʃ La

bashful *adj* SHY VIII.9.2. baʃfʊl St, baʃfə Cu

basket *1. n* [*What do you call that dry mixed feed that you give to your horses?*] *What do you carry this feed to the horses in?* III.5.4. bæskət Man[*basket-work, oval, 2 handles x1*], bæːskɪt So[*wooden, round x1*], baskɪt La Ch[*basket-work, oval*] St, baːskɪt So[*wicker*] Do, baːskət Gl[*wicker, round, with handles*]. ⇒ bag, baiting-sieve, bait sieve, bowl, bowl-dish, box, bucket, bushel-skep, chaff-basket, close sieve, corn-measure, dish, gallon tin, half-bag basket, hod, hopper, kipe, maund, maund-basket, measure, mixing-pan, pail, pan, piggin, pokes, riddle, sack, sack-bag, scoop, scuttle, scuttle-basket, server, sieve, skep, skip, swill, tin, trug, wicker-skep, wisk, wisket; ⇒ also lagging

2. *n* a SOWING-BASKET II.3.6. baskət Du

basket-hive *n* a SKEP IV.8.8(b). baskɪtaɪv Y, baskɪtaᶦv Y

basketweed *n* a COWSLIP II.2.10(a). bæskɪtwiːd Man

basking *v-ing* COUGHING VI.8.2. baskɪn Ch[*old*]

bass *n* a SOWING-BASKET II.3.6. bas Du

bass-broom *1. n* a BESOM I.3.15. bæsbɹʊm Sf[*birch*], bæsbɹuːm Brk

2. *n* a homemade besom. basbɹɪum Nf[*hazel or birch*]

3. *n* a shop-bought besom. bæsbɹʊm Nf Ess[*birch*]

4. *n* a MUCK-BRUSH I.3.14. besbɹuːm K, bæsbɹʊm Ess K Sx, bæsbɹuːm Wa Brk K, basbɹɪuːm Sa, basbɹʊm He Wa L, baːsbɹʊm Wa Mon, baːsbɹuːm W, bɔsbɹuːm Ch

5. *n* a BROOM used for sweeping outdoors V.9.10. besbɹuːm MxL Sr K, bæsbɹʊm Sx, bæsbɹuːm Wa MxL Brk Sr K Sx, basbɹɪuːm Sa, basbɹʊm Sa, basbɹuːm St He Wa Nth Bk Ha, basbɹəum Y, baːsbɹʊm Bk Ess, baːsbɹuːm Wa, baːsbɹuːm W, basbɹuːm O

6. *n* a BRUSH used for sweeping indoors V.9.11. bæsbɹʊm Ess, basbɹuːm C

bass-brush *1. n* a BRUSH used to clean horses III.5.5(a). baːsbɹʌʃ Brk

2. *n* a BROOM used for sweeping outdoors V.9.10. basbɹʌʃ Bk

bassett *n* a MUCK-BRUSH I.3.14. bæsət Sx

bastard-fallow *n* land on which an early crop is grown and which is then left fallow for the rest of the year, ⇐ FALLOW-LAND II.1.1. baːstədfælə Ess

bast-broom *n* a BESOM I.3.15. bastbɹʊm Nf

baste *1. v* to MARK sheep with colour to indicate ownership III.7.9. biːs Nb, bɪast NB, bjɛst Nb, bɪəst Nb, *-ing* be·əstn Nb, bʊst Nb, bʊs Cu

2. *v* to KNEAD dough V.6.4. be·əst L

3. *vt* to BEAT a boy on the buttocks VIII.8.10. beɪst St

bat *1. n* What do you call that small creature with leathery wings that flutters about at dark? IV.7.7. Eng exc. Ch Wo. ⇒ bat-mouse, batty-mouse, bearaway, belly-bat, billy-bat, bit-bat, blind-bat, ekkymowl, flinter-bat, flitter-bat, flitter-mouse, flying-bat, flying-mouse, hairy-bat, hairy-mouse, hat-bat, ink-mouse, leather-bat, leatherin-bat, leathern-bat, leather-wing-bat, leather-winged-bat, mouse-bat, rat-bat, rear-mouse

2. *n* a STICK used to support the shaft of a cart I.11.1. bæt K

3. *n* the SHAFT of a scythe II.9.7. bɛt K, bæt K

4. *n* a WHETSTONE made of stone II.9.10. bɛət Ess, bæt Nf Sf Ess Sr Sx

5. *n* FOOD V.8.2. bat Cu

batch *n* a BROOD of chickens IV.6.12. batʃ We Db Lei Bk Bd

batch-flour *n* MEAL V.6.1(b). batʃflauə Db

batchy *adj* SILLY VIII.9.3. bæːtʃɪ Ess[*old*]

bat-footed *adj* SPLAY-FOOTED VI.10.5. bɛtfʊtɪd Ess, bætfʊtɪd Ess, bætʔfʊtɪd Ess, bætfʊtəd Sf Ess

bath-broom *1. n* a MUCK-BRUSH I.3.14. bæθbɹʊm He, bæθbɹᵁuːm Mon, bæːθbɹuːm Wo, baθbɹuːm Wo, baːθbɹuːm He Wo, baɑːθbɹuːm Wo

2. *n* a BROOM used for sweeping outdoors V.9.10. bæθbɹʊm St, bæːθbɹʊm Wo, bæːθbɹuːm Wo Mon, baθbɹuːm Sa Wo, baːθbɹʊm Sa, baːθbɹuːm Wo, baɑːθbɹuːm Wo

3. *n* a BRUSH used for sweeping indoors V.9.11. bæθbɹuːm Sa

batlings *npl* BOUGHS of a tree IV.12.2. bætʔlənz Sf [*queried ir.r. EMBM*]

bat-mouse *n* a BAT IV.7.7. bætmɛʊs Brk, bætmʌʊs Brk, bætmʊs Brk, batmæʊs W Ha, batməʊs W

bats *npl* BOOTS VI.14.23. bats D

bats-broom *n* a BESOM made of heather I.3.15. bætsbɹuːm Nf

batten-stoop *n* the SHUTTING-POST of a gate IV.3.4. batɪnstuːp La, batənstuːp Cu

batterdock *n* COLT'S-FOOT II.2.7. batədɒk St

batticle *n* a SWINGLE-TREE of a horse-drawn plough harness I.8.3. badɪkɫ Nth, baɹɪkɫ Nth

battle-heads *npl* MINNOWS IV.9.9. badɫɛdz D

battle-twigs *npl* EARWIGS IV.8.11. bɛtɫtwɪgz L, batɫtwɪgz Db*[old x1]* St Nt L, *sg* batɫtwɪg Y, baʔltwɪgz L, batɫtwɪgz Lei

battle-wigs* *npl* EARWIGS IV.8.11. *sg* batɫwɪg L

batty *adj* SILLY VIII.9.3. bætɪ Sr, batɪ O

batty-mouse *n* a BAT IV.7.7. batimæʊs Ha

baulk *1. n* a wooden device with two upright pieces, between which a cow's neck was held in a cow-house, ⇐ TETHER I.3.4. bɔːᵊk Sf
2. n an EVENER on a horse-drawn plough I.8.4. bɔːk Y Nth*[3 horses]*
3. n an evener, the main swingle-tree of a plough harness. bɔːk L, bɔˑək L
4. n a group of furrows 2 feet 6 inches broad in a ploughed field, ⇐ RIDGES II.3.2. bɔːk Ess
5. n a PERCH for hens IV.6.3. bæˑᵊk Nb, baːk Nb Du*[old x1]*, bɔːk Nb, *pl* bɔːks Cu

baulks *1. n* a HAY-LOFT over a cow-house I.3.18. bɔːks La Y Ch Db
2. npl the RIDGES between furrows in a ploughed field II.3.2. bɔːks Ess, *sg* bɔːk Sf, bɔʊks Ess
3. npl HEADLANDS in a ploughed field II.3.3. bɔːks Y

bavin(s) *npl* KINDLING-*WOOD* V.4.2.
no -s: bɛvɪn K, bavɪn Ha
-s: bɛəvnz Ess
pl: bɛvɪnz Sr*[big x1]* K Sx*[large]*, bævɪnz Brk*[large x1]* Sr, bavɪnz Ha

bavin-wood *n* KINDLING-*WOOD* V.4.2. bavɪnwʊd Ha

baw *vi-3prpl* they MOO, describing the noise cows make in the fields III.10.4(b). bɔː La

bawk *1. vi-3prpl* bulls BELLOW III.10.2. bɔːk La, bɔːks La
2. vi-3prpl they MOO, describing the noise cows make during feeding time in the cow-house III.10.4(a). bɔːk La
3. vi-3prpl they MOO, describing the noise cows make in the fields III.10.4(b). bɔːk La

bawky-handed *adj* LEFT-HANDED VI.7.13(a). bɔːkɪ-andɪd Y

bawl *1. vi-3prpl* bulls BELLOW III.10.2. baːlz Wo, baːɫz Gl, *prppl* əbaːlɪn Wo, bɔːl La Y Db St Mon, bɔːlz We, *-ing* bɔːlɪn Nf, bɔːɫ Lei
2. vi-3prpl they MOO, describing the noise cows make during feeding time in the cow-house III.10.4(a). baːɫ D, bɔːl La Y St Mon, bɔːlz Db, bɔːɫ Lei So W
3. vi-3prpl they MOO, describing the noise cows make in the fields III.10.4(b). baːɫ D, baːlz Wo, baːɫz Gl, bɔːl We La Y Ch Db Sa St Mon, bɔːlz Cu, bɔːɫ Lei Nth So W
4. vi-3prpl sheep BLEAT III.10.5. *-ing* baːɫɪn So

5. vi to SCREAM VIII.8.11. bɔːl We Y, *-ing* bɔːlɪn K, bɔːɫ Gl Ess, bɒᵗːʟ̩ Sa

bawling *v-ing* SHRIEKING, describing the shrill noise made by a baby VI.5.15. bɔːlɪn Y Db Nth Bk, əbɔːlɪn Gl Bk, bɔːlən Cu, bɔːɫɪn W

bay *1. n* a STALL in a cow-house I.3.1. bæɪ Ess
2. n a HAYLOFT over a cow-house I.3.18. bæɪ Ess, baɪ Ess
3. n the gangway in a cow-house, used to store hay. beː Sa

beak *1. n* *What does a bird peck its food up with?* IV.6.18. Eng exc. Nb Du Man. ⇒ **beal, bill, crup, neb, pecker, pick**; ⇒ also **geb**
2. vi to CHIP, referring to an egg that is about to hatch IV.6.10. *prppl* biːkɪn K
3. n a NOSE VI.4.6. bɪək Y*[slang]*

beal *1. vi-3prpl* bulls BELLOW III.10.2. biːlz Cu Y, bɪəl La Y, bɪəlz We Y L, *prppl* bɪəlɪn Y, *prppladj* bɪəlɪn Y, *-ing* bɪəlɪn Y L
2. vi-3prpl they MOO, describing the noise cows make during feeding time in the cow-house III.10.4(a). biːl Y, bɪəl Y, bɪˑəlz L
3. vi-3prpl they MOO, describing the noise cows make in the fields III.10.4(b). biːl Cu, bɪəl Du We La Y L
4. vi to CHIP, referring to an egg that is about to hatch IV.6.10. biːɫ Co D, *prppl* biːɫɪn Do, beːl D, beɪɫ D, bɛɪɫ Co D
5. n the BEAK of a bird IV.6.18. biːɫ Co, bɪʊɫ Brk, bɪʊ Sr Sx, bɪᵊɫ So, bɛɪɫ D
6. vi to FESTER, referring to a wound VI.11.8. biːl Nb
7. vi to SCREAM VIII.8.11. bɪˑəl L

beald* *vi* to CHIP, referring to an egg that is about to hatch IV.6.10. *prppl* biːɫdən Co, *?ptppl* bɛɪɫd D

bealing *v-ing* SHRIEKING, describing the shrill noise made by a baby VI.5.15. biːlɪn Du, bɪəlɪn L

beal out *viphr-3prpl* bulls BELLOW III.10.2. bɪəlz aʊt Y, *-ing* bɪəlɪn uːt Y

beam *1. n* the T-SHAPED PLOUGH-BEAM END of a horse-drawn plough I.8.5. biːm Sa He Wo Mon Gl Lei, bjʊm He Wo *[marked ir.r. EMBM]*
2. n the SHAFT of a scythe II.9.7. biːm MxL
3. n the *HORIZONTAL* BAR of a crane over a domestic fire V.3.5(a). biːm Bk Hrt Ess Sr

beam-end *1. n* the T-SHAPED PLOUGH-BEAM END of a horse-drawn plough I.8.5. biːmɛnd St Mon L Ess, bɪimɛnd Brk Ha, bɪˑəmɛnd L; **end of the beam** ɪnd ə ðə beɪm Ess
2. n the CROSS-BEAM END of a cart I.10.1. bɪˑəmɛnd L
3. n a BUMPER of a cart I.10.1(a). bɪiːmɛnd Sx

beam-head *n* the T-SHAPED PLOUGH-BEAM END of a horse-drawn plough I.8.5. bɪiːmhɛd Sr

bean-mouse *n* a SHREW-MOUSE IV.5.2. biːnmɛʊs Sx

beans *n* **full of beans** ACTIVE, describing a child VIII.9.1. fʊɫ ə biːnz O, fʊl ə beɪnz Nf

bear *vt-2prsg Sometimes toothache may get so bad that you think you can hardly ... (it).* VI.5.9. Eng exc. La. ⇒ **abear, abide, abide with, bear with, bide, live through, put up with, stand, stick, suffer**

bearaway *n* a BAT IV.7.7. bɪɹɹəwɛə Y

bear-bind *n* BINDWEED II.2.4. bɪəᵗbəɪn He, bɪəᵗbəɪnd Wo, beːəᵗbaɪn Sa, bɛəᵗbæɪn He, bɛəɹbaɪn St He, bɛəᵗbaɪn Sa, bɛəbɑɪn Ch K, bɛəᵈbɒɪn K, bɛəᵈbɒɪnd K, beːəᵗbɒɪn Wo, bɛəbɔɪn Wo, bɛəbʌɪn Sr, bɛəbəɪn Mon, bɛəᵗbəɪn He Wo Mon Sx, bɑᵗːbɛɪn Sa, bɑᵗːbaɪn Sa, bəᵗːbæɪn He, bəːbɒɪn St, bəᵗːbəɪˤn Wo

beard *1. n If you didn't shave here [point to the chin], you'd soon grow a ....* VI.2.7. Eng. ⇒ **billygoat, billygoat-beard, billygoat-whiskers, goat, nanny, nannygoat-beard, nannygoat's beard, tuffet,** *whisker* ⇒ **whiskers, whiskers**
2. *n* the WATTLES of a hen IV.6.19. bɪəd Sf, bɪəᵗːd̞ So

beard(s) *n* barley AWNS II.5.3.
no -s: bɪəd Ch, bɪəᵗːd̞ So
-s: bɪədz Y St, bɪəᵈdz La, bɪəᵗːd̞z̞ Wo Co

bearer *1. n* a BENCH on which slaughtered pigs are dressed III.12.1. bɛəɹə Ess
2. *n* a BIER VIII.5.9(b). bɪəɹə Cu Nf, bɛːɹə St, bɛəɽə O

bearers *1. npl What do you call the men that carry the coffin?* VIII.5.10. Eng. ⇒ **buriers, carriers, pall-bearers, under-bearers**
2. *n* the BUMPERs of carts 1.10.1(a). bɛᵗːɹəᵗːz̞ D

bearing *n* the metal BUSH at the centre of a cart-wheel I.9.8. bɛᵗːɹɪn W

bear out *vtphr* to AGREE *WITH* somebody VIII.8.12. bɪə ... ᵁuːt We

bear up *vtphr* to AGREE *WITH* somebody VIII.8.12. bɛəɹ ... ʌp He

bear-wind *n* BINDWEED II.2.4. bɑːwaɪnd MxL

bear with *vtphr-2prsg* you BEAR pain VI.5.9. bɪə wɪ La Y, bɛə wɪð Y Ch, bɛə wɪ Y

beast *1. n* **run to beast, want to go to the beast** ON HEAT, describing a cow III.1.6. **run to beast** ɹʌn ʔə biːˈst Nf; **want to go to the beast** *3prsg* wɒnʔ ə gou tə ðə bɪist Nf
2. *n* a BULL III.1.14. biːst Ess, bɪəs Y
3. *n* a BULLOCK III.1.16. biːst Wo
4. *n* a mature bullock. bɹiːst Ess

beast-house *n* a COW-HOUSE I.1.8. biːstʌʊs He Mon, biːstəʊs Mon

beasting *adj* **a-beasting, beasting, on a-beasting** ON HEAT, describing a cow III.1.6. **a-beasting** əbiːstɪn He Wo L; **beasting** biːstɪn Sa He Mon L Nf, biːstn Nf, biistn Nf, bɪˈəstn Nf; **on a-beasting** ɒn əbiːstɪn Wo

beastle *vt* to DIRTY a floor V.2.8. bɛɪsɫ Co

beast-man *n* a COWMAN on a farm I.2.3. biːsmən Y, bɪəsmən Y, bɪəstmən Y, bᵉʊstman Du

beast(s) *n* CATTLE III.1.3.
no -s: biːs Nb Cu Du We La Y Db Wo K, biːst Nb Du Y Ch Db St Wa Nt L Lei R Nth Hu C Bd So W Ha, bjɛs Do, bjɛst Do, bɪʌs W, bɪʌst W, bɪʊs La, bɪəs Cu Du We La Y Db Nt L So W Do Ha, bɪəst Y Ch Nt L, bɛəs Y, beˈəst Du, bɛɪs Db, bɛɪst Du St, bɛəs Y, baɪst Ha, bəɪs Y
-s: biːsts Nb Ch St L MxL W D, bɪˈəsts L, beɪsts Du

beast-shit *n* COW-DUNG I.3.12. bɪəsʃɪt Y

beast-track *n* a PATH made through a field by cattle IV.3.11. biːstɹʌak L

beat *1. vt When a boy had been very naughty indeed, his father might put him across his knee and ... him on the buttocks.* VIII.8.10. biːt Sa*[old]* Wa K, biːd (+V) Co, bjʌt So, bɪət La; **beat him across his arse** bɪət ən əkɽɔːs ɪz aːs Do. ⇒ **bash, baste, beat** *him*, **beat** *him across his arse*, **bensil, bray, cane, clout, dad, dust** *him*, **fettle, flop,** *give him a* **crack,** *give him a good* **bannicking,** *give him a good* **belting,** *give him a good* **hiding,** *give him a good* **lacing,** *give him a good* **leathering,** *give him a good* **licking,** *give him a good* **smack,** *give him a good* **smacking,** *give him a good* **spanking,** *give him a good* **tanning,** *give him a good* **thraping,** *give him a good* **thrashing,** *give him a good* **whacking,** *give him a good* **winding,** *give him a* **hiding,** *give him a* **licking,** *give him a* **smack,** *give him a* **tanning,** *give him a* **thrashing,** *give him some* **strap,** *give him the* **stick,** *give him the* **strap,** *give it a good* **bensilling, hazel, hide, hit, hole, jart, lace, larrup, leather, lick, lowk, mark, pay, pelt, punch,** *put the strap across his arse*, *put the strap athwart his arse*, **quilt, rattle** *his arse*, **rib, scutch, skelp, slap, slap** *him on his behind*, **slap** *his arse*, **slap** *his backside*, **slap** *his behind*, **slap** *his bottom*, **slash, smack, smack** *him*, **smack** *his arse*, **smack** *his backside*, **sole, sole** *his arse*, **sole** *his backside*, **spank, spank** *him*, **spank** *his arse*, **strap, strap** *him*, **stripe, swap, tan, tan** *him*, **tan** *his arse*, **tan** *his arse for him*, **tan** *his seat*, **tank, thrape, thrash, thrash** *him*, *threap* ⇒ **thrape, touse, trounce** *him*, **trounce** *his arse*, **twank, waled, wallop, wallop** *him*, **warm, warm** *his backside*, **whack, whack** *his arse*, **whip, whip** *his backside*, **yark, yuck**
2. *adj* EXHAUSTED, describing a tired person VI.13.8. biːt Sa Bd Ess Sr Co Ha, beɪt Man, bɛɪt Co; **dead beat** dɛd biːt Nth K D, dʒɛd biːt Db

beaten *adj* EXHAUSTED, describing a tired person VI.13.8. biːtn Co

beater *n* a FLAIL II.8.3. biːtəˡ: So

beating-post *n* the SHUTTING-POST of a gate IV.3.4. biːtɪnpɔːs Co

beat it *imp* GO AWAY! VIII.7.9(a). biːt ɪt Man

beat up *vphr* to STOCK a cow III.3.6. biːt ʊp Du

beazled *adj* EXHAUSTED, describing a tired person VI.13.8. bɪiːzʊd Sr*[old]*

beck *n* a RIVULET IV.1.1. bɛk Cu Du We La Y Nt L Nf

bed *1. n* a STALL in a cow-house I.3.1. bed Ch
2. n the CURB-STONE in a cow-house I.3.9. bɛd Ch St
3. n the SOLE of a horse-drawn plough I.8.9. biːd So, bɪd So Sr, bɛd O Bk MxL W Sr Co D Do Ha Sx
4. n the metal BUSH at the centre of a cart-wheel I.9.8. bɛd St
5. n a BUMPER of a cart I.10.1(a). bɛd Wo
6. n the BASE of a stack II.7.4. beɪd D, bɛd Mon Sr Co D, beɪd D
7. n the AFTERBIRTH that comes from a cow's uterus after a calf is born III.1.13. bɛd Ess Co
8. n the UTERUS of a cow III.2.4. bɛd Nb Sa Sf Ess Co

bed-chamber *n* a BEDROOM V.2.3. bɛdtʃeːmbəˡ Sa, bɛdtʃæɪmbə Nf

bedding *1. n* the BASE of a stack II.7.4. bɛdɪn D Do, bɛdən D Do, bɛdn Ha, beɪdɪn D
2. n the AFTERBIRTH that comes from a cow's uterus after a calf is born III.1.13. bɛdn Nf
3. n the UTERUS of a cow III.2.4. bɛdn Nf
4. n **her bedding's come down** she (a cow) shows signs of calving, ⇐ SHOWS SIGNS OF CALVING III.1.12(b). *3prperfsg* hə bɛdnz kʌm dəʊn Nf

bedding-fork *n* a HAY-FORK with a short shaft I.7.11. beˀdnfɔːk Man

bedlam-feet *adj* SPLAY-FOOTED VI.10.5. bɛdləmfiːt Brk

bed-pieces *npl* the BUMPERs of carts I.10.1(a). bɛdpiːsəs He

bed-plate *n* the SOLE of a horse-drawn plough I.8.9. bɛdpleɪt Bk

bed-quilt *n* a QUILT V.2.11. bɛdkwɪlt Y Wo Nf, bɛdkwɪɬ Gl O, bɛdtwɪlt Y

bedroom *n What do you call the one [i.e. room] where you sleep?* V.2.3. Eng. ⇒ **bed-chamber, chamber, kitchen-loft, parlour-loft, room, upstairs room;** ⇒ also **house-chamber, kitchen-chamber, parlour-chamber, sledge-roof chamber**

bedroom slops *n* stale URINE used as fertiliser or insecticide VI.8.8. bɛdɹʊmslɒps Gl

bedspread *n* a QUILT V.2.11. bɛdspɹɛd Nf *[marked u.r. EMBM]*

bee-aviary *n* a HIVE IV.8.8(a). bɪi-ɛɪvəˡɪɪ Brk *[marked u.r. SBM]*

bee-bonnet *n* a SKEP IV.8.8(b). biːbɒnət So

bee-butt *1. n* a wooden HIVE IV.8.8(a). biːbʌt So
2. n a SKEP IV.8.8(b). biːbʌt So Co D Do

bee-coop *n* a SKEP IV.8.8(b). *pl* biːkuːps MxL

beef-dripping *n* DRIPPING V.7.5(a). biːfdɹɪpɪn La, bᵊiːfdɹɪpɪn Bk, bəɪfdɹɪpɪn Y

beef-fat *n* DRIPPING V.7.5(a). bɹiffat Y

beef-house *n* a COW-HOUSE I.1.8. biːfaʊs Man

bee-hackle *n* a SKEP IV.8.8(b). biː-akɬ Do *[queried ir.r. SBM]*

bee-hive *1. n* a HIVE IV.8.8(a). biː-æːv D, biː-æːz D, biː-aːv Y, biːhaɪv So, biː-aɪv Y Ch So, biː-ɑɪv Y D, biː-ɑɪv La Y, biːhɒɪv So, biː-ɒɪv W Do, biː-ɔɪv Wo Bk Do, biˑhʌɪv Nf, biː-ʌɪv Gl, biːhəɪv W, biːjəɪv Wo, bɹi-ɔɪv Ess, bɹihʌɪv Nf, bɹi-əɪv Brk, bɹiː-əɪv Sx, *pl* bɛɪ-ɑɪvz Db, *pl* bɛɪ-ɒːɪvz St, bəɪ-aɪv Y
2. n a SKEP IV.8.8(b). biː-æːv D, biːhəɪv W, biː-əɪv Do, biːjəɪv Wo, bɹihʌɪv Nf

bee-pot *n* a SKEP IV.8.8(b). biːpɒt Do

beer-tub *n* a BARREL VI.13.12. bəətʌb Nf

bee-skep *n* a SKEP IV.8.8(b). biːskɪp Hu*[rushes]* Ess, biːskɛp Y Nf, bɹiskɪp Ess, bɹiskɛp Nf

beesle *n* BEESTINGS V.5.10. biːzɬ Sf

beesning(s) *n* BEESTINGS V.5.10.
no -s: bɪznɪn Bk*[old]* Bd
-s: bɪznɪnz Nth Hu C Bk Bd, bɪznənz C Sf, besnɪnz Db*[old]* L, bɔɪsnɪnz Nth*[rare]*

beesting(s) *n What do you call the first milk of a newly-calved cow?* V.5.10.
no -s: biːstɪn Ch Db Sa St Ess Sx, biːstn Nb, bɪstɪn Sa, beɪstɪn Db
-s: bɹistɪŋz Brk, biːstɪnz Nb Cu We Ch Db Sa St He Mon Gl O L Lei Nth Ess So Sr K Ha Sx, biːstnz Cu Du Nf, biːstənz Nb, bɪastɪnz La Y, beːstɪnz Sa Gl W Do Ha, beːstənz Ha, beɪstɪnz K, beːˡstɪnz Mon, beːstnz Nf, bɛɪstɪnz Y Ch*[old]* Db Sa St Wa*[modern]* Brk K, bæɪstɪnz Gl Brk, baɪstɪnz Sa St Wo Lei, baɪstɪnz Wa, bɒɪstɪnz Sa He*[old]* Wo W, bwɒɪstɪnz Wo, bɔɪstɪnz Wa*[old x1]* Gl O, bɔɪstɪnz Y St Brk

⇒ **afterings, beesle,** *beesling(s)* ⇒ **beestling(s), beesning(s), beest(s), beestling(s), beest-milk, beests-milk, beesty-milk, bisky, bisky-milk, bizzy-milk, brisling, brisling-milk, buss-milk, bussing-milk, bussy-milk, buttermilk, buzzy-milk, calving-milk, cherry-curds, colostrum, colstrap, curdle, curdlings, curdly, curds, custards, first-and-seconds, first milk, first milking(s), ganoos, gleanings, kesnoos, mother-milk, new milk, ropy-milk, sop-milk, streaky-milk, whey-milk**

beestling(s) *n* BEESTINGS V.5.10.
no -s: biːzlən Sf, bɪzlin Hrt
-s: biːstlɪnz Du Y L Lei R Nf, biːslɪnz Nt Lei Nf, biːsɬɪnz Lei, biːsəɬɪnz Lei, bɹiːzlɪnz Ess, biːstlənz

Nb Du, biːstlnz Nf, biːslənz Du, bɪslɪnz Y L, bɪs|ɪnz Y, bɪzlɪnz L Nf Hrt Ess*[old]*, bɪəslɪnz Y L, bɪəzlɪnz Y, beɪzlɪmz Nf, bɛstlɪnz Lei, bɛslɪnz L, bɛsɫɪnz Lei, bɛzlɪnz L, bəɪstlɪnz Y *[beesling(s) and beestlings conflated; considerably intermingled in BM]*

beest-milk *n* BEESTINGS V.5.10. biːstmɪlk Cu, bɪəstmɪlk We La Y, bɪəsmɪlk Y, bəɪstmɪlk Y, bɪʃmɪʊk Sr

beest(s) *n* BEESTINGS V.5.10.
no -s: biːst La Y Ch Db, bɪəst Y, bɛɪst Ch St
-s: biːsts St

beests-milk *n* BEESTINGS V.5.10. bɒɪstɪzmɪɫk W

beesty-milk *n* BEESTINGS V.5.10. bɪstɪmɪɫk Do*[old]*

beetle *1. n* a heavy wooden MALLET I.7.5. biːtl sY He Wo O L Nth Nf, biːtɫ Wo Wa O Lei R Nth Hu C Nf Bd Hrt Ess K Ha, biːtəɫ He Gl O Bk, biːdɫ K Ha, biːʔl O Nf, biːʔɫ C Nf Sf Bk Bd Ess, bɪɪtʔl Nf, biːtʔɫ Ess, bᵊiːʔəɫ Bk Hrt, bɪɪtʊɫ Gl Brk, bɪɪdʊɫ Sx, bɪɪːtʊ Sx bɪtɫ Gl So Sr, bɪdɫ So D Do, bɪʔʊɫ Sr, baɪtɫ So, bɒɪtɫ So, bɒɪdɫ Ha, bɒɪʔɫ So W, bʌɪtəɫ Gl, bəɪdɫ So, bwɒɪtɫ W, bwɒɪdɫ W Ha, bʷɒʊʔɫ W

2. n a wooden mallet of any size. biːdʊɫ K

3. n a wooden mallet of indeterminate size. biːtɫ O Hrt So Brk, biːtʔɫ Sf, bɪˈɪtʔl Nf, biːʔɫ Sf, biːʔʊɫ Bk Brk, bɪɪdʊɫ Ess Sx, bɪɪːdʊ Sr Sx, bɪtɫ Sx, bɪtʊɫ Sr, bɒɪtɫ Brk

before noon *n* THIS FORENOON VII.3.15. bɪfoʊə nɛʊn St, əfʊə nʊɪn Y

beggared *adj* EXHAUSTED, describing a tired person VI.13.8. bɛgəˤd Sa

beggared up *adj* EXHAUSTED, describing a tired person VI.13.8. bɛgəˤːd ʌp Sa

beggar-lice *n* GOOSE-GRASS II.2.5. bɛgələɪs O

beggar off *imp* GO AWAY! VIII.7.9(a). bɛgəɹ ɒf Ch

beggar's-lice *n* GOOSE-GRASS II.2.5. bɛgəzlɔɪs Nth

begins *vi-3prsg* There are two times in the day that every schoolboy knows. One is about 9 in the morning, when school .... VIII.6.2(a). bɪgɪnz Wa, bɪgɪnz Cu Y Ch Sa St He Wo Wa Mon Gl O L Lei R Nth Nf Bk Hrt Ess So W Brk K D Ha Sx, bɪgɪn Nf Sf Ess Do, bɛgɪnz Lei, bəgɪn Sr. ⇒ **commences, gans in, gins, goes in, is open, opens, opens out, starts, takes in** *[uninflected and periphrastic do forms subsumed under inflected forms]*

behind *n* the ARSE VI.9.2. bɪ-aɪnd La, bɪ-ɑˈɪnt L, bɪ-ɒɪn So, bɪhɔɪnd Ess*[polite]*, bɪhɔɪn Ess

belch *vi* to VOMIT, referring to a baby bringing up milk VI.13.14(b). bɛɫʃ Ess

belching *v-ing* What is your word for this *[indicate belching]*? VI.13.13. Eng exc. Du Man Hrt MxL W D Do Ha. ⇒ **barging,** *baulking* ⇒ **boking,** *belching the wind up,* **belching up, belging, belging up, belking,** *belking it up* ⇒ **bulking up, belking up, biking, bloking, blurping, boking, boking about,**

boking up, boking up *the wind,* **boking up** *wind,* **bolking, bolking about, bolking up, breaking up, breaking up** *the wind,* **broaking, bulching, bulching up** *the wind,* **bulging, bulking, bulking** *it* **up, burking, burping, gapping, gaup, gelping, glutch, gulching up,** *gulp* ⇒ **gulping, gulping, gulping** *wind* **up, rifting, rifting** *the wind* **up, rifting up, rosping, vorging up** *wind [there is considerable variation in orthographic treatment between BM volumes]*

belder *vi-3prpl* bulls BELLOW III.10.2. bɛldə Ch St, bɛldəˡz Ch, bɛldəz Db, bɛɫdəz Lei, *prppl* bɛldəɹɪn Ch

belder out *1. vi-3prpl* they MOO, describing the noise cows make during feeding time in the cow-house III.10.4(a). bɛldəɹ æʊt Lei

2. vi-3prpl they MOO, describing the noise cows make in the fields III.10.4(b). bɛldəɹ æʊt Lei

belge *vi* to VOMIT, referring to a baby bringing up milk VI.13.14(b). *prppl* bɛldʒɪn Ch

belging *v-ing* BELCHING VI.13.13. bɛldʒɪn Ch, bɛlʒɪn La *[not a NBM headword]*

belging up *vphr-ing* BELCHING VI.13.13. *no -ing* bɛlʒ ʊp Ch

belking *v-ing* BELCHING VI.13.13. bɛlkɪn Du La Y, bɛlkən Cu We, bɛɫkɪn So W Do, bɛɫkən Co D Ha, bɛɫəkɪn W, *no -ing* bɛʊk So *[not a NBM headword]*

belking up *vphr-ing* BELCHING VI.13.13. bɛlkən ʊp Y *[not a NBM headword]*

bell *1. n* an EAR of oats II.5.2(b). bɛɫ Lei Bk

2. n the BELLY VI.8.7. bɛl Nth

3. vi-3prpl bulls BELLOW III.10.2. bɛl La Db L, bɛlz La Y Wo L, *prppl* bɛlɪn Sa, bɛɫz He Wo

4. vi-3prpl they MOO, describing the noise cows make during feeding time in the cow-house III.10.4(a). bɛl La L

5. vi-3prpl they MOO, describing the noise cows make in the fields III.10.4(b). bɛlz He L, *prppl* əbɛlɪn Wo, bɛɫz He Wo

6. vi to SCREAM VIII.8.11. bɛɫ Wo

bell-bind *n* BINDWEED II.2.4. bɛɫbaɪn Hrt Ess, bɛlbaːnd Y, bɛɫbɔɪn Sf Ess, bɛʊbɔɪn Ess Sr Sx, bɛʊbɔɪnd Ess, bɛʊbʌɪn Sr, bɛɫbɔɪn Hrt, bɛɪɫbɔɪn Brk, bæʊbaɪn K, bʊɫbaɪn Ess

belling *v-ing* SHRIEKING, describing the shrill noise made by a baby VI.5.15. bɛlɪn Wo

bellock *1. vi-3prpl* bulls BELLOW III.10.2. bɛlək Ch, bɛləks He, bɛləks Ch, bɛɫəks He, bɛɫʊks Gl

2. vi-3prpl they MOO, describing the noise cows make during feeding time in the cow-house III.10.4(a). bɛlʊk St

3. vi-3prpl they MOO, describing the noise cows make in the fields III.10.4(b). bɛlʊk St, bɛlək Sa, bɛləks He, bɛɫəks He Mon, bʊɫəks Mon

4. *vi* to SCREAM VIII.8.11. bɛlʊk Wo, bɛlək St*[old]*, *vbln* bɛləkɪn Sa

bellocking *v-ing* SHRIEKING, describing the shrill noise made by a baby VI.5.15. bɛləkɪn St*[=crying]*, əbɛləkɪn St

bellow 1. *vi-3prpl Now tell me your words for the usual cries animals make. Bulls....* III.10.2. bɛlɪz Sa Wo, *prppl* əbɛlɪ-ɪn Wo, bɛlɒʊ Brk, bɛlɒʊz K, bɛɫɒʊ Sr Sx, bɛɫɒʊz Sx, bɛlɔʊ Brk, bɛlɔʊz Ess, bɛɫɔʊz Sx, bɛɫoːz Mon, bɛlou So, *prppl* əbɛlouɪn Brk, bɛluː Du, bɛlə Nb Cu Y Ch Db St Wa Nt Lei R Nth Hu Bk Bd Ess, bɛləz Du Y Db Sa O MxL Brk, bɛlərz Cu, *prppl* bɛləɹɪn Lei, *-ing* bɛləɹɪn Y L K, bɛɫə Lei, bɛɫəz He Gl, *prppl* əbɛləɹɪn Lei Ess, *prppladj* bɛɫəwɪn MxL, bɛləᴶ K, bɛləᴶz Brk, bɛləᶜ Gl Nth Bk Bd So, *inf* bɛləᶜ Sa, bɛləᶜz̩ Sa Gl O Brk, bɛɫəᶜː W Ha Sx, *prppl* bɛɫəᶜːɾɪn Ha, *-ing* bɛɫəᶜːɾɪn W Sx, *prppl* əbɛɫəɾɪn W, baɫəᶜː Ha, bəɫəᶜː So, *adj* bələɾɪn So. ⇒ **baa, baa out, bawk, bawl, beal, beal out, belder, bell, bellock, belve, blare, blart, blodder, blore, blort, blother, croon, cry, growl, holler, moan, moo, mully, roar, rout**

2. *vi-3prpl* they MOO, describing the noise cows make during feeding time in the cow-house III.10.4(a). bɛlɒʊ K, bɛɫɒʊ Sr Sx, bɛɫoː W, bɛlou St, bɛləz Brk, *-ing* bɛləɹɪn K, bɛləᶜ Bk Sx, bɛɫəᶜː W, bɛɫəᶜɾz̩ Sx, baɫəᶜː Ha

3. *vi-3prpl* they MOO, describing the noise cows make in the fields III.10.4(b). bɛlɒʊ K, bɛɫɒʊ Sr, bɛɫoː W, bɛluː Du, bɛlə Nb Cu*[in bad temper]* Y St O L Nth Hu C Bk Bd Hrt Ess, bɛləz Sa, *prppl* bɛləɹɪn Nf, *-ing* bɛləɹɪn K, bɛləᶜ Gl Nth Bk Ha Sx, bɛləᶜz̩ Brk, bɛɫəɾ O, bɛɫəɾz̩ Sx, baɫəᶜː Ha

4. *vi-3prpl* sheep BLEAT III.10.5. bɛlə Wa

bellow about *viphr-3prpl* they MOO, describing the noise cows make in the fields III.10.4(b). *-ing* bɛɫɒʊɪn bɛʊt Sr

bellowing out *vphr-ing* SHRIEKING, describing the shrill noise made by a baby VI.5.15. bɛləɹɪn aːt Y

bellows 1. *n What do you call this [indicate a pair of bellows]?* V.3.10. Eng. ⇒ *a bellows, (a) pair of bellows*, **blow-bellows**

2. *n* the LIGHTS or lungs of a slaughtered animal III.11.5. bɛɫoʊz So, bɛləs Y, bɛləsɪz So

bellowsed up *adj* EXHAUSTED, describing a tired person VI.13.8. bəlɪst ʌp So

bellowsing *v-ing* PANTING VI.8.1. bɛləsən Sf

bells *n* the WATTLES of a hen IV.6.19. bɛɫz Co

bell-vine *n* BINDWEED II.2.4. *pl* bɛlvɑɪnz Hu, bɛɫvɑɪn C Bd, bɛɫvɔɪn Sf

bell-wind *n* BINDWEED II.2.4. bɛʊwɑɪn Sr, bɛɫwɔɪn Bk

belly 1. *n* a LITTER of piglets III.8.3. bɛlɪ Sa He Wo, bɛɫɪ He Wo Co, balɪ Ch Db Sa

2. *n What do you call this [indicate the belly]?* VI.8.7. Eng. ⇒ **bell, gut(s), kite, paunch, pod,** **poddy, stomach, tub, tummy**

3. *v* to remove the entrails from a slaughtered animal. *3prs* bɛləz St

belly/bellies *n* CHITTERLINGS III.12.2.
-*y*: bɛlɪ St, bɛɫɪ Hrt, bɛlᵉɪˑ Wa
-*ies*: bɛlɪz L Nth C Ess, bɛlɪs Sa

belly-ache *vi* to ACHE, referring to a stomach VI.13.3(b). bɛlɪ-ɛˑək L

belly-auger *n* a ROPE-TWISTER II.7.8. bɛlɪ-ɔːgə Nth

belly-band 1. *n What do you call this, going from shaft to shaft to stop the cart tilting up?* I.5.7. bɛlɪbænd Nb Hu Nf Ess So Brk Sx, bɛlɪbæn Man Brk, bɛɫɪbænd He Gl Brk Co, bɛlɪbæn Ha, bɛlɪband Nb Cu Du We La Y Db Sa St Wa Mon Gl O Nth So, bɛlɪbant Nb, bɛlɪban Cu He Bk, bɛɫɪband Mon O W D Do Ha, bɛɫɪban W D, bɛlɪband O, bɛlɪbɒnd Lei Nf Brk, bɛlɪbɒn Nf, bɛɫɪbɒnd He Gl W Ha, bɛlɪbɒn Co, bɛlɪbɔn Sf, bɛɫɪbʊnd St Wo Wa Lei, bɛlɪbʊn Wo Wa, bɛɫɪbʊnd Gl, bɛlɪbənd Y Ch Db Sa Wa O Nt L Lei R Nth, bɛlɪbənt Ch Db L Lei, bɛlɪbən Y Ch Sa He Wo O L Lei Nth Bk, bɛɫɪbənd Mon Lei, bɛlɪbnd Sa Wo, bɛlɪbn Sa He, bɛɫɪbnd Mon, bɛləbənd Nt L, bɛləbən Nt L, balɪband La St, balɪbant La Ch Db, balɪbʊnd O, balɪbənd Ch Db, balɪbən Ch Lei, balɪbnd Sa Wo, balɪbn Sa, bɒlɪbɒnt St, bəɫɪbænd So, bəɫɪbæn So, bəɫɪband So D Do, bəɫɪban D, bəɫɪbɒnd W, bəɫɪbɒn W D. ⇒ **back-strap, belly-beam, belly-bind, belly-chain, belly-girth, belly-strap, belly-tie, belly-wanty, belly-warren, ganty, girth, wanty**

2. *n* the GIRTH of the harness of a cart-horse I.5.8. bɛɫɪbend Sr, bɛlɪbænd Nf Sf Ess, bɛɫɪbæˑnd MxL, bɛlɪbæːənd Nb, bɛlɪband Cu Du We La Y Gl C Bd Hrt, bɛlɪbən L Bd, bɛlɪbənd Y Db Nt R Nth, bɛlɪbɒnd Lei Nf, bɛlɪbɒnt Nf, bɛləbənd Nt, balɪband La, baləband Bd, bəlɪbænd So

belly-bat *n* a BAT IV.7.7. bɛɫibat W

belly-beam *n* the BELLY-BAND of the harness of a cart-horse I.5.7. bɛɫibiːm Co

belly-bind *n* the BELLY-BAND of the harness of a cart-horse I.5.7. bɛɫibaɪ Co

belly-chain *n* the BELLY-BAND of the harness of a cart-horse I.5.7. bɛlɪtʃɛˑɪn Nf, bəɫɪtʃɛɪn D

belly-fat *n* the FAT round the kidneys of a pig III.12.7. bɛlɪfæt Sf

belly-girth 1. *n* the BELLY-BAND of the harness of a cart-horse I.5.7. bɛlɪgɛt Nf, bɛlɪgɛɾːtʔ Nf, bɛlɪgʌt Sf, bɛlɪgəːθ St K, bɛlɪgəːt Nf Sr K, bɛlɪgəːt Ess, bɛlɪgəːɹt Sf, bɛlɪgəᶜθ K, bɛlɪgəᶜːɾt Sr K Sx, bɛlɪgəᶜːɾt̩ Sr Ha Sx

2. *n* the GIRTH of the harness of a cart-horse I.5.8. bɛlɪgɛt Nf, bɛlɪgʌt Sf, bɛlɪgət Nf Ess, bɛlɪgəːt Ess K, bɛlɪgəˑɹt Nth, bɛlɪgəᴶt Brk, bɛlɪgəᶜt K, bɛɫɪgəᶜt̩ Ha, bɛlɪgəᶜːt̩ Ess Sx

33

belly-guts *n* CHITTERLINGS III.12.2. baligʌts Bd

belly-naked *adj* NAKED, describing a person VI.13.20. baɫɪnakɪd Sa

belly-strap *1. n* the BELLY-BAND of the harness of a cart-horse I.5.7.
beɫɪstɹæp Nf, beɫɪstɹæp Mon, beɫiʂtɹ̣æp So, beɫɪstɹap Y, beɫiʂtɹap D
2. n the GIRTH of the harness of a cart-horse I.5.8. beɫɪstɹæp Sf

belly-tie *n* the BELLY-BAND of the harness of a cart-horse I.5.7. bɪɫətəɪ W, beɫɪtɒɪ So, beɫəti: Ha, beɫətəɪ W, bəɫitæɪ So, bəɫita: D, bəɫitaɪ So, bəlitəɪ Do

belly-wanty *n* the BELLY-BAND of the harness of a cart-horse I.5.7. beɫɪwɒntɪ Ess, beɫɪwɒntɪ Sr, beɫɪwɒntɪ Ess, beɫɪwɒntʔɪ Sf

belly-warren *n* the BELLY-BAND of the harness of a cart-horse I.5.7. beɫɪwɒɹən Ess

belt *1. v* to CLEAR grass at the edges of a field II.9.5. beɫt Db
2. vt to BEAT a boy on the buttocks VIII.8.10. beɫt Y Ch Db Sa, beɫt W, beɫʔ Bk, -*ing* beʊtɪn Sx, bæɫt O; **give him a good belting** gɪv ɪm ə gʊd beɫʔɪn Bk

belting *vbln* **give him a good belting** to BEAT a boy on the buttocks VIII.8.10. gɪv ɪm ə gʊd beɫʔɪn Bk

belt-rope* *n* a rope placed round a stack below the eaves, to which are fastened ropes which pass over the thatch, holding it in place, ⇐ ROPES II.7.7(b). beɫtɹɪap Cu, beɫtɹɪəp Cu, beɫtɹe:ᵊp We, beɫtʁøp Nb

belve *1. vi-3prpl* bulls BELLOW III.10.2. beɫv Co D, bəɫv So D
2. vi-3prpl they MOO, describing the noise cows make during feeding time in the cow-house III.10.4(a). beɫv So*[when discontented x1]* Co, bəɫv So D
3. vi-3prpl they MOO, describing the noise cows make in the fields III.10.4(b). beɫv So*[when discontented x1]* Co, bəɫv So D

bench *1. n What do you dress pigs on after killing them?* III.12.1. bɪnʃ Gl, bentʃ Ch Db Sa St Wa Gl Bk Ess, benʃ Ch Sa St He Wo Wa Mon So W Brk Do. ⇒ **bearer, bier, block, butching-stool, clog, cradle, cratch, creel, crouch, dressing-bench, form, greasing-stool, hand-rack, hog-form, hog-stool, jib, killing-block, killing-stock, killing-stool, ladder, pig-bench, pig-block, pig-cratch, pig-creel, pig('s)-form, pig('s)-horse, pig-jib, pig('s)-ladder, pig-rack, pig-scratch, pig-slab, pig('s)-stock, pig('s)-stool, pig('s)-table, pig-trest, pig-trestle, pig-turnel, rack, scat, scrap, scrat, scratch, scrave(-board), scudder, scudding-board, slab, stock, stool, stretcher, thrall, trest, trestle, turnel**
2. n a CUTTING of hay II.9.15. beənʃ Man
3. n a SHEARING-TABLE III.7.8. bentʃ St, benʃ Y Sa He MxL So
4. n a flat surface on which bacon is cured, ⇐

SALTING-TROUGH III.12.5. bentʃ Db*[stone]*, benʃ Sa, beŋk La Y

bend *1. n* the iron TIRE round a cart-wheel I.9.10. bend Co
2. n the GROIN VI.9.4. bend L

bend down *viphr* to DUCK VIII.7.8. ben dæʊn Ha

bender* *n* part of a scythe, ⇐ GRASS-NAIL II.9.9. bendəᶜ Sx *[SBM Edd uncertain on interpretation]*

bends *npl* the RIDGES between furrows in a ploughed field II.3.2. benz So

bennet *n* a TUSSOCK of grass II.2.9. *pl* benəts W

bensil *vt* to BEAT a boy on the buttocks VIII.8.10. bensɪl Y, bensl Du Y, bensəl La

bensilling *vbln* **give it a good bensilling** to BEAT a boy on the buttocks VIII.8.10. gɪv ɪt ə gʊd benslɪn Y

be off *imp* GO AWAY! VIII.7.9(a). bi: ɒf St, bɪ ɒf Y, bi: ɔ:f Sf Ess Brk; **be off with it** bɪi ɔf wɪð ɪt Nf

be-out *adv* WITHOUT V.8.10(a). bɪ-ɛʊt Nth, bɪ-æʊt L*[old]*

berries *npl* GOOSEBERRIES IV.11.2. *sg* be.ɪɪ La

beside *prep Here's the door, and I am standing [stand to one side of it] ... it.* IX.2.5. bɪseɪd Nb Du Ch, bɪsæɪ Man, bɪzæd So, bɪzæ:d Co D, bɪzæɪd So Ha, bɪza:d D, bɪsaɪd Du Sa L Co, bɪzaɪd So, bɪsɑ:d Lei, bɪsaɪd Lei R Sr K, bᵊsaɪd K, bɪsɒɪd St K, bɪzɒɪd So W Co Ha, bɪsɔɪd Wa O Hrt Ess Brk, bəsɔɪd Sf, bɪzɔɪd Sx, bɪsʌɪd W Brk Sr, bɪsʌɪd O, bɪsəɪd Mon Gl Brk, bɪzəɪd So W Do; **beside of** bɪzæ:d ɔ: D, bɪzæ:d o: D, bɪzæ:d əv D, bɪza:d o: D, bɪsaɪd ə Nf, bɪzɒɪd ɒv Ha, bɪzəɪd oʊ Do; **beside on** bɪzəɪd ɒn W. ⇒ *aback on*, **again, against, alongside, alongside** *of*, **alongside** *on*, **anenst, anunst, anunt, aside, aside** *of*, **aside** *on*, **at side, at side** *of*, **at side** *on*, **at** *the* **side, at** *the* **side** *of*, **at** *the* **side** *on*, *backside*, **behind, beside** *of*, **beside** *on*, **broadside, by, by the side, by the** **side** *of*, **by the side** *on*, *close to*, *close up to*, *down* **alongside** *of*, *gain-hand*, *hard up to*, *in back of*, *longside* ⇒ **alongside**, *longside of* ⇒ **alongside**, **next to**, *nigh*, **plum, side, side** *of*, **side** *on*, **sidewards, sideways**, *the* **side**, *the* **side** *of*, **to the side** *of*, **up again**

besom *1. n [Show a picture of a besom.] What do you call this? [Do you make them yourself?] What used they to be made of?* I.3.15.
a. unspecified type of wood or plant used. bɪsəm K, bi:zʊm La Wa, bi:zm Lei R Ess, bi:zəm La Y Db Sa St Wo L Nth Hu C Bk Bd Ess, bɪzɪm W, bɪzʌm Co D, bɪzʊm Gl O Sr, bɪzm Brk Sr K Sx, bɪzəm Du O L Bk Hrt So W Co D, bɛzəm Wo, bɛɪzəm St, bʊzm Brk, bʊzəm Du, bəɪzəm Y

b. made of beech. biːzəm Y L, bɪzm So, bɪzəm Gl

c. made of birch. biːzʊm St Wa, biːzm La Sa Lei Sx, biːzəm Cu We La Y Ch Sa St He Wo Wa Nt Nth Sf Bk, bɪzœm Gl, bɪzʌm Co Ha*[silver-birch]*, bɪzʊm Ch Wo Wa Gl O Ha, bɪzm He Wo Sr Sx, *pl* bɪzmz Brk, bɪzəm Cu We He Mon Gl O L Sf Bk So W K Co D Ha, bɪzn Sr, beːzəm Ch, *pl* bɛzʌmz Mon, bɛzəm So, bɛɪzəm Ch Db St, baɪzəm Y, bəɪzəm Y

d. made of blackthorn. biːzəm Nt

e. made of broom. biːzəm Y, bɪzʊm Ha, bɪzəm He, bɪiːsəm Man, bɛɪzəm St, bʊzəm Nb Cu, bʊsəm Nb

f. made of elm. bɪiːzəm Ess

g. made of fir. bɪzəm So W

h. made of gorse. *pl* biːzəmz Y

i. made of hazel. biːzʊm Nth, biːzəm Y*[hazel or hazel and rushes]* Nth Hu, bɪzm So, bɪzəm Gl, bɛzəm Do, bəɪzəm Y

j. made of heather. biːzʊm La, biːzm Lei R Sx, biːzəm Y Man Ch Db St Nt, bɪzʊm Ha, bɪzm Sr Sx, *pl* bɪzmz Brk, bɪzəm W Co D Do Ha, bɪzn Sr, bɛɪzəm Db, bʊzəm Nb Du, bəzəm Do

k. made of juniper. bɪzəm W

l. made of larch. bɪzʊm Gl, bɪzəm W

m. made of ling. biːzəm La Y, bɪzəm Cu Y, bɛɪzəm Y, baɪzəm Y, bʊzəm Nb Du Y, bəɪzəm Y

n. made of nutwood. bɪzəm W

o. made of snow-berry. biːzm Lei, bɪizəm Y

p. made of willow. biːzʊm Wa, biːzəm Y L, bɛzəm So, baɪzəm Y, bɪzəm Y L So W, bʊzəm Nb

q. made of yew. bɪzəm Ha

⇒ **bass-broom, bast-broom, bats-broom, besom-broom, birch-besom, birch-broom, broom, broom-brush, brush, brush-broom, lawn-broom, leaf-broom, nut-brush, twig-brush, willow-broom, wisk, wisk-broom;** ⇒ also **griglans**

2. *n* a MUCK-BRUSH I.3.14. biːzəm Cu La Y Db Nth Nf, *pl* biːzəmz L, bɪiːzm Ess, bɪzʌm Ha, bɪzʊm O, bɪzm Brk, bɪzəm Y O Sf W D Do Ha, bɛɪzəm Y, baɪzəm Y, bʊzəm Nb Du Y

3. *n* a long-handled BRUSH used for sweeping V.2.14. biːsəm Man, biːzəm Y

4. *n* a BROOM used for sweeping outdoors V.9.10. biːsəm Man, biːzm Sa, biːzəm Cu We Y*[made of ling x1]* Db*[old]* Sa St*[old]* L Nf, bɪzʊm O, bɪʒʊm St, bɪsm Ha*[manufactured]*, bɪzm So Brk, bɪzəm W Do Ha, bɛzəm So, bʊzəm Nb, bəɪzəm Y

5. *n* a BRUSH used for sweeping indoors V.9.11. biːsəm Man, bɪzm Brk

besom-broom *1. n* a MUCK-BRUSH I.3.14. biˈzmbɹʊm Nf

2. *n* a BESOM I.3.15. biːzəmbɹuːm Hrt, bəi:zmbɹəuːm Hrt

besom-brush *1. n* a MUCK-BRUSH I.3.14. biːzəmbɹʌʃ Hu C, biːzəmbɹʊʃ La Y

2. *n* a BROOM used for sweeping outdoors V.9.10. biːzəmbɹʊʃ Y L

besom-shaft *n* the HANDLE of a besom I.3.16. biːzəmʃaft Y

besom-stale *n* the HANDLE of a besom I.3.16. bɛzəmstɛɪɫ Wo

besom-stick *n* the HANDLE of a besom I.3.16. biːzəmstɪk Cu, bɪzʊmstɪk Wo Gl, bɪzmstɪk He, bɪzmstʊk Wo, bɪzəmstɪk Cu Mon, bəɪzəmstɪk Y

bess-cat *n* a TABBY-CAT, the female cat III.13.9. bɛskat Du

best apron *n* a decorative APRON V.11.2(b). bɛst apən Db

best bib and tucker *n* SUNDAY-CLOTHES VI.14.19. bɛs bɪb ŋ tʌkətˑ So

best clothes *n* SUNDAY-CLOTHES VI.14.19. bɛst klɪəz Y, bɛs klɪəz Du Y, bɛs tlʏˑəz Db, bɛs tleaz We La, bɛs kleəz Du, beːs klæʊz Hrt, bɛs tlɒɪz La, bɛs klɒʊðz K Sx, bɛs klɒuz Wo Sr, bɛs kɫɔːz W Ha, bɛst klɒʊðz O, bɛs klɔʊðz Ess Sx, bɛst klɔʊz Lei R, bɛs klɔʊz Lei Hu, bɛs klʌʊz Sf Bk Ess Sr, bɛs kloːᵊðz Mon, bɛst kloːz Wo, bɛs kloːz La Ch Sa He Wo Mon Gl So Do, bɛs kɫɔːz Mon O W Co D Do Ha, bɛst tlɔːz Sa, bɛs tlɔːz Ch Nt, bɛs kloˑʊðz Brk, bɛs klɒuz St He Wo Wa Mon Gl O Lei Nf Bk So Ha, bɛs tlɒuz Nf, beᶦs klous Man, bɛs klʊəz La Y Ch L, bɛs tlʊəz La Y, bɛs kluːz Ch St Wo, bas kɫuːz Ha, bɛs kɫuːz Co D

best room *n* the SITTING-ROOM of a house V.2.2. bɛst ɹuːm Hu*[old]*, bɛs ɹʊm Ess

best things *n* SUNDAY-CLOTHES VI.14.19. bɛs θɪŋz Sf

best tog *n* SUNDAY-CLOTHES VI.14.19. bɛs tɒg Gl So, bɛs tɔg So

best togs *n* SUNDAY-CLOTHES VI.14.19. bɛs tɒgz So W Co, bɛst tɔgz Sf

bes-wind *n* BINDWEED II.2.4. beːzwɒɪn Ha

bethink* *vrefl* to REMEMBER VIII.3.7. bɪθɪŋk Y

beth-wind *n* BINDWEED II.2.4. bɪðwɒɪn Ha, bɛθwɑɪn Bk

bethy-wind *n* BINDWEED II.2.4. bɪðiwaɪn Do, bɪðiwɒɪn Ha, bɪðɪwəɪn Do, bɛθiwɒɪn Ha, bɛðɪwʌɪn Gl

better clothes *n* SUNDAY-CLOTHES VI.14.19. bɛtəᴿ kleːz Nb, bɛtə tleaz We, bɛtə klʊəz Ch, bɛtəᴵ klʊəz La

better suit *n* SUNDAY-CLOTHES VI.14.19. bɛtəᴵ sɪut La, bɛtəɹ sɪuːt Y

betty-cat *n* a TABBY-CAT, the female cat III.13.9. bɛʔɪkɛat Ess, bɛtʔɪkæt Sf, bɛdʔɪkæt Sf, bɛʔɪkæt Nf Ess

betty-wind *n* BINDWEED II.2.4. bɛtɪwɒɪᵊn Gl, bɛdɪwʌɪn Gl

between *1. prep Do you see my teeth? Now I place this pencil … them.* IX.2.11. Eng exc. Hu C. ⇒ **atween, atwixt, atwixt *of*, betwixt, *in*, in atween, in between, in betwixt, in tween, tween,**

twixt

2. prep AMONG IX.2.12. bɪtwiɪn Ess, bɪtwɛɪn St;
in between ɪn bɪtwiːn St, ɪn twiiːn Sx *[marked u.r.*
EM/SBM]

betwixt *1. prep* BETWEEN IX.2.11. bɪtwɪkst Du Y
Sa St*[old x1]* Nt L*[rare x1]* Bd Brk

2. prep **in betwixt** AMONG IX.2.12. ɪn bɪtwɪkst Nf
[marked u.r. EMBM]

bever *1. n* an allowance of food given to a horse
when resting from work, ⇐ BAITING III.5.2. bɪiːvɐ
Ess

2. n a SNACK VII.5.11. biːvə Hrt Ess, biːvə¹ K,
biːvɐɾ O, bɛɪvə Wa Bd, bɛɪvəᵗ Bk

3. n MEAL OUT VII.5.12. bɪiːvə Ess*[very old]*

bevering *adj* **bevering and shivering** COLD,
describing a person VI.13.18. bɪvəɾɪn ən ʃɪvəɾɪn So

bezzle *v* to guzzle a drink, ⇐ GUZZLES VI.5.13(a).
bɛzl Db

bib *n* a long decorative APRON covering the chest
V.11.2(b). bɪb Nf

bib-apron *n* a decorative APRON V.11.2(b).
bɪbɛɪpɹən Ess, bɪbæɪpɹən Ess

biddies *1. npl* LICE IV.8.1(a). bɪdɪz Cu We La
Y*[old x1]*

2. npl NITS IV.8.2. bɪdɪz La

biddy *n* a NESTLING IV.7.1. bɪdɪ Man

bide *1. vt-2prsg* you BEAR pain VI.5.9. bɛɪd Nb Cu,
bæɪd Du, baːd Y, baɪd Cu Du*[old x1]* We La Y, baːd
Y, baɪd La Y Db, bʌɪd Gl

2. vi (**bide home**, **bide at home**) to STAY at home
VIII.5.2. bæːd Co D, bæɪd So, baːd Co D, baɪd Du Gl
So Co, baːd Co, bɒɪd So W Do Ha, -s bɒɪdz Ha, bəɪd
W Do

bidout *adv* WITHOUT V.8.10(a). bɪduːt Y*[old]*

bier *1. n* How is the coffin taken from the house to
the churchyard? VIII.5.9(b). Eng exc. Hu Hrt. ⇒
bearer, bogie, hand-bearer, *hand-bier,* **litter, rack,**
shallow bier, **stretcher, trolley, truck**

2. n a BENCH on which slaughtered pigs are dressed
III.12.1. bɛəɹ K

big *adj* GREAT, describing a mistake IX.1.6. bɪg Sa
L Nf Ess So *[marked u.r. SBM]*

big bellies *n* tripe, ⇐ CHITTERLINGS III.12.2. bɪg
bɛlɪz L

big bodkin *n* an EVENER, the main swingle-tree of
a horse-drawn plough harness I.8.4. bɪg bɒdkɪn W,
bɛg bɒdkɪn Gl

big-coat *n* an OVERCOAT VI.14.6. bɪgkoːt So

big draught *n* an EVENER, the main swingle-tree of
a horse-drawn plough harness I.8.4. bɪg dɹaːf D

big fat head *n* a HEADACHE VI.1.6. bɪg fat ɪəd Y

big finger *n* a THUMB VI.7.6. bɪg fɪŋgə Ess

big-fork *n* a HAY-FORK with a long shaft I.7.11. *pl*
bɪgfɒɹks Y

big ones *npl* A boastful farmer might say: On my farm
we never get small potatoes, but only .... II.4.5. Eng.

⇒ *big potatoes,* **bumpers,** *great big ones,* *great*
ones, large ones, ware potatoes ⇒ **wares, wares**

big post *n* the HANGING-POST of a gate IV.3.3.
bɪg pɔʊs L

big puddings *n* the large intestines of a pig, ⇐
CHITTERLINGS III.12.2. bɪg pʊdɪnz La

big sway-tree *n* an EVENER, the main
swingle-tree of a horse-drawn plough harness
I.8.4. bɪg swɛɪtɹɪ Nth

big swell-tree *n* an EVENER, the main
swingle-tree of a horse-drawn plough harness
I.8.4. bɪg swɛɬtɹɪ Nth Bd, bɪg swɛɬʔɹɪ C Bd

big-swingle-tree *1. n* an EVENER on a
horse-drawn plough I.8.4. bɪgswɪŋgltɹɪ: La Y,
bɪgswɪŋgltɹəɪ Y

2. n an evener, the main swingle-tree of a plough
harness. bɪg swɪŋltɹɪ: Ch Db, bɪg swɪŋgltɹɪ: Db
Wa, bɪg swɪŋɬtɹɪ: Wa, bɪg swɪŋgɬtɹɪ: Wa Nth, bɪg
swɪndltɹ¹i: Nt, bɪg swɪŋgətre: Ch, bɪg swɪŋgltɹɛɪ
Ch Db, bɪg swɪŋgətɹɛɪ Ch

big swivel *n* an EVENER, the main or only
swingle-tree of a horse-drawn plough harness
I.8.4. bɪg swɪvl Gl, bɪg swɪvɬ O

big weigh *n* an EVENER, the main swingle-tree
of a horse-drawn plough harness I.8.4. bɪg wɛɪ Bd,
bɪg wɛɪ Bk

big weigh-tree *n* an EVENER, the main
swingle-tree of a horse-drawn plough harness
I.8.4. bɪg wæɪʔtɹɪ Ess

big whib-tree *n* an EVENER, the main
swingle-tree of a horse-drawn plough harness
I.8.4. bɪg wɪbtɹɪ Bk

big whippens/whippence* *n* an EVENER, the
main swingle-tree of a horse-drawn plough
harness I.8.4. bɪg wɪpənz Ha *[compare*
whippen(s)/whippence(s)]

big whipper *n* an EVENER, the main
swingle-tree of a horse-drawn plough harness
I.8.4. bɪg wɪpəᵗ O

big whipple-tree *n* an EVENER, the main
swingle-tree of a horse-drawn plough harness
I.8.4. bɪg̊ wɪpʔɬtɹᵊi: Bk, bɪg wɪpʔɬtɹɪ Ess, bɪg
wɪbɬtɹɪ: Bk Bds

biking *v-ing* BELCHING VI.13.13. bæɪkən Man

bilberries *npl* What do you call those dark blue
berries the size of a pea, growing on a low plant
on the moors? You make pies with them and the
juice stains your teeth. IV.11.3. bɪlbɛɹɪz Y Wo Nt
Lei R Nth, bɪɬbɛɹɪz Wo O Nth, bɪɬbɛɾɪz O,
bɪʊbɛɹɪz Ess, bɪlbɐʁɪz Nb, bɪlbəɹɪz La Y Ch St
Wa O L Lei Nf, *sg* bɪlbəɹɪ Man, bɪɬbəɹɪz Wa Nf
K, bɪlbɹɪz Ch Db Sa St Wo Wa Nt Lei R, bɪɬbɹɪz
Wo Gl Lei Nth Ess, bɪʊbɹɪz Ess, bɛlbəɹɪz Ch. ⇒
bilberry-berries, **bilbers,** *billberries,*
black-hurts, **blaeberries,** **blueberries,**
bunnums, craw-crooks, dew-berries, filmers,

huckle-berries, hurtle-berries, hurts, whortle-berries, whorts, wimberries, wimble-berries, wimple-berries, winberries

bilberry-berries *npl* BILBERRIES IV.11.3. bɪlbɹɪbe̯ɹɪz Db

bilbers *npl* BILBERRIES IV.11.3. bɪlbə¹ˑz Y

bilboes *n* a TETHER for a cow I.3.4. bɪɫbᵉuz K

bild* *vi* to CHIP, referring to an egg that is about to hatch IV.6.10. bɪɫd So*[old x1]* D, bɪdɫd So

bill *1. n* a HEDGING-BILL IV.2.5. bɪɫ Wo, bɪʊ K
2. n a BILLHOOK IV.2.6. bɪl Y L Hrt Ess*[straight]*, bɪɫ Mon O R Nth Hu C Bk Bd Hrt Ess Ha, bɫ Ess
3. vi to CHIP, referring to an egg that is about to hatch IV.6.10. bɪɫ So W Do, *-ing* bɪɫɪn K, bɪʊ So
4. n the BEAK of a bird IV.6.18. bɪl Nb Du We La Y Man Ch Db St He L Nf, bɪɫ La He Mon Gl Ess*[of duck or goose x1]* So W Brk Co D Do Ha*[of duck]*

billet *n* a SWINGLE-TREE of a horse-drawn plough harness I.8.3. bɪlɪt K, bɪɫɪt K

billhook *1. n* What do you call the short-handled one *[implement used in plashing a hedge]?* IV.2.6. bɪɫɪk W, bɪɫyːk La Ch, bɪɫyk D, bɪɫyːk So D, bɪlʌk Hrt, bɪlouk La, bɪlhʊk Nb Nf Ess*[short straight blade]* So, bɪlʊk La Y Sa St Wo Wa Gl O Nth Hu Bk Ess MxL K Do, bɪɫhʊk Nf Sf Ess So, bɪljʊk Cu We, bɪɫʊk Mon Gl O Ess So W Brk Sr K Co Do Ha, bɪlək Wa Gl O Nth Brk, bɪlɪək Cu We Y, bɪljək We, bɪlhuːk Nb, bɪluːk We La Y Ch St L R Nth, bɪlɪuːk Db, bɪɫuːk K, bɪlʉːk Lei, bɪɫʉːk Lei, bɛluːk Man; **small billhook** smɔːɫ bɪɫʊk Brk. ⇒ *axe*, badging-hook, bagging-hook, bank-hook, bill, bill-knife, broad-hook, broom-hook, browse-hook, brushel, brushing-hook, chopper, clitheroe-bill, *clithero-bill* ⇒ clitheroe-bill, fag-hook, fagging-hook, faggoty-bill, flasher, frith-hook, fur-bill, furze-hook, gorse-hook, grass-hook, *grass-reap* ⇒ grass-rip, grass-rip, hacker, haftern-hook, hand-bill, hand-hook, *hatchet*, hedge-hook, *hedge-reap* ⇒ hedge-rip, hedge-rip, hedging-bill, hedging-hook, hedging-mallet, hook, laying-hook, lea, long-hook, paring-hook, patch-hook, rave-hook, reaf-hook, *reap* ⇒ rip, reap-hook, reaping-hook, rip, rip-hook, scrog-hook, shearing-hook, short-handle slasher, short-hook, sickle, slasher, slash-hook, *small axe*, *small* billhook, spear-hook, steeping-hook, straight-reap, swapple, swatcher, wood-hook; ⇒ also **fag**, **fag up**
2. n an implement with a short straight blade, used for chopping kindling wood. bɪɫhʊk Ess
3. n a HEDGING-BILL IV.2.5. bɪlʌk Sa He, bɪɫʌk Mon, bɪɫʊk He So, bɪʊ-ʊk Sx, bɪlək Sa

billing-hook *n* a HEDGING-BILL IV.2.5. bɪlɪnuːk Y

bill-knife *n* a BILLHOOK IV.2.6. bɪlnɛɪf Nb Du, bɪlnæɪf Y, bɪlnaɪf Du Y

billy-band *1. n* STRING used to tie up a grain-sack I.7.3. bɪlɪban Y *[apparently trade name]*

2. n TWINE used to fasten thatch on a stack II.7.7(b1). bɪlɪband Y

billy-bat *n* a BAT IV.7.7. bɪlɪbæt Ess

billy-buttons *n* GOOSE-GRASS II.2.5. bɪlɪbʊtnz Wa

billygoat *n* a BEARD VI.2.7. bɪlɪgoʊt St

billygoat-beard *n* a BEARD VI.2.7. bɪlɪguːtbɪəd St, bɪlɪgʊətbɪəd Y L, bɪlɪgɒʊtbɪəᵊd̩ Sr *[marked u.r. EMBM]*

billygoat-whiskers *n* a BEARD VI.2.7. bɪlɪgoːtwɪskəz La

bin *1. n* the GANGWAY in a cow-house I.3.7. bɪn He
2. n a CORN-BIN I.7.4. bɪn Nb Cu Du We La Y Man Ch Db Sa St He Wa Mon Gl O Nt Lei Nth Hu Nf Bk Bd Hrt Ess MxL So W Brk Sr Co D Do Ha Sx, biːn He Gl, bɪən Ess, bɛn Ess, bən Do
3. n a wooden corn-bin. bɪn He Wa Mon Gl O So W Brk Sr K Ha Sx; **wooden-bin** *pl* wʊdnbɪnz Ess
4. n a metal corn-bin. bɪn Sa Sf So Brk Sr K Co D
5. n a lidded corn-bin. bɪn So
6. n a corn-bin for storage in a barn or granary. bɪn Cu
7. n a metal container, one half holding chaff, the other corn. bɪn Sr
8. n a dry corner of a barn, partitioned off for storage of corn. bɪn D
9. n a container for cows' fodder. bɪn Sa
10. n a container for meal or cattle-cake. bɪn So
11. n a container for chicken-feed. bɪn So
12. n a dough-bin in which dough is kneaded. bɪn Wa*[wooden]* W Brk
13. n a container, one half holding flour, the other bread. bɪn R
14. n a container. bɪn Man Ess So
15. n a metal container. bɪn Cu Sf Co D Sx
16. n an ASH-MIDDEN V.1.14. bɛn Ess
17. n a container used as a PASTE-BOARD V.6.5. bɪn W*[old]*

bind *1. vt* When you cut corn with a scythe, what do you do after cutting it? II.6.2. bɪnd Nb Cu Du We La Y Lei, bɪn Nb Cu, bæːnd D, bæːn D, bæɪnd Man So, bæɪn Man, baːnd La Co, baːn D, baɪnd Y Sa So Co D, baˑɪn Lei, baːnd La Y D, baːn D, baɪnd La Ch Db Nt Bk K, *-ing* baɪnɪn K, bɒɪnd Sa St So W K Co, bɔɪnd Gl O Sf Hrt Ess Ha Sx, bʌɪnd Brk Sr, bʊnd Sa, bəɪnd Wo Mon Brk Do Sx. ⇒ **bind round**, **bind up**, **bunch up**, **tie**, **tie round**, **tie up**
2. v to PITCH sheaves II.6.10. *3prsg* baˑɪnz Lei, baɪnd Hu Bd
3. n BINDWEED II.2.4. bɪnd L, baɪn Sa, baɪnd Sa, *pl* baɪnz Nf, bɒɪn Nf, bɔɪnd Sf, bʌɪn Nf, bʌɪnd Nf, bəɪnd Sx
4. n the iron TIRE round a cart-wheel I.9.10.

baɪnd Co D

5. n TWINE used to fasten thatch on a stack II.7.7(b1). bəɪᵊn Wo

6. n ROPE used to fasten thatch II.7.7(b2). bæɪnd So*[reed, straw, or grass]* D*[straw] [possibly sg SBM]*

bind-band *n* STRING used to tie up a grain-sack I.7.3. baɪndband Y

binder **1. n* a ROPE-TWISTER II.7.8. baɪndə Ess, baɪndəᴶ Y

2. n a DIAPER V.11.3. bæɪndəᵗ: So, bɔɪndɐ Ess, bʌɪndə Nf, bʌɪndəᵗ Sr *[marked u.r. SBM]*

binder-band *1. n* STRING used to tie up a grain-sack I.7.3. baɪndəband Y, baˑɪndəband L

2. n TWINE used to fasten thatch on a stack II.7.7(b1). baɪndəband Y, baˑɪndəband L

binder-cord *n* STRING used to tie up a grain-sack I.7.3. bæɪndᵊᵗ:kuːɽd D, baɪndəᵗ:kuəᵗːd Co

binder-string *1. n* STRING used to tie up a grain-sack I.7.3. bæɪndəstʰɹɪŋ Man, baɪndəᵗ:s̩tɾɪŋ Co, baɪndəstɹɪng La, bɔɪndəᵗːs̩tɾɪŋ Co Ha, bɔɪndəstɹɪŋ Ess, bʌɪndəᴶstɹɪŋ Sr

2. n TWINE used to fasten thatch on a stack II.7.7(b1). baˑɪndəstɹɪŋ Lei, baɪndəᵗstɹɪŋ Bd, bɔɪndəstɹɪŋ Ess, bʌɪndəstɹɪŋ Nf*[modern]*

binder-twine *1. n* STRING used to tie up a grain-sack I.7.3. bæːndəᵗ:t̩wæːn D, baɪndətwaɪnd Y, baɪndəɹtwaɪn He, baɪndəᵗ:t̩waɪn Co, baːndəᵗ:twaːn D, baɪndətwaɪn MxL, bɔɪndəᴶtwɒɪn K, bɔɪndəᵗ:twɒɪn Ha, bɔɪndətwɔɪn Wa Ess, bɔɪndəᵗtwɔɪn Sx, bʌɪndətwʌɪn Nf, bʌɪndəᵗtwʌɪn Brk Sr, bəɪndətwɔɪn Wa, bəɪndəᵗtwaɪn Brk Sx, bəɪndəᵗ:twəɪn W

2. n TWINE used to fasten thatch on a stack II.7.7(b1). baɪndətwaɪn Y, baɪndətwaɪn La*[for corn-stack]* L K, baɪndəᴶtwaɪn La, baɪndəᵗtwaɪn K, bɒɪndəᴶtwɒɪn K*[old x1]*, bɔɪndəᵗ:twɒɪn W, bɔɪndətwɔɪn Ess, bʌɪndətwʌɪn Nf

binding *n* ROPES used to fasten thatch on a stack II.7.7(b2). bɔɪndɪn Sx

binding-cord *n* TWINE used to fasten thatch on a stack II.7.7(b1). bɔɪndɪnkɔːəᵗɽd Sr

binding-post* *n* the central upright bar of a gate, ⇐ HANGING-POST IV.3.3. bʌɪndɪnpost Nf

binding-string *n* STRING used to tie up a grain-sack I.7.3. bɔɪndɪnstɹɪŋ Sr, bʌɪndɪnstɹɪŋ Sr, bəɪndəns̩tɾɪŋ W

binding-twine *1. n* STRING used to tie up a grain-sack I.7.3. bɔɪndɪntwɔɪn Sx, bəɪːndɪntwəɪːn Wo

2. n TWINE used to fasten thatch on a stack II.7.7(b1). bɔɪndɪntwɔɪn Wa*[modern]*, bəɪːndɪntwəɪːn Wo

bind round *vtphr* to BIND corn into a sheaf II.6.2. bɪnd … ɹaʊnd Y

bind(s) *n* POTATO-HAULMS II.4.4.
no -s: baɪn Ess, bɔɪnd Ess, bɔɪn K
-s: bɔɪnz Ess

bind-turner *n* a ROPE-TWISTER II.7.8. bɪntɐˑnə Nf

bind-twister *n* a ROPE-TWISTER II.7.8. bæɪntwɪstəᵗ: So

bind up *vtphr* to BIND corn into a sheaf II.6.2. bæɪnd .. ʌp So, baɪnd … ʌp So, baɪnd ʌp Ess

bindweed *n [Show a picture of bindweed.] What do you call this?* II.2.4. bɪnwiːd La Y, bɪndwiːd Nb Du Y, bæɪndwiːd Man, baɪnwiːd La Y Ch So, baɪndwiːd Y, baːndwiːd Y, baɪnwiːd L Nth K, baɪndwiːd Y L, baɪndwɛɪd Ch, bɒɪnwiːd St So, bɒɪndwiːd Nf K, bɔɪnwiːd Ha Sx, bʌɪnwiːd Sr, bʌɪndwiːd Nf Brk Sr, bəɪndwiːd Sx. ⇒ **arse-smart, bear-bind, bear-wind, bell-bind, bell-vine, bell-wind, bes-wind, beth-wind, bethy-wind, betty-wind, bind, bind-wood, canary-creeper, columbine, colvudgen, convolvulus, corn-bind, cornflower, devil's-gut, devil's-nightcap, devil's-twine, ground-ivy, ground-lily, lap-love, lily, morning-glory, oxberry-root, reed-bind, robin-run-in-the-hedge, robin-run-the-dike, sheep-bind, shoelaces, sweethearts, vine, wandering-willy, wave-wind, way-bind, way-wind, wheat-bind, wheat-vine, white-runners, widdy-wind, wid-wind, wild convolvulus, wild woodbine, willy-wind, with-wind, withy-wind, woodbine**

bind-wood *n* BINDWEED II.2.4. bɪnwʊd Y

bing *1. n* a TROUGH in a cow-house I.3.6. bɪŋ Nf

2. n the GANGWAY in a cow-house I.3.7. bɪŋ Ch Sa, bɪŋg Ch Db Sa St

3. n the gangway in a cow-house, used to store hay, ⇐ HAY-LOFT I.3.18. bɪŋg Ch St

4. n a CORN-BIN I.7.4. bɪŋ Nb Du La Y Ch Sa He Nt L Lei Nth Hu C Nf Sf Bd, bɪŋg La Sa St Sf, bɪŋk Ch

5. n a wooden corn-bin. bɪŋg La

6. n a metal corn-bin. bɪŋ Du

7. n a container for refuse. bɪŋ Y

8. n a container for straw in a bullock-yard. bɪŋ Sf

9. n a container for flour. bɪŋ Nth

10. n an ASH-MIDDEN V.1.14. bɪŋ L

11. n a container used as a PASTE-BOARD V.6.5. bɪŋ Nth

bing-range *n* the GANGWAY in a cow-house I.3.7. bɪŋɹeːndʒ Sa

bing-wall* *n* the wall at the head of a cow-stall, ⇐ GANGWAY I.3.7. bɪŋwɔːl Ch

bink *n* a SHELF V.9.4. bɪŋk Man

binny *n* a heavy wooden MALLET I.7.5. bɪnɪ Sr

birch *n What do you call that slender tree with the whitish bark?* IV.10.1. Eng; **birch-tree** bɜˑɪtʃtɹɪi Man, bəɪktɹiː Y.

⇒ **birch-*tree*, lady-tree, silver-beech, silver-birch, silver-larch, silvery-birch, white-birch, wych**

birch-besom *n* a BESOM made of birch I.3.15. bəˑtʃbɪzəm Sa

birch-broom *1. n* a MUCK-BRUSH I.3.14. baːtʃbɹʊm Sf, bəˑtʃbɽʏːm So, bəˑɾtʃbɹuːm W Brk Ha Sx

2. n a BESOM I.3.15. baːtʃbɹʊm Sf, baːtʃbɹʊuːm Ess, bʌtʃbɹʌm Sf, bʌˑtʃbɹʊm Ess, bətʃbɹʊm Sx, bəːtʃbɹʊm Sf Ess K, bəːtʃbɹuːm St, *pl* bəːtʃbɹʊuːmz Ess, bəˑtʃbɹʊm Ess K, bəˑtʃbɹuːm Bk Ess K Sx, bəˑtbɽuːm So, bəˑtʃbɹəm Ess

3. n a besom made of birch. bætʃbɹʊm Nf*[birch or broom]*, bætʃbɹuˑm Nf, bætʃbɹʉˑm Nf, bʌtʃbɹʊm Sf, bəːtʃbɹʊm Sf Ess, bəˑtʃbɹuːm Bk Sx, bɐːtʃbɹʉm Nf*[birch and briars]*

4. n a besom made of hazel. bəːtʃbɹʊm Ess

5. n a besom made of elm. bəːtʃbɹʊm Ess

6. n a BROOM used for sweeping outdoors V.9.10. baːtʃbɹʊm Ess, bəˑɪtʃbɹuˑm Brk, bəˑtʃbɹʊm O, bəˑɾtʃbɹʊm Sx*[old]*, bəˑtʃbɹuːm Brk K

7. n a BRUSH used for sweeping indoors V.9.11. bəˑɾtʃbɹuːm Brk

birds *npl What do you call all those things that fly, with feathers?* IV.6.1. Eng. ⇒ also **bird-starving, bird-tenter, bird-tenting, moorbird**

bird-scarer *n* a SCARECROW II.3.7. bəˑɹdskɛəɹə Hu, bəˑdɟskɛəɹə Ess

bird-starving* *v-ing* scaring BIRDS off crops IV.6.1. əbəˑɪdɟstaˑɪvɪn W

bird-tenter* *n* a bird-scarer, ⇐ BIRDS IV.6.1. bɔdtɛntə Nt

bird-tenting* *v -ing* bird-scaring, ⇐ BIRDS IV.6.1. bɔdtɛntɪn L

birle *v* to POUR tea V.8.8. bəːl Cu

birle out* *v* to POUR ale V.8.8. bɔl uːt Y

birns *n* KINDLING-*WOOD* V.4.2. bɒns Man, bɒnz Man

birses *npl* the BRISTLES of a pig III.9.4. bɛɔᵏsɪz Nb, basɪz Cu

biscuit *n* (off her) FOOD V.8.2. bɪskɪt Wo *[marked u.r. WMBM]*

bisky *n* BEESTINGS V.5.10. bɪski D

bisky-milk *n* BEESTINGS V.5.10. bɪskɪmɪłk Do, bɪskɪməłk So D

bit *1. n To do that [i.e. wrap up a parcel] you need not only brown paper, but also a [gesticulate] … (of) string.* VII.2.10. Eng. ⇒ **length, lump, piece,** *some*

2. n a BUMPER of a cart I.10.1(a). *pl* bɪts Nf

3. n a SLICE of bread V.6.10. bɪt Lei *[marked u.r. EMBM]*

4. n the CORE of a boil VI.11.7. bɪt Y

5. n a PINCH of sugar or salt VII.8.6. bɪt Du*[salt]*

Y*[sugar]* St He*[sugar xl]* Wa Lei; **little bit** laːtl bɪt Y, laɪl bɪt Y

6. n a LITTLE amount of milk VII.8.20. **a bit ə** bɪt Sa Mon Nth; **a little bit** ə lɛɪl bɪt Cu

bit-bat *n* a BAT IV.7.7. bɪtbæt Co, bɪtbat Y Ch Sa, bɪʔbat O, bɪʔbaʔ Bk, bɛtbat Ch

bitch *n What do you call the female [dog]?* III.13.2. Eng. ⇒ **stock-dog**

bitch-cat *n* a TABBY-CAT, the female cat III.13.9. bɪtʃkat D

bitch up *viphr* to OVERTURN, referring to a cart I.11.5. bɪʃ ʊp St

bite *n* **bite of eating** MEAL OUT VII.5.12. baɪt ə ɪtɪn Y

biting on *n* a SNACK VII.5.11. baːtɪnɒn Y

bitten-stoop *n* the SHUTTING-POST of a gate IV.3.4. bɪtɪnstuːp Cu, bɪtnstᵁuːp We

bitter *adj* INSIPID, describing food lacking in salt V.7.8. bɪʔəᵗ O

bizzy-milk *n* BEESTINGS V.5.10. bɪzɪməłk Co

blab *n* the TONGUE VI.5.4. blɛb Ess*[old]*

blabbing out *vtphr-ing* PUTTING your tongue OUT VI.5.4. *no -ing* blæb … ɛʊt Ess, blabɪn … ɛʊʔ Hu, blabən ɛʊt C, blabɪn … æʊt L

blackberries *npl What berries do children go picking along the hedgerows in the early autumn?* IV.11.1. Eng exc. Cu We. ⇒ **black-bowowarts, black-bums, blackies, black-kites, black-spice, blag-bers, blags, bowowarts, brambles, brameberries, brumble-kites, brumbles, bumblekites, bumbles-kites, bumly-kites**

black-bowowarts *npl* BLACKBERRIES IV.11.1. blakbʌwəwʌts Nb

black-bums *npl* BLACKBERRIES IV.11.1. blakbʊmz We La

black-currants *npl* RABBIT-DROPPINGS III.13.15. blɛkkʊɹənz Db

black-earth *n* PEAT IV.4.3. blakjɛɹθ Y

blackguarding *1. v-ing* CURSING VIII.8.9(a). əblakgaˑɪdɪn O

2. v-ing SWEARING VIII.8.9(b). ˈblæˌgaːdɪn Nf, blægaːdn Nf, blægaˑɪɽɪn Brk, blakgaˑɪdɪn Bk

black-head *n* a GULL IV.7.5. blakɪˑəd Y, *pl* blakɪˑədz L

black-hurts *npl* BILBERRIES IV.11.3. błakhaˑɪtʃ Ha

blackies *npl* BLACKBERRIES IV.11.1. blakɪz Nb

black-jack *n* CART-GREASE, used to lubricate the wheels of a cart I.11.4. blakdʒak Y

black-kites *npl* BLACKBERRIES IV.11.1. blakkaɪts Cu We, blakaɪts Cu

blackman *n* a BOGEY VIII.8.1. blɛkmɛn Sx, blækmæn Nf Ess Sr, blækʔmæn Nf, blakman Y

St So; **the blackman** ðə blækmæn Ess Sx, dɪ blækmæn Sx*[old]*

black-man *n* **the black-man with no white in his eyes** the DEVIL VIII.8.3. ðə 'blak'man wɪð noː waɪt ɪn ɪz aɪz Sa

black peppermints *n* SHEEP-DUNG II.1.7. blæk pɛpəᵗmɪnts Sx

black pond *n* a CESS-POOL on a farm I.3.11. blɛk pɒ·nd Sr, blɛk pɒn Sx

black pops *1. n* SHEEP-DUNG II.1.7. błak pɒps W
2. npl RABBIT-DROPPINGS III.13.15. błak pɒps W

black-spice *n* BLACKBERRIES IV.11.1. blakspaɪs Y

bladder *vi* to show signs of calving, referring to a cow with a swelling udder, ⇐ SHOWS SIGNS OF CALVING III.1.12(a). bładəᵗː W

bladders *npl* BLISTERS VI.11.5. błædəᵗːz̩ Co, bładəᵗːz̩ Co D

blade *1. n* a SHAFT of a cart I.9.4. bleɪd St
2. n the STEM of a corn-plant II.5.2(a). bleːd He, bleɪd Nf, bleɪd St Lei, bleːɪd Nf, bleˑəd L, blaid Nf

blade-carrier *n* the GRASS-NAIL of a scythe II.9.9. bleːɪdkæɹɪəᵗ Wo

blaeberries *npl* BILBERRIES IV.11.3. bliːbɛrɪz Cu, *sg* bliːbɛʁɪ Nb, bliːbɛɹɪz Nb Cu Du, blˡiːbɛrɪs Man, bliːbaʁɪz Nb Du, bliːbaɹɪz Du, bliːbəɹɪz Du We Y, blɪəbɛɹɪz Cu We Y, blɪəbəɹɪz We Y, bleːbɛʁɪz Nb, bleɪbɛʁɪs Nb, bleɪbəɹɪz Y, *sg* bleˑabɒɹɪ We, *sg* bleˑəbəɹɪ La, bleːbəɹɪz Cu, *sg* bleɪbɛɹɪ Man, blaːbəɹɪz La

blag-bers *npl* BLACKBERRIES IV.11.1. bleːgbəˡˑz Y

blag round *vphr* to CLEAR grass at the edges of a field with a scythe II.9.5. *-ing* blɛgɪn ɹaʊnd He

blags *npl* BLACKBERRIES IV.11.1. blɛgz Y, blagz Y

blain *n* a STYE in the eye VI.3.10. bleːn La Ch

blains *npl* BOILS VI.11.6. bleːnz Y*[old]*, blɛənz Y

blake *1. vi-3prpl* they MOO, describing the noise cows make in the fields III.10.4(b). bleɪk Ess
2. vi-3prpl sheep BLEAT III.10.5. bleːk So, błeːk Do, błeːk W, bleɪks Ess, bleːək So

blake out *1. viphr-3prpl* they MOO, describing the noise cows make in the fields III.10.4(b). błeːk æʊt Do
2. viphr-3prpl sheep BLEAT III.10.5. *-ing* błeːkən əʊt Do

blame *n* a person's own FAULT VIII.9.6. blɪəm Du, bleːm Nb

blank *adj* describing a cow's teat that is dry, ⇐ BLIND TEAT III.2.7. blaŋk Lei

blank quarter *n* a BLIND TEAT III.2.7. blæŋk kɔːtʔə Nf

blank teat *n* a BLIND TEAT III.2.7. blæŋk tɪt Nf

blare *1. vi-3prpl* bulls BELLOW III.10.2. bleɔᴿ Nb, bleɔᴿ Nb, *-ing* blɛɔʁən Nb, *-ing* blɛːɹən Cu, blɛᵗː So, blɛə Cu Hu C Nf Sf Ess, blɛəz Nb L, *prppl* əblɛəɹɪn Ess, blɛəˡ Nf Ha, błɛəᵗː So W Do, błɛəᵗːz̩ Ha, blæː Du, blæːz Du, *-ing* blæːɹən Du, blaːz L, *-ing* blaːɹən L, blaː Nf, blaːɹ Nf, *-ing* blɑːɹɪn Nf
2. vi-3prpl they MOO, describing the noise cows make during feeding time in the cow-house III.10.4(a). blɛːɹ Cu, *prppl* blɛːʈɪn So, blɛə Ess, *-ing* blɛəʁən Nb, blɛəz Y L, blɛəˡ Sr, blɛəˡz Ha, blɛəᵗː So Do, błɛəᵗː D Do, błɛəᵗːz̩ Ha, blaː Du
3. vi-3prpl they MOO, describing the noise cows make in the fields III.10.4(b). bleɔᴿ Nb, bleɔᴿ Nb, blɛˑə Hu C Nf Sf, blɛəz Y L, *-ing* blɛəɹɪn K, blɛərz Cu, blɛəˡ Sr, blɛəˡz Ha, blɛəᵗː So Do, błɛəᵗː D Do, błɛəᵗːz̩ Ha, blɛːəˡ Nf, blæː Du, blaː Du, blɑː Nf
4. vi-3prpl sheep BLEAT III.10.5. blɛː We St, blɛːɹ Cu We, blɛə Nb Cu Du Y L Nth Hu Nf Sf Ess, blɛˑəˡ Bk, blɛəɹ Cu Y, blæː Nf, blæːz Du, *-ing* blaɹən L, blaː L Nf, blaːz Du, blɑː Lei Nf, blɑˡː Nf
5. vi to SCREAM VIII.8.11. blɛˑə C Ess

blare out *viphr-3prpl* they MOO, describing the noise cows make during feeding time in the cow-house III.10.4(a). *-ing* blɛːʈɪn æʊt So

blaring *v-ing* SHRIEKING, describing the shrill noise made by a baby VI.5.15. blɛəʁən Nb, blɛəɹɪn Ess, blɛˑəɹən Ess, blæːɹən We, blɑˑɹɪn Nf, blɑˡːɹən Nf

blart *1. vi-3prpl* bulls BELLOW III.10.2. blaːt St Wa
2. vi-3prpl they MOO, describing the noise cows make during feeding time in the cow-house III.10.4(a). blaːt La Y St
3. vi-3prpl they MOO, describing the noise cows make in the fields III.10.4(b). blaːt Y Ch St Wa, blaːts Wo Sr
4. vi-3prpl sheep BLEAT III.10.5. blæːts Nt, blaːt La Ch Db Wo Wa L Bd, blaːts Sa Gl, *prppl* blaːtɪn St, *-ing* blaːtɪn St, *prppl* əblaᵗːʈɪn Wa, blaːt Ch, blɑːts St Wo
5. vi to SCREAM VIII.8.11. blaːt Wa, blɑːt St

blarting *v-ing* SHRIEKING, describing the shrill noise made by a baby VI.5.15. blaːtɪn Ch Sa St Lei

blash *n* SLUSH VII.6.16. blaʃ Y

blashy *adj* DULL, referring to the weather VII.6.10. blaʃɪ Y

blaspheming *v-ing* SWEARING VIII.8.9(b). blɛsfiːmɪn Sr

blast *v* to STOCK a cow III.3.6. blast Nb*[old]*

blasters* *npl* BLISTERS VI.11.5. błastəᵗːz̩ Ha

blate *1. vi-3prpl* they MOO, describing the noise cows make during feeding time in the cow-house III.10.4(a). błeːt Co

2. *vi-3prpl* they MOO, describing the noise cows make in the fields III.10.4(b). bleːt Sa, bɫeːt Co

3. *vi-3prpl* sheep BLEAT III.10.5. bleːt We La Y Ch Sa Gl, bleːts Db Nt, -*ing* bleːtɪn O, bɫeːt Co, -*ing* bɫeːtən D, bleɪt Du, bleɪʔs Bk, bleːɪts Wo O, bleˑət Y, bleːt St, bleːts Db, bɫeːt Co, bleɪt Ess, blɛˑət Y, blɛˑəʔ Bk

[*not a WMBM headword*]

4. *adj* SHY VIII.9.2. bleːt Nb

blate out* *viphr-3prpl* they MOO, describing the noise cows make in the fields III.10.4(b). *prppl* bleːtɪn aːt Y

blather *n* MUD VII.6.17. blaðə Y, blaðəᴶ Y, blaðəɹ Y

blathering *v-ing* GOSSIPING VIII.3.5(a). blɛðərən Cu, blaðəɹən Nb

blathering out *vtphr-ing* PUTTING your tongue OUT VI.5.4. blaðəɹɪn ... uːt Y

blatherskite *n* a GOSSIP VIII.3.5(b). blaðəskeɪt Du

blay *vi-3prpl* sheep BLEAT III.10.5. bleː Ch, blɛɪ St

bleach *n* stale URINE used for cleaning blankets VI.8.8. bliːtʃ St

bleak *vi-3prpl* sheep BLEAT III.10.5. bliːk So, bɫiːk W Do, -*ing* bɫiːkɪn Ha

bleared up *adj* STICKY, describing a child's hands VIII.8.14. blɪˑəd ʊp Y[*old*]; **bleared up and sticky** blɪəᴶd ʊp ən stɪkɛ Y

bleat 1. *vi-3prpl* [*Now tell me your words for the usual cries animals make.*] Sheep .... III.10.5. Eng exc. Du We Db Wa Gl O R Nf W Do Sx. ⇒ **baa**, *baa-aa* ⇒ **baa**, *bae* ⇒ **baa**, **bawl**, **bellow**, **blake**, **blake out**, **blare**, **blart**, **blate**, **blay**, **bleak**, *bleat and* **baa**, **blurt**, **cry**, **holler**, *hollo* ⇒ **holler**, **maa**, *mae* ⇒ **maa**, **mark**, **mawl**

2. *vi-3prpl* they MOO, describing the noise cows make during feeding time in the cow-house III.10.4(a). bliːt Sf, bɫiːt Co

3. *vi-3prpl* they MOO, describing the noise cows make in the fields III.10.4(b). bɫiːt Co

blebs *npl* BLISTERS VI.11.5. blɛbz Nb La Y[*when not burst x1*], blɛɪbz Nb

blethered *adj* EXHAUSTED, describing a tired person VI.13.8. blɛðəd Y

blewits *npl* MUSHROOMS II.2.11. bluʊːɪts Sr [*probably the type of mushroom*]

blind 1. *adj* A man who cannot see at all is .... VI.3.4. Eng. ⇒ also **blind-ploughman**

2. *adj* describing a cow's teat that is dry, or a cow with a BLIND TEAT III.2.7. blɪnd Cu Y, blɑɪnd Sr[*she's blind in one quarter*] K, blɒɪnd St So

blind-bat *n* a BAT IV.7.7. blɪndbat La, blɪnbat Cu

blind didd *n* a BLIND TEAT III.2.7. *pl* blɛɪn dɪdz Sa

blinders *npl* BLINKERS covering the eyes of a cart-horse I.5.2. blɪndəz Nb Cu Du We Y, blɪndɔᴿz Nb, blɪndɔᴿs Nb, blɪndəᴿz Nb Du, blɪndəɹz Du,

blɪndəɹz Y, blaɪndɔᴿz Nb, bɫɒɪndəᵗːz̩ Ha, blʌɪndəz Nf, blɒɪndəᵗz̩ Gl

blinding 1. *v-ing* CURSING VIII.8.9(a). blɒɪn-ŋ̩ Nf

2. *v-ing* SWEARING VIII.8.9(b). blɑɪndɪn Wa

blind-mouse *n* a SHREW-MOUSE IV.5.2. blɪndmɒʊs Y, blɪndmᵊuːs Cu, blɪnmuːs Y

blind pap *n* a BLIND TEAT III.2.7. blɪnd pap Nb Cu La Y, blɪn pap Cu, blaɪnd pap Y, blɑːnd pap Y, blɑɪnd pap La Y, blɑɪn pap Ch

blind-ploughman *n* a worm, ⇐ BLIND VI.3.4. blaɪnploʊmæn Man

blind quarter *n* a BLIND TEAT III.2.7. blɔɪnd kwɔːtɐ Ess, blɔɪn kwɔːtəˡɹ Sx, blɒɪn kwɔːdəᵗː So, bɫɒɪn kwɔːdəᵗː Do, blɔɪn kwɔːʔəᵗ Brk, blaɪn kwɔᵗːdəᵗː So, blʌɪnd kɔːʔə Nf, blʌɪnd kɔːᴶʔə Nf

blind teat *n* [*Show a picture of a cow.*] What do you call a teat that gives no milk? III.2.7. blɒːɪnd tiːt St, blɔɪn tɪiːt Sr, blɪnd tɪt Cu Du We La Y, blɪnd tɪˑət L, blæɪn tɪt Man, blaɪnd tɪt Y L, *pl* blaɪnd tɪts Sa He, blaɪn tɪt Sa So, blɑːɪnd tɪt St, *pl* blɑːn tɪts Lei, blɑɪnd tɪt La Y Db Lei Nth K, blɑɪn tɪt Nt Lei R Hu Bk Ess, blɑɪn tɪʔ Bk, blɒɪnd tɪt K, *pl* blɒɪnd tɪts Wo, blɒɪn tɪt So, *pl* blɒɪn tɪts Wo, blɔɪnd tɪt Wo, blɔɪn tɪt Wa Sf Ess Ha, blɔɪnd tɪʔ Bk, blʌɪnd tɪt Nf, blʌɪn tɪt Sr, bləɪnd tɪt Sx, *pl* bləɪn tɪts Wo, bləɪn tɪt Mon, bɫəɪn tɪt W, *pl* bləɪn tɪts He, bɫæːn tɛt D, bɫaɪn tɛt D, bɫɒɪn tɛt Ha, blɔɪn tɛt Bk Sx, blɔɪn tɛʔ Bk, bləɪn tɛt W, bɫəɪn tɛt Do. ⇒ **bad pap, bad quarter, bad teat, barrener, barren teat, blank, blank quarter, blank teat, blind, blind didd, blind pap, blind quarter, chamber pap, dead teat, deaf, deaf didd, deaf pap, deaf quarter, deaf teat, dried off, dried teat, dry, dry pap, dry quarter, dry spean, dry teat, dud, dud pap, dud teat, dumb pap, dumb teat, dummy, dummy pap, dummy-teat, false teat, lost quarter, segged quarter, three-quarter cow, three-quarters bag, waster, windy teat, withered teat, wrong, wrong quarter**

blinkers *npl* [*Show a picture of the harness of a cart-horse.*] What do you call this? I.5.2. blɪŋkɔᴿz Nb, blɪŋkɔᴿs Nb, blɪŋkəᴿz Du, *sg* blɪŋkə Cu, blɪŋkəz La Y Ch Db St Wa Mon Nt L Lei R Nth Hu Nf Sf Bd Hrt Ess Sr K, bɫɪŋkəz Mon Hrt, blɪŋkəs Cu Nf, blɪŋkʔəz Nf Sf Bk Ess, blɪŋkʔəs Nf, blɪŋkəᴿz Y, blɪŋkəᴶz La Ch Db He O L Brk Sr K Ha, blɪŋkəᵗz̩ Sa He Wo Wa Mon Gl O Nth Bk Brk Sr K Ha Sr Sx, bɫɪŋkəɹz̩ O, blɪŋkəᵗːz̩ Sa So Sx, bɫɪŋkəᵗːz̩ W Co D Do Ha, blɛŋkəᵗːz̩ Bk, bɫɛŋkəᵗːz̩ W, *sg* blaŋkəᵗː Ha. ⇒ **blinders, bluffs, blufters, bridle-bluffs, cads, eye-blinkers, eye-flop, eye-mop, eye-wings, gloppers, goggles, hoodwinks, mobs, moppers, mops, winkers, winkles**; ⇒ also **mopping-halter**

blishes *npl* BLISTERS VI.11.5. blɪʃɪz Cu We La[old], *sg* blɪʃ Du

blisters *npl* When people who rarely work with their hands use a spade or fork for the first time, what are they likely to get on their hands? VI.11.5. Eng. ⇒ **bladders, blasters, blebs, blishes, blushes, flishes, galls, weals**

bloa* *adj* cold and wet, ⇐ DULL VII.6.10. bluə L

blobbing out *vtphr-ing* PUTTING your tongue OUT VI.5.4. blɒbɪn ... æʊt L

block *1. n* the CLOG on a horse's tether I.4.3. blɑːk? Nf, blɒk Cu Du Y St He Wo Wa Gl L Nth Hu Nf Ess So W Brk Ha Sx, bɬɒk So W Co Do, blɒk? Nf, blɔk C Sf Ess
2. n the HUB of a cart-wheel I.9.7. blɒk Du
3. n a chock, often of wood or stone, placed behind and under a wheel to prevent a cart from going backwards on a hill, ⇐ PROP/CHOCK I.11.2. blɒk Cu Du Y O Hu Nf Bk Bd Hrt Ess So W K Ha Sx, *pl* blɒks St, blɒk? Nf, blɔk Wo C Sf Ess K Ha; **block of wood** bɬɒk ə ʏːd D
4. n a DRAG used to slow a wagon I.11.3. blɒk Nf
5. vt to STOCK a cow's udder III.3.6. bɬɒk Co
6. n a BENCH on which slaughtered pigs are dressed III.12.1. blɑk Bk, blɒk K, kɪɬənblɒk Co, pɪgblɒːk Brk

blodder *vi-3prpl* bulls BELLOW III.10.2. blɒdə We

blog *n* a chock placed behind and under a wheel to prevent a cart from going backwards on a hill, ⇐ PROP/CHOCK I.11.2. blɒg O

bloifing *v-ing* **coughing and bloifing** COUGHING VI.8.2. kɔːfɪn ən blɒːfɪn Nf

bloke *n* **the bloke** my HUSBAND VIII.1.25. ðə blʊʊk So

bloking *v-ing* BELCHING VI.13.13. blʊʊk?n Nf

blood-poison *adj* **turn blood-poison** to FESTER, referring to a wound VI.11.8. təˑn blʌdpɔɪzn Nf

blood-poisoning *n* **get blood-poisoning** to FESTER, referring to a wound VI.11.8. gɪʔ blʌdpɔɪznɪn Hrt

blore *1. vi-3prpl* bulls BELLOW III.10.2. bloˑə Sf, blʊə Nt L, blʊəɹ L, blʊəz La Nt L, *prppl* blʊəɹɪn L, *-ing* bluˑəɹɪn L [[blɑː~blɑː] forms in L Nf taken as **blare**]
2. vi-3prpl they WHINNY, describing the noise horses make during feeding time in the stable III.10.3(a). blɔː La
3. vi-3prpl they MOO, describing the noise cows make during feeding time in the cow-house III.10.4(a). bloˑə Sf, blʊə L, blʊəɹ L
4. vi-3prpl they MOO, describing the noise cows make in the fields III.10.4(b). bloˑə Sf, blʊə Nt L, blʊəɹ L

blort *1. vi-3prpl* bulls BELLOW III.10.2. blɔːt Lei, blɔːts Y
2. vi-3prpl they MOO, describing the noise cows make during feeding time in the cow-house III.10.4(a). blɔːt Nt Lei

3. vi-3prpl they MOO, describing the noise cows make in the fields III.10.4(b). blɔːt Y Lei

blossom(s) *n* POTATO-HAULMS II.4.4.
no -s: blasəm Man
-s: blæsəms Man

blother *1. vi-3prpl* bulls BELLOW III.10.2. blɒðəz Nt
2. vi-3prpl they MOO, describing the noise cows make in the fields III.10.4(b). blɒðə Nt[old]

blow *1. n* an EAR of a corn-plant II.5.2(b). blaʊ Sa
2. v to WINNOW II.8.4. blaʊ Sf, *-ing* blaʊ-ɪn Ess, *-ing* blɔˑ-ɪn Y, *-ing* blɒʊ-ɪn Ess, blʌʊ Sf
3. n a BUMP on someone's forehead VI.1.8. blɔː So Do, bɬɔː Do
4. vi-3prpl they WHINNY, describing the noise horses make during feeding time in the stable III.10.3(a). blɔʊ Ess, blʌʊ Ess
5. vi-3prpl they MOO, describing the noise cows make in the fields III.10.4(b). blɒʊ Wo

blow-bellows *n* BELLOWS V.3.10. blaʊbɛlɪs Sa, blɒʊbɛləz Db, blɔːbɛlɪs Db Sa, blɔːbɛlɪz Ch Db Sa, blɔːbɛləz Sa, blɔːbalɪz Ch, blɒʊbɛlɪz St Wo, blɒʊbɛləz St, blɒʊbalɪz St, bloˑʊbaləz Db, bluːbælɪz Ch, bluːbɛlɪz Ch

blowed *adj* HEAVING *WITH MAGGOTS* IV.8.6. blɔʊd O, blʌʊd K, blɔːd Sa, bɬɔːd Ha, blɒʊd St

blow-flies *npl* FLIES IV.8.5. blæʊflɔɪz Hrt, blɒʊflɑɪz Nf, blɒʊflɒɪz K, *sg* blɒʊflʌɪ Nf, blɔːfliːz Y[bluebottle] L, blɔːflɒɪz Brk, *sg* bɬɔːvɬæː D, blɒʊflɑɪz K, blɒʊflʌɪz Nf

blowing *1. adj* HEAVING *WITH MAGGOTS* IV.8.6. bɬɔːən Co
2. v-ing PANTING VI.8.1. blɛːən Nb, blæˀn Nb, blæʊɪn He Gl, əblæʊɪn Gl, blaːən Du, blɑʊɪn Gl, blɒʊɪn Wo Wa, əblɒʊ-ɪn Nth, blɔːɪn Du Y, bɬɔː-ɪn W, blɔːən Cu Du[old] We, blɒʊ-ɪn L, bɬɔːɪn D, blɔːʷɪn Db, blɒʊɪn He W, əblɒʊ-ɪn W, blɒʊ-ən C, bluːɪn St

blowing-flies *npl* FLIES IV.8.5. blɒʊɪnflaɪz So, blɒʊɪnvlaɪz So

blown *adj* HEAVING *WITH MAGGOTS* IV.8.6. blɑʊn Nf, blɒʊn Sr, blɔʊn St

blow off *vphr* to BREAK *WIND* VI.13.16. *-ing* blɒæən œːf Nb, *-ing* blɑːɪn ɔːf Nf, blɑʊ ɔːf Ess, *-ing* blɒʊ-ɪn ɔːf Nf Sr, *3ptsg* blɔʊd ɔːf Wo, blɔː ɔːf Sa, bluː ɒf St

blow out *vtphr* to WINNOW II.8.4. *-ing* blɔː-ɪn ... ɛʊt Nf

blow-up *n* STOPPING-TIME at the end of a day's work in a brewery VII.5.9. blɒʊ-ʊp St

blow-up-time *n* STOPPING-TIME at the end of a day's work VII.5.9. blɒʊ-ʌptəɪm Sx[old]

blue *adj* RANCID, describing bacon V.7.9. bluː Sx

blue-arse-flies *npl* FLIES IV.8.5. blʉ-ɑˑsflɑˑɪz Nf

blueberries *npl* BILBERRIES IV.11.3. blɪuːbɛrɪz Cu, *sg* bluːbɛɹɪ Y, bluːbɛɽɪz O, bluːbəɹɪz Sx

blue-bottles *npl* FLIES IV.8.5. blɣːbɒʔɫz Nf

blue-bungham *n* CLAY IV.4.2. bluːbʌŋəm MxL *[queried EMBM]*

blue-clay *n* CLAY IV.4.2. bluːklæɪ MxL, bluːklɑɪ Ess

blue-flies *npl* bluebottle FLIES IV.8.5. blɪuːfləɪz Y

bluff *n* a HALO round the moon VII.6.4. blʊf L

bluffs *npl* BLINKERS covering the eyes of a cart-horse I.5.2. blʊfs Lei, bɹɑɪdlblʊfs Ch

blufters *npl* BLINKERS covering the eyes of a cart-horse I.5.2. blʊftəz Db

blundersome *adj* CLUMSY, describing a person VI.7.14. blʌndəˤsʌm Brk

blurping *v-ing* BELCHING VI.13.13. bləˤːpɪn Sr

blurt *vi-3prpl* sheep BLEAT III.10.5. bləːt Lei

blushes *npl* BLISTERS VI.11.5. blʊʃɪz Nb Du, blʊʃəz Nb

boar *n What do you call the male pig?* III.8.7. Eng. ⇒ **boar-pig, brawn, brawn-pig, charlie-pig, hog, hog-pig, johnny-pig, old hog-pig, stag, stock-pig, store-pig**

board *1. n* an END-BOARD of a cart I.10.4. *pl* bɔəᴶdz Brk, bɔːəˤɽd Sr Sx
2. n a flat surface on which bacon is cured, ⇐ SALTING-TROUGH III.12.5. bʊəd L
3. n the THRESHOLD of a door V.1.12. boˑəd We
4. n the FLOOR of a house V.2.7. boːɽd Do, boːəˤːd Do
5. n a PASTE-BOARD V.6.5. bɔːd Sr, bɔᵊd Mon, bɔːəd St, bɔːəˤd Sr, bɔːəˤɽd Sx, boˑəd C, boəˤd Wa Bk, bʊəd L

boaring *adj ON* HEAT, describing a sow III.8.9. bɔˤːrɪn So

boar-pig *n* a BOAR III.8.7. bɔpɪg Ess, bɔːpɪg St Nth, bɔəpɪg Y Nf, boəpɪg Mon, bʊəpɪg L

boar-seg *n* a male HOG III.8.8. bʊəsɛg Y

boar-thistle* *n* a THISTLE, often a large one II.2.2. bɔːθɪsl St, bɔːəfɪsl Sa, bɔːəˤθɪsl Wo, bɔːəˤθɪsʊɫ Gl, bəːθɪsl St *[WMBM headword **burr-**]*

boarward *adj ON* HEAT, describing a sow III.8.9. baɽɪd So, baɽəd So D, bɒɽəd Co D, bɔˤːɽəd Co D, bʌɽɪd D, bʌɽəd So D, bʊɽɪd Co D, bʊɽəd Co D, bʊɽəˤːd Co

boat-ended stack *n* a long stack with rounded ends, ⇐ STACKS II.7.1. bʌʊtɛndəd stæk Sf

boat-shaped stacks *npl* long STACKS with rounded ends II.7.1. bʌʊtʃeːpt stæks Sr

boat-shape stack *n* a long stack with rounded ends, ⇐ STACKS II.7.1. bʌʊtʃɛɪp stæk Ess

boat-stack *n* a long stack with rounded ends, ⇐ STACKS II.7.1. bʊtstæk Sf

boatwright *n* a WRIGHT VIII.4.4. boutɹʌɪt Nf

bob *1. n* the CLOG on a horse's tether I.4.3. bɒb La So, bɔˑb So
2. n **bob of grass** a TUSSOCK of grass II.2.9. bɒb ə gɹəs Y
3. n an ACORN IV.10.3. bɔb Ch
4. n a SHILLING VII.7.5. bœb Du, bœːb Nb, bæb Sx, bɑːb Wo, baˤːb He, bɒb Cu La Y*[old x1]* Man Db Sa St He Gl O Nt L Lei Hu Nf Bk Ess So*[old x1]* K Co Ha, bɔb Cu Du La Wa L Ess So K, bɔːb He
5. vi to DUCK VIII.7.8. bɒb Y Man O Hu Nf Ess Sr D Ha Sx, bɔb C Sf Sr K

bobbin *1. n* the CLOG on a horse's tether I.4.3. bɒbɪn La Ch
2. n a cotton-REEL V.10.6. bɒbɪn Nb Cu We La Y Ch Db St He Wa Nt L Lei R, bɒbn Du, bɒbən Nb Du, bɔbɪn Nb La Y Ch Nt L

bobbing out *vtphr-ing* PUTTING your tongue OUT VI.5.4. bɒbɪn ɛːt Db, bɒbɪn ɛʊt Wo

bobby *n* a BOGEY VIII.8.1. bɒbɪ D, bɒbɪ Y St He, bɔbɪ La Y Ch L, bɔbɛ Y; **the bobby** ðə bɒbɪ D

bobby-dicks *npl* LICE IV.8.1(a). bɒbɪdɪks Nf

bob down *1. viphr* to DUCK VIII.7.8. bɒb dɛʊn Bk Hrt, bɒd dɛʊn Sx, bɒb dæːn Nt, bɒb dæʊn So Ha, bɒb daʊn So, bɒb dʌʊn Brk, bɒb duːn Y, bɒb dəʊn So W Brk Do, bɔb dɛən K, bɔb daʊn L
2. vtph. **bob your head down** bɒb jəˤːɽ ɪd dəʊn Do

bob-grass *n* a TUSSOCK of grass II.2.9. bɒbgɹæˑs So *[marked u.r. SBM]*

bo-boy *1. n* a SCARECROW II.3.7. bɒʊbɒɪ Sr, *pl* bɒʊbɒɪz K, bobɒɪ K
2. n a BOGEY VIII.8.1. bɒʊbɒɪ K

bobtail-mouse *n* a field-vole, ⇐ MOUSE IV.5.1(b). bɒbtɛɪlmɛʊs Nf

bob-weight *n* the CLOG on a horse's tether I.4.3. bɒbwɛɪt Y

bodge *n* a circular TROUGH in a cow-house I.3.6. *pl* bɒdʒɪz K

bodging-hook *n* a HEDGING-BILL IV.2.5. bɒdʒɪnʊk Brk

bodkin *1. n* an EVENER on a horse-drawn plough I.8.4. *pl* bɒdʔkɪnz So
2. n an evener, the main swingle-tree of a plough harness. badkɪn So
3. n a SHEATH or other device used to keep a knitting-needle firm V.10.10. bɒdkɪn R Nf Bd, bɒtkən Nf, bɔdkɪn L, bɔbkɪn L

bodkin(s) *n* a SWINGLE-TREE of a horse-drawn plough harness I.8.3.
sg: bædəkɪn Mon, badkɪn So, bɒdkɪn Gl Do, bɒtkɪn Gl
-s: badkɪnz So, badəkɪnz Mon, batkɪnz So, bɒdkɪnz So W Do, bɒdkənz Do, bɒdkʔɪnz So,

bɒbkɪnz So, bʌtəkɪnz He Mon Gl, bʊtəkɪnz Mon *[-s forms 'undoubted plurals' SBM]*

bods *npl* PALS VIII.4.2. bɒdz La

body *1. n* *What's inside the coffin?* VIII.5.7(a). bɒdɪ Y St He Wo O Lei Nf Ess So W, bɔdɪ Y Wa Ess MxL ⇒ **carcass, corpse,** *dead body,* **dead corpse,** *dead one,* **remains** *[dead body found throughout Eng]*

2. n a PERSON VIII.5.3(a). bɑ·dɪ Wo*[old]*, bɒdɪ Nb Cu Du We La Y Ch Db Sa Wo O Nt Nf D, bɔdɪ Nb Y Wo Wa L*[old x1]*

3. n the body of a stack, ⇐ BASE II.7.4. bɒdɪ K

4. n the VULVA of a cow III.2.3. bɒdɪ Nb

5. n the UTERUS of a cow III.2.4. bɒdɪ L

body-belt *n* the GIRTH of the harness of a cart-horse I.5.8. bɒdɪbeɫt Ess

body-brush *n* a BRUSH used to clean horses III.5.5(a). bɒdɪbɹʌʃ Sr, bɒdɪbɹʊʃ K, bɔdɪbɹʊʃ Ch

body-comb *n* a CURRY-COMB used to clean horses III.5.5(b). bɔdɪkɔm La

body-flannen* *n* a VEST VI.14.9. bɒdɪflanɪn Nb We, bɒdɪflanən Du

body-horse *n* a TRACE-HORSE I.6.3. bɒdɪ-ɔəᴶs Brk

body-jacket *n* a VEST VI.14.9. bɒdɪdʒakət Du

body-sark *n* a VEST VI.14.9. bɒdɪsæːk Du, bɒdɪsaᵏːk Nb, bɒdɪsaᵏːt Du, bɔdɪsaᵏːk Nb

body-shirt *n* a VEST VI.14.9. bɒdɪʃaᵏːt Du, bɒdɪʃət Du, bɔdɪʃɛət Nb

boer yanks *npl* KNEE-STRAPS used to lift the legs of working trousers VI.14.17. bɔə jaŋks La

bofflers *npl* KNEE-STRAPS used to lift the legs of working trousers VI.14.17. bɒfləz Bd

bog *1. n* a TUSSOCK of grass II.2.9. bɒg Ch Sa St

2. n LOW-LYING LAND IV.1.7. bɒg St *[marked u.r. WMBM]*

3. n BOGGY land IV.1.8. bɒg St Bd Brk Sr K, bɔg L

4. n an EARTH-CLOSET V.1.13. bɒg Sr, bɔːg He

bogey *n* *Sometimes, when children are behaving very badly, their mother will tell them that someone will come and take them away. What do you call this mysterious person?* VIII.8.1. bøːgɪ Du, bɒʊgɪ Sr Sx, bɔːgɪ Y, bɔʊgɪ O L R Nth Ess K, bʌʊgɪ Bk Ess, boːgɪ La Mon Nt, boːgi Do, bougɪ St Wa Lei Ha, boːʊgɪ Db Mon Gl, bougi So, buːgɪ Y Ch, bʊəgɪ L; **the bogey** *pl* ðə bʌʊgɪz Bk, ðə buːgi Co; **the old bogey** ð ɔʊd bʊəgɪ L. ⇒ **blackman, bobby, bo-boy, bo-man, bogeyman, bogey-sam, boggart, boggin, bogle, bugabo, bugabowl, copper, elves, hangman, high sprites, hookerman, jenny wisp, old harry, old nick, police, policeman, scug, sprites,** *the* **blackman,** *the* **bobby,** *the* **bogey,** *the bogeyman, the* **constable,** *the* **devil,** *the old* **bogey,** *the old bogeyman, the* **old lad,** *the* **old man,** *the* **old nick,** *the* **policeman,** *thick* **old man, willy with the wisp**

bogey-sam *n* a BOGEY VIII.8.1. buːgɪsam Ch

bogeyman *1. n* a SCARECROW II.3.7. bʌʊgɪman Bk

2. n a BOGEY VIII.8.1. Eng

bog-fern *n* FERN IV.10.13. bɒgfəːn Nf

boggart *n* a BOGEY VIII.8.1. bɒgət La Db, bɒgəd Y Db, bɒgəᴶt La, bɒgəɹt La, bɔgɜᴶːɹt La, bugət Ch

bogged *adj* BOGGY IV.1.8. bœːgd Nb, bɒgɪd W, bɒgd Y Ch St Lei Nf Ess Ha, bɔgd La Ess MxL Sr

boggin *n* a BOGEY VIII.8.1. bɒbɛᵊn Man

boggy *adj* *When a patch of land is water-logged, you say it is....* IV.1.8. bœːgɪ Nb Du, bægɪ Wo Ha, bagɪ Sa, bɑ·gɪ Nf, bɒgɪ Nb Cu Du We La Y Man Ch Db Sa St He Wo Wa Mon Gl O Nt Lei R Nth Hu Nf Bk Bd Hrt Ess Brk Sr K Do Sx, bɒggɪ La Db, bɒgi Nf So W Do Ha, bɒgiː He Wo, bɔgɪ Nb We La Y Ch*[poor x1]* Wa L C Sf Ess MxL Sr K Do Ha. ⇒ **bogged, buggy, clarty, curragh, drowned, flooded, groshy, marshy, miry, oozy, poggy, poshy, puddled, puddly,** *saddened* ⇒ **soddened, sludden** *with water,* **soaked, sobbed out, sodden, soddened, soggy, stagged, staggy, stodgy, stugged, stuggy, suggy, swamp, swamped, swampy, water-logged, water-slog, water-soaked, wet;** ⇒ also **bog, boggy-land, bog-hole, bog-land, marsh**

boggy-land *n* land that is water-logged, ⇐ BOGGY IV.1.8. bɑ·gɪlænd Nf

bog-hole *1. n* a POOL on a farm III.3.9. bɒgoːl Db

2. n BOGGY land IV.1.8. bɔgʊəl L

bog-holes *npl* PUDDLES IV.1.6. bɒgʊəlz Y

bogie *n* a BIER VIII.5.9(b). buːgɪ Y

bog-land *1. n* LOW-LYING LAND IV.1.7. bɒglæːnd Hrt

2. n BOGGY land IV.1.8. bɒglæːnd Hrt

bogle *n* a BOGEY VIII.8.1. bœːgl Nb, bɒgl Nb Cu Du We Y, bɔgl Nb L

boil *vt* to RENDER fat into lard III.12.9. baːɪl St, *-ing* bɒɪlɪn St Brk, bɒɪɫ Wa Ha, *-ing* bɒɪɫɪn Sx, bʷɒɪɫ W Ha, bɔɪɫ Sf, bʌɪɫ D

boil down *vtphr* to RENDER fat into lard III.12.9. baɪɫ ... dæʊn Ha, baɪl ... dɛʊn Bd, baɪɫ dɛʊn C Bk Hrt, bɒɪl ... dɛʊn Bk, *-ing* bɒɪlɪn dɛʊn Bk, bɒɪl ... daʊn He, bɒɪl ... dəʊn So, bɒɪɫ ... dæʏn So D, bɒɪɫ ... daʊn So, bwɒɪɫ ... dæʊn So W, bʷɒɪɫ ... dɒʊn W, bɔɪl ... dɛʊn Nf, bɔɪl dæʊn Ess, bɔɪɫ ... dæᵊn K, *-ing* bʌɪlɪn ... dəʊn Do, bʌɪɫ ... dæʏn D, bʌɪɫ ... dəʊn Do, boil ... dɛʊn Nf

boiled eggs *npl* EASTER EGGS VII.4.9. bɔːɫd ɛᴵgz Ess *[marked u.r. EMBM]*

boiler-can *n* a SCOOP used to take water out of a boiler V.9.9. bɑ·ɪləkan Db, bɔɪləkən Y L

boiler-hook *n* a CRANE on which a kettle is hung over a domestic fire V.3.4. bɔɪləhʊk Ess

boiler-tin *n* a SCOOP used to take water out of a boiler V.9.9. bɔɪlətɪn Y L, bɔɪlɹtɪn L

boils *npl* *What do you call those painful swellings that men often get on the back of the neck; they have to be poulticed?* VI.11.6. Eng exc. C Sf. ⇒ **apses, blains, botches, breeders, carbuncles, glands,** *nabsies* ⇒ **napsies, napsies, pinswells, pouds, pushes, wengs**

boin *n* a BUMP on someone's forehead VI.1.8. bɔɪᵊnd Ess

boisterous *adj* ACTIVE, describing a child VIII.9.1. bɒɪstɹəs K

boke *1. vi* to VOMIT, referring to an adult VI.13.14(a). *prppl* bɔʊkən Nb, bʊək L

2. vi to RETCH VI.13.15. bɒʊk Cu, bɔːk We, -*ing* bɔʊkɪn O, -*ing* bɔʊkən Nb, bʊək L

3. vi to BREAK *WIND* VI.13.16. -*ing* bɔːkɪn So [*marked ir.r. BM*]

boken *1. vi* to VOMIT, referring to an adult VI.13.14(a). bɒʊkən Nb, -*ing* bʊəknɪn Y

2. vi to RETCH VI.13.15. -*ing* bʊəkn̩ɪn Y, -*ing* bʊəknɪn Y

boking *v-ing* BELCHING VI.13.13. baʊkən Du, bɒʊkɪn Sr, bɒʊkən Nb Du, bɔːkɪn Hrt Brk Sr Ha Sx, bɔʊkɪn O MxL, bɔʊkən Nb Du, bɒʊkɪn Brk, bʊəkɪn Y

boking about *vphr-ing* BELCHING VI.13.13. *prppl* bɔːłkən əbæʊt Ha

boking up *1. vphr-ing* BELCHING VI.13.13. bɒʊkɪn ʌp K, *ptppl* bɒʊkt ʏp Du, bɔːkɪn ʌp Sx, *?2prpl* bɔːks ʌp Ha

2. vtphr-ing **boking up (the) wind, boking it up** belching. **boking up (the) wind** *prppl* bɔːkɪn ʌp ðə wɪnd Ha, bɔːkɪn ʌp wɪnd Sx; **boking it up** bɔʊkɪn ɪt? ʌp MxL

bole *1. n* a SHREW-MOUSE IV.5.2. bɒʊł K [*queried BM*]

2. n a tree STUMP IV.12.4. bøːl Nb, bʊəl L

bolking *v-ing* BELCHING VI.13.13. bɒłkɪn K Sx[*old*], bɒłkən D, bɒłəkɪn Brk, bɒʊłkɪn Bk K, bɔłkɪn Ess, bɔːłkɪn Brk Ha, bɔːłkən Ha, bəᵁłkɪn W

bolking about *vphr-ing* BELCHING VI.13.13. *prppl* bɔːłkən əbæʊt Ha

bolking up *vtphr-ing* **bolking it up** BELCHING VI.13.13. *prppl* bɒłkən ɔː t ʌp D

boller *vi-3prpl* they MOO, describing the noise cows make in the fields III.10.4(b). -*ing* əbɒləɹɪn Hrt

bollock-naked *adj* NAKED, describing a person VI.13.20. bɒłəknɛɪkɪd K

bolster *n* a BUMPER of a cart I.10.1(a). baʊstəˡ Sa, bɒʊstəˡ Wo, *pl* boʊłstəz Lei

bolster-end *n* the T-SHAPED PLOUGH-BEAM END of a horse-drawn plough I.8.5. bɒʊstəɹɪnd K

bolt *1. n* an EVENER on a horse-drawn plough I.8.4. bɔʊłt O, bɔʊłʔ O

2. n an evener, the main swingle-tree of a plough harness. bɒʊłt W Sr, bɔʊłt MxL Brk Sr, boːłt W Ha

3. n a LINCH-PIN holding a wheel on a cart I.9.12. boːłt D

4. n a metal linch-pin. bɒʊlt K

5. n a pin keeping a cart-body fixed to the shafts, stopping it from tipping, ⇐ ROD/PIN I.10.3. bɒʊłt Sx

6.1. vt to GOBBLE food VI.5.13(b). -*ing* bɔʊłtɪn Y, -*ing* boːłtɪn So Co D, -*ing* boːłtən Co D Do, -*ing* bɒʊłtɪn So

6.2. v to gobble. bɛʊt Nt, bɒʊłt Wa, -*ing* bɒʊłtɪn K, -*ing* bɔːłtɪn D, *3prsg* bɔʊłts Wa, -*ing* bɔʊłtɪn Ess, -*ing* bɒłtn Du, boːłt W, -*ing* boːłtən Co D, *3prsg* bɒʊłts Lei

7. n the FLAP at the front of old-fashioned trousers VI.14.16. boːłt So

bolt down *1. vtphr* to guzzle a drink, ⇐ GUZZLES VI.5.13(a). -*ing* bɒʊłʔn ... dɛʊn Sx

2. vtphr to GOBBLE VI.5.13(b). -*ing* boːłtɪn ... dæʏn D, -*ing* boːłtɪn ... dəʊn W Brk, boːłtən ... dəʊn Do

bolt-hole *n* a SHEEP-HOLE IV.2.8. bʌʊłtʌʊl Ess

bolting *n* an ARMFUL VII.8.10(c). boːłtɪn Mon

bolt off *imp* GO AWAY! VIII.7.9(a). bɒʊłt ɔːf O

bolt-wagon *1. n* a WAGON without sides I.9.2. boːłtwagən Ha

2. n a wagon with fixed sides. boːłtwagən W

bo-man *n* a BOGEY VIII.8.1. bɒʊmæn K

bon *adj* PRETTY, describing a girl VI.5.18. bɒn Ch

bond *1. n* the metal BUSH at the centre of a cart-wheel I.9.8. bɒnd W

2. n the iron TIRE round a cart-wheel I.9.10. bɒn Co D, bɒnd He Gl So W Brk Co D Ha, bɔːn So W Do, bɔːnd So Do Ha

bond-hook* *n* a ROPE-TWISTER II.7.8. bɒndhʊk Nf

bonding *n* the iron TIRE round a cart-wheel I.9.10. bɒndɪn D

bond-maker *n* a ROPE-TWISTER II.7.8. bɒnmeːˡkəˡ Gl, bɒnmæɪkə MxL, bʊnmeːkəˡ Sa

bond(s) *n* ROPES used to fasten thatch on a stack II.7.7(b2).

no -*s:* bɒnt St, bɒnd Wo[*hay*] Nf[*straw x2, straw x1*], bɒn Sa Wo[*hay*], bɔnd MxL, bʊnt St

-*s:* bɒndz So Ha[*hay*], *sg* bɒnd Ha[*straw*], bɒnz Ha[*straw*] Sx[*straw*], bɒnts Lei[*spun from wet hay*], bɒns Lei, bɔːnd Ha, bɔːnz Ha

[*not a WMBM headword.* **Bond** *marked 'probably material n' EMBM*]

bonds *npl* two iron strips forming the TIRE round a cart-wheel I.9.10. bɒnz Gl

bond-spinner *n* a ROPE-TWISTER II.7.8. bɒntspɪnə Lei, bʊntspɪnə St

bond-turner *n* a ROPE-TWISTER II.7.8. bɒndtɛˑnə Nf

bond-twister *n* a ROPE-TWISTER II.7.8. bɒndtwɪstəˤ: So, bɒnttwɪstə Ch Db St Lei, bɒntwɪstə St, bɒntwɪstəˤ He Wo Wa, bɒntwɪstəˤ: Do, bʊnttwɪstə St R, bʊntwɪstə St, bəntwɪstə St

bond-winch *n* a ROPE-TWISTER II.7.8. bɒnwɪnʃ Sx

bond-winder *n* a ROPE-TWISTER II.7.8. bɒnwɔɪndə O, bɒnwɔɪndəɹ Brk

bonnet *1. n* *What do you mean by* **bonnet***?* VI.14.1. bɒnɪt Wo Nf, bɒnɪt Nb La Y Ch Db Sa St He Wo Wa Mon Gl O*[straw, worn by widows x1]* Nt Lei R Nth Hu Nf Bd Ess So W Brk Sr K Ha Sx, bɒnɪʔ Bk Bd Hrt, bɒnət Nb Cu Du We La Y Man He Gl O Ess So W Brk Co D Do Ha Sx, bɒnə? O Bk, bɒnɪt Nb Y Ch Wo Wa L C Hrt Ess MxL Sr K, *pl* bɒnɪts Nt, bɒnɪʔ MxL, bɒnət Nb La L C Sf Ess, *pl* bɒnəts Y, bʌnət D use:

a. the head-dress of a man or woman. Nb Cu

b. a woman's head-dress. Eng

c. worn outdoors or at work. Ch Db Sa He Wo Wa Mon Gl O L Nth Hrt So W Co D Do Ha Sx

d. worn indoors. Ch Db Sa Wo Gl So W Co D Do Ha Sx

e. worn by older women. L Lei Nth*[black and beaded]* Hu C Nf Sf Bk Ess MxL

f. a sun-hat. L

g. for small children. Mon Hrt

material or construction:

a. with curtain or cover for the neck. Ch Sa St Wa Gl Nt L Lei Nth Nf Hrt Brk Sr D Do Sx

b. made of cloth. Ch Db Sa St He Wo Wa Mon Gl O L Hu Bk*[silk and satin]* Hrt*[felt]*

c. made of cotton. L Lei R Nth Hu Bk Hrt Ess*[worn by maid-servants]*

d. made of calico. Nt L Nth

e. made of straw. Ch Db Sa He Wa O Nt L Nth Hu C Sf Bk Bd Hrt Ess

f. trimmed or with a frill. Nt Lei Nf Sf Bk Ess

g. piece of material tied under chin. Lei R

material/construction and use:

a. straw, for best or Sunday wear. Nth*[trimmed]* Hu*[or stiff cloth]*, Ess

b. flower-trimmed, for best wear. L

⇒ **cotton bonnet, curtain bonnet, cutchy-bonnet, dust-bonnet, fancy bonnet, gook, gook bonnet, granny bonnet,** *hat,* **headgear, hood, milk-bonnet, print bonnet, slouch bonnet,** *slough bonnet* (⇒ **slouch bonnet), soft bonnet, sun-bonnet, tilt, tilt bonnet, wing-bonnet, working-hood**

2. n a zinc plate for increasing the draught in a chimney. bɒnɪt Mon

bonnet-strings *n* WHISKERS VI.2.6. bɒnɪtstɹɪŋz K

bonny *1. adj* PRETTY, describing a girl VI.5.18. bæni Man, bani Sa, bani La, bɒni Nb Cu Du*[old x1]* We*[rare x1]* La Y Man Ch Db Sa He Wo Wa Gl Nt*[old x1]* Nth Bd, bɔni Nb Cu L

2. adv VERY VIII.3.2. bɒni Nb Y; **bonny and** bɒni ən Nb

bonny-looking *adj* PRETTY, describing a girl VI.5.18. bɒniliəkɪn Y

boo *vi-3prpl* they MOO, describing the noise cows make during feeding time in the cow-house III.10.4(a). buː Sa

bool *n* part of a scythe, probably the CRADLE, ⇐ GRASS-NAIL II.9.9. bɔːɫ D, boːɫ So W D, boʊɫ So

boose *1. n* a STALL in a cow-house I.3.1. biˑəs Du, bɪəs We, bɪʊs Cu Y, byːs Ch Db, buːs Cu La Y Db, bʊɪs Y, bʊəs We

2. n the PARTITION between stalls in a cow-house I.3.2. bɪʊs Cu, bʊɪst Y

3. n a TROUGH in a cow-house I.3.6. buːs Lei

boose-hallan *n* the PARTITION between stalls in a cow-house I.3.2. buːsanl Cu

boose-head *n* the PARTITION at the head of a stall in a cow-house I.3.2. buːsɪəd Y

boose-side *n* the PARTITION between stalls in a cow-house I.3.2. bʊɪssaɪd Y, buːssaɪd Y

boose-stake *n* a TETHERING-STAKE in a cow-house I.3.3. byːssteːk La, boussteːk La, bʊɪssteːk Y, bʊuːsstɪak Y, buːssteːk La, buːssteək Y

boosing *1. n* a STALL in a cow-house I.3.1. bjɪʊsɪn Y

2. n a TROUGH in a cow-house I.3.6. bɛʊzɪn Bk, buːzɪn St Wa Lei

boosin-post *n* a TETHERING-STAKE in a cow-house I.3.3. buːzɪnpʊəst La

boosin-stake *n* a TETHERING-STAKE in a cow-house I.3.3. bᴵʉːzɪnstɛɪk Lei, bɛʊzɪnstᴵiːk Db, bɛʊzɪnsteˑɪk Db, bɛʊzɪnstɛɪk St, bɔʊzɪnsteˑᴵk Db, buːzɪnstɛɪk St

boost *n* a STALL in a cow-house I.3.1. byːst La, buːst La Db

boosy *1. n* a STALL in a cow-house I.3.1. bᵁuːzɪ Sa

2. n a TROUGH in a cow-house I.3.6. bɪuːzɪ Sa, byʉzɪ Sa, bʊzɪ He, buːzɪ Ch Sa Wo Wa

3. n the GANGWAY in a cow-house I.3.7. buːzɪ He Wo

boosy-pasture *n* a PADDOCK I.1.10. buːzɪpastjə Ch

boosy-stake *n* a TETHERING-STAKE in a cow-house I.3.3. byʉzɪsteːᵊk Sa, bᵁuːzɪsteːk Ch, *pl* buːzɪsteːks Wo

boot *1. n* the SOLE of a horse-drawn plough I.8.9. buːt L

2. n a SHOE VI.14.22(a). buːt Mon

3. n BOOTS VI.14.23. byːt D

boot and shoemaker *n* a COBBLER VIII.4.5. bɪət ən ʃuːmakə Y

boother *n* a TROUGH in a cow-house I.3.6. buːðə St

boothin-rod *n* a TETHERING-STAKE in a cow-house I.3.3. bᵁuːðɪnɹɒd La

boot-laces *npl What do you call these [indicate boot-laces]?* VI.14.25. bʏtɫeːsɪz Co, bʏtleːɪsəz So, bʏtɫɛːsɪz D, bʏːtɫɛːsɪz D, bɪətlɪəsɪz Y, bɪʊtlɪasɪz Y, bɪʊtlɪəsɪz Y, bɪʊtleːsɪz Y, bɪətlɛəsɪz Y, bʊɪtleːsəz Y, bʊɪtleːsəz Y, bʊɪtlɛəsəz Y, bʊɪtleəsəz Y, bʊɪtleəzəz Y, buːtleːsɪz Mon Brk, buːtɫɛːsəz W, buːʔɫeːsɪz W, buːtleɪsɪs Lei, buːtleɪsɪz St Lei Nf Ess Brk K Sx, bɪuːtleɪsɪz R Brk, bʊuːtleɪzɪs Sr, buːtlɛəsɪz L Sx, buːtlɛəsəz Y, buːtlæɪsɪz K, bᵊuːʔlæɪsɪz Hrt; **leather boot-laces** lɛðə bɪətlɪəsɪz Y. ⇒ **boot-straps, boot-strings, boot-whangs,** *cotton* **laces, laces,** *leather* **boot-laces,** *leather* **laces,** *mohair* **laces, shibbands,** *shoe-***laces, shoe-strings, shoe-ties, shoe-whangs, straps, thongs, whangs**

boot-maker *n* a COBBLER VIII.4.5. buːtmeɪkəᶜ Ha*[makes boots and shoes]*, buːtmɛɪkə K*[makes boots and shoes]*, bʊuːtmɛɪkəᴶ Sr

boots *1. npl What do you call those things that you are wearing [indicate boots]?* VI.14.23. Eng. ⇒ **baffs, bats, boot, high boots, high-lows, high shoes, high ties, high-tops, shoes, shoon, shuff, strong boots, strong shoes, strong shoon**
2. n WHISKERS VI.2.6. bʏːts D *[queried SBM]*

boot-straps *npl* BOOT-LACES VI.14.25. bʊtʂtɹaps Do, buːtʂtɹaps Do*[leather x1]*

boot-strings *npl* BOOT-LACES VI.14.25. bʏːtʂtɹɪŋz So*[leather]*, buːtʂtɹɪŋz Ha*[fibre]*, bʊuːtʂtɹænz So*[leather or fibre]*

boot-whangs *npl* leather BOOT-LACES VI.14.25. buːtwaŋz La

bop *1. vi* to DUCK VIII.7.8. bɒp Nf Ess, bɔp Sf
2. vt **bop your head** to duck. bɔp jə hɛd Sf

bop down *viphr* to DUCK VIII.7.8. bɒp dɛʊn Nf Ess, bɒp dəʊn Nf

bore *1. vt* to BUTT III.2.10. *prppl* bɔɹɪn La, *prppl* bəːʁən Nb
2. v to butt. *-ing* bɔːɽɪn So

bore on *vphr* to BUTT III.2.10. *prppl* bəːʁən œːn Nb

boskin *1. n* the PARTITION between stalls in a cow-house I.3.2. bɒskɪn La Y Ch Db, bɒstɪn La Y, bɒzkɪn St, bɒzgɪn Y Ch Db St, bɔskɪn Y, bɔstɪn La, bɔzgɪn Ch
2. n a wooden partition between stalls in a stable. bɒstɪn La
3. n a TROUGH in a cow-house I.3.6. bɒzgɪn St

boskin-stake *n* a TETHERING-STAKE in a cow-house I.3.3. bɒzgɪnstɛɪk St

bosom *n* a BREAST of a woman VI.8.5. bʌzəm So, bɒʊzm St, bʊzm Nf W Brk Sr Sx *[marked u.r. WM/EM/SBM]*

boss *1. n* the CLOG on a horse's tether I.4.3. bɒs La
2. n **my boss, our boss** my HUSBAND VIII.1.25. **my boss** maɪ bɒs Wa; **our boss** ʊə bɒs Cu Y; **the boss**

ðə bœːs Nb, ðə bɑs Nth Nf, ðə bɑːs Wo Mon Gl, ðə bɒs Du Man Ch Db St He Wo Wa Gl O Lei Nth Hu Nf Bk Bd Ess*[humorous x1]* So Brk Sr K Co Ha, ð bɒs Du Ch, t bɒs Cu La Y Db, ʔ bɒs La, ðə bɔs Nb Wa L C Sf Ess K, t bɔs We La Y, ðə bɔːs Sa Gl Ess So W Co Do Ha, ðə bɒᶜːʂ Sa

boss-eye *adj* CROSS-EYED VI.3.6. bɒsaɪ K

boss-eyed *1. adv* looking in a SQUINTING manner VI.3.5. bɒsɔɪd Ess
2. adj CROSS-EYED VI.3.6. bɑːsʌɪd Nf*[old]*, bɒsaɪd Nf Bd K, bɒzaˑɪd Db, bɒzɒɪd St, bɒsɔɪd Bk Ess*[old x2]* Brk Sr K Ha Sx, bɒsʌɪd Nf Brk Sr*[old x1]*, bɒsəɪd W Brk*[old x1]* Sx*[old x1]*, bɔsaɪd MxL*[impolite]*, bɔsɔɪd Ess*[old x1]* MxL Sr, bɔːsɒɪd Ha, bɔːsəɪd So

boss-eyeded *adj* CROSS-EYED VI.3.6. bɒsʌɪdɪd Sr

botches *npl* BOILS VI.11.6. *sg* bɒtʃ Y*[small x1]*

bothersome *adj* ACTIVE, describing a child VIII.9.1. bæðəsəm Man

bots *1. npl* TICKS on sheep IV.8.3. bɒts Ess *[glossed 'maggots' EMBM, but* **maggots** *used in Nf and elsewhere]*
2. npl SLUGS IV.9.2. bɒts La

bottle and glass *n* the ARSE VI.9.2. bɒʔļ ŋ glɑːs K*[rhyming slang]*

bottle-fish *npl* MINNOWS IV.9.9. *sg* bɒʔļfɪʃ Nf

bottle-haws *npl* HAWS IV.11.6. bɒʔļhɔːz Nf

bottle-lamb *n* a PET-LAMB III.7.3. bɒtʔɫæm Sf, bɔʔɫæm Sr

bottle-ticks* *npl* TICKS on sheep IV.8.3. bɒtɫtɪks K*[larger than sheep-ticks]*

bottom *1. n* the SOLE of a horse-drawn plough I.8.9. bɒdəm Ess
2. n the BUTT of a sheaf of corn II.6.4. bɒtʊm Wa, bɒtəm Wa, bɒˑtʔəm Ess, bɒʔm Nf, bɒdəm O, bɒtəm Nt, bɒtʔəm Sf, bɔːdəm Sf
3. n the BASE of a stack II.7.4. bœːdəm Nb, bætəm Man, bɒtʊm La St Wa*[loose straw x1, old straw for a hayrick/or a cartwheel x1]]*Nth, bɒtəm Y Ch St O Nth Hrt*[straw]*, bɒtm Ess, bɒtʔəm Nf*[straw and brushwood x1]*, bɒʔəm O Bk*[straw and brushwood x3]* Bd, bɒʔm Nf*[straw and brushwood x1]*, bɒdəm Nb Cu Y O Bk, bɒɹɱK, bɒtəm Nb Hrt*[straw]* MxL*[faggots of wood]*, bɔˑtʔəm Sf, bɔdəm Nb C Ess, bɔːdəm C Sf; **straw bottom** stɹɔː bɒtʊm Wa
4. n the ARSE VI.9.2. bɒtəm Nb, bɒtʔəm Nf*[polite]*, bɒdəm Ess
5. v to DITCH IV.2.11. bɒtʔm Nf

bottom arse-board *n* the TAILBOARD of a cart I.10.2. bɒtəm aːsboˑəd Db

bottom back-board *n* the TAILBOARD of a cart I.10.2. bɔtəm bækbɔˑəd Sf

bottom-end *n* the BUTT of a sheaf of corn II.6.4. bɔtəmɛnd L

bottomer* *n* a dried onion, ⇐ ONION V.7.15. *pl* bɒtəməz Wo

bottom-fay *v* to DITCH IV.2.11. *-ing* bɒʔmfʌɪ-ɪn Nf

bottom-ground *n* LOW-LYING LAND IV.1.7. bɒˑtmgɹɛuːnd Wo

bottom-land *n* LOW-LYING LAND IV.1.7. bɒtʊmlænd Wo, bɒtəmland Cu Du La, bɒdəm land La

bottom-mist *n* MIST VII.6.8. bɒdəmmɪst Y

bottom out *vt* to DITCH IV.2.11. bɒtm ... ɛut Nf

bottom-plate *n* the SOLE of a horse-drawn plough I.8.9. bɒtəmplɪət Cu, bɒtəmpleːt Cu, bɒtəmpleɪt Wa, bɒdəmpleːt Cu We, bɒdəmplɛˑət Cu *[marked u.r. NBM]*

bottom(s) *n* LOW-LYING LAND IV.1.7.
no -s: bɒtəm Db
-s: bɒtəmz Cu Du Db, bɒdəmz Du, bɒtnz Hrt, bɔtəmz L

bottoms *n* DREGS left at the bottom of a teacup V.8.15. bɒtʊmz Ch

bottom-tail-board *n* the TAILBOARD of a cart I.10.2. bɒtəmteːlbuəd La

bough *1. n* a BRANCH of a tree IV.12.3. *pl* bɛʊz Ch*[old]* Nf Sf Bk Ess Sx, *-s* béʊz Nf, *pl* baʊz L So*[smaller than branch]*, *pl* buːz La

2. v to LOP a tree IV.12.5. *-ing* bɛʊɪn Db, buː Cu Nt, *-ing* buːɪn La

3. v to cut big boughs back to the trunk. *prppl* buˑɪn Y

4. v to cut large branches from a tree. bɛː Db, *-ing* bɛʊɪn Sx

boughs *npl Now let's talk about the parts of a tree [show a picture]. What do you call these [indicate the boughs]?* IV.12.2. Eng exc. Man. ⇒ **arms**, **batlings**, **big boughs**, **branches**, **brogs**, **broughs**, **butts**, **grains**, *great boughs*, **great branches**, **limbs**, **main branches**, *tree boughs*, **tree-grains**

bough up *1. vphr* to LOP a tree IV.12.5. buː ʊp La

2. vtphr to cut large branches from a tree. *-ing* bɛʊɪn ... ʌp Sr

bounce *1. vi A rubber ball that's punctured won't [indicate bouncing] ....* VIII.7.3. Eng. ⇒ **bound**, **bump up**, **dap**, **glance**, **hop**, **jump**, **play**, **stot**, **tamp**

2. v to BUTT III.2.10. buːns Nb

bound *vi* to BOUNCE VIII.7.3. bæʊnd Ha

boun-tree *n* the bush ELDER IV.10.6. bʊntʁɪ Nb, buːntʁɪ Nb

bourtree *n* the bush ELDER IV.10.6. bɒtʏɪ Y, bɔːtʃɪ La, bɔˀɪːtʃɪ La, bʊətrɪ La, bʊətʃɪ La, bətɪ̃ː Y, bətəʃɪ Y, bəːtʃɪi Cu Du, bəːtrɪ We, bəˀɪːtʃɪ Y*[old]*

bourtree-bush *n* the bush ELDER IV.10.6. bɒtrɪbʊʃ Y, bɒtʃɪbʊʃ Y, bɒtəʃɪbʊʃ Y, bɔˣːtʁɪbʊʃ Du*[old]*, boətrɪbʊʃ Nb, bʊtʃɪbʊʃ Y, bʊtʃɪbʊʃ Y, bəːtrɪbʊʃ Cu*[old]*, bəːtʃɪbʊʃ Du We

bourtree-tree *n* the bush ELDER IV.10.6. bɒtʃɪtʃɪ Y

bout *adv* WITHOUT V.8.10(a). bɪat Y, beat Y, beːt La, bɛat Y, bɛət Y, bæːt Y, bæˑat Y, bæut Y, bæˑət La Y, baːt La Y, baʊt La

bouter *n* the MOULD-BOARD of a horse-drawn plough I.8.8. bəʊtəˡː So

bouters *npl* the RIDGES between furrows in a ploughed field II.3.2. *sg* baʊtəˡː So *[queried SBM]*

bout salt *n* INSIPID, describing food lacking in salt V.7.8. beːt sɔːt La

bow *1. n* a sliding RING to which a tether is attached in a cow-house I.3.5. bɒʊ St

2. n part of a scythe, probably the CRADLE, ⇐ GRASS-NAIL II.9.9. bɔː Co D, bɔˡː Co*[willow]*, boː W Co D Ha*[hazel x1]*, bɒʊ Brk*[wooden x1, wire x1]* K*[wooden]*

3. n **bow of your leg** the CALF of the leg VI.9.7. bɒʊ ə jə lɛg Nb *[queried NBM; probably = **ball** ...]*

4. n a HALO round the moon VII.6.4. bɒʊ Nf

bowdy-legged *adj* BOW-LEGGED VI.9.6. baʊdɪlɛgd Y, bɒʊdɪlɛˑgd K

bowel *n* the PLUCK of a slaughtered animal III.11.6. bɛʊ Sx, bɛʊʊ Sr

bowels *n* CHITTERLINGS III.12.2. baˑəɫz Man

bower-legged *adj* BOW-LEGGED VI.9.6. bɒʊələgd Ch

bow-footed *adj* BOW-LEGGED VI.9.6. bɛʊfʊtɪd Nth

bowk *1. n* the HUB of a cart-wheel I.9.7. bɛʊk Sa, baʊk Sa, bəʊk Gl

2. n the metal BUSH at the centre of a cart-wheel I.9.8. bɛʊk Wo, bæʊk He Mon, bɒʊk He, bʌʊk He Mon, boːk He, bəʊk He Wo Mon

bowl *1. n* the HUB of a cart-wheel I.9.7. bɔːɫ D *[compare Anglo-Welsh **bwl** = 'bowl']*

2. n a SOWING-BASKET II.3.6. bɒʊɫ Gl

3. n a BASKET for carrying horse-feed III.5.4. bɛʊᵊl Ch St, bɒʊl Ch*[with handles]*, bɒʊɫ Brk*[large, metal]*, bɔːl Sa, bɒʊl St

4. n a BREAD-BIN V.9.2. bɔʊl St

5. n a SCOOP used to take water out of a boiler V.9.9. bɛʊːᵊɫ Wo, bæʊl L, baʊɫ Wo Co, bɒʊᵊɫ Gl, bɒʊl Wo K, bɒʊɫ Gl W Sr, bɔːɫ So, bɔʊl St Wo O L, bɔʊɫ O Hu Ess MxL So Brk, bʌʊl Ess, bʌʊɫ C Sf Bk Bd Ess, boːl Sa, boːɫ Mon So W D Ha, boʊl St, boʊɫ Wa Mon Nth C Ess So W, boːʊ Brk

bowl-dish *1. n* a BASKET for carrying horse-feed III.5.4. baʊldɪʃ Ch, boːldɪʃ Ch*[basin, with handles]*

2. n a SCOOP used to take water out of a boiler V.9.9. bæʊɫdɪʃ He, bɒʊɫdɪʃ He Wo, boːldɪʃ Ch Sa, boːɫdɪʃ He So Do, bʊʊldɪʃ St

bow-legged *adj And if [a man's legs are shaped] like this, you say he is ....* VI.9.6. Eng exc. MxL. ⇒ **bandy**, **bandy-kneed**, **bandy-legged**,

bowdy-legged, bower-legged, bow-footed, scrod-legged, straddly- bandy

bowling-egg day* *n* Easter Monday, when EASTER EGGS were bowled VII.4.9. buːlɪnɛg dɛə Y

bowl-turner *n* a ROPE-TWISTER II.7.8. ˈboulˌtənə Nf [i. 'not sure', queried EMBM]

bowowarts *npl* BLACKBERRIES IV.11.1. bʌwəwʌts Nb

box *1. n* a large box with holes in it, fixed on a barn wall, in which pigeons live, ⇐ DOVECOTE I.1.7. bɒks Do
2. n a STALL in a cow-house I.3.1. bɑˑks Nf
3. n a TROUGH in a cow-house I.3.6. bɔks Sf
4. n the HUB of a cart-wheel I.9.7. bɒks He Mon Gl O Nth Ess So W Brk Sr D Do Ha Sx, bɔks Ess K
5. n the metal BUSH at the centre of a cart-wheel I.9.8. bɑˑks Nf, bɒks Wa Gl O Nth Hu Nf Bk Bd Hrt Ess So Brk Sr K Co D Do Ha Sx, bɔks C Sf Hrt Ess MxL
6. n an END-BOARD of a cart I.10.4. bɒks Brk
7. v to BUTT III.2.10. -ing bɒksən So
8. n a BASKET for carrying horse-feed III.5.4. bɒks W
9. n a FASTING-CHAMBER III.11.3. bɒks Nth
10. n a COFFIN VIII.5.7. bɒks St So

box-cart *n* a FARMCART I.9.3. bɒkskaːt Ch

box-hive *n* a HIVE IV.8.8(a). *pl* bɒksɔɪvz Sr

boxing *n* the metal BUSH at the centre of a cart-wheel I.9.8. bɒksɪn Hrt

box-neck *adv* HEAD OVER HEELS IX.1.10. bɒksnɛk He

box-necked *adv* HEAD OVER HEELS IX.1.10. bɒksnɛkt He

box-tree *n* the metal BUSH at the centre of a cart-wheel I.9.8. bɒkstɹi Do [queried ir.r. SBM]

box-wagon *n* a WAGON with sides I.9.2. bɒkswægɪn D

boy *n* a SON VIII.1.4(a). bɒɪ Nth, bɔɪ Nth Nf Sf Ess, bwɔɪ Wa, bɒɪ Nth Hu C Sf Bd Ess, *pl* bɔɪz Bk, bʊɪ Cu

boys *1. npl* Children may be of either sex: they're either ..., or [girls]. VIII.1.3(a). Eng exc. We. ⇒ **chaps, kids, laddies, lads**
2. npl PALS VIII.4.2. bʊɪz Ess, bwaɪz So; **the boys** ðə bwɒɪz So, ðə bʊɪz Sr

brace *1. n* the GRASS-NAIL of a scythe II.9.9. bɹɛɪs MxL
2. n a DIAGONAL BAR of a gate IV.3.7. bɹɛɪs Brk, bɽɛːs D Do Ha, *pl* bɽeːsəz O W, bɹɛˑɪs Man, *pl* bɹɛɪsɪs Nth, *pl* bɹɛɪsɪz Wa, bɽɛɪs O, bɹɛˑəs Bk, *pl* bɹɛəsɪz Y, bɽeːəs So, bɹɛɪs Lei R Nth C Nf Ess Sr K Ha Sx, *pl* bɹɛɪsɪz St Wa O, bɽɛˑɪs Brk, bɽɛːəs So Co [assumes /-əz/ forms to be plurals, not **bracers**]

bracer *n* a DIAGONAL BAR of a gate IV.3.7. bɽeːsəˡ: W Co D, *pl* bɽeːˀsəˡːz̥ So

bracers *n* BRACES VI.14.10. bɹeːsəˡz̥ Sa He Wa Mon Gl W, bɹeːsəˡːz̥ Sa, bɽeːsəˡːz̥ So W Co Do, bɹeɪsəˡz̥ Wo, bɽeɪsəˡːz̥ So, bɹeːɪsəˡz̥ He Wo Mon Gl, bɽeːɪsəˡːz̥ So, bɹeːsəˡz̥ Sa, bɽeːsəˡːz̥ So W, bɽɛɪsəˡːz̥ Ha, bɹeəsəˡˑz̥ O, bɹæsəˡz̥ He Wo, bɹæɪsəˡz̥ Gl, bɹɑˑsəˡz̥ Wo, bɽaɪsəˡːz̥ Ha [r-coloured forms only here; other forms interpreted as **braces**]

braces *n* What do you call these [indicate braces]? VI.14.10. Eng exc. Nb Cu Du Gl Do. ⇒ **bracers**, *gallows* ⇒ **gallowses, gallowses, hames, kicking-straps, slings, suspenders**

bracing-chain *n* an EVENER on a horse-drawn plough I.8.4. bɹeːsɪntʃɛɪn Wo

brack *1. n* the FAT round the kidneys of a pig III.12.7. bɽak Nf
2. vt to CURDLE milk V.5.7. bɹak Sa

bracken *n* [Show a picture of bracken.] What do you call this plant? It grows rank especially on waste ground; it is cut and dried and then used for bedding animals. IV.10.12. Eng exc. Sf. ⇒ **bracketing, brake, fern, fern-brake, furze, heath, tall fern**

bracketing *n* BRACKEN IV.10.12. bɹækətɪn Sx

brackle *adj* BRITTLE, describing cups and saucers which break easily IX.1.4. bɹækl L, bɹakl L, bɹakəl Y, bɹakł L, bɹəkl Y

brackly *adj* BRITTLE, describing cups and saucers which break easily IX.1.4. bɹaklɪ La

bradbury *n* a POUND NOTE VII.7.8. bɹadbəɹɪ Wo, bɹadbɹɪ St, bɹadbəɽɪ O, *pl* bɽadbəɽɪz O, bɽadbɽɪ O

brads *n* MONEY VII.8.7. bɹædz Nf

brae* *n* a steep SLOPE IV.1.10. bʁɪː Nb

brae-full *adj* IN FLOOD, describing a river IV.1.4. bɹɪəfʊl Y

braid *1. vt* to PLASH a hedge IV.2.4. prppl bɹeɪdn Nf, bɹæɪd Nf; **layer and braid** lɛːɹɪ (+V) ... ən bɹeːɪd Nf
2. n a SHELF V.9.4. bɹeːd La

braid down *vtphr* cut off and braid down to PLASH a hedge IV.2.4. kʌʔ ... ɔːf ən bɹæɪd ... dɛun Nf

braid in *vtphr* buck-head and braid in to PLASH a hedge IV.2.4. bʌkhɛd n̩ bɹæɪd ... ɪn Ess

braidler *n* a GRIDIRON V.7.4(a). bɹeːdləˡ Sa [queried WMBM]

brail *vt* to PLASH a hedge IV.2.4. bɹɛɪɫ Ess[old]

brake *1. n* a DRAG used to slow a wagon I.11.3. bɹeːk Ch Mon, bɹeɪk Wo, bɹeːɪk Nf [unevenly marked ir.r. WMBM]
2. n BRACKEN IV.10.12. bɹeɪk Nf, bɹɛɪk Ess K, *pl* bɹeɪks Sf Sx, bɹeːɪk Nf, bɹæɪk Ess

brambles *npl* BLACKBERRIES IV.11.1. bɹæmblz Nf, *sg* bɹæmbł Ess, bʁamblz Nb, bʁambəlz Du, bʁamlz Nb, bʁaməlz Nb, bɹamblz

Nb Du Y Nt L*[old x1]*, bɹambəlz Y, bɹamlz We La Y, bɹaməlz La Y

brame-berries *npl* BLACKBERRIES IV.11.1. bɹɛŋbaɹɪz L

bran *1. n* MEAL V.6.1(b). bɹɛn K, bɹɛən Ess, bɹæn Brk Sx, bɽæn So, bɹan Y St Wo Lei Nth, bɽan W
2. n FRECKLES VI.11.1. bɹæn Ess

branch *n Now let's talk about the parts of a tree [show a picture]. What do you call this [indicate a branch, smaller than a bough]?* IV.12.3. Eng. ⇒ **arm, bough,** *boughs* ⇒ **bough, brash, grain, limb,** *limbs* ⇒ **limb, little bough, little branch, small boughs, spur, twigs**

branches *npl* BOUGHS of a tree IV.12.2. bɹænʃɪs Man, *sg* bɹæˑntʃ Nf, bɹæˑnʃɪz Sr*[large and small]*, bɹænʃ Sf K*[general term]*, bʁanʃɪz Nb, bʁanʃəz Nb Du, bɹantʃɪz Sa Lei Ess, bɹanʃɪz La Y L, bɹanʃəz Y, *sg* bɹanʃ Ch, bɹaːntʃɪz Ess, *sg* bɹaːntʃ Hrt, bɹaːntʃəz Ess, bɹaːnʃɪz Hu Bd Ess, *sg* bɹaːnʃ L Sf, bɹaːnʃəz C Ess, bɹɑːntʃɪz Nf, bɹɑːnʃɪz Ess MxL Sr*[any size]* Sx

brand *1.1. vt* to MARK the horns of sheep with a burn-mark to indicate ownership III.7.9. bɹɛnd Ess, bɹan Ch
1.2. v to mark the horns of sheep with a burn-mark. bɹænd Ha
2.1. vt to mark sheep with colour. bɹænd Nf Hrt Ess Sr, bɹæn Brk, -*ing* bɹændɪn Brk, bɹand Db St Wa Nt L Lei Hu, -*ing* bɹandɪŋ Mon, bɽand W Co D Ha
2.2. v to mark sheep with colour. bɹɛnd Sr, -*ing* bɹɛndɪn Ess, bɹænd Hu Sf Ess Sx, -*ing* bɹændɪn Brk, bʁand Du, bɹand Du Y St Wa O Nt L Lei R Nth C Bk Bd Hrt
3.1. vt to mark sheep in some unspecified way. bɹænd MxL, bɹæːnd Sa Hrt, bɽænd So, bɹand St, bɽand So W Co Do
3.2. v to mark sheep. bɹɛnd K, bɹænd Sf K, -*ing* bɹændɪn Sx, bɹand Y*[with marking-iron x1, on horn(s) x2]* St O, bɽand So, bɹɑnd Ch*[on horns]*, bɹɔnd Y

brand-beetle *n* a small wooden MALLET used for driving wedges I.7.5. bɽɒnbɪtł So

brander *n* a GRIDIRON V.7.4(a). bʁandɔᵏ Nb

brandis *1. n* a CRANE on which a kettle is hung over a domestic fire V.3.4. bɽandɪs So
2. n a GRIDIRON V.7.4(a). bɽandɪs D
3. n a tripod for supporting cooking-pots. bɽandɪs D

brand-new *adj Supposing they [i.e. boots] had never been worn and you'd just got them from the shop, what would you say they were?* VI.14.24. Eng exc. St Lei R. ⇒ *bran-new*, **bran-spanking-new, fire-new, flam-new, grand-new,** *new*, **shop-new, span-fire-new, spanking-new, span-new**

brandreth *n* the BASE of a stack II.7.4. bɹandɹɪf Nt*[mushroom-shaped stones]*, bɹandɹɪ Y*[obsolete/concrete and wooden beams x1, cross-beams on supports x1]*

brandrick *n* the BASE of a stack, made of stones with beams laid across them II.7.4. bɹandɹɪk Db*[very old]*

bran-freckles *n* FRECKLES VI.11.1. bɹanfɹɛkłz Wo Hu

bran-mash *n* FRECKLES VI.11.1. bɹanmaʃ St

bran-meal *n* MEAL V.6.1(b). bʁanmɪːl Du

branny *n* FRECKLES VI.11.1. bɹænɪ Ess

branny-speckles *n* FRECKLES VI.11.1. bɹænɪspɛkłz He

branny-spreckles *n* FRECKLES VI.11.1. bɹænɪspɹɛkłz Wo

brans *n* FRECKLES VI.11.1. bɹænz Brk

bran-spanking-new *adj* BRAND-NEW VI.14.24. bɹanspaŋkɪnnɪu: Db

bran-speckles *n* FRECKLES VI.11.1. bɹænspɛklz He

bran-spots *n* FRECKLES VI.11.1. bɹænspɒts He Hu

brant *adj* STEEP, describing a hill IV.1.11. bɹɛnt Du, bɹɛnt Nb Du Y, brant Cu Y, bɹant We, bɹant Cu We La Y

brash *1. n* a BRANCH of a tree IV.12.3. bɹas Sa*[old] [marked u.r. in WMBM headword list, but not in r. listing]*
2. n twigs. bɹaʃ Sa St Wa
3. n KINDLING-*WOOD* V.4.2. bɹaʃ Ch

brash-lach *n* CHARLOCK II.2.6. bɹæʃlæx Man

brashnachs *n* KINDLING-*WOOD* V.4.2. bɹæˑʃnæxs Man

brashock *n* CHARLOCK II.2.6. bɹaʃək Ch

brass *n* MONEY VII.8.7. bɹæs Y, bɹas Cu Du We La Y Db Sa St L, bɹɑːs Wo

brasthan *n* a PIECE *OF BREAD AND BUTTER* V.6.11(a). bɹæᵊsθən Man

brat *1. n* an alternative to a SOWING-BASKET II.3.6. bʁat Nb *[marked u.r. NBM as not a basket; more closely, an 'apron' or 'sheet']*
2. n a working APRON V.11.2(a). bɹæt Man*[leather x1]*, bɹæt Y, brat Cu, bʁat Nb, bɹat Cu We La Y*[worn by children x1]* Ch Db
3. n a decorative APRON V.11.2(b). bɹat Cu La Y Ch
4. n a cobbler's leather apron. bɹat La

brattice *n* the PARTITION between stalls in a cow-house I.3.2. bʁatɪʃ Nb

brave *1. adj* WELL, describing a healthy person VI.13.1(a). bɹɛːv Co, bɹɛːv Co, bɹɛɪv Co; **pretty brave** pəˡːdi bɹɛːv D
2. adj ACTIVE, describing a child VIII.9.1. bɹɛːv Do

bravish *adj* WELL, describing a healthy person VI.13.1(a). bɹɛːvɪʃ Co

brawl *1. vi-3prpl* they MOO, describing the noise cows make during feeding time in the cow-house III.10.4(a). bɹaːl Y

2. vi-3prpl they MOO, describing the noise cows make in the fields III.10.4(b). bɹaːl Y

brawn *n* a BOAR III.8.7. bʁaːn Nb, bɹaːn Du, bɹɑːn Y Wo, bɹɔːn Ch Db Sa St L Sf, *pl* bɹɔːnz Nf, bɹɔᵗːŋ Sa, bɹɔˑən Y L

brawn-pig *n* a BOAR III.8.7. bɹɔˑənpɪg L

bray *1. vi-3prpl* they WHINNY, describing the noise horses make during feeding time in the stable III.10.3(a). bɹeːz D, bɹɛɪ Brk, bɹɛɪ Co D

2. vi-3prpl they NEIGH, describing the noise horses make in the fields III.10.3(b). bɹeːz D, bɹɛɪ Brk*[old x1, rare x1]*, bɹɛɪ Co D

3. vt to BEAT a boy on the buttocks VIII.8.10. bɹeː Y*[ear x1]*, bɹeː We, bɹɛɪ Y

brazzock(s) *n* CHARLOCK II.2.6. bɹazək Y, bɹazəks Y

bread *n What do you mean by loaf? [Ascertain the pronunciation of loaf and bread.]* V.6.9(b). Eng. ⇒ **tommy**

bread-and-cheese-bush *n* a hawthorn bush, ⇐ HAWS IV.11.6. bɹedəntʃiːzbʊʃ Y

bread-bin *1. n What do you call the large earthenware thing in which people keep, or used to keep, their bread?* V.9.2. bɹɪdbɪn Ess Sr, bɹɛdbɪn Sa St Wa Ess MxL*[modern x1]* K*[modern x1]*, bɹɛdbɪn D, bɹɛbbɪn W. ⇒ **bowl, bread-bing, bread-bowl, bread-box, bread-crock, bread-jar, bread-jowl, bread-mug, bread-pan, bread-pancheon, bread-pankin, bread-pippen, bread-pitcher, bread-pot, bread-stean, bread-trough, bussa, cake-pot, cream-jar, critch, crock,** *dough-trough, dough-tub,* **earthen-pot, jowl, maiden-pot, minging-dish, muffin-pot, mug, pan, pancheon, pankin, pan-mug, pippen, pippen-pot, pot, stean, stugg, urn**

2. n a container for bread, ⇐ CORN-BIN I.7.4. bɹɛdbɪn Y Wa Sf Ess

3. n a metal bread-container. bɹɛdbɪn Wo

4. n a container used as a PASTE-BOARD V.6.5. bɹɛdbɪn St

bread-bing *1. n* a container for bread, ⇐ CORN-BIN I.7.4. bɹɛdbɪŋ Y Nt L

2. n a BREAD-BIN V.9.2. bɹɛdbɪŋ Nt L Lei Nth

bread-board *n* a PASTE-BOARD V.6.5. bʁiːdbɔʁːd Du, bɹɪdbɔʊd Ess, bɹɪʁdbʊəd Y, bɹɪdbuaᵗːd W, bɹɛɪdbœːd Du, bɹɛdbɔːd Cu Lei Sf, bɹɛdbɔᵗːd W, bɹɛdbɔˑəd Nth, bɹɛdbɔəᵈd Ha, bɹɛdboˑəd Db Wo Nf, bɹɛdboːəᵈd Db, bɹɛdbʊəd Y Db*[old x1]*, bɹɛdbuəɹd La

bread-bowl *n* a BREAD-BIN V.9.2. bɹɪədbaʊl Y, bɹɪədbɔʊl Y, bɹɛdbʊl Nf, bɹɛdbʌʊl Nf

bread-box *n* a BREAD-BIN V.9.2. bɹɛdbɒks Wo

bread-crock *n* a BREAD-BIN V.9.2. bɹɪdkɹɒk Ess*[large]* Sr Sx, bɹɪədkɹɒk Y, bɹɪədkɹɔk Y, bɹɛᵊdkrak Man, bɹɛdkɹɒˑk Ha, bɹɛdkɹʊk L K

breadh-agh *n* a SWINGLE-TREE of a horse-drawn plough harness I.8.3. breɪðæx Man

bread-jar *n* a BREAD-BIN V.9.2. bʁiːddʒaʁː Nb

bread-jowl *n* a BREAD-BIN V.9.2. bɹɛddʒaʊl St, bɹɛddʒɒʊl Wo, bɹɛddʒɔʊl Wa, bɹɛddʒɔː Sa*[metal]*

bread-meal *n* MEAL V.6.1(b). bɹɛdmeɪl Du; **bran and breadmeal** bɹan ən bɹɪədmɪəl Y

bread-mug *n* a BREAD-BIN V.9.2. bʁiːdmʌˑg Nb Du, bʁiːdmʊg Nb Du, bɹiːdmʊg Du We*[old x1]*, bɹɪədmʊg La*[old x1]*, bʁɛdmʊg Nb, bɹɛdmʊg La Y Ch Db

bread-pan *n* a BREAD-BIN V.9.2. bɹɪdpɛn Sr Sx, bɹɪdpæn Sx, bɹɪdpæn So, bɹɪdpan So W D Do Ha, bɹɛˑdpæn So, bɹɛdpɛn Ess MxL, bɹɛdpæn He Wo Wa Mon Gl Hrt Ess So Brk Sr K Sx, bɹɛdpæn So, bɹɛdpan Wo Wa Mon Gl O Lei R Nth Bk Bd, bɹɛdpan W D Do Ha, bɹɛdpɑn Bk, bɹɛdpɒn O, bɹɛɪdpan Co, bɹadpan Ha, bəᵗːdpæn So

bread-pancheon *n* a BREAD-BIN V.9.2. bɹɪədpanʃɪn Y, bɹɪədpanʃən Y

bread-pankin *n* a BREAD-BIN V.9.2. bɹɪədpaŋkɪn Y, bɹɛdpaŋkɪn Y*[old]*

bread-paste *n* DOUGH V.6.3. bɹɛdpɪəst Y

bread-pippen *n* a BREAD-BIN V.9.2. bɹɛdpɪpɪn Db L

bread-pitcher *n* a BREAD-BIN V.9.2. briːdpɪtʃər Cu

bread-pot *n* a BREAD-BIN V.9.2. bɹiːdpɒt Cu We, bɹiːdpɒt Cu Y, bɹɪdpɒt Ess, bɹɪdpɒt So, bɹɪədpɒt Cu We La Y Nt, bɹɪədpɒt Y*[old x1]*, bɹɛɪdpɒt Du, bɹɛɪdpɔt Du, bɹɛdpɑːt? Nf, bɹɛdpɒt We Y Db Nf Ess, bɹɛdpɒt? Nf, bɹɛdpɔt Du Y L C Sf Ess

bread-stean *n* a BREAD-BIN V.9.2. bɹɪdstiːn D, bɹɪdsteːn D, bɹɛdstiːn Ch Sa He, bɹɛɪdsteːn Co

bread-trough *n* a BREAD-BIN V.9.2. bɹɛdtɹoː Sa

break *1. vt* **break (the) wind** *What is your word for breaking wind?* VI.13.16. **break wind** *-ing* bɹeɪkɪn wɪnd Lei; **break the wind** *-ing* bɹeɪkɪn ðə wɪnd Ha*[polite].* ⇒ **blow off, boke, break off, crack off, fart, fart** *off,* **fart** *wind,* **prump, put** *wind* **up, rax, rift, trump, trumpet**

2. vt to PEN or FOLD sheep in part of a field III.7.10. bɹɛɪk Wa

3. vi to CHIP, referring to an egg that is about to hatch IV.6.10. bɹeɪk So, bɹɛɪk MxL; **break shell** *-ing* bɹeɪkɪn ʃɛl La

4. vt to WRING the neck of a chicken when killing it IV.6.20. bɹɪk K, bɹeːk Ch O, bɹeːk Ha, bɹɛɪk Wa C Bd Hrt, bɹeˑək Sf, bɹɛk L Nf, bɹeˑk? Nf, bɹeːk D, bɹɛɪk L C Nf Sf Bk Hrt Ess MxL Sr K Sx, *2prpl* bɹɛɪks Brk, bɹɛɪk? Nf Ess, bɹeˑək L, bɹæɪk Hrt Ess, bɹək We

5. vt to CURDLE milk V.5.7. bɹiːk We

6. vi to RETCH VI.13.15. *-ing* bɹɪəkən Y

breakfast *n* MEAL OUT VII.5.12. bɹɛkfəst Ch

breaking *n* is out of breaking SLIP*S* *THE CALF* III.1.11. ʃɹiz əʊt əv bɹeːkɪn Brk

breaking-out-fork *n* a fork used to spread out hay-cocks, ⇐ HAY-FORK I.7.11. bɹɪkənuːtfɔːᵊk Nb

breaking up *1. vphr-ing* BELCHING VI.13.13. bɹɛɪkɪn ʌp Sx
2. vtphr-ing breaking up the wind belching. bɹɛɪkɪn ʌp ðə wɪnd Sr

break off *vphr* to BREAK *WIND* VI.13.16. *-ing* bɹɛˈᴵkn ɔˑf Nf

breaks *1. npl* SNACKs VII.5.11. bɹɛɪks Sr
2. vi-3prsg school FINISHES VIII.6.2(b). bɾɛɪks So

breaks off *viphr-3prsg* school FINISHES VIII.6.2(b). bɹɛɪk ɔːf K

breaks up *viphr-3prsg* school FINISHES VIII.6.2(b). bɾɛɪks ʌp So, bɹɛɪks ʌp Brk

breast *1. n* What do you call this part of a woman [indicate a breast]? VI.8.5. Eng. ⇒ **bosom, bub, chest**
2. n the TEAT of a woman's breast VI.8.6. bɹɛst Nf Ess *[u.r. EMBM]*
3. n the MOULD-BOARD of a horse-drawn plough I.8.8. bɹɪst Nf Sf, bɹɛst Y Nt L Nf Sf Ess K Ha
4. n a SLOPE IV.1.10. bɹəst Cu

breast-bone *n* a WISH-BONE IV.6.22. bʁiːstbøːn Nb, bɹiːstbɪan Cu, bʁiːstbjɛn Nb, briːsbɪən Cu, bʁiːstbɪən Nb Cu, bɹɪstbɪan Du La, bɾɪsboːən So Do, bɾɪsbuːən So, bɹɪəstbɪən Y, bɹɪəstbean We, bɹɛstbɪən Y, bɹɛstbyˑən La, bʁɛsbøᵊn Du, bɹɛsboʊn O Brk, bɹɛstbʌʊn MxL, bɹɛsbʌʊn Ess, bɹɛsboːn Ch Sa He Wo Gl, bɾɛstboːn So, bɾɛsboːn So, bɾɛsboːən So W, bɹɛstboʊn St, bɹɛsboʊn Wo*[modern x1]* Wa Gl, bɾɛsboʊn So, bɹɛstbʊən Y, bɹɛsbʊən Y Ch L, bɾɛsbuːən W, bɹɛɪstbɪan Y, brɛᵊsboːᵘn Man, bɹəstbeˑan Cu, bɹəsbʊən Y

breast-nib *n* the TEAT of a woman's breast VI.8.6. bɹɛstnɪb L

breast-plate *n* the MOULD-BOARD of a horse-drawn plough I.8.8. bɹɛstplɛɪt L

breathing *v-ing* breathing hard, breathing heavy PANTING VI.8.1. **breathing hard** bɹiːðɪn haːd Ess, bɹiiːðən haːd Ess, bɹiːðɪn aᵗːd He, bɾiːðən ɑɾd̥ O; **breathing heavy** bɹiːðɪn hɛvɪ Nf

breathing-tube *n* the WINDPIPE VI.6.5. bɹiˑðɪntɪub Nf

breck *n* a piece of land set aside for grazing sheep, ⇐ PEN or FOLD III.7.10. bʁɪk Nb, brɛk Cu, bɹɛk Y

bred *n* the MOULD-BOARD of a horse-drawn plough I.8.8. bʁɛd Nb, bɹɛd L

breech *1. n* the BREECH-BAND of the harness of a cart-horse I.5.10. bɹɪtʃ Y L Lei R, bɹiːtʃ Lei
2. n a tree STUMP IV.12.4. bɹɪtʃ Hrt

breech-band(s) *n [Show a picture of the harness of a cart-horse.] What do you call this?* I.5.10.

no -s: bɹɪtʃban Sa, bɹɪtʃband Sa St, bɹɪtʃbund St, briːtʃbæn Man, bɹɪtʃbən Sa L, bɹɪtʃbənd Y Ch Db Sa St Nt L Lei, bɹɪtʃbənt Ch, bɹiːtʃbənt Ch, bɹətʃbənd Y

-s: bɹɪtʃbənz Y

⇒ **arse-band, breech, breech-bands, breech-strap, breeching, breechings, breeching-strap, coiler, coilers, hip-straps, seat, stays, strappings, trapping, trappings**

breech-board *n* the TAILBOARD of a cart I.10.2. bɹɪtʃbɔːd Lei, bɹɪtʃbʊəd St

breech-end *n* a tree STUMP IV.12.4. bɹɪtʃɛnd Ess

breecher *n* a SHAFT-HORSE I.6.2. bɹɪtʃəᵗ He

breeches *1. n [What do you call this I'm wearing [indicate trousers]?] Does your word apply to those things shaped at the knees?* VI.14.13(b). Eng exc. We; **a breeches** ə bɹɪtʃɪz Mon. ⇒ **knee-breeches, knickerbockers, riding-breeches, tight breeches**
2. n TROUSERS VI.14.13(a). bɹiːtʃɪz La, bɹiːtʃəz Db*[old]*, brɪtʃɪz Cu, bʁɪtʃɪz Nb, bɹɪtʃɪz Cu Du We*[old]* La Y, bɹɪtʃəz Y Db, brʊtʃɪz Cu, bʁʊtʃɪz Nb, bɹətʃɪz Cu We Y Db, bəᵗːtʃətːz̥ So, briːks Cu, bʁiːks Nb*[old x1]*, bɹiːks Cu

breech-horse *n* a SHAFT-HORSE I.6.2. bɹɪtʃɒs Lei

breeching-horse *n* a SHAFT-HORSE I.6.2. bɾɪtʃɪnaᵗːʂ Do, bɾɪtʃənaᵗːʂ Do, bɹɪtʃɪnɒs Gl, bɾɪtʃɪnɒs So, bəᵗːtʃənɒs Do, bəᵗːtʃɪnɒᵗːʂ So D

breeching(s) *n* the BREECH-BAND of the harness of a cart-horse I.5.10.

no -s: bɹɪtʃɪn Cu Du La Y Ch Db Sa St He Wo Wa Mon Gl O L Lei R Nth Hu C Bk Bd Hrt Ess MxL Brk Sr K Ha Sx, bɾɪtʃɪn O So W Co D Do Ha, bʁiːtʃɪn Nb, bɹiːtʃɪn La Sa K, bʁɪtʃən Nb, bɹɪtʃən Du L Sf Ess, bɾɪtʃən So W Co D Do Ha, bʁiːtʃən Nb, bɾɛtʃɪn K, bɾatʃɪn Ha, bʁʏtʃn Nb, bʁʊtʃən Nb, bʁətʃɪn Nb, bɹətʃɪn We, bəᵗːtʃɪn So W D Do

-s: bɹɪtʃɪnz Cu La Y Nf Sf Ess Sr Sx, bɹɪtʃnz Ess, bɹɪtʃənz C Sf, bɹɪtʃmənz Nf, bɹətʃɪnz Y

breeching-strap *n* the BREECH-BAND of the harness of a cart-horse I.5.10. brɪtʃənstræp Man, bɾɪtʃɪnʂtɾæp So, bɹɪtʃɪnstɹap Ch Wa Gl

breech-piece *n* a BUMPER of a cart I.10.1(a). bəᵗːtʃpiːs So

breech-strap *n* the BREECH-BAND of the harness of a cart-horse I.5.10. bɹɪtʃstɹap Db

breed* *n* a LITTER of piglets III.8.3. bɹiːd Y

breeder *n* a WHITLOW VI.7.12. bɹiːdə Nf

breeders *npl* BOILS VI.11.6. *sg* bɹiːdəᴵ L

breeding *1. adj* IN CALF III.1.10. bɹiːdɪn L
2. n the UTERUS of a cow III.2.4. bɹiːdɪn O

breeding-bag *n* the UTERUS of a cow III.2.4. bɹiːdɪnbɛg Ess MxL Sr K Sx, bɾiːdɪnbɛg D, bɹiːdənbɛg D, bɹiːdɪnbæg Ess Brk Sr Sx, bɹiːdɪnbæg So Co D, bɹiːdɪmbæg So, bɹiːdnbæg Do, bɹiːdɪnbag Wa Gl O Nt L Bk Hrt, bɹiːdɪnbag W D, bɹiːdnbæg Ess, bɹiːdnbag L, bɹiːdnbag W Ha, bɹiːdənbag Co Do, bɹiːdnbaˡg Ha, bɹiːdənbaˡg Co Do Ha

breeding-bed *n* the UTERUS of a cow III.2.4. bɹˀiːdnbɛd Ess

breeding-gut *n* the UTERUS of a cow III.2.4. bɹiːdɪngʊt L

breekin *n* the RIDGE of a house roof V.1.2(a). brɪkɪn Cu

breeze *n* COAL-DUST V.4.1. bɹiːz K*[old]*

brew *v* When you pour the boiling water onto the leaves in the tea-pot, what do you say you do? V.8.9. *vt* bɹɪuː, bɹɪʊ Y, bɾɣː D, bɹuː Y Sx, -*ing* bɹuːɪn St, bɾuː So W

v bɹɪu Du We La, bɹɪʊ St, bɹɪɣ Ch, bɹɪu L Lei Nth Hu Bd Ess, bɹɣ La Ch Db, bɹɛʊ Db Sf, -*ing* bɹuən Man, bʁu Nb, bɹu Du*[?old]* La Ch Sa St He Wa O L Sf Bk Bd Hrt Ess, -*ing* bɹuː-ɪn Sr K Sx, bɾu O*[?beer BM Edd]* So, bɹɯ Nf, -*ing* bɹəʊɪn Nf, bɹəu Hrt

⇒ **brew** *it*, **brew** *the tea*, **damp** *the tea*, **draw**, **draw en**, **draw** *it*, **leave en to soak**, **let it soak**, **make**, **make it**, **make** *tea*, **make** *the tea*, **mash**, **mash** *the tea*, **mask**, **mass**, **mast**, *put en to draw*, *put it soaking*, *put the tea to stand*, **scald**, **scald** *the tea*, **soak**, **soak it**, **soak** *the tea*, **steep**, **steep it**, **steep** *the tea*, **stew**, **wet**, **wet it**, **wet the tea**

breward(s) *n* the BRIM of a hat VI.14.3. *no* -*s*: bɹɪuəˡd La
-*s*: bɹˡɣəɹdz La

brewer's yeast *n* YEAST V.6.2. bɹuwəz jɪst Nf, bɹɪuəz jɛst Y *[probably soft or wet]*

brewis *n* BROTH V.7.20(a). bɹaʊɪs Ch

briar-hook *n* a strong HEDGING-BILL IV.2.5. bɹɪə-uːk Y

briars *1. npl* PEGS used to fasten thatch on a stack II.7.7(a). bɹʌɪəz Gl
2. npl BUSHES IV.10.5. bɹɪˑəz Y, bɹaɪəz Ch

brick bing *n* an artificial CESS-POOL on a farm I.3.11. bɹɪg bɪŋ Nf

brick-earth *n* CLAY IV.4.2. bɹɪkaˑθ Nf, bɹɪkəːθ Nf*[red]*, bɹɪkəˡːθ Nf*[red]*

brick-edge *n* the CURB-STONE in a cow-house I.3.9. bɹɪkɪdʒ Sr

brick-frothers *npl* MINNOWS IV.9.9. brɪkfrɒðəz Man

brick-hole *n* a CESS-POOL on a farm I.3.11. bɹɪkoʊl St

brickle *adj* BRITTLE, describing cups and saucers which break easily IX.1.4. bɹɪkl La Y Sa, bɹɪkəl Y, bɹɪkɫ Mon L Nth W, bɹɪkəɫ He Mon, bɹɪkʊɫ Sx, bɹəkl La *[not a N/SBM headword]*

brickly* *adj* BRITTLE, describing cups and saucers which break easily IX.1.4. bɹɪklɪ Man, bɾɪkɫɪ Do, bɾɪkɫɪ Do

bricks *1. npl* MINNOWS IV.9.9. brɪks Man
2. n a HEARTHSTONE V.3.2. bɹɪks Sr *[marked u.r. BM]*

bridge *n* What do you call the thing built across a river to help you to get from one side to the other? IV.1.2. brɪdʒ Man, bʁɪdʒ Nb Du, bɹɪdʒ La Y Ch Db Sa St He Wo Wa Mon Gl O Nt L Lei R Nth Hu C Nf Sf Bk Bd Hrt Ess MxL Brk Sr K Ha Sx, bɾɪdʒ O So W Co D Do Ha Sx, bɹɪd K, bɹɪtʃ Ess, bɹədʒ Sa, bəˡːdʒ So W D; **footbridge** fʊʔbɹɪdʒ St. ⇒ **brigg**, *foot*bridge, **hatch-bridge**, **truggan**; ⇒ also **clam**, **clammer**, **gantry**, **gout**

bridle *n* the T-SHAPED PLOUGH-BEAM END of a horse-drawn plough I.8.5. breɪdl Cu, bɹɛɪdl Nb, bɹaɪdl Cu, bɹaɪld Cu

bridle-bluffs *npl* BLINKERS covering the eyes of a cart-horse I.5.2. bɹɑɪdlblʊfs Ch

bridle-head *n* the T-SHAPED PLOUGH-BEAM END of a horse-drawn plough I.8.5. bɹaɪdlhˡiːd We

bridle-reested *adj* describing a horse that gets hold of the bit and goes its own way, ⇐ RESTIVE III.5.6. bɹaɪdlɹiːstɪd Y

brigg *n* a BRIDGE IV.1.2. brɪg Cu, bʁɪg Nb, bɹɪg Nb Cu Du We La Y L, bʁɣg Nb *[not a NBM headword]*

brim *n* What do you call this part of a hat [indicate the brim]? VI.14.3. brɪm Cu, brɪm We, bʁɪm Nb Du, bɹɪm Cu Du We La Y*[of bowler hat x1]* Ch Db Sa St He Wo Wa Mon Gl O Nt L Lei R Nth Hu C Nf Sf Bk Bd Hrt Ess Brk Sr K Sx, bɾɪm So W Co D Do Ha, bɹəm La Y, bɾəm So, bəˡːm So. ⇒ **breward(s)**, **brink(s)**, **flap**, **flipe**, **hat-skirts**, **peak**, **poke**, **ridge**, **rim**, **skirt(s)**, **verge**; ⇒ also **neb**, **tippy**

brimming *1. v-ing* on **brimming** ON HEAT, describing a cow III.1.6. ən brɪmən Man *[given as in brimming NBM, but inconsistent with other interpretations of* [ə] *as prep – compare* (on) *riding]*
2. adj ON HEAT, describing a sow III.8.9. əbriːmɪn Cu, bʁiːmɪn Nb, bɹiːmɪn Bd, əbrɪmɪn Cu, əbrɪmən Man, əbʁɪmɪn Nb, bʁɪmən Nb, əbʁɪmən Du, bɹɪmɪn Cu La Y Ch Sa St He Wa Mon Gl Nt L Lei, bɹɪmmɪn La, ɪbɹɪmɪn Y, ɪbɹɪmmɪn La, əbɹɪmɪn Nb Du We La Y Ch Db Sa St He Wo Wa Nt, əbɹɪmmɪn La Y, əbɹɪmən Du Man, əbʁɣmən Nb, əbʁʊmɪn Nb, əbʁʊmən Nb, bɹəmɪn Y Gl, əbɹəmɪn Cu We La Y; **in brimming** ɪ brɪmɪn Ch, ɪ bɹɪmmɪn Db

brimming over *adj* IN FLOOD, describing a river IV.1.4. bɹɪmɪn ɒvə Y

brimward *adj* ON HEAT, describing a sow III.8.9. bɾɪmɪd D

brine-bath *n* a SALTING-TROUGH III.12.5. bɹɑɪnbaθ Y

brine-pan *n* a SALTING-TROUGH made of lead III.12.5. bɹɔɪnpæn Sf

brine-pot *n* a SALTING-TROUGH III.12.5. bɹʌɪnpɒt Nf, bɹʌɪnpɔt Sf

brine-tub *n* a SALTING-TROUGH III.12.5. bɹɑɪntʊb Y, bɹɑɪntʌb K, bɹɔɪntʌb Ess Brk K, bɹʌɪntʌb Nf, bɹɔɪntʌb Sx

bring *vt* **bring the curd** to make curd, ⇐ CURDLE V.5.7. bɹɪŋg ðə kəːd Lei

bring back *vtphr* to VOMIT, referring to a baby bringing up milk VI.13.14(b). bɹɪŋ ... bæːk Gl, bɹɪŋ ... baːk Sa Wo

bring forth (of rabbits) ⇒ **kindle**

bring up *1. vtphr* to VOMIT, referring to an adult VI.13.14(a). bɹɪŋ ... ʊp Ch Wa Lei
2. vtphr to VOMIT, referring to a baby bringing up milk VI.13.14(b). bɹɪŋ ... ʌp Sx, *3prsg* bɹɪŋz ... ʊp Lei

brink* *n* grass at the edges of a field, uncut by the mowing machine, ⇐ CLEAR II.9.5. bɹɪŋk L

brink-mow *v* to CLEAR grass at the edges of a field II.9.5. bɹɪŋkmɔʊ L

brink(s) *n* the BRIM of a hat VI.14.3.
no -s: bɹɪŋk Db Wa L
-s: bɹɪŋks Nt L Nth

briny *adj* RANCID, describing bacon V.7.9. bɹɑːni Co

brisk *adj* TOO HOT V.6.8. bɹɪsk St

brisling *n* BEESTINGS V.5.10. bɹɪzɫɪn W

brisling-milk *n* BEESTINGS V.5.10. bɹɪzɫɪnmɪɫk W

briss *1. n* COAL-DUST V.4.1. bɹɪs D
2. n peat sweepings. bɹɪs D

briss coal *n* COAL-DUST V.4.1. bɹɪs koːɫ D

brissy coal *n* COAL-DUST V.4.1. bɹɪsi koːɫ D

bristle *n* the BRISTLES of a pig III.9.4. bɹɪsl Man, bɹɪsl Y

bristle-broom *n* a BRUSH used for sweeping indoors V.9.11. *pl* bɹɪsʊbɹʊmz Sr

bristle-brush *n* a BROOM used for sweeping outdoors V.9.10. bɹɪsɫbɹʌʃ Bd

bristles *1. npl What do you call the short stiff hairs on the back of a pig?* III.9.4. Eng. ⇒ **birses, bristle**
2. n barley AWNS II.5.3. bɹɪsɫz Sf K, bɹɪsʊz Sr, bɹɪsɫz So, bɹʊslz Y

britchelly *adj* BRITTLE, describing cups and saucers which break easily IX.1.4. bɹɪtʃəlɪ St, bɹɪtʃlɪ St

britcher *adj* BRITTLE, describing cups and saucers which break easily IX.1.4. bɹɪtʃə St

brithin *n* a STYE in the eye VI.3.10. bɹɪθɪn Sa

brittle *adj Thin cups and saucers that come to pieces very easily in your hands, you say are very ....* IX.1.4. Eng exc. Man MxL. ⇒ **brackle, brackly, brickle, brickly, britchelly, britcher, brittled, brittly, *cheapjack*, chippy, crips, delicate, easy broke, easy broken, feckless, femmer, flimsy, fragile, frail,** **frem, jotty, mullum, nesh, *rotten*, semmit, smopple, soft, soon broken, spalt, tender, *thin*, tickle, tingey, *very slender made***

brittled *adj* BRITTLE, describing cups and saucers which break easily IX.1.4. bɹɪtld Du

brittly *adj* BRITTLE, describing cups and saucers which break easily IX.1.4. bɹɪtʔlɪ C, bɹɪtɫɪ Wo Sf, bɹɪtɫi W, bɹɪtɫi W

broaches *npl* PEGS used to fasten thatch on a stack II.7.7(a). bɹɑˑtʃɪz Nf, bɹɒtʃɪz Nf*[willow]*, bɹɔːtʃɪz Nf*[elm]* Ess, bɹɔːtʃəz Sf*[willow or hazel x1, hazel x2]* Ess, bɹɔˑɪtʃəz Nf*[hazel]*, bɹɔˑətʃɪz Nf*[hazel]*, bɹɔˑətʃɪz Nf*[hazel x1, willow or hazel x1]*, bɹɔːətʃəz Nf*[hazel or elder]*, bɹɔˑəʔʃɪz Nf*[hazel]*, bɹɔʊtʃɪz Nf, bɹɔˑʊtʃəz Nf*[willow, hazel, or elder]*

broad *adj* **part-way broad** AJAR IX.2.7. pɛˑʳtwɛɪ bɹɔːd Co

broad-arrowed *adj* SPLAY-FOOTED VI.10.5. bɹɔːdaɹəd So

broad-board *n* the MOULD-BOARD of a horse-drawn plough I.8.8. bɹɑːdbʊə˥d O, bɹɔːdbʊəˡd Bk, bɹɔːdbɔəd O

broad-fall *n* the FLAP at the front of old-fashioned trousers VI.14.16. *pl* bɹɔːdfɔɫz Ess, *pl* bɹɔːdfɔːɫz Ess

broad-footed *adj* SPLAY-FOOTED VI.10.5. bɹɔˑdfʊʔɪd Nf, bɹɔːdfʊtɪd Co, bɹɔːdvʊtɪd Do, bɹɔːdvʊʔɪd W

broad-hook *n* a BILLHOOK IV.2.6. bɹɑːdʌk Sa

broad-legged *adv* ASTRIDE VI.9.8. bɹɔːdlɛˡgɪd So

broad-meads *n* LOW-LYING LAND IV.1.7. bɹɔːdmiːdz Sr

broad-plate *n* the MOULD-BOARD of a horse-drawn plough I.8.8. bɹɔːdplɛːt So

broad-share *n* the SHARE of a horse-drawn plough I.8.7. bɹɔːdʃɪəʳ Sx, bɹɔːdʃɛəʳ K

broad-share-point *n* the SHARE of a horse-drawn plough I.8.7. bɹɔːdʃɛəʳpɒɪnt K

broad-side *n* the MOULD-BOARD of a horse-drawn plough I.8.8. bɹɔːdzæɪd So

broadside *prep* BESIDE a door IX.2.5. bɹʊədsaɪd Y

broad-sower *n* a SOWING-BASKET II.3.6. bɹɔˑədsaʊə Nth

broad-toed *adj* SPLAY-FOOTED VI.10.5. bɹɔːdtoːd Ha

broad-wheel *n* a WAGON with sides I.9.2. bɹɔːdwiːˑəɫ Gl

broaking *v-ing* BELCHING VI.13.13. bɹɔˑkn Nf, bɹɔkʔn Nf, bɹɔːkɪn Nf, bɹɔːkʔn Nf, bɹɔːəkn Nf, bloʊkʔn Nf

brock *n* a BADGER IV.5.9. bʀœk Nb, bʀɒk Nb Du, bɹɒk Du We La Y Db Sa, bɹɒk Do, bʀɔk Nb, bɹɔk L Ess, bɹɔːk Y

brog *1. vt* to CLEAR grass at the edges of a field II.9.5. bɹɒg Y

2. *v* to LOP a tree IV.12.5. bɹɒg Cu

brog about *vphr* to BUTT III.2.10. *-ing* bɹɒgɪn əbæʊt R

brogs *npl* BOUGHS of a tree IV.12.2. bɹɒgz Cu

broke *vt-3ptsg* he/she TAUGHT it III.13.17. bɹoːk Nt, bɹoʊk Wa *[marked u.r. WMBM]*

broke in *vtphr-3ptsg* he/she TAUGHT it III.13.17. bɹɒkn ... ɪn Y, bɹoʊk ... ɪn Wa, bɹʌʊk ... ɪn Bk

broken *1.1. v-ed* HAS NOT HELD, referring to cow that has not conceived III.1.7. bʀœkn Nb, bɹɒkən Cu, bʀɒkən Nb, bɹɒkn Du We La Y Ch Db St, bɹɒkən Cu Du We Ch, bɹɒk Ch Sa, bɹɒʊkn St*[old]*, bʀɒkən Nb, bɹɒkn La Y, bɹoːk Sa, bɹoʊkn St, bɹuːk Ch

1.2. vt-ed has not held. bʀɒkən Nb, bɹɒkn La Y Ch Db, bɹɒkən Nb Y, bɹɒk Cu Y Db, bɹɒʊk Ch; **broken service** bɹʊkən səːvɪs Ch

2. *adj* NOT IN CALF III.1.8. bɹɒkn Y

3. *adj* not in calf but able to conceive. bɹɒkn Y

broken down *vphr-ed* HAS NOT HELD, describing a cow that has not conceived III.1.7. bɹɒkn dɛːn La

bronco* *n* a DONKEY III.13.16. bɹɒŋkɒə L

bronkus *n* a DONKEY III.13.16. bɹɒŋkəs L

broo *n* LOW-LYING LAND IV.1.7. bɹu: Man *[marked sg in headword list, but not in phonetic rr.]*

brood *1. n* What do you call all the chickens you get from one sitting of eggs? IV.6.12. bɹʏːd Ch O, bɾʏːd So Co D, bɹoud Nf, bɹʊd Sf, bruːd Man, bʀuːd Nb Du*[old]*, bʀɪuːd Nb, bɹuːd Cu Du We La Y Ch Sa St He Wa Mon Gl O L Nth Hu C Nf Sf Bk Bd Hrt Ess MxL Brk Sr K Ha Sx, bɹu: Ch, bɾuːd O So W Co Do Ha, bɹɒuːd We La Y Ch Nf Ess Brk Sr Sx, bɹʊɪd Y, bɹʉːd Nf, bɹᶩʉːd Lei. ⇒ **batch, clatch, clecking, cletch, cletching, cluster, clutch, flock, hatch, hatching, laughter, litter, *seating* (⇒ sitting), set, setting, sitting, trip, vatch**

2. *n* a litter of pups. bɾʏːd D

3. *n* a LITTER of piglets III.8.3. bɹiːd Y, bɾʏːd Co D, bɾuːd Co

4. *n* a BROODY HEN IV.6.7. bɹuːd L

brooder *1. n* a BROODY HEN IV.6.7. bɹuːdə Y Nth Nf Sf Hrt Ess, bɹuːdəᵗ K Sx

2. *n* a hen that is sitting on eggs. bɹuːdə Y

brooding hen *n* a BROODY HEN IV.6.7. bɹuːdɪn ɛn Y Nth Hrt

broodster *n* a BROODY HEN IV.6.7. bɹuːstə Y

broody *n* a BROODY HEN IV.6.7. bɹɪuːdɪ Db Sa, bɹᶩʉːdɪ Lei, bɹʏːdɪ La Ch Wa O, bɾʏːdi So Co D, bɹɛʊdɪ Db St, bɹoˑdɪ Nf, bɹoudɪ Nf, bɹʊɪdɪ Y, bʀuːdɪ Nb, bɹuːdɪ La Y*[modern x1]* Ch Sa St He Wo Wa Mon Gl O L Lei R Nth Hu Nf Ess Brk Sr Sx, bɾuːdi So W Do Ha, bɾuːdɪ Do, bɹʉːdɪ Sa Lei

broody chicken *n* a BROODY HEN IV.6.7. bɹɒuːdɪ tʃɪkn Ess

broody fowl *n* a BROODY HEN IV.6.7. bɾʏːdɪ væɫ So, bɾuːdi væʊɫ So

broody hen *n* A hen that wants to sit, you call a .... IV.6.7. bɹᶩuːdɪ ɛn Db, bɹʏːdɪ ɛn Ch Db, bɾʏːdɪ ɪn D, bɾʏːdɪ ɛn D, bɹɛʊdɪ ɛn Db, bɹaʊdɪ ɛn Gl, bɹʊdɪ hɛn Ess, bruːdɪ heᵊn Man, bɹuːdɪ hɪn Nf Sf, bɹuːdɪ ɪn Sx, bɹuːdɪ hɛn Ess MxL, bɹuːdɪ ɛn Y Ch Db Sa He Wo Wa Gl Nt L Lei Nth Hu Bd Hrt MxL Brk Sr Sx, bɹuːdɪ̃ 'n Ess, bɾuːdɪ hɛn So W, bɾuːdɪ ɛn So Ha, bɾuːdɪ ɛn O; **broody old hen** bɹuːdɪ ɔʊd ɛn Y. ⇒ **brood, brooder, brooding hen, broodster, broody, broody chicken, broody fowl, broody *old* hen, clocker, clocking hen, clocky hen, cluck, clucked hen, clucker, cluck hen, clucking hen, clucky, clucky hen, *old* setter, *old* setting hen, *old* sitter, rooking hen, setter, setting hen, setty, setty hen, sitter, sitting hen, sitty hen**; ⇒ also **cluckward**

brook *n* a RIVULET IV.1.1. bɾʏk D, bɹɛʊk St, bɹʌk Sa He Mon Gl O C Bk Bd Hrt, bɾʌk So, bɹʊk La Ch Db Sa St He Wo Wa Mon Gl O Lei R Nth Hu Sf Bk Bd Hrt Ess MxL Brk Sr K, *pl* bɹʊks Ha, bɾʊk O So W Do Ha, bɹuːk La Y Ch St Wo Nt Lei, bɹᶩuːk Sa, bɹʉːk Lei, bɹᶩʉːk Lei, bɹək Gl

brook-land *n* LOW-LYING LAND IV.1.7. bɹʊklænd Sx

brook-meadows *n* LOW-LYING LAND IV.1.7. bɹʊkmɛdəz Lei, bɹʊkmɛdəᵗz̩ Sx

broom *1. n* What do you call this, that you use *[to sweep]* outside the house? V.9.10. bɹɪum Y, bɹʏːm Ch Db, bɾʏːm So Co D, bɹɛʊm St, bɹʌm O*[old]* Sf, bʀʏˑm Nb, bʀʊm Nb Du, bɹʊm Nb Du Y St O Lei Nf Sf Ess Sx, bɾʊm Ha, bɹʊum Y*[old]*, bɹᶩuːm Db Nt, bruːm Man, bʀuːm Nb, bɹuːm Y Ch Db Sa St Mon Gl O L*[old x1]* Lei R Hu C Nf Bk Bd Ess Brk K Ha*[old]*, bɾuːm So W Co Do Ha, bɹᵾm Nf, bɹᵾːm Lei Nf, bɹəuːm Hrt. ⇒ **bass-broom, bass-brush, bath-broom, besom, besom-brush, birch-broom, bristle-brush, brush, cane-broom, cane-brush, causey-brush, green-broom, hard-broom, hard-brush, heath-broom, house-broom, long-broom, rough-broom, rough-brush, scrub, scrub-broom, stiff-broom, stiff-brush, sweeping-brush, swilling-brush, whalebone-broom, whalebone-brush, yard-broom, yard-brush**

2. *n* a MUCK-BRUSH I.3.14. bɹɪum Nf, bɹʏːm Ch, bɾʏːm So Co D, bɹʌm Sf, bʀʊm Nb Du, bɹʊm Du Sa He Gl Nf Sf Bk Ess MxL Sr Sx, bʀuːm Nb, bɹuːm Nb Du We La Y Db Sa St He Wa Gl O Nth Nf Bk Bd Hrt Ess Sr K Ha Sx, bɾuːm So W Co Ha, bɹᵾːm Nf

3. *n* a BESOM I.3.15. bɹʊm Ess, bɹuːm La Y, bɾuːm So

4. *n* a besom made of broom. bɹᵾːm Nf

5. *n* a besom made of birch. bɾʏːm D, bɹuːm Cu Y

6. n a besom made of ling. bɹuːm La

7. n a besom made of heather. bruːm Man

8. n a long-handled BRUSH used for sweeping V.2.14. bɹɪuːm Sa, bɹɛʊm Db St, bɹɪʏːm Ch, bɾʏːm D, bɹʏʉːm Sa, bɹʌm Sf*[old]*, bʁʊm Nb Du, bɹʊm Sa He Wo Wa Gl O Sf Bk Ess K Sx, *pl* bɹʊmz Sr, bɹʊɪm Y*[old]*, bɹᵁuːm We Nt Ess Sr, bɹuːm Y Sa St He Wo Wa Mon Gl Nth Hu C Nf Bk Bd Hrt Ess MxL Brk Sr K Ha Sx, bɾuːm O So W Co

9. n a BRUSH used for sweeping indoors V.9.11. bɹʏːm La, bɹʌm Sa, bɹʊum La, bɹʊm O Sf Ess, bɹʊuːm Y, bɹuːm We Sa St Nth Bk Ess Brk K*[long handle x2]* Sx, bɾuːm W

10. n GORSE IV.10.11. bɹʊm Sf, bʁuːm Nb, bɹuːm We La Y

broom-brush *n* a BESOM made of broom I.3.15. bɹɪəmbɹʊʃ Cu

broom-handle *n* the HANDLE of a besom I.3.16. bɹʊmændɬ Ess, bɹʊnæːndʊ Sx

broom-hook *n* a BILLHOOK IV.2.6. bɹʌmək Sa, bɹʊmˡuːk Sa, bɹʊmʊk St

broom-shaft *n* the HANDLE of a besom I.3.16. bɹʉːmʃɑˑft Nf

broom-stick *n* the HANDLE of a besom I.3.16. bɹʊmstɪk Sf Hrt, bɹuːmstɪk Brk K, bɾuːmstɪk So

broth *n What do you mean by* **broth***?* V.7.20(a). Eng. ⇒ **brewis,** *clear broth,* **glorified soup, hash, keteley broth, kettle-broth, lobby, lob-scouse,** *meat broth,* **shackles, skilly, slingers,** *soup,* **tea-kettle-broth**

brough *n* a HALO round the moon VII.6.4. bʁʌf Nb, bʁʏf Nb, bɹʊf Cu, bʁʊf Nb Du, bɹʊf Nb Du L

broughs *npl* BOUGHS of a tree IV.12.2. bɹɛʊz Nth, bɹæʊz L Lei, bɹaʊz L, *sg* bɹaʊ Lei

brow *1. n* a SLOPE IV.1.10. bɹaʊ La Y, bɹʌʊ Brk, bɹuː La Y, bɾəʊ W *[marked probably ir.r. SBM, probably = 'steep slope' Edd; unmarked NBM]*

2. v to TRIM the sides of hedges IV.2.3. bɹɒˑ Nf

3. v to trim overgrown banks. *-ing* bɹaʊ-ɪn Nf, *-ing* bɹɒː-ɪn Nf

4. n the FOREHEAD VI.1.7. bɹʏː Ch, bɹɛʊ Wo Wa, bɹæʊ St Wo Wa, bɹaʊ Cu La Y St, bɹɑʊ Nf, bʁʌʊ Nb, bɹʌʊ Gl, bʁuː Nb, bɹuː Cu Du We La Y Ch, bɹəʊː Wo

browlock *n* the FORELOCK of a horse III.4.8. bɾævlɒk So

brown-flour *n* MEAL V.6.1(b). bɹeanflɪa Y, bɹɛʊnflɛʊə Hu Bd Hrt Ess, bɹɛʊn flɛʊəˡ Db, bɹɛʊnflɛʊəᵗ Wa Bk, bɹɛʊnflæʊə Ess, bɹæʊnflæʊəᵗ Ess, bɾæʊn vlæʊəᵗ: So, bɹaːnflæʊə L, bɹaːnflaː Y, bɹaɪn flaʊə St, bɹaʊnflaʊə La Y L, bɹaʊnflaʊə Y He, bɹaʊn flaʊəᵗ Sa, bɹʊːnflɪʊə Y, bɹᵁuːn flᵁuːəᵗ Gl, bruːnflʊˑə Cu, bɹuːnflʊə Y L, bɹəʊn fləʊˑə Mon

brown-meal *n* MEAL V.6.1(b). bɹɛʊnmiil Nf, bɹɛənmɛɪl Y, bɹuːnmɪəl Y, bɹuːnmɛɪl Y

brown-sugar-shag *n* a PIECE *OF BREAD AND BUTTER AND JAM/SUGAR* V.6.11(b). bɹuːnʃʊgəʃag Cu

brown wholemeal *n* MEAL V.6.1(b). bɹaʊn oʊlmɪəl Y

brows *npl* the RIDGES between furrows in a ploughed field II.3.2. *sg* bɹʌʊ Brk

browse **1. n* brushwood, ⇐ BASE II.7.4. bɾæʏs D, bɹəus He

2. v to TRIM hedges IV.2.3. bɾæʏs D, *-ing* bɾæʏsɪn So Co, bɾaʊz So

3. n brushwood. bɾæʏs D

browse down *1. vphr* to TRIM hedges IV.2.3. bɾæʏs dæʊn So

2. vtphr to trim a hedge. bɾæʏs ... dæʏn D

browse-hook *1. n* a HEDGING-BILL IV.2.5. bɾæʏsʏk So, bɾæʏsʊk Co

2. n a BILLHOOK IV.2.6. bɾæʏsʏk Co D, bɾæʏzʏk D

browsells *n* SCRAPS left after rendering lard III.12.10. bəᵗːzˌʊɫz K

browse off *vtphr* to TRIM a hedge IV.2.3. *-ing* bɾæʏzɪn ... ɔːf So

browse out *vtphr* to TRIM a hedge IV.2.3. bɾæʏs ... æʏt D

brow-side *n* a SLOPE IV.1.10. bɹuːsaɪd Y

browsing *n* brushwood, ⇐ to TRIM IV.2.3. bɾæʏsɪn D

bruffing *v-ing* COUGHING VI.8.2. bɹʊfɪn Y*[coughing constantly]*; **bruffing and coughing** bɹʊfɪn ən kɒfɪn Y

bruise *n* a BUMP on someone's forehead VI.1.8. bɹˡuˑz Nf, bɾʏːz So, bɹuːz O Brk Sr, bɹʉːz Nf

brumble-kites *npl* BLACKBERRIES IV.11.1. bɹʊmǝlkaɪts Y*[rare]*

brumbles *npl* BLACKBERRIES IV.11.1. bɹʌmblz Nf, bɾʊmlz Cu, bɹʊmlz Y *[not an EMBM headword]*

brun *n* FRECKLES VI.11.1. bɹʌn Ess

brun-spots *n* FRECKLES VI.11.1. bɹʌnspɒts Nf Ess, bɹʊnspɒts C

brunnies *npl* FRECKLES VI.11.1. bɹʌnɪz Nf

brunny *n* FRECKLES VI.11.1. bɹʌnɪ Ess

brunny-spots *n* FRECKLES VI.11.1. bɹʌnɪspɒts Nf Ess, bɹʌnəspɒts Nf*[old]*, bɹʌnɪspəts Sf, bɹʏnɪspɒts Nf, bɹʊnɪspɒts Sf

brush *1. n What do you clean your horses up with?* III.5.5(a). Eng exc. MxL Sx. ⇒ **bass-brush, body-brush,** *broom,* **cane-brush, cuddy-brush, dand-brush, dandy, dandy-brush, horse-brush, kit-brush**

2. n By the way, what do you sweep with? V.2.14. bɾɪːʃ Co D, bɾɪʃ Co D, bɾʏʃ Co, bɾʏːʃ D, bɹʏːʃ Db, bʁʌʃ Nb, bɹʌʃ Sa Mon Gl Nth Hu Nf Bk Bd Hrt K, bɾʌʃ So W Do Ha, bʁʏʃ Nb, bɹʏʃ Nf, bɾʊʃ Cu Man, bʁʊʃ Nb Du, bɹʊʃ Nb Cu Du We La Y

Ch Db St He Wo Gl Nt L Lei R Nth, bɹuʃ Co, bɹəʃ Gl, bɾəᵗːʃ D, bəᵗːʃ So*[old x1]* W Co D. ⇒ **besom, broom, long-brush, soft-broom, sweeping-brush**

3. n What do you call this, that you use [to sweep] inside the house? V.9.11. bɾiːʃ D, bɾɪʃ Co D, bɹʏːʃ Db, bɾʏːʃ Co, bɹʌʃ Mon Hu Nf Sf Bd Ess Brk*[short handle]* K*[short handle x2]*, bɾʌʃ So W Do Ha, bɹʌˡʃ Nf, bʁʏʃ Nb, bɹʊʃ Man, bʁʊʃ Nb Du, bɹʊʃ Nb Cu Du We La Y Ch Db St Wo Nt L Lei R, bɾʊʃ Co, bɹuːʃ Man, bɹəʃ St Gl, bəᵗːʃ So W Co D. ⇒ **bass-broom, bath-broom, besom, birch-broom, bristle-broom, broom, duster, fibre-broom, fibre-brush, hair-broom, hair-brush, hair sweeping-brush, hand-brush, house-broom, house-brush, indoors-broom, kitchen-brush, long-brush, long-handle-brush, scrub-broom, skeeb, smooth brush, soft-broom, soft-brush, sweeping-broom, sweeping-brush**; ⇒ also **bannister-brush**

4. n a BROOM used for sweeping outdoors V.9.10. bɾiːʃ Co, bɹʌʃ Bk, bɾʌʃ So W, bɹʊʃ La Y Ch Db St L Lei Nth, bəᵗːʃ So

5. n a MUCK-BRUSH I.3.14. bɾiːʃ D, bɹʏːʃ Db, bɹʌʃ Nth Hu C Bk Sr, bɾʌʃ So W Co Do, bɹʊʃ Cu We La Y Ch Db St Nt L Lei R Nth, bɹəʃ Gl, bəᵗːʃ So

6. n a BESOM I.3.15. bɹʊʃ C

7. n a besom made of birch or broom. bʁʌʃ Nb

8. v to CLEAR grass at the edges of a field II.9.5. *-ing* bɹɪʃɪn K, *-ing* bɹʌʃɪn K

9. v to TRIM hedges IV.2.3. *-ing* bɹɪʃɪn K Sx, *-ing* bɾɪʃɪn K, bɹʌʃ Sa Sf Ess, *-ing* bɹʌʃɪn Nf, bɹʊʃ Y Ch Db Sa St Wo Wa Lei, *-ing* bɹʊʃɪn K

10. vt to SWEEP V.9.12. bɾʌˡʃ So

11. v to sweep. bɾiːʃ D, *-ing* bɹʊʃən Man, bɹʊʃ Ch, bəᵗːʃ So

brush-broom *n* a BESOM I.3.15. bɹʌʃbɹʊm Ess

brush down *vphr* to CLEAR grass at the edges of a field II.9.5. bɹʌʃ dɛun Sf

brushel *1. n* a HEDGING-BILL IV.2.5. bɾɪʃəl K
2. n a BILLHOOK IV.2.6. bɾɪʃəl K
[SBM Edd notes 'brushel may be a form of brush-bill', but no brush-bill forms recorded]

brush-hook *n* a HEDGING-BILL IV.2.5. bɹɪʃʊk K, bɹʌʃʊk Nf

brushing-bill *n* a HEDGING-BILL IV.2.5. bɹʏʃɪnbɪl Db, bɹʊʃɪnbɪl Y Nt

brushing-hook *1. n* a HEDGING-BILL IV.2.5. bɹɪʃɪnʌk K, bɹʌʃɪnʌk Sa, bɹʊʃɪniuːk Db, bɹʊʃɪnʊk Sa St Wo Wa, bɹʊʃɪnɛʊk Db St, bɹʊʃɪnuːk Ch St
2. n a BILLHOOK IV.2.6. bɹʌʃɪnʌk Sa He, bɹʊʃɪnʊk Wo, bɹʌʃɪnuːk K

brush round *vphr* to CLEAR grass at the edges of a field II.9.5. bɹʌʃ ɹɛund Sf

brush-shank *n* the HANDLE of a besom I.3.16. bɹʊʃʃaŋk Cu

brush-stale* *n* the HANDLE of a besom I.3.16. bɹʊʃstɛɪl La. ⇒ also **stale** *[NBM headword brush-steal]*

brush up *1.1. vtphr* to trim. bɹʊʃ ... ʊp St Wa
1.2. vphr to TRIM hedges IV.2.3. *-ing* bɹʊʃɪn ʊp Db
2.1. vtphr to SWEEP V.9.12. bɾiːʃ ʌp D, bɾɪʃ ... ʌp D, bəᵗːʃ ʌp So, bəᵗːʃ ... əp So
2.2. vphr to sweep. bɹʌʃ ʌp Nf

brushwood *n* KINDLING-*WOOD* V.4.2. bɹɛʃwʊd Ess, bɾʌʃuːd Do

bub *n* a BREAST of a woman VI.8.5. *pl* bʌbz Ess MxL

bubb *n* a NESTLING IV.7.1. bʊb L

bubble *vi* to SCREAM VIII.8.11. bʊbl Nb*[old x1]*

bubbling *n* a NESTLING IV.7.1. bʊblɪn Db Nt L

bubs *1. npl* CHICKENS IV.6.11. bʊbz L
2. npl LICE IV.8.1(a). bʌbs D

bucca *n* a SCARECROW II.3.7. bɒkə Co

buck *1. n* an EVENER on the plough-beam end of a horse-drawn plough I.8.4. bʊk Sa R
2. n the T-SHAPED PLOUGH-BEAM END of a horse-drawn plough I.8.5. *pl* bɒks St, bʊk Nb Du La Y Man Ch Db St Lei, bʊg Ch
3. n a STICK used to support the shaft of a cart I.11.1. bʊk Y
4. v to BUTT III.2.10. bʌk Hrt
5. v to TRIM hedges IV.2.3. bʌk Ess
6. vt to PLASH a hedge IV.2.4. bʌk Ess*[old]*
7. vi to DUCK VIII.7.8. bɒk Sr, bʊk L *[not a SBM headword;* [bɒk] *queried for* **bob** *SBM]*

bucker *n* a PIECE *OF BREAD AND BUTTER* V.6.11(a). bʊkə Db

bucket *n* a container for carrying horse-feed, ⇐ BASKET III.5.4. bʌkɪt He Mon, bʌkʌt So, bʊkɪt Y Db, bʊkət Cu We La Y

buck-fisted *adj* LEFT-HANDED VI.7.13(a). bʌkfɪstɪd C

buck-head *v* to TRIM hedges IV.2.3. *-ing* bʌkhɛdɪn Nf

buckle *1. n* the CLOG on a horse's tether I.4.3. bʌkl Sa
2. vi to WARP, referring to wood IX.2.9. bʌkɫ K, *3prsg* bʌkʊɫz W, *3prsg* bʊkɫz Y

buckles *npl* PEGS used to fasten thatch on a stack II.7.7(a). bʌkɫz He Mon, bʊkɫz Wo

buck over *vphr* to JUMP a wall IV.2.10. bʌk ouvə Nf

bud **1.* *n* a HEIFER up to 1 year old III.1.5. bʏd Nf
**2.* *n* a heifer 1 year old. bod L, bud L
3. n a young castrated bull-calf, ⇐ BULLOCK III.1.16. bʌd Ess, bʏd Nf, bəˈd Nf

budget* *n* a wallet in which a whetstone is carried, ⇐ WHETSTONE II.9.10. bʌdʒət So

buffer *n* a BUMPER of a cart I.10.1(a). *pl* bʌfəᵗːz̞ Do, *pl* bəfəᵗz̞ Gl

buffet *1. n* a TUSSOCK of grass II.2.9. bʊfɪt L

2. n a MILKING-STOOL III.3.3. bʊfɪt Y

buffs *n* the WATTLES of a hen IV.6.19. bʊfs Brk

bugabo *n* a BOGEY VIII.8.1. bʌgɪboː He Mon, bʊgɪboː Sa He Wo, bʊgɪbʊʊ Wo

bugabowl *n* a BOGEY VIII.8.1. bʊgɪbʊʊl Wo

bugalo *n* a SCARECROW II.3.7. bʌgələː Do

buggered *adj* EXHAUSTED, describing a tired person VI.13.8. bʌgəᵗːd̞ So D, bʊgəd Db St

buggered up *adj* EXHAUSTED, describing a tired person VI.13.8. bʌgəᴶd ʌp K, bʌgəᵗd̞ ʌp He, bʌgəᵗːd̞ ʌp Sa W, bʏgəd ʌp Nf, bʊgəᵗd̞ ʊp He Wo Gl, bʊgəᵗːd̞ ʊp Wo, bəgəd ʌp Gl

buggering *v-ing* SWEARING VIII.8.9(b). bʌgəɾɪn So*[old]*

bugger off *imp* GO AWAY! VIII.7.9(a). bəgəɪ ɒf Nt, bʌgəᵗɾ ɑːf He, bʌgəᵗ·ɾ ɒf Sa, bʌgəɪ ɔːf Gl Nf Sf Ess, bʌgəᵗ ɔːf Sa, bʌgəᵗɾ ɔːf Sa He, bʊgɔᴿʁ ɒf Nb, bʊgəɪ ɒf La Y St, bʊgəᵗɾ ɒf Sa He, bʊgəʁ ɔf Nb, bʊgəɪ ɔf L, bʊgəᵗːɾ ɔːf Sa D; **bugger off out of it** bʌgəᵗːɾ ɔːf æʊt ɒv ət Ha

bugger on *imp* GO AWAY! VIII.7.9(a). bʌgəᵗːɾ ɔːn So

buggy* *adj* BOGGY IV.1.8. bʌgi So D

buglug *n* a SCARECROW II.3.7. bʌgɫʌg Do

bugs *1. npl* LICE IV.8.1(a). bʊgz Ch St

2. npl TICKS on sheep IV.8.3. bʌgz Nf Ess, *sg* bʊg St

build *v* to LOAD sheaves onto a wagon II.6.7(a). bɪld Cu

builder *1. n* the LOADER of sheaves onto a wagon II.6.7(c). bɪldə Cu, bɪɫdəᵗ Co

2. n a STACKER who makes sheaves of corn into a stack II.6.11. bɪɫdə Nth Bk Bd Hrt, bɪldər Cu, bɪldəᵗ O, bɪldɾ O, bɪɫdəᵗ O Bk, bɪɫdəᵗː Co, bɪʊɫdəᴶ Brk, bɪʊdəᵗ Sr

buildings *npl* a FARMSTEAD I.1.2. bɪʊdnz Ess

build up *vtphr* to fill gaps in a hedge-bank or hedge with turfs, brushwood, or similar material, ⇐ to PLASH IV.2.4. bɪɫd ... ʌp Co

bulching *v-ing* BELCHING VI.13.13. bɔɫtʃɪn Ess, bɔɫʃn Sf, bʌɫtʃɪn Ess, bʌɫʃɪn Ess, bʌʊtʃɪn Hrt, bʊʊɫtʃɪn Bk, bʊɫʃɪn Hrt, bəɫʃɪn Mon MxL

bulching up *vtphr-ing* **bulching up the wind** BELCHING VI.13.13. bəɫʃɪn ʌp ðə wɪnd MxL

bulging *v-ing* BELCHING VI.13.13. bʌɫdʒɪn Mon, bʊɫdʒɪn He

bulhorns *npl* SNAILS IV.9.3. bʊɫaᵗːn̞z̞ Co

bulk *1.1. vt* to BUTT III.2.10. prppl bʊɫkɪn Co

1.2. v to butt. *-ing* bʊɫkɪn Co

2. n a tree STUMP IV.12.4. bʊɫk Brk

bulking *v-ing* BELCHING VI.13.13. bʌɫkɪn Mon So, *3prsg* bʌɫks Ess, bʌɫʔn Ess, bəɫkɪn So, bəɫkɪn Ess So*[old x1]* W D Do, bəɫkən D Do

bulking up* *vtphr-ing* **bulking it up** BELCHING VI.13.13. *no -ing* bəɫk ɪt ʌp So, bəɫkɪn ʊʊ ət ʌp So

bull *1. n What do you call the male of the cow?* III.1.14. Eng. ⇒ **beast**

2. n **at bull, going to bull, go to bull, on at bull, on bull, ready for the bull, wants the bull** ON HEAT, describing a cow III.1.6. **at bull** ət bʊl O, ət bʊɫ Wa Gl; **going to bull** gʊɪn tə bʊɫ Sf; **go to bull** *3prsg* guː tə bʊɫ Ess, *3prsg* gɒʊ tə bʊʊ Ess; **on at bull** ɒn ət bʊl O, ɑn ət bʊɫ Nth, ɒn ət bʊɫ O, ɑn əʔ bʊɫ Bk, ɒn əʔ bʊɫ Bk, ɒn ət bʊʊ Brk; **on bull** ɒn bʊl Nf, ɒn bʊɫ Bk; **wants the bull** wɒnts ðə bʊɫ O

3. n a pointed steel bar put on an axle to prevent a cart from going backwards on a hill, ⇐ PROP/CHOCK I.11.2. bʊl Y

4. n a WHETSTONE made of stone II.9.10. bʊl Nb

bull-boy* *n* a SCARECROW II.3.7. bʊlbɒɪ K

bull-calf *n* a BULLOCK III.1.16. bʊɫkaːf Ess

bull-dogs *npl* KNEE-STRAPS used to lift the legs of working trousers VI.14.17. bʊldɒgz Hrt

bulled *adj* **not bulled** describing a cow that has not conceived, ⇐ HAS NOT HELD III.1.7. nɔʔ bʊld L

bullets *n* SWEETS V.8.4. bʊlɪts Y, bʊləts Nb Cu Du

bull-face *n* a TUSSOCK of grass II.2.9. bʊlfɪəs Y

bull-forehead *n* a TUSSOCK of grass II.2.9. bʊlfɔɪɪəd Y, *pl* bʊlfʊəɪiːdz Y, bʊlfʊəɪɪəd Y, *pl* bʊlfʊəɪɛdz Y

bull-front *n* a TUSSOCK of grass II.2.9. bʊlfɪʊnt Y

bull-head *n* a STUPID person VI.1.5. bʊlɪəd Y

bull-heads *1. npl* TADPOLES IV.9.5. bʌɫɛdz D, bʊlhiːdz We, *sg* bʊlhiːd Cu, bʊliːdz Cu We*[old]*, bʊlɪədz Cu La Y, bʊlɛɪdz Du, bʊlɛdz Y Sa He Wa Mon So, bʊɫɛdz Lei, bʊlɪɛdz Wa, bʊljɛdz Db Sa St, bʊɫjɛdz Lei, bʊlɛɪdz La

2. npl small fish. bʊlɪədz Y

3. npl MINNOWS IV.9.9. bʊlhiːdz Du, bʊlɪədz Y, bʊlɛdz Sa Wo, bʊljɛdz Sa Wo, bʊɫjœdz Gl, bʊljʊdz Sa He

bullies *1. npl* TADPOLES IV.9.5. bʊlɪz Lei, bʊɪz Lei

*2. npl MINNOWS IV.9.9. bʊlɪz Nt

bulling *adj* **a-bulling, bulling, come along bulling, coming a-bulling, coming in bulling, coming on bulling, in bulling, on a-bulling, on bulling** ON HEAT, describing a cow III.1.6. **a-bulling** əbʊlɪn Ch Db Sa St Wa Gl O Nt L Nth Hu Bk, əbʊɫɪn Gl Lei W Brk Ha Sx; **bulling** bʏɫɪn So, bʊlɪn Nb La Y Ch Sa St He Gl L Lei R Nth C Nf Bk Bd Hrt Ess So*[old x1]* Sr K, bʊɫɪn Gl Lei R Ess So W Brk Sr K D Do Ha Sx*[old x1]*, bʊlən

L Sf Ess K, bʊłən W Do Ha; **come along bulling** kɒm əlɒŋ bʊlɪn Brk; **coming a-bulling** kʊmɪn əbʊlɪn Sa Wa; **coming in bulling** kʊmɪn ɪ bʊlɪn Ch; **coming on bulling** kʌmɪn ɔn bʊlɪn MxL; **in bulling** ɪn bʊlɪn Y Db, ɪ bʊlɪn La Y Ch Db; **on a-bulling** ɒn əbʊlɪn Wo Wa; **on bulling** ə bɒlən Man, ɒn bʊlɪn Bk, ə bʊlɪn Cu We La*[blunt x1]* Y, ɒn bʊłɪn W, ɔn bʊlən Ess, ə bʊlən Nb Du, ɒn bʊłən W *[[ə bʊlɪn] and similar forms taken as on bulling in NBM and retained as such here]*

bull-joats* *npl* TADPOLES IV.9.5. *sg* bʊldʒʊʊt Nt *[queried EMBM]*

bull-lump *n* a TUSSOCK of grass II.2.9. bʊllʊmp Y

bull-nobs *npl* TADPOLES IV.9.5. bɒlnɒbz Ch

bull-nose *n* a TUSSOCK of grass II.2.9. *pl* bʊlnʊəzɪz Y

bullock *When you castrate the male calf, you call it a .... Does he remain a [bullock] till he is slaughtered?* III.1.16. *[Note: 1. below includes references to animals of any age and those for which no age is specified]*

1. *n* a bullock of any or no specified age. *pl* bγłəks Co D, bɒlək Man, bʌlək Sa, *pl* bʌləks O, bʊlɪk Du Y, *pl* bʊłɪks Ess Ha Sx, bʊłœːk Gl, bʊlʊk Cu La St Wo Wa, bʊłʊk Gl Ess, bʊlək Nb Cu We La Y Ch Db Sa St He Wo Wa Mon Gl O Nt L Lei Nth Hu Nf Sf Bk Ess MxL, *pl* bʊləks Sr K, bʊłək He Wo Mon Gl Lei R Nth Ess W K Co, *pl* bʊłəks Sr D Sx

2. *n* a young bullock. bʊłʊk Gl, bʊlək Y

3. *n* a mature bullock. bʊlɪk Ess, bʊlʊk St Wa Nth, bʊlək Du La Y He O L Lei Nth Hu C Nf Sf Bk Bd Hrt Ess Sr, bʊłək Lei Sr

⇒ **beast, bud, bull-calf, stag, steer, steer-calf, stirk, stot**

bullocked *v-ed* CASTRATED, describing a bullock III.1.15. bʊləkt La Db

bullock-man *n* a COWMAN on a farm, often looking after stock other than cows I.2.3. bʊləkmən Cu L

bullock-shed *n* the STRAW-YARD of a farm I.1.9. bʊlək ʃɛd Sa *[not queried WMBM]*

bullock's-yard 1. *n* the STRAW-YARD of a farm I.1.9. bɒłəksjɑ˞ːd D, bʌłəksjɑ˞ːd So, bʊləksjɑ˞ːd D
2. *n* a straw-yard in which cattle are fattened. bʊləksjɑ˞ːd Sa

bullock-walloper *n* a COWMAN on a farm I.2.3. bʊləkwaləpə Y, bʊləkwɒləpə Y

bullocky 1. *n* a COWMAN on a farm I.2.3. bʊləkɪ Cu We Y
2. *n* a person who looks after calves and young stock on a farm. bʊləkɪ Y
3. *n* a person who looks after cattle or other stock on a farm. bʊləkɪ Y
4. *n* a FARM-LABOURER I.2.4. bʊləkɪ K

bullock-yard 1. *n* a FARMYARD I.1.3. bʊləkjɑːd Nf, bʊłəkjɑːd Ess
2. *n* the STRAW-YARD of a farm I.1.9. bʊlɪkjɑːd

Sf, bʊləkjɑːd Nf Sf Bd Hrt Ess, *pl* bʊləkjɑːdz Ch, bʊłəkjɑːd Ess, bʊłɪkjɑːd Ess, bʊləkjɑːd Nf K
3. *n* a straw-yard in which cattle are fattened. bʊləkjɑːd Wa Nf Sf Hrt Ess, bʊləkjɑːd Nf

bull-pate *n* a TUSSOCK of grass II.2.9. bʊlpeːt Du Ch

bull-poll *n* a TUSSOCK of grass II.2.9. *pl* boːpʊʊz Brk, bʊłpoːł W

bull-scalp *n* a TUSSOCK of grass II.2.9. bʊlskɔːp La

bulls'-heads *npl* TADPOLES IV.9.5. bʊlzɛdz Ch

bull-skulled *adj* STUPID VI.1.5. bʊlskʌld Nf, bʊlskʌłd Nf

bull-snout *n* a TUSSOCK of grass II.2.9. bʊlsnuːt Nb

bull-stone *n* a WHETSTONE II.9.10. bʊlstɪn Y, bʊlstɪən Y, bʊlstʊən La Y, bʊlstn Du We La Y, bʊlstən Y Db, bʊlsən Y

bull-topping *n* a TUSSOCK of grass II.2.9. bʊltɒpɪn Y

bull-walloper *n* a person in charge of the bulls on a farm, ⇐ COWMAN I.2.3. bʊlwɔləpə Wo

bullward *adj* ON HEAT, describing a cow III.1.6. bγłəd So*[old]*, bʊlɪd Ess, bʊłɪd Ess Co D, bʊłəd Co D, bʊłə˞ːd Co

bully 1. *v* to PITCH sheaves II.6.10. *-ing* bʊli-ɪn Nf
2. *n* a person who pitches sheaves to the stack. bγlɪ Nf; **standing bully** stændn bʊˑlɪ Nf
3. *n* a person on the stack when stack-building. bʊlɪ Nf

bully-balcher *n* a NESTLING IV.7.1. bʊlɪbɒłʃə Hu

bully-man 1. *n* the FORKER on a wagon who unloads sheaves in a stackyard II.6.9. bʊlɪmæn Nf
2. *n* a person whose job is to PITCH sheaves II.6.10. bʊlɪmæn Nf, bʊləmæn Nf

bullynecks over *adv* HEAD OVER HEELS IX.1.10. bʊlɪnɛks ʊə˩ La

bultree* *n* the bush ELDER IV.10.6. bʊltrˡiː We, bʊltrɪ We

bultree-tree *n* the bush ELDER IV.10.6. bʊltrɪtrɪ Cu, *pl* bʊltəɹɪtɹəɪz Y

bum *n* the ARSE VI.9.2. bɒm K, bʌm Ess Co, bγm Nf

bum-balls 1. *n* SHEEP-DUNG II.1.7. bʌmbłz Gl, bʌmbʊłz Brk, bʊmbłz O; **sheep-bum-balls** ʃɪpbʌmblz O, ʃɪpbʌmbłz O, ʃɪpbʊmbłz Gl Bk, ʃiːpbʊmbəłz O*[polite]*; **sheep's-bum-balls** ʃiːpsbʌmblz O
2. *npl* RABBIT-DROPPINGS III.13.15. bɒmbəłz O, bʌmblz Gl, bʌmbłz O, bʌmbʊłz Brk, bʊmblz O

bumble-fisted *adj* CLUMSY, describing a person VI.7.14. bʌmblfɪstɪd Nf

bumble-hole *n* an ASH-MIDDEN at the back of an earth-closet V.1.14. bʌmbɬʌʊl Ess

bumble-kites *npl* BLACKBERRIES IV.11.1. bʊmblkaɪts Y, bʊmlkaɪts Y, bʊməlkaɪts Y, bʊmlkɑɪts Y, *sg* bʊmlkɒɪt Y

bumbles-kites *npl* BLACKBERRIES IV.11.1. bʊmlskɛɪts Nb

bumby *n* an ASH-MIDDEN V.1.14. bʌmbɪ Sf Ess

bumby-hole *1. n* an ASH-MIDDEN V.1.14. bʌmbɪhʌʊɬ Ess
2. n an EARTH-CLOSET V.1.13. *pl* bʌmbɪ-ɔʊɫz Ess

bumly-kites *npl* BLACKBERRIES IV.11.1. bʊmlɪkaɪts Cu Du We*[old x1]* Y

bump *1. n What do you call that swelling [that comes when a baby hits its forehead on the door]?* VI.1.8. bɒmp K, bʌmp Sa Mon O Lei Hu Nf Sf Bk Bd Hrt Ess MxL So W Brk Sr K Co D Do Ha Sx, bʌmpʔ C, bʏmp Nf, bʊmp Nb Cu Du We La Y Man Ch Db Sa St He Wo Wa Gl O Nt L Lei R Nth Bk Brk K Co D Do, bəmp Gl Sx. ⇒ **blow, boin, bruise, bunch, bunny, cowl, flop, hump, knob, lump, swell, swelling**
2. v to BUTT III.2.10. *-ing* bʊmpɪn He

bumper *1. n [Show a picture of a cart.] What do you call this projecting piece of the beam on which the body rests when tipped up?* (question used after April 1953) I.10.1(a). *pl* bɒmpəᶼz K, *pl* bʌmpəz Ess, *pl* bʌmpəᵗz̗ Sr, bʌmpəᵗː W, *pl* bʌmpəᵗːz̗ Ha, hʊmpə Cu Wa Nt Nth, *pl* bʊmpəz La Ch Db Lei, bʊmpəɹ La, *pl* bʊmpəᶼz Ch Brk, bʊmpəᵗ Wa, *pl* bʊmpəᵗɾz̗ Brk, *pl* bəmpəᵗz̗ Gl. ⇒ **bar, beam-end, bearers, bed, bed-pieces, bit, bolster, breech-piece, buffer,** *buffers* ⇒ **buffer, cart-dog, cart-rest, chockrel, cross-bar, cross-piece, dog, foot-board, fore-buck, front slote, guide, hinder-brig,** *horns* ⇒ **iron, iron, lade-grip,** *lade-grips* ⇒ **lade-grip, lugs, nog, pin, pumble, pumbler, pummel, punder, putt-rester, quarterings, shoot-bat, shoulder, sill, soles, soling-piece, stay, stud, tail-piece, tail-pole, tenant, tib, tip, tipe, tippers, tipping-piece, toe, verge,** *verges* ⇒ **verge, verging**
2. n a SCOOP used to take water out of a boiler V.9.9. bʊmpə Man

bumpers *npl* big potatoes, ⇐ BIG ONES II.4.5. bʊmpəz St

bump up *viphr* to BOUNCE VIII.7.3. bʊmp ʊp Y

bunch *1. v* to BUTT III.2.10. *-ing* bʌnʃɪn Co, *-ing* bʌnʃən Co
2. n a BUMP on someone's forehead VI.1.8. bʌnʃ So

bunch out *vtphr* to THIN OUT turnip plants II.4.2. bʊnʃ ... əʊt He

bunch up *1. vtphr* to BIND corn into a sheaf II.6.2. bʊnʃ ... ʊp Db

2. vtphr-3sg she [a tidy girl] will COLLECT her toys VIII.8.15. bʌnʃ ... ʌp So

bundle *1. n* a SHEAF of corn II.6.3(a). bʌndɬ Mon
2. n a CUTTING of hay II.9.15. bʌndɬ D, bʊndl Du

bundles *npl* SHEAVES of corn II.6.3(b). bʌndɬz Mon, bʊndlz Nb

bung *vt* to BUTT III.2.10. *-ing* bʌŋɪn So

bungersome *adj* CLUMSY, describing a person VI.7.14. bʌŋɡəᵗz̗ʌm W

bungey *n* a COWMAN on a farm I.2.3. bʊŋɡɪ Db St

bunk *n* RUBBISH V.1.15. bʊŋk Ch

bunk down *viphr* to DUCK VIII.7.8. bʌŋk dɛʊn Ess

bunks *n* GOOSE-GRASS II.2.5. bʌŋks Nf

bunkus *n* a DONKEY III.13.16. bʊŋkəs Y

bunnums *npl* BILBERRIES IV.11.3. bʌnʌmz D *[queried SBM]*

bunny *n* a BUMP on someone's forehead VI.1.8. bʌnɪ Nf Sf

bunny-stickles *npl* MINNOWS IV.9.9. bʌnɪstɪkɬz Bk *[marked u.r. and interpreted as 'stickleback' EMBM]*

bunt *1. vt* to BUTT III.2.10. *-ing* bʌntɪn MxL W Ha, *prppl* bʌntən Ha, *-ing* bʌnʔən Ha, *prppl* bʊntɪn Wo, *-ing* bʊntɪn Wo
2. v to butt. bʌnt Sa He, *-ing* bʌntɪn W Brk Sr D Sx, *-ing* bʌntən W Ha, bʌnʔ Bd, *-ing* bʌnʔɪn Bk, *-ing* bʌnʔɪn Bk, bʊnt Sa Wo, *-ed* bʊntɪd St, *-ing* bʊntɪn St Wo Gl O K, *prppl* əbʊntɪn Wo, *-ing* bəntɪn Gl

bunt about *vphr* to BUTT III.2.10. *-ing* əbʌnʔɪn əbɛʊʔ Bk

bunts *n* KINDLING-*WOOD* V.4.2. bʊnts Gl

bup *n* a PIECE *OF BREAD AND BUTTER* V.6.11(a). bʊp Nth

buppy *1. n* a PIECE *OF BREAD AND BUTTER* V.6.11(a). bʌpɪ MxL Sr*[very small child's word]*
2. n a **buppy jam** a PIECE *OF BREAD AND BUTTER AND JAM/SUGAR* V.6.11(b). ə bʌpɪ dʒæm MxL, bʌpɪdʒæm Sr

burdock *n* GOOSE-GRASS II.2.5. bœːdɒk Mon, bœːdʌk Mon, bəɹdɔk Ch, bəᵗːd̗ɒk Sa Mon, bəᵗːd̗ək Sa

burial ground *n* a CHURCHYARD VIII.5.5. bəɹɪʊɬ ɡɹʌʊnd Brk*[near church]*

buried *ptppl A grave is a place in which someone has been ....* VIII.5.11. Eng. ⇒ **laid**

buriers *npl* BEARERS who carry a coffin VIII.5.10. bɛɹɪəz Ess

burking *v-ing* BELCHING VI.13.13. bəːkɪn Ess

burn *1. n* a CUTTING of hay II.9.15. bəᵗːn̗ So

2.1. vt to MARK the horns of sheep with a burn-mark to indicate ownership III.7.9. bɔˈːɹn La, bən Y

2.2. v to mark sheep for ownership. bəːn Y

3. n a RIVULET IV.1.1. bɔʁn Nb, bɔʁən Nb, bɔːᵊn Nb, bɔᵏːn Nb Du, bʊrn Cu, bʊən Du, bʊəɹn Du, bəːn Du

burned *ptppladj* BURNT, describing bread or cakes V.6.7. bœːnd Gl, bɒɹnd Y, bɔnd Y*[old]*, bʊnd Y, bʊɹnd Y, *ptppl* bəːnd Wa, bəˈːnd We La, bəᵗːn̩d̥ Wo Gl Ess So W Co D Do Ha Sx

burnt *ptppladj When your bread or cakes come out all black, then you say they are ....* V.6.7. Eng. ⇒ **burned, kizzened, swinged**

burping *v-ing* BELCHING VI.13.13. bəᵗːpɪn Ess

burr *1. n* a chock placed behind and under a wheel to prevent a cart from going backwards on a hill, ⇐ PROP/CHOCK I.11.2. bɒɹ Y, bɔᵏː Nb, bɔˈɹ Y, bɔːᵊ Nb, bʊɹ Y, bəː Du Y Db, bəˈɹ Y, bəˈː Y

2. n a WHETSTONE made of stone II.9.10. bəᵗː Sa

3. n a whetstone made of unspecified material. bəᵗː So W

4. n a HALO round the moon VII.6.4. bʊr Cu, bʊə Cu, bəɹ Cu We L, bəɾ Nf, bəː Cu We Y L Sf, bəːr We, bəːɹ Cu Hu C, bəᵗː K

5. vi-3prpl they MOO, describing the noise cows make during feeding time in the cow-house III.10.4(a). *prppl* bœːɹən Du

burrow *n* a HALO round the moon VII.6.4. bʌɹə Nth Nf Sf, bʊɹə L R, bəɹə Nf, bəˈɹə Nf, bəɾə Nf

burr(s) *n* GOOSE-GRASS II.2.5.

no -s: bəᵗː Sa

-s: bɔˈːz La, bəːz Bd, bəᵗːz̬ Sa Bk

bursting-jug *n* a round stack, ⇐ STACKS II.7.1. bɒstndʒʊg Nth*[? facetious Edd]*

burst open *vtphr* to shell peas, ⇐ SHELLING V.7.14. bɒst ... oʊpn St

bury *n* a CLAMP in which potatoes are stored out of doors II.4.6. bɛɹiː He Wo, bɛɹɪ St He Wo Wa Gl K

burying-folk *npl* MOURNERS VIII.5.12. bəɹɪ-ɪnfʊək Y

bush *1. n [Show a picture of a farmcart.] What do you call this metal lining in which the axle works?* I.9.8. bʏːʃ Db, bɒʃ Man, bʌʃ Nb K, bʏʃ Nb, bʊʃ Nb Cu Du We La Y Man Ch Db Sa St He Wo Wa Mon Gl O Nt L Lei R Nth Hu C Nf Sf Bk Bd Ess W Brk Sr K Ha. ⇒ **axle-box, axle-case, bearing, bed, bond, bowk, box, boxing, box-tree, cap, clutch, collar, grease-cap, gudgeon-iron, hub, hub-box, iron-box, iron bush, nave, pipe, rim, spindle, steel-casing, steel-plates, stock, wheel-box**

2. n the HUB of a cart-wheel I.9.7. bʏːʃ Db, bɒʃ Man, bʊʃ Nb La Y Ch Db

3. v to BUTT III.2.10. bʏʃ D, *-ing* bʊʃɪn Mon

bushel-skep *n* a BASKET for carrying horse-feed III.5.4. bʊʃlskɛp Nf

bushes *npl Hawthorns and brambles are not trees, but ....* IV.10.5. Eng. ⇒ **briars, busks, scrub, shrubs, stubbs**

bush-hedge *v* to TRIM hedges IV.2.3. *-ing* bʊʃhɛdʒɪn Nf

buskins *npl* LEGGINGS VI.14.18. bʌskɪnz Nf Ess*[leather x1]*, bʌsknz Nf Ess, bʌskənz Nf Sf Ess

busks *npl* BUSHES IV.10.5. bʊsks Y

buss *v* to WEAN a calf III.1.4. bʌs Co

bussa *1. n* a SALTING-TROUGH III.12.5. bʊsə Co

2. n a BREAD-BIN V.9.2. bʊsə Co

bussing-milk *n* BEESTINGS V.5.10. bʌsɪnmɪɫk Co

buss-milk *n* BEESTINGS V.5.10. bʌsmɪɫk D, bʌsməɫk D

bussock* *n* the cough of an animal, ⇐ COUGHING VI.8.2. *pl* bʊsəᵗks Wo

bussocking *1. v-ing* PANTING VI.8.1. bʊsəkɪn Gl*[old]*

2. v-ing COUGHING VI.8.2. bʊsʊkɪn He, bʊsəkɪn Wo*[old x1]* Mon*[old]* Gl*[old x1]*, əbʊsəkɪn Wo, bʊzəkɪn Mon*[old]*

buss up *1. vtphr* to STOCK a cow III.3.6. *ptppl* bʌst ... ʌp Co

2. vphr to stock. *ptppl* bʌst ʌp Co, *ptppl* bʌstəd ʌp Co

bussy-milk *n* BEESTINGS V.5.10. bʌsimɪɫk D

bustion *n* a WHITLOW VI.7.12. bʊstʃən La, bʊʃtən La

busy *1. adj The blacksmith might tell a man who dropped in to see him: I can't stop my work to talk to you now: I'm far too ....* VIII.4.11. Eng. ⇒ **throng**

2. adj ACTIVE, describing a child VIII.9.1. bɪziː W D, bɪzɪ O Nth Nf Sf Ess K

busybody *n* a GOSSIP VIII.3.5(b). bɪzɪbɒdɪ La Y Ch O

but *adv* ONLY VII.8.12. bɒd La, bʌt Sa Ha, bʊt St Wo Nth, bət Wa Lei MxL Ha

butch *n* **piece of butch** a PIECE *OF BREAD AND BUTTER* V.6.11(a). ə piːs ə bʊtʃ Y

butcher *n What do you call the man who buys cattle, kills them, and sells the meat?* III.11.1. Eng. ⇒ **carcass-butcher, cag-mag dealer, dealer butcher, slaughterman, slaughterer**

butching-house *n* a SLAUGHTERHOUSE III.11.4. bʊtʃɪnaʊs Cu

butching-shop *n* a SLAUGHTERHOUSE III.11.4. bʊtʃɪnʃɒp Y

butching-stool *n* a BENCH on which slaughtered pigs are dressed III.12.1. bʊtʃɪnstʊl Cu

butt *1. n What do you call the bottom-end of a sheaf (of corn)?* I.6.4. baːt Wo, bʌt Sa He Mon Gl O Nth Bk Bd Ess MxL So W Sr K Co D Do Ha Sx, bʌʔ O Bk, bʊt Nb Cu Du We La Y Man Db

Sa St He Wo Wa Mon Gl O Nt Lei Nth W Brk Sx, buːt Wo, bət Gl. ⇒ **arse, arse-end, backside, barge-end, base,** *bat* ⇒ **butt,** *bat-end* ⇒ **butt-end, bottom, bottom-end, butt-end, butten-end, dag, dag-end, dowk, hind-end, sheaf-arse, stern-end, stock, stool, stubble- end, stub-end, stump**

2. *v When cows in the field push each other about with their heads, what do you say they do?* III.2.10.

vt -ing bʌtɪn Sr, *-ing* bʌtən Do Ha, *-ing* bʊtɪn L

v bʌt Bk Hrt Ess, *prppl* bʌtɪn Brk, *-ing* bʌtɪn So K Co Sx, *-ing* bʌtən Do Ha, bʌtʔ Ess, bʊt Nb La Nt L Bk, *-ing* bʊtɪn Brk K

⇒ **bore, bore on, bounce, box, brog about, buck, bulk, bump, bunch, bung, bunt, bunt about, bush, doss, dump, dunch, fork, fork about, gore, hake, hanch, hawm, hawm about, hike, hile, hipe, hoke, hook, hook about, horch, horn, horn about, hunch, jar, nush, nuzzle about, pelsh, poke, poke about, prog, puck, push, rip, taunt, toss, tup;** ⇒ also **game, gammock, item about**

3. *n* a PADDOCK I.1.10. bʊt Ha

4. *n* a FARMCART I.9.3. bʌt So Co D

5. *n* a SKEP IV.8.8(b). bʌt D, *pl* bʌts So

6. *n* a tree STUMP IV.12.4. bʌt Sa Ess W Sr Ha, bʌtʔ Nf, bʌʔ Bd, bʊt Wo Wa Lei

7. *n* a CLAMP in which potatoes are stored out of doors II.4.6. *pl* bʊts Man

8. *n* **bread and butt** a PIECE *OF BREAD AND BUTTER* V.6.11(a). ə bɹɛd ən bʊt Y

9. *n* **butt of the lip** a mouth corner, ⇐ MOUTH CORNERS VI.5.2. bʌt ə ðə łɪp Mon

butt-away *n* a SEESAW VIII.7.2. bʌtʔəwei Bf

butt-cart *n* a FARMCART I.9.3. bʌtkɑˤːt So D, bʌtkɑˤːt D

butt-end 1. *n* the T-SHAPED PLOUGH-BEAM END of a horse-drawn plough I.8.5. bʌtɛnd Hrt

2. *n* the BUTT of a sheaf of corn II.6.4. batɛnd Do, bʌtɪnd Sx, bʌtɛn Co D, bʌtɛnd Sa O MxL W Do Ha, bʌʔɛnd Bd, bʊtɪnd R K, bʊtiːnd La, bʊtɛnd Cu Y Sa St Wo Lei R Nth

3. *n* a tree STUMP IV.12.4. bʊtɛnd Lei

butt-end-post *n* the HANGING-POST of a gate IV.3.3. bʊtɛndpɒst Y*[polite]*

butten-end* *n* the BUTT of a sheaf of corn II.6.4. bʌtn̩ɛn Co

butter 1. *n* **bit of butter, piece of butter, round of butter** a PIECE *OF BREAD AND BUTTER* V.6.11(a). **bit of butter** bɪt ə bʌtə Mon; **piece of butter** piːs ə bʊtə Wa; **round of butter** ɹɛund ə bʌʔə Nf

2. *n* **butter and jam** a PIECE *OF BREAD AND BUTTER AND JAM/SUGAR* V.6.11(b). bʌtəɹ ən dʒaːm Mon

3. *n* **bit of butter and cheese** a piece of bread and butter and cheese. bɪt ʌ bʌtə ən tʃiːz Wa

butter-bread *n* a PIECE *OF BREAD AND BUTTER* V.6.11(a). bʊtəbɹɛd L

butter-cake *n* a PIECE *OF BREAD AND BUTTER* V.6.11(a). bʊtəkɪak Y, bʊtəkeːk La, bʊtəkeɪk Man, ə bʊtəkɛək Y

butter-dock *n* the DOCK plant II.2.8. bʌdɑˤːd̥ɒk Co

butter-fingered *adj* CLUMSY, describing a person VI.7.14. bʌʔəfɪŋgəd Nf Ess, bʊtəfɪŋgəd Y

butter-fingers *adj* CLUMSY, describing a person VI.7.14. bʊtəfɪŋəz La Y

butter-haws *npl* HAWS IV.11.6. bʌtəhɔːz Ess, bʌʔəhɔːz Nf

butter-herbs *npl* HAWS IV.11.6. *sg* bʌtəhɑːb Ess, bʌtəhɑˤːbz Ess

butter-kiver *n* a CHURN V.5.5. bʌtəkɪvə Nth

buttermilk 1. *n* CURDS V.5.8(a). bʌtəˡmɪłk Ha

2. *n* WHEY V.5.8(b). bʌʔəˤmɪłk O, bʊtəmɪłk L

3. *n* BEESTINGS V.5.10. bʌdəmɪłk Ess, bʌtəˡmɛłk Brk, bʌdəˤːməłk So *[marked u.r. EMBM]*

butter-shag 1. *n* a PIECE *OF BREAD AND BUTTER* V.6.11(a). bʊtəʃag Cu

2. *n* a PIECE *OF BREAD AND BUTTER AND JAM/SUGAR* V.6.11(b). bʊtəʃag Cu*[bread spread with butter, brown sugar and cream x1]*

butter-tub *n* a CHURN V.5.5. bʌdəˤːtʌb Co*[old x2]* D *[probably a tub in which butter was formerly hand-stirred. Marked u.r. SBM]*

buttery 1. *n* a PANTRY V.2.6. bʌtɹɪ Brk*[old]*, bʌtɹɪ Ess*[very old]* Ha*[in large house]*, bʌʔɹɪ Sf, bʊtəɹɪ La*[old x1]* Y Db, bʊtrɪ Y, bʊtɪɹ La Y Ch, bʊθɹɪ La

2. *n* the DAIRY on a farm V.5.1. bʊtrˤɪ We*[old]*, bʊtɪɹ La Y Ch Db, bʊtəɹɪ La, bʊθəɹɪ La, bʊðɹɪ La*[old]*

butties *1. *npl* FRIENDS VIII.2.7. *sg* bʌtɪ Mon

2. *npl* MATES VIII.4.1. bʌtɪz Gl, bʌtʰɪz Mon*[collier's word]*, bʌʔɪz Brk, bʌtiːz So W, bʌtʰiːz Mon, bʊtɪz Sa Wo Gl, bʊʔɪz Brk

3. *npl* COMPANIONS VIII.4.2. bʌtɪz Mon, bʌtiːz So W, bʊtɪz Mon Gl O

buttons 1. *npl* RABBIT-DROPPINGS III.13.15. bʌtnz Co

2. *n* **hasn't got all his buttons** STUPID VI.1.5. ɛzn gɒt ɔːł ɪz bætnz Sx

buttress *n* the iron stay connecting the beam with the side of a cart, ⇐ CROSS-BEAM END I.10.1. bʊtrəs Cu

buttress-jocks *npl* string KNEE-STRAPS used to lift the legs of working trousers VI.14.17. bʊtɹəsdʒɔks Y

butts 1. *npl* COCKS of hay II.9.12. bʊts Man

2. *npl* BOUGHS of a tree IV.12.2. *sg* bʊt St

butt-shive *n* a PIECE *OF BREAD AND BUTTER* V.6.11(a). ə bʊtʃɑːv Y

butt-stick *n* a STICK used to support the shaft of a cart I.11.1. bʊtstɪk Y

butt up *vphr* to PITCH sheaves II.6.10. bʊt ʊp Wa

butty *1. n* a SLICE of bread V.6.10. bʌtɪ Sa*[old]*
2. n a PIECE *OF BREAD AND BUTTER* V.6.11(a). bʌtɪ Sa, bʊtɪ La Ch Db Sa St He; **bit of butty** bɪt ə bʊtɪ Y*[child's word]*; **bit of bread and butty** bɪt ə bɹɛd ən bʊtɪ Y
3. n a PIECE *OF BREAD AND BUTTER AND JAM/SUGAR* V.6.11(b). bʌtɪ Sa*[with sugar]*

butty-cake *n* a PIECE *OF BREAD AND BUTTER* V.6.11(a). bʊtəkeːk La*[='butty-'],* ə bʊtɪkeək Y

butty-dip *n* a PIECE *OF BREAD AND BUTTER AND JAM/SUGAR* V.6.11(b). bʊtɪdɪp St *[marked u.r. BM]*

butty-treacle *n* a PIECE *OF BREAD AND BUTTER AND JAM/SUGAR* V.6.11(b). bʊtɪtɹiːtl St *[marked u.r. BM]*

buzz off *imp* GO AWAY! VIII.7.9(a). bʌz ɒˑf K, bʌz ɔːf He Ess MxL So Sr K

buzzy-milk *n* BEESTINGS V.5.10. bʌzimɪlk Co, bʌzimɪɫk Co D, bʌzəmɪɫk Co

by *prep* BESIDE a door IX.2.5. bæɪ Man, baɪ St*[old x1],* bɒɪ St, bɔɪ O Ess So, bəɪ Mon

byes *npl* the RIDGES between furrows in a ploughed field II.3.2. bæɪz So, *sg* baɪ So, *sg* bəɪ Do

by-lane *n* a LANE IV.3.13. baɪleːn Sa, baˑɪlɛˑən L, baɪleːn Ch, baɪleːᶦn Db, bɑɪlɛɪn Hrt, bəɪːleːᶦn Wo

byre *n* a COW-HOUSE I.1.8. bɛɪə Y, bɛɪəʁ Du, bæɪəᴶ Man, baɪɔʁ Nb, baɪə Nb Cu Du We, baɪər Cu Du, baɪər Cu, baɪəʁ Nb, baɪəɹ We

byre-grip* *n* a DRAIN in a cow-house I.3.8. baɪəgɹɪəp Du

byre-groop *n* a DRAIN in a cow-house I.3.8. baɪɔʁgʁʊpʰ Nb

byre-man *n* a COWMAN on a farm I.2.3. baɪɔʁmən Nb, baɪəʁmən Nb Du, baɪəmən Nb

by-road *n* a LANE IV.3.13. baːɹʊəd Y, baɪroːəd Ch, baˑɹɹʊəd L, bʌʏɹʊəd O

by the side *prep* BESIDE a door IX.2.5. bɪ ðə zæːd D, bɪ ðə saɪd Nf; **by the side of** baɪ ðə saɪd ɔv MxL, bɒɪ ðə saɪd ə K, bʌɪ ðə sʌɪd ə Sr, bɪ ðə səɪd ə Sx; **by the side on** bɪ t saɪd ɒn Du, bɪ ðə saɪd ɒn Nth, bɪ ðə sɒɪd ən Wo, bəɪ ðə sɒɪd ɒn Wo, bɒɪ ðə sɔɪd ən Wa, bɪ ðə səɪd ɒn Wo, bɪ ðə səɪd ŋ Mon, bə ðə səɪd ŋ Wo, bɪ ðə zəɪd ɒn Gl, bəɪ ðə səɪd ən Wo

by-wash *n* a FORD IV.1.3. baɪwaʃ Du

C

cabbied up *adj* STICKY, describing a child's hands VIII.8.14. kæbɪd ʌp D

cabby *adj* STICKY, describing a child's hands VIII.8.14. kæbi D, kabi D

cack-handed *1. adj* LEFT-HANDED VI.7.13(a). kækəndəd Ess, kækhændɪd Nf Ess, kækændɪd Ess*[old x1]* MxL Brk Sr*[old x1]* K Sx*[old x2]*, kækhændəd Sf, kækændəd Hrt Ess, kakandɪd Bd Hrt Ha, kakandəd Hrt Ha *[not a SBM headword]*
2. adj CLUMSY, describing a person VI.7.14. kækhændɪd Nf, kækhændəd Sf, kakandɪd L, kakandəd L

cack-hander *n* a LEFT-HANDED person VI.7.13(a). kækhændə Sf, kækændə Ess, kækændəˈ Sr, kækændəˈ Brk Ṣr Sx, kakandə Hrt *[not a SBM headword]*

cackling *v-ing* GOSSIPING VIII.3.5(a). kæklɪn Ess, katlɪn Y, katḷɪn Y

cacky *adj* LEFT-HANDED VI.7.13(a). kækɪ MxL

cad *n* a WEAKLING piglet III.8.4. kɛd Ess, kɛəd Ess, kæd Sf Ess, kæˈld Ess, kad Hrt

cad-butcher *n* a KNACKER III.11.9. kadbʊtʃə L, kadbʊtʃɹ L

caddy *n* a WEAKLING piglet III.8.4. kɛdi So

cade *n* a PET-LAMB III.7.3. kiːd Ch, kɪəd Y, keːd La Y Db St Nt, kjeːd Ch, keˈɪd Db, keəd La, keɪd Db Sa St Wa L Lei R C, keˈəd L, kæɪd Wa

cade-lamb *n* a PET-LAMB III.7.3. keːdlæm Sa, keːdlam Y*['a day or two old' x1]* Ch Db Sa Nt, kjeːdlɔm Ch, keədlam La, keːˈldlam Db, kjeːᵊdlam Ch, keɪdlam St Wo Wa L Lei Nth Hu, keədlam L Nth, kædlæm Sf

cades *npl* TICKS on sheep IV.8.3. kjɛdz Nb, *sg* kjɛd Du, kɪadz Y, tɪadz Y, kjadz Cu*[like a spider]*, *sg* kjad Du, kɪədz Nb*[different from ticks x1]* Cu Du Y, keːdz Nb*[different from ticks]* La, keadz Cu We La, keədz Nb Cu, keːədz Du We, kɛdz Db *[form with t- marked as probable error by NBM Edd]*

cadie-lamb *n* a PET-LAMB III.7.3. keɪdɪlam Hu, keɪdɪlam Nth

cadlock *n* CHARLOCK II.2.6. kædlɔk K, kædlək Lei, kadlʊk Lei, kadlɔk Wa, kadlʊk St, kadlək Sa Wo Lei, kadɫək Lei

cadman *n* a KNACKER III.11.9. kadman L, kadmən Nt L

cads *npl* BLINKERS covering the eyes of a cart-horse I.5.2. kadz St

cagmag *1. n* a KNACKER III.11.9. kagmag St
2. n a dealer in poor cattle. kagmag St

3. n a GOSSIP VIII.3.5(b). kɛgmeɪk Sx, kagmag Gl

cag-mag dealer *n* a BUTCHER who buys cattle, kills them, and sells the meat III.11.1. kagmag diːlə St *['presumably facetious' BM Edd]*

cag-magging *v-ing* GOSSIPING VIII.3.5(a). kjagmagɪn Gl, kægmægɪn Gl, *no -ing* kagmag Gl

cagman *n* a KNACKER III.11.9. kagmən Lei R

cagmeg-man *n* a KNACKER III.11.9. kagmɛgman Lei

cake *1. n* a CUTTING of hay II.9.15. keːk Y*[larger than truss]* Wa O*[loose, i.e. untied]* Nt Co D, keɪk Bk Bd, keːək D, kɛɪk Wa Lei R Bk*[loose]*, *pl* kɛɪks Nth, kɛˈək L Nth, kɛːək D
2. vt to FEED cattle with cattle-cake III.3.1. keˈək Bk
3. n a PIECE *OF BREAD AND BUTTER* V.6.11(a). keak La; **bit of cake** bɪt ə kɪək Y, ə bɪt ə keːk Y, keˈək Sf*[currant bread]*, ə bɪt ə kɛək Y, bɪʔ ə keːɪk Nf

cake-bin *n* a container for cattle-cake, ⇐ CORN-BIN I.7.4. kɪəkbɪn So

cake-plate *n* a GIRDLE for baking cakes V.7.4(b). keːkpleːt Ch

cake-pot *n* a BREAD-BIN V.9.2. keːkpɒt Y, keːkpɔt Y

cake-tin *n* a GIRDLE for baking cakes V.7.4(b). *pl* kɛɪktɪnz Sr

cake-tray* *n* a GIRDLE for baking cakes V.7.4(b). keːktɹ̩e W*[modern]*

cakey *1. adj* STUPID VI.1.5. keɪkɪ St
2. adj SILLY VIII.9.3. keːkɪ St, kɛɪkɪ St*[old x1]*

cakey-headed *adj* STUPID VI.1.5. kɛɪkɪjɛdɪd St

cakie *n* a PIECE *OF BREAD AND BUTTER* V.6.11(a). ə keakɪ La

calf *1. n* **in calf** *When you know a calf is on the way, you say the cow ....* III.1.10. ɪn keːv Do, ɪŋ keːv Co Do, ɪn keːəf Co, ɪn keːv Sx, ɪn kæf Brk, ɪn kæᵊf Nb, ɪn kæv He Mon, ɪn kæːf Man Nf So W Sr Co Do, ɪŋ kæːf W D Ha, ɪn kæːv Gl So Co Do, ɪŋ kæːv So D, ɪn kæː Man, ɪn kaf Nb L, ɪn kjaf Gl, ɪn kaːf La Y Ch St Wo Wa Gl O L Lei Nth C Nf Sf Bk Bd Hrt Ess So W Ha, ɪŋ kaːf Nt Nth Hu Bk Bd Hrt Ess So W Co D Do Ha, ɪŋ kjaːf Bd, ɪn kaːv Y Sa He Mon Gl Lei Nf Sf Co D, ɪŋ kaːv Sf So D Do, ən kaːv Nf, ɪn kɪaːv Sa, ɪn kjaːv Gl, ɪn kaˈv Mon, ɪn kaː Brk, ɪn kɑːf St Wo R Nf Ess MxL Brk Sr K Sx, ɪn kɑːv He Wo Nf Ess, ɪn kˈlɑːv Wo, ɪn kɑː Ma, ɪn kɒːf Sx, ɪn kɒʊf Db, ɪn kɔːf Cu

Du We La Y Ch Db Sa St He Nt L, ɪŋ kɔːf La Db Nt, ɪ kɔːf We La Y Ch Db, ɪn kɔᵗːf Sa, ɪn kɔːv La Y Sa He, ɪŋ kɔːv La, ɪ kɔːv La, ɪn kʊəf Nb; **heavy in calf** hɛvɪ ɪn kæf Nf; **by calf** bɪ kɔːv Y; **with calf** wɪ kaːf Du, wʊ kaːf Cu, wɪ kɑːf Y, wɪ kɔːf Cu Du We La Y L, wɪ kɔːv Y, wʊ kɔːf Nb, wə kɔːf Nb; **with the calf** wɪ d kɔːf Cu; **heavy with calf** hɛvɪ wɪ kæːf Nf, ɛvɪ wɪ kɔːf Y. ⇒ **breeding, by calf, calving, downcalving,** *due to* calf, *due to* calve, *going to* calf down, *going to* calve, *has stood* ⇒ stand, **heavy** with calf, **holding,** *in* profit, *is* bad *for calving, is going to* calve, *is heavy in* calf, *is heavy with* calf, *is in* calf, *is* set, *is with* calf, *she's* spring *to calve,* spring *the calf, with* calf, *with the* calf

2. *n* **not in calf** *And so you can say that the cow at that time [i.e. when she has not conceived] is ....* III.1.8. nʏt ɪn kæᵊf Nb, nɒt ɪn kæːv Nf, nɒt ɪŋ kæːf W, nɒd ɪŋ kæːf Ha, nɒʔ ɪn kæːf Nf, nɒd ɪŋ kæːv So D, nɒt ɪn kjaf Gl, nɑt ɪŋ kɑːf Nth, nɒt ɪn kɑːf St O Lei R Ess, nɒt ɪŋ kaːf Ess, nɒd ɪŋ kaːf So, nɒʔ ɪn kaːf O, nɒt ɪŋ kaːf Ess, nɒt ŋ kaːf Ess, nɒd ɪn kaːf So, nɒt ɪn kaːv So, nɒd ɪŋ kaːv So, nɒʔ ɪn kaːv Nf, nɒt ɪn kjaːv Gl, nɒt ɪn kɑːf Nf, nɒt ɪn kɔːf La Sa, nɒt ɪŋ kɔːf Nt, nɒt ɪn kɔːf L, nɒd ɪn kɔːv La, nʊt ɪn kɔːf Cu Y, ŋt ɪ kɔːf Y, nɒt ɪn kɔᵗːf Sa; **isn't in calf** ɪdn ɪŋ keːf Co, ɪdn ɪn kæːf Co, ɪdn ɪn kæːv So, ɪdn ɪŋ kæːv Co, ɪznt ɪn kaːf Lei, ɪdn ɪŋ kaːf D, ɛɪnt ɪn kaːf Lei Ess, ɪdn ɪŋ kaːv D, ɛɪnt ɪn kaːv Lei, ɛɪnʔ ɪn kaːv Nf, ɛɪnt ɪn kɑːf R, ɛnʔ ɪn kɑˑv Nf; **wouldn't be in calf** wʊdn biˑ ɪn kaːv Nf; **not proved in calf** nɒt pɹuːvd ɪŋ kaːf Ess; **not by calf** nət bɪ kɔːv Y; **not with calf** nɒt wɪ kaːf L, nɒt wɪ kɔːf Y, nɒt wɪ kɔːf L, nət wɪ kɔːf Y, nɒt wɪ kɔˑəf L; **isn't with calf** ɪznt wɪ kɔːf L

3. *n* **not in calf** not in calf, but able to conceive. nɒt ɪn kæːf W, nɒt ɪŋ kæːf W, nɒd ɪŋ kæːf D, nɒd ɪŋ kæːv D, nɒt ɪn kaːf St Wo Ess, nɒt ɪŋ kaːf Nt W Ha, nɒd ɪŋ kaːf Do Ha, nɒʔ ɪŋ kaːf W, nɒd ɪŋ kaːv D, ŋˌɒd ɪn kaːv Co, nɒʔ ɪn kɑːv Nf, nʊt ɪn kɔːf Y, nʊt ɪ kɔːf Y, nɒt ɪn kɔːv Sa Nf, nɒt ɪn kɔᵗːf Sa; **isn't in calf** ɪdn ɪŋ keːv Co, eːnʔ ɪŋ kæːf W, ɪdn ɪn kæːv D, ɛɪnt ɪn kaf Lei, ɪdn ɪŋ kaːv D; **not with calf** nɒt wɪ kɔːf Y, nʊt wɪ kɔːf Y; **out of calf** ɛʊt ə kaːf Sf

4. *n* **not in calf** unable to conceive, describing a cow. nɒd ɪŋ kæːf Ha, nɒd ɪn kaːv Do; **isn't in calf** ɛnt ɪn kaːf Lei. ⇒ *a* **barren,** *a* **barrener,** *a* **drape,** *a* **segg, barren, barrener, broken, drape, eald, empty, gast, geld,** gone over, *hasn't held* ⇒ **hold,** *isn't in* calf, **leased, light, naked,** *not by* calf, *not* fit, *not in* calf, *not proved in* calf, *not* served, *not* taken, *not with* calf, *out of* calf, **returned,** *wouldn't be in* calf

5. *npl* **CALVES** III.1.2(a). keːv Do, kæːv D, kaːv Bd, kaʊf St *[not recognized WMBM, queried as error EMBM, given headword status SBM]*

6. *vi* **due to calf** *IN* CALF III.1.10. dɒuː tə kaːf Sr

7. *n* *What do you call this [indicate the calf of the*

leg]? VI.9.7. Eng. ⇒ **back** *of your leg,* **ball** *of my leg,* **ball** *of the leg,* **ball** *of your leg,* **bow** *of your leg,* **calf** *of my leg,* **calf** *of the leg,* **calf** *of thy leg,* **calf** *of your leg*

calf-bag *n* the UTERUS of a cow III.2.4. kæfbæg So, kævbæg He, kæːfbæg D, kæːfbag W, kæːvbɛg D, kæːvbæːg Gl, kæᵊfbæᵊg Nb, kaːfbæg Mon, kaːfbag So, kaːvbaːg Mon, kɑːfbɛg K, kɑːvbˡæg Wo, kɑːvbæg He, kɑːvbɑːg He, kɔːfbag Db L

calf-bed *n* the UTERUS of a cow III.2.4. kˡɑːvbɛd Wo, kjɔːvbɛd Ch, kæːfbɛᵊd Man, kæːvbɛd Gl, kafbɛd Nb, kaːfbɛd Nb Cu Du Y Wo Wa Gl L Lei Nth Hu C Bd, kaːvbɛd Sa He Mon Lei, kaːvbɛɪd D, kɑːfbɛd Wo Ess Sr K, kɒʊfbɛd Db, kɔːfbɛd Nb Cu Du We La Y Ch Db Sa He Wa L, kɔᵗːfbɛd Sa, kɔːvbɛd La Y Sa He

calf-bed-neck *n* the VULVA of a cow III.2.3. kɔːfbɛdnɛk Y

calf-close *n* a PADDOCK I.1.10. kɔːfklʊəs Y

calf down *viphr* **going to calf down** *IN* CALF III.1.10. gwɪn tə kæf dəun Brk

calf-garth *n* a PADDOCK I.1.10. kɔːfgaːθ Y *[for calves up to 6 months old]*

calf keslop* *n* RENNET V.5.6. kɔːf kɛsləp Cu, kɔːf kɛzləp We *[very old x1]* Y

calf-plot *n* a PADDOCK I.1.10. kæːfpɫɒt Ha

calf-poke *1. n* the UTERUS of a cow III.2.4. kaːfpʊək L, kɔːfpʊək L

2. n RENNET V.5.6. kæːvpʊk So *[old]*

calf's-bed *n* the AFTERBIRTH that comes from a cow's uterus after a calf is born III.1.13. kaːvzbɛd Co

calf's maw *n* RENNET V.5.6. kaˑvz mɔː Sa

calf's read *n* RENNET V.5.6. køəfs ʁiːd Nb

calf's stomach *n* RENNET V.5.6. kɔːvz stʊmək La

calf-straps *npl* KNEE-STRAPS used to lift the legs of working trousers VI.14.17. kɔːfstɹaps Y

call *1. vi-3prpl* they MOO, describing the noise cows make during feeding time in the cow-house III.10.4(a). *-ing* əkɔːlɪn Bk

2. vi-3prpl they MOO, describing the noise cows make in the fields III.10.4(b). *-ing* kɔːlɪn Nth, kɔːɫ Nth

3. n CHAT VIII.3.4. kal Y; **bit of a call** bɪt əv ə kal Y; **right call** ɹɛɪt kal Y

4. n a GOSSIP VIII.3.5(b). kal Y

5. n **having a call** GOSSIPING VIII.3.5(a). ɛvɪn ə kal Y

6. vt-2prsg **call to recollection** do you REMEMBER? VIII.3.7. kɔːɫ tə ɹɛkəɫɛkʃən D

call back *vtphr-interrog-2prsg* do you REMEMBER? VIII.3.7. kɔːɫ bæk Brk

caller *n* a GOSSIP VIII.3.5(b). kalə Y, kaləˡ Y, kaləɹ Y, kalɹ L

calleting *v-ing* GOSSIPING VIII.3.5(a). kalətɪn Y

call home* *vtphr-2prsg* do you REMEMBER? VIII.3.7. kɔːɫ ... oːm D

calling *v-ing* GOSSIPING VIII.3.5(a). kalɪn Y L

callosity *n* *What do you call one of these things [point to a callosity] on the hands?* VI.11.4. ⇒ **beat hands**, **callous**, *calloused*, **callous skin**, *callus* ⇒ **callous**, **core**, **corn**, **gaig**, **gall**, **hand-corn**, **hard blister**, **hard core**, **hard flesh**, **hard horn**, **hard knot**, **hard pad**, **hard skin**, *hard-skin* ⇒ **hard skin**, **hard wart**, **hoof**, **horn**, *horny*, **horny buck**, **seg**, **wart**

callous *n* a CALLOSITY VI.11.4. kæləs Sx, *pl* kæləsɪz Brk K, kæɫəs Sr, *pl* kjæɫɪsɪz He, *pl* kalʌsɪz Mon, *pl* kalusəz St, *pl* kaləsɪz Nb Y St*[old x1]* O L Lei, *pl* kaɫɪsəz D, kaɫəs W, *pl* kaɫəsɪz D Ha, *pl* kaɫəsəz D Ha, kouɫəs Ha, kəˈluːsɪz Sx

callous skin *n* a CALLOSITY VI.11.4. kalɪs skɪn Y *[marked u.r. NBM]*

calve *vi* **due to calve**, **going to calve** IN CALF III.1.10. *3prsg* dʏː tə kæːv D, dɪu tə kɑːv Ess, duː tə kɑːv Sr; *prppl* goːn ə kæːv W, goːn ə kæːv W Ha, *3prprogsg* ɡʌn ə kaːv Ess

calves *npl* *[What do you call your animals that give milk?] What do you call the young animals just born?* III.1.2(a). Eng. ⇒ **calf**

calves'-meadow *n* a PADDOCK I.1.10. kaːvzmɛdə Co

calves'-plat *n* a PADDOCK I.1.10. kæːvzpɫat D

calves'-run *n* a PADDOCK I.1.10. kæːvzɾʌn Co

calving *adj* IN CALF III.1.10. kæːvɪn W *[marked u.r. SBM]*

calving-heifer *n* a HEIFER III.1.5. *pl* kɔːvɪnɛfəz Y

calving-milk *n* BEESTINGS V.5.10. kaːvɪnmɪʊk Sx

cam-handed *adj* LEFT-HANDED VI.7.13(a). kamandəd W

camisole *n* a CHEMISE V.11.1. kɛmɪsʊul K

camp *1. n* a CLAMP in which potatoes are stored out of doors II.4.6. kʲæmp Wa, kamp St Wa Nt Lei R Nth Co

2. n CHAT VIII.3.4. kamp La

camping *v-ing* GOSSIPING VIII.3.5(a). kampɪn La

canary-creeper *n* BINDWEED II.2.4. kənɛəʁɪkʁiːpɔʁ Nb

canch *n* a large CUTTING of hay II.9.15. kɛnʃ Ch

candy *n* SWEETS V.8.4. kandɪ L

cane *vt* to BEAT a boy on the buttocks VIII.8.10. kɛɪn Ess, kæɪn Ess

cane-broom *n* a BROOM used for sweeping outdoors V.9.10. kɛɪnbɹuːm O

cane-brush *1. n* a MUCK-BRUSH I.3.14. kɛɪnbɹʊʃ L

2. n a BRUSH used to clean horses III.5.5(a). kɛˈənbɹʊʃ L

3. n a BROOM used for sweeping outdoors V.9.10. kɛːnbrʊʃ Cu, kɛɪnbɹʊʃ L, kɛˈənbɹʊʃ L Nth

cank *1. n* CHAT VIII.3.4. kʲæŋk He

2. n a GOSSIP VIII.3.5(b). kaŋk Wa

canker *1. n* COLT'S-FOOT II.2.7. kaˈŋkə Nf

2. vi to FESTER, referring to a wound VI.11.8. kæŋkə Nf

canker-berries *1. npl* HAWS IV.11.6. kæŋkəbəɹɪz K

2. npl HIPS of the wild rose IV.11.7. kaːŋkətˢbɛɾɪz Ha

cankered *adj* RANCID, describing bacon V.7.9. kæŋkəd Nf

canker-flower *n* COLT'S-FOOT II.2.7. kæŋkʔəflaˈə Nf

cankers *npl* HIPS of the wild rose IV.11.7. kɛŋkəs Ess, kɛŋkəz Ess, kæŋkəz Ess, kæŋkʔəz Sf*[old]*, kæŋkətˢːz̩ Ha, kɹæˈŋkəz Ess

canker-weed *n* COLT'S-FOOT II.2.7. kæŋkʔəwiːd Nf

canking *v-ing* GOSSIPING VIII.3.5(a). kjæŋkɪn He, kæŋkɪn Wo, kaŋkɪn Wa

canny *1. adj* PRETTY, describing a girl VI.5.18. kanɪ Cu

2. adj WELL, describing a healthy person VI.13.1(a). kanɪ Du

3. adv VERY VIII.3.2. kanɪ Nb Y

cant *1. n* a CUTTING of hay II.9.15. kænt K Sx

2. n CHAT VIII.3.4. kʲænt Mon, kaːnt Mon

3. n a GOSSIP VIII.3.5(b). kˡænt He, kjænt Mon, kjant Gl, kænt Mon, kant Ch Sa Mon

canter *n* a GOSSIP VIII.3.5(b). kˡæntətˢ Wo, kjæntətˢ He Gl, kæntətˢ Gl, kantə Db

cant-hook *n* a CRANE on which a kettle is hung over a domestic fire V.3.4. kænthʊk Ess

canting *v-ing* GOSSIPING VIII.3.5(a). kˡæntɪn He, əkˡæntɪn Wo, kjæntɪn He Mon Gl, kjantɪn Gl, kæntɪn He Mon Gl, əkæntɪn Gl, kantɪn Ch*[old]* Db St

cants *npl* the RIDGES between furrows in a ploughed field II.3.2. kænts Sx

canuter* *n* a DONKEY III.13.16. kənyːtətˢː D *[SBM headword queried as **cornutor**, but more probably formed on Canute, English king with reputation for obstinacy]*

cap *n* the metal BUSH at the centre of a cart-wheel I.9.8. kæp Sr, kap Lei, kjap Gl

cap-end stack *n* a long stack with rounded ends, for corn, ⇐ STACKS II.7.1. kæpɪnd stækʔ Nf

capsize *vi* to OVERTURN, referring to a cart I.11.5. kæpsɔɪz Ha, kapˈzəɪz Do

caption *n* the T-SHAPED PLOUGH-BEAM END of a horse-drawn plough I.8.5. kapʃən Nb, kaptʃən Nb, kapsn Nb

captious *adj* INFECTIOUS, describing a disease VI.12.2. kaptʃəs So

car *n* a FARMCART I.9.3. kjətˢː He, kaː Cu We Y, kaːr Cu, kaːɹ Cu We

carbor *n* a WHETSTONE made of stone, with a handle II.9.10. kaᵗbəᵗ Ha

carborundum *n* a WHETSTONE made of stone II.9.10. kɑːbəɹʌndəm Ess, kɑːbəɹɛndum Sx, *pl* kɑːbɔɹʌndəmz Ess, kɑːbəɹʌndəm K, kɑːbəᴶɹʌndəm Sx, kɑɹbərundəm He

carborundum-stone *n* a WHETSTONE II.9.10. kɑːbəɹʊndəmstʊən Y

carbuncles *npl* BOILS VI.11.6. *sg* kæɽɪbʌŋkɬ So, *sg* kaːbʌŋkɬ Mon, kaːbʊŋklz St, *sg* kaᵗːbʌŋkɬ So, kaᵗːbʌkɬz Ha, *sg* kɑːbɒŋkɬ K

carcass *n* a dead BODY VIII.5.7(a). kaːkəs Y

carcass-butcher *n* a BUTCHER who buys cattle, kills them, and sells the meat III.11.1. kaːkəsbʊtʃə Y

care *n* **take care, take care of** LOOK AFTER VIII.1.23. **take care** tɛk kɛˑəᴶˑ L; **take care of** tjɛk kæːəᴿʁ ə Nb

careless *adj* CLUMSY, describing a person VI.7.14. kɪəᴶlɪs K, kɛːlʌs Mon, kɛᵗːləs So, kɛələs Y MxL Sr K, kɛəɫəs Ess, kɛəᵗlɪs Sr, kɛəᵗɬɪs Sr, kɛəᵗləs Ha *[marked u.r. EMBM]*

caretaker *n* a SEXTON VIII.5.4. *-s* kɪətɛˑɪkəz Nf*[at a chapel]*, kɪətakə Y, kɛːᵊtɛɪkə Ess, kɛəteɪkə Nf, kɛətæɪkə Ess, kɛətakə Y

carf *n* a CUTTING of hay II.9.15. kjəɹf He, kɪəᵗːf Sa Wo, kjəᵗːf He Gl W, kjəᵗːv Gl, kəᵗːf Sa He Wo Gl W Ha, kəᵗːv W

car-grease *n* CART-GREASE, used to lubricate the wheels of a cart I.11.4. kaːgɹiːs Cu We, kaˑrgriːs Cu, kaːgɹɪəs Cu We

car-house *n* a CART-SHED I.11.7. kaːɹuːs Cu

carky mawkins *n* GOOSE-GRASS II.2.5. kaᵗːkɪ mɔᵗːkɪnz Sa

carlings *npl* RABBIT-DROPPINGS III.13.15. kaᴿːlənz Nb

carlock(s) *n* CHARLOCK II.2.6.
no -s: kjɛːɹlɪk Gl, kæːlɪk Du C, kaːlɪk L Lei R Nth Hu C Sf Bd Ess, kaᵗːlɒk Wa, kaːlʊk Wa, kaᵗːlʊk Wa, kjaᵗːɫʊk Gl, kaːlək L Nth Sf Hrt Ess, kaᵗːlək Bd, kɪaːlək Wo, kᴵaᵗːlək Wo, kaːlɪk R Nf, kaːɫɪk Ess, kaːlɒk Hrt, kjaᵗlɒk Wo, kaːlək Ess, kaᵗːlək Wo, kᴵaᵗːlək Wo, kəᴶlɪk O, kəᵗːlɪk Bk, kəᵗːlɪk O, kəɽlɪk O, kəɽlɪk O, kəᵗːlʌk Bk, kəᵗːlɒk Sa, kəᵗːlʊk Nth, kaᵗːlʊk Wa kaᵗːlək Bk, kəɹlək He, kəᵗːlək Sa, kᵁəᵗːlək Sa He Wo, kjəᵗːɫək He Mon
-s: kaːlɪks Nf

carman *n* **head carman** a CARTMAN on a farm I.2.2. hɛd kaːmən Sf

carpenter *n* *What do you call the man who makes things out of wood? [Does he distinguish between the two, i.e. carpenter and joiner?]* VIII.4.3. Eng.
a. highly skilled work: Cu Du La Y Ch Db St Wa Mon Gl Nt L Lei Nf Sf Bk Ess So Sx
b. heavier, less skilled work: Du We La Y Ch Sa He Wa Mon O L Nth Hu Nf Sf Bd Ess So W Brk Sr K D Do Ha Sx

c. boat-builder: La Y
d. cabinet-maker: Y
e. makes wagons: O
f. makes tables: MxL
g. works in town: We
h. works outside: Y Sr K Ha
i. old word no longer used: Y
j. modern word: Y
k. refined word: Y St
l. same as joiner: Du La Y Sa St He Wo Wa Mon Gl Nt L Lei R Nth Hu Nf Bk Hrt Ess So W
⇒ **chippy, jobbing carpenter, joiner, rough carpenter, wood-stack carpenter**

car-racks *npl* RUTS made by cartwheels IV.3.9. kaːɹaks Cu

carriers *npl* BEARERS who carry a coffin VIII.5.10. kæɹɪəz Hu Nf Sf, kæɹɪəᵗz̞ O, kaɹɪəz Y Wa*[old]* L Nth Hu C Bk Bd Hrt, kaɹɪəɹz La, kaɹɪəᴶˑz La, *sg* kaɹɪəᴶ L, kaɹɪəᵗz̞ Wa Bk, kaɽɪəᵗz̞ O

carring *1. vt-ing* **carring dung** CARTING DUNG II.1.4. kaᵗːɽən dʌŋ Co, kaːɹɪn dɒŋ K
2.1. v-ing CARTING corn from the field II.6.6. kaᵗːɽɪŋ So, kaᵗːɽən Co, kaᵗːn̩ Do
2.2. vt-ing **carring (of it)** carting corn. kaᵗːɽɪn So

carr-land *n* LOW-LYING LAND IV.1.7. kaːland Y, kaːlənd L

carrs *1. n* LOW-LYING LAND IV.1.7. kaːz L, *sg* kaᴶˑ La
2. n patches of marshy ground. kaːz Y

carry *vt* **carry dung** to cart dung, ⇐ CARTING DUNG II.1.4. kaɽɪ dʌŋ Co

carrying *1. v-ing* CARTING corn from the field II.6.6. kɛɹɪ-ɪn K, kæɹɪ-ɪn MxL, kæˑɽɪn Sr, kaɹɪ-ɪn Ch Sa St Wo Wa O Lei R Nth*[old]* Bk, *inf* kaɹɪ Db, kjaɹɪ-ɪn Db, kaɽɪ-ɪn W Co D
2. vt-ing **carrying (it)** carting corn. kæˑɽᴵɪn Sr

carrying-post *n* the HANGING-POST of a gate IV.3.3. kaɹɪ-ɪnpoːst Ch

carry out *vtphr* **carry out dung** to cart dung, ⇐ CARTING DUNG II.1.4. kɛɹɪ ɛut dɒŋ K

car-saddle *n* the SADDLE of the harness of a cart-horse I.5.6. kaːseːdl Nb, kaːsadl Cu, kaːrsɪədl Cu

car-shed *n* a CART-SHED I.11.7. kaːʃɛd Cu We

cart *n* a FARMCART I.9.3. Eng exc. Nf Sf MxL

cart-arm *1. n* the AXLE of a horse-drawn farmcart I.9.11. *pl* kaːtaːmz St
2. n the iron stay connecting the beam with the side of a cart, ⇐ CROSS-BEAM END I.10.1. kaːtaːm Y

cart-arse *n* the TAILBOARD of a cart I.10.2. kaᴶːtaːs Db, kaᴶːtaᴶːs La

cart-axle *n* the AXLE of a horse-drawn farmcart I.9.11. kaːtaksl Y

cart-dog *n* a BUMPER of a cart I.10.1(a). *pl* kaːtdɔgz Y

cart-door *n* the TAILBOARD of a cart I.10.2. kaːtdʊə Y Db

carter *1. n* a CARTMAN on a farm I.2.2.
no -s: keˈɔᵏtɔᵏ Nb, kæˑˑˀəˡ O, kæˡːtəˡ O, kjæˡːtə Gl, kaɹtə Y, kaːtə Wa Bd Ess, kaːtˀə Bk, kaːtəˡ Wa, kaˡːtə La, kaˡːtəˡ Sa Wo O Nth W, kaˡːˀə Bk, kaˡːˀəˡ Gl O Bk Ha, kˡaˡːtəˡ Wo, kjaˡːtəˡ Gl, kaˡːtəˡː So W Co D Do Ha, kaˡːdəˡː D Ha, kaˡʈəˡ Wo, kaɽtəɣ O, kjaˡʈəˡ Wo, kaːtə St MxL Sr, kaːtˀə MxL Sr, kaːtəˡ K, *pl* kaːˀəˡɽz̦ Sr, kaˡːtəˡ Brk, kaˡːtəˡ Sr K Ha, kaˡːɽtəˡ Sr, kaˡːɽʈəˡ Brk Sx, -s kaˡːɽtəˡz̦ Sr, kaˡːtəˡː Co D, kəˡːɽʈəˡʈ Ha, kˡəˡːtəˡ Wo

2. n the driver of a cart. kaːtəɹ Y, kaˡːtəɹ La

3. n the FORKER of sheaves onto a wagon II.6.7(d). kaɽʈəɣ O

4. n the FORKER on a wagon who unloads sheaves in a stackyard II.6.9. kaˡːtəˡː So

cart-fat *n* CART-GREASE, used to lubricate the wheels of a cart I.11.4. kaˡːʈvat Do

cart-filling *v-ing* loading a cart with dung, ⇐ to LOAD II.1.5. kaˡːtfɛlɪn K

cart-frame(s) *n [Show a picture of a cart.] What do you call the horizontal frame laid on top of the cart and extending beyond the body and wheels?* I.10.6.
no -s: kaˑtfɹeɪm Nf
-s: kaːtfɹeɪmz Ess
⇒ **copse(s), cradles, cratches, dash-boards, dripples, false frame, flake(s), flat-ladders, flat-shelvings, floats, floor-board, frame(s), front carriage, gearing(s), gormers, hay-flake, hecks, ladder-frame, ladders, lade(s), monkey-board, morphrey, morphreydite, outlets, over-rods, racks, rades, rails, rathe(s), rave(s), ravings, ripples, shambles, shelving(s), side-arms, side-board(s), side-hecks, side-ladders, side-lades, side-racks, side-rail(s), side-raves, sides, splash-boards, summers, thrippers, thripples,** *trippers* ⇒ **thrippers,** *tripples* ⇒ **thripples, under-carriage**

cart-grease *n If you don't want your (cart-)wheels to squeak, what do you put on?* I.11.4. kjaːtgɹiːs Ch, kˡaˡːtgɹiːs Wo, kiəˡtgɹiis Ha, kˡəˡːtgɹeːɪs Wo, keɔᵏtgʁiːs Nb, kɛətgɹiːs Du, kæˈtgɹeɪs Man, kaᵏːtgʁiːs Nb, kaːtgɹiːs We Y Wa Lei R Nth Nf Ess, kaˡːtgɾiːs So, kaːtgɹɪəs Y, kaːtgɹɪəs Y Nt L, kaːtgɹeːs Sa, kaˡːtgɾeːs W Ha, kaˈtgɹeɪs Nf, kaːtgɹiːs Nf Ess K, kaɹtgɹiːs He, kaɽʈgɾiːs O, kaˡːtgɹiːs Brk K, kaˡːtgɹiːs K Sx, kaˡːtgɹiːsˡ Sr, kaːtgɹeːs Wo, kaˡːtgɾeːs D, kaːˀgɹɛiːs Hrt. ⇒ **black-jack, car-grease, cart-fat, fat, goose-grease, grease, horse-fat, horse-grease, horse's fat, oil, wagon-grease, wheel-grease, witch-grease**

cart-heck *n* the TAILBOARD of a cart I.10.2. kaːtɛk Y

cart-hoop *n* the iron TIRE round a cart-wheel I.9.10. kaːtᵁuːp Y

cart-horse *n* a SHAFT-HORSE I.6.2. kaːtɒs Y, kaːtɔs Y, kaːtɔːˀs Bd, kaˡːʈhaˡːʂ So, kɑːthɒs Man, kaˡːtɒs D

cart-house *n* a CART-SHED I.11.7. keəthuːs Nb, kæːtaːs La, kæːtʌʊs Y, kæˈtous Man, kæˑˡːtɛʊs La, kæˑˡːtaʊs La, kaːtɛːs Db, kaːtæʊs Sa, kaːtaʊs La Y Sa St, kjaːtaʊs Ch, kaːtɔuːs Du, kaːtuːs We Y, kaːtəs Ess, kaˡːɹtæˑəs La, kaˡːtaʊs La Y, kaˑˡːtᵁuːs We, kaˡːtæʌs So Co, kaˡːdæʌs Co, kaˡːtæʊs So W Ha, kaˡːdæʊs Ha, kaˡːtaʊs Sa So Do, kjaˡːtᵁuːs Gl, kaˡːtəʊs W Do, kˡaˡːtəʊs He Wo, kaˡːdəʊs Do, kaˡːˀəʊs W, kaˡːtəuːs Sa, kjaˡːtəuːs Gl, kaˡːtəs Sa, kaˡːˀəs Bk, kaɹtˀuˑs Y, kaːtæʊs MxL, kaˑˡːtɛʊs Brk, kaˑˡːtʌʊs Brk, kaˡˑtæʊs Ha, kaːəˡɽʈɛʊs Sx

cart-hovel *n* a CART-SHED I.11.7. kæːtɒvɫ C, kæˑˡːˀɒvɫ O, kæˡːtɒvɫ O, kaːtɒvɪl Db St, kjaːtɒvɪl Db St, kaːtɒvl St, kjaːtɒvl St, kaːtɒvɫ Lei Nth Hu Bd Hrt, kaːtɒvl L, kjaːtɒvl L, kaːtɒvɫ C Hrt, kaːɹtɒvɫ Nth, kaˑˡːtɒvl L, kaˑˡːtʊvl L, kaˡːˀɒvɫ O Bk Bd, kaˡːtɒvəɫ W, kaːtɒvɪl Wo, kaˑtɒvɫ Hrt, kaːthɒvɫ Sr, kaːəˡɽʈʌvʊ Sr, kəˡːtɒvɫ O, kjəˡːtɒvl Gl, kˡəˡːtɒbɫ Wo

carting *1. v* **carting dung** *What is your word for getting dung from the dung-heap to the field?* II.1.4. Eng exc. Nb Cu Du He Co. ⇒ **carring** *dung,* **carry** *dung,* **carry out** *dung, carting it, carting manure,* **carting muck, carting your muck, car up** *dung,* **drawing** *dung,* **drawing** *of it* out, *drawmuck* ⇒ **drawing,** *draw out dung* ⇒ **drawing out,** *dray dung* ⇒ **draying dung, draying, draying** *dung,* **draying out,** *dung-cart, dung-carting,* **dung-hauling, dunging, getting out** *muck,* **getting out** *with the manure,* **hauling, hauling** *dung,* **hauling** *muck,* **hauling out** *dung,* **leading, leading** *dung,* **leading** *manure,* **leading** *muck,* **leading** *the muck* **on, lugging** *muck, manure-carting,* **manure-leading, muck,** *muck-carting,* **muck-draw, muck-hauling, muck-leading, muck-lugging, muck-plugging, muck-punching,** *on the* **putt, plugging** *muck,* **pulling** *dung,* **shit-carting**

2. v What is your word for taking the corn from the field? II.6.6. Eng exc. Nb Cu Du We Sa Wa R MxL Co D. ⇒ **barley-cart, carring, carrying,** *carting home, carting out, corn-cart, corn-carting,* **corn-hauling, drawing, draying,** *draying in,* **gathering in, getting, harvest-carrying, harvest-cart, harvest-carting, hauling, housing, leading, lugging, oat-cart, pulling, putting in, saving, wheat-cart**

cart-ladder *n* a rear cart-ladder, ⇐ CART-LADDERS I.10.5. kaːtladə Bd, kaˡːʈladəˡ Bd

cart-ladders *npl [Show a picture of a farm-cart.]*
What do you call these frames that you put on in front
and at the back when you carry hay or corn? I.10.5.
kjaˑˈtɬadəˡz̩ Gl, kaːtlædəz Sf Ess. ⇒ **back-flake,**
back-ladder, back-rail, cart-ladder, cart-rails,
cock-ups, copses, cratches, dibbles, dribbles,
dripples, end-ladder, end-rails, flakes, fore-ladder,
frames, front-flake, front-ladders, front-rail,
gates, gearings, gormers, harvest-rails, hay-flakes,
hay-frames, hay-ladders, hay-rails, hay-raves,
head-ladder, hecks, hind-ladder, ladder, ladders,
laders, lades, leading-rails, levers, loaders, pig-
shelvings, racks, rades, rails, rathes, rathings,
raves, *ravings* ⇒ **rathings, riggers, ripples,**
shelvings, stays, summer, summers, tail-ladder,
thrippers ⇒ **trippers, thripples, trestles, trippers,**
tumble-racks, tumbler-ladders; ⇒ also **standards,**
stipers

cart-leg *n* a STICK used to support the shaft of a cart
I.11.1. kæːtlɛgⁿ La, kæˑʲːɹtlɛg La, kaːtlɛg La Ch, *pl*
kaːtlɛgz Y, kaˑʲːtlɛg La

cart-linhay *n* a CART-SHED I.11.7. kaˡːtɬɪni So,
kaˡːtɬɪni Co D, kaˡːtɬɪni D, kaˡːtɬɪnei So, kaˡːtɬəni
So, kaˡːtɬɪni D, kaˡːtɬɪneː D

cart-lodge *n* a CART-SHED I.11.7. kaːtlɒdʒ Ess,
kaːtlɒdʒ Sf Ess, kaːtlədʒ Ess, kaːtlɒdʒ Ess K,
kaːtlɒdʒ K, kaˑʲːtlɒdʒ K, kaˡːɹtlædʒ Sx

cartman 1. *n What do you call the man in charge of*
the vehicles [on a farm]? I.2.2. keɔᴿtmən Nb,
keɑtmən Nb, kaːtmən Y, kaˡːtman Sa, kaᴿːtmən Nb.
⇒ **bailiff, carter,** *carters* ⇒ **carter, clodhopper,**
draughtsman, foreman, *head* **carman,** *head*
horseman, *head* **wagoner** ⇒ **wagoner(s), hind,**
horse-chap, horse-keeper, horseman, ploughman,
steward, teamer, team-man, teamsman, wag,
wagoner(s), yardman
2. *n* the LOADER of sheaves onto a wagon II.6.7(c).
kaᴿːtmən Nb

cart-pad *n* the SADDLE of the harness of a
cart-horse I.5.6. kaːtpæd Sf Ess, kaˡːtpæd So,
kaˡːtpad W

cart-peg *n* a pin used with a perforated rod in front of
a cart to allow adjustments when tipping, ⇐
ROD/PIN I.10.3. *pl* kaˡːtpɛgz Sa

cart-pin 1. *n* a LINCH-PIN holding a wheel on a cart
I.9.12. kaːtpɪn Hrt
2. *n* a device for keeping a cart-body fixed to the
shafts, stopping it from tipping, ⇐ ROD/PIN I.10.3.
kaːtpɪn Ess

cart-prop *n* a STICK used to support the shaft of a
cart I.11.1. *pl* kjaːtpɹɒps Ch

cart-racks *npl* RUTS made by cartwheels IV.3.9.
kaːtɹæks Sf Ess *[see note at **cart-tracks**]*

car-tracks *npl* RUTS made by cartwheels IV.3.9.
ˈkaːˈtraks Cu *[see note at **cart-tracks**]*

cart-rails *npl* CART-LADDERS   I.10.5.
kæˑtreɪls Man

cart-rakes *npl* RUTS made by cartwheels IV.3.9.
kaːtɹeɪks Ess

cart-rest *n* a BUMPER of a cart I.10.1(a).
kaˡˑtɹɛst Brk

cart-rits *npl* RUTS made by cartwheels IV.3.9.
kaːtɹɪts Y

cart-rucks *npl* RUTS made by cartwheels IV.3.9.
kaːtɹʌks Ess

cart-ruts *npl* RUTS made by cartwheels IV.3.9.
kaːtɹʌuts St*[old x1]*, kaːtɹʌts Ess, kaːtɹuts Y Wa,
kjaːtɹuts Ch, kaˡːtɹævts D, kaˡːtɹɒuts W,
kaˡːtɹʌts Ha, kaˡːʔʌʔs Bk, kaˡːʔɪɛuʔs O,
kaːtɹuts O, kaɹtɹuts O, kaːtɹuts Y, kaˡːtɹœvts D,
kˡəˡːtɹəuts Wo

cart-saddle *n* the SADDLE of the harness of a
cart-horse I.5.6. kˡaˡˑtsædɫ Wo, kɪəˡːtsædɫ Wo,
kjəˡtsædɫ He, kjəˡːtsɒdɫ He, keɔᴿtsadl Du,
kæːtsadl Du, kaˑtsædl Nf, kaːtsædɫ Ess,
kaːtsædəł Mon, kaˡːtsædɫ Mon, kaˡːtsædɫ So,
kaˡːtzædɫ So, kaːtsadl Du Y Wa L, kaːtsadł Mon
Lei, kaᴿtsadl Nb, kaɹtsadl Y, kaˡːtsadl O,
kaˡːtsadəl Sa, kaˡːtsadł Gl, kaˡːtsadł W,
kaˡːtzadł So Do, kaˑtsɛdl Nf, kaˑtsædl Nf,
kaːtsædł Nf, kaːtsadl Y, kaɹtsadl He

cart-shade *n* a CART-SHED I.11.7. keˑəᴿtʃeːd
Nb, kɛətʃɪəd Du, kaˡːtʃeːd So

cart-shed *n What do you call the building where*
you keep your carts and wagons? I.11.7. keɔᴿtʃed
Nb, keˑəᴿtʃeːd Nb, keɔᴿtʃed Nb Du, keɔᴿtʃəd
Nb, kæːtʃed Du C, kæˑtʃɛəd Man, kjærːtʃed Gl,
kaːtʃɪd Y, kaːtʃeːd Y, kaːtʃed Cu Du We Y Ch Db
St Wa Nt L Nth Nf Sf Bk Ess, kjaːtʃed Ch, kaːʔʃed
Bd, kaːtʃeˑəd L, kaːtʃəd Nf, kaːɹtʃed Y, kaˡːtʃed
La Db, kaˡːtʃed So D Do Ha, kaːtʃɪd Ess, kaːtʃed
Y St Nf Hrt Ess Sr K, kaːʔʃed Hrt, kaˑʲˑətʃeˑd Brk,
kaˡːɹtʃɪd Sx, kaˡːtʃed Wo Wa Sr K D Ha,
kaːəˡtʃɪd Sr Sx, kaːəˡɹtʃed Sr, kɜˑʲːɹtʃed La,
kəˡːtʃed Co, *pl* kəˡːtʃedz Wo, kiəˡtʃed Ha. ⇒
barn, car-house, car-shed, cart-house,
cart-hovel, cart-linhay, cart-lodge, cart-shade,
cart-shud, draft-house, helm, hovel, lathe,
linhay, lodge, shed, skeeling, tumbril-shed,
wagon-house, wagon-hovel, wagon-linhay,
wagon-lodge, wagon-shed, wagon-shud,
wagon-skeeling, wain-house

cart-shud *n* a CART-SHED I.11.7. kaːtʃɔd Sf,
kaːtʃʌd Nf, kaːtʃʊd Nf

cart-slip *n* a movable iron hoop that slides along
a cart-shaft and couples it to the projecting end of
the beam on which the cart-body rests, ⇐
ROD/PIN I.10.3. *pl* kaːtslɪps Y

cart-sole *n* the beam of a cart, ⇐ CROSS-BEAM
END I.10.1. *-s* kæːtsʊəlz Du, *-s* kaːtsʊəlz Y

cart-swoes *npl* RUTS made by cartwheels IV.3.9. kæˑɹtswɔːz La

cart-tail *n* the TAILBOARD of a cart I.10.2. kaˑɹtteːl La

cart-track *n* a LANE IV.3.13. kaːttɹak Lei *[marked ir.r. EMBM]*

cart-tracks *npl* RUTS made by cartwheels IV.3.9. kæˑɹttɹaks La, kaːttɹæks Ess, kaːttɹaks We St, kaːtɹaks Sa, kaˑɹttɹaks La, kaˤːttɹaks So, kjaˤːttɹæks Gl *[there may be overlap between these and car-tracks, cart-racks]*

cartwright *n* a WRIGHT VIII.4.4. keəᵏtʁaɪt Nb, *pl* keətɹˡiːts Nb, keərtreɪt Cu, kaːtɹiːt Cu Y, kaːtɹeɪt Cu, kaːtʁaɪt Du, kjaːtɹaɪt Ch, kaːtɹʌɪt Nf, kaːtɹəɪt Y, kaᵏːtʁeɪt Nb, kaːrtreɪt Cu, *pl* kaˑɹtɹiːts Y

car up *vtphr* **car up dung** to cart dung, ⇐ CARTING DUNG II.1.4. kaˤːɾ ʌp dʌŋ Co

carve *v* to WHITTLE a stick I.7.19. *-ing* kaˤːvɪn Sa, *-ing* kɑːvɪn Sx

carwright *n* a WRIGHT VIII.4.4. kaːrˡiːt Cu

cash *n* MONEY VII.8.7. kæʃ Y, kaʃ Y

cask *n* a BARREL VI.13.12. kæsk Nf, kæːsk So, *pl* kasks St Mon, kaːsk He Wa*[18 gallons]* Nf Ess, *pl* kaːskɪz D, kaːst Ess, kɑːsk Nf Hrt Ess Sr, kɑːs Ess

cassen *adj* OVERTURNED, describing a sheep on its back unable to get up III.7.4. kɛsn Nb Cu Du We La, kɛsən Du Y, kasn Nb Cu, kʊsn Nb

cassened *adj* OVERTURNED, describing a sheep on its back unable to get up III.7.4. kɛsnt Cu La

cast *1. v* to PITCH sheaves II.6.10. kast Nb
2.1. v **casts** SLIPS THE CALF III.1.11. *inf* kast Du, kaːsts He, *3ptsg* kast St
2.2. vt **casts** slips the calf. kæsts Mon Gl, *3ptsg* kæst Sa, kjæsts He, kˡæsts Wo, *ptpl* kæstəd He, *ptpl* kast Nb St L, kas St, *ptpl* kaːstɪd He, *ptpl* kʊsn Nb
3. n a dead calf, prematurely born. kaːst He
4. vt to SLIP *A FOAL* III.4.6. *ptppl* kɛst Db, kæst Sa He Mon Gl, kjæst He Mon, *ptppl* kɪæst Wo, kast Cu We Sa St Wo Wa L Lei, *ptppl* kast Y Ch Db, *ptppl* kastɪd St, *3ptsg* kʲast Ch, *ptppl* kʲast Ch, kaːst Sa Mon Ha, *ptppl* kaːst He Wa, *ptppl* kɑːst K
5. vi to KINDLE, describing a rabbit doe giving birth to young III.13.14. kaːst Sf, kɑːst Nf Ess
6. n **in cast** pregnant, describing a doe. ɪn kaːst Ess, ɪn kɑːst Ess
7. adj OVERTURNED, describing a sheep on its back unable to get up III.7.4. kɛst L Lei, kɛɪst R, kæːst Sa Wo Gl Nf Brk, kast St Wo Wa Lei R Nf, kaːst Sa He Wo Wa Gl O L Nth Hu C Nf Sf Bk Bd Hrt Ess So Ha, kjaːst Gl, kɑːs Hrt, kɑːst Nf Ess MxL Brk Sr K, kəst Lei
8. vt to fill gaps in a hedge-bank or hedge with turfs, brushwood, or similar material, ⇐ to PLASH IV.2.4. *-ing* kæːstɪn Co, kaːst Co D
9. v to CUT peat IV.4.4. kast Cu

10. vi-3prpl they MOULT IV.6.13. kɛst Cu We La Y Db, kast Db

cast-calve *?vi* to slip a calf, ⇐ SLIPS *THE CALF* III.1.11. kaskaːv Lei

casted *adj* OVERTURNED, describing a sheep on its back unable to get up III.7.4. kæːstɪd Sf, kæstəˤɾd̩ Brk, kaːstɪt Nf, kaːstɪd O Sf Bk Bd Hrt Ess, kaːstət Sf, kaːstəd C Ess, kɑːstɪd Nf Ess

castrate *v-ed* CASTRATED, describing a bullock III.1.15. kæstɹeːˡt Mon, kæstɹeɪt Ess, kastɹeːɪt Y, kastəɹeɪt Lei, kɑːstɹeːʔ Nf

castrated *v-ed* If you don't want your calf to grow into a bull, you have it .... III.1.15. kæstəɹeˑʔɪd Nf, kaˑstəɹeˑʔtɪd Nf, kaˑstəleˑʔəd Nf, kjæstɹeːtəd He, kæstəɹeːtɪd Brk, kastɹeːtɪd Sa Wo, kaːstɹeːtɪd Mon, kastəɹeːtɪd Mon, kaːştɹeːtɪd Co D Do, kaːştɹeːˑətəd So, kæˑstreɪtɪd Man, kæstɹeɪtəd Man, kæstəɹeɪtɪd Man, kæştɹeɪtəd So, kaːştɹeɪtɪd So, kaˑstɹeɪtʔɪd Nf, kaːstɹeɪtɪd Y, kaːstɹeɪtɪd Wo, kæːştɹeːɪtəd So, kaːstɹeːɪtəd Gl, kɛstɹeɪtɪd Sr, kɛstɹeɪtɪd K, kæstɹeɪtɪd Brk K Sx, kæstəˤɹeɪtɪd Sx, kastɹeɪtəd L, kastəreɪtɪd Lei, kaːstɹeɪtɪd Ess, kaːstəɹeɪtɪd Ess, kɑːstɹeɪtɪd Ess Sr K Sx, kɑːstɹeɪʔɪd Sr, kastəɹeˑətɪd L, kæstəɹæɪtɪd K. ⇒ **bullocked, castrate, cut, cutten, doctored, geld, gelded, nipped, segged, steered**

cast up *vtphr* to fill gaps in a hedge-bank or hedge with turfs, brushwood, or similar material, ⇐ to PLASH IV.2.4. kaːst ... ʌp D

casual labourer *n* a FARM-LABOURER I.2.4. kaʃjuːˑɬ leˑɪbɹə Lei

casual man *n* a FARM-LABOURER I.2.4. kazjʊl mɒn Ch

cat *n* a TOM-CAT, the male cat III.13.8. kat Db

catch *1. n* the CURB-STONE in a cow-house I.3.9. kætʃ So
2. n a device fixing a cart-body to the shafts, stopping it from tipping, ⇐ ROD/PIN I.10.3. kɛtʃ Sf Brk
3. n the LATCH of a door V.1.9. kɪtʃ Ess, kɛtʃ Sf*[old]* Sr K*[modern]* Ha, kætʃ MxL, katʃ Sa
4.1. vt to GROPE *FOR FISH* IV.9.10. *-ing* kɛtʃɪn Wo MxL, kætʃ MxL, *vbln* katʃɪn Ha
4.2. v to grope for fish. *vbln* katʃɪn Y Co

catches *n* the vertical part of a crane over a domestic fire, consisting of a *BAR* or *CHAIN* and a HOOK(*/CROOK*) V.3.5b+c. kætʃɪz W

catch in *1. vtphr* to PITCH sheaves II.6.10. kætʃ ... ɪn Co
2. vphr to pitch. *-ing* katʃɪn ɪn Co

catching *adj* INFECTIOUS, describing a disease VI.12.2. Eng exc. Nb We

cat-choops *npl* HIPS of the wild rose IV.11.7. kattʃuːps Cu

catch out *vphr* to cull sheep, ⇐ CULLING III.11.2. kɛtʃ ɛʊt Ha

catch-pit *1. n* a CESS-POOL on a farm I.3.11. kætʃpɪt Man So, *pl* katʃpɪts Lei, katʃpɪ? Bk
2. n an artificial cess-pool. kɛtʃpɪt He Wo Ha, kætʃpɪt Mon Nf K, katʃpɪt St Wo Lei
3. n a hollow in a muck-yard into which urine drained. kɛtʃpɪt Wa

catch-post *n* the SHUTTING-POST of a gate IV.3.4. kɪtʃpʌʊst Sf, kɛtʃpʌʊst Hrt, kɛtʃpʊəst O

catchy *adj* INFECTIOUS, describing a disease VI.12.2. kɛtʃi D, kætʃi D, katʃɪ Y

cater-amble *adv* DIAGONALLY, referring to harrowing a field IX.1.8. keɪtə-ɒmɪl Db, kɛɪtə-ɒmɪl Db

cater-corner *adv* DIAGONALLY, referring to harrowing a field IX.1.8. kiːtɪkɔːnə Db, keːtɪkɔːnə Y, kɛɪtɪkɔːnə St, katɪkɔːnəᴶ Y

cater-cornered *1. adj* ASKEW, describing a picture that is not hanging straight IX.1.3. keːtɪkɔːnəd Y
2. adv DIAGONALLY, referring to harrowing a field IX.1.8. kiːtəkɔːnəd Ch, keːtɪkɔːnəd Y, keətəkɔːnəd Y, kɛɪtɪkɔːnəd St

cater-cornerways *adv* DIAGONALLY, referring to harrowing a field IX.1.8. kɛɪtɪkɔːnəwiːz St*[old]*

cater-swish *adv* DIAGONALLY, referring to harrowing a field IX.1.8. keːtəswɪʃ Db, kɛɪtəswɪʃ St

cater-way(s) *adv* DIAGONALLY, referring to harrowing a field IX.1.8.
no -s: kɛɪtəᴶwɛɪ K
-s: kɛɪtəwɛɪz Sr*[old x1]* K

cat-face *n* an OWL IV.7.6. katfeːs La

cat-haigs *npl* HAWS IV.11.6. kateːgz Y, katɛgz Y, katɛəgz Y

cat-handed *adj* LEFT-HANDED VI.7.13(a). kæthændɪd Ess

cat-haws *npl* HAWS IV.11.6. katæːᵊz Nb, kataɹz Y, kathaːz Nb, kataːz Du We La Y, kataːz Y, katɔːs Cu, kathɔːz Du, katɔːz Nb Cu We Y Nt L

cat-jugs *npl* HIPS of the wild rose IV.11.7. katdʒʊgz Du

cat-o'-nine-tails *1. npl* EARWIGS IV.8.11. katənaɪnteˑəlz Cu
2. n HAZEL IV.10.8. katənaɪnteːlz Y*[old]*

cat-o'-two-tails *npl* EARWIGS IV.8.11. katətuːteˑəlz Cu

cat-poles *npl* TADPOLES IV.9.5. katpoːɬz W, kaʔpoːɬz W, *sg* kætpoʊɬ So

cat's-head *1. n* an EVENER on the plough-beam end of a horse-drawn plough I.8.4. kɛtsɪd Ess, kɛtzɪd Ess
2. n the T-SHAPED PLOUGH-BEAM END of a horse-drawn plough I.8.5. kætshɛd Ess, kætsɛd Sf Ess, kætsheᶦd Ess, katsɛd K
[the Ess locs which give cat's-head for 1 (and for

which it is marked as u.r.) are not the same as those giving it for 2]

cat's-meat-man *n* a KNACKER III.11.9. kætsmiːtmæn Sx

cattle *n What do you call cows and calves, male and female, all together?* III.1.3. kɛtl Db Sa, kɛʔl Nf, kɛtɫ K Sx, kɛʔɫ Ess Sr K Sx, kɛtʊ Ess Sx, kɛdʊ Sr, kætl Man Sa St Mon L, kˡætl Wo, kædl Sa, kæʔl Nf Ess, kætʔl Nf, kætɫ Wo Wa Mon Gl Sf Hrt Ess So Brk K Ha Sx, kˡætɫ He Wo, kjætɫ He Mon, kætəl He Mon Gl, kˡætəl He, kjætəl He, kædɫ Sf Ess So Sr Co, kjædɫ He, kæʔɫ Nf Sf Bk Ess So Brk Sr Sx, kætʔɫ Ess, kætʊɫ Brk, kjætʊɫ Gl, kædʊɫ Brk Sr Ha Sx, kætʊ Sr, kædʊ Sr, kæʔʊ Sr, katl Nb Cu La Y Ch Db Sa St He Wa O L Lei, kjatl Ch St Gl O, katəl Sa, kadl Sa, kaʔl La Ch O Nf, katɫ Wo Wa Mon Lei R Nth MxL W Co D Ha, katəɫ Mon Gl, kadɫ C So Brk Co D Do Ha, kaʔɫ Gl O Nth Hu C Bk Bd Hrt MxL W Ha, kjaʔɫ Gl Bd. ⇒ **beast(s)**, **stock**

cattle-court *n* the STRAW-YARD of a farm I.1.9. kadɫkɔᶜːt So

cattle-fold *n* the STRAW-YARD of a farm I.1.9. kætəɫfoːɬd Mon, katɫfoʊld St

cattle-man *1. n* a COWMAN on a farm I.2.3. kæˑtɫmən Brk
2. n the man in charge of beef cattle on a farm. kaʔlmən O

cattle-path *n* a PATH made through a field by cattle IV.3.11. kaʔʊpɑːθ MxL

cattle-pen *n* a FASTING-CHAMBER III.11.3. kaʔlpɛn O

cattle-shed *n* a COW-HOUSE I.1.8. katɫʃɛd Mon

cattle-stop *n* a STILE IV.2.9. kæʔɫstɒp Ess *[marked ir.r. EMBM]*

cattle-track(s) *n* a PATH made through a field by cattle IV.3.11.
no -s: kæʔɫtɹæk Sr, katltɹak Y
-s: kaʔɫtɹaks Ha

cattle-trough *n* a TROUGH in a cow-house I.3.6. katltɹɒf Y

cattle-walk *1. n* the GANGWAY in a cow-house I.3.7. kædɫwɔːk Ess
2. n a PATH made through a field by cattle IV.3.11. kæʔɫwɔːk Nf

cattle-yard *1. n* a FARMYARD I.1.3. kæʔɫjaːd Ess
2. n the STRAW-YARD of a farm I.1.9. kæʔɫjaːd Bk, kæʔɫjaᶜːd So, kætʊɫjaᶜːd Gl, kætɫjaːd K, kæʔɫjaːd Ess K, *pl* kæʔɫjaˑəᶜdz Brk, kædʊɫjaᶜːəᶜɽd Sx, kæʔʊjaːd Sr, katljaːd Sa Hu, katɫjaːd Hu, kaʔɫjaːd C Bk, katɫjaᶜːd̩ Wa W, katəɫjaᶜːd̩ Gl, kaʔljaᶜːd̩ O, kaʔɫjaᶜːd̩ Bk W, katɫjaːd MxL, kadɫjaᶜːd̩ D
3. n a straw-yard in which cattle are fattened. kˡætɫjəᶜːd̩ Wo, kæʔɫjaːd Ess, kaʔljaᶜːd̩ O

catty-haws *npl* HAWS IV.11.6. katɪ-ɔːz L

caudle *n* a CRANE on which a kettle is hung over a domestic fire V.3.4. kɔːdɫ Do

caul *n* the FAT round the kidneys of a pig III.12.7. kaʊɫ Hrt, kɔːɫ Hrt

causen* *adj* made of stone flags, describing a FLOOR V.2.7. kɒsən D

causeway *n* the GANGWAY in a cow-house I.3.7. kaᶜːzˌwaɪ Wo

causey-brush *1. n* a MUCK-BRUSH I.3.14. kɔːsɪbɹʊʃ Lei

2. n a BROOM used for sweeping outdoors V.9.10. kɔːsɪbɹʊʃ L*[made of cane x1]* Lei

cave *1. v* to TIP a cart I.11.6. keːᵊv Ch

2. n a CLAMP in which potatoes are stored out of doors II.4.6. keːv So Co D, keɪv So, keːɪv So, kɛːəv D

3. v to WINNOW II.8.4. *-ing* kɛɪvɪn Ess

4. n short pieces of straw left after threshing, ⇐ CHAFF II.8.5. keːf W

5. vi to WARP, referring to wood IX.2.9. keːv Y

cave in *viphr* to WARP, referring to wood IX.2.9. keːv ɪn Y

cavel *n* CHAFF II.8.5. kævɪl Ha, kævʊ Sx

cave over *viphr* to FAINT VI.13.7. keːᵊv ɔə Ch

cave up *vphr* to TIP a cart I.11.6. kiːv ʊp Ch

caving *1. n* CHAFF II.8.5. kʲevɪn W, kjoːvɪn W, kɪəvɪn W, keːvɪn Brk Do, kɛvɪn Gl, kɛfən So, kɛɪvɪn Brk

2. n short pieces of straw left after threshing. kjɛvɪn Gl W, kɪəvɪn W, kɛɪvɪn Brk, keːvɪn Nf Ha, kæɪvn Ess

3. n heads of corn. kʲevɪn W

4. n rubbish such as dust, weed, and seeds, left after threshing. kæɪvn Ess

caving-bar *n* a movable horizontal rod stretching between the shafts of a cart, fixing them to the cart-body and stopping the cart from tipping, ⇐ ROD/PIN I.10.3. kiːvɪnbaː Ch

caving-rod *n* a movable horizontal rod stretching between the shafts of a cart, fixing them to the cart-body and stopping the cart from tipping, ⇐ ROD/PIN I.10.3. kʲeːvɪnɹɒd Ch

cavings *1. n* CHAFF II.8.5. kʲevɪnz Brk, keɪvɪnz So, kæɪvɪnz Hrt

2. n short pieces of straw left after threshing. kɪəvɪnz O, keːvɪnz O, kɛɪvɪnz K

3. n long straw used for bedding for cattle. kɛɪvɪnz Wa

caving-tree *n* a movable horizontal rod stretching between the shafts of a cart, fixing them to the cart-body and stopping the cart from tipping, ⇐ ROD/PIN I.10.3. keːvntɹiː Sa

cawk-fisted *adj* LEFT-HANDED VI.7.13(a). kɔːkfɪstɪd L*[old]*

cawk-handed *adj* LEFT-HANDED VI.7.13(a). kɔːkandɪd L Lei R Nth, kɔːkandəd L

cawk-hander *n* a LEFT-HANDED person VI.7.13(a). kɒkhændə Nf

cawky *adj* LEFT-HANDED VI.7.13(a). kɔːkɪ R

cawky-handed *adj* LEFT-HANDED VI.7.13(a). kɔːkɪ-andɪd Lei R

cellar *n* where food is kept, ⇐ PANTRY V.2.6. sɛlə Y

cellar-head *n* a landing on the cellar steps where food is kept, ⇐ PANTRY V.2.6. sɛləɹɪəd Y, sɛləjed Y

cellar-stone *n* a flat surface on which bacon is cured, ⇐ SALTING-TROUGH III.12.5. sɛləstʊən Y

cemetery *n* a CHURCHYARD VIII.5.5. sɪmətɹɪ Y, sɛmɪtɹɪ K*[away from church]*

centre *n* the HUB of a cart-wheel I.9.7. sɛntə Cu

certain *adj* SURE IX.7.12. sæːtɪn La, saːtɪn Ch, saːtn Cu Y, saːtʔn Nf*[old]*, saːtən Y, saᴵːtn La, sɑːtn Nf, sɑːtʔn Nf*[old]*, sətn Y, səːtən Y, səᶜːtɪn Gl *[marked u.r. NBM]*

cess *n* an artificial CESS-POOL on a farm I.3.11. sɛs He

cess-pit *1. n* a CESS-POOL on a farm I.3.11. sɛspɪt So W Brk Co D

2. n an artificial cess-pool. sɛspɪt He Mon Gl O Ess K

cess-pit-tank *n* a CESS-POOL on a farm I.3.11. sɛspɪttaŋk Gl*[modern]*

cess-pool *1. n Where does it [urine in a cow-house] go? Is it artificial?* I.3.11.
a. unspecified natural or artificial. sɪspʊul Nf, sɪspuːɫ Do, sɛspɔʊɫ Brk, *pl* sɛspɔʊłz Lei, sɛspʊl Nb, sɛspuł K, sɛspuːl Nb Cu Y Nt L, sɛspuːɫ Lei Hu Hrt, sɛspuːɫ Lei, sɛspʊʊ Sx, *pl* sɛspʊʊz Ess, sɛspəɫ Sx
b. artificial. sɪspʊʊ Sx, sɛspᴵɵːɫ Lei, sɛspyːl Ch, sɛspʊɫ O Ess Sr, sɛspuːl Nb Du Y Sa St Mon Nf, sɛspuːɫ Mon Ess MxL So K Sx, zɛspuːɫ So, sɛspʊʊ Ess Brk Sr, *pl* sɛspʊʊz Sx

⇒ **black pond, brick bing, brick-hole, catch-pit, cess, cess-pit, cess-pit-tank, cess-tank, cistern, dew-well, drain, dumb-well, dung-pit, gully-trap, juice cess-pool, lant-hole, little well, midden, midden-stead, midden-sump, mig-hole, mig-tank, mixen, mixen-hole, *mucky pond*** ⇒ **mucky-pound, mucky-pound, piss-tank, pit, pond, pool, saur-hole, saur-tank, sewer-pit, sink, sink-hole, sluice, slush-hole, slush-pit, slush-tank, slutch-tank, soakaway, sockage-hole, sockage-pit, sock-cistern, sock-dike, sock-hole, sock-pit, sock-tank, sock-well, sough, spruce-hole, standjuice-well, sump, sump-hole, sunk-hole, swamp, tank, tank-hole, vault, wash-tank, well, yeddle-hole, yeddle-tank**

2. n an ASH-MIDDEN V.1.14. sɛspuːɫ Bk

cess-tank *n* a CESS-POOL on a farm I.3.11. sɛstæŋk So

chackling *v-ing* GOSSIPING VIII.3.5(a). tʃakɫɪn D

chacks *n* WIPE YOUR MOUTH VI.5.3. tʃaks Co

chafed *adj* CHAPPED VI.7.2. tʃeɪft Bk*[old]*, tʃeɪft Wa Sx

chaff *1. n* What do you call the light stuff blown off *[when threshing]?* II.8.5. Eng. ⇒ *ails* ⇒ **hulls**, **cavel**, **caving**, **cavings**, *chaff and* **pulse**, **cob**, **cosh**, **dust**, **fill-belly**, **flights**, **hinder-ends**, **hucks**, **huds**, **hulls**, **husks**, **offal**, *pulls* ⇒ **pulse**, **pulse**, **pulse** *and chaff*, **racketings**, **screenings**, **shucks**; ⇒ also **cave**, **colder**, **racketing**

2. n What do you call that dry mixed feed that you give to your horses? III.5.3. Eng exc. Cu Du We Man Db Nt R. ⇒ **bait**, *beans and chaff*, *bran and* **chop**, *bran and* **oats**, *chaff*, *chaff and bran*, *chaff and corn*, *chaff and meal*, *chaff and oats*, **chop**, **chop** *and corn*, **chop** *and oats*, **chop** *and oats and beans*, **choppy**, **chuck**, *corn*, *corn and chaff*, *corn chaff*, **crowdy**, *crushed oats*, *cut chaff*, *cut* **meat**, *cut straw*, *dry feed*, *dry* **mash**, **dust**, **dust** *and oats*, **feed**, **fodder**, *grain*, **horse-chop**, **horse-feed**, **horse-mixture**, **licking**, **mash**, *mixed corn*, *mixed* **feed**, *mixed* **meal**, *oats*, *oats and bran*, *oats and chaff*, *provend* ⇒ **provand**, **provender**, **sifting**

3. n DREGS left at the bottom of a teacup V.8.15. tʃaf L

chaff-basket *n* a BASKET for carrying horse-feed III.5.4. tʃɑːfbɑːskət Gl, tʃɑːfbɑːskɪt MxL*[old, carried on back]*

chaff-bin *1. n* a CORN-BIN I.7.4. tʃɑːbən Ess, tʃɑːfbɪn MxL

2. n a container for chaff. tʃɑːfbɪn MxL

chaff-house *1. n* a HAY-LOFT over a stable I.3.18. tʃɑːfus Wa, tʃɑːfəs Wa

2. n the place where hay is stored on a farm. tʃæfaus Sa, tʃafæus L R, tʃɑːfheus Nf, tʃɑːfeus Bk, tʃɑːfʌus Gl, tʃɑːfheus Nf

chain *1. n [What do you call that old-fashioned arrangement for hanging a kettle on to heat it over the fire?] What do you call its parts [b. ref the vertical BAR or CHAIN in or beside the chimney]?* V.3.5(b). tʃiːn Man Ch, tʃɪən La Y O, tʃeːn Nb La Ch Sa St Brk, tʃeɪn Man C Bk Bd So, tʃeːɪn He Wo Mon O, tʃeˑən La, tʃeːn Cu, tʃɛɪn Y Db He Wo Wa Gl O Lei Nth Nf Bd Ess W Brk Sr K Sx, tʃæɪn He Gl O L Ess K, tʃaɪn Nf So Ha. ⇒ **back-crook**, **bar**, **crook**, **cutterlug**, **eye-hook**, **hake**, **handle**, **hanger**, **hangle**, **hangle-iron**, **iron bar**, **jack**, **jib-hook**, **notches**, **pot-bed**, **pot-hanger**, **ratchet**, **reckan**, **recknan**, **rod**, **sneck**, **snotches**, **sway**

2. n a CRANE on which a kettle is hung over a domestic fire V.3.4. tʃeːn Brk, tʃɛɪn Ess, tʃæɪn K

3. n A wrist watch is fastened with a wrist strap, but an ordinary watch with a …. VI.14.12. Eng. ⇒ **albert**,

curb and chain, *watch-chain*, **watch- curb**, **watch-guard**

4. n a chain TETHER for a cow I.3.4. tʃiːn Ch Db St, tʃɪən Y Nt L, tʃeːn Nb La Ch St Gl O Co, tʃeɪn Mon O Bd So W Brk, tʃɛɪn Nb Y St O L Nth Bk Bd Hrt Ess W Sr Co D Sx, tʃɛən Y L, tʃæɪn O Sf Hrt Ess K Do, tʃaɪn Nf So W Do Ha

5. n a chain used to tie up a horse, ⇐ TETHERING-ROPE I.4.2. tʃiːn Ch Lei, tʃɪən La Y L, tʃeːn Sa, tʃeˑn Y, tʃɛɪn He Gl Lei R Sf Ess So, tʃɛˑən L, tʃæɪn Wa Hrt; **head-collar and chain** ɛdkɒlə ən tʃɛɪn St, ɛdkɒɫəɫ n̩ tʃɛɪn Sx; **neck-collar and chain** nɛkkɒləɫ ən tʃɛɪn Ha; **neck-strap and chain** nɛkstɹap ən tʃɛɪn He

6. n a device fixing a cart-body to the shafts, stopping it from tipping, ⇐ ROD/PIN I.10.3. tʃɛɪn (wɪð tuː pɪnz) Sx; **chain and hook** tʃɛɪn ŋ ʊk Sx; **chain and pin** tʃɛɪn ŋ pɪn Sx

7. n a device used to prevent a cart from going backwards on a hill, ⇐ PROP/CHOCK I.11.2. tʃɛɪn Nf

chain and hook *n* a CRANE on which a kettle is hung over a domestic fire V.3.4. tʃeɪn ən ʊk So, tʃɛɪn ən hʊk Ess, tʃɛɪn and *[= ordinary orthography]* ɪk K, tʃæɪn ŋ hʊk Ess

chainer *n* a TRACE-HORSE I.6.3. tʃeːnəɫ: Co, tʃɛɪnəɫ: Co

chain-horse *n* a TRACE-HORSE I.6.3. tʃiːnɒs St Lei, tʃiːnɔːs Ch, tʃɪənɒs La Ch, tʃɪənhɒᵝːs Nb, tʃɪˑənɔs L, tʃɪənhɒᵝs Nb, tʃɪənɔːs La, tʃɪənɔᴶːs La Y Db, tʃeːnɑɫːɹs Brk, tʃeːnɒs Ch St, tʃeːnhɒᵝːs Nb, tʃeːnɔːs Ch Db, tʃeːnɔᴶːs La, tʃeːnɔɫːʂ Sa D, tʃeɪnɑɹs Y, tʃeɪnɔɫːʂ Nth, tʃeənhɒs Du, tʃeənɔːs La, tʃeːnhɒs Cu, tʃeːnɔːs Cu, tʃeɪnɑːs Y, tʃɛɪnɒs Y St Wo, tʃɛɪnɒs Y, tʃɛɪnhɔːs Nb Ess, tʃɛɪnɔːs Y Db St Nth K, tʃɛɪnhɒᵝːs Nb, tʃɛɪnɔɫːʂ Co, tʃɛɪnəs Wa, tʃæɪnɒs Wa, tʃæɪnɔːs MxL K

chaining-pole *n* a TETHERING-STAKE in a cow-house I.3.3. tʃɛɪnɪnpoʊɫ So

chain-post *n* a TETHERING-STAKE in a cow-house I.3.3. tʃaɪnpoːst Do

chain-stake *n* a TETHERING-STAKE in a cow-house I.3.3. tʃɛɪnsteɪk So

chain-tit *n* a TRACE-HORSE I.6.3. tʃiːntɪt Db

chair *1. n* What do you call that you are sitting on? V.2.9. Eng. ⇒ **arm-chair**

2. n a WISH-BONE IV.6.22. tʃeːɫ Sa*[old]*

chalk *n* CHAT VIII.3.4. tʃɔːk L*[old]*

challack-flag *n* a HEARTHSTONE V.3.2. tʃælæxflæg Man

cham *1. vt-1prpl* we CRUNCH apples or biscuits VI.5.12. *-ing* tʃæmɪn Brk Sr*[old]*, tʃam Mon, *-ing* tʃamən Ha, tʃɒm Gl

2. v-1prpl we crunch. *-ing* tʃɛmɪn Sr*[old]* Sx*[old]*, *-ing* tʃæmɪŋ Brk, *-ing* tʃæmɪn Brk*[old]* Sr*[old]* Ha, *-ing* tʃamɪn So, *-ing* tʃamən Ha, *-ing*

tʃɑːmɪn Sr

3. *v* to GOBBLE food VI.5.13(b). *-ing* tʃɛmɪn Sr

chamber *1. n* a HAY-LOFT over a cow-house
I.3.18. tʃeːmbə Y, tʃeːmdə Db, tʃeəmə Y

2. *n* a BEDROOM V.2.3. tʃɪmbəᵗː D, tʃɪməᵗː So D,
tʃɪəmbəᴵ La, tʃɪəmə Y, tʃeːmbə La Y*[upstairs x1,
modern x1]* Ch*[old x1]* Nt*[old x1]*, *pl* tʃeːmbəːɹz La,
tʃeːmbəᵗ Sa, tʃeːmbəᵗː Co*[old x1]*, tʃeːmdə Y*[old]*,
tʃeːᴵmdə Ch, tʃeːmə Y*[obsolete x1]*, tʃeəmbə La Y,
pl tʃeəməz Y, tʃembəᵗː So D, tʃɛːmbə Y, tʃɛːmə Y,
tʃɛɪmbə L, tʃɛˑəmbə L, tʃeəmə Y*[old x1]*, tʃɛˑəmbɹ
L, tʃɛˑəmɹ L, tʃeəməᴵ Y, tʃæməᵗː So, tʃɔːməᴵ
La*[downstairs]* Y

chamberlye *1. n* stale URINE used for cleaning
blankets VI.8.8. tʃeːmblɪ Y, tʃeəmblɪ Y, tʃeəmlɪ Y,
tʃeəmɹɪ Y, tʃeəmɹɪ Y, tʃɪməlɪ Nb, tʃembəlɪ Cu,
tʃeməlɪ Nb Cu Du, tʃemlɪ Cu Du, tʃeəmbəlɪ Y,
tʃeəməlɪ Y, tʃeəmlɪ Y, tʃeəmlɪ Y, tʃamblɪ Nb,
tʃaməlɪ Cu, ʃaməlɪ Nb We, tʃamlɪ Cu We

2. *n* stale urine. tʃɛˑəmbəlaɪ L*[for putting on
chapped hands]*, tʃæɪmbəlʌɪ Nf*[liniment for horses
x1, to cure chilblains x2, embrocation or food additive
for pigs x1]*

chamberlyne *1. n* stale URINE VI.8.8. tʃɛɪmbəlɪn
Nf*[for cleaning blankets]*, tʃɛɪmbəlɛɪn Nf*[to cure
chilblains]*, tʃeəmbəlɪn Y, tʃæɪmbəlʌɪn Nf*[used to
cure chilblains,* tʃæɪmbəlɒɪn Nf, tʃæɪmbəlʌɪn Nf*[for
cleaning blankets x1, to cure chilblains x2] [not a
NBM headword]*

chamber pap *n* a BLIND TEAT III.2.7. tʃeːmbə pap
La Y, tʃembə pap Du, tʃɛːmə pap Y

chamber-water *n* stale URINE used for cleaning
blankets VI.8.8. tʃeːmbəwatə Nt*[also embrocation to
cure scurvy in pigs]*

chammer *1. vt-1prpl* we CRUNCH apples or
biscuits VI.5.12. tʃaməɹ (+V) Db

2. *n* a GOSSIP VIII.3.5(b). tʃæməᵗː So

chamming away *vphr-ing* GOSSIPING VIII.3.5(a).
tʃamɪn əwɛː W

champ *1.1. vt-1prpl* we CRUNCH apples or biscuits
VI.5.12. tʃæmp Sf, tʃamp Du

1.2. v-1prpl we crunch. tʃamp L, *-ing* tʃampɪn O,
-ing tʃampən Co D

2. *v* to GOBBLE food VI.5.13(b). *-ing* tʃæmpɪn Wo,
-ing tʃæmpʔɪn Nf

champ up *vtphr-1prpl* we CRUNCH apples or
biscuits VI.5.12. *-ing* tʃampɪn ... ʊp Y

chamragging *v-ing* GOSSIPING VIII.3.5(a).
tʃamɹagɪn W

cham up *vtphr-1prpl* we CRUNCH apples or
biscuits VI.5.12. *-ing* tʃæmɪŋ ʌp Brk

chance-work man* *n* a casual labourer, ⇐
FARM-LABOURER I.2.4. 'tʃanswəᵗːk maːn Co

change *vi* to CURDLE, referring to milk V.5.9.
tʃeˑəndʒ L

chank *1. vt-1prpl* we CRUNCH apples or
biscuits VI.5.12. tʃæŋk Sf Ess

2. *v-1prpl* we crunch. *-ing* tʃeŋkɪn Sx

channel *n* a DRAIN in a cow-house I.3.8. tʃenɪl
Y, tʃenl Du Sa, tʃenɫ Hrt, tʃenəl Y, tʃænl Nf,
tʃændl Nf, tʃanɪl Y Db, tʃanl Nb Du Y, tʃanɫ O
Nth, tʃanəl Y Sa St Nt, tʃanəɫ Bd

chap *n* my HUSBAND VIII.1.25. **my chap** mɒɪ
tʃap St

chapped *adj In frosty weather, your hands
sometimes get all dry, red and sore, and you say
your hands are ....* VI.7.2. Eng exc. Man Wo Mon
Co D Do. ⇒ **chafed, chappy, charked, chashed,
chilblained, chilled, chipped, chopped, choppy,
cracked, cracked *and sore*, flied, flied *open*, flue,
fly, frayed, frost-bitten, frosted, *full of* keens,
hacked, hacky, hazled, keened, sore, spithey,
sprayed, sprayed *up*, spreathed, spreazed,
spreed, spried**

chappy *adj* CHAPPED VI.7.2. tʃæpi So

chap-rein *n* a TETHERING-ROPE used to tie up
a horse I.4.2. tʃæpɹeɪn Hu

chaps *1. npl [In frosty weather, your hands
sometimes get all dry, red and sore, and you say
your hands are **chapped**.] What do you call those
deep sore places where the skin has broken?*
VI.7.3. tʃeps Ess Sr K Sx, tʃæps Sa He Gl MxL
So Brk Co Sx*[small x1]*, tʃaps Y Sa Wa Mon Gl
O Lei R Nth Bk*[old x1]* Bd So W Co D Do Ha,
tʃaps O. ⇒ **charks, chilblains, chines, chops,
chuns, cracks, cuts, geals, hacks, keens, kins,
kinning, *sore places* ⇒ sores, sores, sprees**

2. *npl* BOYS VIII.1.3(a). tʃaps Wa

3. *npl* PALS VIII.4.2. tʃaps D

char-hole-man *n* a person whose job is to PITCH
sheaves II.6.10. tʃɑˑhoulmæn Nf

charked *adj* CHAPPED VI.7.2. tʃaᴵːkt Y

charks *npl* CHAPS in the skin VI.7.3. tʃaᴵːks Y,
tʃaˑɹks Y

charlie-pig *n* a BOAR III.8.7. tʃɑːlɪpɪg Nf

charlie-turner *n* STRING used to tie up a
grain-sack I.7.3. tʃɑːlɪtɒnəɹ Y *[apparently trade
name]*

charlock *n [Show a picture of charlock.] What do
you call this?* II.2.6. tʃaːlɪk Nth Bk, tʃaᵗːlɪk So Do,
tʃaᵗːɫɪk So W Do Ha, tʃaᵗːl-ɪk W Co D Ha, tʃaːlɒk
Db, tʃaᵗːlɒk So, tʃaᵗːlɒk Gl, tʃaᵗːl-ɒk D, ʃaːlʌk
Mon, tʃaᴵˑlʊk La, ʃaᵗːlʊk Sa, tʃaᵗːlʊkʰ Gl,
ʃaːlək We St, tʃaːlək St Mon Lei, tʃaᵗːlək So,
ʃaᵗːl-ək Gl, ʃaᵗːlək O, tʃaᵗːlək Gl O, tʃaᵗːl-ək
Mon, tʃaːlɪk Brk Ha, ʃaːɹlɪk Sr, tʃaᵗːɫɪk Sr Ha,
tʃaᵗːl-ɪk Brk Co D Sx, tʃaːlɒk Brk, ʃaːlɒk MxL,
ʃaːlək wY Ch St, tʃaːlək wY Man Ess K, tʃaːɫək
Mon K, tʃaᴵːlək Brk K, tʃəɹlək He. ⇒
**brash-lach, brashock, brazzock(s), cadlock,
carlock(s), charnock, dingle, field-kale,**

garlock, gools, kale, katlock(s), kecklet, kecklock(s), kecks, kedlock(s), keglock, kelk, ketlet, ketlock(s), kinkle, mustard, runch(es, wild-kale, yellow-flower, yellow-runch, yellow(s), yellow-top, yellow-weed

charnock *n* CHARLOCK II.2.6. tʃaˤ:ɪnək La

charrow-comb *n* a CURRY-COMB used to clean horses III.5.5(b). tʃaɹʊkoʊm Nth

chashed *adj* CHAPPED VI.7.2. tʃaʃt Y

chat *1. n And when you had both sat down comfortably, you'd start to have a ....* VIII.3.4. Eng exc. Nb Cu Du We Man. ⇒ **call, *bit of a* call, *right* call, camp, cank, cant, chalk, *bit of a chat*, *good old chat*, chatter, chinwag, chitter, chipe, chops, clatter, confab, *old* confab, conflab, conflaberation, conversation, coosh, crack, *bit* crack, *bit of* crack, *right* crack, *bit of* gab, *gnatter* ⇒ natter, gobble, gossip, jaw, larrap, mardle, natter, parl, tale, talk, yarn, *good old* yarn, *right good* yarn**
2. vi to KITTEN III.13.10. tʃat Co, tʃati D, tʃap D*[queried error for* [tʃat] *SBM]*

chats *1. npl* LICE IV.8.1(a). tʃats Y Co
2. n KINDLING-*WOOD* V.4.2. tʃæts Sa He, tʃats Sa*[old]*

chatter *n* CHAT VIII.3.4. tʃætʔə MxL, tʃætəˤ: So, tʃædəˤ: So, tʃatə Y, tʃatəˤ O, tʃatəˤɹ Wa, tʃaʔəɹ O, tʃatəˤ: W

chatterbag *n* a GOSSIP VIII.3.5(b). tʃadəˤ:bɛg D, tʃadəˤ:bag Do

chatter-balls *n* SHEEP-DUNG II.1.7. tʃætəˤbɒɫz Wo

chatterbox *n* a GOSSIP VIII.3.5(b). tʃæʔəbɒks Nf, tʃætəbɒks MxL, tʃæ:dəˤ:bɒks So, tʃaʔəbɒks Bd, tʃatəˤbɒks Sa, tʃatəˤ:bɒks W

chattering *v-ing* GOSSIPING VIII.3.5(a). tʃætʔəɹɪn MxL, tʃaʔəˤ:ɾɪn Ha, tʃadəˤ:ɾən D

chattermag *n* a GOSSIP VIII.3.5(b). tʃatəˤ:mag Do

chatty-balls *1. n* SHEEP-DUNG II.1.7. tʃɛtɪbɒlz Sa
2. npl RABBIT-DROPPINGS III.13.15. tʃætɪbɒɫz He

chaw *vt-1prpl* we CRUNCH apples or biscuits VI.5.12. *-ing* tʃɔ:-ɪn Sx

chaw up *vtphr-1prpl* we CRUNCH apples or biscuits VI.5.12. *-ing* tʃɔ:ən ... ʌp Do

checking *v-ing* THROWING a stone VIII.7.7. tʃɛkɪn He

check-rope* *n* a TETHERING-ROPE used to tie up a horse I.4.2. tʃɛkɹo:p Mon

chee *n* a PERCH for hens IV.6.3. tʃi: K

cheeks *npl* the JAMBS of a door V.1.11. tʃi:ks Nb Cu Du We La

cheese *n What can you make from milk?* V.5.4(b). Eng. ⇒ **sour-milk cheese, white cheese**; ⇒ also **pork-cheese, skim-milk jacks, slip-coat cheese**

chemise *n In your mother's day, what did women wear next to their skin?* V.11.1. ʃɪmi:s Cu Ch, 'ʃɪmi:z St, ʃɪ'mi:z Wo Wa Mon Lei R Nth Nf Ess, tʃɪ'mi:z Sa, ʃɪmi:z St Mon O L K Ha, ʃɪ'mɪi:z Ess, ʃɪmɪi:z Ess Sr Sx, tʃɪmɪi:z Sx, 'ʃɪmɪi:əz Gl, 'ʃɪmɪs Ch, ʃɪ'me:z Ch, ʃɛ'mi:z St, 'ʃɛmɪs St, 'ʃəmi:z St, ʃəmi:z La Man So K, ʃəmɪiz K Ha*[worn over vest]*, tʃəmɪiz Brk, ʃə'mɪi:z Ess, ʃəmɪi:z Ess Sx.
⇒ **camisole, flannel, flannel shirt, flannel vest, sark, shift, shimmy, shimmy-shirt, singlet, smock, undershirt, undervest**

cherks *n* CINDERS V.4.3. tʃəˤ:ks Co

cherries *npl* RABBIT-DROPPINGS III.13.15. tʃəɹɪz Sx*[facetious]*

cherry-curd(s) *n* BEESTINGS V.5.10.
no -s: tʃɛɹɪkəˤ:d̥ O
-s: 'tʃɛɹɪ,kə:z Wo, 'ʃɛɹɪ'kʊz Wo, tʃɛɹɪkəts Bk, tʃɛɹɪkəˤ:dz O, tʃɛɹɪkəˤ:d̥z Wa Gl O Nth, tʃəɹɪkəˤ:d̥z Bk *[s-less form not a WMBM headword]*

chest *n* a BREAST of a woman VI.8.5. tʃɪst Nf *[marked u.r. EMBM]*

chet *vi* to SUCK, describing how a lamb gets its milk III.7.1. *3prsg* tʃɛts Y, *prppl* tʃɛtɪn Y

chew *vt-1prpl* we CRUNCH apples or biscuits VI.5.12. *-ing* tʃævɪn Co D, tʃu: Mon Ess *[marked ir.r. WMBM]*

chewers *npl* MOLARS VI.5.7. tʃu:-əz L

chewing *v-ing* **chewing the rag** GOSSIPING VIII.3.5(a). tʃʊu:ɪn ðə hɹæ:g So

chew up *vtphr-1prpl* we CRUNCH apples or biscuits VI.5.12. *-ing* tʃævɪn ... ʌp Co

chibbles* *1. npl* SPRING ONIONS V.7.16. tʃɪbɫz So Co D, tʃɪpɫz So Co D Do, tʃɪbəɫz Gl
2. npl shoots growing from an old onion. tʃɪbəɫz O

chibblies* *npl* SPRING ONIONS V.7.16. tʃɪbɫɪz Co

chiblings *npl* CHILBLAINS VI.10.6. tʃɪblɪnz Sa

chick *1. vi* to CHIP, referring to an egg that is about to hatch IV.6.10. tʃɪk Nf
2. n a NESTLING IV.7.1. tʃɪk St Sx, *pl* tʃɪks W

chicken *n* a NESTLING IV.7.1. *pl* tʃɪkɪnz Sa

chicken-bin *n* a bin for containing hen-corn, ⇐ CORN-BIN I.7.4. *pl* tʃɪkɪnbɪnz O

chicken-coop *n* a HEN-HOUSE I.1.6. tʃɪkɪnkᵁu:p Y

chicken-house *n* a HEN-HOUSE I.1.6. tʃɪkɪnɛus Bk Sr K Sx, *pl* tʃɪkɪnɛuzɪz Ess, tʃɪkənɛus O, tʃɪkɪnæus Ha, tʃɪknhæus K, tʃɪkɪnaus L, tʃɪkɪnu:s L, tʃɪkɪnhᵊus K, tʃɪkɪnəus K

chicken-hut *n* a HEN-HOUSE I.1.6. tʃɪkɪnʊt L, *pl* tʃɪkənʊts L

chicken(s) *1. npl What comes out of the eggs [of a domestic hen] when they are hatched?* IV.6.11.
no -s: tʃɪkɪn Wa Mon Gl O Bd MxL So W Brk K

Co D Do Ha Sx, tʃɪkən Co D Do, tʃakŋ Ha, tʃakən Ha

-s: tʃɪkɪns La O, tʃɪkɪnz Nb Cu Du We La Y Ch Db Sa St He Wo Wa Mon Gl O Nt L Lei R Nth Hu C Nf Bk Bd Hrt MxL*[when a little older]* So*[when older x1]* Brk Sr K D Ha Sx, *sg* tʃɪkʔɪn Ess, tʃɪkns Man, tʃɪknz Y L Nf Ess, tʃɪkʔnz Nf Sf, tʃɪkəns Man, tʃɪkənz Nb Du We Ch Sa L C Sf Ess So Do, *sg* tʃɪkən Y, tʃɪkʔənz Sf

⇒ **bubs, chick(s), chicken(s), little chickens, little chicks, young chickens**

[incorrect marking of this question as being of phonological significance in one version of the questionnaire may have resulted in undue bias towards chicken(s) responses]

2. *npl* HENS IV.6.2.

no -s: tʃɪkɪn O Ess Brk Sr K Ha Sx, tʃɪkn Sx

-s: tʃɪkɪnz L Bk Ess Brk Sr K Sx, tʃɪknz Nf Ess, tʃɪkənz L

chicken-toed *adj* PIGEON-TOED   VI.10.4.
tʃɪkəntøːd Nb

chick(s) *npl* CHICKENS IV.6.11.

no -s: tʃɪk Ess

-s: tʃɪks Nb Y Ch Db Sa Wo Wa Mon O Nt L Hu Nf Sf Bk Hrt Ess MxL So W Brk Sr K Co D Sx

chid *n* a EWE-LAMB III.6.3. tʃɪd Ha

chid-cat *n* a TABBY-CAT, the female cat III.13.9. tʃɪdkæt Ha

chiel *1. n* a CHILD VIII.1.2(b). tʃiːɫ So Co D, tʃiːˀɫ So Do, tʃiːəɫ So Do, tʃɪɫ So

2. *n* a girl, ⇐ GIRLS VIII.1.3(b). tʃiːɫ So

chiels *npl* CHILDREN VIII.1.2(a). tʃiːɫz D

chig *1. vt* to TOP-AND-TAIL gooseberries V.7.23. tʃɪg La*[modern x1]*

2. *vt* to REMOVE *STALKS* from currants V.7.24. tʃɪg La

chikes *npl* GIPSIES VIII.4.12. tʃəɪks Sx *[queried SBM]*

chilblain *npl* CHILBLAINS VI.10.6. tʃɪʊɫblæɪn K

chilblained *adj* CHAPPED VI.7.2. tʃɪlbleɪnd L, tʃɪlblaɪn Nf

chilblains *1. npl* In frosty weather you may get painful, tingling sores on your feet. What do you call that? VI.10.6. Eng. ⇒ **chiblings, chimblings, chimlings, chilblain, chilbrains, childags, chills, frost-bite**

2. *npl* CHAPS in the skin VI.7.3. tʃɪɫblæɪnz Ess

chilbrains *npl* CHILBLAINS VI.10.6. tʃɪlbɹeːnz Ch Sa, tʃɪɫbɹeːˡnz Gl

child *n* *[In the olden days, families often had up to five or six... [children].] But nowadays many of them have only one .... VIII.1.2(b). Eng exc. Nb Cu Du We Co D.* ⇒ **bairn, chiel, kid, youngster**

childags *npl* CHILBLAINS VI.10.6. tʃɪɫdagz W Do

childern(s) *npl* CHILDREN VIII.1.2(a).

no -s: tʃɪldɪn Nf, tʃɪldn Lei R Nf, tʃɪldən Y Ch Wo

O L Lei Nf, tʃɪlʊn Wo, tʃɪlan St, tʃɪɫdn Lei C Sf Bd, tʃɪɫdən Gl C Sf Bk Hrt So, tʃɪldəɪn L Nth, tʃɪldəˡn Nf, tʃɪɫdəˡn Brk*[rare x1]* K, tʃɪɫdəˡːn Brk*[rare]*, tʃɪɫdəˡn̩ Gl O, tʃɪɫdəˡːn̩ Sa Wo Gl, tʃɪɫdəˡn̩ He Wo Mon, tʃɪɫdəˡːn̩ Wa O Bk Bd So*[old x1]* W Co D Do Ha Sx, tʃɪɫdəˡːrn̩ W Brk Sr Sx, tʃɪɫəˡːn̩ So Co D, tʃʊldn Lei, tʃʊldn Bk, tʃʊɫdn Bk, tʃʊɫdəˡn̩ Bk, tʃəɫdəˡːn̩ So Co D

-s: tʃɪɫdəˡːnz Sr

childer(s) *npl* CHILDREN VIII.1.2(a)

no -s: tʃɪldə La Y*[old x1]* Man Ch Db St Nt, tʃɪɫdə Sf, tʃɪldəɹ La Y*[old]*, tʃɪldəˡ La Y Man Ch, tʃɪɫdəˡ K, tʃɪldəɽ Db, tʃɪldəˡ O*[old]*, tʃɪɫdəˡː So

-s: tʃɪldəz Ess, tʃɪɫdəz Ess

children *npl* In the olden days, families often had up to five or six .... VIII.1.2(a). Eng exc. Nb Cu Du We La R C Bk Co D Do. ⇒ **bairns, chiels, childer(s), childern(s), childs, kiddies, kids, youngsters**

childs *npl* CHILDREN VIII.1.2(a). tʃəɪɫdz Gl

chilled *1. adj* CHAPPED VI.7.2. tʃɪld Lei, tʃɪɫd O Bd

2. *adj* COLD, describing a person VI.13.18. tʃɪɫd Ess

3. *adj* VERY COLD, describing a person VI.13.19. tʃɪʊd So; **chilled most to death** tʃɪʊd mʊʊst tə dɛːθ So

chillicks *n* the WATTLES of a hen IV.6.19. tʃɪlɪks Nb

chills *npl* CHILBLAINS VI.10.6. tʃɪɫz Bk

chilly *1. adj* COLD, describing a room VI.13.17. tʃɪlɪ Ha, tʃɪɫɪ Sr

2. *adj* COLD, describing a person VI.13.18. tʃɪlɪ Ess Brk, tʃɪɫɪ Sr Ha, tʃɪɫɪ D Ha; **cold and chilly** kɔʊd ən tʃɪlɪ Y; **very chilly** wɛɹɪ tʃɪlɪ Nf

chilver *1. n* a EWE-LAMB III.6.3. tʃɪɫvəˡː So Do, *pl* tʃɪɫvəˡːz̩ W

2. *n* a EWE-HOG III.6.4. tʃɪɫvəˡː Gl, tʃɪlvəˡː So, tʃɪɫvəˡː So W

chilver-lamb *n* a   EWE-LAMB   III.6.3. tʃɪɫvəˡːlæm So, tʃɪɫvəˡlam Gl, tʃɪɫvəˡːłam W, tʃɪɫvəˡːłam Do

chimbey* *n* a CHIMNEY V.1.3. tʃɪmbɪ Hu C Nf Sf Ess

chimblet *n* a CHIMNEY V.1.3. tʃɪmblɪt Y

chimbley* *n* a CHIMNEY V.1.3. *pl* tʃɪmbliz K, tʃɪmblɪ La Y Man St Wo Mon L Nf Bk Ess*[facetious x1]* Brk*[old x1]* Sr, tʃɪmbłɪ Gl Ess Brk, tʃɪmblə Nt L Brk

chimblings *npl* CHILBLAINS   VI.10.6. tʃɪmblɪnz Sa, tʃɪmbəlɪnz Sa

chimchamming away *vphr-ing* GOSSIPING VIII.3.5(a). tʃɪmtʃamɪn əwɛː W

chimdey* *n* a CHIMNEY V.1.3. tʃɪmdɪ Ch Db Sa St Wa Nth*[old x1]* Hu C Sf Bd Hrt Ess chimley* *n* a CHIMNEY V.1.3. tʃɪmli Mon So, tʃɪmɫi So W Co D Do Ha, tʃɪmlɪ Nb La Y Ch Sa St He Wo Mon Gl O Nt*[old x1]* L Lei R Nf*[old x1]* Bk Bd Ess Brk Sr K Ha Sx, tʃɪmɫi Mon Gl O Lei W Sr*[old]* Do, tʃɪmlə Nb Cu Du We La Y L, tʃɪmləɹ L, tʃɪmlɪ Y, tʃɪməlɪ Nb Ch Wa O, tʃɪmələ Cu Du, tʃʏmlɪ Nb*[old]*

chimley-piece* *n* a mantel-shelf over a fireplace, ⇐ CHIMNEY V.1.3. tʃɪmləpiːs Cu

chimley-stack* *n* a CHIMNEY V.1.3. tʃɪmlɪstak Wo, tʃɪmləstak Y

chimlings *npl* CHILBLAINS VI.10.6. tʃɪmlɪŋz Sa, tʃɪmlɪnz Sa, tʃɪməlɪnz Sa

chimmock *n* a CHIMNEY V.1.3. tʃɪmʊk He Wo Gl, tʃɪmək He Gl

chimney *n* *[Show a picture of some houses.] What do you call this [indicate a chimney]?* V.1.3. Eng exc. Cu We La Man Db C Bd W Co D. ⇒ **chimbey, chimblet, chimbley, chimdey, chimley, chimley-stack, chimmock, chimney-stack, flue, lum, stack, tun;** ⇒ also **chimley-piece, louvre, louvre-hole, louvre-man**

chimney-bar *n* the *HORIZONTAL* BAR of a crane over a domestic fire V.3.5(a). tʃɪmɫibaᵍ: Nb, tʃɪmɫibaᵗ: W D

chimney-crook *n* the vertical part of a crane over a domestic fire, consisting of a *BAR* or *CHAIN* and a HOOK(/*CROOK*) V.3.5b+c. tʃɪmɫikɾʏk D, tʃɪmlikɾʊk So

chimney-crook(s) *n* a CRANE on which a kettle is hung over a domestic fire V.3.4.
no -s: tʃɪmɫikɾʏk Co D, tʃɪmlikɾʊk So, tʃɪmɫikɾʊk W Co
-s: tʃɪmɫikɾʏks D

chimney-hook *n* the HOOK or *CROOK* of a crane over a domestic fire V.3.5(c). tʃɪmɫi-ʊk Brk

chimney-hook(s) *n* a CRANE on which a kettle is hung over a domestic fire V.3.4.
no -s: tʃɪmlɪ-ʌk Bk
-s: tʃɪmɫi-ʏks D

chimney-soot *n* SOOT V.4.6. tʃɪmɫizʏt D

chimney-stack *n* a CHIMNEY V.1.3. tʃɪmnɪstɛk K, tʃɪmnɪstæk Ess, *pl* tʃɪmɪstæːks Man

chines *npl* CHAPS in the skin VI.7.3. tʃaɪnz Y

chink-cough *1. n* WHOOPING-COUGH VI.8.3. tʃɪŋkɛʊxf La, tʃɪŋkɑːf Wo*[old]*, tʃɪŋkɑːf Gl*[old]*, tʃɪŋkɒf La Db, tʃɪnkɒf La Ch Db Sa St*[old x2]*, tʃɪnkof La, tʃɪŋkʊf La, tʃɪnkʊf La
2. n a sham cough. tʃɪnkɔːf Sa

chinwag *n* CHAT VIII.3.4. tʃɪnwɪg So, tʃɪnwɛˑg Sr, tʃɪnwæg Ess, tʃɪnwag He Wo Gl Nth Do, tʃɪnwaŋ Co

chinwagger *n* a GOSSIP VIII.3.5(b). tʃɪnwagə Sr, tʃɪnwagəᵗ: Ha

chinwagging *v-ing* GOSSIPING VIII.3.5(a). tʃɪnwagɪn Y*[jocular]* Do

chip *1. vi When the young birds [i.e. chickens] show signs of hatching out, you say the eggs are beginning ....* IV.6.10. tʃɪp Nb Cu Du We La Y Man Ch Db Sa St Wo Wa Lei R Hu C Sf Bk Bd Hrt Ess So Brk Sr K Do Ha Sx, dʒɪp Man, tʃɛp Db. ⇒ **beak, beal, beald, bild, bill, break, break shell, build** ⇒ **bild, chick, chit, come off, come out, crack, hatch, hatch off, hatch out, peck, pick, pip, pop, scrat, scratch, spletch, spretch, spring, spurt, stretch, turn**
2.1. v to WHITTLE a stick I.7.19. *-ing* tʃɪppɪn Db
2.2. vt to whittle. *-ing* tʃɪpɪn So W
3. n a SPLINTER VI.7.10. tʃɪp Man
4. n the MOULD-BOARD of a horse-drawn turn-wrest plough I.8.8. tʃɪp Sx
5. n the SOLE of a horse-drawn plough I.8.9. tʃɪp Co Sx

chipe *n* CHAT VIII.3.4. tʃɔɪp Sx

chiplets* *npl* SPRING ONIONS V.7.16. tʃɪpɫəts Ha

chip off *vtphr* **chip a bit off** to WHITTLE a stick I.7.19. *-ing* tʃɪpɪn ... ɒf St

chipped *adj* CHAPPED VI.7.2. tʃɪpt La Y, tʃɪp La

chipping *v-ing* SHEARING sheep III.7.6. tʃɪpɪn La Y

chippy *1. n* a CARPENTER or JOINER VIII.4.3. tʃɪpɪ St*[carpenter, joiner, or wheelwright]* Ess*[heavy, less skilled work]*
2. adj BRITTLE, describing cups and saucers which break easily IX.1.4. tʃɪpɪ Sx

chips *n* KINDLING-*WOOD* V.4.2. tʃɪps Y

chirt out *vtphr* to SUCK, describing how a lamb gets its milk III.7.1. tʃəːt ... ʌʊt Y

chissicking* *v-ing* clearing the throat with a forced cough, ⇐ COUGHING VI.8.2. tʃɪzɪkɪn Ess

chit *1. n* **in chit** pregnant, describing a doe rabbit, ⇐ KINDLE III.13.14. ɪn tʃɪt Do
2. vi to CHIP, referring to an egg that is about to hatch IV.6.10. tʃɪt Nt

chit-cat *n* a TABBY-CAT, the female cat III.13.9. tʃɪtkat Sa

chitter *n* CHAT VIII.3.4. tʃɪdəᵗ: D

chittering *v-ing* GOSSIPING VIII.3.5(a). tʃɪtɹɪn Lei

chitterling(s) *1. n What do you call the small intestines of a pig?* III.12.2.
no -s: tʃɪʔɫɪn Ess
-s: tʃɪtlɪnz Y Sa St He Wo Wa Mon Gl O Lei R Nf Bd Ess MxL Brk K, tʃɪtlənz Ess, tʃɪtɫɪnz He Mon Gl O W Brk K Sx, tʃɪtɫənz W, tʃɪtˌlɪnz Sa, tʃɪtəlɪnz Sa Brk K, tʃɪtəɫɪnz Sx, tʃɪtɔᵗlɪnz He Gl, tʃɪtʔlɪnz Ess, tʃɪdlɪnz Gl Sf Bk Ess So Brk Sr K Ha Sx, tʃɪdlənz Sf, tʃɪdɫɪnz So W Sr Co Do Ha Sx,

tʃɪd|ɪnz Sr, tʃɪklɪnz Y St He Wo Wa Gl Lei Nth,
tʃɪʔlɪnz Gl Bk Hrt K, tʃɪʔlənz O, tʃɪʔɫɪnz W, tʃətɫɪnz
Do

2. *n* the small intestines of a pig when cooked.
tʃɪtlɪnz So, tʃɪklɪnz Y, tʃɪʔlɪnz So, tʃetlɪnz Sa

3. *n* the larger intestines of a pig. tʃɪtlɪnz Y

⇒ **belly/bellies, belly-guts, bowels, chittlets,
entrails, gibblings, gut(s), gut-runners, hides,
hog's-guts,** *innards* ⇒ **inwards, innings, inside,
inwards, knotlings, link-hides, little belly/bellies,
little gut(s), little puddings, little tharms,
pig-bellies, pig's-belly/bellies, pig's-guts, pudding,
puddings, pudding-skin(s), pullings, ropes, ropps,
runners, sausage-hide(s), skins, small bellies, small
guts, small puddings, small ropps, small tharms,
sticking, tharms, thin puddings;** ⇒ **also big bellies,
big puddings, muggets**

chitties *npl* POTATOES II.4.1(a). tʃɪtiːz So, tʃɪdiːz
W, tʃediːz So W, tʃɛʔiːz W

chittlets *n* CHITTERLINGS III.12.2. tʃɪtlɪts L

chitty-haulm(s) *n* POTATO-HAULMS II.4.4.
 no -s: tʃɪdihæm W
 -s: tʃɪti-ɛɫmz So, tʃɛʔi-æmz W

chitty-rinds *npl* potato PEELINGS V.7.22.
tʃɪtiɾɔɪnz So, tʃediɾəɪnz W, tʃɛʔɪɾəɪnz W

chiv *n* a KNIFE I.7.18. tʃɪv St

chobble *v* to GOBBLE food VI.5.13(b). *-ing* tʃɒbɫɪn
He

chock *1. n* the CLOG on a horse's tether I.4.3. tʃɒk
Y Bk

2. *n* a movable iron hoop that slides along a
cart-shaft and couples it to the projecting end of the
beam on which the cart-body rests, ⇐ ROD/PIN
I.10.3. tʃɒk La

3. *n* a chock placed behind and under a wheel to
prevent a cart from going backwards on a hill, ⇐
PROP/CHOCK I.11.2. tʃœːk Nb, tʃɑk O, tʃɒk Nb Cu
Du We La Y Man Brk, tʃɔk Nb We Y L, tʃʌk Bk

chock-holes *npl* PUDDLES IV.1.6. tʃɒkoʊlz St

chockrel *1. n* the CROSS-BEAM END of a cart
I.10.1. tʃɔkɹɪl Ch

2. *n* a BUMPER of a cart I.10.1(a). tʃɒkɹɪl Db,
tʃɒkɹəl Ch

chock-teeth *npl* MOLARS VI.5.7. tʃɒktiːθ Mon,
tʃɒktiːʃ So, tʃɒktɪθ Gl

chog *1. n* a chock placed behind and under a wheel
to prevent a cart from going backwards on a hill, ⇐
PROP/CHOCK I.11.2. tʃɒg Gl W Brk; **chog of wood**
tʃɒg ə wʊd W Ha

***2.** n* a lump of peat, ⇐ to CUT IV.4.4. tʃɒgz W

chog and chain *n* a TETHER for a cow I.3.4. tʃɒg ŋ̩
tʃɛɪn Brk

chog-rope *n* a TETHERING-ROPE used to tie up a
horse I.4.2. tʃɒgɹoʊp O

chog(s) *n* the CLOG on a horse's tether I.4.3. tʃɑːg
Gl, tʃɒg Gl O Ess W Brk Ha, *sg* tʃɒgz Brk, tʃʊg O Sr

choke *1. vt If a man got his fingers round you
here [point to the throat] and slowly squeezed, he
would ... you.* VI.6.4. Eng exc. Lei R. ⇒ **crackle,
garrotte, quackle, stifle, stop** *his wind,* **strangle,
throat, thropple, throttle**

2. *n* a THROAT VI.6.3. tʃʊək L

choker *1. n* a NECKERCHIEF VI.14.4. tʃɒukəˑ
Sr, tʃɒukəᵗ Sr K Sx, *pl* tʃɒukəz Ess, tʃɔukəˑ Brk
K, tʃʌukə Ess, tʃʌukəᵗ K*[silk or linen]*, tʃoˑkə Nf,
tʃoːkəᵗ Ha, tʃɒukə St

2. *n* a long woollen scarf. tʃʌukə MxL

chole *n* the WATTLES of a hen IV.6.19. tʃoːɫ So

choller(s) *n* the WATTLES of a hen IV.6.19.
 no -s: tʃɒləᵗ So, tʃɒtəᵗ So D
 -s: tʃɒləᴿz Nb Du, tʃɒləz Nb Cu Du, tʃɒlərz Cu,
tʃɒləᴿs Nb, tʃɔloᴿz Nb

cholly *n* the WATTLES of a hen IV.6.19. tʃɒti So
D

chom *v* to GOBBLE food VI.5.13(b). tʃɒm Mon

chomble *v* to GOBBLE food VI.5.13(b). tʃɒmbɫ
Wa

chomp *vt-1prpl* we CRUNCH apples or biscuits
VI.5.12. tʃɒmp Db Sa, *-ing* tʃɒmpɪn Y L, *-ing*
tʃɒmpɪn Y L

chomple *v* to GOBBLE food VI.5.13(b). *-ing*
tʃɒmplɪn Sa

chomp up *vtphr-1prpl* we CRUNCH apples or
biscuits VI.5.12. *-ing* tʃɒmpɪn ... ʊp Y

chonks *n* the WATTLES of a hen IV.6.19. tʃɔŋks
Sf

chonnocks *npl* TURNIPS II.4.1(b). tʃɒnəks St

choops *npl* HIPS of the wild rose IV.11.7. tʃɪups
Y, tʃœːps Du, tʃᵁuːps We Y, tʃuːps Nb Cu We Y,
dʒuːps Nb

choosing* *v-ing* CULLING sheep III.11.2.
tʃuːzɪn Brk

chop *1. v* to WHITTLE a stick I.7.19. *prppl*
tʃɒpɪn Brk

2.1. *v* to TOP AND TAIL swedes II.4.3. tʃɒp Db
Bk, tʃɔp Ess

2.2. *vt* to top and tail swedes. tʃɒp Lei

3. *n* feed given to horses in the stable, ⇐
FEEDING III.5.1. tʃɔp L

4. *n* CHAFF fed to horses III.5.3. tʃɒp Nb La Y
Ch Db Sa St L, tʃɔp We La L, tʃʊp Y Man

5. *vt-1prpl* we CRUNCH apples or biscuits
VI.5.12. *-ing* tʃɒpən Co

6. *v* to GOBBLE food VI.5.13(b). *-ing* tʃɒpən Co

chop off *1. vphr* to TOP AND TAIL swedes
II.4.3. tʃɒp ɒf Y

2. *vtphr* to top and tail swedes. **chop the spurns
and tops off, chop the tops and tails off** tʃɒp ...
ɔːf L Lei R Bk, tʃɔp ... ɔf L

chop out *1.1. vtphr* to THIN OUT turnip plants
II.4.2. tʃɑˑpʔ (+syllabic) ... ɛʊt Nf, tʃɒp ... ɛʊt Wo
Wa O L Nth Hu Nf Bk Ess K, tʃɒpʔ (+syllabic) ...

ɛʊt Nf, tʃɔp ... ɛʊt C Sf Ess, tʃɒp ... ɛʊʔ Bk, tʃɒp ... æʊt Wo Lei R W, tʃɔp ... ᵊæʊt L, tʃɒp ... æʊʔ Gl, tʃɒp ... aːt Nt Lei, tʃɒp aʊt So, tʃɔp ... aʊt L, tʃɔp ... aʊʔ L, tʃɔp ... uːt L, *-ing* tʃɒpɪn ... aʊt Sx, tʃɒp ... aʊːt Wo; **chop and single out** tʃɒp ŋ sɪŋgɫ ... ɛuːt Wo

1.2. vphr to thin out turnips. tʃɒp ɛʊt Ess, tʃɔp ɛʊt Ess, *-ing* tʃɔpən æʊt L, tʃɒp aʊt So, tʃɔp aʊt L

2. vtphr to CLEAR grass at the edges of a field II.9.5. tʃɒp ... æʊt R, tʃɒp ... aːt Lei, tʃɔp ... aʊt L

chopped *adj* CHAPPED VI.7.2. tʃɒpt Du We La Y Man Ch Db Sa St He Wo Wa Mon Gl O Nth So W Brk D, tʃɒpɪd Wo D, tʃɔpt Y Wo Wa

chopper *1. n* a HEDGING-BILL IV.2.5. tʃɒpəᴶ K
2. n a BILLHOOK IV.2.6. tʃɒˈpəɹ Brk

choppy *1. n* CHAFF fed to horses III.5.3. tʃœːpɪ Nb, tʃɒpɪ Nb Cu Du, tʃɔpɪ Nb
2. adj CHAPPED VI.7.2. tʃɒpi So, tʃɒpɪ Ch

chops *1. n* the human MOUTH VI.5.1. tʃɒps St*[old x1]* Wa Gl, tʃɔps Wa
2. n WIPE YOUR MOUTH VI.5.3. tʃæps Nf Ess, tʃaps Bk, tʃɒps Ch St Wa*[old]* Mon Nth Bk Ess So Sr, tʃɔps L
3. vt to guzzle a drink, ⇐ GUZZLES VI.5.13(a). *-ing* tʃɒpsɪn Db
4. vt to GOBBLE food VI.5.13(b). *-ing* tʃɒpsɪn Db
5. n CHAT VIII.3.4. tʃɒps Ch*[old]* St Nth Bk*[old x1]* Bd
6. npl CHAPS in the skin VI.7.3. tʃɒps Y Man Sa St He Wo Wa Mon Gl O NthSo W Brk Co D Do

chopsing *v-ing* GOSSIPING VIII.3.5(a). tʃɒpsɪn St*[old]* Bk Bd

chopsing about *vphr-ing* GOSSIPING VIII.3.5(a). tʃɒpsɪn əbɛʊt Bk

chopsticks *n* KINDLING-*WOOD* V.4.2. tʃɒpstɪks Mon Lei

chop-teeth *npl* MOLARS VI.5.7. tʃɒptiːθ Mon *[queried error for chock- WMBM]*

chop up *vtphr* to GOBBLE food VI.5.13(b). *-ing* tʃɒpən ʌp Co

chowls *n* the WATTLES of a hen IV.6.19. tʃæɤɫz D, tʃaʊlz We *[We form interpreted as chawls NBM]*

christmas *n* a HOLLY-bush IV.10.9. kɹɪsməs Nf

christmas-bush *n* a HOLLY-bush IV.10.9. kɹɪsməsbuʃ Nf

christmas eve *n* What specially important days are there during the year? VII.4.8. Eng. ⇒ **ashen-faggot night**

christmas-tree *n* a HOLLY-bush IV.10.9. kɹɪsməstɹɪi Nf

chuck *1. n* the CLOG on a horse's tether I.4.3. tʃʌk Bk, tʃʊk Sx
2.1. vt to PITCH sheaves II.6.10. *3prsg* tʃʊks Bk
2.2. v to pitch. tʃʌk C Sf Hrt, *3prsg* tʃʌks Nb, *-ing* tʃʌkɪn So, tʃʊk La Ch Nt Lei Bd, *3prsg* tʃʊks Y Sa Bk; **fork and chuck** *3prsg* fɒɹks ən tʃʊks Y
3. n CHAFF fed to horses III.5.3. tʃʊk Man

4. n (off her) FOOD V.8.2. tʃʊk Ch
5. n MEAL OUT VII.5.12. tʃʊk Y

chuck about *vtphr* to TED hay II.9.11(a). tʃʌk ... əbɛʊt Bd

chuck across *vtphr* to PITCH sheaves II.6.10. *3prsg* tʃʌks ... əkɾɔːs W

chucker-off *n* the FORKER on a wagon who unloads sheaves in a stackyard II.6.9. tʃʊkəɹɒf La

chucking *v-ing* THROWING a stone VIII.7.7. tʃʌkɪn Ess So W, tʃʌkn Nf*[old]* So, tʃʌkʔn Nf, tʃʌkən Sf, *imp* tʃʌk He Ha, *no -ing* tʃʌk Sx, *ptppl* tʃʌkt Sx, tʃɤkən Nb*[modern]*, tʃʊkɪn Y Ch Db Sa St*[old]* O R, ətʃʊkɪn Wo, tʃʊkn Nb, tʃʊkən Nb We, *no -ing* tʃʊk Du Nth, tʃəkɪn Gl

chucking off *1. vphr-ing* UNLOADING sheaves from a wagon II.6.8. *no -ing* tʃʊk ɒf La
2. vtphr-ing unloading sheaves. tʃʊkɪn ... ɒf Nt

chucking out *vphr-ing* **chucking on out** UNLOADING sheaves from a wagon II.6.8. tʃʌkn ɒ'n ɛʊt Nf

chucking-up-time *n* STOPPING-TIME at the end of a day's work VII.5.9. tʃʌkɪnʌptɒɪm Nf

chuckle(s) *n* the WATTLES of a hen IV.6.19. *no -s*: tʃʌkɫ D
-s: tʃʌkɫz D

chuckle-headed *adj* STUPID VI.1.5. tʃʌkɫhɛdɪd So, tʃʌkɫedəd So

chuckling *v-ing* LAUGHING VIII.8.7. tʃʊklɪn Wo

chuck on *1. vphr* to FORK sheaves onto a wagon II.6.7(b). tʃʊk ɒn La
2. viphr to PITCH sheaves II.6.10. *3prprogsg* tʃʌkɪn ɔːn W

chuck over *viphr* to OVERTURN, referring to a cart I.11.5. *-ed* tʃʊkt ɔvɹ L, tʃʊk oːvəᵗ Sa

chuck up *1. vtphr* to TIP a cart I.11.6. tʃʌk ... ʌp Mon
2. vtphr to LOAD dung into a cart II.1.5. tʃʌk ... ʌp So
3.1. vtphr to FORK sheaves onto a wagon II.6.7(b). tʃʊk ... ʊp Y
3.2. vphr to fork sheaves onto a wagon. *-ing* tʃʊkɪn ʊp La
4. vtphr-3sg **chuck up together** she [a tidy girl] will COLLECT her toys VIII.8.15. tʃʊk ... ʊp təgɪðəᵗ Sa
5. vphr to VOMIT, referring to an adult VI.13.14(a). tʃɤk Nf

chuck-up-time *n* STOPPING-TIME at the end of a day's work VII.5.9. tʃʌkʌptaɪm Sa

chug *n* a chock placed behind and under a wheel to prevent a cart from going backwards on a hill, ⇐ PROP/CHOCK I.11.2. tʃug W

chummies *npl* PALS VIII.4.2. tʃʌmɪz Nf

chump *1. n* the human HEAD VI.1.1. tʃʌmp So

2. vt-1prpl we CRUNCH apples or biscuits VI.5.12. *-ing* tʃʌmpɪn D

chums *1. npl* MATES VIII.4.1. tʃɤmz Nf, tʃʊmz Wo

2. npl PALS VIII.4.2. tʃʌmz MxL So W Sr K D Sx, tʃɤmz Nb Nf, tʃʊmz La Y*[old x1]* O*[old]* Brk, tʃəmz Gl

chunk *1. n* a chock placed behind and under a wheel to prevent a cart from going backwards on a hill, ⇐ PROP/CHOCK I.11.2. tʃʌŋk So

2. n a PIECE *OF BREAD AND BUTTER* V.6.11(a). tʃʌŋk Bd; **chunk of bread** tʃʌŋk ə bɹed Bd, tʃʊŋk ə bɹed L; **chunk bread and butter** tʃʌŋk bɹed n̩ bʌtəᴶ Sr

3. n **chunk bread and jam** a PIECE *OF BREAD AND BUTTER AND JAM/SUGAR* V.6.11(b). tʃʌŋk bɹed n̩ dʒæm Sr

chuns *npl* CHAPS in the skin VI.7.3. tʃʊnz Db

church-clerk *n* a SEXTON VIII.5.4. tʃəᵗːtʃkləᵗːk Ess *[marked u.r. EMBM; see note at* **clerk***]*

churchgarth *n* a CHURCHYARD VIII.5.5. tʃʊətʃga:θ Du*[not usual]*

church-going clothes *n* SUNDAY-CLOTHES VI.14.19. tʃəᵗːtʃgʌʊɪn klʌʊz Ess

church-warden *n* a SEXTON VIII.5.4. tʃœːtʃwɔːdn Mon, tʃəːtʃwɔːdn Bd, tʃəːtʃwɔːdən Nf *[marked ir.r. WM/EMBM]*

churchyard *n What do you call the place where all the tombstones are? [Confirm that he means the place round the church.]* VIII.5.5. Eng. ⇒ **burial ground, cemetery, churchgarth, graveyard, kirkgarth, kirkyard, parson's acre**

churm *1. n* a CHURN V.5.5. tʃəːm Nth*[old]* Bd, tʃə·ɪm C, tʃəᵗːm He Gl Bd So W *[not a SBM headword]*

2. v to churn butter. *prppl* ətʃəᵗːmɪn Wa

churn *n Now in the good old days, what was butter made in?* V.5.5. Eng. ⇒ **butter-kiver, butter-tub, churm, dash-churn, dasher** *[northern [k-] forms are not held separately]*

chuting* *n* the GUTTER of a roof V.1.6. ʃɤːtɪn So D, ʃɤːdɪn D, ʃɤːtən D, ʃɤːdən Co D, ʃʌtɪn So, ʃʌdɪn So, ʃʊtɪn W Do Sx, *pl* ʃʊtɪnz Sr, ʃʊʔn Ha, ʃuːtɪn Mon Gl So W Do Ha Sx*[old x1]*, ʃuːʔn Ha, ʃuːtən Do

cicles *n* ICICLES VII.6.11. sɪkɫz Ess

cinder *n* CINDERS V.4.3. sɪndə Nb Nth, sɪndəᴶ Db Brk, sɪndəᵗ He O Nth Brk

cinder-ashes *n* ASHES from a cold fire V.4.5. sɪndəɹæʃɪs Nf

cinder-bing *n* an ASH-MIDDEN V.1.14. *pl* sɪndəbɪŋz L

cinder-dirt *1. n* ASH in a burning fire V.4.4. sɪndədəᵗːt Ess

2. n ASHES from a cold fire V.4.5. sɪndədə·t Nf, sɪndədəᵗːt Ess

cinder-heap *n* an ASH-MIDDEN V.1.14. sɪndəɹiːp C, sɪndəɹɪəp La, sɪndəᵗɹiːp Sa, sɪndəhɪiːp Ess, zɪndəᵗːɾɛːp W

cinder-hole *n* the ASH-HOLE or other place beneath a domestic fire in which the ashes are collected V.3.3. sɪndəɹoːl Sa, sɪndəɹʊəl L

cinder-midden *n* an ASH-MIDDEN V.1.14. sɪndəmɪdɪn Ch

cinder-muck *1. n* ASH in a burning fire V.4.4. sɪndəmɤk Nf

2. n ASHES from a cold fire V.4.5. sɪndəmʌk Nf, sɪndəmɤk Nf

cinder-pit *n* the ASH-HOLE beneath a domestic fire V.3.3. sɪndəpɪt Nf*[not a hole]*, sɪndəpɛt Sf

cinder-ruck *n* an ASH-MIDDEN V.1.14. sɪndəɹʊk St

cinders *1. n What do you call the red-hot things that fall through the grate when the fire is burning?* V.4.3. Eng. ⇒ **cherks, cinder, clinkers, cokes, embers, gleed(s), greethagh, grubbles, hot coals, smarags**

2. n ASHES from a cold fire V.4.5. sɪndəz L *[marked ir.r. EMBM]*

circle *1. v* to WHITTLE a stick I.7.19. *-ing* sɑːklɪn Ess *[marked u.r. EMBM]*

2. n a HALO round the moon VII.6.4. sœːkɫ Gl, sœːkəɫ Mon, sɑːkʊ Ess, sʌˑkɫ Ess, sɜːkl Man, sɜᴶːkl La, səkl Y, səkəl Y, səᴶkl L, səᴶtl Db, səɹkl Y, səɹkəl Y, səᵗkɫ He, səᵗkʊ Ha, səːkl Y Ch Db Sa St Wa L Hu Bd, səːtl Nt, səːkɫ Wo Wa Lei Nth Bd Hrt Ess K, səːkʔɫ Ess, səːtɫ Lei, səːkʊ Ess MxL, səᴷːkl Nb, səᴶːkl Ch L, səːɹkl St, səːkɫ Lei C, səᴶːkʊ Sr, səᵗːkl Sa Wo Gl, səᵗːkɫ He Wo Wa Mon Gl O Bk Bd Ess So W K Co D, zəᵗːkɫ So, zəᵗːkɾəɫ D, səᵗːkəɫ Mon, səᵗːkʊɫ Wo Gl, səᵗːkʊ Sr K, səᵗːɾkʊɫ W Brk, səᵗːɾkʊ Brk Sx

cistern *1. n* a CESS-POOL on a farm I.3.11. sɪstən Nf, sɛstən Wa

2. n an artificial cess-pool. sɪstən Nth Nf Sf, sɪstəm Nf, sɪstɪənt Y, sɛstn R, sɛstən Nt Nth Ess

3. n an ASH-MIDDEN at the back of an earth-closet V.1.14. sɛstən Db

4. n a SALTING-TROUGH III.12.5. sɛstən Lei

clabby *1. adj* SAD, describing bread or pastry that has not risen V.6.12. kɫabi D

2. adj STICKY, describing a child's hands VIII.8.14. klæbi So, kɫabi D

clacking *v-ing* GOSSIPING VIII.3.5(a). klækʔən Sf

claden *n* GOOSE-GRASS II.2.5. kɫeːdn Do, kleɪdən Do

clagged up *adj* STICKY, describing a child's hands VIII.8.14. klagd ø·p Nb, klagd ʊp Nb Y*[old]*, tlagd ʊp Cu

claggy *adj* STICKY, describing a child's hands VIII.8.14. klagɪ Nb Cu Du La Y, tlagɪ We La

claggy-buttons *n* GOOSE-GRASS II.2.5. klagɪbʊtnz Du

claggy-jack *n* GOOSE-GRASS II.2.5. klagɪdʒak Nb Du La

clairce *n* DANDRUFF VI.1.3. klæəs He *[queried WMBM]*

clam *1. n* a wooden device for holding a cow's head, ⇐ TETHERING-STAKE I.3.3. klam Wa
2. n a CLAMP in which potatoes are stored out of doors II.4.6. kłam Ha
3. n a stone BRIDGE across a stream IV.1.2. kłam D
4. n a wooden footbridge. kłam D
5. vi to go sticky, referring to meat or fish, ⇐ SPOIL V.7.10. tlam Y

clamber *vt* to CLIMB VIII.7.4. klambəˤ Bk*[old]*, tlɒmbəɹ (+V) Wa

clame *n* the AFTERBIRTH that comes from a cow's uterus after a calf is born III.1.13. kłeːm W

clamed up *adj* STICKY, describing a child's hands VIII.8.14. klɛəmd ʊp Y

clam-house *n* a FASTING-CHAMBER III.11.3. klɛmæʊs St, klɛmaʊs Sa, klɛməʊs He, klɛməs St, tlamaɪs Ch, tlamæʊs Nt, tlaməs Db

clammed *1. adj* EXHAUSTED, describing a tired person VI.13.8. kłɛmd W
2. adj HUNGRY VI.13.9. klɛmd Sa*[old]* St, tlɛmd Db Sa, klamd Y*[very hungry x1]* Db Sa Wo, tlamd La*[starving x1]* Db Nt*[old x1]*; **clammed to (the) death** very hungry klɛmd tə dɛθ St, klɛmd tə dʒɛθ Sa, tlɛmd ˤ diːθ Db, klamd tə dɪəθ La Y, klamd tə tˀ dɪəθ Y, klamd tə djeθ Wo, klamd tə dʒɛθ Wo *['very hungry' gloss assumed here for WMBM]*
3. adj THIRSTY VI.13.10. klɛmd L, tlɛmd La, klamd Y, tlamd Y

clammed out *adj* HUNGRY VI.13.9. klamd uːt Y*[old]*

clammed up *adj* THIRSTY VI.13.10. klɛmd ʊp Y

clammer *n* a wooden footbridge, ⇐ BRIDGE IV.1.2. klaməˤː So, kłaməˤː D

clamming-hole *n* a FASTING-CHAMBER III.11.3. klamɪnɔɪl Y, tlamɪnoːl Db, klamɪnʊəl La

clamming-house *n* a FASTING-CHAMBER III.11.3. tlɛmmɪnɛʊs Db, klɛmɪŋgæʊs St, klɛmɪnæʊs Sa St, klɛmɪnaʊs Sa, klɛmɪnaɪs Ch, tlɛmɪnaʊs Db, klamɪnɛʊs Wo

clamming-pen *n* a FASTING-CHAMBER III.11.3. klɛmɪnpɛn St, klamɪnpɛn La, klammɪnpɛn Y *[see note at fasting-chamber]*

clamming-yard *n* a FASTING-CHAMBER III.11.3. klɛmɪnjaˤːɖ Sa *[marked u.r. WMBM]*

clammish *adj* HUNGRY VI.13.9. klamɪʃ Y

clammy *1. adj* SAD, describing bread or pastry that has not risen V.6.12. kłami W
2. adj STICKY, describing a child's hands VIII.8.14. kłæːmi D, klami So

clamp *1. n* When you store the potatoes in the fields for the winter, where do you put them? II.4.6. klɛmp Ess Sr K, klæmp O Nf Sf Bk Ess MxL So Brk Sr K Ha Sx, *pl* klæmps Man, klæːmp Hrt Brk K, tlæmp Nf, klamp Cu Wo L Nth C Nf Bk Hrt So, *pl* klamps Nb Sa, kłamp W D Do Ha, tlamp We La Db Hrt, klɒmp Wo Sx, klʌmp He Mon Ha, tlʌmp Nf, kləmp Sx; **potato-clamp** *pl* tɛɪtəᴶklɛmps Sr. ⇒ **bank, bury, butt, camp, cave, clam,** *clump,* **couch** ⇒ **cwtsh, cramp, cwtsh, foss, grave, hale, heap, hill, hod, hog, hole, pie, pile, pit, potato-bury, potato-camp, potato-cave,** *potato-*clamp, **potato-grave, potato-hale, potato-heap, potato-hog, potato-hole, potato-pie, potato-pile, potato-pit, potato-stack, potato-tump, rick, stack, trench, tump**
2. n a sliding RING to which a tether is attached in a cow-house I.3.5. klamp Y St

clam-pen *n* a FASTING-CHAMBER III.11.3. tlampɛn Db Nt *[see note at fasting-chamber]*

clap *n* a CLOT OF COW-DUNG II.1.6. tlap We

clap-post *n* the SHUTTING-POST of a gate IV.3.4. klæppoust Nf, klappɔʊst L Hu, tlappɔʊst Nth, klappɔʊs L, klappʌʊst L, klappoːst Nt, tlappoːst Nt, klappoʊst C, tlappoːᵁst Db Nt, klappʊəst L, tlappʊəst Nt L, klappʊəs L

clap(s) *n* a wooden device with two upright pieces between which a cow's neck was held in a cow-house, ⇐ TETHER I.3.4.
no -s: klap Nth Bk
-s: klaps Bk
pl: klapsɪz Bk

clap-stump *n* the SHUTTING-POST of a gate IV.3.4. klapstʊmp Ch, tlapstʊmp Db

clapper *n* the SHUTTING-POST of a gate IV.3.4. klapə Y

clapping-gate *n* the SHUTTING-POST of a gate IV.3.4. tlapɪngɪt Ch

clapping-post *n* the SHUTTING-POST of a gate IV.3.4. klɛpɪnpʊst Sr, tlæpnpost Nf, tlæpnpoːs Nf, klæpɪnpoʊst Nf, klæpʔɪnpoust Nf, klæpʔnpoust Nf, tlæpʔɪnpous Nf, klæpnpoˑʊs Nf, tlæpɪnpous Nf, klæpnpʊst Sf, klapɪnpɒst Y, tlapɪnpɒst Y, klapɪnpɔst Y, klapɪnpɔʊst L, tlapɪnpɔʊst Hu, klapɪnpɔʊs Lei R, klapɪnpʌʊs C, klapɪnpoːst Sa, tlapɪnpoːst Ch, klapɪnpoːs Sa, tlapɪnpoːs Ch, klapɪnpoʊst St Wa Bd, tlapɪnpoʊst Nth, klapɪnpoʊs Lei, klapɪnpʊəst Y

clapping-stump *n* the SHUTTING-POST of a gate IV.3.4. klapɪnstʊmp St

clart *1. vt* to DIRTY a floor V.2.8. klaːt Nb, klaᵷːt Nb
2. adj STICKY, describing a child's hands VIII.8.14. klaːt Y

clarted up *adj* STICKY, describing a child's hands VIII.8.14. klaːtɪd ʊp Cu Y, tlaːtʔt ʊp We

clarth *n* DANDRUFF VI.1.3. klaːθ He *[queried WMBM]*

clart(s) *n* MUD VII.6.17.
no -s: klaːt Du
-s: klɛərts Cu, klæːts Du, klaʙts Nb, klaːts Nb Du, klaᴮːts Nb*[thick xl]* Du

clarty *1. adj* BOGGY IV.1.8. klaːtɪ Nb
2. adj STICKY, describing a child's hands VIII.8.14. klatɪ L*[rare]*, klaʔɪ L, klaɹtɪ Y, klaːtɪ Cu La Y*[old xl]* L, tlaːtɪ We La, klaᴮːtɪ Nb

clat *1. n* a CLOT OF COW-DUNG II.1.6. *pl* klæts Brk, klat Bk, *pl* klats Nth; **clat of dung** klat ə dʌŋ W
2. v to break up dry cow-dung and spread it as manure. *-ing* klaʔɪn Bk
3. v to spread cow-dung after rain. *-ing* tlatɪn Wa
4. n a GOSSIP VIII.3.5(b). klat La

clat-can *n* a GOSSIP VIII.3.5(b). klatkan La

clatch *n* a BROOD of chickens IV.6.12. klatʃ La L, tlatʃ La Db Nt

clatted *1. adj* TANGLED, describing hair VI.2.5. kɬatəd Co
2. adj STICKY, describing a child's hands VIII.8.14. kladt La

clatted hedge* *n* a turf bank with a hedge on top, ⇐ HEDGE IV.2.1(a). kɬatəd ɛdʒ D

clatted up *adj* TANGLED, describing hair VI.2.5. kɬatɪd ʌp D, kɬatəd ʌp D

clatter *n* CHAT VIII.3.4. klætʔə MxL

clatting *v-ing* GOSSIPING VIII.3.5(a). klatɪn La

clatty *adj* TANGLED, describing hair VI.2.5. klatɪ So, kɬatɪ D Ha

clat up *vtphr* to fill gaps in a hedge-bank or hedge with turfs, brushwood, or similar material, ⇐ to PLASH IV.2.4. kɬat (...) ʌp D

claumed up *adj* STICKY, describing a child's hands VIII.8.14. klɔːmd ʊp L

claumy *adj* STICKY, describing a child's hands VIII.8.14. klɔːmi So*[old]*

claw *1. n* a PRONG of a fork I.7.10. *pl* klaːz Nb, klɔː Co
2. n the HOOF of a cow III.2.8(a). kɬæː W, klɔː So
3. vt to PULL somebody's hair VI.2.8. klɑː O

clawed *adj* CLOVEN, describing the hoof of a cow III.2.8(b). kɬɔːd W Co

claw-foot *adj* having a CLOVEN hoof, describing a cow III.2.8(b). kɬʊfʊt W, kɬɔːvʏt D, kɬɔːvʊt W, kɬɔːvʏt D

claw-footed *adj* having a CLOVEN hoof, describing a cow III.2.8(b). klɔːfʊtɪd Sx, klɔːvʊtɪd So W, kɬɔːvʏtɪd Co D

claws *1. n* the HOOF of a cow III.2.8(a). klɔːz Y
2. npl the separate parts of a cow's cloven hoof. *sg* klɔː Y, tlɔːz Ch, klɔˑəz Y

3. adj **in claws** CLOVEN, describing the hoof of a cow III.2.8(b). ɪn klɔːz Nf

clay *1. n* *What do you call that heavy sticky earth which doesn't let water through easily?* IV.4.2. Eng. ⇒ **blue-bungham, blue-clay, brick-earth, gault, loam, marl, ooze, puddle, pug**; ⇒ also **clitey, puddle in**
2. n EARTH VIII.5.8. klɛə Y*[layer below surface]*

clean *1.1. v* **clean, clean and top** to TOP AND TAIL swedes II.4.3. **clean** kliːn Wa O Hrt, tliːn Nth, *-ing* kliːnɪn Brk, kleːn Ch O, klɛɪn Wa; **clean and top** kliːn ən tɑp Nth, kliːn ən tɒp Nt, kliːn ən tɒp Nt L
1.2. vt to top and tail swedes. **clean** kliːn O L Lei, tliːn L*[old]* Nth, *-ing* kliˑnən Ess, klɪˈən L, kleːn O, kɬeːn D, kɬɛɪn D; **clean and top** kliːn ən tɒp Wa *[marked ir.r. EMBM]*
2. vt to TOP-AND-TAIL gooseberries V.7.23. tlᵊɪən Ch*[old]*, kleːn Ch, klᵉɪn Du; **clean the tails** klɪˈən ðə tɛˈəlz L *[queried u.r. WMBM]*
3.1. vt to REMOVE *STALKS* from currants V.7.24. kliːn Nb Cu Du Mon Lei R, tliːn Du, *-ing* kɬeːnɪn W, tleːn Ch, *-ing* klɛɪnɪn Y, tlɛɪn Cu, tlɔɪn Y
3.2. v to remove stalks. kliːn Nb Du La R, tliːn Cu Ch
4. v to WINNOW II.8.4. kliːn Nf Bd, *-ing* kliːnɪŋ K, *-ing* kliːnɪn K Ha, *-ing* klɛɪnɪn Ess
5. v to CLEAR grass at the edges of a field II.9.5. kliːn L
6. v to TRIM hedges IV.2.3. *-ing* klˡiːnɪn K
7.1. v to DITCH IV.2.11. kliːn Sa St Sf, *-ing* klɪiːnɪn Ess, klɪən L, *-ing* tlɪənɪn Nt, tlᵊɪən Ch
7.2. vt to ditch. kliːn Nb, *-ing* kliːnɪn La, kɬiːnən Co, kɬeːnɪn D, kɬeːnən Co, kleɪn Man
8. vt to STRAIN milk V.5.2. kliːn Y, klɪən Y

clean-cut hilt* *n* a castrated female pig, ⇐ HOG III.8.8. kleːnkʊt ɪɫt Gl

cleaning(s) *n* the AFTERBIRTH that comes from a cow's uterus after a calf is born III.1.13.
no -s: kliːnɪn Nb Cu We Y Sa Mon O Nth Nf Bk So Sr Sx, kɬiːnɪn Do Ha, tliːnɪn Cu We Nth Nf, kliːnən Nb Du C Sf Ha, kɬiːnən D, klɪənɪn La Y Db, tlɪənɪn La, kleːnɪn O So, kɬeːnɪn D, tleːnɪn Du Gl, kleːŋɪn Sa, kɬeːnən D, tlɛɪnɪn La, klɛɪnən Du, klɔɪnɪn Y, tlɔɪnɪn Y
-s: kliːnɪnz Sa Wo Mon Gl O Nf Sf Bk Ess MxL So Brk Sx, kɬiːnɪnz Mon O W, tliːnɪnz Nf, kliːnɪns Man, kliːnənz Nb, kɬiːnənz Do, kliːnəns Man, tlɪənɪnz La, kleːnənz Ha, klɛnɪnz Ess, klɛɪnɪnz Wa

cleanings *n* STRIPPINGS, the last drops at milking III.3.4. klˡiːnɪnz Gl

clean off *vtphr* to TOP AND TAIL swedes II.4.3. kliːn ... ɔːf R, kɬɛɪn ... ɔːf D *[marked ir.r. EMBM]*

clean out *1.1.* *vphr* to DITCH IV.2.11. kliːn aɪt Ch, tliːn aʊt Ch, -*ing* kliːnɪn aʊt W, kliːᵊn əʊt W

1.2. *vtphr* to ditch. kliːn ... ɛʊt Ch, -*ing* kliənɪn ɛət Y, kɬeːn (...) œʏt D, kɬeːn (...) æʏt D, kɬeːn æʊt D, kɬeːn ... æʊt Ha, kliːn ... æʊt Wa Lei So, -*ing* kliːnɪn ... æʊt Ha, tliːn ... æʊt Nt, kɬiːn (...) æʊt Ha, kliən ... æʊt Y, kliː ... æʊtʔ K, kliin ... ɛʊt K, kliən ... aːt Y, kliːn ... aʊt Sa, -*ing* kliːnɪn ... aʊt La Ch, tliːn aʊt We, tlᵊɪən ... aʊt Ch, kleɪn ... aʊt Y, -*ing* kleɪnɪn ... aʊt La, kliːn uːt Y, kliːn ... uːt Nb Cu, -*ing* kliːnɪn ... uːt Y, tliːn uːt Du, tliːn ... uːt Cu, kliən ... uːt Y, kleɪn (...) ᵊuːt Du, kliːn ... əut Mon, kɬiːᵊn ... əʊt W

2. *vtphr* to RAKE ashes in a domestic fire V.3.8(b). *prppl* kliːnɪn ... ɛuːt Wo

clean pig *1.* *n* a HOG III.8.8. kliən pɪg Y

2. *n* a castrated female pig. kliːn pɪg Db

clean(s) *n* the AFTERBIRTH that comes from a cow's uterus after a calf is born III.1.13.

no *s*: kliːn Nth Hu C Bd Ess, klɛn He Mon

-*s*: kliːnz Lei

cleanse *n* the AFTERBIRTH that comes from a cow's uterus after a calf is born III.1.13. klɛnz Du St He L Lei Bk Bd Hrt Ess So Sr K Sx, kɬɛnz W, tlɛnz Nth

cleansing(s) *n* the AFTERBIRTH that comes from a cow's uterus after a calf is born III.1.13.

no -*s*: klɛnzɪn Nb Cu La Y Ch Db Sa St He Wo Wa Mon Gl O Nt L Nth Hu Bk Ess So Brk Sr K Ha Sx, kɬɛnzɪn He W Co D Do Ha, tlɛnzɪn We Db Sa Wa Nt L, klɛnzɪŋ St, klɛnsɪn Y Wa, klɛnʒɪn Wo, klɛnzən Du Do, klɛnzn Nb Do, kɬɛnzən D Ha, klɛnsən Man, klanzɪn Sa St Wa, tlanzɪn Ch Db

-*s*: klɛnzɪnz Y Sa St L Lei R Bk Ess K, klɛnzənz Ess, klɛənzn̩z Ess

clean up *1.* *vphr* to CLEAR grass at the edges of a field II.9.5. kliːn ʌp Sf

2. *vtphr* to DITCH IV.2.11. -*ing* kɬiːnən ʌp Co

3. *vtphr* to REMOVE *STALKS* from currants V.7.24. kləɪn ... ʊp Y

4.1. *vtphr* to CLEAR the table after a meal V.8.14. kliːn ... ʊp St, kɬiːn ... ʌp Do

4.2. *vphr* to clear the table. kɬeːn ʌp Co

5. *vtphr-3sg* she [a tidy girl] will COLLECT her toys VIII.8.15. kɬeːn ... ʌp W

clear *1.* *v Your mowing machine may leave grass along the edges of the field; so what do you do? (before April 1954: ... what do you do to clear them?)* II.9.5.

vt: klɪɹ (+V) Ess, klɪəɹ (+V) Wo L, klɪəɹ Bd, klɪəᵗɽ (+V) Wo*[with scythe]*, kɬɪəɽ (+V) O

v: klɪə Sa L Sf Ess, -*ing* klɪəɹɪn K, klɪəᴵ La, -*ing* klɪəᴵɹɪn Brk, klɪəᶜ Sa

⇒ **back-cut, back-hack, back-swath, badge, badge out, badge** *the sides* **out, belt, blag round, brink-mow, brog, brush, brush down, brush round, chop** *the edges* **out, chop** *the hedge-bottom*

out, chop *the hedge-sides* out, clean, clean up, clear off, clear out, clear *the outside*, clear up, cut, cut *edges* out, cut *(it) off the borders*, cut *(it) out of the edges*, cut off, cut out, cut out *the backswath*, cut *roads*, cut round, cut *round the edges*, cut *the back-ground* out, cut *the back* out, cut *the back-swath*, cut *the back-swathe*, cut *the back-swath(s)* out, cut *the brink*, cut *the corners* out, cut *the dike-backs*, cut *the dike-backs* out, cut *the edge(s)* out, cut *the headland*, cut *the hedge-backs*, cut *the hedge-sides* out, cut *the oddments*, cut *the road,* cut up *round the edges*, cut up *what's left*, dike-pike, edge out, fash, fetch off, fetch out, fetch out *the mear*, finish, finish off, frim, *go round a-snagging*, hack, hack off, hack out, hack *the dike-backs*, hack *the dike-backs* out, hack *the sides* out, hag out, *have a* back-cut, hob, hob out, hob over, hob round, hob *the sides and corners*, hob *the sides* out, hob up, mop off, mow, mow around, mow down, mow off, mow off *the hedge-backs*, mow out, mow out *the margins*, mow round, mow *the back* out, mow *the back-swath*, mow *the baulks*, mow *the baulks* out, mow *the corners*, mow *the corners and edges*, mow *the corners* out, mow *the dike-back* out, mow *the dike-backs*, mow *the dike-backs* out, mow *the edge* out, mow *the hedge-backs*, mow *the hedge-backs* out, mow *the hedge-bottom* out, mow *the hedge-bottoms*, mow *the hedge-sides* out, mow *them baulks* off, mow *the outside(s)*, mow *the reans*, open out, outside-mow, pare out, pare out *the headland(s)*, pike, pike out, pike *round the edges and dikes*, pike *the sides*, point out, scythe, scythe-mow, scythe *the back*, scythe *the corner*, scythe *the corner and the hedgerows*, scythe *the headlands* out, snag, snag *the wall-bottom*, sneck, sniddle, swap, take *a swathe* away, take out *the dike-back(s)*, take *the back* off, take *the back-swathe* off, take *the dike-backs* out, trim, trim out, trim round, trim *round the edges*, trim up, trut, unedge; ⇒ also **brink, dike-back(s)**

2. *v And after the meal, when you remove the things, what do you say you do?* V.8.14. Eng exc. We. ⇒ **clean** *it* **up, clean** *the table* **up, clean up,** *clear away, clear en away, clear it, clear it away, clear it off, clear it up, clear off, clear table, clear the dishes, clear them, clear them away, clear them off, clear the table, clear the table off, clear the things away, clear up, clear up the table,* **red, red** *the dishes,* **rid off, rid** *the table,* **shift, side, side** *all away,* **side away, siden, side** *table,* **side** *the pots away,* **side** *the table,* **side** *the things away,* **side up, strip** *the table [unclear as to whether vv for which no obj is supplied refer to clearing of table or dishes etc.]*

3.1. *v* to DITCH IV.2.11. -*ing* klɪəɹɪn MxL, klɪəᶜ Sa

3.2. *vt* to ditch. klɪəɹ Y, klɪəᴵ La

4. adv VERY VIII.3.2. klɪəᴵ La

5. vt-3sg she [a tidy girl] will COLLECT her toys VIII.8.15. klɪə Ess

clearance *n* the AFTERBIRTH that comes from a cow's uterus after a calf is born III.1.13. klɪəɹəns, klɪəɹənz Sf

clear away *vtphr-3sg* she [i.e. a tidy girl] will COLLECT her toys VIII.8.15. klɪəᴮ ... əweːᵊ Nb, klɪəɹ (+V) ... əwɛə L Y

clearing(s) *n* the AFTERBIRTH that comes from a cow's uterus after a calf is born III.1.13.

no -s: klɪɹɪn Ess

-s: klɪəɹɪnz Ess

clear off *1. vtphr* to CLEAR grass at the edges of a field II.9.5. klɪəɹ (+V) ... ɒf Y

2. imp GO AWAY! VIII.7.9(a). klɪəɹ ɒf La Y St Wa Lei K, tlɪəɹ ɒf Db, klɪəɹ ɔf La Y L, klɪəɹ ɔːf Wa Mon Gl Lei R C Nf Sf Bd Hrt Ess K, tlɪəɹ ɔːf Nth Nf, klɪəɹ ʊəf L, klɪəᴵɹ ɒːf Sr Sx, klɪəᴵɹ ɔːf Sx, klɪəᶜ ɒf Brk, klɪəᶜɽ ɒˑf W, klɪəᶜɽ ɔːf Sa Wo Wa So, kɬɪəɽ ɒːf Ha, kɬɪəᶜːɽ ɔːf So W, kɬɪəɽ ɔːf O, kɬɪəᶜːɽ ɔːf W D Do Ha, tlɛɪəɹ ɒf Ch; **clear off of here** kɬɪəᶜːɽ ɔːf ə jəᶜː Do; **clear off from here** kɬɪəᶜːɽ ɔːf vɾəm jəᶜː Do; **clear off with you** klɪə ɒf wɪ jə St

clear out *1. vtphr* to CLEAR grass at the edges of a field II.9.5. klɪəɽ (+V) ... ɛʊt Sr

2.1. vphr to DITCH IV.2.11. -*ing* klɪəᴵɹɪn ɛʊt Ha, tlɪəɹ ɛʊt Db

2.2. vtphr to ditch. kɬɪəᶜːɽ œvd D, -*ing* klɪˑəɹɪn ... aʊt L, -*ing* tlɪəɹɪn ... əʊt Y

3. imp GO AWAY! VIII.7.9(a). klɪəɹ ɛʊt Hu Nf Ess MxL K, klɪəɹ æːt Ch, klɪəɹ æʊt Man Lei, klɪˑəɹ aʊt L, klɪəɹ uːt Y[*to lads x1*], klɪəɹ əʊt He K, klɪəᶜːɽ əʊt W Do, kɬɪəᶜːɽ œʏt D, kɬɪəᶜːɽ æʏt D, kɬɪəᶜːɽ æʊt W; **clear on out** kɬɪəᶜːɽ ɔːn æʏt D; **clear out of it** kɬɪəᶜːɽ æʏt oʊ ət So, kɬɪəᶜːɽ æʏd ʌv ɪt Co

clear up *1. vphr* to CLEAR grass at the edges of a field II.9.5. -*ing* klɪəɹɪn ʌp Brk

2.1. vtphr-3sg she [i.e. a tidy girl] will COLLECT her toys VIII.8.15. klɪɹ (+V) ... ʌp Ess, *3prsg* klɪiəz ... ʌp Ess, klɪəɹ (+V) ... ʌp He Nf Ess, klɪəɹ ... ʌp Hu C, *3prsg* klɪəᴵz ... ʌp Sr, klɪˑəɹ (+V) ... ʋp Nf, klɪə ... ʊp Wa, klɪəɹ (+V) ... ʊp Y Nt L Nth, tlɪˑəɹ (+V) ... ʊp L, kɬɪəᶜːɽ (+V) ... ʌp Sa He So, kɬɪəᶜːɽ (+V) ... ʌp W, klɛˑəɹ (+V) ... ʌp C, klɛˑəɹ (+V) ... ʌp Nf

2.2. vphr-3sg she will collect. klɪəɹ ʌp Nth K, klɪəɹ ʊp Lei

cleat *n* a metal LINCH-PIN holding a wheel on a cart I.9.12. klɛt Sa

cleat(s) *n* COLT'S-FOOT II.2.7.

no -s: pl kliːts Cu, klɪət Y L, *pl* tlɪəts Y

-s: klɪəks Y, klɛːps Nt [*kleːps marked EMBM as a possible error for* kleːts]

cleaty *adj* SAD, describing bread or pastry that has not risen V.6.12. kɬiːti D

cleaved *adj* CLOVEN, describing the hoof of a cow III.2.8(b). klɛɪvd Lei

cleaver *n* a TUSSOCK of grass II.2.9. klɪivəᴵ K [*probably a type of grass*]

cleavers *n* GOOSE-GRASS II.2.5. klɪːvəz Y Lei Bk, klɪivəᴵz Brk, klɪvəᶜɽz Sx, klɪiːvəᶜz Brk, kɬiːvəᶜːz Ha, tliːvəᶜːz Sa

cleaves* *n* the HOOF of a cow III.2.8(a). kliˑvz Nf

clecking *n* a BROOD of chickens IV.6.12. klɛkən Nb

clee *n* the HOOF of a cow III.2.8(a). klɪu Y, klɪə Y, tlɪə We, klɛɪ Wa; **cow clee** kaʊ klɪə Y

cleek *n* the vertical part of a crane over a domestic fire, consisting of a *BAR* or *CHAIN* and a HOOK(/*CROOK*) V.3.5b+c. klɪːk Nb[*old*]

cleeky-feet *adj* PIGEON-TOED VI.10.4. klɪkɪfiːt Nb

clees *1. n* the HOOF of a cow III.2.8(a). kliːz L Lei, klɪʊs La, klɪˑəz L, klɛɪz Wo Nth

2. npl the separate parts of a cow's cloven hoof. kliːz St He Wo Mon, *sg* kliː L, tliːz Db, *sg* klɪə La Y, klɪəs Y, klɪəz Y, tlɪəz La, *sg* klɪəɹ La, kleːz Sa, tleːz Sa, klɛɪz Wa, tlɛɪz Wa

3. n **in clees** CLOVEN, describing the hoof of a cow III.2.8(b). ɪn tlɛˑəz Nf, klɛɪz Lei

cleet* *n* the HOOF of a cow III.2.8(a). klɪət La

cleeted *adj* CLOVEN, describing the hoof of a cow III.2.8(b). kliːtɪd St

cleets* *1. n* the HOOF of a cow III.2.8(a). kliːts St, klɪəts Nb

2. npl the separate parts of a cow's cloven hoof. klɪəts Cu Du

cleeve *1. n* a SLOPE IV.1.10. kliːv So, kɬiːv W D[*may be steep*] [*marked prob ir.r. BM, prob = 'steep hill' Edd*]

2. adj STEEP, describing a hill IV.1.11. kliːv So

3. n a steep slope. kliːv So

clef *n* a CUTTING of hay 3 feet square II.9.15. kɬɛf O

cleft *adj* CLOVEN, describing the hoof of a cow III.2.8(b). klɛft Nb Wa O Sf Bk Ess Sx, tlɛft Nt

clent-nail *n* a LINCH-PIN holding a wheel on a cart I.9.12. kɬɛntnɛɪt Ha

clerk *n* a SEXTON VIII.5.4. klaːk Wa Sf, klaᶜːk Sa, klaːk Nf, kləᴵːk O, kləᶜːk Wo Gl [*marked ir.r. EMBM, but note at Nf.13 suggests relevance*]

cletch *n* a BROOD of chickens IV.6.12. klɛtʃ Du Y[*old x1*] L Lei, tlɛtʃ Cu Y Db Nt L

cletching *n* a BROOD of chickens IV.6.12. klɛtʃən Du

clever-clumsy *adj* CLUMSY, describing a person VI.7.14. kɬɪvəᶜːkɬʌmzi D

clevis *n* the T-SHAPED PLOUGH-BEAM END of a horse-drawn plough I.8.5. klɪvɪs Y, tlɪvɪ Db, klɛvɪs St, tlɛɪvz Db

clew* *n* the HOOF of a cow III.2.8(a). klɪu Y

clews* *n* the HOOF of a cow III.2.8(a). klɪʊs La

clibby *1. adj* SAD, describing bread or pastry that has not risen V.6.12. kɬɪbi D
2. adj STICKY, describing a child's hands VIII.8.14. kɬɪbi Co D

click *1. adj* LEFT-HANDED VI.7.13(a). kɬɪk Co
2. n a LEFT-HANDED person VI.7.13(a). kɬɪk Co

clicking *vt-ing* PULLING his ear VI.4.4. klɪkɪn Nb

click-up *v* to hiccup, ⇐ HICCUPING VI.8.4. klɪkʊp L

clicky *1. adj* LEFT-HANDED VI.7.13(a). kɬɪki Co
2. n a LEFT-HANDED person VI.7.13(a). kɬɪki Co

clicky-handed *adj* LEFT-HANDED VI.7.13(a). kɬɪki-andəd Co

clide *1. n* GOOSE-GRASS II.2.5. kɬæːd D, klæɪd So, kɬaɪd D
2. n a pocket, ⇐ POCKETS VI.14.15. klɒɪd So

cliden *n* GOOSE-GRASS II.2.5. klaɪdɪn So, klɒɪdn So, kləɪdn So

clider(s) *n* GOOSE-GRASS II.2.5.
no -s: kɬæːdəᵗ: D, klæɪdəᵗ: So, klɒɪdəᵗ: So, kɬɒɪdəᵗ: So W Ha, gɬɒɪdəᵗ: Co, klɒɪdəᵗ Ha, klʌɪdəˈ Sr, kɬəɪdəᵗ: W
-s: klæɪdəᵗz̨ Sr, kɬɒɪdəᵗ:z̨ Ha, kləɪdəᵗɽz̨ Sx, kɬəɪdəᵗ:z̨ W

clidgy *adj* SAD, describing bread or pastry that has not risen V.6.12. kɬɪdʒi Co D

cliff *n* a HALO round the moon VII.6.4. klɪf Ess

clift *n* a HALO round the moon VII.6.4. klɪft Ess

clifty *adj* STEEP, describing a hill IV.1.11. klɪfti So

climb *vt If a boy wanted to get to the top of a tree, he'd have to ... it.* VIII.7.4. Eng. ⇒ **clamber, climb to, climb up, climmer, climmer up, cline, get up, lumber up, scrawl up, scrawm up, scrim up, shin up, speel, speel up, swarm, swarm it, swarm up**

climbing-stile *n* a STILE with steps IV.2.9. klaɪmɪnstɛɪl Db

climb-stile *n* a STILE with steps IV.2.9. tlaɪmstaɪl Db*[with rails x1]*

climb to *vtphr* to CLIMB VIII.7.4. klaɪm tu: He

climb up *vtphr* to CLIMB VIII.7.4. klɪm œːp Nb, klɪm ʌp So*[old x1]* Do, kɬɪm ʌp W Co Do, klɪm ʊp La Y, tlɪm ʊp We Y, kɬæːm ʌp D, klaɪm ʊp La, tlaɪm ʊp Y, klɑːm ʊp Y, klɑɪm ʌp Nf Ess MxL, klɑɪm ʊp Y, klɒɪm ʊp St, kləɪm ʌp He Mon Gl Sx, kɬəɪm ʌp Mon, kləɪːm ʊp Wo

climmer *vt* to CLIMB VIII.7.4. kɬɪmbəᵗ: D

climmer up *vtphr* to CLIMB VIII.7.4. klɪməᵗ:ɽ ʌp So*[old x1]*

cline *vt* to CLIMB VIII.7.4. klæɪn So

clingy *1. adj* SAD, describing bread or pastry that has not risen V.6.12. kɬɪŋi W Ha

2. adj STICKY, describing a child's hands VIII.8.14. klɪŋi So

clinker-bells *n* ICICLES VII.6.11. klɪŋkəᵗ:bɛɫz So, kɬɪŋkəᵗ:bɛɫz Do, klɪŋkəᵗ:bəɫz So

clinkers *1. n* CINDERS V.4.3. klɪŋkɨs Nf, klɪŋkəˠz K
2. n ICICLES VII.6.11. klɪŋkəᵗ:z̨ So, kɬɪŋkəᵗ:z̨ Do

clip *1. vt* to MARK the ears of sheep with a hole to indicate ownership III.7.9. klɪp La Sr
2. v to TRIM hedges IV.2.3. *-ing* klɪpɪn Ch MxL Sr, *-ing* klɪppɪn La, *-ing* tlɪpɪn Y
3. vt to REMOVE *STALKS* from currants using scissors V.7.24. *-ing* klɪpɪn Y
4. n a haircut, ⇐ *GET YOUR* HAIR *CUT* VI.2.2. klɪp Man L

clipped sheep *n* a sheep from its first to its second shearing, ⇐ GIMMER III.6.5. klɪpt ʃiːp L

clipper *n* the CRUPPER of the harness of a cart-horse I.5.9. kɬɪpəᵗ: W, kɬɛpəᵗ: W

clippers *1. n* hand-operated SHEARS used to cut wool from sheep III.7.7. klɪpəz Ch St Mon Hu Ess, tlɪpəz Y, klɪpəˠz La, tlɪpəɹz La, kɬɪpəᵗ:z̨ Co
2. n electrically-operated SHEARS III.7.7. klɪpəz MxL, tlɪpəz Ch, klɪpəᵗz̨ Bk Ha, klɪpəᵗ:z̨ So

clipping *1. v-ing* SHEARING sheep III.7.6. klɪpɪn Nb Cu La Y Ch*[with machine]* St Nt L Lei Nf MxL Sr K, *no -ing* klɪp Ch Sa, klɪʔpɪn Y, tlɪpɪn We La Y Db Nt L Nf, klɪpɪn Nf, klɪpʔn Nf, klɪpən Nb Cu Du Y L, tlɪpən Cu Du We, kɬɪpən Co*[modern]*, klɛpən Man
2. vt-ing PULLING his ear VI.4.4. klɪpɪn St

clipping-bench *n* a SHEARING-TABLE III.7.8. klɪpɪnbɛnʃ Y

clipping-form *n* a SHEARING-TABLE III.7.8. klɪpɪnfɔːm Cu

clipping-stock *n* a SHEARING-TABLE III.7.8. klɪpɪnstɒk La

clipping-stool *n* a SHEARING-TABLE III.7.8. klɪpɪnstɪyl Cu, *pl* klɪpɪnstɪəlz Y

clit *adj* SAD, describing bread or pastry that has not risen V.6.12. klɪt So, kɬɪt D Do

clitch *n* the GROIN VI.9.4. kɬɪtʃ W

clitchy *adj* STICKY, describing a child's hands VIII.8.14. kɬɪtʃi D

clite *n* GOOSE-GRASS II.2.5.
no -s: klɒɪt O, kɬɔɪt O
-s: klɒʊts W, klɔʊts Gl, klʌʊts Gl, kɬəʊts W

clitey* *adj* clayey, ⇐ CLAY IV.4.2. klɒɪti K

clitheroe-bill *n* a BILLHOOK IV.2.6. klɪðəɹəbil La

clitted up *adj* TANGLED, describing hair VI.2.5. kɬɪtɪd ʌp D

clitter-balls *n* SHEEP-DUNG II.1.7. klɪtəˠbɔəlz Ha

clittied *adj* SAD, describing bread or pastry that has not risen V.6.12. klɪtiːd So

clitty *1. adj* SAD, describing bread or pastry that has not risen V.6.12. klɪti So, kɬɪti W, kɬɪti Do

2. adj TANGLED, describing hair VI.2.5. kɬiːti D, klɪti W Ha, kɬɪti W Do Ha

cliver(s) *n* GOOSE-GRASS II.2.5.
no -s: klæɪvəˈ K, klaɪvə Sr, klɑɪvəˡ K, klɔɪvə Ess, klɔɪvəˡ Sx, klɔɪvəˡ Sx
-s: tlaɪvəz Y, tlɑːvəz Y, klɔɪvəˠz Brk Sr, klɔɪvəˡz̥ O Bk Sx

clives *n* GOOSE-GRASS II.2.5. klaɪvz So

clob *n* the CLOG on a horse's tether I.4.3. klɒb So

clobber *n* ORDINARY CLOTHES VI.14.20. klɒbr̩ O, klɒbə Ess; **old clobber** oʊɫ klɒbəˡ Bk; **week-a-days clobber** wɪkədɛɪz klɒbə Ess

clock* *vi* to be RESTIVE, describing a horse III.5.6. *prppl* klɒkɪn Y

clocker *1. n* a RESTIVE horse III.5.6. klɒkəˈ Y
2. n a BROODY HEN IV.6.7. klɒkɔˠ Nb Du, klɒkə Nb Cu Du La Y, tlɒkə Du We La Y, klɒkər Cu, klɒkəˠ Nb Du, klɒkəɹ La Y, tlɒkəɹ Cu La, klɒkəˈ La, tlɒkəˈ La, klɒkɔˠ Nb, klɒkə Y, klɒkəɹ La Y, klɔkəˈ La Y

clocking *n* a SNACK VII.5.11. klɒkɪn St, tlɒkɪn Db

clocking hen *n* a BROODY HEN IV.6.7. klɒkɪn ɛn Y, tlɒkɪn ɛn Y, klɒkən ɛn Y

clocks *n* a SNACK VII.5.11. klɒks Y

clocky hen *n* a BROODY HEN IV.6.7. klɒki hɛˈn Man*[old]*

clod *vt* to DIRTY a floor V.2.8. klɒd Sr

clodding *v-ing* THROWING a stone VIII.7.7. klɒddɪn La, tlɒddɪn La, klɒdɪn La

clodding off *vtphr-ing* UNLOADING sheaves from a wagon II.6.8. *no -ing* klɒd ... ɒf La

clodhopper *n* a CARTMAN on a farm I.2.2. klɒdɒpə He

clods *n* MUD VII.6.17. klɒdz Sx

clog *1. n [Show a picture of a stable.] What do you call this, at the end of the tether?* I.4.3. klœːg Nb Du, klæg Man, klɒg Nb Cu La Y Sa Mon O Nf Bk Ess Sr, kɬɒg Ha, tlɒg Du We Y Nt Nf, klɔg Y L Sf Hrt Ess Sr, tlɔg Du La. ⇒ **ball, block, bob, bobbin, bob-weight, boss, buckle, chock, chog(s), chuck, clob, dog, dropper, halter-plug, hob-wood, horse-clog, knob ⇒ nob, lob, log, logger, lug, manger-block, nob, nodge, nog, noggin, nug, plug, slip-block, tethering-nob, tie-log, weight, woblet; ⇒ also timbern**

2. n a log of firewood. *pl* klɒgz Y
3. n a chock placed behind and under a wheel to prevent a cart from going backwards on a hill, ⇐ PROP/CHOCK I.11.2. klɒg We, klɔg Ess, tlɔg Y
4. n a DRAG used to slow a cart I.11.3. klɔg Ess
5. n a BENCH on which slaughtered sheep are dressed III.12.1. klɔg Y

cloggy *vt* to DIRTY a floor V.2.8. klɒgI Brk*[old]*

clog-iron *n* the T-SHAPED PLOUGH-BEAM END of a horse-drawn plough I.8.5. klɒgɔɪəˡˈn̩ Wa

cloof *n* the HOOF of a cow III.2.8(a). klɪuf Y, klɪuːf Du

cloot *n* the HOOF of a cow III.2.8(a). tlɪʊt Cu, *pl* kløːts Nb

close *1. n* a small field near a farmhouse, larger than a paddock, ⇐ FIELDS I.1.1. kluəs Nb
2. n a FARMYARD I.1.3. kloəs Cu
3. n a PADDOCK I.1.10. klɔːs Sa, klɔːᵁs O, klʌs C, klʌus Bk, tloːs Nt, kloːs O, klous Nth
4. n PASTURE or a hayfield II.1.3. klʌs C
5. n a MEADOW II.9.2. *pl* klʊɪzɪz Y
6. adj SAD, describing bread or pastry that has not risen V.6.12. kɬoːs Ha
7. vt to SHUT a door IX.2.8. klʌuz Ess, klouz Ha
8. adj NEAR IX.2.10. klɒus K Sx, klɔus O Hu, klʌus Bd Hrt Ess, klos Nf, tlos Nf, klɔːs He Gl Bk Do, kɬoːs O W Co Ha, klous St Wa Gl Brk, tlous Nf, klɔːəs So, klʊs Nf Sf, tlʊs Nf, kluəs Y L; **pretty close** pəˡːdɪ klɔːs So; **very close** vɛɹi klʌus Ess, vɛɹi tlos Nf

close again *prep* NEAR IX.2.10. klɔɪs əgeən Y

close at *adj* NEAR IX.2.10. kloːs æt Sa He Wo Mon, klɔːs at Sa, klɔːs ət He, klɔːʊs æt Mon Gl, tloəs at Nb, tlʊəs at Cu Du

close at hand *adj* NEAR IX.2.10. tlʊəs ət and We

close by *1. adj* NEAR IX.2.10. klʌs bɑɪ Ess, kloːs bəɪ So, klɔːᵊs bɒɪ So, klʊs bʌɪ Sf
2. prep near. kluəs bɑɪ Y

close-hand *prep* NEAR IX.2.10. klɔːsand Y

close handy *adj* NEAR IX.2.10. klʌus ændɪ MxL, kloːs ændɪ Mon; **close handy by** kɬoːs ændɪ bɒɪ Co

close here *adj* NEAR IX.2.10. klous ɪəˡ O

close on *adv* ALMOST VII.7.9. kløˈs ɒn Du, klɔɪs ɒn Y, klʌus ɒn Bk, klʌus ɒn MxL, kloːs ɒn O, klʊs ɔːn Sf

close on to *adv* ALMOST VII.7.9. klʌs ɒn tə Sf

closes *1. npl* the FIELDS of a farm I.1.1. *sg* kløːs Nb*[Scots]*, klɒɪzəz Y, klɔɪsɪz Y, klɔɪzɪz Y, *sg* klʌus Bd, *sg* tloːs Nt Nf, kloːᵁzəz Db, *sg* tloːᵁs Nth, *sg* kloəs Cu, *sg* kluːs Y, *sg* kluəs Y, kluəsɪz Y L, tluəsɪz Nt, *sg* tluəs Y, kluəzɪz L, tluəzɪz L
2. vi-3prsg school FINISHES VIII.6.2(b). Eng exc. Du We O R C So

close sieve *n* a round BASKET with a mesh bottom, for carrying horse-feed III.5.4. klous sɪv Brk

closet *1. n* an EARTH-CLOSET V.1.13. klasɪt Man, klɑːzət Gl, klɒsɪt Nf Ess Brk, klɒzɪt Y Ch Sa St He Wo Wa Mon Gl L Lei R Nth Hu Bd*[polite x1]* Ess So Brk Sr K Sx, klɒzɪʔ Bk, tlɒzɪt Y Db*[polite x1]* Wo*[old]* Nt Nth, klɒsət So, klɒzət

O Ess So Do, klɒzə? Bk, kɫɒzət O*[polite]* So Co D Do, klɔzıt Y*[modern]* Ch*[modern]* Wa L Hrt Ess MxL Sr K, klɔzət L C Sf, klɔːzɪt Sa He, klɔːzət Sx, kləzət So

2. *n* a PANTRY V.2.6. klɒzıt Sr

close to *1. adv* ALMOST VII.7.9. klʌs tⁱuː C, kloʊs tuː Wa; **very close to** vəɹɪ tlᵁuːs tɛʊ Db

2. *adj* NEAR IX.2.10. klɒs tıu: Du, klɒs tᵁuː Sa, tlɒɪs tʊ Y, tlɒɪs tʊuː Y*[old]*, klɔːs tuː Y, klɔʊs tʊ Wa, klɔʊs tuː L, klʌs tıu: C, klʌs tuː Sf, klʌʊs tⁱuː Hrt, kloːs tʏː La Ch, tloːs tɪ Y, tloːs tɪʏ: Ch, tloːs tıu: Ch, tloːs tɛʊ Db, kloːs tuː Sa, tloːs tᵁuː La Ch Nt, kloʊs tıʊ St, tlous tıu Nf, kloʊs tuː St Wo Wa Bk Bd, tloʊs tu Wa, klʊəs tıu Y, klʊəs tuː Du La L, tlʊəs tʊuː La Y, tlᵁuːs tɛʊ Db

3. *prep* near. tlɒɪs tə Y, klʊəs tɪ Y

closet-pit *n* an ASH-MIDDEN V.1.14. klɒzɪʔpɪ? Bk

close up *vtphr* to SHUT a door IX.2.8. kɫuːz ʌp D

clot *1. v* to spread dry cow-dung as manure, ⇐ CLOT OF COW-DUNG II.1.6. -*ing* klɒʔɪn Bk

2. *v* to CURDLE (milk) V.5.7. klɒt Ess

cloth *1. n* a DISHCLOTH V.9.6. klɔːθ Sa O So

2. *n* a DIAPER V.11.3. klɔːθ Nf; **baby's cloth** *pl* beːbız klɔˑðz Nf

clothes-basket *n What do you carry the washed clothes in when you put them out on the line to dry?* V.9.7. Eng exc. We Sf Co D. ⇒ *basket, bath,* **clothes-flask, clothes-flasket, clothes-skep, clothes-swill, clothes-wisket, creel, flask, flasket, linen-basket, maund,** *skep* ⇒ **skip, skip, swill, voider, washbasket, washing-basket, wicker-basket, wisket,** *wooden tub*; ⇒ also **clothes-flake**

clothes-flake* *n* a device on which clothes are dried, ⇐ CLOTHES-BASKET V.9.7. klʊəzflɪək Y

clothes-flask *n* a CLOTHES-BASKET V.9.7. kloːzflæːsk So, kloːzflaːsk So, kɫoːzfɫaːsk D, kɫoːzfɫaːsk D Do*[old]*, kɫoːzvɫaːsk D, kloːzflaːs So

clothes-flasket *n* a CLOTHES-BASKET V.9.7. kɫoːzfɫaːskıt D

clothes-skep *n* a CLOTHES-BASKET V.9.7. klɪəzskɛp Y

clothes-swill *n* a CLOTHES-BASKET V.9.7. tlıasswıl Y, klɪəzswıl Nb, tlıəzswıl Cu, kleazswıl Cu La, tleasswıl We, tleazswıl Cu We, tleˑəzswıl Cu, tlʊəzswıl La

clothes-wisket *n* a CLOTHES-BASKET V.9.7. kloːzwıskıt Sa He, kluːzwıskıt St, klʊəzwıskıt Ch, klʊəzwıskət La, tlʊəzwıskət La

clot of cow-dung *n What do you call the lump of dung that a cow leaves in the field?* II.1.6. ⇒ *baked* **dung, clap, clat, clat** *of dung,* **cow-clap, cow-clat, cow-clot, cow-clud, cow-dab, cow-drop, cowdropping, cow-dung, cow-flop, cow-muck, cowpad, cow-pasty, cow-pat, cow-patch, cow-plat, cow-platter,** *cow's* **dirt,** *cow's* **droppings, cowsharn, cow-shit, cow-shite, cow-slip, cow-slop,**

cow's-**plat,** *cow's* **turd, cow-swat, cow-turd, dirt, dropping, dung, dung-pat, heap** *of cowmuck,* **heap** *of muck,* **hillock** *of cow-muck,* **lump** *of cow-muck,* **lump** *of cow-shit,* **manure, pad, pad** *of cow-shit,* **pancake, plat, pollag, ruck** *of cow-muck,* **ruck** *of dung,* **ruck** *of muck,* **sheddicks, shit, skid, sunburned cake, tump** *of cow-shit,* **turd, turd-stool;** ⇒ also **clot**

clotted *adj* TANGLED, describing hair VI.2.5. klɒtɪd Brk Do*[old]*, kɫɒtəd W

clotting *v-ing* THROWING a stone VIII.7.7. klɒtən Du

cloudy *adj* DULL, referring to the weather VII.6.10. klɛʊdɪ Nf

clough *n* a SLOPE IV.1.10. klʊf Y

clout *1. n* a DISHCLOTH V.9.6. kɫæʊt W, klaʊt Do, tlʌʊt Y, kləʊt Do

2. *n* a DIAPER V.11.3. klɛʊt Nf, klɛʊt Wa O L Nth Nf Sf Hrt Ess, *pl* klɛʊts Hu C Bk Bd Ha, *pl* klɛʊ?s Bk, tlɛʊt Nf, klæʊt L So, *pl* klæʊts Wa, klaːt La, klaıt St, klaʊt Ch St L, *pl* klaʊt Nt, *pl* tlaʊts Ch, tlʌʊt Gl, *pl* klᵁuːts Gl, kləʊt Do, *pl* kləʊts Brk, kɫəʊt W; **baby's clout** *pl* beːⁱbız tlɛːᵊts Db, *pl* beːbız klɛʊts O, *pl* bɛːbız klɛʊts Nf, *pl* bɛˑəbız klaʊts L; **bairn's clout** *pl* bɛˑənz klaʊts L

3. *vt* to BEAT a boy on the buttocks VIII.8.10. klɛʊt Wo, klæʊt Ch St K, kluːt Y

clout-head *n* a STUPID person VI.1.5. klaːtıəd Y

clove *adj* CLOVEN, describing the hoof of a cow III.2.8.(b). klɒʊv K, klɔʊv Brk, kloːv Mon Brk, klɒʊv Wo, kloːʊv Mon

cloved *adj* CLOVEN, describing the hoof of a cow III.2.8.(b). klʌʊvd Ess, kɫoːvd Ha, klɒʊvd Nth

clove-foot *adj* having a CLOVEN hoof, describing a cow III.2.8.(b). kloːvfʊt So, kɫoːvvʏt D

clove-footed *adj* having a CLOVEN hoof, describing a cow III.2.8.(b). kloːvvʊtıd So

cloven *adj [Show a picture of a cow. What do you call this?] Unlike a horse's hoof it is ....* III.2.8.(b). klıvn La, kløːvn Nb, kløːvən Nb, tløːvən Du, klæʊvən Hrt, klɑʊvn Ess, klɒvən Cu Y, tlɒvn We La Y Ch, tlɒvən We, klɒvn Sr K Sx, klɒʊvən Man, klɒvn L, tlɒvn L, klɔːvən Y Ch Ha, tlɔːvən We, klɔʊvn Lei R Ess Ha, klʌʊvn Ess MxL, klʌʊvn Bk Hrt Sr K, kloːvn La Y Ch Sa He Mon Nf So Brk, kɫoːvn W Co, tloːvn Y Ch Db, kloːvən Sa He Mon So, kɫoːvən W D Ha, kloːvm He, kɫoːvm Co D Ha, kloʊvm St He Wo O Lei Nf Bk Brk K, kloʊvm So, tloːᵁvn Db Nt, tloːᵁvən Nth, kluvən Wo, klʊəven Du, klʊəvən L, tlʊəvn Y, kləʊvn Ess. ⇒ **clawed,** *in* **claws, cleaved,** *in* **clees, cleeted, cleft, clove, cloved, clovened, club, clut, cracked, cut, divided, double, open, parted, slit, split, splitten, spread;** ⇒ also **claw-foot,**

claw-footed, clove-foot, clove-footed, cloven-footed, cloven- hoofed, split-hoofed

clovened *adj* CLOVEN, describing the hoof of a cow III.2.8(b). klʌʊvnd Bd

cloven-footed *adj* having a CLOVEN hoof, describing a cow III.2.8(b). klɒʊvnfʊtɪd K

cloven-hoofed *adj* having a CLOVEN hoof, describing a cow III.2.8(b). klɒʊvn̥uːft Sx

cloves *n* the HOOF of a cow III.2.8(a). klɒʊvz St

club *1. adj* CLOVEN, describing the hoof of a cow III.2.8(b). tlʊb Ch

2. n a local FESTIVAL or holiday VII.4.11. klʌb Db He Brk Do Sx, -*s* klʌbs Db, kɬʌb Do, klʊb Db Wa Nth, -*s* klʊbs Db, tlʊb Db; **benefit club** bɛnɪfɪt klʌb Sx; **club day** klʌb deː W, klʌb deː Do, *pl* klʌb deɪ So, klʌb dɛɪ Sx, kɬʌb deː W Do Ha, kɬʌb dɛɪ Co, klʊb deː La, klʊb deɪ Man; **club fair*** klʌb fɛɪəᶜ Sr; **club feast-day** klʌb fiːstdeɪ Brk; **club randy** kɬʌb ɾandi Do; **club's walking** klʊbz wʊʊkɪn St; **club walk** klʌb waːk Mon, klʌb wɔːk He So, kɬʌb wɔːk So, klʊb wɔːk Wa, -*s* klʊb wɔːks St; **Oddfellows' club** ɒdfɛləz klʊb Wa; **Oddfellows' club day** æʊdfɛləz klʊb diː St; **old man's club service** ʊʊɬ mænz klʌb səᶜːvɪs So; **pig club** pɛg kɬʌb W

clubby *adj* STICKY, describing a child's hands VIII.8.14. kɬʌbi D

club-footed *adj* PIGEON-TOED VI.10.4. tlʊbfɣːtɪd La

club-heads *npl* TADPOLES IV.9.5. klʌbɛdz Bk

club-tail *n* a POLE-CAT IV.5.7. tlʊbtɛˑəl L

cluck *1. n* a BROODY HEN IV.6.7. klʌk K, kɬʌk Co

2. adj broody, describing a hen. klʌk Do, kɬʌk Co

clucked hen *n* a BROODY HEN IV.6.7. klʌkt ɪn K

clucker *n* a BROODY HEN IV.6.7. klʌkə K, klʌkəᶜ Sa, klʊkə Y, klʊkəɹ Y

cluck hen *n* a BROODY HEN IV.6.7. klʌk ɛˑn K

clucking hen *n* a BROODY HEN IV.6.7. klʊkɪn ɛn Y, klʊkkɪn ɛn La, kɬʊkɪn ɪn Co

cluckward* *adj* broody, describing a hen, ⇐ BROODY HEN IV.6.7. kɬʌkəd Co *[queried SBM; perhaps clucked]*

clucky *n* a BROODY HEN IV.6.7. klʌki Brk, kɬʌki Co

clucky hen *n* a BROODY HEN IV.6.7. kɬʌki ɛn Co

clumbersome *adj* CLUMSY, describing a person VI.7.14. klɒmbəˡsʊm Brk

clumble-fisted *adj* CLUMSY, describing a person VI.7.14. klʌmbɬvɪstɪd So

clump *n* a TUSSOCK of grass II.2.9. kʰlʌmp Nf, tlʊmp Y

clumsy *adj* Of a person who can't do things properly with his hands, but keeps dropping things and knocking things over, you say he is .... VI.7.14. Eng exc. We C Brk Do. ⇒ **awkward, back-handed, blundersome, bumble-fisted, bungersome, butter-fingered, butter-fingers, cack-handed, careless,**

clever-clumsy, clumbersome, clumble-fisted, *clumsy and unsteady*, coochy, daft, feckless, *fit for nowt with his hands*, foreright, fumble-fingered, fumble-fisted, fumbling, fumbly, gammy, gammy-handed, gaumless, humble-fisted, limp-fingered, loose-fingered, *nervous*, newsy, numb, numb-pawed, numb-thumbed, pizzle-handed, pumble-fisted, scammish, scrammish, scrammy, shaky, *silly*, skiffle-handed, slammocking, slammocky, slipper-fingered, sloven, thumby, tottering, ungain, unheppem, unheppen, wooden

clumsy-head *n* a STUPID person VI.1.5. kɬʌmzi-eɪd D

clunch *n* the top layer of PEAT IV.4.3. klʊnʃ Nth

clunker *n* the WINDPIPE VI.6.5. kɬʌŋkəᶜ Co

cluster *1. n* a TUSSOCK of grass II.2.9. klʊstə Wa

2. n a BROOD of chickens IV.6.12. klʊstə O

clut *adj* CLOVEN, describing the hoof of a cow III.2.8(b). klʌt K

clutch *1. n* the metal BUSH at the centre of a cart-wheel I.9.8. tlʌtʃ Nf

2. n a BROOD of chickens IV.6.12. klɒtʃ Cu, klʌtʃ Nf Ess K Do, tlʌtʃ Nf, klʊtʃ Du La Y Sa L

clutchy *adj* SAD, describing bread or pastry that has not risen V.6.12. kɬʌtʃi Co

clutter *n* RUBBISH V.1.15. klʌtəˡ K

clutty *vt* to DIRTY a floor V.2.8. klʌtɪ Brk, klʌʔɪ Brk

cly *n* GOOSE-GRASS II.2.5. klæɪ So

coal-dirt *n* COAL-DUST V.4.1. kʌʊɬdəᶜːt̠ Ess

coal-dust *n* Before going out for the afternoon, what would you put on the fire to keep it in? V.4.1. kæʊɬdʌs Sx, kɒɬdʌs K, kɒʊɬdʌst K, kɒʊdʌs Sx, kɒʊdəst Sx, kɔʊldɒst Brk, kɔʊɬdʌst Hu, kɔʊɬdʌs Sx, kɔʊɬdʊst R, kɔʊdʌst K, kʌʊl dʌst MxL, kʌʊɬdʌst Ess, koːɬdʌst Brk, koːɬdʌs D, kʊəldʊst Y L, kʉuːɬdʌst Ess. ⇒ **backing, breeze, briss, briss coal, brissy coal, *cinders*, *coal*, coal-dirt, dirty coal, dross, duffy coal, dust, dust coal, dusty coal, firing, light slack, slack, slack coal, slag, slatch, small, small coal(s), smudge, *turf*, *wet* dust, *wet* dust coal, *wet* slack coal**

coal-rake *n* a RAKE used in a domestic fire V.3.8(a). kɔɪlɹeːk Y, kɔɪlɹɛˑᵊk Y

coal-shovel *n* a SHOVEL for a household fire V.3.9. koːʃʊvəɬ O, kʊəlʃʊvl L

coarse-apron *n* a working APRON V.11.2(a). kɔːsɪəpɹɒn Du, kɔːsæɪpɹɒn Ess, kɒᶜːsapəᶜn̩ Sa, kɔəˡsɛɪpəˡˑn Brk, kɔəɾs̠eːpɹɒn O, kɔːəsɛɪpɹ̩n Ess, kɔːəˡsɛɪpɹ̩n Sr, kɔːəᶜɾs̠ɛɪpəᶜːɾn̩ Sx, koːəsɛːɪpɹɒn Db, koˑəs ɛɪpɹɒn Nth, kʊəseˑəpəᶜn̩ Bk, kʊəsapɹɒn Y L, kʊəɹseːpɹɒn La, kuːsɛːbəᶜːn̩ D, kuːsapəᶜːn̩ D

coarse-brat *n* a working APRON V.11.2(a). kɔːsbɹat Cu, koˑᵊsbɹæt Man*[sacking]*, koəsbɹat We, kʊəsbɹat Cu

coarse-flour *n* MEAL V.6.1(b). kɔːsflᵊuːə Cu

coarse meal *n* MEAL V.6.1(b). kʊəs mɪˑəl L

coast *n* a pigeon, ⇐ PIGEONS IV.7.3. koʊəst So *[marked ir.r. SBM]*

coasters *npl* PIGEONS IV.7.3. koʊəstəˡːz̩ So *[marked ir.r. SBM]*

coat *1. n* a JACKET VI.14.5. kˡʏət Ch*[old]*, kʏˑət La*[old]*, køːt Nb, køᵊt Du, kœːət Nb*[modern x1]*, kɒɪt La*[old x1]* Y, kɔːt Cu, kɔɪt Y*[old x1]*, kɔʊt O L, kʌʊt Ess*[old]* Sr, koːt La*[old]* Mon O*[modern]* Co Do, koʊt Man Nth, kwɒt Cu, kʊt Sf, kʊət Nb Cu Du We La Y*[old x4]* Ch*[old]* O L, kwət So, kuːt Ch Db St D, kuːət So D

2. n an OVERCOAT VI.14.6. kɔːt Ha, kɔɪt Y, kɔʊt L Hu O, kʌʊt C Sf Hrt Ess, kout Nf, koutʔ Nf, kwɒt Brk, kwʊt Gl, kʊət Y, kwət Gl, kuːt Sf

coat and breeches *n* a SUIT of clothes VI.14.21. kwʊt ŋ bəˡːtʃəz So

cob *1. n* a SOWING-BASKET II.3.6. kab Ess, kɒb Ess, kɔb Sf Ess

2. n CHAFF II.8.5. kɒb Ess

3. n the WATTLES of a hen IV.6.19. kɒb Co

4. n HAZEL IV.10.8. kɒb Lei

5. v to LOP a tree IV.12.5. kɔb Sf

6. v to TOP-AND-TAIL gooseberries V.7.23. kɒb Bd

7. n a COBBLER VIII.4.5. kɒb Wa

cobbing *v-ing* THROWING a stone VIII.7.7. kɒbɪn Y, kɔbɪn Y

cobbing-fork *n* a HAY-FORK with a long shaft I.7.11. kɒbɪnfɔːk Lei

cobbler *n* What do you call the man who mends boots and shoes? VIII.4.5. Eng. ⇒ **boot and shoemaker, boot-maker, cob, greither, nobby, shoemaker, shoemender, shoe-snob, shoey, snob, snobber, snobbler, snobby, stubby, tacker**

cobble-stick *n* the STRETCHER between the traces of a cart-horse I.5.11. kɒblstɪk Db Nt, kɒbəlstɪk Y, kɔblstɪk L

cobble-tree *n* an EVENER on a horse-drawn plough I.8.4. kɒbltɹiː Y, kɒbltɹəɪ Y

cobbling *v-ing* THROWING a stone VIII.7.7. kɒblɪn Y, kɔblɪn L

cob-handed *adj* LEFT-HANDED VI.7.13(a). kɔbandɪd L

cobs *npl* round STACKS II.7.1. *sg* kɒb Hu, kɔbz C, *sg* kɔb L*[small stack built to dry damp corn]*

cob-wobbly *adj* ASKEW, describing a picture that is not hanging straight IX.1.3. kɒbwɒblɪ St

cock *1. n* an EVENER on a horse-drawn plough I.8.4. kɒk Brk

2. n an evener on the plough-beam end of a horse-drawn plough. kaːk Gl, kɒk Lei R

3. n the T-SHAPED PLOUGH-BEAM END of a horse-drawn plough I.8.5. kɒk Gl O L Lei R Nth Bk Bd

4. n the penis of a horse, ⇐ SHEATH III.4.9. kɒk St W

cock-eyed *1. adj* SQUINTING VI.3.5. kɒkɒɪd St Do, kɒkɔɪd St *[marked u.r. WM/SBM]*

2. adj CROSS-EYED VI.3.6. kaːkəɪd Gl, kɒkiːd Y, kɒkaɪd Nb Cu Du*[old x1]* We La Y Sa*[old]*, kɒkaɪd Ch Wa Nt*[old]* Hu Nf Bd, kɒkɒɪd St So*[old x1]*, kɒkɔɪd Wa Brk Sr, kɒkʌɪd Gl Brk, kɒkəɪd Y Mon W, kɔkiːd Y, kɔkəɪd Nb, kɔkæɪd Y, kɔkaɪd Nb Y L, kɔkaɪd La Y L C

3. adj ASKEW, describing a picture that is not hanging straight IX.1.3. kɒkaɪd Du Y Db, kɒkaˑɪd Y, kɒkɒɪd Co, kɒkɔɪd Hrt, kɔkaɪd Y

cock-foot *n* COLT'S-FOOT II.2.7. kɒkfʊt Wo

cock-hangers *npl* PHEASANTS IV.7.8(b). kɒkaŋəˡːz̩ Ha

cock-kneed *adj* KNOCK-KNEED VI.9.5. kʊkniːd L

cockle *1. n* COUCH-GRASS II.2.3. kɒkł Nf

2. n COLT'S-FOOT II.2.7. kaːkl Nf

cockle-bells *n* ICICLES VII.6.11. kɒkłbełz Co

cockle-buttons *n* GOOSE-GRASS II.2.5. kɒkłbʌtnz Co, kɒkłbʌdnz Co

cockle over *viphr* to OVERTURN, referring to a cart I.11.5. *3prsg* kɒklz aʊə Y

cockles *n* GOOSE-GRASS II.2.5. kɒkłz Co

cock-loft *n* a DOVECOTE I.1.7. kɒklɒft Y, kɒklɔːft So

cock over *viphr* to OVERTURN, referring to a cart I.11.5. *-ed* kɒkt oːə Db

cocks *1. npl* When you put the drying hay into small heaps, e.g. overnight in case of rain, what do you call them? II.9.12. kæks Sx, kɑks O Nth, kɑːks Wo Mon Nf, kɒks Cu La Y Ch Db Sa St He Wo Wa Mon Gl O Nt L Lei R Nth Hu Nf Bk Bd Hrt Ess So W Brk Sr K Ha Sx, kɒkʔs Nf, kɔks Du La Y Wo Wa Nt L C Sf Hrt Ess MxL, *sg* kɔk Sr K, kɔːks Sa Wo; **hay-cocks** eːkɒks Y, eːᵊkɒks Du, hɛɪkɒks Nf, *sg* hɛɪkɒkʔ Nf, əkɒks Y, ɛˑəkɔks L, hæɪkɒks Nf Ess, æɪkɔks Sr

2. npl large cocks. *sg* kakʔ Nf, kɒksəz Ha

⇒ **butts, coils, cops, foot-cocks, foot-coils, fork-cocks, grass-cocks, great-cocks, hay-cocks, hay-pooks, hay-rucks, hay-shocks, heaps, hob-cocks, hoblings, hubbles, hubs, jockeys, lap-cocks, little-cocks, little-huts, pikes, pooks, ricks, rickles, ricklings, rucks, shocks, snooks, summer-cocks, wain-cocks, wappings, waps, wind-cocks;** ⇒ also **jockey-cock**

3. npl round STACKS II.7.1. kɒks Bd*[often with cartwheel as base x1]*, kɔks Hrt*[corn]* Ess*[corn]*

cock's-eye *n* a HALO round the moon VII.6.4. kɒksaɪ Y, kɒksɒɪ Co

cocks-eyed *adj* ASKEW, describing a picture that is not hanging straight IX.1.3. kɒksɔɪd O

cock's-foot *n* COLT'S-FOOT II.2.7. kɒksfʊt Brk, kɒksvʊt W

cock-snails *npl* SNAILS IV.9.3. kɒksnɛɪᵁɫz W

cock's treading *n* TREAD inside a fertile egg IV.6.9. kɔks tɹɛdɪn Ch

cock-ups *npl* CART-LADDERS I.10.5. kɒkʊps Lei

cocky-bells *n* ICICLES VII.6.11. kɒkibɪɫz D

cocoa-string *n* TWINE used to fasten thatch on a stack II.7.7(b1). koʊkoʊstɹɪŋ Lei

coconut-band *n* TWINE used to fasten thatch on a stack II.7.7(b1). kɔːkənut band, koʊkənətbənt St

coconut-string *n* TWINE used to fasten thatch on a stack II.7.7(b1). kɔʊkənʊtstɹɪŋ Wa

cod *n* the scrotum of a horse, ⇐ SHEATH III.4.9. kɒd D, kɔd L Sf

codging *v-ing* DARNING V.10.1. kɒdʒɪŋ St*[not done neatly]*, kɒdʒɪn Wa

cods *npl* the testicles of a horse, ⇐ SHEATH III.4.9. kɒdz Db

coffer *1. n* a CORN-BIN I.7.4. kɒfə St, kʌfəᵗː Sa, kɔːfəᵗ Sa, *pl* kʊːfəz St
2. n a wooden corn-bin. kɒfə Ch, kɔːfəᵗ Sa, koʊfəɹ He, kʊfəᵗ Sa
3. n a corn-bin for mixed corn ready for eating. kɒfə Ch

coffin *n And what is put in the grave?* VIII.5.7. Eng. ⇒ **box**

cogs *npl* the HANDLES of a scythe II.9.8. kɒgz Ch Sa He

cog-wheels *n* GOOSE-GRASS II.2.5. kɒgwiːɫz Wo

coiler(s) *n* the BREECH-BAND of the harness of a cart-horse I.5.10.
no -s: kəɪləᵗ Sx
-s: kwaɪɫəz K, kwɔɪɫəᴶz Sr, kwɔɪɫəᵗɽẓ Sx, kwʌɪɫəᵗẓ Sr, kwəɪɫəᵗẓ Sx

coils *1. npl* COCKS of hay II.9.12. kɛɪlz Nb, kaɪlz Du, *sg* kɒɪl La, kwaɪlz St, kwɒɪlz St
2. npl heaps of hay larger than cocks. *sg* kɛɪl Du, kɒɪlz Db, *sg* kwaɪl Db, kwɒːɪlz St

coin *n* a chock placed behind and under a wheel to prevent a cart from going backwards on a hill, ⇐ PROP/CHOCK I.11.2. kɒɪn Nt

coir *n* a rope used to fasten thatch on a stack, ⇐ ROPES II.7.7(b2). kæɪɑː Man

coir-broom *n* a MUCK-BRUSH I.3.14. kaɪɑᵗːbɽuːm Co

coir-rope(s) *n* ROPES used to fasten thatch on a stack II.7.7(b2).
sg: kæɪɑːrɔːp Man
-s: kaɪɑᵗːɽɔːp Co*[possibly sg SBM]*

cokes *n* CINDERS V.4.3. kɒʊks Y, kɔʊks Y*[also cold] [marked u.r. NBM]*

cold *1. adj What's a room like on a winter's day without a fire?* VI.13.17. Eng. ⇒ **chilly, hunch, parky, shrimpy, snatched**
2. adj [What's a room like on a winter's day without a fire?] And if you were in that room for just a short time, you would be .... VI.13.18. Eng exc. We Nt Nth Sf Bd; **freezing cold** fɹɪiːzɪn koʊld Brk. ⇒ **a-cold, all shivered** *up*, **all shivers, bevering** *and shivering*, **bit cold, chilled, chilly, cold and chilly, foundered, freezed, freezed** *to the bones*, **freezing,** *freezing* **cold, frettishing** *with cold*, **frez, frezen, frosted, frowen, froze, frozen, hunchy,** *main* **cold, mopy, parky, perished, perished** *with cold*, **scrammed, scrammed** *with the cold*, **shaking** *with the cold*, **shivered, shivered** *to death*, **shivering, shivering** *with the cold*, **shivery, shrammed, snatched, starved, starved** *to death*, **starving,** *very* **chilly**
3. adj VERY COLD, describing a person VI.13.19. kɒʊd Sx; **a-freezing cold** əfɹiːzɪn kʌʊld Ess; **cold as ice** kɒʊɫd əz ɒɪst K; **middling cold** mɪdɫɪn kɔʊd K; **rotten cold** ɹɒtn kɛʊd St; **stone cold** ston koʊld Nf; **terrible cold** təɹɪbʊɫ kɒʊɫd K, təɹəbɫ koˑɫd Brk
4.1. vt to COOL tea by blowing on it V.8.11. kæʊɫd He, kɔːɫd So W Do, koʊɫd C So, kuːld Nth
4.2. v to cool tea. kɒʊɫd W, kɔʊld O

cold down *vtphr* to COOL tea by blowing on it V.8.11. kɔːʊld ... daʊn So, kɔːɫd ... dæʊn Ha, koʊɫd ... daʊn So

colden *v* to COOL tea by blowing on it V.8.11. kɔʊdən Y

colder *n* short pieces of straw left after threshing, ⇐ CHAFF II.8.5. koˑldə Nf, koʊldə Nf

cold-shouldered *adj* RESTIVE, describing a horse III.5.6. kɔʊdʃuːðəᴶd La

colg *n* barley AWNS II.5.3. kʊlg Man

collapse *vi* to FAINT VI.13.7. kəlæps Nf

collar *1. n [Show a picture of the harness of a cart-horse.] What do you call this?* I.5.3. kælə Man, kɑˑlə Nf, kɑˑɫə Nf, kɑləᴶ O, kɒlə La Y Man Ch Db St Wa Mon Nt L Lei R Nth Hu Nf Bk Bd Hrt Ess K, kɒɫə Lei Ess, kɒləɹ La Y He, kɒləᴶ La Ch Db St Brk K Ha, kɒɫəᴶ Brk Sr K, kjɒləᵗ Gl, kɒɫəᵗ Sa He Wo Wa Gl O Nth Bk Bd Sx, kɒɫəᵗ He Wo Mon Gl O Brk Sr Sx, kɒləᵗː Sa So Do, kɒɫəᵗː So W Co D Do Ha, kɔlə Y Ch L C Sf Hrt Ess MxL Sr, kɔlɹ L, kɔləᴶ La Wa L, kɔləᵗ Wo K, kɔɫəᵗ K Ha. ⇒ **bargham, head-collar, neck-collar,** *pair of* **barghams**
2. n a HALTER for a cow I.3.17. kɒlə Y
3.1. vt to GEAR a cart-horse I.5.1. kɒləɹ(+V) Ess
3.2. v to gear a horse. kɒɫə Ess
4. n the T-SHAPED PLOUGH-BEAM END of a horse-drawn plough I.8.5. kɒləᴶ K

5. *n* the metal BUSH at the centre of a cart-wheel I.9.8. kɒlə Bd Hrt, kɒləᵗ Wo

collard *n* a LINCH-PIN holding a wheel on a cart I.9.12. kɒləd K *[queried SBM]*

collar-pin* *n* a LINCH-PIN holding a wheel on a cart I.9.12. kɒləpɪn Ess

collar-proud *1. adj* RESTIVE, describing a horse III.5.6. kɒləᵗːpɾaʊd So

2. adj describing a horse which has been out to grass and is fat and unused to harness. kɒləpɹɛʊd Nf

collars *npl* parts of scythes, ⇐ GRASS-NAIL II.9.9. kɒɫəᵗɾz̩ Sx

collar-tree(s) *n* the HAMES of the harness of a cart-horse I.5.4.

no -s: kɒɫəᵗːtɾiː Co

-s: kɒɫəᵗːtɾiːz Co

collar up *vphr* to GEAR a cart-horse I.5.1. kɒɫəɹ ʌp Ess

collect *vt-3sg A tidy little girl, before going to bed, will not leave her toys lying about, but will [indicate collecting]... them.* VIII.8.15. kəlɛkt Sa Wo L Lei Nth K, kəlɛk Brk, *3prsg* kəlɛks Sx, klɛkt Bk, kᵊɫɛkt K, kɫɛkt He; **collect and lay together** klɛkt ... ən læɪ ... təgɛðə Nf. ⇒ **brush aside, bunch up, chuck up** *together*, **clean up, clear, clear away, clear up, collect** *and lay together*, **collect together, collect up, collect up** *together*, **cowl together, fold up, gather, gather** *and put away*, **gather** *together*, **gather up, gather up** *and put away*, **gather up** *together*, **get together, heap up, lap, lap up** *and put tidy*, **lay up, pack away, pack up, pack up** *together*, **pick together, pick up, pick up** *tidy*, **pull together, push up** *together*, **put away, put away** *tidy*, **put by,** *put bye* ⇒ **put by, put together, put up, put up** *tidy*, **put up** *together*, **sam up, sam up** *and side*, **scoop up, scowp up, scrab up, scramble together, scrap up, scrape together, scrape up, side, side away, side by, side up, straighten up, tidy, tidy away, tidy off, tidy up,** *tight up* ⇒ **tidy up**

collect together *vtphr-3sg* she [i.e. a tidy girl] will COLLECT her toys VIII.8.15. klɛkt ... təgɛðə St, klɛkt ... təgɛðəɾ O, klɛkt ... təgɛðəᵗ: So, kɫɛkt ... təgɛðəᵗ: D

collect up *vtphr-3sg* she [i.e. a tidy girl] will COLLECT her toys VIII.8.15. kəlɛkt ... ʌp Nf Sr, *3prsg* kəlɛks ... ʌp Sx, klɛk ... ʌp Bd Brk, *3prsg* klɛks ... ʌp W Sr, kəlɛkt ... ʊp St Wa L, kəlɛkt ... əp Gl, klɛkt ... ʊp Wo, kəɫɛkt ... ʊp Mon, kɫɛkt ... ʌp So W D; **collect up together** klɛkt ... ʌp təgɛðəᵗ: So

collop-fat *n* BACON-FAT V.7.5(b). kɒləpfat Y

colons *n* KINDLING-*WOOD* V.4.2. kɒlənz Y

colostrum *n* BEESTINGS V.5.10. kɒstɹən Bk, kɔʊstɹʊm Ess

colour *1. vt* to MARK sheep with colour to indicate ownership III.7.9. kʌləɾ (+V) Brk

2. n **off colour, off of colour, off it** ILL, describing a person who is unwell VI.13.1(b). **off colour** ɔːf kɒlɒuᴶ K, ɔːf kʌlə Mon Nf, ɒf kʊlə St, ɔf kʊlə Y L, ɔf kʊlɹ L, ɒf kʊləɹ La *[a little unwell];* **off of colour** ɔf ə kʊlɹ L; **off it** ɒf ɪt Y

3. n **off colour, off it** SICK, describing an animal that is unwell VI.13.1(c). **off colour** ɒf kʊlə Y St, ɔf kʊlə L, ɔf kʊlɹ L, ɔːf kəɫəᵗ Sx; **off it** ɒf ɪt Y

colstrap *n* BEESTINGS V.5.10. kɒlstɹəp Y

colt *1. n And when your male foal is older, you call it a ....* III.4.3. Eng exc. Bk. ⇒ **colt-foal, horse-colt, horse-foal, stallion-foal** *[gelding(-foal)] and yearling(-colt) rr. not included]*

2. n a FOAL III.4.1. kɛʊt Ch, kɒɫt Gl O, kɒʊɫt Wa Gl, kɒʊɫ? Bk Bd, kɔʊɫt O, kɔʊt La, kʌʊlt Nf, kʌʊɫt Bk, kʌʊɫ? Hrt, kɒʊɫt O Nth Bk Bd So, kɒʊɫ? Bk

3. n a newborn FOAL. kɒɫ Sr

colt-foal *1. n* a COLT III.4.3. kaʊltfʊəl Y, kaʊtfʊəl Y, kɒltfɔɪl Y, kɒltfɔəl Y, kɒʊltfʊɫd K, kɒʊtfʊəl Nb Cu, kuːltfʊːl Ch

2. n a newborn male horse. kɒɫtfʌʊɫ Bk

colt-foot *n* COLT'S-FOOT II.2.7. kæʊlfʊt Man, kaʊtfʊt Y, kɒltfʊt Y, kɒʊtfʊt We La, kɒʊlfʌt He, kɒʊfʊt Wo, kɔltfʊt Y, kɔʊltfʊɪt Y, kɔʊtfʊt La Y L, kɔʊlfʊt L, kʌʊɫfʊt Sf, koːɫtfʊt Mon, koːɫ?fʊt W, koːlfʊt Db, kɒʊɫfʌt C

colt's-foot *n [Show a picture of colt's-foot.] What do you call this?* II.2.7. Eng exc. Du Hu MxL. ⇒ **backy, batterdock, canker, canker-flower, canker-weed, cleat(s), cock-foot, cockle, cock's-foot, colt-foot, coosil, cow-foot, crow-foot, dishilago, foal-foot, foal's-foot, horse-foot, mugwort, skowl-foot**

columbine *n* BINDWEED II.2.4. kɒləmbaɪn Cu, kɒlənbɑɪn Db

colvudgen* *n* BINDWEED II.2.4. kɒlvʊdʒən La

comb *1. n What do you call this [indicate a hair-comb]?* VI.2.4. Eng. ⇒ **combing,** *hair-comb*, **hair-dasher, lash, lash-comb, rid, ridding-comb;** ⇒ also **combing-comb**

2. n a CURRY-COMB used to clean horses III.5.5(b). kɪəm Nb, kœːᵊm Nb, kɒm Db L, kɔm Db Nt, kɔʊm R, kʌʊm Bd, koːm So, koʊm Lei, koˈəm Do, kʊm He Wa Gl O, kʊəm La, kuːm Sa Brk D Ha, kuːəm W Do Ha, kwɒm Do, kwəm W D

3. n the RIDGE of a stack of corn II.7.2. kaʊm Ess, kʌʊm Sr, kɒʊm Sr Sx

4. n the WATTLES of a hen IV.6.19. kæʊm Hrt, kʌm Sf, kʌʊm Ess, kʊm He, kuːm Sa He *[queried ir.r. EMBM]*

combing *n* a COMB VI.2.4. kʌʊmɪn Ess

combing-comb* *n* a fine-toothed COMB VI.2.4. kɛmɪnkuːm Y

combs *npl* the RIDGES between furrows in a ploughed field II.3.2. *sg* kø:m Nb, *sg* kɒʊm K Co

come *1. imp* **back come here, come again, come back, come by the way, come hauve, come here, come here back, come here hauve, come here hauve a bit, come here hey, come here hoy, come here round, come here way, come here wee, come here woa, come here woot, come hither, come-hither ho, come-hither round, come-hither wee, come hither weet, come hither whup, come hither woy, come-hither-wut, come huggin, come nearer, come on, come over there, come ree, come round, come round here, come to, come to us, come toward, come way, come woa, come ye here, come ye hither, way come here, woa come here, woaf come here, woa come back** the command TURN LEFT!, given to plough-horses II.3.5(a). **back come here** bɒk kʊm ɪə Nt; **come again** 'kʊm əgɛn St; **come back** kʌm bæk Hu, kʊm bæk Gl Nth, kʊ bæk Hu, kʌm bak O Bd W, kʊm bak Ch Db Sa St Wa Gl Lei R Nth Bk; **come by the way** 'kʊm bɛ ðə wəɪ L; **come hauve** kʊm aːv Y, kʊm ɔːv L; **come here** kʌm hɪə So, kʌm ɪə Mon Nf Sf Bk Hrt, kʊm ɪə Cu We La Y Ch Db St L C, kʊn ɪə Y, kɒm ɪəᴵ K, 'kʌm ɪəᴵ Brk, kʊm ɪəᴵ Db, kʊm ɪəɹ La Y, kɒm ɪəᵗ Sa, kʌm ɪəᵗ O Bk Bd, kʊm ɪəᵗ He Wo Mon Gl O, kʌm hɪəᵗ: So W, kʌm ɪəᵗ: So W Co D Do Ha, kʊm ɪəᵗ: D, ke: əᵗ Gl, kʌm jəᵗ: W D Do Ha, kʌm jəᵗ: So; **come here back** 'kʊm 'iː 'bæk Wo, 'kʊm ɪəɹ bæk He, 'kʊm ɪəᵗ 'bæk Wo Gl, kʌm i-əᵗ bak Mon, 'kʊm 'iː 'bak Sa Mon, 'kʊm 'iːəᵗ 'bak Sa; **come here hauve** kʊm ɪ'ə ɔːv L; **come here hauve a bit** kʊm ɪə aːv ə bɪt Y; **come here hey** 'kʌm ɪə ˌheɪ Nf, 'kʊm ɪə hᵊiː Sf; **come here hoy** m ɪə hɔɪ So; **come here round** 'm ɪəᵗ: 'ɾæʊn So, m ɪəᵗ: ɾaʊn So; **come here way** kʊm ɪəᵗ: weɪ So, kʊm iːəᵗ: weɪ So; **come here wee** kʊm ɪ wiː Ess, kʌb ɪ' wiiː Nf; **come here woa** kʊm ɪə woː Db; **come here woot** kʌm ɪ wʌʔ Ess; **come hither** 'kʌm'ɪðəᵗ: W D, kɒmɪðəᴵ K[old], bɪðəᵗɾ Ha, kɒm'ɛðəᴵ Brk, kʌm haːðə Sf, 'kʌm'aðəᵗ: D, kʌm ʌðə Ess, 'kʌm'ʌðəᵗ: D, kʊm ʊðə L, maːðəᵗ Sr; **come-hither ho** mɪðəᵗ: ho: Do[old], mɛðəᴵ-ʊ Sx; **come-hither round** kʊm'ɪðəᴵ ɹəʊnd Brk; **come-hither wee** mɪðəᵗ wiiː Sr, mʊðəᴵ wiiː Sr; **come hither weet** kʌm ʌðə wiiː? Ess; **come hither whup** kʌm ɪðə wʊp Ess, 'mɛðəwəp K; **come hither woy** 'kʊm ɛðə ˌwɔ'ɪ L; **come-hither-wut** mːɑːðəᵗɾwʊt Sx; **come huggin** ˌkʊm 'ʊgɪn Wa[old]; **come nearer** kʊm naːɹə Ch, 'kʊm 'nɔːɹə Sa; **come on** kʊm ɒn Nth; **come over there** kɒm ɒə ðə Man, kʊm ɔ: ðɛə Man; **come ree** kʌm 'ɹi Sf; **come round** 'kʌm 'ɾæʊn W, 'kʌm 'ɾaʊn Do; **come round here** 'kʌm ɾæʊnd 'ɪəᵗ: Ha; **come to** kʌm tu: Bd; **come to us** 'kʊm 'tu: 'ʊs Wo; **come toward** kʊm tɔᵗ:d̩ Wa, kʌm tɔːəd Brk; **come way** kʌm wɪə Ess[on roads]; **come woa** kʊm wɔʊ L; **come ye here** kʌm iː ɪəᵗ: So; **come ye hither** 'kʌm

iː 'ɪðəᵗ: D; **way come here** 'wɛɪ 'kʌm 'ɪəᵗ: Co; **woa come here** wo: kʊm ɪəɹ La, 'wʌɪ kʌm 'ɪəᵗ: Co, 'woːɪ kʌm 'ɪəᵗ: Co, wʊ kʌm ɪə Hrt; **woa come back** wʌ kʊ bæk Hu, wʊ kʊm 'bæk C, 'wʊˌkʊm'bak Nth[to a young horse]; **woa come heller** wo: kʊm ɛlə Sf; **woa come here** wo: kʊm ɪəɹ La, 'wʌɪ kʌm 'ɪəᵗ: Co, 'woːɪ kʌm 'ɪəᵗ: Co, wʊ kʌm ɪə Hrt; **woa come hither** wɔ: kʌm ɪðə Ess, wɔ: kəm ɪðə Ess, wɔ: kʊm ɛðə Ess, 'wɔ: kʌm ˌʌðə Ess; **woaf come here** wɔʊf kʊm ɪə Cu

2. imp **come here, come here back, come hither, come-hither-whup, come hither woy, come out** the command TURN RIGHT!, given to plough-horses II.3.5(b). **come here** kʊm ɪə We, kʊm ɪəɹ Y; **come here back** 'kʌm ɪəᵗ 'bæk Sa; **come hither** kɻ̩ 'ɛðə MxL; **come-hither-whup** 'mɛðəwəp K; **come hither woy** kʊm ɛðə wɔɪ L; **come out** kʊm ᵊʊt Y

3. imp **come along lads, come lads, come on, come on here, come on my lads, come up** the command GO ON!, given to plough-horses II.3.5(d). **come along lads** kʌm əlɒŋ lɛdz Sr; **come lads** 'kʊm 'laːdz Sa; **come on** kɒ: n Sx, kʌm ɒn Nf Co, kʌm ɔːn So, 'kʏm ˌɒn Nf, kʊm ən Man, kʊm aːn He Mon, kʊm ɒn Du Y; **come on here** kʊm 'ɒ'n ɪəᴵ K; **come on my lads** kʊm ɒn mɪ lædz So; **come up** 'kʌm 'ɛp D, kʌm ʌp Nb So D, kʊm ʊp Y

4.1. vt to CURDLE milk V.5.7. kʊm Y; **come the curd** kʊm ðə kɹʊd Ch

4.2. v **come into curd, make it come** to curdle. **come into curd** kʊm ɪntə kəːd St; **make it come** meːk ət kʌm Ha

5. vi to WAX, referring to the moon VII.6.5(a). kʌm Bk, *-ing* kʌmɪn O, kʊm Du La, *prppl* kʊmɪn Y; **comes afresh** *3prsg* kʊmz əfɹɛʃ Ch

come-back *n* the NEAR-HORSE of a pair pulling a wagon I.6.4(a). kʊmbak St

come back *vphr* to VOMIT, referring to a baby bringing up milk VI.13.14(b). kʌm bak Sa

come down *1. vphr* **come down before (her) time, come down early** to slip a calf, ⇐ SLIPS THE CALF III.1.11. *ptppl* kʌm dæʊn bɪfɔ'ə taɪm MxL, *ptpl* kʌm dɛʊn bɪfɔːɹ ə taɪm MxL[calf alive], *ppl* kʌm daʊn əᵗ:ɬi So

2. viphr showing signs of calving, referring to a cow with a swelling udder, or to the udder, ⇐ SHOWS SIGNS OF CALVING III.1.12(a). **coming down in the udder** kʌmɪn dɛʊn ɪn ðɪ ʌdəᵗ Sr; **her udder comes down** əᵗ:ɾ ʌdəᵗ: kʌm dəʊn Do

3. viphr to FARROW, describing a pig giving birth to piglets III.8.10. kʌm dɛʊn MxL, *3prsg* kʌmən dæʊn Ha

4. *viphr* to WANE, referring to the moon VII.6.5(b). *-ing* kʊmɪn dɛːn La *[wrongly listed as **wax** headword NBM]*

come forward *viphr* to WAX, referring to the moon VII.6.5(a). kʊm fɔɹət Cu, *-ing* kʊmən fɔɹəd We

come full *viphr* to WAX, referring to the moon VII.6.5(a). *-ing* kɒmɪn fʊɫ K; **come into full** *-ing* kʊmɪn ɪntə fʊl L; **come to be full** *-ing* kʊmɪn tə bɪ fʊl La; **come to the full** kʊm tə ðə føːl Nb, *-ing* kʊmɪn tə t fʊl Cu Y, *-ing* kʊmən tə ðə fʊl Nb; **come to the full moon** *-ing* kʊmən tə t fʊl mɪʊn Cu; ⇒ also **full**

come off *viphr* to CHIP, referring to an egg that is about to hatch IV.6.10. prppl kʊmɪn ɒf Y

come on *1. vphr* **coming on** *ON* HEAT, describing a cow III.1.6. kɒmɪn ɔːn Sx, kʌmən ɒn Sf
2. viphr-ed **come on again** *HAS NOT* HELD, referring to a cow that has not conceived III.1.7. kʌm ɒn əgɛn
3. viphr to WAX, referring to the moon VII.6.5(a). kʊm ɒn Nt

come out *viphr* to CHIP, referring to an egg that is about to hatch IV.6.10. kʌm ɛʊt Nf

come over *vphr-ed HAS NOT* HELD, referring to a cow that has not conceived III.1.7. kʊm aʊə Y, kʊmd aʊə Y, kʊm ɑʊə Y, kʊm ɒvə Nt, kʊmd ɒvə Y, kʊm ɒʊvə Nth, kʊm ɒʊə Nt Y, kʊmd ɒvə Y, kʊm ɒvəᴵ L, kʊm ɔˑə Y, kʊm ɔᵁwə L, kʊm ɔʊəᴵ L, kʌm ʌʊvə Hrt Ess, kʌm ɒʊvə C; **come over again** kʊm aʊəɹ əgeən Y, kʊm ɑʊəɹ əɪgə Y, kʊm ɑwəɹ əgeən Y, kʊm ɒvə əgɛn Y, kʊm ɒvəɹ əgɛn Nt, kʊm ɒʊəɹ əgɪən Y, *-s* kʊmz ɔvɹ əgɪˑən L, kʊm ɔʊəɹ əgeən Y, *inf* kʊm ɒʊəɹ əgɛn Y, kʌm ʌʊvəɹ əgeɪn Hrt, kɒm ɔˑəɹ əgɛn Db, kʊm ɔˑəɹ əgə Db

comes out *viphr-3prsg* school FINISHES VIII.6.2(b). kʊmz ɛːt Db, kʌmz ɛʊt Ess, kʌm æyt So, kʊmz æʊt Wo, kʌmz æʊt Ess W, kʌm æʊt So, də kʌm æʊt Do, kʌmz aʊt So, kʌm aʊt So, kʊmz aʊt La, kʊz aʊt La O, kʊmz ʌʊt Gl, kʊmz uːt Nb Cu Du, kəmz ᵁuːt Gl, kʌmz əʊt W, kʌm əʊt W, kʊmz əʊːt Gl

come up *viphr* to WAX, referring to the moon VII.6.5(a). kʌm ʌp Sa Mon, *-ing* kʌmɪn ʌp So, kʊm ʊp La Sa Wo, *-ing* kʊmɪn ʊp Y, *-ing* kʊmən ʊp Du; **come up to the full** *-ing* kʊmɪn ʊp tə t fʊl We, *-ing* kʊmɪn ʊp tə ðə fʊɫ He; ⇒ also **full**

comical *adj* STUPID VI.1.5. kɒmɪkəɫ He

coming down *adj IN* FLOOD, describing a river IV.1.4. kʊmən duːn Nb

coming out *adj IN* FLOOD, describing a river IV.1.4. kʊmən aʊt Y; **come out** kʊm ɛʊt Hu *[see note at flood]*

commences *vi-3prsg* school BEGINS VIII.6.2(a). kəmɛnsɪz Brk

companions *npl* PALS VIII.4.2. kʊmpænjəns Man

confab *n* CHAT VIII.3.4. kɒnfab Y, kɔnfab Y; **old confab** ɔʊd kɒnfab Y

conflab *n* CHAT VIII.3.4. kɒnflæb K, kɒnflab Bk

conflabbing *v-ing* GOSSIPING VIII.3.5(a). kɒnflæbɪn Nf

conflaberation *n* CHAT VIII.3.4. kɒnflabəɹeɪʃən Wo

conger *n* a CUCUMBER V.7.17. kɒŋgə Wa*[old]*, kɒŋgəᵗ Wa*[old]*, kʊŋgə Wa*[old]*, *pl* kʊŋgəz Wo, kʊŋgəᵗ Wo

conies *1. npl* RABBITS kept in a hutch III.13.13. kʌʊnɪz MxL
2. npl wild rabbits. *sg* kʌʊnɪ Sr, kɒzˌʊnɪz K

conk *n* a NOSE VI.4.6. kɒŋk Y Sa, kɔŋk MxL*[slang]*

conker-bells *n* ICICLES VII.6.11. kɒŋkəᵗːbɫz So D

conkerooms* *npl* MUSHROOMS II.2.11. *sg* kɒŋkəɹuːm Mon *[WMBM headword conkeroons]*

conkers* *npl* HIPS of the wild rose IV.11.7. kɒŋkəz Ess, *sg* kɒŋkəᵗː W, kɔŋkəz Sf, kɔŋkʔəz Sf

constable *n* **the constable** a BOGEY VIII.8.1. ðə kʊnstəbl L

contagious *adj* INFECTIOUS, describing a disease VI.12.2. kəntɛɪdʒəs Ess, tɛɪdʒəs Wa

contrary *1. adj* RESTIVE, describing a horse III.5.6. kɒn'tɾɛːɾɪ D, ˈkɒntɾɛɾɪ Ha, kɔːntɾəɾɪ So, kɔːntɾɪ So
2. adj STUPID VI.1.5. kɒtɹɛəɹɪ Nf

conversation *n* CHAT VIII.3.4. kɒnvəsɛəʃn Y

convolvulus *n* BINDWEED II.2.4. kɒnvɒlvəs Nb Du Y, kɒnvɒlvləs Y, kʊnvɒlvləs Nb, kənvɒlvəs La Ch Sa, kəvɒljələs Man, kɔnvɒlvəs Y, kənvɔvələs La, kɒnvʊlvɪəs La, kɒnvʊlvʊs Y, kɒnvʊlvəs Nb Cu We La Ch, kɔnvʊlvəs Nb, kənvʊlvəs La, kənvʊlʃəs Ch

coochy *1. adj* LEFT-HANDED VI.7.13(a). kyːtʃɪ D
2. adj CLUMSY, describing a person VI.7.14. kyːtʃɪ So

coochy-gammy *adj* LEFT-HANDED VI.7.13(a). kyːtʃɪgami D

coochy-handed *adj* LEFT-HANDED VI.7.13(a). kytʃɪ-ændɪd D, kytʃɪ-ændəd So, kyːtʃɪ-ændɪd So

coochy-pawed *adj* LEFT-HANDED VI.7.13(a). kyːtʃɪpɔːd D

cooking-board *n* a PASTE-BOARD V.6.5. kukʔnbɔəd Nf, kʊkɪnbuəᵗːd Co

cool *v Some children, if their tea is too hot, blow on it to ....* V.8.11. Eng. ⇒ **cold, cold down, colden, cool down, get cold, make cold, make colder, make cool**

cool down *vtphr* to COOL tea by blowing on it V.8.11. kuːɫ ... dævn Co, kuːɫ ... dæʊn Ha, kuːɫ ... daʊn So

cooler *1. n* a TROUGH in a cow-house, made from a wooden barrel cut in two I.3.6. kuːlə Man

2. n a SALTING-TROUGH III.12.5. kuːlə
Man*[wooden]*, kuːləᵗ Sa*[wooden, stone, unspecified]*, kuːləᵗː Sa*[metal]*, kʏʉːləᵗ Sa

cooms* *n* barley AWNS II.5.3. kuːmz St

coons *npl* RABBITS kept in a hutch III.13.13. kuːnz Sf

coop *1. n* a SLEDGE, 'like a big box on runners', used to carry loads in winter I.9.1. kəʊp Y
2. n a SKEP IV.8.8(b). kuːp MxL
3. imp **coop, coop harley, coop here, coop here harley, coop here holt, coop here wee, coop toward, coop wee** the command TURN LEFT!, given to plough-horses II.3.5(a). **coop** kʏp Nf; **coop harley** ˌkʌˈpaːlə Nf; **coop here** ˈkɛb ˌhɪˈə Nf, kɒp wəː Ess, kʊp iːə L, kʌp ɪə Sf, ˈkʌb ɪə Nf, ˌkʌ ˈbɪə Nf; **coop here harley** ˌkʌb ɪ ˈhælˑi Nf; **coop here holt** ˈkʌp ɪ ˌhoːɬt Nf, ˈkʌb ɪə ˈhɑlt Nf, ˈkʌp ə ˈhɒˑlt Nf, ˌkʌpʔ ɪ ˈhoult Nf; **coop here wee** ˈkʌb iˑ ˈwiː Nf; **coop toward** ˌkʊp ˈtæwəd Ess; **coop wee** ˈkɒp wɪ Ess
4. imp **coop, coop go on*** the command GO ON!, given to plough-horses II.3.5(d). **coop** kʊp O; **coop go on** ˈkʌp ˌgʊ ˈɒn Hu

coopings *1. npl* long gable-ended or round-ended STACKS II.7.1. *sg* kuːpən Y
2. npl long stacks with rounded ends. *sg* kuːpɪn Y

coos *npl* PIGEONS IV.7.3. kuːz L

coosh *n* CHAT VIII.3.4. kuːʃ Man*[old x1]*

cooshies *n* SWEETS V.8.4. koˑʃɪz Nf, koʊʃɪs Nf*[old]*, koʊʃiz Nf, kʊʃɪs Nf

coosil *n* COLT'S-FOOT II.2.7. kəʊsɪl La

coping *1. n* the CURB-STONE in a cow-house I.3.9. koːpɪn He, koːʊpɪn Mon
2. n the RIDGE of a house roof V.1.2(a). koːpɪn Ch He, koʊpɪn So

coping-stones *n* the CURB-STONE in a cow-house I.3.9. koːʊpɪnstʊnz Gl

copper *n* a BOGEY VIII.8.1. kɒpəᵗ Wo

copper-fibre *n* STRING used to tie up a grain-sack I.7.3. kɒpəᵗːfaɪbəᵗː Co

copper-hook *n* a CRANE on which a kettle is hung over a domestic fire V.3.4. kɒpəɹɛʊk Db

copping *v-ing* THROWING a stone VIII.7.7. kɑˑpʔn Nf, kɒpn Nf, kɒpʔn Nf

coppy *1. n* a PADDOCK I.1.10. kɒpɪ Cu
2. n a MILKING-STOOL III.3.3. kɒpɪ Nb Cu Du We La Y
3. n a stool of any kind. kɒbɪ Y

coppy-stool *n* a MILKING-STOOL III.3.3. kɒpɪstɪvl Cu, kɒpɪstɪʊl Cu

cops *1. n* a chain TETHER for a cow I.3.4. kɒps Brk
2. n a sliding RING to which a tether is attached in a cow-house I.3.5. kɒps Do
3. n the T-SHAPED PLOUGH-BEAM END of a horse-drawn plough I.8.5. kɒps O Brk
4. npl the RIDGES between furrows in a ploughed field II.3.2. kɒps St He, *sg* kɒp Db Sa, *-s* kɒsɪz Mon

5. npl COCKS of hay II.9.12. *sg* kɒp K

copse(s) *n* a CART-FRAME I.10.6.
no -s: kɒps Hrt Ess
-s: kɒpsɪz Bd

copses *1. npl* CART-LADDERS I.10.5. kɒpsɪz Ess, koʊpsəz C
2. npl front cart-ladders. kɒpsɪz Hrt, *sg* kɒps Bk, *sg* kɒps Hrt Ess, kɒpsɪz Hrt, koʊpsɪz Hu, koʊpsɪz C
3. nsg a front cart-ladder. kɒpsɪz Bd Hrt

copsil *1. n* an EVENER on the plough-beam end of a horse-drawn plough I.8.4. kɒpsɪl Sa, kɒpsl Sa, kɒpstl Sa
2. n the T-SHAPED PLOUGH-BEAM END of a horse-drawn plough I.8.5. kɒpsəl Sa St

cord *1. n* a TETHERING-ROPE used to tie up a horse I.4.2. kɔəd Wa
2. n STRING used to tie up a grain-sack I.7.3. kɒᵗːd̪ So, koːɘᵗːd̪ So, kuːɽd̪ D, kuɘᵗːd̪ So Co D
3. n a SOWING-BASKET II.3.6. kɔᴶːd K
4. n TWINE used to fasten thatch on a stack II.7.7(b1). kɔːd Db St Hrt, kɒᵗːd̪ Sa So, kɒᵗːɘᵗd̪ Sa
5. n the CORE of a boil VI.11.7. kɔəᴶd Brk, kʊəɹd La
6. n a knee-strap, ⇐ KNEE-STRAPS used to lift the legs of working trousers VI.14.17. kɔᴿːd Du

cords *npl* the REINS of a plough-horse I.5.5. kɔːdz Y, kʊədz Y

core *1. n* *Have you a special word for the centre of a boil?* VI.11.7. Eng exc. Du. ⇒ **bit**, *coke* ⇒ **cork, cork, cord, dot, eye, gore, gowk, grub, gut, head, heart, kernel, pea, pith, root, sitfast, string, tanner, thickfast**
2. n a CALLOSITY VI.11.4. *pl* kɒᵗːz̪ Co

cork* *n* the CORE of a boil VI.11.7. kɔːk Ch, kɔᴿːk Nb

corn *1. n* *What do you mean by* **corn** *here in these parts?* II.5.1.
a. wheat, oats, and barley: Nb Du We La Y Man Ch Db Sa St He Wo Wa Mon Gl Nt L Lei Nth Hu Nf Sf Bk Hrt Ess So W Brk K Co D Do Ha Sx
b. wheat, oats, barley, beans, and peas: Y St O L Lei C Sf Bk Bd Ess MxL Sr K Sx
c. wheat, oats, barley, and rye: La Y Ch He O Nf Bk Ess So Brk Sr K
d. wheat, oats, barley, and beans: He Wo Wa Gl O L Lei R Hu Bk Ess Do
e. oats: Nb Cu Du We La Y Man Db Sa
f. wheat: Du La Sa Gl Nt L
g. wheat and oats: Du La Bk So D
h. wheat, oats, barley, beans, and rye: Wa O Nt Nth So
i. wheat and barley: Bd D
j. wheat, oats, barley, peas, and rye: Y Nf

k. wheat, oats, barley, beans, peas, and rye: L Ess Sr

l. wheat, oats, barley, and indian corn/maize: Y Lei

m. wheat, oats, barley, rye, and linseed: Nf

n. wheat, oats, barley, beans, peas, and linseed: L

o. wheat, oats, barley, beans, peas, rye, and vetches: O

p. wheat, oats, barley, beans, rye, and vetches: Wa

q. wheat, oats, barley, fieldbeans, and fieldpeas: Brk

r. wheat, oats, barley, beans, peas, and buckwheat: Brk

s. wheat, oats, barley, beans, peas, and tares: Nth

t. wheat, oats, barley, beans, peas, maize, and sugarbeet: Sr

u. wheat, oats, barley, beans, indian corn/maize, and peas: Y

v. wheat, oats, and beans: Lei

w. wheat, oats, peas, and beans: Sx

x. wheat, rivet-wheat, and oats: Hrt

y. oats, barley, and rye: Sa

z. oats, barley, beans, peas, and vetches: Sx

2. v to feed corn to horses in the stable, ⇐ FEEDING III.5.1. kɔːn Du, koˑən We

3. n a CALLOSITY VI.11.4. *pl* kaᵗːɳz̧ So W Ha, *pl* kaːnz Wo Mon, *pl* kaᵗːɳz̧ He Wo Mon Gl, *pl* kɒɪnz He, *pl* kɒːnz K, kɔːn St Mon, *pl* kɔːnz C Ess MxL, *pl* kɔˑənz Y L, *pl* kɔᵗːɳz̧ Gl O Brk Ha, kɔːəᴶnz Sr, kɔːəᵗɽɳz̧ Sx

corn-ark *n* a CORN-BIN I.7.4. kɔːnaːk St

corn-bin *n What do you call the container in which you keep the corn for immediate use? [If the answer is bin, ask for additional meanings of bin. If the answer is not bin, ask: Rev. What do you mean by bin?]* I.7.4.

1. material unspecified. kaᵗːɳbɪn Wo So W Brk Do Ha, kaᵗːɳbɪn Wo Mon, kɒɪnbɪn He, kɒᵗɳbɪn O Ha, kɔːnbɪn Cu Y Ch Db Sa St Wa Lei R Hu Sf Hrt Ess MxL Sr K, kɔᵏːnbɪn Du, kɔᴶːnbɪn Db, kɔᵗːɳbɪn Wa Nth Bk So W D Ha, kɔːənbɪn Y K, kɔəᴶnbɪn We La, kɔːəᵗɳbɪn Sx, kʊrnbɪn Cu, kʊənbɪn Y

2. wooden. kaᴶːnbɪn Ha, kaᵗːɳbɪn Wo W Do, kaᴶːnbɪn Brk, kɔːnbɪn Y Man Wa Mon K, kɔᵗːɳbɪn Ha Sx, kɔənbɪn K, kɔəᴶnbɪn Brk Ha, kɔːəᵗɽɳbɪn Sr

3. wooden, lined with tin. kaᵗːɳbɪn Do

4. metal. kaᵗːɳbɪn W, kɔːnbɪn Y Wa Mon, kɔˑəᴶnbɪn Ha

5. for unmixed corn. kɔːnbɪn Ch

6. for hay. kaᴶːnbɪn Brk

⇒ **barrel, bin, bing, chaff-bin, coffer, corn-ark, corn-bing, corn-chest, corn-coffer, corn-hutch, corn-kist, corn-pen, garner, grintern, hutch, keeve, kist, locker, meal-bin, provand-bin, provand-bing, provand-kist, tin-bin, tub, tun,** *wooden-***bin;** ⇒ also **ash-bin, ash-bing, bacon-bing, bread-bin, bread-bing, cake-bin, chaff-bin, chicken-bin, dough-bin, flour-bin, flour-bing, hop-bin, meal-bin, meal-bing, sheep-bing**

corn-bind *n* BINDWEED II.2.4. kɔːnbɪn Y, kɔːnbaɪn Y Nt L Lei, kɔənbaɪn Y L, kɔːnbaːn Lei R, kɔːnbaɪn Db Wa Nt L Lei Nth, kɔːnbaɪnd Nth, kɔːnbɒɪn Lei R, kɔːnbɔɪn Lei Nth Bk, kɔᵗːˀnbɔɪn Nth, kɔᵗːˀnbɔɪn Bk, kʊənbaˑɪn L, kəɹənbaɪn La *[not a NBM headword]*

corn-bing *1. n* a CORN-BIN I.7.4. kaᵗːɳbɪŋ Sa, kaːnbɪŋ Wo, kɔːnbɪŋ Y L Lei R C Nf Bd, kɔənbɪŋ Y Nf, kʊənbɪŋ L

2. n a wooden corn-bin. kɔːnbɪŋ Y

corn-chest *1. n* a CORN-BIN I.7.4. kɔᵗːɳtʃɛst D

2. n a wooden corn-bin. kɔːntʃɪst Du, kɔːntʃɛˑst K

3. n a wooden or iron corn-bin. kɔːntʃɛst K

corn-clean *v* to WINNOW II.8.4. *-ing* kɔːnklᴶɪnɪn K

corn-coffer *n* a CORN-BIN I.7.4. kɔːnkɒfə Ch St

corner *n* from corner to corner DIAGONALLY, referring to harrowing a field IX.1.8. fɹəm kɔɽnəɽ tə kɔɽnəɽ O, fɹɛ kʊənə tə kʊənə Y

corner-end *n* the GABLE-END of a house V.1.5. kaᵗːɳəᵗɽend He

corner-staff *n* the iron stay connecting the beam with the side of a cart, ⇐ CROSS-BEAM END I.10.1. kɔːnəstaf Y

corner-ways *adv* DIAGONALLY, referring to harrowing a field IX.1.8. kɔːnəwɛɪz St Nth Nf Ess*[old]* K, kɔːnəwɛˑəz L, kɔːnəwɔɪz Ess

cornet bag *n* a BAG containing sweets V.8.5. kɔːnɪt bæːg Sr*[old method]*

cornflower *n* BINDWEED II.2.4. kɔːnflæʊə Wa

corn-hauling *v-ing* CARTING corn from the field II.6.6. kaᵗːɳaːɬɪn Gl, kaᵗːɳaːɬɪn He, kaᵗːɳhɔːlən So

corn-hutch *1. n* a CORN-BIN I.7.4. kɔːnhʌtʃ Sf Ess, kɔːnʌtʃ Sf, kɔᵗːɳʌtʃ So D, kɔᵗːɳʊtʃ Co

2. n a wooden corn-bin. kɔːnhʌtʃ Ess, kɔᵗːɳʌtʃ D

corn-kist *1. n* a CORN-BIN I.7.4. kɔənkɪst Y, kʊrnkɪst Cu, kʊənkɪst Cu

2. n a corn-bin in a stable. kʊrnkɪst Cu

corn measure *n* a BASKET for carrying horse-feed III.5.4. kɔːnmɛʒə Du*[like flour-scoop]*

corn-pen *n* a CORN-BIN I.7.4. kɔːnpɛn Ess

corn-yarn *n* TWINE used to fasten thatch on a stack II.7.7(b1). kɔᵗːɳjaᵗːɳ Co*[coarse cord]*

corpse *n* a dead BODY VIII.5.7(a). kœːps Du, kaːps Sa, kaᵗːps So W Ha, kaːps Y Man, kaᴶːps Brk, kaᵗːps He Wo Brk, kɒɪps Y He, kɔːps Cu Du We Y*[modern x1, rare x1]* Ch Db St Wa L Lei R Nth Nf Sf Ess Sr K Ha, kɔᵏːps Nb Du, kɔᴶːps La Y, kɔᵗːps He O Nf So Brk Sr K Sx, kɔəps Y L, kɔˑəᴶps Brk, kɔᵗəps O, kɔːəᵗɽps Sx, kʊəps L, kəːps Man, kəᴶːps L; **dead corpse** dɛd kaᵗːps So

cosh *1. n* a WHIP used for driving horses I.5.12. kɒʃ So

2. n CHAFF II.8.5. kɒʃ Nf

3. n a pea-POD V.7.12. kɔʃ C

coshing *v-ing* SHELLING peas V.7.14. kɒʃɪn Nth, *no -ing* kɒʃ Hu, kɔʃən C*[old]*

cosp *1. n* an EVENER on a horse-drawn plough I.8.4. kɑːsp Mon

2. n an evener on the plough-beam end of a horse-drawn plough. kɑːsp He Gl, kɑˤːʂp Wo, kɒsp He Mon, kɒs Mon, kɔːst He

3. n the T-SHAPED PLOUGH-BEAM END of a horse-drawn plough I.8.5. kɒsp He

cosset *n* a PET-LAMB III.7.3. kɒsɪt Nf, kɔsət Sf Ess

cosset-pet *n* a PET-LAMB III.7.3. kɔsətpɛt Sf

cotmer-handed *adj* RIGHT-HANDED VI.7.13(b). kɔtməɹandəd L *[queried EMBM]*

cotswold-rubbers *n pl* whetstones made of stone, ⇐ WHETSTONE II.9.10. kɒksuɫɹʊbəˤz Brk

cotted *1. adj* TANGLED, describing hair VI.2.5. kɒtɪd Nb Du Nt L, kɔtɪd L; ⇒ also **cottered**

2. adj **nearly cotted** VERY COLD, describing a person VI.13.19. nrˈəlɪ kɔtɪd L

cotter *1. n* a LINCH-PIN holding a wheel on a cart I.9.12. kɒtə St Lei Nth

2. n a metal linch-pin. kɒtə Ch Db St

3. n a pin fixing a cart-body to the shafts, stopping it from tipping, ⇐ ROD/PIN I.10.3. kɒtə Y Db St, *pl* kɒtəz Ch

4. n **of a cotter** TANGLED, describing hair VI.2.5. əv ə kɒtə Y

cottered *adj* TANGLED, describing hair VI.2.5. kɒtəd Cu We St Nt Lei Y, kɒtərd We, kɒtəɹd Y, kɔtəd L, kɔtɪd L; ⇒ also **cotted**

cottered up *adj* TANGLED, describing hair VI.2.5. kɒtəd ʊp Y

cotterel *1. n* a metal LINCH-PIN holding a wheel on a cart I.9.12. kɒtɹɪl Y *[also = 'cotter-pin' Nb, but not defined]*

2. n a CRANE on which a kettle is hung over a domestic fire V.3.4. kɒtɾəɫ Ha

cotterel-pin *n* a LINCH-PIN holding a wheel on a cart I.9.12. kɒtrəlpɪn Cu

cotter-pin *1. n* a LINCH-PIN holding a wheel on a cart I.9.12. kɑˑʔəpɪn Nf, kɒtəpɪn We Y Db St Mon Lei, kɒʔəˤpɪn Bk, kɒtəᵏpɪn Nb

2. n a metal linch-pin. kɒtəpɪn Y Db St, kɒtəɹpɪn La, kɔtəpɪn La Y

3. n a wooden linch-pin. kɔtəpɪn Y

4. n a pin fixing a cart-body to the shafts, stopping it from tipping, ⇐ ROD/PIN I.10.3. kɒtəpɪn Y Db St

cotter-stick *n* a movable horizontal rod stretching between the shafts of a cart, fixing them to the cart-body and stopping the cart from tipping, ⇐ ROD/PIN I.10.3. kɒtəstɪk Db St Nt

cottery *adj* TANGLED, describing hair VI.2.5. kɒtəɹɪ Y

cotton *n* THREAD V.10.2(b). katn Nf, kaːtn Nf, kaːtʔn Nf, kɒtn St Nf Ess, kɒʔn Nf Bk Hrt, kɔtn Ch Wa

cotton-apron *n* a decorative APRON V.11.2(b). kɒtnapɹən Y

cotton bonnet *n* a woman's BONNET VI.14.1. kɒtn bɒnɪt St

cotton-spool *n* a cotton-REEL V.10.6. kɔtnspʊɔl Wa

cotty *adj* TANGLED, describing hair VI.2.5. kɒtɪ Lei R, kɔtɪ L, kɔtʔɪ L

cotty-comb *n* a CURRY-COMB used to clean horses III.5.5(b). kɒtɪkoəm Y, kɔtɪkʊəm L

couch *1. n* COUCH-GRASS II.2.3. kʏːtʃ So, kɛʊtʃ O Bk, kæʊtʃ W Ha, kaʊtʃ W Do, koʊtʃ Brk, kʊtʃ He Mon Gl O, kuːtʃ Cu Gl O Bk So W Brk Sr K Do Ha Sx, kəʊtʃ W Do

2. vt to HIDE something VIII.7.6. kʊtʃ Mon

couch-grass *n* [*Show a picture of couch-grass.] What do you call this?* II.2.3. kʏːtʃgɹaːs D, kɛʊtʃgɹɑːs Ha, kɛʊtʃgɹɑːs MxL Brk, kæʊtʃgɹɑːs Ha, kaʊtʃgɹas L, kɒʊtʃgɹæˑs Man, kʌtʃgɹæs So, kʊtʃgɹæːs So, kʊtʃgɹaːs He Mon Ess, kʊtʃgɹɑːs So, kuːtʃgɹæs Brk, kuːtʃgɹæːs Sx, kuːtʃgɹɑːs So, kuːtʃgɹaːs So W Ha, kuːtʃgɹɹɑːs MxL Sr K. ⇒ **cockle, couch, crouch-grass, dog's-foot-grass, fowl-grass, kesh, quick(s), quick-grass, quitch, scitch, scutch, scutch-grass, scwutch, spear-grass, squitch, squitch-grass, strap-grass, string-couch, string-twitch, stroil, stroily-grass, twicks, twitch, twitch-grass, wick(s), wicken(s), wicken-grass, wick-grass, wilks, wrack**

coughing *v-ing What am I doing now [indicate coughing]?* Eng. ⇒ ***a-coughing*, barking, barking about, basking, bruffing, *bruffing and coughing*, bussocking, *coughing and* bloifing, *got a* hoast, *got the* hisk, hacketing, *hacketing cough*, hacking, *hacking cough*, hackling, hasking, *hawk* ⇒ hawking, hawking, *heckling cough*, hisking, *hoarse cough*, hoasting, hoisting, hoosting, hoozing, *hosk* ⇒ hosking, hosking, huffing in, husking, hussocking, kecking, peghing, peghing *and coughing*, tissicking, tissicking about; ⇒ also **bussock, chissicking, heaze, heckling, hoosk, hoost, hooze, husk, hussock**

coulter *n* [*Show a picture of a horse-drawn plough.] What do you call this?* I.8.6. Eng exc. Gl Sf; **plough-coulter** plɛʊkəʊlʔə Nf, pluːkuːtər Y. ⇒ **coultern, counter, countern, cutter, knife, *plough*-coulter**

coultern *n* the COULTER of a horse-drawn plough I.8.6. koːɫtjəˤn̩ He, kəʊtjən He, kəʊːtjʊn Wo

counter *n* the COULTER of a horse-drawn plough I.8.6. kɛʊntə Sf Hrt Ess, kɛʊntʔə Nf Sf, kɛʊnʔə Nf, kæʊntə Mon Ess, kæʊntəᵗ Mon Gl, kæʊntəᵗ: W, kaʊntəᵗ: So, kɒʊntəᵗ: W, kʌʊnʔə Sf, kʌʊntəᵗ Gl, koːʊntəᵗ Gl, kuːntə Cu Y, kuːntɪ L, kᵁuːntəᵗ Gl, kəʊntə O, kəʊntəᵗ Mon Gl O Brk, kəʊntəᵗ: W

countern *n* the COULTER of a horse-drawn plough I.8.6. kæʊntjən He, kʌʊntjən He Mon, kəʊntjən He

counterpane *n* a QUILT V.2.11. kɛntəpɛɪn Lei, kɛʊntəpɪn Hrt, kɛʊntʔəpɪn Nf, kɛʊnʔəpɪn Nf, kɛʊnʔəpɛn Nf, kɛʊntəpɛɪn MxL, kɛʊntʔəpɛɪn Nf, kɛʊntəpæɪn Ess, kɛʊnʔəpæɪn Nf, kɛʊntəpaɪn Ess, kæːntəpɛɪn St, kæʊntəpiːn Lei, kæʊntəpɛɪn Lei, kæʊntəᵗpɛːən He, kæʊntəpən Man, kaɪntəpiːn St, kaʊnʔəpɛn Nf, kaʊntəpɛɪn St L Lei, kaʊndəpɛɪn Nf, kɒʊntəpɛɪn Lei, kəʊntəpeɪn Mon, kəʊntəpɛ·n K *[marked u.r. N/SBM]*

counter-ways *adv* DIAGONALLY, referring to harrowing a field IX.1.8. kæʊtəˡwæɪz K *[queried SBM]*

coup *1. vi* to OVERTURN, referring to a cart I.11.5. kaʊp Du, kɒʊp Nb Cu Du, kɔʊp Nb

2. v to TIP a cart I.11..6. kɒʊp Nb, kuːp Du

3. vt to SPRAIN an ankle VI.10.8. kɔʊp Nb *[see note at twined]*

4. v **coup over backwards, coup your creel(s)** to turn HEAD OVER HEELS IX.1.10. **coup over backwards** kɒʊp ɒʊə bakwədz Nb; **coup your creel(s)** kɒʊp jə kʁiːlz Du, kɒʊp jə kɹiːl Nb, kɒʊp jə kɹᵉɪlz Du

coup-cart *n* a FARMCART I.9.3. kɒʊpkæˡːt La, kuːpkæːt Du, kuːpkaːt Du

couple of *adj* **a couple of, couple of** A FEW VII.1.19. **a couple of** ə kʌpl ə Nf Ess, ə kʌpəl ə He, ə kʌpɫ ə Ess, ə kʊpl ə Wo, ə kʊpəl ə Y; **couple of** kʌpʔl ə Nf, kʌpɫ ə Ess MxL, kʌpʊ ə So, kʊpʊ ə So

couple of week(s) *n* a FORTNIGHT VII.3.2. kʌpl ə wɪks He, ə kʌpɫ ə wiːks Mon, ə kʊpɫ ə wiːk Mon

couple or three *adj* **a couple or three, couple or three** A FEW VII.1.19. **a couple or three** ə kʌpɫ d̥ɹiː W; **couple or three** kʌpɫ ə d̥ɹii W

coupling *n* the linkage between the swingle-tree and the plough-beam end of a horse-drawn plough, ⇐ EVENER I.8.4. kʊplɪn Lei

couplings *n* **drop in the couplings** referring to a cow, show signs of calving by changes in the pelvic region, ⇐ SHOWS SIGNS OF CALVING III.1.12(b). *3prperfsg* d̥ɹɒpt ɪn ðə kʌplɪnz Ẇa

coupling-stick *n* the STRETCHER between the traces of a cart-horse I.5.11. kʊplɪnstɪk Nth, kʊpᵊɫɪnstɪk Lei

coup over *viphr* to OVERTURN, referring to a cart I.11.5. *-ed* kɒʊpt ɒʊəᴿ Nb

coup up *1. viphr* to OVERTURN, referring to a cart I.11.5. kɔʊp ʊp Nb

2.1. vphr to TIP a cart I.11.6. kɔʊp ʌp Nb, kɔʊp ʊp Nb

2.2. vtphr to tip. kɔʊp ... œːp Nb, kɒʊpt ʏp Nb, kɒʊp ... ʊp Cu, kɒʊp ... əp Du

court *1. n* a FARMYARD I.1.3. kyːɽt D, kɔᵗːt W, koːəᵗːt Ha, kuːɽt D, kuəᵗːt W Co D

2. n the shed of a PIGSTY, distinct from the pen attached to it I.1.5. kɔːt Ess

3. n the STRAW-YARD of a farm I.1.9. kuːɽt D, kuəᵗːt Co

courtain *n* the STRAW-YARD of a farm I.1.9. kuɔᴿːtn Nb, kuətn Nb

courtyard *n* a FARMYARD I.1.3. kɒʊəᵗtjaᵗːd̥ Ẇa, kɔəᵗtjaᵗːd̥ O

cove *n* a DOVECOTE I.1.7. kʊuː Sr

cover *1. n* THATCH on a stack of corn II.7.6. kʊvɔᴿ Nb

2. n a QUILT V.2.11. kɪvəᵗ He *[marked u.r. WMBM]*

covered *adj* HEAVING (WITH MAGGOTS) IV.8.6. kʌvəd Ess, kʊvəd St

covered-in yard *n* the STRAW-YARD of a farm I.1.9. kʌvədɪn jɑːəᵗɽd̥ Sr

covered-yard *n* the STRAW-YARD of a farm I.1.9. kʌvəᵗːdjaᵗːd̥ Co, kʊvəd jaːd St

coverer *n* the THATCHER of a stack of corn II.7.5(b). kʊvəʁɔᴿ Nb

covering *v-ing* THATCHING a stack of corn II.7.5(a). kʌvɔᴿʁən Nb, kʊvɔᴿʁən Nb, kʊvəʁən Nb, kʊvʁən Nb

cover up *vtphr* to HIDE something VIII.7.6. kʊvəɹ ... ʊp Y

cow *1. n [What do you call your animals that give milk?] And one of them?* III.1.1(b). kɛa Y, kɛʊ Y Db Sa Wo Wa Gl O L Lei Nth Hu C Nf Sf Bk Bd Hrt Ess MxL Brk Sr K Ha Sx, kjɛʊ Bd, kɛuː Wo, kɛə Y, kœv D, kæː Y Man Nt Sr, kæ·a Y, kæv So Co D, kæʊ Y Man Ch Sa St He Wo Wa O Nt L Lei R Ess MxL So W Sr K Do Ha, kˡæʊ He, kjæʊ Ch, kæ·ə La Y, kaː La Y Lei, kaʊ La Y Ch Db Sa St Nt L Lei So, kau: Sa, kɑʊ He O Nf, kɒʊ Gl W, kɔʊ Du L, kʌʊ Nb Y He Mon Gl Brk, kᵒuː Du, kᵁuː Nb We Y Sa Gl, kuː Nb Cu Du We La Y L, kju: St, kəʊ Y He Mon Gl O Nf So W Brk K Do Sx, kəʊ: Du Y Wo Gl. ⇒ **dummock, hummock, kye, milk-cow**

2. npl COWS III.1.1(a). kᵋu K

cow-bag *n* the UDDER of a cow III.2.5. kaʊbag Y, kuːbag Y

cow-band *1. n* a TETHER for a cow I.3.4. kaʊband La Y, kuːband We, kuːban Cu

2. n a rope tether. kaʊband La, kuːband We

3. n a chain tether. kuːband Cu

4. n a tether made of rope or chain. kaʊband Y, kuːband Cu Y

5. n an iron tether. kᵒuːband Du, kuːband Du

cowband-stake *n* a TETHERING-STAKE in a cow-house I.3.3. kuːbandsteːk Cu

cow-banger *n* a COWMAN on a farm I.2.3. kaːbaŋə
swY

cow-barton *1. n* a COW-HOUSE I.1.8. kəʊbaˑtːkŋ
W

2. n the STRAW-YARD of a farm I.1.9. kəʊbaˑtːkŋ
Do

cow-bed *n* the UTERUS of a cow III.2.4. kæˑbɛˑəd
Man, kəʊ bɛdːə Y

cow-bing *n* a COW-HOUSE I.1.8. kaʊbɪŋ Sa

cow-boosing *n* a COW-HOUSE I.1.8. kɒʊbɒʊzɪn Gl

cow-broom *n* a MUCK-BRUSH I.3.14. kæʊbɽuːm
Ha

cow-byre *n* a COW-HOUSE I.1.8. kaʊbaɪə St,
kʌʊbaɪə Y, kuːbaɪəᴿ Nb Du, kuːbaɪə Y, kuːbaɪəɹ Cu,
kəʊbaɪə Y

cow-chain *n* a chain TETHER for a cow I.3.4.
kɪatʃɛɪn Y, kɛːtʃɪʊn La, kɛʊtʃeːn Db Sa, kɛʊtʃeɪn Hu
Sx, kɛʊtʃeɪn Wa Hrt Ess Brk Sr Sx, kɛʊtʃæɪn Hu Ess
K, kɛʊtʃaɪn Ess, kæːtʃeːn Nt, kæːᵊtʃeːˡn Db,
kæːᵊtʃɛɪn K, kævtʃeɪn So, kævtʃeɪn D, kæʊtʃɪən Nt,
kæʊtʃeːn Sa W Ha, kæʊtʃeɪn So, kæʊtʃeɪn Nt Lei R
K, kæʊtʃæɪn Nth, *pl* kæʊtʃæɪnz K, kæʊtʃaɪn W Ha,
kaːtʃiːn St Lei, kaːtʃeːn La Nt, kaːtʃɛɪn St Lei,
kaɪtʃiːn Ch, kaʊtʃiːn Db St, kaʊtʃɪən Y, kaʊtʃeːn Db
Sa, kaʊtʃeɪn So, kaʊtʃɛɪn Y Db St Lei, kɔʊtʃɛɪn O,
kʌʊtʃeːn Y, kᵒuːtʃeːn Du, kᵁuːtʃæɪn Gl, kuːtʃiːn Y,
kuːtʃɪən Nb Du Y, kuːtʃeːn Nb, kuːtʃeɪn Y, kuːtʃeən
Nb Y, kuːtʃɛːn We, kuːtʃɛən Y, kəʊtʃeːn Brk,
kəʊtʃɛɪn Gl O, kəʊtʃaɪn W, kᵊuːtʃæɪn Du

cow-chain-pole *n* a TETHERING-STAKE in a
cow-house I.3.3. kæʊtʃeːnpoːɫ Ha

cow-clap *1. n* COW-DUNG I.3.12. kæʊklap Wa
2. n a CLOT OF COW-DUNG II.1.6. kɛːklap La,
kɛaklap Y, kɛəklap Y, kæʊklap Y L, kæˑəklap La,
kaːklap La Y, kaʊklæp Sa, kaʊklap Cu La Y L, *pl*
kaʊtlaps Y, kʌʊtlap Y, kuːklap Cu We Y, kuːtlap Cu
We, kəʊklap Y

cow-clat *n* a CLOT OF COW-DUNG II.1.6. kɛʊtlat
Wa, kɛʊklad Bd, kæʊklæt O, kuːklat Y

cow-clot *n* a CLOT OF COW-DUNG II.1.6.
kɛʊklɒʔ Bk, kæʊklɒt Lei, kaːᵊklɒt Lei, kaʊklɒt R

cow-clud *n* a CLOT OF COW-DUNG II.1.6. *pl*
kəʊklʌdz Brk

cow-court *n* the STRAW-YARD of a farm I.1.9.
kæʊkɔˑːʈ So

cow-crib *1. n* a STALL in a cow-house I.3.1. *pl*
kaʊkɽɪbz So
2. n a TROUGH in a cow-house I.3.6. kæʊkɽɪb D,
kɒʊkɽɪb W, kuːkɽɪb Y
3. n a circular feeding-trough divided into sections.
kɛʊkɽɪb Hrt

cow-crub *n* a TROUGH in a cow-house I.3.6.
kæʊkɽʌb D

cow-dab *n* a CLOT OF COW-DUNG II.1.6. kɛʊdab
Wa Nth, kɒʊdɛb D, kæʊdæb D, kəʊdæb He

cow-drop *n* a CLOT OF COW-DUNG II.1.6.
kaʊdɹɒp La

cow-dropping *n* a CLOT OF COW-DUNG
II.1.6. kæʊdɹɒpɪn K, kæʊdɽɒːpn Ha, kɛːdɹɒpɪn
Db, kɛʊdɹɒpɪn O Hu, kɛʊdɹɒpɪn Sr, *-s*
kɛʊdɹɒpɪnz MxL

cow-dross *n* URINE in a cow-house I.3.10.
kæʊdɽɾɔːs D

cow-dung *1. n* What do you call the other stuff
that you have to sweep up [besides urine, in a
cow-house]? I.3.12. kɛʊdɒŋ K, kɛʊdʌŋ C Nf Hrt
Ess MxL Sr Sx, kɛʊdʊŋ Nth, kɒvdʌŋ D, kævdʌŋ
So Co D, kæʊdʌŋ O Ess So W Do Ha, kæʊdɒŋ
Man, kaʊdʌŋ So, kɒʊdʌŋ W, kɒʊdʊˑŋ Brk,
kəʊdœːŋ Gl. ⟹ **beast-shit, cow-clap, cow-muck,
cow-mush, cow-sharn, cow-shit, cows-muck,
droppings, dung, manure,** *maxen* ⟹ **mixen,
maxhill,** *maxim* ⟹ **mixen, mix, mixen, muck,
sharn, shit, slush, wax**
2. n a CLOT OF COW-DUNG II.1.6. kæʊdʊŋ
Wa L, kaˑᴵdʊŋ La, kaʊdʊŋ Y, kuːdʊŋ Y
3. n dung. kɛʊdʊŋ Nf, kɛʊdʌŋ Nf Ess Sr Sx,
kɛʊdʊŋ Nf, kɛʊdʊŋ Nth Bk, kɒvdʌŋ D, kævdʌŋ
So D, kæʊdʌŋ Nf W Do, kæʊdʊŋ L, kaːdʊŋ La,
kaʊdʌŋ So, kaʊdʊŋ La St, kəʊdʌŋ So Brk Do

cowed *adj* HORNLESS, describing a cow III.2.9.
kaʊd We, kɒʊd La, kɒʊt Cu

cow-engle *n* the GANGWAY in a cow-house
I.3.7. kœɣ-ɛŋgɫ D

cower *vi* to STAY at home VIII.5.2. kɛəɹ (+V) Y,
kaːɹ (+V) Y, kaʊəɹ (+V) Y

cower down *viphr* to DUCK VIII.7.8. kuɔᴿ duːn
Nb

cow-ewer *n* the UDDER of a cow III.2.5. kuːjʊə
Y

cowey *n* a HORNLESS cow III.2.9. kaʊɪ Nb We,
kɒʊɪ Cu We, kɒʊwɪ Nb, kʌʊɪ Nb

cowey-handed *adj* LEFT-HANDED VI.7.13(a).
kɒʊɪhændəd Du, kɒʊɪhaːndəd Du,
kɔʊɪhæːəndəd Nb

cow-faggots *npl* KINDLING-*WOOD* V.4.2.
kɛʊfɛgɪts K*[old]*

cow-fasten *n* a TETHERING-STAKE in a
cow-house I.3.3. *pl* kəʊfɑːznz Brk

cow-flop *1. n* a CLOT OF COW-DUNG II.1.6.
kɛʊflɒp Db Bk, kɛʊflap O, *pl* kæʊflɒps Sa,
kaːflɒp La Y Ch, kaʊflɒp Y Ch Db Sa
2. n a COWSLIP II.2.10(a). kæɣfɬɒp Co D

cow-foot *n* COLT'S-FOOT II.2.7. kɛʊfʊt La Db
Sa Sx

cow-grass *n* a TUSSOCK of grass II.2.9. kuːgɹas
Y

cow-groop *n* a DRAIN in a cow-house I.3.8.
kɛːgɹuːp Db

cow-gutter *n* a DRAIN in a cow-house I.3.8.
kæʊgʌʔə Ess

cow-halter *n* a leather TETHER for a cow I.3.4. kɛu-ɒˑltəˡ K

cow-handed *adj* LEFT-HANDED VI.7.13(a). kaːhandɪt Nb, kaːhandɪd Nb[*old x1*], kɔʊhæˑndəd Nb

cow-heeled *adj* SPLAY-FOOTED VI.10.5. kɛʊhiːld Nf

cow-hemp *n* a HALTER for a cow I.3.17. kəʊhɛmp W

cow-hole *n* a COW-HOUSE I.1.8. kaʊ-ɔɪl Y

cow-house *n* *What do you call the place where you keep the animals that give you milk?* I.1.8. kɛʊ-ɛʊs Wo Nf Hrt Ess MxL Brk Sr, kɛʊhɛʊs Nf Ess, kɛʊ-aʊs Wo, kɛʊəs Sa Wo O Nth C Sf Bk Bd Hrt Ess, kœʏ-œʏz D, kæʏ-æʏs Co, kæʊ-æʊs Y Sa He L W Do, kæʊhæʊs Nf, kæʊ-aʊs Man L, *pl* kæʊ-aʊzɪz St, kæʊ-ʊs O K, kæʊ-ʊz St, kæʊəs Sa O Nt Ess, kaʊ-aʊs Sa Nt L So Do, kaʊəs Y Ch Db Sa St, kɑʊ-ɑʊs He, kɒʊ-aʊs Sa, kʌʊ-ʌʊs Mon, kɒʊ-ɒʊs Brk, koʊ-ɒʊz Brk, kʊʊ-aʊs Sa, kuːs Y, kuːˑuːs Y L, kᵊʊəs Y, kuːəs Cu, kᵊʊhᵋus K, kəʊ-ʌʊs He, kəʊ-əʊs Y He Wo Gl Brk K Do, kəʊhəʊs Man So. ⇒ **beast-house, beef-house, byre, cattle-shed, cow-barton, cow-bing, cow-boosing, cow-byre, cow-hole, cow-hovel, cow-hull, cow- lodge, cow-pen, cow-pine, cow-place, cow-shade, cow-shed, cow-shippon, cow-shud, cow-skeeling, cow-stable, cow-stall, cows'-house, hovel, lathe, milk-shed, milking-byre, milking parlour, mistall, neat-house, shed, shelter, shippon, skeeling**

cow-hovel *n* a COW-HOUSE I.1.8. kɛʊ-ɒvl L, kɛʊ-ɒvł Bd Hrt, kɛʊhɔvł C, kæʊ-ɒvł Lei R, kæʊ-ɔvl L

cow-hull *n* a COW-HOUSE I.1.8. kaʊ-ʊl Y

cow-juice *n* URINE in a cow-house I.3.10. kɛʊdʒɪuːs Ess

cow keslop* *n* RENNET V.5.6. kʌʊ kɛsləp[*old*]

cow-kit *n* a movable wooden TROUGH in a cow-house I.3.6. kɪakɪt Y

cowl *1. n* a RAKE used in a domestic fire V.3.8(a). kaʊl Y

2.1. v to RAKE in a domestic fire V.3.8(b). kaʊl We Y, kaʊ La, kɔʊl Y, kɔʊ Y

2.2. vt to rake. kaʊl We, kɒʊ Y, kɔʊl Y L

3. n a BUMP on someone's forehead VI.1.8. kɪəl Y, kaʊl Y, kuːl Y, kəʊl Y

cowl down *vtphr* to RAKE in a domestic fire V.3.8(b). kaʊl ... duːn Y, *-ing* kɔʊlɪn ... duːn Y, kʊəl ... dᵊuːn Du

cow-lead *n* a HALTER for a cow I.3.17. kæɬɛɪd Co

cowler *1. n* a RAKE used in a domestic fire V.3.8(a). kaʊlə Y

2. v to RAKE coal in a domestic fire V.3.8(b). kɒlə Cu

cowler out *vtphr* to RAKE in a domestic fire V.3.8(b). kɒlə ... uːt Cu

cowler-rake *n* a RAKE used in a domestic fire V.3.8(a). kaʊləɹɪək Y, kɔlʁɪək Nb

cowley-handed *adj* LEFT-HANDED VI.7.13(a). kəʊlɪ-andɪd Y

cow-liquor *n* URINE in a cow-house I.3.10. kəʊlɪkəˡ Gl

cow-lodge *n* a COW-HOUSE I.1.8. kɛʊlɒdʒ K

cowl out *1. vphr* to RAKE in a domestic fire V.3.8(b). kaʊl uːt Y

2. vtphr to rake. *-ing* kaʊlɪn ... uːt Y, *-ing* kaʊɪn ... aʊt La, kɒʊl ... uːt Cu, kɒʊ ... aʊt Y, *-ing* kɔʊlɪn ... aʊt Y, kɔʊlɪn ... jat Y, kɔʊl ... uːt L, kɔʊl ... əʊt Y

cowl-rake *1. n* a RAKE used in a domestic fire V.3.8(a). kɔːlʁɪk Nb, kɔːᶜlʁeːk Nb, kɛʊɹiːk Db, kɛʊɹeːk La, kɛʊɹeːˡk Db, kɛʊəɹeːk Db, kaʊlɹɪək Y, kaʊɹɪk Du, kaʊlɹɪək Du Y, kaʊɹeːk La, kaʊlɹeɪk Db, kaʊlɹeək Du, kaʊlɹeək Y, kaʊɹək We La, kɑʊɹɪək Y, kɒlʁɪk Nb, kɒlʁɪək Nb, kɒlɹɪək Y, kɒləɹɪak Cu, kɒləɹɪək Cu, kɒlɹeːk Nb Y, kɒləɹeːk Cu, kɒləeak Cu, kɒləɹeˑək Cu[*old*], kɒlɹək Cu, kɒləʁəˑᵊk Nb, kɒɹək La, kɒʊlɹɛk Y, kɒʊlɹeːˡk Db, kɒʊɹeːk La Y Db Nt, kɒʊɹeˑək La, kɒʊlɹeːk Y, kɒʊɹək We La Y, kɒʊəɹeːk Y, kɒʊəɹək La, kɔlʁɪˑᵊk Nb, kɔːlʁɪək Du, kɔːlɹək Cu, kɔʊlʁɪək Du, kɔʊlɹɪək Y, kɔʊlɹeːk Y, kɔʊɹeːk La Y, kɔʊlɹeək Y L, kɔʊɹeək La Y, kɔɬɹeɪk Lei, kɔʊlɹeək Y L, kɔʊɹək Y, koːlɹeːk Nt, koːlrɛᵊk Man, kʊʊɹiːk St, kʊəlriːk Cu, kʊəlɹeˑək L, kʊəlɹeək Du, kəːɹeːk Db

2. v to RAKE in a domestic fire V.3.8(b). kɒʊəɹək La

cowl-shovel *n* a SHOVEL for a household fire V.3.9. kaʊlʃʊvəl Y

cowl together *1. vtphr* to RAKE in a domestic fire V.3.8(b). *-ing* kɔʊɪn ... təgɪðə Y

2. vtphr-3sg she [i.e. a tidy girl] will COLLECT her toys VIII.8.15. kɔʊl ... təgəðə Y

cowly *n* a LEFT-HANDED person VI.7.13(a). kɛʊlɪ Y

cow-maid *n* URINE in a cow-house I.3.10. kəʊmɛɪd K [*queried SBM*]

cowman *n* [*Ask what men work on the farm and what each does. If he omits any of the following notions, ask the relevant questions below.*] *What do you call the man who looks after the animals that give you milk?* [*before April 1953: ... looks after the cows?*] I.2.3. Eng exc. L. ⇒ **baiseler, beast-man, bullock-man, bullock-walloper, bullocky, bungey, byre-man, cattle-man, cow-banger, dummock-man, fogger, garth-man, garthy, herdsman, milk-man, stockman, yardman**; also **bull-walloper**

cow-muck *1. n* COW-DUNG I.3.12. kɪamʊk Y, kɛʊmʌk O Hu Bk Hrt Sr, kɛʊmʊk Sa Wo Wa Nth Bk, kɛəmʊk Y, kœʏmʌk D, kæʊmʌk He Ess W

K Ha, kæʊmʊk WY Sa Wo O L Lei R, kæˑəmʊk La
Y, kaːmʊk La Y Lei, kaʊmʌk Sa, kaʊmʊk La Y L,
kɑʊmʌk He, kɒʊmʌk Sa, kɔʊmʊk O, kʌʊmʌk Mon,
kʌʊmʊk Nb Y, kuːmʊk Nb Cu Du We Y L, kəʊmʌk
Mon W, kəʊmʊk Y He Wo O

2. *n* a CLOT OF COW-DUNG II.1.6. kɛʊmʊk Wa,
kaʊmʊk L

3. *n* dung. kɛʊmʊk C, kɛuːmʊk Wo, kæːmʊk La,
kæʊmʊk L R, kaʊmʌk So, kɒʊmʌk W, kuːmʊk Du
Y L

cow-mush *n* COW-DUNG I.3.12. kɛːmʊʃ La

cow-pad *1. n* a CLOT OF COW-DUNG II.1.6.
kɛʊpɛd Sr, kɛʊpæd Ha, kæʊpɒd Wa

2. *n* a PATH made through a field by cows IV.3.11.
kaʊpad La, *pl* kjaʊpadz St

cow-paigle *n* a COWSLIP II.2.10(a). *pl* kɛʊpɛkɫz Hu

cow paps *n* the UDDER of a cow III.2.5. kuː paps Y

cow-parlour *n* the GANGWAY in a cow-house
I.3.7. kæʊpaːlə Ess

cow-pasty *n* a CLOT OF COW-DUNG II.1.6.
kɛːˀpastɪ Db, kaːpastɪ St, kaʊpastɪ St

cow-pat *n* a CLOT OF COW-DUNG II.1.6. kɛʊpɛt
K, kɛʊpæt Ess K, kæʊpæt So, kæʊpat So, kæʊpat Lei
So Ha, kaːpat Lei, kaːˀpat Lei, kaʊpæt So, kəʊpat W

cow-patch *n* a CLOT OF COW-DUNG II.1.6.
kɛʊpatʃ Db, kjæʊpatʃ Ch, kaʊpatʃ Ch St

cow-paw* *n* a LEFT-HANDED person VI.7.13(a).
kɪuːpɔː Cu *[NBM headword -pan]*

cow-pawed *adj* LEFT-HANDED VI.7.13(a).
kɪuːpɔːd Cu, kaːpeːd Nb, kɒʊpæˀd Nb, kɔʊpæˑˀd
Nb

cow-pen *1. n* a COW-HOUSE I.1.8. kæʊpɛn Wa W
Ha, kɛʊpɛn Wa

2. *n* a STALL in a cow-house I.3.1. kɛʊpɛn Sx

cow-piddle *n* URINE in a cow-house I.3.10. kɛʊpɪtl
Sa

cow-pine *1. n* a COW-HOUSE I.1.8. kæʊpaˑɪn So,
kæʊpaɪn Ha

2. *n* a STALL in a cow-house I.3.1. kæʊpæᵁn So,
kæʊpaɪn D

cow-piss *n* URINE in a cow-house I.3.10. kjæʊpɪs
Ch, kɛːpɪs Db, kɛʊpɪs Db Wa O L Nth Hu Nf Sf Bk
Bd Hrt Ess, kœʊpɪs D, kæːpɪs Nt, kæʊpɪs So Co D,
kæʊpɪs He O Nt L Ess So W Ha, kaːpɪs Y, kaʊpɪs La
Y Db Sa So, kʌʊpɪs He Mon Gl, kuːpɪs Nb Cu Du
We Y Gl L, kuːpɪʃ Cu, kəʊpɪs So, kəʊpɪs Y He Mon
Gl So W Do

cow-place *n* a COW-HOUSE I.1.8. kæʊplɛɪs R,
kæʊplɛˑəs L

cow-plat *n* a CLOT OF COW-DUNG II.1.6. kʌʊplat
Y, kᵒʊplat Nb, kᵒuːplat Du, kuːplat Nb Du Y

cow-platter *n* a CLOT OF COW-DUNG II.1.6.
kuːplatə Y

cow-post *n* a TETHERING-STAKE in a cow-house
I.3.3. kaʊpoːst Sa, kəʊpoːst Do

cow-ring *n* a sliding RING to which a tether is
attached in a cow-house I.3.5. kuːɹɪŋ Du Y

cow-rope *n* a TETHER for a cow I.3.4. *pl*
kœʏɾoːps D

cow-run *n* a PATH made through a field by cows
IV.3.11. kɛʊɹʌn Bd

cows *npl* *What do you call your animals that give
milk?* III.1.1(a). kɛɪz Bk, kɛaz Y, kɛʊz Y Db Sa
Wo Wa Gl O L Nth Hu C Nf Sf Bk Bd Hrt Ess
MxL Brk Sr K Ha Sx, kjɛʊz Bd, kɛuːz Wo, kɛəz
Y, kœʏz D, kæːz Db Nt, kæˑaz Y, kæʏz So Co D,
kæʊz Y Sa St He Wo Wa O Nt L Lei R Ess So W
Sr K Do Ha, kᴵæʊz He, kjæʊz Ch, kæus Man,
kæˑəz La, kaːz La Y Db St Lei R MxL, kjaːz Y St,
kaʊz La Y Ch Db Sa St Nt L Lei So, kaʊs Y, kauːz
Sa, kɑʊz He O Nf, kɒʊz Gl W, kɔʊz L, kʌʊz Y
He Mon Gl Brk, kᵒuːz Du, kᵁuːz Nb We Y Sa Gl,
kᵁuːs Nb, kuːz Nb Cu Du La Y L, kjuːz St, kəʊz
Du Y He Mon Gl O So W Brk K Do, kəʊːz Cu Du
Wo Gl. ⇒ **cow, dummocks, hummocks, kine,
kye(s), milch-cows, milk-cows** *[kye/kyes forms
cannot always readily be differentiated from
cow/cows forms]*

cow-seal *n* a chain TETHER for a cow I.3.4.
kaːsɪəl Y

cow-shade *n* a COW-HOUSE I.1.8. kuːʃɪəd Du

cow-sharn *1. n* COW-DUNG I.3.12. kaːʃ3ᴶːɪn
La, kuːskarn Cu

2. *n* a CLOT OF COW-DUNG II.1.6.
kæˑəʃaᴶːɪn La, kaʊʃaᴶɪn La

cow-shed *n* a COW-HOUSE I.1.8. kɛʊʃɛd Nf,
kɛːʃɛd Db, kɛʊʃɪd Ess Sr Sx, kɛʊʃɛd Wo Wa L
Nth Hu C Nf Bk Hrt Ess MxL Sr K, kɛʊʃʏd Nf,
kæːʃɛd Nt K, *pl* kæʏʃɛdz So, kæʊʃɛd St Wo Wa
L Lei R Nth Ess So W K Ha, kæʊʃəd Lei, kaːʃɛd
St Lei, kaʊʃɛd Y St L So, kɒʊʃɛd W, kᴧᵁˑʃɛd Gl,
koʊʃɛd Brk, kəʊʃɛˑd So, kəʊʃɛd Mon Gl O W K
Do

cow-shippon *n* a COW-HOUSE I.1.8. kœʏʃɪpən
D

cow-shit *1. n* COW-DUNG I.3.12. kɛʊʃɪˑt Ess,
kæʏʃɪt Co D, kæʊʃɪt L So W Ha, kaʊʃɪt So, kʌʊʃɪt
Mon, kuːʃɪt Y L, kəʊʃɪt He Mon Gl W

2. *n* a CLOT OF COW-DUNG II.1.6. kɛʊʃɪt L
Nth Hu Hrt, kæʊʃɪt He, kaʊʃɪt L, kʌʊʃɪt Mon,
kuːʃɪt L

3. *n* dung. kɛʊʃɪt Nf Ess MxL, kœʏʒɪt D, kæʏʃɪt
Co D, kæʊʃɪt L So W Ha, kaʊʃɪt St L, kuːʃɪt Y
Gl, kəʊʃɪt W K

cow-shite *n* a CLOT OF COW-DUNG II.1.6.
kuːʃaɪt Y

cows' house *n* a COW-HOUSE I.1.8. kæʏsæʏs
Co, kæʏzæʏs Co, kæʏzæʏz Co

cow-shud *n* a COW-HOUSE I.1.8. kəʊʃœːd Gl,
kaʊʃʊːd Wo

cow-skeeling *n* a COW-HOUSE with one open side I.1.8. kəʊskɪɫɪn W

cowslip *n* [*Show a picture of cowslip, daisy, and dandelion.*] *What do you call these, they are three common flowers that you find in fields?* II.2.10(a). Eng exc. C. ⇒ **basketweed, cow-flop, cow-paigle,** *cow-slop* ⇒ **cow-slip, cow-suckle, cuckoo, horse-buckle, lady-candlestick, paigle**

cow-slip *n* a CLOT OF COW-DUNG II.1.6. kɛʊslɪp Bd, kaʊslɪp Ch Nt

cow-slop *n* a CLOT OF COW-DUNG II.1.6. kæˑəslap Y, *pl* kaːslɒps Y

cow-slush *n* URINE in a cow-house I.3.10. kæʊsɫʌʃ Do

cow's-muck *n* COW-DUNG I.3.12. kɛʊz mʏk Nf, kəʊzmʌk Do

cow-sock *n* URINE in a cow-house I.3.10. kɛuːsɒk Wo

cow-sole 1. *n* a TETHER for a cow, made of rope or chain I.3.4. kaːsɛʊ La
2. *n* a wooden tether. kaʊsʊəl Db

cows'-piss *n* URINE in a cow-house I.3.10. kæʏzpɪs Co, kaʊzpɪs So

cow-stable *n* a COW-HOUSE I.1.8. kɛʊsteˑɪbɫ Ha, kaʊsteːbl Nt, kaʊsteˑəbl L, kuːsteˑəbl L

cow-stall *n* a COW-HOUSE I.1.8. kɛʊstɔːl Sx, kɛʊstɔːɫ Sx, kɛʊstɔːʊ Sr Sx, kæʊstɔːɫ So Do, kəʊstɔːɫ Do

cow-stand *n* a STALL in a cow-house I.3.1. kɪastand Y, kœʏstan D, kaʊstand Y, kuːstand Du Y

cow-standing *n* a STALL in a cow-house I.3.1. kæʊstanɪn R

cow-stool *n* a MILKING-STOOL III.3.3. kuːstɪəl Y

cow-suckle *n* a COWSLIP II.2.10(a). kᵊʊsʊkl Du

cow-sump *n* URINE in a cow-house I.3.10. kuːsʊmp We

cows'-wash *n* URINE in a cow-house I.3.10. kuːzwɛʃ Nb

cow-swat *n* a CLOT OF COW-DUNG II.1.6. kaʊswat La

cows' water *n* URINE in a cow-house I.3.10. kɛuz wɔʔə Nf

cow-tallet *n* a HAY-LOFT over a cow-house I.3.18. kæʏtaɫət D

cow-tie 1. *n* a TETHERING-STAKE in a cow-house I.3.3. kæʊtɒɪ W Do, kaʊtaɪ St, kəʊtəɪ Mon [*marked ir.rr. WBM as referring to a tether]*
2. *n* a TETHER for a cow I.3.4. kʲaʊtaɪ La, kɛʊtɔɪ Sr Ha, kɛʊtʌʏ O, kɛʊtəɪ Sx, kœʏtɒɪ D, kæʏtaɪ D, kæʏtaː Co, kæʊtaˑɪ R, kæʊtɒɪ So, kaʊtaɪ Sa St, kautɛɪ Sa, kʌʊtæɪ He, kʌʊtəɪ Mon, kəʊtəɪ Mon So
3. *n* a rope tether. kɛʊtɔɪ C, kɛʊtʌɪ Nf, kæʊtɔˑɪ L
4. *n* a chain tether. kɛʊtaɪ MxL, kɛʊtɒɪ Sa Wo, kɛʊtɔɪ Wa Ess, kɛʊtəɪ Wo, kɛʊtaɪ Nf, kɛuːtɛɪ Sa, kæʊtaɪ Wa Lei, kæʊtɒɪ He, kæʊtɔɪ Wo, kæʊtəɪ He, kæʊtaɪ Man, kaʊtɒɪ So, kaʊːtaɪ Sa, kaʊtaɪ He, kɒʊtaɪ

Sa, kɒʊtɒɪ W, kʌʊtəɪ Mon, kəʊtɒɪ Wo Gl, kəʊtəɪ He Wo Mon, kᵊʊtæɪ Man
5. *n* a tether made of rope or chain. kɛʊtaɪ Nth
6. *n* an iron tether. kɛʊtaɪ Bd, kæʊtaɪ Nth

cow-tie-chain *n* a TETHER for a cow I.3.4. *pl* kɛʊtɔɪtʃɛɪnz Sx

cow-tier *n* a TETHERING-STAKE in a cow-house I.3.3. kaːʊtaːɪə St [*taken as referring to a tether WMBM]*

cow-track *n* a PATH made through a field by cows IV.3.11. kɛatɹak Y, kɛʊtɹak Bd, kæʊtɹæk Y Ess MxL, kæʊtɹak Wo O, *pl* kjæʊtɹaks Ch, kaːtɹak Y, kaʊtɹak Y St, kɒʊtɹak He, kuːtɹak Y, kəʊtɹak Do

cow-trough *n* a TROUGH in a cow-house I.3.6. kɪatɹɒf Y

cow-tub *n* a movable TROUGH in a cow-house, often made of wood I.3.6. *pl* kaʊtʊbz Cu[*old]*, kuːtʊb We, *pl* kuːtʊbz Cu

cow-turd *n* a CLOT OF COW-DUNG II.1.6. kɛːtəːd Db, kɛʊtəːd Nth Bk Bd Hrt Ess, kɛʊtəᶜːd̪ Sa Wa O Bk Ess Sr K, kɛwtʌd Sf, kœvtəᶜːd̪ D, kæːtɔd Nt, kæʊtɒd Nt L, kæˑətɔd Db, kæʊtəᶜːd̪ So W Ha, kæʊtəᶜːd̪ He, kaːtəːd St, kaʊtəːd Ch St, kaʊtəᴶd L, *pl* kaʊtəᶜːd̪z So, kaʊtəɹd̪ O, kʌʊtəᶜːd̪ Gl, kʌʊtjəᶜːd̪ He Mon, kəʊtœːd Mon Gl, kəʊtəᶜːd̪ He Mon Gl O K Do, kəʊːtᴶəᶜːd̪ Wo

cow-tyal *n* a TETHER for a cow I.3.4. kæʊtaˑɪᵊɫ Lei

cow-tyal-iron *n* a TETHERING-STAKE in a cow-house I.3.3. kæʊtaˑɪᵊɫaˑɪən Lei

cow-walk 1. *n* the GANGWAY in a cow-house I.3.7. kæʊwʊək L
2. *n* a PATH made through a field by cows IV.3.11. kuːwɔːk Y

cow-wash *n* URINE in a cow-house I.3.10. kɛːwɛʃ Db

cow-water *n* URINE in a cow-house I.3.10. kaːwatə La, kaʊweːtə Ch

cow-yard 1. *n* a FARMYARD I.1.3. kɛʊjaːd Ess, kəʊjaᶜːɽd̪ Brk
2. *n* the STRAW-YARD of a farm I.1.9. kɛʊjaːd Ess, kaʊjaᶜːd̪ So, kɔʊjaˑɽd̪ O, kᵁuːjaᶜːd̪ Gl, kəʊjaᶜːd̪ W, kəʊjaˑɽd̪ O
3. *n* a straw-yard in which cattle are fattened. kəʊːjaᶜːd̪ Gl

crab-ankled *adj* KNOCK-KNEED VI.9.5. kɹabaŋkld L

crab-footed *adj* PIGEON-TOED VI.10.4. kʁabfʊtɪt Nb

crab-toed *adj* PIGEON-TOED VI.10.4. kʁabtøːd Nb

crack 1. *vi* to CHIP, referring to an egg that is about to hatch IV.6.10. kɹɛk Sx, kɹæk Gl Nth Hu Nf Sf K, kɽæk So, kɹæːk Wo Hrt, kɹak La Y Ch St Wa Gl L, *3prpl* kɹak He, kɽak W Ha

2. vt to WRING the neck of a chicken when killing it IV.6.20. kɹɛk Sr

3.1. vt-1prpl we CRUNCH apples or biscuits VI.5.12. *-ing* kɹɛkɪn Ess Sr, *-ing* kɹækɪn Sx

3.2. v-1prpl we crunch. *-ing* kɹakən D

4. n CHAT VIII.3.4. krak Cu, kʁak Nb Du, kɹak Nb Cu Du We La*[rare and old x1]* Y*[rare x1, old x1, short x1]*, kɹak Y; **bit crack** bɪt kɹak Du, bɪt kɹɑk Du; **bit of crack** bɪt ə kɹak Y; **right crack** ɹɛɪt kɹak Y

5. n **give him a crack** to BEAT a boy on the buttocks VIII.8.10. gɪb m̩ ə kɹæk Co

cracked *1. adj* CLOVEN, describing the hoof of a cow III.2.8(b). kɹakt Wa Nth

2. adj CHAPPED VI.7.2. kɹɛkt Sr, kɹækt Nf, kɹakt La Y*[with cuts x1]* L, kɹɑkt Y*[old]*; **cracked and sore** kɹakt ən suə Y

3. adj SILLY VIII.9.3. kɹɛkt K

crackers *adj* SILLY VIII.9.3. kɹækəz Hrt MxL, kɹakəᵗːz̩ Do; **real crackers** ɹiːəł kɹækəᵗːz̩ So

cracket *n* a MILKING-STOOL III.3.3. kɹɛkət Du, kʁakɪt Nb, kʁakət Nb

crackle *vt* to CHOKE somebody VI.6.4. kɹæk?ł Ess

crackling(s) *n* SCRAPS left after rendering lard III.12.10.

no -s: kɹaklɪn La

-s: kɹæklɪnz MxL, kraklɪnz Cu, kʁaklənz Nb, kɹaklɪnz La Y Ch

cracknell(s) *n* SCRAPS left after rendering lard III.12.10.

no -s: kɹæknʊ Sx

-s: kʁaknəlz Nb

crack off *vphr* to BREAK *WIND* VI.13.16. *prppl* kɹakɪn ɔːf So

crack out *vtphr* to DIG in the garden with a spade I.7.8. kɹak ... ᵊæʊt L

cracks *npl* CHAPS in the skin VI.7.3. kɹɛks La Db Nf Ess Sr K Sx, *sg* kræk Man, kɹæks La Y He O L Hu Nf Sf Ess MxL Sr K Sx, kɹaks La Y Ch Db Sa St Wa Nt L Nth Hu C Bk Bd Hrt, kəɹaks L, kɹɑks Y, kɹɑks O

craddle* *vt* to CURDLE milk V.5.7. kɹadl Sa

cradle *1. n* a BENCH on which slaughtered pigs are dressed III.12.1. kɹɛdl Du, kɹədl Du

2. n a SAWING-HORSE I.7.16. kɹɛdl La

3. n an END-BOARD of a cart I.10.4. kɹeːdł Do, kɹeɪdł So

4. n a SOWING-BASKET II.3.6. *pl* kʁɛdls Nb

5. n an attachment for a scythe, to collect and bunch cut corn, ⇐ GRASS-NAIL II.9.9. kɹeːdł Ha, kɹɛɪdʊ Sr

cradles *n* a CART-FRAME I.10.6. kɹɛɪdʊz Sr

craffins *n* SCRAPS left after rendering lard III.12.10. kʁafɪns Nb

crag *n* the SCRUFF (of the neck) VI.6.2. kɹag L

cram *v* to STOCK a cow III.3.6. kɹam Y

cramp *n* a CLAMP in which potatoes are stored out of doors II.4.6. kɹæmp Gl, kɹamp Db

cranch *1. vt-1prpl* we CRUNCH apples or biscuits VI.5.12. *-ing* kɹænʃən Man, kranʃ Cu, kɹanʃ Cu We La Y L, *-ing* kɹanʃɪn Ch, kɹɑɪnʃ La

2. v-1prpl we crunch. kɹanʃ Cu Y, *-ing* kɹanʃɪn He

crane *1. n* What do you call that old-fashioned arrangement for hanging a kettle on to heat it over the fire? V.3.4. kɹɪən Nb, kɹɹən La, kʁeːn Nb, kɹeːn Ch Sa, kɹeˑən We La Y, kɹɛːn Cu We, kɹɛɪn Wa Lei Sf Sr K, *pl* kɹɛɪnz Brk, kɹæɪn St K. ⇒ **back-crook, bar, boiler-hook, brandis, cant-hook, caudle, chain, chain and hook, chimney-crook(s), chimney-hook(s), copper-hook, cotterel, *cranes*, crook, crow, dog-hanger, fire-crook, fire-dog, galloper, gate, grid, hake, handimaid, hanger(s), hanging-crook, hanging-hook, hangle(s), hank, hook, hooks and chain, jack, jack-hook, kettle-bar, kettle-crook, kettle-hanger, kettle-hook, kettle-jack, links, pot-bed, pot-crook, pot-hanger, pot-hook, *pot-hooks* ⇒ pot-hook, pot-links, rackem, racken, racken-hook, rack-iron, randle-balk, reckan-crook, reckan-hook, reckan(s), recknan-hook, reddy-pole, roasting-jack, roundabout, slowrie, spit, swape, sway, sway-pole, sweak, swing, swing-bar, swing-peg, trammel, tripod, trivet, yetling-hook**

2. n the *HORIZONTAL* BAR of a crane over a domestic fire V.3.5(a). kɹɪən Y, kɹɛːn Y Sa, kɹeən We Y, kɹɛːn We, kɹɛɪn Wa

3. n the vertical part of a crane over a domestic fire, consisting of a *BAR* or *CHAIN* and a HOOK(*/CROOK*) V.3.5b+c. kɹɛːᵊn La

crank *n* a ROPE-TWISTER II.7.8. kɹæŋk Nf Sf; **pair of cranks** pɛˑɹ ə kɹæŋks Nf

cranky *1. adj* STUPID VI.1.5. kɹaŋkɪ L, kɹaŋkɪ W

2. adj SILLY VIII.9.3. kɹæŋkɪ Ess, kɹaŋkɪ So, kɹaŋkɪ St

crap-house *n* an EARTH-CLOSET V.1.13. kɹapəs Wa

craplings *n* SCRAPS left after rendering lard III.12.10. kɹaplɪnz Y

crapper *n* an EARTH-CLOSET V.1.13. kɹæpəᵗ He Gl, kɹæpəᵗː So

crapping(s) *n* SCRAPS left after rendering lard III.12.10.

no -s: kɹapɪn Y

-s: kɹapɪnz We Y, kɹapənz Du, kɹɒpɪnz Du

crap(s) *n* SCRAPS left after rendering lard III.12.10.

no -s: Y

-s: kɹaps La Y L

cratch *1. n* a HAY-RACK in a stable I.4.1. kɹɛtʃ Sa, kɹætʃ Sa He Mon Gl, kɹatʃ La Ch Db Sa St He Wo
2. v to feed hay to horses in the stable, ⇐ FEEDING III.5.1. kɹatʃ Ch
3. n the TAILBOARD of a cart I.10.2. kɹætʃ Sa, kɹatʃ Sa
4. n an END-BOARD of a cart I.10.4. kɹatʃ Sa
5. n an end-board of a horse-drawn trap. kɹatʃ Wa
6. n a SHEARING-TABLE III.7.8. kɹɛtʃ Y, kɹatʃ Y
7. n a BENCH on which slaughtered pigs are dressed III.12.1. kɹætʃ L, kɹatʃ Y Wa Nt L Lei R Nth

cratches *1. npl* CART-LADDERS I.10.5. kɹætʃɪz He, kɹatʃɪz St, *sg* kɹatʃ Wo
2. n a CART-FRAME I.10.6. kɹatʃɪz Sa

cratchings *n* SCRAPS left after rendering lard III.12.10. kɹatʃɪnz Ch St, kɹatʃənz Ch

cratch-stick *n* the STRETCHER between the traces of a cart-horse I.5.11. kɹatʃstɪk Bd

craunch* *vt-1prpl* we CRUNCH apples or biscuits VI.5.12. kɹɔːnʃ Nth, *-ing* kɹɔːnʃɪn St

craven* *adj* miserly, ⇐ MISER VII.8.9. kɹɪəvən Y

craw *n* the WINDPIPE VI.6.5. kɹɔː St

craw-crooks *npl* BILBERRIES IV.11.3. kʀaːkʀʊks Nb*[old]*

crawlers *npl* LICE IV.8.1(a). kɹɑːɫəᵗːz̦ D

crawling *adj* HEAVING *WITH MAGGOTS* IV.8.6. kʀaːlɪn Nb, kɹaʊlən Cu, krɔːlən Man, kɹɔːlɪn K, kɹɔːɫɪn O

crazy *adj* SILLY VIII.9.3. kɹeˈɪzɪ Db

cream *n When milk stands, what rises to the top?* V.5.3. Eng. ⇒ **head**, **ream**; ⇒ also **cream-stean**

cream-jar *n* a BREAD-BIN V.9.2. kɹiːmdʒaː Nb

cream-stean *n* an earthenware cream-pot, ⇐ CREAM V.5.3. kɹiːmstiːn He, kɹiːmstɪən He

crease *n* the RIDGE of a house roof V.1.2(a). kɹiːs Gl, kɾiːs So, kɾɛɪs Co

creases *npl* wrinkles in the skin, ⇐ to WRINKLE VI.11.2. kɹeˑᵊsɪz Nf

crease up *viphr* to WRINKLE, referring to the skin of very old people VI.11.2. *3prsg* kɹɪəsɪz ʊp Y

cree *n* a PIGSTY I.1.5. kʀiː Nb*[rare]*

creek *n* a RIVULET IV.1.1. kɹiːk Nf Ess

creel *1. n* a SHEARING-TABLE III.7.8. kɹiːl La Y, kɹᵊiˑl We
2. n a BENCH on which slaughtered pigs are dressed III.12.1. kɹiːl We Y, kɹəɪl Y
3. n a CLOTHES-BASKET V.9.7. kɹiːl Y

creep *n* a SHEEP-HOLE IV.2.8. kɹiːp Nf, kɾiːp So, kɾeːp W*[for young sheep]* D Do

creepers *npl* LICE IV.8.1(a). kɹiːpəz Wo

creep-hole *1. n* a SHEEP-HOLE IV.2.8. kɹiːpɒɪl La, kɹiːpoːl Db, kɾiːpoːɫ W D, kɾeːpoːɫ W
2. n a small hole in a pigsty through which piglets can pass to feed. kɾiːpoʊɫ O

creeping *adj* HEAVING *(WITH MAGGOTS)* IV.8.6. kɹiːpɪn Y MxL

creeping-jinny *n* GOOSE-GRASS II.2.5. kɹiːpɪndʒɪnɪ La

creet *n* a rake-like attachment to a scythe, to collect and bunch cut corn, ⇐ GRASS-NAIL II.9.9. kɹiːt K*[3-pronged x2, rounded piece of wood x1]*, kɹɛɪt K*[wooden x1]*

creeve *n* a PIGSTY I.1.5. kʀiːv Nb

creevy *n* a PIGSTY I.1.5. kʀiːvɪ Nb

cress(es) *n What else do you put in salads [besides spring onions, cucumber]* V.7.17(b).
no -es: Eng
-es: kɹiːsɪz K
⇒ **garden-cress**, **water-cress(es)**

crest *1. n* the RIDGE of a stack of corn II.7.2. kɹɛs Wo Gl
2. n the WATTLES of a hen IV.6.19. kɹɛs Gl *[queried ir.r. WMBM, but 'i. insists']*
3. n the RIDGE of a house roof V.1.2(a). kɹɛst He Gl, kɹɛs Sa*[old]* St He Wo Mon Gl

crest-tile *n* the RIDGE of a house roof V.1.2(a). kɹɛsl Sa

crew *n* the STRAW-YARD of a farm I.1.9. kɹɪˑu L, kɹɪu: L

crews *n* the STRAW-YARD of a farm I.1.9. kɹɪuz L, kɹɪuːz L *[presumed sg EMBM]*

crew-yard *1. n* a FARMYARD I.1.3. kɹˡuːjaːd Nth
2. n the STRAW-YARD of a farm I.1.9. kɹɪuːjaːd L Nth, kɹˡuːjaːd Nf, kɹɪuːjaˡːd L, kɹuːjaːd L, kɹʉːjaːd Lei
3. n a straw-yard in which cattle are fattened. kɹɪuːjaːd L Lei
4. n a straw-yard for fattening cattle and producing dung. kɹɪuːjaːd Nt, kɹˡʉːjaːd Lei R, kɹuːjaːd Nt Lei R, kɹʉːjaːd Lei

crib *1. n* a STALL in a cow-house I.3.1. kɾɪb So
2. n the PARTITION between stalls in a cow-house I.3.2. kɹɪb Ess
3. n a TROUGH in a cow-house I.3.6. kɹɪb Y Nt L Nf, kɾɪb So W Co D Do Ha
4. n a HAY-RACK in a stable I.4.1. krɪb Man, kɹɪb L, kɾɪb So *[reference may not be to a rack – SBM Edd note indicates that the picture shown to ii. may have influenced the rr.]*
5. n an allowance of food given to a horse when resting from work, ⇐ BAITING III.5.2. kɾɪb Co
6. n a SNACK VII.5.11. kɾɪb Co D; **a bit of crib** ə bɪd ə kɾɪb D

crib-footed *adj* PIGEON-TOED VI.10.4. kɹɪbfʊtɪd St

crick *1. n* **crick of the mouth** a mouth corner, ⇐ MOUTH CORNERS VI.5.2. kɾɪk ə ðə mæʏð D
2. vt to SPRAIN an ankle VI.10.8. kɹɪk Nth, *-ed* kɹɪkt Co, kɾɪk Do, *-ed* kɾɪkt Co, *-ed* əkɾɪkt Do

criddle *1. vt* to CURDLE milk V.5.8. kɾɪdɫ W
2. v to curdle (milk). kɾɪdɫ So*[old]*

crimmet *n* the VULVA of a cow III.2.3. kɹɪmət Gl, kɹɪmət So, kɹʊmʊt Gl

crimmock* *n* the VULVA of a cow III.2.3. kɹɪmək Gl

crimple *vi* to WRINKLE, referring to the skin of very old people VI.11.2. kʁɪmpl Nb

crine *1. vi* to WARP, referring to wood IX.2.9. kʁɛɪn Nb, kʁɛɪən Nb
2. vi to shrink or shrivel. krɛɪn Cu, *3prsg* kʁɛɪnz Nb

crink *n* a WEAKLING piglet III.8.4. kɹɪŋk Mon

crinkle *vi* to WRINKLE, referring to the skin of very old people VI.11.2. *3prsg* kɹɪŋklz St, kɹɪŋkɫ Bk, *3prsg* kɹɪŋkʊz W

crinkle up *viphr* to WRINKLE, referring to the skin of very old people VI.11.2. *3prsg* kɹɪŋkɫz ʌp Co

crinklings *n* SCRAPS left after rendering lard III.12.10. kɹɪŋklɪnz Bk Bd Hrt, kɹɪŋk?lɪnz Bd Hrt, kɹɪŋ?lɪnz Bk

cripner *n* the CRUPPER of the harness of a cart-horse I.5.9. kɹɪpnəᵗ: So W Do Ha, kɹɪbnəᵗ: So Do

cripper *n* the CRUPPER of the harness of a cart-horse I.5.9. krɪpəᴶ Man, kɹɪpəᴶ Brk, kɹɪpəᵗ Gl O Brk, kɹɪpəᵗ: So W D Do Ha

cripper-gap* *n* a SHEEP-HOLE IV.2.8. kɹɪpəgap Db St, kɹɪpəgjap Ch Db

crippin *n* the CRUPPER of the harness of a cart-horse I.5.9. kɹɪpɪn So, kɹəpɪn So

crippin-horse *n* a TRACE-HORSE I.6.3. kɹɪpɪnɔᵗ:ş So, kɹəpɪnɔᵗ:ş So

cripple* *n* the CRUPPER of the harness of a cart-horse I.5.9. krɪpl Du

cripple-gap *n* a SHEEP-HOLE IV.2.8. *pl* kɹɪplgaps Y, kɹɪplgjap Db

cripple-hole *n* a SHEEP-HOLE IV.2.8. kɹɪplɒɪl Db, kɹɪplɔɪl Y, kɹɪpl‚ʊəl La Y, kɹəplʊəl Y

crips *adj* BRITTLE, describing cups and saucers which break easily IX.1.4. kɹɪps So

crispings *n* SCRAPS left after rendering lard III.12.10. kɹɪspɪnz La, kɹɪspɪnz K

crisps *n* SCRAPS left after rendering lard III.12.10. kɹɪsps Cu

criss-cross *adv* DIAGONALLY, referring to harrowing a field IX.1.8. kɹɪskɹɒs Y, kɹɪskɹɔːs So

crit *n* a WEAKLING piglet III.8.4. kʁɪːt Nb, kʁɪt Nb

critch *n* a BREAD-BIN V.9.2. kɹɪtʃ Do

crits *n* SCRAPS left after rendering lard III.12.10. kɹɪts Ha

crittens* *n* SCRAPS left after rendering lard III.12.10. kɹɪ?nz O Brk

crittlings* *n* SCRAPS left after rendering lard III.12.10. kɹɪtlɪnz Nth, kɹɪt‚ɪnz Ess, kɹɪ?lɪnz Bk Hrt

croaky *adj* HOARSE VI.5.16. kɹɔːkɪ Y

crock *1. n* a SALTING-TROUGH III.12.5. kɹɒk Sr Sx
2. n a GIRDLE for baking cakes V.7.4(b). kɹɒk So Do

3. n a BREAD-BIN V.9.2. krɒk Man, kɹɒk Cu St Ess Brk*[old x1]* Sr K Sx

crock-cake* *n* a scone, ⇐ GIRDLE V.7.4(b). *pl* kɹɒkkjɛks So

crockman *n* a KNACKER III.11.9. kɹɒkman Bk

crock-pot *n* a GIRDLE for baking cakes V.7.4(b). kɹɒkpɒt W

crocky *adj* WEAK, describing a person who has been ill VI.13.2. kɹɔki L

croft *n* a PADDOCK I.1.10. kɹaft Ch Sa St, krɒft Cu, kʁɒft Nb, kɹɒft Cu La Y Ch Db St Nt, kɹɔft La Y

cronch *1. vt-1prpl* we CRUNCH apples or biscuits VI.5.12. kɹɒnʃ La, *-ing* kɹɒnʃɪn K
2. v-1prpl we crunch. *-ing* krɒnʃən Man
[not a SBM headword]

crone* *n* an old toothless EWE past the age of having lambs III.6.6. kɹoun Nf

crone ewe a EWE III.6.6. *pl* kɹʌʊn juːz Ess*[about 5 years old]*, kɹoːʊn jɒu Nf

croning *v-ing* CULLING sheep III.11.2. kɹʌʊnən Sf

cronk *n* a NOSE VI.4.6. kɹɒŋk Sr

crook *1. n* the T-SHAPED PLOUGH-BEAM END of a horse-drawn plough I.8.5. kɹʊk Co *[marked ir.r. SBM]*
2. n the GRASS-NAIL of a scythe II.9.9. kɹʊk Do
3. n a CRANE on which a kettle is hung over a domestic fire V.3.4. kɹɪʏk Cu, kɹɪək Nb Cu We La, krɪʊk Cu, kɹʏk D, *pl* kɹʏks So, kɹʏːk La, krʊk Cu, kɹʊk So Do Ha
4. n the vertical BAR or CHAIN of a crane over a domestic fire V.3.5(b). kɹʏk D, kɹᵁuˑk Y
5. n the HOOK or *CROOK* of a crane over a domestic fire V.3.5(c). kʁɪək Nb, kɹɪək Cu Du Y, krɪʊk Cu, kɹɪuk Y, kɹɪuːk Y, kɹʏk D, kɹʌk So, kɹʊk Gl, kɹʊk So W Ha, kɹuːk Y
6. n the vertical part of a crane over a domestic fire, consisting of a *BAR* or *CHAIN* and a HOOK(*/CROOK*) V.3.5b+c. kɹɪʏk Cu, krɪʊk Cu, kɹɪʊk Cu, *pl* kɹɪuːks Du, kʁɪək Nb, kɹɪək Cu Du We La, kɹʏk So Co D, kɹʏːk La, krʊk Cu, kʁʊk Nb, kɹʊk So W Co Do Ha, kʁuːk Nb, kɹuːk So
7. adj ASKEW, describing a picture that is not hanging straight IX.1.3. kɹʏːk La, kɹᵁuk La

crook down *vtphr* to PLASH a hedge IV.2.4. kɹʏk ... dœyn D, kɹʏk ... dæyn D

crooked *1. adj* ASKEW, describing a picture that is not hanging straight IX.1.3. Eng exc. We Wo Mon R MxL W Brk
2. adv DIAGONALLY, referring to harrowing a field IX.1.8. kɹɪəkt Y, kruːkəd Man, kɹuːkt L

crooked-legged *adj* KNOCK-KNEED VI.9.5. kɹɪəktlɛgd Y

crooking-post *n* the SHUTTING-POST of a gate IV.3.4. kʀʊkɪŋpɔːs Co

crookled *adj* ASKEW, describing a picture that is not hanging straight IX.1.3. kʀuːkld L

crooks *n* **a bit off the crooks, off the crooks** ILL, describing a person who is unwell VI.13.1(b). **off the crooks** ɒf ðə kʀʊks Nb; **a bit off the crooks** ə bɪt ɒf ðə kʀuks Du

crooks and lugs *npl* the parts of the HINGES of a door V.1.11a. kʀʊks ən lʊgz Y

crook-stoop *n* the HANGING-POST of a gate IV.3.3. kʀɪəkstuːp Nb

croon *1. vi-3prpl* bulls BELLOW III.10.2. kʀʏn Cu, kʀʊun Y, kʀʊuːn Du, kʀɪən Du Y, kʀʊnz Cu, kʀʊunz Y, kʀɪənz We, *-ing* kʀʊuːnən Y, kʀuːn Cu, gruːn Nb, *kruːnz* Y*[low noise when bad-tempered]*
2. vi-3prpl they NEIGH, describing the noise horses make in the fields III.10.3(b). kʀɪən La
3. vi-3prpl they MOO, describing the noise cows make in the fields III.10.4(b). krʏn Cu

croop *n* the CRUPPER of the harness of a cart-horse I.5.9. kʀuːp Y

croopin *n* the CRUPPER of the harness of a cart-horse I.5.9. kʀᵁuːpɪn Du We

crooshies *n* SWEETS V.8.4. kʀʊˈʃɪz Nf, kʀʊuʃɪs Nf*[old-fashioned]*

crop *1. n* HARVEST II.6.1. kʀɒp We Y Hrt Ess, kʀɒp So W, kʀɔp Y, kʀɔᵊp Ess
2. v to TRIM hedges IV.2.3. *-ing* kʀæpɪn Wo Gl, kʀɒp Sa He Wo, *-ing* kʀɒpɪn Mon, kʀɒp O, kʀɔp Y, *-ing* kʀɔpɪn Wo
3. v to LOP a tree IV.12.5. kʀap St, kʀɒp St, kʀɔp Ess
4. v to cut small branches from a willow tree. kʀɒp Sa
5. v to cut large branches from a tree. kʀap Ch
6. vt **get cropped, get your hair cropped, have it cropped** *GET YOUR HAIR CUT* VI.2.2. **get cropped** gɪt kʀɒpt Y; **get your hair cropped** gɛt jəɹ ɛə kʀɒpt Y; **have it cropped** æv ɪt kʀaːpt Wo
7. n a haircut. kʀɑp Gl, kʀɒp Du, kʀɒp Y Mon, kʀɔp Nb, kʀɔːp Sa
8. n the WATTLES of a hen IV.6.19. kʀɒp K, kʀɒp So Co D *[queried ir.r SBM]*

cross *1. n* **on the cross** ASKEW, describing a picture that is not hanging straight IX.1.3. ɒn ðə kʀɔːs Nf
2. adv DIAGONALLY, referring to harrowing a field IX.1.8. krɒs Man, kʀɒːs Ha, kʀɔst L; **cross the furrow*** kʀɒs ðə fəʈɒu K; **cross the middle*** kʀɒs mɪdl Y; **on the cross** ɒn ðə kʀɒˈs W, ɒn ðə kʀɔˈs Nf

cross-band *n* a DIAGONAL BAR of a gate IV.3.7. *pl* kʀɒsbanz Y

cross-bar *1. n* a wooden beam across the rear of a cart, ⇐ BUMPER I.10.1(a). kʀɒsbaː St, kʀɔːsbaˤː Sa
2. n a DIAGONAL BAR of a gate IV.3.7. *pl* kʀɑːsbaˤːz̩ Wo, kʀɑːsbaˤː Wo, kʀɒsbæː Du, *pl* kʀɒsbæˡː La, kʀɒsbaː Du Y, *pl* kʀɒsbaːz Db, *pl*

kʀɒsbaɹz Y, *pl* kʀɒsbaˡːz La Y, kʀɒsbaˤː Sa, kɾɒsbaˤː Co D, *pl* kʀɒsbaᴿːz Nb, *pl* kʀɒsbaːz Y L Ess, *pl* kʀɒsbaˡːz La, *pl* kʀɔˈsbaːz Nf, kʀɔːsbaː Wa Sf Ess, *pl* kʀɔːᵊsbaːz Nth, kʀɔːsbaˤː Sa, *pl* kʀɔːsbaˤːz̩ O Bd, kɾɔːsbaˤː So D, kʀɔːsbaː Ess, *pl* kʀɔːsbaːz MxL, kʀɔːsbaˤːɹ Sx, kɾɔːsbaˤː D
3. n the HORIZONTAL BAR of a crane over a domestic fire V.3.5(a). kʀœˈsbaᴿ Nb, kʀɑːsbaˤː He, kʀɔːsbaː K, kɾɔːsbaˤˈ Ha

cross-beam *n* the HORIZONTAL BAR of a crane over a domestic fire V.3.5(a). kʀɔˈsbᵊiːm Hrt

cross-beam end *n* [Show a picture of a cart.] What do you call this projecting piece of the beam on which the body rests? (question used before April 1953) I.10.1. ⇒ **beam-end, buttress, cart-arm, cart-sole, chockrel, corner-staff, dog, ear-board, ear-bray, ear-breed, eaverings, eavering-end, foot-brig, iron-stay, nook-staff, nook-stap, nook-stower, pin, rathe-stay, rod-stick, rung, shove-stay, sole, sole-end, sole-trees, stap, stay, stay-iron, step, strengthener, strut, yard bridge-end** [some interpretation necessitated by uneven treatment between BM vols]

cross-bit *n* a DIAGONAL BAR of a gate IV.3.7. kʀɔːsbɪt Sf

cross-cornered *adv* DIAGONALLY, referring to harrowing a field IX.1.8. kʀɒskɒɹnɹəd He, kʀɔskɔːnəd L, kʀɔskɔˈənəd Y

cross-corner(s) *adv* DIAGONALLY, referring to harrowing a field IX.1.8.
no -s: kʀɔskɔːnə L, kɾɔːskɔˤːŋəˤː D
-s: kʀɔskɔːnəz Y

crossed-eyed *adj* CROSS-EYED VI.3.6. kɾɔːstɒɪd Co

cross-een *adj* CROSS-EYED VI.3.6. kʀɒsiːn Y

cross-eyed *1. n* And a person who sees like that [i.e. squinting] is said to be .... VI.3.6. Eng exc. Nb. ⇒ **across-eyed, boss-eye, boss-eyed, boss-eyeded, cock-eyed, crossed-eyed, cross-een, cross-eyeded, cross-sighted, glee-eyed, gliding, gog-eyed, goggle-eyed, link-eyed, skend, skenning, skew-eyed, skew-whiffty, squint-eyed, squinting, squinty, squinty-een, squinty-eyed, thwart-eyed;** ⇒ also **wall-eyed**
2. adj/adv SQUINTING, looking in a squinting manner VI.3.5. kʀɒsɒɪd St, kʀɒsʌid Nf, kʀɔːsaɪd Hu, kʀɔˈsɒɪd Nf, kʀɔːsɔɪd O Ess, kʀɔːsʌid Nf, kɾɔːsæɪd So, kɾɔːsɒɪd So, kɾɔːsəɪd Do

cross-eyeded *adj* CROSS-EYED VI.3.6. kʀɔːsʌɪdɪd Sr

cross-eyes *adj* SQUINTING VI.3.5. kɾɔːsəɪz Do [marked u.r. SBM]

cross-garnets *npl* the HINGES of a door V.1.11a. kʀɔːsgaˤːɹʈəts Sx

cross-harrowing *adv* DIAGONALLY, referring to harrowing a field IX.1.8. kɪɒsaɪəɹɪn St

cross-harrows *adv* DIAGONALLY, referring to harrowing a field IX.1.8. 'kɪɒːs͵ɛɹəz K

cross-head *n* the T-SHAPED PLOUGH-BEAM END of a horse-drawn plough I.8.5. kɪɒsɛd Lei

crossing *adv* DIAGONALLY, referring to harrowing a field IX.1.8. kɪɒsɪn Brk

cross-lap *n* a DIAGONAL BAR of a gate IV.3.7. *pl* kɪɔːslaps Wo

cross-ledge *n* a DIAGONAL BAR of a gate IV.3.7. kɪɔ'slɛdʒ Nf

cross-leg(s) *n* a SAWING-HORSE I.7.16.
no -s: kɪɒslɛg Y
-s: kɪɒslɛgz Du Y St, kɪɔslɛgz La

cross-nooks *adv* DIAGONALLY, referring to harrowing a field IX.1.8. kɪɒsnɪəks Y

cross-over *adv* DIAGONALLY, referring to harrowing a field IX.1.8. kɪɒsaʊə Y, kɪɒsɑʊə Y, kʁɒsɔʊəᴮ Nb

cross-piece *1. n* a wooden beam across the rear of a cart, ⇐ BUMPER I.10.1(a). kɪɒspiːs Sa St
2. n a movable horizontal rod stretching between the shafts of a cart, fixing them to the cart-body and stopping the cart from tipping, ⇐ ROD/PIN I.10.3. kɪɔːspiːs Wa
3. n an END-BOARD on a cart I.10.4. kɪɔːspiːs Sa
4. n a DIAGONAL BAR of a gate IV.3.7. kɪɑːspiːs He, kɪɒspiːs Y Hrt, *pl* kɪɔspiːsɪz La, kɪɔːspiːs Sf, *pl* kɪɔːspiːsɪz MxL, kɽɔːspiːs So, *pl* kɽɔːspiːsɪz Ha
5. n the THRESHOLD of a door V.1.12. kɪɒspiːs Db

cross-pieces *npl* the horizontal BARS of a gate IV.3.6. kɪɔːspiːsɪz Ch, kɽɔːspiːsəz So

cross-pole *n* the STRETCHER between the traces of a cart-horse I.5.11. kɪɒspɒʊl Y

cross-rail *n* a DIAGONAL BAR of a gate IV.3.7. kɪɒsɹeːl Y Db, *pl* kɪɔːsɹæɪᵊɬz Gl

cross-road(s) *adv* DIAGONALLY, referring to harrowing a field IX.1.8.
no -s: kɪɔsɹʊəd L
-s: kɪɒsɹʊʊdz St

cross-sighted *adj* CROSS-EYED VI.3.6. kɹæ'sseɪtəd Man

cross-slat *n* a DIAGONAL BAR of a gate IV.3.7. *pl* kɪɔːslats Hu

cross-spar *n* a DIAGONAL BAR of a gate IV.3.7. kɪɒsspaː Y, *pl* kɪɔːsspaᵗːz̺ O

cross-spell *n* a DIAGONAL BAR of a gate IV.3.7. *pl* kɪɒsspɛlz Y

cross-stick *1. n* the STRETCHER between the traces of a cart-horse I.5.11. kɪɒsstɪk Y
2. n a movable horizontal rod stretching between the shafts of a cart, fixing them to the cart-body and stopping the cart from tipping, ⇐ ROD/PIN I.10.3. kɪɒsstɪk Lei

3. n a STICK used to support the shaft of a cart I.11.1. kɪɑːsstɪk Wo

cross-tree *n* an END-BOARD on a cart I.10.4. kɪɒstɹi St, kɪɒstɹeɪ St

cross-wards *adv* DIAGONALLY, referring to harrowing a field IX.1.8. kɪɔsəts Ch, kɽɔːswəᵗːdʐ So

cross-way *n* a DIAGONAL BAR of a gate IV.3.7. *pl* kɪɔ'swæɪz Nf

cross-way(s) *adv* DIAGONALLY, referring to harrowing a field IX.1.8.
no -s: kɪɒsweː La Y, kɪɒsweɪ Nth, kɪɒsweə Y, kɪɒswe: Ch, kɪɔːsweɪ O, kɪɔːsweɪ Nth Sf Sr
-s: kʁɒːsweɪz Nb, kɪɑːsweɪz Mon, kɪɑːsweːɪz Wo, kɪɑːsweɪz He, kɪɑːswæɪz He Wo, kɪɑːswaɪz Gl, kɪɑːswəɪz He, kɪɑᵗːʂwaɪz Wo, kʁɒswɪəz Du, kɪɒsweːz La Y, kɪɒsweiz Mon, kɪɒsweəz Du, kɪɒsweɪz St Wo Lei Sx, kɪɒswæɪz Hrt, kɽɒːsweɪz Ha, kʁɒswɪəz Nb, kʁɒsweːz Nb, kɪɔsweːz Y, kɪɔswɛ'əz L, kɪɔːsweɪz Sa O, kɪɔːsweɪz O, kɪɔːsweɪz Y Wa Hu Sf Ess MxL Sr K Sx, kɪɔːswæɪz O Nth Nf Ess MxL, kɪɔːswɔɪz Ess, kɪəswɛ'əz L

cross-ways *1. adj* SQUINTING VI.3.5. kɪɔːsweɪz Wo *[marked u.r. WMBM]*
2. adj ASKEW, describing a picture that is not hanging straight IX.1.3. kɪɔsweɪz L

cross-way(s) on *adv* DIAGONALLY, referring to harrowing a field IX.1.8.
no -s: kɪɔsweə ɒn Y
-s: kɪɔswɛ'əz ɒn L

crotch *n* the GROIN VI.9.4. kɪɒtʃ Nf

crotch-joy *n* GOOSE-GRASS II.2.5. kɪɒtʃdʒɔɪ Ess

crotch-weed *n* GOOSE-GRASS II.2.5. kɪɒtʃwiːd Sf

crouch *1. n* a BENCH on which slaughtered pigs are dressed III.12.1. kɪaʊtʃ Y
2. vt-1prpl we CRUNCH apples or biscuits VI.5.12. *-ing* kɽaʊtʃɪn So

crouch-grass *n* COUCH-GRASS II.2.3. kɪæʊtʃgɪas Y, kɪæʊtʃgəs Y

crounge *v-1prpl* we CRUNCH apples or biscuits VI.5.12. *-ing* kɪaʊndʒɪn La

croup *n* WHOOPING-COUGH VI.8.3. kɪuːp Sa *[old x1]* Ess

crouper *n* the CRUPPER of the harness of a cart-horse I.5.9. kɪuːpə Db

croupy *adj* HOARSE VI.5.16. kʁuːpɪ Nb *[complete loss of voice]*, kɪuːpɪ Y *[of children]*

croust *n* a SNACK VII.5.11. kɽæʏst Co, kɽæʏs Co

crow *1. n* the PLUCK of a slaughtered pig III.11.6. kɪɒʊ Sx; **liver and crow** lɪvəɹ n̩ kɪɒʊ K, lɪvəɹ n̩ kɪɔʊ K
2. n a CRANE on which a kettle is hung over a

domestic fire V.3.4. kɹɒʊ Gl, kɹoʊ Wa

3. n the HOOK or *CROOK* of a crane over a domestic fire V.3.5(c). kɹoː La

4. n a RAKE used in a domestic fire V.3.8(a). kɹoː Sa*[home-made]*

crow-bar *1. n* the *HORIZONTAL* BAR of a crane over a domestic fire V.3.5(a). kɹoːbaːɹ La

2. n a GRIDIRON V.7.4(a). kɹoːbaːɹ La*[old]*

crow-boggart *n* a SCARECROW II.3.7. kɹɔːbɒgəᴵt La, kɹoːbʊgəᴵ't La

crowdy *n* CHAFF fed to horses III.5.3. kɹaʊdɪ Y, kɹəʊdɪ Y

crow-fish *v* to GROPE *FOR FISH* IV.9.10. *-ing* kɹɔˈfɪʃɪn Brk

crow-foot *n* COLT'S-FOOT II.2.7. kɹoːfʊt Ch, kɹoʊfʊt He, kɹuːfʊt Ch

crowkings *n* SCRAPS left after rendering lard III.12.10. kɹaʊkɪnz Cu, kɹɒʊkɪnz We

crowklings *n* SCRAPS left after rendering lard III.12.10. kɹaʊklɪnz Cu We, kɹɒʊklɪnz Cu

crown *n* an EAR of a corn-plant II.5.2(b). kɹɛʊn Nf

crow-toed *adj* PIGEON-TOED VI.10.4. kɹɔʊtɔʊd L Hu

crud *n* the CUD that a cow chews III.2.11. kɽʌd So

cruddings *n* SCRAPS left after rendering lard III.12.10. kɽʊdənz O

cruddy *adj* **be cruddy** to VOMIT, referring to a baby bringing up milk VI.13.14(b). *3prsg* its kɹʊdɪ Nt

crumbs *npl* LICE IV.8.1(a). kɹʊmz Y

crump *vt-1prpl* we CRUNCH biscuits VI.5.12. kɹʌmp Ess

crumpets *n* SCRAPS left after rendering lard III.12.10. kɽʌmpɪts W

crumplings *n* SCRAPS left after rendering lard III.12.10. kɹʌmplənz Ess

crunch *v-1prpl* When, in eating, we crunch apples or biscuits noisily with our teeth, we say we ... (them). VI.5.12. Eng exc. We Man Wo Gl Nt C Bk Bd Hrt Brk Co Do. ⇒ **cham, cham up, chammer, champ, champ up, chank, chaw, chaw up, chew, chew up, chomp, chomp up, chop, chump, crack, cranch, craunch, cronch, crouch, crounge, crump,** *crunch up,* **crunge, crush, crush up, fraunch, gnaw, granch, graunch, graunch up, graunt, graze, gresh, grind, grind up, gronch, gronch up, growdge, grump, grump up, grunch, hanch up,** *manch* ⇒ **maunch, maunch, munch, munge, raunch, scaunch, scranch, scraunch, scrounge, scrump, scrunch, scrunch up, scrunge, scunch**

crunchings *n* SCRAPS left after rendering lard III.12.10. kɹʊnʃənz La

crund *n* CURDS V.5.8(a). krund Man *[queried NBM]*

crunge *vt-1prpl* we CRUNCH apples or biscuits VI.5.12. *-ing* kɽʌnȝən D

crup *1. n* the CRUPPER of the harness of a cart-horse I.5.9. kɹʌp He, kʀʊpʰ Nb, kɹʊp He Mon Gl

2. n the BEAK of a bird IV.6.18. krʊp Man

crupner *n* the CRUPPER of the harness of a cart-horse I.5.9. kɽʌpnəᶜ Do, kɽʊpnəᶜ So

crupper *n* Show a picture of the harness of a cart-horse. What do you call this [indicate the crupper]? I.5.9. kɽɛpəɽ O, kɹɒpə Y St K, kɹɒbə Nf, kɹɒpəᶜ He Wo, kɽɒpəᶜ Co, kʀɔpɔᵏ Nb, kɹɔpə L, kɽɔpəᶜ Ha, kɹɔʊpə Ess, kɹʌpə Mon O Nth Hu Sf Bd Hrt Ess MxL, kɹʌpʔə Sf Bk, kɹʌpəᴵ Sr K, kɹʌpəᶜ Sa He Mon Gl O Bk Bd, kɹʌpəᶜː Sa, kɽʌpəᶜ K, kɽʌpəᶜː D, kɹʌʊpə Nf, kʀʊpɔᵏ Nb, kʀʊpə Nb, kʀʊpəᵏ Du, kɹʊpə Cu We Y Ch Db St Wa Nt L Lei R Nth Hu Nf Hrt Ess, kɹʊb̥ə Nf, kɹʊpʔə C Nf Sf Ess, kɹʊpər La, kɹʊpəɹ La, kɹʊpəᴵ La Db O L Brk Sr K, kɹʊpɪ L, kɹʊpəᶜ Sa Wo Wa Gl O Bk, kɹʊpəᶜː Sa, kɽʊpəȝ O, kɽʊpəᶜː Ha, ʈɽʊpəᶜː Ha, kʀuːpɔᵏ Nb, kɹuːpə Y Db L, kɹuːpəᴵ Ha, kɹuːpɹ L, kɹəpə La Y, kɹəpəᶜ Sa Sr Sx. ⇒ **back-tie-strap, clipper, cripner, cripper, crippin, cripple, croop, croopin, crouper, crup, crupner, cruppon, crup-yard, cupper, dock, dock-strap, hood, tail-band, tail-cripper, tail-cripple, tail-crupper, tail-dock, tail-loop, tail-piece, tail-strap, tail-thong**

cruppon *n* the CRUPPER of the harness of a cart-horse I.5.9. kɹʊpn La, kɹʊpm La, kɹᵊuˈpənd Y

crup-yard *n* the CRUPPER of the harness of a cart-horse I.5.9. kɹʌpjəɹd He, kɹʌpjəᶜd̥ He Mon, kɹʌpijəᶜːd̥ He

crush *vt-1prpl* we CRUNCH apples or biscuits VI.5.12. *-ing* kɽʌʃɪn So, kɹʊʃ R

crush up *vtphr-1prpl* we CRUNCH apples or biscuits VI.5.12. *-ing* kɽʌʃɪn ... ʌp So

crust* *n* a SNACK VII.5.11. kɹʊst Du*[old]*

crut *n* a WEAKLING piglet III.8.4. kʀʊt Nb

crutch *n* the GROIN VI.9.4. kɽʌtʃ So D Ha, kɹʏtʃ Nf *[SBM Edd mark ir.r]*

crutches *npl* the HANDLES of a scythe II.9.8. kɹʊtʃɪz La

crutchings *n* SCRAPS left after rendering lard III.12.10. kɹʌtʃɪnz He, kɹʊtʃɪnz Gl

cruttens *n* SCRAPS left after rendering lard III.12.10. kɹʌʔnz Brk

cry *1. vi-3prpl* bulls BELLOW III.10.2. kɹɔɪ Ess

2. vi-3prpl sheep BLEAT III.10.5. kɹɔɪ O

3. vi to SCREAM VIII.8.11. kɽæɪ So, kɹaɪ We St Nt, kɽaɪ So D, kɹɑɪ La Db Nt Nth Bk Bd Hrt, kɹɒɪ St, kɽɒɪ W, kɹɔɪ Wa O Bk Hrt Ess, kɹʌɪ Nf Sf

crying *v-ing* SHRIEKING, describing the shrill noise made by a baby VI.5.15. kɹɛɪn Brk, kɽæːɪn So D, kraɪən Cu, kʀaɪən Nb Du, kɹaˈ-ɪn L, kɹaɪ-ɪn Ch Sa He Nt L Lei, kɹɑːɪɪn L, kɹɑɪ-ɪn Y Db Wa

cubby-hole

Nt R Nth Hu C Nf Bk Bd Hrt Ess, əkɹɑɪ-ɪn Nth, kɹɑɪ-ən C, kɹɒːɪn St, kɹɒɪ-ɪn St, kɽɒɪ-ɪn W, kɽɒɪjɪn So, kɹɔɪ-ɪn Wa Gl O Ess, əkɹɔɪ-ɪn Gl O, kɹɔɪ-ən Sf, əkɹɔɪ-ən Sf, kɹɔɪŋ Hrt, kɹɔɪn Wo, kɹʌɪ-ɪn Nf, kɹəɪ-ɪn Mon

cubby-hole *n* the ASH-HOLE beneath a domestic fire V.3.3. kɒbɪ-ɔʊɫ Hu

cuckoo *n* a COWSLIP II.2.10(a). kʊkuː L

cuckoo-lamb* *n* a lamb born in April, ⇐ PET-LAMB III.7.3. kʌkuˈlæm So

cucumber *n* *What else do you put in salads? [If necessary show pictures.]* V.7.17. Eng. ⇒ **conger, cumber**

cud *1. n When you see cows lying down and doing this [imitate chewing the cud], what do you say they do? [To chew the ....]* III.2.11. Eng. ⇒ **crud, cuds, quid**
2. v to chew the cud. prppl kʌdɪn Sr, kʊdɪn La, Y, Sr, kʊddɪn La, *-ing* kʊddɪn Db
3. n FOOD V.8.2. kʊd Y

cuddle-me-close *n* GOOSE-GRASS II.2.5. kʊdlmɪkløːs Nb

cuddy *1. n* a SAWING-HORSE I.7.16. kʊdɪ Nb Cu
2. n a DONKEY III.13.16. kʌdɪ Nb, kʌdɪ Nb, kʊdɪ Nb Cu Du We Y
3. n a LEFT-HANDED person VI.7.13(a). kʊdəɪ We

cuddy-brush* *n* a BRUSH used to clean horses III.5.5(a). kʊdɪbɹʊʃ Y

cuddy-comb *n* a CURRY-COMB used to clean horses III.5.5(b). kɒdɪkɪəm Y, kɒdɪkɔəm Y, kɒdɪkʊəm La Y, kɔdɪkɔm La, kɔdɪkʊəm L, kʊdɪkɪəm Nb Du Y, kʊdɪkɔm Wa, kʊdɪkeam Du, kʊdɪkuːm Y, kʊdɪkʊəm Du Y, kədɪkʊəm We

cuddy-handed *adj* LEFT-HANDED VI.7.13(a). kʊdɪhandɪd Du, kʊdɪ-andɪd Du Y

cuddy-wifter *n* a LEFT-HANDED person VI.7.13(a). kʊdɪwɪftə Du

cuds *n* the CUD that a cow chews III.2.11. kɪuːdz Du, kjɪudz Y, kʊdz Y

cuff *n* the SCRUFF (of the neck) VI.6.2. kʌf Nb, kʊf Nb Cu

cull *v* to REMOVE *STALKS* from currants V.7.24. *-ing* kʌɫɪn Brk

culling *v, vt What is your word for picking sheep out of the flock?* III.11.2. Eng exc. Nb Cu Du We Man He Mon Gl Sf Hrt. ⇒ *a-*picking out, catch out, *choose* ⇒ choosing, choosing, *cowl* ⇒ culling, croning, *cull, culling out, culling the best out, culling them sheep out, cull out, cull over, draft* ⇒ drafting, drafting, draft out, *draw* ⇒ drawing, *draw a few out* ⇒ drawing out, drawing, drawing out, *draw out* ⇒ drawing out, *draw the best out* ⇒ drawing out, gleaning out, *grade* ⇒ grading, grading, *herding*, mark out, parting, parting out, *part out* ⇒ parting out, *pick* ⇒ picking, *pick fat ones out* ⇒

picking out, picking, picking *a few good ones* out, picking out, picking over, picking *some* out, picking *the best* out, pick off, *pick out* ⇒ picking out, *pick over* ⇒ picking over, pulling *the sheep* out, *separate* ⇒ separating, separating, *shed* ⇒ shedding, shedding, *sort* ⇒ sorting, sorting, sorting out, sorting over, *sort out* ⇒ sorting out, *sort over* ⇒ sorting over

cullis-ender *n* a long stack with rounded ends, ⇐ STACKS II.7.1. kʊlɪsɛndə Nth

cully-comb *n* a CURRY-COMB used to clean horses III.5.5(b). kʌlɪkoʊm He, kəlɪkɪˈəm Y

cumber *n* a CUCUMBER V.7.17. kʌmbə Lei Sf, kʊmbə Ch Db St

cunny *n* the VULVA of a cow III.2.3. kʌni W

cunny-handed *adj* LEFT-HANDED VI.7.13(a). kʊnɪ-ændɪd Gl

cunt *n* the VULVA of a cow III.2.3. kʌnt D, kʊnt Man Gl Nth

cupboard *n* a PANTRY V.2.6. kʌbʌd Nf, kʌbəd Sf*[old]* Hrt*[in small cottage]* Ess, kʌbət Sf*[old]*

cupper *n* the CRUPPER of the harness of a cart-horse I.5.9. kʊpʔə Ess, kʊpəꜜ Sr Sx, kʊpəꜜ Sx

cur *n* a MONGREL III.13.5. kɔᵏː Nb, kəː St

curb *1. n* the CURB-STONE in a cow-house I.3.9. kɛːᵊb Nt, kœːb Mon, kʌɽb So, kəːb Y St Nt Lei Ess K, kəˡːb Ch L, kəꜜːb Sa He Wa Mon Gl Bk Ess So W Co D Sx, kəꜜːd Wo
2. n the THRESHOLD of a door V.1.12. kəꜜːb Sr

curb and chain *n* a watch-CHAIN VI.14.12. kəːb ən tʃɛɪn Bd

curb-end *n* the CURB-STONE in a cow-house I.3.9. kɪəbɛnd L

curbing *n* the CURB-STONE in a cow-house I.3.9. kəꜜːbɪn Sa Gl D Do

curbing-stone *n* the CURB-STONE in a cow-house I.3.9. kœːbɪnstʊn Gl, kəꜜːbɪnstuːən W, kəꜜːbɪnstwən W

curb-stone(s) *1. n [Show a picture of an old-fashioned cow-house.] What do you call this, at the end of the standing, near the drain? [before April 1955: the curb before at the end]* I.3.9.
no -s: kɛːbstən Nt, kɛˈəbstoʊn L, kəˡbstoʊn L, kəˡbstʊən L, kəːbstoʊn Ess*[usually wooden]*, kəːbstʊən Nt L, kəːbstn Cu, kəꜜːbstoːn Sa, kəꜜːbstoʊn Wo, kəꜜːbstuːn Co D Ha, kəꜜːbstuːən W Co D Do Ha
-s: kœːbstounz Mon, kʊrbstnz Cu, kəꜜːbstoːnz Sa ⇒ **base, bed, brick-edge, catch, coping, coping-stones, curb, curb-end, curbing, curbing-stone, edge, edge** *of the gutter*, **edging, edging-stone, fall-tree, flagstones, fly-stones, footing, grip-stone, grooping, groop-stead, gutter-edging, heading, heel-sill, heel-stone(s),**

heel-tread, heel-tree, hollan-stone, ledge, ligging-stone(s), paving- stones, rib, set-off, settle, settle-stone(s), settle-tree, settling, sill, slab, sleeper, step, stone, thalling, thall-tree

2. *n* the concrete floor of the stalls in a cow-house. kɑːbstən Y

curd *1.1. vt* to CURDLE milk V.5.7. kɛːᵊd Db, kɔːᵊd Nb, kəːd Y Db L Lei Hu, kjəːd Y, kəˡːd L, kəᵗːd̚ Sa O W, kɪʌd Sa Mon, kɹʊd Cu We La Y Mon

1.2. v to curdle. kəːd Cu Db L, kəᵗːd̚ Sa W, kəᵗː K, kɹɪəd Cu, kʁʊd Nb, kɹʊd We La Y

1.3. n **go to curd**, **make it curd**, **turn it curd**, **turn it curds**, **turn it into curd** to curdle milk. **go to curd** gə tə kəːd R; **make it curd** meɪk ət kəᵗːd̚ So, mak ɪt kɹʊd Y; **turn it curd** *3prsg* tɛənz ɪt kɛəd Lei; **turn it curds** təːn ɪt kəːdz Lei; **turn it into curd** tən ɪt ɪntə kɹʊd Y

2.1. vi to CURDLE, referring to milk V.5.9. kɪʌd Sa, kɹʊd La Y, kəd Y

2.2. vt **be curded**, **go curded** to curdle. **be curded** bɪ kɹʊdɪd Y; **go curded** gaː kɹʊdɪt We

curdle *1. v Let's see, you put rennet into the milk in order to ....* V.5.7. Eng exc. We Man Hu C. ⇒ **brack** *it*, **break** *it*, **bring** *the curd*, **clot**, **come** *into curd*, **come** *it*, **come** *the curd*, **craddle** *it*, *cradle it* ⇒ **craddle** *it*, **criddle**, **criddle** *it*, *cruddle it* ⇒ **curdle**, *crud it* ⇒ **curd**, **curd**, **curd** *it*, **curd** *it* up, *go to curd*, **grub** *it*, **help** turn *it*, **make** *it* come, **make** *it* curd, **make** *it* curdle, *make it go loppy*, *make it go sour*, *make it set*, *make it* sour, **quig** *it*, **set** *it*, **sour** *it*, *start it working*, **thicken** *it*, **turn**, *turn it into crud* ⇒ **turn it into** curd, **turn** *it*, **turn** *it* curd, **turn** *it* curds, **turn** *it* sour, **turn** *the milk*, **turn thick**

2. vi In hot weather, fresh milk will soon .... V.5.9. kɛːdl Nf, kadlɪn Nf, kadɬ Sf, kaːdɬ Sf, kɔᵷːdl Nb, kɔˡːdɬ La, kʁɒdl Nb, kʌdl Ess, kɹʊdl Y Nt L, kəːdl Db Hu Nf, kəːdɬ Nth C Hrt MxL, kəˡːdl L, kəᵗːdʊl Brk, kəɾdl̩ Nf, kəᵗːd̩l̩ Sa O, kəᵗːd̩ɬ Wa Bk Ess So W K Sx, kəᵗːɾd̩ʊɬ Sx. ⇒ **be curded**, **be sour**, **change**, **curd**, **curdle up**, **get curdy**, **get sour**, **go bad**, **go curded**, **go loppered**, **go loppy**, **go off**, **go sour**, **go wented**, **go wolpy**, **quig**, **sour**, **turn**, **turn into curd**, **turn off**, **turn sour**, **wolpy**

3. n BEESTINGS V.5.10. kəːgl Nf

4. vi to VOMIT, referring to a baby bringing up milk VI.13.14(b). *-ing* kədlɪn L, kəːdɬ Sf, *3prsg* kɹʊdlz Y, *prppl* kɹʊdlɪn Y, *ptppl* kɹʊdld Y, kɹʊdɬ He

curdle-milk *n* WHEY V.5.8(b). kʊdɬmɪlk Nth

curdle(s) *n* CURDS V.5.8(a).
no -s: kʊdl Nth
-s: kəᵗːɾd̩l̩z̩ Brk, kʁɒdlz Nb

curdles *n* **sheep's-curdles** SHEEP-DUNG II.1.7. ʃiːpskəːd̩ɬz̩ So

curdle up *viphr* to CURDLE, referring to milk V.5.9. *3prsg* kəᵗd̩ɬz̩ ʌp K

curdlings *n* BEESTINGS V.5.10. kəːdɬɪnz MxL

curdly *n* BEESTINGS V.5.10. kɑːd̩ɬi Nf

cur-dog *n* a MONGREL III.13.5. kəːdɒg nmY, kəˑɹdɔg Y

curd(s) *n And when the milk does that [curdles], what do you call the stuff you get? [... and whey]* V.5.8(a).

no -s: kɛəd Lei, kœːd Mon, kaːd Nf Sf, kɔd L, kɔᵷːd Nb La, kɔˡːd L, kɜˡːɹd La, kəd Y, kəɹd Y L, kəɾd Nf, kəːd Cu Du Y Ch Db Nt L Lei Nf Ess, kjəːd Y, kəˡːd Ch Db L, kəˡːɹd Brk, kəᵗːd̚ Sa He Wo Gl O Bk, kəᵗːɾd̚ Sx, kɪʌd Sa Mon, kɾʌd Do, kɹʊd Cu Du Y Ch He Gl L, kɹəd Gl
-s: Eng. ⇒ **buttermilk**, **crund**, **curdle(s)**, **loppered**, **loppered milk**, **milk-curds**, **oast**, **sour-milk**, **wad**

curds *n* BEESTINGS V.5.10. kəˡːdz Brk

curd up *vtphr* to CURDLE milk V.5.7. kɹʊd ... ʊp Y

curdy *adj* **get curdy** to CURDLE, referring to milk V.5.9. gɪt kəːdɪ Sf

curing-stone *n* a flat surface on which bacon is cured, ⇐ SALTING-TROUGH III.12.5. kjuˑəɹənsteˑən Cu

curragh *adj* BOGGY IV.1.8. kʊɹəx Man

currants *1. n* SHEEP-DUNG II.1.7. kʌɹənts Ess, kʌɾənts Co, kəɹənz St; **sheep-currants** ʃiːpkɒɹənz Y He, ʃiːpkəɹənz Y*[polite x1]*

2. *n* RABBIT-DROPPINGS III.13.15. kɒɹʊnz La, kɔɹənz Ch, kʌɹənts Ess, kʌɾənts So, kʊɹənz Db St, kəɹənts Nf Ess, kəˑɹᵊnz Nf

curry *1. n* a WAGON without sides I.9.2. kʌɾi So
2. *n* a wagon for carrying straw. kʌɾi So
3. *n* a CURRY-COMB used to clean horses III.5.5(b). kɒɹɪ Man, kʊɾɪ Man, kʊɹɪ Cu, kəɹɪ Cu

curry-cart *n* a WAGON without sides I.9.2. kʌɾikaᵗːt So

curry-comb *n What do you clean your horses up with?* III.5.5(b). Eng exc. Man. ⇒ **body-comb**, **charrow-comb**, *colly-comb* ⇒ **cully-comb**, **comb**, **cotty-comb**, **cuddy-comb**, **cully-comb**, **curry**, **curry-cope**, **flat comb**, **groom**, **scurry-comb**; ⇒ also **scraper**

curry-cope *n* a CURRY-COMB used to clean horses III.5.5(b). kʊɹɪkɒʊp K *[not a SBM headword]*

cursing *v-ing Of a person who uses a lot of bad language, you'd say: He is always ... [and swearing].* VIII.8.9(a). Eng. ⇒ **a-cursing**, **blackguarding**, **blinding**

curtain bonnet *1. n* a woman's BONNET worn indoors VI.14.1. kəᵗːʈɪn bɒnət So
2. *n* a woman's lace bonnet. *pl* kəᵗːʈən bɒnəts So

cush *n* a HORNLESS cow III.2.9. kʊʃ La Ch St

cushion *1. n What do you call this, on the chair [indicate a cushion]?* V.2.10. Eng. ⇒ **squab**
2. *vi* to show signs of calving, referring to a cow

with a swelling udder, ⇐ SHOWS SIGNS OF CALVING III.1.12(a). *3prprogsg* kʊʃnɪn La

custards *n* BEESTINGS V.5.10. kʊstɪdz L

cut *1. v When you are getting [this] peat, what do you say you do?* IV.4.4.

vt kʌt He Gl So W D Do Ha, *-ing* kʌtɪn Sr, *prppl* kʌʔɪn W, kʌd Co D Ha, kʊt Sa St Wo, *-ing* kʊtɪn O

v to cut peat. kʌt Sa He Mon O Hu Nf Sf Bd Ess MxL So W Brk Sr Co D Ha Sx, *-ing* kʌtɪn K, *-ing* kʌtn Do, kʌʔ Nf, *-ing* kʌʔɪn Hu W, *-ing* kʌʔn Ess K Sx, kʌd D, kʏt Nb, kʊt Nb Cu Du We La Y Man Ch Db Sa St He Wo Wa Mon Gl O Nt L Lei R Nth, kət Gl Sx

⇒ **cast, cut out, cut out** *in spits,* **delve, dig, dig** *for,* **dig out, dig up, get, grave, hod out, pare, peat, peat-dig, peat-raising, spade, spit out, turf, turf-cutting;** ⇒ also **chog**

2.1. vt to WHITTLE a stick I.7.19. *-ing* kʌtɪn So W, *-ing* kʌtn W, *-ing* kʌdən Do, *3prsg* kʊts St, *-s* kʊts Ch, *-ing* kʊtɪn Gl, *-ing* əkʊtɪn He

2.2. v to whittle. kʌt Nth Sf Hrt, *-ing* kʌtɪn He K, kʌʔ Hrt, *-ing* kʌʔɪn Sr, *-ing* kʌʔn K, kʊt La Ch Lei, *3prsg* kʊts R, *-ing* kʊtɪn Y Gl Nth, *-ing* əkʊtɪn Wo [*marked u.r. EMBM*]

3.1. vt to TOP AND TAIL swedes II.4.3. kʌt K

3.2. v to top and tail swedes. kʊt We, *-ing* kʊɹɪn Y

4. v to MOW grass for hay-making II.9.3. kʌt Ess MxL Sr Ha, kʌʔ Nf, kʏʔ Nf, kʊt Nb Cu Du Y St Wa L Lei

5. vt to CLEAR grass at the edges of a field II.9.5. *-ing* kɒtɪn He, kʌt Sa He Mon*[with scythe]* Gl O MxL*[with scythe]* Sr Sx, kʌʔ Nf*[with scythe]* Sr, kʊt Cu Du Y*[with scythe]* Wa O*[with scythe]* L Lei, *-ing* kʊʔn Man

6. n a CUTTING of hay II.9.15. kʌt Mon O Hu Co D, kʌʔ Bd, kʊt Y Man

7. v-ed CASTRATED, describing a bullock III.1.15. kʌt Nb Sa He O Nth Hu C Nf Sf Bk Bd Hrt Ess MxL So W Sr K Co D Do Ha Sx, kʌtʔ Nf, kʌʔ O Nf Bk, kʏt Nf, kʏtʔ Nf, kʊt Nb Cu Du We La Y Ch Db Sa St He Wo Wa Gl O Nt L Lei R Nth C K, kʊʔ Bk, kʊːt He Wo, kət Gl

8. adj CLOVEN, describing the hoof of a cow III.2.8(b). kʊt Y

9.1. vt to MARK the ears of sheep with a cut or hole to indicate ownership III.7.9. kʌt Brk, kʌd (+V) D

9.2. v to mark the ears of sheep. kɒt Man, *-ing* kʌʔn K

⇒ **clip** *their ears,* **clip** *their lugs,* **cut** *a snotch out of their ear,* **cut** *their ears,* **ear-clip, ear-mark, mark, point** *their ears,* **snip** *their ears*

10. v to TRIM hedges IV.2.3. kʌtC So, kʌtɪn K, *-ing* kʌtn Ess, kʊt Nb La Nt L, *-ing* kʊtɪn Y Ch Db

11. v to LOP a tree IV.12.5. kʌt Ess So, *-ing* kʊʔn Man

12. vt **cut the eyes and strigs** to TOP- AND-TAIL gooseberries V.7.23. kʌt ðɪ ɑɪz ŋ stɹɪgz K

cut back *vphr* to TRIM hedges IV.2.3. kʌt bak So, *-ing* kʊtɪn bak Y

cutchy-bonnet *n* a woman's cloth BONNET worn outdoors VI.14.1. kʊtʃɪbɒnət Gl [*queried WMBM*]

cut down *1. vphr* to MOW grass for hay-making II.9.3. kʌʔ ... dɛun Nf

2. vtphr to TRIM hedges IV.2.3. *-ing* kʌtɪn ... dɛun Nf, kʌt ... dævn D, kʊt ... dəʊn Gl [*noted as probably u.rr. EMBM*]

3. vtphr to PLASH a hedge IV.2.4. kʌt ... dæun Ha

cut gilt* *n* a castrated female pig, ⇐ HOG III.8.8. kʊt gɪlt Db, kʊt gɪɫt He

cut hilt* *n* a castrated female pig, ⇐ HOG III.8.8. kʌt ɪɫt He Mon, kʊt ɪlt Gl, kʊt ɪɫt He Mon

cut hog-pig *n* a male HOG III.8.8. kʊt ɒgpɪg Wo

cut-knife *n* a HAY-KNIFE II.9.14(a). kʌtnɑɪf Hu

cut off *1.1. vphr* to TOP AND TAIL swedes II.4.3. kʊt ɒf We

1.2. vtphr **cut the green off and cut the root off, cut the swedes off, cut the top and bottom off, cut the top off, cut the tops and roots off, cut the tops and tails off** to top and tail swedes. kʌt ... ɔːf Hu*[top only]* W, kʊt ... ɒf Db Wa Lei, kʊt ... ɔːv Y

2. vtphr to CLEAR grass at the edges of a field II.9.5. kʌt ... ɔːᶱf Ess, kʊt ... ɔːf Wo

3.1. vtphr to LOP branches from tree IV.12.5. kʌt ... ɔːf So, kʊt ... ɔːf Sa

3.2. vphr to lop branches. kʌt ɔːf Sf

4. vtphr **cut the ends off** to TOP-AND-TAIL gooseberries V.7.23. kʊt ð ɛndz ɔːf La

cut out *1. vphr* to WHITTLE a stick I.7.19. *-ing* kʌtɪn ɛʊt Sx

2.1. vtphr to THIN OUT turnip plants II.4.2. kʌʔ (+fricative) ... ɛʊt O, kʌʔ ... ɛut Nf, kʌt ... æʊt He W Ha, kʌd ... æʊt W, kʊt ... ɑʊt O, kʌt ... ɒʊt W, kʌt ... ʌʊt Brk, kʊt ... ^uːt Gl, kʌt ... oʊt Brk, kʌt ... əʊt W, kʌd ... əʊt W, kʊt ... əʊːt Gl

2.2. vphr to thin out turnips. *prppl* kʌtɪn əʊt Brk

3.1. vtphr to CLEAR grass at the edges of a field II.9.5. kʌʔ ... ɛʊʔ O Bk, kʌd ... œvt D, kʌt ... ævt Co, kʌd ... ævt Co*[with scythe x1]* D*[with scythe x1]*, kʌt æʊt He, kʌt ... æʊt W*[with scythe x1]*, *2prpl* kʌts ... æʊt Ha, kʌd ... æʊt So Do Ha, kʌt aʊt So*[corners]*, kʌt ... aʊt Sa Do, kʌt ... ɒʊt W, kʌt ... ʌʊt Mon, kʌt ... əʊt Mon W Do, *-ing* kʌtɪn ... əʊt He, kʌd ... əʊt W Do, kʊt ... æʊt Wa, kʊt ... ɛʊt Sa, kʊt ... æʊt R, *-ing* kʊtɪn ... æʊt Lei, kʊt ... aːᶱt Lei, kʊt ... ʌʊt Mon, kʊt ... uːt Nb, kʊt əʊt He Wo Gl

3.2. vphr to clear grass. kʌt ɛʊt O, *-ing* kʌtɪn ɛʊt Sx, *-ing* kʌʔn ɛʊt Ess, kʌt æʊt Ha, *-ing* kʌtɪn æʊt W

4. vphr **cut out and chuck back** to TRIM hedges

IV.2.3. kʌt aʊt ən tʃʌk bæk So

5. *vtphr* to CUT peat IV.4.4. kʌd ... æɤt D, *-ing* kʌdn ... æɤt So, kʌt ... æʊt Ess, kʌt ... aʊt So, kʌd ... əʊt Do, kʊt ... æʊt Wa; **cut out in spits** kʌt ... ɛʊt ɪn spɪts MxL

cut pig *n* a male or female HOG III.8.8. kʌt pɪg Sf

cut round *1. vtphr* to CLEAR grass at the edges of a field II.9.5. kʌd (+V) ... ɽœɤn D

2. *vphr* to clear grass. kət ɹᵁuːn Gl

cuts *npl* CHAPS in the skin VI.7.3. kʌts Sa MxL

cut sow* *n* a castrated female pig, ⇐ HOG III.8.8. kʊt sæʊ Wo

cutten *v-ed* CASTRATED, describing a bullock III.1.15. kʊtn Nt, kʊʔn L

cutter *1. n* the COULTER of a horse-drawn plough I.8.6. kʌtə Hrt, kʌtəᵗː So, kʊtə We Y Ch *[taken as* **coulter** *not* **cutter** *in N/WMBM]*

2. *n* a HAY-SPADE II.9.14(b). kʌtəˡ K

cutterlug *n* the vertical BAR or CHAIN of a crane over a domestic fire V.3.5(b). kʊtəˡlʊg Brk

cutting *n What do you call the amount of hay you cut off [from the stack] at a time for your own use?* II.9.15. kʌtɪn He, kʌtn Nf Sf, kʊtɪn St L. ⇒ **bank, bench, bundle, burn, cake, canch, cant, carf, clef, cleft, cut, cutting-down, dess, flake, flap, forkful, hay-truss, heading, keech, kelf, load, pad, pitch, quarter, sess, slab, slice, slipe, slysh, spit, square, tod, ton, top, truss, vult, wad, yafful**

cutting-down *n* a CUTTING of hay II.9.15. kʊtɪndaʊn La

cutting-knife *1. n* a HAY-KNIFE II.9.14(a). kʌtɪnnaɪf Sa, kʌtɪnnaɪf Hu, kʌtɲnaɪf C Nf, kʌtɲnɒɪf Nf, kʌtɪnnɔɪf Gl O, kʌtɲnɔɪf Sf Ess Ha, kʌʔɪnnɔɪf Bk, kʌʔɲnɔɪf Sf Ess Ha, kʌttɪnnʌɪf Bd Brk, kʌtɲnʌɪf Nf Sf Ess, kʌtʔɪnnʌɪf Nf, kʌtʔɲnʌɪf Nf, kʌʔɲnʌɪf Nf, kʌʔɪnnʌɪf O, kʌtɪnnəɪf He W, kʌʔɪnnəɪf W, kʌʔɲnəɪf W, kɤtɲnʌɪf Nf, kʊtɪnnæɪf Sa, kʊtɪnaɪf Sa, kʊtɪnnaɪf Db Sa L Lei, kʊtɪnnaːf Lei, kʊtɪnaɪf Nt, kʊtɪnnaɪf Y Ch Db Wa O Nt L Lei R Nth, kʊtɲnaɪf C, kʊtɪnnɒɪf Sa St, kʊtɪŋgnɒɪf St, kʊtɪnnɔɪf Wa L Nth, kʊtɪnnəɪf Wo Gl, kətɪnnæɪf He, kətɪnnʌɪf Gl

2. *n* a HAY-SPADE II.9.14(b). kʌtɪnnɛɪf Sa, kʌtənnɔɪf Sf, kʌtɲnɔɪf Sf, kʌtɪnnəɪf Sx, kʊtɪnnaˑɪf L

cutting-spade *n* a HAY-SPADE II.9.14(b). kʊtɪnspeːd Y

cut up *1. vtphr* to CLEAR grass at the edges of a field II.9.5. kʌd ʌp So

2. *vphr* to clear grass. kʌʔ ʌp Nf

cutwith *n* a SWINGLE-TREE of a horse-drawn plough harness I.8.3. kʌtwɪθ O

cwtsh* *1. n* a CLAMP in which potatoes are stored out of doors II.4.6. kʊtʃ He

2. *n* a PANTRY V.2.6. kʰʊtʃ Mon

cyst *n* a STYE in the eye VI.3.10. sɪs Nf

D

dab *vt* to MARK sheep with colour to indicate ownership III.7.9. dɛb Ess, dæb He Sx, dab D *[not a SBM headword]*

dabs *n* sheep-dabs SHEEP-DUNG II.1.7. ʃiːpdabz D

dab-toed *adj* PIGEON-TOED VI.10.4. dæbtʌʊd Ess *[queried EMBM]*

dack *1. n* a PET-LAMB III.7.3. dæk So
2. n a WEAKLING piglet III.8.4. dæk So

dacky *n* a PIGLET III.8.2. dækɪ Sa

dad *vt* to BEAT a boy on the buttocks VIII.8.10. dad Nb

daddy-long-leg(s) *1. n* What do you call those insects with small thin bodies and thin legs, that fly up and down the window-pane? IV.8.10.
no -s: dædɪlɒŋlɛg Brk, dadɪlɒŋlɛg Y, dadɪlɒŋlɛg La
-s: Eng exc. We He Mon R
⇒ **daddy-long-tails, davy, davy-long-legs, gnats, gramfer-long-legs, grandfather-fly, harry-eight-legs, harry-long-legs, harvest-men, hobhouchin, jacka-legs, jacka-long-legs, jacky-long-legs, jenny-long-legs, jenny-spinner(s), jen-spinners, jerry-long-legs, jimmy-long-legs, johnny-long-legs, lady-milord, long-legged-gnat, long-legged-harry, long-legged-jacks, long-legged-tailor(s), longleg-tailors, may-maid, nanny-long-legs, nanny-spinner, spindle-shanks, spinning-dicky, tailor, tailor-tartan, tommy-long-legs, tommy-spinner, tommy-tailor(s), tom-spinner, tom-tailor(s), tom-tailor-legs, willy-biter**
2. n a long-legged spider. dædɪlɒŋlɛgz Nf, dædɪlɒŋlɛgz Nf, dædɪlɒŋlɛgz Ess

daddy-long-tails *n* DADDY-LONG-LEGS IV.8.10. dadɪlɒŋtɛˑəlz L

daddy-roughs *npl* MINNOWS IV.9.9. dadɪɹʊfs Wo

daff in *imp* HELP YOURSELVES!, said to invite visitors to eat V.8.13. daf ɪn Nb

daffy *1. n* the YIELD of milk from a cow III.3.5. dɛəfɪ Ess
2. adj SILLY VIII.9.3. dæˑfɪ Brk

daft *1. adj* STUPID VI.1.5. dɛft Y, dɛːft Sx, dæft He Wo Brk, dæf Brk, dæːft Gl So W, dæːf So, daft Nb We La Y Ch Db St Wo O L Lei, daːft Sa He Mon Gl C Ess Do Ha, daːf Ess So Co D Do, dɑft Y, dɑːft Wo Hrt MxL K Sx
2. adj CLUMSY, describing a person VI.7.14. dæːf So
3. adj SILLY VIII.9.3. Eng exc. MxL Sx

dafty *1. adj* SILLY VIII.9.3. dæːfti So
2. n a silly person. daftɪ Y

dag *1. n* the BUTT of a sheaf of corn II.6.4. dɛg So
2. n DEW VII.6.7. dɛɪg Ess, dæg Sf*[old x1]* Ess*[early morning mist x1, old x1, occasional x1]*, dæᶦg Ess*[old x1]*, daɪg Ess
3. n MIST VII.6.8. dæg Nf

dag-end *n* the BUTT of a sheaf of corn II.6.4. dægɛnd So, dagɛnd So

dagg *vi* to FESTER, referring to a wound VI.11.8. dɛg Y

dagger *n* a DIAGONAL BAR of a gate IV.3.7. *pl* dagəz Y

daggers *n* ICICLES VII.6.11. dægəᶜz̩ Wo, dagəz L, dagəᶜz̩ Bk

daggings *n* sheep-daggings SHEEP-DUNG II.1.7. ʃɪpdægɪnz He

daglers *n* ICICLES VII.6.11. dægləᶜɾz̩ Ha

daglets *n* ICICLES VII.6.11. dɛgləts Sx*[old]*, dæglɪts W, dægləts W Brk Sr*[old]*, dægɫəts Brk, dagləts W, dagɫəts W

dags *n* sheep-dags SHEEP-DUNG II.1.7. ʃɪpdægz He*[balls of dung in sheep's wool x1]*

dairy *1. n* What do you call the place where in the old days you kept the milk? V.5.1. Eng exc. Cu. ⇒ **buttery**, *cellar*, **dairy-house, larder,** *milk-cellar*, **milk-dairy, milk-house, milking-dairy, milk-parlour, milk-shed,** *on the cellar-head,* **pantry,** *safe*
2. n a PANTRY V.2.6. dɪˈəɹɪ L, deˈəɹɪ L, deːɹɪ We*[on farm]*, dɛɪɹɪ Gl, dɛɪəᶜːɾɪ D Ha, dɛəɹɪ We*[on farm]* La Y*[in old house x1, old x1]* Nt L, dɛəɾi Co D, dɛəᶜːɾɪ Co*[in farmhouse x1, old x1]* D, daːɹɪ Y, dəːɹɪ Wa*[in farmhouse]*

dairy bench *n* a flat surface on which bacon is cured, ⇐ SALTING-TROUGH III.12.5. dɛəɹɪ bɪnʃ Nt

dairy-house *n* the DAIRY on a farm V.5.1. dɛːɾɪ-æʊs Do

daisy *n* *[Show a picture of cowslip, daisy, and dandelion.]* What do you call these, they are three common flowers that you find in fields? II.2.10(b). Eng. ⇒ **dog-daisy**

daker *n* a WHETSTONE made of stone II.9.10. deːkəᶜː Do

dall* *n* a WEAKLING piglet III.8.4. dæˑɫ Brk

dall-pig *n* a WEAKLING piglet III.8.4. daʊpɪg So

dam *1. n* a POOL on a farm III.3.9. dam Y *[hilly locality]*

2. *n* a POND IV.1.5. dæm Man, dam Y

dam-holes *npl* PUDDLES IV.1.6. *sg* dʊmɒil La

damn *adv* VERY VIII.3.2. dæm Nf, dam St L

damned *adv* VERY VIII.3.2. dɛmd Ess, dæmd He Sx, dæmnd He, damd L

damp *1. vt* to BREW tea V.8.9. *-ing* dʌmpin Brk

2. *n* MIST VII.6.8. dæmp Nf

dams *npl* PUDDLES IV.1.6. dæms Man

dand *n* DANDRUFF VI.1.3. dænd Ess

dand-brush *n* a BRUSH used to clean horses III.5.5(a). dandbɹʊʃ L

dandelion *n [Show a picture of cowslip, daisy, and dandelion.] What do you call these, they are three common flowers that you find in fields?* II.2.10(c). Eng. ⇒ **dando, dandy, dog-stink(er), pee-bed, piddle-your-bed, pissabed, piss-bed, piss-mare, pissy-bed, pissy-moor, pissy-mother, pissy-moul, pithabed, pittle-bed, shitabed** *[some examples of primary stress on 3rd syllable in EMBM and SBM, but probably not always recorded]*

dando *n* a DANDELION II.2.10(c). dændou Nf

dandruff *n What do you call the white powdery stuff that falls onto the shoulders?* VI.1.3. dɛndɹʌf Sr K, dændɹʌf Ess K, dæːndɹʌf Hrt MxL, dændrʊf Man, dandrɪf Co, dandɹʌf Mon, dandrʌf D Ha, dandɹʊf Y, dandɹəf Y. ⇒ **clairce, clarth, dand, dry scurf, fruzzings, hurf, rift, rummet, scale, scruff, scruffy, scurf, scurfy, scurvy, snow**

dandy *1. n* a DANDELION II.2.10(c). dandɪ La

2. *n* a BRUSH used to clean horses III.5.5(a). dændi Co, dandɪ Bk

dandy-brush *n* a BRUSH used to clean horses III.5.5(a). dɛndɪbɹʌʃ Sr K Sx, dɛndɪbɹʊʃ K, dɛndɪbɹəʃ Sx, dæːndɪbɹʌʃ He Mon Hu Nf Sf Hrt Ess MxL Brk Sr K Ha Sx, dændɪbrʌʃ So D, dændɪbɹʊʃ Sa Wo K, dændɪbrʊʃ Co, dændɪbɹəʃ Sx, dændɪbəˤːʃ So, dandibɾiːʃ D, dandibɾɪʃ Co D, dandɪbɹʏːʃ Db, dandɪbɾʏːʃ D, dandɪbʀʌʃ Nb, dandɪbɹʌʃ Sa He Mon O Bk Bd Hrt, dandibɾʌʃ So W Do Ha, dandɪbʀʊʃ Nb Du, dandɪbɹʊʃ Cu Du We La Y Ch Db St Wa Gl O Nt L, dandɪbɹəʃ Gl, dandibəˤːʃ So, dandɪbɾʊʃ O

daniel *n* a WEAKLING piglet III.8.4. dænʊɫ K

dannockins* *n* children's mittens, small GLOVES with only the thumb separate VI.14.7. dænɪkɪnz Nf

dannocks* *n* mittens, GLOVES with only the thumb separate VI.14.7. dænɪks Nf*[working gloves x1]*, dænəks Nf, danəks Nf

dap *1. vt* to MARK sheep with colour to indicate ownership III.7.9. dæp So, dap W

2. *vi* to BOUNCE VIII.7.3. dæp He Mon*[old x1]* Gl So W*[old x1]*, dap Mon Gl W, daːp Mon

dap on* *vt* to put colour on sheep to MARK them for ownership III.7.9. dap ... ɔːn Ha

dappy *adj* SILLY VIII.9.3. dæpɪ Ess

daps *1. n* a copy, referring to someone who RESEMBLES someone else VIII.1.9. dæps D, daps Co D

2. *n* **the daps of** a resemblance to someone. ðə daps əv W D

dark *adj* DULL, referring to the weather VII.6.10. daːk Y, dɑːk Man, dɜ˔ːɹk La, dəˤːk O

darkies *npl* GIPSIES VIII.4.12. daˤːkɪz D

dark rubber *n* a WHETSTONE made of stone II.9.10. daˤːk ɹʌbəˤ O

darksome *adj* DULL, referring to the weather VII.6.10. daʁːksəm Nb

darling *n* a WEAKLING piglet III.8.4. daˤːɫɪn W, daˤːɫən W Ha, daːlɪn Sr, dɑːlɪŋ Sr, dɑːɫɪn Sr K, dɑˤːlɪn Brk, daˤːɾɫɪn Sx

darn* *adv* VERY VIII.3.2. daˤn̩ Ha *[SBM headword* **darned***]*

darning *v-ing What is your word for mending socks?* V.10.1. Eng. ⇒ **codging, mending**

darning-needle *n* a NEEDLE V.10.2(a). daːnɪnnɪdl Ch *['presumably this kind was shown' WMBM Edd]*

darrel *n* a WEAKLING piglet III.8.4. daɾəɫ Ha, daˤːɾəɫ W

dash *n* **a little dash** a LITTLE amount of milk VII.8.20. ə ɫɪdɫ daɪʃ D

dash-board *1. n* an END-BOARD on a cart I.10.4. *pl* dɛʃbɔˤːdz̩ Sa, dæʃbɔːˤˤːd̩ He, dæʃbɔːəd Mon, dæʃboːəˤd̩ Sa He Wo Mon Gl, dæʃbəˤːd̩ He, daʃbɔːəˤd̩ Wo, daʃbəˤːd̩ Sa

2. *n* a side-board on a cart. *pl* dæʃbɔːdz He, *pl* dæʃbɔːɹdz He

dash-boards *n* a CART-FRAME I.10.6. dæʃbɑːˤd̩z̩ Wo

dash-churn *n* a CHURN with a handle which moved up and down V.5.5. daʃtʃəːn Ch

dasher *n* a CHURN with a rotating fan V.5.5. daʃə St

dateless *adj* SILLY VIII.9.3. deːkləs Y, deːkl̩əs Y

daub *vt* to DIRTY a floor V.2.8. dɔːb Y

daubed *adj* STICKY, describing a child's hands VIII.8.14. dɔːbd Y

daubed up *adj* STICKY, describing a child's hands VIII.8.14. dæːbd ʌp So, daːbt ʊp Y, daʊbd ʊp Lei, dɔːbd ʊp La

dauby *adj* STICKY, describing a child's hands VIII.8.14. dɔːbɪ Y

daughter *n [Show a picture of a family. Who are the members of this family?] She [point to the girl] is their [point to the father and mother] ....* VIII.1.4(b). Eng. ⇒ **girl, lass, lassie, little maid, maid, wench**

davy *n* a DADDY-LONG-LEGS IV.8.10. deɪvɪ He

davy-long-legs *n* DADDY-LONG-LEGS IV.8.10. deɪvɪlɒŋlɛgz He

dawk *n* the human HAND VI.7.1. *pl* dɔːks Y

dawks *n* **get down in the dawks, fall at the dawks** referring to a cow, show signs of calving by changes in the pelvic region, ⇐ SHOWS SIGNS OF CALVING III.1.12(b). *3prsg* gɛts dɛən ɪ t dɔːks Y; *3prprogsg* fɔːlɪn ə tʔ dɔːks Y

dawl *n* a WEAKLING piglet III.8.4. dɔːɫ Ha

dawling *n* a WEAKLING piglet III.8.4. dɒɫɪn Sx, dɔːɫɪn Sr Sx; **little dawling** lɪtɫ dɔːlɪn K

dawl-pig *n* a WEAKLING piglet III.8.4. dɔːɫpɪg Sx, dɔᶜːɫpɪg Ha

dawzles *n* TREMORS suffered by a person who cannot keep still VI.1.4. dɒzɫz O

day *adv* **the day** AGO VII.3.1. ðə deː Nb

day-man *n* a FARM-LABOURER I.2.4. deːmæn Wo, deːman O W, deːmɒn O, deːmɒn Gl, deɪmæˈn Man, deːˡmɒn Gl, dɛɪmæn Brk, dɛɪmən Ess, dæɪmən Ess, daɪmən Ess

daytalman *n* a FARM-LABOURER I.2.4. deːtəlman Y, deːtlman La, deːtlmən Du La, deˈətlmɒn Y, dɛətəlman Y, dɛətlman Y

daytal workman *n* a FARM-LABOURER I.2.4. deːtl wɜˡːkmən La

dazed *adj* SAD, describing bread or pastry that has not risen V.6.12. dɛzd Du

dead *1. adv* VERY poisonous IV.11.5. deːd D, dɛd La Y Hrt Sr

2. adj SAD, describing bread or pastry that has not risen V.6.12. dɛd Y

dead-fallow(s) *n* FALLOW-LAND II.1.1.
no -s: dɛdfalə Lei, dɛdfɒtə Lei
-s: dɛdfɒləz Nth

dead-land *n* FALLOW-LAND II.1.1. dɛdlænd Brk

deadly *adv* VERY poisonous IV.11.5. diːdlɪ Nb Cu Du We La, dɪədlɪ Cu We La Y Db, dɛdlɪ Nb Du We La Y Ch Db Sa St He Wo Wa Mon Gl O Nt L Nth C Nf Sf Bk Bd Hrt Ess MxL So Brk Sr K Ha Sx, dɛdɫɪ He Mon Gl O Sr Do Ha, dʒɛdlɪ Ch Gl, dɛdlɪ So K, dɛdɫɪ W Co D Ha, dʒədlɪ Gl. **very deadly** vaɪə dɪədlɪ La, vɛɪ dɛdlɪ Ess

deadman *n* a KNACKER III.11.9. dʒɛdmɒn St

dead teat *n* a BLIND TEAT III.2.7. dɛd tɪt Hu

deaf *1. adj When a man is hard of hearing, we say he is* .... VI.4.5. Eng. ⇒ **dunch, dunny, luggy, stone-deaf**

2. adj describing a cow's teat that is dry, or a cow with a BLIND TEAT III.2.7. diːf Nb*[x1 she's deaf of a pap]* La Db St, diːv D, dɪəf We Y*[x1 she's deaf on a teat]*, dɛf St

deaf didd *n* a BLIND TEAT III.2.7. dʒɛf dɪd Ch

deaf pap *n* a BLIND TEAT III.2.7. diːf pap Nb We, dɪəf pap La Y Db, dɛf pap Nb Y Ch Db

deaf quarter *n* a BLIND TEAT III.2.7. dɪəf kwaːtə Y

deaf teat *n* a BLIND TEAT III.2.7. diːftɪt Du We, diːv tɪt Co D, diːf tɪd Co, dɪəf tɪt Y Nt L, dɛf tɪt St Nt L, diːv tɛt So Co D

dealer butcher *n* a BUTCHER who buys cattle, kills them, and sells the meat III.11.1. dɪɪlə bʊtʃə Nf

deathly *adv* VERY poisonous IV.11.5. dɪəθlɪ La Y, dɛθlɪ L

decent *adj* PRETTY, describing a girl VI.5.18. dɪəsnt Y

decline *vi* to WANE, referring to the moon VII.6.5(b). dɪtlaɪn Nt

decrease *vi* to WANE, referring to the moon VII.6.5(b). *-ing* dɪɪkɹiːsɪn Sx

degs *npl* WEAKLING piglets III.8.4. dɛgz Gl

de-horned *adj* HORNLESS, describing a cow III.2.9. diːhaᶜːn̩d So, diːˈɔᶜːn̩d D Ha

delf *n* a QUARRY IV.4.6. dɛlf La Y

delf-hole *n* a QUARRY IV.4.6. dɛlfɔɪl Y

deliberate *adv* **deliberate careless** ON PURPOSE IX.1.5. dɪlɪbəɹət kɛələs K *[marked u.r. SBM]*

deliberately *adv* ON PURPOSE IX.1.5. dɪlɪbəɹətlɪ W, dɪlɪbɹətlɪ Brk, dɪlɪbɾəʔłɪ So

delicate *adj* BRITTLE, describing cups and saucers which break easily IX.1.4. dɛlɪkɪt Nf, dɛlɪkət Nf *[marked u.r. EMBM]*

delve *1. v* to DIG in the garden with a spade I.7.8. dɛlv Nb Cu Du La Ch, *prppl* dɛlvɪn Y, *-ing* dɛlvɪn Wa, dɛl Cu

2. v to dig a deep hole. dɛlv Db

3. v to CUT peat IV.4.4. *vbln* dɛlvɪn La

demon *n* DEVIL VIII.8.3. diːmən Wa

dennis *n* a fishermen's word for a pig, ⇐ PIGS III.8.1. dɛnəs Nb

dense *adj* STUPID VI.1.5. dɛns L

desperate *adv* VERY VIII.3.2. dɛspɹət Y

dess *1. n* a CUTTING of hay II.9.15. dɛs Nb Cu Du We La Y, dɛz Y

2. n a cutting extending across a stack from one side to the other. dɛs Nb Du Y

devil *1. n What do you call that other mysterious person we think of as having horns and a tail?* VIII.8.3. Eng. ⇒ **demon, old devil, old harry, old lad, old nick,** *old* **satan, old** *sir* **nick, satan,** *the* **black-man** *with no white in his eyes,* **the devil,** *the* **old boy,** *the* **old chap,** *the* **old devil,** *the* **old fellow,** *the* **old lad,** *the* **old man**

2. n **the devil** a BOGEY VIII.8.1. ðə dɛvʊ Ess

devil-guts *n* GOOSE-GRASS II.2.5. dɪvlgʊts Ch

devilment *n* **for devilment** ON PURPOSE IX.1.5. fə dɛvɪlmənt Y *[marked u.r. NBM]*

devil's-gut *n* BINDWEED II.2.4. dɪvlzgʊt Y, dɛvɪlzgʊt Y, dɛvəlzgʊt Y

devil's-nightcap *n* BINDWEED II.2.4. dɪvlzniːtkap Cu

devil's-twine *n* BINDWEED II.2.4. dɛvlztwɑːn La

devon *n* a PASTE-BOARD V.6.5. dɛvn L *[queried EMBM]*

dew *n* *On other days, especially in late summer, the grass in the early morning is very wet. What has there been during the night?* VII.6.7. Eng. ⇒ **dag, flop, heavy water, rime, slab, water-frost**

dew-berries *npl* BILBERRIES IV.11.3. dʒæʊbɛɹɪz Gl, dɪuːbɛɹɪz Nf Ess, dɪɹbəɹɪz Nf, *sg* dʒuːbɛɹɪ Wo

dew-bit *n* a SNACK VII.5.11. duːbɪt Ess

dew-crook *n* the GRASS-NAIL of a scythe II.9.9. dʏːkɾʏk So, dʏːkɾʊk So

dew-dasher* *n* a SPLAY-FOOTED person VI.10.5. dɪuːdaʃə L

dew-footed *adj* SPLAY-FOOTED VI.10.5. dʌufʊʔɪd Nf

dew-pond *1. n* a POOL on a farm III.3.9. dɪʊpɔːn Co, djuːpɔnd K, d¹uːpɒ·nd K, dʒuːpɒnd W, dʒuːpɔːnd Ha, *pl* dʏːpɔːnz D, duːpɒnd Sx, *pl* duːpɔːndz Sr

2. n a POND IV.1.5. dʒuːpɒnd Wa

dew-sweeper* *n* a SPLAY-FOOTED person VI.10.5. d¹uːswiːpə Ess, dɪuːswiːpɹ L

dew-well *n* an artificial CESS-POOL on a farm I.3.11. dʒuːwɛɬ Ess

diagonal *adv* DIAGONALLY, referring to harrowing a field IX.1.8. dɔɪ-ægnəɬ Ess

diagonal bar *n* *What do you call this [indicate the diagonal bar of a gate]?* IV.3.7. ⇒ **angle-board, bar, brace, bracer, cross-band, cross-bar, cross-bit, cross-lap, cross-ledge, cross-piece, cross-rail, cross-slat, cross-spar, cross-spell, cross-way, dagger, drag-bar, gate-lace, gate-ledge, gate-sag, gate-strip, helper, hold-fast, lace, lacet, lacing, lacing-bar, ledge, muntons, panel, rail, sag-bar, sheath, slanting-bar, slat, slote, spar, spell, splice, spline, spreader, sprun, spur, squinway-rail, start, stave, stay, stay-bar, stay-rod, strainer, straining-larra, strap, strapping, strengthener, strengthener-bar, strengthening-bar, strengthening-piece, stretcher, stride, strip, strut, support, swate-bar, swin-bar, swing-bar, swint-bar, sword, top-bar, upright**

diagonally *adv* *To harrow a field, you can go this way [gesticulate going along the side], but sometimes you go [indicate going diagonally]* .... IX.1.8. dɔɪ-ægnəlɪ Ess. ⇒ **across**, *across the corner*, *across the furrow* ⇒ **cross**, *across the middle* ⇒ **cross**, *all a*slosh, askew, *a*slantways, *a*swint, athwart, athwart-ways, cater-amble, cater-corner, cater-cornered, cater-cornerways, cater-swish, cater-way(s), corner-ways, counter-ways, criss-cross, crooked, cross, cross-corner(s), cross-cornered, cross-harrowing, cross-harrows, crossing, cross-nooks, cross-over, cross-road(s), cross-wards, cross-way(s), cross-way(s) on, diagonal, *from* corner *to* corner, longways, nooky-way, oblong, *on a* slant, *on the* cross, *on the* hover, *on the* skew, *on the* slew, *on the* sosh, over-thwart(s), over-thwarting, quy-ways, sideways, skew, skew-across, skew-cornered, skew-harrow, skewing it, skewting across, skew-wamped, skew-way(s), skew-whiff, skwin-ways, slant, slant-across, slantaway, slantaways, slanting, slanting-way across, slant-road, slant-way(s), slanty, slew-ways-over, slosh, sosh-ways, squint-roads, squint-way on, squint-ways, swint, swint-way(s), swint-ways on, swin-way(s), swish, swish-way(s), three-cornered, thwart, thwart *and* across, thwarting it, thwart-ways**

diaper *n* *What do you call the cloth a mother puts round her baby's legs to keep it clean?* V.11.3. dɑɪpə K, dɔɪpə Wa. ⇒ **barrow, binder, cloth, clout, double(s), flannel pilch, flannels, gauze,** *gauzes* ⇒ **gauze, hipping(s), nap, napkin, nappin, nappy, packer, packing-cloth, pilch, pilcher, roller, shitting-clout, whittle;** ⇒ *also* **back-skirt, flannel clout, hipping-pin, square, swather**

dibble *n* a DRINK (of milk) given to a kitten III.13.12. dɪbɬ Ess

dibbles* *npl* CART-LADDERS I.10.5. dɪbɬz Mon

dibby *adj* SILLY VIII.9.3. dɪbɪ L

dick-and-daniel *n* a FLAIL II.8.3. dɪkn̩dænjəl Nf, dɪkəndænjəl Nf

dick-cat *n* a TOM-CAT, the male cat III.13.8. dɪkkat Wa Nth, dɪkkaʔ Bk, dɪkkjaʔ Bk

dickies *npl* LICE IV.8.1(a). dɪkɪz Y Hu

dickoys* *npl* GIPSIES VIII.4.12. ˈdɪkɒɪz Sa

dicks *1. npl* LICE IV.8.1(a). dɪks Nb Y*[old x1]* Nt L*[old]* Lei Nth*[old x1]*

2. npl NITS IV.8.2. dɪks La

dicky *1. n* a DONKEY III.13.16. dɪkɪ Nf*[female x1]* Sf Ess, dɪkʔɪ Nf Sf Ess

2. adj ILL, describing a person who is unwell VI.13.1(b). dɪkɪ So W, dɪkɪ O Ess; **a bit dicky** ə bɪt dɪkɪ Sr

3. adj SICK, describing an animal that is unwell VI.13.1(c). dɪkɪ So, dɪkɪ Ess; **pretty dicky** pɹɪtɪ dɪkɪ Wo

4. adj WEAK, describing a person who has been ill VI.13.2. dɪkɪ Y

5. adj SLIPPERY VII.6.14. dɪki So*[old]*

dicky-birds *npl* LICE IV.8.1(a). dɪkɪbɒdz Lei

diddies *npl* GIPSIES VIII.4.12. dɪdiːz Ha, dɪdɪz O Sr*[old]*

diddikies *npl* GIPSIES VIII.4.12. dɪdɪkeɪz Mon So, dɪdɪkæːz D, dɪdɪkæɪz Mon Gl So Sr, dɪdɪkjæɪz Mon, dɪdɪkaɪz Y*[most natural, old]* So Co D, dɪdɪkɑɪz Hu*[modern]* Bd K*[old]*, dɪdɪkʌɪz

Gl Brk*[full form of diddies]*, sg dɪdɪkʌʏ O*[old]*, dɪdɪkəɪz Mon Gl W Do Sx*[old x1]*, dɛdɪkəɪz W, dədɪkaɪz So

diddikites *npl* GIPSIES VIII.4.12. dɪdɪkæɪts So, dɪdɪkʌɪts Sr, dɪdɪkəɪts Brk

diddikoys* *npl* GIPSIES VIII.4.12. dɪdɪkɒɪz Gl Nf So*[old x1]* W Do Ha Sx, dɪdɪkɔɪz He Wa*[old x1]* O Nf*[old x1, rare x1]* Sf*[old]* Ess*[rare x1, facetious and rare x1]* Sr*[old]* Ha*[old x1]* Sx, dɪdɪkouz Bk, dɛdɪkɔɪəz St

diddiks *npl* GIPSIES VIII.4.12. dɪdɪks D

diddiky *n* a TINKER VIII.4.9. dɪdɪkɔɪ Nf

diddling *n* a WEAKLING piglet III.8.4. dɪdlɪn O, dɪdḷɪn MxL

didds *npl* the TEATS of a cow III.2.6. dɪdz Ch Sa

diddy *n* the TEAT of a woman's breast VI.8.6. dɪdɪ Sa

die *vi* to WANE, referring to the moon VII.6.5(b). *-ing* dəɪ-ɪn Mon

die down *viphr* to WANE, referring to the moon VII.6.5(b). dɔɪ dæʊn O

die out *viphr* to WANE, referring to the moon VII.6.5(b). *prppl* daɪ-ɪn æʊt Ha, *-ing* dɒɪn ɛʊt K

dies away *viphr-3prsg* it WANEs, referring to the moon VII.6.5(b). diːz əweᵊ Ch

diet *n* (off her) FOOD V.8.2. dɔɪət Ess

dig *1. v What do you do in the garden with a spade?* I.7.8.
1.1. v Eng
1.2. vt dɪg So W Do Ha, *prppl* ədɪgɪn So
⇒ **crack out, delve, dig over, dig up, fork, fork up, grave, howk, spade up, spit, spit up, turn, turn over, turn up, work**
2. v to ROOT, what a pig does when it digs the ground with its snout III.9.2. *-ing* dɪgɪn Sr
3. vt to DITCH IV.2.11. *-ing* dɪgɪn So
4.1. vt to CUT peat IV.4.4. dɪg Wo Mon Ha, *-ing* dɪgɪn O So K
4.2. v to cut peat. dɪg Nb Cu Du We Gl O L C Ess W Do Ha, *prppl* dɪgɪn Brk, *-ing* dɪgɪn Brk Sx; **dig for** *-ing* dɪgɪn fɒɹ Y

digger *n* the WINDPIPE VI.6.5. dɪgəˡː So

digging *1. v-ing* SCRATCHING VI.1.2. dɪgɪn Co D, dɪgŋ D, dɪgən Co
2. vrefl-ing scratching. dɪgɪn D
3. vt-ing scratching. dɪgɪn So Co D, dɪgŋ D, dɪgən Co

dight *1. v* to WINNOW II.8.4. diːt Cu We, dɛɪt Nb Cu
2. vt to DIRTY a floor V.2.8. dɹit La

dighting-barn *n* a BARN where corn is winnowed I.1.11. dɛɪtnbaᵍːn Nb

dig out *1. vtphr* to DITCH IV.2.11. dɪg ... uːt Y
2.1. vtphr to CUT peat IV.4.4. dɪg ... æʊt So, dɪg ... əʊt Do
2.2. v to cut peat. dɪg aʊt So

dig over *vtphr* to DIG in the garden with a spade I.7.8. dɪg ... ɔwə L

digs *npl* DUCKS IV.6.14. dɪgz La

dig up *1. vtphr* to DIG in the garden with a spade I.7.8. dɪg (...) ʌp Nf So, dɪg ... ʏp Nf, dag ʌp Ha
2. vtphr to ROOT, what a pig does when it digs the ground with its snout III.9.2. *-ing* dɪgən ... ʌp Ha
3. vtphr to CUT peat IV.4.4. dɪg ... ʌp W, dɪg ... ʊp Ch

dike *1. n What do you mean by dike?* IV.2.2.
a. ditch, drain. Du We La Y Ch Db Sa St He Wo Wa Gl O Nt L Lei R Nth Hu C Nf Bk Hrt Ess MxL So W Brk Sr K Co D Do Ha Sx
b. embankment. So
c. fence. Y
d. field-boundary. St So W Sr K
e. hedge. Nb Cu Du We La Y Man
f. (derelict) pit (i.e. ?coal-mine) hole. Wa*[very hesitant]*
g. pond, pool. Y Sa Mon
h. privy (i.e. outside lavatory). Mon Gl O Bk
i. swamp. So
j. wall. Nb Cu Du Y
k. watercourse (stream etc.). Y Ch Db Sa St He Wo Wa O Nt Nf So W Sr Do
l. wire fence. Cu
2. n a POOL on a farm III.3.9. daɪk Y
3. n a RIVULET IV.1.1. daɪk Y L, daːk Y, daɪk Y Db Nt L, dɒɪk K*[3–6 feet wide]*, dɔɪk O*[smaller than brook]*, dʌɪk Nf*[smaller than drain x1]*
4. n an artificial rivulet. dɔɪk Nf, dʌɪk Nf
5. n a HEDGE IV.2.1(a). dɛɪk Nb*[bushes x1, hawthorn x1]* Cu*[thorns or wire x1]* Du, dæɪk Du*[quickthorn]*, daɪk Cu*[thorn x1]* Du We*[thorn]* La*[thorn x1]*
6. n a WALL IV.2.1(b). dɛɪk Nb*[stone x2]*
7. n a DITCH IV.2.1(c). dɪk K, dɛɪk L, daˑɪk L So, daɪk L, *pl* dɒˑɪks R, dʌɪk Nf, *pl* dʌʏks Hu, dəɪk W
8. v to TRIM hedges IV.2.3. *-ing* daɪkɪn Y
9. vt to PLASH a hedge IV.2.4. *-ing* daɪkɪn La
10. v to DITCH IV.2.11. *-ing* diːkɪn Nf, *-ing* dɪkɪn K, *-ing* dɛɪkɪn L Lei, *-ing* dæɪkɪn Y, *-ing* daɪkɪn La Y L R, daɪk Nth Hu, *-ing* daɪkɪn La Db Nt L, *-ing* dɒɪkɪn Nf K, dɔɪk L, dʌʏk Hu
11. n an EARTH-CLOSET V.1.13. daɪk Gl, dɔɪk Gl O Bk Ess*[old]*, dʌɪk Gl*[old]*, dəɪk Mon

dike-back(s)* *n* grass at the edges of a field, uncut by the mowing machine, ⇐ CLEAR II.9.5.
no -s: dɛɪkbak Nb
-s: dɛɪkbaks Nb

dike-draw *v* to DITCH IV.2.11. *-ing* diːgdɹɔˑɹɪr. Nf

dike-open *v* to DITCH IV.2.11. *-ing* daɪkɒpn̩ɪn Y

dike-pike *v* to CLEAR grass at the edges of a field II.9.5. *-ing* daɪkpaɪkɪn Y

dike-slasher *n* a HEDGING-BILL IV.2.5. daɪkslaʃə We

diller *n* a SHAFT-HORSE I.6.2. dɪɫəᵗ: W

dillerd *n* a SHAFT-HORSE I.6.2. dɪɫəᵗ:d̩ W

diller-horse *n* a SHAFT-HORSE I.6.2. dɪɫəᵗ:ɾɔᵗ:ş W; ⇒ also **diller**

dilling *n* a WEAKLING piglet III.8.4. dɪlɪn Wa Gl O Lei Nth Hu Bk Bd Brk, dɪɫɪn Gl O, dɪɫən So Brk

dimmy *adj* SILLY VIII.9.3. dɪmɪ L

dingle *1. n* CHARLOCK II.2.6. dɪŋgl Nf
2. n a small RIVULET IV.1.1. dɪŋgɫ He
3. n LOW-LYING LAND IV.1.7. dɪŋgl Sa

dingy *adj* STUPID VI.1.5. dɪŋɪ Y

dining-room *n* the SITTING-ROOM of a house V.2.2. dæɪnɪnɾγ:m So, dəɪnɪnɹu:m Brk

dinky *n* a DONKEY III.13.16. dɪŋkɪ Ess

dinloes *npl* GIPSIES VIII.4.12. dɪnɫo:z Ha *[queried SBM]*

dinner *n* MEAL OUT VII.5.12. dɪnɔᴿ Nb, dɪnə Nb Cu Du We La Y Ch Db Wa Nt L Lei R Nth Hu C Nf Sf Bk Bd Hrt Ess MxL Sr K, dɪnɹ L, dɪnəɹ La Y He, dɪnəᴶ La Ch L Nf Brk Sr K Ha, dɪnər Cu, dɪnəɾ O, dɪnəᵗ Sa Wo Wa Gl O Nth Bk W Brk Sr K Sx, dɪnəᵗ: So W Co D Do Ha, dɛnəᵗ: Co; **dinner out** dɪnəɹ ɛʊt Ess

dip *1. n* a POND IV.1.5. dɪp So
2. n DRIPPING V.7.5(a). dɪp Y
3. n BACON-FAT V.7.5(b). dɪp Du La Y Db*[soaked up in bread]* St L
4. vt to RINSE clothes V.9.8. dɪp Mon
5. vi to DUCK VIII.7.8. dɪp Lei Co D

dip down *viphr* to DUCK VIII.7.8. dɪp dæʋn Co, dɪp dœʋn D

dip fore *viphr* to DUCK VIII.7.8. 'dɪp 'vɔᵗ: Co

dipper *n* a SCOOP used to take water out of a boiler V.9.9. dɪpəᴶ Brk, dɪpəᵗ: So W Co D Do Ha, dɛpəᵗ: Co

dipping *n* BACON-FAT V.7.5(b). dɪpɪn Y

dipping-bowl *n* a SCOOP used to take water out of a boiler V.9.9. dɪpɪnbɔ:ʊɫ So

dipping-bread* *n* bread dipped in BACON-FAT V.7.5(b). dɪpɪnbɹɪəd Y

dippo *n* BACON-FAT V.7.5(b). dɪpoʊ Wa*[very old]*

dippy *adj* STUPID VI.1.5. dɪpɪ Nf

dips *npl* PUDDLES IV.1.6. dɪᵊps Ess

direction *n* If you wanted to know where the wind was coming from, you would ask: What ... is the wind? VII.6.26. dɪɹɛkʃn Nf, dɪɹɛkʃən Ess, dɪɹɛktʃnz Brk, dɑɪɹɛkʃn Sr K, dəɹɛkʃən Ess, dɪɹæktʃn Brk. ⇒ **art, eaver, part, quarter, road, sail**

dirt *1. n* a CLOT OF COW-DUNG II.1.6. də˙t Nf; **cow's dirt** kɛuz da:t Nf
2. n ASHES from a cold fire V.4.5. də:t Nf *[marked u.r. EMBM, but compare* **cinder-dirt***]*

3. n MUD VII.6.17. dəᵗ:t So

4. n EARTH VIII.5.8. dʌt Sf Hrt, dərt Y, dəᴶt Ch Db, də:t Db St Wa Nt Sf Bd Hrt Ess Sr, də:t? Ess, dəᴶ:t St Brk K, də:ɹt C, dəᵗ:t He Wo Wa Mon Gl Ess So W K D Do Ha, dəᵗ:ɾt W Brk Sr Ha Sx, dəᵗ:? O Bk
5. vt to DIRTY a floor V.2.8. dɛət Nb, dəᵗ:t Co Ha, dəᵗ:? Bd

dirt-bing *n* an ASH-MIDDEN V.1.14. dʌtbɪŋ Sf

dirty *1. vt* If you walked on a clean floor in boots that weren't clean, you'd be certain to ... it. V.2.8. dɛəti L Lei, dœ:ti Mon, *-ing* da't?i-ɪn Nf, dɔti Nt L, dɔᴿ:tɪ Nb Du, dʌti Sf*[old]* Ess, dʌt?ɪ Sf, dʋᵊrti Cu, dɜ:ti Man, dəti We Sf, dəˤtʃɪ La, dərti Cu, də:ti Y Ch Db St Wo Wa Lei R Nth Hu Sf Hrt Ess MxL, də:t?ɪ C Nf Hrt, də:?ɪ Nf, dəᴶ:tɪ La*[modern]* Db He O Brk K, dəᴶ:t?ɪ Nf, dəᵗ:tɪ Sa He Wo Wa Mon Gl O Nth Ess Sr K Do Ha, dəᵗ:ɾtɪ Sr Sx, dəᵗ:?ɪ O Bk, dəᵗ:ti So W D Do, dəᵗ:dɪ So Co D;
2. adj **make dirty** maɪk ... dʌtɪ Ess, mɛɪk ... də:tɪ Ess*[polite x1]* MxL Sr, me:k ... də:ɾtɪ O, me:k ... dəᵗ:tɪ Do, mɛɪk ... dəᵗ:tɪ Ess K, me:k ... dəᵗ:tʃɪ W, me:g ... dəᵗ:tʃɪ D, meɪk ... dəᵗ:tʃi So, maɪk ... dəᵗ:tʃi He, mɛ:g ... dəᵗ:dʒɪ D

⇒ **balm up, beastle, clart, clod, cloggy, clutty, daub, dight, dirt, dirty up, filthy, *make a* mess, *make a* mess *of*, *make a* mess *on*, *make a* muck *on*, *make a tidy* mess, *make* dirty, *make* slushy, mark, mess up, muck, muck up, mucky, mucky up, mud up, nasty, paddle, paddle up, smalm up, stabble**

3. adj DULL, referring to the weather VII.6.10. dɔᴿ:tɪ Du, dəɹttɪ La, dəti Cu, də:tɪ St, dəᵗ:tʃɪ Wa *[marked as emotive and therefore u.r. NBM]*

dirty coal *n* COAL-DUST V.4.1. dəᵗtʃɪ kɔʊ Ha

dirty up *vtphr* to DIRTY a floor V.2.8. da:tɪ ... ʌp? Nf, dəɹti ... ʋp Nf

dish *n* a container for carrying horse-feed, ⇐ BASKET III.5.4. dɪʃ Nb

dishcloth *n* And what do you rub them [i.e. pots and pans] with [when washing them]? V.9.6. Eng exc. Nb Cu Du We. ⇒ **cloth, clout, dish-clout, dish-rag, dwile, *piece of rag*, swab, washing-up-cloth, *wire sponge***

dish-clout *n* a DISHCLOTH V.9.6. dɪʃklɛ:t La, dɪʃtlɛ:t Db, dɪʃkɛɪt Bk*[old]*, dɪʃklɛat Y, dɪʃklɛʊt Nth Bd Ess*[old x1]* Brk Sr Sx, dɪʃklɛət Y, dɪʃklæʏt So, dɪʃklæʏt So D, dɪʃklæʊt Y Ch Lei So, dɪʃtlæʊt Nt, dɪʃklæʊt W Do Ha, dɪʃklæət L, dɪʃtlæ˙ət La, dɪʃkla:t Y Db St, dɪʃtla:t La, dɪʃklaɪt St, dɪʃklaʊt Cu La Y Ch St L So, dɪʃtlaʊt La Y Nt, dɪʃtlʌʏt Y, dɪʃklu:t Nb Cu Du Y L, dɪʃtlu:t Cu We, dɪʃkləʊt Y Mon Do, dɪʃkɫəʊt W Do, dʋʃklu:t Nb

dishes* *npl* PUDDLES IV.1.6. *sg* dɪʃ Y

dishilago *n* COLT'S-FOOT II.2.7. dɪʃəlagɪ Nb

dish-rag *n* a DISHCLOTH V.9.6. dɪʃɹaːg Gl

dismal *adj* DULL, referring to the weather VII.6.10. dɪzməl We La Y, dɪzmǝł Gl, dɪzmʊ Sr *[marked as emotive and therefore u.r. N/WM/SBM]*

ditch *1. n What do you separate two fields by?* IV.2.1(c).

a. separating fields: dɪtʃ Ch Db Sa*[small x1]* St He Wo Wa Mon Gl O Nt L Lei R Nth C Nf Sf Bk Bd Hrt Ess MxL So W Brk Sr K Co D Do Ha Sx, dæɪtʃ He, daɪtʃ Ch Sa*[large x1]* St, dɒɪtʃ Sa

b. also recorded, but as drainage channel: dɪtʃ Hu, dɛɪtʃ Ch

⇒ **dike, furrow, gripe, gully, gurt, gutter, hent, holl, rean, water-furrow;** ⇒ also **water-table**

2. vt From time to time the ditches need clearing out; what do you say you do? IV.2.11. dɪtʃ Nb Cu Du La Y Man Ch*[large stretch, annually]* Db Sa St Wo Wa7 Gl O Nt Nth C Sf Bk Bd Hrt Ess, *prppl* dɪtʃɪn Brk Do, *vbln* dɪtʃɪn D, *-ing* dɪtʃɪn He Mon Lei R Nf So W Brk Sr K D Ha Sx, *prppl* dɪtʃən So Do, *vbln* dɪtʃən W Ha, *-ing* dɪtʃən W Co D Do Ha, *vbln* ədɪtʃɪn Bk, *-ing* ədɪtʃɪn Wo Wa Bk Hrt, *-ing* ədæɪtʃɪn Ch, dæɪtʃ He, *-ing* datʃɪn Ha, daɪtʃ Sa, *-ing* daɪtʃɪn St, daɪtʃ Db. ⇒ **barge, bottom, bottom-fay, bottom out, clean, clean out, clean up, clear, clear out, dig, dig out, dike, dike-draw, dike-open, ditch-clean, ditch out, do out, drain, fay, flush, grub out, grup, gutter, hut out, muck out, mud out, open out, out-holl, road,** *scoop out* ⇒ **scowp out, scour, scour out, scowp out, shovel out, skip out, slub, sludge out, slutch, slutch out, throw, throw out, throw up, trim** *and flash*; ⇒ also **grubber**

3. n a DRAIN in a cow-house I.3.8. dɪtʃ Sr

4. n a RIVULET IV.1.1. dɪtʃ Nf Hrt Ess Brk

5. vt to DRAIN wet land IV.1.9. dɪtʃ K

6. n HEADLANDS in a ploughed field II.3.3. dɪtʃ Co

ditch-clean *v* to DITCH IV.2.11. *-ing* dɪtʃkliːnɪn Sx, *-ing* dɪtʃ-tlɪǝnɪn Bd

ditch-hole *n* a SHEEP-HOLE IV.2.8. dɪtʃoːł So

ditch out *vtphr* to DITCH IV.2.11. dɪtʃ ... ɛʊt Sa, dɪtʃ ... ɛuːt Wo, dɪtʃ æʏt Co, dətʃ ... ǝʊt He

ditch up *vtphr* to fill gaps in a hedge-bank or hedge with turfs, brushwood, or similar material, ⇐ to PLASH IV.2.4. dɪtʃ ... ʌp Sa

dithers *n* TREMORS suffered by a person who cannot keep still VI.1.4. dɪðəz Y Ch Db Wa L Sf, dɪðǝᴵ·z La Db, dɪðǝɹz La, dɪðǝᵗz He, dɪðǝᵗːz Sa, *-ing* dɪðǝɹɪn La; **dither and plop** dɪðǝɹ ən plǝp L; **the dither and pop** ðǝ dɪðǝɹ ən pɒp L; **the dithers** ðǝ dɪðǝᴵz K, ðǝ dɪðǝᵗz He, ðɪ dɪðǝᵗːz Wo, ðǝ dɪðǝᵗːz Sa

ditherums *n* TREMORS suffered by a person who cannot keep still VI.1.4. dɪðǝɹǝmz La Y, dɪdǝɹǝmz We; **the ditherums** ðǝ dɪðǝɹǝmz He Wo

dithery *adj* VERY COLD, describing a person VI.13.19. dɪdǝɹɪ Nf

ditters *n* TREMORS suffered by a person who cannot keep still VI.1.4. dɪtǝz Y

dive in *imp* HELP YOURSELVES!, said to invite visitors to eat V.8.13. daɪv ɪn Du

divided *adj* CLOVEN, describing the hoof of a cow III.2.8(b). dɪvaɪdɪd Du

division *n* the PARTITION between stalls in a cow-house I.3.2. dɪvɪʒǝn Sr

dizzy *1. adj* feeling FAINT VI.13.7. dɪzɪ Sr
2. adj GIDDY IX.1.11. dɪsɪ Man, dɪzi Man, dɪzɪ Cu We La Y Ch*[old x1]* Db Sa St O*[old x1]* Nt L Lei R Nth Hu C Nf Sf Ess Brk Sr Ha Sx, dɪzɛ Y, dɪzɛ Y, dɛzɪ Db, daɪzi Ha, dʌzɪ Nb, dʊzɪ Nb Du Db*[old]*, dǝzɪ Nf

dizzy-headed *adj* GIDDY IX.1.11. dɪzɪ-ɪdɪd Sr

doak *n* a STUPID person VI.1.5. dɔːk Co

dob *vi* to DUCK VIII.7.8. dɒb O

dob down *viphr* to DUCK VIII.7.8. dɒb dɛʊn Ess

dobbie *n* a SEXTON VIII.5.4. dɒbɪ La

dock *1. n [Show a picture of a dock plant.] What do you call this?* II.2.8. dæk Brk, dak Sa, dak O Nth Bk, daːk He Mon Gl, dɒk La Y Ch Db Sa St He Wo Wa Mon Gl O Nt L Lei R Nth Hu Nf Bk Bd Hrt Ess So W Brk Sr K Co D Do Ha Sx, dɒkʔ Nf, dɔk La Y Wo Wa L C Sf Hrt Ess MxL Sr K, dɔːk Sa So Sx. ⇒ **butter-dock, docken,** *dockin* ⇒ **docken, dock-stanners, dock-weeds, field-dock, sour-dock**

2. n the CRUPPER of the harness of a cart-horse I.5.9. dɒk So*[under tail x1]* Co*[under tail x1]*, D

3. v to TOP AND TAIL swedes II.4.3. dɒk Man

4. n a tree STUMP IV.12.4. dɒk Nf*[old x1]*, dɒkʔ Nf

5. v to LOP a tree IV.12.5. dɒk Y*[old]*

docken *n* the DOCK plant II.2.8. dœːkən Nb, dɒkɪn Nb Cu Du We La Y, dɒkn Du Y, dɒkən Nb Cu Du We, dɔkɪn Y L, dɔkn L, dɔkən Nb Y L, dɔʔn L

dock-stanners *n* the DOCK plant II.2.8. *?pl* dɒkstanǝz Y

dock-strap *n* the CRUPPER of the harness of a cart-horse I.5.9. dɒkʂtɹæp So

dock-weeds *npl* DOCK plants II.2.8. dɒkwiːdz So

docky *1. n* food given to a horse when resting from work, ⇐ BAITING III.5.2. dɒkɪ Nth, dɔkɪ C
2. n a SNACK VII.5.11. dɒkɪ Nth Hu, dɒkʔɪ Nf, dɔkɪ C, dɔkʔɪ Sf
3. n MEAL OUT VII.5.12. daːkʔɪ Nf, daːgɪ Nf*[not local]*, dɔkʔɪ Sf

docky-bag *n* a nosebag used for BAITING a horse when resting from work III.5.2. daːkʔɪbæg Nf

doctored *v-ed* CASTRATED, describing a bullock III.1.15. dɒktɨd Nf, dɒktəd Nf Ess, dɒˈkʔtəd Nf, dɔktəd Ess MxL, dɔːktʔəd Sf

dod *n* a HORNLESS cow III.2.9. dɔd La

dodded *adj* HORNLESS, describing a cow III.2.9. dɒdɪd Y

dodder-mans *npl* SNAILS IV.9.3. dɑˈdəmənz Nf, *sg* dɑˈdəmən Nf, *sg* dɒdəmən Nf

dodders *n* TREMORS suffered by a person who cannot keep still VI.1.4. dɒdəz Y Nt, dɒdəˡz O *[not a NBM headword]*

doddings *n* sheep-doddings SHEEP-DUNG II.1.7. ʃiːpdɒdɪnz Y

doddy *n* a HORNLESS cow III.2.9. dɒdi Y

doddy-bag *n* a nosebag used for BAITING a horse when resting from work III.5.2. dɒdɪbæg Nf

dodge *1. vi* to DUCK VIII.7.8. dɒdʒ Y Ess So K, dɔdʒ Y, dʌdʒ So
2. vt to duck. **dodge your head** dɒdʒ jəˡɹ ɪd Sx *[marked u.r. EMBM and some occurrences in SBM]*

dod-mans *npl* SNAILS IV.9.3. dɒdmɹ̩z Nf, dɒdmənz Nf, *sg* dɒdmən Nf

dodny-hornies *npl* SNAILS IV.9.3. dɒdnəhɔːnɪz Nf

dods *n* SWEETS V.8.4. dɔdz Ess

dog *1. n* a TETHERING-STAKE in a cow-house I.3.3. dɒg Man
*2. n the CLOG on a horse's tether I.4.3. dɒg St
3. n the iron stay connecting the beam with the side of a cart, ⇐ CROSS-BEAM END I.10.1. *pl* dɒgz Du
4. n a BUMPER of a cart I.10.1(a). dɒg Du, *pl* dɒgz Nb We La Y

dog-berries *npl* HIPS of the wild rose IV.11.7. dɒgbɛɹɪz He, dɔgbɛɹɪz He

dog-choops *npl* HIPS of the wild rose IV.11.7. dɒgtʃɔups Y

dog-chows *npl* HIPS of the wild rose IV.11.7. dɒgtʃɔuz Y

dog-chumps *npl* HIPS of the wild rose IV.11.7. dɒgtʃʊmps Y

dog-daisy *n* a DAISY II.2.10(b). dɔgdɛɪzɪ L

dogging-up-straps *npl* KNEE-STRAPS used to lift the legs of working trousers VI.14.17. dɒgɪnʌpstɾaps O

dog-hanger *n* a CRANE on which a kettle is hung over a domestic fire V.3.4. dɒgaŋəˡ O

dog-hips *npl* HIPS of the wild rose IV.11.7. dɒːghɪps Nb

dog-joops* *npl* HIPS of the wild rose IV.11.7. dɒgdʒɔups Y

dog-jumps *npl* HIPS of the wild rose IV.11.7. dɒgdʒʊmps Y

dog-noses *npl* HIPS of the wild rose IV.11.7. dɒgnoːzɪz Ch

dog-pig *1. n* a male HOG III.8.8. dɒgpɪg Cu We La
2. n a hog. dɒgpɪg Cu La Y

dog-rose-berries *npl* HIPS of the wild rose IV.11.7. dɒgɹɒuzbɛɹɪz Wo, dɒgɹoːzbɛɹɪz Ch Wo Mon, dɒgɹɒuzbɛɹɪz Wo, dɔːgɹoːzbɛɹɪz He

dog's-foot-grass *n* COUCH-GRASS II.2.3. dɒgzfʊtgɹɑːs Ess

dog-snouts *npl* HIPS of the wild rose IV.11.7. dɒgsnᵊuːts Du

dog-stink(er) *n* a DANDELION II.2.10(c). dɒgstɪŋk Y, dʊgstɪŋkə Y

dog-thistle *n* a variety of THISTLE II.2.2. dɑˈgθɪsl Nf

dog-tired *adj* EXHAUSTED, describing a tired person VI.13.8. dœːgtaɪɔᴿd Nb

dog-tree *n* the bush ELDER IV.10.6. dɔgtɹiː La

doing(s) *n* a person's own FAULT VIII.9.6.
no -s: duˈɪn La Y L Nf
-s: duˈɪnz Wa So

doles *npl* the HANDLES of a scythe II.9.8. dɛʊɫz K, dɒɫz K, dɒʊɫz Sr K, dɒʊz Sr Sx, dɔʊz Sr, dɔʊɫz K

doll *n* a PIGLET III.8.2. daɫ O

dollies *npl* FARTHINGS VII.7.2. dɒlɪz K

dollocker *n* a LEFT-HANDED person VI.7.13(a). *pl* dɒləkəz Y, dɒləkəˡ Y

dollock-handed *adj* LEFT-HANDED VI.7.13(a). dɒləkændəd Y

dolly *1. n* a PET-LAMB III.7.3. dɒɫɪ Sx
2. n a WEAKLING piglet III.8.4. dɒlɪ O Sx
3. vt to RINSE clothes V.9.8. dɒlɪ Nf*[old]*
4. n a THIMBLE V.10.9. dɒɫi W

dolly-crow *n* a SCARECROW II.3.7. dɒɫɪkɾɔː W

dolly-pawed *adj* LEFT-HANDED VI.7.13(a). dɒlɪpɔːd Y

dolly-pig *n* a WEAKLING piglet III.8.4. dɒlɪpɪg Bk K

domiciled *adj* SHY VIII.9.2. dɒməsɔɪl Wo *[queried WMBM]*

dominie *n* a TEACHER VIII.6.5. dɒmɪnɪ Nb *[marked u.r. NBM]*

done *1. v-ed* FINISHED, referring to a store of potatoes V.7.21. diːn Nb, dɪən Nb, dɪʏn Nb, djʏn Du, dɪʊn Cu Y, djʊn Du, dɪən Nb Cu Du We Y, dʌn Sa He Mon Gl O Hu C Nf Sf Bk Bd Ess MxL W Co Sx, dʏn Nf, dʏːn Nb, dʊn Cu We La Y Ch Db Sa St Wo Gl Nt L Lei R C Bk; **all done** ɔːl dɒn Man, ɔːl dʌn Nf, ɔːɫ dʌn So Co Do, aːɫ dʊn Gl, ɒʊ dʊn St, ʊəl dʊn L; **done for** dʌn vaᵗː So, dʊn fɔː Y Db, dʊn fə: St; **done in** dʊn ɪn Lei; **done with** dʌn wɪð Sf, dʊn wɪθ Wa, dʊn wɪð Lei, dʊn wɪ Y Nth; **gone done** gɒn dʊn La
2. adj EXHAUSTED, describing a tired person VI.13.8. dɪʊn Y, dɪən Nb Y, dʌn Sa Hu So Co Do Ha, dʊn Y Gl Nt L

done for *adj* EXHAUSTED, describing a tired person VI.13.8. dʌn vɔᵗː So, dʊn fɔː Db

done in *adj* EXHAUSTED, describing a tired person VI.13.8. dɒn ɪn K, dʌn ɪn Nf Hrt Ess So W Brk Sr Co D Ha Sx, dʊn ɪn St Wo Wa Mon Lei; **done right in** dʌn ɹʌiʔ ɪn Nf

done off *adj* EXHAUSTED, describing a tired person VI.13.8. dɪən ɒf Du

done out *adj* EXHAUSTED, describing a tired person VI.13.8. dɒn out Man, dʌn ɛʊt Sx, dʌn æʊt Ha

done up *adj* EXHAUSTED, describing a tired person VI.13.8. dʌn ʌp Sa He Mon Gl O Nth Sf Ess So W Brk K Co D Do Ha Sx, dʊn ɒp Man, dʊn ʌp Bk, dʊn ʊp La Y Ch Sa St He Wo Wa Gl O Nt L, dən əp Gl

donk *n* a DONKEY III.13.16. dɒŋk W

donkey *1. n* *What do you call the animal that makes a noise like hee-haw?* III.13.16. dæŋkɪ Mon, daŋkɪ Sa, dɑːŋkɪ He Wo Mon Gl O, dɒŋkɪ Eng, dɒŋkʔɪ O Nf Bk, dɒŋkɪ We La Y Wa L Ess MxL So Sr K Ha, dɔːŋkɪ Sa He Ess Sr Do Ha, dɒŋkʔɪ C Sf Hrt, dʌŋkɪ Bk Bd Ess So W Co D, dʊŋkɪ La He Lei. ⇒ **ass**, *bronkaw* ⇒ **bronco, bronco, bronkus, bunkus, canuter,** *cornutor* ⇒ **canuter, cuddy, dicky, dinky, donk,** *fussanock* ⇒ **fuzzanock,** *fussock* ⇒ **fuzzock, fuzzadick, fuzzanock, fuzzock, hick-horse, jackass, jasock, jason, jerusalem, moke, mokus, mule, nazareth, neddy, nirrup, nussock, pronkus, yoke;** ⇒ also **jack-donkey, jack-nirrup,** *jenny* ⇒ **jinny,** *jenny-donkey* ⇒ **jinny-donkey, jinny, jinny-donkey**

2. n a SAWING-HORSE I.7.16. dɒŋkɪ Y Ch Db Wo

donkeys *npl* LICE IV.8.1(a). dɒŋkɪz Hu

donny* *n* the human HAND VI.7.1. dɒnɪ St*[used to children]*

door *n* the TAILBOARD of a cart I.10.2. dɔːᵊ Db, dɔːə Db

door-board *n* the THRESHOLD of a door V.1.12. dɪuəbɔəd La

door-case *n* the JAMBS of a door V.1.11. dɔːkɛɪs St *[reference apparently to whole door-frame]*

door-cheeks *npl* the JAMBS of a door V.1.11. dɪuːətʃəɪ·ks We, dʏ·ətʃiːks Db, dɔːᵊrtʃiːks Cu, doətʃiːks Nb, *sg* do·ətʃiːk Db, doəɹtʃiːks La, duoᴿtʃiːks Nb, dᵁuːətʃiːks We, duətʃiːks Cu Du Ch, duətʃɛɪks St, duəɹtʃiːks La

door-durns *npl* the JAMBS of a door V.1.11. *sg* dɔ·ədaːn L, duːɾdəᴸːnẓ D, *sg* duədəᴸ·ɪn L, duəᴸːdəᴸːnẓ Ha, *sg* du·ədaːn L, duːəᴸːðəᴸːnẓ So

door-frames *npl* the JAMBS of a door V.1.11. *no -s* dɔːfɹɛɪm R, dɔᴸːfɾɛːmz W, *no -s* dɔ·əfɪɑɪm Sf, *no -s* dɔːᵊfɪɑɪm Ess, duəfɪɛɪmz Lei, *no -s* duəfɪɛɪm L R, du·əfɪɛ·əmz L, *no -s* duəᴸfɪɛɪm Sx, *no -s* duəᴸːfɾɛːm W *[reference in s-less or perhaps all cases apparently to whole door-frame]*

door-hangings *npl* the HINGES of a door V.1.11a. duəᴸːɾæŋɪnz Co

doorings *npl* the JAMBS of a door V.1.11. dɔːɾɪnz So, dɔᴸːɾɪnz W *[headword queried SBM]*

door-key *n* a KEY V.1.10. dɪəkaɪ Y

door-posts *npl* the JAMBS of a door V.1.11. dɔːpɛusts Sr, dɔːpʌus Ess, dɔːəpʌusts Ess, *sg* dɔːpoust St, dɔᴸːpoːstɪz W, dɔ·ᵊpɒst Sf, dɔəpɒus K, dɔəpɒustɪz K, dɔə⁴pɔəstɪz Brk, dɔə⁴pusts Ha, dɔəᴸpoːstɪz Brk, dɔːə⁴pɒusts Sr, dɔːəᴸpɒusts Sx, dɔːəᴸɾpɒusts Sx, dɔuɐpɔusts Ess, dɔuə⁴pɔus Brk, dɔuə⁴pɒustɪz Brk, dɔuəᴸpɒustɪz Sx, do·əpʌusts Bd Hrt, dɔəpousts Mon Bd, do·əpo·əsts Nth, dɔːəpust Sf, dɔəᴸpoːstɪz Brk, dɔ·əᴸpo·əst Bk, dɔːəᴸpoːs He Mon, dɔːəᴸpoːsɪz Sa Wo, *sg* dʊəpuəst L, duəᴸpɒusts Sx, *sg* duəᴸpɔust O, duəᴸːpoːsts Ha

door-sill *n* the THRESHOLD of a door V.1.12. dɛuəsɪl St, dɔːsɪl St Wa, dɔːsɪu Sr, dɔəsɪu K, dɔəsɛl K, dɔ·əɹsɪl He, dɔuəᴸsɪu Sx, do·əsɪł Bk*[old]*, dɔːəᴸsɪl Sa, dɔːuəɾʂɪł Gl, duəsɪl Ch St Wa, duəsɪł Lei, duəᴸsɪu Sx, duəᴸːʂɪł Ha

door-sneck *n* the LATCH of a door V.1.9. dɪəsnɛk Y, duəsnɛk Y

door-stalls *npl* the JAMBS of a door V.1.11. dɔəstɔ·lz Nf, dɔəstls Nf, dɔə⁴stls Nf, doəstɔlz Nf, doəstɔːlz Nf, *sg* do·əstɔːł C, doəstlz Nf, doə⁴stɔ·lz Nf, doə⁴stɔːłz Nf, dɔːəstɔłz Nf

door-stanchels* *npl* the JAMBS of a door V.1.11. duəstɛnʃəlz Y

door-stands *npl* the JAMBS of a door V.1.11. dɔːstændz Ess

door-steads *npl* the JAMBS of a door V.1.11. doəstɪdz Nf

door-step *n* the THRESHOLD of a door V.1.12. dɔːstɛp St Lei Ess, dɔəstɛp Hrt MxL, dɔːəstɛp Ess K, do·əstɛp Hrt, duəstɪp Wo, duəstɛp St Lei, duəᴸːstɛp So Co, dəːstɛp St

door-studs *npl* the JAMBS of a door V.1.11. duəstudz La

door-threshel *n* the THRESHOLD of a door V.1.12. dɔːəθɹɛʃł Ess, dɔːəθɹɛsł Ess

door-threshwood *n* the THRESHOLD of a door V.1.12. duəθɹɛʃət La

do out *vtphr* to DITCH thoroughly every 5–6 years IV.2.11. du ... ɛʊt Nf

dopey *1. adj* STUPID VI.1.5. dʌupɪ MxL, dɔːpɪ Ch

2. adj SILLY VIII.9.3. doupɪ Wa

dormant *1. adj* STUPID VI.1.5. dɔːmənt Y

2. adj DULL, referring to the weather VII.6.10. dɔᴸːmənt Co *[marked as emotive and therefore u.r. SBM]*

dormouse *n* a SHREW-MOUSE IV.5.2. daᴸːmaʊs So, dɔːᵊmɛus K, dɔːmʌus Y, dɔːmʊu·s Y

dorrel *n* a WEAKLING piglet III.8.4. dɒɾəł W Ha

doss *1.1. vt* to BUTT III.2.10. *-ing* dɒʃɪn Nf, *-ing* dɒsn Nf, *prppl* dɒːsɪn Nf
1.2. v -ing to butt. dɑːsɪn Nf, *-ing* dɒsɪn Nf, dɒʃ Hrt, *-ing* dɒʃɪn Nf, *-ing* dɒːsɪn Nf, dɔˑs Sf, dɔʃ C Sf
2. n **have a doss** LIE DOWN VIII.3.6(a). av ə dɔs Wa

dot *1. v* to MARK sheep with colour to indicate ownership III.7.9. dɒˑʔ Nf, dɔt Sf
2. n the CORE of a boil VI.11.7. dɔt Y

dother(s) *n* TREMORS suffered by a person who cannot keep still VI.1.4.
no -s: dɒðɔᴮ Nb, dɒðə Cu
-s: dɒðɔᴮz Nb, dɒðəz Du Y, dɒdðəz Cu, dɔðəz Cu

dotherums *n* TREMORS suffered by a person who cannot keep still VI.1.4. dɒdəɹəmz We Y

dotherum-shakums *n* TREMORS suffered by a person who cannot keep still VI.1.4. dɒdəɹəmʃeːkəmz We

dotlings *1. n* SHEEP-DUNG II.1.7. dɒtlɪnz Cu
2. n RABBIT-DROPPINGS III.13.15. dɒtlɪnz Cu

dottles *1. n* SHEEP-DUNG II.1.7. dɶtls Nb, dɶtlz Nb Du, dɒtlz Nb Du We, dɔtls Nb, dɔtlz Nb
2. n RABBIT-DROPPINGS III.13.15. dɶːtls Nb, dɶːtlz Nb Du, dɒtlz Nb, dɒʔtlz Du, dɒdlz Du, dɔtlz Nb

dottrel *n* a ring-dove, ⇐ DOVES IV.7.4. dɒtɹəł Hu, dɒʔɹəł Hu [*marked 'sic' EMBM*]

dotty *adj* SILLY VIII.9.3. dɒtɪ Y Db Hrt, dɔtɪ La

double *adj* CLOVEN, describing the hoof of a cow III.2.8(b). dʌbl Sa, dʊbl La

double-barrelled shit-house* *n* an EARTH-CLOSET with two holes V.1.13. dʌblbæɹəld ʃɪteʊs Nf [*[ɪ] in [ʃɪteʊs] from fw recording book; EMBM incorrect*]

double draught *n* an EVENER, the main swingle-tree of a horse-drawn plough harness I.8.4. dʌbł dɹɑːf D

double-grid *n* a GRIDIRON V.7.4(a). dʊbəlgɹɪd Y

double heel-tree *n* an EVENER, the main swingle-tree of a horse-drawn plough harness I.8.4. dʊbl iːltɹi L, dʊbl ɪltɹi L, dʊbł ɪłtɹi Nth

double-horse draught *n* the main swingle-tree or EVENER of the harness of a plough pulled by two horses I.8.4. dʌbł͵ɒs dɹɑːf D

double-horses *n* a TEAM of two horses I.6.1. dʌbł͵aᶜːşɪz W

double-knappers *npl* MOLARS VI.5.7. *sg* dʊblnapəɹ La

double(s) *1. n* a DIAPER V.11.3.
no -s: dʊbl La Y Ch
-s: dʊblz Du La Y
pl: dʌbłz Bk, dʊblz Db, dʊbłz Lei
2. v to put a diaper on a baby. dʊbl Ch

double stub *adj* FLEDGED IV.7.2. dʌbł stʌb So

double swell-tree *n* an EVENER, the main swingle-tree of a horse-drawn plough harness I.8.4. dʌbł swɛłtɹɪ Hu

double-swingle-tree *n* an EVENER, the main swingle-tree of a horse-drawn plough harness I.8.4. dʊblswɪŋltɹiː La, dʊbl swɪŋgltɹiː Db, dʊblswɪŋltɹɪ La, dʊblswɪŋgltɹɪ La, dʊbl swɪndltɹɛɪ Db [*northern forms with -tree given this definition, although NBM data less specific*]

double tailboard *n* an END-BOARD on a cart I.10.4. dʌbł tɛɪlbɔːd Nf, dʌbl tɛɪłbɔəd Nf, dʌbl tæɪlbɔəd Nf

double-teeth *npl* MOLARS VI.5.7. dʌblti:θ Sa He Wa Gl Nf, dʌbłti:θ Mon O Hu C Sf Bk Bd Hrt Ess MxL So W Sr Ha, dʌbʊtɹi:θ Sr K Sx, dʌbłti:f Bd So, dʌbłtɪθ He Wa W, dʏblti:θ Nf, dʊblti:θ Nb Du La Y Ch Db St Wo Wa Nt L Nth, dʊbəlti:θ Y, dʊbłti:θ He Wa O R Nth Bk, dʊbltɪθ Sa Wo, dʊbłtɪθ He Wo Gl, dʊbłtᶦɣ:θ Ch, dʊbltɛɪθ Ch St

double-theave *1. n* a GIMMER III.6.5. dʌbłθɛɪv Bk, dʊblθiːv R, *pl* dʊbl θɛɪvz St
2. n a sheep one year older than a gimmer. dʊbl θiːv Db
3. n a ewe between its first and second lambing. dʊbłθɛɪv Nth

double threave *n* a GIMMER III.6.5. dʊbł θɹeᵊv Ch

double-tree *n* an EVENER, the main swingle-tree of a horse-drawn plough harness I.8.4. dʌbltʁi: Nb, dʊbltʁɛɪ Nb [*see note at double-swingle-tree*]

double-whip *n* an EVENER, the main swingle-tree of a horse-drawn plough harness I.8.4. dʌbłwɪp Co, dʌbłwɛp Co, dʌbłwʌp Co, dʊbłwɛp Co

double-whippen *n* an EVENER, the main swingle-tree of a horse-drawn plough harness I.8.4. dʌbłwɪpən Co

double-whipper *1. n* an EVENER on a horse-drawn plough I.8.4. dʌbłwɪpəᶜː D
2. n an evener, the main swingle-tree of a horse-drawn plough harness. dʌbłwɪpəᶜː D

dough *1. n* What do you call all that stuff together *[ingredients for making bread], when you've mixed it up?* V.6.3. Eng. ⇒ **bread-paste, leaven, paste**
2. n MONEY VII.8.7. dɒʊ Sx, dɔː La, do: So, doʊ So

dough-bake *n* a STUPID person VI.1.5. dɔːbeɪk So, doʊpeɪk So

dough-bin *1. n* a container in which dough is kneaded, ⇐ CORN-BIN I.7.4. dɔʊbɪn O, doʊbɪn O Lei
2. n a container used as a PASTE-BOARD V.6.5. dɔʊbɪn O, doʊbɪn O Lei

dough-board *n* a PASTE-BOARD V.6.5. dɒʊbɒʊəᶜd̪ Wa, dɔːbuəᶜːd̪ Co, dʌʊbɔːd Ess

dough-kiver *n* a container used as a PASTE-BOARD V.6.5. dɒυkɪvəᵗ O, dɔυkɪvəᵗ O, doυkɪvəᵗ Wa*[wooden, like a chest]* Nth

dough-punching *v-ing* kneading dough, ⇐ to KNEAD V.6.4. dɒυpʌnʃɪn W, dʌυpʌnʃɪn Bd

dough-skeel *n* a lidded wooden tub used as a PASTE-BOARD V.6.5. dɔυskɪl Wo

dough-trough *n* a container used as a PASTE-BOARD V.6.5. dαυtɹɑυ Gl, dɔυtɹυf Wa, doːt̥ɹ̥oː W, do'υtɹoυf Nth

dough up 1. *vtphr* to KNEAD dough V.6.4. dæυ ... υp He

doughy *adj* SAD, describing bread or pastry that has not risen V.6.12. dæυɪ He, dɒυɪ Gl, dɒυi W, dɒfɪ St, dɔːi W D, dɔfɪ Ch, dʌυɪ Ess, doːɪ Co, doυɪ So W Ha, doːυi So W Do, dυfɪ Sa, dυəfɪ La

douthy 1. *adj* ILL, describing a person who is unwell VI.13.1(b). dɔυθɪ Nb

2. *adj* SICK, describing an animal that is unwell VI.13.1(c). dɔυθɪ Nb

dovecote *n* What do you call the place where you keep the birds that go [imitate cooing]? I.1.7. dʌkət Bk, dʌvkyːt D, dʌvkɒt W Sx, dʌvkɒut Sr, dʌvkut O, dυkət Nb Du, dυfkɪt Nt, dυvkɪt L, dυfkɒt Nth, dυvkɒt We Man Ch, dυvkət L, dυvkɔut L, dυfkoυt St, dυvkυt Wa, dυvkuːt Ch, dυvkυət Nt L, dυfkət St Nt Nth, dυvkət Sa L Lei R. ⇒ **box, cock-loft, cove,** *dovecot* ⇒ **dovecote, dove-house, locker, loft, pigeon-box, pigeon-coop,** *pigeon-cot* ⇒ **pigeon-cote, pigeon-cote, pigeon-cove, pigeon-cub,** *pigeon-dovecot* ⇒ **pigeon-dovecote, pigeon-dovecote, pigeon-dove- house, pigeon-duff, pigeon-duffer, pigeon-hole, pigeon-holes, pigeon-house, pigeon-hull, pigeon-hut, pigeon-locker, pigeon-loft, pigeon-pen, pigeon-roost, pigeons'-holes, pigeons'-house, tallet**

dove-house *n* a DOVECOTE I.1.7. dʌfɛυs Bd, dʌvɛυs Hu, dʌfəs O Nth Hu Sf Bk Bd Hrt Ess, dʌvəs Hrt Ess, dυfɛuːs Wo, dυfɛυs Nth, dυvæυs Wo Wa, dυvυs Wa, dυfəs Nth C

dove(s) *n* What do you call those very tame birds, just like pigeons, only with ring markings round their necks? IV.7.4.

no -s: dʏv Nb, dυv St Wo Wa Gl, dəv Gl

-s: Eng

⇒ **ring-doves, turtle-doves;** ⇒ also **dottrel**

dowan *n* a SNACK VII.5.11. dαυən Du*[very old]*

dowdy *adj* DULL, referring to the weather VII.6.10. dəυdɪ W *[marked as emotive and therefore u.r. SBM]*

dowk *n* the BUTT of a sheaf of corn II.6.4. daυk L

dowl *adj* DULL, referring to the weather VII.6.10. dɔυɫ Sx, dʌυɫ K

dowly 1. *adj* ILL, describing a person who is unwell VI.13.1(b). daυlɪ Y, dɑυlɪ Y; **a bit dowly** ə bɪt daυlɪ Y

2. *adj* DULL, referring to the weather VII.6.10. daυlɪ Du Y, dɒυlɪ Du

down 1. *adj* SAD, describing bread or pastry that has not risen V.6.12. dɛυn O

2. *adj* **bit down, down in the dumps** ILL, describing a person who is unwell VI.13.1(b). **bit down** bɪt dɛυn Nf; **down in the dumps** dɛυn ɪn ðə dʌmps Nf, duːn ɪt dυmps Y *[down in the dumps marked ir.r. EMBM]*

3. *adj* SICK, describing an animal that is unwell VI.13.1(c). dɛυn Bk Bd, dæγn Co; **gone down** gɔːn dɛυn C

downcalve 1. *vi* to show signs of calving, ⇐ SHOWS SIGNS OF CALVING III.1.12. *3prprogsg* dɛυnkaːvɪn Nth, *-ing* daυnkɔːvɪn L

2. *vi* give birth to a calf. *-ing* dɛυnkaːvɪn MxL

down-calver *n* a cow that is showing signs of calving, ⇐ SHOWS SIGNS OF CALVING III.1.12. dæυnkaːvə Wa

downcalving *adj* IN CALF III.1.10. dæυnkaːvɪn Lei

downright *adv* VERY VIII.3.2. daυnɹɛɪt L, dəυnɹəɪt Y

dozy 1. *adj* STUPID VI.1.5. doːᵘzɪ Db, dυəzɪ La, dυəzə Y

2. *adj* SILLY VIII.9.3. dɔəzɪ Y, doːzɪ Db

drab-thread *n* strong linen twine for sewing buttons on, ⇐ THREAD V.10.2(b). dɹæbθɹed Nf

draft-house *n* a CART-SHED I.11.7. dɹɪftəs Sa

drafting *v-ing* CULLING sheep III.11.2. dɹæːftɪn Nf, dɹaftɪn La, dɹaftɪn Y, d̥ɹaːftɪn ... Co D, dɹɑːftɪn ... K

draft out *vtphr* to cull sheep, ⇐ CULLING III.11.2. dɹaːft ... ɛυt Nf

drag 1. *n* What do you put underneath the wheel to stop a wagon going too fast downhill? I.11.3. dɹæg Ess, dɹag Sa. ⇒ **block, brake, clog, drag-shoe, drug, drug-back, drug-bat, drug-shoe, fish, roller, scut, shoe, shoe-drug, skid, skid-pan, sled, sledder, sledge, slew, slid, slide, slider, slip, slipper, slod, sprag, trash, vake, wagon-shoe, wagon-slod, wheel-drug, wheel-shoe**

2. *n* a device used to prevent a cart from going backwards on a hill, ⇐ PROP/CHOCK I.11.2. dɹæg Sf

3. *n* a SLEDGE used to carry loads in winter I.9.1. d̥ɹag Co

drag-bar *n* a DIAGONAL BAR of a gate IV.3.7. dɹagba Y, *pl* dɹagbaˡːz La, dɹagbaː Cu

draggings *n* STRIPPINGS, the last drops at milking III.3.4. dɹagɪnz Wa

drag on *vtphr* to PULL somebody's hair VI.2.8. dɹag ɔn L

drag-shoe *n* a DRAG used to slow a wagon I.11.3. dɹægʃəu Ha, d̥ɹagʃʏ Co

drag-way *n* a LANE IV.3.13. dɹægwæi Nf

drail *1. n* an EVENER on the plough-beam end of a horse-drawn plough I.8.4. dˌɹaɪᵊɬ Do

2. n the T-SHAPED PLOUGH-BEAM END of a horse-drawn plough I.8.5. dˌɹɛɪᵊɬ Gl, dˌɹɛɪᵊɬ W, dˌɹaɪɬ Do Ha, dˌɹaɪᵊɬ W Do

drain *1. n [Show a picture of an old-fashioned cow-house.] What do you call this?* I.3.8. dˌɹɪən O L, dˌɹeːn Mon, dˌɹeːn Ha, dˌɹeɪn Mon, dˌɹeɪn So W Ha, dˌɹeːɪn Sa Wo, dˌɹɛɪn Sa Wo L Lei Ess Brk Sr K Sx, dˌɹɛɪn W Co D, dˌɹæɪn He Nf Hrt Ess K, dˌɹæɪn So, dˌɹaɪn Gl Nf, dˌɹaɪn So W Do Ha. ⇒ **alley, back part, byre-grip, byre-groop, channel, cow-groop, cowgutter, ditch, drainage gutter, draining-gutter, drip, drop, dung-passage, grip, groop, grooping, gullet, gully, gully-way, gutter, guttering, muckchannel, muck-drain, slack, sock-hole, sough, sullage-place, trench, valley, water-drain**

2. n a CESS-POOL on a farm I.3.11. dˌɹɛɪn So, dˌɹɛɪn D *[Edd note in SBM that this is strictly u.r. – probably so for D, but unclear for So]*

3. v To get water away from land that is wet and boggy, you must ... it IV.1.9.

vt dˌɹiːn St, dˌɹiˑən L, dˌɹɛɪn Sa Mon O Brk, dˌɹeːn W, dˌɹeɪn Mon Gl Hu C Bk Hrt, dˌɹɛɪn O So Ha, dˌɹeːɪn Db He Wo, dˌɹeːən So, dˌɹeːn W, dˌɹɛɪn St He Wa Gl L Lei R Nf Bk Hrt Ess MxL Sr K Ha Sx, dˌɹɛɪn W Sr Co D Ha, dˌɹæɪn He Mon Gl Nf Hrt Ess MxL K, dˌɹaɪn Wo Gl, dˌɹaɪn W D Do Ha, dˌɹɒɪn He

v dˌɹiːn Ch Db Lei, *prppl* ədˌɹiːnɪn St, *ptppl* dˌɹiːnd St, dˌɹɪən Y, dˌʁɪən Nb, dˌɹɪən Du Y O Nt L, dˌɹeːn Cu, dˌɹeːn Nb La, dˌʁeːn Nb Du, dˌɹeːn Du We La Y Ch Db Sa Mon O Nt Brk, *ptppl* dˌɹeːnd D, dˌɹeɪn Man, dˌɹeɪn Y He Wo Wa O Bk Bd, dˌɹeɪn So, dˌɹeːˡn Db Sa, dˌɹeːn So Do, dˌɹeən La, dˌɹeˑən Du, dˌɹeˑən Cu La, dˌʁeən Nb Du, dˌɹeən Du La Y Sf, dˌɹeːn Cu We, dˌɹeːn Cu We, dˌɹɛɪn Y Sa St Wo Wa L Lei Nth Hu C Nf Sf Bk Bd Ess Brk Sr K Sx, dˌɹɛɪn W Co D Ha, dˌɹeən La Y, dˌɹæɪn Gl Nth Nf K, dˌɹaɪn Nf, dˌɹaɪn W Ha, *ptppl* dˌɹaɪnd So.

⇒ **ditch, drain away, drain off, drain out, grip, groop, gutter, land-ditch, land-drain,** *make a drain*, **pipe, sough, under-drain**

4. v to DITCH IV.2.11. dˌʁeːn Nb, *-ing* dˌɹeːnən Co, *-ing* dˌɹæɪnɪn Nf K *[marked u.r. EMBM]*

5. n a RIVULET IV.1.1. dˌɹɛɪn Nf, *pl* dˌɹeˑənz L *[marked ir.r. EMBM]*

drainage gutter *n* a DRAIN in a cow-house I.3.8. dˌɹɛɪnɪdʒ gʊtʔə C

drain away *vtphr* to DRAIN wet land IV.1.9. dˌɹaɪn ... əwaɪ W

draind *n* a DRAUGHT of air V.3.11. dˌɹɑːɪnd He *[queried WMBM]*

draining-gutter *n* a DRAIN in a cow-house I.3.8. dˌɹæɪnɪngʊtəˡ K

draining(s) *n* STRIPPINGS, the last drops at milking III.3.4.

no -s: dˌɹæɪnɪn Gl

-s: dˌɹɪənənz Du, dˌɹeɪnɪnz So, dˌɹɛɪnɪnz St, dˌɹɛɪnənz Ess

drainings *n* WHEY V.5.8(b). dˌɹeɪnɪnz Nf *[marked u.r. EMBM]*

drain off *vtphr* to DRAIN wet land IV.1.9. dˌɹɛɪn ... ɔːf Wo, dˌɹæɪn ... ɔːf K

drain out *vtphr* to DRAIN wet land IV.1.9. dˌɹɛɪn ... æʊt W

drains *n* DREGS left at the bottom of a teacup V.8.15. dˌɹɛɪnz So, dˌɹɛɪnz K

dram *n* a row or SWATH of mown grass cut for hay-making II.9.4. dˌɹæm Co, dˌɹam Co

drang-way *1. n* the GANGWAY in a cow-house I.3.7. dˌɹæŋweɪ D

2. n a narrow passage between walls or houses, ⇐ LANE IV.3.13. dˌɹaŋweɪ So

drape *1. adj* NOT IN CALF III.1.8. dˌɹeɪp L, dˌɹɛˑəp L

2. adj not in calf but able to conceive. dˌɹeːp Nt

3. n a cow that is not in calf. dˌɹeɪp L, dˌɹɛˑəp L

4. n a cow that is not in calf but that can conceive. dˌɹeːp Nt

5. n a cow that cannot conceive. dˌɹeːp Nt, dˌɹeːp Y, dˌɹɛˑəp L

6. adj DRY, describing a cow with no milk III.1.9. dˌɹɛˑəp L

7. n a dry cow. dˌɹɪəp Y, dˌɹeːp Y*['old drape']*, dˌɹeɪp L Nth, dˌɹɛəp Y*['old drape' x1]*

8. n a old, unproductive cow. dˌɹɛəp Y

drash *v* to TRIM hedges IV.2.3. dˌɹæʃ Mon, *-ing* dˌɹaʃɪn Mon

drash down *vtphr* to TRIM hedges IV.2.3. *-ing* dˌɹaʃɪn ... dəʊn He

drash-hook *n* a HEDGING-BILL IV.2.5. dˌɹæʃʊk Mon

drashing-bill *n* a HEDGING-BILL IV.2.5. dˌɹaʃɪnbɪl He

drashing-hook *n* a HEDGING-BILL IV.2.5. dˌɹæʃɪnʊk Mon, dˌɹaʃɪnʊk Mon

draught *1. n If you open the window and the door, what are you bound to feel coming through the room?* V.3.11. Eng. ⇒ **draind, fease, through-draught**

2. n a TEAM of horses I.6.1. dˌɹaft Y

3. n a team of two horses. dˌɹaʊt We

4. n an EVENER, the main swingle-tree of a horse-drawn plough harness I.8.4. dˌɹaːf D, dˌɹɔːt Ha

5. n an evener on the plough-beam end of a plough. dˌɹaːf So

6. n the T-SHAPED PLOUGH-BEAM END of a horse-drawn plough I.8.5. dˌɹaːf D

7. n a SHAFT of a cart I.9.4. dˌɹɔːt Ess

draught-beam *n* the T-SHAPED PLOUGH-BEAM END of a horse-drawn plough I.8.5. dɹɑːftbɹiːm Sr

draught-board *n* the THRESHOLD of a door V.1.12. draftbʊəd Cu

draught-horse *n* a SHAFT-HORSE I.6.2. dɹɔːtaᵗːʂ Do

draught-leg *n* a STICK used to support the shaft of a cart I.11.1. dɹɔːtleˡg Ess

draught(s) *n* a SWINGLE-TREE of a horse-drawn plough harness I.8.3.
sg: dɹaːf D
-*s*: dɹaːfs D, dɹaːvz So

draughts *npl* the SHAFTS of a cart I.9.4. dɹɔːts Ess, dɹɔːts Do, dɹɔːəts Ess

draughtsman *n* a CARTMAN on a farm I.2.2. dʁʊtsmən Du

draught-stick *n* a STICK used to support the shaft of a cart I.11.1. dɹɔːtstɪk Ess

draught-stopper *n* the THRESHOLD of a door V.1.12. dɹaftstɒpə Ch*[rare] [queried ir.r. WMBM]*

draw *1. vt* **draw udder** to show signs of calving, referring to a cow with a swelling udder, ⇐ SHOWS SIGNS OF CALVING III.1.12(a). *3prprogsg* dɹɔːən ... ʌdəᵗː Co, *3prprogsg* dɹoːɪn ʌdəᵗː D
2. v to SUCK, describing how a lamb gets its milk III.7.1. dɹɔː Sf
3. v to PLUCK a dead chicken of its feathers IV.6.21. dɹɔː Sa *[queried ur.r. WMBM. Object unclear, and may frequently be 'feathers', not 'chicken']*
4.1. v to RAKE in a domestic fire V.3.8(b). dɹɔː Ess
4.2. vt to rake. dɹɔː Ess
5. v to BREW tea V.8.9. dɹɔː O Nf Sf Ess, dɹɔə MxL
6. vt to leave tea to stand to become strong before pouring. dɹɔː K, dɹɔː Co
7. v to stand, referring to tea left to become strong before pouring. dɹaː Bk, dɹɔː Co Ha
8. vi to WARP, referring to wood IX.2.9. dɹɔː Nf

draw back *viphr* to show signs of calving, ⇐ SHOWS SIGNS OF CALVING III.1.12(a). *prppl* dɹɔːn bæk So

draw-bar *1. n* an EVENER on the plough-beam end of a horse-drawn plough I.8.4. dɹɔːbaː Lei, dɹɔːbɑː K, dɹɔːbɑᵗːɹ Sx, dɹɔːbaᵗː So, dɹɔᵗːbaᵗː Sa
2. n the T-SHAPED PLOUGH-BEAM END of a horse-drawn plough I.8.5. dɹɔːbaː O
3. n a movable horizontal rod stretching between the shafts of a cart, fixing them to the cart-body and stopping the cart from tipping, ⇐ ROD/PIN I.10.3. dɹɔːbaː We, dɹɔːbaː St Nth, dɹɔːbaᵗː O

draw-bolt *n* a movable horizontal rod stretching between the shafts of a cart, fixing them to the cart-body and stopping the cart from tipping, ⇐ ROD/PIN I.10.3. dɹaːbɔʊt Nb

draw down *vtphr* to RENDER fat into lard III.12.9. dɹɔˑɹ (ɪt) dɛʊn Nf

draw in *vtphr* to guzzle a drink, ⇐ GUZZLES VI.5.13(a). -*ing* dɹɔːən ... ɪn Sr

drawing *1. vt-ing* **drawing dung, draw muck** CARTING *DUNG* II.1.4. **drawing dung** dɹɔːən dʌŋ Co, dɹɔːn dʌŋ D; **draw muck** dɹɔː mʊk Ch *[but interpreted as **throw** in SBM at locality D.10]*
2. v-ing CARTING corn from the field II.6.6. dɹɔːɪn O, dɹɔːɪn Co
3. n STRIPPINGS, the last drops at milking III.3.4. dɹɔɪn Hrt
4. v-ing CULLING sheep III.11.2. dʁæːən Nb, *v* draː Cu, dʁaːən Nb Du, dɹaˑɪn Y, dɹaːən Du, *v* dɹaː La, dɹɑːɪn Wo Mon, dɹɑːɪn ... Gl, dɹɔːən Du, *v* dɹɔː We, dɹɔːɪn Cu La Sa St Nt L Nf, dɹɔːɪn ... Sa He, ðɹɔːɪn La, dɹɔːɹɪn St Nth, dɹɔːɹən L, *v* dɹɔː Wa, *v* dɹɔᵗː Sa, dɹɔːɪn ... So

drawing-bone *n* a WISH-BONE IV.6.22. dɹɔːɪnbɔːn Sa

drawing out *1. vtphr-ing* **drawing out, draw out dung** CARTING *DUNG* II.1.4. **drawing (of it) out** dɹæːɪn ... æɤt So; **draw out dung** dɹɔː œɤt dʌŋ D
2. vphr-ing CULLING sheep III.11.2. *vt* dɹaː ... ᵊuˑt Y, dɹɑːɪn ... ɛʊt Wo, dɹɑːɪn ... ʌʊt Mon, dɹɑːɪn ... aʊt He, ədɹɑːɪn ... əʊ Wo, dɹɔːɪn ... ɛʊt O Nf, dɹɔːɹɪn ... ɛʊt Nf, dɹɔɪn ... ɛʊʔ O, *vt* dɹɔː ... ɛʊt Sr, *vt* dɹɔː ... æʊt Nt, *v* dɹɔː aʊt Sa, dɹɔˑ-ɪn ... uːt Y

drawing-stend *n* the STRETCHER between the traces of a cart-horse I.5.11. dɹɔːɪnstɛn Ch

draw on *vphr* to LOAD a cart with dung II.1.5. θɹiː ɒn Nf *[queried BM]*

draw-pin *n* a LINCH-PIN holding a wheel on a cart I.9.12. dɹʊpɪn He

draw up *viphr* to show signs of calving, referring to the swelling udder of a cow, or to the cow, ⇐ SHOWS SIGNS OF CALVING III.1.12(a). *3prsg/periphrastic* ʌdəᵗːn də dɹɔː ʌp Co; **draw up for calving** *3prprogsg* ʃiːz dɹɔːən ʌp fəᵗː kæːvən Co

draw-way* *n* a SHEEP-HOLE IV.2.8. dɹɔːweː W *[BM headword **through-way**, queried SBM]*

dray *1. n* a SLEDGE used to carry loads in winter I.9.1. dɹeɪ So*[10 feet by 3 feet x1]*, dɹeɪ Ha
2. n a WAGON I.9.2. dɹeː Ch Db Sa, dɹeːɪ Wo, dɹeɪ St Lei, dɹeə Cu, dɹeˑə L, dɹæɪ Sr, dɹaɪ So
3. n a wagon with sides. dɹaɪ Wo
4. n a wagon with detachable sides. dɹeˑə L
5. n a wagon without sides. dɹeː Y Sa, dɹeːɪ Wo, dɹeɪ St L Lei Ha, dɹæɪ He
6. n a light wagon. dɹeː Y

draying *1.1. v-ing* CARTING *DUNG* II.1.4. *prppl* dɹeːn D
1.2. vt-ing **draying dung** carting dung. dɹeːn dʌŋ So*[old]*, dɹeːɪn dʌŋ Co D, dɹeːən dʌŋ Co D, dɹeɪ-ɪn dʌŋ D

2. v-ing CARTING corn from the field II.6.6.
d̪ɹeːɪ-ɪn D, d̪ɹeːən D

draying in *1. vphr-ing* CARTING corn from the
field II.6.6. d̪ɹeːɪn ɪn Co

2. vtphr-ing carting corn. d̪ɹeːən ... ɪn D

draying out *vtphr-ing* CARTING *DUNG* II.1.4.
d̪ɹæːɪn ... æʏt So

dreary *adj* DULL, referring to the weather VII.6.10.
dʁɪɐʁɪ Nb, dɹɪəɹɪ Y Db St He Wo O Nth Ess, dɹɪəɾɪ
O, dɾɪəˤːɾɪ So, dɹeɪəɹɪ Man *[marked as emotive and
therefore u.r. BM]*

dredging *n* STRIPPINGS, the last drops at milking
III.3.4. dɹɛdʒɪn He

dregs *n What is left at the bottom of your teacup when
you've finished drinking the tea?* V.8.15. dɹɪgz Nf Sf
Ess Sr, drɛgs Man, drɛgz Cu Y, dʁɛgz Nb*[old]*, dɹɛgz
Du Y Db Sa St He Wo Wa Nt L Lei Nth Nf Ess MxL
Brk Sx, d̪ɹɛgz So, dɹægz Nf, dɹæɪgz Hrt. ⇒ **bottoms,
chaff, drains, drugs, grains, gregs, grogs, grounds,
groushans, grouts, grummets, leaves, monkeys,
slop(s), tea-dregs, tea-grains, tea-grounds, tea-
grouts, tea-leaves, tea-slops, tea-wiffs**

dress *1. vt* to TOP AND TAIL swedes II.4.3. dɹɛs Nt

2. v to WINNOW II.8.4. dɹɛs La Nt L Nth Hu C Nf
Sf Bd Hrt Ess, drəs Y, drəs We La, dɹəs We, *-ing*
dɹəsɪn La

3. v to TRIM hedges IV.2.3. *-ing* dɹɛsɪn La Y, drəs
We, dɹəs Cu

4.1. vt to PLUCK a dead chicken of its feathers
IV.6.21. *prppl* dɹɛsɪn Wa

4.2. v to pluck. dɹɛs St, *-ing* dɹɛsɪn L

dress-apron *n* a decorative APRON V.11.2(b).
dɹɛsapəˤn̩ Sa

dressing-bench *n* a BENCH on which slaughtered
pigs are dressed III.12.1. dɹɛsɪnbɛnʃ Mon

dressing-hook *n* a HEDGING-BILL IV.2.5.
dɹɛsɪnuːk Ch

dress-pinny *n* a decorative APRON V.11.2(b).
dɹɛspɪnɪ L

dribble(s) *n* STRIPPINGS, the last drops at milking
III..3.4.
no -s: dɹɪbł Wo
-s: ðɹɪblz La

dribbles* *npl* CART-LADDERS I.10.5. dɹɪbłz Mon

dribblings *n* STRIPPINGS, the last drops at milking
III.3.4. dɹɪblɪnz C, dɹɪbłɪnz He

driddles *n* STRIPPINGS, the last drops at milking
III.3.4. drɪdlz Cu

dried *adj* DRY, describing a cow with no milk III.1.9.
dɹaˈɪd Lei, dɹaˈɪd Lei

dried off *1. adj* DRY, describing a cow with no milk
III.1.9. d̪ɹæɪd ɔːf So, dɹɑːd ɒf Y, dɹɑɪd ɔːf Nth Hu
K, dɹɔɪd ɒf Sr, dɹɔɪd ɒːf Sx, dɹɔɪd ɔːf Sx, dɹʌɪd
ɔːf Sr, dɹʌʏd ɔːf O, dɹəɪd ɑːf Wo, dɹəɪd ɒːf Sx, d̪ɹəɪd
ɔːf W

2. adj describing a cow with a BLIND TEAT
III.2.7. dɹəɪd ɔːf Sx*[she's dried off in one spean]*

dried teat *n* a BLIND TEAT III.2.7. dɹɒɪd tiːt K

dried up* *adj* DRY, describing a cow with no
milk III.1.9. dɹɔɪd ʌp Ess, dɹəɪd ʌp Brk

drift *n* a LANE IV.3.13. dɹɪft Nf*[shorter than
lane x2, closed end x1, fenced x2]* Sf

drift-way *n* a FORD IV.1.3. dɹɪftwæiˈ Nf

drill *1. n* a RIVULET between 1 and 3 feet wide
IV.1.1. dɹɪł K

2. n a GRIDIRON V.7.4(a). dɹɪl St

drills *npl* the RIDGES between furrows in a
ploughed field II.3.2. dʁɪlz Nb

drink *n That kitten seems to be thirsty; do you
think it could have a ... OF MILK.* III.13.12. drɪŋk
Man, drɪŋk Cu, dʁɪŋk Nb, dɹɪŋ Ess, dɹɪŋk La Y
Ch Db Sa St He Wo Wa Mon O Nt L Lei Nf Sf Bk
Hrt Ess MxL Brk Sr K Sx, d̪ɹɪŋk So W Co D Do
Ha, dɹɪŋk? Nf Sf, d̪ɹɛŋk W. ⇒ **dibble**, *dish*, **drop,
lap, lick,** *little* **drop,** *saucer, saucerful,* **spot, sup,
swat**

drinking *v-ing What am I doing now [indicate
drinking]?* V.8.1. Eng. ⇒ **golloping,** *having a
drink,* **supping, swigging;** ⇒ also **mopping**

drinking-dip *n* a POND IV.1.5. dɾɪŋkɪndɪp So

drinking-pond *n* a POND IV.1.5. dɹɪŋkɪnpɒnt
MxL

drinking(s) *n* a SNACK VII.5.11.
no -s: drɪŋkɪn Y, drɪŋkɪn La Y, dɹɪŋkɪn La Y
-s: dɹɪŋkɪnz La Y L

drinkings *n* MEAL OUT VII.5.12. dɹɪŋkɪnz La
Y*[nearly obsolete x1]*

drip *1. n* a DRAIN in a cow-house I.3.8. dɹɪp He
Wa Bd

2. n DRIPPING V.7.5(a). dɹɪp Y Sx

3. n BACON-FAT V.7.5(b). dɹɪp Y

4. n a LITTLE amount of milk VII.8.20. dɹɪp Sx

dripping *n* LARD made from the fat of a pig
III.12.8. drɪpn Nf, drɛpən Man

dripping(s) *1. n What do you call the fat from
roasting meat?* V.7.5(a).
no -s: Eng
-s: dɹɪpɪnz Nf, dɹɪpnz Nf
⇒ **beef-dripping, beef-fat, dip, drip, drippy, fat,
gravy, grease, lard**

2. n BACON-FAT V.7.5(b). dɹɪpɪn Nf

3. n STRIPPINGS, the last drops at milking
III.3.4.
no -s: dɹɪpɪn O Hu Brk Sx
-s: dɹɪpɪnz La Ch Db Sa St Wo Wa O Bk Bd Hrt
Brk K, dɹɪppɪnz Db, dɹɪp?ɪnz Ess, d̪ɾɪpɪŋz Ha,
d̪ɾɪpənz Co Ha

dripples *1. npl* CART-LADDERS I.10.5.
dɹɪpəlz He, drɪpłz Mon, dɹɪpłz He Mon Gl

2. n a CART-FRAME I.10.6. dɹɪpəlz He, dɹɪpłz
He Gl

dripplings *n* STRIPPINGS, the last drops at milking III.3.4. dɹɪpɬɪnz Nth

drippy *n* DRIPPING V.7.5(a). dɹɪpɪ Y

drips *n* STRIPPINGS, the last drops at milking III.3.4. dɹɪps Nth Brk

driving-lines *npl* the REINS of a cart-horse I.5.5. dɹaɪvɪnlaɪnz Y

driving-reins *npl* the REINS of a cart-horse I.5.5. dɹʌɪvɪnɹɛˑɪnz Brk

drock *n* the SOLE of a horse-drawn plough I.8.9. dɹɒk He Mon

droop *vi* to DUCK VIII.7.8. **droop your head** dɹʏːp jəᵗːɹ ɪd D

droopy *adj* ILL, describing a person who is unwell VI.13.1(b). dɹuːpɪ Ha

drop *1. n* a DRAIN in a cow-house I.3.8. dɹɒp Hu, dɹɒp So
2.1. vt to SLIP *A FOAL* III.4.6. *ptppl* dɹɒpt Bk Ess, *ptppl* dɹɒpt So
2.2. v to slip a foal. *-ed* dɹɒpt So
3. vi to FARROW, describing a pig giving birth to piglets III.8.10. *3prsg* ədɹɒpɪn Brk; **drop a litter** dɹɒp ə lɪtə Y *[regarded as referring to pregnancy and therefore u.r. SBM]*
4. n a DRINK (of milk) given to a kitten III.13.12. dɹap D, dɹap Nth Hu Bk, dɹap? C, dɹɑːp Mon Gl, dʁɒp Nb, dɹɒp Y, dɹɒp La Y Ch Sa St He Wo Wa Mon Gl O Nt L Lei R Nth Hu Bk Bd Ess Brk Sr, dɹɒp O, dɹɒp So W D Ha, dɹɒp? Nf Bk, dɹɒ? Nf, dɹɔp Y L Sf Ess, dɹɔp So, dɹɔp? C, dɹɔːp Sa
5. n a LITTLE amount of milk VII.8.20. **drop** dɹæp W, dɹap Nth, dɹɒp Y Gl L Lei Brk K Ha, dɹɒp Co, dɹɔp L Ess; **a drop** ə dʁœːp Nb, ə dɹap D, ə dɹap La Gl Bk, ə dɹɑːp He Wo Mon Gl, ə dɹɑᵗːp Wo, ə drɒp Cu, ə dʁɒp Du, ə dɹɒp Nb Du La Y*[old x1]* Ch Db Sa St He Wo Wa Mon Gl Nt L Lei Nf Hrt Ess, ə ðɹɒp La, ə dɹɒp So W Co D Do Ha, ə dɹɒp La Y He Wa L C Sf Ess Sr K, ə dɹɔp So, ə dɹæp Wa; **a little drop** ə lɪtl dʁœːp Nb, ə lɪdl dʁœp Nb, ə ɬɪtɬ dɹap So, ə lɪdɬ dɹap So, ə ɬɪdɬ dɹap D, ə lɪtl dɹap Wa, ə laɪl drɒp Cu Y, ə lɪtl dɹɒp La St, ə lɪtɬ dɹɒp Ha, ə lɪ?ɬ dɹɒp Bk Bd, ə laɪl dɹɒp Y, ə ɬɪtɬ dɹɒp O, ə ɬɪdɬ dɹɒp W Co D Do Ha, ə tɪ?ɬ dɹɒp Ha, ə ɬɪɬ dɹɒp Co, ə lɪtl dʁɔˑp Nb, ə lɪtl dɹɔp Ch Wo L, ə lɪ?dḷ dɹɔp Ess, ə lɪdɬ dɹɔp Ess, ə laɪl dɹɔp Y; **a small drop** ə smɑːɬ dɹɑːp Mon, ə smɔːl dɹɒp He, ə smɔːɬ dɹɒp So W Do, ə smɔːl dɹɒp Sf MxL, ə smɔː dɹɔp K, ə smɔːɬ dɹɔːp MxL, ə smɔɬ dɹɔˑp O; **a wee drop** ə wiː dɹɒp D; **little drop** lɪdɬ dɹap So, ɬɪdɬ dɹap W, lɪtl dɹɒp Ch, lɪtl dɹɒp Lei, ɬɪdɬ dɹɒp W D, lɪ?ɬ dɹɒp W, lɪ?l dɹɔp Y; **small drop** smɔːɬ dɹɒp Sx, smɔːɬ dɹɒp So, zmɔːɬ dɹɒp So D, smɔːɬ dɹɔˑp Sf

drop back *viphr* to WANE, referring to the moon VII.6.5(b). *3prsg* dɹɔps bak Y

drop-door *n* the FLAP at the front of old-fashioned trousers VI.14.16. *pl* dɹɔpdʊəz L

drop-latch *n* the LATCH of a door V.1.9. dɹɒplatʃ Wa

dropper *n* the CLOG on a horse's tether I.4.3. dɹɒpəɹ La

drop-pin *n* a metal LINCH-PIN holding a wheel on a cart I.9.12. dɹɒppɪn Sa, dɹɒppɪn La

dropping *n* a CLOT OF COW-DUNG II.1.6. dɹɑːp?n̩Nf, *-s* dɹɒpɪnz St; **cow's droppings** kæʊz dɹɒpɪnz Ess

dropping-post *n* the SHUTTING-POST of a gate IV.3.4. dɹɒpɪnpoˑᵊst So

droppings *1. n* COW-DUNG I.3.12. dɹɒpɪnz Brk*[polite x1]*, dɹɒpnz Nf
2. n SHEEP-DUNG II.1.7. dɹɒpɪŋz K, dɹɒpɪnz St Lei Ess K Sx, dɹɒp?nz Nf, dɹɒp?mz Ess; **sheep-droppings** ʃɪpdɹɒpɪnz Nth Bk, ʃiːpdɹɒpɪnz Y Db St Mon O L Lei Bk Brk K, ʃiˑpdɹɒpnz Nf, ʃɪpdɹɒpɪnz Sa He Mon Lei Nth Hu Bk Bd, ʃɛpdɹɒpɪnz Mon, ʃɛɪpdɹɒpɪnz Db, ʃiːpdɹɔpɪnz Y Sr, ʃiːpdɹɔpənz L, ʃɪpdɹɔpɪnz Ess, ʃɪpdɹɔpənz Ess; **sheep's-droppings** ʃiːps dɹɑːp?nz Nf, ʃiːpsdɹɒpɪnz Wa, ʃiːpsdɹɒpɪnz D, ʃiˑᵊps dɹɒpmz Ess, ʃiːps dɹɔpɪnz Ess, ʃɪps dɹɔːpnz Sf *[droppings marked u.r. SBM]*
3. n RABBIT-DROPPINGS III.13.15. dɹapɪnz Nth, dɹɒpɪŋz Sx, dɹɒpɪnz St Mon L Lei Bk Brk Sr K Sx, ðɹɒpɪnz La, dɹɒp?nz Nf, dɹɒpənz Do, dɹɔpənɪz L

dropping-stoop *n* the SHUTTING-POST of a gate IV.3.4. dɹɒpɪnstuːp Y

drops *n* **sheep-drops** SHEEP-DUNG II.1.7. ʃiːpdɹɒps Ch

dross *n* COAL-DUST V.4.1. dɹɒs Nth

drought *1. n [Some years the summer months have almost no rain. So the summer has been very (dry)] And you say there has been a long and serious ....* VII.6.20. Eng. ⇒ **droughty spell, drouth, dry spell, dry summer, dry time, dryth**
*2. *adj DRY, referring to a summer VII.6.19. dɹəʊt Y

drought-struck **adj* very THIRSTY VI.13.10. dɹuːtstɹʊk Y

droughty *1. adj* THIRSTY VI.13.10. dɹuːtɪ Y
2. adj DRY, referring to a summer VII.6.19. dɹaʊtɪ Y, dʁɒʊtɪ Du, dʁɔʊtɪ Nb, dʁʊθɪ Nb, drʊftɪ Cu, drʊftɪ Cu We*[very old]*, dɹʊftɪ La Y*[old x1]*, drᵊuːtɪ Du, drʊːtɪ Nb We, dʁuːtɪ Nb*[old]* Du*[old]*, dɹuːtɪ Cu Du We La Y, dʁuːθɪ Nb, dɹaʊtɪ Y
3. adj drying, describing a wind. dɹʊftɪ Y

droughty spell *n* a DROUGHT VII.6.20. dɹuːtɪ spɛl Y

drouth *n* a DROUGHT VII.6.20. dɹɛʊθ Wo Wa Bk Ess, dɹæːθ D*[old x1]*, dɹæɣθ D, dɹæʊθ Wo, dɹaʊθ So, dɹɒʊθ W, dɹɔːθ K Sx, dɹɔːθ So, dʁuːθ

Nb, dɹəʊθ He Wo Gl *[not a N/WM/SBM headword]*

drove *n* a LANE IV.3.13. dɹɔːv W, dɹ̥ɔːv W Do Ha, dɹəʊv C Nf, dɹuˑv Nf

drowned *adj* BOGGY IV.1.8. dɹæʊndɪd Ess, dɹæʊntɪd L

drowsy *adj* ILL, describing a person who is unwell VI.13.1(b). dɹaʊzi So

drucken *adjpred* DRUNK VI.13.11(a). dɹʊkn Y, dɹʊxn Y*[old]*

druffen *adjpred* DRUNK VI.13.11(a). dɹʊfn La Y, dɹʊfən Y

drug *1. n* a SLEDGE used to carry loads in winter I.9.1. dɹ̥ʊg Co

2. n a WAGON used for carrying timber I.9.2. dɹʊg Db

3. n a DRAG used to slow a wagon I.11.3. dɹ̥ʌg D, dɹ̥ʌg Co D Do Ha, dɹ̥ʊg Co

drug-back *n* a DRAG used to slow a wagon I.11.3. dɹ̥ʌgbak W

drug-bat *n* a DRAG used to slow a wagon I.11.3. dɹ̥ʌgbat W Ha, dɹʊgbæt Brk, dɹʊgbat O

drugs *n* DREGS left at the bottom of a teacup V.8.15. dɹʌgz C, dɹʊgz Sa

drug-shoe *1. n* a device on a wheel to prevent a cart from going backwards on a hill, ⇐ PROP/CHOCK I.11.2. dɹ̥ʌgʃʊu: So

2. n a DRAG used to slow a wagon I.11.3. dɹ̥ʌgʃʌ: Co, dɹ̥ʌgʃʌ: So D, dɹ̥ʌgʃu: So W Do Ha, dɹʊgʃu: Gl O Brk, dɹ̥ʊgʃʌ: D, dɹ̥ʊgʃu: So

drum-up *n* a SNACK VII.5.11. dɹʊmʊp Ch

drunk *adjpred When a man has had too much beer, you might say he is ....* VI.13.11(a). Eng. ⇒ **drucken, druffen, drunken**

drunken* *adjpred* DRUNK VI.13.11(a). dɹʊŋkn Wa

dry *1. adj What do you say of a cow that has stopped giving milk or has not given any for some time? She is ....* III.1.9. dɹɛɪ Db Sa, ðɹɛɪ La, dɹ̥æ: D, dɹæɪ Man, dɹæɪ Man, dɹ̥æɪ So, dɹɑ: Y, dɹ̥ɑ: Co D, dɹaɪ Cu Du Y, dɹaɪ Nb Cu We La, dʁaɪ Cu Du La Y Ch Db Sa St He Nt L, ədɹaɪ La, dɹ̥aɪ So Co, dɹɑˑɪ L Lei, dɹaːɪ Y Sa, dɹɑ: Y, dɹ̥ɑ: D, dɹɑɪ La Y Ch Db St Nt Nth Hu C Nf Bk Bd Hrt Ess MxL Sr K, dɹɑˑɪ L Lei R, dɹɒɪ Sa St Wo Wa Gl K, dɹ̥ɒɪ So W Co D Do Ha, dɹɒːɪ St, dɹɔɪ Wo Wa Gl O Nth C Sf Bk Ess Brk K Ha, dɹʌɪ He Gl O Nf Sf Brk Sr, dɹəɪ He Wo Mon Gl Brk Sx, dɹ̥əɪ So W Do. ⇒ **barren, barrener, drape, dried, dried off, dried up, drybag, drybagged, empty, geld, grake, lease, sined, veer;** ⇒ also **leaser, sew, sine**

2. adj describing a cow's teat that is dry, or a cow with a BLIND TEAT III.2.7. dɹ̥ɒɪ Ha*[dry on one quarter]*, dɹɒːɪ St, dɹʌɪ Sr*[she's dry in one quarter]*

3. adj Some years the summer months have almost no rain. So the summer has been very .... VII.6.19. Eng. ⇒ **a-dry, drought, droughty, hask, hasky**

4. adj THIRSTY VI.13.10. dɹi Y, dɹɛɪ Db, ðɹɛɪ La,

---

dɹæɪ Man, dɹæɪ Ch, dɹ̥æɪ So, dɹaɪ Cu Du We, dɹaɪ Nb Cu We La, dʁaɪ Nb Du, dɹaɪ Cu Du We La Y*[old x1]* Ch Sa Nt L, dɹ̥aɪ So, dɹɑ: Y, dɹ̥ɑ: Co, dɹɑɪ La Y Ch*[old x1]* Db Nt L Lei Nth Hu C Bk*[old]* Bd Hrt Ess MxL Sr K, dɹɒɪ St, ədɹɒɪ K, dɹ̥ɒɪ So W Do Ha, dɹɔɪ St Wa O Nth*[old]* Sf Bk Ess*[old x1]* Brk Sr K Ha Sx, ədɹɔɪ Ess Brk, dɹ̥ɔɪ So, dɹʌɪ Gl Nf Bk Brk Sr, ədɹʌɪ Brk, dɹʌʏ O*[old]*, dɹ̥ʌʏ O, dɹəɪ W Brk Sx, dɹ̥əɪ So W Do

dry-ask *n* a NEWT IV.9.8. dɹaɪ-ask Cu We

drybag *1. adj* DRY, describing a cow with no milk III.1.9. dɹaɪbag Y, dɹaɪbag La Y, dɹaɪbag La
2. n a dry cow. dɹaɪbag Y

drybagged *adj* DRY, describing a cow with no milk III.1.9. dɹaɪbagd Du, dɹaɪbagd We La, dɹaɪbagt Cu, dɹaɪbagd We

dry down *vtphr* to RENDER fat into lard III.12.9. dɹɑ: ... dɛʊn Nf, dɹʌɪ (...) dɛʊn Nf Sf

drying-pen *n* a FASTING-CHAMBER III.11.3. dɹɑˑɪnpɛn L *[see note at fasting-chamber]*

dry pap *n* a BLIND TEAT III.2.7. dɹɛɪ pap Db, ðɹɛɪ pap La, dɹaɪ pap Y, dɹɑ: pap Y

dry quarter *n* a BLIND TEAT III.2.7. dɹaɪ kwɔːtə Wa MxL, dɹʌɪ kwɔːtəᵗ Gl, dɹ̥əɪ kwɔːdəᵗ: Do

dry-reach *v* to RETCH VI.13.15. *-ing* dɹəɪɹiːtʃn Mon

dry scurf *n* DANDRUFF VI.1.3. dɹʌɪ skəˑf Nf

dry spean *n* a BLIND TEAT III.2.7. dɹɔɪ spiːn K

dry spell *n* a DROUGHT VII.6.20. dɹeɪ spɛᵊl Man, dɹɛɪ spɛl Ch, ðɹɑ: spɛl: La, dɹaɪ spɛl Y, dɹɑ: spɛl Y, dɹɑɪ spɛl Y, dɹɔɪ spɛl Wa, dɹɔɪ spɛɫ Wa, dɹ̥ɔɪ spɛʊ O

dry-stone-wall *n* a WALL IV.2.1(b). ˈdɹæːˈstoːnən ˈwɔːɫ D, dɹaɪstɪənwɔːl Y, dɹaɪstənwɔːl Y

dry teat *n* a BLIND TEAT III.2.7. dɹ̥æɪ tɪt So, dɹaɪ tɪt Hrt, dɹɒɪ tɪt K, dɹ̥ɒɪ tɪt W, dɹ̥ɒɪ tɪt? So, dɹɔɪ tɪt Ess Brk, dɹɔɪ tiʔ Bk, dɹ̥ɔɪ tɪt Ha, dɹʌɪ tɪt Gl, dɹəɪ tɪt Mon, dɹ̥ɒɪ tɛt W Ha, dɹ̥ɔɪ tɛt O, dɹ̥əɪ tɛt W

dryth *n* a DROUGHT VII.6.20. dɹ̥aɪθ Co, dɹaɪθ K, dɹ̥ɒɪθ Co, dɹəɪθ Mon *[not a WMBM headword]*

dry time *n* a DROUGHT VII.6.20. dɹ̥æ: tæːm D, dɹaɪ taɪm La, dɹaɪ taɪm Y Ch Db Nt L, dɹɑˑɪ taːm Lei, dɹɑɪ taɪm L*[old x1]* Hu Ess Sr, dɹɔɪ tɔɪm Sf

dry-wall *n* a WALL IV.2.1(b). dɹaɪwɔːl Y, dɹɑ:wɔːl

dry-wizened *adj* go dry-wizened to WRINKLE, referring to the skin of very old people VI.11.2. *3prsg* gʊəz dɹɑˑɪwɪzn L

dry-yard *n* the STRAW-YARD of a farm I.1.9. dɹ̥əɪjaᵗːd̥ Do

dry yeast *n* YEAST V.6.2. dɹaɪ jiːst Ch

dub *1. n* a POOL on a farm III.3.9. dʊb Cu Man

2. *n* a POND IV.1.5. dʊb Cu Man*[artificial x1]*

3. *v* to TRIM a privet hedge IV.2.3. -*ing* dʊbɪn Ch

dubbings *npl* PUDDLES IV.1.6. dʊbɪnz Y

duberous *adj* AFRAID VIII.8.2. duːbəɹəs Brk

dub-holes *npl* the HOOF-MARKS of a horse IV.3.10. dʊbɔɪlz La

dubs *1. npl* PUDDLES IV.1.6. dʊbz Cu We La Y

2. *npl* pools in a stream where sheep might be washed. *sg* dʊb Cu

duck *1. vi* If you saw a stone coming straight for your head, you'd at once [indicate ducking] .... VIII.7.8. Eng. ⇒ **bend down, bob, bob down, bop, bop down, buck, bunk down, cower down, dip, dip down, dip fore, dob, dob down, dodge, droop,** *duck down,* **hop down, mind, pop down, quat, quat down, squat, stoop**

2. *n* a GRIDIRON V.7.4(a). *pl* dʌks K

duck-feet *adj* PIGEON-TOED VI.10.4. dʊkfiːt Lei

duck-footed *1. adj* PIGEON-TOED VI.10.4. dʌkfʊtɪd Sr

2. *adj* SPLAY-FOOTED VI.10.5. dʌkvytɪd D, dʌkvytəd D, dʌkfʊtɪd Sr, dʊkfyːtɪd La, dʊkfʊtɪd Du Ch, dʊkfʊtəd Db

duck-frost *n* HOAR-FROST VII.6.6. dʊkfɹɒst L

duck-nebbed *adj* PIGEON-TOED VI.10.4. dʊknɛbd Nb

duck-pond *n* a POOL on a farm III.3.9. dʊkpɒnd St

ducks *npl* What do you call those birds that you see swimming about the pond of a farmstead? IV.6.14. Eng. ⇒ **digs, wids**

duck-toed *adj* PIGEON-TOED VI.10.4. dʊktøᵊd Du

ducky-feet *adj* SPLAY-FOOTED VI.10.5. dʌkivɪt D

dud *n* a BLIND TEAT III.2.7. dʌd Sa Ess K, *pl* dʌdz He, dʏd Nf, dʊd St, *pl* dʊdz Sa He Wo

duddekin *n* an EARTH-CLOSET V.1.13. dʌdɪkɪn W, dʌdəkən Ess

dud-man *n* a SCARECROW II.3.7. dʌdmən O, dʊdmən Gl O

dud pap *n* a BLIND TEAT III.2.7. dʊd pap Ch Db St

dud teat *n* a BLIND TEAT III.2.7. dʌd tɪt Sf, dʌd tɛt Do

duffing *adj* ILL, describing a person who is unwell VI.13.1(b). dʊfɪn L *[queried EMBM]*

duffty *adj* INSIPID, describing food lacking in salt V.7.8. dʌftɪ Nth

duffy coal *n* COAL-DUST V.4.1. dʊfɪ køˈəl Nb

dug *n* the UDDER of a cow III.2.5. dʌg Nf, dʏg Nf

duggled *adj* EXHAUSTED, describing a tired person VI.13.8. dʌgɫd Gl

dug up *vtphr* to STOCK a cow III.3.6. -*ing* dʌgn ... ʌp Nf

duke *n* a FIST VI.7.4. dɪuˑk Nf*[facetious]*

dulbert *n* a STUPID person VI.1.5. dʊlbət Cu

dull *1. adj* When it is dark and gloomy, what sort of a day do you say it is? VII.6.10. Eng exc. Man. ⇒ **blashy, cloudy, dark, darksome, dirty, dismal, dormant, dowdy, dowl, dowly, dreary, gammy, gloomy, glummy, hazely, heavy, howery, louring, melancholy,** *mirky* ⇒ **murky, miserable, mucky, muggy, murky, overcast, part-shitting, poor, rawky;** ⇒ also **bloa, hashy, hezzly, howery, slattery**

2. *adj* SAD, describing bread or pastry that has not risen V.6.12. dʌɫ So

3. *adj* **rather dull** ILL, describing a person who is unwell VI.13.1(b). ɹɑːðə dʌɫ K

dullard *n* a STUPID person VI.1.5. dʌlɔᴷt Nb

dullish *n* GRUEL V.7.2. dʊlɪʃ Man

dumb *adj* STUPID VI.1.5. dʌm Ess, dʊm Nt

dumb pap *n* a BLIND TEAT III.2.7. dʊm pap Nb

dumb teat *n* a BLIND TEAT III.2.7. dʌm tɪt Co, dʊm tɪt Du Nt L

dumb-well *1. n* a CESS-POOL on a farm I.3.11. dʌmwɛəɫ Hrt

2. *n* an artificial cess-pool. dʌmwɛɫ Bd

dum-hole *n* a POOL on a farm III.3.9. dʊmɒɪl La

dumlocks *n* SHEEP-DUNG II.1.7. dʊmlʊks Wo

dummel *adj* STUPID VI.1.5. dʌmɫ Gl, dʊmɫ Gl, dəmɫ Gl

dummel-head *1. adj* STUPID VI.1.5. dʊml̩ ɪəd We

2. *n* a STUPID person VI.1.5. dʊml̩ ᴵiːd Cu

dummock *n* a COW III.1.1(b). dʌmɪk Sx

dummock-man *n* a COWMAN on a farm I.2.3. dʌmɪkmæn Sx

dummocks *npl* COWS III.1.1(a). dʌmɪks Sx

dummy *n* a BLIND TEAT III.2.7. dʌmi O C Bd, dʏmi Nf, dʊmi Nb La Y Gl O L Lei Nth

dummy pap *n* a BLIND TEAT III.2.7. dʊmi pap La Y

dummy-teat *n* a BLIND TEAT III.2.7. dʌmi tɪt Nf W, dʏmi tɪt Nf, dʊmɪtɪt Db, *pl* dʊmɪtɪts Wo, dʊmɪ tɪt Cu Du Lei Nth

dump *1. v* to BUTT III.2.10. dʊmp Cu

2. *n* an ASH-MIDDEN V.1.14. dʌmp Mon Sx, dʊmp Mon, dəmp Gl

dump-heads *npl* TADPOLES IV.9.5. dʌmpiːdz D

dumps *n* SWEETS V.8.4. dʌmps So

dumpy *adj* SAD, describing bread or pastry that has not risen V.6.12. dʊmpɪ Ch Gl

dunch *1. v* to BUTT III.2.10. dɔːns Ess, dʊnʃ Nb We

2. *adj* DEAF VI.4.5. dʌnʃ So*['they can't hear, and don't wish to']*

dung *1. n* COW-DUNG I.3.12. dɒŋ Man K, dɒŋg St, dʌŋ He O Nf Bk Bd Hrt Ess So W Brk Sr Co D Do Ha Sx, dʏŋ Nf, dʊŋ L, dʊŋg Ch St, dəŋ Gl

2. *n* a CLOT OF COW-DUNG II.1.6. dʌŋ Nf;
baked dung bɛɪkt dʌŋ Brk
3. *n* dung. dʌŋ Man Brk
4. *n* SHEEP-DUNG II.1.7. dʌŋ Nf Sr; **sheep's-dung** ʃiːpsdʌŋ So Co D Do, ʃiːps dʌŋ Nf, ʃiːps dʏŋ Nf *[dung marked u.r. SBM]*
5. *n* RABBIT-DROPPINGS III.13.15. dʌŋ Sr Ha Sx, dʌŋk Sf, dʌŋg Brk, dʊŋ Wo*[modern]*
dung-brush *n* a MUCK-BRUSH I.3.14. dɒŋbɹʌʃ K, dʌŋbɹ̩iːʃ D
dung-cart *n* a FARMCART I.9.3. dɒŋkɑːt K, dɒŋkɑˑ̍ːt K, dɒŋkəˑ̍ˑt̪ K, dʌŋkaˤːt̪ So Ha, dʌŋkaˤːʔ O, dʌŋkɑːt K, *pl* dʌŋgɑːts K, dʌŋkaˤːt̪ Sr Ha Sx, dʌŋkaˤːə̍ˤt̩t Sx, *pl* dʊŋkæːɹt̩s̪ Brk
dung-filling *v-ing* loading a cart with dung, ⇐ to LOAD II.1.5. dʌŋfɪlɪn Ess
dung-fork *n* a MUCK-FORK I.3.13. dœːŋvaˤːk Gl, dʌŋfaˤːk So, dʌŋfɒˤk Ha, dʌŋfɔːk Hrt Ess MxL K, dʌŋfɔˤːk He O Bk So D, dʌŋfɔːəˤk Sr Sx, dʌŋfəɹk He, dʊŋfɒɹk O, dʊŋfɔˤːk Bk, dəŋvɔˤːk Gl
dung-hauling *v-ing* CARTING *DUNG* II.1.4. dʊŋɑːɫn He Gl, dʌŋhɔːlɪn So, dʌŋhɔːlən So, dʌŋɔːlɪn Gl, dʌŋɔːɫən Do, dəŋɔːlɪn Gl
dung-hill *n* an ASH-MIDDEN V.1.14. dʌŋɪɫ Bk
dung-hook* *n* a bent fork used to pull muck from a cart, ⇐ MUCK-FORK I.3.13. dʊnʊk Sa
dunging *v-ing* CARTING *DUNG* II.1.4. dʌŋɪn Ha
dung-passage *n* a DRAIN in a cow-house I.3.8. dɒŋpɛsɪdʒ K
dung-pat *n* a CLOT OF COW-DUNG II.1.6. dɒŋpɛt K
dung-peek* *n* a MUCK-FORK I.3.13. dʌŋpiːk So
dung-pick *n* a MUCK-FORK I.3.13. dʌŋpɪk So D Do
dung-pit 1. *n* an artificial CESS-POOL on a farm I.3.11. dʌŋpɪt D
2. *n* an ASH-MIDDEN V.1.14. dʊŋpɪt Co
dung-prong *n* a MUCK-FORK I.3.13. dʌŋpɾaŋ Co, dʌŋpɾɒŋ W Co D Ha
dung-putt *n* a FARMCART I.9.3. dʌŋpʊt Do, dʌŋpʌt Ha
dung-spud *n* a MUCK-FORK I.3.13. dɒŋspɒd K, dɒŋspʌd K, dʌŋspʌd Sx, *pl* dʌŋspʌdz Sr
dung-yard *n* the STRAW-YARD of a farm I.1.9. dɒŋjɑːd K, dɒŋjaˑ̍ːd Brk, dʌŋjaːd Ess, dʌŋjaˤːd̩ Bk, dʌŋjaˑ̍ːd Brk, dʌŋjaːəˤt̩d̩ Sr
dunnek *n* an EARTH-CLOSET V.1.13. dʌnɪk W Sx
dunnekin *n* an EARTH-CLOSET V.1.13. dɒnɪkɪn D, dʌnɪkɪn Bk W Brk D Ha, *pl* dʌnɪkɪnz Sx, dʌnɪkŋ Ha, dʌnəkɪn Bk*[old]* Bd Hrt Ess, *pl* dʌnəkɪnz K, dʌnkɪn W, dʌŋkɪn Ess, dʊnəkɪn Bk, *pl* dʊnəkɪnz Y*[old]*
dunny *adj* DEAF VI.4.5. dʊnɪ Brk
durns 1. *npl* GATE-POSTS IV.3.2. dɪənz Y
2. *npl* the JAMBS of a door V.1.11. daːnz L, daˤːn̩z̪ So Co, dəˤːn̩z̪ So W Co D Do, ðəˤːn̩z̪ So

durrum *n* the TAIL of a cow III.2.2. dʊɹʊm Gl
dust 1. *n* *In summer when there has been no rain for a long time, the country roads are covered with* .... VII.6.18. Eng. ⇒ **mud**, silt, smeech, stew, stour
2. *n* CHAFF II.8.5. dœʏs D, dæʏs So Co D, dæʊs So, daʊs So, dʌst So, dʌs So Do
3. *n* CHAFF fed to horses III.5.3. dæʊs So; **dust and oats** dæʊs ən uːəts W
4. *n* SMOKE from a chimney V.1.4. daʊs So, dʌs So
5. *n* COAL-DUST V.4.1. dʌst Nf Sf Ess So Brk K Ha, dʌs So, dʏst Nf, dʊst Lei So, dəst Ess; **wet dust** wɛt dʌs Nf
6. *n* ASH in a burning fire V.4.4. daʊs So, dʌst So
7. *vt* to BEAT a boy on the buttocks VIII.8.10. dʌst Sr*[old]*
dust-bonnet *n* a woman's cloth BONNET worn indoors VI.14.1. dʊstbɒnɪt Db
dust coal *n* COAL-DUST V.4.1. dʌs kɒʊɫ Sx, dʌst kʌʊə̍ɫ Sf, dʌs koːl Nf, dʌs koːɫ Do, dʌst koul Nf, dʌs koul Nf, dʊs kɒʊɫ K; **wet dust coal** wɛt dʌs koul Nf
duster *n* a BRUSH used for sweeping indoors V.9.11. dʌstəᴮ Nb*[long handle x1, soft x1]*
dust-heap *n* an ASH-MIDDEN V.1.14. dʌstⁱiːp K
dust-hole *n* an ASH-MIDDEN V.1.14. dʌstɒʊ K*[hole in a wall]*, dʌstʌʊɫ Ess, dʊstɔʊɫ Lei, dʊstoʊɫ Wa
dust-pan *n* a SHOVEL for a household fire V.3.9. dʌspæn Sf Ess, dʌspn Nf*[long-handled x1, small x1]*, dʌspən Sf Ess, dʊstpan Db Nt, dʊspan Nt L Nth*[large x1]* *[marked ir.r. WMBM]*
dust-pit *n* an ASH-MIDDEN V.1.14. dʌspɪt Nf
dusty coal *n* COAL-DUST V.4.1. dʌstɪ kɒʊɫ Sx, dʌstɪ kɒʊ Sr, dʌstɪ kʌʊɫ Hrt Ess, dɪstɪ koːɫ Co, dʌstɪ koʊɫ Bk Ha
dutch-apron *n* a decorative APRON V.11.2(b). dʊtʃɛɪpɹən St
dutch-barn *n* the place where hay is stored on a farm, ⇐ HAY-LOFT I.3.18. dʌtʃ baːn Ess, dʌtʃ baˤːn̩ W, dʊtʃbaːn Y
dutch yeast *n* YEAST V.6.2. dʊtʃ ɹ̍əst L
dwile *n* a DISHCLOTH V.9.6. dwʌɪl Nf
dwindle away *viphr* to WANE, referring to the moon VII.6.5(b). *-ing* dwɪndlɪn əweː Y
dwindled *adj* **get dwindled** to WRINKLE, referring to the skin of very old people VI.11.2. gɛʔ dwɪndld Nf
dwindler *n* a WEAKLING piglet III.8.4. dwɪndlə Wa
dyed eggs *npl* EASTER EGGS VII.4.9. daɪd ɛgz La

E

ea *n* a RIVULET IV.1.1. iː L

eagles *npl* HAWS IV.11.6. iːglz La, iːgɟz Co

eald *adj NOT IN* CALF III.1.8. iːld Nb

ear *1. n What do you call the parts of the fully-grown plant (of corn, except peas and beans) while still green? There's the root and the ....* II.5.2(b). iːə St Ess, ɪəᴿ Nb, ɪə Du La Y Ch Db St Wa Nt L Lei R Nth Hu C Nf Sf Bk Bd Hrt Ess MxL, *pl* ɪəz Sr, hɪə Y St Lei, ɪəɹ La Y L Brk, ɪəᴵ La St L Brk K, *pl* ɪəᴵz O, jɪəᴵ Brk, ɪəᶜ Sa He Wo Wa Mon Gl O Bk Bd Brk Sr K, *pl* ɪəᶜz Ha, jɪəɾ Brk, hɪəᶜ O, ɪəᶜɾ Sx, jɪəᶜɾ Ha, *pl* jɪəᶜɾz Brk, ɪəː Ha, jəᶜː He Wo Mon Gl O So W Co D Do Ha, eɪəᴵ Man, eəɹ(+V) Nf, eˑə Hrt, ɛɪəᶜ K, ɛə Nf Hrt Ess, ɛˑəᴵ Nf. ⇒ **blow, crown, head, [hud], top**; also **bell, hackle, jag, lobe**

2. n an ear of barley, oats, or wheat. ɪəᶜ So, *pl* jəᶜːz̥ So

3. n an ear of barley or wheat. ɪə C, iɪəɹ Man, ɪəᶜ K, jəᶜː So

4. n an ear of oats or wheat. ɪə Y

5. n an ear of wheat. ɪəᶜ O

6. n an ear of any corn other than oats. jəᶜː W

7. n an EVENER on a horse-drawn plough I.8.4. ɪəᶜ Sa

8. n the GRASS-NAIL of a scythe II.9.9. jəᴵː Y

ear-bake *n* an EAR-HOLE VI.4.3. jəᶜːbeːk D

ear-board *n* the CROSS-BEAM END of a cart I.10.1. ɛəbʊəd Y

ear-bolt *n* an EAR-HOLE VI.4.3. jəᶜːboːɬt D

ear-bosom *n* an EAR-HOLE VI.4.3. jəᶜːbʊzəm D

ear-bray *n* the iron stay connecting the beam with the side of a cart, ⇐ CROSS-BEAM END I.10.1. ɪəbɹeː Y, ɪəbɹe Y *[marked u.rr. in NBM headword list, but unmarked in phonetic listings]*

ear-breed *n* the CROSS-BEAM END of a cart I.10.1. ɪəbɹiːd Y L, ɪəlbɹiːb Y, ɪəbɹɪəd Y, ɪəbɹɪd La Y, ɛəbɹiːd Y, ɛəbɹiːð Y *[note at La.8 suggests that r. there perhaps better interpreted as **bumper**]*

ear-buss *n* an EAR-HOLE VI.4.3. *pl* jəᶜːbʌsəz D

ear-clip *vt* to MARK the ears of sheep with a hole to indicate ownership III.7.9. *-ing* ɪəᴵklɪpɪn K, jəᶜːkɬɪp W

ear-hole *n What do you call this, inside [the ear]?* VI.4.3. Eng exc. Cu. ⇒ *drum*, **ear-bake, ear-bolt, ear-bosom, ear-buss,** *ear-drum*, **ear-lug, ear-trumpet, flap-hole, glob, lug, lug-hole, tab-hole, wicker-hole**

ear-lug *n* an EAR-HOLE VI.4.3. ɪˈəlʊg L

early-wigs *npl* EARWIGS IV.8.11. jaᶜːɬɪwɪgz Ha, əːɹlɪwɛgz Brk, əᶜːɬɪwɪgz W, *sg* əᶜːɬɪwɪg Sr, əːɾlɪwɪgz Brk, əᶜːlɪwɪgz Sr*[old]*, *sg* əᶜˈlɪwɪg K, əᶜːɾlɪwɪgz Brk, jɪəᶜɾlɪwɪgz Brk, jəᶜːlɪwɪgz Gl, əᶜːɬɪwɪgz Ha, əᶜːɾɬɪwɪgz Sx*[old x2]*

ear-mark *1. vt* to MARK the ears of sheep with a hole or cut to indicate ownership III.7.9. ɪəᴵmɑᴵˈk Brk

2. v to mark the ears of sheep with a hole or cut. ɪəmaːk Db Nt Lei, *pt* ɪˈəmaːkt L, *-ing* ɪəᴵmaːkən Man

3. vt to mark the ears of sheep in some unspecified way. ɪəᶜːmaᶜːk Co, jəᶜːmaᶜːk So D, jəᶜːmaᶜːk D

4. v to mark the ears of sheep in some unspecified way. ɪəmaːk Cu*[hill sheep]* Y, jəᶜːmaᶜːk W Co Ha, *-ing* ɪəᴵmɑᴵːkɪn K, ɪəᶜɾmaᶜːk Sr

earned *vt-3sgperf Talking of a man's living, you can say: That man is a regular wastrel, he has never ... his living.* (Version 4 of Questionnaire: *A mother looks after the house, but the money she spends comes from the father; and he doesn't steal it, of course, but he ... it.*) VIII.1.26. Eng exc. We. ⇒ **addled,** *doed a stroke of work, done a day's work, done a good day's work, done any good, done anything, done aught, done no regular work, done nothing, done no work,* **earn, get, got nought, got no work,** *he don't break many tools, he never does a day's work, he never works,* **tried to earn, worked, worked** *for,* **works** *for,* **works hard** *for,* **wrought** *for*

earning *n* RENNET V.5.6. əᴵːnɪn L

ear-punch *v* to MARK the ears of sheep with a hole to indicate ownership III.7.9. ɪəpʊnʃ Db

ears *1. npl What do you call these [indicate the ears]?* VI.4.1. Eng exc. Nb Cu Du We. ⇒ **flappers, harkeners, harkers, listeners, lugs, tabs, tags, wickers;** ⇒ also **lug-root**

2. n barley AWNS II.5.3. ɪəᶜz̥ Gl, jəᶜːz̥ Gl

3. n the WATTLES of a hen IV.6.19. ɪˈəz Ess, jəᶜːz̥ So *[queried ir.r. EM/SBM]*

earth *n What's a grave filled in with?* VIII.5.8. eːθ Co D, eːəθ So*[old]* Co D, ɛᶜːθ Co, ɛəθ Lei, ɛəᶜθ Sr, ɛːəθ D, œːθ Mon, ɑːθ Nf Ess, ɔᴿːθ Nb, ʌf Mon, ɜːθ Man, ɜᴵːɹθ La, əθ Du Y, əᴵθ L, əɪθ He Nth Hu*[old]*, əᶜθ He Ha, əɾθ O Nf, əːθ Y Ch Db St Wa Lei R Nth Hu Nf Hrt Ess, əᴵːθ L Ess Brk K, əːᴵθ Ch, əᶜːθ Sa He Wa Bk Bd Ess So W Sr K Co D, jəᶜːθ Ha, həᶜːθ Sr, əᶜːɾθ Sx, həᶜːɾθ Brk; **earth**

and clay əːθ ən kleː Y. ⇒ **clay, dirt, earth** *and clay*, **mould(s), muck,** *sand, sand and gravel,* **soil, soil** *or clay*

earth-closet *n* What's your word for the old-fashioned W.C. [i.e. water-closet or lavatory]? V.1.13. ɛˈəθtlɒzət Cu, ɔːθklɒzət Du, əːθklɒzɪt Ess K, əˡːθklɒzɪt Sa Sr K. ⇒ **bog, bumby-hole,** *bumby-holes* ⇒ **bumby-hole, closet, crap-house, crapper, dike, duddekin, dunnek, dunnekin, earth-lavatory, garden-house, house of commons, houses-of-parliament, lavatory, lavvy, little-house, lobby, middy, mixen, mizzen, necessary, nessy, netty, out-house, petty, petty-hole, petty-house, piss-house, privy, shite-house, shit-hole, shit-house, shitting-house, thyeveg, vault;** ⇒ also **double-barrelled shit-house**

earthen-pot *n* a BREAD-BIN V.9.2. aːθənpɒt Ess, aːθnpɔt Sf, ɑˈθənpɒt Nf, əːθənpɒt Ess

earthenware pot *n* a SALTING-TROUGH III.12.5. əˈθənwɛˈə pɑˈt? Nf

earth-lavatory *n* an EARTH-CLOSET V.1.13. əːθlavətɹɪ St

earth-worms *npl* WORMS IV.9.1. əɹθwəɹmz He

ear-trumpet *n* an EAR-HOLE VI.4.3. ɪətɹʊmpɪt St

earwigs *npl* What do you call those insects, reddish-brown, with feelers and a tail like a pair of pincers? (before April 1954: that you think might creep into this [point to the ear]? in place of reddish-brown ... pincers?) IV.8.11. iiwɪgz Man, *sg* ˡɪəwəg Man, ɪəwɪgz Cu We La Y Ch Db Sa St Lei R Nth Nf Hrt Ess, *sg* ɪəwɪg Wo Wa L MxL, hɪəwɪgz Nth, *sg* hɪəwɪg Du, ɪərwɪgz Cu, ɪəɹwɪgz La, *sg* ɪəɹwɪg Y, ɪəˡwɪgz La K, *sg* ɪəˡwɪg Y, *sg* ɪəˡɹwɪg Sx, ɪəˡwɪgz Sa O Sr Ha Sx, *sg* ɪəˡwɪg He, jəˡwɪgz Mon, *sg* jəˈːwɪg Y, ɪəˡːwɪgz So, *sg* ɪəˡːwɪg Co, jəˡːwɪgz Mon Gl So W Co D Do Ha, *sg* jəˡːwag Ha, iiːəˡːwɪgz Sa, eˈəwɪgz Sf, ɛəwɪgz Nf, *sg* ɛəɹwɪg Ess, ɛəˡwɪgz He, *sg* ɛəˡwɪg K, œːwɪgz Mon. ⇒ **battle-twigs,** *battle-wig* ⇒ **battle-wigs, battle-wigs, cat-o'-nine-tails,** *catonine-tails* ⇒ **cat-o'-nine-tails, cat-o'-two-tails,** *catotwo-tails* ⇒ **cat-o'-two-tails, early-wigs, eary-wigs, forking-robins, forky-tails, harry-wiggles, harry-wigs, kutchy-bells, lug-wigs, pincher-bobs,** *pincher-wig* ⇒ **pincher-wigs, pincher-wigs, skutchy-bells, twinges, twitch-bells, twitchy-bells, urrins**

eary-wigs *npl* EARWIGS IV.8.11. iːɹɪwɪgz Sa He Wo Mon, *sg* iːɹɪwɪg Wa, iːɹəwɪgz Sa, ɹɪɪwɪgz Ess, ɪəɹɪwɪgz Wa Lei Bk Hrt[old] K, *sg* ɪəɹɪwɪg Sa[old] He O Nth, ɪəˡʷwɪgz K, *sg* ɪəʇɪwɪg O, ɪəˡʈɪwɪgz Sa Sr, ɪəˡːʈɪwɪgz Co D, jəˡːʈɪwɪgz W D, jœɹɪwɪgz Mon, jəɹɪwɪgz He, əˡːʈɪwɪgz Gl

ease *imp* **ease up** the command GO ON!, given to plough-horses II.3.5.(d). iːz ʌp W, iːz ʊp Nb

easing *1. n* the RIDGE of a house roof V.1.2(a). iːzɪn St

2. n the GUTTER of a roof V.1.6. iːzɪn Sa

easing-pipe *n* the GUTTER of a roof V.1.6. iːzɪŋpaɪp St

easing-rope* *n* a rope placed round a stack below the eaves, to which are fastened ropes which pass over the thatch, holding it in place, ⇐ ROPES II.7.7(b). iːznʁøːp Nb

easing(s) *n* the EAVES of a stack of corn II.7.3. *no -s:* iːsɪŋ Man, iːzɪn Nb Cu Du We Db Sa St Wa, iːzɪn Nb, iːzən Nb Du, ɪəsɪn Y, ɪəzɪn We La Y, eːzɪn Ch Db Sa Wo, heɪzn Du, heɪzən Du, eɪzən Man, ɛɪzɪn Y Ch Db Wo

-s: iːzɪnz Db St L, jɪzɪnz Y, ɪuːzn̩z Sf, ɪəzɪnz Cu Y L, ɛɪzɪnz Db

easing-spout *n* the GUTTER of a roof V.1.6. ɪəzɪnspaʊt Y, eːzɪnspæʊt Ch

easing-stick *n* a STICK used to support the shaft of a cart I.11.1. iːznstɪk Nb

easing-trough *n* the GUTTER of a roof V.1.6. jɪzɪntɹɒf Y, jɛzɪntɹɒf Y, ɪəzɪntrɒf Y, ɛʊzɪntɹɒf Y[modern], ɛʊzɪntɹɒx Y[old]

easses *npl* WORMS IV.9.1. jɛsiːz So

easter eggs *npl* During one of these festivals [Easter etc.] children, especially, eat hard-boiled eggs. What do you call them? VII.4.9. Eng exc. Nb Cu Du We La. ⇒ **boiled eggs, dyed eggs, hard-boiled eggs, hollowed eggs, pace eggs;** ⇒ also **bowling-egg day**

eastoft leggings *npl* KNEE-STRAPS used to lift the legs of working trousers VI.14.17. ɪˈəstɒft lɛgɪnz L [queried facetious EMBM]

easy broke *adj* BRITTLE, describing cups and saucers which break easily IX.1.4. iːzɪ bɹoʊk St

easy broken *adj* BRITTLE, describing cups and saucers which break easily IX.1.4. ɪəzɪ bɹɒkn Y, jɛzɪ bɹɒkən Y, iːzɪ bɹɒkn Ch, iːzɪ bɹɒkən Nb

eatage *n* pasture, ⇐ HIRE *PASTURAGE* III.3.8. ɪətɪdʒ Y

eating *1. n* the **eating** pasture, ⇐ HIRE *PASTURAGE* III.3.8. ð iːtɪn St

2. n FOOD V.8.2. ɛɪtɪn Y

3. n MEAL OUT VII.5.12. iːtn We

eating-ground *n* PASTURE II.1.3. ɛɪdɪngɹæʊn Co

eave *n* a EWE-HOG III.6.4. *pl* iːvz St

eave-knife *n* a HAY-KNIFE II.9.14(a). iːvnɑɪf Hu

eaver *n* the DIRECTION from which the wind blows VII.6.26. iːðəɹ La

eavering-end *n* the CROSS-BEAM END of a cart I.10.1. *pl* ɪvɹɪnɛndz La

eaverings *n* the beams of a cart, ⇐ CROSS-BEAM END I.10.1. *pl* ɪəvʁənz Du

eave(s) *n* [*Show a picture of some stacks.*] *What do you call this?* II.7.3.

no -s: iːv Gl O L Nf Sf Sr, ɪiːv Sx, iiːf Sx, ɪˈəv Y L
-s: iːvz Nb La Y Sa St He Wo Wa Mon Gl O Nt L Lei R Nth Hu C Nf Bk Bd Hrt Ess MxL So W K Do Ha, iːz Y, ɪiːvz Lei Nf Ess Brk Sr K Sx, ɪəvz Y Nt L Bk, ɪəz Y, eːvz Ch Wo Gl O W Ha, eɪvz Nf, ɛɪvz La Wo Wa Nth Bd Ess

⇒ **easing(s), foth, hips, oaves,** *office* ⇒ **oaves, ouse, ousing, shoulder(s), square**

[*The following marked as ir.rr. or u.rr. and omitted: eave-laying, oaves-line, ring-lain, roof-end. BM also queries foth and square, included here.*]

eave-troughing *n* the GUTTER of a roof V.1.6. iːvtɹɔːvɪn Ess

ebber *n* an EVENER on a horse-drawn plough I.8.4. ɛbəᵗ Sa

ebb-place *n* a FORD IV.1.3. ɛbpleːs Ch

edder *1. vt* to fill gaps in a hedge-bank or hedge with turfs, brushwood, or similar material, ⇐ to PLASH IV.2.4. *-ing* ɛðəᵗɹɪn He
2. n a thin willow-stick woven into a hedge after laying. *pl* ɛðəʈz̩ O

eddidge* *n* AFTERMATH, a second crop of grass II.9.17. ɛdɪdʒ Db

eddish *1. n* STUBBLE remaining in a cornfield after harvesting II.1.2. ɛtʃ Ess
2. n AFTERMATH, a second crop of grass II.9.17. ɛdɪʃ La Y Db Sa[*clover*] Nt L Lei R Nth Hu C Nf, hɛdɪʃ C, ɛdɪtʃ La Db St

edge *n* the CURB-STONE in a cow-house I.3.9. eɪdʒ So, ɛdʒ Brk; **edge of the gutter** ɛdʒ ə ðə gʌtɔᵏ Nb

edgeland(s) *n* HEADLANDS in a ploughed field II.3.3.

no -s: ɛdʒlənt Lei
-s: ɛdʒlənts Lei

edge out *vphr* to CLEAR grass at the edges of a field II.9.5. ɛdʒ ʌut O

edging *n* the CURB-STONE in a cow-house I.3.9. ɛdʒɪn Lei R

edging-stone *n* the CURB-STONE in a cow-house I.3.9. ɛdʒɪnstoːᵘn He

e'er-a-one* *pron* EITHER VII.2.13. iəɹəwɒn K, ɛɹəwʊn Bk, ɛːɹəwʊn Wa, ɛəɹɪwʌn Bd, ɛəɹəwʊn Wa, aɹiwʌn D, aᵗːwʌn So W Ha, aᵗːn̩ W Ha, əᵗːn̩ So; **e'er-a-one a one*** aᵗːn̩ ə wʌn Nth, aᵗːn̩ ə wʊn Nth

eff *n* a NEWT IV.9.8. ɛf Gl O Bk Hrt Ess

eft *n* a NEWT IV.9.8. ɛft Y[*preferred*] O

egg-cups *n* hiccups, ⇐ HICCUPING VI.8.4. ɛgkʌps So, æɪgkʌps So

eggle-berries *n* HAWS IV.11.6. ɛgɫbɛɹɪz D

eggles *npl* HAWS IV.11.6. ɛgɪʊɫz Ha

eglets *npl* HAWS IV.11.6. ɛgɫəts Co D

eglons *npl* HAWS IV.11.6. ɛgɫənz Co

eiderdown *n* a QUILT V.2.11. aɪdəɹdaʊn He, aɪdədɛʊn Hrt MxL, aɪdədæːn MxL, aɪdədæʊn Ch,

aɪdədaːn MxL, ɒɪdədaɪn St, ɔɪdədɛʊn Ess, ɔɪdədæʊn Wo O

eighting *v-ing* making a stook of eight sheaves, ⇐ STOOKING II.6.5. aɪtɪn Co

eights* *n* eight furrows, ⇐ RIDGES II.3.2. æɪts Ess

eight up *vphr* to make a stook of eight sheaves, ⇐ STOOKING II.6.5. aɪt ʌp Co

either *pron* [*I don't think he'd stop at a third of the pie, or even half of it; he'd want the (whole of it).*] *And a less greedy boy will say: It doesn't matter, I'll have ....* VII.2.13. Eng; **either a one** iːðəɹ ə wʌn Sf; **either one** iːðəᵗː wʌn D, æːðəᵗː wan D, æɪ wan So, aːðəᵗː wan D, aːðəᵗː wʌn Co D, aɪðəᵗː wʌn Co, aːðəᵗː wan D, aːðəᵗː wʌn Co D, aɪðə wʏn Nf, ɒɪðəᴶ wɒn K, ʌðəᵗː wan Co D, ʌðəᵗː wʌn So Co D; **either piece** aɪ pɪs So. ⇒ *awther* (⇒ **either**), either *a one,* either *of it,* either *of them,* either *one,* either *one of it,* either *one of them,* either *piece of it,* ever, e'er-a-one, e'er-a-one *a one,* e'er-a-one *of en,* e'er-a-one *of it,* e'er-a-one *of them,* ever-a-one ⇒ e'er-a-one, *other one* ⇒ either *one, other one of it* ⇒ either *one, other one of them* ⇒ either *one*

ekkymowl *n* a BAT IV.7.7. ɛkimæɥ̈ɫ Co

elder *1. n* What do you call that tall bush with the cluster of dark berries from which you can make wine? IV.10.6. Eng exc. C. ⇒ **alder, alder-berry, alder-tree, aldern, aldern-berry, aldern-tree, boun-tree, bourtree, bourtree-bush, bourtree-tree, bultree, bultree-tree, dog-tree,** *elderberry, elderberry-tree,* **elder-bush, eldern,** *eldern-berries* ⇒ **eldern-berry, eldern-berry, eldern-bush,** *eldren* ⇒ **eldern,** *ellren* ⇒ **eldern, saugh, scaw, scaw-tree, tremming-tree**
2. n the UDDER of a cow III.2.5. ɪldə L, ɪldɪ L, ɛldə La Y Ch Db St Nt Lei, ɛɫdə Ch Sf, ɛldəɹ La He, ɛldəᴶ La Ch L, ɛldəɾ Db, ɛldəᵗ Sa Wo, ɛᵗdəᵗ He Mon, ɛɫdəᵗː Sa, ɛɫðəɹ La, ɒɫdəᵗ He

eldern *n* the bush ELDER IV.10.6. ɛɫʊn He Gl, ɛɫʊm Gl, *pl* ɛldənz L, ɛldɹən L, ɛlɹən L, ɛɫdən Hu C, ɛɫən Mon Gl, ɛɫdɹən Gl, ɛləᵗn̩ Sa, ɛɫdəᵗn̩ Gl Bk, ɛɫəᵗn̩ He, ɛldəᵗːn̩ W, ɛləᵗːn̩ Sa

eldern-berry *n* the bush ELDER IV.10.6. ɛldəᵗn̩bɛ.ɪɪ O, *pl* ɛɫdəᵗːn̩bɛɾiːz W

eldern-bush *n* the bush ELDER IV.10.6. ɛlənbʊʃ Wo, ɛɫdnbʊʃ Nth

elder-stick *n* a SHEATH or other device used to keep a knitting-needle firm V.10.10. ɛˈldəstɪk Nf

elder up *viphr* to show signs of calving, ⇐ SHOWS SIGNS OF CALVING III.1.12(a). *-ing* ɛldəɹɪn ʊp La

elding *n* KINDLING-*WOOD* V.4.2. ɛldɪn Y

eleveners *n* a morning SNACK VII.5.11. ɫɛmnəᵗːz̩ Co

elevenpence-halfpenny *adj* STUPID   VI.1.5.
lɛvn̩pənsɛɪpnɪ Sx

elevens *n* a morning SNACK VII.5.11. lɛvənz Ess,
lɛvnz Ess, lɛbmz Ess

elevenses *n* a morning SNACK VII.5.11. ɪlɛvənzɪz
Y*[modern]*, lɛvənzɪz He Ess Ha*[modern]*, lɛvnzɪz
Lei Ess, łɛvənzɪz O*[modern]*, łɛvnzəz Ha, lɛbmzɪz
Sf Ess

elk *n* a YOUNG SOW III.8.5. ɛłk W Do

eller *n* an ELM tree IV.10.4. ɛlə Cu *[queried ir.r.
NBM]*

ellerd *n* the UDDER of a cow III.2.5. ɛləd Y

elm *n* What do you call that other tree with hard
wood, which is often used for making coffins and
clogs; when old, it's easily blown over? IV.10.4. Eng;
elm-tree ɛləmtɹiː La Y Ess, *pl* ɛlʌmtɹiːz So, *pl*
ɛlm,tɹɛɪz Lei, ɛʊmtɹiː Sr. ⇒ **eller, elm-*tree*, holm**

elp *n* a YOUNG SOW III.8.5. ɛłp W

elt *n* a YOUNG SOW III.8.5. ɛłt So W Do Ha, əłt D

elve *1. vi-3prpl* they MOO, describing the noise
cows make during feeding time in the cow-house
III.10.4(a). ɛłv Co

2. vi-3prpl they MOO, describing the noise cows
make in the fields III.10.4(b). ɛłv Co
[queried SBM]

elves *npl* BOGEYs VIII.8.1. ɛłvz Hu

embers *n* CINDERS V.4.3. ɪmbəᵗːz̩ Sa*[old, usual]*,
ɪʊməᵗːz̩ Co, ɛmbiz Nf, ɛmbəz St Nth K, ɛmbəᴶz K

emery-stone *n* a WHETSTONE II.9.10. ɛmɹɪstɒʊn
Sx, ɛmɹɪstoːn Sa, ɛməɹstʊən Y, ɛmbɹɪstʌʊn Ess,
ɛmlɪstɪən Nb

emmet-banks *npl* ANT-HILLS   IV.8.13.   *sg*
ɛmətbɛŋk D, ɛmʌtbæŋks Co, ɛməʔbaŋks Bk

emmet-batches *npl* ANT-HILLS   IV.8.13.   *sg*
ɛmətbætʃ So, jɛmətbætʃɪz So, jamətbatʃəz So

emmet-butts *npl* ANT-HILLS IV.8.13. ɛmətbʌts So
Do

emmet-casts* *npl* ANT-HILLS   IV.8.13.   *sg*
ɛmɪtkaːst K, *sg* æmɪtkæˑst K, *sg* æmɪtkaːst K

emmet-heaps *npl* ANT-HILLS IV.8.13. jɪmətiːps
So, ɛmɪtiips Ha, *sg* ɛmɪthiːp Sr, ɛmʌtiːps W,
ɛmətiːps Co, ɛməʔiːps Bk, ɛməthaɪps Do, amətiːps
D, jamətiːps So

emmet-heaves *npl* ANT-HILLS IV.8.13. ɛmətiːvz
D

emmet-hills *npl* ANT-HILLS IV.8.13. ɛmɪtɪʊz Sr
Sx, *sg* ɛmɪtɪʊ Brk, ɛmʊtɪʊłz Brk, ɛmʊtɪʊz Sx,
ɛmətɪłz O, ɛmətɪłz O W Co D Ha, ɛməʔɪłz O, *sg*
ɛmətɪʊ Brk, æmɪthɪłz K, *sg* æmɪthɪʊł K, æmɪtɪʊz K,
sg amətiːł D, amətɪłz D, jamətɪłz So Ha

emmet-humps* *npl* ANT-HILLS   IV.8.13.   *sg*
ɛməthʌmp So. ⇒ also **emmet-tumps** *[it is not
possible to distinguish -humps and -tumps forms with
certainty]*

emmet-knolls* *npl* ANT-HILLS   IV.8.13.   *sg*
ɛmʌtnoːł W, *sg* ɛmətno:ł W

emmet-moulds *npl* ANT-HILLS   IV.8.13.
ɛmʌtmoːłdz W, ɛmətmoːłdz W

emmet-mounds *npl* ANT-HILLS   IV.8.13.
ɛmɪtmɛʊnz Brk Ha, *sg* ɛmɪtmɛʊn Sx,
ɛmətmæʊnz Ha, *sg* ɛmʊtmʌʊnd Gl

emmets *npl* ANTS IV.8.12. jɪməts So, ɛmɪts Lei
Brk Sr*[old x2]* K*[old x1]* Ha Sx*[old x1]*, ɛmʌts W
Co, *sg* ɛmʌt So, ɛmʊts Gl Brk Sx, ɛməts Mon Gl
O Bk So W Brk Co D Do Ha, jɛməts So*[old x1]*
D, ɛməʔs Bk, æmɪts K, æməts Sx, aməts D, *sg*
amət Ha, jaməts So Ha

emmets'-batches *npl* ANT-HILLS   IV.8.13.
ɛmətsbætʃəz So

emmets'-butts *npl* ANT-HILLS   IV.8.13.
ɛmətsbʌts Do

emmets'-casts *npl* ANT-HILLS   IV.8.13.
ɛmətskaːstɪz Sr

emmets'-heaps *npl* ANT-HILLS   IV.8.13.
ɛmətsiːps Co

emmets'-heaves* *npl* ANT-HILLS IV.8.13. *sg*
ɛmətsiːv Co

emmets'-hills *npl* ANT-HILLS   IV.8.13.
ɛmətsiːłz D, *sg* ɛmʊtsɪʊł Brk, *sg* æmətsɪʊ Sx

emmets'-nests *npl* ANT-HILLS IV.8.13. *sg*
ɛmətsnɪst Gl, jɛmətsnɛstɪs D, *sg* amətsnɛst Ha

emmets'-patches *npl* ANT-HILLS   IV.8.13.
ɛmɪtspætʃəz So, jəmətspætʃɪz So

emmet-tumps *npl* ANT-HILLS   IV.8.13.
ɛmʌtʌmps So, ɛməttʌmps Mon, ɛmətʌmps So W,
jɛmətʌmps So, *sg* ɛmətʊmp Mon, ɛməttəmps Gl.
⇒ also **emmet-humps** *[it is not possible to
distinguish -tumps and -humps forms with
certainty]*

empier *n* the FORKER on a wagon who unloads
sheaves in a stackyard II.6.9. ɛmpɪə Hu

empt *vt* to TIP a cart I.11.6. *-ing* ɛmptɪn Brk

empter *n* the FORKER on a wagon who unloads
sheaves in a stackyard II.6.9. ɛmtə Nth, ɛmptəᵗ O
Nth, ɛmʔtəᵗ Bk

emptier *n* the FORKER on a wagon who unloads
sheaves in a stackyard II.6.9. ɛmtɪə Hu Bd, ɛmptɪə
O C

empting *1. v-ing* UNLOADING sheaves from a
wagon II.6.8. ɛmptɪn O, ɛmtɪn Nth, *prppl* ɛmtɪn
Wa, *prppl* ɛntɪn Brk, *no -ing* ɛmt Wa Nth,

2. vt-ing unloading sheaves. ɛmtɪn Nth, ɛmʔtɪn
Bk, *no -ing* ɛmp Hu

empting-fork *1. n* a HAY-FORK with a long
shaft I.7.11. ɛmtɪnfɔːk Nth

2. n a hay-fork with a short shaft. *pl* ɛmtɪnfɔːks
Nth

empt out *vtphr* to POUR tea V.8.8. ɛmp aʊt So

empty *1. v* to PITCH sheaves II.6.10. ɛmtɪ O

2. adj HAS NOT HELD, describing a cow that
has not conceived III.1.7. ɛmptɪ Nf, ɛmtɪ Lei

3. adj NOT IN CALF III.1.8. ɛmptɪ Nf Sf Bk Ess,

εmpt?ɪ Sf, εmtɪ Sa L Lei Hu

4. *adj* not in calf but able to conceive. εmptɪ Hu C, εmtᵊɪ Bd, εm?ti W

5. **adj* DRY, describing a cow with no milk III.1.9. εmti Co

6. *adj* HUNGRY VI.13.9. εmptɪ O Nf; **empty in the hole** εmtɪ ɪn ðə ʊəl L

emptying *v-ing* UNLOADING sheaves from a wagon II.6.8. *no -ing* εmptɪ O, εmtɪ-ɪn Hu[old] Bd, *no -ing* εmtɪ Du O[rare] L Nth, *no -ing* εmpɪ Nb Y

en *objpron* HIM IX.2.4. ŋGl So W Brk Co Do Ha Sx, ən So W Co D Ha, ŋCo Ha

enclosure-yard *n* a FARMYARD I.1.3. ɪŋklʌʊӡəjaːd Ess

end 1. *n* the GABLE-END of a house V.1.5. εnd O Nt L Ess, εɪnd Ess; **end of the house** εnd ə t uːs Y, εnd ə d uːs Y [marked u.r. EMBM]

2. *vt* to TOP-AND-TAIL gooseberries V.7.23. εnd Du

end-board 1. *n* [Show a picture of a cart.] What do you call this piece which you put on top of the tailboard when you want to carry a bigger load, e.g. turnips? I.10.4. εndbaᵗːd̩ Wo, εndbɔːd Cu Du Y, εnbɔːd Hrt, εndbɔᴿːd Nb Du, εndbʷɔˑəd Cu, εndboəd We, εnboəᵗd̩ Ha, εndbʊəd Du La Y L, hεndbʊəd We, εndbʊəᴵd La O, εnbuːɽd̩ D, εnbuəᵗːd̩ Co. ⇒ **back-board, back-cage, back-end-board, back-heck, back-shelving, back-side-board, back-stay, board, box, cradle, cratch, cross-piece, cross-tree, dash-board, double tailboard, end-door-top, extension, extra tailboard, false-board, false-rave, fast-board, flacker-board, fruit-board, grain-board, heck, heck-board, high-ladder, high-tailboard, hind-board, hind-door, hinder-end-board, hood, jack, jack-board, ladder,** *ladders* ⇒ **ladder, lade, leaf-board, little board, little-end-board, loader, rack, rade, rail, rathe, rave, rave-board, scrat-board, shelving, side-board, slip-on, small tailboard, spare-board, spare tailboard, splash-board, tailboard, tail-heck, tail-ladder, top, top arse-board, top back-board, top-board, top-tail, top tailboard**

2. *n* the TAILBOARD of a cart I.10.2. εndbœːd Du, εndbɔːd Cu, εndbuəd Nb Cu We, εndbʷəd Cu

end-door *n* the TAILBOARD of a cart I.10.2. εnddɪuːə Y, εnddεʊə Y, εnddʊə Y L

end-door-top *n* an END-BOARD of a cart I.10.4. εnddʊətɒp Y

end-heck *n* the TAILBOARD of a cart I.10.2. εndhεk Du, εndεk Du We, hεndεk Du

end-ladder *n* a rear cart-ladder, ⇐ CART-LADDERS I.10.5. ɪnladəᵗ Bk

end over end *adv* HEAD OVER HEELS IX.1.10. εnd aʊəɪ εnd Y, εnd ɔʊəɪ εnd Y

end over heels *adv* HEAD OVER HEELS IX.1.10. εnd ɔvəɪ iːlz L, εnd ɔʊəɪ iːlz L

end-rails *npl* CART-LADDERS I.10.5. εndɪεəlz Y

ends *vi-3prsg* school FINISHES VIII.6.2(b). ɪndz Ess Sr Sx, εᵊnds Man, εndz Lei R Brk, εnz Sa Wa Ess So W

end-wall *n* the GABLE-END of a house V.1.5. εndwɔːɫ Gl

energetic *adj* ACTIVE, describing a child VIII.9.1. εnədӡεtɪk Y Ch Sa Wa Mon Gl L Ess Sr K Ha, εnəᵗdӡεtɪk Sa Gl Nth, εnəᵗːdӡεtɪk Ha Sx, εnəᵗːdӡεdɪk W

energy *n* **full of energy** ACTIVE, describing a child VIII.9.1. fʊl ə εnədӡɪ Nf

engine-wright *n* a WRIGHT VIII.4.4. ɪndӡɪnᴿaɪt Du, εndӡɪnᴿεɪt Du

english thistle *n* a variety of THISTLE II.2.2. ɪŋglɪ∫ θɪsl St

enough *n* If you are fed up with all these questions, you might say to me: Stop, I've had .... IX.11.5. Eng. ⇒ **plenty**

ent 1. *vt* to TIP a cart I.11.6. εnt Brk

2. *v* to POUR tea V.8.8. εnt Co

ent out *vtphr* to POUR tea V.8.8. εnt (...) æʏt Co

entilage *n* AFTERMATH, a second crop of grass II.9.17. ɪntəlɪdӡ Sa [queried WMBM]

entire *n* a STALLION III.4.4. εntæɪə Y, ɪntaɪəᵗː So D, εntæəᵗ He, ɪntaɪə Db Nt, εntaɪə Nb Cu Du We La Y Db St L Lei, hεntaɪə Du La, εntaɪəɪ La L, εntaɪəᵗ Sa, ɪntaɪɔːː D, εntaɪɔːː W, εntaː C Ess MxL, ɪntaɪə Nth, εntaɪə Lei Sf Ess K, εntaɪəᴵ La K, εntaɪəᵗ Bd, ɪntɔɪə St, εntɔɪə St, εntɔɪəᵗː W, εntɔɪə O Sf Ess, εntɔɪəᴵ Ha, εntɔɪəᵗ Gl, ɪntəˑɽ Brk, ɪntaɪəᵗ Sx, εntaɪəᵗ He Mon Sx

entire-horse *n* a STALLION III.4.4. taˑəhaːs Nf, taːəhɔːs Nf, taɪəhɔˑs Nf, ɪntæɪəᴵɒs Man, ɪntaɪəɪɒs Y, εntaɪəhɔːs Sf, ɪntaːɪɔs L, εntaː-ɔs Ess, ɪntaː-ɔːs MxL, ɪntaːhɔːs MxL, əntaɪəhaˑs Nf, *pl* εntaˑɪə-ɒsɪz Lei, εntaɪəhɒˑs Nf, εntaɪəhɔˑs Nf, εntaɪəɪɔːs Nth

entrails 1. *n* the PLUCK of a slaughtered animal III.11.6. ɪntɹəlz Wo

2. *n* CHITTERLINGS before being cleaned for eating III.12.2. ɪntɹʊɫz Brk

esk *n* a NEWT IV.9.8. εsk Y

ess-hook 1. *n* the GRASS-NAIL of a scythe II.9.9. εsʊk St

2. *n* the HOOK or *CROOK* of a crane over a domestic fire V.3.5(c). εshʊk Nf, εsuːᵊk Gl

ettidge *n* AFTERMATH, a second crop of grass II.9.17. εtɪdӡ L

even *n* EVENING VII.3.11(c). iːvn Brk

evener *n* [Show a picture of a (horse-drawn) plough.] What do you call this, for equalizing the pull of the horses? I.8.4. iːvnəᵗ Wo. ⇒ **advantage bodkin, back bodkin, back lantree, back whipper, balancer, baulk, big bodkin, big**

draught, big sway-tree, big swell-tree, big-swingle-tree, big swivel, big weigh, big weigh-tree, *big whibble-tree* ⇒ big whipple-tree, big whib-tree, big whippens/whippence, big whipper, big whipple-tree, bodkin, bolt, bracing-chain, buck, cat's-head, cobble-tree, cock, copsil, cosp, coupling, double-draught, double heel-tree, double-horse draught, double swell-tree, double-swingle-tree, double-tree, double-whip, double-whippen, double-whipper, drail, draught, draw-bar, ear, ebber, gampus, gauge, gear, great-sway, grid, gridiron, guider, harr-tree, hake, hind weigh, horse-tree, irons, kibble-tree, lanes, links, main-sway, main-swingle-tree, master-man, master-swingle-tree, master-tree, middle whipper, nicks, nose-piece, notcher, plough-cock, pole, pound-tree, pratt, pulling-tree, pull-tree, pummel-tree, pundle-tree, pun-tree, regulator, rock-tree, setter, shape, strut-beam, sway, sway-cosp, sway-tree, swingle- tree, swivel, tail bodkin, three-horse baulk, three-horse-pulling-tree, three-horse swingle-tree, three-horse whipper, threep-tree, thribble swell-tree, thrib-tree, totrils, traverse, two-horse baulk, two-horse bit, two-horse horse-tree, two-horse tree, two-horse weigh-tree, two-horse whipple-tree, vantage-whippens, wang, weigh, weigh-bar, weigh-beam, weigh-tree, whipple-tree, wild ducks, wing, wing-swell-tree

evening *1. n What do you call the various parts of the day?* VII.3.11(c). Eng. ⇒ **even**
2. n AFTERNOON VII.3.14. iːvnɪn Mon

evening-apron *n* a decorative APRON V.11.2(b). iːvnɪneːpəˁːŋ Sa

evening clothes *n* ORDINARY CLOTHES VI.14.20. [I]iːvnɪn kloːʊz Gl*[worn at night after work]*

ever *1. pron* EITHER VII.2.13. aˁː W
2. det EVERY VII.8.19. ɪvəɹ Y *[s.w. NBM]*

ever-slit *n* a LOOSE *PIECE OF* SKIN at the bottom of a finger-nail VI.7.11. ɛvəˁslɪt Sr

ever so *adv* VERY VIII.3.2. ɛvə sæʊ Hrt, ɛvə soʊ St, ɛvə sə Wa Nth Hu Sf Bk Ess, ɛvəˁː zə Do

ever-split *n* a LOOSE *PIECE OF* SKIN at the bottom of a finger-nail VI.7.11. ɛvəˁsplɪt Sr *[marked as mistake by fw SBM]*

every *det You don't milk the cows on Tuesdays and Fridays only, you milk them ... day.* VII.8.19. Eng. ⇒ **ever**

everyday clothes *n* ORDINARY CLOTHES VI.14.20. ɛvʁɪde klɪəz Nb, ɪvɹɪdeː tlɪəz Nb Du, ɪvɹɪdɛɪ kloʊz L, ɪvɹɪdə: kloːz Db, ɛvɹɪdeː[I] kloːz Sa, ɛvɹɪdeː kloːz Ch, ɛvɹɪdeːɪ kloːz He, ɛvɹɪdæɪ kloːz He, ɛvɹɪdeː kloːz Mon, ɛvɾɪdeɪ kloːz So, ɪvɾɪdeɪ kɫoːz So, ɛvɹɪdeː kɫoːz Mon, ɛvɾɪdeː kɫoːz Co, ɛvɹɪdeː tloːz Ch, ɪvɹɪdeɪ kloʊz St, ɛvɹɪdɛɪ kloʊðz Ha, ɛvɹɪdɛɪ kloʊz Wa, ɛvɹɪdeːɪ kloˑʊðəz Brk, ɛvɹɪdeː

kloːʊz Gl, ɛvɹɪdiː tl[U]uːz Db, ɛvɹɪdɛɪ kluəz Bk, ɪvɹɪdeˑə kluəz L, ɪvəɹɪdɛə kluəz Y, ɛvɹɪdeː kluəz La Ch, ɪvɹɪdeː tluəz La, ɛvɹɪdeː tluəz La

everyday things *n* ORDINARY CLOTHES VI.14.20. ɪvɹɪdiː θɪŋgz Db

everyday wear *n* ORDINARY CLOTHES VI.14.20. ɛvɹɪdɛɪ weə Nf

evet *n* a NEWT IV.9.8. eːvət D, ɛfɪt Brk Sr K, *pl* ɛfɪts Sx, *pl* ɛvɪts So Sx, ɛvʌt W, ɛfʊt Brk, -*s* ɛfʊts Sx, ɛvʊt Brk, ɛfət Sr Sx, ɛvət Mon Gl So W Co D Do Ha, ɛbət So Do, ɛɪvət D, abət D

evil *1. n* a MUCK-FORK I.3.13. iːvɫ Co D, iːvəɫ D
2. n a four-pronged fork used in farming, ⇐ FORKS I.7.9. iːvɫ Co

ewe *1. n And [what do you call a female sheep] after that [i.e. the second shearing]?* III.6.6. Eng. ⇒ **crone ewe, full-mouthed ewe, old ewe, theave**; ⇒ also **crone, old crone**
2. n a EWE-LAMB III.6.3. jɪu Mon Nf, juː St
3. n a EWE-HOG III.6.4. jɪˑu Nf, ɪuː Nf, juː Wo Ess *[marked u.r. WMBM]*
4. n a GIMMER III.6.5. jæʊ He, jɔʊ L, jɔː So W D, joʊ O, juː Wo Nf So, jɯ: Nf *[queried u.r. SBM]*
5. n a TABBY-CAT, the female cat III.13.9. jɔː Co D

ewe-cat *n* a TABBY-CAT, the female cat III.13.9. jɔːkæt Co, jɔːkat D, joːkæt So, joːkat D

ewe-hog *1. n [What do you call the animals that give us wool? And the female?] And then what is it until the first shearing?* III.6.4. jɛʊ-ɒg La, ɛʊ-ɒg La, jɒuhɒg Cu, jɒu-ɒg Nt, jɔː-ɒg D, jɔː-ʌg So D, jɔʊhœˑg Nb, joːhɒg So, joː-ɒg D, joː-ʌg So D, juː-ɒg Db Sa Lei. ⇒ **chilver, eave, ewe, ewe-hogget, ewe-lamb, ewe-teg, feave, first shearling, first-year ewe, gimmer, gimmer-hog, hog, hogget, lamb, lamb-hog, maiden, maiden-lamb, one-shear, seave, shearing, shearling, shearling ewe, sheeder, sheeder-hog, she-hog, tag, teg, teg-lamb, theave, threave, two-teeth, two-tooth, wether, yearling, yearling-ewe, yearling-lamb, young ewe**; ⇒ also **maiden-ewe**
2. n a GIMMER III.6.5. jɔː-ʌg So

ewe-hogget *1. n* a EWE-HOG III.6.4. jɯhɒˑgət Nf
2. n a sheep from its first to its second shearing, ⇐ GIMMER III.6.5. jɯhɑˑgɪt Nf

ewe-lamb *1. n And [what do you call] the female [lamb when newly born]?* III.6.3. Eng exc. We. ⇒ **chid, chilver, chilver-lamb, ewe, gimmer, gimmer-lamb, lamb, nanny-lamb, sheeder, sheeder-lamb, she-lamb, theave-lamb**
2. n a EWE-HOG III.6.4. jaʊłam Ha, joːłam Do, joʊłæ·m Ha, juːłam W, ɯːłam Lei

ewer *n* the UDDER of a cow III.2.5. jaʊə Cu, jaʊəɹ La, jɒʊəɹ La, jɔʊɔᵍ Nb, juɔᵍ Nb Du, juəɹ Y, juˈə Nb Cu Du Y, juˈər Cu Y

ewe-tag *n* a GIMMER III.6.5. jɒʊtæg Sr

ewe-teg *1. n* a EWE-HOG III.6.4. jɒʊtɛg Sx, jʌʊtɛg K, juːtɛg He*[at 9 months]*, uːtɛg Brk K

2. n a GIMMER III.6.5. juːtɛˈg K, uːtɛg K

ewt *n* a NEWT IV.9.8. ɹuːt Bd, ɹuːʔ Bd, ɛʊt C

exhausted *adj You might say: Look, I've carried this heavy bag all that distance; I must have a rest, I'm absolutely ....* VI.13.8. ɪgzɔːstɪd Ess Brk, ɛgzhɔːstɪd Mon. ⇒ **beat, beaten, beazled, beggared, beggared up, bellowsed up, blethered,** *buggared* ⇒ **buggered,** *buggared up* ⇒ **buggered up, buggered, buggered up, clammed,** *dead* **beat, dog-tired, done, done for, done in, done off, done out, done** *right* **in, done up, duggled, fagged, fagged out,** *fair* **whacked, faldered,** *fed* **up, finished, finished off, flagged out, flopped out, gone in, harrowed, harrowed** *to dead,* **harrowed** *to death,* **jaded, jaded out, jiggered, jiggered out, jiggered up, jossed up, knocked, knocked out, knocked up, lagged out, maggled, mucked, paggered, paid out, paid** *to the world,* **pegged out, played out, pole-fagged, pootled, razzored,** *run down,* **shot at, shotted, spunned up, spun out, tewed out, through, tired, tired out, tired** *to death,* **useless, weared out, whacked, wore out, worn out**

expand *vi* to WAX, referring to the moon VII.6.5(a). *-ing* ɪkspɛndɪn Sr

extension *n* an END-BOARD of a cart I.10.4. ɪkstɛnʃən Bk

extra *adv* VERY VIII.3.2. ɛkstɹɪ Sf

extra tailboard *n* an END-BOARD of a cart I.10.4. ɛkstɹə teːᵊlboˈəd Ch, ɛkstɹə teɪᵊɫbɔːᵊd Hu

eye *1. n* the CORE of a boil VI.11.7. aɪ Sa D, əɪ Mon

2. n a HALO round the moon VII.6.4. aɪ Co

3. n **give eye to, keep an eye on, keep your eye on** LOOK AFTER VIII.1.23. **give eye to** gɪv əɪ tə Sx; **keep an eye on** kiːp ə aɪ ɔn La; **keep your eye on** kiːp jəɹ ɑˈɪ ɒn Lei, kiːp jəɹ əɪj ɒn Mon

eye-and-stalk *vt* to ⟶ TOP-AND-TAIL gooseberries V.7.23. əɪŋstʊk Wo

eye-blinkers *npl* BLINKERS covering the eyes of a cart-horse I.5.2. aɪblɪŋkəz Nth, ɔɪblɪŋkəz Ess

eyebrees *npl* EYEBROWS VI.3.9. iːbɹiːz Y

eyebrows *npl What do you call these [indicate the eyebrows]?* VI.3.9. Eng. ⇒ **eyebrees, eyelashes, hoods**

eye-flop *n* a blinker, ⟵ BLINKERS covering the eyes of a cart-horse I.5.2. aɪfɫɒp D

eye-hook *n* the vertical BAR or CHAIN of a crane over a domestic fire V.3.5(b). aɪhuːk Nb

eyelashes *npl* EYEBROWS VI.3.9. iːlaʃɪz Y, iːlaʃəz Y*[rare]*, aɪlaʃɪz Y, ɑˈɪlæʃɪz Nf, ɔɪlæʃɪz Ess

eye-mop *n* a blinker, ⟵ BLINKERS covering the eyes of a cart-horse I.5.2. aɪmɒp D

eye-tag *n* the TAG of a boot-lace VI.14.26. aɪtæg So *[queried SBM]*

eye-teeth *npl* MOLARS VI.5.7. aɪtiːθ Nb Du We Db, ɑɪtiːθ Y Lei K, ɒɪtiːθ K, ɒɪteːθ Ha, ɔɪtiːθ Sf Sx, hɔɪtɪθ Ha, əɪtiːθ Mon Brk

eye-wings *npl* BLINKERS covering the eyes of a cart-horse I.5.2. ʌɪˈwɪŋz Nf

F

fa *n* FATHER VIII.1.1(a). faː Nf, faːə Nf

face *n* **the face of** a resemblance to someone, ⇐ he RESEMBLES VIII.1.9. ðə fiːᵊs ɒv Cu

face-ache *n* TOOTHACHE VI.5.8. feɪseɪk Nf, feɪseɪk Ess, fæɪsæɪk K

face in *vtphr* to TRIM hedges IV.2.3. feɪs ... ɪn Ess

fade *vi* to WANE, referring to the moon VII.6.5(b). *3prsg* feːdz Ch, feɪd Wa, *-ing* feɪdɪn L

fade away *viphr* to WANE, referring to the moon VII.6.5(b). *-ing* feɪdɪn əweɪ Bk, *-ing* vaɪdn əweː Ha

fady *adj* **get fady** to SPOIL, referring to meat or fish V.7.10. gɪt veːdi D, gɪd veːdi D

fag *v* to cut corn with a sickle, ⇐ BILLHOOK IV.2.6. *prppl* fagɪn O

fagged *adj* EXHAUSTED, describing a tired person VI.13.8. fægd Ess, fagd L

fagged out *adj* EXHAUSTED, describing a tired person VI.13.8. fɛgd ɛut K, fɛgd ɛət K, vɛgd æʏt D, fɛgd aut So, fɛgd əut So Sx, fægd ɛut Hu Nf Sf Ess Brk, fægd æʏt So Co, fægd æut So, fægd aːt Y, fægd aut So, fægd əut Nf, vægd əut W, fagd ɛat Y, fagd ɛut Ch Wo Nth Ess, fagd ɛuʔ Bk, fad ɛuʔ Bk*[queried error for* fagd *EMBM]*, fagd ɒʏt D, fagd æut St Wa Ha, fagd æʊd W, fagd æˑət La, fagd aːt St, fagd aɪt Ch, fagd aut Y Ch St, fagd ɒut W, fagd uːt Cu Y L, fagd əut Y Mon Do

fagging-hook *1. n* a BILLHOOK IV.2.6. fæginhʊk Brk, fæginʊk Wo Sr, væginʊk Brk
2. n a sickle for cutting corn. væginʊk Brk, faginʊk O, vaginʊk W

faggot(s) *n* KINDLING-*WOOD* V.4.2.
no -s: fægɪt Nf, fækʌt So, fakət Co D, fagət Hrt*[large bundle]*
-s: fɛgəts Ess MxL, fæˑgəʔs Hrt
pl: fɛgɪts K, vɛgəts D, fægɪts K Sx*[old]*, vægɪts Brk, vægəts Brk, fakəts D

faggoty-bill *n* a BILLHOOK IV.2.6. fakətɪbɪɫ Gl

fag-hook *n* a BILLHOOK IV.2.6. fɛgʊk Sr*[for trimming]* Sx, vagʊk W Ha*[for trimming x1]*

fag(s) *n* the layer of turf overlying PEAT IV.4.3.
sg: vɛg D
-s: vɛgz D*['turfs of peat' x1]*, vagz D

fags *npl* TICKS on sheep IV.8.3. fagz Nt L

fag up *vphr* to use a BILLHOOK IV.2.6. *prppl* fagɪn ʊp Wa

fail *vi* **fail for calve, fail for calving** to show signs of calving, ⇐ SHOWS SIGNS OF CALVING III.1.12. *3prprogsg* feːlɪn fə kɔːv La; *3prprogsg* feːlɪn fə kɔːvɪn La

faint *vi* *Sometimes there are so many people in a room and it gets so hot, that you think you are going to ....* VI.13.7. Eng. ⇒ cave over, collapse, *come over on a faint, dizzy, drop in a* ruck, faint away, faint off, faint over, fainty, flop out, giddy, go off, groggy, pass out, sile away, stifle, swarf, swimmy, swimy, swoon, tawm over, topple over, tumble over, type over, walt over, warm away

faint away *viphr* to FAINT VI.13.7. fɛnt əwæɪ Gl, feɪnt əweɪ L, fɛˑənt əweːˑə L

faint off *viphr* to FAINT VI.13.7. feɪnt ɒf Lei

faint over *viphr* to FAINT VI.13.7. fiːnt ouə St

fainty *1. adj* **go fainty** to SPOIL, referring to meat or fish V.7.10. gʊ fɛˑənti L
2. adj WEAK, describing a person who has been ill VI.13.2. feːɪnti Mon
3. vi to FAINT VI.13.7. feɪnti Co
4. ?adj feeling faint. fæɪnti W Sr Sx

fair *1. n* a local FESTIVAL or holiday VII.4.11. fɪə L Nf, feˑə Sa Hrt, feˑəɪ We La, feːɪəˡ He, fɛː We, feːɹ Cu, fɛˡː So W D Ha, veˡː D, feɪəˡ Sr, vɛɪəˡ Gl, fɛə Nb Cu We La Y Wa L Nf Sf MxL Sr, *pl* fɛəz Du Ess, fɛər Cu, fɛəˡ L K, fɛəɪ La Y He, fɛəˡ Sa Mon Sr K Ha, fɛəˡː He Co D Sx, vɛəˡː D, fæɪəˡ Gl, fɜˡːɹ La, fəː-əˡ Sa; **club fair*** klʌb feɪəˡ Sr; **dead man's fair** dɛd manz feːəˡ Sa*[November]*; **fair friday** veˡː vɹaːdi D; **goosey fair** gʏːzi vɛəˡː D; **horse fair** ɔˡːʂ feːəˡ Sa; **St Giles' fair** snt dʒaɪɫzɪz fɛəˡ O; **sheep fair** ʃiːp feəˡ Ha; **wool fair** wʊl feːəˡ Sa
2. adv VERY VIII.3.2. veˑɹ (+V) Y, fɛə Du Y

fairly *adv* VERY VIII.3.2. fɛəlɪ Y

fake *vi* to hurt, ⇐ HURTS VI.13.3(a). feːk Y

fake up *vtphr* to STOCK III.3.6. *-ing* feɪkɪn ... ʌp K *[marked u.r. SBM]*

faldered *adj* EXHAUSTED, describing a tired person VI.13.8. faldəd Y

fall *1. n* a SLOPE IV.1.10. fɔːɫ Ess, fɔu Ess *[marked ir.r. EMBM]*
2. n the FLAP at the front of old-fashioned trousers VI.14.16. fɔːl St, *pl* fɔːlz L
3. n AUTUMN VII.3.7. faːɫ Mon Gl, vaːɫ D, fɔːl La Y Wa O*[old]* L Nth*[old and rare]*, fɔːɫ Nth Bk Bd Ess So*[old x1]* W Co Do Ha, vɔːɫ So*[old x1]* W Co D, fɔəl L; **fall of the leaf** fɔːl əv ðə liːf K, fɔːl ə ðə liːf L Sf Ess, fɔːᵊɫ ə ðə liːᵊf Sf, fɔːl ə ðə lɪˑəf L, fɔːl ə t lɪˑəf Y L; **fall of the leaves** fɔːl ə ðə lɪˑəvz; **fall of the year** vaːɫ ə ðə ɪəˡ Gl, fɔːl

ə ðə jɪə Wa L Bd[old], fɔːl ə ðə jɪˈəɹ L, fɔːl əv ðə jɪəᴶ K, fɔːl ə t ɪˈə Y, fɔːl ə ðə jəᵗ Ha, vɔːl ə ðə jəᵗː So, fɔːl ə ðə jəːᵗː Gl So W Do, vɔːɫ ə ðə jəᵗː So W D

4. vi to WANE, referring to the moon VII.6.5(b). -*ing* fɔːɪn Ch; **on the fall** ɔn ðə fɔˈəl L

fall-downs *npl* FLAPs at the front of old-fashioned trousers. fɔːɫdæɤnz Co

fallen *adj* SAD, describing bread or pastry that has not risen V.6.12. fan Nb

faller *n* the SHUTTING-POST of a gate IV.3.4. faːɫəᵗ Gl

fall-front *n* the FLAP at the front of old-fashioned trousers VI.14.16. fɔːlfɹɒnt K, fɔːɫfɹʌnt Ess, fɔːlfɹʊnt Y

falling-post *n* the SHUTTING-POST of a gate IV.3.4. vaːɫɪnpɔːs D, faːlɪnpʊʊst Wo, faːɫɪnpoːst Wo, faːlɪnpoːs He Wo Mon, faːlɪnpoːus Mon, fɔːlɪnpɒst Y, vɔːlɪnpoːst So, vɔːlɪnpoːst D, vɔːlənpoːs D, fɔːlɪnpost Wa, fɔːlɪnpoːst Sa He, vɔːlɪnpoːst W, vɔːlɪnpoːst So W, vɔːlɪnpoːst So, fɔːlɪnpoːst Wo, vɔːɫɪnpoːst W Do, fɔːlɪnpoːs He, fɔːlɪnpoʊst Wa So, vɔːlɪnpoust So, vɔːɫɪnpoːəst So Do, vɔːɫɪnpwʊst Gl, vɔːɫənpuːst D

falling-stoop *n* the SHUTTING-POST of a gate IV.3.4. fɔːɪnstuːp Cu, fɔːənstuːp We

fall over *viphr* to OVERTURN, referring to a cart I.11.5. fɔːl ɔvə L

fallow-ground *1. n* FALLOW-LAND II.1.1. væləᵗːgɹævn So, væɫəᵗːgɹæʊn So, væloʊgɹəʊn So, væɫəᵗgɹəʊn Sx, faləgɹɛːᵊn Wa, faɫəgɹɒʊn W, vaɫəᵗːgɹəʊn Do, fɒləgɹaʊnd Sa, fɒɫəᴶgɹɛʊn Sr

2. n land cleared for cultivation. fæləgɹɛʊnd Ess

fallowing *n* FALLOW-LAND II.1.1. vɒɫəɹɪn K

fallow-land *1. n What do you call the land that you have ploughed but that you leave unsown for some time?* II.1.1. fæləlɛnd Ess, fæloːlænd Sa, fæləlænd He Ess, fæləˈlænd Brk, væɫəᴶlæˈn Brk, fæloʊland So, fæɫəlaːnd Mon, faloʊlæːnd Man, faloland Sa, faləland La Y Sa Wo, vaɫəᵗːɫaːn W, fɒləlɛᵊn Man, fɒləlænd Wo Hrt Ess Brk, fɒləᵗlænd Wo K, fɒləᵗlæn Wo, fɒɫəᴶlænd Sr

2. n land cleared for cultivation. fæləlænd Ess

⇒ **bare-fallow(s), bare-faugh, barren-field, barren-ground, barren-land, bastard-fallow, dead-fallow(s), dead-land, fallow(s), fallow-ground, fallowing, fallow-piece, fare-fallow, furrow-land, groot, groot-land, half-fallow, lea(s), lea-ground, long-fallow, long-summer-land, long-summer-leas, pin-fallow, ploughed-fallows, plough-ground, stale-furrow, summer-fallow(s), summer-fallowing, summer-land, summer-lea, summer's-fallow, summer-till, summer-tilling, summer-working, through-fallow, through-faugh**

fallow-piece *n* FALLOW-LAND II.1.1. fɒləpiːs Wo

fallow(s) *n* FALLOW-LAND II.1.1.

no -s: fæɫʌʊ MxL, fæloʊ K, væloʊ Ha, fæloː He, fæloʊ So, fælə Sf Ess MxL Sr, væləɹ Brk, fæloʊ Sr Sx, fæloʊ So, fæɫəᵗ He Mon, vælə Gl Sr, faloˑ Sa, faloʊ St He Mon So, falə Nb Cu Du We La Y Ch Db Sa St Gl O L Lei Nth Nf Bk, valə Gl So Ha, faləᴷ Nb, faləᵗ Bk, valəᵗː So, faɫə O Lei K Co, vaɫə W Co D, vaɫəᵗ Gl, faɫəᵗː Ha, vaɫəᵗː W D Do Ha, faɹə Du, fɒlə Du C, fɒlo He, fɒloʊ St, fɒlə Db St Wo Wa Lei Nth Hu Bk Bd Hrt, vɒlə Brk, fɒləᴶ K, fɒləᵗ Wo Nth Bk, vɒlɒʊ Sx, fɒɫʊ Gl, fɒɫə He Lei Ess, vɒɫəᴶ K, fɒɫəᵗ He Gl, vɒɫəᵗ Sx, fɔlə Wo Wa O C Hrt Ess

-s: fæloːʊz Brk, faləs We L, faləz La Y Nt L R Ha, vaɫəz W, fɒləz Lei R Nth

pl: faləz Gl, faləᵗz O, fɔləz O

fall to *imp* HELP YOURSELVES!, said to invite visitors to eat V.8.13. vɔːɫ tʏ So

fall-tree *1. n* the CURB-STONE in a cow-house I.3.9. fɔːltɹiː Y, fɔːtɹiː La

2. n a wooden curb-stone. fɔːltɹiː Y

false *adj* RESTIVE, describing a horse III.5.6. faːɫs He, fɒls Sa, fɒɫs O, fɔːls Sa, fɔːɫs So Do

false-board *n* an END-BOARD of a cart I.10.4. fɔːlsboˈəd Nth, vɔːɫsbuːɽd̥ D

false frame *n* a CART-FRAME I.10.6. fɒls fɹeɪm Nf

false link *n* a sliding RING to which a tether is attached in a cow-house I.3.5. fals lɪŋk Nf

false-rave *n* an END-BOARD of a cart I.10.4. *pl* fɒɫsɹeːvz W

false teat *n* a BLIND TEAT III.2.7. fɒɫs tɪt Ess, vɔːɫs tɛt W

famished *1. adj* HUNGRY VI.13.9. fæmɪʃt Ess, famɪʃt Cu Du Y[old x1] Ch L

2. adj very THIRSTY VI.13.10. fæmɪʃt Nf

famishing *adj* HUNGRY VI.13.9. famɪʃɪn Y

fammelled *adj* HUNGRY VI.13.9. famɫd O[old x1]

fancy-apron *n* a decorative APRON V.11.2(b). fɛnsɪ-ɛɪpɹɪ̩n Ess, fɛnsɪ-ɛɪpəᵗːɽn̩ Sx, fɛnsɛpəᵗːn̩ Sr, fænsɪ-æɪpɹən K, fansɪ eːpʁən Nb, *pl* fansɪ-eːpəᵗːn̩z Co, fansɪ-ɛɪpɹən St L

fancy bonnet *n* a woman's lace-trimmed BONNET worn indoors VI.14.1. fansɪ bɒnɪt O

fancy-pinner *n* a decorative APRON V.11.2(b). fansɪpɪnə Nt

fang *1. n* a PRONG of a fork I.7.10. *pl* faŋz Ch

2. n a ROOT of a tree IV.12.1. *pl* faŋz L[old] [*BM note seems to imply some kind of collective*]

fare *1. n* a PIGLET III.8.2. vɪəᵗː Co D, vjɛᵗː Co, *pl* vɛəᵗːz̩ Co

2. n a LITTER of piglets III.8.3. vjɛᵗː Co, fɛə Sf Ess, vɛəᵗː Do

3. vi to FARROW, describing a pig giving birth to piglets III.8.10. vɪəᵗː D, vɛːɽ Do, vɛᵗː Do, vjɛᵗː

Co, fɛə Sf, fæˡ K, væɽ So, væˡ: So, vaˡ: So Ha, fɑːɽ Sr, *prppladj* vɑːɽɪn So

fare down *viphr* to FARROW, describing a pig giving birth to piglets III.8.10. fæˡˑ dəʊn K, væˡ: dæʊn So, vaˡ: dæʊn So, veːɽ dəʊn Do, vɛˡ: dæʊn Do, vɛˡ: d̯æʊn W, vɛˡ: dəʊn Do, fɑːɽ dɛʊn Sx, faˡ:ɽ dɛʊn Sr Sx, faˡ:ɽ d̯ɛʊn Sr

fare-fallow *n* FALLOW-LAND II.1.1. ˈfɛəˈfælɐ K *[queried for bare- SBM]*

fares *npl* the HOOF-MARKS of a horse IV.3.10. fɛːz Ch St

far-horse *1. n When you have two horses pulling a wagon side by side, how do you distinguish them?* I.6.4(b)*[the righthand horse].* faˑɹɑɹs Y, faɹɒs Y, faːɹɒs Y Wo Bd, faːɹɔs Du L, faːɹɔːs Db L, faːɹɔˡ:ʂ Sa, faːɹɔəˡs La, faᴿːhɒᴿːs Nb, faᴿːhɔᴿːs Nb, faˡːɹɒs La, faˡːɽaˡːʂ Sa So W, vaˡːɽaˡ:ʂ W, vaˡːɽɒs W, faˡːɔˡːʂ Sa, faˡːɽɔˡːʂ Sa. ⟹ **farside, farside-horse, farthermost-horse, from-horse, furrow-horse, furrowside-horse, further-horse, gee-back, off, off-horse, offside, offside-horse, offside-tit, off-tit, offward-horse, offward-side, outside-horse, righthand-horse, shaft-horse, shortline-horse**

*2. *n* the FURROW-HORSE of a ploughing team II.3.4(a). faːɹɒs Y *[taken as **furrow-horse** NBM, but compare **farside-horse**]*

faring *n* a LITTER of piglets III.8.3. vɛːɽən Do

farm *1. n* a FARMSTEAD I.1.2. fɛəˡm La, fæːm C, fæˡːm La, faːm Cu We Y Ch Db Sa St Wa Mon Lei Nth Sf Bk Ess, faɹm Y He, faˡːm La, faˡːm Sa He Wo Wa Mon Gl Bd So Do, vaˡːm Gl So D Do Ha, *pl* faɹmz O, faˡm O Ha, faːm Ch St Wo Hrt Ess Sr K, faˡːm Brk, faˡːm Wo Sx, vaˡːm D, fɜˡːɹm La, fəˡːm Wo, *pl* fəˡːɽəmz Gl

2. *n* the VULVA of a cow III.2.3. faːm Nt

farm-building *n* a FARMSTEAD I.1.2. faˡːmbɪʊdɪn Sr

farm-buildings *npl* a FARMSTEAD I.1.2. fæˑmbɪldəns Man, faːmbɪldɪnz StL, faːmbɪʊdnz Ess, faˡːmbɪɫdɪnz Wa So, faːmbɪɫdɪnz K, faːmbɪʊɫdɪnz Ess, faːmbɪʊdɪnz Ess, faˡːmbɪʊɫdɪnz Brk K, faˡːmbɪʊɫdɪnz Sx, faˡːmbɪʊdɪnz Sr Sx, faːəˡɽmbɪʊɫdɪnz Sr, faˡːˈəˡɽmbɪʊdɪnz Sr

farmcart *n [Show a picture of a (tipping) farmcart.] What do you call this?* I.9.3. faːmkaːt Y Nth Ess, faːmkaːʔ Bd, faːmkaˑɹt Y, faˡːmkaˡːɽ Mon, faːmkaːt Nf Ess, *pl* faːmkaːʔs Hrt, faˡːɽmkaˡːɽʈ Sx. ⟹ **box-cart, butt, butt-cart, car, cart, coup-cart, dung-cart, dung-putt, hay-cart, long-cart, luggage-cart, manure-cart, muck-cart, putt, putt-cart, rade-cart, scotch-cart, shandry, shit-cart, stiff-cart, tip-cart, tip-tumbler, trolley, truck,** *tumble* ⟹ **tumbril,** *tumble-cart* ⟹ **tumbril-cart, tumbler, tumbril, tumbril-cart**

farmer-man *n* a FARM-LABOURER I.2.4. fɛˑəməman Y

farmer's friend *n* STRING used to tie up a grain-sack I.7.3. faːməzfɹɛnd Y *[apparently trade name]*

farmer's glory *n* STRING used to tie up a grain-sack I.7.3. faɹməɹz gloːɹɪ He *[apparently trade name]*

farmer's-man *n* a FARM-LABOURER I.2.4. faːməzmæn Y, faːməzman Y, faˡːməzman Y

farm-garth *n* a FARMYARD I.1.3. faᴿːmgaᴿːθ Nb

farm-hand *n* a FARM-LABOURER I.2.4. faɹmand He, faːmænd Sf, faːmand Y, faˡːmand Bk, faːmaːnd Lei, faːmhænd MxL, faːmænd MxL Sr; **general farm-hand** dʒɛnɹəɫ faˡːmand Bk

farmhouse *n* a FARMSTEAD I.1.2. fɛˑəmæˑəs Y, faːmhɛʊs Nf, faːmaɪs Ch, faːmaʊs Y, faˡːmɛʊs Sa, faˡːmæʏs So Co, vaˡːmæʏs D, vaˡːmæʏz Co, faˡːmæʊs So Ha, vaˡːmæʊs W Do Ha, faˡːmaʊs Sa So, vaˡːməʊs W Do, *pl* faɽmaʊzɪz O, *pl* faɽməʊzɪz O, faːmhɛʊs Nf, faːmɛʊs Nf, faːmhɛʊs Nf, faːmaɪs St, faːmhəʊs Nf, vaˡːmœʏs D, vaˡːmæʏz Co; **farmhouse and buildings** faːmhɛʊs ən bɪɫdnz Sf

farmhouse-yard *n* a FARMYARD I.1.3. faːmuːsjaːd Y

farm-labourer *n What do you call the man who is put on to any sort of task on a farm? [before April 1953: ... any task and does general work on a farm]* I.2.4. fæˡːmlɛɪbəɹə O, faːmleːbəɹə Y Db, faːmleːbɹə Y Ch Sa Mon Nt, faːmleɪbəɹə Bk Hrt, faːmleːbəɹə We La Y, faːmlɛɪbəɹə Wa Nth Hu Ess, faːmlɛɪbɹə St R Nf Ess, faːmlɛəbəɹə Y, faːmleˑəbɹə L, faˡːmleːbəɹəˡ La, faˡːmleːbɹəˡ Sa vaˡːmɫeːbɽəˡ: Ha, faˡːmlɛɪbəɹəˡ Bk, faˡːmlɛɪbəɽəˡ: So, faˡːmlɛɪbəˡ: So, faˡːmlɛɪbɽə So, faˡːmlɛɪbɽəˡ: So, faːmlɛɪbɹə Nf Sr, faːmlɛɪbɹə St, faːmlæɪbɹə Hrt, vaːɽmleɪbɽ̩ Sx, *pl* faˡːmlɛɪbɹ̩z Sr, faˡːɽmlɛɪbɽ̩ Sx, faˡːɽmlɛɪbɹə Sr Sx, faˡːɽmlɛɪbɹəˡ Sx, *pl* faˡːmlɛɪbɹəˡz Sr, fəˡːmleːbɹəˡ Gl; **all-round farm-labourer** ɔːlɹɛʊn faːmlɛɪbəɹə Hu. ⟹ **agricultural labourer, all-rounder, all-round farm-hand,** *all-round* **farm-labourer, all-round labourer, all-round man, all-works, bullocky, casual labourer, casual man, day-man, daytalman, daytal workman, farmer-man, farmer's-man, farm-hand, farm-man, farm-servant, farm-souk, farm-worker,** *general* **farm-hand,** *general* **farm-worker,** *general* **knockabout,** *general* **labbet,** *general* **labourer,** *general* **man,** *general* **worker,** *general* **workman, handy-labourer, handy-man, hind, hobny-man, husband-man, jack-of-all-trades, job-about, jobbing-man, job-man, job-workman, knockabout, labbet, labourer, labouring-man, lackey, loose-man, man, man-of-all-jobs, odd-bloke, odd-job-man,**

odd-man, oddy, ordinary labourer, piece-worker, regular-man, scut, servant-man, slinger, spade-hind, spade-man, spades-man, stand-to-work-man, strapper, tommy-aught, workman, yob; ⇒ also chance-work man

farm-man *n* a FARM-LABOURER I.2.4. faːmman He, faːmman Cu Y Nt, faːmmæˑn Ess

farm-place *n* a FARMSTEAD I.1.2. faːmplɛəs Y

farm-premises *npl* a FARMSTEAD I.1.2. faˈmprɛmɪsɪz Nf

farm-servant *n* a FARM-LABOURER I.2.4. faːmsaɹvənt Y, faːmsaːvnt Y

farm-souk *n* a FARM-LABOURER I.2.4. faːmsaʊk Cu

farm-speckles *n* FRECKLES VI.11.1. faːmspɛkəlz Y

farm-spot *n* a FARMSTEAD I.1.2. faːmspɒt Y

farmstead *n [Show an aerial photograph of a farmstead and surrounding fields.] What do you call this?* I.1.2. fæːmsteɪd Du, fæˑ꞉msted O, fæˑ꞉mstɛd La, fæəˑmstɛd Ha, faːmstiːd Nb Cu Du We, faːmstɪd Cu Db Lei Hrt Ess, faʶːmstiːd Du, faʶːmstɪd Nb, faˤːmstɪd O, faːmstɪəd Y Nt L, faˑːmstɪəd La, faːmstɛd La Y Ch Db Wo Wa Nt L Nth Hu Sf Ess*[big]*, faˑːmstɛd La Db, faˤːmstɛd O Nth Bk, vaˤːmstɛd Gl, faːmstəd St Nt Ess, faːmstəɪd Y, fɑːmstɪd Ess K, fɑˑːmstɪd K, fɑˤːmstɪd Brk Sx, fɑːmstɛd Ess MxL Sr K, fɑˑːmstɛd Sr, fɑˈəꭇmstiːd Brk, fɜˑːmstɛd La, fəˤːmsted Gl. ⇒ **buildings, farm, farm-building, farm-buildings, farmhouse, farmhouse** *and buildings*, **farm-place, farm premises, farm-spot, farm-steading, home-farm, homestead, house, house** *and buildings*, **living-house, onstead, place, steading**

farm-steading *n* a FARMSTEAD I.1.2. faːrmstɛdɪn Cu

farm-street *n* a FARMYARD I.1.3. fæːmstʰriːt Man

farm-worker *n* a FARM-LABOURER I.2.4. faːmwəːkə St; **general farm-worker** dʒɛnɹəl faːmwəːkə Db, dʒənɹəl faˑːmwəːkə We

farmyard *1. n [Show an aerial photograph of a farmstead and surrounding fields.] What do you call this?* I.1.3. fɛˑəmjɛˑəd Y, fɛˑəmjad Y, fæˑːmjæˑd La O, fæˑːmjaˑːɹd La, fæːmjæːd Du C, fæˤːmjæˤːd O, fæəˑmjɑːəˑd Ha, faːmjæːd Du, faːmjaːd Cu Du We La Y Ch Db Sa St Wa Mon Nt L Lei R Nth Hu Nf Sf Bk Bd Hrt Ess, faːrmjaːrd Cu, faʶːmjeːʶd Nb, faʶːmjaʶːd Nb Du, faːmjaˑd NwY L, faːꭇmjaːd Y, faˑːmjaˑːd We La Db L, faˤːmjaˤːd Sa He Wa Mon Gl O Bk Bd So W Co, vaˤːmjaˤːd Gl W, faːmjaːd Nf, faˤːmjaˤːd Sa He Wo, fɑːmjaːd Nf, fɑːmjaːd Ch St Wo Nf Hrt Ess MxL Sr K, fɑˑːmjaːd K, fɑˑːmjaˑːd Brk K, faːmjaːˤd Sr, faˤːmjaˤːd Wo O Brk Sr Ha Sx, fɑˑːmjəˑːd K, faˤːmjəˤːd He, fɜˑːꭇmjɔˑːꭇd La, fɜˑːꭇmjɜˑːꭇd La, fəˤːmjəˤːd Gl. ⇒ **back-court, back-yard, barton, bullock-yard, cattle-yard,** close, court, courtyard, cow-yard, crew-yard, enclosure-yard, farm-garth, farmhouse-yard, farm-street, fold, folder, fold-yard, house-yard, laying-yard, muck-yard, open-yard, stock-yard, stone-yard, yard, yards

2. n the STRAW-YARD of a farm I.1.9. faːmjaːd Nth, faˤːmjaˤːd̩ Bk, fɑˑːmjɑˑːd Brk

far off *adv* **none so far off, not far off** ALMOST VII.7.9. **none so far off** nʊən sə faːꭇ ɒf Y; **not far off** nat faˑ꞉ ɔf La, nə fəːꭇ ɔf Ch

farrow *1. vi And when she [i.e. a sow] is going to have young ones, you say she is going ....* III.8.10. Eng exc. Cu Nth Hu C Sf MxL Sr Do. ⇒ *after pigging*, **come down, drop** *a litter*, **fare, farrow down,** *farrowing*, **farrowing down, farthe,** *for pig*, **furrow,** *going down, going to fare, going to fare down, going to farrow, going to farrow down, going to litter, going to pig, has come to farrowing, have a litter, have her pigs, have pigs, hoo's going to pig, in fare, in farrow, in litter, in pig, is a-dropping, is coming down* ⇒ **come down,** *is due to pig, is faring down* ⇒ **fare down,** *is farrowing, is going to fare, is going to farrow, is going to* **farrow down,** *is going to pig, is in fare, is in farrow,* **kindle, pig, pig down,** *pigging, she's farrowing, she's in farrow, she's in pig, to* **farrow,** *to* **farrow down,** *to* **litter,** *to* **pig,** *to* **pig down, vally**

2. n a LITTER of piglets III.8.3. fæꭇɪ Wo Gl, væꭇɪ Mon Gl, væꭇiː He, fæꭇɒʊ Sx, fæꭇoː Mon, fæꭇɪə Sf K, faꭇɪ Sa St Wo Wa, vaꭇɪ Gl, faꭇə Ha, vaꭇə D Ha

3. vi to KINDLE, describing a rabbit doe giving birth to young III.13.14. fɛꭇɪ Cu, fəꭇɪ Cu We La Y, fəꭇə Cu Y

farrow down *viphr* to FARROW, describing a pig giving birth to piglets III.8.10. fæꭇɪ dɛʊn Ess, fæꭇə dæʊn Sr, fæꭇɒʊ dɛʊn Sx, faꭇɪ dɛʊn O, vaꭇɪ dœʏn D, vaꭇɪ dæʏn Co, vaꭇə dæʏn Co, vaꭇɪ dæʊn So, vaꭇə dæʊn W Ha, faꭇə dæʊn Ha, faˤꭇɒʊ dɛʊn Sx

farside *1. n* the FAR-HORSE of a pair pulling a wagon I.6.4(b). faːsaɪd We L, faːsɔˑꭇd L, faʶːsɛɪd Nb, faʶːsaɪd Nb, faˑˑsaˑɪd L, faˤːʂɔɪd Wa, fəˤːʂɔɪd O, fəˤːʂʌɣd O

2. n the FURROW-HORSE of a ploughing team II.3.4(a). faʶːsɛɪd Nb, fəˤːsʌɣd O, fəˤːsɔɪd Gl O

farside-horse *1. n* the FAR-HORSE of a pair pulling a wagon I.6.4(b). fæˑːsaɪdɔˑːs La, faːsaɪdhɒs Du, faːsaːdɒs Y, faːsaɪdɒs Cu Y, faːsaɪdɒs Y Nt L, faːsaɪdɔːs Cu, faːsaɪdɔːs Ch, faʶːsɛɪdhɒˤːs Nb, faʶːsɛɪdhɒʶːs Nb, faˑꭇsaɪdɔːs La, faˑꭇsaɪdɔˑːs We La Y, faːꭇsaɪdɒs Y, faˤːʂaɪdɒs Gl, faˑꭇʂɔɪdaꭇʂ O, fəˤːʂɔɪdɒs Wa, fəˤːʂɔɪdɔˤːʂ Gl

2. n the FURROW-HORSE of a ploughing team

II.3.4(a). faˑᴵsaɪdɔˑᴵːs La, faːsaɪdɒs Y, faːsaɪdɒɹs Y, faːsaɪdhɔᵏːs Nb, faˑᴵːsaɪdɔˑᴵːs La, fɑˑɾsɔɪdɑɾʂ O, fətːsɔɪdɔtːʂ Wa, vətːzʌɪdɒs Gl

fart 1. n the ARSE VI.9.2. faᵗːt̠ Co

2. vi **fart, fart off, fart wind** to BREAK *WIND* VI.13.16. Eng

farth n a LITTER of piglets III.8.3. faˑᴵːθ La, vatːθ So, vatːf So, faːəθ La

farthe vi to FARROW, describing a pig giving birth to piglets III.8.10. faˑᴵːð La

farthermost-horse n the FAR-HORSE of a pair pulling a wagon I.6.4(b). fatːðəmʊsatːʂ Wo

farthings npl A halfpenny is worth two .... VII.7.2. Eng. ⇒ **dollies,** *farthing*

far-welted adj OVERTURNED, describing a sheep on its back unable to get up III.7.4. faːwɛltɪd L, faˑᴵːwɛlʔɪd L, faˑᴵ·wɛltɪd L

fash 1.1. v to TOP AND TAIL swedes II.4.3. faʃ La Ch

1.2. vt to top and tail swedes. faʃ Ch

2. v to CLEAR grass at the edges of a field II.9.5. -*ing* faʃɪn La

fast-board n an END-BOARD of a cart I.10.4. faːstbɔə K

fasten vt to SHUT a door IX.2.8. vasn Co

fastener n the SHUTTING-POST of a gate IV.3.4. fæˑsnətː So

fastening-pen* n a FASTING-CHAMBER III.11.3. faːsnɪn-pɛn Bd [taken as error for **fasting-pen** *EMBM*]

fastening-post 1. n a TETHERING-STAKE in a cow-house I.3.3. fɛsnɪnpʊəst Y

2. n the SHUTTING-POST of a gate IV.3.4. fæsnɪnpʊust Ha, fæsnɪnpwʊst Brk, fasnənpøːst Nb, fasənɪnpɒst Y, fasnɪnpʊst Gl, fasənɪnpʊəs Y, faːsnɪnpʌust Hrt, faːsɪnɪnpʌus Ess, faːsnɪnpoːst So, faːsnɪnpoːs Mon, faːsnɪnpoust O Nth Bk, faːsnɪnpoːʊᵊst Gl, faːsnɪnpoːʊs Gl, vaːsnɪnpoːʊs Gl, faːsnənpʊst Sf, fɑːsn̩ɪnpʊust Sr, fɑːsnɪnpʊust Brk, fɑːsnɪnpɒus Sx

fastening-rod n a movable horizontal rod stretching between the shafts of a cart, fixing them to the cart-body and stopping the cart from tipping, ⇐ ROD/PIN I.10.3. faːsnɪnɾɒd W

fastening-stoop n the SHUTTING-POST of a gate IV.3.4. fasnɪnstɛʊp Db, fasənɪnstɔʊp Y, fasənɪnstuːp La, fasnɪnstʊuːp La

fastening-stub n the SHUTTING-POST of a gate IV.3.4. fasnɪnstʊb· La

fastening-stump n the SHUTTING-POST of a gate IV.3.4. fasnɪnstʊmp Db

faster-house n a FASTING-CHAMBER III.11.3. fastəɹuːs Y

fast-house n a FASTING-CHAMBER III.11.3. fastuːs Y

fasting-chamber n What place does the butcher put them before killing? III.11.3. fæstɪntʃæɪmbəᵗ Brk. ⇒ **box, cattle-pen, clam-house, clamming-hole, clamming-house, clamming-pen, clamming-yard, clam-pen, drying-pen, fastening-pen, faster-house, fast-house, fasting-house, fasting-pen, fasting-shed, fasting-stall,** *fold, horse-box,* **house, hovel, hunger-house, hunger-hull, hungering-house, hungering-pen, hunger-shed, killing-house, lair, loose-box,** *paddock,* **pen, penthouse, pine-hole, pine-house, pining-fold, pining-hole, pining-house, pining-pen, pound, shambles, shed, sheep's-house, shippon, slaughterhouse, slaughtering-pen, stall, starving-pen, starving-place, store-house, yard** ['them' refers back logically to 'sheep' in question III.11.2, whereas the intention had been to refer principally to earlier 'cattle' in question III.11.1; (-)pen forms may relate specifically to sheep]

fasting-house n a FASTING-CHAMBER III.11.3. fæstənæʏs Co, fæːstənæʏs Co, fastɪnɛʊs Y, fastɪnuːs Y, faːstɪnɛʊs Sa Wa O, vaːstənœʏs D, faːstənæʏs Co, faːstənæʏz Co, fatːʂt̠nɛuːs Wo, faːsənæuːs Man

fasting-pen n a FASTING-CHAMBER III.11.3. fæstɪnpɛn Mon K, fæːstɪnpɛn Sa He Wo Gl Co, fastɪnpɛn Sa St Wo Wa Lei R, faːstɪppɛn Nth, faːstɪnpɛn Sa He Wo Wa Mon Gl O Nth Bk Bd D, faːstənpɛn D, vaːstənpɛn D Ha, vatːʂt̠npɛn Gl, fɑːstɪnpɪn K, pl fɑːstɪnpɛnz K, fɒstɪnpɛn He [see note at **fasting-chamber**]

fasting-shed n a FASTING-CHAMBER III.11.3. faːstɪnʃɛd Mon

fasting-stall n a FASTING-CHAMBER III.11.3. fɑːstɪnstɔːɫ Brk

fat 1. n What do you call the inner layer of fat round the kidneys of a pig? III.12.7. fɛt Ess K, fæt Man Nf Ess, fæt? Nf, fat Sa He Mon. ⇒ **apron, belly-fat, brack, caul,** *cowl* ⇒ **caul, flare, flea(s),** *fleck* ⇒ **flick, fleed, flick, fry-fat, heeld,** *hele* ⇒ **heeld, kell, kells, kidney-fat, kircher, lard, lard-saim,** *lard-seam* ⇒ **lard-saim, leaf, leaf-fat, leaf-grease, leaf** of fat, **leaves, mort, near-fat, pig-fat, pig's-leaf, reeding, reef, rough fat, rutting fat, saim,** *seam* ⇒ **saim, shawl, spine, suet**

2. n CART-GREASE, used to lubricate the wheels of a cart I.11.4. fæt So, fat Y, fatʰ Mon

3. n LARD made from the fat of a pig III.12.8. fat La

4. n DRIPPING from mutton V.7.5(a). fat Nb Cu

5. n BACON-FAT V.7.5(b). fɛt Sr, fæt Nf K, fat Lei C W Do, vat Ha, fɑt Y

father n [Show a picture of a family. Who are the members of this family?] Who are the two most

important members of a family? [mother and ...]
VIII.1.1(a). Eng. ⇒ **ayer, fa**

fat-hogget *n* a WETHER III.6.8. fæthɒgət Nf
[marked u.r. EMBM]

fat-sheep *n* a WETHER III.6.8. fætʃiːp Nf *[marked
u.r. EMBM]*

fattening-pen *n* the STRAW-YARD of a farm I.1.9.
fæʔnɪnpɛn K, fæʔnənpɛn Ha

fattening-yard *n* the STRAW-YARD of a farm I.1.9.
fæʔnɪnjɑːəᵗd̥ Sx, fatənɪnjaɪd Y, fatnɪnjaːd Sa,
fatnɪnjaᵗːd̥ Sa Gl

fatting-stall *1. n* the STRAW-YARD of a farm I.1.9.
-*s* fæʔn̥stɔuz Sx
2. n a shed where bullocks were formerly fattened in
winter. fætɪnstɔːɬ Sx

fatting-yard *n* the STRAW-YARD of a farm I.1.9.
fætɪnjɑːəᵗd̥ Sr

fatty-land *n* LOW-LYING LAND IV.1.7. fatɪland Y

fault *n* *If a foolish man, in spite of your advice, does
something and comes to grief and nobody else is to
blame, you could say: Well, it serves him right, it's his
own .... VIII.9.6.* Eng. ⇒ *a dish of his own cooking*,
blame, *damned fault*, **doing(s)**, **look-out**, **seeking**

favours *vt-3prsg he* RESEMBLES VIII.1.9. feːvəz
Nb Cu Y Ch Db Mon Nt, feːvə Nt, feːvəᴵz La, feːvəᵗz̥
O, feɪvəz He O Hu C Bd, *prppl* feɪvəɹən Man,
feɪvəᵗz̥ O, feːᴵvəz Db, feˑəvəz Bk, feˑəvəᵗz̥ Bk,
fɛɪvəz L Hu C Bk Hɪt Ess Sr*[old x1]* K, fɛɪvə St Sf
Ess, fɛɪvəᴵz Brk K, fɛɪvəᵗz̥ O Sr, fɛəvəz Y L, fɛˑəvəɹ
(+V) L, fæɪvəz Ess, fæɪvə Ess, fæɪvəᴵz̥ K, favəz La
Y Ch Db, favəᴵz La Db, favəɹz La

fay *1. v* to WINNOW II.8.4. fɛɪ Y, fæɪ Y, -*ing* fɑi-ɪn
Nf
2. v to DITCH IV.2.11. *prppl* fʌɪ-ɪn Nf, -*ing* fʌɪ-ɪn
Nf

feal *vt* to HIDE something VIII.7.6. fɪəl Y*[rare x1,
very old x1]*

feared *adj* AFRAID VIII.8.2. fɪɔᴿd Nb*[old]*, fɪət Ch,
fɪəd Y Ch, fɪəᵗːd̥ So, vɪəᵗːd̥ D

fease *n* a DRAUGHT of air V.3.11. vɛɪz Co

feast *n* a local FESTIVAL or holiday VII.4.11. fiːst
Nb He O Nt Lei R Nth Hu C Bk Bd Co, fɪəst Y Nt L
Nth Bk Do, fɛɪst Du, fɛɪst Co; **coffee feast** kɔfɪ fɪəst
La; **Foresters' feast** fɒɹəstəᵗːz̥ fiːst Sa; **club
feast-day** klʌb fɪistdeɪ Brk

feather *1. n* a metal LINCH-PIN holding a wheel on
a cart I.9.12. fɛðəɹ La
2. n PASTURE II.1.3. *pl* fæˑðəz Sf *[queried u.r.
EMBM]*
3. vt to PLUCK a dead chicken of its feathers
IV.6.21. fɪðəᵗɾ̥ (+V) Sa He, vɪðəᵗɾ̥ (+V) He, fɛðəɹ
(+V) St He Mon, fɛðəᵗɾ̥ (+V) He Mon, vɛðəᵗɾ̥ (+V)
He
4. n a LOOSE *PIECE OF* SKIN at the bottom of a
finger-nail VI.7.11. fɛðəᵗ He

feathered *adj* FLEDGED IV.7.2. fɛðɔᴿd Nb,
fɛðəd Nb Cu Y Db Wa Ess Ch, fɛdðəd La, fɛðət
Ch, fɛðəᴵd Brk, fɛðəᵗd̥ Wa O, fɛðəᵗːɾɪd D

feathered-up *adj* FLEDGED IV.7.2. fɛðədʌp Bd

feathering *adj* FLEDGED IV.7.2. fɛðəɹɪn O
[queried WMBM]

features *vt-3prsg he* RESEMBLES VIII.1.9.
fiːtʃəz Du Y Ch Db Sa St He Wa Mon Gl Nth Hrt
MxL, fiːtʃə St, fɪitʃəᴵz Brk, fiːtʃəᵗz̥ He Wo Wa
Mon Gl, viːtʃəᵗz̥ Gl, fiːtʃəᵗ Wa, fiːtʃəᵗːz̥ Ha,
viːtʃəᵗːz̥ D, feːtʃəᴵz Ch, feːɪtʃəᵗz̥ Sa Gl,
veːtʃəᵗːz̥ W Ha, fɛɪtʃəᵗz̥ Wo, fɛɪtʃəz Ch Wo,
vɛɪtʃəᵗːz̥ D

feave *n* a EWE-HOG III.6.4. fiːv Sa

feckles *n* FRECKLES VI.11.1. fɛklz Y, fɛkɬz Wa,
vɛkɬz Gl

feckless *1. adj* STUPID VI.1.5. fɛkləs Cu Du
2. adj CLUMSY, describing a person VI.7.14.
fɛkləs La
3. adj SILLY VIII.9.3. fɛkləs La
4. adj BRITTLE, describing cups and saucers
which break easily IX.1.4. fɛkləs Cu*[rare]*

feeble *adj* WEAK, describing a person who has
been ill VI.13.2. fiːbl L

feed *1. v* *[In looking after your cows, in the
old-fashioned way, tell me what do you do?]* To
keep the cattle from going hungry, the cowman has
to ... THEM (before April 1955: *To keep the cattle
from starving, ...*). III.3.1. Eng. ⇒ **bait**, **bait** *them*,
cake *them*, *feed it*, *feed round*, *feed the cattle*, *feed
them*, **fodder**, **fodder down**, **fodder** *the beast*,
fodder *them*, **fodder** *them* **up**, **fodder up**, **hay**
them, **keep feeding** *them*, **meat**, **meat** *them*, **mow
up**, **provand**, **rack** *them*, **sarrow**, **sarrow** *them*,
serve, **tub** *[forms without object marked u.rr.
WM/EM/SBM]*
2. n CHAFF fed to horses III.5.3. fiːd Mon, fɪid
Ha; **dry feed** dɹɑˑɪ fiːd Lei; **mixed feed** mɪks fɪiˑd
Nf *[feed marked u.r. WMBM]*
3. n FOOD V.8.2. fiːd Cu We La Y Sa Gl O C Nf
Bk Ess So W K Co D Do Ha, viːd Co D, fɪid Nf
Brk, fɪiːd We Y Ess Sr Sx, fɛɪd Db
4. v to PITCH sheaves II.6.10. fiːd Wa Nth,
3prsg fiːdz La O Ha, *prppl* fiːdɪn La, -*ing* fiːdɪn
W Sr
5. n the YIELD of milk from a cow III.3.5. fiːd
Sa

feeder *1. n* a SOWING-BASKET II.3.6. fiːdəᵗː
W
2. n the FORKER on a wagon who unloads
sheaves in a stackyard II.6.9. fiːdə St, fɹiːdəᵗ Sr

feeding *1. v-ing* *What is your word for giving
horses their food in the stable?* III.5.1. ⇒ **baiting**,
baiting up, **corn**, **cratch**, *feed in* ⇒ **feeding in**,
feeding in, **feeding round**, **feeding up**, *feed*

round ⇒ feeding round, foddering, foddering up, *fodder up* ⇒ foddering up, *get fed*, *give a bit of* grub, *give a feed*, *give a sifting*, *give* chop, *give his* grub, *give their* grub, *giving their feed*, *giving their licking*, *giving their* snapping, *grub* ⇒ grubbing, grubbing, grubbing up, *grub up* ⇒ grubbing up, hay up, mangering, *meat* ⇒ meating, meating, provand, racking, rack up, *sarrow* ⇒ sarrowing, sarrowing, *serve* ⇒ serving, serving, *stable up* ⇒ stabling up, stabling up, supper up, supping up, *tend* ⇒ tending, tending, troughing

2.1. *v-ing* BAITING a horse when resting from work III.5.2. fiːdɪn La Y Mon Bk Ess W Brk Sr, fiːdn Nb Ess, *prppl* viːdən D, *v* fiːd Ch St Nth, *v* fɛɪd St

2.2. *vt-ing* baiting. fiːdɪn So, *v* viːd Co

feeding-alley 1. *n* the GANGWAY in a cow-house I.3.7. fiːdɪnalɪ Wa, fəiːdɪnælɪ Hrt

2. *n* the gangway in a cow-house, used to store hay, ⇐ HAY-LOFT I.3.18. fiːdɪnalɪ Wa

feeding-block *n* the GANGWAY in a cow-house I.3.7. fɪiːdɪnblɒk Brk

feeding in* *vtphr-ing* FEEDING horses in the stable III.5.1. fidn ... ɪn K

feeding-pan *n* a TROUGH in a cow-house I.3.6. fiːdɪnpæ'n Ess

feeding-passage 1. *n* the GANGWAY in a cow-house I.3.7. fiːdɪnpæsɪdʒ Brk Sr K, fiːdɪnpasɪdʒ Y St O W Sr, viːdɪnpasɪdʒ Co, fiːdnpasɪdʒ Ha, viːdənpasɪdʒ Ha, fɪidɪnpɛsɪdʒ Sx

2. *n* the gangway in a cow-house, used to store hay, ⇐ HAY-LOFT I.3.18. fiːdɪpasɪdʒ Sr [*not defined in SBM; interpreted from I.3.7*]

feeding-path *n* the GANGWAY in a cow-house I.3.7. fiːdɪnpaːθ So, viːdɪnpaːθ D, viːdɪnpaːf So, fiːdɪnpaːθ Ess Ha, vɛɪdɪnpaːθ D

feeding-pen *n* the GANGWAY in a cow-house I.3.7. fɪiːdɪnpɪn Sx

feeding round* *vphr* FEEDING horses in the stable III.5.1. vɪidɪn ɹæʊn Ha

feeding-trough *n* a TROUGH in a cow-house I.3.6. fiːdɪntɹɒf Y, fiːdɪntɹɔːf Ess, fiːdəntɹɔːf Co

feeding up *vphr-ing* FEEDING horses in the stable III.5.1. fiːdɪn ʊp Nth, *v* fiːd ʊp Nt

feeding-yard *n* the STRAW-YARD of a farm I.1.9. fidɪnˈjəʲːd̪ Wo

feed out *vphr* to put cattle on hired pasture, ⇐ HIRE *PASTURAGE* III.3.8. fiːd ɛʊt O

feed-shed *n* the place where hay is stored on a farm, ⇐ HAY-LOFT I.3.18. fiːdʃed Lei

feed-walk *n* the GANGWAY in a cow-house I.3.7. fiːdwɔːk So

feet 1. *n* [*What do you call this (indicate the foot)?] And both of them?* VI.10.1(b). Eng. ⇒ **foots, shammocks**

2. *n We don't say a boy is 60 inches tall, but we usually say he is 5 ....* VI.10.10. fiːt Nb Du La Y Man

Db St Mon O L Lei R Nf MxL Sr K, fɪt Ess Sx, vɪt Co, fɪit Brk K Ha, fɪiːt Ess Brk Sr Sx, fɛɪt Db, fəiːt St, fᵊiːʔ Hrt, fəɪt Y. ⇒ **foot**

3. *n* the HOOFS of a horse III.4.10(b). fiːt La Y Wa O Sr, feːt Ch, fɛɪt Ch

feeting* *npl* the HOOF-MARKS of a horse IV.3.10. fiːtn Nf

feetings *npl* the HOOF-MARKS of a horse IV.3.10. fiːtɪnz Nt L Sr, fiːtnz Nf Sf, fɪtɪnz C

feet-markings *npl* the HOOF-MARKS of a horse IV.3.10. fiːtmaːkɪnz L

feet-marks *npl* the HOOF-MARKS of a horse IV.3.10. fiːtmæˡːks La, fiːtmaːks Cu Y Ch Lei Nth Nf Ess, fiːtmaᵷːks Nb, fiːtmaˡːks La, viːtmaˤːks Ha, *sg* fiːtmaˡːk K, fɹiːtmɑːəˤks Sr, vɪtmaˤːks So

feg *n* a TUSSOCK of grass II.2.9. fɛg St

felfs* *npl* FELLIES, the sections of the wooden rim of a cart-wheel I.9.9. fɛlfs Y L

felks* *npl* FELLIES, the sections of the wooden rim of a cart-wheel I.9.9. fɛlks La Y

fell 1. *vt* to PLASH a hedge IV.2.4. fɛl Cu

2. *n* RENNET V.5.6. vɛl D

fellies 1. *npl* [*Show a picture of a farmcart.] What do you call these sections of the wooden rim [of the wheel]?* I.9.9. fɪlɪz Lei Sf Ess, fɪłɪz Sx, vɪliːz Do, vɪłiːz W Ha, fɛlɪz Nb Cu Du We La Y Ch Db Sa St He Wo Wa Mon O Nt L Lei R Nth Hu C Nf Sf Bk Bd Hrt Ess MxL, fɛlɪs Nb La Sa He, fɛłɪz He Ess Sr Sx, fɛlz He, vɛlɪz Wo Gl O Bk Brk Sx, vɛłɪz O Co D, vɛliːz So W, vɛłiːz W Ha, fɛləz La Y Man Sa Nt L Nth Nf Sf, fɛləs Man Nf, fɛłəz Co, fɛłɹz L, vɛləˤːz̩ So, vɛłəˤːz̩ Do, fæłɪz Hrt, væłɪz So Brk, vætɪz He Mon Gl Co, fałɪz Db Hrt, valɪz O, vałɪz Gl Co D, faləz Bd, *sg* fałɪ O, vʌłɪz D, vʌləz So, vʌłəˤːz̩ Do, vəliːz So, vəłiːz D, vələˤːz̩ So Do, vəłəˤːz̩ So. ⇒ **felfs, felks, felloes, felves, ferrules, spellies, thellies**

2. *npl* the SPOKES of a cart-wheel I.9.6. fɪlɪz Ess

fellmonger *n* a KNACKER III.11.9. fɛlmʌngə Nf, fɛlmʊngə Y [*old x1, polite x1*], fɛłmʊngə Lei, fɛlmʊngɹ L

felloes* *npl* FELLIES, the sections of the wooden rim of a cart-wheel I.9.9. fɛłʊz Lei, fɛlʌʊz Sr, fɛlouz St, vɛlouz So

fellow *n* my HUSBAND VIII.1.25. **my fellow** mɪ fɛlɪ Y

felon *n* a WHITLOW VI.7.12. fɛlʌn Mon, fɛlən Mon

felt 1. *n* the PELT of a sheep III.11.8(b). fɛlt Sa

2. *vt* to HIDE something VIII.7.6. fˡiːld We, fɛlt Y [*old x1*]

felve* *npl* FELLIES, the sections of the wooden rim of a cart-wheel I.9.9. fɛlvz Y

female cat *n* a TABBY-CAT, the female cat III.13.9. fiːmɛł kat Mon

femmer *1. adj* WEAK, describing a person who has been ill VI.13.2. fɛmə Du

2. adj BRITTLE, describing cups and saucers which break easily IX.1.4. fɛmə Nb*[old]* Du Y*[old x1]*

fen *n* LOW-LYING LAND IV.1.7. fɛn L Hu

fence *1. vt* to PEN or FOLD sheep in part of a field III.7.10. fɛns Nb We*[on turnip-field]* La Y Ch Db Wa

2. n a HEDGE IV.2.1(a). fɪns Man, fɛns Du*[bushes]* La Ch*[thorn]* Db Wa*[white-thorn x1, split wood or thorn x1]* Nf, *pl* fɛnsɪz Y, fɛnts Sf, fɛ⁹ns Man*[on stone and sod foundation]*

fence in *vtphr* to PEN or FOLD sheep in part of a field III.7.10. fɛns ... ɪn Y Nf

fence off *1. vtphr* to PEN or FOLD sheep in part of a field III.7.10. fɛns ... ɒf Nb Y Db St Nt, fɛns ... ɔf Y, fɛns ... ɔːf Nth

2. vtphr to divide a field with wire and stakes. fɛns ... ɒf Db

fen-land *n* LOW-LYING LAND IV.1.7. fɛnlænd Nf, fɛnland L

fern *1. n [Show a picture of fern.] What do you call this plant? It grows on moist ground; its leaves are long and feathery.* IV.10.13. Eng. ⇒ **bog-fern, fur, tongue-fern**; ⇒ also **fern-crooks**

*2. n GORSE IV.10.11. fœːn Mon *[queried error for [fœːz] WMBM Edd]*

3. n BRACKEN IV.10.12. fiːn Ch, fiː⁹n Lei*[old, obsolete]*, fɪən St, fɪərən Man, vɛɪəᵗːn̩ D, fɛən Ch, fjɛəᵗn̩ He, fœːn Mon, fɪan Sa, vaᵗːn̩ D, fjaːn Ch Sa, fjaᵗːn̩ Sa, vɑᵗːn̩ D, fɜⁿːn La, fjəᵗn̩ He Mon, fəːn Ch Db*[old]* St Bd*[old x1]* Hrt, fəᵗːn̩ Sa Wo Mon Gl Bk*[old x1]* Bd*[old x1]* W Co, vəᵗːn̩ So W Co D Ha, fɪəᵗːn̩ Sa Wo, vɪəᵗːn̩ So Co D Ha, fjəᵗːn̩ He, vjəᵗːn̩ He

fern-brake *n* BRACKEN IV.10.12. *pl* fəːnbɹɛɪks Sx

fern-crooks* *npl* FERN-fronds IV.10.13. fəːnkɹʊks He

fern-tickles *n* FRECKLES VI.11.1. fɛəʁntɪklz Nb, fæː⁹ntɪklz Du, fantɪkls Nb, fantɪklz Cu Du We La Y*[old x2]*, faːntɪklz Nb Du, faːᵘːntɪklz Nb, fəˑrntɪklz Cu, fəʁəntɪklz Nb

ferny-tickles *n* FRECKLES VI.11.1. fɛɔᴿnɪtɪklz Nb, fɛəʁnɪtɪklz Nb, faᴿːnɪtɪklz Nb, fəʁnɪtɪklz Nb*[old]*

ferrules *npl* FELLIES, the sections of the wooden rim of a cart-wheel I.9.9. fɛɹɪlz Y, fɛɹʊlz Wo *[queried 'mistake' in NBM, marked ir.r. WMBM]*

fest *vi* to FESTER, referring to a wound VI.11.8. fɛst L

fest out *1. vtphr* to put cattle on hired pasture, ⇐ HIRE *PASTURAGE* III.3.8. fɛst ... aʊt Y, fɛst ... uːt We

2. vphr to put cattle on hired pasture. fiːst uːt Cu, fɛst aʊt Y, fɛst uːt We

fester *1. vi If you don't keep the dirt out of a wound, what is it likely to do?* VI.11.8. Eng exc. Bd Hrt. ⇒ **beal, canker, dagg, fest,** *fester up,* **fewster, gather,** **gather up,** *get* **blood-poisoning,** *get* **septic,** *go* **septic,** *go the wrong road,* **matter, poison, rangle, suppurate,** *take bad ways, turn* **blood-poison,** *turn* **poison,** *turn* **poisonous,** *turn* **septic,** *turn to a bad place, turn to* **poisoning**

2. n a WHITLOW VI.7.12. fɪəstə Y, fɛstə St, fɛstəᵗ Brk, *pl* fɛstəᵗːz̩ So, fəˑstə Nf

3. n PUS VI.11.9. fɛstə Ess

festerlow *n* a WHITLOW VI.7.12. *pl* fɪstloːz Mon, θɪslʌʊ Ess*[on thumb]*, fɪstɪloʊ St, fɛstɪloʊ St, vɛstəloː D

fester-stuff *n* PUS VI.11.9. fɛstəstʌf Ess

festival *n What do you call your local festival or holiday?* VII.4.11. fɛəstəvl Man. ⇒ **Ash Wednesday, barnaby,** *benefit* **club, club, club** *day,* **club fair, club feast-***day,* **club randy, club's** *walking,* **club walk,** *coffee* **feast,** *dead man's* **fair, fair, fair** *friday,* **feast, feast** *sunday,* **fete, fete** *day,* **flower show, flower show** *day,* **Foresters' dinner,** *Foresters'* **feast,** *Foresters'* **fete, friendly society,** *goosey* **fair, harvest** *festival,* **harvest frolic,** *harvest* **hockey, harvest-***home,* **hiring, hockey,** *horse* **fair, horse races,** *June* **fair,** *March* **fair, may day,** *May Day* **fair, May Day** *week, May* **fair,** *May* **statutes, mop, Oak-apple Day,** *Oddfellows'* **club,** *Oddfellows'* **club** *day,* **old roy,** *Palmsun* **fair, picnic,** *pig* **club, primrose day, randy, revel, roast, rout, rush-bearing,** *St Giles's* **fair,** *St James's Day* **fair, sales, school treat,** *September* **fair,** *sheep* **fair, shick-shack day, show, show** *day,* **sports, sports** *day, statis* ⇒ **statutes, statute(s),** *summer* **fair, thump,** *village* **club,** *village* **fair,** *village* **fete, wake(s), walk, well-dressing,** *Whitmonday* **fair,** *Whitmonday* **old man's club service,** *Whitsun* **club, Whitsunday,** *Whitsun* **fair,** *Whitsuntide* **feast,** *Whitsuntide* **frolic,** *wool* **fair** *[information on dates and activities given variously in BM]*

fetch off *1. vtphr* **fetch bits off** to WHITTLE a stick I.7.19. *-ing* fɛtʃɪn ... ɒf Y

2. vtphr to CLEAR grass at the edges of a field II.9.5. fɛtʃ ... ɒf Y

fetch out *vtphr* to CLEAR grass at the edges of a field II.9.5. fɛtʃ ɛʊt Gl, fɛtʃ ... æʊt O

fetch up *1. vtphr* to VOMIT, referring to an adult VI.13.14(a). fɛtʃ ... ʌp Ess K

2. vphr to vomit. fɛtʃ ʌp Ess

3. vphr to VOMIT, referring to a baby bringing up milk VI.13.14(b). fɛtʃ ʌp Ess

fete *n* a local FESTIVAL or holiday VII.4.11. feːt Ha, veːt Ha, fɛɪt Db, fæɪʔ Hrt; **fete day** fɛɪt dɛɪ Brk, vɛɪt deː D*[modern]*; **Foresters' fete** fɒɹəstəᵗːz̩ faɪt Ha

fetlings *npl* the HOOF-MARKS of a horse IV.3.10. fɛtlɪŋz Nth

fettle *1. vt* to LAY the table V.8.12. *-ing* fɪtlɪn Y, fɛtl Y

2. n **in the fettle*** WELL, describing a healthy person VI.13.1(a). ɪn ðə fɛtl Nb

3. n **in bad fettle, in poor fettle, in very bad fettle, not in good fettle, out of fettle*** ILL, describing a person who is unwell VI.13.1(b). **in bad fettle** ɪn bæᵊd fɛtl Nb, ɪ bad fɛtl Cu; **in poor fettle** ɪ pʊə fɛtl Y; **in very bad fettle** ɪ varɪ bad fɪtl Y; **not in good fettle** nʊt ɪ gʊd fɛtl Y; **out of fettle** ʌʊt ə fɛtl Y

4. n **out of fettle** SICK, describing an animal that is unwell VI.13.1(c). uːt ə fɛtl Y, uːt ə fɛtəl Y

5. vt to BEAT a boy on the buttocks VIII.8.10. fɛtl Y St

fettling-apron* *n* a APRON worn when black-leading V.11.2(a). *pl* fɛtlɪnapɹənz Y

few *1. adj* **a few** *You might say to somebody: I'm not going away for long, not even for a week, but just for … days.* VII.1.19. Eng exc. MxL. ⇒ *a couple of, a couple or three days, a day or two, a few days, a few of, a lite, a little few, a lock of, a tidy time, a two or three, a two–three, couple of, couple of days, couple or three, day or two, few days, one or two, short period, three or four, three or four days, two or three, two or three days, two–three*

2. adj A FEW VII.1.19. fjɑʊ Gl, fju Nf Sx, fɪu Nf Co Ha, fju: Nb We Y Man Wo Wa Mon L Hrt W Brk K Sx, fɪu: Y L Sf Ess Sr, vju: So W Do Ha, fɛu· Nf, vjaʊ W, vɤ: Co, fu: Nth, vu: Co, fəʊ Nf

3. pron **a few** *I might ask you if there are any foxes round here, and you might answer: Yes, but only ….* VII.8.21. ⇒ *a little few, a lite, a lock, an odd one, an odd one one, an odd one or two, a scattering, a skittering, a two-or-three, a two-three, few, odd ones, one or two, two or three, two-three, very few*

few of *adj* **a few of** A FEW VII.1.19. ə fɪu ə Du, ə fju: ə La Y L

fewster *vi* to FESTER, referring to a wound VI.11.8. fju:stəᵗ: Do, vɤːstəᵗ: Co D

fezzle *n* a LITTER of piglets III.8.3. fazl St

fibre-broom *n* a BRUSH used for sweeping indoors V.9.11. fɔɪbəᵗbɹuːm Bk

fibre-brush *n* a BRUSH used for sweeping indoors V.9.11. faˈɪbəbɹʊʃ L

fiddle *n* an alternative to a SOWING-BASKET II.3.6. fɪdl Lei Do*[modern]* *[marked u.r. SBM]*

fidget(s) *n* **on the fidget(s)** ACTIVE, describing a child VIII.9.1. **on the fidget** ɒn t fɪdʒɪt Y; **on the fidgets** ɔn ðə fɪdʒɪts L Ess *[marked u.r. N/EMBM]*

fidgets *n* **the fidgets** TREMORS suffered by a person who cannot keep still VI.1.4. ðə fɪdʒɪts He, dɪ fɪdʒəts Sx

fidgety *adj* ACTIVE, describing a child VIII.9.1. fɪdʒɪtɪ Ch Db St He Wo Wa L Ess K, fɪdʒɪtʔɪ Sf, fɪdʒɪʔɪ Bd, fɪdʒɪdɪ Nf, fɪdʒətɪ La He L Nf Sf Bk Hrt, fɪdʒəʔɪ Bk *[marked u.r. NBM]*

field *1. n* PASTURE II.1.3. fiːld La, viːᵊłd Gl, fɪəłd Gl

2. n a MEADOW II.9.2. fiːld Nb*[old]*

field-dock *n* the DOCK plant II.2.8. fɪildɒk Nf

field-gate *n* a GATE between fields IV.3.1. fiːłdgɛɪt Lei, fiːlgɛːt Nf, fɪʊłgɛɪt Ess, fɪlgɛːt Nf

field-kale *n* CHARLOCK II.2.6. fiːldkɪəl Cu, fiːldkeal Cu We, fiːlkeːᵊl We

field-mouse *n* a SHREW-MOUSE IV.5.2. *pl* fiᵊłdmɑɪs K, viːłmɒʏs D, viːłdmæʊs W, viːᵊłdmæʊs W, viːłmæʏs Co D, *pl* fiːlmɑɪs La, fiːldmɑːs La Y, fiːlmɑːs Y, fiːldmaʊs La Y, fiːlmaʊs Ch Sa, fiːłdmaʊs So, fiːlmɛʊs Db, viːłdmɒʊs W, fiːldmuːs Cu Y, fiːlmuːs Y, fⁱiːldmᵁuːs Cu We, fɪʊłdmaːs MxL, fɪəłmɛʊs MxL, fɪəłdmæʊs Ha, fɪəłmæʊs Ess Ha, vɪəłmæʏs So, *pl* vɪəłdmɑɪs So, fɪʊmæʊs K, fɪəłdmaʊs Y, fɪəlmuːs Y, veːłmæʊs Ha, fɛɪldmᵊuːs Du, fɛɪldmᵊuːs Y, fəɪldmaʊs Y, fəɪlmuːs Y, fᵊiːᵊłmɛʊs Hrt

fields *npl* *[Show an aerial photograph of a farmstead and surrounding fields.] What do you call these?* I.1.1. Eng. ⇒ **closes, grounds, leas;** ⇒ also **close, garth, ground, home-close**

field-way *n* a PATH through a field IV.3.11. fɪʊdwɛɪ Sr

fierce *adj* TOO HOT V.6.8. fɪəs Nth Nf K, fiːiəˡs Sr, fɪəᵗʂ Ha

fifer's dance *n* TREMORS suffered by a person who cannot keep still VI.1.4. fəɪfəᵗːz̦ dans W; **saint fifer's dance** sən vɒɪfəᵗːz̦ dans Ha; **the fifer's dance** ðə fəɪfəᵗːz̦ dans W

fifth-quarter *n* the PLUCK of a slaughtered animal III.11.6. fɪfkwɔːtəˡ K; **fifth-quarter pluck** fɪθkwɔːtəˡ plʌk K

filbert *n* HAZEL IV.10.8. fɪlbət St

file *n* ⇐ WHETSTONE II.9.10. *pl* fɒɪłz So, vɒɪᵊłz So, fɔɪʊ O

fill *1.1. v* to LOAD a cart with dung II.1.5. fɪl Nb Cu Du La Y Man Ch Db Sa St Wo Wa Gl O Nt*[old xl]* L Nth Hu C Nf Sf Bk Sr, *prppl* fɪlɪn Sx, *-ing* fɪlɪn Sx, vɪl Gl, *-ing* vɪlɪn Ha, fɪł He Wa Mon O Nth Hu C Sf Bd Hrt Ess, fɛł Ess*[old]*

1.2. vt to load. fɪl Db Sa St He Wa L C Nf Bk Ha, fɪł He Wo Gl Sf Hrt Ess, vɪł He, fɛl Db

1.3. vt to load dung into a cart. fɪl Y Nth Nf Bk, *-ing* fɪlɪn La Nt L, fɪł Hrt, *-ing* fælɪn Ess

[it is often not clear from BM that 1. and 2. refer to cart]

2.1. vt to STOCK a cow's udder III.3.6. *-ed* vɪłd D

2.2. v to stock. *-ing* fɪlɪn St

3. vi to WAX, referring to the moon VII.6.5(a). fɪl Bk, *-ing* fɪlɪn Y Sx, fɪł Bd, *-ing* fɪłɪn Ha, *-ing* vɪłən Ha

fill-belly *n* CHAFF II.8.5. fɪlbɛlɪ Y

filler *n* a SHAFT-HORSE I.6.2. fɪlɪ Ess, fɪlə St Wa O Nth Nf Sf Ess, fɪləˠ O Brk, fɪləˠ Wo Wa O Bk, vɪləˠ Gl, fɪˠəˠ Sr, fɪˠəˠ He Wo, vɪˠəˠ Gl, vɪˠəˠː W Do, fɛlə Ess

filler-horse *n* a SHAFT-HORSE I.6.2. fɪləhɔs Nf, fɪlɹɔːs Nth, fɪˠəˠ-aˠːɾʂ Brk, fɪˠəˠ-ɔːəˠʂ Brk

fillers *npl* the SHAFTS of a cart I.9.4. fɪˠəˠɾz̩ Brk

fill in *1. vtphr* to LOAD dung into a cart II.1.5. fɪl ... ɪn La

2. vphr to PITCH sheaves II.6.10. *-ing* vɪˠən ɪn Ha

fillis *n* STRING used to tie up a grain-sack I.7.3. fɪlɪs Ha*[strong and fluffy]* Sx*[soft, also for mending sacks]*, fɪˠəz Ha*[very soft, also for mending sacks]*

fillis-string *n* STRING used to tie up a grain-sack I.7.3. fɪlɪsstɹɪŋ Nf Brk*[very soft]*, fɪləsstɹɪŋ Sf, fɪˠəsstɹɪŋ Sx

fillist *n* a SHAFT-HORSE I.6.2. fɪlɪst Bd Hrt, fɪləs Hrt Ess, fɪləz Ess

fillist-horse *n* a SHAFT-HORSE I.6.2. fɪləshɔs Ess, fɪləshɔːs Ess, fɪlɪstɔːᵊs Hu

fill out *viphr* to WAX, referring to the moon VII.6.5(a). *prppl* vɪˠɪn æʊt Ha

fill up *1. vtphr* to LOAD a cart with dung II.1.5. fɪˠ ... ʌp Mon, vɪˠ ... ʌp Gl

2. vtphr to STOCK III.3.6. *-ing* fɪlɪn ... ʌp

3. vtphr **cut and fill the gaps up** to PLASH a hedge IV.2.4. kʌʔ ən fɪl ðə gæpʔs ʌp Nf

4. vtphr to fill gaps in a hedge-bank or hedge, probably with turfs, brushwood, or similar material. vɪˠ ... ʌp So W *[SBM Edd uncertain as to precise meaning]*

5. viphr to WAX, referring to the moon VII.6.5(a). *prppl* fɪlɪn ʊp Y

filly *1. n* And *[what do you call the young horse] when a female?* III.4.2. fɪlɪ Man Nf So K Do, fɪˠɪ He So W Co D Do Ha, vɪˠɪ W D Ha, ðɪˠɪ W, fɪlɪ Nb Cu Du We La Y Ch Db Sa St Wo Wa Mon Gl O Nt L Lei R Nth Hu C Nf Sf Bd Hrt Ess MxL Brk Sr K Ha Sx, vɪˠɪ Gl Brk Ha, fɪˠɪ He Wo Gl O Hrt Ess Sr K Do Ha, fɪlɛ Nf, fɪlə Y, vəˠɪ Do. ⇒ **filly-colt, filly-foal, mare-colt, mare-foal, young mare**

2. n a MARE III.4.5. fɪlɪ Nf

filly-colt *n* a FILLY III.4.2. fɪlɪkɐʊt Ch, fɪˠɪkɒˠt Gl, fɪlɪkɒʊˠt Wa, fɪlɪkɔʊˠ? Bk, fɪlɪkɔʊˠt Wa O, fɪlɪkɔʊt La, fɪlɪkʌʊt Sf, fɪlɪkɔːlt Sa, fɪlɪkɔʊˠt O Nth

filly-foal *n* a FILLY III.4.2. fɪlɪfʊʊl Wo, fɪˠɪfʊʊˠ Sr, fɪlɪfɔɪl Y, fɪlɪfɔʊˠ O, fɪlɪfəəl Y, fɪlɪfʌʊˠ Bk Ess, fɪlɪfoːl Ch He, fɪˠɪfoːˠ Mon, fɪlɪfoː He, fɪlɪfoul Nf, fɪlɪfoʊˠ Bk, fɪlɪfoːul Nf, vɪˠɪvoːʊˠ Gl, fɪlɪfuːl Ch, fɪlɪfual Y, fɪlɪfʊəl Du La Y

filmers *npl* BILBERRIES IV.11.3. fɪlməz L *[queried EMBM]*

filth *n* WEEDS, unwanted plants that grow in a garden II.2.1. fɪˠθ O So

filthy *1. vt* to DIRTY a floor V.2.8. fɪˠθi So

2. adj STICKY, describing a child's hands VIII.8.14. fɪʊθi MxL

fine *1. adj* PRETTY, describing a girl VI.5.18. faɪn Cu La Y, faɪn L

2. adj WELL, describing a healthy person VI.13.1(a). faɪn Lei Ha, fəɪn Mon Gl

fine-looking *adj* PRETTY, describing a girl VI.5.18. faɪnlʊkɪn Y, faɪnlʊkɪn Ess, fɒɪnlʊkɪn Sa So, fɔɪnlʊkɪn Wa

finger-friend *n* a LOOSE *PIECE OF* SKIN at the bottom of a finger-nail VI.7.11. *pl* fɪŋɡəfɹɛnz Mon

fingerful *n* a PINCH of sugar or salt VII.8.6. fɪŋəfʊl Y

fingerin *n* a decorative APRON V.11.2(b). fəniʁən Nb

finish *1. v* to CLEAR grass at the edges of a field II.9.5. fɪnɪʃ L, *-ing* fɪnəʃən Man *[with scythe]*

2. n STOPPING-TIME at the end of a day's work VII.5.9. fɪnɪʃ Db

finished *1. v-ed* Your wife in bringing in the last of the old potatoes onto the table, might say: *Now the old potatoes are .... And what would you yourself have said? [Idiom]* V.7.21. fɪnɪʃt Nb Cu Y Ch Db Sa St He Wo Wa Mon Gl O Nt L Lei Nth Nf Sf Bk Bd Ess MxL So Brk Sr K Ha Sx, vɪnɪʃt D Ha, fɛnəʃt Man, fənɪʃt So, vənɪʃt So D Do; **all finished** ɔːl fɪnɪʃt Sa, ɔːˠ fənɪʃt Co, ɔːˠ vənɪʃt D Dʊ; **finished with** fɪnɪʃt wɪð Mon W; **finished up** fɪnɪʃt ʊp Bk. ⇒ **all done, all gone, done, done for, done in, done with, gone, gone done, got done, napood, over, used up** *[also wide range of extended phrasal rr., from which material has been extracted]*

2. adj EXHAUSTED, describing a tired person VI.13.8. vɪnɪʃt D

finished off *adj* EXHAUSTED, describing a tired person VI.13.8. fɪnɪʃt ɔːf R

finishes *vi-3prsg [There are two times in the day that every schoolboy knows. One is about 9 in the morning, when school ...], and the other is about 4 o'clock when school ....* VIII.6.2(b). Eng exc. Man Nt R Hu C MxL. ⇒ **breaks, breaks off, breaks up, closes, comes out, ends, gets out, gives out, gives over, goes home, goes out,** *is out,* **knocks off, leaves, leaves off, leaves out,** *looses* ⇒ **lowses, lowses, lowses out, shuts, shuts up, stops, turns out** *[uninflected and periphrastic do forms subsumed under inflected forms]*

finishing-time *n* STOPPING-TIME at the end of a day's work VII.5.9. fɪnɪʃɪntaɪm We La L, fɪnɪʃɪntaˑɪm L, fɪnɪʃɪntɒɪm St, fɪnɪʃɪntɔɪm Gl, fɪnɪʃɪntəɪm Gl

finish off *vtphr* to CLEAR grass at the edges of a field II.9.5. fɪnɪʃ ... ɔːf Wo

fins *n* barley AWNS II.5.3. fɪnz Ch

fire *n* LIGHTNING VII.6.22. faɪɔᵏ Nb*[old x1, very old x1]*, faɪə Nb

fire-crook *1. n* a CRANE on which a kettle is hung over a domestic fire V.3.4. væɪəᵗːkɾɤk So

2. n the vertical part of a crane over a domestic fire, consisting of a *BAR* or *CHAIN* and a HOOK(/*CROOK*) V.3.5b+c. vɒɪəᵗːkɾɤk D

fire-dog *n* a CRANE on which a kettle is hung over a domestic fire V.3.4. faːdɒg Hrt

fire-grid *n* a GRIDIRON V.7.4(a). vəɪəᵗːgɾɪd W

fire-hoe *n* a RAKE used in a domestic fire V.3.8(a). faːɹʌʊ Ess, vɒɪəᵗːɾoː Ha

fire-hole *n* the ASH-HOLE beneath a domestic fire V.3.3. faɪə-ɔɪl Y

fire-hook *n* a RAKE used in a domestic fire V.3.8(a). faːɹʊk C

fire-lighting *n* KINDLING-*WOOD* V.4.2. fɔɪəlɔɪtʔn Ess; **fire-lighting wood** faɪəlɔɪtɪn wʊd Ess

fire-new *adj* BRAND-NEW VI.14.24. fɒɪəᵗnjuː Wo

fire-pan *n* a SHOVEL for a household fire V.3.9. faɪəpn Nf*[large]*, faːəpn Nf*[short-handled x1, small x1]*, fɒɪpn Nf

fire-point *n* a POKER V.3.6. faːpɔɪnt Y, faˑɹpɔɪnt Y, faᴶːpɔɪnt Y

fire-rake *n* a RAKE used in a domestic fire V.3.8(a). faːɹɛɪk MxL, faɪəɹɛɪk Nth, faɪəᵗɾeɪk Ha

fire-shovel *n* a SHOVEL for a household fire V.3.9. fæɪəʃʊvl Ch, fæɪəʃʊvəl Y, faɪɔᵏʃʊl Nb, faɪəʃʊvl L, faɪəʃʊvəl Y, faɪəʃuːl Cu Y, faɪəʃəʊl Y, fɔɪəʃʌvɬ Ess*[long-handled x1]*, fɔɪəʃʊvəl Wa, vʌɪəᵗʃəvɬ Gl

fire-sticks *n* KINDLING-*WOOD* V.4.2. faɪəstɪks Cu Y Sa, faɪəstɪks Ch, fɒɪəᵗstɪks Wo, fəɪəᵗstɪks Wo

fire-tongs *n* TONGS V.3.7. fæɪətʊnz Ch, faːtɒnz MxL, vəɪəᵗtɒnz Gl

firewood *n* KINDLING-*WOOD* V.4.2. fæɪəwʊd Y, fæɪəᵗwʊd He, faːwʊd Y, faɪəwʊd Y, vaɪəᵗːwʊd So, faɪəwʊd Wa Nth, faɪəɹwʊd La Bk, fɒɪəwʊd Wo, fɒɪəᵗwʊd Wo, fɔɪəᵗwʊd Wa, fɔɪəᴶɹʊd Bk, vʌɪəɾʊd Gl, fəɪəᵗwʊd Wo Mon, vəɪəᵗːɾʊd W

firing *1. n* COAL-DUST V.4.1. fɒɪəɾɪn W

2. n KINDLING-*WOOD* V.4.2. faːᴶɹɨn Nf

firkin *n* a BARREL that holds 4½ gallons VI.13.12. fəᵗːkɪn Ess

firking *v-ing* SCRATCHING VI.1.2. feːkɪn Db, fəːkɪn St; **firking about** *prppl* fəᵗːkɪn W

first-and-seconds *n* BEESTINGS V.5.10. fəᴶˑsɹsɛʔnz Brk

first-horse *n* a TRACE-HORSE I.6.3. fɒstɒs Y Db, fɒstɒs L, fɔstɔs L

first milk *n* BEESTINGS V.5.10. fəɹst mɪlk He, fəːst mɪʊk Sr, fəᵗˑʂt mɪɬk Ha, vəᵗːʂ məɬk Do

first milking(s) *n* BEESTINGS V.5.10.
no -s: vəᵗːʂ mɪɬkən Do
-s: fʌs məɬkɪnz So

first rate *adj* WELL, describing a healthy person VI.13.1(a). fɒst ɹɛət Y

first shearling *n* a EWE-HOG III.6.4. fʊst ʃɪəᵗɬɪn Wo

first-year ewe *n* a EWE-HOG III.6.4. fəstɪˑə juː Y

fish *n* a DRAG used to slow a wagon I.11.3. fɪʃ Ess

fish-grill *n* a GRIDIRON V.7.4(a). fɪʃgɹɪʊ K

fish-tickle *v* to GROPE *FOR FISH* IV.9.10. *?vbln* fɪʃtɪklɪn Hrt, *prppl* fɪʃtɪklɪn Sa

fist *n* What do you call this [indicate a (closed) fist]? VI.7.4. Eng exc. Du We; **double fist** dʊbl fɪst We. ⇒ **doubled fist** ⇒ **double** fist, *double* fist, **duke, mauler, neive, puncher**

fistful *n* a HANDFUL VII.8.10(a). fɪstfʊl Cu Y, fɪsfʊl La, fɪstfl Cu*[?old]*, fɪsfəl Sa

fistle on *viphr* to show signs of calving, ⇐ SHOWS SIGNS OF CALVING III.1.12. *3prog* fɪslən ɒn Nb

fit *1. adj* not fit *NOT IN* CALF, but able to conceive III.1.8. nɒʔ fɪʔ So

2. adj WELL, describing a healthy person VI.13.1(a). fɪt Nb Cu Du We La Y Ch Db Sa St He Wo Wa Mon Gl Nt L Nth Nf Sf Bd Hrt Ess MxL So W Sr K Co D Ha, fɪʔ O Bk Hrt, vɪt So W Co D Do Ha, fɪət Ess; **fit and well** fɪt ən wiːl Y; **well and fit** wɛɬ ən fɪt O; **pretty fit** pəᵗːdɪ vɪt Do

3. adj **not very fit** ILL, describing a person who is unwell VI.13.1(b). nɒt vɛɹɪ fɪt He

4. adj READY VIII.1.16. fɪt Y Wo L Ess MxL So K, vɪt D; **fit and ready** vɪt ən ɾedi D

fitch *n* a POLE-CAT IV.5.7. fɪtʃ Co D, vɪtʃ So D

fitch-colour *adj* dark-coloured, describing a POLE-CAT IV.5.7. fɪtʃkʌləᵗː So, vɪtʃkʌləᵗː So

fitcher *n* a POLE-CAT IV.5.7. fɪtʃəᵗ Wa, fɪtʃəᵗː Co *[WMBM headword fitchew]*

fitchet *1. n* a POLE-CAT IV.5.7. fɪtʃət Sa*[old]*, fɪtʃəɹt He

2. n a ferret. fɪtʃɪt He

fitchet-ferret *n* a ferret used to hunt the POLE-CAT IV.5.7. fɪtʃəɹtfɛɹət He

fitchew *n* a POLE-CAT IV.5.7. fɪtʃuː Co

fitchock *n* a POLE-CAT IV.5.7. fɪtʃʌk Mon, fɪtʃəɹk He, fɪdʒək Mon

fitchy *1. n* a POLE-CAT IV.5.7. fɪtʃi D*[black x1]*, vɪtʃi So Co D

2. n a ferret. vɪtʃi So*[dark-coloured x1]*, *pl* fɪtʃɪz D

3. adj dark-coloured. vɪtʃɪ So

fit-for-nought *n* a STUPID person VI.1.5. fɪtvəᵗːnɔᵗːt Co

fitty *1. adj* WELL, describing a healthy person VI.13.1(a). vɪti So*[old]* Co D, vɪdi Co

2. adj **not very fitty*** SICK, describing an animal that is unwell VI.13.1(c). ɪdn vɛɾi vɪdi D

five-foot prong *n* a HAY-FORK with a short shaft I.7.11. fʌɪvvət pɹɒŋ Gl

five-grained fork *n* a   MUCK-FORK   I.3.13.
faɪvgɹeːnt fɔːk Ch
five-tine-fork* *n* a   MUCK-FORK   I.3.13.
fɔɪvtɔɪnfɔːɪəˠk Sr
fixture-plough *n* a PLOUGH with two wheels of
unequal size I.8.1. fɪkstjəˠpləʊ Brk
flacker-board *1. n* the TAILBOARD of a cart
I.10.2. flakəbʊəd La, flakəɹbʊəɹd La
2. n an END-BOARD of a cart I.10.4. flakəbʊəd La,
flakəɹbʊəɹd La
flacket *n* the FLAP at the front of old-fashioned
trousers VI.14.16. flakɪt St
flag *1. n* the STEM of a corn-plant II.5.2(a). flag Lei
2. n a leaf of a corn-plant. *pl* flægz Ess
3. n the THRESHOLD of a door V.1.12. flæg Man
[queried ir.r. NBM]
4. n a HEARTHSTONE V.3.2. flɛg Brk Sr
5. n the place in which the ashes are collected
beneath a domestic fire, ⇐ ASH-HOLE V.3.3. flɛg
Sr
flagged out *adj* EXHAUSTED, describing a tired
person VI.13.8. flægd ɛʊt Sf Ha
flags *1. npl* the RIDGES between furrows in a
ploughed field II.3.2. *sg* flæg Nf
2. n PEAT IV.4.3. flægz Nf
flagstone *n* a HEARTHSTONE V.3.2. flɛgstɒʊn Sr
flagstones *1. npl* the stone THRESHOLD of a door
V.1.12. flɛgstɒʊnz Sx
2. n the CURB-STONE in a cow-house I.3.9.
flɛgstɒʊnz Sr, flægstɒʊnz K
flail *1. n [Show a picture of a flail.] What did they
thresh with before machines came in?* II.8.3. fleːɪl Nb
Cu La Y Sa*[striking part]* Nt, fleɪɫ So*[striking part]*,
fleɪəɫ Man Bk, *pl* fleˑalz La, fleəl Du La Y, *pl* fleˑəlz
Cu, fleːˤl Sa, fleːˤɫ O, fleːɪl Cu We, fleɪl St*[striking
part]*, *pl* fleɪlz St, vɫeɪɫ D, *pl* vɫeɪɫz Ha, fleɪʊ Sr, fleəl
Cu La Y*[striking part x1]*, fleˑəl L, flæɪɫ Ess, flæɪˤɫ
Ess, vɫaɪɫ D, vlaɪəl So, væɪəɫ So, *pl* vaɪˤɫz Do, vɒɪəɫ
Do, *pl* vʌɪəɫz Gl, vəˤːɫ Do. ⇒ **beater, dick-
and-daniel, *drashel* ⇒ threshel, flay, frail, *furl* ⇒
flail, nile, paddle, stick-and(-a)- half, swingle,
swipper, swipple, swivel, swopple, thrail, thresher,
thrashet, thrave, threshel, threshel-nile,
threshing-flail ⇒ threshing-frail, threshing-frail,
threshing-stick, threshing-thrail, wimble, wippet**
2. v to THRESH corn II.8.1. fɹeɪl L, fleˑəl L
flake *n* a CUTTING of hay II.9.15. fliːk Hu C, fleɪk
St Wa Lei Sx
flake(s) *n* a CART-FRAME I.10.6.
no -s: fleɪk La
-s: fleɪks La
flakes *1. npl* CART-LADDERS I.10.5. fleːks La,
fleɪks La
2. npl HURDLES used to pen sheep in part of a field
III.7.11. fliːks Db St Lei, fleːks Nt, fleɪks Y Lei, *sg*
fleɪk Nt

flambergasted *adj* STUPID VI.1.5. flaməgastɪd
O
flam-new *adj* BRAND-NEW VI.14.24. fɫæmnɪʊ
Co, fɫamnɪʊ Co, fɫamnɪ Co
flams *n* LOW-LYING LAND IV.1.7. flæmz Brk
flank *n* the GROIN VI.9.4. flæŋk Wo *[marked
ir.r. WMBM, but perhaps connected with **lank***]*
flannel *1. n* a CHEMISE V.11.1. flanəl Db Wo
2. n a VEST VI.14.9. flænɫ Sf, flænʊ Sr, flanɪl Y
Db, flanəl Wa*[old]*, flanɫ Gl MxL, fɫanəl Co,
vlanɫ Gl, vɫanəl Co
flannel clout* *n* a wrapper worn over a DIAPER
V.11.3. flænəl tlɛʊt Nf
flannel pilch *n* a DIAPER V.11.3. flanl pɪlʃ L
flannels *n* a DIAPER V.11.3. flɛnʊz Sr
flannel-sark *n* VEST VI.14.9. flanəlsaˠːk Nb
flannel-shirt *n* a VEST VI.14.9. flæˑnəɫʃəːt
MxL*[old, worn by men]*, flænʊ ʃəˤˑt Sr, flanɪlʃɛt
Nt L, flanɪlʃɒt L, flanlʃɒt L, flanɪlʃəˠːɹt La,
flanɪlʃət Y, flanlʃət L, flanɫʃəːt C Bd, flanɪlʃəˠt
L, flanlʃəˠːt O, flanɫʃəˑɹt C, flanəlʃəˤːt Wo,
flanlʃəˤːʔ O*[old]*, flanɫʃəˤːʔ Bk, flanəɫʃəˤːʔ Bk,
fɹanəɫʃəˤːʔ Bk, flanɫʃəˤːt Wa O*[very old]*,
fɫanəɫʃəɻt O
flannel shirt *n* a CHEMISE V.11.1. flanəl ʃɒt L,
ˌflænɫ ˈʃəɻt Nf
flannel-singlet *n* a VEST VI.14.9. flanlsɪŋlət La
flannel-undershirt *n* a   VEST   VI.14.9.
flanəɫʌndəʃəˤːʔ   Bk,   flanɪlʊndəʃəˠːɹt   La,
flanɪlʊndəʃəˠt Y
flannel vest *n* a CHEMISE V.11.1. flænʊɫ vɛst
Ha *[marked u.r. SBM]*
flannen* *n* a VEST VI.14.9. flanɪn Cu We La Y
flannen-shirt *n* a VEST VI.14.9. flanɪnʃɛt Y*[old]*
L, flanɪnʃɒt L, flanɪnʃəˠt L *[not a NBM
headword]*
flap *1. n Trousers today are fastened up in front
by buttons. But the old-fashioned trousers had a
....* VI.14.16. Eng. ⇒ **bang-down, barn-door,
barn-doors ⇒ barn-door, barn's-door, bolt,
broad-fall, drop-door, fall, fall-downs, fall-
front, flacket, flap-door, flap-front, *flap-fronts*
⇒ flap-front, flap-helds, flap-hole, flappet,
flapping-front ⇒ flopping-front, flap-ups, flop,
flopping-front, fly, fly-away, fly-ballups,
fly-fall, fly-flap, fly-flapper, fly-front, full-fall,
heck-board, lap, lap-over, midden-doors, old
falls,   pig's-door,   pigsty-door,   piss-lap,
sideboards** *[pl forms may relate to two- or
three-piece flap arrangements]*
2. n a CUTTING of hay II.9.15. flæp So, flap Y
So Do, fɫap W, flɒp So
3. n the BRIM of a hat VI.14.3. flap Y
flap-door *n* the FLAP at the front of old-fashioned
trousers VI.14.16. flæpduəˤː So

flap-front *n* the FLAP at the front of old-fashioned trousers VI.14.16. vlæpfɹɒnts Brk, *pl* flapfɹʊnts Y L, flɑpfɹʊnt Y

flap-helds *n* the FLAP at the front of old-fashioned trousers VI.14.16. flapɛlz Y

flap-hole *1. n* an EAR-HOLE VI.4.3. flɛəpɔʊɫ Ess
2. n the FLAP at the front of old-fashioned trousers VI.14.16. flapoːᵁl Db

flappers *npl* EARS VI.4.1. flɑːpəz Ess

flappet *n* the FLAP at the front of old-fashioned trousers VI.14.16. *pl* flapəts O

flap-ups *npl* FLAPs at the front of old-fashioned trousers VI.14.16. fłapʌps Co

flare *n* the FAT round the kidneys of a pig III.12.7. flɪəᵗ O Bk, fleəˢ O, flɛə Sf Bk Bd Hrt Ess Sr, flɛəᵗ O Bk Bd

flash *1. v* to TRIM hedges IV.2.3. flæʃ Sf
2. adj INSIPID, describing food lacking in salt V.7.8. flɛʃ Ess, flɛːəʃ Ess, flæʃ Sf Ess, fłæʃ Sf
3. adj PRETTY, describing a girl VI.5.18. flaʃ Y

flasher *1. n* a HEDGING-BILL IV.2.5. flæʃə Nf Sf
2. n a BILLHOOK IV.2.6. flæˑʃə Sf
3. n a PRETTY girl VI.5.18. flæʃəᵗ Brk

flashing fire *n* LIGHTNING VII.6.22. flaʃn faɪə Du

flask *n* a CLOTHES-BASKET V.9.7. flæːsk So, flɑːsk So, fłɑːsk D

flasket *n* a CLOTHES-BASKET V.9.7. fłæskɪt Co, fłæːskɪt Co, flaskɪt St, fłaskɪt Co, flaːskɪt He*[old]*, fłaːskɪt Co D, fłaːskət D

flat *1. adj* SAD, describing bread or pastry that has not risen V.6.12. flɛt Ess K Sx, flæt Man Sa Nf Sf Ess MxL So Brk Sr K, flæʔ Sr, flat Nb Cu We La Y Ch St He Wa Mon O Hrt, flaʔ Bk Bd
2. adj INSIPID, describing food lacking in salt V.7.8. flat C Hrt
3. n **flat of your hand** the PALM of the hand VI.7.5. flæt ə jəᵗː hænd So, flat ə jər han Cu

flat comb *n* a CURRY-COMB used to clean horses III.5.5(b). flæt kɒʊm Sx

flat-footed *adj* SPLAY-FOOTED VI.10.5. flætfʊtɪd Nf Ess MxL K Sx, flætfʊtəd Sf, flætvʊtɪd So, flatvʏtəd So

flat-jack *n* a GIRDLE for baking cakes V.7.4(b). fłatdʒak Ha

flat-ladders *n* a CART-FRAME I.10.6. flætlædəz K

flat-lands *n* LOW-LYING LAND IV.1.7. flætlænz Ess

flats *n* LOW-LYING LAND IV.1.7. flæts Nf

flat-shelvings *n* a CART-FRAME I.10.6. flatʃɪlvɪnz Y

flaught *n* a flat piece of PEAT IV.4.3. flaʊt Y

flaughts *n* the top layer of PEATS IV.4.3. flaʊts Y

flavourless *adj* INSIPID, describing food lacking in salt V.7.8. flæɪvələs MxL

flay *1. n* the MOULD-BOARD of a horse-drawn plough I.8.8. vłaɪ D
*2. n a FLAIL II.8.3. fleː Mon

flay-boggle *n* a SCARECROW II.3.7. flɛəbɒgl Y, flɛəɹbɒgl Y

flay-crow *n* a SCARECROW II.3.7. fleːkʀøː Nb, fleːkra: Cu, fleːkʀa: Nb Du, fleːkɹa: Du We La Y, fleːkɹɑ: Du, fleːkɹɔ: Cu La Y, fleːkɹɔ: Nb, fleːkrɔ: Cu, fleːkɹɔ: Cu We, flɛɪkɹɔ: Y, flɛəkɹɔ: Y

flayed *adj* AFRAID VIII.8.2. fleːt Nb*[old]* Cu We, fleːd Nb Du La Y, fleˑət Cu, fleˑəd Du La, flɛːt Cu We, flɛːd Cu, flɛɪd Y

flayth* *npl* FLEAS IV.8.4. flɛɪθ La

flea(s) *n* the FAT round the kidneys of a pig III.12.7.
no -s: flɪi: Sr Sx, fłi: O, fłeː Ha, fłeɪ Ha, flɛɪ Ess MxL Brk Sr Sx
-s: flɪiːs Brk, flɛɪz Brk

fleas *1. npl What do you call those little black insects that jump about and bite you?* IV.8.4. Eng. ⇒ *bed-fleas,* **flayth, flecks, fleffs, flen(s), fyoff,** *hopping-flea,* **jumpers, lopperds, lops, midgens, midgets**
2. npl LICE IV.8.1(a). fliːz MxL

flecks *npl* FLEAS IV.8.4. flɛks La Db *[not a NBM headword]*

fled *adj* FLEDGED IV.7.2. flɛd Wo Mon, fłɛd W D

fledged *adj When the young wild birds have got their feathers and are ready to go, you say they are* .... IV.7.2. flɛdʒd Nb La*[rare x1]* Y Ch Sa St He Wo Wa Mon O Nt L Lei R Nth Sf Bk Bd Hrt Ess MxL So Brk Sr K Ha Sx, fłɛdʒd Gl O W Ha. ⇒ **double stub, feathered, feathered-up, feathering,** *fit for flying, fit to fly,* **fled,** *fledge,* **fledged, fledged up, fledgers,** *fledging* ⇒ **fledgings, fledgings,** *fledgling* ⇒ **fledglings, fledglings, fleeters, flegged,** *flew,* **flidged, flidgings, flied,** *fliers* ⇒ **flyers, flig, fligged, fligged-flyers, fligged up, fliggers, fliggies,** *fligging,* **flish, flished, flitch, flitched, flitters, floppers,** *flown,* **flush, flushed, flushed up,** *flushing, fly,* **flyers, full-feathered, full-fledged, full-floppers, full-flushed, full-flyers, fully-feathered, fully fledged,** *getting onto the wing,* **half-flyers,** *in full plumage,* **nest-ripe,** *on the point of flushing, on the wing, on wing,* **ready,** *ready for fligging, ready for flushing, ready for flying, ready for off, ready to flig, ready to flit, ready to fly, starting to fly,* **wing-feathered, young fledglings**

fledged up *adj* FLEDGED IV.7.2. flɛdʒd ʊp Sa

fledgers *npl* young FLEDGED birds IV.7.2. flɛdʒəˡz K

fledging *n* a NESTLING IV.7.1. vłɪdʒɪn D, flɛdʒɪn Y Ess K, *pl* flɛdʒɪnz St So, *pl* vlɛdʒɪnz So, flɛdʒən Ess, flɛtʃɪn Mon *[marked ir.r. WM/EMBM]*

fledgings *npl* young FLEDGED birds IV.7.2. flɛdʒɪnz Ch O Ess, *sg* flɛdʒɪn K, *sg* flɛdʒən Ess

fledglets *npl* NESTLINGs IV.7.1. flɛdʒləts So

fledgling *n* a NESTLING IV.7.1. flɪdʒɫɪn Sr, flɛdʒlɪn Lei Nf Ess Brk K, *pl* flɛdʒlɪnz MxL So, *-s* flɛdʒlɪnz Hrt, flɛdʒɫɪn So, *pl* flɛdʒɫɪnz Gl, flɛdʒlən Nb *[marked ir.r. WM/EMBM]*

fledglings *npl* young FLEDGED birds IV.7.2. flɛdʒɫɪŋz Wa, flɛdʒlɪnz We Y Sa Wa, *sg* flɛdʒlɪn La Db, *no -s* flɛdʒɫɪn Nth Brk Sr K, flɛdʒɫɪnz Ess

fleece *n* a SHEEPSKIN III.11.8(a). fliːs St Lei Nf Sf Ess So, fɫiːs D

fleeced hide *n* the PELT of a sheep III.11.8(b). flɪˈəst ɑːd Y

fleed *1. n* the FAT round the kidneys of a pig III.12.7. fliːd Wo Sr K Sx

2. *n* SCRAPS left after rendering lard III.12.10. vɫiːd Ha *[queried ir.r. SBM]*

fleet *1. n* URINE in a cow-house I.3.10. vɫɪt D, vɫɛɪt D

2. *n* mixed dung and urine. vɫɛɪt D

fleeters *npl* young FLEDGED birds IV.7.2. fliːtəz Cu

fleffs *npl* FLEAS IV.8.4. flɛfs La Ch, *sg* flɛf St*[old]* *[not a NBM headword]*

flegged* *adj* FLEDGED IV.7.2. flɛgd Hrt

flegger *n* a NESTLING IV.7.1. *pl* flɛgəz Du

flen(s) *npl* FLEAS IV.8.4.

no -s: flɛn Sa*[old x1]* He Wo, vlɛn He, fɫɛn He

-s: flɛnz Sa*[old x1]* He Wo

flesh-flies *npl* bluebottle FLIES IV.8.5. flɛʃflɛɪz Y, flɛʃflɑɪz Y

flesh-meat *n* MEAT V.8.3. flɛʃmiːt Du

flick *1. n* a FLITCH or side of bacon III.12.3. flɪk Nb Cu Du We La Y Db Wa Nt L Lei Bd So, flɪkʰ Nb Du Y, flɪək Nb Y, fleːkʰ Nb, flɛkʰ Nb, fɫɛk W *[flick of bacon forms included here]*

2. *n* the FAT round the kidneys of a pig III.12.7. flɪk Mon Gl So W Do Ha, vlɪk So, fɫɪk Do, vɫɪk W D Do Ha, fɫɛk W, vɫɛk W Ha

flicking out *vtphr-ing* PUTTING your tongue OUT VI.5.4. fɫɪkən əʊt Do, vɫɪkən əʊt Do*[old]*

flidged *adj* FLEDGED IV.7.2. flɪdʒd Ess Sr *[not a SBM headword]*

flidgings *npl* young FLEDGED birds IV.7.2. flɪdʒɪnz Cu

flied *1. adj* FLEDGED IV.7.2. fɫæːd D, vɫæɪd D, fɫaɪd D

2. *adj* CHAPPED VI.7.2. fɫaɪd D; **flied open** fɫæɪd oːpn D

flies *npl* You cover up meat in the pantry, to keep what away? IV.8.5. Eng. ⇒ **blow-flies, blowing-flies, blue-arse-flies, blue-bottles, blue-flies, flesh-flies, mawk-flies, mawky-flies, meat-flies** *[fly recorded MxL and Sx with no indication of wordclass status]*

flig *adj* FLEDGED IV.7.2. flɪg Wa L Lei

fligged *adj* FLEDGED IV.7.2. flɪgd Nb Y Db Nt L Nth Hu C Bd

fligged-flyers *npl* young FLEDGED birds IV.7.2. flɪgdflɑɪəz Hu

fligged up *adj* FLEDGED IV.7.2. flɪgd ʌp Hrt

fliggers *npl* young FLEDGED birds IV.7.2. flɪgəz Y R

fliggies *npl* young FLEDGED birds IV.7.2. flɪgɪz Du

flights *n* CHAFF II.8.5. flaɪts Y

flimsy *adj* BRITTLE, describing cups and saucers which break easily IX.1.4. flɪmsiˈ Nf

fling *1. v* to PITCH sheaves II.6.10. flɪŋ Ess

2. *vt* to SLIP A FOAL III.4.6. vlɪŋ Gl

flinging *v-ing* THROWING a stone VIII.7.7. flɪŋɪn Y Wo Sf Ess So, flɪŋən Sf Ess, fɫɪŋɪn W, fɫɪŋən Ha, vɫɪŋɪn W D, vɫɪŋən D Do Ha

fling over *viphr* to OVERTURN, referring to a cart I.11.5. flɪŋ ᴅʊə Du

flinter-bat *n* a BAT IV.7.7. flɪntəˈbæˑt K

flint-stone *n* a WHETSTONE II.9.10. flɪntston Nf

flipe *1. n* the BRIM of a hat VI.14.3. flɛɪp Nb, flæɪp Y, flaɪp Nb Du Y

2. *n* the peak of a cap. flɛɪp Du

flipping out *vtphr-ing* PUTTING your tongue OUT VI.5.4. fləpɪn ... æʊt So

flirt open *vtphr* to shell peas, ⇐ SHELLING V.7.14. fləːt ... oʊpn St

flish* *adj* FLEDGED IV.7.2. fɫiːʃ Co D

flished* *adj* FLEDGED IV.7.2. fɫiːʃt D, flɪʃt Brk, fɫɪʃt Ha

flishes *npl* BLISTERS VI.11.5. flɪʃɪz Y*[can develop into a full blister]*, *sg* flɪʃ Y

flitch *1. n* What do you call the side of a pig when salted and cured? III.12.3. flɪtʃ La Y Man Ch Db Sa St He Wo Wa Mon Gl O Nt L Lei R Nth Hu Nf Sf Bk Bd Hrt Ess So W Brk Sr K Ha Sx, vlɪtʃ He Gl So Brk Do, fɫɪtʃ Mon W Co D, vɫɪtʃ Gl W Co D Do Ha, flɛtʃ Nb, vlɛtʃ Brk, vɫɛtʃ Ha. ⇒ **flick, flick of bacon, flitch of bacon, picture, side, side of bacon, side-piece** *[flitch of bacon forms included here]*

2. *adj* FLEDGED IV.7.2. fɫɪtʃ Ha

flitched *adj* FLEDGED IV.7.2. fɫɪtʃt Ha

flitter-bat *n* a BAT IV.7.7. flɪtəᶜbæt Sx

flitter-mouse *n* a BAT IV.7.7. flɪtəˈmɛʊs Sx, flɪʔəmɛʊs Nf*[small, light brown]*, flɪtəmæʊs K, flɪtəmuːs Y, flɪtəˈməʊs K

flitters *1. n* SCRAPS left after rendering lard III.12.10. flɪtəz Hu Bd Ess, flɪtʔəz C, flɪʔəz Hu

2. *npl* young FLEDGED birds IV.7.2. flɪtəˈz K*[old]*

floats *n* a CART-FRAME I.10.6. flᴅʊts K

flobbers *v-3prsg* he GUZZLES a drink VI.5.13(a). flᴅbəᶜz Gl

flock *n* a BROOD of chickens IV.6.12. flɒk Ch Sa

flood *1. n* in (a) **flood, up flood** *After very heavy rains a river becomes swollen, and so you say the river is* .... IV.1.4. **in flood** ɪn flɪʊd Cu, ə flɪʊd Cu, ɪn flɪəd Cu Y, ɪn flød Nb, ɪn flʌd Sa He Mon O Nf Bd Hrt Ess So Sr K Ha, ɪn fɬʌd Co D, ɪn vɬʌd D, ɪn flɤd Du Nf, ɪn flʊd Nb Du We La Y Man St Nt L Brk K, ɪ flʊd La*[=overflowing x1]* Y Wo Wa Mon, ɪn fɬʊd He; **in a flood** ɪn ə flʊd Cu; **up flood** ʌp flʌd Brk. ⇒ **aflood**, *bang* **full, bank-high, brae-full, brimming over,** *broke the banks, broke through, burst the bank, come out* ⇒ **coming out, coming down, coming out,** *flooded,* **flooded out, flooded over, flooded up, flooding, flooding over, flowing over, full, full-flooded, full up,** *getting very* **strong, high, high-tide,** *in a* **flood,** *in* **spate, out, over-banked, over-flood, over-flowed, over-flowing, over-flown, risen, rising, rose, rose up, runned over, running full, running over,** *rushing over the banks,* **sprung up, swelled, swelled up, swole up, swollen,** *swollen up* ⇒ **swole up,** *there's a big flood out,* **thickening, up,** *up* **flood, up** *high, well* **out,** *well* **up** *[question was intended to refer to a swollen river only, not to one that is overflowing: however, several terms, most notably those with* **over** *and* **out,** *apparently refer to overflowing, and these are variably marked as u.r. in the BM volumes]*
2. v to STOCK a cow III.3.6. *-ing* flʊdɪn St

flooded *adj* BOGGY IV.1.8. flʌdɪd So *[marked u.r. SBM]*

flooded out *adj IN* FLOOD, describing a river IV.1.4. flʊdɪd ɛʊt Wo *[see note at* **flood***]*

flooded over *adj IN* FLOOD, describing a river IV.1.4. flʊdɪd ʊvə Lei *[see note at* **flood***]*

flooded up *adj IN* FLOOD, describing a river IV.1.4. flʊdɪd ʊp Lei

flooding *adj IN* FLOOD, describing a river IV.1.4. flʌdɪn So K, *prppl* flʌdɪn Hrt, flʊdɪn St Wo

flooding over *adj IN* FLOOD, describing a river IV.1.4. *prppl* flʌdn ouvə Sf *[see note at* **flood***]*

flood-meadows *n* LOW-LYING LAND IV.1.7. fɬʌdmɛdoːz Mon, flʌdmɛdəᵗz̩ Sa Mon, flʊdmɛdəz Sa

floods *n* A LOT (of money) VII.8.7. flʌdz So

floor *1. n* What do you call this *[indicate the floor of a house]?* V.2.7. Eng; **house-floor** aɪsflʊə St. ⇒ **board,** *house-floor;* ⇒ also **causen, floor-cloth, quarry-floor, planching**
2. n the GROUND IV.4.1. flɪə Y, flɪ'ːə Ch, fly·əᴵ Db, flɛʊə Ch Db, flɔː Wa, flɔə Nf, floː Wa, floːə Db C, flo·əᵗ Wa Nth, flʊə Y*[old x1]* Db Nt, flᵁuə Ch, flʊəᴵ La, flᵁuːəɪ La
3. vt to cut large branches from a tree, ⇐ to LOP IV.12.5. *-ing* flɔːɹɪn Sx *[queried SBM]*

floor-board *n* a CART-FRAME I.10.6. flʊəbʊəd St

floor-cloth* *n* linoleum, ⇐ FLOOR V.2.7. flɔəᴵklɒːθ Brk

flop *1. adj* SAD, describing bread or pastry that has not risen V.6.12. flɒp La
2. n a BUMP on someone's forehead VI.1.8. flɒp So
3. n the FLAP at the front of old-fashioned trousers VI.14.16. flɒp Bk, fɬɒp D, vɬɒp D, *pl* flɒps L
4. n DEW VII.6.7. flɒp Wa O*[old]* Bk
5. vt to BEAT a boy on the buttocks VIII.8.10. flɒp L

flop out *viphr* to FAINT VI.13.7. flɒp ɛʊt Sx

flop over *viphr* to turn HEAD OVER HEELS IX.1.10. flɒp oə Ch

flopped out *adj* EXHAUSTED, describing a tired person VI.13.8. flɒpt ɛʊt K

floppers *npl* young FLEDGED birds IV.7.2. flɑ·pəz Nf, flɒpʔəs Nf

flopping-front* *n* the FLAP at the front of old-fashioned trousers VI.14.16. *pl* flɒpɪnfɹʊnts La

flour *1. n* What do you make your white bread out of? V.6.1(a). Eng. ⇒ **wheat-flour, white-flour**
2. n MEAL V.6.1(b). flɛʊə Db*[bran added]*, flɛʊəᵗ Sx

flour-bin *1. n* a container for flour, ⇐ CORN-BIN I.7.4. flæʊəbɪn Y Ess, flaʊəbɪn Y, flʊ·əᴵbɪn Y, fluəbɪn Du Y
2. n a wooden flour-container. flᵊuːəbɪn We

flour-bing *1. n* a container for flour, ⇐ CORN-BIN I.7.4. flɪu·əbɪŋ L, flaʊəbɪŋ L, fluəbɪŋ Y, flu·əbɪŋ Nb
2. n a wooden flour-container. flu·əbɪŋ Y

flour-lithe *vt* to THICKEN gravy V.7.7. flaʊəlaɪð La

flower show *n* a local FESTIVAL or holiday VII.4.11. flɛʊəᵗ ʃʊʊ K, vlaʊəᵗː ʒoʊ So, flaːᵊ ʃʌʊ Ess, flʌʊə ʃaʊ Gl; **flower show day** flɛʊəᵗ ʃʊʊ dɛɪ K, flaː ʃʊu dɛɪ K

flowing over *adj IN* FLOOD, describing a river IV.1.4. floːɪn oəɹ La, floːən oəɹ La *[see note at* **flood***]*

flows *n* the top layer of PEAT IV.4.3. flɪ'əz Y

flue *1. n* the VULVA of a cow III.2.3. flɪʊʊː Ess
2. n a CHIMNEY V.1.3. fɬɪʊ Co
3. adj CHAPPED VI.7.2. flɪuː Ess *[queried EMBM]*

flush *1. v* to clean a DITCH by running water down it IV.2.11. flʌʃ Sa
2. adj FLEDGED IV.7.2. flœːʃ Gl, flʌʃ He Mon Gl So Do, fɬʌʃ W Do, flʊʃ Ch Db Sa St*[old x2]* He Wo

flushed *adj* FLEDGED IV.7.2. flyːʃt La, flʌʃt Sa He So, fɬʌʃt W Co Do Ha, vɬʌʃt Do, flʊʃt La Db He Wo Mon Gl, fɬʊʃt Co

flushed up *adj* FLEDGED IV.7.2. flʌʃt ʌp W

flush up *vtphr* to STOCK a cow III.3.6. fluʃ ... ʊp L

fly *1. adj* CHAPPED VI.7.2. flɒɪ So*[rare]*

2. n the FLAP at the front of old-fashioned trousers VI.14.16. flæɪ Man*[rare]*, flaɪ Nb*[old]* Y*[old x1]* So, flaɪ Y Lei, *pl* vɫɒɪz Ha, flɔɪ O, *pl* flɔɪz Ess

fly-away *n* the FLAP at the front of old-fashioned trousers VI.14.16. flaɪ-əwɛɪ St

fly-ballups *n* the FLAP at the front of old-fashioned trousers VI.14.16. *?pl* flaɪbɛləps Nb

fly-blowed *1. adj* HEAVING *WITH MAGGOTS* IV.8.6. flaɪblɔːd Sa, flaːɪblʊʊd St, flɑːblʊʊd Lei, flɑ·ɪblʊʊd Lei, flɒɪblʊʊd Wo, flɒɪblɔːd Sa, flɒːɪblʊʊd St Lei, flɔɪblɑʊd Ess, flɔɪblɔːd Wa, flʌɪblʊʊd Sr, flɛɪblɛʊd Sx, flɛɪblæʊd Brk, flɛɪblʊʊd Sx, flɛɪblʊʊd Wo

2. adj **get fly-blowed** to SPOIL, referring to meat or fish V.7.10. *3prsg* gɛts flɔɪblʊʊd Wo

fly-blown *adj* HEAVING *WITH MAGGOTS* IV.8.6. fliːblɔːn L, vliːblu·ən So, flaɪblʊʊn Nf K, flɑ·ɪblɔʊn Lei, flɒɪblʊʊn K, flɔɪblʊʊn Brk Sr Sx, flɔɪblɔʊn Ess K Sx, flɔɪblʌʊn Ess, flɔɪ·blʊʊn Ha, flʌɪblʊʊn Nf, flʌɪblɔ·ʊŋ Brk, vlɛɪbɫɒn W, flɛɪblʊʊn Sx

flyers *npl* young FLEDGED birds IV.7.2. flaɪəz L Nth Sf Bd Ess, flaɪəᵗz̧ K, flɔɪəz Ess, flɔɪəᴶz O, flʌi-əs Nf, flʌɪ-əz Nf

fly-fall *n* the FLAP at the front of old-fashioned trousers VI.14.16. flaɪfɔːl La

fly-flap *n* the FLAP at the front of old-fashioned trousers VI.14.16. flaɪflap Cu

fly-flapper *n* the FLAP at the front of old-fashioned trousers VI.14.16. flaɪflapəᴿ Nb

fly-front *n* the FLAP at the front of old-fashioned trousers VI.14.16. flæɪfɾʌnt So, flaɪfɹʊnt Nb Y*[modern x2]*, flaɪfɾʌnt So, *pl* flaɪfɹʊnts L, *pl* flaɪfɹʊnts Ch, flɒɪfɾʌnt Do, flɔɪfɾʌnt Do, vlɔɪvɾʌnt Do

flying-bat *n* a BAT IV.7.7. flaɪnbat Y, *pl* flʌi-ɪnbæts Nf

flying-mouse *n* a BAT IV.7.7. flʌɪ-ɪnməʊs Nf

fly-stones *n* the CURB-STONE in a cow-house I.3.9. flaɪsto·əns Man

fly-strucken *adj* HEAVING *WITH MAGGOTS* IV.8.6. flaɪstɹʊkn L

foal *n Now let's talk about horses. What do you call the young animal?* III.4.1. Eng; **horse-foal** ɑsfʊʊl C. ⇒ **colt**, *horse-foal*

foal-foot *n* COLT'S-FOOT II.2.7. fɪalfʊt Cu, føːlfʊt Nb Du, fœːlfʊt Nb, fɒɪlfɾiːt Y, fɔːlfɪət Cu Y, fɔːlfʊt Du Y, fɔːlfʊt Lei, fɔɪlfʊt Y, fɔɪlfʊɪt Y, fɔʊlfʊt L, fɔʊfʊt Nth Hu, foːlfɪət We, foːlfʊt Du Y Db Nt, foʊlfʊt Db C, foʊfʊt Lei, fuəlfʊt We, fuəlfʊt Nb Cu Du Y Nt L

foal's-foot *n* COLT'S-FOOT II.2.7. fʊʊlsfʊt Nth, fɔʊɫzfʊt Lei Hu, foulzfʊt Nf

fodder *1.1. vt* to FEED cattle III.3.1. fɒdə Db, -s fɒdəz Y, fɒdəɹ (+V) Y Db St R Bk*[hay or straw]*, fɒdəɽ (+V) O, fɒdəᴶɹ Sr, fɒdɹ Y Db, fɒdəᵗɽ Bk*[hay]*, fɒdðə We*[hay and/or straw]*, fɒðə Nb Cu Du We*[hay and/or straw]* St*[hay]*, *3prsg* fɒðəz Y, fɒðəɹ (+V) La*[hay and/or straw]* Y Ch*[hay x1]* Nt*[hay or seeds]*, fɒðəᵗ Sx, fɔdəɹ (+V) Y Ch C*[hay or straw]*, fɔdəᴶ (+V) La, fɔdəɽ (+V) K*[hay and straw, last meal of night]*, fɔðə Nb, *3prsg* fɔðəz L, fɔðɹ L, fɔðəɹ (+V) Y L

1.2. v to feed cattle. fadəᴶ O*[old]*, fɒdɔᴿ Nb, fɒðɔᴿ Nb*[old]*, fɒdə Cu Du La*[hay and/or straw]* Y Db*[hay x1]* O*[in fields]* L Bd*[hay or straw]*, fɒdɹ Y, fɒdəɹ La*[hay and/or straw]*, fɒdðə Cu, *prppl* fɒðð.ɪɪn La*[hay and/or straw]*, fɒðə Nb Du La*[hay and/or straw]* Y O*[old]* Hu, fɔðɔᴿ Nb, fɔðə Y Sr, fɔðə Y L, fɔðəɹ L

2. n CHAFF fed to horses III.5.3. fɒðə Y

fodder-bin *n* the GANGWAY in a cow-house I.3.7. fɔdəbɪn Ch

fodder-bing *1. n* the GANGWAY in a cow-house I.3.7. fɒdəbɪŋ Db St

2. n the gangway in a cow-house, used to store hay, ⇐ HAY-LOFT I.3.18. fɒdəbɪŋg Db

fodder down *vtphr* to FEED cattle III.3.1. fɒðəɹ (+V) ... daːn Y

fodder-field *n* a MEADOW II.9.2. fɔðɹfiːld L

fodder-gang *n* the GANGWAY in a cow-house I.3.7. fɒdəgaŋ We La Y, fɒdəᴶgɛŋk Db, fɒdðəgaŋ Cu We La

fodder-house *n* part of a cow-house partitioned off for the storage of hay, ⇐ HAY-LOFT I.3.18. fɒdəᵗːɾæʊs Ha, fɒdəᵗːɾæʏs Co

foddering *1.1. v-ing* FEEDING horses in the stable III.5.1. *v* fadə Nth*[hay, at night]*, *v* fɒdə Cu*[hay]* We*[hay]* La*[hay x1]* Y Db*[hay x1]* Nt*[hay]* Bd*[hay]*, *v* fɒdɹ Y, fɒdəᴶɹɪn Sr*[hay in racks]*, fɒðə.ɹɪn Cu*[hay x2]* Y*[old x1]* St, fɒðəʁən Nb*[last meal of day x1]*, *v* fɒðə Du*[hay x1]* We*[hay]* La*[hay]* Nt*[clover or hay]* Hu*[hay]*, fɔðə.ɹɪn Y Ch, fɔðɔʁən Nb, fɔðəʁən Nb, *v* fɔðə Y, *v* fɔðɹ L, *v* fɔðəᴶ La

1.2. vt-ing feeding horses. fɒðəɹ (+V) Sr

2. v-ing BAITING a horse when resting from work III.5.2. *prppl* əfɒdəᴶɹɪn Brk, *v* fɒdə Db, *v* fɔðə L, *v* fɔðəɹ Wa

foddering-ginnel* *n* the GANGWAY in a cow-house I.3.7. fɒdə.ɹɪngɪnəl Y

foddering-passage* *n* the GANGWAY in a cow-house I.3.7. fɒdə.ɹɪnpasɪdʒ Y

foddering up **1.1. vphr-ing* FEEDING horses in the stable III.5.1. fɒðə.ɹɪn ʊp Y

*1.2. vtphr-ing feeding horses. fɒdə.ɹɪn ... ʊp Y, fɔðə.ɹɪn ... ʊp Y

2. vtphr-ing BAITING a horse when resting from work III.5.2. fɔðə.ɹɪn ... ʊp L

fodder out *vphr* to bait a horse when resting from work, ⇐ BAITING III.5.2. fɒdəˡ əʊt Brk

fodder-run *n* the GANGWAY in a cow-house I.3.7. fɒdəɹʊn Y *[queried NBM; possibly a form of fodderum]*

fodderum *n* the GANGWAY in a cow-house I.3.7. fɒdərəm Y, fɒdɹəm Y Db

fodder up *1. vtphr* to FEED cattle III.3.1. *-ing* fɒdɹɪn ... ʌp L*[hay]*, fɒðəɹ (+V) ... ʊp Y*[hay and/or straw x1]*, fɔðəɹ (+V) ... ʊp Y
2. viphr to feed cattle. fɒdəɹ ʊp Y, *ptppl* fɒðəd ʊp Y
3. vphr to feed cattle. fɒdəɹ ʌp Sr, *-ing* fɒðəɹɪn ʊp L

fodder-yard *n* the STRAW-YARD of a farm I.1.9. fɒddəjaːd Db

fog *1. n* When it is really thick outside, especially in November, you call it.... VII.6.9. Eng. ⇒ **mist, rawk, rime**
2. n MIST VII.6.8. faːg Nf, fɒg St Wa Nf, vɔːg So
3. n a TUSSOCK of grass II.2.9. fɒg Lei; **old fog** oʊɫ fɒg Lei
4. n AFTERMATH, a second crop of grass II.9.17. fœːg Nb Du, fɒg Nb Cu Du We La Y, fɔg Cu Y L
5. n dead grass left over winter. fɒg L

fogger *n* a COWMAN on a farm I.2.3. fɑgɹ O, *pl* fɒgəˡz Brk, fɒgəˡ Brk

foggy-frost *n* HOAR-FROST VII.6.6. fɒgɪfɹɔːs Bd

fold *1. v* If you want to confine your sheep to only one part of a field, how do you do it? III.7.10.
vt faːd Du, fɒʊld Nf*[temporarily x1]*, fɒʊɫd Co Sx, fɔːld Cu, fɔːd Du, fɒʊɫd Hu K, fɒʊd L, fʌʊɫd Bd Ess, *-ing* fʌʊɫdɪn Hrt, foːld W, voːɫd Co Ha, *-ing* foʊldn Nf, foʊl Brk, *-ing* foʊɫdɪn So, voʊld W
v fæʊd Sa, vaʊɫd Gl, fɒʊld Y Nf*[temporarily x1]* K*[on turnips, corn, or hay]*, fɒʊɫd Sr K Sx, fɒʊɫ Sx, fɒʊd Nt Sr, fɔːld We, fɔːd Y*[for clipping or dipping]*, fɔʊld Y L, fɔʊl Wo, fɒʊɫd Lei R Nth Hu Sf Ess, *pt* fɔʊɫdɪd MxL, *-ing* fɔʊɫdɪn K, vɔʊɫd Ha, fɔʊd L Ess, fɔˑəd Y, *-ing* fɔˑədɪn Y, fʌʊɫd C Sf Bd Hrt Ess, fʌʊd Sf Bk, foːld Sa, foːɫd O So Brk, *ptppl* əvoːɫdəd Ha, foʊld St Nf, foʊɫd Lei C Bk Bd Ha, *prppl* foʊɫdɪn So, *-ing* foʊdɪn St*[on turnips x1]*, foˑəld Man
⇒ **bar up, break, fence, fence in, fence off, fold back, fold in, fold off, fold on, fold** *on the back,* **fold up,** *give a* **breck,** *hit* **hurdles** *up,* **hold, hurdle, hurdle in, hurdle off, hurdle off** *in a pen,* **hurdle out, hurdle up, mound, mound off, net, net off, part, part** *the field,* **part** *the field with hurdles,* **pen, pen in, pen off, pen up, pinfold, pitch, pitch** *a fold,* **pitch** *a* **pen, pitch** *a sheep-fold,* **pound,** *put a* **breck** *up, put in a pen, put into a pen, put on the* **breck,** *set a fold for,* **wattle**
2. vt-3prpl they KEEP hens IV.6.2. fɔʊd Nb
3. n a FARMYARD I.1.3. fɛʊd Sa, fɒʊɫd Mon, fɔːld We, fɔʊd Y, foːld Cu He
4. n the STRAW-YARD of a farm I.1.9. fæʊd He, fæˑd Nb, faːd Nb Du, fɒʊɫd Co, fɔːd Du, fɔʊd Y, *pl* fɔədz Y, foːɫ He, fəʊd He
5. n a straw-yard in which cattle are fattened. fɛʊd Sa, faʊd Sa He, foːɫd He
6. n a PADDOCK I.1.10. fɔːˑd Du

fold back *vtphr* to PEN or FOLD sheep in part of a field III.7.10. voːɫd ... bak D

folder *n* a FARMYARD I.1.3. vɒʊɫdəˡ Gl

fold-garth *n* the STRAW-YARD of a farm I.1.9. fɔˑədgaːθ Y

fold in *1. vtphr* to PEN or FOLD sheep in part of a field III.7.10. fɒʊd ... ɪn L, fʌʊld ... ɪn Ess
2. vphr to pen or fold sheep. voːɫd ɪn D

fold off *1. vtphr* to PEN or FOLD sheep in part of a field III.7.10. fɒʊld ... ɔːf Nf, *-ing* fɒʊdɪn ... ɔːf Sr, fɔʊɫd ... ɔːf Sr, fɔʊd ... ɒf Y, fʌʊld ... ɔːf Nf, voːɫd ... ɔːf W Ha
2. vphr to pen or fold sheep. *-ing* fɒʊɫdɪn ɒːf Sx

fold on *vtphr* to PEN or FOLD sheep in part of a field III.7.10. *-ing* fɔədɪn ... ɒn Y

fold up *1. vtphr* to PEN or FOLD sheep in part of a field in winter III.7.10. fɒʊd ... ʊp Nt
2. vtphr to WRAP a parcel VII.2.9. fɒʊld ʊp K, *-ing* fɒʊdɪn ... ʌp Sx, foːd ... ʌp W, vɒʊld ... ʌp W, fɒʊld ... ʊp Wo
3. vtphr-3sg she [i.e. a tidy girl] will COLLECT her toys VIII.8.15. fɔʊɫd ... ʌp O, fʌʊɫd ... ʌp Sf *[marked u.r. WMBM]*

fold-yard *1. n* a FARMYARD I.1.3. faʊldjaːd Y, fɒʊdjaːd Nt, fɔːdjaːd Y, fɔʊldjaːd Y, foʊldjaːd St, foʊldjəˡːd̩ Wo
2. n the STRAW-YARD of a farm I.1.9. fɛʊtjaːd St, faːdjæːd Du, faʊdjaˡːd̩ Sa, faʊljaːd Y, fɒʊdjaːd Db, fɔːdjɛˑəd Y, fɔːdjaːd Y, fɔʊljaɪd Y, fɔʊldjaːd Y, fɔʊdjaːd Y L, fɔədjaːd Y, foːldjaˡːd̩ Sa, foʊldjaːd St, foʊldjaːd St, foʊdjaːd St, foʊdjaːd Wo, foʊdjəˡːd̩ Wo, foʊljəˡːd̩ Wo, fuːldjaːd St, fʊədjaːd Y
3. n a straw-yard in which cattle are fattened. fɛʊdjaːd Db Nt, fæʊdjəˡːd̩ He, fɒʊɫdjaˡːd̩ He, fɒʊdjaːd Nt
4. n a straw-yard in which cattle are kept to produce dung. fɔʊljaːd Wa

foliage *n* the STEM of a corn-plant II.5.2(a). fɒʊlɪdʒ K

folk(s) *npl* PEOPLE VIII.2.12.
no -s: føːk Nb, føək Nb, fœːˀk Nb, fɒk Y, fɒʊk La Y, fɔːk Nb Cu We, vɔːk So W Do, fɔʊk La Y Wo R Brk, fɔək Cu, fʌk C*[old]*, fʌʊk C, foːk Du La Ch Db Sa, vɒːk Gl So W D Do Ha, foʊk St He Lei, voːˀk Gl, foək Nb Cu We La Y Ch L, fuːk Ch, fʊək Cu Du We La Y Ch L
-s: føˀks Du, fɛʊks Ch, fœːks Nb, fɒʊks Db He Wo Wa Nth Sr Sx, fɔːks We, vɔːks D, fɔʊks Y St Wo Wa O Lei R Nth, fʌʊks L Bk*[old x1]* Bd Hrt Ess, foːks Du La Y Ch Sa He Wo Gl Brk, voːks

So Co D Ha, foʊks St He Wo Wa*[old x1]* Lei Nth Nf Bk Bd So, voʊks Ha, foːʊks Db He Mon Gl Nt, foəks Du Y Db, fʊks Nf, fʊəks Nb We Y Ch Db Nt L, fuːks Ch, vuːks D

followers *npl* MOURNERS VIII.5.12. vɒɫəˤːɾəˤːz̩ Ha

follows *vt-3prsg* he RESEMBLES VIII.1.9. fɒloːz He, fɒləz L, fɒləz Wa

fond *1. adj* STUPID VI.1.5. fɒnd Y

2. *adj* SILLY VIII.9.3. fœˑnd Nb*[old]*, fɒnd Y

fond-brazen *adj* STUPID VI.1.5. fɒndbɹaznd Y

food *1. n* If a child wasn't well and didn't want anything to eat, you might say she was off her .... V.8.2. Eng exc. Cu Co. ⇒ **appetite, bait, bat, biscuit, chuck, cud, diet, eating, feed, grub, hooks, meat,** *off colour, off* **food,** *off* **hooks,** *off of her* **food,** *off of the* **hooks,** *off side, off the* **hooks,** *out of sorts*, **peck, pick, snap, stomach, tommy, victual(s);** ⇒ also **hand-meat, kysty**

2. *n* **food for the day** MEAL OUT VII.5.12. fuːd fə tʔ deː Y

food-cellar *n* a PANTRY V.2.6. fuːdsɛlə Y

food-cupboard *n* a PANTRY V.2.6. fuːdkʌbəd Nf

fool *1. n* a STUPID person VI.1.5. fuːl St

2. *n* a SILLY person VIII.9.3. fɪvl Nb

foolish *adj* SILLY VIII.9.3. fuːlɪʃ Ess

foor-head(s) *n* HEADLANDS in a ploughed field II.3.3.

no -s: vɒɾiːd So, vɔˤːɾɪd So Co D, vɔˤːɾɛd Co

-s: vɔˤːɾiːdz So, vɔˤːɾɪdz D, vɔˤːɾədz So

foorings *n* HEADLANDS in a ploughed field II.3.3. vɔˤːɾɛnz Co, vɔˤːɾənz Co *[also interpretable as foor-ends]*

foot *1. n* the HANDLE of a besom I.3.16. fʊt Man

2. *n* the SHAFT of a hay-fork I.7.12. fʊt Man

3. *n* the SOLE of a horse-drawn plough I.8.9. fʌt Sa, fʊt Ch Sa St He Wo Lei So, vʊt So

4. *n* the BASE of a stack II.7.4. fʊt K Sx

5. *n* the HOOF of a cow III.2.8(a). *pl* fɪt O, fɪʊt Cu, fʊt Mon Nf, fᵁuːt La

6. *n* the HOOF of a horse III.4.10(a). fɪʊt Cu, fʊt Y Ch Wa O, fɪət Y

7. *n* the measurement FEET VI.10.10. fɪt Cu, fɪʊt Cu Y, fɪət Y, vʏt So Co D, fʌt Sa He Mon O Hu Bd Hrt, fʌʔ Bk, fʏt Nb Nf, fʊt Eng exc Bd W Brk D Do, fʊʔ O Bk, vʊt Gl So W Co Do Ha, fʊɪt Y, fᵁuːt La, fuːt La Ch Brk, fət Y, vət Gl *[[ɪə] forms in Y all interpreted as foot, though those at Y.2/11/16 could be feet according to foot/feet VI.10.1]*

8. *vt* **foot it** to WALK VIII.7.10. fʌt ɪt Sa, fʊt ɪt St Brk Sx

foot-board *n* a BUMPER of a cart I.10.1(a). vʊtboːəˤːd̩ So

foot-bridge *n* a STILE IV.2.9. fʊtbɹɪdʒ St *[queried u.r. WMBM]*

foot-brig *n* the CROSS-BEAM END of a cart I.10.1. fʊtbɹɪg L

foot-cocks *npl* COCKS of hay II.9.12. fɪtkɒks Cu, *sg* fɪʏtkɒk Cu Du, fɪʊtkɒks Cu, fɪʊtkɒk Y, fɪuːtkɒks Y, fɪətkɒks We La Y, *sg* fɪətkɒk Cu, fɪətkɔks We, fʊtkɒks Du Y Ch Nt, *sg* fʊtkɒk Nb, fʊtkɔks Y, fuːtkɒks La, fuːtkɔks Ch

foot-coils *npl* COCKS of hay II.9.12. fʊtkɒɪlz Db

foot-gate *n* a PATH through a field IV.3.11. fʊɪtgeːt Y*[for cattle or people x1]*, fʊɪtgeət Y

foot-holes *npl* the HOOF-MARKS of a horse IV.3.10. fʊtɔʊlz Nth, vʊtoːɫz W, fʊtoʊlz Nf, fʊtoʊɫz So, fʊtoːᵁlz Db, fʊthʊəlz Nb, fʊtʊəlz Y

foot-horse *n* a SHAFT-HORSE I.6.2. fuːtɔːs La, fuːtɔᴶːs La

footing *1. n* the CURB-STONE in a cow-house I.3.9. fʊtɪn Y

2. *n* the BASE of a stack II.7.4. fʊɪtɪn Y*[made of saddle-wood, ?= staddle-wood]*

footings *npl* the HOOF-MARKS of a horse IV.3.10. fɪtnz Cu, fɪətɪnz Y, fʊtɪnz Db St K, *sg* fʊtn Nf

footlings *npl* the HOOF-MARKS of a horse IV.3.10. fʌtlɪnz Bd Hrt, fʊtlɪŋks St, fʊtlɪnz St Lei Bd

foot-marks *npl* the HOOF-MARKS of a horse IV.3.10. fɪətmaːks We Y, vʏtmaˤːks Co D, vʏtmaˤːks D, fʌtmaːks Nth, *sg* fʌtmaᴮːk Nb, fʌtmaˤːks Sa, fʌʔmaˤːks Bd, fʊtmæːks Du, fʊtmaːks Cu Du Y Ch St Sf Hrt Ess, fʊtmaˤːks O Bk Brk, fʊʔmaˤːks Bk, vʊtmaˤːks Ha, vʊtmaˤːkṣ Do, fʊtmaːks Db St Nf Ess MxL, *sg* fʊʔmaːk Hrt, fʊtmaᴮːks Nb, fʊtmaˤːks Brk, fʊtmɑːəˤks Sx, fʊɪtmaːks Y, fuːtmæᴶːks La, fuːtmaᴶːks La *[[fɪət-]-form at Y16 ambiguous, problem of interpretation being common to east and north Y; no feet-marks headword in NBM, but some forms are interpreted as such by reference to VI.10.1. foot/feet]*

foot-pad *n* a PATH through a field IV.3.11. fʊtpad La Y Db Nt L Lei Nth, fuːtpad La

foot-pads *npl* the HOOF-MARKS of a horse IV.3.10. *sg* fʊtpad Hu

foot-path *n* a PATH through a field IV.3.11. fɪˈətpaθ Y, vʏtpaːθ So Co D, fɒtpæˀθ Man, fʌtpa:θ O Nth, fʌˀpaːf Bd, fʏtpæθ Nf, fʊtpæθ Nb Wa, fʊʔpæːθ So, vʊtpæːθ So Do, fʊtpaθ Cu Du Y Db St He Ha*[for people]*, fʊtpað Nb, fʊtpaːθ Db Wa Gl O Nth Hu C Sf Bk Hrt Ess, *pl* fʊtpaːðz Bd, vʊtpaːθ W Do Ha, vʊtpaːf Do, fʊtpaːθ O Nf Ess MxL Sr Ha Sx, fʊtpaːð Sr Sx, vʊtpaːð Sx, fʊʔpɑːθ Hrt, fʊɪtpaθ Y, fətpaθ Nb, vətpaːθ Gl

foot-plough *1. n* a PLOUGH I.8.1. fʊtpleʊ Ess K Sx

2. *n* a heavy plough. fʊtpleʊ K

3. n a plough with no wheels. fʊtpleʊ K, fʊtplæu K

foot-prints *npl* the HOOF-MARKS of a horse IV.3.10. fʊtprɪnts Cu, fʊtpɹɪnts We Y Db St L Ess K, fuːtpɹɪnts La

foot-road *n* a PATH through a field IV.3.11. fɪətɹʊəd Y*[for people]*, fʊtɹʊd Wo, fʊtɹoːd Ch, fʊtɹoʊd St Wa, fʊtɹʊəd Y L, *pl* fuːtɹʊədz Y

foots *n* FEET VI.10.1(b). fʌts O, fʊts L

foot-spade *n* a SPADE I.7.6. fʊtspeɪᵊd C

foot-steps *npl* the HOOF-MARKS of a horse IV.3.10. fʊtstɛps C Ha

foot-stile *n* a STILE IV.2.9. fʊtstaɪl Nth

foot-stump *n* the HANGING-POST of a gate IV.3.3. fʊtstʊmp Ch

foot-track *n* a PATH through a field IV.3.11. fʊttʁak Nb*[old]*

foot-trod *n* a PATH through a field IV.3.11. fɪttrɒd Cu, fʊttrɒd Cu, fʊttrɒd Cu, fʊttɹɒd Y*[for people x1]*

foot-walk *n* a PATH through a field IV.3.11. fʊtwɒk Man, fʊtwɔːk Ch

ford *n Sometimes there is no bridge [across a river]. What do you call that shallow place where you can walk across?* IV.1.3. Eng. ⇒ **by-wash, drift-way, ebb-place, fording-place, ford-stead, forge, gap, gully, low place, ope-way, scour, shallow(s), shallow-shop, shallow spot, shallow water, sluice, splash, splosh, wash, wash-way, water-splash, water-wash, water-way, wath, wath-stead;** ⇒ also **leapings**

fording-place *n* a FORD IV.1.3. fɔɹdɪnpleːs He

ford-stead *n* a FORD IV.1.3. faːdstˡiːd Du

fore *1. prep* TILL IX.2.2. vɔt: D
2. prep IN FRONT OF a door IX.2.6. fɔːɹ (+V) K

fore-acre(s) *n* HEADLANDS in a ploughed field II.3.3.
no -s: fɒɹɪkəˡ K, fəɹɪkəˡ K*[old]*
-s: foˑɹɪkəˡz K

fore-bay *1. n* a TROUGH in a cow-house I.3.6. vɔt:baɪ So *[queried SBM]*
2. n the GANGWAY in a cow-house I.3.7. fɔt:beɪ So, vɔt:beɪ So, vɔt:baɪ So D Do, foˑətbæɪ Gl

fore-buck *n* a BUMPER of a cart I.10.1(a). fɔːbʊk Lei *[marked ir.r. EMBM]*

forecap *n* the FORELOCK of a horse III.4.8. fɔətkæp Sx

fore-cock *n* a subsidiary SWINGLE-TREE of a horse-drawn plough harness I.8.3. fɔəkɔk MxL

fore-end *n* (the) fore-end of the year the season of SPRING VII.3.6. **fore-end of the year** fɔɹ end ə t jəˡ: Y; **the fore-end of the year** t fɔɹ ɛnd ə t jɪə Y

forehead *n When a baby hits its head on the door, there might be a slight swelling on [point to the forehead]....* VI.1.7. Eng exc. Nb We. ⇒ **brow**, *head*

fore-horse *n* a TRACE-HORSE I.6.3. fɒɹɔːs Wa, fɒɹəs Hrt, fɔːɹɔːs St Wa, vɔt:rɒs D, vɔt:rɔt:ʂ So D, fɔəhɔˑs Nf, fɔəˡɹɒˑs Nf, vɔətrɔˑətʂ Ha, fɔˑəɹɒs Nth,

fɔˑəɹɔˑᵊs Nth, foˑəɹɔs C, foˑəɹɔːɹəs Hu, foˑəɹɒs Ess, voːətrɒs He, fʊəɹɒs L, vuːətrɒt:ʂ So, fəːɹɒs

fore-house *n* the LIVING-ROOM of a house V.2.1. fʊəɹæʊs Y

foreigners *1. npl* STRANGERS VIII.2.10. vaɹɪnət:ʐ Do, fɒɹɪnə K, *sg* vɒrɪnət:ʐ So D, fɒɹənəɹ O, fɔɹɪnəz Ess, fɔːɹɪnəˡ Sx, fəɹɪnəˡz K
2. npl town people. fɒɹənətʐ Ha, vɒɹənətʐ Ha

fore-ladder *1. n* a front cart-ladder, ⇐ CART-LADDERS I.10.5. fɔt:ladə Nth, fɔˑəladət Bk, fɔˑəɹ (+ V) ... lædə Sr, *pl* fɔːəˡɹ (+ syllabic) ... lɛdətʐ Sr, fɔːətˡ lædət: Sr, foˑəlædə Bk MxL, fɔəladət Bk
2. n a front ladder on a wagon. foˑətladət Wa, fət:ladə Gl

forelock *1. n [Show a picture of a horse.] What do you call this?* III.4.8. faːlɒk Sa, vat:ɫɒk W, vat:ɫɒk W, faːtɒk Mon, fɒtˑlɒk Ha, fɔːlɒk Ch Sa St Nth Ess, fɔːtɒk Ess, fɔːrɫɒk Brk, fɔt:lɒk Sa So, vɔt:lɒk So, fɔt:ɫɒk So, fɔt:tɒk Co Ha, vɔt:tɒk W D Do, vɔt:ɫɒk W Co D Ha, vɔt:lɔk So, fɔt:lɔːk So, vʌt:lɔːk Do, fɔt:lək Sa, fɔəlɒk Nf, vɔəˡlɒk Ha, fɔˑəlɒk? Nf, fɔˑəɹlɒk He, fɔːətɒk Ess, fɔːətˡlɒk Sa, fɔːətˡlək Sa, foːlɒk Mon, fɔəlɒk? Nf, fɔəlɒk Ch Nf, fɔəlɒk? Nf, foˑəlɒk Sf Ess, fɔːətˡlɒk Wo, fʊəlɒk Y St, fʊəlɔk L, fʊəɹlɒk La, vuət:ɫɒk Co, fəˡ:lɒk Ch. ⇒ **browlock, forecap, foremane, foretop, fringe, front mane, mane, maun**, *tassle* ⇒ **tossel, tossel, topknot, toppet, topping, topple, tussock**
2. n a LINCH-PIN holding a wheel on a cart I.9.12. vɔt:ɫɒk Co

foreman *n* a CARTMAN on a farm I.2.2. fɔːmən Hu, fɔəmən Nf, fɔːəmn̩ Nf, foəmən Nf, fʊəmən Cu Y L *[marked as u.r. NBM, but not EMBM, where several rr. marked as having general rather than specific application]*

foremane *n* the FORELOCK of a horse III.4.8. fɔt:maɪn W, vɔt:maɪn W, fət:meːᵊn Wa

foremost *n* a TRACE-HORSE I.6.3. fɔːmʊst Wa, fɔːməst O, fɔt:məst O

foremost-horse *n* a TRACE-HORSE I.6.3. fat:məstat:ʂ Wo Gl, fatməstatʂ Wo, fat:məstat:ʂ Gl, fat:mʊstat:ʂ Wo, fat:məstɒs Wo. fət:məstɔt:ʂ Gl

forenoon *1. n* MORNING VI.3.11(a). fɒnɪən Y, fɒuɛnuːn K, fɒnʊɪn Y, fɔənʊɪn Y, fɔːnɪʊn Y*[old]*, fɔːnɪʉn Nf, fɔːnɪən Cu, fɔːnuːn Wa, vɔt:n̩ʏːn Co D, fɔt:n̩uːn Co, vɔt:n̩uːn Co, foənɪən We*[breakfast to dinner-time]*, foˑᵊnɛʊn Db, foənuːn Man Ch, fʊənɪən Y, fʊənuːn Ch
2. n tomorrow forenoon TOMORROW MORNING VII.3.13. təmɔɹɔə fɔːnuːn Wa
3. n THIS FORENOON VII.3.15. fɔːnˡʉn Nf*[old]*, fɔːnuːn St, fət:n̩uːn Bk*[rare]*, fɔənɪʊn Nf*[old]*, fɔənʉn Nf, fɔənuːn K, fɔːəˡnʊuːn Sr,

foəᶜn̩ᴵuːn Nf, fuənuːn L; **in the forenoon** ɪ t fɒnʊɪn Y, ɪ t fɒnuːn Y, ɪ ðə fɔᴿːnjʊn Du, ɪ t fɔənɪun Y, ɪ t fɔˑənɪən Y, ɪ t fɔənʊɪn Y, ɪ t fɔənuːn Y, ɪn ðə fɔəᴵnʊuːn Brk, ɪ t fʊənɪən Y, ə t fʊənɪən Y, ɪ t fʊənuːn Ch, ə ðə fʊənuːn L; **the forenoon** ðə fɔᴿːnɪən Nb

forenoon-drinking(s) *n* a morning SNACK VII.5.11.

no -s: fɒɪnuːndɹɪŋkɪn Y, fɔənʊɪndɹɪŋkɪn Y, fɔənuːndɹɪŋkɪn Y, fɔənʊɪndɹɪŋkɪn Y, fuənʊɪndɹɪŋkɪn Y, fɜˑɪnᵁuːdɹɪŋkɪn La*[old]*
-s: fɔənuːndɹɪŋkɪnz Y

forenoons *n* a morning SNACK VII.5.11. vɔᶜːn̩ɣːnz So

forenoon-snap *n* MEAL OUT VII.5.12. fɔənuːnsnap Y

fore one *n* a TRACE-HORSE I.6.3. foˑəɹ ən C, voːəᶜɾ ən He *[one marked u.r. WMBM]*

fore-part *n* **the fore-part of the year** the season of SPRING VII.3.6. t fʊə paːt ə t jɪə Y

fore-post *n* the SHUTTING-POST of a gate IV.3.4. vɔᶜːpɔːs Co, vɔᶜːpoːs D, vuəᶜːpɔːs Co

foreright 1. *adj* STUPID VI.1.5. fɔᶜːɾaɪt Co
2. *adj* CLUMSY, describing a person VI.7.14. vɔᶜːɾaɪt So

fore-stall *n* the GANGWAY in a cow-house I.3.7. fɔᶜːʂtɔːɫ So, vɔᶜːʂtɔːɫ W

Foresters' dinner *n* a local FESTIVAL or holiday VII.4.11. fɒɹəstəz dɪnə Wo

foretop *n* the FORELOCK of a horse III.4.8. faᶜːtɒp Wo, vaᶜːtɒp Ha, faᶜːɾtɒp Brk, vaᶜːtɑp Gl, fɔɹtɒp Nth, fɔːtɒp Wa Hrt Ess, fɔːtɒp Ess Sr, fɔˑᴵtɒp K, fɔᶜːɾtæp Sx, fɔᶜːtɑp Nth, fɔᶜːtɒp Wa Bk W, fɔᶜːtɒp Co, vɔᶜːtɒp W, fɔəᴵtɒp Brk K, fɔəᶜtɒp Sx, fɔˑətɒp Sf Ess MxL K, fɔˑəɾtɒp O, fɔːətɒp Ess, fɔːəᴿtɒp Sr, fɔːəᴵtɒp Sr, fɔːəᶜtɒp Sr Sx, fouətɒp K, fɔəᶜtap Bk, fɔəᶜtɒp O Bk, foˑətɑp Nth, foˑətɒp Hu Bd Hrt, foˑətɒp C Hrt, voˑəᶜtap Gl, fɔːəᶜtɒp Gl, fʊəᶜtɒp O, fʊəᶜtəp Wo, fətᶜːtɑp Gl

fore-tree *n* the SHUTTING-POST of a gate IV.3.4. fɔəθɹeɪ Y

fore-walk *n* the GANGWAY in a cow-house I.3.7. vɔᶜːwɔːk Do

forge *n* a FORD IV.1.3. faᶜːdʒ Wo, fɔːdʒ Ess, vɔᶜːdʒ Gl *[queried WMBM, taken as ford EMBM]*

fork 1. *v* There you have the stooks and there the wagon *[gesticulate]. Now what exactly do you do [to lift the sheaves onto the wagon]?* II.6.7(b). fɒɹk Y, fɒᴿːk Nb, fɔːk Cu Y, *-ing* fɔːkən Man, *prppl* fɔːɾkn Cu, fɔᴿːk Nb, fəᴵːk L. ⇒ **chuck on, chuck up, fork in, fork on, fork up, pick, pitch, pitch in, pitch on, pitch up, reach, reach up** *[see note at **load**]*
2. *n* a MUCK-FORK I.3.13. faᶜːk Wo Gl So Do, faːk Y, faᴵːk O Brk, faᶜːk He Wa, fɒɹk Y*[4 prongs]*, fɔɹk Cu, fɔːk Y*[2 prongs]* Db St Wa Mon Nt L Lei R Nf Sf Bk Hrt Ess, fɔᴵːk La Brk, fɔᴵːɪk La, fɔᶜːk Sa

Wa O So, fɔəᴵk We La, fɔːəᴵk Sr, fɔːəᶜk Sr, fəᴵːk L

3. *n* the SHAFT of a spade I.7.7. vaᶜːk W
4. *vt* to DIG in the garden with a spade I.7.8. fɔᶜːk D
5. *n* a PRONG of a fork I.7.10. fɔːk Man
6. *v* to PITCH sheaves II.6.10. *3prsg* fɔːks Y, *3prsg* fɔᴵːks La
7.1. *vt* to BUTT III.2.10. *prppl* fɔːkɪn Y
7.2. *v* to butt. fɔːk Nt
8. *n* the GROIN VI.9.4. fɔᶜːk So, vɔᶜːk D *[marked ir.r. SBM]*

fork about *vtphr* to BUTT III.2.10. fɔːk … əbaʊt Nt

fork back *vphr* to PITCH sheaves II.6.10. fɔːk bak Cu

fork-cocks *npl* COCKS of hay II.9.12. fɒɹkkɒks Y

forker 1. *n* [There you have the stooks and there the wagon [gesticulate]. Now what exactly do you do [to lift the sheaves onto the wagon]?] Who does it? II.6.7(d). fɒɹkə Y, fɒᴿːkɔᴿ Nb, fɔᴿːkɔᴿ Nb, fɔᴿːkə Nb, fjɔᴿːkəᴿ Du, fɔːkə Cu Du We Y L, fɔːkəɹ Man, fɔːɹkə Cu, fɔᴵːkə La, fɔᴵːkəᴵ K, *pl* fɔᴵːkəᴵz Y, fəᴵːkə L. ⇒ **carter, forker-up, *headcarter*, loader, picker, pitcher, pitcher-on, pitcher-up, reacher, wagoner**
2. *n* [Show a picture of three men unloading a wagon of sheaves in a stackyard.] Who is this on the wagon? II.6.9. faᶜːkəᶜː So, fɒᴿːkɔᴿ Nb, fɒtᴿːkə Nb, fɒɹkəɹ Y, fɔːkə Cu Du We Y, fɔˑɹkə Cu, fɔᴿːkɔᴿ Nb, fɔᴿːkə Nb, fɔᴿːkəᴿ Du, fɔˑɹkə Y, fəᴵːkə L. ⇒ **bully-man, carter, chucker-off, empier, empter, emptier, feeder, forker-off, heaver, labourer, lader, loadener, loader, picker, picker-off, pitcher, pitcher-off, pitching-off-man, reacher, sheaf-turner, stacker's mate, teemer, unempter, unemptier, unlader, unloadener, unloader, unpitcher, unteemer, wagoner**

forker-off *n* the FORKER on a wagon who unloads sheaves in a stackyard II.6.9. fɒᴵkəɹɒf Y, fɒəkəɹɒf Y, fɔːkəɹɒf Cu Du We, fɔᴵːɹkəɹɒf La, fɔːkəɹɒf Cu

forker-up *n* the FORKER of sheaves onto a wagon II.6.7(d). fɔᴵːɹkəɹʊp La, fəᴵːkəɹʊp L

forkful *n* a CUTTING of hay II.9.15. fɔˑkfʊl Nf *[marked u.r. EMBM]*

fork-grain *n* a PRONG of a fork I.7.10. *pl* fɔːkgɹeːɪnz Db

fork-handle *n* the SHAFT of a hay-fork I.7.12. fɔːkændʊ Sr

fork in *vphr* to FORK sheaves onto a wagon II.6.7(b). *-ing* fɔːkɪn ɪn Y

forking *v-ing* UNLOADING sheaves from a wagon II.6.8. fɒᴿːkn Nb, fɔːkən We

forking off *1. vphr-ing* UNLOADING sheaves from a wagon II.6.8. fɒᴿːkən ɔf Nb, fɔːkən ɒf Cu, *no -ing* fɔːk ɒf Du, *no -ing* fɔːrk ɒf Cu, fɔˑɹːɹkɪn ɒf La Y *2. vtphr-ing* unloading sheaves. *no -ing* fɒɹk ... ɒf Y, *no -ing* fɔːk ... ɒf Y, fɔːkɪn ... ɔf Y

forking-off-fork *n* a HAY-FORK with a long shaft I.7.11. fɔːkɪnɒffɔːk Cu

forking-on-fork *n* a HAY-FORK with a short shaft I.7.11. fɔːkɪnɒnfɔːk Cu

forking-robins *npl* EARWIGS IV.8.11. fɒɹkɪnɹɒbɪnz Y, *sg* fɒˑkɪnɹɒbɪn Y

fork on *1. vtphr* to FORK sheaves onto a wagon II.6.7(b). fɒrk ... ɒn Y, fɔːk ... ɒn Y
2.1. vtphr to PITCH sheaves II.6.10. *3prsg* fɒɹks ... ɒn Y
2.2. vphr to pitch. *3prsg* fɔːks ɒn Y

forks *npl [Show a picture of forks (i.e. the farming implements) of various kinds.] What are these?* I.7.9. fœːks Du, *sg* fæːk Man, faːks Man, *sg* faˑːk O, faˤːks Sa Wo Gl So W Brk Co Do, vaˤːks Gl W Ha, faːks Y Wo Mon, fɑˑks Brk, *sg* fɑˑːk O, faˤːks He Wo Wa Mon, *sg* fɑˤːk Sx, vaˤːk He, fɒᴿːk Nb, fɒɹks Y He, fɒɾks O Ha, fɔːks Cu Du We La Y Ch Db St Wa Mon O Nt L Lei R Nth Hu C Nf Sf Bk Bd Hrt Ess MxL Sr K Sx, fɔːrks Cu, fɔᴿːks Nb Du, fɔˑːks We La Y Db Brk Sr, *sg* fɔˑːk L, fɔˤːks Sa He Wa O Nth Bk So Sr Co D Sx, *sg* fɔˤk Wo, vɔˤːks Gl So W Co D, *sg* vɔəˤk Ha, fuəks Lei, *sg* fuək L, fəːks Du, *sg* fəːk Y Db, fəɹks Du, fəˑːks L, *sg* fəˑːk K, fəˤːks Gl, *sg* fəˤk O. ⇒ **peeks, picks, prongs, spuds;** ⇒ also **evil, grip**

fork-tine *n* a PRONG of a fork I.7.10. *pl* fɑˤːktəiːnz Wo

fork up *1. vtphr* to DIG in the garden with a spade I.7.8. fɔˤːk ... ʌp So
2. vtphr to FORK sheaves onto a wagon II.6.7(b). fɔːk ... ʊp Cu, *prppl* fɔːkɪn ʊp Y, *-s* fɔːks ʊp Y, fɔᴿːk ... ʌp Nb
3.1. vtphr to PITCH sheaves II.6.10. fɒrks ... ʊp Y, fɒɹks ... ʊp Y, fɔːks ... ʊp Y
3.2. vphr to pitch. *prppl* fɒˑkɪn ʊp Y

forky-tails *npl* EARWIGS IV.8.11. *sg* fɔᴿːkɪteːl Nb[old], *sg* fɔᴿːkɪtɪəl Du, *sg* fɔᴿːkɪteəl Nb

form *n* a BENCH on which slaughtered pigs are dressed III.12.1. fɔːm St, fɔəˤm Sx, foˑəˤm Nth

form-peckles* *n* FRECKLES VI.11.1. fɔˑːɹmpɛklz La

form-speckles* *n* FRECKLES VI.11.1. fɔːmspɛklz Sa St

form-specks* *n* FRECKLES VI.11.1. fɔːmspɛks St

forn-peckles* *n* FRECKLES VI.11.1. fɔːnpɛklz Ch

forn-speckles* *n* FRECKLES VI.11.1. fɔːnspɛklz Ch[old]

forrest *n* a TRACE-HORSE I.6.3. fɒɹɪst Bk Bd, fɒɹəst O Nth Bk Hrt, fɔɹɪst Hrt, fɔɹəst O, foəɹəst Ess

forrest-horse *n* a TRACE-HORSE I.6.3. fɒɹəstɔˑᵊs Hu

forth *adv* FORWARDS IX.1.7(b). vɔˤːθ Co

fortnight *n* a fortnight *And if it [i.e. the event] was twice that time [i.e. a week] back? [You'd say: It happened] A ... ago.* VII.3.2. Eng. ⇒ *(a)* **couple of week(s), two weeks**

forward *adv* FORWARDS IX.1.7(b). føəwəd Nb, faˤːwəd Co, vaˤːwəd Do, vaˤːwəˤːd̪ So, vaˤːɾəd So W Ha, vaˤːɾəˤːd̪ Do, faɹəd Nth, fɑˤːɾwəd W, fɒwəd La, fɒɹwəd Y, fɒᴿɒt Nb, fɒɹʊd La Gl, fɒrəd Man, fɒᴿət Nb, fɒɹət Cu We La Ch Sa, fɒᴿəd Du, fɒɹəd Nb Cu Du[rare] La Y Man Db Sa St Wa Mon Lei R Nth Nf Ess W Brk Sr K Sx, vɒɹəd He Gl, fɒɾəd O K Ha, vɒɾəd So, fɒɹəˑˑd Brk, fɒɹəˤd̪ Bk, vɒɹəˤd̪ Brk, fɒˤwəˤd̪ Ha, fɒɾəˤd̪ Sr, fɔᴿɒᴿd Nb, fɔɹəd La Y L Hrt Ess K, vɔɾəˤːd̪ So, fɔːwʊd St, fɔːwəd Du St Nf Hrt Ess MxL Sr K, fɔˑːɹwəˤd̪ Ha, fɔːɹəd K, vɔːɾəd So W, fɔˤːwəd Sr, fɔˤːɾwəd Sx, fɔˤːwəˤːd̪ Sa Co, vɔˤːwəˤːd̪ Co Do, fɔˤːɾəd Co Ha Sx, vɔˤːɾɪd D, vɔˤːɾəd So Co D Do Ha, vɔˤːɾəˤːd̪ So, fɔəwəˤd Brk, foəwəd Nf, fuɹəd Man Lei Sx, vuːɾwəd So, vuəˤːwəd Co, vuəˤːwəˤːd̪ D, fəɹəd Ch, fəːwəd Du

forwards *adv* Here are two ways of walking. This way, I'm walking [backwards]. And this way, ... IX.1.7(b). Eng exc. Cu Man Co D Do Ha Sx. ⇒ **forth, forward, frontwards, frontways**

foss *n* a CLAMP in which potatoes are stored out of doors II.4.6. vɔːs So

foster-lamb *n* a PET-LAMB III.7.3. fəˑstəˤlæm Brk

fotes *npl* the HANDLES of a scythe II.9.8. fʌʊts Sf [queried EMBM]

foth *n* the EAVES of a stack of corn II.7.3. vɔːf So

fother-bin* *n* the GANGWAY in a cow-house I.3.7. fɒðəbɪn Ch St

fother-bing* *n* the GANGWAY in a cow-house I.3.7. fɒðəbɪŋ St, fɒðəbɪŋg St

fother-drift* *n* the GANGWAY in a cow-house I.3.7. fɒðədɹɪft Nb

fother-gang* *n* the GANGWAY in a cow-house I.3.7. fɒðəgaŋ Cu We La Y

fother-house* *n* a place close to or adjoining a cow-house, used to store hay, ⇐ HAY-LOFT I.3.18. fɒðəɹaʊs L

fothering-gang *n* the GANGWAY in a cow-house I.3.7. fɒðəɹɪngaŋ Y

fothering-hole *n* the GANGWAY in a cow-house I.3.7. fɒðəɹɪnɔɪl Y

fothering-passage *n* the GANGWAY in a cow-house I.3.7. fɒðəɹɪnpæsɪdʒ K

fotherum *1. n* the GANGWAY in a cow-house I.3.7. fɒðəɹəm Y Nt, fɒðəɹəm Y L, fɔːðəɹəm Lei
2. n a HAY-LOFT over a cow-house I.3.18. fɒðəɹm, Lei, fɒðəɹəm Nt, *pl* fɒðəɹəmz Lei,

fɔðəɹəɐ̯t L

3. n a place close to or adjoining a cow-house, used to store hay. fɒðəɹəm Y Nt

foths *n* HEADLANDS in a ploughed field II.3.3. vɔːfs So

foumart *n* a POLE-CAT IV.5.7. fɛlmət Ch, fɣːmət Db, fɔːmət Y, fʊməd Nt*[old x1]* L*[old x1]*, fʊəmət Y, fʊməd Y, fᵁuːmaːt Cu, fuːmət Nb Cu*[same as a stoat x1]* Du*[old x1]* We La*[very old x1]* Y, fuːmərt Cu, fɪuːməɹt La, fjuːməɹ Y, fuːməᴵt La*[old]*

foundation *n* the BASE of a stack II.7.4. fɛʊndæɪʃn Hrt, faʊndɛɪʃən St

foundered *1. adj* COLD, describing a person VI.13.18. fʊnərt Cu

2. adj **foundered to death** VERY COLD, describing a person VI.13.19. fʊnərt tə diːd Cu

four-grain *n* a MUCK-FORK I.3.13. fɒʊəɡɹæɪn Gl, fɒʊəɡɹaɪn Gl, fɔᵗːɡɹeːn Ha

four-grained-fork *n* a MUCK-FORK I.3.13. foəᵗɡɹæɪndfaːk Brk, fɔəᵗɡɹeːndfaᵗːk Brk, fɒᵗːɡɹeɪndfɒᵗːk Ha, fɔˈəᵗɡɹeɪnd fɔɾk O

four-grained-prong *n* a MUCK-FORK I.3.13. voˈəᵗɡɹæɪnd pɹɑŋ Gl, fɔəᴵɡɹɜˈɪndpɹɒŋg Brk

four-grainer *n* a MUCK-FORK I.3.13. vɔᵗːɡɹaɪnəᵗː Ha

four-grain-prong *n* a MUCK-FORK I.3.13. vɔᵗːɡɹaɪnpɾɒŋ W Do

four-legged-emmet *n* a NEWT IV.9.8. fɔəᵗːɫegɪdɛmʌt Co *[queried error SBM]*

four-legged-evet *n* a NEWT IV.9.8. vɔᵗːɫegɪdɛvət Co

four-legged stool *n* a MILKING-STOOL III.3.3. foəlɛgɪd stuːɫ Wa

four o'clock *1. adj* SPLAY-FOOTED VI.10.5. fæʊəᵗ əklɒk Brk

2. n an afternoon SNACK VII.5.11. foˈəɹətlək Nth

four-prong-peek* *n* a MUCK-FORK I.3.13. fɔᵗːpɾɒŋpiːk So, *pl* fuəᵗːpɾɒŋpiːks So

fourses *n* an afternoon SNACK VII.5.11. faʊəzɪz Ess, faːzɪz Nf*[old-fashioned]*, faᴶːzɪz Nf, fɔːzɪz Nf Ess, fɔːzəz Nf, fɔᴶːzɪz Nf, fɔːəzɪz Hu, fɔˈəzəz Sf, foəᵗz̩ɪz Nf

four-speaned-spud *n* a MUCK-FORK I.3.13. fɔːəᵗspiːndspʌd Sx

four-teeth *n* a sheep from its first to its second shearing, ⇐ GIMMER III.6.5. vɔᵗːʈiːθ D

fourths *n* MEAL V.6.1(b). fɔwəts L

four-tined dung-fork *n* a MUCK-FORK I.3.13. fɔətaɪnd dʌnfɔːk MxL

four-tined fork *n* a MUCK-FORK I.3.13. fɔʊətɔɪnd faᵗk Wo, fɔːtaɪnd fɔːk R, fɔːətɔɪnd fɔːk Ess, foəᵗtɔɪnd fɔᵗːᵊk Bk

four-tine dung-fork *n* a MUCK-FORK I.3.13. foətaɪn dʌnfɔːᵊk Hrt

four-tine fork *n* a MUCK-FORK I.3.13. faːtaɪn fɔˈk Nf, faːtʌɪn fɔːk Nf, fɔˈtaɪn fɔːk Nf, fɔːtaːɪn fɔːk Lei,

fɔətaɪn fɔːk Nth Bd Ess, foətaɪn fɔːk Nf Bd, foˈətɔɪn fɔːk Wa, fɔˈətɔɪn fɔːᵊk Sf

four-toe-spike *n* a MUCK-FORK I.3.13. vɒʊəᵗːʈoːspaɪk D

four-tooth *1. n* a sheep from its first to its second shearing, ⇐ GIMMER III.6.5. vɔᵗːʈɣːθ D, fɔᵗːʈuːθ Co

2. n a 2-year-old sheep, ⇐ TOOTH VI.5.6(b). *pl* fɔᵗːʈʊθs Ha

fowl-cote *n* a HEN-HOUSE I.1.6. fɛʊlkɔːt Ch, faʊlkɔːt St, faʊlkoʊt St

fowl-grass *n* COUCH-GRASS II.2.3. fɛʊlɡɹaːs Nf, fɛʊlɡɹaˈs Nf, fʌʊlɡɹaːs Nf

fowl-house *n* a HEN-HOUSE I.1.6. fɛːlɛːs Db, fɛʊlɛʊs Nf, fɛʊlɛʊs Wo O Hrt, fɛʊlhɛʊs Ess, *pl* fɛʊlhɛʊzən Nf, fɛʊlɛʊs Sr, *pl* fɛʊlɛʊzɪz K, vɛʊlɛʊs Ha, vœʏlœʏs D, vœʏlœʏz D, væɣlæʏs So D, væɣlæʏz D, fæʊlæʊs Wo K, fæːᵁlæːᵁs Db, fæʊlæʊs Nth, fæʊlæʊs He, væʊəlæʊs So W Ha, fæʊlaːᵊs Lei, faːlæːs Nt, faːᵊlaːᵊs Lei R, faʊlaʊs Sa Nt L, *pl* faʊlaʊzɪz St, faʊlaʊs So, vaʊlaʊs So Do, fɒʊloʊs Brk, fᴬʊlᴬʊs Gl, fʌʊlʌʊs He Mon, foʊloʊs Brk, vᵁuːɫᵁuːs Gl, fæʊləʊs He Mon, fæʊləʊs He Mon Gl, fəʊːləʊːs Wo, vəʊəɫəʊs W Do

fowl-hut *n* a HEN-HOUSE I.1.6. fɛʊlhʌt Nf

fowl-pen *n* a HEN-HOUSE I.1.6. fɛʊːlpɛn Wo, fæʊlpɛn Wo, *pl* fæʊlpɛnz Wa, fæʊlpɛn Wa, faʊlpɛn St Wa Lei, faʊɫpɛn Lei

fowl-roost *n* a HEN-HOUSE I.1.6. fɛʊlɹuːst Wo Wa, fɛʊɫɹuːst Wa, faʊlɹuːst St, fɒʊɫɹuːst Gl

fowl(s) *npl* HENS IV.6.2.

no -s: fɛʊl La Ch Wo, fɛʊɫ Wa Nth Hu, fɛʊᵊɫ Wa O Nth C Bk, fɛʊːɫ Wo, fæʊl Sa St Wo Wa, fæʊɫ Wa O Lei, fæʊəɫ Ha, faʊl La Ch Sa St, fʌʊɫ Mon Gl, foʊɫ Brk, vᵁuːᵊɫ Gl, fəʊɫ Wo, fəʊːᵊɫ Gl

-s: fɛʊlz Nf, fɛːlz Db, fɛʊlz Sa Nf Bk, fɛʊɫz Wo Nth Sf Bd Hrt Ess MxL, fɛʊʊz Sx, vœɣɫz D, fæɣɫz Co, væɣɫz So Co D, væɣəɫz So Co, fæʊlz St He L Ess, fæʊɫz He Ha, væʊɫz So W Ha, væʊəɫz So W Do Ha, faːlz Y, faʊlz Sa St L, faʊɫz Wo MxL, vaʊɫz So, faʊz MxL, faʊəɫz So, vaʊəɫz So Do, faʊɫz So, fɒʊəɫz So, vɒʊɫz Co, vɒʊᵊɫz W, voʊəɫz So, fᵁuːᵊɫz Gl, fəʊlz Y Mon, vəʊɫz Do, fəʊᵊɫz He Gl, vəʊəɫz W Do

fowls'-house *n* a HEN-HOUSE I.1.6. fɛʊlzhɛʊs Nf, vœɣɫzœʏs D, fæɣɫzæʊs Co, væɣɫzæʏz Co D, fæʊlzhæʊs Nf, væʊɫzæʊs Do, væʊɫzhæʊs So, vaʊəɫzhaʊs So, vɒʊɫzæʏz Co D, vɒʊəɫzɒʊs W, fɒʊəɫzhaʊs So, fəʊɫzəʊs Gl, vəʊəɫzəʊs W

fowls'-run *n* a HEN-HOUSE I.1.6. faʊɫzɾʌn So, vaʊɫzəᵗːn̩ So

fox *n What do you call that sly animal that is hunted with hounds?* IV.5.11. fœks Nb Du, fœːks Nb, fæks Man Wo Ha, faks O Nth Nf, vaks Gl So, faːks Mon Nf, faᵗːks Wo, fɒks Nb Cu Du We La

Y Ch Db St He Wo Wa Mon Gl O Nt L Lei R Nth Hu Nf Bk Bd Hrt Ess So Brk Sr K Co Ha Sx, vɒks So W Co D Do Ha, fɔks Nb We La Y Ch Wo Wa O L C Sf Hrt Ess MxL Sr K, fɔːks Man Ess So, vɔːks Do. ⇒ *renard* ⇒ **reynard, renny, reynard, reynold(s)**

frackens *n* FRECKLES VI.11.1. fɹakənz Y

fragile *adj* BRITTLE, describing cups and saucers which break easily IX.1.4. fɹeːgɑɪl La, fɹædʒæɪʊ Sr, fɹædʒɑɪl MxL, fɹædʒʊɫ K, fɹeɪgɑɪɫ K, fɹædʒɑɪl Nf Ess, fɹædʒɑɪɫ Sf Ess Sr*[polite]*, fɹædʒɑɪʊ Ha, fɹædʒɔɪɫ Hrt Ess, fɹægɫ He, fɹæːgɒɪl So, fɹadʒɑɪl Y St, fɹadʒɑˑɪɫ Lei, fɹagɒɪl Wa, fɹadʒɔɪɫ Bk, fɹadʒəiɫ Mon

fraid *adj* AFRAID VIII.8.2. fɹeːd MxL, fɾeːd D, vɾeːd D, fɹeɪd Wa, fɾeɪd So, fɹeɪd St Sr, fɾɛɪd Co, vɾɛɪd Co D, fɹæɪd Nf Sr

frail *1. n* a FLAIL II.8.3. fɹˡiːɫ Lei, fɹeːl We La Y Db Nt, *pl* fɹeːlz Sa, fɹeˑɫ Wo, *pl* freɪls Man, fɹeɪɫ Hu, fɹeːˡl Db, fɹeɪəl He, *pl* fɹeɪᵊlz C, fɹeɪᵊɫ Bk, fɾeɪᵊɫ So, vɾeɪᵁɫ Ha, fʁeəl Nb, fɹeəl Du Y*[striking part x1]*, fɹeːᵊl Gl O, fɾeˑʊ O, fɹeːl Du, fɹeɪl Y L Nf, *pl* fɹɛɪlz St, fɹeɪɫ St Lei R K*[striking part x1]*, *pl* fɹɛɪɫz Sf, fɾeɪɫ Ha, fɹeɪᵊɫ Wa Nth C Bk Bd Ess, *pl* fɹeɪᵊɫz Sf, vɹeɪʊɫ Ha, *pl* vɹeɪʊɫz Brk, fɹeɪʊ Ess Sr Sx, *pl* fɹeɪʊz Brk, fɹeəl Y L, *pl* θɹeəɫz O, fɹeᵊɫ O, θɹæɪl Wa, fɹæɪl Nf Ess K, fɹæɪɫ Lei Ess K*[striking part]*, *pl* fɹæɪɫz K, θɹæɪᵊɫ Nth, fɹæɪᵊɫ Nth Sf Ess, fɹæɪʊ Ess Brk Sx, fɹɑɪɫ Wo Ess, fɾɑɪɫ Ha, vɾɑɪɫ W D, fɹɑɪəl MxL, fɹɑɪᵊɫ Ess MxL Sr, fɾɑɪᵊɫ W, vɾɑɪᵊɫ Do, fɹɑɪʊ K, fɹɑɪəɫ Sf, *pl* vɾɑɪᵊɫz Do

2. adj BRITTLE, describing cups and saucers which break easily IX.1.4. fɹeːl Cu Y Sa Mon, fɹeɪəɫ Bk Bd, fɹeˑəl Y, fɹeɪɫ Wa Lei, fɹeˑəl L, fɹɑɪʊ MxL

framble *n* a sliding RING to which a tether is attached in a cow-house I.3.5. fɹambəl Y

frame *n* the BASE of a stack II.7.4. fɹeɪm Lei

framed *vi-3ptsg* he TRIED VIII.8.4. fɹeːmd Y

frame(s) *n* a CART-FRAME I.10.6.

no -s: fɹeːm Mon, fɹeˑɪm Nf, fʁeːᵊm Nb, fʁeəm Nb, fɾɛːm Co

-s: fʁeːᵊmz Nb, fɹeɪmz Sr

frames *1. npl* CART-LADDERS I.10.5. fɹeəmz L

2. npl the horizontal BARS of a gate IV.3.6. fɹeəmz Du

3. npl the JAMBS of a door V.1.11. fɹeːmz Sa, *sg* fɹeːm Ch He, *no -s* Nt, *no -s* fɹeɪm Hu Brk, fɹeɪmz Wa Hrt, *sg* fɹeɪm St, *no -s* Lei C Ess, fɹæɪmz Wa *[ref in s-less or perhaps all cases apparently to whole door-frame]*

frammle *n* a sliding RING to which a tether is attached in a cow-house I.3.5. fɹamɪl La

frampot *n* a sliding RING to which a tether is attached in a cow-house I.3.5. fɹampɪt Db, fɹamfət Db, fɹamət La

fran-freckles *n* FRECKLES VI.11.1. fɹanfɹɛklz Nt L

fran-tickles *n* FRECKLES VI.11.1. fɹantɪtlz Y, fɹantɪklz We

fraunch *vt-1prpl* we CRUNCH apples or biscuits VI.5.12. fɹɔːnʃ C

frawed out *adj* HEAVING *WITH MAGGOTS* IV.8.6. fɹɑːd ɛʊt Ess *[queried EMBM]*

frayed *adj* CHAPPED VI.7.2. fɹeɪd O

freckened *adj* AFRAID VIII.8.2. fɹɪkənd La, frɛkənt Man

freckles *n* What do you call the brownish marks or spots that some people have in the skin on their faces, and especially ginger-haired people? VI.11.1. Eng exc. Hu C Do. ⇒ **bran, bran-freckles, bran-mash, branny, branny-speckles, branny-spreckles, brans, bran-speckles, bran-spots, brun, brunnies, brunny, brunny-spots, brun-spots, farm-speckles,** *fawm-speckles* ⇒ **form-speckles,** *fawm-specks* ⇒ **form-specks,** *fawn-peckles* ⇒ **forn-peckles,** *fawn-speckles* ⇒ **forn-speckles, feckles, fern-tickles, ferny-tickles, form-peckles, form-speckles, form-specks, forn-peckles, forn-speckles, frackens, fran-freckles, fran-tickles,** *freckly,* **moulds, muffles, murfles,** *pawm-pettles* ⇒ **porm-pettles,** *paw-pettles* ⇒ **por-pettles, porm-pettles, por-pettles, reckles, speckles, spreckles, summer-freckles, summer-moles, summer-moulds, summer-spots, summer-voys, sun-freckles, sun-speckles, sun-spots**

free-stone *n* a WHETSTONE II.9.10. fʁeɪstɪən Nb

freestone-sconce *n* a flat surface on which bacon is cured, ⇐ SALTING-TROUGH III.12.5. friːstnskɒns Cu

freet *adj* AFRAID VIII.8.2. fɹiːt Db

freetened *adj* AFRAID VIII.8.2. frˡiːtnd Du, fɹiːtnt La Y Db*[old]*, fɹiːtnd Cu Du We La Y Db Nt L, fɹiːtənd Y, fɹɪtnt La, fɹɪtnd La *[not a N/EMBM headword]*

freezed *1. adj* COLD, describing a person VI.13.18. fɹiːzd K, vɹɑɪst So; **freezed to the bones** vɹɑɪst tə ðə boːnz So

2. adj VERY COLD, describing a person VI.13.19. fɹiːzd Sx, vɾiːzd So D; **freezed stiff** vɾiːzd stɪf; **freezed to death** vɾiːzd tə dɛθ So D, vɾʏːzd tə dɛθ Co; **most freezed** mɔːst vɾiːzd So

freezed up *adj* VERY COLD, describing a person VI.13.19. fɾiːzd ʌp Co

freezing *1. adj* COLD, describing a person VI.13.18. vɾiːzɪn Co D, fɾiːzən Co, vɾiːzən Co D

2. adj VERY COLD, describing a person VI.13.19. fɹiːzɪn Wo Ess Sr Sx

frem *adj* BRITTLE, describing cups and saucers which break easily IX.1.4. fɹɛm Lei

fremd bodies* *npl* STRANGERS VIII.2.10. *sg* fʁɛmd bɒdɪ Nb

fresh *1. adj* INSIPID, describing food lacking in salt V.7.8. fɹɪʃ Nf, fɾɛɪʃ So, fɹɛʃ Nth Nf So, fɾɛʃ So W Co Do Ha, fɾɛɪʃ So Co D, vɾɛɪʃ D, fɾaᵗːʃ So, fɾaɪʃ So W Co D Do; **too fresh** tuː fɹɛʃ Brk K, tʏː fɾɛʃ So, tuː fɾɛʃ So, tuː fɹɛⁱʃ Nf, tʏː fɾɛɪʃ D
2. adj ACTIVE, describing a child VIII.9.1. fʁɛʃ Nb

frettishing *adj* **frettishing with cold** COLD, describing a person VI.13.18. fʁɛtɪʃən wɪ kaːɹd Nb

frez *1. adj* COLD, describing a person VI.13.18. fɹɛz C Bk Bd
2. adj VERY COLD, describing a person VI.13.19. Nth; **frez to death** fɹɛz tə deθ Bd, fɹɛz tə dɛθ Bk Bd
[not an EMBM headword]

frezen *adj* COLD, describing a person VI.13.18. fɹɛzn C

friendly society *n* a local FESTIVAL or holiday VII.4.11. vɾɛnɫi səzæɹɪəti So, vɾɛnɫi səzəɹɪəti W

friends *1. npl If you know some people very well, and like them, you speak of them as your....* VIII.2.7. Eng. ⇒ **butties,** *butty* ⇒ **butties, mates,** *old* **pals, pals**
2. n RELATIONS VIII.2.4. fʁiːnz Nb
3. npl PALS VIII.4.2. fɹɛndz Y, fɹɛnz St Nf Ess, fɾɛnz So

friggan *n* a LOOSE *PIECE OF* SKIN at the bottom of a finger-nail VI.7.11. fɹɪɡən Man

frigging *1. n* a NESTLING IV.7.1. *pl* fɹɪɡɪnz Y
2. vt-ing robbing a nest of its eggs. fɹɪɡɪn Y

fright *adj* AFRAID VIII.8.2. fɹɒɪt Wo

frightened *1. adj* AFRAID VIII.8.2. fɹˀeɪtnd Du, fʁɛɪtnd Nb, fʁɛɪtnd Nb Du, fɹɛɪtnt Db St, fɹɛɪtnd Y Ch Db Sa St, fɹɛɪʔnd L, fɹæɪtnd He, fɹæɪʔnd Sr K, fɹaɪtnd Cu, fʁaɪtnd Nb, fɹaɪtnd Db, fɹaɪtnd Y St Nt, fɹaˑɪtənd L, fɹɑɪtnd Nt L Nth Ess MxL, fɹɑɪʔnd Bd, fɹɑˑɪtənd Lei, fɹɒɪtnd St Wo Wa, fɾɒɪtnd So, fɾɒɪʔnd So, fɹɔɪtnt Ess, fɹɔɪʔnt Ess, fɹɔɪtnd Wa Gl L Sf Ess, fɹɔɪtʔnd Sf Ess, fɹɔɪʔnd O Sf Hrt Ess Sx, fɹɔɪtənd Wo, fɹʌɪtnd Wa Gl Nf, fɹʌɪʔnd Nf, fɹʌɪʔnd Gl Nf Sr, fɹʌɪtənd Nf, fɹʌʏtnd O, fɹəɪtnd Y He Wo Mon Gl, vɹəɪtnd Gl, fɹəɪʔnd W Brk, fɹəɪtənd Y
2. adj SHY VIII.9.2. fɹiːtnd Y *[marked u.r. NBM]*

frightful *adv* VERY VIII.3.2. fɾɒɪtfʊɫ Nb

frim *1. v* to CLEAR grass at the edges of a field II.9.5. *-ing* fɹɪmɪn Sx
2. adj ACTIVE, describing a child VIII.9.1. fɹɪm Lei

fringe *n* the FORELOCK of a horse III.4.8. fɹɪndʒ Y Lei Brk, fɹɪnʒ La O L

frinny *vi-3prpl* they WHINNY, describing the noise horses make during feeding time in the stable III.10.3(a). fɹɪnɪ La

frisky *adj* ACTIVE, describing a child VIII.9.1. fʁɪskɪ Nb

frit *adj* AFRAID VIII.8.2. fɹɪt La Db Sa St*[old]* Wo Wa Lei R Nth Hu C Bd Hrt, fɹɪʔ C Bk Bd, fɾɪt O

fritened *adj* AFRAID VIII.8.2. fɹɪtnd Ch Sa O

frithe *vi* to VOMIT, referring to a baby bringing up milk VI.13.14(b). *-ing* fɹɔɪðɪn Ha *[queried SBM]*

frith-hook *n* a BILLHOOK IV.2.6. vɾaɪθʏk D

fritted *adj* AFRAID VIII.8.2. fɹɪtɪd R

fritten* *adj* AFRAID VIII.8.2. fɹɪtn Sa

fritters *n* SCRAPS left after rendering lard III.12.10. fɹɪtəz Ess, fɹɪtʔəz Sf, fɹɪʔəsɪz Sf

frizzified *adj* TANGLED, describing hair VI.2.5. fɹɪzɪfaɪd Sa

frizzled *adj* VERY COLD, describing a person VI.13.19. fɹɪzɫd MxL

frizzled up *adj* VERY COLD, describing a person VI.13.19. fɹɪzɫd ʌp MxL

frizzle up *viphr* to WRINKLE, referring to the skin of very old people VI.11.2. *3prsg* fɹɪzɫz ʌp MxL

fro *prep* FROM VIII.2.11. fʁɪ Du, fʁeˑ Nb, fɹeː Cu Du We La Y*[old x1]* Ch, fɹeːv Y, fɹeə Du Y, frɛ Cu, fʁɛ Nb Du, fɹɛ Nb Cu Du We La Y, fɹɛː Cu We, fɹɛə Y L, fʁæ Nb, fɹoː La, fɹuː La Y Db, fɹə La Y L, fɹəv Du Y

frog *vt* **frog it** to WALK VIII.7.10. fɹɒɡ ɪt La Y, fɹɔɡ ɪt Y

frog-foot *n* the GRASS-NAIL of a scythe II.9.9. vɾɒɡvʏt So

frog-gender *n* frog-spawn, ⇐ FROGS IV.9.6. fɹɒɡdʒɛndəᵗ He

froggy *adj* HOARSE VI.5.16. fɹɒɡɪ Sx

frogs *npl What do they (tadpoles) grow into?* IV.9.6. Eng. ⇒ **jackies, jacky-toads, paddocks;** ⇒ also **frog-gender**

frolic *n* a local FESTIVAL or holiday VII.4.11. fɹɒlɪk Nf; **harvest frolic** hɑːvəst fɹɒlɪk Nf

from *prep You might say: Who's that queer-looking stranger over there? I wonder where he comes ....* VIII.2.11. Eng. ⇒ **fro, thro**

from-horse *n* the FAR-HORSE of a pair pulling a wagon I.6.4(b). vɾɒmhɔᵗːʂ So *[queried SBM]*

fromward* *1. adj* turning to the right, ⇐ TURN RIGHT! II.3.5(b). vɾaməᵗːd̩ W
2. imp the command TURN RIGHT!, given to a cart-horse. vɹæməᴶd Brk

front carriage *n* a frame with two wheels, attached to a cart to convert it into a wagon, ⇐ CART-FRAME I.10.6. fɹʌnt kæɹɪdʒ Nf

front-flake *n* a front cart-ladder, ⇐ CART-LADDERS I.10.5. fɹʊntfleɪk Y

front-horse *n* a TRACE-HORSE I.6.3. fɹʌnthɔˑs Nf

front-house *n* the SITTING-ROOM of a house V.2.2. fɹʌnʔɛʊs Bk, fɹʊntʌʊs Gl, fɹʊnthuːs Cu

front-kitchen *1. n* the LIVING-ROOM of a house V.2.1. fɹʊntkɪtʃɪn Y
2. n the SITTING-ROOM of a house V.2.2. fʁʊntkɪtʃɪn Nb

front-ladders *npl* front cart-ladders, ⇐ CART-LADDERS I.10.5. fɹʊnʔladəᵗz̩ Bk

front mane *n* the FORELOCK of a horse III.4.8. vɹʊnt meːn Brk

front of *prep* IN FRONT OF a door IX.2.6. fɹʊnt ə Sx, fɹʌnt ɒv Nf, fɹʌnt əv Nf, fɹʌnt ə He Ess MxL, fɹʊnt əv L, fɹʊnt ə L; **the front of** ðə fɹʌnt ɒv Nf

front on *prep* IN FRONT OF a door IX.2.6. fɹʌnʔ ɔn Sf, fɹʊnt ɒn Db

front one *n* a TRACE-HORSE I.6.3. fɹʌnt ən Mon *[one marked u.r. WMBM]*

front-parlour *n* the SITTING-ROOM of a house V.2.2. fɹʊntpaːlə Y Ch

front-post *n* the HANGING-POST of a gate IV.3.3. fɹɒntpɔʊst Ess

front-rail *n* a front cart-ladder, ⇐ CART-LADDERS I.10.5. fɹʊntɹɛˑəl L

front-room 1. *n* the LIVING-ROOM of a house V.2.1. fɹɒntɹuːm Sx *[queried ir.r. SBM]*
2. *n* the SITTING-ROOM of a house V.2.2. fɾʌntɾʏːm So D, fɾʌnʔɾʏːm So, vɾʌntɾʏːm Co D, fɹʌntɹʊm O C Nf Sf Ess*[old x1]*, fɹʌnʔɹʊm Sf Hrt Ess, fɹʌntɹuːm He Nth Nf Brk Sr K Ha, fɹʌnʔɹuːm Bk Hrt Ess, vɾʌntɾʊm Ha, fɾʌntɾʏːm So W Do, fɹʌnthɾuːm So, vɾʌntɾʊːm W Ha, vɾʌnʔɾʊːm W, fɹʌntɹɪːm Nf, fɹʊntɹɪuːm Sa, fɹʊntɹɛʊm St, fɹʊntɹʊm L, fʁʊntʁuːm Du, fɹʊntɹuːm Y*[facing street x1, modern x1]* Ch St Wo Gl L, fɹʊnʔɹuːm Nth, fɹəntɹʊm Gl

front slote *n* a BUMPER of a cart I.10.1(a). fɹʊnt slʊʊt St

front-stick *n* a vertical rod in front of a cart, perforated to allow adjustments when tipping, ⇐ ROD/PIN I.10.3. fɹʊntstɪk Du

frontwards 1. *adv* FORWARDS IX.1.7(b). fɹʌntwʊdz Mon, fɹʌntədz Sf, fɹʌnʔədz C Sf, fɹʌntəᵗdz O, fɹʌnʔəᵗdz Bk, fɾʌntwəᵗːdz So, fɾʌntəᵗːdz So, vɾʌntəᵗːdz Ha, fɹʊntədz Db St Wo Wa, vɹʊntədz Gl
2. *prep* IN FRONT OF a door IX.2.6. fɹʌnʔəᵗdz Bk

frontways *adv* FORWARDS IX.1.7(b). fɹɒntweɪs Man

frost *n* HOAR-FROST VII.6.6. fʁɒːst Nb, vɾæːst So, vɾɑːst Ha, vɾaːs Co D, fɹɑːst He Wo Mon Gl, fɹɑːs Gl, vɹɑːst Gl, fɹɑᵗːʂt Wo, fɹɒst Y Ch Db Sa St He Wo Mon Nt Lei R Nf Ess W Brk Sr Ha, fɹɒs Lei, fɾɒst O Ha, vɾɒst So W, fɹɔːst La Db Sa He Wo Wa L Hu Nf Ess MxL Sx, fɹɔːs Nf Bd Ess, fɾɔːst So Co, *pl* fɾɔːstɪz Ha, fɾɔːs Co, vɾɔːst So W Co D Do Ha, vɾɔːs So W Co D

frost-bite *npl* CHILBLAINS VI.10.6. fɹɒsbɒɪt St

frost-bitten *adj* CHAPPED VI.7.2. fɹɒsbɪtn Y, fɹɒsbɪtən Ch, fʁɒsbɪtn Nb

frosted 1. *adj* CHAPPED VI.7.2. fʁɒstɪt Nb, fʁɒstɪd Nb
2. *adj* COLD, describing a person VI.13.18. vɾɔːstɪd So

frosted up *adj* VERY COLD, describing a person VI.13.19. vɾʌstɪd ʌp D

frost-rind *n* HOAR-FROST VII.6.6. fʁœːstʁɛɪnd Nb, fʁɒstʁaɪnd Du, fʁɒsʁaɪnd Nb, fɹɒstɹɪnd Nb

frosty rime *n* HOAR-FROST VII.6.6. fɹɒstɪ ɹaɪm Cu

frowen 1. *adj* COLD, describing a person VI.13.18. fɹɔːən Sf
2. *adj* **frowen to death***, **frowen with cold***, **frowened with cold*** VERY COLD, describing a person VI.13.19. **frowen to death** fɹɔːˑən tə dɛθ Sf; **frowen with cold** fɹɔːn ə kʌʊd Ess; **frowened with cold** fɹɔˑənd ə kʌʊɫd Sf

froze 1. *adj* COLD, describing a person VI.13.18. vɾɔːz W, fɹʊʊz St, fɾʊʊz So *[not a WMBM headword]*
2. *adj* VERY COLD, describing a person VI.13.19. fɹɒʊz Sr Sx, fɹɔz Ess, fɹʊʊz O, fɹʌz Nf Ess, fɹɔːz Mon Brk, fɾɔːz O, vɾɔːz So, fɹʊʊz O Ess; **froze stiff*** fɹʌʊz stɪf Ess; **froze to dead*** fɹʊz tə dɛd Sf; **froze to death** fɹɔz tə dɛθ L, fɹʌʊz tə dɛθ Hrt, fɹɔːz tə dɛθ Brk, fɹɔːz tə djɛθ Gl; **froze with cold*** fɹʌz ə kʌʊɫd Ess; **nearly froze** njəᵗːɫi vɾɔːz W; **very nigh froze** vəᵗː nɒi vɾɔːz Ha *[not a WMBM headword]*

frozed *adj* VERY COLD, describing a person VI.13.19. vɾɔːzd Do, fɹʊʊzd St *[not a WMBM headword]*

frozen 1. *adj* COLD, describing a person VI.13.18. fɹɒzn Cu Du O, fɹɔzn L*[occasional x1]*
2. *adj* VERY COLD, describing a person VI.13.19. fɹœːzn Nb, fʁɒzn Nb, fʁɒzən Nb, fɹɒzn Y, fɹɒzən Y, fɹɒʊzn Sr, fɹɔzən L, fɹɔːzn Y, fɹɔʊzn Brk, fɹɔʊzən Ess, fɹʌʊzn K, fɹɔːzn Mon, vɹɔːzn He, vɾɔːzn Do, fɹʊʊzn St Ha, fɹʊʊzən Nf, fɹʊzn Nf; **frozen stiff** fɹɒzn stɪf O, fɹɔzn stɪf Y, fɹʊʊzn stɪf St; **frozen to death** fʁœːzn tə dɛθ Nb, fɹɒzn tə diːθ Cu Du, fɹɒzn tə dɪθ Du, fɹɒzn tə dɪəθ Cu Y, fʁɒzn tə diːθ Nb, fɹɔzn tə dɪˑəθ L, fɹʌzn tə dɛθ Sf; **frozen to the death** fɹɔzn tə t dɪəθ Y, fɹɔzn tə tʔ dɪəθ Y

froze up* *adj* VERY COLD, describing a person VI.13.19. fɹʌʊz ʌp MxL

fruit-board *n* an END-BOARD of a cart I.10.4. *pl* fɹuˑtbɔˑdz K

fruzzings *n* DANDRUFF VI.1.3. fɹʊzɪnz Y

fry 1. *n* the PLUCK of a slaughtered animal III.11.6. fɹɑɪ Y, fɹɔɪ Ess, fɹʌɪ Nf
2. *n* the pluck of a slaughtered pig. fɹɑɪ Nt Ess, fɹɔɪ Wa, fɹʌɪ Nf
3. *n* the pluck of a slaughtered pig, without the lungs. fɹɔɪ Wa

fry-fat *n* the FAT round the kidneys of a pig III.12.7. fɹɔɪfæt Ess

frying-pan *n* a GIRDLE for baking cakes V.7.4(b). fɹaɪ-ɪnpan Y*[short sides, hung over fire]*, fɹaɪ-ɪnpɒn Ch, fɹa·ɪnpan L, fɹaɪ-ɪnpan L, fɹɑ·ɪnpan L, fɹɔɪnpan Wa, fɹʌɪ-ɪnpæn Nf

fuddled *1. adj* STUPID VI.1.5. fʌdɫd Sr, fədɫd Sx
2. adj GIDDY IX.1.11. fʋdld Nf*[old]*

full *1.1. v* to LOAD a cart with dung II.1.5. fʋl We
1.2. vt to load. fʌɫ Sf
1.3. vt to load dung into a cart. -*ing* fʋlən We
[it is not clear from BM that 1. and 2. refer to cart]
2. adj IN FLOOD, describing a river IV.1.4. fʋl Y Wo Nf, vʋɫ W; **bang full** baŋ fʋl Sa
3. vi to WAX, referring to the moon VII.6.5(a). -*ing* faːlən Nb, fʋɫ Gl, -*ing* vʋɫɪn W D, -*ing* vʋɫən W Ha
4. n **the full** the state of appearing fully grown, referring to the moon. ðə føːl Nb, θ fʋl Db, t fʋl We La Y Ch, ðə fʋl Nb Ess, ðə fʋɫ He, ðə vʋɫ W, ðə fʋuː Ess; ⇒ also **come full, come up, get full, get up**
5. n **past its full** waning, referring to the moon, ⇐ to WANE VII.6.5(b). paːst ɪts fʋɫ He

fullard *n* a POLE-CAT IV.5.7. fʋɫəd Lei

full-bagged *adj* showing signs of calving, describing a cow with a swollen udder, ⇐ SHOWS SIGNS OF CALVING III.1.12(a). fʋlbagd Cu

full-fall *n* the FLAP at the front of old-fashioned trousers VI.14.16. fʋlfɔːl Y

full-feathered *adj* FLEDGED IV.7.2. fʋlfɛðəd L Nth C Nf, fʋɫfɛðəd Sf Ess, fʋʋfɛðəᵗɹd Sx

full-fledged *adj* FLEDGED IV.7.2. fʋlflɛdʒd St

full-float *adj* swollen, describing the udder of a cow that SHOWS SIGNS OF CALVING III.1.12(a). fʋʋflɔʋt Ess

full-flooded *adj* IN FLOOD, describing a river IV.1.4. fəflʋdəd Db

full-floppers *npl* young FLEDGED birds IV.7.2. fʋlfla·pəz Nf, fʋlflaːp?əs Nf, fʋlfla·p?əz Nf, fʋlflɒpəz Nf, fʋɫflɒpəz Nf, fʋlflɒp?əs Nf, fʋlflɒp?əz Nf

full-flushed *adj* FLEDGED IV.7.2. fʋɫfɫʌʃt Ha

full-flyers *npl* young FLEDGED birds IV.7.2. fʋlflaɪəz Nf, fʋlfla·ɪz L, fʋlflʌɪ·əz Nf, fʋɫflʌɪəz Sf

full-mouthed ewe *n* a EWE III.6.6. fʋlmaʋθt joːᵁ O

full-pitch *n* a HAY-FORK with a long shaft I.7.11. fʋʋpɪtʃ Sx

full-pitch-prong *n* a HAY-FORK with a long shaft I.7.11. fʋɫpɪtʃpɾɒŋ Ha

full up *1. adj* IN FLOOD, describing a river IV.1.4. fʋl ʋp Y, fʋl ʌp K, fʋɫ ʌp Brk Sr, vʋɫ ʌp Ha
2. viphr to WAX, referring to the moon VII.6.5(a). -*ing* vʌɫən ʌp D

fully-feathered *adj* FLEDGED IV.7.2. fʋlɪfɛðəd Y Hu Nf

fully fledged *adj* FLEDGED IV.7.2. fʋlɪ flɛdʒd Sr

fumble-fingered *adj* CLUMSY, describing a person VI.7.14. fʌmbɫfɪŋɡəd Ess

fumble-fisted *adj* CLUMSY, describing a person VI.7.14. fʌmbɫfɪstɪd Nf Hrt, fʌmbʋfɪstɪd Sr

fumbling *adj* CLUMSY, describing a person VI.7.14. fʋmlɪn La

fumbly *adj* CLUMSY, describing a person VI.7.14. fʋməlɪ La

funnel *n What do you call the thing [indicate a funnel] used for pouring liquid from a basin into a bottle?* V.9.3. Eng exc. Db St He Mon. ⇒ **tinner, tinniger, tun-dish, tun-mill, tunnel, tunniger, tunning-dish, tun-pail**

funnified *adj* SICK, describing an animal that is unwell VI.13.1(c). fʌnɪfɔɪᵊd Sf

funny *adv* VERY VIII.3.2. fʌnɪ Nf

fur *1. n* FERN IV.10.13. fəː Ess *[queried ir.r. EMBM]*
2. vt to pull, ⇐ PULLING his ear VI.4.4. fəᵗː Co

fur-bill *n* a BILLHOOK IV.2.6. fəɹbɪl L, fəᴶbl L, fəːbɪl Nt L, fəᴶːbɪl L, fəᴶːbl L

furbish* *v* to TRIM hedges IV.2.3. fɔəbɤʃ Nf

furbobs *n* GOOSE-GRASS II.2.5. fəːbɒbz We

fur-bush *n* GORSE IV.10.11. fəːbʋʃ Nf, fəᴶːbʋʃ Nf

furra-bush *n* GORSE IV.10.11. fəɹəbʋʃ Nf*[old]*

furrow *1. n What do you call the track made by a plough?* II.3.1. Eng. ⇒ **furrow-hole, plough-furrow, plough-seam, rean**. ⇒ also **reaning**
2. vi to FARROW, describing a pig giving birth to piglets III.8.10. fʋɹɒʋ Brk, fʋɹə Man, fəɹə Nf, fəɹəᴶ K *[not a N/EMBM headword]*
3. n a DITCH IV.2.1(c). fʌɹɒʋ K
4. vi to WRINKLE, referring to the skin of very old people VI.11.2. *3prsg* fʌɹəz MxL

furrow-board *n* the MOULD-BOARD of a horse-drawn plough I.8.8. θəɹəboˈəd Bk

furrow-hole *n* a FURROW II.3.1. fɔˈɹɔɪl Y, fəˈɹɔɪl Y

furrow-horse *1. n When you use two horses for ploughing, what do you call each one? [The horse walking in the furrow.]* II.3.4(a). Eng exc. MxL. ⇒ **far-horse, farside, farside-horse, furrow-tit, furrow-walker, further-horse, leader, muddy-horse, off, off-horse, offside, offside-horse, outside, rean-horse**
2. n the FAR-HORSE of a pair pulling a wagon I.6.4(b). færə-ɔːs Man, fɒɹɒs Y, fʌɹəᵗ:-ɒᵗ:ʂ Sa *[first element of forms at Man and Y may be **far-**]*

furrow-land *n* FALLOW-LAND II.1.1. fæɹəlænd Mon, fɒɹəland Ch

furrow-lands *n* HEADLANDS in a ploughed field II.3.3. fɔələnz Y

furrows *npl* RUTS made by cartwheels IV.3.9. *sg* fʋɹɒ Brk, vuːɾẓ D

furrowside-horse *n* the FAR-HORSE of a pair pulling a wagon I.6.4(b). fɔˈːɹsɑːdɔˈːɹs La *[first element may be far-]*

furrow-tit *n* the FURROW-HORSE of a ploughing team II.3.4(a). fəɹətɪt Db, fəːtɪt Y

furrow-walker *n* the FURROW-HORSE of a ploughing team II.3.4(a). fʌɹəwɔːkəˤ He, fʌɹəwɔˤːkəˤ Sa

further-horse 1. *n* the FURROW-HORSE of a ploughing team II.3.4(a). fəˤːðəˤːɽɒs Co, vəˤːd̺əˤːɽɒs Co, vəˤːd̺əˤːɽɔˤːʂ Co

2. *n* the FAR-HORSE of a pair pulling a wagon I.6.4(b). fəˤːðəˤːɽaˤːʂ Co, fəˤːðəˤːɽɒs Co, vəˤːd̺əˤːɽɒs Co D

furze 1. *n* GORSE IV.10.11. fɛz Ess, fʌz O Bk Hrt Ess*[old x1]* MxL So Brk*[old]* Sr Co, vʌz So*[old x2]* W Co D Do Ha, foəz Nb, fʊz Gl Bk Brk Ha, fʊˤz̞ Wo, fəz O K Sx, vəz So, fəːz Y Nf Sf Bk Ess*[correct x1]* MxL K, fəˈːz O Sr, fəˤːʂ Co, fəˤːz̞ Ess Sr Co Ha Sx, fəˤːɽz̞ Sr Sx

2. *n* BRACKEN IV.10.12. fʌz So, fəz Gl Sf *[queried error WMBM; queried ir.r. EMBM; no marking SBM]*

furze-bush *n* GORSE IV.10.11. fʌzbʊʃ Bk

furze-hook *n* a BILLHOOK IV.2.6. fəˤːʂʊk Co*[for cutting furze x1]*

furzen-faggot* *n* KINDLING-*WOOD* V.4.2. fəˤːʂənfægət Co *[SBM headword furze-]*

furze-pig *n* a HEDGEHOG IV.5.5. vʌzpɪg D

fusty *adj* RANCID, describing bacon V.7.9. fʌsti So, fʌstɪ Sf, fʌistɪ Nf

fuzzanock* *n* a DONKEY III.13.16. fʊzanək Y

fuzzart* *n* a POLE-CAT IV.5.7. fʊzət Y

fuzzazick *n* a DONKEY III.13.16. ˌfʊzˈazɪk L

fuzzock* *n* a DONKEY III.13.16. fʊzək Y

fuzzy *adj* TANGLED, describing hair VI.2.5. fʊzɪ Y

fyoff* *npl* FLEAS IV.8.4. fjɒf Sa

G

gab *n* bit of gab CHAT VIII.3.4. bɪt ə gab Y

gabber *n* a GOSSIP VIII.3.5(b). gæˑbəˑ Brk

gabbing *v-ing* GOSSIPING   VIII.3.5(a).   gæbɪn
Brk*[old]*

gabble *1. v* to GOBBLE food VI.5.13(b). *-ing*
gæblɪn Man, gæbᵊɫ Gl *[not a WMBM headword]*
2. n a GOSSIP VIII.3.5(b). gæbɔʊ Brk *[queried
SBM]*

gable *n* the GABLE-END of a house V.1.5. geːbl Ch,
geːbɫ D, geɪbɫ Bk So, geːɪbɫ Wo, geabl Cu, geɪbl St
L, geɪbɫ O Ess K Ha, geɪbuɫ Brk Sx, geɪbʊ Ess Sr K
Sx, gæɪbl̩ Hrt, gæɪbɫ Ess, *pl* gæɪbɫz K *[not a NBM
headword]*

gable-end *n* *[Show a picture of some houses.]* What
do you call this [indicate a gable-end]? V.1.5. Eng
exc. Man Mon. ⇒ angle-end, corner-end, end, end
of the house, end-wall, gable, gavel-end, house-end,
pine-end, pining-end, *pinion-end* ⇒ pining-end,
pointed-end, *point-end* ⇒ pine-end, pointen-end,
pointing-end ⇒ pining-end, side-wall

gable-ended stacks *npl* long   STACKS   II.7.1.
gɪəbl̩endɪd staks Y

gable stack *n* a long stack with square ends, ⇐
STACKS II.7.1. geɪblstæk Ess

gaby *n* a foolish lout, ⇐ STUPID VI.1.5. gɔːbɪ Y

gad *n* a GOSSIP VIII.3.5(b). gad Y

gaffer *n* my HUSBAND VIII.1.25. gafə St; the
gaffer t gæfə Y, ðə gæfəᵗ Sa He Wo Mon, ðə gᵗæfəᵗ
He Wo, ðə gjæfəᵗ He Gl, ðə gæfəᵗː W, ðə gafə Nb
Ch St*[old x1]* Mon Nt L Lei, t gafə Cu We Y, ðə gafəɹ
He*[old and rare]*, ʔ gafəɹ La, ðə gafəᵗ Sa*[old x1]* Wo,
ðə gjafəᵗ Gl, ðə gafəᵗː So W D

gafferman *n* my   HUSBAND   VIII.1.25.   the
gafferman ðə gafəᵗmɒn Wo

gaig *n* a CALLOSITY VI.11.4. *pl* gɛgz Man

gain *1. vi* to WAX, referring to the moon VII.6.5(a).
prppl gainən Do
2. adj NEAR IX.2.10. geːn Y Nt, gɛˑən L

gain enough *adv* ALMOST VII.7.9. gɛˑən ənʊf L

gainer *n* a GANDER IV.6.16. geːnɔᴿ Nb, geənɔᴿ Nb

gain-hand *adj* NEAR   IX.2.10.   geːnand Y Nt,
gɛˑənand Y L

gaiters *npl* LEGGINGS VI.14.18. gˡitəs Man,
gˡɛːdəᵗːz̩ D, gɪətəᵗːz̩ W, geːtəz Ch O, geːtəᵗz̩ Gl O,
geːʔəᵗz̩ W, geːtəᵗːz̩ W Ha, geːdəᵗːz̩ Do, geitəz
Mon, geitəᵗz̩ Ha, geiʔəᵗz̩ O Bk, geitəᵗːz̩ So,
geəʔəᵗz̩ O, geːtəz St Ess Sr, geitəᴶz Sr, geiʔəᴶz Sr,
gɛːitəᵗz̩ Sr, gɛiʔəᵗz̩ Bk, geitəᵗɾz̩ Brk Sx, gɛːitəᵗːz̩
Ha, gɛːidəᵗɾz̩ Brk, gaitʔəz Ess, gaitəᵗːz̩ Ha

gale *vt* to STOCK a cow III.3.6. *ptppladj* geːɫd D

gale-hook *n* the HOOK or *CROOK* of a crane over
a domestic fire V.3.5(c). *pl* gɛɪlʊks St

gale up *1. vtphr* to STOCK III.3.6. *-ing* geːɫɪn ...
ʌp Co
2. vphr to stock III.3.6. *ptppl* geːɫd ʌp Co

gall *n* a CALLOSITY VI.11.4. *pl* gaɫz Co D, gɔːɫ
Co Do, *pl* gɔːɫz So D

gallied *adj* AFRAID VIII.8.2. gaɫiːd Do, gaɫɪd
Do

gallivanter *n* a GOSSIP VIII.3.5(b). kalɪvantə Ch

gallivanting *v-ing* GOSSIPING   VIII.3.5(a).
kaləvantɪn So

gallock *n* a LEFT-HANDED person VI.7.13(a).
galɪk Y

gallock-handed *adj* LEFT-HANDED
VI.7.13(a). galɪkandɪd Y, galəkandɪd Y,
galətandɪd Y

gallon tin *n* a metal container for carrying
horse-feed, ⇐ BASKET III.5.4. gæɫɪn tɪn Co

gallop down *vtphr* to GOBBLE food VI.5.13(b).
-ing gaɫəpən ... dəʊn Do

galloper *1. n* a CRANE on which a kettle is hung
over a domestic fire V.3.4. galəpə Y
2. n the *HORIZONTAL* BAR of a crane over a
domestic fire V.3.5(a). galəpə Y

galloper-hook *n* the vertical part of a crane over a
domestic fire, consisting of a *BAR* or *CHAIN* and
a HOOK(*/CROOK*) V.3.5b+c. galəpə-uːk Y

gallows *adv* VERY poisonous IV.11.5. gæləs Brk

gallowses *n* BRACES   VI.14.10.   gæləsəs
Man*[old]*, galɪsɪz Y, galʊzɪz La, galəsɪs Cu,
galəsɪz Nb Cu Du We La*[old x1]* Y L*[rare x1]*,
galəzɪz La, galəsəz Nb Du Y*[rare]* Db

galls *npl* BLISTERS VI.11.5. gaɫz D, gɔːɫz So D
Do

gally-bagger *n* a   SCARECROW   II.3.7.
gæɫibægəᵈ Brk, gæɫibægəᵗɾ Ha, galibagəᵗː Do,
gaɫibagəᵗː W Ha

gally-balk *n* the *HORIZONTAL* BAR of a crane
over a domestic fire V.3.5(a). gæɫibɔːk Nf,
galɪbɔːk Y L, galəbɔːk Y L

gally-bar *n* the *HORIZONTAL* BAR of a crane
over a domestic fire V.3.5(a). gæɫibɑ Nf, galibɑː
L, galəbɑːɹ L

gally-crow *n* a SCARECROW II.3.7. gaɫikɾɔː
Do

gally-handed *adj* LEFT-HANDED VI.7.13(a).
galɪ-andɪd Y

galt* *n* a castrated female pig, ⇐ HOG III.8.8. gɒʊt Sa, gɔːt Sa St
gambo *n* a flat-topped horse-drawn vehicle with vertical poles at each corner, and with two wheels, ⇐ WAGON I.9.2. gæmboː Sa, gæmbəᶫ Mon, gæmbɫ Gl, gamboː Sa Mon
gambol over *viphr* **gambol right over** to turn HEAD OVER HEELS IX.1.10. gambouɫ ɹaˑɪt ʊwə Lei
game *v* to play, referring to cows in a field, ⇐ to BUTT III.2.10. *-ing* əgeːmɪn Wa, *-ing* gɛɪmɪn Sx
gammed up *adj* STICKY, describing a child's hands VIII.8.14. gamd ʌp W
gammock *v* to jump about playfully, referring to cows in a field, ⇐ to BUTT III.2.10. *-ing* gamɪkɪn St, *-ing* gamәkɪn Ch
gammy *1. n* a LEFT-HANDED person VI.7.13(a). gæmi So
2. adj CLUMSY, describing a person VI.7.14. gæmi So D
3. adj DULL, referring to the weather VII.6.10. gamɪ Y
4. adj STICKY, describing a child's hands VIII.8.14. gæmɪ Sx, gami W Ha
gammy-fisted *adj* LEFT-HANDED VI.7.13(a). gamɪfɪstɪd Sa
gammy-handed *1. adj* LEFT-HANDED VI.7.13(a). gæmihændɪd So, gæmi-ændɪd So, gamɪ-andɪd Gl, gæmihandɪd So, gami-andɪd So, gami-andәd W
2. adj CLUMSY, describing a person VI.7.14. gami-andәd W
gammy-pawed *adj* LEFT-HANDED VI.7.13(a). gamɪpɔːd Ch
gamp *n* GRANDDAD VIII.1.8(a). gamp O*[baby talk]*
gampus *n* an EVENER on a horse-drawn plough I.8.4. gambәs Wo
gamy *adj* **go gamy** to SPOIL, referring to meat or fish V.7.10. gʊ geːmɪ Y, *3prsg* gʊәz geәmɪ Y
gan *imp* **gan to hell**, **gan your ways** GO AWAY! VIII.7.9(a). **gan to hell** gan tә hɛl Du; **gan your ways** gan ðɪ weːz Y
gan away *imp* GO AWAY! VIII.7.9(a). gan әwɛә Y
gander *n What do you call the male (goose)?* IV.6.16. Eng. ⇒ **gainer**, **gandy**, **steg**
gandy *n* a GANDER IV.6.16. gandɪ Y
gang *n* the GANGWAY in a cow-house I.3.7. gæŋg La, gaŋ La, gaŋk La
gang-hole *n* a GANGWAY in a cow-house, closed at one end I.3.7. gaŋɔɪl Y
gangingfolk *npl* GIPSIES VIII.4.12. gaŋәnfoәk Cu
gangway *1. n [Show a picture of an old-fashioned cow-house.] What do you call the passage in front of the cows from which they are fed?* I.3.7. gɛŋgwæɪ K, gæŋwɛɪ Nf*[none in old cow-house]* Ess Co, gæŋgwɛɪ Wa, gæŋwæɪ Gl, gaŋgwiː St, gaŋwɪә Du, gaŋweː Nb Du La Y, gaŋgweː Wo, gaŋweɪ Wa, gaŋweːә Cu Du, gaŋwɛɪ Y Wa Lei Co, gaŋwɛә Y, gaŋwæɪ Gl O, gaŋwaɪ Gl W D Ha. ⇒ **alley**, **alley-way**, **bing**, **bing-range**, **boosy**, **cattle-walk**, **causeway**, **cow-engle**, **cow-parlour**, **cow-walk**, **drang-way**, **feeding-alley**, **feeding-block**, **feeding-passage**, **feeding-path**, **feeding-pen**, **feed-walk**, **fodder-bing**, ***fodder-drift*** ⇒ **fother-drift**, **fodder-gang**, **foddering-ginnel**, **foddering-passage**, ***fodder-room*** ⇒ **fodderum/fotherum**, **fodder-run**, **fodderum**, **fore-bay**, **fore-stall**, **fore-walk**, **fother-bin**, **fother-bing**, **fother-drift**, **fother-gang**, **fothering-gang**, ***fothering-ginnel*** ⇒ **foddering-ginnel**, **fothering-hole**, **fothering-passage**, **fotherum**, **gang**, **gang-hole**, **hay-bay**, **hay-bing**, **hay-hole**, **hay-house**, **hay-walk**, **head-walk**, **passage**, **passage-walk**, **passage-way**, **path**, **range**, **roadway**, **run**, **shed-alley**, **walk**, **walking-path**; ⇒ also **bing-wall** *[there is inconsistent BM treatment of **fodder/fother-** forms, with **fothering-** used for* [ð] *and* [d] *forms with **-ing** but **fodder** used for non **-ing** forms:* [ð] *and* [d] *forms have here been consistently separated. **Bin** and **bing** forms have also been separated.]*
2. n the gangway of a cow-house, used to store hay, ⇐ HAY-LOFT I.3.18. gaŋwæɪ O
gan home *imp* GO AWAY! VIII.7.9(a). gan ʊәm Y
ganning-on *n* **full of ganning-on** ACTIVE, describing a child VIII.9.1. fʊl ә 'gan'œn Nb
ganny *n* GRANNY VIII.1.8(b). ganɪ Cu
gan off *imp* GO AWAY! VIII.7.9(a). gan œf Du
gan on *imp* GO AWAY! VIII.7.9(a). gan ɒn Nb Du, gan ɔn Du
ganoos *n* BEESTINGS V.5.10. gәnuːs Man
gansey *n* a VEST VI.14.9. ganzɪ L
gans in *viphr-3prsg* school BEGINS VIII.6.2(a). ganz ɪn Nb Cu Y, ganz ɤn Nb
gant *adj* HUNGRY VI.13.9. gant Y
gant-hook *n* the GRASS-NAIL of a scythe II.9.9. gantʊk Sr
ganting *v-ing* YAWNING VI.13.4. gantn Nb*[old x1]* Du
gantry *1. n* a flat surface on which bacon is cured, ⇐ SALTING-TROUGH III.12.5. gantɹɪ L*[bricks x1, stone x1]*
2. n a light BRIDGE of planks with handrails for pedestrians IV.1.2. gantʈi D
ganty *n* the BELLY-BAND of the harness of a cart-horse I.5.7. ganti Do
gap *1.1. vt* to THIN OUT turnip plants II.4.2. gap Y L
1.2. v to thin out turnips. gap La
2. n a FORD IV.1.3. gæp Ess

3. vt to fill gaps in a hedge-bank or hedge, probably with brushwood or similar material, ⇐ to PLASH IV.2.4. *-ing* gæ·pɪn Hrt, *?2prpl* gæːps Hrt, *-ing* gapɪn So *[regarded as 'only a part of the operation' of plashing, EMBM; SBM Edd uncertain as to precise meaning]*

4. n a SHEEP-HOLE IV.2.8. gɛp Nf MxL Sr K, gɛəp Man Ess, gæp He Nf Ess MxL So Brk Sr K Co Sx, gæpʔ Nf, gᵁæp He Wo, gjæp He Gl, gap La Y[open at top x1] Ch Sa St Wa O Nt L Lei So W[in hedge x1] Co D Do Ha, gʊap Wo

5. n a GATEWAY IV.3.8. gap Y Db

gapes *1. vi-3prsg If someone looks steadily in astonishment with his mouth open, you say he ....* VI.3.7. Eng exc. Ch Sa Lei R. ⇒ *a-gaping about, flabbergasted, gaping about, gauming* ⇒ **gaums, gaums, gaups, gauves,** *gawking* ⇒ **gawks, gawking about, gawks,** *gawping* ⇒ **gaups,** *gawps* ⇒ **gaups, gazes,** *gazing* ⇒ **gazes, geeking, glapes, glares,** *glaring* ⇒ **glares, glops, glores, gnat-catching,** *gollied, gorming* ⇒ **gaums,** *looking aghast, looks a-gazed* ⇒ **gazes,** *looks amazed, squinting about,* **stags, stares, stares** *with his chops open,* **stares** *with his mouth open, staring* ⇒ **stares, yaums, yaups, yawning about** *[-ing forms in NBM taken as prppls]*
*2. npl **the gapes** a fit of YAWNING VI.13.4. ðə gæəps Ess

gap-hole *n* a GATEWAY IV.3.8. gapɔɪl Y, gapʊəl Y

gaping *1. v-ing* YAWNING VI.13.4. giːpɪn Ch, giːpən Cu, gɪɛpən Nb Cu Du, gɪapɪn Y, gɪapən Du La, gɪəpɪn Y, gɪəpən Cu, geːpɪn La[old x1] Y Ch[old x1] Db He Wo Mon Gl O Nt[old x1] D Ha, geːpən Co, geɪpɪn Db Wo O Bk Bd, geɪpʔɪn Hu, geɪpən Man, geapɪn La, geapən Cu We, geəpɪn La Y Bk, geəpən Nb We, geːᶦpɪn Db Mon Nt, geːᵊpɪn Ch Wa, əgeːᵊpɪn Wa, gɛɪpɪn St[old x1] Wa O L Lei Nth Hu C Bk[old] Hrt Ess, gɛɪpʔn Sf, gɛɪpʔən Sf, gɛɪpm Ess, *no -ing* gɛɪp Brk, geˑəpɪn Y L Nth, geˑəpn Sf, geˑəpən C, gæpɪn[old] Brk, gæpm Ess, gæːpʔn Nf[old x1], gæɪpɪn Ess MxL Sr, gapɪn D, gapən Co
2. v-ing shouting. gɪəpən Cu

gap out *vtphr* to THIN OUT turnip plants II.4.2. gap ... ɛʊt L, gap ... æʊt L, *-ing* gapɪn ... aʊt L, gap ... uːt Y

gapping *1. v-ing* BELCHING VI.13.13. *no -ing* gap Ess, gjapən Gl
*2. v-ing GOSSIPING VIII.3.5(a). gæpɪn Brk

gap-spot *n* a GATEWAY IV.3.8. gapspɒt Db

gap-stead *1. n* a SHEEP-HOLE IV.2.8. gapstɪˑəd Y, gapstɛd Nt
2. n a GATEWAY IV.3.8. gapstiːd Du, gapstɪəd La, gapstɛɪd Du

gap-stop *vtphr* to fill gaps in a hedge-bank or hedge, probably with turfs, brushwood, or similar material, ⇐ to PLASH IV.2.4. gæpstɒp Ess, gæpstɔp Ess

[regarded as 'only part of the operation' of plashing EMBM]

gap up *vtphr* to fill gaps in a hedge-bank or hedge with turfs, brushwood, or similar material, ⇐ to PLASH IV.2.4. gap ʊp Sa

gap-way *n* a SHEEP-HOLE IV.2.8. gæpweɪ Brk, gapweɪ Ha*[wide]*

garbage *n* RUBBISH V.1.15. gaːbɪʃ Cu, gaːbɪdʒ Sr

garden-cress *n* CRESS V.7.17(b). gaːdnkɹes Ess, gaːdnkɹes Nf, gaᶜ·dṇkɹes Ha

garden-house *n* an EARTH-CLOSET V.1.13. gaᶜːdṇæus Do*[old]*

garlock *n* CHARLOCK II.2.6. gaːlɪk Nth Bd, gaᴵːɹlək La, gaːlɪk Nf, gaᶜːɹɫək Sx, gjaᶜːɫək He

garner *n* a CORN-BIN I.7.4. gaːnə St

garrotte *vt* to CHOKE somebody VI.6.4. gaɹɪt St

garters *npl* KNEE-STRAPS used to lift the legs of working trousers VI.14.17. *sg* gaɹtəɹ Y*[strap]*, gaɪtəz Y, gaːʔəs Nf

garth *1. n* a small field, ⇐ FIELDS I.1.1. gaːθ Y
2. n a PADDOCK I.1.10. gaθ Du Y, gaᴮːθ Nb Du, gaːθ Nb Cu We Y

garth-man *1. n* a COWMAN on a farm I.2.3. gaθman L, gaθmən Nt L
2. n a man who looks after store cattle on a farm. gaθmən Nt

garthy *n* a COWMAN on a farm I.2.3. gaθɪ Nt, gaːθɪ Y

gasbag *n* a GOSSIP VIII.3.5(b). gæsbæg Brk, gasbag Sa

gast *adj NOT IN* CALF, or not in foal III.1.8. gaːst Sf

gate *1. n If you want to take your cart from one field to another, what have you to open first?* IV.3.1. Eng. ⇒ **field-gate**
2. n a GATEWAY IV.3.8. geːt So, geət La Y, jat Y, jət Y
3. n a CRANE on which a kettle is hung over a domestic fire V.3.4. geɪt Lei
4. v to put cattle on hired pasture, ⇐ HIRE *PASTURAGE* III.3.8. gɪət Y, geət Du

gate-back *nsg* the horizontal BARS of a gate IV.3.6. geɪtbæk K *[queried ir.r. SBM]*

gate-cheeks *npl* stone GATE-POSTS IV.3.2. jattʃeɪks Y

gate-clap *n* the SHUTTING-POST of a gate IV.3.4. geːttlap Db

gate-heads *npl* GATE-POSTS IV.3.2. geˑətɪˑədz L

gate-hole *n* a GATEWAY IV.3.8. geːtɒɪl La Y, geːtɔɪl Y, geːtoːl La Db, geətɔɪl Y, jeətɔɪl Y, gɛətʊəl Y L, jətʊəl Y

gate-lace *n* a DIAGONAL BAR of a gate IV.3.7. *pl* geɪtleɪsɪz St

gate-lackses *npl* the horizontal BARS of a gate IV.3.6. geːtɬaksəz D *[queried SBM]*

gate-laths *npl* the horizontal BARS of a gate IV.3.6. gɛɪtlɑːθs Sx

gate-ledge *n* a DIAGONAL BAR of a gate IV.3.7. geːɪtlɛdʒ Nf*[no special word]*

gate-ledges *npl* the horizontal BARS of a gate IV.3.6. geːtlɛdʒɪz Nt, geːɪtlɛdʒɪz Nf, geˑətlɛdʒɪz L

gate-opening *n* a GATEWAY IV.3.8. geːtoːpnɪn Nt, geɪtʌʊpnɪn MxL

gate out *vtphr* to put cattle on hired pasture, ⇐ HIRE PASTURAGE III.3.8. -*ing* gɪatɪn ... ʌʊt Y, gɪət ... uːt Y, geˑat ... ᵒuːt Du
2. *vphr* to put cattle on hired pasture. geˑət əʊt Y*[old]*

gate-place *n* a GATEWAY IV.3.8. geːtpleːs Ch, geːᴵtpleːᴵs Db, geɪtpleɪs St, gjeɪtpleɪs St

gate-post *1. n* the HANGING-POST of a gate IV.3.3. gɪətpoʊst So, geːtpʊəst Y, geɪtpoust Nf
2. *n* the SHUTTING-POST of a gate IV.3.4. gɪᵊtpous Man, geːtpʊəst Y, gjətpʊəs He

gate-posts *npl [Show a picture of a gate and posts.]* *What do you call these [indicate the gate-posts]?* IV.3.2. Eng exc. Cu We Ch. ⇒ **durns, gate-cheeks, gate-heads, gate-stoops, gate-stubs, gate-stumps, heads, pillars, *posts*, stoops, stubs, stumps, uprights**

gate-rails *npl* the horizontal BARS of a gate IV.3.6. geːɪtɹeːɪɬz Mon, geətɹeəlz Y, gᴵɛtɹaɪəɬz W

gates *1. npl* CART-LADDERS I.10.5. geːts Nb*[not locally]*, geːɪts He
2. *npl* HURDLES used to pen sheep in part of a field III.7.11. jeːts Y

gate-sag *n* a DIAGONAL BAR of a gate IV.3.7. *pl* geːtsagz Nt

gate-shivers *npl* the horizontal BARS of a gate IV.3.6. geːətʃɪvəˡːz̩ Co

gate-shuttles *npl* the horizontal BARS of a gate IV.3.6. geətʃʌdɬz So

gate-slices *npl* the horizontal BARS of a gate IV.3.6. geətslaɪsɪz Y

gate-spells *npl* the horizontal BARS of a gate IV.3.6. geətspɛlz Y, jatspɛlz Y

gate-spot *n* a GATEWAY IV.3.8. geːtspɒt Db

gate-stead *n* a GATEWAY IV.3.8. gɪatstiːd Nb Du, geːtstiːd Nb We Y, geːtstɛd Nt, geətstɛd Du Y, gjetstiːd Du, jetstiːd Cu, gjetsteɪd Du, geətstɪəd Y L, jatstiːd Cu We, gɪatstɪəd Y, jatstɪəd Y*[old x1]*, jatstɛd Y*[old]*, jətstɪˑəd Y

gate-stoops *npl* GATE-POSTS IV.3.2. gɪatstʊʊˑps Y, gɪətstuːps Cu, geːtstᵁuːps Db, geətstɔʊps Y*[old]*, geətstuːps La Y, gjetstuːps Du, jetstuːps Nb Cu, geətstuːps Y, jatstɪəp Y, jatstaʊps Y, jatstuːps We*[old x1]* Y, *sg* jatstuːp Cu*[usually slate]*, no -s jatstuːp Cu Y, *sg* jətstuːp Y

gate-strip *n* a DIAGONAL BAR of a gate IV.3.7. *pl* geɪtstɹɪps Lei

gate-stubs *npl* GATE-POSTS IV.3.2. geːtstʊbz La

gate-stumps *npl* GATE-POSTS IV.3.2. geːtstʊmps Ch

gateway *n* *What do you call this space [show a picture] between the two posts [of a gate]?* IV.3.8. Eng exc. We MxL. ⇒ **gap, gap-hole, gap-spot, gap-stead, gate, gate-hole, gate-opening, gate-place, gate-spot, gate-stead, opening, road**

gather *1. n* an ASH-MIDDEN V.1.14. gæθə Sf *[queried BM]*
2. *vi* to FESTER, referring to a wound VI.11.8. gɪðə La*[old x1]*, -*ing* gɪðəɹən Cu We, -*ing* gɪdðəɹɪn We La, gɪdəɹ Y, gɛðɔᴿ Nb, gɛðə Nb Cu Du*[old x1]* We La Y Ch Db Wo Wa L K, -*ed* gɛðət Cu, *pt* gɛðəd Nth, -*ing* gɛðəɹɪn Bd, gjɛðə Gl, -*ing* gjɛðəɹɪn Ch, gɛddə Cu We, gɛðɪ L, gɛðəɹ La, gɛddəɹ Cu, gɛðər Cu, -*ing* gɛðᴿən Nb, gɛðəᴿ Du, gɛðəᴵ Db, gɛðəˡ Mon Nth Bk*[old x1]* Sx, gjɛðəˡ Gl*[old x1]*, -*ing* gɛdəɹɪn Y, gæðə Hu Nf Ess, -*ing* gæðəɹən Man, -*ed* gæðəᴵd Brk, gaðə Y Db St Wa Mon Nt*[old x1]* L Nth C Nf Bd Hrt, -*ing* gaðəɹɪn La, gjaðə Db*[old]*, gaðəɹ Y, gaðəˡ Wo Wa Mon Bk, gaðə Nf
3. *vi* to WAX, referring to the moon VII.6.5(a). -*ing* gæðəɹɪn Nf, -*ing* əgæðəɹɪn Ess
4. *vt-3sg* she [i.e. a tidy girl] will COLLECT her toys VIII.8.15. gɛðɔᵊ Nb, gɛðə Du We Db, gɛðəᴿ Nb Du, gɛðəɹ Y, gæðə Man Ess, gaðəɹ (+V) La, gaːðə Mon; **gather and put away** gæðəɹ (+V) ... ən pʊt ... əwɛɪ MxL; **gather together** gaðə ... təgɛðə St

gathering *n* a WHITLOW VI.7.12. gɛðəɹɪn Y Db L Bk*[any festering place]*, gjɛðəɹɪn Ch, gæðəɹɪn Nf, gæðəɾɪn So, gæðəˡːɾɪn So, gaðəɹɪn Y L Nf, gadəɹɪn Y, gaðəˡːɾɪn W

gathering in *vphr-ing* CARTING corn from the field II.6.6. gaːðəɹɪn ɪn Mon

gatherings *npl* the RIDGES between furrows in a ploughed field II.3.2. *sg* gæðəɾɪn Sr

gather up *1. viphr* to FESTER, referring to a wound VI.11.8. gɛðəɹ ʊp Wa, gæðəɹ ʌp Nf, *prppl* gaðəɹɪn ʌp He, *3prsg* gaðəɹz ʌp He
2. *vtphr-3sg* she [i.e. a tidy girl] will COLLECT her toys VIII.8.15. gɪðɹ (+V) ... ʊp L, gɪðəɹ (+V) ... ʊp Y, *3prsg* gɛðəz ... ʌp Ess, gɛðə ... ʊp Cu We, gɛðəᴿ ... ʊp Du, gɛðəɹ (+V) ... ʊp La Y Ch Db St L, gɛðəᴵɹ (+V) ... ʌp Ha, gɛðəˡɾ (+V) ... ʊp Sa, gjɛðəˡɾ ʌp He, gæðə ... ʌp MxL, *3prsg* gæðəs ... ʊp Man, gæðəɹ (+V) ... ʌp Nf K, gæðəˡɾ ... ʌp He, gᴵæðəˡɾ (+V) ... ʌp He, gjæðəˡɾ (+V) ... ʌp Mon, gjæðəˡɾ (+V) ... ʊp Gl, gæðəˡːɾ (+V) ... ʌp So, gaðɔᴿ ... ʌp Nb, gaðə ... ʊp Nb St, *3prsg* gaðəz ... ʊp Y, gaðɹ (+V) ... ʊp Wa, gaðəɹ (+V) ... ʊp Y St

Nt, gaðəɽ (+V) ... ʌp Ha, gaðəˡːɽ (+V) ... ʌp Do Ha, gɒðəᴶɹ (+V) ... ʊp Brk; **gather up and put away** gɛðəɹ (+V) ... ʊp ŋ pʊt ... əwɛˑə L; **gather up together** gaðəˡːɽ (+V) ... ʌp təgɛðəˡː W

gauge *1. n* an EVENER on the plough-beam end of a horse-drawn plough I.8.4. geɪdʒ So, gɛɪdʒ Sx
2. n the T-SHAPED PLOUGH-BEAM END of a horse-drawn plough I.8.5. gɛɪdʒ Sr

gault *1. n* CLAY IV.4.2. gɒlt Nf*[heavy blue clay]*, gɒɫt Hu, gɔɫt C
2. v to remove topsoil, dig up clay, and spread it on fields. *-ing* gɒɫtɪn Hu, gɒɫʔɪn Hu

gaumless *1. adj* STUPID VI.1.5. gaʊmləs Y, gɔːmlɪs La Y, gɔːmləs Cu Du La Y, gɔːmləz Y, gɔᴶːɹmləs La
2. adj CLUMSY, describing a person VI.7.14. gɔːmləs Du
3. adj SILLY VIII.9.3. gɔːmlɪs Du Y, gɔːmləs Du La Y, gɔəmlɪs Y

gaums *vi-3prsg* he GAPES VI.3.7. *no -s* gɔːm Cu, *prppl* gɔːmɪn Ch L

gaumy *1. adj* STUPID VI.1.5. gɔmɪ Y
2. adj SILLY VIII.9.3. gɔːmɪ St

gaunge *vt* to GOBBLE food VI.5.13(b). *-ing* gɔːnʒɪn Y

gaunges *vt-3prsg* he GUZZLES a drink VI.5.13(a). *-ing* gɔːnʒɪn Y

gaup *1. vi* to belch, ⇐ BELCHING VI.13.13. gɔʊp Ess, gʌʊp Ess
2. vi to laugh, ⇐ LAUGHING IX.2.14. gɔːp Y

gaups *vi-3prsg* he GAPES VI.3.7. gɪɑːps Wo, gjɑːps He Gl, gjɑˡːps He, gɑːps Wo Mon Gl, *prppl* gɑːpɪn Nf MxL, *prppl* əgɑːpɪn Nf, *prppl* gɑːpn Nf Ess*[old]*, gɒps Sa, gɪɔːps Sa He, gjɔːps He*[old x1]*, *prppl* əgjɔːpɪn Wa, gɔːps Ch Db Sa St L Lei R Bk, *no -s* gɔːp Cu Y, *prppl* gɔːpɪn La Y Wa O Nt Nth Nf Bd K, *prppl* əgɔːpɪn Wa, *prppl* gɔːpən Du Y, *prppl* gjɔːpɪn Gl, gɔˡːps Sa

gaustering *1. v-ing* LAUGHING VIII.8.7. gɒstɹɪn Y*[immoderate laughter]* Db*[old]*, gɔːstɹɪn L*[rare x1]*, gɔːstrən We, gɔːstəɹɪn La*[noisy laughter]*
2. v-ing LAUGHING IX.2.14. gɔːstəɹɪn L

gauves *vi-3prsg* he GAPES VI.3.7. *prppl* gɔːvɪn Y

gauze* *n* a DIAPER V.11.3. *pl* gɑːzəˡz̩ Sx *[queried SBM]*

gavel-end *n* the GABLE-END of a house V.1.5. gɪvlɛnd Nb, gɪəvlɛnd Nb Cu, geːvlɛnd Nb Cu, geɪvɫɛnd C, geavlɛnd La, geavlɛnd We, geavəlɛnd We, geəvələᵊnd Nb, gɛvlɛnd Nb*[old]*, gᴶɛvəlɛnd Du, gavlɛnd L, gɪavlɛnd Du, gjavlɛnd Y, gɪavəlɛnd Cu *[not a NBM headword]*

gawbosh *adj* ASKEW, describing a picture that is not hanging straight IX.1.3. ˌgaːˈbɔʃ L

gawison *adj* ASKEW, describing a picture that is not hanging straight IX.1.3. gaːˈwɛsn L

gawk *n* a STUPID person VI.1.5. gɔːk Co D

gawk-handed *adj* LEFT-HANDED VI.7.13(a). gɔːkandəd Y

gawk-hander *n* a LEFT-HANDED person VI.7.13(a). gɔːkandə Y

gawking *v-ing* SQUINTING VI.3.5. gɔːkɪn Gl

gawking about *viphr-ing* gaping, ⇐ GAPES VI.3.7. gɔːkɪn əbɛut K

gawks *vi-3prsg* he GAPES VI.3.7. gjɑːks He Gl, gɑːks Mon, *prppl* gɒʊkɪn Du, gɔːks Cu Gl, *prppl* gɔːkɪn Mon Sr K, *prppl* gɔːkən Co

gawky *1. adj* STUPID VI.1.5. gɔːki Co D
2. n a LEFT-HANDED person VI.7.13(a). gɔːkɪ Y
3. adj **proper gawky** SILLY VIII.9.3. pɽɒpəˡː gɔˡːki D

gawky-handed *adj* LEFT-HANDED VI.7.13(a). gɔːkɪ-andɪd Y

gawp *v* to GOBBLE food VI.5.13(b). *-s* gɔʊps Y

gawp-handed *adj* LEFT-HANDED VI.7.13(a). gɔːpandɪd Y

gawping *v-ing* YAWNING VI.13.4. gaːpɪn Bk Ess, gjaːpɪn Gl, gaːpm Ess, gɑːpɪn Wo Nf, gᵁɑːpɪn Wo*[old x1]*, əgᴵɑːpɪn Wo, gjaːpɪn He Gl, gɒpɪn Sa, gɔːpɪn La Sa St*[old x1]* Nt L, gɪɔːpɪn Sa, gjɔːpɪn Gl, gɔˡːpɪn Sa, gjɔˡːpɪn He

gawps *1. vt-3prsg* he GUZZLES a drink VI.5.13(a). ptppl gɔʊpt Y
2. v-3prsg he guzzles. gɔʊps Y

gay *1. imp* the command TURN LEFT!, given to plough-horses II.3.5(a). geɪ Sx
2. adj WELL, describing a healthy person VI.13.1(a). geɪ Brk*[old x1]*
3. adv VERY VIII.3.2. geː Nb Cu Du We La Y, geˑə Cu, gɛː Cu We, gɛə Y

gayly *adv* VERY VIII.3.2. geːlɪ Cu We La, gɛːlɪ Cu We

gazes *vi-3prsg* he GAPES VI.3.7. *prppl* geːzɪn W, geɪzɪz Hu, gɛɪzɪz Nth, *prppl* geɪzɪn St Sx, *pt* gɛəzd Y; **looks a-gazed** ɫuks əgeːzd W

geal *1. vi* to WARP, referring to wood IX.2.9. gɪɛˑl Cu, geal We
2. vi to dry or split. geal We, geˑəl We, dʒeˑəl La

geals *npl* CHAPS in the skin VI.7.3. geːlz La

gear *1. Before your horse in the stable can pull the cart, what must you do with it?* I.5.1.
vt giːɹ (+V) St, gɪəɹ (+V) La Y Db St L, gɪəˡɽ (+V) Sa He Wo Mon, gjəˡɽ (+V) He, gɪəˡːɽ (+V) Sa He, gjəˡːɽ (+V) Wo Mon, gᵊʊəɹ (+V) Du
v gɪə Nb Cu Du We Y Ch Db L Nth Hu, *-ing* gɪəɹɪn St, gɪəᴷ Du, gɪəɹ We La, gɪəˡ Sa Wo Bk, gjəˡ He, gɪəˡː Sa
n harness for a cart-horse. gɪəɹ (+V) Cu La Y, gɪəᴶɹ (+V) Sr
⇒ **collar, collar up, gear up, get geared, get gears on, get the gearing on, get yoked up, harness, harness up, put gears on, put harness on, put**

some gears on, *put some tack on him*, *put tackle on*, *put the gear on*, *put the gear on to*, *put the gears on*, *put the gee-ho tackle on*, *put the harness on*, *put the tackle on*, saddle, tackle, tackle up, yoke, yoke in, yoke out, yoke up

2. *n* an EVENER on a horse-drawn plough I.8.4. gɪəᵗ Gl

gear-horse *n* a TRACE-HORSE I.6.3. gɪəɹɒs Y Nt Lei, gɪəɹɔs Nt L, gɪəɹɔːs Y L Lei Nth

gearing *n* the harness of a cart-horse, ⇐ to GEAR I.5.1. gɪəɹɪn Y

gearing(s) *n* a CART-FRAME I.10.6.
no -s: gɪəɹɪn St Wa Lei, gɛɪəɹɪn Ch
-s: gɪəɹɪnz Wa Lei Nth

gearings *npl* CART-LADDERS I.10.5. gɪəɹɪnz St Wa Lei

gears *1. n* the harness of a cart-horse, ⇐ to GEAR I.5.1. gɪəz Y Ch St Mon L, gɪəᴮz Du, gɪəɹz He
2. *n* the traces of a cart-horse harness. gɪəz L
3. *n* the harness of a plough-horse. gɪəz Lei

gears-horse *n* a TRACE-HORSE I.6.3. gɪəzɒs Lei R, gɪəzɔːs Lei R

gear up *1. vtphr* to GEAR a cart-horse I.5.1. gɪəɹ (+V) ... ʌp He Ess, gɪəɹ (+V) ... ʊp We La Y Db St L, *-ing* gɪəɹɪn ... ʊp Ch, gɪəᵗɾ (+V) ... ʊp Sa
2. *vphr* to gear a horse. gɪəɹ ʊp La Ch Db
3. *vtphr* to yoke a horse to a cart. gɪəɹ (+V) ... ʊp Y

geb* *n* the mouth of a hen, ⇐ BEAK IV.6.18. gɛb Y

gee *1. imp* gee, gee back, gee up the command TURN LEFT!, given to plough horses II.3.5(a). gee dʒiː Y; gee back dʒiː bak Y; gee up dʒiː ʊp Y *[non-farming informant]*
2. *imp* gee, gee about, gee again, gee back, gee back gee again, gee gee again, gee ho, gee hoot, gee ho round, gee off, gee over, gee up*, gee whup, gee woa gee, gee woot, gee wug the command TURN RIGHT!, given to plough-horses II.3.5(b). gee dʒiː Nb*[to Scottish horses x1]* We La Y*[move only a little x1]* Db He Wo Gl Nt L Bd Ess Sr K Sx, dʒɪ L, dʒəɪ Y; gee about dʒiː əbuːt Nb; gee again dʒiː əgen St Nt, 'dʒiː gɛn St Wa, dʒiː gɪn Wa, 'dʒɪ gɛn Lei; gee back tʃiː bɛk Man, dʒiː bɛk Db, dʒiː bæk Man He Gl Nth, dʒiː bak Du La Y Ch Db Sa St Wo Wa Gl O Nt L Lei Nth Bk, dʒɪ bak L Lei, dʒiː bɑk Y; gee back gee again dʒiː bak dʒiː əgen La; gee gee again dʒiː dʒiː əgɛn La; gee ho dʒiː ɛʊ Bd, dʒiː ʌʊ Bd Hrt, dʒiː ɔʊ Hu, dʒiː oː Ch, dʒiː oʊ Wa Hrt, 'dʒəɪ 'æʊ Hrt; gee hoot dʒiː uːt K; gee ho round dʒiː ɔʊ ɹɛʊn Hu, dʒiː oʊ ɹɛʊn C; gee off dʒiː ɒf Y, dʒɪ ɒf Ch, dʒiː ɔːf He Nth Co D, dʒɪ ɔːf So; gee over dʒɪ oəᴵ Ch, dʒiː oˑəᵗ Sa; gee up dʒiː ʊp L; gee whup dʒiː wʊp He Bk; gee woa gee dʒiː wəː di Sf; gee woot dʒiː wʊt Bk Sr; gee wug dʒiː wʊg Sr
3. *imp* gee, gee back, gee here, gee lads, gee up, gee up there the command GO ON!, give to plough-horses II.3.5(d). gee dʒiː Wa Gl Lei Nth Sf

Ess Brk; gee back 'dʒiː 'bak W; gee here dʒɪ əː St; gee lads 'dʒiː 'ladz Wo; gee up dʒiː ɪp Ess, dʒiː ɛp Hrt, dʒiː œːp Mon, dʒiː ʌp Sa He Wa Mon Gl O L Hu Nf Sf Bk Bd Hrt Ess So W Brk Sr K Co D Do Ha Sx, ˌdʒiː 'ʋp Nf, tʃiː ʊp Mon Gl, dʒiː ʊp Nb Cu Du La Y Ch Db Sa St He Wo Wa Gl O L, dʒiː əp Y Gl So W Ha Sx, dʒiː p Lei Co, dʒɪ ʌp Bk Ess, dʒɪ ʊp Nb Du We La Y Db Wa Lei R Nth Brk, dʒɪ əp Ch Lei Ess Sr K Sx, dʒɪ p Ess So, dʒɛː ʊp Wo, dʒɛɪ ʊp Y, dʒəɪ ʌp Hrt, dʒəɪ ʊp Y; gee up there dʒiː ʊp ðɛə Y *[gee back queried ir.r. SBM]*

gee-back *n* the FAR-HORSE of a pair pulling a wagon I.6.4(b). dʒiːbak St

gee back *imp* the command stop! or WOA!, given to plough-horses II.3.5(c). 'siː 'bæk He

gee-ho-lines *1. npl* the REINS of a cart-horse I.5.5. dʒɪoləɪnz Wo, dʒɪoːlaɪnz Sa, dʒɪoːləɪnz He, dʒoːlaɪnz Sa
2. *npl* the reins of a plough-horse. dʒɪoːlɒɪnz Wo, dʒɪoːləɪnz He Wo, dʒɪoːɫəɪnz Mon, dʒɪəɫəɪnz Mon, dʒoʊlaɪnz He

geeking *1. vi-ing* gaping, ⇐ GAPES VI.3.7. *prppl* giːkən Co
2. *v-ing* PEEPING VI.3.8. giːkən Co

geese *npl* *What do you call those hissing birds that waddle about in flocks?* IV.6.15(a). Eng. ⇒ **gooses**

gee-waw *adj* ASKEW, describing a picture that is not hanging straight IX.1.3. dʒɪwaʊ Cu

gee-wom *adj* ASKEW, describing a picture that is not hanging straight IX.1.3. dʒaɪwɒm Cu

gee-y *adj* ASKEW, describing a picture that is not hanging straight IX.1.3. dʒiːwaɪ Nb

gegged *adj* THIRSTY VI.13.10. gɛgd Y*[old]*

geld *1. adj* NOT IN CALF III.1.8. gɛld Nb Cu Du We La Y, gɛlt We La
2. *adj* not in calf but able to conceive. gɛld Nb Cu Du We La Y, gɛl Cu, gɛlt La
3. *adj* unable to conceive, describing a cow. gɛld Du La Y
4. *adj* DRY, describing a cow with no milk III.1.9. gɛld Nb Du
5. *v-ed* CASTRATED, describing a bullock III.1.15. gɛld Nb Cu Du We La Y, gɛlt We La
6. *n* a YOUNG SOW III.8.5. gɛld La

gelded *v-ed* CASTRATED, describing a bullock III.1.15. gᴵɛldɪd He*[chiefly horses]*, gjɛldɪd Ch, gɛldɪd Nb Cu Du We La Y Nf, gɛldɪt Cu, gɛldəd Man Db

gelping *v-ing* BELCHING VI.13.13. gɛɫpɪn Ess

germ *n* TREAD inside a fertile egg IV.6.9. dʒɑˑm Nf, dʒɔˑm St

german yeast *n* dry, hard, crumbly YEAST V.6.2. dʒəˑmən jiːst Ess

gesling *n* a GOSLING IV.6.17. gɛslɪn Nb La Y, gɛzlɪn Nb Cu Du We La Y Ch Db St L, gɛzlən Nb Du, gɛzʝɪn Y

get *1. imp* **get hither, get off back, get over** the command TURN RIGHT!, given to plough-horses II.3.5(b). **get hither** gɛt 'ɪðəᶜ Ha; **get off back** 'gɪd ɔːf 'bak Ha; **get over** gɪd ɔːvəᶜː So

2. imp **get, get on, get ready, get up, get up there** the command GO ON!, given to plough-horses II.3.5(d). **get** gɪt Brk; **get on** gɪd ɒn So, gɪɹ ɒːn Y, 'gɪd 'ɔːn So, gɛt œːn Nb; **get ready** 'gɛt 'ɹɛdɪ Sa; **get up** gɪt ʊp Cu Y Lei, gɪd ʌp Sf Bk Ess So Co D Ha, gɪd ʊp Nb Cu We, gɪd əp Nb Ess, gɪɹ ʊp Cu We La Y, gɛɹ ʊp La Y, gəɹ ʊp We La; **get up there** 'gɪd ʌp ðɛəᶜ Ha, gɪɹ ʊp ðɛə Y

3. v to CUT peat IV.4.4. *prppl* gɪtɪn Y, gɛt La

4. vt to earn, ⇐ EARNED VIII.1.26. gɪt Y, gɛt La Y, *3prsg* gɛt He

get away *imp* GO AWAY! VIII.7.9(a). gɛt əwɪˑə Du, gɪt əweˑə Du, get əweə Nb, gɛt əweːə Nb, gɛd əweː Nb, gɪt əwɛː We, gɪt əwɛɪ St, gɪɹ əwɛˑə Y; **get away home** gɛʁ əweə hjɛm Nb; **get away out** gɪt əweː uːt Cu; **get yourself away** gɪt jəsɛl əweː We, gɪt ðɪsɛl əweː Cu; **go on get yourself away** gø: œːn gɛt jəsɛl əwɪə Nb

get big *viphr* to WAX, referring to the moon VII.6.5(a). *-ing* gɛtən bɪg Nb; **get bigger** gɪt bɪgə L, get bɪgə Db Nth, *prppl* gɛtɪn bɪgə Y, *-ing* gɛɹɪn bɪgə Y, gɛʔɪn bɪgə Bd, *-ing* gɪtn bɪgə Y Sr, get bɪgəᶜ Gl, *-s* gets bɪgəʈ O, *-ing* gɪdən bɪgəᶜː Co

get full *viphr* to WAX, referring to the moon VII.6.5(a). *prppl* gɪtɪn fʊl Y, get fʊl Lei, *-ing* gɛʔn fʊl Man, *-ing* gɪtɪn fʊl MxL, *-ing* gɛdɪn fʊl So, *-ing* gɛdən vʊl Do, *-ing* gɪtɪn fʊʊ Ess Sr, *-ing* gɪʔn fʊʊ Sx, *-ing* gɛtɪn fʊʊ Brk, *-ing* gɛʔn fʊʊ Brk; **get for full*** *-ing* gɛʔɪn fəᶜ fʊl O; **get fuller** *-ing* gɛʔn fʊɫəᴶ Ha, *-ing* gɛtɪn fʊɫəᴶ Sr; **get full moon** *-ing* gɪʔɪn fʊʊ muːn Sx; **get on the full** *-ing* gɛtɪn ɒn ðə fʊl Ess; **get to the full** *-ing* gɛtɪn tə ðə vʊl W; ⇒ also **full**

get going *imp* GO AWAY! VIII.7.9(a). gɪt gɔːʊ-ŋ Ess, gɪt əgu-ɪn Sx

get-hither *imp* **get hither there** the command TURN LEFT!, given to plough-horses II.3.5(a). 'tɪðəᶜː ðɛᶜː Ha *[queried SBM]*

get larger *viphr* to WAX, referring to the moon VII.6.5(a). get laʁːdʒɔʁ Nb, *-ing* gɛʔŋ lɑˑdʒə Nf

get less *viphr* to WANE, referring to the moon VII.6.5(b). get lɛs Nb

get liler *viphr* to WANE, referring to the moon VII.6.5(b). *-ing* gɪtn laɪlə Y

get off *imp* GO AWAY! VIII.7.9(a). get ɑːf He, gɛd ɑːf Gl, gɛɹ ɑːf Wo Gl, gɪt ɒf Cu Wo, get ɒf St Nt Brk, gɛɹ ɒf La Y Ch St, gɪt ɔf L, gɛɹ ɔf L, gɪd ɔːf D, gɪɹ ɔːf Sr, get ɔːf Ess W, gɛd ɔːf O Nth, gɛɹ ɔᶜːf Sa; **get off out of it** get ɒf aːt əv ɪt Lei; **get off out the road** gɪt ɒf æʊt ðə ɹʊɐ Lei

get older *viphr* to WAX, referring to the moon VII.6.5(a). *prppl* gɛʔn oʊɫdəᶜ W

get on *imp* GO AWAY! VIII.7.9(a). get ɑːn Mon, gɪd ɔːn So D; **get on home** gɪd ɔn oʊm So; **get on out of it** gɪd ɔːn aʊt oʊ ət So

get out *imp* GO AWAY! VIII.7.9(a). gɪt ɛʊt Ess, gɪd ɛʊt Hrt Ess, get ɛʊt Ess, gɛɹ ɛʊt Wa, gɛɹ æːt Y, gɪd æɤt Co, gɛɹ æˑət La, gɪt aʊt Y, get aʊt Db L, gɛɹ aʊt Nt, gɛɹ ʌʊt Y, gɪt uːt Nb, get uːt Nb, gɛɹ uːt L; **get on out** gɪd ɔːn æɤt D; **get on out of it** gɪd ɔːn æɤd əv ɪt Co, gɪd ɔːn aʊt oʊ ət So, gɪd ɔːn aʊt əv ɪt Do; **get out of it** gɛɹ ɛʊˀ əv ɪˀ Bk, gɪd œɤd ɔː t D, gɪd æɤd ɔː t Co, gɪd æɤd ʌv ɪt Co, gɛd aʊt əv ɪt So, get ʌʊt əv ɪt Mon; **get out of the way** gɛʔ ɛʊˀ ə ðə weɪ Nf; **get out on it** get ɛʊt ɒn ɪt Sa, get æʊt ɒn ət W, get aːt ɒn ɪt Y, get aʊt ɒn t So, gɛɹ aːt ɒn ɪt Y, gɪd uːt ɒn ɪt Cu, gɛʔ əʊʔ ɒn ɪt W; **get yourself out** gɪt ðɪsɛl ᵁuːt We

get smaller *viphr* to WANE, referring to the moon VII.6.5(b). *-ing* gɪtɪn smɔːlə MxL, *-ing* gɪtn smɔːlə Sr, *-ing* gɪdɪn zmɔːɫəᶜː D, *-ing* gɪdən smɔːɫəᶜː Co *[not an EMBM headword]*

gets out *viphr-3prsg* school FINISHES VIII.6.2(b). gɪts uːt Cu

getting *v-ing* CARTING corn from the field II.6.6. gɛtɪn Db

getting on for *adv* ALMOST VII.7.9. gɪtɪn ɒn fəɹ Y

getting out *vtphr-ing* **getting out muck, getting out with the manure** CARTING *DUNG* II.1.4. **getting out muck** gɪtən ᵊuːt mʊk Y; **getting out with the manure** gɪtɪn ɛʊt wɪ ðɪ mənjuəᶜ Sr

get together *vtphr-3sg* she [a tidy girl] will COLLECT her toys VIII.8.15. gɛɹ (+V) ... təgɛðə Y

get up *1. vtphr* to STOCK a cow's udder III.3.6. gɪt ... ɤp Nf

2. vtphr to VOMIT, referring to an adult VI.13.14(a). get ... ʊp St

3. viphr to WAX, referring to the moon VII.6.5(a). gɪt ʊp Y, get ʌp Sa, *-ing* gɛtɪn ʌp He; **get up for the full** *-ing* gɪtɪn ʊp fə t fʊl La; **get up full** *-ing* gɛɹɪn ʊp fʊl La; **get up to the full** *-ing* gɪtn ʊp tə t fʊl La; ⇒ also **full**

4. vtphr to CLIMB VIII.7.4. gɛɹ ʊp Lei

gib *n* a GOSLING IV.6.17. gɪb Nt L

gibble-fisted *adj* LEFT-HANDED VI.7.13(a). gɪblfɪstɪd Db

gibbles *1. npl* SPRING ONIONS V.7.16. dʒɪbɫz Gl *[old x1]* So W D, sɪbɫz So, dʒɪbəɫz Gl, dʒɪbuɫz So W, dʒɪbʊz So

2. npl shoots growing from an old onion. dʒɪblz Gl

gibblets *npl* SPRING ONIONS V.7.16. dʒɪbɫəts W

gibblings *n* CHITTERLINGS III.12.2. gɪblənz Ess *[queried EMBM]*

gibbons *npl* SPRING ONIONS V.7.16. dʒɪbʌnz Mon, dʒɪbənz He Mon

gibby-lamb *n* a PET-LAMB III.7.3. gɪbilam So

gib-fork *n* a HAY-FORK with a long or short shaft I.7.11. gɪbfɔːk Nf

giblets *n* the WATTLES of a hen IV.6.19. gɪblɪts Wo

giblicks *n* the WATTLES of a hen IV.6.19. dʒɪblɪks Wo

giddy *1. adj When you turn round and round, you soon begin to feel ....* IX.1.11. gɪdɪ Mon So W K Co D Do Ha, gɪdɪ La Y*[old]* Ch Db Sa St He Wo Wa*[old x1]* Mon Gl O L Lei Nth Hu Nf Sf*[old x1]* Bk Bd Hrt Ess MxL W Brk Sr K Do Ha Sx, gjɪdɪ St, gɛdi D. ⇒ **dizzy, dizzy-headed, fuddled, giddy-headed, headlight, mazy, swimmy, swimmy-headed, swimy, wanky** ⇒ **wonky, whirly, wonky, wooden**
2. adj feeling FAINT VI.13.7. gɪdɪ Sr

giddy-headed *adj* GIDDY IX.1.11. gɪdi-ɛɪdəd Co

giggling *v-ing* LAUGHING VIII.8.7. gɪglɪn L Ess, gɪdlɪn Db

gill *n* a RIVULET small enough to jump over IV.1.1. gɪl Y

gill(s) *n* the WATTLES of a hen IV.6.19.
no -s: gɪɫ So
-s: gɪlz L Nf, gɪɫz Gl O L Hu C Nf Sf Bk Bd Hrt Ess So Do, gɪᵊɫz Gl O, gɪʊɫz K, gɪʊz Brk

gills *1. npl* MOUTH CORNERS VI.5.2. gɪlz Y Nf
2. n the WINDPIPE VI.6.5. gɪɫz K

gilt *1. n* a YOUNG SOW III.8.5. gɪlt Nb Cu Du We La Y Man Ch Db Sa St He Wo Wa Mon Nt L Lei R Nf Ess, gɪɫt He Wo Wa L Lei R Nth Sf Bk Ess MxL So W Brk K Co D Ha, gɪɫʔ Bk, gɪʊlt K, gɪʊɫt O Sr Ha Sx, gɪʊt Ess Sr K Sx, gʌlt Nb
2. n a young sow after she has been served by a boar. gɪɫt O
3. n a castrated female pig, ⇐ HOG III.8.8. gɪɫt Wo

gilt pig *n* a YOUNG SOW III.8.5. gɪlt pɪg Y

gimmer *1. n [What do you call the animals that give us wool? And the female?] What is it until the second shearing?* III.6.5. gɪmᵊᴿ Nb, gɪmə Nb Cu Du Y Man Db St Nt L, gɪmbə L, gɪmᵊᴶ La Y O, gɪmᵊᵗ Db Sa. ⇒ **clipped sheep, double-theave, double threave, ewe, ewe-hog, ewe-hogget, ewe-tag, ewe-teg, four-teeth, four-tooth, gimmer-shearling, hog, hogget, lamb, maiden, one-shear, over-year hogget, second-shearling, second-shearling ewe, second-theave, second-tooth, second-year ewe, shearer, shear-hog, shearing, shearling, shearling-ewe, shearling-gimmer, shear-sheep,** *sheep***, tag, teg, theave, threave, twinter, two-shear, two-shear ewe, two-shear gimmer, two-teeth, two-teeth ewe, two-tooth, two-tooth ewe, two-year-old, wether, yearling, yearling ewe, young ewe**
2. n a EWE-HOG III.6.4. gɪmə Cu Y Nt, gɪmɹ L,

gɪmᵊɹ Y, gɪmᵊᵗː Ha *[taken by SBM Edd to refer to sheep after first shearing,* ⇒ *gimmer III.6.5]*
3. n a EWE-LAMB III.6.3. gɪmə Y, gɪmᵊɹ Y

gimmer-hog *n* a EWE-HOG III.6.4. gɪmᵊhɒg Nb Du, gɪmᵊɹɒg Cu We La Y, gɪmᵊɹɔg La Y

gimmer-lamb *n* a EWE-LAMB III.6.3. gɪmᵊᴿlam Nb, gɪmᵊlam Nb Cu Du We La Y Nt, gɪmᵊrlam Cu, gɪmᵊɹlam La Y

gimmer-shearling *n* a GIMMER III.6.5. gɪmᵊʃɪᵊlɪn Y, gɪmᵊʃɪᵊlən Du

gimmicker *n* a LEFT-HANDED person VI.7.13(a). gɪmɪkᵊᵗː So

gins *vi-3prsg* school BEGINS VIII.6.2(a). gɪnz O

gippies *npl* GIPSIES VIII.4.12. dʒɪpɪz Ess

gippoes *npl* GIPSIES VIII.4.12. dʒɪpɒuz Wo K Sx, dʒɪpɔːz Y L, dʒɪpᵊuz O L Nth Hu Ess Ha, dʒɪpʌuz Bk Bd Ess*[facetious and rare x1]* MxL K, dʒɪpʔʌuz Sf, dʒɪpoːz Sa*[old x1]* He Wo Mon Gl Nt So W Brk*[old x1]* Co D Do Ha, dʒɪpouz St*[old x1]* Wo Wa O, dʒɪpouz Lei Nth Nf, dʒɪpʔouz Ess, dʒɪpuːz Ch Sf, dʒɪpʔʊ'z Sf, dʒɛpɔːz W

gippots *npl* GIPSIES VIII.4.12. dʒɪputs He

gips *npl* GIPSIES VIII.4.12. tʃɪps Wo, dʒɪps L

gipsies *npl What do you call those dark-skinned people who move about the country in caravans?* VIII.4.12. Eng exc. He Mon W D. ⇒ **chikes, darkies,** *dickies* ⇒ **dickoys, dickoys, diddies, diddikies, diddikites, diddiks, diddikoys, dinloes, gangingfolk, gippies, gippoes, gippots, gips, long companies, muggers, pikeys, potters, romanies, romeos, tallies, tally-gipsies, tinks, travellers, turnpike-road-sailors, turnpike-sailors**

gipsies' stools *npl* MUSHROOMS II.2.11. dʒɪpsɪz styːɫz D

girdle *1. n And [what do you call] that iron plate that cakes were baked on over the fire?* V.7.4(b). gɪᵊdl La, geᵊᴿdl Nb, geːdl Db Nt Nf, geːdɫ Lei, geᵊᴿdl Nb, geᵊdl Nb La, gerḷ Cu, gœːdl Du, gœːdɫ Gl, gᵊᴿːdl Nb Du, gʌdɫ Ess, gʊrdl Cu, gɜᴿːdl La, gᵊdl Du Y, gᵊɹdl He, gᵊɾdɫ O, gᵊːdl Cu Du We La Y Db St Nt L, gᵊːdɫ Wa Gl*[not used]* Lei Sf Bd Ess MxL Sr, gᵊᴿːdl Nb, gᵊᴶːdl La Ch L, gᵊᴶːdɫ O, gᵊᵗːdḷ Sa, gᵊᵗːdɫ Wo Wa Bk So W K Do Ha, gᵊᵗːdʊ Sr, gᵊᵗːɾdɫ Brk Ha Sx, gᵊᵗːɾdʊ Sx. ⇒ **backstone, baker, bakestone, baking-iron, baking-tin, cake-plate, cake-tin, cake-tray, crock, crock-pot, flat-jack, frying-pan, girdle-plate, girdle-stone, grid, griddle, gridiron, grill, hang-on-oven, hot-plate, oven-shelf, pan, plate, pot, shelf;** ⇒ also **crock-cake, haver-bread**
2. n a GRIDIRON V.7.4(a). gᵊᵗːdḷ D
3. n the GIRTH of the harness of a cart-horse I.5.8. gᵊːdɫ Ess

girdle-iron *n* a GRIDIRON V.7.4(a). gəᵗːd̲ᶤ̣ɒɪəᵗːn̩ D

girdle-plate* *n* a GIRDLE for baking cakes V.7.4(b). gəːdlpleˑət Cu

girdle-stone *n* a GIRDLE for baking cakes V.7.4(b). gəːdlstoʊn St

girl *n* a DAUGHTER VIII.1.4(b). gɛl Nf, gɛɫ Wa Nth Sf Bd Ess, *pl* gɛɫz Bk, gɛᵊɫ Sf Bk, gæɫ Nth, gal C, gəɹl Nth, gəˑɹɫ C, gəːl Wa, gəᵗːļ Gl*[usual]*

girls *npl* Children may be of either sex: they're either *[boys]*, or .... VIII.1.3(b). Eng exc. Cu La. ⇒ **bairn, chiel, lasses, lassies, maidens, maids, mawr, mawther, wenches, young bitch**

girth *1. n [Show a picture of the harness of a cart-horse.] What do you call this, for fastening the saddle on the horse?* I.5.8. Eng exc. MxL. ⇒ **back-strap, belly-band, belly-girth, belly-strap, body-belt, girdle, girth-band, girther, girthing, girths, girth-strap, pad-strap, saddle-belly-band, saddle-girth, saddle-strap, under-strap**
2. n the BELLY-BAND of the harness of a cart-horse I.5.7. gəˑt Nf, gəːɹt Sf, gəᵗːr̩θ Ha, gəᵗːrt Sr Sx

girth-band *n* the GIRTH of the harness of a cart-horse I.5.8. gɒθbənt Ch, gʊʔband Bk, gəːθband Y, gəːtbən L

girther *n* the GIRTH of the harness of a cart-horse I.5.8. gœːθəᵗ Gl

girthing *n* the GIRTH of the harness of a cart-horse I.5.8. gəθɪn Y, gəːθɪn Db

girths *nsg* the GIRTH of the harness of a cart-horse I.5.8. gəᶨːts Brk

girth-strap *n* the GIRTH of the harness of a cart-horse I.5.8. gəᶨθstɹap Ch, gɜᶨːθstɹap La

gissy *n* a STYE in the eye VI.3.10. gɪsɪ Du

gist *1. v* to put cattle on hired pasture, ⇐ HIRE *PASTURAGE* III.3.8. dʒᶨiːst We, -*ing* dʒɪstɪn Y, dʒaɪst La Y L Lei, -*ing* dʒaɪstɪn Nt, dʒɑːst Y dʒaɪst Db Nt Nth Bd, -*ing* dʒɑɪstɪn La L, dʒaɪs Hu, -*ing* dʒaɪsɪn Y, dʒɒɪst Nt Nth, -*ing* dʒɒɪsɪn La, dʒɔɪst L, -*ing* dʒɔɪstɪn Lei, dʒɔɪs Db C
2. n hired pasture. dʒɑːst Y, dʒɑɪst Bd, dʒɔɪs L

gister out *vtphr* to put cattle on hired pasture, ⇐ HIRE *PASTURAGE* III.3.8. -*ing* dʒaɪstəɹɪn ... uːt Y

gisting *n* hired pasturage, ⇐ HIRE *PASTURAGE* III.3.8. dʒɔɪstɪn Lei R

gistment *n* hired pasture, ⇐ HIRE *PASTURAGE* III.3.8. gɪstmənt Y

gist out *1. vtphr* to put cattle on hired pasture, ⇐ HIRE *PASTURAGE* III.3.8. -*ing* gɪstɪn ... aːt Y, -*ing* dʒɛɪstɪn ... uːt Y, dʒaɪst aʊt La, -*ing* dʒaɪstɪn ... aʊt Y, -*ing* dʒaˑɪstɪn ... ɔʊt L, dʒaɪstɪn ... uːt L
2. vphr to put cattle on hired pasture. -*ing* dʒaɪsɪn uːt Y

gives out *viphr-3prsg* school FINISHES VIII.6.2(b). gɪvz æʊt Ha

gives over *viphr-3prsg* school FINISHES VIII.6.2(b). gɪz aʊə Y, gɪvz ɔʊə Ch

giving *v-ing* THAWING, referring to snow VII.6.15. gɪvɪn He Sr K D, gɪvən Co, gɪjɪn So

giving out *vphr-ing* THAWING, referring to snow VII.6.15. gɪvən œʏt D, gɪvɪn æʊt So, gɪvɪn aʊt So*[old x1]*, gɪvɪn əʊt So*[old]*, gɪjɪn aʊt So*[old]*

giving-out-time *n* STOPPING-TIME at the end of a day's work VII.5.9. gɪvɪnɛʊʔtʌʏm O

giving-over-time *n* STOPPING-TIME at the end of a day's work VII.5.9. gɪvɪnaʊataɪm Y, gi-ɪnaʊataɪm Y, gɪvɪnɑʊətaɪm Y, gɪvɪnɒvətɑːm Y, gɪvɪnɒvətaˑɪm L, gɪvɪnɒvətɒɪm Lei, gɪvɪnɒʊəteɪm Nb, gɪvnɒʊəteɪm Cu, gɪvɪnɒʊətɑːm Y, gi-ɪnɒʊətɑːm Y, gɪiːnɒʊətaɪm Cu, gi-ɪnɔˑətaɪm Y, gɪvɪnɔʊəᵍteɪm Nb, gɪvɪnɔʊətaɪm Y, gɪvɪnɔʊətaᶨm Ch, gɪvɪnɔəɹtaɪm La, gɪvɪnɔəɹtɑɪm La, gɪvɪnɔːəɹtɑːm La, gɪvɪnɒʊətaᶨm Ch

giving way *vphr-ing* THAWING, referring to snow VII.6.15. gɪvɪn weː Sa, giːɪn wiː St

gizzard *1. n* a THROAT VI.6.3. gɪzəᵗːd̲ So
2. n the WINDPIPE VI.6.5. gɪzɒᵍd Nb, gɪzəd Cu*[old]* Du We La Y Ess, gɪzər Cu, gɪzəɹd Y, gɪzəᵗd̲ He Wo, gɪzəᵗːd̲ Sa Gl So W Co D Do Ha

gizzen *vi* to WARP, referring to wood IX.2.9. gaɪzn Nb

gizzened* *adj* dried and split, describing unseasoned wood, ⇐ WARP IX.2.9. gaɪznd Nb

glance *vi* to BOUNCE VIII.7.3. gɫans Co D

glands *npl* BOILS VI.11.6. glænz Ess *[queried u.r. EMBM]*

glapes *vi-3prsg* he GAPES VI.3.7. *prppl* glɛːpən Cu

glares *vi-3prsg* he GAPES VI.3.7. *prppl* klɛəɹɪn Ess, *prppl* glaːɹən Du *[queried N/EMBM]*

glat *1. vt* to fill gaps in a hedge-bank or hedge with turfs, brushwood, or similar material, ⇐ to PLASH IV.2.4. glat Sa He
2. n a SHEEP-HOLE IV.2.8. glɛt Sa, glæt He Mon*[not man-made x1]*, gɫæt He Mon Gl, glat Sa*[man-made x1, not man-made x2]* Mon
3. n a break in a hedge. glat He
4. v to stop up holes in a hedge. -*ing* glætɪn Mon

glaur *n* MUD VII.6.17. glaː Nb, glaᵍː Nb, glaːᵍ Nb, glɔʊəᵍ Nb

glazing *v-ing* PEEPING VI.3.8. gɫeːzən Co

glazy *adj* SLIPPERY VII.6.14. gleɪzɪ Brk

gleaning out *vphr-ing* CULLING sheep III.11.2. dliˑnɪn ... ɛʊt Nf

gleanings *n* BEESTINGS V.5.10. gliənɪnz Y

gleed(s) *n* CINDERS V.4.3.
no -s: gliːd St, glɛɪd St
-s: gliːdz Ch St, glɛɪdz Ch*[old]* St

glee-eyed *adj* CROSS-EYED VI.3.6. gliː-iːd Du, gliː-aɪd Nb Cu*[old x1]* Du

gleeing *v-ing* SQUINTING VI.3.5. gliːən Cu Du

glib *adj* SLIPPERY VII.6.14. glɪb C

gliding *prppladj* CROSS-EYED VI.3.6. glaɪdɪn So

gliffed *adj* AFRAID VIII.8.2. glɪft Nb

glining *v-ing* LAUGHING IX.2.14. glaɪnɪn So

glirry *vi* to SLIDE VIII.7.1. glətɪ O*[old]*

glob *n* an EAR-HOLE VI.4.3. glɒb Sa *[queried WMBM]*

globe *n* a SKEP IV.8.8(b). *pl* gloˑʊbz Nf*[reeds]*

gloomy *adj* DULL, referring to the weather VII.6.10. glɤːmi So, gluːmɪ O C Nf Sx

gloppers *npl* BLINKERS covering the eyes of a cart-horse I.5.2. glɒpəz La, glɒpəᴶz We

glops *vi-3prsg* he GAPES VI.3.7. *no -s* dlɔːp We

glores *vi-3prsg* he GAPES VI.3.7. *prppl* glɔːɹən Du, *prppl* gloəɹən We, *no -s* glʊə Cu, *prppl* glʊəɹɪn Y, *-ing* glʊəɹɪn La Y*[old x1]*, *prppl* glʊəɹən We Y

gloring* *v-ing* PEEPING VI.3.8. glʊəɹɪn Y, *no -ing* glʊə Cu

glot *n* the WATTLES of a hen IV.6.19. gɫɒt W

gloves *n* *And what else [do you put on in very cold weather], to keep your hands and fingers warm?* VI.14.7. Eng. ⇒ **mittens**; ⇒ also **dannockins**, **dannocks, mitts**

glummy *adj* DULL, referring to the weather VII.6.10. glʊmɪ Sf

glut *v* to GOBBLE food VI.5.13(b). *-ing* glʌtɪn Brk Sr Sx, *-ing* glʌʔɪn W Sx, *-ing* glʊtn Nt *[Nt form taken as **glutton** WMBM; cp **glut down**]*

glutch *1. v* to guzzle a drink, ⇐ GUZZLES VI.5.13(a). *-ing* gɫʌtʃɪn W

2. v to GOBBLE food VI.5.13(b). *-ing* gɫʌtʃɪŋ Brk, *-ing* gɫʌtʃɪn Do, *-ing* gɫʌtʃən Do Ha

3. vi to belch, ⇐ BELCHING VI.13.13. glʌtʃ So

glutch down *vtphr* to GOBBLE food VI.5.13(b). *-ing* glʌtʃɪn ... dæʊn W

glut down *vtphr* to GOBBLE food VI.5.13(b). *-ing* gɫʌtn ... dæʊn Ha *[could be **glutton**; see note at **glut**]*

gluts *1. vt-3prsg* he GUZZLES a drink VI.5.13(a). *prppl* glʊtən Man

2. v-3prsg he guzzles. *prppl* glʊtn Cu, *-ing* glʊtɪn Wo

glutton *1. v* to guzzle a drink, ⇐ GUZZLES VI.5.13(a). *-ing* glʊtnɪn Db

2. n a person who guzzles. glʊtn St

3.1. vt to GOBBLE food VI.5.13(b). *3prsg* glʊtnz St

3.2. v to gobble. *-ing* glʌʔɲɪn Brk, glʊtn Ch *[Ch form taken as **glutting** EMBM]*

glutton down *vtphr* to GOBBLE food VI.5.13(b). *-ing* glʊtnɪn ... dæʊn St

gnarred *adj* TANGLED, describing hair VI.2.5. næːd Nf *[queried EMBM]*

gnat-catching *vi-prppl* gaping, ⇐ GAPES VI.3.7. natkɛtʃən W

gnats *n* DADDY-LONG-LEGS IV.8.10. *no -s* nɛt Nf, næts Nf *[size and referent uncertain]*

gnaw *1.1. vt-1prpl* we CRUNCH apples or biscuits VI.5.12. neɪ So, nɔː So, nɔˑɹ (+V) Nf, nɔəᴶₑᶜᴶ (+V) Brk

1.2. v-1prpl we crunch. *-ing* nɔˑɹɪn Nf

2. vi to ACHE, referring to a stomach VI.13.3(b). *prppl* nɔːɹɪn Nf

go *1. imp* **go off** the command TURN LEFT!, given to plough-horses II.3.5(a). gʊ ˈɔːf MxL

2. imp **go fromward, go hither, go off, go over** the command TURN RIGHT!, given to plough-horses II.3.5(b). **go fromward** goʊ ˈfɹɒməᶜḍ Ha; **go hither** ˈgoʊ ˈɪðəᶜɹ Wo; **go off** goː ɒf Db; **go over** gu ʌʊvə Sf

3. imp **go forward, go up gee** the command GO ON!, given to plough-horses II.3.5(d). **go forward** goʊ ˈfɒɹəd Ha; **go up gee** ˈgoʊ ˌᵞp ˈdʒiː Nf

4. vi to WANE, referring to the moon VII.6.5(b). *-ing* goɪn Brk; **begin to go** *prppl* bɪgɪnɪn tə gʊə Y

5. imp GO AWAY! VIII.7.9(a). gʊː St; **be going** bɪ gaː-ɪn La, bɪ gʊɪn Y; **you'll have to be going** ðuːl ɛ tə bɪ gaːn Y

6. n **full of go, on the go** ACTIVE, describing a child VIII.9.1. **full of go** fʊɫ əv gʌʊ MxL; **on the go** ɒˑn ðə gɒu K, ɒn t gɔː Cu, ɒn ðə gɒu Hu, ɒn ðə gɒu Wa L, ɒn ðə gʌʊ Hrt, ɒn ðə goː Nt, ɔˑn ðə goː Sa, ɒn ðə gou St Nth, ɒːn ðə gou Ha, ɒn ðə goːᵁ He Nt So, ɒn t goːᵁ Db, ɒn ðə gu: Ch, ɒn t gʊː La Y, ɒn ðə guː Sf Ess, ɔːn ðə gu: Co, ɒn ðə gʊˑə Y, ɒn t gʊə Y, ɒn ðə gʊə L *[marked u.r. BM]*

goat *n* a BEARD VI.2.7. gʌʊt Ess

goating *v-ing* STOOKING II.6.5. gᵧːtɪn D, gᵧːtən D

go away *1. imp* *To get rid of someone quickly who was being a bit of a nuisance, you'd say:* .... VIII.7.9(a). gaː əweː We, gɑː əweː Y, goː əweː Db, gaː əwɛː Cu, gʊ əwɛː Y, gɒʊ əwɛɪ Sr, gɒʊ əwɛɪ L, gʊə əwɛˑə L, gɒʊ əwæɪ K, guː wæɪ K. ⇒ **away** *with you*, **beat it**, **beggar off**, *be going*, *be going* on, **be off**, **be off** *with it*, **bolt off**, **bugger off**, **bugger off** *out of it*, **bugger on**, *bugger you*, **buzz off**, **clear off**, **clear off** *of here*, **clear off** *with you*, **clear out**, **clear out** *of it*, **gan away**, **gan off**, **gan on**, **gan** *to hell*, **gan** *your ways*, **get** *agoing*, **get away**, **get away** *home*, **get away** *out*, **get going**, **get off**, **get off** *out of it*, **get off** *out the road*, **get off** *with thee*, **get off** *with you*, **get on**, **get on** *home*, **get on** *I've had enough of you*, **get** *on* **out**, **get** *on* **out** *of it*, **get out**, **get out** *of it*, **get out** *of the way*, **get out** *on it*, **get out** *with you*, *get you from here*, **get** *yourself* **away**, **get** *yourself* **out**, *get your ways*, **go**, **go on**, *go on get yourself away* ⇒ **go on** + **get away**, **hadaway** *be going*, **hadaway** *with you*, **hike**, **hook it**, **hop it**, **hop it** *you*, **hop off**, **jert it**, **mess off**, **mizzle**, **muck off**,

off you go, *out you go boy*, pack off, *pick your* hook, potter off, push it, push off, scoot, scram, shift, shift on, skeedaddle, *sling your* hook, *sling your* hook *you*, slip off, *take thy hook* ⇒ *take your* hook, take your hook, *take your* hooks, way *with you*, *you* clear *on* out, *you'd better be going*, *you'd better* be off, *you* get off, *you had better* clear off, *you had better* clear off *from here*, *you had better* get on, *you had better* get on *out of it*, *you* hammer off *out the way*, *you'll have to be going*, *you* scram

2. *viphr* to WANE, referring to the moon VII.6.5(b). -*ing* gɔːɪn əwɛː Mon, guː əwɛː Sa

gob *1. n* the human MOUTH VI.5.1. gœb Nb Du, gɒb Cu Du*[vulgar x1]* We*[vulgar x2]* La Y*[slang/vulgar x1, vulgar x1, old x2]* Db L Nf*[vulgar x1]*, gɔb Du We Y Ch L*[impolite]*, gɔːb Nb

2. *n WIPE YOUR* MOUTH VI.5.3. gœb Nb, gœːb Nb, gɒb Nb*[vulgar]* Cu We La Y, gɔb L

3. *n* the WINDPIPE VI.6.5. gɔb L

go back *viphr* to WANE, referring to the moon VII.6.5(b). -*ing* gwiːn bak So, gɤː bak Db, -*ing* geːn bak Co, -*ing* gweːn bak D, -*ing* gwaɪn bæk So, -*ing* gwæɪn bak So, ga bak We La Y, gan bak Nb Cu Du We, *prppl* gaːn bak La Y, *prppl* gwaɪn bak So, -*ing* gwaɪn bak So Do, -*ing* gɒɪn bak W, gɒʊ bak Wo, -*ing* gɒʊən bæˑk Man, *3prsg* gʌʊz bak K, *prppl* gɔːn bak So, -*ing* gɔːn Bak So, -*ing* gɔən baːk W, *prppl* gɔːɪn bak So, -*ing* gɔːɪn bak So D Do, -*ing* gɒɪɪn bak Do, gʊ bak Nb La Ch Db, *prppl* gʊɪn bak Y, -*ing* gʊɪn bak Y, guː bak Db, -*ing* gᵿːɪn bak Lei

gobble *1. v [If a man drinks noisily and greedily, you say he ....] And if he eats in the same way?* VI.5.13(b). Eng exc. Du We Man R MxL Brk Co D Do. ⇒ **bolt, bolt down, cham, champ, chobble, chom, chomble, chomple, chop, chops, chop up** *his grub, eats it greedily*, **gabble, gallop down, gaunge, gawp, glut, glutch, glutch down, glut down, glutton, glutton down,** *gobble back*, *gobble down*, *gobble up*, **golk, gollop, gollop down, gollops down, golp, golsh, gorge, gorge down, gormandise, granch, graunch, growdge,** *growge* ⇒ **growdge, growze, gubble, guggle, gullett, gulf, gullop, gulp, gut, gut back, gut down, guts, guts down, guttle, gut up, guzzle, hog, hog down, larp, maunch,** *mundge* ⇒ **munge, munge, munge away, pig, push down, rattle down, scoff up, scrump, scrunch, slabber, slawp, slobber, slop,** *slorp* ⇒ **slawp, slotch, slother, slubber, slush, sluther, smack, smack***ing your gills*, **soss, stuff, sup, wolf down, wolf** *his food*

2. *n* CHAT VIII.3.4. gɒbł So*[old]*

gobble down *vtphr* to guzzle a drink, ⇐ GUZZLES VI.5.13(a). -*ing* gɒblɪn ... dæʊn Lei, -*ing* gɒbłɪn ... dæʊn W, gɒbłɪn ... daʊn O

gobbler *n* the WATTLES of a hen IV.6.19. gɔbłə Ess

gobble(s) *n* the WATTLES of a hen IV.6.19.

?*sg*: gɒbl Y

-*s*: gɒblz Sa, gɒbłz Wo

gobbles *1. vt-3prsg* he GUZZLES a drink VI.5.13(a). -*ing* gɔbłɪn La

2. *v-3prsg* he guzzles. gɒblz La Sa, *no* -*s* gɒbl St O Nt, -*ing* gɒblɪn Y St Nf, -*ing* gɒbəlɪn K, *inf* gɔbl Y, -*ing* gɔblɪn L

gobble up *vtphr* to guzzle a drink, ⇐ GUZZLES VI.5.13(a). -*ing* gɔbłɪn ... ʊp Wo

go bigger *viphr* to WAX, referring to the moon VII.6.5(a). -*ing* gʊɪn bɪgəɪ La

goblet(s) *n* the WATTLES of a hen IV.6.19.

no -*s*: gɒblət So

-*s*: gɔblɪts Wo, gɔbləts Ess

godling* *n* a GOSLING IV.6.17. gɒːdlɪŋ Sx

godmother's wish *n* a LOOSE *PIECE OF* SKIN at the bottom of a finger-nail VI.7.11. *pl* gɒdmʊðəz wɪʃɪz La

go down *viphr* to WANE, referring to the moon VII.6.5(b). -*ing* gweɪn dæʊn He, goː dɛʊn Sa, goː daʊn Sa, goː dəʊn Mon, -*ing* gɔːɪn dæʊn He, -*ing* goˑɪn dəʊn He, goʊ dɛʊn Wo, -*ing* gʊɪn daːn Y

goes home *viphr-3prsg* school FINISHES VIII.6.2(b). guːz uːm Ha

goes in *viphr-3prsg* school BEGINS VIII.6.2(a). gaːz ɪn Cu La, gʌʊz ɪn Ess, goːz ɪn Sa Gl, goː ɪn W, də goː ɪn Do, goʊ ɪn So, gʊz ɪn La Db, gʊəz ɪn Y

goes out *viphr-3prsg* school FINISHES VIII.6.2(b). gʊz uːt Cu

gog-eyed *adj* CROSS-EYED VI.3.6. gɒgɒɪd K

goggle *n* the WATTLES of a hen IV.6.19. gɒgł Gl *[marked 'sg' and queried mass noun WMBM]*

goggle-eyed *adj* CROSS-EYED VI.3.6. gɔgłaˑɪd L

goggles *1. npl* BLINKERS covering the eyes of a cart-horse I.5.2. gœːglz Nb

2. *v-3prsg* he GUZZLES a drink VI.5.13(a). -*ing* gɒglɪn Nt Brk, -*ing* gɒgłɪn Co

goggles down* *vphr-3prsg* he GUZZLES a drink VI.5.13(a). gɒgłɪn ... dæʌn Co

going-home-time *n* STOPPING-TIME at the end of a day's work VII.5.9. gɔːɪnʊəmtaɪm Nt

goldering *v-ing* LAUGHING VIII.8.7. gɒləɹən We

go less *viphr* to WANE, referring to the moon VII.6.5(b). -*ing* gɤːɪn lɛs La, -*ing* gʊɪn lɛs La Ch

golk *1. vt-3prsg* to guzzle a drink, ⇐ GUZZLES VI.5.13(a). -*ing* gɒłkən Co

2. *vt* to GOBBLE food VI.5.13(b). -*ing* gɒłkɪn D, -*ing* gɒłkən Co

golk down *vtphr* to guzzle a drink, ⇐ GUZZLES VI.5.13(a). gɒłk ... dæʌn D, -*ing* gɒłkən ... dæʌn Co

gollacker *n* the human MOUTH VI.5.1. gɔləkə L

golling *n* a GOSLING IV.6.17. gɒlɪn Bk, *pl* gɒlɪnz So

gollop *1. n* a NESTLING IV.7.1. gɒləp Y, gʊləp Y
2.1. vt to GOBBLE food VI.5.13(b). gɒləp Cu, *prppl* gɒləpɪn Y, *-ing* gɒləpɪn Y
2.2. v to gobble. gɒləp Cu Du Ch Db Wa O Nth Hu, *3prsg* gɒləps Mon Lei R, *-ing* gɒləpɪn La Y St, *-ing* gɒɫəpn Ha, *-ing* gɔləpɪn Y

gollop down *vtphr* to GOBBLE food VI.5.13(b). *-ing* gɒɫəpn ... dæʊn Ha, *-ing* gɔləpɪn ... dɛʊn MxL *[not a SBM headword]*

golloping *v-ing* DRINKING V.8.1. gʌləpɪn Mon

gollops *1. vt-3prsg* he GUZZLES a drink VI.5.13(a). gɒləps Man
2. v-3prsg he guzzles. *no -s* gɒlʊp Wa, gɒləps He O Nt Lei R Nth, *inf* gɒləp La, *no -s* gɒləp Ch Wa Bd, *-ing* gɒləpɪn Y St Bk Bd K, gɒɫəps Hrt, *-ing* gɒɫəpn Ha, gɔləps L, *no -s* gɔləp O C Sf, *-ing* gʌləpɪn Mon, gʊləps Nth

gollops down *vtphr* to GOBBLE food VI.5.13(b). gɒləps ... dæʊn Ch

golly *n* a NESTLING IV.7.1. gɒlɪ Y, gɔlɪ Y

golly-handed *adj* LEFT-HANDED VI.7.13(a). gɒlɪ-andɪd Y

golp *1. v* to guzzle a drink, ⇐ GUZZLES VI.5.13(a). gɒɫp Wa, *-ing* gɒɫpɪn Gl K, *-ing* əgɒɫpɪn Brk, gɔˈlps Man, gɔɫp Hrt, *-ing* gɔɫpɪn Brk Ha *[not a NBM headword]*
2. v to GOBBLE food VI.5.13(b). gɒɫp Wa, *-ing* gɔʊlpən Nb

golp down *vtphr* to guzzle a drink, ⇐ GUZZLES VI.5.13(a). *-ing* gɒɫpən ... dæʏn Co

golp up *vtphr-3prsg* to guzzle a drink, ⇐ GUZZLES VI.5.13(a). gɒɫp ... ʌp Ha

golsh *v* to GOBBLE food VI.5.13(b). *-ing* gɒlʃɪn Y

gone *1. v-ed* FINISHED, referring to a store of potatoes V.7.21. gɑːn He Wo Gl Nf, gɑᵗːŋ Wo, gɒn La Y St He Wo Wa Gl Nt Nth So, gɔːn Sa O Hu Bk Hrt Ess MxL So W Sr K D Do Ha, gʊən Y; **all gone** ɔːl gɪən Y, ɑːl gɒn He, ɔːl gɒn Wa Nth, ɔː gɒn Ch, ɔːl gɒn Wa L, ɔːl gɔːn So, ɔːɫ gɔːn So W Co D Do; **gone done** gɒn dʊn La
2. adj SILLY VIII.9.3. gɔːn So

gone in *adj* EXHAUSTED, describing a tired person VI.13.8. gɒn iːn D

gone over *viphr-ed* HAS NOT HELD, referring to a cow that has not conceived III.1.7. gɒn ɔvə L, gɒn ɔʊwə L, gɔːn ʌʊvə C Sf Ess, gɒn ɒʊvə Bd, gɒn ʊvə Lei; **gone over again** gɒn ɔvəɪ əgɛn L

gongog *n* GRANDDAD VIII.1.8(a). gɒŋgɒg He*[baby word]*

good *1. adj* WELL, describing a healthy person VI.13.1(a). gʊd So K, gᵁuːd Gl
2. adj **not so good**, **not too good** ILL, describing a person who is unwell VI.13.1(b). **not so good** nɒt so gʊd Mon; **not too good** nɔt tuː gʊd MxL K

good bit *n* **a good bit** A LOT (of money) VII.8.7. ə gʊd bɪt Du So

goodies *n* SWEETS V.8.4. gʊdɪz Cu We Y St Nt L, gʊdəz Co

good-like *adj* PRETTY, describing a girl VI.5.18. gʊdlaɪk Y

good-looking *adj* PRETTY, describing a girl VI.5.18. gʌdlʌkɪn Sa, gʊdlɪəkɪn Y, gʊdlɪuːkən Cu, gʊdlɪːkɪn Ch, gʊdlʊkɪn La St He Wa Mon Ess Sr Ha, gʊdlʊkən Nb, gʊdluːkɪn Y L

good tidy *adv* VERY VIII.3.2. gʊd tʌɪdɪ Nf

goody *n* SWEETS V.8.4. gʊdɪ Y

goody-packet *n* a BAG containing sweets, twisted from a square piece of paper V.8.5. gʊdɪpakɪt Y

go off *1. viphr* to FAINT VI.13.7. gan ɒf Du
2. viphr to WANE, referring to the moon VII.6.5(b). *-ed* gɒn ɒːf Man

gook *n* a woman's BONNET VI.14.1. guːk Co*[worn outdoors x1]*

gook bonnet *n* a woman's BONNET worn outdoors VI.14.1. guːk bɒnət Co

gooky *n* a STUPID person VI.1.5. gʏːkɪ D

gools *n* CHARLOCK II.2.6. guːlz La

go on *1. imp* **go on**, **go on gee** *[When you want your horses to stop, what do you say?]* And start (before April 1954: *And go on*)? II.3.5(d). **go on** gɒʊ ɒn K, ˈgɒ ˈɒn Nf, ˈgoː ˈɔːn W, gou æn Man, gou ɒn St Nth Nf, gʊ œˑn Nb, gʊ ɑn O, gʊ ɒn La Y Db St Wa Nt Nth Nf K, gʊβ ɒn Nf, gʊ ɒn La L C MxL, gʊ ən Db, guː ɒn Lei Nf Ess, guː ɔn C, guː ɔːn W Co Do; **go on gee** gʊ ɒn dʒi: St. ⇒ *all* **right**, come *along* **lads**, come **lads**, come *on*, come *on here*, come *on my lads*, come *up*, **coop**, **coop** *go on*, *cup go on* ⇒ **coop**, ease *up*, **gee**, **gee** *back*, **gee** *here*, **gee** *lads*, **gee** *up*, **gee** *up there*, **get**, **get** *on*, **get** *ready*, **get** *up*, **get** *up there*, **go** *forward*, **go on gee**, **go** *up* **gee**, hold *fast*, **pull** *up*, **right**, **right** *away*, **right** *ho*, **start**, **tick** *lads here*
2. imp GO AWAY! VIII.7.9(a). goː ɒn La, gʊ ɒn La Nt Ess, gɒʊ ɔːn O, goː ɔːn Ha; **go on get youself away** gø œːn gɛt jəsɛl əwɪə Nb; **be going on** bɪ gan ɒn We

gooseberries *npl* What do you call those berries with a sharp taste and a hairy skin that grow on prickly bushes in gardens? IV.11.2. Eng. ⇒ **berries**, **goose-bobs**, **goose-gobs**, **goose-gogs**, **grozers**

goose-bobs *npl* GOOSEBERRIES IV.11.2. gᵁuːsbɒbz La Y

goose-footed *adj* SPLAY-FOOTED VI.10.5. gɪuːsfʊtɪd Du

goose-gobs *npl* GOOSEBERRIES IV.11.2. gɪʊsgɒbz Y, gɪəsgɒbz We Y, gʏzgɒbz D, gʏːzgɒbz D, gʊɪsgɒbz Y*[modern x1, old x1]*, gʊɪzgɒbz Y, gʊɪzgɔbz Y, guːsgɒbz Cu Y,

175

guːzgɒbz Y, gᵁuːsgɒbz Du We La Y, gᵁuːzgɒbz La*[old]* Nt, guːsgɔbz Y, gᵁuːsgɔbz We

goose-gogs *npl* GOOSEBERRIES IV.11.2. gɪəsgɒbz Y, gʏːzgɒgz D, gʏːzgʌgz So, gousgɒgz La, gʊzgɑːgz Mon, gʊzgɒgz St He Wo Wa*[old x1]* Mon Gl*[old x2]* O Nth Nf*[children's word]* Sf*[children's word x1]* Bd*[children's word x1]* W Brk*[old x1]* K Do Sx, gʊzgɒgz Wa Ess*[children's word]* MxL*[old]*, gʊzgɔːgz Do, *sg* gʊzgɔːg Sa, guˈzgɑgz Nf*[children's word]*, guːsgɒgz Y St L Nf*[children's word]*, guːzgɒgz Ch Sa Lei Co, guːsgɔgz L, guːzgɔgz La, gᵁuːzgɒgz La*[old x1]*, gəusgɔgz Y

goose-grass *n [Show a picture of goose-grass.] What do you call this?* II.2.5. gɪusgɹas Y, gɪəsgɹas Y, gɔˡːsgɹæs So, gʌsgɹæs Sa K, guːsgɹɛs L, guːsgɹɛˀs Man, guːsgɹæs Sa K, guːsgɹæːs So Co, guːsgɹas Y La L, guːsgɹɑːs So Do, guːsgəs Y, gʊɪsgɹɛs Y, gʊɪsgɹas Y, gʊɪsgəˡːs Y. ⇒ **beggar-lice, beggar's-lice, billy-buttons, bunks, burdock, burr(s), carky mawkins, claden, claggy-buttons, claggy-jack, cleavers, clide, cliden, clider(s), clite(s), cliver(s), clives, cly, cockle-buttons, cockles, cogwheels, creeping-jinny, crotch-joy, crotch-weed, cuddle-me-close, devil-guts, furbobs, gosling-grass, gully-grass, gum-weed, hairif, hairip, hairis, hair-weed, *hay-riff* ⇒ hairif, jack-by-the-hedge, meg-many-feet, nut-grass, policeman's-buttons, pricklies, prickly-back, robin-run-in-the-hedge, robin-run-the-dike, robin-run-up-the-dike, scratch-grass, scratch-weed, soldier's-buttons, sticky-back, sticky-bobs, sticky-buttons, sticky-dick, sticky-grass, sticky-jack, sticky-stinking-joe, sweet-heart(s), swine-grass, teasels, tongue-weed**

goose-grease *n* CART-GREASE, used to lubricate the wheels of a cart I.11.4. gɪusgɹɪəs Y

gooseling* *n* a GOSLING IV.6.17. guːslɪn Sa

goose-neck tack *n* the lower of the two HANDLES of a scythe II.9.8. gɯsnɛk tɛk Nf

goose-quill *n* a SHEATH or other device used to keep a knitting-needle firm V.10.10. gɛuskwɪl Db

gooses *npl* GEESE IV.6.15(a). guːsɪz Sa

go over 1. *viphr* to OVERTURN, referring to a cart I.11.5. gʊ ɒʊə Y, gʌu ʌuvə Bd, *3prsg* gʌuz ʌuvə K, *ptppl* gɒn oːvəˡ Gl Brk, guː ouvə C, *ptppl* gɒn ouvə St, *ptppl* gɑˑn ouvə Nf
2. *viphr* to fail to conceive, referring to a cow, ⇐ *NOT IN* CALF III.1.8. ppadj gɔːn ʌuvə Ess

gorbet *n* a NESTLING IV.7.1. *pl* gɔːbəts Nb

gore 1. *vt* to BUTT III.2.10. *prppl* gʊəɹɪn Y
2. *v* to butt. *prppl* gɔᴿːʁən Nb, *prppl* gʊəɹɪn Y
3. *n* the CORE of a boil VI.11.7. gɔˑəˡ Gl, gʊə Ch L

gorge *v* to GOBBLE food VI.5.13(b). gɔːdʒ Mon, gɔˡːdʒ O, *-ing* gɔədʒɪn K

gorge down *vtphr* to GOBBLE food VI.5.13(b). *-ing* gɔːdʒɪn ... dæʊn Ess, *3prsg* gɔˡːdʒəz ... dæʊn So

gorging-grubs *npl* SLUGS IV.9.2. gɔˡːdʒəngɹʊbz La

gorling *n* a NESTLING IV.7.1. gɔːᵊlɪn Nb, *pl* gɔˑrlɪŋz Cu

gormandise *v* to GOBBLE food VI.5.13(b). *-ing* gɔːmənɑːzɪn La

gormers 1. *npl* CART-LADDERS I.10.5. gaˡːməˡːz̩ Sa, gɔːməz Y Db St Nt L Lei, gɔːmɹz L, dɔːməˡz̩ Sa, gɔˡːməz Db L, gɔˡːməˡz̩ Sa, gɔəməz Y
2. *npl* the posts at the corners of a cart. gɔːməz L
3. *n* a CART-FRAME I.10.6. gɔːməz Nt, gɔˡːməˡz̩ Sa

gorse *n What do you call that prickly bush with bright yellow flowers, sometimes said to be in bloom all the year round?* IV.10.11. gaˡːʂ W, gaːs Man Mon Gl, gaːst Mon, gaᴶːs Brk, gaˡːʂ Mon, gaːəˡʂ Gl, gaˡːʂt He Mon, gɒs Y Ch Db Sa St*[old x1]* Wo Wa Gl O Nt L Lei R Nth*[old x1]* Nf Bk Bd Brk K, gɒst Sa He Wo Gl, gɒsp He, gɒs Wa O Nt L Ess, gɔːst He, gɔːs La Y Man Ch Db St Wa Nt Nth C Nf Ess*[refined x1]* W, gɔːᵊs Nth Hu Nf Ess Sx, gɔːst He, gɔːz Y Db*[old]* Nth Bd Ess MxL K, gɔːᵊz Mon Bd, gɔːθ Y, gɔᴿːs Du, gɔᴶːs La Y Bɪk, gɔːəᴶs Ha, gɔᴶːz La, gɔᴶɹɪs La, gɔˡːʂ Sa So, gɔːəˡʂ Sr, gɔˡːʂt Sa He, gɔˡːʂk Sa, gɔəs Y K, gɔəɹs La, gous St, gʊəs Y, gɛːs St, gəᴶːs L. ⇒ **broom, fern, fur-bush, furra-bush, furze, furze-bush, gorse-bush, whin, whin-bush**; ⇒ also **gorse-birns, gorse-stubs**

gorse-birns 1. *n* KINDLING-*WOOD* V.4.2. gɔːsbɒnz Man
*2. *npl* dried GORSE-branches used as firewood IV.10.11. gɔːsbɒnz Man

gorse-bush *n* GORSE IV.10.11. *pl* gɒsbʊʃəz Nt, gɔːsbʊʃ Nf

gorse-hook *n* a BILLHOOK IV.2.6. gɒsʊk Wa Lei, gɒsᶦuːk Db, gɒsuːk St Lei Nth, gɒsɯːk Lei, gɔːsɛuk Db

gorse-stubs* *npl* dead pieces of GORSE used for lighting a fire IV.10.11. gɔːstʌbz Sa

gosling *n What do you call the young bird [i.e. goose]?* IV.6.17. Eng. ⇒ **gesling, gib, godling, golling, gooseling, gozzy, gull, gully, gutling, swaddling**

gosling-grass *n* GOOSE-GRASS II.2.5. gɒzlɪngɹɑːs Hrt, gɒzlɪŋgɹɑːs Hrt

go small *viphr* to WANE, referring to the moon VII.6.5(b). *-ing* goʊn smɔːɫ Lei

gossip 1. *n [What is your word for spending a lot of time doing this (i.e. chatting and spreading*

tales?)] And have you a special word for a woman who does this? VIII.3.5(b). Eng exc. Man Mon C Bk W Co D Do Ha. ⇒ **blatherskite, busybody, cagmag, call, caller, cank, cant, canter, chammer, chatterbag, chatterbox, chattermag, chinwagger, clat, clat-can,** *fair old gossip,* **gabber, gabble, gad, gallivanter, gasbag,** *gnatterer* ⇒ **natterer, gossiper, gossipmonger,** *gossips,* **jaffock, jaffocker, magger, mischief-maker, nagger, natter, natterer, newsagents, news-bag, news-canter, newser, newsgag, newsmonger, newsmongerer, nosey-parker,** *old* **cant,** *old* **chatterbox,** *old* **chinwagger,** *old* **gasbag,** *old* **gossip,** *old* **gossiper,** *old* **nagger,** *old* **newsmonger,** *old* **newspad,** *proper old* **chatterbag,** *proper old* **gossiper,** *rare old gossip, rare old* **gossiper, rattlebox, rattler, rattle(s),** *regular old* **cant,** *regular old* **houser, scandalmonger,** *scandlemonger* ⇒ **scandalmonger, tale-pyet, taler, tattler, tongue-wag, windbag, yapper**
2. *n* having a gossip GOSSIPING VIII.3.5(a). ɛvɪn ə gɒsəp Y
3. *n* CHAT VIII.3.4. gɒsəp Y O Ha, gɒʃəp O*[old],* gɔsəp Sr

gossiper *n* a GOSSIP VIII.3.5(b). gɑ'səpəᵗ Wo, gɒsɪpə Y Nf Ess, gɒzɪpə Y, gɒsʌpə Mon, gɒsəpə Nb Du La Y Db St Nt L Nth Hu Nf Bd Hrt Ess, gɒzəpə Y, gɒsɪpəˀ La*[modern],* gɒsəpəˀ La Y Sr, gɒsəpɹ La Y, *?pl* gɒsɪpəᵗz̩ Bk, gɒsəpəᵗ Sa He Wo Gl*[old]* O Nth Bk Bd W Ha Sx, gɒsəpə O, gɒʃəpəᵗ O, gɒsɪpəᵗ: Do, gɒsəpəᵗ: W Co D Do Ha, gɔsɪpə Y L Ess, gɔsəpə Y L C Sf Ess, gɔspə Ess, gɔsɪpɹ L, gɔsɪpəˀ L, gɔsəpəᵗ K, gɔːsəpəᵗ He, gɔːzəpəᵗ Sa, gɔːsəpəᵗ: Ha

gossiping *v-ing What is your word for spending a lot of time doing this [i.e. chatting] and spreading tales?* VIII.3.5(a). Eng. ⇒ *a*-canting, *a-gossiping,* *a*-nagging, **back-biting, blathering, cackling,** *cag-mag* ⇒ **cag-magging, cag-magging, calleting, calling, camping, canking, chackling, chamming** away, **chamragging, chattering, chewing** *the rag,* **chimchamming** away, **chinwagging, chittering, chopsing, chopsing** about, **clacking, clatting, conflabbing, gabbing, gallivanting,** *gaping* ⇒ **gapping, gapping,** *gnatter* ⇒ **nattering,** *gnattering* ⇒ **nattering, grinding** out *the time,* **hamchammering,** *having a* call, *having a* gossip, *having a* mag, *having a* natter, **hawching, jaffocking, jawing, magging,** *making* **mischief, nagging, nattering, neighbouring, newsbagging, newsing, newsmongering, prossing, raking, raning, rattling, spinning** *yarns, spreading* tales, **tale-telling,** *telling the tale* ⇒ **tale-telling, tick-tatting, tongue-wagging, yaddering, yapping, yarning**

gossipmonger *n* a GOSSIP VIII.3.5(b). gɒsɪpmɒŋgəᵗ Brk

gote 1. *n* a RIVULET IV.1.1. gɒɪt Y, gɔɪt Y*[side stream]*
2. *n* a SHEEP-HOLE IV.2.8. gʊət Cu

got to *vaux-2sg* you MUST do it IX.4.11. gɒt tʏː Co, gɒt tə Man So W K, gɒʔ ə O Bk, gɔt ə C; **have got to** əv gɒt tu St

go up *viphr* to WAX, referring to the moon VII.6.5(a). gʊ ʊp Wa

gout *n* a BRIDGE over a ditch at a field gateway, made of stone or planks covered with earth and stones IV.1.2. gaʊt So

governor *n* my HUSBAND VIII.1.25. **the governor** ðə gʌvnə Nf Bd Hrt Ess*[humorous x1]* MxL Sr, ðə gʌvɪnəᵗː So, ðə gʌvnə Nf, ðə gʊvnəɹ O

gowk *n* the CORE of a boil VI.11.7. gaʊk Y, gɒʊk Cu We, gɔːk Du Y, gɔ'ək Y, gʊək Y

gowpen *n* a HANDFUL VII.8.10(a). gɔʊpɪn Nb

gowpenful *n* a HANDFUL VII.8.10(a). gɔʊpɪnfə Nb

gozzy *n* a GOSLING IV.6.17. gɒzɪ Y

grab 1. *vt* to GROPE *FOR FISH* IV.9.10. gɹæb Nf
2. *vt* to PULL somebody's hair VI.2.8. gɹæb Sa

gradely 1. *adj* PRETTY, describing a girl VI.5.18. gɹeɪdɪ Lei *[queried EMBM]*
2. *adv* VERY VIII.3.2. gɹeːdlɪ La Ch, gɹe'ədlɪ Y

grading *v-ing* CULLING sheep III.11.2. gɹeːdɪn Y, gɹeədɪn Y, gɹeɪdɪn St L Lei, gɹæɪdɪn Sr

graft 1. *n* the SHAFT of a spade I.7.7. gɹɑːft Nth
2. *n* the SHAFT of a hay-fork I.7.12. gɹɑːft Nth
3. *n* WORK VIII.4.8(a). gɹɑːft Nf

grafting-shovel *n* a SPADE I.7.6. gɹaftɪnʃʊvl Ch

grails *n* SCRAPS left after rendering lard III.12.10. gɹeːɫz Co

grain 1. *n* a PRONG of a fork I.7.10. gɹiːn Ch, *pl* gɹiːnz St Brk, *pl* gʁɪənz Nb, *pl* gɹɪənz Du, greːn Cu, *pl* gʁeːnz Nb, gɹeːn La Y Ch, *pl* gɹeːnz Du Db Sa St Nt Brk, gɹeːn W Ha, gɹeɪn Db, gɹeɪn Ha, gɹe'ən Cu We La Y, *pl* gɹeənz Du, gɹeːn Cu, *pl* gɹɛːnz We, gɹɛːn W, gɹɛɪn Gl Sr, *pl* gɹɛɪnz Sa St Brk K Ha, *pl* gɹɛɪnz O W, gɹɛən O, gɹæɪn Gl, *pl* gɹæɪnz O, gɹaɪn W Do Ha
2. *vi-3prpl* they MOO, describing the noise cows make during feeding time in the cow-house III.10.4(a). gɹɛ'ən Cu
3. *n* a BRANCH of a tree IV.12.3. *pl* gɹɛənz Y

grain-board *n* an END-BOARD of a cart I.10.4. gɹeːnbʊəd Ch

grainer *adj* RANCID, describing bacon V.7.9. greɪnə Man

grains 1. *npl* BOUGHS of a tree IV.12.2. gɹeːənz Y*[old],* gɹɛːnz We, gɹɛənz Y*[old]*

2. n DREGS left at the bottom of a teacup V.8.15. gɹɛɪnz Lei Bk Ess Sx, gɹæɪnz Ess

graip *n* a MUCK-FORK I.3.13. gʁeːp Nb, gɹeːp Nb, gʁeəp Nb, gɹeɪp Cu, gʁɛɪp Nb Du, gɹɛɪp Cu

grake *adj* DRY, describing a cow with no milk III.1.9. gɹeːk Nt

gramfer-long-legs *n* DADDY-LONG-LEGS IV.8.10. gɹamfɪlɒŋlɛgz So, gɹamfəˤːlɒŋlɛgz So, gɹamfəˤːɫʌŋɫɛgz Co D

grammer *n* GRANNY VIII.1.8(b). gɹæməˤː So, gɹamə O *[not a SBM headword]*

grammy *n* GRANNY VIII.1.8(b). gɹamɪ L

gramp(s) *n* GRANDDAD VIII.1.8(a).

no -s: gɹæmp Mon Gl Brk*[old x1]*, gɹamp Mon Gl O Nth Bk, gɹamp O W

-s: gɹæmps Brk

grampy *n* GRANDDAD VIII.1.8(a). gɹampɪ O*[old x1]* Nth Bk Bd

gran *1. n* a GRANDMOTHER VIII.1.7(b). gɹæn So
2. n GRANDDAD VIII.1.8(a). gɹæn Sx
3. n GRANNY VIII.1.8(b). gɹɛm Sr, gɹæn He Mon Gl Nf Sf Hrt Ess W Brk*[old x1]* Ha, gɹæn So, gɹan We St Wo Gl O Lei, gɹan O So W D Do, gɹɒn La

granary *n* a HAY-LOFT over a cow-house I.3.18. gɹeːnəɹɪ Y

granch *1.1. vt-1prpl* we CRUNCH apples or biscuits VI.5.12. gɹænʃ He Wo Gl, gɹanʃ Sa, *-ing* gɹanʃɪn La, gɹaːnʃ Wo Wa
1.2. v-1prpl we crunch. *-ing* gɹænʃɪn He, *prppl* gɹanʃɪn Sa
2. v to GOBBLE food VI.5.13(b). *-ing* gɹænʃɪn Wo

grand *1. adj* PRETTY, describing a girl VI.5.18. gɹand Y
2. adj WELL, describing a healthy person VI.13.1(a). gɹænd Nf, gɹand Sa
3. adj **not very grand** ILL, describing a person who is unwell VI.13.1(b). nɒt vɛɹɪ gɹand Mon, nɒʔ vɛɹɪ gɹand St
4. n GRANDDAD VIII.1.8(a). gɹænd W

grand-ayer *n* GRANDDAD VIII.1.8(a). grændɛə Man

grandda *n* GRANDDAD VIII.1.8(a). græˑndə Man, granda Cu, gʁanda Nb, gɹanda Du We, gʁanda: Nb Du, gɹanda: Nb Cu Du We*[rare]*

granddad *1. n [Show a picture of a family. Who are the members of this family?] And, to call them [i.e. his grandfather and grandmother] into a room, the boy would shout: Come in .... [and granny].* VIII.1.8(a). Eng exc. Man Mon O So Co D Do. ⇒ **gamp, gongog, gramp(s), grampy, gran, grand, grand-ayer, grandda, grandfa, grandfather, grandfer, grandpa, grandpap, grandpop,** *grandsire* ⇒ **gransh/gransher/granshy, granf,** *granfer* ⇒ **grandfer,** *granfey* ⇒ **granfy, granfy, gransh, gransher, granshy, pap, pappy, pop, taid**
2. n a GRANDFATHER VIII.1.7(a). gɹændæd Nf

Sf Ess*[modern x1]*, gɹandad Y*[modern x1, usual x1]* He Wo, gɹandad O So Ha, gɹɒndad Wo

grandfa *1. n* a GRANDFATHER VIII.1.7(a). gɹɛnfɑː Nf, gɹænfɑː Nf, gɹændfɑːə Nf, gɹænfɑːə Nf, gɹæfə Nf*[old]*, gɹanfɑːə Nf
2. n GRANDDAD VIII.1.8(a). gɹænfɑ Nf

grandfather *1. n [Show a picture of a family. Who are the members of this family?] This boy speaks of him [i.e. his grandfather] as his ....* VIII.1.7(a). Eng. ⇒ **granddad, grandfa, grandfer, grandpa**
2. n GRANDDAD VIII.1.8(a). gɹænfɑːðə Hu Ess, gɹanfɛəðə Y, gɹanfɛəðəɹ Y, granfadðə Cu, gɹanfaðəɹ Y, gɹanfaðə Y, gɹanfaðəɹ La, gɹanfadðə We, gʁanfɛðəʁ Nb, gɹanfɛdðə Cu, gɹɒnfeːðə Db, gɹɒnfaðə Y Db, gɹɒnfaðəᴶ Y

grandfather-fly *n* a DADDY-LONG-LEGS IV.8.10. gɹænfɑːðəflɔɪ Ess

grandfer *1. n* a GRANDFATHER VIII.1.7(a). gɹæmfəˤː So, gɹanfəˤː D Ha, gɹamfəˤː Co D
2. n GRANDDAD VIII.1.8(a). gɹænfəᴶ Brk*[old x1]*, gɹænfəˤ He W Ha, gɹænfəˤː So, gɹæmfəˤː So, gɹanfəɹ Y, gɹanfəˤ Sa, gɹanfəˤː So W Do Ha, gɹanvəˤː Ha, gɹamfəˤː So W Co D Do

grand-looking *adj* PRETTY, describing a girl VI.5.18. gɹandlɪuːkɪn Y

grandma *1. n* a GRANDMOTHER VIII.1.7(b). gɹæˑmaː So, gɹændmɑː Nf, gɹændmɑː Nf, gɹæməˤː So, gɹanmaː Y, gɹanmaː D
2. n GRANNY VIII.1.8(b). gɹɛnmaː Ess, gɹɛnma Ess, gɹɛnmaɣ Ess, gɹɛnmɑː Sr, grænmæ Man, gɹænmæ Sx, gɹænma L, gɹænma: He Sf Ess, gɹænma: So, gɹanma: Nf Ess MxL Sr K, gɹæmmaᴶˑ Brk, gɹænmaˤ: Wo, gɹænmə W, gʁanma Nb, gɹanma Du La Y Nt L Nth, gɹanma: Nb Cu Du Y Ch Sa Wa Nt L Lei, gɹanma: Y*[polite x1, modern x1]* Lei, gɹanmə La, gɹama: Du Y Bk, gɹam:ə Y, gɹɒnma: La Db, gɹɒnma Y

grandmam *n* GRANNY VIII.1.8(b). gɹanmam Y Ch Sa

grandmayer *n* GRANNY VIII.1.8(b). grænmɛə Man

grandmother *1. n [Show a picture of a family. Who are the members of this family?] This boy speaks of her [i.e. his grandmother] as his ....* VIII.1.7(b). Eng. ⇒ **gran, grandma, granny**
2. n GRANNY VIII.1.8(b). gɹænmʌðə Sf, gɹandmʊðə Y, gɹanmʊðə Y, gɹanmʊdðə We, gɹɒnmʊðə Y, gɹɒnmʊðəᴶ Y

grandmother-jag *n* a LOOSE *PIECE OF* SKIN at the bottom of a finger-nail VI.7.11. *pl* gɹanmʊðədʒagz La

grandmum *n* GRANNY VIII.1.8(b). gɹɛnmʌm Ess, gɹænmʌm Ess Sx

grand-new *adj* BRAND-NEW VI.14.24. gɹannu Ch

grandpa *1. n* a GRANDFATHER VIII.1.7(a). gɹænpa Ess

2. n GRANDDAD VIII.1.8(a). gɹænpə Sr, gɹænpaː Ess, gɹænpaː Nf Sr Ha, gɹæːnpɑː Hrt, gɹanpaː Lei, gɹanpə Gl, gɹɒnpaː La

grandpap *n* GRANDDAD VIII.1.8(a). gɹanpap Wa

grandpop *n* GRANDDAD VIII.1.8(a). gɹænpɒp K

granf *n* GRANDDAD VIII.1.8(a). gɹæmf So, gɹaˑmf So

granfy *n* GRANDDAD VIII.1.8(a). gɹanfɪ Gl, gɹaːmfɪ So

granny *1. n [Show a picture of a family. Who are the members of this family?] And, to call them [i.e. his grandfather and grandmother] into a room, the boy would shout: Come in [granddad and].... VIII.1.8(b). Eng. exc. Man Mx L ⇒ **baba, ganny, grammer, grammy, gran, grandma, grandmam, grandmayer, grandmother, grandmum, nan** ⇒ **nan(s), nanna, nannies, nanny, nan(s)**

2. n a GRANDMOTHER VIII.1.7(b). gɹæni So, gɹanɪ Y St He Wo, gɹani So Co D Ha, gɹanɪ O

3. n a LOOSE *PIECE OF* SKIN at the bottom of a finger-nail VI.7.11. gɹanɪ Y

granny bonnet *n* a woman's BONNET VI.14.1. *pl* gɹænɪ bɒnɪts Ha

granny's bonnet-strings *n* WHISKERS VI.2.6. gɹɛnɪz bɒnɪtstɹɪŋz Sx[old]

gransh* *n* GRANDDAD VIII.1.8(a). gɹænʃ Mon

gransher* *n* GRANDDAD VIII.1.8(a). gɹænʃə Mon, gɹænʃəˡ Mon Gl

granshy* *n* GRANDDAD VIII.1.8(a). gɹanʃɪ Gl

grapes *n* SHEEP-DUNG II.1.7. gɹeːps Ha

grapple *v* to GROPE *FOR FISH* IV.9.10. gɹapl Cu We, gɹapəl Y, *vbln* gɹaplɪn La Y, *vbln* gɹaplən Nb Du, gɹabl We

grass-bit *n* the GRASS-NAIL of a scythe II.9.9. gɹaːsbɪt He

grass-bool *n* part of a scythe, probably the CRADLE, ⇐ GRASS-NAIL II.9.9. gɹæːsboːɬ D, gɹæːsbouɬ So, gɹaːsboːɬ W Ha

grass-close *1. n* PASTURE II.1.3. gɹaskluəs L

2. n a MEADOW II.9.2. gɹesklɔɪs Y

grass-cocks *npl* COCKS of hay II.9.12. gɹæskɒks So

grass-crook *n* the GRASS-NAIL of a scythe II.9.9. gɹaːskɾʊk Do

grass-field *1. n* PASTURE II.1.3. gɹaːsfɪˀɬd O, *pl* gɹaːsfiːˀɬz Wa

2. n a MEADOW II.9.2. gɹɛsfˡiːld Nt, gɛsfiːld Y[never ploughed], gɹaːsfiːɬd Wa Gl[never ploughed] O Hu, gɹaːsfɪɬd Bk, gɹaːsfɪəɬd O, gɹaːsfɪᵁd Ess

grass-ground *n* PASTURE II.1.3. gɹaːsgɹᵁuːn Gl, *pl* gɹaːsgɾəunz Do

grass-guide *n* the GRASS-NAIL of a scythe II.9.9. gɹasgɒɪd Wo

grass-hook *1. n* the GRASS-NAIL of a scythe II.9.9. gɹɪəsʊk La, gɹɛsɪuːk Db, gɹɛsyːk Ch Db, gɹɛsɛʊk Db, gɹɛsʊk Db Lei, gɹɛsuːk La Y Ch[old x1] Db St Nt L, græˀsuːk Man, gɹæsʌk Sa, gɹæsʊk He, gɹæːsʊk Sf, gʁasuːk Nb, gɹasyːk La, gɹasʊk St, gɹasuːk La Ch St, gɹasək Sa, gɹaːsʏ̠k Sa, gɹaːsʌk Sa Hrt, gɹaːshʊk Ess, gɹaːsʊk Sa He Wo Wa Gl Nth Sf Bk Hrt Ess, gɹaːsək Sa, gɹaːsʌk Hrt, gɹɑːshʊk Ess, gɹɑːsʊk Ess Sr, gəˡːsuːk Y

2. n a BILLHOOK IV.2.6. gɹasuːk L, gɾaːshʊk W

grassing *n* pasture, ⇐ HIRE *PASTURAGE* III.3.8. gɹasn Nb

grass-keeping *n* pasture, ⇐ HIRE *PASTURAGE* III.3.8. gɹaːskiːpɪn Nth Bd

grass-land *1. n* PASTURE II.1.3. gɹesland L, gɹaˑslænd Nf, gɹasland L

2. n a MEADOW II.9.2. gɹɑːslænd Nf

grass-lea *1. n* PASTURE II.1.3. gɹaːslɛɪ Ess

2. n a MEADOW II.9.2. gɹaːslæɪ Ess

grass-meadow *n* a MEADOW II.9.2. gɹɑːsmɛdə Ess

grass-mouse *n* a SHREW-MOUSE IV.5.2. gɹɛsmæʊs L, gɹɛsmuːs L, *pl* gɹæsmɔɪs Sx, gɹæsmʌʊs Brk, gɹæsmous Brk, gɾæːsmæʊs So Ha, gɹæːsmeʊs Sx, gɹæːsmə̃ʊs Sx, gɾæːsməʊs W, gɹasmuːs Du[?old] Y L, gɾaːsmæys D, gɾaːsmæyz Co, gɹaːsmeʊs Wa O Bk Bd Hrt Ess, gɾaːsmeʊs O, gɹaːsmæʊs O, gɾaːsməʊs W, gɹɑːsmeʊs Brk, *pl* gɹɑːsmʌɪs Brk, gɹɑːsməʊs Brk

grass-nail *n [Show a picture of a scythe.] What do you call this [indicate the grass-nail]? II.9.9. Eng exc. Man Ch Db St Hrt MxL So K Co D Do. ⇒ **back-wire, bail, bender, *bendle* ⇒ bender, blade-carrier, bool, bow, brace, collars, cradle, creet, crook, dew-crook, ear, ess-hook, frog-foot, gant-hook, grass-bit, grass-bool, grass-crook, grass-guide, grass-hook, grass-pin, grass-wire, guide, guide-bar, heel-iron, hook, nail, quinet, scythe-hook, scythe-nail, stay, streak-iron, support, swarth-turner, swath-bool, swather, tiddly-wag, wire-hook, worm; ⇒ also **grass-bool**

grass-pin *n* the GRASS-NAIL of a scythe II.9.9. gɾaːspˡɛn W

grass-rip* *n* a BILLHOOK with a long, slightly curved blade IV.2.6. gɹaːsɹɪp Ess

grass-snake *n* an ADDER IV.9.4. gɹassneək Y, gɹassnɛək Y

grass-string *n* STRING made of straw, used to tie up a grain-sack I.7.3. gɹaːsstɹɪŋ Sr

grass-wire *n* the GRASS-NAIL of a scythe II.9.9. gɾæːswɒɪəˡː Ha

grass-worm *n* an ADDER IV.9.4. gəswəm Y

grate *1. n* the place in which the ashes are collected beneath a domestic fire, ⇐ ASH-HOLE

V.3.3. gʁeːᵊt Nb *[marked u.r. NBM]*

2. *vt* to RAKE in a domestic fire V.3.8(b). gɹeːt Y

3. *n* a GRIDIRON V.7.4(a). gʁɪət Du

grate-hole *n* the ASH-HOLE beneath a domestic fire V.3.3. greːtɒɪl Y, gɹɛɪtouɫ Lei, gɹɛətɔːl Y

grating *n* a GRIDIRON V.7.4(a). gɹɛɪtɪn Wa

gratton *n* STUBBLE remaining in a cornfield after harvesting II.1.2. gɹæʔn K

gratton-land *n* land on which nothing grows, ⇐ PASTURE II.1.3. gɹæʔnlæn Sx

graunch *1.1. vt-1prpl* we CRUNCH apples or biscuits VI.5.12. gɹɔːntʃ Sa, gɹɔːnʃ Ch Db St Wa Nt
1.2. v-1prpl we crunch. gɹɔːntʃ Wa, gɹɔːnʃ Ch, -*ing* gɹɔːntʃɪn St, -*ing* gɹɔːnʃɪn St Nt, əgɹɔːnʃɪn Wa
2. *v* to GOBBLE food VI.5.13(b). gɹɔːntʃ Sa

graunch up* *vtphr-1prpl* we CRUNCH apples or biscuits VI.5.12. -*ing* gɹɔːntʃɪn ... ʊp St

graunt *vt-1prpl* we CRUNCH apples or biscuits VI.5.12. -*ing* gɹɔːntɪn Lei

gravat *n* a NECKERCHIEF VI.14.4. gɹavət Nb

grave *1. v* to DIG in the garden with a spade I.7.8. gɹɪav Y, -*ing* gɹɪəvɪn Y, greːv Cu La Y, greav Cu We La, greˑəv Cu, -*ing* grɛəvɪn Y
2. *n* a CLAMP in which potatoes are stored out of doors II.4.6. gɹeːv Do, gɹeːɪv Do, gɹɛɪv L, gɹɛˑəv L
3. *v* to CUT peat IV.4.4. -*ing* gɹɪavɪn Y, gɹɪəv Y, gɹɛˑav We La, gɹɛᵊv Y, -*ing* gɹɛˑəvən Cu, *prppl* gɹɛˑəvɪn L, -*ing* gɹɛˑəvɪn L

grave-digger *n* a SEXTON VIII.5.4. gɹɪəvdɪgəɹ Y, gɹɛɪvdɪgə Hrt, gɹɛɪvdɪgəˡ Sx

graveyard *n* a CHURCHYARD VIII.5.5. gɹɪəvjaːd Y, gɹɛːvjæˡːd La, gɹeːvjaːd Y St Mon, gɹeːvjaˡːd Y, gɹeːvjaˡːd̪ Gl, gɹɛɪvjaːd Hu*[round a chapel]* Nf, greɪvjaːd Man, gɹɛɪvjaːɹd He, gɹɛɪvjaˡːd̪ Bk, gɹɛːɪvjaˡːd̪ So, gʁeəvjaːd Nb, gɹɛɪvjaːd St L Nth Ess, gɹɛɪvjaːd Nf Ess MxL Brk K, gɹɛˑɪvjaˡːd Brk*[not always near church]*, gɹɛɪvjaˡːd̪ Sr, gɹɛɪvjaˡːəˡˌɽd̪ Sx, gɹɛəvjaːd Y

gravy *n* DRIPPING V.7.5(a). gɹɛːvɪ La Sa Wo Gl, gɹɛːɪvɪ Wo*[old x1, warm x1]* Mon Gl

graze *1. v* to put cattle on hired pasture, ⇐ HIRE *PASTURAGE* III.3.8. -*ing* gɹeɪzn Nf, gɹɛɪz Sf Hrt Ess Sr*[horses only]*, -*ing* gɹæɪzɪn Hrt
2. *v-1prpl* we CRUNCH apples or biscuits VI.5.12. -*ing* gɹɛɪzɪn K

graze-land *n* PASTURE II.1.3. gɹɛɪzlæn Brk, gɹɛɪzland St

graze out *vtphr* to put cattle on hired pasture, ⇐ HIRE *PASTURAGE* III.3.8. -*ing* gɹɛˑɪzɪn ... ɛʊt Nf

grazing *1. n* PASTURE II.1.3. greːzɪn Ch, gɹɛˑəzɪn Bk, gɹɛɪzɪn Lei, gɹɛˑəzɪn L
2. *n* pasture, ⇐ HIRE *PASTURAGE* III.3.8. gɹeɪzɪn Bd Hrt, gɾeɪzɪn Ha, gɹɛəzɪn O, gɹɛɪzɪn Sr K, gɹɛɪzɪn Ess

grazing-field *n* PASTURE II.1.3. gɹeːzɪnfɪʊɫd Brk, gɹeːzɪnfɪəɫd Gl, *pl* gɹeɪzɪnfiːɫz Hu, gɹeɪzɪnfiːᵊld Nth Hu

grazing-grass *n* PASTURE II.1.3. gɹɛəzɪngɹas Y

grazing-ground *n* PASTURE II.1.3. gɾeːzɪngɾæʏn D, gɹeɪzɪngɹɛʊnd Nth Ess, gɹɛɪzɪngɹæʊn Lei, gɹæɪzɪngɹɛʊnd Ess

grazing-land *n* PASTURE II.1.3. gɹiːzɪnland Lei, gɹeːzɪnland Ch, gɾeːzɪnłand W, greɪzɪnlæn Man, gɹeɪzɪnland Bd, gɹɛɪzɪnlænd Ess MxL Sr, gɹeɪzɪnlæːn K, gɹɛɪzɪŋland L, gɹɛɪzɪnland St Wa Lei R Nth Bk, gɹeːɪzɪnlan Lei, gɹɛˑəzɪnland L

grease *1. n* CART-GREASE, used to lubricate the wheels of a cart I.11.4. griːs Man Mon, griːs Cu, gʁiːs Nb, gɹiːs Nb Cu Du Y Ch Db Sa St He Wa Mon Gl O Nt L Lei R Nth Hu C Nf Sf Bk Bd Hrt Ess MxL Brk Sr K Sx, gɹiːz Sr, gɾiːs O So W Co Do Ha, gʁɪəs Du, gɹɪəs We La Y St Nt L C Nf Bk Bd, gɹeːs La Ch Db Sa Wo Gl O, gɾeːs W Co D Ha, gɹeɪs Du O, gɹeːɪs Sa Wo, gɹeɪs Ch Db St Wo Nth Sf Bk Bd, gɾeɪs Co D, gɾaɪs D Ha, gɾəɪs So
2. *n* LARD made from the fat of a pig III.12.8. gɹɪəs Y
3. *n* DRIPPING V.7.5(a). gʁiːz Nb, gɹiːs Ess, gɹɪis Nf, gɹɪˑəs L
4. *n* BACON-FAT V.7.5(b). gʁiːs Nb, gʁiːz Nb, gɹiːs Nf Sf Ess Sx, gɾiːs So, gɹɪˑəs L, gɹɛɪs Wa*[very old]* Nf*[old]*, gɾɛɪs D

grease-cap *n* the metal BUSH at the centre of a cart-wheel I.9.8. gɹəiːskæːp Hrt

greasing-stool *1. n* a SHEARING-TABLE III.7.8. gɹɪəzɪnstɪʊl Y, gɹˡɪəznstɪʊl Du
2. *n* a BENCH on which slaughtered pigs are dressed III.12.1. gɹɪəzɪnstɪʊl Y

greasy *adj* SLIPPERY VII.6.14. gɹiːsɪ St Brk, gɹiːzɪ K, gɾeːsi Do, gɹeɪsɪ St Brk*[old]*

great *adj To marry the wrong woman isn't a little mistake, but a ... mistake.* IX.1.6. Eng. ⇒ **big**

great branches *npl* BOUGHS of a tree IV.12.2. gət bɹanʃɪz Y

greatcoat *n* an OVERCOAT VI.14.6. gɹɪətkʊət Y, gɹeɪtkɔʊt Brk, gəˡːtkwɒt Brk, gəˡːʈkɒʊt Sr, gəˡːʈkoːət So*[old]*, gəˡːɽʈkoːt Brk, gəˡːɽʈkoʊt Ha, gəˡːɽʈkwʊt Brk, gəˡːʈkwət Do, gəˡːɽʈkwət W

great-cocks *npl* very large COCKS of hay II.9.12. gətkɒks We

great-pitch *n* a HAY-FORK with a long handle I.7.11. gəˡːɽʈpɪtʃ Sx

great-sway *n* an EVENER, the main swingle-tree of a horse-drawn plough harness I.8.4. gətsweɪ La

greaves *n* SCRAPS left after rendering lard III.12.10. gɾiːvz W

green-broom *n* a BROOM used for sweeping outdoors, made of broom V.9.10. *pl* gɹiːnbɹʊmz Sx

green-meat *n* clover used as food for cows, ⇐ MEAT V.8.3. gɹiːnmɪət Y

green onions *npl* SPRING ONIONS V.7.16. gɹiːn ɒnjənz Nf K, gɹiːn ɒɪnʊnz Gl, gɹiːn ɔɪnʊnz Wa, *sg* gɹiᵊiːn ɔɪnɪɪc Bk, gɹiːn ʌnjənz Nf Ess K Sx, gɹiin ʏnjənz Nf, gɹiːn ʊnɪənz Cu La Y, gɹiːn ʊnjənz L, *sg* gɹiˡiːn ʊnjən Db, gɹiən ʊnɪənz Y, *sg* gɹɛɪn ʊnjən St, gɹəɪn ʊnɪənz Y, *sg* gɹiːn ʊɪnʊn Gl

green straw *n* the STEM of a corn-plant II.5.2(a). gɹiːn stɹɔː Nth

greensward *1. n* a grass field for grazing, ⇐ PASTURE II.1.3. gɹɪnsəd O
2. n a MEADOW II.9.2. gɹɪnsəd O

greet *vi* to SCREAM VIII.8.11. gʁiˑt Nb, gɹiːt*[= cry]*, gʁɪt Nb*[prolonged]*

greeter *n* the MOULD-BOARD of a horse-drawn plough I.8.8. gɹiːtəᵗ: Co

greethagh *n* CINDERS V.4.3. ˈgriːðæx Man *[marked u.r. NBM]*

greeting *v-ing* SHRIEKING, describing the shrill noise made by a baby VI.5.15. gʁiːtn Nb

gregs* *1. n* DREGS left at the bottom of a teacup V.8.15. gɹɛgz Lei, gɹɛˡgz Ess
2. n dregs of coffee. gɹɛgz Brk

greither *n* a COBBLER VIII.4.5. greɪðə Man

gresh *vt-1prpl* we CRUNCH apples or biscuits VI.5.12. gɹɛɪʃ La

grey-mont *n* a SQUIRREL IV.5.8. *pl* gɹɛɪmɒnts Bk *[headword queried EMBM]*

gribbles *n* SCRAPS left after rendering lard III.12.10. gɹɪbɫz D

grid *1. n* an EVENER on the plough-beam end of a horse-drawn plough I.8.4. gɹɪd Brk
2. n a CRANE on which a kettle is hung over a domestic fire V.3.4. gɹɪd Ha
3. n a GRIDIRON V.7.4(a). gʁɪd Nb, gɹɪd Cu Du We La Y Ch Db Sa St He Wo Wa Mon Gl Nt L Lei R Nth Hu Nf Sf Bk Bd Hrt*[for cooking herrings]* Ess Brk, *pl* gɹɪdz Sr, gɹɪd O So W D Ha
4. n a GIRDLE for baking cakes V.7.4(b). gɹɪd St MxL*[modern]*, gɽɪd Do

gridder *n* a GRIDIRON V.7.4(a). gɹɪdᵊ La Db, gɹɪdəᵗ: Ha *[not a WMBM headword]*

griddle *1. n* a GRIDIRON V.7.4(a). gɹɪdl St, kɽɪdɫ So, gɽɪdɫ Co D Do
2. n a GIRDLE for baking cakes V.7.4(b). gɹɪdl St L, gɹɪdɫ Ess MxL K Sx, gɹɪdʊɫ K, gɹɪdʊ Sr Sx, gɽɪdɫ So W Do, gɽɪdɫ̩ Brk, gɽɪdʊɫ Brk Sr
3. n a girdle for cooking meat. gɽɪdɫ So

griddle-iron *n* a GRIDIRON V.7.4(a). gɹɪdɫˌəɪən Sf

griddles *n* SCRAPS left after rendering lard III.12.10. gɹɪdɫz D

gridge-iron *n* a GRIDIRON V.7.4(a). gɽɪdʒaɪəᵗ:n̩ Do, *pl* gɹɪdʒəɪəᵗɹn̩ˌ Sx

gridger *n* a GRIDIRON V.7.4(a). gɽɪdʒəᵗ: Do

grid-hole *n* the ASH-HOLE beneath a domestic fire V.3.3. gɹɪdoʊl St

gridiron *1. n What do you call that thing with bars you use in cooking a fish over the fire?* V.7.4(a). gɹɪdɛɪən La, gʁɪdɛɪʁən Nb, gɹɪdɛɪəɹən Y, gɹɪdaɪɹən Cu, gʁɪdaɪʁən Nb, gɹɪdæɹən Y Ch, gɹɪdæɹən Y, gɹɪdaɪən We Y*[old x1]* Sa St L, gɹɪdaɪəɹn La, gɹɪdaɪɹɛn Du, gɹɪdaɪɹən Y, gɹɪdaɪɹən Cu Y L, gɹɪdaɪəᵗn̩ Sa, gɹɪdaɪəᵗːn̩ Sa, gɽɪdaɪəᵗːn̩ So Co D, gɽɪdaɪəᵗ: Co, gɹɪdaːn Y Hu Nf MxL, gɹɪdaːᵊn Nf Sr, gɹɪdaɪən La Lei Nf Ess K, gɹɪdaɪəᴵn La Y Sr, gɹɪdaɪəᵗn̩ Sx, gɹɪdɒɪᵊn Wo, gɽɪdɒɪəᵗːn̩ W D Do Ha, gɹɪdɔɪn Ess, gɹɪdɔɪən Wo O Sf Hrt Ess, gɹɪdɔɪəᴵn Brk K, gɹɪdɔɪəᵗn̩ Bk Ha, gɹɪdʌɪəᴵn Brk, gɹɪdʌɪəᵗn̩ Sr*[old x1]*, gɹɪdəɪʊn Wo, gɹɪdəɪən Mon, gɹɪdəɪəᵗn̩ He Wo Mon Gl Sx, gɽɪdəɪəᵗ: W Do. ⇒ **bars, braidler, brander, brandis, crow-bar, double-grid, drill, duck, fire-grid, fish-grill, girdle, girdle-iron, grate, grating, grid, gridder, griddle, griddle-iron, gridge-iron, gridger, grill, griller, grill-iron, hanger, herring-roaster, roaster, roasting-jack, trippet, trivet**
2. n a GIRDLE for baking cakes V.7.4(b). gɹɪdaɪən St, gɹɪdɔɪən Ess, gɽɪdaɪəᵗ: D, gɽɪdɒɪəᵗːn̩ W, gɽɪdəɪəᵗːn̩ W
3. n an EVENER on the plough-beam end of a horse-drawn plough I.8.4. gɹɪdʌɪəᴵn Brk

griglans* *n* heather, ⇐ BESOM I.3.15. gɽɪgɫənz Co

grill *1. vt* to STOCK a cow III.3.6. -*ing* gɹɪɫɪn Ess
2. n a GRIDIRON V.7.4(a). gʁɪɫ Du, gɹɪɫ La Y Sa St He Mon L, gɹɪɫ La O L Lei Nth Nf Bd Hrt Ess MxL Sx, gɹɪʊ Ess Sr K Sx, gɽɪɫ O So D, gɽɪʊ So Ha, gɹəɫ Y
3. n a GIRDLE for baking cakes V.7.4(b). gɹɪɫ Ess

griller *n* a GRIDIRON V.7.4(a). gɹɪlə We, gɹɪɫəᵗ He, gɽɪɫəᵗ: W Co D

grill-iron *n* a GRIDIRON V.7.4(a). gɹɪlaːᵊn C

grind *1. vt-1prpl* we CRUNCH apples or biscuits VI.5.12. gʁɪnd Nb, -*ing* gɽæːndɪn D, gɹaɪnd Sa L, gɹaːɪnd La, -*ing* gɹɒɪndɪn St, -*ing* gɽɒɪndɪn W, gɽɒɪn So, -*ing* gɹɔɪndɪn MxL, gɹʌɪnd Gl, -*ing* gɹʊɪndɪn Y, gɹənd La, -*ing* gɹəɪndɪn W, gɽəɪnd Do, -*ing* gɽəɪndɪn W
2. v-1prpl we crunch. -*ing* gɽæːndɪn D, gɹaˑɪnd L, -*ing* gɹaˑɪndɪn L, gɹaˑɪn L, *prppl* gɹʌɪndɪn Gl, gɹəɪndɪn Wo

grinder *n* a GRINDSTONE IV.2.7. gɹaɪndə MxL

grinders *npl* MOLARS VI.5.7. gʁɪndᵊʁz Nb, gʁɛɪndᵊʁz Nb, gɹɛɪndᵊʁz Nb, gɹæːndəᵗːẓ D, gɹæɪndəᵗːẓ So, gɹaɪndəz Y Ch Db Sa L Lei, gɹaɪnəz Lei, gɹaɪndᵊʁz La, gɹaɪndɹz L, gɹaˑɪndəᵗːẓ Sa, gɹaɪndəᵗːẓ So*[old x1]* Co, gɹaːndəᵗːẓ D, gɹaɪndəz Y Ch Db L Lei Nth Hu

C*[old]* Nf Hrt MxL Sr K, gɹɑɪndəˡz̩ *[old]*, gɹɒɪndəz St Nf, gɹɒːɪndəɹz St, gɾɒɪndəˡːz̩ Ha, gɹɔɪndəz Ess, gɹɔɪndəˡz K, gɹɔɪndəˡz̩ Bk K Ha Sx, gɹʌɪndəz Nf, gɹʌɪndəˡz Sr, gɹʊndəz Du, gɹəɪndəz Mon, gɹəɪndəˡz̩ Mon Gl Brk Sx, gɾəɪndəˡːz̩ W

grinding out *vphr-ing* grinding out the time GOSSIPING VIII.3.5(a). gɾæɪndɪn æʊt ðə tæɪm So

grinding-stone *1. n* a WHETSTONE II.9.10. gɹɔɪndɪnstoʊn Wa, gɹəɪndɪnstoun Mon

2. n a GRINDSTONE IV.2.7. gʁɪndənstən Nb, gɾæːndɪnstuːn D, gɾæːndɪnstuən D, græɪnənstoːn Man, græɪnəstoˈən Man, gɾæːɪnɪnstoːən So, gɾæɪndɪnstuːn D, gɾæɪnɪnstuːən So, gɹɑːɪndɪnstoːn La, gɹɑˈɪnɪnstoʊn L, gɹɑˈɪnɪnstuən L, gɾɑːnɪnstuːn D, gɾɑːnɪnstuːən Co, gɾaɪndɪnstoːn So Co Do, gɾaɪnɪnstoːn So, gɾaɪnɪnstoun So, gɾaɪnɪnstoːən So, gɾaɪndɪnstuːn Co, gɾaɪnɪnstuːən So*[old]*, gɾaɪnʔənstuːən Ha, gɹɑɪndɪnstoːn La, gɾɑːndɪnstuːn Co, gɾɑːnɪnstuːn D, gɹɑɪndɪnstoːn La Nt, gɹɑˈɪndɪnstən R, gɹɑˈɪndɪnstoʊn L R Hu, gɹɑˈɪnɪnstoʊn L, gɹɑˈɪndɪnstuən L, gɹɑɪndɪnstuən La, gɾɒɪndɪnstʌn Ha, gɾɒɪndɪnstuːn Ha, gɾɒɪndənstuːn Ha, gɾɔɪndɪnstoʊn Ha, gɹʌɪnɪnstoʊn Sr, gɹəɪndɪnstoun Mon, gɾəɪndɪnstoːən W Do, gɾəɪndɪstoːən Do, gɾəɪnɪnstoːən Do, gɾəɪnənstoːən Do, gɾəɪnɪnstuːən W, gəˡːn̩ɪnstuːən D

grindle-stone *1. n* a WHETSTONE II.9.10. gɹɪndlstoʊn Wa, gɹɪnəlstən Ch

2. n a GRINDSTONE IV.2.7. gɹɪndɬstoʊn Wa Nth Hu, gɹɪndlstoːn La Ch Sa, gɹɪnlstoːn Db, gɹɪndɬstoːn He Wo, gɹɪndlstoʊn Wo, gɹɪndɬstoun Nth C, gɹɪndɬstuːn Wo, gɹɪndlstuən Y, gɹɪndəlstuən Y, gɹɪnlstuən La, gɹɪnəlstuən La Y, gɹɪndlstuːn Sa, gɹɪndlstn Sa Wo, gɹɪndlstən Ch Db Sa St Nt, gɹɪndəlstən Y, gɹɪnlstn Y, gɹɪnlstən La Ch

grindstone *1. n What do you call that big round thing which you turn to sharpen your tools on?* IV.2.7. Eng exc. Ch R Hu. ⇒ **grinder, grinding-stone, grindle-stone, rub**

**2. n* a WHETSTONE II.9.10. gɹaɪnstoun He, gɹɔɪnstoːn O, gɹʌɪnstwən Gl

grindstone-rub *n* a WHETSTONE made of sandstone, used to give a blade a fine edge II.9.10. gɹɪnstənɹʌb Ess

grind up *1. vtphr-1prpl* we CRUNCH apples or biscuits VI.5.12. *-ing* gɹaɪndɪn ... ʊp Y, *-ing* gɾaɪndɪn ... ʌp So, gɹɑˈɪnd ... ʊp L, *-ing* gɹʊndɪn ... ʊp Y

2. vphr-1prpl we crunch. gɾaɪndɪn ʌp Co

grintern *n* a CORN-BIN I.7.4. gɾɪntən Do

grip *1. n* a DRAIN in a cow-house I.3.8. gɾɪp Man, gʁɪt Nb, gʁɪp Nb, gɹɪp Y Db Lei K, gɾɪbə Man, gʁɪəpʰ Nb, gɹɪəp Nb Cu We La Y, gɾeb Man

2. n a shallow drain round a stack of corn. gɹɪp La

3. vt to DRAIN wet land IV.1.9. gɹɪp Nt L Nth*[with surface channels]*, gɹəp Y

4. v to make a drain. gɹɪp Y, *-ing* gɹɪpɪn L

5. n a MUCK-FORK I.3.13. gɾɪp Man, gɾɛp Man

6. n a four-pronged fork used in farming, ⇐ FORKS I.7.9. gɾɛp Man

gripe *1. n* a MUCK-FORK I.3.13. gɹæɪp Y, gɾaɪp Cu, gʁaɪp Nb Du, gɹaɪp Cu Du We Y

2. n a narrow DITCH IV.2.1(c). gɹɔɪp Brk

3. v to GROPE *FOR FISH* IV.9.10. *-ing* gɹɑɪpɪn K

4. vi to ACHE, referring to a stomach VI.13.3(b). gɹaɪp Cu, *3prsg* gɹɔɪps Ess; **to be griped** to be gripped by a pain in the stomach *1prsgpass* gɹaɪpt Cu

grips *1. npl* wooden grips on the handles of a horse-drawn plough, ⇐ HANDLES I.8.2. gɹɪps Wa

2. npl the HANDLES of a scythe II.9.8. *sg* gɾɪp Man, gɹɪps Y Mon Bd Brk, gɾɪps So W Co, *sg* gɾɪp Brk

grip-stone *n* the CURB-STONE in a cow-house I.3.9. gɹɪpstɪan We

gripy *adj* SICK, describing an animal that is unwell VI.13.1(c). gɹʌɪpɪ Sr

grist *n* MEAL V.6.1(b). gɹɪst Db

gristle(s) *n* the ligaments in the pelvic region of a cow, ⇐ SHOWS SIGNS OF CALVING III.1.12(b). **give in her gristle** *v-ing* gɪvɪn ɪn əɹ gɹɪsl La; **her gristles go** *3prpl* ə gɹɪslz gʊəz Nt, *3prpl* ə gɹɪslz əz gɒn Nt; **her gristles drop** *3prpl* ə gɹɪslz ɪz dɹɒpt L

grit-hole *n* the ASH-HOLE beneath a domestic fire V.3.3. gɹɪtl Db

grizzle *n* SCRAPS left after rendering lard III.12.10. gɾɪzɬ So

grizzling *v-ing* LAUGHING VIII.8.7., IX.2.14. gɾɪzɬɪn Co

groan *vi-3prpl* they MOO, describing the noise cows make in the fields III.10.4(b). gɹoːn O

groats *n* PORRIDGE V.7.1. gɹɒts Nf

grob* *v* to GROPE *FOR FISH* IV.9.10. *vbln* gɹɒbɪn Y

grobble *v* to GROPE *FOR FISH* IV.9.10. *-ing* gɹɒblɪn Y, *vbln* gɹɒblɪn Y*[modern]*

groggy *1. adj* ILL, describing a person who is unwell VI.13.1(b). gɹɒgɪ Y, gɾɒgi W

2. adj SICK, describing an animal that is unwell VI.13.1(c). gɹɒgɪ Y W Sr, gɾɒgi W, gɾɔgi So

3. adj WEAK, decribing a person who has been ill VI.13.2. gɹɒgɪ Y Sa He Sx

4. adj feeling FAINT VI.13.7. gɹɒgɪ W

grogs *n* DREGS left at the bottom of a teacup V.8.15. gɹɔgz Cu

groin *1. n What do you call this [indicate the groin]?* VI.9.4. græɪn Man, gɹæɪn He Gl Ess Ha Sx, gɹaɪn La Db Sa St Wo, *pl* gɹaɪnz Ch, gɾaɪn So W D Do Ha, gɹɑɪn La Ch Db Gl Nth Hu Bk Bd Ess, gɹɒɪn La Y Db Sa St He Wo Mon Gl Nt Brk

Sr K Sx, gɾɒɪn So W Co D Do Ha, gɹɔɪn La Y St He Wa Mon L Lei R Nth Nf Sf Bk Ess MxL Sr K Sx, gɾɔɪn O Ha, gɹʌɪn Brk Sr, gɾʌɪn Co, gɹʌʊn Ess, gɹɔːn He, gɹʊʊn Wa Gl, gɹʊɪn Y, gɹʊən Y, gʊəɹɪn Y, gɹəɪn Mon Gl Sx, gɾəɪn So W Do. ⇒ **bend**, **clitch**, **crotch**, **crutch**, **flank**, **fork**, **groind**, **lank**, **lesk**, **lisk**, **lock-hole**, **stifle**

2. *n* the SNOUT of a pig III.9.1. gɹɪuːn Du nwY, gɹɪən Nb Du, gɹɔːn Y, gɹɔɪn Y, gɹʊnd Du, gɹʊɪn Y

groind *n* the GROIN VI.9.4. gɹaɪnd Ch L, gɹɑɪnd Ch L Nth Hu C Bd Hrt, gɹɔɪnd Wa O Lei C Sf Bk Ess, gɹʌɪnd Gl Sf, gɹʌɪnt Bk, gɹɔɪnd O

gronch *vt-1prpl* we CRUNCH apples or biscuits VI.5.12. gɹɒnʃ Ch Nt, *-ing* gɹɒnʃɪn L

gronch up* *vtphr-1prpl* we CRUNCH apples or biscuits VI.5.12. gɹɒnʃ ... ʊp Sa

groom *n* a CURRY-COMB used to clean horses III.5.5(b). gɹuːm St

groop 1. *n* a DRAIN in a cow-house I.3.8. gɹɪʏp Cu, gɹɪʊp Cu Y St, gɹɪuːp Du Ch, gɹʏːp La Ch Db, gɹɛʊp Db St, gɹoup La, gɹʏp Nf, gɹʊp Cu Nf, gɹuːp La Y Ch Db St L

2. *vt* to DRAIN wet land IV.1.9. gɹʏp Nf

3.1. *vt* to GROPE *FOR FISH* IV.9.10. *-ing* gɾʏːpɪn D, *-ing* gɹʊːpɪn Ch

3.2. *v* to grope for fish. *prppl* gɾʏːpɪn D, *-ing* gɾʏːpɪn Co D, *-ing* gɹuːpən Co

[not a WMBM headword]

grooping 1. *n* a DRAIN in a cow-house I.3.8. gɹɪʏ̈ːpɪn Sa, gɹᴿʊupɪn La

2. *n* the CURB-STONE in a cow-house I.3.9. gɹuˈpɪn Brk *[queried ir.r. SBM]*

groops *npl* PUDDLES IV.1.6. gɹʌps Nf

groop-stead *n* the CURB-STONE in a cow-house I.3.9. gʀʊpstiːd Nb *[queried u.r. NBM]*

groot *n* FALLOW-LAND II.1.1. gɾʏːt D

grooter *n* the MOULD-BOARD of a horse-drawn plough I.8.8. gɾuːtəᵗː Co, gɾuːdəᵗː Co

groot-land *n* FALLOW-LAND II.1.1. gɾʏːtɫand D

groot-reest *n* the MOULD-BOARD of a horse-drawn plough I.8.8. gɾʏːtɪs D, kɾʏːtɪs D, gɾʏːdɪs Co D

grop *n* the WATTLES of a hen IV.6.19. gɹɒp Ha *[queried ir.r SBM]*

grope *v* You sometimes catch fish, especially trout, with your hand. What's your word for that? IV.9.10. *vt* gɹoːᵁp Db

v vbln gɹɪapɪn Y, *vbln* gɹɪəpɪn Y, gɹeap We*[old]*, gɹoːp Db Sa He, *-ing* gɾoːpɪn So D, *-ing* gɾoːpən D, *-ing* gɹoupɪn St Ha, *vbln* gɹʊəpɪn Y

⇒ **catch**, **catch** *by hand*, **catch** *with your hands*, **crow-fish**, *fish for*, **fish-tickle**, *fish-tickling* ⇒ **fish-tickle**, **grab**, **grapple**, **grapple** *for*, **gripe**, **grob**, *grobb* ⇒ **grob**, **grobble**, **groop**, **grope**, **grope** *for*, **gropple**, **grovel**, **guddle**, **gumf**, **hand-tickle**, **kittle**, **snare**, **stroke**, **tickle**, **tickle on**, **tickle up**, **tiddle**,

tittle, **trout**

[prep for not regularly recorded by fws]

gropple *v* to GROPE *FOR FISH* IV.9.10. *vbln* gɹɒplɪn Y

groshy *adj* BOGGY IV.1.8. gɹɒʃɪ Y

ground 1. *n* When apples fall from the tree, where do they fall? [To the ....] IV.4.1. Eng. ⇒ **floor**

2. *n* a large arable field, ⇐ FIELDS I.1.1. gɹɛʊn Ha

3. *n* a MEADOW II.9.2. *-s* gɹəʊːᵊnz Gl*[sometimes ploughed]*

4. *n* the SOLE of a horse-drawn plough I.8.9. gɹɛʊnd Ess, gɹɛwnd Sf, gɹæʊnd Ess

ground-car *n* a SLEDGE used to carry loads in winter I.9.1. gɹəʊːnkᴵɑᵗː Wo

ground-cart *n* a SLEDGE used to carry loads in winter I.9.1. gɹaʊnkaᵗːt Sa

ground-down *n* MEAL V.6.1(b). gɹʊndæʊn Y

ground-frost *n* HOAR-FROST VII.6.6. gɹɛʊnfɹɔːst K Sx, gɹæᵁnfɹɔːs K, gɹaɪnd fɹɒst La, gɹaʊndfɹɒst Y, gɹʊndfɹɒst Y, gɾəʊnfɹɒst Sx

ground-iron *n* the SOLE of a horse-drawn plough I.8.9. gɹɛʊndaɪən Sf

ground-ivy *n* BINDWEED II.2.4. gɾœʏnæːvi D, gɾæʏndæːvi Co D, gɾæʏndæːvi D, gɾæʏndaːvi Co D, gɾæʏnaɪvi Co, gɾæʏndɑːvi Co

ground-lily *n* BINDWEED II.2.4. gɾæʊnlɪlɪ Ha

ground-mist *n* MIST VII.6.8. gɹuːndmɪst Y

ground-mouse *n* a SHREW-MOUSE IV.5.2. gɹɪuːnmaʊs Y, gɹɛʊnmeʊs Sa, *pl* gɹɛʊnmɔɪs Ha, gɾœʏnmœʏs D, gɾæʏnmæʏz D, gɾæʊnmæʊs So, gɹaʊnmaʊs Sa

ground-reest 1. *n* the SHARE of a horse-drawn plough I.8.7. gɹʌʊnɹɪst Brk

2. *n* the MOULD-BOARD of a horse-drawn plough I.8.8. gɹɛʊnɹʌɪs Sr, gɹæʊndɹɑɪs Sr, gɹʌʊnɹɪst Brk

3. *n* the SOLE of a horse-drawn plough I.8.9. gɹɛʊnɹɪst Wa, gɾæʊndɾɪst Ha, gɾæʏnɾɪs So*[on right-hand side]*, gɹʌʊndɹɛst Gl, gɾəʊnɾɛs Do

ground-rise *n* the right-hand side of the SOLE of a horse-drawn plough I.8.9. gɾəʊnɾəɪz Do

grounds 1. *npl* the FIELDS of a farm I.1.1. gɾæʊnz So W Ha, *sg* gɾæʊn Do, gɹæʊndz Wo, *sg* gɾaʊn So, gɾaʊnd So, gɾɒʊnz W, *sg* gɹʌʊnd Gl, gɹᴿʊːnz Gl, gɾəʊnz So Do, *sg* gɾəʊn W

2. *n* DREGS left at the bottom of a teacup V.8.15. gɹɛʊndz Ess, gɹɛʊnz Ch Wo Wa C Bk Ess MxL K, gɹɛʊdz K, gɹæʊnz Wo, gɾæʊnz W, gɹaʊnz Ch, gɾaʊndz So, gɹɑɪndz Ch, gɹʌʊnz He Mon, gʀʊndz Nb Du, gʀʊnz Nb, gɹʊnz Y, gɹuːnz Y, gɹɹəʊndz Mon, gɹəʊnz He Wo Mon

ground-side *n* the SOLE of a horse-drawn plough I.8.9. gɾəʊnzəɪd W

ground-sill *n* the THRESHOLD of a door V.1.12.
gɹʌnsɨł Brk, gɹʌnsł Ess, gɹʌnsəł Ess*[old]*, gɹʌnsɪʊ
Ess, gɹʊnsɨł Brk, gɹʊnsɪʊ Brk Sr, gɹʊnsəł Brk,
gɹəʊnsɪʊ Brk

ground-stool* *n* the THRESHOLD of a door V.1.12.
gɹʌnstʊuː Ess

groushans *n* DREGS left at the bottom of a teacup
V.8.15. gɹævʒənz Co, gɹævdʒənz Co

grouts *n* DREGS left at the bottom of a teacup
V.8.15. gɹɛɪts Bk, gɹɛʊts Wa Bk Bd Hrt Ess*[old]* Brk
Sr*[old x1]* Ha Sx, gɹɛʊʔs Hrt, gɹɛʊts O, gɹɛˑᵊts Ess,
gɹævts Co, gɹæʊts MxL Sr K Ha, gɹæʊts So W Do
Ha, gɹɑʊts Sa, gɹɑʊts So, gɹɒʊts O, gɹɒʊts W, gɹʌts
W, gɹʌʊts Gl, *sg* gɹɔːt W, gɹəʊts Brk, gɹəʊts So W
Do

grovel *v* to GROPE *FOR FISH* IV.9.10. *prppl*
gɹɔvlən Du

groves *n* SCRAPS left after rendering lard III.12.10.
gɹɔːvz Co

grow *vi* to WAX, referring to the moon VII.6.5(a).
-ing gɹɛʊɪn Sx, gɹæʊ He Gl, gɹɑʊ Gl, əgɹɑʊ-n̩ Ess,
-ing gɹɒː-ɪn Nf, *-ing* gɹɒʊɪn He Sr K Sx, *prppl* gɹɔːɪn
So W, *-ing* gɹɔːɪn D, *-ing* gɹɔːən Co, *vbln* gɹɔːn Co,
-ing gɹɔːn Co D, *-ing* gɹɔɪ-ɪn Wa, gʁɔʊ Nb, gɹɔʊ Hu,
-ing gɹɔʊɪn L Ess K, gɹʌʊ Nf Ess, gɹoː He Mon Gl,
prppl gɹoːɪn So W, *-ing* gɹoːɪn D Do, *prppl* gɹoːən D,
-ing gɹoːən D, *prppl* gɹoːn Do, *-ing* gɹoːɪn D, gɹoˑʊ
Db Mon, *-ing* gɹoʊɪn St Ha, *-ing* gɹoʊɪn So W, *prppl*
gɹoːʊɪn So, *prppl* gɹoːʊən Do, *-ing* gɹoːʊɪn So; **he's
on the grow** ɪz ɒn ðə gɹoː He; **in his growing** ɪn ɪz
gɹoːʊɪn So

grow big *viphr* to WAX, referring to the moon
VII.6.5(a). *-ing* gɹoʊɪn bɪg Y

growdge *1. v-1prppl* we CRUNCH apples or biscuits
VI.5.12. gɹæʊdʒ L
2. v to GOBBLE food VI.5.13(b). *3prsg* gɹæʊdʒɪz
Brk

grow fuller *viphr* to WAX, referring to the moon
VII.6.5(a). *-ing* gɹɒʊən fʊlə Cu

growl *vi-3prpl* bulls BELLOW III.10.2. gɹʌʊl Nf

grow less *viphr* to WANE, referring to the moon
VII.6.5(b). *-ing* gɹɒʊɪn lɛs Y

growze *v* to GOBBLE food VI.5.13(b). *-ing* gɹaʊzɪn
St

grozers *npl* GOOSEBERRIES IV.11.2. gʁøːzəz Nb,
gʁœːzəz Nb, gʁɔːzɔᵏs Nb, gʁɔːzɔᵏz Nb, gɹɔːzəz
Nb, gʁɔːzəᵏz Du, gɹɔːzəz Du, gɹʊəzəz Du, gʊˑzɔᵏz
Nb, gʁuːzəᵏz Du

grub *1. n* feed given to horses in the stable, ⇐
FEEDING III.5.1. gɹʌb So
2. n FOOD V.8.2. gɹœːb Gl, gɹʌb He*[rare]* Nth
Nf*[older than* feed*]* Sf Bd Hrt Ess MxL, gɹʌb So W
Co D Do Ha, gʁʊb Nb Du, gɹʏb Nf*[older than* food*]*,
gʁʊb Nb, gɹʊb Cu Du We La Y Ch Db St*[older than*
food*]* Wa Nt Nth Bk, gɹəb Gl
3. n MEAL OUT VII.5.12. gɹʌb Bk Bd Ess, gɹʌb So

W Co D Do, gɹʊb Y Db St Wo L Bk
4. vt to CURDLE milk V.5.7. gɹʊb Nth
5. v to ROOT, what a pig does when it digs the
ground with its snout III.9.2. gɹʌb Bk, *-ing* gɹʌbɪn
O MxL Sr Sx, *-ing* gɹʌbɪn Ha, gɹʊbɪn Brk, gɹəbɪn
Sr
6. n the CORE of a boil VI.11.7. gɹʊb Y

grubber *n* a tool for clearing out ditches, ⇐
DITCH IV.2.11. gɹʌbəᵗ Sx

grubbing* *vt-prppl* FEEDING horses in the
stable III.5.1. gɹʌbən Co

grubbing up* *vtphr-ing* FEEDING horses in the
stable III.5.1. gɹʌbən ʌp Co

grubbles *n* CINDERS V.4.3. gɹʌbɫz So*[old]*

grub out *vtphr* to DITCH IV.2.11. gɹʌb ... əʊt Sx

grubs *1. npl* TICKS on sheep IV.8.3. gɹʌbz Mon
2. npl WORMS IV.9.1. gɹʌbz Sa*[old x3, usual
x4]* Mon, gɹʊbs Ch*[usual]*, gɹʊbz La Ch*[usual]*
Sa*[usual]* Wo*[usual]*

grub up *vphr* to ROOT, what a pig does when it
digs the ground with its snout III.9.2. *-ing* gɹʌbən
ʌp Ha

gruel(s) *1. n [For breakfast, some people eat
oatmeal boiled in water or milk. What do you call
it when it's thick?] And when it's very thin? V.7.2.
no -s:* Eng
-s: gɹuˑɪlz Y

⇒ **dullish, lumpy-dicks, meal-gruel, posset,
skilly, skilly and wack, skimdick, slack, slop,
swill, thin porridge, wet-pot;** ⇒ also **oatmeal,
onion-gruel, slutter**
2. n gruel made from onions and milk thickened
with flour. gɹuˑəl Bd, gɹˡuːəl Bd, gɹuːəł Nth Bk
Bd, gɹɪuːəł Ess

gruels *n* SCRAPS left after rendering lard
III.12.10. gɹʏːɫz D

grummets *n* DREGS left at the bottom of a teacup
V.8.15. gɹʌməts Sx

grummy *adj* INSIPID, describing food lacking in
salt V.7.8. gɹʊmɪ Ch *[queried WMBM]*

grump *vt-1prpl* we CRUNCH apples or biscuits
VI.5.12. gɹʊmp St, *-s* gɹʊmps Lei, *-ing* gɹʊmpɪn
Wo

grump up* *vtphr-1prpl* we CRUNCH apples or
biscuits VI.5.12. *-ing* gɹʊmpɪn ... ʊp Wo

grunch *1. vt-1prpl* we CRUNCH apples or
biscuits VI.5.12. gɹʌnʃ Mon, gɹʌnʃ So, gʁʊnʃ Nb,
gɹʊnʃ La*[old x1]* St Wo Gl
2. v-1prpl we crunch. *prppl* gɹʊnʃɪn Wo

grunters *npl* PIGS III.8.1. gɹʌntəz Hrt

grunt on *viphr-3prpl* they MOO, describing the
noise cows make during feeding time in the
cow-house III.10.4(a). *-ing* gʁʊntn œːn Nb

grup *v* to DITCH IV.2.11. gʁʊp Nb

guard *n* a THIMBLE V.10.9. gɑːd Ess

gubble *1. vt* to guzzle a drink, ⇐ GUZZLES VI.5.13(a). *-ing* gʌbɫɪn So
2. *v* to GOBBLE food VI.5.13(b). gʊbl La

guddle *v* to GROPE *FOR FISH* IV.9.10. gʊdl Nb, *prppl* gʊdlən Cu

guddle down *vtphr* to guzzle a drink, ⇐ GUZZLES VI.5.13(a). *-ing* gʌdlɪn ... daʊn So, *-ing* gʌdɫɪn ... dæʊn Do, *no -s* gʌdɫ ... dəʊn Do

guddles *1. vt-3prsg* he GUZZLES a drink VI.5.13(a). *-ing* gʌdɫən Do
2. *v-3prsg* he guzzles. *-ing* gʌdlɪn So, *no -s* gʌdɫ So, *-ing* gʌdɫɪn So D Do, *-ing* gʊdl La

gudgeon-iron *n* the metal BUSH at the centre of a cart-wheel I.9.8. gʊdʒənɑːən Y

gudgeons *npl* MINNOWS IV.9.9. gʌdʒənz Nf Ess, gʊdʒɪnz Y *[marked ir.rr. N/EMBM]*

guggle *1. v* to GOBBLE food VI.5.13(b). *-ing* gʌglɪn Sx*[old]*, *-ing* gʌgɫɪn W, gʊgl L
2. *n* a THROAT VI.6.3. gʌgʊ Sx*[old]*
3. *n* the WINDPIPE VI.6.5. gʊgl St

guggle down *vtphr* to guzzle a drink, ⇐ GUZZLES VI.5.13(a). *-ing* gʌgɫɪn ... dæʊn W

guggle in *vtphr* to guzzle a drink, ⇐ GUZZLES VI.5.13(a). *-ing* gʌgɫɪn ... ɪn W

guggles *1. vt-3prsg* he GUZZLES a drink VI.5.13(a). *-ing* gʌgɫɪn Ha
2. *v-3prsg* he guzzles. *-ing* gʌglɪn Gl Sx*[old]*, *-ing* gʊglɪn O L, gʌgɫz So, *-ing* gʌgɫɪn W, gʌgɫz Nf, *-ing* gʊgɫɪn Ch, *-ing* gʊgɫɪn Brk

guide *1. n* a BUMPER of a cart I.10.1(a). gəɪd Do *[queried ir.r. SBM]*
2. *n* the GRASS-NAIL of a scythe II.9.9. gəɪd Do*[forked stick]*

guide-bar *n* the GRASS-NAIL of a scythe II.9.9. gɑːdbaːɹ Y

guider *n* an EVENER on a horse-drawn plough I.8.4. gɒɪdəˡ· So

guile-dish *n* a SCOOP used to take water out of a boiler V.9.9. gaːldɪʃ L

gulch *vi* to VOMIT, referring to a baby bringing up milk VI.13.14(b). *-ing* gʊltʃɪn St

gulching up *vphr-ing* BELCHING VI.13.13. gɒlʃɪn ʊp Y

gulf **1.* n* a GULL IV.7.5. gʌlf Sa
2. *vt* to GOBBLE food VI.5.13(b). *-ing* gɒlfɪn Y, *-ing* gʊlfɪn Y

gulfs *1. vt-3prsg* he GUZZLES a drink VI.5.13(a). *-ing* gʊlfɪn Y
2. *v-3prsg* he guzzles. *-ing* gʊlfɪn Y

gull *1. n* What do you call that big greyish-white bird you sometimes see following the plough? IV.7.5. gɒl Sa, *pl* gɒɫz K, gʌl Sa O Nf K, *pl* gʌlz So, gʌɫ Gl Hu C Sf Bk Bd Hrt Ess MxL So Brk Sr K Co Do, *pl* gʌʊz Hrt, gʏl Nb Du, *pl* gʏlz Nf, gʊl Nb Cu Du La Y Db St Wo Nt L, *pl* gʊls Man, *pl* gʊlz We Sa, gʊɫ Man Wo Wa Mon Gl Lei R Nth Bk K, *pl* gʊɫz La O, gəl Sa. ⇒

black-head, petch, scouting-pewit, sea-crow, sea-gull, sea-mall, sea-martin, sea-maw, white bird, white crow
2. *n* a GOSLING IV.6.17. gɒɫ He, gʌl Sa He, gʌɫ He Mon, *pl* gʌɫz Gl, gʊl Sa Wo, gʊɫ He Wo, gəl Sa

gullantine *n* long-handled pruning shears, ⇐ HEDGING-BILL IV.2.5. gʊləntaɪn Db

gullet *1. n* a DRAIN in a cow-house I.3.8. gʌlɪt Sa
2. *n* the GUTTER of a roof V.1.6. gʌɫət So
3. *n* the WATTLES of a hen IV.6.19. gʌlɪt Nf, gʌɫɪt Ha, gʌɫət Ess, gʊɫət Sx *[queried ir.r. SBM]*
4. *n* a THROAT VI.6.3. gʌlɪt C Nf Ess, gʌlət Sf Ess, gʌɫət Co Ha, gʊlɪt Y Lei, gʊlət Du
5. *n* the WINDPIPE VI.6.5. gʌlɪt Ess Brk K, gʌlət O Ess Sr, gʌlaʔ Hrt, gʌɫɪt Nf Sr Ha, gʌɫət D Ha, gʊlɪt La Y L Lei, gʊlət Du La, gʊɫɪt Lei K

gullets *npl* large PUDDLES IV.1.6. gʌləts

gullett *v* to GOBBLE food VI.5.13(b). gʊlət La

gulley *n* a THROAT VI.6.3. gʌlɪ Nf

gullies *n* the PLUCK of a slaughtered animal III.11.6. gʊlɪz Nb

gullock *n* the WINDPIPE VI.6.5. gʌɫɪk Ess, gʌɫək Ess

gullop *v* to GOBBLE food VI.5.13(b). *-ing* gʊləpɪn Y, *-ing* gʊləpən We

gulls *1. npl* PUDDLES IV.1.6. gʌɫz Sf
2. *n* PORRIDGE V.7.1. gʊlz Y

gull-thivel *n* a PORRIDGE-STICK V.9.1. gʊlθaɪbəl Y

gully *1. n* a DRAIN in a cow-house I.3.8. gʌlɪ Nf Bk Ess K, gʌɫɪ Ess Sr Ha Sx, gʊlɪ Du O L R Nth, gʊɫɪ Gl
2. *n* a FORD IV.1.3. gʊlɪ La
3. *n* a DITCH IV.2.1(c). gʌɫɪ D
4. *n* a LANE IV.3.13. gʊlɪ Brk
5. *n* a GOSLING IV.6.17. gʌlɪ Sa, gʊlɪ Ch Sa St
6. *n* a NESTLING IV.7.1. *pl* gʊlɪz Sa
7. n the WINDPIPE VI.6.5. gʊlɪ Y

gully-grass *n* GOOSE-GRASS II.2.5. gʊlɪgɹas Sa

gully-hole* *n* the WINDPIPE VI.6.5. gʊlɪ-ʊəl Y

gully-trap *n* a CESS-POOL on a farm I.3.11. gʌɫɪtʈap Do

gully-way *n* a DRAIN in a cow-house I.3.8. gʌlɪweɪ Sf

gulp *1. vt* to GOBBLE food VI.5.13(b). *-ing* gʊlpɪn Y
2. *v* to gobble. gʌlp Ess, *3prsg* gʌɫps Ess, gʊlp Du

gulp back *vtphr* to guzzle a drink, ⇐ GUZZLES VI.5.13(a). *-ing* gʌɫpɪn ... baˑk So

gulping *v-ing* BELCHING VI.13.13. gʌlpn Nf, *no -ing* gʌlp Mon, gʌləpɪn Sf, gʌɫpɪn Ess, gʌɫpən Sf, gʌɫtʔn Nf

gulping up *vtphr-ing* **gulping wind up** BELCHING VI.13.13. gʌlpɪn wɪnd ʌp Nf

gulps *1. vt-3prsg* he GUZZLES a drink VI.5.13(a). *-ing* gʌɫpɪn K D, *-ing* gʌɫpən Do

2. v-3prsg he guzzles. *no -s* gʌlp Bd, *-ing* gʌlpɪn Nf, gʌɫps Ess, gʊlps Cu Du La, *inf* gʊlp We, *-ing* gʊlpɪn Y

gumf *v* to GROPE *FOR FISH* IV.9.10. *vbln* gʊmfən Nb

gumny *adj* STICKY, describing a child's hands VIII.8.14. gʌmnɪ K

gump *v* to GROPE *FOR FISH* IV.9.10. *vbln* gʊmpən Nb

gum-weed *n* GOOSE-GRASS II.2.5. gʊmwˡiːd Sa

gurgle *v* to guzzle a drink, ⇐ GUZZLES VI.5.13(a). *-ing* gəɫːɾglɪn Sx

gurry-wagon *n* a WAGON without sides I.9.2. gʌɾiwægɪn D

gurt* *n* a DITCH IV.2.1(c). gəɫːt̞ Co

gut *1. v* to GOBBLE food VI.5.13(b). *3prsg* gʊts Nt
2. n the CORE of a boil VI.11.7. gʌt He

gut back *vtphr* to GOBBLE food VI.5.13(b). *-ing* gəʔn ... bæk

gut down *vtphr* to GOBBLE food VI.5.13(b). *-ing* gʌtɪn ... dæʊn Ha

gutling* *n* a GOSLING IV.6.17. gʊtlɪn Wo

gut-runners *n* CHITTERLINGS III.12.2. gʌtɹʌnəz K

gut(s) *1. n* CHITTERLINGS III.12.2.
no -s: gʌt Ess
-s: gʌts O Nth Bk Bd Ess So Sr Do Ha, gʌʔs Bk, gʊts Nb Y Man St Wo Wa Nth K, gʊʔs Bk, gəts Gl Sx
2. n the BELLY VI.8.7.
no -s: gʌt Nth Sf W, gʊt Wa
-s: gʌts Gl Nf So Sr K Sx, gʌʔs Bk, gʏts Nf, gʊts Y Wa Gl L, gəts Sx

guts *1.1. vt* to guzzle a drink, ⇐ GUZZLES VI.5.13(a). *-ing* gʌtsən D, gʊts St
1.2. v to guzzle. gʌts Mon, *-ing* gʌtsɪn D, gʊts Ch
2. v to GOBBLE food VI.5.13(b). gʌts He, *-ing* gʌtsɪn So, *-ing* gʌtsən Co, *-ing* gʊtsɪn St

guts-ache *vi* to ACHE, referring to a stomach VI.13.3(b). gʊtsɛˑək L

guts down *1. vtphr* to guzzle a drink, ⇐ GUZZLES VI.5.13(a). *-ing* gʌtsən ... dœvn D
2. vtphr to GOBBLE food VI.5.13(b). *-ing* gʌtsɪn ... dævn D, *-ing* gʌtsɪn ... dəʊn W, *-ing* gʊtsɪn ... dɛʊn Sa

gutter *1. n* What do you call this, to prevent the rain-water dripping off the roof? V.1.6. gʌtə Sf Bd Ess MxL Sr, *pl* gʌtəz Hrt, gʌtəˡ Brk Ha, *pl* gʌtəˡz K, gʌtəɫ Brk Sx, gʌtʔəɫ Ha, gʌdəɫː D, gʌʔəʔː W Ha, *pl* gʌdəɫːz̞ So Co, gʊtə Y Man Nt L, *pl* gʊʔəz L, gʊtʁ Nb, gʊtɹ L, gʊtəˡ La Man, gʊʔəˡ L, gʊtəɫ Gl, gʊʔəɫ Bk. ⇒ **chuting, easing, easing-pipe, easing-spout, easing-trough, eave-troughing, gullet, guttering,**

gutter-work, house-easing box, launder, laundering, piping, rain-shoot, shoot, *shooting* ⇒ **chuting, spout, spouting, trough, troughing, water-spout, water-trough**

2. n the drainage channel between the roofs of adjoining houses. gʊtɹ L

3. n a TROUGH in a cow-house I.3.6. gʌdəɫː So

4. n a DRAIN in a cow-house I.3.8. gʌtəʁ Nb, gʌtə C Nf Bk Bd Hrt Ess MxL Sr, *pl* gʌtəz K, gʌtʔə Nf Sf Ess, gʌʔə Nf Hrt Ess K, gʌtəɹ He Brk, gʌtəˡ K, gʌtəɫ He Mon Gl O Brk Sx, gʌtəɫː Sa So W D Ha, gʌdəɫː So W Co D Do, gʌʔəɫː W, gʊtə Y Sa St Wa Nt L Lei R Nth, gʊtər Y, gʊtɹ L, gʊtəˡ L Brk, gʊtəɫ Sa He Wo Wa Mon Gl O, gʊʔəɫ Bk Ha, gətəɫ Gl

5.1. vt to DRAIN wet land IV.1.9. gʌtəɫːɾ So

5.2. v to drain land. gʊtə Y, gʊtər Cu

6. n a DITCH IV.2.1(c). gʌtəɫ Sa, *pl* gʌtəɫːz̞ D, gʌdəɫː D, gʊtəˡ Brk

7. v to DITCH IV.2.11. *-ing* gʌtəɫɾɪn Sa, *-ing* gʌdəɫːɾɪn D, gʊtə Cu Du We, *-ing* gʊtəɹɪn La Y, *-ing* gʊtʁən Nb

8. v to dig a new ditch. gʊtə We

9. n an ASH-MIDDEN V.1.14. gʌtə Ess, gʌʔə Sf

gutter-dike *n* an ASH-MIDDEN V.1.14. gʌtəɫdɪk Sx*[old]*

gutter-edging *n* the CURB-STONE in a cow-house I.3.9. gʌtəɫːɾedʒɪn So

gutter-hole *n* an ASH-MIDDEN V.1.14. gʌtʔəhoʊl Nf, gʌʔəhoʊl Nf

guttering *1. n* a DRAIN in a cow-house I.3.8. gʌtəɹɪn Mon MxL, gʌtəɾɪn So, gʌdəɫːɾən Co, gʌʔəɹɪn Bk

2. n the GUTTER of a roof V.1.6. gʌtəɹɪn He*[rare]* K, gʌtʔəɹɪn K, gʌtəˡɹɪn Brk Sr Sx, gʌtɹɪn K, gʌtɹɪn Mon Bd Ess Brk Sr K, gʌʔəɹɪn Bd Hrt, gʌtəɫɾɪn Mon, gʌtəɫːɾɪn Ha, gʌdəɫːɾɪn D, gʌtəɹən MxL, gʌʔəɹn̩ Ess, gʌʔɹɪn Ess, gʌtəɾɪn So, gʌʔəɾɪn O, gʌtɾɪn W, gʌtəɫːɾən W, gʊtəɹɪn L, gʊtɹɪn O Lei, gʊtəɾɪn O, gətɹɪn Gl

gutter-work *n* the GUTTER of a roof V.1.6. gʊtəwʊk Lei

guttle *1. v* to guzzle a drink, ⇐ GUZZLES VI.5.13(a). gʊtl Db
2.1. vt to GOBBLE food VI.5.13(b). *-ing* gʊtlɪn Y
2.2. v to gobble. *-ing* gʊtlɪn St

gut up *vtphr* to GOBBLE food VI.5.13(b). *3prsg* gʌts ... ʌp Ess*[old]*

guy *n* a SCARECROW II.3.7. gɒɪ Co, gɔɪ Sf Bk Ess

guzzle *1. n* a wet pit forming an ASH-MIDDEN V.1.14. gʌzʊɫ

2.1. vt to GOBBLE food VI.5.13(b). *-ing* gʊzˌlɪn Y, *-ing* gʊzlɪn St, *3prsg* gʌzlz He

2.2. *v* to gobble. gɒzl Sa, gʌzl Sa, gʊzl We La Wo O, *-ing* gʊz|ɪn Y, *-ing* gʊzlɪn Ch St L, gʊzł He, gəzl Gl

3. *n* a THROAT VI.6.3. gʊzl St, gʊzł Co

4. *n* the WINDPIPE VI.6.5. gɒzl Y, gʌzł So, gʊzl Y Sa St Wa, gʊzł Wo Co, gʊzəł Gl

guzzle-hole *n* an ASH-MIDDEN V.1.14. gʌzʊłɒuł Brk, gʌzʄɔuł Brk, gʌzʊłoːł Brk

guzzles *v-3prsg* *If a man drinks noisily and greedily [indicate], you say he ....* VI.5.13(a). Eng exc. Nb Du We Man Ch R Sf Hrt Do. ⇒ **balk, bezzle, bolt down, chops, draw in, flobbers, gaunges, gawps,** *glut* ⇒ **gluts, glutch, gluts, glutton,** *gobble* ⇒ **gobbles, gobble down, gobbles, gobble up,** *goggle* ⇒ **goggles, goggles, goggles down, golk, golk down,** *gollops* ⇒ **gollops, gollops, golp, golp down, golp up, gubble,** *guddle* ⇒ **guddles, guddle down, guddles,** *guggle* ⇒ **guggles, guggle down, guggle in, guggles, gulfs,** *gulp* ⇒ **gulps, gulp back, gulps, gurgle, guts, guts down, guttle,** *guzzle away, guzzle down, guzzle up, he's a glutton, he's a-goggle on the throat,* **hog, quilt, slabbers, slapes, slatches, slawps, slobbers, slodders,** *sloop* ⇒ **sloops, sloops, sloop up, slooshes,** *slop* ⇒ **slops, slop down, slops,** *slorps* ⇒ **slawps, slotches, slothers, slouse down, slubbers,** *slurps* ⇒ **sloops, slurrup, slurrup down,** *slush* ⇒ **slushes, slush down, slushes, slutches, sluthers, slutters, snorks, soss,** *sossle* ⇒ **sossles, sossles, suck down, sucks, sucks up,** *suck up* ⇒ **sucks up,** *sup* ⇒ **sups, sup in, sups, sup up, swabbles, swallows, swig, swill**

H

haaves *npl* HAWS IV.11.6. hɛːvz So, haːvz Ess Do, aːvz Bd Hrt Do, hɑːvz K, ɑːvz Hrt Ess K *[not a SBM headword]*

habes *npl* HAWS IV.11.6. eːbz Do

hack *1.1.* *vt* to CLEAR grass at the edges of a field II.9.5. hak We, ak Db
1.2. *v* to clear grass. hak Cu Du We, -*ing* hakən Nb, ak Db
2. *vt* to TURN hay II.9.11(b). æk Hu

hacked *adj* CHAPPED VI.7.2. hækt Nb, hakt Nb Cu Du, akt Cu, hakɪt Cu, hakd Cu

hacker *n* a BILLHOOK IV.2.6. ækəˡ Sa Wo, akə Mon

hacketing *v-ing* COUGHING VI.8.2. hɛkətɪn Do, ɛkətɪn Gl, ækətɪn So*[old]*

hacking *v-ing* COUGHING VI.8.2. ɛkən D, hækɪn Ha*[rough cough]*, jakɪn Ch

hackle *1.* *n* the T-SHAPED PLOUGH-BEAM END of a horse-drawn plough I.8.5. hɛkl Cu
2. *n* an EAR of oats II.5.2(b). hækɫ So, -*s* aklz Wo, -*s* akɫz Wa
3. *vt* to TURN hay II.9.11(b). akɫ Wa

hackling *v-ing* COUGHING VI.8.2. aklɪn Lei, jaklɪn St, hakɫɪn W*[short cough]*

hack off *vtphr* to CLEAR grass at the edges of a field with a scythe II.9.5. akk ... ɒf Ch

hack out *1.* *vtphr* to CLEAR grass at the edges of a field II.9.5. -*ing* aˑkɪn ... aːt Db, hak ... uːt Du
2. *vphr* to clear grass. -*ing* ækɪn əuːt Wo*[old]*

hack over *vtphr* to TURN hay II.9.11(b). ak ... ʊvə Lei

hacks *npl* CHAPS in the skin VI.7.3. hæks Nb, haks Nb

hacky *adj* CHAPPED VI.7.2. hakɪ Nb

hadaway *imp* **hadaway be going, hadaway with you** GO AWAY! VIII.7.9(a). **hadaway be going** hadəweː bɪ ganən Nb; **hadaway with you** haɹəweː wɪ ðə Du

haft *n* the HANDLE of a besom I.3.16. ɛft L

haftern-hook *n* a BILLHOOK IV.2.6. aːftəˡːŋɤːk D *[queried SBM]*

hagags *npl* HAWS IV.11.6. agagz Ha

haggard *n* the STACKYARD of a farm I.1.4. hækət Man, hægət Man

haggles *npl* HAWS IV.11.6. aɪgaɫz Ha, aɪgaɫdz Ha

hag-haws(es) *npl* HAWS IV.11.6.
no -es: eɪgɔːz Bk, ɛguːz MxL, agaːz O, agaˡːẓ O
-es: agaːzɪz Bk

haglets* *npl* HAWS IV.11.6. agɫəts Co

haglons* *npl* HAWS IV.11.6. agɫənz Co

hag out *vphr* to CLEAR grass at the edges of a field II.9.5. æg əuᵊt Gl

hags *npl* HAWS IV.11.6. ɛgz Db St, ɛgɪs Sx*[rare]*

hag-worm *n* an ADDER IV.9.4. agwɒrm Y, *pl* agwʊrmz Cu, agwʊrəm Cu, agwɜˡːm La, agwəm Y, agwəɹm Y, agwəɹəm Y, agwəːm Cu, *pl* hagwəːmz We, *pl* agwəːmz Du, agwəˡːm Cu, *pl* agwəˡːmz Y

haig-berries *npl* HAWS IV.11.6. eːgbɛɹɪz Ch

haigiemint* *n* MIST which comes at sunset and is a sign of fine weather VII.6.8. heːgɪmɪnt Y

haigins *npl* HAWS IV.11.6. eːgɪnz Y

haigs *npl* HAWS IV.11.6. eːgz La Y

haig-tree *npl* a hawthorn bush, ⇐ HAWS IV.11.6. eːgtɹɪ Y

hailstones *npl* RABBIT-DROPPINGS III.13.15. hæɪlstonz Nf *[queried facetious EMBM]*

haining *v-ing* THROWING a stone VIII.7.7. ɛnɪn So

hair *1.* *n* What do you call this *[indicate hair]*? VI.2.1. Eng. ⇒ *hure*, **lug**, **mop**, **squitch**, **tow**
2. *n* **get your hair cut** You go to the barber's to *[indicate cutting the hair]* .... VI.2.2. ⇒ *a haircut*, *be* **polled**, *for a haircut*, *get a* **clip**, *get a* **crop**, *get a* **hair-crop**, *get a haircut*, *get an haircut*, *get a* **poll**, *get a* **trim-up**, *get cropped*, *get haircut*, *get it cut*, *get it* **polled**, *get my hair cut*, *get my hair* **polled**, *get* **polled**, *get the hair cut*, *get your hair clipped*, *get your hair* **cropped**, *get your hair cut*, *get your hair cut off*, *get your hair* **cutten**, *get your hair* **polled**, *get your hair* set back, *get your tow cut*, *haircut*, *have a* **crop**, *have a* **hair-crop**, *have a haircut*, *have a* **hair-trim**, *have a* **poll**, *have a* **trim-up**, *have haircut*, *have his hair cut*, *have it* **cropped**, *have it cut*, *have it trimmed*, *have my hair cut*, *have their hair cut*, *have thy hair cut*, *have your hair clipped*, *have your hair cut*, *have your hair* **polled**
3. *n* the WOOL of a sheep III.7.5. ɛə Y

hair-broom *n* a BRUSH used for sweeping indoors V.9.11. heːᵊbɹʊm Ess, eːˡbɹʊm Sa, ɛːbɹuːm Wa, hɛɪəˡbɹuːm Brk K, ɛɪəˡbɹuːm Brk, ɛɪəˡbɹuːm Sx, ɛəbɹʊm Bk Ess, ɛəbɹuːm Wo Bd Hrt K, ɛəˡɪbɹʊm Sx, hɛəˡbɹʊuːm Sr, ɛəˡbɹʊuːm Sr, ɛəˡbɹʌm O, hɛəˡbɹʊm O, ɛəˡbɹʊm O Sx, ɛəˡːbɹʊm Wo, hɛəˡbɹʊuːm Sr, hɛəˡɾbɹʊuːm Sx, ɛəˤbɹuːm Wa Brk K Sx, ɛəˤˤbɹuːm Ha *[Ha form with* *[ɛəˤˤ] seems suspect]*

hair-brush *n* a BRUSH used for sweeping indoors V.9.11. ɛˈəbɹʌʃ Bk, hɛəbɹʊʃ L, ɛəbɹʊʃ Nt, ɛˈəˤbɽʌʃ So

hair-crop *n* a haircut, ⟸ GET YOUR HAIR CUT VI.2.2. ɛːəˤkɹɑp Wo

hair-dasher *n* a COMB VI.2.4. ɛədaʃə Y *[old]*

hairif *n* GOOSE-GRASS II.2.5. ɛɹɪf Y Ch Db Sa St Wa O Nt Lei R Nth, hɛɹɪf Wa, ɛːɹɪf Ch Wa, ɛɹɹɪf St Wo Gl, ɛəɹɪf Y Nt L Nth, ɛəɹəf Y, æɹɹɪf He Gl O, aɹɹɪf Wo

hairip* *n* GOOSE-GRASS II.2.5. hɛɹəp Y, ɛəɹəp Y, aːɹəp Y

hairis* *n* GOOSE-GRASS II.2.5. ɛˈəɹɪs Y, ɛəɹəs Y

hair-trim *n* a haircut, ⟸ GET YOUR HAIR CUT VI.2.2. hɛˈətɹɪm Ess

hair-weed *n* GOOSE-GRASS II.2.5. hɛəwiːd Nf Sf

hair sweeping-brush *n* a BRUSH used for sweeping indoors V.9.11. ɛˈə swiːpɪnbɹʊʃ L

hairy-bat *n* a BAT IV.7.7. ɛəˤːɽibat D *[queried SBM]*

hairy-mouse *n* a BAT IV.7.7. ɛəɽimævz Co *[queried SBM]*

hait *1. imp* **hait, hait up, woa hait** the command TURN LEFT!, given to plough-horses II.3.5(a). **hait** iːt Sa, ɛˈt Wo, ɛɪt St; **hait up** ɛt ʊp O; **woa hait** woː hɛɪt W *[at end of field]*

2. imp **hait, hait again, hait up, woa hait** the command TURN RIGHT!, given to plough-horses II.3.5(b). **hait** iːt La L Nth *[old]*, ɛɪt L R, ɑɪt Nth; **hait again** ˈiːt əgɪn Lei, ˈɛːɪt əgɪn Lei; **hait up** əɪt ʊp L; **woa hait** ˈwɔʊ ɛɪt Brk

hake *1. n* an EVENER, the main swingle-tree of a horse-drawn plough harness I.8.4. hɛɪk Sf Ess

2. v to BUTT III.2.10. *-ing* hɪəkən Nb, hɛːk We, ɛɪk Ch, *prppl* hɛɪkən Nb

3. n a CRANE on which a kettle is hung over a domestic fire V.3.4. hɛɪk Nf, hɛːɪk Nf

4. n the vertical BAR or CHAIN of a crane over a domestic fire V.3.5(b). *pl* hɛɪks Nf, hɛɪk Nf, hɛːⁱk Nf

5. n the HOOK or *CROOK* of a crane over a domestic fire V.3.5(c). hɛˈɪk Nf, *pl* hɛːɪks Nf

hake-bar *n* the *HORIZONTAL* BAR of a crane over a domestic fire V.3.5(a). hɛːⁱkbaː Nf

hake(s) *n* the notches on the T-SHAPED PLOUGH-BEAM END of a horse-drawn plough I.8.5.

no -s: hɛɪk C Nf, hɛːⁱk Nf, hɛɪk Sf, hɛːɪk Nf
-s: hɛːks Nf, hɛɪks Nf, hɛːⁱks Nf

hakes *npl* the HANDLES of a scythe II.9.8. hɛɪks C

hale *n* a CLAMP in which potatoes are stored out of doors II.4.6. hɛˈl Nf, hɛɪl Nf, hæˈɪl Nf

hale out *1. vtphr* to POUR tea V.8.8. ɛːɫ ... əʊt Do *[old]*

2. vphr to pour tea. *?-ing* hɛːɫən æʊt Do

hales *npl* the HANDLES of a horse-drawn plough I.8.2. ɛːlz Nt, ɛəlz Y, ɛɪlz L, ɛɪɫz Lei R Nth, ɛəlz Y L, aɫz Co D

half-a-crown *n What do you call this [indicate* *half-a-crown]?* VII.7.6. Eng. ⟹ **half-a-dollar,** *half-crown*

half-a-dollar *n* HALF-A-CROWN VII.7.6. ɛːfədɒlə Y, haːfədɒlə Ess *[slang x1]*

half-after-eights *npl* KNEE-STRAPS used to lift the legs of working trousers VI.14.17. haːfaːtəɹæɪts Sf

half-bag basket *n* a round BASKET with handles, for carrying horse-feed III.5.4. hæːfbæˈg bæːskɪt So

half-cracked *adj* SILLY VIII.9.3. hæːfkɽækt So

half-daft *adj* STUPID VI.1.5. æːfdæːft W, aːfdaːf Co, ɑːf dɑːft Wa, aˈfdaˈft K

half-fallow *n* FALLOW-LAND, apparently left fallow for a restricted period II.1.1. ɑːffɒɫə Ess, ɑːfθɒɫə Ess *[definition follows EMBM note]*

half-flyers *npl* young FLEDGED birds IV.7.2. ɑːffləɪəz Ess

halfpenny *n [Show a halfpenny.] What do you* *call this?* VII.7.1(a). Eng. ⟹ **make, meg**

halfpenny's-worth *n* a HALFPENNYWORTH VII.7.1(b). ɔːpnɪzwəθ Ch

halfpennyworth *n If a child went into a shop to* *buy some sweets for a halfpenny, what would she* *ask for?* VII.7.1(b). Eng. ⟹ **halfpenny's-worth** *[halfpennyworth/ha'porth not differentiated]*

half-pitch *n* a HAY-FORK with a long handle I.7.11. ɑːfpɪtʃ Sx

half-pitcher *1. n* a HAY-FORK with a shaft of medium length, about 5 feet long I.7.11. hæfpɪtʃəⁱ Ha

2. n a hay-fork with a short shaft. hɑːfpɪtʃəⁱ K

half-pitching-pick *n* a HAY-FORK with a short shaft I.7.11. aːfpɪtʃɪnpɪk Gl

half-pitch-prong *n* a HAY-FORK with a long shaft I.7.11. æːfpɪtʃpɹɒŋ Sx, aːfpɪtʃpɽɒŋ Ha

half-sharp *adj* SILLY VIII.9.3. aːfʃaːp Hu

hall *n* the SITTING-ROOM of a house V.2.2. ɔːɫ Co

hallan *1. n* the PARTITION between stalls in a cow-house I.3.2. halən Cu

2. the partition at the head of a cow-stall. halən Nb

halls *npl* HAWS IV.11.6. hɔːɫs Do

halo *n What can you sometimes see round the* *moon?* VII.6.4. ɛːlɔː Y, ɛːɫɔː O, ɛːloː Sa Nt, ɛːɫoː D, hɛˈɪlo So, hɛɪlou So, ɛɪlɔu Ess, hɛɪlʌʊ Ess, ɛɪlou St, ɛɪɫou So, ɛəlɔː Y, æɫo He, hæːluː Man *[rare]*, alɔː Y, halo: Du, aːlo Db. ⟹ **ball, bar, bluff, bow, brough, burr, burrow, circle, cliff, clift, cock's-eye, eye, mist, rim, ring, wagon-wheel, weather, weather-sign, wheel**

halse *n* HAZEL IV.10.8. ɒɬs D, ɔːɬs So D

halse-bushes *npl* HAZEL-bushes IV.10.8. hɔːɬsbʊʃɪz So

halt *imp* the command stop! or WOA!, given to plough-horses II.3.5(c). hɒlt Nf

halter *1. n What would you lead a cow by?* I.3.17. hɛltɒᵏ Nb Du, ɛltə Cu We La Y Db Nt L, hɛltə Nb Cu Du We Y, ɛltər Cu, hɛltər Cu, ɛltər Y, ɛltəɹ La Y L, hɛltəɹ Y, ɛˑɪltə Lei, æʊɬtəˡ He, æʊtəˡ He Gl, altə Y, aːɬtəˡ Co, aʊtəˡ Wo, haltə Nf, haˑlʔə Nf, aːɬtəˡ He Mon, ɒltə Y Ch Db St Nt Lei R, hɒltə Man Mon, hɒltʔə Nf, hɒlʔə Nf, ɒɬtə Ch Wa Mon Lei R Nth, hɒɬtə Mon Nth, ɒɬʔə Hu C Bd, ɒltər Y, ɒltəᴶ Y, ɒlʔəᴶ O, ɒltəˡ Sa Wo Mon, ɒɬtəˡ He Wo Gl Bk, ɒɬtəˡ W Co D, hɒːɬtəˡ W, ɒldəˡ Co, ɒʊɬtəˡ He Wa Mon Gl, ɒʊtəˡ He Gl, ɔltə L, hɔldə Nf, hɔltʔə Nf, hɔɬtʔə C Nf Sf, hɔɬʔə Sf, ɔltər Ch, ɔltəᴶ Wa L, ɔɬʔəˡ O, ɔːltə St K, hɔːltə Man, ɔːɬtə Wa Hrt MxL, hɔːɬtə Sf Ess Sr, ɔːtə La Ch Db, ɔːtʔə Bk, ɔːtəɹ Ch Db He, ɔːɬtəᴶ Brk K, ɔːtəɹ La Sr Ha, ɔːɬtəˡ Sa Wo O, ɔˡːɬtəˡ Sa, ɔːɬtəˡ He Wo Gl O Sr K Ha Sx, hɔːɬtəˡ Brk, ɔːtəˡ So K Sx, hɔːɬtəˡ So W Co D Do Ha, hɔːɬtəˡː So W, hɔːtəˡː So, ɔːɬʔəˡː W, hoːɬtəˡː W Do, oʊtə St, hoʊɬtəˡː So; **cow-halter** kɛʊ-ɒɬtə Nth, kɛʊ-ɒɬʔə Nth, kuː-ɛltə Y, kᵊuː-ɛltəɹ Y. ⇒ **collar, cow-halter, cow-hemp, cow-lead, halter-and-rope, head-stall, hemp, hempen-halter, hemp-halter, lead, leading-rein, neck-rope, rope, rope-halter, single-halter, slip**
2. n a chain TETHER for a cow I.3.4. hɒˑlʔə Nf, ɔːltəᴶ K, ɔːɬtəᴶ K
3. n a TETHERING-ROPE used to tie up a horse I.4.2. ɛltə La L, ɛltər Y, ɛltɪ L, ɛltəɹ Y, æɬdəˡː Ha, haltəᴮ Nb, aːɬtəˡː Co, hɑltʔə Nf, ɒltə Gl, ɒlʔəᴶ O, hɒltə Mon Nth, ɒɬtə Wa Gl, hɒɬtəᴶ K, ɒɬtəˡ Wa Nth Bk, ɒɬʔəˡ Bk, hɒɬtəˡː W, ɒɬtəˡː Co D Ha, ɒʊɬtə Wa, ɔltəˡ O, hɔɬtə Sf, ɔɬtə Ess, hɔˑɬʔə Sf, ɔɬtəˡ Wo, ɔːltəˡ Sx, ɔːltɛ K, hɔːɬtə Ess, ɔːtə Bk, ɔːɬtəᴶ K, ɔːɬtəˡ So Brk, ɔːtəˡ So Sr, hɔːɬtəˡː So, ɔːɬtəˡː So W Co D Do Ha, ɔːɬʔəˡː W, hɔʊʔə Ess, hoːɬtəˡː W, oʊɬtəˡ Brk, hoʊɬtəˡː So; **neck-strap and halter** nɛkstɹæp ŋɔːɬtəˡ Sr

halter-and-rope *n* a HALTER for a cow I.3.17. ɔːtəˡn̩ˌɹʊʊp Sr

halter and shank *n* a TETHERING-ROPE used to tie up a horse I.4.2. ɔːtəᴶ ŋ̍ ʃɛŋk Sr

halter-chain *n* a TETHERING-ROPE or chain used to tie up a horse I.4.2. ɛltətʃɛɪn Y, ɔːltətʃeːn Ch

halter-plug *n* the CLOG on a horse's tether I.4.3. hɛltɒᵏplʊg Nb

halter-rope *n* a TETHERING-ROPE used to tie up a horse I.4.2. ɒɬtəɹoːᵁp Nth, ɔːɬʔəˡɹɔup O, ɔːɬtəɹʌʊp MxL, ɔːtəɹɹoːp La

halter-shank *n* a TETHERING-ROPE used to tie up a horse I.4.2. hɛltɒᵏʃaŋk Nb Du, hɛltəʃaŋk Cu Du We, ɛltəʃaŋk Cu Du We La Y Db Nt, hɛlʔəʃaŋk Nb,

hɛltərʃaŋk Du, hɛltəʁʃaŋk Nb, ɛltəɹʃaŋk Y, ɒltəʃaŋk Db, ɔːtəʃaŋk La Db, ɔːtəɹʃaŋk La, ɔːtəᴶʃaŋk La

halves *npl* the HANDLES of a horse-drawn plough I.8.2. aɬvz Co

hamchammering *v-ing* GOSSIPING VIII.3.5(a). hæmtʃæməˡːɹɪn So

hames *1. n [Show a picture of the harness of a cart-horse.] What do you call this [indicate the hames]?* I.5.4. ɪmz Sa, jeəmz Du, jɛmz Cu, jɛmzəz So W, ɪamz Y, jamz Cu Du We La Y, ɪəmz Du Y, hɪəmz Cu, jəmz Y O, eːmz La Y Ch Db Sa Mon Gl O Nt W Co Do Ha, eːmzɪz Gl Co, heːmzɪz Do, eːmzəz Gl W D Do, heːmzəz W, eɪmz Db He Wo Wa Mon Gl O Hu C Bk Bd Hrt Ha, heɪmz Nf, heɪmzɪz So, eɪmzəz So, heɪmzəz So, eəmz La Y Nth Bk Bd, ɛmzɪz D, hɛmzɪz So, ɛmziːz So, ɛmzəz So D, ɛːmz Co, ɛːmzəz So D, ɛɪmz St Wo Wa O L Lei R Nth Hu C Nf Bd Hrt Ess Brk Sr K Sx, hɛɪmz Wa Nf Sf Ess Sr K Ha, ɛɪmzəz Co D, ɛʊmz La, ɛəmz Y L, hæmz Nf, æmɪz Sx, æɪmz Hrt Ess K, hæɪmz Nf Ess MxL Sr K, æɪmzɪz He, amz We La, amzəz Co, aɪmz Ess K Ha, ɒʊmz La, ɔːmzɪz Gl, ɔʊmz La, oːmz La Ch Sa He Wo Mon, oːmzɪz He, oːmzəz He, oʊmz La St He Wo Wa Mon, hoʊmz Man, oːʊmzɪz Gl, ʊːmz Wo, ʊəmz La. ⇒ **collar-tree(s), hame-sticks, hame-woods, jambles, seals, sill-hanks, tees, tug-hames, tugs**
2. n BRACES VI.14.10. hɪəmz W

hame-stick *n* a STICK used to support the shaft of a cart I.11.1. ɛˑɪmstɪk L

hame-sticks *n* the HAMES of the harness of a cart-horse I.5.4. jɛmstɪks Nb Du, hjɛmstɪks Du, jamstɪks Du, hɪəmstɪks Nb Du, heːmstɪks Nb

hame-woods *n* the HAMES of the harness of a cart-horse I.5.4. ɛɪmʊdz K, ɛɪmədz Sr, æmʊdz Sx, æmədz Sx

hammer off *imp* **hammer off out the way** GO AWAY! VIII.7.9(a). aməˡːɹ ɔːf æʊt ðə waɪ Ha

hamper *n* a SOWING-BASKET II.3.6. ampə Nth

hample-tree(s) *n* a SWINGLE-TREE of a horse-drawn plough harness I.8.3.
sg: hæməʔtɹ̍ɪ Nf
-s: hæmpltɹɪz Nf, hæməkʔlz Nf

ham(s) *n* LOW-LYING LAND IV.1.7.
no -s: hæm So, æm So, ham So Do, am D
-s: hæmz So, æmz Co D, hamz So W, amz W Co D

hanch *1. vt* to BUTT III.2.10. *-ing* ɔːnʃɪn Wa, *-ing* ɒˡːn̩ʃɪn D, *-ing* ɒˡːn̩ʃən D
2. v to butt. *-ing* ɑːnʃɪn Gl, ɔːntʃ Wa, ɔːntʃɪn Bk, *-ing* ɔːnʃɪn So, *-ing* ɒˡːn̩ʃɪn O

hanch up *vtphr-1prpl* we CRUNCH apples or biscuits VI.5.12. *-ing* anʃɪn ... ʊp Y

hand *1. n What do you call this [indicate the (human) hand]?* VI.7.1. Eng. ⇒ ***danny*** ⇒ **donny,**

dawk, donny, mauler, neive

2.1. *vt* to PITCH sheaves II.6.10. æn Co, *-ing* ændın Co, *-ing* andın Co

2.2. *v* to pitch. hænd Sf, *-ing* andın La, *-ing* handən Du

hand-bearer *n* a BIER VIII.5.9(b). hændbɪəɹə Nf

hand-bill *n* a BILLHOOK IV.2.6. ɛndbɪʊ K, æ·nbɪɬ K, ænbɪʊ Sr Sx, andbɪl Y Nt, anbɪl Y

hand-bowl *n* a SCOOP used to take water out of a boiler V.9.9. hɛndbɒʊɬ Sr, ɛndbɒʊɬ K, hɛnbɒʊɬ Sr K, hɛnbɔʊɬ Ess Sx, ændbæʊᵊɬ Gl, ænbæʊɬ He Gl, *pl* ænbæʊz Sx, ænbaʊl Wo, hændbɒʊl Nf, ændbɒʊl K, hændbɒʊɬ K, ænbʊɬ He, ænbʊ Sr, hænbɔʊɬ So Brk, æ·nbɔʊɬ Brk, ænbɔʊ Sr K, hænbʌʊɬ Ess, ænbo:ɬ He Mon So, ændbou Brk, anbaʊɬ Co, anbɑʊəl Gl, hanbʊʊᵊɬ Wa, anbʊʊᵊɬ Wa, anbɔʊl Wa, anbɔʊɬ Ha, anbɔʊ Ha, anbʌʊɬ Bd Hrt, anbo:l O, hanbo:ɬ So W Do, anbo:ɬ D Do Ha, ambo:ɬ Ha, andbʊʊl St, hanbouᵊl Mon, anbʊʊl He Wo Wa, hanbʊʊɬ So*[old x1]*, anbʊʊɬ Nth Bk

hand-brush *n* a short-handled BRUSH used for sweeping indoors V.9.11. ænbɹʌʃ Brk

hand-clippers *n* hand-operated SHEARS used to cut wool from sheep III.7.7. andklɪpəz St Lei

hand-corn *n* a CALLOSITY VI.11.4. *pl* æ:ndkɔ:əᵗɹ̩nz̩ Sx

hand-cup *n* a SCOOP used to take water out of a boiler V.9.9. hændkʌp Nf, hænkʌp Nf Sf, hænkʌp? Nf, hænkʊp Nf

hand-fed-lamb *n* a PET-LAMB III.7.3. hændfɛdlæm Nf

hand-fork *1.* *n* a HAY-FORK I.7.11. anfɔ·ək L, hanfə·ᴵ:k L, anfə·ᴵ:k L

2. *n* a hay-fork with a short shaft. hændfɔ·k Nf, ænfɔ:ᵊk Hu, andfɔ:k Nt L Lei R Nth, anfɔ:k Db, anfɔᵗ:ᵊk Bk, andfə·ᴵ:k L, anfə·ᴵ:k L

3. *n* a ROPE-TWISTER II.7.8. hanfɔ:k Du

handful *n* What do you call this *[indicate a handful]*? VII.8.10(a). Eng. ⇒ **fistful, gowpen, gowpenful, hantle, mittful, neiveful**

hand-grips *npl* the HANDLES of a scythe II.9.8. andgɹɪps Y

hand-hoe *vt* to THIN OUT turnip plants II.4.2. 'an'o:ʊ W

hand-hook *n* a BILLHOOK IV.2.6. hɛndhʊk Nf, hændhʊk Nf Sf, hænʊk So, ændʊk He, anʏk D, a'ndʊk Sa, ɒndʊk He

hand-hooks *npl* the HANDLES of a scythe II.9.8. andu:ks Y

handimaid *n* a CRANE on which a kettle is hung over a domestic fire V.3.4. andimɛɪd D

handkerchief *n* a NECKERCHIEF VI.14.4. ɛŋkəᵗtʃɪf Sx, *pl* æŋkatʃɪfs W, hæŋkətʃi:f Man, hæŋkətʃɪf Ess, æŋkətʃɪf Sr*[silk]*, æŋktʃəf K, æŋkə?tʃə Y, æŋkɪtʃəᵗ: So, hæŋkəᵗ:tʃəᵗ: So, hæŋktʃəᵗ: So, aŋkɪtʃɪf Ch, aŋkɪtʃə Ch L, aŋkətʃ Y,

aŋkətʃi:f Y, aŋktʃi:f L, aŋkətʃɪf L, aŋktʃɪf L, antʃɪf W, aŋətʃɪf Wa, aŋkəᵗ:tʃɪf W Ha, aŋkətʃəɪf Y, aŋkʊtʃə Y, aŋkʊtʃəɪ Y, aŋkətʃə Y, aŋkətʃəɪ Y, aŋətʃəᵗ O, aŋkəᵗ:tʃəᵗ: Do, aŋktʃəᵗ: Do

handkerchiefs *n* a silk NECKERCHIEF VI.14.4. ænkəᴵtʃɪfs Brk

handle *1.* *n* *[Show a picture of a besom.] What do you call this part?* I.3.16. ɛndɬ K, *pl* ɛndʊɬz Ess, ɛ·ndʊ K, hændl Man Nf, ændɬ He C Bk Hrt So Brk K D, hændɬ Sf Ess MxL So, ændəɬ He Mon Gl Ess, hændəɬ Sf Ess, ændʊɬ Brk Sr Sx, ændʊ Brk Sr K Sx, hændʊ Ess Sr, ænɬ So Co, andl Y St Mon L Nth, handl Y, andɬ Wa Gl O Lei Bk W Co D Do Ha, handɬ Nf W Do, andəɬ O, andʊɬ Gl Ha, anl We, anəl Y, ɒndl He; **besom-handle** bɪzəmandɬ O W. ⇒ **besom-shaft, besom-stale, besom-stick, broom-handle, broom-shaft, broom-stick, brush-shank, brush-stale, *brush-steal*** ⇒ **brush-stale, foot, haft, shaft, shank, stake, stale, stave, steal, stem, stick, stub, stump**

2. *n* the SHAFT of a spade I.7.7. ɛndʊɬ Ess K, hɛndʊɬ Ess, ɛndʊ Sr Sx, æ·ndl K, hændl Man Nf, ændɬ Hu Bk Ess K, hændɬ Sf Ess So K, ændʊɬ Gl Brk Sr K Sx, ændʊ Sr K, hændʊ Ess Sr Sx, ændəɬ Mon, anl L, anɬ Wo Co Do, andl Gl O L, andɬ Wa Mon Gl O Lei Nth Bk Hrt W Co D Do Ha, handɬ O So W Ha, handᵁɬ W, anəl Y, andəɬ Gl, aŋəl Y, ɒndl La

3. *n* the SHAFT of a hay-fork I.7.12. ɛndʊɬ K, ɛndʊ Sr, æ·ndl K, hændl Man Nf, ænɬ So, ændɬ He Bk Ess So Brk K D, ændəɬ Mon Ess, hændɬ Sf Ess So, ændʊɬ Gl Sr K Sx, hændʊɬ Sx, ændʊ Sr K Sx, hændʊ Sr, anəl Y, andl Db Gl O, anɬ Co D Do, hanɬ So, andɬ Wa Gl O W Co D Do Ha, andəɬ Gl Bk, handɬ So W Do, handəɬ O

4. *n* the left-hand handle of a horse-drawn plough, ⇐ HANDLES I.8.2. ɛʊndʊ Ess, hændɬ Sf

5. *n* the SHAFT of a scythe II.9.7. hændl Man Nf, hændɬ So, ændʊɬ Brk, ændəɬ Bk, handɬ Do, handəɬ O, andl L, andɬ Gl O Bk Bd W Ha, anl Y

6. *n* the vertical BAR or CHAIN of a crane over a domestic fire V.3.5(b). hændɬ Sf

handle-bowl *n* a SCOOP used to take water out of a boiler V.9.9. ændʊbɒʊ Sx

handle-cup *n* a SCOOP used to take water out of a boiler V.9.9. hændlkʌp Nf, hændlkʏp Nf, handlkʏp Nf

handle-dish *n* a SCOOP used to take water out of a boiler V.9.9. ɛndʊdɪʃ K*[old]* Sx, hændʊɬdɪʃ Sx, ændʊɬdɪʃ Sx

handles *1.* *npl* *[Show a picture of a (horse-drawn) plough.] What do you call these [indicate the handles]?* I.8.2. ɛndlz Sa, ɛndʊɬz Ess K Sx, *sg* hɛndʊɬ Ess, ɛndʊz Sr Sx, ænlz Y, ænɬz So, ændlz He L, hændls Man Nf, hændlz Nf Sf, ændɬz He

Hu Hrt Ess So K D, hændɫz Nf Sf Ess MxL So, ændəɫz Mon Gl Bk Ess, ændʊɫz Gl Brk Sx, hænduɫz Ha, ænduz Sr K Sx, hænduz Ess, anlz La Y Wo, hanlz Nb We, anəlz Y Sa, anɫz Co D Do, andlz Y Ch Db Sa St Wo Wa Gl O L Nth, aːndəlz Sa, andɫz Wa Mon Gl O Lei R Nth Hu C Bk Bd Hrt So W Co D Do Ha, andəɫz Gl Bk Bd Hrt, andᵁɫz W, aŋlz Y, ɒndlz La, ɒndɫz He Gl; **plough-handles** plɛʊ-ɛndɫz K, plɛʊhændɫz Ess, plɛʊ-ændɫz Ess, plɛʊ-ændʊɫz Sx, plɛʊ-ænduz Sx, plau-æ·ndlz K, pɫæʊ-andɫz W, pɫæʊ-andᵁɫz W, pɫəʊ·-andəɫz O, pləʊ-a·nduɫz Ha. ⇒ **hales, halves, holds, plough-hales, *plough*-handles, plough-shafts, plough-stilts, plough-tails, shafts, shanks, stilts, tails;** ⇒ *also* **grips, handle, hands, staff, stave**

2. *npl* grips on the handles of a horse-drawn plough. ændlz Wo, hændlz Nf, andlz He Nt *[also apparently La, but no phonetics given]*

3. *npl [Show a picture of a scythe.] What do you call these?* II.9.8. ɛnduz Sr, hændlz Nb Nf, hæendls Man Nf, ændlz L, hændɫz Nf Ess So, ændɫz Wo Sf Hrt Ess MxL, ændəɫz Mon Gl Bk, ænduɫz Gl Brk, *sg* ænɫ Co, handlz Nb Du, handls Du, andlz Cu La Y Ch Db Sa St Wo Wa O Nt L, andəlz Y, handɫz So W D, andɫz Ch Wa Lei R Nth Bk Bd W D, *sg* andɫ Gl Ha, anduɫz Ha, hanlz Nb Cu Du We, anlz Cu La Y, anəlz La Y, hanls Nb, *sg* anl We, ɒndlz La, ɒndɫz Wo; **scythe-handles** saɪðandɔlz Y, saːðandlz Y, *sg* sɔɪðændɫ Ess, zəɪᵊθændʊɫz Gl. ⇒ **cogs, crutches, doles, fotes, goose-neck tack, grips, hakes, hand-grips, hand-hooks, hand-pins, hand-tings, hilts, horn, kags, lea-nibs, lugs, nebs, nibbles, nibs, nippets, nipples, nips, noggets, noggins, nogs, *scythe*-handles, scythe-nibs, snogs, straight-handles, tack, tacks, tholes, toggers, tugs**

handle-shaft *n* the SHAFT of a hay-fork I.7.12. æ·ndɫʃɑːft K

hand-meat* *n* concentrated animal feed, ⇐ FOOD V.8.2. anmɪət Y

hand on *vtphr* to PITCH sheaves II.6.10. and ... ɒn La

hand over *vtphr* to PITCH sheaves II.6.10. *3prsg* ænz ... ʌʊvə K

hand-pins *npl* the HANDLES of a scythe II.9.8. ænpɪnz Co, anpɪnz Co D

hand-prong *n* a HAY-FORK I.7.11. æːndpɹɒːŋ Sx

hand-rack *n* a BENCH on which slaughtered pigs are dressed III.12.1. anɹak Hrt

hands *npl* grips on the handles of a horse-drawn plough, ⇐ HANDLES I.8.2. andz Nt

hand-shears *n* hand-operated SHEARS used to cut wool from sheep III.7.7. hænʃɪəz Nf, hændʃɪəz Nf, hæ·nʃɪəᴶs Man, ænʃɪəᵗz He, ænʃɪəᵗːz So, hænʃeəz Nf, anʃɪəz Ch St Bd, andʃɪə·z Y, anʃɪəᵗz Bk, anʃɪəᵗːz W Co, aːnɜɪəᵗːz Ha, anʃɪəᵗz Ha

hand sledge-knife *n* a HAY-SPADE II.9.14(b). ɛn slɪdʒnɑːf Lei, ɛn slɪdʒnɑ·ɪf Lei *[queried EMBM]*

handsome *adj* PRETTY, describing a girl VI.5.18. hɛnsəm Nf, ænsəm Wo, ansəm Y Nth

handsome-looking *adj* PRETTY, describing a girl VI.5.18. ænsəmlʊkɪn Ess Sx

hand-tickle *v* to GROPE *FOR FISH* IV.9.10. *vbln* andtɪtlɪn La

hand-tings *npl* the HANDLES of a scythe II.9.8. antɪŋz D

hand-wrist *n* a WRIST VI.6.9. hæenhɹɪst So, hæenhɹɪs So, hænɹəs So, hænəᵗːʂt So, ænɹɪs So, æ·ndɹɪst MxL, hæːnɹɪst So, hanəᵗːʂt So, andɹɪst O, andɹəst We, anɹɪst O Bk, anɹɪst D, anɹɪs So, ha·nɹɪst So, haːnɹɪs So

handy *adj* NEAR IX.2.10. handɪ We, andɪ He; **pretty handy** pəᵗːdɪ ændɪ Co

handy-labourer *n* a FARM-LABOURER I.2.4. andɪleːbɹəᵗ Gl

handy-man *n* a FARM-LABOURER I.2.4. hændɪmæn Sf, ændɪmæn Hu, ændɪmɒn He Wo, handɪman W, andɪman Y Bd Do, ɑndɪman Ch, ɑ·ndɪmɑːn Ha

hang *v* **hang in** to AGREE with somebody VIII.8.12. aŋ ɪn Nth

hang-bow *n* the HANGING-POST of a gate IV.3.3. aŋbæʋ Co

hange *n* the PLUCK of a slaughtered animal III.11.6. hɪndʒ So W Do, ɪndʒ So Co Do Ha, ɪnʒ Gl, ɛndʒ W Co D, ændʒ So, hæntʃ So, andʒ D

hanger 1. *n* the HANGING-POST of a gate IV.3.3. hæŋəᵗː So, æŋəᵗ He, aŋəᵗ Sa
2. *n* the vertical BAR or CHAIN of a crane over a domestic fire V.3.5(b). haŋəᵗ W, aŋgə Wa
3. *n* a GRIDIRON hung in front of the bars of a fire V.7.4(a). aŋə Nth *[marked u.r. EMBM]*

hanger(s) *n* a CRANE on which a kettle is hung over a domestic fire V.3.4.
no -s: ɛŋəᵗː D, hæŋgə Sf, aŋə C, aŋgə Wa, aŋəᵗ O Bk, aŋəᵗ O, haŋəᵗː So W, aŋəᵗː W Ha
-s: æŋəᵗːz̩ D, aŋəᵗːz̩ W

hangers *npl* the HINGES of a door V.1.11a. æŋəᵗːz̩ D*[old]*, haŋəᵗːz̩ So

hanging* *v-ing* THROWING a stone VIII.7.7. hæŋɪn So

hanging-crook 1. *n* a CRANE on which a kettle is hung over a domestic fire V.3.4. aŋɪnkɽʏk D
2. *n* the HOOK or *CROOK* of a crane over a domestic fire V.3.5(c). aŋɪnkɽʏk D

hanging-gate *n* the HANGING-POST of a gate IV.3.3. ɛŋgɪngɪt Ch

hanging-hook *n* a CRANE on which a kettle is hung over a domestic fire V.3.4. aŋɪnʊk Bd

hanging-nail *n* a LOOSE *PIECE OF* SKIN at the bottom of a finger-nail VI.7.11. *pl* aŋɪnneɪᵊɫs Nth

hanging-post *n What do you call this, to which the gate is attached?* IV.3.3. Eng exc. Cu We Ch. ⇒ **arse-end-post, big post, butt-end-post, carrying-post, crook-stoop, foot-stump, front-post, gate-post, hang-bow, hanger, hanging-gate, hanging-stoop, hanging-stub, hanging-stump, hang-post, hang-stump, harr-tree, head of the gate, head-post, heel, heel-post, heel-stump, hind-post, hingeing-stump, hinge-post, hinge-stoop, hinging-post, hinging-stoop, hing-post, hurl, post, slinger, standard, standard-post, stand-post, strinding-post, swinging-post, swing-post**; ⇒ also **binding-post, hangs-tree, hinge-tree**

hangings *npl* the HINGES of a door V.1.11a. ɛŋɪnz D, ɛŋənz D, æŋɪnz So Co, aŋənz Co

hanging-stoop *n* the HANGING-POST of a gate IV.3.3. aŋgɪnstɛʊp Db, haŋənstuːp Nb Du, aŋɪnstuːp La Y

hanging-stub *n* the HANGING-POST of a gate IV.3.3. aŋgɪnstʊb La

hanging-stump *n* the HANGING-POST of a gate IV.3.3. ɛŋgɪnstʊmp Ch Db, aŋɪnstʊmp St

hangle *n* the vertical BAR or CHAIN of a crane over a domestic fire V.3.5(b). hæŋgɫ Brk, haŋ^{ʊ}ɫ W

hangle-iron *n* the vertical BAR or CHAIN of a crane over a domestic fire V.3.5(b). hæŋɫʌɪə^{ɹ}n Sr

hangle(s) *n* a CRANE on which a kettle is hung over a domestic fire V.3.4.
no -s: æŋgʊ Sr
-s: hæŋʊɫs So, haŋɫz W, haŋʊɫz W

hangman *n* a BOGEY VIII.8.1. aŋman Y

hang-nail *n* a LOOSE *PIECE OF* SKIN at the bottom of a finger-nail VI.7.11. ɛŋnɛɪɫ K, hɛŋnɛɪʊ Ess*[broken nail x1]*, ɛŋnɛɪʊ Ess, *pl* hɛŋnæilz Nf, ɛŋgnæɪɫ K, hæŋnɛɪl Nf, *pl* æŋnɛɪlz L, hæŋnɛɪɫ Nf, æŋnɛɪ^{ə}ɫ Ess, hæŋnæɪl Nf, hæŋnæɪɫ Ess MxL, *pl* hæŋnæɪɫz Ess, hæŋnæɪ^{ə}ɫ Sf, æŋnæɪ^{ə}ɫ Sf, *pl* æŋnæɪ^{ə}ɫz Hu Ess, hæŋnaɪl Nf, hæŋnaɪɫ Ess, æŋnaɪʊ K, æŋnɑˑɪɫ Ess, *pl* aŋneːlz La, haŋneɪ^{ə}ɫ C, *pl* aŋneɪ^{ə}ɫz Hu Bd, aŋneɪʊɫ Ha, aŋneəl Cu Du, aŋnɛːl We, *pl* aŋnɛːlz Cu, aŋnɛɪɫ O, aŋnɛɪ^{ə}ɫ C, *pl* aŋnɛˑəlz L, aŋnæɪ^{ə}ɫz Wa, aŋnaɪɫ Ha

hang-on-oven *n* a GIRDLE for baking cakes, hung from a hook in a chimney V.7.4(b). hæŋɒnɤvən Nf

hang-post *n* the HANGING-POST of a gate IV.3.3. aŋpʌʊst L, aŋpɔʊst L, aŋpoː^{ʊ}st Nt, aŋpʊəst Nt L, aŋpʊəs L

hangs* *n* barley AWNS II.5.3. haŋz Cu, aŋz La

hang-stoop *n* the SHUTTING-POST of a gate IV.3.4. haŋkstuːp Nb

hangs-tree* *n* the part of a gate that has the hinges on it, ⇐ HANGING-POST IV.3.3. æŋstɹiː He, æŋstɹɪ He, aŋstɹiː He

hang-stump *n* the HANGING-POST of a gate IV.3.3. aŋstʊmp Ch

hank *1. n* a sliding RING to which a tether is attached in a cow-house I.3.5. aŋk Db
2. n a CRANE on which a kettle is hung over a domestic fire V.3.4. hæŋk Nf
3. n the HOOK or *CROOK* of a crane over a domestic fire V.3.5(c). hæŋk Nf

hantle *1. n A* LOT (of money) VII.8.7. antl St
2. n a HANDFUL VII.8.10(a). antl Ch*[old]* St, ɑntl St*[old]*, ɒntl St

hap up *vtphr* to HIDE something VIII.7.6. hap ... ʌp Nb

har *imp* the command TURN RIGHT!, given to plough-horses II.3.5(b). ɑ^{ɻ}ː Wo, ɔ^{ɻ}ː Sa

hard blister *n* a CALLOSITY VI.11.4. *pl* aːd blɪstəz L

hard-boiled eggs *npl* EASTER EGGS VII.4.9. haːbɔɪɫd ɛ^{ɪ}gz Ess *[marked u.r. EMBM]*

hard-broom *1. n* a MUCK-BRUSH I.3.14. haːdbruːm Mon, aːdbɹuːm Bd, a^{ɻ}ːɖbɹuːm Sa Gl, a^{ɻ}ːɖ bɽuːm So, ɑːdbɹəuːm Hrt
2. n a BROOM used for sweeping outdoors V.9.10. aːdbɹɪəm Y, aːdbɹʊm Hrt Ess, haːdbɹuːm Mon, aːdbɹuːm Y Sa Mon Hrt, a^{ɻ}ːɖbɹʊm Mon Gl, a^{ɻ}ːɖbɹuːm Wo Gl, a^{ɻ}ːɖ bɽuːm Do, hɑːd bɹuːm K, ɑːdbɹʊm Ess, ɑ^{ɻ}ːɖbɹʊm He

hard-brush *1. n* a MUCK-BRUSH I.3.14. aːdbɹʊʃ Mon Nth, a^{ɻ}ːɖ bɽɪʃ D, a^{ɻ}ːɖbɹʊʃ Gl
2. n a BROOM used for sweeping outdoors V.9.10. aːdbɹʊʃ Y Sa Nth, a^{ɹ}ːdbɹʊʃ Y, a^{ɻ}ːɖ bɽiːʃ Co, a^{ɻ}ːɖbɹʊʃ He Gl, a^{ɻ}ːɖbɹəʃ Gl

hard core *n* a CALLOSITY VI.11.4. haːd koˑə Sf

harden-apron *n* a working APRON V.11.2(a). aːdɳɛˑəpɹən L, haːdɳapɹən Du, *pl* aːdɪnapɹənz Y, aːdɳapɹən Y L, aːdɪnapɻən Y, əːdɳɛɪpɹən Wa, əːdɳɛɪpənd St, əːdənapən Wa, ə^{ɻ}ːɖɳˌeːpə^{ɻ}ːɳ He, ə^{ɻ}ːɖɳˌɛːpə^{ɻ}ːɳ O, ə^{ɻ}ːɖɳˌapɹən Wa

hard flesh *n* a CALLOSITY VI.11.4. aːd flɛʃ Nth

hard horn *n* a CALLOSITY VI.11.4. *pl* aːd ʊənz Y

hard knot *n* a CALLOSITY VI.11.4. *pl* ha^{ɻ}ːɖ nɔts So

hard pad *n* a CALLOSITY VI.11.4. *pl* a^{ɻ}ːɖ padz W, hɑˑd pæd Nf

hard skin *n* a CALLOSITY VI.11.4. hæːd skɪ^{ə}n Sf, haːdskɪn Sf Ess, ˈaːd skɪn St Lei R, ˌaːd ˈskɪn St Wa L Nth, ˈaːd ˈskɪn L R, haːd skɪn Ess, aːd skɪn Y Ch Db St Wo Wa Nt L Lei Nth Hu C Sf Bd Hrt Ess, ha^{ʁ}ːd skɪn Nb Du, ha^{ʁ}ːʁəd skɪn Nb, a^{ɹ}ˑd skɪn L, a^{ɻ}ːɖskɪn Nth, ˈa^{ɻ}ːɖ ˌskɪn Sa He, ˈa^{ɻ}ːɖ ˈskɪn Sa He Wo Gl, ˌa^{ɻ}ːɖ ˈskɪn Wo Bk, ha^{ɻ}ːɖ skɪn So W, a^{ɻ}ːɖ skɪn Wa Mon O Bk W Do Ha, hɑːdskɪn Ess, ˈɑːd ˈskɪn Hrt, ˌhɑːd ˈskɪn Nf, hɑːd skɪn Ess, ɑːd skɪn St Wo, ˈɑ^{ɻ}ːɖ skɪn He Gl, ˈɑ^{ɻ}ːɖ ˈskɪn Wo, ˌɑ^{ɻ}ːɖ ˈskɪn Wo, ɑ^{ɻ}ːɖ skɪn O K D, ɑ^{ɻ}ːɽɖ skɪn Sx *[marked u.r. N/SBM, note in EMBM asserts relevance]*

hard-stone *n* a WHETSTONE II.9.10. aᵗːdˌṣtoʊn So

hard up *adj* ILL, describing a person who is unwell VI.13.1(b). haˑʁd ʊp Nb

hard wart *n* a CALLOSITY VI.11.4. aːd wɔːᵊts Bd, *pl* haːd wɔːts Nf, *pl* haːd wʊəts Nf

hardy *adj* ACTIVE, describing a child VIII.9.1. aᵗːɾdˌɪ Brk *[marked u.r. SBM]*

hardy-mouse *n* a SHREW-MOUSE IV.5.2. æᵗːdˌɪmɛʊs O, aːdɪmɛʊs Wa Nth, aᵗːdˌɪmɛɪs Bk, aᵗːdˌɪmɛʊs Wa Nth Bk, haːdɪmɛʊs Wa*[old]*

hardy-shrew *n* a SHREW-MOUSE IV.5.2. aːdɪsɹæʊ Wo Gl, aᵗːdˌəsɹɒf Sa, aːtɪsɹoʊ Wo

hardy-shrew-mouse *n* a SHREW-MOUSE IV.5.2. aːdɪʃɹɔʊmæʊs Wo, aːdɪsɔʊmæʊs Wo

hardy-strow* *n* a SHREW-MOUSE IV.5.2. aɹdɪstɹɔː He, aːtɪstɹæʊ He, aːdɪstɹoː Wo, aːtɪstɹɔː Mon, aᵗːdˌɪstɹæʊ He, aᵗːdˌɪstɹaʊ Wo, aᵗːdˌɪstɹɪɑ Gl, aᵗːtˌɪstɹɑ Mon Gl, aᵗːdˌɪstɹɒʊ He, aᵗːdˌɪstɹɔː He, aᵗːtˌɪstɹɔː Gl, aᵗːdˌɪstɹɔː Sa, aᵗːtˌɪtɹɔː Sa, aᵗːtˌɪstɹɔːʊ Mon, aːdɪstɹɔː St, aːtɪstɹɒʊ Wo, aᵗːtˌɪstɹɑ He

hare *n* *What do you call that animal like a rabbit, but larger and stronger?* IV.5.10. Eng. ⇒ **auntie, aunt sally, jenny, neddy, old jerk, old masker,** *old sall* ⇒ **sal, sal,** *old sal, sall* ⇒ **sal, sally, sarah-annie**

harkeners *npl* EARS VI.4.1. aᵗːkənəᵗːzˌ Sa, aᵗːknəᵗːzˌ Sa*[old]*

harkers *npl* EARS VI.4.1. aːkəᴶz K

harness *1. vt* to GEAR a cart-horse I.5.1. haːnəs Nf Ess, aːnɪs Y St Gl, aːnɪʃ Wo Mon, haʁːnɪs Nb, haʁːnəs Nb, haᵗːn̩ɪs So W, aᵗːn̩ɪs Gl W D Do Ha, aᵗːn̩ɪʃ Gl, hanəs Nf, aᵗn̩əs Ha, haːnɪs Nf MxL, haːnəsᴶ Sr, aːnɪs St Ess K, aᵗːn̩ɪs D, aᵗːnɪʃ Wo, *prppl* aᵗːɾn̩ɪsɪn Sr, *-ing* aᵗːɾn̩ɪsɪn Brk Sx, əᵗːn̩ɪs Gl

2. v to gear a horse. *-ing* hæˑnəsən Man, æːnəs Du C, hæˑᴶːnɪs O, *-ing* æːɹnɪsɪn Brk, aᵗn̩ɪs O, haːnɪs Cu Ess, haːnəs Nb Du Sf Ess, *?-ed* haːnəst Sf, aːnɪs Y Ch Db St Wa Nt L Nth Hu C Bk Bd Hrt, aːnɪʃ Wa, aːnəs We Y Ess, haʁːnɪs Nb, haʁːnəs Nb, haᵗːn̩ɪs So W, haᵗːn̩əs O, aᵗːn̩ɪs Wa Bk So, aᵗːnəs O, haˑnɪs Nf, *-ing* aːnɪsɪn Ess K, haˑᴶːɪnɪs Ha, *-ing* əhaˑᴶːnɪsɪn K, haᵗːn̩ɪs Sr, *prppl* aᵗːɾn̩ɪsɪn Sr Sx, *-ing* aᵗːɾn̩əsən Sx, əᵗːn̩ɪs O

harness-horse *n* a TRACE-HORSE I.6.3. aᵗːn̩ɪsɔᵗːṣ D

harness up *1. vtphr* to GEAR a cart-horse I.5.1. aɾn̩ɪs ... ʊp O, haːnɪs ... ʊp Nf, haːnəs ... ʌp Ess, aːnʌs ... ʌp Mon, haᵗːn̩ɪs ... ʌp W Do, aᵗːn̩ɪs ... ʌp So W Co D Do Ha, aᵗːn̩əs ... ʌp Co, haːnəs ... ʌp Nf, *prppl* aːnɪsɪn ... ʌp Brk, aːnəs ... ʌp Hrt, aᵗːn̩ɪs ... ʌp D Sx, aᵗːɾn̩əs ... ʌp Sx

2. vphr to gear a horse. aᵗːn̩ɪs ʌp W D, aːnɪs ʌp K, *-ing* haˑᴶːnɪsɪn ʌp K, aᴶːnɪs ʌp K, aᴶːnɪs ʊp K, haᵗːɾn̩ɪs ʌp Sx, aᵗːn̩ɪs ʌp Brk Co, *-ing* aᵗːɾn̩ɪsɪn ʌp Sx

harney *vi* to SCREAM VIII.8.11. haᵗːn̩ɪ So*[also = 'to bray', of a donkey] [queried SBM]*

harridges *npl* the RIDGES between furrows in a ploughed field II.3.2. *sg* haɹɪdʒ Cu

harrowed *adj* EXHAUSTED, describing a tired person VI.13.8. aɹəd Nt*[old]* L; **harrowed to dead** aɹəd tə dɪˑəd L; **harrowed to death** aɹəd tə dɪˑəθ L, aɹəd tə dɛθ L

harr-tree *1. n* an EVENER, the main swinge-tree of a horse-drawn plough harness I.8.4. aːtɹɪ Cu *[northern forms with -tree given this definition, although NBM data less specific]* *2. n* the HANGING-POST of a gate IV.3.3. haᴶθɹɛɪ Y, aːtɹɪ Y

harry *n* a WEAKLING piglet III.8.4. aɹɪ Bd Hrt; **little harry** lɪʔɫ aɹɪ Bd

harry-eight-legs *n* DADDY-LONG-LEGS IV.8.10. aɾɪ-aɪtɫɪgz Co

harry-hog *n* a WEAKLING piglet III.8.4. æɹɪ-ɒg Hrt

harry-long-legs *n* DADDY-LONG-LEGS IV.8.10. æɹɪlɒŋlɛgz Sa He, æɹɪlʊŋlɛgz He Wo Gl, aɹɪlaŋɫɛgz Gl, aɹɪlaŋglɛgz St, aɾɪlɒŋlɛgz So, aɾɪɫɒŋɫɛgz So, aɹɪlɒŋlɛgz Ch Db Sa Wa Gl Lei, aɹɪlɒŋglɛgz Sa St, aɾɪlɒŋlɛgz O, aɾɪɫʌŋɫɛgz Co D, aɹɪlʊŋlɛgz Ch Db St Wo Wa Nth, aɹɪlʊŋglɛgz Sa Wo, ɒɹɪlʊŋlɛgz He

harry-pig *n* a WEAKLING piglet III.8.4. æɹɪpɪg Ess, aɹɪpɪg Bd Hrt

harry-wiggles *npl* EARWIGS IV.8.11. ɛɹɪwɪgɫz Sf, *sg* aɹɪwɪgl L, aɹɪwɪgɫz C, aɹəwɪgɫz Nth

harry-wigs *npl* EARWIGS IV.8.11. ɛɹɪwɪgz Sa, ɛɹɪwɪgz Sa*[old]* He Wo Wa Gl O Hu Sf Bk K, *no -s* ɛɹɪwɪg He, jɛɹɪwɪgz Wo, ɛɾɪwɪgz O, ɛəɹɪwɪgz Wo*[old]* Lei, ɛəᴶɹɪwɪgz Brk, æɹɪwɪgz O Hu, *sg* æɹɪwɪg Sf, aɹɪwɪgz Bk Hrt, *sg* aɹɪwɪg Nth C Bd, jaɾɪwɪgz W *[not a WMBM headword]*

harvest *1. n* *When your fields have done well, you say: We've had a good ....* II.6.1. Eng. ⇒ **crop, yield**
2. n **harvest festival, harvest-home** a local FESTIVAL or holiday VII.4.11. **harvest festival** aːvɪs fɛstɪvəl Mon; **harvest-home** haᵗːvɪshoːʊm So

harvest-carrying *v-ing* CARTING corn from the field II.6.6. aᴶːvɪskəɹɪ-ɪn K

harvest-carting *v-ing* CARTING corn from the field. aːɹvɪskaᴶːtɪn Brk, aᵗːɾvɪskaᵗːtʃɪn Sx, aːɾvɪskaːəᵗɾ̩tɪn Sr, *vbln* aᵗːvɪskaᵗːt W

harvest-men *n* DADDY-LONG-LEGS IV.8.10. *sg* hæːvəstmən C, hæːvəsmən Sf, haːvɪstmən Ess*[old]*, *sg* haːvəstmæn Nf, haːvəstmən Nf, aːvəstmən Nf *[size and referent uncertain]*

harvest-mouse *n* a SHREW-MOUSE IV.5.2. *pl* aᵗːvɪsmæyzɪz D

harvest-rails *npl* CART-LADDERS I.10.5. hæˑvɪsreɪls Man

harvest-shrew *n* a SHREW-MOUSE IV.5.2. aᵗːvɪstɹɑː Gl, aᵗːvɪssɹɒʊ Gl, aᵗːvɪstɹɔː Gl, haᵗːvɪstɹ̩ɔː W*[large]*, aᵗːvɪstɹ̩ɔː W

harvest-time *n* AUTUMN VII.3.7. aːvɪsttaɪm Y

hash *n* BROTH V.7.20(a). aɪʃ Db *[queried WMBM]*

hashy* *adj* showery, ⇐ DULL VII.6.10. haʃɪ Nb

hask *adj* DRY, referring to a summer VII.6.19. ask St

hasking *v-ing* COUGHING VI.8.2. hæːskɪn So

hasky *adj* DRY, referring to a summer VII.6.19. askɪ St

haslet *n* the PLUCK of a slaughtered animal III.11.6. aːsɫɪt Ha

hasp *n* the LATCH of a door V.1.9. hæps So Ha, æps So, haps So W Co Do, aps So W Co D Ha; **hasp and staple** *n* asp ən steːpl Ch *[last marked u.r. WMBM]*

hasping-post *n* the SHUTTING-POST of a gate IV.3.4. æpsənpuːəs Co, apsɪnpɔːs D, apsənənpɔːs D

hasp-post *n* the SHUTTING-POST of a gate IV.3.4. hapspoːst W, apspɔːs D

hassock *n* a TUSSOCK of grass II.2.9. hæsɪk C, asɪk L, *pl* asɪks Nth Bk, asɒk Lei, asʊk Wa, asək Db O L Lei R Bk, *pl* asəks Nt, -s asəks Bd, azək L

hasty-pudding *n* thick PORRIDGE V.7.1. eːstɪpʊdɪn Db

hat-bat *n* a BAT IV.7.7. atbat Db Sa St Nt

hatch *1. vi* to CHIP, referring to an egg that is about to hatch IV.6.10. ɛtʃ Y, -*ing* ɛtʃɪn Sr Sx, hætʃ W, -*ing* hætʃɪn Ha, hatʃ Du Y, atʃ La Y L So, *prppl* atʃɪn D, haːtʃ So
2. n a BROOD of chickens IV.6.12. ɛtʃ Sx, hætʃ Nf MxL, ætʃ Sa He Wo Mon Gl Sr, hatʃ O, atʃ La Db Sa St*[old x1]* He Wo Wa Mon Lei R
3. n the LATCH of a door V.1.9. hætʃ Ess

hatch-bridge *n* a BRIDGE IV.1.2. ætʃbɹɪdʒ Sr

hatchel *n* stale URINE used for cleaning blankets VI.8.8. aːtʃɪl Db *[queried WMBM]*

hatching *n* a BROOD of chickens IV.6.12. ɛtʃɪn Ess, ætʃɪn Wa, hatʃɪn Cu, atʃɪn Y Ch St Nt Lei R Nth Bk, hatʃn Nb, hatʃən Nb Du

hatch off *viphr* to CHIP, referring to an egg that is about to hatch IV.6.10. hætʃ ɔˑf Nf

hatch out *viphr* to CHIP, referring to an egg that is about to hatch IV.6.10. -*ing* hɛtʃɪn ɛʊt K, ɛtʃ ɛʊt Ess, -*ing* ɛtʃɪn ɛʊt Sr, -*ing* ɛtʃɪn œʏt D, ætʃ aʊt MxL, -*ing* ætʃɪn ʌʊt Brk, -*ing* ætʃɪn əʊt Brk

hat-rack *n* the HIP-BONE of a cow III.2.1. *pl* ætɹæks Ess*[facetious]*

hat-skirts *n* the BRIM of a hat VI.14.3. atskəˡts L

hattock *n* a stook of eight sheaves of corn, ⇐ STOOKING II.6.5. atək La Y, *pl* atəks Ch

hattocking *v-ing* STOOKING II.6.5. atəkɪn La

haugh *n* a flat field, ⇐ LOW-LYING LAND IV.1.7. haf Cu

haugh-land *n* LOW-LYING LAND IV.1.7. hafland Nb

haugh(s) *n* LOW-LYING LAND IV.1.7.
no -s: hæˑf Nb, haf Nb Du, hɔʊf Nb
-s: hafs Nb *[-s form not a NBM headword]*

hauling *1.1. v-ing* CARTING *DUNG* II.1.4. hɔːlɪn So, hɔːɫɪn So
1.2. vt-ing **hauling dung**, **hauling muck** carting dung. **hauling dung** hɔːlɪn dʌn So, ɔːlɪn dʌn So, hɔːɫɪn dʌn So, ɔːɫɪn dʌn So D Do; **hauling muck** aːɫɪn mʌk He, *no -ing* ɔːl mʊk Db
2.1. v-ing CARTING corn from the field II.6.6. aːɫɪn He Mon*[old x1]* Gl, hɔːlɪn So, ɔːlɪn Gl, hɔːɫɪn W Do, ɔːɫɪn He So W Ha
2.2. vt-ing carting corn. ɔːɫɪn Do

hauling out *vtphr-ing* **hauling out dung** CARTING *DUNG* II.1.4. ɔːɫən əʊt dʌn Do

haulm *n* STRAW II.8.2. hɑːm Brk

haulm(s) *1. n* POTATO-HAULMS II.4.4.
no -s: hɛlm So, hɛɫm Ess Do, ɛɫm Do, hɛləm Cu, ɛːm Sx, ɛɪm K, aɫm O Ha, ham W, am Gl Ha, haːm Bk Ess*[old]*, aːɫm Brk Sx, aːʊm Brk, hɑːm Ess Brk, aːm Mon Sr K, aᵗːɹ̩m Sr Sx, hɒləm Du, hɔːɫm So, ɔːɫm K Ha, hɔːm Ess K, ɔːm He Wo, əɫm So, əɫəm So
-s: eɪmz Bk, ɛɫmz Gl O Bk So, ɛləmz Sa, hɛmz Nf, ɛʊmz Y, ɛɪmz Brk, æɫmz So K, aləmz Nt*[modern]* Bk, hamz W, amz Gl W Ha, haːmz Sf, aːmz Wo O W, aᵗːmz Gl, aʊmz O, hɑːmz Sr, ɑːmz Wo Hrt Sx, aᵗːmz Wo, ɒɫmz Bd D, hɒləmz Nb, ɒmz He Wo Mon Gl, ɒʊmz La, ɔːɫmz D, hɔːmz Nf Ess, ɔːmz La Y*[modern]* Ch Db Sa St He Wa Mon L, ɔᵗːmz Sa, hɔʊɫm MxL*[polite]*, ɔʊmz Ha, oʊmz St, ʊmz Sa, ɪuːmz L, juːmz St
2. n barley AWNS II.5.3.
no -s: hɛlm So
-s: hæːmz Nf, haːmz Nf, ɛɫmz Bd, ɔːmz Wa Nth, jɔːmz Lei
[not a WMBM headword]

haulms *n* STUBBLE remaining in a cornfield after harvesting II.1.2. ɛɫmz Brk, heːɫmz Brk, ɛʊɫmz Brk

haunch *n* the human HIP-BONE VI.9.1. hɛnʃ Du

haunch-bone *1. n* the HIP-BONE of a cow III.2.1. ɒntʃbɒʊn Wo
2. n the human HIP-BONE VI.9.1. hɪnʃbɪən Nb*[old]* Cu, hɪnʃbøːn Nb*[old]*, henʃbeːn Nb, ʊnʃbɪan Cu

hauve *1. imp* **hauve**, **hauve again**, **hauve back**, **hauve come again**, **hauve come here**, **hauve left**, **hauve up a bit**, **hauve way**, **hauve woot** the command TURN LEFT!, given to plough-horses II.3.5(a). **hauve** aːf Y, aːv Y, aː Y, hɔːf Du, hɔː Y, ɔːv Y Db Nt L; **hauve come here** aːv kʊm ɪə Y, aː kʊm ɪə La, aː kʊm ɪəˡ La, ɔːv kʊm ɪə Db; **hauve left** ɔːv lɛft L; **hauve up a bit** 'ɔːv ʊp ə bɪt Lei; **hauve again** 'aːv əgɪn R, 'ɔːv əgɪn Lei, ɔːv əgen Nt; **hauve back** ɔːv bak Y; **hauve come again** ɔː

kʊm əgɛn La; **hauve come here** aːv kʊm ɪə Y, aː kʊm ɪə La, aː kʊm ɪəˡ La, ɔːv kʊm ɪə Db; **hauve left** ɔːv lɛft L; **hauve up a bit** 'ɔːv ʊp ə bɪt Lei; **hauve way** aːf weɪ Du; **hauve woot** 'ɑː wʊt MxL

2. *imp* **hauve, hauve right, hauve way, hauve wee, hauve woa** the command TURN RIGHT!, given to plough-horses II.3.5(b). **hauve** haːv Y, aːv Y; **hauve right** ɔːv ɹaɪt L; **hauve way** ɔː weː Y*[non-farming informant]*; **hauve wee** aː wiː Y; **hauve woa** aː woː Y

havels *n* barley AWNS II.5.3. hɛːbɫz Nf, hɛɪvəɫz Sf Ess, ɛɪvɫz Sf, ɛɪbʊz Ess

have over *vtphr* to OVERTURN, referring to the load on a cart I.11.5. *pt* æd ... ɒʊvəˡ Sx

haver *n* OATS II.5.1. avə Cu We, avəɹ Cu, havə Cu We

haver-bread* *n* oat-cakes, ⇐ GIRDLE V.7.4(b). avəbɹɪəd Y

havermeal-crowdy *n* PORRIDGE V.7.1. avəmˡiːlkɹaʊdɪ We

have to *vaux-2sg* you MUST do it IX.4.11. hɛf tʊuː Ess, hɛv tuː Ess, hɛf tə Ess, hɛv tə Nb Cu Ess, ɛv tə Y L, hɛ tə Du, ɛ tə Y L, æf tuː Brk, hæv tʉˑ Nf, hæf tə Nf, æf tə Sx, hæv tə Ess, hæʔ ə Nf*[old x1]*, av tə L Lei

haw *imp* **haw up** the command TURN LEFT!, given to plough-horses II.3.5(a). 'ɔː ˌwʊp Ch

haw-berries *npl* HAWS IV.11.6. hɔːbəɹiːz So, ɔːbəɹɪz L

hawching *v-ing* GOSSIPING VIII.3.5(a). atʃɪn St

hawking *v-ing* COUGHING VI.8.2. *v* ɑːk St, hɔːkɪn W*[short cough]* Co

hawm *v* to BUTT III.2.10. ɔːm Nth

hawm about *vphr* to BUTT III.2.10. *-ing* ɔːmɪn əbaʊt L

haws(es) *npl* You know that bush which has white flowers in May and red berries in autumn and winter. What do you call its berries? IV.11.6.
no -es: hæːz Nb, haːz Nb Cu Du, aːz Bk Hrt Sr, ɑːz Gl, ɒɪz K, hɔːs Nb Man, hɔːz Nf Ess So K, ɔːz Cu La Y Ch Db Sa St He Wa Gl O Nt L Lei R Nth Hu C Bk Bd Hrt So W K Sx, ɒˡːz Sa Wa, hɔːəz Nb Nf, hɔːᵊz Ess, ɔːᵊz L Lei Nth Hu Ess, hɔːᵊˡz So, ɔːᵁz So, hʌʊz Sf, ʊəz L
-es: hæːzɪz Sf, aːzɪz Gl O, hɔːzɪz Nf Sf Ess, hɔːzəz Sf, ɔːzɪz Bk K, hɔɪzɪz Nf.

⇒ **aglons, ahzygahzies, bottle-haws, butter-haws, butter-herbs, canker- berries, cat-haigs, cat-haws, catty-haws, eagles, eggle-berries, eggles, eglets, eglons, haaves, habes, hagags, haggles, haghaws(es), haglets, haglons, hags, haig-berries, haigins, haigs, halls, haw-berries, hawthornberries, hay-heggs, hays,** *heagles* ⇒ **eagles, hedge-berries, herbs, higs, hip- haws, hips, hipsy-haws, hobs, hogasses, hoggans, hog-hazels, may-berries, nick-and-haws, pig-berries, pighales, pig-haws, pig-shells, quick-berries, skegs,** **thorn-berries;** ⇒ also **bread- and-cheese-bush, haig-tree, hawsy wine**

hawsy wine *n* hawthorn wine, ⇐ HAWS IV.11.6. hɔːzɪ wɔɪn Ess

hawthorn-berries *npl* HAWS IV.11.6. aθənbɛɹɪz Sa St, ɑːðɑːnbɛɹɪz Wo, aːθʊnbɛɹɪz Wo, aːθənbɛɹɪz He Mon, aːðənbɛɹɪz Wo Mon, aːðəˡŋbɛɹɪz He, aˡːθəˡŋbɛɹɪz He, ɒθənbɛɹɪz Wo, hɔˑθɔənbɛɹɪz Nf, ɔːθɔːnbɛɹɪz Ch St Wa Mon Nt, ɔːθɔˡːŋbɛɹɪz St, ɔːθɔˡːŋbəɹiːz So, ɔːθənbɛɹɪz Sa, ɔːθənbɛɹɪz Sa He, ɔːθəˡŋbɛɹɪz He, ɔːðəˡːŋbɛɹɪz Gl, ɔˡːθənbɛɹɪz Sa, ɔˡːθənbɛɹɪz Sa, ɔˡːθəˡŋbɛɹɪz Sa

hawthorn dike *n* a HEDGE IV.2.1(a). haːθɔᴮːn dɛɪk Nb

hawthorn fence *n* a HEDGE IV.2.1(a). haːθɔᴮːn fɛns Nb

hay 1. *n* And [what do cows feed on] in the cow-house? II.9.1(b) Eng. ⇒ **long hay**
2. *vt* to FEED cattle III.3.1. haɪ W *[presumably with hay only; queried u.r. SBM]*

hay-band(s) *n* ROPES used to fasten thatch on a stack II.7.7(b2).
no -s: eːbænd Mon*[obsolete x1]*, eːband Sa*[straw x1]*, æɪbænd Gl, æɪbæn He Mon Gl
pl eːbænz Sa
-s: eɪbanz Bk, eːɪbændz Wo, hɛɪbɛndz Nf*[straw]*, ɛɪbandz L, ɛɪbanz Lei Bk, ɛˑəbandz Y L
[hay-band marked u.r. WMBM as mass n]

hay-band-maker *n* a ROPE-TWISTER II.7.8. æɪbænmeːˡkəˡ He

hay-band-twister *n* a ROPE-TWISTER II.7.8. eːɪbæntwɪstəˡ Wo

haybarn *n* a BARN used for storing corn I.1.11. *pl* ɛɪbaːnz St

hay-barton *n* the STACKYARD of a farm I.1.4. eɪbaˡːʈʔn̩ So

hay-bay 1. *n* the GANGWAY in a cow-house I.3.7. ɛɪbeɪ Gl
2. *n* the gangway of a cow-house, used to store hay, ⇐ HAY-LOFT I.3.18. ɛɪbeɪ Gl

hay-bing 1. *n* the GANGWAY in a cow-house I.3.7. iːbɪŋ Db St
2. *n* the gangway of a cow-house, used to store hay, ⇐ HAY-LOFT I.3.18. iːbɪŋ Db St
3. *n* a HAY-RACK in a stable I.4.1. hɛˑɪbɪŋ Nf

hay-bogey *n* a WAGON without sides I.9.2. heːbʊgɪ Nb *[marked u.r. NBM]*

hay-bond(s) *n* ROPES used to fasten thatch on a stack II.7.7(b2).
sg ɛɪbɒnd Wo*[straw]*, aɪbɒnd W
no -s: ɛɪbʊn Wo, æɪbɒnd He, æɪbɒn He
-s: 'ɛɪ 'bɒndz Wo, ɛɪbɒnz Gl, æɪbɒnz He Gl
[hay-bond not a WMBM headword: taken as hay-band and marked u.r. as mass n]

hay-boose *n* a HAY-LOFT over a cow-house I.3.18. heːbɪuːs Du, heːbɪəs Nb

hay-cart *n* a FARMCART I.9.3. eːkaːt Y, eəkaːt Y, ɛɪkaːt Y, ɛɪkɑːɾt Brk, eəkaːt Y, hæɪkaːt Ess, aɪkaːt Ess

hay-chamber *n* a HAY-LOFT over a cow-house I.3.18. hæiˑtʃæɪmbə Nf

hay-cratch *n* a HAY-RACK in a stable I.4.1. eːkɹatʃ Ch

hay-cutter *n* a HAY-KNIFE II.9.14(a). eɪkʌʔə Bd, ɛɪkʌtəˑ Sr, hɛɪkʌtəˑ K, æɪkʌtəˡ Sx

hay-field *n* a MEADOW II.9.2. heːfiˑld Nb, eːfeːld Ch*[sometimes ploughed]*, eːfiːl Sa*[never ploughed]*, -s eːfiːɫz Ch, *pl* eːfᵁilz Ch, eɪfiːᵊɫd Bd, eɪfɪəɫd O, hɛifiːld Nf*[sometimes ploughed]*, ɛɪfiːld L Lei Hu, ɛɪfiːɫd Wa*[never ploughed, also for grazing]*, ɛɪfiːᵊɫd Wa Bk*[never ploughed]* Bd*[never ploughed]*, ɛɪfiːɫ Co, ɛˑəfiːld L, hæɪfiːld Nf, hæɪfiːl Nf, hæɪfɪːɫ Nf, æɪfɪʊɫ K Sx

hay-flake *n* a CART-FRAME I.10.6. eːfleːk La

hay-flakes *npl* CART-LADDERS I.10.5. *sg* ɛəfleɪk Y

hay-fork *n* *What do you call a fork [farming implement] with two prongs? [Ascertain its use according to length of shaft.]* I.7.11.

1. unspecified length. iːfɔːk Db, hɪəfɔːk Du, hɪəfɔᴮːk Du, eːfɑːk Y, heːfɒᴮːk Nb, heːfɒɹk Y, eːfɒɹk Y, heːfɔːk Du, eːfɔːk Y Db, heːfɔˑrk Cu, heːfɔᴮːk Nb Du, eːfɔˡːk La, heːfɔˡːk O, heːfɔˑək We, eːfəːk Y, heːfəɹk Du, heɪfaˑk Man, heɪfɔːk Bk, ɛɪfɔːk Bk Bd, eəfœːk Du, eəfɒrk Y, eəfɔːk Cu Y, heəfɔᴮːk Nb, eˑəfɔˡːk La, heːfɒrk Y, ɛːfɒɹk Y, heːfɔːk We, ɛːfɔːk Y, ɛɪfaˡːɾk Brk, ɛɪvaˡːk W, ɛɪfɑːk Wo, hɛɪfɔːk Ess, ɛɪfɔːk Y St Wa L Lei Nth Bk K, ɛɪfɔˡːk Wa, ɛɪvɔˡːk Gl, ɛɪvɔˡːk D, ɛɪfʊək L, ɛəfɒɹk Y, eəfɔɹk Y, ɛˑəfɔːk Y L, ɛˑəfɔˡːk L, ɛˑəfəˡːk L, hæɪfɔːk Nf Sf Ess Sr, æɪfɔːk Hu, haɪvaˡːk So, aɪfaˡːk Ha

2. long shaft. eːfɔːk La, eːfɔˡːk La, eːfɔˡːk O, heːfɔːk Cu

3. short shaft. *pl* ˡiːfɔːᵊks Lei, eːfaˡːk Wa, eːfɔːk Y Nt, eːfɔəˡk La, eɪfɒˡk Ha, eɪfɔˡːk Bk, eɪfɔːᵊk Bk Bd Hrt, ɛɪfɒɾk O, ɛɪfɔːk Wa L Lei Nth C Bk Bd Hrt Ess, ɛɪfɔəˡk Brk, hæɪfɔːk Sf K, æɪfɔːᵊk Ess, haɪfɔːk MxL, aɪfɔːk Ess

4. long, medium, or short shaft. æɪfɔːk St

⇒ **bedding-fork, big-fork, cobbing-fork, empting-fork, five-foot prong, forking-off-fork, forking-on-fork, full-pitch, full-pitch-prong, gib-fork, great-pitch, half-pitch, half-pitcher, half-pitching-pick, half-pitch-prong, hand-fork, hand-prong, haymaking-fork, hay-peek, hay-pick, hay-pikel, hay-pitching-pick, hay-prong, little-fork, little hay-fork, little-prong, loading-fork, loading-pike, long-fork, long-handled-prong, mowing-fork, mule, mule-fork, nine-mealer, nine-point-fork, peek, pick, pick-fork, picking-fork, pike, pike-fork, pikel, pitcher, pitch-fork, pitching-fork, pitching-pick, pitching-pike, pitching-pikel, pitching-prong, pitch-prong, prong, putting-in-pikel, putting-off-pikel, reacher, reaching-fork, reaching-pikel, rick-fork, rick-prong,** *ruching-pikel* ⇒ **rucking-pikel, rucking-pikel, sheaf-fork, sheppeck, short-fork, small pitch-fork, stacking-fork, stover-fork, straw-fork, strawing-fork, tedding-fork, three-quarter, three-quarter-fork, two-grain, two-grained-fork, two-grain-fork, two-grain-prong, two-spean-prong, two-sprong-peek, two-tined-fork, two-tine-fork, two-tine-short-fork, underhanded-prong, unloading-fork;** ⇒ also **breaking-out-fork, longhandled-spud, long tom, two-spean-spud**

use of implement, irrespective of term:

a. long shaft. pitching Db Sa St He Wo Mon Nf Ess Sr Co; moving straw St; 'for corn' Nf

b. medium length shaft. haymaking St; unloading St

c. short shaft. loading Sa St He Wo Nf Ess; turning hay St Wo Mon Sr; making hay-cocks Db St Wo; stacking Nf Sr; unloading Nf; feeding cattle St

[reason for designating long or short shaft often unclear in BM headword lists: in such cases length of shaft not recorded]

hay-frames *npl* CART-LADDERS I.10.5. heːfʁeːmz Nb

hay-grass *n* a MEADOW II.9.2. eːgɹɛs Ch

hay-heggs *npl* HAWS IV.11.6. eːɛgz La

hay-hole *1. n* the GANGWAY in a cow-house I.3.7. ɛɪ-ʌʊl Bk*[not in older buildings]*

2. n a HAY-LOFT over a cow-house I.3.18. heːhoːl Nb, ɛɪ-ʌʊɫ Bk

3. n a place adjoining a cow-house, used to store hay. heəhøːl Nb

hay-house *1. n* the GANGWAY in a cow-house I.3.7. ɛɪ-əs Bk

2. n the place where hay is stored on a farm, often at one end of a cow-house, ⇐ HAY-LOFT I.3.18. heːhuːs Nb Du, heː-əʊs Brk, eː-æʊs Co, heɪ-æys So, ɛɪ-æʊs So, ɛɪ-oʊs Brk, ɛɪ-əs Bk, ɛɪ-əs Bk, hæɪhɛʊs Nf, hæɪ-ɛʊs Nf, aɪ-æys Co, aɪ-æʊs Do, aɪ-əʊs Do

hay-knife *1. n* *What do you cut hay from the stack with?* II.9.14(a). Eng exc. Hu C Nf Sf. ⇒ **cut-knife, cutting-knife, eave-knife, hay-cutter, knife, mow-cutter, spade-knife**

2. n a HAY-SPADE II.9.14(b). eːnɑːf Y, ɛɪnɔɪf Sx, hɛɪnɔɪf Ess, æɪnɑɪf K, hæɪnɔɪf Ess

hay-ladders *npl* CART-LADDERS I.10.5. eɪɫadəˡːz̩ W, ɛɪlædəˡz K

hay-loft *1. n* *[Show a picture of an old-fashioned cow-house.] Where do you store your hay, if you have it inside?* I.3.18. iːlɒft Db, eːlɒft La, heːlɔft

Nb, heːɬɔːft W, eːɬɔːft Ha, eːlɔːf Sa, heɪlæf Man, heɪlɒf K, eɪlɔːft So, heɪlɔːf Man, eɪɬɔːf W, hɛɪlɒft Nf K, ɛɪlɒft St Sx, ɛɪlɒf Lei Brk, hɛɪlɒf K, heɪlɔːft Ess, ɛɪlɔːft Bd Sr K Sx, ɛɪɬɔːft Co, ɛɪlɔːf Sx, ɛɪɬɔːf W Co D, ɛəlɒft Y, ɛˈəlɔft L, hæɪlɒft Ess, æɪlɒft K, *pl* æɪlɒˈfs Brk, hæɪlɒft Nf, hæɪlɔːft Ess, æɪlɔːft K, aɪlɑːft Gl, haɪɬɔːft W, haɪlɔːf Do, haɪɬɔːf W, aɪlɔˈft K, aɪɬɔːf W Ha

2. *n* a hay-loft over a stable. heɪlɔːft O, hæɪlɔːft Ess. haɪlɔːft MxL

⇒ *balks* ⇒ baulks, barn, baulks, bay, bing, chaff-house, chamber, cow-tallet, dutch-barn, feeding-alley, feeding-passage, feed-shed, fodder-bing, fodder-house, *fodderum* ⇒ fotherum, fother-house, fotherum, gangway, granary, *hay-barn* ⇒ barn, hay-bay, hay-bing, hay-boose, hay-chamber, hay-hole, hay-house, hay-mow, hay-pen, hay-place, hay-shed, hay-stall, hovel, lathe, loft, loose-box, lote, mow, mow-stead, pen, range, roost, *shade* ⇒ shed, shed, skaffats, stall, standing, store-place, tallent, tallet, walk

hayly-gayly *n* a SEESAW VIII.7.2. eːlɪgeːlɪ Sa *[queried WMBM]*

haymaking-fork *n* a HAY-FORK I.7.11. haɪmakɪnvaˤːk So

hay-math *n* AFTERMATH, a second crop of grass II.9.17. ɪməθ Wo *[queried WMBM]*

hay-meadow *n* a MEADOW II.9.2. eːmɛdə Y, heɪmɛdə Ess, ɛɪmɛdə Gl*[sometimes ploughed]* L*[sometimes ploughed]*, æɪmɛdəˤ He*[never ploughed x1]*, aɪmɛdə Wo

hay-mow 1. *n* a HAY-LOFT over a cow-house I.3.18. eːmɪu Y

2. *n* the place in a barn where hay is kept. eːmʌʊ Y, eːmu La Y, ɛɪmʊf Y, ɛɪmʊx Y

3. *n* a HAYSTACK II.9.13. eːmɪu Y, eːməʊ Mon, heɪməu Mon

hay-peek* *n* a HAY-FORK I.7.11. heɪpiːk So, ɛɪpiːk Co

hay-pen *n* an empty stall in a cow-house, used to store hay, ⇐ HAY-LOFT I.3.18. ɛɪpɪn Sx

hay-pick 1. *n* a HAY-FORK I.7.11. ɛɪpɪk Gl D, heɪpɪk So, eɪpɪk So, haɪpɪk So Do, aɪpɪk Do

2. *n* a hay-fork with a long shaft. heɪpɪk So, eɪpɪk So, ɛɪpɪk D, aɪpɪk Do

3. *n* a hay-fork with a short shaft. heɪpɪk So, eɪpɪk So, aɪpɪk Do

hay-pikel *n* a HAY-FORK I.7.11. eːpaɪkɪl La, eːpaɪkɪl La

hay-pitching-pick *n* a HAY-FORK I.7.11. eɪpɪtʃɪnpɪk So

hay-place 1. *n* a HAY-LOFT over a cow-house I.3.18. ˡiːpleɪz Lei, ɛɪpleɪs Lei, ɛˈəplɛˈəs L

2. *n* an empty stall in a cow-house, used to store hay. eˈəplɛˈəs L

3. *n* a place close to or adjoining a cow-house, used to store hay. ɛɪpleɪs C

hay-pooks *npl* COCKS of hay II.9.12. ɛɪpuːks Co

hay-prong 1. *n* a HAY-FORK I.7.11. heːpɾɒŋ W, ɛɪpɾɛŋ D, heːpɾɒŋ W, ɛːpɾɒŋ W, ɛɪpɾɛŋ D, heɪpɹɒŋ Ess Ha, ɛɪpɹɒŋ Gl, æɪpɹɒŋ Gl, haɪpɾɒŋ W, aɪpɾɒŋ W Ha

2. *n* a hay-fork with a long shaft. ɛɪpɹɒŋ Sx, haɪpɾɒŋ Do

3. *n* a hay-fork with a short shaft. eːpɹɒŋ Brk, aɪpɾɒŋ Ha

hay-rack *n* *[Show a picture of a stable.]* *What do you call this, where you put the hay for the horse to eat?* I.4.1. iːɹak St, *-s* eːrɛks Brk, eːɹæk Mon, eːɾæk Co, eːɹak Y O L, *pl* eːɾaks D, heɪɹæˈk Man, heɪɾæːk So, heɪɾak So, ɛːɹak Y, ɛɪɹɛk Brk Sr K, hɛɪɹɛk Ess Sx, ɛɪɹæk Brk Sr Ha Sx, hɛɪɹæk Nf Sf Ess, *sg* ɛɪɹæks Brk, ɛɪɾæk Co D, ɛɪɹak St Wo Lei R Nth, hɛɪɹak C, ɛɪɾak O W Co D, ɛˈəɹak L, æɪɹɪk K, æɪɹɛk K Sx, hæɪɹɛk Nf Ess K, æɪɹæk Gl Hrt Brk, hæɪɹæk Nf Ess Sr, aɪɹæk Wo Ess MxL K, haɪɹæk Sf MxL, aɪɾæk Co Do, aɪɾak W Do Ha, haɪɾak W. ⇒ cratch, crib, hay-bing, hay-cratch, heck, horse-rack, manger, rack, scratch

hay-rails *npl* CART-LADDERS I.10.5. heːʁeːlz Nb

hay-rake *n* a ROPE-TWISTER II.7.8. heːʁɪəkʰ Nb, eːɹeːk Y

hay-raves *npl* CART-LADDERS I.10.5. eɪɾeːvɹ O

hay-rick *n* a HAYSTACK II.9.13. iːɹɪk St, eːɹɪk Mon, eɪɹɪk He Bk, *pl* eɪɹiːks Bd, *pl* heɪɾɪks So, eɪɾɪk O Ha, eɪɹiːk Bk, eɪɹiːks Hrt, eːɹɪk Wo, hɛɪɹɪk Sx, ɛɪɹɪk Wo Wa Gl Nth Bk Bd Brk Sr Ha, ɛɪɾɪk Co, hæɪɹɪk Nf Ess, æɪɹɪk He Wa Mon Gl Nth, æɪɹɛk He Wo, aɪɹɪk Wo Gl, *pl* aɪɾɪks W

hay-ropes *n* ROPES used to fasten thatch on a stack II.7.7(b2). *sg* ɛːɹɪəp Y

hay-rucks *npl* COCKS of hay II.9.12. ɛɪɹʊks St

hays *npl* HAWS IV.11.6. ɛɪz St

hay-shed *n* the place where hay is stored on a farm, ⇐ HAY-LOFT I.3.18. heɪʃɛd So, hɛɪʃɛd Wa Nth, ɛɪʃɛd Lei Bk, aɪʃɛd Do

hay-shocks *npl* COCKS of hay II.9.12. ɛɪʃɒks L

hay-spade *n* *What do you cut hay from the stack with?* II.9.14(b). hˡɪspeɪd Man, hɪəspɪəd Du, eːspɪad Y, heːspɪad Y, eːspɪəd Y, heːspɪəd Nb, eːspeːd La Y Ch Brk, heːspeːd Du, eːspead We La, eːspeəd Du Y, heɪspeɪd Man, heəspɪəd Du, eəspeəd La Y, heəspeəd Nb, ɛːspead We, heːspead Cu, heːspeːd We, ɛːspeəd Y, ɛəspɪad Y, ɛəspeəd Y. ⇒ cutter, cutting-knife, cutting-spade, hand sledge-knife, hay-knife, rick-knife, spade, spade-hay-knife, spade-knife, toss-cutter haystack *n* How do you store the hay outside for use over the winter? II.9.13. h^Iistæ^ək Man, iːstak Ch Db Lei, ɪəstak Du, heːstak Nb Y, eːstak La Y Ch Db Sa Nt, eː^əstak Du Y, heɪstæk Man, eɪstæk Hu, *pl* eɪstaks Bd, eː^Istak Sa, heˈəstak Du, heəstak Nb, eəstak Y, ɛːstak Cu Y, *pl* hɛɪstɛks Ess, ɛɪstɛk Sr K, *pl* hɛɪstɛəks Ess, heɪstæk Nf Sf Ess K, ɛɪstæk Nth Ess Sx, ɛɪstak Y St L Lei R Nth Bk, *pl* ɛɪstaks C Hrt, ɛəstak Y L, hæɪstɛk Ess, æɪstɛk K, hæɪstæk Nf Sf Ess, æɪstæk Hrt Sr K, *pl* æɪstæks Sx, hæɪstæk? Nf, æɪstak Nth, aɪstæk Ess K, *pl* aɪstæks MxL. ⇒ **hay-mow, hay-rick, mow, rick, ruck, stack**

hay-stall *n* a stall in a cow-house, used to store hay, ⇐ HAY-LOFT I.3.18. eːstɔːl Y

hay-truss *n* a CUTTING of hay II.9.15. haɪt̠ʌs Do

hay-tweezers *n* a ROPE-TWISTER II.7.8. aɪtwiːzə^tz̩ Wo

hay-twister *n* a ROPE-TWISTER II.7.8. eːtwɪstə Mon, eːtwɪstə^t Sa Mon, eːtwɪstə^td̩ Sa, eːɪtwɪstə^t Sa, ɛɪtwɪstə^t Wo Gl Nth, hæɪtwɪstə Ess, æɪtwɪstə He, æɪtwɪstə^t Wo Gl

hayty-bayty *n* a SEESAW VIII.7.2. eːdɪbeːdɪ Sa

hay up *vtphr* to feed horses in the stable at night, ⇐ FEEDING III.5.1. ɛɪ ... ʊp Nth

hay-walk *n* the GANGWAY in a cow-house I.3.7. ɛɪwɔːk Nth

haze *n* MIST VII.6.8. eːz Ch, heɪs Man, heɪz Man, heɪz K, ɛɪz K

hazel 1. *n* Do you know a bush that bears catkins, and then nuts later on? IV.10.8. ⇒ **cat-o'-nine-tails**, *catonine-tails* ⇒ **cat-o'-nine-tails, cob, filbert, halse, halse-bushes,** *hazel-bush,* **hazel-nut, hazel-nut-bush, hazel-nut-tree, hazel-stool,** *hazel-tree,* **hazel-wood, new-nut-tree, nitall, nitall-bush, nit-bush, nit-halse, nut, nut-bough, nut-bush, nuthall-bush, nut-halse, nut-hazel, nut-stab, nut-stems, nut-stool, nut-stub,** *nuttery-wood* ⇒ **nut-tree-wood, nut-tree, nut-tree-bush, nut-tree-wood, nut-wood, wood-nut, wood-nut-bush, wood-nut-tree**

2. *vt* to BEAT a boy on the buttocks VIII.8.10. ɛzəl Y

3. *vt* to beat somebody. ɛzl L

hazel-bands *n* ROPES used to fasten thatch on a stack II.7.7(b2). aslbandz La*[about 6 feet long, ends pushed into stack]*

hazel-nut *n* HAZEL IV.10.8. ɛzlnʊt L, heːɪzłnʌt Nf, hæɪzlnʌt Nf, hæɪzłnʌt Ess, azlnʊt Db

hazel-nut-bush *n* HAZEL IV.10.8. heːzɪlnʌtbʊʃ Nf

hazel-nut-tree *n* HAZEL IV.10.8. ɛzlnʊttʃɪ L

hazel-stool *n* HAZEL IV.10.8. eːzłstaʊəł W

hazel-wood *n* HAZEL IV.10.8. ɛɪzʊwʊd Ess Brk

hazely *adj* DULL, referring to the weather VII.6.10. aɪzłi Ha

hazled *adj* CHAPPED VI.7.2. azłd Wa

he *objpron* HIM IX.2.4. iː Ess Brk*[old]* D

head 1. *n* What do you call this [indicate the (human) head]? VI.1.1. Eng. ⇒ **chump, napper, noddle, scalp**

2. *n* the T-SHAPED PLOUGH-BEAM END of a horse-drawn plough I.8.5. hɪd K, ɪd Sx, hɛd Sr Sx, ɛd L Hu C Bd Hrt W Brk Sr Ha, heɪd Ess, jəd Gl

3. *vt* **head and tail, tail and head** to TOP AND TAIL swedes II.4.3. **head and tail** jəd ən tæɪl Gl; **tail and head** tæɪl n̩ ɛd K

4. *n* an EAR of a corn-plant II.5.2(b). iːd Cu Y, hiːd Nb Cu We, jɛd La Y Ch Db Sa St, jœːd Gl, ɪəd We La Y L, jəd Cu Gl, heɪd Du, ɛd Y Ch Db Sa St He Wo Mon Nt L Lei R Nth Sf Bk K Co, hɛd Y Lei Sf Ess Ha, ɛɪd La Co, *pl* ʌdz Bk

5. *n* an ear of a corn-plant, especially oats. *pl* hɛdz Man

6. *n* an ear of barley. ɛd Lei, *pl* ɛdz O

7. *n* an ear of a corn-plant when being threshed. ɪəd Y

8. *n* the SHUTTING-POST of a gate IV.3.4. ɪd Sr, ɛd St Sx

9.1. *vt* to LOP a tree IV.12.5. hɪd So

9.2. *v* to lop. ɛd Bd

10. *n* CREAM V.5.3. ɛɪd D

11. *vt* to REMOVE *STALKS* from currants V.7.24. -*ing* hɛdn Man

12. *n* the CORE of a boil VI.11.7. ɪˈəd Y, ɛd Sa, heɪd Ess

13. *n* **off his head** SILLY, describing a man VIII.9.3. ɔːf ɪz ɛd Wa

headache *n* When you don't feel too well here [point to the head], what do you say you've got? VI.1.6. Eng exc. Cu We. ⇒ *a* **bad head,** *a* **big fat head,** *(the)* **headwarch,** *(a/a bit/a terrible/the)* **headwark,** *(a)* **sick head,** *(a/the)* **skullache,** *(a)* **sore head**

head-and-bottoms *n* HEADLANDS in a ploughed field II.3.3. hɛdnbɒtəmz So

head and heels *adv* HEAD OVER HEELS IX.1.10. jɛd ən ɪɪlz Ch, jɛd ən ɪəlz Wa, hɛd ən ɪəłz MxL

head-and-tail 1. *vt* to TOP-AND-TAIL gooseberries V.7.23. ɪədnteːɪl Nt, ɛd n̩ teɪł So, jɛdənteːɪl Sa, ɛdnteːɪɫ Wo, ɛdnteɪl L, -*ing* ɛdənteɪlɪn L, ɛd n̩ teɪł Co, ɛd ən teɪł W Ha

2. *v* to top-and-tail gooseberries. jɛdəntiːɪl Db, hɛdnteɪł Man, ɛdnteːɪł Lei K, ɛdənteɪ^əł Nth, -*ing* ɛd n̩ teɪʊłɪn Sr, ɛdnteˈəl L, ɛ·d n̩ tæɪł K

3. *vt* to REMOVE *STALKS* from currants V.7.24. ɪədnteːl Nt

head-and-toe *vt* to TOP-AND-TAIL gooseberries V.7.23. ɪədntoː La

head-butt(s) *n* HEADLANDS in a ploughed field II.3.3.

no -*s*: adbʊt La

-*s*: ɪədbʊts La, adbʊts La Ch

head-chain *n* a TETHER for a cow I.3.4. ɛdtʃeɪn Ha

head-collar *1. n* a TETHERING-ROPE used to tie up a horse I.4.2. ɛdkɒlə St, jɛdkɒlə St, ɛdkɒɫəᵗ Brk [*queried ir.r. WMBM*]

2. n the COLLAR of the harness of a cart-horse I.5.3. ɪədkɔlə Y, ɛdkɒlə Y, ɛdkɒlɘɹ He

head-collar rope *n* a TETHERING-ROPE used to tie up a horse I.4.2. ɛdkɒlɘɹuːp Ch

head-gear *n* the T-SHAPED PLOUGH-BEAM END of a horse-drawn plough I.8.5. ɛdgɪəᵗː Co

head-grow *n* AFTERMATH, a second crop of grass II.9.17. ɛdgɹʏ̈: Sa, ɛdgɹoː Sa, ɛdgɹu: Ch

head-halter *n* a TETHERING-ROPE used to tie up a horse I.4.2. ɪdɔːɫtəᵗ Do, ɛdɔːtəᴵ Sr

heading *1. n* the CURB-STONE in a cow-house I.3.9. ɛdɪn St [*marked ir.r. WMBM*]

2. n HEADLANDS in a ploughed field II.3.3. ɛdɪnz So

3. n a CUTTING of hay II.9.15. ɛdɪn St

head-ladder *n* a front cart-ladder, ⇐ CART-LADDERS I.10.5. *pl* ɛd ... læɘdəᵗz̩ Brk, *pl* hɛˑd ... læɘdəᴵz Ha, *pl* hɛd ... ɫadəᵗːz̩ W Ha, ɛdɫadəᵗː W, *pl* ɛd ... ɫadəᵗːz̩ W Ha

headland(s) *n* *What do you call the strips of land left unploughed at the ends of a field but afterwards ploughed at right angles?* II.3.3. Eng exc. Cu Du We Co. ⇒ **baulks**, **ditch**, **edgeland(s)**, *foor-ends* ⇒ **foorings**, **foor-head(s)**, **foorings**, **fore-acre(s)**, **foths**, **furrow-lands**, **head-and-bottoms**, **head-butt(s)**, **headings**, **head-ridges**, **head-rigg(s)**, **heads**, **side-baulks**, **top-and-bottoms**, **voryer**

head-light *adj* GIDDY IX.1.11. ɛdɫaɪt Co

head-lines *npl* the REINS of a cart-horse I.5.5. hɛdɫəɪnz W

head of the gate *n* the HANGING-POST of a gate IV.3.3. hɪd ə ðə geˑɪt Nf

head over heels *adv In going backwards downhill, you might stumble and go over like this [indicate a somersault with your arms]. How?* IX.1.10. Eng exc. Du Gl W Brk D Do Sx. ⇒ **arse backwards**, **arse first**, **arse over appetite**, **arse over backwards**, **arse over end**, **arse over head**, **arse over head** *backwards*, **arse over heels**, **arse over hips**, **arse over shit**, **arse over tip**, **arse over** *your* **head**, **arsewards**, **back over**, **backward(s) over**, **backwards-road**, **backwards-road over**, **backwards-way first**, **backwards-way over**, **box-neck**, **box-necked**, **bullynecks over**, **coup** *over backwards*, **coup** *your creel(s)*, **end over end**, **end over heels**, **flop over**, **gambol** *right* **over**, **head and heels**, *head first*, **headlong**, **head over shoulders**, **head over tails**, *head over the heel*, **head over tip**, **head and heels**, **heels over head**, **kilt** *your creels*, **kitbolch**, **mountybank over**, **neck over nothing**, **neck over shit**, *over backwards*, **over head**, **over-noddles**, **over** *the* **head**, **over** *your* **head**, **pitch** *a* **somersault**, **pitch-falling**, **pitch-poll**, **pitch-poll** *over*, **roll over** *backwards*, **roly-poly**, **somersault**, **tail over end**, **tail over head**, **tip and tail**, **tipple** *a monkey-bank*, **tipple** *backwards*, **tipple** *over top-tail*, **tipple-stail**, **toppling over**, **topsy-turvy**, **top-tail**, **towpy-tails**, **towtil**, **tumble** *neck and heels*, **tumble** *the wild-cat*, **turn** *a* **somersault**, *turn a* **somerset**

head over shoulders *adv* HEAD OVER HEELS IX.1.10. hɛd ouvə ʃɛuldəz Nf

head over tails *adv* HEAD OVER HEELS IX.1.10. ɪəd aʊə teəlz Y

head over tip *adv* HEAD OVER HEELS IX.1.10. ɛd ɒʊəᴵ tɪp K, hɛd ʌuvə tɪp Ess

head-pole *n* a TETHERING-STAKE in a cow-house I.3.3. ɛɪdpoːɫ D

head-post *1. n* the HANGING-POST of a gate IV.3.3. ɪˑədpʊəst L

2. n the SHUTTING-POST of a gate IV.3.4. ɪədpɒst Y, ɛdpɔːs Co, hɛdpoʊst So, ɛdpoʊst Wo, ɛdpoˑəst Gl, ɛdpʊəst L, ɛdpuˑəs Nth, hɛdpʊst Sf

head-rail *n* the T-SHAPED PLOUGH-BEAM END of a horse-drawn plough I.8.5. hɪdɾaɪɫ So

head-ridges *n* HEADLANDS in a ploughed field II.3.3. hɪdɾʌdʒɪz So

head-rigg(s) *n* HEADLANDS in a ploughed field II.3.3.

no -*s*: hiːdɾɪg Cu, iːdrɪg Cu, hiːdʁɪg Nb Du, hiːdɹɪg Nb[*old*] Cu, heɪdɹɪg Du, ɛɪdɹɪg Y, ɪədɹɪg La Y

-*s*: hiːdʁɪgz Nb, hiːdɹɪgz Cu Du We, iːdɹɪgz Cu We, heːdɹɪgz Du, ɪədɹɪgz We La Y, jədɹɪgz Cu

heads *1. npl* the RIDGES between furrows in a ploughed field II.3.2. heᴵdz Ess, ɛˑᴵdz Ess

2. n HEADLANDS in a ploughed field II.3.3. hɛdz So

3. npl GATE-POSTS IV.3.2. ɪˑədz L

heads and heels *adv* HEAD OVER HEELS IX.1.10. ɛdz ən ɪʊz K

head-slip *n* a TETHERING-ROPE used to tie up a horse I.4.2. ɛdslɪp St [*queried ir.r. WMBM*]

head-stall *1. n* a TETHER for a cow I.3.4. hɛdstɔːl K, ɛdstɔːɫ Sr K

2. n a chain tether. hɛdstɫ Ess, ɛdstɔːɫ Brk

3. n a HALTER for a cow I.3.17. ɛdstɔːɫ W

4. n a TETHERING-ROPE used to tie up a horse I.4.2. ɪdstɔʊ Sx, ɛdstɒl Sa, ɛdstɔːl St Wo Mon O, hɛdstɔːɫ Do, ɛdstɔːɫ W Brk Ha Sx, ɛdstɔː O, hɛdstɔʊ Ha Sx, ɛdstɔʊ Sx, ɛdstəɫ O, jədstɫ O

headstall-chain *n* a chain used to tie up a horse, ⇐ TETHERING-ROPE I.4.2. ɛdstɔːɫtʃeɪn Lei

headstall-cord *n* a TETHERING-ROPE used to tie up a horse I.4.2. ɛkstɹəɫkɔːd Ess

headstall-halter *n* a TETHERING-ROPE used to tie up a horse I.4.2. ɛstəɫɔːɫtə Ess, ɛsˌtɾəɫɔːɫtə Ess

headstall-line *n* a TETHERING-ROPE used to tie up a horse I.4.2. hɛdstɬlɔɪn Ess

headstall-rein *n* a TETHERING-ROPE used to tie up a horse I.4.2. ɛdstɔːɬɹeɪn Bk, ɛdstɬɹeɪn Hrt, ɛdstəɬɹæɪn Hrt, ɛstəɬɹæɪn Ess, ɛstɹəɬɹæɪn Ess

headstall-rope *n* a TETHERING-ROPE used to tie up a horse I.4.2. hɛdstɬɹʌʊp Ess

head-stoop *n* the SHUTTING-POST of a gate IV.3.4. hˡiːstᵁuːp Cu

head-stump *n* the SHUTTING-POST of a gate IV.3.4. ɛdstʊmp Ch St, jɛdstʊmp Ch

head-tow *n* the T-SHAPED PLOUGH-BEAM END of a horse-drawn plough I.8.5. ɛdtɔː Co D, ɛtə Co, ɛɪdtɔː D, ɛɪdtoː D

head-walk *n* the GANGWAY in a cow-house I.3.7. hɛdwɔːk Man W

head-wang *n* the T-SHAPED PLOUGH-BEAM END of a horse-drawn plough I.8.5. ɛdwaŋ D, ɛɪdwæŋ D

headwarch *n* a HEADACHE VI.1.6. ɪədwæˡːtʃ La, jɛdwæˡːtʃ La*[old]*, jɛdwaːtʃ Db, jɛdwaˡːtʃ Db, jɛdwɜˡːɹtʃ La, ɛɪdwæˡːɹtʃ La, ɛɪdwaːtʃ La, ɛɪdwaˡːtʃ La *[not a NBM headword]*

headwark *n* a HEADACHE VI.1.6. hiːdwaːk Nb Cu Du We Y, iːdwaːk Cu Du, hiːdwaːɹk Du, hiːdwaᴳːk Nb, jɪdwaːk Y, ɪədwæˡːɹk La, ɪədwaːk Y, ɪədwaˡːk We La, heɪdwæːk Du, jɛdwaːk Y, jɛdwɜˡːɹk La, ɛɪdwæˡːɹk La

heaks *1. npl* long STACKS II.7.1. iːks Du
2. npl long STACKS with rounded ends II.7.1. hiːks Y*[corn]*, *sg* hiːk Du, iːks Y*[corn]*, *sg* heɪk Du

heak-stacks *npl* long STACKS II.7.1. *sg* iːkstak Nb

healing *n* the AFTERBIRTH that comes from a cow's uterus after a calf is born III.1.13. ɪəlɪn Y

healthy *1. adj* WELL, describing a healthy person VI.13.1(a). hɛlθɪ Nf, hɛɬfɪ Ess
2. adj ACTIVE, describing a child VIII.9.1. hɛɬθi So *[marked u.r. SBM]*

hean *n* the SHAFT of a spade I.7.7. eːn Ch

heap *1. n* **heap of (cow-)muck** a CLOT OF COW-DUNG II.1.6. ɪəp ə mʊk Y, jʊːp ə kæʊmʊˑk Wo
2. n a CLAMP in which potatoes are stored out of doors II.4.6. iːp Cu Ha, hiːp We, *pl* hiːps Nb, hiːpʰ Cu, ɪp Gl
3. n an ASH-MIDDEN V.1.14. iːp Sa, hɪiːp Ess, ɪiːp Sx

heaps *1. npl* COCKS of hay II.9.12. ɪˈəps L
2. npl ANT-HILLS IV.8.13. *sg* iːp Sa
3. n A LOT (of money) VII.8.7. hɪips Ha

heap up *vtphr-3sg* she [a tidy girl] will COLLECT her toys VIII.8.15. *3prsg* ɪiːps ... əp Sx

heart *n* the CORE of a boil VI.11.7. aᵗːt D

hearth *1. n* a HEARTHSTONE V.3.2. aɹθ He, haːθ Cu Du We Sf Ess, aːθ Cu Y St Wa O Nt L Lei Nth Hu Bk Hrt Ess, aːf Ess, haᴳːθ Nb Du, haᵗːθ So, aᵗːθ He

Wa Mon Gl O Co Ha, haːθ St Nf Ess Sr K, aːθ St MxL K, aːf Wo MxL, aˡːθ Brk, haᵗːθ Nf Sx, aᵗːɾθ Sx, haːəᵗɾθ Sx, aᵗːəᵗɾθ Sx, əᵗːθ Gl
2. n the place in which the ashes are collected beneath a domestic fire, ⇐ ASH-HOLE V.3.3. haːθ Nf, haᴳːθ Nb, haːθ Nf, aːθ Sr, haːəᵗɾθ Sx

hearth-flag *n* a HEARTHSTONE V.3.2. aːθflag We

hearth-pan *n* the container or place in which the ashes are collected beneath a domestic fire, ⇐ ASH-HOLE V.3.3. aᵗːɾθpæn Brk

hearth-slab *n* a HEARTHSTONE V.3.2. aːθslab L Nth

hearthstone *n What do you call this large flat thing [beneath and in front of a household fire]?* V.3.2. Eng exc. Hu Hrt MxL Sx. ⇒ **bricks, challack-flag, flag, flagstone, hearth, hearth-flag, hearth-slab, hearthstone-flag, slab, slab-stone**

hearthstone-flag *n* a HEARTHSTONE V.3.2. astnflag Y, aɹsənflag Y, aːθstən flag Ch, aːstənflɛg Y

hearty *adj* HUNGRY VI.13.9. aːtɪ Wo

heat *1. vi If hay is stacked too green, what do you say it does in the stack?* II.9.16. **take heat** teɪk hiːt Man, *-s* teɪks heɪt Man. ⇒ **catch fire, come too hot, fire, get fusty, get heated, get hot, get over-heated, get swelt, get the hot, get too hot, get warm, go fusty, go mouldy, heat up, mould, mowburn, overheat, roak, set fire, set light, steam, sweat, take heat;** ⇒ also **mowburnt**
2. n **in heat, in the heat, on heat** *When a cow is ready for service, you say she is ....* III.1.6. **in heat** ɪn ɪət La; **in the heat** ɪ t iːt Y; **on heat** ɒn iːt St Mon, ɒn hɪiːt Ess. ⇒ **a-beasting, a-beasty, a-bulling, amiss, at bull, beasting, bulling, bullward,** *come along* **bulling,** *comed on* **riding,** *coming a-*bulling, *coming in* bulling, *coming on* ⇒ **come on,** *coming on* bulling, *going to* bull, **gone wild, go to bull,** *in* bulling, **in kine,** *in* **season,** *in* **use,** *on a-*beasting, *on a-*bulling, *on at* bull, *on* brimming, *on* bull, *on* bulling, *on* riding, *on* stock, *on* store, **ready** *for mating,* **ready** *for the bull,* **ready** *to go to store,* **revelling, riding, roining, romping, rummaging,** *run to* beast, **stocking, storing, troublesome,** *wants the* bull, *want to go to the* beast, **wild**
3. n **on heat, at heat, on at heat, in heat** *When the sow is ready for service, you say she is ....* III.8.9. **on heat** ɒn hiːt Nf, ɒn iːt La St O K, ɒn jɛt So; **at heat** ət iːt L; **on at heat** ɒn əʔjɛʔ O; **in heat** ɪn iːt Sx. ⇒ **abrimming,** *ahogging,* **amiss, apigging,** *astoring,* **at heat,** *at* **use, boaring, boarward, brimming, brimward,** *coming on* hogging, *coming on storing* ⇒ *on* store, **hogging, hogward,** *in* brimming, *in* heat, *in* season, *in*

store, *in* use, on, *on* abrim, *on* abrimming, *on at* heat, *on at* hog, *on at* use, *on* hog, *on* hogging, *on* stock, *on* store, ranting, ready *for service*, ready *for the boar*, ready *for the hog*, ready *to go to store*, run *to store* ⇒ *on* store, *she wants the pig*, storing

4. *n What makes you sweat? Not the cold, but [the]* .... VI.13.6. Eng. ⇒ hot

heated *adj* get heated to HEAT, referring to a haystack II.9.16. *3prsg* gɛt hɪiːtɪd Ess

heath *n* BRACKEN IV.10.12. hɛθ Sf

heath-broom *1. n* a MUCK-BRUSH I.3.14. ɪiθbɹuːm Ha, hɪiːθbɹuːm Sx

2. *n* a BROOM used for sweeping outdoors V.9.10. hɪiːθbɹɒuːm Sr Sx, ɪiːθbɹuːm Sx, *pl* ɪiːθbɹɒuːmz Sx, *pl* ɪiːθbɹʊmz Sr

heat up *viphr* to HEAT, referring to a haystack II.9.16. *3prsg* iːts ʊp Ch, *3prsg* hɪiːts ʌp Ess, *3prsg* jɛts ʊp Y, *3prsg* ɪəts ʊp Y, *-ing* hɛɪtɪn ʊp Y

heave *1. n* all of a heave HEAVING *WITH MAGGOTS* IV.8.6. ɔːɫ əv ə heːv Do

2. *vi* to VOMIT, referring to a baby bringing up milk VI.13.14(b). *prppl* ɪəvɪn Y

3. *vi* to RETCH VI.13.15. hᴵiːv We, iːv Cu Sa Wo Wa Mon Nt, *-ing* iːvɪŋ St, *-ing* iːvɪn La Ch Db St He Gl L Nth Hu K, *-ing* ɪəvɪn La Y, eːv Sa Gl, *-inf* eːvɪn Ch Db, ɛɪv La Wa, *-ing* ɛɪvɪn Y Db*[old x1]* St; **heave at the heart** *-ing* ɛɪvɪn ət θ æːt La

heave about *vtphr* to TED hay II.9.11(a). eːv ... əbæyt D

heaved *adj* OVERTURNED, describing a sheep on its back unable to get up III.7.4. hiːvd So

heave on *vtphr* to LOAD dung into a cart II.1.5. *-ing* hiːvɪn ... ɒn Man

heaver *n* the FORKER on a wagon who unloads sheaves in a stackyard II.6.9. ɛɪvə La

heave up *vphr* to RETCH VI.13.15. *-ing* iːvɪn ʊp La

heaving *1. adj When the bluebottles get at the meat or fish, you'll soon find it ... WITH MAGGOTS.* IV.8.6. hiːvɪn Ess So W Ha, iːvɪn Sa So W Sr Co, hᴵiːvən Du, iːvən Co, ɪəvɪn Y, heːvɪn W Do, eːvɪn W Co, heːvən Do, ɛɪvɪn So, ɛɪvɪn La Bk D, ɛɪvən Co. ⇒ alive, alive *with eggs*, alive *with maddocks*, alive *with maggots*, all alive, *all* alive, *all* live *with maggots*, all *maggots*, all *of a* heave, ate up *with maggots*, blowed, blowed *with flies*, blowing *with maggots*, blown, blown *with flies*, blown *with maggots*, covered *with maggots*, crawling, crawling *with maggots*, crawling *with mawks*, crawling *with quicks*, creeping *with maggots*, creeping *with mawks*, fly-blowed, *fly-blowed and all* alive, fly-blown, fly-strucken, frawed out, *full of* maddocks, *full of* maggots, *full of* mawks, go bad, *going* maggoty, go maggoty, gone maggoty, *heave with maggots* ⇒ heaving, heaving *by maggots*, heaving up, heaving *with maggot*, heaving *with maggots*, heaving *with mawks*, jumping *with maddocks*, lifted *with mawks*, lifting *with maggots*, lifting *with mawks*, live, live *by maggots*, live *with maggots*, live *with mawks*, lousy, lousy *with mawks*, maggoted, *maggot in it*, maggots, maggoty, manky, mawked, mawky, moving *with maggots*, moving *with mawks*, on *the* lift, quick, quick-crawling *with mawks*, quicked, quick *with maggots*, quick *with mawks*, ready *to walk*, rotten *with mawks*, shugging *with mawks*, stricken *with maggots*, strucken, swarming *with maggots*, swarming *with mawks*, tainted, *that'll all turn to maggots*, walking *with maggots*, walking *with mawks*, working *with maggies*, working *with maggots*, working *with mawks*

2. *v-ing* PANTING VI.8.1. hiːvɪn Ess

3. *v-ing* THROWING a stone VIII.7.7. hiːvn Nb, eːvɪn Co, eːvən D, ɛɪvən Co

heaving off *vtphr-ing* UNLOADING sheaves from a wagon II.6.8. *no -ing* ɛɪv ... ɒf La

heaving up *adj* HEAVING *WITH MAGGOTS* IV.8.6. hɛɪvɪn ʌp So

heavy *1. adj* STEEP, describing a hill IV.1.11. hɛvɪ Du

2. *adj* SAD, describing bread or pastry that has not risen V.6.12. ɪvɪ Ess, hɛvɪ Mon Nf So Do, ɛvɪ Co D Do Ha, ɛviː Wo W, hɛvɪ Nb C Nf Sf Ess Sr K Ha Sx, ɛvɪ Y Sa He Wo Wa Mon Gl*[old x1]* Nth*[old]* Bk Bd Hrt K Do Ha, ɛbɪ Sa; **too heavy** tuː ɛvɪ Sx

3. *adj* DULL, referring to the weather VII.6.10. hɛvɪ W, ɛvɪ Sa Gl Bd

heavy-coat *n* an OVERCOAT VI.14.6. ɛvɪkʊət Y

heavy land *n* LOW-LYING LAND IV.1.7. hɛvɪ læn Ess *[noted as 'prob merely descriptive' in EMBM]*

heavy water *n* DEW VII.6.7. hɛvɪ watə We, ɛvɪ watə Cu, ɛvɪ watəɹ Y

heaze* *1. vi* to cough, describing the COUGHING of cows VI.8.2. hɪəs Nb

2. *n* the cough of a cow. hɪəs Nb

heck *1. n* a HAY-RACK in a stable I.4.1. ɛk La Y Db Nt L , hɛk Nb Cu Du, jɛk Cu

2. *n* the TAILBOARD of a cart I.10.2. hɛk We Y, ɛk We La Y

3. *n* an END-BOARD of a cart I.10.4. ɛk Y

4. *imp* heck, heck in the command TURN LEFT!, given to plough-horses II.3.5(a). **heck** hɛk Nb*[to Scottish horses x1]*; **heck in** hɛk ɪn Nb

5. *v* to bait a horse when resting from work, ⇐ BAITING III.5.2. hɛk Nb *[not clear from BM that r. in fact verbal]*

heck-board *1. n* the TAILBOARD of a cart I.10.2. hɛkbøːd Nb, hɛkbɔᴿːd Nb Du, hɛkbɔᴿːd Nb

2. n an END-BOARD of a cart I.10.4. hɛkbɔᴿːd Nb, ɛkbʊəd La, ɛkbʊəɹd La

3. n the FLAP at the front of old-fashioned trousers VI.14.16. hɛkbɔːd Nb, *pl* hɛkbɔᴿːdz Du *[queried facetious NBM]*

hecketing *v-ing* HICCUPING VI.8.4. ɛkətɪn O

heckling* *v-ing* COUGHING, of animals VI.8.2. ɛkɬɪn W

hecks *1. npl* CART-LADDERS I.10.5. hɛks Cu, ɛks Y L

2. n a CART-FRAME I.10.6. ɛks Y

hedge *1. n What do you separate two fields by?* IV.2.1(a). Eng exc. Cu

material/construction:

a. quickthorn: Y

b. whitethorn: O

c. hawthorn: K Sx

d. thorn: L W

e. elm: Nf

f. stakes and heather: Sr

g. stone: Co

h. stone wall filled with earth: Co

i. stone with small hedge on top: Co

j. grown on sods on a stone foundation: Man

k. often combined with a fence: Nf

⇒ **dike, fence, hawthorn dike, hawthorn fence, hedgerow, quick-fence, quick-hedge, quickthorn fence, riddle-hedge, stake-hedge, thorn-dike, thorn-fence, thorn-hedge;** ⇒ also **clatted hedge, hedge-peas**

2. v to TRIM hedges IV.2.3. *-ing* hɪdʒɪn Sr, hɛdʒ Sf, *-ing* hɛdʒɪn Nf Ess, ɛdʒ Hu, *-ing* ɛdʒɪn Bk, *-ing* ɛdʒn Ess

hedge-berries *npl* HAWS IV.11.6. ɛdʒbɛɹɪz Ch

hedge-bill *n* a HEDGING-BILL IV.2.5. ɪdʒbɪʊ Sx, ɛdʒbɪl Sa He, ɛdʒbɪɬ He Gl

hedge-brush *v* to TRIM hedges IV.2.3. *vbln* hɛdʒbɹʌʃɪn Ess, *-ing* ɛdʒbɹʌʃɪn He, ɛdʒbɹʊʃ Lei, *-ing* ɛdʒbɹʊʃɪn St Wo Wa

hedge-crop *v* to TRIM hedges IV.2.3. *-ing* ɛdʒkɹæpɪn Gl

hedge-cropper *n* a HEDGING-BILL IV.2.5. ɛdʒkɾɒpəˡ O

hedge-cut *v* to TRIM hedges IV.2.3. hɛdʒkʌtʔɪn Nf

hedgehog *n What do you call the animal with the prickly back that rolls itself up when frightened?* IV.5.5. Eng exc. Sa. ⇒ **furze-pig,** *hedge-boar* ⇒ **hedgy-boar, hedge-pig, hedgy-boar, prickly-backed-urchin, prickly-back-urchin, prickly-black-urchin, prickly-pig, prickly-urchin, prick-urchin, pricky-back-urchin, pricky-black-urchin, pricky-urchin, urchin**

hedge-hook *1. n* a HEDGING-BILL IV.2.5. hɛdʒʊk Nf, ɛdʒʊk La Gl Hrt, ɛdʒuːk La Y

2. n a BILLHOOK IV.2.6. ɛdʒʏk D, ɛdʒuːk L, ɛɪdʒʏk D

hedge-knife *n* a HEDGING-BILL IV.2.5. hɛdʒnɛɪf Nb, ɛdʒnaˑɪf L, ɛdʒnɑɪf Nt L Nth

hedge-peas* *npl* wild plums, ⇐ HEDGE IV.2.1(a). ɛdʒpiːz Sx

hedge-pig *n* a HEDGEHOG IV.5.5. ɛdʒpɪg O, *pl* ɛdʒpɪgz Brk

hedger *n* a HEDGING-BILL IV.2.5. ɛdʒə Y

hedge-rip* *n* a BILLHOOK IV.2.6. hɛɪdʒɹɪp Ess

hedgerow *n* a HEDGE IV.2.1(a). ɛdʒɹoʊ St Wa

hedge-slasher *n* a HEDGING-BILL IV.2.5. hɛdʒslæʃə Nf, ɛˑdʒslæʃəᴶ K, hɛdʒslaʃə Y, ɛdʒslaʃə Y Bk, ɛdʒslaʃəˡ K

hedge-splasher *n* a HEDGING-BILL IV.2.5. ɛdʒsplaʃəˡ Nth

hedge-sticks *n* KINDLING-*WOOD* V.4.2. ɛdʒstɪks Wa

hedge-stopper *n* a HEDGING-BILL IV.2.5. ɛdʒstɒpə R

hedge-top *v* to TRIM hedges IV.2.3. *-ing* ɛdʒtɔpən L

hedge-topper *n* a HEDGING-BILL IV.2.5. ɛdʒtɒpə Nth, ɛdʒtɔpɹ L

hedge-trimmer *n* a HEDGING-BILL IV.2.5. ɛdʒtɹɪməˡ O

hedge up *vtphr* to fill gaps in a hedge-bank or hedge with turfs, brushwood, or similar material, ⇐ to PLASH IV.2.4. adʒ ... ʌp Co

hedging-bill *1. n What do you call the long-handled implement you use [when plashing a hedge]?* IV.2.5. ɛdʒɪnbɪl La Y, ɛdʒɪnbɪɬ So. ⇒ **back-slasher, barging-hook, bill, bill-hook, billing-hook, bodging-hook, briar-hook, browse-hook, brushel, brush-hook, brushing-bill, brushing-hook, chopper, dike-slasher, drash-hook, drashing-bill, drashing-hook, dressing-hook, flasher, hedge-bill, hedge-cropper, hedge-hook, hedge-knife, hedger, hedge-slasher, hedge-splasher, hedge-stopper, hedge-topper, hedge-trimmer, hedging-hook, hedging-knife, hook, knife, lazy-back, long flasher, long-handle bill-hook, long-handled hook, long-handle hook, long-hook, long-shafted-hook, long slasher, long-staled brushing-hook, long-staled hook, quick-hook, rip, shredding-hook, sickle, slanching-hook, slash, slasher, slash-hook, slashing-hook, slash-knife, splasher,** *splash-hook* ⇒ **slash-hook, splashing-hook, splosher, staff-hook, swiver, tommy-hook, trimming-hook, trouncing-hook;** ⇒ also **gullantine**

2. n a BILLHOOK IV.2.6. ɛdʒɪnbɪl Y Db, adʒɪnbɪl Db

hedging-hook *1. n* a HEDGING-BILL IV.2.5. hɛdʒɪnhʊk So, ɛdʒɪnʊk Wo Gl Bd Ess MxL Ha, adʒɪnᵁuk Db

2. *n* a BILLHOOK IV.2.6. hɪdʒɪnhʊk Do, hɛdʒɪnhʊk Ess, ɛdʒɪnuːk La

hedging-knife *n* a HEDGING-BILL IV.2.5. ɛdʒɪnnɑɪf L Nth

hedging-mallet *n* a BILLHOOK IV.2.6. hɛdʒənmalət C

hedgy-boar* *n* a HEDGEHOG IV.5.5. ɛdʒɪbuəˤː D

heeder *1.* *n* a MALE LAMB III.6.2. iːdə L, iːðə R

2. *n* a WETHER III.6.8. *pl* iːdəz Nt

3. *n* a TOM-CAT, the male cat III.13.8. iːdəⁱ L

heeder-hog *n* a WETHER III.6.8. iːdəɹɒg Nt

heeder-lamb *n* a MALE LAMB III.6.2. iːdəɹlam L

heel *1.* *n* the SOLE of a horse-drawn plough I.8.9. hiːɫ Nf, iːɫ Gl, ɾiːʊ Sx

2. *n* the HANGING-POST of a gate IV.3.3. iːl St

heeld *n* the FAT round the kidneys of a pig III.12.7. hiːɫd D

heel-iron *1.* *n* the SOLE of a horse-drawn plough I.8.9. hiːlɑən Nf, hiilɑɪən Nf

2. *n* the GRASS-NAIL of a scythe II.9.9. hiːlɑːᵊn Nf

heel-plate *n* the SOLE of a horse-drawn plough I.8.9. ɪɫpleɪt K, iiɫpɫeɪt K, iːʊɫplæɪt K, ɪʊpleɪt K, ɾiˈʊpleɪt K

heel-post *n* the HANGING-POST of a gate IV.3.3. iːɫpoːs Ch, iːlpoːᵊst Sa, iːlpoʊst St O*[the 'bigger post']*

heel-sill *n* the CURB-STONE in a cow-house I.3.9. ɛɪlsɪl Db

heels over head *adv* HEAD OVER HEELS IX.1.10. iːlz oˈə jɛd Db

heel-stone(s) *n* the CURB-STONE in a cow-house I.3.9.
no -s: hiːlstɪən Nb, iːlstʊən La Y, iːlstən Y, ɪlstən Db, ɛɪlstən Db St
-s: iːlstoːᵁnz Db, iːlstʊənz La

heel-stump *n* the HANGING-POST of a gate IV.3.3. iːlstʊmp St

heel-tread *n* the CURB-STONE in a cow-house I.3.9. iːltɹɛd Ch

heel-tree *n* the CURB-STONE in a cow-house I.3.9. iːltɹiː Ch

heel-tree(s) *n* a SWINGLE-TREE of a horse-drawn plough harness
sg: hiˈltɹi Nf, iːltɹiː Nt L Lei, iːɫtɹiː Lei R, ɪltɹɪ L, ɾɫtɹɪ Nth
-s: iːltɹiːz Nt L, iːɫtɹiːz R, ɪltɹiːz L

heel up* *vtphr* to KNEAD dough V.6.4. *-ing* ɾiːlɪn … ʌp Brk *[queried ir.r. SBM]*

heelway *adv* BACKWARDS IX.1.7(a). hⁱiːlwɛ We*[old]*

heffering *v-ing* LAUGHING noisily VIII.8.7. hɛfəʁən Nb

heft *1.* *vt* to WEIGH something I.7.1. hɛˈft Ha

2. *vt* to lift something in order to estimate its weight I.7.1. hɛftʰ Mon

3.1. *vt* to STOCK a cow III.3.6. *ptppl* hɛftɪt Cu; **the**

bag is hefted ðə bagz ɛftɪd Y

3.2. *v* to stock. hɛft Nb Cu Du*[old x1]*

4. *n* the SHAFT of a scythe II.9.7. ɛft L

heifer *1.* *n* *What do you call the female [of cattle] when it stops being a calf?* III.1.5. eːfəˤ He Wo Mon Gl, *pl* eːfəˤɾz̩ Brk, eɪfəɹ He, eːɪfəˤ He Mon Gl, eəfəⁱ K, hɛfəᵍ Nb, hɛfə Nb Cu Du We Y Man Wa Nf Sf Ess MxL, ɛfə Cu We La Y Ch Db St Wa Mon Nt L Lei R Nth Hu C Bk Bd Hrt Ess Sr K, hɛfər Cu, ɛfɹ L, ɛfəɹ La Y St He, hɛfəⁱ K, ɛfəⁱ La Y Db St L Brk Sr K Ha, ɛfəɾ Db, hɛfəˤ Sr, ɛfəˤ Sa He Wo Wa O Nth Bk Brk K Ha Sx, hɛfəˤː So W Do Ha, ɛfəˤː Sa So W Co D Do Ha, jɛfəˤː So D, ɛɪfəˤ Gl, ɛɪfəˤː W, hɛəfə Man, hæfə Nf, *pl* æfəs Brk, æfəˤ Gl, æfəˤɾ Sx, æɪfəˤ He Gl, hafə Nf, jafəˤː Co D, aːfəˤ Mon, aɪfəˤ Sa Gl, hɛfə Nf

2. *n* a heifer 1 year old. ɛfəɹ Y, ɛfəˤː W

3. *n* a heifer 2 years old. ɛfə La, ɛfəɾ Y

4. *n* a heifer from 2 to 3 years old. ɛfəɹ Y

5. *n* a heifer 2½ to 3 years old. ɛfə L

6. *n* a heifer 3 years old. ɛfə St

7. *n* a heifer until 6 years old. ɛfə Y

8. *n* a heifer until it calves. ɛfə Y St, ɛfəɾ O

9. *n* a heifer when in calf. ɛfə Y, ɛfəⁱ La

⇒ **bud, calving-heifer, heifer-stirk, heifer-yearling, maiden heifer, quey, quey-calf, stirk, twinter,** *whye* ⇒ **quey,** *whye-calf* ⇒ **quey-calf, yearling, yearling heifer**

heifer-stirk *n* a HEIFER 9 to 12 months old III.1.5. ɛfəstək Y, ɛfəstəɹk Y

heifers'-yard *n* a STRAW-YARD for heifers I.1.9. ɛfəzjaːd Ess

heifer-yard *n* the STRAW-YARD of a farm I.1.9. hɛɪfəⁱjaːd Ess

heifer-yearling *n* a HEIFER 12 months old III.1.5. jɛfəˤːjəˤːɫɪn D

height *n* *Now we have discussed the man from head to foot. The distance from a man's head to his feet, you call his ….* VI.10.9. hiːt Nb Cu Du, iːt Cu Y, heɪt Man, hɛɪt Nb Cu We Sf, ɛɪt Cu We La Y Ch Db St Nt L, æːɪt D, hæɪt Du, æɪt Y, haɪt Nb Du So, aɪt Cu Du La Y Db Sa Nt L Lei Co D, aɪʔ Sa, ɑɪt Db Nt L Lei R Nth Sr K, ɑɪʔ Hrt, hɒɪt K, ɒɪt St Lei D Ha, hɔɪt Sf Ess, ɔɪt Nth Bk Ha, hʌɪt Nf, ʌɪt O, həɪt Du Mon Sx, əɪt Y Mon, hɛɪt Nf. ⇒ **heighth, length**

heighth *n* HEIGHT VI.10.9. eːⁱʔθ He, ɛtθ Wa O, ɛkθ Wa, hɛɪtθ Sf, ɛɪtθ D, æːɪtθ D, hæɪtθ Ess, æɪtθ Ch He So, æɪʔθ He, aɪtθ Sa St He Lei So Co D, aɪʔθ Sa Wo, haɪtθ Hu Ess, ɑɪtθ Db Wa L Lei Nth Hu C Bk Bd Hrt Ess MxL Sr K Sx, ɑɪθ K, hɒɪtθ So W, hɒɪtf Do, hɒɪθ So, ɒɪtθ St W K Do Ha, ɒɪʔθ So, ɒɪʔθ Sa Wo, ɒɪθ K, hɔɪtθ C Ess Sr, ɔɪtθ Wo Wa Gl O L Nth Sf Bk Hrt Ess Brk K Ha Sx, ɔɪʔθ Bk K, ɔɪθ K, hʌɪtθ Nf, ʌɪtθ Gl Brk Sr, ʌɪtθ O Hu, ʌɪʔθ He, həɪtθ Mon W Do, əɪtθ He Mon W Brk Do Sx, əɪʔθ He Wo Mon Gl, hɐɪtθ Nf

he-lamb *n* a MALE LAMB III.6.2. iːlæm MxL, iːlam L Lei Nth C Bk, hiˑlæm Nf

held *v-ed* **has not held** *When the cow has been to the bull and has not conceived, you say she* .... III.1.7.
vi-ed **has not held** ᵁuːz nɒd ɛld La, ɛznt ɛld Du Y L, ɛnt ɛld L, aznəɹ ɛld Db, anə ɛlt St, anəɹ ɛld Sa, avnt ɛɫd Ha, ɛzn ɛɫd K, æzn ɛʊd K; **has not holded** ɛnt ɔʊdɪd L; **not held** nœː hɛld Nb, nɒt ɛld St, nɒt ɛɫd Brk; **is not holding** ɪdn ɒʊɫdɪn Co; **not holding** ɪznt ɒdɪn Y, nɒt hœːldn Nb
vt-ed **has not held** ɛɪnʔ hɪld Nf, æˑsnt ɛəld Man; **not held** næt hɛl Man

⇒ *a-turned* again, barren, broken, broken *down*, broken *the bull*, broken *to the bull*, come over, come over *again*, come over *again in bulling*, comes over *again*, *did not* stand, *didn't take it* ⇒ taken, empty, gone over, gone over *again*, has *a-returned*, has *a-turned*, *has* broken, *has (?is)* broken *bull*, *has* broken *her*, *has* broken *service*, *has (?is)* broken *the bull*, *has* broken *the bulling*, *has (?is)* broken *to the bull*, *has* come on *again*, *has* come over, *has* come over *again*, *has* come over *again in bulling*, *has* gone over, *has* missed, *has not* held, *has not* held *the bull*, *has not* sped, *has not* stood ⇒ stand, *has not* taken, *has not* taken on, *has not* taken *the bull*, *has not took* ⇒ taken, *hasn't* held, *hasn't* held *the bull*, *hasn't* holded ⇒ held, *hasn't* stood ⇒ stand, *hasn't took* ⇒ taken, *hasn't took the bull* ⇒ taken, *has* overrun, *has* returned, *has* run*ned* over, *has* run over, *has* slipped, *has* slipped over, *has* turned, *has* turned *again*, *has* turned *on the bull*, *is a* barren, *is a* barrener, *is* barren, *is* empty, *is not holding* ⇒ held, *is not in season*, *is not on*, *is not served*, *is not speeded* ⇒ sped, *is* riding *again*, missed, missed *holding*, *never took* ⇒ taken, *not* bulled, *not* held, *not* held *the bull*, *not holding* ⇒ held, off, overrun, ran over, ran over *her time*, returned, *returns service* ⇒ returned, run*ned* over, run over, turned, turned *to the bull*, won't hold, *won't stand*

helk *n* a YOUNG SOW III.8.5. hɛɫk W

hell out *vtphr* to POUR tea V.8.8. hɛɫ ... əʊt Do*[old]*, ɛɫ ... əʊt Do

helm *1. n* the SHAFT of a spade I.7.7. hɛɫəm Sf
2. n a CART-SHED I.11.7. ɛləm Y

helm-stones *n* the BASE of a stack II.7.4. ɛlmstɪənz Y

help *vt* to AGREE *WITH* somebody VIII.8.12. ɛlp St

helper *n* a DIAGONAL BAR of a gate IV.3.7. *pl* hɛlpʔəz Sf

help out *vtphr* to AGREE *WITH* somebody VIII.8.12. ɛlp ... aʊt St, ɛlp ... uːt Y

help yourselves! *imp What do you say to your visitors at table when you want them to begin eating?*

V.8.13. ⇒ *come on* muck in, daff in, dive in, fall to *then*, lean to, muck in, reach *for it*, reach out, reach till, reach to, reach to *and help yourselves*, reach up, reach up *and help yourselves*, set to, set to *now*, start on, tuck in, wade in, wire in, work *it* back *[also wide range of extended phrasal rr. from which above material has been extracted]*

helve *n* the SHAFT of a spade I.7.7. ɛɫv Wa Bk

hemmel *1. n* the STRAW-YARD of a farm I.1.9. hɛml Nb
2. n a shed for cattle adjoining a straw-yard. hɛml Nb
3. n the covered part of a straw-yard. hɛml Nb

hemmel(s) *n* the BASE of a stack II.7.4.
no -s: ɛməl Y*[raised, for straw]*
-s: ɛməlz Y*[wooden beams and straw]*

hemmels *npl* long STACKS II.7.1. ɛmlz Y

hemp *n* a HALTER for a cow I.3.17. hɛmp W

hempen-halter *1. n* a TETHER for a cow I.3.4. ɛmpənɔɫtə Ess
2. n a HALTER for a cow I.3.17. ɛmpʔɳɔɫdə Ess, ɛmpənɔɫtə Ess, hɛmpnhɔːɫtə Ess, hɛmpmhɔːɫtə Ess, ɛmpm,ɔːtətᶜ So, ɛmpʔənɔːᵊtʔə Bk, hɛmptnhɔʊtə Ess, hæmpnhɒtʔɐ Ess, hæmpʔmhɔːɫtʔə Ess
3. n a TETHERING-ROPE used to tie up a horse I.4.2. ɛmpənɔɫtə Ess, hɛmpmhɔːɫtə Ess, hɛmpm,hɔːɫtətᶜ: So, ɛmpm,ɔːɫtətᶜ: So

hemp-halter *1. n* a HALTER for a cow I.3.17. ɛmpɛltɹ L, ɛmpɒɫtə Nth Hu Bd, ɛmpɒɫʔə Bk Bd, ɛmpɔːɫtə Hrt, ɛmpɔːɫtəᶜ O So Ha, ɛmpɔːɫʔəᶜ Bk, ɛmpɔːʔəᶜ Bk, ɛmpɔːθə La
2. n a TETHERING-ROPE used to tie up a horse I.4.2. ɛmpɒɫtə Nth, ɛmɒɫtə Bd, ɛmpɒɫʔə Bd, ɛmpɒᵁɫtətᶜ: W, ɛmpɔːltəᴶ K, ɛmpɔːθə La

hemplands *n* a PADDOCK I.1.10. ɛmplʊnz Wo

hen-baulk *n* a PERCH for hens IV.6.3. hɛnbaːk Cu *[above cattle in cow-house]*, *pl* hɛnbɔːks Cu

hen-coop *n* a HEN-HOUSE I.1.6. ɛnkᵁuːp La

hen-cote *n* a HEN-HOUSE I.1.6. ɛnkɒt Y He, ɛnkɒɪt La, ɛnkɔːt La, ɛnkɔɪt Y, ɛnkoːt La Ch Db, ɛnkoʊt St, ɛnkʊat Y, ɛnkʊət La

hen-cree *n* a HEN-HOUSE I.1.6. ɛnkɹiː Du, hɛnkʁi: Nb Du, hɛnkʁɪə Nb

hen-crow *n* a HEN-HOUSE I.1.6. ɛnkɹoʊ La, ɛnkɹuː La

hen-hole *n* a HEN-HOUSE I.1.6. ɛnɒɪl Y, ɛnɔɪl Y, ɛnʊəl Y

hen-house *n What do you call the place where you keep the birds that lay eggs for you?* I.1.6. ɪnɛʊs K Sx, hɪnɛʊs Ess, *pl* hɪnhɛʊzɪz Ess, ɪnəs Ess, hɪnəs Sf Ess, hɛnɛʊs Nf, ɛnɛʊs O Nth Hu Bk Hrt MxL Sr, hɛnɛʊs Nf Ess Sx, hɛnhɛʊs Nf Ess, ɛnæʊs L R Ess Ha, hɛnhæʊs Nf, ɛnaːs La Lei, ɛnaʊs La Y Sa St L So, hɛnaʊs Man So, ɛnɑʊs He O, ɛnʌʊs Y, ɛnʊs O, ɛnuːs Cu We La Y Sa L, hɛnuːs Nb Cu Du Sa, hɛnhuːs Nb, ɛnəs Y Sa O Hu C Bk Bd Hrt Ess, hɛnəs Sf Ess, ɛnəʊzɪz Brk, *pl* ɛnəʊzɪz Y. ⇒ **chicken-coop, chicken-house, chicken-hut, fowl-cote, fowl-house, fowl-hut, fowl-pen, fowl-roost, fowls'-house, fowls'-run, hen-coop, *hen-cot* ⇒ hen-cote, hen-cote, hen-cree, hen-crow, hen-hole, hen-hull, hen-hut, hen-loft, hen-pen, hen-place, hen-roost, hen-run, hen-shed, hens'-house, hens'-hut, hens'-shed, poultry-house, run, shade**

hen-hull *n* a HEN-HOUSE I.1.6. ɛnʊl We La Y, hɛnʊl Cu Du We

hen-hut *n* a HEN-HOUSE I.1.6. hɪnzhʌt Nf, ɛnʊt Y L

hen-loft *n* a HEN-HOUSE I.1.6. ɛnlɒft Cu, hɛnlɒft Nb

hen-pen *n* a HEN-HOUSE I.1.6. ɛnpɛn Y Ch St Wa

hen-perk* *n* a PERCH for hens IV.6.3. *pl* ɛnpɪəks Y

hen-place *n* a HEN-HOUSE I.1.6. ɛnpleəs La, ɛnpleɪs Lei Nth

hen-roost *n* a HEN-HOUSE I.1.6. ɛnɹʏːst Sa, ɛnɹɛʊst Db, ɛnɹuːs K, ɛnɹuːst Ch Sa St Wo Wa Nt L Lei Nth, ɛnɹʊst Sa, hɛᵊnruːs Man

hen-run *n* a HEN-HOUSE I.1.6. ɛnɾʊn O

hen(s) *npl Some people have a shed and a wire-netting run at the bottom of their garden in which they [keep]* .... IV.6.2.

no -s: hɛən Man

-s: hɪnz Nf Sf Sr, ɪnz Ess Sr K Sx, hɛnz Nb Cu Du We Y Nf Sf Ess So, ɛnz Cu We La Y Ch Db Sa St Wa Mon O Nt L Lei R Hu C Bk Bd Hrt Ess Brk K Ha Sx, hɛˑəns Man, hɛˑᵊnz Nb

⇒ **chicken(s), fowl(s), poultry**

hen-shed *n* a HEN-HOUSE I.1.6. *pl* ɛnʃɛdz Wo

hens'-house *n* a HEN-HOUSE I.1.6. hɪnzhɛʊs Nf, hɛnzhaʊs So, hɛnzhʌʊs Nf

hens'-hut *n* a HEN-HOUSE I.1.6. hɪnzhʌt Nf

hens' roost *n* a PERCH for hens IV.6.3. *pl* ɛnz ɾʏːstəz D

hens'-shed *n* a HEN-HOUSE I.1.6. hɛnzʃɛd Nf

hen-stick *n* a PERCH for hens IV.6.3. hɛnstɪk Du

hent *n* a DITCH less than a yard wide IV.2.1(c). ɪnt Brk

hen-toed *adj* PIGEON-TOED VI.10.4. ɪntɔʊd O, ɪntoːd W, ɛntæʊd Hrt, ɛntɔʊd O Brk, ɛntʌʊd Bk Bd Hrt, ɛntoːd He Wo Wa Gl O W, ɛntoʊd Wo Wa Gl Bk Brk, ɛntuːd Wo

he-pig *n* a HOG III.8.8. iːpɪg La

herbs *1. npl* HAWS IV.11.6. həːbz Ess, əːbz Ess

2. npl PALS VIII.4.2. əˑɾbz Brk

herd *n* a SHEPHERD I.2.1. heɔᴿd Du, heəd Nb, hɛ̞ʁd Nb, hɛʁəd Nb

herdsman *1. n* a COWMAN on a farm I.2.3. əᴵdzmən Ch, həːdzmən Du, əᵗːɾd̠z̠mən Sr, həᵗːd̠z̠mən So

2. n a man who looks after bullocks or other cattle on a farm. əᵗːɾd̠z̠mən Ha Sx

herring-roaster *n* a GRIDIRON V.7.4(a). haʁənʁøᵊstəᴿ Du*[old]*

hessian-apron *n* a working APRON V.11.2(a). ɛsɪnæɪpɹən K

hetch *n* the TAILBOARD of a cart I.10.2. ɛtʃ Y

hew *1. vt* to WHITTLE a stick I.7.19. *-ing* juːɪn He

2. v to LOP a tree IV.12.5. huːwɪn K *[queried SBM]*

hezzly* *adj* foggy and rainy, ⇐ DULL VII.6.10. ɛzlɪ L

hibbin *n* IVY IV.10.10. hɪbən Man

hiccuping *v-ing What am I doing now [indicate hiccuping]?* VI.8.4. Eng exc. Brk Do Sx. ⇒ **click-up, egg-cups, *got the hiccups*, hecketing, *hiccup(s)*, yewking, *you've got the hiccups*, *you've got the yewcums [wordclass for click-up and egg-cups uncertain]***

hick-horse *n* a DONKEY III.13.16. ɪkɒːs L

hid *vt* to HIDE something VIII.7.6. iːd Y, ɪd La Y

hiddy *vt* to HIDE something VIII.7.6. ɪdɪ Y

hide *1. vt A dog buries a bone because he wants to … it.* (Version 4 of Questionnaire: *If the naughty boys [who were robbing an orchard] happened to catch sight of the owner as they left the orchard, they'd no doubt slip the apples into their pockets in order to … it.*) VIII.7.6. Eng. ⇒ **couch, cover *them up*, feal *it*, feal *them*, felt *it*, felt *them*, hap *it* up, hid *it*, hid *them*, hid *them out of sight*, hid *them* up, hiddy *it*, hiddy *them*, *hide en*, *hide en away*, *hide her*, *hide him*, *hide it*, hide *it* up, *hide them*, *hide them out of sight*, hod *it*, keep *it*, keep *it safe*, keep *them out of sight*, keep *them out of the sight*, lay *it* up, save *it*, squat**

2. n What do you call the skin of a cow? III.11.7. ɛɪd Cu Ch Db, heɪd Nb Du, æːd D, æɪd He So D, hæɪd Man So, aːd Y Co D, aɪd Cu Du We La Y Ch Sa St L Lei Co, *pl* kjæʊ-aɪds Ch, haɪd Cu Du We Y Db So, ɑːd Y Co D, ɑɪd La Y Ch Db He Nt L Lei R Nth Hu C Bk Bd Hrt Ess MxL K, hɑɪd Du Nth Ess Sr, ɒɪd Sa St Wo Wa Gl W K Co Ha, hɒɪd So W Do, ɔɪd Wa O Nth Bk Hrt Ess K Ha Sx, kæʊzɔɪd Wo Wa, hɔɪd C Nf Sf Ess Brk Sr Ha Sx, ʌɪd Gl O Sf Brk Sr, hʌɪd Nf Sf Sr, əɪd He Wo Mon Gl So W Brk Do Sx, həɪd W Brk Do. ⇒ *cow-***hide, pelt, skin**

3. n a SHEEPSKIN III.11.8(a). heɪd Nb, aɪd La Sa, haɪd So, ɑːd Y, ɑɪd Hu Bd, hɒˑɪd Nf, ɔɪd Nth, ʌɪd O, hʌɪd Nf, əɪd Sx

4. n the PELT of a sheep III.11.8(b). ɛɪd Cu, heɪd Nb, aɪd Cu Du La Y Sa, ɑɪd Nth, ɒɪd St, ɒːɪd St, ɔɪd Nth Sx, hɔɪd Ess Sr, ʌɪd O Sr, hʌɪd Nf, əɪd Brk Sx, həɪd Brk

5. *vt* to BEAT a boy on the buttocks VIII.8.10. aɪd Y

hide away *vtphr* to HIDE something VIII.7.6. iːd ... əwɛɪ Co*[old]*

hides *n* CHITTERLINGS III.12.2. hʌɪdz Nf

hide up *vtphr* to HIDE something VIII.7.6. hɔɪd ... ʌp Sf Ess, hʌɪd ... ʌp Nf Sf

hiding *vbln* **give him a (good) hiding** to BEAT a boy on the buttocks VIII.8.10. aɪd Y; **give him a good hiding** gɪv ɪm ə gʊd aɪdɪn La, gɪv ɪm ə gʊd aɪdɪn Y, gɪ ɪm ə gʊd aɪdɪn L, gɪv ɪm ə gʊd aɪdən Y, giː ŋ ə gʊd hɒɪdɪn So, gɪv ɪm ə gʊd ɒːɪdɪn St, gɪv ɪm ə gʊd ɔɪdɪn He, gɪ ɪ n ə gʊd əɪdn Do; **give him a hiding** gɪv ɪm ə ɒɪdɪn K, giː ən əɪdn Do

hid up *vtphr* to HIDE something VIII.7.6. ɪd ... ʊp Y

hie *imp* **hie**, **hie way***, **hie wee**, **woa hie** the command TURN LEFT!, given to plough-horses II.3.5(a). **hie** haɪ Nb; **hie way** aː weː La, ɑː weː Y, hæː weɪ Du; **hie wee** aː wiː Du Y; **woa hie** woː haɪ Cu

high *1. adj* IN FLOOD, describing a river IV.1.4. aɪ Co, ɑɪ Ch, ɔɪ O, ʌʏ O
2. adj **go high** to SPOIL, referring to meat or fish V.7.10. gʊ iː Y

high boots *npl* BOOTS VI.14.23. ɛɪ buːts La

high-ladder *n* an END-BOARD of a cart I.10.4. *pl* aɪɫadəˤːz̩ W

high-lows *npl* BOOTS VI.14.23. haɪlɒuz Nf, hʌɪlɒuz Nf*[ankle-height x2, hob-nailed x1]*

highly strung *adj* ACTIVE, describing a child VIII.9.1. aːɫi ʂt̠ɹʌŋ Co *[marked u.r. SBM]*

highroad *n* a ROAD IV.3.12. haɪɹoʊd Nf, ɔɹæʊd Hrt

high shoes *npl* BOOTS VI.14.23. ɒɪ ʃuːz Wo

high sprites *npl* BOGEYs VIII.8.1. hʌɪ spɹʌɪts Nf

high-tailboard *n* an END-BOARD of a cart I.10.4. aɪ teɪɫboːˤd Bd, *pl* aɪtæɪɫbɔədz K

high-tide *adj* IN FLOOD, describing a tidal river IV.1.4. hʌɪˑtʌɪˑd Nf

high ties *npl* BOOTS VI.14.23. ɛɪ tɑɪz Y

hightle *n* a SEESAW VIII.7.2. ɛɪtl L, aɪtl L, ɔɪtl L

high-tops *npl* BOOTS VI.14.23. hɔɪtɔps Sf

highty *n* a SEESAW VIII.7.2. aɪtɪ Nt

highty-tighty *n* a SEESAW VIII.7.2. aɪtɪtaɪtɪ Nt L

highway-road *n* a ROAD IV.3.12. hɒɪwɛɪɹoːˤd Nf

higs *npl* HAWS IV.11.6. ɪgz La Db *[not a NBM headword]*

hike *1. imp* the command TURN LEFT!, given to plough-horses II.3.5(a). hɛɪk Nb
2. imp the command TURN RIGHT!, given to plough-horses II.3.5(b). hæɪk Ess, hɔɪk L, ɔɪk L
3.1. vt to BUTT III.2.10. aɪk Sa, *prppl* aɪkɪn La Y Wo
3.2. v to butt. *prppl* haɪkən Nb Y, aɪk Sa Wo, *prppl* aɪkɪn La Y Ch St, *-ing* aɪkɪn Ch L, *-ing* aɪkkɪn Db, *prppl* aɪkən Du We, *-ing* aˑɪkɪn L Lei, *-ing* aːɪkɪn St, *prppl* ɑɪkɪn Wa, *-ing* ɑɪkɪn Ch Wa, aˑɪk Db, *-ing*

aˑɪkɪn L Lei R, ɒɪk St, *-ing* ɔˑɪkɪn Lei
4. imp GO AWAY! VIII.7.9(a). ɔɪk Brk
5. vt **hike it** to WALK VIII.7.10. əɪk ɪt Do

hike for *vtphr* LOOK FOR it III.13.18. *-ing* hʌɪkɪn fɔɹ (+V) Nf

hile *1. vt* to BUTT III.2.10. *-ing* æɪlɪn He, æɪɫɪn He, əɪɫɪn Wo
2. v to butt. *-ing* æɪɫɪn He Mon, aɪlɪn he, əɪɫɪn Wo Mon

hiling *v-ing* STOOKING II.6.5. *inf* æɪʊɫ Ha, haɪɫɪŋ So, haɪɫɪn Do, aɪɫɪn W Ha, *3prs* hɒɪɫz Ha, həɪɫɪn W

hill *1. n* a CLAMP in which potatoes are stored out of doors II.4.6. hɪl Nf, *pl* ɪlz L
2. n a SLOPE IV.1.10. hɪl Nf, hɪlː Nf, ɪl La Y, hɪɫ Wa Lei Nf Ess, ɪɫ Lei R Hrt

hillock *1. n* **hillock of cow-muck** a CLOT OF COW-DUNG II.1.6. ɪlʊk ə kəʊːmʊːk Wo
2. n a TUSSOCK of grass II.2.9. ɪɫək K

hillside *n* a SLOPE IV.1.10. ɪlsaɪd Y

hilly *adj* STEEP, describing a hill IV.1.11. ɪlɪ L, ɪɫɪ Ess *[noted as probably u.r. EMBM]*

hilt *1. n* the SHAFT of a spade I.7.7. hɪɫt Ess, ɪɫt Co
2. n the SHAFT of a hay-fork I.7.12. ɪɫt Co
3. n a YOUNG SOW III.8.5. hɪɫt W

hilts *npl* the HANDLES of a scythe II.9.8. ɪlts Y

him *1. objpron* If you've lost your way and someone comes along, you'd go up to him and [ask] .... IX.2.4. Eng exc. Du Co Do. ⇒ **he, en, someone**
2. n my HUSBAND VIII.1.25. ɪm Y

hime *n* HOAR-FROST VII.6.6. aɪm Y Db*[old]*, aɪm Y

himy frost *n* HOAR-FROST VII.6.6. aɪmɪ fɹɔst Y, ɑːmɪ fɹɔst Y

hind *1. n* a CARTMAN on a farm I.2.2. heɪnd Nb, haɪnd Du
2. n a FARM-LABOURER I.2.4. heɪnd Nb, haɪnd Nb Cu, aɪnd Y
3. n a farm-labourer who is the tenant of a farm cottage. hɛɪənd Nb
4. n a ploughman who is the tenant of a farm cottage. hɛɪnd Nb
5. n the working farm-manager. aɪnd Y, ɑɪnd Cu
6. n a farm-bailiff. aɪnd La Y, haɪnd Cu
7. n a foreman. haɪnd Y, aːˡnd Y
8. n/adj the LAST sheep through a gate VII.2.2. hæɪn Man, hɔɪnd Sf, hɔɪn Ess, ɔɪn K*[adj]*, həɪn W*[adj]*
9. n HOAR-FROST VII.6.6. aɪnd Y

hind-board *1. n* the TAILBOARD of a cart I.10.2. hæɪnboˑəd Man, aɪntbʊəd L, aˑɪndbɔəd Hu
2. n an END-BOARD of a cart I.10.4. hæɪnbɔəd Man, aˑɪntbʊəd L, aɪnbʊəˤːd̟ Co, ɑɪndbʊəd Nt

hind-door *1. n* the TAILBOARD of a cart I.10.2. aˈɪntdʊə L, aɪntdʊəˡ L

2. n an END-BOARD of a cart I.10.4. aɪntdʊə Y

hind-end *n* the BUTT of a sheaf of corn II.6.4. aˈɪntɛnd L

hind-end-board *n* the TAILBOARD of a cart I.10.2. hɪnɛndbɔːd Cu

hinder *n/adj* the LAST sheep through a gate VII.2.2. aɪndəˡː Co*[adj]*, hɒɪndə Nf*[old]*, ɒɪndəˡː Co*[adj]*, hɔɪndəˡ Ha, hʌɪndə Nf

hinder-brig *n* a BUMPER of a cart I.10.1(a). ɪndəbɹɪg Lei

hinder-end *n* the ARSE VI.9.2. hɪntɔᴿʁɛnd Nb*[polite]*

hinder-end-board *n* an END-BOARD of a cart I.10.4. hɪndəɹɛndbʊəd We, ɪndəɹɛndbʊəd Y

hinder-end-door *n* the TAILBOARD of a cart I.10.2. ɪndəɹɛnddʊə Y

hinder-ends *n* CHAFF II.8.5. ɪndɹɛndz L

hindermost *n/adj* the LAST sheep through a gate VII.2.2. ɪndəˡməst He

hind-horse *n* a SHAFT-HORSE I.6.2. ɒɪndɔːs K, ɔɪndɒˡːş Sx, əɪndaˡːş Gl, əɪndɔːs Sx, əɪnɔəˡɹs Sx, əɪnɔəˡːş Sx

hind-ladder *n* a rear cart-ladder, ⇐ CART-LADDERS I.10.5. aɪndlædə Hu, *pl* aɪndladəz Hu, aɪnladə C Bd Hrt, ɔɪnladəˡ Bk

hindmost *n/adj* the LAST sheep through a gate VII.2.2. hɪnməst Du

hind one *n* a SHAFT HORSE I.6.2. aɪnd ən C

hind-post *n* the HANGING-POST of a gate IV.3.3. aɪnpɔːs Co

hind-skin *n* RENNET V.5.6. *pl* aɪənskɪnz Db*[from a lamb's liver] [queried WMBM]*

hindward *n/adj* the LAST sheep through a gate VII.2.2. haɪnəˡːd̦ So

hind weigh *n* an EVENER, the main swingle-tree of a horse-drawn plough harness I.8.4. ɔɪn weɪ Bk, ɔɪn wæɪ Hrt

hindy frost *n* HOAR-FROST VII.6.6. aɪndɪ fɹɒst Y

hingeing-stump *n* the HANGING-POST of a gate IV.3.3. ɪndʒɪnstʊmp La

hinge-post *n* the HANGING-POST of a gate IV.3.3. ɪndʒpɔːst W

hinges *npl* [*Show a picture of some houses.] What do you call these on which the door turns?* V.1.11a. Eng. ⇒ **bands, crooks and lugs, cross-garnets, door-hangings,** *door-hinges,* **hangers, hangings, hingings, hingles, irons, jimmers**

hinge-stoop *n* the HANGING-POST of a gate IV.3.3. hɪndʒstuːp Nb

hinge-tree* *n* the part of a gate that has the hinges on it, ⇐ HANGING-POST IV.3.3. ɪnʒtɹiː He

hinging-post *n* the HANGING-POST of a gate IV.3.3. hɪŋənpɒst Du, ɪŋɪnpoːst Nt, ɪŋgɪnpoːst Db, ɪŋgɪnpoʊst St, ɪŋɪnpʊəst L

hingings *npl* the HINGES of a door V.1.11a. ɪŋɪnz La Y, hɪndʒɪnz Nf, ɪndʒɪnz L, ɪndʒənz C, ɛndʒɪnz L

hinging-stoop *n* the HANGING-POST of a gate IV.3.3. ɪŋɪnstɒʊp Y, ɪŋɪnstoʊp Y, hɪŋɪnstᵁuːp Du We, ɪŋɪnstᵁuːp We La Y, hɪŋɪnstuːp Cu Du We, ɪŋɪnstuːp Cu La Y, hɪŋənstᵁuːp Cu Du, hɪŋənstuːp Cu, ɪŋənstuːp Cu

hingles *npl* the HINGES of a door V.1.11a. hɪndʒəlz Nf, hɪndʒɫz Ess, hɪnʒɫz Nf Sf, hɪnʒəɫz Nf

hing-post *n* the HANGING-POST of a gate IV.3.3. ɪŋpoːᵁst Db

hip *1. n* the HIP-BONE of a cow III.2.1. hɪp Wa Nth Nf Sf Hrt Ess, ɪp Y Ch Db St He Wa Gl O Nth Hu C Bk Bd Hrt Ess, *pl* ɪps Sa, ɛp Db

2. n the human HIP-BONE VI.9.1. hɪp Nb Cu Du We C Nf Sf Ess, ɪp We La Y Ch Db Sa St Wa Gl O Nt L R Nth Hu C Bk Bd Hrt K Co D, jɪp Gl

hip-and-haws *npl* HIPS of the wild rose IV.11.7. ˈɪpɪˈnɔˡːz̩ Sa

hip-berries *npl* HIPS of the wild rose IV.11.7. ɪpbɛɹɪz Gl

hip-bone *1. n [Show a picture of a cow.] What do you call this [indicate the hip-bone]?* III.2.1. ɪpbɪan Du, ɪpbean We, ɪpbɛʊn St, hɪpbɶˈn Nb, ɪpbɒn Sx, *pl* hɪpbɒʊnz Ess, ɪpbɒʊn Nth Sr K Sx, *pl* hɪpbɔʊnz Ess, ɪpbɔʊn Wa O L K, *pl* ɪpbɔʊnz Brk Sx, hɪpbʌn Sf, ɪpbʌn C Ess, hɪpbʌʊn Ess MxL Sr, ɪpbʌʊn Bk Bd K, hɪpbon Nf, *pl* hɪbboˈnz Nf, hɪpʔboˈn Nf, hɪpboːn Mon, ɪpboːn La Ch Db Sa He Wo O Bk So W Brk Ha, *pl* ɪpboːnz Mon, hɪpboʊn Nf So, ɪpboʊn St Wo Wa Lei R Bk Bd So Brk Ha, *pl* ɪpboːʊnz Mon Gl, hɪpboˈən Man, hɪpboᵊn K, hɪpbʊn Sf, *pl* ɪpbʊnz Gl, ɪpbuːn St, ɪpbuən Db L W, *pl* ɪpbwənz He Wo, ɪpbuːn Ch Db Wo Ha, hɪpbuːən W, *pl* ɛpbɒʊnz Sx. ⇒ **aitch-bone, hat-rack, haunch-bone, hip, hook, hook-bone, huckle-bone, huggin, huggin-bone, huvvon, huvvon-bone, pin, pin-bone, rump, rump-bone, tout-bone**

2. n What do you call this [indicate the human hip-bone]? VI.9.1. Eng exc Nth Hu C Bk. ⇒ **haunch, haunch-bone, hip,** *hook* ⇒ **huck, huck, huck-bone, huckle, huckle-bone, huggin, huggin-bone, oxter-bone, pin, pin-bone, thigh, thigh-bone, whirl-bone**

hipe *1. v* to BUTT III.2.10. *prppl* æɪpɪn Y, aɪp Y

2. v to butt. *prppl* ɛɪpɪn Y, haɪp Du, *prppl* haɪpən Cu We, aɪp We Y, *prppl* aɪpɪn La, *prppl* aɪpən La, *prppl* ɑːpɪn Y

3. v to push, describing cows going through a gateway. *prppl* aɪpɪn Cu

hip-haws *1. npl* HAWS IV.11.6. hɪpɔɪz Nf, ɪpɔːz St Bd

2. npl HIPS of the wild rose IV.11.7. ɪpɔːᵊz Bd

hipnies *npl* HIPS of the wild rose IV.11.7. ɪpnɪz St

hipping-pin* *n* a safety-pin, ⇐ DIAPER V.11.3. ɪpɪnpɪn Y

hipping(s) *n* a DIAPER V.11.3.
no -s: hɪpɪn Nb Cu We Y, ɪpɪn Cu La Y Db St, ɪpn Du, hɪpən Nb Du, hɛpən Nb
-s: hɪpɪns Nb, hɪpɪnz Nb Cu, ɪpɪnz Cu La Y, hɪpənz Nb Du, ɪpənz Du

hips *1. npl What do you call the berries that grow on the wild-rose bush?* IV.11.7. Eng exc. We. ⇒ **canker-berries, cankers, cat-choops, cat-jugs, choops, conkers, dog-berries, dog-choops, dog-chows, dog-chumps, dog-hips, dog-joops, dog-jumps, dog-noses, dog-rose-berries, dog-snouts, hip-and-haws, hip-berries, hip-haws, hipnies, hipsen(s), hipsies, hipsons** ⇒ **hipsen(s), hipsy-haws, hipsy-pipsies, horse-haws, imps, itching-berries, itchy-backs, itchy-berries, pig-noses, pips, rose-bubs, rose-hips, rose-pips, shoops**
2. npl HAWS IV.11.6. ɛps Db
3. n the EAVES of a stack of corn II.7.3. ɪps Ha

hipsen(s) *npl* HIPS of the wild rose IV.11.7.
no -s: ɪpsn O
-s: ɪpsnz Brk

hipsies *npl* HIPS of the wild rose IV.11.7. ɪpsɪz Bk

hip-stack *n* a square stack, ⇐ STACKS II.7.1. hɪpstæk Ess

hip-straps *n* the BREECH-BAND of the harness of a cart-horse I.5.10. ɛpstɹæps Sx

hipsy-haws *1. npl* HAWS IV.11.6. hɪpsɪ-ɔːz Ess
2. npl HIPS of the wild rose IV.11.7. ɪpsɪ-ɔɪz MxL Brk, ɪpsɪjɔɪz MxL *[queried EM/SBM]*

hipsy-pipsies *npl* HIPS of the wild rose IV.11.7. ɪpsɪpɪpsɪz Bk

hire *v, vt* **hire pasture** *When you arrange to put your cows on somebody else's field, what do you say you do?* III.3.8. ⇒ **agist, agrist, buy a keep, buy some keep, buy the grazing, feed out, fest out, gate, gate out, get out, get out to keep, gist, gister out, gist out, gist the beast, got to graze-field, graze, graze out, have out at tack, hire, hire feed, hire grazing, hire meadow, hire off, hire out, hire pasture, hire the feed, hire the feeding, hire the field, hire the grazing, hire the ground, hire the ground for their feed, hire the keep, hire the marsh, lea, lead out, lea out, let, let out, let out grazing, let out on keep, let out to keep, let the feed, let the field, let the grass-keeping, let the keep, let the pasture, marsh-let, on tack, out to keep, out to lea, out to tack, pad off, pay for lea, put down to keep, put on a lea, put on tack, put on the keep, put out, put out at lea, put out at tack, put out for keep, put out for keeping, put out for to keep, put out on hire, put out on tack, put out to gist, put out to gistment, put out to grass, put out to graze, put out to grazing, put out to keep, put out to lea, put out to pasture, put out to tack, raise out, rent, rent a piece, rent it, rent out, rent pasture, rent the feed, rent the keep, send out to graze, stint, summer, summer-graze, swarth, tack, tack out, take a field, take a meadow, take gisting, take grass, take grassing, take keep, take keeping, take land, take out to gist, take some eatage, take the eating, take the grazing, take the keep, they'd be on gist, took some keep** ⇒ *also* **take, turn out to keep, turn out to score** *[pragmatic decisions have sometimes been taken on obj of verb, and definitions framed accordingly:* **agrist** *and* **swarth** *remain particularly unclear. Incomplete information also available in BM on relevance of terms to hiring of pasture for horses and sheep]*

hire off *vtphr* to HIRE PASTURAGE III.3.8. ɑːɽ (+V) ... ɔːf Ess

hire out *vtphr* to put cattle on hired pasture, ⇐ HIRE PASTURAGE III.3.8. *-ing* ɑɪɽən ... æət K

hiring *n* a local FESTIVAL or holiday at which workers were hired VII.4.11. haɪəʁɪn Nb

hisk *1. n* a cough, ⇐ COUGHING VI.8.2. hɪsk So, hɪs So
2. n the cough of a cow. hɪsk Y

hisking *v-ing* COUGHING VI.8.2. hɪskɪn So*[old]*

hisky *adj* HOARSE VI.5.16. iːski D

hiss *imp* the command stop! or WOA!, given to plough-horses II.3.5(c). s: Nb*[to Scottish horses]*

hit *vt* to BEAT a boy on the buttocks VIII.8.10. ɪt R

hitch *n* the T-SHAPED PLOUGH-BEAM END of a horse-drawn plough I.8.5. hɪtʃ So

hitchings *n* the T-SHAPED PLOUGH-BEAM END of a horse-drawn plough I.8.5. hɪtʃɪnz So

hitch-off-time *n* STOPPING-TIME at the end of a day's work, when horses were unhitched from the plough VII.5.9. ɪtʃɔːftəɪm W

hither *imp* the command TURN LEFT!, given to plough-horses II.3.5(a). ɪðə K, ɪðəˡ K

hither-naked *adj* NAKED, describing a person VI.13.20. hɪðərniːkɪt Cu

hive *1. n What do you keep those insects in that make honey for you?* IV.8.8(a). Eng exc. Nb Cu Du We Man. ⇒ **bee-aviary, bee-butt, bee-hive, box-hive, skep, wood-hive**
2. n a SKEP IV.8.8(b). aɪv La Y L, ɑːv La, ɑɪv La Nt L Nth Hu, *pl* ɑɪvz Bk, *pl* hɒɪvz So, ɒɪvz So W, hɔɪv C Sf Ess, ɔɪv Nth Bk, ʌɪv Brk, əɪv W Sx

ho *1. imp* the command TURN RIGHT!, given to plough-horses II.3.5(b). oː Sa
2. imp the command stop! or WOA!, given to plough-horses II.3.5(c). ɒʊ Co, hoʊ Co
3. adv NO VIII.8.13(b). hʌʊ Sf

hoarder *n* a MISER VII.8.9. hɔədə Nf

209

hoar-frost *n When in spring or autumn it has been cold at night, what may you see on the ground next morning?* VII.6.6. ɔːfɪɒst Bk Brk, ɔːfɪɒs Lei, hɔᴷːfʁɒst Du, hɔːfɪɔːst Ess, ɔːfɪɔːst Ess, hɔːfɪɔːs Ess, ɔᶜːfɪɔːst Wa, hɔəᴶfɪɒst K, ɔəᴶfɪɒˈst Brk, ɔəᴶfɪɔˈst K, hɔːəfɪɒs Hrt, ɔˈəɹfɪɒst La, ɔəᶜːvɪɔːst Ha, ɔːəᶜfɪɒst Sx, hɔːɐfɪɒːst Ess*[on trees]*, ɒʊəᶜːvɪɔːst So, oˈəfɪɒst Db, hɔəfɪɒs Man, oˈə fɪɒs Man, oˈəɹfɪɒst La, ɔəᶜɾfɪɒˈst W, hɔːəᶜːvɪɔːst So, hɔːəᶜːvɪɔːs So, ʊəfɪɒst La Y, ʊəᴶfɪɒst La, ʊəfɪɔst L, ʊəɹfɪɔst L, huːəᶜːvɪɔːst So, uəᶜːvɪɔːst Co. ⇒ **duck-frost, foggy-frost, frost, frost-rind, frosty rime, ground-frost, hime, himy frost, hind, hindy frost, hoary-frost, rag, raggy-frost, rime, rime-frost, rimer, riming, rimy-frost, rind, rindy-frost, rye-frost, water-frost, water rime, white-frost, white-hime, white hind, white-hoar-frost, white rag, white-rime, white rind**

hoarse *adj When a man has a cold here [point to the throat] and it affects his voice [indicate hoarseness], you say he is ....* VI.5.16. Eng. ⇒ **croaky, croupy, froggy, hisky, *his throat is sore*, hoarsed, hoarsed up, *hoarst* ⇒ hoarsed, hoarsty, hoarsy, *hoast* ⇒ hoarsed, *hoasty* ⇒ hoarsty, hoizy, hooze, hoozed, hoozed up, hoozy, husk, husky, rapy, rawky, rouped, roupy, thick, throaty, wheezy**

hoarsed *adj* HOARSE VI.5.16. ɑᶜːʂt He, ɔːst Du We Y, ɔːɹst Cu, ɔʊst L, ɔəst Y, hɔəᶜʂt Nf, oːst Nt, oˈəst Nt Nth, ʊəst La Y Nt L, uːəᶜːʂt D

hoarsed up *adj* HOARSE VI.5.16. uəᶜːz d̩ ʌp Co

hoarsty* *adj* HOARSE VI.5.16. ɒʊstɪ Nth, ɔːstɪ O*[old]*, ɔʊstɪ L, ʊəstɪ L

hoarsy *adj* HOARSE VI.5.16. ɔəsɪ Wa, uəᶜːzi D

hoary-frost *n* HOAR-FROST VII.6.6. jaːɹɪfɪɒst Ch*[old]*, hɔɹɪfɹɔːᵊst Sf, ɔːɹɪfɪɔːst K, ɔːɾɪfɪɒːst K, hɔəɹɪfɪɒˈst K, ɔːəᶜɾɪfɪɒst Sx

hoast *1. n* a cough, ⇐ COUGHING VI.8.2. ɒst Db, hɒs K, uːst St

2. n the cough of an animal. ɛʊst Sa, hɒst Db, ɒst Db, uːst St

hoasting *v-ing* COUGHING VI.8.2. ɒstɪn St, oʊstɪn St

hob *1.1. vt* to CLEAR grass at the edges of a field II.9.5. ɔb Nt

1.2. v to clear grass. ɒb Nt, ɔb Nt

2. v to WEAN a calf III.1.4. *-ing* ɒbɪn Sr

*3. v to foster a PET-LAMB III.7.3. *-ing* ɒbɪn Sr

hobby *n* a PET-LAMB III.7.3. ɒbi Co

hobby-lamb *n* a PET-LAMB III.7.3. ɒbiłæm Co

hob-cocks *npl* large COCKS of hay II.9.12. hɒbkɒks We

hobhouchin *n* a DADDY-LONG-LEGS IV.8.10. ˈɒbɛʊtʃɪn Bd

hob-lamb *n* a PET-LAMB III.7.3. hɒblɛm Sr, hɒblæm Sx, ɒblæm Sr Sx

hoblings *npl* COCKS of hay II.9.12. ɒblɪnz Db

hobny-man *n* a FARM-LABOURER I.2.4. hɒbnɪmæn So

hob out *1. vtphr* to CLEAR grass at the edges of a field II.9.5. *-ing* ɒbɪn ... æʊt Nt, ɔb ... æᵊt Y

2. vphr to clear grass. ɒb ɛːt Db, ɒb aːt Y

hob over* *vtphr* to CLEAR grass at the edges of a field II.9.5. *-ing* ɔbɪn ɔvə L

hob round *vphr* to CLEAR grass at the edges of a field II.9.5. ɒb ɹæːnd Nt

hobs *npl* HAWS IV.11.6. ɒbz Wo Wa O*[old]*

hob-thistle *n* a variety of THISTLE II.2.2. ɒbθɪsł Ch

hob up *vphr* to CLEAR grass at the edges of a field II.9.5. ɒb ʊp Nth

hob-wood *n* the CLOG on a horse's tether I.4.3. ɒbwʊd Y

hock *n* the HOOF of a cow III.2.8(a). *pl* ʌks So *[queried SBM]*

hock about *vphr* to ROOT, what a pig does when it digs the ground with its snout III.9.2. *-ing* ɒkɪn əbaʊt O, *-ing* ɒkɪn əbaʊt O

hockey *n* a local FESTIVAL held at harvest-time VII.4.11. hɔːkɪ Nf, hɔːkʔɪ Sf, hɔːᵊkʔi Nf; **harvest hockey** haːvəst hɔːəkʔɪ Nf*[old]*

hocksing *v-ing* THROWING a stone VIII.7.7. ɒksɪn Hu

hock up* *vphr* to ROOT, what a pig does when it digs the ground with its snout III.9.2. *-ing* ɒkɪn ʌp Brk

hod *1. n* a SOWING-BASKET II.3.6. hɒd Nf Ess, hɒˈdə Nf, hɒd Sf Ess

2. n a CLAMP in which potatoes are stored out of doors II.4.6. ɒd Sa

3. n a metal container for carrying horse-feed, ⇐ BASKET III.5.4. ɒd Lei

4. n the ASH-HOLE beneath a domestic fire V.3.3. hɒd Nf*[old]*

5. n a block of PEAT cut for drying IV.4.3. hɒd Nf

6. vt to HIDE something VIII.7.6. ɒd La

hodding *v-ing* SHELLING peas V.7.14. hɒdn̩ Ess

hoddy-doddies *npl* brown SNAILS IV.9.3. ɒdɪɒdɪz Bk

hoddy-dods *npl* SNAILS IV.9.3. hɔdɪdɔdz Sf*[small]*, hɔdɪdʌdz Ess

hodmandod *n* a SCARECROW II.3.7. *pl* ˈʌdmɪdʌdz W, ˈʊdmɪˌdʊd Brk

hodmedods *npl* SNAILS IV.9.3. hɒdmɪdɒdz Ess*[old ×1]*, *sg* hɒdmɪdɒd Nf, *sg* ɒdmədɒd Ess*[old]*, hɒdɪmɪdɒdz Ess, hɒdnɪdʌdz Ess, hɒbnɪdʌdz Ess, hɔdmɪdɔdz C*[brown]* Sf, ɔdmədɔdz Sf, ɔbmɪdɔdz Ess, *sg* ɔdnɪdɒd C*[brown]* Ess, ɔdn̩ɪdɔdz Ess, hʌdmɪdʌdz Ess

hod out *vtphr* to CUT peat IV.4.4. hɒd ... ɛʊt Nf

hoe *1.1. vt* to THIN OUT turnip plants II.4.2. ɛʊ St, aʊ We, hɒʊ Cu We, ɔː Sa, ɔːɹ(+V) Sa, oː So

Co D, oʊ St

1.2. v to thin out turnips. *-ing* æʊˈɪn Hrt, haʊ Du, hɒʊ Cu, ɔᶜːɽ Sa, oː Sa

2. n a RAKE used in a domestic fire ·V.3.8(a). hɛʊ Sr, hɒʊ Nf, hɔʊ Ess, ɔʊ Hu, hʌʊ Sf, ʌʊ Ess*[old]*

3. vt to RAKE in a domestic fire V.3.8(b). hɒʊ Nf

hoe out *1. vtphr* to THIN OUT turnip plants II.4.2. hɒˈ ... ɛʊt Nf, oʊ ... ɛʊt Wo, oʊ ... ɛʊʔ Bd, oː ... œɤt D, ɔː ... æɤt So Co, oː ... æɤt Co D, hoː ... æʊt Do, oː ... æʊt He So, haʊ ... aʊt Y, hoː ... aʊt So, æʊ ... ʌʊt He, æʊ ... əʊt He, haʊ ... əʊt Y, oː ... əʊt He

2. vtphr to RAKE in a domestic fire V.3.8(b). *-ing* hɒˈɪn ... ɛʊt Nf

hog *1. n What do you call a pig when castrated? Does that word apply to the female as well?* III.8.8. Eng exc. Hu C Bk Bd Hrt D. ⇒ **bacon-hog, bacon-pig, barrener, barrow, barrow-hog, barrow-pig, boar-seg, clean pig, cut hog-pig, cut pig, dog-pig, he-pig, hogget, hog-pig, pig, pigs, rig, stag, store, store-pig;** ⇒ also **clean-cut hilt, cut gilt, cut hilt, cut sow, galt, gilt, sow-pig, splayed hilt**

2. n a BOAR III.8.7. ɒg Gl Nth Bk, hɒg Nf Ess Sr, ɔg Sr, hɔg Sf Ess, ʌg Hu, ʊg Nth

3. n **on hog, on at hog** *ON* HEAT, describing a sow III.8.9. ɒn hɒg Ess, an ɒg Bk, ɒn hɔg Ess, ɔn hɔg Sf, an əʔ ɒg Bk, ɒn ət ɒg O Brk, ɒn əʔ ɒg O

4. vt to STOCK III.3.6. *-ing* ɒgɪn St Lei

5. n a sheep before its first shearing, ⇐ EWE-HOG III.6.4. hœːg Nb, hɒg Nb Cu We Y Sa, ɒg We La Y Ch Db Sa St L Co, *pl* ɒgz Cu, ɔg La Y L, hɔːg Do, ʌg So Co D

6. n a sheep from its first to its second shearing, ⇐ GIMMER III.6.5. hɒg So, ɒg Db Do, hʌg So

7. n a WETHER III.6.8. hœˈg Nb Du, hɒg Y So, ɒg Cu La Y Db St Nt L Lei, ɔg La*[to 6 months old x1]* Y L, ʊg Lei *[queried u.r. SBM on grounds of age and castration]*

8. n a CLAMP in which potatoes are stored out of doors II.4.6. ɒg La Y Ch Db Sa St, ɔg We La Ch, *pl* ʊgz La

9. v to guzzle a drink, ⇐ GUZZLES VI.5.13(a). *pt* hɒgd Nf, *-ing* hɒgn Nf

10.1. vt to GOBBLE food VI.5.13(b). *-ing* hɒgn Nf

10.2. v to gobble. hɒg Nf, *-ing* ɔgɪn L

hogasses *npl* HAWS IV.11.6. ɛgaʃəz Ha, ɛɪgaːsɪz Sr Sx, ɒgæˈsɪz Sr, ɒgaːsɪz Sr Sx, ɒgaːzɪz Sx

hog down *vtphr* to GOBBLE food VI.5.13(b). hɒg ... dɛʊn Ess

hog-form *n* a BENCH on which slaughtered pigs are dressed III.12.1. ɒgfɔᶜːᵊm Bk

hoggans *npl* HAWS IV.11.6. ɒgənz Co

hog-gap *n* a SHEEP-HOLE IV.2.8. ɒggap Cu

hogget *1. n* a sheep before its first shearing, ⇐ EWE-HOG III.6.4. haːgət Nf, hɒgɪt Nf, *pl* hɒgɪts K*[rare]*, hɒkɪt Ess, hɒˈgət Nf, ɒgɪt Ch Hrt, *pl* ɒgɪts K, ɒgət Co, hɔˈgət Sf, hɔgɪt Sf, *pl* hɔkəts Sf, ɔgɪt C,

ʌgɪt Hu, ʌgət Co, ogɪt L

2. n a sheep from its first to its second shearing, ⇐ GIMMER III.6.5. hɒkɪt Ess, *pl* hɒgɪts Sr, hɒgət Ess, ʊgɪt Ch

3. n a WETHER III.6.8. hɒgɪt Nf, *pl* ɒgɪts Nth, hɒgət Ess, ɒgət Mon, ɔgɪt Ess*[old]*, hɔgət Ess, *pl* hɔgəts Sf

4. n a HOG III.8.8. ɔgət K

hogging *adj ON* HEAT, describing a sow III.8.9. hɒgɪn Ess So Sr Do Ha, əhɒgɪn W, hɒgən W Do, *prppl* əhɒgən Ha, ɒgɪn Wa Gl Nt Lei R Nth Hu Bk Bd So W Brk Sr K Do Ha Sx, *prppl* ɒgɪn K, ɒgən Do Ha, hɔgɪn So, *prppl* hɔgɪn Sr, ɔgɪn L C Hrt Ess MxL, *prppl* ɔgɪn K, ɔgən Ess, *prppl* ɔgən Ha, hɔːgən Do, ʊgɪn Nth; **on hogging** ɒn hɒgɪn W, ɔːn hɒgɪn W, an ɒgɪn Bk, ɒn ɒgɪn Bk Bd Hrt W Brk, ɒn ɒgən Ha, ɔn hɔːgən Sf, ɒn ɔːgən Ha

hog-hazels *npl* HAWS IV.11.6. ɒgɛɪzʊɫz K, ɒgɛɪzʊz Sx

hog-hole *n* a SHEEP-HOLE IV.2.8. hɒgwɒl We, hɒgwʊl Cu, ɒgʊəl We La

hog-house *n* a PIGSTY I.1.5. ɔgæʊs Ha

hog-lamb *n* a MALE LAMB III.6.2. ʊglam Lei

hog-mouse *n* a SHREW-MOUSE IV.5.2. *pl* ɒgmaɪs Hu, ʌgmɛʊs Bd, ɒgmɛʊs Nth, ʊgmɛʊs Nth

hog-pig *1. n* a BOAR III.8.7. ɒgpɪg Y

2. n a male or female HOG III.8.8. ɒgpɪg Wo

3. n a male hog. aːgpɪg Gl, hɒgpɪg Cu Nf W, ɒgpɪg Y Ch Sa He Wo Wa Mon O Nt Nth, hɔgpɪg C, ɔgpɪg Y Wa

4. n a hog. hœːgpɪg Nb, ɑgpɪg O, hɒgpɪg Du Y Mon, ɒgpɪg Y Sa O L Nth, *pl* ɒgpɪgz Wo, ɔgpɪg La L

5. n a castrated female pig. ɔgpɪg Wo

hogs *npl* PIGS III.8.1. ɒgz Hrt, hɒgz Nf, ʌgz Bk Bd, ʊgz Bd

hog's-guts *n* CHITTERLINGS III.12.2. ɒgzgʌts Hrt

hog-stool *n* a BENCH on which slaughtered pigs are dressed III.12.1. hɒgstʉːl Nf, hɒgstuːʊ Ess

hog-sty *n* a PIGSTY I.1.5. ʌgstaɪ Bd, ʌgstɔɪ Bk

hog up *vphr* to STOCK a cow III.3.6. *-ed* ɒgd ʊp Ch

hogward *adj ON* HEAT, describing a sow III.8.9. hɒgəd Ess, hɔgəd Ess

hoisting *v-ing* COUGHING VI.8.2. *no -ing* hɒɪst Nb, *no -ing* hɔɪst Nb*[coughing badly]*

hoizy *adj* HOARSE VI.5.16. ɒɪzi Co *[queried SBM]*

hoke *v* to BUTT III.2.10. *-ing* hɔːkɪn So, *-ing* hoːkɪn So

hold *1. imp* **hold off** the command TURN RIGHT!, given to plough-horses II.3.5(b). ɔʊɫd ɔːf O

2. imp **hold fast** the command GO ON!, given to

211

plough-horses II.3.5(d). 'hoːɫ 'vaːs So, 'oːɫ 'vaːst Ha, 'oːɫ vaːs Do, 'oː 'vaːst Do

3. *vi* to conceive, referring to a cow, ⇐ *NOT IN CALF* III.1.8. *3prperfsg/neg* ɛznt ɛld Ch, *3prperfsg/neg* aznəɹ ɛld Ch

4. *vt* to PEN or FOLD sheep in part of a field III.7.10. ɒd La

5. *v* to AGREE with somebody VIII.8.12. hʌʊɫd Sf Ess, hʌʊɫ Ess, oːɫ D, houl Nf, ɔʊɫd Hu, ɔʊd La

holders *npl* sheaths or other devices used to keep a knitting-needle firm, ⇐ SHEATH V.10.10. oʊldəz St

hold-fast *n* a DIAGONAL BAR of a gate IV.3.7. oʊɫdfæst Brk, oʊɫdfæ·s Brk

hold in *vphr* to AGREE with somebody VIII.8.12. ɒld ɪn Gl, hʌʊɫd ɪn Ess

holding *adj* IN CALF III.1.10. ɒldɪn Y, ɒdɪn La *[Y form may be v-ing]*

holds *npl* the HANDLES of a horse-drawn plough I.8.2. ɔːɫz D, hɔːɫz So, ɔːɫdz So

hold tight *vphr imp* the command stop! or WOA!, given to plough-horses II.3.5(c). 'hʌʊɫ ˌtɔɪt Ess

hole *1. n* a PIGSTY I.1.5. *pl* ɒɪlz Db

2. *n* a CLAMP in which potatoes are stored out of doors II.4.6. oːl La

3. *n* a POOL on a farm III.3.9. hoəl Nb

4. *n* a SHEEP-HOLE IV.2.8. oʊl St

5. *n* an ASH-MIDDEN V.1.14. ɒʊɫ Sr*[old]*

6. *vt* to BEAT a boy on the buttocks VIII.8.10. hɒɪl Cu

holes *npl* PUDDLES IV.1.6. *sg* houl Nf

holiday *n* On election day the school is often used for polling, and the children get a .... VIII.6.3. Eng. ⇒ **hollie**

holl *1. n* an artificial RIVULET IV.1.1. hɒl Nf

2. *n* a DITCH IV.2.1(c). hɒl Nf*[larger than ditch x1]*, hɒɫ Nf, hʌl Nf

hollan *n* a POOL on a farm III.3.9. ɒɫən Co

holland-apron *n* a working APRON V.11.2(a). ɒləndeɪpɹən He

hollan-stone *n* the CURB-STONE in a cow-house I.3.9. ɔʊlnstʊən La *[interpretation questioned NBM]*

holler *1. vi-3prpl* bulls BELLOW III.10.2. hɒlə Nf, ɒlə Nth, ɒɫə Hrt

2. *vi-3prpl* they WHINNY, describing the noise horses make during feeding time in the stable III.10.3(a). ɒlə Hrt

3. *vi-3prpl* they NEIGH, describing the noise horses make in the fields III.10.3(b). ɒlə Hrt, ɒləz Wa, ɒɫəˤɹz Sx

4. *vi-3prpl* they MOO, describing the noise cows make during feeding time in the cow-house III.10.4(a). ɒɫi D, ɒlə O Hrt, *-ing* ɒɫəˡɹɪn Sr

5. *vi-3prpl* they MOO, describing the noise cows make in the fields III.10.4(b). ɒɫi D, hɒləz O, ɒlə Gl O, ɒɫə Hrt

6. *vi-3prpl* sheep BLEAT III.10.5. ə-ɒləɹɪn Hrt, *-ing*

ɒɫən D

7. *vi* to SCREAM VIII.8.11. hɒlə Cu Ess, *-ing* ɒləɹɪn K, hɒɫəˤː Do

hollering *v-ing* SHRIEKING, describing the shrill noise made by a baby VI.5.15. hɒləˤɪn So, ɒləɹɪn K, ɒləˡɹɪn Brk, *3prsg* ɒɫəz K

hollie *n* a HOLIDAY VI.6.3. hɒlɪ Man

hollin *n* a HOLLY-bush IV.10.9. hɒlɪn We, ɒlɪn Cu La Y Db, hɒlən Man

hollin-bush *n* a HOLLY-bush IV.10.9. ɒlɪnbʊʃ Y

holling *v-ing* THROWING a stone VIII.7.7. ɒlɪn Db

hollin-tree *n* a HOLLY-bush IV.10.9. ɒlɪntɹiː Y, ɒlɪntɹəɪ Y

hollow *1. n* LOW-LYING LAND IV.1.7. ɒlo· Sa, ɒlə St

2. *n* **hollow of your hand** the PALM of the hand VI.7.5. hɒlə ə jə hænd Nf, ɒlə əv jə and Cu

3. *adj* HUNGRY VI.13.9. ɒɫəˤː Ha

hollowed eggs *npl* EASTER EGGS VII.4.9. *sg* ɒɫəˤɾd̩ ɛg Sx

hollows *1. npl* PUDDLES IV.1.6. ɔləz L

2. *n* the WINDPIPE VI.6.5. ɒɫəs Mon *[queried WMBM]*

hollow-teeth *npl* MOLARS VI.5.7. hɒləti:θ Ess

holls *npl* PUDDLES IV.1.6. *sg* hɒl Nf

holly *n* At Christmas time we decorate our rooms with branches from what bush? IV.10.9. Eng; **holly-bush** hɒlɪbʊʃ Nf, ɒlɪbʊʃ Y He Wo Lei, ɒɫɪbʊʃ O Ha, ɒləbʊʃ L, ɔlɪbʊʃ La Wa Ess, ɔɫɪbʊʃ K. ⇒ **christmas, christmas-bush, christmas-tree, hollin, hollin-bush, hollin-tree, holly-berry, holly-*bush*, holly-tree, holm-bush, hulver, hulver-bush, prick-holly** *[-bush and -tree elements of compounds may not always have been recorded by fws]*

holly-berry *n* a HOLLY-bush IV.10.9. ɔlɪbəɹɪ L

holly-tree *n* a HOLLY-bush IV.10.9. hɒlɪtɹiː So, ɒlɪtɹi Y Wo, hɒlɪtɹɛɪ Y, ɒlɪtɹəɪ Y, ɔlɪtɹi Y Ch Wa MxL, ɔɫɪtɹiː Sr K

holm *n* an ELM tree IV.10.4. ɔːm We Y, oːm Y

holm-bush *n* a HOLLY-bush IV.10.9. ɔːmbɤʃ So*[old]*

holm-land *n* LOW-LYING LAND IV.1.7. ɒʊmland La, ɔʊmland La

holm(s) *n* LOW-LYING LAND IV.1.7. *no -s*: aʊm Y, hɒʊm We, hɔʊm Nb*['more a Cu word']*, ɔʊm La Y

-s: ɛʊmz La, haʊmz We*[field-name]*, ɒʊmz Cu La Y, hɔʊmz Nb, ɔʊmz La Y, oːmz Y

home-bred lamb *n* a PET-LAMB III.7.3. oːmbɹɛd ɫɑːm O

home-close *1. n* a field near a farmhouse, ⇐ FIELDS I.1.1. oʊmklous Bd

2. *n* a PADDOCK, the field nearest to the farm I.1.10. hoʊmklous O

home-farm *n* a FARMSTEAD I.1.2. ʌmfaːm C

home-ground *n* a PADDOCK I.1.10. hoʊmgrəʊnd So

home-paddock *n* a PADDOCK I.1.10. ɔʊmpadək R, ʊmpadək Lei

homer *n* a pigeon, ⇐ PIGEONS IV.7.3. houmə Nf

homestead *n* a FARMSTEAD I.1.2. jamstɛd Cu, æʊmstɪd Hrt, ɒʊmstɪd Db K, ɔmstɪd Nt, ɔʊmstɪd Lei R, ɔʊmstɛd Hu, ʌʊmstɪd Bk Bd, hʌʊmstɪd Ess, hʌʊmstɛd MxL, ʌʊmstɛd Ess[small], oːmstɪd Db, oːmstɛd Ch W, oʊmstɛd Lei Bd, oʊmstɛd Y St Wa O, oʊmstəd St Wa, ʊmstɪd Lei, ʊːmstɛd Y, wʊmstɛd St, ʊəmstɪəd Y, ʊəmstɛd Y

home-time *n* STOPPING-TIME at the end of a day's work VII.5.9. ʊəmtaɪm L

hone *v* to TRIM hedges IV.2.3. oːn He *[queried WMBM]*

hood *1. n* the CRUPPER of the harness of a cart-horse I.5.9. hʊd So

2. n an END-BOARD of a cart I.10.4. hʊd Sf

3. n a THIMBLE V.10.9. hʌd W

4. n a woman's cotton BONNET VI.14.1. hʊd L

hoods *npl* EYEBROWS VI.3.9. ʌdz Co

hoodwinks *npl* BLINKERS covering the eyes of a cart-horse I.5.2. ʌdwɪŋks Sa, ʌdɪwɪŋks Sa, ʊdwɪŋks Ch St, ʊdɪwɪŋks Sa

hoof *1. n* [Show a picture of a cow.] What do you call this [indicate a hoof]? III.2.8(a). Eng; **cow hoof** kuː uːf Y. ⇒ **claw, claws, cleaves, clee, clees, cleet, cleets, clew, clews**, *clivs* ⇒ **cleaves, cloof, cloot**, *cloots* ⇒ **cleets, cloves**, *cow* **clee**, *cow* **hoof, foot, hock, trotter**

2. n [Show a picture of a horse.] What do you call this [indicate a hoof]? III.4.10(a). Eng. ⇒ **foot**

3. vt **hoof en, hoof it** to WALK VIII.7.10. **hoof en** hʌf ən So[old]; **hoof it** ʊf ɪt He, uːf ɪt Wa[old]

4. n a CALLOSITY VI.11.4. *pl* ɪəfs Y, *pl* ʊufs Y Db Nt, ʊuvz Y

hoof-holes *npl* the HOOF-MARKS of a horse IV.3.10. uːfɔʊlz L, uːfoʊɫz Wa Nth, uːfʊəlz Y L

hoofings *npl* the HOOF-MARKS of a horse IV.3.10. uːfɪnz La

hoof-marks *npl* What do you call the holes the horse makes in the ground as it walks along? IV.3.10. ɪəfmaːks Y, ʏːfmaˡːks La, ʏːfmaˡːks So Co D, ɛʊfmaːks Db, ʌfmaˡːks Sa He Mon Bk, ʌfmaːks Hrt, ʌfməˡːks Sa, hofmaːks Nf, oʊfmaˡːks La, hʊfmaːks Ess, ʊfmaːks Y Mon Lei Brk, hʊˑfmaʁːks Nb, *sg* hʊfmaʁːk Du, hʊfmaˡːks O So Sr Ha, ʊfmaˡːks Sa Wa Mon Gl O Bk So W Ha, ʊfmaˡːks He, ʊfmaˡːks K, ʊfmarks O, hʊfmaːks MxL, ʊfmaːks Wo Ess K, ʊfmaˡːks He Brk Sr Sx, ʊfmaˑəˡks Brk, ʊfmaˡːəˡks Sx, ʊfməˡːks He Wo Gl, ˡuːfmæːks La, ᵁuːfmaˡːːks La, huːfmaːks Du Ess, uːfmaːks Y Db St Wa Nt L Lei, huːfmaʁːks Nb Du, huːfmaˡːks So W Do, huːfmaˡːkṣ Do, uːfmaˡːks Wa Co Ha, uːfmaːks He, uːfmaːks K, uːfmaˡːks Co Sx, huːfmaːəˡks Sr, uːfməˡːks Sa, ʉːfmaːks Lei. ⇒ **dub-holes, fares, feetings, feet-markings, feet-marks, fetlings, foot-holes, footings, footlings**, *foot-links* ⇒ **footlings, foot-marks, foot-pads, foot-prints, foot-steps, hoof-holes, hoofings, hoof-pits, hoof-prints, hoofs-marks, hoops, horse-feetings, horse-footings, horse- footlings, horse-foot-marks, horse-holes, horse-marks, horse-pads, horse's-feeting, horse's feet-marks, horse's-footings, horse's foot-marks, horse-shoe-marks, horse-staupings, horse-staups, horse-steppings, horse's tracks, horse-tracks, marks, muck-holes, pot-holes, prints, shoe-marks, spits, stabbles, staup-holes, staupings, step-holes, steppings, stepplings, tracks, trod-marks**; ⇒ also **track, tread**

hoof-pits *npl* the HOOF-MARKS of a horse IV.3.10. ʏːfpɪts D

hoof-prints *npl* the HOOF-MARKS of a horse IV.3.10. ʏːfpr̩ɪnts So D, ʊfpɹɪnts Mon, uːfpr̩ɪnts Co

hoofs *npl* [Show a picture of a horse. What do you call this?] And four of them? III.4.10(b). hᵁuːfs We, hɪvfs Nb, hjʏfs Du, hjʊfs Cu, ɪufs Y, jʊfs Cu Du, ɪuːfs Db Sa, hɪuːfs Du, ɪəfs Cu Y, hɪəfs Nb Du, jəːfs Du, ʏːfs La Ch Db, ʏʉːfs Sa, ɛʊfs Y Db, ʌfs Bk Bd Hrt W Co, hʌfs Sa Nf, hofs Nf, hʏfs Nf, ʊfs La Y Sa He Wo Wa Mon Gl O C Bk Bd Hrt Ess W Brk Sr K Ha Sx, hʊfs Nb C Nf Sf Ess MxL So Sr K, uːfs We La Y Ch Db St Wo Wa Mon Nt L Lei Nth Hu So W Brk K Co Do Ha Sx, huːfs Nb Cu Du We C Nf Ess So W Sr K Do Ha. ⇒ **feet, hooves**

hoofs-marks *npl* the HOOF-MARKS of a horse IV.3.10. ʊfsmaˡːks Wa

hook *1. n* [What do you call that old-fashioned arrangement for hanging a kettle on to heat it over the fire?] What do you call its parts [c. referring to the HOOK (CROOK) in or beside the chimney]? V.3.5(c). ɪuk Y, jʊk Y, hjuːk Y, ˡuːk Db, ɪək Y, ʏːk La Ch Db, ʌk Sa Bk Bd, ouk La, hʊk O Nf Sf Ess Brk Sr K, ʊk He Wo Wa Mon Gl O Lei Nth C Bk Bd Ess W Brk Sr K Sx, huːk Nb Man, uːk La Y Db Nt L Lei R, ʉːk Lei. ⇒ **chimney-hook, crook, crow, ess-hook, gale-hook, hake, hanging-crook, hank, link, iron hook, pot-hook, reckan, reckan-crook, reckan-hook, sway-link, trammel-hook**

2. n [What do you call that old-fashioned arrangement for hanging a kettle on to heat it over the fire?] What do you call its parts [b+c. referring to the BAR or CHAIN and the HOOK (CROOK) in or beside the chimney]? V.3.5(b+c). hɪʏk Nb, jʊk Nb, hʊk MxL, ʊk Ha, *pl* ʊks Sr, huˑk Nb, uːk Y Ch, *pl* ʉːks Lei[2 hooks]. ⇒ *back-crooks* ⇒

back-crook, catches, chimney-crook, cleek, crane, crook, fire- crook, galloper-hook, *hooks, pot-hooks* ⇒ pot-hook, reckan, reckan-crook

3. *n* a CRANE on which a kettle is hung over a domestic fire V.3.4. hʊk Sf Ess MxL, ʊk Mon Nth Bk Ess, ᶦuːk Db, uːk Y L

4. *n* a hook used in place of the *HORIZONTAL* BAR of a crane over a domestic fire V.3.5(a). hʊk MxL, ʊk Ess

5. *n* a ROPE-TWISTER II.7.8. ɤːk Db

6. *n* a HEDGING-BILL IV.2.5. hjʊk Cu, hʊk C Sf, ʊk Gl Hu W, uːk L*[curved]*

7. *n* a BILLHOOK IV.2.6. ɤk So, hʊk Cu Nf Sf Ess*[curved]* So, ʊk La Wo Mon O Bk MxL, ᵁuːk La

8. *vt* to PLASH a hedge IV.2.4. hʊk Sf

9. *n* the GRASS-NAIL of a scythe II.9.9. ʊk St Wa O Hu K

10.1. *vt* to BUTT III.2.10. -ing hʊkən Do, -ing ʊkɪn W

10.2. *v* to butt. -ing hʊkɪn Ha, -ing ʊkɪn W

11. *n* the HIP-BONE of a cow III.2.1. hjɤk Du, hjʊk Du, jʊk Nb Cu Du We Y, ɪuk Y, hɪuːk Nb, hɪək Nb We, *pl* jəks Y, ʊk L, huːk Nb, juːk Cu

hook about *vphr* to BUTT III.2.10. *prppl* hʌkən əbæʊt Ha, -ing hʌkən əbæʊt Ha

hook-bone *n* the HIP-BONE of a cow III.2.1. hiːᵊkbɪən Du, hɪʊkbœːn Nb, hjʊkbɪən Cu, jʊkbɪən Du Y, hjʊkbøːn Nb, jʊkbuːn Y, *pl* hɪəkbeˈanz La, hʊkbɪˈᵊn Cu, uːkbɪan Y

hookerman *n* a spirit reputed to drag children into a pond, ⇐ BOGEY VIII.8.1. ʊkəman Hu

hook it *imp* GO AWAY! VIII.7.9(a). ʊk ɪʔ Bk, uk ɪt K, uːk ɪt L

hook out *vtphr* to RAKE in a domestic fire V.3.8(b). ʊk ... əʊt Brk

hook(s) *n* **pick your hook, sling your hook, take your hook, take your hooks** GO AWAY! VIII.7.9(a). **pick your hook** pɪk ði: ʊk So; **sling your hook** slɪŋ jəɹ ʊk Ess, sɫɪŋ ði: ʊk W; **take thy hook** teːɪk jəˡɽ ʌk Mon, teɪk jəɹ ʌk Bk, teɪk jəɹ ʊk Bk Bd, teɪk jəˡ ʊk Wo, tɛk jəɹ ʊk Wa, tɛɪk jəɹ ʊk Hu, tɛk jəɹ uːk Y Ch L, tɛk ði uːk Y, tak ði uːk Y L, tɛ ði ᵁuːk La, tak jəɹ uːk Y, tak ði uːk Y; **take your hooks** teː ði ʊuks Y

hooks 1. *n* (off her) FOOD V.8.2. ᶦuːks Db, ɛʊks St, uks St, uːks Nt L

2. *n* **off the hooks** ILL, describing a person who is unwell VI.13.1(b). ɒf ð uks St, ɒf t uːks Y, ɒf ʊuks Y

3. *n* **a bit off the hooks, off the hooks** SICK, describing an animal that is unwell VI.13.1(c). **a bit off the hooks** ə bɪt ɒf əv ʊks St; **off the hooks** ɔf ðə uːks L

hooks and chain *n* a CRANE on which a kettle is hung over a domestic fire V.3.4. ʊks ŋ tʃɛɪn Brk

hook-toed *adj* PIGEON-TOED VI.10.4. hʊktɔʊd Hu

hooly *adj* ILL, describing a person who is unwell VI.13.1(b). jʊlɪ Du

hoop *n* the iron TIRE round a cart-wheel I.9.10. ɪuːp nwY Db Sa, jʊp Cu Du We, hjɤp Nb Du, ɪəp Y, hɪəp Nb Du, ɤːp La Ch Db, ɛʊp Db St, ʌp Sa, uːp Cu We La Y Ch Db Sa St Wo Gl Nt L Lei Bd, huːp Nb Cu We Man

hooping *n* the iron TIRE round a cart-wheel I.9.10. ʊupɪn Y

hoops *npl* the HOOF-MARKS of a horse IV.3.10. uːps Y *[queried NBM]*

hoose* *n* the cough of an animal, ⇐ COUGHING VI.8.2. ɤːs D

hoosk* *n* the cough of an animal, ⇐ COUGHING VI.8.2. ɤːsk D, jɤːsk D

hoost* *n* the cough of sheep, ⇐ COUGHING VI.8.2. ɤːs Co D, uːs Co

hoosting *v-ing* COUGHING VI.8.2. ɤːstɪn D, ɤːstən Co*[light cough]*, ɤːsən D*[animals]*, ʊəstɪn Y, uːstɪn St*[old x1]*

hoot 1. *imp* **hoot, hoot off*** the command TURN RIGHT!, given to plough-horses II.3.5(b). **hoot** ɒʊt Sx, huːt K Sx; **hoot off** 'uːt 'ɑːf He *[taken as woot- WMBM]*

2. *vi-3prpl* they MOO, describing the noise cows make in the fields III.10.4(b). uːt Wa

hooves* *npl* the HOOFS of a horse III.4.10(b). hɪɤvz Nb, ɪuvz Y St, hɪəvz Nb We, ɤːvz So Co D, hnuːvz K, hʊvz Ess, uːvz La Y Ch Db St Wa L Lei R Nth K Co Do Sx, huːvz Nb Cu Ess So W, ʉːvz Lei

hooze 1. *adj* HOARSE VI.5.16. uːz La D

*2. *n* the cough of a cow, ⇐ COUGHING VI.8.2. ɤːz D*[animal]*, jʊz Y*[also sheep x1]*, jəz Y, ʊəz Y, ʊuːz Y

hoozed *adj* HOARSE VI.5.16. uːzd Co

hoozed up *adj* HOARSE VI.5.16. ɤːzd ʌp Co

hoozing *v-ing* COUGHING VI.8.2. ɤːzɪn D*[animals]*, no -ing ɤːʃ D, jʊzɪn Y, jʊzn We*[persistently]*, jʊzən Du*[cows]*, juːɹsən Cu*[cows]*, ʊuːzɪn Y*[cows]*, ʊəzɪn Y

hoozy *adj* HOARSE VI.5.16. ɤːzi D, uːzi Co D

hop 1. *imp* **hop in** the command TURN LEFT!, given to plough-horses II.3.5(a). ɒp ɪn We

2. *imp* **hop, hop back, hop over** the command TURN RIGHT!, given to plough-horses II.3.5(b). **hop** hɒp Nb, ɒp Cu; **hop back** hɒp bak We, hɒ bak Cu We; **hop over** ɒp ɒuə Cu

3. *vi* to BOUNCE VIII.7.3. hɒp So, ɒp So*[old]* Co D Do

hop-bin *n* a storage container for hops, ⇐ CORN-BIN I.7.4. *pl* ɒpbɪnz K

hop down *viphr* to DUCK VIII.7.8. ɒp dɛʊn K

hopeless *adj* STUPID VI.1.5. ɔːpləs Y

hop it *imp* GO AWAY! VIII.7.9(a). ɒp ɪt La Y Db St O So Sr D Sx, ɒp ɪʔ Hrt Ess, ɔp ɪt Ch K

hop off *imp* GO AWAY! VIII.7.9(a). ɒp ɑːf Wo

hop over *vphr* to JUMP a wall IV.2.10. hɒp ɔːvəᵗ: So W, ɒp ɔːvəᵗ: W, ɒp oːvəᵗ Mon, hɒp ouvəᵗ: So

hopper *1. n* a SOWING-BASKET II.3.6. ɑpə Wa, hɒpə Cu Wa*[zinc]* Mon, ɒpə Cu We La Y Ch*[tin or wood x1]* Db St Wa Nt Lei R, hɒpəˀ Man, ɒpəˀ La Y Ch*[tin]* Nth, ɒpəɹ La Y St He, hɒpəᵗ Wa, ɒpəᵗ Ch Db Sa St He Wo Wa*[wood x1]*, ɒpəᵗ: Sa, ɔpə Y Wa L Ess, ɔpəˀ La L, ɔpɹ L, ɔpəɹ Y, ɔpəᵗ Wo
2. n a BASKET for carrying horse-feed III.5.4. ɒpə R
3. n a SKEP IV.8.8(b). *pl* ɒpəz Db

hoppet *1. n* a PADDOCK I.1.10. hɒpət Ess
2. n a SOWING-BASKET II.3.6. ɒpɪt La

hop-spud *n* a MUCK-FORK I.3.13. ɒpspʌd Sx

hop-string *n* TWINE used to fasten thatch on a stack II.7.7(b1). ɒpstɹɪŋ K

horch *1. vt* to BUTT III.2.10. ɔᵗ:tʃ D, *-ing* ɔᵗ:tʃɪn So
2. v to butt. *-ing* ɔᵗ:tʃɪn D

horn *1. npl* a handle of a scythe, ⇐ HANDLES II.9.8. *sg* ɔᴶ:ɹn La
2.1. vt to BUTT III.2.10. *prppl* hɔːnən Man, *-ing* hɔːnən Nf, *prppl* ɔːnɪn L, *-ing* ɔːnɪn L Ess, *-ing* ɔᵗ:n̩ɪn So Co D, *-ing* ʋənɪn L
2.2. v to butt. *prppl* hœːnən Du, *-ing* aᵗ:n̩ɪn Gl, *-ing* hɔːn Ess, *-ing* hɔːnɪn Nf, ɔːn Ess, *prppl* ɔːnɪn Y Mon L, *-ing* ɔːnɪn Nt L Nth Hu, ɔᴶ:ɹn La, ɔᵗ:n̩ O, *-ing* ɔᵗ:n̩ɪn Gl Bk Co D, *-ing* ʋənɪn L
3. v to MARK the horns of sheep in some unspecified way to indicate ownership III.7.9. huən Nb*[old]*
4. n a CALLOSITY VI.11.4. hœːn Du, hɔːn Du, *pl* ɔːnz Db, hɔᵏ:n Du, *pl* ɔˑənz Y, *pl* hoənz Nb, ʋən Y

horn about *vtphr* to BUTT III.2.10. *prppl* ɔᵗ:n̩ɪn ... əbævt D

horn-burn *v* to MARK the horns of sheep with a burn-mark to indicate ownership III.7.9. ɔːnbɒn Y*[hill sheep x1]*, hɔːnbɔːn Du, hɔᵏ:nbɔᵏ:n Nb, *-ing* hɔːnbəːnɪn Y, ɔːnbəːn We Y, ɔᴶ:ɹnbɔᴶ:ɹn La, ɔᴶ:ɹnbəᴶ:n La, ɔəᴶnbɔᴶ:n La, ɔᴶ:ɹnbəᴶ:n We Y, ɔːnbʋən Y, hoənbəːn Nb

hornless *adj When a cow has no horns, you say it is* .... III.2.9. aᴶ:nləs Brk, aᵗ:n̩lɪs Wo, aᵗ:n̩tɪs Gl, aᵗ:n̩ləs Gl, haᵗ:nləs So, aᵗ:n̩təs W Ha, aᵗ:n̩təs W Ha, haᵗ:n̩təs W, ɑːnlɪs Wo, aᵗ:n̩lɪs Wo Wa, ɑːntɛs Mon, aᵗ:nlɛs He Wo Mon, aᵗ:ntɛs He, ɔːnlɪs Sa Wa MxL, hɔːnlɪs Ess, ɔᵗ:n̩lɪs He O, ɔˑn̩tɪs O, ɔᵗ:n̩lɛs Sa, ɔːnləs St, ɔᵗ:n̩ləs Sa O So Sx, hɔᵗ:n̩ləs So, ɔᵗ:n̩təs So, hɔᵗ:n̩təs So, ɔᵗ:n̩təs Co D Sx. ⇒ **cowed, cowey, cush, de-horned, dod, dodded, doddy, hummel, hummelled, mailie, mooldy, not, not-cow, not-horn-cow, notted, poll, poll-beast, poll-cow, polled, polled-cow, poller, poller-cow, pollow, polly, polly-cow, scotty**

horn-mark *v* to MARK the horns of sheep in some unspecified way to indicate ownership III.7.9. aᵗ:n̩maᵗ:k Do

horns *n* barley AWNS II.5.3. hœːnz Du, haːnz Nf, haːnz Nf, hɔːnz Cu Du We, hɔˑrnz We, hɔənz Nf

horny buck *n* a CALLOSITY VI.11.4. ɔəni bʊk Y

horse *1. n* **horse in the cart** a SHAFT-HORSE I.6.2. ɒs ɪ t kaːt Y
2. npl HORSES I.6.5. hɒsˑ Nf, ɔs L
3. n a SAWING-HORSE I.7.16. ɑːs Mon, ɒs St L, ɔːs St L Hrt, ɔᴶ:ɹs La, hɔᵗ:ʂ So, ɔᵗ:ʂ Sa
4. n a STALLION III.4.4. aᵗ:ʂ So, ɒs Du Y Lei R, hɒˑs Nf, ɔːs Ch St Lei R Hrt, ɔᵗ:ʂ So

horse-ants *npl* ANTS IV.8.12. aᵗ:ʂæːnts Gl

horse-brush *n* a BRUSH used to clean horses III.5.5(a). ɒsbɹɪʃ Co, ɒsbɹʌʃ W, ɒsbɹʊʃ Y, ɒsbɹʊʃ Y St, ɔsbɹʊʃ Y L, ɔᴶ:sbɹʊʃ La

horse-buckle *n* a COWSLIP II.2.10(a). *pl* ɔːsbɒkɫz K

horse-chap *n* a CARTMAN on a farm I.2.2. ɒstʃap D

horse-chop *n* CHAFF fed to horses III.5.3. ɔstʃɔp L

horse-clog *n* the CLOG on a horse's tether I.4.3. ɒsklɒg Y, ɒɹsklɒg Y, ɔsklɒg Y

horse-colt *n* a COLT III.4.3. aᵗ:ʂkoːɫt Brk, ɒskɛʊt Ch, ɒskɒɫt Gl, hɔskʌʊt Sf, hɔˑskʌult Nf, ɔːskɒɫt K, ɔːskʊult Wa, hɔˑskoult Nf*[3 years old]*, ɔːskoʊɫt Nth, ɔːskoʊɫ? Bd, ɔːzkoːɫt Sa, ɔᴶ:ɹskɔut La, ɔᵗ:ʂkɒɫt Gl O, ɔᵗ:ʂkɒuɫt O, ɔᵗ:ʂkɔult Wa, ɔᵗ:ʂkoːɫt D, ɔᵗ:ʂkoʊɫt O, ɔᵗ:ʂkouɫ? Bk, ɔːˀskɒuɫ? Bd, ɔːˀskʌuɫʰ Hrt, ɔᵗ:ˀskɒuɫ? Bk

horse-fat *n* CART-GREASE, used to lubricate the wheels of a cart I.11.4. hɒsfæt Nf

horse-feed *n* CHAFF fed to horses III.5.3. hɒsfiːd Cu, ɒsfiːd Cu

horse-feetings *npl* the HOOF-MARKS of a horse IV.3.10. ɒsfiːtɪnz Nt

horse-foal *n* a COLT III.4.3. hɔˑsfoul Nf, ɔːsfʌʊɫ Bk, ɔᵗ:ʂfouɫ Bk

horse-foot *n* COLT'S-FOOT II.2.7. ɔːsfʊt MxL

horse-footings *npl* the HOOF-MARKS of a horse IV.3.10. ɒsfʊtɪnz St, hɒsfʊtnz Sf, ɔsfʊtɪnz L

horse-footlings *npl* the HOOF-MARKS of a horse IV.3.10. *sg* ɔːˀsfʊ?lɪn Hrt

horse-foot-marks *npl* the HOOF-MARKS of a horse IV.3.10. ɒsfɪətmaːks Y, ɔːs fʊtmaːks Wa, ɔᴶ:sfʊuːtmaᴶ:ks Y

horse-grease *n* CART-GREASE, used to lubricate the wheels of a cart I.11.4. ɒsgɹɪəs Y, hɔsgɹɪis Nf

horse-haws *npl* HIPS of the wild rose IV.11.7. hɒshɔːz Nf

horse-hoe *vt* to THIN OUT turnip plants II.4.2. ˈɒsoː D

horse-holes *npl* the HOOF-MARKS of a horse IV.3.10. ɒsᴅɪlz La, ɔˑⱼɹsoːlz La

horse-keeper *n* a CARTMAN on a farm I.2.2. ɒskiːpə Nth Bd, ɒskiːpə C Ess, hɔːskiːpə Ess, ɔːskiːpə Nth Hu C Bd

horseman *n* a CARTMAN on a farm I.2.2. ɑsmən C, hɑːsmən Ess, aᵗːʂmæn Co, hɒsmən Cu Du, hɒsmæˑn Man, ɒsmæn Co, ɒsmən Cu La Y Co D, hɔsmən Sf Ess, ɔsmən Y, hɔːsmən We Sf Ess, ɔːsman Y, ɔːsmən Cu Y Hrt Ess, hɔᵝːsmən Nb, ɔˑⱼːsmen La, ɔˑⱼːsmən La, ɔᵗːʂmæn Co; **head horseman** hɛd hɑːsmən Ess, hɪd hɔsmən Sf, hɛd hɔːsmən Ess, hɪd hɔːsmən Nf, hiːd hɔːᵊsmən Sf *[NBM also has **head-** form in Y, but undefined and not a headword]*

horse-marks *npl* the HOOF-MARKS of a horse IV.3.10. ɒsmɑːks Y, ɔsmaːks Ch, ɔːsmaːks Wa, ɔᵗːʂmaᵗːks Sa

horse-mixture *n* CHAFF fed to horses III.5.3. hɔːəᵗʂmɪkstjəᵗ Sr*[old]*

horse-needle* *n* a dragonfly, ⇐ NEEDLE V.10.2(a). hɔːᵊsniːdɬ Ess

horse-pads *npl* the HOOF-MARKS of a horse IV.3.10. ɔᵗːʂpadz O

horse-pightle *n* a PADDOCK I.1.10. hɒspɪtɬ Ess

horse-plough *n* a PLOUGH I.8.1. hɒsplæʊ Lei, ɒsplaʊ Lei, ɔːsplæʊ St, ɔːsplaːᵊ Lei

horse races *n* a local FESTIVAL or holiday VII.4.11. hɒᵗːʂ ɾeɪsɪz So

horse-rack *n* a HAY-RACK in a stable I.4.1. ɔᵗːʂɹæk Wo

horses *npl* Many farmers now use tractors and have sold most of their .... I.6.5. Eng. ⇒ **horse, tits**

horse's fat *n* CART-GREASE, used to lubricate the wheels of a cart I.11.4. hɔˑsɪz fæt Nf

horse's-feeting *n* the HOOF-MARKS of a horse IV.3.10. hɔˑsɪzfiːtn Nf, hɔsəzfɪtn Sf

horse's feet-marks *npl* the HOOF-MARKS of a horse IV.3.10. ɒsɪz fɪtməᵗːks Wo, ɔˑⱼˑsɪz fɪtmaːks

horse's-footings *npl* the HOOF-MARKS of a horse IV.3.10. *sg* hɒˑsɪzfʊtn Nf, ɔːᵊsəzfʊtɪnz Hu

horse's foot-marks *npl* the HOOF-MARKS of a horse IV.3.10. ɔːsɪz fʊtmaːks Ch Wa

horse-shoe-marks *npl* the HOOF-MARKS of a horse IV.3.10. ɔːsʃuːmaːks K

horse-slaughterer *n* a KNACKER III.11.9. hɑːsslɔːʔəɹə Nf, hɒsslɔʔəɹə Nf, hɒsslɔːʔəɹə Nf, hɒsslɔːʔːə Nf, hɒsslɔˑtʔə Nf, hɔːsslɔːʔə Nf, hɒsslɔˑᵊdəɹə Sf

horse-snails *npl* large black SNAILS IV.9.3. ɔːssneːlz Db

horse-staupings *npl* the HOOF-MARKS of a horse IV.3.10. ɒsstaːpɪnz Y, ɒsstɔːpɪnz Y *[-au- spelling from NBM headword list, but IM note in Y gives 'cow-stowps']*

horse-staups *npl* the HOOF-MARKS of a horse IV.3.10. ɒsstɔups Y *[see note at **horse-staupings**]*

horse-steppings *npl* the HOOF-MARKS of a horse IV.3.10. ɔːᵊsstɛpɪnz Bk

horse's tracks *npl* the HOOF-MARKS of a horse IV.3.10. ɒsɪztɹæks He

horse-team *n* a TEAM of horses I.6.1. haᵗːʂtiːm W

horse-tie *n* a TETHERING-ROPE used to tie up a horse I.4.2. ɑːstiː Y, hɒstæɪ Man, ɒstəɪ He, ɔːᵊstɑɪ Nth

horse-tracks *npl* the HOOF-MARKS of a horse IV.3.10. aᵗːʂtɹæks Gl, aᵗːʂtɹaks Sa, aᵗːʂtɹæks He, hɒˑstɹækʔs Nf, ɒstɹæks Wo Gl, ɒstɹæks Co, ɒstɹaks Wo Gl, ɒstɹaks Co D, ɒʂtɹaks D, ɔstɹæks Ess, ɔːstɹæks Sa, ɔːstɹaks Ch Sa

horse-tree *n* an EVENER, the main swingle-tree of a horse-drawn plough harness I.8.4. ɑːstɹiː C, hɒstɹɪ Nf, hɒːstɹɪ Nf, ɒstɹiː L, hɔːstɹiː Nf, hɔːstɹɪ Nf

horse-tree(s) *n* a SWINGLE-TREE of a horse-drawn plough harness I.8.3.
sg: hɑstɹɪ Nf, hɒstɹɪ Nf, hɔˑstɹɪ Nf
-s: hɑːstɹəs Nf, hɒˑstɹɪs Nf, ɒstɹiːz L

horse-whip *n* a WHIP used for driving horses I.5.12. ɒswɪp Ha

horse-yard *1. n* a FARMYARD I.1.3. ɔːsjaːd Nth
2. n the STRAW-YARD of a farm I.1.9. hɒsjaᵗːd̪ W*[few cows kept]*

hosking *v-ing* COUGHING VI.8.2. ɒskɪn La

hot *1. adj* And why have they [i.e. bread or cakes] been burnt? Because the oven has been TOO .... V.6.8. ⇒ Eng *overheated*, *over hot*, *too* brisk, *too* fierce
2. adj come too hot, get hot, get the hot, get too hot to HEAT, referring to a haystack II.9.16. **come too hot** *3prsg* kʌmz tyː hɒt MxL; **get hot** gɪt jat Y, gɛt jat Y, gɛt ɒt St; **get the hot** gɛt ðə hɒt Ess; **get too hot** gɛt tuː ɑt Gl, *3prsg* gⱼɛts tuː ɒt Ch
3. n HEAT VI.13.6. ɒʔ O, ɔt L
4. adj STUPID VI.1.5. hɒt W

hot coals *n* CINDERS V.4.3. hɒt kʌʊɫz Ess

hot-plate *n* a GIRDLE for baking cakes V.7.4(b). ɒtpleːt Sa, ɒtpɫeːt W, ɒtpleɪt Hu

hough-bands *npl* KNEE-STRAPS used to lift the legs of working trousers VI.14.17. hɒfbands Nb, *sg* hɒfband Du

hound-man *n* a KNACKER III.11.9. huːndman Nb

house *1. n* [Show a picture of some houses. What do you call these?] And one of them? V.1.1(a). Eng. ⇒ **hovel, housen**
2. n the LIVING-ROOM of a house V.2.1. jas Y, hɛʊs Ess, ɛʊs Nth*[single downstairs room]* Hrt*[old]*, ɛas Y, æˑas Y, æʊs L*[single downstairs room]*, æʊz Lei, aːs La Y Lei, aʊs Y Db, uːs Y L, əʊs Y

3. n the SITTING-ROOM of a house V.2.2. hɛʊs Sf, aʊs Y

4. n a FARMSTEAD I.1.2. hɛus Nf; **house and buildings** æʊs ən bɪɫdɪnz Nth, aʊs ən bɪldɪnz Nt

5. n a FASTING-CHAMBER III.11.3. æʏz D

house-broom *1. n* a BROOM used for sweeping outdoors V.9.10. uːsbɹuːm Y

2. n a BRUSH used for sweeping indoors V.9.11. hɛʊsbɹʊm Ess, hɛʊsbɹuːm Ess, ɛʊsbɹuːm Sa Nth, æʊsbɹuːm St, æʊsbɹuːm O, aʊsbɹʊm Sa, aʊsbɹuːm Sa St He, ʌʊsbɹuːm Gl

house-brush *n* a BRUSH used for sweeping indoors V.9.11. ɛʊsbɹʌʃ Nth, aɪsbɹʊʃ Ch, haʊsbəᵗːʃ So, aʊsbɹʊʃ La Nt, uːsbɹʊʃ Y

house-chamber* *n* a BEDROOM over a living-room V.2.3. aʊstʃeːmbə Db

house-crease *n* the ridging-tiles of a house roof, ⇐ RIDGE V.1.2(a). ᵁuːskɹiːs Gl

house-easing box *n* the GUTTER of a roof V.1.6. *pl* huːsiːzn bɒksɪz Nb

house-end *n* the GABLE-END of a house V.1.5. ɛʊsɛnd O, æʊsɛnd L, əʊːˀsɛnd Gl

house-meadow *n* a PADDOCK I.1.10. hᵆusmɛdɐ K

housen* *n* a HOUSE V.1.1(b). aʊzən Mon

house of commons *n* an EARTH-CLOSET V.1.13. hɛus ə kɒˈmənz Nf

house-place *1. n* the LIVING-ROOM of a house V.2.1. ɛːspleˈɪs Db, aːspleːs Y, aɪspliːs St, aʊspleɪs St Lei

2. n the SITTING-ROOM of a house V.2.2. ɛːspleːˡs Db

houser *n* a GOSSIP VIII.3.5(b). æʏzəᵗː Co

house-snails *npl* SNAILS IV.9.3. æʏssnɛɪɫz Co

houses-of-parliament *n* an EARTH-CLOSET V.1.13. aʊzəz əv paᵗːlɪmənt So, uːsɪzəpaːlɪmənt Y

housing *v-ing* CARTING corn from the field II.6.6. aːzɪn La*[old]*, aʊzɪn La

hovel *1. n* a COW-HOUSE I.1.8. *pl* ʊvʊlz Sx

2. n the place where hay is stored on a farm, ⇐ HAY-LOFT I.3.18. ɒvɫ Bd, ɔvl L

3. n a CART-SHED I.11.7. hɒvəl Nf

4. n a FASTING-CHAMBER III.11.3. ɒvɫ Wa Bd

5. n a HOUSE V.1.1(b). ɒvəl Sa

hover *n* **on the hover** DIAGONALLY, referring to harrowing a field IX.1.8. ɒn ðə hʌvə Nf

how *n* **in this how, this how** IN THIS WAY IX.10.7. **in this how** ə ðɪs aʊ La, ə ðɪs uː Y L; **this how** ðɪs æʊ L, ðɪs ɔʊ L

howery *1. adj* DULL, referring to the weather VII.6.10. aʊɹɪ L

*2. adj drizzly. aʊɹɪ L

howk *1. v* to DIG in the garden with a spade, or to dig a hole in the ground I.7.8. hɔʊkʰ Nb

2. v to ROOT, what a pig does when it digs the ground with its snout III.9.2. ɒʊk Cu, hɒʊk Nb, hɔʊkən Nb, hɔʊkn Du, *3prs* hɒʊks Nb, ʊkɪn W Ha, hʊkɪn W

3. vt to RAKE in a domestic fire V.3.8(b). haʊk Du, hɔʊk Du

howk about *vphr* to ROOT, what a pig does when it digs the ground with its snout III.9.2. *-ing* hʊkn əbæʊt Ha

howking *v-ing* building peats into a round stack containing about 100 turves, ⇐ PEAT IV.4.3. aʊkɪn La

howk up *1. vphr* to ROOT, what a pig does when it digs the ground with its snout III.9.2. hɒʊk ʊp Cu

2. vtphr to root. *-ing* hʊkɪn ... ʌp W

howl *vi* to SCREAM VIII.8.11. hɛʊl Nf, ɛʊl Sa, hɛʊɫ Hu Sf Ess, ɛʊɫ Wa O Hu Sr, ɛʊʊ K, œʏɫ D, hœˈʊl Nb, æʊl L, *-ing* hæʊɫɪn W, aʊl Du We La Db, hɔʊl Du, ʊʊl Y, ˡuːˀɫ Gl, *-ing* əʊlɪn He, əʊɫ Mon, həʊˀɫ Do, əʊəɫ W

howling *v-ing* SHRIEKING, describing the shrill noise made by a baby VI.5.15. hɛʊlɪn Nf Ess, ɛʊlɪn C, œʏɫən D, æʊɫən Ha, aʊlɪn Y

hoying *v-ing* THROWING a stone VIII.7.7. *no -ing* hɔɪ Du, hɔɪən Nb*[old]*

hub *1. n* [Show a picture of a farmcart.] What do you call this wooden part to which all the spokes are fixed? I.9.7. ɒb Sa Lei Brk, hɒb Nf, ɔʊb R, ʌb Sa Gl O Hu C Bk Bd Hrt Ess So W Brk K Ha Sx, hʌb Sa Mon Hu Nf Sf Ess MxL So Sr Sx, hʏb Du, ʊb Cu La Y Db Sa St Wo Wa Gl O Nt L Lei R Nth C Brk, ʊːb Wo Gl, hʊb Wa Ha. ⇒ **axle-box, block, bowk, bowl, box, bush, centre, masterpiece, nathe, nave, nave-stock, nose, nub, nut, stock, wheel-block, wheel-box, wheel-stock**

2. n the metal BUSH at the centre of a cart-wheel I.9.8. ʌb Sx, ʊb La

hubbles *npl* large COCKS of hay II.9.12. ʊblz St

hub-box *n* the metal BUSH at the centre of a cart-wheel I.9.8. hʌbbɒks Nf

hubs *npl* COCKS of hay II.9.12. ʊbz La*[large]* Y*[large x1]*

huck *1. n* a pea-POD V.7.12. ʌk K

2. n the human HIP-BONE VI.9.1. hɪək La, ʊk L, jʊk Cu Y

huck-bone *n* the human HIP-BONE VI.9.1. hɪəkbɪən Nb, hɪʊkbɪən Y

hucking *1. vt-ing* SHELLING peas V.7.14. hʊkɪn W

2. v-ing shelling. hʌkɪn W, ʊkɪn Ha

huckle *n* the human HIP-BONE VI.9.1. hʌkɫ So

huckle-berries *npl* BILBERRIES IV.11.3. ʌkɫbɛɹɪz Bk, ʌkɫbəɽɪz K

huckle-bone *1. n* the HIP-BONE of a cow III.2.1. hʌkɫbuːən So

2. n the human HIP-BONE VI.9.1. hʌkɫboːən So Do, hʌkɫbuːən W

hucks *1. n* barley AWNS II.5.3. ʌks MxL
2. *n* CHAFF II.8.5. ʌks Sr
hud *1. n* a pea-POD V.7.12. hʌd Brk, *pl* ʊdz O
2. *n* a NOSE VI.4.6. hɔːd So *[queried SBM]*
hudding *vt-ing* SHELLING peas V.7.14. ʌdɪn Brk
huds *n* CHAFF II.8.5. hʊdz So
huffing *v-ing* PANTING VI.8.1. hʌfɪn Ess, ʌfɪŋ Sx
huffing in *vphr-ing* COUGHING VI.8.2. hʌfɪn ɪn Ha
huggin *1. n* the HIP-BONE of a cow III.2.1. ʊgɪn We La Y Nt L, ʊgn Y, ʊgən Y
2. *n* the human HIP-BONE VI.9.1. ʊgɪn La
huggin-bone *1. n* the HIP-BONE of a cow III.2.1. ʊgɪnbɪan Y, ʊgɪnbɔːn Nt, ʊgɪnbʊən La Y Nt, ʊgnbʊən Y L, ʊgənbʊən Y L
2. *n* the human HIP-BONE VI.9.1. ʊgɪnbʊən La
huh *n* one huh, on one huh, on the huh, on the one huh ASKEW, describing a picture that is not hanging straight IX.1.3. one huh wʌn ʊf Ess; on one huh ɒn wɒn hə̃ Ess; on the huh ɒn ðə h˞ː Nf, ɒn ðə h˞ʊˑ Nf; on the one huh ɒn ðə wʌn h˞ʊ Ess
hulkings *n* barley AWNS II.5.3. ɛʊkɪnz Nth
hull *1. n* a pea-POD V.7.12. *pl* hjeˑlz Nb, hʌl Sa*[old]*, *pl* hʌlz Nb, ʌl Sa, *pl* hʊlz Nb, ʊl Sa Wo, *pl* ʊlz Ch St
2. *v* to TOP-AND-TAIL gooseberries V.7.23. *prppl* ɪɬɪn He
hulling *1.1. vt-ing* SHELLING peas V.7.14. ʊlɪn Ch
1.2. v-ing shelling peas. hjeˑlən Nb, hʌlɪn Nb, ʌlɪn Sa, ʊlɪn Ch Db St Wo*[old]*
2. *v-ing* THROWING a stone VIII.7.7. hʌlɪn Nf, hʌln̩ Nf, əhʌlən Sf, *3ptsg* hʌɬd Sf
hulls *1. n* barley AWNS II.5.3. ʌɬz Mon, ʌʊɬz Bk *[queried WMBM]*
2. *n* CHAFF II.8.5. ɒʊɬz Sx, ɔːɬz Do Sx, ɔːɬvz Ha, ʌɬz Gl
3. *n* short rough bits of straw. hɔəɬz Ha
[taken as ails SBM]
hulver *n* a HOLLY-bush IV.10.9. hʌlvə Nf*[old-fashioned x1]*
hulver-bush *n* a HOLLY-bush IV.10.9. hʌlvəbʊʃ Nf
hum *1. vi-3prpl* they WHINNY, describing the noise horses make during feeding time in the stable III.10.3(a). hʌm Sf
2. *vi-3prpl* they MOO, describing the noise cows make during feeding time in the cow-house III.10.4(a). hʊm We, ʊm La*[contented murmur x1]* Db, *-ing* ɪmɪn Y*[low soft noise]*
humble-fisted *adj* CLUMSY, describing a person VI.7.14. hʌmblfɪstɪd Nf
hummel *adj* HORNLESS, describing a cow III.2.9. wʊml Y, ʊmbl Y
hummel-ended stacks *npl* long STACKS with rounded ends II.7.1. ʊmlɛndɪd staks Y
hummelled *adj* HORNLESS, describing a cow III.2.9. ʊmld Y*[artificially de-horned only x1]*, hʊmld Du, ʊməld Du Y, hʊməld Y

hummer *1. vi-3prpl* they WHINNY, describing the noise horses make during feeding time in the stable III.10.3(a). hʌmɪ Sf*[old]* Ess, hʌmə Sf Ess, ʌmə Hrt Ess
2. *vi-3prpl* they NEIGH, describing the noise horses make in the fields III.10.3(b). hʌmə Sf Ess
hummock *1. n* a COW III.1.1(b). hʌmɪk Ha
2. *n* a MILKING-STOOL III.3.3. ɒmʊk Gl *[queried WMBM]*
hummocks *npl* COWS III.1.1(a). hʌmɪks Ha, ʌmɪks Ha
humour *n* PUS VI.11.9. jɪməˤː So, jɛməˤː D, jʏːməˤː So, ɪʊməˤː Co, jʊuːməˤ Sr, jʊuːməˤ Sx, hjuːmə So, juːməɹ Wa*[old]*, juːməˤ Sr Sx
hump *1. n* a SLOPE IV.1.10. hʌmp So *[marked probably ir.r. SBM]*
2. *n* a BUMP on someone's forehead VI.1.8. ʌmp D
humpty *adj* ILL, describing a person who is unwell VI.13.1(b). ʌmptɪ Bd *[queried EMBM]*
hunch *1.1. vt* to BUTT III.2.10. *prppl* ʌnʃɪn O W
1.2. v to butt. ʌnʃ O, *-ing* ʌnʃɪn Brk
2. *n* a SLICE of bread V.6.10. hʌnʃ So, ʌnʃ W
3. *n* hunch of bread and cheese a piece of bread and cheese, ⇐ PIECE *OF BREAD AND BUTTER AND JAM/SUGAR* V.6.11(b). ɔːnʃ ə bɹɛd ŋ̩ tʃiːz Bk
4. *adj* COLD, describing a room VI.13.17. ʊnʃ L
hunchy *adj* COLD, describing a person VI.13.18. ʌntʃɪ C
hunger* *adj* HUNGRY VI.13.9. ʌŋgəˤː Co
hungered *adj* HUNGRY VI.13.9. hʌŋgəd Ess, hʌŋgəˤːd̺ So, ʌŋgəˤːd̺ So Co D, hʊŋᵏt Nb, hʊŋəd Du We, ʊŋəd La Y, hʊŋəᵏd Nb; **hungered to death** very hungry ʊŋəd tə dɪəθ Cu Y
hunger-house *n* a FASTING-CHAMBER III.11.3. hʌŋɔᵏhuːs Nb, ʊŋəɹʌʊs La Y, ʊŋɡəɹʌʊs Y, ʊŋəɹʌʊs Y, hʊŋɔhuːs Nb, hʊŋɔᵏhuːs Nb Du, hʊŋəhᵒuːs Du, hʊŋəhuːs Nb Du We, hʊŋəɹᵊuːs Du, ʊŋəɹuːs Du Y, ʊŋəɹʌʊs Y
hunger-hull *n* a FASTING-CHAMBER III.11.3. hʊŋəɹʊl La
hungering-house *n* a FASTING-CHAMBER III.11.3. ʊŋəɹɪnᵊuːs We
hungering-pen *n* a FASTING-CHAMBER III.11.3. hʊŋəɹɪnpɛn Cu, hʊŋəʁənpɛn Nb *[see note at fasting-chamber]*
hunger-shed *n* a FASTING-CHAMBER III.11.3. ʊŋəʃed Cu
hungry *1. adj* If you haven't eaten any food for a long time, you're bound to be very .... VI.13.9. Eng exc. Co Do. ⇒ **clammed, clammed out, clammish, empty, empty in the hole, famished, famishing, fammelled, gant, hearty, hollow, hunger, hungered, lear, leary, peckish, pined, sinking, starved, starving, thirl, thirly, wallow,**

yap
2. adj miserly, ⇐ MISER VII.8.9. ʊŋəɹɪ Y

hunk *1. n* a SLICE of bread V.6.10. hʌnk So*[thick x1]*, ʌŋk W*[old x1]*
2. n **hunk of bread, hunk of bread and butter** a PIECE *OF BREAD AND BUTTER* V.6.11(a). **hunk of bread** hʌŋk əv bɹɛd Sr, hʌŋk ə bɹɛd Nf, ʌŋk ə bɹɛd Ess; **hunk of bread and butter** hʌŋk ə bɹɪd ŋ bʌdəᵗ: Do, ʌŋk ə bɹɛd ŋ bʌdəᵗ: W
3. n **hunk of bread and jam** a PIECE *OF BREAD AND BUTTER AND JAM/SUGAR* V.6.11(b). ʌŋk ə bɹɛd ŋ dʒam W

hunky *n* **hunky of bread** a PIECE *OF BREAD AND BUTTER* V.6.11(a). ʊŋkɪ ə bɹɛd O*[old]*

hunt *vt* LOOK FOR it III.13.18. ʌnt He, ʊnt Ch

hunt for *vtphr* LOOK FOR it III.13.18. hʌnt fɔɹ Nf, hʌnt? fɔɹ Nf, hʌnt fɔːɹ Sf, hʌn? fɔːɹ Sf, hʌn? vɔᵗ: So, ʌnt vɔᵗ:ɽ Do, ʌnt fəᴶ Ha, ʊnt fɔɹ He, ʊnt fəɹ Wo

hunt up *vtphr* LOOK FOR it III.13.18. ʊnt ... ʊp Y

hurdle *1. vt* to PEN or FOLD sheep in part of a field III.7.10. *-ing* əːdl Db Wa, əːdlɪn Ch, əːdɫ Wa, əˈɹdl He, əᵗ:dl̩ Sa, həᵗ:dɫ So, əᵗ:dɫ So W D, jəᵗ:dɫ So D
2. v to pen or fold sheep. həᵗ:dɫ So
3. n HURDLES used to pen sheep in part of a field III.7.11. əːdəl Y *[wc needed]*

hurdle-gates *npl* HURDLES used to pen sheep in part of a field III.7.11. əᵗ:dɫgɪəts D

hurdle in *vtphr* to PEN or FOLD sheep in part of a field III.7.10. həᵗ:dɫ ... ɪn W

hurdle off *1. vtphr* to PEN or FOLD sheep in part of a field III.7.10. hadl ... ɔːf Nf, əᵗdl ... ɔːf Wo, əᵗ:dɫ ... aːf Wo, həᵗ:dɫ ... ɔːf Do, əᵗ:dɫ ... ɔːf W Co D Do Ha, jəᵗ:dɫ ... ɔːf Co D
2. vphr to pen or fold sheep. əᵗ:dɫ ɔːf D
3. vtphr to divide a field for grazing sheep. əᵗ:dɫ ... ɔːf Do

hurdle out *1. vtphr* to PEN or FOLD sheep in part of a field III.7.10. əᵗ:dɫ ... æʏt So, əᵗ:dɫ ... aʊt Do
2. vtphr to divide a field for grazing sheep. həᵗ:dɫ ... aʊt So

hurdles *npl What do you make your pen/fold of?* III.7.11. Eng. ⇒ **bar-hurdles, bars,** *fence, fencing,* **flakes, gates,** *hemp nets and stakes,* **hurdle, hurdle-gates,** *hurdles and stakes,* **iron hurdles, iron-wheel hurdles,** *large poles and wire,* **lift-hurdles,** *net and posts, net and stakes,* **nets, nets and stakes, netting, netting and stakes, posts,** *posts and railings, posts and rails, posts and sheepnet, posts and wire-netting,* **raff-hurdles, rift-hurdles,** *rope nets and stakes,* **sheep-bars, sheep-flake, sheep-gates, sheep-hurdles,** *sheep-nets,* **sheep-netting, sheep-trays, stack-bars,** *stakes and hurdles,* **stakes and sheep-net,** *stakes and sheep-netting, stakes and twine-nets, stakes and wire,* **stuckins** *and* **nets, stumps, trays,** *turnip-rails,* **wattle-gates, wattle-hurdles, wattles, wicker-hurdles, wind-**

hurdles, *wire, wire-netting, wire-netting and stakes,* **wooden hurdles, wood hurdles**

hurdle up *vtphr* to PEN or FOLD sheep in part of a field III.7.10. əᵗ:dɫ ... ʌp Co

hurf *n* DANDRUFF VI.1.3. ʊɹf Y, əːf Y

hurked up *adj* KNOCK-KNEED VI.9.5. əːkt ʊp Wa

hurl *n* the HANGING-POST of a gate IV.3.3. həːɫ Sr

hurt *vi* to ACHE, referring to a stomach VI.13.3(b). *prppl* həᵗ:ʈɪn So

hurtle-berries *npl* BILBERRIES IV.11.3. *sg* əᵗɫbəɹɪ Sr, əᵗ:ɫɫbəɹɪz Co

hurts *1. vi-3prsg* Supposing you have a bandage taken off a wound and it is not done gently, you would probably cry: Stop, it ...! VI.13.3(a). Eng. ⇒ **fake,** *hurt, is* **tart,** *jerts,* **lames, pains, pulls, rankles, smarts, yucks**
2. npl BILBERRIES IV.11.3. aᵗ:ʦ Do, əᵗ:ʦ So Sr Co D Ha Sx, əᵗ:ɹʦ Sr Sx

husband *n And if you asked Mrs. Smith if you could have a sack of potatoes or a load of dung, she'd probably say: It's nothing to do with me, you'll ... [have to ask MY HUSBAND].* VIII.1.25. hʌzbən Ess, ʊzbʊn Wo; **my husband** mɪ hɒsbənd Man, mɔɪ ɒsbənd Brk, mʌɪ hʌzbənd Sf, maɪ hʌzbənd Nf, mɪ hʌzbən Ess*[very rare x1]*, mɪ hʌzbən Ess, maɪ hʌzbən K, mʌɪ hʌzbən Nf, məɪ hʌzbən Ess, məɪ ʌzbʌnd Mon, miː ʌzbənt Co, mʌɪ ʌzbənd Brk, məɪ ʌzbənd W, mɪ ʌsbən K, mɔɪ ʌsbən Brk, mɪ ʌzbən Sr Sx, mɔɪ ʌzbən O Hrt, məɪ ʌzbən Sx, mɔɪ ʌzbənd Sx, mɪ ʌzbən Ha, maɪ ʌzbən K*[polite]*, mʌɪ ʌzbən Brk, mʌʏ ʌzbən O, mɪ hʌzbn Ess, mɪ ʊzbʊnd La, məɪ hʊzbənd W, maɪ ʊzbənt Y, maɪ ʊzbənd Du, mɒɪ ʊzbənd St, mɔɪ ʊzbənd Wa*[polite]*, mɪ ʊzbənd La Y Nt L, mɪ ʊzbən Y Ch, mɪ ʊzbnd La; **the husband** ðə hʌzbənd Nf, ðə hʌzbən Ess Sr, ðə ʌzbənd K, ð ʌzbənd Brk, ðɪ ʌsbən Sx, ðə ʌsbən K, ðɪ ʌzbən Ess Sx, ðə ʌzbən Sx, ð ʌzbən Sx, ðə ʌzbən Brk, θ ʊzbənd St, ðɪ ʊzbən K. ⇒ **bloke, boss, chap, fellow, gaffer, gafferman, governor, him, man, master,** *Mr Smith,* **old chap, old fellow, old man**

husband-man *n* a FARM-LABOURER I.2.4. ʊzbəndman Cu

husk *1. n* a pea-POD V.7.12. hʌsk Sf, ʌsk Ess*[empty x1]*, ʊsk Db St
2. adj HOARSE VI.5.16. ʊsk O
3. n a cough, ⇐ COUGHING VI.8.2. ʌsk Sa
4. n the cough of an animal. ɒsk Ch, hʌsk W, ʌsk Sa Mon W Ha, ʊsk He Wa Gl, əsk Gl

husking *1. v-ing* SHELLING peas V.7.14. ʌskən Ess
2. v-ing COUGHING VI.8.2. hʌskɪn Ess, hʌskən Sf, ʌskɪn Bk*[calves]* W*[animals]* D*[animals]*, *prppl* ʊskɪn He*[animals]*, ʊskɪn

Y*[cows]* Sa*[old]* He*[old]*, ʊskən Y*[cows]*, *prppl* əskɪn Y

husks *n* CHAFF II.8.5. ʌsks So Sr, ʊsks St

husky *adj* HOARSE VI.5.16. hʌski Mon Nf, ʌski W, hʌskɪ Nf Sf Ess, ʌskɪ O Bd K Ha Sx, ʊski Co, ʊskɪ La Ch Wa Nth Bk

hussock* *n* a cough, ⇐ COUGHING VI.8.2. ʊsək He

hussocking *v-ing* COUGHING VI.8.2. ʌsəkɪn Bd*[old]*, *prppl* ʊsəkɪn He*[animals]*

hut *n* a TUSSOCK of grass II.2.9. *pl* hɔts Nb, hʊt Nb

hutch *1. n* a CORN-BIN I.7.4. hɒtʃ So, hʌtʃ Sf So, ʌtʃ So Co D, ʊtʃ Co
2. n a wooden corn-bin. hʌtʃ So, ʌtʃ So Co D

hut out *vtphr* to DITCH IV.2.11. hʊt ... uːt L

huvvon *n* the HIP-BONE of a cow III.2.1. ʊvn Y

huvvon-bone *n* the HIP-BONE of a cow III.2.1. ʊvnboən Y, ʊvnbʊən Y L

I

ice-bugs *n* ICICLES VII.6.11. ɛɪsbʊgz Y

ice-candles *n* ICICLES VII.6.11. æɪskandlz Y, æɪskanlz Y, aɪskandlz L, aˈɪskanlz L, aɪskandɫz Do, əɪskandɫz Do

ice-daggles *n* ICICLES VII.6.11. ʌɪsdægɫz Brk

icelets *n* ICICLES VII.6.11. ɒɪsɫəts W

ice-lick *n* ICICLES VII.6.11. aˈɪslɪk L

ice-shackles* *n* ICICLES VII.6.11. aɪsʃaklz La Y

ice-shockles* *n* ICICLES VII.6.11. ɛɪsʃɒkls Du, ɛɪsʃɒklz Nb, ɛɪsʃʊklz Cu, aɪsʃɒklz Cu Du We La Y, aɪsʃʊklz Y

ice-shoggles *n* ICICLES VII.6.11. ɛɪsʃɒglz Nb Du, ɛɪsʃɔglz Nb, aɪsʃɒglz Nb Du, aɪʃɒglz Y, aɪsʃʊglz Du

icicles *n In winter when water freezes, what can you sometimes see hanging down from the spouts?* VII.6.11. Eng exc. Du. ⇒ cicles, clinker-bells, clinkers, cockle-bells, cocky-bells, conker-bells, daggers, daglers, daglets, ice-bugs, ice-candles, ice-daggles, icelets, ice-lick, ice-shackles, ice-shockles, ice-shoggles, ickles, icy-bells, izles, snipes, tankles, tanklets

ickles *n* ICICLES VII.6.11. ɪklz Db, ɛkəlz Y

icy-bells *n* ICICLES VII.6.11. *sg* aɪsɪbɛɫ D, aɪsɪbəlz D, ɒɪsɪbɛɫz D

idle-back *n* a LOOSE *PIECE OF* SKIN at the bottom of a finger-nail VI.7.11. aɪdlbak L, *pl* aɪdlbaks Nt, aɪdlbak Nt L

idle-feg *n* a LOOSE *PIECE OF* SKIN at the bottom of a finger-nail VI.7.11. *pl* ɔɪdɫfɛgz Bk

idleman* *n* a STICK used to support the shaft of a cart I.11.1. ʌɪdɫmɛn Gl

idle-wheal *n* a LOOSE *PIECE OF* SKIN at the bottom of a finger-nail VI.7.11. aɪdɫwɛɪəɫ Nth

ill *1. adj When you are not well, then you are ....* VI.13.1(b). ɪl Man L Nf, ɪɫ La Lei C Sf Ess MxL W K*[rare x1]* Ha, ɪʊɫ Brk Sr Sx, ɪʊ Ess Brk Sr K Sx. ⇒ *a bit* dicky, *a bit off the* crooks, *a bit out of* sorts, *a bit* seedy, ailing, *ain't very* well ⇒ *not very* well, *aught but* right, bad, badly, *bit* down, *bit* off, *bit* rough, dicky, douthy, dowly, down *in the dumps*, droopy, drowsy, *feeling* badly, *feeling* duffing, *feeling* rotten, *feeling* sadly, groggy, hard up, hooly, humpty, *in bad* fettle, *in poor* fettle, *in very bad* fettle, knocked out, middling, middling *fair*, moal, moody, *nobbut a bit* dowly, *nobbut* middling, *none so* well, *not in good* fettle, *not so* good, *not so* well, *not too* good, *not too* special, *not too* well, *not up to* much, *not very* fit, *not very* grand, *not very* well, nought-cracky, *off* colour, *off it* ⇒ *off* colour, *off of* colour, *off the* crooks, *off the* hooks, *out of* fettle, *out of* sorts, poorly, queer, *rather* dull, *right* bad, rotten, rough, seedy, sick, sickly, sicky, slight, unfit, unhealthy, unwell, *very* mangey, *very* middling, wallowish, wisht
2. adj SICK, describing an animal that is unwell VI.13.1(c). ɪl Sa L Nf, ɪɫ Gl C Ess W

ilt *1. n* a YOUNG SOW III.8.5. ɪɫt He Wo Wa Mon Gl O Nth Bk So W, ɪɫʔ Bk, ɪʊlt O, ɪʊɫt W Brk
2. n a young sow before she has been served by a boar. ɪɫt O

image *1. n* a SCARECROW II.3.7. ɪmɪdʒ Co
2. n a copy, referring to someone who RESEMBLES someone else VIII.1.9. ɪmɪdʒ Nb Y L Nf Ess W Sr K Co; **spit and image** spɪt ən ɪmɪdʒ Y, spɪt n̩ ɪmɪdʒ Du Y, spɪʔ n̩ ɪmɪdʒ Y

imps *npl* HIPS of the wild rose IV.11.7. ɪmps Sa Sr

in *prep* AMONG IX.2.12. ɪn St Nf Ess W K Sx *[marked u.r. EM/SBM]*

in atween *prep* BETWEEN IX.2.11. ɪn ətwiːn Nb Du We Ess

in between *prep* BETWEEN IX.2.11. ɪn bɪtwiːn Ch He Wo Wa O Lei R Nth Nf So W Brk K Ha, ɪn bɪtwɪn Wo

in betwixt *prep* BETWEEN IX.2.11. ɪn bɪtwɪkst Nf, ɪn bɪtwɪks W

incline *n* a SLOPE IV.1.10. ɪnklæɪn Sr, ɪŋklaɪn So, ɪnklaɪn Y Nt, ɪŋklɑɪn Wa Nth, ɪnklɑɪn Nf K, ɪŋklɒɪn St, ɪnklɒɪn St*[mining term]*, ɪŋklɔɪn Bk Ess, ɪnklɔɪn Wa

increase *vi* to WAX, referring to the moon VII.6.5(a). *-ing* ɪŋkɹiiːsɪn Sx

indoors-broom *n* a BRUSH used for sweeping indoors V.9.11. ɪndɔːzbɹʊm Ess

industrious *adj* ACTIVE, describing a child VIII.9.1. ɪndʊstɹəs St *[marked u.r. WMBM]*

infecting *adj* INFECTIOUS, describing a disease VI.12.2. ɪnfɛktɪn Sx

infectious *adj Any disease that you can easily get from other people must be very ....* VI.12.2. ɪnfɛkʃʌs Mon, ɪnfɛkʃəs Nb Y St O L Nf Hrt Sr Ha, ɪnfɛkᵗjəs K, ɪnfɛkʃəz Y O Nt L, əfɛkʃəs Ch, fɛkʃəs So Sx, fækʃəs Brk. ⇒ captious, catching, catchy, contagious, *dangerous*, *easily catched*, *easily caught*, infecting, infective, latching, smitting, smittle, smittling, taking

infective *adj* INFECTIOUS, describing a disease VI.12.2. ɪnfɛktɪv Y, əfɛktɪv So

infernal *adv* VERY VIII.3.2. fəˤːŋəɫ So, fəˤːŋɫ So

in front *prep* IN FRONT OF a door IX.2.6. ɪn fɹʌnt He Mon Nf Sr, ɪn vɹʌnt Brk, ɪn fɹʌnʔ O, ɪn fɾʌnt So Co Do, ɪm fɾʌnt So, ɪn vɾʌnt So W Co D Do, ɪ fɹʊnt St, ɪn fɾʊnt Co

in front of *prep [Here's the door, and I am standing beside it.] And now [stand sideways in front of it] … it.* IX.2.6. ɪn vɾɪnt ɔː D, ɪn vɾɪnt oː D, ɪn fɹɒnt ɒv Sx, ɪn fɹɒnt əv K, ɪn fɹɒnt ə Brk K Sx, ɪn fɹɒn əv K, ɪn fɹɒnʔ ə Ess Sr, ɪn fɹʌnt ɒv Sa, ɪn fɹʌnt ɒv O, ɪn fɹʌnt əv Sa He Mon O Nth Nf Sf Bd Hrt Ess MxL K, ɪn fɹʌntʔ əv Ess, ɪn fɹʌnʔ əv Bk Bd Hrt, ɪn fɹʌnt ə Nth Nf Ess, ɪn fɹʌn ə Ess, ɪn fɹʌnʔ ə Bd Brk, ə fɹʌnt ət Ess, ɪn fɾʌnt ɒv Co, ɪn fɾʌnt oː W, ɪn fɾʌnt oʊ So, ɪn fɾʌnt əv Ha, ɪn fɾʌnt ə Co, ɪn vɾʌnt ɒ W, ɪn vɾʌnt ɔː So D Ha, ɪn vɾʌnt oː D, ɪn vɾʌnt oʊ So, ɪn vɾʌn oʊ Do, ɪn vɾʌnt ə D, ə fɹʏnt əv Lei, ɪn fɹʊnt ɒf St, ə fʁʊnt ə Nb, ə fɹʊnt ɒv Wa, ɪn fɹʊnʔ ɔːv O, ɪn fɹʊnt əv La St Wa Nt L Lei R, ɪn fɹʊnt ə Lei, ə fɹʊnt əv Y Lei R, ə fɹʊnt ə Y Lei R, ɪn vɹʊnt əv Gl, ɪn fɾʊnt ɒv O; **in the front of** ɪn ðə fɹɒnt ə Gl. ⇒ **afore, afore** *on*, **afront on**, *again*, **anent, at front of, at front on, at** *the* **front of, at** *the* **front on**, *back on door, behind, facing*, **fore, front of, front on, frontwards**, *hind*, **in front, in front on, in** *the* **front of, in** *the* **front on**, *opposite, side of it, sideways to the door, the* **front of**

in front on *prep* IN FRONT OF a door IX.2.6. ɪn fɹɒnt ɒn Sf, ɪn fɹʌnt æn Sx, ɪn fɹʌnʔ an Bk, ɪn fɹʌnt ɑn C, ɪn fɹʌnʔ an Bk, ɪn fɹʌnt ɒn Sa He Mon O Hu, ɪn fɹʌnʔ ɒn Nf, ɪn fɹʌŋ ɒn Bd, ɪn fɾʌnt ɒn So Ha, ɪn vɾʌnt ɒn W Ha, ɪn fɹʌnt ɒn Sf, ɪn fɹʌnʔ ɒn C Sf Hrt, ɪn fɹʌnt ʌn O[old] Ess, ɪn fɹʌnt ŋ He Mon, ɪn fɹʌnt ən O, ɪn fʁʊnt ɒn Nb, ɪn fɹʊnt an Nth, ɪn fʁʊnt ɒn Nb, ɪn fɹʊnt ɒn Cu Du We La Ch Db Sa St He Wo Wa Mon Gl Nt Nth, ɪ fɹʊnt ɒn Db, ŋ fɹʊnt ɒn L, ɪn fɹʊnt ɒn L, ɪn fɹʊnʔ ɒn L, ɪn fɹʊnt ən Ch Wo Wa, ɪn vɹʊnt ŋ He Gl, ɪn fɹənt ɒn Nf; **in the front on** ɪn θ fɹʊnt ɒn St, ɪ t fɹʊnt ɒn Y Db, ə θ fɹʊnt ɒn St

ings *n* LOW-LYING LAND IV.1.7. ɪŋz Y

ink-mouse *n* a BAT IV.7.7. ɪŋkməʊs Do

innings *n* CHITTERLINGS III.12.2. ɪnɪnz Ess

inside *1. n* the LAND-HORSE of a ploughing team II.3.4(b). ɪnsaːɪd St
2. n CHITTERLINGS III.12.2. ɪnsəɪd Mon
3. n **inside of the hand** the PALM of the hand VI.7.5. ɪnsaɪd ə t and Y

inside-horse *1. n* the NEAR-HORSE of a pair pulling a wagon I.6.4(a). ɪnsaɪdɒs Du
2. n the LAND-HORSE of a ploughing team II.3.4(b). ɪnsəɪdɔːəˤɹ̩s Sx

insipid *adj If you haven't put enough salt into your food, you say it is ….* V.7.8. ɪnsɪpɪd St Mon Lei Nf Bk MxL, ɪnsɛpɪd Man. ⇒ *a bit* **weak, bitter, bout kick, bout salt, duffty, flash, flat, flavourless, fresh**, *got*

no taste, **grummy**, *I haven't put enough salt in, it tastes of nought, it wants salt, it wasn't* **salt**, **mawkish**, *mush*, **nasty, no taste, no taste to it**, *not enough salt, not enough salt in, not proper taste, not* **salt** *enough, not salted enough, not salty enough, putrid, raw, rotten*, **saltless, sappy**, *short of salt, short of seasoning*, **sipid, swaffy, tame, tasteless**, *there isn't enough salt in, there's no taste in it, there's no taste to it, this hasn't got no taste, 'tisn't* **salt** *enough, 'tisn't salty enough, too* **fresh, unseasoned, waff, waffly, waffy, wairish, wairsh, wallow**, *wallowish* ⇒ **walsh, walsh, walshy**, *wants salt*, **watery, waugh, waughy, welsh, worrish**

intentionally *adv ON* PURPOSE IX.1.5. ɪntɛnʃənlɪ Nf

in tween *prep* BETWEEN IX.2.11. ɪn twiːn Hrt Co Sx

inwards *1. n* the PLUCK of a slaughtered animal III.11.6. ɪnwəˤːd͡z So
2. n CHITTERLINGS III.12.2. ɪnədz Brk K, ɪnəɾd͡z O, ɪnwəˤːd͡z So Do, ɪnəˤːd͡z So

iron *1. n* a TETHERING-STAKE in a cow-house I.3.3. aɪəⁿn La, ɑˑən Nf
2. n a BUMPER of a cart I.10.1(a). *pl* ɔˑənz K, *pl* ɔːəˤnz̩ Sr Sx, ʌɪəˤn̩ Sr

iron band *n* the iron TIRE round a cart-wheel I.9.10. ɔɪən band Wa, əɪ-ən band Mon

iron banding *n* the iron TIRE round a cart-wheel I.9.10. ɒɪəˤn̩ bændɪn Wo

iron-bar *n* a TETHERING-STAKE in a cow-house I.3.3. æɪənbaː Y, aɪənbaː Y, ɔɪən baː Wa

iron bar *1. n* the *HORIZONTAL* BAR of a crane over a domestic fire V.3.5(a). aɪən baː Lei, aɪən baː K, ɒɪən baˑ Nf, ɒɪəˤn̩ baˤː So, ɔɪəⁿn baⁱː Brk
2. n the vertical BAR or CHAIN of a crane over a domestic fire V.3.5(b). ɑːn baː Ess

iron beam *n* the *HORIZONTAL* BAR of a crane over a domestic fire V.3.5(a). ɑːn biːm Sr

iron-box *n* the metal BUSH at the centre of a cart-wheel I.9.8. ɒɪəˤːŋbɒks Ha, əɪəˤːŋbɒks W

iron bush *n* the metal BUSH at the centre of a cart-wheel I.9.8. aɪən bʊʃ Ch

iron hook *n* the HOOK or *CROOK* of a crane over a domestic fire V.3.5(c). ɒɪəˤn̩ ʊk So, ɔɪəˤɾn̩ hʊk Sx, ʌɪəⁿn ʊk Sr

iron-horse *n* a STICK used to support the shaft of a cart I.11.1. ɒɪəˤɾn̩ɔːəˤ͡s Sx *[marked u.r. SBM]*

iron hurdles *npl* HURDLES used to pen sheep in part of a field III.7.11. ɑˑən hʌdlz Nf, ɒɪən hʌdɫz Nf, aɪən hədlz Nf, aɪən həːdlz Nf, ɒɪən həːdlz Nf

iron-loop *n* a sliding RING to which a tether is attached in a cow-house I.3.5. aɪəɹnluːp La

iron pin *n* a LINCH-PIN holding a wheel on a cart I.9.12. ɒɪəˤn̩ pɪn So

iron-rim *n* the iron TIRE round a cart-wheel I.9.10. ɑˑənɹɪm Nf

iron-rod *n* a TETHERING-STAKE in a cow-house I.3.3. æɹɹənɹɒd Y

irons *1. n* an EVENER on the plough-beam end of a horse-drawn plough I.8.4. ɔːənz Sx *[queried SBM]* *2. npl* the HINGES of a door V.1.11a. aɹənz Db *3. npl* KNEE-STRAPS used to lift the legs of working trousers VI.14.17. ɑːᵊnz Hrt

iron standards *n* the BASE of a stack II.7.4. ɒɹᵊn stændədz Nf*[occasional]*

iron stands *n* the BASE of a round stack II.7.4. ɑˑən stæˑnz Nf

iron-stay *n* the iron stay connecting the beam with the side of a cart, ⇐ CROSS-BEAM END I.10.1. aɹən steɪ He, aɹəɹn steɪ He, ɑɹəˡnsteː La *[WMBM does not have definition as NBM; forms assumed to be identical]*

iron-tire *n* the iron TIRE round a cart-wheel I.9.10. ɑːntɑː MxL, hɑːntɑː Ess, haˑɹəntɑɹə Lei

iron-wheel hurdles *npl* HURDLES used to pen sheep in part of a field III.7.11. aɹənwiːl həːdlz Nf

irritable *adj* ACTIVE, describing a child VIII.9.1. əˡːtəbɫ D *[marked u.r. SBM]*

isaac *n* STRING used to tie up a grain-sack I.7.3. aɪzək La *[apparently trade name]*

issue *n* the VULVA of a cow III.2.3. ɪʃuː C

itching-berries *npl* HIPS of the wild rose IV.11.7. *sg* ɪtʃɪnbɛɹɪ Db

itchy-backs *npl* HIPS of the wild rose IV.11.7. ɪtʃɪbɛks Db

itchy-berries *npl* HIPS of the wild rose IV.11.7. *sg* ɪtʃɪbɛɹɪ La, ɪtʃɪbəɹɪz La

item about *vphr* to play, referring to cows in a field, ⇐ to BUTT III.2.10. *-ing* aɪtəmɪn əbaʊt So

ither *n* the UDDER of a cow III.2.5. ɪðə L

ivory *n* IVY IV.10.10. aɪvəɹɪ Nth Hu, ɔɪvəɹɪ Sf, ɔɪvɹɪ Ess, ʌɪvɹəɹɪ Nf, ʌɪvɹɪ Nf

ivy *n What do you call that evergreen plant that climbs up walls and trees?* IV.10.10. Eng; **ivy-tree** *pl* ɪvɪtɹeɪz St. ⇒ **hibbin, ivory, ivy-*tree***

izles *n* ICICLES VII.6.11. əɪsʉɫz Brk

J

jack *1. n* a SAWING-HORSE I.7.16. dʒak Y
2. n an END-BOARD of a cart I.10.4. dʒæk Nf Sf Ess, dʒæk? Nf
3. vt to slip a calf, ⇐ SLIP*S THE CALF* III.1.11. dʒakt Nth*[old]*
*4. vi to be RESTIVE, describing a horse III.5.6. *prppl* dʒakɪn Y
5. n a WEAKLING piglet III.8.4. dʒak Y
6. n a CRANE on which a kettle is hung over a domestic fire V.3.4. dʒæk So, dʒak Nb La Y Db So Ha
7. n the vertical BAR or CHAIN of a crane over a domestic fire V.3.5(b). dʒak Sa

jacka-legs *n* DADDY-LONG-LEGS IV.8.10. dʒakəlɛgz He

jacka-long-legs *n* DADDY-LONG-LEGS IV.8.10. dʒækəlɒŋlɛgz He

jackass *n* a DONKEY III.13.16. dʒakas L

jack-bannocks *npl* MINNOWS IV.9.9. dʒakbanəks St

jack-board *n* an END-BOARD of a cart I.10.4. dʒækbɔəd Nf

jack-by-the-hedge *n* GOOSE-GRASS II.2.5. dʒakbɪtɛdʒ swY

jack-donkey* *n* a male DONKEY III.13.16. dʒak dɒŋki Ha, dʒak dɔːŋki Do

jacket *n What do you call this [indicate a jacket]?* VI.14.5. Eng. ⇒ **coat, swinger**

jack-hook *n* a CRANE on which a kettle is hung over a domestic fire V.3.4. dʒakʊk Bd

jackies *npl* FROGS IV.9.6. dʒɛɪkɪz Ess, dʒækɪz Sf

jacking-off-time *n* STOPPING-TIME at the end of a day's work VII.5.9. dʒakɪnɔːftʌʏm O

jacking-up-time *n* STOPPING-TIME at the end of a day's work VII.5.9. dʒakɪnʌptæɪm So, dʒakɪnʌptaɪm Bd, dʒakɪnʌptɒɪm W

jack-nirrup* *n* a male DONKEY III.13.16. dʒak nɪɾʌp W Ha

jack-of-all-trades *n* a FARM-LABOURER I.2.4. dʒækəfɔˑltɪɛːᴵdz Nf, dʒækʔə-ɔːtreːdz Nf

jack-off-time *n* STOPPING-TIME at the end of a day's work VII.5.9. dʒakɔːftəɪm Do

jack-out-time *n* STOPPING-TIME at the end of a day's work VII.5.9. dʒakæʊttɒɪm W

jacks *1. npl* large MUSHROOMS II.2.11. dʒaks Wo
2. npl MOLARS VI.5.7. dʒaks Co

jack-sharps *npl* MINNOWS IV.9.9. dʒɛkʃaᴵːps Db, dʒakʃæːps La, dʒakʃæᴵːps La, dʒakʃaːps Ch St, dʒakʃɑːps Ch *[marked u.rr. NBM]*

jack-teeth *npl* MOLARS VI.5.7. dʒæktɪiːθ Brk, dʒakti:θ Co

jack-up-time *n* STOPPING-TIME at the end of a day's work VII.5.9. dʒakʌptæːm D, dʒakʌptaːm D, dʒakʌptɒɪm W, dʒakʌptəɪm W

jack-weasel *n* a WEASEL IV.5.6. dʒakwiːzl Cu La

jacky-bull-heads *npl* TADPOLES IV.9.5. dʒakɪbʊlhiːdz Du

jacky-long-legs *n* DADDY-LONG-LEGS IV.8.10. dʒækɪlɒŋɬɛgz He Mon, dʒækɪlɒŋɬɛgz Mon, dʒækɪɬɒŋɬɛgz Mon, dʒækɪluŋlɛgz He, dʒakɪlɒŋlɛgz Mon, dʒakɪlɒŋlɛgz Gl

jacky-toads *npl* FROGS IV.9.6. dʒækɪtʌʊdz Ess

jacobite *n* a variety of THISTLE II.2.2. dʒækəbaɪt Ess

jade *n* a RESTIVE horse III.5.6. dʒeɪd Nf, dʒeːᴵd Nf, dʒɛˑɪd Nf; **old jade** oul dʒɪːd Nf, oˑul dʒɛːᴵd Nf

jaded *adj* EXHAUSTED, describing a tired person VI.13.8. dʒɛɪdɪd St

jaded out *adj* EXHAUSTED, describing a tired person VI.13.8. dʒeːdəd aːt Y

jaffock *n* a GOSSIP VIII.3.5(b). dʒavək La

jaffocker *n* a GOSSIP VIII.3.5(b). dʒafəkəᴶ La

jaffocking *v-ing* GOSSIPING VIII.3.5(a). dʒafəkɪn La, dʒavəkɪn La

jag *1. n* an EAR of oats II.5.2(b). dʒag O W, djʌg O
2. n a LOOSE *PIECE OF* SKIN at the bottom of a finger-nail VI.7.11. dʒag Ch
3. n **on the jag** AJAR IX.2.7. ɒn ðə dʒag St

jaggers *n* **the jaggers** TREMORS suffered by a person who cannot keep still VI.1.4. ðə dʒagəᶜz̩ Wo

jam *n* a PIECE *OF BREAD AND BUTTER AND JAM/SUGAR* V.6.11(b). dʒɛm Ess, dʒæm Nf

jambles *n* the HAMES of the harness of a cart-horse I.5.4. dʒamblz La*[chains permanently attached x1]*

jam-bread *n* a PIECE *OF BREAD AND BUTTER AND JAM/SUGAR* V.6.11(b). dʒambɪed L

jambs *npl [Show a picture of some houses. Indicate a door-frame.] What do you call these uprights?* V.1.11. dʒæmz Sa He Wo Mon Gl Ha, dʒæːmz MxL Sr K, dʒamz Cu Du Y Sa St Wo Wa Gl O*[old x1]* L Nth Bk W Ha, *sg* dʒam Bd, dʒaːmz La*[old x1]* Y Ch Sa St Nt L Bk, dʒaːz Nt, dʒaʊmz Y, dʒɑːmz Hrt, dʒɒmz He Wo, *sg* dʒɒʊm Db, dʒɔːmz Cu We La Y Ch Db St Nt L Lei Bd, dʒɔˈəmz L, dʒoɔmz Y, *sg* dʒoən Man; **door-jambs** dɪədʒamz Y, dɪədʒɔːmz Y, dɪuədʒamz Y, dɔːdʒamz Wa, *sg* dɔːdʒam St, dɔˠːdʒæmz So, dɔəɹdʒamz He, doːədʒæmz Nf, duədʒamz Y Wo Wa, *sg* duədʒaːm L, duədʒɒːmz L, duədʒɔːmz Y St L, dᵿuəɹdʒaːmz La. ⇒ cheeks, door-case, door-cheeks, *door-durn* ⇒ **door-durns, door-durns,** *door-frame* ⇒ **door-frames, door-frames, doorings,** *door-*jambs, **door-posts, door-stalls, door-stanchels,** *door-stanchions* ⇒ **door-stanchels, door-stands, door-steads, door-studs, durns,** *frame* ⇒ **frames, frames, joists, lintels, posts, stanchels,** *stanchions* ⇒ **stanchels, standards, steals, studs, uprights**

jam-bucker *n* a PIECE *OF BREAD AND BUTTER AND JAM/SUGAR* V.6.11(b). dʒambʊkə Db

jam-butty *n* a PIECE *OF BREAD AND BUTTER AND JAM/SUGAR* V.6.11(b). ə dʒambʊtɪ La, dʒambʊtɪ La Ch Db

jam-cake *n* a PIECE *OF BREAD AND BUTTER AND JAM/SUGAR* V.6.11(b). ə dʒamkeak La, ə dʒamkɛək Y

jam-shag *n* a PIECE *OF BREAD AND BUTTER AND JAM/SUGAR* V.6.11(b). dʒamʃag Cu

jam-shive *n* a PIECE *OF BREAD AND BUTTER AND JAM/SUGAR* V.6.11(b). ə dʒamʃɑːv Y

jangles *n* TREMORS suffered by a person who cannot keep still VI.1.4. dʒæŋʊz Sr

jar *1. v* to BUTT III.2.10. *-ing* dʒəːɹɪn Db
2. *adj* AJAR IX.2.7. dʒaˠ Db; **a little jar*** ə lɪtɫ dʒaˠːəɽ Sx; **on a jar** ɒn ə dʒaː Sa Hu, ɒn ə dʒaˠː Sa, ɒn ə dʒəˠ Sa; **on jar** ɒn dʒaˠː Co; **on the jar** ɑn ðə dʒaː Ess, ɒn ðə dʒaː Ch Sa He Wa Ess*[old x1]*, ɔn ðə dʒaː Sf Ess, ɒn ðə dʒaˠː Sa So*[old x1]* W Co D Do, ɔːn ðə dʒaˠː W D Do, ɒn ðə dʒaː Wo Ess K, ɒn ðə dʒaˠ Kʲ K, ɒn ðə dʒaˠː He D, ɔn ðə dʒaˠ Kʲ K, ɒːn ðə dʒaːəᴶ Brk Sr, ɒn ðɪ dʒaˠəˠ Sx, ɒːn ðə dʒaːəˠ Sr Sx, ɒn ðə dʒaːəˠɽ Ha, ɔːn ðə dʒaːəˠɽ Sr

jart *vt* to BEAT a boy on the buttocks VIII.8.10. dʒaːt Y

jasock *n* a DONKEY III.13.16. dʒazək L

jason *n* a DONKEY III.13.16. dʒazn L, dʒazm L

jaw *n* CHAT VIII.3.4. dʒɔː Ess Sr Sx, dʒɔːə Nf*[old]* Sf Hrt Ess

jaw-ache *n* TOOTHACHE VI.5.8. dʒaʊ-ɛɪk Sf, dʒɔː-eːk Brk, dʒɔː-ɛɪk St*[old x1]*, dʒɔːɹɛɪk St Nf, dʒɔː-ɛˈək L

jawer *n* a SNACK VII.5.11. dʒaʊəˠ Gl

jawing *v-ing* GOSSIPING VIII.3.5(a). dʒɔˈɪn K, dʒɔːɹɪn Ess

jaws *n* WIPE YOUR MOUTH VI.5.3. dʒaːz Sf Ess

jaws-ache *n* TOOTHACHE VI.5.8. dʒæːzeːk So, dʒaːzeːk Do, dʒaːzeɪk So, dʒaːzeːək So, dʒaːzeɪk Sf Ess, dʒɔːzeːk W Co D Ha, dʒɔːzeɪk So Ha, dʒɔːzeɪk Nf Brk Sr Sx, dʒɔːzaɪk Ha, dʒɔːəᴶzeɪk Sr

jaw-teeth *npl* MOLARS VI.5.7. dʒæːtiːð So*[old]*, dʒaːtiːθ So Do, dʒaːtiːð So, dʒɔːtiːθ So W Co D Do Ha, dʒɔːtiːf Do, dʒɔːteːθ D, dʒɔːtɛɪθ Co, dʒɔˠːtiːf So

jay-legged *adj* KNOCK-KNEED VI.9.5. dʒeːlɛgd Y

jelly bread *n* bit jelly bread a PIECE *OF BREAD AND BUTTER AND JAM/SUGAR* V.6.11(b). bɪt dʒɪlɪ bʁiːd Nb*[old]*

jelly-piece *n* a PIECE *OF BREAD AND BUTTER AND JAM/SUGAR* V.6.11(b). dʒɪlɪpiːs Nb

jen *n* a TABBY-CAT, the female cat III.13.9. dʒɪn Y

jenny *1. n* a ROPE-TWISTER II.7.8. dʒɪnɪ Bk
2. *n* a HARE IV.5.10. dʒɪni Ha

jenny-cat *n* a TABBY-CAT, the female cat III.13.9. dʒɪnɪkat Y

jenny-long-legs *n* DADDY-LONG-LEGS IV.8.10. dʒɪnɪlaŋlɛgz Du We La Y, dʒɪnɪlɒŋlɛgz Y, dʒɛnɪlaŋlɛgz Nb

jenny-owl *n* an OWL IV.7.6. dʒɪnɪ-uːl Cu

jenny-owlet* *n* an OWL IV.7.6. dʒɪnɪ-aʊlɪt Y*[large, grey]*, dʒɪnɪ-ʊlɪt Y, dʒɪnɪ-ʊlət Y, dʒɪnɪ-juːlət Y, dʒɪnɪ-uːlət Cu Du, dʒɛnɪhuːlət Nb

jenny-spinner(s) *n* DADDY-LONG-LEGS IV.8.10.
no -s: dʒɪnɪspɪnə Cu We La Y*[old x1]* Db, dʒɪnɪspɪnəᴮ Nb, dʒɪnɪspɪnəɹ La Y, dʒɛnɪspɪnɔᴮ Nb, dʒɛnɪspɪnə Cu
-s: dʒɪnɪspɪnəz St
pl: dʒɪnɪspɪnərz Cu

jenny wisp *n* a BOGEY VIII.8.1. dʒɪnɪ wɪsp Nth

jen-spinners *n* DADDY-LONG-LEGS IV.8.10. dʒɪnspɪnəz St

jerking *v-ing* THROWING a stone VIII.7.7. dʒəᴶːkɪn Brk

jerry-long-legs *n* DADDY-LONG-LEGS IV.8.10. dʒeʁɪlaŋlɛgz Du

jert it *imp* GO AWAY! VIII.7.9(a). dʒɜᴶːt ɪd La

jerusalem *n* a DONKEY III.13.16. dʒəˈɹuːzləm L

jib *1. n* the STRETCHER between the traces of a cart-horse I.5.11. dʒɪb Sx
2. *n* a RESTIVE horse III.5.6. dʒɪb Man Sf Ess K
3. *v* to be RESTIVE, describing a horse III.5.6. *prppl* dʒɪbɪn La Wo, *prppl/adj* dʒɪbən Ha, *ptppl* dʒɪbd Wa
4. *n* a BENCH on which slaughtered pigs are dressed III.12.1. dʒɪb Do
5. *n* the WATTLES of a hen IV.6.19. dʒɪb Sa *[marked 'sg' and queried mass noun WMBM]*
6. *n* **hanging a jib** PUTTING your tongue OUT VI.5.4. aŋɪn ə dʒɪb Sa

jibber *n* a RESTIVE horse III.5.6. dʒɪbɔᴮ Nb, dʒɪbʌ Ess, dʒɪbə Cu Du La Y Man Ch Db St Wa

Nt L Lei R Nth Hu C Nf Sf Bk Bd Hrt Ess MxL Sr, dʒɪbbə Db, dʒɪbɹ L, dʒɪbəɹ Du La Y, dʒɪbəˡ La Y Man Ch St L Nf Brk Sr K, dʒɪbr̩ O, dʒɪbbr̩ Db, dʒɪbəˡ Sa He Wo Wa Mon Gl O Nth Bk Bd Brk Sr K Ha Sx, dʒɪbəˡː Sa Wo So W Co D Do Ha, dʒɪbɐ Nf Ess

jibby *adj* RESTIVE, describing a horse III.5.6. dʒɪbɪ Y

jib-hook *n* the vertical BAR or CHAIN of a crane over a domestic fire V.3.5(b). dʒɪbʊk Ess

jibs *npl* MOUTH CORNERS VI.5.2. dʒɪbz Sa

jig *imp* jig, jig again the command TURN RIGHT!, given to plough-horses II.3.5(b). jig tʃɪk Sa; jig again 'dʒɪk 'gɛn Sa, 'dʒɪg ə'gɛn St

jiggered *adj* EXHAUSTED, describing a tired person VI.13.8. dʒɪgɔᴿt Nb, dʒɪgɔᴿd Du, dʒɪgət Cu We, dʒɪgəd Cu We La Y St L, dʒɪgəᴿd We, dʒɪgəˡt Db, dʒɪgəɹt La, dʒɪgəɹd La, dʒɪgəˡːd̩ Sa

jiggered out *adj* EXHAUSTED, describing a tired person VI.13.8. dʒɪgəd æʊt L

jiggered up *adj* EXHAUSTED, describing a tired person VI.13.8. dʒɪgət ʊp Ch, dʒɪgəd ʊp Du La Db, dʒɪgəˡːd̩ ʌp Sa

jiggin *imp* jiggin, jiggin off the command TURN RIGHT!, given to plough-horses II.3.5(b). jiggin 'dʒɪ,gɪn Wa*[old]*; jiggin off 'dʒɪgɪn 'ɑːf Wo

jimmers *npl* the HINGES of a door V.1.11a. dʒɪmɪz Nf*[old x1, small x1, large hinges on barn doors x1]*, dʒɪməz We Y L Nf, dʒɪməɹ Y, dʒɪməˡz Nf, dʒɛmæz We Y*[large hinges on barn doors x1]*, dʒɛmɪsɪz Y, *sg* dʒamə Cu*[very old]*, dʒamɪsəz Y

jimmy 1. *n* the human MOUTH VI.5.3. dʒɪmɪ Sf
2. *n* a NOSE VI.4.6. dʒɪmɪ Sf *[recorded at VI.5.3 MOUTH; some doubt over interpretation]*

jimmy-long-legs *n* DADDY-LONG-LEGS IV.8.10. dʒɪmɪlaŋlɛgz Cu

jinny* *n* a female DONKEY III.13.16. dʒɪnɪ Y

jinny-donkey* *n* a female DONKEY III.13.16. dʒɪni dɒŋki Ha

jitters *n* TREMORS suffered by a person who cannot keep still VI.1.4. dʒɪtəz Db; the jitters ðə dʒɪtəz Nf, ðə dʒɪtəːz St, ðə dʒɪdəˡːz̩ D

jo *n* little jo a WEAKLING piglet III.8.4. lɪtɫ dʒoː Brk

job-about *n* a FARM-LABOURER I.2.4. dʒɔbəbaːt La

jobbing carpenter *n* a CARPENTER or JOINER who does heavy, less skilled work VIII.4.3. dʒɔbɪn kaːpntə Sf

jobbing-man *n* a FARM-LABOURER I.2.4. dʒɒbɪnman D, dʒɒbənman Cu

joblets *n* the WATTLES of a hen IV.6.19. dʒɒbləts He

job-man *n* a FARM-LABOURER I.2.4. dʒɒbman Wa, dʒɒbmən Db Ess

job-workman *n* a FARM-LABOURER I.2.4. dʒɒbwəˡːkmən D

jock *n* MEAL OUT VII.5.12. dʒɒk Y*[rare x1]*, dʒɔk Y*[farmer's word x1]*

jock-bit *n* MEAL OUT VII.5.12. dʒakbɪt La

jockey-cock* *vt* to make hay into medium-sized cocks, ⇐ COCKS II.9.12. dʒɒkɪkɒk La

jockeys *npl* COCKS of hay II.9.12. dʒɒkɪz Y, dʒɔkɪz Y*[large]*

joe-worms* *npl* large WORMS IV.9.1. *sg* dʒoʊwəˡːm Wo

joey 1. *n* a WEAKLING piglet III.8.4. dʒo-ɪ Brk, dʒoʊ-i So
2. *n* a THREEPENNY-BIT VII.7.3(a). dʒoʊɪ K*[old]*, dʒʌʊɪ K, dʒoː-i Ha, dʒoːɪ Gl, dʒoʊɪ Ha
3. *n* SIXPENCE VII.7.4. joʊɪ O

joggle-pin *n* a movable horizontal rod stretching between the shafts of a cart, fixing them to the cart-body and stopping the cart from tipping, ⇐ ROD/PIN I.10.3. dʒɒglpɪn Y, dʒɒgəlpɪn Y

joggle-stick *n* a movable horizontal rod stretching between the shafts of a cart, fixing them to the cart-body and stopping the cart from tipping, ⇐ ROD/PIN I.10.3. dʒɒglstɪk Y

johnny-long-legs *n* DADDY-LONG-LEGS IV.8.10. dʒɒnɪlɒŋlɛgz So, dʒɒniɫʌŋɫɛgz D, dʒɒnɪlɒŋlɛgz Y, dʒɒnɪlɒŋlɛgz L

johnny-pig *n* a BOAR III.8.7. dʒɒnɪpɪg Nf

joiner *n* What do you call the man who makes things out of wood? [Does he distinguish between the two, i.e. carpenter and joiner?] VIII.4.3. Eng.
a. highly skilled work: Du Y Ch Sa He Wo Wa Mon O L Nth Hu Nf Sf Bd Ess MxL So W Brk Sr K D Do Ha Sx
b. heavier, less skilled work: Cu Du La Y Ch Sa St Mon Gl Nt Lei Nf Ess So Sx
c. makes furniture: Sx
d. makes wheels: St O
e. undertaker: Wa Nth
f. also makes coffins: Wo
g. works inside: Y Sr Ha
h. apprentice carpenter: Brk
i. old word: Cu Y
j. same as carpenter: Du La Y Sa St He Wo Wa Mon Gl Nt L Lei R Nth Hu Nf Bk Hrt Ess So W
⇒ carpenter, chippy, jobbing carpenter, rough carpenter, wood-stack carpenter

joists *npl* the JAMBS of a door V.1.11. dʒaɪsts Y

jokers *npl* PIGLETs III.8.2. dʒoːkəˡz̩ Brk

jolly *adv* VERY VIII.3.2. dʒɒlɪ Sa Sx, dʒɒɫɪ Ess Sr

jossed up *adj* EXHAUSTED, describing a tired person VI.13.8. dʒɒst ʊp La

jotty *adj* BRITTLE, describing cups and saucers which break easily IX.1.4. dʒɒtɪ Ch

jowl *n* a BREAD-BIN V.9.2. dʒɛʊ St, dʒaʊl St, jaʊl St*[queried error for* [dʒaʊl] *WMBM]*, dʒɔʊl Wa, dʒoʊl St

jowl(s) *n* the WATTLES of a hen IV.6.19.
no -s: dʒaʊˀɫ W
-s: dʒoʊlz St

juggle-stick* *n* a device hanging down under a cart to prevent it from going backwards on a hill, ⇐ PROP/CHOCK I.11.2. dʒʊglstɪk Nth

juice *1.* *n* URINE in a cow-house I.3.10. dʒɪuːs Nth Hu C Ess, dʒuːs Bk Bd Ess
2. *n* hand-operated SHEARS used to cut wool from sheep III.7.7. dʒˀus Man *[probably = deuce]*

juice cess-pool *n* a CESS-POOL on a farm I.3.11. dʒˡuːs sɛspuːl Nth

jumbles *n* SWEETS V.8.4. dʒʌmblz Gl

jump *1.* *v A sheep wouldn't use a stile; it would [gesticulate] ... the wall.* IV.2.10. dʒɒmp Man, dʒʌmp Sa He Wa Mon O Nth Hu C Nf Sf Bk Bd Hrt Ess MxL So Brk Sr K D Do Ha Sx, *prppl* ədʒʌmpɪn Bk, dʒʌmp? Hrt, dʒʏmp Nf, dʒʊmp Nb We La Y Man Ch Db Sa St He Wo Wa Mon Gl O Nt L Lei R Nth Bk K, dʒəmp Gl. ⇒ **buck over**, *go over the top*, **hop over**, **jump over**, **leap**, **leap over**, **loup**, **loup over**; ⇒ also **loup-hopper**
2. *vi* to BOUNCE VIII.7.3. dʒʌmp Sf

3. *n* the SHAFT of a diking-spade I.7.7. dʒʏmp Nf *[queried EMBM]*

jumpers *npl* FLEAS IV.8.4. dʒʌmpɐz Ess

jumping *adj* HEAVING *(WITH MAGGOTS)* IV.8.6. dʒʊmpɪn Ch

jump over *vphr* to JUMP a wall IV.2.10. dʒʌmp ʌʊvə Ess MxL Sr, dʒʌmp ɔːvəˡ: So W Co D Do Ha, dʒʌmp ɔʊvəᴶ K, dʒɛmp ɔːvəˡ He, dʒʊmp ɔːvəˡ He Wo, dʒʌmp ɔːvəˡ: So W Co D, dʒʌmp oʊvə Nf Ha, dʒʏmp oʊvə Nf, dʒʊmp oʊvəˡ Wo, dʒʌmp oʊvəˡ: So, dʒʌmp ɔːʊvəˡ Gl, dʒʊmp oə Db

junk *1.* *n* RUBBISH V.1.15. dʒʌŋk Ess So K, dʒʏŋk Nf, dʒʊŋk Y *[modern x1]* Wa
2. *n* a thick SLICE of bread V.6.10. *pl* dʒʌŋks D

just *adv* ONLY VII.8.12. dʒʊst Nb Cu Du Y

just about *adv* ALMOST VII.7.9. dʒʊst abuːt Nb

just on *adv* ALMOST VII.7.9. dʒʌs ɒn So

just short of *adv* ALMOST VII.7.9. dʒʊs ʃaːt əv Man, dʒʊst ʃɔːt əv Y

just under *adv* ALMOST VII.7.9. dʒʌst ɒndə Nf, dʒʌst ʌndəˡ Sr

jye *adj* ASKEW, describing a picture that is not hanging straight IX.1.3. dʒaɪ Nb Cu

K

kaggy-fisted *adj* LEFT-HANDED   VI.7.13(a).
kægɪfɪstɪd Wo, kagɪfɪstɪd Sa

kaggy-handed *adj* LEFT-HANDED   VI.7.13(a).
kægɪ-ændɪd Wo, kægɪ-ɒndɪd Wo, kagɪ-andɪd St Wo
Wa Mon, kagi-andəd Ha, kagɪ-ɒndɪd Sa*[old x1]*
St*[old x1]* Wo *[not a SBM headword]*

kags *npl* the HANDLES of a scythe II.9.8. kɛgz C

kale *n* CHARLOCK II.2.6. kɪal Y, kɛ·əl Y

katlock(s) *n* CHARLOCK II.2.6.
no -s: katlʊk La
-s: katləks La

kay-fist *adj* LEFT-HANDED VI.7.13(a). keːfɪst La

kay-fisted *adj* LEFT-HANDED VI.7.13(a). keːfɪstɪd
La, keəfɪstɪd La, keɪfɪstɪd La

kay-fister *n* a LEFT-HANDED person VI.7.13(a).
keːfɪstəˠ La

kay-legged *adj* KNOCK-KNEED VI.9.5. keːlɛgd
Y*[old]*, keɪlɛgd Y, kaɪɫɛgd Ha, kaɪɫɛgɪd Ha

kay-neive *adj* LEFT-HANDED VI.7.13(a). kɛɪnɛɪv
Y

kay-neived *adj* LEFT-HANDED   VI.7.13(a).
kɛɪnɛɪvd Y

kay-paw *n* a LEFT-HANDED person VI.7.13(a).
kiːpɔː Ch, keɪpɔː La

kay-pawed *adj* LEFT-HANDED VI.7.13(a). kiːpɔːd
Ch, keːpɔːd La, keɪpɔːd La

keb-footed *adj* PIGEON-TOED VI.10.4. kɛbfɪtɪd
Cu

keb-legged *adj* PIGEON-TOED VI.10.4. kɛblɛgd
Cu

keck *1.* *v* to TIP a cart I.11.6. kɛk Cu We La Y
2. *vt* to tip. kɛk La

keck-bar *n* a vertical rod in front of a cart, perforated
to allow adjustments when tipping, ⇐ ROD/PIN
I.10.3. kɛkbaː Cu, kɛkbaːɹ We, kɛkbaˠː La Y
[compare kecker-bar in WMBM]

kecker *1.* *n* a vertical rod in front of a cart, perforated
to allow adjustments when tipping, ⇐ ROD/PIN
I.10.3. kɪkə Man, kɪkəˠ (+V) Man, kɛkkə La, kɛkəɹ
La, kɛkkəɹ La *[compare kecker-bar in WMBM]*
2. *n* the WINDPIPE VI.6.5. kɛkəˡ Gl

kecker-bar *n* a movable horizontal rod stretching
between the shafts of a cart, fixing them to the
cart-body and stopping the cart from tipping, ⇐
ROD/PIN I.10.3. kɛkəˡbaˠː Db *[compare kecker and
keck-bar in NBM]*

keck-fisted *adj* LEFT-HANDED   VI.7.13(a).
kɛkfɪstɪd He Mon

keck-handed *adj* LEFT-HANDED   VI.7.13(a).
kɛkɛndɪd Ess*[old x1]* Sr K, kɛkændɪd Brk K,
kɛkandɪd O Nth Bk Bd*[old x1]* Do, kɛkandəd W

keck-handeder *n* a LEFT-HANDED person
VI.7.13(a). kɛkɛndɪdəˠ Sr

keck-hander *n* a LEFT-HANDED person
VI.7.13(a). kɛkɛndə Ess, kɛkɛndəˠ K, kɛkɛndəˡ
Sr, kɛkændəˠ Brk K, kɛkændəˡ Brk, kɛkandə Bd,
kɛkandəˡ Bk

keck-hand man *n* a LEFT-HANDED person
VI.7.13(a). kɛkænd mæn Brk

kecking *v-ing* COUGHING VI.8.2. kɛkɪn Bk W,
kɛkən Ha, kækɪn So*[short cough]*

kecklet* *n* CHARLOCK II.2.6. *pl* kɛkləts L *[not
an EMBM headword]*

kecklock(s*) *n* CHARLOCK II.2.6.
no -s: kɛklək Y, *pl* kɛkləks Db
-s: kɛkləks Y

keck over *viphr* to OVERTURN, referring to a
cart I.11.5. kɛk oər La

keck-paw *n* a LEFT-HANDED person
VI.7.13(a). kɛkpaː O

keck-rod *n* a vertical rod in front of a cart,
perforated to allow adjustments when tipping, ⇐
ROD/PIN I.10.3. kɛkɹɒd La

kecks *n* CHARLOCK II.2.6. kɛks Y

keck-stick *n* a vertical rod in front of a cart,
perforated to allow adjustments when tipping, ⇐
ROD/PIN I.10.3. kɛkstɪk La Y

keck up *1.* *viphr* to OVERTURN, referring to a
cart I.11.5. *-ed* kɛkt ʊp La
2.1. *vphr* to TIP a cart I.11.6. kɛk ʊp Y
2.2. *vtphr* to tip. kɛk ... ʊp We La Y

kecky *n* a LEFT-HANDED person VI.7.13(a).
kɛkɪ Sa

kecky-fisted *adj* LEFT-HANDED   VI.7.13(a).
kɛkɪfɪstɪd Mon

kecky-handed *adj* LEFT-HANDED VI.7.13(a).
keːkɪ-æːndɪd Sa, kɛkɪ-andɪd Sa Wa Nth

kecky-hander *n* a LEFT-HANDED person
VI.7.13(a). kɛkɪ-andə Wa Nth

kedlock(s) *n* CHARLOCK II.2.6.
no -s: kɛdɫɔk Sr, kɛdlʊk Sa St, kɛdlək Y Db Sa
St Lei
-s: kɛdləks Y

keech *n* a CUTTING of hay II.9.15. kiːtʃ Sa He
Wo, kœːtʃ Gl

keedle *n* a PORRIDGE-STICK V.9.1. kiːdl
Cu*[old]*

keeking *v-ing* PEEPING VI.3.8. kiːkɪn Nb, kiːkən Nb Cu

keel over *viphr* to OVERTURN, referring to a cart I.11.5. kiːl oːvəᵗ Sa, keːl oːvəᵗ Sa, keːl oːəᵗ Sa

keel up *viphr* to OVERTURN, referring to a cart I.11.5. kɛɪl ʌp Sa

keened *adj* CHAPPED VI.7.2. kiːnd Nb Du*[cracked]*

keens *1. npl* **full of keens** CHAPPED VI.7.2. fʊl ə kiːnz Nb

*2. npl CHAPS in the skin VI.7.3. kiːnz Nb Cu Du We

keep *1. vt-3prpl Some people have a shed and a wire-netting run at the bottom of their garden in which they ... hens.* IV.6.2. *Eng* ⇒ **fold, has, have, have some, keep a few, keep a lite, keep some in, keep their, keep the old, you keep a few**

2. n pasturage, ⇐ HIRE *PASTURAGE* III.3.8. kiːp Man St O Lei Sf Bk So W Brk Sr K Co D Do Ha Sx, kɪp So W Co D Do, keːp W Ha

3. vi to STAY at home VIII.5.2. kiːp Sf Ess

4. vt **keep ... out of sight, keep ... out of the sight** to HIDE something VIII.7.6. kiːp ... uːt ə siːt Y, kiːp ... aʊt ə saɪt Y, kiːp ... æʊt əv sɔɪt Wo, kiːp ... aːt ə t siːt Y, kiːp ... aʊt ə t siːt Y

keeping *n* pasture, ⇐ HIRE *PASTURAGE* III.3.8. kiːpɪn Lei R

keeve *1. n* a lidless barrel in a stable, containing one day's supply of feed, ⇐ CORN-BIN I.7.4. kiːv D

2. n a SALTING-TROUGH III.12.5. kiːv Co

keggy *1. adj* LEFT-HANDED VI.7.13(a). kɛgɪ Db St*[old x1]* O

2. n a LEFT-HANDED person VI.7.13(a). kɛgɪ Db Wa O

keggy-handed *adj* LEFT-HANDED VI.7.13(a). kɛgɪ-andɪd La Wa Lei, kɛgɪ-andəd Db Wa, kɛgɪ-ɒndɪd St

keggy-hander *n* a LEFT-HANDED person VI.7.13(a). kɛgɪ-andə Wa

keg-handed *adj* LEFT-HANDED VI.7.13(a). kɛghændɪd Nf

keglock* *n* CHARLOCK II.2.6. kɛglək Y

kegman *n* a KNACKER III.11.9. kɛgmən Lei, *pl* kɛgmɛn St *[WMBM headword cagman]*

kegman-chap *n* a KNACKER III.11.9. kɛgməntʃap Lei

keg-pawed *adj* LEFT-HANDED VI.7.13(a). kɛgpoʊd St

keiked *vt-ed* sprained, ⇐ to SPRAIN an ankle VI.10.8. kɛkt La, *inf* kɛɪk La

kelf *n* a square CUTTING of hay II.9.15. *pl* kɛlvz Y

kelk *n* CHARLOCK II.2.6. kɪʊk Sr K Sx

kell(s) *n* the FAT round the kidneys of a pig III.12.7.
no -s: kɛl L Nth
-s: kɛlz L

kelt *1. v* to TIP a cart I.11.6. kɛlt Cu *[queried NBM]*

2. n MONEY VII.8.7. kɛlt La Y

kelt-bar *n* a vertical rod in front of a cart, perforated to allow adjustments when tipping, ⇐ ROD/PIN I.10.3. kɛltbaː Cu *[queried NBM on grounds that kelt = 'to overturn']*

kelter *1. n* WEEDS, unwanted plants that grow in a garden II.2.1. kɛltər Y

2. n RUBBISH V.1.15. kɛltə Cu*[rare]* Du We Y*[obsolete x1]* L, kɛɬə Nth*[old]*, kɛlʔə L Nth*[old]*, kɛltər Cu*[rare]* Y, kɛltɪ L, kɛltəɪ Y L, kɛlʔəᴶ L

kelterment *n* RUBBISH V.1.15. kɛltəmənt Nb Du Y

kennel-man *n* a KNACKER III.11.9. kɛnlmən Nb

kennel's-man *n* a KNACKER III.11.9. kɛnəlzmən Nb

kenner *n* STOPPING-TIME at the end of a day's work VII.5.9. kɛnə Du

kenspeck* *1. n* a sheep recognition-mark, ⇐ MARK III.7.9. kɛnspɛk La

2. n a marked sheep. kɛnspɛk La

kent *n* **a kent of wood** a bundle of wood, ⇐ KINDLING-*WOOD* V.4.2. ə kɛnt ə wʊd K

kent-plough *1. n* a PLOUGH I.8.1. kɛntpleu K, kɛntpləʊ K

2. n a wheeled plough. kɛntpleʊ K, kɛnpleʊ K, kɛntplæʊ K

kep *n* a SKEP IV.8.8(b). kɛp La, *pl* kɛps Cu

kepping-post *n* the SHUTTING-POST of a gate IV.3.4. kɛpɪnpøːst Nb, kɛpnpøːst Nb, kɛpənpøːst Nb

kep-stick *n* a vertical rod in front of a cart, perforated to allow adjustments when tipping, ⇐ ROD/PIN I.10.3. kɛpstɪk Nb

kernel *n* the CORE of a boil VI.11.7. kɔᴶːnəl La

kesh *n* COUCH-GRASS II.2.3. kɛʃ We

keslop(s) *n* RENNET V.5.6.
no -s: kɛsləp Cu Y, kɛzləp Y*[old x1]*
-s: kɛzləps Y*[old]* L *[marked 'probably pl' N/EMBM]*

kesnoos *n* BEESTINGS V.5.10. kəsˈnuːs Man

kessen *vi* to WARP, referring to wood IX.2.9. kɛsn Du*[old]*

ket *1. n* WEEDS, unwanted plants that grow in a garden II.2.1. kɛt Cu Y

2. n RUBBISH V.1.15. kɛt Cu Du*[old]* We*[not common x1]* La Y*[old x1]*

3. n food which has gone bad. kɛt We Y

4. n rotting organic matter. kɛt Nb

5. n weeds. kɛt Y

6. n offal. kɛt Y

ket-dealer *n* a KNACKER III.11.9. kɛtdɪələᴶ La

keteley broth *n* BROTH V.7.20(a). kɪdɬi bɾɔːθ Co

ket-house-man *n* a KNACKER III.11.9. kɛtuːsman Y

ketlet* *n* CHARLOCK II.2.6. kɛtlət La *[not a NBM headword]*

ketlock(s) *n* CHARLOCK II.2.6.
no -s: kɛtlɪk La, kɛtlɒk Y Wa, kɛtlɔk L, kɛʔlɔk L, kɛtlək La Y Nt L
-s: kɛtləks La Y, kɛʔlək L

ketman *n* a KNACKER III.11.9. kɛtman Y

ketment *n* RUBBISH V.1.15. kɛtmənt Y

kettle *n* *You boil water for tea in a ....* V.8.7. Eng;
tea-kettle tɛɪkɛtɬ Nth. ⇒ **pompey, pot, suke, sukey,** *tea-kettle;* ⇒ also **kettle-wedge**

kettle-bar *n* a CRANE on which a kettle is hung over a domestic fire V.3.4. kɛtɬbaᵗ: Gl

kettle-broth *n* BROTH V.7.20(a). kɪdɬ bɾɔːθ Co D Do Ha, kɛtlbɹɔːθ Gl, kɛtlbɹɔᵗ:θ Sa

kettle-crook *n* a CRANE on which a kettle is hung over a domestic fire V.3.4. kɛdɬkɾʊk Ha

kettle-hanger *n* a CRANE on which a kettle is hung over a domestic fire V.3.4. kɪtɬhæŋgə Sf, kɪdɬaŋəᵗ: Ha, kɪʔɬaŋəᵗ: W, kɛʔɬaŋəᵗ: W

kettle-hook *n* a CRANE on which a kettle is hung over a domestic fire V.3.4. kɛʔɬʊk Gl

kettle-jack *n* a CRANE on which a kettle is hung over a domestic fire V.3.4. kɛʔɬdʒak Ha

kettle-wedge* *n* a log on which a KETTLE is boiled over a fire V.8.7. kɛʔɬwɛdʒ So

kewny *adj* RANCID, describing bacon V.7.9. kɪʊni Co

key *1. n What do you lock a door with?* V.1.10. Eng. ⇒ **door-key, locking-key**
2. n a LINCH-PIN holding a wheel on a cart I.9.12. kiː C, *pl* kiːz R, kʰiː Mon, kəɪ Y
3. n a metal linch-pin. kɹiː Sx

key-pin *n* a pin keeping a cart-body fixed to the shafts, stopping it from tipping, ⇐ ROD/PIN I.10.3. kiːpɪn So, keːpɪn W

key-stick *n* a movable horizontal rod stretching between the shafts of a cart, fixing them to the cart-body and stopping the cart from tipping, ⇐ ROD/PIN I.10.3. kiːstɪk O Bk MxL Brk Sr Ha, keːstɪk Ha, kaɪstɪk W Ha

kibble-tree *n* an EVENER, the main swingle-tree of a horse-drawn plough harness I.8.4. kɪbltɹiː Y *[northern forms with -tree given this definition, although NBM data less specific]*

kick *1.1. v* to TIP a cart I.11.6. kɪk Ch Db
1.2. vt to tip. kɪk Man
2. vt to TED hay II.9.11(a). kɪk Co
3. n **bout kick** INSIPID, describing food lacking in salt V.7.8. baːt kɪk Y
4. vi to RETCH VI.13.15. kɪk Brk

kicking-straps *1. n* BRACES VI.14.10. kɪkɪnstɾaps So

2. npl KNEE-STRAPS used to lift the legs of working trousers VI.14.17. kɪkɪnstɹæps MxL

kick out *vtphr* to TED hay II.9.11(a). kɪk ... eʊt Nf

kick up *1. vphr* to TIP a cart I.11.6. kɪk ʌp Sf Ess
2. vtphr to tip. kɪk ... ʌp Nf Ess, kɪk ... ʊp Db

kid *1. n* **in kid** pregnant, describing a doe rabbit, ⇐ KINDLE III.13.14. ɪn kɪd W *[queried SBM]*
2. n a CHILD VIII.1.2(b). kɪd La Y Db St He Mon Gl L Lei Nf Ess So W

kiddies *npl* CHILDREN VIII.1.2(a). kɪdɪz La St Wa*[familiar]* Nt L MxL Ha Sx

kiddle *vi* to VOMIT, referring to a baby bringing up milk VI.13.14(b). kɪdl Sa, kɪdɬ He Wo

kidney-balchin *n* a NESTLING IV.7.1. *pl* kɪdnɪbɔɬtʃɪnz O

kidney-fat *n* the FAT round the kidneys of a pig III.12.7. kɪdnɪvat Do

kids *1. n* KINDLING-*WOOD* V.4.2. kɪdz L Lei
2. npl CHILDREN VIII.1.2(a). kɪdz La Y Ch Db St He Wo Wa*[familiar x1]* Mon Gl L Nth Hu Nf Sf Bk Ess, kɪədz Ess So Sr D Ha
3. npl BOYS VIII.1.3(a). kɪdz St

kill-house *n* a SLAUGHTERHOUSE III.11.4. kɪɬævz Co

killing-block *n* a BENCH on which slaughtered pigs are dressed III.12.1. kɪɬənblɒk Co

killing-house *1. n* a FASTING-CHAMBER III.11.3. kɪlɪnəʊs W
2. n a SLAUGHTERHOUSE III.11.4. kɪɬənœvs D, kɪɬɪnævs Co, kɪɬənævs Co, kɪlənhuːs Nb

killing-shop *n* a SLAUGHTERHOUSE III.11.4. kɪlɪnʃɒp Y

killing-stock *n* a BENCH on which slaughtered pigs are dressed III.12.1. kɪɬɪnstɒk Co, kɪɬənstɒk Co

killing-stool *n* a BENCH on which slaughtered pigs are dressed III.12.1. kɪlɪnstɪəl Nb Cu, kɪlɪnstuːɬ Bk, kɪɬɪnstuːɬ W Ha, kɪlɪnstuːʊ Brk, kɪlənstɪʏl Nb, kɪlənstuːl Nb, kɪlənstuːɬ Sf

kilt *vt* **kilt your creels** HEAD OVER HEELS IX.1.10. *-ing* kɪltn jə kʙiːlz Nb

kimit *adj* SILLY VIII.9.3. kjaɪmət He

kin *n* RELATIONS VIII.2.4. kɪn Nb La Y L Nf

kind *n* (what) SORT VII.8.17. **(what) kind** kɛɪnd Nb Cu Du, kɛɪn Cu, kæːn D, kaːnd La Co, kaɪnd Du La Y Ch Lei, kaˑɪn Lei, kɑɪnd La L Lei R Nth Bd K, kɒɪnd St So W, kɒɪn K, kɔɪnd Wa O Bk Ess Brk, kʌɪnd Brk Sr, kəɪnd He Mon W Sx, kəɪn W;
(what) kind (of) kæːnd D, kaɪnd Co, kɑɪnd Ch L, kɒɪnd Nf, kʌɪnd Nf; **(what) kind (of a)** kɔɪnd Wo;
(what) kind (of) + obj kɒɪnd So, kɔɪnd Sr K Ha Sx, kʌɪnd Brk, kəɪnd Brk

kinders *n* KINDLING-*WOOD* V.4.2. kɪndəz Ch

kinding-sticks *n* KINDLING-*WOOD* V.4.2. kɪndɪnstɪks Db

kindle *1. vi When the [rabbit] doe is going to have a family, you say she is going* .... III.13.14. kɪndl La Y Ch Db Sa St He Wo Wa Mon Gl Nt L, kɪndəl Y, kɪnl Nb Du We La Y L, kɪnəl Y, kɪndɫ Ch He Wo Wa Mon Gl O Lei Nth Bk Bd Hrt So W K, kɪndəɫ He Gl O Sf Bk Bd Hrt, kɪnɫ Nth Hrt, kɪndʊ K, kɪŋgl Ch, kɛnɫ Ess, kɛnʊ Ess. ⇒ **cast, farrow,** *going to have a litter, going to have her young, going to have her young ones, going to have some young ones, going to have young, going to* **kindle down,** *have a breed, have a litter, have a young one, have her young, have her young ones, have rabbits, have some young, have some young ones, have some young rabbits, have young, have young ones, in* **cast,** *in* **kid,** *in* **kindle,** *in* **kit,** *in* **young,** *is going to have a bear of young, is going to have a trip, is going to have her young, is going to have young, is going to have young ones, is in* **chit,** *is in* **kindle,** *is in* **young, kindle down, kit, kit down, kittle, lay down, litter, litter down, rabbit,** *she's having her young ones, she's in* **cast,** *she's in* **kindle,** *to have a litter, to have a stop, to have young, to have young ones, to* **kindle,** *to* **kit down,** *to* **kittle,** *to* **litter down, worry, young**

2. n in **kindle** pregnant, describing a doe. ɪn kɪndl Wa, ɪn kɪndɫ Wa So Sr, ɪŋ kɪndɫ So Ha, ɪn kɪndʊ Sr, ɪn kɪndʊɫ K Ha, ɪn kɛnʊ Ess

3. vi to FARROW, describing a pig giving birth to piglets III.8.10. kɪndəɫ Hrt

4. vi to WHELP III.13.3. kɪndɫ Ess, kɛnʊ Ess

5. n in **kindle** pregnant, describing a bitch. ɪn kɪndɫ K

6. vi to KITTEN III.13.10. kɪndəɫ Hrt

7. n KINDLING-*WOOD* V.4.2. kɪndɫ Ess W

kindle down *1. viphr* to KITTEN III.13.10. kɪndɫ dæʊn Ha

2. viphr to KINDLE, describing a rabbit doe giving birth to young III.13.14. kɪndɫ dəʊn W, kɪndɫ dæʊn W Ha, kɪnɫ dɛʊn Ess, kɛnɫ dæʊn Ess

kindler *n* KINDLING-*WOOD* V.4.2. kɪnləˀ La

kindle-wood *n* KINDLING-*WOOD* V.4.2. kɪndɫwʏd D, kɪndlwʊd O, kɪndʊwʊd Sr Sx

kindling *n What do you light your fire with in the morning?* V.4.2. Eng exc. Man St Wo Gl Bk Hrt W Sr D Do Ha Sx. ⇒ *a bit of furze,* **bavin(s), bavin-wood, birns,** *bit of* **stick, brash, brashnachs, brushwood, bunts, chats, chips,** *chopped-sticks* ⇒ **chopsticks, chopsticks, colons, cow-faggots,** *dried* **wood, elding, faggot(s), fire-lighting, fire-lighting** *wood,* **fire-sticks, firewood, firing, furzen-faggot, gorse-birns, hedge-sticks, kids, kinders, kinding-sticks, kindle, kindler, kindle-wood,** *kindlings,* *kindling-sticks, kindling-wood,* **light-fire, lighting-wood, lords, morning-sticks, morning's-wood, morning-wood, nickies, pimp(s), puffs, scrap-faggots, small wood,** *some* **stick, spray, spray-faggot(s), spray-sticks, spray-wood, stick(s),** **tindlers, tindling-sticks,** *top* **wood** *off the hedges,* **twigs, wood, wood** *for morning;* ⇒ also **kent**

kindred *n* RELATIONS VIII.2.4. kɪndɹəd Du, kɪnəːˀd So

kine **1. npl* COWS III.1.1(a). kaɪn Cu Y

2. n in **kine** ON HEAT, describing a cow III.1.6. ɪŋ kæːn D, ɪŋ kæɪn D

3. n a WEASEL IV.5.6. kiːn K, kəɪn Sx*[very small]*

kink *1. vt* to SPRAIN an ankle VI.10.8. kɪŋk L*[old]*, -*ed* kɪŋkt Y

2. n got a kink SILLY VIII.9.3. gɒt ə kɪŋk Sx

kink-cough *1. n* WHOOPING-COUGH VI.8.3. kɪŋkœːf Nb*[old]*, kɪŋkɒf Nb Du We La Y, kɪŋkɔf We, kɪnkɔst Y, kɪŋkɔʊf Nb, kɪŋkʊf La*[old]*

2. n a heavy cold. kɪŋkɒf Y

kinkle *n* CHARLOCK II.2.6. kɪŋkɫ K, kɪŋkʊɫ K

kinning *n* a chap in the skin, ⇐ CHAPS VI.7.3. kɪnɪn Y

kins *npl* CHAPS in the skin VI.7.3. kɪnz Nb Cu We La Y*[old x1]*

kinsfolk *n* RELATIONS VIII.2.4. kɪnzfʊək Y

kinsmen *n* RELATIONS VIII.2.4. kɪnzmən Nf

kip* *n* a SKEP IV.8.8(b). kɪp Sa, *pl* kɪps Y

kipe *n* a round wicker BASKET for carrying horse-feed III.5.4. kjæɪp He

kircher *n* the FAT round the kidneys of a pig III.12.7. kəˀːtʃəˀː So D

kirkgarth *n* a CHURCHYARD VIII.5.5. keəᵏkgaᵏːθ Nb*[very old]*, kəːkgaːθ Y*[old]*

kirkyard *n* a CHURCHYARD VIII.5.5. keəᵏkjaᵏːd Nb, keəᵏkjaᵏːd Nb*[old]*, kəɹkjaːrd Cu, kəɹkjaˡːd La

kist *1. n* a CORN-BIN I.7.4. kɪst Cu Du We La Y

2. n a wooden corn-bin. kɪst Cu Du

3. n a wooden chest. kɪst La Y

kisty *adj* SAD, describing bread or pastry that has not risen V.6.12. kɪsti Ha

kit *1. vi* to KITTEN III.13.10. kɪt C Nf Sf Bd Ess So Brk, kɪtʔ Nf, kɪʔ Sf Hrt

2. n in **kit** pregnant, describing a she-cat. ɪn kɪt O L Ess W Brk

3. n a KITTEN III.13.11. kɪt Gl

4. vi to KINDLE, describing a rabbit doe giving birth to young III.13.14. kɪt Nth C Nf Bk Ess, kɪtʔ Nf, kɪʔ Bk

5. n in **kit** pregnant, describing a doe rabbit. ɪn kɪt Brk Sr Sx

kitbolch *adv* HEAD OVER HEELS IX.1.10. kɪtbɒlʃ L

kit-brush *n* a BRUSH used to clean horses III.5.5(a). kɪtbɹʊʃ St

kitchen *n* the LIVING-ROOM of a house V.2.1. kɪtʃɪn Nb Cu Du We La Y Ch Db Sa St He Wo Wa Mon Gl O Nt L Lei R Nth Hu C*[in small house x1]* Nf Bk Bd Hrt Ess MxL So W Sr K Co D Do

Ha Sx, kɪtʃʊn La, kɪtʃn Nb Du Sx, kɪʔtʃn L, kɪtʃən Nb Du La Db Sa Gl Nt L Sf Hrt So W Co D Do Ha

kitchen-brush *n* a BRUSH used for sweeping indoors V.9.11. kɪtʃənbɽʌʃ W, kɪtʃɪnbɹʊʃ Gl

kitchen-chamber* *n* a BEDROOM over a kitchen V.2.3. kɪtʃɪntʃeːmbə Db

kitchen-loft *n* a BEDROOM V.2.3. kɪtʃɪnlɒft Cu

kit down *1. vphr* to KITTEN III.13.10. kɪt dɛʊn Sr, kɪt dæʊn MxL

2. viphr to KINDLE, describing a rabbit doe giving birth to young III.13.14. kɪt dəʊn Brk

kite *n* the BELLY VI.8.7. kaɪt Y

kiting *v-ing* PEEPING VI.3.8. kɒɪʔn Ha

kittagh-hand *adj* LEFT-HANDED VI.7.13(a). kɪðəhæˑn Man

kittaghy *adj* LEFT-HANDED VI.7.13(a). kɪðəgiː Man, kɛθəgɪ Man

kitten *1. vi When she [i.e. a she-cat] is going to have young ones, you say she is going ....* III.13.10. kɪtn Nb Du La Y Ch Db Sa St He Wo Wa Mon Gl O Nt L Lei R Ess W Sr Do Sx, kɪtən Y Sa He Mon, kɪtʔn Ess, kɪtʔən So, kɪʔn Man Ch O L Nf Bd Ess Brk Sr K. ⇒ *after kitting, bound to kittle, going to chat, going to have kittens, going to have some kittens, going to have young, going to kitten, going to kitten down, have her kittens, have kitlings, have kittens, have some kitlings, have some kittens, have some young ones, in kit, in kitten, in kittle, is going to chat, is going to have her kittens, is going to have kits, is going to have kittens, is going to have some kittens, is going to kindle down, is in kitten, kindle, kit, kit down, kitten down, kittle, pup, she's in kit, to have kittens, to have some kittens, to kit, to kitten, to kittle*

2. n in kitten pregnant, describing a she-cat. ɪn kɪʔn Ess So Sr Ha

3. n What do you call a young cat? III.13.11. kɪtn Nb Du Y Ch Db Sa St He Wo Wa Mon Gl O Nt L Lei R Nth Hu C Nf Sf Bd Ess MxL So W Sr Co D Do, *pl* kɪtnz La K Ha Sx, kɪdn So Co D Do, kɪʔn Man O L Nf Sf Bk Hrt Ess So W Brk K Do Ha Sx, *pl* kɪʔnz Bd Sr, kɪtʔn Nf Sf Ess, kɪtən Y Sa He Mon Lei, *pl* kɪtənz Y Wo Wa, kɪtʔən So W. ⇒ **kit,** *kitling* ⇒ **kittling, kitty**

kitten down *viphr* to KITTEN III.13.10. kɪtn dæʊn Ess Ha*[old ladies' expression x1]*, kɪʔn dæʊn Ha, kɪtn dæən K, kɪtn dɑʊn O, kɪtn dəʊn O

kittle *1. vi* to KITTEN III.13.10. kɪtl Nb*[old x1]* Cu Du We*[old x1]* La Y Ch*[frequent x1]* Db*[rare x1]* Sa St Nt*[rare x1, old x1]* L*[old x1]*, kɪtɫ Ch Lei R Nth

2. n in kittle pregnant, describing a she-cat. ɪn kɪtɫ Brk

3. vi to KINDLE, describing a rabbit doe giving birth to young III.13.14. kɪtl Nb Cu Du La Nt L, kɪtɫ Lei R Nth Hu, kɪdɫ So

4. v to GROPE *FOR FISH* IV.9.10. kɪtl Cu Du

kittling *n* a KITTEN III.13.11. kɪtlɪn Nb Cu We La Y Ch Db Sa, *pl* kɪtlɪnz Du St L, kɪt|ɪn La wY, kɪtlən Nb, *pl* kɪtlənz Du

kitty *n* a KITTEN III.13.11. kɪtɪ Nf

kitty-bags *npl* LEGGINGS made of sacking VI.14.18. kɪdɪbægz Co

kiver *1. v* make sheaves of corn into stooks, ⇐ STOOKING II.6.5. kjɪvəɪ Ch

2. n a stook of corn. kɪvə St, *pl* kɪvəz Ch, *pl* kjɪvəz Ch St

3. n a container used as a PASTE-BOARD V.6.5. kɪvə Nth Bk, kɪvəˡ Nth

kiver-top *n* the top of a container used as a PASTE-BOARD V.6.5. kɪvəˡtap Bk, kɪvəˡtɒp Bk

kizzened *ptppladj* BURNT, describing bread or cakes V.6.7. kɪznt Cu, kɪznd Y

knacker *n Suppose a cow dies on your farm, who comes to take the carcass away?* III.11.9. Eng exc. Bk Bd Hrt MxL Sr Sx. ⇒ **cad-butcher, cadman, cagmag, cagman, cagmeg-man,** *cagmen* ⇒ **cagman, cat's-meat-man, crockman, deadman, fellmonger, horse-slaughterer, hound-man, kegman, kegman-chap, kennel-man, kennel's-man, ket-dealer, ket-house-man, ketman,** *knacker-bloke, knacker-chap,* **knacker-dealer,** *knacker-fellow, knacker-killer, knacker-man, knacker's-man,* **knackery, slaughterer(s), slaughterman, slink-butcher, slink-chap, slink-dealer, slink-fellow,** *slink-fellows* ⇒ **slink-fellow, slinkman, tallowman;** ⇒ also **scrug**

knacker-dealer *n* a KNACKER III.11.9. nakədiːlə Db St

knacker-killer *n* a KNACKER III.11.9. nakəˡkɪləˡ Wo

knacker-kneed* *adj* KNOCK-KNEED VI.9.5. nakəniːd Y *[under knack-kneed NBM]*

knackery *n* a KNACKER III.11.9. nakʙɪ Nb *[queried as meaning a knacker's yard NBM]*

knack-kneed *adj* KNOCK-KNEED VI.9.5. nækniːd Man Gl Co Ha Sx, nakniːd Nb Du Wo Co D, nɑkniːd O Nth, naːkniːd Wa Mon Gl *[not a WMBM headword]*

knacky-kneed* *adj* KNOCK-KNEED VI.9.5. nakɪniːd Nb Du, nakɪneɪd Nb *[under knack-kneed BM]*

knap-kneed *adj* KNOCK-KNEED VI.9.5. nɛpniːd Nf, næpniːd Hu Nf Sf Ess, næpʔniːd Nf, napniːd Ch L Nth Hu C Sf So D, napneɪd Du

knapper *n* a RESTIVE horse III.5.6. napə Lei

knapper-kneed *adj* KNOCK-KNEED VI.9.5. napəneːd Ch

knappy *adj* RESTIVE, describing a horse III.5.6. napɪ Wa L Lei

knappy-kneed *adj* KNOCK-KNEED VI.9.5. napɪniːd Db, napɪneɪd Ch

knead *v* *What do you do to the dough before you roll it?* V.6.4.

vt niːd Ch St He Wa Mon O So Sr K Co D Do Ha, *2prpl* niːdz Wo, *-ing* niːdɪn ɒn t W, nɪid Brk, nɪiːd Brk Sr, *-ing* nɪiːdɪn Sx, *-ing* nɪiːdn Sx, neːd Db W D Ha, *-ing* neːɪdɪn Wo, nɛɪd St, nᵊɪd We

v niːd Nb Cu Du Y Man Ch Db Sa St Wo Wa Mon Gl O Nt L Lei R Nth Hu C Nf Sf Bk Bd Hrt Ess MxL So W K Co D Do Ha, iːd Hrt, nɪd Sa, nɪid Y Nf Ess Brk K, *-ing* nɪidn Ha, nɪiːd Du We Mon Gl Ess Sx, *-ing* nɪiːdɪn Brk Sr, nɪəd Cu We La Y Nt L, neːd Ch*[old x1]* Sa Gl W Ha, neɪd Du O Nf, neːɪd He, nɛd Nb Bk, *-ing* nɛdn Man, nɛːd Nf, nɛɪd La Y Ch Db St Wo Sf Bk Co, nəɪd Y, nᵊiːd Sf Bd Hrt

⇒ **baste, dough-punching, dough up,** *draw up* ⇒ **dough up,** *heal up* ⇒ **heel up, heel up, knead up, knock, knodden, lie, lie in, mix, mix up, mould, mould up, munge, pommel, pound, punch, punch about, ruck up and punch, work, work up**

kneading-board *n* a PASTE-BOARD V.6.5. niːdɪnbɔːd Wa, niːdɪnboˈəd Bd, nɪidɪnbɔəᶦd Brk, nɛɪdɪnbʊəɹd La, nɛɪdɪnbʊət La

kneading-trough *n* a container used as a PASTE-BOARD V.6.5. nɪidɪntɹɒf K, nᶦidntɹɒˈf K, nɪiːdɪntɹɒʊ Sr*[big x1]* Sx, nɪiːdntɹɔːf Ess, nɪiːdntɹɔːθ Ess, *pl* nɪiːdntɹɔːᵊz Ess, nɪiːdntɹʌʊ Ess, nɪiːdɪntɹɒʊ Brk Ha

knead up *vtphr* to KNEAD dough V.6.4. niːd ... ʌpʰ Mon, nɪiːd ... ʌp Nf Sx, nɪəd ... ʊp Y, neːd ... ʊp Wo, nɛɪd ... ʊp Y

knee-breeches *n* BREECHES VI.14.13(b). niːbɹiːtʃɪz La Ch, niːbɹiːtʃəz Db, niːbʁɪtʃɪz Nb, niːbɹɪtʃɪz Cu Du We La Wa, niːbɹɪtʃəz Y Db, nᶦiːbrʊtʃɪz Cu, niːbɹətʃɪz We, neːbɹɪtʃɪz Ch, neːbɹeːɪtʃɪz Ch*[old]*, nɛɪbɹɛɪtʃɪz Ch*[old]*, nəɪbɹətʃɪz Y

knee-nabbed *adj* KNOCK-KNEED VI.9.5. niːnæbɪd D, niːnabd D, niːnabɪd D

knee-napped *adj* KNOCK-KNEED VI.9.5. niːnæpəd So, niːnapɪd D, niːnapəd So Co

knee-nocked *adj* KNOCK-KNEED VI.9.5. niːnɒkt Do

knee-straps *npl* *What do some workmen wear below the knees [point] to lift the trouser-legs up?* VI.14.17. niːstɹɛps K, *sg* niːstræp Man, niːstɹaps O L Nth Bk Bd, *sg* niːstɹap Lei. ⇒ *a bit of* **string, band,** *bit of* **band,** *bit of* **string, boer yanks, bofflers, bull-dogs, buttress-jocks, calf-straps, cord, dogging-up-straps, eastoft leggings, garters, half-after-eights, hough-bands, irons, kicking-straps, leather garters, leeds-and-yorks, leg-straps, lijahs, london-and-yorks, londons, london-to-yorks, london-yorks, navvy-straps, norwichers,** *piece of* **string, pitsies, rennies, shay-garters, spitsies, strads, straps, tie-ups, upchurchers, wallies,**

warricks ⇒ **warwicks, warwicks, whangers, whirlers, yelks, yorkers, yorkies, yorks**

knetter *n* soft STRING used to tie up a grain-sack I.7.3. nɛtəᵗ Sx

knickerbockers *n* BREECHES VI.14.13(b). nɪkəbɔkəz Y

knicky *adj* WELL, describing a healthy person VI.13.1(a). nɪki D*[used in negative only]*

knife 1. *n* *[Show a picture of a knife.] What do you call this?* I.7.18. Eng. ⇒ **chiv**
2. *n* the COULTER of a horse-drawn plough I.8.6. naɪf Y
3. *n* a HAY-KNIFE II.9.14(a). naɪf Cu, nɔɪf Hrt
4. *n* a straight HEDGING-BILL IV.2.5. naɪf L

knitted up *adj* TANGLED, describing hair VI.2.5. nɪdɪd ʌp D

knitting-bag *n* a SHEATH or other device used to keep a knitting-needle firm V.10.10. nɪtɪnbag Y

knitting-bobbin *n* a SHEATH or other device used to keep a knitting-needle firm V.10.10. nɪtɪnbɒbɪn Y

knitting-fish *n* a SHEATH or other device used to keep a knitting-needle firm V.10.10. nɪtnfɪʃ Du

knitting-holder *n* a SHEATH or other device used to keep a knitting-needle firm V.10.10. nɪtɪnɒʊldə La

knitting-pad *n* a SHEATH or other device used to keep a knitting-needle firm V.10.10. nɪtɪnpæd Y, nɪtɪnpad Y Nt L Db

knitting-peg *n* a SHEATH or other device used to keep a knitting-needle firm V.10.10. nɪtɪnpeg La

knitting-pen *n* a SHEATH or other device used to keep a knitting-needle firm V.10.10. nɪtɪnpɛn La

knitting-pig *n* a SHEATH or other device used to keep a knitting-needle firm V.10.10. nɪtɪnpɪg Y

knitting-pin-holder *n* a SHEATH or other device used to keep a knitting-needle firm V.10.10. nɪtɪnpɪnɒʊldə Wa

knitting-quill *n* a SHEATH or other device used to keep a knitting-needle firm V.10.10. nɪtɪnkwɪl Cu La, nɪtɪntwɪl Cu

knitting-shear *n* a SHEATH or other device used to keep a knitting-needle firm V.10.10. nɪtɪnʃɪə Y, nɪtɪntʃɛː St

knitting-sheath *n* a SHEATH or other device used to keep a knitting-needle firm V.10.10. nɪtɪnʃiːθ Y C, nɪtnʃiːθ Nb, nɪtɪnʃiːf L, nɪtɪnʃɪəθ La Y, nɪtɪnʃeːθ Co, nɪtənʃeːθ Co D, nɪtnʃeɪð Nf, nɪtɪnʃɛθ Y O, nɪtɪnʃəɪθ Y, nətɪnʃɪːf So

knitting-shield *n* a SHEATH or other device used to keep a knitting-needle firm V.10.10. nɪtɪnʃiːl La, nɪtɪnʃiːɫd Co, nɪtɪnʃɪəld Nt, nɪtɪnʃɪət O, nɪtɪnʃiːəɫd Nth, nɪtɪnʃɛɪld Ch

knitting-shuttle *n* a SHEATH or other device used to keep a knitting-needle firm V.10.10. nɪtɪnʃʊtl Y

knitting-socket *n* a SHEATH or other device used to keep a knitting-needle firm V.10.10. nɪtɪnsɒkɪt Db

knitting-stick *n* a SHEATH or other device used to keep a knitting-needle firm V.10.10. nɪtɪnstɪk We La Y, nɪtnstɪk Nb Cu Du We, nɪʔnstɪk Man

knob *n* a BUMP on someone's forehead VI.1.8. nʌb Co

knob-pin *n* a PIN V.10.8. nɒbpɪn Db St

knock *v* to KNEAD dough V.6.4. nɔk Sf

knockabout *n* a FARM-LABOURER I.2.4. nɒkəbaʊt La, nɒkəbuːt Cu We; **general knockabout** dʒɛnəɹəl nɒkəbuːt Y, dʒɛnɹəl nɒkəbᵁuːt We

knockabout clothes *n* ORDINARY CLOTHES VI.14.20. nɒkəbɛʊt klɒʊðz K

knocked *adj* EXHAUSTED, describing a tired person VI.13.8. nɔkt MxL

knocked-kneed* *adj* KNOCK-KNEED VI.9.5. nɒkɪdniːd Y *[under knock-kneed NBM]*

knocked out *1. adj* ILL, describing a person who is unwell VI.13.1(b). nɔkt æʊt MxL
2. adj EXHAUSTED, describing a tired person VI.13.8. nɒkt ɛʊt Nf Ess, nɔkt ɛʊt Sf MxL, nɔkt aʊt L

knocked up *adj* EXHAUSTED, describing a tired person VI.13.8. nɒkt ʌp Nf Bd Hrt Ess, nɒkt ʏp Nf, nɒkt ʊp L, nɔkt ʌp C Sf Hrt Ess MxL, nɔkt ʊp L C

knocker-kneed *adj* KNOCK-KNEED VI.9.5. nɒkəniːd La Y, nɒkəᴵniːd La, nɒkənɛɪd Ch St, nɒkənəɪd Y, nɔkəniːd Y Ch L, nɔkəɹniːd L, nɔkəᴵniːd La, nɔkənəɪd Y *[not a NBM headword]*

knocking-off-time *n* STOPPING-TIME at the end of a day's work VII.5.9. Eng exc. Nb Cu Du We D Do Sx

knocking-time *n* STOPPING-TIME at the end of a day's work VII.5.9. nakɪntaɪm La

knock-kneed *adj Of a man whose legs are shaped like this [indicate knock-kneed], you say he is ....* VI.9.5. Eng exc. Du Hu C Co. ⇒ **bandy-legged, cock-kneed, crab-ankled, crooked-legged, hurked up, jay-legged, kay-legged,** *key-legged* ⇒ **kay-legged, knacker-kneed, knack-kneed, knacky-kneed, knap-kneed, knapper-kneed, knappy-kneed, knee-knocked, knee-nabbed, knee-napped, knocked-kneed, knocker-kneed, knocky-kneed, knuckle-kneed, straddle-legged**

knock-off *n* STOPPING-TIME at the end of a day's work VII.5.9. nɒkɒf Db St, nɒkɔːf Sa

knock off *vtphr* **knock the top off and the tail** to TOP AND TAIL swedes II.4.3. nɒk ... ɒf Du

knock-off-time *n* STOPPING-TIME at the end of a day's work VII.5.9. nakɔːftaːm Co, nɒkɒftaɪm Sa, nɒkɒftɔɪm Ha, nɒkɒftəɪm W Brk, nɒkɔːftaɪm Co, nɒkɔːftaːm Co, nɒkɔːftaɪm K, nɒkɔːftɒɪm W Ha, nɒkɔːftɒɪm Ess Brk K, nɒkɔːftʌɪm Brk Sr, nɒkɔːftəɪm W Do Sx, nɔkɔːftaɪm K

knock out *vtphr* to THIN OUT turnip plants II.4.2. nɒk ... ɛʊt Ess, nak ... æʏt Co, nɒk ... əʊt Y

knock-out-time *n* STOPPING-TIME at the end of a day's work VII.5.9. nɒkkaʊttəɪm So

knocks off *viphr-3prsg* school FINISHES VIII.6.2(b). nɒks ɑːf He

knocky-kneed* *adj* KNOCK-KNEED VI.9.5. nɒkɪnᴵiːd We La, nɒkɪnɛɪd Y, nɒkɪnəɪd Y, nɔːkɪniːd Y *[under knock-kneed NBM]*

knodden *v* to KNEAD dough V.6.4. nɒdn Y*[old] [marked by fw as ptppl at one Y locality]*

knot *n* **a knot of bread** a very thick SLICE of bread V.6.10. ə nɒt ə bɾɛːd So

knotchery *adj* TANGLED, describing hair VI.2.5. nɒtʃi

knotlings *n* CHITTERLINGS III.12.2. nɛtɫɪnz Do, næɫ ɪnz So, natlɪnz So, natɫɪnz So D, natɫənz Co D, nadlɪnz So, nadɫɪnz D Do, nadɫənz Co D, nɒtɫənz Co, nɒdlənz So, nɔtlɪnz So

knots *n* **full of knots** TANGLED, describing hair VI.2.5. fʊl ə nɒts Nf

knotted *adj* TANGLED, describing hair VI.2.5. næt?ɪd Nf, nɒtɪd Y Mon Gl Nth Nf So Do, nɒt?ɪd Nf, nɒʔɪd O

knotted up *adj* TANGLED, describing hair VI.2.5. næ?ɪd ʏp Nf, natəd ʌp D

knotty *adj* TANGLED, describing hair VI.2.5. nati So D, nadi D, nɒtɪ Du La Y Db Gl Ess, nɒti So W, nɒt?ɪ Nf, nɒɹɪ Sr, nɔtɪ La

knuckle-kneed *adj* KNOCK-KNEED VI.9.5. nʌkɫnᵊiːd Sf

kutchy-bells *npl* EARWIGS IV.8.11. *sg* kʊtʃɪbɛl So

kye *1. n* a COW III.1.1(b). kiː Ch, kɛː La Db, *poss.sg* kɛːz Nt, kɛɪ Ch Bk, kaɪ Cu Y Ch St
2. npl COWS III.1.1(a). kɛɪ Ch St, kaɪ Nb Cu Du We Y *[kye/kyes forms cannot always readily be differentiated from cow/cows forms]*

kye-man* *n* a COWMAN on a farm I.2.3. kɛɪmən Bk, kaɪmʊn Ch, kaɪmən Ch

kyes* *npl* COWS III.1.1(a). kᵊiːz Ch, kɛːz La Db K, kɛɪz Ch

kysty* *adj* fastidious about food, describing a child, ⇐ FOOD V.8.2. kaɪstɪ We

L

labbered up *adj* STICKY, describing a child's hands VIII.8.14. lɒbəd ʊp Y

labbet *n* a FARM-LABOURER I.2.4. ɫæbət Co, ɫabət Co; **general labbet** dʒɪŋəɫ ɫabət Co

labourer *1. n* a FARM-LABOURER I.2.4. leːbəɹə La Y Db Nt, leːbəɹəˑɹ La, leːbəɹəᵗ Gl, leːbəɹəᵗː Sa, ɫeːbəᵗːɾə W Co D, ɫeːbəᵗːɾəᵗː Co, leːbɹə Du La Sa Nf, leːbɹəᵗ He Wo Brk, ɫeːbɾə D, ɫeːbɾəᵗː W Co D Do Ha, leibʌɹə Mon, leɪbəɹə C Hrt, leɪbɾˌəᵗː So, leɪbɹə Db Nf, leɪbɾə So, leɪbɾəᵗː So, leːbəɹə Nf, leːᵊbɹə Nf, leɪbəɹə Wa L C Nf Sf Ess, leɪbəɹəᵗ Wa, leɪbɹə St Lei R Ess Sr, leɪbɹəᵗɾ Ha, leɪbɾˌ K, lɛˑəbɹə Y L, lɛˑəbəɹɛɹ L, lɛˑəbɹə Y L, lɛˑəbɹeɪɹ L, lɛˑəbɹəᴶ L, læɪbɹə Nf Hrt; **general labourer** dʒɛnɹəl leːbɹə Sa Gl, dʒɛnɹəl leˑɪbɹə Db, dʒɛnɾəɫ leɪbəɾəᵗ O, dʒɛnɾəɫ leɪbəɾəᵗː So, dʒɛnɹəl leːbɹə Nf, dʒɛnɹəl leɪbɹə St, dʒɛnɹəɫ leɪbəɹəᵗ Wa, dʒɛnɹəɫ leɪbɹə Nth, dʒɛnɹəɫ leɪbɹə Lei, dʒɛnɹɫ leˑɪbɹə Lei, dʒɛnɹəl leəbɹə Y L; **ordinary labourer** ɔːdnɹɪl lɛˑəbɹə L

2. n the FORKER on a wagon who unloads sheaves in a stackyard II.6.9. leɪbəᵗɾəᵗ Sx

labouring-man *n* a FARM-LABOURER I.2.4. leɪbɹɪnman Hu, leɪbɹɪnman Lei

lace *1. n* a DIAGONAL BAR of a gate IV.3.7. leːs Mon Gl, *pl* leːsɪz He, leːɪs He, *pl* leˑɪsəz Db, lɛɪs Wa, *pl* lɛɪsɪz St, *pl* lɛɪsəz St

2. vt to PLASH a hedge IV.2.4. leɪs So

3. vt to BEAT a boy on the buttocks VIII.8.10. lɪəs Nb

lace-apron* *n* a decorative APRON worn on Sunday V.11.2(b). leːsapɹən Y

laces *npl* BOOTLACES VI.14.25. Eng exc. R

lace-stoop *n* the SHUTTING-POST of a gate IV.3.4. leːsstuːp Nb

lacet *n* a DIAGONAL BAR of a gate IV.3.7. *pl* lɛɪsɪts Lei

lace-tab *n* the TAG of a boot-lace VI.14.26. *pl* lɛˑəstabz L

laches *npl* PUDDLES IV.1.6. leːtʃɪz La

lacing *1. n* a DIAGONAL BAR of a gate IV.3.7. *pl* liːsɪnz Ch, *pl* leːsɪnz Ch, *pl* leɪsɪŋz St, leːɪsɪn He Mon, lɛɪsɪn Wo, *pl* lɛɪsɪnz St Wa

2. vbln **give him a good lacing** to BEAT a boy on the buttocks VIII.8.10. lɪəs Nb; gɪb ṃə gʊd leɪsɪn So

lacing-bar *n* a DIAGONAL BAR of a gate IV.3.7. leːsɪnba: Ch, leːsɪnbaᵗː Sa

lacings *npl* the horizontal BARS of a gate IV.3.6. leːsɪnz Sa

lackey *n* a FARM-LABOURER I.2.4. lækɪ Ess

lackses *npl* the horizontal BARS of a gate IV.3.6. ɫɛksɪz D, ɫaksəz D *[queried SBM]*

lad *n* a SON VIII.1.4(a). lad Nb Cu*[usual x2]* Du*[usual x1]* We*[usual x1]* La Y*[old x1]* Ch Db Wa Nt*[old-fashioned x1]* L

ladder *1. n [Show a picture of a ladder.] What do you call this?* I.7.14. lɛðəᴿ Nb Du, lɛdə L Ess, lɛðə Y Nt L Nf, lɛdəᴿ Du, lɛðəᴿ Nb, lɛdəᴶ Sr K, lɛðəᴶ L, lɛdəᵗ Sr K Sx, lɛdəᵗː So, ɫɛdəᵗː D, lædə Man Wa Mon Nf Sf Bk Hrt Ess MxL Sr K, læðə Wa Hu Nf, lædəᴶ Brk Sr K, lædəᵗ He Wo Mon Gl Brk Sr Sx, *pl* læˑdəᵗz̩ Ha, lædəᵗ Sa He Wo, lædəᵗː So, ɫædəᵗː So Co D, ladəᴿ Nb, laðəᴿ Nb, ladə Nb Cu Du We La Y Ch Db St Wa Mon Nt L Lei R Nth Hu C Nf Bd Hrt Ess, laðə Du La Ch Db St Nth C, laðəʳ Cu, laðəᴿ Nb Du, ladəɹ We La Y He, ladəᴶ La Db O L, ladðəɹ La, laðəᴶ La, ladəᵗ Sa Wo Wa Gl O Nth Bk Bd, ɫadəɾ O, laðəᵗ Sa Wo, ladəᵗː W Do, ɫadəᵗː W Co D Do Ha, lɑdə Ch, lɑdəᴶ L, ladəᵗ Wo Ha, lɒdəᵗ Wo. ⇒ **stee, ladders**

2. n a vertical rod in front of a cart, perforated to allow adjustments when tipping, ⇐ ROD/PIN I.10.3. ɫædəᵗː Co

3. n an END-BOARD of a cart I.10.4. *pl* lædəz Ess, ɫadəᵗː Ha *[marked ir.r. EMBM]*

4. n a rear cart-ladder, ⇐ CART-LADDERS I.10.5. *pl* læˑdez Hrt, ladə Hrt

5. n a BENCH on which slaughtered pigs are dressed III.12.1. lɛdəᵗː So*[about 3 feet wide]*, pɪgɫɛdəᵗː D, pɪgɫædəᵗː D, pɪgzlɛdəᵗː So, pɪgzɫɛdəᵗː D

6. n a STILE IV.2.9. laðə St

ladder-frame *n* a CART-FRAME I.10.6. lædəfɹɛɪm Ess

ladder-round *n* a RUNG of a ladder I.7.15. ɫadəᵗːɾɒʊnd W

ladders *1. n* a LADDER I.7.14. lædəᴶz Brk Ha, ladəz L

2. npl CART-LADDERS I.10.5. lɛdəz Ess Sx, lɛdəᵗz̩ Sx, lɛðəᵗz̩ Sr, leðəz Nf, lædəz Nf Sf Ess Sr K, lædᵊz Nf, lædəᴶz Brk Sr K Ha, lædəᵗz̩ Wo Gl Brk Sr, lædəᵗːz̩ So, ladəz Nf Ess, *sg* ladə O, ladəᵗz̩ Gl O Ha, ɫadəᵗːz̩ W Ha, laðəᵗz̩ Sa

3. npl (cart-)ladders on a wagon. ladəz Gl

4. n a CART-FRAME I.10.6. lædəz Sf Ess

ladder-stall* *n* a RUNG of a ladder I.7.15. *pl* ɫædəᵗːstɔːɫz D

ladder-stay *n* a RUNG of a ladder I.7.15. *pl* ɫadəˡːs̩teːz D

ladder-stile *n* a STILE IV.2.9. laðəstɑɪl Hu

ladder-tree *n* a vertical rod in front of a cart, perforated to allow adjustments when tipping, ⇐ ROD/PIN I.10.3. ɫadəˡːtɹiː Co

laddies *npl* BOYS VIII.1.3(a). ladɪz Nb, *sg* ladɪ Du

lade *1. n* an END-BOARD of a cart I.10.4. ɫeːd D, *pl* ɫeːdz Co, *pl* leɪdz So

2. *v* to LOAD a cart with dung II.1.5. *v-ing* lɛɪdɪn Y

3. *v* to LOAD sheaves onto a wagon II.6.7(a). lɪəd Nb Y, leˑad Cu Du We La, leˑəd We, *prppl* leˑədn Cu

4. *v* to POUR tea V.8.8. leːd Ch

lade-bowl *n* a SCOOP used to take water out of a boiler V.9.9. lɛɪdbɔʊl St

lade-can *n* a SCOOP used to take water out of a boiler V.9.9. leːɪdkan Db, lɛɪdkan St, lɛɪtkan Lei

lade-grip* *n* a BUMPER of a cart I.10.1(a). *pl* ɫeːdgɾɪps D

laden *1. v* to LOAD a cart with dung II.1.5. lɛˑədn Y

2. *v* to LOAD sheaves onto a wagon II.6.7(a). lɪədn Cu, *prppl* lɪədnɪn Y, lɪədn̩ɪn Y, leadn Cu

3. *v* to POUR tea V.8.8. leːdn Ch

ladener *n* the LOADER of sheaves onto a wagon II.6.7(c). lɪədnə Y, lɪədn̩ə Y

lader *1. n* the LOADER of sheaves onto a wagon II.6.7(c). lɪədə Nb, lɪədðə Cu, leadə Cu*[old x1]* Du We La, leˑədə Cu, leˑədðə We

2. *n* the FORKER on a wagon who unloads sheaves in a stackyard II.6.9. lɛˑədə Y

3. *n* a SCOOP used to take water out of a boiler V.9.9. leːdə Nt, lɛɪdə L

laders *npl* CART-LADDERS I.10.5. leːᵊdəˡːz̩ Do, ɫeːðəˡːz̩ Do, leɪdəˡːz̩ So

lader-tin *n* a SCOOP used to take water out of a boiler V.9.9. lɛɪdətɪn Lei

lade(s) *n* a CART-FRAME I.10.6.

no -s: lɛɪd Sx, lɛɪ Brk

-s: lɛɪdz Sr K Sx, lɛɪz Brk, læɪdz K Sx

lades *npl* CART-LADDERS I.10.5. leːdz So, ɫeːdz Co D Do, ɫeːədz Co D, leɪdz So

lade up *vtphr* to LOAD sheaves onto a wagon II.6.7(a). lɛˑəd ... ʊp Y

lading-bowl *n* a SCOOP used to take water out of a boiler V.9.9. liːdɪnbɛʊl Ch

lading-can *n* a SCOOP used to take water out of a boiler V.9.9. liːdɪnkan Db, leːdɪŋkan Ch Db, leːdɪnkan Db, leːdɪnkjɔn Ch

lading-pot *n* a SCOOP used to take water out of a boiler V.9.9. lɪədnpɒt Du

lading-tin *n* a SCOOP used to take water out of a boiler V.9.9. liːdɪntɪn Ch, leːdɪntɪn Nt, lɛˑədɪntɪn L

ladle *1. n* a PORRIDGE-STICK V.9.1. leːdɫ W, ɫeːdɫ D Ha, leɪdl St*[old x1]* L Nf, lɛɪdʊɫ Brk*[old]*, lɛɪdʊ Sx, ladɫ Do

2. *n* a SCOOP used to take water out of a boiler

V.9.9. lɪədl Du, leːdl Nb, leːdɫ Co, leːˡdl Db, leɪdɫ Bk, leədl Nb Y, leˑədəɫ Bk, lɛɪdl St L, lɛɪdɫ Lei R, lɛɪdʊ MxL, lɛˑədl L, læɪdɫ Lei K

ladle-can *n* a SCOOP used to take water out of a boiler V.9.9. leːdlkan Nt

ladling-can *n* a SCOOP used to take water out of a boiler V.9.9. leːdlɪnkan La

lads *1. npl* BOYS VIII.1.3(a). *sg* lɛd Sr, lædz Nb Y He*[old]* Mon, *sg* læd Sa MxL, *sg* læːd Ess K Ha, ladz Nb Cu Du We La Y Ch Db*[old x1]* Sa*[old x1]* St*[old x1]* Wa Mon Nt L Lei

2. *npl* PALS VIII.4.2. lædz Ess; **the lads** ðə lædz Sx

lady-candlestick *n* a COWSLIP II.2.10(a). leːdɪkanlstɪk We

lady-heads *npl* TADPOLES IV.9.5. leːdɪjɪdz Y

lady-milord *n* a DADDY-LONG-LEGS IV.8.10. leɪdɪmɪlɔːd Nf

lady-tree *n* a BIRCH tree IV.10.1. leədɪtɹiː Y

lagged out *adj* EXHAUSTED, describing a tired person VI.13.8. lægd ʌʊt Brk

lagging* *n* a stave of a tub, ⇐ BASKET III.5.4. lagɪn Y

lagging out *vtphr-ing* PUTTING your tongue OUT VI.5.4. *no -s* lag ... uːt Y

laid *1. adj* OVERTURNED, describing a sheep on its back unable to get up III.7.4. lɛɪd Sx; **laid fast** lɛəd fast Y

2. *ptppl* BURIED VIII.5.11. læɪd Nf

lair *1. n* a FASTING-CHAMBER III.11.3. lɛəᴵ K *[queried u.r. SBM]*

2. *n* a SLAUGHTERHOUSE III.11.4. lɛəᴵ K*[rare]*

lait *vt* LOOK FOR it III.13.18. leːt Cu We La Y, leət Y, lɛːt Cu We, lɛət Y

lait up *vtphr* LOOK FOR it III.13.18. leat ... ʊp La

lake *vi* to PLAY VIII.6.4. *prppl* lɪəkɪn Y, leːk Nb Cu Du We La Y, leˑak La, leək Du La Y, leːᵊk Cu Y, lɛːk Cu We, *-ing* lɛɪkɪn Y, lɛək Y

lake about *viphr* to PLAY VIII.6.4. *3prpl* leːk əbaːt Y, leːk əbuːt Y, *-ing* lɛəkɪn əbuːt Y

lakes* *npl* PUDDLES IV.1.6. *sg* leːk La

lalling *1. vt-ing* PUTTING your tongue OUT VI.5.4. lalɪn Y

2. *v-ing* PANTING VI.8.1. lalɪn L*[old]*

lalling out *vtphr-ing* PUTTING your tongue OUT VI.5.4. lalɪn ... aʊt Y L, lalɪn ... əʊt Y, lalən ᵊuːt ... We

lamb *1. n* a MALE LAMB III.6.2. lɛm Nf, læm Man Nf Brk, lam La St Mon R So

2. *n* a EWE-LAMB III.6.3. læm Nf, lam St

3. *n* a sheep before its first shearing, ⇐ EWE-HOG III.6.4. lɛm K, læm Sr, lam Ch St Mon Bk, ɫam D Do

4. *n* a sheep from its first to its second shearing,

⇐ GIMMER III.6.5. łam W

5. n a PET-LAMB III.7.3. læːm Hrt

lamb-hog *n* a sheep before its first shearing, ⇐ EWE-HOG III.6.4. lamɒg Lei, lamɔg L

lames *vi-3prsg* it HURTS VI.13.3(a). lɪəmz Y*[old]*, *prppl* lɪəmɪn Y, leːmz Ch, leˑams La, *inf* leˑəm La, *no -s* leəm We

lamp-oil *n* OIL used for lighting V.2.13(a). lɛmpʔɔil Nf, lamppɛɪl Db, lampɔɪl Y

land-ditch *vt* to DRAIN wet land IV.1.9. lændɪtʃ Ess

land-drain *v* to DRAIN wet land IV.1.9. lændɹɛɪn Ess, *-ing* læːnddɹæɪnɪn Ess

land-horse *1. n When you use two horses for ploughing, what do you call each one? [The horse walking on the unploughed land.]* II.3.4(b). Eng exc. Hu MxL Do. ⇒ **inside, inside-horse, landside-horse, land-tit, line-horse, near, near-horse, nearside, nearside-horse, one on top, outside-horse,** *rigg-horse* ⇒ **rig-horse, rig-horse, string-horse, swath-horse, top-horse**

2. n the NEAR-HORSE of a pair pulling a wagon I.6.4(a). læˑnɔːs Man, landɒs Y

land-ledge *n* the SOLE of a horse-drawn plough I.8.9. łanłedʒ D

land-mouse *n* a SHREW-MOUSE IV.5.2. lanmuːs Y

land-plate *n* the SOLE of a horse-drawn plough I.8.9. læːnplɛɪt Sr, lanpleːt Gl

land-race *n* the SOLE of a horse-drawn plough I.8.9. landʁeːs Nb

land-rise *n* the SOLE of a horse-drawn plough I.8.9. lanɾæɪz So, lɔːnɾəɪz Do*[left-hand side]*

land(s) *n* a SLOPE IV.1.10.

no -s: lɒnt St

-s: lanz Lei

lands *npl* the RIDGES between furrows in a ploughed field II.3.2. lændz Brk Sx, lanz Y Wo Wa, landz Wa, laːnz Ha, lɒnts Db, lɔnz Wo

land-side *1. n* the MOULD-BOARD of a horse-drawn plough I.8.8. læːnzæɪd So

2. n the SOLE of a horse-drawn plough I.8.9. lænzaɪd So, łænzaɪd D, landsɑˑɪd Lei, łanzɒɪd Ha, łanzəɪd W*[on left x1]*, łaːnzɒɪd Ha, lɒndzaɪd So, łɒnzɒɪd Do, łɒnzəɪd W, łɔːnzɒɪd Do Ha, łɔːnzəɪd W

landside-horse *n* the LAND-HORSE of a ploughing team II.3.4(b). læᵊndsɛɪdhoᴿːs Nb, lansaːdɒs Y, landsaɪdɒs Ch, lansɑɪdɔːs Bd, lansɔɪdɔːs Wa

land-slide *1. n* the MOULD-BOARD of a horse-drawn plough I.8.8. lænslʌɪd Brk

2. n the SOLE of a horse-drawn plough I.8.9. lenslɔɪd Ess, lɛnslʌɪd Sr, lænslɒɪd Wo, læːnslɔɪd C Hrt, lænslʌɪd Sr, lænsləɪd Brk Sx, landslɪd Wo, lanslæɪd Sa, lanslaɪd St, landslɑːd Lei, landslaɪd Lei Nth Bk, lanslɑɪd Db Wa Lei Hu C Bd Hrt, landslɒɪd St, landslɔɪd Nth, lansɔɪd Wa Nth Bk, lɑnslaɪd Hu

land-slip *n* the SOLE of a horse-drawn plough I.8.9. łænsłɪp D

land-slipe *n* the SOLE of a horse-drawn plough I.8.9. lændslɑɪp Nf

land-tit *n* the LAND-HORSE of a ploughing team II.3.4(b). lantɪt Db

lane *1. n If a road is narrow and between hedges, you call it a ....* IV.3.13. Eng exc. Cu. ⇒ **by-lane, by-road, cart-track, drag-way, drift, drove, gully, loan, loaning, loke, mear, narrow loke, twitten;** ⇒ also **drang-way**

2. n a row of sheaves in a rick. łeːn D

lanes *1. n* an EVENER on the plough-beam end of a horse-drawn plough I.8.4. lɛˑənz L *[probably refers to notches on the end of the evener; marked u.r., as are all such, in EMBM]*

2. n the notches on the T-SHAPED PLOUGH-BEAM END of a horse-drawn plough I.8.5. leːnz Nt, lɛˑənz L

lank *n* the GROIN VI.9.4. łaŋk D, lɒŋk Sa St He Wo

lant *1. n* URINE in a cow-house I.3.10. lant La

2. n stale URINE used for cleaning blankets VI.8.8. lant La Ch Db Sa St, land La; **old lant** ɒʊd lant La, ɔʊd land La, ɔʊd laŋ La

lant-hole *n* a CESS-POOL on a farm I.3.11. lantoːl La

lantree(s) *n* a SWINGLE-TREE of a horse-drawn plough harness I.8.3.

sg: lantɹiː He

-s: læntɹiːz Sa He Wo, lɛntɹiz He, lantɹiz Sa

lanyard *n* a TETHER for a cow I.3.4. łænjəɭːd̪ Co

lap *1. n* a SOWING-BASKET II.3.6. lap Nb

2. n the FLAP at the front of old-fashioned trousers VI.14.16. *pl* laps Db

3. n a DRINK (of milk) given to a kitten III.13.12. ljɛp Nb, lɪəp Nb, lɛp Cu We, læp Sf Ess, lap Cu Du We La Y Gl O Nt L Nth C Bk So, lɒp Ch

4. vt to WRAP a parcel VII.2.9. lɛp Cu, læp He Wa, lap Nb*[old x1]* Cu Du We La Y Ch*[with cloth x1]* Db*[very old x1]* Sa St Wo*[old]* Wa Gl O Nt L Nth

5. vt-3sg she [i.e. a tidy girl] will COLLECT her toys VIII.8.15. lap Ch

lap-cocks *npl* small COCKS of hay II.9.12. lapkɒks Y

lap-love *n* BINDWEED II.2.4. laplʊv St

lap-over *n* the FLAP at the front of old-fashioned trousers VI.14.16. lapʊəᴿ Du

lapper *n* the TONGUE VI.5.4. læpəɭ (+V) So*[old]*

lapping *vt-ing* PUTTING your tongue OUT VI.5.4. łæpɪn Co

lapping out *vtphr-ing* PUTTING your tongue OUT VI.5.4. leːpɪn ... ɛat Y, læpɪn ... ɛʊt K, ɫapɪn ... æɤt Co, ɫapən ... œɤt D, ɫapən ... æɤt Co

lap round *vtphr* to WRAP a parcel VII.2.9. lap ... ɹaːnd La, lap ... ɹaʊnd Y L

lap up *1. vtphr* to WRAP a parcel VII.2.9. læp ... ʌp He, læᵊp ... ʊp Nb, læp ... ʊp He Wo, lap ... ʊp Nb, lap ... ʊp Nb Cu Du La Y Ch St Wo Wa L, *ptppl* lapt ... ʊp Lei, lap ... ʊp Y

2. vtphr-3sg **lap up and put tidy** she [i.e. a tidy girl] will COLLECT her toys VIII.8.15. lap ... ʊp ən pʊt ... taɪdɪ Y

lard *1. n* *What do you make from this fat [round the kidneys of a pig]?* III.12.8. Eng. ⇒ **dripping, fat, grease, pork-saim, seam, saim**

2. n the FAT round the kidneys of a pig III.12.7. læːd La, laːd Du, ɫaᶜːd̪ D

3. n DRIPPING V.7.5(a). laːd Mon

4. n BACON-FAT V.7.5(b). laːd Y, ɫaᶜːd̪ Co

larder *1. n* a PANTRY V.2.6. læˑdə Sf*[in old house]*, læᶜːd̪əᶜ Bk, ɫaɽdəɽ O, laːdə Y Ch*[modern]* Db Wa*[in farmhouse]* L Ess*[refined x1]*, laᶜːd̪ə O Nth*[in farmhouse]*, laᶜːd̪əᶜ O Bk Ha, laᶜːd̪əᶜː So W, ɫaᶜːd̪əᶜː Co D Do Ha, laɹdəɹ He, laːdə Man*[old x1]* St Wa*[modern]* Hrt Ess, laːdəᴶ K, laːdəᶜ Gl Sr, laᴶːdəᴶ Brk, laᶜːɽdəᴶ Sr, laᶜːɽdəᶜ Brk Sx, ɫaᶜːd̪əᶜː D*[modern x1]*, lɔːdəᶜ Sa*[modern]*

2. n the DAIRY of a cottage V.5.1. laːdə Ess

lard-saim *n* the FAT round the kidneys of a pig III.12.7. laːdsiːm Nf

large tooth *n* a molar, ⇐ MOLARS VI.5.7. laᶜːdʒ tuːθ O

larp *v* to GOBBLE food VI.5.13(b). laːp Mon

larrap *1. n* the human MOUTH VI.5.1. laɹəp Sa *[queried WMBM]*

2. n CHAT VIII.3.4. laɹəp Sa

larras *npl* the horizontal BARS of a gate IV.3.6. ɫaᶜːz̪ Y

larrup *vt* to BEAT a boy on the buttocks VIII.8.10. læɹəp MxL

larry *n/adj* the LAST sheep through a gate VII.2.2. laɹɪ Cu

lash *1. n* the YIELD of milk from a cow or from a herd of cows III.3.5. laʃ Y

2. n a COMB VI.2.4. laʃ Cu

lash-comb *n* a COMB VI.2.4. læɪʃkuːm Y

lashing-chain *n* a chain used to tie up a horse, ⇐ TETHERING-ROPE I.4.2. læʃɪntʃæɪn K

lass *n* a DAUGHTER VIII.1.4(b). las Nb Cu*[usual x2]* Du*[usual x1]* We La Y*[old x1]* Db Nt*[old-fashioned x1]* L

lasses *npl* GIRLS VIII.1.3(b). *sg* læs Ha, lasɪs Y, lasɪz Nb Cu Du We La Y Sa Nt L, lasəz Nb Du Y Db*[old x1]*Nt L. ⇒ also **lassies** *[taken as lassies EMBM. Note at NBM suggests lassies only likely where laddies is*

recorded for boys: this interpretation is accepted here]

lassie *n* a DAUGHTER VIII.1.4(b). lasɪ Cu

lassies *npl* GIRLS VIII.1.3(b). lasɪz Nb, lasəz Nb. ⇒ also **lasses**

last *n/adj [Let's talk about the order in which you put things. Here are nine sheep coming through a gate [indicate]. (before April 1952: Here are nine dots.)] And the one at the back [indicate the last one]? (before April 1953: Which is this [indicate the last one]?)* VII.2.2. Eng. ⇒ **hind, hinder, hindermost, hindmost, hindward, larry, latter, tail** *[only SBM marks definite cases of adj in this notion; wordclass for unmarked forms substantival]*

last evening *n* LAST NIGHT VII.3.9. ɫeːs iːbmən Co, ɫaːs eːvnən D

last night *n [If you wanted to tell me that something happened seven days back from now, you'd say: It happened ....] If yesterday, but about 9 p.m. or so?* VII.3.9. Eng. ⇒ **last evening, tonight, yesterday afternoon, yesterday night, yester night**

lat *n* a RUNG of a ladder I.7.15. *pl* lats L

latch *1. n What do you fasten a door with?* V.1.9. ɫeɪtʃ D, lɛtʃ Gl Ess Sr K Sx, lætʃ Man Sa He Wo Mon Gl O L*[old]* Hu C Sf Hrt Ess MxL So Brk Sr K Ha Sx, læ Brk, ɫætʃ Mon Co, læᴵtʃ So, latʃ La Ch Db Sa St He Wo Wa Mon Gl O L Lei R Nth Hu C Bk Bd Hrt So Do, ɫatʃ O W D Do Ha, ɫaɪtʃ Co D, lɒtʃ Mon; **door-latch** dʊəlatʃ La. ⇒ **catch,** *door*-**latch, door-sneck, drop-latch, hasp, hasp and staple, hatch, sneck, thumb-latch, wooden latch**

2. vt to SHUT a door IX.2.8. latʃ Wo *[marked u.r. WMBM]*

latching *adj* INFECTIOUS, describing a disease VI.12.2. laksɪn La

latching-post *n* the SHUTTING-POST of a gate IV.3.4. ɫɛtʃənpɔːs D, lætʃɪnpoʊst Wo, latʃɪnpɔʊst O

latch-post *n* the SHUTTING-POST of a gate IV.3.4. lætʃpʌʊst Sf, lætʃpʌʊs Ess, latʃpɔʊst Nth, latʃpɔʊs Wo

lathe *1. n* a COW-HOUSE I.1.8. lɪəð Y

2. n a BARN I.1.11. lɪaθ Y, lɪəð Y, lɪˑə Y, leːθ Y, leːð Y, leaθ Cu We, leəð We Y, leəð Y, lea Y, lɛəð Y, lɛəd Y

use:

a. for storing corn: Cu We Y

b. for storing hay: Cu We Y

c. for storing tools and/or implements: Cu Y

d. for housing cows: Y

e. for threshing in: Y

location:

adjoining or near farmhouse: Cu We

3. n the place where hay is stored on a farm, ⇐ HAY-LOFT I.3.18. lɪaθ Y, leːð Y, leaθ We, leað We, leəð Y

4. n a CART-SHED I.11.7. lɪaθ Y

lathered up *adj* STICKY, describing a child's hands VIII.8.14. laðəd ʊp L

laths *npl* the horizontal BARS of a gate IV.3.6. lɑːθs Hrt, lɑːðz Sx

lats *npl* the horizontal BARS of a gate IV.3.6. lats Db

latter *n/adj* the LAST sheep through a gate VII.2.2. lætəᴶ Brk*[old]*

latter end *n* AUTUMN VII.3.7. lætəɹ ɛnd K

latter-cut *n* AFTERMATH, a second crop of grass II.9.17. lætəɹkʊt Brk

latter-math *n* AFTERMATH, a second crop of grass II.9.17. lɛtəmaθ Wa, ɫɛtəᵗːmɔːθ W, lætəᵗmæθ He Wo, lætəᵗmæːθ Gl, lætəmaːθ Nth, lætəᵗmaːθ Gl, lætəᴶmɒθ Brk, lætəᵗmɒθ Brk, lætəməθ Mon, ɫætəməθ Mon, lætəᵗməθ He Mon, latəmaːθ Wo Wa O, laʔəmaːθ Bk, latəᵗmaːθ Wa Gl O Nth, latɪmɒθ Lei, ɫatəɹmɔ·ɽθ O, latəmʌθ Mon, ɫatəᵗːmʌθ W, latəmʊθ Lei, latəɹməθ He, latəᵗməθ O, ladəᵗməθ Bk, laʔəməθ Bk Bd, laʔəᵗməθ Bk, ɫatəᵗːməθ W, latɪmə Lei

laugh *vi-3prpl* they WHINNY, describing the noise horses make during feeding time in the stable III.10.3(a). læːfs Gl

laughing *1. v-ing What am I doing now [indicate laughing]?* VIII.8.7. Eng. ⇒ **a-laughing**, **chuckling**, **gaustering**, **giggling**, **goldering**, **grizzling**, **heffering**, **nickering**

2. v-ing [Smith was so bad at riding that he fell off his horse.] Some of those who saw it thought it rather funny and just couldn't help [indicate laughing] .... IX.2.14. Eng. ⇒ **a-laughing**, **bursting out a-laughing**, *but* **gauster**, *but* **gaup**, *but* **laugh**, **gaustering**, **glining**, **grizzling**

laughter *1. n* a LITTER of piglets III.8.3. laʊtə Du

2. n a BROOD of chickens IV.6.12. laftə Cu We La Y*[occasional x1]*, laftər Cu, laʊtə Nb We, lɔːtə Wa

launder *n* the GUTTER of a roof V.1.6. laːndəɹ Y, lɔːndə Db, ɫɔːndəᵗː Co

laundering *n* the GUTTER of a roof V.1.6. lɔːndɹɪn Db

lavatory *n* an EARTH-CLOSET V.1.13. lavətɹi Mon

laving-can *n* a SCOOP used to take water out of a boiler V.9.9. leːvɪnkan La

laving-tin *n* a SCOOP used to take water out of a boiler V.9.9. leavəntɪn Du

lavvy *n* an EARTH-CLOSET V.1.13. lavɪ Lei

lawn-broom *n* a BESOM I.3.15. lɔːnbɹʊm Sx

lay *1. vt When you put things on the table ready for a meal, what do you say you do?* V.8.12. Eng exc. Nb Du We Nt Hu Sf. ⇒ **fettle** *the tea*, **get the table ready**, **get the table** set, **get the tea ready**, **lay en**, **lay it**, **lay table**, **lay the board**, **lay the cloth**, **lay the cloth and get the things out**, **lay the dinner**, **lay the table**, **lay the table out**, **lay the tea**, **lay thick table**, **lie the table**, **lie the table-cloth**, **put the cloth on**, **put the dishes out**, **put the table-cloth on**, **put the things on the table**, **set out** *the table*, **set** *table*, **set the table**, **set** *the table out*, **set** *the table* **up**, **set** *the tea*, **set the tea out**, **spread** *the table*, **spread** *the tea-table*

2. vt to PLASH a hedge IV.2.4. liː St, leː Nb Cu Du La Y Ch Db Sa O, ɫeː W D, *-ing* ɫeːɪn O, leɪ Y O Hu C Bk Bd So, *-ing* leɪ-ɪn Man Brk K Ha, leːɪ He Wo Gl, *-ing* ɫeɪ-ɪn O, lɛː Y, lɛɪ St Wo Gl L Lei R Nth Hu C Nf Sf Bk Bd Hrt Ess Sr Sx, *-ing* lɛɪ-ɪn Wo K Ha, *-ing* əlɛɪ-ɪn Brk, ɫɛɪ D, lɛə Y L Bd, *iæː* D, læɪ He Gl Nf Sf K, *-ing* læɪ-ɪn Ess MxL, laɪ Du La Wo Gl, ɫaɪ Ha, lɑɪ Du, ɫɒɪ Do; **buck-head and lay** bʌkhɛd n̩ læɪ Ess; **cut and lay** kʊt ən liː St, *-ing* kʊtɪn ən lᴵiː-ɪn Lei, kʌt n̩ leː Brk, kʌt ən leː O, kʊt n leː Y, kʌt ən ɫeː Ha, kʌʔ ən leɪ O, kʊt ən leɪ Nth, kʊt n̩ leˑɪ Lei, kʊt ən lɛɪ St Wa Lei R Nth, kʌt ən ɫɛɪ W, *-ing* kʌtən ... ən ɫɛɪən Co, kʌt ən laɪ W, kʌt ən ɫaɪ W Ha; **cut down and lay** *ppl-adj* kʊt daʊn ən ɫeɪd O, *3prpl* kʌts ... dɛʊn n̩ lɛɪz Ha; **make and lay** meːᵊk ... ən leɪ So

3. vt **bank up and lay** to fill gaps in a hedge-bank and plash the hedge. bæŋk ... ʌp ən leɪ So

4. v-imp LIE DOWN VIII.3.6(a). leɪ Nf *[see note at lie down]*

lay-down *n* have a lay-down LIE DOWN VIII.3.6(a). ɛv ə leɪdɛʊn Bd, hæv ə leɪdɛʊn Nf, av ə leɪdɛʊn O Bk, hɛv ə leɪdɛʊn Ess, ɛv ə leɪdɛʊn Nth Hu, hæv ə leɪdɛʊn Nf, ɛv ə leɪdæʊn Ess *[see note at lie down]*

lay down *1. vphr* to KINDLE, describing a rabbit doe giving birth to young III.13.14. leːᴵ dᵁuːn Gl

2. vtphr to PLASH a hedge IV.2.4. læːᵊ ... dɛʊn Nf, leː ... dɛuːn Sa, ɫeː ... dæʊn Ha, læɪ ... dæʊn Wa, ɫaɪ ... dæʊn Ha, leɪ ... daʊn So, leɪ ... daʊn L, *ʔptppl* lɛd daʊn So, leɪ ... dəʊn He

3.1. vphr-imp LIE DOWN VIII.3.6(a). Eng exc. Cu Du Man Db He Gl Nt R Hu So Co

3.2. vphr-refl-imp **lay you down**, **lay yourself down** lie down. **lay you down** leː ðɪ daɪn Y, leː ðə dɛːn La; **lay yourself down** leː ðɪsɛn dæʊn Ch, leː ðɪsɛn daːn Y, leə ðɪsɛn daːn Y *[see note at lie down]*

layer *vt* to PLASH a hedge IV.2.4. leɪəᵗ Bk, *-ing* leəɹɪn Y, leˑəᴵɹ (+V) Bk, leˑəᵗ Bk, *-ing* lɛɪəɹɪn K Sx, *-ing* lɛɪəᴶɹɪn Sr, lɛɪjəɹ (+V) Lei, læˑəɹ (+V) Nf

laying-hook *n* a BILLHOOK IV.2.6. leːᵊnhuːk Nb, leːɪnᵁuːk La

laying-yard *n* a FARMYARD I.1.3. lɛɪ-ɪnjɑˑd Nf

lay up *1. vtphr* to HIDE something VIII.7.6. leː ... ʊp La

2. *vtphr-3sg* she [a tidy girl] will COLLECT her toys VIII.8.15. leː ... ʊp La

lazy-back *1. n* a HEDGING-BILL IV.2.5. ɬeːzɪbak Do *[queried SBM]*

2. *n* a LOOSE *PIECE OF* SKIN at the bottom of a finger-nail VI.7.11. *pl* lɛɪzɪbaks L

lazy-flake *n* a LOOSE *PIECE OF* SKIN at the bottom of a finger-nail VI.7.11. *pl* leːzɪfleːks O

lea *1. n* PASTURE II.1.3. liː So, leː Mon, leˑə Nb, lɛɪ St Nf Sr, læɪ Hrt

2. *n* a clover-field used as pasture after being cut. lɛɪ Ha

3. *n* a MEADOW II.9.2. liː Cu, leɪ He, lɛɪ Y*[ploughed periodically]* St*[sometimes ploughed]* Wo*[sometimes ploughed]* Sr*[on high ground]*, lɛːə Nf, læɪ K*[cut 3 years running]*; **new lea** nuˑ leɪ Nf

4. *n* LOW-LYING LAND IV.1.7. liː St, lɛɪ Man Brk

5. *n* a SCYTHE II.9.6. lⁱi Du, lɪə Cu Y, leː Y, lɛɪ We La Y, læɪ Y, laɪ Y, ləɪ Y

6. *n* a BILLHOOK IV.2.6. læɪ Sf

7. *v* to put cattle on hired pasture, ⇐ HIRE *PASTURAGE* III.3.8. liː Ch St, leː Ch Db, lɛɪ La St

8. *n* hired pasture. liː Db St, leː Ch Sa, lɛɪ St, læɪ St

lead *1. n* a HALTER for a cow I.3.17. liːd K

2. *n* a TETHERING-ROPE used to tie up a horse I.4.2. lⁱiːd Ess; **headstall and lead** hɛdstɔːl ŋ liːd K, ɛdstɔːɬ ən liːd K; **neckstrap and lead** nɛkstɹæp ən liːd K

3. *n* a SALTING-TROUGH III.12.5. *pl* lⁱiːdz We, lɪəd Y, lɛd O Nth Bk Bd

lead-bowl *n* a SALTING-TROUGH III.12.5. lɪədbaʊl Y, lɪˑədbaʊl Y, lɪədbɔʊl Y, lɛdbaʊl Du Y, ləɪdbaʊl Y

leader *1. n* a TRACE-HORSE I.6.3. liːdə We MxL K, liːdəɹ He, lⁱidəᴶ Brk, liːdəᵗ Sa He Wo Gl K Sx, liːdəᵗː Sa So, ɬiːdəᵗː W Co, *pl* lɪˑədəz Y, leːdə Ch

2. *n* the FURROW-HORSE of a ploughing team II.3.4(a). lⁱiːdə Ess

lead-horse *n* a TRACE-HORSE I.6.3. liːdaᵗːʂ Mon, liːdɔːs Cu

leading *1.1. v-ing* CARTING *DUNG* II.1.4. liːdn Nb, *no -ing* liːd Cu Y, lɪədɪn La L, *no -ing* lɪəd We, ləɪdɪn Y

1.2. vt-ing **leading dung, leading manure, leading muck** carting dung. **leading dung** lⁱiːdɪn dʌŋ Sr; **leading manure** liːdɪn mənjʊə Y, liːdɪn manɹ L; **leading muck** liːdɪn mœːk Nb, *no -ing* liːd mʌk Nb; liːdɪn mʊk Y Db L, liːdn mʊk Nb Du We, *no -ing* liːd mʊk Cu, *no -ing* lᵉɪd mʊk Du, lɪədɪn mʊk Y*[old x1]* L, *no -ing* lɪəd mʊk Cu La, ləɪd mʊk Y

2.1. v-ing CARTING corn from the field II.6.6. liːdɪn We Y St Nt L Lei*[old x1]* R*[old x1]*, liːdn Nb Cu Du We, lɪədɪn La Y L, lɪədn Cu, *vt* lɪəd Db, *v* lɪəd We Nt, lɛɪdɪn Y, ləɪdɪn Y

2.2. vt carting corn. liːdɪn Lei, *v* lɪəd Db

leading-horse *n* a TRACE-HORSE I.6.3. liːdŋɔs L, lⁱiːdɪnɔˑəᵗɽʂ Sx

leading on *vtphr-ing* **leading the muck on** CARTING *DUNG* II.1.4. liːdɪn t mʊk ɒn Y

leading-rails *npl* CART-LADDERS I.10.5. liːdɪnɹeəlz Y

leading-rein *1. n* a HALTER for a cow I.3.17. lⁱidɪnɹɛˑɪn Brk

2. *n* a TETHERING-ROPE used to tie up a horse I.4.2. liːdɪnɹeɪn Bd

lead-tray *n* a SALTING-TROUGH III.12.5. *pl* lɪdtɹɛɪz Sr

lead out *vt* to put cattle on hired pasture, ⇐ HIRE *PASTURAGE* III.3.8. *-ing* lⁱiːdɪn ... ɛʊt Ess

leaf *n* the FAT round the kidneys of a pig III.12.7. liːf Nb Cu Du We La Y Ch Db Sa St He Wo Wa Mon Gl O L Lei R Nth Hu C Nf Sf Bd Ess, ɬiːf He Mon, lɪəf Cu We La Y Db L Nth Bk, leːf Gl, leɪf Du, lɛɪf Ch, ləɪf Y; **leaf of fat** liːf ə fat Ch Sa

leaf-board *n* an END-BOARD of a cart I.10.4. liːfboˑəᵗd̥ Bk

leaf-broom *n* a BESOM made of hazel and willow I.3.15. liːfbɹɥːm Nf

leaf-fat *n* the FAT round the kidneys of a pig III.12.7. liːffæt Nf, liːfat Nt, liːffat Cu Y Db Nt Hrt, lɪəfat La L, lɪəffat La Y Nt L, lɛɪffat Db

leaf-grease *n* the FAT round the kidneys of a pig III.12.7. lɪəfgrɪəs Y, lɪəvgrɪəs Y

lea-ground *1. n* FALLOW-LAND II.1.1. ɬeːgɹæɪnd Co, ɬeːgɹæɪn Co

2. *n* PASTURE II.1.3. leːgɹəʊn Do, leɪgɹæʊn So

lea-land *1. n* PASTURE that is ploughed up after two or three years II.1.3. leɪland Ha

2. *n* a MEADOW II.9.2. liːlæᵊnd Nb*[ploughed occasionally]*, lɛɪlænd Sx

lea-nibs *npl* the HANDLES of a scythe II.9.8. læɪnɪbz Y, laɪnɪbz Y

lean to *imp* HELP YOURSELVES!, said to invite visitors to eat V.8.13. lɛɪn tᵁuː La

lea out *vphr* to put cattle on hired pasture, ⇐ HIRE *PASTURAGE* III.3.8. liː ɛːt Db, leː ɛːt Db, leˑɪ ɛːt Db

leap *v* to JUMP a wall IV.2.10. liːp La Y Wa L So, lⁱiːp Ess Sr, lɪəp La, lɛp Mon, lɛɪp La, leˑəp La

leapings *n* stepping-stones across a shallow place in a stream, ⇐ FORD IV.1.3. lɛpɪnz Y *[stepping-stones is also a Y r.]*

leap over *vphr* to JUMP a wall IV.2.10. *ptppl* lɪpən ɒvə Y, lɪəp ɔʊə Y, lᵊɪːp ʌʊvə Ess, liːp ɔːvəɹ (+ V) He, liːp ouvə St, liːp ʊːvə St

lear *adj* HUNGRY VI.13.9. lɪəᴶ Brk Sr, lɪəᵗ Bk*[old]* Brk Sx*[old]*, lɪəᵗɽ Sr*[very hungry]* Ha Sx*[old and rare x1]*, lɪəᵗː So, ɬɪəᵗː W Ha

learnt *vt-3ptsg* he/she TAUGHT it III.13.17. Eng exc. MxL Sr

leary *adj* HUNGRY VI.13.9. lɪəɻi So Do, ɬɪəɻi Do Ha, lɪəᵗːɻi So, ɬɪəᵗːɻi W Co D, ɬeːɻi Do

lea(s) *n* FALLOW-LAND II.1.1.
no -s: ɬeː Co Do, lɛɪ Sr, ɬɛɪ W
-s: ɬeːz Co

leas *npl* the FIELDS of a farm I.1.1. lɛɪz St

lea-scythe *n* a SCYTHE II.9.6. lⁱiːsaɪð We

lease *1. n* a TEAM of horses I.6.1. lɪiːs Ess
2. adj DRY, describing a cow with no milk III.1.9. ɬiːz Co

leased *adj NOT IN* CALF III.1.8. ɬeːzd D

lease-lines *npl* the REINS of a plough-horse I.5.5. liːslɔɪnz Ess

leaser* *1. n* a DRY cow III.1.9. ɬeːzəᵗː Co
2. n a cow that is becoming dry. ɬeːzəᵗːɻ (+V) D

lea-shaft *n* the SHAFT of a scythe II.9.7. læɪʃaft Y, laɪʃaft Y

leasing *n* STUBBLE remaining in a cornfield after harvesting II.1.2. ɬeːzɪn Do *[queried ir.r. BM]*

lea-stone *n* a WHETSTONE II.9.10. liːstean Cu, lɛɪstn La

leather *vt* to BEAT a boy on the buttocks VIII.8.10. lɛðəɹ (+V) Cu La, lɛðəᵗː So, ɬɛðəᵗːɻ (+V) W

leather bams *npl* LEGGINGS VI.14.18. ɬɛðəᵗː bamz W

leather-bat *n* a BAT IV.7.7. lɪðəᵗːbæt He, lɛðəᵗbæt He Wo Mon, *pl* lɛðəᵗːbæts So, lɛðəbat Wo, lɛðəᵗbat Sa Wo, læðəᵗbæt He

leather garters *npl* KNEE-STRAPS used to lift the legs of working trousers VI.14.17. lɛðə gɑːʔəs Nf

leather-halter *n* a TETHERING-ROPE used to tie up a horse I.4.2. lɛðəɹɔːltəˡ K

leatherin-bat *n* a BAT IV.7.7. lɪðəɹɪnbat Wa, lɛðəɹɪnbæt He Gl, lɛðɹɪnbæt Wo Gl, lɛðɹɪnbæːt Wo, lɛðəᵗɻɪnbæt Wo Gl, lɛðəᵗːɻɪnbæt So, lɛðəɹɪnbat Sa St Wa *[So form taken as **leathern-bat** in SBM]*

leathering *vbln* **give him a good leathering** to BEAT a boy on the buttocks VIII.8.10. gɪv ɪm ə gʊd lɛðəɹɪn Y, gi n ə gʊd lɛðəᵗːɻɪn So

leathern-bat *n* a BAT IV.7.7. lɛðəᵗːn̩bæt So, lɛðəᵗːn̩bat So

leather-wing-bat* *n* a BAT IV.7.7. lɛðəwɪnbæt Nb, lɛðəwɪŋbat Du

leather-winged-bat *n* a BAT IV.7.7. lɛðəwɪŋdbat Du

leaven *n* DOUGH V.6.3. lɛvn St*[old]*

leave-off-time *n* STOPPING-TIME at the end of a day's work VII.5.9. ɬiːvɔːftɒɪm Ha, liːvɔːftɔɪm O K Sx, ɬeːvɔːftæːm D, ɬeːvɔːftɒɪm Ha, ɬɛɪvɔːftæːm D

leaves *1. n* the FAT round the kidneys of a pig III.12.7. liːvz We Y Sf Ess, lɪəfs Y L, lɪəvz Du Y L
2. n DREGS left at the bottom of a teacup V.8.15. liːvz Nb St Wo Nf So, lɪəvz Y, leːˡvz Gl
3. vi-3prsg school FINISHES VIII.6.2(b). liːvz Y Wa O Nt, lɪəvz Y Nt, lɛɪvz Ch, ɬɛɪvz Co

leaves off *viphr-3prsg* school FINISHES VIII.6.2(b). liːvz ɔːf Sx

leaves out *viphr-3prsg* school FINISHES VIII.6.2(b). ɬeːv æʏt Co, də ɬeːv æʏt Co, ɬeː ðəm æʏt Co

leave-work-time *n* STOPPING-TIME at the end of a day's work VII.5.9. ɬiːvwəᵗːktæːm D, ɬeːvwəᵗːktæːm D, ɬeːvwəᵗːktaːm D, ɬeːwəᵗːktaɪm Co, ɬeːvwəᵗːktɑːm D, lɛfwəᵗːktæɪm So, ɬɛfwəᵗːktaːm D, lɛfwəᵗːktaɪm So, ɬɛɪvwəᵗːktaːm Co

leaving-off-time *n* STOPPING-TIME at the end of a day's work VII.5.9. lɪivɪnɒːftaɪm K, liːvɪnɔːftæɪm He, liːvɪnɔftaˑɪm L, liːvɪnɔːftaɪm Nth C Bd Ess, liːvɪnɔːftaɪm L, liːvɪnɔːftɒɪm Nf, liːvɪnɔːftɒɪm Wa Ess Brk Sr Sx, liːvənɔːftɔɪm Sf, liːvɪnɔːftʌɪm Nf, liːvənɔːftʌɪm Sf, lɪˑəvɪnɔftaˑɪm L, leˑvɪɔ̩ˑftʌɪm Nf, lɛɪvɪnɔːftʌɪm Nf, leɪvɪɔ̩ˑftʌɪm Nf, lɛɪvənɔːˑᵊftɔɪm Sf

leaving-time *n* STOPPING-TIME at the end of a day's work VII.5.9. liːvɪntaɪm Nt, lɪəvɪntaːm Y, lɪəvɪntaɪm We La Y, lɪˑəvɪntaˑɪm L

leaving-work-time *n* STOPPING-TIME at the end of a day's work VII.5.9. ɬɛvmwəᵗːktaɪm Co

ledge *1. n* the CURB-STONE in a cow-house I.3.9. lɪdʒ Sx, lɛdʒ Du Y
2. n a DIAGONAL BAR of a gate IV.3.7. lɛdʒ Nf

ledges *npl* the horizontal BARS of a gate IV.3.6. lɛdʒɪs Nf, lɛdʒɪz L Nf*[old x1, preferred x1]*, lɛdʒəz Sf Ess, leˡdʒɪz Sf

leeds-and-yorks *npl* KNEE-STRAPS used to lift the legs of working trousers VI.14.17. liːdzənjɔːks Y

lees *n* brewer's YEAST V.6.2. ɬiːz D

left-couch *1. adj* LEFT-HANDED VI.7.13(a). lɛftkɛʊtʃ Nf, lɛfkɛʊtʃ Nf
2. n a LEFT-HANDED person VI.7.13(a). lɛftkɛʊtʃ Nf, lɛfkɛʊtʃ Nf

left-couched *1. adj* LEFT-HANDED VI.7.13(a). lɛftkɛʊtʃt Nf*[old]*
2. n a LEFT-HANDED person VI.7.13(a). lɛftkɛʊtʃə Nf, lɛfkɛʊtʃə Nf

left-hand *adj* LEFT-HANDED VI.7.13(a). lɛftæˑnd K

left-hand afore *n* a LEFT-HANDED person VI.7.13(a). lɛfthænd əfɔə Nf

left-handed *adj Of a man who does everything with this [show your left hand], you say he is ....* (October 1956: *Get the noun for* **left-hander** *also.*) VI.7.13(a). Eng exc. Man Wo Gl Lei R Nth Bk Brk Co D Do.

LEFT-HANDED ⇒ **back-handed, ballock-handed, bang-hand, bang-handed, bawky-handed, buck-fisted, cack-handed, cacky, cam-handed, cat-handed, cawk-fisted,** cawk-handed, cawky, cawky-handed, click, clicky, clicky-handed, cob-handed, coochy, coochy-gammy, coochy-handed, coochy-pawed, cow-handed, cowey-handed, cowly-handed, cow-pawed, cuddy-handed, cunny-handed, dollock-handed, dolly-pawed, gallock-handed, gally-handed, gammy-fisted, gammy-handed, gammy-pawed, *gar-handed* ⇒ cow-handed, *gar-pawed* ⇒ cow-pawed, gawk-handed, gawky-handed, gawp-handed, gibble-fisted, golly-handed, kaggy-fisted, kaggy-handed, kay-fist, kay-fisted, kay-neive, kay-neived, kay-pawed, keck-fisted, keck-handed, kecky-fisted, kecky-handed, keggy, keggy-handed, keg-handed, keg-pawed, kittagh-hand, kittaghy, left-couch, left-couched, left-hand, left-kaggy, left-keck, left-kegged, left-keggy, left-kelly, left-pug, marlborough-handed, north-handed, scoochy, scram-handed, scrammy-handed, scroochy, scrummy-handed, skay-pawed, skiffle-handed, skiffy, skiffy-handed, skivvy-handed, south-pawed, squiffy, squippy, squivver-handed, watted, watty, watty-handed.

LEFT-HANDER (person) ⇒ back-hander, cack-hander, cawk-hander, click, clicky, cowly, cow-paw, cuddy, cuddy-wifter, dollocker, gallock, gammy, gawk-hander, gawky, gimmicker, kay-fister, kay-paw, keck-handeder, keck-hander, keck-hand man, keck-paw, kecky, kecky-hander, keggy, keggy-hander, left-couch, left-coucher, left-hand afore, left-handeder, left-handed squiffy, left-hander, left-hand man, left-hand scroochy, left-keck, left-keg, marlborough-hand, right-hand afore, squippies, wat-man

left-handeder *n* a LEFT-HANDED person VI.7.13(a). lɛftɛndɪdəˑ Sr

left-handed squiffy *n* a LEFT-HANDED person VI.7.13(a). ɬɪfandəd skwɪfi W

left-hander *n* a LEFT-HANDED person VI.7.13(a). lɪftɛndə Ess, lɛftɛndə Ess, lɛfhændə Nf Sf, lɛftændə Ess, lɛftændəˑ K, lɛftændəˈ Sx, lɛfthandə Nf, lɛftandə Nt Nth C Bd Hrt, lɛftandəˈ Wa

lefthand-horse *n* the NEAR-HORSE of a pair pulling a wagon I.6.4(a). lɛftændɔːs K, lɛftandɒs Y

left-hand man *n* a LEFT-HANDED person VI.7.13(a). lɛfthænd mæˑn Nf

left-hand scroochy *n* a LEFT-HANDED person VI.7.13(a). ɬɪftan skɽyːtʃi D

left-kaggy *adj* LEFT-HANDED VI.7.13(a). lɛfkagɪ Wo

left-keck* *1. adj* LEFT-HANDED VI.7.13(a). lɛftkɛk Ch
2. n a LEFT-HANDED person VI.7.13(a). lɛfkɛk Sa He

left-keg *n* a LEFT-HANDED person VI.7.13(a). lɛfkɛg Db

left-kegged *adj* LEFT-HANDED VI.7.13(a). lɛftkɛgd Db

left-keggy *adj* LEFT-HANDED VI.7.13(a). lɛftkɛgɪ St, lɛfkɛgɪ L

left-kelly *adj* LEFT-HANDED VI.7.13(a). lɛfkɛlɪ Ch

left-pug *adj* LEFT-HANDED VI.7.13(a). lɛftpʌg Nf

leg *1. n* a STICK used to support the shaft of a cart I.11.1. lɛg La Y Ch Sa St Mon O Nf Sf Bk Ess Sx, *pl* lɛgz Db Nth Brk, ɬɛgz Ha, *pl* lɛɪgz Sf, lɛəg Man
2. n the BASE of a stack II.7.4. lɛg St

legders *npl* LEGGINGS VI.14.18. lɛgdəˈz K *[queried SBM]*

leggings *npl* *What do you sometimes wear below the knee to protect the legs?* VI.14.18. ɬɪgɪnz D, lɛgɪns Nb, lɛgɪŋz Ha, lɛgɪnz Nb Cu We La Y Ch Db Sa St He Wo Wa Mon Gl O Nt L*[worn over breeches x1]* Lei R Nth Hu C Nf Bk Bd Hrt Ess MxL So Brk Sr K Ha Sx, ɬɛgɪnz He Mon O W Co D Do Ha, lɛgəns Man, lɛgnz Du Sf, lɛgənz Nb Du La Y Sa Wo C Sf, ɬɛgənz Co, lɛgəms Nb, lɛgəmz Nb Du Y, lɛᵁgɪnz Ess*[cloth x1]* So, ɬɛˈgɪnz D, lɛˈgnz Ess, lægɪnz So, læɪgɪnz So, ɬagɪnz Do, ɬaˈgɪnz Do. ⇒ **bams, buskins, gaiters, kitty-bags, leather bams, legders, leg-straps, spats, splats, yanks**; ⇒ also **strads**

leg-rest *n* a STICK used to support the shaft of a cart I.11.1. lɛgɹəst Y

leg-stick *n* a STICK used to support the shaft of a cart I.11.1. lɛgstɪk Db St Lei Sr

leg-straps *1. npl* KNEE-STRAPS used to lift the legs of working trousers VI.14.17. lɛgstɹæps Nf MxL Brk, *sg* lɛgstɹæp Sf Ess, lɛgstɹaps Y Db L C, *sg* lɛgstɹap O, lɛɪgstɹæps Ess
2. npl LEGGINGS VI.14.18. lɛgstɹaps Nt *[marked ir.r. BM]*

lend *vt* *You want a spade for a short time, and yours is broken, so you ask your neighbour: Will you ... me yours?* VIII.2.2. Eng. ⇒ **let**, *let us have a loan of*, **loan**

length *1. n* HEIGHT VI.10.9. lɛŋθ Ch Wo
2. n a BIT (OF string) VII.2.10. lɛnθ Du Y Mon, lɛŋθ Y Ch L Nf Bd Brk, lɛŋt L

lesk *n* the GROIN VI.9.4. lɛsk Nt L, lɛs L

let *1. v* to HIRE *PASTURAGE* III.3.8. lɛt Wa Gl*[whole field]* Sf Ess, lɛʔ Nf Bk Hrt
2. vt to LEND VIII.2.2. lɛt Cu We La Y*[old]*

let out *1. vtphr* to put cattle on hired pasture, ⇐ HIRE *PASTURAGE* III.3.8. *-ing* lɛʔn ... ɛʊt Brk, *-ing* lɛtɪn æʊt Wo, *prppl* lɛtɪn ... əʊt Brk
2. vphr to put cattle on hired pasture. lɛʔ ɛʊʔ Bk, *-ing* lɛtɪn æʊt Wo, lɛt aʊt Cu

let up *vtphr* to TIP a cart I.11.6. lɛt ... ʌp Do
level *n* LOW-LYING LAND IV.1.7. lɛvʊ K

lever *n* a device fixing a cart-body to the shafts, stopping it from tipping, ⇐ ROD/PIN I.10.3. liːvə Wa Bk*[iron] [exact definition queried WMBM, definition not known EMBM]*

levers *npl* CART-LADDERS I.10.5. lɛvəz L

lewze *n* a PIGSTY I.1.5. lyːz So, łyːz So, luːz So

lice *1. npl When a child scratches its head a lot, what is it likely to have in its hair?* IV.8.1(a). *[If you [i.e. fieldworker] get lice [as a response], ask for the name of one of them.]* IV.8.1(b). Eng. ⇒ **biddies, bobby-dicks, bubs, bugs, chats, crawlers, creepers, crumbs, dickies, dicks, dicky-birds, donkeys, fleas, head- lice, lice-bub, lices, louses, nannies, nits, titties, vermin** *[sg forms from IV.8.1(a) show only one lexical item (lice-bub) not in pl list from IV.8.1(b); only this sg form treated]*

2. npl TICKS on sheep IV.8.3. læɪs Y, lɑɪs Db, lɒɪs Nf, lɔɪs Ess

lice-bub *n* a LOUSE IV.8.1(b), ⇒ LICE IV.8.1(a). łæːsbʌb D

lice-eggs *npl* NITS IV.8.2. laɪsɛgz Y

lices *npl* LICE IV.8.1(a). liːsɪz Ess

lick *1. n* a DRINK (of milk) given to a kitten III.13.12. lɪk La

2. vt to BEAT a boy on the buttocks VIII.8.10. lɪk Nb La Y

licking *1. n* feed given to horses in the stable, ⇐ FEEDING III.5.1. lɪkɪn Ch

2. n CHAFF fed to horses III.5.3. lɪkɪn St

3. vbln **give him a (good) licking** to BEAT a boy on the buttocks VIII.8.10. lɪk Nb La Y; **give him a good licking** gɪv ɪm ə gʊd lɪkɪn La; **give him a licking** gɪ n ə lɪkɪn So

licking out *vtphr-ing* PUTTING your tongue OUT VI.5.4. lɪkɪn ... æʊt Sa, lɪkɪn ... aːt St

lick-trough *n* a TROUGH in a cow-house I.3.6. lɪktɪɔf Y

lid *n* **lid of the bin** the lid of a container used as a PASTE-BOARD V.6.5. lɪd ə ðə bɪn Wa

lide *vt* to THICKEN gravy V.7.7. laɪd Y*[old]*

lie *1. v* to KNEAD dough V.6.4. lɑˑɪ Y

2. v-imp **lie and rest** LIE DOWN VIII.3.6(a). læɪ ən ɹɛst *[see note at lie down]*

lie back *viphr* to WANE, referring to the moon VII.6.5(b). *-ing* laɪ-ɪn bak Y

lie-down *n* **have a lie-down, have you a lie-down** LIE DOWN VIII.3.6(a). **have a lie-down** hɛv ə læɪdɛʊn Ess, ɛv ə læɪdɛʊn Sf, hæv ə læɪdɛʊn Nf, ɛv ə laɪduːn Cu, av ə laɪduːn Y, av ə laɪdæʊn Ch, æv ə lɒɪdaʊn So, hɛv ə lɔɪdɛʊn Sf; **have you a lie-down** æv jə ə ləɪdɛʊn Wo *[see note at lie down]*

lie down *1. vphr-imp You might say to your visitor: If you are not feeling well, here's the sofa, why not come and ....* VIII.3.6(a). Eng exc. We C Bd MxL Brk

2. vphr-refl-imp **lie you down, lie yourself down** lie down. **lie you down** laɪ ðɪ dɛʊn Db, laɪ ðɪ daːn Db,

laɪ ðə daʊn La, lɑː ðə daːn La, lɑɪ ðɪ dɛːn Db, lɑɪ ðə daːn La, lɑɪ ðɪ daɪn Ch, lɒɪ ðɪ daɪn St, lɒːɪ jə daʊn St; **lie yourself down** laɪ jəsɛl duːn Nb

⇒ *a lay-down, have a doss, have a lay-down, have a lie-down, have you a lie-down, lay, lay down, lay you down, lay yourself down, lie and rest, lie you down, lie yourself down, lig down, lig you down, lig yourself down, quat down, rest yourself for a bit [SBM raises problem of interpretation of [æɪ] forms as either lay or lie]*

lie in *vtphr* to KNEAD dough V.6.4. *-ing* lɑˑɪn ... ɪn Y

life *n* **full of life** ACTIVE, describing a child VIII.9.1. fʊl ə lɛɪf Nb, vʌł ə łəɪf Gl

lift *1. vt* to PITCH sheaves II.6.10. *3prsg* łɪfts O

2. n a STILE IV.2.9. lɪft Ess

3. n **on the lift** HEAVING *WITH MAGGOTS* IV.8.6. ɒn ðə lɪft Wa

4. vi to RETCH VI.13.15. lɪft Db

lifted *adj* HEAVING *(WITH MAGGOTS)* IV.8.6. lɪftɪd Y

lifter *1. n* a vertical rod in front of a cart, perforated to allow adjustments when tipping, ⇐ ROD/PIN I.10.3. łɪftəᵗˑ Co

2. n a SCOOP used to take water out of a boiler V.9.9. lɪftɔᴿ Nb, lɪftə Cu We

lift-hurdles *npl* HURDLES used to pen sheep in part of a field III.7.11. lɪftʰɛˑdlz Nf*[wooden]*

lifting *adj* HEAVING *(WITH MAGGOTS)* IV.8.6. lɪftɪn La Y Wo Nt L So, əlɪftɪn Wa, lɪftn Nb Du, lɪftən Du

lig *vt* to PLASH a hedge IV.2.4. lɪg Cu We La Y L; **cut and lig** kʊt ən lɪg Y; **fell and lig** fɛl ən lɪg Cu

lig down *1. vtphr* to PLASH a hedge IV.2.4. lɪg duːn Y

2.1. vphr-imp LIE DOWN VIII.3.6(a). lɪg dæˑən La, lɪg daʊn Cu La Y Nt L, lɪg dɔʊn L, lɪg dʌʊn Y, lɪg duːn Du We Y*[old x1]* L

2.2. vphr-refl-imp **lig you down, lig yourself down** lie down. **lig you down** lɪg ðɪ dɛʊn Db*[old]*, lɪg ðɪ dɛən Y, lɪg ðɪ dæʊn Y, lɪg ðɪ dæˑən Y, lɪg ðɪ daːn Y*[old x1]*, lɪg ðə daːn Y, lɪg ðɪ daʊn Y, lɪg ðə daʊn La Y, lɪg ðə dᵊun Y; **lig yourself down** lɪg ðɪsɛl daʊn La Y, lɪg ðɪsɛl duːn Y, lɪg ðɪsɛn duːn Y

liggies *npl* MINNOWS IV.9.9. lɪgɪz Cu*[old]*

ligging-away-time *n* STOPPING-TIME at the end of a day's work VII.5.9. lɪgɪnəweːtaɪm Y

ligging-off-time *n* STOPPING-TIME at the end of a day's work VII.5.9. lɪgənɒftaɪm La

ligging-stone(s) *n* the CURB-STONE in a cow-house I.3.9.

no -s: lɪgɪnstɪˈən Y, lɛgɪsən Y*[formerly could be wooden]*

-s: lɪgɪnstnz Y*[old]*

light *1. adj NOT IN* CALF III.1.8. lʌit Nf

2. *adj* not in calf but able to conceive. lʌit Nf

light-fire *n* KINDLING-*WOOD* V.4.2. ˈlɒitvɒiəˡː So, ˈɬəitvəiəˡː Do

lighting *n* LIGHTNING VII.6.22. laɪtʔn̩ Ess, lɔitn Sf

lighting-wood *n* KINDLING-*WOOD* V.4.2. ləitɪnwʊd Sx

lightning *n Before we hear the thunder, we see ....* VII.6.22. Eng. ⇒ **fire, flashing fire, lighting**

lights *n What do you call the lungs of a slaughtered animal?* III.11.5. liːts Nb Cu Du We La Y Ch Db, leits Man, lɛits Nb Cu Y Ch Db Sa St, læːts D, læits Man Sa So, ɬæts D, laits Ch Sa He L Lei So, ɬaits Co D, laˈɪʔs L, laːts Lei R, lɑits La sY Ch Db Nt L Lei Nth Hu C Bk Bd Hrt MxL Sr K, lɑiʔs Bd, lɒits Sa St Wo Wa Lei R So K, ɬɒits W Co D Do Ha, lɔits Wo Wa Gl O L Lei Nth Sf Bk Hrt Ess Brk Sr K Ha Sx, lɔiʔs Bk Hrt, lʌits Gl O Hu Nf Sf Brk Sr, ləits Du We Y He Wo Mon Gl So Brk Do Sx, ɬəits Mon W Do. ⇒ **bellows, lungs, melt, pipe, pluck,** *smelt* ⇒ **melt**

light slack *n* COAL-DUST V.4.1. ləit slæːk Gl

lig in *vtphr* to PLASH a hedge IV.2.4. lɪg ɪn Y

lijahs *npl* KNEE-STRAPS used to lift the legs of working trousers VI.14.17. laidʒəz Nf, lɔˡdʒəz Sf, lʌidʒəz Nf

likeness *n* **a likeness to** a resemblance to someone, ⇐ he RESEMBLES VIII.1.9. ə laːknəs tʊ Y, ə lɔiknəz tʊ Ha

like so *adv-phr IN THIS* WAY IX.10.7. laɪk sʌʊ K

like that *adv-phr IN THIS* WAY IX.10.7. lɔɪk ðɛt Ess, lɑɪk ðæt Ess MxL, lɔɪk ðæt Ess, lʌik ðæt Nf, lʌɪkʔ ðæʔ Nf, ləɪk ðæt Sx, lɛik ðat Nb, læɪk ðat So, laɪk ðat Cu Sa, laˈɪk ðaʔ L, ɬaɪk ðat D, lɑːk ðat Db Lei, laˈɪk ðat Y, lɒɪk ðat Wa, ɬɒɪk ðat W Ha, ləɪk ðatʰ Mon, ɬəɪk ðat Do

like thick *adv-phr IN THIS* WAY IX.10.7. ləɪk ðɪk W

like this *adv-phr IN THIS* WAY IX.10.7. Eng exc. Man; **like this here** laɪk ðɪs ɪə L, laɪk ðɪz iːə Ess, læɪk ðɪs jəˡː So, lʌɪk ðɪs jɪəˡ Brk, ləɪk ðɪs iəˡ Brk, ɬəɪk ðɪs jəˡː W

lilly-pin *n* a metal LINCH-PIN holding a wheel on a cart I.9.12. lɪlɪpɪn Ch

lily *n* BINDWEED II.2.4. lɪlɪ Sx

limb *1. n* a BRANCH of a tree IV.12.3. *pl* lɪmz Mon Gl, *pl* ɬɪmz Ha

2. *v* to LOP a tree IV.12.5. lɪm Cu We Y Sf, *-ing* lɪmɪn K Sx

3. *v* to cut large branches from a tree. lɪm Y L, *-ing* lɪmɪŋ Brk, *-ing* lɪmɪn K, *prppl* lɪmən Man

limber *n* a SHAFT of a cart I.9.4. lɪmɔᴿ Nb, lɪmə Nb Du, lɪməᴶ Du, lɪməᴶ La

limber-horse *n* a SHAFT-HORSE I.6.2. lɪmɔᴿhɒᴿːs Nb

limber-prop *n* a STICK used to support the shaft of a cart I.11.1. lɪməpɹɒp Du *[but hesitantly, not found locally]*

limbers *npl* the SHAFTS of a cart I.9.4. lɪmɔᴿs Nb, lɪmɔᴿz Nb, lɪməz Nb Du La Y, lɪməᴿz Nb Du, lɪməᴶz Y, ɬɪmbəˡːz̩ So W

limb out *vtphr* to cut large branches from a tree, ⇐ to LOP IV.12.5. lɪm ... aʊt Ch

limbs *npl* BOUGHS of a tree IV.12.2. lɪms Man, lɪmz Cu Y*[old x1]* Man Ch St He Wo*[old]* Wa Mon Gl L Ess MxL So*[thick x1, large and small x1]* Brk Sr*[large x1]* K*[very big x1]* Do Sx*[big x1]*, ɬɪmz W Co D Do Ha

limb up *1. vtphr* to LOP a tree IV.12.5. lɪm ... ʌp So

2. *vtphr* to cut large branches from a tree. *-ing* lɪmɪn ... ʊp Ch

limp-fingered *adj* CLUMSY, describing a person VI.7.14. ɬɪmpvɪŋgəˡːd̩ W

lim-pin *1. n* a LINCH-PIN holding a wheel on a cart I.9.12. lɪmpɪn Cu Du We Y Db Sa He Wo Nt L Lei R

2. *n* a metal linch-pin. lɪmpɪn Y Db Sa Wo

3. *n* a wooden linch-pin. lɪmpɪn Y Sa St *[not a N/EMBM headword]*

4. *n* a pin fixing a cart-body to the shafts, stopping it from tipping, ⇐ ROD/PIN I.10.3. lɪmpɪn Nb

limpin-pin *n* a LINCH-PIN holding a wheel on a cart I.9.12. lɪmpɪnpɪn Db

linch *1. n* a LINCH-PIN holding a wheel on a cart I.9.12. lɪnʃ K

2. *n* a metal linch-pin. lɪnʃ K

linch-pin *1. n How is the wheel [of a cart] kept on the axle?* I.9.12. lɪnʃpɪn Man Wa Mon Gl O Nt L Lei R Nth Nf Sf Bd So W Brk Sr K, ɬɪnʃpɪn O W Co D Do Ha, lɪntʃpɪn O Nth Hu Bk Hrt Ess, ɬɪntʃpɪn Hrt

2. *n* a metal linch-pin. lɪnʃpɪn Cu He Mon So Brk

3. *n* a wooden linch-pin. lɪnʃpɪn Db Mon Ha

⇒ **axle-pin, bolt, cart-pin, cleat, clent-nail, collard, collar-pin, cotter, cotterel, cotterel-pin, cotter-pin, draw-pin, drop-pin, feather, forelock, iron pin, key, lilly-pin, lim-pin, limpin-pin, linch, link-pin, lin-nail, lin-pin, linse, linse-pin,** *lins-pin* ⇒ **linse-pin, lintel, lint-pin,** *lints-pin* ⇒ **linse-pin, nave-pin, peg, pin, plug, prid, spindle, split-pin, ward-pin, wheel-pin**

4. *n* a pin fixing a cart-body to the shafts, stopping it from tipping, ⇐ ROD/PIN I.10.3. lɪnʃpɪn Sf

linchy-lunch *n* a SEESAW VIII.7.2. ɬɪnʃɪɬʌnʃ Co

line *1. n* a TETHERING-ROPE used to tie up a horse I.4.2. lɔɪn Ess

2. vt to PLASH a hedge IV.2.4. -*ing* lɔɪnɪn Ess

3. n **out of line** ASKEW, describing a picture that is not hanging straight IX.1.3. ᵊuːt ə lɛɪn Du

line-horse *1. n* the NEAR-HORSE of a pair pulling a wagon I.6.4(a). laɪnhɒˑs Nf

2. n the LAND-HORSE of a ploughing team II.3.4(b). laɪnɒs Y, laˑɪnɔs L, laɪnɑs C, laɪnɒs Y, laˑɪnɔs L, laɪnɔːs Hu, lɔɪnhɔˑs Nf

linen-basket *n* a CLOTHES-BASKET V.9.7. lɪnɪnbæːskɪt Nf, lɪnːbæˑskɪt Nf, lɪnɪnbɑːskɪt Nf Ess, lɪnənbɑːskɪt Nf Ess, lɪnənbɑːskət Sf Ess, lɪnɪnbɑːskɪt Nf, lɪnn̩bɑːskɪt Nf, lɪnənbɑːskɪt Ess, lɪnənbɑːskət Nf, lɪnˑbaˑskɪt Nf

lines *1. npl* the REINS of a cart-horse I.5.5. laˑɪnz L, laˑɪnz L, lɔɪnz Ess

2. npl the reins of a plough-horse. læɪns Man, lɔɪnz He

lings *n* LOW-LYING LAND IV.1.7. lɪŋz Y

linhay *1. n* a CART-SHED I.11.7. lɪneɪ So

2. n a lean-to shed. ɬɪni D

link *1. n* a sliding RING to which a tether is attached in a cow-house I.3.5. lɪŋk Cu, lɪŋkʰ Nb

2. n the HOOK or *CROOK* of a crane over a domestic fire V.3.5(c). *pl* lɪŋks Wa

link-eyed *adj* CROSS-EYED VI.3.6. lɪŋkiːd Y, lɪŋkaɪd Y

link-hides *n* CHITTERLINGS III.12.2. lɪŋkhʌɪdz Nf

link-pin *1. n* a LINCH-PIN holding a wheel on a cart I.9.12. lɪŋkpɪn Nf Sf

2. n a wooden linch-pin. lɪŋkpɪn Wo

links *1. n* the linkage between the swingle-tree and the plough-beam end of a horse-drawn plough, ⇐ EVENER I.8.4. lɪŋks St Lei

2. n a CRANE on which a kettle is hung over a domestic fire V.3.4. ɬɪŋks W

linkum-jinkum *n* a SEESAW VIII.7.2. lɪŋkəmdʒɪŋkəm Man

lin-nail *n* a LINCH-PIN holding a wheel on a cart I.9.12. lɪnneəl Y, *pl* lɪŋneəlz Y

lin-pin *1. n* a LINCH-PIN holding a wheel on a cart I.9.12. lɪnpɪn Nb Cu Du We Y Nt Lei

2. n a metal linch-pin. lɪnpɪn Y

linse *1. n* a LINCH-PIN holding a wheel on a cart I.9.12. lɪns Ess So K, ɬɪns Do, lɪnts C Hrt

2. n a metal linch-pin. lɪns Sr K

linse-pin *1. n* a LINCH-PIN holding a wheel on a cart I.9.12. lɪnspɪn Nb Wa Gl O Nth C Sf Bd Ess So, ɬɪnspɪn W Co D Do Ha, lɪntspɪn Wa O Nf Bk Bd Hrt, lɪnspɪən Ess

2. n a metal linch-pin. lɪnspɪn Man He Brk Sr K Ha Sx

3. n a wooden linch-pin. lɪnspɪn Wa

4. n a linch-pin holding a wheel on a plough. lɪnspɪn Hrt

[not an EMBM headword; NBM headword lins-pin]

lintel* *n* a LINCH-PIN holding a wheel on a cart I.9.12. lɪntl Cu *[queried NBM]*

lintels *npl* the JAMBS of a door V.1.11. lɪntʔɬz Ess, *no -s* lɪntəɬ Nth, lɛntlz Man, lɛntɬz Mon *[marked ir.r. EMBM]*

lint-pin *n* a wooden LINCH-PIN holding a wheel on a cart I.9.12. lɪntpɪn St

liquid manure *n* URINE in a cow-house I.3.10. lɪkwɪd mənəuə Nf

liquor *1. n* URINE in a cow-house I.3.10. lɪkuɹ Ch

2. n BACON-FAT V.7.5(b). lɪkə Ch

lises *n* POTATO-HAULMS II.4.4. laɪzɪz La *[queried error for wises NBM]*

lish *adj* ACTIVE, describing a child VIII.9.1. lɪʃ Du We La Y

lisk *n* the GROIN VI.9.4. lɪsk Nb Cu Du We La Y Nt L Lei, lɪst Nb We L*[animals]*

lissom *adj* ACTIVE, describing a child VIII.9.1. lɪsm Brk Sr, lɪsəm W Brk, lɪzəm St

listeners *npl* EARS VI.4.1. lɪsnəz St

lite *1. adj* **a lite** A FEW VII.1.19. ə laɪt La

2. pron A FEW VII.8.21. **a lite** ə laɪt La, ə lɑɪt La

lithe *vt* to THICKEN gravy V.7.7. laːð Y, laɪð Y Nt L, lɑɪð La Nt L

lithen *1. vt* to THICKEN gravy V.7.7. laɪðɪn La, laɪðən Y, laːɪðn L, lɑːðən Y

2. n thickening for gravy. laɪðn Y

lithening *n* thickening for gravy, ⇐ to THICKEN V.7.7. laːðnɪn Y

lither *imp* **lither wee** the command TURN LEFT!, given to plough-horses II.3.5(a). ləðəᴵ wiː Sr

lithing *n* thickening for gravy, ⇐ to THICKEN V.7.7. laɪðɪn Y

litter *1. n* *What do you call all the young ones [i.e. piglets] in a family together?* III.8.3. Eng exc. Wa Do. ⇒ **belly, breed, brood, fare, faring, farrow, farth, fezzle, laughter, strain, team, trap, trip, troop, vally**

2. vi to FARROW, describing a pig giving birth to piglets III.8.10. lɪtə Sr, lɪʔəᵗ Brk

3. vi to WHELP III.13.3. lɪtʔəᵗ K

4. vi to KINDLE, describing a rabbit doe giving birth to young III.13.14. lɪtə Man, lɪtəᵗ Sx

5. n a BROOD of chickens IV.6.12. lɪʔə Nf

6. n a BIER VIII.5.9(b). lɪtə Nth

litter down *viphr* to KINDLE, describing a rabbit doe giving birth to young III.13.14. lɪtə dæun Sr, lɪtəᵗ dɛun Sx, lɪtʔəᵗ dæun Ha

little *n* *If you are asked whether you take milk in your tea, you might answer: Yes, but only ....* VII.8.20. lɪtl Man Sa K, lɪtʔl Nf, lɪʔtl Nb, lɪʔl Nf, lɪtɬ He Lei R Ess W Brk K Ha Sx, lɪtuɬ Sr, lɪtʊ Sr

Sx, lɪʔɫ C Sf Hrt Ess, lɪdɫ Brk Sx, lɪdʊ Sx, ɫɪdɫ D; **a little** ə lɪtl Nb Sa St Wo L Nth Nf, ə lɪtʔl Nf, ə lɪʔl L Nf, ə lɪtɫ Wo Mon Nth Ess K Sx, ə lɪtʔɫ Ess, ə lɪʔɫ Hu Bk Bd Hrt Ess, ə lɪʔət Bk, ə lɪʔdl Ess, ə lɪdɫ Sf Ess So, ə ɫɪtɫ Ha, ə ɫɪʔɫ W, ə ɫɪdɫ Co D Do Ha; **a very little** ə vɛɾɪ lɪtɫ Ha, ə vəɹɪ lɪtʊɫ Sx; **very little** vaʁɪ lɪtl Nb, wɛɹɪ lɪʔl Nf, vaʁɪ lɪʔl Du, vɛɹɪ lɪtɫ Nth, vaɹɪ laɪl Y. ⇒ *a bit, a little bit, a little dash, drip, drop, a drop, little drop, a little drop, small drop, a small drop, a wee drop, a little, very little, a very little, a little lock, a small quantity, a spoonful, a spot, a little spot, sup, a sup, a little sup*

little-bars *npl* the horizontal BARS of a gate IV.3.6. lɪtlbaːz L

little belly/bellies *n* CHITTERLINGS III.12.2.
-*y*: lɪtɫ bɛlɪ Wa
-*ies*: lɪtl bɛlɪz L, lɪtɫ bɛlɪz Hu, lɪʔɫ bɛlɪz Hu Sf

little bird *n* a NESTLING IV.7.1. *pl* lɪtl bəːdz Ch, *pl* laɪl bəːdz We, *pl* laɪl bəˑːdz Y

little blindy *n* a SHREW-MOUSE IV.5.2. lɪtəl blɪndɪ Y

little board *n* an END-BOARD of a cart I.10.4. lɪtl buːəd St

little bough *n* a BRANCH of a tree IV.12.3. lɪtl buː Y

little branch *n* a BRANCH of a tree IV.12.3. *pl* lɪtəl bɹantʃɪz Y, laːl bɹanʃɪz We

little chickens *npl* CHICKENS IV.6.11. lɪʔɫ tʃɪˀknz Nf

little chicks *npl* CHICKENS IV.6.11. lɪʔl tʃɪks Nf

little-cocks *npl* COCKS of hay II.9.12. laɪlkɒks We La

little cropper *n* a SHREW-MOUSE IV.5.2. *pl* ɫɪdɫ kɾɒpəˀːz̩ Do

little-end-board *n* an END-BOARD of a cart I.10.4. laːlɛndbʊəd Cu

little few *adj* **a little few** A FEW VII.1.19. ə lɪtl fjuː Cu

little-fork *n* a HAY-FORK with a short shaft I.7.11. *pl* lɪtl fɔˡːks Db, *pl* laɪlfɔɹks Y

little gut(s) *n* CHITTERLINGS III.12.2.
no -*s*: lɪtɫ gʌt Sx, lɪʔl gʌʔ Nf, lɪtl gʊt L
-*s*: lɪtɫ gʌts Hu

little hay-fork *n* a HAY-FORK with a short shaft I.7.11. lɪtl ɛɪfɔːk Wa

little heel-tree *n* a subsidiary SWINGLE-TREE of a horse-drawn plough harness I.8.3. lɪʔl iːltɹɪ L

little hog *n* a THREEPENNY-BIT VII.7.3(a). laɪl ɒg Cu [*in headword list for* **threepenny-bit** *but in IM for* **threepence**]

little-house *n* an EARTH-CLOSET V.1.13. lɪʔlhɛʊs Sf, lɪtɫhɛʊs K

little-huts *npl* very large COCKS of hay II.9.12. laɪlʊts Y

little johnny *n* a THREEPENNY-BIT VII.7.3(a). lɪtəl dʒɒnɪ Y

little maid *n* a DAUGHTER VIII.1.4(b). lɪdɫ maɪd So

little onions *npl* SPRING ONIONS V.7.16. lɪdʔɫ hɪnənz Sf

little pasture *n* a PADDOCK I.1.10. lɪdɫ pastʃə Ess

little pig *n* a PIGLET III.8.2. lɪtl pɪg Du La Y Db He Wa, *pl* lɪtl pɪgz Sa St L, lɪʔl pɪg O Nf, lɪtɫ pɪg Wo Wa Mon Hrt MxL, *pl* lɪtɫ pɪgz Nth Bd Ess, lɪdɫ pɪg C, *pl* lɪdɫ pɪgz W, lɪʔɫ pɪg Nth Bk Bd, *pl* lɪʔɫ pɪgz C Sf Ess, lɪʔət pɪg Bk, *pl* lɪtʊɫ pɪgz Sr, laːtl pɪg Y, laɪl pɪg We

little-prong *n* a HAY-FORK with a short shaft I.7.11. lɪtɫpɹɒŋ Sx

little puddings *n* CHITTERLINGS III.12.2. lɪtl pʊdɪnz Nt L

little ram *n* a MALE LAMB III.6.2. lɪdɫ ɾaˑm Do

little stool *n* a MILKING-STOOL III.3.3. lɪtɫ stʰuːɫ Mon

little sucker *n* a PIGLET III.8.2. ɫɪdɫ zʌkəˡː D

little swell-tree *n* a subsidiary SWINGLE-TREE of a horse-drawn plough harness I.8.3. lɪʔɫ swɛɫtɹɪ Bd

little tharms *n* CHITTERLINGS III.12.2. lɪtl θaːmz L

little weigh *n* a subsidiary SWINGLE-TREE of a horse-drawn plough harness I.8.3. lɪʔɫ weɪ Bd

little well *n* an artificial CESS-POOL on a farm I.3.11. lɪʔl wɛl Nf

litty *1. adj* WELL, describing a healthy person VI.13.1(a). lɪtɪ So
2. adj ACTIVE, describing a child VIII.9.1. lɪtɪ So

live *1. adj* HEAVING *WITH MAGGOTS* IV.8.6. leɪv So, ɫæːv D, lɒɪv So, ɫɒɪv Do, lɔɪv C Sf, lʌɪv Nf, ləɪv He Wo Sx, ɫəɪv W
2. vt to THICKEN gravy V.7.7. laɪv Du L
3. n the QUICK of a fingernail VI.7.9. laɪv So

lively *adj* ACTIVE, describing a child VIII.9.1. ɫæːvlɪ D, laɪvlɪ Nb We, ɫaɪvɫɪ Co, lɑɪvlɪ Ch Db Wa, lɒɪvlɪ St, lɔɪvlɪ O Ess Sx, lʌɪvlɪ Gl Brk, ləɪvlɪ Sx, ləɪvɫɪ Gl

liven *vt* to THICKEN gravy V.7.7. laːvn Y, laːvən Y

livening *n* thickening for gravy, ⇐ to THICKEN V.7.7. laɪvnɪn Y

liversick *n* a LOOSE *PIECE OF* SKIN at the bottom of a finger-nail VI.7.11. lɪvəˡsɪk Brk, lɪvəˡsɪk Brk, lɪvəˡɾʂɪk Sx, lɪvəˡksɪk Sx

liverslick *n* a LOOSE *PIECE OF* SKIN at the bottom of a finger-nail VI.7.11. *pl* lɪvəˡslɪks Sx

live through *vtphr-2prsg* you BEAR pain VI.5.9. lɪv θɹəu Nf

living-house *n* a FARMSTEAD I.1.2. lɪvɪnɛʊs Nf

living-kitchen *n* the LIVING-ROOM of a house V.2.1. lɪvɪnkɪtʃɪn Y

living-place *n* the LIVING-ROOM of a house V.2.1.
lɪvɪnpleːs Ch, lɪvɪnplɛ'əs L

living-room *1. n [Now let's talk about the inside of
a house of the old-fashioned type.] What do you call
this part of the house we're in now?* V.2.1. lɪvɪnɹum
Gl Nf Hrt Ess Sr, lɪvɪnɹʊn Sr, lɪvɪnɹuːm Ess Sr,
lɪvɪnɹuːm Y*[modern x2]* Ch St Wa Mon L Lei R C*[in
large house]* Bk Ess*[in large house x1]* Brk K,
lɪvnɹuːm Ess, lɪvɪnɹʉːm Lei, lɪvɪnɹəuːm Hrt Ha. ⇒
**back-house, back-kitchen, back-place, back-room,
fore-house, front-kitchen, front-room, house,
house-place, kitchen, living-kitchen, living-place,
parlour, sitting-room;** ⇒ also **back-hole**
2. n the SITTING-ROOM of a house V.2.2.
lɪvɪnɹuːm Y Ess

lizard *n* a NEWT IV.9.8. lɪzʊd Wo, lɪzəd Nf *[queried
ir.r. WMBM]*

load *1. v, vt What do you do first [when getting dung
from the dung-heap to the field]?* II.1.5. Eng exc. Nb
Cu Du We Nth Hu C Sf. ⇒ **cart-filling, chuck up,
draw on, dung-filling, fill, fill** *a load,* **fill** *dung,* **fill
en, fill in, fill** *it,* **fill** *muck,* **fill** *the cart,* **fill** *the muck,*
fill up, fill *with muck,* **full, full** *it,* **full** *muck,* **heave**
it on, **lade, laden, loaden, loaden** *it,* **load** *it,* **load**
muck, **load up, muck-cart-filling, muck-filling,
muck-plugging, pitch, plug** *muck,* **put** *it* onto *the
tumbril,* **put** *your muck* on, **throw, throw up**
*2. v There you have the stooks and there the wagon
[gesticulate]. Now what exactly do you do [to pack
the sheaves onto the wagon]?* II.6.7(a). Eng exc. Cu
We Man Bd Brk. ⇒ **build, lade, laden, lade up,
loaden,** *load on, load up,* **loave, make** *the load,* **make**
load, **take in, tread** *[it is necessary to divide rr. for
this notion between* **load** *and* **fork** *headwords. The
object of those forms known to be transitive is
frequently unclear and may be 'sheaves' or 'wagon',
so that the definitions used may be inaccurate]*
3. n a CUTTING of hay II.9.15. lo'ʊd Nf *[marked
u.r. EMBM]*

loaden *1.1. v* to LOAD a cart with dung II.1.5. lʊədn
L
1.2. vt to load. lɔʊdn Ess, loudn Nf, lʊədn L
1.3. vt to load dung into a cart. -*ing* lʊədnɪn L
[it is not clear from BM that 1. and 2. refer to cart]
2.1. vt to LOAD a wagon with sheaves II.6.7(a).
lʊədn Y
2.2. vt to load sheaves onto a wagon. loudn Ha
2.3. v to load sheaves onto a wagon. lɒudɪn Sx,
lɔːdɪn Gl, lɔudɪn L Ess Brk, lɔudn Ess, lʌudn Bd
Ess, lʌʊdn Ess, loːdɪn Wo, loːdn Nt, ɫoːdən Do, ɫoːən
D, loʊdɪn He Wo Nf Bd, luːdən Y, lʊədɪn L, lʊədn
Y Db Nt L, ɫuːdɪn D
[many of these may be **loading** *rather than* **loaden,**
especially [-ɪn] *forms and* [-ən, -n] *forms in WM/SBM,
where* **loaden** *is not a BM headword]*

loadener *1. n* the LOADER of sheaves onto a
wagon II.6.7(c). lɔədnə Y, loːdn̩ʲ Nt, luːdənə Y,
lʊədnə Y Nt L, lʊədn̩ə Y L, lʊədnəˡ L
2. n the FORKER on a wagon who unloads
sheaves in a stackyard II.6.9. lʊədnə Y, lʊədn̩ə Y

loader *1. n [There you have the stooks and there
the wagon [gesticulate]. Now what exactly do you
do [to pack the sheaves onto the wagon]?] Who
does it?* II.6.7. Eng exc. We Man R MxL. ⇒
**builder, cartman, ladener, lader, loadener,
load-maker, load-stacker, loaver,** *man on the
top,* **packer, stacker, stern-loader, treader**
2. n the FORKER of sheaves onto a wagon
II.6.7(d). loːᵊdə Du, loudəˡ So
3. n the FORKER on a wagon who unloads
sheaves in a stackyard II.6.9. lɔudəˡ O, loːdə Mon,
loːdəˡ So, loudəˡ So, lʊədə La
4. n an END-BOARD of a cart I.10.4. loudəˡ
So, *pl* loːʊdəˡːz̩ So

loaders *npl* CART-LADDERS I.10.5. loudəˡːz̩
So

loading-fork *n* a HAY-FORK with a short shaft
I.7.11. lɔudnfɔːk Ess, lʌʊdɪnfɔːk Bk, loudɪnfɔ'k
Nf, luːdɪnfɔːk Db

loading-pike *n* a HAY-FORK with a short shaft
I.7.11. loːʊdɪnpəɪk Gl

load-maker *n* the LOADER of sheaves onto a
wagon II.6.7(c). ɫuːdmɛːkəˡ D, ɫuːdmɛːkəˡ Co D

load-stacker *n* the LOADER of sheaves onto a
wagon II.6.7(c). loːᵊdstakəˡ So

load up *vtphr* to LOAD a cart with dung II.1.5.
loud ... ʊp St

loam *n* CLAY IV.4.2. lɔʊm Ess, lʊm Ess

loan *1. n* a LANE IV.3.13. lɒɪn La Y, lɔɪn Y, loːn
La Db, lʊən Nb La Y *[Y forms variously
interpreted as* **loan** *and* **lane** *by NBM fws]*
2. vt to LEND VIII.2.2. lɔʊn Brk, lʌʊn MxL

loaning *n* a LANE IV.3.13. lœ'nən Nb, lɒnɪn Nb
Cu We La Y, lɒnən Nb Du, lɔnɪn Nb Cu We, lɔnən
Nb, lʊənɪn Y

loave *v* to LOAD sheaves onto a wagon II.6.7(a).
ɫoːv D

loaver *n* the LOADER of sheaves onto a wagon
II.6.7(c). ɫoːvəˡ D

lob *1. n* the CLOG on a horse's tether I.4.3. lɒb
Sx
2. v to TRIM hedges IV.2.3. lɒb Y
3. v to LOP a tree IV.12.5. lɒb Y

lobby *1. n* an EARTH-CLOSET V.1.13. lɔ'bɪ Sf
2. n BROTH V.7.20(a). lɒbɪ Ch

lobe *n* an EAR of barley II.5.2(b). lʊəb Y

lobe(s) *n* the WATTLES of a hen IV.6.19.
no -s: loːb Mon *[marked 'sg' and queried mass
noun WMBM]*
-s: lɒubz K, lɔʊbz Ess, ɫoːbz D

lob off *vtphr* to LOP a tree IV.12.5. lɒb ... ɒf St*[old]*

lobs *n* the WATTLES of a hen IV.6.19. lɒbz Y He

lob-scouse *n* BROTH V.7.20(a). lɒbskɛʊs Ch

lock *1. n* **a lock** A LOT (of money) VII.8.7. ə lɒk Cu We

2. n an ARMFUL VII.8.10(c). lɒkʔ Nf

3. n **a little lock** a LITTLE amount of milk VII.8.20. ə laːᵏˡl lɒk Cu

4. pron A FEW VII.8.21. **a lock** ə lɒk We

locker *1. n* a space or compartment inside the gable-end of a barn, in which pigeons live, ⇐ DOVECOTE I.1.7. lɒkə Nf, lɒkʔə Nf; ⇒ also **pigeon-locker**

2. n a CORN-BIN I.7.4. *pl* lɔkəz Ess

lock-hole *n* the GROIN VI.9.4. lɔkʊəl L

locking-key *n* a KEY V.1.10. lɑ·kʔnkɹi Nf

lockings *n* **go in the lockings**; **drop her lockings** referring to a cow, show signs of calving by changes in the pelvic region, ⇐ SHOWS SIGNS OF CALVING III.1.12(b). *3prperfsg* gɔːn ɪn ðə ɬɒkɪnz Co; *3prprogsg* dɹɒpən əᵗː ɬɒkənz Co

lock of *adj* **a lock of** A FEW VII.1.19. ə lɒk ə La

lodge *1. n* a CART-SHED I.11.7. lɒdʒ K

2. n a POOL on a farm III.3.9. lɒdʒ La

3. n a POND IV.1.5. lɒdʒ La

4. n a mill dam. lɒdʒ La

loft *1. n* a DOVECOTE I.1.7. lɒft We Y Nf Bk, lɔːf So, ɬɔːf W D, lɔːft Nf So, ɬɔːft W

2. n a HAY-LOFT over a cow-house I.3.18. lœːft Nb, lɑᵗːft Wo, lɒft Nb Cu Du We La Y Ch Db St Nf, lɒf St Lei, lɒft Y, *pl* lɒfs Ch, lɔːft La Wa Gl C Sf Bk So W Sr, ɬɔːft Co Ha, lɔːf Wo So Sr Ha, *pl* lɔːfs Sa, ɬɔːf Ha

3. n a hay-loft over a stable. lɑːft O, lɒft Wa, lɔːft Wa Nth Bk Ess K, lɔːf So

log *1. n* the CLOG on a horse's tether I.4.3. lœːg Nb, lɑːg He Wo Mon Gl, ɬɑːg Wo, lɒg Nb Cu Du Db Sa He Wo Mon Lei, ɬɒg W, lɔg L Sf MxL *[not a SBM headword]*

2. v to cut large branches from a tree, ⇐ to LOP IV.12.5. lɒg Wa

log-beetle *n* a heavy wooden MALLET I.7.5. lɒgbɹiːdɬ Ess

logger *n* the CLOG on a horse's tether I.4.3. lɑːgəᵗ Gl, lɒgəᵗ Wo Bk, ɬɒgəᵗː W

logger-heads *npl* TADPOLES IV.9.5. ɬɒgəᵗːɹɛdz Ha

loke *1. n* a LANE IV.3.13. lo·k Nf*[fenced, shorter than drift]*, louk Nf*[shorter and narrower than* lane *x1, cul-de-sac x1]*, louk? Nf*[shorter and narrower than drift]*

2. n a fenced footpath or track. louk Nf

loller *n* the TONGUE VI.5.4. lɒləɹ (+V) Y

lolliker *n* the TONGUE VI.5.4. lɒlɪkə Y, lɒlɪkəɹ (+V) Du, lɒləkə Y, lɒlɪkəɹ La, lɔlɪkə L, lɔlɪkəɹ (+V) L, lɔləkə L

lolling out *vtphr-ing* PUTTING your tongue OUT VI.5.4. lɒlɪn ... ɛʊt Nf, lɒlɪn ... aʊt Y, lɒlən ... uːt Nb, lɔlən ... æʊt L

lolliper *n* the TONGUE VI.5.4. lɒlɪpəɹ (+V) Du, lɔləpəɹ (+V) L

lolliping out *vtphr-ing* PUTTING your tongue OUT VI.5.4. lɔləpɪn ... uːt L

lompers* *npl* TEETH VI.5.6(a). lɒmpəz Y

london-and-yorks *npl* KNEE-STRAPS used to lift the legs of working trousers VI.14.17. ɬʌndənənjaᵗːks W, lʊndənənjɔːks Y, lʊndənənjɔᴿːks Du

londons *npl* KNEE-STRAPS used to lift the legs of working trousers VI.14.17. lʊndənz Cu

london-to-yorks *npl* KNEE-STRAPS used to lift the legs of working trousers VI.14.17. lʊndəntəjɔːks Y, lʊndəntəjɔ·əks Y

london-yorks *npl* KNEE-STRAPS used to lift the legs of working trousers VI.14.17. lʌndənjɔːks Hu, lʊndənjɔːks Y L, lʊndənjɔ·əks Nth, lʊndənjɔᴿːks Nb, lʊndənjɔ·ɹks Y, lʊndʊnjaᵗːks Gl, lʊndənjɔᵗːks Sa

long-bar *n* the *HORIZONTAL* BAR of a crane over a domestic fire V.3.5(a). lʊŋba Wo

long-broom *n* a BROOM used for sweeping outdoors V.9.10. lɒŋbɹɹ·m Nf

long-brush *1. n* a long-handled BRUSH used for sweeping V.2.14. lɒŋbɹʊʃ Y

2. n a BRUSH used for sweeping indoors V.9.11. laŋbɹʊʃ Y, lɑ·ŋbɹʌʃ Nf, lɒŋbɹʌʃ Nf, lɒŋbɹʊʃ Y, lɔŋbɹʊʃ L

long-cart *n* a FARMCART I.9.3. laŋkeɔᴿt Nb, lɒŋkɑᵗːɹt Brk *[there are other* **long-cart** *forms in N/SBM not given as rr. to I.9.3;* **long-cart** *may not strictly refer to a tip-cart]*

long companies *n* GIPSIES VIII.4.12. lʊŋ kəmpənɪz Sa

long-fallow *n* FALLOW-LAND II.1.1. lɒŋfɛəɬə Ess

long flasher *n* a HEDGING-BILL IV.2.5. lɔ·ŋ vlæ·ʃə Sf

long-fork *n* a HAY-FORK with a long shaft I.7.11. laŋfœːk Du, laŋfɔːk Nf, lɒŋfɔ·ək Nf, lɒŋfɔːᵊk C, lɔŋfəᴶːk L, *pl* lʊŋ fɔᴶːks Db

long-handle bill-hook* *n* a HEDGING-BILL IV.2.5. lɒŋandɬ blɒk Mon *[queried* **bill-hook** *BM]*

long-handle-broom* *n* a MUCK-BRUSH I.3.14. lɒŋhɛndlbɹʊm Nf *[-handled- EMBM]*

long-handle-brush **1. n* a MUCK-BRUSH I.3.14. lɒŋhændlbɹʌʃ Nf *[-handled- EMBM]*

2. n a BRUSH used for sweeping indoors V.9.11. lɒŋhændlbɹʏʃ Nf

long-handled-fork *n* a MUCK-FORK I.3.13. lɒŋænɬd faᵗːk Gl, lɒŋændʊdfɔːəᵗɹk Sx

long-handled hook *n* a HEDGING-BILL IV.2.5. ɬʌŋandɬd ʏk D, ɬʌŋanɬd ʏk D, lɒŋæ·ndʊɬd ʊk

Brk, ɫɒŋænɫd ʊk Co, ɫɒŋhandɫd hʊk W, ɫɒŋandɫd ʊk Co, lɔŋhændɫd hʊk Ess, lɔŋaŋdld ʊk Wa

long-handled-prong *1. n* a MUCK-FORK I.3.13. lɒŋandɫdprɒŋ W

2. n a HAY-FORK with a long shaft I.7.11. lɒŋɛndʊdpɹɒŋ Sr

longhandled-spud *n* a fork used for dung-lifting, ⇐ HAY-FORK I.7.11. lɒŋændʊɫdspʌd Sx

long-handle hook *n* a HEDGING-BILL IV.2.5. ɫʌŋanɫ yk D, ɫɒŋænɫ ʊk Co, ɫɒŋandɫ ʊk W, ɫɒŋanɫ ʊk Co

long hay *n* HAY II.9.1(b). lɒŋ hæi Nf

long-hook *1. n* a HEDGING-BILL IV.2.5. lɒŋyːk D, ɫɒŋyːk D, ɫʌŋyːk D

2. n a BILLHOOK IV.2.6. lɑˈŋ hʊk Nf

long-legged-gnat *n* a DADDY-LONG-LEGS IV.8.10. lɔŋlɛgɪdnæt Ess

long-legged-harry *n* DADDY-LONG-LEGS IV.8.10. *pl* lɒŋlɛgddɛ.ɪɪz La

long-legged-jacks *n* DADDY-LONG-LEGS IV.8.10. lɒŋlɛgʊddʒæks Gl

long-legged-tailor(s) *n* DADDY-LONG-LEGS IV.8.10. *no -s*: laŋlɛgdtɪəlɪə Nb, laŋlɛgdtalɪə Du *pl*: laŋlɛgdtalɪəz Du

longleg-tailors *n* DADDY-LONG-LEGS IV.8.10. laŋlɛgteːlɔᵏz Nb

long rick *n* a long stack, ⇐ STACKS II.7.1. lɒˈŋ ɹɪk K*[old]*

long-shafted-hook *n* a HEDGING-BILL IV.2.5. laŋʃaftɪduːk La

long slasher *n* a HEDGING-BILL IV.2.5. lɒŋ slæːʃəᵗ Sx

long-snead *n* the SHAFT of a scythe II.9.7. laŋsnɛd Nb

long stacks *n* long STACKS II.7.1. *sg* lɒˈŋ stɛk K, laŋ staks Cu*[uncommon x1]* Y, We*[dry hay and corn]* La*[hay]*, *sg* lɒŋ stak La*[corn and hay]*, lɔŋ staks Y L*[fodder]*, *sg* lʊŋ stak La*[hay]*

long-staled brushing-hook *n* a HEDGING-BILL IV.2.5. lʊŋstɛɪld bɹʊʃɪnʊk Wo

long-staled hook *n* a HEDGING-BILL IV.2.5. lɒŋsteːld ˡuːk Sa, lʊŋsteːɪld ʊk Wo

long-staple *n* a TETHERING-STAKE in a cowhouse I.3.3. lɒŋsteːpɫ So, lɒŋsteɪpɫ So

long-summer-land *n* FALLOW-LAND, apparently left fallow for a restricted period II.1.1. lɔŋsʌmɫən Sf *[definition follows EMBM note]*

long-summer-leas *n* FALLOW-LAND, apparently left fallow for a restricted period II.1.1. lɒŋsʌməlɪz Nf *[definition follows EMBM note]*

long tom *n* a fork with a 7ft shaft, used for finishing off a stack, ⇐ HAY-FORK I.7.11. lɒŋ tɒm Y

long-trough *n* a SALTING-TROUGH III.12.5. lɒˈŋtɹoʊ Brk

longways *adv* DIAGONALLY, referring to harrowing a field IX.1.8. laŋwɛəz Y

look *1. n* **a look of, the look of** a resemblance to someone, ⇐ he RESEMBLES VIII.1.9. **a look of** ə lʊk əv Y; **the look of** ðə lʊk ə Nf

2. vt **look out to, look till, look to** LOOK AFTER VIII.1.23. **look out to** lʊk æʊt tə So; **look till** lɪʊk tl Cu; **look to** lɯːk tə Lei

look after *1. vtphr* Mary had to leave the baby at home while she went out shopping, so she said to her husband: Jack, will you ... the baby? VIII.1.23. Eng exc. R. ⇒ **give eye** *to*, *keep an* **eye** *on*, *keep your* **eye** *on*, **look out** *to*, **look** *till*, **look** *to*, **mind**, **see** *after*, **see** *to*, **sit with**, **stay with**, *take* **care**, *take* **care** *of*, **watch**, **watch** *over*

2. vtphr LOOK FOR it III.13.18. lʊk ætəᵗɾ Wo, lʊk aftəɹ Wo, lʊk ɑːftəᵗ Wo

looker *n* a SHEPHERD I.2.1. lʌkəᴶ K, lʊˈkəᴶ K

look for *1. vtphr* If your dog was missing, you'd go out at once and ... it. III.13.18. Eng exc. Man. ⇒ **find**, **find** *him*, **find** *it*, **hike for** *him*, **hunt for** *en*, **hunt for** *him*, **hunt for** *it*, **hunt** *him*, **hunt** *him* **up**, **lait** *it*, **lait** *it* **up**, **lait** *of it*, **look**, **look about**, **look about for** *it*, **look after** *him*, **look after** *it*, **look deedy for** *it*, **look for** *en*, **look for** *her*, **look for** *him*, **look for** *it*, **look** *it* **up**, **look round for** *en*, **search**, **search around for** *it*, **search for** *him*, **search for** *it*, **search** *it*, **see for** *en*, **see if you can find** *it*, **see if you could find** *it*, **seek** *him*, **seek** *it*, **seek on** *him*, **shout** *him*, **try and find** *him*, **try and find** *it*, **try to find** *en*, **try to find** *him*, **try to find** *it*, **whistle**, **whistle and shout for** *him*, **whistle** *en*, **whistle** *him*, **whistle** *it*

2. viphr **look for calf** to show signs of calving, ⇐ SHOWS SIGNS OF CALVING III.1.12. *3prprogsg* ɫʊkən fəᵗ keːf Co

looking *v-ing* PEEPING VI.3.8. lɪəkən Y, lɪʊkɪn Y, lʊkɪn He Sr, lʊkn MxL *[marked u.r. WM/EMBM]*

look-out *n* a person's own FAULT VIII.9.6. lyːkˈɛːt La, lʊkæʊt Lei

looks like *vphr-3prsg* he RESEMBLES VIII.1.9. lɪəks laɪk We, lʊks lɛɪk Y, lʊks læɪk Y, lʊks laɪk Nt L, lʊks laɪk La Lei, lʊks lɔɪk Ess, lʊk lɔɪk Ess, lʊk lʌɪk Nf, luːks lɑˈɪk L Lei R, lɯːks lɑˈɪk Lei, lɯːks lɑːk Lei, lɯːks lɑˈɪk Lei; **looks just like** lʊk dʒɛs lɔɪk Ess

loony *1. adj* SILLY VIII.9.3. lˡuːnɪ Ess, ɫuːni W, lɯˈnɪ Nf, lˡɯːnɪ Nf

2. n a silly person. ə luːnə Man*[condemnatory]*

loop *1. n* a sliding RING to which a tether is attached in a cow-house I.3.5. luːp St Nt

2. v to TOP AND TAIL swedes II.4.3. luːp Nb

3. v to LOP a tree IV.12.5. luːp Sa*[top branches]*, *-ing* lʊuːpɪn Y

4. v to cut small branches from a tree. *prppl* lʊpən Man

loop-hole *n* a man-made SHEEP-HOLE in a wall IV.2.8. *pl* luːpoʊlz Wo

loopy *adj* SILLY VIII.9.3. luːpɪ Ess Ha Sx

loose-all *n* STOPPING-TIME at the end of a day's work VII.5.9. luːsɔːl St

loose-box *1. n* the place where hay is stored on a farm, ⇐ HAY-LOFT I.3.18. luːsbɒks O Nth

2. n a FASTING-CHAMBER III.11.3. lʉsbɒks Nf

loose-fingered *adj* CLUMSY, describing a person VI.7.14. łuːsvɪŋgəˡːd̩ Ha

loose-halter *n* a TETHERING-ROPE used to tie up a horse I.4.2. luːsɒłtə Hu

loose-head *n* the T-SHAPED PLOUGH-BEAM END of a horse-drawn plough I.8.5. łuːsɛd Ha

loose-it *n* STOPPING-TIME at the end of a day's work VII.5.9. luːsɪt St

loose-man *n* a FARM-LABOURER I.2.4. lɑʊsman Nb, luːsman Nb

loose-pen *n* the STRAW-YARD of a farm I.1.9. lʊuːs'pɛn So

loose skin *n What do you call this, at the bottom of the nail?* VI.7.11. luːs skɪn Y L Lei; **bit of loose skin** bɪt əv lɑʊs skɪn Y, bɪt ə lʊs skɪn Y, bɪt ə luːs skɪn Y He Wo, bɪt luːs skɪn Nb; **bit of skin** bɪt ə skɪn Y Lei, *pl* bɪts ə skɪn Ch Db; **loose bit of skin** lɑʊs bɪt ə skɪn Y, lɔːs bɪt ə skɪn Y, luːs bɪt ə skɪn Y; **loose piece of skin** lʊuːs pɪiːs ə skɪn Sx; **piece of loose skin** piːs ə lɑʊs skɪn Y. ⇒ *ang-nail* ⇒ hang-nail, anger-nail, **angry-nail, angry wheal, back-biter, back-fiend, back-flea, back-friend,** *back-friends* ⇒ **back-friend, back-fringe,** *bit of* loose skin, *bit of skin* ⇒ **loose skin,** *dry skin,* **ever-slit, ever-split, feather, finger-friend, friggan, godmother's wish, grandmother-jag, granny, hanging-nail, hang-nail, idle-back, idle-feg, idle-wheal, jag, lazy-back, lazy-flake, liversick, liverslicks, loose** *bit of* **skin, loose** *piece of* **skin, nail-hang, nail-spring, nang-nail, peel, peeler,** *piece of* **loose skin,** *proud-flesh,* **quick, quick-backs, quick-flaw, quick-nail, ravel-back, ravelling-back, rebble-back, rebblings, revel-back, ring-nail, rivel-backs, rivelling, rivels,** *rough skin,* **ruggle-back, scurf, skinning, snag, springs, spring-wart, step-father, step-mother, stepmother-jack, stepmother-jag, stepmother's blessing, stepmother's jag, wart-spring, wartywell**

loose-yard *n* the STRAW-YARD of a farm I.1.9. luːsjæːd Man, luːs jaːd St, luːsjɑːd Man

lop *1. v When you take off the branches of a growing tree, what do you say you do?* IV.12.5. Eng exc. Man Sf. ⇒ **bark, barken, bough, bough up, brog, cob, crop, cut, cut off, dock, floor, head, hew, limb, limb out, limb up, lob, lob off, log, loop, lop down, lop off, lop up, nop, poll, prime, prume, prune, shroud,** shrove, slat out, snag, snare, sned, snib, stow, strip, take off, tod, top, trim, trim out, trim up

2. v to TRIM hedges IV.2.3. lɒp St, *-ing* lɒpɪn Y

3.1. v to TOP AND TAIL swedes II.4.3. lɒp La

3.2. vt to top and tail swedes II.4.3. łɒp Co

4. vt to TOP-AND-TAIL gooseberries V.7.23. lɔp Y

5. vi to STAY at home VIII.5.2. lɒp K

lop down *1. vtphr* to LOP a tree IV.12.5. lɒp dæʊn Do

2. vphr to lop. lɒp dɛan Y

lop-ended *adj* ASKEW, describing a picture that is not hanging straight IX.1.3. lɒpɛndɪd Wo

lop off *vtphr* to cut large branches from a tree, ⇐ to LOP IV.12.5. lɒp ... ɔːf Wa

lopperds *npl* FLEAS IV.8.4. *sg* lɒpəd Y

loppered *1. n* CURDS V.5.8(a). lɒpəd Hu

2. adj **go loppered** to CURDLE, referring to milk V.5.9. gaːn lɒpəd*[sour and solid]*, gɔʊ lɒpəd Hu*[old]*

loppered milk *n* CURDS V.5.8(a). lɒpɪt mɪlk Nf

loppy *1. adj* **make it go loppy** to CURDLE milk V.5.7. mɛk ɪt gɔʊ lɒpɪ L

2. adj **go loppy** to CURDLE, referring to milk V.5.9. gɔʊ lɒpɪ L

lops *1. n* the WATTLES of a hen IV.6.19. lɒps Gl, lɔps Y

2. npl FLEAS IV.8.4. lœps Nb, lɒps Nb Du*[old x1]* La Y, lɔps Y L*[rare x1]*

lopsided *adj* ASKEW, describing a picture that is not hanging straight IX.1.3. łɒpzæːdəd D, lɒbsæɪdɪd Man, lɒpsaːdɪd Y, lɒpsaɪdɪd Y Sa, lɒbsaɪdɪd We La, lɔbsaɪdɪd L, lɒbsɑːdəd Y, lɒbsɑɪdɪd La, lɔpsaɪdɪd C Ess MxL, lɒbsɒɪdɪd St, lɒpsɒːɪdɪd St, lɒpsɔɪdɪd Ess, lɒbsɔɪdɪd Ess, lɔpsɔɪdɪd Ess K

lop up *vtphr* to LOP a tree IV.12.5. lɒp ... ʌp So, *-ing* lɒpɪn ... ʌp He, łɒp ... ʌp D

lords *npl* KINDLING-*WOOD* V.4.2. lɔːdz K

lorry *1. n* a WAGON I.9.2. lɒʁɪ Du, lɒɹɪ Cu Sa St Mon, lɔɹɪ La, lɔɽɪ Ha, lʌɹɪ Sa, lʊɹɪ La Ch Sa, ləɹɪ La

2. n a wagon with sides. lɒɹɪ Ch Ess

3. n a wagon with detachable sides. lɒɹɪ La Sa Wa, lɒɽɪ So, lʊɹɪ We Ch, ləɹɪ We La Y Db

4. n a wagon without sides. lɒɹɪ Ch St He Wo Wa Ess, łɒɹɪ O, lʊɹɪ St, ləɹɪ Cu We La Ch

lose *vi* to WANE, referring to the moon VII.6.5(b). luːz O, *-ing* lʊuːzɪn Ess; **lose size** *-ing* əluːzɪn səɪz Wo

lost quarter *n* a BLIND TEAT III.2.7. lɒs kwaˡːɹtəˡ Brk, lɒs kwɔːtəˡ Brk, lɒs kwɒˡːtəˡː So

lot *n a lot A man is rich when he has ... of money.* VII.8.7. lɒt Lei Hrt Ess Brk Sr Sx, lɒʔ Nf, lɒɹ (+V) W, łɒd (+V) D; **a lot** ə lœ·t Nb, ə lat O, ə lɒt Nb Cu Du La Y Man Ch Db St He Wa Mon Nt L Lei

R Nth Nf Ess Brk Sr K Sx, ə lɒ? Nf Ess, ə lɒd Hu Ess, ə ɫɒt O, ə ɫɒd O, ə lɔt Nb L Sf MxL Sr, ə lɔ? L MxL, ə lɔɹ (+V) Sf Ess, ə lɔd Ess. ⇒ *a good bit, a lock, a mint, any amount, a plenty, a pocketful, bags, floods, hantle, heaps, lots, middling, plenty, pots, tons*

lote *n* a HAY-LOFT over a cow-house I.3.18. loʊt Ha

lots *n* A LOT (of money) VII.8.7. lɒts Ha Sx, lɔts La

lounge *n* the SITTING-ROOM of a house V.2.2. lɛʊndʒ Ess

loup *v* to JUMP a wall IV.2.10. laʊp Du We Y, *-ing* laʊpɪn La, lɑʊp Nb Y, lɒʊp Nb Cu Du We La Y, lɔːp Y, lɔʊp Nb Y L, lᵊuːp Du

loup-hopper* *n* a hobble used to prevent a sheep from jumping, ⇐ JUMP IV.2.10. lɔːpɒpə Y

loup over *vphr* to JUMP a wall IV.2.10. lɔːp ɒvə Y, loːp ɒvə Y, *pt* lɔʊpd ɒvɹ L, lɔʊp ɔʊə Y, laʊp ɔʊɹ Y, lɔʊp ɒwə L, lɔʊp ʊəvə L

louring *adj* DULL, referring to the weather VII.6.10. laʊɽɪn So

louses *npl* LICE IV.8.1(a). laʊːzəz Sa

lousy *adj* HEAVING *WITH MAGGOTS* IV.8.6. lɛʊzɪ Ess, laʊzɪ Y

louvre* *n* the flue of a CHIMNEY V.1.3. lʊvəɹ La

louvre-hole* *n* the hole of the flue of a CHIMNEY V.1.3. lʊvəɹɔɪl Y

louvre-man* *n* a CHIMNEY-sweep V.1.3. lʊvəman Y

lovely-looking *adj* PRETTY, describing a girl VI.5.18. ɫʊvlɪɫʊkɪn O

low *1. vi-3prpl* they MOO, describing the noise cows make during feeding time in the cow-house III.10.4(a). laᵁ Sa, lɔʊ L, *-ing* lɔʊɪn Y, lʌʊ Bk Ess, lou Nf
2. vi-3prpl they MOO, describing the noise cows make in the fields III.10.4(b). lʌʊ Ess, loː Sa

lowance *n* a SNACK VII.5.11. lɛəns Y, laːns Y*[probably old]*, laʊənz Y, lʊəns Y*[old x2]*

low boot *n* a SHOE VI.14.22(a). lɔʊ bʊɪt Y

low ground(s) *n* LOW-LYING LAND IV.1.7.
no -s: loː gɹaʊn So
-s: ləʊ gɹʌʊnz Brk

lowk *vt* to BEAT a boy on the buttocks VIII.8.10. laʊk Y

low-land-meadow *n* LOW-LYING LAND IV.1.7. lɔʊlænmɛdə Ess

low-land(s) *n* LOW-LYING LAND IV.1.7.
no -s: lɒʊlɛnd K, lɔːland We, lɔʊland Ch L, lɔʊlan Ch, loːlænd He, loːland Sa; *piece of low-land* piːs ə lɔʊland Wo
-s: ɫɒʊɫanz Gl, lɔʊlənz Y, loʊlanz St

low-lying ground *n* LOW-LYING LAND IV.1.7. loːləɪ-ɪn gɹæʊn He

low-lying land *n* *What do you call that low-lying flat land in the bend of a river, generally very fertile?* IV.1.7. lʌʊlɑɪ-ɪn lænd MxL, loːləɪ-ɪn lænd He,

loːlaɪ-ɪn læn Sa, loʊlaɪ-ɪn lænd So, læʊlɔɪn læːnd Hrt, loːʊləɪ-ɪn læːnd Gl, lɒʊlɪgɪn land Y, lɒʊlaɪ-ɪn land Y, loːlaɪ-ɪn land Sa. ⇒ *bog, bog-land, bottom(s), bottom-ground, bottom-land, broad-meads, broo, brook-land, brook-meadows, carr-land, carrs, dingle, fatty-land, fen, fen-land, flams, flat-lands, flats, flood-meadows, ham(s), haugh(s), haugh-land, heavy land, hollow, holm(s), holm-land, ings, lea, leigh* ⇒ *lea, level, lings, low-ground(s), low-land(s), low-land-meadow, low-lying ground, low-meadows, low-pasture, lows, marsh(es), marsh-land, marshy-land, mead(s), meadow(s), meadow-land, meadow-marsh-ground, middle-marsh, mires, moor-land, moors, mosses, moss-land, nesses, new grounds, pastures, piece of low-land, river-ground, river-land, river-meadows, riverside land, scour, slang, spilly, swamps, swampy ground, swampy patch, tack, warp, warp-land, warpy-land, wash, water-mead(s), water-meadow(s), watery-meadows, wet land, yelland;* ⇒ also **haugh** *[headword noted as 'probably merely descriptive' in EMBM]*

low meadow *n* PASTURE II.1.3. *pl* lʌʊ mɪdəz Sf

low-meadows *n* LOW-LYING LAND IV.1.7. lʌʊmɪdəz Sf

low-pasture *n* LOW-LYING LAND IV.1.7. lɔʊpastə Y

low place *n* a FORD IV.1.3. lo pleːs Ch *[marked u.r. WMBM]*

lows *n* LOW-LYING LAND IV.1.7. lʌʊz Sf

lowse *n* STOPPING-TIME at the end of a day's work VII.5.9. laʊz Nb, lɒʊz Nb Du, lɔʊz Nb Du

lowses *1. npl* RUTS made by cartwheels IV.3.9. lɔʊsɪz Sx*[not used]*
2. vi-3prsg school FINISHES VIII.6.2(b). laʊzɪz Du Y, laʊzəz Du, *v* laʊz Nb, lɒʊzɪz Y, lɔːsɪz La Y, lɔːzɪz La*[old x1]*, lɔːzəz Y, lɔʊzəz Y, loːsɪz La, luːsɪz La Y, luːzɪz Y

lowses out *viphr-3prsg* school FINISHES VIII.6.2(b). laʊzɪz ʌʊt Y

lowse-time *n* STOPPING-TIME at the end of a day's work VII.5.9. laʊztaɪm Du, lɔʊztɛɪm Nb

low shoe *n* a SHOE VI.14.22(a). loʊ ʃɪu C, loː ʃY La, loʊ ʃʊu Y, lɔʊ ʃuː Y, lʌʊ ʃuː Sf, loː ʃu Db Gl, lɔː ʃᵁuː Du We, laː ʃᵊuː Y

lowsing-off-time *n* STOPPING-TIME at the end of a day's work VII.5.9. lɒʊznɒftaɪm Cu

lowsing-out-time *n* STOPPING-TIME at the end of a day's work VII.5.9. laʊznaʊttaɪm Cu

lowsing-time *n* STOPPING-TIME at the end of a day's work VII.5.9. laʊzntɛɪm Du, laʊzɪntaːm Y, laʊzɪntaɪm We La Y, laʊzɪntaːm Y, lɒʊzntɛɪm Nb, lɒʊzɪntaɪm Y, lɒʊzntaɪm Cu, lɔːsɪntaɪm La*[old]*, lɔːsɪntaːm La, lɔʊzntɛɪm Nb, lɔʊzɪntaɪm

L[horse-man, at 2pm], lʌʊzntɛɪm Nb[old], loːzɪntɑɪm La, luːzɪntaɪm Y

lozenges n SWEETS V.8.4. lɒsɪndʒəˡːz̩ Gl, lɒsəndʒəˡːz̩ So

lucky-bone n a WISH-BONE IV.6.22. lʌkɪbɒʊn Sx, lʌkɪbʌʊn Bk, lʌkɪboːn He, lʌkiboːən Do, lʌkiboʊn So, lʌkɪbʊn Sf, lʊkɪbɪan Cu Y[old], lʊkɪbɪən Y, lʊkɪbeˑan Cu La, lʊkɪbɔʊn L Nth, lʊkɪboːn La Db Sa, lʊkɪbʊʊn Db St Wo, lʊkɪbʊən La Y

lug 1. n the CLOG on a horse's tether I.4.3. lʌg Brk
2. n HAIR VI.2.1. lʊg Y
3. vt to PULL somebody's hair VI.2.8. lʌg Hu Ess, lʊg Y Ch Db St Wa Nt L Nth, 3prpl lʊgz La
4. n an EAR-HOLE VI.4.3. lʌg Brk, lʊg Nb Cu La

luggage cart n a FARMCART I.9.3. lʊgɪdʒkɑːt St

lugged up adj TANGLED, describing hair VI.2.5. lʊgd ʊp Y

lugging 1. vt-ing lugging muck CARTING DUNG II.1.4. lʌgɪn mʌk Sa He, lʊgɪŋg mʊk St, lʊgɪn mʊk Sa
2.1. v-ing CARTING corn from the field II.6.6. lʌgɪn Sa He, lʊgɪn Sa St Wo
2.2. vt-ing carting wheat. lʊgɪn Wo
3. vt-ing PULLING his ear VI.4.4. lʌgɪn Nth, lʌgən Ess, lʊgɪn La St Nth

lugging out vtphr-ing PUTTING your tongue OUT VI.5.4. lʊgɪn ... ɛʊt Db

luggy 1. adj TANGLED, describing hair VI.2.5. lʊgɪ Du[old] La[old x1] Y Ch Db Sa St Wa Nt, lʊgɛ Y
2. adj DEAF VI.4.5. lʌgɪ Nf, lʏgɪ Nf[not completely deaf x1]

lug-hole n an EAR-HOLE VI.4.3. lɒgɒʊɫ K, lʌghøːl Nb, lʌgɒʊɫ Sr K, lʌgɔʊɫ K, lʌgʌʊɫ Sf Bd, ɫʌgoːɫ W, lʌgoʊɫ So, lʏghøːl Nb, lʏghoul Nf, lʏgoul Nf, lʏgoʊɫ Nf, lʊghøːl Nb, lʊghœːl Nb, lʊgɒɪl La Y, lʊgɔːl Cu Du, lʊgɔɪl La Y, lʊgɔʊl L, lʊgoːl La Db, lʊgoəl Cu Du, lʊgwɒl We, lʊghʊəl Nb Cu, lʊgʊəl Cu Du We La Y L[old x1]

lug-mark v to MARK the ears of sheep in some unspecified way to indicate ownership III.7.9. lʊgmaːk Y

lug-root* n the lobe of an ear, ⇐ EARS VI.4.1. lʊgɹɪət Nb

lugs 1. n BUMPERs of carts I.10.1(a). ɫɒgz W
2. npl the HANDLES of a scythe II.9.8. lʊgz St
3. npl EARS VI.4.1. lɛgz Ess[old], lœːgz Nb, sg lɒg

K, lʌgz Nb Nf[old x1] Sf Bd Ess[old] Sr K[old], lʏgz Nb Nf[old x1], lʊgs Man lʊgz Nb[vulgar x1] Cu Du We La[old x1] Y Ch Db St Wa[children's word] Gl O[old] L[old x2], sg lʊg Man
4. n the WATTLES of a hen IV.6.19. lʊgz K

lug-wigs npl EARWIGS IV.8.11. sg lʊgwig Y[facetious]

lum 1. n a CHIMNEY V.1.3. lœːm Nb[rare]
2. n the flue of a chimney. lʌm Nb

lumber n RUBBISH V.1.15. lʌmbə Nf, lʊmbə Ch, lʊmbəɪ Y[old], lʊmbəˠ La

lumber up vtphr to CLIMB VIII.7.4. lʊmbəɪ ʊp Y

lump 1. n lump of cow-muck, lump of cow-shit a CLOT OF COW-DUNG II.1.6. **lump of cow-muck** lʌmp ə kəumʌˑk Mon; **lump of cow-shit** lʌmp ə kɛʊʃɪt Nf, ɫʌmp ə kæʏʃɪt Co, ɫʌmp ə kæʊʃɪt W
2. n a BUMP on someone's forehead VI.1.8. lɒmp K, lʌmp Nb Sa He Mon Gl Hu Nf Bk Ess So Sx, ɫʌmp Sf, lʏmp Nf, lʊmp Nb Cu Du We La Y Man Ch Db Sa St He Wo Mon Gl Nt L Lei R C
3. n a BIT (OF string) VII.2.10. lʊmp Nb Cu Du We La Y Db St Nth

lump-head n a STUPID person VI.1.5. lʊmpɪˑəd Y

lumpy-dicks n thin, lumpy GRUEL V.7.2. lʊmpɪdɪks Y [marked u.r. NBM]

lumpy-toms n PORRIDGE V.7.1. lʊmpɪtʊmz Ch[thick porridge] Db[old]

lunch 1. n a SNACK VII.5.11. lʌntʃ C Nf Bk Ess, lʌnʃ Sa O Nf Bk Ess So W Brk Sr K Do Ha Sx, ɫʌnʃ W D Do, lʏntʃ Nf, lʏnʃ Nf, lʊntʃ La Db Wa Gl O Lei, lʊnʃ Du We Y Man Ch Sa St Wo Wa Nt[old x1] L Lei R Nth So, lʊɲʃ Nth; **a little lunch** ə lɪtl lʊnʃ St; **bit of lunch** bɪt ə ɫʌnʃ Do
2. n MEAL OUT VII.5.12. lɒnʃ Man, lʌnʃ Sa Mon So W Sr K[rare x1], ɫʌnʃ D Ha, lʊnʃ Cu La[modern] Man Sa He Wa L
3. n a SEESAW VIII.7.2. ɫʊnʃ Co

lunchy* n springy, describing a bog, ⇐ SEESAW VIII.7.2. ɫʌnʃi Co

lungs n the LIGHTS or lungs of a slaughtered animal III.11.5. lɒŋs Man, lɒŋgz K, lʌŋz Sa He Ess, ɫʌŋz W, lʊŋgz Sa

luny 1. adj STUPID VI.1.5. luːnɪ Man
2. n a STUPID person VI.1.5. luːnə Man

M

maa *vi-3prpl* they BLEAT, describing the noise sheep make III.10.5. meː Nb Sa Nt, meːz Du Y, mɛː Y D, meːz St, mɑːz Brk

maddocks *npl* MAGGOTS IV.8.6. madəks Ch L

maff *n* a RIDGEL III.4.7. maf Cu

mag *n* having a mag GOSSIPING VIII.3.5(a). ɛvɪn ə mag Y

magger *n* a GOSSIP VIII.3.5(b). magəˡ Gl

maggies *npl* MAGGOTS IV.8.6. magɪz Y

magging *v-ing* GOSSIPING VIII.3.5(a). magɪn Y

maggled *adj* EXHAUSTED, describing a tired person VI.13.8. magɫd Bk

maggoted *adj* HEAVING *WITH MAGGOTS* IV.8.6. magətɪd St L

maggots *1. npl When the bluebottles get at the meat or fish, you'll soon find it HEAVING WITH ....* IV.8.6. Eng exc. Du R Brk Sx. ⇒ **maddocks, maggies, mawks, quicks**
2. npl TICKS on sheep IV.8.3. mɪgəts Sx, mɛgɪts D Sx*[smaller than ticks]*, mɛgəts Sx, mægɪts Nf Ha, mædʒɪts Wo, mægəts Nf So, magʌts W, magəts D

maggoty *adj* HEAVING *WITH MAGGOTS* IV.8.6. mɛgətɪ K, mægətɪ Nf Ess K, mægət?ɪ Nf Sf, mægədɪ Ess, magɪtɪ Lei R, magətɪ Y St Nt R *[marked u.r. NBM]*

maid *n* a DAUGHTER VIII.1.4(b). meɪd So, mɛɪd Co, mæɪd Gl

maiden *n* a female sheep that has had no lambs, ⇐ EWE-HOG III.6.4, and GIMMER III.6.5. meːdn Brk, mæɪdn K

maiden-ewe* *n* a female sheep before she lambs, ⇐ EWE-HOG III.6.4. meɪdnjʌʊ K

maiden heifer *n* a HEIFER III.1.5. meːdn ɛfəˡ Sa, meɪdnhɛfəˡ Sr

maiden-lamb *n* a female sheep that has had no lambs, ⇐ EWE-HOG III.6.4. meɪdnlæm Sr

maiden-pot *n* a BREAD-BIN V.9.2. meːdɪnpɒt Y

maidens *npl* GIRLS VIII.1.3(b). meɪdnz So, mɛɪdnz Co D, maɪdnz So W Do, maːɪdənz So

maids *npl* GIRLS VIII.1.3(b). meːdz D, meːd Co, *sg* meɪd So, mɛɪdz Co D, *sg* mɛɪd St So Do, *sg* mæɪd So, maɪdz W Do, maɪd So

maid's-water *n* URINE in a cow-house I.3.10. mɛɪdzwɔːtəˡ K*[rare]*

mailie *adj* HORNLESS, describing a cow III.2.9. meɪlɪ Man, mɜːlɪ Man

main *1. adv* VERY poisonous IV.11.5. meːn Brk, mɛɪn Brk, maɪn W Ha

2. adv VERY VIII.3.2. meːn W*[old]*, mɛːn W, mɛɪn Brk, mæɪn W, maɪn W Ha

main branches *npl* BOUGHS of a tree IV.12.2. meːn bɹanʃəz Y

mainly *adv* VERY poisonous IV.11.5. mɛɪnlɪ Brk

main-sway *n* an EVENER, the main swingle-tree of a horse-drawn plough harness I.8.4. mɛənsweɪ La

main-swingle-tree *n* an EVENER, the main swingle-tree of a horse-drawn plough harness I.8.4. meːnswɪŋltɹi: La Db, meːnswɪŋltʁeɪ Nb, meːnswɪŋltɹəɪ We, meːnswɪnltɹəɪ Y, me·ənswɪŋltɹiː La, me·ənswɪŋltɹɪ La, mɛɪn swɪŋɫtɹi: Wa *[northern forms with **-tree** given this definition, although NBM data less specific]*

make *1. vt* make (the) load to LOAD sheaves onto a wagon II.6.7(a). meːk ðə ɫuːd Co, meːk ɫuːd Co

2. vt to STOCK a cow's udder III.3.6. mɛk Y

3.1. vt to BREW tea V.8.9. meːk He Wo O*[polite xl]* Do, *-ing* meːkɪn W Brk, meɪk So, *-ing* meɪkn Man, meːˡk Gl, 2prpl meːɪks Wo, *-ing* meːɪkɪn So, *-ing* mɛkɪn So, meːk So, meɪk Wo Sx, *-ing* mɛɪkɪn Sr K, mæɪk Sr, mak Y Sa

3.2. v to brew tea. meːᵊk Wa, meɪk Bk, *-ing* meɪkɪn Mon, meːˡk Gl, *-ing* mɛkɪn Nf, mɛkn Nf Ess, mɛɪk Hrt Ess, mɛɪkɪn Nf, mɛɪk?n Nf, mæɪk Ess

4. vt to PLASH a hedge IV.2.4. *-ing* meˑɪkɪn K; **cut and make** kʌt ən meːk W

5. vi to WAX, referring to the moon VII.6.5(a). *prppl* mɛkɪn La, mɛɪk Hrt Ess, *-ing* mɛɪkɪn K; **he's making himself** iːz əmeːɪkɪn ɪmsɛɫf Wo; **on the make** ɒn ðə mɛɪk Nf Ess

6. n a HALFPENNY VII.7.1(a). mɪək Y

7. n (what) SORT VII.8.17. (**what**) **make** mak Cu

make up *1.1. vtphr* to STOCK a cow's udder III.3.6. *-ing* makɪn ... ʊp Y

1.2. vphr to stock. mɛk ʊp La

2. vtphr to PLASH a hedge IV.2.4. mɛːk ... ʌp D

male lamb *n What do you call the male (sheep) when newly born?* III.6.2. *pl* meɪl lamz Wo. ⇒ **heeder, heeder-lamb, he-lamb, hog-lamb, lamb, little ram, male-tup, pur-lamb, ram-lamb, tup-lamb, wether-lamb, young ram, young tup**

male-tup *n* a MALE LAMB III.6.2. mɛɪltʊp St

mallet *n What's your word for a wooden hammer?* I.7.5.

1. n the heavy implement. mɛlɪt La Y L K, mɛlət La, mælɪt K, mælæd Man, mǽlət Man, malɪt La Y Db Sa St O L Lei Nf, *pl* malɪts R, malʊt Gl, malət Du So Do, maɫət O W Co D Do, maɫəɾt O

2. n the small implement. mɛlɪt Y, mɛlət Cu La, mɛtət Ess, mɛlə? Bk, mælɪt C Nf Ess K, mǽlɪt Gl, mælʌt So, mæɫʊt Gl, mælət Hu Nf Sf Bk Ess So Sx, mæɫət He, mælə? Nf, malɪt Du Y Ch Db Sa St He Wo Wa L Lei Nth Bk Bd Hrt, maɫɪt W Ha, malɪ? O, malət Nb Cu Du We La Gl C Ess So, maɫət Gl W D Ha, malə? Bk

3. n an implement of any size. mɛlɪt Nt K, mælɪt Nf K, malɪt Ch Db Wa Nt Lei Nth Hu, malət Gl, maɫət W D

4. n an implement of indeterminate size. mɛlət La, mɛləd L, mælɪt Wo Nf Hrt Sx, mæɫɪt Sr, mælɪk Nf, mæːlɪ? Hrt, mæɫʊt Gl, mælət Sf Ess, mæɫət Brk Co Sx, mæləd Brk, mælʌt So, malɪt Y St Wa L Lei Bk MxL, malət Nb La O So, maɫət So W Co D Do Ha, mɒɫət D

⇒ **beetle, binny, brand-beetle, log-beetle, maul, mauler, mell, pile-maul, ring-beetle, stake-beetle, stake-maul, stake-mell, stake-riddle**

man *1. n* a FARM-LABOURER I.2.4. mæn MxL K, man Y; **general man** dʒɛnɹəl man Ch, dʒɛnɹəl mɒn Db

2. n my HUSBAND VIII.1.25. **my man** mɪ mæˑn Nb, maɪ mæˑn So, maː man Nb, maɪ man Cu Du, maɪ man Du

mancreeper *n* a NEWT IV.9.8. mæːnkriːpə Man

mane *n* the FORELOCK of a horse III.4.8. meːn Sa Mon, meːɪn He, mɛɪn He, mæɪn He Mon Gl

mange *n* **the mange** *You know how dogs and cats sometimes lose their hair in patches. What would you say they had got?* III.13.7. Eng. ⇒ **moult**, *reef* ⇒ **riff, riff, rift, scurvy,** *the mange,* **the rift**

manger *1. n* a TROUGH in a cow-house I.3.6. meːndʒə Nt, meːndʒəˤ O, meːŋʒəˤ Mon, meːndʒəˤː W D Do, meɪndʒə Hu C Bd Hrt, meɪndʒəɪ He, meɪndʒəˤ O Nth Bk, meɪnʒəˤ Bk, meɪndʒəˤː So, meːɪndʒə Db, meːɪndʒəˤ He Wo, meːɪnʒəˤ Mon Gl, meəndʒə Y, meˑəndʒəˤ Bk, mɛndʒə Nf, mɛːndʒəˤː D, mɛɪndʒə Db St Wa L Lei R Nth C Nf Sf Bd Hrt Ess, mɛɪnʒə L, mɛɪndʒəᴶ O Ha, mɛɪndʒəˤ He Wa O Bk Sr, mɛɪnʒəˤ Gl, mɛɪndʒəˤː Co, meəndʒə Y L, mɛənʒə L, mɛːˀndʒəˤ Wo, meəndʒəᴶ La, mænʒə Mon, mænʒəˤ Mon, mæɪndʒə St Hu Nf Hrt Ess Sr, mæɪnʒə Nf, mæɪndʒəᴶ K, mæɪndʒəˤ He Gl O, mæɪnʒəˤ Mon Gl, manʒə Nf, maɪndʒə Ess MxL K, maɪnʒə Gl, maɪndʒəˤ Wo, maɪnʒəˤ Gl, maɪndʒəˤː W Do Ha, mɒndʒəˤː Do, mɔːndʒə Y

2. n a HAY-RACK in a stable I.4.1. meːndʒə Y, meːɪndʒəˤː Do, meɪndʒəˤː So, mɛndʒəˤː So, mɛːɪndʒəˤː So, mɛəndʒə Y, mɑːndʒəˤː So,

mɔːndʒəˤː So *[reference may not be to a rack – SBM note indicates that the picture shown to ii. may have influenced the rr.]*

manger-block *n* the CLOG on a horse's tether I.4.3. mɛːnʒəblɒk We

manger-halter *n* a TETHERING-ROPE used to tie up a horse I.4.2. meːndʒəˤːɾɔːɫtəˤː Ha, meɪndʒəᴶɹɔːɫtəᴶ Brk, mandʒəˤːɾpʊɫtəˤː W

mangering *v-ing* FEEDING horses in the stable III.5.1. meɪndʒəɹɪn St

manger-post *n* a TETHERING-STAKE in a cow-house I.3.3. meɪndʒəpɒʊs K

manger-string *n* a TETHERING-ROPE used to tie up a horse I.4.2. mæɪndʒəstɹɪŋg K

mangey *adj* **very mangey** ILL, describing a person who is unwell VI.13.1(b). vɛɹi mandʒi Mon

manilla *n* TWINE used to fasten thatch on a stack II.7.7(b1). mənɛlə Y

manky *adj* HEAVING *WITH MAGGOTS* IV.8.6. mæŋkɪ Brk

man-of-all-jobs *n* a FARM-LABOURER I.2.4. manəvɔːldʒɒbz St

mantle *n* a working APRON V.11.2(a). mænt?l Nf*[for heavy work]*, mæn?l Nf, mænt?ɫ Nf*[for hard work]*, mæn?ɫ Sf, mɛntl Nf*[for rough work]*, mɛntɫ Sf, mɛn?l Nf

manure *1. n* COW-DUNG I.3.12. mʌnjuˑə Mon, mənᴸüːə Ess, mənjuə Y Ess

2. n a CLOT OF COW-DUNG II.1.6. mənjuə Man

3. n SHEEP-DUNG II.1.7. mənuːəˤ Sx; **sheep-manure** ʃɹiːpmənjuə Ess *[manure marked u.r. SBM]*

manure-cart *n* a FARMCART I.9.3. manəkaːt L

manure-fork *n* a MUCK-FORK I.3.13. mənjuəˤfɔˤːɾk Sx

manure-leading *v-ing* CARTING *DUNG* II.1.4. manəliːdɪn L

maphrodite *n* a RIDGEL III.4.7. mæpɹədaɪt Ess

marbles *n* SHEEP-DUNG II.1.7. maːbɫz D

mardle *n* CHAT VIII.3.4. maːdl Nf, maːdl Nf

mare *n What do you call the fully-grown female (of the horse)?* III.4.5. Eng. ⇒ **filly, mare-beast**

mare-beast *n* a MARE III.4.5. mᵊɹəbiːst Du

mare-colt *n* a FILLY III.4.2. meaˤkoʊɫt Bk, meˑəˤkɒʊ? Bk, mɛˤːkɒɫt O, meəkɛʊt Ch, meəkoːɫt Mon, meaˤːkoːɫt D, meːəˤːkoːɫt So

mare-foal *n* a FILLY III.4.2. meɪəˤfoˑəl Man, meˑəˤfʌʊɫ Bk, meəfʌʊɫ Bk, meəᴶfʊʊɫ Sr, meəᴶfʊʊ K, meˑəfoul Nf, meˑəfoːʊl Nf, meːəˤfʊʊl Wo

mark *v How do you mark your sheep to tell them from somebody else's?* III.7.9.

1. vt to MARK the ears of sheep with a hole or cut to indicate ownership. maᴶːk Brk

2. *vt* to MARK sheep with colour to indicate ownership. mæᵗːk Wa, maːk Db Sa Nf Ess, -*ing* maːkɪn St, maᵗːk Sa He Mon Gl So W Co Ha, maɹ̥k O, maːk He Wo Nf, -*ing* maːkɪn Ess, -*ing* maˑᴶːkn K, maᵗːk He Gl Sr, maᵗːɻ̥k Ha Sx, maːəᴶk Sr, məᵗːk Wo

3. *v* to mark sheep with colour. -*ing* mæˑkən Man, mark We, maːk Nb Cu We Y Db Wa Nt L Lei Nth Sf Db Ess, -*ing* maːkɪn St, maᴶːk La, maᵗːk Wa Gl O Bk W, maːk Man Nf, -*ing* maːkɪn Ess

4. *vt* to mark sheep in some unspecified way. maᵗːk W Do, maˑᴶːk Brk, maᵗːk D

5. *v* to mark sheep. maɹk Du, maːk La Y Lei Ess, maᵗːk Do, -*ing* maːkɪn K, -*ing* maᵗːkɪn K, *prppl* maᵗˑɻ̥kɪn Sx, -*ing* maᵗːɻ̥kɪn Sx, *ptppl* maᵗːkt D

⇒ with a cut or hole: **clip** *their ears*, **clip** *their lugs*, **cut**, **cut** *a snotch out of their ear*, **cut** *their ears*, **ear-clip**, **ear-mark**, **ear-punch**, **lug-mark**, **point** *their ears*, **punch**, **punch** *a hole*, **punch** *a hole in the ear*, **punch** *the ear*, **punch** *the ears*, **punch** *their ears*, **punch** *the lug*, **snip** *their ears*

⇒ with a burn-mark: **brand**, **burn**, **burn** *on the horns*, **burn** *the horns*, **burn** *their horns*, **horn**, **horn-burn**

⇒with colour: **baste**, **brand**, *buist* ⇒ **baste**, **colour**, **dab**, **dap**, **dap on**, **dot**, **paint**, **pick**, **pitch**, **pitch-mark**, *put a brand on*, **raddle**, **raddle-mark**, **red**, **reddle**, **riddle**, **rud**, **ruddle**, **sheep-mark**, **smit**, **stamp**, **tar**, **tar-iron**, **tar-mark**, **tiver**

⇒ unspecified method: **brand**, **ear-mark**, **horn-mark**, **lug-mark**, **smit**, **stamp**, **stock-mark**

⇒ also **kenspeck**

6. *vt* to DIRTY a floor V.2.8. maːk Mon, maᵗːɻ̥k Sx *[marked u.r. SBM]*

7. *vt* to BEAT a boy on the buttocks VIII.8.10. maᵗːk O

8. *vi-3prpl* they BLEAT, describing the noise sheep make III.10.5. maːks Mon

9. *n* **up to the mark** WELL, describing a healthy person VI.13.1(a). ʊp tə ðə maːk L *[marked u.r. EMBM]*

10. *n* **none up to the mark** SICK, describing an animal that is unwell VI.13.1(c). nʊən ʊp tə t maːk Y

mark out *vphr* to cull sheep, ⇐ CULLING III.11.2. *?ptppl* maᵗːɻ̥kt ɛʊt Sx

marks *npl* the HOOF-MARKS of a horse IV.3.10. maːks Ch Sa

marl *n* CLAY IV.4.2. maːl St

marlborough-hand *n* a LEFT-HANDED person VI.7.13(a). mɔːɫbɹ̥əhand W

marlborough-handed *adj* LEFT-HANDED VI.7.13(a). mɒlbɹ̥ɔʊ-ændɪd Brk*[old]*, mɔːɫbɹ̥ə-andəd W

married *adj* If your son Jack is not single, he must be .... VIII.1.17. Eng. ⇒ **tied up**, **wed**, **wedded**

marrows *npl* MATES VIII.4.1. maʀəz Nb*[down the pit, i.e. mine]*, *sg* maʀə Du, *sg* maɹə Cu

marrying-bone *n* a WISH-BONE IV.6.22. maɹɪ-ɪnbʌʊn Bd

marsh 1. *n* a MEADOW II.9.2. maːʃ Ess*[reclaimed land]*

2. *n* pasture, ⇐ HIRE *PASTURAGE* III.3.8. mæːʃ Nf

3. *n* BOGGY land IV.1.8. maːʃ K

marsh(es) 1. *n* marsh used as PASTURE II.1.3. *no -es*: maːʃ Nf
-es: maːʃɪz K

2. *n* LOW-LYING LAND IV.1.7. *no -es*: mɛɪʃ D, mæʃ Ess, maːʃ Cu Ch L Nf, mɜᴶˑɹʃ La
-es: maːʃɪz L, maᴶːʃɪz La*[near sea]*, maᵗːʃɪz So

marsh-grass *n* PASTURE II.1.3. maːʃgɹɑˑs Nf

marsh-land 1. *n* PASTURE II.1.3. maːʃlænd Ess

2. *n* LOW-LYING LAND IV.1.7. mæːʃland La, maːʃlænd Nf, maːʃland Wa L, maᴶːɹʃland La, maᵗʃland Ha

marsh-let *v* to HIRE *PASTURAGE* for cattle in summer on a marsh III.3.8. -*ing* maːʃlɛtn Nf

marshy *adj* BOGGY IV.1.8. mæʃɪ Brk, mæᴶːʃɪ La, maːʃɪ Y Sa Wa Ess, maᵗːʃɪ Sa, maːʃɪ K, maᵗːɻ̥ʃɪ Sx

marshy-land *n* LOW-LYING LAND IV.1.7. maːʃɪland Y

mash 1. *n* CHAFF fed to horses III.5.3. mæʃ Nf Sx, maʃ Y Ch; **dry mash** dɹɒɪ mæˑʃ K *[mash marked u.r. SBM]*

2.1. *vt* to BREW tea V.8.9. -*ing* mɛʃɪn Y, -*ing* mæˑʃɪn Brk, maʃ Nb*[old]* Du*[rare x1]* La Y St*[old x1]* Wo Wa, -*ing* maʃɪn L, -*ing* maʃən We

2.2. *v* to brew tea. mɛʃ Ess, mæʃ Wo C Nf*[old x1]*, maʃ Db Sa St Wo Wa O Nt L Lei R Nth Bd Hrt*[old]*

mashlum *n* MEAL V.6.1(b). maʃləm Du

mask* *vt* to BREW tea V.8.9. mask Nb Cu

mass 1. *n* an ACORN IV.10.3. meːˀs So, meːəz So, mæːsk So, maːs So D

*2. *vt* to BREW tea V.8.9. mas Cu We*[old x1]*, -*ing* masɪn La*[old]*

massed *adj* TANGLED, describing hair VI.2.5. mæst Nf

massey-harris* *n* STRING used to tie up a grain-sack I.7.3. masɪ-aɹɪs Y *[apparently trade name]*

mast* *vt* to BREW tea V.8.9. mast Du*[old x1]*

master 1. *n* my HUSBAND VIII.1.25. meːstaᵗː Co D, mɛstə Ch*[rare]*, meːstər Y; **our master** aː mɛstə Y Db; **the master** ðə mɪəstaᵗː So, ðə meːstər Cu Du, t meːstər Cu, t meːstər We, t meːstəɹ La, ðə meːstaᵗː So*[old]* W Co D Do, ðə mɛɪəstəᵗː So, ðə meˀəstoᵝ Nb, t mɛəstə Cu, ðə mɛstə L Ch, ð mɛstə Db Nt, t mɛstə Y Db, ðə mɛstɪ L, ʔ mɛɪstə Y, ðə mɛˑəstə Nt L, t mɛəstə

Y, ðə mɛˈəstɹ L, t mɛəstəɹ Y, ðə mɛˈəstəˈ L, ðə mæːstəˡ Ha, ðə mæɪstə Lei, ðə mastə St Wa Nt L Lei R, t mastə Ch, ðə mastəˡ Wa, ðə maːstə Wa L Lei Nth Hu Sf*[old x1]* Bd Hrt Ess, ðə maːsʔə Nf, ðə maːstɹ O, ðə maːstəˡ Sa Mon O Bk, ðə maːstəˡ: So, ðə maːstə Nf, ðə maːstəˈ K

2. *n* a TEACHER VIII.6.5. meːstə Cu, meːstəˡ: W Do, meəstəˡ: Do, mɛːstə We, mɛːstər Du, mɛːstəˡ: So, mɛːˈstəˡ: So, mɛəstə Y, mæːstəˡ: Co, maːstə Ess, maːstəˡ: D, mɑːstəˈ Brk K, mɑːstəˡ Sx*[old]*

3. *adv* VERY VIII.3.2. maːstəˡ: D

Master *n* MR. VIII.2.3(b). meəstɔᴿ Nb, meːstə Du, meːstəˡ: Co, mɛstə La Y Ch Db St Nt L Lei Hu, mɛstɹ L, mɛstəɹ La, mɛstəˈ Ch L Brk, mɛsθəɹ La, mɛstəˡ Bk Brk, mɛəstə Y L, mɛəstəɹ Y, mæstə St, mæːsθə Man, mæɪstʰə Man, mastə St L, mastəˡ Bk, maːstəˡ O Bk, maːstə Lei Ess, maːskə Bd*[obsolete]*, mɑːstə K*[old]*, mɑːstəˈ Brk*[old]* Sr*[old]*, maːs Sr*[old]* Sx, mʌstə C Bd Hrt, mʊstə Wa Nth C, məstə Y, məstəˡ: So Do

master-man *n* an EVENER, the main swingle-tree of a horse-drawn plough harness I.8.4. maˡːʂtəmən Sa

master-piece *n* the HUB of a cart-wheel I.9.7. maˡːstəˡːpiːs So

master-swingle-tree *n* an EVENER, the main swingle-tree of a horse-drawn plough harness I.8.4. meːstəswɪŋltɹiː u, meːstɔᴿswɪŋltᴮei Nb, meːstəswɪŋltᴮei Nb, mɛəstəswɪŋltᴮiː Du, mɛˈəstəswɪŋltɹəɪ Y, mastə swɪŋgltɹiː St*[3 horses only]*, mastə swɪŋgltɹɛɪ St, maːstəswɪŋltɹiː Du *[northern forms with -tree given this definition, although NBM data less specific]*

master-tree *n* an EVENER, the main swingle-tree of a horse-drawn plough harness I.8.4. mæstətᴮi Nb, mastəᴮtᴮi Nb *[northern forms with -tree given this definition, although NBM data less specific]*

mat *n* **all in a mat, all of a mat, in a mat** TANGLED, describing hair VI.2.5. **all in a mat** ɔːɫ ɪn ə mæt So; **all of a mat** ɔːl əv ə mæt Brk; **in a mat** ɪn ə mæɪt Sx, ɪn ə mat Man

mate(s) *npl* PALS VIII.4.2.
sg: meət Nb, meːɪʌt So, mɛət Sx
no -s: mɛɪt Ess
-s: mɪəts Du Do, mjɛts Do, meːts Nb Cu La*[old x1]* Y Gl W Do, meɪts Wo W, meːɪts Gl So, meɪəts So, meəts La Bk, meːəts Nb Du So Co Do Ha, mɛts Sf, mɛːts Cu We, mɛɪts St L Nf Sf Ess Brk Sr K, mɛəts Y, maɪts W, mæɪts Ess

mates *1. npl* *What is your word for the men that you work with?* VIII.4.1. Eng exc. Man R Hu. ⇒ **butties, chums, marrows, old chummies, pals, work-mates, work-pals** *[BM headword work-mates]*
2. npl FRIENDS VIII.2.7. meːts Y, *sg* meːt Gl, mɛɪts Sx

matted *adj* TANGLED, describing hair VI.2.5. mɛtɪd K*[horse's coat]*, mɛətəd Ess, mætɪd Sa He Wo

Mon Hrt Ess So Brk Sr K Co Sx, mætʔɪd Ess, mæʔɪd Nf, mætəd Man He Ess*[if dirty x1]* So, matɪt Cu, matɪd Nb Cu Du La Y Ch Db Sa St Wo Wa O L Nth Bd W Sr Ha, maʔɪd O Bk, madɪd D, matəd Nb Db Sa Wo, matʔəd C Sf, maʔəd W

matted together *adj* TANGLED, describing hair VI.2.5. mætɪd təgɛðəˡ Wo, mæʔɪd təgɛðə Nf, matɪd təgɪðə Y, matɪd tgɛðə St, matəd təgɛðə Y; **matted up together** matɪd ʌp təgɛðəˡ: W

matted up *adj* TANGLED, describing hair VI.2.5. mætɪd ʌp Mon K, mæʔɪd ʌp Nf, mæʔɪd ʏp Nf, mætɪd ʊːp Gl, matɪd ʌp W, matɪd ʊp We Y Sa, matəd ʊp Y Gl; **matted up together** matɪd ʌp təgɛðəˡ: W

matter *1. vi* to FESTER, referring to a wound VI.11.8. matər Y, madəˈ Y, madəˈ Y
2. n PUS VI.11.9. Eng

matty *adj* TANGLED, describing hair VI.2.5. matɪ La Y L Do, maːdɪ Gl

maul *1. n* a chock placed behind and under a wheel to prevent a cart from going backwards on a hill, ⇐ PROP/CHOCK I.11.2. mɔˡːl̩ Sa
2. n a heavy wooden MALLET I.7.5. mɔːɫ He, mɒl Sa, mɔː La Ch Db St, mɔːl La Y Ch Sa St Nt Hu Ha, mɔːɫ Ess Sx, mɔˡːl Sa, mɔʊl Y
3. n a small wooden mallet. mɔːɫ W Co
4. n a wooden mallet of any size. mɔːl Y
5. n a wooden mallet of indeterminate size. maʊ St, mɔː Ha, mɔːɫ Ha

mauler *1. n* a heavy wooden MALLET I.7.5. *pl* mɔːləz Y
2. n the human HAND VI.7.1. mɔːlə St, *pl* mɔːləz Ch
3. n a FIST VI.7.4. mɔːlə MxL

maun *n* the FORELOCK of a horse III.4.8. mɒn Sa, mɔːn Sa

maunch **1.1. v-1prpl* we CRUNCH apples or biscuits VI.5.12. mɔːnʃ Hu
1.2. v-1prpl we crunch. -ing mɔːnʃɪn Db
2. v to GOBBLE food VI.5.13(b). -ing mɔːnʃən Co

maund *1. n* a BASKET for carrying horse-feed III.5.4. mɔːnd *[small, wicker]* K*[round, holds about 2 bushels]*, mɔːn So*[round, wood x1; round, wicker, with handles x1; round, wicker, with handles x1; round x1]* Co D*[wicker, no handles x1; wicker x1; wicker, round x1]*, mɔːən Co*[wicker]*
2. n a CLOTHES-BASKET V.9.7. mɔːn D

maund-basket *n* a wicker BASKET holding 5 bushels, for carrying horse-feed or hops III.5.4. mɒʊnbaːskɪt K

maupy *adj* STUPID VI.1.5. mɔːpɪ Y

maw *1. vi-3prpl* they MOO, describing the noise cows make during feeding time in the cow-house III.10.4(a). mɔː La, mɔːz W

2. *vi-3prpl* they MOO, describing the noise cows make in the fields III.10.4(b). mɔː Brk, mɔːz W

3. *n* MOTHER VIII.1.1(b). mɒˑə Nf

mawked *adj* HEAVING *WITH MAGGOTS* IV.8.6. maːkɪt Cu, mɔːkt Cu Y *[marked u.r. NBM]*

mawk-flies *npl* FLIES IV.8.5. maːkfliːz La*[bluebottle]*, mɔːkfliːz Cu*[bluebottle]* We*[bluebottle]*, *sg* mɔːkfleɪ Nb*[bluebottle]*, mɔːkflaɪz L, mɔːkflɑˈɪz L

mawkin *n* a SCARECROW II.3.7. mæʊkɪn He, mjæʊkɪn He Mon, maˤːkɪn Sa, mjaʊkɪn He, mɑːkɪn He Wo Gl, maˤːkɪn Wo, mɔːkɪn Y Ch Sa St He Wo Wa L Lei Nth Bd Ess, mɔˤːkɪn Sa, mɔːkʔɪn Nf, mɔːxɪn L, mɔːkn Nf, mɔːkən Nf, mɔːkʔn Nf, mɔːkʔən C Nf Sf, mɔːgən Hrt, *pl* mɔːkmz Ess, mɔˑkʔəm Nf, moˑəkɪn Nth

mawkish *adj* INSIPID, describing food lacking in salt V.7.8. maːkɪʃ W

mawks *npl* MAGGOTS IV.8.6. mæˑᵊks Nb maːks Nb Cu Du La Y, mɔːks Nb Cu Du We La Y Nt L

mawky *adj* HEAVING *WITH MAGGOTS* IV.8.6. mɔːkɪ Y L *[marked u.r. NBM]*

mawky-flies *npl* bluebottle FLIES IV.8.5. maːkɪfliːz Nb, maːkɪfleɪz Nb, maːkɪfleɪz Nb

mawl 1. *vi-3prpl* sheep BLEAT III.10.5. mɔːł D

2. *vi-3prpl* cats MEW III.10.6. maːł D, *prppl* maːłɪn So, *-ing* maːłɪn So

mawpin *n* a SCARECROW II.3.7. mɔːpɪn Y

mawr *n* a girl, ⇐ GIRLS VIII.1.3(b). mɔː Sf, mɔːə Nf, moːə Nf

mawther *n* a girl, ⇐ GIRLS VIII.1.3(b). mɔːðə Nf*[an older girl x1]* Sf

maxhill *n* a dung-heap, ⇐ COW-DUNG I.3.12. mɛkstəl K, mækstəł K

may-berries *npl* HAWS IV.11.6. meibɛɹiz Mon, maɪbəɹɪz So

may day *n* a local FESTIVAL or holiday at the beginning of May VII.4.11. mei dei Mon, mɛɪ dɛɪ Ess, mɛˑə dɛə L, mæɪ dæɪ Ess; **may day week** mɛˑə də wiːk L

mayer *n* MOTHER VIII.1.1(b). meɪə Man*[informal]*

may-maid *n* a DADDY-LONG-LEGS IV.8.10. mɛˑəmɛɪd Ess *[queried EMBM]*

mazed 1. *adj* STUPID VI.1.5. meːzd D, meɪzd So

2. *adj* SILLY VIII.9.3. meːzd Co

mazger *n* the mazger a TOM-CAT, the male cat III.13.8. ðə mazgə L

mazy *adj* GIDDY IX.1.11. meːzɪ La Y, meəzɪ La, mɛɪzɪ St, mɛəzɪ Y

mead 1. *n* a PADDOCK I.1.10. miːd Ess Brk

2. *n* PASTURE II.1.3. miːd Ess D, mɪɛd Do, mɪəd W

meadow 1. *n* What do you call the field where grass is grown for hay-making? [Ascertain whether this applies to a field that is never ploughed.] II.9.2. Eng

exc. O. ⇒ **close, field, fodder-field, grass-close, grass-field, grass-land, grass-lea, grass-meadow, greensward, ground, hay-field, hay-grass, hay-land, hay-meadow, lea, lea-land, marsh, mead(s), meadow-field, meadow-land, meadow-lea, mow-field, mowing-field, mowing-grass, mowing-ground, mowing-meadow, mowing-piece,** *new* **lea, old-grass field,** *old* **old-land,** *old* **swarf, pasture, seed-field, upland, upland hay**

2. *n* cow-pasture liable to flooding. mɛdə O

3. *n* a PADDOCK I.1.10. mɪdə Nf, mɛdoʊ Nf, mɛdə Nf Ess K Co

4. *n* PASTURE II.1.3. mɪdə Nf Sf, mɛdoʊ So, mɛdə Y Db Sa Gl O L R C Nf Bk Hrt Ess, *pl* mɛdəz Sf, mɛdəˤ Do Ha

5. *n* permanent pasture. *pl* mɛdəz St

6. *n* pasture near a stream or river. mɛdə Ch Wa O, *pl* mɛdəz Ess

7. *n* pasture, ⇐ HIRE *PASTURAGE* III.3.8. mɛdə Nf

meadow-field 1. *n* PASTURE II.1.3. *pl* mɛdəfeːldz Ch

2. *n* a MEADOW II.9.2. mɪdəfiːld L, mɪdəfəɪld Y*[never ploughed]*, mɛdəfiːld L*[never ploughed x2]*, mɛdəfɪəl O*[never ploughed]*

meadow-land 1. *n* PASTURE II.1.3. mɛdɒʊlænd Sx, mɛdəlænd Nf, mɛdəland Db, mɛdəˤlænd Sx

2. *n* a MEADOW II.9.2. mɛdəlæːn Hrt, mɛdə ˡlæn Sr, mɛdəland Nth

3. *n* LOW-LYING LAND IV.1.7. mɛdəland Ch Wa Nth Bd

meadow-lea *n* a MEADOW II.9.2. mɛdəɹlɛɪ Brk

meadow-marsh-ground *n* LOW-LYING LAND IV.1.7. mɛdəmaːʃgɹɛʊnd Nf

meadow-pasture *n* PASTURE II.1.3. *-s* mɛdəpaːstjəz Sr

meadow(s) *n* LOW-LYING LAND IV.1.7.

no -s: mɛdə Ch He Wa O Nt Bk Hrt Ess, mɛdəˤː W

-s: mɪdəz Sf, mɛdoʊz He So, mɛdəz Man*[for hay]* Ch Wa O Lei R Nth Ess W Sr K, mɛdəˤz̩ Sa Wo Mon Bk

mead(s) 1. *n* a MEADOW II.9.2.

no -s: miːd Ess*[never cut x1]* So*[never cut x2, old x1]* Brk*[old]* D Ha, mɪʌd W, mɪəd W Do, meːd D Ha

sg: mɪidz Brk*[old]*

-s: mɪiːdz Brk*[where water is plentiful]*

2. *n* LOW-LYING LAND IV.1.7.

no -s: miːd So

-s: miːdz Gl

meal 1. *n* [What do you make your white bread out of?] And your brown bread? V.6.1(b). Eng. ⇒ **barley-meal, batch-flour, bran,** *bran and*

257

bread-meal, bran-meal, bread-meal, brown-flour, brown-meal, brown wholemeal, coarse-flour, coarse meal, flour, fourths, grist, ground-down, mashlum, middlings, oatmeal, offal, pollard, rye-flour, sharps, sharps-flour, *toppings and* pollard, wheat-meal, wholemeal, wholemeal-flour

2. *n* **mixed meal** CHAFF fed to horses III.5.3. mɪkst mɛɪl Nf

3. *n* the YIELD of milk from a cow III.3.5. miːl Nb Cu We Y Ch Db Sa St Nt, miːɬ He So Co D, miːᵊɬ Wa So, mɪəl Du Y*[old x1]* Wa L, meːl Sa, meːɬ D, meɪl Du, mɛɪl Y*[old x1]* Ch Db St, mɛɪɬ D

4. *n* the yield of milk from a herd of cows. miːl Du Y Sa St, miːɬ He D, miːᵊɬ So, mɪəl Y*[old x1]*, meɪl Du, meəl Y, mɛɪl Y*[old]* St

5. *n* a yield of milk. miːl Nb La Db St Nt L, miːɬ Ch So Co D, miːəɬ Do, mɪal Y, mɪəl Nb La Y Nt L, mjɛl Nb, meːl Ch, meːɬ D, meal Du We

meal-bin 1. *n* a CORN-BIN I.7.4. meɪlbɪn Man *[marked u.r. NBM]*

2. *n* a container for meal for pigs and fowls. mɪʊbɪn K

3. *n* a pig-meal container. *pl* mɪəlbɪnz Y, mɪəɬbɪn Ha

4. *n* a container for meal. miːᵊɬbɪn Ess, mɪəlbɪn Y, mɪʊbɪn Sr, meɪlbɪn Man, mɛɪlbɪn Y, məɪəɬbɪn Hrt

meal-bing *n* a container for meal, ⇐ CORN-BIN I.7.4. mɪəlbɪŋ Y

meal-gruel *n* GRUEL V.7.2. mɛɪlgɹɪʊɪl Y

mealing-board *n* a PASTE-BOARD V.6.5. mɪiːlɪnbɔəᴵd Brk

meal out *n* *What do you call the food you take to work with you as a meal?* VII.5.12. mɪˈəl aʊt L. ⇒ **bagging, bait, bever, bite** *of eating,* **breakfast, chuck, dinner, dinner** *out,* **docky, drinkings, eating, food** *for the day,* **forenoon snap, grub, jock, jock-bit, lunch, meat, nammet, nunch, nuncheon, packing, packing-up grub, sandwich(es), snack, snap, snapping, tommy, victual(s)**

meal-porridge *n* PORRIDGE V.7.1. mɛɪlpɒɹɪdʒ Y

mear *n* a LANE IV.3.13. mɪə Lei

measles *n* *What do you call that very common disease that children get; you know, with spots?* VI.12.1. Eng. ⇒ **measlings**

measlings *n* MEASLES VI.12.1. mᴵiːzlɪnz Nf, mɪːzlɪnz Nf

measure *n* a BASKET for carrying horse-feed III.5.4. mɛʒɔᴮ Nb

measure grove *n* a PADDOCK I.1.10. mɛʒəᶜː gɹoːv So

meat 1. *n* *Some people eat only vegetables and never touch....* Eng. ⇒ **flesh-meat**; ⇒ *also* **green-meat**

2. *n* (off her) FOOD V.8.2. miːt Nb Cu Du We Y Ch, mɪət La Y Nt, meːt Sa, mɛɪt Cu La Y *[not including form at Co, which was not recorded in phr context]*

3. *n* MEAL OUT VII.5.12. meːt Ch, mɛɪt La*[old x1]*

4.1. *vt* to FEED cattle III.3.1. meːt Co

4.2. *v* to feed cattle. miːt Co*[pigs]*, meːt Co

5. *n* cut meat CHAFF fed to horses III.5.3. kʌt miːt K, kʊt mɪˈət L, kʊʔ mɪˈəˀ L

meat-flies *npl* FLIES IV.8.5. mᴵiːtflɒɪs Nf, meːtvlʌɪz Gl, mɛːtflʌɪz Nf

meating* 1. *v-ing* FEEDING horses in the stable III.5.1. meːtɪn Co

2. *vt-ing* feeding horses. meːtɪn Co

meat-standard *n* a SALTING-TROUGH III.12.5. miːtstandəᶜːd̥ D

meg 1. *n* a PET-LAMB III.7.3. mɛg Man

2. *n* a HALFPENNY VII.7.1(a). mɛg Y*[old x1]*

meg-lamb *n* a PET-LAMB III.7.3. mɛglæˈm Man

meg-many-feet *n* GOOSE-GRASS II.2.5. mɛgmɛnɪfiːt Cu

meg-owl *n* an OWL IV.7.6. mɛgaʊl L

meg-owlet *n* an OWL IV.7.6. mɛguːlɪt L

megrim *n* a RESTIVE horse III.5.6. meːgɹəm Y

melancholy *adj* DULL, referring to the weather VII.6.10. maɬənkɒɬi W *[marked as emotive and therefore u.r. SBM]*

mell 1. *n* a heavy wooden MALLET I.7.5. mɛl Nb Cu Du We La Y Nt L

2. *n* a small wooden mallet. mɛl La, mal L

3. *n* a wooden mallet of any size. mɛl Nb Cu Du We La Y L

4. *n* a wooden mallet of indeterminate size. mɛl Nb Y L

melt 1. *vt* to RENDER fat into lard III.12.9. mɛl Y, mɛɬt Mon Gl Ess, mɛʊt So Ha, məɬt D

*2. *n* the LIGHTS or lungs of a slaughtered animal III.11.5. mɛlt St *[WMBM headword* **smelt***]*

3. *n* the TONGUE VI.5.4. mɛlt Y

melt down *vtphr* to RENDER fat into lard III.12.9. mɪɬt dœvn D, mɪɬt ... dævn Co, *-ing* əmɛltɪn ... dæʊn Wo, mɛlt ... duːn Y, mɛɬt ... dɛʊn Ess, mɛɬt ... dæʏn Co D, mɛɬt ... dæʊn W Do Ha, *prppl* mɛɬtɪn ... dæʊn So, *-ing* mɛltɪn dæʊn So, mɛɬt ... daʊn So, mɛɬt ... dɑʊn O, mɛɬt ... dʌʊn Brk, mɛɬt ... dəʊn Mon Gl, mɛɬʔ ... dəʊn W, mɛᵁɬt ... dɛʊn Ess, mɛʊɬt ... dæʊn Sr, mɛʊt ... dæʊn Sr Ha, mɛʊt ... daʊn So, məɬt ... dæʏn So D

melting *v-ing* THAWING, referring to snow VII.6.15. mɛltn Nb, mɛɬtɪn So W, mɛɬʔɪn Bk, mɛɬʔn Ess, məɬtɪn D

mending *v-ing* DARNING V.10.1. mɛndɪn Ch MxL

mental *adj* STUPID VI.1.5. mɛntʰəl Mon

mere 1. *n* a POOL on a farm III.3.9. miːə St, mɪə Db

2. *n* a POND IV.1.5. mɪə Db

merry-bone *n* a WISH-BONE IV.6.22. məɹɪbean We, maɹɪbʊən Y

merry-thought *n* a WISH-BONE IV.6.22. mɛɹɪθɔːt Sa Wa

mess *n* **make a mess (of/on)**; **make a tidy mess** to DIRTY a floor V.2.8. meːk ə mɛs W Ha, *?ptppl* mɛɪd ə meːs Sr, mɛɪk ə mɛəs Sx, mɛɪk ə mɛs əv St, mɛk ə mɛs ɒn Sa, *pt* mɪəd ə mɛs ɒn Y; meːk ə tɒɪdɪ mɛs Ha

messed up *adj* STICKY, describing a child's hands VIII.8.14. mɛst ʊp Y Lei

mess off *imp* GO AWAY! VIII.7.9(a). mɛs ɒf Ch, mɛs ɔf La, mɛs ɔːᵊf Sf

mess up *vtphr* to DIRTY a floor V.2.8. mɛs ... ʌp Nf Ess MxL So, mɛs ... ʌpʔ Nf, mɛs ... ʊp Cu Du Ch

messy *adj* STICKY, describing a child's hands VIII.8.14. meːɪsɪ So, mɛsɪ La Ha

mew *1. vi-3prpl* [*Now tell me your words for the usual cries animals make.*] *Cats....* III.10.6. miːʊ Co, mɪʏːz O, mjʏː So D, mɪʊ Sx, mɪuː Nb Cu Du La Y Db O Nt L Nth Hu C Sf Bk Bd Ess Sr, mɪuːz Sa He Sx, mɪuːz Cu La Db L Sr, mjuː Cu Nf W Brk Sr K Sx, mjuːz W, mjuːz Y Ch Brk K, mjəʊz Brk, mʊuz Y, muː K, məʊˈ Nf, məuːz K, məʊɪ Hrt. ⇒ **mawl, miaow, mow, row, scrawl, squall, squawk, wow, yawl, yell, yow, yowl**
2. vi-3prpl they MOO, describing the noise cows make during feeding time in the cow-house III.10.4(a). mjuː W, mjuːz Ch Ha [*not a WMBM headword*]
3. vi-3prpl they MOO, describing the noise cows make in the fields III.10.4(b). mjuː W, mjuːz Ha

mewt *n* a NEWT IV.9.8. mjæʊt Wo Gl, mjuːt Wo

miaow *vi-3prpl* they MEW, referring to cats III.10.6. mɪʏːz O, mɪɛʊ Y Ess, mɪɛʊz Sa, mɪɛʊz Y Db Wa Ha, mjɛʊ La Y Wa Nth Sf, mjɛʊz Y Wa, mɪæʊ Y St R Sr, *inf* mɪæʊ Sa, mɪæʊz Sa He Wo Mon, mɪæʊz Ha, mɪæʊs Man, mɪjæʊz He, *-ing* mɪæuːwən Man, mjæʊ He Wa Gl Do Ha, mjæʊz Mon Gl, mɪaʊ Nb Cu We La Sa St O Lei R MxL So W K Do, mɪaʊz Sa Wo, mɪaʊz Du We Y Ch Sa Wo Bk, mɪjaʊz Wo, mjaʊ Du Ch St Wo Wa Gl O W D Do Ha, mjæʊz Ch, mjaʊz Db He Wa Gl Sr, mɪaʊ Nf, mjaʊ Nf, mɪɒʊ Cu Nf, mjɒʊ Gl Nf, mjɒʊz Gl, mɪɔʊ Nb, mɪɔʊz Y, mjɔʊ Y, mɪ-ʌʊ Nf, ˌmjuːˈaʊz Y, mɛæʊ Brk K, mɛˈaʊ St, mwaːz He

mice *n* a MOUSE IV.5.1(b). miːs Ess, maɪs Hrt

mice(s) *npl What do you call the small animals that cats are fond of catching?* IV.5.1(a)
no -s: Eng
-s: miːsɪz Ess, maɪsɪz Co, mɑˈɪsɪz R
⇒ **mouses**; ⇒ also **michaels**

michael *n* STRING used to tie up a grain-sack I.7.3. maɪkl We, maɪkəl We [*apparently trade name*]

michaels *npl* house-mice, ⇐ MICE IV.5.1(a). mɑɪkɬz K

michael-string *1. n* STRING used to tie up a grain-sack I.7.3. maɪklstɹɪŋ Cu

2. n string used to bind sheaves of corn. maɪklstɹɪŋ Cu
[*apparently trade name*]

midden *1. n* a CESS-POOL on a farm I.3.11. mɪdɪn La, mɪdn Nb
2. n a dunghill into which urine drained. mɪdɪn Y Ch, mɪdn Db [*1. and 2. may be the same*]
3. n an ASH-MIDDEN V.1.14. mɪdɪn Cu La Y Wa, mɪdn Nb[*old x1*] Du, mɛdn Man

midden-doors *n* the FLAP at the front of old-fashioned trousers VI.14.16. mɪdɪndɔəɹz La

midden-hole *n* an ASH-MIDDEN V.1.14. mɪdɪnʊəl La

midden-stead *n* a CESS-POOL on a farm I.3.11. mɪdɪnstiːd Cu, mɪdɪnstɛd La

midden-sump *n* a CESS-POOL on a farm I.3.11. mɪdnsʊmp Cu

middle *1. n* **middle of my/thy* hand** the PALM of the hand VI.7.5. mɪdl ə mɪ and We, mɪdɬ ə mɪ hæn So, mɪdl ə ðɪ ænd Y, mɪdl ə ðɪ and Db *[*[ðɪ] taken as **your** BM]*
2. n **in the middle** AMONG IX.2.12. ɪn ðə mɪdʊɬ K

middle-marsh *n* LOW-LYING LAND IV.1.7. mɪdl̩mɑˡːʃ L

middle whipper *n* an EVENER, the main swingle-tree of a horse-drawn plough harness I.8.4. mɪdl wɪpəˡ O

middling *1. adj* very WELL, describing a healthy person VI.13.1(a). mɪdlɪn Db
2. adj ILL, describing a person who is unwell VI.13.1(b). mɪdlɪŋ St, mɪdlɪn Nb La Y Sa St He Wo Wa O Nth Bk Bd So, mɪdlɪn Y, mɪdɬɪn He Mon Gl Nth, mɪdəlɪn Mon, mɪdəɬɪn He; **very middling** vɛɹɪ mɪdlɪn Sa; **middling fair** mɪdɬɪn fæɪəˡ Gl
3. adj SICK, describing an animal that is unwell VI.13.1(c). mɪdlɪn La Y Ch St Wa Gl O
4. n A LOT (of money) VII.8.7. mɪdlɪn La[*bilberries*] Y

middlings *n* MEAL V.6.1(b). mɪdɬɪnz Ha

middy* *n* an EARTH-CLOSET V.1.13. mɪdɪ Wa

midfeather-pole *n* a pole separating two cows in a double cowstall, ⇐ PARTITION I.3.2. mɪdfɛðəpʊ Y

midgens *npl* FLEAS IV.8.4. mɪdʒəns Man

midgets *npl* FLEAS IV.8.4. mɪdʒɪts Brk

midst *n* **in the midst of** AMONG IX.2.12. ɪn ðə mɪdst ə W

mig *n* URINE in a cow-house I.3.10. mɪg Y, mɛg Y

mig-hole *n* a CESS-POOL on a farm I.3.11. mɪgʊəl Y

might *vaux-3sg Smith said to you: It didn't rain yesterday, though you thought it would. You said:*

True, but it very easily ... have done. IX.4.14. Eng. ⇒ **could**, **may**, **mud**, **would**

mighty *adv* VERY VIII.3.2. meıtı Man, mʌytı O, məıtı Sx

mig-tank *n* a CESS-POOL on a farm I.3.11. mıgtaŋk Y

milch-cows *npl* COWS III.1.1(a). mılʃkuːz Y, mıʊtʃkɛʊz Sx

mildewed *adj* RANCID, describing bacon V.7.9. mıldɵːd Nf

milk-bag *n* the UDDER of a cow III.2.5. mılkbæg Nf, mıɫkbæːg Ess

milk-bonnet *n* a woman's BONNET VI.14.1. mılkbɔnıt L

milk-bowl *n* a SALTING-TROUGH III.12.5. mılkbaʊl Du *[presumably = a milk-bowl used as a salting-trough]*

milk-cow *n* a COW III.1.1(b). mılkkuː Y

milk-cows *npl* COWS III.1.1(a). mılkkuːz Y

milk curds *n* CURDS V.5.8(a). mıɫkkṛıdz D

milk-dairy *n* the DAIRY on a farm V.5.1. mılkdɪˑəɹı L, mılkdɛˑəɹı Y L

milk-gathering *n* a WHITLOW VI.7.12. mıɫkgaðəᶜːṛın So*[caused by milking x1]*

milk-house *1. n* a PANTRY V.2.6. mılkæˑəs La*[on farm]*, mılkaıs Ch, mılkhuːs Nb*[combined with dairy x1]* Cu, mılkəs Nb Cu*[old x1, in farmhouse x1]* Du*[old x1]* We*[old]* Y*[old and rare x1]*

2. n the DAIRY on a farm V.5.1. mıɫkɛʊs Ha, mılkæʊs Y, mılkæˑəs La, mılkaıs Ch*[on cheese-making farm x1]*, mılkaʊs La Ch Sa*[old x1]* St, mıɫkʊs Gl, mılkhuːs Nb Cu, mılkuːs Y, mılkəs Nb*[old x2]* Cu Du We Y Db, mıɫkæʊs Do, məɫkæʊs Do

milking *1. n* the YIELD of milk from a cow III.3.5. mılkın Cu La Y Sa Wo Gl, mılkən Nb, mıɫkın He Wo Gl MxL

2. n the yield of milk from a herd of cows. mılkın Sa Wo, mıɫkın He Wo Gl

3. n a yield of milk. mılkın Cu We LaSa, mılkən Sa, mıɫkın Mon Gl

milking-buffet *n* a MILKING-STOOL III.3.3. mılkınbʊfıt Y

milking-byre *n* a COW-HOUSE I.1.8. mıɫkınbæıəᶜ Brk

milking-dairy *n* the DAIRY on a farm V.5.1. *pl* mılkındɪˑəɹız L

milking parlour *n* a COW-HOUSE I.1.8. mıɫkʔn paːlə Ess

milking-stool *n* When he [the cowman] milked them [the cows], what did he sit on? III.3.3. mılkınstɪəl Y, mılkınstıul Y, mılkınstᶦuːl Db, mılkınstɤː La Ch Db, mılkınstɛʊl Db, mılkınstʊl Cu Sa, mılkınstou La, mılkınstʊıl Y, mılkınstʊəl Y, mılkınstuːl La Y Ch Db Sa Wo Mon L, mılkənstuːl Man Sa L, mılkınstuːəl Sa, mılkınstuːɫ Sa Wo Lei R, mılkınstuː La Ch Brk, mılkınstɵːɫ Lei, mılkŋstuːᵊɫ Ess, mıɫkənstɣːɫ D, mıɫkınstɒʊɫ K, mıɫkınstuːl Mon, mıɫkınstuːɫ Wa Nth Bk MxL Brk K Ha, mıɫkənstuːɫ Co Ha, mıɫknstuːɫ C Ess, mıɫʔnstuːɫ Ess, mıɫkınstuːᵊɫ Wa O Ess, mıɫkınstuːəɫ W, mıɫknstuːᵊɫ Ess, mıɫkənstuːᵊɫ Hu Ess Do Ha, mıɫkınstuːʊ Ess Brk Sx, mıɫkʔnstʊu: Ess, mıɫkınstɵːɫ Lei, mıʊɫkınstuːʊ Ha, mıʊkınstuːɫ K, mıʊkınstuːʊ Ess Sr K Sx, mıʊknstʊuʊ Ess, mɛɫkınstuːɫ Brk K, mʊʊlknstuːl Nf, məɫkınstɣːɫ D, məɫkınstɣːəɫ So, məɫkınstuːəɫ W Do; **three-legged milking-stool** θɹiːlɛgd mılkınstuːɫ L, θɹiːlɛgıd mılkınstuːl Wa. ⇒ **buffet**, **coppy**, **coppy-stool**, **cow-stool**, **cracket**, **four-legged stool**, **hummock**, **little stool**, **milking-buffet**, **milk-stool**, **stool**, *three-legged* milking-stool, three-legged milk-stool, three-legged stool

milk-lead *n* a SALTING-TROUGH III.12.5. mılklıəd La, mıɫklɛd Bk *[presumably = a milk-lead used as a salting-trough]*

milk-man *n* a COWMAN on a farm I.2.3. mılkmn̩ Nf, mıɫkmən Sf

milk-parlour *n* the DAIRY on a farm V.5.1. mılkpaːlə Y

milk-rising* *n* a WHITLOW VI.7.12. *pl* mıɫkṛɒızınz So, *pl* mıɫkṛəızınz Do

milk-shed *1. n* a COW-HOUSE which is open at the back I.1.8. mıɫkʃɛd Nth

2. n the DAIRY on a farm V.5.1. mılkʃɛd Db

milk-stool *n* a MILKING-STOOL III.3.3. mılkstıəl Y, mılkstuːl Man, mıɫkstuːɫ Nth

milk-water *n* WHEY V.5.8(b). mılkwɔtˀə Nf

millwright *n* a WRIGHT VIII.4.4. mılɹiːt Cu Du, mılʁɛıt Nb Du, mılɹɛıt Cu Db, mılɹaıt Cu Du St L, mılɹɑıt Du La Y, mıɫɹaıt Ess, mıʊɹɑıt K, mıɫɹɔıt Wa Sf Ess Brk, mıɫɹɔıʔ Bk Hrt, mıʊɹɔıt Sr Sx, mıəɫṛɔıt Ha, mılɹʌıt Nf, mıʊɫɹʌıt Brk, mılɹᵊıˑt We, mıɫɹəıt Brk, mıʊɹəıt Brk Sx

mimseys *npl* MINNOWS IV.9.9. mımzız Co

mind *1. v* LOOK AFTER VIII.1.23. mɛınd Nb Du*[probably old]*, mæːn D, mæınd Du*[old]* He, mæın Man, maːnd Y, maːn Y Co D, maınd Cu Du We Y Ch Db Sa He L*[old x1]* So K, maın We Sa Co, maːn Y, mɑːn D, mɑınd La L Lei R Hu C Ess MxL K, mɒınd St Wo So W Do, mɒın Sa Wo Ha, mɔınd St Wo Wa Nf Ess Brk Sr Ha Sx, mɔın Bk Ess, mʌınd Nf Sf, -*ing* mʌındın Sr, məınd He Wo Gl W Brk Do Sx, məın Gl W

2. vt-2prsg do you REMEMBER? VIII.3.7. mɛınd Nb Du, mæːn D, mæınd Du So, maːnd Y, maːn Co D, maınd Cu Du We, maın Co, mɑːn Co D, mɑınd Ess, mɒınd So Ha, mɒın Co, mɔınd Ha*[old]*, mʌınd Gl Nf

3. vi to DUCK VIII.7.8. mɔınd Hrt *[marked u.r. EMBM]*

mind of *vtphr-2prsg* do you REMEMBER? VIII.3.7. mɛɪnd ə Nb, maɪnd ə Cu

mind on *vtphr-2prsg* do you REMEMBER? VIII.3.7. mɛɪn ɒn Cu

mingies *npl* MINNOWS IV.9.9. mɪndʒiːz So D, mɪndʒɪz Co D

minging-dish *n* a BREAD-BIN V.9.2. mɪŋɪndɪʃ Nf

minnies *npl* MINNOWS IV.9.9. mɪniːs So, mɪniːz So W D Do Ha, mɪnɪs La So, mɪnɪz Y Ch Db He Wo Wa Mon Gl O Nt Lei R Nth Sf Ess Brk Co D Sx, mɪmɪz Ess, mɛnɪz Y *[taken as minnows N/WMBM]*

minnims *npl* MINNOWS IV.9.9. mɪnɪnz Hrt, mɪnəmz Nb Cu Du La Sf Co, *sg* mɪnəm Y, mɛnəmz Nb Du We

minnits *npl* MINNOWS IV.9.9. mɪnɪts Mon

minnows *npl* What do you call those small fish in rivers that children like to catch with glass jars? IV.9.9. mɪns So, mɪniːs So, mɪniːz So W D Do Ha, mɪnɪs La So, mɪnɪz Cu Du Y Ch Db He Wo Wa Mon Gl O Nt Lei R Nth Sf Ess Brk Co D Sx, mɪmɪz Ess*[old]*, mɪnɒuz K Sx, mɪnoːz Sa He Mon Gl W D Ha, mɪnouz Nth So Brk Ha, mɪnoːuz Gl, mɪnuz Ch, mɪnəz Du We La Y Ch Db Sa St He Wa Mon O Nt L Nth Nf Bd Hrt Ess So Co, mɪnədz Nth, mɪnəɹz La Y Brk, mɪnəˡz O, mɪnəˡz̩ He O Bk*[3 inches long]* K, mɪnəˡːz̩ Sa Ha, mɛnɪz Y, mɛnəz Y, mɛnədz Y, maɪnəz St. ⇒ **ban-stickles, bantams, banty-tickles, battle-heads, bottle-fish, brick-frothers, bricks, bull-heads, bullies, bunny-stickles, daddy-roughs, gudgeons, jack-bannocks, jack-sharps, liggies,** *little fish,* **mimseys, mingies, minnies, minnims, minnits, pallies, pennywinkles, pin-heads, pinks, prickly-backs, pricky-backs, shrimps, sickle-backs, silver-bellies, soldiers, sparlings, spriddle-backs, squibs, stannicles, stan-sickles, sticklebacks, stricklebacks, striddle-backs, struts, stuts, stuttle, stuttle-fish, tan-tickles, tiddle-brats, tiddlers, tiddles, tin-tattles, tittle-brats, tittlers, tommy-lie-lodgers, tommy-loachers, tommy-lodgers, tommy-minnims, whirligigs;** ⇒ also **strut**

mint *n* a mint A LOT (of money) VII.8.7. ə mɪnt Cu

mire *n* MUD VII.6.17. maɪˡ Y

mires *n* LOW-LYING LAND IV.1.7. maɪəz We

miry *adj* BOGGY IV.1.8. maɪəɹɪ Cu

mischief *n* making **mischief** GOSSIPING VIII.3.5(a). makɪn mɪstʃiːf Y

mischiefful *adj* ACTIVE, describing a child VIII.9.1. mɪstʃɪfəł Ess, mɪstɪfʊl W *[marked u.r. EM/SBM]*

mischief-maker *n* a GOSSIP VIII.3.5(b). mɪstʃiːfmakə Y

mischievous *adj* ACTIVE, describing a child VIII.9.1. mɪstʃɪvəs Lei So, mɪs'tʃɪ·vəs Nf, mɪstʃiːvɪəs R *[marked u.r. EM/SBM]*

mise* *v* to hoard money, ⇐ MISER VII.8.9. maɪz Ess

miser *n* What do you call a man who has a lot of money, but still goes on saving every penny? VII.8.9. Eng. ⇒ **hoarder, miserd, scrawmer, screw, screwer, scrounger, skinflint, skinger, skinner,** *a* **tight one;** ⇒ also **craven, hungry, mise, near, niggardly**

miserable 1. *adj* DULL, referring to the weather VII.6.10. mɪzɹʊbl La, mɪzəɹəbl Y, mɪzɹəbl Y L Nth, mɪzɹəbɫ Bd Hrt MxL, mɪzəbɫ Ess *[marked as emotive and therefore u.r. N/EMBM]*

2. *adv* VERY VIII.3.2. mɪzəˡɾəbɫ Ha

miserd *n* a MISER VII.8.9. mæɪzəˡːd̩ D, maːzək La, maɪzəd Y, maɪzət Cu, maɪzəˡːd̩ D, maɪzəˡːt̩ Sa, mɑːzəɹt La, mɑ·ɪzəd L, mɒɪzʊd Wo, mɒɪzəˡːd̩ Wo, məɪzəˡd̩ He G *[not a NBM headword]*

misfluke *n* the miscarriage of a foal, ⇐ SLIP A FOAL III.4.6. mɪsfluːk Sx

misk *n* MIST VII.6.8. mɪsk O So W Do

mislaid *adj* OVERTURNED, describing a sheep on its back unable to get up III.7.4. mɪsleɪd K, mɪslæɪd K

missed *vi-ed* HAS NOT HELD, referring to a cow that has not conceived III.1.7. mɪst Nb Du La Y Man St L Ess Brk K Sx; **missed holding** mɪst ɔʊdɪn La

missis 1. *n* my WIFE VIII.1.24. **missis** mɪsɪs Co, mɪsɪz Y St Co; **my missis** maː mɪsɪs Y, *poss* maɪ mɪsɪsɪz Db, maːɪ mɪsɪs St, mɑɪ mɪsɪs Ch L, mɔɪ mɪsɪs O, məɪ mɪsəs W, mɔɪ mɪsʊs Brk, mɪ mɪsɪz Wa Lei, mæ mɪsɪz Sx, maɪ mɪsɪz Y He Lei, mɒɪ mɪsɪz Co, mʌɪ mɪsɪz Brk; **our missis** æˡː mɪsɪz La; **the missis** ðɪ mɪsɪs Nth, ðə mɪsɪs Nb Du La Y Ch Sa St He Wo Wa Mon Gl O Nt L Nth Hu C Nf Sf Bk Bd Hrt Ess So W Sr Co D Do Ha, ð, mɪsɪs Ch Db St, t mɪsɪs Cu Du We La Y Db Nt L, ʔ mɪsɪs La, ðə mɪsʊs Brk*[old]*, ðə mɪsəs Sf Bk Ess MxL Sr, ðə mɪsɪz La Ch St He Wo Mon O L Lei R Nth Hu C Nf Sf Bk Hrt Ess MxL So W Brk D Do Ha, t mɪsɪz La Y Ch Db, ʔ mɪsɪz Y, ðə mɪsəz O Sf Sx, ðə mɪzɪs So, ðə mɪzɪz Ess D Do, ðə mɛsɪz W, ðə məsɪs So W Co, ðə məsɪz D Do Ha, ðə məzɪs So, ðə məzɪz So

2. *n* a TEACHER VIII.6.5. mɪsɪs We So *[not a NBM headword]*

mist 1. *n* In patches of low-lying ground near rivers, what do you sometimes see, especially in the early morning or the evening? VII.6.8. ⇒ **bottom-mist, dag, damp, fog, ground-mist, haze, misk, murk, murky, racks, rawk, rime, steam;** ⇒ also **haigiemint**

2. *n* FOG VII.6.9. mɪst Nb Y

3. *n* a HALO round the moon VII.6.4. mɪst Gl

mistall *n* a COW-HOUSE I.1.8. mɪstəl Y, mɪstl Y

mistress 1. *n* my WIFE VIII.1.24. **the mistress** ðə mɪstrəs Cu*[old]*, ðə mɪstʀəs Nb, ðə mɪstɹəs

Nb*[very old]*; **my mistress** mɒɪ mɪstəs K *[taken as missis SBM]*

2. *n* a TEACHER VIII.6.5. mɪstrɪs Cu, mɪstɹɪs Ess

Mistress *n* MRS. VIII.2.3(a). mɪstʁəs Nb Du*[very rare x1]*, mɪstɹəs Nb

mite *n* a PINCH of sugar VII.8.6. mɒːɪt St

mittens 1. *n* GLOVES VI.14.7. mɪtənz Y, mɪtnz So, mɪʔnz L*[with half-fingers]*So K

2. *n* gloves with only the thumb separate. mɪtɪnz Ch Sa St He Wo, mɪtnz Mon Nf MxL, mɪʔnz O L Hrt

3. *n* gloves with only thumb and index finger separate. mɪtənz Nf

[It is likely that forms in 1. above generally refer to gloves without separate fingers, as in 2. and 3.]

mittful *n* a HANDFUL VII.8.10(a). mɪtfʊl Y

mitts* *n* GLOVES with only the thumb separate VI.14.7. mɪts St, mɪəts Ess

mivet *n* a MOUSE IV.5.1(b). mɪvət Sf *[queried BM]*

mix 1. *n* COW-DUNG I.3.12. mɪs So

2. *v* to KNEAD dough V.6.4. mɪks Db K

mixen 1. *n* an artificial CESS-POOL in a farm-yard I.3.11. mɪksn Do

2. *n* a dunghill into which urine drained on a farm. mɪksn Ch Sa, mɪksən Sa He *[1. and 2. may be the same]*

3. *n* COW-DUNG I.3.12. mɪksən K, mæksn K, mæksɪm K

4. *n* a dung-heap. mɪksən So, mæksən K

5. *n* a hole beneath and behind an EARTH-CLOSET V.1.13. mɪskɪn Wa

6. *n* an ASH-MIDDEN V.1.14. mɪksn St, mɪskɪn St Wa, mɪksn So, mɪksən Sa He Do, mʌksən So

mixen-hole 1. *n* a hole in a straw-yard on a farm, into which urine drained instead of into a CESS-POOL I.3.11. mɪksɹ̩ɒːl Sa

2. *n* an ASH-MIDDEN V.1.14. mɪksɪnoʊl Wa

mixing-pan *n* a round metal container with handles, for carrying horse-feed, ⇐ BASKET III.5.4. mɪksɪnpan Sa

mix up *vtphr* to KNEAD dough V.6.4. mɪks ... ʊp Y, *2prpl* mɪksɪz ... ʊp Wo

mizzen* *n* an EARTH-CLOSET V.1.13. mɪzən He

mizzle *imp* GO AWAY! VIII.7.9(a). mɪzl L

moal 1. *adj* ILL, describing a person who is unwell VI.13.1(b). mɔːl Man

2. *adj* WEAK, describing a person who has been ill VI.13.2. mɔːl Man

moan 1. *vi-3prpl* bulls BELLOW III.10.2. mɔːn Nf

2. *vi-3prpl* they WHINNY, describing the noise horses make during feeding time in the stable III.10.3(a). moʊn Nth

3. *vi-3prpl* they MOO, describing the noise cows make during feeding time in the cow-house III.10.4(a). mɪ·ən Y, mɪʊn Cu Du, *prppl* mɔənɪn Y, mɔːn La Gl, moʊn Wa, mʊən Du, mʊənz Cu, *-ing* mʊənɪn*[low noise made by over-fed cows x1, made by cows being fattened for slaughter x1]*

4. *vi-3prpl* they MOO, describing the noise cows make in the fields III.10.4(b). mɔːnz Sa

moan out *viphr-3prpl* they MOO, describing the noise cows make during feeding time in the cow-house III.10.4(a). *-ing* mɔənən aʊt Y

mobs *npl* BLINKERS covering the eyes of a cart-horse I.5.2. mɒbz Y, mɔbz Y

mochyns *npl* PIGS III.8.1. mɒkɪnz Ch

mock *n* a TUSSOCK of grass II.2.9. mɒk Do; **mock of grass** mɒk ə gɹæːs So, mɒk ə gɹaːs So Do

model *n* a copy, referring to someone who RESEMBLES someone else VIII.1.9. mɒdəl Y

moggy 1. *n* a SCARECROW II.3.7. mɒgɪ Hu Bd

2. *n* a TABBY-CAT, the female cat III.13.9. mɒgɪ Nf

moke *n* a DONKEY III.13.16. mɪʊːk Db, mɔːk La Y, mɔʊk L, mʌʊk Bk Bd Hrt Ess, moːk W, moʊk Db St He O Sf K, mʊək L

mokus *n* a DONKEY III.13.16. mɔːkəs Do, moːkʌs Co D Do, moːkəs Ha, moːks Ha

molars *npl* *What do you call the teeth at the back?* VI.5.7. møːləz Nb, *sg* mæʊlə Hrt, mɒləz Sa, mɒʊlɛz K, mɒʊɫɛz K, mɒʊləˤz Sx, mɒʊtəˤz Sr, mɔːlæs Man, mɔːləz Nb Y L Ess, mɔːləˠz Brk, mɔːləɹz La Y, mɔːɫəˤz He, mɔːləˤːz Sa, mʌʊləz Ess*[modern]*, mʌʊɫəz MxL, moːləz Mon, moːləɹz La, moːləˤːz Sa, mʊələz Y, *sg* mʊələ L, mʊələ˥z La. ⇒ **axles, axle-teeth, back-teeth, chewers, chock-teeth, chop-teeth, double-knappers,** *double ones*, **double-teeth, eye-teeth, grinders, hollow-teeth, jacks, jack-teeth, jaw-teeth, large tooth, mole-teeth, mummers, mushers, tuck,** *tushies, wisdom, wisdom-teeth*

mole *n* *What do you call the animal that throws up small mounds of earth in the fields?* IV.5.4. Eng exc. Nb Cu Du We Mon Gl Nt. ⇒ **mole-warp, mould, mouldard, moulden, mouldwarp, mouldy, mouldy-rat, mouldy-warp, mouldy-worm, mouly, mouly-rat, mouly-warp, unt, want, yule**

mole-mouse *n* a SHREW-MOUSE IV.5.2. mæɣəɫmævz D, mɒʊlmɛʊs K, *pl* mɒʊɫmɒɪs K, mɒʊmɛʊs Sr, moːəlmæʊs Man

mole-teeth *npl* MOLARS VI.5.7. mɔːɫtɹiθ Brk

mole-warp* *n* a MOLE IV.5.4. *pl* mæʊlwaːps Y, mɒʊlwæ˥ːɹp La, mɒʊlwaːp Y

mommet *n* a SCARECROW II.3.7. mɒmɪt Wo Gl So W D, mɒmɪk So, mɒmət So D

money *n* *A man is rich when he has (a lot of)* .... VII.8.7. Eng. ⇒ **brads, brass, cash, dough, kelt, rattle**

money-dust *n* ASHES from a cold fire V.4.5. mʌnidʌst Nf*[facetious]* *[marked u.r. EMBM]*

mong *prep* AMONG IX.2.12. mɒŋ Sx, mɔŋ L, mʌŋ Nf Co, mʊŋ Nth Sf *[not a SBM headword]*

mongrel *n What do you call a dog with half a dozen breeds in it?* III.13.5. mœŋgʀəl Nb, maŋəɹəl Nb, mɒŋgə˥l Nf, mɒŋgɹl Nf, mɒŋgɹɪl Y Sa, mɒŋɪɹl Y, mɒŋgəɹɪl La, mɒŋgɹʊɫ K, mɒŋgrəl Man, mɒŋəɹ| Cu, mɒŋʀəl Nb, mɒŋgʀəl Du, mɒŋgəʀəl Du, mɒŋgɹəl Du La Y Sa Nf K, mɒŋgɹəɫ He Wa Gl O Nth K Ha, mɒŋgɹəɫz Brk, mɒŋəɹəl Cu Du, mɒŋgɹəɫ So Do, mɒŋgɹɪl L, mɔŋgʀəl Nb, mɒŋɹəl L, mʌŋgʌɫ W, *pl* mʌŋgʊz Sx, mʌŋgəl Nf Sx, mʌŋgəɫ O Hrt Ess D Ha, mʌŋgɫ Bd, mʌŋgɹɪl Sa, mʌŋgɹʊɫ Hrt, mʌŋgɹʊ Ess Brk Sr Sx, mʌŋəʀəl Nb, mʌŋɹəɫ Mon Hu, mʌŋgɹl Nf, mʌŋgɹəl Mon Nf mʌŋgɹəɫ He O Lei R Nth Hu C Sf Bk Bd Hrt Ess MxL Brk K Sx, mʌŋgɽl Ess, mʌŋgɽəɫ So W Sr Co D Do Ha, mʌŋgɽɫ K, mʏŋgəl Nf, mʊŋɹɪl Y Ch St L, mʊŋgɹɪl La Y Ch Db Sa St Wo Nt L, mʊŋgɹɪɫ Wo Lei, mʊŋəɹɪl La Y L, mʊŋgɹɪl Y, mʊŋgɹʊɫ Brk, mʊŋgrəl Man, mʊŋərəl Cu, mʊŋɹəl Cu, mʊŋʀəl Nb, mʊŋəʀəl Nb, mʊŋɹəl La Y L, mʊŋgɹəl Du La Ch Db St Wa Nt L, mʊŋgɹəɫ Ch He Wo Wa Mon Gl O Lei C Bk, mʊŋəɹəl Cu We La Y, mʊŋəɹəɫ Wo Wa, mʊŋgɹəl Y Sa L, mʊŋgəɹɫ Lei, mʊŋgɽəɫ O So Co, məŋɹəl Gl, məŋgɹəɫ Gl. ⇒ **cur, cur-dog**

mongst *prep* AMONG IX.2.12. mɒŋst Brk K, mɒŋgst K, mʌŋst Ess Sr K Sx, mʌŋs W Sr Co D, mʊŋst Nt; **in mongst** ɪn mɒŋst Sr, ɪn mʌŋst Sr Sx, ɪn mʌŋs Co *[not a SBM headword]*

monkey-board *n* a CART-FRAME I.10.6. mɒŋkibɔəd Nf

monkeys *n* a children's word for DREGS left at the bottom of a teacup V.8.15. mʊŋkɪz Du

monstrous *adv* VERY VIII.3.2. mʌnʃəz D

moo *1. vi-3prpl [Now tell me your words for the usual cries animals make.] Cows, during feeding-time in the cow-house, ...* III.10.4(a). Eng exc. Cu We Co. ⇒ **bawk, bawl, beal, belder out, bell, bellock, bellow, belve, blare, blare out, blart, blate, bleat, blore, blort, boo, brawl, burr, call, elve, grain, grunt on, holler, *hollo* ⇒ holler, hum, low, maw, mew, moan, moan out, *moon* ⇒ moan, moonge, mumble, murmur, murr, nim *themselves*, rawt, roar, sing**

2. vi-3prpl [Now tell me your words for the usual cries animals make. Cows, during feeding-time in the cow-house, ...] And in the fields, and when they want attention, they .... III.10.4(b). mʏː D, mɒʊ St, mou La, *-ing* mʊˈɪn Y, muː Nb La Y Man St O L Lei R Nth Nf Bk Ess So W Brk K Do Ha Sx, muːz Sa He Wo Mon Gl MxL Sr, muˈə Y. ⇒ **baw, bawk, bawl, beal, belder out, bell, bellock, bellow, bellow about, belve, blake, blake out, blare, blart, blate, blate out, bleat, blore, blort, blother, blow, boller, brawl, call, croon, elve, groan, holler, *hollo* ⇒ holler, hoot, low, maw, mew, moan, rawt, roar**

3. vi-3prpl bulls BELLOW III.10.2. mʌʊ Ess, muː Ess Do

moody *adj* ILL, describing a person who is unwell VI.13.1(b). muːdi So

mooldy *1. n* a HORNLESS cow III.2.9. muːɫdi Co

2. adj hornless, describing a cow. muːɫdi Co

moonge *vi-3prpl* they MOO, describing the noise cows make during feeding time in the cow-house III.10.4(a). mɪənʒ We, meənʒ We, muːndʒ Nb, muːnʒ Nb Du We

moont* *v* to ROOT, what a pig does when it digs the ground with its snout III.9.2. *-ing* mʊntɪn Mon

moorbird* *n* a grouse, ⇐ BIRDS IV.6.1. mʊəbəːd Y

moor-land *n* LOW-LYING LAND IV.1.7. mɔəlænd Nf

moors *n* LOW-LYING LAND IV.1.7. moˈəz Ch, muːəᵗːz̩ So

moot *1. v* to ROOT, what a pig does when it digs the ground with its snout III.9.2. muːt He Mon Gl, *-ing* muːtɪn So

2. n a POND IV.1.5. muːt Brk

3. n a tree STUMP IV.12.4. mʏːt D, muːt So Brk D

mop *1. n* a TUSSOCK of grass II.2.9. mɒp So D; **mop of grass** mɒp ə gɹæːs So, mɒp ə gɹaːs So W D

2. n HAIR VI.2.1. mɔp Wa

3. n a local FESTIVAL or holiday VII.4.11. mɒp Wo O W, mɔp Wo Wa

mop off *vtphr* to CLEAR grass at the edges of a field with a scythe II.9.5. mɒp ... ɔˈf Nf

moppers *npl* BLINKERS covering the eyes of a cart-horse I.5.2. mɒpəᵗːz̩ Co D

mopping* *v-ing* DRINKING beer V.8.1. mɒpɪn He

mopping-halter* *n* a bridle, ⇐ BLINKERS I.5.2. mɒpɪnɔːɫtəᵗːɽ (+V) D

mops *1. npl* BLINKERS covering the eyes of a cart-horse I.5.2. mɒps Co

2. n a HALTER I.3.17. mɒps Co

3. n a bridle. mɒps Co

mopy *adj* COLD, describing a person VI.13.18. moːpi So

more *1. n* a ROOT of a tree IV.12.1. mɒᵗː Co D, *pl* mɒᵗːz̩ So, mɔːəᵗː Do, *pl* mɔːəᵗːz̩ So, *pl* muːɽz̩ D, muəᵗː Co, *pl* muəᵗːz̩ D, *pl* muːəᵗːz̩ So

2. n a tree STUMP IV.12.4. mɔəᵗː Ha

more than *adv* VERY VIII.3.2. mɒᵗː n̩ So

morn *1. n* MORNING VII.3.11(a). maᵗːn So, mɔːn Ess, mɔᴿːʀəᵗn Nb, mɔ˥n Y, mɔən Y

2. n **at morn, in the morn, the morn morning, the morn's morn, the morn's morning, tomorrow morn** TOMORROW MORNING VII.3.13. **at morn** ət mɔən Y; **in the morn** ɪ t mɔᵗn Db, ɪ t mɔən Y; **the morn morning** ðə mɔᴿˈn

263

mɔᴿ·nən Nb; **the morn's morn** ðə mɔᴿːnz mɔᴿːn Nb, ðə mɔʁanz mɔᴿ·ᵊn Nb; **the morn's morning** ðə mɔᴿːnz mœːnən Nb, ðə muəᴿnz muəᴿnɪn Nb; **tomorrow morn** təmɒɹə mɔːn Man, tɪmɒɹə muən Y

3. *n* **the morn** TOMORROW VII.4.1. ðə mɔʁn Nb, ðə mɔʁən Nb, ðə mɔʁːn Nb Du

morning 1. *n What do you call the various parts of the day?* VII.3.11(a). Eng. ⇒ **forenoon, morn**

2. *n* **at morning, early in the morning, first thing in morning, first thing in the morning, in the morning, morrow morning, next morning, the morning, the morrow morning** TOMORROW MORNING VII.3.13. **at morning** ət mɔ·ᵊnən Du, ət muənɪn Y; **early in the morning** əːlɪ ɪ t mɔənɪn Ch; **first thing in morning** fɒst θɪŋ ɪ mɔ·ənɪn Y; **first thing in the morning** fəs θɪŋ ɪn ðə maᵗːn̩ɪn Nth, fɒst θɪŋ ɪ t mɔːnɪn St, fast θɪŋ ɪ t mɔːnɪn Y, fast θɪŋg ɪ ð mɔːnɪn Db, fəᵗşţ θɪŋ ɪn ðə mɔːnɪn K, fəɹst θɪŋ ɪn ðə mɔ·ɹnɪn He, vʌs ðɪŋ ɪn ðə mɔᵗːn̩ən Co, fɒst θɪŋ ɪ t mɔənɪn Y, fəst θɪŋ ɪ t mɔənɪn Y, fast θɪŋ ə t muənɪn Y; **in the morning** ɪn ðə maᵗːn̩ɪn So, ɪn ðə maᵗn̩ɪn Wo, ɪn θ mɔːnɪn La, ɪn ðə mɔːnɪn St Wa L Hu C Bd Ess[old x1] MxL, ɪn ðə mɔːnən Nt C Ess, ɪn ðə mɔːn̩ Sf, ɪn ð mɔːnɪn Db, ɪ ð mɔːnɪn L, ɪn t mɔːnɪn Y Db, ɪ t mɔːnɪn Y Db, ɪ ðə mɔᴶːnɪn L, ɪ t mɔᴶːnɪn Y, ɪn t mɔᴶːɪnɪn La, ɪn ðə mɔᵗːn̩ɪn So, ɪn ðə mɔᵗːᵊnɪn Bk, ɪn ðə mɔːᵊnɪn Nth Bk Hrt, ɪn t mɔːᵊnɪn We, ɪn ðə mɔᵊnɪn L, ɪ t mɔənɪn Y, ɪn t mɔ·ənən Du, ɪ t mɔːəᴶɪnɪn La, ɪn ðə mɔᵗənɪn O, ɪ t muənɪn Y, ɪ ðə mu·əᴿnɪn Nb, ɪn t muəᴶnɪn La; **morrow morning** maᵗː maᵗːn̩ɪn W Do Ha, mɒɹə maᵗːn̩ɪn O W, maɹə maᵗːn̩ən Co, maᵗː maᵗːn̩ən Do Ha, mɒɹə maᵗːn̩ən W, mɔᵗː maᵗːn̩ɪn W, mɒɹə mɔɹn̩ɪn O, mɒɹə mɔᵗːn̩ɪn D, maɹə mɔᵗːn̩ɪn Co, maᵗː mɔᵗːn̩ɪn Co, mɔᵗː mɔᵗːn̩ɪn So D Do Ha, mɒɹə mɔᵗːn̩ən Co, mɔːɹ mɔᵗːn̩ən Sx, mɔᵗːɹəᵗː mɔᵗːn̩ən D, mɔᵗː mɔᵗːn̩ən Co D, mɒɹəᴶ mɔəᴶnɪn Brk, mɒᵗːɹ mɔːəᵗn̩ɪŋ Sx, mɔᵗː muːɹn̩ən D; **next morning** nɛks mɔːnɪn K; **the morning** ðə mɔᴿːnən Nb Du; **the morrow morning** ðə mɒʁə mɔᴿːnən Du, ðə mɒɹə mɔəᴿnɪn Cu, ðə mɒɹə muənɪn Nb

3. *n* THIS FORENOON VII.3.15. mɔːnɪn St, mɔːnən Nf, mɔᵗːn̩ən So; **in the morning** ɪn ðə maᵗːn̩ɪn So, ɪn ðə mɔːnɪn Ess MxL; **mid morning** mɪd mɔənɪn K; **the morning** ðə mɔːnən Ess, ðə mɔᵗənən O

morning-glory *n* BINDWEED II.2.4. mɔᴿːnənglɔːʁɪ Nb, mɔᴶːɹnɪnglɔəɹɪ La

morning-sticks *n* KINDLING-*WOOD* V.4.2. maᵗːn̩ɪnstɪks Sa, mɔːnɪnstɪks Sa, mɔᵗːn̩ɪnstɪks Sa

morning's-wood *n* KINDLING-*WOOD* V.4.2. maᵗːn̩ɪnzwʊd W, maᵗːn̩ɪnzʊd Gl[old], mɔːnɪnzwʊd Ess, mɔᵗːɹn̩ɪnzwʊd Sx

morning-wood *n* KINDLING-*WOOD* V.4.2. maᵗːn̩ɪnʊd Gl, maːnɪnʊd Mon, maᵗːn̩ɪnʊd He Gl, mɔːnɪnwʊd Ess K, məᵗːn̩ɪnʊd He

morphrey *n* a frame with two wheels, attached to a cart to convert it into a wagon, ⇐ CART-FRAME I.10.6. mɒfɹɪ Nf, mɔːfɹɪ Nf, mɔːfɹə Nf

morphreydite *n* a frame with two wheels, attached to a cart to convert it into a wagon, ⇐ CART-FRAME I.10.6. mɔ·fɹɪdʌit Nf

morrow *n* TOMORROW VII.4.1. maɹə W Co, maᵗːɹə W, maːɹə Ess, mɒɹɒʊ Brk, mɒɹɒʊ W Ha, mɒɹə O So Co D, m̩ᵐɒɹə W, mɔᵗː Do Ha; **the morrow** ðə mɒɹə Cu, ðə mɒʁə Du

morsel 1. *n* a SLICE of bread V.6.10. maᵗːşəl Co, *pl* maᵗːşłz̩ Co; **bit of morsel** *n* a bit of bread bɪd ə mɔːsəl Co

2. *n* a PIECE *OF BREAD AND BUTTER* V.6.11(a). mɒsł Co; **bit of morsel** bɪd ə mɒsł Co

3. *n* a SNACK VII.5.11. mɒsł Co

4. *n* a PINCH of salt VII.8.6. mɒsəl Y

mort *n* the FAT round the kidneys of a pig III.12.7. mɔᵗːt Co, mɔᵗːd̩ D

mosses *n* LOW-LYING LAND near the sea IV.1.7. mɒsɪz La

moss-land *n* LOW-LYING LAND IV.1.7. mɒsland Cu

mossro *n* a SHREW-MOUSE IV.5.2. mʊsɹɒʊ St

most *adv* ALMOST VII.7.9. mɔʊs Brk, mʌʊst Ess Sr K, mɔːst Co, mɔːs D, mɔʊst He So, mɔʊəst So; **e'en most** iːn məs Brk[old]

most bad *adjsup* WORST VI.12.5. mʌʊst bɛːd MxL

mother *n* MOTHER VIII.1.1(b). [*Show a picture of a family. Who are the members of this family?*] *Who are the two most important members of a family?* [*father and ...*] VIII.1.1(b). Eng. ⇒ **maw, mayer**

mother-milk *n* BEESTINGS V.5.10. mʌðəᴶmɪʊłk K

mould 1. *n* **mould of grass** a TUSSOCK of grass II.2.9. mɒʊłd ə gɹɛːs Sx

2. *n* a MOLE IV.5.4. maʊld Ch[old], mɒʊld Ch, mɔʊłd Lei, mɔːld Ch, mɔːłd W D Do Ha, mɒʊld So, mɒʊłd Lei So, mɒʊd O

3.1. *vt* to KNEAD dough V.6.4. mɔːłd So, mɒʊłd So [*queried ir.r. SBM*]

3.2. *v* to knead. mʌʊłd Ess

mouldard *n* a MOLE IV.5.4. maːdət La, maːðət La, maːᴶːɹbət La, maʊldəd Y, maʊdət La, maʊdəɹt La

mould-board *n* [*Show a picture of a (horse-drawn) plough.*] *What do you call this* [*indicate the mould-board*]? I.8.8. mɛlbɔːᵊᵗd̩ Sa, mɛʊldbɔ·əd Nf, mæʊłbɔːd Hrt, mæʊːlbɒuəᴶ Man, maːlbɔ·əd Ch, maʊldbœːd Du, maʊldbɔːd Du, maʊlbɔːd Du, maʊlbɔːə Man, maʊlbuəd We Y Ch, maʊdbɔːd Y, maʊdbuəd La, mɒʊlbuəd Y, mɑʊdbɒəd Nb, mɑʊdbuəd Y, mɒʊldbɔːd Nb, mɒʊldbᵂɔrd Cu, mɒʊlbɔᵗːd̩ Sa, mɒʊlbɒəd Nth

K, mɒʊlbʊəd La Db, mɒʊlbərd Cu, mɒʊɬbɔːəᴉd K*[on foot plough]*, mɒʊɬboˑəd Bk Hrt, mɒʊɬbʊˑəᶜd̪ Bk, mɒʊdbɔːd Cu, mɒʊdbɔəd Cu, mɒʊdbɔəd La, mɒʊdbʊəd Cu We La Y, mɔʊldbøəd Nb, mɔʊldbɔᵝːd Nb Du, mɔʊldbʊəd Nb Y, mɔʊlbʊəd Y, mɔʊɬboˑəd Hrt, mɔʊɬdbʊəᴉd O, mɔʊɬbɔːd K, moːlbɔᶜːd̪ Sa, moːlbəᶜd̪ Sa, moːɬbɔᶜːd̪ Ha*[wooden]*, moːɬbɔːəd Mon. ⇒ **bouter, breast, breast-plate, bred, broad-board, broad-plate, broad-side, chip, flay, furrow-board, greeter,** *greet-reest* ⇒ **groot-reest, grooter, groot-reest, ground-reest, land-side, land-slide, mould-bred, mould-cast, moulding-board, mouldy-board, pitch, plat, plate, plough-board, plough-breast, plough-reest, plough-slipe, reest, share-board, shell-band, shell-board, shell-iron, shelve-reest, slipe, swath-board, swath-turner, turn-burrel, turner, turn-furrow, wing**

mould-bred *n* the MOULD-BOARD of a horse-drawn plough I.8.8. mɒʊlbɹeːd Db

mould-cast *n* the MOULD-BOARD of a horse-drawn plough I.8.8. mɒʊɬkaːst C

moulden *n* a MOLE IV.5.4. mɛʊɬdɪn Wa*[old]*

moulding-board *n* the MOULD-BOARD of a horse-drawn plough I.8.8. mɔʊdnbɔːʁd Nb

mould(s) *n* EARTH VIII.5.8.
no -s: mɛʊld Nf, mɛʊl Nf, mɛʊɬd Nf, mæʊl Man, mæʊɬ He Mon*[old]* Gl, mɒʊd Y*[old]*, mɔʊɬ Nth, mɔʊd MxL, moːɬd Mon, moːɬ Mon, moːʊɬd Gl, məʊl Nf, məːʊld Nf
-s: mɛʊɬz Sf

moulds *1. npl* ANT-HILLS IV.8.13. *sg* mɒʊld Nf, *sg* mɔʊld Nf, mʊʊlz Ch
2. n FRECKLES VI.11.1. moːɬdz W

mould up *vtphr* to KNEAD dough V.6.4. mɔːɬd ... ʌp Brk *[queried ir.r. SBM]*

mouldwarp *n* a MOLE IV.5.4. mɔʊldwaːp Y

mouldy *n* a MOLE IV.5.4. mɛʊdɪ Db, maʊdɪ Cu Du We La Y, mɑʊdɪ Nb, mɒʊdɪ Cu We La Y Db, mɔʊldɪ Y, mɔʊdɪ Nb Y

mouldy-board *n* the MOULD-BOARD of a horse-drawn plough I.8.8. maʊdɪbœːd Nb, mɔʊldbɔᵝːd Nb

mouldy-rat *n* a MOLE IV.5.4. mɒʊdɪʁat Du, mɔʊdɪʁat Nb

mouldy-warp *n* a MOLE IV.5.4. mɪʊdɪwaːp Y, mʏːdɪwaᴉːp Db, mɛʊdɪwaːp Nt, mɛʊdɪwɔːp Db St, maʊdɪwæːp Du, maʊdɪwaːp Y*[old x1]*, maʊdɪwaːp Y, *pl* maʊdɪwɔːps St, maʊdɪwaːp Y, mɒʊldɪwaːp Y, mɒʊdɪwaːp Cu Y Db Nt, mɒʊdɪwaᴉːp La, mɒʊdɪwaɪp Nt, mɔʊldɪwaːp Y, mɔʊdɪwaːp Y L Lei R, mɔʊdɪwɔːp R

mouldy-worm *n* a MOLE IV.5.4. maʊdɪwɛᶜːm Sa

moult *1. vi-3prpl When hens start to lose their feathers, you say they ....* IV.6.13. Eng. ⇒ **cast,** *drop into the moult, going into the moult, going into the*

mount, *in the moult, lose their feathers,* **moulter, mount, mounter,** *off into the* **mount,** *on the moult, on the* **mount**
2. n MANGE, which causes dogs and cats to lose their hair III.13.7. muːt Y; **the moult** ðə muːt Nb

moulter *1. n* a ridging PLOUGH I.8.1. muːtəɹ He
2. vi-3prpl they MOULT IV.6.13. *vbln* mʏːʈɾɪn D, *-ing* mʏːʈɾɪn D, *-ing* maʊltɹɪn R, *-ing* maːltəᶜʈɾɪn Gl, *-ing* mɒltəɹɪn Lei, *prppl* əmɒltəɹɪn Lei, *-ing* mɒʊɬtəɹɪn Gl, *-ing* mɔʊltɹɪn L, *-ing* mɔʊltɹən L, *-ing* mɔʊɬʔɹɪn O, *-ing* mɔʊɬʔəᴉɹɪn Brk, mʌʊɬʔə C, *-ing* moːɬd̪ɾɪn D, *-ing* moːʈɾɪn W, *inf* moʊltə L, moʊɬtɹə Wo, *prppl* əmoːɬtɹɪn Wo, *-ing* əmoʊɬtɹɪn Wa, *-ing* moʊɬʔəɾɪn O, moːʊɬtɹə Gl

mouly *n* a MOLE IV.5.4. maʊlɪ Y, mɔlɪ L

mouly-rat *n* a MOLE IV.5.4. mɒʊlɪʁat Nb, mɔʊlɪʁat Du

mouly-warp *n* a MOLE IV.5.4. mɔʊlɪwaːp Y*[very rare]*, moʊlɪwɔːp Lei

mound *1. vt* to PEN or FOLD sheep in part of a field III.7.10. məʊnd Brk
2. n a SLOPE IV.1.10. maʊnd So *[marked probably ir.r. SBM]*

mound off *vtphr* to PEN or FOLD sheep in part of a field III.7.10. məʊn ... ɔːf Brk

mounds *npl* ANT-HILLS IV.8.13. mɛʊndz Ess, mɛʊnz MxL

mount *1. vi-3prpl* they MOULT IV.6.13. mɛʊnt Sf, maʊnt La, *prppl* maʊntɪn Y, *prppl* maʊntən Y, muːnt Cu Y, *-ing* mᵁuːntɪn Gl, *prppl* muːntn We, *-ing* məʊntɪn W
2. n the state of moulting. mɛʊnt Nf, muːnt Y

mounter *vi-3prpl* they MOULT IV.6.13. *-ing* muːntɹɪn Gl

mounting-swing *n* a SEESAW VIII.7.2. mæʏntɪnswɪŋ D

mountybank over *viphr* to turn HEAD OVER HEELS IX.1.10. *-ing* mᵊʊntɪbaŋkɪn aʊə Y

mourners *npl What do you call the relatives and friends who attend a funeral?* VIII.5.12. Eng. ⇒ **burying-folk, followers,** *moaners [moaners-forms only separated in NBM, and difficult to separate from* **mourners** *with certainty]*

mouse *n And [what do you call] one of them [i.e. mice]?* IV.5.1(b). Eng. ⇒ **mice, mivet;** ⇒ also **bobtail-mouse**

mouse-bat *n* a small BAT IV.7.7. mɛʊsbæt Nf

mouse-hunter *1. n* a WEASEL IV.5.6. mɛʊshʌntə Nf*[small]*, mɛʊshʌnʔə Nf*[small x4, brown throat and 'thicker' than weasel x1]*, mɛʊsʌntə Nf*[small]*, mɛʊshʏntʔə Nf*[small]* Ess*[small, old term]*, məʊshʌntʔə Nf*['more colour' than weasel]*
2. n a stoat. mɛʊshʌntʔə Nf

mouse-mole *n* a SHREW-MOUSE IV.5.2. mɛʊsmɒʉɫ K

mouses *npl* MICE IV.5.1(a). mɪəsɪz Y, mæʏzɪz Co D, mæʊziːz So, maʊsɪz L, mʌʊsɪz Brk, muːsɪz L

mouth *1. n What do you call this [indicate the (human) mouth]?* VI.5.1. Eng. ⇒ **chops, gob, gollacker, larrap, mug, mun, yap**
2. n When a child, while eating, gets all smeared with jam here [point to the mouth], its mother will say [gesticulate]: [wipe your] .... VI.5.3. Eng. ⇒ **chacks, chops,** *face,* **gob, jaws, jimmy,** *lips,* **mun, munge, muss, wykings**

mouth-bag *n* a nosebag used for BAITING a horse when resting from work III.5.2. muːθbag Cu

mouth corners *npl What do you call these parts of the mouth [indicate the mouth corners]?* VI.5.2. Eng exc. We Man Ch St Mon Hu C Nf Sf Bk Ess MxL So Sr Co Do. ⇒ **butt** *of the lip, corner of mouth, corner of my mouth, corner of your chops, corners, corners of my mouth, corners of the mouth, corners of thy mouth, corners of your mouth, crick of the mouth, edge of the mouth, edges of the mouth, end of your lips, end of your mouth, gills, jaws, jibs, lip corners, lips, mouth sides, quick of your lips, side of my mouth, side of the mouth, side of your lip, sides of his mouth, sides of the gob, sides of the mouth, sides of your mouth,* **wicks,** *wicks of its mouth, wicks of thy mouth,* **wykings**

mouthing *v-ing* PUTTING your tongue OUT VI.5.4. mᵘuːðɪn Gl

mouth-poke *n* a nosebag used for BAITING a horse when resting from work III.5.2. mᵊuːθpʊək Du

move *1. vt* to PITCH sheaves II.6.10. *3prsg* muːvz Bk
2. n **on the move** ACTIVE, describing a child VIII.9.1. ɒn ðə muːv Y, ɒn t muːv Y *[marked u.r. NBM]*

moving *adj* HEAVING *(WITH MAGGOTS)* IV.8.6. myʉːvɪn Sa, mɛʊvɪn Db, moːvɪn Sa, muːvɪn Y Sa He Wo Mon Gl Nth Hu Nf, muːvən Nb Cu Man

mow *1. v In hay-making, what do you do first?* II.9.3. Eng. ⇒ **cut, cut down, reap**
2.1. vt to CLEAR grass at the edges of a field II.9.5. mə: Nb, mɒ: Nf, mɒʊ Sa Wa Nf*[with scythe x1, by hand x1]*, mɔ: Y*[with scythe]* L, mɔʊ Nth Brk*[with scythe]*, mʌʊ C Bk Bd, mo: Ch Nt, mɒʊ Nth
2.2. v to clear grass. mɔ: Y L, mʌʊ Bk Hrt*[with scythe]* Ess
3. n a HAY-LOFT over a cow-house I.3.18. mʊx Y
4. n a hay-loft over a stable. mɒʊ W
5. n a stook of corn, ⇐ STOOKING II.6.5. *pl* mɛʊz St, maʊ Sa St Wo
6. n a HAYSTACK II.9.13. mʏ: D, *pl* maʊz So
7. vi-3prpl they MEW, referring to cats III.10.6. mæʏ Co, mæʊ Y Sf Ess Co Sx, mæʊz Sr, mɛʊ La, mɛʊ La Y Db L Nth Hu C Bk Bd Hrt Ess K, mɛʊz

Sa, mɛʊz Y O Ess Sx, mɛʊwz L, -*ing* mɛʊɪn St, maʊ Du La Y Db St Nth Sf So D, maʊz Wo, maʊz Nb Cu We La Y Mon
8. n a SLOPE IV.1.10. mæʊ W *[queried SBM]*

mow around *vphr* to CLEAR grass at the edges of a field II.9.5. -*ing* moːɪn əræʏn D

mow-barken *n* the STACKYARD of a farm I.1.4. mᵘuːbaᶜːkn Gl

mow-barton *n* the STACKYARD of a farm I.1.4. mɒʊbaᶜːtn So, məʏbaᶜːtɪn So

mow-bed *n* the BASE of a stack II.7.4. mʏːbeɪd D

mowburn *vi* to HEAT, referring to a haystack II.9.16. moˑbəᶜːn̩ Sa

mowburnt* *adj* overheated, describing a haystack, ⇐ HEAT II.9.16. mᵘuːbɹʊnt La

mow-cutter *n* a HAY-KNIFE II.9.14(a). mɛʊkʌtəᴶ Sr

mow down *1. vtphr* to CLEAR grass at the edges of a field II.9.5. mɔ: ... duːn L
2. vphr to clear grass. -*ing* mæʊɪn dɛʊn Hrt

mow-field *n* a MEADOW II.9.2. mɒʊfɛɪld St

mow-hay *1. n* the STACKYARD of a farm I.1.4. mʏːeː Co D, mæʏ-eː Co, moː-eː Co
2. n the STRAW-YARD of a farm I.1.9. mæʏ-eː Co

mowing *v-ing* STOOKING II.6.5. maʊɪn Sa

mowing-field *n* a MEADOW II.9.2. *pl* mɔˑɪnfiːlz Y, mɔˑɪnfɪəld Y, mɒʊɪnfiːɫd Lei*[never ploughed]*, mʌʊɪnfᵊiːɫd Bk, moˑɪnfiːld He, *pl* moːɪnfiːlz Ch, mo-ɪnfɪʊɫd Brk, *pl* mɒʊɪnfiːldz St, mɒʊɪnfiːld St*[never ploughed]*, mɒʊɪnfiːᵊɫd Nth*[sometimes ploughed x1]* Bd W*[seldom ploughed]*, mʊɪnfiːld St

mowing-fork *n* a HAY-FORK with a short shaft I.7.11. mʊɪnfɔᴶːk La

mowing-grass *n* a MEADOW II.9.2. mɔ-ɪngɹɛs Y

mowing-ground *n* a MEADOW II.9.2. mæʊɪngɹəʊːn Gl*[sometimes ploughed]*, mɒʊɪngɹᵘiːnd Gl, mɔˑɪngɹʊnd Y, moːɪngɹᵘuːn Gl, mɒʊɪngɹaʊnd So

mowing-meadow *n* a MEADOW II.9.2. moˑɪnmɛdɒʊ He

mowing-piece *n* a MEADOW II.9.2. moːɪnpiːs Ch

mow-maker *n* a STACKER who makes sheaves of corn into a stack II.6.11. mʏːmeːkəᶜː D, mʏːmɛːkəᶜː Co, mæʏmeːkəᶜː Co, maʊmækəᶜː So, maʊmeɪkəᶜː So, mɒʊmᶥekəᶜː So, mᵘuːmeːkəᶜ Gl, məʊmeːkəᶜ Mon, məʊmeːᶥkəᶜ Gl

mow-man *n* a STACKER who makes sheaves of corn into a stack II.6.11. muːman Co

mow off *vtphr* to CLEAR grass at the edges of a field II.9.5. mɔ: ... ɒf Y, moː ɒf Ch

mow out *1. vtphr* to CLEAR grass at the edges of a field II.9.5. maː ... uːt Du, mɒʊ ... ɛʊt Nf, *-ing* mɒʊɪn ɛʊt Sx, mɒʊ ... ɛʊt Wa, mɔː ... ʌʊt Y, mɔː ... uːt Y*[with scythe x1]* L, mɔʊ ... aːᵊt Lei, mɔʊ ... aʊt L, moː ... œʏt D, moː ... æʏt So D, moː ... æʊt Ha, moʊ ... ɛʊt Wa Nth, moʊ ... æʊt Lei So

2. vphr to clear grass. maʊ ɛʊt Sf, *-ing* mɒʊɪn ɛʊt Sx, moː æʊt W, moʊ ɛʊt Wa Nth

mow-pen *n* the STACKYARD of a farm I.1.4. mᵁuːpɛn Gl

mow-pins *npl* PEGS used to fasten thatch on a stack II.7.7(a). mæʏpɪnz Co

mow-plat *n* the STACKYARD of a farm I.1.4. mʏːpɫat D

mow-plot *n* the STACKYARD of a farm I.1.4. mʏːpɫɒt D

mow round *1. vphr* to CLEAR grass at the edges of a field II.9.5. mɔː ɹaːnd Y*[with scythe]*, mɔʊ ɹɛʊn Hu, mʌʊ ɹɛʊnd Ess

2. vphr -ing mɔːɪn ɹæˈənd Y

mows *1. npl* STACKS II.7.1. mʏːz Co, *sg* mʏː D, mæʏz D, *sg* mæʏ Co*[smaller than rick and made in field x1]*, maʊz So, *sg* maʊ Sa*[6 sheaves]*, məʊz Mon*[hay and corn]* Gl*[hay and corn]*, *sg* mᵁuː Gl

2. npl round stacks. mʏːz D, mæʏz So, *sg* mæʏ Co

mowsing *v-ing* STOOKING II.6.5. maʊzɪn St

mow-stage *n* the BASE of a stack, a wooden platform raised about 2 feet II.7.4. mʏːstɛɪdʒ D

mow-stead *1. n* the STACK-YARD of a farm I.1.4. mʏːsteːd D, mʏːstɛd D

2. n a HAY-LOFT over a cow-house I.3.18. mɪəfstɛd Y, muːstɪəd Y

3. n the place in a barn where hay is kept. mɪuːstɪəd Y

4. n the BASE of a stack II.7.4. mʏːstiːd Co, mæʏsteːd Co

mow up *vphr* to FEED cattle III.3.1. *-ing* mᵁuːɪn ʊp La

mow-yard *n* the STACKYARD of a farm I.1.4. məʊjaˡːd̩ Gl

Mr. *n [Among friends you speak of your neighbour as Mary White, but among strangers you speak of her as Mrs. White.] And of her husband as ... White.* VIII.2.3(b). Eng. ⟹ **Master**

Mrs. *n Among friends you speak of your neighbour as Mary White, but among strangers you speak of her as ... White.* VIII.2.3(a). Eng. ⟹ **Mistress**

muck *1. n* URINE in a cow-house I.3.10. mʌk W D

2. n COW-DUNG I.3.12. mʌk Sa Gl O Nth Hu C Nf Sf Bk Bd Ess So D, mʏk Nb Nf, mʊk Nb Cu Du We La Y Ch Db St Wa Nt L Lei Nth

3. v to cart dung, ⟸ CARTING *DUNG* II.1.4. mʌk Ess

4. n **sheep-muck** SHEEP-DUNG II.1.7. ʃiːpmʌk Sa Mon Sf W, ʃɪpmʌk Sa He Sf Bk Bd, ʃiːpmʊk We La Y Man Db St Nt Lei R, ʃɪpmʊk Ch Sa St Wo Wa Lei R Nth, ʃeːpmʊk Ch, ʃɛɪpmʊk Ch Db

5. n RABBIT-DROPPINGS III.13.15. mʏk Nf, mʊk St R

6. n RUBBISH V.1.15. mʌk So K Sx, mʊk Y

7.1. vt to DIRTY a floor V.2.8. mʌk K D, mʊk We La Y Man

7.2. n **make a muck on** to dirty a floor. meːk ə mʌk ɒn W, meːk ə mʊk ɒn Ch

8. n MUD VII.6.17. mʌk Bk W Co D, mʊk Du We La Y Nt Lei Nth, mək Gl

9. n EARTH VIII.5.8. mʌk Hu MxL So, mʏk Nb, mʊk La Y Db St L C, mək Gl

muck-bin *n* an ASH-MIDDEN V.1.14. mʌkbin Nf, mʌgbin Nf

muck-bing *n* an ASH-MIDDEN V.1.14. mʌkbiŋ Nf, mʏkbiŋ Nf

muck-broom *n* a MUCK-BRUSH I.3.14. mʌkbɹuːm He Brk, mʊkbɹʏᵿːm Sa, mʊkbɹuːm Y Wo

muck-brush *n What do you sweep the dung [in a cow-house] up with?* I.3.14. mʌkbɹʌʃ Sa Mon, mʌkbɾʌʃ W, mʊkbɹʊʃ Y Sa Wo, mʊkbɹəʃ He. ⟹ **bass-broom, bassett, bath-broom, besom, besom-broom, besom-brush, birch-broom, broom, brush, cane-brush, causey-brush, coir-broom, cow-broom, dung-brush, hard-broom, hard-brush, heath-broom, long-handle-broom, long-handle-brush, muck-broom, rough-broom, stable-broom, stable-brush, stiff besom, stiff-broom, stiff-brush, stiff-yard-brush, strong-brush, whalebone, whalebone-brush, yard-broom, yard-brush**

muck-cart *n* a FARMCART I.9.3. mʌkkaˡːt So

muck-cart-filling *v-ing* loading a cart with dung, ⟸ to LOAD II.1.5. mʏkkɑˈtfɪlɪn Nf

muck-channel *n* a DRAIN in a cow-house I.3.8. mʌktʃænəɫ Ess

muck-drain *n* a DRAIN in a cow-house I.3.8. mʌkd̩ɾɛɪn D

muck-draw *v* to cart dung, ⟸ CARTING *DUNG* II.1.4. mʊkdɹɔː Ch

mucked *adj* EXHAUSTED, describing a tired person VI.13.8. mʊkt Ch

mucked up *adj* STICKY, describing a child's hands VIII.8.14. mʌkt ʌp Ess

muck-filling *v-ing* loading a cart with dung, ⟸ to LOAD II.1.5. mʌkfiltin Nf, mʊkfilin Wa L

muck-fold *n* the STRAW-YARD of a farm I.1.9. mʊkfɔʊd Y

muck-fork *n What do you remove it [cow-dung in a cow-house] with?* I.3.13. mʌkfaˡːk Sa, mʌkfɑːk Mon, mʌkfaˡːk He Mon, mʌkfɔːk Hu C Nf Bd Ess Sr K, mʌkfɔˡːk Sa He O Bk, mʌkfɔəᴶk Brk, mʏkfɔˈk Nf, mʊkfaˡːk Wo, mʊkfɑːk Y He Mon C, mʊkfaˡːk He Wo, mʊkfɔɹk Y, mʊkfɔːk La Y Ch Db Sa St Wo Wa Nt L R Nth, *pl* mʊkfɔːks Lei, mʊkfɔˈːk La Y Db, mʊkfɔᵗːk Sa Wa Nth, mʊkfʊəˈk L, mʊkfəːk Ch, mʊkfəˈːk L; **four-tine muck-fork** fɔˈətɔɪn mʌkfɔːˤk Sf, fɔwətaɪn mʊkfəˈːk L; **three-tine muck-fork** θɹiːtɑˈɪn mʊkfɔˈək L. ⇒ **American-tine fork, dung-fork, dung-peek, dung-pick, dung-prong, dung-spud, evil, five-grained fork, five-tine-fork, fork, four-grain, four-grained-fork, four-grained-prong, four-grainer, four-grain-prong, four-prong-peek,** *four-prong-pick* ⇒ **four-prong-peek, four-speaned-spud, four-tined dung-fork, four-tined fork, four-tine dung-fork, four-tine fork,** *four-tine* **muck-fork, four-toe-spike, graip, grip, gripe, hop-spud, long-handled-fork, long-handled-prong, manure-fork, mucking-fork, muck-spud, peek, pick, pitch-fork, prong, sheppeck, shit-prong, spring-tine fork, spud,** *three-tine* **muck-fork, two-tined fork, yelve;** ⇒ also **dung-hook, scraper** *[shovel and spade forms omitted]*

muck-hauling *v-ing* CARTING *DUNG* II.1.4. mʌkɑːɬɪn He Mon, mʌkɔːɬɪn He, mʊkɑːɬɪn He Mon Gl

muck-heap *n* an ASH-MIDDEN V.1.14. mɤkhɪip Nf
muck-hill ⇒ **muck-hole, muckle**
muck-hole *1. n* an ASH-MIDDEN V.1.14. mʌkhoʊl Nf, mʌkhoʊɬ So, mɤkhoʊl Nf
2. n the ASH-HOLE or other place in which the ashes are collected beneath a domestic fire V.3.3. mʊkʊəl Y

muck-holes *npl* the HOOF-MARKS of a horse IV.3.10. mʊkʊəlz Y
muck in *imp* HELP YOURSELVES!, said to invite visitors to eat V.8.13. mʌk ɪn MxL, mɤk ɪn Nf*[facetious]*

mucking-fork* *n* a MUCK-FORK I.3.13. mʊkɪnfɔˈːk La

muck-juice *n* URINE in a cow-house I.3.10. mʌkdʒˡuːs Ess, mʌkdʒuːs Ess

mucklagh *n* a PIGSTY I.1.5. mʊklæx Man

muckle *n* an ASH-MIDDEN V.1.14. mʌkɬ O, mʌkəɬ Bd, mʊkɬ Nth *[pres. taken as* **muck-hill** *EMBM]*

muck-leading *v-ing* CARTING *DUNG* II.1.4. mʊkliːdɪn Y L, əˈmʊkliːdɪn Nt, mʊkliːdn Nb, mʊkliədn La Y L

muck-lugging *v-ing* CARTING *DUNG* II.1.4. mʌklʌgɪn He, mʊklʊgɪn Sa*[old x1]*

muck off *imp* GO AWAY! VIII.7.9(a). mʊk ɒf Ch
muck out *vtphr* to DITCH IV.2.11. *-ing* mʌkɪn ... ɛʊt Ess

muck-pit *n* the ASH-HOLE or other place in which the ashes are collected beneath a domestic fire V.3.3. mʌkpɪt Nf

muck-plugging *1. v-ing* CARTING *DUNG* II.1.4. mʊkplʊgɪn Y
2. v-ing loading a cart with dung, ⇐ to LOAD II.1.5. mʊkplʊgɪn Y

muck-punching *v-ing* CARTING *DUNG* II.1.4. mʌkpʌntʃɪn Ess

muck-rake *n* a RAKE used to clean the flue of a domestic fire V.3.8(a). mʊkɹeːk O

muck-ruck *n* an ASH-MIDDEN V.1.14. mʊkɹʊk St

muck-spud *n* a MUCK-FORK I.3.13. mʌkspʌd Sr

muck up *vtphr* to DIRTY a floor V.2.8. mʌk ʌp Bk W Sr, *?ptppl* mʌkt ʌp K, mʌk ... ʌp Sa O Hu Nf Bk Bd Ess So Co D, mʌk? ... ʌp Nf, mʌk ... əp Ess, mʊk ... œˈp Nb, mʊk ... ʊp Nb Cu We La Y Ch Db St Wa Gl L, mək ... əp Gl

muck-water *n* URINE in a cow-house I.3.10. mʊkweːtə La

mucky *1. vt* to DIRTY a floor V.2.8. mʌkɪ Nb O Brk, mɤkɪ Nb, mʊkɪ Nb Cu Du La Y Ch Db Sa St*[old x1]* Nt L Lei Nth, mʊk?ɪ C*[old]*
2. adj DULL, referring to the weather VII.6.10. mɑːkɪ Ess, mʌkɪ Hrt, mʌkɪ So D, mʊkɪ La Y St Nth *[marked as emotive and therefore u.r. NBM, EMBM, SBM]*
3. adj STICKY, describing a child's hands VIII.8.14. mʊkɪ Y Wo, məkɪ Gl

muck-yard *1. n* a FARMYARD I.1.3. mʊkjaːd Nth, mʊkjaᵗːɖ Wa
2. n the STRAW-YARD of a farm I.1.9. mʌkjaːd Bd, mʊkjaːd Nth, mʊkjaᵗːɖ Wa
3. n a straw-yard in which cattle are fattened. mʌkjaːd Ess

mucky-pound* *n* a CESS-POOL on a farm I.3.11. mʊkɪpaʊnd Y *[taken as* **mucky pond** *NBM]*

mucky up *vtphr* to DIRTY a floor V.2.8. mʊkɪ ... ʊp L

mud *1. n* When you walk along a country road after a heavy rain, your boots may get covered with .... VII.6.17. Eng exc. Du. ⇒ **blather, clart(s), clods, dirt, glaur, mire, muck, plother, puddle, slough, slub, slud, sludder, sludge, slurry, sluss, slutch, sluther, squad, sump**
2. n SLUSH VII.6.16. mɤd Nf
3. vaux-3sg it MIGHT have done IX.4.14. mɛd Cu, mʊd Cu We La Y, məd Y

mudded lamb *n* a PET-LAMB III.7.3. mʌdɪd ɬam Ha

muddle *v* to ROOT, what a pig does when it digs the ground with its snout III.9.2. mʌdɬɪn K Sx, mʌdɬɪn K

muddled *adj* STUPID VI.1.5. mʌdld Nf

muddy-horse *n* the FURROW-HORSE of a ploughing team II.3.4(a). mʌdɪɔːs K

mud-lamb *n* a PET-LAMB III.7.3. mʊdlæm Ha

mud out *1. vphr* to DITCH IV.2.11. mʌd aʊt Sa
2. vtphr to ditch. mʊd ... æʊt St

mud-pools *npl* PUDDLES IV.1.6. mʊdpuːlz L

mud up *vtphr* to DIRTY a floor V.2.8. mʏd ... ʌp Nf

muffin-pot *n* a BREAD-BIN V.9.2. mʊfɪnpɒt Y

muffler *1. n* a NECKERCHIEF VI.14.4. mʌflɔᴿ Nb, mʌflə Mon O Nth Ess, mʌfɫə Mon, mʌfləɹ He, mʌfləᵗ Sa He O Brk Sx, mʌfɫəᵗ Mon W Brk Sr, mʌfləᵗː Sa So*[silk x1]*, mʌfɫəᵗː W Co D Do Ha, mʏflɔᴿ Nb, mʏflə R, mʊflɔᴿ Nb Du, mʊflə Cu Du We La Y Ch*[old x1]* Db St Wo Wa Lei Nth, mʊfɫə Y Wa, mʊflər Cu, mʊfləᴿ Nb Du, mʊfləᴵ La Y Db L, mʊfɫəᴵ La, mʊfləɹ La Y, mʊfləᵗ Sa He Wo Bk, mʊfɫəᵗ Mon Gl, mʊfɫəɽ O*[silk]*, məfləᵗ Gl

2. n. a long woollen scarf. mʌflə C, mʊflə Nb Cu Du We

muffles *n* FRECKLES VI.11.1. mʌfɫz Co

mug *1. n* a container used as a PASTE-BOARD V.6.5. mʊg Ch

2. n a BREAD-BIN V.9.2. mʏˑg Nb

3. n the human MOUTH VI.5.1. mʏg Nf, mug St

muggers *npl* GIPSIES VIII.4.12. mʏgɔᴿz Nb

muggets *n* the intestines of a calf, ⇐ CHITTERLINGS III.12.2. mʌgəts So

muggy *adj* DULL, referring to the weather VII.6.10. mʌgɪ Nf Sf Bk, mʌgi So D, mʊgi Nb La Y Ch L, məgɪ Gl

mugwort *n* COLT'S-FOOT II.2.7. mʊgwəᵗːt̬ Co, mʊgəᵗːd̬ Co

mule *1. n* a HAY-FORK with a long shaft I.7.11. mɪuːl L

2. n a DONKEY III.13.16. *pl* mjulz St

mule-fork *n* a HAY-FORK I.7.11. mɪuːlfəᴵːk L

mullock *n* WEEDS, unwanted plants that grow in a garden II.2.1. mʌlək Bk, mʊlək Wa

mullocks *n* RUBBISH V.1.15. mʊləks Nth

mullum *adj* BRITTLE, describing cups and saucers which break easily IX.1.4. mɒləm Man *[queried NBM]*

mully *vi-3prpl* bulls BELLOW III.10.2. *-ing* mʌliˑ-ɪn Nf*[referring to an angry bull]*

mumble *vi-3prpl* they MOO, describing the noise cows make during feeding time in the cow-house III.10.4(a). mʊmbɫ O

mummers *npl* MOLARS VI.5.7. mʌməᵗːz̬ Ha

mun *1. n* the human MOUTH VI.5.1. mʊn Cu La Y

2. n WIPE YOUR MOUTH VI.5.3. mʊn Cu*[very old]* We La Y

3. vaux-2sg you MUST do it IX.4.11. mɒn La Ch, mɒn La, mʌn Sa, mʊn Nb Cu Du*[old x1]* We La Y Ch Db Sa St L, mən Nb Cu La Y Db St L

munch *1. vt-1prpl* we CRUNCH apples or biscuits VI.5.12. *-ing* mʊnʃɪn Y

2. v-1prpl we crunch. mʌnʃ Nb Sx, *-ing* mʌnʃɪn Co, *-ing* mʌnʃən Co

mundle *n* a PORRIDGE-STICK V.9.1. mʌndl Sa, mʊndl Ch, mʊndɫ He

munge *1. v* to KNEAD dough V.6.4. mʌnʒ Co

2. n WIPE YOUR MOUTH VI.5.3. mʊnʒ Ch

3.1. vt-1prpl we CRUNCH apples or biscuits VI.5.12. mʌndʒ Mon, *-ing* mʌnʒən D, *-ing* mʊndʒɪn Ha

3.2. v-1prpl we crunch. *-ing* mʌnʒən Co

4. v to GOBBLE food VI.5.13(b). *-ing* mʌndʒɪn W, *-ing* mʊndʒɪn He

munge away *vphr* to GOBBLE food VI.5.13(b). *-ing* mʌndʒɪn əweɪ W

muntons *npl* diagonal bars on a gate, ⇐ DIAGONAL BAR IV.3.7. mʌntənz Do *[queried ir.r. SBM]*

murfles *n* FRECKLES VI.11.1. məᵗːfɫz Co D

murk *n* MIST VII.6.8. mʊək L

murky *1. n* MIST VII.6.8. mʊəkɪ L

2. adj DULL, referring to the weather VII.6.10. mɑːkɪ Ess, məːkɪ Y, məᴵːkɪ Y, məᵗːki D

murmur *vi-3prpl* they MOO, describing the noise cows make during feeding time in the cow-house III.10.4(a). *-s* məːməz Y

murphies *npl* POTATOES II.4.1(a). məᵗːfɪz K

murr *1. vi-3prpl* they WHINNY, describing the noise horses make during feeding time in the stable III.10.3(a). məᵗːz̩ He

2. vi-3prpl they MOO, describing the noise cows make during feeding time in the cow-house III.10.4(a). mə: Db

muryan-banks* *npl* ANT-HILLS IV.8.13. *sg* mʌɾɪənbæŋk Co

muryans *npl* ANTS IV.8.12. mʌɾɪənz Co

mushers *1. npl* MUSHROOMS II.2.11. mʌʃəᵗɽz̩ Ha

2. npl MOLARS VI.5.7. mʊʃəz Y

mushrooms *npl* [*Show a picture of mushrooms.*] *What do you call these; you can eat them?* II.2.11. Eng. ⇒ **blewits, conkerooms, gipsies' stools, jacks, mushers, mushroons,** *rooms* ⇒ **roons, roons**

mushroons* *npl* MUSHROOMS II.2.11. mɛʃəɹuːnz K, mæʃɹuːnz He, mʌʃɹuːnz Ess K Sx, *sg* mʌʃɹuːn Sr, mʌʃəɹuːnz Ess Brk K, mʌʃɽuːnz Co Ha, mʌʃəᵗːɽuːnz So W Ha Sx, mʊʃɹuːnz K, *sg* mʊʃəɹuːn Gl

muslin apron *n* a decorative APRON V.11.2(b). mʌzlɪneɪpɹən He

muss *n* WIPE YOUR MOUTH VI.5.3. mʊs Y Db

must *vaux-2sg You needn't do that job today if you don't want to, but tomorrow you really ... do it.* IX.4.11. Eng. ⇒ **got to,** *have got to,* **have to, mun,** *ought to,* **shall have to,** *should,* **will have to, you'll have to, you'll have to do,** *you're boun to*

mustard *n* CHARLOCK II.2.6. mʊstəd Cu

musty *adj* RANCID, describing bacon V.7.9. mʌstɪ K Sx

mutter *vi-3prpl* they WHINNY, describing the noise horses make during feeding time in the stable III.10.3(a). mʊtə Nb

mutter out *viphr-3prpl* they WHINNY, describing the noise horses make during feeding time in the stable III.10.3(a). mʊtər ɛʊt Du

muzzle *v* to ROOT, what a pig does when it digs the ground with its snout III.9.2. mʌzl Sa, mʌzł D, *-ing* mʌzłən Co, *-ing* mʌzłən Co, *-ing* mʊzłin Co, *-ing* mʊzłən Co

muzzle up *vphr* to ROOT, what a pig does when it digs the ground with its snout III.9.2. *prppl* mʌzlən ʌp D

muzzy *adj* STUPID VI.1.5. mʊzi Y

myself *adv* *If you had done something without the help of anybody else, you could say: I did it all ....* IX.11.3. mɪsɛlf Sa St He Wo Wa Nf, mɑɪsɛlf Nf, mʌɪsɛlf Nf, məsɛlf Nf, məɪsɛlf Gl, mɪsɛłf Ch He Wo Wa Mon Gl O Nth Hu C Sf Bk Bd Hrt Ess MxL So K Co, mɒɪsɛłf W, mʌɪsɛłf Sf, mɔɪsɛłf Ess, məsɛłf Mon Sf, mɪsɛʊf Ess MxL Sr K Ha, mɑɪsɛʊf MxL, mɪzɛłf Gl So Co Ha, mɪzɛłf W D Do, mɪsæłf O, mʌʏsæłf O, mɪzəłf So; **by myself** bɪ mɪsɛlf St L, bɑɪ mɪsɛlf Sa, bɑɪ mɑɪsɛlf Nf, bɒɪ məsɛlf Nf, bʌɪ mʌɪsɛlf Nf, bə məsɛlf Nf, bəɪ mɪsɛlf Mon Gl, bɑː miːsɛlf St, bɪ mɪsɛłf Wa Lei R Nth C So Co Ha, bɪ məsɛłf Sf, bæ mɑɪsɛłf K, bɑɪ mɪsɛłf He Co, bɑɪ mɪsɛłf Nth Hu K, bɒɪ mɪsɛłf W, bɔɪ mɪsɛłf Ess, bə mɪsɛłf Ess, bəɪ mɪsɛłf Mon Gl, bɪ mɪsɛʊłf Brk, bɪ mɪsɛʊf Sr Sx, bɔɪ mɪsɛʊf Ess Sx, bɪ mɪzɛłf So W D Do Ha, bɑɪ mɪzɛłf D, bɒɪ mɒɪzɛłf W, bʌɪ mɪzɛłf Gl, bɪ mɪsałf O, bɪ mɪzəłf So D, bɪ mɪzəʊf W; **my own self** mɑɪ oun sɛlf Nf; **with myself** wɪ mɪsɛlf Y, wɪ mɪzɛłf So W. ⇒ *alone*, *by myself*, *by mysell*, *by mysen*, *my own self* ⇒ *myself*, **mysell**, **myseln**, **mysen**, *on my own*, *single-handed*, *with* **myself**

mysell *adv* *BY* MYSELF IX.11.3. mɪsɛl Nb Cu Du We La Y Ch Db Sa, mɪzɛł Co, mɪssl Y, mæɪsɛl Man, mɔɪsɛł Hrt, mɔɪsɛʊł Brk Hrt, mɪsɛʊ Sr Ess, mɪzəł D; **by mysell** bɪ mɪsɛl Nb Cu La Y Ch, bɪ mɪsɛł K, bɪ mɪsɛʊ W Brk K, bɪ mɪzɛʊ Ha, bəɪ məɪsɛʊ Brk Sx, bæ mæɪsɛl Man, bɪ mɪzəł So D

myseln *adv* *BY* MYSELF IX.11.3. mɪsɛln Y

mysen *adv* *BY* MYSELF IX.11.3. mɪsɛn Y Db St Nt L; **by mysen** bɪ mɪsɛn Y Db Nt L Lei R*[old x1]*

N

nadder *n* an ADDER IV.9.4. nædə Nf

nagger *n* a GOSSIP VIII.3.5(b). nɛgə Ess, nægəˠː So

nagging *v-ing* GOSSIPING VIII.3.5(a). nægɪn So, *prppl* ənagən Ha

naiglet *n* the TAG of a boot-lace VI.14.26. nɛglɪt La Db, nɛglət Nb, næglət La, naglət La

nail *n* the GRASS-NAIL of a scythe II.9.9. nɛɪɫ Co

nailbourn *n* an intermittent RIVULET IV.1.1. næɪɫbən K

nail-hang *n* a LOOSE *PIECE OF* SKIN at the bottom of a finger-nail VI.7.11. nɛɪɫhæŋ Ha

nail-spring *n* a LOOSE *PIECE OF* SKIN at the bottom of a finger-nail VI.7.11. *pl* neːɫspɾɪŋz D, nɛɪɫspɾɪŋ D, *pl* nɛɪɫspɾɪŋz Co, *pl* naɪɫspɾɪŋz Co

nail-wart* *n* a WHITLOW VI.7.12. *pl* nɛɪɫwəˠːʈʂ D

naked *1. adj By the way, if a person had no clothes on at all, you would say he was ....* VI.13.20. Eng exc. C Hrt. ⇒ **belly-naked, bollock-naked, hither-naked,** *naked to the skin,* **nude, star-bone naked, stark-bellied, stark-bellied-naked, stark-belly-naked, stark-naked, star-naked, start-naked, starve-naked, stone-naked, strip-naked, stripped**
2. adj NOT IN CALF III.1.8. nɛɪkɪd Ess

naked-feet *adj* BARE-FOOT VI.10.2. nɛikɪdfiɪt Nf

naked-foot *adj* BARE-FOOT VI.10.2. neːkɪdvuːt Do, nɛikɪdvut Sx

nammet *n* MEAL OUT VII.5.12. namət W Do*[tea-time]* Ha, namɪk Ha, nɒmət So, nʌmət So Do

nammet(s) *n* a SNACK VII.5.11.
no -s: næmət Ha, namɪk Ha, namət W D Do, nɔmət Do, nʌmɪk So, nʌmɪt D, nʌmət So
-s: næmɪts Brk, næməts W

nang-nail *n* a LOOSE *PIECE OF* SKIN at the bottom of a finger-nail VI.7.11. naŋneːl La

nanna *n* GRANNY VIII.1.8(b). nænə Ess, nanə He Mon Ha

nannies *1. npl* LICE IV.8.1(a). nanɪz Y
2. n GRANNY VIII.1.8(b). nænɪz Brk

nanny *1. n* a BEARD VI.2.7. nanɪ St
2. n GRANNY VIII.1.8(b). nænɪ Nf, nanɪ Sa

nannygoat-beard *n* a BEARD VI.2.7. nɛnɪgɒutbiəˠd K

nannygoat's beard *n* a BEARD VI.2.7. nanɪgoʊts bɪəd St

nanny-lamb *n* a EWE-LAMB III.6.3. *pl* nanɪlamz Wo

nanny-long-legs *n* DADDY-LONG-LEGS IV.8.10. nanɪlɒŋlɛgz Ch, nanɪluŋlɛgz Ch

nanny-spinner *n* DADDY-LONG-LEGS IV.8.10. nanɪspɪnə Y

nan(s) *n* GRANNY VIII.1.8(b).
no -s: næˈn Nf
-s: nænz Brk*[old]*

nants* *npl* ANTS IV.8.12. nants Nb

nap **1. v* to TOP-AND-TAIL gooseberries V.7.23. nap La
2. n a DIAPER V.11.3. *pl* næps Sx, nap Do

nape *n* the SCRUFF (of the neck) VI.6.2. neːp Y, neɪp Ha, nɛɪp R MxL

napkin *n* a DIAPER V.11.3. nɛpkɪn Ess K Sx, *pl* nɛːpkɪnz Brk, næpkɪn Sa He Wo Mon Gl Hu Ess MxL So Sr, næpʔkɪn Nf, næpkjɪn Gl, næpkən Man Sf Ess So, napkɪn Y Ch Sa St He Wo Wa Mon Gl Nt Lei Nth Bk Bd So W Ha, napkən So

napood *v-ed* FINISHED, referring to a store of potatoes V.7.21. napuːd Y

napper *n* the human HEAD VI.1.1. næpəˠ Sa Mon

nappin* *n* a DIAPER V.11.3. napɪn He

napping* *v-ing* cutting off clotted wool before shearing, ⇐ SHEARING sheep III.7.6. næpɪn So

nappy *n* a DIAPER V.11.3. nɛpɪ Sr K Sx, næpi So, næpɪ Sa He Mon Ess MxL So Brk Sr K Ha Sx, næpʔɪ Nf, napi So W Co Ha, napɪ La Y Db Sa St Wo Wa O Nt Lei R Nth Bk Bd Hrt D Do Ha; **baby's nappy** babɪz napɪ Wo

napron* *1. n* a working APRON V.11.2(a). neɪpɹən Nf, napɹən Y
2. n a decorative APRON V.11.2(b). neɪpɹən Nf

napsies* *npl* BOILS VI.11.6. *sg* næpsɪ Brk

narrow loke *n* a LANE IV.3.13. næɹə loʊk Nf

naskgel *n* a NEWT IV.9.8. naˈskgʊɫ Wo

nasty *1. vt* to DIRTY a floor V.2.8. nastɪ La
2. adj **go nasty** to SPOIL, referring to meat or fish V.7.10. guː naːstɪ Do

nathe *n* the HUB of a cart-wheel I.9.7. neːθ La, neːð La Ch St Nt, nɛɪð Db St, naθ Nb La Y Db

natter **1. n* CHAT VIII.3.4. nɛtɐ Ess, nætəˠ Sx, nædɐ Ess, natəˠː W
2. n **having a natter** GOSSIPING VIII.3.5(a). avən ə natəɾ O
3. n a GOSSIP VIII.3.5(b). natəˠ O

natterer* *n* a GOSSIP VIII.3.5(b). nætəˠɾəˠ Sx

nattering *v-ing* GOSSIPING VIII.3.5(a). næʔəˠᴵɹɪn Brk, næʔɹɪn Ess, natəɹɪn He, natəɾ̥ɪn O, natəˠːɾɪn Ha, nadəˠːɾɪn D

nattery* *adj* RESTIVE, describing a horse III.5.6. næʔəɹɪ Nf

naught *pron* NOTHING VII.8.14. nɛʊt La Ch Db Sa St Wa Nt Lei Nth Brk Sr K*[old]* Ha Sx, næʊt Du La Ch Sa St L Lei R So Ha, naᵗːʈ Co, naɪt Ch, naʊt Nb Cu Du We La Y Sa St Lei So*[old x1]*, naʊt La Y, nɒʊt Nb Cu Du We La Y Ch Db Nt Nth Nf, nɔːt Y W Brk Sx, nɔᵗːʈ So Co D, nɔʊt Nb La Y Ch Wa O L*[old x1]* Lei R, nɔʊʔ L, nʌʊt L Ess Brk, nɔət Nb, noːt Sa, noʊt St*[old x1]* Wa O Lei Nth Bd, nʊˑt L, nʊət L, nəʊt Y Brk Do, nəʊːt Wo

naunt *n* an AUNT VIII.1.12(b). neːnt Sa, nænt Gl, nant Ch Db, nɒnt Y, nɔnt Y Db

nave *1. n* the HUB of a cart-wheel I.9.7. niːv Ch, neːv Ch Db Sa Nt Co, neav We, neɪəv Man, nɛɪv St L Sf Ess K, nɛəv L, nɛˑəf L, næɪv K, nav Cu La Y, naf Nb Cu Du We La Y Nt

2. n the metal BUSH at the centre of a cart-wheel I.9.8. næf Y, naf Y

nave-pin *n* a LINCH-PIN holding a wheel on a cart I.9.12. nafpɪn Y

nave-stock *n* the HUB of a cart-wheel I.9.7. neːvstɒk D, neːəvstɒk D

navvy scarf *n* a NECKERCHIEF VI.14.4. nævɪ skaᵗːɹf Ha

navvy-straps *npl* KNEE-STRAPS used to lift the legs of working trousers VI.14.17. navɪstɹaps Wa

nay *adv* NO VIII.8.13(b). niː Cu Du We Y, nɪə Y, neː Cu La*[contradicting x1]* Y Ch, neˑa Cu La, neːə La, nɛː Y, nɛɪ Lei, na Nb Du

nazareth *n* a DONKEY III.13.16. nazɹəθ Db

near *1. adv* Our house is not far away; so it must be .... (early (fourth) version of questionnaire: Here are two telegraph poles [draw them]. A car stops here, rather far from this one, but quite ... that one.) IX.2.10. Eng exc. Nt Hu C. ⇒ **again, anent, anigh, at, close, close again, close at, close at hand, close by, close-hand, close handy, close handy** *by***, close here, close to, gain, gain-hand, handy, near at, near at hand, nearby, near-hand, near on, near till, near to, neighbour, nigh, nigh-hand,** *pretty* **close,** *pretty* **handy,** *pretty* **near,** *tidy* **near,** *very* **close**

2. adv **near about** ABOUT VII.2.8. nɪəᵗɹ bɛʊt Sx

3. adv ALMOST VII.7.9. nɪəɹ (+V) MxL, nɪəᴵ La, nɪəᵗːɹ Ha; **near as could be** nɪəɹ əs kʊd biː Ess; **damn near** dæm nɪəᵗ Mon; **gayly near** gɛːlɪ nɪə Cu; **gay near** geː nɪəᴿ Nb, gɛː nɪə Cu; **pretty near** pɹɪtɪ nɪəɹ Y, pɹətɪ nɪəɹ (+V) Sr, pɹətɪ nɪəᵗ Ha, pɹɪ nɪəᴵ Sr, pɹɪ nɪəᵗ Sr, pədɪ nɪəᵗːɹ (+V) Ha, pəɹ̥tɪ nɪəᵗ O, pəᵗːdɪ nɪəᵗ So D, pəᵗːdɪ nɪəᵗːɹ (+V) Co D Do, pəᵗːdɪ njəᵗːɹ (+V) D, pəᵗːdɪ nəᵗːɹ D, pəᵗːʈ ɳɪəᵗːɹ W, pəᵗːd̥ nɪəᵗː So, pəᵗː ɳɪəᵗː Ha, pəᵗː ɳɪəᵗːɹ (+V) D, pəᵗːɳ ɳɪəᵗːɹ (+V) So, pəᵗː ɳəᵗːɹ D; **very near** Eng exc. Man Sa Hu Do; **welly near** wɛlɪ nɪə St; **wholly near** hʌlɪ nɪə Sf, hʊlɪ nɪə Sf

4. n the NEAR-HORSE of a pair pulling a wagon

I.6.4(a). nɪəɹ St, nɪəᵗ Brk, nɪəᵗː So; **near one** nɪəᵗːɹ ən So

5. n the LAND-HORSE of a ploughing team II.3.4(b). nɪəɹ(+V) St, nɪəᴵ K

6. adj miserly, ⇐ MISER VII.8.9. nɪəɹ Y

near about *adv* ALMOST VII.7.9. nɪəɹ əbᵃᵉus Man

near at *adj* NEAR IX.2.10. nɪəʁ at Nb

near at hand *adj* NEAR IX.2.10. nɪɔᴿʁ ət hæᵊnd Nb, nɪɔᴿʁ ət hand Nb, nɪəʁ ət haˑnd Du, nɪəɹ ət and Y, naɪr ət hand Cu

nearby *adj* NEAR IX.2.10. nɪəbɑɪ Nth

near enough *adv* ALMOST VII.7.9. nɪɪ ənʌf Ess, nɪəʁ ɪnɪəf Nb, nɪəɹ ənɪʊf Cu, nɪəɹ ɪnɪəf Y, nɪəɹ ənɪəf Y, nɪəɹ ənʌf He Sf Ess, nɪəᴵ ənʊf La, nɪəɹ ɪnʊf Y L Lei, nɪəɹ ənʊf La Y Db Nt, nɪəɹ ənəf Gl, nɪəᴵ ənʌf Brk, nɪəᴵ nʌf K, nɪəɹ nʌf K, nɪəᴵɹ nʌf Brk Sx, nɪəᵣ ənʏf Ha, nɪəᵗ ənʌf O, nɪəᵗːɹ ɪnʊf Wo, nɪəᵗːɹ nʌf Ha, njəᵗːɹ ənʌf He, nɪəᵗːɹ ɪnʌf Co, naɪr ənʊf Cu, naᵗːɹ ɪnʊf Db, nəᵗːɹ ənəˑf Gl

near-fat *n* the FAT round the kidneys of a pig III.12.7. nɪəfat Y Nt

near-hand *1. adj* NEAR IX.2.10. nɪɔᴿhæˑnd Nb, nɪɔᴿhaˑnd Nb, nɪəhæːᵊnd Nb, nɪəɹand Y O *2. prep* near. nɪəɹand Y

nearhand *adv* ALMOST VII.7.9. nɪə-and Y, nɪəɹand Y; **pretty nearhand** pʁɛtɪ nɪəhæːᵊnd Nb; **very nearhand** vaɹɪ nɪɔᴿhæᵊnd Nb, vɛɹɪ nɪəɹand Y, vaɹɪ nɪɔɹand Y

nearhand-horse *n* the NEAR-HORSE of a pair pulling a wagon I.6.4(a). nɪərandɒs Y

near-horse *1. n* When you have two horses pulling a wagon side by side, how do you distinguish them? I.6.4(a)[the lefthand horse]. nɪɔᴿhɒᴿːs Nb, nɪɔᴿhɔᴿːs Nb, nɪəɹɑːs Mon, nɪəɹɑɹs Y, nɪəhɒˑs Nf, nɪəɹɒs La Y Ch Db St Bd Ess, nɪəɹɔs Du L C Hrt, nɪəhɔːs Nf Sf Ess, nɪəhɔːəs Nb, nɪəɹɔːs Db St Wa L Nth Hrt Ess K, nɪəᵣɔːs K, nɪəɹɔᴵːs La, nɪəᴵ-ɑᴵːs Brk, nɪəᴵɔːs Sx, nɪəᴵ-ɔəᴵs Brk, nɪəᴵɹɔːəᴵs Sr, nɪəᴵɹɔːəᵗɹ̥s Sr, nɪəᵗɹɑᵗːʂ Sa Wo Gl So, nɪəᵗːhaᵗːʂ So, nɪəᵗːɹɑᵗːʂ W Co Do Ha, nɪəᵗɑᵗʂ Wo, nɪəᵗɹɑᵗːʂ He, nɪəᵗɹɒs Sa Wo Mon Gl, nɪəᵗːɹɒs W Co D Do Ha, nɪə-ɔᵗːʂ Sa, nɪəɹɔᵗːʂ O K Ha, nɪəɹɔᵗːʂ Sa, nɪəᵗ-ɔːəᵗʂ Sr Sx, nɪəᵗːɹɔːəᵗʂ Ha Sx, nɪəᵗːhɔᵗːʂ So, nɪəᵗːɹɔᵗːʂ So D Do Ha, nɛəhɒs Nf, nɛˑəhɔˑs Nf, nɛə-ɔˑs Nf, naɪəᵗːɹɒs Ha. ⇒ **come-back, inside-horse, land-horse, lefthand-horse, line-horse, near, nearhand-horse, near** *one***, nearside, nearside-horse, nearside-tit, near-tit, rein-horse**

2. n the LAND-HORSE of a ploughing team II.3.4(b). nɪəᴵ-ɑᴵːs Brk, nɪəᵗːɹɑᵗːʂ W Do, nɪəᵗɹɑᵗːʂ Wa, nɪəɹɒs Y, nɪəᵗːɹɒs W Co D Do Ha, nɪəɹɔːs Cu Wa Bk K, nɪəᵗɔːs Bk, nɪəᵗɔᵗʂ Sr Ha, nɪəᵗːɹɔᵗːʂ So Co D Do, nɪəᵗːhɔᵗːʂ So, nɪəᴵɹɔːəᵗʂ Sr, nɪəᵗ-ɔːəᵗɹ̥ʂ Sx

nearish *adv* ALMOST VII.7.9. nıəɻɪʃ O

nearly *adv* ALMOST VII.7.9. nıəlı Y St Wa L Lei Hu Nf Ess Sr, nıəˡlı La Brk Sr K, nıəˡlı Sx, nıəˡlı O Brk, nıəˡɬı Sr, nıəˡɬı Mon, nıəˡːɬı So, nıəˡːɬi Co D, njəˡːli So, njəˡːɬi So Ha, njəˡːɬi D Ha, njəˡːɬı Gl W, neılı Nf; **very nearly** vɛɹı nıəlı Nth Hrt, vəɹı nıəlı Hu Ess, vɛɹı nıəˡɬı Sr

near on *prep* NEAR IX.2.10. nıəɹ ɒn Y*[old]*

nearside *1. n* the NEAR-HORSE of a pair pulling a wagon I.6.4(a). nıɔᴿsɛıd Nb, nıəsɛıd Nb Ch, nıəsaːd Y, nıəsaıd Nb We Y, nıəsɒıd St, nıəsɒːıd St, nıəsɔıd Wa, nıəsʌyd O, nıəˡsɔıd O, nıəˡsɔıd O, naːsaıd We, naːsɒıd St

2. n the LAND-HORSE of a ploughing team II.3.4(b). nıɔᴿsɛıd Nb, nıəsaıd St, nıəsaıd Nth Ess, nıəsɒıd St, nıəsɔıd O Sf Ess, nıəɹsɔıd Brk, nıəˡsɔıd Gl O Bk, nıəˡsʌyd O

nearside-horse *1. n* the NEAR-HORSE of a pair pulling a wagon I.6.4(a). nıəsaıdaːs Y, nıəsaːdɒs Y, nəıəsaıdhɒs Du, nıəsaıdɒs Cu Du La Y, nıˈəsaːdɒs Y, nıəsaıdɒs Db Nt Nth Bd, nıəsɔıdɒs Bk, nıəseıdhɒᴿːs Nb, nıəsaıdɒs Y Nt L, nıəsaıdɔs Nt, nıəsɔıdhɔs Sf, nıəsɔıdɒs Sf, nıəseıdhɔːs Du, nıəsaıdɔːs Cu, nıəsaːdɔːs Lei, nıəsaıdhɔˑs Nf, nıəsaıdɔːs Ch Wa Nth Hu Bk Hrt Ess, nıəsɔıdhɔːs Ess, nıəsɔıdɔːs Wa Ess MxL, nıəsʌıdhɔːs Sf, nıəseıdhɔᴿːs Nb, nıəsaıdɔˡːs We La Y Db, nıəsaıdɔˡːs La, nıəsaıdɒˡːʂ Sr, nıəsɔıdɒˡːʂ Bk, nıəˡsaıdɔs L, nıəˡsaıdɔːs La, nıəˡsaıdɔˡːs La, nıəɹsaıdɔːs La, nıəɹsaıdɔɹs He, nˡiːəˡsɛıdɔˡːʂ Sa, nıəˡʂɒıdaˡːʂ Mon Gl, nıəˡzˌɔıdaˡːʂ Gl, nıəˡsəıdaˡːɻʂ Brk, nıəˡʂɒıdaˡːʂ Wo, nıəˡsɔıdaˡːʂ Wa O, nıəˡsaıdɒs Bd, nıəˡsɔıdɒs Wa, nıəˡʂəıdɒs He Wo Gl, nıəˡɻsəıdɒs Mon, nıəˡsaıdɒˡʂ Ha, nıəˡsaıdɔːs Sa, nıəˡsəıdɔːs He, nıəˡsæıdɔˡːʂ He, nıəˡʂaıdɔˡːʂ Sa, nıəˡsɔıdɔˡːʂ Nth, nıəˡsɔıdɔˡːʂ Gl, nıəˡʂəıdɔˡːʂ Wo, nıəˡʂəıdɔəˡːʂ Sx, neəsaıdɒs L, nɛısaːdɒs Ch, naːsaıdɒs We, naːsaıdɔːs Ch, naːɹsaːdɔˡːɹs La

2. n the LAND-HORSE of a ploughing team II.3.4(b). nısʌıdhɔːs Sf, nıəsaıdɒs Y, nıəsaıdɒɹs Y, nıəsaıdɒs Y, nıəsɔıdhɔs Sf, nıəsaıdɔːs Y Ch, nıəsaıdɔːs Ch Bk Hrt MxL, nıəsɒıdɔːs St, nıəsɔıdɔːs Wa, nıəsɔıdhɔːs Ess, nıəseıdhɒᴿːs Nb, nıəsaıdɔˡːs La, nıəsɔıdɒˡːʂ Bk, nıəɻsɔıdaɻʂ O, nıəˡsɔıdɔˡːʂ Wa Sr, nıəˡzʌıdɒs Gl, nıəˡːsɒıdaˡːʂ W, naˡːsaıdɔˡːs La, naˡːsaıdɔˡːs La

nearside-tit *n* the NEAR-HORSE of a pair pulling a wagon I.6.4(a). nıəsaıdtıt Db

near till *adj* NEAR IX.2.10. nıə tıl Cu

near-tit *n* the NEAR-HORSE of a pair pulling a wagon I.6.4(a). nıəɹtıt St

near to *adj* NEAR IX.2.10. nıə tıuː Hu, nıə tɛʊ St, nıə tuː La Y St Nt L Nth, nıəˡ toᵘ Man, nıəɹ tᵁuː La, nıəˡ tuː Wa

neat-house *n* a COW-HOUSE I.1.8. nɛtəs Nf, nɛtʔəs Nf Sf

neat-tree *n* a TROUGH in a cow-house I.3.6. niːtɹiː St

neb *1. n* the BEAK of a bird IV.6.18. nɛb Nb Cu Du We La Y*[old x3, of hen x1]* L*[old x1, uncommon x1]*

*2. n the peak of a cap, ⇐ BRIM VI.14.3. nɛb Y

nebbed *adj* PIGEON-TOED VI.10.4. nɛbd Cu

nebbing in *adj* PIGEON-TOED VI.10.4. nɛbən ın We

nebby *adj* PIGEON-TOED VI.10.4. nɛbı Cu

neb-footed *adj* PIGEON-TOED VI.10.4. nɛbfʊtıd Cu

nebs *npl* the HANDLES of a scythe II.9.8. nɛbz Gl Bk Bd Hrt, *sg* nɛb O, næːbz Hrt

necessary *n* an EARTH-CLOSET V.1.13. nɛsısɛɹı Y*[old]*

neck *1. n Where do you wear your collar [gesticulate to the neck]? Round your ....* VI.6.1. Eng. ⇒ **neck-hole**, **niddick**, **poll**, **throat**, **thropple**

2. n a THROAT VI.6.3. nɛk Y Sr

3. vt to kill a chicken by wringing its neck, ⇐ to WRING IV.6.20. nɛk Du La Sa He

neck-band *n* a rope TETHER for a cow I.3.4. nɛkband La

neck-chain *1. n* a TETHER for a cow I.3.4. nɛktʃeːᵊn Ch, nɛktʃɛın Ess K, nɛktʃæın K

2. n an iron tether. nɛktʃɛˈən L

3. n a chain which, together with a steel-chain, comprises a tether or head-stall. nɛktʃɛın Ess

4. n a chain used to tie up a horse, ⇐ TETHERING-ROPE I.4.2. nɛktʃiːn Db, nɛktʃıən Y, nɛktʃeːn Ch Sa

neckcloth *n* a NECKERCHIEF VI.14.4. nɛkləθ We

neck-collar *1. n* a TETHERING-ROPE used to tie up a horse I.4.2. nɛkkɒlə St

2. n the COLLAR of the harness of a cart-horse I.5.3. nɛkkɒlə La Y, nɛkkɒlər Y, nɛkkɒləɹ La

neckerchief *n What do men sometimes wear round their necks instead of a collar; not that long woollen thing?* VI.14.4. nɛkətʃiːf Y Lei R Hrt Ess, nɛktʃiːf Man, nɛkətʃɪf Sa, nɛkəˡtʃɪf K, nɛkəˡtʃɪf Wa*[old]*, nɛkəˡːtʃɪf Co D. ⇒ **choker**, **gravat**, **handkerchief**, **handkerchiefs**, **muffler**, **navvy scarf**, **neckcloth**, **neck-handkerchief**, **neck-hanky**, **necking**, **necklet**, **neck-tie**, **neck-wrapper**, **scarf**, *silk* **handkerchief**, **slip**, **swetagg**, **wrap**, **wrapper**

neck-handkerchief *n* a NECKERCHIEF VI.14.4. ˈnɛkˌhɛkətʃɪf Ess, nɛkæŋktʃıif Brk, nɛkæntʃˤiːf Ess, nɛkhæŋkətʃɪf Ess, nɛkæŋkətʃəf Hu, nɛkæŋkıtʃə Sa, nɛkæŋkətʃə Hu Nf Sf, nɛkaŋkətʃiːf Nt*[old x1]* L Nth Bd, nɛkaŋətʃiːf L C, nɛkaŋtʃiːf Hrt, nɛkaŋkətʃɪf L C Bd, nɛkaŋətʃɪf L Hrt, nɛkaŋkıtʃəf We, nɛkaŋkɪtʃəˡ Wa, nɛkaŋkətʃəˡ O, nɛkaŋkətʃə Y Db Bd*[old]*, nɛkaŋkətə L*[?error for* nɛkaŋkətʃə *BM Edd]*, nɛkaŋətʃə L

neck-hanky *n* a NECKERCHIEF VI.14.4. nɛkhæntʃɪ Sf*[old]*, nɛkaŋkɪ Y L

neck-hole *1. n* the NECK of a person VI.6.1. nɛkɔɪl Y, nɛkʊəl Y

2. *n* the WINDPIPE VI.6.5. nɛkhɒʊɫ K, nɛkʊɫ K

necking *n* a NECKERCHIEF VI.14.4. nɛkɪn Nf

necklet *n* a NECKERCHIEF VI.14.4. nɛklət Db*[silk]*, nɛklθət Cu *[Cu form taken as* **neck-cloth** *NBM]*

neck over nothing *adv* HEAD OVER HEELS IX.1.10. nɛk oə nʊθɪn Ch

neck over shit *adv* HEAD OVER HEELS IX.1.10. nɛk ɔvə ʃɪt Y

neck-rope *1. n* a HALTER for a cow I.3.17. nɛkɪɒʊp K

2. *n* a TETHERING-ROPE used to tie up a horse I.4.2. nɛkɪoːp Mon

neck-stall *n* a TETHERING-ROPE used to tie up a horse I.4.2. nɛkstɑːɫ Wo *[queried ir.r. WMBM]*

neck-strap *1. n* a TETHER for a cow I.3.4. nɛkstɪap Sf

2. *n* a TETHERING-ROPE used to tie up a horse I.4.2. nɛkstɪæp Sa He, nɛkstɪap Y Sa St Wo *[queried ir.r. WMBM]*

neck-tie *1. n* a TETHERING-ROPE used to tie up a horse I.4.2. nɛktaɪ Sa St, nɛktəɪ He *[queried ir.r. WMBM]*

2. *n* a NECKERCHIEF VI.14.4. nɛktəɪ Gl

neck-wrapper *n* a NECKERCHIEF VI.14.4. nɛkɪæpə Nf Ess

neddy *1. n* a DONKEY III.13.16. nɛdɪ Du Y L So Ha, *pl* nɛdɪz Ess

2. *n* a HARE IV.5.10. nɛdɪ La

need *n* **stand need to** OUGHT TO IX.4.6. *3prsg* standz niːd tə L

needle *1. n* What do you call this *[indicate a needle and thread]?* V.10.2(a). Eng. ⇒ **darning-needle**, **thread-needle**; ⇒ also **bag-needle, horse-needle, needle and thread, needle-holes, poke-needle, poking-needle**

2. *n* **needle already threaded, needle and cotton, needle and thread, needle of thread, needle ready, needle ready-threaded, needle threaded, needle threaded ready, threaded needle** a NEEDLEFUL of cotton or thread V.10.5. **needle already threaded** niːdɫ ɔːɫɪedɪ θɪedɪd Bk; **needle and cotton** niːdʊɫ ŋ kɒʔn K; **needle and thread** niːdl ən θʁiːd Nb, niːdl ən θɹiːd Nb, niːdl ən θʁɪˈəd Nb, niːdl ən θɹɪəd Y, niːdl ən θʁɛd Nb, niːdl ən θɹɛd Db Nth, niːdɫ ən θɹɛd Wo Wa Nth C, neːdl ən θɹɪd Ch; **needle of thread** niːdl ə θɹɛd O; **needle ready** neːdl ɹɪdɪ Ch; **needle ready-threaded** niːdl ɹɛdɪ θɹɛdəd Nt, niːdɫ ɹɛdɪθɹɛdɪp Wa, nɛɪdl ɹɛdɪθɹɛdɪp Db; **needle**

threaded niːdl θɹɪədɪd La, niːdl θɹɪədt La, niːdl θɹɛdɪd Y L, niːdɫ θɹɛdɪd Gl Hu Bd Hrt Ess, niːdɫ θɹɛdəd Sf, nɪdl θɹɛdɪd Gl; **needle threaded ready** niːdl θɹiːdəd ɹɛdɪ Db; **threaded needle** θʁiːdɪd niːdl Nb, θɹiːdɪd niːdl Du, θɹiːdəd niːdl Y, θɹɛɪdɪd niːdl La, θʁɛdəd niːdl Du, θɹɛdɪd niːdl Cu La Sa Nt, θɹɛdəd niːdl Sa Nt, θɹɛdɪd niːdɫ Wa Nth C Bd, θɹɛdɪd niːdət Bk, θɹɛdəd neːdl Sa

needle and thread* *n* bed, ⇐ NEEDLE V.10.2(a). niːdɫ ən θɹɛd MxL

needleful *n* What do you call this *[indicate a threaded needle]?* V.10.5. Eng exc. Nb Nt Nth C MxL. ⇒ **bit of thread, hank of thread, length, length of thread, lump of thread, needle** *already* **threaded, needle** *and cotton*, **needle** *and thread*, **needleful** *of cotton*, **needleful** *of thread*, **needle** *of thread*, **needle** *ready*, **needle** *ready-threaded*, **needle** *threaded*, **needle** *threaded ready*, **piece, piece of cotton, piece of thread, strand, strind, threaded-ful,** *threaded* **needle** *[material culture notes in BM]*

needle-holder *n* a SHEATH or other device used to keep a knitting-needle firm V.10.10. nɪɪdlhɒʊldə Nf, neɪdlɔʊldə St

needle-holes* *npl* ventilating holes in barns, ⇐ NEEDLE V.10.2(a). nəɪdlʊalz Y

needle-rest *n* a SHEATH or other device used to keep a knitting-needle firm V.10.10. niːdlɹest Ch

needle-shield *n* a SHEATH or other device used to keep a knitting-needle firm V.10.10. niːdlʃiːld Y

neigh *1. vi-3prpl* they NEIGH, describing the noise horses make in the fields III.10.3(b). neː Nb La Ch Sa Ha, neːɪz Mon Brk, neɪ Y Mon O Bk So Do Ha, neːɪ Man, neːɪz He Wo Gl O, *-ing* neɪən Man, neɪ Y Db St He Wo Wa L*[modern x1]* Lei Nth Nf Sf Bk Bd Hrt Ess Brk Sr Co D Ha Sx, nɛɪz Gl, *3prsg* nɛɪz K, *-ing* nɛɪ-ɪn K, nɛə L*[modern]* Ess, næɪ Du Y Gl Nf Sf Ess Sr K, næɪz He Mon, naɪ Co, naɪz Wo Gl, nɑɪ Y. ⇒ **bray, croon, holler,** *hollo* ⇒ **holler, hummer, nicker, nucker, nutter, rinny, shriek, snicker, snork, squeal, whicker, whinny, whistle, winker**

2. *vi-3prpl* they WHINNY, describing the noise horses make during feeding time in the stable III.10.3(a). neː Nb Ch Db Ha, neɪ La Mon Gl Bk So Ha, neːɪz O, neːɪ Man, neɪ Y He Wo L*[modern]* Lei Nth Sf Bk Bd Ess St Brk Sr Co D Sx, nɛɪz Wa, nɛə Ess, næɪ Du Y Gl Nf Sf Ess K, naɪ MxL Co Ha, naɪz K

neighbour *adj* NEAR IX.2.10. nɛɪbə K

neighbouring *v-ing* GOSSIPING VIII.3.5(a). nɛəbəɹɪn Y

neive *1. n* the human HAND VI.7.1. nɪəf We

2. *n* a FIST VI.7.4. niːv Nb Cu Y, niːf Nb Cu Du

We, nɪəv Y, nɪəf Cu We La Y, neɪf Du, nɛɪv La Y

neiveful *n* a HANDFUL VII.8.10(a). nɪəvfʊl Y, nɪəvfəl Y, nɪəffʊl Cu We La, nɪəfʊl La, nɪəffl Du Y

nep* *v* to TOP-AND-TAIL gooseberries V.7.23. nɛp We La

nerve(s) *n* TREMORS suffered by a person who cannot keep still VI.1.4.

no -s: nœːv Mon

-s: nœːvz Mon, naːvz Nf, nɑːvz Nf, nɑˑvz Nf, nəːvz Ch St Lei R Nf Ess, nəˤːvz So W Sr Co D; **the nerves** ðə nəːvz St

nervous *1. adj* ACTIVE, describing a child VIII.9.1. nɑːvəs Nf *[marked u.r. EMBM]*

2. adj SHY VIII.9.2. nɛəvəs Y, naːvəs Y, naᵞːvəs Nb, nəːvəs Y Ess, nɛˑvəs Nf

nervy *adj* SHY VIII.9.2. nɛˤːvi Co

nesh *adj* BRITTLE, describing cups and saucers which break easily IX.1.4. nɛʃ St He

nesp *1. v* to TOP-AND-TAIL gooseberries V.7.23. nɛsp La Y

2. v to REMOVE *STALKS* from currants V.7.24. nɛsp La

nesses *n* LOW-LYING LAND IV.1.7. nɛsɪz La

nessy *1. n* an EARTH-CLOSET V.1.13. nɛsɪ Cu Du We Y*[old x1]*

2. n an ASH-MIDDEN V.1.14. *pl* nɛsɪz Y

nestle *1. n* **on the nestle for calving** showing signs of calving, ⇐ SHOWS SIGNS OF CALVING III.1.12. ɒnt nɛsl fə kɔːvɪn Y

2. n WEAKLING piglet III.8.4. nɛzł So

nestle-bird *n* a WEAKLING piglet III.8.4. nɪsłbəˤːd̪ D, nɛsłbəˤːd̪ D

nestle-draf *n* a WEAKLING piglet III.8.4. nɪsłd̪ɾaːf D, nɪzłd̪ɾaːf D, nɛsłd̪ɾaːf D, nɛzłd̪ɾaːf D, nɛsłd̪ɾaːf Co D

nestle-dredge *n* a WEAKLING piglet III.8.4. nɛsłd̪ɾʏdʒ D, nɛzłd̪ɾʏdʒ D

nestle-drish* *n* a WEAKLING piglet III.8.4. nɪsłd̪ɾɪʃ Co, nɪzłd̪ɾɪʃ D

nestle-tripe *n* a WEAKLING piglet III.8.4. nɪsłt̪ɾaɪp D, nɪzłt̪ɾaɪp D, nɪzłt̪ɾɒɪp Do, nɛsłt̪ɾaɪp So, nɛsłt̪ɾɒɪp So, nɛsłt̪ɾəɪp W, nɛzłt̪ɾæɪp So, nɛzłt̪ɾaɪp So

nestling *n* What do you call the young wild bird just out of the egg? IV.7.1. nɛslɪŋ Man Sr, nɛslin Nb Y Db Sa St Wo L Nf So Brk K*[rare x1]*, nɛsłɪn Mon Ess Ha, nɛstlɪn Nb, nɛstłɪnz Ess, nɛstlən Ess. ⇒ **balch bird, balcher, balchin, bald-arse, bald one, baldy, bare-arse, bare-balchin, bare-bubb, bare-bubbling, bare-golling, bare-golly, biddy, bubb, bubbling, bully-balcher, chick, chicken, fledging, fledglets, fledgling, flegger, frigging, gollop, golly, gorbet, gorling, gully, kidney-balchin,** *lile bird* ⇒ **little bird, little bird,** *naked* **young one, new-hatched one, pudding-kite, raw-golly, raw-gorbet, red-raw kellick, skinny ball, squab, squabber, squeaker, tabby-balcher, young, young bird, young fledging, young one**

nest-ripe *adj* FLEDGED IV.7.2. nɛsɾaɪp So*[old]*

nests of pissymires* *npl* ANT-HILLS IV.8.13. *sg* nɛst ə pɪʃəmɪəz Nf

net *v* to PEN or FOLD sheep in part of a field III.7.10. nɛt Db

net off *vtphr* to PEN or FOLD sheep in part of a field III.7.10. nɛt ... ɔf L

netting *n* stale URINE used as a cure for chilblains VI.8.8. nɛtɪn Nt

netty *n* an EARTH-CLOSET V.1.13. nɛtɪ Nb Cu Du*[common x1]* Y*[polite]*

never-a-one *pron* NONE VII.1.18. neəˤn̩ wʌn O, nɛɹʊn Wo, naɾiwʌn D, naˤːwʌn Ha, naˤːn̩ W Do Ha, nɒɾiwʌn D, nʊɹən Gl*[old]*, nəˤːn̩ So W Do

new grounds *n* LOW-LYING LAND reclaimed from a river IV.1.7. njuː gɹᵁuːnz Gl

new-hatched one *n* a NESTLING IV.7.1. nuː-atʃt ən La

new-lea *n* PASTURE grown after barley II.1.3. nᵼleɪ Nf

new milk *n* BEESTINGS V.5.10. nɪʊ mɪłk Co, nɪuː mɪłk Sf, nju: mɪłk So, nju: məłk Do

new-nut-tree *n* HAZEL IV.10.8. njuːnʊtt̪ɹi: Y

news-agents *npl* GOSSIPs VIII.3.5(b). nɪʊzeːdʒənts Co

news-bag *n* a GOSSIP VIII.3.5(b). njʏːzbæg So, nʏːzbɛg D, nʏːzbæg So D, nʏːzbag Co D, njuːsbæˑg Man, njuːzbæg So, nɪuːzbag L, njuːzbag St W

newsbagging *v-ing* GOSSIPING VIII.3.5(a). nʏːzbægɪn So

news-canter *n* a GOSSIP VIII.3.5(b). njuːzkantəˤ Gl

newser *n* a GOSSIP VIII.3.5(b). nʏːzəˤː Co D, njuːzəˤː So

newsgag *n* a GOSSIP VIII.3.5(b). njuːzgæg W *[queried error for news-bag SBM]*

newsing *v-ing* GOSSIPING VIII.3.5(a). nɪuːzɪn L, njuːzɪn So Do, nʏːzɪn So

newsmonger *n* a GOSSIP VIII.3.5(b). nɪʊzmɒŋgə Ess, nɪʊzmʌŋgə Nf, *pl* nɪʊzmʌŋgəˤːz̩ Co, njuːzmɒŋgəᵞ Nb, nɪuːzmʌŋgə C, njuːzmʌŋgəˤ Sx, njuːzmʌŋgəˤː So W, nɪuːzmʊŋgə Du, nʏːzmʌŋgəˤː Co, nuːzmʌŋgəᴶ K

newsmongerer *n* a GOSSIP VIII.3.5(b). nʏːzmʌŋgəˤːɾəˤː D

newsmongering *v-ing* GOSSIPING VIII.3.5(a). njuːzmʌŋgəˤːɾɪn So

newspad *n* a GOSSIP VIII.3.5(b). njuːzpad W

newsy *adj* CLUMSY, describing a person VI.7.14. njuːzɪ Brk *[queried BM]*

newt *n* What do you call that small four-legged, long-tailed creature, blackish on top; it darts *about in ponds?* IV.9.8. nɪʊt Y L Nf Ess Co, *pl* nɪʊts La, nɪʊːt Nb La Y Db Sa Wo Nt L Nth Hu C Bd Ess, njuːt Du Y*[modern x1]* Man Db St Wa Nt L Lei R K, *pl* njuːts Nb, *pl* njᵊuːʔs Hrt, nᴵʉt Nf, njʉːt Lei, nɛʊt La Y Db Wa*[old x1]* Nth, nuːt Y*[modern]* Db St Lei Nth Bk MxL K, *pl* naʊts St, nᵊuːt Wo Wa. ⇒ ask, asker, askert, askgel, aster, dry-ask, eff, eft, esk, evet, ewt, four-legged-emmet, four-legged-evet, lizard, mancreeper, mewt, naskgel, *padgetty-pow* ⇒ padgy-poll, padgy-poll, swift, tiddlywink, water-ask, water-evet, water-lizard, water-swift, wet-eff, wet-evet, yellow-belly, yolt

next to *prep* BESIDE a door IX.2.5. nɛks tʉ Nf

nib *1.1. vt* to TOP-AND-TAIL gooseberries V.7.23. nɪb So D, *-ing* nɪbɪn Co

1.2. v to top-and-tail gooseberries. nɪb Nf

2.1. vt to REMOVE *STALKS* from currants V.7.24. nɪb Co D, *-ing* nɪbɪn So

2.2. v to remove stalks. nɪb D

3. n the TAG of a boot-lace VI.14.26. *pl* nɪbz Sf

nibble *n* the TEAT of a woman's breast VI.8.6. nɪbl St Nth

nibbles *npl* the HANDLES of a scythe II.9.8. nɪbɫz Nth

nib off *vtphr* to TOP-AND-TAIL gooseberries V.7.23. nɪb ... ɔːf Co

nibs *1. npl* PEGS used to fasten thatch on a stack II.7.7(a). nɪbz La*[wooden x2]*

2. npl the HANDLES of a scythe II.9.8. nɪbs Do, nɪbz Cu We La Y Ch Db St He Wo Wa O L Lei Nth Hu Bk W Brk Do Ha Sx

nice *adj* PRETTY, describing a girl VI.5.18. neɪs Man, naɪs Y L, nɑɪs La Y, nɒɪs St Ha, nɔɪs Wo O Brk, nʌɪs Nf, nʌɪs O; **nice pretty** naɪs pɽɪdi So; **nice young** nɔɪs jʌŋ Ha

nice-looking *adj* PRETTY, describing a girl VI.5.18. neɪslʊkn Du, nɑːslʊːkɪn Y, nɑɪslʊkɪn Wa MxL, nɒɪslʊkɪn W, nɔɪslʊkɪn Gl O Sx, nɔɪsɫʊkɪn O, nɔɪslʊkn Ess, nʌɪslʊkɪn He Brk, nʌɪsləkɪn Gl, nəɪslʊkɪn Sx, nəɪsɫʊkɪn W

nick-and-haws *npl* HAWS IV.11.6. 'nɪkɪ'nɔᶜːz̩ Sa

nicker *1. vi-3prpl* they WHINNY, describing the noise horses make during feeding time in the stable III.10.3(a). nɪkɔᴮ Nb, nɪkə Cu Du Y O, *3prpl* nɪkərz Cu

2. vi-3prpl they NEIGH, describing the noise horses make in the fields III.10.3(b). nɪkɔᴮ Nb, nɪkə Du, nɪkərz Cu

nickering *v-ing* LAUGHING VIII.8.7. nɪgəɹɪn St, nɪgɹɪn St

nickies *npl* KINDLING-*WOOD* V.4.2. nɪkɪz Ha

nicks *1. n* an EVENER on the plough-beam end of a horse-drawn plough I.8.4. nɪks Lei

2. n the notches on the T-SHAPED PLOUGH-BEAM END of a horse-drawn plough I.8.5. nɪks Wa Lei R Nth

niddick *n* the NECK of a person VI.6.1. nɪdɪk Co D, nɛdɪk Co D

niddy-noddy *adj* STUPID VI.1.5. nɪdɪnɒdi D

niggardly* *adj* miserly, ⇐ MISER VII.8.9. nɪgədlɪ Y

nigh *1. n* a PADDOCK I.1.10. næɪ Man

2. imp the command TURN LEFT!, given to plough-horses II.3.5(a). nɒɪ K *[queried SBM]*

3. adv ALMOST VII.7.9. nəɪ Sx; **pretty nigh** pətɪ nɑɪ MxL, pɹɪ nɔɪ Sr, pɹɪ nəɪ Sx; **very nigh** vəɹɪ nɛɪ Db, vəɽɪ næː D, vɛɹɪ næɪ He, vɛɹɪ naɪ Y, vaɹɪ naɪ Y, vəɹ nɑˑɪ L, vɛɹɪ nɒɪ Wo, vɛ nɒɪ Ha, vəᶜː n̩ɒɪ Sx, vɛɹɪ nɔɪ Ess, wɛɹɪ nʌɪˑ Nf, vəɽɪ nʌɣ O

4. adj NEAR IX.2.10. næɪ So*[old]*, nᵊaɪ Du, nɑɪ Ess MxL Sr*[old]*, ənɒɪ So, nɔɪ Ess Brk*[rare]* Sr*[old]* Sx*[old x1]*, nʌɪ Nf W Brk*[old]* Sr*[old]*, nəɪ W Brk*[old]* Sx

nigh enough *adv* ALMOST VII.7.9. nɑɪ ənʌf Hrt MxL, nʌɪ ənʌf Nf, nʌɪ ənɣf Nf, nəɪ nʌf Sx

nigh-hand *prep* NEAR IX.2.10. nɛɪhæᵊnd Nb, naɪhaˑnd Du

nigh on *adv* ALMOST VII.7.9. næː ɒn D, nɒɪ ɒn Wo, nəɪ ɒn W, nəɪ ɔːn W

night *n What do you call the various parts of the day?* VII.3.11(d). Eng. ⇒ **night-time**

night-halter *n* a TETHERING-ROPE used to tie up a horse I.4.2. naɪtɔːɫtəᶜː D, naɪtɔltəᴵ Ch

night-time *n* NIGHT VII.3.11(d). nʌɪttaɪm Hu

nile *1. n* a FLAIL II.8.3. næɪɫ He Mon, nɒɪᵊɫ Gl, nɔɪəɫ Wo, nʌɪᵊɫ He, nəɪɫ Mon, nəɪᵊl Gl

2. n the striking part of a flail. naɪl Wo, nɒɪɫ He, nəɪᵊɫ Gl

nim *vi-3prpl* **nim themselves** they grunt, describing the satisfied noise cows make after feeding time in the cow-house, ⇐ MOO III.10.4(a). *-ing* nɪmɪn ðəsɛnz Y

nimble *adj* ACTIVE, describing a child VIII.9.1. nɪmbl St, nambɫ Ha

nimpingang *n* a WHITLOW VI.7.12. nɪpɪngeːn So, nɪmpɪŋgɛŋ D, nɪpɪŋgɛŋ D, nɪpɪngɛŋ Co D

nine-mealer *n* a HAY-FORK with a long shaft I.7.11. naɪnmiːlə L

nine-point-fork *n* a HAY-FORK with a long shaft I.7.11. naɪnpaɪntfəᴵːk L

nineses *n* a morning SNACK VII.5.11. nɔɪnzɪz Sf, nʌɪnzɪz Nf

nip *1. v* to TRIM hedges IV.2.3. nɪp W

2.1. vt to TOP-AND-TAIL gooseberries V.7.23. nɪp La Y Db Co

2.2. v to top-and-tail gooseberries. nɪp La O

3. vt to REMOVE *STALKS* from currants V.7.24. nɪp Du Co

4. n a PINCH of sugar or salt VII.8.6. nɪp Cu*[old, salt]* Du*[old x1, salt x2]* Y Wa L Lei R Nth Hu C Nf Ess

nip out *vtphr* to RINSE clothes V.9.8. nɪp ... aʊt L

nipped *v-ed* CASTRATED, describing a bullock III.1.15. nɪpt Y

nippets *npl* the HANDLES of a scythe II.9.8. nɪpɪts W

nipple *1. vt* to TOP-AND-TAIL gooseberries V.7.23. nɪpl Nb
2. *n* the TEAT of a woman's breast VI.8.6. nɪpl Cu Man Nf, nɪpɫ Sf Ess, nɪpʔɫ Ess, nɪpʊɫ W Brk Ha, nɪpʊ O Ess Sr K Sx, nɛpɫ Man

nipples *npl* the HANDLES of a scythe II.9.8. nɪpʊɫz Gl

nips* *npl* the HANDLES of a scythe II.9.8. nɪps O

nirrup *n* a DONKEY III.13.16. nɪɾʌp W Ha, nəɾʌp Do

nisgal *n* a WEAKLING piglet III.8.4. nɪzgl Sa, nɪzgəl Sa He, nɪzgəɫ He Wo, nɪzgʊɫ He Wo

niskral *n* a WEAKLING piglet III.8.4. nɪskɹəɫ Mon

niskwal *n* a WEAKLING piglet III.8.4. nɪskwɛɫ He, nɪskwʊɫ He, nɛskwɑːɫ Mon

nitall *n* HAZEL IV.10.8. nɪtaɫ Co, nɪdaɫ Co

nitall-bush *n* HAZEL IV.10.8. nɪtɔɫbyʃ D

nit-bush *n* HAZEL IV.10.8. *pl* nɪtbyʃɪz D

nit-halse *n* HAZEL IV.10.8. nɪdɔːɫs D

nither *vi* to WRINKLE, referring to the skin of very old people VI.11.2. nɪðə Nb

nithered *adj* VERY COLD, describing a person VI.13.19. nɪðəd Y

nits *1. npl What do you call its (the louse's) eggs?* IV.8.2. Eng. ⇒ **biddies, dicks, lice-eggs, ticks**
2. *npl* LICE IV.8.1(a). nɪts Y

no *1. adv If I asked you: Have you met that man, you could say: [Yes,] ....* VIII.8.13(b). Eng. ⇒ **ho, nay, why no**
2. *adv* NOT IX.7.11. nø: Nb, nœ: Nb, no: Nb

nob *n* the CLOG on a horse's tether I.4.3. nɒb Y St Mon Ess W Do, nɔːb Do

nobbut *adv* ONLY VII.8.12. nɒbət Nb Cu Du We La Y Db, nɒbəd Du We Y, nɔbət La Y L, nɔbəd La *[not a WMBM headword]*

nobby *n* a COBBLER VIII.4.5. nɒbɪ Sa

nod *n* the SCRUFF (of the neck) VI.6.2. nɒd Sx

noddering *n* TREMORS suffered by a person who cannot keep still VI.1.4. nɒðəɾɪn So, nɒðəᵗːn̩ So

nodding *n* TREMORS suffered by a person who cannot keep still VI.1.4. nɒdɪn K D, nɒdn Sx

noddle *n* the human HEAD VI.1.1. nɒdɫ So

noddlings *n* **the noddlings** TREMORS suffered by a person who cannot keep still VI.1.4. ðə nɒdlɪnz Lei

noddy *adj* SILLY VIII.9.3. nɒdɪ Ess

nodge *n* the CLOG on a horse's tether I.4.3. nɒdʒ Sa

nog *1. n* the CLOG on a horse's tether I.4.3. nɑg O Bk, nɒg Ch Db St Wa Nt Lei R Nth Bk, nɔg Wa L
2. *n* a BUMPER of a cart I.10.1(a). nɒg Nt

noggen *adj* SILLY VIII.9.3. nɒgən Ch

noggets *npl* the HANDLES of a scythe II.9.8. nɔgəts So

noggin *1. n* the CLOG on a horse's tether I.4.3. nɒgɪn Y Db Sa St Lei R, nɔgɪn L
2. *n* a PIECE *OF BREAD AND BUTTER AND JAM/SUGAR* V.6.11(b). nɔgɪn Wa
3. *n* a slice of bread and cheese. nɒgɪn St; **noggin of bread and cheese** nɒgɪn ə bɹɛd n̩ tʃiːz Wa
4. *n* **a noggin and lard** a piece of bread and lard. ə nɒgɪn ən laːd Hu

noggin-head *n* a STUPID person VI.1.5. nɒgɪnjɛd Ch

noggins *npl* the HANDLES of a scythe II.9.8. *sg* nɒgɪn Gl

nogs *npl* the HANDLES of a scythe II.9.8. nɒgz He Mon W

noither *n* a WHETSTONE made of stone II.9.10. nɔɪðə Wa Gl *[queried WMBM]*

none *1. pron If you had two apples and then ate them both, how many would you have left?* VII.1.18. Eng. ⇒ **never-a-one**
2. *adv* NOT IX.7.11. nɪn We, njɛn Nb, nɪən Nb Cu Du We La Y, nean Du, ne·ən La, nɒn La Db St, no·ən Db, nʊən La Y L

non-high *adj* SAD, describing bread or pastry that has not risen V.6.12. noːnaɪ So, noːnaːˡ So

nonpower *adj* **turned nonpower** OVER-TURNED, describing a sheep on its back unable to get up III.7.4. təᵗːn̩d nʌmpʊʊəᵗː D

noodle *n* a STUPID person VI.1.5. nuːdl St

nook-staff *n* the iron stay connecting the beam with the side of a cart, ⇐ CROSS-BEAM END I.10.1. nɪəkstaf Nb, nuːkstaf Y

nook-stap *n* the iron stay connecting the beam with the side of a cart, ⇐ CROSS-BEAM END I.10.1. nɪʊkstap Cu

nook-stower *n* the iron stay connecting the beam with the side of a cart, ⇐ CROSS-BEAM END I.10.1. nɪʊkstaʊə Y, nɪəkstaʊə Cu We, nɪəkstɔʊəᴿ Nb

nooky-way *adv* DIAGONALLY, referring to harrowing a field IX.1.8. nɪakɪweː La

nop *1. v* to cut small branches from a tree, ⇐ to LOP IV.12.5. *-ing* nɒpɪn Sx
2.1. vt to TOP-AND-TAIL gooseberries V.7.23. nɒp Nb Cu La
2.2. *v* to top-and-tail gooseberries. nɒp Nb*[old]* Cu Du We La
3.1. vt to REMOVE *STALKS* from currants V.7.24. nɒp Nb
3.2. *v* to remove stalks. nɒp Cu Du

nope *n* the SCRUFF (of the neck) VI.6.2. nɒʊp He

nor *prep* THAN VI.12.4. nɪ Lei, nə Cu We La Y Ch Db Wo Wa O L Lei Nth Bk, nəɹ (+V) Nt Ess, nəɹ We La*[rare x1]* Y, nəɾ O, ə Nb Cu Y Sf *[Sf* [ə] *treated as **than** in EMBM]*

norn *pron* NOTHING VII.8.14. nɔːn Sx
north-handed *adj* LEFT-HANDED VI.7.13(a). nafandɪd L, nɔːθandɪd L, nɔˑəθandɪd L
norwichers *npl* KNEE-STRAPS used to lift the legs of working trousers VI.14.17. nɒɹɪdʒəᵗɽz̩ Sx*[old]* *[queried SBM]*
nose *1. n What's your ordinary word for this [indicate the nose]?* VI.4.6. Eng. ⇒ **beak, conk, cronk, hud, jimmy, pecker, sneck, snitch, snitcher, snotter, snout, trunk**
2. n the SNOUT of a pig III.9.1. nɔʊz L, nʌʊz Ess, nʊəz La Y L
3. n the SHARE of a horse-drawn plough I.8.7. nøːz Nb
4. n the HUB of a cart-wheel I.9.7. noːz D
5. vt to TOP-AND-TAIL gooseberries V.7.23. nɔːz Co
nose-and-tail *vt* to TOP-AND-TAIL gooseberries V.7.23. nɔʊzəntæɪɫ Hu
nose-bait *n* an allowance of food given when BAITING a horse when resting from work III.5.2. nʊəzbɛət Y
nose-gay *n* the T-SHAPED PLOUGH-BEAM END of a horse-drawn plough I.8.5. noːzgeː Co
nose-holes *npl* NOSTRILS VI.4.7. nøːzhøːlz Nb, nᵆuzɒulz K, nɒzəɫ Lei, nɒʊzɒʊɫz Sx*[old x1]*, *sg* nɒuzɒuɫ K, nɒʊzʊɫz K, nɔʊzɔʊlz Wa*[old]* L, nɔʊzɔʊɫz Lei R Sx, nʌʊzʌʊɫz Bk Bd Hrt Ess MxL, *sg* nʌʊzhoʊl Sf, nʌʊzəʊɫz Sr, noːzɒɪlz Db, noːzoːlz La Ch*[old x1]* Db Sa Gl Nt Nth Bk, noʊzɔʊɫz Lei, nouzhoulz Nf, noʊzoʊlz St Nf, noʊzoʊɫz Wo Wa Lei Bd, noːᵁzoːᵁlz Db, noəzoəlz Y L, nʊːzoʊlz St, nʊːzʊːlz St, nuazwɔlz We, *sg* nʊəsɒɪl La, nʊəzɒɪlz La*[old x1]* Y, nʊəzɔɪlz La Y, nʊəzʊalz Y, nʊəzʊəlz La Y Ch Nt L, *sg* nʊˑəzʊəɫ Bk, nᵁuːzoːlz Db
nose-piece *n* an EVENER on the plough-beam end of a horse-drawn plough I.8.4. noːzpiːs So
nosey-parker *n* a GOSSIP VIII.3.5(b). nʊəzɪ paːkə Y, nɒʊzɪpɑᵗːkəᵗ Sr
nossro *n* a SHREW-MOUSE IV.5.2. nɒsɹoʊ St, nɒsɹᵁuː Ch, nʌʃɹoː Sa, nosɹoʊ St, nʊsɹoː Sa, nʊsɹoʊ St
nossrol *n* a SHREW-MOUSE IV.5.2. nʊsɹəɫ Ch
nostrils *npl What do you call these [indicate the nostrils]?* VI.4.7. Eng exc. Lei R. ⇒ ***holes in the nose, nose-end*, nose-holes, smellers, snout-holes**
not *1. adv If you were angry about what I said [accusing you of being drunk], you might say: Get away, I'm ... drunk.* IX.7.11. Eng exc. Db C Bk. ⇒ **no, none** *[also unstressed forms recorded at some locs]*
2. n a HORNLESS cow III.2.9. nat Co D, nɒt Gl So W D Do Ha
3. adj HORNLESS, describing a cow III.2.9. nɒt W *[no adj headword BM]*
notch *1. v* to WHITTLE a stick I.7.19. *-ing* nɒtʃɪn K
2. vt to whittle. *3prsg* nɒtʃɪz K
notcher *n* an EVENER of the plough-beam end of a horse-drawn plough I.8.4. natʃə St
notch(es) *n* the notches (or a notch) on the T-SHAPED PLOUGH-BEAM END of a horse-drawn plough I.8.5.
no -es: nɒtʃ Wa
-es: natʃɪz St Wa, natʃəz Db, nɒtʃɪz St Wa Nth, nɒtʃəz Nt, nɔtʃɪz Wo
notches *n* the vertical BAR or CHAIN of a crane over a domestic fire V.3.5(b). nɒːtʃɪz Ha
notching-bar *n* the T-SHAPED PLOUGH-BEAM END of a horse-drawn plough I.8.5. nɒtʃɪnbaᵗː W
not-cow *n* a HORNLESS cow III.2.9. nɒtkæɤ So Co, nɒtkæʊ So Do, nɒtkəʊ W Do
nothing *pron What's in my pocket [show an empty pocket]?* VII.8.14. Eng exc. Cu Du We La Db. ⇒ **naught, norn**
nothing but *adv* ONLY VII.8.12. nʌðɪn bʌt So
not-horn-cow *n* a HORNLESS cow III.2.9. nɒthaᵗːɳkəʊ So
notted *adj* HORNLESS, describing a cow III.2.9. nɒtɪd So
nought *adv* ONLY VII.8.12. nɔːt Y, nɔːət Y, nɔʊt Y
nought but *adv* ONLY VII.8.12. nɛʊt bət Ch, naʊt bət Y, nɒʊt bət Nb Nt, nɔᵗːʈ bʌt Co D, nɔᵗːʈ bʌd D, nɔᵗːʈ bʌd(+V) So Co D
nought-cracky *adj* ILL, describing a person who is unwell VI.13.1(b). nɔʊtkɹakɪ Y
nought only *adv* ONLY VII.8.12. nɔʊt ɔːnɪ L
nub *1. n* the HUB of a cart-wheel I.9.7. nʌb Do
2. vt to TOP-AND-TAIL gooseberries V.7.23. nʊb C
nub-and-tail *v* to TOP-AND-TAIL gooseberries V.7.23. nʌbəntɛɪəɫ C
nucker *1. vi-3prpl* they WHINNY, describing the noise horses make during feeding time in the stable III.10.3(a). *-ing* nʌkəɹɪn K, nʌkəᴵɹ Sx, nʌkəᵗ Sr Sx, *-ing* nʊkəɹɪn K, nʊkəᴵ K, nəkəᵗ Sx
2. vi-3prpl they NEIGH, describing the noise horses make in the fields III.10.3(b). nʌkəᴵɹ Sx
nude *adj* NAKED, describing a person VI.13.20. nᵊuːd Hrt
nug* *n* the CLOG on a horse's tether I.4.3. nʌg Bk, nʊg Lei
numb *adj* CLUMSY, describing a person VI.7.14. nʊm Nb Cu Du We La
numbed *adj* VERY COLD, describing a person VI.13.19. nʌmd So
numb-head *n* a STUPID person VI.1.5. nʊmɪəd Y

numb-pawed *adj* CLUMSY, describing a person VI.7.14. nʊmpæᵊd Nb

numbskull *n* a STUPID person VI.1.5. nʊmskʊl Nb Y Db

numb-thumbed *adj* CLUMSY, describing a person VI.7.14. nʊmθʊmd We

nunch *1. n* a SNACK VII.5.11. nʌnʃ W Ha, nʊntʃ Nth*[old]*
2. n MEAL OUT VII.5.12. nʌnʃ So Do

nuncheon *1. n* a SNACK VII.5.11. nʌnʃɪn W Brk, nʌnʃn Sx*[old]*, nʊnʃɪn Wa Brk
2. n MEAL OUT VII.5.12. nʌnʃɪn Brk, nʌnʃən W Ha, nʊnʃɪn Brk

nuncle *n* an UNCLE VIII.1.12(a). nʊŋkl Y Ch*[rare]* Db Sa, nəŋkl Gl

nunk *n* an UNCLE VIII.1.12(a). nʌŋk So*[name]*, nʊŋk Ch Wa*[old]*

nursed-lamb *n* a PET-LAMB III.7.3. noəsdlam Nb

nush *v* to BUTT III.2.10. *prppl* nʊʃʃɪn La

nussock *n* a DONKEY III.13.16. nɛsʊk Gl, nʊzʊk Db

nut *1. n* the HUB of a cart-wheel I.9.7. nʌt So Do
2. n HAZEL IV.10.8. nʊt Lei R

nut-bough *n* HAZEL IV.10.8. nʌtbɛʊ Ess, nʌtbʌʊ Ess

nut-brush *n* a BESOM made of hazel I.3.15. nʌtbɹʌʃ Nf

nut-bush *n* HAZEL IV.10.8. nʌtbʊʃ He Nf Sf W, *pl* nʌtbʊʃɪz O So, nʌʔbʊʃ Bk, nʏtbʊʃ Nf, nʊtbʊʃ Y St He Wo Wa, *pl* nʊtbʊʃɪz Lei

nut-grass *n* GOOSE-GRASS II.2.5. nʊtgɹas Wo

nuthall-bush *n* HAZEL IV.10.8. nʌtɔːɬbyʃ D

nut-halse *n* HAZEL IV.10.8. nʌtɔːɬs Co

nut-hazel *n* HAZEL IV.10.8. nʌteɪzɫ Bd, nʌteɪzɫ

Hrt, nʌtʔɛɪzɫ Ess, nʌʔɛɪzɫ Bk Hrt, nʌteɪzʊ Sx, nʌthæɪzɫ Ess, nʌtæɪzəl Ess

nutmeg *n* a SHEATH or other device used to keep a knitting-needle firm V.10.10. nʊtmɛg St

nut-stab *n* HAZEL IV.10.8. *pl* nʌtstɛbz Sf

nut-stems *npl* HAZEL-bushes IV.10.8. nʌtstɛmz Ha

nut-stool *n* HAZEL IV.10.8. nʌtstaʊəɫ W

nut-stub *n* HAZEL IV.10.8. nʌtstʌb Ess

nutter *1. vi-3prpl* they WHINNY, describing the noise horses make during feeding time in the stable III.10.3(a). *-ing* nʌtəᴵɹɪn Sx, nʊtəɾ O, nʊtəᵗ O, nʊtəᵗz̩ He Gl, nʊtəᵗːz̩ Wo
2. vi-3prpl they NEIGH, describing the noise horses make in the fields III.10.3(b). *-ing* nʌtəɹɪn Brk*[rare]*, nʊtəɾ O

nut-tree *n* HAZEL IV.10.8. nʌʔɹi Nf, nʌttɪi: He O C Sf Ess K, nʌtɹᴵi: Mon, nʌʔtɹi: Bk, nʌttɾi: Ha, nʌttɹi Sf, nʌtɹi Sa*[old]*, nʌtʔɹi Nf, nʊttɹi: La Y Sa Wo Wa Gl Lei Nth, nʊtɹi: Sa*[old]* He, nʊtɹi Sa, nʊttɾi: O, nəttɹi: Gl

nut-tree-bush *n* HAZEL IV.10.8. nʊtɹɪbʊʃ Sa

nut-tree-wood* *n* HAZEL IV.10.8. nʊʔɹiwʊd Brk

nutty *adj* SILLY VIII.9.3. nʊti L, nəti Sx

nut-wood *n* HAZEL IV.10.8. nʌtwʊd Ess Brk*[old]*

nuzzle *v* to ROOT, what a pig does when it digs the ground with its snout III.9.2. *-ing* nɒzlɪn Hrt, *-ing* nʌzɫɪn So, *-ing* nʌzɫɪn So, *-ing* nʌzɫən Do

nuzzle about *vtphr* to BUTT III.2.10. *-ing* nʌzɫən … əbæʊt Do

nuzzle-tripe* *n* a WEAKLING piglet III.8.4. nʌzɫtɾæɪp So, nʌzɫtɾaɪp So, nʌzɫtɾəɪp Do

O

oak *n What do you call that sturdy tree which gives us our best wood?* IV.10.2. Eng; **oak-tree** jaktɹiː Y, ɒʊktɹiː Sr, *pl* ɔːkʈʈiːz W, *pl* ɔʊktɹiːz L, ɔʊktɹiː Ess, oʊktɹiː Lei, wʌkʈʈiː So, wʊkʈʈiː So, ʊəktɹiː Y, ʊəktɹəɪ Y. ⇒ **oak-*tree***

oak-apple day *n* a local FESTIVAL or holiday on 29 May VII.4.11. oʊkapɫ deː Wo

oak-cratching *n* an ACORN IV.10.3. *pl* eːkɹatʃɪnz Ch, *pl* oːkkɹatʃɪnz Ch

oak-fillip *n* an ACORN IV.10.3. *pl* ɔʊkfɪləps L *[queried BM]*

oast *n* CURDS V.5.8(a). ʊast Y

oat *n* OATS II.5.1. oːt La Mon, oːᵁt Db, wʊt Ch

oat-cart *vbln* CARTING corn from the field II.6.6. wʌtkaʵːʈ Ha

oat-gratton* *n* STUBBLE remaining in a field after oats have been harvested II.1.2. ɒʊtgræʔn Sx

oatmeal *1. n* MEAL V.6.1(b). ɔʊtmiːl L, ʌʊtmɪəɫ Ess, wɒtmɛɪl Y, ʊətmɛɪl Y

*2. *n* GRUEL V.7.2. uːtmiːɫ Co

oatmeal-porridge *n* PORRIDGE V.7.1. ʊətmɪəlpɒdɪʃ Y

oats *n [What do you mean by corn here in these parts?] What other kinds of cereals do you know?* II.5.1. Eng. ⇒ **haver, oat**

oaves *n* the EAVES of a stack of corn II.7.3. ɒfɪs So, ɔːvz So W, hɔːvz Brk, ɔːvɪs So Co D, ɔːfɪs So Co D, ɔːfɪz So, ɔːvəs D, ɔːfəs D, ɔʊvəs Ha, oːvɪs Co Do, oʊvəs Ha

oblong *adv* DIAGONALLY, referring to harrowing a field IX.1.8. ɒblɒŋ Nf *[queried u.r. EMBM]*

obstinate *adj* RESTIVE, describing a horse in a stable III.5.6. ɒbstnət So

odd *adj* **an odd one, an odd one one, an odd one or two, odd ones** *A* FEW VII.8.21. **an odd one** ən ɒd n̩ Cu*(='very few' x1)*, ə ɒd n̩ St, ən ɔd n̩ L; **an odd one one** ən œːd n̩ ən Nb; **an odd one or two** ən ɔd n̩ ə tuː L; **odd ones** ɒd n̩z Cu Du*(='one or two' x1)* We Y Db, ɒd ənz La Y Db Nt L, ɔd n̩z Nb L, ɔd ənz La

odd-bloke *n* a FARM-LABOURER I.2.4. ɒdbɫoːk Ha

odd-job-man *n* a FARM-LABOURER I.2.4. ɒddʒɒbmæn Nf, ɒddʒɒbman Y, ɒddʒɒbmɒn St

odd-man *1. n* a FARM-LABOURER I.2.4. œːdman Nb, ɒdmæn He Hrt Brk Sr K Sx, hɒdmæn So, ɒdman Y Ch Sa O Bk W Do Ha, ɒdmaːn Mon, ɒdmɒn Sa St He Wo, ɒdmn Mon, ɒdmən O Lei, ɔdmɔn Wo, ɔdmæn K, ɔːdmæn Sa

2. n a domestic handy-man, ⇐ FARM-LABOURER I.2.4. ɒdman He

oddy *n* a FARM-LABOURER I.2.4. ɒdɪ K

off *1. n* the FAR-HORSE of a pair pulling a wagon I.6.4(b). ɒf St Brk, ɔːf So Ha

2. n the FURROW-HORSE of a ploughing team II.3.4(a). ɒf St, ɔːf K

3. adj HAS NOT HELD, describing a cow that has not conceived III.1.7. ɔːf Nf

4. adj **go off, turn off** to CURDLE, referring to milk V.5.9. **go off** goː ɔːf W, guː ɔːf Co; **turn off** təʵːn̩ ɒf He, təʵːn̩ ɔːf So D

5. adj RANCID, describing bacon V.7.9. ɒːf Ess, ɔːf C Nf MxL Sr K Do Ha *[marked u.r. EM/SBM]*

6. adj **go off, turn off** to SPOIL, referring to meat or fish V.7.10. **go off** goː ɒf Sa Brk, goʊ ɒf He Mon, guː ɒf Y, gɒʊ ɒːf Sr K, gəʊ ɒːf Ess, gʏː ɔːf So, *3prsg* gɛʊz ɔːf Sr, gɒʊ ɔːf K, gɔː f MxL, gəʊ ɔːf Ess Brk K Ha, gʌʊ ɔːf Bd MxL Sr, *-ing* gʌʊɪn ɔːf Ess, goː ɔːf W Do, goʊ ɔːf Nf Bd So, *3prpl* goʊz ɔːf K, gʊ ɔːf Ess, *3prsg* gʊz ɔːf Wa, guː ɔːf Ess W Co D Ha; **turn off** təʵːn̩ ɔːf So Do

7. adj **bit off** ILL, describing a person who is unwell VI.13.1(b). bɪt ɔːf Sx

offal *1. n* CHAFF II.8.5. ɒfəɫ Hrt

2. n the PLUCK of a slaughtered animal III.11.6. œːfəl Nb, ɒfɪl Ch, ˌɒf'al Du, ɒfʊɫ Lei, ɒfl La Db St, ɒfɫ Nth, ɒvɫ Wo So, ɒfəl Y St, ɒfəɫ So, ɔːfʊɫ Brk, ɔːfʊ Sr Sx, ɔːfl Nf, ɔːfəl Nf So, ɔːfəɫ So W Ha

3. n the pluck of a cow. ɒfl Y, ɒfəl Y

4. n a butcher's term for the pluck of a slaughtered sheep or pig. ɔːfɫ Ha

5. n RUBBISH V.1.15. ɒfɫ Sx

6. n MEAL V.6.1(b). ɒfʊ Brk

offals *n* the PLUCK of a slaughtered animal III.11.6. ɒflz Gl, ɒfɫz Bd, ɔflz L

off-horse *1. n* the FAR-HORSE of a pair pulling a wagon I.6.4(b). ɑːfɑːs Mon, ɑːfaʵːs He, ɑːfaʵːʂ He, ɑːfɒs He, ɒfaʵːʂ So, ɒfɒs Ch Db Sa St, ɒ'fhɔːs K, ɒfɔːs Sa St Hrt K, *pl* ɒfɔʵːʂəz Ha, ɔfɔːs Wa K, ɔːfhaʵːʂ So, ɔːfaʵːʂ W Do Ha, ɔːfaʴːs Brk, ɔːfaʵʂ Wo, ɔːfhɒs Nf, ɔːfɒs Gl Nf Ess W Co D Do Ha, ɔːfhɔˑs Nf Ess, ɔːfɔːs Db Hrt Ess Sx, ɔˑfɔˑʴs K, ɔːfhɔʵːʂ So, ɔːfɔʵːʂ Sa O So D Do Ha, ɔːfɔːəʴs Brk Sr, ɔːfɔːəʵʂ Sr Sx

2. n the FURROW-HORSE of a ploughing team II.3.4(a). ɒfaʵːʂ W, ɒfɔːs Cu, ɒːfɔːəʵʈʂ Sx, ɔːfaʵːʂ Do, ɔːfaʴːs Brk, ɔːfɒs W D Do Ha, ɔːfhɔːs Ess, ɔːfɔːs Bk, ɔːfhɔˡːʂ So, ɔːfɔˡːʂ So Sr D Ha, ɔːfɔːəˡʂ Sr Sx

off-loading *v-ing* UNLOADING sheaves from a wagon II.6.8. ɔfluədn L

off-side *adj* ASKEW, describing a picture that is not hanging straight IX.1.3. ɔfsaːd Y

offside *1. n* the FAR-HORSE of a pair pulling a wagon I.6.4(b). aːfsɔɪd O, ɒfsɛɪd Ch, ɒfsaɪd We Y Lei, ɒfsaːd Lei, ɒfsaˑɪd Lei R, ɒfsɒɪd St, ɔfsaːd Y, ɔːfsaɪd Bk Bd Ess, ɔːfsɔɪd O Sf Bk Ess Brk

2. n the FURROW-HORSE of a ploughing team II.3.4(a). ɒfsaɪd St, ɒfsɒːɪd St, ɔːfsaɪd Nth Ess, ɔːfsɔɪd O Sf Bk Ess Brk, ɔːfsʌɪd Sr

offside-horse *1. n* the FAR-HORSE of a pair pulling a wagon I.6.4(b). aːfsəɪdaˡːʂ Mon Gl, aːvzəɪdaˡːʂ Gl, aːfsɒɪdaˡːʂ Wo, aːfsəɪdɒs Wo Mon, ɒfsaːdɒs Y, ɒfsaɪdɒs We Y, hɒfsaɪdɒs Du, ɒfsaːdɒs Y Ch, ɒfsaɪdɒs Db Nt, ɒfsɔɪdɒs Bk, ɒfsəɪdɒs He Mon, ɒfsaɪdɔs Nt, ɒfsaɪdɔːs He, ɒfsaɪdɔːs Cu, ɒfsaɪdɔːs La Ch Wa, ɒfsɛɪdɔːᵊs Nb, ɒfsɛɪdɔᵝːs Du, ɒfsaɪdɔˡːs La, ɒfsaɪdɔˡːs La, ɒfsaɪdɔˡːʂ Sa, ɔfsaɪdɔs Y L, ɔfsaɪdɔːs Ch, ɔfsaɪdɔˡːs La, ɔːfsəɪdaˡːʈʂ Brk, ɔːfsaɪdɒs La, ɔːfsaɪdɒs L Nth Bd, ɔˑfsaɪdaːs Y, ɔːfsɔɪdaˡːʂ Wa, ɔːfsaɪdɒˡˑʂ Ha, ɔˑfsaɪdhɔˑs Nf, ɔːfsɔɪdhɔs Sf, ɔːfsɔɪdɔs Sf, ɔˑfsʌɪdhɔs Nf, ɔːfsaɪdɔːs Wa Nth Hu Bk Hrt Ess, ɔːsɔɪdhɔːs Ess, ɔːfsɔɪdɔːs Wa Ess MxL, ɔːfsʌɪdhɔːs Sf, ɔːfsəɪdɔːs He Mon, ɔːfsaɪdɔˡːs Db, ɔːfsæɪdɔˡːʂ He, ɔːfsaɪdɔˡːʂ Sa, ɔːfsaɪdɔˡˑʂ Sr, ɔːfsɔɪdɔˡːʂ Nth Bk, ɔːfsəɪdɔˡːʂ Wo, ɔːfsəɪdəəˡːʂ Sx

2. n the FURROW-HORSE of a ploughing team II.3.4(a). ɒfsaɪdɒs Y, ɒfzɒɪdɒs Ha, ɒfsaɪdɔːs Ch, ɒfsɒɪdɔːs St, ɒfsaɪdɔˡːs La, ɔfsaɪdɔːs Ch, ɔːfsɒɪdaˡːʂ W, ɔːfzəɪdaˡːʂ W, ɔːfsɔɪdhɔs Sf, ɔːfsʌɪhɔːs Sf, ɔːfsaɪdɔːs Y, ɔːfsaɪdɔːs Bk Hrt MxL, ɔːfsɔɪdɔːs Wa, ɔːfsɔɪdɔˡːʂ Bk Sr, ɔːfsəɪdɔːəˡʈʂ Sx

offside-tit *n* the FAR-HORSE of a pair pulling a wagon I.6.4(b). ɒfsaɪdtɪt Db

off-tit *n* the FAR-HORSE of a pair pulling a wagon I.6.4(b) ɒftɪt St

offward-horse *n* the FAR-HORSE of a pair pulling a wagon I.6.4(b). ɔːfədɔs C Hrt

offward-side *n* the FAR-HORSE of a pair pulling a wagon I.6.4(b). ɔːfədsaɪd C

oil *1. n Before gas and electricity came in, people had to use what [to light their homes]?* V.2.13(a). Eng. ⇒ **lamp-oil**, **paraffin**, **paraffin-oil**

2. n CART-GREASE, used to lubricate the wheels of a cart I.11.4. ɛɪl Ch, aɪl St, aɪl La, ɔɪl Y Nf, ɔɪɫ Mon *[these rr. probably conditioned by the broad nature of the question]*

oils *n* **in oils** TANGLED, describing hair VI.2.5. ɪn ɒɪɫz Brk *[queried fw's error for **in coils** SBM]*

old *1. adj I am a young man, and you are ....* VIII.1.20. Eng. ⇒ **oldy**

2. adj **get old** to SPOIL, referring to meat or fish V.7.10. *-s* gɛts ɔʊd La

old boy *n* **the old boy** the DEVIL VIII.8.3. ðə ɒʊɫ bɒɪ K, ðə ɔʊɫ bɒɪ K

old chap *1. n* my HUSBAND VIII.1.25. **the old chap** t ɛʊd tʃap Db

2. n **the old chap** the DEVIL VIII.8.3. ðə ɒʊᵊɫ tʃæp Gl, ðə ɔʊɫ tʃæp Sr

old chummies *npl* MATES VIII.4.1. ɔʊl tʃʌmɪz Nf

old clobber *n* ORDINARY CLOTHES VI.14.20. ɔʊɫ klɒbəˡ Bk

old clothes *n* ORDINARY CLOTHES VI.14.20. ɔːd klɪəz Y, aːld tleaz La, aːd tleaz La, ɔːɫ kloːz So, ɔʊl tlouz Nf, ɒʊd kluəz Y; **old weekday clothes** ʌuld wiːkdeɪ klʌuz Ess

old crone* *n* an old toothless EWE past the age of having lambs III.6.6. ɒʊld kɹoʊn Nf, ɔʊld kɹoʊn Nf

old devil *n* DEVIL VIII.8.3. ould dɛvl Nf; **the old devil** ðɪ ɔʊɫ dɛvʊ K Ha Sx

old dutch *n* my WIFE VIII.1.24. **the old dutch** VIII.1.24. ðɪ ʌʊɫ dʌtʃ MxL

old ewe *n* a EWE III.6.6. aːd jɒʊ Nb, ɒˑʊ jɒˑʊ Nf, ɔʊl jɔʊ Wo

old falls *n* the FLAP at the front of old-fashioned trousers VI.14.16. ɒʊɫ fɔːz So, ɔʊ fɔːz So *[queried SBM]*

old fellow *1. n* my HUSBAND VIII.1.25. **our old fellow** aːɹ ɒʊd fɛlə Y

2. n **the old fellow** the DEVIL VIII.8.3. ðə aʊd fɛlə Sa

oldfield *n* AFTERMATH, a second crop of grass II.9.17. oːɫviːᶷɫd W

old girl *n* my WIFE VIII.1.24. **the old girl** ð ɔʊɫ gɛəɫ W

old-grass field *n* a MEADOW II.9.2. aːdgʁɛs fiːld Nb

old harry *1. n* a BOGEY VIII.8.1. ʌʊɫd æɹɪ MxL, ɔʊɫ aɹɪ Nth

2. n DEVIL VIII.8.3. ɒʊd æɹɪ He, ɔːɫd æɹɪ Mon, ɔʊɫ aɹɪ Nth

old hog-pig *n* a BOAR III.8.7. ɔʊld ɒgpɪg Wo

old jerk *n* a HARE IV.5.10. ɔːd dʒəˑɹk Y

old lad *1. n* **the old lad** a BOGEY VIII.8.1. ð ɒʊd lad L

2. n DEVIL VIII.8.3. aʊd lad Sa, ɒʊd lad La, ɔʊd lad Y L, ɔˑəd lad Y; **the old lad** t ɔʊd læd Y, θ ɛʊd lad La Ch, ð ɛʊd lad Ch Db, t ɛʊd lad Db, t aːld lad La Y, ðə aʊd laˑd Sa, ð ɒʊd lad Nt, t ɒʊd lad Y, θ ɔʊd lad La Y, ð ɔʊd lad La L, t ɔʊd lad Y, t ɔəd lad Y

old lady *n* my WIFE VIII.1.24. **the old lady** ð ɔʊl lɛɪdɪ St

old-land *1. n* PASTURE II.1.3. ɒlən Nf

2. *n* grass-land that has been cut. ɒlənd Nf, ɔːlən Nf

3. *n* a hayfield used for grazing after cutting. ɒlən Nf

4. *n* **old old-land** a MEADOW II.9.2. oul ɒlən Nf*[sometimes ploughed]*

old man *1. n* my HUSBAND VIII.1.25. æʊd mɒn St; **my old man** mɪ ʊɫ mæn K, mæɪ ɔːɫ man D, mɔɪ ɔuld mɒn Wo; **the old man** ðɪ ʌʊɫ mæn Ess, ð oːɫ mæn Co, ð oʊɫ mæn So, ðɪ ɒʊɫ mæːn Sx, ðə woʊɫ mæ'n So, ð ɒʊɫ man W, t ɔːld man We, ð ɒud man L, ð oːɫ man D Ha, ðɪ oʊɫ man So, ð oʊɫ man Wa W, ð oːɫ maːn So Ha, ðə woːɫ maːn Do, ðə æʊɫ mɒn He

2. *n* a BOGEY VIII.8.1. **the old man** ðɪ ɔʊɫ mæn K, ðə ʌʊɫ mæn Ess; **thick old man** ðɪk ɒʊɫ man Gl

3. *n* **the old man** the DEVIL VIII.8.3. ðə oːɫ maːn Mon, ðɪ æʊᵊɫ mɒn Gl, ðə aʊl mɒn Wo

old masker *n* a HARE IV.5.10. ɑːd maskə Y

old mob *n* a SCARECROW II.3.7. ɔ'əd mɒb Y

old nick *1. n* a BOGEY VIII.8.1. ɒʊɫ nɪk Wa, ɔʊɫ nɪk Ess, oʊɫ nɪk So*[old]*; **the old nick** ðɪ ɔʊɫ nɪk Ha, t ɔəd nɪk Y *[not a WMBM headword]*

2. *n* **old nick, old sir nick** DEVIL VIII.8.3. **old nick** ɛud nɪk Sa St, æʊɫd nɪk He, æʊɫ nɪk Gl, ɛud nɪk St He, aːld nɪk We La, aːl nɪk Cu, aːd nɪk Nb Du*[very old x1]* La, aʊd nɪk La Sa, ɒuld nɪk Nb, ɒʊɫd nɪk He Mon, ɒul nɪk K, ɒʊɫ nɪk Gl, ɒud nɪk La Y Db Sa He Wo, ɔːld nɪk Cu*[old x1]*, ɔːd nɪk Du Y, ɔuld nɪk Y, ɔʊɫ nɪk Lei, ɔud nɪk Y, ɔəd nɪk Y, ʌʊɫ nɪk Ess, oːl nɪk He, oːɫ nɪk Co Do, oːd nɪk Nb, ould nɪk Nf, oʊɫd nɪk W, oʊɫ nɪk Lei Nf So, oud nɪk St, ou nɪk So; **old sir nick** oːɫ səʳɫ n̩ɪk Co

old roy *n* a local FESTIVAL or holiday VII.4.11. aːd ɹɔɪ Y

old shep *n* a SHEPHERD I.2.1. oːɫ ʃɛp W Ha, oʊɫ ʃɛp W

old sow *n* a SOW III.8.6. aːd sɪu Y, ɔːd sɪuː Y, ɒʊl sɛu Nf, o'uld səu Nf

old togs *n* ORDINARY CLOTHES VI.14.20. ʌʊɫ tɔgz Sf

old woman *n* my WIFE VIII.1.24. **my old woman** mæː oːɫ wʌmən D, maː oːɫd ʌmən D, miː oːɫ wumən Co, maɪ oːɫ wumən Co, mæɪ oʊɫ umən So, mɒɪ ɒuld umən So; **the old woman** ð oːɫ wʌmən D, ð oːɫd ʌmən D, t ɛud wumən Db, ð æud wumən St, t ɒud wumən Y, t ɔːld wumən We, ð ɔud wumən L, t ɔ'əd wumən Y, ð oːɫ wumən D, ð oʊɫd wumən So, ð aud umən W, ðə woːld umən So, ðɪ oʊɫ umən So*[old]*

oldy *adj* OLD VIII.1.20. oːɫdi Co

olves* *n* barley AWNS II.5.3. ɔːɫvz Ha

on *1. adj* **is not on** HAS NOT HELD, describing a cow that has not conceived III.1.7. ɪnəʊ ɔːn Wo

2. *adj* ON HEAT, describing a sow III.8.9. ɒn So W

one *pron* **one or two** A FEW VII.8.21. jɪn ə twiː Cu, jan ə twˡi: Du, jan ə twɪə Y, jan ə tʊə Y, jan ə tuː Y, wɒn ə tæʊ St, wɒn ə tuː Y Sa, wɔn əɹ tuː L, wʊn ə tuː Y, wʊn əᵗː tuː Wo

one-haw *adj* ASKEW, describing a picture that is not hanging straight IX.1.3. wɒn'əᵗːɹ Sx

one on top *n* the LAND-HORSE of a ploughing team II.3.4(b). wʌn ɒn tɒp Ess

one or two *adj* A FEW VII.1.19. jan ə tuː Y

oner *n* **all of a oner** ASKEW, describing a picture that is not hanging straight IX.1.3. ɔːl əv ə wʌnə O

one-shear *1. n* a sheep before its first shearing, ⇐ EWE-HOG III.6.4. wɒnʃɪə Wa *[taken by BM Edd to refer to sheep after first shearing, ⇒ gimmer III.6.5]*

2. *n* a sheep from its first to its second shearing, ⇐ GIMMER III.6.5. wɒnʃɪə Wa L, wʊnʃɪə Y, wʊnʃɪəᵗ Brk

one side *adj* ASKEW, describing a picture that is not hanging straight IX.1.3. wʌn zæɪd So, wʌnsɔɪd O; **on one side** ə wɒn sɒːɪd St; **to one side** tə wɒn saɪd L

one-stoner *n* a RIDGEL III.4.7. wʌnstʌnə Nf

onion *n* What do you call that vegetable with the thin brown skin that makes your eyes water? V.7.15. Eng. ⇒ also **bottomer**

onion-gruel* *n* GRUEL made from onions and milk thickened with flour V.7.2. ɪŋəngɹuˑəɫ Bd, ɑɪnəngɹuːəl Bk, ɔɪnəngɹuːəɫ Bk, ʌɲɪngɹʊəɫ Ess, ʌɲɪngɹɪuːᵊɫ C, ʌɲɪngɹuːəɫ Hrt, ʌɲəngɹuːəɫ Ess, ʌɲəngɹuˑəɫ Sf, ʌɲəngɹɹːɫ Nf, ʊɲɪngɹuˑəɫ C

only *adv* If your little girl Mary did something wrong, you wouldn't be so hard on her as on a grown-up, you'd say: After all, Mary is … a child. VII.8.12. Eng exc. Cu Du We. ⇒ **but, just, nobbut, nothing but, nought, nought but, nought only**

onstead *n* a FARMSTEAD I.1.2. ɒnstɪd Nb, ɒnstiːd Nb Du, ɒnstiːd Nb, ɒnstɛd Nb

ooze *n* CLAY IV.4.2. ʉːz Nf

oozle *1. n* a THROAT VI.6.3. ʌzɫ Co

2. *n* the WINDPIPE VI.6.5. ʌzɫ Co

oozy *adj* BOGGY IV.1.8. ʉːzɪ Nf

ope *adj* **a bit ope, half ope, half-way ope** AJAR IX.2.7. **a bit ope** ə bɪd ɔːp D; **half ope** aːf ɔːp D; **half-way ope** aːfwɛɪ ɔːp D

open *1. adj* CLOVEN, describing the hoof of a cow III.2.8(b). ɒpn Y, hɒpn Cu, oːpn Wo, oːpm Do, oupn Nth

2. *adv* ASTRIDE VI.9.8. ɒpn Y*[old]*, ɒpn L; **feet wide open** fiːt waɪd ʌupn Bd; **legs gaping open** lɛgz gɪəpɪn ɒpn Y; **legs open** lɛgz ɒpn La, lɛgz ɒpn Y Ch, lɛgz oupn Nf; **legs wide open** lɛgz waːd ɒpn La, lɛgz waɪd ɒpn Y, lɛgz waːd ɒpən Y, lɛgz waɪd ɒpən Y, lɛgz waɪd ɒpn Ch, lɛgz waɪd ɒpm La; **wide open** waːɪd ɒpn La

3. *adj* AJAR IX.2.7. ɒpn La, ɔupn R, upn Lei; **a bit of way open** ə bɪt ə weː ɒpn Nt, ə bɪt ə wɛ'ə ɔpn L; **a bit open** ə bɪt øːpən Du, ə bɪt ɒpn Du La

Y Ch, ə bɪt ɒpən Du La, ə bɪt ɔpn Y; **a little bit open** ə laːl bɪt ɒpn Cu, ə lɪtl bɪt ɒpən Y, ə laɪl bɪt ɔpn Y; **a piece of way open** ə piːs ə weː ɔpn Nt*[old]*; **a shade open** ə ʃeːd ɔpn Y; **half open** eːf ɒpn Ch, ɔːf ɒpn Y, ɔːf ɒpən Y, aːv ɒbm Co D, aːf oːpn Gl, æf oːpm Brk, æːf oʊpn So; **half-way open** heːfwaɪ oːpn W, aːfweː oːpm Co; **half-ways open** aːfweɪz oːpm So; **open a bit** ɒpən ə bɪt Y; **partly open** paːtlɪ ɒpn Y, paːtlɪ ɒpən Y, pɛətlɪ ɔpən Y; **part open** pæᴶːt ɒpn La, paːt ɒpn Db, paᴿːt ɔpən Nb, paːt oːpn Ch; **part-way open** pɛᵗːtweɪ oːpən Co; **piece of the way open** piːs ə ðə weː oʊpən Man; **wee bit open** wiː bɪt ɔpn Nb *[open marked u.r. EMBM]*

opened out *adv* ASTRIDE VI.9.8. ɒpnd uːt Y

opening *n* a GATEWAY IV.3.8. øːpnən Nb, ɒpnɪn Y, ɒpn̩ɪn Y, ɒʊpnɪn Sx, ɔpnɪn Y, ʌʊpn̩ɪn MxL, oʊpnɪn St

open-legged *adv* ASTRIDE VI.9.8. ɒpnlɛgd Y

open-legs *adv* ASTRIDE VI.9.8. ɒpnlɛgz Y

open out *1.1. vtphr* to CLEAR grass at the edges of a field II.9.5. ɒpn ... aʊt Y, ɒpn ... ᵊuːt Y

1.2. vphr to clear grass. ɒpm aʊt Y *[marked u.r. NBM]*

2. vtphr to DITCH IV.2.11. *-ing* ɒpnən uːt We, oʊpn ... æʊt St

opens *vi-3prsg* school BEGINS VIII.6.2(a). Eng exc. Du Mon O Hrt Brk Ha

open shed *n* the STRAW-YARD of a farm I.1.9. oʊpn ʃɛd St

opens out *viphr-3prsg* school BEGINS VIII.6.2(a). ɒpnz uːt Y

open-toed *adj* SPLAY-FOOTED VI.10.5. ɔpntʊəd Y

open-yard *1. n* a FARMYARD I.1.3. ɔpnjaːd L

2. n the STRAW-YARD of a farm I.1.9. *pl* ɔʊpnjaːdz Hu, oːpn jaɪd He, oːpn jaᵗːd̩ Sa

ope-way *n* a FORD IV.1.3. oːpwɛɪ D

ordinaries *n* ORDINARY CLOTHES VI.14.20. ɔᴿːdnɛʁɪz Du

ordinary clothes *n What do you call the things you wear on weekdays?* VI.14.20. ɔᴿːdnəʁɪ kleəz Nb, ɔːdɪnəɹɪ klæʊz Hrt, ɔːdnɹɪ klɔʊz Nth, ɔːdɹ̩ɪ klʌʊz MxL. ⇒ **clobber, evening clothes, everyday clothes, everyday things, everyday wear, knockabout clothes, old clobber, old clothes, old togs, old** *weekday* **clothes, ordinaries, rough clothes, roughs, rough tog, shifting clothes, warday clothes, warday suit, wearing clothes, week-a-day clothes, week-a-days, week-a-days clobber, week-a-days clothes, weekday clothes, weekdays, weekday suit, weekday things, weekday togs, weekenday clothes, workaday clothes, work clothes, workday clobber, workday clothes, working clobber, working clothes, working-day clothes, working suit, working tack, working tackle, working things, working togs, worky clothes**

orphan *n* a PET-LAMB III.7.3. ɔːfn Sf, *pl* ɔːfənz Ess *[marked u.r. EMBM]*

osier *n* WILLOW IV.10.7. ʌʊʒə Sr, oʊʒɪ Nf, oʊʒə Man Nf*[for basket making]*, *pl* oːʊʒɪz Nf, *-s* ɪəzɪəz L*[pliable]*

osier carr* *n* a plantation of osiers on wet, boggy ground, ⇐ WILLOW IV.10.7. oʊʒə kaː Nf

ossed *vi-3ptsg* he TRIED VIII.8.4. ɒst Y, ɔst Y

ought *vaux-3pl* OUGHT TO IX.4.6. aːt He Wo Mon Gl, aᵗːt̩ Wo Gl, ɒʊt Db Nt, ɔːt Ch Sa He Mon Gl O Ess D, ɔːd D, ɔːʔ O, ɔᵗːt̩ Sa, ɔʊt L

ought to *vaux-3pl Children are always expected to help their parents in their old age, but if they don't, other people will say they certainly ... help them.* IX.4.6. Eng. ⇒ **ought, should,** *sould* ⇒ **should,** *stand* need *to*

ouse *n* the EAVES of a stack of corn II.7.3. ɛʊs Y, ɔʊs Y

ousing *n* the EAVES of a stack of corn II.7.3. ɛʊzɪn Y, aʊzɪn La

ousing-tin *n* a SCOOP used to take water out of a boiler V.9.9. aʊzɪntɪn Y

out *1. adj* IN FLOOD, describing a river IV.1.4. ɛːt Db, æʏt D, æʊt Wo Wa; **well out** wiːl aʊt Y *[see note at flood]*

2. adv WITHOUT V.8.10(a). æʏt So

3. adv legs out ASTRIDE VI.9.8. lɛgz æʊt Wo

out-holl *v* to DITCH IV.2.11. *-ing* ɛʊtʰɒlɪn Nf, *-ing* əʊtʰɒˈlɪn Nf, *-ing* əʊtʰɒˈlən Nf

out-house *n* an EARTH-CLOSET V.1.13. ɛʊtʰɛʊs Ess

out-inner *adj* ASKEW, describing a picture that is not hanging straight IX.1.3. 'æʊt'ɪnəᵗ Do

outlet *n* a PADDOCK I.1.10. aʊtlɛt Ch

outlets *n* a CART-FRAME I.10.6. ɛʊtlɛts K

outside *n* the FURROW-HORSE of a ploughing team II.3.4(a). aʊtsaːɪd St

outside-horse *1. n* the FAR-HORSE of a pair pulling a wagon I.6.4(b). ᵓuːtsaɪdɒs Du

2. n the LAND-HORSE of a ploughing team II.3.4(b). əʊtsəɪdɒs Gl

outside-mow *v* to CLEAR grass at the edges of a field II.9.5. *-ing* əʊtsaɪdmoˑɪn Brk

oval-hive *n* a SKEP IV.8.8(b). ɒvʊ-əɪv Sx

oval rick *n* an oval stack, ⇐ STACKS II.7.1. oʊvʊ ɾɪk Brk

oven-shelf *n* a GIRDLE for baking cakes V.7.4(b). ʊvnʃɛlf Nt L

over *1. adv* overturned, referring to a cart, ⇐ to OVERTURN I.11.5. oʊvə St

2. adv TOO *HOT* V.6.8. aʊə Cu Du Y, aʊəɪ We, aʊə Nb Y, ɒvə Y, ɒʊr Cu, ɒʊə Nb Cu Du La, ɒʊɹ (+V) We Y, ɒʊəɾ Cu, ɒʊəᴿ Du, ɒʊəɹ Du We, ɒʊwəɹ (+V) L, ɔvəɹ (+V) L, ɔwəɹ (+V) L, ɔʊəᴿ

Nb, ɔʊə Nb Y, ɔʊəɹ (+V) L, ɔʊwəɹ (+V) Y L

3. *adj* FINISHED, referring to a store of potatoes V.7.21. ɒʊə Nt, ɔwə L, oʊvəᶜ Wo, oʊvəᶜː So; **all over** ɔːɫ ɔːvəᶜː W

4. *adj* **all over** TANGLED, describing hair VI.2.5. ɔːl ʌʊvə Ess

over-banked *adj IN* FLOOD, describing a river IV.1.4. oːvəbaːŋkt Mon *[see note at flood]*

overcassen *adj* OVERTURNED, describing a sheep on its back unable to get up III.7.4. ɒʊəkɛsn We

overcast 1. *adj* OVERTURNED, describing a sheep on its back unable to get up III.7.4. ɒvəkast Y L, ovəᶜkæst Brk, uːvəkjast Ch

2. *adj* DULL, referring to the weather VII.6.10. aʊəkɛst Y, ɔʊvəkɑːst Wa, oːvəᶜkæst Brk

overcoat *n When you go out in very cold weather, what else do you put on [over a jacket]?* VI.14.6. æʊvəkæʊ? Hrt, ɑʊəkʊət Y, ɒvəkʊət Y*[refined x1]* Nt, ɒʊəkɒʊt K, ɒʊvəᴶkɒʊt Sr K, ɒʊəᴶkɒʊt Sr, ɒʊvəᶜkɒʊt Sr Sx, ɒʊvəkoʊt K, ɒʊvəkoˑᵊt Man, ɔvəkʊət L, ɔːvəᶜːkɔːt Ha, *pl* ɔːvəkɔˑəts Y, ɔːvəᶜːkoːt So Co D, ɔːvəᶜːkuːt Co D, ɔːvəkwæt So, ɔːvəᶜːkuət W D, ɔːivəᶜːkuːət W Co D Do, ɔʊvəkɔʊt Lei R Hu Ess, ɔʊvəᴶkɔʊt K, ɔʊvəᶜkɔʊt Sx, ɔʊvəkʌʊt Ess, ʌʊvəkʌʊt Sf*[old x1]* Hrt Ess MxL Sr K, ʌʊvəkʊt Sf, oːvəkoːt Mon So, oːvəᶜkoːt Sa He Wo Mon, oːvəᶜːkoːt So W Co Ha, woːvəᶜːkoːt Ha, oːvəᶜːkoːət Do, oːvəᶜːkuːt Co Ha, oːvəᶜːkwət Do, oːvəᶜːkuːət Ha, oʊvəᶜːkoːt So, oʊvəkɔʊt Man St Mon Lei C Nf Ha, oˑʊvəkoʊt? Nf, oʊvəkoʊ? Nf, oʊvəᴶkoʊt Brk, oʊvəᶜkoʊt Wo Mon So, oʊəᶜkɔʊt So, oʊvəkuːt St, oːʊvəᶜkoːʊt Gl, oʊvəkʊət Nth, oːʊvəkwət Gl, ʊvəkɔʊt Lei, ʊvəkoʊt Lei, ʊvəkət Lei. ⇒ **big-coat, coat, greatcoat, heavy-coat, topcoat**

over-flood *adj IN* FLOOD, describing a river IV.1.4. oːvəᶜːfɫʌd Ha *[see note at flood]*

over-flowed *adj IN* FLOOD, describing a river IV.1.4. ɒvəflɔʊd L, ɒʊvəflɒʊd Wa, ɒʊvəᴶflɒʊd Sr, ɔːvəᶜːvlɒʊd W, ɔːvəᶜːvlɔːd W Ha, ɔʊvəflɔʊd Hu, ɔʊvəɹflɔʊd O, ʌʊvəflʌʊd C Sf Bd Ess, ovəflʌʊd Nf, oːvəflʊʊd Gl, oːvəfloːd Ch, oːvəᶜːfɫɔːd D, oːvəᶜːvɫoːd Ha, oːᵊfloːd Ch, oʊvəfloʊd St Wa Gl C, ʊəvəflɔʊd L *[see note at flood]*

over-flowing *adj IN* FLOOD, describing a tidal river IV.1.4. ɒʊvəflɒʊɪn Sx, ɒʊvəᶜflɒʊɪn Sx, ɔˑvəᴶflɒʊɪn Brk, ɔʊwəflɒʊ-ɪn L, oːəɹfloːɪn La, *prppl* ɔʊvəflaˑ-ɪn Nf, *prppl* ɔʊvəflɒʊ-ɪn Nf, *prppl* ɔʊvəflaˑɪn Nf, ɔʊvəflɔʊɪn O, *inf* ɔʊvəflɔʊ Ess *[see note at flood]*

over-flown *adj IN* FLOOD, describing a river IV.1.4. ɒʊvəflɒʊn Nth, ɒvəfloːᵁn Db, ɔʊvəflɔʊn Nth, ɔwəflɔʊn L, ʌʊvəflʌʊn Bd Ess, oːvəᶜːvɫɔːn D, oʊvəflɔʊn Wa *[not a SBM headword. See note at flood]*

over head *adv* HEAD OVER HEELS IX.1.10. ʌʊvə ɹɛʊ ɛd Bk; **over the head*** ɒʊə t ɹəd Y; **over your head** ɒvəɹ jəɹ ɪˑəd Y

overheat *vi* to HEAT, referring to a haystack II.9.16. æʊvɹəiˑ? Hrt, *3prsg* ɒvəɹiˑəts Y, *3prsg* ɔvəɹiːts L, ɔʊvəɹiːit Hu, ɔʊvəᴶ-ɪit Brk, oːvəᶜːhiːt So, oːvəᶜːɹiˑit W, *-ing* oːvəᶜːɹɛːʔn Ha, *3prsg* oʊvəɹiːts St

over-heated *adj* **get over-heated** to HEAT, referring to a haystack II.9.16. *3prsg* ɡɪts ɔːvəᶜːɹiːtɪd D, *3prsg* ɡɪts ɔʊvəᶜhiːtɪd Sx, ɡɛt oʊvəᶜːɹiːtɪd So

overlaid *adj* OVERTURNED, describing a sheep on its back unable to get up III.7.4. ɒʊvəᴶlæɪd K, ɒʊvəᶜlɛzɹɪd Sx, oʊvəlɛɪd St, oʊvəlæɪd K

overload *v* to STOCK a cow III.3.6. oːvəᶜloːd Sa

over-noddles *adv* HEAD OVER HEELS IX.1.10. ɒʊənɒdlz We

over-reach *vi* to RETCH VI.13.15. oːvəᶜɹiːtʃ He

over-rods *n* a CART-FRAME I.10.6. oʊvəᴶ-ɹɒˑdz Ha

over-rolled *adj* OVERTURNED, describing a sheep on its back unable to get up III.7.4. ɒvəɹɒld St Nt, oˑəɹɒld Db

over-ropes *n* ROPES used to fasten thatch on a stack II.7.7(b2). ɒʊəɹeˑaps Cu

overrun *vi-ed* HAS NOT HELD, referring to a cow that has not conceived III.1.7. oːvəᶜɹʌn Sa, oʊvəɹʏn Nf

overstrung *adj* describing a cow which SHOWS SIGNS OF CALVING III.1.12. ɒvəᶜstɹʌŋ Brk

overthrow *vi* to OVERTURN, referring to a cart I.11.5. *-ed* æʊvəθɹæʊd Hrt, ʌʊvəθɹʌʊ Hrt, ɒʊəθɹɔʊ C

overthrowed* *adj* OVERTURNED, describing a sheep on its back unable to get up III.7.4. ɒʊəɹɔʊd St, oˑəθɹʊt Db

overthrown *adj* OVERTURNED, describing a sheep on its back unable to get up III.7.4. ɑʊəθɹɔːn Y, ɒvəθɹɔʊn L, ɔʊəθɹuːn Y, ɔwɔθɹɔʊn L, ɔwɔθɹuːn L, oːvəθɹɔːn Db, oəθɹɔːᵁn Db, oʊvəθɹɔʊn St

over-thwarting *adv* DIAGONALLY, referring to harrowing a field IX.1.8. oˑʊvəwɔːət?n Nf

over-thwart(s) *adv* DIAGONALLY, referring to harrowing a field IX.1.8.
no -s: oʊvəwɔˑət Nf
-s: aʊəkwaːts Y

over-tip *vi* to OVERTURN, referring to a cart I.11.5. oːʊvəᶜtɪp Gl

overturn *vi Suppose your cart goes over accidentally, what would you say it does?* I.11.5. ʌʊvətaːn Sf, ɒʊətəːn K, ʌʊvətəːn Ess, *-ed* æʊvətəːnd Hrt, ɒʊvətəːɪn Nth, *-ed* oːvəᶜːtəᶜːnd̩ So W, *-ed* oːvəᶜːtəᶜːnd̩ D Do, *-ed* ʌʊvətəᶜːnd̩ Ess, oːvəᶜtəᶜːn He Gl, *-ed* oːvəᶜːtəᶜːnd̩ W, oʊvəᶜtəᶜːn Wo. ⇒ **arse-over-head, atilt over,**

balch over, *been* upset, bitch up, capsize, chuck over, cockle over, cock over, coup, coup over, coup up, fall over, fling over, *go arse-over-head*, *gone arse over head* ⇒ arse-over-head, go over, *go upside-down*, *had the load over* ⇒ have over, *he's gone arse over head* ⇒ arse-over-head, *is* over, *it's gone arse over head* ⇒ arse-over-head, keck over, keck up, keel over, keel up, over, overthrow, overtip, put over, skell, skell over, skell up, slip over, throw over, throw *the cart*, throw *the cart over*, tilt, tip, *tip arse over head* ⇒ arse-over-head, tipe, tipple, tipple over, tip over, tip up, topple over, tumble over, turn *it* over, turn over, turn *the cart over*, upset, uptip, walt, walt over, *went arse over head* ⇒ arse-over-head

overturned *adj Sometimes a sheep gets turned over on its back and can't get up, so you say the sheep is* .... III.7.4. ɔːvəˡːtəˡːn̩d D, oːvəˡːtəˡːn̩d W. ⇒ award, aweld, awkward, cassen, cassened, cast, casted, far-welted, *fast on his back, gone on his back, got on his back, got over on his back, has got onto its back*, heaved, laid, laid *fast*, mislaid, *on her back, on his back, on its back, on the back, on their back*, overcassen, overcast, *over-hulled* ⇒ over-rolled, overlaid, *over on his back, over on its back*, over-rolled, overthrowed, overthrown, rean-wawted, rigged, rig-welted, saddle-backed, straddled, thrown, *turned* nonpower, unpowered

over-year hogget *n* a sheep from its first to its second shearing, ⇐ GIMMER III.6.5. ouvəjɪə hɒˈɡɪt Nf

owl *n What do you call that bird with large round eyes; it flies about at night?* IV.7.6. Eng. ⇒ barn-owl, cat-face, *howlet* ⇒ owlet, *jenny-howlet* ⇒ jenny-owlet, jenny-owl, jenny-owlet, meg-owl, meg- owlet, owlet, *polly-howlet* ⇒ polly-owlet, polly-owlet, screet-owl

owlet *n* an OWL IV.7.6. ʊlɪt La Y, hʊlɪt Y, ʊlət Cu We La Y Sa, ʊləˡt La He, ʊləˡːt̩ Sa, huːlət Nb Cu, uːlət Cu Y*[young]*, *pl* juːlɪts Y, juːlət We Y, juːləd Y

oxberry-root *n* BINDWEED II.2.4. azbɹɪɹuːt Ch *[queried WMBM]*

oxter *n* an ARMPIT VI.6.7. œːkstɔᴿ Nb, ɒkstɔᴿ Nb Du, ɒkstə Nb Cu*[very old and rare x1]* Du We*[old and rare]* Y*[old x1]*, hɒkstə Du, ɒksθə Du, ɒkstər Cu Du, ɒkstəɹ Cu Y, ɔkstɔᴿ Nb, ɔkstə Y*[old]*, okstɔᴿ Nb, ʊkstər Cu

oxter-bone *n* the human HIP-BONE VI.9.1. ʊkstəbɪən Y

P

pace eggs *npl* EASTER EGGS VII.4.9. piːs ɛgz Cu, pjɛst ɛgz Nb Du, pɪas ɛgz Cu*['broader' dialect]* Y, pɪast ɛgz Du Y, pɪəs ɛgz Nb Cu We, *sg* pɪəs ɛg Du, pɪəst ɛgz Du Y, peːs ɛgz Cu La Y Db, peːᵊs ɛgz Nb Cu, peːst ɛgz Nb La, peas ɛgz Cu We La, peast ɛgz Du, peəs ɛgz La, peəst ɛgz Du, pɛəs ɛgz Y

pack away *vtphr-3sg* she [i.e. a tidy girl] will COLLECT her toys VIII.8.15. pæk ... əwɛɪ MxL, pak ... əwiː Db, pak ... əwɛɪ O L D

packer *1. n* the LOADER of sheaves onto a wagon II.6.7(c). pækə Man, pækəɹ Man

2. n a DIAPER V.11.3. pækʔə Nf

packet *n* a BAG containing sweets V.8.5. pækɪt Wo Nf, pæˑkʔɪt Nf, pækət Nf, pækʔət Nf, pakɪt Wo Mon O L, pakət Nb Cu

packing *1. n* a SNACK VII.5.11. pakɪn Y

2. n MEAL OUT VII.5.12. pakɪn Y

packing-cloth *n* a DIAPER V.11.3. pækʔɪnklɔθ Nf

packing-up grub *n* MEAL OUT VII.5.12. pækɪnʌp gɹʌb Ess

packing-up-time *n* STOPPING-TIME at the end of a day's work VII.5.9. pækɪɪʌptaɪm Sa, pækɪnʌptɑɪm Hu, pækʔɪnʌptʌɪm Nf, pækɪnʌptəɪm Brk, pakɪnʊptɑˑɪm L

packman *n* a snail, ⇐ SNAILS IV.9.3. pakmən R

pack off *imp* GO AWAY! VIII.7.9(a). pak ɔːᵊf Nth

pack round *vphr* to PITCH sheaves II.6.10. *-ing* pakɪn ɽæʊn Ha

pack up *1. vtphr* to STOCK III.3.6. *-ing* pakən ... ʊp Cu

2. vtphr-3sg she [i.e. a tidy girl] will COLLECT her toys VIII.8.15. pɛk ... ʌp Sr, *3prsg* pɛks ... ʌp Sx, pæk ... ʌp Hu Ess So W K, pækʔ ... ʌp Nf, pæk ... ʏp Nf, pækʔ ... ʏp Nf, pak ... ʌp O Bd Hrt W Do Ha, pak ... ʊp Ch Sa Nt L Lei Nth, pag (+V) ... ʊp Y; **pack up together** pak ... ʊp təgɪðəᵗ Sa

pad *1. n* the SADDLE of the harness of a cart-horse I.5.6. pɛd Sr Sx, pæd So Sr K, pad Gl O So Ha, pɑˑd Ha

2. n the SOLE of a horse-drawn plough I.8.9. pɛd Ess

3. n a CLOT OF COW-DUNG II.1.6. pɛd Ess; **pad of cow-shit** pæd ə kævʃɪt Co

4. n a CUTTING of hay II.9.15. pad D

5. n a SHEATH or other device used to keep a knitting-needle firm V.10.10. pæd Nf, pad L

6. n a PATH through a field IV.3.11. pæd Sa, pad Du La Ch Sa L Lei R Nth

7. n a path made by animals. pæd Nf

8. vt **pad the hoof** to WALK VIII.7.10. pæd ðə hʊf Sf*[very rare, old]*

paddick-gallon *n* a SCOOP used to take water out of a boiler V.9.9. padɪgalən Nb*[very old]*

padding *n* a PATH through a field IV.3.11. padɪn Wa

paddle *1. n* the SOLE of a horse-drawn plough I.8.9. pædʊ Sr *[marked ir.r. SBM]*

2. n a FLAIL II.8.3. pædł So

3. vt to DIRTY a floor V.2.8. padl St, padł Lei

paddle up *vtphr* to DIRTY a floor V.2.8. padl ... ʊp St

paddock

1. n *What do you call the small enclosed piece of pasture near the farmhouse, the place where you might put a cow or a pony that's none too well?* I.1.10. Eng exc. Co. ⇒ **back-meadow, boosy-pasture, butt, calf-close, calf-garth, calf-plot, calves'-meadow, calves'-plat, calves'-run, close, coppy, croft, fold, garth, hemplands, home-close, home-ground, home-paddock, hoppet, horse-pightle, house-meadow, little pasture, mead, meadow, measure grove, nigh, outlet, paddocks, paddy, park, parrock, pasture-field, patch,** *piddle* ⇒ **pightle, pightle, pigs'-meadow, pinfold,** *plack* ⇒ **pleck/plock, plat, pleck, plock, plot, screech, sheep's-meadow, sick-field, slipe, small plat, splat**

2. n a small field near a farmhouse, in which animals are exercised. padʌk Mon

3. n a TOAD IV.9.7. padək Cu

paddocked *adj* THIRSTY VI.13.10. padəkt La

paddocks *1. n* a PADDOCK I.1.10. *sg* pædɪks Sx

2. npl FROGS IV.9.6. padɪks Nb Du, *sg* padɪk Cu, padəks We La, *sg* padək Nb Cu

paddock-stool *n* a toadstool, ⇐ TOAD IV.9.7. padɪkstɪəl Cu La, *-s* padɪkstɪəlz We, padəkstɪəl Cu, padəkstuːl Cu

paddy *n* a PADDOCK I.1.10. pade Y

padgy-poll* *n* a NEWT IV.9.8. pædʒɪpʊł Co

pad off *vtphr* to put cattle on hired pasture, ⇐ HIRE *PASTURAGE* III.3.8. pɛd ... ɔːf Ess

pad-road *n* a PATH through a field IV.3.11. padɹʊəd La

pad-strap *n* the GIRTH of the harness of a cart-horse I.5.8. pɛdstɹæˑp K

pad-walk *n* a PATH through a field IV.3.11. padwɔːk La Y, *pl* padwɔːks St

paggered *adj* EXHAUSTED, describing a tired person VI.13.8. pagəd Y

paid *adj* **paid to the world** EXHAUSTED, describing a tired person VI.13.8. peːd tə ðə wəld Y

paid out *adj* EXHAUSTED, describing a tired person VI.13.8. peːd aʊt Y, peːd ʌʊt Y, peːd uːt Nb Du, pɛəd uːt Y

paigle *n* a COWSLIP II.2.10(a). pɛgɫ Hrt Ess, *pl* pɛgɫz Sf, pegʊ Ess, pɛɪgɫ C Ess, pæɪgɫ Ess, pæɪgʊ Ess

pail *n* a container for carrying horse-feed, ⇐ BASKET III.5.4. pɪəl Nb*[wooden]*, peːl Du, pe·əl Du, *pl* peəlz Y

pails *n* barley AWNS II.5.3. piːlz Ch, pɛɪlz St*[old]*, peːlz Sa, peːᵊlz Ch Sa

pain *1.1.* *vi* to show signs of calving, ⇐ SHOWS SIGNS OF CALVING III.1.12. *3prprogsg* peːnən Cu, peːnɪn Y Bk; **a-pain for calving** *3prprogsg* əpeɪnɪn fə kaːvɪn Nth
1.2. *vrefl* to show signs of calving. *3prprogsg* piːnɪn əsɛl Db, *3prprogsg* pɪənən həsɛl Du
2. *vi* to ACHE, referring to a stomach VI.13.3(b). pæɪn Nf, *3prsg* pæɪnz Ess

pains *vi-3prsg* it HURTS VI.13.3(a). pæɪnz Nf

paint *1.* *vt* to MARK sheep with colour to indicate ownership III.7.9. peɪnt So K Ha, peɪnt Ess, *2prpl* pæɪnts Sx
2. *v* to mark sheep with colour. peːnt La, pɛənt Y, pæɪnt K

pair *n* a TEAM of two horses I.6.1. pe·ɔᴿ Nb, pe·əᴿ Nb, peɪəᴵ Man, peː St Wa So, pɛə Nb Y Mon Nf Ess K, pɛəɹ St, pɛəᵗ Wa; **pair of horses** pɛɹ əv ɔːsɪz K, pɛᵗːɾ ɒsəz Ha

pall-bearers *npl* BEARERS who carry a coffin VIII.5.10. pɔːlbɛəᵊɹəs Man

pallies *npl* MINNOWS IV.9.9. palɪz Cu*[old]*

palm *n* What do you call this [indicate the palm of the hand]? VI.7.5. Eng. ⇒ **ball**, **ball** *of the hand*, **ball** *of your hand*, **flat** *of your hand*, **hollow** *of your hand*, **inside** *of the hand*, **middle** *of my hand*, **middle** *of your hand*, *palm of my hand*, *palm of the hand*, *palm of their hand*, *palm of thy hand*, *palm of your hand*, **pane**, **pane** *of your hand*

palmer-worms* *npl* caterpillars, ⇐ WORMS IV.9.1. pɔːlməᵗːwəᵗːms So

pals *1. npl* [What is your word for the men that you work with?] And, when you were a young man, what did you call those you went about with when you weren't at work? VIII.4.2. Eng. ⇒ **bods**, **boys**, **butties**, **chaps**, **chums**, **chummies**, *clique*, **companions**, **friends**, **herbs**, **lads**, **mate(s)**, *old pals*, **playmates**, **sweats**, *the* **boys**, *the* **lads** *[BM headword companions]*
2. npl FRIENDS VIII.2.7. pɛɫz Sx, palz Y*[men x1]* Db L Lei, *sg* pal Gl, paɫz Ha; **old pals** ɔʊd palz Y

3. npl MATES VIII.4.1. pæɫz Nf, palz Y St L, *sg* pal Cu La

palsy *n* TREMORS suffered by a person who cannot keep still VI.1.4. palzɪ Sa, pɒlsɪ Y, pɒlzɪ Y Sa St L Nf, pɒlzɪ La L, pɔɫzɪ Sf, pɔːlzɪ St Ha, pɔːɫzɪ Wa, pɔəlzɪ L, pɔʊzɪ Sr; **the palsy** ðə paɫzɪ Co, ðə pɔːɫzɪ Sr; **the shaking palsy** ðə ʃeːkən pɒɫzi Co

pan *1.* *n* a container for carrying horse-feed, ⇐ BASKET III.5.4. pan Sa D
2. *n* a SALTING-TROUGH III.12.5. pæn Nf Ess*[earthenware]*, pan Hrt
3. *n* a GIRDLE for baking cakes V.7.4(b). pæn He, pan L Lei
4. *n* a container used as a PASTE-BOARD V.6.5. pæn Ess, pan Gl*[earthenware]*
5. *n* a BREAD-BIN V.9.2. pɛn Sr, pæn So Brk, pan Sa Wa Gl O Hrt D

pancake *n* a CLOT OF COW-DUNG II.1.6. pɛnkɛɪk Sr, *pl* pɛnkɛɪks Ess, *pl* pænkeːks Gl, pæŋkɛɪk Sf Sr K, *pl* pæŋkɛɪks Sx, pæŋkɛɪk Sf Ess, pæŋkæɪk Ess, pankeːk O, paŋkɛɪk He, panke·ək Bk, pankɛɪk C, pɒnkeːᵊk Ch *[sometimes glossed 'facetious' or 'children's word']*

pancheon *1.* *n* a container used as a PASTE-BOARD V.6.5. panʃən St Nt L Lei
2. *n* a BREAD-BIN V.9.2. panʃɪn Y Lei, panʃn Lei R Hu, *pl* panʃnz L, panʃən Db St*[old x1]* Lei Nth, pansən Y

pane *n* the PALM of your hand VI.7.5. peːn D; **pane of the hand** peːn ə jəᵗːɾ an D

panel *n* a DIAGONAL BAR of a gate IV.3.7. *pl* panɫz O

pankin *n* a BREAD-BIN V.9.2. paŋkɪn Y, pankɪn Y*[old]*, panɪkɪn Cu

panking *v-ing* PANTING VI.8.1. pæŋkɪŋ So, pæŋkɪn So Brk Ha, paŋkɪn O Bk So W D Ha, paŋkn̩ Ha, paŋkən Ha; **pank and blow** paŋk ən blʌʊ Bk

pan-mug *1.* *n* a container used as a PASTE-BOARD V.6.5. pɒnmʊg Ch
2. *n* a BREAD-BIN V.9.2. pɒnmʊg La*[old]* Ch

pan-shelf *n* a SHELF V.9.4. panʃɛlf Y

panting *v-ing* What do you call this [indicate panting, not gasping]? VI.8.1. Eng exc. We Hu C. ⇒ *a*-**blowing**, **bellowsing**, **blowing**, **blowing** *very hard*, **breathing** *hard*, **breathing** *heavy*, **bussocking**, *gasping*, **heaving**, **huffing**, **lalling**, *out of breath*, *out of puff*, *out of wind*, *pank and blow* ⇒ **panking**, **panking**, *panting for breath*, **puffed out**, **puffing**, **puffing** *and blowing*, **puffing** *and panting*, **pumping**, *short-winded*, *taking thy breath*, **thocking**, **tifting**, **waffing**

pantony *n* a PANTRY V.2.6. pæntnɪ Brk, pantnɪ Gl*[old]*, panʔn̩ɪ W, panʔənɪ W

pantry *1. n Where do you keep your food?* V.2.6.
Eng. ⇒ back-house, buttery, cellar, cellar-head,
closet, *couch* ⇒ cwtsh, cupboard, cwtsh, dairy,
food-cellar, food-cupboard, larder, milk-house,
pantony, scullery, *top of the cellar-steps*
2. n the DAIRY on a farm V.5.1. pantʁɪ Du, pantɹ I
Db*[old x1]* L

pantry-bench *n* a flat stone surface on which bacon
is cured, ⇐ SALTING-TROUGH III.12.5.
pantrɪbɛntʃ Db

pants *n* TROUSERS VI.14.13(a). pænts So

pap *1. n* the TEAT of a woman's breast VI.8.6. pæp
He, pap Nb Cu Du We La Y Ch Db C, *pl* paps Wa L
2. n a mother's milk. pap Y
3. n GRANDDAD VIII.1.8(a). pap Nth

paper funnel *n* a BAG containing sweets V.8.5.
pɛɪpʔə fʌnɫ Ess

paper-packet *n* a BAG containing sweets V.8.5.
peːpəpakət Nb

paper-parcel *n* a BAG containing sweets, made from
newspaper in the shape of a horn V.8.5. pɛəpəpasɪl Y

pappy *n* GRANDDAD VIII.1.8(a). papɪ Nth

paps *npl* the TEATS of a cow III.2.6. paps Nb Cu Du
We La Y Ch Db St L Nth Bd, *sg* pap Wa

paraffin *n* OIL used for lighting V.2.13(a). pæɹəfɪn
Hrt Ess, pæɹɪfiːn Sx, pæɹəfiːn Sx, paɹəfiːn L,
paɹəfɪn Y Bk

paraffin-oil *n* OIL used for lighting V.2.13(a).
pæɹəfiːnaɪɫ Hu, pæɹɪfiːnɒɪl Sx, paɹəfɪnaɪl Y Db,
paɹafɪnɒɪɫ Lei, paɹəfɪnɔɪl Y, paɹafɪnɔɪɫ Lei,
paɹəfɪnɔɪɫ Lei, paɹəfɪn əɪl Ch

parched *adj* THIRSTY VI.13.10. paːtʃt Hrt

parched up *adj* THIRSTY VI.13.10. paːtʃt ʊp Y

pare *1.1. v* to WHITTLE a stick I.7.19. *-ing* pɜˡːɹɪn
La
1.2. vt to whittle. *-ing* pɛˡːɹ in Co D, *-ing* pɛəɹ in Wa,
-ing əpɛəɹ in Wo
2. v to TRIM hedges IV.2.3. pɛˡː Co D, pɛˡːɹ(+V)
So, pɛəˡː Co
3. v to CUT peat IV.4.4. *-ing* pɛəɹ in Y

pare out *1. vtphr* to CLEAR grass at the edges of a
field II.9.5. pɛˡːɹ ɑʏt So
2. vphr to clear grass. *-ing* pɛːɹɪn æʏt So

pare up *vphr* to WHITTLE a stick I.7.19. *-ing* pɛəɹ in
ʌp K

paring-hook *n* a BILLHOOK IV.2.6. pɛːɹɪnʏk
D*[light, for finishing]*, pɛˡːɹənʏk D

parings *npl* potato PEELINGS V.7.22. pɪəɹɪnz Y,
pɛːɹɪnz St Wa, pɛəɹɪnz Y*[old]* L Lei R Nth*[old]* Nf,
pɛəˡɹɪnz He, pɛəˡːɹɪnz Sa, paɹɪnz O, paˡːɹɪnz Wo

parish-clerk *n* a SEXTON VIII.5.4. paɹɪʃklaɹk He

park *n* a PADDOCK I.1.10. paˡːk Co Do

park yourself *imp* SIT DOWN VIII.3.3. paˡːɹk
ðɪsɛʊf

parky *1. adj* COLD, describing a room VI.13.17.
paˡːkɪ Nth

2. adj COLD, describing a person VI.13.18.
paːkɪ Sr

parl *n* CHAT VIII.3.4. paːl L

parlour *1. n* the LIVING-ROOM of a house
V.2.1. paːlə Man
2. n the SITTING-ROOM of a house V.2.2. peːlə
Y*[old]*, pɛələɹ Y, pæˡːlə La, paɹləɹ He*[old]*, paːlɔ
Nb, paːlə Cu Du*[old x1]* We Y Ch*[old x1]* Db St
Wa Mon Nt*[old x1]* L Lei R Nth Hu*[old x1]* C Sf
Bd Hrt*[in larger house]* Ess*[old x1]*, paːɫə Mon
Lei, paːləɹ La Y, paːləˡ La Y, paːləˡ Sa He Wo
Wa Bk, paᵏːlɔᵏ Nb, paᵏːləᵏ Nb, paˡːlə La Ch,
paˡːləɹ La, paˡːləˡ La*[old x1]* Db, paˡːləˡ Sa Wa
Gl, paˡːləˡ Bk, paˡːɫəˡ He Mon, paˡːləˡː So,
paˡːɫəˡː So, paˡːɫəˡː W Co D Do Ha, paɹɫəɹ O*[in
large house or public house]*, paːlə Y Man St Wa
Lei Ess MxL Sr*[old]* K, *pl* paːləz Wo, paːɫə R,
paːləˡ Wo Sx, paːɫəˡ Mon Gl*[old x1]*, paˡːlə K,
paˡːləˡ Brk K, paˡːləˡ Wo, paˡːɫəˡ Sx, paˡːɫəˡː
Co D, paˡːɹɫəˡ Ha, paˡːɹɫəˡ Sx, poːləˡ Sa, poːɫəˡː
D, pɜˡːɹlə La, pɜˡːɹləɹ La

parlour-chamber* *n* a BEDROOM over a
parlour V.2.3. paːlətʃeːmbə Db

parlour-loft *n* a BEDROOM V.2.3. paːləlɒft Cu

parrock *n* a PADDOCK I.1.10. pæɹɪk So, pæɹʌk
So, paɹɪk So, paɹək La Y

parson's acre *n* a CHURCHYARD VIII.5.5.
paːsənz ɛːkə Cu

part *1.1. vt* to divide a field in order to PEN or
FOLD sheep III.7.10. paˡːt D
1.2. v to divide a field for grazing sheep. paˡːt Gl
[assuming the obj of the Gl verb is the field]
2. n the DIRECTION from which the wind blows
VII.6.26. paˡːt Nth, paˡːɹt Sx

parted *adj* CLOVEN, describing the hoof of a
cow III.2.8(b). paːtɪd Wo L Hu, paˡːtɪd Gl O,
paˡːd̪ɪd So

parting *1. n* the PARTITION between stalls in a
cow-house I.3.2. pɛətɪn Y, pæːᵊtn Du, paːtɪn Y,
paːtn Nf Ess, *pl* paːtənz L, paˡːtɪn L, paˈəˡtɪn Brk,
paˡːtɪn Wo Mon Gl So W Co D Do Ha, paˡːd̪ɪn
Co D, paˡːtən Ha, paˡːʔn Ha, paɹtɪn He, paɹtɪn
O, paːtɪn K, paˡːtɪn K, paˡːtɪn Wo Gl Sr D,
paˡːtən D, *pl* paˡːɹtɪnz Sx, pəˡːtɪn O
2. n the partition between stalls in a stable.
paɹtɪn O
3. v-ing CULLING sheep III.11.2. paːtn Ess

parting out* *vphr-ing* CULLING sheep III.11.2.
paˡːɹtɪn ɛʊt Sx

parting-stone *n* a small PARTITION within a
stall, separating two cows I.3.2. paːtɪnstuːn Ch

partition *n* *[Show a picture of an old-fashioned
cow-house.] What do you call this, between the
stalls?* I.3.2. patɪʃn Nf Ess, paːtɪʃn Nf, pətɪʃn Nth
Hu Nf Ess So W Brk Sr K Co Ha Sx, pətɪʃən Nb
Cu Sa St He Wo Wa Mon Gl O Nth Hu Nf Bk Hrt

Ess MxL So K Ha, pəɹtıʃən He, pəˑɪ̩ˑtıʃən O, pəˈt̬ɪ̩ʃən He, pət̬ːtɪʃn So W, pət̬ːtɪʃən He; **wood partition** wʊd pətıʃn Nf; **wooden partition** wʊdn paˈtıʃn Nf. ⇒ **bail, boose, boose-hallan, boose-side, boskin, brattice, crib, division, hallan, parting, partment, partning, pen, post, rail, rail partition, russling, skell-board, skell-boose, stall, stall-board, stallboards, stall-posts, stanchions, stand, standing, standing-board, standing-parting, standing-post, stand-side, stoothing, studdle, tail-post, trevice,** *wood* **partition,** *wooden* **partition;** ⇒ also **boose-head, midfeather-pole, parting-stone, stall-post**

partles *1. n* SHEEP-DUNG II.1.7. paːtlz Cu; **sheep-partles** ʃiːppaːtlz Cu

2. npl RABBIT-DROPPINGS III.13.15. paːtlz Cu

partlicks *n* SHEEP-DUNG II.1.7. paːtlɪks We

partment *n* the PARTITION between stalls in a cow-house I.3.2. paːtmənt Ess

partnicks *npl* RABBIT-DROPPINGS III.13.15. paːtnɪks We

partning *n* the PARTITION between stalls in a cow-house I.3.2. pɛt̬ːtn̩ɪn So

partridge(s) *n What do you call those birds that are shot during the shooting season?* IV.7.8(a).

no -s: peːtɹɪdʒ Y, peətɹɪdʒ Y, pætɹɛdʒ Man, pætɹɪdʒ Ess, pæːtɹɪdʒ La, pæːt̬ɹɪdʒ Co, pæˑʲ:ʔɹɪdʒ La, patrɪdʒ Cu, patʀɪdʒ Nb, pat̬ɹɪdʒ So W[old], paᵏtʀɪdʒ Nb, paɹt̬ɹɪdʒ Y, paːtrɪdʒ Cu Du, paːtrɪdʒ Cu We, paːtʀɪdʒ Nb, paːtɹɪdʒ Nb Cu Du We La Y Ch Db Sa St He Wa Mon Gl Nt L Lei Hu, paːtˀɹɪdʒ L, paːʔɹɪdʒ Db Lei C Bk, paᵏːtʀɪdʒ Nb, paᵏˑʔʀɪdʒ Du, paˑʲːtɹɪdʒ La Y L, paˑʲːɹtɹɪdʒ La, pat̬ːt̬ɹɪdʒ Sa He Mon Gl, pat̬ːʔɹɪdʒ Bk, pat̬ːt̬ɹɪdʒ So W D Ha, pat̬ːʔt̬ɹɪdʒ So, paɹt̬ɹɪdʒ O, paːtrɪdʒ Man, paːtɹɪdʒ St Wo Sr Sx, paːʔɹɪdʒ Ess Brk Sr K, paːʔt̬ɹɪdʒ K, pət̬ːt̬ɹɪdʒ Wo, pət̬ːʔɹɪdʒ O *pl:* Eng exc. Man

⇒ **stumpers, stumpies**

part-shitting *adj* DULL, referring to the weather VII.6.10. paːt-ʃɪtɪn Nf [*marked as emotive and therefore u.r. EMBM*]

party *n* a PERSON VIII.5.3(a). paˑʲːtɪ Brk, pət̬ːt̬ɪ Sr

pass *v* to PITCH sheaves II.6.10. *-ing* pasɪn Lei, paːs Wa; **sheaf-catch and pass** *-ing* ʃiːvkatʃɪn ən pasɪn Co

passage *1. n* the GANGWAY in a cow-house I.3.7. pɛsɪdʒ Sr K, pæsɪdʒ Sa Hu[*not in older sheds*] Nf Ess Sr K Co Sx, pæsɪtʃ Nf, pasɪdʒ Nb Du Y Wo O Nt L R Nth Bd W D, paːsɪdʒ Ha

2. n the VULVA of a cow III.2.3. pæsɪdʒ Sr

passage-walk *n* the GANGWAY in a cow-house I.3.7. pæsɪdʒwɔːk Sx

passage-way *n* the GANGWAY in a cow-house I.3.7. pæsɪdʒwɛɪ Sr

pass away *viphr* to WANE, referring to the moon VII.6.5(b). pas əwæɪ O

pass out *viphr* to FAINT VI.13.7. pæːs æɤt Co

pass over *vtphr* to PITCH sheaves II.6.10. *-ing* paːsn ... oʊvə Nf

past *1. prep* [*What time is this (indicate a quarter to twelve)?*] *And this* [*indicate half past seven*]? VII.5.4. Eng. ⇒ **after**

2. adv AGO VII.3.1. pæst Brk

paste *n* DOUGH V.6.3. pjɛst Nb[*old*], pɪast Cu[*old x1*] La[*old*] Y, pɪəst Nb[*old x2*] Cu Y[*old x1*], peːst Cu, peast We[*old x1*], pɛˑəst L

paste-board *n What do you call that flat wooden thing you knead the dough on?* V.6.5. pɪastbɔːd Y, pɪəstbʊəd Y, peːstbɔːd St, peːsbɔˀːd̬ Sa W, peːstbɔˑəˀːd̬ Sa, peːsbʊəd Ch Nt, peːsbʊᵊṛd̬ O, peːstbɔːəˀd̬ Sa, peːsbɔːəˀd̬ He, peːsbɔːəˀːd̬ So, peːsbʊʊəˀd̬ Wo Gl, peːstbʊəd Y Ch, peːsbʊəd Nt, peːsbuːṛd̬ D, peːsbuəˀːd̬ D, peːsbuːəˀːd̬ So, peɪstbʊˑəd C, peɪsbʊəd Db Nf, peːɪsbɔːəˀːd̬ Wo, peːɪsbʊʊəˀd̬ Wo, peːˀstbuˑəd Db, peəstbʊəd Y, peːəsbɔˀːd̬ Co, pɛɪstbɔːd St Lei R, pɛɪsbɔːd L Lei, pɛɪstbɔˑəd Ess, pɛɪstbʊəd L, pɛɪsbʊəd L, pɛəstbʊəd Y L, pɛˑəsbʊəd L, pɛːsbuəˀːd̬ D, pɛːəsbuəˀːd̬ Co, peɪstbɔːəˀṛd̬ Sx. ⇒ **bakeboard, baking-board, bin, bing, board, bread-bin, bread-board, cooking-board, devon, dough-bin, dough-board, dough-kiver, dough-skeel, dough-trough, kiver, kiver-top, kneading-board, kneading-trough, lid** *of the bin,* **mealing-board, mug, pan, pancheon, panmug, paste-board, pastry-board, pasty-board, plaster-board, rolling-board, slab, slick-board,** *table,* **tray, trough, trough-top, wooden slab**

pastry-board *n* a PASTE-BOARD V.6.5. peːstɹɪbɔːd Nf, peːstɹɪbɔˀːd̬ Sa, peːstɹɪbɔˀːd̬ W Ha, peːstɹɪbɔːəˀd̬ Sa He, peːstɹɪbʊəd Ch, peːstɹɪbɔːəd Mon, peːstɹɪbɔːəˀd̬ Sa He Wo Mon Gl, peːʂtɹɪbɔːṛd̬ Do, peːstɹɪbʊəˀːd̬ Do, peːʂtɹɪbuːṛd̬ D Ha, peːəʂtɹɪbuːṛd̬ D, peːʂtɹɪbʊəˀːd̬ W Co, peɪstɹɪbɔːd Nf, peɪstɹɪbʊˑɹd He, peɪstɹɪbɔˀːd̬ So, peɪstɹɪbɔˑəṛd̬ O, peɪstɹɪbɔːəˀːd̬ So, peːɪstʊbɔːəˀd̬ He Wo, peːˀstɹɪbɔːᵘəˀd̬ Mon, peːstɹɪbʊəˀːd̬ W, peːʂtɹɪbuːṛd̬ D, peːəʂtɹɪbuːṛd̬ D, peːʂtɹɪbuːəˀːd̬ D, pɛɪstɹɪbɔːd St Sr K, pɛɪstɹɪbɔːəd Wo Ess, pɛɪstɹɪbɔːəˀd̬ Sr, pɛɪstɹɪbʊəˀṛd̬ Brk Sx, pɛɪstɹɪbuːəd St, pæɪstɹɪbɔːd MxL, pæɪstɹɪbɔəd K, pæɪstɹɪbʊəd K

pasture *1. n What do you call the grass-land where you graze your cattle?* II.1.3. pæstjə Brk, pæˑstjəʲ Brk K, pæstjət̬ He, pæstʃət̬ Mon, pæstʃət̬ː Co, pæstət̬ Wo, pæːstjə Man Sa, pæːstjəɹ He, pæːstjət̬ Wo Sx, pæːstʃət̬ Gl, pæːstʃət̬ː So W, pastjɔᵏ Nb, pastoᵏ Nb, pastjə Du Y Ch Sa St Wo Wa Nt L, pastjəɹ La Y L, pastjəʲ L, pastʃə St Lei Nf, pastə Nb Cu Du We La Y Ch Db Nt Bk, pastθə Y, pastər Nb Cu Du Y, pastər

Y, pastəɹ La Y, pastə˧ La Y, paʃtjə St, paʃtʃə St, pɑːstjə Sa Wo Wa O L Nth Sf Bk, pɑːstjəᵗ Sa He Wo Wa Gl O Bk Ha, pɑːstʃə Wa Nf Hrt Ess, pɑːstʃəᵗ Sa Wo Mon Gl Bk, pɑːstʃəᵗː So W Co D Do Ha, pɑːstə Sf, pɑːstəᵗ Gl Bk, paᵗːs̗tjə Sa, paᵗːs̗tʃəᵗː Do, paᵗːs̗tə· Sa, pɑːstjə Ess MxL Sr K Sx, pɑːstjə˧ Brk K, pɑːstʃə Nf, *pl* pɑːstʃəz Sr, pɑːstʃəᵗː D; **cow-pasture** kaʊpastə La, kuːpastə Y, kuːpastəɹ Cu

2. *n* permanent pasture. pɑːstjəᵗ Ha

⇒ **bare pasture, close,** *cow***-pasture, eating-ground, feather, field, grass-close, grass-field, grass-ground, grass-land, grass-lea, gratton-land, graze-land, grazing, grazing-field, grazing-grass, grazing-ground, grazing-land, lea, lea-ground, lea-land,** *leigh* ⇒ **lea, low meadow, marsh, marsh-grass, marsh-land, mead, meadow, meadow-field, meadow-land, meadow-pasture, new-lea, old-land, pasture-field, pasture-land, pasturing-land, sward, swath, swath-field, swath-land, turf, upland field, upland-pasture;** ⇒ *also* **greensward**

3. *n* a MEADOW II.9.2. pɑːstɪə Hrt*[usually too damp to be ploughed]*

pasture-field *1. n* a PADDOCK I.1.10. pɑːstʃəᵗːviːɫ D

2. *n* PASTURE II.1.3. pastjəfiːld La Ch, *pl* pastəfiːlz Y, pastərfiːl Cu, pɑːstjəfɪəɫ Ess

pasture-land *1. n* PASTURE II.1.3. pæːstjəlænd C, pæː·stʃəᵗːlæːnd So, pastjəland Y, pastjə˧land La, pɑːstjəland Bd, pɑːstjəᵗland Bk, pɑːstʃəlænd Ess, pɑːstjəᵗlæːnd Sr

2. *n* pasture for sheep. pastəland Y

pastures *n* LOW-LYING LAND IV.1.7. pɑːstjəᵗz̗ He

pasturing-land *n* PASTURE II.1.3. pastəɹɪnland Y

pasty-board *n* a PASTE-BOARD V.6.5. pɛɪstɪbɔ·əd Hu

pasty-footed *adj* SPLAY-FOOTED VI.10.5. pastɪfʊtɪd La

pat *n* a small round TROUGH in a cow-house I.3.6. pæ·t K

patch *1. n* a PADDOCK I.1.10. patʃ Sa

2. *n* a TUSSOCK of grass II.2.9. pætʃ Ess, patʃ So

patch-hook *n* a BILLHOOK IV.2.6. pætʃʊk Co, patʃʊk Co

pate *n* a BADGER IV.5.9. pɛ·ət Y

path *1. n What do you call a track made by cows or sheep or human beings through a field?* IV.3.11. pɛ·θ K, pæθ Brk, pæːθ Sa He Wo Sf So W Brk, pæːð So, pæːf So, pæˀθ Man, paθ Nb Du La Y Ch Db Sa St, pɑːθ Sa He Wo Wa Mon Gl O Lei C Sf Bk Bd Hrt Ess So W Co D Do Ha, pɑːf Do, paᵗːθ Sa, pɑːθ Wo Nf MxL Brk Sr K*[made by human beings x1]* Sx, *pl* pɑːðz Ess, pɑːf Ess. ⇒ **beast-track, cattle-path, cattle-track(s), cattle-walk, cow-pad, cow-run, cow-track, cow-walk, field-way, foot-gate, foot-pad, foot-path, foot-road, foot-track, foot-trod,**

foot-walk, pad, padding, pad-road, pad-walk, path-way, rack, roadway, sheep-pad, sheep-run, sheep-track, sheep-walk, stile-road, track(s), track-way, trail, trod, walk

2. *n* the GANGWAY in a cow-house I.3.7. pæːθ Nf, pæːf So

path-way *n* a PATH through a field IV.3.11. pɑːθwaɪ Nf, pɑːθwæɪ Ess

patter *n* a PORRIDGE-STICK V.9.1. pætə˧ Brk

paunch *n* the BELLY VI.8.7. pænʃ He, panʃ Gl, pɑːnʃ Gl, pɒntʃ Ess

pausle *vt* to TED hay II.9.11(a). pɔːzl Cu

paving-stones *n* the CURB-STONE in a cow-house I.3.9. pɛːvɪnstɪənz Cu

paw-heads *npl* TADPOLES IV.9.5. pɔːhiːdz Du

pay *vt* to BEAT a boy on the buttocks VIII.8.10. *-ing* pɛɪ-ɪn Ess*[old]*

pea *n* the CORE of a boil VI.11.7. pɛɪ La

peach *n* a PRETTY girl VI.5.18. piːtʃ So

pea-cod *n* a pea-POD V.7.12. pɛɪkɒd Y, pɛɪkɔd Y

pea-hod* *n* a pea-POD V.7.12. *pl* pɛː-ɒdz W

pea-huck *n* an empty pea-POD V.7.12. *pl* pɛː-ʊks W

pea-hud *n* a pea-POD V.7.12. piː-ʌd So

pea-husk *n* a pea-POD V.7.12. pɹiː·hʌsk Nf

peak *n* the BRIM of a hat VI.14.3. pɹiːk Ess

peaked-nose *n* a SHREW-MOUSE IV.5.2. pɹiːkɪdnɔʊs Sx

pea-mouse *n* a SHREW-MOUSE IV.5.2. piːmɛʊs O

pea-posh *n* a pea-POD V.7.12. *pl* piːpɒʃɪz Nth

pea-pusket* *n* a pea-POD V.7.12. *pl* pɛɪpʌskəts Sf*[children's word]*

peascod *n* a pea-POD V.7.12. pɛːɪzkɒd Nf*[old]*

pea-shell *n* a pea-POD V.7.12. *pl* piːʃɛlz St, piːʃɛɫ Do, *pl* piːʃɛɫz So, pɹiːʃɛɫ Ess*[empty]*, *pl* pɛːʃɛɫz Gl

pea-shuck *n* a pea-POD V.7.12. piːʃʌk MxL Sr, *pl* pɹiːʃʌks Brk, *pl* pɛːʃʌks W Ha

pea-shull *n* a pea-POD V.7.12. piːʃʊl Ch

pea-stick* *n* a movable horizontal rod stretching between the shafts of a cart, fixing them to the cart-body and stopping the cart from tipping, ⇐ ROD/PIN I.10.3. pɹiːstɪk Sr

pea-swad *n* a pea-POD V.7.12. piːswad Y, *pl* pɪəswadz Y, *pl* pɛəswadz Cu, pɛswad Y, pɛswɒd Y, pɛɪswad La Y

pea-swath* *n* a pea-POD V.7.12. pɛɪswaːθ Y

peat *1. n What do you call that dry black stuff that people cut into sods and burn for fuel?* IV.4.3. Eng exc. Hu. ⇒ **black-earth, flags, peat-moss, scag, sess, turf(s), turves** ⇒ *also* **clunch, fag(s), flaught, flaughts, flows, hod, howking, peat-dubs, peat-hag, peat-pot, stook, turf-dole**

2.1. *vi* to CUT peat IV.4.4. *vbln* piːtɪn Y,

vbln pɪətɪn Y, *-ing* pɪətɪn Y

2.2. *v* to cut peat. *-ing* pi:tɪn St, *prppl* pi:ʔɪn O

peat-dig *v* to CUT peat IV.4.4. *vbln* pᵊi:ʔdɪgɪn Hrt, *-ing* pɪi:tdɪgɪn Sr

peat-dubs *npl* holes where PEAT is dug IV.4.3. pi:tdʊbz Nb

peat-hag *n* a PEAT hole IV.4.3. pɪəthag Y

peat-moss *n* PEAT IV.4.3. pi:tmɒs Cu La, pi:tmɔs Ch, pi:tmɔ:s Sa, pɪətmɒs Y

peat-pot *n* a PEAT hole IV.4.3. pɪətpɒt Y

peat-raising *vbln* cutting peat, ⇐ to CUT peat IV.4.4. pᵊi:ʔɹæɪzɪŋ Hrt

peck *1. vi* to CHIP, referring to an egg that is about to hatch IV.6.10. pɛk W, *ptppl* pɛkt Sr

2. *n* (off her) FOOD V.8.2. pɛk Y L

peck-basket *n* a SOWING-BASKET II.3.6. pɛk'bæ:skɪt So

pecker *1. n* the BEAK of a bird IV.6.18. pɛkəˤ: So W Do

2. *n* a NOSE VI.4.6. pɛkɐ Ess*[old]*

peckish *adj* HUNGRY VI.13.9. pɛkɪʃ Ch St So K

pedlar *n* a TINKER VIII.4.9. pɛdlə Ess

pee *n* stale URINE used for cleaning blankets VI.8.8. pɪi: Ess

pee-ants *npl* ANTS IV.8.12. pi:-ants Sa

pee-bed *n* a DANDELION II.2.10(c). pi:bed Sa

peek *1. n* a MUCK-FORK I.3.13. pi:k So

2. *n* a HAY-FORK I.7.11. pi:k So

3. *n* a hay-fork with a long shaft. pi:k So

peeking *v-ing* PEEPING VI.3.8. pi:kɪn C Bk Hrt Ess, pi:kn Ess, pᵊi:kɪn Hrt, pᵊi:kən Sf*[old x1]*, pɪəkn Nf, pe·kn Nf, pe:kʔn Nf, pe:ᶦkɪn Nf

peeks *npl* FORKS used in farming I.7.9. pi:ks So

peek-stick *n* the SHAFT of a hay-fork I.7.12. pi:kstɪk Co

peel *1.1. v* to WHITTLE a stick I.7.19. *-ing* pi:lɪn Y, *-ing* pi:ɫɪn W, *-ing* pɪəlɪn Y

1.2. *vt* to whittle. *-ing* pi:lɪn Wa

2. *n* a LOOSE *PIECE OF* SKIN at the bottom of a finger-nail VI.7.11. pɪʊɫ K

peeler *n* a LOOSE *PIECE OF* SKIN at the bottom of a finger-nail VI.7.11. pi:ɫəˤ Gl

peeling *＊1. v-ing* SHELLING peas V.7.14. pi:lən Cu

2. *n* potato PEELINGS V.7.22. pi:lɪn Nb La, pɪi:lɪn Nf Ess Brk, pɪlɪn Brk, pɛɪlɪn Y

peelings *npl What do you call the strips [indicate peeling] that you take off potatoes before boiling them?* V.7.22. Eng exc. MxL Do. ⇒ **chitty-rinds, parings, peel(s), peeling, potato-parings, potato-peel(s), *potato-peelings*, potato-rind(s), potato-skins, rind(s), skin(s), spud-peelings**

peel off *vtphr* peel the bark off to WHITTLE a stick I.7.19. *-ing* pᵊi:lɪn ... ɔ:f Hrt *[marked u.r. EMBM]*

peel(s) *n* potato PEELINGS V.7.22.

no -s: pɪ:l Mon, pɪ·l Nf, pɪiɫ K, pɪʊɫ Sr, pɪʊ Sx

npl: pi:lz Db Hrt, pi:ᵊlz Nth, pi:ɫz Co, pi:ᵊɫz Nth Sf Bk Bd Ess, pɪʊɫz K, pɪʊz Sr, pɪɫz Wa L, pɪiɫz Ess

peep-eyeing *v-ing* PEEPING VI.3.8. pi:pɔɪ-ən Ess

peeping *1. v-ing What am I doing now through the keyhole [indicate peeping]?* VI.3.8. Eng exc. We He Hu Hrt. ⇒ **geeking, glazing, gloring, *glowering* ⇒ gloring, *having a* squint, keeking, kiting, looking, peeking, peep-eyeing, peering, pimping, quizzing, skenning, spying, squinting**

2. *v-ing* SQUINTING VI.3.5. pi:pɪn L *[marked u.r. EMBM]*

peer down *vtphr* to RENDER fat into lard III.12.9. *-ing* pɪəᵗɹɪn ... dɛʊn Ha

peering *v-ing* PEEPING VI.3.8. pɪəɹɪn K, peɪəɹən Man

peg *1. n* a metal LINCH-PIN holding a wheel on a cart I.9.12. pag Ch

2. *n* a PIN used with a perforated rod in front of a cart to allow adjustments when tipping I.10.3. pɛg Ch Sa Wo Wa Mon, pɛd Ch

pegged out *adj* EXHAUSTED, describing a tired person VI.13.8. pɛgd u:t Nb We

pegging *v-ing* THROWING a stone VIII.7.7. pɛgɪn Ch

peghing *v-ing* COUGHING VI.8.2. bɛfɪn Y; **peghing and coughing** pɛfɪn ən kɒfɪn Y

pegs *npl [Show a picture of some stacks. What do you call this (i.e. thatch)?] What do you fasten it down with? [Pegs driven into stack.]* II.7.7(a). pɛgz Du We La, pɛgz Nb We La Y Ch*[hazel x2]* Db*[wooden x2]* Sa St*[hazel x1, usually elder x1]* He Wo Wa*[willow x1, hazel x1, wooden x2]* Mon Gl O Nt*[hazel or ash x1, ash or elm x1]* L Lei R Nth Bk Hrt Ess So*[willow]* Brk K, *sg* pagᵊ Db, paᶦgz So; **stack-pegs** stækpɛgz Nf*[willow]*, stakpɛgz Y*[wooden, 15 inches long]* L; **withy pegs** wɪðɪ pɛgz St. ⇒ **briars, broaches, buckles, mow-pins, nibs, prickers, prods, rawters, rick-pegs, rick-spars, rick-sprays, scollops, sparrers, spars, spats, speaks, spears, spelks, spicks, spilk, spindles, spits, splinters, splints, sporrels, sprays, sprindles, springers, springles, spurs, stack-brods, *stack*-pegs, stack-pins, stack-pricks, stack-prods, stack-spelks, stack-stobs, stakes, sticks, stobs, thacking-pegs, thack-pegs, thatching-pegs, thatch-pegs, thatch-pricks, *withy* pegs**

peg-toed *adj* PIGEON-TOED VI.10.4. pɛgtɒʊd W

pellets *1. n* sheep-pellets SHEEP-DUNG II.1.7. ʃɪi:ppɛɫɪts Sr

2. *npl* RABBIT-DROPPINGS III.13.15. pɛɫɪts W, pɛləts Ess, pɛlts St

3. *n* SWEETS V.8.4. pɛləʔs Bk

pelsh *v* to BUTT III.2.10. *-ing* pɛlʃɪn Gl

pelt *1. n* [What do you call the skin of a cow? And of a sheep?] And when the wool is off? III.11.8(b). pɛlt Nb Cu Du We La Y Man Ch Db Sa St He Nt L Lei R, pɛɫt Ch He Wo Wa Mon Gl O L Lei So Brk Sr K Co D Ha, pɛɫʔ Sf, pɛʊɫt Ess Brk, pɛʊt K Sx, pɛlət Cu, pɪlt̬ Man, pəɫt So D; **sheep-pelt** ʃiːppɛlt Y. ⇒ **felt, fleeced hide, hide,** *pellet* ⇒ **pelt, sheep-pelt, sheep's-apron, sheep's-hide, sheepskin, shorn skin, skin, slack, trim-hide**

2. n a SHEEPSKIN III.11.8(a). pɛlt La Y St, pɛʊt K, pəɫt D

3. n an under-layer of skin on a sheep, under the top skin. pɛɫt O

4. n the HIDE of a cow III.11.7. pɛlt La Y L, pɛɫt Ch Gl

5. vt to BEAT a boy on the buttocks VIII.8.10. pɛlt La

pelting *v-ing* THROWING a stone VIII.7.7. pɛltɪn Y St Nt L Nth, pɛlʔɪn L, pɛltn Nb Nf, *pt* pɛltɪd Du, *no -ing* pɛlt La, pɛɫʔn̩ C

pen *1. v* If you want to confine your sheep to only one part of a field, how do you do it? III.7.10.
vt pɛn La[for clipping or dipping x1] Nf Bk So W Sr[in market] Ha
v pɪn Ess[in farmyard only x1] Sr[rare x1], pɛn Cu Du We La[for clipping or dipping x1] Y[in a market x1, at sheepdog trials and markets x1, at sheep sales x1, temporarily x1] Man Ch[when sorting x1, on turnips near farm x1] Db[when sorting x1] Sa St He Wo Wa[in yard ready for sale x1, on turnips x1, on swedes x1] Mon Gl[in small pen for veterinary treatment x1] O[at market x1] Nt L Lei R Nth[when dipping x1] Hu[for medicinal purposes x1, temporarily for sending to market x1] C Nf[when culling x1] Sf[for shearing or giving medical treatment] Bk Bd[when culling x1] Hrt Ess[when shearing x1, when culling x1, temporarily at market x1] So Brk Sr[small] K[for confining when slaughtering x1] Ha[at market] Sx[temporarily, usually for health check], pɛˡn MxL, pɛˑən Man. ⇒ **bar up, break, fence, fence in, fence off, fold, fold back, fold in, fold off, fold on, fold** *on the back***, fold up,** *give a* **breck,** *hit hurdles up***, hold, hurdle, hurdle in, hurdle off, hurdle off** *in a pen***, hurdle out, hurdle up, mound, mound off, net, net off, part, part** *the field***, part** *the field with hurdles***, pen in, pen off, pen up, pinfold, pitch, pitch** *a fold***, pitch** *a pen***, pitch** *a sheep-fold***, pound,** *put a* **breck** *up***,** *put in a* **pen,** *put into a* **pen,** *put on the* **breck,** *set a fold for***, wattle**

2. n a STALL in a cow-house I.3.1. *pl* pɪnz K, pɛn Wa So Sr K Sx

3. n the PARTITION between stalls in a cow-house I.3.2. pɛn Sx

4. n the place where hay is stored on a farm, ⇐

HAY-LOFT I.3.18. pɛn Wa Sx

5. n a FASTING-CHAMBER III.11.3. pɪn Sr, pɛn Nb Cu La Wa Gl O Nth Hu C Nf Sf Bk Hrt Ess MxL So W Brk Sr K Co D Ha Sx, pɛɪn Co D [see note at **fasting-chamber**]

6.1. vt to STOCK III.3.6. *ptppl* əpɪnd D, *-ing* peːnɪn D, pɛn So, *-ing* pɛnɪn W D Do, *-ing* pɛnən Do, *-ed* pɛnd W Ha, *-ed* peˡnd D, pɛɪn D

6.2. v to stock. pɛn So W

pen in* *vtphr* to PEN or FOLD sheep in part of a field III.7.10. pɛn ... ɪn Y

penis *n* the penis of a horse, ⇐ SHEATH III.4.9. piːnɪs W

penny-wagtails *npl* TADPOLES IV.9.5. pɛnɪwægtæɪ³lz Sf

pennywinkles *npl* MINNOWS IV.9.9. pɛnɪwɪŋkɫz Sf [marked u.r. EMBM]

pen off *1. vtphr* to PEN or FOLD sheep in part of a field III.7.10. pɛn ... ɑːf He, pɛn ... ɒf Du Y, pɛn ... ɔːf Nf Co

2. vphr to pen or fold sheep. *-ing* pɛnɪn ɒf Brk

penthouse *n* a FASTING-CHAMBER III.11.3. pɛntəʊs Do, pɛntəs Lei

pen-toed *adj* PIGEON-TOED VI.10.4. pɛntʊd L Lei R, pɛntʌʊd L, pɛntoʊd Nt Lei, pɛntʊəd Y Nt L [taken as **pin-** NBM]

pen up *1. vtphr* to STOCK a cow III.3.6. *-ing* pɛnɪn ... ʌp W, *ptppl* pɛnd ... ʌp W

2.1. vtphr to PEN or FOLD sheep in part of a field III.7.10. pɛn ... ʌp He Mon, pɛn ... ʊp Y Wo Gl L[when dipping or clipping x1]

2.2. vphr to pen or fold sheep. pɛn ʊp Nth K

people *npl* If your wife comes home from a meeting and you want to know if it was well attended, you'd ask her: Were there many ... there? VIII.2.12. Eng exc. Cu We Db Bd Hrt. ⇒ **folk(s)**

pepman *n* a WEAKLING piglet III.8.4. pɛpʔm Nf

peps *n* SWEETS V.8.4. pɛps Nth

perch *n* What do hens rest on at night? IV.6.3. Eng exc. We. ⇒ **baulk, chee, hen-baulk, hen-perk,** *hen-perch* ⇒ **hen-perk, hens' roost, hen-stick,** *peark* ⇒ **perk, perk, polley, prop, roost, roosting-baulk, stick**

perished *1. adj* COLD, describing a person VI.13.18. pɛrɪʃt Cu, pɛ.ɹɪʃt Mon Nf Sf Bk, pə̢rɪʃt W; **perished with cold** pɛ.ɹɪʃt ə kʌʊɫd Hrt

2. adj VERY COLD, describing a person VI.13.19. pɛ.ɹɪʃt Y Nf Bk Ess Brk Sr Ha, pə.ɹɪʃt Sr Do Sx, pə̢rɪʃt D; **perished to dead** pɛ.ɹɪʃt tə dɛɪd Sf; **perished to death** pə.ɹɪʃt tə dɪəθ Y; **perished to the bone** pɛ.ɹɪʃt tə ðə boʊn Nf; **perished with cold** pɛ.ɹɪʃt ə kʌʊɫd Ess

perishing *adj* VERY COLD, describing a person VI.13.19. pɛɹɪʃɪn Nf; **perishing with cold** pɛɹɪʃən ə kʌʊɫd Ess

perk *n* a PERCH for hens IV.6.3. pɪək We La Y L, pɪəɹk La, *pl* peːɪks Nf, *pl* pɛːɪks Nf, pəɾk Nf, pəːk Nf, pəˑɹk Sf, pəᴵˑk Nf

person *n* He [i.e. the parson] came along with his wife; she is a very nice .... VIII.5.3(a). Eng exc. Nb Cu Du We. ⇒ **body**, **lady**, **party**, **soul**, **tart**, **woman**

perspire *3prsg* you SWEAT VI.13.5. pɛspɔɪə Ess, pɹɛspɔɪəᴵ Brk, *-ing* pəᵗˑspaɪɽɪn K[modern]

pert *1. adj* WELL, describing a healthy person VI.13.1(a). pɪəᵗːt Sa
2. *adj* ACTIVE, describing a child VIII.9.1. pɪəᵗɽt Sx[old]

pestle *n* a PORRIDGE-STICK V.9.1. pɛstəɫ So

pet *n* a PET-LAMB III.7.3. pɛt Nb Y Gl O [marked u.r. NBM]

petch *n* a GULL IV.7.5. pɛtʃ La

pet-lamb *n* [Sometimes a lamb has to be brought up in the house because its mother has died.] What do you call such a lamb? III.7.3. Eng exc. Man Db Sa Nt Lei R Hu Sf D Do. ⇒ **bottle-lamb**, **cade**, **cade-lamb**, **cadie-lamb**, **cosset**, **cosset-pet**, **dack**, **dolly**, **foster-lamb**, **gibby-lamb**, **hand-fed-lamb**, **hobby**, **hobby-lamb**, **hob-lamb**, **home-bred lamb**, **lamb**, **meg**, **meg-lamb**, **mudded lamb**, **mud-lamb**, **nursed-lamb**, **orphan**, **pet**, **sock-lamb**, **sucker**, **suck-lamb**, **suckle-lamb**, **suckler**, **suckler-lamb**, **suckling**, **suckling-lamb**, **tame lamb**, **tiddler**, **tiddling**; ⇒ also **cuckoo-lamb**, **hob**, **sucklet**

petman *n* a WEAKLING piglet III.8.4. pɛtmən Nf, pɛtn Nf

petty *n* an EARTH-CLOSET V.1.13. pɛtɪ Cu We La Y[old x1] Ch[old x1] Db[polite x1] Sa St[old x1] He Wo Wa O Nt[old x1] L[old x1] Lei Nth[old x1] Hu[old x1] Nf Bd, pɛtʔɪ Nf Sf Ess, pɛʔtɪ Nf, pɛʔɪ O L[old x1] Nf, patɪ Nth[old]

petty-hole *n* an EARTH-CLOSET V.1.13. pɛtɪ-oːᵁl Db

petty-house *n* an EARTH-CLOSET V.1.13. pɛtɪ-əʊs He[polite]

pheasant(s) *n* What do you call those birds that are shot during the shooting season? IV.7.8(b).
no -s: fɛzʌnt So W, fɛzʊnt He Wo, fɛznt Nb Du Y Sa St L Ess Sr K, fɛznʔ Bk, fɛzənt Nb Y Ch O Lei So Co, vɛzənt Ha, fɛzən Man
pl: Eng
⇒ **cock-hangers**

pick *1. n* a MUCK-FORK I.3.13. pɪk Gl So D Do
2. *n* a HAY-FORK I.7.11. pɪk So D
3. *n* a hay-fork with a long shaft. pɪk So
4. *n* a hay-fork with a short shaft. pɪk So
5. *v* to FORK sheaves onto a wagon II.6.7(b). pɪk We Y Nt L

6. *v* to PITCH sheaves II.6.10. pɪk Du Y L [not a NBM headword]
7.1. *v* **picks** SLIP*S THE CALF* III.1.11. pɪks La St, *ptppl* pɪkt Nb
7.2. *vt* **picks** slips the calf. pɪks Cu Du Y Sa, *ptppl* pɪkt Nb We La Man Ch St Nt, *no -s* pɪk Man Ch L, *3ptsg* pɪkt Ch Db St Nt L
8.1. *v* to SLIP *A FOAL* III.4.6. pɪk St, *ptppl* pɪkt Y, *-ed* pɪkt Nb Cu
8.2. *vt* to slip a foal. pɪk Du We[old x1] La Man Nt L, *3prsg* pɪks Y, *-s* pɪks Y, *ptppl* pɪkt Nb Cu Y Db St, *-ed* pɪkt Nb Y Sr
9. *vi* to CHIP, referring to an egg that is about to hatch IV.6.10. pɪk So
10. *n* the BEAK of a bird IV.6.18. pɪk Sa [queried error for **beak** EMBM]
11.1. *vt* to PLUCK a dead chicken of its feathers IV.6.21. pɪk Wo Gl So W Co D Do Ha, *-ing* pɪkɪn O Brk Sr
11.2. *v* to pluck. pɪk Wo Wa Gl O Nth Hu Bk Bd[old x1] Hrt[old x1] MxL So W Co Do Ha Sx, *-ing* pɪkɪn Sr K
12.1. *vt* to TOP-AND-TAIL gooseberries V.7.23. pɪk L, *-ing* pɪkɪn Y; **pick the noses of them** pɪk ðə noːzɪz oʊ ən So; **pick the stems out of them** pɪk ðə stɛmz æʊt oʊ əm So
12.2. *v* to top-and-tail gooseberries. pɪk Nb Cu La Nt
13.1. *vt* to REMOVE *STALKS* from currants V.7.24. pɪk La Y L Lei Nth Bk Sx, *-ing* pɪkɪn W Brk K
13.2. *v* to remove stalks. pɪk Cu La Y Nt L Nth Hu C Bk Bd, *-ing* pɪkən Du
14. *n* FOOD V.8.2. pɪk Nt L
15. *v* to MARK sheep with colour to indicate ownership III.7.9. pɪk Y

pick-and-clean *vt* to TOP-AND-TAIL gooseberries V.7.23. pɪkənkliən Y

pick-and-snout *v* to TOP-AND-TAIL gooseberries V.7.23. pɪkənsnɛʊʔ O

pick-calve *v* to slip a calf, ⇐ SLIP*S THE CALF* III.1.11. *ptppl* pɪkkaˑft Nb[old], *pt* pɪkkɔvd L[old], *ptppl* pɪkkɔːft Nb La

picker *1. n* the FORKER of sheaves onto a wagon II.6.7(d). pɪkə We Y Db Nt L Lei R, pɪkəᴵ L, pɪkəɹ La, pɪkɪ L [not a N/WMBM headword]
2. n the FORKER on a wagon who unloads sheaves in a stackyard II.6.9. pɪkə We, pɪkəɹ La

picker-off *n* the FORKER on a wagon who unloads sheaves in a stackyard II.6.9. pɪkəɹɒf Db, pɪkkəɹ ɒf Db

pick-foal *1. v* to SLIP *A FOAL* III.4.6. *ptppl* pɪkfɒːld Nb, *ptppl* pɪkfoːlt La, *ptppl* pɪkfʊald Cu, *ptppl* pɪkfʊəld L, *-ed* pɪkfʊəld Du
2. *n* a prematurely-born foal. ˈpɪkfɒʊɫ Sr

pick-fork *1. n* a HAY-FORK I.7.11. pɪkfɒ.ɪk Y, pɪkfɔːk Y, pɪkfəᴶːɪk Y

2. n a hay-fork with a long shaft. pɪkfɔːk Nt R, pɪkfəᴶːk L, *pl* pɪktfɔːks Lei

3. n a hay-fork with a short shaft. pɪkfəᴶːk L

pick-grate *n* the ASH-HOLE beneath a domestic fire V.3.3. pɪkgɹeːt W

pick-handle *n* the SHAFT of a hay-fork I.7.12. pɪkhandɫ So

picking *1. v-ing* CULLING sheep III.11.2. pɪkɪn Y Wa Lei, pɪkɪn ... Ha, *prppl* pɪkɪn Sx, pɪkən Man, *v* pɪk Hu

2. v-ing SHELLING peas V.7.14. pɪkɪn Nth

picking-fork *1. n* a HAY-FORK I.7.11. pɪkɪnfəᴶːk L

2. n a hay-fork with a long shaft. pɪkɪnfɔːk Y Db Nt L, pɪkkɪnfɔːk Db

3. n a hay-fork with a short shaft. pɪkɪnfœːᵊk Du

picking off *vphr-ing* UNLOADING sheaves from a wagon II.6.8. pɪkɪn ɒf Db

picking out *vphr-ing* CULLING sheep III.11.2. pɪkɪn ɛʊt Sr, pɪkɪn ... ɛʊt Wo Nf Ess Sx, pɪkɪn ... ɛʊt Nf Ess, əpɪkən ... ɛʊt Sf, *v* pɪk ɛʊt Wa Hrt MxL, pɪkɪn ɛʊʔ Bd, *v* pɪk ɛʊʔ Bk Hrt, pɪkʔn ... ɛʊt Nf, pɪkən ... œʏt D, *3futpl* pɪk ... æat Y, pɪkɪn æʏt So D, pɪkɪn ... æʏt So Co D, pɪkɪn æʊt W, pɪkɪn ... æʊt L Lei So W, pɪkən ... æʊt Ha, *v* pɪk ... æʊt Ess, pɪkɪn aɪt Ch, *vt* pɪk ... aʊt Lei So, *v* pɪk aʊt So, pɪkɪn ... aʊʔ L, pɪkɪn ... ɒʊt W, pɪkɪn ʌʊt He, pɪkɪn ᵁuːt Gl, pɪkɪn ... əʊt W Brk Sx, pɪkɪn əʊt He, əpɪkən əʊt Brk, pɪkɪn əʊːt Gl, pɪkən ... əʊt Do, *vt* pɪk ... əʊːt Gl

picking over *vphr-ing* CULLING sheep III.11.2. pɪkɪn ... ɒvə Lei, pɪkɪn ... ɔːvəᵗ so, *vt* pɪk ... ɔːvəᵗː D

pickle *n* a PINCH of sugar or salt VII.8.6. pɪkl Nb*[rare x2, salt x1]*, pɪkəl Cu

pickle-pot *n* an earthenware SALTING-TROUGH III.12.5. pɪkʔɫpɒt Sf

pickle-tub *n* a SALTING-TROUGH III.12.5. pɪkʊtʌb Sr

pickling-cask *n* a wooden SALTING-TROUGH III.12.5. pɪklɪnkaːsk Ha

pickling-pan *n* a SALTING-TROUGH III.12.5. pɪklɪnpæn Ess

pickling-tank *n* a SALTING-TROUGH III.12.5. pɪkɫɪntæŋk K

pickling-trough *n* a SALTING-TROUGH III.12.5. pɪkɫɪntɹɒʊ Nf, pɪklɪntɹoʊ Brk

pickling-tub *n* a SALTING-TROUGH III.12.5. pɪkɫɪntʌb Ess, pɪk]ɪntʌb Nf, pɪkləntʏːb Nb, pɪklɪntʊb Nb Y

pick off *1. vphr* to cull sheep, ⇐ CULLING III.11.2. pɪk ɔːf K

2. vtphr **pick the heads and tails off** to TOP-AND-TAIL gooseberries V.7.23. pɪk ð ɪ·ədz ŋ tɛ·əlz ɔf L

3. vtphr to REMOVE *STALKS* from currants V.7.24. pɪk ... ɔːf So Co D, *-ing* pɪkɪn ... ɔːf W

pick over *vtphr* to REMOVE *STALKS* from currants V.7.24. pɪk ... ɔwə L, pɪk ... ɔːvəᵗː D, pɪk ... ɔʊvə L, *-ing* pɪkɪn ... oːvəᵗː So

picks *npl* FORKS used in farming I.7.9. pɪks So D Do

pick-stale *n* the SHAFT of a hay-fork I.7.12. pɪkstɛɫ D, pɪkstaːɫ D

pick-stem *n* the SHAFT of a hay-fork I.7.12. pɪkstɪm Do, pɪkstɛm So

pick together *vtphr-3sg* she [i.e. a tidy girl] will COLLECT her toys VIII.8.15. pɪk ... təgəðə Y

pick up *vtphr-3sg* she [i.e a tidy girl] will COLLECT her toys VIII.8.15. pɪk ... ʌp O Ess So W Brk Co D Do Ha, pɪk ... ʊp Nb Wo Gl Lei R Nth; **pick up tidy** pɪk ... ʌp taːdi Co

picnic *n* a local FESTIVAL or holiday VII.4.11. pɪknɪk Du

picture *1. n* a FLITCH or side of bacon III.12.3. pɪkʃəᴿ Du

2. n a copy, referring to someone who RESEMBLES someone else VIII.1.9. pɪktɔᴿʀ (+V) Nb, pɪktə Y

piddle *n* stale URINE VI.8.8. pɪdl Nth*[embrocation for horses]*, pɪdʊ Ha*[for cleaning blankets]*

piddles *npl* RABBIT-DROPPINGS III.13.15. pɪdlz St

piddle-your-bed *n* a DANDELION II.2.10(c). pɪdɫjəbɛd Ess*[facetious]*

piddling *n* stale URINE used for cleaning blankets VI.8.8. pɪdɫɪn Sr

pie *n* a CLAMP in which potatoes are stored out of doors II.4.6. paː Y, paɪ Du Y L, pɑː Y, paɪ Db Nt L Lei, *pl* paˑɪz Y, pɒɪ K, pʌɪ Sr, *pl* pəɪz Sx

piece *1. n* What might a child ask for when it's hungry, e.g. on coming home from school? V.6.11(a). ə piːs Nb La Man, piːs Nb Cu Db*[old]* Sa St Wo Wa, pɛɪs St. ⇒ *a bit of bread, a bit of bread and butter, a chunk, a chunk of bread, a piece of bread, a piece of bread and butter, bit bread, bit bread and butter, bit bread and butty, bit butter and bread, bit of bread, bit of bread and butter, bit of butter, bit of butty, bit of cake, bit of morsel, bit of scrat, bit of victuals, brasthan, bread and butt, bread and butter, bucker, bup, buppy, butter-bread, butter-cake, butter-shag, butt-shive, butty, butty-cake, cake, cakie, chunk bread and butter, chunk of bread, crust of bread, crust of bread and butter, hunk of bread, hunk of bread and butter, hunky of bread, lump of bread, lump of bread and butter, lump of butter and bread, morsel, piece, piecie, piece bread and butter, piece bread and cream, piece of bar, piece of bread, piece of bread and butter, piece of* butch, *piece of* butter, *piece of crust and butter*, round *of bread*, round *of bread and butter*, round *of* butter, shive *of bread and butter*, *short-cake*, *slice bread and butter*, *slice of bread*, *slice of bread and butter*, *slice of bread with a bit butter on it*, snobbler, snoul *of bread*, *some bread and butter*

2. *n* a PIECE *OF BREAD AND BUTTER AND JAM/SUGAR* V.6.11(b). piːs Db St Wa*[treacle and bread x1]*, pɛɪs St; **piece of jam** piːs ə dʒam Wa; **bit jam and piece** ə bɪt dʒam ən piːs Nb. ⇒ *a bit of bread and butter and jam, a bit of bread and butter and treacle, a bit of bread and jam, a bit of bread and sugar,* a **buppy** jam, *a chunk and a bit of cheese, a* **noggin** and lard, *a piece of bread and butter with some jam, a slice of bread and butter and jam, bit bread and berries, bit bread and butter and treacle, bit bread and jam, bit jam and bread, bit jam and piece, bit* **jelly-bread**, *bit of bread and butter and sugar, bit of bread and cheese, bit of bread and cream, bit of bread and dripping, bit of bread and jam, bit of bread and lard, bit of bread and saim, bit of bread and sugar, bit of bread and syrup, bit of bread and treacle, bit of* butter *and* cheese, *bit of jam and bread, bread and brown sugar, bread and butter and jam, bread and butter with a bit of sugar on, bread and cheese, bread and jam, bread and lard, bread and lard and sugar, bread and sugar, bread and treacle,* **brown-sugar-shag**, butter *and jam,* **butter-shag**, **butty**, **butty-dip**, **butty-treacle**, **chunk** *bread and jam, crust of bread and jam, dripping,* hunch *of bread and cheese*, hunk *of bread and jam,* jam, *jam and bread, jam and cake,* **jam-bread**, **jam-bucker**, **jam-butty**, **jam-cake**, **jam-shag**, **jam-shive**, **jelly-piece**, *lard, little bit of cheese, lump of bread and butter and jam, lump of bread and butter and preserves, lump of bread and jam, lump of bread and sugar, lump of jam and bread, morsel of cream and jam,* **noggin**, noggin *of bread and cheese*, piece, *piece of bread and brown sugar, piece of bread and butter and jam, piece of bread and butter and some jam, piece of bread and dripping, piece of bread and jam, piece of bread and lard, piece of bread and lard and sugar, piece of bread and sugar, piece of bread and treacle, piece of crust and jam, piece of crust and sugar,* piece *of jam, piece of jam and bread, piece of lard, piece of* **treacle-bar**, round *of bread and drippings*, round *of bread and jam, round of bread and treacle, round of dripping, round of treacle,* **serve-cake**, *slice of bread and butter, slice of bread and butter and jam, slice of bread and cheese, slice of bread and jam, slice of bread and sugar, slice of bread and treacle, slice of fat and bread, some bread and butter and jam, some bread and jam, some jam and bread, some jam and cake,* **sugar-bread**, **sugar-bread** *and* **butter**, **sugar-buppy**, **sugar-butty**, **sugar-sandwich**, **sugar-shag**, *treacle*, **treacle-buck**, **treacle-butty**, **treacle-shag**

3. *n* a SLICE of bread V.6.10. piːs Sa He, pɛɪs Ch *[marked u.r. WMBM]*

4. *n* a BIT (OF string) VII.2.10. piːs Nb Du La Y Ch Db Sa St He Wo Wa Mon Gl O Nt L Nth Nf Sf Ess MxL So W Brk Sr K Co D Do Ha Sx, pɪs Ess So, peːs Ch, peɪs Ess, pɛɪs Db St, pəɪs Y

piece-worker *n* a FARM-LABOURER I.2.4. piːswəˤːkəˤː So

piecie *n* a PIECE *OF BREAD AND BUTTER* V.6.11(a). pʰiːsɪ Gl

pig 1. *n* PIGS III.8.1. pɪg L

2. *n* a PIGLET III.8.2. pɪg Nf, *pl* pɪgz Sf Co

3. *n* a male or female HOG III.8.8. pɪg Nth Sf, *pl* pɪgz Wa*[no special word] [marked u.r. WMBM]*

4. *n* a male hog. pɪg Sf

5. *n* a hog. pɪg Nb Y C*[no special word]* Nf

6. *vi* to FARROW, describing a pig giving birth to piglets III.8.10. pɪg Nb Cu Du We La Y Ch Db Sa St He Wa Gl O Nt L Nth Hu C Nf Sf Bk Bd Ess Sr Co Ha, pɪgi Co; **for pig** fə pɪg Ch

7. *v* to GOBBLE food VI.5.13(b). *3prsg* pɪgz L

pig-bellies *n* CHITTERLINGS III.12.2. pɪgbɛlɪz Ess

pig-bench 1. *n* a BENCH on which slaughtered pigs are dressed III.12.1. pɪgbɛntʃ Db St, pɪgbɛnʃ Y Ch Sa He Wo Wa Mon Gl Lei Brk K Ha

2. *n* a flat surface on which bacon is cured, ⇐ SALTING-TROUGH III.12.5. pɪgbɛnʃ Wo

pig-berries *npl* HAWS IV.11.6. pʰɪgbɛɹɪz Mon, pɪgbɛɹiːz W, pɪgbəɹɪz W, pɛgbəɹiːz W

pig-block *n* a BENCH on which slaughtered pigs are dressed III.12.1. pɪgblɒːk Brk

pig-cote *n* a PIGSTY I.1.5. pɪgkyˈət La, pɪgkɒt He Gl, pɪgkɒɪt La, pɪgkɔɪt Y, pɪgkoːt La Ch Db Nt, pɪgkoʊt St, pɪgkʊət mY

pig-court *n* a PIGSTY I.1.5. *pl* pɪgkɔːts Ess

pig-cratch *n* a BENCH on which slaughtered pigs are dressed III.12.1. pɪgkɹɛtʃ Y, pɪgkɹatʃ L

pig-cree *n* a PIGSTY I.1.5. pɪgkʁiː Nb Du, pɪgkɹiː Du, pɪgkʁɪə Nb

pig-creel *n* a BENCH on which slaughtered pigs are dressed III.12.1. pɪgkɹiːl La Y, pɪgkɹəɪl We Y

pig-crow *n* a PIGSTY I.1.5. pɪgkɹoː Cu, pɪgkɹoʊ La, pɪgkru: La Db

pig down *viphr* to FARROW, describing a pig giving birth to piglets III.8.10. pɪg dɛʊn Bk Ess Sr Ha, pɪg dæʊn R Ess, pɪg daːˀn Lei, pɪg dəʊn Brk

pigeon-box 1. *n* a DOVECOTE I.1.7. pɪdʒɪnbɒks Cu Sa Mon Lei, pɪdʒənbɒks Do, pɪdʒɪnbɔːks Sa

2. *n* a box fixed on a wall, in which pigeons live. pɪdʒɪnbɒks Sa Wo Brk

pigeon-coop *n* a DOVECOTE I.1.7. *pl* pɪdʒɪnkuːps Brk, pɪdʒənkuːp L

pigeon-cote *n* a DOVECOTE I.1.7. pɪdʒɪnkɑːt Mon, pɪdʒɪnkɒt He Mon, *pl* pɪdʒɪnkɒts Sx, pɪdʒənkɒt Y, pɪdʒɪnkɒɪt Y, pɪdʒənkɒɪt La Y, pɪdʒɪnkʊut K, pɪdʒənkɔt MxL, pɪdʒənkɔːt La, pɪdʒənkɔɪt Y, pɪdʒənkɔʊt L, pɪdʒənkʌʊt K, pɪdʒɪnkoːt La Ch Db Sa He, pɪdʒənkoːt Db, pɪdʒɪnkout St Wa, pɪdʒənkoˈət Du, pɪdʒənkʊət Y, pɪdʒɪnkʊət Y Nt L, pɪdʒʊnkʊət La, pɪdʒənkʊət La Y L, pɪdʒɪnkʊət La, pɪdʒɪnkəʊt Wa

pigeon-cove *n* a DOVECOTE I.1.7. pɪdʒɪnkɔʊ K, pɪdʒɪnkʊuː Sr K Sx, pɪdʒənkuː K, pɪdʒɪnkuːv Sx

pigeon-cub *n* a DOVECOTE I.1.7. pɪdʒɪnkʌb O

pigeon-dovecote *n* a DOVECOTE I.1.7. pɪdʒɪndʊkət Nb, pɪdʒəndʊkət Nb Cu Du, pɪdʒɪndʊfkɪt Nt, pɪdʒɪndʊvkət Lei

pigeon-dove-house *n* a DOVECOTE I.1.7. pɪdʒɪndʌf Ess, pɪdʒɪndʌfə Ess, pɪdʒɪndʌfəs C Ess, pɪdʒɪndʌvəs Ess, pɪdʒəndʌfəs Sf, pɪdʒndʌfəs Ess, ˈpɪdʒɪnˌdufʊs Wa

pigeon-duff* *n* a DOVECOTE I.1.7. pɪdʒɪndʌf Ess

pigeon-duffer* *n* a DOVECOTE I.1.7. pɪdʒɪndʌfə Ess

pigeon-footed *adj* PIGEON-TOED VI.10.4. pɪdʒənvʊtɪd W

pigeon-hole *n* a DOVECOTE I.1.7. pɪdʒənɒɪl Y, pɪdʒɪnɔɪl Y, pɪdʒənɔɪl Y, pɪdʒənʊəl Y

pigeon-holes *npl* holes built into a wall, in which pigeons live, ⇐ DOVECOTE I.1.7. *no -s* pɪdʒɪnoːɫ Mon, pɪdʒənoːɫz W Co D, pɪdʒənouls Man

pigeon-house *n* a DOVECOTE I.1.7. pɪdʒɪnɛʊs Wo Wa O, pɪdʒɪnæus He, pɪdʒɪnaʊs Sa, pɪdʒɪnʌus He, pɪdʒɪnəʊs He Wo, pɪdʒənəʊs O W

pigeon-hull *n* a DOVECOTE I.1.7. pɪdʒɪnʊl Cu, pɪdʒənʊl We

pigeon-hut *n* a DOVECOTE I.1.7. pɪdʒɪnʌt Brk, pɪdʒənhʌt So

pigeon-locker *n* a space or compartment inside the gable-end of a barn, in which pigeons live, ⇐ DOVECOTE I.1.7. pɪdʒɪnlɑːkʔə Nf, pɪdʒɪnlɒkə Nf, pɪdʒɪnlɒkʔə Nf

pigeon-loft *n* a DOVECOTE I.1.7. pɪdʒɪnlɑːft Gl, pɪdʒɪnlɒf Lei, *pl* pɪdʒɪnlɒfs K, pɪdʒɪnlɒft Cu We La Y Ch Db Sa St He Wa Nf Bk K, pɪdʒʊnlɒft La, pɪdʒənlɒft La Y Ch Db Bk, pɪdʒənɫɒft Ha, pɪdʒɪnloft St, pɪdʒɪnlɔːf Gl Bk Ess, *pl* pɪdʒɪnlɔːfs So, pɪdʒɪnɫɔːf Do Ha, pɪdʒənlɔːf So, pɪdʒənɫɔːf W D Ha, pɪdʒɪnlɔːft Gl O Sf Ess Sr Ha, pɪdʒənlɒft L, pɪdʒənlɔːft La Sf Ess So W, pɪdʒənɫɔːft W Ha

pigeon-pair *n* a family comprising a son and a daughter, ⇐ PIGEONS IV.7.3. pɪdʒɪnpɛː St, pɪdʒɪnpɛə Hu Nf

pigeon-pen *n* a DOVECOTE I.1.7. pɪdʒɪnpɛn St Lei

pigeon-roost *n* a DOVECOTE I.1.7. pɪdʒɪnɹuːs Gl

pigeon(s) *npl* *What do you call those birds that coo [imitate] and can be trained to fly distances?* IV.7.3. *no -s*: pɪdʒɪn Gl Nt Nth Brk K Ha, pɪdʒən Wo L Sf Hrt Co D

-s: Eng exc. Sa

⇒ **coast, coasters, coos, homer, quist, quists**; ⇒ also **pigeon-pair**

pigeons'-holes *npl* holes built into a wall, in which pigeons live, ⇐ DOVECOTE I.1.7. pɪdʒənzoːɫz Co D

pigeons'-house *n* a DOVECOTE I.1.7. pɪdʒɪnzhɛɪs Nf, pɪdʒɪnzəʊs Brk

pigeon-toe *adj* PIGEON-TOED VI.10.4. pɪdʒəntou Man, pɪdʒɪntuː Nf

pigeon-toed *adj* A *man who walks like this [indicate pigeon-toed], you say is ….* VI.10.4. Eng exc. Db He Wa Gl O Nt Lei R Nth Hu Bk Bd. ⇒ **chicken-toed, cleeky-feet, club-footed, crab-footed, crab-toed, crib-footed, crow-toed, dab-toed, duck-feet, duck-footed, duck-nebbed, duck-toed, hen-toed, hook-toed, keb-footed, keb-legged, nebbed, nebby, neb-footed, nebbing in, peg-toed, pen-toed, pigeon-footed, pigeon-toe, pincered, pincer-toed, pince-toes, pincher-toe, pincher-toed, pinch-toed, pinchy-toed, pinson-toed, pin-toed, pumple-footed, spraw-footed, *sprawled out*, timber-toed, timber-toes, timble-toed, tip-toed, toes-in, tosie, troll-footed, trow-footed, turkey-toed, turn-toed, twang-toed, twill-toed, twilly-toed, twinny-toed, web-footed**

pig-fat *n* the FAT round the kidneys of a pig III.12.7. pɪgfat Cu

pig-form *n* a BENCH on which slaughtered pigs are dressed III.12.1. pɪgfɔːm Db C, pɪgfɔˠːm K, pɪgfɔˠːm D, pɪgfɔːəɽm Sr, pɪgfɔˠːɽm Sx, pɪgfəːm Cu

piggery 1. *n* a PIGSTY I.1.5. pɪgɹɪ Wo L[large] Ess Sr, *pl* pɪgɹɪz St Lei Brk, pɪgəɹɪ Y St Nf Ess[large], *pl* pɪgəɹɪz L Brk K Sx, pɪgəˠɹɪ Ha Sx, pɪgɽi So W, pɪgəɽi So W Ha, pɛgəɽi W

2. *n* a group of pigsties. pɪgəɹɪ Ess

piggin 1. *n* a movable wooden bucket used as a TROUGH in a cow-house I.3.6. pɪgɪn La

2. *n* a wooden container for carrying horse-feed, ⇐ BASKET III.5.4. pɪgɪn La Y[*tub with projecting stave as handle x2*]

3. *n* a SCOOP used to take water out of a boiler V.9.9. pɪgɪn Y

piggy-whidden *n* a WEAKLING piglet III.8.4. pɪgiwɪdn Co

pig-hales *npl* HAWS IV.11.6. pɪgɛɪɫz W, pɪgɛɪᵁɫz W, pɪgaɪɫz Do

pig-haws *npl* HAWS IV.11.6. pɪgɔːz W, pɛgɔːz So W

pig-hole *n* a PIGSTY I.1.5. pɪgɒɪl La Y Db, pɪgɔɪl Y, pɪgoʊl St, pɪgʊəl Cu La Y

pig-horse *n* a BENCH on which slaughtered pigs are dressed III.12.1. pɪgɒs D, pɛgɒs Co

pig-house *n* a PIGSTY I.1.5. pɪguːs Y, pɪghuːs Nb Du

pig-hovel *n* a PIGSTY I.1.5. pɪgɒvɫ Nth

pightle *n* a PADDOCK I.1.10. pɪdʊɫ Brk, paɪkəɫ Bd, paɪkɫ Hu Bd, pɔɪkəɫ Bk, pɔɪkɫ C Sf Ess, pʌɪtʔl Nf, pʌɪkʔl Nf, pʌiʔl Nf

pig-hull *n* a PIGSTY I.1.5. pɪgʊl Cu Du We La Y, pɪghʊl Cu

pig-jib *n* a BENCH on which slaughtered pigs are dressed III.12.1. pɪgdʒɪb So*[2 feet 6 inches x 2 feet x 5 feet, handles at ends]* Do

pig-ladder *n* a BENCH on which slaughtered pigs are dressed III.12.1. pɪgɫedəᵗː D, pɪgɫædəᵗː D

piglet *n* *What do you call a newly born pig?* III.8.2. Eng exc. Cu We Ch Hu C Bd Co. ⇒ **dacky, doll, fare, jokers,** *little ones,* **little pig, little pigs, little sucker, pig, pigs, pigling, shoots, slip, sucker, sucking-pig, suckler, sucklers, suckling, suckling-pig, suck-tit, wiggle,** *young one,* **young pig, young piglet, young suckers**

pigling *n* a PIGLET III.8.2. pɪglɪn Ch, pɪgɫɪn Mon, pɪgɫɪn K

pig-noses *npl* HIPS of the wild rose IV.11.7. pɪgnoːzɪz Ch

pig-pat *n* a TROUGH for pigs III.9.3. pɪgpɛˑt K

pig-pound *1.* *n* a PIGSTY I.1.5. pɪgpɛʊn Sx, *pl* pɪgpɛʊnz K, pɪgpɛʊnd Sx, pɪgpᵊund K

2. *n* an enclosure in which pigs are kept on a farm. pɪgpʊnd He *[Sx notes suggest K/Sx rr. = 'sty'; perhaps attached to building]*

pig-rack *n* a BENCH on which slaughtered pigs are dressed III.12.1. pɪgɹæk Hrt Ess, pɪgɹak Bk, pɛgɾak Co

pigs *npl* *What do you keep in sties?* III.8.1. pɪgs Nb Man, pɪgz Eng, pɛgz Gl Bk W Co D, *poss.sg* pɛgz Ha, pæɡz Ha, pagz Ha. ⇒ **dennis, grunters, hogs, mochyns, pig, swine, urks**

pig's-belly/bellies *n* CHITTERLINGS III.12.2.
-*y:* pɪgzbɛlɪ Lei Ess, pɪgzbalɪ Lei
-*ies:* pɪgzbɛlɪz Sf Ess

pigs'-cote *1.* *n* a PIGSTY I.1.5. pɪgzkɑːt He, pɪgzkɒt He Wo Mon Gl

2. *n* the shed of a pigsty, distinct from the pen attached to it. pɪgzkɒt He

pig's-court *n* a STYE in the eye VI.3.10. pɪgzkɔːt Ess*[old]*

pigs'-court *1.* *n* a PIGSTY I.1.5. pɪgzkɔːᵊt Ess
2. *n* the shed of a pigsty, distinct from the pen attached to it. pɪᵊgzkɔːt Ess

pig-scratch *n* a BENCH on which slaughtered pigs are dressed III.12.1. pɪgskɹɛtʃ Y, pɪgskɹatʃ Y Nt Nth *[possibly pig's-cratch]*

pigs'-crow *n* a PIGSTY I.1.5. pɪgzkɾæʋ Co

pig's-door *n* the FLAP at the front of old-fashioned trousers VI.14.16. pɪgzduəᵗː D

pig's-foot *n* a STYE in the eye VI.3.10. pɪgzfʊt Gl

pig's-form *n* a BENCH on which slaughtered pigs are dressed III.12.1. pɪgzvɔᵗːm D

pig's-guts *n* CHITTERLINGS III.12.2. pɪgzgʌts Ess So D

pig-shells *npl* HAWS IV.11.6. pɪgʃɛɫz So*[old]*

pig-shelvings *npl* CART-LADDERS I.10.5. pɪgskɛlvɪnz Cu

pig's-horse *n* a BENCH on which slaughtered pigs are dressed III.12.1. pɪgzhaᵗːʂ So

pigs'-house *n* a PIGSTY I.1.5. pɪgzhɛʊs Nf, pɪgzœʋs D, pɪgzœʋz D, pɪgzæʋs D, pɪgzæʋz Co D, pɛgzæʋz Co

pig-sill *n* a flat surface on which bacon is cured, ⇐ SALTING-TROUGH III.12.5. pɪgsɪl St

pig-slab *n* a BENCH on which slaughtered pigs are dressed III.12.1. pɪgsɫab Ha

pig's-ladder *n* a BENCH on which slaughtered pigs are dressed III.12.1. pɪgzɫedəᵗː So, pɪgzɫedəᵗː D

pig's-leaf *n* the FAT round the kidneys of a pig III.12.7. pɪgzlɪˑəf L

pigs'-lewze *n* a PIGSTY I.1.5. pɪgzlʏːz So D, pɪgzɫʏːz So, pɪgzluːz So, pɪgzɫuːz D

pigs'-meadow *n* a PADDOCK I.1.10. pɪgzmɛdə Co

pig's-nut *n* an ACORN IV.10.3. *pl* pɪgznʌts So

pigs'-pound *n* an enclosure in which pigs are kept on a farm ⇐ PIGSTY I.1.5. pɪgzpæʊn He

pig('s)-stock *1.* *n* a TROUGH for pigs III.9.3. pɪgstɒk K

2. *n* a BENCH on which slaughtered pigs are dressed III.12.1. pɪgstɒk La Y Co, pɛgstɒk D, pɪgzstɒk D

pig('s)-stool *n* a BENCH on which slaughtered pigs are dressed III.12.1. pɪgstɪʏl Nb Cu, pɪgstɪʊl Cu Du Y Nf, pɪgstɪəl Cu We, pɪgstʊːɫ O Nf Sf Ess MxL Brk Sr Do Ha, pɪgstʊːl Nf, pɛgstuːɫ Ha, pɪgstuːʊ Sr Ha, pɪgzstuːɫ Co

pig's-table *n* a BENCH on which slaughtered pigs are dressed III.12.1. pɪgs-teɪbl Man

pig-stall *n* a PIGSTY I.1.5. pɪgstɔːɫ So

pigsty *n* *[Show an aerial photograph of a farmstead and surrounding fields] What do you call the various buildings? [If necessary, ask the relevant question below.] What do you call the place where you keep the animals that go [imitate grunting]?* I.1.5. Eng exc. Cu We. ⇒ **court, cree, creeve, creevy, hog-house, hog-sty, hole, lewze, mucklagh, pig-cote, pig-court, pig-cree,** *pig-crew* ⇒ **pig-crow, pig-crow, piggery, pig-hole, pig-house, pig-hovel, pig-hull, pig-pound, pigs'- cote, pigs'-court, pigs'-crow, pigs'-house, pigs'- lewze, pigs'-pound, pig-stall, pig-yard, sty**

pigsty-door *n* the FLAP at the front of old-fashioned trousers VI.14.16. pɪgstɪduˑə Db

pig-stye *n* a STYE in the eye VI.3.10. pɪgstiː La, pɪgstaɪ Nb, pɪgstɑɪ C MxL Sr, pɪgstɒɪ K, pɪgstɔɪ Wa O Bk Ess*[humorous x1]* Brk K Sx, pɪgstʌɪ Sr, pɪgstəɪ He Brk Sx

pig-trest *n* a BENCH on which slaughtered pigs are dressed III.12.1. pɪgtɹɛst La, pɪgtrɛst La, pɪgtɹɛs Db

pig-trestle *n* a BENCH on which slaughtered pigs are dressed III.12.1. pɪgtrɛsl La

pig-trough *n* a SALTING-TROUGH III.12.5. pɪgtɹʌʊ MxL

pig-turnel *1. n* a SALTING-TROUGH III.12.5. pɪgtəːnə Ch

2. n a BENCH on which slaughtered pigs are dressed III.12.1. pɪgtəːnə Ch

pig-yard *n* the place where pigs are kept on a farm ⇐ PIGSTY I.1.5. pɪgjaːd Ess

pike *1. n* a HAY-FORK I.7.11. pæɪk He, paɪk Co, pɒɪk Wo, pɔɪk Gl, pəɪk He Mon Gl

2. n a hay-fork with a long shaft. paɪk Co, pəɪk He Wo Mon

3. n a hay-fork with a short shaft. pæɪk Mon, pəɪk He Wo

4. n a hay-fork with a long or short shaft. pæɪk Mon, pəɪk He Wo

5. v to glean. *prppl* paɪkɪn Ch

6. n a pointed iron stick hanging down behind an axle to prevent a cart from going backwards on a hill, ⇐ PROP/CHOCK I.11.2. paˑɪk L

7.1. vt to CLEAR grass at the edges of a field II.9.5. paɪk La, pɑːk Y

7.2. v to clear grass. paɪk We La Y, *2prpl* paɪks La

8. n a STYE in the eye VI.3.10. pɛːk La Db, pæᵊk La, paɪk La Ch

pike-fork *1. n* a HAY-FORK I.7.11. paɪkfɔˑːk La

2. n a hay-fork with a long shaft. pɑɪkfət La

pike-handle *n* the SHAFT of a hay-fork I.7.12. pəɪkændəɬ Mon

pike-hilt *n* the SHAFT of a hay-fork I.7.12. paɪkɪɬt Co

pikel *1. n* a HAY-FORK I.7.11. pɛɪkɪɬ Ch, pɛɪkl Ch, pæɪkɪl He, paɪkɪl Ch Sa St, paɪkl La Sa, paɪtl He, paɪkəl Sa He, pɑɪkɪl Ch, pɑɪkl La Ch, pɒɪkɪl St, pɒːɪkɪl St, pɒɪkl Sa, pɒɪkəl Sa

2. n a hay-fork with a short shaft. paɪtl La, *pl* paɪtlz La

3. n a hay-fork with a long or short shaft. paɪkɪl Sa

4. n a hay-fork with a long, medium length, or short shaft. paɪkɪl St, pɑɪkl St

pike out *vphr* to CLEAR grass at the edges of a field II.9.5. -*ing* paɪkɪn ᵊuːt Du

pikes *1. npl* round STACKS II.7.1. pæɪks Y, paɪks Y*[hay and corn x1]*, *sg* pʌɪk Nf*[uncommon]*

2. npl large COCKS of hay up to 12 feet in height II.9.12. *sg* pɛɪk Nb, paɪks La Y, pɑːks La

pikeys *npl* GIPSIES VIII.4.12. pɒɪkɪz K*[old x1]*, pɔɪkɪz Ess K, pʌɪkɪz Sr*[old x1]*, pəɪkɪz Sx*[old x1]*

pilch *1. n* a DIAPER V.11.3. pɪlʃ La Y L, pɪltʃ Nf, pɪɬʃ L MxL K, pɪɬtʃ Ess So, pɪʊɬʃ K Ha, pɪʊʃ Brk

2. n a wrapper worn over a diaper. pɪlʃ Sa, pɪltʃ Wa Nf, pɪɬʃ Brk Sr

3. n a cloth put on a mother's lap for protection while holding a baby. pɪlʃ Sa

[SBM Edd suggest all forms may refer to an outer wrapper]

pilcher *n* a DIAPER V.11.3. pɪʊɬtəᴵ Brk *[SBM Edd suggest may refer to outer layer]*

pile *n* a CLAMP in which potatoes are stored out of doors II.4.6. paɪɬ Co

pile-maul *n* a heavy wooden MALLET I.7.5. paɪlmɔːl Db

piles *n* barley AWNS II.5.3. pæɪɬz He, paɪlz Sa, pɒɪlz Sa Wo, pɒːɪlz St, pɔɪlz Wa, pəɪlz Wo, pəɪɬz He Wo

pillars *npl* stone GATE-POSTS IV.3.2. pɪləs Man

pills *1. n* **sheep-pills** SHEEP-DUNG II.1.7. ʃɪppɪlz Wa

2. npl RABBIT-DROPPINGS III.13.15. pɪlz St Nt*[facetious]* Nf, pɪʊɬz Brk

pimping *v-ing* PEEPING VI.3.8. pɪmpɪn Ch, pɪmpən Du

pimple *n* a STYE in the eye VI.3.10. pɪmpʊ Ess

pimp(s) *n* KINDLING-*WOOD* V.4.2.

no -s: pɪmp Hrt*[bundle of sticks]*

-s: pɪmps Hrt

pl: pɪmps Sx*[small, for stoves x1]*

pin *1. n* What do you call this [indicate a pin]? V.10.8. Eng. ⇒ **knob-pin**

2. n a LINCH-PIN holding a wheel on a cart I.9.12. pɪn Nb Du We La Y Ch Db St Wo Wa Nt L Lei Nf Sf Bk Ess MxL Sx

3. n a metal linch-pin. pɪn Cu La Y Sa Wa Sr Sx

4. n a wooden linchpin. pɪn We Wa

5. n the iron stay connecting the beam with the side of a cart, ⇐ CROSS-BEAM END I.10.1. pɪn La

6. n a BUMPER of a cart I.10.1(a). pɪn Sx *[queried ir.r. SBM]*

7. n a pin fixing a cart-body to the shafts, stopping it from tipping, ⇐ ROD/PIN I.10.3. pɪn Wo Mon O So Sr

8. n a pin used with a perforated rod in front of a cart to allow adjustments when tipping. pɪn St Wo Mon Gl, *pl* pɪnz Sa

9. n the HIP-BONE of a cow III.2.1. pɪn Co, *pl* pɪnz D

10. n the human HIP-BONE VI.9.1. pɪn D

pinafore *1. n* a working APRON V.11.2(a). pɪnəfɔːə Ess*[with bib x2]*, pɪnɪfʊə L

2. n a decorative APRON V.11.2(b). pɪnɪfaᶜː W, pɪnɪfʊʊəᶜ Wa, pɪnɪvʊʊəᶜ Gl, pɪnɪfɔː Wa Mon, pɪnəfɔː St Wa MonSf, pɪnɪfɔᵗ: So W D Ha, pɪnɪvɔᵗ: W D, pɪnəfɔᵗ: So Co Ha, pɪnɪfɔə L Nf K, pɪnəfɔˑə Nf Sf, pɪnɪfɔˑəɪ He, pɪnəfɔəˡ Brk K, pɪnɪfɔəᵗ Sx, pɪnəfɔəɽ O, pɪnɪfɔʊəᵗ O, pɪnɪfɔːə Ess, pɪnəfɔːə Nf Ess[covers bosom x1, covers back and front x1, covers arms and bosom x1, overall with sleeves x1], pɪnɪfɔə Db[for little girl x1] Nth Nf, pɪnəfoˑə Hu C Nf[with shoulder straps], pʰɪnɪfou Mon, pɪnɪfoˑə Bd Hrt, pɪnəfoə Wa Ess, pɪnɪfɔəˡ O, pɪnɪfoəᵗ Brk, pɪnəfoːᵊ Man Db, pɪnɪfoːəᵗ Mon, pɪnəfoːəᵗ He Bk, pɪnɪfʊə Nt L Bk, pɪnəfʊə Y L, pɪnɪfʊəᵗ O, pɪnəfuːəᵗ Gl, pɪnɪfəᵗ Gl, pɪnəfəᵗ Mon

pin-bone *1. n* the HIP-BONE of a cow III.2.1. pɪnboːn So Co, *pl* pɪnboʊnz Ha, pɪnboːən So Do, pɪnbwʊn Gl, pɪnbuːn Co D Ha, pɪnbuːən So W Co D Do Ha
2. n the human HIP-BONE VI.9.1. pɪnboːən So Do, pɪnbuːn D

pincered *adj* PIGEON-TOED VI.10.4. pɪnsɜˡːɽ La

pincer-toed *adj* PIGEON-TOED VI.10.4. pɪnsətɪəd Y, pɪnsətʊəd La Y

pince-toes *adj* PIGEON-TOED VI.10.4. pɪnstʊəz Y

pinch *1. n What do you call a very small quantity of sugar or salt [gesticulate]?* VII.8.6. Eng exc. R C. ⇒ **bit, fingerful,** *little* **bit, mite, morsel, nip, pickle, snip, spoonful, spoontle, toothful**
2. vi-3prpl burglars STEAL VIII.7.5(a). pɪnʃ Wa K
3. vt-3prpl burglars STEAL things VIII.7.5(b). pɪntʃ St, pɪnʃ Nb Ch Bd K

pinched up *adj* VERY COLD, describing a person VI.13.19. pɪnʃt əp Sx

pincher-bobs *npl* EARWIGS IV.8.11. pɪnʃəˡbɒbz Sr

pincher-toe *adj* PIGEON-TOED VI.10.4. pɪnʃətʊə Y

pincher-toed *adj* PIGEON-TOED VI.10.4. pɪnʃətɪəd Y, pɪnʃətʊəd Y L

pincher-wigs* *npl* EARWIGS IV.8.11. *sg* pɪnʃəˡwɪg Ha

pinching* *vt-ing* PULLING his ear VI.4.4. pɪnʃɪn Y, *no -ing* pɪnʃ Brk

pinch-toed *adj* PIGEON-TOED VI.10.4. pɪnʃtɪˑəd Y, pɪnʃtoʊd O

pinchy-toed *adj* PIGEON-TOED VI.10.4. pɪnʃɪtɪəd Y

pindy *adj* **get pindy, go pindy** to SPOIL, referring to meat or fish V.7.10. **get pindy** gɪt pɪndɪ D, gɪd pɪndi D; **go pindy** guː pɪndi D

pine **1. n* a group of furrows 20 feet broad, ⇐ RIDGES II.3.2. pæɪn Ess
2. vi to WARP, referring to wood IX.2.9. paːn Y, paɪn Y
3. vi to shrink. pɛɪn Nb Du[dry and shrink], paɪn Du

pined *adj* HUNGRY VI.13.9. paɪnd Y; **pined to death** very hungry. paɪnd tə dɪəθ Y

pine-end *n* the GABLE-END of a house V.1.5. pæɪnɛnd Mon, paɪnɛnd Gl, pɒɪnɛnd So W, pʌɪnɛnd Gl, pəɪnɛnd Mon Gl

pine-hole *n* a FASTING-CHAMBER III.11.3. paɪnɔɪl Y, paɪnʊəl Y

pine-house *n* a FASTING-CHAMBER III.11.3. paɪnɒus L, paɪnuːs Y, paˑɪnæus L

pin-fallow *n* FALLOW-LAND II.1.1. pɪnfałə Lei

pinfold *1. n* a PADDOCK I.1.10. pɪnfaːd Nb
2. vt to PEN or FOLD sheep in part of a field III.7.10. pɪnfɒuld Y

pin-heads *npl* MINNOWS IV.9.9. pɪnɛds Y

pin-horse *n* a TRACE-HORSE I.6.3. pɪnɒːs K

pining-end *n* the GABLE-END of a house V.1.5. pɪnənɛnd Do, paɪnɪn ɛnd So

pining-fold *n* a FASTING-CHAMBER III.11.3. paˑɪnɪnfɔuld L [marked u.r. EMBM]

pining-hole *n* a FASTING-CHAMBER III.11.3. paɪnɪnɔɪl Y, paˑɪnɪnɒɪl Y

pining-house *n* a FASTING-CHAMBER III.11.3. paˑɪnɪnaʊs Nt L, paˑɪnɪnuːs L, paɪnɪnæʊs Nt L

pining-pen *n* a FASTING-CHAMBER III.11.3. paɪnɪnpɪn Y, paɪnɪnpɛn L, paˑɪnɪnpɛn L Lei *[error in EMBM headword, giving dining-. See note at fasting-chamber]*

pinks *npl* MINNOWS IV.9.9. pɪŋks He

pinnacle *n* the RIDGE of a house roof V.1.2(a). pɪnɪkł Ess

pinner *1. n* a pin fixing a cart-body to the shafts, stopping it from tipping, ⇐ ROD/PIN I.10.3. pɪnəᵗ: So
2. n a working APRON V.11.2(a). pɪnə Lei, pɪnəᵗ Sx
3. n a decorative APRON V.11.2(b). pɪnə Ch Db St Wo Gl Lei Sf So, pɪnəɪ St, pɪnəᵗ Sa He Wo O Nth Bk, pɪnəᵗ: Do

pinnerette *n* a decorative APRON V.11.2(b). pɪnɪrɛˡt Nf, pɪnərɛt St Ess[with a bib]

pinnock *n* a very small RIVULET IV.1.1. pɪnʊk K

pinny *1. n* a working APRON V.11.2(a). pɪnɪ We Y Nf
2. n a decorative APRON V.11.2(b). pɪnɪ Nb Cu Du We La Y[with a bib x1] Ch Sa St Wo Wa Mon Gl O Nt L Nth Hu Nf[worn by children] Bk Bd K Ha, pɪnɪ So W Co D Do Ha, pəni D

pinson-toed *adj* PIGEON-TOED VI.10.4. pɪnʃntˡyːəd Ch, pɪnʃəntoːd Ch

pinswells *npl* BOILS VI.11.6. pɪnzwɪłz D, *sg* pɪnswəł Do, pɪnzwəłz D, *sg* pɪnzł So, pɪnzəłz So

pin-toed *1. adj* PIGEON-TOED VI.10.4. pɪntʊd Sx, pɪntɔud Wa O Lei Nth Brk, pɪntʌud C Bk Bd MxL Sr, pɪntoːd He Brk Ha, pɪntoʊd Db St Wa Gl O Nth Nf Bk Bd, pɪntʊəd Nt L, pɪntuːd

Db St Ha

2. *adj* SPLAY-FOOTED VI.10.5. pɪntɒud Sx

pip *1. vi* to CHIP, referring to an egg that is about to hatch IV.6.10. pɪp Sa He Wo Wa Mon Gl O Nth Bk So W K, *ptppl* pɪpt Ha

2. *vt* to TOP-AND-TAIL gooseberries V.7.23. pɪp He, *prppl* pɪpɪn Gl, pɛp Co

3. *vt* to REMOVE *STALKS* from currants V.7.24. pɛp Co

pipe *1. n* the metal BUSH at the centre of a cart-wheel I.9.8. pəɪp Mon

2. *n* the LIGHTS or lungs of a slaughtered animal III.11.5. paːɪp St

3. *vt* to DRAIN wet land IV.1.9. paɪp MxL

piping *n* the GUTTER of a roof V.1.6. pəɪpɪŋ Mon

pipman *n* a WEAKLING piglet III.8.4. pɪpʔmən Sf, pɪpmn̩ Nf, pɪpʔmn̩ Nf, pɪpʔn Nf, pɪpm Sf

pippen *n* a BREAD-BIN V.9.2. pɪpɪn L Lei

pippen-pot *n* a BREAD-BIN V.9.2. pɪpɪnpɒt Nt

pips *npl* HIPS of the wild rose IV.11.7. pɪps Mon Nth Bk

pirl *n* a cotton-REEL V.10.6. pɒl Y, pəl Y

pirls *n* SHEEP-DUNG II.1.7. pyʁəlz Nb; **sheep-pirls** ʃiːppəɹəlz Cu

pirn *n* a cotton-REEL V.10.6. pɛʁən Nb

piss *1. n* URINE in a cow-house I.3.10. pɪs Nb Y St Mon O L Lei R Nf Sf Ess MxL So W Brk Sr K Do Ha, pɪst Man

2. *n* stale URINE used for cleaning blankets VI.8.8. pɪs Y Db He*[used as fertilizer or insecticide]* Mon Gl*[used as fertilizer or insecticide]* O L*[cure for chilblains or embrocation for animals]* Ess MxL*[fertilizer]* So W Sr K Co D Do Ha; **old piss** ɒud pɪs Y; **stale piss** stˡil pɪs Man

pissabed *n* a DANDELION II.2.10(c). pɪsəbɛd Y O, pɪsəbiˑd So *[Y rr. taken as **pissy-bed** NBM]*

piss-annats *npl* ANTS IV.8.12. pɪsanəts Ch

piss-annats'-nests *npl* ANT-HILLS IV.8.13. *sg* pɪsanətsnɛst Ch

piss-ants *npl* ANTS IV.8.12. pɪsænts Sa Wo Sf, pɪʃænts Nf, pɪsants Ch Sa L Nth C Bd Hrt Ess, pɪsaːnts Ess

piss-ants'-nests *npl* ANT-HILLS IV.8.13. pɪsaːntsnɛsts C

piss-bed *n* a DANDELION II.2.10(c). pɪsbɛd Y Ch

piss-emmet-banks *npl* ANT-HILLS IV.8.13. pɪsɛmətbaŋks Bk, pɪsɛməʔbaŋks Bk

piss-emmet-heaps* *npl* ANT-HILLS IV.8.13. *sg* pɪsɛməʔɪəp Bk

piss-emmet-mounds* *npl* ANT-HILLS IV.8.13. *sg* pɪsɛmətmɛund O

piss-emmets *npl* ANTS IV.8.12. pɪsɛməts Bk, pɪsɛməʔs Bk

pisser *n* the VULVA of a cow III.2.3. pɪzəˤː Do

piss-hills *npl* ANT-HILLS IV.8.13. pɪsɪlz L

piss-hole* *n* a hole in the wall of a byre through which urine drains, ⇐ URINE I.3.10. pɪsʊəl Y

piss-house *n* an EARTH-CLOSET V.1.13. pɪsəus Do

piss-lap *n* the FLAP at the front of old-fashioned trousers VI.14.16. *pl* pɪslaps Db

pissle *1. n* the penis of a horse, ⇐ SHEATH III.4.9. pɪsʊɫ Brk, pɪsʊ Sx

2. *n* stale URINE used as garden fertilizer VI.8.8. pɪsɫ Ess

piss-mare *n* a DANDELION II.2.10(c). pɪsmɛˑə Y

piss-mice *npl* ANTS IV.8.12. pɪsmaɪs La

pissmice-nests *npl* ANT-HILLS IV.8.13. *sg* pɪsmaɪsnɛst La

pissmire-heaps *npl* ANT-HILLS IV.8.13. pɪsmaɪəɹiːps Nt, pɪsmaɪəɹiːps Nth

pissmire-hills *npl* ANT-HILLS IV.8.13. pɪsmæɪə-ɪlz Y, pɪsmaɪəɹɪlz Y Nt L, *sg* pɪsmaˑɪəɹɪl L

piss-mires *npl* ANTS IV.8.12. pɪʃmɪəz Nf, pɪʃmeəz Nf, pɪsmæɪəz Y, pɪsmaɪəz Du Nt L*[old x1]*, pɪsmaɪəz L*[old x1]* Nth Hu, pɪʃmaɪəz Nf, pɪsməɪ-əz Mon *[not a WMBM headword]*

pissmower-nests* *npl* ANT-HILLS IV.8.13. *sg* pɪsmaʊəˡnɛst La

piss-mowers* *npl* ANTS IV.8.12. pɪsmaʊəz La, pɪsmaʊəˡz La

piss-tank *n* an artificial CESS-POOL on a farm I.3.11. pɪstaŋk Y

pissy-ants *npl* ANTS IV.8.12. pʌsɪ-ants Sa

pissy-bed *n* a DANDELION II.2.10(c). pɪsɪbɛd Nb Cu Du We La Y

pissy-beds *npl* ANTS IV.8.12. pɪsɪbɛdz Ch Sa

pissymare-nests *npl* ANT-HILLS IV.8.13. *sg* pɪsɪmɛənɛst La

pissy-mares *npl* ANTS IV.8.12. pɪsɪmɪəz Nb, pɪʃəmɪəz Nf, *sg* pɪsɪmɛə La, pɪʃəmɛəz Nf *[not a EMBM headword]*

pissymer-heaps *npl* ANT-HILLS IV.8.13. pɪsɪməɹiːps Cu

pissymer-hills *npl* ANT-HILLS IV.8.13. pɪsɪməɹɪlz We Y

pissymer-nests *npl* ANT-HILLS IV.8.13. *sg* pɪsəmənɛst Y

pissy-mers *npl* ANTS IV.8.12. pɪsɪməz Cu We Y, pɪsəməz Y

pissy-mice(s) *npl* ANTS IV.8.12. *no -s:* pɪsɪmaːs La *-s:* pɪsɪmaɪsɪz Ch[old]

pissymire-heaps *npl* ANT-HILLS IV.8.13. *sg* pɪsɪmɪəhiːp Nb*[fist-size]*, pɪsɪmaɪəɹiːps Du Lei, pɪsɪmaɪəɹiːps Lei R, pɪsəmaˑɪəɹiːps Lei, pɪsəmaˑɪəˡiːps Lei

pissymire-hills *npl* ANT-HILLS IV.8.13.
pɪsɪmaɪəɹɪlz La Y Nt, *sg* pɪsɪmaɪə-ɪl Y, pɪsɪmɑˈɪəɹɪlz L

pissymire-nests *npl* ANT-HILLS IV.8.13. *sg* pɪsɪmaɪənɛst Y

pissy-mires *npl* ANTS IV.8.12. *sg* pɪsɪmæɪə Y, pɪsɪmaɪəz Du La Y Nt*[old]* Lei, *sg* pɪsɪmaɪəɹ Y, pɪsɪmɑɪəz Db Lei R, pɪsəmɑˈɪəz Lei, pɪzəmɒːɪəz St, pɪʃəmɒɪəz Nf

pissymoo-nests *npl* ANT-HILLS IV.8.13. *sg* pɪsɪmuːnɛst Nb*[for 'smaller' ant]*

pissy-moor *n* a DANDELION II.2.10(c). pɪsɪmɛʊə Y *[queried error NBM]*

pissymoor-heaps *npl* ANT-HILLS IV.8.13. pɪsɪmʊəɹɪəps La

pissymoor-hills *npl* ANT-HILLS IV.8.13. pɪsɪmʊəɹɪlz Cu

pissymoor-nests *npl* ANT-HILLS IV.8.13. pɪsɪmʊənɛsts We

pissy-moors *npl* ANTS IV.8.12. pɪsɪmʊəz Nb*[old x1]* Cu Du*[old]* We La, *sg* pɪsɪmʊəɹ Y

pissymoors'-hills *npl* ANT-HILLS IV.8.13. pɪsɪmʊəzhɪlz Du

pissy-moos *npl* ANTS IV.8.12. *sg* pɪsɪmuː Nb*[old]*

pissymote-rucks *npl* ANT-HILLS IV.8.13. pɪsəmoːtɹʊks Ch

pissy-motes *npl* ANTS IV.8.12. pɪsɪmɒʊts Db*[old]*, pɪsɪmɒʊts Ch, pɪsəmoːts Ch

pissy-mother *n* a DANDELION II.2.10(c). pɪsɪmʊðə Cu

pissymother-hills *npl* ANT-HILLS IV.8.13. pɪsɪmɣðɔᴿhɪls Nb, pɪsɪmʊðəɹɪlz Cu

pissy-mothers *npl* ANTS IV.8.12. *sg* pɪsɪmɣðɔᴿ Nb, pɪsɪmʊðəz Cu

pissymothers'-nests *npl* ANT-HILLS IV.8.13. *sg* pɪsɪmʊðəznɛst Cu

pissy-moul *n* a DANDELION II.2.10(c). pɪsɪmɔʊl Nb

pissymower-hillocks *npl* ANT-HILLS IV.8.13. pɪsɪmaʊəɹɪləks La

pissymower-hills *npl* ANT-HILLS IV.8.13. pɪsɪmaʊəɹɪlz La

pissy-mowers *npl* ANTS IV.8.12. pɪsɪmaʊəz Y, pɪsɪmaʊəɹz La, *sg* pɪsɪmaʊəᴶ Y

pit *1. n* a CESS-POOL on a farm I.3.11. pɪt Nf So W K Co Do

2. n an artificial cess-pool. pɪt Wa O Bd So W Do, *pl* pɪts Lei, *pət* So

3. n a POOL on a farm III.3.9. pɪt Ch Db Sa St Wa L Lei Nth Nf So W Co D Do, *pət* So

4. n a POND IV.1.5. pɪt La Ch Db Sa Wa L Lei Nf So Do

5. n a QUARRY IV.4.6. pɪt Y L Nf Sf Bk Bd Hrt Ess Sr, *pɛt* Ess

6. n a CLAMP in which potatoes are stored out of doors II.4.6. pɪt Nb Cu Du Y Db Gl O Lei Hu C Bd

MxL So W Brk K Do, pɪtʰ Nb Du, pɪʔ O Bk

7. n an ASH-MIDDEN V.1.14. pɪʔ Bk

8. n the ASH-HOLE beneath a domestic fire V.3.3. pɪt Gl

pitch *1. v [Show a picture of three men unloading a wagon of sheaves in a stackyard.] What does this man [the middle man, pitching the unloaded sheaves onto the stack] do?* II.6.10.
vt -ing pɪtʃɪn Do
v pɪtʃ Man Sa St He Wo Mon Gl Lei Sf Bk Hrt Ess So Brk Sr K Sx, *vbln* pɪtʃɪn Ch, *vbln* pɪtʃən Co
⇒ bind, bully, butt up, cast, catch in, chuck, chuck across, chuck on, chuck *the sheaves*, empty, feed, fill in, fling, fork, *fork and* chuck, fork back, fork on, fork up, hand, hand on, hand over, hand *sheaves*, hand *the sheaves*, *labour*, lift, move *the sheaves*, pack round, pass, pass *them* over, pick, pitch, pitch *it* up, pitch off, pitch on, pitch up, put, put *it* back, put *it to him*, put *it to them*, reach, serve, *sheaf-catch and* pass, sheaf-turn, shift, shoot on, stack-heed, take, take away, take in, take off, take *them*, take *the sheaves*, throw, throw across, throw back, throw *it* across, *throw on and* sheaf-turn, toss, turn, turn *sheaves*, turn *the sheaf*, turn *the sheaves*, unempt, wait *on the stacker*; ⇒ also bully-man, char-hole-man, *standing*-bully, taker-away

2.1. v to LOAD dung into a cart II.1.5. pɪtʃɪn Man

2.2. vt to load dung. pɪtʃ Wo

3. v to FORK sheaves onto a wagon II.6.7(b). pɪtʃ Man Ch Db St Wa Gl O Nth C Nf Sf Bk Bd Hrt Ess So W K Co Do Sx, *3prsg* pɪtʃɪz He, *-ing* pɪtʃɪn Brk Sr D Ha, *prppl* əpɪtʃɪn Wo

4. n a CUTTING of hay II.9.15. pɪtʃ Ha

5. n the MOULD-BOARD of a horse-drawn plough I.8.8. pɪtʃ Brk

6. n the SOLE of a horse-drawn plough I.8.9. pɪtʃ W Ha

7. vt to slip a calf, ⇐ SLIP*S THE CALF* III.1.11. *-ed* pɪtʃt K

8. vt to set up hurdles in a field in order to PEN or FOLD sheep III.7.10. pɪtʃ So Sr, *2prpl* pɪtʃəz Ha

9.1. vt to MARK sheep with colour to indicate ownership III.7.9. pɪtʃ Sa He Mon

9.2. v to mark sheep with colour. pɪtʃ Db So

10. n a SLOPE IV.1.10. pɪtʃ He Mon Gl

11. n a very steep hill. pɪtʃ Gl

pitch away *viphr* referring to a cow, to show signs of calving by changes in the pelvic region, ⇐ SHOWS SIGNS OF CALVING III.1.12(b). *3prperfsg* pɪtʃt əweɪ So

pitch-balls *npl* RABBIT-DROPPINGS   III.13.15. pɪtʃbaːɫz He

pitch-band *1. n* STRING used to tie up a grain-sack I.7.3. pɪtʃbænd Ess

2. n TWINE used to fasten thatch on a stack II.7.7(b1). pɪtʃbænd Ess

pitcher *1. n* a HAY-FORK with a long shaft I.7.11. pɪtʃəᴶ Ha

2. n the FORKER of sheaves onto a wagon II.6.7(d). pɪtʃə Man Ch Db St Wa Mon Gl O Lei R Nth Hu C Nf Sf Bk Bd Hrt Ess MxL K, pɪtʃəᴶ St O Brk Sr K Ha, pɪtʃəɹ St He Brk Sr, pɪtʃəᵗ Sa He Wo Wa Mon Gl O Bk Brk Sr Ha Sx, pɪtʃəᵗː Sa So W Co D Do Ha, pʏtʃəᵗː Co, pətʃəᵗː So

3. n the FORKER on a wagon who unloads sheaves in a stackyard II.6.9. pɪtʃə Man, pɪtʃəᴶ Brk K, pɪtʃəᵗ Sr Sx, pɪtʃəᵗː So W Co D, pɪtʃɐ K

pitcher-off *n* the FORKER on a wagon who unloads sheaves in a stackyard II.6.9. pɪtʃəɹɒf La, pɪtʃəɹɔf Ch, pɪtʃəɹɔːf Ess Sr, pɪtʃəɾɔːf Gl Sr Sx, pɪtʃəᵗːɾˈɔːf So D, ˈpɪtʃəᵗːɾɔːf Ha, ˈpɪtʃəᵗːɾˈɔːf D Do

pitcher-on *n* the FORKER of sheaves onto a wagon II.6.7(d). pɪtʃəɹɒn St

pitcher-up *n* the FORKER of sheaves onto a wagon II.6.7(d). pɪtʃəᵗ-ʌp Sx, pɪtʃəɹup Nt

pitch-falling *adv* HEAD OVER HEELS IX.1.10. pɪtʃfɔːɫɪn W

pitch-fork *1. n* a MUCK-FORK with four prongs I.3.13. pɪtʃvaᵗːk Gl, pɪtʃfɔːk L

2. n a HAY-FORK I.7.11. pɪtʃfɔrk Cu, pɪtʃfɔːk Cu Du Y Lei Hrt Ess K, pɪtʃfɔᵗːk Ha

3. n a hay-fork with a long shaft. pɪtʃfaˑk Man, pɪtʃfaᵗːk So, pɪtʃfaᵗːk Wa, pɪtʃfɔɾk O, pɪtʃfɔːk Man Db St Wa L Lei R Nth Hu Nf Sf Bk Bd Hrt Ess MxL Sr K, pɪtʃfɔᴶːk La K, pɪtʃfɔᵗːk Wa Bk Ha, pɪtʃfɔəᴶk Brk

4. n a hay-fork with a short shaft. pɪtʃfɔːk Cu La K

pitch-handle *n* the SHAFT of a hay-fork I.7.12. pɪtʃændɫ Brk

pitch in *1. vtphr* to FORK sheaves onto a wagon II.6.7(b). pɪtʃ ... ɪn Ch

2. viphr referring to a cow, to show signs of calving by changes in the pelvic region, ⇐ SHOWS SIGNS OF CALVING III.1.12(b). *-es* pɪtʃəz ɪn Co, *3prprogsg* pɪtʃɪn ɪn So W Do, *-ing* pɪtʃɪn ɪn So W D Do Ha, *3prprogsg* pɪtʃən ɪn So D Ha, *-ing* pɪtʃən ɪn So, *3prperfsg* pɪtʃt ɪn W D, *-ed* pɪtʃt ɪn D, *-ing* pətʃən ɪn Do; **pitch in behind** *3prprogsg* pɪtʃɪn ɪn bɪˈæɪnd So; **pitch in to the pins** *-ing* pɪtʃən ɪn tə ðə pɪnz Do

pitching *1. v-ing* UNLOADING sheaves from a wagon II.6.8. pɪtʃɪn O W K

2. v-ing THROWING a stone VIII.7.7. pɪtʃɪn Y, pɪtʃən Man, *inf* pɪtʃ Mon

pitching-fork *n* a HAY-FORK with a long shaft I.7.11. pɪtʃɪnfaᵗːk Brk, pɪtʃɪnvaᵗːk So, pɪtʃənfɒᵗk Ha, pɪtʃɪnfɔːk Db C K, pɪtʃɪnfɔək Brk, pɪtʃɪnfəᵗːk Gl

pitching off *1. vphr-ing* UNLOADING sheaves from a wagon II.6.8. pɪtʃɪn ɒf La, pɪtʃɪn ɔːf Sr K Co D Sx, pɪtʃən ɔːf Co D

2. vtphr-ing unloading sheaves. pɪtʃɪn ... ɔːf So D

pitching-off-man *n* the FORKER on a wagon who unloads sheaves in a stackyard II.6.9. pɪtʃɪnɔːfmæn Sx

pitching-pick *n* a HAY-FORK with a long shaft I.7.11. pɪtʃɪnpɪk Gl

pitching-pike *n* a HAY-FORK with a long shaft I.7.11. pɪtʃɪnpaɪk He, pɪtʃɪnpəɪk Gl

pitching-pikel *n* a HAY-FORK with a long shaft I.7.11. pɪtʃɪnpɒːɪkɪl St

pitching-prong *1. n* a HAY-FORK I.7.11. pɪtʃɪnpɾɒŋ Ha

2. n a hay-fork with a long shaft. pɪtʃɪnpɹɒŋ O Brk, pɪtʃɪnpɾɒŋ W

pitchmark *1. vt* to MARK sheep with colour to indicate ownership III.7.9. pɪtʃmaᵗːk Gl So

2. v to mark sheep with colour. pɪtʃmaᵗːk So D

pitch off *1. vphr* to PITCH sheaves II.6.10. pɪtʃ ɒf K, *-ing* pɪtʃɪn ɔːf K Sx

2. viphr referring to a cow, to show signs of calving by changes in the pelvic region, ⇐ SHOWS SIGNS OF CALVING III.1.12(b). *-ed* pɪtʃt ɔːf W

pitch on *1. vtphr* to FORK sheaves onto a wagon II.6.7(b). pɪtʃ ... ɒn La Wa Nf

2. vphr to PITCH sheaves II.6.10. *3prsg* pɪtʃəz ɔːn D, *-ing* pɪtʃɪn ɔːn Ess

pitch-poll *adv* HEAD OVER HEELS IX.1.10. pɪtʃpæʊəɫ Gl, pɪtʃpɒʊɫ Gl; **pitch-poll over** pɪtʃpæʊɫ oːvəᵗ He

pitch-prong *1. n* a HAY-FORK I.7.11. pɪtʃpɹɒŋ Ess

2. n a hay-fork with a long shaft. pɪtʃpɹɒŋ Sr Sx, pɪtʃpɾɒŋ W Ha

pitch up *1.1. vtphr* to FORK sheaves onto a wagon II.6.7(b). pɪtʃ ... ʌp Wa W, *prppl* pɪtʃɪn ... ʌp So, *-ing* pɪtʃɪn ... ʌp Ess, pɪtʃ ... ʏp Nf

1.2. vphr to fork sheaves onto a wagon. *-ing* pɪtʃɪn ʌp K, pɪtʃ ʊp Wa Nt Lei

2.1. vtphr to PITCH sheaves II.6.10. *3prsg* pɪtʃɪz ... ʌp MxL

2.2. vphr to pitch sheaves. pɪtʃ ʌp He Sx, *-ing* pɪtʃɪn ʌp Nf, pɪtʃ ʊp Nth, əpɪtʃɪn ʊp Wa

pit-grate *1. n* the ASH-HOLE beneath a domestic fire V.3.3. pɪtgreːᵊt Gl

2. n the grating above an ash-hole. pɪtgɹeːt Gl

pith *1. adj* wrinkled, describing the skin of very old people, ⇐ WRINKLE VI.11.2. pɪθ Brk

2. n the CORE of a boil VI.11.7. pɪθ Nf

pithabed *n* a DANDELION II.2.10(c). pɪθəbɛd Y

pit-hole *n* a POOL on a farm III.3.9. pɪtɒɪl La, pɪthoul Nf, pɪtoːl Sa, pɪttoːl Db

pit in *viphr* referring to a cow, to show signs of calving by changes in the pelvic region, ⇐ SHOWS SIGNS OF CALVING III.1.12(b). *3prprogsg* pɪtɪn ɪn Do, *3prperfsg* pɪtəd ɪn Co

pitman *n* a WEAKLING piglet III.8.4. pɪtmən Nf

pits *npl* PUDDLES IV.1.6. pɪts So Co D

pitsies *npl* KNEE-STRAPS used to lift the legs of working trousers VI.14.17. pɪtsɪz Ess *[queried EMBM]*

pittle-bed *n* a DANDELION II.2.10(c). pɪtlbɛd Y L

pizzle *n* the penis of a horse, ⇐ SHEATH III.4.9. pɪzl Sa St He, pɪzɫ MxL, pɪzəł Ess, pɪzʊł Ess, piːzł Wo

pizzle-handed *adj* CLUMSY, describing a person VI.7.14. pɪzɫhændɪd Nf

place *1. n* a FARMSTEAD I.1.2. pleɪs Man
2. n a STALL in a cow-house I.3.1. pɫɛːəs D
3. n the VULVA of a cow III.2.3. pleɪs St

planching* *n* a wooden upstairs FLOOR V.2.7. pɫanʃɪn Co, pɫanʃən Co

plane *n* the SOLE of a horse-drawn plough I.8.9. pleːn Y

plant out *vphr* to THIN OUT turnip plants II.4.2. *-ing* plæntɪn ɛʊt Sr

plash *vt [When you take the rough growth off your hedges, what do you say you do to them?] But if your hedge is overgrown and there are gaps in the bottom of it, what do you do to it?* IV.2.4. plæʃ So, plaʃ Nt L. ⇒ *bank up and* lay, *block the gaps*, braid, brail, buck, *buck-head and* braid, *buck-head and* lay, build up, *bung the holes up*, cast, cast *the hedge*, cast up, clat up, clat up *the gaps*, crook down, *cut and* fill *the gaps* up, *cut and* lay, *cut and* lay *the hedge, cut and* lig, *cut and* make, cut down, *cut down and* lay, *cut off and* braid down, dike, ditch up, edder, fell, *fell and* lig, fill up, gap, gap-stop, gap up, glat, hedge up, hook, lace, lay, lay *a hedge*, lay down, layer, layer *a hedge*, *layer and* braid, layer *to the ground*, lie ⇒ lay, lig, lig down, lig in, line, make *a hedge, make and* lay, make up, pleach, pleach down, plush, plush down, reave, re-lay, re-lig, rise *the hedge*, set up, set up *the gap*, slash, slipper, spale *gaps* up, splash, splawter, splay, splet, *splice*, splish, splisher, *split down*, splitter, split *the hedge*, steep, steep down, steep *the hedge*, steep *the hedge* down, stop, stop *shards*, stop *the gap*, stop *the gaps* up, stop *the shards*, stop up, stop up *gaps*, tine, wreath down; ⇒ also steepers

plaster-board *n* a PASTE-BOARD V.6.5. plæstəbɔːd Ess

plat *1. n* a PADDOCK I.1.10. pleˑt K, plæt Sr K Sx, pɫat Co D
2. n the MOULD-BOARD of a horse-drawn plough I.8.8. plæt Nf
3. n a CLOT OF COW-DUNG II.1.6. plat Nb;

cow's-plat kᵊuːzplat Du
4. n the THRESHOLD of a door V.1.12. pɫæt Co

plate *1. n* the MOULD-BOARD of a horse-drawn plough I.8.8. pɫeːət Co D, pɫɛət D, pɫɛːət D
2. n the SOLE of a horse-drawn plough I.8.9. pɫeɪt So
3. n a GIRDLE for baking cakes V.7.4(b). pleːt Sa He

platform *n* a SHEARING-TABLE III.7.8. platfɔᵗːm Sa*[trestle table]*

plaw-footed *adj* SPLAY-FOOTED VI.10.5. plaːfʊtɪd La, plaːfᵁuːtɪd La

play *1. vi In their holidays some children like to work, but most like to ....* VIII.6.4. Eng exc. We. ⇒ lake, lake about, play about, play them, play themselves
2. vi to BOUNCE VIII.7.3. pleɪ St

play about *viphr* to PLAY VIII.6.4. pleː əbaːt La, pleː əbuːt Y, pɫɛɪ əbœvt D, plæɪ əbəuːᵊt Gl, pɫaɪ əbæʊt W Ha, pɫaɪ əbəʊt W, plɒɪ əbæʊt So

played out *adj* EXHAUSTED, describing a tired person VI.13.8. pleːd ɛət Y

playmates *npl* PALS VIII.4.2. pliːmɛɪts St, pleɪmeɪts St

play them *virefl* to PLAY VIII.6.4. *-ing* pliːn ʊm Db, *prppl* pliːɪn əm Db, pleː ʊm La, pleːᶦ əm Db

play themselves *virefl* to PLAY VIII.6.4. *prppl* pleː-ɪn ðəsɛlz La

pleach *vt* to PLASH a hedge IV.2.4. pliːtʃ Ch Db Sa St He Wo Mon Nt, pɫiːʃ D, pleːtʃ Sa Wo*[old]*, pleːɪtʃ He Wo, plɛtʃ Nb, plɛɪtʃ Db Wo Nt, *-ing* pleɪʃɪn Sx*[old]*

pleach down *vtphr* to PLASH a hedge IV.2.4. pliːtʃ ... daɪn St, pɫiːs dœvn D

pleck* *n* a PADDOCK I.1.10. plɛk Mon

plenty *1. n* A LOT (of money) VII.8.7. Eng exc. Lei R Sr; *a plenty* ə plɛnʔɪ Nf
2. n ENOUGH IX.11.5. plɛntɪ Nb Cu Du Y

plim *vi* to WARP, referring to wood IX.2.9. pleːm W

ploat *1. v* to PLUCK a dead chicken of its feathers IV.6.21. pløːt Nb Du*[old x1]*, plœːt Nb Du, plɔːt Du Y, ploət Nb Du We, plʊət Nb*[old]* Cu Du We Y*[old x1]*
2. vt to PULL somebody's hair VI.2.8. plɔːt Y

plock* *n* a PADDOCK I.1.10. plɒk He

plook *n* a WHITLOW VI.7.12. pluːk Y

plot *n* a PADDOCK I.1.10. plɒt Sa Do, pɫɒt D Do, plɔːt Do

plother *n* MUD VII.6.17. plɒðə Y, plɒðəɪ Y

plough *1. n [Show a picture of a (horse-drawn) plough.] What do you call this?* I.8.1. Eng. ⇒ foot-plough, horse-plough, kent-plough, sole, sull, sully, sully-plough, swing-plough, turnrice, wheel- plough; ⇒ also fixture-plough,

moulter, **plough-pad,** *reest-plough* ⇒ **rice-plough/turn-reest-plough/turnrice, rice-plough, tommy-plough, turn-reest-plough, wooden dick**
[uneven presentation between BM volumes, with some data as rr. in one volume but bracketed in another; some bracketed material incorporated]
2. *v* to ROOT, what a pig does when it digs the ground with its snout III.9.2. *-ing* pɫæʊɪn Ha

plough-beam *n* the T-SHAPED PLOUGH-BEAM END of a horse-drawn plough I.8.5. plɛʊbiːm MxL, pɫæʊbɪˈəm L, plaʊbiːm Sa, pləʊːbiːm Wo *[marked ir.r. EMBM]*

plough-board *n* the MOULD-BOARD of a horse-drawn plough I.8.8. plɛʊboˈəᵗd̩ Bk, pɫəʊboːəᵗd̩ Mon, pləʊbɔəɹd He

plough-bottom *n* the SOLE of a horse-drawn plough I.8.9. plɛʊbɒdəm Ess, plɛʊbɒtəm Hrt

plough-breast *n* the MOULD-BOARD of a horse-drawn plough I.8.8. plɛʊbɹɛst C, plæʊbɹɛst Ess, pluːbɹɛst Y

plough-bridle *n* the T-SHAPED PLOUGH-BEAM END of a horse-drawn plough I.8.5. plɹuːbɹaɪdl Cu

plough-buck *n* the T-SHAPED PLOUGH-BEAM END of a horse-drawn plough I.8.5. pluːbʊk La

plough-cock *1. n* an EVENER on the plough-beam end of a horse-drawn plough I.8.4. plæʊkɔk L
2. *n* the T-SHAPED PLOUGH-BEAM END of a horse-drawn plough I.8.5. plɛʊkɒk O Bk, plæʊkɔk L

plough-cords *npl* the REINS of a plough-horse I.5.5. *no -s* plɹəfkʊəd Y, plɛʊkɔːdz Ess

ploughed-fallows *n* FALLOW-LAND II.1.1. pɫæʊdvaɫəz W

plough-furrow *n* a FURROW II.3.1. plæʊfʊɹə Wo

plough-ground *n* FALLOW-LAND II.1.1. plaʊɡɹəʊn So *[queried ir.r. SBM]*

plough-hales *npl* the HANDLES of a horse-drawn plough I.8.2. pɫæv-aɫz D, plæʊ-ɛɪlz L, plæʊ-ɛˈəlz L, plaʊ-ɛəlz Y, pluː-ɛəlz Y L

plough-head *n* the T-SHAPED PLOUGH-BEAM END of a horse-drawn plough I.8.5. plɛːjed Db, plɛʊ-ɛd Hrt Ess, plɛʊhɛˡd Ess, plæʊ-ɛd R, plaʊ-ɛd L, plɹuː-iːd Cu, pluːhiːd Nb, pluː-ɹəd We La Y, plᵘuː-ˡiːd We, plᵊuː-eɪˈd Du

plough-lines *npl* the REINS of a plough-horse I.5.5. plɛʊlaɪnz Nf Hrt, *sg* plɛʊlɔɪn Ess, *sg* plɛʊlʌɪn Nf, plæʊlaˈɪnz L, plaːˈᵊloˈɪnz Lei, plaulʌɪnz Nf, pluːlaɪnz L

ploughman *n* a CARTMAN on a farm I.2.2. plɛʊmən Hrt

plough-nose *n* the SHARE of a horse-drawn plough I.8.7. plɹʊnʊəz Y

plough-pad *n* the saddle on a plough-horse, ⇐ PLOUGH I.8.1. pluːpad Y, pləʊpad Ch

plough-point *1. n* the SHARE of a horse-drawn plough I.8.7. pɫəʊpʌɪnt Do, pləʊpwəɪnˀ Do

2. *n* the pointed end of the SHARE of a horse-drawn plough. plæʊpɔɪnt K

plough-reest *n* the MOULD-BOARD of a horse-drawn plough I.8.8. pluːɹiːst La

plough-seam *n* a FURROW II.3.1. pluːsɪəm Y

plough-shafts *npl* the HANDLES of a horse-drawn plough I.8.2. plæʊʃɑːvz Sr

plough-share *n* the SHARE of a horse-drawn plough I.8.7. plɛʊʃɹə Nf, plɛʊʃɛə Nf Hrt, plɛʊʃɑᵗ: Bd, plɛuːʃeːəᵗ Wo, plɛuːʃɔᵗ: Wo, plᵊæʊʃɪˈə L, plæʊʃɪəᵗ He, plæʊʃɛəᵗ Ha, pɫæʊʃɔᵗ: Do, plʌʊʃɪəᴶ Brk, plʌʊʃɪəᵗ Mon, pluːʃɛə Y, pləʊʃɛə Y

plough-share-slide *n* the SOLE of a horse-drawn plough I.8.9. pɫaʊʃɪəɽsɫaɪd O

plough-shoe *n* the SOLE of a horse-drawn plough I.8.9. plɛʊʃu: Ess, pɫæʊʃʏ: Co

plough-slead *n* the SOLE of a horse-drawn plough I.8.9. plɛʊsliːd Ess

plough-sled *n* the SOLE of a horse-drawn plough I.8.9. plɛʊslɛd Nf

plough-slide *n* the SOLE of a horse-drawn plough I.8.9. plæʊslaɪd MxL

plough-slipe *n* the MOULD-BOARD of a horse-drawn plough I.8.8. pluːslæɪp Y, pluːslaɪp Y

plough-sock *n* the SHARE of a horse-drawn plough I.8.7. pluːsʊk La, pləʊsɒk He

plough-stilts *npl* the HANDLES of a horse-drawn plough I.8.2. plɹəfstɪlts Y, pluːstɪlts Y

plough-tails *npl* the HANDLES of a horse-drawn plough I.8.2. plɛʊtɛɪlz Nf, plɛʊːteːɪɫz Wo

plough-top-share *n* the SHARE of a horse-drawn plough I.8.7. plʌʊtɒpʃɛəᴶ Brk

plough up *vtphr* to ROOT, what a pig does when it digs the ground with its snout III.9.2. *prppl* pɫæʊɪn ... ʌp Ha

pluck *1. n* What do you call the lungs, liver and heart [of a slaughtered animal] together? III.11.6. plʊk Man, plʌk Nb Sa He O R Nth Hu C Nf Sf Bk Bd Hrt Ess MxL Brk Sr K Ha Sx, pɫʌk Ess Co D Ha, plʏk Nf, plʊk Nb Cu Du We La Y Ch Db Sa St Wo Wa Gl O Nt L Lei R Nth C Bk Brk K, pɫʊk O

2. *n* the pluck of a slaughtered pig. plʊk La Y Db
3. *n* the pluck of a slaughtered sheep. plʌk Nf, plʊk Y Wa Nt
4. *n* the pluck of a slaughtered pig or sheep. plʊk L
5. *n* the lungs of a slaughtered animal. plʊk Y
⇒ **bowel, crow, entrails, fifth-quarter, fifth-quarter** *pluck,* **fry, gullies, hange, haslet, inwards,** *liver and* **crow, offal, offals, plucktow, race, spleen, whole-pluck**
6. *n* the LIGHTS or lungs of a slaughtered animal III.11.5. plʊk L Lei

7. v What do you say you do when you strip the feathers off a dead chicken? IV.6.21. Eng exc. Nb Co Do. ⇒ **draw, dress, feather, pick, ploat, pug, pull, strip** *[object unclear, and may frequently be 'feathers', not 'chicken']*

8. v to TOP-AND-TAIL gooseberries V.7.23. plʊk Nt

9. v to REMOVE *STALKS* from currants V.7.24. plʊk Nt, *-ing* plʊkɪn Gl

10. vt to PULL somebody's hair VI.2.8. plʊk Db

plucking *vt-ing* PULLING his ear VI.4.4. plʊkkɪn Ch

plucktow *n* the head, liver, lungs, and any general waste from a slaughtered animal, ⇐ PLUCK III.11.6. plʊktoʊ Man

pluffy *adj* SAD, describing bread or pastry that has not risen V.6.12. plʌfi D

plug *1. n* the CLOG on a horse's tether I.4.3. plɒg K, plʌg Bk Bd Hrt So Sr K Sx, plʌg Hrt Co D, plʊg Cu La L Nth So, plʊgːⁿ La

2. n a wooden LINCH-PIN holding a wheel on a cart I.9.12. plʌg K

3. vt to LOAD dung into a cart II.1.5. *-ing* plʊgɪn Y L

4. vt to PULL somebody's hair VI.2.8. plʌg Sa, plʊg Ch Sa

plugging *1. vt-ing* **plugging muck** CARTING DUNG II.1.4. plʊgɪn mʊk Y Nt, plʊgən mʊk Du

2. vt-ing PULLING his ear VI.4.4. plʌgɪn Sa, plʊgɪn Sa

pluggy *adj* TANGLED, describing hair VI.2.5. plʊgɪ La Ch

plum *prep* BESIDE a door IX.2.5. plʌm Ess *[queried EMBM]*

plumb *adj* **a bit plumb** STEEP, describing a hill IV.1.11. ə bɪt plʊm Y

plunder-bar *n* a rod fixing a cart-body to the shafts, stopping it from tipping, ⇐ ROD/PIN I.10.3. plʌndəbaᵗː Bd

plush *vt* to PLASH a hedge IV.2.4. plʌʃ Do, plɫʌʃ Do, *-ing* plɫʌʃɪn Co, *-ing* plʌʃən So, *-ing* plɫʌʃən Co, *-ing* pləʃɪn Sr

plush down *vtphr* to PLASH a hedge IV.2.4. plʌʃ ... dəʊn Do, plɫʌʃ dəʊn Do, *-ing* plʊʃɪn dæʌn Co

plut-holes *npl* PUDDLES IV.1.6. plʌtoːlz Sa

pob-holes *npl* PUDDLES IV.1.6. pɒbɔɪlz Y

pobs *n* PORRIDGE V.7.1. pɔbz Y

pocketful *n* **a pocketful** A LOT (of money) VII.8.7. ə pɒkɪtfʊl St

pocket-handkerchief *n* the WATTLES of a hen IV.6.19. pɒkətaŋkətʃiːf W

pockets *npl What do you call these [indicate pockets]?* VI.14.15. Eng. ⇒ **clide, pouches**

pod *1. n [Show a peapod with peas.] What do you call this?* V.7.12. Eng exc. Cu La Nt Hu. ⇒ **cosh, huck, hud, hull, husk, pea-cod, pea-huck, pea- hod, pea-hud, pea-husk,** *pea-pod***, pea-posh, pea-pusket,**

pea-puss-coat ⇒ **pea-pusket, peascod, pea-shell, pea-shuck, pea-shull, pea- swad,** *pea-swarth* ⇒ **pea-swath, pea-swath, posh, shell, shuck, shull, slough, swad;** ⇒ also **swath**

2. n the BELLY VI.8.7. pɒd Ess, pɔd Sf Ess

podding *v-ing* SHELLING peas V.7.14. pɑːdɪn Gl, pɒdɪn Gl So

poddy *n* the BELLY VI.8.7. pɒdɪ Ess

podge-holes *npl* PUDDLES IV.1.6. pɒdʒoʊłz Lei

podges* *npl* PUDDLES IV.1.6. pɒdʒɪz R

pod-thistle *n* a variety of THISTLE II.2.2. *pl* pɔdθɪslz Wo

poggy *adj* BOGGY IV.1.8. pɒgɪ Db

point *1. vt* to WHITTLE a stick I.7.19. *-ing* pɔɪntən Ha

2. n the SHARE of a horse-drawn plough I.8.7. pɑɪnt Ch Hrt, pɒɪnt St Wa, pʷɒɪnt He, pɔɪnt K, pwəɪn? Do *[marked ir.rr. WMBM]*

3. n the pointed end of the SHARE of a horse-drawn plough. pɒɪnt K

4. vt to MARK the ears of sheep with a cut or hole to indicate ownership III.7.9. *-ing* pɔɪntɪn K

5. n a SPLINTER VI.7.10. pɒɪn? Nf

pointed-end *n* the GABLE-END of a house V.1.5. paɪntɪdɛnd So

pointen-end *n* the GABLE-END of a house V.1.5. pɒɪ?n̩end So

point out *vphr* to CLEAR grass at the edges of a field II.9.5. *-ing* pɔɪntɪn ɛʊt Sr

poison *1. adj* POISONOUS IV.11.4. pɛɪzn Ch Db, pɛɪzən Sa, pæɪzn Brk, paɪzn Ch Sa Gl L D, paɪzən La, pɑːzn La, pɑɪzn La Y Db Nth Hu Bd, pɒɪzʊn Wo, pɒɪzn Cu Du La Y Db Sa St Wa Gl Nt Nth Bk Bd Hrt So W Sr K Do Ha Sx, pwɒɪzn W Do, pɒɪzən Wo So, pɔɪzn Nb Du Y Gl O L Nf Sf Bk Hrt Ess So, pɔɪzən La Y Nf MxL K, pʌɪzn Nf W Co D Ha, pwʌɪzn Do, poɪzn We Wa O C Sf Bd, poɪzən Sf, pʊzn Nb Cu *[rare x1]* We La *[old x1]*, pʊzən Y, pʊzəm Y, pʊɪzn Y, pəɪzn So, pəɪzən He Wo Gl

2.1. vi to FESTER, referring to a wound VI.11.8. pɔɪzn Ess, pɔɪzən Ess

2.2. adj **turn poison** to fester. təᵗːn̩ pɒɪzn Ha

poisoning *n* **turn to poisoning** to FESTER, referring to a wound VI.11.8. *3prsg* təːnz tə pɔɪzənɪn Wo

poisonous *1. adj If you know a berry will kill you if you eat it, you say it is* .... IV.11.4. Eng exc. C Bd. ⇒ **poison**, *very deadly*

2. adj **turn poisonous** to FESTER, referring to a wound VI.11.8. tɑˑn pɔɪznəs Nf

poke *1. n* a SACK in which grain is weighed I.7.2. pøːkʰ Nb, pœːk Nb, poːk Du, poʊk Nf, poək We, pʊak Y, pʊək Nb Cu We Y

2. n an alternative to a SOWING-BASKET

II.3.6. poək Nb *[marked u.r. NBM]*

3. *v* to BUTT III.2.10. *-ing* pʊʊkɪn K, *prppl* pʊʊkən Du, *-ing* pɔʊkɪn O, *-ing* pʌʊkɪn Bd

4. *n* a POKER V.3.6. poːk Ha

5. *n* the BRIM of a hat VI.14.3. pɔʊk Wo, pʌʊk Ess, pʊʊk St

poke about *vphr* to BUTT III.2.10. *-ing* pʌʊkɪn əbɛʊʔ Bk, *-ing* poːkɪn əbaːt Nt

poke-needle* *n* a NEEDLE for mending sacks V.10.2(a). pʊəkniːdl Y

poker *n What do you call this [indicate a poker]?* V.3.6. Eng. ⇒ **fire-point, poke, potter, proker, purr, wottle**

pokes *npl* large sacks for carrying horse-feed, ⇐ BASKET III.5.4. pʊʊks Sx

poking-needle* *n* a NEEDLE for mending sacks V.10.2(a). pʊəkɪnnɛɪdl Y

poking out *vtphr-ing* PUTTING your tongue OUT VI.5.4. pɔːkɪn ... əʊt Do, pɔːkən ... œʏt D, *no -ing* pɔːk ... aʊt So, pɔʊkɪn ... ɛʊt Brk, poːkɪn ... ɛʊt Sa, poːkɪn ... æʏt D, poːkɪn ... æʊt W, poːkŋ ... æʊt Ha, poːkən ... æʊt Ha, poːkɪn ... aʊt O So, poːkɪn ... ʊʊt W, poːkɪn ... əʊt Mon Brk, əpoːkɪn ... əʊt Wo, pʊʊkɪŋ ... ɛʊːt Wo, pʊʊkɪn ... ɛʊt Wo O, pʊʊkɪn ... ɛʊʔ O Bk, pʊʊkʔn ... ɛʊt Nf, pʊʊkɪn ... aʊt So

pole *1. n* a TETHERING-STAKE in a cow-house I.3.3. pʊʊl Y Sr, pʊʊɫ Sr, pɔʊl Y, poːɫ Mon W D Ha, pʊʊᵊɫ Gl, pʊʊ Ha

2. *n* the STRETCHER between the traces of a cart-horse I.5.11. pɔʊɫ Brk, pɔʊ Brk, pʊʊ K

3. *n* an EVENER on a horse-drawn plough I.8.4. pʊʊɫ So

4. *n* a STICK used to support the shaft of a cart I.11.1. poʊl Nf, pʊʊ K

5. *n* the SHAFT of a scythe II.9.7. pɛʊl La, pɛʊ La Ch Db, paʊ We, pʊʊl Y Db, pʊʊ We La Y, pɔʊl Y L, pɔʊɫ Y, pɔʊ La, poːl Ch, pʊːl St

6. *n* the *HORIZONTAL* BAR of a crane over a domestic fire V.3.5(a). pʊʊɫ Wa, pɔʊl O

pole-cat *1. n What do you call that similar animal [to a weasel] with a bushy tail, darkish, as large as a ferret; it stinks and kills poultry, but is rather rare now?* IV.5.7. Eng exc. Co. ⇒ **club-tail, fitch, fitcher, fitchet, fitchew, fitchock, fitchy, foumart, fullard, fuzzart, pole-cat-ferret, skunk, stoat, vairy**; ⇒ also **fitch-colour, fitchet-ferret**

2. *n* a cat that has gone wild. pʊʊlkat St

pole-cat-ferret *1. n* a POLE-CAT IV.5.7. *pl* pʊʊlkɛt fəɹɪts K, *pl* pʊʊkæt fəɹɪts Sx, pɔʊkɛtfɛɹəts Ess, pɔːʊkæt fəɹət Ha, pʌʊɫkætfɛɹɪt Ess MxL, *pl* pʌʊɫkætfɛɹəts Ess, poʊlkætfɛɹɪt Nf

2. *n* a ferret used to hunt the POLE-CAT IV.5.7. *pl* pɔʊlkætfəɹɪts Y

pole-fagged *adj* EXHAUSTED, describing a tired person VI.13.8. pʊʊfagd La

pole-hook *n* a RAKE used in a domestic fire V.3.8(a). pɔʊlʊk Hu

police *n* a BOGEY VIII.8.1. pɒləs Du

policeman *n* a BOGEY VIII.8.1. pɫiːsmæn Co, pliːsman He, pəliːsmən Lei, pliːsmən Y St He Mon Nf Hrt Ess So Sr, pɫiːsmən O; **the policeman** ðə pliˑsmən Nf, ðə pɫiːsmən Ha

policeman's-buttons *n* GOOSE-GRASS II.2.5. pɫiːsmənzbʌdnz Co

poll *1. adj* HORNLESS, describing a cow III.2.9. pʊʊɫ Bd, pɔl L, pʌʊɫ Sf Ess, poːlˑ Nf

2. *n* a HORNLESS cow III.2.9. pøːl Nb, *pl* pœːlz Nb, pɒl Y Db St, pʊʊɫ Wa Bk Bd K Sx, pɔːɫ Ess, pʊʊɫ O Brk Sx, pʌʊɫ C Sf Bd Hrt, poːl Sa, poːɫ Gl W Brk D Do, poʊl St, *pl* poʊlz Wo, poʊɫ Wa Nth Bk Brk, poʊ Brk

3. *v* to LOP a tree IV.12.5. paʊl Y

4. *vt* **be polled, get it polled, get my hair polled, get polled, get your hair polled, have your hair polled** *GET YOUR* HAIR *CUT* VI.2.2. **be polled** bɪ paʊld Y, bɪ pʊʊd La, bʊ pʊʊld Y, bɪ pɔʊd La; **get it polled** gɛt ɪt pʊʊd Y*[old]*; **get my hair polled** gɛt mɪ jʊə pʊld Ch; **get polled** gɛt pyːd Ch, gɛt pɛʊld La, gɛt pɛʊd La*[old x1]*, gɪt paʊld We Y, gɪt paʊd La, gɛt pʊʊld Y, gɪt pʊʊld Du, gɪt pʊʊd We Y, gɛt pʊʊd Y Db, gɪt pɔʊld Y, gɛt pɔʊld Nb, gɛt pʊʊd Nb La; **get your hair polled** gɛt ðɪ hɛə pʊʊld Nb, gɛt jə hɪɔᴿ pʊʊd Nb; **have your hair polled** ɛv jəɹ ɜᴶːɹ paʊd La

5. *n* a haircut. paʊl Du, pʊʊl Nb We, pʊʊ La Y Db*[old]*, pɔʊl Y, pɔʊ Nb La

6. *n* the NECK of a person VI.6.1. pʊʊ Sx, pɔʊɫ Sx, poːɫ Brk

7. *n* the SCRUFF (of the neck) VI.6.2. pʊʊɫ Gl, pɔʊɫ O, pɔʊ O Sr, poːɫ So W Do, poːʊɫ So, pʊɫ Brk *[precise reference to 'scruff' or 'neck' uncertain except for Brk]*

pollag *n* a CLOT OF COW-DUNG II.1.6. pɒləg Man

pollard *n* MEAL V.6.1(b). pɒləd Hu K, pɒɫəɽd O; **toppings and pollard** tɒpɪnz ən pɒlaᶜːɖ O

poll-beast *n* a HORNLESS cow III.2.9. pɔʊbiːst Sr, poːɫbiːst Mon

poll-cow *n* a HORNLESS cow III.2.9. pæʊɫkɛʊ Hrt, pɒlkæːᵊ Nt, pɒlkæʊ Lei, pʊʊɫkɛʊ Nth Sr, *pl* pʊʊɫkɛʊz Sx, pəlkaʊ L, pɔʊlkæʊ Wa, pʌʊɫkæʊ MxL, poːlkauː Sa, poːɫkəʊ W, poulkɛʊ Nf

polled *adj* HORNLESS, describing a cow III.2.9. pøːld Nb, pœːld Nb, paʊd Du, pɒld Cu Du We La Y Db St Nt Nf, pɒɫd Bk, pɒɫəd Ess, pʊʊld Du Nf, pʊʊɫd Sr, pʊʊʊd Sx, pʊʊt Cu, pɔld Cu Y L, pɔɫd Sf, poːɫd D, pɔʊɫd O Hu, pɔʊd K, poːld Sa, poːɫ Co, poːɫd D, pʊʊld Wo Nf, poʊɫd Wa C So, pʊʊd Ch, pʌʊld Nf, pʌʊɫd Bk Ess, pʌʊd Bk

polled-cow *n* a HORNLESS cow III.2.9. pɔɫdkɛˑʊ Sf

poller *n* a HORNLESS cow III.2.9. pɒulə Nth, pɒulə¹ K, pɔulə Hu

poller-cow *n* a HORNLESS cow III.2.9. pɒuləkeu Nth

polley *n* a PERCH for hens IV.6.3. *pl* pɒlɪz Nf

pollow *adj* HORNLESS, describing a cow III.2.9. pɔuɫɔu Sx

polly *1. adj* HORNLESS, describing a cow III.2.9. pɒlɪ Y Lei R Nf, pɔlɪ L, pʌulɪ Ess
2. n a HORNLESS cow III.2.9. pœːlɪ Nb, pɒlɪ We La Y Ch Db Sa St Wa, pɒulɪ K Sx, pɒuɫɪ Bd Sr, *pl* pɒuɫɪz Sx, pɔlɪ La Y L, pɔuɫɪ Nth, poɫɪ Mon, poːlɪ Nb Sa, pouɫɪ Nth Ess K

polly-cow *n* a HORNLESS cow III.2.9. pɒlɪkæʊ Lei, *pl* pɒlɪkæʐʊz Ch, pɒuɫɪkeʊ Sr, pɔlɪkaʊ L

polly-owlet* *n* an OWL IV.7.6. pɒlɪ-uːlət Y

polly-wags *npl* TADPOLES IV.9.5. pɔlɪwæˑgz Ess

polly-wigs *npl* TADPOLES IV.9.5. pɒlɪwɪgz Ess, *sg* pɒlɪwɪəg Ess, pɔlɪwɪgz Sf Ess

pommel *v* to KNEAD dough V.6.4. pɔml L

pompey *n* a KETTLE V.8.7. pɔmpɪ Ch

pond *1. n* What do you call that place on a farm filled with water, smaller than a lake? IV.1.5. pœːnd Nb Du, paːn D, pɑnd Nth, pɒnd Nb Cu Du We La Y Ch Db Sa St Wo Mon Gl O Nt Lei R Nth Hu Nf Bk Bd Hrt Ess So W Brk Sr K Ha Sx, pɒn Cu Man Db He Ess W K Sx, pɒːnd Ess Brk Sr, pɔnd Nb Cu We Y Wa L C Sf Hrt Ess MxL So Sr K, pɔːnd Y So W Do Ha, pɔːn So W Co D Do Ha. ⇒ **dam, dew-pond, dip, drinking-dip, drinking-pond, dub, lodge, mere, moot,** *mot* ⇒ **moot, pit, pool, pound, round pond, water-pit**
2. n a CESS-POOL on a farm I.3.11. pɔːn So
3. n a POOL on a farm III.3.9. pœːnd Nb Du, pɑnd Nth, pɒnd Nb Cu Du We La Y Db Sa Wa O Nt L Lei R Nth Hu Nf Bk Bd Hrt Ess So W Brk Sr K Ha Sx, pɒn Man He Brk Sr K Ha Sx, pɔnd Nb We Y Ch L C Sf Hrt Ess MxL Sr, pɔːnd So W D Ha, pɔːn So Co D Do Ha

pond-hole *n* a POOL on a farm III.3.9. pɒndʌuɫ Ess, pɔnduəl Y

pooks *npl* COCKS of hay II.9.12. pʏks Co D, pʏːks So D, *sg* poːk D, pʊks So W Brk Co D Do Ha, puːks Co

pool *1. n* In a field, what do you call the hollow filled with water where your cattle go to drink? III.3.9. pɪəl Du, pʏːɫ D, pʏː Ch, peʊ St, puːl Y Sa He Wo O, *pl* puːlz L, puːɫ He Wo Mon So Brk Co, puːˀl Man Sa, puːˀɫ He Wo Wa Mon Gl. ⇒ **bog-hole, dam, dew-pond, dike, dub, duck-pond, dum-hole, hole, hollan, lodge, mere, pit, pit-hole, pond, pond-hole, pooly-pit, pound, stell, water-hole, watering-hole, watering-place, watering-spot;** ⇒ also **water-place**
2. n a CESS-POOL on a farm I.3.11. puːɫ Do
3. n a POND IV.1.5. pɪəl Nb, pʏːɫ D*[bigger than*

pond], puːl Y Sa St Wo, pᵁuːɫ Mon, puːɫ He Wo Mon Nth Co, puːˀɫ Wo Wa Mon Gl, puː Ch

pools *npl* PUDDLES IV.1.6. *sg* pɪʊl Cu, *sg* pɪəl Nb, *sg* pʏːl Db, puːlz Cu Y Nth Ess, *sg* puːl Nb, puːˀz Hu, *sg* puːɫ L

pooly-pit *n* a POOL on a farm III.3.9. pʏːɫɪpɪt D

poor *1. adj* **rather poor** SICK, describing an animal that is unwell VI.13.1(c). ɹɑːðə pʊə K
2. adj DULL, referring to the weather VII.6.10. pʊə Y *[marked as emotive and therefore u.r. NBM]*

poorly *1. adj* ILL, describing a person who is unwell VI.13.1(b). pɒuˀlɪ K, pɔːlɪ Ess MxL, pɔˀlɪ L, poˑəlɪ Wa Nf Bd, pʊəlɛ Y, pʊələ Y, pʊəɹlɪ La
2. adj SICK, describing an animal that is unwell VI.13.1(c). poːlɪ Hrt Ess, poːɫɪ Ess, poʊəlɪ Man, pʊəlɪ Y St Ha, pʊəɽlɪ O

pootled *adj* EXHAUSTED, describing a tired person VI.13.8. pᵁuːtld We

pop *1. vi* to CHIP, referring to an egg that is about to hatch IV.6.10. pɒp W
2. n GRANDDAD VIII.1.8(a). pɒp Brk

pop down *viphr* to DUCK VIII.7.8. pɒp dæʊn Do

pop-hole *n* a SHEEP-HOLE IV.2.8. pɒpoːɫ W, pɒpoːʊɫ Mon

pop-noddles* *npl* TADPOLES IV.9.5. pɒpnɒdlz L

pops *n* SWEETS V.8.4. pɒps So*[old x1]* Do*[old x1]*, pɔps So

pork-cheese* *n* brawn, ⇐ CHEESE V.5.4(b). pʊəktʃiːz L

pork-fat *n* BACON-FAT V.7.5(b). poəkfæˀt Man

pork-saim *n* LARD made from the fat of a pig III.12.8. pɔːksɛːɪm Nf

pormpettles* *n* FRECKLES VI.11.1. pɔːmpetlz La*[obsolete]*

porpettles* *n* FRECKLES VI.11.1. pɔˀɹpetlz La

porridge *n* For breakfast, some people eat oatmeal boiled in water or milk. What do you call that when it's thick? V.7.1. Eng. ⇒ **groats, gulls, hasty-pudding, havermeal-crowdy, lumpy-toms, meal-porridge, oatmeal-porridge, pobs, skilly, stir-pudding, thickans, thick-dicks;** ⇒ also **set on**

porridge-slice *n* a PORRIDGE-STICK V.9.1. pɒɹɪʃslaɪs Db

porridge-spoon *n* a PORRIDGE-STICK V.9.1. pɒɹɪdʒspuːn Lei Brk

porridge-stick *n* What do you call the wooden thing for stirring your porridge in the pan (before April 1954: What do you call the wooden stick...)? V.9.1. pɒɹɪdʒstɪk Brk K, pɒdɪʃstɪk La. ⇒ **gull-thivel, keedle, ladle, mundle, patter, pestle, porridge-slice, porridge-spoon, porridge-**

thivel, pot-stick, skimmer, spatula, speltle, spoon, stick, stirrer-up, stirring-spoon, thivel, thivel-stick, wooden-fork, wooden-ladle, wooden-porridge-spoon, wooden-spoon, wood-spoon

porridge-thivel *n* a PORRIDGE-STICK V.9.1. pɒdɪʃθaɪbl Y

posh **1. n* a pea-POD V.7.12. pɒʃ Nth
2. *adj* PRETTY, describing a girl VI.5.18. pɒʃ L

poshing *v-ing* SHELLING peas V.7.14. *no -ing* pɒʃ Nth

poshy *adj* BOGGY IV.1.8. pɒʃɪ Y

posset *1. n* GRUEL V.7.2. pɒsɪt Brk*[old]*
2. *vi* to VOMIT, referring to a baby bringing up milk VI.13.14(b). pɒsɪt La Db Nt, *3prsg* pɒsɪts Y, pɒzɪt Db, *3prsg* pɒzɪts Y, *-ing* pɒzɪtɪn La Y, pɒsət We*[old x1]* La, pɒzət Cu We, *3prsg* pɒzɪts Y, *-ing* pɒzɪtɪn Y

post *1. n* the PARTITION between stalls in a cow-house I.3.2. pɒst Du *[marked technically u.r. NBM, but **standing-post** unmarked EMBM, **stall-posts** unmarked WMBM]*
2. *n* a TETHERING-STAKE in a cow-house I.3.3. pɒst La, pɒʊst Sr Sx, pɒʊs Sr Sx, pɔːst So, pɔʊst R Ess Sx, pʌʊst Bk Hrt Ess, post Nf, pɔːst Sa So D, poust Nf, poʊs Nf K, pɔːəst So, pʊst Sf, pʊəst L
3. *n* a STICK used to support the shaft of a cart I.11.1. pɒst Cu
4. *n* the HANGING-POST of a gate IV.3.3. pʊːs Y

posts *npl* the JAMBS of a door V.1.11. pɒʊstɪz Sr, pɒʊsɪz Nth, pɔʊsts Ess K, pʌʊsts Bk, pʌʊstɪz MxL, pʌʊs Ess K, pʌʊsɪz Bd*[old]*, pɔːst Ha, poːs Mon O, poːsɪs Sa, poːsɪz Sa, poːᵁs Mon, poˑəsts Bd, pʊsts Ess*[old]*, pʊstɪz Ess*[old, not used]*

pot *1. n* a SALTING-TROUGH III.12.5. pɒt Nf, pɒt? Nf*[earthenware]*
2. *n* a GIRDLE for baking cakes V.7.4(b). pɒt W
3. *n* a KETTLE V.8.7. pɒt Brk
4. *n* a BREAD-BIN V.9.2. pɔt Sf

pot-and-pan man *n* a TINKER VIII.4.9. pɒtn̩pæn mæn W

potato-bind(s) *n* POTATO-HAULMS II.4.4.
no -s: teɪtəbaɪn K, pəteɪtebaɪn K
-s: tɛɪtəbɔɪnz Ess

potato-bogle *n* a SCARECROW, especially in a potato field II.3.7. teːtɪbøːgl Nb, teːtɪbœːgl Nb, tatɪbøːgl Nb

potato-bury *n* a CLAMP in which potatoes are stored out of doors II.4.6. teːtəˡbɛɹiː Wo, teːtəˡbɛrɪ O, *pl* teːᵊtəbɛɹɪz Wa, tæɪtəbɛɹɪ Wa

potato-camp *n* a CLAMP in which potatoes are stored out of doors II.4.6. tɛdikamp Co

potato-cave *n* a CLAMP in which potatoes are stored out of doors II.4.6. tɪdikeːɪv So, tɛdikeːv So Co D, tɛdikeɪv So

potatoes *npl* *What root-crops do you grow?* II.4.1(a). Eng. ⇒ **chitties, murphies, spuds**

potato-grave *n* a CLAMP in which potatoes are stored out of doors II.4.6. tɛˑətɪgɹɛˑəv L

potato-green *n* POTATO-HAULMS II.4.4. tɪdigɹiːn Do

potato-hale *n* a CLAMP in which potatoes are stored out of doors II.4.6. teˑᵊˡ ʔəheɪl Nf

potato-haulage *n* POTATO-HAULMS II.4.4. tæɪ ʔəhɔˑlɪdʒ Nf

potato-haulm(s) *n* *What do you call the stems and leaves of a potato plant?* II.4.4.
no -s: tɪdi-ɛɫm So, teːti-æm W, teːtəˡ ɹ̩am Ha, teːdəˡ ɹ̩am Ha, teːtəˡ ɹ̩aːm He, teːtəˡ ɹɔːm Sa, teːdəˡ ɹ̩ɔːɫm Ha, teɪtə-am Wa, teɪtəˡɔːm Wo, tɛtiham W, tɛdi-əɫm So, pəteɪtəɹɛʊm Sr*[refined]*, tɛɪtəɹɛʊɫm K, tɛɪtəˡ-æəm Sx, pəteɪtəɹaːm Sr, tɛɪtə-aːm MxL, tɛɪtəˡɹaːm Sr, tɛɪ ʔəˡ-aˑɫm Brk, tɛɪtəhɔːm Ess, tɛɪtə-ʌɫm MxL
-s: teːtəˡ ɹ̩æmz Gl, teːɪtəˡ ɹ̩æmz Gl, teːti-amz W Ha, pəteːtə-ɔːmz Ch, teːtəˡ ɹɔːmz Sa, teːətəˡ ɹɔːmz Sa, teɪtəˡ ɹ̩æmz So*[old]*, teɪtəˡ-ɔʊmz O, teːɪtəˡ ɹɒmz He, tɛdi-eːmz Do, tɛdi-ɔːɫmz D, teːtəˡ ɹɒmz He, teːtɪ-ɔʊmz Y, tɛɪtəhaːmz Ess*[rare]*, pəteɪtə-aːmz Brk, tɛɪtəˡ ɹ̩aːmz Sx, tɛɪtəɹaːmz Ess, tɛɪtəɹɔːmz St, tɛˑətɪ-ɔːmz L
⇒ **bind(s)**, **blossom(s)**, **chitty-haulm(s)**, **haulm(s)**, **lises**, **potato-bind(s)**, **potato-green**, **potato-haulage**, **potato-husks**, **potato-rise**, **potato-shaws**, **potato-stalks**, **potato-stands**, **potato-stems**, **potato-top(s)**, **potato-vine**, *potato-wisels* ⇒ **potato-wyzles**, **potato-wises**, **potato-wyzles**, **rames**, **shaws**, **stalk(s)**, *stams* ⇒ **staums**, **tops**, **vines**, **weasums**, **wises**, **wyzles**

potato-heap *n* a CLAMP in which potatoes are stored out of doors II.4.6. teːtɪ-iːp Cu

potato-hog *n* a CLAMP in which potatoes are stored out of doors II.4.6. *pl* tiːtəɹɒgz Ch, *pl* teːtɪ-ɒgz Cu

potato-hole *n* a CLAMP in which potatoes are stored out of doors II.4.6. pɹeːtə-ɔːl La

potato-husks *n* POTATO-HAULMS II.4.4. teːtəˡ ɹ̩ʊsks Wo

potato-parings *npl* potato PEELINGS V.7.22. tɛɪtəpeəɹɪnz MxL, tɛətɪpeəɹɪnz Y L*[old x1]*

potato-peel(s) *n* potato PEELINGS V.7.22.
no -s: tɪdipiːɫ W
npl: tɛdipiːɫz Co, pəteɪtəpiːᵊɫz Ess, tɛɪtɪpɪɫz L

potato-pie *n* a CLAMP in which potatoes are stored out of doors II.4.6. teːtəpaɪ Nt, teətɪpaɪ Y, tɛətɪpaɪ Y L, teːtɪpaː Y, teːtɪpaɪ Y, tɛətəpaɪ Nt, tɛətɪpaɪ L, *pl* teːtəˡpɔɪz Sx

potato-pile *n* a CLAMP in which potatoes are stored out of doors II.4.6. tɛdipɒɫ Co

potato-pit *n* a CLAMP in which potatoes are stored out of doors II.4.6. teːdəˡpɪt Do, *pl* tɛtɪpɪts Nb, tɛdipɪt D, tɛɪtəˡpɪt Brk

potato-rind(s) *n* potato PEELINGS V.7.22.
no -s: teːtiʈɒɪn W, pəteɪtəɹɑɪn K, tɛɹɹəɹɹæɪn Brk
npl: tɪdiʈɒɪnz Ha, tɪdihʈɒɪnz So, tɪdiʈəɪnz W, tɪdiʈəɪnz Do, teːdiʈɒɪnz Do, teːtəˡːʈɒɪnz Ha, teːtəɹʌɪnz Gl, teːtiʈəɪnz W, teːdiʈəɪnz Do, tɛdiʈæːnz D, tɛdiʈæɪnz So, tɛdiʈaːnz D, tɛdiʈaɪnz So, tɛdiʈəɪnz Do

potato-rise *n* POTATO-HAULMS II.4.4. teːtəˡːʈɒɪs Sa

potato-shaws *n* POTATO-HAULMS II.4.4. teːtiʃaːz Nb

potato-skins *npl* potato PEELINGS V.7.22. tɛdiskɪnz So Co D

potato-stack *n* a CLAMP in which potatoes are stored out of doors II.4.6. tætəˡstæk He

potato-stalks *n* POTATO-HAULMS II.4.4. tɪdistɔːks So D Do, tɪdistɔːks Do, tɛdistałks Co D, tɛdistołks D, tɛdistɔːks Co D, tɛɪtəstɔːks L, tɛˈətɪstʊəks L

potato-stands *n* POTATO-HAULMS II.4.4. tɛdistɔːnz So*[old]*

potato-stems *n* POTATO-HAULMS II.4.4. teːdistɛmz Co

potato-top(s) *n* POTATO-HAULMS II.4.4.
sg: teɪtətɒp Bd, tɛʔətapʔ Nf
no -s: teːtɪtɒp Y, teətɪtɒp Y, tɛətɪtɒp Y, tɛətɪtɒp Y
-s: pəteɪtətɒps St, pʊtɛətətɒps Y, tɪətɪtɒps Du, teːtɪtœːps Nb, teːtɪtɒps Nb Cu Du We La Y, teːtətɒps Cu Y Db Nt, teːditɒps Co, teˈᵊʔətɒps Nf, teːtəˡɒps O, teːᵊtəˡːtɒps Wa, teːtəˡːtɒps Sa, teːtɪtɒps Y, teɪtətɒps Hu Hrt, teɪtʔətɒps Nf, teːˡtətɒps Db, teətɪtɒps Du Y, teˈətəˡtɒps Nth, teˈəʔəˡtɒps Bk, tɛditɒps Co, tɛtɪtɒps Cu, tɛːʔətaps Nf, tɛːʔətaˈpʔs Nf, tɛːʔːtɒps Nf, tɛːtɪtɒps We Y, tɛɪtətaps Nth, tɛɪtɪtɒps L, tɛɪtətɒps Db St Wa Lei R Nth Hu, tɛɪtɪtɔps L, tɛɪtətɔps C Sf, tɛɪtʔətɒps Sf Hrt, tɛətətaps Nth, tɛətɪtɒps Y, teˈətɪtɔps L*[old x1]*, teˈəʔɪtɒps L, tæɪtətɔːps Hrt, pɹeːtətɒps La, pɹeːtətɔps La

potato-tump *n* a CLAMP in which potatoes are stored out of doors II.4.6. teːtətʌmp Mon, *pl* teːtəˡtʌmps Sa

potato-vine *n* POTATO-HAULMS II.4.4. tæɪtəvaˈɪn Ess

potato-wises *n* POTATO-HAULMS II.4.4. teːtɪwaɪzəz Y*[old]*, teːtɪwaːzəz Y, pɹeːtəwaɪsɪz La, təːtɪwɔːzəz Y, teɪtɪwɔːzəz Y

potato-wyzles *n* POTATO-HAULMS II.4.4. tiːtəweɪzlz Ch, teːtəˡwiːzlz Sa, teːtəweɪzlz Ch, teːtəwaɪzlz Ch, pɹeːtəwaːzlz La

pot-bed *1. n* a CRANE on which a kettle is hung over a domestic fire V.3.4. pɔtbæd Sr *[headword queried SBM]*
2. n the vertical BAR or CHAIN of a crane over a domestic fire V.3.5(b). pɔtbæd Sr *[queried SBM]*

pot-crook *n* a CRANE on which a kettle is hung over a domestic fire V.3.4. pɒtkɹʊk Do

pot-hanger *1. n* a CRANE on which a kettle is hung over a domestic fire V.3.4. pɒtaŋəˡː Ha
2. n the vertical BAR or CHAIN of a crane over a domestic fire V.3.5(b). pɒtʌŋə Ess

pot-holes *1. npl* PUDDLES IV.1.6. pœːthøːlz Nb, pætoʊłz Ha, pathoulz Nf, pɒdɒłs Man, pɒtɒulz K, pɒthɒułz K, pɒtɒułz Wo Sr, pɒʔɒułz Sr, pɒtɔːłz W, pɒtɔulz Y, pɒtɔułz Lei Ess, pɒʔɔułz Brk*[deeper than puddles]*, pɒtɔuz Ess, pɒthʌułz Ess, pɒtʌulz Hrt*[bigger than puddles]*, pɒtoːlz La Sa, pɒtoːłz He Wo Mon Gl W Co Do Ha, pɒdoːłz He So W Co D Do Ha, pɒʔoːłz W, pɒthoulz Nf, pɒtoulz St He Wo Nf, pɒtoułz Wo Wa Lei So, pɒdoułz So, pɒʔoułz O, pɒtoːułz Mon Gl, pɒthoəlz Nb, pɒtuːlz St, pɒtʊəlz Du La Y, pɒtwɒlz We, pɒdɒłs Man, pɒdłz K D, pɒtłz So, pɔtɔulz Wa, *sg* pədouł So, pɔthuəlz Nb, pɔtuəlz Wo L, *sg* pʌtɒuł K
2. npl the HOOF-MARKS of a horse IV.3.10. pɒthʌułz Ess, pɒdoułz So *[marked u.r. EMBM]*

pot-hook *1. n* a CRANE on which a kettle is hung over a domestic fire V.3.4. pɒtɛuk Db, *pl* pɒtɛuks St, pɒtʌk Bd Hrt, pɒʔʌk Bk*[old]* Bd, pɒtuk Gl Nth Hu K Sx, *pl* pɒtʊks Lei R, pɒʔuk Bk, pɒtuːk Nt Lei, *pl* pɒtuːks R, pɒtɨːk Lei, pɔtuk Wo, pəduk C, pʊtuk Ess Sx
2. n the HOOK or *CROOK* of a crane over a domestic fire V.3.5(c). pɒtʌk Hrt, pɒthʊk Nf, pɒtuk Nth Hu Sx, pɒtʔuk Hu, pɒtuːk L Nth, *pl* pɒtɨːks Lei, pɔtuk C Ess, pɔtʔuk Hrt, pɔtuːk L
3. n the vertical part of a crane over a domestic fire, consisting of a *BAR* or *CHAIN* and a HOOK(/*CROOK*) V.3.5b+c. *pl* pɒtuks K

pot-ladles *npl* TADPOLES IV.9.5. pɒtleˑdlz Nf, pɒtleɪdlz Nf, pɒdleːɪdlz Nf

pot-links *n* a CRANE on which a kettle is hung over a domestic fire V.3.4. pɒtlɪŋks Ch

pot-noddles *npl* TADPOLES IV.9.5. pɔʔnɒdlz L

pots *n* A LOT (of money) VII.8.7. pɒts Lei

pot-skimmings* *n* fat taken off when bacon is boiled, ⇐ BACON-FAT V.7.5(b). pɒtskɪmɪnz L

pot-stick *n* a PORRIDGE-STICK V.9.1. patstɪk Man, pɒtstɪk Man

potter *n* a POKER V.3.6. pɒtə Db Y, pɒtəᴵ La Db, pɔttə Ch

potter off *imp* GO AWAY! VIII.7.9(a). pɒtəɹ ɒf St

potters *1. npl* GIPSIES VIII.4.12. pɒtərz Cu, pɔtəɹz Y
2. npl dealers in second-hand goods. pɒtəz We

pottle-ladles *npl* TADPOLES IV.9.5. pɒʔlleɪdlz Nf

potty *1. adj* STUPID VI.1.5. pɒtɪ Du La Y, pɔtɪ L
  2. adj SILLY VIII.9.3. pɒtɪ Wa O Nth, pɔˈtɪ Ess

pouch *n* the scrotum of a horse, ⇐ SHEATH III.4.9. pɛʊtʃ L Bk, pæʊtʃ W

pouches *npl* POCKETS VI.14.15. puːtʃɪz Nb, puːtʃəz Nb

pouds *npl* BOILS VI.11.6. pɛʊdz Sx[old]

pouk *1. n* an ASH-MIDDEN V.1.14. pɒuk K[old x1, deep hole x1]
  2. n a STYE in the eye VI.3.10. pɛʊk Ch Db Sa, pæʊk Sa, paʊks La Y Db, *pl* paʊks Wo, poːk Sa He[old x1] Wo, pʊʊk Wo, pʊk Wo
  3. n a pimple. paʊk We Ch, pʊək We

poultry *npl* HENS IV.6.2. pæʊɫɹɪ He, paʊɫɹɪ Y, pɒʊɫɹɪ La, pɔʊɫɹɪ Y, poːɫɹɪ He, pʊɫtrɪ Cu, pʊɫtɹɪ Y

poultry-house *n* a HEN-HOUSE I.1.6. pæʊɫɹɪ-əʊs Brk, pɔʊɫtɹɪ-æʊs Ch L, pʌɫtɹɪhɛʊs Ess, pʊɫtrɪhᵊʊːs Du, pʊɫtɹɪ-ᵊʊːs Du

pound *1.1. vt* to STOCK III.3.6. -*ing* pæʊndɪn Sa
  1.2. v to stock. pæʊnd Sa, paʊnd Sa
  2. n a POOL on a farm III.3.9. paʊnd Y, paʊənd Nb
  3. n a POND IV.1.5. paʊnd Y, pʊənd Y
  4. vt to KNEAD dough V.6.4. pɛʊnd Sx
  5. v to PEN or FOLD sheep in part of a field to be ready for dipping III.7.10. -*ing* pəʊnɪn K
  6. n a FASTING-CHAMBER III.11.3. pɛʊnd Nf Ess, pɛʊn Nf, pæʊnd K[concrete shed adjoining slaughterhouse]

pound note *n* What do you call this [indicate a pound note]? VII.7.8. Eng. ⇒ **bradbury, *pound*, pound paper, quid note, sovereign paper**

pound paper *n* a POUND NOTE VII.7.8. pɛʊn pɛɪpə Nf Ess, pɛʊn pɛɪpʔə Sf

pound-tree *n* an EVENER, the main swingle-tree of a horse-drawn plough harness I.8.4. pʌʊnʔɹɪ Sf

pound up *vtphr* to STOCK III.3.6. paʊnd ... ʌp Sa

pour *v* To get the tea from the tea-pot into the cup, what do you say you do? V.8.8. Eng exc. Du We La Db. ⇒ **birle, empt out, ent, ent out, hale out, hell out, lade, laden, pour in, *pour out*, shoot out, teem, teem in, teem out, teem up, *toom* ⇒ teem; ⇒** also **birle out**

pour in *vtphr* to POUR tea V.8.8. pævɣ ... ɪn Co, pɔˈʈ ... ɪn Ha, pɒtː ... ɪn So, pʊːʈ ... ɪn D
  2. vphr to pour tea. *2prpl* pʊʊᵊtz ɪn Ha

pouse *n* RUBBISH V.1.15. pɛʊs St

pratt *1. n* an EVENER on the plough-beam end of a horse-drawn plough I.8.4. pɹæt K, pɹæt K Sx
  2. n the T-SHAPED PLOUGH-BEAM END of a horse-drawn plough I.8.5. pɹæt K Sx [apparently forms one piece with the **evener** in at least some localities]

pratt-footed *adj* SPLAY-FOOTED VI.10.5. pɹætfʊtɪd K, pɹætfʊtɪd K

preaching clothes *n* SUNDAY-CLOTHES VI.14.19. pɹɪˈətʃɪn kluəz L

press *vi* to show signs of calving, referring to a cow with a swollen udder, ⇐ SHOWS SIGNS OF CALVING III.1.12(a). -*ing* pɹɛsən Man

pretty *1. adj* Of a good-looking girl, you might say: That's a very ... girl. VI.5.18. Eng exc. Cu We Man Db Wo. ⇒ *a flasher*, **attractive, bon, bonny, bonny-looking, canny, decent, fine, fine-looking, flash, good-like, good-looking, gradely, grand, grand-looking, handsome, handsome-looking, lovely-looking, nice, *nice bit of* stuff, nice *pretty*, nice *young*, not a bad piece of stuff, posh, *pretty little*, *rather* stirring, she's a peach, smart, smartish, smart-looking, smashing, sweet; ⇒** also **tart**
  2. adv VERY VIII.3.2. pɹɪtɪ He Wa Mon L Lei Ess, pɹɪʔɪ Sf MxL, pɹɪdɪ Sa, pɹətɪ He, pʊtɪ Mon, pətɪ MxL, pəɾʈɪ O, pətːdɪ Sa

prick *n* the penis of a horse, ⇐ SHEATH III.4.9. pɾɪk So

pricker *n* a SPLINTER VI.7.10. pɹɪkkəˈɹ La

prickers *npl* PEGS used to fasten thatch on a stack II.7.7(a). pɹɪkəᵗz Bk

prick-holly *n* a HOLLY-bush IV.10.9. pɹɪkɒlɪ L

prickles *n* barley AWNS II.5.3. pɾɪkɫz W

pricklies *n* GOOSE-GRASS II.2.5. pɹɪklɪz Wo

prickly-back *n* GOOSE-GRASS II.2.5. pɹɪk|ɪbak Y

prickly-backed-urchin *n* a HEDGEHOG IV.5.5. pɹɪklɪbaktəːtʃən Du

prickly-backs *npl* MINNOWS IV.9.9. pɹɪklɪbaks Y, pɹɪk|ɪbaks La [marked u.r. NBM as presumably referring to 'stickleback']

prickly-back-urchin *n* a HEDGEHOG IV.5.5. pɹɪklɪbakɒtʃɪn Y, pɹɪklɪbakəːtʃənt Du

prickly-black-urchin *n* a HEDGEHOG IV.5.5. pɹɪtlɪblakɒtʃɪn Y

prickly-pig *n* a HEDGEHOG IV.5.5. pɹɪklɪpɪg Y

prickly-urchin *n* a HEDGEHOG IV.5.5. pɹɪk|ɪ-ɔtʃən Y, pɹɪklɪ-əɹtʃən Y

prick-urchin *n* a HEDGEHOG IV.5.5. pɹɪkɒtʃən L

pricky-backs *npl* MINNOWS IV.9.9. pɹɪkɪbaks Y [marked u.r. NBM as presumably referring to 'stickleback']

pricky-back-urchin *n* a HEDGEHOG IV.5.5. pɹɪkɪbakɒtʃɪn Y, pɹɪkɪbakɒtʃən Y, pɹɪkɪbakəːtʃɪn Y

pricky-black-urchin *n* a HEDGEHOG IV.5.5. pɹɪkɪblakɒtʃɪn Y, pɹɪkɪblakɒtʃən Y, pɹɪkɪblakɒtʃən Y

pricky-urchin *n* a HEDGEHOG IV.5.5. pɹɪkɪ-ɒtʃən Y, pɹɪkɪ-ɔtʃɪn L, pɹɪkɪ-ɔdʒɪn L, pɹɪkɪ-ɔtʃən L

prid *n* a metal LINCH-PIN holding a wheel on a cart I.9.12. pɹɪdᵊ La

prill *n* a RIVULET IV.1.1. pɹɪɫ Mon*[smaller than brook x1]*

prime *v* to LOP a tree to improve its appearance IV.12.5. pɹɔɪm Ess

primrose day *n* a local FESTIVAL or holiday on 19 August VII.4.11. pɹɪmɹouz dɛːɪ Nf

print bonnet *1. n* a woman's cotton BONNET VI.14.1. *pl* pɹɪnʔ bɒnɪʔs L

2. n a woman's bonnet with a sun-flap at the back of the neck, worn at work in the fields. *pl* pɹɪnʔ bɒnəʔs Bk

prints *npl* the HOOF-MARKS of a horse IV.3.10. pɹɪnts MxL

privy *n* an EARTH-CLOSET V.1.13. pɹɪvɪ Du Y*[polite x2, vulgar x1, old x1]* Ch He O Nt L Nth Nf Sf Bk Bd*[old]* Ess MxL Brk K Ha, pɹɪbɪ Bd*[polite]* Ess, pɽɪvɪ O Ha, pɽɪvɪ So W, pɹəvɪ Y, pɽəvɪ So, *pl* pɽəviːz Do

privy-midden *n* an ASH-MIDDEN V.1.14. pɹɪvɪmɪdɪn Y

prods *npl* PEGS used to fasten thatch on a stack II.7.7(a). pɹɒdz Du We Y*[hazel]*, pɹɔdz La*[willow]* Y

profit *n* **in profit** IN CALF III.1.10. ɪn pɹɔfɪt L

prog *v* to BUTT III.2.10. *-ing* pɹɑgɪn Nth, pɹɒg Nth

progger *n* a SNACK VII.5.11. pɹɒgəᴶ K

projine *n* RENNET V.5.6. pɹəˈdʒaɪn Man *[queried NBM]*

proker *n* a POKER V.3.6. pɹoːkə Ch, pɹoukə Db St

prong *1. n* *[Show a picture of forks (i.e. the farming implements) of various kinds.] What do you call this?* I.7.10. *pl* pɽɪnz D, pɽɛŋ D, *pl* præŋs Man, *pl* pɹaŋz Ch, pɹɑːŋ Mon, pɹɒŋ Man, *pl* pɹɒŋz Cu, pʁɒŋ Nb, *pl* pʁɒŋz Du, pɹɒŋ We La Db Mon Gl Lei Nf Hrt Ess Sx, *pl* pɹɒŋz Y St He Wa K, pɽɒŋ So D Do, *pl* pɽɒŋz O, *pl* pɹɔŋz La, pɽɔːŋz Do, pɽʌŋ D, *pl* pɽʌŋz So, pɹuŋ Lei, *pl* pɹuŋz La, *pl* pɹuŋgz Wa. ⇒ **claw, fang, fork, fork-grain, fork-tine, grain, prong-grain, spean, spline, sprong, tang, tine, toe**

2. n a MUCK-FORK I.3.13. pɽaŋ Co, pɹɒŋ Sr, pɹɒːŋ Ha

3. n a HAY-FORK I.7.11. pɽɛŋ D, pɹaŋ O, pɹɒŋ O Sr

4. n a hay-fork with a long shaft. pɹɒŋ Sr Sx

5. n a hay-fork with a short shaft. pɹɒŋ Bk Sr Sx

prong-grain *n* a PRONG of a fork I.7.10. pɽɒŋgɽɛːn W

prong-handle *n* the SHAFT of a hay-fork I.7.12. pɹɒŋænduɫ Sx, pɹɒŋhænduɫ Sx, pɽɒŋandɫ Ha

prongs *1. npl* FORKS used in farming I.7.9. pɽɛŋz D, pɽaŋz Co, pɹɒŋz Gl O Brk, pɽɒŋz W Co D Ha

2. n TONGS V.3.7. pɽɒŋz Co

prong-steal *n* the SHAFT of a hay-fork I.7.12. pɹɒˑŋstiʊɫ Ha

pronkus *n* a DONKEY III.13.16. pɹɔŋkəs L, pɹɔːŋkəs L

proon *n* a RUNG of a ladder I.7.15. pɹuːn Du

prop *1. n* a STICK used to support the shaft of a cart I.11.1. pɹɑp Nth Bk, pɹɑːp Gl, pʁɒp Nb, pɹɒp Cu*[not local]* La Y Ch Db Sa St Wo Wa O L Lei R Nth Hu Bd Hrt Ess, pɽɒp So Co D, pɹɔp L Sf Ess

2. n a device used to prevent a cart from going backwards on a hill, ⇐ PROP/CHOCK I.11.2. pɹɒp Y, pɹɔp L Ess

3. n a PERCH for hens IV.6.3. pɹɒp Du

prop/chock *n* *What do you use to prevent your cart going backwards when you stop on a hill? Describe it (*added April 1955). I.11.2. ⇒ **block, block** *of wood*, **blog,** *brick*, **bull, burr, chain, chock, chog, chog** *of wood*, **chug, chunk, clog, coin, drag, drug-shoe,** *joggle-stick* ⇒ **juggle-stick, juggle-stick,** *log*, **maul, pike, prop, prop-stick, reel, roller, scot, scotch,** *scote* ⇒ **scot, set-stick, shoe, skid,** *slead* ⇒ **sled, sled, slide, slipper, slod, sprag, spragger, squat, squat-bat, squat-roller,** *stone*, **stop-block, strut, topping, trig, trigger, trug, wheel-block, wood-chuck, wood-roller;** ⇒ also **scotch up, scot up, trig up, trug up** *[information on material generally omitted, since often n.r. in BM or stated as anything available. Some rr., especially in WMBM, interpreted as 'chock'-responses in absence of particular evidence]*

prop-staff *n* a STICK used to support the shaft of a cart I.11.1. pɹɒpstɑːf Sr

prop-stick *1. n* a STICK used to support the shaft of a cart I.11.1. pʁɒpstɪk Nb, pɹɒpstɪk Du Y O Nt Lei Bk Hrt Ess Sr Sx, pɽɒpstɪk W Do, pɹɔpstɪk Y L MxL K

2. n a device hanging down under a cart to prevent it from going backwards on a hill, ⇐ PROP/CHOCK I.11.2. pɹɒpstɪk Bk

proper *1. adj* WELL, describing a healthy person VI.13.1(a). pɽapəᵗː Co

2. adv VERY VIII.3.2. pɹɒpəᴶ O, pɹɔpə L

propper *n* a STICK used to support the shaft of a cart I.11.1. pɹɑːpʔə Nf

propping *adv* ASTRIDE VI.9.8. pɹɒpɪn St

prossing *v-ing* GOSSIPING VIII.3.5(a). pɹɒsən Du

proud *adj* SLIPPERY VII.6.14. pɹɛʊd Ess

provand *1.1. vt* to FEED cattle with cake or similar food in a tub or trough III.3.1. pɹɒvɪn La

1.2. v to feed cattle. pɹɒvɪn La, pɹɒvən La

2. v to feed horses in the stable, ⇐ FEEDING III.5.1. pɹɒvɪn We*[food other than hay]* La

3. v to bait a horse when resting from work, ⇐ BAITING III.5.2. pɹɒvɪn La

4. n CHAFF fed to horses III.5.3. pɹɒvɪn We La Y*[old x1]*, pɹɒvn La

provand-bin *n* a CORN-BIN I.7.4. pɹɒvɪnbɪn La

provand-bing *n* a CORN-BIN I.7.4. pɹɒvɪnbɪŋ La, pɹɒvɪnbɪŋ La

provand-kist *n* a CORN-BIN I.7.4. pɹɒvɪnkɪst La

provender *n* CHAFF fed to horses III.5.3. pɹɒvɪndə We, pɹɒvndə We

provin-bucket *n* a TROUGH in a cow-house I.3.6. *pl* pɹɒvn̩bʊkɪts La

provin-trough *n* a TROUGH in a cow-house I.3.6. pɹɒvɪnθɹɛʊf La

provin-tub *n* a TROUGH in a cow-house I.3.6. pɹɒvɪntʊb La

prume *v* to LOP a tree IV.12.5. pɹəʊm Nf *[queried blend of prune and prime EMBM]*

prump *vi* to BREAK *WIND* VI.13.16. prppl pɹʊmpɪn Y

prune *1. vt* to LOP a tree IV.12.5. pɾuːn W

2. *v* to lop. pɹɪyn La, pɹɪun La Nf, pʁɪuːn Nb, pɹɪən Cu, pʁuːn Nb Du, pɹuːn Wo L Ess, -*ing* pɹuːnɪn St Mon Brk*[light cut x1]*, pɾuːn So

3. *v* to cut small branches from a tree. pɹɪun La Y, -*ing* pɹyːnɪn Ess, pɹuːn Y, -*ing* pɹuːnɪn He MxL Sr K Sx

4. *v* to cut branches from fruit trees. pɹɪyːn La, pɹɪuːn Nt L Nth C, -*ing* pɹɛunɪn Nf, pɹuːn Cu Du Y Wa Nth Bk Hrt Ess, *ptppl* pɹuːnd Nb, pɹʊn Db

puck *1. vt* to BUTT III.2.10. pʊk Sx

2. *v* to butt. -*ing* pʊkɪn Sx

puddeny* *adj* SAD, describing bread or pastry that has not risen V.6.12. pʊdn̩ᶦ W, pʊdni W Ha

pudding *n* CHITTERLINGS III.12.2. pʊdən Nb

pudding-kite *n* a NESTLING IV.7.1. *pl* pʊdɪnkaɪts La

puddings *1. n* CHITTERLINGS III.12.2. pʊdɪnz Cu We La Y Ch Nt, pʊdnz Nb Cu Du

2. *n* the large intestines of a pig. pʊdɪnz Y

pudding-skin(s) *n* CHITTERLINGS III.12.2.

no -s: pʊdɪnskɪn Ch

-s: pʊdnskɪnz Co

puddle *1. n* CLAY IV.4.2. pʌdł So

2. *n* SLUSH VII.6.16. pʌdł Sf

3. *n* MUD VII.6.17. pʊdl Cu We*[thin]* Y*[mud and water x2]*

puddled *1. adj* BOGGY IV.1.8. pʊdld Cu

2. *adj* SILLY VIII.9.3. pʌdʊłd Sx

puddle-holes *npl* PUDDLES IV.1.6. pɒdʲoːlz Nt, pʌdʲoːlz Sa, *sg* pɤdlhœːl Nb, pʊdʲɒɪlz La Y, pʊdʲɒulz Ch, pʊdʲɔːlz Y, pʊdʲɔɪlz Y, pʊdələɔɪlz Y, *sg* pʊdlhoəl Nb*[muddy]*, pʊdʲoːlz Du La Ch Sa Nt, *sg* pʊdʲoːl Db, pʊdʲoulz St Wa L, pʊdłoulz Wa, pʊdłoułz Lei, pʊdʲoːᶷlz Db, pʊdłuːłz Lei, pʊdʲuəlz Y, pʊdlhuəlz Du, *sg* pʊdlhuəl Cu, pʊdʲuəlz Du Y L, puɡʲuəlz Y

puddle in* *n* to line a pond with CLAY IV.4.2. pʌdł ... ɪn So

puddles *npl* What do you call those small hollows in the road, filled with water after rain? IV.1.6. pæᶦdłz Sf, pʌdlz Sa He Bd Ess So, *sg* pʌdl Nf, pʌdłz Mon O Hu C Sf Bk Bd Hrt Ess MxL So W K D Do Ha Sx, *sg* pʌdł Sr, pʌdəłz Bk, pʌdułz Brk Sx, pʌdʊz Sr, *sg* pʌdʊ K Sx, pɤdlz Nb Du, pʊdlz Nb La Y Db Sa Wo Wa L*[without water x1]* Bk, *sg* pʊdl Du We Ch Nt, pʊdłz Ch Wo Wa Gl O Lei R Nth Brk Co Ha, *sg* pʊdł C Bk, pʊdəłz Mon O, pʊdułz Brk K Sx, *sg* pʊdułz Brk, puːdls Man, pədlz Gl, pədłz Sx, pədułz Sx. ⇒ **bog-holes, chock-holes, dam-holes, dams, dips,** *dish* ⇒ **dishes, dishes, dubbings, dubs, groops, gullets, gulls, holes, hollows, holls, laches,** *lake* ⇒ **lakes, lakes, mud-pools, pits, plut-holes, pob-holes,** *poddles* ⇒ **pot-holes, podge-holes, podges, pools, pot-holes,** *pottles* ⇒ **pot-holes, puddle-holes, pudge-holes, pudgells, pudges, slap-holes, slop-holes, splashes, swellies,** *swelly* ⇒ **swellies, swidges, water-dubs, water-holes**

puddly *1. adj* BOGGY IV.1.8. pʌdłɪ K

2. adj slushy, ⇐ SLUSH VII.6.16. pʌdlɪ Nf

pudge-holes *npl* PUDDLES IV.1.6. pʊdʒʊlz L, pʊdʒuəlz L

pudgells *npl* PUDDLES IV.1.6. pʌdʒłz Nth

pudges *npl* PUDDLES IV.1.6. pʊdʒɪz L

puffing *v-ing* PANTING VI.8.1. pʌfɪn Sa Hu C Nf Bk Bd Hrt Ess MxL So Sr K Sx, pʌfn Nf Ess, pʌfən Ess, pɤfɪn Nf, pʊfɪn La Y Ch Db St Wo Wa Gl Nt Nth K, pʊfən Nb Du We Y; **puffing and blowing** pʌfn ŋ blaːᶷn Nf, pʌfn ən blɒːɪn Nf, pʌfɪn ŋ̩ blɒu-ɪn Nf, pʌfɪn ən błoːn Do, pʊfən ən blaːɪn Cu, pʊfɪn ən blaːɪn Y, pʊfɪn ən blɒuɪn He, pʊfɪn ən blɔˑɪn La Y L, pʊfɪn ən blɒu-ɪn L, pʊfɪn ən blɒːɪn Sa, pʊfɪn ən blouɪn Wo; **puffing and panting** pʊfɪn ən pantɪn L Nth

puffs *npl* KINDLING-*WOOD* V.4.2. pʌfs Brk*[very small brushwood x1]*

pug *1. n* CLAY IV.4.2. pɛɡ Ess, pɒɡ K, pʌɡ Ess MxL*[heavy soil]* K*[clay for bricks]*

2. *vt* to PLUCK a dead chicken of its feathers IV.6.21. pʊɡ He

3. *vt* to PULL somebody's hair VI.2.8. pʌɡ He Mon, pʊɡ He Mon

pugging *vt-ing* PULLING his ear VI.4.4. pʌɡɪn He Mon, pʊɡɪn He Wo Mon, əpʊɡɪn Wo

puggled *adj* STUPID VI.1.5. pʌɡłd W

puke *1. vi* to VOMIT, referring to an adult VI.13.14(a). -*ing* pjuːkɪn Y

2. *vi* to VOMIT, referring to a baby bringing up milk VI.13.14(b). -*ing* pjuːkən Du

pull *1. vt* When two little girls get cross with each other, what do they often do? They [indicate pulling hair] ... EACH OTHER'S hair. VI.2.8. ⇒ **claw, grab, lug, ploat, pluck, plug, pug, rive, sclow, scrum, tag, tear, towse, tug, work**

2.1. v to TOP AND TAIL swedes II.4.3. pʊl Db*[pulling, cleaning and topping combined]*, -*ing* pʊlɪn Y, pʊł Bk Bd*[tops only]*

2.2. vt to top and tail swedes. *-ing* pʊlɪn K, *-ing* pʊlən Ess *[marked ir.r. WMBM, u.r. Bd]*

3. vt to REMOVE *STALKS* from currants V.7.24. *-ing* pʊlɪn Ess

4. vt to WRING the neck of a chicken when killing it IV.6.20. pɛʊ Db, pɒl Man, pʊl Nb Cu Du We La Y Ch Sa St Wo Wa Gl L Nf, pʊɫ Lei Bd So W Brk, puː Ch

5. v to PLUCK a dead chicken of its feathers IV.6.21. pʊl Cu We Y L

6.1. v to RAKE in a domestic fire V.3.8(b). pʊl Cu Ch, pʊɫ Sf

6.2. vt to rake. pɣl Nb, pʊl Nb Nt L Hu Db

pull forward *vtphr* to RAKE in a domestic fire V.3.8(b). pʊl ... fɔɹəd Y

pulling *1. vt-ing And when someone does this [indicate pulling a person's ear] to someone else, you say he is ... [his ear].* VI.4.4. Eng. ⇒ **clicking, clipping, fur, lugging,** *lug-pulling,* **pinch** ⇒ **pinching, pinching, plucking, plugging, pugging,** *pulling on, pulling out,* **screwing, skewing, tugging, tugging at, tweaks, twist,** *weet* ⇒ **weeting,** *wring* ⇒ **wringing, wringing, yarking**

2. vt-ing PUTTING your tongue OUT VI.5.4. puˈɪn La

3. vt-ing CARTING *DUNG* II.1.4. pʊɫɪn dʌŋ Co, pʊɫən dʌŋ Co

4. v-ing CARTING corn from the field II.6.6. pʊɫən Co

pulling-bone *n* a WISH-BONE IV.6.22. puːlɪnboːn Sa*[old]*

pulling out *1. vphr-ing* CULLING sheep III.11.2. pʊlɪn ... ʌʊt Gl

2. vtphr-ing PUTTING your tongue OUT VI.5.4. pɣːɪn ... ɛːt La, pɣːɪn ... aɪt Ch, pʌlɪn ... aʊt Sa, pʊlɪn ... ɛːt Db, pʊlɪn ... ɛʊt Db, pʊlɪn ... æʊt MxL, pʊlɪn ... aʊt La Sa, puːlɪn ... ɛʊt Sa, puːlɪn aʊt Sa, pᵁuːɪn ... aːt La, puːɪn ... aʊt La

pullings *n* CHITTERLINGS III.12.2. puːlɪnz Y

pulling-tree *n* an EVENER, the main swingle-tree of a horse-drawn plough I.8.4. pʊlɪntɹiˈ Nf, pʊlɪntɹɪ Nf, pʊlɪnʔ-tɹɪ Nf

pull off *vtphr* to REMOVE *STALKS* from currants V.7.24. pʊl ... ɔf L

pull out *1. vtphr* to WRING the neck of a chicken when killing it IV.6.20. pɣɫ ... ævt So, pɣː ... ɛʊt Db, pɣː ... aːt La, pʊl ... ɛːt Db, pʊl ... ɛʊt Nth, pʊl ... æʊt Sa Wa L Lei, pʊl ... æət L, pʊl ... aːt Db St Nt, pʊl ... aɪt Ch, pʊl ... aʊt La Y Ch, pʊl ... uːt Y Gl, pʊɫ ... ɛʊt Nth, pʊɫ ... æʊt Lei R W, pʊɫ æʊd (+V) Do, pʊɫ ... aːˀt Lei, pʊɫ ... aʊt So, pʊɫ ... əʊt W Do, puːl ... aʊt Sa, puː ... aʊt La Y

2. vtphr to RAKE in a domestic fire V.3.8(b). pʊl ... ʌʊt Gl, pʊl ... ˀuːt Du, *-ing* pʊlɪn ... uːt Y

pull-rail *n* a movable horizontal rod stretching between the shafts of a cart, fixing them to the cart-body and stopping the cart from tipping, ⇐ ROD/PIN I.10.3. pʊlɹeːl Y

pulls *vi-3prsg* it HURTS VI.13.3(a). pʊɫz Nth

pull to *vtphr* to SHUT a door IX.2.8. pʊl ... tuː Y

pull together *vtphr-3sg* she [a tidy girl] will COLLECT her toys VIII.8.15. pʊl ... təgjɛðəɽ He

pull-tree *n* an EVENER, the main swingle-tree of a horse-drawn plough harness I.8.4. pʊltʔɹɪ Nf

pull up *imp* the command GO ON!, given to plough-horses II.3.5(d). pʌɫ ʌp Sx, pʊɫ ʌp He Brk Sr Do Sx

pully-bone* *n* a WISH-BONE IV.6.22. pʊlɪboʊn St

pulse *1. n* CHAFF II.8.5. pʊlts L, pʊɫts Lei, pʊɫps Lei, pʊlz Y; **chaff and pulse*** tʃaf ən pʊlts L; **pulse and chaff** pʊls ən tʃaf L

2. n short pieces of straw left after threshing. pʊlts L, pʊlz Y

pumble *n* a BUMPER of a cart I.10.1(a). *pl* pʌmbəlz Ess, *pl* pʌmbəɫz Hrt Ess, *pl* pʌmbɫz C Hrt Do

pumble-fisted *adj* CLUMSY, describing a person VI.7.14. pʌmbɫvɪstɪd So

pumbler *n* a BUMPER of a cart I.10.1(a). pʌmblə C

pummel *n* a BUMPER of a cart I.10.1(a). pɒmɫ O Nth, pʌməɫ Bk Bd, pʌmɫ Bk, pʌmʊɫ Brk, pʊmɫ Wa Gl Bk, *pl* pʊmɫz Nth, *pl* pʊmʊɫz Brk

pummel-tree *1. n* a large SWINGLE-TREE of a horse-drawn plough harness I.8.3. pʌmʊtɹiː Ess

2. n an EVENER, the main swingle-tree of a horse-drawn plough harness I.8.4. pʌmɫtɹɪ Sf

pumping *v-ing* PANTING VI.8.1. pʊmpɪn St

pumple-footed *1. adj* PIGEON-TOED VI.10.4. pʌmɫvʊtɪd So, pʌmɫvʏtəd So, pʌmɫvʊtɪd So

2. adj SPLAY-FOOTED VI.10.5. pʌmɫvʊtɪd So, bʌmbɫfʊtɪd So

punch *1.1. vt* to MARK the ears of sheep with a hole to indicate ownership III.7.9. pɒnʃ Man, pʌnʃ So K Ha, *3prpl* pʌnʃɪz Sx, *-ing* pʌnʃɪn K, pʊnʃ Y Db Gl, *-ing* pʊnʃɪn Sa

1.2. v to punch holes in the ears of sheep. pʊnʃ L, *-ing* pʊnʃɪn K

2.1. vt to KNEAD dough V.6.4. pʌnʃ So W D Ha

2.2. v to knead. pʌnʃ O*[old x1]* Bd W D, *-ing* pʌnʃɪn Brk, pʊnʃ Du Gl L*[old x1]* Nth Bk

3. vt to BEAT a boy on the buttocks VIII.8.10. pʊnʃ La

punch about *vtphr* to KNEAD dough V.6.4. pɒnʃ ... əbæʊt L, pʌnʃ ... əbɛʊt Nf

puncher *n* a FIST VI.7.4. pʌnʃə Nf

punder *1. n* a BUMPER of a cart I.10.1(a). pʌndə Bd *[queried ir.r. EMBM]*

2. n a ROD keeping a cart-body fixed to the shafts, stopping it from tipping I.10.3. pʌndə C Bd, pʊndə Nth Hu

punder-stick *n* a ROD keeping a cart-body fixed to the shafts, stopping it from tipping I.10.3. pʌndəstɪk C

pundle-stick *n* a ROD keeping a cart-body fixed to the shafts, stopping it from tipping I.10.3. pʌndlstɪk Nf

pundle-tree *n* an EVENER, the main swingle-tree of a horse-drawn plough harness I.8.4. pʌndltɹi Nf

pun-tree *n* an EVENER, the main swingle-tree of a horse-drawn plough harness I.8.4. pʌntɹi· Nf

pup *1. vi* to WHELP III.13.3. pɒp Man Nf, pʌp Sa Wo O Nf Sf Bk Bd Hrt Ess Sr K, pɣp Nb Nf, pʊp Nb Cu Du We La Y*[modern x1]* Ch Db St Wa O Nt L Lei, pəp Sx

2. n **in pup** pregnant, describing a bitch. ɪn pʌp Mon Ess So Brk Sr Co Do, ɪn pʊp St L Brk

3. n **with pups** pregnant, describing a bitch. wɪð pʌps D

4. vi to KITTEN III.13.10. pʌp Ess

pup down *viphr* to WHELP III.13.3. pʌp dɛʊn O Ess, pʌp dæʊn Sr Ha, pʌp dəʊn Brk

puppies *npl* PUPS or young dogs III.13.4. pɒpɪz Nf, pɒpɪs Man, pʌpiːz So W D Do, pʌpɪs Nf, pʌpʔɪs Nf, pʌpɪz Gl O Sf Bk Bd Ess Brk Sr K Co D Ha Sx, pʌpʔɪz Hu C Sf, pɣpʔɪs Nf, pʊpɪz Cu Y Wa O Nt Lei R Nth Bk Brk, pəpɪz Gl, *sg* pəpɪ Sx

pups *1. npl* *What do you call the young ones [of the bitch or female dog]?* III.13.4. pɒps Ha, pʌps He Mon O Hu Nf Sf Bk Bd Hrt Ess MxL So W Brk Sr K Co D Do Ha Sx, pɣps Nb Nf, pʊps Cu La Y Man Ch Db St Wo Wa O Nt L Lei Nth C So Brk, pəps Gl

2. npl young dogs older than yelps III.13.4. pʌps So ⇒ **puppies, whelps, yelps**

pur *n* a WETHER III.6.8. pəˡːɽ Ha *[queried u.r. SBM on grounds of age]*

pure *adv* VERY VIII.3.2. pjʊuəˡː So

purgat *n* the ASH-HOLE beneath a domestic fire V.3.3. pəˡːgət Sa

purgat-hole *n* the ASH-HOLE beneath a domestic fire V.3.3. pəˡgɪtɒʊl Wo, pəˡːgɪtoʊl Wo, pəˡːgɪtoʊɫ Wo

purgatory *1. n* the ASH-HOLE beneath a domestic fire V.3.3. pʊgətɹi: He, pəːgətəɹɪ Wo, pəˡːgɪtɛɹɪ Wo, pəˡːgətɛɹɪ He

2. n the place in which ashes are collected. pəˡːgətoːɹɪ He, pəˡːgətoˑəɹɪ Nth

purgy-hole *n* the ASH-HOLE beneath a domestic fire V.3.3. pəˡːgɪ-oːl Sa

pur-lamb *n* a MALE LAMB III.6.2. pəˡːɬam Do

purpose *n* **on purpose** *If in drying the cups and saucers, someone breaks four or five cups, you might begin to think he was doing it ....* IX.1.5. Eng **for a purpose** fəɹ ə paːpʔəs Sf, fəɹ ə pɔːpəs Hu; **for purpose** fə paːpəs Nf, fə pɔːpəs Ess, fə pəːpʔəs Sf, fəˡ pəˡːpəs K, fəˡ pəˡːpəs Sr, vəˡː pəˡːpəs W Co; **for the purpose** fə ðə paːpəs Nf, fə ðə paːpʔəs Sf, fə ðə paːpəs Nf Ess, fə ðə pɔːpəs Sf, fə ðə pʌpəs Nf Ess, fə ðə pəɹpəs He C, fə ðə pəˡpəs He Mon Nf, fəˡ ðə pəˡpəs He, fəˡː ðə pəˡpəs He, fə ðə pɔːpəs Nf Hrt Ess, fə ðə pəˡːpəs Brk, fəˡ· ðə pəˡːpəs Sr, fə ðə pəˡːpəs Sa He Wo Ess, fəˡ ðɪ pəˡːpəs K, fəˡː ðə pəˡːpəs Co, vəˡː ðə pəˡːpəs Co, fəˡ ðə pəˡːpʊs He Wo Gl, fə ðə pɐˑpəs Nf; **on a purpose** ɔn ə pəˡːpəs L; **to the purpose** tə ðə pəˡːpʊs Wo; **with a purpose** wɪð ə pɔːpəs K. ⇒ *awkwardways, carelessly, deliberate careless, deliberately, for devilment, intentionally, purposely, wilful, wilfully*

purposely *adv* ON PURPOSE IX.1.5. poᴮːpəslɪ Nb, pəɹpəslɪ Y, pəˡpəsɬɪ O Ha, pəːpəslɪ Y Ch Db St Nt Nth Hu Ess, paːpəsɬɪ Ess Sr, pəˡːpəslɪ Mon O Bk Ess Sx

purr *n* a POKER V.3.6. pɔː Du, pɔːr Cu, poᴮː Nb, pɔːɹ Cu, pɔˑəɹ Cu Du Y*[old]*

purse *n* the scrotum of a horse, ⇐ SHEATH III.4.9. pʌs Nf Bk W Ha, pʊs St, pəs Nf, pəɹs Nth, pəɽs Nf, pəːs Nth Hu, pəːɹs Sf, pəˡːʂ Gl Bk So W D Ha Sx

pus *n* *What do you call the white stuff that comes out of it [a boil]?* VI.11.9. pʌs Mon Ess Brk D, pʊs Du St Brk, pəs Nf Sx. ⇒ **atter, fester, fester-stuff, humour, matter,** *varmint* ⇒ **vermin, vermin**

push *v* to BUTT III.2.10. *prppl* pɒʃən Man

push down *vtphr* to GOBBLE food VI.5.13(b). pʊʃ ... daːn Db

pushes *npl* BOILS VI.11.6. pʊʃɪs Nf, pʊʃɪz Nf Sf Hrt Ess*[old x2]*, pʊʃəs Nf, pʊʃəz C Sf Hrt Ess

push fast *vtphr* to SHUT a door IX.2.8. pɣʃ ... væːs D

pushing *adv* ALMOST VII.7.9. pʊʃɪn Sa

pushing out *vtphr-ing* PUTTING your tongue OUT VI.5.4. pʌʃɪn ... aʊt Mon Gl, pʊʃɪn ... æʊt He So, *3prsg* pʊʃɪz æʊt Ha, pʊʃɪn ... ʌʊt Mon, pʊʃɪn ... əʊt He Mon Gl

push it *imp* GO AWAY! VIII.7.9(a). pʊʃ ɪt Wo

push off *imp* GO AWAY! VIII.7.9(a). pɣʃ ɔːf D, pʊʃ ɒf Gl, pʊʃ ɔːf Wa

push up *vtphr-3sg* **push up together** she [a tidy girl] will COLLECT her toys VIII.8.15. pʊʃ ... ʌp təgɛðəˡ Mon

pussy *n* a TABBY-CAT, the female cat III.13.9. pʊsi St

put *vt* to PITCH a sheaf II.6.10. pʊt R Nth Sf, *3prsg* pʊts Wa

put away *vtphr-3sg* she [a tidy girl] will COLLECT her toys VIII.8.15. pʌt ... əweː Sa, pʌd (+V) ... əwɛɪ D, pɣt ... əwɪə Nb, pʊɹ (+V) ... əweː Y, pʊd (+V) ... əweɪ So, pʊʔ ... əweːˡ O, pʊt ... əwɛɪ Wa Gl Sf, pʊɹ (+V) ... əweːˑə L, pʊd (+V) ... əwæɪ Ess, pʊɹ (+V) ... əwæɪ K, pʊd (+V) ... əwaɪ

Do, pʊd (+V) ... əwɒɪ So, pət ... əwɛɪ Sx; **put away tidy** pʊt ... əwɛɪ tɑɪdɪ K

put back *vtphr* to PITCH sheaves II.6.10. pʊt ... bak Wa

put by* *vtphr-3sg* she [a tidy girl] will COLLECT her toys VIII.8.15. pʊt ... bɑɪ Du *[NBM headword put bye]*

put on, put onto *vtphr* to LOAD dung into a cart II.1.5. pʊt ... ɒn Nf, pʊʔ ... ɒnt Nf

put out *1. vtphr* to put cattle on hired pasture, ⇐ HIRE *PASTURAGE* III.3.8. pʊt ... eʊt Nf, pʊt ɛːt Db, pʌt ... ɛʊt O Ha Sx, pʊt ɛʊt Sf Bk, pʊt ... ɛʊt Wo Wa Nf MxL Sr Sx, *-ing* pʊtn ... ɛʊt K, pʊʔ ... ɛʊʔ Bk, pʌt ... ɛuːt Sa, pʊt ... ɛuːt Wo, pʏd (+V) ... œʏt D, pʊd (+V) ... œʏt D, pʏd (+V) ... æʏt So D, pʌd (+V) ... æʏt Co D, pʊd (+V) ... æʏt So Co, pʌt ... æʊt He, pʊt ... æʊt St Wa O L W, pʊd (+V) ... æʊt So W Do Ha, pʊt ... aːt St, pʌt ... aʊt Sa, pʊt ... aʊt Sa St L So, pʊd (+V) ... aʊt So, pʊt ... ɒʊt W, pʊt ... ʌʊt He Brk, pʊt uːt Nb, pʊt ... uːt Nb Du, pʊɹ (+V) ... uːt Y, pʊt ... ᵊʊt K, *-ing* pʊtɪn ... ᵊuːt Ch, pʌt ... əʊt Brk, pʊt ... əʊt He Wo Mon Gl W, *-ing* pʊtɪn ... əʊt K, *-ing* pʊʔn ... əʊt Nf, pʊd (+V) ... əʊt W Do

2. vtphr to WRING the neck of a chicken when killing it IV.6.20. pʊt ... oʊt Man

3. vtphr to SPRAIN an ankle VI.10.8. pʌt ... aʊt Sa, pʌt ... əʊt Mon

put over *viphr* to OVERTURN, referring to a cart I.11.5. *ptppl* pʊt oʊvə Man

putrid *adj* **go putrid** to SPOIL, referring to meat or fish V.7.10. goʊ pɪʊtɹɪd Ha

putt *1. n* a FARMCART I.9.3. pɒt Do, pʌt So Do, pʊt So Ha

2. n **on the putt** CARTING *DUNG* II.1.4. ɔːn ðə pʊt So *[marked u.r. SBM]*

putt-cart *n* a FARMCART I.9.3. pʊtkaᶜːt So

puttice *n* a WEASEL IV.5.6. pʌtɪs K

putting in *vphr-ing* CARTING corn from the field II.6.6. pɒtən ɪn Man *[queried u.r. NBM]*

putting-in-pikel *n* a HAY-FORK with a short shaft I.7.11. pʊdɪnɪnpaɪkl La

putting-off-pikel *n* a HAY-FORK with a shaft of medium length I.7.11. pʊdɪnɒfpaɪkl La

putting-on *n* a SNACK VII.5.11. pʊtɪnɒn Y

putting out *vtphr-ing* What am I doing now [indicate putting your tongue out in derision]? VI.5.4. Eng exc. Mon C. ⇒ **blabbing out, blathering out, blobbing out, bobbing out, flicking out, flipping out,** *girning,* **hanging a jib, lagging out, lalling, lalling out, lapping, lapping out, licking out, lolling out, lolliping out, lugging out, mouthing, poking out, pulling, pulling out, pushing out, shooting out, shoving out, slaking, slaking out, slapping out, slarking, slicking, snicking out, sticking out, tipping, wagging**

put to *vtphr* to SHUT a door IX.2.8. pʊt ... tuː La

put together *vtphr-3sg* she [a tidy girl] will COLLECT her toys VIII.8.15. pʊt ... təgeðə Db, pʊd (+V) ... təgeðəᶜː Do

putt-rester *n* a BUMPER of a cart I.10.1(a). pɒtɹɛstəᶜː Do

putt-stick *n* a movable horizontal rod stretching between the shafts of a cart, fixing them to the cart-body and stopping the cart from tipping, ⇐ ROD/PIN I.10.3. pɒtstɪk W Do Ha

put up *1. viphr* to be RESTIVE, decribing a horse III.5.6. *ptppl* pʊt ʌp Ess

2. vphr to VOMIT, referring to an adult VI.13.14(a). pʊt ʊp Man

3. vtphr to VOMIT, referring to a baby bringing up milk VI.13.14(b). *-ing* pʊʔn ... ʊp Man

4. vtphr **put wind up** to BREAK WIND VI.13.16. *-ing* pʊʔən wɪnd ʊp Man

5. vtphr-3sg she [a tidy girl] will COLLECT her toys VIII.8.15. pʌt ... ʌp Sa Mon, pʊt ... ʌp Gl, pʊt ... ʊp Sa St Wa Gl; **put up tidy** pʊt ... ʊp tɔɪdɪ O; **put up together** pʊt ... ʊp təgɪðə Wo

put up with *vtphr-2prsg* you BEAR pain VI.5.9. pʌt ʌp wɪð K Sx, pʌt ʌp wɪ Gl, pʌd ʌp wiː Ha, pʊd ʌp wiː Ha, pʊt ʌp wɪð O Ess Brk K Ha Sx, pʊʔ ʏp wɪð Nf, pʊt ʊp wɪð Ch Wo

Q

quackle *vt* to CHOKE somebody VI.6.4. kwæk?l Nf

quailaway *n* a STYE in the eye VI.3.10. kwɪɫəweː D, kwɛːɫəwɛɪ Co, kwɛɪɫəwɛɪ Co, kweːɫəwɛɪ D

quantity *1. n* the YIELD of milk from a cow III.3.5. kwɒnətɪ K

2. n the yield of milk from a herd of cows. kwɒnʔəʔɪ Bk

3. n a yield of milk. kwɒntət³ɪ Bd, kɒntʔətɪ Nf

4. n **a small quantity** a LITTLE amount of milk VII.8.20. ə smɔl kɒntɪdɪ Nf, ə smɔl kɒnʔətɪ Nf

quarrel *n* a QUARRY IV.4.6. kwaɹɪl Y, waɹɪl Y

quarry *1. n* *Coal is got out of a mine, but stone out of a ....* IV.4.6. Eng. ⇒ **delf, delf-hole, pit, quarrel, quarry-hole, quarry-pit, stone-hole, stone-pit, stone-quarry**

2. n a paving-stone on a kitchen floor. *pl* kwɒɹɪz St

quarry-floor* *n* a tiled FLOOR V.2.7. kwɒɹɪflɔː St

quarry-hole *n* a QUARRY IV.4.6. kwaɹɪ-ʊəl La

quarry-pit *n* a QUARRY IV.4.6. kwɔɽɪpɪt Sr

quart *1. n* *What is your word for two pints?* VII.8.1. Eng. ⇒ **quartern**

2. n a SCOOP used to take water out of a boiler V.9.9. kwaːt Nb

quarter *1. n* a CUTTING of hay II.9.15. kʷɔːʔə Nf

2. n the DIRECTION from which the wind blows VII.6.26. kwatə L, kwaːtə We Y L, kwaːtər Y, kwaːtəɹ (+V) Y L, kwaːtɪ L, kwaˡːtəˡ He, kwɔːtə Hrt Sr

quarterings *npl* the five cross-beams of a cart-body, ⇐ BUMPER I.10.1(a). kwaˡːtɹɪnz Wo

quartern *n* a QUART VII.8.1. kwaːtn L, kwɔːtn Lei

quarter-past-nine *adj* SPLAY-FOOTED VI.10.5. kwɔːdəˡ paːs næɪn So

quarters *npl* the TEATS of a cow III.2.6. kwaˡːtəˡːz̡ W, kwaˡːtəˡz̡ Gl, kwɔˡːdəˡːz̡ So

quarter-to-five *adj* SPLAY-FOOTED VI.10.5. kwaˡːdəˡː d̡ə vəɪv W

quarter-to-four *adj* SPLAY-FOOTED VI.10.5. kɔːtʔəfɑˑə Nf

quarter-to-nine *adj* SPLAY-FOOTED VI.10.5. kwaːtətənɑɪn La, kwɔˡːtə nɑɪn Co

quarter-to-three *adj* SPLAY-FOOTED VI.10.5. kwaːt³təθɹɪ Y, kwaːttəθɹɪ Y, kwaˡːdəˡː tə d̡ɹɪ Co, kwaˡːtə θɹɪ Co, kwaˡːdə d̡ɹɪ W*[facetious]*, kwɔˑɹdəɹtəθɹɪ He, kwɔˡːtətəθɹɪ Sa, kwɔˡːd̡əˡː tə d̡ɹɪ D

quarter-to-three feet *1. adj* SPLAY-FOOTED VI.10.5. kwɔˡːt̡ətəθɹɪː fiːt Sa, kwɔˡːt̡əˡt̡əθɹɪː fiːt Sa

2. n a splay-footed person. kwaːttəθɹɪːfiːt Y

quarter-to-two *adj* SPLAY-FOOTED VI.10.5. kwaːtətətu: Y, kwaˡːt̡ə tu: W, kwɔˡːd̡əˡː tə tʏː D

quart-tin *n* a SCOOP used to take water out of a boiler V.9.9. kwɛərttɪn Du, kwarttɪn Cu

quat *vi* to DUCK VIII.7.8. kwat Co

quat down *viphr* to DUCK VIII.7.8. kwad dæʏn Co

queagle *n* a SEESAW VIII.7.2. kwiːgl Db St

queen *n* a TABBY-CAT, the female cat III.13.9. kwiːn Nb Du D, *pl* kwiːnz Cu, wɪən Y

queen-cat *n* a TABBY-CAT, the female cat III.13.9. kwiːnkat Nb Du Y

queeny *n* a TABBY-CAT, the female cat III.13.9. kwiːni Ha

queer *1. adj* ILL, describing a person who is unwell VI.13.1(b). kwɪə Nf Sf Ess, kwɪəᴵ K, kwɪəˡ Brk

2. adj SICK, describing an animal that is unwell VI.13.1(c). kwɪə Wa Nf Sf Ess MxL; **pretty queer** pətɪ kwɪə MxL; **very queer** vɛɹɪ kweˑə Nf

3. adj SILLY VIII.9.3. kwɪəˡ So

quey *1. n* a HEIFER III.1.5. waɪ Cu Du We La Y, hwaɪ Nb

2. n a heifer calf. waɪ Y, hwaɪ Nb

3. n a heifer approximately 2 years old. kwaɪ Nb

4. n a cow that has had only one calf. hwaɪ Nb

quey-calf *n* a HEIFER-calf III.1.5. waɪkaːf Y, waɪkɔːf Cu La Y

quick *1. n* *Some boys have a habit of biting their nails down [gesticulate] TO THE ....* VI.7.9.

no -s: kwɪk Cu Man Ch Db Sa St He Wo Wa Mon Gl O Nt L Lei R Nth Hu C Nf Sf Bk Bd Hrt Ess MxL So W Brk Sr K Co D Do Ha Sx, kwak Ha

-s: kwɪks Nf Ess Brk Sr

⇒ **live**, *red quick* ⇒ **red wick, red wick, wartywell, wick**; ⇒ also **till**

2. n a LOOSE *PIECE OF* SKIN at the bottom of a finger-nail VI.7.11. kwɪk Sa Wo Mon Bd Hrt Ess Sr, *pl* kwɪks Bk

3. n **quick of your lips** MOUTH CORNERS VI.5.2. kwɪk ə jə lɪps Sr

4. adj HEAVING *WITH MAGGOTS* IV.8.6. wɪk We La Y *[quick alone marked u.r. NBM]*

5. adj ACTIVE, describing a child VIII.9.1. kwɪk St

quick-backs *npl* loose pieces of skin at the bottom of a finger-nail, ⇐ LOOSE *PIECE OF* SKIN VI.7.11. kwɪkbaks Ha

quick-berries *npl* HAWS IV.11.6. kwɪkbɛɽiz So

quick-crawling *adj* HEAVING *(WITH MAGGOTS)* IV.8.6. hwɪkskɹɑʊlən Du

quicked *adj* HEAVING *WITH MAGGOTS* IV.8.6. wɪkt Cu *[marked u.r. NBM]*

quick-fence *n* a HEDGE IV.2.1(a). kwɪkfɛns Nf

quick-flaw *1. n* a LOOSE *PIECE OF* SKIN at the bottom of a finger-nail VI.7.11. wɪkflo: Db
2. n a WHITLOW VI.7.12. wɪkflu: Cu*[old]*

quick-grass *n* COUCH-GRASS II.2.3. kwɪkgɹɪs La

quick-hedge *n* a HEDGE IV.2.1(a). wɪkɛdʒ Y

quick-hook *n* a HEDGING-BILL IV.2.5. kwɪkʊk C

quicklaw *n* a WHITLOW VI.7.12. kwɪklɑʊ Nb*[old]*

quick-nail *n* a LOOSE *PIECE OF* SKIN at the bottom of a finger-nail VI.7.11. kwɪknæɪl Nf

quick(s) *n* COUCH-GRASS II.2.3.
no -s: kwɪk Nf*[not local]*
-s: kwɪks Nf

quicks *1. npl* TICKS on sheep IV.8.3. wɪks La
2. npl MAGGOTS IV.8.6. wɪks Cu

quickthorn-fence *n* a HEDGE IV.2.1(a). kwɪkθɔ:nfɛns Y

quid *n* the CUD that a cow chews III.2.11. kwɪd Ess So W Sr K D Do Sx

quid note *n* a POUND NOTE VII.7.8. kwɪd nɛʊt St

quiet *adj* SHY VIII.9.2. kweːt Co *[queried u.r. SBM]*

quig *1. vt* to CURDLE milk V.5.7. kwɪg Man
2. vi to CURDLE, referring to milk V.5.9. kwɪg Man

quill *n* a SHEATH or other device used to keep a knitting-needle firm V.10.10. kwɪl Cu Y Db St Wa L, kwɪɫ Lei

quilt *1. n What do you call the top-covering on a bed?* V.2.11 Eng. ⇒ **bed-quilt**, **bedspread**, **counterpane**, **cover**, **eiderdown**
2. v to guzzle a drink, ⇐ GUZZLES VI.5.13(a). *-ing* kwɪɫʔən Ha
3. vt to BEAT a boy on the buttocks VIII.8.10. twɪlt Y

quilter *1. n* a THROAT VI.6.3. kwɪɫtəˤ Brk, kwɪɫtəˤ: W
2. n the WINDPIPE VI.6.5. kwɪɫtəˤ: W, kwəɫtəˤ: D

quinet *n* the GRASS-NAIL of a scythe II.9.9. kwɪnət O

quist *1. npl* PIGEONS IV.7.3. kwɪst He Mon Gl, kwɪs Mon, kwɛɪs Sa, kwæɪst He, kwaɪst Sa, kwaɪs Sa, kwɒɪs Sa Wo, kwəɪːs Wo, kwəɪst Wo, kwəɪs Wo Gl
2. npl wood-pigeons. *sg* kwiːs Ch, *sg* kwɪst He Gl, *sg* kwɪs Gl, kwɛɪs Wo, kwaɪs Ch

quists *1. npl* PIGEONS IV.7.3. kwɪsts He, kwaɪzɪz Sa, kwəɪsɪz Gl
2. npl wood-pigeons. kwɪsts He

quitch *n* COUCH-GRASS II.2.3. kwəːtʃ Hrt

quivers *n* TREMORS suffered by a person who cannot keep still VI.1.4. kwɪvəz Db

quizzing *v-ing* PEEPING VI.3.8. kwɪzən Ess

quy-ways *adv* DIAGONALLY, referring to harrowing a field IX.1.8. kwʌɪwɛɪz Sr

R

rabbit *vi* to KINDLE, describing a rabbit doe giving birth to young III.13.14. ɹabət Mon

rabbit-balls *npl* RABBIT-DROPPINGS III.13.15. ɾabətbɔːɫz So

rabbit-bum-balls *npl* RABBIT-DROPPINGS III.13.15. ɾabɪtbɒmbəɫz O, ɹabɪʔbʌmbɫz Bk, ɹæbʊtbʊmbɫz Gl

rabbit-currants *npl* RABBIT-DROPPINGS III.13.15. ɹabɪtkɒɹənz Y He, ɹabɪtkəɹənz Y

rabbit-dirt *n* RABBIT-DROPPINGS III.13.15. ɹabɪtdəːt St

rabbit-dottles *npl* RABBIT-DROPPINGS III.13.15. ʁabətdʏtlz Nb

rabbit-droppings *npl What do you call the little black balls rabbits leave behind them in the fields?* III.13.15. ɹabɪtdɹɒpɪnz Nth, ɹabɪʔdɹɒpɪnz Bk, ɹɛbɪtdɹɒˈpɪnz K, ræbətdɹɒpəns Man, ɹæbɪtdɹɒpɪnz He Ess, ɹabɪtdɹɒpɪnz Y Sa Wa Mon Lei Nth, ɹabɪʔdɹɒpɪnz O Bd, ɹabətdɹɒpɪnz Cu, ɹæbɪtdɹɔpɪnz Ess MxL, ɹæbətdɹɔpənz Ess. ⇒ black-currants, black pops, bum-balls, *bum-bals* ⇒ bum-balls, buttons, carlings, chatty-balls, cherries, currants, dotlings, dottles, droppings, dung, hailstones, muck, partles, partnicks, pellets, piddles, pills, pitch-balls, rabbit-balls, rabbit-bum-balls, rabbit-currants, rabbit-dirt, rabbit-dottles, rabbit-dung(s), rabbit-muck, rabbit-partles, rabbit-pellets, rabbit-pills, rabbits'-currants, rabbits'-dirt, rabbits'-droppings, rabbits'-dung(s), rabbit-shit, rabbits'-muck, rabbits'-pills, rabbits'-shit, rabbits'-trottles, rabbits'-turds, *rabbit-tricklings* ⇒ rabbit-trittlings, rabbit-triddles, rabbit-triddlings, *rabbit-tridlings* ⇒ rabbit-triddlings, rabbit-trittlings, rabbit-trottles, rabbit-trunlings, *rabbit-trunlins* ⇒ rabbit-trunlings, rabbit-turd(s), raisins, triddlings, trimlings, trindlings, trottles, truckles, trunlets, trunlings, turd(s)

rabbit-dung(s) *n* RABBIT-DROPPINGS III.13.15.
npl: ɹæbɪtdʊŋz Sa
n: ɹæbɪtdʌŋ Ess, ɹabəʔdʌŋ Bk, ɾabɪtdʌŋ W Ha, ɾabətdʌŋ W

rabbit-muck *n* RABBIT-DROPPINGS III.13.15. ɹɛbɪtmʌk Sa, ɹæbɪtmʌk Sa Ess, ɹæbətmʌk Mon, ɹabɪtmʌk Sa, ɹabətmʌk Mon, ɹabəʔmʌk Bd, ɾabɪtmʌk W, ɹæbɪtmʊk Wo Gl, ɹabɪtmʊk Y Ch St Wo Wa Nt, ɹabətmʊk Du We, ɹapɪtmʊk La Ch Db, ɹapətmʊk La

rabbit-partles *npl* RABBIT-DROPPINGS III.13.15. ɹabətpaːtlz Cu

rabbit-pellets *npl* RABBIT-DROPPINGS III.13.15. ɾabʌtpɛɫɪts W

rabbit-pills *npl* RABBIT-DROPPINGS III.13.15. ɹæˑbətpɪɫz Sf, ɹabɪtpɪlz Wo*[old]*, ɹabəʔpɪɫz Bd, ɾabətpɪɫz Co

rabbits *npl What animals do you keep in a hutch?* III.13.13. *sg* ɹɪbɪt Ha, ɹɛbɪts Sa Ess Sr K Sx, ɹɛəbəts Ess, ræbəts Man, ɹæbɪts Sa He Wo Mon Gl L Hu Nf Sf Bk Ess Brk Sr K Ha Sx, ɹæˈbɪʔs Hrt, ɾæbɪts So Co, *sg* hɾæbɪt So, ɾæbʌts So, ɹæbʊts Gl, ɹæbəts He Mon O Nf Sf Ess Brk Ha Sx, ɾæbəts So, *sg* ɾæbət Ha, ʁabɪts Nb, ɹabɪts La Y Ch Db Sa St He Wo Wa Mon O Nt L Lei R Nth Hu C Bk Hrt MxL Ha, ɹapɪts La Ch Db, ɹabɪʔs L Bk Bd Hrt, ɾabɪts O So W Co D Do Ha, hɾabɪts So, ɾabʌts W, hɾabʌts So, ɹabʊts Gl, rabəts Cu, ʁabəts Nb Du, ɹabəts Nb Cu Du We La Y Mon Gl O L C Bd, ɹapəts La, ɹabəʔs Bk, *sg* ɹabəʔ Bd, ɾabəts So W Co D Do Ha, ɹɒbɪts He Lei, *sg* ɹɒbət Brk. ⇒ conies, coons *[three forms in SBM may be collectives or singulars – see SBM note; taken as sg here]*

rabbits'-currants *npl* RABBIT-DROPPINGS III.13.15. ɾabətskʌɾənts D

rabbits'-dirt *n* RABBIT-DROPPINGS III.13.15. ɹæbɪtsdɛˑt Nf

rabbits'-droppings *npl* RABBIT-DROPPINGS III.13.15. ɹæbɪtsdɹɒˈpʔnz Nf, ɹæbɪtsdɹɒpmz Ess, ɾæbətsd̥ɾɒpɪnz So

rabbits'-dung(s) *n* RABBIT-DROPPINGS III.13.15.
npl: ɾabətsdʌŋz So
n: ɹæbɪtsdɒŋ K, ɹæbɪtsdʌŋ Ess, ɾæbɪtsdʌŋ So, ɾabɪtsdʌŋ Do, ɾabətsdʌŋ Co Do Ha

rabbit-shit *n* RABBIT-DROPPINGS III.13.15. ræbətʃɪt Man, ɹæbɪtʃɪt He

rabbit-smoot *n* a SHEEP-HOLE IV.2.8. ɹabətsmuːt La

rabbits'-muck *n* RABBIT-DROPPINGS III.13.15. ɹæbɪtsmʌk Sf, ɹæbɪtsmʊk Nf

rabbits'-pills *npl* RABBIT-DROPPINGS III.13.15. ɾabɪtspɪɫz D

rabbits'-shit *n* RABBIT-DROPPINGS III.13.15. ɾabɪtsʃɪt W Co, ɾabətsʃɪt D, ɾabətsʃɪd D

rabbits'-trottles *npl* RABBIT-DROPPINGS III.13.15. ɹæbɪtsʈɹʌʔls Nf

rabbits'-turds *npl* RABBIT-DROPPINGS III.13.15. ɹæbɪtstɛːdz Nf, ɹæˈbɪtstʌdz Nf, ɹæbɪtstəːdz Ess MxL, ɹabʊtstœːdz Gl, ɽæbɪtstəɽːɖʐ Ha, ɽabɪtstəɽːɖʐ So W D Do Ha, ɽabʌtstəɽːɖʐ W, ɽabətstəɽːɖʐ Co D Ha, ɹabəʔstəɽːɖʐ Bd

rabbit-triddles *npl* RABBIT-DROPPINGS III.13.15. ɹabʊttɹʊdłz Hu

rabbit-triddlings *npl* RABBIT-DROPPINGS III.13.15. ɹabɪttɹɪdlɪnz Y, ɹabəttɹɪdlɪnz La, ɹabɪʔtɹɪdlɪnz C

rabbit-trittlings* *npl* RABBIT-DROPPINGS III.13.15. ɹæbɪttɹɪtlɪnz Sa

rabbit-trottles *npl* RABBIT-DROPPINGS III.13.15. ɹabɪttɹɒtlz Nt, ɹabɪttɹɔtlz L, ɹabɪttɹɔʔlz L, ɹabəttɹɔtlz L

rabbit-trunlings *npl* RABBIT-DROPPINGS III.13.15. ɹabɪttɹʊnlɪnz Wa

rabbit-turd(s) *n* RABBIT-DROPPINGS III.13.15. *npl*: ɹabɪttɪədz Y, ɹabəʔtɛːɹdz C, ɹæbəttaːdz Sf, ɹabɪttɒdz Y, ɹabɪttɔdz Y Nt L, ɹabɪttʌdz Hrt, ɹabəttʊəɹdz La, ɹabɪttədz Y, ɹabɪttəːdz Y Db St Wa, ɹapɪttəːdz Db, ɹæbɪttəːdz Hu Ess Sr, ræbɪttɹəɽːɖʐ Wo, ɹæbɪttəɽːɖʐ He Wo K, ɽæbɪttəɽːɖʐ So, ɹabɪttəɽːɖʐ Sa Mon K, ɹabəttəɽːɖʐ Gl, ɹabəʔtəɽːɖʐ Bk, ɽabɪttəɽːɖʐ Ha
n-mass: ɹæbɪttəɽɖ Nf, ɹabɪttəːd Wa L, ɹabɪttəɽːɖ Wa

rab-footed *adj* SPLAY-FOOTED VI.10.5. ɹɛdfʊtɪd Ess, ɹæbfʊtɪd Ess *[queried EMBM]*

race *n* the PLUCK of a slaughtered animal III.11.6. ɹiːs Wo, ɹeːs Sa He Mon Gl, ɹeːɪs He Mon Gl

rack *1. n* a HAY-RACK in a stable I.4.1. ɹɛk Du Db Gl K Sx, ræk Man, ɹæk He Wo Wa Mon Gl L Nth Hu C Nf Sf Bk Hrt Ess Sr K, ɽæk So W Co Do, hɽæk So, rak Y, ʁak Nb Du, ɹak Cu Du We La Y Ch Sa St Wo Wa Gl O Nt L Lei Nth Bk Bd Hrt, ɽak So W Co D Do Ha, ɽɑˑk Wo
2. vt to FEED cattle III.3.1. ɹæk Sf*[hay]*
3. n a SAWING-HORSE I.7.16. ɹak Y
4. n the T-SHAPED PLOUGH-BEAM END of a horse-drawn plough I.8.5. ɹak Y
5. n an END-BOARD of a cart I.10.4. ɽɛk Do, ɽæk Do, ɽak So W
6. n a BENCH on which slaughtered pigs are dressed III.12.1. ɹæk C Sf Ess, ɹak Bk Bd Hrt
7. n a flat surface on which bacon is cured, ⇐ SALTING-TROUGH III.12.5. ɽæk So*[presumably]*
8. n the *HORIZONTAL* BAR of a crane over a domestic fire V.3.5(a). ɹak Db
9. n a SHELF V.9.4. ɹæk Ess, ɽæk So, hɽæk So, ɹak L *[marked u.r. EMBM]*
10. n a BIER VIII.5.9(b). ɹak Hrt
11. n a WEAKLING piglet III.8.4. ɹæk C, ɹak C
12. n a PATH through a field IV.3.11. ɹæk He

rackem *n* a CRANE on which a kettle is hung over a domestic fire V.3.4. ɹakəm Nth

racken* *n* a CRANE on which a kettle is hung over a domestic fire V.3.4. ɹakən La

racken-hook *n* a CRANE on which a kettle is hung over a domestic fire V.3.4. ɹakɪnuːk Nt L, ɹakənuːk L

racketing *n* short pieces of straw left after threshing, ⇐ CHAFF II.8.5. ɹækətɪn Sx

racketings *n* CHAFF II.8.5. ɹækətnz Sr

racking *v-ing* FEEDING horses in the stable III.5.1. ɹakɪn St

rack-iron *1. n* a CRANE on which a kettle is hung over a domestic fire V.3.4. ɹakɑˑɪən L
2. n the *HORIZONTAL* BAR of a crane over a domestic fire V.3.5(a). ɹakɑˑɪən L

rackling *n* a WEAKLING piglet III.8.4. ɹaklɪn Nth

racks *1. npl* CART-LADDERS I.10.5. ɹɛks K, *sg* ɽɛk Do, ɹaks Y St, ɽaks W
2. npl cart-ladders on a wagon. ɹaks Wa
3. n a CART-FRAME I.10.6. ɹaks St
4. npl RUTS made by cartwheels IV.3.9. ɹæks Sf Ess, ʁaks Nb, raks Cu, ɹaks Cu We
5. n MIST VII.6.8. ɹaks Y

rack-stick *n* the STRETCHER between the traces of a cart-horse I.5.11. rakstɪk Cu

rack up *1. v* to feed horses in the stable, ⇐ FEEDING III.5.1. ɹak ʌp Bk*[with hay at night]*, ɽak ʌp Do
2. vt to feed horses. ɹæk ... ʌp Nf, ɽak ... ʌp Do *[queried u.r. SBM]*

raddle *1. vt* to MARK sheep with colour to indicate ownership III.7.9. ɹadl Sa St
2. v to mark sheep with colour. ɹadl Y Db, ɹaːdl Sa

raddle-head *n* an ACTIVE child VIII.9.1. ɽadɬɛɪd Co

raddle-mark *v* to MARK sheep with colour to indicate ownership III.7.9. ɹadlmaːk Db

rade *n* an END-BOARD of a cart I.10.4. ɹɛɪd Brk

rade-cart *n* a FARMCART I.9.3. ɹɛɪdkɑɹːt Brk

rades *1. npl* CART-LADDERS I.10.5. ɹɛɪdz Brk
2. n a CART-FRAME I.10.6. ɹeːdz O, ɽeːdz Ha, ɹeɪdz O, ɹæɪdz MxL

raff-house* *n* an old cellar where junk is kept, ⇐ RUBBISH V.1.15. ˈɹafˌuːs Y

raff-hurdles *npl* HURDLES used to pen sheep in part of a field III.7.11. ɽæfhəɽːɖɬʐ So

rafty *adj* RANCID, describing bacon V.7.9. ɹæːftɪ Nf, ɽæːfti W, hɽæːfti So, ɽæːftɪ So, ɽaːfti W Do, hɽaːfti So, ɽaːftɪ O

rag *n* HOAR-FROST VII.6.6. ɹag Cu We La

raggy frost *n* HOAR-FROST VII.6.6. ɹagɪ fɹɔst La

rail *1. n* the PARTITION between stalls in a cow-house I.3.2. ɹeəɫ O
2. n a TETHERING-STAKE in a cow-house I.3.3. ɹɛɪəɫ Sf
3. n a RUNG of a ladder I.7.15. ɹeil Mon

4. n an END-BOARD of a cart I.10.4. ɹeɪᵊɬ So

5. n a DIAGONAL BAR of a gate IV.3.7. ɹeːl Nb Cu, ɹeəl Y

rail partition *n* the PARTITION between stalls in a cow-house I.3.2. ɹɛil pɑtɪʃn Nf

rails *1. npl* CART-LADDERS I.10.5. rˡilz Man, reɪls Man

2. n a CART-FRAME I.10.6. ɹeːɬz D, ɹeɪəɬz So

3. npl the horizontal BARS of a gate IV.3.6. ʁeːlz Nb, ɹeːlz La Y, ɹeːˡɬz He, ʁeəlz Nb, *sg* ʁeˈəl Du, ɹeəlz Y*[wooden x1]*, *sg* ɹeˈəl La, ɹeˈəlz Cu, ɹeˈəɬz Bk, ɹeəɬz O, ɹeːəɬz O, ɹeːᵊɬz O W, ɹeːlz Cu, ɹɛɪɬz Brk, ɹɛɪᵊɬz Gl Nth C Bk, ɹɛɪʊɬz Brk, ɹɛˈəlz Cu, *sg* ɹɛˈəl L, ɹæɪlz Nf, ɹæɪᵊɬz Gl, ɹæɪʊz Brk

rail-stake *n* a TETHERING-STAKE in a cow-house I.3.3. ɹeːlsteːk Ch

rain-shoot *n* the GUTTER of a roof V.1.6. ɹeɪnʃʌt So

raise out *vphr* to put cattle on hired pasture, ⇐ HIRE PASTURAGE III.3.8. *-ing* ɹeɪzɪn ɛʊʔ Bk

raisins *npl* RABBIT-DROPPINGS III.13.15. ɹeəzɪnz Y

rake *1. n* *What do you call this [indicate a rake used in a domestic fire]?* V.3.8(a). ɹɪək Y, ɹeːk Mon Gl Nt Brk, ɹeːk O So W Co D Do Ha, ɹeɪk St He Bk Bd, ɹeɪk So Do, ɹeːˡk Gl, ɹeːɪk Do, ɹeək O Bd, ɹeːək D, ɹɛːk W D, ɹɛɪk St Wa L Lei R Nth Sf Bk Hrt Ess Brk Sr K Ha Sx, ɹɛˈək L, ɹɛːək So Co D, ɹæɪk Hrt Ess MxL Sr K. ⇒ **ash-rake, coal-rake, cowl, cowler, cowler-rake, cowl-rake, crow, fire-hoe, fire-hook, fire-rake,** *fire-shovel,* **hoe, muck-rake, pole-hook, raker, scrape, scraper, soot-rake**

2. v *What do you do with it [i.e. the rake used in a domestic fire]?* V.3.8(b). Eng exc. Du Man C. ⇒ **clean** *the ashes* **out,** *clean the flue-holes, clean the flues,* **cowl, cowler, cowler** *the ashes* **out, cowl** *it* **down, cowl out, cowl-rake, cowl** *the ash,* **cowl** *the ashes,* **cowl** *the ashes* **out, cowl** *the ash* **out, cowl** *the cinders,* **cowl** *the cinders* **down, cowl** *the cinders* **out, cowl** *the coals,* **cowl** *the cokes* **out, cowl** *the fire* **together, cowl** *them* **down, cowl** *the muck* **out, draw, draw** *the ash,* **grate** *the cokes,* **hoe** *the coal,* **hoe** *the soot,* **hoe** *the soot* **out, hook** *it* **out, howk** *the* **ashes, howk** *the coals,* **pull, pull** *cinders,* **pull** *the* **ashes, pull** *the ashes* **out, pull** *the cinders,* **pull** *the cinders* **out, pull** *the coal,* **pull** *the coal* **forward, pull** *the coals onto the fire, rake cinders out, rake coal out, rake it, rake it out, rake it up, rake out, rake out the ashes, rake out the cinders, rake out the old ashes, rake the ash, rake the ashes, rake the ashes out, rake the ash out, rake the backing, rake the back of the fire out, rake the cinders, rake the coal, rake the fire, rake the muck out, rake the soot, rake the soot out, rake your ashes out,* **riddle, riddle** *the cinders,* **scrape, scrape out, scrape** *the ash,* **scrape** *the ashes,* **scrape** *the ashes* **out, scrape** *the ash out on the flues,* **scrape** *the ash* **up, scrape** *the chimney,*

scrape *the cinders,* **scrape** *the cinders* **in, scrape** *the flue,* **scrape** *the muck* **out, scrape** *the soot,* **scrape** *the soot and ash,* **scrape** *the soot* **down, scrat** *coal* **down, sift** *the cinders*

3. n a ROPE-TWISTER II.7.8. ɹɪək Nb

4. n a RIDGEL III.4.7. ɹeɪk O

5. n an ACTIVE child VIII.9.1. ɹeˈək Bk

rake out *vtphr* to TED hay II.9.11(a). ɹɛːk ... æʏt D

rake over *vtphr* to TURN hay II.9.11(b). ɹɛɪk ... oʊvə Wa

raker *n* a RAKE used in a domestic fire V.3.8(a). ɹeːkəˡ Sa Mon, ɹeɪkəˡ Ha, ɹeːɪkəˡ Wo, hɹeːˡkəˡː So, ɹɛɪkə St, ɹɛɪkʔə Ess, ɹɛɪkəᴶ Brk, ɹɛɪkəˡ Sx, ɹæɪkəᴶ K

raking *1. vt-ing* SCRATCHING VI.1.2. ɹeːkən Do

2. v-ing GOSSIPING VIII.3.5(a). ɹeːkɪn La

ram *1. n* *When the male lamb grows up, you call it a ....* III.6.7. ɹɛm Nf Ess Sr K, ɹɛəm Ess, ɹæm O Nf Sf Hrt Ess Brk Sr K Ha Sx, ɹæm So Co, hɹæm So, ræᵊm Man, ræːm Man, ɹam La Y Ch St Wo Gl O L Hu Nf Bk Bd Hrt Ha, ɹam So W Co D Do Ha, ɹɑm O, ɹɔm Ch. ⇒ **tup, tup-hog**

2. adj RANCID, describing bacon V.7.9. ʁam Du

ram-cat *n* a TOM-CAT, the male cat III.13.8. ɹamkat D

rames *n* POTATO-HAULMS II.4.4. ɹɪəms So, ɹeɪᵊmz So

ram-lamb *n* a MALE LAMB III.6.2. ɹɛmlɛm Sr K, ɹɛmlɛəm Ess, ɹɛəmlɛəm Ess, ɹæˈmlɛm K, ɹæmlæm O Sf Ess MxL Brk Sr K Ha Sx, ɹæmlæm So, hɹæmlæm So, ɹæmɬæm So Co, ɹamlam La Y St Wa Gl O Hu Bk Bd, ɹamlam So D Do, ɹamɬam W Co D Do Ha, ɹamlɑm Ha, ɹamlɑm O

rammel *1. n* WEEDS, unwanted plants that grow in a garden II.2.1. ɹaml La

2. n RUBBISH V.1.15. ɹamɪl Y Db*[old]* Nt L, ɹaml Nt L, ɹaməl St, ʁʊml Nb

ramp *vt* to SPRAIN an ankle VI.10.8. ɹamp Nb

ramped *adj* SICK, describing an animal that is unwell VI.13.1(c). ɹampt La

ramp-pole *n* a TETHERING-STAKE in a cow-house I.3.3. *pl* ɹampəɬz So, ɹamppoːɬ W, ɹampoːɬ W

rance *n* a RUNG of a ladder I.7.15. *pl* ɹansɪz Cu

rancid *adj* *If the bacon has gone yellow and has a strong nasty taste, you say the bacon is ....* V.7.9. ɹensɪd Sr K, ɹænsɪd Mon Nf Sf Ess Brk Sr K, ɹansɪd Sa Nt, ɹanst Y. ⇒ **bad, blue, briny, cankered,** *dainty* ⇒ **tainty, fusty, grainer, kewny, mildewed, musty, off, rafty, ram, randed, rank, rash, rasty, reachy, reased,** *reast* ⇒ **reased, reasted, reasty, reazy, rindy,** *rotten,* **rusted, rusty, rutchy, sappy, smeeky, sour,**

stale, *stinky*, **tainted**, **tainty**, **tallowy**, **twangy**, **windy**, *wrong*, **yenky**

randed *adj* RANCID, describing bacon V.7.9. ɹandɪd Cu

randle-balk *1. n* a CRANE on which a kettle is hung over a domestic fire V.3.4. ɹanlbɔːᵊk Cu
2. n the HORIZONTAL BAR of a crane over a domestic fire V.3.5(a). ɹanlbɔːk Du, ɹanəlbɔːk Y

randle-tree *n* the HORIZONTAL BAR of a crane over a domestic fire V.3.5(a). ɹanltriː Cu, ɹanlʧiː Cu, ʁaŋltʁiː Nb

randy *n* a local FESTIVAL or holiday VII.4.11. ɹandi Do; **club randy** kɫʌb ɹandi Do

range *1. n* a STALL in a cow-house I.3.1. ɹɔːnʒ La *[queried u.r. NBM]*
2. n the GANGWAY in a cow-house I.3.7. ɹeːndʒ La, ɹeːnʒ Mon, ɹeɪndʒ He Mon, ɹeːɪnʒ He Mon, ɹɛnʒ He, ɹænʒ He, ɹɔːnʒ La, ɹoːnʒ La
3. n the gangway of a cow-house, used to store hay, ⇐ HAY-LOFT I.3.18. ɹeɪndʒ Mon

rangle *vi* to FESTER, referring to a wound VI.11.8. ɹæŋgəɫ He

raning *v-ing* GOSSIPING VIII.3.5(a). ʁɪənɪn Nb

rank *1. adv* VERY poisonous IV.11.5. ɹɛŋk K Sx, ɹæŋk Nf Sf Ess, ʁaŋk Nb, ɹaŋk Cu Y St Wa O*[old x1]* Nf, ɹɒŋk Ch Sa
2. adj RANCID, describing bacon V.7.9. ɹɛəŋk Ess, ɹæŋk Sf Ess Sx, ɹæːŋk Nf Hrt, ɹaŋk Hrt, ɹaŋk Ha
3. adj **go rank** to SPOIL, referring to meat or fish V.7.10. gʊ ɹɒŋk O

rankles *vi-3prsg* it HURTS VI.13.3(a). ʁaŋklz Nb

rank place *n* a TUSSOCK of grass II.2.9. ɹæŋk pleːˡs Nf

ranny *n* a SHREW-MOUSE IV.5.2. ɹɛnɪ Nf Sf Ess, ɹɛəni Ess, ɹæni Nf Sf Ess*[old x1, common x1]*, ɹani Hu C Nf

ranny-mouse *n* a SHREW-MOUSE IV.5.2. *pl* ɹɛnɪmɛʊsɪz Ess*[old]*, ɹænɪmɛʊs Ess

ran over *viphr-ed HAS NOT* HELD, referring to a cow that has not conceived III.1.7. ɹæn oʊvə Nf

ran-stake *n* a TETHERING-STAKE in a cow-house I.3.3. ɹansteːk Ch

rant *n* a SEESAW VIII.7.2. ɹant Y

ranting *adj ON* HEAT, describing a sow III.8.9. ɹantɪn D

ranting-board *n* a SEESAW VIII.7.2. ɹantɪnbʊəd Y

rantipole *n* a SEESAW VIII.7.2. ɹantɪpɔʊl Y

ranty *1. n* a SEESAW VIII.7.2. ɹantɪ Y L, ɹante Y
2. n a period of seesawing. ɹantɪ Y

rap-stick *n* a wooden implement, greased and sanded, used to sharpen a scythe, ⇐ WHETSTONE II.9.10. ɹapstɪk Lei R Nth, ɹaθstɪk L

rapy *adj* HOARSE VI.5.16. ɹæːpɪ Y

rare *adv* VERY VIII.3.2. ɹɪˈə L, ɹɛə Y L K

rash *adj* RANCID, describing bacon V.7.9. ɹæɪʃ So

rasher-fat *n* BACON-FAT V.7.5(b). ɹeɪʃəˡːvat D, ɹæʃəˡfæt Brk, ɹaʃəˡfat Bk, ɹaʃəˡːvat Do

rasty *adj* RANCID, describing bacon V.7.9. ɹæstɪ He, ɹæːstɪ Gl, ɹæːsti So, ɹastɪ Gl, ɹasti Mon, ɹaːstɪ Mon Gl, ɹaˡːʂʧɪ Gl

rat *n What do you call the animal larger than a mouse, with a long tail; it lives in stacks and sewers?* IV.5.3. Eng. ⇒ **ratten**

rat-bat *n* a BAT IV.7.7. ɹætbæt Sf

ratchet *n* the vertical BAR or CHAIN of a crane over a domestic fire V.3.5(b). ɹatʃət Db

ratch-stake *n* a TETHERING-STAKE in a cow-house I.3.3. ɹatʃsteːk Ch

rathe *n* an END-BOARD of a cart I.10.4. *pl* ɹɛɪz Brk

rathe(s) *n* a CART-FRAME I.10.6.
no -s: ɹeˈɪð Db
-s: ɹˡiːðz Db, ɹeːðz Db, ɹeːɪz He, ɹɛɪðz St Lei

rathes *npl* CART-LADDERS I.10.5. ɹɛɪθs St, ɹɛɪðz St Lei *[not an EMBM headword – taken as raves]*

rathe-stay *n* the iron stay connecting the beam with the side of a cart, ⇐ CROSS-BEAM END I.10.1. ɹɛɪvstɛɪ L *[EMBM treats simply as* **cross-beam end**]

rathings* *npl* CART-LADDERS I.10.5. ɹɛɪðɪnz Lei

rath-stake *n* a TETHERING-STAKE in a cow-house I.3.3. ɹaθsteːk Y

ratling *n* a WEAKLING piglet III.8.4. ɹatlɪn Sa Hu

rat-runs *n* **get rat-runs** referring to a cow, show signs of calving by changes in the pelvic region, ⇐ SHOWS SIGNS OF CALVING III.1.12(b). *3prperfsg* gɔʔ ɹæʔɹʌnz Sf

ratten *n* a RAT IV.5.3. ʁatn Nb*[young x1]*, ɹatn Cu Du We La Y, *pl* ɹatənz Y, ɹaʔn La

rattle *1. n* MONEY VII.8.7. ɹatɫ W, ɹadɫ D
2. vt **rattle his arse** to BEAT a boy on the buttocks VIII.8.10. ɹatl ɪz aːz Ch, ɹatl ɪz aˡːʂ Sa

rattlebox *n* a GOSSIP VIII.3.5(b). ɹætɫbɒks He

rattle down *vtphr* to GOBBLE food VI.5.13(b). *-ing* ɹadɫɪn ... dæʊn Do

rattler *n* a GOSSIP VIII.3.5(b). ɹatlə St

rattle(s) *n* a GOSSIP VIII.3.5(b).
no -s: ɹatl Sa
-s: ɹatɫz Lei

rattling *v-ing* GOSSIPING VIII.3.5(a). ɹatlɪn Lei, ɹatɫɪn Lei

raunch *vt-1prpl* we CRUNCH apples or biscuits VI.5.12. ɹɔːᵊnʃ Hrt

rave *n* an END-BOARD of a cart I.10.4. ɹeːv Do, *pl* ɹeːvz W Ha, *pl* ɹeɪvz So, *pl* hɹeːɪvz So

rave-board *n* an extension board raising the side of a cart, ⇐ END-BOARD I.10.4. ɹeːvboˈəˡd̚ Gl

rave-hook *n* a BILLHOOK IV.2.6. ɹeˈɪvhʊk Nf

ravel-back *n* a LOOSE *PIECE OF* SKIN at the bottom of a finger-nail VI.7.11. *pl* ɹavɫbaks W

ravelled *adj* TANGLED, describing hair VI.2.5. ɹɒvɫd He

ravelling-back *n* a LOOSE *PIECE OF* SKIN at the bottom of a finger-nail VI.7.11. hɹavlınbæk So

rave(s) *n* a CART-FRAME I.10.6.
no -s: ɹeɪv Nf, ɹɛˑəv L, ɹaɪv Wa
-s: ɹeːvz Gl O, ɾeːvz W Do Ha, ɹeɪvz Wo Nth Hu C, ɾeɪvz So Ha, ɹɛɪvz Wa O L Lei Nth Hu, ɹɛəvz Y L, ɹæɪvz Sr

raves *1. npl* CART-LADDERS I.10.5. ɹeːvz Gl, ɹeɪvz Nf, ɾeɪvz So, hɾeɪvz So, ɹeːɪvz Wo, rɛɪvz O*[not found locally]*, ɹɛɪvz L Lei R Brk Sr, ɹɛˑəvz L
2. npl fixed side-boards on a cart. ɹɛɪvz Sf
3. npl upright (cart-)ladders on a wagon. ɹɛɪvz Hu

ravings *n* a CART-FRAME I.10.6. ɹɛˑɪvɪnz L

raw *adj* INSIPID, describing food lacking in salt V.7.8. ɹaː Bd, ɾɔː W

raw-golly *n* a NESTLING IV.7.1. ɹaːgʊlɪ Du

raw-gorbet *n* a NESTLING IV.7.1. ʀæˑəgɔːbət Nb

rawk *1. n* MIST VII.6.8. ɹaʊk Cu, ɹɔːk Y*[wet]*, ɹɔːk Nf, ɹʊək Y
2. n FOG VII.6.9. ɹɒʊk Cu

rawky *1. adj* HOARSE VI.5.16. ɹʊəkɪ Y
2. adj DULL, referring to the weather VII.6.10. ɹəʊkɪ Y

rawt *1. vi-3prpl* they MOO, describing the noise cows make during feeding time in the cow-house III.10.4(a). ɹɔːt Y
2. vi-3prpl they MOO, describing the noise cows make in the fields III.10.4(b). ɹɔːt Y

rawters *npl* PEGS used to fasten thatch on a stack II.7.7(a). ɹɔːtəz Ess*[old] [queried EMBM]*

rax *1. vi* to RETCH VI.13.15. **rax himself** *-ing* ɹaksın ızsɛl Y
2. vi to BREAK *WIND* VI.13.16. *-ing* ɹaksın Y

raxed *vt-ed* sprained, ⇐ to SPRAIN an ankle VI.10.8. ɹakst We, *inf* ɹaks Du*[old]*

razzored *adj* EXHAUSTED, describing a tired person VI.13.8. ɹazəd Db

reach *1. v* to FORK sheaves onto a wagon II.6.7(b). ɹɛɪtʃ Ch, *3prsg* ɹɛɪks Y
2. v to PITCH sheaves II.6.10. *3prsg* ɹiːtʃɪz Ch, ɹɪtʃ Sa, ɹɛɪtʃ La
3. n a row or SWATH of mown grass cut for hay-making II.9.4. ɹiˑtʃ Nf
4. imp **reach for it** HELP YOURSELVES!, said to invite visitors to eat V.8.13. ɹɪətʃ fɔɹət La

reacher *1. n* a HAY-FORK with a long shaft I.7.11. ɹɛɪtʃə Ch
2. n the FORKER of sheaves onto a wagon II.6.7(d). ɹiːtʃə Ch, ɹiːtʃəˠ Db, ɹeːtʃə Ch, ɹɛɪtʃə La Ch, ɹɛɪtʃəˠ La, ɹɛɪtʃəɹ La
3. n the FORKER on a wagon who unloads sheaves in a stackyard II.6.9. reːtʃə Ch

reaches *npl* the RIDGES between furrows in a ploughed field II.3.2. ɹɛɪtʃɪz Ha

reaching-fork *n* a HAY-FORK with a long shaft I.7.11. ɹɛɪtʃɪnfɔˠːk La
2. n a hay-fork with a long shaft. *pl* ɹiːtʃɪnfɔˠːks Db, ɹɛɪtʃɪnfɔˠːk La
3. n a hay-fork with a short shaft. ɹɛɪtʃɪnfɔˠːk La

reaching-pikel *n* a HAY-FORK with a long shaft I.7.11. *pl* ɹiːtʃɪnpaɪkɪlz Ch, ɹɛɪtʃɪnpaɪkl La, ɹɛɪtʃɪnpaɪtl La

reach out *imp* HELP YOURSELVES!, said to invite visitors to eat V.8.13. ʀiːtʃ uːt Nb

reach till *imp* HELP YOURSELVES!, said to invite visitors to eat V.8.13. ɹiːtʃ tɪl Cu

reach to *imp* HELP YOURSELVES!, said to invite visitors to eat V.8.13. ɹiːtʃ tɪuː Db, ɹiːtʃ tuː Y, ɹɪətʃ tɪə Du Y, ɹɪətʃ tuː Cu Y, ɹɛɪtʃ tiː Du, ɹɛɪtʃ tᵁuː La, ɹɛɪk tuː Y

reach up *1. vtphr* to FORK sheaves onto a wagon II.6.7(b). ɹɛɪtʃ ... ʊp La
2. imp HELP YOURSELVES!, said to invite visitors to eat V.8.13. ɹiːtʃ ʊp Nb Cu We, ɹɪətʃ ʊp We Y

reachy *adj* RANCID, describing bacon V.7.9. ɹɪtʃɪ Wo O, ɹɛɪtʃɪ Wa

ready *1. adj* Jack, waiting to go out with Mary, shouts: Have you got your things on yet? And she answers: Yes, I'm quite .... VIII.1.16. Eng. ⇒ **fit, fit** *and* **ready**
2. adj **ready for mating**, **ready for the bull**, **ready to go to store** ON HEAT, describing a cow III.1.6. **ready for mating** ɹɛdɪ fə meɪtɪn MxL; **ready for the bull** ɹɛdɪ fə ðə bʊl Nf; **ready to go to store** ɹɛdɪ tə gou tə stoˑə Nf
3. adj ⇐ ON HEAT, describing a sow III.8.9. **ready for service** rɛdɪ fə sɜːvɪs Man, ɹɪdɪ fəᵗ səᵗːvɪs Sr; **ready for the boar/hog** ɹɛdɪ fə ðə boˑə Nf, ɹɛdɪ fə ðɪ ɒg MxL; **ready to go to store** ɹɛdɪ tə gou tˀə stoˑə Nf
4. adj **ready to walk** HEAVING *WITH MAGGOTS* IV.8.6. ɹɛdɪ tə wɔːk Sa

reaf-hook *n* a BILLHOOK IV.2.6. ɹiːfhʊk Nf*[curved blade x1]*, ɹeˑfhʊk Nf, ɹeɪfhʊk Nf

real *adv* VERY VIII.3.2. ɹiːl Cu, ɹɪəl Y L, ɹɪəɫ C Bk Bd MxL, ɹɪʊ Sr K

really *adv* VERY VIII.3.2. ɹɪəlɪ Wa MxL, ɹɛəlɪ Nf

ream *n* CREAM V.5.3. ɾɪːm Co, ɹɪəm Y, ɾɛːm D

rean *1. n* a FURROW II.3.1. ɹɪən La
2. n a wide or double furrow. ɹiːn St He, ɹɪən La Ch Db Sa, ɹɛːn Sa
3. n the bottom of a furrow. ʀiːn Nb
4. n a DITCH without a hedge IV.2.1(c). ɾiːn So

rean-horse *n* the FURROW-HORSE of a ploughing team II.3.4(a). ɹɪənɔˠːs La Db, ɹeːnɔːs Ch

reaning *n* a wide or double FURROW II.3.1. ɹiːnɪn He

rean-wawted *adj* OVERTURNED, describing a sheep on its back unable to get up III.7.4. ɹiːnwaːtɪd Ch, ɹiːnwɔːtɪd Ch St, ɹɪənwɔːtɪd La Ch, ɹɪənwɔˈːtɪd La

reany* *adj* undulating, ⇐ SLOPE IV.1.10. ɹeənɪ Y

reap *v* to MOW grass for hay-making II.9.3. *-ing* riːpən Man, *-ing* ɹˤiˈpɪn Hrt, ɹɪəp smY L

reaper-rulley *n* a WAGON with sides about 4 inches high I.9.2. ɹɪəpəɹʊlɪ Y

reap-hook *n* a BILLHOOK IV.2.6. ɹˡiːpʌk Mon Gl, ɹiːpʊk He Brk, ɾiːpʊk So Do, ɾiːpɣːk So, ɹɪɪphʊk Nf*[short curved blade x1]*, ɹeɪphʊk Nf, ɹɛəphʊk Nf *[Brk form marked ir.r. by fw]*

reaping-hook *n* a BILLHOOK IV.2.6. ɹiˈpɪnhʊk Nf

rear-mouse *n* a BAT IV.7.7. ɾɛːɾmæʊs W

rear up *vtphr* to make sheaves of corn into stooks, ⇐ STOOKING II.6.5. ɹɪəɹ (+V) ... ʊp St, ɹɛəɹ (+V) ... ʌp Ch

reased *adj* RANCID, describing bacon V.7.9. ɹiːst La, ɹiːzd Y

reasted *adj* RANCID, describing bacon V.7.9. ʁiːstɪt Nb, ʁiːstɪd Nb, ɹiːstɪd Nb Cu Du We La, ɹɪəstɪd La Y

reasty *adj* RANCID, describing bacon V.7.9. riːstɪ Cu Man, ʁiːstɪ Nb Du, ɹiːstɪ Cu Du We La Ch Db Sa St Wa Nt L Lei R Nth Hu C Nf Bd K, rɪstɪ So, ɾɪstɪ Co D, ɹɪəstɪ La Y Nt L, ɹeːstɪ Ch Sa He Wo Mon Nf, ɹeɪstɪ Du, ɹeːˡstɪ Db Wo Mon Gl, ɹeːˡzdɪ Db, ɹɛːstɪ La, ɹɛɪstɪ La Ch Db St*[old x1]* He, ɹɛɪzdɪ Db, ɹɛːˤstɪ Wo, ɹaɪstɪ St, ɹəɪstɪ Y

reave *1. vt* to PLASH a hedge IV.2.4. *-ing* ɾiːvən D *2. vi* to RETCH VI.13.15. *-ing* ɹˡiːvɪn Gl

reave up* *vtphr* to RETCH VI.13.15. *-ing* ɹiːvɪn ... ʊp La

reazy* *adj* RANCID, describing bacon V.7.9. ɹiːsɪ Wa, ɹiːzɪ Wa O Nth Sf Bk Bd, ɹɛɪzɪ St

rebble-back *n* a LOOSE *PIECE OF* SKIN at the bottom of a finger-nail VI.7.11. *pl* hɾɛbɫbæks So, ɾɛbɫbak So

rebblings *npl* loose pieces of skin at the bottom of a finger-nail, ⇐ LOOSE *PIECE OF* SKIN VI.7.11. ɾɛblɪnz So

reckan *1. n* the vertical BAR or CHAIN of a crane over a domestic fire V.3.5(b). ɹɛkɪn Y, ɹɛkn Y, ɹɛkən Y *2. n* the HOOK or *CROOK* of a crane over a domestic fire V.3.5(c). ɹɛkn L *3. n* the vertical part of a crane over a domestic fire, consisting of a *BAR* or *CHAIN* and a HOOK(*/CROOK*) V.3.5b+c. ɹɛkn Y, ɹɛkən Du Y

reckan-bar *n* the *HORIZONTAL* BAR of a crane over a domestic fire V.3.5(a). ɹɛkɪnbaː Y L, ɹɛkənbaˡː Y

reckan-crook *1. n* a CRANE on which a kettle is hung over a domestic fire V.3.4. akənkɹuːk La *2. n* the HOOK or *CROOK* of a crane over a domestic fire V.3.5(c). ɹɛkɪnkɹɪʊk Y, akənkɹuːk La *3. n* the vertical part of a crane over a domestic fire, consisting of a *BAR* or *CHAIN* and a HOOK(*/CROOK*) V.3.5b+c. akənkɹuːk La

reckan-hook *1. n* a CRANE on which a kettle is hung over a domestic fire V.3.4. ɹɛkɪnuːk L, ɹɛkɲuːk L, ɹɛkənuːk L *2. n* the HOOK or *CROOK* of a crane over a domestic fire V.3.5(c). ɹɛkɲək Y, ɹɛkɲuːk Y

reckan-hook-bar *n* the *HORIZONTAL* BAR of a crane over a domestic fire V.3.5(a). ɹɛkɪnuːkbaː L

reckan(s) *1. n* a CRANE on which a kettle is hung over a domestic fire V.3.4. *no -s*: ɹɛkɪn Y L, ɹɛkn Y, ɹɛkən Du Y L *-s*: ɹɛkɪnz Du, ɹɛkənz Du Y *2. n* the *HORIZONTAL* BAR of a crane over a domestic fire V.3.5(a). *no -s*: ɹɛkn La *-s*: ɹɛkɪnz Du

reckles *n* FRECKLES VI.11.1. ɹɛklz L

recklien *n* a WEAKLING piglet III.8.4. ɹɛklɪən Y, ɹɛkɭɪən Y

reckling *n* a WEAKLING piglet III.8.4. rɛklɪn Cu, ʁɛklɪn Nb, ʁɛklən Du, ɹɛklɪn Nb Cu Du We La Y Nt L R Nf, ɹɛkɭɪn La Y, ɹɛklən Du L

recknan *n* the vertical BAR or CHAIN of a crane over a domestic fire V.3.5(b). ɹɛknɪn L

recknan-hook *n* a CRANE on which a kettle is hung over a domestic fire V.3.4. ɹɛknɪnuːk L

recollect *vt-2prsg* do you REMEMBER? VIII.3.7. ɹɛkələkt La Y Db Sx, ɹɛkələk Brk

red *1. v* to MARK sheep with colour to indicate ownership III.7.9. *ptppl* ɾɛdəd D, ɹəd La *2. n* the YOLK of an egg IV.6.5. ɹɪəd Y *3.1. vt* to CLEAR dishes from the table after a meal V.8.14. ʁɛd Nb*[old]* *3.2. v* to clear the table. ʁɛd Nb *['dishes' or 'table' unclear]*

reddin-stake *n* a TETHERING-STAKE in a cow-house I.3.3. ɹɛdɪnsteːk Y

reddle *1. vt* to MARK sheep with colour to indicate ownership III.7.9. ɹɛdl Db *2. v* to mark sheep with colour. ɹɛdl Db, ɹɛdɫ Bk, ɹədl Y

reddy-pole *1. n* a CRANE on which a kettle is hung over a domestic fire V.3.4. ɹɛdɪpʊɫ Wa *2. n* the *HORIZONTAL* BAR of a crane over a domestic fire V.3.5(a). ɹɛdɪpʊʊl Nth

rediwilly *n* a sliding RING to which a tether is attached in a cow-house I.3.5. ɹɛdɪwɪlɪ Du

red-raw kellick *n* a NESTLING IV.7.1. *pl* ʁiːdʁaː kɛlɪz Du

reds *n* the WATTLES of a hen IV.6.19. ɹɛdz O

redster *n* a TETHERING-STAKE in a cow-house I.3.3. ɹɛdstəɹ Y, ɹədstə Y *[compare rood-stower]*

red wick* *n* the QUICK of a fingernail VI.7.9. ɹɪd wɪk Y *[NBM headword red quick]*

red-withie *n* a TETHERING-STAKE in a cow-house I.3.3. ɹədɪwɪdɪ Du

red yolk *n* the YOLK of an egg IV.6.5. ɹɛd juˑk Ch

reed *1. n* STRAW II.8.2. ɼiːd So
2. n the UTERUS of a cow III.2.4. ɹiːd Ch Db Nt L, ɹɛɪd Db

reed-beam *n* a straw rope used to fasten thatch on a stack, ⇐ ROPES II.7.7(b2). ɼiːdbiːm D

reed-bind *n* BINDWEED II.2.4. ɹiidbɔɪnd Brk

reeden-rope *n* straw ROPES used to fasten thatch on a stack II.7.7(b2). ɼiːdənɼoːp D*[possibly sg SBM]*

reeding *n* the FAT round the kidneys of a pig III.12.7. ɹɪdn Nb

reed-rope *n* straw ROPES used to fasten thatch on a stack II.7.7(b2). ɼiːdɼoːp D*[possibly sg SBM]*

reef *1. n* the SOLE of a horse-drawn plough I.8.9. ɹiˑf Nf
2. n the FAT round the kidneys of a pig III.12.7. ɹiːf Sf

reek *1. n* SMOKE from a chimney V.1.4. riːk Cu, ʁiːk Nb, ɹiːk Nb Cu Du Y, ɹˡiːk Du, ɹɪˑək Y, ɹɛɪk Y, ɹɔɪk Y
2. n tobacco smoke. ɹiːk Y
3. n the smell of tobacco smoke. ɹiːk Y
4. vi to smoke, describing a fire. *-ing* ɹɪkɪn Y
5. vi to smoke, describing a chimney. *3prsg* ɹiːks Y, *prppl* ɹəɪkɪn Y

reel *1. n* What do you call this *[indicate a cotton-reel]?* V.10.6. riːl Man, ʁiːl Nb, ɹiːl Y Db Sa St Wa L Nf, ɹiːɫ Ch He Wo Wa Mon L Lei Nf Sf MxL Sr K, ɼiːɫ So Co D Ha, hɼiːɫ So, ɹiːʊɫ K, ɼiːᵁɫ W Ha, ɹiːʊ Ess K, ɹiil Nf, ɹiɫ K, ɹiˑᵊɫ Ess, ɹiiːl Sa Nf, ɹˡiːɫ Mon Nf, ɹiiːʊ Ess Sx, ɹiˑᵊl Sa, ɹiˑᵊɫ He Wo Wa Mon Gl Lei Nth Hu C Sf Bk Bd Hrt Ess, ɼiˑᵊɫ So W Do, hɼiˑᵊɫ So, ɹəiːɫ Hrt, *pl* ɹɪɫz O, *pl* ɹiəlz Lei, ɹiəɫ O MxL Ha, ɼɪəɫ O Ess So, hɼɪəɫ So, ɹiʊɫ Brk Sx, ɹiʊ MxL Brk Sr K Ha Sx, ɹeˑəɫ Sf, ɹɛil Y Ch, ɼaɪᵊɫ Ha, ɹəil Ch; **cotton-reel** kɒt?nɼiːᵊɫ Do, kɒdnɼiːᵊɫ So, kɒ?nɼiːᵁɫ W. ⇒ **bobbin**, *cotton-*reel, cotton-spool, pirl, pirn, reeler, spool
2. n a device used to prevent a cart from going backwards on a hill, ⇐ PROP/CHOCK I.11.2. ɹɪʊ Brk

reeler *n* a cotton-REEL V.10.6. ɹiːlə Sf

reest *1. n* the MOULD-BOARD of a horse-drawn plough I.8.8. ɹiːst La K*[on Kent plough x1]*, ɹiːs K, ɹɪst Sx*[on one-way plough]*, ɹeːst Ch, ɹɛst Brk, ɹɛist La, ɹɑɪst K*[on foot plough]*, ɹɑɪs K, ɹəst Sr, ɹəɪs Sx
***2. vi** to be RESTIVE, describing a horse III.5.6. *prppl* ɹɪəstɪn Y

reest-board *n* the SOLE of a horse-drawn plough I.8.9. ɹɔɪsbɔːd Hrt

reested *adj* RESTIVE, describing a horse III.5.6. riːstɪd Cu, ʁiːstɪd Nb, ʁiːstɪt Nb, ɹiːstɪd Nb Du, ɹɪəstɪd Y

reester *n* a RESTIVE horse III.5.6. ʁiːstɔᵝ Nb, ɹiːstə Db, ɹɪəstə Y, ɹɪəstəɹ Y

reesty *adj* RESTIVE, describing a horse III.5.6. ɹiːstɪ Y, ɹɪəstɪ Y

refuge *n* RUBBISH V.1.15. ɹɛfjuːdʒ La St, ɹɛfuːdʒ Brk

regular *adv* ALWAYS VII.3.17. ɹɛgjələ St, ɹɛglə L, ɹɛgləᶜ Sa Wo O *[marked u.r. EMBM]*

regular-man *n* a FARM-LABOURER I.2.4. ɹɛgləman Y, ɹɛgləᶜ man Wo

regulating bar *n* the T-SHAPED PLOUGH-BEAM END of a horse-drawn plough I.8.5. ɹɛgjəɫeɪtɪnbaᶜː So

regulator *1. n* an EVENER on a horse-drawn plough I.8.4. ɹɛgleːɪtəᶜ Wo
2. n an evener on the plough-beam end of a plough. ɹɛgəlæɪtə Hrt

rein-horse *n* the NEAR-HORSE of a pair pulling a wagon I.6.4(a). ɹeːnɔːs Db

reinies *npl* the REINS of a cart-horse I.5.5. reːnɪz Ch

reinings *npl* the REINS of a cart-horse I.5.5. ɹiːnɪnz Ch, ɹɪənɪnz La Y, reɪnɪnz St

reins *npl Show a picture of the harness of a cart-horse. What do you pull to make a horse turn?* I.5.5. Eng. ⇒ reins of cart-horse: **driving-lines, driving-reins, gee-ho-lines, head-lines, lines, reinies, reinings**; reins of plough-horse: **cords, gee-ho-lines, lease-lines, lines, plough-cords, plough-lines, strings, whippin-lines, whippin-strings** *[Although the cart/plough distinction is sometimes well marked, especially in WMBM, it is not always so, apparently because it was not recorded. The above separation is based on the BM evidence available.]*

relations *n If people are connected with you by birth, they are your ....* VIII.2.4. Eng. ⇒ **friends, kin, kindred, kinsfolk, kinsmen, relatives** *[BM headword relatives]*

relatives *n* RELATIONS VIII.2.4. ɹɪˈleːtɪvz Brk, ɼɪˈɫeːtɪvz W, ɹɪˈleɪtɪvz Sr, ɹɪlətɪvz K, ɹɛlətɪvz Y*[polite x1]* Ch*[old x1]* Db St Wa Mon O Nth Nf Bk Ess Brk K, ɹɛlətəvz Nb, ɼɛlətɪvz So*[modern]* Ha, ɼɛlətɪvz W

re-lay *1. n* AFTERMATH, a second crop of grass II.9.17. ɹiiːleɪ Sr *[queried ir.r. SBM]*
2. vt to PLASH a hedge IV.2.4. ɹiiːlæɪ Ess

re-lig *vt* to PLASH a hedge IV.2.4. ɹiːlɪg Y

remains *n* a dead BODY VIII.5.7(a). ɹɪmæɪnz Nf

remember *vt-2prsg In talking over with an old friend the happy times you had together long ago,* *you'd ask him from time to time: DO YOU ... how we ...?* VIII.3.7. Eng exc. Nb Cu Du Co. ⇒ **bethink, call back, call home, call** *to recollection*, **mind, mind of, mind on, recollect, tell, tell of, think on**

remove *v* **remove stalks** *What is your word for removing the stalks from red or black currants after you've gathered them?* V.7.24. ⇒ *a*-**strip, chig, clean, clean** *them*, **clean up, clip, cull,** *do, get the stalks off*, **head, head-and-tail,** *knip* ⇒ **nip,** *knop* ⇒ **nop, nesp, nib, nib** *them*, **nip** *them*, **nop, pick, pick-and-clean, pick over, pick** *stalks*, **pick** *them*, **pick** *them from the stalks*, **pick** *them* **off, pick** *them* **over, pick** *the noses off them*, **pick** *the stalks*, **pip** *them*, **pluck, pull, pull** *stalks* **off, screg** *them*, **scrig** *them* ⇒ **screg** *them*, **shed, shred, skin** *them*, **slip** *them*, **slough, snip, snout, snuff, snuff** *them*, **spray, stalk, stalk** *them*, **stalk** *them* **off, stem, stem** *them*, **strig, strig** *them*, **string, string** *them*, **strip, stripe, strip** *them*, **strip** *them off the stalk*, **strip** *them* **over, tail** *them*, *take stalks off, take the ends off, take them off the risps, take the stalks off, take the stems off*, **thread, tip** *them*, **top, top-and-tail, top** *them*, **top** *them* **over, trim, unstring**

removing stalks ⇒ **remove**

rench* *1. vt* to RINSE clothes V.9.8. ɹɛnʃ Y L C
2. *v* to rinse. ɹɛnʃ Du Y L Nf Hrt

rench out* *vtphr* to RINSE clothes V.9.8. ɹɛnʃ ... ʌʊt Y, ɹɛnʃ ... uːt L

rend *vt* to RENDER fat into lard III.12.9. *-ing* ɹɪndɪn Sx, *-ing* ʁɛndən Du, ɾɛnd D, ɹɛn Y, ʁɛɪnd Nb, *-ing* ɾɛəndən Man

rend down *vtphr* to RENDER fat into lard III.12.9. *-ing* ɹɛndɪn ... duːn Y, ɹɛn .. dɛʊn Sx

render *vt How do you make lard out of this fat [from round the kidneys of a pig]?* III.12.9. ɹɪndə Du, ɾɛndə Cu, ʁɛndəᴿ Nb, ʁɛndəᴿ Nb Du, ɹɛndə Nb Cu Du We La Y Ch Db St Wa Gl Nt L Lei R Nth Hu C Sf Bd Hrt Ess K, ɹɛndəɹ (+V) He MxL, *-ing* ɹɛndɹɪn St, ɹɛnðə La, ɹɛndər Du, ɹɛndɹ L. ɹɛndəɹ La Y, ɹɛndəᴶ La O L Brk, ɹɛndəᴶɹ (+V) Sr, ɹɛndəᵗ Sa He Wo Wa Mon Bk Brk, ɹɛndəᵗ: Sa, ɾɛndəᵗ O, ɾɛndəᵗ: So, ɾɛndəᵗːɾ (+V) Do, ɾændəᴶ Man. ⇒ **boil, boil down, draw down, dry down, melt, melt down, peer down, rend, rend down, render down, rind, run, run down, separate, simmer, simmer down, squeeze, try down, try up**

render down *vtphr* to RENDER fat into lard III.12.9. ɹɛndə dɛʊn Db Nth Sf, ɹɛndəɹ (+V)... dɛʊn Nf Ess, ɹɛndə duːn Y, ɹɛndəɹ (+V)... dæʊn Y Ch Wa L Sr, ɹɛndəɹ (+V)... dæːᵊn K, ɹɛndəɹ (+V)... daːn La Nt, *2prsg* ɹɛndəz ... daːn Y, ɹɛndəɹ (+V)... daɪn Ch, ɹɛndɹ (+V)... daʊn L, ɹɛndəɹ (+V)... daʊn La Y St L, ɹɛndəɹ (+V)... duːn Y, ɹɛndəᴶ dɛʊn K, *pt* ɹɛndəᵗd̥ d̥ɛʊn Sr, ɹɛndəᵗɾ (+V)... dɛuːn Wo, ɹɛndəᵗ (+V)... dəʊn Mon, *-ing* ɹɛndəᵗɾɪn dəʊn He, ɹɛndəᵗɾ (+V)... dəʊːn Wo, ɾɛndɾ, (+V)... dæʊn So, ɾɛndəᵗ: ... dævn D, ɾɛndəᵗːɾ (+V) dæʊn W, ɾɛndəᵗːɾ (+V)... daʊn So

rendles *n* RENNET V.5.6. ɹʊndłz Lei

rennet *n And when you made cheese, what did you put into the milk?* V.5.6. Eng exc. Hu Hrt. ⇒ **bag-skin, calf keslop, calf-poke,** *calf's keslop* ⇒ **calf keslop, calf's maw, calf's read, calf's stomach, cow keslop,** *cow's keslop* ⇒ **cow keslop, earning, fell, hind-skin, keslop(s), projine, rendles,** *rennets*, **renning, renty, sour buttermilk, steep-skin, stiffening**

rennies *npl* string KNEE-STRAPS used to lift the legs of working trousers VI.14.17. ɹɛnɪz La

renning *n* RENNET V.5.6. ɹɛnɪn Sa

renny *n* a FOX IV.5.11. ɹɛnɪ Du Y

rense *1. vt* to RINSE clothes V.9.8. ʁɛɪnz Nb[*old*], rɛns Man, ɹɛns Y Ch Db L Nf Sr, ʁɛɪnz Nb
2. *v* to rinse. ɹɛns Y Ch Wa L Lei Nth Nf, ɹɛnts Nth
[not a N/WM/EMBM headword]

rense out* *vtphr* to RINSE clothes V.9.8. ɹɛnz ... ᵊuːt Y

renty *n* RENNET V.5.6. ɹɛntɪ Y

resembles *vt [Show a picture of a family.] Look at their faces now. Don't you think this boy ... his grandfather?* VIII.1.9. ʁɪzɛmblz Nb Du, ʁɪzɛmbl Nb, ɹɪzɛmblz Gl, ɹɪzɛmbl Nf, ɹɪzɛmbłz Sr, ɹɪzɛmbł Nf. ⇒ *bears a* **likeness to,** *be the* **daps** *of, exactly like*, **favours,** *feature one another*, **features, follows, follows** *him in looks*, **got the daps** *of*, **has a** *look of*, **has a resemblance to, has got the** *look of*, **has the very** *face of*, **he's got a fair** *likeness to*, **he's like, he's the** *daps of*, **he's the** *image of*, **he's the** *spit of*, **he's the splitten image** *on*, **he's the very** *daps of*, **he's the very** *image of*, **image** *of*, **is a** *likeness of*, **is just like, is like, isn't he like, is rather like, is really like, is terrible like, is the** *image of*, **is the** *model of*, **is the** *picture of*, **is the real** *spit of*, **is the spit, is the spit** *and* **image** *of*, **is the spit** *and* **image** *on*, **is the spit** *of*, **is the spit** *on*, **is the very** *daps of*, **is the very** *picture of*, **is the very** *spit of*, **is very much** *like*, *just like*, **like,** *looks just like, looks like*, **runs back** *into*, **sembles, takes after, takes like, takes to,** *the daps of*, *the spit of*, **turns after**

rest *n* a STICK used to support the shaft of a cart I.11.1. ɹɛst La Sa Nth, *pl* ɹɛsts K, *pl* ɾɛsts W *[pl headword SBM]*

rest-bar *n* the *HORIZONTAL* BAR of a crane over a domestic fire V.3.5(a). ɹɛstbaː Nth

rester *n* a STICK used to support the shaft of a cart I.11.1. ɹɛstər Du, ɹɛstəᵗ Gl O, *pl* ɹɛstəᵗz̥ Brk, *pl* ɹɛstəᵗːz̥ So W

resting-pin *n* a STICK used to support the shaft of a cart I.11.1. ɹɛstnpɪn Cu

resting-pole *n* a STICK used to support the shaft of a cart I.11.1. ɹɛstɪnpoːł Mon

resting-staff *n* a STICK used to support the shaft of a cart I.11.1. ɾɛstɪnstɑːf D

resting-stick *n* a STICK used to support the shaft of a cart I.11.1. ɹɛstɪnstɪk Nf Brk

restive *adj* A horse that is stubborn and refuses to move, you say is .... III.5.6. ɹɛstɪv Ch, ɾɛstəv So. ⇒ **awkward, bad-collared, clock, clocker,** *clocking* ⇒ **clock, cold-shouldered, collar-proud, contrary, false,** *gnattery* ⇒ **nattery, jack,** *jacking* ⇒ **jack, jade, jib,** *jibbed* ⇒ **jib, jibber,** *jibbing* ⇒ **jib, jibby, knapper, knappy, megrim, nattery, obstinate,** *old* **jade, put up, reest, reested, reester,** *reesting* ⇒ **reest, reesty, restless, rough, stall,** *stalled* ⇒ **stall, staller,** *stalling* ⇒ **stall, stecked, stetched, stomachy, strunter, stubborn, stupid, sulky, tetched, tinkler, wooden;** ⇒ also **bridle-reested**

restless *1. adj* RESTIVE, describing a horse III.5.6. ɹɛstləs Sa
2. adj ACTIVE, describing a child VIII.9.1. ɹɪstləs Du, ɹɛstlɪs Wo, ɹɛslɪs Sa Wa Ess, ɹɛstɪs Sr, ɹɛslɛs Wo, ɹɛsɫɛs Mon, ɹɛstləs Y Sa, ɹɛsləs Y Ch Sa Nt K, ɹɛsɫəs He, ɾɛsɫəs So Co; **never at rest** nɛvəɾ ət ɹɛst Wo *[marked u.r. SBM]*

rest-pole *n* a STICK used to support the shaft of a cart I.11.1. ɹɛspʊᵊɫ Gl

rest-stick *n* a STICK used to support the shaft of a cart I.11.1. ʁɛststɪkʰ Nb, ɾɛsstɪk Co D Ha

retch *1. vi* When you have already vomited and are straining without bringing anything up, what do you call that? VI.13.15. Eng exc. Gl. ⇒ **altch, boke, boken, break, dry-reach,** *fetch your wind up,* **haltch** ⇒ **altch, heave, heave** *at the heart,* **heave up, kick, lift, over-reach, rax** *himself,* **reach** ⇒ **retch, reave, reave up,** *reeve it up* ⇒ **reave up, rick, rift, strain, strain** *the guts,* **urge** ⇒ **retch, vellop, vomp, vope, yuck**
2. vi to VOMIT, referring to an adult VI.13.14(a). ɹiːtʃ Ess
3. vi to VOMIT, referring to a baby bringing up milk VI.13.14(b). ɹiːtʃ He MxL

retch up *vtphr* to VOMIT, referring to a baby bringing up milk VI.13.14(b). *-ing* ɹiːtʃɪn ... ʌp MxL

retling *n* a WEAKLING piglet III.8.4. ɹɛtlɪn Nt, ɹɛʔlɪn L

returned *1.1. v-ed* HAS NOT HELD, referring to a cow that has not conceived III.1.7. ɹɪtəːnd Wa, ɹɪtəɾːɾn̩d Brk Sr, ɾɪtɑɾːn̩d Co, ɾɪtəɾːn̩d So Co D
1.2. vt-ed **returns service** has not held. ɹɪtəɾn̩ səɾːvɪs K
2. adj NOT IN CALF III.1.8. ɾɪtəɾːn̩d So

revel *n* a local FESTIVAL or holiday VII.4.11. ɾɛvɫ D

revel-back *n* a LOOSE *PIECE OF* SKIN at the bottom of a finger-nail VI.7.11. ɾɛvɫbak Do, *pl* ɾɛvɫbaks W, *pl* ɾɛvᵁɫbaks W

revelling *v-ing ON* HEAT, describing a cow III.1.6. ɹɛvlɪn St

reynard *n* a FOX IV.5.11. ʁɛnᵘᵏt Nb, ɹɛnəd Cu*[read in newspapers]* Y St L Ess, ɹɛnəɹd La, ɹɛnəɾd He Mon Gl

reynold(s) *n* a FOX IV.5.11.
no -s: ɹɛnɔʊɫt MxL, ɹɛnəɫd He, ɹaɪnəl Sa
-s: ɹɛnəlz Nf, ɾɛnəɫz W, ɹænəlz Nf

rezzle *n* a WEASEL IV.5.6. ɹɛzəl Y

rib *1. n* the CURB-STONE in a cow-house I.3.9. ɹɪb Ess
2. n the RIDGE of a stack of corn II.7.2. ɹɪəb Ess
3. vt to BEAT a boy on the buttocks VIII.8.10. ɹɪb Nb

rice-plough *n* a reest-plough, a one-way PLOUGH with a movable mouldboard I.8.1. ɹɑɪsplɛʊ Sr

rick *1. n* a CLAMP in which potatoes are stored out of doors II.4.6. ɹɪk Sf
2. n the BASE of a stack II.7.4. ɹɪk Ess
3. n a HAYSTACK II.9.13. ɹɪk St O Ess*[not used locally x1]* Brk Sx, *pl* ɹɪks Nf K, ɾɪk So W Co D Do Ha, *pl* ɾɪks O, *pl* hɾɪks So
4. n a WEAKLING piglet III.8.4. ɹɪk Y
5. vt to SPRAIN an ankle VI.10.8. ɹɪk O Lei C Sf Bk*[old]* Bd Hrt Ess K, *-ed* ɹɪkt Y L Nf MxL Brk Sr*[old x2]* Sx, ɹɪg Wa, *-ed* ɹɪgd O, ɾɪk So W Co Do, *-ed* ɾɪkt D Ha, *-ed* əɾɪkt W, hɾɪk So
6. vi to RETCH VI.13.15. ɹɪk Db

rick-barken* *n* the STACKYARD of a farm I.1.4. ɾɪkbaɾːkn̩ W Do, *pl* ɾɪkbaɾːknz W

rick-barton *n* the STACKYARD of a farm I.1.4. ɾɪkbaɾːtɪn So D, ɾɪkbaɾːtn̩ So

rick-bed *n* the BASE of a stack, made of browse (= brushwood) II.7.4. ɾɪkbɛd D

rick-bottom *n* the BASE of a stack II.7.4. ɹɪkbatəm Nth, ɹɪkbɒtm Sa, ɹɪkbɒtəm St Wa*[straw x1]* Bd*[straw and brushwood x1]*

rick-builder *n* a STACKER who makes sheaves of corn into a stack II.6.11. ɹɪkbɪldə Gl Nth, ɹɪkbɪldəɾ Sa Wo Wa, ɾɪkbɪldəɾ Ha, ɹɪkbɪɫdə Wa Nth Bk, ɾɪkbɪɫdəɾ O, ɹɪkbɪɫdəɾ He Wo Wa Gl Bk, ɾɪkbɪɫdəɾː Co D Ha, ɹɪkbɪʊɫdəᴵ Ha, ɹɪkbɪʊdəɾ Sr Sx

ricker *n* a STACKER who makes sheaves of corn into a stack II.6.11. ɹɪkə St Wa, ɹɪkəɹ St, ɹɪkəᴵ St

rickess *n* the STACKYARD of a farm I.1.4. ɹɪkɪs Ha, ɹɪkəs Ha

rick-fold *n* the STACKYARD of a farm I.1.4. ɹɪkfʊɫd Mon

rick-fork *n* a HAY-FORK with a short shaft I.7.11. ɹɪkfaɾːk Brk

rick-knife *n* a HAY-SPADE II.9.14(b). ɹɪknɒɪf K

rickles *1. npl* COCKS of hay II.9.12. ɹɪkəlz Y
2. npl cocks larger than footcocks but smaller than pikes. *sg* ɹɪkl La

rickling *n* a WEAKLING piglet III.8.4. ɹɪklɪn La Db St Wo, ɹɪkļɪn Y

ricklings *npl* COCKS of hay II.9.12. ɹɪklɪnz Y

rick-maker *n* a STACKER who makes sheaves of corn into a stack II.6.11. ɽɪkmˡekəᵗ: So, ɽɪkmɪəkəᵗ: W, ɹɪkmeːkə Mon Gl, ɹɪkmeːkəᵗ Sa He Mon Gl, ɽɪkmeːkəᵗ: So W D Do Ha, ɹɪkmeɪkəɹ He, ɽɪkmeɪkəᵗ: So, hɽɪkmeˡkəᵗ: So, ɹɪkmeːˡkəᵗ He Mon, ɽɪkmeːkəᵗ: So W D Do, ɹɪkmɛɪkəɹ Brk, ɹɪkmæɪkə Hrt, ɹɛkmeːkəᵗ He, ɹɛkmeːkəᵗ He

rick-man *n* a STACKER who makes sheaves of corn into a stack II.6.11. ɹɪkmən Brk

rick-park *n* the STACKYARD of a farm I.1.4. ɽɪkpɑᵗːk D

rick-pegs *npl* PEGS used to fasten thatch on a stack II.7.7(a). ɹɪkpɛgz Wo O Bk MxL

rick-prong *n* a HAY-FORK with a short shaft I.7.11. ɹɪkpɽɒŋ Brk

ricks *1. npl* STACKS II.7.1. ɹiːks Hrt, *sg* ɹiːk O MxL, ɹɪks Ch Db Sa*[old x1]* St*[old x1]* He*[hay and corn]* Wo Wa Mon*[hay and corn]* Gl*[hay and corn x1]* Lei R Nth Nf Bk Hrt Ess*[hay x1]* Brk Sr*[old x1]* K*[modern x1, rare x1]* Sx*[old x1]*, *sg* ɹɪk O MxL Ha, ɽɪks O So W D Do Ha, *sg* ɽɪk Co*[always x1]*, hɽɪks So

2. npl long stacks with square ends. ɹiːks Bk Hrt*[old x1]*, ɹɪks Ch*[hay and corn]* He Wa Nth Bk*[hay and corn x3]* Bd Hrt, ɽɪks O

3. npl round stacks. ɹɪks Ch*[hay and corn]* Wo*[rare x1]* Wa*[hay and corn x1, corn x2]* Mon*[hay and corn]*, ɹɪk Gl*[hay and straw x1]*, hay Gl*[hay x1]*, ɽɪks O, ɹɛks He*[hay and corn]* Mon*[old, hay and corn]*

4. npl square stacks. ɹɪks Ch*[hay and corn]* Wo Wa*[corn]* Mon*[hay and corn]*, ɽɪks Co D, ɹɛks He*[hay and corn]* Mon*[hay and corn]*

5. npl COCKS of hay II.9.12. rɪks Man, *sg* ɹɪk Nf

6. n a RIDGEL III.4.7. ɹɪks Nf

rick-saddle *n* the BASE of a stack II.7.4. ɹɪksadl St

rickser *n* a RIDGEL III.4.7. ɹɪksə Nf

rick-spars *npl* PEGS used to fasten thatch on a stack II.7.7(a). ɹɪkspɑːəᵗɽz̩ Sr

rick-sprays *npl* PEGS used to fasten thatch on a stack II.7.7(a). *sg* ɹɪkspɽeɪ O

rick-staddle *n* the BASE of a stack II.7.4. ɹɪkstadl Sa*[hedge-brushings]*, ɹɪkstɪdʊɫ Sx*[raised wooden platform]*, ɹɪkstɪdʊ Sr

rick-stones *n* the BASE of a stack II.7.4. ɹɪkstənz Ess

rick-stool *n* the BASE of a stack II.7.4. ɹɪkstuːl St, ɹɪkstuːɫ He, ɹɛkstuːɫ He

ricksy *n* a RIDGEL III.4.7. ɹɪksɪ Nf

ricksy-horse *n* a RIDGEL III.4.7. ɹɪksɨhaˑs Nf

rickyard *n* the STACKYARD of a farm I.1.4. ɹɪkɪt Hu, ɹɪkjaːd Ch Db St Wo Wa Mon Lei Nth Hu Bk Bd Hrt, ɹɪkjaɹd He, ɹɪkjaᵗːd Sa He Wa Mon Gl O Nth Bk Bd, ɽɪkjaᵗːd̩ So W D Do Ha, ɹɪkjaːd Wo MxL Sr K, ɹɪkjaᵗd̩ Wo, ɽɪkjaᵗd̩ Ha, ɹɪkjaˑːd Brk, hɽɪkjaᵗːd̩ So, ɹɪkjaᵗːɽd̩ Brk Sx, ɹɪkjaːəˡd Sr, ɹɪkjaːəɽd̩ Brk Sr Sx, ɹɪkjaᵗːəɽd̩ Brk Sx, ɹɪkjəd Sa, ɹɪkjəᵗːd̩ He Wo Gl, ɹɪkəˡd O, ɹɪkaᵗd̩ O Bk, ɹɪkəᵗːd̩ Wo, ɹɛkjaᵗːd̩ He, ɹɛkjəᵗːd̩ He, ɽakjaᵗːd̩ Ha

rick-yark *n* the STACKYARD of a farm I.1.4. ɹɪkjaːəᵗk Sx

rid *1. vt* to CLEAR the table after a meal V.8.14. ɹɪd He

2. n a COMB VI.2.4. rɪˈd Cu

rid back *vtphr* to TRIM a hedge IV.2.3. ɹɪd ... bak Gl

ridding-comb *n* a COMB VI.2.4. ɹɛdɪnkɒm St

riddings *n* SCRAPS left after rendering lard III.12.10. ɹɪdnz Nb, ʁʊdnz Du

riddle *1. v* to WINNOW II.8.4. ɹɪdl Y, ɹɪdɫ C

2. n a BASKET for carrying horse-feed III.5.4. ɹɪgl Y

3.1. vt to MARK sheep with colour to indicate ownership III.7.9. ɽɪdɫ W

3.2. v to mark sheep with colour. ɹɪdl La Y

4.1. v to RAKE in a domestic fire V.3.8(b). ɹɪdl Db

4.2. vt to rake. rɪdl Cu, ɹɪdl Db

riddle-hedge *n* a HEDGE of brushwood bundles held together by stakes IV.2.1(a). *pl* ɹɪdɫɛdʒɪz K

riddle-stick *n* a TETHERING-STAKE in a cow-house I.3.3. ɽɪdɫstɪk D

ridge *1. n [Show a picture of some stacks.] What do you call this [indicate the ridge]?* II.7.2. rɪdʒ Man, ʁɪdʒ Nb, ɹɪdʒ Du La Y Ch Db Sa St He Wo Wa Mon Gl O Nt L Lei R Nth Hu C Nf Sf Bk Bd Hrt Ess MxL Brk Sr K Ha Sx, ɽɪdʒ O So W Co D Do Ha, hɽɪdʒ So, ɹʊdʒ Gl O, ɹədʒ O, əᵗːdʒ So. ⇒ **back, comb, crest, rib, ridge-piece, ridge-top, ridging, rig, *rigg* ⇒ rig, rigging, top, top corner, top of the roof**

2. n [Show a picture of some houses.] What do you call this [indicate the ridge of a roof]? V.1.2(a). Eng exc. Cu We Mon. ⇒ **barge, breekin, coping, crease, crest, crest-tile, easing, house-crease, pinnacle, ridge-tile, ridge-tree, ridging, rigg, rigging, roof, top, top *of the slates***

3. n a SLOPE IV.1.10. hɽɪdʒ So, ɽʌdʒ W *[marked probably ir.r. SBM]*

4. n the ROOF of a house V.1.2. ɹɪdʒ L

5. n the BRIM of a hat VI.14.3. ɹɪdʒ Ch

ridgel *n What do you call a male horse when only half castrated?* III.4.7. ɹɪdʒɪl Ch Sa St Wo, ɹɪdʒɪɫ Wo R, wɪdʒɪɫ Wo, ɹɪdʒʊl Wa, ɹɪdʒʊɫ Wa, ɹɪdʒəl Sa He Wa, ɹɪdʒɫ̩ Gl, ɹɪdʒəɫ Wo Lei R, ɹʌdʒəɫ He Mon, ɹʊdʒɪl Sa, ɹʊdʒʊɫ Wo Gl, ɹʊdʒɫ̩ Gl O, ɹʊdʒəɫ He Wa Gl, ɹədʒəl Sa, əᵗːdʒəɫ So. ⇒ **maff, maphrodite, one-stoner, rake, ricks, rickser, ricksy, ricksy- horse, ridgeller, ridger, rig, riggel, rigger, rigging, riggold, riggot, rigling, will-do, will-jill**

ridgeller *n* a RIDGEL III.4.7. ɹɪdʒɪləˡ Sa

ridge-piece *n* the RIDGE of a stack of corn II.7.2. ɹɪdʒpiːs Wo

ridger *n* a RIDGEL III.4.7. ɽɪdʒəˡː Co D, ɽʊdʒəˡː Co

ridges *npl What do you call the raised parts in a ploughed field?* II.3.2. ɹɪdʒɪs Man, ʁɪdʒɪz Nb, ʁɪdʒəz Nb, ʁɪdʒəs Nb, ɹɪdʒɪz La Ch Sa St He Wo Wa Mon Gl L Lei Nth Hu C Nf Sf Bk Bd Hrt Ess MxL Brk Sr K Sx, ɹɪdʒəz Ch Db Sa Wo Gl Nf Sf Hrt Ess, *sg* ɹɪdʒ Cu Du Y O Nt, ɽɪdʒɪz So W Co D Ha, hɽɪdʒɪz So, ɽɪdʒəz So W Co D Ha, *sg* ɽɪdʒ Do, ɹʌdʒɪz Gl, ɾʌdʒɪz W, ɹʊdʒɪz La, *sg* ɹʊdʒ O, ɾʊdʒɪz O. ⇒ **backs, baulks, bends, bouters, brows, byes, cants, combs, cops, drills,** *feerings* ⇐ **veerings, flags, gatherings, harridges, heads, lands, reaches, riggs, rows, seams, stetches,** *stitches* ⇒ **stetches, tops, veerings;** also **baulk, pine, rove;** ⇒ also **eights**

ridge-tile *n* the RIDGE of a house roof V.1.2(a). ɹɪdʒtɑɪl K

ridge-top *n* the RIDGE of a stack of corn II.7.2. ɽɪdʒtɒp So

ridge-tree *n* the RIDGE of a house roof V.1.2(a). ɹɪdʒtɹiː Lei

ridging *1. n* the RIDGE of a stack of corn II.7.2. ɹɪdʒɪn La Db, ɹʊdʒɪn La
2. n the RIDGE of a house roof V.1.2(a). ɹɪdʒɪn La Y Ch Db Sa St Wa Nf Hrt Brk K, ɹɪdʒən Ess

riding *1. v-ing* **comed on riding, on riding, riding** *ON* HEAT, describing a cow III.1.6. **comed on riding** kɒmd əˡ ɹɑɪdɪn Y; **on riding** ə ɹɑːdɪn La, ə ɹɑɪdɪn Y; **riding** ɹɑːdɪn Y *[comed represented in BM as* **come***]*
2. vi-ing **riding again** *HAS NOT* HELD, referring to a cow that has not conceived III.1.7. ɹɑːdən əgən Y

riding-breeches *n* BREECHES VI.14.13(b). ʁɛɪdnbʁɪtʃɪz Nb, ʁɛɪdnbʁɪtʃəz Du, ɹɑɪdɪnbɹɪtʃɪz La, ʁɑɪdnbʁʊtʃɪz Nb, ɹɑɪdɪnbɹiːtʃɪz La, ɹɑɪdɪnbɹɛɪtʃəz Db, ʁɛɪdnbʁiːks Nb

ridling *n* a WEAKLING pig III.8.4. ɹɪdlɪn La

rid off *vphr* to CLEAR the table after a meal V.8.14. ɹɪd ɒf St

rid-widdy *n* a sliding RING to which a tether is attached in a cow-house I.3.5. ɹɪdwədɪ We

riff* *n* MANGE, which causes dogs and cats to lose their hair III.13.7. ɹɪf He

rifle *1. n* a wooden implement, greased and sanded, used to sharpen a scythe, ⇐ WHETSTONE II.9.10. ɹəɪfʊɫ Sx
2. n emery cloth attached to wood, used to sharpen a scythe. ɹɔɪfʊ Sr

rift *1. n* MANGE, which causes dogs and cats to lose their hair III.13.7. ɹɪft Wa L; **the rift** ðə ɹɪft L
2. n DANDRUFF VI.1.3. ɹɪft L
3. vi to VOMIT, referring to an adult VI.13.14(a). ɹɪft L
4. vi to RETCH VI.13.15. ɹɪft We, *-ing* ɹɪftɪn St

5. vi to BREAK *WIND* VI.13.16. *-ing* ɹɪftən Man, *-ing* ɹɪftɪn Y Lei

rift-hurdles *npl* HURDLES used to pen sheep in part of a field III.7.11. ɹɪfthəːdlz Nf *[split ash]*

rifting *v-ing* BELCHING VI.13.13. ɹɪftn Cu Du, ʁɪftn Nb, ʁɪftən Nb, ɹɪftn La Y Db *[old]* St Nt L, ɹɪˈfɪn Man, ɹɪftn We, ɹəftɪn Y *[old]*

rifting up *1. vphr-ing* BELCHING VI.13.13. ɹɪftɪn ʊp Y
2. vtphr-ing **rifting the wind up** belching. ɹɪftɪn ðə wɪnd ʊp Lei

rig *1. n* the RIDGE of a stack of corn II.7.2. ʁɪg Nb Du, ɹɪg Y Db Nt L Lei R Nf
2. n a RIDGEL III.4.7. ɹɪg Cu We La Y Man Ch Db St He Wa Mon Gl O Nt L Lei Nth Hu C Nf Sf Bk Bd Hrt Ess MxL Brk Sr K Ha Sx, ɽɪg O So W Do Ha, hɽɪg So
3. n a HOG III.8.8. ɹɪg L

rigg *n* the RIDGE of a house roof V.1.2(a). ɹɪg Y Db Nt L Lei

rigged *adj* OVERTURNED, describing a sheep on its back unable to get up III.7.4. ɹɪkt Y, ɹɪgd Du La Y, ɹɪkɪt Y

riggel *n* a RIDGEL III.4.7. ɹɪgɪl Y, ɹɪgl Cu Du La, ɹɪgɫ Gl, ɹɪgəl Y *[not a NBM headword]*

rigger *n* a RIDGEL III.4.7. ɹɪgə Db, ɹɪgəɹ Y, ɹɪgəˡ He Mon, ɽɪgəˡː Do *[not a SBM headword]*

riggers *npl* CART-LADDERS I.10.5. ɽɪgəˡːz Co

riggin *n* the RIDGE of a stack of corn II.7.2. ɹɪgɪn Cu, ʁɪgɪn Nb, ɹɪgɪn Cu We La Y Db, ɹɪgən Du, ʁəgɪn Nb

rigging *1. n* a RIDGEL III.4.7. ɹɪgɪn Cu, ɹɪgⁿ La
2. n the RIDGE of a house roof V.1.2(a). ʁɪgɪn Nb, ɹɪgɪn Nb Cu Du We La Y Db L, ɹɪgn Du, ɹɪgən Du, ʁʏgɪn Nb *[not a NBM headword]*

riggold *n* a RIDGEL III.4.7. ɹɪgɫd Du, ɹɪgɫt Cu La, ɹɪgəɫt Nb

riggot *n* a RIDGEL III.4.7. ɹɪgɪt Y, ʁɪgət Nb Du, ɹɪgət Du We La Y, ɹɪkɪt Y, ʁɪkət Nb, ʁɛkət Nb

riggots *npl* RUTS made by cartwheels IV.3.9. ɹɪgʊts La *[old]*

riggs *npl* the RIDGES between furrows in a ploughed field II.3.2. ɹɪgz Cu, ʁɪgz Du, *sg* ʁɪg Nb, ɹɪgz Nb Du We La Y Db Nt Lei R Nf, *sg* ɹɪg Cu L

rig-horse *n* the LAND-HORSE of a ploughing team II.3.4(b). ɹɪghɑːs Nf

right *1. imp* the command TURN RIGHT!, given to plough-horses II.3.5(b). ɹʌɪt Nf
2. imp **all right, right, right away, right ho** the command GO ON!, given to plough-horses II.3.5(d). **all right** ˈɔː ˈɽɒɪt Ha; **right** ɾæɪt So, ɹəɪt Wo Mon; **right away** ɹɔɪd əwɛɪ Ess; **right ho** ˈɹəɪt ˈoː He
3. adv VERY (poisonous) IV.11.5. ɹæɪt Man
4. adj **all right** WELL, describing a healthy person VI.13.1(a). ɔːl ɹɔɪt Wa

5. adj **aught but right** ILL, describing a person who is unwell VI.13.1(b). æʊt bət ɹiːt Ch

6. adj **none right, not right** SICK, describing an animal that is unwell VI.13.1(c). **none right** nʊən ɹɛɪt Y; **not right** nʊt ɹiit Y, nʊt ɹɛɪt Y, nət ɹɛɪt Y, eɪnt ɹʌɪt Nf, ɛɪnt ɹʌɪt Nf

7. adv VERY VIII.3.2. ɹiːt La Y Ch Nt, rɛɪt Y, ɹɛɪt La Y Db Sa L, ɹaɪt Sa, ɹɒɪt Sa Wo, ɹɔɪt Ess, ɹʌɪt Nf, ɹəɪt Y Wo

right-hand *adj* RIGHT-HANDED VI.7.13(b). ɹiːtant La, ɹiːtand La, ɹɛɪtand Y, ɹɑɪtæ·nd K

right-hand afore *n* a LEFT-HANDED person VI.7.13(a). ɹʌɪthænd əfɔ·ə Nf

right-handed *adj [Of a man who does everything with this [show your left hand], you say he is ....]* And with the other hand [show your right hand]? VI.7.13(b). Eng. ⇒ **cotmer-handed, right-hand, right-hander, (a) right-hand man**

righthand-horse *n* the FAR-HORSE of a pair pulling a wagon I.6.4(b). ɹɛɪtandɒs Y, ɹɑɪtændɔːs K

rigling *n* a RIDGEL III.4.7. ɹɪglɪn Cu, ɹɪd̩lɪn Y, ɹɛglɪn Cu

rig-welted *adj* OVERTURNED, describing a sheep on its back unable to get up III.7.4. ɹɪgwɛltɪd Y L

rim *1. n* a RUNG of a ladder I.7.15. *pl* ɹɪmz Y

2. n the metal BUSH at the centre of a cart-wheel I.9.8. *pl* əːmz Ess *[queried EMBM]*

3. n the iron TIRE round a cart-wheel I.9.10. ɹɪm Y Ch St Wo Wa Nt L Lei R Nth Nf Bk Ess Sx

4. n the BRIM of a hat VI.14.3. rɪm Man, ʁɪm Nb, ɹɪm Cu Du La Y Ch Sa St He Wo Mon Gl O Hu Nf Sf Bd Hrt Ess MxL W Brk Sr K Ha Sx, ɽɪm O So W D Do Ha, ɹɪəm Ess, ɹəm La Y

5. n a HALO round the moon VII.6.4. ɹɪm Y L

rime *1. n* HOAR-FROST VII.6.6. ɹɛɪm Cu, ɹaɪm Cu Du We Y[rare x1] He L, ɹɑːm Lei, ɹɑɪm Db Nt L Lei Nth Hu C Bd, ɹɒɪm Sa[old] St Lei Nf, ɹɔɪm Wo Wa Nth[heavy frost on trees] Ess, ɹʌɪm Nf

2. n DEW VII.6.7. ɹɑɪm Nf

3. n MIST VII.6.8. ɹaɪm Y

4. n FOG VII.6.9. ɹaɪm Y

rime-frost *n* HOAR-FROST VII.6.6. ɹaɪm fɹɒst Y, ɹaɪmfɹɒst L, ɹɑ·ɪmfɹɒst L, ɹɑ·ɪmfɹɔːst L, ɹɑɪmfɹɔ·st Ess, ɹɑ·ɪmfɹəst L, ɹɒɪmfɹɔːst Nf, ɹɔɪmfɹɒst Ess, ɹɔɪmfɹɔːst Sf MxL, ɹʌɪmfɹɔːst Nf

rimer *n* HOAR-FROST VII.6.6. ɹʌɪmə Nf

riming *n* HOAR-FROST VII.6.6. ɹaɪmɪn Y

rimy-frost *n* HOAR-FROST VII.6.6. ɹaɪmɪfɹɒst He, ɹaɪmɪ fɹɒst Y, ɹɑɪmɪfɹəst Db, ɹɑɪmɪfɹɒst Wa Lei, ɹɑɪmɪfɹɔːst Hrt Sr K, ɹɒɪmɪfɹɑːst Wo, *pl* ɹɒːɪmɪfɹɒsɪz St, ɹɔɪmɪfɹɔːst Wo Wa O Bk, ɹɔɪmɪfɹɔːᵊs Sf, ɹʌɣmɪfɹɔːst O

rinch *1. vt* to RINSE clothes V.9.8. ɹɪnʃ Y Db L Ess, ɽɪnʃ D

2. v to rinse. ɹɪntʃ O, ɹɪnʃ La Y Man Nt L Bd

rinch off *vtphr* to RINSE clothes V.9.8. ɽɪnʃ ... ɔːf Ha

rinch out *vtphr* to RINSE clothes V.9.8. ɹɪnʃ ... æ·ət Y, ɹɪnʃ ... aːt Y, ɹɪnʃ ... uːt Y

rind *1. n* What do you call the outer skin of bacon? III.12.6. Eng. ⇒ **bacon-rind, scram, skin, sward, swath**

2. vt to RENDER fat into lard III.12.9. ɹaɪnd Cu

3. n HOAR-FROST VII.6.6. ʁɛɪnd Nb, ʁɛɪn Nb, ɹaːnd Y, rain Cu, ɹaɪn Y, ɹɑɪn Du

4. n the iron TIRE round a cart-wheel I.9.10. ɹɪnd O

5. v to WHITTLE a stick I.7.19. *prppl* ɽɒɪnən So

rindle *n* a RIVULET IV.1.1. ɹɪndl St

rind(s) *n* potato PEELINGS V.7.22.

no -s: ɹɪnd K[old], ɽæːn D, ɹæɪn Brk, ɹɑɪnd K Ha, ɹɔɪnd O, ɹɔɪn Ha, ɽɔɪn Ha, ɹəɪᵊnd Gl, ɽəɪn Do

npl: ɽɒɪnz So W, hɽɒɪnz So, ɹɔɪnz Bk Ess Brk, ɽɔɪnz So, ɹəɪnz Mon

rindy *adj* RANCID, describing bacon V.7.9. ɹɔɪnɪ Ess

rindy frost *n* HOAR-FROST VII.6.6. ɹaːndɪ fɹɒst Y, ɹaɪndɪ fɹɔst Y, ɹaɪnɪ fɹɒst Du

ring *1. n [Show a picture of an old-fashioned cow-house.] What do call this iron thing that slides on the [tethering-]stake? I.3.5.* rɪŋ Man, ʁɪŋ Nb Du, ɹɪŋ Cu Du We La Y Ch Sa St He Wo Wa Mon Gl Nt L Lei R Nf Sf Bk Hrt Ess Brk Sr K Ha Sx, ɹɪŋg La Ch Db Sa St Wa Lei Sx, ɽɪŋ So W Co D Do Ha, hɽɪŋ So, rɛŋ Man Ch

2. n a ring fixed to a manger or partition in a cow-house, to which a tether is attached. ɹɪŋ O Nt L Nth Hu MxL, ɽɪŋ O

⇒ sliding: **angle-iron, bow, clamp, cops, cow-ring, false link, framble, frammle, frampot, hank, iron-loop, link, loop, rediwilly, rid-widdy, ring, ringle, ring-widdy, round-hank, runner, shackle, sliding swivel, swivel, stiddle-ring, *studdle-ring* ⇒ stiddle-ring, thrampwith, thrampwith-ring, torret, widdy, wid-ring**; fixed: **ring, ringle**

3. n a HALO round the moon VII.6.4. ʁɪŋ Nb[probably old x1], ɹɪŋ Du We La Y Ch Db Sa He Wa Mon Gl Nt L Lei R Nth Sf Bk Hrt Ess MxL Brk K Ha Sx, ɹɪŋg La Y Ch[old] Db Sa St, ɽɪŋ O So W Co D Do Ha, ɽɪn So, hɽɪŋ So[old x1], rɛŋ Man, ɹɛŋ Ch Gl, ɽæŋ So

ring-beetle *n* a heavy wooden MALLET I.7.5. ɹɪŋbɪtɬ Mon, ɹɪŋbɪtəɬ He Mon, ɹɪŋbɪtʊɬ Gl

ring-doves *npl* DOVES IV.7.4. ɹɪŋdɛʊz Sf Ess, ɹɪŋdɒuz Nf, ɹɪŋdʌvz C Nf Ess, *sg* ɹɪŋdʌʊ Nf, ɹɪŋdvvz Nf, ɹɪŋdʊvz Y L

ringe *1. vt* to RINSE clothes V.9.8. ʁɪnʒ Nb[old x1], ɹɪnʒ Cu, ʁɪənʒ Nb

2. v to rinse. rɪnʒ Cu, ɹɪnʒ Cu

ringle *1. n* a sliding RING to which a tether is attached in a cow-house I.3.5. ɹɪŋgl Nf, ɹɪŋgɬ Nf Sf Ess K, ɹɪŋgəɬ Ess, ɹɪŋgʊ Ess, ɹɪŋkɬ Ess

2. *n* a ring fixed to a manger or partition in a cow-house, to which a tether is attached. ɹɪŋɫ Nf Ess, ɹɪŋgʊ Ess, ɹɪŋkɫ Ess

ring-nail *n* a LOOSE *PIECE OF* SKIN at the bottom of a finger-nail VI.7.11. *pl* ɹɪŋnæɪɫz Ess

ring-post *n* a TETHERING-STAKE in a cow-house I.3.3. ɹɪŋpoːst Ch

ring-widdy *n* a sliding RING to which a tether is attached in a cow-house I.3.5. ɹɪŋwɪdɪ We La

rinkling *n* a WEAKLING piglet III.8.4. ʁɪŋklən Nb, ɹɪŋklɪn St Lei *[NBM has -g, WMBM and EMBM have no -g]*

rinnick *n* a WEAKLING piglet III.8.4. ɹɪnək Mon Gl, ɾɪnɪk W

rinny *vi-3prpl* they NEIGH, describing the noise horses make in the fields III.10.3(b). ɹɪnɪ La, ɹɪnəɪ La

rinse *v* If some of the clothes you've washed are still sticky with soap, what do you say you do with them? V.9.8. Eng exc. Mon. ⇒ **dip, dolly, nip out, range** ⇒ **ringe, rench, rench out, rense, rense out, rinch, rinch off, rinch out, ringe, rinse out, sind, sipe, slush, stream, stream out, swill, swill out, swill through**

rip *1. v* to BUTT III.2.10. *-ing* ɾɪpən Co

2. *n* a HEDGING-BILL IV.2.5. ɹɪp Sf

3. *n* a BILLHOOK IV.2.6. ɹɪp ɹɪp Ess*[curved blade x2, for trimming x1]*

rip-hook *1. n* a BILLHOOK IV.2.6. ɹɪpʊk Brk, ɾɪpʊk W Ha, həɾːpʊk W

2. *n* an implement used for reaping or for cutting grass. ɹɪpʊk Brk Sx, ɾɪpʊk Do *[Brk/Sx forms designated 'reap-' SBM]*

ripings* *n* big CINDERS from a previous night's fire V.4.3. ɹaɪpɪnz Y

ripples *1. npl* CART-LADDERS I.10.5. ɹɪplz Sa

2. *n* a CART-FRAME I.10.6. ɹɪplz Sa

ripplet *n* a RIVULET IV.1.1. ɹɪplɪt Sr

rise *1. n* a SLOPE IV.1.10. ræɪs Man, ræɪz Man, ɹæɪz Nf, ɾæɪz So, ʁaɪz Nb, ɹaɪz Cu Du We La Y Sa, ɹɑːz Y, ɹɑɪz La Y L Nf Sf Hrt MxL, ɹɔɪz O Hrt Ess, ɾɔɪz O Ha, ɹʌɪz Nf, ɹʌʏz O, ɹəɪᵊz Gl

2. *vt* to put turfs, brushwood, or similar material into a hedge in order to fill gaps, ⇐ to PLASH IV.2.4. *-ing* ɾaːzɪn Co

3. *v* **hasn't risen, hasn't rose, isn't rose, not risen** SAD, describing bread or pastry that has not risen V.6.12. **hasn't risen** ɛznt ɹəzn La; **hasn't rose** ɛnʔ ɹaʊz Ess, hæsnt roːs Man, ɛn t ɹoʊz Wa; **isn't rose** jent ɹoːz Gl; **not risen** noˈ ɹʊzn Cu

4. *n* the season of SPRING VII.3.6. **rise of leaf** ɹaˈɪz ə lɪˈəf L; **the rise of the leaf** ðə ɹɔɪz ə ðə lᵊiːf Sf Ess; **the rise of the year** ðə ɹaˈɪz ə ðə jɪˈə L, ðə ɹɑɪz ə ðə jɪə Bd*[old]*, ðə ɹɔɪz ə ðə jɔɾː Gl *[the rise of the year Gl abstracted from phrase* **the rise and fall of the year**]

5. *vi* to WAX, referring to the moon VII.6.5(a). ʁaɪz

Nb, ɹaɪz L, *prppl* ɹaɪzɪn Y, *-ing* ɹaɪzn We, ɹɑɪz L Nth C, *-ing* ɹɑɪzɪn Ch, *-ing* ɹɒɪzɪn Lei, ɹɔɪz O, ɹəɪz Gl, *-ing* ɹəɪzɪn He, *-ing* əɹəɪzɪn Wo; **on the rise** ɒn ðə ʁaɪz Nb, ɔn ðə ʁaɪz Nb, ɔn ðə ɹaˈɪz L, ɔn ðə ɹɑɪz L Ess, ɒn ðə ɹɑɪz Nth

risen *adj IN* FLOOD, describing a river IV.1.4. ɹɪzn St

risen-on *adj* VERY COLD, describing a person VI.13.19. ɹɪzɒn St

rise up *viphr* to WAX, referring to the moon VII.6.5(a). *-ing* ɹɑɪzɪn ʊp La

rising *1. adj IN* FLOOD, describing a river IV.1.4. *prppl* ɾæːzɪn D, hɾaɪzɪn So, ɹɒɪzɪŋ St, ɾəɪzɪn Do

2. *n* a WHITLOW VI.7.12. ɾɒɪzɪn Do

rising ground *n* a SLOPE IV.1.10. ɹaɪzɪn gɹʊnd Y

risk *n* a STYE in the eye VI.3.10. hɾɪsk So

rissle *n* a SLOPE IV.1.10. ɹɪzl L

risy* *adj* sloping, ⇐ SLOPE IV.1.10. ɾɒɪzi Ha

rit *n* a WEAKLING piglet III.8.4. ɹɪt La Ch St

ritch *n* a TUSSOCK of grass II.2.9. ɹɪtʃ Sa

ritching *vt-ing* to SPRAIN an ankle VI.10.8. ɹɪtʃɪn K *[queried BM]*

rithers *npl* stooks of corn, ⇐ STOOKING II.6.5. ɹaɪðəˡz Db, ɹɛɪðəz Ch

ritling *n* a WEAKLING piglet III.8.4. ɹɪtlɪn La

rits *npl* RUTS made by cartwheels IV.3.9. ɹɪts Du We La Y Db St Lei *[not a WM/EMBM headword]*

rittings *npl* RUTS made by cartwheels IV.3.9. ɹɪtɪnz Y

rive *vt* to PULL somebody's hair VI.2.8. ɹaɪv Y, *-ing* ɹaɪvɪn We, ɹɑːv Y

rivel *vi* to WRINKLE, referring to the skin of very old people VI.11.2. *3prsg* ɹɪvɫz Wo, ɹɪvəl Gl, *3prsg* ɹɪvɫz Wa, ɹɪvəɫ Gl, *prppl* əɹɪvəɫɪn Gl

rivel-backs *npl* loose pieces of skin at the bottom of a finger-nail, ⇐ LOOSE *PIECE OF* SKIN VI.7.11. ɾɪvɫbaks Do

rivelled *adj* wrinkled, describing the skin of very old people, ⇐ WRINKLE VI.11.2. ɹɪvəld Wo

rivelling *n* a LOOSE *PIECE OF* SKIN at the bottom of a finger-nail VI.7.11. ɾɪvlɪn So

rivelly *adj* wrinkled, describing the skin of very old people, ⇐ WRINKLE VI.11.2. ɹɪvəlɪ Wo

rivels *npl* loose pieces of skin at the bottom of a finger-nail, ⇐ LOOSE *PIECE OF* SKIN VI.7.11. ɾɪvɫz Do

rivel up *viphr* to WRINKLE, referring to the skin of very old people VI.11.2. ɹɪvɫ ʌp O

rive out *vtphr* to WRING the neck of a chicken when killing it IV.6.20. ɹaɪv ... uːt Y

river *n* a RIVULET IV.1.1. ɾɛvəɾː Co

river-ground *n* LOW-LYING LAND IV.1.7. ɹɪvəˡgɹaʊnd Sa

river-land *n* LOW-LYING LAND IV.1.7. ɹɪvəland Db

riverlet *n* a RIVULET IV.1.1. ɹɪvəˈlət K

river-meadows *n* LOW-LYING LAND IV.1.7. ɹɪvəˈmɛdəz Mon, ɹɪvəˈmɛdəˈz̩ Gl

riverside land *n* LOW-LYING LAND IV.1.7. ɹɪvəsaˈɪd land L *[noted as 'prob merely descriptive' in EMBM]*

rivet-wheat *n* WHEAT II.5.1. ɹɛvɪʔ-wəiːʔ Hrt

riving *adj* ACTIVE, describing a child VIII.9.1. ɹaɪvɪn Y

riving about *vphr-ing* ACTIVE, describing a child VIII.9.1. ɹaːvɪn əbuːt Y, ɹaɪvɪn əbaʊt La, ɹaɪvɪn əbuːt Y *[marked u.r. NBM]*

rivulet *n* *What do you call any running water smaller than a river?* IV.1.1. ⇒ **beck, brook, burn, creek, dike, dingle, ditch, drain, drill, ea, gill, gote, holl, nailbourn, pinnock, prill, rindle, ripplet, river, riverlet,** *running* **stream, sike, slade, stell, stream, trench**

rize-stake *n* a TETHERING-STAKE in a cow-house I.3.3. ɹaɪzsteːk Y

road *1. n To get from this village to the next in your car, you wouldn't go across the fields, you'd go by ....* IV.3.12. Eng. ⇒ **highroad, highway-road**

2. v to clear reeds annually from a DITCH IV.2.11. ɹoud Nf

3. v to clear weeds from a dike of running water. *-ing* ɹoʊdɪn L

4. n a GATEWAY IV.3.8. ɹoud Brk

5. n the DIRECTION from which the wind blows VII.6.26. ɹɪəd Y, ɹæud Gl, ɹoːd La Ch Db Sa Nt, ɹoud St Wo Wa, ɹuəd La Y, ɹuːd Ch

6. n **in that road, in this road, this road** *IN THIS WAY* IX.10.7. **in that road** ə ðat ɹuəd La; **in this road** ə ðɪs ɹuəd Y L; **that road** ðat ɹuəd Y; **this road** ðɪs ɹoːd La Ch, ðɪs ɹoud St Wo, ðɪs ɹoːᵁd Db He Gl, ðɪs ɹuəd Cu La Y L

roadway *1. n* the GANGWAY in a cow-house I.3.7. ɹoudweːɹ Wo

2. n a PATH through a field IV.3.11. ɹɒdwæi Nf *[marked u.r. EMBM]*

roar *1. vi-3prpl* bulls BELLOW III.10.2. ʁœᴿː Nb, ɹɔː St Wa, ɹɔːz Sr, *-ing* əɹɔːɹɪn Hrt, ɹɔːə Sa St Nf Sf Hrt Ess, ɹɔːəz Ess K, *-ing* ɹɔːəɹɒn Ess, ɹɔːəˈ Sr K, ɹɔːəˈz Sr, ɹɔəɹz He, ɹɔːeᵗ Sr, ɹɔɔᵗz̩ Ha, ɹɔːəᵗ: So W D Do Ha, ɹoːə Ch Sa Nf Sf Hrt Ess, ɹoːəz Mon, ɹoəˈ Nf, ɹoəˈz Brk, ɹoəɹ La, ɹoːeᵗ Sa O Bk, ɹoːəᵗz̩ Sa He Wo Mon Gl Bk, ɹoueᵗz̩ Wo, ɹoˈəɹz̩ O, *-ing* ɹoueəɹən Man, ɹoˈʊəs Man, ɹoʊəˈ K, ɹoʊəᵗ Wa, ɹʊə St, ɹɪəz Y, ɹʊəɹ La, ɹuəᵗː Co D, *pt* ɹuːəᵗːd̩ Co, *prppl* ɹuəᵗːɹɪn D

2. vi-3prpl they MOO, describing the noise cows make during feeding time in the cow-house III.10.4(a). ɹɔːə Ess, *-ing* ɹɔːɹɪn So, ɹɔːəᵗːz̩ Sa, ɹuəᵗː Co D

3. vi-3prpl they MOO, describing the noise cows make in the fields III.10.4(b). ɹɔəɹz He, ɹɔːə Sa Nf Ess, *-ing* ɹɔːɹɪn So, ʁʊɔᴿs Nb, ɹuəᵗː Co D

4. vi to SCREAM VIII.8.11. ɹoˈᵁə Nth, ɹʊə Y*[= 'cry', of a child x2]* L, ɹʊəˈ L, ɹʊəɹ La Y*[=cry x1, old x1]* L, *-ing* ɹʊəɹɪn Y*[crying, of a child]*

roaring *v-ing* SHRIEKING, describing the shrill noise made by a baby VI.5.15. ɹɒʊɹɪn Wa*[old]*, ɹɔːɹɪn So, ɹɔˈəɹˈɔɹ Hu, ɹoˈəɹɪn Nth, ɹoəˈɹɪn Ha, ɹʊəɹɪn La Y*[low loud cry x1]* L

roast *n* a local FESTIVAL or holiday VII.4.11. ɹoʊst Wa

roaster *n* a GRIDIRON V.7.4(a). roustə Man

roasting-bar *n* the *HORIZONTAL* BAR of a crane over a domestic fire V.3.5(a). ɹoustɪnbaː L

roasting-jack *1. n* a CRANE on which a kettle is hung over a domestic fire V.3.4. ɹoustɪndʒek Ess

2. n a GRIDIRON V.7.4(a). ɹeustɪndʒek K

rob *vi-3prpl* burglars STEAL VIII.7.5(a). ɹɒbz Sr

robin-run-in-the-hedge *1. n* BINDWEED II.2.4. ɹɒbɪnɹʊnɪθɛdʒ La, ɹɒbɪnɹʊnɪðɛdʒ La, ɹɒbɪnɹʊnɪnðɛdʒ Ch, ɹɒbɪnɹʊnɪʔɛdʒ Db

2. n GOOSE-GRASS II.2.5. ɹɒbɪnɹʊnɪθɛdʒ La, ɹɒbɪnɹʊnɪnðɛdʒ Y, ɹɒbɪnɹʊnɪtθɛdʒ La, ɹɒbɪnɹʊnɪtɛdʒ La Y, ɹɒbɪnɹʊnɪʔθɛdʒ La, ɹɒbɪnɹʊnɪʔɛdʒ Db, ɹɒbɪnɹʊnɪnðɛdʒ La

robin-run-the-dike *1. n* BINDWEED II.2.4. ʁœːbənʁənðədeɪk Nb

2. n GOOSE-GRASS II.2.5. ʁɒbɪnʁʊnðədeɪk Nb, ɹɒbɪnɹʊnðədaɪk We, ʁɒbɪnʁʊnðədeɪk Nb, ʁɒbnʁʊnðədeɪk Nb

robin-run-up-the-dike *n* GOOSE-GRASS II.2.5. ɹɒbɪnɹʊnuptdaɪk Cu

rock-tree *1. n* a SWINGLE-TREE of a horse-drawn plough harness I.8.3. ɹɔktɹiː Y

2. n an EVENER, the main swingle-tree of a horse-drawn plough harness I.8.4. ɹɒktɹiː Y, ɹɒktɹəɹ Y, ɹɔktɹiː Y *[northern forms with -tree given this definition, although NBM data less specific]*

rod *1. n* a TETHERING-STAKE in a cow-house I.3.3. ʁɒːd Nb, ɹɒd Wa Nt Nf, ɹɒd Y

2. n a SHAFT of a cart I.9.4. ɹɒd Sr K Sx, ɹɒd K

3. n a movable horizontal rod stretching between the shafts of a cart, fixing them to the cart-body and stopping the cart from tipping, ⇐ ROD/PIN I.10.3. ɹɒd Wa Bk*[wood]* Brk

4. n a STICK used to support the shaft of a cart I.11.1. ɹɒd Bk

5. n the *HORIZONTAL* BAR of a crane over a domestic fire V.3.5(a). ɹɒd Db, ɹɒd O

6. n the vertical BAR or CHAIN of a crane over a domestic fire V.3.5(b). ɹɒd Y

rod-horse *n* a SHAFT-HORSE I.6.2. ɹɒdɔːs K, ɹɒdˈɹˈs K, ɹɒdəs K, ɹɒdɔəs K

rod/pin *n* *[Show a picture of a cart.] What do you call this, for keeping the cart-body fixed to the shafts so as to stop it tilting up?* I.10.3. ⇒ **bar, bolt, cart-peg, cart-pin, cart-slip, catch, caving-bar, caving-rod, caving-tree, chain, chain** *and hook,* **chain** *and pin,* **chock, cotter, cotter-pin, cotter-stick, cross-piece, cross-stick, draw-bar, draw-bolt, fastening-rod, front-stick,** *handle and two cleets,* **joggle-pin, joggle-stick, keck-bar, kecker, kecker-bar, keck-rod, keck-stick, kelt-bar, kep-stick, key-pin, key-stick, ladder, ladder-tree, lever, lifter, lim-pin, linch-pin, pea-stick, peg, pin, pinner, plunder-bar, pull-rail, punder, punder-stick, pundle-stick, putt-stick, rod, set-stick, shoot-stick, slip, sliper, slip-iron, slot, slot-bar, slot-stick, sluver, snubber, spindle, spreader-bar, sprig, standard, stander, standle-pin, stay, stick, straight-stick, strap-stick, sword, sword-peg, sword-pin, tinge-bat, tip-bar, tipe-stick, tipper, tip-pin, tipping-bar, tip-stick, toe-stick, tongue, tongue-peg, tongue-pin, trap, trapping-iron, trap-iron, trap-stick, trigger-bar, trigger-bat, trigger-stick, trip-stick, tumbril-stick** *[definitions reflect frequent lack of precise evidence of material culture in BM]*

rods *1. npl [Show a picture of some stacks. What do you call this (i.e. thatch)?] What do you fasten it down with? [Wood laid over thatch.]* II.7.7(b3). ɹɒdz Mon K. ⇒ **spars, straps, stretchers, thatching-rods, thatch-rods**

2. npl the SHAFTS of a cart I.9.4. ɹɒdz Sr K Sx, ɹɔdz K

rod-stake *n* a TETHERING-STAKE in a cow-house I.3.3. ɹɒdstiːk Db, ɹɒdstɪək Y, ɹɔdsteːk Db, *pl* ɹɒtstɛɪks St

rod-stay *n* a STICK used to support the shaft of a cart I.11.1. *pl* ɹɒdstɛɪz Sx

rod-stick *n* the iron stay connecting the beam with the side of a cart, ⇐ CROSS-BEAM END I.10.1. ɹɔdstɪk Y

roining *adj* ON HEAT, describing a cow III.1.6. ɹɑɪnɪn Ch

roller *1. n* a device used to prevent a cart or wagon from going backwards on a hill, ⇐ PROP/CHOCK I.11.2. ɹɒʊlə Gl, *pl* ɹɒʊɫəˡz Sr, ɹɒʊləˡ Wa, ɽɒʊɫəˡ: W, ɹɔʊlə L Lei, ɹɔʊɫə Ess, ɹɔʊlɪ L, ɹɔʊɹəl L, ɹɔʊləˡ Brk, ɹɔʊɫə Sx, ɽoːɫəˡ: So W Co D Do Ha, ɾoʊɫəˡ: So *[probably a chock, but definition 'special implement' SBM]*

2. n a DRAG used to slow a wagon I.11.3. ɹɒʊlə Lei

3. n a DIAPER V.11.3. ɹɔʊlə Ess

rolling-board *n* a PASTE-BOARD V.6.5. ɹoːɫɪnboəˡɽd Brk

roll over *viphr* **roll over backwards** to turn HEAD OVER HEELS IX.1.10. *pt* ɹɛʊlt ʊəɹ bakəːɹts La

roll up *vtphr* to WRAP a parcel VII.2.9. ʁɔʊ … ʌp Nb

roly-poly *adv* HEAD OVER HEELS IX.1.10. ɹoːlɪpoːlɪ Sa

romanies *npl* GIPSIES VIII.4.12. ɹɒmnɪz Y L, ɹʌʊmənɪz Ess, ɹoʊmənɪz Wo Nf

romeos *npl* GIPSIES VIII.4.12. ɹʌʊmiːʌʊz Ess, ɾoːmɪjoːz Do

romping *v-ing* ON HEAT, describing a cow III.1.6. ɹɔːmpɪn Ch

rood-post *n* a TETHERING-STAKE in a cow-house I.3.3. ɹʊdpɒst Cu

rood-stake *n* a TETHERING-STAKE in a cow-house I.3.3. ɹɪdstɪək We Y, ɹɪdsteak We, ɹɪʊdstɪɛk Cu, ɹɪədstɪək Cu, ɹʊdstɪək Y, ɹʊdstɪək We Y, ɹʊdsteːk Y, ɹʊdstɛək Y, ɹədstɹak Cu, ɹədstɪək Y, ɹədsteak Cu We La, ɹədstɛːˈək Y

rood-stower *n* a TETHERING-STAKE in a cow-house I.3.3. ɹədstaʊə Du *[compare **redster**]*

roof *1. n [Show a picture of some houses.] What do you call this [indicate a roof]? [Is **thack** used?]* V.1.2. Eng. ⇒ **ridge, thack, thatch, thatch-roof**

2. n the RIDGE of a house roof V.1.2(a). ʁɪːf Du

rook *v* to ROOT, what a pig does when it digs the ground with its snout III.9.2. ɹuːk Bk

rooking hen *n* a BROODY HEN IV.6.7. ɹʊkɪn ɛn Y

rook-scarer *n* a SCARECROW II.3.7. ɹʊkskɛˈəɹə Ess

rooky *adj* bit rooky SILLY VIII.9.3. bɪt ɹʊkɪ Sx

room *1. n* the SITTING-ROOM of a house V.2.2. ʁʊm Du, ʁuːm Nb*[old]*, ɹuːm Y*[modern x1]* Nt L Hu

2. n a BEDROOM V.2.3. ɹɪːm La

roons* *npl* MUSHROOMS II.2.11. ɹuːnz Gl Ess *[EMBM headword **rooms**, but response **roons**]*

roost *1. n* a HAY-LOFT over a cow-house I.3.18. ɹᵁuːs La

2. n a PERCH for hens IV.6.3. ɾYːst Co D, hɾʌst So, ɹʊst He Mon Gl Sf, ɾuːs Man, ɹuːst St Mon Gl L C Ess Brk K Sx, ɹuːs Bk Ess Sx, *pl* ɹuːsəz St, ɾuːst So W Co

roosting-baulk *n* a PERCH for hens IV.6.3. ɹuːstɪnbɔːk Y

root *1. v* You know how the pig uses its snout for digging up the ground. What do you say it does? III.9.2. ɹɪʏt Cu, ɹɪʊt Y St, *-ing* ɹɪʊtn Cu, ɹɪuːt Ch Db Wo, *-ing* ɹɪuːtɪn Sa, ɹɪuːtn Du, *-ing* ɹᵁuːtʔn Nf, *-ing* ʁɪətn Nb, ɹɪət Cu We La Y, *-ing* ɹɪətn Nb Du, ɹɪʏt La Ch, *-ing* ɹʊʏːtɪn La, *-ing* ɾʏːtɪn D, *-ing* ɾʏːdɪn D, *-ing* ɾʏːtən D, *-ing* ɹʏuːtɪn Sa, ɹɛʊt Db Sa Wo Wa O Nth, *-ing* ɹɛʊtɪn Y St, ɹɛʊʔ Bk, *-ing* ɹɛʊʔɪn O, *-ing* ɹæʏtɪn D, ɹæʊt He Wa, *-ing* ɹæʊtɪn Wo, ɾæʊt W, *-ing* ɾæʊtɪn So Do, *-ing* ɾæʊtən Ha, *-ing* ɹaʊtn Ha, ɹaʊt Sa Wo, *-ing* ɹaʊtɪn W, ɹɒʊt Gl, ɾɒʊt W, *-ing* ɹʌʔn K, ɹʌʊt Gl, ʁʊt Du, *-ing* ʁʊtn Nb, ɹʊt Cu C Sf Ess, *-ing* ɹɪtɪn O, *-ing* ɹʊtn Nf, *prppl* ɹʊʔn Ess, *-ing* ɹʊʔn Ess, *-ing* ɹʊɪtɪn Y, *-ing* ruːʔn Man, ɹuːt La Y Ch Db Sa St Gl O Nt L Lei R Nth Ess K, *3prsg* ɹiuts Brk, *-ing* ɹuːtɪn He Wa MxL Brk Sr, *-ing* ɹuːʔɪn L Bd, *-ing* ɹuːtn Du Nf, *-ing* ɽuːtɪn So K Do, *-ing* hɽuːtɪn So, *-ing* ɽuːtən Do, ɹɤːt Lei Nf, ɹəʊt Gl, *-ing* ɹəɪtɪn Brk, *-ing* ɽəɪtɪn W, *-ing* ɹəɪːtɪn Wo. ⇒ **dig, dig up, grub, grub up, hock about, hock up**, *hook* ⇒ **howk**, *hook about* ⇒ **howk about**, *hook up* ⇒ **howk up, howk, howk about, howk up, moont, moot, muddle, muzzle, muzzle up**, *mwnt* ⇒ **moont, nuzzle, plough, plough up, rook, root about, rootle, root up**, *rout* ⇒ **root**, *rout up* ⇒ **root up, rox up, snout**

2. *n Now let's talk about the parts of a tree [show a picture of a tree]. What do you call this [indicate a root]?* IV.12.1. Eng. ⇒ **fang, more, toe**

3. *n* the CORE of a boil VI.11.7. ɹʊɪt Y

root about *vphr* to ROOT, what a pig does when it digs the ground with its snout III.9.2. *-ing* ɹʊʔn əbɛʊt Ess

root-butt *n* a tree STUMP IV.12.4. ɽuːtbʌt So

rootle *v* to ROOT, what a pig does when it digs the ground with its snout III.9.2. ɹʌʔɬ Hrt, ɹʊtɬ Sf, ɹʊʔɬ C Sf, *-ing* ɹʊʔɬɪn Hrt, *-ing* ɹʊtʊʔɬən Ess, ɹuːtl Nth Nf, *-ing* ɹuːtlɪn Bd, ɹᵁuʔəl Nf, *-ing* ɹuːʔlɪn Bd, ɹuːtɬ Nth Hu, ɹuːʔɬ Nth Hu

root up 1. *vphr* to ROOT, what a pig does when it digs the ground with its snout III.9.2. *-ing* ruːʔən ʊp Man

2. *vtphr* to ROOT III.9.2. *-ing* ɹʊətɪn ... ʊp Y, *prppl* ɽæʊtɪn ... ʌp W, *-ing* rautɪn ... ʌp Ha, *-ing* rʊɪtɪn ... ʊp Y

rope 1. *n* a TETHER for a cow I.3.4. ɹʌʊp Sf

2. *n* a HALTER for a cow I.3.17. ɹʊəp L

3. *n* a TETHERING-ROPE used to tie up a horse I.4.2. ɹʌʊp C Sf, ɹoːp La Ch Db Nt, ɽoːp O, ɹʊʊp Wa Lei, ɹʊəp La Y

rope-halter *n* a HALTER for a cow I.3.17. ɹoːpɔːtəɹ La

ropekin *n* TWINE used to fasten thatch on a stack II.7.7(b1). ɹʌʊpkɪn Ess

rope-maker *n* a ROPE-TWISTER II.7.8. ɹeːᵊpmakə Du, ɹeapmakə We

rope(s) *n* [*Show a picture of some stacks. What do you call this (i.e. thatch)?] What do you fasten it down with? [Material tied over thatch.]* II.7.7(b2).

no -s: ɽoːp Co D, ɽuːp Co*[straw] [possibly sg BM]*
-s: ɹiaps Y, rɪˑᵊps Cu, ɹiəps Nb*[straw]*, *sg* ɹiəp Cu Du*[hay]*, *sg* ɹeap We, ʁøːps Nb, ɹoːps Brk, ɽoːps So*[straw]* D, ʁʊps Nb, ɹʊəps Y, ɽuːps Co D*[straw]* ⇒ **bands, bind, binding, bond(s), coir, coir-rope(s), hay-band(s), hay-bonds, hay-ropes, hazel-bands, over-ropes, reed-beam, reeden- rope, reed-rope, scud(s), simes, stack-bands, straw, straw-band(s), straw-bond(s), straw- rope(s), suggan, tar-rope, thatch-rope, thimes, thumb-beans, thumb-binds, thumb-bonds,**

thumble-beams, thumble-bean, thumb-ropes, thumb-simes; ⇒ also **belt-rope, easing-rope** [*separation of ropes and twine terms is problematical: see also twine*]

ropes *n* CHITTERLINGS III.12.2. ɹʌʊps Sf, ɹoːps Ch, ɹʊups St Sf [*taken as ropps WMBM*]

rope-tie *n* a TETHERING-ROPE used to tie up a horse I.4.2. ɹɔptɑɪ L, rʊuptæɪ Man

rope-twister *n What do you make a straw rope with?* II.7.8. roˈuptwɪstə Man. ⇒ **band-hook, band-maker**, *band-spinner* ⇒ **bond-spinner, band-twirler, band-twister, band-winder, belly-auger, binder**, *bind-hook* ⇒ **bond-hook, bind-turner, bind-twister, bond-hook, bond-maker, bond-spinner, bond-turner, bond-twister, bond-winch, bond-winder, bowl-turner, crank, hand-fork, hay-band-maker, hay-band-twister, hay-rake, hay-tweezers, hay-twister, hook, jenny**, *pair of cranks*, *pair of twisters*, **rake, rope-maker, rope-winder, scud, scud-winder, sime-twiner, sime-twister**, *sked* ⇒ **scud, sked-binder, sked-winder, spindle-hook, spinner, spinning-jenny, straw-hook, straw-rope-twister, straw-spinner, straw-turner, straw-twiner, straw-twister, straw-whipple, straw-winder, swintle, swivel, thime-spinner, thraw-crook, turnel, turner, turner-up, tweezers, twiddler, twiner, twister(s), twisting-wire, twizzler, whankie, whim-wham, whipple, wimble, winch, winder, windlass, wink**

rope-winder *n* a ROPE-TWISTER II.7.8. ɹʊəpwaˈɪndə L

rope-yarn *n* STRING used to tie up a grain-sack I.7.3. ɹɔʊpjɑːn Ess, ɹʌʊpjən Ess

ropps 1. *n* CHITTERLINGS III.12.2. ɹaps Db St Lei, ɹɒps La Ch Db Nt, ɹɔps La Y

2. *n* the large intestines of a pig. ɹɒps La

ropy-milk *n* BEESTINGS V.5.10. ɹoupɪmɛłk Brk

rose *adj* IN FLOOD, describing a river IV.1.4. ɹoʊz O

rose-bubs *npl* HIPS of the wild rose IV.11.7. ɽoːzbʊbz Co

rose-hips *npl* HIPS of the wild rose IV.11.7. ɹʊʊzɪps Wa, ɹoːzɪps Y, ɹoʊzhɪps Nf

rose-pips *npl* HIPS of the wild rose IV.11.7. ɹoːzpɪps La, ɹoʊzpɪps Nf

rose up *adj* IN FLOOD, describing a river IV.1.4. ɽoːz ʌp Co

rosping *v-ing* BELCHING VI.13.13. ɹɔːspɪn Sf

rot *vi* to SPOIL, referring to meat or fish V.7.10. ɹɔt MxL

rotten 1. *adj* HEAVING (*WITH MAGGOTS*) IV.8.6. ɹɒtn Y

2. *adj* **go rotten** to SPOIL, referring to meat or

fish V.7.10. ga ɹɒtn Y, goʊ ɹɒtn Wa, gʊə ɹɒʔn Y, *3prsg* ganz ɹɒtən Y

3. *adj* BAD, describing an egg V.7.11. ræʔn Man, ʀœːtn Nb, ɹɑtn Gl*[old]*, ɹɑːʔtn Nf, rɒtn Cu, ʀɒtn Nb Du, ɹɒtn Cu Du We La Y Ch Db*[old x1]* Nf, ɹɒtən Y, ɹɒʔn Y O Nf Bd Sr Sx, ʀɔtn Nb, ɹɔtn La Y Ch L K Ha, ɹɔʔn L C Ess

4. *adj* ILL, describing a person who is unwell VI.13.1(b). ɹɒtn Y St*[old]*, ɹɒʔn Y K, ɹɔtn La Wo

rough 1. *adj* RESTIVE, describing a horse III.5.6. ɹʊf Ch *[marked u.r. WMBM]*

2. *adj* TANGLED, describing hair VI.2.5. ɹʊf Y He O; **all rough** ɔːl ɹʌf Ess

3. *adj* ILL, describing a person who is unwell VI.13.1(b). ɹʌf Ess, ɽʌf W D Do Ha, ɹəf Gl; **bit rough** bɪt ɽʌf Co, bɪd ɽʌf D

4. *adj* SICK, describing an animal that is unwell VI.13.1(c). ɹʌf Ess, ɽʌf So W D Do; **bit rough** bɪt ɽʌf Co D

rough-apron *n* a working APRON V.11.2(a). ɹʌfeːɹən Sa, ɹʌfeːpəˡːn̩ Sa

rough-brat *n* a working APRON V.11.2(a). ɹʊfbɹat We La Y

rough-broom 1. *n* a MUCK-BRUSH I.3.14. ɹʌfbɹuːm Sa

2. *n* a BROOM used for sweeping outdoors V.9.10. ɹʌfbɹʊm Sa He, ɹʌfbɹuːm Sa

rough-brush *n* a BROOM used for sweeping outdoors V.9.10. ɹʊfbɹʊʃ Y He

rough carpenter *n* a CARPENTER or JOINER who does heavy, less skilled work VIII.4.3. ɹʊf kaːpntə L

rough clothes *n* ORDINARY CLOTHES VI.14.20. ɹʌf kloʊz C

roughed up *adj* **all roughed up** TANGLED, describing hair VI.2.5. ɔːɫ ɹʌft ʌp Ha

roughet *n* a TUSSOCK of grass II.2.9. ɽʌfɪt D

rough fat *n* the FAT round the kidneys of a pig III.12.7. ɹʊf fat Db St

rough grass *n* a TUSSOCK of grass II.2.9. ɹʌf gɹaːs Ess, ɽʌf gɹaːs Ha; **old rough grass** ʌuˑl ɹʌf gɹæːs Nf; **patch of rough grass** patʃ ə hɹʌf gɹæːs So; **piece of rough grass** piːs ə ɹʊf gɹas eY *[rough grass marked u.r. SBM but not EMBM – probably a type of grass]*

rough patch *n* a TUSSOCK of grass II.2.9. ɹʌf patʃ Nth

roughs *n* ORDINARY CLOTHES VI.14.20. ɹʌfs Bd

rough-stone *n* a WHETSTONE II.9.10. ɽʌfstoːn Do

rough tog *n* ORDINARY CLOTHES VI.14.20. ɹəf tɒg Gl

rouk *n* **on the rouk** ACTIVE, describing a child VIII.9.1. ɒn ðə ɹaʊk Y *[marked u.r. NBM]*

round 1. *adj* A ball isn't square, it is .... IX.1.1. Eng. ⇒ **rounden, roundy**

2. *n* a RUNG of a ladder I.7.15. ɹɛʊn Wo Bk Ess Sr Sx, *pl* ɹɛʊnz Sa Wa Nth Hu Bd Hrt Brk K, ɹɛʊnd Wa O Hrt Sx, *pl* ɹɛʊndz C Ha, *pl* ræʊnz Ha, ɹæʊn He Lei,

pl ɹæʊnz Wo MxL Ha, ɽæʊn W, *pl* ɽæʊnz Ha, *pl* ɹæʊndz St Wa O, ɽæʊnd Ha, ɹaʊn Sa Wo, *pl* ɽaʊnz So, ɹaʊnd St, ɽʊʊnd W, *pl* ɹʌʊndz Brk, ɹəʊn Sa He Wo Gl, *pl* ɹəʊnz Brk, *pl* ɽəʊnz W, ɹəʊnd He, *pl* ɹəʊndz Brk

3. *n* a SLICE of bread V.6.10. ɹɛʊnd Nf*[old x2]*, *pl* ɹɛʊndz C, *pl* ɹæʊndz L, ɹaʊnd Ch L, ɹəʊnd He

4. *n* **round of bread, round of bread and butter, round of butter** a PIECE *OF BREAD AND BUTTER* V.6.11(a). **round of bread** ɹɛʊnd ə bɹɪˑd Nf, ɹɛʊnd ə bɹɛd Nf; **round of bread and butter** ɹɛʊnd ə bɹɛd n̩ bʌʔə Nf; **round of butter** ɹɛʊnd ə bʌʔə Nf

5. *n* **round of bread and jam** a PIECE *OF BREAD AND BUTTER AND JAM/SUGAR* V.6.11(b). ɹɛʏnd ə bɹɛd n̩ dʒam Nf

6. *adj* SLIPPERY VII.6.14. ɹaʊnd Sa

roundabout *n* a CRANE on which a kettle is hung over a domestic fire V.3.4. ɹəʊndəbəʊt Mon

roundel *n* a SLICE of bread V.6.10. ɹɛʊndɫ Sf

rounden *adj* ROUND, describing a ball IX.1.1. ɽæʏndən Co

round-hank *n* a sliding RING to which a tether is attached in a cow-house I.3.5. ɹaʊndaŋk La Y, ɹaʊndɒŋk La, ɹəʊndaŋk Y

round mow *n* a round stack, ⇐ STACKS II.7.1. ɽœʏn mʏː D

round pond *n* a POND IV.1.5. ɹæʊnd pɒnd L

round ricks *n* round STACKS II.7.1. ɹɛʊnd ɹɪks MxL*[corn and hay]*, *sg* ɹɛʊn ɹɪk Brk K*[old]*, ɽœʏn ɽɪks D, *sg* ɹæʊn ɹɪk Wa, *sg* ɹæʊnd ɹɪk Wa, *no -s* ɹaʊnd ɹɪk St

roundy *adj* ROUND, describing a ball IX.1.1. ɹɔʊndɪ L, ɹuːndɪ L

rouped *adj* HOARSE VI.5.16. ɹᵊupt Y

roupy *adj* HOARSE VI.5.16. ʀuːpɪ Nb, ɹuːpɪ Du

rout 1. *vi-3prpl* bulls BELLOW III.10.2. ɹɔːts Y, ɹʊəts Y, *-ing* ɹʊətɪn Y

2. *n* a local FESTIVAL or holiday VII.4.11. ɹʊt St

rove* *n* a group of furrows 2 feet broad, ⇐ RIDGES II.3.2. ɹʌʊv Ess

row 1. *n* a row or SWATH of mown grass cut for hay-making II.9.4. ɹɒʊ Nf, ɹuː Sr, ɽuː So

2. *n* a swath of grass cut for hay-making, dried, and ready for carting. ɹɒʊ Sr

3. *vi-3prpl* they MEW, referring to cats III.10.6. *-ing* ɹɛʊŋ Ess

rowen(s) 1. *n* AFTERMATH, a second crop of grass II.9.17.

no -s: ɹɛʊɪn Hrt K, ɹæʊɪn Hrt Ess

-s: ɹɛʊɪnz K Sx, ɹɛʊwɪnz Sx, ɹæʊwɪnz K, ɹaʊənz Sf, ɹɒʊ-ɪnz Sx

2. *n* a third crop of grass. ɹɛʊwɪnz K

rowet *n* a TUSSOCK of grass II.2.9. ɹəwət Brk

rows *npl* the RIDGES between furrows in a ploughed field II.3.2. ɹɒʊz Sx

rox up *vtphr* to ROOT, what a pig does when it digs the ground with its snout III.9.2. *-ing* ɽɪksɪn ... ʌp Ha

rub *1. n* a WHETSTONE made of stone II.9.10. ɹɛb Sf Ess, ɹʌb Nf Sf Ess, ɹʊb Nf, ɹʏb Nf

2. n a whetstone made of unspecified material. ɹɛb Sf, ɹʌb Sf Ess

[see note at rubber]

3. n a GRINDSTONE IV.2.7. ɹʌb Ess

rubber *1. n* a WHETSTONE made of stone II.9.10. ɹʌbə Bk MxL, *pl* ɹʌbɐz K, ɹʌbəɹ He, ɹʌbəˡ Sr K, ɹʌbəˡ Sa He Nth Bk Brk Sr Sx, ɽʌbəˡː W Ha, ɹʊbə Wo Wa, ɹʊbəˡ Brk K, ɹʊbəˡ Sa He Wo Wa Brk Sx

2. n a wooden implement, greased and sanded, used to sharpen a scythe. ɹʌbəˡ Sr

3. n a whetstone made of unspecified material. ɹʌbə Mon Bk Hrt, ɹʌbəˡ K, ɹʌbɽ O, ɹʌbəˡ Mon O Brk Sr K, ɽʌbɽ O, ɽʌbəˡː W Ha, ɹʊbəˡ Brk K, ɹʊbəˡ Wa Mon Gl O Bk, ɽʊbɽ O, ɹəbəˡ Gl

[Rub is treated as 'of stone' in EMBM, but sometimes marked as 'material unspecified'; rubber, similarly treated in SBM, receives Edd note that it is not stone at one locality in Sr. Some local stone-names given ('silt', 'white stone', etc). Entries for rub and rubber are here simplified to stone/grease and grit/metal/unspecified, avoiding dubious division by stone-type.]

rubbing *v-ing* SCRATCHING VI.1.2. ɹʌbɪn Nf

rubbish *1. n What do you call any worthless stuff that you throw away?* V.1.15. Eng. ⇒ **bunk, clutter, garbage, junk, kelter, kelterment, ket, ketment, lumber, muck, mullocks, offal, pouse, rammel, refuge,** *refuse* ⇒ **refuge, rummage, salvage, slink, slush, waste, waste stuff;** ⇒ also **raff-house**

2. n WEEDS, unwanted plants that grow in a garden II.2.1. ɹɒbɪʃ K, ɹʌbɪʃ O Hu C Sf Bk Hrt Ess K Ha, ɹʌbɪdʒ Sx, ɐʏbɪʃ Nb, ɹʏbɪtʃ Nf, ɐʊbɪʃ Nb, ɹʊbɪʃ We La Y Db Nt L Lei Nth, ɹʊbɪdʒ L

rubbish-bin *n* an ASH-MIDDEN V.1.14. ɹəbɪʃbɪn Sr

rubbish-dump *n* an ASH-MIDDEN V.1.14. ɹʌbɪʃdʌmp Ess*[modern]*

rubbish-heap *n* an ASH-MIDDEN V.1.14. ɹʌbɪʃiːp He Hrt, ɹʌbɪʃɛɪp Bk, ɽʌbɪʃhaɪp Do, ɹʊbɪʃiːp Wa, ɹʊbɪʃɪəp La

rubbish-hole *n* an ASH-MIDDEN V.1.14. ɹʌbɪʃɔʊɫ Brk

rub-stone *n* a WHETSTONE II.9.10. ɹʌbstɛʊn Hrt, ɹʌbstɔʊn Hu, ɹʌbstʌʊn Hrt, ɹʌbstən C Bd Hrt, ɹʏbston Nf, ɹʊbstɔn L, ɹʊbstɔʊn L R Hu, ɹʊbstʊʊn L Lei, ɹʊbstʊn C, ɹʊbstʊən L, ɹʊbstən L Lei R Nth

ruches *npl* RUTS made by cartwheels IV.3.9. ɹʊtʃɪz La

ruck *1. n* **ruck of dung, ruck of (cow-)muck** a CLOT OF COW-DUNG II.1.6. **ruck of dung** ɹʌk ə

dʌŋ Sa; **ruck of muck** ɹʌk ə mʌk Sa, ɹʊk ə mʊk Sa Wo; **ruck of cow-muck** ɹʊk ə kɛuːmʊk Wo

2. n a TUSSOCK of grass II.2.9. *pl* ɹʊks Wa

3. n a HAYSTACK II.9.13. *pl* ɹʊks Cu, ɹʊk Du*[round]*, *pl* ɹʊks Du*[usually inside]*

4. n an ASH-MIDDEN V.1.14. ɹʊk Wa

5. vi to WRINKLE, referring to the skin of very old people VI.11.2. ɹʊk Nf

6. n **drop in a ruck** to FAINT VI.13.7. dɹɒp ɪn ə ɹʌk Sa

rucking-pikel* *n* a HAY-FORK with a short shaft I.7.11. ɹʊkɪnpaɪkɪl Ch

rucks *1. npl* STACKS II.7.1. ɹʌks Sa, *sg* ɹʊk Du*[rare]*

2. npl long stacks for hay. *sg* ɹʊk Du

3. npl round stacks. ɹʊks Cu*[corn and hay]*, *sg* ɹɪk Du*[corn and hay]*

4. npl COCKS of hay II.9.12. ɹʊks Man, ɹʊks Db St

5. npl large cocks consisting of three footcocks. *sg* ɹʊk Ch

6. npl RUTS made by cartwheels IV.3.9. ɹʌks Mon Sf Hrt Ess

ruck up and punch *vtphr* to KNEAD dough V.6.4. ɹʊk ... ʊp ən pʊnʃ ... St

rud *v* to MARK sheep with colour to indicate ownership III.7.9. ɹʊd Cu*[on sheep kept in fields]* Y, ɹuˑd Nb

rudder *n* the UDDER of a cow III.2.5. ɹʊdəˡ Wo

ruddicks *n* SCRAPS left after rendering lard III.12.10. ɹʊdɪks Du

ruddle *v* to MARK sheep with colour to indicate ownership III.7.9. ɹʊdl La Y, ɽʊdɫ O

ruffled *adj* TANGLED, describing hair VI.2.5. ɹʌfɫd MxL, ɹʊfəld Y

ruffled up *adj* TANGLED, describing hair VI.2.5. ɹʊfəlt ʊp Ch

ruggle-back *n* a LOOSE *PIECE OF* SKIN at the bottom of a finger-nail VI.7.11. ɽʌgɫbak Do

rulley *1. n* a WAGON I.9.2. ɹɒlɪ Du, ɐʊlɪ Nb, ɹʊlɪ Y, *pl* ɹʊlɪz Du, ɹəlɪ Y

2. n a wagon with detachable sides. ɐɒlɪ Nb, ɐʌlɪ Nb, ɹʊlɪ Nb

3. n a wagon without sides. ɐalɪ Nb, ɐɒlɪ Nb, ɐʌlɪ Nb, ɹʊlɪ Du Y

rum *adv* VERY VIII.3.2. ɹʌm Nf

rummage *n* RUBBISH V.1.15. ɽʌmɪdʒ So Co D, hɽʌmɪdʒ So

rummage-heap *n* an ASH-MIDDEN V.1.14. ɽʌmɪdʒiːp D

rummager *n* an ACTIVE child VIII.9.1. ɽʌmɪdʒəˡː Co

rummage-shed *n* an ASH-MIDDEN V.1.14. hɽʌmɪdʒʃed So

rummaging *v-ing ON* HEAT, describing a cow III.1.6. ɽʌmədʒɪn D

rummet *n* DANDRUFF VI.1.3. ɽʌmət D

rump *1. n* the HIP-BONE of a cow III.2.1. ɹʏmp Nf *[marked as u.r. in BM, but* **hip, hook, huggin, huvvon, pin** *all recorded as rr. without -bone]*
2. n the ARSE VI.9.2. ɹʌmp Ess Sr

rump-bone *n* the HIP-BONE of a cow III.2.1. ɹʌmpbʌʊn Ess, ɹʌmpbon Nf, ɹʊmpbʊən Y

run *1. n* a HEN-HOUSE I.1.6. əˤːn So
2. n the GANGWAY in a cow-house I.3.7. ɽʌn Co
3. n a SHEEP-HOLE IV.2.8. ɹʊˈn Brk
***4. n* a RUNG of a ladder I.7.15. ɹʌn Sa, *pl* ɹʌnz Sr
5. vt to RENDER fat into lard III.12.9. ɹʌn O

runch(es) *n* CHARLOCK II.2.6.
no -es: ʁʌnʃ Nb, ʁʏnʃ Nb ʁʊnʃ Nb, ɹʊnʃ Du Y
-es: rʊnʃɪz Cu

run down *vtphr* to RENDER fat into lard III.12.9. ɹʌn ... dɛʊn O Nf Sr K, *-ing* ɹʌnɪn dɛʊn Nf Sx, *-ing* ɹʌnɪn dəʊn Sx, ɽʌn ... dœʏn D, ɽʌn ... dæʏn Co, ɹʏn ... dɛʊn Nf, ɹʊn ... dəʊn K

rung *1. n [Show a picture of a ladder.] What do you call this [pointing to a rung]?* I.7.15. *pl* rɒŋs Man, ɹɒŋ Mon Gl, ɽɒŋ W D Do, *pl* ɽɒŋz So Ha, ʁʌŋ Nb, ɹʌŋ He Mon O Hrt Ess, *pl* ɹʌŋz Nth Hu Bk MxL Brk Sr K, ɽʌŋ So Ha, *pl* ɽʌŋz D, hɽʌŋ So, *pl* ʁʏ·ŋz Nb, rʊŋ Y, ʁʊŋ Nb, *pl* ʁʊŋz Du, ɹʊŋ Cu Du La Y He Mon Gl, *pl* ɹʊŋz Nb We Wa, ɹʊŋg Sa Lei, *pl* ɹʊŋgz La Ch St, *pl* ɽʊŋz O, *pl* ɹəŋz Gl; **ladder-rung** *pl* ɫɛdəˤːɽɒŋz D.
⇒ **bar, ladder-round,** *ladder-*rung, *ladder-stales* ⇒ **ladder-stall, ladder-stall, ladder-stay, lat, prʊʊn, rail, rance, rim, round, run, spar, spell, spindle, spoke, stab, stabber, staff, stale, stall, stap, stave,** *staver* ⇒ **stabber/stavver, stavver, stay, stee-spell, stee-step, step, stower, tread**
2. n the CROSS-BEAM END of a cart I.10.1. ɹʊŋ L

runned over *adj* IN FLOOD, describing a river IV.1.4. ɹʌnd ʌʊvə Sf *[see note at* **flood***]*

runner *1. n* a sliding RING to which a tether is attached in a cow-house I.3.5. rʌnə Mon, ɹʊnəɹ Y, ɹʊnəˤ Sa
2. n a TETHERING-ROPE used to tie up a horse I.4.2. ʁʊnɔʁ Nb, ɹʊnə L
3. n the STEM of a corn-plant II.5.2(a). ɹʌnə Nf

runners *1. n* CHITTERLINGS III.12.2. ɹʌnəz Nf, ɹʌnəˤz̩ Bk, ɹʊnəz Nt
2. n small chitterlings used as sausage-skins. ɹʌnəz Nf

running full *adj* IN FLOOD, describing a river IV.1.4. ɹʌnɪn fʊʊ Ha

running over *adj* IN FLOOD, describing a river IV.1.4. prppl ɹʌnɪn ʊʊvə Nf, ɹʊnɪn oːvə Ch, ɹʊnɪn ʊəᴶ Ch *[see note at core entry]*

runnings *n* URINE in a cow-house I.3.10. ɹʌnənz Sf

run over *viphr-ed HAS NOT* HELD, referring to a cow that has not conceived III.1.7. ɹʌn ʊʊvə Nf Sf; **runned over** ɹʌnd ʊʊvə Nf Sf

runs back *vphr-3prsg* **runs back into** he RESEMBLES VIII.1.9. ɹʌnz bæk ɪntʊ MxL

runt *n* a WEAKLING piglet III.8.4. ɹʌnt Sa Ess, ɹʊnt Db St Lei K, ɽʌnt Ha

runtling *n* a WEAKLING piglet III.8.4. ɹʊntlɪn Lei

run-through *n* a SHEEP-HOLE IV.2.8. ɹʊnθɹuː Lei K

runts *npl* SPRING ONIONS V.7.16. ɹɔːnts Bd

run up *viphr* to WARP, referring to wood IX.2.9. ɹʊn ʊp Db St

rush-bearing *n* a local FESTIVAL or holiday VII.4.11. ɹʊʃbəɹɪn La

russling *n* the PARTITION between stalls in a cow-house I.3.2. ɽʌslɪn So *[queried SBM]*

russling-post *n* a TETHERING-STAKE in a cow-house I.3.3. rʌslɪnpʊʊst So

rusted *adj* RANCID, describing bacon V.7.9. ɽəstɪt O

rusty *1. adj* RANCID, describing bacon V.7.9. ɹaʊstɪ Ch*[old]*, ɹʌstɪ MxL Brk*[old x2]* Sr Ha Sx, ɽʌstɪ Do, ɽʌsti So Co D Do Ha, ɹʊstɪ Brk, ɽəstɪ O
2. adj **go rusty** to SPOIL, referring to meat or fish V.7.10. gɔʊ ɹʌstɪ Brk

rut *n* a WEAKLING piglet III.8.4. ɹʊt St Lei

rutchy *adj* RANCID, describing bacon V.7.9. ɹʊtʃɪ Gl

rut-holes *npl* RUTS made by cartwheels IV.3.9. ɹʊtʊəlz Y

rutling *n* a WEAKLING piglet III.8.4. ɹʊtlɪn Db Lei

ruts *npl What do you call those lines left behind by the cartwheels when the ground is soft?* IV.3.9. Eng exc. Nb Sf. ⇒ **car-racks, car-tracks, cart-racks, cart-rakes, cart-rits, cart-rucks, cart-ruts, cart-swoes, cart-tracks, furrows, lowses, racks, riggots, rits, rittings, ruches, rucks, rut-holes, sporring-marks, spurlings, spurns, tracks, wheelings, wheel-lowses, wheel-marks, wheel-rakes, wheel-ruts, wheel-spurlings, wheel- spurns, wheel-tracks, wheel-treads**

rutting-fat *1. n* the FAT round the kidneys of a pig III.12.7. rʊtɪnfat Y
2. n the fat round the intestines of a pig. rʊtɪnfat Y

rye-flour *n* MEAL V.6.1(b). ɹaɪflaʊə L

rye-frost* *n* HOAR-FROST VII.6.6. ɹʌɪfɹɔ·st Nf

S

sack *1. n* *What would you weigh grain in?* I.7.2. Eng. ⇒ **bag**, **poke**, **sack-bag**

2. n a container for carrying horse-feed, ⇐ BASKET III.5.4. sɛk MxL, zak Co *[marked u.r. EMBM]*

sack-apron *n* a working APRON V.11.2(a). *pl* sɛkɛɪpɹənz Ess

sack-bag *1. n* a SACK in which grain is weighed I.7.2. sɛkbag Nt L, sækbæg He, sakbaˑg Wa

2. n a container for carrying horse-feed, ⇐ BASKET III.5.4. sakbaˑg Wa

sacking-apron *n* a working APRON V.11.2(a). sækɪnɛpəˑɽɳ Brk, sækənɛɪpɹən Sf, sæk?ɳɛɪpɹn Nf, zakənjɛpəˑɳ W

sacking-mantle *n* a working APRON V.11.2(a). sæk?ɪnmænt?ɬ Nf

sackless *adj* STUPID VI.1.5. sakləs Y

sack-string *n* STRING used to tie up a grain-sack I.7.3. sakstɹɪŋ Bk

sack-tie *n* STRING used to tie up a grain-sack I.7.3. sæktɑɪ MxL, sæˑktɔɪ Brk, zaktəɪ W *[marked u.r. SBM]*

sack-tiers *npl* pieces of STRING used to tie up grain-sacks I.7.3. zaktɒɪəˑⁱːz̩ Ha *[marked u.r. SBM]*

sack-ties *npl* pieces of STRING used to tie up grain-sacks I.7.3. sɛktɔɪz Sx, sɛktʌɪz Sr, sæktɑɪz K, zaktəɪz W *[marked u.r. SBM]*

sack-twine *n* STRING used to tie up a grain-sack I.7.3. sæktwʌɪn Nf Brk

sack-tying-twine *n* STRING used to tie up a grain-sack I.7.3. sæktɑɪ-ɪntwɑɪn K

sad *adj* *When your bread or pastry has not risen, you say it is ....* V.6.12. sɛd Sr, sæd Y He L Hu Nf, sæˑd Man Sa Brk K Ha, sæˑᵊd Nb, sad Nb Cu Du We La Y Ch Db Sa St Wo Wa Gl O Nt L Lei R Nth Hu C Bk; **sad and tough** sad ən tɹəf Y. ⇒ **clabby**, **clammy**, **cleaty**, **clibby**, **clidgy**, **clingy**, **clit**, **clittied**, **clitty**, **close**, **clutchy**, **dazed**, **dead**, **doughy**, **down**, **dull**, **dumpy**, **fallen**, **flat**, **flop**, *hasn't rose* ⇒ **rise**, **heavy**, *isn't rose* ⇒ **rise**, **kisty**, **non-high**, *not risen* ⇒ **rise**, **pluffy**, **puddeny**, *pudding-bread*, **puddingy** ⇒ **puddeny**, **sad** *and tough*, **slack baked**, **sodden**, **soddened**, **soddle**, **soddled**, **sodly**, **soggy**, **sour**, **sunk**, **thodden**, *too* **heavy** *['resulting' copula* **gone** *forms (***flat**, **flop**, **sad**, **thodden***) are subsumed: these strictly suggest 'fallen' rather than 'not risen']*

saddle *1. n* *[Show a picture of the harness of a cart-horse.] What do you call this [indicate the cart-saddle]?* I.5.6. siːdl Nb, sɪədl Cu, sedl Nb, sɛdɬ K, *pl* sɛdɬz Ess, sɛdʊɬ Ess Sr K Sx, sɛdʊ Ess, sædl Man Sa He Nf K, sædɬ He Wo Wa Mon Gl Hu Nf Sf Bk Hrt Ess MxL So Brk Sr K Co, zædɬ So D, sædʊɬ Gl Brk Sr K Ha Sx, sædʊ Sr Sx, sadl Nb Cu Du We La Y Ch Db Sa St Wo Gl O Nt L Nth, sadɬ Wo Wa Mon Lei R Nth Hu C Bk Bd Hrt Ess Co, sadəɬ O Bk, zadɬ Gl W Co D Do Ha, sɑdɬ Wo, sɒdɬ Wo. ⇒ **car-saddle**, **cart-pad**, **cart-saddle**, **pad**

2. v to GEAR a cart-horse I.5.1. sæːdɬ Hrt

3. n the BASE of a stack II.7.4. sadl Sa

4. n the THRESHOLD of a door V.1.12. sadl Cu

saddle-backed *adj* OVERTURNED, describing a sheep on its back unable to get up III.7.4. sadlbakt Y

saddle-belly-band *n* the GIRTH of the harness of a cart-horse I.5.8. sadlbɛləbənd Nt

saddle-girth *n* the GIRTH of the harness of a cart-horse I.5.8. sædlgʌt Ess, sædɬgʌˑt Nf, sædlgəɽt Nf, sædʊɬgəːɽt Sx, sadlgaːθ Y Nt, sadɬgʌt Hrt, sadlgəːθ Db St, sadlgəːt Db, sadɬgəˑɹt Hu

saddle-strap *n* the GIRTH of the harness of a cart-horse I.5.8. sædlstɹæp Nf, sædɬstɹæp Ess, sadlstɹap Y Ch

sadly *adj* ILL, describing a person who is unwell VI.13.1(b). sædlɪ Nf

sag *vi* to WARP, referring to wood IX.2.9. *-ing* sæggɪn La

sag-bar *n* a DIAGONAL BAR of a gate IV.3.7. sagbaː Nt L, sagbaˡː L

sail *n* the DIRECTION from which the wind blows VII.6.26. sɛɪl Y

saim *1. n* the FAT round the kidneys of a pig III.12.7. sɪiˑm Nf, sɪəm Du, seːm Nb Cu, seəm Nb, sɛːm Cu

2. n LARD made from the fat of a pig III.12.8. seːm Nb Cu Y, sɛːm Cu We, sɛˑəm L

saint fifer's dance *n* TREMORS suffered by a person who cannot keep still VI.1.4. sən vɒɪfəˡːz̩ dans Ha

saint viper's dance *n* TREMORS suffered by a person who cannot keep still VI.1.4. sən vɒɪpəˡːz̩ dans Ha

saint vitus' dance *n* TREMORS suffered by a person who cannot keep still VI.1.4. sənt vaɪtəsɪs daːns Sa

sal* *n* a HARE IV.5.10. sæl Sf; **old sal*** ʌʊɬ sæl Sf

salad onions *npl* SPRING ONIONS V.7.16. *sg* saləd ʌnjən K

sales *n* a local FESTIVAL or holiday on which sheep were sold VII.4.11. sealz We

sallow *n* WILLOW IV.10.7. sælɪ Man Sa He, sæłɪ He Mon, sælə Ess, salɪ Man Sa Wo, salə Y Lei Nf*[round leaves]*, sɒłɪ Wo

sallow-tree *n* WILLOW IV.10.7. sæˑlətɹᵊiː Sf

sallow-willow *n* WILLOW IV.10.7. saləwɪlə Lei

sally *n* a HARE IV.5.10. sɛli Nf, sælɪ Nf Ess*[nickname]*

salt *adj* **it wasn't salt, not salt enough, 'tisn't salt enough** INSIPID, describing food lacking in salt V.7.8. **it wasn't salt** ɪt wʌznt sɒlt Nf; **not salt enough** nɒʔ sɒlt ənʌf Nf, ɛɪnʔ salʔ ənʌf Nf, ɪzn sɒlt ɪnʏf Nf, eɪnt sɒlt ənʏf Nf, eɪnʔ sɒłt ənʌf Bk, eɪnʔ sɒłʔ ənʌf Hu, ɛnt sɒłt ənʌf Nth, nat sɒlt ənuf Gl, nɒt sɒłt ɪnuf Lei, nɒt sɔːłt ɪnʌf Brk, nɒt sɔːłt ənʌf MxL, nɒt sɔːłt ənuf Wa; **'tisn't salt enough** tɪzn sɒłt ɪnʌf Sr, tɪn sɔːłt ɪnʌf So, tɪn zɔːłt ɪnʌf Do

salter *1.* *n* a SALTING-TROUGH III.12.5. sɔːltəᶜ: So*[leaden or wooden]*, sɔːłtəᶜ: So, zɔːłtəᶜ: So D Do, zʌłtəᶜ: Do

2. *n* a salting-trough or flat surface of undetermined kind. sɒltə St, sɔːltə St

salting-bin *n* a SALTING-TROUGH III.12.5. sɔːłtɪnbɪn W, sɔːᵊtɪnbɪn Bk

salting-board *n* a flat surface on which bacon is cured, ⟸ SALTING-TROUGH III.12.5. sɔːltɪnbɔːəᶜd He, sɔːłtɪnbɒᶜːd W*[presumably]*

salting-bowl *n* a SALTING-TROUGH III.12.5. zɒłtɪnbɒuł W

salting-form *n* a flat surface on which bacon is cured, ⟸ SALTING-TROUGH III.12.5. zɔːłʔnvɒᶜːm Ha

salting-keeve *n* a SALTING-TROUGH, usually half of a large barrel III.12.5. zɒłtənkiːv Co

salting-lead *1.* *n* a SALTING-TROUGH III.12.5. saːltnlɛd Gl, sɒłtɪnlɪd Nth*[lead-lined]*, sɒłtɪnlɛd Hu Bd, sɔłtɪnlɪd Wa*[concrete]*, sɒłʔnlɪd Ess*[wooden, lead-lined]*, sɔłtɪnlɛd Wo*[metal]*, sɔłtnlɛd L, sɔːłtɪnlɪd Hu*[lead-lined]*, sɔːłtɪnlɛd Wa O

2. *n* a flat surface on which bacon is cured. sɒłtɪnlɛd Wa

salting-pan *n* a SALTING-TROUGH III.12.5. salʔnpæn Nf, sɔːłtɪnpæn Ess Sx, zɔːłtənpan D Ha

salting-slab *n* a SALTING-TROUGH or flat surface on which bacon is cured III.12.5. saːłtɪnslæːb Gl, saːłtɪnsłaːb Mon, sɔːltɪnslæb Sa

salting-standard *n* a SALTING-TROUGH III.12.5. sɒłtɪnstandəᶜːd D

salting-stean *n* a SALTING-TROUGH III.12.5. saːltɪnstiːn He

salting-stone *1.* *n* a SALTING-TROUGH III.12.5. sɔłtɪnstʊːn Ch

2. *n* a flat surface on which bacon is cured. sɒłtɪnstoːn Nt, sɒłtɪnstoːn Mon, sɒłtɪnstoʊn He, sɒʊttɪnstᵁuːn Db, sɔːtɪnstoːn La

3. *n* a salting-trough or surface of undetermined kind. saːłtɪnstoːn He Mon, saːłtɪnstʊn Gl, sɒłtɪnstoːn He, sɒłtɪnstoːn He Wo, sɒłtɪnstoːʊn Wa, sɔːłtɪnstoːn He, sɔːłtɪnstoʊn St, *pl* sɔːłtɪnstʊːnz St, sɔːtɪnstuːn Db *[WMBM definition in 3. probably over-particular]*

salting-stool *n* a SALTING-TROUGH III.12.5. sɔːłʔnstuːł Ha

salting-table *n* a flat surface on which bacon is cured, ⟸ SALTING-TROUGH III.12.5. sɒłtɪnteːbl Sa

salting-trough *n* What do you call the thing you cure bacon in? III.12.5. sɒłtɪntɹɒf Lei R, sɒłtɪntɹɒf Brk, sɒłʔɪntɹɔːf Bk, sɒłtɪntɹɒuf Nth, sɒłtɪntɹʌf Sa, sɒłtɪntɹoʊf Nth, sɒłtɪntɹoʊf Wa, sɒłtɪntɹʊf Lei, sɔːłtɪntɹɔːf L, sɔːłtɪntɹɒf Lei, *pl* sɔːłtɪntɹɔːfs Sx, sɔːłʔɪntɹoʊf O, sɔːłtɪntɹoʊf Wa, sɔːłtɪntɹʊf Lei, sɔːłtɪntɹuf Lei R, saːłtɪntɹɒʊ Gl, sɒłtɪntɹaʊ Gl, sɒłʔɪntɹoʊ Bk, sɒłtɪntɹɒ Brk, sɔˑtɪntɹoʊ Brk, sɔːłtɪntɹɒʊ Sx, sɔːtɪntɹɒʊ Sr, sɔːłtɪntɹʌʊ Sr, sɔːtɪntɹʌʊ Sr, sɔːłtɪntɹoʊ Brk, sɔːłtɪntɹoʊ So*[lead-lined]*. ⟹ **bench, board, brine-bath, brine-pan, brine-pot, brine-tub, bussa, cellar-stone, cistern, cooler, crock, curing-stone, dairy-bench, earthenware pot, freestone-sconce, gantry, keeve, lead, lead-bowl, lead-tray, long-trough, meat-standard, milk-bowl, milk-lead, pan, pantry-bench, pickle-pot, pickle-tub, pickling-cask, pickling-pan, pickling-tank, pickling-trough, pickling-tub, pig-bench, pig-sill, pig-trough, pig-turnel, pot, rack, salter, salting-bin, salting-board, salting-bowl, salting-form, salting-keeve, salting-lead, salting-pan, salting-slab, salting-standard, salting-steen, salting-stone, salting-stool, salting-table, salting-tub, salting-vat, salt-lead, salt-pan, salt-stone, salt-trough, scalding-tub, sconce, settless, sill, silt, sink-trough, skill, slab, slate, slate-tank, slop-stone, standard, steen, stone, stone-flag, stone-slab, stone-table, table, thrall, trendle, trindle, trough, trundle, tub, turnel, vat, whey-lead, yot** *[it is not always clear when reference is to 'containers' or 'slabs']*

salting-tub *n* a SALTING-TROUGH III.12.5. saːtntʏb Nb, saltntʏb Nf, sɒltɪntʊb Y L, sɒłtɪntʊb O, sɔłtɪntʊb Nt L, sɔlʔɪntʊb L, sɔłtntʊb L, sɔłtəntʊb L, sɔːłʔɪntʌb O

salting-vat *n* a SALTING-TROUGH III.12.5. sɒłtɪnvat St

salt-lead *n* a SALTING-TROUGH III.12.5. saːłtłɛd Wo

salt-pan *n* a SALTING-TROUGH III.12.5. sɔːłtpæn Ess

sal-tree *n* a TETHERING-STAKE in a cow-house I.3.3. zaɫtɾiː D, zɒɫtɾiː Co

salt-stone *n* a flat surface on which bacon is cured, ⇐ SALTING-TROUGH III.12.5. sɒltstoˈʊn Nt

salt-trough *n* a SALTING-TROUGH III.12.5. sɒltɹɒuf Nth

salvage *n* RUBBISH V.1.15. sɛɫvɪdʒ K, sælvɪdʒ So*[modern]*

sam up *vtphr-3sg* she [a tidy girl] will COLLECT her toys VIII.8.15. sam ... ʊp Y; **sam up and side** sam ... ʊp ən saːd ... Y

sand-stone *n* a WHETSTONE II.9.10. sanstɪən Y, sanstʊən La, sandstn Cu

sandwich(es) *1. n* a SNACK VII.5.11.
no -es: sanwɪdʒ Y
-es: samwɪdʒɪz La
2. n MEAL OUT VII.5.12.
no -es: sanwɪdʒ Y
-es: sanwɪdʒɪz Y

sap *vi* **sap and crack** to WARP, referring to a branch IX.2.9. sap ən kɹak St

sapey* *adj* **go sapey** to SPOIL, referring to meat or fish V.7.10. goˈ seːpɪ Sa*[old x1]*, gʊ seːpɪ Gl*[old]*, goʊ sɛɪpɪ St, gʊ sɛɪpɪ St

sappy *1. adj* INSIPID, describing food lacking in salt V.7.8. seːpɪ Sa, sapɪ Wa
2. adj RANCID, describing bacon V.7.9. seːpɪ Sa

sarah-annie *n* a HARE IV.5.10. sɛˈɹˡænɪ Nf

sark *1. n* a CHEMISE V.11.1. sark Cu, saːk We, saᴿːk Nb
2. n a SHIRT VI.14.8. seˈəᴿk Nb, sæːk Du, saɹk Du, saːk Nb Cu Du, saˈrk Cu, saᴿːk Nb

sarrow *1. vt* to FEED cattle III.3.1. saᵗːɾ (+V) So Do
2. v to feed cattle. saᵗː So W*[pigs]* Do, zaᵗː W

sarrowing* *v-ing* FEEDING horses in the stable III.5.1. saʀə Du*[old]*, saɹə Du, saᵗːɾɪn So, *v* saᵗː Do *[not a NBM headword]*

satan *n* **satan**, **old satan** DEVIL VIII.8.3. **satan** sɛɪtn Nf, seɪtən Man, sɛɪtən O, sɛɪˀn Ess Sx, sɛˈəʔŋ L, sæɪʔŋ Ess, saɪʔn Ha; **old satan** ɔːɫ seɪtn Brk

saucy *adj* SLIPPERY VII.6.14. saːsɪ Do, sɔːˀsɪ Hrt

saugh *1. n* the bush ELDER IV.10.6. sɔːg Y *[queried ir.r. as meaning 'willow' NBM]*
2. n WILLOW IV.10.7. saf Nb

saur *n* URINE in a cow-house I.3.10. sɔˈə Y, sɔˈɹ Y

saur-hole *n* a CESS-POOL on a farm I.3.11. sɔəɹɒl Y

saur-tank *1. n* a CESS-POOL on a farm I.3.11. sɔˈətaŋk Y
2. n an artificial cess-pool. sɔˈətaŋk Y

sausage-hide(s) *n* CHITTERLINGS III.12.2.
no -s: saːsɪdʒhʌɪd Nf
-s: sɒsɪdʒhʌɪdz Nf

saving *v-ing* CARTING corn from the field II.6.6. seːvɪn D, seːvən D

saw-bench *n* a SAWING-HORSE I.7.16. saːbɛnʃ Nb, saːbɛntʃ He, sɒbɛntʃ Wo, sɔːbɛntʃ St Nf, sɔːbɛnʃ Y Man Wa, sɔəˈbɛnʃ K

saw-buck *n* a SAWING-HORSE I.7.16. saːbʌk He

saw-coom *n* SAW-DUST I.7.17. saːkəum Y

saw-dust *n* What falls to the ground as you saw? I.7.17. Eng. ⇒ **saw-coom, wood-dust**

saw-frame *n* a SAWING-HORSE I.7.16. sɔˈəfɹɛˈəm L

saw-horse *n* a SAWING-HORSE I.7.16. saːhɒs Cu, saː-ɒs Y, saː-ɔs Y, saːhoᴿːs Du, saː-ɔˡːs La Y, saː-əs Y, saːaːs Mon, saː-aᵗːʂ He, saː-ɒs He Wo, zaː-ɒs Gl, sɒ-ɔᵗːʂ Sa, sɔ-ɔəˡs Brk, sɔəɹɔes Brk, sɔːˀəɹas C, sɔː-aˡːs Y, sɔːhɒs Du We, sɔː-ɒs Cu We La Y Ch Db Sa St, zɔː-ɒs Gl So D Ha, sɔːhɒs Du, sɔː-ɔs Y Nt L, sɔːɹɔs Ess, sɔːhɔːs Cu We Ess, sɔː-ɔːs Cu Ch Wa, sɔː-ɔˡːs We La Y K, sɔː-ɔeəˡs Ha, sɔː-ɔᵗːʂ He, zɔː-ɔᵗːʂ D, sɔːˀs Sa, sɔᵗːɹɔːᵗːʂ Wa

sawing-block *n* a SAWING-HORSE I.7.16. sɔːɪnblɒk Ch Sa

sawing-cratch *n* a SAWING-HORSE I.7.16. sɔːɪnkɹatʃ Db

sawing-horse *n* What do you call the frame on which you saw a log of wood? I.7.16. zaːnaᵗːʂ W, saːɪnɔᵗːʂ O Bk, saːɪnəᵗːʂ O, savənhɒs Sf, saːɪnaᵗːʂ Gl, saːɪnaᵗːʂ Mon, saːɪnɒs Wo Gl, zaːɪnɒs Gl, saːɪnɒs O, sɒˈ-ɪnɒs Y, sɔ-ɪnaˈəˡs Brk, sɔ-ɪŋhɔəᵗʂ Sx, sɔɫɪnɔːəᵗʂ Sx, sɔːɪnhaᵗːʂ So, zɔːɪnhaᵗːʂ So, sɔːɪnaᵗːʂ Sa So W Brk Ha, sɔːənaᵗːʂ Co, zɔː-ɪnaᵗːʂ W, zɔːɪnaᵗːʂ Do, sɔːɪnaᵗːʂ Wa Brk, sɔːɪnhɒs So, zɔː-ɪnhɒs W, sɔːɪnhɒs Nf Ess, sɔːɪnɒs Y Ch St Nt Lei R Co, sɔːənɒs Co Ha, zɔːɪnɒs W D, zɔːɪənɒs W Co, zɔːɪnɒs Co D Ha, sɔːɹɪnɒs Nth Bd Ess, sɔˈɪnɒᵗʂ O, sɔˈənɒᵗʂ Ha, sɔˈɪnhɔs Sr, sɔːɪnhɒs Sf, sɔːɹɪnhɔs Sf, sɔːɪnɒs Y Nt L, sɔːwɪnɒs L, sɔːənɒs Ess, sɔːˀɹɪnɒs Hrt, sɔːɹənɒs Sf, sɔˈɹnɒs He, sɔːɪnhɔːs Nf Ess MxL K, sɔːənhɔːˀs Sf, sɔːɹɪnhɔːs Nf Ess, sɔːɪnɔːs Ch Wa Nt Lei C Bk Hrt K, sɔːwɪnɔːs Db K, sɔːənɔːˀs Hrt, sɔːɹɔːs Ess Sx, zɔːnɔːs Do, sɔːɹɪnɔːs Wa Mon Nth Hu Sf Bd Ess, sɔːɪnhɔᵗːʂ So, zɔːɪnhɔᵗːʂ So, sɔːɪnɔᵗːʂ Sa Wa Gl O Nth Bk, sɔːənɔᵗːʂ Ha, zɔːɪnɔᵗːʂ So W D Do, zɔːɪnɔᵗːʂ So Do, zɔːənɔᵗːʂ D, sɔːlɪŋɔᵗːʂ O, sɔː-ɪnɔːəˡs Sr, sɔː-ɪŋɔːəᵗʂ Sr, sɔː-ɪnɔːəᵗʂ Sr Sx, sɔː-ɳɔːəᵗɹʂ Sx, sɔːɪnəˡːs L, sɔᵗːɪnɔᵗːʂ Sa, zɔᵗːɳɔːs Do. ⇒ **cradle, cross-leg(s), cuddy, donkey, horse, jack, *pair of* three-legs, rack, saw-bench, saw-buck, saw-frame, saw-horse, sawing-block, sawing-cratch, sawing-jack, sawing-stand, sawing-stock, sawing-stool, sawing-trestle, saw-jack, saw-stall, saw-stand, saw-stock, saw-stool, saw-table, saw-trestle, seesaw, stick-horse,**

three-legs, trestle, wooden-horse, wood-horse, wood-stock

sawing-jack *n* a SAWING-HORSE I.7.16. sɔːˀɹɪndʒak Hrt

sawing-stand *n* a SAWING-HORSE I.7.16. sɔːɹɪnstan Hu

sawing-stock *n* a SAWING-HORSE I.7.16. sɔˑ-ɪnstɒk Y

sawing-stool *n* a SAWING-HORSE I.7.16. sɔɹɪnstʉːl Nf, sɔːɹɪnstʉːl Nf, sɔːɹɪnstəul Nf

sawing-trestle *n* a SAWING-HORSE I.7.16. sɔːɪntɹɛsl Db

saw-jack *n* a SAWING-HORSE I.7.16. sɑːdʒæk Wo, sɔːdʒak St Wo

saw-stall *n* a SAWING-HORSE I.7.16. sɔːstɔːl Y

saw-stand *n* a SAWING-HORSE I.7.16. sɔːstand Wa Lei

saw-stock *n* a SAWING-HORSE I.7.16. sɔːstɒk La

saw-stool *n* a SAWING-HORSE I.7.16. sɔːstuːl L

saw-table *n* a SAWING-HORSE I.7.16. sɔːtɪəbl Y

saw-trestle *n* a SAWING-HORSE I.7.16. sɔːtɹɛsl Y

scag *n* PEAT IV.4.3. skæg K *[queried SBM]*

scald *1. vt* to BREW tea V.8.9. skald Y, *-ing* skadn Nb, skaːd Du*[old]*, *-ing* skɒld Y, *-ing* əskɒɫdɪn Wo, skɔːld Sa St, *-ing* skɔːɫdɪn Brk, skɔːd We*[very old]*, *-ing* skɔːdɪn Y*[old]* Sr Ha
2. v to brew tea. skɑːld Wo, skɒld Sa, skɒɫd Sf, skɔːld Sa, *-ing* skɔːldɪn K, skɔːd Ch St, skʌʊɫd Ess

scalding-tub *n* a SALTING-TROUGH III.12.5. skɔːɫdɪntʌb Ha, skɔːdɪntʊb Y

scale *1. vt* to WEIGH something I.7.1. skɛɪɫ Brk
2. vt to TED hay II.9.11(a). skeːl Cu We La, skɛːl Cu We
3. n DANDRUFF VI.1.3. skeːl Ch

scallions *1. npl* SPRING ONIONS V.7.16. skɛlɪənz MxL, skɛljənz Ess, skæljənz Ess, skalɪənz Nb Du We La Y*[old x1]* Db Bd, skaljənz Bd Hrt, *sg* skalɪən Cu, skɛlɪənz Db, skɛljənz Man, *sg* skaljən L
2. n shoots growing from an old onion. skæljənz Hu Ess, skalɪənz La O Hu, skaljənz O Hrt

scallops *n* SCRAPS left after rendering lard III.12.10. skɛləps So, skaɫəps D

scally onions *npl* SPRING ONIONS V.7.16. skalɪ-ʊnɪənz La*[old x1]* Y Db

scalp *n* the human HEAD VI.1.1. skɔːp Y

scammish *adj* CLUMSY, describing a person VI.7.14. skamɪʃ Do

scandalmonger *n* a GOSSIP VIII.3.5(b). skɛndɫmʌŋgəl Sr, skændɫmʌŋgə Sf, skændɫmʌŋgəl Sx, skandɫmʌŋgəlː Do, skandlmʊŋgə Y St

scanning *v-ing* SQUINTING VI.3.5. skɛnɪn Ch Db St, skanɪn St

scarecrow *n What do you put up in a field to frighten birds away?* II.3.7. Eng exc. Cu We Sa Wo. ⇒ **bird-scarer, bo-boy, bogeyman, bucca**, *bull-boy* ⇒

bo-boy, bugalo, buglug, crow-boggart, dolly-crow, dud-man, flay-boggle, flay-crow, gally-bagger, gally-crow, guy, hodmandod, image, mawkin, mawpin, moggy, mommet, old mob, potato-bogle, rook-scarer, shay, shuft

scared *adj* AFRAID VIII.8.2. skɪəˡːd̩ So, ske·əd Sf, skeːəˡd̩ Wo, skɛt Ess, skɛːd Nf, skɛˑət Sf, skɛəd Y Wa Ess, skɛəᴵd K, skɛəˡːd̩ Sa, skaɹd Y, skaːd Y L

scarf *n* a NECKERCHIEF VI.14.4. skæːf La Man C Nf, ska:f Cu Du We Y Ch Db Sa St He Nt, skjaːf He Gl, skaᴵːf La, skaˡːf Sa W Co D Do, skᴵaˡːf He Wo, skjaˡːf Gl, ska:f St*[old]* Nf Brk, skɑː Sx, skᴵaˡːf Wo, skjaˡːf He, skəˡːf Wo, skᴵəˡːf Wo, skjəˡːf Gl

scat *n* a BENCH on which slaughtered pigs are dressed III.12.1. skat Y

scattering *pron* **a scattering** A FEW VII.8.21. ə skatɹɪn Ch

scaunch* *v-1prpl* we CRUNCH apples or biscuits VI.5.12. skɔːˀntʃ Bd, *-ing* skɔːnʃɪn Bk *[queried errors for scranch/scraunch EMBM]*

scaw *n* the bush ELDER IV.10.6. skæʏ Co

scaw-tree *n* the bush ELDER IV.10.6. skæʏtɹiː Co

school-boss *n* a boys' name for a TEACHER VIII.6.5. skɪuːlbɒs Sa

school-master *n* a TEACHER VIII.6.5. skʏːɫmɛːstəˡ Co, skuːlmeːstə Y, skuːɫmeːstəˡː W, skuʊmeːstəˡ Sx, skuːlmæˑsθə Man, skuːmastə Lei, skuːlmɑˑstə Nf, skuʊmɑːstəˡ Sr

school-missis *n* a TEACHER VIII.6.5. skʏːɫmɪsɪs So*[old]*, skuːɫmɪsɪs Co

school treat *n* a local FESTIVAL or holiday VII.4.11. skʏːl tɹiːt La

scitch* *n* COUCH-GRASS II.2.3. skɪtʃ Wo

sclow *vt* to PULL somebody's hair VI.2.8. skɫæʏ Co

scoff up *vtphr* to GOBBLE food VI.5.13(b). *-ing* skɔːfn ... ʌp Nf

scollops *1. npl* PEGS used to fasten thatch on a stack II.7.7(a). skɒlps Mon
2. n SCRAPS left after rendering lard III.12.10. skɒləps So, skɒɫəps So Co Do

sconce *n* a stone shelf in a dairy, on which bacon is cured, ⇐ SALTING-TROUGH III.12.5. skɒns Cu

scoochy *adj* LEFT-HANDED VI.7.13(a). skʏːtʃi D

scoop *1. n What do you use to take the hot water out of the boiler?* V.9.9. skaʊp Cu, skʊʊp Cu Wa, skɔʊp Y L, skʊp Sf, skuːp Nb Bk Bd Co. ⇒ **baler**, *basin*, **boiler-can, boiler-tin, bowl, bowl-dish,** *bucket*, **bumper, dipper, dipping-bowl, guile-dish, hand-bowl, hand-cup, handle-bowl, handle-cup, handle-dish,** *jug*, **lade-bowl,**

lade-can, lader, lader-tin, lading-bowl, lading-can, lading-pot, lading-tin, ladle, ladle-can, ladling-can, laving-can, laving-tin, lifter, *mug*, ousing-tin, paddick-gallon, piggin, quart, quart-tin, skimmer, spudgel, tin bowl, two-quart-can

2. *n* a SOWING-BASKET II.3.6. skʊp Ess

3. *n* a BASKET for carrying horse-feed III.5.4. skɒʊp Cu We[*ladle-shaped x1*], sku:p Nb Du Y

4. *n* a SHOVEL for a household fire V.3.9. sku:p Brk[*old x1*]

scoop up *vtphr-3sg* she [a tidy girl] will COLLECT her toys VIII.8.15. sku:p ... ʊp Wo Wa

scoot *imp* GO AWAY! VIII.7.9(a). skʊt Gl

scopping *v-ing* THROWING a stone VIII.7.7. skɒpən Cu[*old and rare x1*]

score *n* pasture, ⇐ HIRE *PASTURAGE* III.3.8. sko:ə La

scorp *n* the SCRUFF (of the neck) VI.6.2. skɔˠ:ɹp Sx

scot *1. n* a chock placed behind and under a wheel to prevent a cart from going backwards on a hill, ⇐ PROP/CHOCK I.11.2. skɑ:t Wo Gl, skɒt La Sr, skɔt La Man Ess, skɔ:t Bk, sko:ʊt Gl

scotch *1. n* a chock placed behind and under a wheel to prevent a cart from going backwards on a hill, ⇐ PROP/CHOCK I.11.2. skætʃ Brk, skɑtʃ Nth, skɑ:tʃ Wo, skɒtʃ La Y Ch Db Sa St Wo Wa Mon Gl O L Lei R Nth Bd Sr, skɔtʃ La Wa L C Sf Hrt Ess Sr, skɔ:tʃ Nt, skʌtʃ Sa[*with handle*], skʊtʃ Cu

2. *vt* to chock a wheel. skɒtʃ Y

3. *v* to TRIM hedges IV.2.3. skɒtʃ Nt[*5–6 years' growth*] L[*2–3 years' growth*], -*ing* skɒtʃɪn R

scotch-cart *n* a FARMCART I.9.3. skɒtʃkɑɻt O

scotchman *n* a variety of THISTLE II.2.2. skɒtʃmən Ess

scotch-stick *n* a STICK used to support the shaft of a cart I.11.1. skɒtʃstɪk Bd

scotch up* 1. *vphr* to chock a wheel to prevent a cart from going backwards on a hill, ⇐ PROP/CHOCK I.11.2. skætʃ ʌp Brk

2. *vtphr* to chock a wheel. skɒtʃ ... œ:p Gl, skɒtʃ ... ʌp Do

scote *n* a STICK used to support the shaft of a cart I.11.1. skɔ:t Gl

scotty *n* a HORNLESS cow III.2.9. skɒtɪ Cu

scot up* *vtphr* to chock a wheel to prevent a cart from going backwards on a hill, ⇐ PROP/CHOCK I.11.2. *2pr* skɑˠ:t ... ʊp Wo

scour *1. n* a FORD IV.1.3. skaʊə St

2. *n* LOW-LYING LAND IV.1.7. skaʊə St

3. *v* to DITCH IV.2.11. -*ing* skɛʊəɹɪn K, skɔ:ɹ (+V) Ess

4. *n* stale URINE used to scour cloth at a mill VI.8.8. skaʊə Y

scour out *vtphr* to DITCH IV.2.11. skɛʊəɹ (+V) ... ɛʊt Ess

scouting-pewit *n* a GULL IV.7.5. *pl* skɛʊtnpi'wɪts Nf

scow *n* the SHEATH of skin covering the penis of a horse III.4.9. skaʊ Y

scowp out *1. vphr* to DITCH IV.2.11. -*ing* skɔʊpɪn aʊt Y

2. *vtphr* to ditch. skɔʊp ... aʊt Y, skoʊp ... aʊt St

scowp up *vtphr-3sg* she [a tidy girl] will COLLECT her toys VIII.8.15. skɒʊp ... ʊp La

scrabble-footed *adj* SPLAY-FOOTED VI.10.5. skɹabɫvʊtɪd So

scrab up *vtphr-3sg* she [a tidy girl] will COLLECT her toys VIII.8.15. skɹæb ... ʌp Sf

scrafting *v-ing* SCRATCHING VI.1.2. skɹæftɪn W [*queried SBM*]

scraggly *adj* TANGLED, describing hair VI.2.5. skɹɛglɪ Brk, skɹæglɪ Sx

scram *1. n* the RIND of bacon III.12.6. skram Cu, skɹam Cu

2. *imp* GO AWAY! VIII.7.9(a). skɹæm Ess, skɹam St He

scramble together *vtphr-3sg* she [a tidy girl] will COLLECT her toys VIII.8.15. skɹambl ... təgɛðə Y

scram-handed *adj* LEFT-HANDED VI.7.13(a). skɹæmhændɪd So, skɹamandəd Do

scrammed *1. adj* COLD, describing a person VI.13.18. skɹæ:md So; **scrammed with the cold** skɹæmd wɪ ðə koʊɫd So

2. *adj* VERY COLD, describing a person VI.13.19. skɹamd So; **damn nigh scrammed** dam nəɪ skɹamd Do; **scrammed to death** skɹamd tə dɛθ D; **scrammed with the cold** skɹamd wɪ ðə ko:ɫ D, skɹamd wɪ ðə ko:ɫd So, skɹamd wɪ ðə koʊɫd So

scrammed up *adj* VERY COLD, describing a person VI.13.19. skɹamd ʌp So D

scrammish *adj* CLUMSY, describing a person VI.7.14. skɹʌmɪʃ Do

scrammy *adj* CLUMSY, describing a person VI.7.14. skɹami Do

scrammy-handed *adj* LEFT-HANDED VI.7.13(a). skɹamɪhandɪd So, skɹamɪ-andəd Do

scran *n* a SNACK VII.5.11. skɹan L

scranch *1. vt-1prpl* we CRUNCH apples or biscuits VI.5.12. skʁanʃ Du, skɹanʃ Du

2. *v-1prpl* we crunch. -*ing* skʁanʃən Nb Du, skɹanʃ Du

scranchems *n* SCRAPS left after rendering lard III.12.10. skʁanʃəmz Du

scranchings *n* SCRAPS left after rendering lard III.12.10. skɹɔ:nʃənz Db

scrap *n* a BENCH on which slaughtered pigs are dressed III.12.1. skɹap Bd

scrape *1. n* a RAKE used in a domestic fire V.3.8(a). skɹeːp He

2.1. v to RAKE in a domestic fire V.3.8(b). skɹeːp
Ch O, skɽeːp O, skreɪp Man, skɹeɪp Mon Gl, skɽeˑɪp
O, skrɛᵊp Man, skɹɛɪp St Wa, skɹɛəp Nth

2.2. vt to rake. skɹiːp St, skʁɪəp Nb, skɹeːp Sa He
Mon Gl, *-s* skɹeːps Wo Mon, skɹeɪp C Nf, skɹeːɪp He
Mon, *-s* skɹeːˡps Gl, skɹeˑəp Nth Bk, skɹeːp Nf,
skɹeɪp St Wo, skɹeˑəp L

scrape down *vtphr* to RAKE soot in a domestic fire
V.3.8(b). skɹeːp ... dɛʊn Sa

scrape in *vtphr* to RAKE in a domestic fire V.3.8(b).
skɹeˑəp ... ɪn L

scrape out *vtphr* to RAKE in a domestic fire
V.3.8(b). skɹeːp ... æʊt O, skɽeːp æʊt D, skɹeɪp ... ɛʊt
Brk, skɹeˑəp ... aʊt L

scraper *1. n* a wooden implement used to remove
cow-dung in a cow-house, ⇐ MUCK-FORK I.3.13.
skɹeːpəˡ Sa

2. n a wooden instrument with rubber teeth, used to
clean horses, ⇐ CURRY-COMB III.5.5. skɹeɪpə
Mon

3. n a RAKE used in a domestic fire V.3.8(a).
skʁeːpɔᴿ Nb, skɹeːpə Ch, skɹeːpəˡ Sa He Wo Mon
Gl*[modern, for flues x1]* O, skɽeːpɽ O, skɽeːpəˡ O,
skɽeːpəˡː W Co D Do, skreɪpə Man, skɹeɪpə Mon Nf,
skɹeɪpʔə Nf, skreɪpəᴶ Man, skɹeɪpəɹ He, skɽeɪpəˡː
So, skɹeːɪpəˡ He Mon Gl, skɹeˑəpə Nth, skɹeəpəˡ Bk,
skɹɛɪpə St Wo Lei Ess, skɹɛɪpəɹ Brk, skɹɛɪpəˡ Sa Wa,
skɹɛˑəpə L Nth, skɹɛˑəpɹ L, skɽaɪpəˡː Ha

scrape together *vtphr-3sg* she [a tidy girl] will
COLLECT her toys VIII.8.15. skɹɛəp ... təgɪðə L

scrape up *1. vtphr* to RAKE ash in a domestic fire
V.3.8(b). skɹɛɪp ... ʊp St

2. vtphr-3sg she [i.e. a tidy girl] will COLLECT her
toys VIII.8.15. skɹiːp ... ʊp Ch

scrap-faggots *n* KINDLING-*WOOD*   V.4.2.
skɹɛpfɛəgəts Ess

scrappings *n* SCRAPS left after rendering lard
III.12.10. skɹæpɪnz Sr, skɹapɪnz Y, skɹapənz Du

scrap(s) *n When the hot fat is drawn off [when
rendering lard], what is left behind?* III.12.10.
no -s: skɹæp Sf Ess K
-s: skɹeps Ess Sr K Sx, skræps Man, skɹæps Nf Sf Ess
Sr Ha Sx, skɽæps So, skɹaps Cu La Y Db Nt L R Nth
C, skɽaps So W Do Ha, skɹʊps Y
⇒ **browsells, crackling(s), cracknell(s), craffins,
crap(s), craplings, crapping(s), cratchings,
crinklings, crispings, crisps, crits, crittens,** *crittings*
⇒ **crittens, crittlings, crowkings, crowklings,
cruddings, crumpets, crumplings, crunchings,
crutchings, cruttens, fleed, flitters, fritters, grails,
greaves, gribbles, griddles, grizzle, groves, gruels,
riddings, ruddicks, scallops, scollops, scranchems,
scranchings, scrappings, scratch, scratching(s),
screeds, scridlings, scrippings, scrips, scrittlings,**
scroompings ⇒ **scrumpings, scroves, scrummets,**

**scrumpings, scrumps, scrutchings, scruttings,
scutchings, shrimps, skirtings**

scrap up *vtphr-3sg* she [i.e. a tidy girl] will
COLLECT her toys VIII.8.15. skɹæp ... ʌp Sf

scrat *1. n* a BENCH on which slaughtered pigs
are dressed III.12.1. skɹat Hu

2. vi to CHIP, referring to an egg that is about to
hatch IV.6.10. skɹat L

3. n **bit of scrat** a PIECE *OF BREAD AND
BUTTER* V.6.11(a). bɪt ə skɹat Wa

scrat-board *n* an END-BOARD of a cart I.10.4.
skɹætbɔːəˡd̥ Gl

scratch *1. n* a HAY-RACK in a stable I.4.1.
skɹatʃ La

2. n a BENCH on which slaughtered pigs are
dressed III.12.1. skɹætʃ Hu, skɹatʃ Y Nt Lei Nth

3. n SCRAPS left after rendering lard III.12.10.
skɹatʃ St

4. vi to CHIP, referring to an egg that is about to
hatch IV.6.10. skɹadʒ Nth

scratch-grass *n* GOOSE-GRASS   II.2.5.
skɹætʃgɹaːs Hu Hrt, skɹatʃgɹaːs C Hrt

scratching *v-ing What am I doing now [scratch
your head]?* VI.1.2.

v-ing skɹætʃɪn Nf Ess Sr K Sx, skɽɛtʃɪn So,
skɽɛtʃən D, skrætʃən Man, skɹætʃɪn He Gl Hu Nf
Sf Hrt Ess MxL Brk Sr K Ha Sx, skɹætʃn Brk,
skɹætʃən Sf Ess, skɽætʃɪn So, skɽæːtʃɪn So,
skɽætʃən Co, skætʃən Man, skʁatʃɪn Nb, skʁatʃn
Nb, skʁatʃən Nb Du, skɹatʃɪn La Y Db Sa He Wa
Mon Gl O Nt L Lei Nth Hu C Bk Hrt Sr K Ha,
skɹatʃən L C, skɽatʃɪn So W Co D Do Ha, skɽatʃn
O, skɽatʃən Co D Do Ha, skɹʌtʃɪn K
vt-ing skɹætʃɪn Nf

⇒ **digging, firking, firking** *about*, **raking,
rubbing, scrafting, scratting**

scratching(s) *n* SCRAPS left after rendering lard
III.12.10.
no -s: skɹatʃɪn Db O
-s: skɹɛtʃɒnz Db, skɹætʃɪnz Sa He Wo Wa Gl Nth
Sx, skɹatʃɪnz We La Ch Db Sa St He Wo Wa O Nt
Lei R Nth Hu Bk Bd, skɹatʃənz Db

scratch-weed *n* GOOSE-GRASS   II.2.5.
skɹætʃwiːd Hu Nf

scrat down *vtphr* to RAKE coal in a domestic fire
V.3.8(b). *-ing* skɹatɪn ... dæʊn Ch

scratting *v-ing* SCRATCHING VI.1.2. skɹætɪn
He Wo Mon Gl, əskɹætɪn He Wo, skratn Cu,
skʁatn Nb, skɹatɪn Cu La*[old x1]* Y*[old x1]* Ch
Db*[very old x1]* Sa St He Wo Wa Mon Nt L Lei
R Nth Bd Hrt, skɹattɪn La Ch Db, skɹaʔɪn O L Bk,
skɹatn Cu Du We Sa Gl, skɹatən We La Wa L,
skaːtn Nb*[very old]*, skaᴿːtn Nb *[not a NBM
headword]*

scraunch* *1. vt-1prpl* we CRUNCH apples or
biscuits VI.5.12. skɹɒnʃ Bk, skɹɔˑntʃ Nf, skɹɔːnʃ

O Nth C Nf Bk Bd, -ing skɹɔːnʃɪn Gl Hrt, skɹɔɪnʃ O
2. v-1prpl we crunch. -ing skɹɒnʃɪn K, skɹɔːntʃ Nf, skɹɔːᵊnʃ Bd Hrt, -ing skɹɔːᵊnʃɪn Bk

scrave *n* a BENCH on which slaughtered pigs are dressed III.12.1. skɹeɪv Nf, skɹeɪv Ess

scrave-board *n* a BENCH on which slaughtered pigs are dressed III.12.1. skɹeɪvbɔːəd Ess

scrawking *v-ing* SHRIEKING, describing the shrill noise made by a baby VI.5.15. skɹaːkɪn La

scrawl *vi-3prpl* they MEW, referring to cats III.10.6. -ing skɽaːɫən Co

scrawling *v-ing* SHRIEKING, describing the shrill noise made by a baby VI.5.15. skɽaːɫən D, skɽɔːɫɪn So

scrawl up *vtphr* to CLIMB VIII.7.4. skɹɑːɫ ʌp Mon

scrawmer *n* a MISER VII.8.9. skɹoʊmə St *[queried WMBM]*

scrawm up *vtphr* to CLIMB VIII.7.4. skɹɔːm ʊp Y

scream *vi If a child nipped her fingers in a door very badly, she'd most likely begin at once to ....* VIII.8.11. skriːm Cu Man, skɹiːm Du Y Sa St He Wo Wa Mon L Lei R Nf Sf Hrt Ess MxL W Brk Sr K Sx, sɹiim Ha, skɽiːm So W Co D Do, skɹɪəm La Y Nt L, skɽeːm W D Ha, skɽeɪm Ha; **scream and roar** skɹɪəm ən ɹʊə Y. ⇒ **bawl, beal, bell, bellock, blare, blart, bubble, cry, greet, harney, holler, howl, roar, scream** *and* **roar, scream out, screech, screech out, screet, shout, shriek, shriek out, skrike, skrike out, snoodle, squall, squall out, squawk, squawk out, squeal, tune, whinge, yell,** *yell and scream,* **yeller, yell out, yelp out, yowl**

screaming *v-ing* SHRIEKING, describing the shrill noise made by a baby VI.5.15. skriːmən Man, skɹiːmɪn Y Sa He Wo Mon Lei R Nf Ess MxL Brk Sr K Sx, skɹiːmən Cu Du Mon, skɽiːmɪn So W D, skɽiːmən Co D Do Ha, skɹɪəmɪn We La Y Nt L, skɹɪəmən Du, skɽeːmɪn W, skɽeːmən W

scream out *viphr* to SCREAM VIII.8.11. skɽiːm æʊt So

screech *1. n* a PADDOCK I.1.10. skɹɪitʃ Ess *[queried EMBM]*
2. vi to SCREAM VIII.8.11. skɽiːtʃ Co D, skɽɪtʃ Co, skɽɛɪtʃ Co, -ing skɹətʃɪn Y

screeching *v-ing* SHRIEKING, describing the shrill noise made by a baby VI.5.15. skɹiːtʃɪn Y Sr, skɽiːtʃɪn Do, skɽiːtʃən Co D Do, skɽɪtʃɪn D, skɽeːtʃən Co D

screech out *viphr* to SCREAM VIII.8.11. skɽɪtʃ œʏt D

screeds *n* SCRAPS left after rendering lard III.12.10. skɽiːdz Co

screeking *v-ing* SHRIEKING, describing the shrill noise made by a baby VI.5.15. skɹiːkɪn Y L

screen *v* to WINNOW II.8.4. skɹiːn Nf Bd

screenings *n* CHAFF II.8.5. skɹɪinɪnz Nf

screet *vi* to SCREAM VIII.8.11. skɹiːt La

screeting *v-ing* SHRIEKING, describing the shrill noise made by a baby VI.5.15. skɹiːtɪn La, skɽiːtɪn W, skɹɛɪtɪn Db

screet-owl *n* an OWL IV.7.6. skɹiːtuːl Y *[presumably particular, but not noted as such in NBM]*

screg* *vt* to REMOVE *STALKS* from currants V.7.24. -ing skɹɛgɪn K *[SBM queried headword* **scrig***]*

screw *1. n* a SHREW-MOUSE IV.5.2. skɽʏː Co, skɽuː Co
2. vt to WRING the neck of a chicken when killing it IV.6.20. *3prpl* skɹuz Mon, skɹu: La Y Ch Wa Nth Sr; **screw and tug** skɹuː ŋ tʌg Sr
3. n a MISER VII.8.9. skɽuː W
4. n **all of a screw, on the screw** ASKEW, describing a picture that is not hanging straight IX.1.3. **all of a screw** ɔːl əv ə skɽuː So; **on the screw** ɒn ðə skɹuː Sx

screwel *n* a SHREW-MOUSE IV.5.2. skɽɪʊɫ Co, skɽuːəɫ Co

screwer *n* a MISER VII.8.9. skɹuuːəᴶ Brk

screwing *vt-ing* PULLING his ear VI.4.4. skɹuː-ɪn Sx

screw-jye *adj* ASKEW, describing a picture that is not hanging straight IX.1.3. skɹuːdʒaɪ Y

screw out *vtphr* to WRING the neck of a chicken when killing it IV.6.20. skɹɪuː ... æːt Nt, skɹuː ... ɛːt Db, skɹuː ... aːt St

screw round *vtphr* to WRING the neck of a chicken when killing it IV.6.20. skɹɪu ... ɹɛand Y, skɹɪu ... əɹɛənd Y, skɹɪu ... ɹaːnd Y, skɹɪu ... ɹaʊnd La, skɹuː ... ɹaʊnd Ch L, skɹʏː ... ɹɛːnd La, skɹuː ... ɹaːnd Y, skɹuː ... ɹɔʊnd L

screw-ways *adj* ASKEW, describing a picture that is not hanging straight IX.1.3. skɹuːwɛɪz Sr Sx, skɽuːweːz Ha, skɽuːwaɪz Ha

screw-whiff *adj* ASKEW, describing a picture that is not hanging straight IX.1.3. skɽʏːwɪf D, skɽuːwɪf So Do

screwy *adj* ASKEW, describing a picture that is not hanging straight IX.1.3. skɽʊɪ Do

scrickings *n* STRIPPINGS, the last drops at milking III.3.4. skɹɪkɪnz Sx *[Edd note on possible error SBM]*

scridlings *n* SCRAPS left after rendering lard III.12.10. skɽɪdɫɪnz Co, skɽɪdəɫənz D

scrimmed up *adj* **scrimmed right up** VERY COLD, describing a person VI.13.19. skɽɪmd ɽæːd ʌp Co

scrim up *vtphr* to CLIMB VIII.7.4. skɹɪm ʊp Y *[old x1, scramble x1]*

scrippings *n* SCRAPS left after rendering lard III.12.10. skɽɪpənz D

scrips *n* SCRAPS left after rendering lard III.12.10. skɹɪps Gl Ess

scrittlings* *n* SCRAPS left after rendering lard III.12.10. skɹɪtlɪnz Ess

scrod-legged *adj* BOW-LEGGED VI.9.6. skɽɒdlɛgɪd So

scrod out *adv* ASTRIDE VI.9.8. skɽɒd aʊt So

scrog-footed *adj* SPLAY-FOOTED VI.10.5. skɹɒgfʊtəd Sf *[queried EMBM]*

scrog-hook *n* a BILLHOOK with a curved blade IV.2.6. skɹɒkhʊk Ess

scroochy *adj* LEFT-HANDED VI.7.13(a). skɽʏːtʃi D

scrounge *vt-1prpl* we CRUNCH apples or biscuits VI.5.12. *-ing* skɽæʏndʒɪn D

scrounger *n* a MISER VII.8.9. skɹɔːndʒə St *[marked u.r. WMBM]*

scroves *n* SCRAPS left after rendering lard III.12.10. skɹoːvz Co

scrub *1. n* BUSHES IV.10.5. skɹʌb Nf *[marked ir.r. EMBM]*

2. n a BROOM used for sweeping outdoors V.9.10. skɹuːb Wo

3. n the SCRUFF (of the neck) VI.6.2. skɹʌb Nf

scrub-broom *1. n* a BROOM used for sweeping outdoors V.9.10. skɹʌbbɹʊm Sa, skɹʌbbɹuːm Brk

2. n a BRUSH used for sweeping indoors V.9.11. skɹʊbbɹuːm Bk

scruck *n* the SCRUFF (of the neck) VI.6.2. skɹʊk Du

scruff *1, n* *If someone takes hold of a man here [point to the scruff of the neck], he will take him (by the) ... (of the neck).* VI.6.2. Eng exc. Ch Wo O Nt Lei R Sr. ⇒ **back, cuff, crag, nape, nod, nope, poll, scorp, scrub, scruck, scruffle, scruft, scuff, scuffle, scuft, scurf** *[forms generally + of the/his neck]*

2. n DANDRUFF VI.1.3. skɹɪʊf Cu, skɹɪuːf Du, skɹɪəf Nb We, skɹʏːf Db, skɐʌf Nb, skɹʌf Sa Mon Ess, skɽʌf So Co D, skɐɒf Nb, skɐʏf Nb, skɹʊf Cu Man*[old, common]*, skɐʊf Nb Du, skɹʊf Cu Du We La Y Ch*[old x2]* Sa He, skɹuːf La, skɹəf Gl *[not a NBM/WMBM headword]*

scruffle *n* the SCRUFF (of the neck) VI.6.2. skɹʊfl Y

scruffy *n* DANDRUFF VI.1.3. skɽʌfi D *[queried ir.r. SBM]*

scruft *n* the SCRUFF (of the neck) VI.6.2. skɹʊft La Y

scrug* *n* poor cattle, ⇐ KNACKER III.11.9. skɹʊg St

scrum *vt* to PULL somebody's hair VI.2.8. skɽʌm Co

scrummets *n* SCRAPS left after rendering lard III.12.10. skɽʌməts So

scrummy-handed *adj* LEFT-HANDED VI.7.13(a). skɹʌmɪ-ændɪd Mon

scrump *1. vt-1prpl* we CRUNCH apples or biscuits VI.5.12. *-ing* skɹʌmpɪn Brk

2. v to GOBBLE food VI.5.13(b). skɹʊmp Gl

scrumpings* *n* SCRAPS left after rendering lard III.12.10. skɹʊmpɪnz So

scrumps *n* SCRAPS left after rendering lard III.12.10. skɹəmps Gl

scrunch *1.1. vt-1prpl* we CRUNCH apples or biscuits VI.5.12. skɹʌnʃ Bk Bd Ess, *-ing* skɹʌnʃɪn K, skɽʌnʃ Do Ha, *-ing* skɽʌnʃɪn So D, *-ing* skɽʌnʃən D, skɹʊnʃ Gl

1.2. v-1prpl we crunch. *-ing* skɽæʊnʃɪn W, skɹʌnʃɪn Sr K, *-ing* skɽʌnʃɪn So W D, *-ing* skɽʌnʃən Co D

2. v to GOBBLE food VI.5.13(b). *-ing* skɹʊnʃɪn He

scrunch up *vtphr-1prpl* we CRUNCH apples or biscuits VI.5.12. *-ing* skɹʌnʃɪn ... ʌp Sr, *-ing* skɹʊnʃɪn ... ʊp O

scrunge *v-1prpl* we CRUNCH apples or biscuits VI.5.12. *-ing* skɽʌndʒɪn Ha

scrush-footed *adj* SPLAY-FOOTED VI.10.5. skɽʌʃvʊtɪd Do

scrutchings *n* SCRAPS left after rendering lard III.12.10. skɹʌtʃɪnz Mon, skɹʊtʃɪnz He

scruttings *n* SCRAPS left after rendering lard III.12.10. skɹʊtnz Gl

scud* *n* a ROPE-TWISTER II.7.8. skəd Ess *[EMBM sked, but compare scud-winder]*

scudder *, n* a BENCH on which slaughtered pigs are dressed III.12.1. skʌdə Ess

scudding-board *n* a BENCH on which slaughtered pigs are dressed III.12.1. skʌdnbɔːəd Ess

scud(s) *n* straw ROPES used to fasten thatch on a stack II.7.7(b2). skʌdz Sf

scud-winder *n* a ROPE-TWISTER II.7.8. skʌdwɔɪndə Sf, skʌdwʌɪndə Sf

scuff *n* the SCRUFF (of the neck) VI.6.2. skɒf Ha, skʌf Sa O Nth Nf Sf Bk Bd Hrt Ess W Brk Sr K Sx, skʊf Cu Du We La Y Ch Db Sa St He Wo Wa Gl L Lei R Nth

scuffle *1. vt* to THIN OUT turnip plants II.4.2. *2prpl* skʌflz Sa

2. n the SCRUFF (of the neck) VI.6.2. skʌfɫ Ess

scuffling-apron *n* a working APRON V.11.2(a). skʌflɪnɛɪpɹn K

scuft *n* the SCRUFF (of the neck) VI.6.2. skʌft Sf, skʊft La Y Ch Db Sa St Nt L Lei

scug *n* a BOGEY VIII.8.1. skʊg Ch

scuggy *n* a SQUIRREL IV.5.8. skʌgi Ha

scullery *n* a PANTRY V.2.6. skʌləɹɪ MxL Sr, skʊləɹɪ La Y

scummer *n* a SHOVEL for a household fire V.3.9. skʊmə Y

scunch *v-1prpl* we CRUNCH apples or biscuits VI.5.12. *-ing* skʌnʃən D

scurf *1. n* DANDRUFF VI.1.3. Eng exc. We Man

2. n the SCRUFF (of the neck) VI.6.2. skɹəᵊːf Sa, skaᵊːf Do Ha, skɔᵊːf Brk, skəːf Wo MxL Sr, skəᴶf

Sr, skəᶜf Sr, skəɽf O, skəᶜːf He Gl W Sr K Sx *[not an EMBM headword]*

3. *n* a LOOSE *PIECE OF* SKIN at the bottom of a finger-nail VI.7.11. skəᶜːɽf W

scurfy *n* DANDRUFF VI.1.3. skəᶜːfɪ K *[queried ir.r. SBM]*

scurry-comb *n* a CURRY-COMB used to clean horses III.5.5(b). skʌɾikuːəm W

scurvy *1. n* MANGE, which causes dogs and cats to lose their hair III.13.7. skəːvɪ Nf

2. *n* DANDRUFF VI.1.3. skɔᴶːvɪ La, skuɹvɪ Y, skəːvɪ Y, skəᴶˑbɪ Nf

scut *1. n* a FARM-LABOURER I.2.4. skʊt Man

2. *n* the TAILBOARD of a cart I.10.2. skʊt Cu La

3. *n* a DRAG used to slow a wagon I.11.3. skʊt La

scutch *1. n* COUCH-GRASS II.2.3. skʌtʃ Sa He, skʊtʃ Ch Sa St He Wo Mon

2. *vt* to BEAT a boy on the buttocks VIII.8.10. skʊtʃ Man

scutch-grass *n* COUCH-GRASS II.2.3. skʌtʃgɹaːs He

scutchings *n* SCRAPS left after rendering lard III.12.10. skʊtʃɪnz Mon

scuttle *1. n* a SOWING-BASKET II.3.6. skɪtɫ Hrt, skʌtɫ Hu Hrt, skʌʔɫ Hu, skʊtl Du L, skʊʔɫ C

2. *n* a container for carrying horse-feed, ⇐ BASKET III.5.4. skʊtɪl Y*[wicker, no handles]*, skʊtl Cu*[basket-work x2, 'a swill with 2 handles and an open mouth at the front' x1]* La*[basket-work, like a flour-scoop]* Y*[willow, oval, no handles x1; metal, bowl-shaped x1]* L*[oval, metal, with handles]*, skʊtɫ Wo*[round, wicker]* Lei*[metal, with handles x2; metal x1]*, skʊtəɫ Gl*[metal]*

scuttle-basket *n* an oval basket-work BASKET for carrying horse-feed III.5.4. skʊtlbaskɪt Wo

scwutch *n* COUCH-GRASS II.2.3. skwʊtʃ Gl

scythe *1. n [Show a picture of a scythe.] What do you call this?* II.9.6. sɛɪð Du Sa, zæːð D, zæːv D, zæː Co D, sæɪð Man He So, zæɪð So, zæɪv So, saːð Y, saɪð Nb Cu Du We La Y Ch Db Sa St He Wo Nt L Lei So, zaɪð So, saɪθ Du, saɪv So, zaɪv So, saɪ Cu We Co, zaɪ Co, saːð La Y, saːθ Db, saɪð La Y Ch Db Wa Nt L Lei R Nth Hu C Nf Bk Bd Hrt Ess MxL Sr K, saˑɪθ Lei, saɪ Lei K, sɒɪð Sa St Wo Gl Nf So K Ha, zɒɪð So Ha, sɒɪv So W, zɒɪv So W Do Ha, zɒɪ Co, sɔɪð Wo Wa O Nth Sf Bk Hrt Ess Brk Sr K Ha Sx, sɔɪθ Gl, sɔɪv Nth Sf, zɔɪv So, sɔɪz Bk Ess, sɔəð L, sʌɪð Wa O Nf Sf Brk Sr, sʌɪv Gl, zʌɪv Gl, sʌɪz Nf Sr, sʌɪ Nf Sr, sʌʌɣð O, səɪð He Wo Mon Gl Brk Sx, zəɪð Gl Do, səɪθ He, zəɪᵊθ Gl, səɪv He Mon, zəɪv W Do, səɪz Sx. ⇒ **lea**, **lea-scythe**

2.1. vt to CLEAR grass at the edges of a field II.9.5. saɪv So, saɪð Nt Bd, sɔɪð Bk

2.2. v to clear grass. sɔɪz Bk

scythe-bat *n* the SHAFT of a scythe II.9.7. sɒɪðbɛt K

scythe-handle *n* the SHAFT of a scythe II.9.7. saɪvhændʊ So, zɒɪvandɫ W, sɔɪðændʊɫ Brk, zɔɪvændɫ So, zəɪvandɫ W

scythe-hook *n* the GRASS-NAIL of a scythe II.9.9. saɪðʊuk Y, saɪðᵁuːk Nt

scythe-mow *v* to CLEAR grass at the edges of a field II.9.5. *-ing* zʌɪvmaʊɪn Gl*[with scythe]*

scythe-nail *n* the GRASS-NAIL of a scythe II.9.9. saˑɪðnɛɪl L

scythe-nibs *npl* the HANDLES of a scythe II.9.8. sɔɪðnɪbz Wa

scythe out *vtphr* to CLEAR grass at the edges of a field II.9.5. sʌɪzɪn ... ɛʊt Sr

scythe-pole *n* the SHAFT of a scythe II.9.7. saɪðpɛʊ La Ch Db, saɪðpʊ Y, saɪðpɔʊl Y, saːðpɔʊl Y, saɪðpɛʊ Ch, saɪðpɔʊl Y

scythe-rubber *n* a WHETSTONE made of unspecified material II.9.10. saːɪðɹʊbə St

scythe-snathe* *n* the SHAFT of a scythe II.9.7. zæːsneːv D

scythe-snead *n* the SHAFT of a scythe II.9.7. zæɪvsniːd So, sɔɪðsnɛd Wa, sʌɪðnɪəd Brk, zəɪvsnjed Do, zəɪvsnɪəd W *[Brk form queried SBM]*

scythe-stave *n* the SHAFT of a scythe II.9.7. zəɪvsteːv W

scythe-steal *n* the SHAFT of a scythe II.9.7. saːðstɛɪl Y

scythe-stick *1. n* the SHAFT of a scythe II.9.7. saɪðstɪk Wa L Nth Hu Nf, sɒɪðstɪk Gl Nf, zɒɪðstɪk So, zɒɪvstɪk So, sɔɪðstɪk O Sf, sɔɪθstɪk Gl Ess, sʌɪðstɪk Nf Sf Brk, zʌɪvstɪk Gl, zəɪðstɪk Gl Do

2. *n* a wooden implement, greased and sanded, used to sharpen a scythe, ⇐ WHETSTONE II.9.10. saˑɪðstɪk L, saˑɪstɪk Lei

3. *n* sandpaper attached to wood, used to sharpen a scythe. saɪðstɪk Db

scythe-stone *n* a WHETSTONE II.9.10. saɪðstoːn Db, saɪðstʊən Y, saːðstoːn La, saːðstʊən Y, saɪðstʌʊn Bd, saɪðstoːn La Ch, saɪðstoːᵁn Nt, saɪðstən Db Nt Lei, saˑɪstən Lei, saˑɪðstɔʊn Lei, saˑɪðstoˑʊn Db, sɒːɪðstən St, sʌɪðstʊun Sr, səɪðstoːn Mon Brk, zəɪᵊθstʊn Gl, zæːvstuːən D, zæːstuːn D, zæɪvstoːən So, zæɪvstuːn So, zæɪvstuːən So

scythe-strick *n* a wooden implement, greased and sanded, used to sharpen a scythe, ⇐ WHETSTONE II.9.10. saˑɪðstɹɪk L

sea-crow *n* a GULL IV.7.5. siːkɹɒʊ Gl, *pl* siːkɹɔːz O, siːkɹʌʊ Sf, sɪˑəkɹɔːᵊz Y, *pl* seɪkʁaːz Nb, seɪkɹʌʊ Sf

sea-gull *n* a GULL IV.7.5. Eng exc. Man

seal *1. n* a TETHER for a cow, made of rope or chain I.3.4. sɪəl La Y

2. *n* a chain tether. sɪəl Y

3.1. vt to STOCK III.3.6. *-ing* siːlɪn Y, sɪʊɫ K

3.2. v to stock. sɪəl Y

4. n WILLOW IV.10.7. sɪəl We La Y

seal-chain *n* a chain TETHER for a cow I.3.4. sɪəltʃɛɪn Y

sealing-iron *n* a TETHERING-STAKE in a cow-house I.3.3. siːlɪnɛɪəɪn La

sealing-post *n* a TETHERING-STAKE in a cow-house I.3.3. siːlɪnpʊəst Y

seals *n* the HAMES of the harness of a cart-horse I.5.4. sɪlz Nf, siːᵊlz Sf Ess, sɪiːʊz Ess, seˑlz Nf, seɪlz Nf, sɛɪᵊlz Sf, seˑɪlz Nf

seal-stake *n* a TETHERING-STAKE in a cow-house I.3.3. sɪəlsteːk Y

seal up *1. vtphr* to STOCK III.3.6. *3prpl* siːl ... ʊp Y, *-ing* siːlɪn ... ʊp Y, *-ing* sɪəlɪn ... ʊp La Y

2. vphr to stock. *ptppl* sɪəld ʊp La

seam **1. n* LARD made from the fat of a pig III.12.8. siːm L Lei Nth Nf, sɪəm Nb Cu Du Y L

2. n a STITCH V.10.4. siːm St

sea-mall *n* a GULL IV.7.5. *pl* siːmɔˑəlz L

sea-martin *n* a GULL IV.7.5. *pl* siːmaᶜʔənz O

sea-maw *n* a GULL IV.7.5. sɪəmaː La, sɪˑəmɔː L, sɪːəmʊ Nf

seams *npl* the RIDGES between furrows in a ploughed field II.3.2. *sg* sɪˑəm L

search *vt* LOOK FOR it III.13.18. siːtʃ La, səːtʃ Ch

search around for *vtphr* LOOK FOR it III.13.18. səᶜːtʃ əɹɛʊnd fəˡɹ Sr

search for *vtphr* LOOK FOR it III.13.18. səːʃ fəɹ Man, səʃ Man, səɹᶜtʃ fɔɹ Nf, səᶜtʃ fɔːɹ K, səːtʃ fɔɹ Wa Nf, səˡɹtʃ fɒɹ Brk, səˡːtʃ fəˡːɹ Sr, səˡːtʃ fəˡɹ Sr, səᶜːtʃ fəɹ K

season *1. n* **in season** ON HEAT, describing a cow III.1.6. ɪn siːsən Man, ɪn siːzn So

2. n **in season** ON HEAT, describing a sow III.8.9. ɪn siːzn Mon Nf Ess So

3. n **any season** ANY TIME VII.3.16. ɛnɪ sɪizən Nf

seat *1. n* the BREECH-BAND of the harness of a cart-horse I.5.10. siːt So

2. n a tree STUMP IV.12.4. siːt St

3. n the ARSE VI.9.2. sɪˑət L

seave *n* a EWE-HOG III.6.4. *pl* sɛɪvz St

seck *n* (what) SORT VII.8.17. **(what) seck** sɛk Cu; **(what) seck (of)** sɛk We

seckie *n* a SEXTON VIII.5.4. sɛkɪ Y

second-crop *1. n* AFTERMATH, a second crop of grass II.9.17. sɪknkɹɒp Ess, sɛknd kʁœːp Nb, sɛknkɹap Nf, sɛknkɹapʔ Nf, sɛkən krɒp Man, sɛkndkɹɒp L, sɛknd kɹɒp La Ch, sɛkənd kɹɒp O, sɛkəntkɹɒp Bd, sɛknkɹɒp Nf Hrt Ess Sr K, sɛŋkɹɒp Ess, sɛkən kɹɒp Ch, sɛkənkɾɒp W Co Ha, sɛknd kʁɒp Nb, sɛknkɹɔp Sf Ess

2. n a second crop of clover or clover and sainfoin. sɛknkɹɒp Hrt, sɛkndkɹɔp L, sɛkʔnkɹɒp Sf

second-cut *1. n* AFTERMATH, a second crop of grass II.9.17. zɛkʌnkʌt W, sɛknkʌt Ess Sr K Sx, sɛkŋkʌt Ess, sɛknkʌʔ K, zɛknkʌt W, sɛkəndkʌt MxL, sɛkənkʌt MxL Sr K Do Ha, zɛkənkʌt Ha

2. n a second crop of clover or clover and rye-grass. sɛknkʌt C, sɛkənkʌt Ess

second cutting *n* AFTERMATH, a second crop of grass, cut for silage II.9.17. sɛkən kʊtən Man

second-grass *n* AFTERMATH, a second crop of grass II.9.17. sɛkəngɹaːs Do

second-growth *n* AFTERMATH, a second crop of grass II.9.17. sɛkəngɹɔːθ Co

second-hay *n* AFTERMATH, a second crop of grass II.9.17. sɛknhɛɪ Ess

second shearling *n* a sheep from its first to its second shearing, ⇐ GIMMER III.6.5. sɛkənd ʃɪəᶜlɪn Wo *[taken in WMBM to refer to sheep after second shearing, and hence 'perhaps' u.r.]*

second shearling ewe *n* a GIMMER III.6.5. sɛkəndʃɪəᶜlɪn jʌʊ K

second-theave *n* a GIMMER III.6.5. sɛkəntθiːθ Lei

second-tooth *n* a sheep from its first to its second shearing, ⇐ GIMMER III.6.5. sɛkntuːθ Sx

second-year ewe *n* a GIMMER III.6.5. sɛkndɪˑə juː Y

see **1. imp* **see, see back, see off, see off a bit** the command TURN RIGHT!, given to plough-horses II.3.5(b). **see** sˡiː Gl; **see back** 'sˡiː bæk Mon, siː bak Mon; **see off** 'siː 'ɑːf Mon, 'siː ɒf He; **see off a bit** ʃiː ɔːf ə bɪt Mon

2. vt **see after, see to** LOOK AFTER VIII.1.23. **see after** sɪi ɑːftə Nf; **see to** sɪi tu Nf*[polite]*, zɪː tə W

seed *1. vi* to show signs of calving, referring to a cow with a swollen udder, ⇐ SHOWS SIGNS OF CALVING III.1.12(a). *3prprogsg* siːdɪn Nb, *3prprogsg* siːdn Nb

2. n TREAD inside a fertile egg IV.6.9. siːd He MxL

seed-apron *n* an alternative to a SOWING-BASKET II.3.6. siːdeːpʁən Du *[marked u.r. NBM]*

seed-basket *n* a SOWING-BASKET II.3.6. siːdbaskɪt Ch L, sɪiːdbaːskɪt Ess, siːdbɑskɪt L, səɪdbaskɪt Y

seed-bodge *n* a SOWING-BASKET II.3.6. siːdbɒdʒ K

seed-box *n* a SOWING-BASKET II.3.6. sɪidbɒks Sx

seed-brat *n* an alternative to a SOWING-BASKET II.3.6. siːdbɹat Cu La *[marked u.r. NBM]*

seed-cob *n* a SOWING-BASKET II.3.6. sɪiːdkɔᵊb Ess, siːdkəp K seed-cord *n* a SOWING-BASKET II.3.6. siːdkɔːd K, sɪidkɔˑ᠌ʲːd K, sɪidkɔəˑ᠌ʲd K

seed-cot *n* a SOWING-BASKET II.3.6. siːkʌʔ Bk, sɪdkʌʔ O Bk, sɪdkət Brk

seed-cup *n* a SOWING-BASKET II.3.6. sɪdkʌp O *[not a WMBM headword, and apparently taken as seed-cot; seed-cup a queried EMBM headword, though forms in Bk seem more like seed-cot and have been treated as such]*

seed-field *n* a MEADOW II.9.2. siːdfiːld L*[ploughed annually]*, siːdfiːl Man

seed-hopper *n* a SOWING-BASKET II.3.6. siːɒpəɹ La, siːdɒpəᵗ Sa Sx, siːɔpəᵎ La, sɛidɒpə St

seed-lift* *n* a SOWING-BASKET II.3.6. siːdlɪft Mon, sɪdlɪft Mon, sɪdlɪf He Mon, sɪdɫɪf Mon, zɪdɫɪf Gl *[taken as seed-lip BM]*

seed-lip *n* a SOWING-BASKET II.3.6. siːdlɪp O*[made of iron, kidney-shaped]* Bk So Brk Sr*[galvanised metal x1]* Sx, sɪidɪp Brk, ziːdlɪp So Ha, siːdɫɪp Co Ha, ziːdɫɪp So W Co D Do Ha, siːdɫæp Co, siːdɫəp Co, ziːˑᵊdləp So, ziːɫəp D, sɪdlɪp Gl O Brk Sr Sx, zɪdlɪp Gl, *pl* zɪdlɪps So, sɪdɫɪp O, zɪdɫɪp W Do Ha, zɪɫɪp D, sɪdlʌp Nf, sɪdlʊp Wa Nf, sɪdɫʊp Gl, sɪdləp Nf Sx, sɪdlət Nf, zɪdlək Ha, sɛdlɪt Hrt, sɛdɫʊp Nf, sɛdlʌp Nf, sɛdləp Nf, zɛɪdɫɪp Co, sædlʌp Nf, sædlʊp Nf, sædᵗʊp Nf, sɪblɪt Nth, sɛblɪt Nth*[very old]* Bd, sɪbɫʊk Gl, sɛplɪt C, zɪɫəp D, zɛɫʌp D, zɛɫəp Co D, zʌɫəp Do

seed-scuttle *n* a SOWING-BASKET II.3.6. sˤiːdskʌʔɫ Bk

seed-sheet *n* a canvas alternative to a SOWING-BASKET II.3.6. sɪiːdʃiːt Sr*[a Scots idea] [marked u.r. SBM]*

seed-skep *n* a SOWING-BASKET II.3.6. siːdskɛp L, sɪiːdskɔˑᵊb Ess

seed-tray *n* a SOWING-BASKET II.3.6. sɪiːdtɹɛɪ Ess

seed-trug *n* a SOWING-BASKET II.3.6. sɪiːdtɹʊg Sx

seedy 1. *adj* ILL, describing a person who is unwell VI.13.1(b). siːdi D, sɪiˑdɪ Nf; **a bit seedy** ə bɪt ziːdi D
2. *adj* SICK, describing an animal that is unwell VI.13.1(c). zeːdi Ha

see for *vtphr* LOOK FOR it III.13.18. siː faᵗː Co

seek *vt* LOOK FOR it III.13.18. siːk La Y Db L, sɛɪk Db, səɪk Y

seeking *n* a person's own FAULT VIII.9.6. siːkɪn So

seepy* *adj* **go seepy** to SPOIL, referring to meat or fish V.7.10. gou siːpɪ St

seesaw 1. *n Children also like to play on a [indicate action of a seesaw].* VIII.7.2. Eng. ⇒ **butt-away, hayly-gayly, hayty-bayty, hightle, highty, highty-tighty, linchy-lunch, linkum-jinkum, lunch, mounting-swing, queagle, rant, ranting-board, rantipole, ranty, seesaw-plank, shaddle, sharrow, shiggly, shuggy, swaygog, sweepole, tee-totter,** **tiddy-bump, tikant, tintant, tintitant, tippen-totter, tippeny-totter, tippety-totter, tittema-totter, titter, tittery, tittery-tot, tweedle, tweezle;** ⇒ also **lunchy**
2. *n* a SAWING-HORSE I.7.16. sᵎiːsɔᵗː Sa

seesaw-plank *n* a SEESAW VIII.7.2. siːsɑːplaŋk Wo

seg *n* a CALLOSITY VI.11.4. sɛg Cu La Y Sa, *pl* sɛgz We Man Ch*[old x1]* Db St, *pl* sagz Sa

segg *n* a cow that is NOT IN CALF and is unlikely to conceive III.1.8. sɛg Y

segged *v-ed* CASTRATED, describing a bullock III.1.15. sɛgd Ch St, sɛg Db

segged quarter *n* a BLIND TEAT III.2.7. sɛgd kwatəɹ Y

self-binder-string *n* STRING used to tie up a grain-sack I.7.3. sɛɫfbɑɪndəᵗstɹɪŋ Ha

sembles *vt-3prsg* he RESEMBLES VIII.1.9. sɛmblz Nf, sɛmbɫ Ess, də zɛmbɫ Co *[not a SBM headword]*

semmit 1. *n* a VEST VI.14.9. sɪmət Cu
2. *adj* BRITTLE, describing cups and saucers which break easily IX.1.4. sɛmɪt Y

sensitive *adj* SHY VIII.9.2. sɛnsɪtɪf Ch

separate *vt* to RENDER fat into lard III.12.9. sɛpəᵗɹɛɪt Sx

separating *v-ing* CULLING sheep III.11.2. sɛpəɹeitɪn Mon, *vt* sɛpəɹɛɪt Ess

septic *adj* **get septic, go septic, turn septic** to FESTER, referring to a wound VI.11.8. **get septic** gɛʔ sɛptɪk W, *3prsg* gɛts sɛptɪk Sr; **go septic** goˑ sɛptɪk Mon, gou sɛptɪk St, gʊ sɛptɪk Sa, guː sɛptɪk Y*[modern]* He, gə sɛptɪk Lei, *-ing* gwɪn sɛptɪk Sr; **turn septic** tœːn sɛptɪk Mon, təːn sɛptɪk St Lei, *3prsg* təːnz sɛptɪk Wa Ess, təᵗːn̩ sɛptɪk Ess So W K Ha

servant-man *n* a FARM-LABOURER I.2.4. saːvəntman Y

serve 1. *v* to PITCH sheaves II.6.10. səᵗːv Sa Gl
2.1. *vt* to FEED cattle III.3.1. saːv Y
2.2. *v* to feed cattle. saːv Y

serve-cake *n* a PIECE OF BREAD AND BUTTER AND JAM/SUGAR V.6.11(b). ə saːvkɛək Y

served 1. *v-ed* **is not served** HAS NOT HELD, referring to a cow that has not conceived III.1.7. jʊnt sjəᵗːvd Wo
2. *adj* **not served** NOT IN CALF, but able to conceive III.1.8. nɒt səᵗːvd W

server 1. *n* a BASKET for carrying horse-feed III.5.4. sɛəvə R*[wicker, round]*, saːvə Y*[old x1]* St*[basket-work x1]* Nt*[wicker, no handles]* L*[metal x1]*, səːvə St*[round x1, basket-work x1, old x1]* Nt*[metal]* Lei R, səᵗːvəᵗ Sa*[metal]*
2. *n* a container for taking corn out of a bin. saːvə Y

347

3. n a container for measuring corn for horse-feed. saɹvəɹ Y

serving* *v-ing* FEEDING horses in the stable III.5.1. saːvin Y

sess *1. n* a CUTTING of hay II.9.15. sɛs Ch Db St

2. n PEAT IV.4.3. sɛs C

set *1. adj* IN CALF III.1.10. sɛʔ Nf

2. n a BROOD of chickens IV.6.12. sɛt Man

3.1. vt to CURDLE milk V.5.7. sɛt Y, *3prsg* sɛts Man

3.2. vi **make it set** to curdle milk. mɛk ɪt sɛʔ Nf

4. vt to LAY the table V.8.12. sɪʔ Nf, sɛt Nb Cu Du We La Y Ch Db St Nt L Lei R Nth Hu C Nf Sf Bd Ess So K*[old]*, sɛtʔ Nf, sɛʔ Nf Bk Hrt, sɛʔɪn Hu Ess; **get the table set** gɛt ʔ tɹabl sɛt Y

5. vi to WANE, referring to the moon VII.6.5(b). *-ing* əsɛtɪn Wo

set back *vtphr* **get your hair set back** *GET YOUR HAIR CUT* VI.2.2. gɪt jəɹ ɛəᴵ sɛt bɛk K

set down *imp* SIT DOWN VIII.3.3. sɛt dɛʊn Sr, sɛʔ dɛʊn O C Nf Sf Bd, sɛ dɛʊn C Nf Ess, sɛd dɛʊn Sf Ha, sɛt dæyn Co, sɛd dæyn Co, zɛt dæʊn Ha, zɛd dæʊn Ha, sɛt daʊn O, sɛt dʌʊn Gl Brk, *inf* sat dæyn Co

set-off *n* the CURB-STONE in a cow-house I.3.9. sɛtɔːf Lei

set on *viphr* to stick to the bottom of a pan, said of PORRIDGE V.7.1. *3prprogsg* sɛtɪn ɒn

set out *1.1. vtphr* to THIN OUT turnip plants II.4.2. sɛt ... ɛʊt Nth Sf MxL Sr Sx, sɛt ... ɛʊʔ Bd Hrt, *-ing* sɛʔn ... ɛʊt K, sɛʔ ... ɛʊʔ Bk, zɛt ... æʊt Ha, sɛt ... əʊt Sx

1.2. vphr to thin out turnips. sɛt ɛʊt Hrt, sɛtʔ ɛʊt Bk

2. vtphr to LAY the table V.8.12. sɛt ... uːt Nb Cu Y, sɛt ᵊuːt Du

set-screw *n* the T-SHAPED PLOUGH-BEAM END of a horse-drawn plough I.8.5. zɛtskɽuː So *[marked ir.r. SBM]*

set-staff *n* the STRETCHER between the traces of a cart-horse I.5.11. sɛtstaf Lei

set-stick *1. n* the STRETCHER between the traces of a cart-horse I.5.11. sɪtstɪk Ess, sɛtstɪk L C Nf Sf Ess, sɛtʃstɪk Nf

2. n a movable horizontal rod stretching between the shafts of a cart, fixing them to the cart-body and stopping the cart from tipping, ⇐ ROD/PIN I.10.3. sɛtstɪk Wa Nf Ess

3. n a STICK used to support the shaft of a cart I.11.1. sɛtstɪk Y L C Nf Sf Hrt Ess

4. n a device used to prevent a cart from going backwards on a hill, ⇐ PROP/CHOCK I.11.2. sɛtstɪk L

setter *1. n* the STRETCHER between the traces of a cart-horse I.5.11. sɛtə R Nth Hu, sɛtəɹ La

2. n an EVENER on a horse-drawn plough I.8.4. sɛʔəᴵ Brk

3. n a BROODY HEN IV.6.7. sɛtə Hrt, sɛtʔə Nf MxL, sɛʔə Bk, sɛtəᵗ O, sɛʔəᵗ O Bk; **old setter** ʌʊl sɛʔə Nf

setter-bar *n* the STRETCHER between the traces of a cart-horse I.5.11. sɛtəᴵbaᴵː La

setter-stick *n* the STRETCHER between the traces of a cart-horse I.5.11. sɛtəstɪk L Lei Nth

setting *n* a BROOD of chickens IV.6.12. sɛtn Sf, sɛʔn Ess

setting hen *n* a BROODY HEN IV.6.7. sɛtn hɪn Nf, sɛtn hɛn Sf Ess, sɛtʔn hɪn Nf, sɛʔn hɛn Ess; **old setting hen** oʊl sɛtn hɪn Nf

setting-stick *1. n* the STRETCHER between the traces of a cart-horse I.5.11. sɛtnstɪk Nf

2. n a STICK used to support the shaft of a cart I.11.1. sɛtnstɪkʰ Nb

setting up *vphr-ing* STOOKING II.6.5. sɛtɪn (...) ʊp La Y, *inf* sɛt ʊp Ch St, *v* sɛt ʊp Db, zɛtɪn ʌp W, zɛtən ʌp W, zɛdɪn ʌp D

settle *n* the CURB-STONE in a cow-house I.3.9. sɛtl Du

settless *n* a flat surface on which bacon is cured, ⇐ SALTING-TROUGH III.12.5. sɛtlɪs Sa*[stone]*, sɛtləs Ch*[stone]* St

settle-stone(s) *n* the CURB-STONE in a cow-house I.3.9.

no -s: sɛtlstɪan We, sɛtlstɪən Y, sɛtlstʊən Y, sɛtlstn Cu Du We, sɛtlstən Cu We La Y

s: sɛtlstɪnz Y, sɛtlstɪənz Y, sɛtlstnz La Y

settle-tree *1. n* the CURB-STONE in a cow-house, made of wood or stone I.3.9. sɛtəltɹiː Y

2. n a wooden curb-stone in a cow-house. sɛtltɹiː Y, sɛtlθɹiː La

settling *n* the CURB-STONE in a cow-house I.3.9. sɛtlɪn Nb

settly *adj* BAD, describing an egg V.7.11. sɛtlɪ Brk

set to *imp* HELP YOURSELVES!, said to invite visitors to eat V.8.13. sɛt tuː Sa Ess, sɛʔ tʉ Nf*[old]*

setty *1. n* a BROODY HEN IV.6.7. sɛtɪ W Ha, sɛtɪ Brk

2. adj broody, describing a hen. sɛʔɪ Brk

3. adj BAD, describing an egg V.7.11. sɛtɪ Brk

setty hen *n* a BROODY HEN IV.6.7. sɛtɪ hɛn W, sɛtɪ ɛn W Ha, zɛtɪ ɛn Ha, sɛtɪ ɛn Ha, sɛʔɪ ɛn O

set up *1. vtphr* to fill gaps in a hedge-bank or hedge with turfs, brushwood, or similar material, ⇐ to PLASH IV.2.4. zɪd ʌp D, zɛd (...) ʌp D

2. vtphr to LAY the table V.8.12. *-ing* sɛtɪn ... ʊp La

set yourself down *imp* SIT DOWN VIII.3.3. zɛt ðɪzɛɫf dæʊn Ha, sɛt ðɪsɛl dᵊuːn Du

sew *1. v What do you say you do with your needle and thread?* V.10.3. Eng. ⇒ **stitch**

*2. n a DRY cow III.1.9. zʏː D

sewer *n* URINE in a cow-house I.3.10. sɪuːə Cu

sewer-pit *n* an artificial CESS-POOL on a farm I.3.11. suːəˡpɪt Brk

sexton *n* *What do you call the man who looks after the church building, and keeps it warm and clean?* VIII.5.4. Eng. ⇒ **caretaker, church-clerk,** *church-sexton,* **church-warden, clerk, dobbie, grave-digger, parish-clerk, seckie, verger, warden**

shackle *1. n* a TETHER for a cow I.3.4. ʃɛkʊ Ess
2. n a sliding RING to which a tether is attached in a cow-house I.3.5. ʃɛkəl Nb, ʃakl Cu Ch, ʃakəl We
3. n a WRIST VI.6.9. ʃɛkl Nb Y, ʃakl Nb La Y, ʃakəl Y
4. n an ANKLE VI.10.7. ʃakl Y

shackle(s) *n* the T-SHAPED PLOUGH-BEAM END of a horse-drawn plough I.8.5.
no -s: ʃɛkl We, ʃæku Sr, ʃakl Nb We Y, ʃakəl Y
-s: ʃaklz Y

shackles *n* BROTH V.7.20(a). ʃækɫz So, ʃækɒuz Sx, ʃaklz O*[old x1]*, ʃakɫz Wa So Do

shaddle *n* a SEESAW VIII.7.2. ʃadl La

shade *n* a HEN-HOUSE I.1.6. ʃeːd La

shaft *1. n* *What do you call the part between the handle and the metal spade?* I.7.7. ʃɛˑəft Ha, ʃæft So, ʃæːf Sx, ʃæːft Gl, ʃaf Y Lei, ʃaft Nb Cu Du We La Y Ch Db Sa St Wa O Nt L Lei R, ʃaːf O Nth Hu Bk So, ʃaːft Sa He Wa L Nth C Nf Bk Bd Ess W, *pl* ʃaːfs Sf, *pl* ʃaːvz Sf, ʃaːf Nf Hrt Sx, ʃaːft Nf MxL Ha. ⇒ **fork, graft, handle, hean, helm, helve, hilt, jump, shank, shovel-hilt, spade-handle, spade-shaft, spade-stick, spade-tree, span,** *spean* ⇒ **span, spittle-tree, staff, stale,** *steal* ⇒ **stale, stem, stick, stock, strap, tiller, tree**
2. n *[What do you call a fork with two prongs?] What do you call this part [the handle]?* I.7.12. ʃɛˑəft Ha, ʃæːft Gl Nf, ʃaf Lei Brk, ʃaft Nb Cu Du We La Y Db St Wa Nt L Lei R, ʃaːf Hu Nf Sf So, ʃaːft O L Nth C Nf Bk, ʃaːf Nf Hrt Ha, ʃaːft Nf MxL Sr. ⇒ **foot, fork-handle, graft, handle, handle-shaft, hilt, peek-stick, pick-handle, pick-stale,** *pick-steal* ⇒ **pick-stale, pick-stem, pike-handle, pike-hilt, pitch-handle, prong-handle, prong-steal, shank, staff, stake, stale, stale, steal, stem, stick, stock**
3. n *[Show a picture of a scythe.] What do you call this [the handle]?* II.9.7. ʃæːft C, ʃaft Cu Du We Y Nt L, ʃaf Lei, ʃaːft Wo Mon O L Nth Bk, ʃaːf Bk; scythe-shaft saːðʃaft Y. ⇒ **bat, beam, handle, heft, lea-shaft, long-snead, pole, scythe-bat, scythe-handle, scythe-pole,** *scythe*-shaft, **scythe-snathe, scythe-snead, scythe-stave, scythe-steal, scythe-stick, sheath, snathe, snead, sneath, stave, steal, stem, stick**
4. n the HANDLE of a besom I.3.16. ʃæft So, ʃaft Cu We Y Db Nt L R, ʃaːft L Nf, ʃɑːft Sr
5. n *[Show a picture of a farmcart. What do you call these?] And one of them?* I.9.4. ʃɛːf Gl, ʃæf Sa He Wo Mon Sr K, ʃæv He Brk, ʃæft Wo Mon Ess So Sx, ʃæːf Man Sa Gl So W Co D Ha, ʃæːv Wo Gl Do, ʃæːft O C Nf So W, ʃaf Y Sa St Wo L Lei R, ʃav L Lei, ʃaft Nb Cu We La Y Ch Db Sa St Wa Mon Nt L Lei, ʃaːf Sa He Wo Wa Gl O Lei Nth Hu C Nf Sf Bk Bd Hrt Ess So W Co D Do Ha, ʃaːv He Nth So D Do Ha, ʃaːft Sa He Wo Wa Mon O L Lei R Nth Nf Sf Ess So W Do Ha, ʃaː Brk, ʃaːt Ess, ʃaːf Nf Hrt Ess Sr Sx, ʃɑːv Brk, ʃɑːft Wo Nf MxL Sr K Sx, ʃɒf He. ⇒ **blade, draught, limber, rod, sharp, sill, stang, till**
6. n a SHAFT-HORSE I.6.2. ʃaft Du

shafter *n* a SHAFT-HORSE I.6.2. ʃæftə Wa, ʃæftəˡ Sa He Wo Mon, ʃaftə Nb Ch St Lei R, ʃaftəɹ He, ʃaftəˡ L, ʃaftəˡ Sa Wo, ʃaftəˡː Co, ʃaːftəˡ Sa Mon

shafter-horse *n* a SHAFT-HORSE I.6.2. ʃatəɹɔːs Lei, ʃaːftəɹɔːs Lei

shaft-horse *1. n* *[Show a picture of two horses in tandem.] What do you call this?* I.6.2. ʃæftaˡːʂ So Co, ʃæftaˡːʂ He, ʃæftɒs He Mon, ʃæftəəˡʂ Sx, ʃæˑfhɒs Nf, ʃæˑfthɒs Nf, ʃæˑftɒˑs Nf, ʃæːfthaˡːʂ So, ʃæːfthɒs So, ʃæːfɔˡːʂ D, ʃaftœːs Du, ʃaftaɹs Y, ʃaftaːs Y, ʃaftɒs Cu Du We La Y Ch Db St Nt Lei R, ʃafthɒs Cu Du, ʃafthɒᴮːs Nb, ʃaftɒs Du Y Nt L, ʃaftɔːs Cu We La Y Ch Db St L Lei, ʃafthɒᴮːs Nb, ʃaftɒᴶːs La Y Db, ʃaftɔˡːʂ Sa D, ʃaːfas C, ʃaːftaːs Mon, ʃaːfɒs Co D, ʃaːtɒs L, ʃaːftɒs L, ʃaːftɔːs Mon R Nth Hu Nf Sf, ʃaːfɔˡːʂ So D, ʃaːfhɒˡːʂ So, ʃaːftɔˡːʂ So D, ʃafhɒs Nf, ʃaˑfthɒˑs Nf, ʃaˑvhɔˑs Nf, ʃaˑfthɒˑs Nf, ʃaːfhaːs Nf, ʃaːftɒˑs Nf, ʃaːftɒs Sr, ʃaːfɔːs Ess, ʃaːftɔːəᴶs Brk, ʃaːvɔːəˡʂ Sr. ⇒ **breecher, breech-horse, breeching-horse, cart-horse, diller, dillerd, diller-horse, draught-horse, filler, filler-horse, fillist, fillist-horse, foot-horse, hind-horse, hind one, horse** *in the cart*, **limber-horse, rod-horse, shaft, shafter, shafter-horse, shaft-tit, sharper, sharp-horse, string-horse, thiller, thiller-horse, thill-horse, thrill, thrill-horse**
2. n the FAR-HORSE of a pair pulling a wagon I.6.4(b). ʃaːftɔˡːʂ Sa

shaft-leg *n* a STICK used to support the shaft of a cart I.11.1. *pl* ʃaːflɛɪgz Ess

shaft-pin *n* a STICK used to support the shaft of a cart I.11.1. ʃaːftpɪn Mon

shaft-prop *n* a STICK used to support the shaft of a cart I.11.1. ʃæfpɹɒp Mon, ʃaftpɹɒp St, ʃaːfpɹɒp Nth, ʃaːvpɹɒp D

shaft-rest *n* a STICK used to support the shaft of a cart I.11.1. ʃæːfɹɛs Sa, ʃaˑfɹɛs Sa, ʃɑːftɹɛst Sx, ʃɑːfɹɛst Brk Sr

shafts *1. npl* *[Show a picture of a farmcart.] What do you call these?* I.9.4. ʃɛːfs Sx, ʃɛːvz Gl, ʃæfs Man Sa He Mon Ess Sr K, ʃævz He Wa Mon Ess Brk K, ʃæːfs Nf So, ʃæːvz Man Wo Gl O C Nf Sf Ess So W D Do Ha, ʃafs Cu We La Y Ch Db

Sa St Wa Nt L Lei, ʃavz Y Db St Wo Nt L Lei R Do, ʃafts Nb Cu We Y St, ʃaːf Sa, ʃaːfs Sa He Wa O R Nth Sf Hrt Ess, ʃaːvz Sa He Wo Wa Mon Gl O L Lei R Nth Hu C Nf Sf Bk Bd Ess So W Brk Co D Do Ha, ʃaːfts Lei Ess, ʃaːts Ess, ʃaːfs Nf Ess K, ʃaːvz He Wo Nf Hrt Ess MxL Brk Sr Sx; **cart-shafts** kaːtʃafs Y. ⇒ **cart-shafts, draughts, fillers, limbers, rods, sharps, stangs, thills, tills**

2. *npl* the HANDLES of a horse-drawn plough I.8.2. ʃæˑvz So, ʃafs Y, ʃaːvz Sr

shaft-stick *n* a STICK used to support the shaft of a cart I.11.1. ʃæːfstɪk Man Ha, ʃaːfstɪk Sr

shaft-tit *n* a SHAFT-HORSE I.6.2. ʃafttɪt Db

shaft-trap *n* a STICK used to support the shaft of a cart I.11.1. ʃaːvtɹæp Sf

shake *vt* to TED hay II.9.11(a). ʃeːk La Y O, ʃɛk Y, ʃɛɪk Nth Sf, -*ing* ʃɛɪkɪn MxL, ʃæɪk Hrt, ʃak Cu Y Nt

shake about *vtphr* to TED hay II.9.11(a). ʃeɪkʔ ... əbɛʊt Nf, ʃeɪk ... əbɛʊt Nf, ʃeːk ... əbæʏt So, ʃeːk ... əbaʊt Sa, ʃeːk ... əbaʊt O, ʃeːk ... əbəʊt O, ʃak ... əbuːt Y

shake out *vtphr* to TED hay II.9.11(a). ʃeːk ... ɛʊt Db Wa, ʃeɪk ɛʊt Ess, ʃeɪk ... ɛʊt Wa Nth Hu C Sf Sr, ʃeɪk ... əət K, ʃɛk ... æʊt Nt, ʃeɪk ... æʊt Ess, *pt* ʃakt ... æʊt Y, ʃeːk ... aːt La, ʃɛk ... aːt La Y, ʃɛk ... aʊt Y, ʃeɪk ... aʊt St, ʃak ... aʊt Y, ʃeːk uːt Cu, ʃak ... uːt Y L

shake over *vtphr* to TED hay II.9.11(a). ʃeɪk ʌʊvə Ess

shakers *n* TREMORS suffered by a person who cannot keep still VI.1.4. ʃeˀkəᴶz La

shakes *n* TREMORS suffered by a person who cannot keep still VI.1.4. ʃɹəks Du, ʃeːks Nb La Ch Sa W Brk, ʃeɪks Man Db Bk Bd, ʃeəks Nb La, ʃɛɪks St Lei R Hu Nf Bk Ess Brk Sr K Sx, ʃɛˑəks L, ʃaks Y, ʃʊks Gl; **the shakes** ðə ʃeːks Sa Wo Mon Gl Nt Co D Do Ha, ðə ʃeɪks So, ðə ʃeːɪks He Wo, ðə ʃeːəks D, ðə ʃɛɪks Wo Wa Lei Ess Sr K Sx, ðə ʃɛəks Wa, ðə ʃœːks Mon, ðə ʃʊks He

shake up *vtphr* to TED hay II.9.11(a). ʃɪˑk ... ʌpʔ Nf, ʃɛk ... ʌp He, ʃɛɪk ... ʌp Ess, ʃæɪk ... ʌp Hrt, ʃɛk ... ʊp Y, ʃɛɪk ... ʊp Wa, ʃɛək ... ʊp La, ʃak ... ʊp Y

shakiness *n* TREMORS suffered by a person who cannot keep still VI.1.4. ʃeːkɪnɪs D

shaking *adj* **shaking with the cold** COLD, describing a person VI.13.18. ʃeɪkɪn wɪ ðə koʊɫd So

shaking(s) *n* TREMORS suffered by a person who cannot keep still VI.1.4.

no -s: ʃeːkɪn La, ʃeɪkɪn So

-s: ʃeːkɪnz Do

shaky *1. adj* CLUMSY, describing a person VI.7.14. ʃakɪ Y

2. *adj* WEAK, describing a person who has been ill VI.13.2. ʃiˑkɪ Man, ʃɹəkɪ So, ʃeːkɪ Nb He Ha, ʃeɪkɪ Man, ʃeɪkɪ So, ʃeˀkɪ Du, ʃeɪkɪ St Sf Ess Brk Sr, ʃɛɪkɪ So, ʃɛˑɪgɪ Nf, ʃɛˑəkɪ L, ʃæɪkɪ Hrt, ʃakɪ Cu Y

shalling* *v-ing* SHELLING peas V.7.14. ʃalɪn O

shallots *npl* SPRING ONIONS V.7.16. ʃalɒts Ch, ʃaˡːləts Wo, ʃaːləts Wa, ʃəlæts Man, ʃəlɒts Y He Wo Lei, *sg* ʃəlɒt Cu, ʃəlɒts Y Ch Wa *[marked u.r. WM/EMBM, and queried NBM]*

shallow(s) *n* a FORD IV.1.3.

no -s: ʃælɒʊ Brk

-s: ʃælɒʊz Brk

shallow-shop *n* a FORD IV.1.3. ʃaləʃɒp Y

shallow spot *n* a FORD IV.1.3. ʃalə spɒt Cu

shallow water *n* a FORD IV.1.3. ʃælɒʊ wɔːtəᴶ K, ʃalə wɔːdəˡ W *[marked u.r. SBM]*

shambles *1. n* a CART-FRAME I.10.6. ʃambɫz Bk

2. *n* a FASTING-CHAMBER III.11.3. ʃamɫz So

shame-faced *adj* SHY VIII.9.2. ʃɛːmfɛːɪst Nf, ʃɛˑɪmfɛˑɪst Nf*[old]* *[marked u.r. EMBM]*

shammocks *n* FEET VI.10.1(b). ʃæmʌks So, ʃamʊks Wa

shandry *n* a sprung cart that does not tip, ⇐ FARMCART I.9.3. ʃandɹɪ Ch

shank *1. n* the HANDLE of a besom I.3.16. ʃaŋk Nb Cu Du We Y, ʃaŋkʰ Nb Y

2. *n* the SHAFT of a spade I.7.7. ʃaŋk Nb Du Y, ʃaŋkʰ Nb Cu

3. *n* the SHAFT of a hay-fork I.7.12. ʃaŋk Nb Cu Du Y, ʃaŋkʰ Nb

4. *n* the STEM of a corn-plant II.5.2(a). ʃaŋk Du

5. *n* a TETHERING-ROPE used to tie up a horse I.4.2. ʃaŋk Nb La Y

6. *vt* **shank it** to WALK VIII.7.10. ʃaŋk ɪt Cu La Y

shanks *npl* the HANDLES of a horse-drawn plough I.8.2. *sg* ʃæŋk O

shanks'-mare *vt* **shanks'-mare it** to WALK VIII.7.10. ʃaŋksmɛəɹ ɪt Y

shanks' pony *n* **go on shanks' pony, walk (it) on shanks' pony** to WALK VIII.7.10. **go on shanks' pony** goː ɒn ʃaŋksɪz poːnɪ Gl; **walk on shanks' pony** wɒʊk ɒn ʃaŋksɪz pʊʊnɪ St; **walk it on shanks' pony** wɔːk ɪt ɒn ʃaŋksɪz pʊʊnɪ St

shape *1. v* to WHITTLE a stick I.7.19. *-ing* ʃɛˑɪpɪn Lei *[marked u.r. EMBM]*

2. *n* an EVENER on a horse-drawn plough I.8.4. ʃɛɪp Sr

3. *vi* to show signs of calving, ⇐ SHOWS SIGNS OF CALVING III.1.12. *3prprogsg* ʃeəpɪn Y; **shape to calve** *3prprogsg* ʃeːɪpɪn tə kɔːv La

4. *n* the VULVA of a cow III.2.3. ʃeːp Ch Db Sa St He Wo Wa Mon Gl, ʃeɪp Bd, ʃeːɪp Db He Wo Mon, ʒeːɪp Gl, ʃɛɪp St Wa C Sf, ʃap Db

shard *1. n* a SHEEP-HOLE IV.2.8. ʃaˡːd̪ Gl*[in hedge or wall]* So W, ʃaːɹd Brk, ʃaˡːd̪ Gl, ʃɔːd Mon*[larger than glat]*, ʃɔˡːd̪ So*[in hedge x1]*, ʃɔˡːd̪ So*[made by animals x1]*

2. *n* a place in a hedge trodden down by cows. ʃaˡːd̪ So

shard-way *n* a SHEEP-HOLE IV.2.8. ʃaᵗd̥weɪ Ha, ʃaᵗːd̥we: Ha*[narrower than* gap-way*]*

share *n* [*Show a picture of a (horse-drawn) plough.*] *What do you call this?* I.8.7. ʃɪə Y Db Mon Nt L Nth C Nf Sf Hrt Ess MxL, ʃɪəᴶ O Brk, ʃɪəᵗ He Wo Mon Gl O Bk Brk Sr K Sx, ʃɪəᵗː So W Co D Do Ha, ʃeɪəᴶ Man, ʃeə Y Bk Bd Ess, ʃeːəᵗ Sa Wo, ʃeəᵗː So, ʃɛː Db St Wa, ʃɛːɹ Db, ʃɛᵗː Bk, ʃɛə Y Ch Db St Wa O Nt L Lei R Nth Hu Nf Sf Bd Hrt Ess Sr K, ʃɛəɹ Y, ʃɛəᴶ L K, ʃɛəᵗ Sa He Wa Nth Bk Sr K Sx, ʃɛəᵗː So W Co D Ha, ʃæːᵊ Du, ʃaːᵊ Lei, ʃaᵗː He, ʃəᵗː He Wo Gl. ⇒ **broad-share, broad-share-point, ground-reest, nose, plough-nose, plough-point, plough-share, plough-sock, plough-top-share, point, share-point, sock, turn-furrow**

share-board *n* the MOULD-BOARD of a horse-drawn plough I.8.8. ʃɪəᵗbaᵗːd̥ Gl, ʃəᵗːboːəᵗd̥ He

share-grass *n* a TUSSOCK of grass II.2.9. ʃəːgəs Y; **lump of share-grass** lump ə ʃəːgəs Y *[probably a type of grass]*

share-point *n* the pointed end of the SHARE of a horse-drawn plough I.8.7. ʃɪəpɔɪnt Wo

sharn *n* COW-DUNG I.3.12. ʃɛʁən Nb, ʃeˑɔᴿn Nb, ʃeˑəʁən Nb

sharp *1.1. v* to WHITTLE a stick I.7.19. ʃaːp Nf, *-ing* ʃaːpɪn Mon

1.2. vt to whittle. *-ing* ʃaᵗːpɪn Co D, *-ing* ʃaᵗːpən Do, *-ing* ʃɾapn Ha, *-ing* ʃaᵗːpən D

[-ing forms assumed; may be infinitive **sharpen***]*

2. n a SHAFT of a cart I.9.4. ʃaːp Bk Hrt Ess, ʃaᵗːp Bk Bd So Co D, ʃaᵗːp D Ha Sx

3. adj STEEP, describing a hill IV.1.11. ʃaːp K

4. adj ACTIVE, describing a child VIII.9.1. ʃaːp Wa

sharpen *1. v* to WHITTLE a stick I.7.19. ʃaːpn Sf, *prppl* ʃaːpənɪn Y, *vbln* ʃaːpnɪŋ Mon, *-ing* ʃaːpnɪn Y Lei Hu, *-ing* əʃaːpnɪn St, ʃaᵗːpn Sa, *-ing* ʃaᵗːpnɪn Wa Brk, *-ing* əʃaᵗːpnɪn He, *-ing* ʃaᵗːpnɪn Wo, *-ing* əʃaᵗːpnɪn Wo

2. vt to whittle. ʃaᵗːpn Sa, *-ing* ʃaᵗːpnɪn So Ha, *-ing* ʃaᵗːpmɪn Do, *-ing* ʃaᵗːbmɪn D, *-s* ʃaːpənz Ch, *-ing* ʃaᵗːpnɪn Wo, *-ing* ʃaᵗːpmən D, *-ing* ʃəᵗːpnɪn Wo *[marked u.r. N/WM/EMBM]*

sharpening-stone *n* a WHETSTONE II.9.10. ʃaᵇːpn̥ənstɪən Nb, ʃaᵇːpnənstøːn Nb

sharpen out *vtphr* to WHITTLE a stick I.7.19. *-ing* ʃaᵗːpmɪn æʏt D, *-ing* ʃaᵗːbmɪn æʏt Co, *-ing* ʒaᵗːbmɪn æʏt D, *-ing* ʃaᵗːpmən ... œʏt D

sharper *n* a SHAFT-HORSE I.6.2. ʃaᵗːpəᵗː Co

sharp-horse *n* a SHAFT-HORSE I.6.2. ʃaᵗːpɒs Co D, ʃaᵗːpɔᵗːʂ So, ʃaːphɔːs Ess

sharping-stone *n* a WHETSTONE II.9.10. ʃaːpɪnstɪən Cu, ʃaːpənstɪən Nb, ʃaᵇːpɪnstɪən Nb, ʃaᵇːpənstøːn Nb

sharp out *vtphr* to WHITTLE a stick I.7.19. *-ing* ʃəᵗːpən æʏt W *[-ing forms assumed; may be infinitive* **sharpen out***]*

sharps *1. npl* the SHAFTS of a cart I.9.4. ʃaːps Bk Bd Hrt Ess Ha, ʃaᵗːps Bk Bd So Co D, ʃaᵗːps O D Ha Sx

2. n barley AWNS II.5.3. ʃaːps Cu

3. n MEAL V.6.1(b). ʃaːps L

sharps-flour *n* MEAL V.6.1(b). ʃaːpsfluˑə Cu

sharrow *n* a SEESAW VIII.7.2. ʃaɹə La

shatter-dadders *n* TREMORS suffered by a person who cannot keep still VI.1.4. ʃatədadəz Y

shave *v* to WHITTLE a stick I.7.19. ʃeːv Ch Sa Wa Gl, *-ing* ʃeːvɪn Y O W, ʃeɪv O, *-ing* ʃeɪvɪn So, *-ing* ʃeɪvn Nf, ʃeːᴵv Db, *-ing* ʃeːᴵvɪn Mon, *-ing* ʃeəvɪn Du Y, ʃɛɪv Wa K, *-ing* ʃɛɪvɪn Lei Ess, *prppl* ʃɛəvɪn Y, *-ing* ʃɛəvɪn Y, *-ing* ʃæɪvɪn Ess K, *-ing* ʃaɪvɪn Y, *-ing* ʃʌvɪn He

2. vt to whittle. ʃeːv Sa, *-ing* ʃeːvɪn He Mon Gl D, *-ing* ʃeːvən Co, *-ing* ʃeɪvɪn He So, *-ing* ʃeːɪvɪn Gl So, *-ing* ʃɛɪvɪn K, ʃav Y

shave down *vtphr* to TRIM a hedge IV.2.3. *-ing* ʃɛɪvɪn ... dɛun K

shave up *1. vphr* to WHITTLE a stick I.7.19. ʃeˑəv ʌp Bk

2. vtphr to whittle. *-ing* ʃɛɪvɪn ... ʌp Sx, *-ing* ʃɛɪvən ... ʌp Sf

shaw *v* **shaw, root and shaw** to TOP AND TAIL swedes II.4.3. **shaw** *-ing* ʃæːɪn Nb, ʃaː Nb, ʃɔː Cu; **root and shaw** ʁʌt ən ʃaː Nb, *-ing* ʁut n̩ ʃaːn Nb

shawl *n* the FAT round the kidneys of a pig III.12.7. ʃɔːᵊɬ Ess

shaws *n* POTATO-HAULMS II.4.4. ʃaːz Nb Du*[old]*, ʃɔːz Cu

shay *n* a SCARECROW II.3.7. ʃɛɪ Sf

shay-garters *npl* KNEE-STRAPS used to lift the legs of working trousers VI.14.17. ʃeːgaᵗːd̥əᵗːz D *[queried SBM]*

she *n* a TABBY-CAT, the female cat III.13.9. ʃiː Nb Du O So W Co D Do Ha, ʃəɪ nY *[marked u.r. N/WMBM]*

sheaf *1. n* [*When you cut corn with a scythe, what do you do after cutting it? to bind*] *Into what?* II.6.3(a). Eng. ⇒ **bundle**

*2. n the SHEATH of skin covering the penis of a horse III.4.9. ʃiːf Cu We Db Sa St He Wo Mon Gl O Nt L Hu C Nf Sf Bd Ess So Brk Sr Do Ha Sx, ʃɪʊf Y, ʃɪˑʊv Nth, ʃɪəf La Y, ʃɪəv Y, ʃɛf Ch O Sx, ʃɛɪf Db

*3. n the VULVA of a cow III.2.3. ʃiːf Bk

sheaf-arse *n* the BUTT of a sheaf of corn II.6.4. ʃiːfaːs L, ʃɪˑəfaːs L, ʃafaːs Y, ʃavaːs Y, ʃɒfaːs Ch

sheaf-fork *n* a HAY-FORK with a short shaft I.7.11. ʃɪəffɔᴶːk La

sheaf-turn *v* to PITCH sheaves II.6.10. *-ing* ʃiːvtəᵗːn̩ɪn D; **throw on and sheaf-turn** *-ing* d̥ɹoːən ... ɔːn ən ʃiːvtəᵗːn̩ən D

sheaf-turner *n* the FORKER on a wagon who unloads sheaves in a stackyard II.6.9. ʃiːftɒnə Db, ʃɪftəːnə St, ʃɛɪftəːnə Db

shear *1. v* to TRIM hedges IV.2.3. ʃiːəᵗ So, *-ing* ʃəᵗːɽɪn So Do

2. n a SHEATH or other device used to keep a knitting-needle firm V.10.10. ʃɪaɹ Y, ʃɪəᵗ So

shearer *n* a sheep from its first to its second shearing, ⇐ GIMMER III.6.5. ʃɪaɹə Wa

shearers *n* hand-operated SHEARS used to cut wool from sheep III.7.7. ʃɪaɹəz Ch, ʃɪaɽəɽz So

shear-hog *1. n* a sheep from its first to its second shearing, ⇐ GIMMER III.6.5. ʃaɹʊg Wa

2. n a WETHER III.6.8. ʃaɹəg Wa, ʃəɽəg O

shearing *1. v-ing* What is your word for taking the wool off [sheep]? III.7.6. Eng exc. Cu Du We. ⇒ **chipping, clipping,** *sheep-shearing*; ⇒ also **napping**

2. n a sheep before its first shearing, ⇐ EWE-HOG III.6.4. ʃɪaɹɪn Y

3. n from its first to its second shearing, ⇐ GIMMER III.6.5. ʃɪɔʁən Nb, ʃɪaɹɪn Du We La Y, ʃɪəᵗːɽɪn So

shearing-bench *n* a SHEARING-TABLE III.7.8. ʃɪaɹɪnbɛnʃ Db, ʃɪəɽɪnbɛnʃ K[*old x1*], ʃɪəᵗɽɪnbɛnʃ Sa He Mon, ʃɛaɹɪnbɛnʃ Mon

shearing-hook *n* a BILLHOOK IV.2.6. ʃəᵗːɽɪnhʊk Dʊ

shearing-rack *n* a SHEARING-TABLE III.7.8. ʃɪaɹɪnɹæːk Hrt, ʃɪaɹɪnɹak Wa

shearing-stock *n* a SHEARING-TABLE III.7.8. ʃɪəᵗːɽɪnstɒk D

shearing-stool *n* a SHEARING-TABLE III.7.8. ʃɪaɹɪnstuːɬ Sr[*rare*], ʃɪəᵗːɽənstuːɬ Ha[*long narrow stool*]

shearing-table *n* What do you do it [i.e. *sheep-shearing*] on? III.7.8. ʃɪaɹəntɪəbɬ So, ʃɪəᵗɽɪnteːbl Sa. ⇒ **bench, clipping-bench, clipping-form, clipping-stock, clipping-stool, cratch, creel, greasing-stool, platform, shearing-bench, shearing-rack, shearing-stock, shearing-stool, sheep-cratch, sheep-creel, sheep-stock, sheepstool, stand, stock, stool, table, trestle, tubs.** [*other rr. for this notion concern shearing done on the floor or on other surfaces*]

shearling *1. n* a sheep before its first shearing, ⇐ EWE-HOG III.6.4. ʃɪalɪn Y Man Ch St L Bk Ess, *pl* ʃɪalɪnz La, ʃɪəᶨlɪŋ Man, ʃɪəᶨlɪn La, *pl* ʃɪəᵗlɪnz Sx, ʃɪəᵗːlɪn So, ʃeˑəlɪn O, ʃɛələn Man, ʃəːlɪn Lei, ʃəᵗːɪn Do, ʃəᵗːɬən Co [*taken in WM/EM/SBM to refer to sheep after first shearing,* ⇒ **gimmer** III.6.5]

2. n a sheep from its first to its second shearing, ⇐ GIMMER III.6.5. ʃɪəᵏlən Nb, ʃɪəlɪn Nb Cu Du We La Y Db St L Nf, *pl* ʃᶨəːlɪnz Ess, ʃɪəᶨlɪn La Nf, ʃɪəᵗɬɪn Wo, ʃɪəᵗːlɪn So, ʃɪəᵗːɬɪn So, ʃeˑələn Sf, ʃəːlən Du, ʃəᵗːɭɪn Sa Wo Wa, ʃəᵗːɬɪn He Wo Mon W, ʃəᵗːɬən

Ha

3. n a shorn ewe that has not lambed. ʃəɹlɪn He

shearling-ewe *1. n* a EWE-HOG III.6.4. ʃɪəᵗlɪn jʌʊ K [*taken in SBM to refer to sheep after first shearing,* ⇒ **gimmer** III.6.5]

2. n a GIMMER III.6.5. ʃɪəlɪnjuː Nf, ʃɪəlɪnɪuː Sf, ʃɪˑəlɪnjɯ Nf, ʃəᵗːɭɪn juː Sa

shearling-gimmer *n* a GIMMER III.6.5. ʃɪˑəlɪngɪmɹ L

shear-mouse *n* a SHREW-MOUSE IV.5.2. ʃɪəᵗmɛʊs Sx

shear(s) *n* [*What is your word for taking the wool off (sheep)?*] *And what do you do it with?* III.7.7. *no -s:* ʃɪə Db O, ʃɪəᵗː D, ʃɛəᶨ Brk

-s: Eng

⇒ **clippers, hand-clippers, hand-shears, juice,** *pair of* **shears, shear, shearers, sheep-clippers, sheep-shears**

shear-sheep *n* a sheep from its first to its second shearing, ⇐ GIMMER III.6.5. ʃaˑɹʃiːp Y

sheath *1. n* [*Show a picture of a horse.*] *What do you call this* [*the skin covering the penis*]? III.4.9. ʃiːθ Nb Cu We La Y Man Ch Db Sa St He Wo Wa Mon Gl O Nt L Lei R Nth Hu Nf Sf Bk Bd Hrt Ess MxL So Brk Sr K Ha Sx, ʃɪəθ Cu We La Y Nt L Bk, ʃeːθ Ch, ʃeɪθ Du O, ʃɛθ Nb Du Y Gl, ʃɛːθ Ch, ʃɛɪθ Y, ʃʊθ Wa O. ⇒ **scow, sheaf, shell, shield, steer;** ⇒ also **bag, ball-bag, cock, cod, cods, penis, pissle, pizzle, pouch, prick, purse, tool**

2. n the VULVA of a cow III.2.3. ʃeːθ D

3. n To help you to keep your knitting-needle firm, you use a .... V.10.10. ʃiːθ Nb Du Y Sa Wo Nf So Brk Sr K Sx, ʃiːf Wo Lei Hu, ʃɪəθ Y L, ʃɛθ Sa, ʃɛf Du, ʃɛɪθ Db St. ⇒ **bodkin, elder-stick, goose-quill, holders, knitting-bag, knitting-bobbin, knitting-fish, knitting-holder, knitting-pad, knitting-peg, knitting-pen, knitting-pig, knitting-pin-holder, knitting-quill, knitting-shear, knitting-sheath, knitting-shield, knitting-shuttle, knitting-socket, knitting-stick, needle-holder, needle-rest, needle-shield, nutmeg, pad, quill, shear, shield, shuttle, socket, steller, straw-pad, straw-wad** [*material culture notes in BM*]

4. n the SHAFT of a scythe II.9.7. ʃiːθ K

5. n a DIAGONAL BAR of a gate IV.3.7. ʃɛθ Nb

sheaths *npl* the horizontal BARS of a gate IV.3.6. ʃɛθs Du, *sg* ʃɛθ Nb

sheaves *npl* [*When you cut corn with a scythe, what do you do after cutting it? to bind*] *Into what?* II.6.3(b). Eng. ⇒ **bundles**

she-cat *n* a TABBY-CAT, the female cat III.13.9. ʃiːkjæt He Wo Mon, 'ʃiːkɪ'at Wo, ʃiːkjat Wo Wa Gl Bd, ʃiːkjaʔ Bk, ʃiːkɛt Nf Sr K Sx, ʃɪtʐiːkɛət Ess, ʃiːkæt Y Sa He Wa Mon Gl L Hu C Nf Sf Bk Ess MxL So Brk Sr K Sx, ʃiːkat Nb Cu Du We La

Y Ch Db Sa St He Wa Gl O Nt L Lei R Nth Hu C Hrt So W D Do Ha, ʃiːkatʰ Nb Y Bd, ʃiːkaʔ O Bk, ʃɛɪkjat St, ʃɛɪkat Db St, ʃəiːkæːʔ Hrt, ʃəɪkat Y

shed *1. n* a COW-HOUSE I.1.8. ʃeˑd So

2. n the place where hay is stored on a farm, ⇐ HAY-LOFT I.3.18. ʃeːd K, ʃɛd Gl Nt Lei Ess, ʃɛɪd Sf

3. n a CART-SHED I.11.7. ʃɛd Y

4. n a FASTING-CHAMBER III.11.3. ʃɛd Cu Y Wa L Nf Sf Bd Ess, ʃɛˡd D

5. n an ASH-MIDDEN V.1.14. ʃɛd Mon *[marked u.r. BM]*

6. n a row or SWATH of mown grass cut for hay-making II.9.4. ʃɛd Nb

7. vt to REMOVE *STALKS* from currants V.7.24. *-ing* ʃɛdɪn Mon

shed-alley *n* the GANGWAY in a cow-house I.3.7. ˈʃɛdˈɛlɪ Ess

sheddicks *n* a CLOT OF COW-DUNG II.1.6. ʃɛdɪks Nf *[possibly pl]*

shedding* *v-ing* CULLING sheep III.11.2. ʃɛdn Du, *v* ʃɛd Nb

sheeder *1. n* a EWE-LAMB III.6.3. ʃiːdə L R, ʃiːdɹ L

2. n a EWE-HOG III.6.4. ʃiːdə Lei Nth, *pl* ʃiːdəz Nt

3. n a TABBY-CAT, the female cat III.13.9. ʃiːdə sY, ʃiːdəˡ L *[NBM headword sheder]*

sheeder-cat *n* a TABBY-CAT, the female cat III.13.9. ʃiːdəkat Nt L

sheeder-hog *n* a EWE-HOG III.6.4. ʃiːdəɹɒg Nt, ʃiːdəɹɒg L

sheeder-lamb *n* a EWE-LAMB III.6.3. ʃiːdəlam Nt, *pl* ʃiːdəlamz L, ʃiːdɹlam L, ʃiːdəɹlam L

sheeling *v-ing* SHELLING peas V.7.14. ʃiːlɪn La K, ʃiːlən Nb, ʃiːɫɪn He, ʃiʊɫɪn K *[not a SBM headword]*

sheep *npl* What do you call the animals that give us wool? III.6.1. ʃiːp Nb Cu Du We La Y Man Ch Db Sa St He Wo Wa Mon O Nt L Lei R Nth Nf Sf Hrt Ess MxL So W Brk Sr K Co D Do Ha Sx, ʒiːp D, ʃɪp Db Sa St He Wo Wa Mon Gl O L Lei R Nth Hu C Sf Bk Bd Hrt Ess So W Brk D Ha Sx, ʃɪəp Y L, ʃeːp Ch W Ha, ʃɛp Mon So Ha, ʃɛɪp Du Y Ch Db Lei, ʃəɪp We Y. ⇒ **sheeps**

sheep-bars *npl* HURDLES used to pen sheep in part of a field III.7.11. ʃiːbaːz Y

sheep-bind *n* BINDWEED II.2.4. ʃɪpbɔɪn Ess

sheep-bing *n* a feeding-trough for sheep, ⇐ CORN-BIN I.7.4. *pl* ʃiːpbɪŋz Nf

sheep-bugs *npl* TICKS on sheep IV.8.3. ʃiːpbʌgz MxL, ʃiːpbʊgz Y

sheep-cades *npl* TICKS on sheep IV.8.3. ʃiːpkɪədz Y, ʃəɪpkjadz Y, ʃəɪpkɪədz Y

sheep-cags *npl* TICKS on sheep IV.8.3. ʃiːpkɛgz Wa

sheep-clippers *n* hand-operated SHEARS used to cut wool from sheep III.7.7. ʃiːpklɪpəz Y, ʃiːptlɪpəz Y

sheep-cratch *n* a SHEARING-TABLE III.7.8. ʃəɪpkɹatʃ Y

sheep-creel *n* a SHEARING-TABLE III.7.8. ʃiːpkɹiːl Y Ch, ʃəɪpkɹəɪl We Y

sheep-dicks *npl* TICKS on sheep IV.8.3. ʃɪpdɪks Gl

sheep-dung *n* What do you call the little balls that sheep leave behind? II.1.7. ʃiːpdɒŋ Man K, ʃiːpdʌŋ Ess So W Brk Sr K D Do Ha, ʃɪpdʌŋ C Bd Ess Brk, ʃɪpdʌŋk Sf, ʃiˑpdʏŋ Nf, ʃiːpdʊŋ Wa Lei. ⇒ **black peppermints, black pops, bum-balls,** *bum-bals* ⇒ **bum-balls, chatter-balls, chatty-balls, clitter-balls, currants, dotlings, dottles, droppings, dumlocks, dung, grapes,** *lamb's*-**turds,** *lamb*-**turds, manure, marbles, partles, partlicks, pirls,** *sheep*-**bum-balls,** *sheep*-**currants,** *sheep*-**dabs,** *sheep*-**daggings,** *sheep*-**dags,** *sheep*-**doddings,** *sheep*-**droppings,** *sheep*-**drops,** *sheep*-**dung,** *sheep*-**manure,** *sheep*-**muck,** *sheep*-**partles,** *sheep*-**pellets,** *sheep*-**pills,** *sheep*-**pirls,** *sheep's*-**bum-balls,** *sheep's*-**curdles,** *sheep's*-**droppings,** *sheep's*-**dung,** *sheep*-**shit,** *sheep's*-**shit,** *sheep's*-**treddles,** *sheep's*-**turd,** *sheep's*-**turds,** *sheep*-**trickles,** *sheep*-**tricklings,** *sheep*-**triddles,** *sheep*-**tridlings,** *sheep*-**trimlings,** *sheep*-**trinlings,** *sheep*-**trinnions,** *sheep*-**troddles,** *sheep*-**trotters,** *sheep*-**trottles,** *sheep*-**truckles,** *sheep*-**turd,** *sheep*-**turds, tathe, thrindlings, treddles, tridlings, trinlings, trotlings, trottles, truckles, truddles, trundlets, trunlings, turds, wad**

sheep-fags *npl* TICKS on sheep IV.8.3. ʃiːpfagz L, *sg* ʃiːpfag Nt, ʃɪpfagz L

sheep-flake *n* a hurdle used when penning sheep in part of a field, ⇐ HURDLES III.7.11. ʃiːpfleɪk Nt

sheep-fly *n* TICKS on sheep IV.8.3. ʃiiːpflɔɪ Ess *[queried collective n EMBM]*

sheep-gap *n* a SHEEP-HOLE IV.2.8. ʃiːpgap Lei R, ʃɪpgap Lei

sheep-gate *n* a SHEEP-HOLE IV.2.8. ʃiːpgeːt Y

sheep-gates *npl* HURDLES used to pen sheep in part of a field III.7.11. ʃiːpgɛɪts K

sheep-hide *n* a SHEEPSKIN III.11.8(a). ʃɪpæɪd He, ʃɪpɑɪd Nth Hu, ʃɪpəɪd He

sheep-hole *n* What do you call the small opening made in the bottom of a wall or fence or hedge to let the sheep through? IV.2.8. ʃiiːpɒʊɫ Sx, ʃiːpwɒl Cu, ʃiːphʊəl Nb, ʃɪpuːl St, ʃiːpɔɪl Y; **sheep's-hole** ʃiːpsoːɫ Co, ʃiːpsoʊɫ So. ⇒ **bolt-hole, creep, creep-hole,** *creeper-gap* ⇒ **cripper-gap, cripper-gap, cripple-gap, cripple-hole, ditch-hole, draw-way, gap, gap-stead, gap-way, glat, gote, hog-gap, hog-hole, hole, loop-hole, pop-hole, run, run-through, shard, shard-way, sheep-gap, sheep-gate, sheep-run,**

sheep's-creep, sheep's-hole, sheep-smoot, sheep-walk, smoot, smoot-hole, smuft-hole, thirl, thirl-hole, *through-way* ⇒ draw-way, wash; ⇒ also bank-hole, rabbit-smoot, slip-rail, smoose-hole

sheep-hurdles *npl* HURDLES used to pen sheep in part of a field III.7.11. ʃɪpəːdlz Wa, ʃiːpəˤːdɬz̩ W

sheep-lice *npl* TICKS on sheep IV.8.3. ʃiːpleɪs Man, ʃiːpleɪs Db, *sg* ʃiːpleʊs Nf, ʃiːplæɪs Y Ch, ʃiːplaɪs La Y Db Sa, ʃiːplɑːs La Y, ʃiːplɑɪs La Nt L MxL, ʃiːplɒɪs St, ʃiiːplɔɪs Ess, ʃɪpliːs Sf, ʃɪplaɪs He

sheep-man *n* a SHEPHERD I.2.1. ʃiːpmæn So

sheep-mark *v* to MARK sheep with colour to indicate ownership III.7.9. ʃəɪpmaːk Y

sheep-pad *n* a PATH made through a field by sheep IV.3.11. ʃiːppad La St

sheep-pelt *n* a SHEEPSKIN III.11.8(a). ʃiːppɛlt Y

sheep-run 1. *n* a SHEEP-HOLE IV.2.8. ʃiːprɒn Man, ʃiːpʁʊn Nb, ʃiːpɹʊn Cu Lei R

2. *n* a PATH made through a field by sheep IV.3.11. ʃɪpɹʌn Bd

sheeps *npl* SHEEP III.6.1. ʃiːps Cu Brk, ʃɪps Sa

sheep's-apron *n* the PELT of a sheep III.11.8(b). *pl* ʃiːpsɛpəns L

sheep's-creep *n* a SHEEP-HOLE IV.2.8. ʃiːpskɹiːp D

sheep's-fleece *n* a SHEEPSKIN III.11.8(a). ʃiːpsfliːs Wa

sheep-shears *n* hand-operated SHEARS used to cut wool from sheep III.7.7. ʃiːpʃɪəz Y L Nf Ess Sr, ʃiːpʃɪəˡz La, ʃiːpʃɪəˤːz̩ So Co, ʃiiːpʃɪəˤɾz̩ Sx, ʃɪpʃɪəz St Hu, ʃɪpʃɪəˤz̩ Wo O Bk, ʃɪpʃeˑəz Gl Ess, ʃɪpʃəˤːz̩ Wo Gl, ʃeɪpʃeːz Db

sheep's-hide 1. *n* a SHEEPSKIN III.11.8(a). ʃiːpshɛɪd Nb, ʃiːpsaɪd Ch Nt, ʃiˑpshʌɪd Nf, ʃɪpsaɪd Bk Bd, ʃɪpsɔɪd Bk, ʃɪpshɔɪd Ess, ʃɪpshʌɪd Sf, ʃeɪpsaɪd Db

2. *n* the PELT of a sheep III.11.8(b). ʃiːpsaɪd Nt, ʃiːpsʌɪd O, ʃɪpsaɪd Bk Bd, ʃɪpsɒɪd Sa, ʃɪpsɔɪd Bk, ʃɪpsʌɪd Gl, ʃɪpsəɪd Wo

sheep's-house *n* a FASTING-CHAMBER for sheep III.11.8. ʃiːpsæʊs Ha *[marked u.r. SBM as being specific to sheep]*

sheepskin 1. *n [What do you call the skin of a cow?] And of a sheep?* III.11.8(a). Eng exc. Hu MxL. ⇒ fleece, hide, pelt, sheep-hide, sheep-pelt, sheep's-fleece, sheep's-hide, sheep's-pelt, skin, wool skin

2. *n* the PELT of a sheep III.11.8(b). ʃiːpskɪn Nb Cu La Y Ch Db O Nt L Lei Nth Nf Hrt Ess So W K D Do Ha Sx, ʃɪpskɪn Wo Wa O Lei Nth C Sf Bk Bd Hrt Ess W Ha, *pl* ʃɪpskɪnz St, ʃɪəpskɪn Y, ʃɛɪpskɪn Db St

sheep's-lice *npl* TICKS on sheep IV.8.3. ʃiˑpslʌɪs Nf, *sg* ʃɪpslɛws Sf

sheeps'-meadow *n* a PADDOCK I.1.10. ʃiːpsmɛdə Co

sheep-smoot *n* a SHEEP-HOLE IV.2.8. ʃiːpsmuːt Y
sheep's-pelt *n* a SHEEPSKIN III.11.8(a). ʃiːpspɛlt L

sheep-stock *n* a SHEARING-TABLE III.7.8. ʃiːpstɒk La Y, ʃəɪpstɒk Y*[old x1]*

sheep-stool *n* a SHEARING-TABLE III.7.8. ʃiːpstʊl Cu, ʃiːpstɪəl Nb*[not found locally]* Cu We La, ʃˤɪpstɪəl We

sheep-tegs *npl* TICKS on sheep IV.8.3. *sg* ʃiˑptɛg Nf

sheep-track *n* a PATH made through a field by sheep IV.3.11. ʃiːptɹæk Y MxL, ʃiːptʁak Nb, ʃiːptɹak Y Ch St He O L, ʃɪptɹæk Ess, ʃɪptɹak Wo Wa Bd, ʃɪptɾak W, ʃiiːptɹɛək Ess, ʃiiːptɹæk Sr, ʃəɪptɹak Y

sheep-trays *npl* HURDLES used to pen sheep in part of a field III.7.11. ʃɪptɹeɪz R, ʃiːptɹeˑəz L*[for patching holes in fences x1]*

sheep-walk 1. *n* a SHEEP-HOLE IV.2.8. ʃiːpwaːk Nb

2. *n* a PATH made through a field by sheep IV.3.11. ʃiːpwɔːk Y St Nf

sheery *n* a SHREW-MOUSE IV.5.2. ʃəɾi So

sheet *n* an alternative to a SOWING-BASKET II.3.6. ʃiːt Nb Cu *[marked u.r. NBM]*

she-hog *n* a EWE-HOG III.6.4. ʃiːɒg Nt L, *pl* ʃiːɔgz L

she-lamb *n* a EWE-LAMB III.6.3. ʃiːlæm L Nf, ʃiːlam L Nth Hu

shelf 1. *n What do you call this, on which you keep your pans?* V.9.4. Eng. ⇒ bink, braid, pan-shelf, rack, tack

2. *n* a GIRDLE for baking cakes V.7.4(b). ʃɛlf Wo L, ʃɛɫ Nf

shell 1. *n* the SHEATH of skin covering the penis of a horse III.4.9. ʃɛɫ He Mon Gl

2. *n* a pea-POD V.7.12. ʃɛl Man Sa Wa Nf, ʃɛɫ Wa Nth Hrt Ess, *pl* ʃɛɫz Sf, ʃɛʊ Sr

shell-band *n* the MOULD-BOARD of a horse-drawn plough I.8.8. ʃɛlbən R

shell-board *n* the MOULD-BOARD of a horse-drawn plough I.8.8. ʃiːlboːəˤɫd He, ʃɪɫbɑˤːd He Wo, ʃɪɫbʷɑˤːd Wo, ʃɪlbɒˤːd Sa Wo, ʃɪlboːəˤɫd Wo, ʃɪɫbɑˤɫd Wa, ʃɛɫbɑˤːd Gl, ʃɛɫbwɑˤːd Wo, ʃɛlboːd Db St Wa Lei Nth, ʃɛɫbɔːd Lei, ʃɛlbɔˤːd Sa, ʃɛɫbɔˤːd Wa, ʃɛlbɔəd Wa, ʃɛlbɔːəd St, ʃɛɫbɔːˤəd He Lei, ʃɛɫbɒʊəˤːd Wa, ʃɛlbɔəd Ch Db Wa, ʃɛɫboˑəd Nth, ʃɛɫboːəˤɫd Wo Gl, ʃɛlbʊəd Ch St, ʃɛlbəd Db Lei R, ʃɛɫbəd Lei, ʃɛlbəˤɫd Sa, ʃɛʊlbɔəd Wa, ʃuːlbɔəd Wo

shelling *v What is your word for taking the peas out of the pod?* V.7.14. Eng. ⇒ burst open, coshing, flirt open, hodding, hucking, hucking *them*, hudding *them*, hull ⇒ hulling, hulling, husking, peel ⇒ peeling, peeling, picking, podding, poshing, *shaling* ⇒ shalling, shalling, *sheel* ⇒ sheeling, sheeling, shelling *them* out, shilling, shill out, sholling, shucking, shucking *them*, **shucking** *the peas*, **shulling**, *swad* ⇒ **swadding, swadding**

shelling out* *vt-ing* SHELLING peas V.7.14. *no -ing* ʃɛɫ ... æɪt So D, ʃɛɫɪn ... æʊt Do

shell-iron *n* the MOULD-BOARD of a horse-drawn plough I.8.8. ʃɛlɑɪəᶜn Nth

shell-snag *n* a snail, ⇐ SNAILS IV.9.3. ʃɛʊsnɛg Sx

shell-snail *n* a snail, ⇐ SNAILS IV.9.3. ʃɛʊsnɛɪʊ Sr

shelter *n* a COW-HOUSE I.1.8. ʃɪɫtəᶜː Co

shelve *v* to TIP a cart I.11.6. ʃɛɫv Sx, *-ing* ʃɛʊɫvɪŋ Sx, ʃɛʊv K Sx

shelve out *vtphr* to empty a cart by tipping it, ⇐ TIP I.11.6. *-s* ʃɛʊvz ... ɛʊt Sx

shelve-reest *n* the MOULD-BOARD of a horse-drawn plough I.8.8. ʃɛɫvɹiːs K

shelve up *vtphr* to TIP a cart I.11.6. ʃɛɫv ... ʌp K, ʃɛʊɫv ... ʌp K

shelving *n* an END-BOARD of a cart I.10.4. *pl* ʃɪlvɪnz Nb

shelving(s) *n* a CART-FRAME I.10.6.
no -s: ʃɪlvɪn Du La, ʃɛlvɪn Cu L Nf, skɛlvɪn Cu
-s: ʃɪlvɪnz Nb Cu Du We La Y, ʃɪlvənz Du, ʃɛlvɪnz Nb Cu Y Db Nt L, ʃɛlvənz Nb, skɪlvɪnz Cu

shelvings *npl* CART-LADDERS I.10.5. ʃɪlvɪnz Cu Y, ʃɛlvɪnz Y Nt

shep *n* a SHEPHERD I.2.1. ʃɪp Y, ʃɛp Db Nt L D Do

shepherd *n* [*Ask what men work on the farm and what each does. If he omits any of the following notions, ask the relevant questions below.*] *What do you call the man who looks after those animals that give us wool?* I.2.1. Eng. ⇒ **herd, looker, old shep, sheep-man, shep**

she-pig *n* a YOUNG SOW III.8.5. ʃiːpɪg Man

sheppeck *1. n* a MUCK-FORK with four prongs I.3.13. ʃʊpɪk Wo
2. n a HAY-FORK I.7.11. ʃʌpɪk O, ʃʊpiːk Wo, ʃʊpɪk Wo Gl O, ʃʊpʊk Wo
3. n a hay-fork with a long shaft. ʃʊpɪk Gl
4. n a hay-fork with a long or short shaft. ʃʊpɪk Wo

sherra-crop *n* a SHREW-MOUSE IV.5.2. ʃɛɾəkɾɒp D

shevel up *viphr* to WARP, referring to wood IX.2.9. *prppl* ʃɛvələn ʊp Man

shewd *n* a SHREW-MOUSE IV.5.2. ʃuːd Mon [*queried WMBM*]

shibbands *npl* BOOT-LACES VI.14.25. ʃɪbɪnz Y[*old x1, leather x1, leather or fibre x1*], ʃɪvɪnz Y[*leather or fibre*], ʃɪbənz Y[*leather or fibre*], ʃʊvn Y[*old*]

shick-shack day *n* a local FESTIVAL or holiday VII.4.11. ʃɪkʃæk dɛɪ Brk

shield *1. n* the SHEATH of skin covering the penis of a horse III.4.9. ʃiːld Nf, ʃiːᵊɫd Nth, ʃiid Nf
2. n a SHEATH or other device used to keep a knitting-needle firm V.10.10. ʃiːld Y St L Nf, ʃiːᵊl L,

ʃiːɫd Sa Lei, *pl* ʃiiɫdz K[*old*], ʃiːᵊɫd Wa Sf W, ʃiːᵊɫ C, ʃiːʊɫd K, ʃiʊɫd Brk, ʃəɪld Y

shift *1. v* to PITCH sheaves II.6.10. ʃɪft Ch
2. n a CHEMISE V.11.1. ʃɪft Nb Cu Du We La Y Ch Db St Wo Wa O L Hu Nf Bk Ess MxL Sr, ʃɪf Man Sr
3. n a SHIRT VI.14.8. *pl* ʃɪfs Brk
4. imp GO AWAY! VIII.7.9(a). ʃɪft Y

shifting clothes *n* ORDINARY CLOTHES VI.14.20. ʃɪftɪn tloːz Db

shift on *imp* GO AWAY! VIII.7.9(a). ʃɪft ɔːn So

shiggles *n* the shiggles TREMORS suffered by a person who cannot keep still VI.1.4. ðə ʃɪgɫz W

shiggly *n* a SEESAW VIII.7.2. ʃɪgɫɪ Mon

shillard *n* a SHILLING VII.7.5. ʃɛɫəᶜːd̩ Co

shilling *1. n* What do you call this [*indicate a shilling*]? VII.7.5. Eng. ⇒ **bob, shillard**
2. n short of a shilling STUPID VI.1.5. ʃɔːt əv ə ʃɪlɪn Sx
*3.1. vt-ing SHELLING peas V.7.14. ʃɪlɪn Y Nf K, ʃɪln̩ Nf, ʃɪɫɪn Co D, ʃɪɫən Do
3.2. v shelling. ʃɪlɪn La Y Db Nt L Lei Brk Sr K, ʃɪln̩ Cu Nf, ʃɪlən Cu Du We Sf, ʃɪɫɪn Sx, ʒɪɫɪn D, ʃɪɫən Co D, ʒɪɫən D

shill out *vtphr* to shell peas, ⇐ SHELLING V.7.14. ʃɪl ... aʊt Y

shimmy *n* a CHEMISE V.11.1. ʃɪmiː Du Y He Mon, ʃɪmi So W Co D Do Ha, ʃɪmɪ Nb Cu Du We La Y Ch Db Sa St He Wo Wa Gl O Nt L[*worn over flannel shirt x1*] Lei Nth Hu C Nf Sf Bk Bd Hrt Ess Brk Sr K Do Ha Sx, tʃɪmɪ Wo Sr, ʃɛmi So, ʃəmi: Du, ʃəməɪ Y

shimmy-shirt *n* a CHEMISE V.11.1. ʃɪmɪʃəːt K

shin up *vtphr* to CLIMB VIII.7.4. ʃɪn ʊp Y

shippon *1. n* a COW-HOUSE I.1.8. ʃɪpɪn La Ch Sa So D, ʃɪpʊn La, ʃɪppʊn La, ʃɪpən La Y Ch Db St Co D, ʃɪbən D, ʃɪpn La Y Db St, ʃɪpm La, ʃʊpʊn La, ʃʊpn La Y, ʃʊpm We La Y
2. n the part of a cow-house where fodder is kept. ʃɪpɪn Co
3. n a FASTING-CHAMBER III.11.3. ʃɪpɪn Ch

shipwright *n* a WRIGHT VIII.4.4. ʃɪpɹɑɪt La K, ʃɪpɹɑɪʔ MxL, ʃɪpɹɔɪt Ess Ha, ʃɪpɹʌɪt Sr

shire-horse *n* a STALLION III.4.4. ʃɪəhɔˑs Nf

shiresmen *npl* STRANGERS VIII.2.10. ʃɪəᴶzmən K

shirl *vi* to SLIDE VIII.7.1. ʃɔːl Nb[*old*], ʃɒl Y, ʃəl Y[*old*], ʃəɪl We, *-ing* ʃəɹlɪn Y, ʃəːl Cu Du[*old*] We Y

shirp out *vtphr* to WHITTLE a stick I.7.19. *-ing* ʃəᶜːpən æʊt W

shirrow *n* a SHREW-MOUSE IV.5.2. ʃɛɹə Lei, ʃəɹə Db

shirt *n* What do you call this [*indicate a shirt*]? VI.14.8. Eng. ⇒ **sark, shift**

shit *1. n* COW-DUNG I.3.12. ʃɪt Y L Lei Ess W Brk, ʃɪtʔ So

2. n a CLOT OF COW-DUNG II.1.6. ʃɪt Man

3. n **sheep-shit, sheep's-shit** SHEEP-DUNG II.1.7. **sheep-shit** ʃiːpʃɪt Mon W, ʃɪpʃɪt He Gl; **sheep's-shit** ʃiːpsʃɪt D

shitabed *n* a DANDELION II.2.10(c). ʃɪdəbiːd D, ʃɪdəbeɪd D

shit-cart *n* a FARMCART I.9.3. ʃɪtkaᵗːt W

shit-carting *v-ing* CARTING *DUNG* II.1.4. ʃɪtkaᵗːɽtɪn Sx

shite-house *n* an EARTH-CLOSET V.1.13. ʃaɪtaʊs Y*[vulgar]*, ʃɔɪtɛʊs Bk *[not an EMBM headword]*

shithers *n* **the shithers** TREMORS suffered by a person who cannot keep still VI.1.4. ðə ʃɪðəz St

shit-hole *n* an EARTH-CLOSET V.1.13. ʃɪtɔɪl Y*[vulgar x1]*

shit-house *n* an EARTH-CLOSET V.1.13. ʃiteːs Db, ʃɪthɛʊs Sf, ʃɪtɛʊs Hu Ess, ʃɪtæːs St, ʃɪtæʏs So, ʃɪdæʏs Co D, ʃɪtæʊs Wo W, ʃɪdæʊs So Ha, ʃɪtaːs Y*[vulgar]* St, ʃɪtaɪs St, ʃɪtaʊs La*[vulgar]* So, ʃɪtʊs Wo, ʃɪtuːs Y Gl, ʃɪtəs Db Sa Bd, ʃɪtəʊs He Mon W, ʃɪdəʊs W, ʃɪtəʊːs Wo Gl*[old x1]*

shit-prong *n* a MUCK-FORK I.3.13. ʃɪtpɽɒŋ W

shitting-clout *n* a DIAPER V.11.3. *pl* ʃɪʔɪnklɛʊts Hu

shitting-house *n* an EARTH-CLOSET V.1.13. ʃɪtɲəs Sf

shittles *npl* the horizontal BARS of a gate IV.3.6. ʃedɫz D, ʒedɫz D

shive *1. v* to WHITTLE a stick I.7.19. *-ing* ʃaɪvɪn Y

2. n a SLICE of bread V.6.10. ʃeɪv La Ch Db, *pl* ʃæɪvz Ch, ʃaɪf Y, ʃaɪv Nb Cu Du*[rare x1]* We*[old x1, rare x2]* La Y Ch, ʃɑːv Y, *pl* ʃɑːvz La, ʃaɪv La Db, ʃaːv Y

3. n **shive of bread and butter** a PIECE *OF BREAD AND BUTTER* V.6.11(a). ʃaɪv ə bʁiːd n bʊtəᴮ Nb

4. n a SPLINTER VI.7.10. ʃɪv Y

shivelly *adj* **get shivelly** to WRINKLE, referring to the skin of very old people VI.11.2. *3prsg* gɛts ʃɪvəɫi So

shiver *n* a SPLINTER VI.7.10. ʃɪvə L Nf, ʃɪvɹ L, ʃɪβɐ Nf

shivered *1. adj* COLD, describing a person VI.13.18. ʃɪvəᵗːd̩ D; **all shivered up** ɔːɫ ʃɪvəᵗːd̩ ʌp D; **shivered to death** ʃɪvəᵗːd̩ tə dɛθ D

2. adj VERY COLD, describing a person VI.13.19. ʃɪvəᴵd Ess

shivering *adj* COLD, describing a person VI.13.18. ʃɪvəᵗːɽɪn W Co, ʃɪvəᵗːɽən Co; **shivering with the cold** ʃɪvəʁən wɪ ðə kæᵊd Nb

shivers *1. npl* the horizontal BARS of a gate IV.3.6. ʃɪvəᵗːz̩ Co D, ʃɛvəᵗːz̩ Co

2. n TREMORS suffered by a person who cannot keep still VI.1.4. ʃɪvəz Nth, ʃɪvəᵗz̩ Mon; **the shivers** θ ʃɪvəz St, ðə ʃɪvəz Mon, ðə ʃɪðəz St

3. n **all shivers** COLD, describing a person VI.13.18. ɔːɫ ʃɪvəᴵz K

shivery *adj* COLD, describing a person VI.13.18. ʃɪvɹi Ess Sx, ʃɪvəɽi So W, ʃɪvɽi So W

shock *1. n* a stook of corn, ⇐ STOOKING II.6.5. ʃɒk O Lei Ess, *pl* ʃɒks St Bk Hrt, ʃɔk Wa Ess, ʃʊk Wo, *pl* ʃʊks St Wa

2. vt to TED hay II.9.11(a). ʃʊk Gl

shocking *v-ing* STOOKING II.6.5. ʃɒkɪŋ Nf Hrt, ʃɒkɪn Db St Gl O Lei Nth Nf Bk Bd Hrt Ess Brk Sr K Co Ha Sx, əʃɒkɪn Hu Bk, ʃɒkʔɪn Nf, ʃɒkɪn Nf, ʃɒkən Nf Co, ʃɔkɪn C Ess MxL, ʃɔkn Sf, ʃɔkən Sf, ʃɔkʔn Sf, *inf* ʃɔk Sr, *3prs* ʃɔks Hrt, ʃʌkɪn Brk, ʃʊkɪn St Wa Lei, ʃɰːkɪn Lei

shocking up *vphr-ing* STOOKING II.6.5. ʃaːkn ... ʌp Nf, ʃɒkɪn ʌp Sr Sx, *inf* ʃɒk ʌp Co, *inf* ʃɒk ... ʌp W Ha, ʃɒkʔɪn ʏp Nf, ʃɒkʔɳ̩ ʌp Nf, ʃɒkʔɳ̩ ... ʌp Nf, ʃɔkɪn ... ʌp Ess, *inf* ʃɔːk ʌp Sr

shocks *npl* COCKS of hay II.9.12. ʃɒks L Nth Hu, ʃɔks C

sho-croach *n* a SHREW-MOUSE IV.5.2. ʃoːkɽoːtʃ So *[queried SBM]*

sho-crop *n* a SHREW-MOUSE IV.5.2. ʃoːkɽɒp W Do, ʃoʊkɽɒp So, ʃəᵗːkɽəb So

shoddy *adj* WEAK, describing a person who has been ill VI.13.2. ʃɒdɪ K

shod-tire *n* the iron TIRE round a cart-wheel I.9.10. ʃɒdtaɪə Nth

shoe *1. n* the SOLE of a horse-drawn plough I.8.9. ʃʏː So Co D, ʃɛu Y, ʃuː La Y Wo Gl O So Brk K Co

2. n a chock placed behind and under a wheel to prevent a cart from going backwards on a hill, ⇐ PROP/CHOCK I.11.2. ʃuː La

3. n a DRAG used to slow a wagon I.11.3. ʃɪu Ch Nf, ʃɪuː C Sf, ʃʏː Ch So, ʃɛˑu Y, *pl* ʃʊuːz Sr, ʃuː Nb Du We La Y Man*[not found]* St Wa Gl L Hu Bk Ess So Brk, ʃəʊ Y

4. n a SHOE VI.14.22(a). Eng. ⇒ **boot, low boot, low shoe, shoon, shuff**

shoe-drug *n* a DRAG used to slow a wagon I.11.3. ʃuːdɽʊg Co

shoe-laces *n* BINDWEED II.2.4. ʃuːlæɪsɪz K

shoeless *adj* BARE-FOOT VI.10.2. ʃuːləs K

shoemaker *n* a COBBLER VIII.4.5. ʃɪmkə Nf, ʃɪmɛkə Nf*[old]*, ʃɪməkə Nf, ʃʏːmeːkəᵗː D, ʃʏːmɛkəᵗː So D, ʃɒumiːkər Cu, ʃʌməkə Nf, *pl* ʃɔmɛkəz Nf, ʃʊməkə Nf, ʃuˑmakʔə Sf*[makes shoes]*, *poss* ʃuːmɪkəᵗːz̩ Sa, ʃuːmeːkəᵗ W Brk, ʃuːmeɪkə Sr*[makes boots and shoes]*, ʃuːmeˑəkə Cu, ʃuːmɛkə La Y L Lei Nf, *pl* ʃuːmɛkəz Y, ʃuːmɛkəᴵ La, ʃuːmeɪkə Ess, ʃuːmeɪkəᵗ Sx, ʃuːmakə La Y, ʃəməkə Nf

shoe-marks *npl* the HOOF-MARKS of a horse IV.3.10. ʃɒumaːks Cu, ʃuːmaːks Cu, ʃuːmɑːks K

shoemender *n* a COBBLER VIII.4.5. ʃuːmɛndə Ess, ʃuːmændəˡ Brk

shoes *npl* BOOTS VI.14.23. ʃɒʊz Cu, ʃuːz La Mon Gl Ess, ʃɪuːz C

shoe-snob *n* a COBBLER VIII.4.5. ʃuːsnɒb Gl O W

shoe-strings *npl* BOOT-LACES VI.14.25. ʃuːstɹɪŋz La*[old]* Sa*[fibre]*, ʃuːʂʈɹɪŋz Ha

shoe-ties *npl* BOOT-LACES VI.14.25. ʃɪʉtʌɪz Nf

shoe-whangs *npl* BOOT-LACES VI.14.25. ʃuːwaŋz Cu*[leather]* We*[leather]* La*[leather x1, fibre x1, old x1]* Y*[leather]*, ʃᵊuwɪŋz Y*[leather]*

shoey *n* a COBBLER VIII.4.5. ʃʏːi So

sholling* *vt-ing* SHELLING peas V.7.14. ʃɒlɪn St

sho-mouse *n* a SHREW-MOUSE IV.5.2. ʃɔːmæʊs So, ʃɔːmaʊs So

shoon *1. n* a SHOE VI.14.22(a). ʃʊn Y, ʃʊɪn Y, ʃuːn La *[not a NBM headword]*
2. npl BOOTS VI.14.23. ʃʊn La Y*[old x1, modern x1]*, ʃuːn Y*[old x1]* Db, ʃᵁuːn La

shoops *npl* HIPS of the wild rose IV.11.7. ʃaʊps La, ʃɒʊps La Y, ʃɔʊps Y, ʃᵁuːps We, ʃuːps Y

shoot *1. n* the STEM of a corn-plant II.5.2(a). ʃuːt Man
2.1. v to TIP a cart I.11.6. ʃˡuːt Db
2.2. vt to tip. ʃʊɪt Y, ʃʊuːt Y
3. n a SLOPE IV.1.10. ʃuːt Ha *[marked probably ir.r. SBM; prob ='steep slope' Edd]*
4. n the GUTTER of a roof V.1.6. ʃʏːt D, *pl* ʃʏːts Co, ʃʌt So, ʃʊt Do, ʃuːt Do Sx

shoot-bat *n* a BUMPER of a cart I.10.1(a). ʃʊtbæt Sr *[marked ir.r. SBM]*

shooting *v-ing* THROWING a stone VIII.7.7. ʃʊtn Du

shooting out *vtphr-ing* PUTTING your tongue OUT VI.5.4. ʃætɪn æʏt D, ʃʌtn ... uːt Nb

shoot on *vphr* to PITCH sheaves II.6.10. -*ing* ʃʌtɪn ɔːn Ha, -*ing* ʃʌtn ɔːn Ha

shoot out *1. vtphr* to empty a cart by tipping it, ⇐ TIP I.11.6. ʃʊt ... ɛʊt Sf
2. vphr to POUR tea V.8.8. ʃʌt aʊt So

shoots *npl* piglets, ⇐ PIGLET III.8.2. ʃəts Sx

shoot-stick *n* a movable horizontal rod stretching between the shafts of a cart, fixing them to the cart-body and stopping the cart from tipping, ⇐ ROD/PIN I.10.3. ʃuːtstɪk O

shoot up *1. vphr* to TIP a cart I.11.6. ʃuːt ʊp Db
2. vtphr to tip. ʃɪʊt ... ʌp Nf, ʃuːt ... ʌp O Bd Sx, ʃɪuːʔ ... ʏp Nf, ʃʊʔ ... ʏp Nf, ʃuːt ... ʏp Nf, ʃʏːt ... ʊp Ch, ʃʏːt ... ʊp Db, ʃʊɪt ... ʊp Y, ʃuːt ... ʊp Y St Nt

shop *n* the VULVA of a cow III.2.3. ʃɒp Db St Nth

shop-new *adj* BRAND-NEW VI.14.24. ʃɒpnjuː He

shorn skin *n* the PELT of a sheep III.11.8(b). ʃɔɪn skɪn He

short *adj* **a bit short, a button short** SILLY VIII.9.3. ə bɪt ʃɔːəˡt Sx, ə bʌtn ʃaˡːt So

short-fork *n* a HAY-FORK with a medium-length or short shaft I.7.11. ʃɔːt fɔːk St, ʃɔːtfɔːk C Nf

short-handle slasher *n* a BILLHOOK IV.2.6. ʃɔːthændl slæʃə Nf

short-hook *n* a BILLHOOK IV.2.6. ʃaːtʊk Wo, ʃaˡːtʊk He, ʃɔːtʊk He

shortline-horse *n* the FAR-HORSE of a pair pulling a wagon I.6.4(b). ʃɔˑtlaɪnhɒˑs Nf

short-shovel *n* a SHOVEL for a household fire V.3.9. ʃɔːtʃʌvɫ Ess

short-side *n* the SOLE of a horse-drawn plough I.8.9. ʃɔːəˡʈsəɪd Sx

shot at *adj* EXHAUSTED, describing a tired person VI.13.8. ʃɒt at La Y

shots *npl* the horizontal BARS of a gate IV.3.6. ʃɒts Ha

shotted *adj* EXHAUSTED, describing a tired person VI.13.8. ʃɒtɪt Db *[queried WMBM]*

should *vaux-3pl* OUGHT TO IX.4.6. ʃøːd Nb, ʃʏˑd Nb, ʃʊd Nb Cu Du We La Y Ch St Wa L Bd Ess MxL W Brk Sr K Ha Sx, sʊd La Y *[marked u.r. NBM, SBM]*

shoulder *n* a BUMPER of a cart I.10.1(a). ʃɛʊɫdə Nf

shoulder(s) *n* the EAVES of a stack of corn II.7.3.
no -s: ʃɒʊldə Ch
-s: ʃᵊuːldəz Du
[shoulder marked u.r. WMBM, but shoulders not so marked NBM]

shout *vi* to SCREAM VIII.8.11. ʃuːt Du

shouting *v-ing* SHRIEKING, describing the shrill noise made by a baby VI.5.15. ʃɛʊtɪn Sr, ʃaʊtɪn So

shovel *1. n What do you call this [indicate a shovel for a household fire]?* V.3.9. Eng. ⇒ **coal-shovel, cowl-shovel, dust-pan, fire-pan, fire-shovel, scoop, scummer, short-shovel, shuddy, sifter, slice, spittle**
2. n a SPADE I.7.6. ʃaˡːvəl Sa, ʃʊvl Ch, ʃəvɫ Gl

shovel-footed *adj* SPLAY-FOOTED VI.10.5. ʃʊvlfʊtɪd Nt L, ʃʊvlfʊʔɪd L

shovel-hilt *n* the SHAFT of a spade I.7.7. ʃæʏɫɪt Co, ʒʌvɫɪɫt D

shovel out *vtphr* to DITCH IV.2.11. ʃɛʊl ... ɛʊt Wa, ʃʊvl ... æʊt Wo

shove off *imp* GO AWAY! VIII.7.9(a). ʃʌv ɒˑf Ha, ʃʌv ɔːf Nf So W Co Sx, ʃʊv aːf Gl, ʃʊv ɔːf Wa

shove-stay *n* the iron stay connecting the beam with the side of a cart, ⇐ CROSS-BEAM END of a cart I.10.1. ʃʌvstæɪ K *[BM treats simply as cross-beam end]*

shove to *vtphr* to SHUT a door IX.2.8. ʃʊv ... tʊuː Y

shoving out *vtphr-ing* PUTTING your tongue OUT VI.5.4. ʃʌvɪn æɤt So, ʃʌvɪn ... æɤt D, ʃʌvən æɤt Co, ʃʌvɪn aʊt So, ʃʊvɪn ... ɛːt Db, ʃʌfɪn ... ɛʊt Ess, ʃʊvɪn ... ɛʊt Nth, ʃʊvɪn ... aːt Y, ʃʊvɪn ... aʊt Y L, ʃʊvɪn ... ʌʊt He, ʃʊvɪn uːt Y, ʃʊvn ... uːt Nb, ʃəvɪn ᵁuːt Gl

show *n* a local FESTIVAL or holiday VII.4.11. ʃʌʊ MxL, ʃoː Du; **show day** ʃoː deː D

showed *vt-3ptsg* he/she TAUGHT it III.13.17. ʃoːd So, ʃoʊd St *[marked u.r. WMBM]*

shows signs of calving *phr When a cow shows signs of giving birth, you say she ....* III.1.12, III.1.12(a), III.1.12(b)

1. referring to imminence of calving, III.1.12: *about at calving, about calving, a-going to calve, a-heading for her calving, begins to fidget, calving, calving down, calving is coming on her, coming close, coming on, downcalving* ⇒ **downcalve,** *due to calf, due to calve, fares for calving, faring a-calving, faring on calving, getting close, getting restless, going to calve, has* sickened *for calving, has started, has started calving, her time's up, is about calving, is about to calve, is a* down-calver, *is after calving, is a-going to calve, is a-paining for calving, is bad for to calve, is* boun *to calve, is calving, is close on calving, is coming down, is coming down for calving, is coming on, is coming on calving, is coming on for calving, is coming on to calve, is coming up to calve, is distressed, is down-calving* ⇒ **downcalve,** *is down to calve, is due, is due to calf, is due to calve, is* failing *for calve, is* failing *for calving, is faring a-calving, is faring calving, is faring for calve, is faring for calving, is faring for to calve, is faring on calving, is faring to calve, is fistling on* ⇒ **fistle on,** *is getting close to calving, is getting down to it, is getting uneasy, is going to calf, is going to calf down, is going to calve, is going to calve down, is going to come down, is like calving, is likely for calving, is like to calve any day, is* looking *for calf, is making ready, is near calving, is near her time, is near to her calving, isn't going to be long before she's going to calve, is on calving, is on the job, is on the* nestle *for calving, is on the way to calving, is* paining, *is* paining *herself, is ready for calving, is ready to calve, is restless, is right for calving, is shaping* ⇒ **shape,** *is shaping to calve* ⇒ **shape,** *is sick on, is sick on the calf, is sitting, is soon going to calve, is starting to calve, is uneasy, is uneasy a bit, is upon calving, is wanting to calve, is warming down for calving, labours, looks like calving, near calving, on calving, overstrung,* paining *herself, ready for calving, restless, shows signs,* sickens *for calving, straining, uneasy, unsettled, will be calving directly, will be downcalving directly* ⇒ **downcalve,** *will calve, will calve any time, will not be long, will not be long before she calves, will not be long on calving, will soon calve, will soon start to calve*

2. referring to swelling of the udder, III.1.12(a): *are* springing, *a-springing, a-springing to calf, a-springing up, bagged up, bagging up, bag up, coming down in the udder* ⇒ **come down,** *drawing back, filling, getting full-float, has got a good show, has sprung* ⇒ **spring,** *her bag is dropping, her bag is swelling, her milk has come, her milk is coming, her milk is coming down, her udder comes down, her udder draws up, her udder gets stiff, her udder is springing, her udder is springing to calf, is a-springing, is bagging up, is drawing her udder, is drawing udder, is drawing up for calving, is springing, is springing her udder, is springing to calf, is springing udder, milk has come, milk up, she's bagging, she's bagging up, she's cushioning, she's eldering up, she's full-bagged, she's pressing, she's seeding, she's springing, she's stocking up, she's swollen hard, springing, springing her udder, springs her udder, swelling up, the flues are swollen, the milk begins flowing, the milk is sprung* ⇒ **spring,** *the udder is springing, udder drops, would* bladder

3. referring to pelvic slackening, III.1.12(b): *a-dropping, all slunk* ⇒ **slink,** *bones drop, drop in, drop in the hips, dropped, dropped in, dropping, dropping in behind, drops in, fallen away, falls in, giving in the bone, has dropped, has dropped for calving, has dropped in, has dropped in the* couplings, *has dropped in the haunches, has dropped round the tail, has gone at bone, has gone in the bone, has gone in the bones, has gone off in the bone, has gone off in the hips, has got* rat-runs, *has* pitched *away, has* pitched *in, has* pitted *in, has slackened for calving, has* slinkt, *has sunk* ⇒ **sink,** *have gone in the* lockings, *her barren has dropped, her bedding's come down, her bones are coming off, her bones are down, her bones are dropped, her bones are fallen apart, her bones are going, her bones are gone, her bones are open, her bones are parting, her bones are slackened off, her bones are splitting, her bones be dropped, her bones be dropping, her bones be gone, her bones drop, her bones have dropped, her bones have given way, her bones have gone, her bones is dropping, her bones is going, her bones is gone, her gristles goes* ⇒ **gristle(s),** *her gristles is dropped* ⇒ **gristle(s),** *her gristles is gone* ⇒ **gristle(s),** *her hips have dropped, her joints are gone, her muscles is going, her* slacks *are dropping, her* slacks *are going down, her* slacks *drop, her strings are down, her strings are dropped, her strings are going, her strings are going down, her strings are gone, her strings are slackening, hips be gone, is a-dropping, is* *a-ginning to open, is dropping, is dropping down, is dropping for calving, is dropping her lockings, is dropping in, is dropping in behind, is dropping in its slacks, is dropping in the bone, is falling in, is giving, is giving way, is going in on her back, is going in the bone, is looking hollow, is loose behind, is off at the hips, is off on the hips, is pitching in, is pitching in behind, is pitting in, is sinking, is sinking in, is spreading, is springing, is tight in calf, parted, pitched in, pitched off, pitches in, pitching in, pitching in to the pins, she drops down, she falls, she gets down in the dawks, she goes down in the slacks, she has dropped her slacks, she has dropped in the slacks, she has dropped the slacks, she has given in her gristle ⇒ gristle(s), she has gone slack, she has slipped, she has slipped her bones, she has slipped in her strings, she is down in her bones, she is down in the bones, she is dropping, she is dropping in the slacks, she is falling at the dawks, she is falling in her strings, she is going in the slacks, she is gone down in the slacks, she is gone in her slacks, she is gone in the slacks, she is loosening, she is sinking, she is slackening, she is slackening at the slacks, she is slipping, she is slipping in her strings, she is through with her bones, sinks in each side of the tail, sinks in the hips, slinkt, springing, springs behind, starts spreading, strings are gone, swelled behind, swelling in the barren, the bones are opening, the bones are slipped, the bones be gone, the bones drop, the bones go, the slacks are going, the slacks are gone, the strings are gone, the water has broke, they've dropped*

shrammed *1. adj* COLD, describing a person VI.13.18. ʃʈæmd So

2. adj VERY COLD, describing a person VI.13.19. ʃʈæmd So, ʃʈamd W D Ha, ʂʈamd Ha, ʒʈamd Ha; **shrammed to death** ʃʈamd tə dɛθ W, ʒʈamd tə dɛθ Ha; **shrammed with the cold** ʃʈæmd wɪ ðə koʊłd So, ʃʈamd wɪ ðə kɒʊłd W, ʃʈamd wɪ ðə koːłd W, ʂʈamd wɪ ðə koːłd Ha; **very nigh shrammed** vəˤː n̩ɒɪ ʃʈamd Ha

shred *1. v* to TRIM hedges IV.2.3. sɹɪd Gl

2.1. vt to REMOVE *STALKS* from currants V.7.24. ʃɹɪd Gl

2.2. v to remove stalks. *-ing* ʃɹɪdɪn Sr

shredding-hook *n* a HEDGING-BILL IV.2.5. sɹɪdɪnʊk Gl

shrew *n* a SHREW-MOUSE IV.5.2. sɹɪyː La Ch, ʃɹɪʊ Y, sɹɪʊ O, ʃɹɪuː Nt, sʃɹɪuː Y L Ess, sɹɪuː Nt L Ess, ʃɹɪʉː Nf, ʃʈyː So D, ʃəʀøː Nb, ʃɹɛʊ La Y, sʃɹɛʊ La, sɹɛʊ Y Db, ʃəʀœː Nb, ʃɹaʊ La, ʃɹɔʊ Y, sɹoʊ Lei, ʃʀuː Nb, sʃʀuː Nb, ʃəʀɪʊ Nb, ʃəʀuː Nb Du, ʃɹuː Cu We La Y Db Sa St Wa Nt Ess K Sx, ʃəɹuː Cu We, sɹuː Ch Db Lei R Nf Sr, *pl* sɹuːz K, ʃɹʉː Lei, sɹʉː Lei

shrewd* *n* a SHREW-MOUSE IV.5.2. ʃəɹuːd Nb [*NBM headword* **shewd**]

shrewd-mouse *n* a SHREW-MOUSE IV.5.2. ʃʈyːdmʏːz D, *pl* ʃɹuːdmɛɪs Cu

shrew-mouse *n* *What do you call that small kind of mouse with the long snout; it eats insects and lives outside?* IV.5.2. sɹɪuːmɛws Sf, sɹɪuːmæːs Nt, ʃɹɪuːmaʊs L, sɹɪuːmaʊs L, ʃɹuːmɛʊs Wa, sɹɪuːmɛʊs Ess, səɹuːmɛʊs Ess, sɹuːːmæɪs Ch, ʃɹuːmæʊs Lei, ʃʈuːmaʊs So, *pl* sɹuːmɑˑɪsɪz R, ʃɹʉːmæʊs Lei, sɹʉːmæʊs Lei. ⇒ **bean-mouse, blind-mouse, bole, dormouse, field-mouse, grass-mouse,** *groin-mouse* ⇒ **ground-mouse, ground-mouse, hardy-mouse, hardy-shrew, hardy-shrew-mouse, hardy-strow, harvest-mouse,** *harvest-row* ⇒ **harvest-shrew, harvest-shrew, hog-mouse, land-mouse, little blindy, little cropper, mole-mouse, mossro, mouse-mole, nossro, nossrol, peaked-nose, pea-mouse, ranny, ranny-mouse, screw, screwel,** *shear-crop* ⇒ **sho-crop, shear-mouse, sheery, sherra-crop, shewd, shirrow, sho-croach, sho-crop, sho-mouse, shrew, shrewd, shrewd-mouse, shrow-crop, shrow-mouse, sow-mouse, strickling, white-belly-mouse**

shriek *1. vi-3prpl* they NEIGH, describing the noise horses make in the fields III.10.3(b). ʃɹiːk Sf Ess, *-ing* sɹiˑkʔɪn Nf[*very loud*]

2. vi to SCREAM VIII.8.11. ʃɹiːk Y, sɹiːk Nf Ess, ʃɹɪk Sf, sɹɪk Ess[*old*], *prppl* əʃɹɪkən Sf

shrieking *v-ing* When a baby wakes up and starts making loud, shrill noises, you say the baby is .... VI.5.15. ʃɹiːkɪn Y Sa Wa Lei K, sɹiːkɪŋ Brk, sɹiːkɪn Nf Ess, ʃɹɪkɪn Ess, sɹɪkɪn Ess, sɹɪkŋ̩ Ess, sɹɪkən Ess. ⇒ **bawling, bealing, belling, bellocking, bellowing out, blaring, blarting, crying, greeting, hollering, howling, roaring, scrawking, scrawling, screaming, screeching, screeking, screeting, shouting, siking, skelling, skriking, squalling, squawking, squeaking, squealing, twining on, twisting, whauping, whinging, whinnocking, yarking, yarming, yawling, yawning, yelling, yelling out, yelping, yiling, yowling**

shriek out *viphr* to SCREAM VIII.8.11. ʃɹiːkʔ ɛʊt Nf

shrimped *adj* VERY COLD, describing a person VI.13.19. ʃʈɪmpt D

shrimped up *adj* VERY COLD, describing a person VI.13.19. ʃʈɪmpt ʌp W D; **shrimped right up** ʃʈɪmpt ɹɑːd ʌp D; **shrimped up with the cold** ʃʈɪmpt ʌp wɪ ðə koːłd Co

shrimps *1. n* SCRAPS left after rendering lard III.12.10. ʃɹɪmps Mon

2. npl MINNOWS IV.9.9. ʃɹɪmps Sa [*marked u.r. WMBM*]

shrimpy *adj* COLD, describing a room VI.13.17. ʃʈɪmpi W

shrink *1. vi* to WRINKLE, referring to the skin of very old people VI.11.2. ʃɹɪŋk La

2. *vi* to WANE, referring to the moon VII.6.5(b). *-ing* ʃʈɪŋkɪn So, *-ing* ʂʈɪŋkɪn D

3. *vi* to WARP, referring to wood IX.2.9. ʃɹɪŋk Y Ch Wa Mon Gl L Lei Sr Do Sx, sʃɹɪŋk O L, sɹɪŋk Sa He Wo Mon Gl O Lei C Nf Sf Hrt Ess Sr Sx, *3prsg* sɹɪŋks MxL, *-s* sɹɪŋks Wa, sɹɪŋk? Bd, ʃʈɪŋk So W Co D Do, ʂʈɪŋk Co D Ha, ʃɹɛŋk He, ʒɾɛŋk Ha

shrinked up *adj* **shrinked right up** VERY COLD, describing a person VI.13.19. ʃʈɪŋkt ɾæːd ʌp D

shrip *vt* to WHITTLE a stick I.7.19. *-ing* ʃʈɪpɪn W

shrivel *vi* to WRINKLE, referring to the skin of very old people VI.11.2. sɹɪvəl Gl, sɹɪvɬ He Gl, ʃɹɪvəɬ Bk, *3prsg* ʃɹɪvəɬz K, *prppl* əsɹɪvəɬɪn Gl, *3prsg* sʈɪvəɬz O, ʃʈɪvɬ So

shrivelled *adj* wrinkled, describing the skin of very old people, ⇐ WRINKLE VI.11.2. ʃʈɪvɬd So, ʃʈɪvʊd So, sɹɪvʊd Ess

shrivelled up *adj* **shrivelled up with the cold** VERY COLD, describing a person VI.13.19. ʃʈɪvɬd ʌp wɪ ðə kʊʊɬd Co

shrivel up *viphr* to WRINKLE, referring to the skin of very old people VI.11.2. ʃɹɪvɬ ʌp Bk, *3prsg* sɹɪvəɬz ʌp Ess, ʃʈɪvɬ ʌp Do, *3prsg* ʃʈɪvɬz ʌp So D

shroud *1. vt* to LOP a tree IV.12.5. ʃɾaʊd So, ʃɹəʊd W

2. *v* to lop. *-ing* ʃɾæʊdn W, ʃɹᵁuːd Gl

shrove *v* to cut large branches from a tree, ⇐ to LOP IV.12.5. *-ing* sɹoʊvɪn K

shrow-crop *n* a SHREW-MOUSE IV.5.2. ʃɾoːkɾɒp Do

shrow-mouse *n* a SHREW-MOUSE IV.5.2. ʃɾoːməʊs W

shrubs *npl* BUSHES IV.10.5. *sg* ʃɹʌb Sr, ʃɹʌbz Sx, sɹʌbz Sr K, ʃɾʌbz So, sʈʌbz Ha, ʃɹʊbz Y Man L, sɹʊbz L *[Sx form apparently marked ir.r. by fw]*

shuck *n* a pea-POD V.7.12. ʃʌk Brk Ha Sx*[old x1]*, *pl* ʃʌks Ess*[old x1, empty x1]* Sr, *pl* ʃəks Sx

shucking *v-ing* SHELLING peas V.7.14. ʃʌkɪn Sr Ha, ʃʌkɳ Ha, ʃʌkən Ha

2. *v* shelling. ʃʌkɪn Bk Brk Sr Ha Sx, ʃəkɪn Sx

shucks *n* CHAFF II.8.5. ʃʌks Sr *[marked ir.r. by fw]*

shuddered *adj* **shuddered with the cold** VERY COLD, describing a person VI.13.19. ʃʌdəᵗːɖ wɪ ðə koːɬd D

shuddering *adj* VERY COLD, describing a person VI.13.19. ʃʌdəɾɪn So

shudders *n* **the shudders** TREMORS suffered by a person who cannot keep still VI.1.4. ðə ʃudəᵗz Gl

shuddy *n* a child's word for a SHOVEL for a household fire V.3.9. ʃʌdɪ Bk

shuff *n* a SHOE VI.14.22(a). ʃʊf La Ch *[not a NBM headword]*

2. *npl* BOOTS ʃʊf Ch*[old, also sg]*

shuft *n* a SCARECROW II.3.7. ʃʌft Bk

shugging *adj* HEAVING *(WITH MAGGOTS)* IV.8.6. ʃʊgən Nb

shuggy *1. n* a SEESAW VIII.7.2. ʃɤʒɪ Nb, ʃʊgɪ Nb*[old x1]* Du

2. *n* a swing. ʃʊgɪ Du

shull *n* a pea-POD V.7.12. ʃʊl Db, *pl* ʃʊlz Ch

shulling *1. vt-ing* SHELLING peas V.7.14. ʃʊlɪn Ch St Wo

2. *v-ing* shelling. ʃʊlɪn Y Ch*[old x1]* Db Sa St *[not a NBM headword]*

shut *1. vt* If the door blew open on a cold day, you'd get up at once and ... it. IX.2.8. Eng. ⇒ **close, close up, fasten, latch, pull to, push fast, put to, shove to, shut up, sneck, tine**

2. *adj* **half shut** AJAR IX.2.7. haːf ʃʊt Man

shut-post *n* the SHUTTING-POST of a gate IV.3.4. ʃɛtpʊʊst O, ʃʌtpoːst Brk

shuts *vi-3prsg* school FINISHES VIII.6.2(b). ʃɛt Nf, ʃʌts C Bk MxL So D Do, ʃʌʔs Bk, ʃʌt Sf So Do, ʒʌt D, ʃʊts We Y Db Nt L Lei C Ch, dʊ ʃət Gl

shuts up *viphr-3prsg* school FINISHES VIII.6.2(b). ʃʌts ʌp MxL, ʒʌd ʌp Ha, ʃʊts ʊp La Y Db

shutting-post *n* What do you call the other one *[i.e. the gate-post opposite the hanging-post]?* IV.3.4. ʃɛtɪnpʊʊs K, ʃɛʔnpʊʊst O, ʃɛtʔnpʌʊst Ess, ʃɛʔɪnpoˑəs Bd, ʃɛʔnpʊəst O, ʃʊtɪnpʊʊst K, ʃʌtɪnpæʊs Hrt, ʃʌtɪnpʊʊs K, ʃʌ?npʊʊs Sx, ʃʌ?ɳpʊʊst Ess, ʃʌ?npʊʊs Ess, ʃʌtɪnpʌʊs Sr, ʃʌʔɪnpʌʊst Bk Bd, ʃʌʔɳpʌʊst Ess, ʃʌtɪnpoːst Sa Ha, ʃʌdɪnpoːst Ha, ʃʌtɪnpoːst W, ʃʌʔnpoːst W, ʃʌtɪnpoːəst W, ʃʌtənpoːəst Ha, ʃʌtɪnpoʊs K, ʃʌtɪnpʊəst O, ʃʌʔɪnpʊəst O Bk, ʃʊ?npʊʊs K, ʃʊtɪnpoːs O, ʃʊtɪnpʊəst La Bk, ʃʊtɪnpʊəs Y, ʃətɪnpɒst Sx, ʃətɪnpʊʊst Sx, ʃəʔnpʊʊst Sx, ʃətɪnpʊʊst Sx, ʃətɪnpoˑʊst Brk. ⇒ **back-post, batten-stoop, beating-post, bitten-stoop, catch-post, clapper, clapping-gate, clapping-post, clapping-stump, clap-post, clap-stump, crooking-post, dropping-post, dropping-stoop, faller, falling-post, falling-stoop, fastener, fastening-post, fastening-stoop, fastening-stub, fastening-stump, fore-post, fore-tree, gate-clap, gate-post, hang-stoop, hasping-post, hasp-post, head, head-post, head-stoop, head-stump, kepping-post, lace-stoop, latching-post, latch-post, shut-post, shutting-stoop, shutting-stub, shut-to-post, slammer, slamming-post, slapping-post, slap-stump, snecking-post, sneck-post, sneck-stoop, stopping-post, swinging-post, swinging-stump, taking-post, tie- stoop, tying-stoop**

shutting-stoop *n* the SHUTTING-POST of a gate IV.3.4. ʃʊtɪnstʊʊp Y, ʃʊtɪnstɔʊp Y, ʃʊtɪnstuːp Cu Du We La Y

shutting-stub *n* the SHUTTING-POST of a gate IV.3.4. ʃʊttɪnstʊb La

shuttle *n* a SHEATH or other device used to keep a knitting-needle firm V.10.10. ʃʊtl He

shuttles *npl* the horizontal BARS of a gate IV.3.6. ʃʌdɬz So Co

shut-to-post *n* the SHUTTING-POST of a gate IV.3.4. ʃɛttuːpʌʊs Ess, ʃʌttuːpʌʊst Ess, ʃʌttuːpʌʊs Ess, ʃʌttuːpoʊst Ess

shut up *vtphr* to SHUT a door IX.2.8. ʃʌd ... ʌp Bk, ʃʌʔ ... ʋp Nf, ʃʊd ... ʊp O

shy *adj* *Some children are very quiet and easily blush in company, because they are far too ....* VIII.9.2. Eng. ⇒ **bash**, **bashful**, *blate*, *domiciled*, **frightened**, **nervous**, **nervy**, **quiet**, **sensitive**, **shame-faced**, **timid**

shying *v-ing* THROWING a stone VIII.7.7. ʃɔɪ-ɪn Ha, ʃəɪ-ɪn W

sick *1.* *adj* *If one of your animals isn't well, then you say it is ....* VI.13.1(c). sɪk Nb La Y Man Mon L Nf Ess So W Brk Sr K Co Ha Sx, zɪk So D Ha, səɪk Y. ⇒ *a bit off the* **hooks**, **ailing**, *ain't right* ⇒ *not* **right**, *ain't well* ⇒ *not* **well**, **bad**, **badly**, *bit* **rough**, **dicky**, **douthy**, **down**, *feeling* **sick**, **funnified**, *gone* **down**, **gripy**, **groggy**, **ill**, *isn't very fitty* ⇒ *not very* **fitty**, *isn't very well* ⇒ *not very* **well**, **middling**, *nobbut* **middling**, *none* **right**, *none so* **well**, *none up to the* **mark**, *not* **right**, *not so* **well**, *not very* **fitty**, *not very* **well**, *not* **well**, *off* **colour**, *off it* ⇒ *off* **colour**, *off* **sorts**, *off the* **hooks**, *out of* **fettle**, *out of* **sorts**, **poorly**, *pretty* **dicky**, *pretty* **queer**, **queer**, **ramped**, *rather* **poor**, **rough**, **seedy**, **sickly**, *taken* **bad**, *very* **queer**, **wisht**, **wrong**

2. *adj* ILL, describing a person who is unwell VI.13.1(b). siːk Lei, sɪk La Y Ess Sx, zɪk So Ha

3.1. *vi* to VOMIT, referring to an adult VI.13.14(a). sɪk Lei R Nf *[marked u.r. as adj SBM]*

3.2. *adj* **be sick** to vomit. biː sɪk Lei Sx, bɪ sɪk Y Sa Lei R Ess Brk Sr K Sx, bɪ zɪk So

4.1. *vi* to VOMIT, referring to a baby bringing up milk VI.13.14(b). sɪk St Mon Lei R Nf Sf *[marked u.r. SBM, presumably as adj]*

4.2. *adj* **be sick** to vomit, referring to a baby. biː sɪk Sa Ess, bɪ sɪk Cu Du La Y Ch Db Sa Wa Mon Gl O Nt Lei Nth Hu C Sf Bk Bd Hrt Ess Brk Sr K, bə sɪk Gl, *ptppl* biːn sɪk W, *ptppl* bɪn sɪk W, *ptppl* bɪn zɪk D, *-ing* biːɪn sɪk Nf, *3prsg* hiːz sɪk Nf, *3prsg* iːz sɪk W, *3prsg* ɪts sɪk Nb He Wo L, *3prsg* ɪz sɪk Nf, *3prsg* z sɪk He Wo

sicken *vi* **sicken for calving** to show signs of calving, ⇐ SHOWS SIGNS OF CALVING III.1.12. *3prperfsg* sɪkənd fə kɪaːvɪn Sa, *3prperfsg* sɪknd fə kaːvɪn Sa, *3prperfsg* sɪknd fə kaːvɪn Wo, *3prperfsg* sɪknd fə kɔːvɪn Sa, *3prsg* sɪknz fə kɔːvɪn He, *3prperfsg* sɪknd fə kɔᵗːvɪn Sa

sick-field *n* a PADDOCK I.1.10. sɪkfiːld St

sick head *n* a HEADACHE VI.1.6. sɪk ɛd MxL, sɪk heᵊd Man

sickle *1.* *n* a HEDGING-BILL IV.2.5. sɪkl Sa, sɪkɬ Man

2. *n* a BILLHOOK IV.2.6. sɪkl Y Man Sa

sickle-backs *npl* MINNOWS IV.9.9. sɪkɬbæks Ess *[marked u.r. and interpreted as 'stickleback' EMBM]*

sickly *1.* *adj* ILL, describing a person who is unwell VI.13.1(b). sɪklɪ Hrt

2. *adj* SICK, describing an animal that is unwell VI.13.1(c). sɪkɬi So

sick on *adj* showing signs of calving, ⇐ SHOWS SIGNS OF CALVING III.1.12. sɪk ɒn Man; **sick on the calf** sɪk ɒn ðə kæː Man

sick up *vtphr* to VOMIT, referring to a baby bringing up milk VI.13.14(b). sɪk ... ʌp Nf, *3prsg* sɪks ... ʌp Ha, *-ing* sɪkɪn ... əp Sx, *3prsg* sɪks ... ʊp Lei, *-s* sɪks ... up St

sicky *1.* *adj* ILL, describing a person who is unwell VI.13.1(b). sɪkɪ Sx

2. *vi* to VOMIT, referring to an adult VI.13.14(a). zɪki So

side *1.* *n* a FLITCH or side of bacon III.12.3. saːd Y, zaːd D, saɪd La Y, zaɪd So, saɪd La Db C Nf Bk Bd Hrt Ess MxL Sr K, sɒɪd St K, zɒɪd So W Co Ha, sɔɪd Wo O Sf Ess Sx, *pl* sɔɪdz Ha, sʌɪd Nf Sf, zʌɪd Gl, səɪd Mon Sx, zəɪd W *[side of (a) bacon forms included here]*

2. *v* to TRIM hedges IV.2.3. *-ing* zaɪdɪn So

3.1. *vt* to CLEAR the table after a meal V.8.14. saːd La Y, saɪd La Y*[old x1]* L, saːd Y, saɪd La Db

3.2. *vt* to clear dishes from the table. saɪd Y

3.3. *v* to clear the table. saɪd Cu Du We La Y Db, saɪd Du La Ch *['dishes' or 'table' unclear]*

4. *v* to AGREE with somebody VIII.8.12. seɪd Nb*[old]* Sa, saːd Y, saɪd Du Y Sa St L, saɪd K, sɒɪd St, zɒɪd So, sɔɪd Bk*[old]*

5. *vt-3sg* she [a tidy girl] will COLLECT her toys VIII.8.15. saːd La, saɪd Cu La Y, saːd La Y, saɪd La Ch

6. *prep* BESIDE a door IX.2.5. zaːd D, saɪd K, sɒɪd K, sɔɪd Ess K, səɪd Sx; **side of** zaːd ɒv D, zaɪd ɔː Co, saɪd əv K, saɪd ə Nf MxL, sɔɪd əv K, sʌɪd əv Nf, zəɪd oː W; **side on** saːd ɒn Y, saˑɪd ɔn L, zaɪd ɒn Co, saˑɪd ɒn Db, saˑɪd ɔn L, zɒɪd ɒn Ha, sʌɪd ɒn Nf, sʌɪd ɔn Sf; **the side** ðə sɔɪd Bk; **the side of** ðə sɔɪd ə Brk Ha

side away *1.1.* *vtphr* to CLEAR dishes from the table after a meal V.8.14. saːd ... əweː Y, saɪd ... əweː Y, *-ed* saɪdɪd ... əweə Y

1.2. *vphr* to clear dishes. saːd əwɛə Y, *-ing* saɪdɪn əweː Y, *-ind* saɪdɪn əwɛə Y, saɪd əwɛɪ L *['dishes' or 'table' unclear]*

2. *vtphr-3sg* she [a tidy girl] will COLLECT her

toys VIII.8.15. saːd ... əwɛə Y, saɪd ... əweː Y, saɪd ... əweə Du, saɪd ... əweː Ch

side-arms *n* a CART-FRAME I.10.6. saɪdaːmz Sa

side-baulks *n* HEADLANDS in a ploughed field II.3.3. saɪdbɔːks Y

side-beard(s) *n* WHISKERS VI.2.6.
no -s: sɒɪdbiəˡːd̥ W, sʌɪdbɪəd Nf
-s: saɪdbɪˈəz Y

side-bits *n* WHISKERS VI.2.6. saɪdbɪts Nf

side-blinders *n* WHISKERS VI.2.6. saɪdblaɪndəz Db

side-blinds *n* WHISKERS VI.2.6. saːdblaːnz La, saɪdblaɪnz Wo, saɪdblaɪnz La

side-board *1. n* an END-BOARD of a cart I.10.4. *pl* zɛdbuːɽd̥z̥ D, sɛɪdbɔˡːd̥ Sa, sɛɪdboᴿːd Nb, sɛɪdboəd Nb, zæːdbuəˡːd̥ D, sæɪdbouəˡd Wo, *pl* saɪdbɔːdz Cu, saɪdbɔˡːd̥ Sa, zaɪdbɔˡːd̥z̥ So, *pl* saɪdboˈəˡːd̥z̥ So, zaɪdbuəˡːd̥ Co, *pl* zaɪdbuəˡːd̥z̥ D, *pl* saɪdbɔːdz K, *pl* saɪdbɛuədz Ch, *pl* saɪdboədz Ch Db K, sɒɪdbɔːd St, *pl* sɒɪdbɔˡːd̥z̥ So Ha, sɒɪdboədz K, sɒɪdbuəd St, zɒɪdbuːɽd̥ D, zɒɪdbuəˡːd̥ Co, *pl* sɔɪdbɔˡːd̥z̥ O, sɔɪdbɔːəd Sx, sɔɪdboəˡd̥ Ha, *-s* səɪdboːdz Mon, səɪdboːəˡd̥ He Mon *[apparently refers to a general side extension, often in a set – hence frequent pls]*
2. n WHISKERS VI.2.6. sɔɪdbɔːd Ess

side-board(s) *1. n* a CART-FRAME I.10.6.
sg: saɪdbɔəd St
no -s: saˈɪdbɔːd Lei
-s: zæːdbuːɽd̥z̥ D, saˈɪdbɔːdz Lei, zaɪdbɔːˡd̥z̥ So, saˈɪdbuədz L, saɪdbuəˡːd̥z̥ Co, zaɪdbuəˡːd̥z̥ D, saɪdbuːəˡːd̥z̥ So, saˈɪdbɔːdz Lei R, saˈɪdbuədz Lei, sɒɪdbouədz St, zɒɪdbuːɽd̥z̥ Ha, sɔɪdbɔːədz Sx *[at 45 degrees]*, səɪdbɔːəˡd̥z̥ He, zəɪdbuəˡːd̥z̥ W
2. n WHISKERS VI.2.6.
mass n: sɔɪdbɔːd Nf
-s: Eng exc. R MxL Co D

sideboards *npl* FLAPs at the front of old-fashioned trousers VI.14.16. zaɪdbuːɽd̥z̥ D *[queried ir.r. SBM]*

side-braids *n* WHISKERS VI.2.6. saɪdbɹeːdz Db

side by *vtphr-3sg* she [i.e. a tidy girl] will COLLECT her toys VIII.8.15. sɛɪd ... baɪ Cu, saɪd ... baɪ Cu We Y

side-chats *n* WHISKERS VI.2.6. saɪdtʃats Y

side-end *n* the GABLE-END of a house V.1.5. səɪdɛnd He

side-hecks *n* a CART-FRAME I.10.6. saɪdɛks Y

side-ladders *n* a CART-FRAME I.10.6. saɪdladəˡːz̥ W, saɪdlædəz K, sɔɪdlɛdəz Ess, sɔɪdlædəz Ess, səɪdlædəˡz̥ Brk

side-lades *n* a CART-FRAME I.10.6. zæɪdleːʰdz So, zaɪdleːdz So, saɪdleɪdz So, zɒɪdɫeːdz D, sɔɪdleɪdz Sx

side-lights *n* WHISKERS VI.2.6. sɔɪdlɔɪts Sf

side-lines *n* WHISKERS VI.2.6. saɪdlaɪnz Nf, sɒɪdlɒɪnz Nf, sʌɪdlʌɪnz Nf

sideling **1. adj* sloping, ⇐ SLOPE IV.1.10. zɪdɫɪn D, zæːdɫɪn D, saɪdlɪn So
2. adj STEEP, describing a hill IV.1.11. zəɪdlɪn W, zəɪdɫɪn W

sidelings *n* a SLOPE IV.1.10. sɔɪdlənz Ha, səɪdlənz Sx

side-locks *n* WHISKERS VI.2.6. saɪdlɒks Cu

siden *v* to CLEAR the table after a meal V.8.14. saɪdən Y *['dishes' or 'table' unclear]*

side-piece *n* a FLITCH or side of bacon III.12.3. sʌɪdpiːs Sr

side-props *n* WHISKERS VI.2.6. saɪdpɹɒps Db

side-racks *n* a CART-FRAME I.10.6. zəɪdɽaks Do

side-rail(s) *n* a CART-FRAME I.10.6.
no -s: saˈɪdɹeɪɫ Lei
-s: zæːdɽeɪɫz D, zæɪdɽeɪᵊɫz So, sɒɪdɹeɪlz St

side-rails *n* WHISKERS VI.2.6. saɪdɹeəlz La

side-raves *n* a CART-FRAME I.10.6. saˈɪdɹeɪvz L, saˈɪdɹeˈəvz L, zɒɪdɽeːvz Ha, səɪdɹeɪvz Brk, zəɪdɽeːvz W

siders *n* WHISKERS VI.2.6. sɛɪdɔᴿs Nb

sides *n* a CART-FRAME I.10.6. sɔɪdz Ess

side up *1. vphr* to CLEAR the table after a meal V.8.14. saɪd ʊp Y, saːd ʊp Y *['dishes' or 'table' unclear]*
2. vtphr-3sg she [i.e. a tidy girl] will COLLECT her toys VIII.8.15. saːd ... ʊp La Y, saɪd ... ʊp Cu La Y L, saˈɪd ... ʊp Lei

side-walls *n* WHISKERS VI.2.6. zəɪdwɔːɫz Do

sidewards *prep* BESIDE a door IX.2.5. sɔɪdəˡd̥z̥ Bk

sideways *1. adv* looking in a SQUINTING manner VI.3.5. sɔɪdwæɪz MxL
2. adj ASKEW, describing a picture that is not hanging straight IX.1.3. zaɪdwɛɪz So
3. adv DIAGONALLY, referring to harrowing a field IX.1.8. səɪdwɛɪz Sx *[marked u.r. SBM]*
4. prep BESIDE a door IX.2.5. sɔɪdwɛɪz Sr

sie *1. vt* to STRAIN milk V.5.2. sæɪ He, saɪ Sa St, saɪ Db, sɒːɪ St, səɪ Wo
2. v to strain milk. saɪ Db Sa

sieve *1. n* a SOWING-BASKET II.3.6. sɪv Gl
2. n a BASKET for carrying horse-feed III.5.4. sɪf Nf *[willow, round]*, sɪv Y Wo *[wicker, round x1; basket-work, round x1]* Wa *[basket-work, oval x1; wooden, oval x1; wicker, oval x1]* Mon *[flat-bottomed, wicker, round]* O *[straw or split cane x1; wicker x1; split cane bottom x1]* Nt *[wooden, cane bottom, round x1; basket-work, oval x1]* L *[cane bottom, round x2; basket-work bottom, round x1; lath bottom x1; wooden x1; willow, plaited bottom x1; wooden, cane bottom, round x1; wooden, round x1; cane bottom x1]* Lei *[wicker]* Nth *[wicker, round x1; basket-work, round x1; basket-work, round, no handles x2]*

Hu*[basket-work, round, willow x1; wooden, cane bottom, round x1]* C*[wooden, cane-bottom, round x1; wooden, round, wicker bottom x1]* Nf*[wooden, round, willow or nutwood bottom x1; cane bottom, round x5; wooden, cane bottom x1; wooden, cane bottom, round x2; round x4]* Sf*[basket-work x1; split willow, round x1; wooden, cane bottom, round x1; cane bottom, round x1]* Bk*[wooden, round, no handles x1; rush bottom, round, cane sides x1; round, split cane x1; wooden, cane bottom, round x1; cane bottom, round x1]* Bd*[round, split cane x1; wooden, cane bottom x1; wooden, cane bottom, round x1]* Hrt*[rush bottom, round x1; wicker, round x1]* Ess*[wooden, cane bottom, round x2; basket-work, round x1; wooden, rush bottom, round x2; wooden, round x2; round x2; rush bottom x1]* Brk*[basket-work x1; basket-work, round x1]* Sr*[wooden, round, no handles x1; beech, cane bottom, round x1; cane bottom, round x1, rush bottom x1]* K*[round x1; rush bottom, round x1]* Ha*[round, wooden, no handles x1; cane bottom, round x1]* Sx*[cane bottom x1; rush bottom x1; cane bottom, round x2]*, sɪəv Ess*[wooden, cane bottom, round x1; rush bottom, round x1]*, ziːv Do*[round x2]*, zɪv So*[round, handles]* W*[round, no handles x1; round x1; basket-work x1; wicker, round, no handles x1; round, mesh bottom x1; wicker x1]* Do*[round x1; wicker x1]* Ha*[wooden, round, wicker bottom x1]*

3.1. *vt* to STRAIN milk V.5.2. sɪv Y Db Sa St He Wo, sɛv Wo

3.2. *v* to strain milk. sɪf Db, sɪv La*[old x1]* Ch Sa Wa Sf

sieve out *vphr* to WINNOW II.8.4. -*ing* sɪvɪn ɛʊt Nf

sieve up *vtphr* to STRAIN milk V.5.2. sɪv ... ʊp Ch

sift *1. v* to WINNOW II.8.4. sɪft Hrt*[by hand, with sieve]*, -*ing* sɪftn Ess

2. *vt* to RAKE cinders in a domestic fire V.3.8(b). sɪft Du

sifter *n* a SHOVEL for a household fire V.3.9. sɪftə L K*[small]*, sɪftɹ L, sɪftəˈ K*[old]*

sifting *1. n* a feed given to horses in the stable, ⇐ FEEDING III.5.1. sɪftɪn Nf, ʃɪftn Ess *[*ʃɪftn*] queried as error for* [sɪftn] *EMBM]*

2. *n* CHAFF fed to horses III.5.3. sɪftɪn Nf

sig *1. n* URINE in a cow-house I.3.10. sɪg So

2. *n* stale URINE used for cleaning blankets VI.8.8. sɛg W

sighing *v-ing* YAWNING VI.13.4. saɪkɪn Db, sɔɪ-ɪn Ess, səɪ-ɪn Mon

sike *n* a small RIVULET IV.1.1. sɛɪk Du, saɪk Cu We Y

siking *v-ing* SHRIEKING, describing the shrill noise made by a baby VI.5.15. saɪkɪn Sa

sile *1. vt* to STRAIN milk V.5.2. sɛɪl Nb Du, saːl Y, saɪl Nb Cu La Y Nt L, saˈɪɫ Lei, saːl Y L, saɪl L R, saˈɪɫ R

2. *v* to strain milk. sɛɪl Nb Cu, saːl Y, saɪl Nb Cu Du We La Y Db L, -*ing* saɪlɪn Man, saːl La Y, saɪl Du La Db Nt L

sile away *viphr* to FAINT VI.13.7. saˈɪl əwɛˈə L

sill *1. n* the CURB-STONE in a cow-house I.3.9. sɪɫ Wo Gl*[stone or wood]* Lei

2. *n* a SHAFT of a cart I.9.4. sɪl St

3. *n* a BUMPER of a cart I.10.1(a). sɪl St, *pl* sɪlz Nf

[in WMBM noted as referring to **shaft** *and therefore marked ir.r.; accepted as* **bumper** *EMBM]*

4. *n* a flat surface on which bacon is cured, ⇐ SALTING-TROUGH III.12.5. sɪl St

5. *n* the THRESHOLD of a door V.1.12. sɪl Db Sa Gl O L, ʃɪl L, sɪɫ He Wo Wa Gl O Nth Bk Bd Hrt Ess*[old]* W Ha, zɪɫ Gl Ha, sɪᵊɫ Wa O, sɪʊɫ Sx, sɪʊ Ha Sx*[wooden x1]*, sɛʊ Sr K Sx

sill-hanks *n* the HAMES of the harness of a cart-horse I.5.4. sɪlaŋks Y

silly *1. adj* A man who is always doing ridiculous things and behaving stupidly, you say is quite .... VIII.9.3. sɪli So, sɪɫɪ W Co Ha, sɪlɪ Nb Y Db St Wa Gl O Lei R Nf Hrt Ess Brk K Sx, sɪɫɪ Sr K. ⇒ *a bit* **short**, *a* **dafty**, *a button* **short**, **addled**, **addle-headed**, *a* **fool**, *a luny* ⇒ **loony**, **awkward**, **barmy**, **batchy**, **batty**, *bit* **rooky**, **cakey**, **cracked**, **crackers**, **cranky**, **crazy**, **daffy**, **daft**, **dafty**, **dappy**, **dateless**, **dibby**, **dimmy**, **dopey**, **dotty**, **dozy**, **feckless**, **fond**, **foolish**, **gaumless**, **gaumy**, **gone**, *got a* **kink**, **half-cracked**, **half-sharp**, **kimit**, **loony**, **loopy**, *luny* ⇒ **loony**, **mazed**, **noddy**, **noggen**, **nutty**, *off his* **head**, **potty**, *proper* **gawky**, **puddled**, **queer**, *real* **crackers**, **simple**, **soft**, **soppy**, **stupid**, **touched**, **touched** *in the* **head**, **wappy**, **wet**

2. *adj* STUPID VI.1.5. sɪlɪ Wo Mon Gl O Lei R Ess, sɪɫɪ Ess

silt *1. n* a SALTING-TROUGH III.12.5. zɪɫt So*[wooden or leaden]* W*[wooden or leaden]* Do Ha, zɪʊt So*[wooden or leaden]*

2. *n* DUST on a road VII.6.18. sɪlt Nf

silver-beech *n* a BIRCH tree IV.10.1. sɪlvəbiːtʃ La, sɪlvəbɪətʃ Y

silver-bellies *npl* MINNOWS IV.9.9. sɪlvəbalɪz Db

silver-birch *n* a BIRCH tree IV.10.1. sɪlvəbəᴿːtʃ Nb, sɪlvəbəˡtʃ Ch, sɪlvəbəɹk Y, sɪlvəbəːtʃ Y Nf, sɪlvəbəˡːtʃ Nf, sɪɫvəbəːtʃ Nf, sɪɫvəᵗbəˡtʃ Sr Ha, sɪɫvəᵗbəˡːtʃ Bk *[Sr form apparently specific]*

silver-larch *n* a BIRCH tree IV.10.1. sɪɫvəlaːk Hrt *[queried ir.r. EMBM]*

silvery-birch *n* a BIRCH tree IV.10.1. sɪlvəɹɪbəːtʃ Nf

simes *n* ROPES used to fasten thatch on a stack II.7.7(b2). saɪmz Cu We

sime-twiner *n* a ROPE-TWISTER II.7.8. sɛɪmtwɛɪnə Cu, saɪmtwaɪnə Cu

sime-twister *n* a ROPE-TWISTER II.7.8. saɪmtwɪstə Cu

simmer *vt* to RENDER fat into lard III.12.9. sɪmɔᵿ Nb

simmer down *vtphr* to RENDER fat into lard III.12.9. sɪməɹ (+V)... dɛʊn Ess

simmon thatcher *n* the THATCHER of a stack of corn II.7.5(b). sɑːmn̩ θætʃə Nf *[queried EMBM]*

simple *1. adj* STUPID VI.1.5. sɪmpl Y Nf, sɪmpɫ O Ess Do

2. *adj* SILLY VIII.9.3. sɪmpl St L, sɪmpʊ Brk

simple-minded *adj* STUPID VI.1.5. sɪmpʊməɪndɪd Brk

sin *adv* AGO VII.3.1. sɪn Cu Du We La Y Ch Db St Nt L, sɛn Cu Du We La Y St

since *adv* AGO VII.3.1. sɪns Nb Du Y L, sɪnts Db

sind *1. vt* to RINSE clothes V.9.8. -*ing* sɪndɪn Cu
2. *v* to rinse. sɪnd Cu Du We La Y

sine **1. v* to make a cow DRY, so that it gives no milk III.1.9. *1prprog* saɪnɪn We
2. *adv* AGO VII.3.1. sᵊiːn Du, sɛɪn Nb

sined *adj* DRY, describing a cow with no milk III.1.9. saɪnd We

sing *vi-3prpl* they MOO, describing the noise cows make during feeding time in the cow-house III.10.4(a). sɪŋ Cu, sɪŋz Wo Gl

single *1. vt* to THIN OUT turnip plants II.4.2. sɪŋl Nb Cu Du Y Db, sɪŋəl Y, sɪŋgl La Man Ch Sa St He Wo Wa Nt L Nth Nf, -*ing* sɪŋglɪn K, sɪŋgəl Y, zɪŋɫ So, sɪŋgɫ Wa Mon Lei R C Ess So Do, zɪŋgɫ W Do, sɪŋgʊɫ K
2. *v* to thin out turnips. sɪŋl Nb He, sɪŋəl Y, sɪŋgl Db Sa Nt, -*ing* sɪŋglɪn Man St Brk, sɪŋɫ Wa Nth Hu C Sf Bk Bd Hrt Ess, -*ing* sɪŋgɫ,ɪn O

singled onions *npl* SPRING ONIONS V.7.16. sɪŋɫd ʌŋənz Sf

single-halter *1. n* a HALTER for a cow I.3.17. sɪŋglhælt?ə Nf, sɪŋglhal?ə Nf, sɪŋglhɒltə Nf
2. *n* a TETHERING-ROPE used to tie up a horse I.4.2. sɪŋglhælt?ə Nf, sɪŋglhaˑlt?ə Nf

single out *1. vtphr* to THIN OUT turnip plants II.4.2. sɪŋgl ... ɛʊt Sa Nf Sf, sɪŋgɫ ... ɛʊt Wo Nth Sf Bk Ess Sr, sɪŋɫ ... ɛʊ? Bk, sɪŋgɫ ... ɛʊ? Bd, zɪŋgɫ ... æʏt D, -*ing* sɪŋlɪn ... æʊt Y, sɪŋgl ... æʊt Sa, sɪŋgɫ ... æʊt He Lei So Ha, sɪŋl ... aɪt Ch, sɪŋəl ... aʊt Y, sɪŋgl ... aʊt L, sɪŋgɫ ... aʊt Lei, sɪŋgl ... aːʊt St, sɪŋgɫ ... ʌʊt Mon, sɪŋgɫ ... əʊt He Mon Do, zɪŋgɫ ... əʊt W
2. *vphr* to thin out turnips. -*ing* sɪŋgɫɪn ɛʊt Sr, -*ing* sɪŋglɪn aːt Y

singler *n* a VEST VI.14.9. sɪŋgləᵗ Sa

single-sway *n* a SWINGLE-TREE of a horse-drawn plough harness I.8.3. sɪŋəlswɛɪ La

singlet *1. n* a CHEMISE V.11.1. sɪŋglət Nt
2. *n* a VEST VI.14.9. sɪŋlɪt La Y*[old x1]* Ch*[old x1]*

Db Nt L, sɪŋglɪt Y Ch Db Sa St*[old x1]*, sɪŋlɪt Y, sɪŋlət Cu We*[old x1]* La Y Man Sa, sɪŋglət La Sa, sɪŋgɫət Mon
3. *n* a WAISTCOAT VI.14.11. sɪŋlɪt Y*[old]*

single-tree *n* a SWINGLE-TREE of a horse-drawn plough harness I.8.3. sɪŋltʁiː Nb

sink *1. n* URINE in a cow-house I.3.10. sɪŋk Man
2. *n* a CESS-POOL on a farm I.3.11. zɪŋk So *[noted as u.r. SBM]*
3. *vi* referring to a cow, show signs of calving by changes in the pelvic region, ⇐ SHOWS SIGNS OF CALVING III.1.12(b). *3prprogsg* sɪŋkɪn Wo, *3prperfsg* sʊŋk Sa, səŋk Gl
4. *vi* to WANE, referring to the moon VII.6.5(b). sɪŋk Sa
5. *vi* to WARP, referring to wood IX.2.9. sɪŋk He Wo Wa

sink-hole *1. n* a CESS-POOL on a farm I.3.11. sɪŋkɒʊɫ Sr
2. *n* an ASH-MIDDEN V.1.14. zɛŋkoːɫ Ha

sink in *viphr* referring to a cow, show signs of calving by changes in the pelvic region, ⇐ SHOWS SIGNS OF CALVING III.1.12(b). *3prprogsg* ʂɪŋkɪn ɪn Co

sinking *adj* HUNGRY VI.13.9. sɪŋkɪn Sx

sink-trough *n* an earthenware SALTING-TROUGH III.12.5. sɪŋktɹɒʊ Sx

sipe *v* to RINSE clothes V.9.8. saɪp La *[queried u.r. NBM]*

sipid *adj* INSIPID, describing food lacking in salt V.7.8. sɪpɪd O

sipings *n* URINE in a cow-house I.3.10. sæɪpɪnz Y, saɪpɪnz La

sire *n* a STALLION III.4.4. sɒɪəᵗˑ So

sit *1. vi* to show signs of calving, ⇐ SHOWS SIGNS OF CALVING III.1.12. *3prprogsg* sɪtn Sa
2. *vi* to STAY at home VIII.5.2. sɪt Nb Cu Y Lei, sɛt? Nf Sf

sit down *imp* And what do you say when you offer him *[i.e. a visitor]* a chair? VIII.3.3. Eng exc. Db C. ⇒ **park yourself, set down, set yourself down,** *sit thissen down* ⇒ **sit yourself down, sit you down, sit yourself down, squat down, squat yourself down** *[th- forms subsumed under y-forms; other idioms also recorded in BM]*

sitfast *n* the CORE of a boil VI.11.7. sɪtfast Nb*[old x1]* Cu Du We Y, sɛtfast Nb Cu*[old x1]* Du We Y

sitter *n* a BROODY HEN IV.6.7. sɪtə Y Wa L Nth C Hrt, sɪt?ə Nf, sɪ?ə Bd, sɪtəɹ Y, sɪtəᵗ He Wa Sx, sɪ?əᵗ Bk Bd; **old sitter** ɒul sɪt?ə Nf, ɒul sɪt?ə Nf

sitting *n* a BROOD of chickens IV.6.12. sɪtɪn He, sɪɪt?n Nf

sitting hen *n* a BROODY HEN IV.6.7. sɪtɪn ɛn Wa O L, sɪt?ɪn ɛn C, sɪtn hɪn Sf, sɪtn hɛn Sf, sɪt?n hɛn Ess, sɪt?n ɛn Ess

sitting-room *1. n What do you call the one [i.e. room] where you would entertain company?* V.2.2. sɪdɪnʧːm So D, zɪdənʧːm D, sɪtɪnɹoum La*[modern]*, sɪtɪnrʊm Cu, sɪtɪnɹʊm He Ess Sr Sx, sɪtnʁʊm Nb, sɪtnɹʊm Du O Sf, sɪtɪnruːm Man, sɪtɪnɹuːm La*[modern]* Y St O L Lei Sr K Sx, sɪtɪnɹʊuːn Sr, sɪʔɪnɹuːm O Brk, sɪtɪnʧːm So W Ha, sɪʔɪnʧːm W, sɪdɪnʧuːm So, sɪtnʁuːm Nb, sɪtnɹuːm Ess*[rare]* Ha*[modern]*, sɪʔnɹuːm Brk Sr*[old x1]* Sx, sɪtənɹuːm Y*[modern]*, sɪtnʧuːm O, sɪdənʧuːm Co, sɪtɪnɹɨːm Lei, sɪtnɹɨˑm Nf, sədɪnhʧuːm So. ⇒ **best room**, **dining-room**, **front-house**, **front-kitchen**, **front-parlour**, **front-room**, **hall**, **house**, **house-place**, **living-room**, **lounge**, **parlour**, **room**

2. n the LIVING-ROOM of a house V.2.1. sɪʔɪnɹʊm Sx, sɪtɪnɹuːm Sr K, sɪtʰɪnɹuˑm Mon, sɪʔnɹuːm Ess Sr*[old]*

sitty hen *n* a BROODY HEN IV.6.7. sɪti ɛn W, zɪti ɛn Ha, sɪtɪ ɪn Sr, sɪtɪ ɛn O

sit with *vtphr* LOOK AFTER VIII.1.23. sɪt wɪð Sr

sit you down *imp* SIT DOWN VIII.3.3. sɪt ðɪ dɛːn Db, sɪt ðə dɛːn La, sɪt ðɪ dɛan Y, sɪt jə dɛʊn Sa, sɪt ʃə dɛʊn Bd, sɪt ðɪ dɛʊn Db Sa, sɪt ðɪ dɛan Y, sɪt ʃə dæːn St, sɪt ðɪ dæːn Y, sɪt ðə dæˑan Y, sɪt jə dæʊn St St Wa Lei, zɪt ðɔ̈ː dæʊn W, sɪt ðɪ dæʊn Y, sɪt ðə dæˑən La, sɪt jə daːn St, sɪt ðɪ daːn La Y Ch St, sɪt ðə daːn La Y, sɪt jə daɪn Ch, sɪt ðɪ daɪn St, sɪt jaː daʊn L, sɪt jə daʊn Y, sɪt ðɪ daʊn La Y Db, sɪt ðə daʊn La Y Sa, sɪt ðɪ duːn Y, sɪt ðə duːn We Y, sɪt jə dəʊn He, zɪt ðɪː dəʊn So, sɪt ðə dəʊn Y Gl, zɪt ðɪ dəʊn So

sit yourself down *imp* SIT DOWN VIII.3.3. sɪʔ jəsɛɬf dɛɪn Bk, sɪt ðɪsɛlf dæʊn Wo, zɪt ðɪsɛɬf dæʊn So, sɪt ðɪsɛn daːn Y, sɪt jəsɛlf daʊn Sa, sɪt ðɪsɛl daʊn Cu La, sɪt ðɪsɛn dɔʊn L, sɪt ðɪsɛl dʌʊn Y, sɪt jəsɛl duːn Nb, sɪt ðɪsɛl duːn Cu Du La Y, sɪt ðɪsɛn duːn Y

six-days *npl* WORKDAYS VII.4.6. sɪksdɛɪz K, sɪksdæɪz Ess

sixpence *n What do you call this [indicate sixpence]?* VII.7.4. Eng. ⇒ **joey**, **sixpen**, **sixpenny-bit**, **sixpenny-joey**, **sprasey**, **tanner**

sixpenny-bit *n* SIXPENCE VII.7.4. sɪkspnɪbɪt Cu, sɪkspənɪbɪt Y

sixpenny-joey *n* SIXPENCE VII.7.4. sɪkspnɪjoʊɪ O

six-tooth *n* a 3-year-old sheep, ⇐ TOOTH VI.5.6(b). *pl* zɪkstʊθs Ha

skaffats *npl* a HAY-LOFT over a cow-house I.3.18. skafəts La

skate *n* the SOLE of a horse-drawn plough I.8.9. skeɪt Wo *[queried WMBM]*

skay-pawed *adj* LEFT-HANDED VI.7.13(a). skiːpɔːd Ch

sked-binder *n* a ROPE-TWISTER II.7.8. skɛdbɔɪndə Ess

sked-winder *n* a ROPE-TWISTER II.7.8. skɛdwaɪndə Sf

skeeb *n* a BRUSH used for sweeping indoors V.9.11. skiːb Man

skeedaddle *imp* GO AWAY! VIII.7.9(a). skɪdadl Y

skee-head *n* the T-SHAPED PLOUGH-BEAM END of a horse-drawn plough I.8.5. skɪiː-ɪd Ess

skeeling *1. n* a COW-HOUSE I.1.8. skɪɬɪn W*[one open side x1]*

2. n a CART-SHED I.11.7. skɪljən Brk

skegs *npl* HAWS IV.11.6. *sg* skɛg Man

skeithing-iron *n* the SOLE of a horse-drawn plough I.8.9. skeːðɪnɑːən Y

skell *1. vi* to OVERTURN, referring to a cart I.11.5. skɛl L

2. v to TIP a cart I.11.6. skɛl Y L

skell-board *n* the PARTITION between stalls in a cow-house I.3.2. skɪalbʊəd Cu, skɪəlbʊəd Cu, skɛlbʊəd Cu We

skell-boose *1. n* the PARTITION between stalls in a cow-house I.3.2. skɪəlbɪəst Y, skɛlbɪəs We Y, skɛlbɪəst Y, skɛlbɪus Y, skɛlbjɪus Y, skɛlbʊəs We, skɛlbuːs La Y

2. n the partition at the head of a cow-stall. skɛlbuuːs Y

skeller *vi* to WARP, referring to wood IX.2.9. skɛlə La Y Db, skələᴵ La; **go skellered** go skɛlɪd St

skeller up *viphr* to WARP, referring to wood IX.2.9. skɛləɹ ʊp Y

skellet *vi* to WARP, referring to wood IX.2.9. skɛlət La

skelling *v-ing* SHRIEKING, describing the shrill noise made by a baby VI.5.15. skɛələn Nb

skell over *viphr* to OVERTURN, referring to a cart I.11.5. *3prsg* skɛlz aʊə Y, *-ed* skɛld aʊə Y, *-ed* skɛld ɔwə L

skell up *1. viphr* to OVERTURN, referring to a cart I.11.5. *3prsg* skeəlz ʊp Y, skɛl ʊp Y

2.1. vphr to TIP a cart I.11.6. skɛl ʊp Y

2.2. vtphr to tip. skɛl ... ʊp Y L

skelp *1.1. v* to TIP a cart I.11.6. skɛlp L

1.2. vt to tip. skɛlp L

2. vt to BEAT a boy on the buttocks VIII.8.10. skɛlp Nb*[old x1]* Cu We Y*[old x1]*

skench *vt* to SPRAIN an ankle VI.10.8. skɛnʃ St*[old]*

skend *adj* CROSS-EYED VI.3.6. skɛnd La

skenning *1. prppladj* CROSS-EYED VI.3.6. skɛnɪn St, skɛnnɪn La

2. v-ing PEEPING VI.3.8. skɛnɪn La Y

skep *1. n [What do you keep those insects in that make honey for you?] Is that the word for one of the old-fashioned straw hives?* IV.8.8(b). skɛp Nb Cu Du We La Y Man Sa St O Nt L Lei R Nf Sf Hrt Brk K, *pl* skɛps Wa R Ess, *pl* skaps Db. ⇒ **basket-hive**, **bee- bonnet**, **bee-butt**, **bee-coop**, bee-hackle, bee-hive, bee-pot, bee-skep, *bee-skip* ⇒ bee-skep, butt, coop, globe, hive, hopper, kep, kip, oval-hive, *skep-hive* ⇒ skip-hive, skip-hive, straw-bee-hive, straw-hive, *straw-skeps* ⇒ straw-skip, straw-skip, thatched- hive, *thatched skep* ⇒ thatched skip, thatched skip

2. *n* a tray in the bottom of a hive. skɛp Ess

3. *n* a basket. skɛp Ess

4. *n* a large basket for bobbins. skɪp Y

5. *n* a HIVE IV.8.8(a). skɪp W

6. *n* a SOWING-BASKET II.3.6. skɛp We L

7. *n* a container for carrying horse-feed, ⇐ BASKET III.5.4. skɛp Y[*wooden x2; round, 2 handles x1; metal x1; wicker x1*] St Lei[*wicker x1*] Nf[*modern x1*], *pl* skɛps Y[*basket-work*]

8. *n* a container for carrying chopped turnips to cows. skɛp Nt

[*not a WMBM headword*]

skew *1. adv* looking in a SQUINTING manner VI.3.5. skɪuː Ess

2. *adj* ASKEW, describing a picture that is not hanging straight IX.1.3. skjuː Wo Wa Mon, skɪuː Nb Hu Bd[*old*] Hrt, ʂkɤː Co; **on a skew** ɒn ə skɪu Y, ɒn ə skɪuː Ess, ɔn ə skɪuː Ess; **on the skew** ɒn ðə skjæʊ He, ɒn ðə skɪu Ess Ha, ɒːn ðɪ skɪu Sx, ɔn ðɪ skɪu K, ɒn ðə skjuː St Gl So W Brk Sr K, ɒn dɪ skjuː Sx, ɔːn ðə skjʊu Sx[*old*], ɒn ðə skɪu Nth Ess K, ɒn t skɪu We, ɔn ðə skɪu Sf

3. *adv* DIAGONALLY, referring to harrowing a field IX.1.8. skjuː Gl So, skˡuː Bd, skɤː Co; **on the skew** ɒn ðə skɪu Sa Ess K, ɒn t skɪu Y

4. *vi* to WARP, referring to wood IX.2.9. skɪu Y

skew-across *adv* DIAGONALLY, referring to harrowing a field IX.1.8. skjuː-əkɹɔːs Wa

skew-cornered *adv* DIAGONALLY, referring to harrowing a field IX.1.8. skjuːkəˡːnʊd Wo

skewdy-whiff* *adj* ASKEW, describing a picture that is not hanging straight IX.1.3. skjuːdɪwɪf Mon

skew-eyed *adj* CROSS-EYED VI.3.6. skɪuː-ɔɪd Ess

skew-footed *adj* SPLAY-FOOTED VI.10.5. skjæʊfʊtɪd He

skew-harrow *adv* DIAGONALLY, referring to harrowing a field IX.1.8. skjæʊ-aˡːw (+V) He

skewing *vt-ing* PULLING his ear VI.4.4. skɪuːɪn La

skewing it *adv* DIAGONALLY, referring to harrowing a field IX.1.8. skjuː-ɪn ɪt W

skewting across *adv* DIAGONALLY, referring to harrowing a field IX.1.8. skɪuːtɪn əkɹɔːs Sa

skew-wamped *adv* DIAGONALLY, referring to harrowing a field IX.1.8. skˡuːwɒmpt Bk

skew-way(s) *1. adj* ASKEW, describing a picture that is not hanging straight IX.1.3.

no -s: skjuːwɛɪ O, skjuːwaɪ W

-s: skjuːwɛɪz Sr Sx, skˡuːwæɪz Wo; **on the skew-ways** ɒn ðə skjuːwaɪz W; **all to a skew-ways** ɔːɬ tɤː ə skɤːwɪz D

2. *adv* DIAGONALLY, referring to harrowing a field IX.1.8.

no -s: skɪuːwɛɪ Nth Hrt Ess

-s: skɪywɛɪz Ess, skɪuwæɪz Sf Ess MxL, skjuːwɛːz St, skju:weɪz Wo, skɪuːweɪz Hu Bd Hrt, skjuːwɛɪz Wa, skɪuːwɛɪz Ess, skjuːwæɪz Gl, skɪuːwæɪz Ess, skuːwɛɪz Bk

skew-whiff *1. adj* ASKEW, describing a picture that is not hanging straight IX.1.3. skjɪuwɪf Mon, skɪʊwɪf Co, skjuːwɪf St He Mon Bk[*old*] So W Do, skɪuːwɪf La Y Sa, skɤːwɪf So Co D, skuːwɪf Lei R, skˡʉːwɪf R, skɵːwɪf Lei [*WMBM headword skew-wiff*]

2. *adv* DIAGONALLY, referring to harrowing a field IX.1.8. skjuːwɪf Bk, skˡuːwɪf Nth Bk

skew-whiffed *adj* ASKEW, describing a picture that is not hanging straight IX.1.3. skɪiwɪft La, skɪɤːwɪft Ch, skɪuːwɪft Sa Wa, skjuːwɪft St K, əskjuːwɪfət W; **on the skew-whiffed** ɒn ðə skjuː-ɪft He, ɒn ðə skɪuːwɪft Sa [*WMBM headword skew-wiffed*]

skew-whiffty *adj* CROSS-EYED VI.3.6. skjuːwɪftɪ St

skew-whifted* *adj* ASKEW, describing a picture that is not hanging straight IX.1.3. skjuːwɪftɪd St He, skɪuːwɪftɪd Sa, skju:-ɪftɪd He Wo, skɪuː-ɪftɪd Wo

skew-whish *adj* ASKEW, describing a picture that is not hanging straight IX.1.3. 'skɤː'wɪʃ So

skewy *adj* ASKEW, describing a picture that is not hanging straight IX.1.3. skjuːi ha, skɤːi So; **on the skewy side** ɔːn ðə skjuːi zɒɪd Ha

skid *1. n* the SOLE of a horse-drawn plough I.8.9. skɪd So

2. *n* a chock placed behind and under a wheel to prevent a cart from going backwards on a hill, ⇐ PROP/CHOCK I.11.2. skɪd Y

3. *n* a DRAG used to slow a wagon I.11.3. skɪd La Man Ch St O Nth Nf Bk Bd Hrt Ess Brk, *pl* skɪdz Sr

4. *n* a CLOT OF COW-DUNG II.1.6. *pl* skɪdz Sr

5. *vi* to SLIDE VIII.7.1. skɪd Co

skidder *vi* to SLIDE VIII.7.1. skɪdəˡː Co D

skiddle *vt* to WHITTLE a stick I.7.19. *-ing* skɪdɬɪn Sx

skid-pan *n* a DRAG used to slow a wagon I.11.3. skɪdpen Sr K Sx, skɪdpæn Wo Mon MxL Brk Sr K Sx, skɪppæn Wo K, skɪpæn K, skɪdpan He Wa, skɪpan Wa, skɪdpɑn Ha, skɪpən Wa

skid(s) *n* a SLEDGE used to carry loads in winter I.9.1.

no -s: skɪd He Gl O Nth Brk

-s: skɪdz W

skiffle-handed *1. adj* LEFT-HANDED VI.7.13(a). skɪfɬændɪd So

2. *adj* CLUMSY, describing a person VI.7.14. skıfɫændıd So

skiffy *adj* LEFT-HANDED VI.7.13(a). skıfi So

skiffy-handed *adj* LEFT-HANDED VI.7.13(a). skıfihændıd So

skill *n* a SALTING-TROUGH III.12.5. skıl Wo

skilly *1. n* PORRIDGE V.7.1. skılı L *[marked u.r. EMBM]*

2. *n* GRUEL V.7.2. skıli So, skıɫi So Co D, skılı Nb Du Y*[old x1, slang x1]* Db St*[unintentionally thin]* Wa Lei*[very thin]* Nf Sf Bd Hrt Ess MxL Brk K*[old x1]* Ha Sx, skıɫı Mon*[very thin]* Sr, skəli So

3. *n* BROTH V.7.20(a). skılı St Sx, skıɫı Sx

skilly and wack *n* GRUEL V.7.2. skılı ən wak St

skimdick *1. n* WHEY V.5.8(b). skımdık Sa Sx

2. *n* GRUEL V.7.2. skımdık St

skimmer *1. n* a PORRIDGE-STICK V.9.1. skımə˺ K

2. *n* a SCOOP used to take water out of a boiler V.9.9. skımə˺ O

skim-milk jacks* *n* a kind of CHEESE V.5.4(b). skımmılk dʒæks Nf

skimmings *n* BACON-FAT V.7.5(b). skımınz L

skin *1. vt* to WHITTLE a stick I.7.19. skın So

2. *n* the HIDE of a cow III.11.7. skın St So

3. *n* a SHEEPSKIN III.11.8(a). skın Nb We La Y Ch Sa St He Mon Gl Nt L Nf Sf Ess MxL W Sr Ha

4. *n* the PELT of a sheep III.11.8(b). skın Nb Y Ch Db Sa St Wa Mon Gl O L Lei R Hu Nf Bd Ess MxL So Sr D

5. *n* the RIND of bacon III.12.6. skın Nb Co

6. *vt* to REMOVE *STALKS* from currants V.7.24. *-ing* skının So

skinflint *n* a MISER VII.8.9. skınflınt La Y Wo, skınvlınt So, skınvɫınt W Do

skinger *n* a MISER VII.8.9. skındʒə˺: So

skinner *n* a MISER VII.8.9. skınə˺: So

skinning *n* a LOOSE *PIECE OF* SKIN at the bottom of a finger-nail VI.7.11. skının K

skinny ball *n* a NESTLING IV.7.1. *pl* skını baːɫz Gl

skin(s) *n* potato PEELINGS V.7.22.

no -s: skıˑn Nf

npl: skınz L W Co D

skins *n* CHITTERLINGS III.12.2. skınz Nf, skıns La

skip *1. n* a SOWING-BASKET II.3.6. skıp Y Db Bd Hrt MxL Sr *[not a N/EM/SBM headword]*

2. *n* a container for carrying horse-feed, ⇐ BASKET III.5.4. skıp La*[basket-work]* Y*[wicker, 2 handles]* Db*[oval, metal x1; oval, wooden x1]*, *pl* skıps*[round, rush]* Sa*[round, wicker]* St*[wooden]* Wa*[wooden]* Lei*[with handles x1; wicker x3]* Sf*[wooden, basket-work bottom]* Bk*[round, with handles]* *[not an EMBM headword]*

3. *n* a SKEP IV.8.8(b). skıp Nb Cu Du La Y Ch Db Sa St He Wo Wa Mon Gl O Lei C Nf Sf Bk Hrt Ess So W Brk Sr K D Ha Sx*[old x1]*, *pl* skıps Man L Bd Do

4. n a CLOTHES-BASKET V.9.7. skıp Man[old]*

skip-hive* *n* a SKEP IV.8.8(b). skıpaıv Db, *pl* skıpaːvz Y, *pl* skıpɑıvz Bd, skıpɔıv Gl

skip-jack *n* a WISH-BONE IV.6.22. skıpdʒak Nb Du Y O

skip out *vtphr* to DITCH IV.2.11. skıp ... ɛʊt Sa

skirl *vi* to SLIDE VIII.7.1. skʊrl Cu, skərl Cu

skirr *vi* to SLIDE VIII.7.1. *-ing* skəːɹın La, skɜ˺ː La

skirtings* *n* SCRAPS left after rendering lard III.12.10. skɜ˺ːɹtınz La

skirt(s) *n* the BRIM of a hat VI.14.3.

no -s: skət L

-s: skɛts L, skə˺ːts L

skittering *pron* a skittering A FEW VII.8.21. ə skıtəɹın St

skivvy-handed *adj* LEFT-HANDED VI.7.13(a). skıvihandıd So

skob *v* to WHITTLE a stick I.7.19. *-ing* skɒbən Man

skowl-foot* *n* COLT'S-FOOT II.2.7. skoʊlfʊt Wa

skrike *vi* to SCREAM VIII.8.11. skɹaık La Y Ch Sa, skɹɑık La Ch, skɹɒık St

skrike out *viphr* to SCREAM VIII.8.11. skɹaık aʊt Sa, skɹɒık aıt St

skriking *v-ing* SHRIEKING, describing the shrill noise made by a baby VI.5.15. skɹeıkın La Ch Sa, skɹaːkın La, skɹaıkın La Ch Sa, skɹɑıkın La Y Ch

skullache *n* a HEADACHE VI.1.6. skʌleık Nf, skʌleːk Nf, skʌlɛık Nf Sf, skʌɫɛık Sf Ess*[old x2]*, skʌlæık Ess*[old x1]*

skumjot *adj* ASKEW, describing a picture that is not hanging straight IX.1.3. skjɒmdʒɒʊt Gl

skunk *n* a POLE-CAT IV.5.7. skʌŋk Sx

skutchy-bells *npl* EARWIGS IV.8.11. *sg* skʊtʃıbɛl Nb

skwift *adj* ASKEW, describing a picture that is not hanging straight IX.1.3. skwıft Mon

skwin-ways *adv* DIAGONALLY, referring to harrowing a field IX.1.8. skwınweːz Cu

sky-bald *adj* ASKEW, describing a picture that is not hanging straight IX.1.3. skaıbɔːld Y

sky-wannock *adj* ASKEW, describing a picture that is not hanging straight IX.1.3. skwɑˑıwanık L

sky-wobbled *adj* ASKEW, describing a picture that is not hanging straight IX.1.3. skwɑıwɒbld L

slab *1. n* the CURB-STONE in a cow-house I.3.9. slæb Hu

2. *n* a CUTTING of hay II.9.15. sɫɒb Do

3. *n* a BENCH on which slaughtered pigs are dressed III.12.1. slæb K, sɫæb O*[lead, shallow sides]*

4. *n* a flat surface on which bacon is cured, ⇐

SALTING-TROUGH III.12.5. slab Cu Y Wa*[stone]*
5. n a stone salting-trough or surface of
undetermined kind. slab Wa

6. n the THRESHOLD of a door V.1.12. slæb Mon
Ess

7. n a HEARTHSTONE V.3.2. slɛb K, sɫæb Co,
sɫab Co

8. n a PASTE-BOARD V.6.5. slæb K

9. n a SLICE of bread V.6.10. *pl* slæːbz So

10. n DEW VII.6.7. slab Y

slabber *v* to GOBBLE food VI.5.13(b). *-ing*
slæbəˈɹɪn Sx, slɑbəɹ La *[not a SBM headword]*

slabbers *v-3prsg* he GUZZLES a drink VI.5.13(a).
slæbəz Ess, *no -s* slɑbəɹ La *[not an EMBM
headword]*

slab-stone *1. n* the THRESHOLD of a door V.1.12.
slæbstoːn He

2. n a HEARTHSTONE V.3.2. slabstʊən L

slack *1. n* a DRAIN in a cow-house I.3.8. slæk He

2. n the PELT of a sheep III.11.8(b). slæk Sf

3. n COAL-DUST V.4.1. slɪək Nb, slɛk We La
Y*[old x1]* Man Ch Db*[old x1]* Sa St Nt L Lei MxL Sr
K, slæk Man Ch Sa He Wo Mon Gl Hu*[modern]* Nf
Sf Hrt Ess MxL So Brk Sr K Ha, sɫæk So Co, slak Nb
Cu Du We La Y Ch Db Sa St He Wo Wa Gl O Nt L
Lei R Nth Bk Bd Hrt So, sɫak O W D Ha

4. n GRUEL V.7.2. slɛk Brk

slack baked *adj* SAD, describing bread or pastry that
has not risen V.6.12. slak beɪkt Wo

slack coal *n* COAL-DUST V.4.1. slɛkkɔɪl Y, slɛk
koːl Db, slæk oːl He, slæk koːɫ He, slæk oːɫ He, sɫak
koːɫ W Co, zɫak koːɫ Ha, slak koʊɫ Nth, slɛkkʊəl Y,
slɛk kʊəl L; **wet slack coal** wɛt slækʔ koul Nf

slacks *n* **the/her slacks go/go down, go in/of her/the
slacks, gone down in the slacks, her slacks drop,
drop her slacks, drop in the/its slacks, slacken at
the slacks** SHOWS SIGNS OF CALVING
III.1.12(b). **the/her slacks go/go down** *3prpl* t slaks
ɪz gaːn We, *3prpl* t slaks ɪz gɒn La, *3prpl* ʔ slaks əz
gɒn La, *3prprogpl* ə slaks ɪz gʊɪn daʊn La; **go in/of
her/the slacks** *3prsg* gɒn əv ə slaks Y, *3prprogsg*
gʊɪn ɪ t slaks Y; **gone down in the slacks** *3prsg* gɒn
dæˈən ɪt slaks La, *3prsg* gʊz daʊn ɪn t slaks Y; **her
slacks drop** *3prpl* ə slaks dɹɒps La, *3prprogpl* ə slaks
ɪz dɹɒpɪn Y; **drop her slacks** *3prprogsg* dɹɒpt əɹ
slaks La; **drop in the/its slacks** *3prprogsg* dɹɒpɪn ɪ t
slaks La, *3prperfsg* dɹɒpt ɪ t slaks La, *-ing* dɹɒpɪn ɪn
ɪts slaks La; **slacken at the slacks** *3prprogsg* slaknən
ət slaks Y

slade *n* a RIVULET IV.1.1. slɛɪd Ess

slads *npl* the horizontal BARS of a gate IV.3.6. sɫædz
Co, sɫadz Co

slag *n* COAL-DUST V.4.1. slɛg Sr, slæg O, slag Y

slake *adj* SLIPPERY VII.6.14. sleːk Wo, sleːɪk Wo

slaking *v-ing* PUTTING your tongue OUT VI.5.4.
slɛɪkɪn K *[marked u.r. SBM]*

slaking out *vtphr-ing* PUTTING your tongue
OUT VI.5.4. sliːkən ... aʊt Sa, sleːkɪn ... ɛʊt Db,
sleːkɪn ... aːt Y, slɛəkən ... æʊt Y

slammer *n* the SHUTTING-POST of a gate
IV.3.4. slaməˡ Sa

slamming-post *n* the SHUTTING-POST of a
gate IV.3.4. slæmɪnpoːst Sa, slæmɪnpoːs He,
slamɪnpoːst Sa, slamɪnpoʊst St

slammocking *adj* CLUMSY, describing a person
VI.7.14. slamkɪn So

slammocky *adj* CLUMSY, describing a person
VI.7.14. slamɪkɪ So, sɫʌmɪkɪ Do

slanch *v* to TRIM the sides of hedges IV.2.3. slanʃ
Ch

slanching-hook *n* a HEDGING-BILL IV.2.5.
slanʃɪnyːk Ch

slang *n* LOW-LYING LAND IV.1.7. slang Db

slant *1. n* a SLOPE IV.1.10. slænt Nb, slant Db,
slɑːnt Ess

2. adj ASKEW, describing a picture that is not
hanging straight IX.1.3. slant Du Y; **all of a slant**
ɔːl əv ə slant Y; **on a slant** ɒn ə slant La; **on the
slant** ɒn ðə sɫant W, ɒn ðə slaːnt Nf, ɒn ðə slɑːnᵗ
K

3. adv DIAGONALLY, referring to harrowing a
field IX.1.8. slant Nb; **on a slant** ɒn ə slɑːnt Wa

slant across *adv* DIAGONALLY, referring to
harrowing a field IX.1.8. slant əkʁɑs Nb, slant
əkɹɒs Y

slantaway *n* a SLOPE IV.1.10. slantəweː Y

slant-away(s) *adv* DIAGONALLY, referring to
harrowing a field IX.1.8.
no -s: slantɪweː Y, slantəweː Y
-s: slantəweːz Nb

slanting *1. adj* ASKEW, describing a picture that
is not hanging straight IX.1.3. slantɪn La Db,
slantn Du, slaːnʔn Sf, slɑːntʔn Nf

2. adv DIAGONALLY, referring to harrowing a
field IX.1.8. slantɪn Y Db, slantn Du

slanting-bar *n* a DIAGONAL BAR of a gate
IV.3.7. slaˈnʔɲbaː Ess

slanting-way across *adv* DIAGONALLY,
referring to harrowing a field IX.1.8. slantɪnweː
əkɹɒs Y

slant-road* *adv* DIAGONALLY, referring to
crossing a room IX.1.8. slantɹʊəd Y

slant-way(s) *adv* DIAGONALLY, referring to
harrowing a field IX.1.8.
no -s: slantweː Nb Db
-s: slantweːz Cu Y Ch, əslantweˈəz Nb, slantwɛəz
Y

slanty *1. adj* ASKEW, describing a picture that is
not hanging straight IX.1.3. slæntɪ Nb

2. adv DIAGONALLY, referring to harrowing a
field IX.1.8. slæntɪ Nb, slantɪ Y

slap *vt* to BEAT a boy on the buttocks VIII.8.10. slæp
He Gl Hu Ess, slæpʔ Nf, slap Cu We La Y Db Sa Wa
Gl Nth So Ha; **slap his arse** slæpʔ ɪz æːs Nf, slæp ɪz
æːs Nf, slæp ɪz aːs He Hu Sf, slæp ɪz ɑːs Nf, *ʔinf*
slæpn ɪz ɑːs Nf, slap ɪz aːs Db Sa St, słap ɪz aːs Do
Ha; **slap his backside** slæˑp ɪz bæˑksʌɪd Brk; **slap
his behind** slap ɪz bɪ-ɒːɪnd St; **slap his bottom** slæp
ɪz bɒtʔm Nf, slap ɪz bɒtəm St

slape *1. adj* BALD VI.2.3. sleəp Y
  2. adj SLIPPERY VII.6.14. slɪap Y, slɪəp Du*[old]*
Y, sleːp Cu We La Y Db Nt, sleap We La, sleəp Cu
Du*[old x2]* La Y, sleːp Cu We, sleɪp L, sleəp Y L

slapes *v-3prsg* he GUZZLES a drink VI.5.13(a). *-ing*
sleːpən Du

slap-holes *npl* PUDDLES IV.1.6. slapɒɪlz Y,
slapɔɪlz Y, slapʋəlz Y Nt

slappery *adj* SLIPPERY VII.6.14. slapɹɪ So*[old]*,
słapɹɪ Ha

slapping out *vtphr-ing* PUTTING your tongue OUT
VI.5.4. slapɪn ... aːt Y

slapping-post *n* the SHUTTING-POST of a gate
IV.3.4. slæpɪnpɒʋst Sr, slapɪnpoːst Sa, slapɪnpoʋs
Man

slap-stump *n* the SHUTTING-POST of a gate
IV.3.4. slapstʋmp La

slapy *adj* SLIPPERY VII.6.14. sleəpɪ Y

slare *vi* to SLIDE VIII.7.1. sleː Ch, slaː Ch

slarking *vt-ing* PUTTING your tongue OUT VI.5.4.
slaːkɪn La

slash *1. v* to TRIM hedges IV.2.3. slæʃ L So, slaʃ Nb
Cu Du We La Y Ch L Bk*[1–2 years' growth]*, *-ing*
slaʃɪn Bd, *-ing* ʃlaʃɪn Y
  2. vt to PLASH a hedge IV.2.4. slæʃ Man
  3. n a HEDGING-BILL IV.2.5. slaʃ Cu We
  4. n a SLICE of bread V.6.10. *pl* slaʃɪz We
  5. n SLUSH VII.6.16. sleʃ Sf, slæʃ Hrt, slaʃ Ess
  6. vt to BEAT a boy on the buttocks VIII.8.10. slaʃ
Nth

slash down *vphr* to TRIM hedges IV.2.3. *-ing* slæʃɪn
dɛun Nf *[noted probably u.rr. EMBM]*

slasher *1. n* a HEDGING-BILL IV.2.5. slɛʃə Ess,
slɛʃəˡ Sr, slɛʃəᵗ Sr Sx, slæʃə Man L Nf Sf Ess, slæʃəˡ
Brk Sr Ha, slæʃəᵗ Brk Sr, slæʃəᵗː So, slaʃəᴿ Nb,
slaʃə Nb Cu Du We La Y L Lei Nth C Bk Bd K, slaʃər
Cu, slaʃəɪ Y, slaʃəˡ L, slaʃəᵗ Gl O Bk, slaʃəᵗː W,
słaʃəɾ O, słaʃəᵗː W Do, słaɪʃəᵗː W Ha
  2. n a BILLHOOK IV.2.6. slaʃəᵗː W

slash-hook *1. n* a HEDGING-BILL IV.2.5. slæʃuːk
Wa, slaʃuːk St, slaʃɵːk Lei
  2. n a BILLHOOK with a straight blade IV.2.6.
slæʃʋk Nf

slashing-hook *n* a HEDGING-BILL IV.2.5.
slæˑʃɪŋʋk Brk, slaʃɪnɪːk Ch, slaʃɪnʋk Wo Wa Bk,
slaʃɪnuːk La Y St, słaɪʃɪnʋk Ha

slash-knife *n* a HEDGING-BILL IV.2.5. slaʃnɛɪf Du

slash off *vtphr* **slash the muck off** to TOP AND
TAIL swedes II.4.3. slaʃ ... ɔf Y *[marked u.r.
NBM]*

slat *n* a DIAGONAL BAR of a gate IV.3.7. slat
Bd, *pl* slats Hrt

slatch *n* COAL-DUST V.4.1. słatʃ Do

slatches *v-3prsg* he GUZZLES a drink
VI.5.13(a). *-ing* slatʃən Cu

slate *1. vt* to THIN OUT turnip plants II.4.2. *-ing*
slɛɪʔn K, *-ing* slæɪʔn K *[queried SBM]*
  2. n a SALTING-TROUGH III.12.5. sleːt Gl

slate-tank *n* a SALTING-TROUGH III.12.5.
slɛɪttɛŋk K

slat out *vtphr* to LOP a tree IV.12.5. slat ... æʋt L

slats *npl* the horizontal BARS of a gate IV.3.6.
slɛts K, slæts Nf K Sx, słæts K, slats Hu Bd

slattery* *adj* drizzly, ⇐ DULL VII.6.10. slatɹɪ L

slaughterer *1. n* a BUTCHER who buys cattle,
kills them, and sells the meat III.11.1. slaftəɹə Y
  2. n a KNACKER III.11.9. slɔːtəɹə Nf, *-s*
slɔːtəɹəz Y, slɔːʔəɹə Nf

slaughterhouse *1. n* a FASTING-CHAMBER
III.11.3. slɔːdəᵗːɹævs So, słɔːdəᵗːhæus Do,
zlɔːdəᵗːhæus So, slɔːdəᵗːɹæus So, słɔːdəᵗːɹæus
Do, słɔːtəᵗːɹæus W, słɔːtəᵗˑɹaus So, slɔːtəɹəus
Mon, słɔːdəᵗːɹəus W
  2. n And where does he *[i.e. the butcher]* kill them
[i.e. animals]? III.11.4. ⇒ **butching-house,
butching-shop, kill-house, killing-house,
killing-shop, lair, slaughter-place, slaughter-
shop**

slaughtering-pen *n* a FASTING-CHAMBER
III.11.3. slɔːtɹɪnpɛn C, slɔːᵊʔəɹɪnpɛn Hrt *[see
note at fasting-chamber]*

slaughterman *1. n* a BUTCHER who buys
cattle, kills them, and sells the meat III.11.1.
slɔːtəˡmən K
  2. n a KNACKER III.11.9. slaːtəmən Nb,
slɔːtəmæn Ess, slɔːtəmən Hrt Ess, slɔːʔəmɪn Nf,
slɔːtʔəmən C

slaughter-place *n* a SLAUGHTERHOUSE
III.11.4. slɔːtəᵗpleɪs Sr

slaughter-shop *n* a SLAUGHTERHOUSE
III.11.4. slɔːʔəʃɒp Nf

slawp *1. vt* to GOBBLE food VI.5.13(b). *-ing*
slɑʋpɪn Y, *imp* slɑʋp Y
  2. v to gobble. slɔːp Nb

slawps *1. vt-3prsg* he GUZZLES a drink
VI.5.13(a). *-ing* slɑʋpɪn Y, *3ptsg* slɑʋpt Y
  2. v-3prsg he guzzles. *-ing* slɑʋpɪn Y, *-ing*
slɑʋpɪn Y, slɔːps Nb, *-ing* slɔːpən Du

sled *1. n* a SLEDGE used to carry loads in winter
I.9.1. slɪd Man, sliːd Ess, slɪəd L Ess, slɛd Nb Cu
Du We La Y Man Db Sa*[not found locally]* Nt L
Lei Nf Sf Bk Sr, slɛɪəd Sf, slæɪd So, slɔd Sf
  2. n an iron runner chained to a cart, on which a

cart-wheel could slide to prevent the cart from going backwards or too fast on a hill, ⇐ PROP/CHOCK I.11.2. slɛːd Nf, slɛ^Id Nf

3. *n* a DRAG used to slow a wagon I.11.3. slɛd La Nt L Nf

sledder *n* a DRAG used to slow a cart I.11.3. slɛdə Db

sledge *1. n When in winter you can't use a cart with wheels, what do you use for carrying heavy loads?* I.9.1. slɪdʒ Ess Sx, zɫɪdʒ D, sledʒ L, slɛdʒ Nb Cu Du La Y Ch Db Sa St*[flat bottom, iron skids, same shape as cart]* He Wo Wa Mon Gl O Nt L Lei R Hu C Nf Sf Bk Bd Hrt Ess So Brk K Do Sx, sɫɛdʒ Mon O So W Co D Do Ha, zɫɛdʒ Ha, slɛɪdʒ Ess So Sr, sɫɛɪdʒ D, slæɪdʒ So, sɫadʒ Ha, sɫaɪdʒ D. ⇒ **coop, drag, dray, drug, ground-car, ground-cart, skid(s),** *slead* ⇒ **sled, sled, sleigh,** *slide* ⇒ **sled, trail-cart**

2. *n* a DRAG used to slow a wagon I.11.3. slɛdʒ Nb Cu La Y L

sledge-roof chamber* *n* a BEDROOM in the gable of a house V.2.3. slɛdʒɹuːf tʃɛˈəmbə L

sleeper *1. n* a railway sleeper, used as the CURB-STONE in a cow-house I.3.9. *pl* sliipə^Jz Ess

2. *n* a tree STUMP IV.12.4. slɛːəpʔə Nf

sleigh *n* a SLEDGE used to carry loads in winter I.9.1. sleː Ch La*[none locally]*, sleɪ Y*[none locally]*, slɛɪ Ch, *pl* sleˈɪz L, sɫɛɪ D, zɫɛɪ D

slender *vt* to THIN OUT turnip plants II.4.2. slɛndə^J (+V) La

slew *1. n* a DRAG used to slow a wagon I.11.3. sɫʏː Co

2. *n* **on the slew** DIAGONALLY, referring to harrowing a field IX.1.8. ɒn ðə sluː K

slewed *n* ASKEW, describing a picture that is not hanging straight IX.1.3. sl^əuːd Du; **on a slew** ɔn ə slɪu Y

slewing *v-ing* THROWING a stone VIII.7.7. sluːɪn So *[queried SBM]*

slew-ways-over *adv* DIAGONALLY, referring to harrowing a field IX.1.8. slɪuwɛəzɑʊə Y

slice *1. n What do you call the thin piece you cut off from the loaf with the bread-knife?* V.6.10. Eng. ⇒ **bit, butty, hunch, hunk, junk, morsel, piece, round, roundel, shive, slab, slash, slipe,** *slish* ⇒ **slishe, slishe, slithag, sliver,** *slysh* ⇒ **slishe, square, stull;** ⇒ also **knot, slive**

2. *n* a CUTTING of hay II.9.15. sɫɔɪs So, slɔɪs So

3. *n* a SHOVEL for a household fire V.3.9. slʌɪs Gl

slices *npl* the horizontal BARS of a gate IV.3.6. slaɪsɪz Y*[excluding top bar x1]*

slick *adj* SLIPPERY VII.6.14. slɪk He Mon Gl, sɫɪk Gl

slick-board *n* a PASTE-BOARD V.6.5. slɪkboːə^ɾd̥ Gl

slicking *vt-ing* PUTTING your tongue OUT VI.5.4. slɪkn Man

slid *1. n* a DRAG used to slow a wagon I.11.3. slɪd Nf, slʏd Nf

2. *vi* to SLIDE VIII.7.1. slɪd Y

slide *1. vi When children find the footpaths or the playground covered with ice, they will at once begin to ....* VIII.7.1. Eng exc. We. ⇒ **glirry, shirl, skid, skidder, skirl, skirr, slare, slid,** *slide about*, **slider, slire, slip, slither, slur, slur about**

2. *n* the SOLE of a horse-drawn plough I.8.9. slɛɪd Sa, sɫæːd D, slæɪd So Sr, slɑɪd Lei Ess K, slɒɪd St Wo, slɔɪd Wa L1ei Sf, slʌɪd Brk

3. *n* a chock chained to a cart, which could be placed behind and under a wheel to prevent the cart from going backwards on a hill, ⇐ PROP/CHOCK I.11.2. slɑɪd Mon

4. *n* a DRAG used to slow a cart I.11.3. slɛ^Id Nf, slɑɪd Nth Hu C Bk Bd Hrt, slɔɪd Wa Gl O Sf Hrt Ess, slʌɪd Wa Sf Ess, slɔɪd He Mon Gl, sɫɔɪd Mon

slider *1. n* a DRAG used to slow a wagon I.11.3. slʌɪdə^ɾ Bk, slɔɪdə^ɾ Bk

2. *vi* to SLIDE VIII.7.1. sɫaɪdə^ɾː Co

sliding swivel *n* a sliding RING to which a tether is attached in a cow-house I.3.5. slɔɪdɪn swɪvɫ Ess

slight *adj* ILL, describing a person who is unwell VI.13.1(b). sɫaɪt Co

slike *1. vt* to TOP AND TAIL swedes II.4.3. slaɪk Sa

2. *adj* SLIPPERY VII.6.14. slaɪk He, slə̆ɪk He

sling *1. n* the STRETCHER between the traces of a cart-horse I.5.11. slɪŋ Ess

*2. *?pt/ptppl* to slip a calf, ⇐ SLIPS *THE CALF* III.1.11. slʌŋ Sx

slinger *1. n* a FARM-LABOURER I.2.4. *pl* sɫɪŋə^ɾːz̩ Co *[queried u.r. SBM]*

2. *n* the HANGING-POST of a gate IV.3.3. slɛŋə Man

slingers *n* BROTH V.7.20(a). sɫɪŋə^ɾːz̩ So D

sling-gear-horse *n* a TRACE-HORSE I.6.3. slɪŋgɪəɹɒs Db

slinging *v-ing* THROWING a stone VIII.7.7. slɪŋɪn Y K

sling(s) *n* a SWINGLE-TREE of a horse-drawn plough harness I.8.3.

sg: slɪŋ Ess

-s: slɪŋz Sf

slings *npl* BRACES VI.14.10. sɫɪŋz Co

sling-tit *n* a TRACE-HORSE I.6.3. slɪŋtɪt Db

slink *1.1. v* to slip a calf, ⇐ SLIPS *THE CALF* III.1.11. slɪŋk Ch; **slunk** slʌŋk K*[before 7 months]*

1.2. *vt* to slip a calf. slɪŋk Ch K, *-ed* slɪŋkt K; **slanked** slæŋkt K

2. *vi* referring to a cow, show signs of calving by changes in the pelvic region, ⇐ SHOWS SIGNS OF CALVING III.1.12(b). *-ed* slɪŋkt K Sx, *ppl* ɔːl slʌŋk K

3. vt to SLIP *A FOAL* III.4.6. slɪŋk K, *-ed* slɪŋkt K
4. n RUBBISH V.1.15. slɪŋk La
5. vi to SPOIL, referring to meat or fish V.7.10. slɪŋk St

slink-butcher *n* a KNACKER III.11.9. slɪŋkbʊtʃə Db
slink-chap *n* a KNACKER III.11.9. slɪŋktʃap La
slink-dealer *n* a KNACKER III.11.9. slɪŋkdɪələ La
slink-fellow *n* a KNACKER III.11.9. *-s* slɛŋkfɛləz Y
slinkings *n* the AFTERBIRTH that comes from a cow's uterus after a calf is born III.1.13. slɪŋkɪnz K
slinkman *n* a KNACKER III.11.9. slɪŋkmɒn St
slip *1. v* **slips the calf** *When the cow calves before her time, you say she ....* III.1.11. ⇒ **aborted,** *calved a dead calf, calved before her time, calves before her time, cast calf,* **cast-calve, cast** *her calf,* **casts, casts** *a* **calf, casts** *her* **calf, casts** *it,* **draws** *her* **calf** ⇒ **throw,** *had a slip, has a slip, has a-*warped, has calved before time, has cast, has casted her calf, has cast her calf, has come down before her time, has come down early, has had a slip, has picked, has picked calf, has picked her calf, has picked it, has slipped, has slipped calf, has slipped her calf, has slipped it, has slipped the calf, has strat her calf, has stratted calf, has throwed her calf before time, have slipped her calf, is out of* breaking, jacked, pick, **pick** *calf,* **pick-calved,** picked, **picked** *calf,* picked *her* calf, picks, **picks** *a* calf, **picks** *calf,* picks *her* calf, picks *it,* picks *its* calf, **picks** *the* calf, pitched *her* calf, slanked *calf* ⇒ slink, **slink,** slinked *her* calf, slinked *it,* slinked *the* calf, **slink** *her* calf, slip *calf,* **slip-calve, slip-calved,** slip *her* calf, slipped, slipped *calf,* slipped *her* calf, slipped *her* calf *afore* time, slipped *her* calf *early,* slipped *it,* slipped *the* calf, slips, slips *a* calf, slips *calf,* slips *her* calf, slips *him,* slips *the* calf, slung *the* calf ⇒ sling, slunk ⇒ slink, throwed *her* calf, warped, warped *the* calf, **warped** *the* calf
2. v **to slip a foal** *What do you say if the mare gives birth before the proper time?* III.4.6. ⇒ **came before time,** *cast a colt,* **cast** *a* **foal, cast** *her* colt, **cast** *her* foal, cast *the* foal, **come down** *before* time, drop *a* foal, dropped, drop *the* foal, fling *her* colt, foal *before her* time, foaled *before her* time, foaled *before* time, had *a* misfluke, had *a* slip, has aborted, has *a-*foaled *before her* time, has *a-*slipped *foal,* has cast *a* foal, has cast *her* colt, has cast *her* foal, has cast *it,* has dropped *her* colt, has foaled *before her* time, has foaled *before* time, has picked *a* foal, has picked *her* foal, has slip *a* foal, has slip-foaled, has slip *her* foal, has slipped, has slipped *a* foal, has slipped *before* time, has slipped colt, has slipped *foal,* has slipped *her* colt, has slipped *her foal,* has slipped *the* colt, has strat *her* colt, has strat *her* foal, has throwed *a* colt, has throwed *her* colt, has throwed *the* colt, have *a* slip, he came *before his* time, it came *before* time, pick, **pick** *a* foal, picked *the* foal,

pick-foal, pick *foal,* pick *her foal,* pick *its* colt, pick *its foal,* pick *the foal,* slink *a foal,* slinkt *her foal* ⇒ slink, *slinkt it* ⇒ slink, slip, slip *a* colt, slip *a* foal, slip colt, **slip-foal,** slip *foal,* slip *her* colt, slip *her* foal, slip *its* foal, slipped, slipped *a* colt, slipped *a* foal, slipped colt, slipped *foal,* slipped *her* colt, slipped *her foal,* slipped *the foal,* slipping *her* colt, slips *her* foal, slips *the* foal, slip *that there foal,* slip *the* colt, slip *the foal,* slip *their foal,* throw *a* foal, throw *a* foal *early,* throwed *her* colt, throw *her* foal, *to* cast *her* colt, warp, warped, warped *her* colt, warped *the foal,* warp *her foal*

3. n a PIGLET III.8.2. slɪp So, sɫɪp W
4. n a TETHER for a cow I.3.4. slɪp Nf K
5. n a chain tether. slɪp Nf
6. n a tether made of rope or chain. slɪp Nf
7. n a leather tether. slɪp Nf
8. n a bridle for a cow, to which a tie or tether can be clipped. slɪp Nf
9. n a HALTER for a cow I.3.17. slɪp Nf
10. n a TETHERING-ROPE used to tie up a horse I.4.2. slɪp St L Nf K Sx, *pl* slɪps Sa *[queried ir.r. WMBM]*
11. n the SOLE of a horse-drawn plough I.8.9. slɪp Nf Sf, sɫɪp D
12. n a movable horizontal rod stretching between the shafts of a cart, fixing them to the cart-body and stopping the cart from tipping, ⇐ ROD/PIN I.10.3. slɪp Cu
13. n a movable iron hoop that slides along a cart-shaft and couples it to the projecting end of the beam on which the cart-body rests, ⇐ ROD/PIN I.10.3. slɪp Cu Du Y
14. n a DRAG used to slow a wagon I.11.3. slɪp L
15. vi to SLIDE VIII.7.1. slɪp Ess *[marked u.r. EMBM]*
16. v to REMOVE *STALKS* from currants V.7.24. *-ing* slɪpɪn Sx
17. n a decorative APRON V.11.2(b). slɪp C
18. n a NECKERCHIEF VI.14.4. sɫɪp Do
slip-block *n* the CLOG on a horse's tether I.4.3. slɪpblɒk? Nf
slip-chain *n* a chain used to tie up a horse, ⇐ TETHERING-ROPE I.4.2. slɪptʃeːn Nt
slip-coat cheese* *n* a kind of cream CHEESE V.5.4(b). *-s* slɪpkʊət tʃɪˈəzɪz L
slipe *1. n* a PADDOCK I.1.10. slaɪp C
2. n the MOULD-BOARD of a horse-drawn plough I.8.8. slæɪp Y, slaɪp Y
3. n the SOLE of a horse-drawn plough I.8.9. sɫæːp D, slæɪp Y, slaɪp Y Db L, slɑɪp Db Nt L Lei R Nth, slɔɪp L
4. n a CUTTING of hay II.9.15. slæɪp So, slaɪp

So, sɫɒɪp D

5. *n* a SLICE of bread V.6.10. slæɪp So

sliper *n* a movable iron hoop that slides along a cart-shaft and couples it to the projecting end of the beam on which the cart-body rests, ⇐ ROD/PIN I.10.3. slɑːpə Y *[queried NBM]*

slip-iron *1. n* a TETHERING-STAKE in a cow-house I.3.3. slɪpɒɪən Nf

2. n a movable iron hoop that slides along a cart-shaft and couples it to the projecting end of the beam on which the cart-body rests, *or* a movable horizontal rod or bar stretching across the shafts, ⇐ ROD/PIN I.10.3. slɪpaɪɹən Du

sliply *adj* SLIPPERY VII.6.14. slɪplɪ Ch

slip off *imp* GO AWAY! VIII.7.9(a). slɪp ɔːf Nf*[to a child]*

slip-on *n* an END-BOARD of a cart I.10.4. 'slɪp'ɒn L

slip over *viphr* to OVERTURN, referring to a cart I.11.5. -*ed* slɪpt ɔwə L

slipped *vi-ed* HAS NOT HELD, referring to a cow that has not conceived III.1.7. slɪpt Brk

slipped over *viphr-ed* HAS NOT HELD, referring to a cow that has not conceived III.1.7. slɪpt ɔuvə Ess

slipper *1. n* the SOLE of a horse-drawn plough I.8.9. slɪpə Y

2. n a chock placed behind and under a wheel to prevent a cart from going backwards on a hill, ⇐ PROP/CHOCK I.11.2. slɪpəᵗ He

3. n a DRAG used to slow a wagon I.11.3. slɪpə Cu Du We La Y Db St Nt L Lei R Nth, slɪpəɹ Y, slɪpɹ La L, slɪpəɹ La Y He, slɪpəᴶ Y Db, slɪpəᵗ Sa He Wo Wa Nth, slɪpəᵗː Sa

4. vt to PLASH a hedge IV.2.4. -*ing* slɪpəᴶɹɪn Sx

5. adj SLIPPERY VII.6.14. sɫɪpəᵗː Co D*[old x1]*, sɫɛpəᵗː Co

slipper-fingered *adj* CLUMSY, describing a person VI.7.14. sɫɪpəᵗːvɪŋɡəᵗːḑ Co

slippery *adj* When the ground is frozen, you must take care, because the roads are very.... VII.6.14. Eng exc. Cu Du We Ch Db R. ⇒ **dicky, glazy, glib, greasy, proud, round, saucy, slake, slape, slappery, slapy, slick, slike, sliply, slipper, slippy, slittery, strickly, tricky**

slippy *adj* SLIPPERY VII.6.14. slɪpɪ Nb Du La Y Ch Db Sa St He Wo Wa Gl O Nt L Lei R Nth Sf Bk Bd Ess Brk, sɫɪpɪ O, slɪppɪ La Db, slɪʔpɪ Nb, slɪpʔɪ Sf, slʌpɪ Nb

slip-rail *n* a low rail across a gateway, that can be removed to let sheep pass through, ⇐ SHEEP-HOLE IV.2.8. slɪpɹɛːl Ch, *pl* slɪpɹɛɪlz St

slip-shank *n* a TETHERING-ROPE used to tie up a horse I.4.2. slɪpʃaŋk Y

slip-stile *n* a narrow gap between two stone pillars, forming a STILE IV.2.9. slɪpstɑɪl Db

slip-tie *n* a TETHERING-ROPE used to tie up a horse I.4.2. slɪptʌɪ Nf

slire *vi* to SLIDE VIII.7.1. slaɪər Cu

slishe* *n* a SLICE of bread V.6.10. sɫæɪʃ D, *pl* slaɪʃəz Y, *pl* sɫaɪʃəz D, slɑːʃ Y, sləɪʃ Gl

slit *adj* CLOVEN, describing the hoof of a cow III.2.8(b). slɪt Y Wa

slithag *n* a SLICE of bread V.6.10. 'slɪðəg Man

slither *1. n* a SPLINTER VI.7.10. slɪðə Ess

2. vi to SLIDE VIII.7.1. slɪðə Y Man St L, slɪðəᴶ L, slɪðɹ L, slɪðəɹ He, slɪðəᵗ Sa He Wo Mon, sɫɪðəᵗ He, slɛðə Wo, slɛðəᵗ Wo, sɫɛðəᵗ He

slits *npl* the horizontal BARS of a gate IV.3.6. slɪts K Sx

slittery *adj* SLIPPERY VII.6.14. slɪʔəᵗɹɪ Sx

slive* *n* a SLICE of beef V.6.10. slaɪv Y

sliver *1. n* a SLICE of bread V.6.10. slaɪvə Y

2. n a SPLINTER VI.7.10. slɪvə C Sf Ess*[old x1]*, slɪvəᴶ K, slɪvəᵗ Sx

slob *n* SLUSH VII.6.16. slɒbː La

slobber *v* to GOBBLE food VI.5.13(b). slɒbəᵗ Bk, -*ing* sɫɒbəᵗːɽɪn Ha, sɫɔːbə Sf

slobbers *1. vt-3prsg* he GUZZLES a drink VI.5.13(a). *prppl* slɒbəɹɪn La

2. v-3prsg he guzzles. slɒbəz Wa Mon, *no* -*s* slɒbə Gl, -*ing* slɒbəɹɪn La, -*ing* slɒbɹɪn St, slɒbəᵗz̩ Wo Bk

slod *1. n* the SOLE of a horse-drawn plough I.8.9. slɒd Nf, slɔd Sf

2. n a device used to prevent a cart from going backwards on a hill, ⇐ PROP/CHOCK I.11.2. slɔd Sf

3. n a DRAG used to slow a wagon I.11.3. slɔd Sf Ess

slodders *v-3prsg* he GUZZLES a drink VI.5.13(a). slɒdə We, -*ing* slɒdəɹɪn Y, -*ing* slɒdðəɹən We, -*ing* slɔdərən Cu

sloops *1. vt-3prsg* he GUZZLES a drink VI.5.13(a). -*ing* sɫʏːpən Co, -*ing* slʌpn Nf

2. v-3prsg he guzzles. slɔups L, -*ing* slupn Nf, sluːps L, -*ing* ʃluːpn Nf

sloop up *vtphr* to guzzle a drink, ⇐ GUZZLES VI.5.13(a). -*ing* sɫuːpən ... ʌp Co

slooshes *v-3prsg* he GUZZLES a drink VI.5.13(a). *inf* sluʃ We, *inf* sluːʃ Nb

slop *1. n* GRUEL V.7.2. slɔp Ess

2. v to GOBBLE food VI.5.13(b). slɒp Cu, *3prsg* slɒps Ess

3. n SLUSH VII.6.16. slɒp Nf Bd Ess So, slɔp Y

slop barm *n* soft brewer's YEAST V.6.2. slɒp baːm Nt

slop down *vtphr* to guzzle a drink, ⇐ GUZZLES VI.5.13(a). -*ing* slɒpɪn ... dæən L

slope *1. n* If the land is not level, what do you call a part that goes up gently? IV.1.10. Eng exc. Mon R. ⇒ **bache, bank, breast, brow, brow-side, cleeve, clough, fall, hill, hillside, hump, incline, land(s), mound, mow, pitch, ridge, rise, rising**

ground, rissle, shoot, sidelings, slant, slantaway, sprint, swoop; ⇒ also **bachy, brae, reany, risy, sideling, stickle**

2. *n* **on the slope** ASKEW, describing a picture that is not hanging straight IX.1.3. ɒn t slɒʊp We

slop-holes *npl* PUDDLES IV.1.6. slɒpɔɪlz Y, slɒpoʊlz St *[not a NBM headword]*

slop(s) *n* DREGS left at the bottom of a teacup V.8.15.

no -s: slɒp Y

-s: slœ˙ps Nb, slæps He, slaps Man, slɒps Cu Y Lei So, sɫɒps D, slɔps L Ess

slops *1.1. vt-3prsg* he GUZZLES a drink VI.5.13(a). *-ing* slɒpɪn Y, *-ing* slɒpn Nf

1.2. v-3prsg he guzzles. *-ing* slɒpɪn Db L

2. *n* stale URINE used for cleaning blankets VI.8.8. slɒps We Gl*[fertilizer or insecticide]* Ha Sx

slop-stone *n* a SALTING-TROUGH III.12.5. slɒpstən St

slosh *1. n* SLUSH VII.6.16. slɒʃ Y Ch Db Sa St He Lei Bk Ess*[old x1]* Brk K Sx, slɔʃ Y L C MxL Sr, sɫɔʃ Ha

2. *adv* DIAGONALLY, referring to harrowing a field IX.1.8. slɔʃ L, əslɔʃ L

slot *n* a movable horizontal rod stretching between the shafts of a cart, fixing them to the cart-body and stopping the cart from tipping, ⇐ ROD/PIN I.10.3. slɒt We Y, slɔt We

slot-bar *1. n* a movable horizontal rod stretching between the shafts of a cart, fixing them to the cart-body and stopping the cart from tipping, ⇐ ROD/PIN I.10.3. slɒtbaː Y

2. *n* the *HORIZONTAL* BAR of a crane over a domestic fire V.3.5(a). slʊtbaː Db

slotch *1. v* to GOBBLE food VI.5.13(b). slɒtʃ Ch

2. *n* SLUSH VII.6.16. slɒtʃ La

slotches *v-3prsg* he GUZZLES a drink VI.5.13(a). slɒtʃɪz Ch, *-ing* slɒtʃɪn Y

slote *n* a DIAGONAL BAR of a gate IV.3.7. sloʊt Bk

slother *v* to GOBBLE food VI.5.13(b). slɒðə Cu

slothers* *v-3prsg* he GUZZLES a drink VI.5.13(a). *-ing* slɒðəɹɪn La

slot-stick *n* a movable horizontal rod stretching between the shafts of a cart, fixing them to the cart-body and stopping the cart from tipping, ⇐ ROD/PIN I.10.3. slɒtstɪk Y Nt, slɔtstɪk Y L

slotten *adj* AJAR IX.2.7. slɔtən L

slot up *vtphr* to TIP a cart I.11.6. slɔt ... ʊp L

slouch-bonnet* *n* a woman's BONNET worn outdoors VI.14.1. slɛʊtʃbɒnət O

slough *1. n* a pea-POD V.7.12. slʊf Y*[old]*

2.1. vt to TOP-AND-TAIL gooseberries V.7.23. slʊf Y

2.2. v to top-and-tail gooseberries. slʊf Y

3.1. vt to REMOVE *STALKS* from currants V.7.24. slʊf Y L

3.2. v to remove stalks. slʊf Y

5. *n* SLUSH VII.6.16. slaʊ St, sləʊ He

6. *n* MUD VII.6.17. sləʊ Gl

slouse down *vtphr* to guzzle a drink, ⇐ GUZZLES VI.5.13(a). *-ing* slɐʊsn ... dɛʊn Nf

sloush* *n* SLUSH VII.6.16. sɫœʏʃ D, slæʏʃ So, sɫæʏʃ Co D, slæʊʃ So, sɫæʊʃ W, slaʊʃ So Do*[old]*, sɫaʊʃ Do, sɫɒʊʃ W, sɫəʊʃ Do*[old]*

sloven *adj* CLUMSY, describing a person VI.7.14. slʊvn L

slow *adj* STUPID VI.1.5. slɒʊ Sr, slo˙ʊ Nth

slowrie *n* a CRANE on which a kettle is hung over a domestic fire V.3.4. slæʊɾɪ Man, slaʊɾɪ Man

slub *1. v* to DITCH IV.2.11. *-ing* slʌbn Nf

2. *n* SLUSH VII.6.16. slʌ˙b Nf

3. *n* MUD VII.6.17. slʏb Nf

slubber *v* to GOBBLE food VI.5.13(b). slubə Y

slubbers *1. vt-3prsg* he GUZZLES a drink VI.5.13(a). *-ing* slʊbəɹɪn Y, *3ptsg* slubəd Y

2. *v-3prsg* he guzzles. *-ing* slʌbəɹɪn MxL

slud *1. n* SLUSH VII.6.16. slʏd Nf*[old]*

2. *n* MUD VII.6.17. slɛd Ess, slʌd Sf Hrt Ess

sludden *adj* **sludden with water** BOGGY IV.1.8. slə?n wɪ waʔəˀ L

sludder *1. n* SLUSH VII.6.16. slʌdə Bk

2. *n* MUD VII.6.17. slʌdə Hu*[old]* C

sludge *1. n* SLUSH VII.6.16. slʌdʒ Sa Nth, slʏdʒ Lei, slʊdʒ Y Sa He Wo Gl L Lei R Nth

2. *n* MUD VII.6.17. slʊdʒ Cu La Y Ch Db St Nt L Nth

sludge out* *1. vphr* to DITCH IV.2.11. slʊdʒ uːt Y

2. *vtphr* to ditch. slʊdʒ ... uːt Y

slugs *npl* *What do you call those small slimy whitish things that feed on your cabbages and greens?* IV.9.2. Eng. ⇒ **bots, gorging-grubs, snails, spitters, white slugs, white snails, young snails**

sluice *1. n* a shallow CESS-POOL on a farm I.3.11. sluːs Ess

2. *n* a FORD IV.1.3. slʊuːʃ Sr *[queried ir.r. BM]*

slur *vi* to SLIDE VIII.7.1. *-ing* slɔɹɪn Y, slɔˡːɹ La, slɜˡː La, slɜˡːɹ La, *-ing* sləɹɪn Y, sləː Y Ch Db St, sləˡː Y Ch Db L

slur about *viphr* to SLIDE VIII.7.1. sləˀɹ əbæʊt Ch

slurrup *vt* to guzzle a drink, ⇐ GUZZLES VI.5.13(a). *-ing* slʊɹəpɪn Wa

slurrup down *vphr* to guzzle a drink, ⇐ GUZZLES VI.5.13(a). *-ing* slʊɹəpɪn dæʊn Wa

slurry *1. n* URINE in a cow-house I.3.10. slʌɹɪ O, sɫʌɾi W D Ha, sləɹɪ Ha

2. *n* mixed dung and urine. slʌɹɪ Sa

3. *n* thin mud. sləɹɪ O

4. *n* SLUSH VII.6.16. slʌɹɪ Sa, sɫʌɹɪ Mon, slʊɹɪ

La, sluɹiː Wo

5. *n* MUD VII.6.17. slʌɹı He, sɫʌɾi D, sluɹı Ch

slush *1. n* When the frost breaks and the snow becomes very wet, what might you have to walk through? VII.6.16. Eng. ⇒ **blash, mud, puddle, slash, slob, slop, slosh, slotch, sloush, slough, slub, slud, sludder, sludge, slurry, slushy, sluss, slutch, snow-broth;** ⇒ also **puddly**

2. *n* URINE in a cow-house I.3.10. sɫʌʃ W Ha, slʌs Nf, slʊʃ Brk, sluːʃ L

3. *n* mixed dung and urine. sɫʌʃ Ha

4. *n* COW-DUNG I.3.12. slʌʃ Brk

5. *n* RUBBISH V.1.15. sɫʌʃ Do

6. *vt* to RINSE clothes V.9.8. slauʃ So

7. *v* to GOBBLE food VI.5.13(b). slɔˑʃ Sf

slush down *vtphr* to guzzle a drink, ⇐ GUZZLES VI.5.13(a). slʊʃ ... dɛʊn Wa

slushes *1. vt-3prsg* he GUZZLES a drink VI.5.13(a). *-ing* slɔʃən Sf, *-ing* slʌʃın Nf

2. *v-3prsg* he guzzles. *inf* slʊʃ We

slush-hole *1. n* a CESS-POOL on a farm I.3.11. slʌʃɒuɫ Brk, slʊʃɔuɫ Brk

2. *n* an artificial cess-pool. slʌʃɒuɫ Sx, slʌʃoːɫ Do, sɫʌʃoːɫ Ha

slush-pit *n* an artificial CESS-POOL on a farm I.3.11. slʌʃpıt Ha

slush-tank *n* a CESS-POOL on a farm I.3.11. sɫʌʃtaŋk W

slushy *1. adj* **make slushy** to DIRTY a floor V.2.8. mɛˑık ... slʌʃı Nf *[marked u.r. BM]*

2. *n* SLUSH VII.6.16. sləʃı Sr

sluss *1. n* SLUSH VII.6.16. slʌs Nf

2. *n* MUD VII.6.17. slʌs Nf

slutch *1. v* to DITCH IV.2.11. *-ing* slʊtʃın La

2. *n* SLUSH VII.6.16. slʊtʃ La Y Ch

3. *n* MUD VII.6.17. slʊtʃ La Y Ch Db

slutches *v-3prsg* he GUZZLES a drink VI.5.13(a). *-ing* slʊtʃın Y

slutch out *vphr* to DITCH IV.2.11. *-ing* slʊtʃın ... æʊt Y, *-ing* slʊtʃın ... aıt Ch *[wet ditch] [not a NBM headword]*

slutch-tank *n* an artificial CESS-POOL on a farm I.3.11. slʊtʃtaŋk Y

sluther *1. v* to GOBBLE food VI.5.13(b). slʊðə Y

2. *n* MUD VII.6.17. slʊðə Cu

sluthers *v-3prsg* he GUZZLES a drink VI.5.13(a). slʌðəˡːz̩ Sa

slut's-hole *n* an ASH-MIDDEN V.1.14. slʌtsɔuɫ Sx

slutter* *n* GRUEL for calves V.7.2. slʊtər Nb

slutters *v-3prsg* he GUZZLES a drink VI.5.13(a). *-ing* slʊtəʁən Nb

sluver *n* a movable iron hoop that slides along a cart-shaft and couples it to the projecting end of the beam on which the cart-body rests, ⇐ ROD/PIN I.10.3. *pl* slʊvəz Y

sly-footed *adj* SPLAY-FOOTED　　VI.10.5. slæıfʊtət Man

slysh* *n* a CUTTING of hay II.9.15. sɫaıʃ D

smack *1. v* to GOBBLE food VI.5.13(b). *-ing* smækn Nf; **smacking your gills** smæk?ın jɔˑ gılz Nf

2. *vt* to BEAT a boy on the buttocks VIII.8.10. smɛk Db K, smæk Sa Sf Ess K, smæk? Nf, smak Nb Du La Y Ch Db Sa St Wa Mon Gl O Nt L Lei Nth C Bk Hrt; **give him a good smack** gıv ım ə gʊd smæk Nf; **give him a smack** giː n ə smak Ha; **smack his arse** smæk ız æs Mon, *?3prsg* smæks ız æːs Wo, smæk ız aːs He Mon Gl Nf Sf, smæk ız aˡːʂ Wo, smæk ız aːs Nf, smæk iiːz aˡːɽʂ Sx, smak ız aːs Db St Nt L So W Co D, smak ız aˡːʂ Gl; **smack his backside** smak ız baksaˑıd L

smacking *vbln* **give him a good smacking** to BEAT a boy on the buttocks VIII.8.10. gıv ım ə gʊd smakın St

small *n* COAL-DUST V.4.1. smɔːᵊɫ Bk

small bellies *n* CHITTERLINGS III.12.2. smɔl bɛliz Nf

small boughs *npl* branches of a tree, ⇐ BRANCH IV.12.3. smɔːɫ bɛʊz Sx

small coal(s) *n* COAL-DUST V.4.1.

no -s: smaːl kəˑl Nb, smaːl kəəl Nb Du, smɔːɫ kɒuɫ W, smɔː kɔːl Cu, smɔːl kɔul O L, smɔːl kɔuɫ Hu Brk, smɔːɫ kʌuɫ C Sf Bk Ess, smɔːɫ koːl He Gl, smɔːɫ koːɫ Mon, smaːɫ koːɫ Mon, smɔːl koːl O, smɔːɫ koːl So, smɔːl koːɫ O, smɔːɫ koːɫ So W Co D Do Ha, zmɔːɫ koːɫ W, smɔːɫ koː O, smɔːɫ kouɫ Mon Bk So, smaː koːuɫ Gl, smaːl koəl Du, smɔː koəl Nb Cu, smɔː kʊal Y, smaːl kʊəl Du, smaːl kʊəl Y, smɔːl kʊəl Y Nt, smɔː kʊəl Nb Cu Du, smɔː kwɒl Cu

-s: smaː kʊəlz Cu

small guts *n* CHITTERLINGS III.12.2. smɔːl gʌts He, smɔːɫ gʊts Wa C

small pitch-fork *n* a HAY-FORK with a short shaft I.7.11. smɔːl pıtʃfɔːk K

small plat *n* a PADDOCK I.1.10. smɔːɫ plæt Sx

small puddings *n* CHITTERLINGS III.12.2. smɔːl pʊdınz La Y St L, smaːl pʊdnz Du

small ropps *n* CHITTERLINGS III.12.2. smɔːl ɹaps R, smɔːɫ ɹaps Lei, smɔː ɹɒps Ch

small tailboard *n* an END-BOARD of a cart I.10.4. smɔːɫ tɛıᵊɫboˑəˡd̩ Nth

small tharms *n* CHITTERLINGS III.12.2. smɔːl θaːmz L

small weigh-tree *n* a subsidiary SWINGLE-TREE of a horse-drawn plough harness I.8.3. smɔːl wæıʔtɹı Ess

small wood *n* KINDLING-*WOOD*　　V.4.2. smɔːlwʊd O, smɔːɫ wʊd Hrt, smɔːɫ wʏd Co, smɔːɫ ʊd Ha, smɔːɫ uːd W Do

smalm up *vtphr* to DIRTY a floor V.2.8. smam ... ʌp Ha

smalmy *adj* STICKY, describing a child's hands VIII.8.14. smami Ha

smarags *n* CINDERS V.4.3. sməˈɹɛgs Man *[marked u.r. NBM]*

smart *adj* PRETTY, describing a girl VI.5.18. smaːt Y Mon L Nf Ess, smaᴷːt Nb, smaᶜːṭ Mon Gl So Sr, smɑːt Nf MxL K, smɑːʔ Hrt, smɑᴷːt Nb, smɑᴶːt K

smartish *adj* PRETTY, describing a girl VI.5.18. smaᶜːṭɪʃ So

smart-looking *adj* PRETTY, describing a girl VI.5.18. smaːtlʊkən We, smaːtluːkɪn Y, smaᶜːṭlʌkɪn Sa, smɑːtlukɪn K

smarts *vi-3prsg* it HURTS VI.13.3(a). *no -s*: smaːt Ess

smashing *adj* PRETTY, describing a girl VI.5.18. smæʃɪn Ess

smeared up *adj* STICKY, describing a child's hands VIII.8.14. smɪəᶜḍ ʌp K

smeech *1. n* SMOKE from a chimney V.1.4. smiːtʃ Co D, zmiːtʃ D*[smoke and dust]*, smɪtʃ Co*[sooty]* D, smaɪtʃ So*[old]*

2. vi to smoke, describing a lamp. *prppl* smiːtʃən D

3. n DUST on a road VII.6.18. smiːtʃ So D, smɪtʃ So, smaɪtʃ Do

smeeky *1. adj* RANCID, describing bacon V.7.9. smiˑkɪ Ess

2. adj **go smeeky** to SPOIL, referring to meat or fish V.7.10. gʌʊ smiːkɪ Ess

smellers *npl* NOSTRILS VI.4.7. smɛləᶜẓ Brk

smit *1. v* to MARK sheep with colour to indicate ownership III.7.9. smɪt Cu La

2. v to mark sheep in some unspecified way. *ptppl* ṣmʌtɪd D

smitting *adj* INFECTIOUS, describing a disease VI.12.2. smɪtn Y L, smɪʔɪn L, smɪtn Du

smittle *adj* INFECTIOUS, describing a disease VI.12.2. smɪtl Nb*[old x1]* Cu*[old x1]* Du*[old x1]* We La Y

smittling *adj* INFECTIOUS, describing a disease VI.12.2. smɪtḷɪn Y, smɪtlɪn Y*[old x1]* L, smɪtlən Cu

smock *n* a CHEMISE V.11.1. smɒk So D

smoke *n [Show a picture of some houses.] What do you call this [indicate smoke from a chimney]?* V.1.4. Eng. ⇒ **dust, reek, smeech, smother**; ⇒ also **smoke-jack**

smoke-jack* *n* a large spit on which meat is roasted, ⇐ SMOKE V.1.4. smʌʊkdʒæk Sr

smoose-hole *n* a hole in a wall, fence, or hedge made by hares or rabbits, ⇐ SHEEP-HOLE IV.2.8. *pl* smʊʊːsɒɪlz Y

smoot *1. n* a SHEEP-HOLE IV.2.8. smuːt Nb Du Y

2. n a hole in a wall, fence, or hedge made by hares or rabbits. smuːt We La Y*[or for overflow water]*, *pl* smuːts Cu

3. n a hole in a hedge-bottom. smuːt Y

smooth brush *n* a BRUSH used for sweeping indoors V.9.11. smuːv bʈʌᴵʃ So

smoot-hole *1. n* a SHEEP-HOLE IV.2.8. smuːthøːl Du, *pl* smuːthøːlz Nb, smuːtɒɪl Y, *pl* smᵓuːthoːlz Du, smuːtwɒl We, smuːthʊəl Nb Cu, *pl* smᵊuːthʊəlz Du, smuːtʊəl La Y*[made by sheep x1]*

2. n a hole in a wall, fence, or hedge made by hares or rabbits. *pl* smuːthoəlz Du, smuːtʊəl Y

smopple *adj* BRITTLE, describing cups and saucers which break easily IX.1.4. smɒpl Y

smother *n* SMOKE from a chimney V.1.4. smʌðəᶜ Co

smothered up *adj* STICKY, describing a child's hands VIII.8.14. smʌðəd ʌp MxL

smudge *n* COAL-DUST V.4.1. smʊdʒ Y

smuft-hole *n* a SHEEP-HOLE IV.2.8. smʊftɒɪl La

snack *1. n Tell me, do you have anything to eat between meals?* VII.5.11. snɛk Man Sr K Sx, snæk Man Nf So Sr, snak Cu Y Sa St Wa Mon L MxL So W Do Ha; **bit of a snack** bɪt əv ə snak Y; **snack of lunch** snæk ə lʊnʃ So*[old].* ⇒ *a bit of* **crib,** *a little* **lunch, bagging(s), bait,** *beaver* ⇒ **bever, bit** bait, **bite** *of* ten o'clock, biting on, *bit of a* snack, *bit of a* snap, *bit of* bait, *bit of* lunch, **breaks, clocking, clocks, crib, croust, crust, dew-bit, docky, dowan, drinking(s), drum-up, eleveners, elevens, elevenses, forenoon-drinking(s), forenoons, four-o'clock, fourses, jawer, lowance, lunch, morsel, nammet(s), nineses, nunch, nuncheon,** *nunching* ⇒ **nunching** ⇒ **nuncheon, packing, progger, putting-on, sandwich(es), scran, snack-bit, snack** *of lunch,* **snap, snapping, sup-and-a-bite, tenner, ten-o'clock(s), tenses, threeses, tommy**

2. n MEAL OUT VII.5.12. snɛk Ess K, snæk Ess, snæːk Hrt, snak Bd So

snack-bit *n* a SNACK VII.5.11. snakbɪt Sa

snag *1. v* to TOP AND TAIL swedes II.4.3. snag Cu We La Y

2.1. vt to CLEAR grass at the edges of a field II.9.5. *-ing* snagɪn Y

2.2. v to clear grass. *prppl* snægɪn He, snag La Sa; **go round a-snagging** gʊ ɹaːnd əsnagɪn La*[with scythe]*

3. v to TRIM hedges IV.2.3. snag La, *-ing* snagɪn Y

4. v to LOP a tree IV.12.5. snag La*[old]*, *prppl* snagɪn Y

5. n a LOOSE *PIECE OF* SKIN at the bottom of a finger-nail VI.7.11. snæːg MxL

snags *npl* SNAILS IV.9.3. snɛgz K Sx*[old]*, snægz K

snails *1. npl [What creatures live in and on the soil in your garden?] What do you call those slow slimy things that carry their houses about with them; they come out after rain?* IV.9.3. Eng. ⇒ **bulhorns, cock-snails, dodder-mans, dod-mans, dodny-hornies, hoddy-doddies, hoddy-dods, hodmedods, horse-snails, house-snails, packman, shell-snag, shell-snail, snags, snarl-gugs, sniggles**

2. npl SLUGS IV.9.2. sniːlz Db St, snɪəlz Y, *sg* sneːl Db, snaːlz Y

snake *n* an ADDER IV.9.4. sniːk Ch, sneɪk Wo

snap *1. n* (off her) FOOD V.8.2. snap Y

2. n a SNACK VII.5.11. snæp Y Gl Hu Nf Ess So, snap Y Db St Nt Lei Bk So; **bit of a snap** bɪt əv ə snap St

3. n MEAL OUT VII.5.12. snɛp K*[coal-miner's term]*, snæp K, snap Y*[collier's word x1]* Db St Lei

snapping *1. n* feed given to horses in the stable, ⇐ FEEDING III.5.1. snapɪn St

*2. n a SNACK VII.5.11. snapɪn Db

3. n MEAL OUT VII.5.12. snapɪn Ch Sa St

snare *1. v* to GROPE *FOR FISH* IV.9.10. *vbln* snɛˈəɹɪn Man

2. v to LOP a tree IV.12.5. *prppl* snɛəɹɪn Y, snɛˈəɹɪə L, *-ing* snɛˈəɹɪn L

snarled *adj* TANGLED, describing hair VI.2.5. snaᵗːɫd So, snaᵗːl̩d So, snaᵗːɫd̩ So*[old]*

snarl-gugs *npl* SNAILS IV.9.3. snaᵗːɫgʌgz So*[old]*

snarly *adj* TANGLED, describing hair VI.2.5. snæːᵊlɪ Sf, snaːɫɪ Ess*[when knotted]*

snatch *n* a TETHERING-STAKE in a cow-house I.3.3. *pl* snatʃəz W

snatched *1. adj* COLD, describing a room VI.13.17. snætʃt Sx

2. adj COLD, describing a person VI.13.18. snætʃt Sx

snathe *n* the SHAFT of a scythe II.9.7. sneθ Nt, sneᵊθ Y, sneːð Db, sneːð Nt Db Ha, sneːv D, snɛɪθ Lei K, snɛɪð Db, snɛəθ Ess, snɛːᵊθ Lei, snaːθ Bd Hrt Ess, snaːf Ess, snaːθ Hrt, snaːf Ess

snaze *v* to TRIM hedges IV.2.3. sneːz La

snead *n* the SHAFT of a scythe II.9.7. sniːd Nb Du St He Mon O So Brk Co D, zniːd D, sniːəd So W, snɪiːd Ess Brk Sr Ha, snɪd Du, snɪəd So W, sneːd So W Co D Do Ha, zneːd D, snɛd Nb Cu Du Y Ch Sa St He Wo Wa O Nth Bk Co, snɛɪd St Co D, snɛːəd D

sneath *n* the SHAFT of a scythe II.9.7. sniːθ Lei R, sniːð Db St Lei Bd Ha, sniːv Ha, snɪið Brk, snɪiːθ Sr, snɪiːð Sx, snɪiːz Sx

sneck *1. v* to CLEAR grass at the edges of a field II.9.5. snɛk La

2. n the LATCH of a door V.1.9. snɛk Nb Cu Du We La Y Nt L Nf, snɛɪk Nf, snæk Nf, snak L

3. n **just off the sneck, off the sneck** AJAR IX.2.7. **just off the sneck** dʒʊst ɒf t snɛk Y; **off the sneck** ɒf t snɛk Cu*[old]*

4. vt to SHUT a door IX.2.8. snɛk La *[marked u.r. NBM]*

5. n the vertical BAR or CHAIN of a crane over a domestic fire V.3.5(b). snɛk Sf

6. n a NOSE VI.4.6. snɛk Nb*[vulgar x1]*

snecked *adj* **not snecked** AJAR IX.2.7. nʊt snɛkt We

snecking-post *n* the SHUTTING-POST of a gate IV.3.4. snɛkənpøːst Nb, snɛkɪnpʊəst Y

sneck-post *n* the SHUTTING-POST of a gate IV.3.4. snɛkpɒst Du, snɛkpʊəst L

sneck-stoop *n* the SHUTTING-POST of a gate IV.3.4. snɛkstuːp Nb Du La

sned *1. v* to TOP AND TAIL swedes II.4.3. snɛd Nb

2. v to LOP a tree IV.12.5. snɛd Nb Cu

snedgers *npl* TURNIPS II.4.1(b). snɛdʒəz Du

snib *v* to LOP a tree IV.12.5. snɪb Nb

snicker *1. vi-3prpl* they WHINNY, describing the noise horses make during feeding time in the stable III.10.3(a). snɪkəᵗː Ha

2. vi-3prpl they NEIGH, describing the noise horses make in the fields III.10.3(b). snɪkəᵗ Ha

snicking out *vtphr-ing* PUTTING your tongue OUT VI.5.4. snɪkɪn ... aʊt Ch

sniddle *v* to CLEAR grass at the edges of a field II.9.5. snɪdl Ch

sniggles *npl* SNAILS IV.9.3. snɪgɫz Wa*[old]*

snip *1. vt* to cut the tails off swedes, ⇐ TOP AND TAIL II.4.3. snɪp MxL *[marked u.r. EMBM]*

2. vt to MARK the ears of sheep with a cut or hole to indicate ownership III.7.9. snɪp La

3.1. vt to TOP-AND-TAIL gooseberries V.7.23. Wa

3.2. v to top-and-tail gooseberries. snɪp Wa Nth Bd Hrt

4.1. vt to REMOVE *STALKS* from currants V.7.24. snɪp Lei

4.2. v to remove stalks. snɪp La, *-ing* snɪppɪn Db

5. n a PINCH of sugar or salt VII.8.6. snɪp L

snipes *n* ICICLES VII.6.11. snaɪps Nth

snitch *n* a NOSE VI.4.6. snɪtʃ La*[vulgar x1]* Y*[old x1]* Ch*[facetious]* K

snitcher *n* a NOSE VI.4.6. snɪtʃə Y Bd*[vulgar]*, snɪtʃəᵗ Sa

snob *n* a COBBLER VIII.4.5. snɑb Nth, snɑːb He Wo Mon Gl, snɒb Y*[old]* St*[old]* He Wo*[occasional x1, old x1]* Wa*[rare x1, old x1]* Mon Gl O Nth*[old x1]* Hu Nf*[not used x1]* Bk*[old]* Bd*[old x1]* Hrt Ess So W Brk Sr K*[old x1]* D Do Ha Sx, snɒb C*[old]* Sf*[old x1]* Hrt Ess*[old x1]* MxL So Brk Sr K, snɔːb He Ess So Sx, snʌb So

snobber *n* a COBBLER VIII.4.5. snɒbə Nf, snɒbəᵗ He

snobble *vt* to kill chickens by hitting them on the head, ⇐ to WRING IV.6.20. -*s* snɒbɬz Gl

snobbler *1. n* a PIECE *OF BREAD AND BUTTER* V.6.11(a). snɒbɬəᶜ Mon
2. *n* a COBBLER VIII.4.5. snɒbɬəᶜ Gl, snɒbɬəᶜ: D*[a nickname]*

snobby *n* a COBBLER VIII.4.5. snɒbi W Do Ha, snɒbɪ Brk

snogs *npl* the HANDLES of a scythe II.9.8. snɒgz Ha

snoodle *vi* to SCREAM VIII.8.11. snʏ:dɬ D *[queried SBM]*

snooks *npl* COCKS of hay II.9.12. snuu:ks Sx

snoring *v-ing What am I doing now [indicate snoring]?* VI.5.14. Eng. ⇒ *a-snoring*, **snorking**, **snorting**

snork *vi-3prpl* they NEIGH, describing the noise horses make in the fields III.10.3(b). snɔːks Sx

snorking *v-ing* SNORING VI.5.14. snɔᶜːrgɪn Sx

snorks *v-3prsg* he GUZZLES a drink VI.5.13(a). -*ing* snɔːkən Du

snort *vi-3prpl* they WHINNY, describing the noise horses make during feeding time in the stable III.10.3(a).G snaᶜːr̥t̥ʂ Brk, snəːt Ch

snorting *v-ing* SNORING VI.5.14. snaᶜːt̥ɪn So, snɔᶜːt̥ɪn So, snɔᶜːt̥ən D, snɔᶜːʔn So

snotches *1. n* the notches on the T-SHAPED PLOUGH-BEAM END of a horse-drawn plough I.8.5. snɒˈtʃɪz Nf
2. *n* the vertical BAR or CHAIN of a crane over a domestic fire V.3.5(b). snɒtʃɪz Sx, snɒtʃəz W

snotter *n* a NOSE VI.4.6. snɒtə St, snɒtəᶜ Sa

snoul *1. n* a tree STUMP IV.12.4. snɒʊəl So
2. *n* **snoul of bread** a PIECE *OF BREAD AND BUTTER* V.6.11(a). snɒʊᵊɬ ə bɹɛd Gl

snout *1. n What do you call this part of a pig [gesticulate]?* III.9.1. snᵊʏːt La, snɛːt Db, snɛʊt La Y Ch Db Sa St Wo Wa O L Nth Hu C Nf Sf Bd Hrt Ess MxL Brk Sr K Ha Sx, snɛʊʔ O Bk Bd Hrt, snœvt D, znœvt D, snæːt La Y Nt K, snæʏt So Co D, znæʏt D, snæʊt Y Man Ch St He Wo Wa Nt L Lei R Ess So W Sr Do Ha, znæʊt W, snaːt La Y Lei Bk, snaʊt Cu La Y Ch Db Sa St Nt L Lei So, znaʊt So, snɑʊt He O, snɒʊt W, snɔʊt L, snʌʊt Y He Mon Gl Nf Brk, snuːt Nb Cu Du We Y Sa He Wo Gl L, snəʊt Y He Wo Mon Gl Nf W Brk K Do. ⇒ **groin, nose**
2. *v* to ROOT, what a pig does when it digs the ground with its snout III.9.2. -*ing* snɛʊtɪn Sx
3. *n* a NOSE VI.4.6. snɛʊt Nf*[vulgar x1]* Hrt*[vulgar]* Ess*[humorous x1, old x1]* Sr*[facetious]*, snæʊt St L So Sr, snæʏt So, snaʊt Cu Y*[vulgar x1]* Sa St L So, snᵊuːt Du, snʌʊt Y*[old]* Brk, snuːt Nb Cu Du*[vulgar]* We Y*[slang x1, old x1]* L, snəʊt Y*[old]*
4.1. *v* to TOP AND TAIL swedes II.4.3. snɛʊt C*[roots only]* Hrt*[roots only]*, -*ing* snɛʊtɪn Hrt
4.2. *vt* to top and tail swedes. snaːt Lei
5.1. *vt* to TOP-AND-TAIL gooseberries V.7.23.

snɛʊt Nth, snaʊt Sa, -*ing* snɛʊtn Nf
5.2. *v* to top-and-tail gooseberries. snɛʊʔ Bk
6. *v* to REMOVE *STALKS* from currants V.7.24. -*ing* snɛʊʔɪn Bk

snout-holes *npl* NOSTRILS VI.4.7. snɛʊthoˈʊlz Nf, snɛʊtoʊlz Nf, snɛʊtoʊɬz Nf*[old-fashioned x1]*, *sg* snaʊtʊəl L, snʊuˈtʊəlz Y*[old]*

snow *n* DANDRUFF VI.1.3. snoː Sa

snow-broth *n* SLUSH VII.6.16. snaːbɹɒθ La Y*[old]*, snɔːbɹɒθ La Y, snɔːbɹɒθ Y, snɔːbrɔːθ La, snɔːbɹɒθ Db, snoːbɹɔːθ La

snub *1. vt* to TOP-AND-TAIL gooseberries V.7.23. snʊb Ch St Wa
2. *v* to top-and-tail gooseberries. snʊb Du Ch St

snubber *n* a movable iron hoop that slides along a cart-shaft and couples it to the projecting end of the beam on which the cart-body rests, ⇐ ROD/PIN I.10.3. *pl* snʊbəz Y, snʊbəɪ Y

snuff *1. v* to TOP AND TAIL swedes II.4.3. -*ing* snɒˈvɪn Ha
2.1. *vt* to TOP-AND-TAIL gooseberries V.7.23. snɒf Lei, -*ing* snɒːvɪn Ha, -*ing* snɒfɪn Do, snɔːf W Do, snʌf So*[old x1]* Do Ha, snʊf Y St*[old x1]* Gl Lei R; **snuff and tail** snʌf ən taɪɬ W
2.2. *v* to top-and-tail gooseberries. snʊf Y Db O Lei
3.1. *vt* to REMOVE *STALKS* from currants V.7.24. Y Lei
3.2. *v* to remove stalks. snʊf Du Y1

snuffle *vi-3prpl* they WHINNY, describing the noise horses make during feeding time in the stable III.10.3(a). -*ing* snʌft̥ɪn Ess

snuft *1. vt* to TOP-AND-TAIL gooseberries V.7.23. snʊft St Lei
2. *v* to top-and-tail gooseberries. *prppl* snʊftɪn St

snut *vt* to TOP-AND-TAIL gooseberries V.7.23. snʏt Nb

so *adv* IN THIS WAY IX.10.7. sʌʊ Ess, soː Mon, soʊ St, sʊə Y

soak *1. n* URINE in a cow-house I.3.10. soːk Sa, soʊk He
2.1. *vt* to BREW tea V.8.9. zɔːk So W D, soːk So, zoːk W Co D Do, zuːk D
2.2. *v* to brew tea. -*ing* zɔːkən D
3. *v* to stand, referring to tea left to become strong before pouring. zɔːk Co, -*ing* zɔːkən D, -*ing* zoːkɪn D, zʊk So

soakaway *1. n* a CESS-POOL on a farm I.3.11. zɔːkəweː Ha
2. *n* an artificial cess-pool. soʊkəweɪ Ha

soaked *1. adj* BOGGY IV.1.8. soʊkt Nf
2. *adj* WET VII.6.24. zɔːkt So, zoːkt W

soaking *adj* WET VII.6.24. zoːkɪn So

soaking wet *adj* WET VII.6.24. zɔːkɪn wɛt W

sobbed out *adj* BOGGY IV.1.8. zɒbd æʊt W

sock

sock *1. n* URINE in a cow-house I.3.10. sɒk Ch Db Sa St He Wo Wa L Lei, sɔk Wa Nt L, sʌk Sa, sʊk Sa Wo

2. n the SHARE of a horse-drawn plough I.8.7. sœk Nb Du, sɒk Nb Cu Du Y Man, sɔk Nb Cu We Y, sʌk Sa, sʊk We La Ch Sa St

sockage *n* URINE in a cow-house I.3.10. sɒkɪdʒ Wo Wa, sɔkɪdʒ Wo

sockage-hole *n* a CESS-POOL on a farm I.3.11. sɒkɪdʒɔʊɫ Wo

sockage-pit *n* an artificial CESS-POOL on a farm I.3.11. sɒkɪdʒpɪt Wo

sock-cistern *n* a CESS-POOL on a farm I.3.11. sɒksɛstən St, sɔksɪstən Wa

sock-dike *n* a CESS-POOL on a farm I.3.11. sɔkdaˑɪk L

sock-hole *1. n* a DRAIN in a cow-house I.3.8. sʊkoːl Sa, sʊkoʊl Wo

2. n a CESS-POOL on a farm I.3.11. sɒkoʊl St

3. n an artificial cess-pool. sɒkoːᵁl Db

socking *v-ing* THROWING a stone VIII.7.7. sɒkɪn Nth

sock-lamb *n* a PET-LAMB III.7.3. sɒklɛˑm K, sɒklæm K

sock-pit *1. n* a CESS-POOL on a farm I.3.11. sɒkpɪt St, *pl* sɒkpɪts Ch

2. n an artificial cess-pool. sɒkpɪt Sa Wo Wa

sock-tank *n* an artificial CESS-POOL on a farm I.3.11. sɒktaŋk Ch St

sock-well *n* an artificial CESS-POOL on a farm I.3.11. sɒkwɛl St

sod-and-stone-dike *n* a WALL IV.2.1(b). sɒdnsteˑandaɪk Cu

sodden *1. adj* BOGGY IV.1.8. sɒdn St Nf Ess Sx

2. adj SAD, describing bread or pastry that has not risen V.6.12. sɒdn La St K, sɔdn La

soddened *1. adj* BOGGY IV.1.8. sɒdnd Ch, sɒdənd Gl, ʃɒdnd Brk, sadənd Y

2. adj SAD, describing cake that has not risen V.6.12. sɒdnd Brk

soddle *adj* SAD, describing bread or pastry that has not risen V.6.12. sɒdɫ Co

soddled *adj* SAD, describing bread or pastry that has not risen V.6.12. sɒdɫd Co

sodly *adj* SAD, describing bread or pastry that has not risen V.6.12. sɒdɫi Co

soft *1. adj* STUPID VI.1.5. sɒft Lei R, sɔːft So

2. adj SILLY VIII.9.3. sɒft Y Man Nt Lei Nf, sɔft L, sɔːft Nth Nf

3. adj BRITTLE, describing cups and saucers which break easily IX.1.4. zɑːft Gl, sɔːft Wa Nf *[marked u.r. EMBM]*

soft bonnet *n* a woman's BONNET *pl* sɔft bɒnɪts Ch

soft-broom *1. n* a BRUSH used for sweeping indoors V.9.11. sɑːfbɹʊm He Gl, sɑːfbɹuːm Wo Mon Gl, sɒfbɹʊm He, sɒfbɹuːm Sa Wo, sɒːf bɹuːm K,

sɔfbɹʊm Ess, sɔfbɹuːm MxL, sɔftbɹʊm Y, sɔːfbɹʊm Sf Hrt Ess He, sɔːftbɹuːm Wo, sɔːfbɹuːm C Ess MxL Wa O

2. n a long-handled BRUSH used for sweeping V.2.14. sɒft bɹuːm Lei

soft-brush *n* a BRUSH used for sweeping indoors V.9.11. sɑːfbɹʊʃ He Mon Gl, sɒfbɹʌʃ Mon, sɒftbɹʊʃ Cu We La Y, sɒfbɹʊʃ Cu La Sa He, sɔftbɹʊʃ L, sɔːf bɾiːʃ Co, sɔːfbɹʌʃ Hu Bd, sɔːf bɾʌʃ D, sɔːᵊfbɹʊʃ Nth, sɔːfbɹəʃ Gl, sɔːf bəᶜːʃ So

soft-rub *n* a WHETSTONE made of sandstone II.9.10. sɔˑfɹʏb Nf

sogged *adj* WET VII.6.24. zɒgd Ha

soggy *1. adj* BOGGY IV.1.8. sagɪ Gl, sɒgɪ Y Wo Sf

2. adj SAD, describing bread or pastry that has not risen V.6.12. sɒgɪ He

soil *n* EARTH VIII.5.8. sɛɪl La, sæɪl Man Ch*[old]*, saɪl Ch Db Sa, sɑːl Ch, sɑɪl La Ch Db, sɒɪl Nb Cu Du We La Y Db Sa St Nt L Brk, sɒɪᵊl Wo, sɒɪɫ He O, sɒɪᵊɫ Wo Wa Nth Bd W, sɒɪʊ Sr Sx, sɔɪl Nb La Y Ch Db St Wa O Nt L Nf, sɔɪɫ O Lei Nth MxL Brk Sr, sɔɪʊ Ha, sɔɪl Y, sɔɪɫ O; **soil or clay** sɔɪl əˡ kleː La

solderer *n* a TINKER VIII.4.9. sɔːðɛɹə La, sɔːdəᶜːɾəᶜ Co

soldiers *npl* MINNOWS IV.9.9. sʌʊdʒəz Sf

soldier's-buttons *n* GOOSE-GRASS II.2.5. sœːldʒəzbʏtnz Nb

sole *1. n [Show a picture of a (horse-drawn) plough.] What do you call this, the flat iron foundation?* I.8.9. søːl Nb, sœːl Nb, sɒʊɫ K Sx, sɔʊl O, soːl Du La Db, soːɫ He, soʊɫ Wo, sʊəl Nb Du We Y L;* **plough-sole** plɛʊsoːl Db. ⇒ **bed, bed-plate, boot, bottom, bottom-plate, chip, drock, foot, ground, ground-iron, ground-reest,** *ground-rest* ⇒ **ground-reest, ground-rise, ground-side, heel, heel-iron, heel-plate, land-ledge, land-plate, land-race, land-rise, land-side, land- slide, land-slip, land-slipe, pad, paddle, pitch, plane, plate, plough-bottom, plough-share-slide, plough-shoe, plough-slead, plough-sled, plough-slide,** *plough*-**sole, reef, reest-board, shoe, short-side, skate, skeithing-iron, skid, slide, slip, slipe, slipper, slod, sole-cleap, sole-clout, sole-plate, strake, strip, throck, wing-plate**

2. n the bottom of a furrow. sʊəl Y

3. n a PLOUGH I.8.1. zʏːɫ D, zæʏɫ D, zoːɫ So, zuːɫ So D

4. n a wooden plough. *pl* sʊʊz Brk

5. n the beam of a cart, ⇐ CROSS-BEAM END I.10.1. soːəl Man, sʊəl We

6. n the THRESHOLD of a door V.1.12. soːl Man

7. n a TETHER for a cow I.3.4. sʏˑɪl Db

378

8. *n* a rope tether. sɔʊ L

9. *vt* to tether a cow. *3prpl* sɔʊz La

10. *vt* to BEAT a boy on the buttocks VIII.8.10. sɔʊl Nf, sʊəl Y; **sole his arse** sʌʊɬ ɪz aːs Ess; **sole his backside** sɔʊɬ ɪz bæksɔɪd Ess

11. *vt* to beat somebody. sɔʊl Nf, sʊəl L

sole-cleap *n* the SOLE of a horse-drawn plough I.8.9. sɔːlkleːp La

sole-clout *n* the SOLE of a horse-drawn plough I.8.9. sɔɪlklaʊt La, sʊəlklaʊt La

sole-end *n* the CROSS-BEAM END of a cart I.10.1. sʊəlɛnd L, *pl* sʊəlɛndz Du La

sole-plate *n* the SOLE of a horse-drawn plough I.8.9. søːlpleˑət Nb, soːlpleːt La Ch, soːəlpleɪ Man, soʊlpleɪᵗ Man, sʊəlplɪət Y, sʊəlpleːt La Ch, sʊəlpleat We La, sʊəlpleˑət La, sʊəlpleːt Cu

soles *npl* BUMPERs of carts I.10.1(a). sɒʊɫz K, sɔʊɫz Hu

sole-trees *n* the beams of a carts, ⇐ CROSS-BEAM END I.10.1. *pl* sɔəltriːz Nb

soling-piece *n* a BUMPER of a cart I.10.1(a). soːlɪnpiːs So, soːlɪnpɪs So

some *adv* VERY VIII.3.2. sʌm Sf Co, zʌm Co

somersault 1. *adv* HEAD OVER HEELS IX.1.10. sʌməsalt Nf

2. *n* **pitch a somersault, turn a somersault** turn head over heels. **pitch a somersault** pɪtʃ ə sʌməsɔːɬt Ess; **turn a somersault** tɒn ə suməsɔlt Nt *[grammatically undefined:* sʌməsɒɬt Hu, suməsɔːlt St, sumæsɔːɬt Lei*]*

somerset *n* a somersault, ⇐ HEAD OVER HEELS IX.1.10. suməsɛt Y L

something 1. *pron But in this one [show a full pocket] there's not nothing, there's ....* VII.8.15. Eng exc. Du We La Db Gl Nt Hrt. ⇒ **somewhat(s)**

2. *adv* VERY VIII.3.2. sʌmpɪn Nf

somewhat(s) *pron* SOMETHING VII.8.15.

no -*s*: sɒmət Y, zʌmɪt W, sʌmʌtʰ Mon, sʌmət Sa He Mon Gl O Nth Bk Bd Hrt Ess MxL So W Brk Sr Ha Sx, zʌmət So W Co D Do Ha Sx, sʌmɒᵗt̚ He Mon, sʌməʔ Bk Bd, sʊmʊt La Wo Wa Gl, zʊmʊt Gl, sʊmʊːt He Wo Gl, sʊmət Nb Cu*[uncommon x1]* Du We La Y Ch Db Sa St Wo Wa Mon Gl O Nt L Lei R Nth Bk, zʊmət Gl W, sʊməᵗt̚ He Wo Gl, zʊmɒᵗt̚ He Gl, sʊmək Du, sʊməʔ Ch O, səmət Sa Gl, zəmət Gl -*s*: sʊməts Nt L

son *n [Show a picture of a family. Who are the members of this family?] He [point to the boy] is their [point to the father and mother] ....* VIII.1.4(a). Eng. ⇒ **boy, lad**

soon broken *adj* BRITTLE, describing cups and saucers which break easily IX.1.4. sɪun bɹɒkən Y

soot *n What do you call the black stuff that comes down the chimney?* V.4.6. Eng. ⇒ **chimney-soot**

soot-rake *n* a RAKE used in a domestic fire V.3.8(a). sɸt̚ʔɹɛːʊk Nf, sɪtɹeʊk Nf, sɪtɹæʊk MxL

sop-milk *n* BEESTINGS V.5.10. sɒpmɪlk Ess

sopping wet *adj* WET VII.6.24. sɒppɪn wiːt Db

soppy 1. *adj* STUPID VI.1.5. sɒpˡɪ Wa

2. *adj* SILLY VIII.9.3. sɒpɪ MxL

sore *adj* CHAPPED VI.7.2. sɛə Y

sore head *n* a HEADACHE VI.1.6. seɔᴮ hiːd Nb*[rare x1]*, sɛər hiːd Cu, sœː hiːd Nb

sores *npl* CHAPS in the skin VI.7.3. sʊəz Lei; **sore places** sʊə pleˑəsɪz L

sort *n You go into a bootshop and say you want some boots. The shopman would at once ask you: WHAT...?* VII.8.17. Eng exc. Lei R. ⇒ **kind, kind of, kind of a, make, seck, sort of** *[BM headword* **kind***]*

sorting *v-ing* CULLING sheep III.11.2. saᵗ̚tɪn ... So, sɒɾ̚tɪn ... O, sɔːtɪn Ch Db Sa St He Lei Nth K, sɔːtɪn ... Lei K, sɔːt̚ʔɪn Bd, sɔːtn Cu We Sf Ess, *v* sɔːt Nt, sɔᵗ̚tɪn Sa Wa, zɔᵗ̚tɪn ... D, sɔᵗ̚ˑʔɪn Bk, sɔᵗɾ̚ʔ? ... O, sɔːᵗʔɪn Hrt, soˑətn Ch Bd, soətn Nb Cu, *v* soˑət Db, soːəˡtɪn Db, soˑəᵗ̚ʔɪn Bk, sʊətɪn La Y Db L, sʊətɪn ... Ch, sʊətn Nb Cu We, zʊəᵗ̚tɪn Co, zuːəᵗ̚tɪn ... Co, sɜːtɪn Y, sɜːʔən Man

sorting out *vphr-ing* CULLING sheep III.11.2. zaᵗ̚tɪn ... æʊt W, *ptppl* zaᵗ̚təd æʊt Ha, saᵗ̚tən ... əʊt Do, saᵗ̚tɪn ... ɛuːt Wo, saᵗ̚tɪn ... əʊt Wo Gl, sɔːʔtn ... ɛut Nf, *v* sɔːt ɛʊt Sf, sɔˡtn ... ɛuʔ Nf, sɔᵗ̚tɪn ɛut K, *vt* sɔᵗ̚ɾt ... ɛut Sx, sɔːəᵗɾ̚ʔn ... ɛut Sx, sɔətn ... uːt Y, sʊətɪn ... aːt Y, sʊətən ... aʊt Y, sʊətɪn ... uːt Y

sorting over* *vphr-ing* CULLING sheep III.11.2. sɔːəᵗ̚tɪn ... ɒʊvəᵗ Sr, sʊətɪn ... ɒvə Y

sort out *vtphr* to THIN OUT turnip plants II.4.2. sʊət ... æʊt Y

sorts 1. *n* **a bit out of sorts, out of sorts** ILL, describing a person who is unwell VI.13.1(b). **a bit out of sorts** ə bɪt uːt ɪ sʊəts Y; **out of sorts** aʊt ə saᵗ̚tʃ So, ɛut əv sɔːts Ess, ɛut ə sɔːts Ess*[rare x1]*, aːt ə sɔːts St, aɪt ə sɔːts St, aʊt əv sɔᵗ̚tʃ Sa, aʊt ə sɔᵗ̚tʃ Sa, ɛut ə sɔəˡts Brk, ɛut əˡ sɔəᵗ̚tʃ Ha, ɛut əv sɔːəᵗtʃ Sr, aɪt ə soʊts St, aʊt ə sʊats Y, æʊt ə sʊats Y L, aʊt ə sʊats L, uːt ə sʊats Y, aʊt ə suːəᵗ̚tʃ So, aʊt ə zuːəᵗ̚tʃ So, ʌʊt ə səːɪts Y

2. *n* **off sorts, out of sorts** SICK, describing an animal that is unwell VI.13.1(c). **off sorts** ɒf sʊats Y; **out of sorts** əʊd ə zaᵗ̚tʃ W, ɛut əv sɔːts Ess, ɛut ə sɔːts Ess, aːt ə sɔːts St, uːt ə sɔᴮːts Du, aʊt ə sʊats Y, ɛat ə sʊats Y, æʊt ə sʊats L, aːt ə sʊats Y, aʊt ə sʊats L, uːt ə sʊats Y

sosh 1. *n* **on the sosh** ASKEW, describing a picture that is not hanging straight IX.1.3. ɒn ðə sɒʃ Nf

2. *n* **on the sosh** DIAGONALLY, referring to harrowing a field IX.1.8. ɒn ðə sɒʃ Nf

sosh-way *adj* ASKEW, describing a picture that is not hanging straight IX.1.3. sɒʃwɛɪ Nf

sosh-ways *adv* DIAGONALLY, referring to harrowing a field IX.1.8. sɒʃweɪz Nf, sɒʃwɛɪz Nf, sɒʃwæɪz Nf, sɒʃwʌɪz Nf

soss *1. v* to guzzle a drink, ⇐ GUZZLES VI.5.13(a). sʌs Sf
2. v to GOBBLE food VI.5.13(b). sʌs Sf

sossles *v-3prsg* he GUZZLES a drink VI.5.13(a). *inf* sɒzl Y, *no -s* sʌzł Sf Ess

sough *1. n* a DRAIN in a cow-house I.3.8. sʌf Sa, sʊf Sa St
2. n a CESS-POOL on a farm I.3.11. sʊf Ch
3. n an artificial cess-pool. sʊf Ch
4.1. vt to DRAIN wet land IV.1.9. sʊf Db St
4.2. v to drain land. sʊf Db, *prppl* sʊfɪn St
5. n a drain. sʊf St

soul *n* a PERSON VIII.5.3(a). sɔːł D

sour *1. vt* to CURDLE milk V.5.7. sæʊəɹ (+V) Ch, saʊəɹ (+V) St Nt
2. adj **make it go sour, make it sour, turn it sour** to curdle milk V.5.8. **make it go sour** mæɪk ɪt gʊ sæʊə Ess, meːk ət goː zæʊəᵗ: W; **make it sour** meɪk ɪʔ sɛʊᵗ Bk, mɛk ɪt sɛʊə Db, maɪk ɪt zaʊəᵗ: So; **turn it sour** tʃɜᴶːn ɪt sɛːəɹ La, təːn ɪt sæʊə Ess Sr, təːn ɪt saʊə Y St, tɜᴶːn ɪt saʊəɹ La, teˑn ɪt sɑə Nf, tɛˑn ɪt saːᵊ Nf, tɛən ɪt saˑʊə Lei, tɒn ɪt sʊə Y, tɔᴿn ɪt suˑɔᴿ Nb
3. adj **be sour, get sour, go sour, turn sour** to CURDLE, referring to milk V.5.9. Eng
4. adj SAD, describing bread or pastry that has not risen V.6.12. sʊɔᴿ Nb*[old]*
5. adj RANCID, describing bacon V.7.9. sɑː Man
6. adj **go sour** to SPOIL, referring to meat or fish V.7.10. *3prsg* gʊz sæʊəᵗ Wo, *ptppl* gɒn saʊə Y, goː saʊəᵣO, gou zaʊəᵗ: So, go sɑː Man, gou sɑˑə Nf, gan sʊɔᴿ Nb, goː zᵁuːəᵗ Gl, guː zəʊəᵗ: W
7. n VINEGAR V.7.19. sʊə Y

sour buttermilk *n* RENNET V.5.6. sʊə bʊθəmɪlk Y

sour-dock *n* the DOCK plant II.2.8. saʊədɒk Cu

sour-grass *n* **lump of sour-grass, patch of old sour-grass** a TUSSOCK of grass II.2.9. **lump of sour-grass** *pl* lʌmps ə sɒːəgɹɑːs Nf; **patch of old sour-grass** pætʃ ə ɒʊl saːəgɹæs Nf

sour-milk *n* CURDS V.5.8(a). saˑəmɪlk Nf

sour-milk cheese *n* CHEESE V.5.4(b). saəmɪlk tʃiˑz Nf

south-pawed *adj* LEFT-HANDED VI.7.13(a). suːθpɔːd Cu

sovereign paper *n* a POUND NOTE VII.7.8. sɒvɹɪn pɛɪpə Hrt

sow *1. n* What do you call a female (pig) after she has had her first litter? III.8.6. Eng. ⇒ **old sow, yilt, young sow**
2. n a female pig after she has had her second litter. sɛʊ Ess
3. n a YOUNG SOW III.8.5. sɛʊ Nf, zœʏ D, zæʏ So, saʊ So

sow-cat *n* a TABBY-CAT, the female cat III.13.9. sɛʊkɛt Sr*[old word, not used now]*

sowing-basket *n* What do you call the container for the seeds used for sowing by hand (before April 1955: What do you call the basket ...)? II.3.6. sɒʊɪnbæskɪt So. ⇒ **basket, bass, bowl, brat, broad-sower, cob, cord, cradle, feeder, fiddle, hamper, hod, hopper, hoppet, lap, peck-basket, poke, scoop, scuttle, seed-apron, seed-basket, seed-bodge, seed-box, seed-brat, seed-cob, seed-cord, seed-cot, seed-cup, seed-hopper, seed-lift, seed-lip, seed-scuttle, seed-sheet, seed-skep, seed-tray, seed-trug, sheet, sieve, skep, skip, sowing-sheet, trough, trug, wisket**

sowing-sheet *n* a SOWING-BASKET II.3.6. søːənʃiːt Nb *[marked u.r. NBM]*

sow-mouse *n* a SHREW-MOUSE IV.5.2. sɛʊmɛʊs Ess *[queried EMBM]*

sow-pig *1. n* a YOUNG SOW III.8.5. sɛʊpɪg Sx
***2. n* a castrated female pig, ⇐ HOG III.8.8. saʊːpɪg Sa

sow-stacks *npl* long STACKS II.7.1. sᵁuːstaks Nb, *sg* suːstak Nb*[common type x1]*

sow-thistle *n* a variety of THISTLE II.2.2. sɛʊθɪsł Wo Ess, sæʊθɪsl L, sæʊθɪsł Wo, saʊθɪsl Ch Sa, θɛʊθɪsl Nf

spade *1. n* What do you dig the ground with? I.7.6. Eng. ⇒ **foot-spade, grafting-shovel, *sharevil* ⇒ shovel, shovel, spade-shovel, spit, spitter, spittle**
2. n a HAY-SPADE II.9.14(b). spɪəd We, speːd La, spɛˑəd L
3. v to CUT peat IV.4.4. *-ing* speɪdɪn So

spade-handle *n* the SHAFT of a spade I.7.7. speɪdaˑndł Ha, speəᵗɾdændu Sx, spæɪdændł Ess

spade-hay-knife *n* a HAY-SPADE II.9.14(b). speːdeːnaɪf La

spade-hind *n* a FARM-LABOURER I.2.4. spɪədhɛɪnd Nb Du

spade-knife *1. n* a HAY-KNIFE II.9.14(a). speːdnɑːf Y
2. n a HAY-SPADE II.9.14(b). spɛˑədnaɪf L

spade-man *n* a FARM-LABOURER I.2.4. spɪədmən Nb, speːdmən Nb

spade-shaft *n* the SHAFT of a spade I.7.7. speədʃaft Y

spade-shovel *n* a SPADE I.7.6. speːdʃʌvł Gl, spjədʃəvł Gl

spades-man *n* a FARM-LABOURER I.2.4. speədzmən La

spade-stick *n* the SHAFT of a spade I.7.7. speːɪdstɪk He So, spɛdstɪk He

spade-tree *n* the SHAFT of a spade I.7.7. speːdtɹiː He, speɪdtɹiː Lei, speəᵗːdtɾiː Do

spade up *vtphr* to DIG in the garden with a spade I.7.8. speːd ... ʌp D

spale *n* a SPLINTER VI.7.10. speˑal Cu, speɪl Cu

spale up *vtphr* to close gaps in a hedge, ⇐ to PLASH IV.2.4. speɪɫ ... ʌp K

spalt *adj* BRITTLE, describing cups and saucers which break easily IX.1.4. spɒult Nf

span **1. n* the SHAFT of a spade I.7.7. span D

2. vt to STOCK III.3.6. *-ing* spænɪn So, *-ing* spanɪn So

spane *v* to WEAN a calf III.1.4. spjɛn Du, spɪan Cu We Y, spɪən Nb Cu Du Y, speːn Y, spean Cu Du We La Y, speən Nb Cu Y, spɛən Y

span-fire-new *adj* BRAND-NEW VI.14.24. ˈspɒnfaɪˈnjɤ Ch

spank *vt* to BEAT a boy on the buttocks VIII.8.10. spɛŋk Sr Sx, spæŋk Sa Ess MxL K, spæŋkʔ Sf, spæᶦŋk Ess, spaŋk Nb*[old x1]* Cu Du*[old x1]* We La Y Ch Db Sa St He Wo Wa Gl Nt L Lei Hu C Bd Hrt; **spank his arse** spaŋk ɪz aːs L

spanking *vbln* **give him a good spanking** to BEAT a boy on the buttocks VIII.8.10. gɪv ɪm ə gʊd spaŋkɪn Hu

spanking-new *adj* BRAND-NEW VI.14.24. spaŋkɪnnɪu Y Bd, spaŋkənnɪu Cu*[old]*

span-new *adj* BRAND-NEW VI.14.24. spaŋnɪu Cu, spɒnnɪu Ch, spɒnnɪu La

spar *1. n* a RUNG of a ladder I.7.15. *pl* spaᵗːz O, spəᵗ Gl

2. n a DIAGONAL BAR of a gate IV.3.7. *pl* spaᵗːz Bk, spaːɾ Sr

spare-board *n* an END-BOARD of a cart I.10.4. spɛəᵗbɔːəᵗɾd Sx

spare tailboard *n* an END-BOARD of a cart I.10.4. spɛə tɛɪuɫbɔːd Ess

sparlings *npl* MINNOWS IV.9.9. spaᴶːlənz La

sparrers *npl* PEGS used to fasten thatch on a stack II.7.7(a). spaɾəz Sr

spars *1. npl* PEGS used to fasten thatch on a stack II.7.7(a). spaᵗːz So*[willow, hazel, or nutwood x5, willow x1]* W*[willow x1; willow, hazel, or nutwood x2; hazel or nutwood x1]* D Do*[hazel or nutwood x2; willow, hazel, or nutwood x1]* Ha, spaᵗːz Sr Ha*[hazel or nutwood x1]*, spaᵗːɾz Brk Sx*[hazel or nutwood x1]*, spaːəɾz Sr Ha Sx, spaᵗːəᵗɾz Sx

2. npl RODS laid on thatch to fasten it on a stack II.7.7(b3). spaᵗːz So*[old method]*

3. npl the horizontal BARS of a gate IV.3.6. spaːz Y L, *sg* spaː Y*[top bar only]* Wa, spaᵗːz O, *sg* spaᵗː Wo, spaːz MxL Brk, spaəᴶz Brk, spaːəᵗɾz Brk

spat *n* the STRETCHER between the traces of a cart-horse I.5.11. spæt K*[rare]*

spate *n* **in spate** IN FLOOD, describing a river IV.1.4. ɪ speːt La, ɪn speˑət Nb D

spats *1. npl* PEGS used to fasten thatch on a stack II.7.7(a). spaʔs Bk

2. npl LEGGINGS VI.14.18. spɛts Sx, spæts Sx

spatula *n* a PORRIDGE-STICK V.9.1. spatʃələ St

speaks *npl* PEGS used to fasten thatch on a stack II.7.7(a). spiːks So, *sg* spiːk Gl *[not a SBM headword]*

spean *n* a PRONG of a fork I.7.10. spiːn K Sx, *pl* spiiːnz Sr, speɪn Sr

speans *1. npl* the TEATS of a cow III.2.6. spiːnz K, spɛnz Sx

2. npl the horizontal BARS of a gate IV.3.6. speːnz Ha

spear-grass *n* COUCH-GRASS II.2.3. spɪəgɹaːs Sf, spɪəgɹaˑs Nf, spɛˑəgɹæs Nf, spɛˑəgɹaːs Nf

spear-hook *n* a BILLHOOK IV.2.6. spɪəᵗːɾʏk Co

spears *1. n* barley AWNS II.5.3. spɪəᵗːz̩ So

2. npl PEGS used to fasten thatch on a stack II.7.7(a). spɪəᵗːz̩ Co D*[hazel or nutwood x1; willow, hazel, or nutwood x1]*

special *adj* **not too special** ILL, describing a person who is unwell VI.13.1(b). nɒt tuː spɛʃət Ha

speckles *n* FRECKLES VI.11.1. spɛtlz Db, spɛklz Cu La Ch Db St O Nt L, spɛkɫz He Wo Mon O W, spɛkʊz Ess Sx

sped *vi-ed* **has not sped, is not speeded** HAS NOT HELD, referring to a cow that has not conceived III.1.7. **has not sped** avm spɛd Co; **is not speeded** ɪdn spiːdəd Co

speel *1. v* to WHITTLE a stick I.7.19. *-ing* spɪələn Nb

2. n a SPLINTER VI.7.10. spiːl We La Y L, spɪˑᵊl Cu

3. vt to CLIMB VIII.7.4. spiːl Nb*[old x1, up a smooth tree-trunk x1]*

speel up *vtphr* to CLIMB VIII.7.4. spiːl ʊp Nb

speer *v* to ASK IX.2.4. spɪər Cu

spelch *n* a SPLINTER VI.7.10. spɛlʃ Y

spelk *n* a SPLINTER VI.7.10. spɛlk Nb Cu Du We La Y

spelks *npl* PEGS used to fasten thatch on a stack II.7.7(a). spɛlks Y, spɛləks Y*[wooden, 2 feet long x1]*

spell *1. n* a RUNG of a ladder I.7.15. *pl* spɛlz*[round x1]* Y L

2. n a DIAGONAL BAR of a gate IV.3.7. *pl* spɛlz Y

3. n a SPLINTER VI.7.10. spɛl Nb Cu Du La Y Db L, spɛɫ Cu La

spellies *npl* FELLIES, the sections of the wooden rim of a cart-wheel I.9.9. spɛləz Y

spells *npl* the horizontal BARS of a gate IV.3.6. spɛlz Y

speltle *n* a PORRIDGE-STICK V.9.1. spɛltl Nb

spew *1. vi* to VOMIT, referring to an adult VI.13.14(a). spɪʏ La Ch Db, spjʏ So, spɪu Nb La Y Db O Nf Co Do, *-ing* spɪuɪn Sr K Ha, *-ing* spju-ɪn MxL, spɪu Nb*[old x1]* Cu Du We La Y Ch*[when drunk x1]* Db*[old x1]* Sa Wo Wa Gl O Nt L Nth

Hu C Nf Sf Bk Bd Hrt Ess, -*ing* spɪuːɪn Ha, spjuː Nb Du*[old x1]* Sa St*[old x1]* He Wo Wa Mon Gl O Bk So W K Do Ha Sx*[old]*, -*ing* spjuːɪn Y L MxL Sr, -*ing* spjuːwɪn Brk, -*ing* spjuːŋ Brk, *pt* spjuːd L, spɛʊ La St, spʏ: Co D, -*ing* spʏːɪn So, spuː Db St*[old]* Nth Sf Bk Do, -*ing* spuːɪn O Sx, -*ing* əspuˑɪn Ess, 2*prpl* spuːn St, ?*ptppl* spuːd K, spəʊ Nf

2. *vi* to VOMIT, referring to a baby bringing up milk VI.13.14(b). -*ing* spɪuɪn Y, spɪuː Nb Cu L Ess, spjuː So W Do, -*ing* spjʏːɪn So, -*ing* spʏːɪn So, spəʊ Nf

spew back *vtphr* **spew back again** to VOMIT, referring to a baby bringing up milk VI.13.14(b). -*ing* spjuˑɪn ... bak əgɛn Wa

spew up 1. *vphr* to VOMIT, referring to an adult VI.13.14(a). spɪʏː ʊp Ch, spjuː ʌp K, spjuː ʊp Du*[vulgar]*, -*ing* spjuːɪn ʊp St, spʏː ʌp D

2. *vtphr* to vomit. *pt* spɪud ... ʌp Ha, spjuː ... ʌp Mon So, spjuː ... ʊːp Gl, spəʊ ... ʌp Nf, spʏː ʌp D, spʏː ... ʌp D

3. *vtphr* to VOMIT, referring to a baby bringing up milk VI.13.14(b). spʏː ʌp D

spice *n* SWEETS V.8.4. spaɪs Y L, spɑːs Y, spaɪs Db

spicks *npl* PEGS used to fasten thatch on a stack II.7.7(a). spɪks Gl W*[hazel or nutwood x1]* *[not a WMBM headword]*

spider *n* *What do you call that insect that spins a web?* IV.8.9. Eng. ⇒ **arain, attercrop**; ⇒ also **spinny-web**

spikes *n* barley AWNS II.5.3. spəɪks Sx

spile *n* a SPLINTER VI.7.10. spaːl La, spɑːl La, spaɪl La, spəɪl Y

spilk *n* a peg used to fasten thatch on a stack, ⇐ PEGS II.7.7(a). spɪłk Co*[hazel or nutwood]*

spill *n* a SPLINTER VI.7.10. spɪl Sa He, spɪł He

spill back *vtphr* to VOMIT, referring to a baby bringing up milk VI.13.14(b). spɪł ... baːk Gl

spilly *n* LOW-LYING LAND IV.1.7. spɪlɪ Brk *[queried SBM]*

spindle 1. *n* a RUNG of a ladder I.7.15. spɪnl Y, *pl* spɪnlz La, *pl* spɪndłz R

2. *n* the metal BUSH at the centre of a cart-wheel I.9.8. spɪndʊł Brk, spɪndəł O *[queried ir.r. in SBM, u.r. in WMBM]*

3. *n* a LINCH-PIN holding a wheel on a cart I.9.12. spɪndʊł Brk

4. *n* a pin fixing a cart-body to the shafts, stopping it from tipping, ⇐ ROD/PIN I.10.3. spɪndl St *[queried WMBM]*

spindle-hook *n* a ROPE-TWISTER II.7.8. spɪnʃuːkʰ Y

spindles *npl* PEGS used to fasten thatch on a stack II.7.7(a). spɪndłz K*[rods or staples about 2 feet long]*

spindle-shanks *n* DADDY-LONG-LEGS IV.8.10. spɪnlʃaŋks Y

spine *n* the FAT round the kidneys of a pig III.12.7. spaɪn D

spinner *n* a ROPE-TWISTER II.7.8. spɪnə St, spɪnnə Db, spɪnəᵗ Brk, spɪnəᵗ: D

spinning *v-ing* **spinning yarns** GOSSIPING VIII.3.5(a). spɪnɪn jɑːnz Nf

spinning-dicky *n* DADDY-LONG-LEGS IV.8.10. spɪnɪndɪkɪ La

spinning-jenny *n* a ROPE-TWISTER II.7.8. spɪnɪndʒɪnɪ Brk, spɪnɪndʒɛnɪ Nf

spinny-web* 1. *n* a spider's web, ⇐ SPIDER IV.8.9. spɪnɪwɛb Y

2. *n* small dew-covered spider's web on hedges. spɪnɪwɛb Y

spit 1. *n* a SPADE I.7.6. spɪt Nb

2. *vt* to DIG in the garden with a spade I.7.8. spɪt So, *ptppl* əspɪt So, spət So

3. *n* a row or SWATH of mown grass cut for hay-making II.9.4. spɪt L

4. *n* a CUTTING of hay II.9.15. *pl* spɪts Bd

5. *n* a CRANE on which a kettle is hung over a domestic fire V.3.4. spɪt Bk Brk

6. *n* a copy, referring to someone who RESEMBLES someone else VIII.1.9. spɪt Y Ch Wo L Nf K Ha; **spit and image** spɪt ən ɪmɪdʒ Y, spɪt ŋ ɪmɪdʒ Du Y, spɪʔ ŋ ɪmɪdʒ Y

spithey *adj* CHAPPED VI.7.2. spaɪðɪ Ha

spit out *vtphr* to CUT peat IV.4.4. spɪt ... ɛʊt Sx, spɪt ... uːt Y

spits 1. *npl* PEGS used to fasten thatch on a stack II.7.7(a). spɪts Nth*[hazel]* Hu C*[hazel x1]* Bd*[hazel x1, willow x1]* Hrt

2. *npl* the HOOF-MARKS of a horse IV.3.10. spɪts So

spitsies *npl* KNEE-STRAPS used to lift the legs of working trousers VI.14.17. spɪtsɪz Ess *[queried EMBM]*

spitter *n* a SPADE I.7.6. spɪtəᵗ Gl

spitters *npl* SLUGS IV.9.2. spɪtəz Y

spittle 1. *n* a SPADE I.7.6. spɪtł He, spɪtəł He Mon

2. *n* a SHOVEL for a household fire V.3.9. spɪtəl Y

spittle-tree *n* the SHAFT of a spade I.7.7. spɪtłtɹiː Wo

spit up *vtphr* to DIG in the garden with a spade I.7.8. spɪt ... ʌp W Co

splab-footed *adj* SPLAY-FOOTED VI.10.5. splæbvʊtɪd So

splal-footed *adj* SPLAY-FOOTED VI.10.5. splalfʊtɪd Cu

splare-footed *adj* SPLAY-FOOTED VI.10.5. splɛəᵗfʊtɪd Sx

splar-footed 1. *adv* ASTRIDE VI.9.8. splɑᵗːɹfʊtɪd Sx *[marked ir.r. SBM]*

2. *adj* SPLAY-FOOTED VI.10.5. splɑːfʊtɪd Sr Sx

splash *1. n* a FORD IV.1.3. splɛʃ Sr, splæʃ O Sr Sx
2. v to TRIM hedges IV.2.3. splaʃ Cu La Wa Lei Nth, *-ing* splaʃɪn R
3. vt to PLASH a hedge IV.2.4. splaʃ Hrt

splash-board *n* an END-BOARD of a cart I.10.4. splæʃboːʊəᵗd̞ Gl, splaʃboːʊəᵗd̞ Gl

splash-boards *n* a CART-FRAME I.10.6. splæʃbɔːᵊᵗd̞z̞ He *[queried for dash-boards WMBM]*

splasher *n* a HEDGING-BILL IV.2.5. splaʃə Wa O Lei R

splashes *npl* PUDDLES IV.1.6. splɛʃɪz Sr

splashing-hook *n* a HEDGING-BILL IV.2.5. splaʃɪnʊk Wa, splaʃɪnuːk La

splash up *vtphr* to TRIM a hedge IV.2.3. splaʃ ... ʊp Wa

splat *n* a PADDOCK I.1.10. splæt So, splat So, spɫat D

splather-footed *adj* SPLAY-FOOTED VI.10.5. splaðəfʊtɪd Du Y Ch, splaðəᵗfʊtɪd Sa, splɑːðəfɪətɪd Y

splats *npl* LEGGINGS worn over trousers VI.14.18. splats L

splatter-foot *adj* SPLAY-FOOTED VI.10.5. splatəfʊt Lei

splatter-footed *adj* SPLAY-FOOTED VI.10.5. splætəᵗvʊtɪd Gl, splatəfoʊtɪd La, splatəfʊtɪd St Lei, splatəfʊtəd Db

splaudered *adv* ASTRIDE VI.9.8. splɔːðəd Y

splauder-legged *adv* ASTRIDE VI.9.8. splɔːðəlɛgd Y, splɔːðəlɛgd Y

splauder-legs *adv* ASTRIDE VI.9.8. splɔːðəlɛgz Y

splaw *adv* ASTRIDE VI.9.8. splaː Cu

splawdered *adj* SPLAY-FOOTED VI.10.5. splɔːdəd L

splawder-foot *adj* SPLAY-FOOTED VI.10.5. splɔːdəfɪˈət Y

splawder-footed *adj* SPLAY-FOOTED VI.10.5. splɔːdəfɪətɪd Y, splɔːdəfʊtɪd Y L, splɔːdɹfʊtɪd L, splɔːdəɹfʊtɪd Y, splɔːdəfʊtɪd Y

splawdy-footed *adj* SPLAY-FOOTED VI.10.5. splɔːdɪfʊtəd Nt

splaw-foot *adj* SPLAY-FOOTED VI.10.5. splaːfuːt La, splɔːfʊt Db Nf

splaw-footed *adj* SPLAY-FOOTED VI.10.5. splæᵊfiːtɪd Nb, splæːfʊdət Nb, splaːfɪtɪd Cu, splaːfɪʊtɪd Cu, splaːfʊtɪt Nb, splaːfʊtɪd Nb Cu We La Y, splaːfʊtəd Nb Du, splaːfʊdəd Du, splɔːfɪtəd Sa, splɔːfɪətɪd We, splɔːfʌtɪd Sa, splɔːfʊtɪd Y Ch L Lei R Nth Ess, splɔːfʊʔɪd L, splɔːfʊɪtɪd Y, splɔːfʊtəd Db

splawter *vt* to PLASH a hedge IV.2.4. *-ing* splɔːtəɹɪn K, splɔːˡtəɹɪn K

splay *vt* to PLASH a hedge IV.2.4. splɛɪ Sr*[old]*

splayed-footed *adj* SPLAY-FOOTED VI.10.5. spleːdfʌtɪd Sa

splayed hilt* *n* a castrated female pig, ⇐ HOG III.8.8. *pl* splæɪd ɪɫts Gl

splay-foot *adj* SPLAY-FOOTED VI.10.5. spleːfʊt Nb

splay-footed *adj* *[A man who walks like this [indicate pigeon-toed], you say is ....] And the opposite way [indicate splay-footed]?* VI.10.5. spliːfʊtɪd St, splɪˈəfʊʔɪd So, spleːfʌtɪd Sa, spleːfʊtɪd Nb Y Wo Mon, spleːfuːtɪt Ch, spɫeːvʏtəd D, spleɪfʊtɪd Mon Nth, spɫeɪfʊtɪd Ha, splɛɪfʊtɪd Wa Nth K Sx, splæɪfʊtɪd Nth, splaɪfʊtɪd Ess, spɫaɪvʊtɪd Do. ⇒ **bat-footed, bedlam-feet, broad-arrowed, broad-footed, broad-toed, cow-heeled, dew-footed, duck-footed, ducky-feet, flat-footed, four o'clock, goose-footed,** *he turns his feet out a good bit,* **open-toed, pasty-footed, pin-toed, plaw-footed, pratt-footed, pumple-footed, quarter-past-nine, quarter-to-five, quarter-to-four, quarter-to-nine, quarter-to-three, quarter-to-three feet, quarter-to-two, rab-footed, scrabble-footed, scrog-footed, scrush-footed, shovel-footed, skew-footed, sly-footed, slab-footed, splal-footed, splare-footed, splar-footed, splather-footed, splatter-foot, splatter-footed, splawdered, splawder-foot, splawder-footed, splawdy-footed, splaw-foot, splaw-footed, splayed-footed, splay-foot, splay-toed, splod-footed, splother-footed, spraw-footed, sprawl-footed, sprawling-feet, sprawly-footed, sprawly-hocked, sprayed-footed, spray-footed, spread-eagled, spread-feet, sprog-hocked, sprottle-footed, squab-footed, straddle, straddle-foot, straddle-footed, stroddle-footed, swab-footed, sweepy,** *swiping his feet out,* **ten-minutes- to-two, ten to two, timble-toed,** *turn his feet out, turning his feet out,* **turn-toed, web-footed, wem-footed, wednesday-and-thursday, wide-feet, wide-foot, wide-footed;** ⇒ also **dew-dasher, dew-sweeper**

splay-toed *adj* SPLAY-FOOTED VI.10.5. spleːtʊəd Y

spleats *npl* the horizontal BARS of a gate IV.3.6. splɪiːts Sr

spleen *n* the PLUCK of a slaughtered animal III.11.6. spliːn Sa

splet *vt* to PLASH a hedge IV.2.4. splɛt Y

spletch *vi* to CHIP, referring to an egg that is about to hatch IV.6.10. splɛtʃ Y

splice *1. n* a DIAGONAL BAR of a gate IV.3.7. splɔɪs Bk
2. n a SPLINTER VI.7.10. splɛɪs Nb

spline *1. n* a PRONG of a fork I.7.10. spɫaɪn K
2. n a DIAGONAL BAR of a gate IV.3.7. *pl* splʌɪnz Nf

splint *n* a SPLINTER VI.7.10. splɪnt Y Ch Db Sa St He Wo Wa Nth, spɫɪnt D, splɛnt Ch St

splinter *n What do you call a very small piece of wood that has got into your finger?* VI.7.10. Eng exc. Nb Cu Du We C. ⇒ **chip, point, pricker, shive, shiver, slither, sliver, spale, speel, spelch, spelk, spell, spile, spill, splice, splint, spliver,** *spoal* ⇒ **spool, spool, spreel, sprint, stob**

splinters *npl* PEGS used to fasten thatch on a stack II.7.7(a). splɪntəz Ess*[hazel x1]*, splɪn?əz Ess

splints *npl* PEGS used to fasten thatch on a stack II.7.7(a). splɪnts Hrt*[old]*

splish *vt* to PLASH a hedge IV.2.4. -*ing* ʂpɬɪʃən D

splisher *1. vt* to PLASH a hedge IV.2.4. -*ing* splɪʃəᴸɹɪn Sx*[old]*, splɪʃəᵗ Sx
2. v to drive stakes into a hedge to close a gap. -*ing* spliːʃəɽɪn Sr
3. n a stake used to close a gap in a hedge. *pl* spliːʃəᵗz̩ Sr

split *1. adj* CLOVEN, describing the hoof of a cow III.2.8(b). splɪt Nb Cu Du We La Y Man Db Sa St He Wo Wa Mon Gl O Nt L Nth Hu C Nf Sf Bd Hrt Ess MxL Brk Sx, splɪ? L Bk, spɬɪt Gl O W Co Do Ha, spɬɪ? So, splɛt Nb
2. v to TRIM hedges IV.2.3. splɪt Ess *[noted probably ur.r. EMBM]*
3. vt to PLASH a hedge IV.2.4. splɪt Brk

split-hoofed *adj* having a CLOVEN hoof, describing a cow III.2.8(b). splɪtuːvd L *[may refer to animal not hoof]*

split-pin *1. n* a LINCH-PIN holding a wheel on a cart I.9.12. splɪtpɪn Gl Bk, splɪ?pɪn Hrt
2. n a metal linch-pin. splɪtpɪn Sx

splitten *adj* CLOVEN, describing the hoof of a cow III.2.8(b). splɪ?n L

splitten image *n* a copy, referring to someone who RESEMBLES someone else VIII.1.9. splɪ?ɪn ɪmɪdʒ Sx

splitter *vt* to PLASH a hedge IV.2.4. -*ing* splɪtəᴸɹɪn Sr

split up *vtphr* to TRIM a hedge severely IV.2.3. splɪt ... ʌp *[noted probably ur.r. BM]*

spliver *n* a SPLINTER VI.7.10. splɪvə C

splod-footed *adj* SPLAY-FOOTED VI.10.5. splɔdfʊtɪd

splosh *n* a FORD IV.1.3. spɬɒʃ Co

splosher *n* a HEDGING-BILL IV.2.5. splɒʃə O, splɒʃəᴸ O

splother-footed *adj* SPLAY-FOOTED VI.10.5. splɒðəfʊtɪd Db Sa St, splɒðəfʊtəd Db

spoil *vi In hot weather your meat or fish will soon ....* V.7.10. spɒɪl Sa, spɒɪɬ Wo, spɔɪl Y Ess, spɔɪɬ Ess. ⇒ *bad*, **clam,** *fady*, **get** fady, **get** fly-blowed, **get** old, **get** pindy, **get** sticky, **get** taint, **get** tainted, **go all** tainty, **go** bad, **go** fainty, **go** gamy, **go** high, **go** maggoty, **go** mawky, **go** nasty, **go** off, **go** pindy, **go** putrid, **go** quick, **go** rank, **go** rotten, **go** rusty, **go** sapey, **go** sappy ⇒ **go** sapey/seepy, **go** seepy, **go** slimy, **go**

smeeky, **go** sour, **go** stale, **go** sticky, **go** stinking, **go** taint, **go** tainted, **go** tainty, **go** wrong, *hum*, *mawk*, *pindy*, rot, slink, *smell*, *stink*, taint, *tainty*, turn, *turn* bad, *turn* off, *whistle*, *wrong*

spoke *n* a RUNG of a ladder I.7.15. *pl* spɹəks Y, *pl* spɔːks Cu, *pl* spɔʊks Ess, spʌʊk Sf, *pl* spoʊks Wo

spokes *npl [Show a picture of a farmcart.] What do you call these [indicate the spokes]?* I.9.6. Eng. ⇒ **arms, fellies, staves, wheel-spokes**

spone *v* to WEAN a calf III.1.4. spʊən La

spool *1. n* a cotton-REEL V.10.6. spɛʊl St, spɒʊl St, spoːl Sa, spoʊl St, spo·ʊɬ Db, spʊɪl Y, spʊəl Y, spuːl Man Sa St, *pl* spuːlz L, spuːʊ Brk
2. n a SPLINTER VI.7.10. spʊəl Y[old x1]*

spoon *n* a PORRIDGE-STICK V.9.1. spɪʏn Nb, spʊən St, spᴸuːn Db, spɪən Nb Y, spyːn La Ch O So Co D, spɛʊn Db, spʊn Nb Cu Sa Sf Ess, spuːn La Y St Mon Gl Nt L Nth Nf Hrt Ess So W Brk Co Ha

spoonful *1. n* a PINCH of sugar VII.8.6. spuːnfʊl Wo Wa
2. n a LITTLE amount of milk VII.8.20. **a spoonful** ə spuːnfʊl Ch

spoontle *n* a PINCH of sugar or salt VII.8.6. spɛʊntl St

sporrels *npl* PEGS used to fasten thatch on a stack II.7.7(a). spɒɹəlz K

sporring-marks *npl* RUTS made by cartwheels IV.3.9. spɔʁənmaːks Nb

sports *n* a local FESTIVAL or holiday at which sporting competitions take place VII.4.11. spɔːts St Nf, spɔᴮːts Nb, spɔːɘᵗʂ Sr; **sports day** spoəts dɛːᵊ We *[marked u.r. WM/SBM]*

spot *1. n* a DRINK (of milk) given to a kitten III.13.12. spɒt Ch Nth
2. n TREAD inside a fertile egg IV.6.9. spɒt Wa
3. n a LITTLE amount of milk VII.8.20. **a spot** ə spɒt Ch Nt; **a little spot** ə lɪtl spɒt St

spout *n* the GUTTER of a roof V.1.6. spɪʏt Nb*[broad dialect, old]*, speʊt Nf, spɛʊt O L, spæ·at Y, spæʊt St L, spaːt La Y, spaɪt Ch*[old]* St, spaʊt Cu La Y Ch L, spuːt Nb Cu Du We Y L, *pl* spuːts La, spəʊt Y

spouting *n* the GUTTER of a roof V.1.6. speʊtɪn Db Sa Wo Wa O Nth Hu C Bk Hrt Brk, spɛʊ?ɪn Bk Bd, speʊtn C, speuːtɪn Wo, speətɪn Y, spæːtɪn St Nt, spæʊtɪn Ch St He Wo Wa L Lei R, spaːtɪn St Nt Lei, spaɪtɪn Ch St, spaʊtɪn Y Db Sa St Wo Nt L, spʌʊtɪn Y Gl Brk, spuːtɪn Nb Cu We Y Gl, spuːtn Du, spəʊtɪn He Gl W, spəʊːtɪn Wo Gl

sprack *1. adj* ACTIVE, describing a child VIII.9.1. spɹæk So, spɾak W
2. adj quick, bright, clever. spɾæk So, spɾak So

sprad-legged *adv* ASTRIDE VI.9.8. spʁadlɛgd Nb

sprag *1. n* a device used to prevent a cart from going backwards on a hill, ⇐ PROP/CHOCK I.11.2. spɹag Nt L

2. n a device put into the spokes of a wheel to prevent a cart from going backwards. spɹag Nt

3. n a chock placed behind and under a wheel to prevent a cart from going backwards. spɹag Cu

4. n a DRAG used to slow a wagon I.11.3. spɹag Bd

spragger *n* a stick hanging down under a wagon to prevent it from going backwards on a hill, ⇐ PROP/CHOCK I.11.2. spɹægə Hu

sprain *vt When your ankle goes over like this [indicate], what have you done to it?* VI.10.8. Eng exc. We MxL Co Do. ⇒ *acricked, aricked, crab-ankle,* crick, cricked, cowp*ed*, keiked, kink, kink*ed*, put out, ramp*ed*, raxed, rick, rick*ed*, ritching, skench, spray, spring, *sprung* ⇒ spring, strain, strain*ed*, turned, turned over, *turning* ⇒ turned, twined, twined over, twist, twist*ed*, walted, wemble, wrench, wrench*ed*, *wricked* ⇒ rick, wring

sprasey *n* SIXPENCE VII.7.4. spɹɑːzɪ MxL

sprawed-footed *adv* ASTRIDE VI.9.8. spɾɔːdvʊtɪd W

spraw-footed *1. adj* PIGEON-TOED VI.10.4. spɹɔːfʊtɪd La, spɾɔːfʊtɪd So

2. adj SPLAY-FOOTED VI.10.5. spɹɑːfʊtɪd We, spɹɑːvʊtɪd Gl, spɹɔːfʊtɪd O Brk Sr, spɹɔːfʊʔɪd Hu Bk, spɹɔːvʊtɪd Gl, spɾɔːvʊtɪd So W Do Ha, spɾɔːvʊʔɪd W, spɾɔːvʊtəd W Ha

sprawled *adv* ASTRIDE VI.9.8. spɹɔːɬd C

sprawled out *adv* ASTRIDE VI.9.8. spɹɑːld aʊt Y, spɹɔːld əʊt Mon

spraw-legged *adv* ASTRIDE VI.9.8. spɹɔːlɛgd La Y Gl, spɾɔːlɛgɪd So

sprawl-footed *adj* SPLAY-FOOTED VI.10.5. spɾɑːɬvʏtɪd D, spɹɔːlfʌtʔəd C, spɹɔːlfʌʔɪd Bd, spɹɔːlfʊtəd Db, spɹɔːɬfʊtɪd Hrt, spɹɔːɬfʊʔɪd Hu C, spɹɔːɬfʊtəd Sf, spɾɔːɬvʊtɪd W, spɾɔːɬvʊtəd Co

sprawling *adv* ASTRIDE VI.9.8. spɹɑːɬɪn Gl, spɹɔːlɪn Wa, *prppl* spɹɔːlɪn K

sprawling-feet *adj* SPLAY-FOOTED VI.10.5. spɹɔːlɪnfɪit Brk

sprawling out *adv* ASTRIDE VI.9.8. spɹɑːlən aʊt Cu

sprawly-footed *adj* SPLAY-FOOTED VI.10.5. spɹɔːlɪfʊtɪd Ch, spɹɔːlɪfʊtəd Nt

sprawly-hocked *adj* SPLAY-FOOTED VI.10.5. spɾɔːɬi-ɒkt Ha

spray *1. n* KINDLING-*WOOD* V.4.2. spɹæɪ K

2. vt to REMOVE *STALKS* from currants V.7.24. spɹæɪ He, spɹaɪ Wo*[pulling them off the sprays]*

3. vt to SPRAIN an ankle VI.10.8. spɹæɪ He, spɹaɪ Wo

sprayed *adj* CHAPPED VI.7.2. spɾɛɪd W, spɾɛd D, spɾɛɪd Co D; **sprayed up** spɾɛɪd ʌp D

sprayed-footed *adj* SPLAY-FOOTED VI.10.5. spɹæɪdvətɪd O

spray-faggot(s) *n* KINDLING-*WOOD* V.4.2.
no -s: spɹɛɪfɛgət Sx
pl: spɹɛɪfægəts Sr*[old]*

spray-footed *adj* SPLAY-FOOTED VI.10.5. spɹɛːfʌtɪd Gl, spɹɛːfʊtɪd Mon, spɹɛːfʊʔɪd O, spɹɛɪfʌtɪd Hrt, spɹɛɪfʊtɪd Wo Mon Bk, spɾɛɪfʊʔɪd O, spɹɛːɪfʌtɪd Mon, spɹɛːɪfʊtɪd He Wo, spɹɛɪfʌʔɪd Bk Bd, spɹɛɪfʊtɪd Wa O Bd Sr, spɹɛɪfʊʔɪd Nf Bk, spɾɛɪvʊtɪd W, spɹæɪfʌtɪd He, spɹæɪvʌtɪd He, spɹæɪfʊtɪd He Wa Gl Hrt, spɹaɪfʊtɪd Wo

spray-legged *adv* ASTRIDE VI.9.8. spɹɛɪlɪgd Sr

sprays *1. npl* PEGS used to fasten thatch on a stack II.7.7)a). spɹɛːz Brk, spɾɛɪz O, spɹɛɪz Wa*[wooden]*, spɹæɪz O, spɹaɪz Gl*[withies or hazel]*

2. npl pegs used to fasten thatch on a house. spɹɛɪz Bk, spɹæɪz Bk

spray-sticks *n* KINDLING-*WOOD* V.4.2. spɾɛɪstɪks D

spray-wood *n* KINDLING-*WOOD* V.4.2. spɾɛɪwʏd D, spɾɛɪ-yd D, spɹɛɪwʊd Sr*[old x1]* Sx

spread *1. vt* to TED hay II.9.11(a). spɹɪəd Y, spɹɛd Y, spɹɛɪd La

2. vi to show signs of calving, ⇐ SHOWS SIGNS OF CALVING III.1.12(b). *3prprogsg* spɹɛdn Ess; **starts spreading** *3prsg* stɑːəˁːtʂ spɹɪdɪn Sx

3. adj CLOVEN, describing the hoof of a cow III.2.8(b). spɹɛd He Mon

4. vt to LAY the table V.8.12. spɹɪəd Y, *-ing* spɹɛdn Nf

5. adv ASTRIDE VI.9.8. spɹɛd Wa

spread-addled *adv* ASTRIDE VI.9.8. spɾɛdædɬd So

spread-apron *n* a working APRON V.11.2(a). spɹɛdeɪpɹən Ha

spread-bat *n* the STRETCHER between the traces of a cart-horse I.5.11. spɹɛdbɛt K, spɹɛdbæt K

spread-eagled *adj* SPLAY-FOOTED VI.10.5. spɹɛdiːgld St

spreader *1. n* the STRETCHER between the traces of a cart-horse I.5.11. spɹiːdəɹ He, spɹiːdəˁ Sa He Mon Gl, spɾiːdəˁː D, spɹɪdə Wa, spɹɛdə Bk, spɹɛːdəˁ Sa, spɹɛːˡdəˁ Sa Gl, spɹɛdə St He Wa Mon Hrt MxL Sr, spɹɛdəˡ Brk Sr, spɹɛdəˁ Sa He Wo Wa Mon Gl O Nth Bk Brk Sr Ha Sx, spɾɛdəˁ O Ha, spɹɛdəˁː Sa, spɾɛdəˁː So W Co D Do Ha, spɾɛɪdəˁː Co D, spɾadəˁː Ha

2. n a STICK used to support the shaft of a cart I.11.1. spɾɛdəˁː Do *[marked ir.r. SBM; perhaps **spreader** used as stick]*

385

3. n a DIAGONAL BAR of a gate IV.3.7. spɹɛdəᶜ Mon

spreader-bar *n* a movable horizontal rod stretching between the shafts of a cart, fixing them to the cart-body and stopping the cart from tipping, ⇐ ROD/PIN I.10.3. spɹɛdəᶜbaᶜ: Bk

spreaders *n* a SWINGLE-TREE of a horse-drawn plough harness I.8.3. spɹɛdəᶬz Brk *[queried ir.r. SBM]*

spreader-stick *n* the STRETCHER between the traces of a cart-horse I.5.11. spɹɛdəstɪk Lei

spread-feet *adj* SPLAY-FOOTED VI.10.5. spɹɛdfiːt Man

spreading *v-ing* **spreading tales** GOSSIPING VIII.3.5(a). spɽɛdɪn teɪɫz So

spread-staff *n* the STRETCHER between the traces of a cart-horse I.5.11. spɹɛdstaf St

spreathed *adj* CHAPPED VI.7.2. spɹiːðd Mon, spɽiːðd W Ha

spreazed *adj* CHAPPED VI.7.2. spɹiːzd Gl*[old x1]*, spɽiːz W *[queried SBM]*

spreckles *n* FRECKLES VI.11.1. spɽɛklz Cu, spɹɛklz La*[old x1]* Y

spreed *adj* CHAPPED VI.7.2. spɹiːd Gl W*[old]*, spɽiːd D Do Ha *[not a WMBM headword]*

spreel *n* a SPLINTER VI.7.10. spɹiːl L

sprees *npl* CHAPS in the skin VI.7.3. spɹiiz Brk

spretch *vi* to CHIP, referring to an egg that is about to hatch IV.6.10. spɹɛtʃ Y Nt L, spɹætʃ L, spɹatʃ L

spriddle-backs *npl* MINNOWS IV.9.9. spɹɪdɫbæks Hu *[marked u.r. and interpreted as 'stickleback' EMBM]*

spried *adj* CHAPPED VI.7.2. spɽaɪd W Do

sprig *n* a device fixing a cart-body to the shafts, stopping it from tipping, ⇐ ROD/PIN I.10.3. spɹɪg Brk

sprightly *adj* ACTIVE, describing a child VIII.9.1. spʁæɪtlɪ Du, spɽæːɫi D

sprindles *npl* PEGS used to fasten thatch on a stack II.7.7(a). spɹɪntɫz Ess*[hazel]*, spɹɪndɫz Ess*[rare, hazel x1; willow or hazel x1]*

spring *1. vi* to show signs of calving, referring to a cow with a swelling udder, or to the udder, ⇐ SHOWS SIGNS OF CALVING III.1.12(a). *3prprogsg* spɹɪŋɪn La Y Sa Mon O Nt L Lei Nf Bk, *3prprogpl* spɹɪŋɪn Ha, *-ing* spɹɪŋɪn La Ch Wa Gl O Nt Nth Hu Bk Bd, *3prprogsg* əspɹɪŋɪn Wa Gl L C, *-ing* əspɹɪŋɪn Wa Bk, *3prprogsg* spɹɪŋgɪn Wa, *-ing* spɹɪŋgɪn Ch Db St Wa, *3prprogsg* spɽɪŋɪn So W D Do, *-ing* spɽɪŋɪn So W Brk Do, *3prprogsg* spɽɪŋɪn D, *3prprogsg* spɹɪŋən Cu Du We Nf Sf, *3prprogsg* spɽɪŋən D Do, *3prprogpl* spɽɪŋən Ha, *-ing* spɽɪŋən Do Ha, *3prprogsg* spɽɪŋən Co, *3prperfsg* spɹʊŋ L; **spring to calf** *-ing* əspɽɪŋɪn tə kæːf W, *3prprogsg* spɽɪŋən tə kaːf Ha; **spring to calve** *3prprogsg* spɽɪŋɪn tə kaːv D, *3prprogsg* spɽɪŋən tə kæːv; **the**

milk is sprung ðə mɪɫk spɹʊŋ Gl

2. vt **spring (her) udder** to show signs of calving. *3prprogsg* spɽɪŋɪn ʌdəᶜ: D, *3prsg* spɽɪŋz əᶜːɽ ʌdəᶜ: D, *3prsg* spɽɪŋz əᶜːɽ ʌdəᶜ: D, *3prprogsg* spɽɪŋɪn əᶜːɽ ʌdəᶜ: D, *prppl* spɽɪŋən əᶜːɽ ʌdəᶜ: D, *3prprogsg* spɽɪŋən əᶜːɽ ʌdəᶜ: D

3. vi to show signs of calving, referring to the opening of the pelvic bones, ⇐ SHOWS SIGNS OF CALVING III.1.12(b). *-ing* spɹɪŋɪŋ Sr, *3prprogsg* spɹɪŋɪn Ch Mon; **spring behind** *3prsg* spɹɪŋz bɪ-ɔɪnd O

4.1. vi **spring to calve** to be IN CALF III.1.10. *3prprogsg* spɹɪŋɪn tə kaːf Mon

4.2. vt **spring the calf** to be in calf. *-ing* spɹɪŋɪn ðə kaːf Sx *[marked ir.r. SBM]*

5. vi to CHIP, referring to an egg that is about to hatch IV.6.10. spɹɪŋ Nf Sf

6. vt to SPRAIN an ankle VI.10.8. spɹɪŋ L, *-ed* spɹʊŋ Y

7. n If *[you wanted to tell me that something happened]* in the season after winter, *[you'd say: it happened] in....* VII.3.6. Eng; **spring of the year** spɹɪŋ ə ðə jɪə Nt R Nth, spɹɪŋ ə t jɪˑə L, spɹɪŋ ə t jɜᶬːɹ La, spɹɪŋ ə ðə jəᶜ Mon, spɽɪŋ ə ðə jəᶜː So; **the spring of the year** ðə spɹɪŋ əv ðə jɪə Lei, ðə spɹɪŋ ə ðə jɪə Lei, t spɹɪŋ ə t jɪə Y, ðə spɹɪŋ ə ðə jɪəᶜɽ Sx, ðə spɹɪŋ ə ðə ɪəᶜ Sa, ðə spɹɪŋg ə ðə jəᶜ: Wo, ðə spɽɪŋ ə ðə jəᶜ: C; **spring of year** spɹɪŋ ə jɪə Y; **the spring** ðə spɹɪŋ Sa He Wa Gl O L Nth Nf Bk Ess MxL Sr K Ha, ðə spɹɪŋg Wa, t spɹɪŋ Nt, ðə spɽɪŋ W Co D Ha. ⇒ **fore-end** *of the year*, **rise** *of leaf*, **spring** *of the year*, **spring** *of year*, *the* **fore-end** *of the year*, *the* **fore-part** *of the year*, *the* **rise** *of the leaf*, *the* **rise** *of the year*, *the* **spring**, *the* **spring** *of the year*

springers *1. npl* PEGS used to fasten thatch on a stack II.7.7(a). spɹɪŋkəz Ch

2. npl SPRING ONIONS V.7.16. spɽɪŋəᶜːz̩ Ha

springles *npl* PEGS used to fasten thatch on a stack II.7.7(a). spɹɪndʒɫz Ess

spring onions *npl* What do you call them *[i.e. onions]* when they are young and used in a salad? V.7.16. Eng exc. Nb We Man Mon Gl So Co D Do. ⇒ **chibbles, chibblies,** *chibboles* ⇒ **chibbles, chiplets, gibbles, gibblets, gibbons, green onions, little onions, runts, salad onions, scallions, scally-onions, shallots, singled onions, springers, stallions, tripples, young onions;** ⇒ also **tripolis**

springs *npl* loose pieces of skin at the bottom of a finger-nail, ⇐ LOOSE *PIECE OF* SKIN VI.7.11. spɹɪŋz So

spring-tine fork *n* a MUCK-FORK I.3.13. spɹɪŋtɔɪn fɔːk Ess

spring up *1. vtphr* to TIP a cart I.11.6. spɹɪŋ ... ʌp Ess

2. *viphr* to show signs of calving, referring to a cow with a swelling udder, ⇐ SHOWS SIGNS OF CALVING III.1.12(a). -*ing* əspɹɪŋɪn ʌp Hrt

spring-wart *n* a LOOSE *PIECE OF* SKIN at the bottom of a finger-nail VI.7.11. *pl* spʁɪŋwaːts Nb

sprinkle *n* a YIELD of milk III.3.5. spɹɪŋkɫ Hrt

sprinkling *n* a YIELD of milk III.3.5. *pl* spɹɪŋklɪnz Hrt

sprint *1. n* a SLOPE IV.1.10. spɹɪnt Y
2. *n* a SPLINTER VI.7.10. spɹɪnt Ch

sprites *npl* a BOGEY VIII.8.1. spɹʌɪts Nf

sprog-hocked *adj* SPLAY-FOOTED VI.10.5. spɹɒgɒkt St

sprong *n* a PRONG of a fork I.7.10. spɾɒŋ So K, *pl* spɾɒŋz D, spɾʌŋ D, *pl* spɾʌŋz So

sprottle-footed *adj* SPLAY-FOOTED VI.10.5. spɹɒtlfʊtəd Y

spruce *1. n* URINE in a cow-house I.3.10. spɹʏːs Db *[queried WMBM]*
2. *adj* WELL, describing a healthy person VI.13.1(a). spɹɪuːs L

spruce-hole *n* a CESS-POOL on a farm I.3.11. spɹʏːsoːl Db

sprun *n* a DIAGONAL BAR of a gate IV.3.7. *pl* spɹʊnz Db *[queried WMBM]*

sprung up *adj* IN FLOOD, describing a river IV.1.4. spɹʊŋ ʊp L

spry *adj* ACTIVE, describing a child VIII.9.1. spɾəɪ Do

spud *n* a MUCK-FORK I.3.13. spʌd K

spudgel *n* a SCOOP used to take water out of a boiler V.9.9. spʊdʒʊɫ Ha

spud-peelings *n* potato PEELINGS V.7.22. spʌdpiːlɪnz MxL

spuds *1. npl* FORKS used in farming I.7.9. spʌdz Sr K Sx, spʊdz K, spədz Sx
2. *npl* POTATOES II.4.1(a). spʌdz Ess MxL W Sr Sx, spʊdz St Wo Lei Sx, spədz Sr Sx

spunned up *adj* EXHAUSTED, describing a tired person VI.13.8. spʌnd ʌp W

spun out *adj* EXHAUSTED, describing a tired person VI.13.8. spʌn əʊt So

spunyarn *n* TWINE used to fasten thatch on a stack II.7.7(b1). spʌnjən Ess*[oiled, thick]*

spur *1. n* a DIAGONAL BAR of a gate IV.3.7. spəᶜː W Sr Do
2. *n* a BRANCH of a tree IV.12.3. spəˀːz La

spurlings *npl* RUTS made by cartwheels IV.3.9. spɛəlɪnz Du, spœːlənz Du, spɒlənz Nb, spɔːlɪnz Nb, spɔːləns Du, spɔːlənz Nb Du, spoəlɪnz Nb, spəːlɪnz Y, spəːlənz Du

spurns *npl* RUTS made by cartwheels IV.3.9. spɔʁːnz Nb

spurs* *npl* PEGS used to fasten thatch on a stack II.7.7(a). spəˀːz K

spurt *vi* to CHIP, referring to an egg that is about to hatch IV.6.10. spəᶜːț W

spying *v-ing* PEEPING VI.3.8. spaɪ-ɪn Y L, spaɪən Du We, spɑɪ-ɪn MxL, spɒɪ-ən Ha, spɔɪ-ɪn Ess Sx, spɔɪŋ Ess, spʌɪ-ɪn Nf

squab *1. n* a NESTLING IV.7.1. skwɔb K
2. *n* a CUSHION V.2.10. skwɒb K

squabber *n* a NESTLING IV.7.1. skwɒbəᴵ K

squabble *n* a WEAKLING piglet III.8.4. skwɒbəɫ Gl

squab-footed *adj* SPLAY-FOOTED VI.10.5. skwabfʊtəd Db, skwɒbfʊtɪd Sa

squad *n* MUD VII.6.17. skwad L*[old]*

squall *1. vi-3prpl* they MEW, referring to cats III.10.6. skwaːɫ Co D, skwɔːɫz Ha
2. *vi* to SCREAM VIII.8.11. skwaːɫ Gl, swaᶜːɫ Wo, skwɔːl Y Sa, skwɔːɫ Gl So Do Ha, *3prsg* skwɔːɫz Sx

squalling *v-ing* SHRIEKING, describing the shrill noise made by a baby VI.5.15. skwæˑˀlən Nb, skwaːlɪn Y, skwaːlən Nb Cu, skwaːɫɪn Gl, skwaːɫən Co, skwɑːlɪn Wo, skwaːɫɪn He Wo Gl, skwɒɫɪn He, skwɔːlɪn Sa Wa Gl Bk Sr Ha, skwɔːɫɪn So W K Ha, *prppl* skwɔːlən Ha

squall out *viphr* to SCREAM VIII.8.11. skwɔːɫ æʊt W, skwɔːɫ əʊt W

square *1. n* the EAVES of a stack of corn II.7.3. skwɜːᴵ La, skwɜᴵːɹ La
2. *n* a CUTTING of hay II.9.15. skwɛˑə L Lei Sf, skwɛˑəᴵ L, skwaːɹ Du
3. *n* a SLICE of bread V.6.10. *pl* skwɛəɹz Cu
*4. *n* a wrapper worn over a DIAPER V.11.3. skwɛə Ess

square-ender *n* a long stack with square ends, ⇐ STACKS II.7.1. skwɛəɹendə Nth

square ricks *npl* square STACKS II.7.1. skwɛə ɹɪks MxL, *sg* skwɛəᴵ ɹɪk Brk

square stacks *1. npl* long STACKS for hay II.7.1. skwɛː staks Cu
2. *npl* long stacks with square ends. *sg* skwɛə stæk Ess

squat *1. n* a STICK used to support the shaft of a cart I.11.1. skwɒt K
2. *n* a chock, sometimes specially shaped, placed behind and under a wheel to prevent a cart from going backwards on a hill, ⇐ PROP/CHOCK I.11.2. skwæt He, skwat Wo, skwɒt Sa He Wo Mon Sr K Sx
3. *vt* to HIDE something VIII.7.6. skwat La
4. *vi* to DUCK VIII.7.8. skwat Y

squat-bat *n* a device used to prevent a cart from going backwards on a hill, ⇐ PROP/CHOCK I.11.2. *pl* skwɒtbɛts K

squat down *imp* SIT DOWN VIII.3.3. skwæt dæʊn He, skwɒt dɛʊn Sr

squat-roller *n* a device on a chain behind a wheel to prevent a cart from going backwards on a hill, ⇐ PROP/CHOCK I.11.2. skʷɒtɹɒləᴸ K

squat-stick *n* a STICK used to support the shaft of a cart I.11.1. skʷɒtstɪk K

squat yourself down *imp* SIT DOWN VIII.3.3. skwɒt ðɪsɛɫf daʊn So

squawk *1. vi-3prpl* they MEW, referring to cats III.10.6. skwɔːk Bk

2. vi to SCREAM VIII.8.11. skwɑːk He, skwɔːk He O*[old]*

squawking *v-ing* SHRIEKING, describing the shrill noise made by a baby VI.5.15. skwaːkɪn La Ch St*[old x1]*, *prppl* əskwaːkɪn St, skwaːkɪn Mon Sx, *no -ing* skwɑːk Wo, skwɔːkɪn St He Wa Nt So, swɔːkɪn Nt

squawk out *viphr* to SCREAM VIII.8.11. skwɑːk əʊːt Wo

squeaker *1. n* a WEAKLING piglet III.8.4. skwiːkəᵗ So W Do

2. n a NESTLING or a young pigeon IV.7.1. skwiːkə MxL

squeaking *v-ing* SHRIEKING, describing the shrill noise made by a baby VI.5.15. skwiːkɪn Nf

squeal *1. vi-3prpl* they NEIGH, describing the noise horses make in the fields III.10.3(b). skweːtz Gl

2. vi to SCREAM VIII.8.11. skwiːl Nb Y L, skwiːɫ Wo Lei K Co, skwiːᵊɫ He Mon Gl Nth Do, skwɪiːʊ Brk, skwɪəl Y Man St Wa O Nt L, skwɪᵊɫ O, skwɪʊ O Sx, skweːɫ Do, skweːᵊl Ch, skeːᵊɫ Gl, skwɛɪl Wa*[old]*

squealing *v-ing* SHRIEKING, describing the shrill noise made by a baby VI.5.15. skwiːlɪn St Brk Sx, skwiːlən Man, skwiːɫɪn Gl So, skwɪʊɫɪn K, skwɪəlɪn Y L, skweːlɪn So Do, skweːɫən Co, skweːɪlɪn Wo, skwɛːlɪn So

squeeze *vt* to RENDER fat into lard III.12.9. *-ing* skwiːzɪn K

squibs *npl* MINNOWS IV.9.9. skwɪbz L

squiffy *adj* LEFT-HANDED VI.7.13(a). skwɪfi W

squinking *1. v-ing* SQUINTING VI.3.5. skwɪŋkɪn Ess

2. vbln blinking. skwɪŋkɪn Ess

squint *1. adj/adv* SQUINTING VI.3.5. skwɪnt L W K Sx

2. n **having a squint** PEEPING VI.3.8. ɛvɪn ə skwɪnt Y

3. adj ASKEW, describing a picture that is not hanging straight IX.1.3. skwɪnt Cu Nth; **on a squint** ɒn ə skwɪnt Cu; **on the squint** ɒn ð skwɪnt Ch

squint-eyed *1. adj* SQUINTING VI.3.5. skwɪntɒɪd So, skwɪntɔɪd Hrt, skwɪntəɪd W, skwəntæɪd So

2. adj CROSS-EYED VI.3.6. skwɪntiːd Y, skwɪntæɪd So, skwɪntaɪd Cu Y He, skwɪntaɪd Db, skwɪntɒɪd W Do Ha, skwɪntɔɪd Ess, skwɪntəɪd W Sx

squinting *1. v-ing* What is your word for seeing like this [squinting, indicate with your fingers]? VI.3.5.

Eng. ⇒ **cock-eyed, cross-eyed, cross- eyes, cross-ways, gawking, gleeing,** *looking* **boss-eyed,** *looking* **cross-eyed,** *looking* **sideways,** *looking* **skew, peeping, scanning, squinking, squint, squint-eyed, squinty, squinty-eyed, winkly-eyed**

2. prppladj CROSS-EYED VI.3.6. skwɪntɪn Du

3. v-ing PEEPING VI.3.8. skwɪntɪn Cu La Y Ch*[old x1]* Db Sa St He Wo Wa Mon Gl O Nt L Nth Hu So W Sr Co D Do, skwɪnʔɪn O Bk, skwɪnɪn Co, skwɪntn Nb Cu Du We Nf Sf, skwɪntʔn Nf, skwɪnʔn Nf Sf Ess So, skwɪntən Cu Du We D Do Ha, skwɪntʔən Sf, skwɪnʔən Ha, skwɪnən Co, skwəntɪn So

squinting about *viphr-ing* gaping, ⇐ GAPES VI.3.7. skuːnɪn əbəʊt K

squint-roads *adv* DIAGONALLY, referring to harrowing a field IX.1.8. skwɪntɹoːdz Ch, skwɪntɹʊədz Ch

squint-way on *adv* DIAGONALLY, referring to harrowing a field IX.1.8. skwɪntweə ɒn Y

squint-ways *adv* DIAGONALLY, referring to harrowing a field IX.1.8. skwɪntweːz Ch, skwɪntwaɪz W

squinty *1. adj* SQUINTING VI.3.5. skwɪntɪ Ess Ha Sx

2. adj CROSS-EYED VI.3.6. skwɪntɪ Co

3. adj ASKEW, describing a picture that is not hanging straight IX.1.3. skwɪntɪ Nt

squinty-een *adj* CROSS-EYED VI.3.6. skwɪntɪ-iːn Y

squinty-eyed *1. adj* SQUINTING VI.3.5. skwɪntɪ-ʌɪd Sr

2. adj CROSS-EYED VI.3.6. skwɪnɪ-ɔɪd Sf, skwɪnɪ-ʌɪd Nf

squinway-rail *n* a DIAGONAL BAR of a gate IV.3.7. skwɪnweːɹeˑəl Cu

squippies *npl* LEFT-HANDED people VI.7.13(a). skwɪpɪz W

squippy *adj* LEFT-HANDED VI.7.13(a). skwɪpɪ W

squirrel *n* What do you call that friendly little animal with a bushy tail; it skips about in trees? IV.5.8. Eng. ⇒ **grey-mont, scuggy, squirret, tree-rat**

squirret* *n* a SQUIRREL IV.5.8. *pl* skwəɾəts Sx, skəɾət Sx

squitch *1. n* COUCH-GRASS II.2.3. skwɪtʃ Ch Sa St Wo Wa Gl O Nth Bk

2. n HAIR VI.2.1. skwɪtʃ St

squitch-grass *n* COUCH-GRASS II.2.3. skwɪtʃgɹaːs Wa

squittle *v* to WHITTLE a stick I.7.19. skwɪtl Gl

squivver-handed *adj* LEFT-HANDED VI.7.13(a). skwɪvəᵗːɹandɪd Do

stab *n* a RUNG of a ladder I.7.15. stab Y

stabber* *n* a RUNG of a ladder I.7.15. *pl* stabəz L, stabə¹ L *[EMBM treats as staver]*

stabble *vt* to DIRTY a floor V.2.8. stæbʊł Ha

stabbles *npl* the HOOF-MARKS of a horse IV.3.10. stæbʊłz Ha

stable-broom *n* a MUCK-BRUSH I.3.14. stɛɪbʊbɹuːm Sr, stæɪbʊbɹuːm Sx

stable-brush *n* a MUCK-BRUSH I.3.14. steɪbəlbɹʌʃ Nf

stabling up* *1. vphr-ing* FEEDING horses the last meal of the day in the stable III.5.1. *v* stɪəbl ʊp Y
2. vtphr-ing stɪəblɪn ... ʊp Y

stack *1. n* a CLAMP in which potatoes are stored out of doors II.4.6. stak Bd
2. n a HAYSTACK II.9.13. stɛk Sr, *pl* stɛks Db, stæk L Hu Nf Ess, *pl* stæks C Sf, stækʔ Nf, stak Nb Cu Du We La Y Db Sa St L, *pl* staks Ch, ʂtak D*[following [ðəᵗ:]]*
3. n a CHIMNEY V.1.3. stæk So, staːk Brk

stack-bands *n* ROPES used to fasten thatch on a stack II.7.7(b2). stakbanz Y*[coconut fibre]*

stack-bars *npl* HURDLES used to pen sheep in part of a field III.7.11. stakbaːz Y, stakba·ɹz Y

stack-bed *n* the BASE of a stack, made of old planks and tree stumps II.7.4. stakbɛd Y

stack-bottom *n* the BASE of a stack II.7.4. stækbɑːʔm Nf, stækbɒtm Nf*[straw]* Ess, stækbɒtʔm Ess, stækʔbɒtʔm Nf, stækbɒʔm Nf, stækbɒtəm Hu, stækbɒtʔəm Nf*[straw]*, stækbɒdəm Ess, stækbɒtm Ess, stækbɔdəm Ess*[straw x1]*, stækbɔːdʔəm Sf, stakbɒtʊm Ch, stakbɒtʊn St, stakbɒtm La Sa Lei, stakbɒtəm Nb Cu Du We La Y Ch Db Sa*[stones and wood x1]* Nth, stakbɒdm Sa, stakbɒdəm Nb Cu Du We La Y*[straw or thorns]*, stakbɔtəm Y Ch, stakbɔdəm Y, stakbɔðəm Y

stack-brandrick* *n* the BASE of a stack, made of oak beams on 2-foot high supports II.7.4. stakbɹandɹɪ Y

stack-brods *npl* PEGS used to fasten thatch on a stack II.7.7(a). stakbɹɒdz Y

stack-builder *n* a STACKER who makes sheaves of corn into a stack II.6.11. *pl* stɛkbɪʊdəᵗz̩ Sr, stækbɪʊdə¹ Sr, stakbɪldəᵗ Sa

stack-croft *n* the STACKYARD of a farm I.1.4. stakkɹɒft La

stacker *1. n* [*Show a picture of three men unloading a wagon of sheaves in a stackyard.*] *Who is this?* II.6.11. stɛkə Ess, stɛkkə Db, stɛkə¹ Sr K, stɛkəᵗ Sr, stækə Man L Hu C Nf Sf Ess MxL K, stækʔə Nf Sf Ess, stækə¹ Man K, stækəᵗ Brk Sr K Sx, stækəᵗ: So, stakoᴿ Nb, stakə Nb Cu Du We La Y Ch Db St Nt L Lei R Nth Hu C Nf Bd MxL, stakər Cu, stakəᴿ Du, stakɹ L, stakəɹ La Y, stakə¹ We La Db L, stakəᵗ Sa Bk. ⇒ **builder**, **mow-maker**, **mow-man**, **rick-builder**, **ricker**, **rick-maker**, **rick-man**, **stack-builder**, **stack- maker**, **stack-man**

2. n the LOADER of sheaves onto a wagon II.6.7(c). stækəᵗ: So

stacker's mate *n* the FORKER on a wagon who unloads sheaves in a stackyard II.6.9. stækəz mæɪt Ess *[marked u.r. EMBM]*

stack-frame *n* the BASE of a stack II.7.4. stakfɹeːm Sa

stack-garth *n* the STACKYARD of a farm I.1.4. stakgaːθ Cu Y, stakgaᴿ:θ Nb, stagaːθ Cu, staggaːθ We, stagaᴿ:θ Nb Du, stagəθ Nb Du We Y

stack-heed *v* to PITCH sheaves II.6.10. stakhiːd Nb

stacking *v-ing* STOOKING II.6.5. stækɪn He Wo, stakɪn Y Wo W D, stɑːkɪn Gl

stacking-fork *n* a HAY-FORK with a long shaft I.7.11. stakɪnfɔːk Db
2. n a hay-fork with a short shaft. stækɪnfɔ·k Nf

stack-maker *n* a STACKER who makes sheaves of corn into a stack II.6.11. stakmeːkə Ch*[in team of three]*, stakmeːkəᵗ Sa

stack-man *n* a STACKER who makes sheaves of corn into a stack II.6.11. stækmən Ess, stakman Sa Wa, stakmɒn Wa, stakmən St

stack-pins *npl* PEGS used to fasten thatch on a stack II.7.7(a). stakpɪnz Du

stack-plat *n* the STACKYARD of a farm I.1.4. stɛkplɛt K, stɛkplæ·t K

stack-pricks *npl* hazel PEGS about 2 feet long, used to fasten thatch on a stack II.7.7(a). stakpɹɪks Y

stack-prods *npl* PEGS used to fasten thatch on a stack II.7.7(a). stakpɹɒdz La*[hazel]* Y*[often willow, 2 feet long x1; hazel, 2 feet long x1]*, stakpɹɔdz La*[hazel]*

stacks *1. npl* [*Show a picture of some stacks.*] *What are these?* [*Ascertain the names according to size and shape and materials.*] II.7.1. stɛks Db Ess Sr K Sx, stæks La Man*[hay x1]* L C Nf Sf Ess So K Sx, stækʔs Nf, staks Nb Cu Du We La Y*[hay x1]* Ch*[old x1]* Db*[hay and corn x1]* Sa St Nt L Lei R Nth Hu Bk*[corn]*, *sg* stak C
2. npl long stacks. stæks La*[hay and corn]* Man, staks Cu*[corn and hay x1]* La*[corn and hay x1]* Y, *sg* stak Du
3. npl long stacks with rounded ends. stæks Sf, stækʔs Nf*[corn x1]*, staks C, *sg* stak Db*[corn]* L; **round-ended stacks** ɹæʊndɛndɪd staks L
4. npl long stacks with square ends. staks Ch*[corn and hay]*, *sg* stak Db
5. npl round stacks. stɛks Db*[hay and corn x1, corn x1]*, stæks Nf*[corn]* Sf*[wheat, beans]*, *sg* stæk Sf*[straw base]* Ess, staks Cu We*[corn x1]* La*[hay in small quantities x1]* Y Ch*[corn x2, hay and corn x1]* Mon*[small, rare]*, *sg* stak Du*[corn]*; **round stacks** *sg* ɹɛʊn stɛk K, *sg* ɹɛʊnd stæk Nf, ɹɛʊnd stæks Ess*[all grain except barley x1]*, *sg*

ɹɛʊn stæk Ess, *sg* ɹæʊnd stæk Sr, ɹəʊnd stæks Nf*[obsolete]*, ɹɛ:n staks Db*[corn]*, *sg* ɹa:nd stak La*[corn]*, ɹaʊnd staks La, ʁʊnd staks Nb, ru:nd staks Cu*[corn and hay]*, ʁu:nd staks Nb*[corn and hay x1]*, *sg* ʁu:nd stak Du, ɹu:nd staks Cu*[corn x1]* We*[wet hay and corn]* La*[corn]* Y*[corn and hay]* L, *sg* ɹu:nd stak Du, ɹəʊnd staks Y, ɹᵊu·nd stak Ch

6. *npl* square stacks. stæks Sf*[barley]* Ess*[barley and oats]*, stæk?s Nf, staks Ch*[hay and corn]* Mon; **square stacks** *sg* skwɛəᴶ stɛk K*[hay and corn]*, skwɛə stæks Ess, skwɛə stæks Ess, *sg* skwɛə stæk Nf, skwɛ·ə staks L

⇒ **barged-up rick, barn stacks, boat-ended stack, boat-shaped stacks, boat-shape stack, boat stack, bursting-jug, cap-end stack, cob, cocks, coopings, cullis-ender, gable-ended stacks, gable stack, heaks, heak-stacks, hemmels, hip-stack, hummel-ended stacks, long rick, long stacks, mows, oval rick, pikes, ricks,** *round-ended* **stacks, round mow, round ricks,** *round* **stacks, rucks, sow-stacks, square-ender, square ricks,** *square* **stacks, thurran, tovven**

stack-spelks *npl* hazel PEGS used to fasten thatch on a stack II.7.7(a). stakspɛlks Y

stack-staddle *n* the BASE of a stack II.7.4. *pl* stakstɛdəlz Y, stakstadəl Y

stack-stobs *npl* PEGS used to fasten thatch on a stack II.7.7(a). stakstɒbz Y*[wooden, 21 inches long x1; usually hazel, 3 feet long x1]*

stack-twine *n* TWINE used to fasten thatch on a stack II.7.7(b1). staktwaɪn We

stackyard *n [Show an aerial photograph of a farmstead and surrounding fields.] What do you call this?* I.1.4. stɛkja:d Nf, stɛk?ja:d Nf, stɛkjaᴶ:d Db, stɛkja:d Ess K, stɛkja:əɾḏ Sx, stækjæ·ᴶ:d La, stækja:d C Nf Sf Ess, stækjaᶜ:ḏ Sa So, stækja:d Nf Hrt Sr K, stæk?ja:d Nf, stækjaᴶ:d Ess K, stækjaᶜḏ K, stækjaᶜ:ɾḏ Sx, stækja:ə-ᴶd Sr, stækja:əᶜɾḏ Sr, stækjaᶜ:əᶜḏ Sx, stækjəd Nf Ess, stakjɛəᴿd Nb, stakjɛəᴿd Nb, stakjæ:d Du La Y C, stakjæ·ᴶ:d La, stakja:d Nb Cu Du Y Ch Db Sa St Nt L Lei R Nth C Bd Hrt, stakjaᴿ:d Nb, stakjaᴶ:d We La Y L, stakjaᶜ:ḏ Sa Bd, stakja:d St, stakjə·ᴶ:d La, stakjəd Sa, stakjərd Cu. ⇒ **barton, barton- yard, haggard, hay-barton, mow-barken, mow-barton, mow-hay, mow-pen, mow-plat, mow-plot, mow-stead, mow-yard, rick-barken, rick-barton, rickess, rick-fold, rick-park, rickyard, rick-yark, stack-croft, stack-garth, stack-plat**

staddle-bottom *n* the BASE of a stack II.7.4. stadlbɒtəm La

staddled *adv* ASTRIDE VI.9.8. stædʊd Sr*[old]*

staddle(s) *n* the BASE of a stack II.7.4.
no -s: stɛdl Du*[on stone or metal legs]* Y*[straw x1]* L Nf*[iron frame]*, stɛdəl Y, stɛdɫ Lei So K*[faggots]* Ha*[straw, formerly stone, green wood x1]*, stɛ?ɫ

K*[brushwood, bracken]*, stɛdʊ Sr*[wooden platform on steel spikes x1]* K*[stone pillars]*, stædɫ He*[of browse = small branches x1]* Wo So*[hay and brushwood on wooden frame raised on mushroom shaped stones x1]* D*[frame raised on stone pillars x1, brushwood x1]*, stædəɫ Mon Gl, stædʊɫ Gl, stadl La Y Db*[hedge brushings and old straw x1]* Wo Wa Gl*[stones or old straw]* O*[straw, or staddle-stones]* Nt*[old wood and thorns x1, straw and brushwood x1]*, stadɫ Wo Wa*[old x1, for corn x2, stones and beams x1]* Gl O*[very old x1, straw or stones + timber x1]* Lei R So W*[thorns]* Do Ha, stadəɫ Gl, stabᵁɫ W
-s: stɪdʊz Sx*[a stand]*, stɛdlz Nt, stɛdɫz Sr*[lumps of chalk, bricks, iron]*, sta?lz O

staddle-stones* *n* stones, one placed at each corner of a stack, with poles across and faggots underneath, as the BASE of a stack II.7.4. stadlstɔʊnz O

staddling *n* the BASE of a stack II.7.4. steadlɪn Cu, stɛdlɪn La Nt*[straw and brushwood]* L, stædlɪn So, stadlɪn La Y Db Nt*[straw and brushwood]*, stadɫɪn W

staff *1. n* the SHAFT of a spade I.7.7. sta:f Nf
2. *n* the SHAFT of a hay-fork I.7.12. sta:f D
3. *n* a RUNG of a ladder I.7.15. staf Y, stav Y, *pl* stavz Db Nt, stæ:f Sx, *pl* sta:vz Sx. ⇒ also **stave**
4. *n* the adjustable right-hand handle of a horse-drawn plough, ⇐ HANDLES I.8.2. sta:f Sf
5. *n* a STICK used to support the shaft of a cart I.11.1. sta:f Sa

staff-hook *n* a HEDGING-BILL IV.2.5. stæ:fhʊk So Do, sta:fʏk Co D, sta:fʏ:k So D, sta:vʏk D, sta:vʏ:k So, sta:fhʊk So, sta:fʊk So Do

stag *1. n* a mature BULLOCK III.1.16. stæg So
2. *n* a BOAR III.8.7. stæg Sa So
3. *n* a male HOG III.8.8. stɛg Ha, stæg Sa
4. *n* a hog. stɛg D
5. *v* to TRIM hedges IV.2.3. *-ing* stagɪn O, *ptppl* stagd O
6. *v* to trim hedges to within 2 or 3 feet of the ground. stag Bk
7. *v* to trim the tops of hedges. stag Bk

stagged *1. adj* BOGGY IV.1.8. stægd Co
2. *adj* bogged down. stægd Co *[assumed reference to cart]*

staggy *adj* BOGGY IV.1.8. stægi Co

stags *vi-3prsg* he GAPES VI.3.7. sta·gz Wo

stair *1. adj* STEEP, describing a hill IV.1.11. stɪə Db Nth, stɪəᶜ Sa Nth
2. *adj* steep, describing a roof. stɪəᶜ Wa

stake *1. n* a TETHERING-STAKE in a cow-house I.3.3. stɪək Y, *pl* stɪəks Du Sa Gl, ste:k Nb Sa Gl, steɪk So, stɛɪk Lei K
2. *n* the HANDLE of a besom I.3.16. ste:k W,

steɪk K

3. *n* the SHAFT of a hay-fork I.7.12. steɪk D

stake-beetle *1. n* a heavy wooden MALLET I.7.5. steːkbɪtəɬ Mon, steːkbɪtɬ Mon, steːɪkbɪtəɬ Mon, steɪkbiːdʊɬ Sx

2. *n* a wooden MALLET of indeterminate size. steːˡkbɪtəɬ Gl

stake-hedge *n* a HEDGE made of strong thorn stakes and brushwood IV.2.1(a). steɪkɛdʒ Nth

stake-maul *1. n* a heavy wooden MALLET I.7.5. steːkmɑːɬ Wo

2. *n* a wooden MALLET of indeterminate size. steːkmɑːɬ Gl

stake-mell *n* a heavy wooden MALLET I.7.5. steːkmɛl Y

stake-riddle *n* a wooden MALLET of indeterminate size I.7.5. steɪkɹɪdʊɬ Sx *[queried SBM]*

stakes *npl* PEGS used to fasten thatch on a stack II.7.7(a). steːks Gl, steɪks Sf Ess

stale *1. n* the HANDLE of a besom I.3.16. steːl La Ch Db Sa Wo Nt, steːɬ Wo, steːˡl Wo, steːɪɬ He, steːʊɬ Brk, steˑəɬ Bk, stɛɬ D, stɛɪl La Y St Wo Wa, stɛɪɬ Wa Lei R, steɪˀɬ Wa Nth Sf Bk Bd Hrt Ess, stæɪɬ He, staːɬ D, stɔɪɬ Hrt

2. *n* the SHAFT of a spade I.7.7. stiːl Ch St, steːl Ch Sa St Wo, steːɬ He, steːɪl Wo, steːɪɬ He Wo, steɪˀɬ Hrt, stɛɬ D, stɛɪl Y St Wa, stɛɪɬ Ess, staɬ D, stɔɪl Y

3. *n* the SHAFT of a hay-fork I.7.12. steːl Ch Db Sa St Wo, steːɬ Db He O, steɪl Nf, steɪɬ Bd Hrt, steːɪl Wo, steːɪɬ He Wo, steˑəɬ Bk, steːʊ Brk, stɛɪl La Y St Wo Wa, stɛɪɬ Wa Lei R Nth Sf Bk Ess K, stæɪɬ Lei Hrt, staɬ D, staːɬ D

4. *n* a RUNG of a ladder I.7.15. *pl* steɪlz K, *pl* steɪɬz K, stæɪl K, *pl* stæɪɬz K, *pl* stæɪʊɬz K

5. *adj* RANCID, describing bacon V.7.9. steɪʊ Ess

6. *adj* **go stale** to SPOIL, referring to meat or fish V.7.10. guː steːɬ Co

7. *adj* BAD, describing an egg V.7.11. steɪɬ Sx, steɪʊ Sx

stale-furrow *n* FALLOW-LAND II.1.1. stɛɪɬvʊɹʊ Brk

stale(s) *n* URINE in a cow-house I.3.10.

no -s: steɪˀɬ Nth, stɛɪɬ Lei, stɛˑəl L

-s: stɛɪɬz Brk

stalk *1. n* the STEM of a corn-plant II.5.2(a). staɬk Co D, staˑk Nb, staːk Mon Gl O, stɒlk Co, stɒɬk Co D, stɔːk Nb Cu We La Y Man Db Sa Mon Gl O Nt L Lei Nth Ess So W Brk Sr Co D Ha Sx, stɔːg Ha, stɔˤːk Sa, stɔːɬk D, stoʊk St, stɔːˀk Nf Hrt Ess

2.1. *vt* to TOP-AND-TAIL gooseberries V.7.23. staːk Wo

2.2. *v* to top-and-tail gooseberries. staːk Du

3.1. *vt* to REMOVE *STALKS* from currants V.7.24. staːk He Wo, *-ing* stɒkɪn Sa, stɔːk La Y He Wa Lei Nf, *-ing* stɔːkɪn Ha Sx, stɔˤːk Sa

3.2. *v* to remove stalks. stæˀk Nb, staːk Gl, stɔːk We Y Ch Db, *-ing* stɔːkɪn Wa Nth Hu Nf

stalk off *vtphr* to REMOVE *STALKS* from currants V.7.24. stɒɬk ... ɔːf Co

stalk(s) *n* POTATO-HAULMS II.4.4.

no -s: stɔːk We, stɔːɬk D

-s: staːks O, stɔːks Nf So Co D Do, stɔːɬks D

stall *1. n* [*Show a picture of an old-fashioned cow-house.*] *What do you call this?* I.3.1. staːl Nb Du Sa, staːɬ Gl Co D, staː Cu, staːɬ He Wo Mon Gl, staˤːɬ Wo, staːˀ Gl, stɔːl Nb Cu We La Y Man Ch Db Sa St Wo Nt L Nf K, stɔːɬ He Wa Mon Gl O Nth Hu C Nf Sf Bk Bd Hrt Ess MxL So W Brk K Co D Do Ha, stɔˤːɭ Sa, stɔː Nb La Ch He Gl Bk K, stɔʊɬ Ess, stɔːʊ Ess Brk Sr K Ha Sx; **cattle-stall** katlstɔːl Ch; **cow-stall** kɛustɔˑl Nf, kɛustɔːɬ Ess, kɛustɔːʊ Sr, kæustɔːɬ So Do Ha, kaustɔːl St So, kaustɔːɬ So, kɒustɔːɬ W, kəustɔːɬ W. ⇒ **bay, bed, boose, boosing, boost, boosy, box,** *cattle***-stall, cow-crib, cow-pen, cow-pine,** *cow***-stall, cow-stand, cow-standing, crib, pen, place, range, stand, standing**

2. *n* the PARTITION between stalls in a cow-house I.3.2. staːl Du Sa, staːɬ Mon, stɔːl Man Ch Sa St Mon, stɔːɬ Ess, stɔːʊ Brk, stɔˤːɭ Sa, stɔːˀɬ Sf, stʊəl L

3. *n* a device consisting of one fixed and one moving pole, in which a cow's head was fastened in a cow-house, ⇐ TETHERING-STAKE I.3.3. stɔːɬ O

4. *n* a stall in a cow-house, used to store hay, ⇐ HAY-LOFT I.3.18. staːl Du

5. *n* a FASTING-CHAMBER III.11.3. stɔːɬ W Brk

*6. *n* a RUNG of a ladder I.7.15. *pl* stɔːɬz D *[included with* **stale**-*forms in SBM]*

7. *n* a STALLION III.4.4. stæɬ Co

8. *vi* to be RESTIVE, describing a horse III.5.6. *-ing* stɔː-ɪn La, *ptppl* stɔːld St, *ptppl* stɔːd St, *ptppl* stoʊd St

stall-board *n* the PARTITION between stalls in a cow-house I.3.2. stɔːɬbuəˤːd̥ D

stall-boards *n* the PARTITION between stalls in a cow-house I.3.2. stɔːlbɔədz K, stɔːlbɔːˀd̥z Wo, stɔːɬbɔːˀːd̥z So

staller *n* a RESTIVE horse III.5.6. stɔːlɚ La

stallin *n* a TETHERING-STAKE in a cow-house I.3.3. staɬɪn D

stallion *n And* [*what do you call the male colt] when it is fully grown?* III.4.4. Eng exc. Lei R MxL; **horse-stallion** hɒsstæljən Man. ⇒ **entire, entire-horse, horse,** *horse***-stallion, shire-horse, sire, stall, stock-horse, stone-horse, whole-horse, young entire**

stallion-foal *n* a COLT III.4.3. stalɪənfɔːl Ch

stallions *npl* SPRING ONIONS V.7.16. staljənz O

stall-post *1. n* a post supporting the PARTITION between stalls in a cow-house I.3.2. stɔːlpoːst Ch
2. n a TETHERING-STAKE in a cow-house I.3.3. staːɫpoʊst Wo, stɔːɫpoːst Do

stall-posts *n* the PARTITION between stalls in a cow-house I.3.2. stɔːlpoːsɪz Sa

stall-tree *n* a TETHERING-STAKE in a cow-house I.3.3. stɔːɫtɽiː So

stall up *vtphr* to STOCK a cow's udder III.3.6. *prppl* stɔːlɪn ... ʊp Ch

stamp *1.1. vt* to MARK sheep with colour to indicate ownership III.7.9. stamp W D
1.2. v to mark sheep with colour. stæmp Sf, stamp Y Wo Wa Lei Nth D
2.1. vt to mark sheep in some unspecified way. *prppl* stɛəmpn Ess, stæmp Ess, stamp Do
2.2. v to mark sheep. stamp Ha

stanchels* *npl* the JAMBS of a door V.1.11. stɪənʃəls Du, steːndʒəlz Nb, steːnʃəlz Du, steənʃəlz Nb, stɛnʃlz Du, stɛnsɪlz Y

stanchion *n* a TETHERING-STAKE in a cow-house I.3.3. stantʃən Sa

stanchions *n* the PARTITION between stalls in a cow-house I.3.2. stɒnʃənz St *[but marked 'presumably posts' WMBM Edd]*

stand *1. n* a STALL in a cow-house I.3.1. stænd C, stan D, *pl* stanz Bk, stand Nb Du Y Nth
*2. n the PARTITION between stalls in a cow-house I.3.2. stænd Ess
3. n a STICK used to support the shaft of a cart I.11.1. stænd He, stæn He Wo, stand We La St Wo Wa So, stan Sa, *pl* stanz Wa
4. n a SHEARING-TABLE III.7.8. staˑnd Ha
5. v **did not stand**, has not/hasn't stood HAS NOT HELD, referring to a cow that has not conceived III.1.7. **did not stand** dɪdnt stand Wa; **has not stood** aznt stʊd O Hu, ʃɪz nɒt stʊd Mon, hæzn stʊd Ess, ævnt stʊd He, avn stʊd Mon, ænə stʊd He, anə stʊd Gl, ɛzn stʊd K, ɛdn stʊd Ess, ɛɪnt stʊd Hu Ess
6. vi of a cow, to become pregnant, ⇐ IN CALF III.1.10. *3prperfsg* stʊd K
7. vt-2prsg you BEAR pain VI.5.9. stænd Gl K Co Sx, stand Y Sa St*[old x1]* Mon L So, stan Wa L C Bk, stɒnd Wo

standard *1. n* a TETHERING-STAKE in a cow-house I.3.3. stændəˡːɽd̩ Sx
2. n a pin fixing a cart-body to the shafts, stopping it from tipping, ⇐ ROD/PIN I.10.3. standəd Nb Du
3. n a SALTING-TROUGH III.12.5. stændəˡːd̩ D
4. n the HANGING-POST of a gate IV.3.3. stæˑndəᴵˑd Brk

standard-post *n* the HANGING-POST of a gate IV.3.3. stɛndədpoʊst Ess

standards *1. npl* the posts at the corners of a cart, ⇐ CART-LADDERS I.10.5. stɛndədz K
2. npl the JAMBS of a door V.1.11. stɛndəˡd̩z̩ Sr

stand by *vphr* to AGREE *WITH* somebody VIII.8.12. stɛnd bɔɪ Ess, stand baɪ St, stand bɒɪ Db, stan baɪ Ch, stan bɒɪ So, stɒnd bəɪ Gl, stɒn baɪ Ch

stander *n* a pin fixing a cart-body to the shafts, stopping it from tipping, ⇐ ROD/PIN I.10.3. *-s* standəᵏz Nb

standing *1. n* a STALL in a cow-house I.3.1. stænɪn Wa Hu, stændɪn Wo Wa Sr, stanɪn Y Db Wa O Nt L Lei R Nth Bk, standɪn Y Ch Db St He Nt Lei Bd Hrt, stanən L, standən Nb L
2. n the PARTITION between stalls in a cow-house I.3.2. stændɪn Wa Brk, stænɪn Wa, stæːndɪn Ess, standɪn St Bd, standən Y, stanɪn Y Wa O Nt Lei R
3. n the partition between stalls in a stable. *pl* stanɪnz O
4. n a stall in a cow-house, used to store hay, ⇐ HAY-LOFT I.3.18. stanɪn L R, stanən L

standing-board *n* the PARTITION between stalls in a cow-house I.3.2. *pl* stanɪnbɔːdz Lei R, *pl* stanənbɔːdz L, standɪnbɔːᵊd Lei, stanɪnbɔːᵊd Lei, stanɪnbʊəd Y Nt L, *pl* stanɪnbʊədz Lei, stanənbʊəd L, standɪnbuːᵊd Lei, stanɪnbuːᵊd Lei

standing-parting *n* the PARTITION between stalls in a cow-house I.3.2. stanɪnpaːtɪn Y

standing-post *1. n* the PARTITION between stalls in a cow-house I.3.2. stanɪnpoːst Nt, stanɪnpʊəst L
2. n a TETHERING-STAKE in a cow-house I.3.3. stanɪnpoʊs Lei, stanɪnpʊəst Y

standjuice-well *n* a CESS-POOL on a farm I.3.11. stændʒuːswɛl Ess

stand-leg *n* a STICK used to support the shaft of a cart I.11.1. stanlɛgːⁿ La

standle-pin *n* a pin fixing a cart-body to the shafts, stopping it from tipping, ⇐ ROD/PIN I.10.3. standlpɪn Nb

stand-post *n* the HANGING-POST of a gate IV.3.3. stanpʊəst L

stand-side *n* the PARTITION between stalls in a cow-house I.3.2. stansaɪd Y

stand-to-work-man *n* a FARM-LABOURER I.2.4. stantəwəˡːkman D, stantəwəˡːkmən D

stang *n* a SHAFT of a cart I.9.4. staŋ Cu We La Y

stangs *npl* the SHAFTS of a cart I.9.4. staŋz Cu We La Y

stank *1. n* URINE in a cow-house I.3.10. staŋk Y
2.1. vt to STOCK III.3.6. *-ing* stæŋkɪn He Wo, staŋk Sa Wo, *-ing* staŋkɪn He
2.2. v to stock. stæŋk Sa He Gl, *-ing* stæŋkɪn He

Wo Mon, staŋk Sa Wo Mon Gl, -ing staŋkɪn St Mon

stank up *1. vtphr* to STOCK III.3.6. -ing staŋkɪn ... ʌp Sa, -ing staŋkɪn ... ʊp Wa

2. vphr to stock. *pt* staŋkt ʊp Wa

stannicles *npl* MINNOWS IV.9.9. stænɪklz Nf [*marked u.r. and interpreted as 'stickleback' EMBM*]

stan-sickles *npl* MINNOWS IV.9.9. stænsɪklz Nf [*marked u.r. and interpreted as 'stickleback' EMBM*]

stap *1. n* a RUNG of a ladder I.7.15. *pl* staps Cu We

2. n the iron stay connecting the beam with the side of a cart, ⇐ CROSS-BEAM END I.10.1. stɛp Y

staple *1. n* a TETHERING-STAKE in a cow-house I.3.3. steːpł W Ha

2. n a staple used in place of the *HORIZONTAL* BAR of a crane over a domestic fire V.3.5(a). stæɪpł Ess

star-bone naked *adj* NAKED, describing a person VI.13.20. staːbʌn nɛɪkɪd Sf

stares *vi-3prsg* he GAPES VI.3.7. stɛːz St Mon, stɛˤːz̩ So, *prppl* stɛˤːɾən Co, stjɛᵊrs Man, -ing stɛəɹɪn Y Ess K, -ing stɛəɾɪn O

stark-bellied *adj* NAKED, describing a person VI.13.20. staːkbalɪd Ch

stark-bellied-naked *adj* NAKED, describing a person VI.13.20. staːkbalɪdneːkɪd Ch

stark-belly-naked *adj* NAKED, describing a person VI.13.20. staɹkbɛlineˡːkɪd He, staˡːkbalɪneːkt Db

stark-naked *adj* NAKED, describing a person VI.13.20. stæːkneɪkəd Man, staːkneːkɪd Ch, staˤːkneːkɪd Wa, staːkneɪkɪd Hrt, staˤːkneˑəkɪd Bk, staːkneɪkɪd L, staːknɛˑəkəd L, staˤːkneːəkɪd So, staːknæɪkɪd MxL, stæˡːkneːkt La, staːknɪəkt Y, staːkneːkt Y Db Nt, staːkneəkt Y, staːkneəkt Y L, staˡkneˑəkt L, staːkneəkt Y, st3ˡːkneːkt La

star-naked *adj* NAKED, describing a person VI.13.20. stæːneɪkɪd C, staˤːneˑəkɪd Bk, staːneɪkɪd Ess, staːnɛɪkɪt Sf, staːnɛɪkəd Sf, staˑneɪkɪd Nf

stars *npl* What can you see in the sky on a clear night? [*Ascertain the existence of* **stern**.] VII.6.3(a). Eng. ⇒ **starn** ⇒ **stern**, stern

start *1. imp* the command GO ON!, given to plough-horses II.3.5(d). stʌt Sf

2. n a DIAGONAL BAR of a gate IV.3.7. stəˤːt̩ Co

start-naked *adj* NAKED, describing a person VI.13.20. staːtneːkɪt Ch, staːtneɪkɪd Hrt, staˤːt̩neɪkɪd Bk

start on *imp* HELP YOURSELVES!, said to invite visitors to eat V.8.13. staˤːt̩ ɔːn Ha

starts *vi-3prsg* school BEGINS VIII.6.2(a). Eng exc. We Hu Sf Do

starved *1. adj* very HUNGRY VI.13.9. staˤːvd Ha

2. adj COLD, describing a person VI.13.18. stæːvd Du, stæˡːvt La, stæˡːvd La, staːvt We, staːvd Nb Cu Du We Y Ch Db Sa St Wa Nt L Nth Hu, staᴮːvd Nb Du, staˡːvt La, staˡːvd We La Db, staˤːvd Sa Wa Gl Nth, staˤːd̩ Wa, staːvd Man St Wo Nf, st3ˡːɹvt La, st3ˡːɹvd La, stəˤːvd Sa; **starved to death** stavd diəθ St

3. adj VERY COLD, describing a person VI.13.19. staːɹvd Y He, staːvd Y Sa St Lei R, staˡːvd La, stɑːvd Lei R; **starved stiff** stavd stɪf St, staᴮːvd stɪf We; **starved to dead** staːvd tɪ dɪəd Y, staːvd tə dɪəd Y Nt L, staːvd tə dɛd L Nth, staːrvd tə diːd Cu; **starved to death** stæːvd tə dɪəθ La, stæːvd tə dɛθ Du, stæˡːvd tə dɪəθ La, stæˡːɹvd t dɪʊθ La, stavt ʔ diːθ Ch, stavd ʔ diːθ Db, staːvt tə dˡiːθ Y, staːvd tə diːθ Nb Cu Du We Db, staːvd ʔ diːθ Db, staːvd tə dɪəθ Y Nt L, staːvd tə dɛθ Du Ch Db Wa Nt Nth Hu, staːvd tə dɛf Mon, staːvd tə dʒɛθ Ch Wo, staːd tə dʒɛθ Sa, staːvd tə djɛθ Wa, staːvd tə dʒʌθ He, staːvd tə dʒəθ Gl, staːvd tə djəθ Wa, staːvd tə dəɪθ Y, staᴮːvd tə diːθ Nb Du, staˡːvd tə dɪəθ La, staˡːvd ʔ dɛθ Db, staˤːvd tə dɛθ Sa Mon, staˤːvd tə dʒɛθ Sa He Wa, staˤːvd tə djɛθ Wo Nth, staˤːvd tə dʒʌθ Sa, staˤːvd tə dʒʊθ Gl, staˤːd̩ tə dʒʊθ Wa, staˤːvd tə djʊθ Gl, staˤːvd tə dʒəθ Gl, staːvd tə dɛθ MxL, staːvd tə dʒɛθ Wo, staːvd tə dʒʊθ He, staˤːvd tə dʒˡɛθ Wo, staˤːvd tə dʒʌθ He, staˤːvd tə djʊθ He, st3ˡːɹvd tə dɪəθ La, staˤːvd tə dɛθ He, staˤːvd tə dʒʊθ Wo, staˤːvd tə dʒəˤːθ Wo; **starved to death with cold** staːvd tə dɛθ ə kɔʊłd Hu; **starved to the bone** staːvd tɪ t boːn Du; **starved to the death** stæˡːvt tə ʔ dɪəθ La, staːvd tə tʔ dɪəθ Y, staˡːɹvd tə ʔ dɪəθ La, st3ˡːɹvt tə ʔ dɪəθ La

starved out *adj* VERY COLD, describing a person VI.13.19. staːvd uːt Y

starved through *adj* VERY COLD, describing a person VI.13.19. staːvd θɹʊf L

starved up *adj* VERY COLD, describing a person VI.13.19. stæˤːd̩ ʌp O, staˤːvd ʌp Mon

starven *adj* **starven to death** VERY COLD, describing a person VI.13.19. staːvnt tʔ dɪəθ Ch [*compare* **starving (to death)**]

starve-naked *adj* NAKED, describing a person VI.13.20. staːvneɪkɪd Bd, staːvnɛɪkɪd C, stæːvneːkt La, staːfneakt We, staˡːfneˑakt La, staˡːvneakt La

starving *1. adj* HUNGRY VI.13.9. staːvɪn Ess, stəˤːvɪn W

2. adj COLD, describing a person VI.13.18. staːvn Cu, staːvən Nb, staᴮːvən Nb

3. adj VERY COLD, describing a person VI.13.19. staˤːvɪn Sa O; **starving cold** staːvɪn koːłd Mon; **starving to death** staːvn tə diːθ Cu

starving-pen *n* a FASTING-CHAMBER III.11.3. staˡːvɪnpɛn O, staˤːvɪnpɛn Bk [*see note at* **fasting-chamber**]

starving-place *n* a FASTING-CHAMBER III.11.3. staːvɪnpliːs Ch

statute(s) *n* a local FESTIVAL or holiday at which workers were hired VII.4.11.

no -s: stætɪ Ess, staʔɪ Bd[*old, no reference to*

hiring]

-*s*: statʃits St, statɪs Y Nt, statəs L Hu

staums* *n* POTATO-HAULMS II.4.4. stɔːmz Wa

staup-holes *npl* the HOOF-MARKS of a horse IV.3.10. stʊʊphʊəlz Du, stɔːpɔɪlz Y *[see note at* **horse-staupings***]*

staupings *npl* the HOOF-MARKS of a horse IV.3.10. staːpɪnz Y *[see note at* **horse-staupings***]*

staups *adj* STUPID VI.1.5. stɔːps Du

stave *1.* *n* the HANDLE of a besom I.3.16. steˑɪv Ha
2. *n* a RUNG of a ladder I.7.15. stiːv Db, steːv Sa Nf Co, *pl* steːvz Y Ch Db St Nt D, steɪv Nf, *pl* steɪvz Db C, steːvz Co Sx, *pl* steˑəvz L, steɪv Lei Nf Sf Ess K, *pl* steɪvz St Nth Sx, stæɪv Ess, stav Y, *pl* stavz Db Nt. ⇒ also **staff**
3. *n* the right-hand handle of a horse-drawn plough, ⇐ HANDLES I.8.2. steɪv Ess
4. *n* the SHAFT of a scythe II.9.7. steːv W
5. *n* a DIAGONAL BAR of a gate IV.3.7. steːv Sa

stavel *n* the BASE of a stack II.7.4. stavɫ Gl*[wood and straw]*, stavəɫ W*[on stavel stones x1]*

staves *1.* *npl* the SPOKES of a cart-wheel I.9.6. steɪvz Ess
2. *npl* the horizontal BARS of a gate IV.3.6. steːvz Y, steɪvz St

stavver* *n* a RUNG of a ladder I.7.15. *pl* stavəz L R, stavəˡ L, stavɹ L

stay *1.* *vi [What do good people do on Sunday?]* But some lazy people like to read the Sunday papers, and so they ... at home. VIII.5.2. steː La Y Sa He W Brk D, -*s* steːz Mon, steɪ Y Wa Mon O Bk So W Ha, steː Y, steɪ St Wa Lei R Bk Ess Brk Sr K Ha Sx, -*s* steɪz Brk Sx, steə Y, stæɪ He Nf Ess K, staɪ So. ⇒ **bide** *home*, **bide** *at home*, **cower** *at home*, **keep** *at home*, **lop** *about home*, **set** ⇒ **sit**, **sit** *at home*, **stay** *home*, **stay** *at home*, **stay** *by home*, **stop** *home*, **stop** *at home*, **stop** *in*, **are stopped** *at home*
2. *n* a TETHERING-STAKE in a cow-house I.3.3. steː La, *pl* steːᵊz Nb, steɪ Wa, stæɪ Nf Ess
3. *n* a RUNG of a ladder I.7.15. *pl* steɪz R, *pl* stæɪz K
4. *n* the iron stay connecting the beam with the side of a cart, ⇐ CROSS-BEAM END I.10.1. steː Nb, *pl* steːz Y, *pl* steːᵊz Du, stæɪ Sr K *[forms at He and Sr/K interpreted as relevant: WMBM marks u.r., SBM includes as* **cross-beam end***]*
5. *n* a BUMPER of a cart I.10.1(a). *pl* stˡiːz Lei, *pl* steːz W, stɛˑɪ Lei
6. *n* a device fixing a cart-body to the shafts, stopping it from tipping, ⇐ ROD/PIN I.10.3. steɪ St
7. *n* a STICK used to support the shaft of a cart I.11.1. steː Y*[not locally]*, steɪ So Ha, steɪ Sx, staɪ W Do
8. *n* the GRASS-NAIL of a scythe II.9.9. steː Nb, steɪ So, steː W, steɪ W, stæɪ Gl
9. *n* a DIAGONAL BAR of a gate IV.3.7. steː Y Sa

Mon, *pl* steːz Nb Db, steɪ So, *pl* steɪz C Bd, steːɪ Wo So, *pl* steːɪz Gl, *pl* steˑəz La Y, steː W, *pl* steːz We, steɪ Sa Lei Nth Ess W Co, *pl* steɪz L Hu Brk, *pl* steəz Y L, stæɪ Gl Sf, *pl* stæɪz Nf, staɪ Wo W Do Ha, *pl* staɪz Gl Nf

stay-bar *n* a DIAGONAL BAR of a gate IV.3.7. stɛɪbaˡː W

stay-iron* *n* the iron stay connecting the beam with the side of a cart, ⇐ CROSS-BEAM END I.10.1. steː-aɪən Y

stay-rod *n* a DIAGONAL BAR of a gate IV.3.7. *pl* steˑɔɹdz L

stays *1.* *n* the BREECH-BAND of the harness of a cart-horse I.5.10. steːz Cu, steːz Cu We, steːs Cu
2. *npl* CART-LADDERS I.10.5. steːz Y

stay-stick *n* a STICK used to support the shaft of a cart I.11.1. stɛɪstɪk D

stay with *vtphr* LOOK AFTER VIII.1.23. steɪ wɪð Sx

stead *n* the BASE of a stack II.7.4. stiːd Co*[wooden platform on short granite posts x1, made of browse = brushwood x1]*, steːd Co

steading *n* a FARMSTEAD I.1.2. stiːdɪn We, stɛdn Nb

steal *1.* *vi-3prpl* What do burglars do? They break into houses and .... VIII.7.5(a). Eng. ⇒ **pinch**, **rob**, *stealen*, *steals*
2. *vt-3prpl [What do burglars do? They break into houses and ....]* So you can say: We ordinary people buy the things we need, but *[burglars]* ... *[them]*. VIII.7.5(b). Eng. ⇒ **pinch**, *steals*, **thieven**
3. *n* the HANDLE of a besom I.3.16. stiːl Nb Ch Db St, stiːɫ He Hu, stɪʊ Ess, stɪəl La Y
4. *n* the SHAFT of a hay-fork I.7.12. stiːl Ch St, stiːɫ He Wo Mon Lei, *pl* stiiːɫz Ess, stɪəl La St,
5. *n* the SHAFT of a scythe II.9.7. stɛɪl La

steals *npl* the JAMBS of a door V.1.11. stəɹᵊɫz W

steam *1.1.* *vt* to STOCK III.3.6. -*ing* stɛɪmɪn Y
1.2. *v* to stock III.3.6. -*ing* stɛmɪn Y
2. *n* MIST VII.6.8. stɛm Wo

steam up *1.* *vtphr* to STOCK a cow III.3.6. -*ing* stiiːmɪn ... ʌp Sx, stɪəm ... ʊp La, stɛɪm ... ʊp Y
2. *vphr* to stock. *ptppl* stɪəmd ʊp Y

stean *1.* *n* a BREAD-BIN V.9.2. stiːn Sa St He Wo, stiːən Sa, stɪən He, steːn Sa*[old]* D
2. *n* a container for butter. steːn D

stecked *adj* RESTIVE, describing a horse III.5.6. stɛkt We La Y

stedding *n* the BASE of a stack II.7.4. stɛdɪn Y

stee *1.* *n* a LADDER I.7.14. stiː Nb Cu Du We La Y L, stɛɪ Y, staɪ Y, stɔɪ We Y
2. *n* a STILE IV.2.9. stiː Cu We La Y

stee-hole *n* a STILE IV.2.9. stiː-ɒɪl Y, stiː-ɔɪl Y, stiː-oːl Db

steel* *n* a STILE IV.2.9. stiːl Cu La Y Man L

steel-casing *n* the metal BUSH at the centre of a cart-wheel I.9.8. stɪiːʊkɛɪsn Ess

steel-chain *n* a chain which, together with a neck-chain, comprises a tether or headstall, ⇐ TETHER I.3.4. stɪˈəɫtʃɛɪn Ess

steel-hole* *n* a STILE IV.2.9. stiːlɔɪl Y, stiːloːl La

steel-plates *n* the metal BUSH at the centre of a cart-wheel I.9.8. stiːlpleːᵊts Ch

steen *n* a SALTING-TROUGH in which ham is cured in brine III.12.5. stiːn Wo

steep *1. adj* If the road up a slope is not like this [indicate gentle rise], but like this [indicate steep rise], you say it is .... IV.1.11. stiːp Nb Cu Du La Y Man Ch Db Sa St He Wo Wa Mon Gl O Nt L Lei R Nth Hu C Nf Sf Bk Bd Hrt Ess MxL So W Sr K Co D Do Ha, stɪip Y Nf Ess Brk K Ha, stɪiːp Y Sa Wo Wa Mon Gl Nt L Nf Ess Brk Sr Sx, stᵊiːp Sf Bk Bd Hrt Ess, stɪəp La Y Db L, steːp Ch Gl O So W D Do Ha, steɪp Du Ess, stɛːp W D, stɛɪp La Ch Db St D, stəɪp We Y. ⇒ *a bit* **plumb, banky, brant, cleeve, clifty, heavy, hilly, sharp, sideling, stair, steepy, steepy** *sideling,* **stickle, stiff, stunt, upright,** *very* **steepy**

2. vt to PLASH a hedge IV.2.4. stiːp D

3.1. vt to BREW tea V.8.9. stiːp La Co, *-ing* stiːpɪn Mon W

3.2. v to brew tea. stiːp Wa*[modern]* Bk MxL, *-ing* stiːpɪn Co

steep down *vtphr* to PLASH a hedge IV.2.4. stiːp ... dæʊn D

steepers* *npl* boughs laid horizontally when hedging, ⇐ to PLASH IV.2.4. stiːpəᵗːz D

steeping-hook *n* a BILLHOOK IV.2.6. stiːpɪnyk D

steep-skin *n* RENNET V.5.6. stiːpskɪn St

steepy *adj* STEEP, describing a hill IV.1.11. stiːpi So; **very steepy** vɛɹi stɪəpɪ Y; **steepy sideling** stiːpi zæɪdlɪn So

steer *1. n* a BULLOCK III.1.16. stɪɔᴿ Nb, stɪə La Y St Gl Nt L Lei Nth Nf Sf Bk Ess K, stɪəɹ He, stɪəᴵ Y L Brk Sr K, stɪəᵗ Gl O Brk Sr Ha Sx, stɪəᵗɾ Ha Sx, stɪəᵗː So W Co D Do Ha

2. n a young bullock or bull-calf. stɪə Y Nt L Nth Hu C Nf Bk Bd Ess Sr, stɪəᴵ Sr, stɪəᵗ Wa O Nth Bk, steˈə Nf, stɛˈə Nf, *pl* stɛˈəz Nt

3. n a mature bullock. stɪə Y Nf, stiːəᵗ Gl, stjəᵗː Gl *[detail of data varies between BM volumes]*

4. n the SHEATH of skin covering the penis of a horse III.4.9. stɪə Nf

steer-calf *n* a young BULLOCK III.1.16. stɪəkaːf Nth, stɪəkaːv Nf, stɪəɹkaːv He, stɪəᵗːkæːf So

steered *v-ed* CASTRATED, describing a bullock III.1.15. stɪəᵗːd̩ So

stee-spell *n* a RUNG of a ladder I.7.15. *pl* stiːspɛlz Y

stee-step *n* a RUNG of a ladder I.7.15. *pl* stiːstɛps Y

steeved *adj* VERY COLD, describing a person VI.13.19. stiːvd Co; **steeved with the cold** stiːvd wɪ də koːɫ Co

steg *n* a GANDER IV.6.16. stɛg Nb Cu Du We La Y

stelch *1. n* a TETHERING-STAKE in a cowhouse I.3.3. stɪlʃ Sa, stɛltʃ St, stɛɫtʃ He, stɛlʃ Sa He Wo, stɛɫʃ He, stəɫtʃ Wo

2. v to STOCK III.3.6. *-ing* stɛltʃɪn Sa

stell *1. n* a POOL on a farm III.3.9. steˈəl Y

2. n a RIVULET IV.1.1. stɛl Du

3. n an open drain. stɛl Y

steller *n* a SHEATH or other device used to keep a knitting-needle firm V.10.10. stɛlə Nt

stem *1. n* What do you call the parts of the fully-grown plant (of corn, except peas and beans) while still green? There's the root and the .... II.5.2(a). stem Nf, stɛm Nb Cu Du We La Y Ch Db Sa St He Wo Wa Mon Gl O Nt L Lei R Nth Hu Nf Sf Bk Bd Hrt Ess So W Sr K Co D Do Ha Sx, stɛːm He Wo Gl, stɛᴵm Sf Ess, stɑːm Wo, stɒm Wo. ⇒ **blade, flag, foliage, green straw, runner, shank, shoot, stalk,** *stam* ⇒ **stem, stock, stool, strand, straw, straw-stem**

2. n a tree STUMP IV.12.4. stɛm Sx

3. n the HANDLE of a besom I.3.16. stɛm So Do

*4. n the STRETCHER between the traces of a cart-horse I.5.11. stɛm Ch.

5. n the SHAFT of a spade I.7.7. stɛm So D Do

6. n the SHAFT of a hay-fork I.7.12. stɛm So Do

7. n the body of a stack, ⇐ BASE II.7.4. stɛm W Brk Sr D Ha Sx, stæm Sx

8. n the SHAFT of a scythe II.9.7. stɛm Ess

9.1. vt to REMOVE *STALKS* from currants V.7.24. stɛm So D, *-ing* stɛmɪn W Do, *-ing* stɛmən Co

9.2. v to remove stalks. *-ing* stɛmɪn Ha

10. v to STOCK III.3.6. stɛm La

stem up *vphr* to STOCK III.3.6. stɛm ʊp Y

stend *n* the STRETCHER between the traces of a cart-horse I.5.11. stɛn La Ch St

step *1. n* the CURB-STONE in a cow-house I.3.9. stɛp Nb La Wa Nt L Ess

2. n a RUNG of a ladder I.7.15. stɛp Nf, *pl* stɛps Cu Du We La Y*[flat x1]* Wa*[flat x1]* L

3. n the CROSS-BEAM END of a cart I.10.1. stɛp Ess

4. n the THRESHOLD of a door V.1.12. stɛp Sa He Wo*[cement x1]* Mon Lei So Sr Co

step-board *n* the THRESHOLD of a door V.1.12. stɛpbʊəd Y

step-father *n* a LOOSE *PIECE OF* SKIN at the bottom of a finger-nail VI.7.11. *pl* stɛpfaðəz Y

step-holes *npl* the HOOF-MARKS of a horse IV.3.10. stɛpoːɫz W

step-ladder *n* a STILE IV.2.9. stɛpladə Bd, stɛpladəˤ W

step-mother *n* a LOOSE *PIECE OF* SKIN at the bottom of a finger-nail VI.7.11. stɛpmʊðə La Y

stepmother-jack* *n* a LOOSE *PIECE OF* SKIN at the bottom of a finger-nail VI.7.11. *pl* stɛpmʊðədʒaks Y

stepmother-jag *n* a LOOSE *PIECE OF* SKIN at the bottom of a finger-nail VI.7.11. stɛpmʊðədʒag La Y, stɛpmʊðəᴶdʒag La

stepmother's blessing *n* a LOOSE *PIECE OF* SKIN at the bottom of a finger-nail VI.7.11. stɛpmʊðəz blɛsɪn La, *pl* stɛpmʊðəz blɛsɪnz Db

stepmother's jag* *n* a LOOSE *PIECE OF* SKIN at the bottom of a finger-nail VI.7.11. *pl* stɛpmʊðəz dʒagz La

steppings *npl* the HOOF-MARKS of a horse IV.3.10. stɛpɪnz O Lei R

stepping-stile *n* a STILE IV.2.9. stɛpɪnstɑˈɪɫ Lei, stɛpɪnstɒɪl St, stɛpɪnstɒɪɫ So

stepplings *npl* the HOOF-MARKS of a horse IV.3.10. stɛplɪnz Lei

steps *n* a STILE IV.2.9. stɛps St

step-stile *n* a STILE IV.2.9. stɛpstɑɪl Db

stern *1. n* the ARSE VI.9.2. stɑːn Nf*[vulgar]*

2. npl STARS VII.6.3(a). stɑːn Cu*[very rare]*, stɑᴿːn Nb, staˤːn̩ O*[old]*

stern-end *n* the BUTT of a sheaf of corn II.6.4. stɑˈnɪnd Nf

stern-loader *n* the LOADER of sheaves, standing on the back of a wagon II.6.7(c). stanloˈʊdə Nf

stetched *adj* RESTIVE, describing a horse III.5.6. stɛtʃt Cu

stetches *1. npl* the RIDGES between furrows in a ploughed field II.3.2. stɛtʃɪz Ess, *sg* stɪtʃ Ess

2. npl a group of furrows, ⇐ RIDGES II.3.2. stɛtʃəz Ess, *sg* stɛtʃ Ess*['group of furrows 7 feet 2 inches. broad']*

stew *1. v* to BREW tea V.8.9. stɪuː Sa, stuː Bk

2. n DUST on a road VII.6.18. stɪuː Cu*[old x1]*

steward *n* a CARTMAN on a farm I.2.2. stəːᵊd Nf, stəəᴶd Nf, stəᴶːd Nf

stick *1. n [Show a picture of a farm-cart.] What do you call this, for supporting the shaft to give the horse a rest?* I.11.1. stɪk Nb We La Y O L Ess So Sr Do. ⇒ **back-rest, balancer, bat, buck, butt- stick, cart-leg, cart-prop, cross-stick, draught- leg, draught-stick, easing-stick, hame-stick, idleman,** *idlemen* ⇒ **idleman, iron-horse, leg, leg-rest, leg-stick, limber-prop, pole, post, prop, propper, prop-staff, prop-stick, rest, rester,** *resters* ⇒ **rester, resting-pin, resting-pole, resting-staff, resting-stick, rest-pole,** *rests* ⇒ **rest, rest-stick, rod, rod-stay,** *rod-stays* ⇒ **rod- stay, scotch-stick, scote, set-stick, setting-stick, shaft-leg, shaft-pin, shaft-prop, shaft-rest, shaft-stick, shaft-trap, spreader, squat, squat-stick, staff, stand, stand-leg, stay, stay-stick, stop-stand, strap-stick, team-stick, trap-stick, trigger, trig-stick, upright**

2. n the HANDLE of a besom I.3.16. stɪk La Man He Mon Gl O Nth Hu C Ess So Co D

3. n the SHAFT of a spade I.7.7. stɪk He Gl C, stɪːk Wo

4. n the SHAFT of a hay-fork I.7.12. stɪk Sa He C Hrt Ess So Co D, stɪːk Wo

5. n a vertical rod in front of a cart, perforated to allow adjustments when tipping, ⇐ ROD/PIN I.10.3. stɪk La *[queried NBM]*

6. n the SHAFT of a scythe II.9.7. stɪk Gl L Nth C Nf Sf So

7. n a PERCH for hens IV.6.3. stɪk Cu

8. n a PORRIDGE-STICK V.9.1. stɪk Wa

9. vt-2prsg you BEAR pain VI.5.9. stɪk St He Wa Gl Hrt So K Co D Sx

10. n **give him the stick** to BEAT a boy on the buttocks VIII.8.10. gɪ ɪm ðə stɪk Lei

stick-and(-a)-half *n* a FLAIL II.8.3. stɪkɳ̩haːf Ess, stɪkəŋaːv Co

stick-horse *n* a SAWING-HORSE I.7.16. stɪkɒs St

stickied up *adj* STICKY, describing a child's hands VIII.8.14. stɪkɪd ʊp Y St L

sticking *1. v-ing* STOOKING II.6.5. stɪkɪn Ch Sa He Wo W D

2. n CHITTERLINGS III.12.2. stɪkɪn Ess

3. adj **sticking together** TANGLED, describing hair VI.2.5. stɪkɪn təgɪðəˤ Sa

sticking out *vtphr-ing* PUTTING your tongue OUT VI.5.4. stɪkɪŋ ... ɛʊt Sr, stɪkɪn ... ɛʊt C Bd Ess, stɪkn ... ɛʊt Sf Ess, stɪkən ... ɛʊt Sf, *3prpl* stɪk ... ɛʊt Sx, stɪkɪn ... æʊt Wa W Ha, stɪkɪn ... æˈət Y, stɪkɪn ... aːt La, stɪkɪn ... aɪt Ch St, stɪkɪn ... aʊt Y L, stɪkɪn ... ʌʊt Mon, stɪkɪn ... uːt Y, stɪkən ... uːt We, stɪkɪn ... əʊːt Gl

stickings *n* STRIPPINGS, the last drops at milking III.3.4. stɪkɪnz Co

sticking up *v-ing* STOOKING II.6.5. stɪkɪn ʊp Ch, stɪkɪn ... ʊp St

stickle **1.* *adj* sloping, ⇐ SLOPE IV.1.10. stɪkɫ D

2. adj STEEP, describing a hill IV.1.11. stɪkɫ So D Do

sticklebacks *npl* MINNOWS IV.9.9. stɪklbaks Y, stɪtlbaks Y *[marked u.r. and interp as 'sticklebacks' NBM]*

stick(s) *n* KINDLING-*WOOD* V.4.2.

no -s: stɪk St Lei Do; **bit of stick** bɪd ə stɪk So; **some stick** səm stɪk So

-s: stɪks Nb Du La Y Ch Db St Wo Wa Mon Lei Nth Nf Hrt Ess, stɛks Db

sticks *npl* PEGS used to fasten thatch on a stack II.7.7(a). stɪks So

stick up for *vphr* to AGREE *WITH* somebody VIII.8.12. stɪk ʊp fə La Y

sticky *1. adj When eating bread and treacle, a little girl's hands would soon get....* VIII.8.14. Eng exc. Du We. ⇒ balmed up, balmy, bleared up, bleared up *and sticky,* cabbied up, cabby, clabby, clagged up, claggy, clamed up, clammy, clart, clarted up, clarty, clatted, claumed up, claumy, clibby, *climy* ⇒ clammy, clingy, clitchy, clubby, daubed, daubed up, dauby, filthy, gammed up, gammy, gumny, labbered up, lathered up, messed up, messy, mucked up, mucky, smalmy, smeared up, smothered up, stickied up, stucked up, stuck up, tacky, targy

2. *adj* get sticky, go sticky to SPOIL, referring to meat or fish V.7.10. get sticky gɪt stɪkɪ K; go sticky gɒʊ stɪkɪ K

sticky-back *n* GOOSE-GRASS II.2.5. stɪkɪbak Cu

sticky-bobs *n* GOOSE-GRASS II.2.5. stɪkɪbɒbz Y

sticky-buttons *n* GOOSE-GRASS II.2.5. stɪkibʌtnz Co, stɪkibʌdnz Co, stɪgibʌdnz D

sticky-dick *n* GOOSE-GRASS II.2.5. stɪkɪdɪk La

sticky-grass *n* GOOSE-GRASS II.2.5. stɪkɪgɹas Cu

sticky-jack *n* GOOSE-GRASS II.2.5. stɪkɪdʒak Du

sticky-stinking-joe *n* GOOSE-GRASS II.2.5. stɪkɪstɪŋkɪndʒo: La

stiddle-ring* *n* a sliding RING to which a tether is attached in a cow-house I.3.5. stɪdɬɽɪŋ Co

stiff *adj* STEEP, describing a hill IV.1.11. stɪf Co

stiff besom *n* a MUCK-BRUSH I.3.14. stɪf bɪzəm W

stiff-broom *1. n* a MUCK-BRUSH I.3.14. stɪfbɹʊm Sf, stɪfbɹu:m Y, stɪf bɹu:m So

2. *n* a BROOM used for sweeping outdoors V.9.10. stɪfbɹʊm Sf, stɪfbɹʊu:m Ess

stiff-brush *1. n* a MUCK-BRUSH I.3.14. stɪfbɹʏʃ La, stɪf bɽʌʃ Do, stɪfbɹʊʃ La

2. *n* a BROOM used for sweeping outdoors V.9.10. stɪfbɹɪy:ʃ La, stɪf bɽʌʃ Do, stɪf bɽʌ¹ʃ So, stɪfbɹʊʃ We La Y Lei

stiff-cart *n* a FARMCART I.9.3. stɪfkæːt Man

stiffening *n* RENNET V.5.6. stɪfənɪn K

stiff-yard-brush *n* a MUCK-BRUSH I.3.14. stɪfjæːdbɹʊʃ La

stifle *1. vt* to CHOKE somebody VI.6.4. stɔɪfɬ Ess

2. *viphr* to FAINT VI.13.7. stɪfɬ So, stɔɪfɬ Ess

3. *n* the GROIN VI.9.4. stəɪfʊʊ Brk

stile *n What do you call that thing, sometimes with steps, by which we get across a wall or fence?* IV.2.9. Eng exc. We. ⇒ cattle-stop, climbing-stile, climb-stile, foot-bridge, foot-stile, ladder, ladder-stile, lift, slip-stile, stee, stee-hole, steel, steel-hole, step-ladder, stepping-stile, steps, step-stile, *stile-hole* ⇒ steel-hole, stone-ladder, sty, sty-hole

stile-road *n* a PATH through a field IV.3.11. staɪlɹo:d La *[marked as presumably for humans only NBM Edd]*

stilts *1. npl* the HANDLES of a horse-drawn plough I.8.2. stɪlts Nb Cu Du We La Y Ch Db Sa St Wa Nt Lei, stɪɬts Wa Lei, stɛlts Ch

2. *n* the wooden BASE of a stack II.7.4. stɪlts Y

stine *n* a STYE in the eye VI.3.10. stɛən Lei, staɪn Cu We Db Nt L, staɪən Cu, stɑːn Lei, staɪn Db Wa Nt Lei R

stint *v* to put cattle on hired pasture, ⇐ HIRE *PASTURAGE* III.3.8. stɪnt Cu Du

stipers *npl* poles stuck in the sides of a cart in place of CART-LADDERS I.10.5. stɒɪpə¹z K

stirk *1. n* a HEIFER III.1.5. stəɹk Y, *pl* stəɹks L, stəːk Ch, stəˤːk W

2. *n* a heifer immediately after the calf stage. stɜ¹ːk La, stək Y, stəɹk Y, stə¹k Ch, stə¹ːk Y

3. *n* a heifer 1 year old. stəɹk Y, stəˤːk Bk

4. *n* a heifer up to 18 months old. steɔᵏk Nb, stək Y, stəːk Y

5. *n* a heifer from 12 to 18 months old. stəɹk Y, stə¹ːk La

6. *n* a heifer from 1 to 2 years old. stəɹk Y, stəːk Y St

7. *n* a heifer up to 2 years old. stəːk St

8. *n* a heifer 2 years old. stəːk St, stəˤːk W

9. *n* a large, strong heifer. stəˤk Sr

10. *n* a young bullock. steˑək Du

11. *n* a young BULLOCK III.1.16. steɔᵏk Du, stə¹ːk St

stir-pudding *n* PORRIDGE V.7.1. stəːpʊdɪn St

stirrer-up *n* a PORRIDGE-STICK V.9.1. stəɹə-ʊp Y

stirring *adj* rather stirring PRETTY, describing a girl VI.5.18. ɹʌðə stɛˑəɹɪn Nf

stirring-spoon *n* a PORRIDGE-STICK V.9.1. stəɹɪnspuːn Brk

stitch *1. n What do you call this [imitate sewing]; you do one at a time?* V.10.4. Eng. ⇒ seam

2. *v* to SEW V.10.3. stɪtʃ Ch St L

stitching *v-ing* STOOKING II.6.5. stɪtʃɪn So D Do, stɪtʃən D, stɛɪtʃɪn Ch

stitching up *v-ing* STOOKING II.6.5. *inf* stɪtʃ ʌp D, *inf* stɪtʃ ... ʌp So

stithy *1. n* an ANVIL VIII.4.10. stɪðɪ Y, stɪdɪ Cu*[old x1, rare x1]* Du*[old]* La*[old x1]* Y*[old x3, cutler's anvil x1]* L*[square x1, old x1, new x1]*, stɛdɪ Du Y, stʊdɪ Nb*[old x4, rare x1]* Y, stədɪ Y

2. *n* the wooden block supporting an anvil. stɪdɪ Nb Y, stədɪ Nb

3. *n* a smithy. stɪdɪ Y

stoat *1. n* a WEASEL IV.5.6. stoːt Ch *[marked ir.r. WMBM]*

2. *n* a POLE-CAT IV.5.7. stɛʊt Ess, stɔ¹ːt La, stʌʊt Ess, stoːt La, stoʊt St, stʊːt St

stob *n* a SPLINTER VI.7.10. stɒb Y*[old]*

stobs *npl* PEGS used to fasten thatch on a stack II.7.7(a). stɒbz Du Y*[hazel]*, stɔbz Y

stock *1. v* People leave a cow unmilked before she goes to market, in order to make her udder look bigger. What do you call this? III.3.6.

vt stɒk Wa Gl So W Ha, *-ing* stɒkɪn Y St D, *-ing* stɔkɪn Sr

v stɒk Cu Du We*[modern]* Gl O Lei Bk, *-ing* stɒkɪn St, *-ing* stɒkən Co, *-ing* stɔkɪn L

⇒ bag, bag *her* up, bag *it* up, bag *them* up, bag up, beat up, *been neglected at being milked*, blast, block *her udder*, buss *her* up, buss up, cram, *don't milk her*, dug up, fake *them* up, fill, fill *her udder*, fill *them* up, flood, flush up, *full-milk, full-uddered*, gale, gale *them* up, gale up, get *the bag* up, grill, heft, hog, hog up, *leave, leave her bag to fill, leave the bag, leave them a meal in, left, left unmilked*, let bag up, make *the bag* up, make *their bags*, make up, *not milked*, overload, *overstocked*, pack *it* up, pen, pen *her*, pen *her udder*, pen *her* up, pen *their udder*, pen *them*, pound, pound up, seal, seal *her ewer* up, seal *her* up, seal *their teats*, seal *them*, seal *the paps* up, *she hasn't been milked, she's been left*, span *her*, span *the udder*, stall *its bag* up, stank, stank *her bag* up, stank *the milk*, stank up, steam, steam *her* up, steam *of her*, steam up, stelch, stem, stem up, stock *her*, stock *her bag*, stock *her udder*, stock *her* up, stock *his udder*, stock *it* up, stock *she* up, stock *the bag*, stock *them*, stock *them* up, stock up, stop up, *the bag is hefted, they don't milk her, they don't milk them, they haven't milked her out, with a full bag*

2. n a wooden device fitted round the neck of an animal to tether it in a cow-house, ⇐ TETHERING-STAKE I.3.3. stɒk Gl

3. n a round TROUGH in a cow-house I.3.6. stɒk K

4. n the SHAFT of a spade I.7.7. stɒk Brk

5. n the SHAFT of a hay-fork I.7.12. stɒˑk Brk

6. n the HUB of a cart-wheel I.9.7. stɒk Sa He Mon Sr Do Ha, *pl* stɒks Sx, stɔːk He, stʌk Bk

7. n the metal BUSH at the centre of a cart-wheel I.9.8. stɒk W Ha

8. n the STEM of a corn-plant II.5.2(a). stɒk Wo W Do *[taken as* **stalk** *SBM]*

9. n the BUTT of a sheaf of corn II.6.4. stʌk Gl

10. n CATTLE III.1.3. staˑkʔ Nf, stɒk Ch Sa St Wa O Nth Sr

11. n **on stock** *ON* HEAT, describing a cow III.1.6. ɒn stɒk Nf, ɔn stɔk Sf

12. n **on stock** *ON* HEAT, describing a sow III.8.9. ɔn stɔk Sf

13. n a SHEARING-TABLE III.7.8. stɒk La Y D

14. n a BENCH on which slaughtered pigs are dressed III.12.1. stɒk La Y, stɔk Y, kɪɬɪnstɒk Co, kɪɬənstɒk Co, pɪgstɒk La Y Co, pɛgstɒk D, pɪgzstɒk D

stock-dog *n* a BITCH, the female dog III.13.2. stɒkʔdɔːg Nf

stock-horse *n* a STALLION kept for breeding III.4.4. stɒkaˤːʂ Brk, stɒkɒs Ha

stocking *1. v-ing* STOOKING II.6.5. stɒkɪn Mon, *3prs* stɒks Brk, stɔːkɪn Ess, stɔːkn Ha, *prppl* stɔːkən Ha

2. v-ing ON HEAT, describing a cow III.1.6. stɒkɪn Sx *[queried ir.r. SBM]*

stockman *1. n* a COWMAN on a farm I.2.3. stakmən Nth, stɒkmən Du St O Nth Ess Brk, stɔkmən nwY Ess

2. n a man who looks after animals on a farm. stɒkmən Cu La Nf

3. n a man who looks after beef cattle or cattle generally on a farm. stɒkmən Lei Bk K, stɔkmən Sf

stock-mark *v* to MARK sheep in some unspecified way to indicate ownership III.7.9. stɒkmaˑrk Cu

stock-pig *n* a BOAR III.8.7. stɒkpɪg Nf

stock up *1. viphr* to show signs of calving, referring to a cow with a swelling udder, ⇐ SHOWS SIGNS OF CALVING III.1.12(a). *-ing* stɒkən ʊp Man

2.1. vtphr to STOCK III.3.6. stɒk ... ʌp Do Ha, *-ing* stɒkɪn ... ʌp Sr K, *-ing* stɒkn ... ʌp W, (əˤːẓ) ʂtɒkt ʌp D, stɒk ... ʊp O Lei, *-ing* stɒkɪn ... ʊp K, *-ing* stɔkɪn ... ʊp Y

2.2. vphr to stock. stɒk ʌp Bk, *-ing* stɒkɪn ʌp Ess K Sx, *-ed* stɒkt ʌp Sx, stɒk ʊp Db Nth Bk, *-ing* stɒkɪn ʊp La, *-ed* stɒkt ʊp Man, stɔk ʌp Ess

stock-yard *1. n* a FARMYARD I.1.3. stɒkjaːd Ess

2. n the STRAW-YARD of a farm I.1.9. stɒkjæˑ¹ːd O, stɒkjaːd Ess, stɒkjaːd Hrt K, stɒkjaˤːd D, stɒkjɑːəˤɽd Sr, stɒkjaˤːəˤd Sr, stɒkjəˤːd Wo O, stɒkjəˤːɽd Brk, stɒkjæːd C, stɔkjaˑ¹ɹd Ch, stɔkjaːd Sf, stɔkjaˤˑd Ha

3. n a straw-yard in which cattle are fattened. stɒkjaːd Sa*[for young stock]*, stɒkjaˤːd Nth, stɒkəˤːd O

4. n a straw-yard in which cattle are kept to produce dung. stɒkjaːd Mon, stɒkjaˤːd Mon

stodgy *adj* BOGGY IV.1.8. stɒdʒɪ K

stomach *1. n* (off her) FOOD V.8.2. stʌmɪk So, (əˤː) ʂtʌmɪk D, stʌmək Nf

2. n the BELLY VI.8.7. stɒmɪk Sx, stɒmək Man Ess Sr, stʌmɪk Nf Ess Sx, stʌmʌk W, stʌmək Nf, stʌmɐk Mon, stʊmək O

stomachy *adj* RESTIVE, describing a horse III.5.6. stʌmɪkɪ W *[queried u.r. SBM]*

stone *1. n* the CURB-STONE in a cow-house I.3.9. stɪən Y, stʊən Y

2. n a WHETSTONE II.9.10. stɪan Du, stɪən Y, stɒʊn Sr, stɔʊn Lei R, stoʊn St, stoːʊn Db So, stoːˀn Db, stuːn St Lei, stʊən Du Y L

3. n a flat stone, 6 inches thick and with rounded corners, resting on bricks, on which bacon is cured, ⇐ SALTING-TROUGH III.12.5. stʊən Y

4. n the THRESHOLD of a door V.1.12. stuːn Wo*[old]*

stone-deaf *adj* DEAF VI.4.5. stʌndɛf Sf, stʊəndɪˑəf L

stone-dike *n* a WALL IV.2.1(b). stɪəndɛɪk Nb Du, stɪəndaɪk Cu, steːndɛɪk Nb

stone-fence *n* a WALL IV.2.1(b). stɪənfɛns Y, *pl* stoːnfɛnsəz Co

stone-flag *n* a flat surface on which bacon is cured, ⇐ SALTING-TROUGH III.12.5. stʊənflag Y*[in cellar]*, stʊən flag La*[in buttery]*

stone-hedge *n* a WALL IV.2.1(b). stɔʊnhɪdʒ Ess

stone-hole *n* a QUARRY IV.4.6. stɒʊnɔʊɫ K

stone-horse *n* a STALLION III.4.4. stʊnəs Ess

stone-ladder *n* a STILE IV.2.9. stoːnənlaðəˡ: W

stone-naked *adj* NAKED, describing a person VI.13.20. stoʊnneɪkɪd Bk, stoːneˀkəd Du, stɪənneːkt Y, stanneːkt Y, stjɛnnɛkt Nb, stjɛnnjɛkt Nb, stɪannɪakt Y, stɪənnɪəkt Nb Cu Du, stɪanneakt Cu, steanneakt Cu We, stʊənneˑakt La, stɪənneəkt Du

stone-pit *n* a QUARRY IV.4.6. stɔʊnpɪt L R Ess Sx, stʌnpɪt Sf, stʌʊnpɪʔ Bk, stʌʊmpɪt Ess, stonpɪt Nf, stoːnpɪt Brk, *pl* stoːnpɪʔs Bk, stounpɪt Nf, stʊnpɪt R Nth Nf Sf, stʊənpɪt L, stʊənpɪʔ Bk*[old]*

stone-quarry *n* a QUARRY IV.4.6. stɔʊnkwɒɹɪ Lei, stɔʊnkwɔːɹɪ Sx, stʌʊnkwɒɹɪ K, stʷoːnkwɒˡ: W, stʊnkwæɹɪ Wo, stʊnkwɒɹɪ Wo Wa, stʊnkwɔɹɪ Wo, stuːənkwaɹɪ W, stuːənkwɒɹɪ W

stone-slab *n* a flat surface on which bacon is cured, ⇐ SALTING-TROUGH III.12.5. stʊənslab La Y*[in dairy x1, in cellar x1]* Nt

stone-table *n* a flat surface on which bacon is cured, ⇐ SALTING-TROUGH III.12.5. stʊənteəbl Y

stone-wall *n* a WALL IV.2.1(b). stɪanwɔːl Y, stɪanwɔː Cu We Y, stɪənwɔːl Y, stɪənwɔː Cu, *pl* stɪənwɔːz We, steˑanwɔː Cu, støːnwaːl Nb, *pl* stɔʊnwɔːlz Wa*[not dividing fields]*, *pl* stʌʊnwɔːɫz K*[not local]*, *pl* stʌʊnwɔːz K*[not local]*, *pl* stʊnwaːɫz Gl, stʊənwɔːl Y, stʊənwɔːɫ O, stwənwɔːɫ W, stʊənwɔː Ch, stᵁunwɒʊ Db

stone-yard *n* a FARMYARD I.1.3. stɔʊnjɑːd Ess

stoning *v-ing* THROWING a stone at somebody VIII.7.7. steanən Cu

stook *1. n* a stack of PEAT about 6 feet high, comprising one cartload IV.4.3. staʊk La

2. n a tree STUMP IV.12.4. stɛʊk Sa *[queried WMBM]*

stooking *v-ing* What is your word for putting sheaves together in the harvest field for drying? II.6.5. stɪuːkən Du, stɪəkən We Y, stʏːkɪn La, stʏːpɪn Db, stʌkɪn He Mon, *inf* stʌk O, stʊkɪn He Wo Mon Gl Bk So Brk Sx, stuːkɪn Nb We La Y Ch Sa Nt L So, stuːkən Nb Cu Du We Man, *inf* stuːk Sr, stəkɪn Gl. ⇒ **eighting, eight up, goating, hattocking, hiling, kiver, mowing, mowsing,** *putting some* **rithers** *up,* *putting them in a* **kiver,** *putting them in* **mows,** *rear them* up,*rear them* up *into* kivers, *setting the* kivers *up,* **setting up, setting up** *corn,* **setting up** *in a* **hattock, shocking, shocking up, stacking, sticking,** *sticking them up in* **shocks,** *sticking the sheaves into* **mows, sticking up, stitching, stitching up, stocking, stowking, thraving, tiling;** ⇒ also **thrave**

stool *1. n* the STEM of a corn-plant II.5.2(a). stɪuːl Db

2. n the BUTT of a sheaf of corn II.6.4. stɛʊl Db, staːɫ Gl

3. n the BASE of a stack II.7.4. stuːl He*[hedge trimmings x1]*, stuːɫ Wo Mon

4. n a MILKING-STOOL III.3.3. stɪʊl Nb Du, stɪʊl Cu Du Y, stɪuːl Du Y Sa, stˡuːɫ Wa, stɪɵːl Nf, stˡɵːɫ Lei Nf, stɪəl Nb Cu Du We Y, stʏːl Ch, stʏː La Ch Db, stʏːl Co D, stʏːˀɫ So D, stʏɵːl Sa, stɛʊl Db St, stɛʊ St, *pl* stɒʊɫz K, stʊɫ Mon Bk, stwʊɫ Gl, stʊɪl Y, stuːl Nb La Y Db Sa St He Nt L Nth Nf, stuːɫ He Wo Wa Mon O R Nth Hu Nf Sf Bk Bd Ess So W Brk Sr Co, stuːˀɫ He Wo Wa Mon Gl O C Sf Bk Bd Hrt Ess So W, stuːəɫ So W Co Do Ha, stuː La Ch Sr Sx, stɵːl Nf, stɵːɫ Lei, stəʊl Nf

5. n a SHEARING-TABLE III.7.8. stɪʊl Cu, stʊʊl Nf, stuːʊ Sx

6. n a BENCH on which slaughtered pigs are dressed III.12.1. stɪəl Nb, stjʏl Du, stjʊl Nb, steul Nf, stuːl Nb Nf W K, stuːɫ O Sf Ess MxL W Brk, stuːʊ O Brk Sr Sx

7. n a tree STUMP IV.12.4. stʏːɫ D, stɛʊl La*[rare]* St*[very short]*, staʊl Sa*[very low]*, stæʊəl Gl Ha, staʊɫ Wo, stauəɫ So, stɒʊˀɫ Gl*[old]*, stʊʊʊ Sr, stuːl Nb*[rare x2, sawn off 2 feet high x1]* Cu*[rare]* Du Y*[sawn off x2, sawn off at ground level x1, of a felled tree x1, old x1]* Ch Sa*[old x1]* St*[at ground level x1]* He Wo*[old x1]* L*[old x1]* Nf*[not used]* K, stˡuːɫ Db*[not used]*, stuːɫ He O*[sawn off x2, sawn off close to ground x1, sprouting x1]* Lei Bk Ess Brk*[sawn off]* K*[sawn off x1, old x1]* Co Do, stuʊ Sx, stəʊl Nf*[not used x1]*

8. n a spur on an uncovered root of a tree. *pl* stuːˀɫz Lei

9. n a stub in a hedge when laid. stuːɫ R Bk

stoop *vi* to DUCK VIII.7.8. stʊp Ess

stoops *npl* GATE-POSTS IV.3.2. stɒʊps Y, stɔʊps Y, stuːps Du We La Y, *sg* stuːp Cu

stoothing *n* the PARTITION between stalls in a cow-house I.3.2. stɪuːðən Du, stɪəðən Du

stop *1. vt* to fill gaps in a hedge-bank or hedge, probably with turfs, brushwood, or similar material, ⇐ to PLASH IV.2.4. *-ing* stapın So, stɒp So W Ha *[SBM Edd uncertain as to precise meaning]*

2. vt **stop his wind** to CHOKE somebody VI.6.4. stɒpˀ ız wınd Nf

3. vi to STAY at home VIII.5.2. stɒp Nb Cu Du We La Y Ch Db Sa St He Wo Wa Mon Gl O Nt L Lei Nth Hu Nf Bk Bd Hrt Ess So Sr Sx, *3prpl* stɒps Ha, *-s* stɒps Db Gl O, *-ed* stɒpt Brk, stɒb D, stɔp Nb La Y Ch L C Sf Hrt Ess MxL Sr, stɔpˀ Sf; **stop in** stɒp ın Y

stop-block *n* a chock placed behind and under a wheel to prevent a cart from going backwards on a hill, ⇐ PROP/CHOCK I.11.2. stɒpbłɒk So

stopping-post *n* the SHUTTING-POST of a gate IV.3.4. stɒpmpʌʊst Ess, stɔpınpʌʊst MxL

stopping-time *n* *What do you call the time when you stop work for the day?* VII.5.9. stɔpənteɪm Nb. ⇒ **blow-up, blow-up-time, chucking-up-time, chuck-up-time, finish, finishing-time, giving-out-time, giving-over-time, going-home-time, hitch-off-time, home-time, jacking-off-time, jacking-up-time, jack-off-time, jack-out-time, jack-up-time, kenner, knocking-off-time, knocking-time, knock-off, knock-off-time, knock-out-time, leave-off-time, leave-work-time, leaving-off-time, leaving-time, leaving-work-time, ligging-away-time, ligging-off-time, loose-all, loose-it,** *loosing-time* ⇒ **lowsing-time, lowse, lowse-time, lowsing-off-time, lowsing-out-time, lowsing-time,** *my time,* **packing-up-time, taking-off-time, time, time** *to give out,* **time** *to go home,* **time** *to knock off,* **time** *to leave off,* **time** *to leave work*

stops *vi-3prsg* school FINISHES VIII.6.2(b). stɒps D

stop-stand *n* a STICK used to support the shaft of a cart I.11.1. stɒpstand So

stop up *1. vphr* to STOCK III.3.6. *-ing* stɒpən ʌp Co

2. vtphr to fill gaps in a hedge-bank or hedge, probably with turfs, brushwood, or similar material, ⇐ to PLASH IV.2.4. *-ing* stapın ʌp So, stɒp … ʌp Ess So, stɒpˀ … ʌpˀ Nf *[EM/SBM Edd uncertain as to precise meaning]*

store *1. n* **on store** ON HEAT, describing a cow III.1.6. ɒn stɔːə Ess

2. n **in store, on store** ON HEAT, describing a sow III.8.9. **in store** ın stɔːə Ess; **on store** ɒn stɔːˀə Ess, ɒn stɔˀə Nf, ɔn stɔˀə Sf, ɒn stoə Nf, ɒn stoəˡ Nf, ɔn stɒʊə Sf; **come on storing** *3prprogsg* kʊmən ɒn stɔːɹın L; **run to store** ɹʌn tˀə stoˀə Nf *[on storing taken to be the adj phr, on analogy with* **on hogging** *(where* **coming on hogging** *is subsumed without comment)]*

3. n a male or female HOG III.8.8. stɔˀə Hu, stoˀəˡ Bd

4. n a hog. *pl* stɔːz Ess

store-house *n* a FASTING-CHAMBER III.11.3. stɔːɾɛʊs O

store-pig *1. n* a BOAR III.8.7. stɔˀpɪg Nf, stuˀəpɪg Nf

2. n a male or female HOG III.8.8. stɔˡːpɪg So, stɔˀəpɪg Sf Ess*[but females no longer cut],* stɔˀᵁəpɪg Ess, stoˀəpɪg Nth Hu Bk Bd Hrt, stoˀəˡpɪg Bk

3. n a male hog. stɔːpɪg Du, stɔˀˀpɪg Nf

4. n a hog. stɔːpɪg Nf, stoˀəpɪg Bd*[males and uncut females]*

store-place *n* the place where hay is stored on a farm, ⇐ HAY-LOFT I.3.18. stʊəplɛˀəs L

store-stock-yard *n* the STRAW-YARD of a farm I.1.9. stɔəˡɪstɒkjɑˡːɾd̦ Sx

store-yard *n* the STRAW-YARD of a farm I.1.9. stɔːjɑˡːd̦ So

storing *1. v-ing* ON HEAT, describing a cow III.1.6. stɔˀəɹın Hu

2. v-ing ON HEAT, describing a sow III.8.9. stɔˀɹın Nf, stɔːɹn̦ Nf, stɔəɹın Nf, stoːɹın Nf, əstʊəɹən L

stortle *vi-3prpl* they WHINNY, describing the noise horses make during feeding time in the stable III.10.3(a). stɔːtł Ess

stot *1. n* a BULLOCK III.1.16. stœːt Nb, stɔt Du*[young]*

2. vi to BOUNCE VIII.7.3. stœt Nb, stœːt Nb, stɒt Nb Cu Du, stɔt Nb, stʌt Nb

stour *n* DUST on a road VII.6.18. staʊə Du, stuˀᵏ Nb*[old x1]*, stuˀə Nb*[old]* Cu Du*[old]* We, stuˀər Cu, stuˀˀᵏ Nb*[old]*, stuəɹ Cu Du

stoven *1. n* a tree STUMP IV.12.4. stɔːvɪn Lei, stɔːvn R*[old]*

2. n a stump in a hedge. stɒbɪn Lei, stɔʊvɪn Lei, *pl* stɔːvɪnz Lei, stɔːvn Lei R

stover-fork *n* a HAY-FORK with a short shaft I.7.11. stʌvəfɔːˀk Sf

stow *1. vt* to LOP a tree IV.12.5. *-ing* stəː-ın Nf

2. v to lop. stɛʊ Sf

stower *1. n* a TETHERING-STAKE in a cow-house I.3.3. staʊə Du, staʊə Nb

2. n a RUNG of a ladder I.7.15. staʊə Y, *pl* staʊəɹz Y, *pl* staʊəz Y

stowking *v-ing* STOOKING II.6.5. stæːˀkın Nt, stæʊkın Nt L Lei R, staʊkın La Db Nt L Lei R, *inf* staʊk Y, stɛʊkın Nth Hu, *inf* stɛʊk L, stɒʊkən Cu, *inf* stɒʊk La, stoʊkın La

straddle *1. n* the BASE of a stack II.7.4. stʁadl Nb, stɹadł Lei

2. adv ASTRIDE VI.9.8. stɹɛdʊł Sr, stɹædł Gl Sf Ess, stɹædʊł Sr, stɹædʊ K, ştɹadł W Co

3. adj SPLAY-FOOTED VI.10.5. stɹædł K

straddled *1. adj* OVERTURNED, describing a sheep on its back unable to get up III.7.4. stɹadłd Ch

2. adv ASTRIDE VI.9.8. stɹɛədɫd Ess, stɹædɫd Ess, stɹædʊɫd W Ha, stɹadlt Db, stɹadld La Gl Nt, stɹadɫd Wa C, ʂtɹadɫd Ha

straddled out *adv* ASTRIDE VI.9.8. stɹædʊɫd ɛʊt Sx

straddle-foot *adj* SPLAY-FOOTED VI.10.5. stɹædlfʊt Nf

straddle-footed *adj* SPLAY-FOOTED VI.10.5. stɹædɫvʊtɪd Ha, ʂtɹadɫvʊtɪd D

straddle-leg *adv* ASTRIDE VI.9.8. stɹædǀlɛg Nf

straddle-legged *1. adj* KNOCK-KNEED VI.9.5. stɹɒdɫlɛgd Lei *[queried ir.r. EMBM]*

2. adv ASTRIDE VI.9.8. stɹædǀlɛgd Nf, stɹædɫlɛgd K, stɹadǀlɛgd Y Ch Db Sa St*[old]*, stɹadəllɛgd La Y, stɹadɫlɛˑˡgd MxL, ʂtɹadɫlɛgd Ha

straddle-legs *adv* ASTRIDE VI.9.8. stɹædǀlɛgz Nf, stɹædǀlɛgz Nf, stɹadǀlɛgz Y L

straddle-stick *n* the STRETCHER between the traces of a cart-horse I.5.11. stɹadɫstɪk Lei

straddling *adv* ASTRIDE VI.9.8. stɹædlɪn Nf Brk K, stɹædɫən Sf Ess, stɹadlɪn Ch Db St Gl Nt L Bd*[old]*, *prppl* stɹadɫɪn Ha, stɹaːdlən Ess, ʂtɹadɫɪn Do Ha

straddly *adv* ASTRIDE VI.9.8. stɹɛdɫɪ Ess

straddly-bandy *adj* BOW-LEGGED VI.9.6. stɹædɫɪbændɪ K

strads *1. npl* KNEE-STRAPS used to lift the legs of working trousers VI.14.17. ʂtɹadz D

*2. npl wooden gaiters for protection when using a sickle, ⇐ LEGGINGS VI.14.18. ʂtɹadz So

3. n leather pieces for protecting a thatcher's knee. ʂtɹædz So

strad-stick *n* the STRETCHER between the traces of a cart-horse I.5.11. stɹædstɪk Lei, stɹɛtstɪk Lei, stɹadstɪk Lei

straggy *adj* TANGLED, describing hair VI.2.5. stɹɛgɪ Ess

straighten up *vtphr-3sg* she [a tidy girl] will COLLECT her toys VIII.8.15. stɹɛɪtn ... ʊp Db, stɹɛɪtən ... ʊp Ch

straight-handles *npl* the HANDLES of a scythe II.9.8. ʂtɹaɪthandɫz So

straight-rip *n* a BILLHOOK with a long straight blade IV.2.6. stɹaɪtʔɹɪp Ess *[EMBM headword -reap]*

straight-stick *n* a movable horizontal rod stretching between the shafts of a cart, fixing them to the cart-body and stopping the cart from tipping, ⇐ ROD/PIN I.10.3. stɹɛtstɪk Lei

straik *1. n* a WHETSTONE made of stone II.9.10. stʁeːk Nb

2. n a wooden implement, greased and sanded, used to sharpen a scythe. stʁɪək Nb, stʁeːk Nb

strain *1. v* What do you do with the milk as soon as it has come from the cow-house? V.5.2. Eng exc. Nb Cu We Ch Db Nt R. ⇒ **clean, sie, sieve, sieve up, sile,** *strain out*

2. n a LITTER of piglets III.8.3. stɹɛɪn Ha

3. vt to SPRAIN an ankle VI.10.8. striːn Cu, stʁiːn Nb*[old]*, stɹiːn Db, *-ed* stɹiːnd Du St, *-ed* stɹɪənd We, stɹɪən La Y*[broad x1]* L, stʁeːn Nb, stɹeːn Cu Ch Db, *-ed* stɹeːnd La Mon, stɹeɪn C Bd, *-ed* ʂtɹeɪnd So, *-ed* stɹeˑənd Y, stɹeːn Cu, *-ed* stɹeɪnd Y MxL, *-ed* ʂtɹeɪnd D, stɹeɪn Sf *[one form at D [ʂtɛɪnd], taken as error by SBM Edd]*

4. vi to RETCH VI.13.15. *-ing* stɹɪənɪn Y, *-ing* stɹeɪnɪn He, *-ing* ʂtɹeɪnɪn So, stɹeɪn Ess, *-ing* stɹeɪnɪn Y St; **strain the guts** *-ing* stɹeːnɪn t gʊts Y

strainer *n* a DIAGONAL BAR of a gate IV.3.7. stɹeɪnəˡ Gl

straining-larra *n* a DIAGONAL BAR of a gate IV.3.7. ʂtɹeɪnɪnɫaˑ: D

strake *n* the SOLE of a horse-drawn plough I.8.9. stɹɪək Y, stɹeːk Y, stɹɛək Y

strakes *1. npl* pieces of iron forming the sections of the TIRE round a cart-wheel I.9.10. stɹeːks Sa He Wo, ʂtɹeːks W, stɹeːk 'nailed on outside of wheel' Gl *[taking all as pl and as 'sections', but there are not fw notes for all; Wo reference could be to whole tire. See note at strigs]*

*2. n STRIPPINGS, the last drops at milking III.3.4. ʂtɹeːks Do

strand *n* the STEM of a corn-plant II.5.2(a). ʂtɹɔːn So

strange *adv* VERY poisonous IV.11.5. stɹeˑənʒ L

strangers *npl And if you don't know certain people at all, you say they are ....* VIII.2.10. Eng. ⇒ **foreigners, fremd bodies,** *fremd body* ⇒ **fremd bodies, shiresmen, uncouth, undercreepers**

strangle *vt* to CHOKE somebody VI.6.4. stɹæŋgl Nf, stɹæŋgɫ Hrt Ess MxL Sr K, stʁaŋl Du, stɹaŋl Y L, stɹaŋgl St He Wo Wa, stɹaŋgɫ Mon

strap *1. n* a TETHERING-ROPE used to tie up a horse I.4.2. stɹap Sa L *[queried ir.r WMBM]*

2. n the SHAFT of a spade I.7.7. ʂtɹap So

3. n a DIAGONAL BAR of a gate IV.3.7. ʂtɹap So

4. vt to BEAT a boy on the buttocks VIII.8.10. stɹæp Ess, ʂtɹæp So; **give him some strap** gɪv ɪm sʊm stɹap Y; **give him the strap** giː n ðə ʂtɹæp So, gɪb m, ðə ʂtɹæp So, gɪ ɪm ðə stɹap Lei; **put the strap across his arse** pʊʔ ðə stɹæp əkɹɒst hɪz aː:s Nf; **put the strap athwart his arse** pʊt ðə ʂtɹæp əðəˡːt ɪz æs So

strap-grass *n* COUCH-GRASS II.2.3. ʂtɹapgɹæ:s Ha, ʂtɹapgɹaːs Do

strapper *1. n* a FARM-LABOURER I.2.4. ʂtɹapəˡː Co

2. n a casual labourer. stɹapəˡ O

strapping *n* a DIAGONAL BAR of a gate IV.3.7. *pl* stɹapɪnz Db

strapping(s) *n* STRIPPINGS, the last drops at milking III.3.4.

no -s: stɹapın L, stɹapən L, ʂtɹapm Ha

-s: stɹæpınz Nf, stɹæpʔnz Nf, stɹapınz L Lei R Nth Hu, ʂtɹapınz W Do, stɹapənz C, ʂtɹapənz Ha

strappings* *n* the BREECH-BAND of the harness of a cart-horse I.5.10. stɹapınz Y

straps *1. npl* green willow RODS laid on thatch to fasten it on a stack II.7.7(b3). stɹaps Wo*[obsolete]*

2. npl KNEE-STRAPS used to lift the legs of working trousers VI.14.17. stɹeps Sx, stɹɛəps Ess, stɹæps Nf Sf Hrt Ess MxL K Sx, *sg* səɹæp Man, *sg* stʁap Nb, stɹaps Y Wa L Lei R Nth, *sg* stɹap Ha

3. npl BOOT-LACES VI.14.25. stɹæps Ha*[leather]*, ʂtɹaps Do

strap-stick *1. n* a rod keeping a cart-body fixed to the shafts, stopping it from tipping, ⇐ ROD/PIN I.10.3. stɹæpstık Sf Hrt Ess, stɹapstık Hrt

2. n a STICK used to support the shaft of a cart I.11.1. stɹæpstık Ess

strat *1. vt* to slip a calf, ⇐ SLIPS *THE CALF* III.1.11. *ptppl* stɹæt Co, *ptppl* ʂtɹad (+V) Co, *ptppl* ʂtɹadəd Co

2. vt to SLIP *A FOAL* III.4.6. ʂtɹæt Co, ʂtɹæd (+V) Co

straw *1. n* When you've got the grain out [by threshing the sheaves], what's left? II.8.2. stɹiː Nb, stɹɪa Y, strɪə Cu Y, strɪə Cu We La, stʁɪə Du, stɹɪə Cu Du We La Y, stʁeː Nb, ʂtɹɛɪ So, ʂtɹæː W, stɹaː Y, stʁa: Nb Du, stɹaː Du Y Gl O Bk Ess, stɹau Sf, stɹ ɑː Y, stɹɑ: He Wo Mon Gl, stɹɑᵗ: Wo, strɔː Man, stʁɔː Nb, stɹɔː Du La Y Ch Db Sa St He Wo Wa Mon Gl O Nt L Lei R Nth Hu C Nf Sf Bk Bd Hrt Ess MxL Brk Sr K Ha Sx, stɹɔᵗ: Sa, stɹɔ: O, ʂtɹɔ: So W Co D Do Ha, stɹʌʊ Ess, ʂtɹɔ: Co, stɹou St, ʂtɹou So Co, stɹuə Y. ⇒ **haulm, reed**

2. n the STEM of a corn-plant II.5.2(a). stɹɪə La Y, stʁeːˡ Nb, stɹaː Du, stɹɔː La Y Ch Db St Wo Wa O Nt L Nth C Nf Bd Hrt Ess Brk Sr K Sx, strɔ: O, ʂtɹɔ: So W Ha, stɹɔːə L Ess MxL Brk Sr Sx, stɹou St

3. n ROPES used to fasten thatch on a stack II.7.7(b2). stɹɔ: Gl *[marked u.r. as mass noun WMBM]*

straw-band(s) *n* ROPES used to fasten thatch on a stack II.7.7(b).

sg: stɹɔːband Y

no -s: stɹɔːban Bk*[straw]*

-s: stɹɔ·bændz Nf, strɔːbæːnz Hrt, stɹɔːəbænz Sr, stɹɔːbanz Lei Bd

[straw-band marked probably material n EMBM]

straw-barton *n* the STRAW-YARD of a farm I.1.9. ʂtɹɔːbaᵗːtn̩ So, ʂtɹɔːbaᵗːkŋ Do

straw-bee-hive *n* a SKEP IV.8.8(b). stɹɔːbi:-aıv Ch

straw-bond(s) *n* ROPES used to fasten thatch on a stack II.7.7(b2).

sg: stɹɔːbɒnd K, ʂtɹɔːbɒnd W

no -s: stɹɒːbɒnd Nf, stɹɔ·bɒnd Nf*[old x2, old-fashioned x1]*

-s: stɹɔːbɒnz K, stɹɔːbɔnz K, ʂtɹɔːbɒnz W

[straw-bond marked probably material n EMBM]

straw-bonnet* *n* a round floppy BONNET worn at work in the fields VI.14.1. *pl* stɹɔːbɒnəʔs Bk

straw-fork *1. n* a HAY-FORK I.7.11. stɹɔːfɔːk Y

2. n a fork with long prongs. *pl* stɹɔːfɔɹks Y

straw-hive *n* a SKEP IV.8.8(b). *pl* stɹɔː-aːvz Y, stɹɔː-aıv Y, stɹɔː-ɑːv Y, stɹɔː-aıv La Y, *pl* stɹɔː-aıvz Ch, stɹɔːɬɔıv Sx

straw-hook *n* a ROPE-TWISTER II.7.8. stɹɔʊ-ʊuk Y

strawing-fork *n* a HAY-FORK with a short shaft I.7.11. stɹɔːınfɔˡ:k La

straw-pad *n* a SHEATH or other device used to keep a knitting-needle firm V.10.10. ʂtɹɔːpæd Co

straw-rope(s) *n* ROPES used to fasten thatch on a stack II.7.7(b2).

sg: strɔːro:p Man

no -s: ʂtɹɔːɹo:p D*[possibly sg SBM]*

-s: stɹɪəɹɪəps Cu, stʁeːʁøːps Nb, stʁaːʁøːps Nb, stɹɔːɹɒʊps Sr, ʂtɹɔːɹoːps D

straw-rope-twister *n* a ROPE-TWISTER II.7.8. stɹɔːɹoːptwıstəᵗ: So

straw-skip *n* a SKEP IV.8.8(b). *pl* stɹɔːskıps K

straw-spinner *n* a ROPE-TWISTER made from a bucket-handle II.7.8. stɹɔːspınə Y

straw-stem *n* the STEM of a corn-plant II.5.2(a). stɹɔːstɛm Bk

straw-turner *n* a ROPE-TWISTER II.7.8. stɹɪətɔˡːnəɹ La

straw-twiner *n* a ROPE-TWISTER II.7.8. stɹɔːtwaːnə Y

straw-twister *n* a ROPE-TWISTER II.7.8. stɹɔːtwıstə Lei Ess, stɹɔᵗːtwıstəᵗ Sa, stɹɔ·ətwıstɹ L

straw-wad *n* a SHEATH or other device used to keep a knitting-needle firm V.10.10. ʂtɹɔːwɒd Co

straw-whipple *n* a ROPE-TWISTER II.7.8. stɹɔːwıpɬ K

straw-winder *n* a ROPE-TWISTER II.7.8. stɹɔːᵊwɑınə Nth

straw-yard *1. n* What do you call the yard in which cattle are kept, especially during the winter, for fattening, and for producing dung? [Verify the kind of cattle and the purpose.] I.1.9. ʂtɹæːjaᵗːd Ha, stɹɔːjæˡːd La, stɹɔːjaːd Y Ch Db Wa, stɹɔːjɑːd K, stɹɔːjəᵗːd K, ʂtɹɔːjaᵗːd So W Co D Do Ha, ʂtɹɔːjaᵗːd D, stɹɔʊjaːd St.

2. n a straw-yard in which cattle are fattened. stɹɔːjaᵗd Wo

3. n a straw-yard in which cattle are kept to produce dung. stɹɔːjaːd Wa

⇒ *barken* ⇒ barton, barton, bullock-shed, bullock-yard, bullocks'-yard, cattle-court, cattle-fold, cattle-yard, court, courtain, covered-in yard, covered-yard, cow-barton, cow-court, cow-yard, crew, crews, crew-yard, dry-yard, dung-yard, farmyard, fattening-pen, fattening-yard, fatting-stall, fatting-yard, feeding-yard, fodder-yard, fold, fold-garth, fold-yard, heifer-yard, heifers'-yard, hemmel, horse-yard, loose-pen, loose-yard, mow-hay, muck-fold, muck-yard, open shed, open-yard, stock-yard, store-stock-yard, store-yard, straw-barton, yard, yard-run

streak-iron *n* the GRASS-NAIL of a scythe II.9.9. ʂtɹeɪkaɪəᵗːn̩ So

streaks *npl* pieces of iron forming the sections of the TIRE round a cart-wheel I.9.10. stɹiːks Sf Ess Ha *[see note at strigs]*

streaky-milk *n* BEESTINGS V.5.10. stɹeɪkɪmɪʊk Ess

stream *1. n* a RIVULET IV.1.1. stʰrɪiːm Man, stɹiːm St Wa*[very small x1]* Mon O Nt L Lei Nth Nf Sf Bk Ess MxL K Ha, ʂtɹiːm So W Co D Do Ha, stɹɪɪiːm Nf Ess*[smaller than brook x1]* Brk Sr K Sx, strɪəm La*[smaller than beck]*, stɹɪəm La Y L, stɹeːm Gl, ʂtɹeːm W Ha, stʰreɪm Man, stɹeɪm Ess, stɹɛm He; **running stream** ɹʌnɪn stɹii'm Nf

2.1. vt to RINSE clothes V.9.8. ʂtɹiːm Co D, ʂtɹeːm Co

2.2. v to rinse. ʂtɹiːm D

stream out *vtphr* to RINSE clothes V.9.8. ʂtɹiːm ... æʏt Co, ʂtɹeɪm ... æʏt D

strengthener *1. n* the iron stay connecting the beam with the side of a cart, ⇐ CROSS-BEAM END I.10.1. stɹɛnθənə Y

2. n a DIAGONAL BAR of a gate IV.3.7. *pl* stɹɛnθənəz Y, *pl* stɹɛnθnəz Y, stɹɛŋθnə Hrt, *pl* stɹɛŋθnəz La Ch

strengthener-bar *n* a DIAGONAL BAR of a gate IV.3.7. stɹɛŋθnəbɑː Hrt

strengthening-bar *n* a DIAGONAL BAR of a gate IV.3.7. *pl* stɹɛŋθnɪnbæːz La, stɹɛnθn̩ɪnbaː Mon, stɹɛŋθnɪnbaː Y, *pl* stɹɛŋθnɪnbaːz Ch

strengthening-piece *n* a DIAGONAL BAR of a gate IV.3.7. *pl* stɹɛnθnɪnpiːsɪz Y

stretch *1. vi* to CHIP, referring to an egg that is about to hatch IV.6.10. stɹɪtʃ Y*[old]*, stɹɛtʃ L *[queried error for **spretch** NBM]*

2. vt to WRING the neck of a chicken when killing it IV.6.20. stɹɛtʃ La L, ʂtɹɛtʃ Co

stretcher *1. n [Show a picture of the harness of a cart-horse.] What do you call the wooden rod that keeps the traces apart?* I.5.11. stɹɪtʃə Nb Cu We La Y, stɹɪtʃəɹ La, stʁɪtʃɔᴿ Nb, stɹɪtʃə Nb Cu Du Y, stɹɪtʃəɹ La Y, stretʃə Du Y Man, stɹɛtʃə La, stʁɛtʃə Nb, stʁɛtʃɔᴿ Nb, stɹɛtʃə Du Y Ch L, stɹɛtʃəɹ La Y, stɹɛtʃəᴶ La O, stɹɛtʃəᵗ Db Sa Wo, strətʃə Y, stʁətʃɔᴿ

Nb, stɹətʃə We Y. ⇒ cobble-stick, coupling-stick, cratch-stick, cross-pole, cross-stick, drawing-stend, jib, pole, rack-stick, set-staff, set-stick, setter, setter-bar, setter-stick, setting-stick, sling, spat, spread-bat, spreader, spreader-stick, spread-staff, stem, stend, straddle-stick, strad-stick, stretcher-stick, stretching-stick, stretch-staff, stretch-stick, swingle-tree, tawtree, team-stick, trace-stick, trap-stick, tread-stick, truss-stick, tween-stick, whipper

2. n a DIAGONAL BAR of a gate IV.3.7. *pl* stɹɛtʃəz St, stʁətʃə Du

3. n a BENCH on which slaughtered pigs are dressed III.12.1. stɹɛtʃə Y Ess

4. n a BIER VIII.5.9(b). stʁɛtʃɔᴿ Nb

stretchers *npl* RODS laid on thatch to fasten it on a stack II.7.7(b3). ʂtɹɛtʃəᵗːz̩ So*[thorn-sticks x1, briars x1]*

stretcher-stick *n* the STRETCHER between the traces of a cart-horse I.5.11. stʁɪtʃəstɪk Du, stɹɪtʃəstɪk Y

stretching-stick *n* the STRETCHER between the traces of a cart-horse I.5.11. strɪtʃənstɪk Nb

stretch-staff *n* the STRETCHER between the traces of a cart-horse I.5.11. stɹɛtʃstaf Db St, stɛtʃstaf St

stretch-stick *n* the STRETCHER between the traces of a cart-horse I.5.11. stɹɛtʃstɪk Bd

strew *vt* to TED hay II.9.11(a). stɹɪu: Y, *-ing* stɹeː-ɪn Nf, stɹɑː Y, stɹɑʊ We Y Sf, strɒʊ Nb, *ptppl* stʁɒʊd Du, stɹɒʊ Du We, stɹɔː La

strew out *vtphr* to TED hay II.9.11(a). stɹɑʊ ... aʊt Y

strick *n* a wooden implement, greased and sanded, used to sharpen a scythe, ⇐ WHETSTONE II.9.10. stɹɪk L

stricken *adj* HEAVING *(WITH MAGGOTS)* IV.8.6. strɪkn Y

strickle *n* a wooden implement, greased and sanded, used to sharpen a scythe, ⇐ WHETSTONE II.9.10. strɪkl Cu Du, stʰrɪgl Man, stʰrɪgɬ Man, strɪkl Cu We, stʁɪkl Nb, stɹɪkl Cu Du We La Y Db Nt L, stɹɪkəl Nb Y Cu, stɹɪkl Cu Du We La Y, strəkl Y, strəkl We La Y, stɹəkl Cu La

strickle-backs *npl* MINNOWS IV.9.9. stɹɪklbaks Y *[marked u.r. and interpreted as 'stickleback' NBM]*

strickling *n* a SHREW-MOUSE IV.5.2. stɹɪklɪn Mon

strickly *adj* SLIPPERY VII.6.14. ʂtɹɪkɬi W

striddle-backs *npl* MINNOWS IV.9.9. stɹɪdlbaks Y, stɹɪdɬbaks Hu *[marked u.r. and interpreted as 'stickleback' N/EMBM]*

striddled *adv* ASTRIDE VI.9.8. strədlt Cu, stʁədlt Nb, stʁədld Nb, stɹədld Cu

striddled out *adv* ASTRIDE VI.9.8. stɹɪdld aʊt L;
legs striddled out lɛgz stɹɪdld uːt Y

striddle-legged* *adv* ASTRIDE VI.9.8. stɹɪdǀlɛgd
Du Y

striddle-legs *adv* ASTRIDE VI.9.8. stʁɪdǀlɛgz Nb,
stɹɪdǀlɛgz We

striddling *adv* ASTRIDE VI.9.8. stɹɪdlɪn Cu,
strɪdlən Du, strɪdlɪn We, strɪdlən We, stʁɪdlən Nb,
stɹɪdlɪn Cu We La Y L, stɹɪdlən Nb, stʁədlən Du,
stɹədlən Cu

stride *1. n* a DIAGONAL BAR of a gate IV.3.7.
stɹaɪd So *[queried SBM]*
2. adv ASTRIDE VI.9.8. stɹaɪd Y, stɹaɪd Co, stɹɔɪd
Ess

stride-legged *adv* ASTRIDE VI.9.8. stɹaɪdɫɛgd D

striding *adv* ASTRIDE VI.9.8. stɹaɪdɪn Sa

strid-legged *adv* ASTRIDE VI.9.8. stʁɪdlɛgd Du,
stɹɪdlɛgd Du

stridlings *adv* ASTRIDE VI.9.8. stɹɪdlɪnz Cu Du L

strig *1. n* STRIPPINGS, the last drops at milking
III.3.4. st^hrɪg Man
2. vt to TOP-AND-TAIL gooseberries V.7.23. stɹɪg
K
3.1. vt to REMOVE *STALKS* from currants V.7.24.
-*ing* stɹɪgɪn K
3.2. v to remove stalks. -*ing* stɹɪgɪn Sr K Sx

strigs *npl* pieces of iron forming the sections of the
TIRE round a cart-wheel I.9.10. stɹɪgz Brk *[reference
may be to tire or to sections. There are ambiguous fw
notes for **strakes/streaks/strigs** rr., and all are
probably pl, referring to sections of tire.]*

strike *1. vt* to THIN OUT turnip plants II.4.2. stɹaɪk
Y L, stɹɑːk Y, stɹɑɪk Db Nt
2. v to thin out turnips. stɹaɪkɪn Y, stɹɑɪk Db

strike out *vtphr* to THIN OUT turnip plants II.4.2.
stɹɪk ... ævt Co, stɹaɪk ... ævt Co, stɹaɪk aːt Y, stɹaɪk
... uːt Y L
2. v to thin out turnips. *pppl* stɹʊk aːt Y

striker *n* a wooden implement. greased and sanded,
used to sharpen a scythe, ⇐ WHETSTONE II.9.10.
stɹaɪkə La

strikings *n* STRIPPINGS, the last drops at milking
III.3.4. stɹaɪkənz D

strime out *vtphr* to THIN OUT turnip plants II.4.2.
stɹɑɪm ... æːt Nt

strind *n* a NEEDLEFUL of cotton or thread V.10.5.
stɹɛɪn St

strinding-post *n* the HANGING-POST of a gate
IV.3.3. stʁɪndənpøːst Nb

string *1. n* What would you tie the *[grain-]sack up
with?* I.7.3. strɪn Cu Man, strɪng Man, srɪn Man, strɪn
We La, strɪng La, stʁɪn Nb Du, stɹɪn Nb Du We La
Y Ch Db Sa He Wo Wa Mon Gl O Nt L Lei R Nth Hu
C Nf Sf Bk Bd Hrt Ess Brk Sr K Sx, *pl* stɹɪnz St, stɹɪng
La Ch Db Sa St Wo Wa Lei Sf, sθɹɪng La, stɹɪn So
W Co Do, z̧ˌtrɪn Ha, strɛng Man, stˌtrɛn W, stˌtræn So,
stˌtraŋ Ha. ⇒ **bagging, bagging-string, bag-tie,
ball-string, band, billy-band, bind-band,
binder-band, binder-cord, binder-string,
binder-twine, binding-string, binding-twine,
charlie-turner, copper-fibre, cord, farmer's
friend, farmer's glory, fillis, fillis-string,
grass-string, isaac, knetter, massey-harris,
massie-harris** ⇒ **massey-harris, michael,
michael-string, pitch- band, rope-yarn,
sack-string, sack-tie, sack- ties, sack-tiers,
sack-twine, sack-tying-twine,
self-binder-string, tarred-string, tar-rope,
tarry rope-yarn, thacking-string, thatching-
string** ⇒ **thacking-string, tiers, twine, warby,
wattle, yarn**
2. n TWINE used to fasten thatch on a stack
II.7.7(b1). strɪn Nb, *pl* strɪnz La, strɪng La, stɹɪn
Du We La Y Sa He Wo*[modern]* Wa Mon Gl O
Nt L Lei R Nth Hu Nf Sf Bk Bd Hrt Ess Brk
K*[recent x1]* Sx, stɹɪng Ch Db St Wo, stˌtrɪn
So*[modern]* W; **thick rough string** θɪk ɹʊf stɹɪn
Lei
3. n **(a) bit of string, piece of string** a knee-strap
used to lift the leg of working trousers, ⇐
KNEE-STRAPS VI.14.17. **(a) bit of string** bɪt ə
stʁɪn Nb, ə bɪt əv stɹɪn Lei; **piece of string** pɛɪs
ə stɹɪng Db *[piece of string marked u.r. WMBM]*
4.1. vt to REMOVE *STALKS* from currants
V.7.24. stɹɪn Mon Nf Sx, -*ing* stɹɪnɪn MxL, -*ing*
stɹɪnɪn Ess Sr, -*ing* ʃtɹɪnɪn Nf, stɹɪngɪn Brk, stˌtrɪn
So W Ha
4.2. v to remove stalks. -*ing* stɹɪnɪn Nf Sf Bk Ess
Sr, stˌtrɪn So*[old]*
5. n the CORE of a boil VI.11.7. stɹɪng La

string-couch *n* COUCH-GRASS   II.2.3.
stɹɪnk^ʊuːtʃ Gl

string-horse *1. n* the LAND-HORSE of a
ploughing team II.3.4(b). stɹɪnəs Y L
2. n a SHAFT-HORSE I.6.2. stˌtrɪnhɔˑtˑːş So
[marked ?error SBM]
3. n a TRACE-HORSE I.6.3. stˌtrɪnaˑtˑːş Do,
stˌtrɪnɒs Do

strings *1. npl* the REINS of a plough-horse I.5.5.
sg stɹɪn Y
2. n ⇐ SHOWS SIGNS OF CALVING by
changes in the pelvic region (of a cow) III.1.12(b).
slip in/of her strings *3prprogsg* slɪpən əv ə strɪnz
We, *3prperfsg* slɪpt əv ə stɹɪnz Cu; **(the/her)
strings go** *3prpl* stɹɪnz ə gaːn Cu, *3prpl* t stɹɪnz
əz gɒn We, *3prprogpl* ə stɹɪnz ɪz gʊɪn Y, *3ptpl* ə
stɹɪnz ɪz gɒn Y; **her strings are down** ə stɹɪnz ə
d^ʊuːn Du, **her strings drop** *3prpl* ə stɹɪnz ɪz dɹɔpt
Y; **fall in/of her strings** *3prprogsg* fɔːlɪn əv ə
stɹɪnz Y; **her strings slacken** *3prprogpl* ə stɹɪnz
ə slakənɪn Y

string-twitch *n* COUCH-GRASS II.2.3. stɹɪŋtwɪtʃ Ess

strint out *vphr* to strip the last drops of milk from a cow, ⇐ STRIPPINGS III.3.4. *-ing* strɪntɪn aʊt La

strints *n* STRIPPINGS, the last drops at milking III.3.4. strɪnts La

strip *1. n* the SOLE of a horse-drawn turn-wrest plough I.8.9. stɹɪp Sx

2. *n* STRIPPINGS, the last drops at milking III.3.4. stɹɪp K

3. *n* a DIAGONAL BAR of a gate IV.3.7. *pl* stɹɪps Wa, s̯tɹ̯ɪp So

4.1. *v* to PLUCK a dead chicken of its feathers IV.6.21. *-ing* s̯tɹ̯ɪpɪn D

4.2. *v* to pluck a chicken. stɹɪp La, s̯tɹ̯ɪp D

5. *v* to LOP a tree IV.12.5. stɹɪp MxL

6. *v* to cut small branches from a tree. *-ing* stɹɪpɪn Y

7. *vt* to TOP-AND-TAIL gooseberries V.7.23. *-ing* stɹɪpɪn Ess

8.1. *vt* to REMOVE *STALKS* from currants V.7.24. strɪp Cu, stɹɪp La Y Sa He Wo Wa, *-ing* stɹɪpɪn Mon Gl, *-ing* strɪpɪn O, s̯tɹ̯ɪp D Do, s̯tɹ̯ɪb (+V) D, *-ing* s̯tɹ̯ɪpɪn So W Co, s̯tɹ̯ɪpən Co, *-ing* stʁəpɪn Nb, stɹəpən La

8.2. *v* to remove stalks. strɪp Cu, *-ing* strɪpɪn We, stʁɪp Nb, stɹɪp Db Sa Wo O Sf Bd Hrt Ess, *-ing* stɹɪpn Nf, stθɹɪp La, s̯tɹ̯ɪp Ha, *-ing* stʁʏpən Nb

9. *vt* to CLEAR the table after a meal V.8.14. stɹɪp Ess

stripe *1. vt* to REMOVE *STALKS* from currants V.7.24. stɹaɪp We

2. *vt* to BEAT a boy on the buttocks VIII.8.10. stɹəɪp Mon

strip-naked *adj* NAKED, describing a person VI.13.20. stɹɪpniːkɪd Ch

strip out *vtphr* to drain a cow of its last drops of milk, ⇐ STRIPPINGS III.3.4. stɹɪp ... æʊt Wa Ess, stɹɪp ... uːt Y, *-ing* stɹɪpɪn ... uːt Cu, *imp* s̯tɹ̯ɪp ... æʊt Ha, *2prperf* s̯tɹ̯ʊp ... əʊt Do

strip over *vtphr* to REMOVE *STALKS* from currants V.7.24. *-ing* stɹɪpɪn ... ɒʊvəˡ Sx*[old]*

stripped *adj* NAKED, describing a person VI.13.20. stɹɪpt Ess K

stripper *n* a cow that does not produce much milk, ⇐ STRIPPINGS III.3.4. stɹɪpə Y

stripping(s) *n What do you call the last drops [from a cow that is being milked]?* III.3.4.

no -s: strɪpn Cu, strɪpɪn La, strɪpən We, stɹɪpɪŋ Sr, stɹɪpɪn Y He Wo O Ess Sr Sx, stɹɪppɪn Mon, stɹɪpn Nf Sf Ess, stɹɪpm Ess, stɹɪpən Du, stɹɛpn Nf, stʁəpɪn Nb, stʁəpən Du

-s: strɪpɪnz Cu Y, strɪpnz Du, strɪpənz Cu, stʰrɪpəns Man, strɪpənz Nb Cu We, stʁɪpəns Nb, stʁɪpənz Nb, stɹɪpɪnz La Y Ch Db Sa St He Wo Wa Mon Gl Nt Lei Nth Sf Bk Bd Ess MxL Brk Sr K Sx, s̯tɹ̯ɪpɪnz So W Sr D Ha, stɹɪpnz Nf Ess K, stɹɪpmz Ess, stɹɪpʔnz Sf,

stɹɪpənz Du Sa Ess, stɹɪpʔənz Sf, s̯tɹ̯ɪpnz Ha, s̯tɹ̯ɪpəns Co, s̯tɹ̯ɪpənz Co Do, stʁɛpɪns Nb, stʁʏpɪnz Nb, strəpɪnz Y, strəpɪnz Cu, strəpənz We, stʁəpəns Nb, s̯tɹ̯əpɪnz So

⇒ **afterings, cleanings, draggings, draining(s), drawing, dredging, dribble(s), dribblings, driddles, dripping(s), dripplings, drips, scrickings, stickings, strakes, strapping(s),** *streaks* ⇒ **strakes, strig, strikings, strints, strip, stroking(s), stroos, strop, stropping(s), swattings**; ⇒ *also* **strint out, strip out, stripper, swat off**

stroddle *adv* ASTRIDE VI.9.8. stɹɒdl Sa, stɹɒdɫ Lei Sx, s̯tɹ̯ɒdɫ O, s̯tɹ̯ɒdɫ D, stɹɔdɫ MxL

stroddled *adv* ASTRIDE VI.9.8. stɹɒdld Wa*[old]*, stɹɒdɫd Gl Bk Hrt, s̯tɹ̯ɒdɫd W

stroddle-footed *adj* SPLAY-FOOTED VI.10.5. s̯tɹ̯ɒdɫvʊtɪd So

stroddle-legged *adv* ASTRIDE VI.9.8. stɹɒdl̩lɛgd Db Sa St Wo, stɹɒdɫlɛgd He Wa, stɹɒdɫlɛgɪd Mon, s̯tɹ̯ɒdɫlɛgɪd So, stɹɔdɫlɛgd Sr K

stroddling *adv* ASTRIDE VI.9.8. stɹɒdlɪn He, stɹɒdlɪn Sa St He Wo Nth Bk, stɹɒdɫɪn Bk, stɹɒdɫɪn He Mon Gl Sx, s̯tɹ̯ɒdɫɪn W, *prppl* s̯tɹ̯ɒdɫɪn So, s̯tɹ̯ɒdɫən Do, stɹɔdlɪn Hrt, *prppl* stɹɔdɫɪn K, stɹɔdɫɪn MxL

stroddling out *adv* ASTRIDE VI.9.8. stɹɒdɫɪn ɛʊt K

strog-legged *adv* ASTRIDE VI.9.8. stɹɒglɛgd Sa

stroil *n* COUCH-GRASS II.2.3. s̯tɹ̯aɪɫ D, s̯tɹ̯ɒɪɫ So Co D

stroily-grass *n* COUCH-GRASS II.2.3. s̯tɹ̯eːɫɪgɹæːs Co

stroke *vt* to GROPE *FOR FISH* IV.9.10. stɹɔʊkɪn O

stroking(s) *n* STRIPPINGS, the last drops at milking III.3.4.

no -s: stɹɒkɪn K

-s: stɹɒkɪnz K, s̯tɹ̯ɒkənz Co D, s̯tɹ̯ɔːkɪnz So D Do, s̯tɹ̯ɔːkənz D, s̯tɹ̯ɔːkɪnz So D, s̯tɹ̯ɔːkənz Do

strong *1. adj* **getting very strong** (IN) FLOOD, describing a river IV.1.4. gɛɹɪn vaɹɪ stɹɒŋ Y

2. *adv* VERY poisonous IV.11.5. straŋ Cu, stɹɒŋ Sa

strong boots *npl* BOOTS VI.14.23. stɹaŋ bɪʊts Cu, straŋ bɪəts We

strong-brush *n* a MUCK-BRUSH I.3.14. stɹɒŋbɹʊʃ Nt

strong shoes *npl* BOOTS VI.14.23. stɹʊŋ ʃʏːz La, stɹɒŋ ʃˡʏːz Ch, straŋ ʃᵁuːz We

strong shoon *npl* BOOTS VI.14.23. stɹɔŋ ʃuːn La

stroos *n* STRIPPINGS, the last drops at milking III.3.4. strᵁuːz We

strop *n* STRIPPINGS, the last drops at milking III.3.4. stɹɒp K

stropes *npl* large pieces of metal forming the TIRE of a wagon-wheel I.9.10. stɹoʊps St

stropping(s) *n* STRIPPINGS, the last drops at milking III.3.4.
no -s: stɹɒpɪn L
-s: stɹɒpɪnz Y Nt L Lei, stɹɒpʔnz Nf, stɹɒpɪnz L

strucken *adj* HEAVING *WITH MAGGOTS* IV.8.6. stɹʊkn L

struddle *adv* ASTRIDE VI.9.8. stɹʊdʊɫ Brk

strunter *n* a RESTIVE horse III.5.6. stɹʊntə Y

strut *1. n* the CROSS-BEAM END of a cart I.10.1. *pl* ʂtɹʌts Ha
2. n a wooden device used to prevent a cart from going backwards on a hill, ⇐ PROP/CHOCK I.11.2. stɹʌʔ Ess
3. n a DIAGONAL BAR of a gate IV.3.7. stɹʌt Nf Sx, *pl* stɹʌts Sr K, ʂtɹʌt Ha, stɹʌtʔ Nf, stɹʌʔ Nf, stɹʊt Cu, *pl* stɹʊts La Y
*4. vi to fish for MINNOWS IV.9.9. *vbln* stɹʊtɪn L

strut-beam *n* an EVENER on the plough-beam end of a horse-drawn plough I.8.4. ʂtɹɒdbiːm W

struts *npl* MINNOWS IV.9.9. stɹʊts L

stub *1. n* the HANDLE of a besom I.3.16. stʌb Ha
2. n a tree STUMP IV.12.4. stʌb Sa He Sf K, stʊb Wo Ha Sx, stəb Ess
3. n a root of a laid hedge. stʌb K

stub-end *n* the BUTT of a sheaf of corn II.6.4. stʌbɛnd Bd, stʌbeɪn D, stʊbɛnd Nth

stubber *n* AFTERMATH, a second crop of grass II.9.17. stʊbə Hrt

stubble *n* *What is left in a cornfield after harvesting?* II.1.2. stɒbəl Wo, stɒbɫ He Wo K, stɒbʊɫ Brk, stʌbl Nb Sa O Nf, stʌbɫ He Mon Gl O Nth Hu C Nf Sf Bk Bd Hrt Ess MxL So W Sr K Co D Do Ha, stʌbʊɫ Brk Sx, stʌbʊ Ess Brk Sr K Sx, stɒbɫ Nth, stʏbəl Nf, stʊbɪl Db, stʊbl Nb Cu Du We La Y Man Ch Db Sa St Wa Nt L, stʊbɫ Man Ch He Wo Wa Mon Gl Lei R Nth C, stʊbʊɫ Gl, stʊbʊ Sx; **corn-stubble** kaᶜːŋstʌbɫ So. ⇒ **arrish, corn-stubble, eddish, gratton, haulms, leasing, stub(s), stubbles, stubbling;** ⇒ also **oat-gratton**

stubble-end *n* the BUTT of a sheaf of corn II.6.4. stʌbɫɛnd So D, stʌbɫeɪn D, stʊbɫɛn Ch, stʊbʊɫɛnd Brk

stubbles *n* STUBBLE remaining in a cornfield after harvesting II.1.2. stʌblz He Nf, stʌbɫz Mon Bk So W Do Ha, stʌbʊɫz Brk Ha, stʊblz Nb Cu Y Nt L, stʊbɫz Gl, stəbʊz Sx

stubbling *n* STUBBLE remaining in a cornfield after harvesting II.1.2. stʌblɪn Sa, stʊblɪn Ch

stubborn *adj* RESTIVE, describing a horse III.5.6. stɒbən Man, stʌbɔːn Mon, stʌbn Sx, stʌbən Mon Ess Sx, stʌbəᶜːŋ So W Co Do Ha

stubbs *npl* BUSHES IV.10.5. stəbz Ess

stubby *n* a COBBLER VIII.4.5. stʌbi Ha

stub(s) *n* STUBBLE remaining in a cornfield after harvesting II.1.2.
no -s: stʌb O
-s: stʌbz Gl O So W Brk, stʊbz O L R

stubs *npl* GATE-POSTS IV.3.2. stʊbz La

stucked up *adj* STICKY, describing a child's hands VIII.8.14. stʌkt ʌp Gl

stuckins *npl* stakes used to support netting, used to pen sheep in part of a field, ⇐ HURDLES III.7.11. stɒkənz Nb, stʌkənz Nb

stuck up *adj* STICKY, describing a child's hands VIII.8.14. stʊk ʊp Y

stud *1. n* a BUMPER of a cart I.10.1.(a). stʊd Ha
2. n the BASE of a stack II.7.4. stʌd Ess
3. n the TAG of a boot-lace VI.14.26. stʌd So

studdle *1. n* the PARTITION between stalls in a cow-house I.3.2. stɪdʊɫ Sx
2. n a TETHERING-STAKE in a cow-house I.3.3. stɪdɫ Co D, stʌdɫ Co, stʊdɫ Co

studs *npl* the JAMBS of a door V.1.11. stʌdz Sf

stuff *1. v* to GOBBLE food VI.5.13(b). *-ing* stʌfɪn O
2. n **bit of stuff, piece of stuff** a girl, ⇐ PRETTY VI.5.18. **bit of stuff** bɪt ə stʊf L; **piece of stuff** pɪiːz ə stʌf W

stugg *n* a BREAD-BIN V.9.2. stʊg Co

stugged *1. adj* BOGGY IV.1.8. stʌgd D
2. adj bogged down. stʌgd Co *[assumed reference to cart]*

stuggy *adj* BOGGY IV.1.8. stʌgi Co D, stʊgi D

stull *n* a SLICE of bread V.6.10. stʌɫ Sf

stump *1. n* *[Show a picture of a tree.] Suppose the tree had blown down and broken off there [point], what would you call the part left?* IV.12.4. Eng; **tree-stump** tɹiːstʌmp He. ⇒ **arse-end, bole, breech, breech-end, bulk, butt, butt-end, dock, moot, more, root-butt, seat, sleeper, snoul, stem, stook, stool, stoven, stub, timber-stub, tree-butt, tree-dog, tree-stool, *tree*-stump**
2. n the HANDLE of a besom I.3.16. stʌmp So
3. n the BUTT of a sheaf of corn II.6.4. stʊmp Nb

stumpers *npl* PARTRIDGES IV.7.8(a). stʌmpəᶜːz Ha

stumpies *npl* PARTRIDGES IV.7.8(a). stʌmpiːz Ha

stumps *npl* GATE-POSTS IV.3.2. stʊmps Ch Db St Wa

stunt *adj* STEEP, describing a hill IV.1.11. stʌnt Hu, stʌnʔ Hu Hrt, stʊnt Nth

stupid *1. adj* *A man who can never do things in the right way is quite* .... VI.1.5. stjʏːpəd Db, stʏːpɪd D, stjʊpɪd He Wa, stɪupɪd K, stɪuːpɪd Sa Nt L Ess, stɪuːpəd Nt Sf, stju:pɪd Nb Cu Man Ch Db Sa St He Wo Mon O L So Brk Sr K, stɪuːpʌd Sa, stju:pət Du, stju:pəd Nb Du Man, stu:pɪd Db Sa Wa Hu Ess K

2. *n* a stupid person. stju:pɪd Brk

⇒ **addle-headed**, *a* **niddy-noddy** *heller*, *a* **numb one**, *a* **stupid, awkward, barmy, bull-head, bull-skulled, cakey, cakey fool, cakey-headed, chuckle-headed, clout-head, clumsy-head, comical, contrary, cranky, daft, daft** *wap*, **dense, dingy, dippy, doak, dopey, dormant, dough-bake, dozy, dulbert, dullard, dumb, dummel, dummel-head, elevenpence-halfpenny, feckless, fit-for-nought, flambergasted, fond, fond-brazen, fool, foreright, fuddled, gaby, gaumless, gaumy, gawk, gawky,** *going wrong*, **gooky,** *got a* **tile** *loose*, **half-daft,** *hasn't got all his* **buttons,** *he's* **half-daft, hopeless,** *hopeless at doing aught*, **hot, lump-head, luny, maupy, mazed, mental, muddled, muzzy, noggin-head, noodle, numb-head, numbskull, potty, puggled, sackless,** *short of a* **shilling, silly, simple, simple-minded, slow, soft, soppy, staups, thick-head, thick-headed, tool, touched, touched** *in the head*, **uncouth, useless,** *wanky* ⇒ **wonky, wonky, wooden, wooden-headed, yampy**

3. *adj* SILLY VIII.9.3. stɪupɪd Ess, stju:pɪd Y L So, stu:pɪd Brk Sr K, stju:pət Nb, stju:pəd Man

4. *adj* RESTIVE, describing a horse III.5.6. stɪupɪd Y

stuts *npl* MINNOWS IV.9.9. stʊts L

stuttle *npl* MINNOWS IV.9.9. stʌʔl Nf

stuttle-fish *npl* MINNOWS IV.9.9. stʌʔ|fɪʃ Nf

sty 1. *n* a PIGSTY I.1.5. steɪ So, staɪ Nb, *pl* staːɪz St, staɪ Nt Ess, stɒɪ So Ha, stɔɪ O Ha, *pl* stɔɪz Sx

*2. *n* a STILE IV.2.9. staɪ Y, staɪ La, stəɪ We Y *[headword created in light of sty-hole headword WMBM]*

styany *n* a STYE in the eye VI.3.10. staɪnaɪ Nth, staɪni Nf, staɪnə Nf, stɒɪnə Nf, stɔɪnə Sf, stʌɪni Sf, stʌɪnə Nf, stʌɪnəᴶ Nf

stye *n What do you call that red, sore place with a white centre [point to the eye]?* VI.3.10. Eng exc. Y St Wo Nt Bd MxL Sx. ⇒ **blain, brithin, cyst, gissy, pig's-court, pig's-foot, pig-stye, pike, pimple, pouk, quailaway, risk, stine,** *styan* ⇒ **stine, styany, ulcer, west, wilk, wilt, wisk, wisp, wist, wiss** *[q not asked before March 1953]*

sty-hole *n* a STILE IV.2.9. staɪ-ɔɪl Y, stəɪ-ʊəl Y *[a WMBM headword, but the form in Db is stee-hole]*

such *predet You might go on to say: What a fool! You can't get any sense out of him at all. I've never come across ... a fool.* VIII.9.7. Eng. ⇒ **suchan**

suchan *predet* SUCH VIII.9.7. sɪtʃn Y L, sɪtʃən Y, sʊtʃn Du Y L, sʊtʃən Y, saɪkn Y

suck *v How does the newly-born lamb gets its milk?* III.7.1. zʏk Co D, sɛʊk Y, zœːk Gl, saʊk Cu La Y, sɒk Brk, sɒʊk La, sʌk Sa He Mon Gl O Nth Hu C Nf Sf Bk Bd Hrt Ess MxL So W Brk Sr K Ha Sx, zʌk So W Co D Do Ha, sʏk Nf, sʊk Cu Du La Y Man Ch Db Sa St He Wo Wa Mon Gl O Nt L Lei R Nth C Bk Co,

suːk Nb Cu Du We Y Nt, sʊːkʰ Nb Cu, sək Gl O, zək Gl, sʌk its mʌðə Nf. ⇒ **chet, chirt out, draw, suckle, suck out**

suck down *vtphr* to guzzle a drink, ⇐ GUZZLES VI.5.13(a). *-ing* sʌkɪn ... dɛʊn MxL, *-ing* sʌkɪn ... dæʊn Ess

sucker 1. *n* a PET-LAMB III.7.3. zʌkəˤː W Do, sʊkə Y

2. *n* a PIGLET III.8.2. zʏkəˤː So Co D, sʌkə Nf*[to 8 weeks old]*, sʌkəˤ Sa O, zʌkəˤː So W D Do, *pl* zʌkəˤːz̩ Ha, sʊkə Y*[to 8 weeks old x1]* Ch Db Nt L Nth, sʊkɹ L, sʊkəɹ La He L, sʊkkəɹ La, sʊkəᴶ La Ch, *pl* sʊkəᴶz Db, sʊkəˤ He Wa, *pl* sʊkəˤz̩ Bk, zʊkəˤ Gl, sʊkəˤɽ Brk, sʊkəˤː Co

suckers *n* SWEETS V.8.4. sʌkəz Sf Bd Hrt Ess Sr, sʌkʔəz Sf Ess, sʌkəˤz̩ O Bk

sucking-pig *n* a PIGLET III.8.2. sæʊkɪnpɪg Y, sʌkɪnpɪg O Hu Sr Sx, sʌkənpɪg Ha, zʌkɪnpɪg So, sʊkɪnpɪg Y L

suck-lamb *n* a PET-LAMB III.7.3. sʌklɛm K, zʌklæm So, zʌklam So Do, zʌkłam W D Do

suckle 1. *vt* to WEAN a calf III.1.4. sʊkl St

2. *v* to SUCK, describing how a lamb gets its milk III.7.1. sʌkł O Sf, sʌkʔł Sf, *3prsg* sʌkʊz K, *-ing* sʏkļn Nf, sʊkl Ch St Wo, sʊtl Db, sʊkł K

3. *vt* to suck its mother, referring to the action of a feeding lamb. *3prsg* sʊklz Y

suckle-lamb *n* a PET-LAMB III.7.3. sʌkʊlæm Sx

suckler 1. *n* a PET-LAMB III.7.3. sʌklə K

2. *n* a PIGLET III.8.2. sʌklə Nf, sʌkłəˤ Mon, sʌkłəˤz̩ K

suckler-lamb *n* a PET-LAMB III.7.3. zʌkəłəłam W

sucklet* *n* a lamb unable to drink without help, ⇐ PET-LAMB III.7.3. sʌklɪt K

suckling 1. *n* a PET-LAMB III.7.3. zʌkļɪn W

2. *n* a PIGLET III.8.2. sʌklɪn Nf Sr, sʊklɪn Cu Y L, sʊtlɪn La, səklɪn K

suckling-lamb *n* a PET-LAMB III.7.3. sʌkļɪnlæːm K

suckling-pig *n* a PIGLET III.8.2. sʌklɪnpɪg Ess Brk, sʊkłɪnpɪg Lei

suck out *vphr* to SUCK, describing how a lamb gets its milk III.7.1. zʌk æʊt W

suck(s) *n* SWEETS V.8.4.

no -s: sʌk He, sʊk St He Wo Wa

-s: sʌks Sa, sʊks St Wa Nth

sucks *vt-3prsg* he GUZZLES a drink VI.5.13(a). *-ing* sʌkɪn Ess

sucks up* *vtphr-3prsg* he GUZZLES a drink VI.5.13(a). sʊks ... ʊp Lei

suck-tit *n* a PIGLET III.8.2. *pl* zʊktɪts Gl*[to 8 weeks old]*, zəktɪt Gl

suction *n* URINE in a cow-house I.3.10. sʊkʃən Du

suet *n* the FAT round the kidneys of a pig III.12.7. sɪuət Sf Ess, sø-ɪt Nf, suˑɪt Nf, suːət Man Ess, səː-ɪt Nf

suffer *vt-2prsg* you BEAR pain VI.5.9. sʌfəˡɽ (+V) Sa

suffering *adv* VERY VIII.3.2. sʌfɹɪn Nf

sugar *n You sweeten tea with ....* V.8.10. Eng. ⇒ also **sugar-baby**, **sugar-head**, **sugar-sop**

sugar-baby* *n* a person who likes sugar, ⇐ SUGAR V.8.10. ʃugəbɛɪbɪ Lei

sugar-bread *n* a PIECE *OF BREAD AND BUTTER AND JAM/SUGAR* V.6.11(b). ʃugəˡbɹɛˑd K; **sugar-bread and butter** ʃugəˡbɹɪd ŋ bʌtəˡ Sr

sugar-buppy *n* a PIECE *OF BREAD AND BUTTER AND JAM/SUGAR* V.6.11(b). ʃugəbʌpɪ K

sugar-butty *n* a PIECE *OF BREAD AND BUTTER AND JAM/SUGAR* V.6.11(b). ʃɒgəˡbɒtɪ Man K, ʃʌgəˡbʌtɪ Sa, ʃugəˡbʌtɪ K, ʃugəˡbʌtɪ Sa

sugar-head* *n* a simpleton, ⇐ SUGAR V.8.10. sɪugəɹɪəd Y

sugar-sandwich *n* a PIECE *OF BREAD AND BUTTER AND JAM/SUGAR* V.6.11(b). ə ʃugəsandwɪdʒ Y

sugar-shag *n* a PIECE *OF BREAD AND BUTTER AND JAM/SUGAR* V.6.11(b). ʃugəʃag Cu[*bread spread with sugar x1*] We

sugar-sop* *n* bread soaked in water and sugar, ⇐ SUGAR V.8.10. ʃugəsɒp Nf

sugg *n* a WHETSTONE made of stone II.9.10. *pl* zʌgz So

suggan *n* a rope used to fasten thatch on a stack, ⇐ ROPES II.7.7(b2). sɒgɛən Man

suggy* *adj* BOGGY IV.1.8. sʌgɪ Sr

suit *1. n What do you call jacket and trousers together when they match?* VI.14.21. Eng. ⇒ **coat and breeches**, *suit of clothes*
2. n SUNDAY-CLOTHES VI.14.19. bɛs sɪut Y Ess, bɛs sɪuːt Nb Ess, bɛs sy:ʔ O, bɛst suːt St, bɛs suːt Wa MxL So W K, bɛs sʉːt Nf

suke *n* a KETTLE V.8.7. ʃʊk O

sukey *n* a KETTLE V.8.7. sɪukɪ Y[*rare*], sʊkɪ O, ʃʊkɪ Gl[*old*] O, suːkɪ Bd Hrt K, sjəʊːkɪ Hrt

sulky *adj* RESTIVE, describing a horse III.5.6. sʌlkʔɪ Nf, sʌɫkɪ Ess K, sʌɫki W D

sull *n* a PLOUGH I.8.1. zʌɫ So, zʊɫ So

sullage-place *n* a DRAIN in a cow-house I.3.8. sʊlɪdʒplɛɪs K

sully* *n* a PLOUGH I.8.1. zɛloʊ So, zɛɫoʊ So

sully-plough *n* a PLOUGH I.8.1. sʌɫɪpleʊ K

summer *v* to put cattle on hired pasture, ⇐ HIRE *PASTURAGE* III.3.8. sʊmə We, -*ing* sʊməɹɪn Du La, *ptppl* sʊməd Du

summer-cocks *npl* large COCKS of hay II.9.12. sʊməɽkɒks O

summer-fallowing *n* FALLOW-LAND, apparently left fallow for a restricted period II.1.1. zʌməˡːvaɫɪn D [*definition follows EMBM note*]

summer-fallow(s) *n* FALLOW-LAND, apparently left fallow for a restricted period II.1.1. *no* -*s*: sʌməfælə Sf, sʌməˡvalə Ha, zʌməˡːvaɫəˡː Do, sʊməfalə Cu Y Db Nt, sʊmərfalə Cu, sʊməɹfalə La
-*s*: sʊməfaləz L Lei, sʊməfaləs Cu, sʊmɹfaləz L, sʊməfʊləz Lei
[*definition follows EMBM note and SBM note at Do.4*]

summer-freckles *n* FRECKLES   VI.11.1. zʌməˡːvɹakɫz W

summer-graze *v* to put cattle on hired pasture, ⇐ HIRE *PASTURAGE* III.3.8. -*ing* sʊməgɹeːzɪn La, -*ing* sʊməgɹɛˑəzɪn L

summer-land *n* FALLOW-LAND,   apparently left fallow for a restricted period II.1.1. sʌmlən Sf

summer-lea *n* FALLOW-LAND, apparently left fallow for a restricted period II.1.1. sʌməlɪ Nf [*definition follows EMBM note*]

summer-moles *n* FRECKLES   VI.11.1. zʌməˡːmoːɫz D Do

summer-moulds *n* FRECKLES   VI.11.1. sʌməˡːmoːɫdz Do, zʌməˡːmoːɫdz W Do

summers *1. npl* CART-LADDERS   I.10.5. sʊməz Nth
2. npl flat front cart-ladders. sʌməz Hu
3. n a CART-FRAME I.10.6. sʊməz Nth

summer's-fallow* *n* FALLOW-LAND, apparently left fallow for a restricted period II.1.1. sʊməzfɔlə Wa [*definition follows EMBM note*]

summer-spots *n* FRECKLES   VI.11.1. sʊməˡspɒts Mon

summer-till *n* FALLOW-LAND, apparently left fallow for a restricted period II.1.1. sʌmətɪl Nf [*definition follows EMBM note. Also recorded ?adj summer-tilled W*]

summer-tilling *n* FALLOW-LAND, apparently left fallow for a restricted period II.1.1. sʌmətɪlɪn Nf, sʌmətɪlŋ Nf [*definition follows EMBM note*]

summer-voys *n* FRECKLES   VI.11.1. sʌməˡːvɒɪz So, zʌməˡːvɒɪz So

summer-working *n* FALLOW-LAND, apparently left fallow for a restricted period II.1.1. sʊməwɜˡːkɪn La [*definition follows EMBM note*]

sump *1. n* URINE in a cow-house I.3.10. sʊmp Cu We
2. n a CESS-POOL on a farm I.3.11. sʊmp Cu Nt
3. n an artificial cess-pool. sʊmp Cu Y St
4. n MUD VII.6.17. sʊmp Y

sump-hole *1. n* a CESS-POOL on a farm I.3.11. *pl* sʌmpɔʊɫz Ess, sʊmpoʊl St
2. n an artificial cess-pool. sʊmpʊəl Y, zʊmpoːʊl Gl

sun-bonnet *1. n* a woman's BONNET VI.14.1. sʊnbɒnɪt L

2. n a woman's cotton bonnet. sʊnbɔnət L

3. n a woman's cloth or straw bonnet worn when working. sʌnbɒnəʔ O

4. n a woman's cloth bonnet with a curtain or cover for the neck. sʊnbɒnɪt O

sunburned cake *n* a CLOT OF COW-DUNG II.1.6. sʌnbəːnd kɛɪk Nf*[facetious]*

sunday-apron *n* a decorative APRON V.11.2(b). sʌndɪ-ɛːpɹ,n Nf, sʊndə-eːpɹən La

sunday best *n* SUNDAY-CLOTHES VI.14.19. sʌndɪ bɛst Brk K, sʊndɪ bɛst Y, sʊndə bɛst Y

sunday best clothes *n* SUNDAY-CLOTHES VI.14.19. zɪndi bɛs kɫuːəz D, sʌndɪ bɛs klɒʊðz Sx

sunday-clobber *n* SUNDAY-CLOTHES VI.14.19. sʊndɪklɒbə Db

sunday-clothes *n* *What do you call the things that you wear on Sundays?* VI.14.19. Eng exc. He Mon Co D Do. ⇒ **best bib and tucker, best clothes, best suit,** *best sunday-clothes, best* **sunday** *go-to-meeting* **togs, best things, best tog, best togs, better clothes, better suit, church-going clothes, preaching clothes, sunday best, sunday best clothes, sunday-clobber,** *sunday go-meeting clothes,* **sunday's best, sunday-suit, sunday-things, sunday-togs**

sunday's best *n* SUNDAY-CLOTHES VI.14.19. sʊndɪz bɛst Brk

sunday-suit *n* SUNDAY-CLOTHES VI.14.19. sʌndɪsɪut Nf, sʌndɪsɪuːt Ess Ha, sʌndɪsuːt Sr K, sʌndɪsʉːt Nf, sʊndəsɪut Y, sʊndəsɪuːt L, sʊndɪ suːt St

sunday-things *n* SUNDAY-CLOTHES VI.14.19. sʌndɪθɪŋz Ess

sunday-togs *n* SUNDAY-CLOTHES VI.14.19. sʌndɪtɒgz K, sʊndɪtɒgz Y St Nth; **best sunday go-to-meeting togs** bɛs sʌndɪ goutəmiːtɪŋ tɒgz Ha

sun-freckles *n* FRECKLES VI.11.1. sʌnfɹɛkʊz Sr, zʌnvɹ̥ɛkɫz So, sənfɹɛkɫz Gl

sunk *adj* SAD, describing bread or pastry that has not risen V.6.12. sʌŋk O Ess, sʊŋk Y

sunk-hole *n* a CESS-POOL on a farm I.3.11. sʊŋkɒɪl Y

sun-speckles *n* FRECKLES VI.11.1. zənspɛklz Gl

sun-spots *n* FRECKLES VI.11.1. sʊnspɒts Lei

sup *1. n* a DRINK (of milk) given to a kitten III.13.12. sʌp Nb Sa, soːp La, sʏp Nb, sʊp Nb Cu Du We La Y Db Nt L

2. n a LITTLE amount of milk VII.8.20. sʊp Nt L; **a sup** ə sʊp Db Nt; **a little sup** ə lɪtl sʊp Du L, ə laːl sʊp Cu We, ə laɪl sʊp We La Y; **little sup** lɪtl sʊp Nb

3. v to GOBBLE food VI.5.13(b). *3prsg* sʊps Ess

sup-and-a-bite *n* a SNACK VII.5.11. sʊpənəbaɪt Y

sup in *vtphr* to guzzle a drink, ⇐ GUZZLES VI.5.13(a). *-ing* sʊpən ... ɪn Sr

supper up *1. vphr* to feed horses in the stable, ⇐ FEEDING III.5.1. sʌpəɹ ʌp Hu*[with hay]*, sʊpəɹ ʊp Nt*[at night]*

2. vtphr to feed horses the last meal of the day. sʊpəɹ (+V) ... ʊp Y

supping *v-ing* DRINKING V.8.1. sʌpɪn Sa O Bk, sʊpɪn Nb Du La Y Ch Db*[old x1]* Sa St Wo O Nt L*[old x1]*, sʊppɪn La Db*[old x1]*, sʊpn Sf, sʊpən Nb Cu Du We La Man, *no -ing* sʊp So

supping up *vtphr-ing* FEEDING horses in the stable III.5.1. sʊpɪn ... ʊp St

support *1. n* the GRASS-NAIL of a scythe II.9.9. səpɔˈət K, səpɔːəˈt Sr

2. n a DIAGONAL BAR of a gate IV.3.7. *pl* səpɔːts Du, *-s* səpɔːts Sf, *pl* səpɔʁːts Nb, *pl* səpɔːɹts La, səpɔəˈt Brk

3. vt to AGREE *WITH* somebody VIII.8.12. səpɒʊəˤt̚ Wa, səpɔːt Y Nf Ess, səpɔʁːt Nb Du, sʌpɔˤːt̚ So

suppurate *vi* to FESTER, referring to a wound VI.11.8. sɛpɹət O

sups *v-3prsg* he GUZZLES a drink VI.5.13(a). sʌps Mon, sʊps Ess, *no -s* sʊp Sf, *-ing* sʊpɪn St, *-ing* sʉːpən Co, *-ing* səpɪn Sx

sup up *vtphr* to guzzle a drink, ⇐ GUZZLES VI.5.13(a). *-ing* sʊpɪn ... ʊp St, *-ing* sʉːpən ... ʌp Co

sure *adj* *If asked whether the postman had been, and you were somewhat doubtful, you'd say [using his own words from IX.7.11]: I'm not .... IX.7.12. Eng.* ⇒ **certain**

suspenders *n* BRACES VI.14.10. sʊspɛndəz Y

swab *n* a DISHCLOTH V.9.6. swɒb Brk

swabble *n* the *HORIZONTAL* BAR of a crane over a domestic fire V.3.5(a). swæbəɫ He

swabbles *v-3prsg* he GUZZLES a drink VI.5.13(a). swɒblz La

swab-footed *adj* SPLAY-FOOTED VI.10.5. swabfʊtɪd L

swad *n* a pea-POD V.7.12. swad Nb Cu La Y*[old x1]* Db L*[old x2]*, *pl* swadz Du*[old x1]* We Nt, *pl* swɒdz Nt, swɒd L

swadding *v-ing* SHELLING peas V.7.14. swadɪn La Nt

swaddling *n* a GOSLING IV.6.17. swɒdɫɪn Sr

swaffy *adj* INSIPID, describing food lacking in salt V.7.8. swafɪ Db

swailing* *v-ing* THROWING a stone VIII.7.7. swɛəlɪn Y

swallows *v-3prsg* he GUZZLES a drink VI.5.13(a). *inf* swɛlɪ Nb, *-ing* swɛlɪ-ən Nb

swamp *1. n* a CESS-POOL on a farm I.3.11. swɒmp So

2. adj BOGGY IV.1.8. swamp Du

swamped *adj* BOGGY IV.1.8. swɒmpt Gl So, swɔmpt MxL

swamps *n* LOW-LYING LAND IV.1.7. swɔːmps W

swampy *adj* BOGGY IV.1.8. swampɪ Cu Du We Y Ch L, swɒmpɪ La Sa St He Ess K, swɔmpɪ MxL, swɔːmpi So Ha

swampy ground *n* LOW-LYING LAND IV.1.7. swɔːmpi gɹaʊnd So

swampy patch *n* LOW-LYING LAND IV.1.7. swɔːmpɪ pɛtʃ Ess *[noted as 'probably merely descriptive' in EMBM]*

swap *1. v* to CLEAR grass at the edges of a field II.9.5. *-ing* swɒpɪn Sr

2. v to TRIM hedges IV.2.3. *-ing* swɒpɪn Sx

3. vt to BEAT a boy on the buttocks VIII.8.10. swɒp Bk

swape *n* a CRANE on which a kettle is hung over a domestic fire V.3.4. sweːp La

swapple *n* a BILLHOOK IV.2.6. swɒpʊɫ Sx *[queried SBM]*

sward *1. n* PASTURE II.1.3. swɔːd He

2. n the RIND of bacon III.12.6. swad Nb Du We Y, swaˑᴶːd La Y, swaᶜːd̩ Gl, swaᶜːd̩ He Wo Gl, sɒʊəd Db, sɔːᵊd Sa, sɔᶜːd̩ Sa, swɔᶜːd̩ Sa He, sɔːd Db, soəd Ch Db, soʊəd St Wo, soːᵊᴶd Db, sʊəd Y Db St, sʊəɹd La, sʊəᴶt Db, sʊəɽd̩ La, swɜːᴶːɹd La

swarf *1. n* old swarf a MEADOW II.9.2. ɒʊd swaːf Db *[never ploughed]*

2. vi to FAINT VI.13.7. swaˑᴶːf La

swarm *vt* to CLIMB VIII.7.4. swaɹm L, swaːm Y Db L, swaɪm L, swɔɹm He *[up tree without branches]*, swɔᶜːm Sa; **swarm it** swaːm ɪt Y

swarming *adj* HEAVING (WITH MAGGOTS) IV.8.6. swɛˑəmɪn Y, swaːmɪn La, *no -ing* zwaᶜːm D, swɔᶜːmɪn Sa

swarm up *vtphr* to CLIMB VIII.7.4. swæːm ʊp La, swaːm ʊp Y Ch, swɜːᴶːɪm ʊp La

swarth *v* to HIRE *PASTURAGE* III.3.8. swɒf Ch

swarth-turn *vt* to TURN hay II.9.11(b). *-ing* zwɔːftəᶜːn̩ɪn W, zwɔᶜːːtəᶜːn̩ D

swarth-turner *n* the GRASS-NAIL of a scythe II.9.9. zwɒᶜːːtəᶜːn̩əᶜː D

swat *n* a DRINK (of milk) given to a kitten III.13.12. swat Y

swatcher *n* a BILLHOOK IV.2.6. swatʃə Cu

swate-bar *n* a DIAGONAL BAR of a gate IV.3.7. *pl* sweːətbaᴶːz Y *[queried for swape- NBM]*

swath *1. n* *What do you call a row of mown grass?* II.9.4. swiːθ Nb, swiːð Nb Cu Y, swiːd Nb K, swɪaθ Y, swɪað Y, swɪəθ Du Y, swɪəð Du Y, sweːθ Cu La, sweːð Cu We La Y Nt, sweːd Nb La, sweːv Co, sweɪθ Man, sweɪ Man, sweaθ La, swe̜að We, sweəð Y, swɛθ Nf Sf, *pl* swɛθs Man, swɛð He, swɛːð Cu We, swɛːf So, swɛɪð Sf K, swɛɪd K, swɛəθ L, swɛəð La Y L, swæθ He Wo Mon Gl, swæð Wo, swaθ Nb Du Y Ch Db Sa St Wo Wa Gl Nt L Lei R, swaf Du Lei, swaᴶθ Ch, swaːð Sa, zwaᶜː Co D, swaːθ Y Wa Mon Nf, swaːð Wo Gl, swɒθ Db Sa St Mon Lei Brk Ha, swɒf So, *pl* swɒvz O, swɔːθ Wa Gl O L Nth Hu C Nf Sf Bk Bd Hrt Ess So Brk Sr K Ha Sx, zwɔːθ W Ha, swɔːð O Nth Bk Bd Hrt Ess MxL W Sr Do, *pl* swɔːðz So Brk, zwɔːð Ha, swɔːf Gl Nth Bk Hrt Ess So W Do Sx, zwɔːf W Do, swɔːv So, zwɔːv Ha, *pl* swɔːz So Sr Ha, zwɔː W, swɔᶜːθ So Sr Ha, swɔᶜːð So, swɔᶜː So Co, zwɔᶜː Co D, swʊəθ L.

⇒ **dram, reach, row, shed, spit,** *swarth* ⇒ **swath,** *swathe* ⇒ **swath,** *sweath* ⇒ **swath, wagon-row, wake, wally, windrow**

2. n PASTURE II.1.3. swaθ Y

3. n pasture used for grazing and as a hayfield in alternate years. swɛɪð Bd

4. n the RIND of bacon III.12.6. swaθ Cu We Y Nt L, swaːf Y

**5. n* a bean-POD V.7.12. swaθ L

swath-board *n* the MOULD-BOARD of a horse-drawn plough I.8.8. swæθboːəᶜd̩ He

swath-bool *n* part of a scythe, probably the CRADLE, ⇐ GRASS-NAIL II.9.9. swɔːfboːɫ So

swather *1. n* part of a scythe, probably the CRADLE, ⇐ GRASS-NAIL II.9.9. swɒfəᶜː So, swɔːθəᶜː So

**2. n* a wrapper worn over a DIAPER V.11.3. swɛɪðə L

swath-field *n* PASTURE II.1.3. swaθfiːld Y

swath-horse *n* the LAND-HORSE of a ploughing team II.3.4(b). swaθɔːs Y

swath-land *1. n* PASTURE II.1.3. swaθland L

2. n pasture for cows and horses. swaθland Y

swath-turn *vt* to TURN hay II.9.11(b). swaθtɛən Lei, swaθtəːn St Lei, *-ing* swɒftəᶜːn̩ɪn So, swɔːftəᶜːn̩ Gl So

swath-turner *n* the MOULD-BOARD of a horse-drawn plough I.8.8. swaθtənə Y

swat off *vtphr* to drain cows of their last drops of milk, ⇐ STRIPPINGS III.3.4. swæt ... ɔˑf Y

swattings *n* STRIPPINGS, the last drops at milking III.3.4. swætɪnz Y

sway *1. n* an EVENER, the main swingle-tree of a horse-drawn plough harness I.8.4. swaɪ Wo

2. n a CRANE on which a kettle is hung over a domestic fire V.3.4. swiː St, sweː Nb Sa Mon, sweːɪ He Wo Mon, sweɪ Nb Ch Sa St Gl, swæɪ He Gl, swaɪ Wo

3. n the *HORIZONTAL* BAR of a crane over a domestic fire V.3.5(a). sweː Sa, sweːɪ Mon, sweɪ Ch

4. n the vertical BAR or CHAIN of a crane over a domestic fire V.3.5(b). sweɪ Wo

sway-bar *n* the *HORIZONTAL* BAR of a crane over a domestic fire V.3.5(a). sweɪbaː Wo

sway-cosp *n* an EVENER on a horse-drawn plough I.8.4. sweɪkaːsp He

swaygog *n* a SEESAW VIII.7.2. sweɪgɔg Sr, sweɪgɔg K *[old]*

sway-head *n* the T-SHAPED PLOUGH-BEAM END of a horse-drawn plough I.8.5. swɪi-əd Ess

sway-link *n* the HOOK or *CROOK* of a crane over a domestic fire V.3.5(c). *pl* swæɪlɪŋks Gl

sway-pole *1. n* a CRANE on which a kettle is hung over a domestic fire V.3.4. swɛːpoːl Sa, sweɪpoʊl He, swaːˡpoʊl He*[old]*

2. n the *HORIZONTAL* BAR of a crane over a domestic fire V.3.5(a). sweɪpoʊl He

sway(s) *n* a SWINGLE-TREE of a horse-drawn plough harness I.8.3.

sg: swɛɪ La

-s: swɛɪz La

sway-tree *1. n* a SWINGLE-TREE of a horse-drawn plough harness I.8.3. swɛɪtɹiː Lei, swɛɪtɹi Nth, swɛɪʔɹɪ Nth

2. n an EVENER, the main swingle-tree of a horse-drawn plough harness I.8.4. swɛɪtɹiː Nth

sweak *1. n* a CRANE on which a kettle is hung over a domestic fire V.3.4. swiːk Ch St, swiːt St, swɪk Sa, swɛːk Sa, swɛk Sa

2. n the *HORIZONTAL* BAR of a crane over a domestic fire V.3.5(a). swiːk Ch

sweal up *viphr* to WRINKLE, referring to the skin of very old people VI.11.2. swiːɬ ʌp O

swearing *v-ing Of a person who uses a lot of bad language, you'd say: He is always [cursing and] ....* VIII.8.9(b). Eng. ⇒ **abusing, blackguarding, blaspheming, blinding, buggering**

sweat *vi* to HEAT, referring to a haystack II.9.16. swɪət Cu Y, *3prsg* swɪəts We La, swɛt Ch Db Sa, *3prsg* swɛts Y *[N/WMBM Edd note that sweat probably refers to a different aspect of the process from heat, though Cu informant regards them as 'the same thing']*

sweat(s) *3prsg On a very hot day, you [gesture wiping your forehead]....* VI.13.5.

no -s: Eng

-s: swɛts O, swɛʔs O

⇒ **perspire**

sweats *npl* PALS VIII.4.2. swɛʔs Hrt

swede-clean *v* to TOP AND TAIL swedes II.4.3. *-ing* swiːdklɛɪnɪn Bk *[marked ir.r. EMBM]*

swede-trim *v* to TOP AND TAIL swedes II.4.3. *-ing* swɪiːdtɹɪmɪn Sr

sweep *v What do you do with a brush?* V.9.12. Eng. ⇒ **brush, brush up, sweep out, sweep up**

sweeping-broom *n* a BRUSH used for sweeping indoors V.9.11. swiːpɪnbɹuːm Y Wa Sr, swˡiːpɪnbɹɪuːm Sa

sweeping-brush *n* a long-handled BRUSH used for sweeping V.2.14. swiːpɪnbɹʏːʃ La, swiːpɪnbɹʌʃ Mon, swiːpɪnbɹʊʃ Y L, swɪpɪnbɹʊʃ Gl, swɛɪpɪnbɹʊʃ St

2. n a BROOM used for sweeping outdoors V.9.10. swɛɪpɪnbɹʊʃ St

3. n a BRUSH used for sweeping indoors V.9.11.

swiːpɪnbɹɪʏːʃ La, swiːpɪnbɹʏːʃ La, swiːpɪnbɹʌʃ Mon, swiːpɪnbɹʊʃ Cu, swiːpɪnbɹʊʃ Y Db Nt L Nth, swiːpɪnbəˡːʃ So, swɪipɪnbɹʌʃ Nf, swˡiːpɪnbɹʊʃ We, swɪəpɪnbɹʊʃ Y, swɛɪpɪnbɹʊʃ St, swəɪpɪnbɹʊʃ Y

sweepole *n* a SEESAW VIII.7.2. swɛɪpoʊl Y

sweep out *vphr* to SWEEP V.9.12. *-ing* swiːpɪn æʊt Wo

sweep up *1. vtphr* to SWEEP V.9.12. swiːp ʌp So, zwiːp ... ʌp Do, zweːp ... ʌp Co, swɛɪp ... ʊp St

2. vphr to sweep. swiːp ʌp Nf So W Co Do Ha Sx, zwiːp ʌp So W Co D Do Ha, swiːp ʏp Nf, swiːp ʊp Y Ch Wo, swiːpʔ ʌpʔ Nf, swɪp ʌp So Ha, zwɪp ʌp W D Ha, swɪp ʊp He, zweːp ʌp D Ha, swɛp ʌp W, swɛɪp ʊp St, swəɪp ʊp Y

sweepy *adj* SPLAY-FOOTED VI.10.5. swɪpɪ W

sweet *1. n* SWEETS V.8.4. swɪit Ess

2. adj PRETTY, describing a girl VI.5.18. swiːt So

sweet-heart(s) *n* GOOSE-GRASS II.2.5.

no -s: swiːtaːt Y, swiːthaːt Nf Ess, swiːtʔaːtʰ Bk, swiːtaːt Nf, swiːthaːt Nf

-s: swiːtaːts Y Ch Bd Ess, swiːtaɪts He, swiːtaˡːts Gl So, swiːʔaˡːʔs Bk, swiːthaːts Nf, swiːʔaːts MxL, swiːtəˡːts Wo

sweet-hearts *n* BINDWEED II.2.4. swiːtaːts Db

sweeties *n* SWEETS V.8.4. swiːtɪz Cu Sf MxL Ha*[said to small child]*

sweets *n If you wished to please a child, you might say: Here's 3d, go and buy yourself [some] ....* V.8.4. Eng exc. Nb Du We Y Nth Hu C Bk Bd. ⇒ *a bag of sweets, a bit of suck, a few bullets, a few goodies, a few lollies, a few sweets, a pennyworth of suck, cooshies, crooshies, goodies, some balsers, some bullets, some candy, some cooshies, some crooshies, some dods, some dumps, some goodies, some goody, some humbugs, some jumbles, some lollies, some lollipops, some lozengers* ⇒ **lozenges**, *some lozenges, some pellets, some peppermints, some peps, some pops, some spice, some suckers, some suck(s), some sweet, some sweeties, some toff, some toffee, some toffee-nobs, some toffees, some tommy-dods, spice, what you want [terms identified as referring to types of sweet not given headword status: some other terms, e.g. pops, may also belong to this category]*

swell *1. n* a BUMP on someone's forehead VI.1.8. swɛl Db

2. vi to WAX, referring to the moon VII.6.5(a). *prppl* swəɬɪn D, *-ing* swəɬɪn D

3. vi to WARP, referring to wood IX.2.9. swɛl Nf

swelled *adj IN* FLOOD, describing a river IV.1.4. swɛld Nf, zwɛɬd Gl

swelled up *adj* IN FLOOD, describing a river IV.1.4. swɛld ʊp Y

swellies* *npl* PUDDLES IV.1.6. *sg* swɛlɪ Nb

swelling *n* a BUMP on someone's forehead VI.1.8. swɛlɪŋ K

swell-tree(s) *n* a SWINGLE-TREE of a horse-drawn plough harness I.8.3.
sg: swɛłtɹɪ Nth Hu, swɛł?ɹɪ C Bd
-*s*: swɛłtɹɪz Nth

swelt *adj* get swelt to HEAT, referring to a haystack II.9.16. *3prsg* gɪt swɪłt Sx

swetagg *n* a NECKERCHIEF VI.14.4. swɛtæg Man

swibble-tree *n* a SWINGLE-TREE of a horse-drawn plough harness I.8.3. swɪbłɹɪ Bk

swidges *npl* PUDDLES IV.1.6. swɪdʒɪz Nf, swɪdʒɪs Nf

swift *n* a NEWT IV.9.8. swɪft Nf Sf Ess, swɪf Ess

swig *v* to guzzle a drink, ⇐ GUZZLES VI.5.13(a). -*ing* swɪgɪn Mon

swigging *v-ing* DRINKING V.8.1. swɪgɪn Mon

swill *1. n* a BASKET for carrying horse-feed III.5.4. swɪl Nb*[wicker x1; old x1]* Du We*[wicker]* La*[basket-work x1; wooden, with projecting stave as a handle x1]* Y*[basket-work x1]*, swʊl Nb*[wicker x1]*
2. n a basket for carrying turnips to cattle. swɪl Du
3. n a CLOTHES-BASKET V.9.7. swɪl Du Y*[made of rushes]*
4. n a basket for carrying turnips and potatoes. swɪl We
5.1. vt to RINSE clothes V.9.8. swɪl St Wa Gl O So, swɪł He Wo Mon Gl
5.2. v to rinse. swɪl La*[old]* Sa Wo Wa L*[old]* So, swɪł Wa Mon W
6. n GRUEL fed to pigs V.7.2. swɪł Sf
7. v to guzzle a drink, ⇐ GUZZLES VI.5.13(a). -*ing* swɪlɪn Nf, swɪł Ess
8. n old swill stale URINE used for cleaning blankets VI.8.8. aːd swɪl La, ɒʊd swɪl La

swilling-brush *n* a BROOM used for sweeping outdoors V.9.10. swɪlɪnbɹʊʃ Y

swill out *vtphr* to RINSE clothes V.9.8. swɪł ... əʊt Mon, swəł ... æʊt So

swill through *vtphr* to RINSE clothes V.9.8. swɪl ... θɹu: Sa, zwɪł ... dɹᵘu: Gl

swimmers *npl* TADPOLES IV.9.5. swɪməz Sf

swimmy *1. adj* feeling FAINT VI.13.7. swɪmɪ Sr*[old]* Sx*[old x1]*
2. adj GIDDY IX.1.11. swɪmɪ Ess Sr

swimmy-headed *adj* GIDDY IX.1.11. swɪmɪ-ɛdɪd K

swimy *1. adj* feeling FAINT VI.13.7. swɔɪmɪ Sr*[old]*, swəɪmɪ Sx*[old x1]*
2. adj GIDDY IX.1.11. swɑɪmɪ K, swɒɪmɪ Wo*[old]*, swɔɪmɪ Gl K Sx*[old]*, swʌɪmɪ Sr, swəɪmɪ Sx*[old x1]*

swin *n* on the swin ASKEW, describing a picture that is not hanging straight IX.1.3. ɒ t swɪn We

swin-bar *n* a DIAGONAL BAR of a gate IV.3.7. swɪnbaː We

swine *n* PIGS III.8.1. swɛɪn Nb, swaɪn Y Ch*[rare]*, swɒːɪn St

swine-grass *n* GOOSE-GRASS II.2.5. swɑɪngɹɛs Db

swing *n* a CRANE on which a kettle is hung over a domestic fire V.3.4. swɪŋ St

swing-bar *1. n* a DIAGONAL BAR of a gate IV.3.7. *pl* swɪŋbaːz Cu We*[old]*, swɪŋbaːɹ Cu
2. n a CRANE on which a kettle is hung over a domestic fire V.3.4. swɪŋbaː Db
3. n the *HORIZONTAL* BAR of a crane over a domestic fire V.3.5(a). swɪŋbaː Ch

swing-beam *n* a large SWINGLE-TREE of a horse-drawn plough harness I.8.3. swɪŋbɪiːm Ess

swinged *ptppladj* BURNT, describing bread or cakes V.6.7. swɪnʒd La

swinger *n* a JACKET VI.14.5. swɪŋə L

swinging-post *1. n* the HANGING-POST of a gate IV.3.3. swɪŋɪnpʌʊs Ess, swɪŋɪnpoust Nf, swɪŋɪnpous Nf, swɪŋɪnpʊəst Y
2. n the SHUTTING-POST of a gate IV.3.4. swɪŋɪnpoust St, swɪŋɪnpous Nf

swinging-stump *n* the SHUTTING-POST of a gate IV.3.4. swɪŋɪnstʊmp Db

swingle *n* a FLAIL II.8.3. swɪnʒł Bk

swingle-tree **1. n* the STRETCHER between the traces of a cart-horse I.5.11. swɪŋgłɹɪ: St
2. n an EVENER, the main swingle-tree of a horse-drawn plough harness I.8.4. swɪŋłɹɪ: Y Ch Wo Wa, swɪŋgłɹɪ: St, swɪŋəłɹɪ: Y, swɪŋtɹɪ Cu, swɪŋəłɹɪ Y *[northern forms with -tree given this definition, although NBM data less specific]*

swingle-tree(s) *n [Show a picture of a horse-drawn plough.] What do you call this?* I.8.3.
sg: swɪŋltri: Du Man, swɪŋgltri: Man, swɪŋłtɹɪ: Cu We La, swɪŋłtɹɪ: Nb Du, swɪŋłtɹɪ: Nb Cu Du La Y Ch Db Sa St Wo Wa L, swɪŋłtɹɪ: Wo Wa K, swɪŋgłtɹɪ: La Y Db Sa St Wa O, swɪŋgłtɹɪ: Wo Wa Lei Nth, swɪŋəłtɹɪ: Y, swɪŋgəłtɹɪ: Y, swɪndltɹˡi: Nt, swɪŋłtʁɛɪ Nb, swɪŋłtʁɛɪ Nb, swɪŋłtɹɪ La, swɪŋgłtɹɪ La, swɪŋgłtɹɛɪ Ch Db St, swɪŋgətɹɛɪ Ch, swɪndltɹɛɪ Db, swɪŋłtɹəɪ Y, swɪŋłtɹəɪ Y, swɪnłtɹəɪ Y, swɪŋəłtɹəɪ Y, swʊŋłtɹɪ: La
-*s*: swɪŋłtɹi:z Nb, swɪŋłtɹɪ:z Nb Cu We La Y Ch Db L, swɪŋgłtɹɪ:z Y Sa St, swɪŋgłtɹɪ:z Lei, swɪnłtɹɪ:z Y, swɪŋəłtɹɪ:z Y, swɪŋłtɹɪz Ch, swɪŋgətre:z Ch, swɪŋgłtɹɛɪz St, swɪŋgłtɹɛɪz Lei, swɪŋgətɹɛɪz St.

⇒ **barraquail, batticle, billet, bodkin(s), breadh-agh, cutwith, draught(s), fore-cock, hample-tree(s), heel-tree(s), horse-tree(s),** lantree(s), little heel-tree, little swell-tree, little weigh, pummel-tree, rock-tree, single-sway, single-tree, sling(s), small weigh-tree, spreaders, sway(s), sway-tree, swell-tree(s), swibble-tree, swing-beam, swingling, swivel, swupple-trees, tawtree(s), weigh(s), *whibble-tree(s)* ⇒ whipple-tree(s), whip, whippen(s)/whippence(s), whippen-tree(s), whipper(s), whipples-tree, whipple-tree(s) *[at interviews a set of swingle-trees was shown to ii. and this appears to have influenced rr., some referring to the set as a unit, some to one of the set only; it cannot reliably be inferred that -s forms are pls having corresponding sgs]*

swingling *n* a SWINGLE-TREE of a horse-drawn plough harness I.8.3. swıŋlın Cu

swing-peg *n* a CRANE on which a kettle is hung over a domestic fire V.3.4. swıŋpɛg Gl

swing-plough *1. n* a PLOUGH I.8.1. swıŋpləʊ Ch
2. n a plough with no wheels. swıŋplɛʊ Brk, swıŋplᵃ̈ːu: Man
[two further forms, in Brk and Sr, recorded as special in some (undefined) way; also in Y, with note at one locality that it is for 'scrattin the soil over']

swing-post *n* the HANGING-POST of a gate IV.3.3. swıŋpoᵁst Db, swıŋpʊəst L

swint *adv* DIAGONALLY, referring to harrowing a field IX.1.8. swınt La, əswınt La

swint-bar *n* a DIAGONAL BAR of a gate IV.3.7. *pl* swıntbaɹz Y

swintle *n* a ROPE-TWISTER II.7.8. swıntɬ Ess

swint-way *adj* ASKEW, describing a picture that is not hanging straight IX.1.3. swıntweː La, swıntwɛə La

swint-way(s) *adv* DIAGONALLY, referring to harrowing a field IX.1.8.
no -s: swıntweː Cu La, swıntweː Cu
-s: swıntweːz La

swint-ways on *adv* DIAGONALLY, referring to harrowing a field IX.1.8. swıntweːz ɔn La

swin-way(s) *adv* DIAGONALLY, referring to harrowing a field IX.1.8.
no -s: swınweː We La, swınwɛː Cu We
-s: swınweːz Nb Cu Du, swınweːz Cu

swipe *v* to WHITTLE a stick I.7.19. *prppl* swaɪpın La

swipper *n* a FLAIL II.8.3. swıpə St, *pl* swıpəz Ch

swipple *n* a FLAIL II.8.3. swıpl Db Sa St

swish *1. adj* ASKEW, describing a picture that is not hanging straight IX.1.3. swıʃ Nt
2. adv DIAGONALLY, referring to harrowing a field IX.1.8. swıʃ Lei R

swish-way(s) *adv* DIAGONALLY, referring to harrowing a field IX.1.8.
no -s: swıʃweː Nt
-s: swıʃweːz Nt, swıʃwɛız L, swıʃwɛˑəz L

switch *1. n* the TAIL of a cow III.2.2. swıtʃ Y
2. v to TRIM hedges IV.2.3. swıtʃ Nb Cu Y

swite *v* to WHITTLE a stick I.7.19. *prppl* swaɪtın Y, *-ing* swaɪtın La, swaɪt Db, *pt* swɔɪtıd Wo

swivel *1. n* a sliding RING to which a tether is attached in a cow-house I.3.5. swıvl La, swıvəl Y, swıbəl Y, swıvəɬ So, swıvʊ Ess, swiːvəl Y *[queried ir.r. SBM]*
2. n a SWINGLE-TREE of a horse-drawn plough harness I.8.3. swıvl Gl O
3. n an EVENER, the main swingle-tree of a horse-drawn plough I.8.4. swıvɬ O, swıbɬ O
4. n the T-SHAPED PLOUGH-BEAM END of a horse-drawn plough I.8.5. swıvəɬ W, swıbɬ Nth *[marked ir.r. EM/SBM]*
5. n a ROPE-TWISTER II.7.8. swıvəl Y
6. n a FLAIL II.8.3. *pl* swıvlz Sa, swıvɬ Lei
7. n the striking part of a flail. swıvəɬ D
8. n the *HORIZONTAL* BAR of a crane over a domestic fire V.3.5(a). swıvɬ Sf, swıθəɬ Lei

swiver *n* a HEDGING-BILL IV.2.5. swɛıvə Nf

swole* *adj IN* FLOOD, describing a river IV.1.4. swoːl ʊp Sa*[old]*

swollen *adj IN* FLOOD, describing a river IV.1.4. swoʊlən Man

swoon *vi* to FAINT VI.13.7. swuːn Y

swoop *n* a SLOPE IV.1.10. swuːp L

swopple *n* a FLAIL II.8.3. *pl* swɒplz Sa

sword *1. n* a movable horizontal rod stretching between the shafts of a cart, fixing them to the cart-body and stopping the cart from tipping, ⇐ ROD/PIN I.10.3. sɔᵗːd̩ W, zuəᵗːd̩ W
2. n a vertical rod in front of a cart, perforated to allow adjustments when tipping. sɒuəᵗd̩ Wa, sɔːd St Wo Wa, sɔːɹd St, sɔᵗːd̩ Sa Wa O, zɔᵗːd̩ So, sɔəd Y, sɔːᵊᵗd̩ Wo, zɔːᵊᵗːd̩ Do, sɔuəd Wa, sɔːd Ch, sɔəd Ch, soːəd Mon, soːᵊᵗd̩ Sa Wo Mon Gl, zoˑᵊᵗd̩ Gl, soːᵊᵗːd̩ So, zoːᵊᵗːd̩ So W Do, sɒuəd St, sɒuəᵗd̩ Wo Wa, soːʊəᵗd̩ Gl, zoːʊəᵗd̩ Gl, suəᵗːd̩ Co, zuəᵗːd̩ So, zuːəᵗːd̩ So D, swaːd Mon, swəᵗːd̩ Sa
[WMBM all forms vertical; SBM, one horizontal, one implied horizontal, some vertical, most unmarked]
3. n a DIAGONAL BAR of a gate IV.3.7. sɔᵏːd Nb

sword-peg *n* a pin used with a perforated rod in front of a cart to allow adjustments when tipping, ⇐ ROD/PIN I.10.3. *pl* soːᵊᵗd̩pɛgz He

sword-pin *n* a pin fixing a cart-body to the shafts, stopping it from tipping, ⇐ ROD/PIN I.10.3. soəᵗːd̩pın So

swupple-trees *n* a SWINGLE-TREE of a horse-drawn plough harness I.8.3. swʊbltɹız Wo

swush-way *adj* ASKEW, describing a picture that is not hanging straight IX.1.3. swʊʃwɛə L

T

tab *n* the TAG of a boot-lace VI.14.26. tæb Y MxL, *pl* tæbz Ha, tab Nb Cu We La Y L Nth Bk

tabby *n* a TABBY-CAT, the female cat III.13.9. tabɪ La

tabby-balcher *n* a NESTLING IV.7.1. tabɪbɒɫʃə Hu

tabby-cat *n* What do you call the female [cat]? III.13.9. tæbɪkæˑt Man, tabɪkatʰ Nb. ⇒ **bess-cat, betty-cat, bitch-cat, chid-cat, chit-cat, ewe, ewe-cat, female cat, jen, jenny-cat, moggy, pussy, queen, queen-cat, queeny, she, she-cat, sheeder, sow-cat, tabby, tib, tibby-cat, tib-cat, tit, titty**

tab-end *n* the TAG of a boot-lace VI.14.26. tabɛnd Y

tab-hole *n* an EAR-HOLE VI.4.3. *pl* tabɔɪlz Y, tabo:l Nt

table *1. n* a SHEARING-TABLE III.7.8. tɛɪbɫ Brk, tɛˑəbl L

2. n a flat surface on which bacon is cured, ⇐ SALTING-TROUGH III.12.5. te:bl Mon

tabs *npl* EARS VI.4.1. tabz Y Db*[old x1]* St Nt L, *sg* tab Lei

tack *1. n* harness for a cart-horse, ⇐ to GEAR I.5.1. tak Wo

2. n the upper of the two HANDLES of a scythe II.9.8. tɛk Nf

3. v to put cattle on hired pasture, ⇐ HIRE *PASTURAGE* III.3.8. tæk Sa Gl, -*ing* tækɪn He Wo, tak Mon

4. n pasturage. tæk Sa He Wo Mon Gl, tak Sa Wo Wa Gl W

5. n LOW-LYING LAND IV.1.7. tæk Gl

6. n a SHELF V.9.4. tæk So, tæːk So

7. n a mantelpiece. tæk So

8. n the TAG of a boot-lace VI.14.26. tak Ch

tacker *n* a COBBLER VIII.4.5. tækəᵗː So

tackle *1. vt* to GEAR a cart-horse I.5.1. tækl Wo, takl St L, takɫ Wa Lei R

2. v to gear a horse. takl Db St Wa L, takɫ Wa

3. n the harness of a cart-horse. takl Wa, takɫ Lei R

tackle up *vtphr* to GEAR a cart-horse I.5.1. takɫ ... ʌp So

tack out *vtphr* to put cattle on hired pasture, ⇐ HIRE *PASTURAGE* III.3.8. tæk ... aʊt So, tæk ... ʌʊt Mon, tæk ... əʊt He, tak ɛʊt Wa, *pt* takt ... æʊt Wa, tak ... aʊt He

tacks *npl* the HANDLES of a scythe II.9.8. tæks Nf Sf, tækʔs Nf

tacky *adj* STICKY, describing a child's hands VIII.8.14. tækɪ Sa, takɪ Sa*[old x1]*

taddies *npl* TADPOLES IV.9.5. tadɪz Y*[children's/familiar word x2]*

tadpoles *npl* What do you call those active little creatures in ponds that have large heads and wriggle their tails? IV.9.5. Eng. ⇒ **bull-heads, bullies, *bull-joat* ⇒ bull-joats, bull-joats, bull-knobs, bulls'-heads, *bully-heads* ⇒ bull-heads, cat-poles, club-heads, dump-heads, jacky-bull-heads, lady-heads, logger-heads, paw-heads, penny-wagtails, polly-wags, polly-wigs, pop-noddles, pot-ladles, pot-noddles, pottle-ladles, swimmers, taddies, *tad-tail* ⇒ tad-tails, tad-tails, tagpoles, tiddlers, toads, tom-gudgeons, tommy-toddies, tom-thumbs, tom-toddies, young frogs**

tad-tails* *npl* TADPOLES IV.9.5. *sg* tɛdtæɪɫ K

taffled *adj* TANGLED, describing hair VI.2.5. tæːfɫd So, tæːfʊɫd So

taffled up *adj* TANGLED, describing hair VI.2.5. tafɫd ʌp Do

taffles *n* in taffles TANGLED, describing hair VI.2.5. ɪn tafɫz Do

tag *1. n* What do you call this [indicate the tag of a boot-lace]? VI.14.26. tɪg Sx, tɛg Y Man Nf Ess Sr K D Ha Sx, *pl* tɛgs So, tɛəg Ess, tæg Nb Man Sa He Wo Wa Mon Gl O Nth Hu Nf Sf Hrt Ess MxL So W Brk Sr K Co D Do Ha, *pl* tægz Db, tæːg Wo Gl Brk, tæˡg Nf Sf Ess, *pl* tæˡgz So, tag Nb Cu Du We La Y Ch Db Sa St Wo Wa Mon Gl O Nt L Lei R Nth C Bk Bd Hrt W Co D Ha, *pl* tagz He, taːg Mon, taˡg Ess Co Do Ha, tɑg Y. ⇒ **eye-tag, lace-tab, naiglet, nib, stud, tab, tab-end, tack, tag-end, taglet, tib, tip, tug**

2. n a sheep before its first shearing, ⇐ EWE-HOG III.6.4. tæg So Do, tag W

3. n a sheep from its first to its second shearing, ⇐ GIMMER III.6.5. tæg So, tag Do Sx*[12 months old]*

4. n a WETHER III.6.8. tæˑg Brk *[queried u.r. SBM on grounds of age and castration]*

tag at *vtphr* to PULL somebody's hair VI.2.8. tag ət Bd

tag-end *n* the TAG of a boot-lace VI.14.26. tagɛnd Y L

taggled *adj* TANGLED, describing hair VI.2.5. tagəld Cu

taglet *n* the TAG of a boot-lace VI.14.26. taglət Du

tagpoles *npl* TADPOLES IV.9.5. tagpoːlz Ch

tags *npl* EARS VI.4.1. tagz Lei

taid *n* GRANDDAD VIII.1.8(a). taɪd Sa*[old]*

tail *1. n [Show a picture of a cow.]* What do you call this? III.2.2. Eng; **cow-tail** kæʊtæɪl Y. ⇒ **cow-tail, durrum, switch**

2. *n* the TAILBOARD of a cart I.10.2. teɪɬ Ha

3. *vt* to TOP-AND-TAIL gooseberries V.7.23. *-ing* teːɬən Co

4. *vt* to REMOVE *STALKS* from currants V.7.24. teʊɬ O, tɛɪl O, tɛɪɬ Brk D

5. *n/adj* the LAST sheep through a gate VII.2.2. tɛɪɬ Sx, taɪɬ W*[adj]*

tail-band *n* the CRUPPER of the harness of a cart-horse I.5.9. tɪəlband Du Y, teːlband La Y, teːlbənd Y, teəlband Cu Du Y, teəlbənd Y, tɛːlband We, tɛɪlbənd Y, tɛəlband Y, tɛəlbənd Y L

tailboard *1. n [Show a picture of a farmcart.]* What do you call this? I.10.2. Eng exc. Du We Db. ⇒ **arse-board, back-board, back-door, bottom arse-board, bottom back-board, bottom-tail-board, breech-board, cart-arse, cart-door, cart-heck, cart-tail, cratch, door, end-board, end-door, end-heck, flacker-board, heck, heck-board, hetch, hind-board, hind-door, hind-end-board, hinder-end-door, scut, tail, tail-cratch, tail-door, tail-gate, toe-board, tumbril-board**

2. *n* an END-BOARD of a cart I.10.4. tiːlboˑəd Db, tɪəlbʊəd Nb, teːlbɔ^ʁːd Nb, teːlboəɹd La, teːlboːəˡd Sa, teːlbʊəd Y, teːlbʊəˡɹd La, teɪ^əłbɔːd Bk, teɪɬbɔəˡd̩ Ha, tɛɪɬbɔːd Lei R, tɛɪʊbɔəˡɹd̩ Sx, tɛəlbʊəd Y, tæɪɬbo^əd K

tail bodkin *n* an EVENER, the main swingle-tree of a horse-drawn plough harness I.8.4. tɛɪ^əɬ bɒdkɪn Gl

tail-cratch *n* the TAILBOARD of a cart I.10.2. teːlkɹatʃ Sa

tail-cripper *n* the CRUPPER of the harness of a cart-horse I.5.9. teːlkɹɪpə Nb

tail-cripple* *n* the CRUPPER of the harness of a cart-horse I.5.9. teəlkʁɪpl Nb

tail-crupper *n* the CRUPPER of the harness of a cart-horse I.5.9. teːlkɹʊpəɹ Y, tɛilkɹʊpə Nf

tail-dock *n* the CRUPPER of the harness of a cart-horse I.5.9. taɪɬdɒk Do

tail-door *n* the TAILBOARD of a cart I.10.2. teːlduˑə Nt, tɛˑəldʊə L, tɛˑəldʊə^ɹ L

tail-gate *n* the TAILBOARD of a cart I.10.2. tɛɪʊgeɪt Sr

tail-heck *n* an END-BOARD of a cart I.10.4. teːlɛk Y

tail-ladder *1. n* an END-BOARD of a cart I.10.4. tɛɪɬladəˡː W, taɪɬladəˡː W

2. *n* a rear cart-ladder, ⇐ CART-LADDERS I.10.5. *pl* tɪʊ lɛdəˡz̩ Sr, teɪ^əɬlædə Bk, *pl* teʊ lædəˡz̩ Brk, tɛɪɬ lædə Sr, tɛɪɬladəˡː W, *pl* tɛɪʊ lædəˡz Ha, tɛɪʊ lædəˡ Sr, taɪllædə MxL, *pl* taɪɬladəˡːz̩ W, *pl* taɪɬ ladəˡːz̩ W Ha

tail-loop *n* the CRUPPER of the harness of a cart-horse I.5.9. tɛːlluːp Cu

tailor *n* DADDY-LONG-LEGS IV.8.10. tɪlɪə Nb

tailor-tartan *n* DADDY-LONG-LEGS IV.8.10. teːlɔtaˡ^ʁːtn Nb

tail over end *adv* HEAD OVER HEELS IX.1.10. tɛˑəl ɔwəɹ ɛnd L

tail over head *adv* HEAD OVER HEELS IX.1.10. tɛˑəl ɑvɹ ɪˑəd L*[old]*, tɛˑəl ɑvɹ ɛd L

tail-piece *1. n* the CRUPPER of the harness of a cart-horse I.5.9. teːlpiːs Cu, tæɪlpiːs K

2. *n* a BUMPER of a cart I.10.1(a). teɪɬpiːs So

tail-pole *n* a BUMPER of a cart I.10.1(a). tiːlpɛʊ Db

tail-post *n* the PARTITION between stalls in a cow-house I.3.2. teːlpɒst Y *[marked technically u.r. NBM, but **standing-post** unmarked EMBM, **stall-posts** unmarked WMBM]*

tails *1. npl* the HANDLES of a horse-drawn plough I.8.2. teːlz Sa, teːɬz Mon, teɪlz He, teːɪlz Wo, teːɪɬz Wo Mon, tɛˑɪlz Nf, tɛɪɬz He, tæɪlz Nf, tæɪɬz He Nf, taɪlz Sa, taɪɬz Wo

2. *n* barley AWNS II.5.3. teːlz Ch

tail-strap *n* the CRUPPER of the harness of a cart-horse I.5.9. teəlstɹap Y

tail-thong *n* the CRUPPER of the harness of a cart-horse I.5.9. tɛɪlθɒŋ Nf

taint *1. vi* to SPOIL, referring to meat or fish V.7.10. teːnt Ch, tɛɪnt St Bk, tɛɪn? Bk, tɛˑənt L, tæɪnt Gl

2. *adj* **get taint, go taint** to spoil. **get taint** gɛt tɛɪnt Nth; **go taint** gə tɛɪnt Lei

tainted *1. adj* RANCID, describing bacon V.7.9. tɛntɪd Cu

2. *adj* **get tainted, go tainted** to SPOIL, referring to meat or fish V.7.10. **get tainted** *3prsg* gɛts teəntəd Y, *ptppl* gɒt tɛntɪd Co, gɛt tɛɪntɪd K; **go tainted** gʌʊ tɛɪntɪd K, goː tɛɪntɪd St, gʊ tɛɪntɪd L, gə tɛɪntɪd Lei, goː taɪntəd W

tainty *1. adj* RANCID, describing bacon V.7.9. tɛːnti W D, tɛɪntɪ K, dɛɪntɪ Brk

2. *adj* **go all tainty, go tainty** to SPOIL, referring to meat or fish V.7.10. **go all tainty** goː ɔːɬ tɛnti Do; **go tainty** gɔʊ tɛɪnti Sx, gou tæɪnt?ɪ Nf, guː taɪnti Ha

take *1.1. vt* to PITCH sheaves II.6.10. *3prsg* teɪks Bk, *3prsg* tɛɪks Bk

1.2. v to pitch. tɛɪk Sf

2. *v* to HIRE *PASTURAGE* III.3.8. tɪək Nb, teɪk Bd, tɛk Cu Lei R, tak Y, *pt* tʊk Hu *[following NBM Edd,* [tak] *regarded as **take** rather than **tack**]*

take away *1. vphr* to PITCH sheaves II.6.10. *3prsg* teːks əweː O, teɪk əweɪ Bd, tɛk əweː Nt, tɛk əweɪ Lei Nth, *3prsg* tɛks əweɪ L, tɛk əweˑə L, *3prsg* tɛɪks əweɪ Sr, tɛɪk əweɪ Hu, tak əweː Nt

2. *vtphr* **take a swathe away** to CLEAR grass at

the edges of a field II.9.5. *-ing* tɛˑkɪn ə swɛθ əwɛɪ Nf

take in *1. vtphr* to LOAD sheaves onto a wagon II.6.7(a). *3prsg* tɛks ... iːn D

2.1. vtphr to PITCH a sheaf II.6.10. teːks ... ɪn W

2.2. vphr to pitch. teːk ɪn Gl, *-ing* tɛɪkɪn ɪn Ha

taken *1.1. vi-ed* **has not taken/took, never took** *HAS NOT* HELD, referring to a cow that has not conceived III.1.7. **has not taken/took** ɛzn tæɪkn K, aːn teɪkŋ Do, ʃɪz nɒt tʊk K, eɪnt tʊk Nf, ɛɪn tʊk Sx, ɛznt tʊk MxL, ant tʊk O; **never took** nɛvəˤː tʊk So

1.2. vt-ed **has not taken/took, did not take** has not held. **has not taken/took** aznt tʊk Wo Nth; **did not take** dɪdn tɛɪk Ess

2. adj **not taken** *NOT IN* CALF, but able to conceive III.1.8. nɒt tæɪʔŋ K

taken on *viphr-ed* **has not taken on** *HAS NOT* HELD, referring to a cow that has not conceived III.1.7. aznt teːkn ɒn O

take off *1. vtphr* **take the back off, take the back-swathe off** to CLEAR grass at the edges of a field II.9.5. tɛɪk ðə bɛk ɔːf Ess, tɛk ʔ bakswɛːð ɒf La *[with reaper]*

2. vtphr to PITCH sheaves II.6.10. teːk ... ɔːf Wa

3. vtphr to WEAN a calf III.1.4. tɛk ... ɒf L

4. vphr to LOP a tree IV.12.5. *-ing* tɛkɪn ɒf La

5. vphr to cut large branches from a tree. *-ing* tɛkɪn ɒf Y

take out *vtphr* **take out the dike-back(s), take the dike-backs out*** to CLEAR grass at the edges of a field II.9.5. teːk uːt ðə dɛɪkbak Nb, tɛk uːt ðə dɛɪkbaks Nb, teək ðə dɛɪkbaks uːt Nb

taker-away *n* a person whose job is to PITCH sheaves II.6.10. teɪkəɹəweɪ Bd, tɛkɛɹəwɛɪ L, tɛkəɹəwɛɪ L, tɛkəɹəwɛˑə L

takes after *vphr-3prsg* he RESEMBLES VIII.1.9. tjeːks aftɐʁ Nb, tjɛks ɛftɒʁ Nb, tjɛks aftə Nb, teːks æftəˤ Sa, teːks aftəˤː Sa, teːks aːftəˤ Sa, teːks aˤːftə Sa, teːk aˤːftəˤ Sa, teɪks aˤːt̞əˤ Bk, teɪkʔ aˑftə Nf, teˑək aːtʔə Sf, tɛks ɛftɪ Cu La, *inf* tɛk ɛftə We, tɛks ɛftər Cu, tɛks ɛftɪ L, tɛks aftə Cu La Y L Lei, tɛks aftəɪ(+V) L Lei, tɛks aftɪ L, tɛks aːtə Nth, tɛɪks aːftəɪ (+V) K, tɛɪks aːtə MxL, tɛˑɪk aːtʔəˡ Nf, tɛɪks aːftəˤ Sx, tæɪks aːftə Hrt, tæɪk aːftə Hrt, taks ɛftə Cu Du We*[old]* Y, taks ɛftər Du, taks ɛftər We, taks ɛftəɪ Y, taks aftə We La Y, taks aftəɪ L, taks aftɪ Y, taks əftə Y

takes in *viphr-3prsg* school BEGINS VIII.6.2(a). tɛks ɪn La

takes like *vphr-3prsg* he RESEMBLES VIII.1.9. tɛɪks lɔɪk Sf

takes to *vphr-3prsg* he RESEMBLES VIII.1.9. tɛks tʊ Y, tɛks təv Cu

taking *adj* INFECTIOUS, describing a disease VI.12.2. takən Cu

taking-off-time *n* STOPPING-TIME at the end of a day's work VII.5.9. tɛkɪnɒftaɪm Nt

taking-post *n* the SHUTTING-POST of a gate IV.3.4. teːkɪnpoːst Mon

tale *n* CHAT VIII.3.4. tɛɪᵊɫ Ess

tale-pyet *n* a GOSSIP VIII.3.5(b). teːlɪpaɪət Cu

taler *n* a GOSSIP VIII.3.5(b). teːɫəˤː Do

tale-telling *v-ing* GOSSIPING VIII.3.5(a). tæɪɫtɛlɪn K; **telling the tale** tɛlɪn ʔ teəl Y

talk *n* CHAT VIII.3.4. tæˑᵊk Nb, taːk Wo, tɔːk La Y Wa O Nt*[old]* Lei Nf Ess So W Brk K Do, tɔːək Nf Bd Hrt, tɔːɫk D

tallent *n* a HAY-LOFT over a cow-house I.3.18. tælənt Sa, talənt Sa, tɒlənt Sa He

tallet *1. n* a DOVECOTE above a cowshed or stable I.1.7. tɒɫət D

2. n a HAY-LOFT over a cow-house I.3.18. tælɪt He Wo, tæɫɪt Wo Gl, tæɫœt Gl, tælət So, tæɫət He Gl, talɪt Wo, talət So Do, taɫət So W Co D Ha, tɒɫɪt He, tɒlət He, tɒɫət He Mon D, tɒləɪt He, tɒɫəˤt̞ He

3. n a hay-loft over a stable. tælət Brk, talɪt Gl, taɫɪt W, talʊt Gl, talət Gl O So, taɫət O So Ha, tɒlət Mon

tall fern *n* BRACKEN IV.10.12. *pl* tɔˤːl̩ fəˤːn̩z̩ Sa

tallies *npl* GIPSIES VIII.4.12. talɪz Bk

tallowman *n* a KNACKER III.11.9. taɫəmman D *[fw erased* [man]*, giving* [taɫəm]*]*

tallowy *adj* RANCID, describing bacon V.7.9. tʌləɹi Nf

tally-gipsies *npl* GIPSIES VIII.4.12. talɪdʒɪpsɪz Bk

tame *adj* INSIPID, describing food lacking in salt V.7.8. teːm D

tame lamb *n* a PET-LAMB III.7.3. teːm lam So, teːm ɫam Co D, teːm lam So, teːᵊm lam So, teːm ɫam Co D, taɪm ɫam Ha

tamp *vi* to BOUNCE VIII.7.3. tæmp Mon, tamp Mon, tʰamphʰ Mon

tan *vt* to BEAT a boy on the buttocks VIII.8.10. tæn Man Ess So Sr K Sx, tan Y St He W D; **tan his arse** tæn ɪz æːs Gl So Co, tæn ɪz aˤːʂ He, tan ɪz æːs Co, tan ɪz as W, tan ɪz aːs So W D Do Ha, tan iːz aːs D; **tan his arse for him** tæn ɪz aːs vɔˤː ŋ So; **tan his seat** tæn ɪz siːʔ Ess

tandem-horse *n* a TRACE-HORSE I.6.3. tandəmɒs Cu

tang *n* a PRONG of a fork I.7.10. teŋ Du, *pl* taŋz Ch Sa

tangle *n* **in the tangle** TANGLED, describing hair VI.2.5. ɪn ðə tɛŋgʊ Sx

tangled *adj* If you don't comb long hair, it quickly gets .... VI.2.5. tɛŋgɫd D, tɛŋgʊd Sr Sx, tæŋgld Sf, tæŋɫd He K, tæŋgɫd Nth Sf Ess*[if clean x1]* So Co, tæŋgʊɫd Gl, tæŋgʊd So, tæˡŋgɫd Ess, taŋgld Y Gl O, taŋgɫd Wa Mon O Nth C Bk Bd Hrt Co Do. ⇒ *all in a* mat, *all in* whorls, *all of a* mat, *all* over, *all* rough, *all* roughed up, *all* whorled up, angly, baked, clatted, clatted up, clatty, clitted up, clitty, clotted, cotted, cottered, cottered up, cottery, cotty, frizzified, *full of* knots, fuzzy, gnarred, *in a* mat, *in* oils, *in* taffles, *in the* tangle, knitted up, knotchy, knotted, knotted up, knotty, lugged up, luggy, massed, matted, matted together, matted up, matted up together, matty, *of a* cotter, pluggy, ravelled, rough, ruffled, ruffled up, scraggly, snarled, snarly, sticking *together*, straggy, taffled, taffled up, taggled, tangled, tangled up, *tangles*, tangly, tatted, tatty, tazzled, tazzled together, tousled, tousy, towy, twisted, wangled, whorled up

tangled up *adj* TANGLED, describing hair VI.2.5. tæŋgld ʌpʔ Nf, tæŋɫd ʌp Hu, taːŋɫd ʌp Mon

tangly *adj* TANGLED, describing hair VI.2.5. tɛŋɫi D, tɛŋɫi K, tæŋɫi D, tæŋɫi So, tæŋɫi K, taŋɫi Co

tank *1. n* URINE in a cow-house I.3.10. taŋk Cu La Y

2. n a CESS-POOL on a farm I.3.11. tɛŋk Sx, tæŋk Man, taŋk Du La Y Db St O

3. n an artificial cess-pool. tɛŋk Sr, tæŋk La Nf, taŋk Nb Cu We La Y Db St Nt

4. vt to BEAT a boy on the buttocks VIII.8.10. taŋk St

tank-hole *n* a CESS-POOL on a farm I.3.11. taŋkɒil Y

tanking *n* URINE in a cow-house I.3.10. tæŋkɪn La

tankles *n* ICICLES VII.6.11. taŋklz Nb

tanklets *n* ICICLES VII.6.11. taŋkləts Nb

tank-water *n* URINE in a cow-house I.3.10. taŋkwatə Y Nt, taŋkwatəɹ La

tanner *1. n* the CORE of a boil VI.11.7. tɛnə Du

2. n SIXPENCE VII.7.4. tɛnə MxL, tɛnəˤ Sx, tɛənə Ess, tænə Y Man Hu Nf Sf Ess, tænəɹ La, tænəᴶ K, tænəˤ Sa He, tænəˤː So*[old x1]*, tanoᴿ Nb, tanə Nb Cu Du We La Y*[old x1]* Ch Db St Wa Nt L Lei Nth Hrt, tanər Cu*[old]*, tanəᴿ Du, tanɹ L, tanəɹ La Y*[slang x1]* He, tanəᴶ La Y, tanəɾ O, tanəˤ Db Sa Wo Wa Gl O Nth Bk Ha, tanəˤː W D, taːnə Nf

tanning *vbln* give him a (good) tanning to BEAT a boy on the buttocks VIII.8.10. give him a good tanning gɪ ɪm ə gʊd tanɪn Y; give him a tanning gɪv ɪm ə tænɪn Ess

tan-tittles *npl* MINNOWS IV.9.9. tænti?|z Nf *[marked u.r. and interp as 'stickleback' EMBM]*

tar *1. vt* to MARK sheep with colour to indicate ownership III.7.9. tæɹ (+V) Sx

2. v to mark sheep with colour. tæː Du, taː St, taːɹ Y, -*ing* taɹɪn Y

tar-band *n* TWINE used to fasten thatch on a stack II.7.7(b1). taɹband Y, taːband Y Nt L

tar-cord *n* TWINE used to fasten thatch on a stack II.7.7(b1). taɹkɔːd C

targy *adj* STICKY, describing a child's hands VIII.8.14. taᴶːgɪ La

tar-iron *v* to MARK sheep with colour to indicate ownership III.7.9. taˤːɾɒiəˤːn̩ So

tar-line *n* TWINE used to fasten thatch on a stack II.7.7(b1). taːlain Nf, taːlɒin Nf, taːlʌin Nf

tar-mark *v* to MARK sheep with colour to indicate ownership III.7.9. tæːmæːk Du, tæːmaːk La, taːmaːk Cu We Y Ch, taːmaɹk Du, tɜᴶːmɜᴶːk La

tar-marl *n* TWINE used to fasten thatch on a stack II.7.7(b1). taːmaːl L*[obsolete]*

tar-marl-band *n* TWINE used to fasten thatch on a stack II.7.7(b1). taːmaːlband L

tar-marl-string *n* TWINE used to fasten thatch on a stack II.7.7(b1). taːmaːɫstɹin Lei

tarred band *n* TWINE used to fasten thatch on a stack II.7.7(b1). taˤːd̪ bæːnd Sr *[possibly sg, SBM]*

tarred-line *n* TWINE used to fasten thatch on a stack II.7.7)b1). taːdlʌin Nf

tarred string *n* STRING used to tie up a grain-sack I.7.3. taˈɾd̪ stɹin Brk

tarred-twine *n* TWINE used to fasten thatch on a stack II.7.7(b1). taᴶːdtwain La, taˤd̪ twain K

tar-rope *1. n* STRING used to tie up a grain-sack I.7.3. təᴶːɹoup Brk

2. n rope used to fasten thatch on a stack, ⇐ ROPES II.7.7(b2). taːɹʌup C Sf, taːɹoup Sf *[marked 'probably material n' EMBM]*

tarry-band *n* TWINE used to fasten thatch on a stack II.7.7(b1). taːɹiband Y

tarry rope-yarn *n* STRING used to tie up a grain-sack I.7.3. taːɹi ɹoupjaːn Ess

tar-string *n* TWINE used to fasten thatch on a stack II.7.7(b1). taːstɹin L, taˤːɾʂtɹin Sx

tart **1.* n* a girl, ⇐ PRETTY VI.5.18. taːt Y

2. adj (it) is tart it HURTS VI.13.3(a). s tiəˤt Gl

tar-twine *n* TWINE used to fasten thatch on a stack II.7.7(b1). tæᴶːtwain La, taᴶːtwʌin Brk

tassels *n* the WATTLES of a hen IV.6.19. tɒsəɫz Bd

tathe *n* SHEEP-DUNG II.1.7. teiθ Nf, tɛːiθ Nf

tatted *adj* TANGLED, describing hair VI.2.5. tatid Nb

tattler *n* a GOSSIP VIII.3.5(b). tɛətɫɛ Ess

tatty *adj* TANGLED, describing hair VI.2.5. tatɪ Nb Cu Du, tatʔɪ Du

taught *vt-3ptsg That dog knows some clever tricks. I expect it was its owner that ... it.* III.13.17. taʊt Y, taːt Man, taʊt Y, tʊut La Db, tɔːt St Wo Wa Mon Gl O Nth Hu Ess MxL So Sr K Do Ha Sx, *ptppl* tɔːt Brk, tɔːʔ Nf Hrt, tɔˤːt Sa, tɔut Y, tʊut St. ⇒ broke, broke in, *broken it in* ⇒ broke in, *learned* ⇒ learnt, learnt, showed, teached, trained, trained up

taunt *vt* to BUTT III.2.10. *3prpl* tɔːnts

tawm over *viphr* to FAINT VI.13.7. tɒɹm aʊə Y, tɔːm ʊə St

tawtree *n* the STRETCHER between the traces of a cart-horse I.5.11. *pl* tɔːtɒɹɪz Sa

tawtree(s) *n* a SWINGLE-TREE of a horse-drawn plough harness I.8.3.
sg: tɔːtɹɪ Sa
-*s*: tɔːtɹiːz Ch, tɔːtəɹɪz Sa, tɔᵗːt̩əɹɪz Sa

tazzled *adj* TANGLED, describing hair VI.2.5. tazɫd Hu

tazzled together *adj* TANGLED, describing hair VI.2.5. tazəld təgɛðə La

tea-apron *n* a decorative APRON V.11.2(b). tiː-eːpʁən Nb

teached *vt-3ptsg* he/she TAUGHT it III.13.17. tiːtʃt Du, tɹiːtʃt Brk Sx*[old]*, tɹiːtʃ Sx*[old]*, teːtʃt Do, tɛɪtʃt La D

teacher *n* At school, the class is taken by the .... VIII.6.5. Eng. ⇒ **dominie, master, missis, mistress, school-boss, school-master, school-missis,** *school-teacher*

tea-dregs *n* DREGS left at the bottom of a teacup V.8.15. tiːdɹɛgz L Nf, tɹiˑdɹægz Nf

tea-grains *n* DREGS left at the bottom of a teacup V.8.15. tiːgɹeɪnz Y, tiːgɹæɪnz Sf Ess, teːgɹeːnz La

tea-grounds *n* DREGS left at the bottom of a teacup V.8.15. tiːgɹɛʊnz Wa, tiːgɹaʊndz St, tiːgɹaʊnz La, tiːgɹaʊnz Ch He, tiːgɹʌʊnts Mon, tiːgɹʊnz Y, tiːgɹuːnz Y, tiːgɹəʊnz Mon Gl*[old]*, tɹəgɹaʊnz La, tɹəgɹʊnz Y, teːgɹɛʊndz O, teːgɹɛʊnz Sa, teːgɹaːndz La, teːgɹaʊnz La, teːgɹəʊnz Gl, teɪgɹɛuːnz Wo, teˑ¹gɹəʊnz Gl, teˑəgɹaʊnz La

tea-grouts *n* DREGS left at the bottom of a teacup V.8.15. tiːgɹɛʊts Wa K, tiːgɹæᵗʊts K, tiːgɹəʊts Do, teːgɹæʊts Ha, teːgɹɔːts W, teɪgɹævts Co

tea-kettle *n* a KETTLE V.8.7. tɛɪkɛtɫ Nth

tea-kettle-broth *n* BROTH V.7.20(a). tiːkɛtɫbɹɔːᵊθ, teːkɛtɫbɹɔːθ Gl, tɛɪkɛtɫbɹɔːθ Wa

tea-leaves *n* DREGS left at the bottom of a teacup V.8.15. tiːliːvz Nb Cu Du We Sa St He Gl O Nt Lei R Nth Hu So Do Sx, tiːɫiːvz W Sr Ha, tiːlɪəvz La Y L Nth, tiːlɪˑəvz L, tiːleːvz Gl, tɹəlɪəvz Y Db, teːliːvz Ch Db, teːɫiːvz W Co D Ha, teːlɪəvz La O, teːleːvz La, teɪliːvz Nb O So*[old x1]* So, teɪleɪvz Du, teɪliːvz Cu Wa Nth, tɛɪɫiːvz Brk Co D, tɛɪlɪəvz Y, tɛɪlɛɪvz Du Db Bk, taɪɫeːvz Ha, təɪliːvz So, təɪlɪəvz Y, təɪləɪvz Y

team *1. n* [Show a picture of two horses in tandem.] When you have more than one horse pulling a heavy load, what do you call them? I.6.1 tiːm Eng (exc La Y Man O), tiːm ɒsəz Co, tiːm ə ɒsəz Co, tiːm əv ɔᵗːʂəz Co, tɹiːm ɔːsɪz Sx, tɹəm Nb Cu We La Y Db Nt L Bk Ess, teːm Ch Wo Gl O Nf W D Ha, teːm ɔᵗːʂəz D, teɪm Du Nf, tɛɪm Ch Db St Nf Sf, təɪm Y, tʃɛm Sa; **team of horses** tiːm ɒsəz Co, tiːm ə ɒsəz Co, tiːm əv ɔᵗːʂəz Co, tɹiːm ɔːsɪz Sx, teːm ɔᵗːʂəz D.

⇒ **draught, horse-team, lease;** ⇒ also **double-horses, pair** *[team horses in Co D Sx may contain elided 'of' or represent 'horses that work as a team']*

2. n a LITTER of piglets III.8.3. tɹiːm K

teamer *n* a CARTMAN on a farm I.2.2. tɹəmə Y

team-man *n* a CARTMAN on a farm I.2.2. teɪmmən Nf, tɛɪmən Nf, tɛːɪmən Nf

teamsman *n* a CARTMAN on a farm I.2.2. tiːmzmɒn La, tiːmzmən Ch St, tɹəmzmən La

team-stick *1. n* the STRETCHER between the traces of a cart-horse I.5.11. tɛˑɪmstɪk Nf

2. n a STICK used to support the shaft of a cart I.11.1. tɛɪmstɪk Nf *[queried EMBM]*

tear *vt* to PULL somebody's hair VI.2.8. tɪˑə L, tɛə Ch, tɛəᵗ Gl

tear-down *n* an ACTIVE child VIII.9.1. tɹˑəduːn L

teasels *n* GOOSE-GRASS II.2.5. teːzɫz Wo

tea-slops *n* DREGS left at the bottom of a teacup V.8.15. tˡiːslɒps We

teat *1. n* What do you call the part [of a woman's breast] the child actually sucks? VI.8.6. tiːt Nb St Wo Gl L Nf, teɪt Du ⇒ **breast, breast-nib, diddy, nibble, nipple, pap, tet, tetty, tit, titty**

2. n a WHITLOW VI.7.12. tiːt So

teats *npl* [Show a picture of a cow.] What do you call these? III.2.6. tiːts St L Nf Ess MxL Sr Sx, *sg* tiːt K, tɪts Nb Cu Du We La Y Man Ch Db Sa St He Wo Wa Mon Gl O Nt L Lei R Nth Hu C Nf Sf Bk Hrt Ess MxL So W Brk Sr K Co D Ha Sx, tɪʔs Bk, tɛts O C Bk Bd So W Brk K Co D Do Ha Sx, *sg* tɛt Sr. ⇒ **cow paps, didds, paps, quarters, speans,** *tits* ⇒ **teats, udders**

tea-wiffs *n* DREGS left at the bottom of a teacup V.8.15. tiːwɪfs Gl

ted *1. vt* When the grass has been mown for haymaking, what do you do next? II.9.11(a). -*ing* tɪdɪn D, tɪt Do, tɛd Nb Cu La Y Ch Db Sa St He Wo Wa Mon Gl O Nth Sf Bk Bd So W Brk K Ha, -*ing* tɛdɪn Sx, -*ing* tɛdn Nf; **hay-ted** -*ing* ɛɪtɛdɪn Co. ⇒ **chuck about,** *hay-ted,* **heave about, kick, kick out, pausle, rake out, scale, shake, shake about, shake out, shake over, shake up, shock, spread, strew, strew out, ted about, tedder, teddy, teddy out, ted out, ted over, teth, tether, throw out, topple up, toss, turn**

2. vt to TURN hay II.9.11(b). tɛd Nb

ted about *vtphr* to TED hay II.9.11(a). tɛd ... əbævt So, tɛd ... əbəʊt Do

tedder *vt* to TED hay II.9.11(a). tɛdə Hrt, -*ing* tɛdəɹɪn Y MxL, tɛdə¹ Brk

tedding-fork *n* a HAY-FORK with a short shaft I.7.11. tɛdɪnfɔːk Db, tɛddɪnfɔːk Db

teddy *vt* to TED hay II.9.11(a). tɛdi Mon

teddy out *vtphr* to TED hay II.9.11(a). *3prsg* tɛdɪz ... ɛʊt K

ted out *vtphr* to TED hay II.9.11(a). tɛd ... æʊt Wa

ted over *vtphr* to TED hay II.9.11(a). tɛd ... ɔːvəᵗ: W, tɛd ... oːvəᵗ: Co

teem *1. vt* to POUR tea V.8.8. tiːm Nb La Y, tɪəm Y, tɛɪm Du

2. v to pour tea. tiːm Nb*[old]* Du La Db Nt L, tⁱiːm Cu Du We Y Nt, tɪəm We La Y*[old x1]* Nt L, tɪʊm Cu, teːm Ch, tɛɪm Db, tam Db*[old]*, təɪm Y

teemer *n* the FORKER on a wagon who unloads sheaves in a stackyard II.6.9. tiːmə Y Nt L Lei R, tiːməᴵ L, tɪmə Nt L, tɪəmə Y Nt L, tɪəməɹ Y L

teem in *vtphr* to POUR tea V.8.8. tiːm ... ɪn Y

teeming *1. v-ing* UNLOADING sheaves from a wagon II.6.8. tiːmɪn Y Nt L R, tiːmən Nb, tɪəmɪn Y Nt*[old]* L, *no -ing* tɛɪm Du

2. vt-ing unloading sheaves. tiːmɪn Lei

teem out *vtphr* to POUR tea V.8.8. tiːm ... eat Y, tiːm ... æʊt L, tiːm ... aːt La Y Db, tiːm ... aʊt La L, tɪəm ... æːt Y, tɪəm ... aːt Y, tɪəm ... uːt Y, tɪəm ... uːt Y, *-ing* tɪəmən ... uːt Cu We, tɛɪm ... aʊt Y, tam ... ɛːt Db, təɪm ... ᵊuːt Y

teem up *vtphr* to POUR tea V.8.8. tiːm ... ʊp L, tɪəm ... ʊp Y

tees *n* the HAMES of the harness of a cart-horse I.5.4. tiːz Nf Sf

teeth *npl* *What do you call these [point to your teeth]?* VI.5.6(a). Eng. ⇒ **lompers, teeths, tooths, tushers, tushes,** *tushies* [⇒ **tushes], tushy-megs**

teeth-ache *n* TOOTHACHE VI.5.8. tiːθeːk Wa O, tiːðeːk Co D, tiːθeːɪk Hrt Ha, tiːθeːɪk So, tiːðɛɪk D, tiːθɛɪk Sr, tɪiθɛɪk Nf Brk Ha, tɪiːθɛɪk Brk Sx, tiːθɛ·ᵊk Nth

teeths *npl* TEETH VI.5.6(a). tɪθs Brk

teeth-wark* *n* TOOTHACHE VI.5.8. tiːθwaːk We, tiːθwaᴵːk La

tee-totter *n* a SEESAW VIII.7.2. tiːtɔːᵊtʔə Sf

teg *1. n* a sheep before its first shearing, ⇐ EWE-HOG III.6.4. tɪg Sr, tɛg Db Sa St He Wo Wa*[12 months old x1]* Gl O Lei Nth Bk Bd Hrt So W Brk Sr K Ha Sx, tɛəg Ess

2. n a sheep from its first to its second shearing, ⇐ GIMMER III.6.5. tɛg St Wa Gl Bk So Brk Sr K Ha Sx, tɛəg Ess

3. n a WETHER III.6.8. tɛg Sa St He*[old]* Wo Wa Mon Gl Lei R Nth Hu Bd*[old x1]* W, *pl* tɛgz Hrt Ess MxL *[queried SBM on grounds of age and castration]*

teg-lamb *n* a EWE-HOG III.6.4. tɛglam Bk

tegs *npl* TICKS on sheep IV.8.3. tɛgz Ess

tell *vt-2prsg* do you REMEMBER? VIII.3.7. tɛl Du We La Y

tell of* *vtphr-2prsg* do you REMEMBER? VIII.3.7. tɛl ə Y

tenant *n* a BUMPER of a cart I.10.1(a). tɛnənt Lei

tender *adj* BRITTLE, describing cups and saucers which break easily IX.1.4. tɛndə Nf Sf, tɛndɹ L

tending* *v-ing* FEEDING horses in the stable III.5.1. tɛndɪn Co

ten-minutes-to-two *adj* SPLAY-FOOTED VI.10.5. tɛnmɪnɪtstətᵁu La

tenner *n* a morning SNACK VII.5.11. tɛnəᵗ: Ha

ten-o'clock(s) *n* a morning SNACK VII.5.11. *no -s*: tɛnəklœk Nb Du, tɛnəklɒk Nb Cu Du We St, tɛnətlɒk Nb We; **bite of ten-o'clock** baɪt ə tɛnəklɒk Cu

-s: tɛnəklɒks Cu Y, tɛnəklɔks Cu Y

tenses *n* a morning SNACK VII.5.11. tenzɪz Nf, tɛnzəz Y*[modern]*

ten to two *adj* SPLAY-FOOTED VI.10.5. tɛɪn tə tʏː D

terrible *1. adv* VERY poisonous IV.11.5. taᵗːbł D

2. adv VERY VIII.3.2. tɛrəbl Cu Man, tɛɹəbl O, tɛɹəbəł MxL, taɾɪbł Ha, taʁbl Nb, taʁːbl Nb, taᵗːbł Ha, tərəbl Cu, tɑrbl Y, tɑɹbl Cu We La, tɑɹbəl Y, təɾɪbł So, təɾbł Do, təːbl Y, təːbəl Y, təᴵːbl La, təᴵːbəl La, təᵗːɾəbł Ha, təᵗːbł So

terribly *adv* VERY VIII.3.2. tɛɹɪblɪ Y, tɛɹəblɪ Y, taᵗːbli So

tet *n* the TEAT of a woman's breast VI.8.6. tɛt O So W Sr Co D Do Ha, *pl* tɛts MxL, tɛtʔ MxL, tɛʔ Bk, tat Ha

tetched *adj* RESTIVE, describing a horse III.5.6. tɛtʃt Cu

teth *vt* to TED hay II.9.11(a). tɛð W

tether *1. n [Show a picture of an old-fashioned cow-house.] What do you call this? What is it made of?* I.3.4. tɛðəᵗ: So

2. n a chain tether. tɛðəᵗ: So
⇒ **baikie-band, band, bilboes, chain, chog and chain, cops, cow-band, cow-chain, cow-halter, cow-rope, cow-seal, cow-sole, cow-tie, cow-tie-chain, cow-tyal, halter, head-chain, head-stall, hempen-halter, lanyard, neck-band, neck-chain, neck-strap, rope, seal, seal-chain, shackle, slip, sole, tether-chain, tie, tie-chain, tie-up, yoke;** ⇒ also **baulk, clam, clap(s), stall, steel-chain, stock**

3. n a TETHERING-ROPE used to tie up a horse I.4.2. tɛðəᵗ: So

4. vt to TED hay II.9.11(a). tɛðəɹ (+V) Y K

tether-chain *n* a TETHER for a cow I.3.4. tɛðətʃɛɪn Nf

tethering-cord *n* a TETHERING-ROPE used to tie up a horse I.4.2. tɛðɹɪnkɑᵗːd̢ Wo

tethering-nob *n* the CLOG on a horse's tether I.4.3. tɛðɹɪnnɑːb Wo

tethering-pole *n* a TETHERING-STAKE in a cow-house I.3.3. tɛðəɾɪnpoːł So

tethering-rope *n* *[Show a picture of a stable.] What do you call this, that you tie up the horse with?* I.4.2. tɛðəɹɪnɹɔːp Y. ⇒ **chain, chap-rein, check-rope, chog-rope, cord, halter, halter and shank, halter-chain, halter-rope, halter-shank, head-collar,** *head-collar and* **chain,** *head-collar and* **rope, head-collar rope, head-collar rope, head-halter, head-slip, head-stall,** *head-stall and* **lead, headstall-chain, headstall-cord, headstall-halter, headstall-line, headstall-rein, headstall-rope, hempen-halter, hemp-halter, horse-tie, lashing-chain, lead, leading-rein, leather-halter, line, loose-halter, manger-halter, manger-string, neck-chain, neck-collar,** *neck-collar and* **chain, neck-rope, neck-stall, neck-strap,** *neck-strap and* **chain,** *neck-strap and* **halter,** *neck-strap and* **lead, neck-tie, night-halter, rope, rope-tie, runner, shank, single-halter, slip, slip-chain, slip-shank, slip-tie, strap, tether, tethering-cord, tie, tie-chain, tie-cord, tie-rope, tie-slip, tie-up, tie-up-line, tyal-chain, under-halter**

tethering-stake *1. n [Show a picture of an old-fashioned cow-house.] What do you call this, for tethering?* I.3.3. **bar, boose-stake,** *boosing-stake* ⇒ **boosin-stake, boosin-post, boosin-stake, boosy-stake, boothin-rod, boskin-stake, chaining-pole, chain-post, chain-stake, cowband-stake, cow-chain-pole, cow-fasten, cow-post, cow-tie, cow-tier, cow-tyal-iron, dog, fastening-post, head-pole, iron, iron-bar, iron-rod, long-staple, manger-post, pole, post, rail, rail-stake, ramp-pole, ran-stake, ratch-stake, rath-stake, reddin-stake, redster, red-withie, riddle-stick, ring-post, rize-stake, rod, rod-stake, rood-post, rood-stake, rood-stower, russling-post, sal-tree, sealing-iron, sealing-post, seal-stake, slip-iron, snatch, stake, stallin, stall-post, stall-tree, stanchion, standard, standing-post, staple, stay, stelch, stower, studdle, tethering-pole, tethering-stump, tether-post, tie- iron, tiens, tie-pole, tie-post, tier, tie-rod, tie-stake, tie-up, trace-pole,** *tyer* ⇒ **tier, upright, wooden- post;** ⇒ also **baulk, clam, clap(s), stall, stock, yoke**

2. n a stake to which cows are tethered in a field. tɛðəɹɪnstɛɪk Ess

tethering-stump *n* a TETHERING-STAKE in a cow-house I.3.3. tɛðəᴶɹɪnstʊmp Wo

tether-post *n* a TETHERING-STAKE in a cow-house I.3.3. tɛðəpoust Nf

tetty* *n* the TEAT of a woman's breast VI.8.6. *pl* tɛdɪz Ha

tewed *vi-3ptsg* he TRIED VIII.8.4. tɛʊd Y

tewed out *adj* EXHAUSTED, describing a tired person VI.13.8. tɹuːt uːt Cu

thack *1. n* THATCH on a stack of corn II.7.6. θɛk Bd, θæk Nth Hu C, θak Nb Cu Du We La Y Db St Wa Nt L Lei R Nth

2. n the ROOF of a house V.1.2. θæk Nth, θak Cu*[obsolete]* La Y*[generic x2]* Db*[obsolete x1]* Sa L

3. n a thatched roof. θak Lei R

thack-cord *n* TWINE used to fasten thatch on a stack II.7.7(b1). θakkʊəᴶd Y

thacker *n* the THATCHER of a stack of corn II.7.5(b). θɛkə Bd, θɛkəᵗ Bd, θækə Nth, θæˑkʔᵊ C, θakɔᵏ Nb, θakə Nb Cu Du We La Y Db St Wa Nt L Lei R Nth, θakɹ L, θakəɹ La Y L, θakkəɹ La, θakəᴶ La Db L, θakəᵗ Nth

thacking *1. v-ing* THATCHING a stack of corn II.7.5(a). θeːᵊkɪn Gl, θɛkɪn Bd Hrt, θækɪn Nth Hu, θæˑkʔɪn C, θakɪn Cu La Y Db St Wa Nt L Lei R Nth C, θakkɪn La Db, θakən Cu Du We

2. n THATCH on a stack of corn II.7.6. θakɪn Wa *[thack(ing) not differentiated from thatch(ing) NBM and WMBM]*

thacking-band *n* TWINE used to fasten thatch on a stack II.7.7(b1). θakɪnband Db*[matting-type string]*

thacking-pegs *npl* PEGS used to fasten thatch on a stack II.7.7(a). θakɪnpɛgz Y

thacking-string *1. n* STRING used to tie up a grain-sack I.7.3. θakɪnstɹɪŋ Lei

2. n TWINE used to fasten thatch on a stack II.7.7(b1). θækɪnstɹɪŋ Nth, θakɪnstɹɪŋ Lei Nth

thack-pegs *npl* PEGS used to fasten thatch on a stack II.7.7(a). θakpɛgz Y Nt L*[ash x1, old x1]*, *sg* θakpɛg Lei, θakpagz Db

thalling *n* the CURB-STONE in a cow-house I.3.9. θoʊɪn St

thall-tree *1. n* the CURB-STONE in a cow-house I.3.9. θɔːltɹiː Y, θɔːtɹiː Db, ɔːtɹiː Y Db

2. n a wooden curb-stone. θɔːtɹiː Ch

than *1. prep So, putting it another way, you can say that diphtheria is much worse ... mumps.* VI.12.4. Eng. ⇒ **as, nor, till, to**

2. prep TILL IX.2.2. ðən Ch

tharms *n* CHITTERLINGS III.12.2. θaːmz L

that *1. pron [In asking the next questions, you must stand at the informant's side. Put a coin close to the informant, and another a little further away.] Say which you'll have. You'll have [point to the further one] ....* IX.10.1. Eng. ⇒ *that one,* *that one over there, that there, the further one, the one over there,* **thick, thick** *here,* **thick** *one,* **thick** *there,* **thicky, thicky** *one,* **thicky** *there, this, this here,* **thuck, thucker,** *tother,* **yon**

2. pron **that (over there)** *[In asking the next questions, you must stand at the informant's side. Put a coin close to the informant, another a little further away, and another further away still.] Now you can choose [point to the furthest one] ....* IX.10.3. Eng exc. Nb Cu We So W D Do. ⇒ **thick,**

thick *one*, thicky, thon, thon *one*, thuck, thucker, yon, yond, yonder *one*, yon *one*, yons

thatch 1. *n* [*Show a picture of some stacks.*] *What do you call this?* II.7.6. ðeɪtʃ D, deɪtʃ D, θɛtʃ Y Ch Sa Wa O Bk Bd Hrt Ess Brk Sr K Sx, ðɛtʃ W Ha, vɛtʃ So, dɛtʃ D, θɛətʃ Ess, θætʃ Y Man Sa He Wo Mon Gl O Hu C Nf Sf Bk Hrt Ess MxL So Brk Sr K Co Sx, ðætʃ He Gl So Brk Ha, fætʃ Mon, vætʃ He So, tʰætʃ Man, dætʃ D, θatʃ Nb Du La Y Ch Db Sa St He Wo Wa Mon Gl O Nt L Hu Bk W Ha, ðatʃ Gl So W Co D Do Ha, vatʃ Do, datʃ Co, ðaɪtʃ D, daɪtʃ D. ⇒ **cover**, *rushes*, *straw*, **thack, thacking, thatching, theak, theaking**

2. *n* the THATCHER of a stack of corn II.7.5(b). θatʃ Gl

3. *n* the ROOF of a house V.1.2. θætʃ Sx, θæːtʃ Brk, θatʃ Wa

4. *n* a thatched roof. θatʃ Lei

thatch-band *n* TWINE used to fasten thatch on a stack II.7.7(b1). θatʃbant Ch[*thick waterproofed string*]

thatch-cord *n* TWINE used to fasten thatch on a stack II.7.7(b1). θatʃkɔːd St, θatʃkoˑəd Ch Db[*coconut string*]

thatched-hive *n* a SKEP IV.8.8(b). θætʃtɔɪv Ha

thatched skip *n* a SKEP IV.8.8(b). θatʃt skɪp Wo

thatcher *n* [*What is your word for covering a stack with a roof of straw?*] *What do you call the man who does it?* II.7.5(b). ðeɪtʃəᵗ: D, deɪtʃəᵗ: D, θɛtʃə Y Ch Hrt Ess, θɛtʃəᴶ Brk Sr K, θɛtʃəᵗ Sa Wa O Bk Sr Sx, ðɛtʃəᵗ: W Ha, vɛtʃəᵗ: So, dɛtʃəᵗ: D, θɛətʃə Ess, θætʃə Y Mon O Hu C Nf Sf Bk Hrt Ess MxL K, *pl* θætʃəs Man, ðætʃə He, tʰæˑtʃə Man, θætʃəᴶ Brk Sr K, θætʃəᵗ Sa He Wo Mon Gl O Brk Sr, *pl* θætʃəᵗz̩ Sx, ðætʃəᵗ Gl Brk, fætʃəᵗ Mon, vætʃəᵗ He, θætʃəᵗ: So Co, ðætʃəᵗ: So Ha, vætʃəᵗ: So, dætʃəᵗ: D, θatʃɔᴿ Nb, θatʃə Du Y Ch Db St Wa Mon Lei Hu, θatʃəᴿ Du, θatʃəɹ La St He, θatʃəᴶ La Db St O, θatʃəᵗ Sa Wo Wa Mon O Bk Ha, ðatʃəᵗ Gl, θatʃəᵗ: Sa W Ha, ðatʃəᵗ: So W Co D Do Ha, vatʃəᵗ: Do, datʃəᵗ: Co, ðaɪtʃəᵗ: D, daɪtʃəᵗ: D. ⇒ **coverer, simmon thatcher, thacker, thatch, theaker**

thatching 1. *v-ing What's your word for covering a stack with a roof of straw?* II.7.5(a). ðeɪtʃən D, deɪtʃən D, θɛtʃɪn Y Ch Wa Gl O Bk Hrt Ess Brk Sr K Sx, əθɛtʃɪn O Bk, ðɛtʃɪn Ha, vɛtʃɪn So, ðɛtʃən W D Ha, dɛtʃən D, θætʃɪn Y Man Sa He Wo Mon Gl O Hu Nf Bk Hrt Ess MxL So Brk Sr K Sx, ðætʃɪn He Gl So Brk, fætʃɪn Mon, vætʃɪn He So, dætʃɪn D, θætʃn C Sf Ess, θætʃən Sf Co, ðætʃən Ha, tʰæˑtʃən Man, dæɪtʃɪn D, θatʃɪn Du La Y Ch Db Sa St He Wo Wa Mon O Nt L Lei Hu Bk W Ha, ðatʃɪn Gl So W Co D Ha, vatʃɪn W Do, datʃɪn Co, θatʃn Du, ðatʃn Gl, θatʃən Nb Du, ðatʃən So W D Do, vatʃən Do, datʃən Co, ðaɪtʃɪn D, daɪtʃən D. ⇒ **covering, thacking, theaking**

2. *n* THATCH on a stack of corn II.7.6. θɛtʃɪn Bk, θætʃɪn MxL K, θatʃɪn Wa

thatching-cord *n* TWINE used to fasten thatch on a stack II.7.7(b1). θɛtʃɪnkɔːd Ess, θɛtʃɪnkɔᵗːd̩ Sa, θɛtʃɪnkoːd Ch, θatʃɪnkɔᵗːd̩ Sa

thatching-line *n* TWINE used to fasten thatch on a stack II.7.7(b1). θatʃənlaɪn Du

thatching-pegs *npl* PEGS used to fasten thatch on a stack II.7.7(a). θætʃɪnpɛᶦgz Ess, θatʃɪnpegz Y[*wooden*], θatʃɪnpɛgz He[*split willow*]

thatching-rods *npl* RODS laid on thatch to fasten it on a stack II.7.7(b3). θɛtʃɪnɹɒdz K[*'staples', old*]

thatching-string *n* TWINE used to fasten thatch on a stack II.7.7(b1). θatʃɪnstɹɪŋ Sa He

thatch-pegs *npl* PEGS used to fasten thatch on a stack II.7.7(a). θatʃpɛgz Ch Db Wo Wa Nt[*hazel*] Lei

thatch-pricks *npl* PEGS used to fasten thatch on a stack II.7.7(a). θatʃpɹɪks La[*old*]

thatch-rods *npl* RODS laid on thatch to fasten it on a stack II.7.7(b3). θɛtʃɹɒdz Sx

thatch-roof *n* the ROOF of a house V.1.2. θɛtʃɹuːf Sr Sx, θætʃɹuf Brk

thatch-rope *n* hay ROPES used to fasten thatch on a stack II.7.7(b2). θatʃɹoːp Db [*marked u.r. as mass n WMBM*]

thawing *v-ing When it begins to get warm again and the snow begins to melt, what do you say it is doing?* VII.6.15. Eng. ⇒ **a-thawing, giving, giving out, giving way,** *in thaw*, **melting,** *thawing out*, **wasting**

theak *n* THATCH on a stack of corn II.7.6. θiːk Nb Cu, θɪək Y, θɛɪk Y

theaker *n* the THATCHER of a stack of corn II.7.5(b). θiːkɔᴿ Nb, θiːkə Nb Cu We Y, θɪkər Cu, θɪəkə Y, θɪəkəɹ Y, θɛɪkə Y

theaking 1. *v-ing* THATCHING a stack of corn II.7.5(a). θiːkɪn Nb Cu Y, θiːkən Nb We, θɪkɪn Cu, θɪkən Nb, θɪəkɪn Y, θɛɪkɪn Y, θɛɪkən We

2. *n* THATCH on a stack of corn II.7.6. θɪəkɪn Y

theaking-band *n* TWINE used to fasten thatch on a stack II.7.7(b1). θɪəkɪnband Y

theave 1. *n* a EWE-HOG III.6.4. θiːv Sa He Wa L R, θiːθ Lei, θɪˑəv L, θeːv Sa Mon Gl, θɛɪv Wa Nth Bk, *pl* θɛɪvz St

2. *n* a GIMMER III.6.5. θiːv Db St[*2 years old x1*], θeːv Gl O[*having had only one lamb*], θɛɪv Db St Wa[*maiden x1*] O[*2 years old*]

3. *n* a EWE III.6.6. θeːv Sa

theave-lamb *n* a EWE-LAMB III.6.3. θiːvlam Sa

thellies* *npl* FELLIES, the sections of the wooden rim of a cart-wheel I.9.9. θɪlɪz Ha, ðɪɬiːz W, ðəɬiːz Do

them 1. *pron* THOSE IX.10.4. ðɛm Nb Cu Du We La Y Man Ch Db St He Wo Wa Gl O Nt L R

Nth Hu C Nf Sf Bk Bd Hrt Ess MxL So[old x1] Brk Sr K Sx

2. *pron* THESE IX.10.5. ðɪm Ess, ðɛm Nb L Lei Nf Sr, təm Ess [queried u.r. EMBM]

3. *pron* THOSE over there IX.10.6. ðɛm Du Y Man Ch Db Sa St He Wo Wa Mon Gl O Nt L Nth Hu C Nf Sf Bk Bd Hrt Ess MxL So Brk Sr K Co Sx

there *1. adv* **(that)** **over there** [In asking the next questions, you must stand at the informant's side. Put a coin close to the informant, another a little further away, and another further away still.] Now you can choose [point to the furthest one] .... IX.10.3. ⇒ **over yon**, **over yonder**, **yonder**

2. adv **(those)** **over there** [In asking the next questions, you must stand at the informant's side. Put two coins at each place [i.e. two close to the informant, two a little further away, two further away still].] Now you can choose [point to the furthest pair] .... IX.10.6. ⇒ **over thonder**, **over yon**, **over yonder**, **yonder**

these *pron* [In asking the next questions, you must stand at the informant's side. Put two coins at each place [i.e. two close to the informant, two a little further away, two further away still].] Now you can choose [point to the closest pair] .... IX.10.5. Eng. ⇒ *that lot, that two, theasum* ⇒ **theseum**, *the first two*, **them**, **them** *ones*, **them** *others*, **the near one**, **these here**, *these lot*, **these ones**, **these** *two*, **these** *twos*, **theseum**, **theseun**, **they**, **they** *back there*, **they** *over there*, **they** *two*, **thick**, *thick lot*, **thick ones**, **thick** *two*, *thicky lot*, **thir**, **thir** *here*, **thir** *two*, *this lot*, *this two*, **tho**, **those**, *tother lot*, **tothers**

theseum* *pron* THESE IX.10.5. ðiːzəm W, ðɪəzəm W

theseun *pron* THESE IX.10.5. ðˡiːzn Sa

they *1. pron* THOSE IX.10.4. ðeː W Brk Ha, ðeɪ So W Do, ðɛɪ Gl W Brk[old x1] Sr Co D Ha Sx, ðæɪ Gl Sf Ess, ðaːɪ So

2. pron THESE IX.10.5. ðeː Brk Do Ha, ðeɪ So Do, ðɛɪ Ess W Brk Sr[old] D, ðaːɪ So

3. pron THOSE over there IX.10.6. ðeː W Brk Ha, ðeɪ So Do, ðɛɪ Gl Ess W Brk Sr Ha Sx, ðæɪ Gl Sf Ess, ðaɪ Ess So

thick *1. adj* **turn thick** to CURDLE (milk) V.5.7. təːn θɪk MxL

2. vt to THICKEN gravy V.7.7. θɪk C

3. adj HOARSE VI.5.16. θɪk Brk

4. n **thick of the/your leg**, **thick part of your leg** the THIGH VI.9.3. **thick of the leg** θɪk ə ðə lɛg Sa, θɪk ə t lɛg Y; **thick of your leg** θɪk ə jə lɛg Nt Nf Bk0; **thick part of your leg** θɪk paːt ə jə lɛg Ess

5. pron THAT IX.10.1. ðɪk He So W Do, ðək Gl

6. pron THIS IX.10.2. ðɪk He So W Do Ha

7. pron THAT over there IX.10.3. ðɪk He Mon Gl So W Do Ha

8. pron THOSE IX.10.4. ðɪk So

9. pron THESE IX.10.5. ðɪk He Gl So

10. pron THOSE over there IX.10.6. ðɪk He Mon Gl So

thickans *n* PORRIDGE V.7.1. θɪknz Y

thick-dicks *n* PORRIDGE V.7.1. θɪkdɪks We

thicken *1. vt* If you see that your gravy is too thin, what do you do to it? V.7.7. ⇒ **flour-lithe** *it*, **lide** *it*, **lithe** *it*, **lithen** *it*, **live** *it*, **liven** *it*, **liven** *it with flour*, **make it thick**, **make it thicker**, **put lithen in**, **put some lithening in**, **put some livening in**, **put thickening in it**, **stiffen it**, **thicken en**, **thicken her**, **thicken her up**, **thicken him**, **thicken him up**, **thicken it**, **thicken it up**, **thicken it with flour**, **thicken it with lithing**, **thicken it with some flour and water**, **thick it**

2. vt to CURDLE milk V.5.7. *3prsg* θɪknz K

thickening *prppl-adj IN* FLOOD, describing a river IV.1.4. θɪkənɪn Y

thickfast *n* the CORE of a boil VI.11.7. θɪkfast Du

thick forenoon *n* THIS FORENOON VII.3.15. ðɪk foːəᵗnuːn W

thick-head *n* a STUPID person VI.1.5. θɪkɪəd Y

thick-headed *adj* STUPID VI.1.5. θɪkɪədəd Y

thick morning *1. n* THIS MORNING VII.3.10. ðɪk maᵗːɾŋ ɪn W

2. n THIS FORENOON VII.3.15. ðɪk maᵗːŋ ɪn W

thicky *1. pron* THAT IX.10.1. ðɪki So D

2. pron THIS IX.10.2. ðɪki So Co D

3. pron THAT over there IX.10.3. ðɪki Co

thieven *vt-3prpl* burglars STEAL things VIII.7.5(b). ðeɪvn St

thigh *1. n* What do you call this [indicate the thigh]? VI.9.3. Eng. ⇒ **thick** *of the leg*, **thick** *of your leg*, **thick** *part of your leg*

2. n the human HIP-BONE VI.9.1. θʌɪ Nf [marked u.r. EMBM]

thigh-bone *n* the human HIP-BONE VI.9.1. θiːbɔːn Y

thiller *n* a SHAFT-HORSE I.6.2. θɪlə Nf MxL, θɪləᵗ Wa Gl O Bk Ha, θɪɬəᴶ Sr, θɪɬəɾ O Ha, θɪɬəᵗː W, ðɪɬəᵗː W Ha

thiller-horse *n* a SHAFT-HORSE I.6.2. θɪləᴶ-aˑːs Brk, θɪɬə-ɔːəᵗɾ̩ʂ Sx, θɪɬəᵗaᵗːʂ Gl, θɪɬəᵗ-ɔːəᵗːʂ Sr

thill-horse *n* a SHAFT-HORSE I.6.2. θɪɬaᵗːʂ Ha, θɪɬɔːəᵗɾʂ Sx, tɪlhɒs Man

thills *npl* the SHAFTS of a cart I.9.4. θɪlz Nf

thim *n* a THIMBLE V.10.9. θɪm Nt

thimble *n* What do you call this [indicate a thimble]? V.10.9. Eng. ⇒ **dolly**, **guard**, **hood**, **thim**

thimes *n* ROPES used to fasten thatch on a stack II.7.7(b2). θaɪmz We

thime-spinner *n* a ROPE-TWISTER II.7.8. θaɪmspɪnə La

thin *1. vt* to THIN OUT turnip plants II.4.2. θɪn Nb Cu We La Y Ch Db Wo Wa Gl MxL So Brk K, ðɪn So D Ha, tʰɪn Man

2. v to thin out turnips. θɪn Nb Cu La Ch, *-ing* θɪnɪn St

think on *vtphr-2prsg* do you REMEMBER? VIII.3.7. θɪŋk ɒn Cu We

thin out *v At first your young turnip plants are too close together, so what do you do?* II.4.2.

1. vtphr θɪn ... aɪt Ch, θɪn ... ɛʊt Wa Nth Brk Sr, ðɪn ... ɛʊt Ha, θɪn ... ɛʊ? O Bd, ðɪn ... œyt D, ðɪn ... æyt So Co D, θɪn ... æʊt Wa Ess Ha, ðɪn ... æʊt So W Ha, θɪn ... aʊt La Sa St So, ðɪn ... aʊt So, θɪn ... uːt Nb Du Y, ðɪn ... ᵁuːt Gl, θɪn ... əʊt W, ðɪn ... əʊt Gl So, θɪn ... əʊːt Gl

2. v -ing θɪnɪn ɛʊt Sx, θɪn aːt La, θɪn aʊt La, *-ing* θɪnɪn aʊt So, θɪn uːt Du Y

⇒ **bunch out**, **chop** *and single* **out**, **chop out**, **cut out**, **gap**, **gap out**, *get singled*, **hand-hoe**, **hoe**, **hoe out**, **horse-hoe**, **knock out**, **plant out**, **scuffle**, **set out**, **single**, **single out**, **slate**, **slender**, **sort out**, **strike**, *strike and single*, **strike out**, **strime out**, **thin** *[terms not always synonymous, relating to stages in process]*

thin porridge *n* GRUEL V.7.2. θɪn pɒɹɪdʒ Bk, θɪn pɒɹɪdʒ Nth Bk

thin puddings *n* CHITTERLINGS III.12.2. θɪn pʊdɪnz Y

thir *1. pron* THIS IX.10.2. ðʊə Du

2. pron THESE IX.10.5. ðɪə Y, ðɪəɹ (+V) Y, ðəː Du

thirl *1. n* a SHEEP-HOLE IV.2.8. θəl Y, *pl* ðəɹəlz Y

2. adj HUNGRY VI.13.9. ðɛɽəł Co, θʌɽəł Co, ðʌɽəł Co*[especially cattle x1]*, ðəˤːɽəł Co, ðəˤːdɫ D, vəˤːdɫ D

thirl-hole *n* a SHEEP-HOLE IV.2.8. θəlʊəl Y, θəːlʊəl Y

thirly *adj* HUNGRY VI.13.9. ðəˤːłi Co

thirsty *adj If you haven't drunk anything for a long time, you're bound to be very ....* VI.13.10. Eng. ⇒ *a-*dry, **clammed**, **clammed up**, **droughty**, **dry**, **famished**, **gegged**, **paddocked**, **parched**, **parched up**; ⇒ *also* **drought-struck**

this *pron [In asking the next questions, you must stand at the informant's side. Put a coin close to the informant, and another a little further away.] Say which you'll have. You'll have [point to the closer one] ....* IX.10.2. Eng. ⇒ **he**, **that**, **that one**, **thick**, **thick** *one*, *thick over there*, **thick** *here*, **thicky**, **thicky one**, **thicky** *there*, **thir**, *this here here*, *this here one*, *this here one here*, *this one*, *this one here*, *this here*, **thuck**, *tother*

this forenoon *1. n You will see him again today, between 9 and 12 noon, so....* VII.3.15. ðɪs fʏənʏːn La, ðəs fœːnɪvn Nb, ðɪs fœːnjvn Du, ðɪs fɒnɪən Y*[old]*, ðɪs fɒnʊɪn Y, ðɪs fɒnᵁuːn Db, ðɪs fɒvɛnuːn K, ðɪs fɒnɪuːn Y, ðɪs fɒnʊɪn Y, ðɪs fɒnᵁuːn Nt, ðɪs fɔːnɪʊn Y Nf*[old]*, ðɪs fɔːnɪən Cu We, ðɪs fɔːnɪuːn Y Db, ðɪs fɔːnɛʊn St, ðɪs fɔːnuːn St Wa Nt Lei R Nf Ess Sr, ðəs fɔᵏːnjvn Nb, ðəs fɔᵏːniːn Nb, ðɪs fɔᵏːnɪən Nb, ðɪs fɔᵏːnjʊn Du, ðɪs fɔᴶːnɪən La, ðɪs fɔᴶːnʊuːn We Y, ðɪs fɔˤːɳuːn Sa Co, ðɪs vɔˤːɳuːn Co, ðɪs fɔənɪɰːn Nf*[old x1]*, ðɪs fɔənʊɪn Y, ðɪs fɔᵊnʊn Sf, ðɪs fɔənuːn K, ðɪs fɔːənuːn Bd Ess, ðɪs fɔəᴶnuːn Brk, s fɔːəᴶnʊuːn Sr, dɪs fɔəˤːɳuːn Sx, ðɪs vɔəˤːɳɳəuːn Ha, ðɪs fɔːəˤnʊuːn Sr Sx, ðɪs fɔːəˤːɳuːn Sx, dɪs fɔːəˤːɳuːn Sx, ðɪs fɔənɪʊn Nf, ðɪs fɔənɪən We, ðɪs fɔəɹnʊn Cu, ðɪs fɔːənyːn Ch, ðɪs fo·ənɛʊn Db, ðɪs fo·əɹnyːn La, ðɪs fɔəᴶnuːn Brk, s fɔəˤnəuːn Brk, ðɪs fɔːəˤɳuːn Sa Brk, ðɪs fɔʊənɛʊn St, ðɪs fʊənɪʊn Cu Y, ðɪs fʊənɪən Cu Du We Y, ðɪs fʊənuːn La L, ðɪs fʊəɹnʊɪn Cu, ðɪs fʊəɹnyːn La, ðɪs fʊəᴶnᵁuːn La, ðɪs fʊəˤɳʊn O, ðɪs fɜᴶːɪnᵁuːn La, ðɪs fəːnjvn Du, ðɪs fəːnɪuːn Du, ðɪs fəːnɛʊn St, ðɪs fəᴶːnuːn L. ⇒ **afore dinner**, **afore noon**, *afore the* **dinner**, **before noon**, **forenoon**, *in the* **forenoon**, *in the* **morning**, *mid* **morning**, **morning**, *some time* **before noon**, *the* **forenoon**, *the* **morning**, **thick forenoon**, **thick morning**, **this morn**, **this morning**

2. n THIS MORNING VII.3.10. ðɪs fɒnɪuːn Y, ðɪs fɒnɪən Y, ðɪs fɔːnɪʊn Y Nf, ðɪs fɔːnɪən Cu, ðɪs ɖʊənuːn La

this morn *1. n* THIS MORNING VII.3.10. ðɪs mɔᴶːn Db

2. n THIS FORENOON VII.3.15. ðɪs mɔᴶːn Db

this morning *1. n [If you wanted to tell me that something happened seven days back from now, you'd say: It happened ....] If in the early part of today?* VII.3.10. Eng. ⇒ *afore noon*, *at morn*, *forenoon*, *fore part of the day*, *in the forenoon*, *in the morn*, *in the morning*, *the fore end of the day*, **thick morning**, **this forenoon**, **this morn**

2. n THIS FORENOON VII.3.15. Eng exc. Cu We Brk Sr Sx.

thistle *n [Show a picture of a thistle.] What do you call this?* II.2.2. θɪsl Nb Cu Du We La Y Ch Db Sa St He Wa O Nt L Nf Ess, θɪstl Cu, θɪsɫ Nb He Wo Wa Mon Gl O Lei R Nth Hu C Nf Sf Bk Bd Hrt Ess MxL So W Brk Sr K Ha, θɪsʊł Brk K, *pl* θɪsʊłz Hrt Ha Sx, θɪsʊ Ess Sr K Ha Sx, *pl* θɪzłz Lei, θɪsə Bk, θɛsəł Hrt, θaɪsł Co, θʏsəl Nb, θəsl Sa, θəsł Wo, ðɪsł Gl W Do Ha, *pl* ðɪsłz Gl So, ðɪsʊł Brk, *pl* ðɪsʊz Brk, ðɪzł Gl Ha, *pl* ðɪzłz So, *pl* ðɪzʊłz Ha, *pl* ðəsłz So, θɹɪsl Cu, *pl* θʙɪzˌslz Nb, θɹɪsl Nb Du, sɪsł Mon, sɪsʊł Sx, *pl* sɪzʊlz Sx, fɪsl Sa, fɪsł He Wo Mon Lei Ess So, vɪsł He Do, vɪzł So, tʰɪsl Man, *pl* tɪsłz Lei R, tɹɪsəl Y, dɪsł So W, *pl* dazłz Bk, daɪʃɫ Co D, daɪzł Co. ⇒ **boar-thistle**, *burr-thistle* ⇒ **boar-thistle**, **dog-thistle**, **english thistle**, **hob-thistle**, **jacobite**, **pod-thistle**, scotchman, sow-thistle, *thow-thistle* ⇒ sow-thistle

thithers *n* TREMORS suffered by a person who cannot keep still VI.1.4. ðɪðəz La Y

thivel *1. n* a PORRIDGE-STICK V.9.1. θaɪvl Nb Cu Du We, θaɪvəl Nb Cu, θɹaɪvl We, saɪvl Nb, θaɪbl Cu We La Y, θaɪbəl Y, θɑːbl Y, *pl* θɔːblz Y
2. n a wooden stick for lifting clothes from boiling water during washing. θaɪvl Nb

thivel-stick *n* a PORRIDGE-STICK V.9.1. θaɪvlstɪk Nb

tho *1. pron* THOSE IX.10.4. ðɔ:ᴶ Y, ðoə Nb
2. pron THESE IX.10.5. ðoə Nb, ðʊɹ Y, ðʊə Du
3. pron THOSE over there IX.10.6. ðʊəɹ (+V) La

thocking *v-ing* PANTING VI.8.1. θœːkɪn Nb, θɒkən Nb

thodden *adj* SAD, describing bread or pastry that has not risen V.6.12. θɒdn La Ch Db *[not a WMBM headword]*

tholes *npl* the HANDLES of a scythe II.9.8. θɒʊłz Sx, θoʊłz Ess, ðoʊłz Ha, θɔʊz Ess, θʌʊłz Ess, fʌʊłz Ess, θoʊłz Sf, θəʊłz Ess

thon *1. pron* THAT over there IX.10.3. ðœn Nb, ðɒn Du
2. pron THOSE over there IX.10.6. ðɒn Nb Du

thond* *n* a WHIP used for driving horses I.5.12. θɒnd Nf

thonder *adv* **over thonder** those OVER THERE IX.10.6. oʊvə ðɪndə Nf*[old]*

thongs *npl* BOOT-LACES VI.14.25. θɒŋz O, θʊŋz La, θʊŋks La Ch Sa St*[old x1]*

thorn-berries *npl* HAWS IV.11.6. ðɔˡːn̩bəɹɪz D, *sg* ðɔˡːn̩bəɹi So

thorn-dike' *n* a HEDGE IV.2.1(a). θɔːndaɪk Cu We, θɔᴿːndɛɪk Du, θoəndɛɪk Nb, θʊəndɛɪk Nb

thorn-fence *n* a HEDGE IV.2.1(a). θɔːnfɛns Nf

thorn-hedge *n* a HEDGE IV.2.1(a). *pl* θɔːnɛdʒɪz L, θɔːᴶːnɛdʒ Y

those *1. pron* [In asking the next question, you must stand at the informant's side. Put two coins at each place [i.e. two close to the informant, two a little further away, two further away still].] Now you can choose [point to the middle pair] .... IX.10.4. ðʏːz La, ðɛuz Sr, ðæuz Hrt, ðɒus K, ðɒʊz Wo Gl K Sx, ðɔʊz Lei R Ess, ðʌʊz Ess Sr K, ðoːs W, ðoːz La Sa He Wo Mon So Co D, ðoʊz St He Wo Wa Mon Gl Lei Nf So Ha, ðᵁuːz La.* ⇒ *both them, that, that lot, that two, them, them here, the middle one, them ones, them there, them two, the others, these, these here, the second lot, they, they over there, they two, thick, thick lot, thick over there, thick two, thicky lot, thicky lot there, this two, tho, those ones, those two, thoseun, tho two, thuck lot, tother lot, tothers, totherum, yon*
2. pron THESE IX.10.5. ðæuz Hrt, ðɔʊz L, ðoːz So *[queried ir.r. EMBM]*
3. pron **those (over there)** [In asking the next

questions, you must stand at the informant's side. Put two coins at each place [i.e. two close to the informant, two a little further away, two further away still].] Now you can choose [point to the furthest pair] .... IX.10.6. ðʏːz La, ðæuz Hrt, ðɒuz Wo K, ðɔʊz L Lei R Ess, ðʌʊs Ess, ðʌʊz MxL Sr K, ðoːz Sa He Wo Mon, ðoᵘs Man, ðoʊz St He Wo Wa Gl Lei Ha, ðʊz Lei. ⇒ **them, they, thick, tho, thon, thoseun, thuck, yon, yond, yonder, yons**

thoseun *1. pron* THOSE IX.10.4. ðoːzn Sa
2. pron THOSE over there IX.10.6. ðoːzn Sa

thow *imp* **thow wee** the command TURN LEFT!, given to plough-horses II.3.5(a). 'ðɒʊ ˌwiː Sr

thrail *n* a FLAIL II.8.3. θɹiːl Db, θʁeːl Nb, θɹeːl La, θɹeɪł Hu, θɾeɪł Ha, θɹeɪəl Wa, θɹeɪᵊł Bd, *pl* θɹeɪᵊłz Bk, dɹeɪᵊł W, θɹeəl Du, *pl* θɹeəłz O, θɹeˑəł Nth Bk, θɹeːᵊl Sa, θɹeːᵊł O, θɹeːʊł Brk, θɹeɪl Wa L, θɹeɪł Lei, θɹeɪᵊł Wa Nth C Bk, *pl* θɹeɪᵊłz Hu Hrt, dɹeɪᵊł W Ha, *pl* θɹeɪʊłz Brk, *pl* dɹeɪᵁłz W, θɹeɪʊ Sr Sx, θɹeəl Y, *pl* θɹeəłz O, θɹæɪl Wa, *pl* θɹæɪłz Hrt, θɹeɪᵊł Nth, *pl* dɹaɪᵊłz So

thrall *1. n* a BENCH on which slaughtered pigs are dressed III.12.1. θɹɔːl St
2. n a flat surface on which bacon is cured, ⇐ SALTING-TROUGH III.12.5. θɹɔːl Db*[stone]* St Wa*[brick]*, θɹɔːł Lei*[stone, in dairy x1]*

thrampwith *n* a sliding RING to which a tether is attached in a cow-house I.3.5. θɹɒmpɪk St, ɹaʊmpɛn Db

thrampwith-ring *n* a sliding RING to which a tether is attached in a cow-house I.3.5. ðɹampətɹɪŋ Ch

thrape *vt* to BEAT a boy on the buttocks VIII.8.10. θɹeːᶦp He, θɹeɪp St*[old x1]*, θɹeəp Y

thraping *vbln* **give him a good thraping** to BEAT a boy on the buttocks VIII.8.10. gɪ ɪm ə gʊd θɹeːpɪn Wa, gɪv ɪm ə gʊd θɹeɪpɪn Wo

thrash *vt* to BEAT a boy on the buttocks VIII.8.10. θɹɛʃ Y Sr K Sx, *-ing* θɹɛʃɪn Ess, ɹɛʃ Y, dɹɛʃ Brk Ha, dɹɛɪʃ D, θɹæʃ W Sr, dɹæʃ Brk, θɹaʃ Y Sa St L, θɾaʃ O, ɹɹaʃ Nf, θɹɒʃ Ess

thrashet *1. n* a FLAIL II.8.3. θɹaʃət St
2. n a pair of threshing-sticks, one of which is held in each hand. θɹaʃət Ch

thrashing *1. v-ing* winnowing, ⇐ to WINNOW II.8.4. *-ing* θɹaʃɪn Mon
2. vbln **give him a (good) thrashing** to BEAT a boy on the buttocks VIII.8.10. **give him a good thrashing** gɪ ɪm ə gʊd θɹɛʃɪn L, gɪv ɪm ə gʊd ɹɛʃɪn Y, giː m ə gɹd dɹɛɪʃən D, gɪv ɪm ə gʊd θɹaʃɪn Wo; **give him a thrashing** gɪv n̩ ə dɹɛʃɪn Brk, gɪv ɪm ə θɹaʃɪn Mon

thrave *1. n* a stook of corn, ⇐ STOOKING II.6.5. tɹɛɪv Ess
2. *n* a FLAIL II.8.3. θɹɛːv Ch, *pl* θɹɛɪvz St

thraving *v-ing* STOOKING II.6.5. tɹæɪvɪn Ess, tɹɛɪvɪn Ess, tɹɛɪvn Ess, tɹɛɪvən Ess

thraw-crook *n* a ROPE-TWISTER II.7.8. θʀaːkʀʊk Nb, θʀaːkrək Nb

thread *1. n* What do you call this [indicate a needle and thread]? V.10.2(b). Eng. ⇒ **cotton, drab-thread**
2. *v* to REMOVE *STALKS* from currants V.7.24. dɹɛd So

threaded-ful *n* a NEEDLEFUL of cotton or thread V.10.5. θɹɛdɪdfʊɫ Ess

thread-needle *n* a NEEDLE V.10.2(a). θɹɛdniiˈdl Nf

threave *1. n* a EWE-HOG III.6.4. θɹeˑᵊv Ch, θɹeːᵊv Gl *[not a WMBM headword]*
2. *n* a GIMMER III.6.5. θɹeːᵊv Gl

three-cornered *adv* DIAGONALLY, referring to harrowing a field IX.1.8. θɹiːkɔᵊnəd Y

three-horse baulk *n* the main swingle-tree or EVENER of the harness of a plough pulled by three horses I.8.4. θɹiː-ɒs bɔᵊk L, θɹiː-ɒs bɔːk Nt

three-horse-pulling-tree *n* the main swingle-tree or EVENER of the harness of a plough pulled by three horses I.8.4. θɹiˈhɒspʊlɪntɹi Nf

three-horse swingle-tree *n* the main swingle-tree or EVENER of the harness of a plough pulled by three horses I.8.4. θɹiː-ɒs swɪŋgltɹi St, θɹɛɪ-ɒs swɪŋgətɹɛɪ St

three-horse whipper *n* the main swingle-tree or EVENER of the harness of a plough pulled by three horses I.8.4. θɹiː-ɔrʂ wɪpəɾ O

three-legged milk-stool *n* a MILKING-STOOL III..3.3. θɹiːɫɛgɪd mɪɫkstuˈʊ O

three-legged stool *n* a MILKING-STOOL III.3.3. dɹiːɫɛgɪd styːɫ D, θɹɛɪɫɛgd stɛʊl Db, θɹiːlɛgd stʊɪl Y, θɹiːlɛgd stuːɫ L Nf, θɹiːleˡgd stuːɫ Ess, θɹiːlɛgɪd stuːɫ Wa Bd Ess Ha, θɹilɪgəd stuːɫ Ess, θɹiːlɛgd stuːᵊɫ Ess, θɹiileˡgɪd stuːᵊɫ Ess, dɹiːɫɛgɪd stuːəɫ W, dɹiːlɛgɪd stuːəɫ So, dɹiːlagɪd stuːəɫ Do, dɹiːɫagɪd stuːəɫ Ha, dɹiːɫagəd stuːəɫ W. θɹəiˑlɛgəd stəuːɫ Hrt

three-legs *n* a SAWING-HORSE I.7.16. θɹiːlɛgz Du; **pair of three-legs** pɛəɹ ə θɹiːlɛgz Y

three or four *adj* A FEW VII.1.19. θɹiː ə fauə Y, θɹiː ə fauə Y, θɹiː ə fɔuə Y, dɹiː ə vauəˡː So, dɹiː ə vɒuəˡː W, dɹiː əˡː vɒuəˡː D

threepenny-bit *n* What do you call this [indicate a threepenny-bit]? VII.7.3(a). Eng. ⇒ **joey, little hog, little johnny, threepenny-jimmy, threepenny-joe, threepenny-joey, threepenny-piece, threepenny-tag, tizzy**

threepenny-jimmy *n* a THREEPENNY-BIT VII.7.3(a). θɹʊpnɪdʒɪmɪ Y

threepenny-joe *n* a THREEPENNY-BIT VII.7.3(a). θɹɛpnɪʒoʊ St

threepenny-joey *n* a THREEPENNY-BIT VII.7.3(a). θɹɪpnɪdʒʌʊɪ Sr, θɹɛpnɪdʒɒ-ɪ Brk, θɹəpnɪdʒɒ-ɪ Sx, θɹɛpnɪdʒoʊɪ He Wo

threepenny-piece *n* a THREEPENNY-BIT VII.7.3(a). θɹɪpnɪpiːs K, θɾɪpmɪpiːs Ha, θɹɛpnɪpiːs Nf Ha, θɹʌpnɪpiːs Sf Hrt, θɹʊpnɪpiːs K, θʀəpnɪpiːs Nb, θɹəpnɪpiːs O L Ess, θɹəpʔnɪpiːs Ess, θɹɪpnɪpiis K, θɹʊpnɪpiis K, θɹɪpnɪpiːs Sr Ha, θɹɪnɪpiːs Sr, θɹɪpn̩ɪpiːs Nf, θɹʊpnɪpiːs Sx, θɹəpnɪpiːs Sr Sx, θɹɪpnɪpeɪs Ess,

threepenny-tag *n* a THREEPENNY-BIT VII.7.3(a). θɹɪpnɪtag Y

threep-tree *n* an EVENER, the main swingle-tree of a horse-drawn plough harness I.8.4. θʀiːptʀiː Nb, θɹiːptri Cu, θɹiːptri Cu, θɹᵊiːptrˡi We, θɹiːptɹi Nb Cu We

three-quarter *n* a HAY-FORK with a short shaft I.7.11. θɹiːkwɔːᵊtʔə Sf

three-quarter cow *n* a cow with a BLIND TEAT III.2.7. θɹiːkwɔːtəˡ kɛʊ Sx

three-quarter-fork *n* a HAY-FORK with a shaft of medium length I.7.11. θɹiˑkʷɒˡtəfɔˑk Nf

three-quarters bag *n* the udder of a cow with a BLIND TEAT III.2.7. θɹɪkwɔːtəˡz̩ bæg Sx *[not defined in SBM]*

threeses *n* an afternoon SNACK VII.5.11. θɹᵊiːzɪz Sf

thresh *1. v [Get the informant to describe the old-fashioned way of threshing. If he omits any of the following notions, ask for them.] To get the grain out, what do you do with the sheaves?* II.8.1. Eng. ⇒ **flail**
2. v to TOP AND TAIL swedes II.4.3. θɹɛɪʃ La
3. *n* the THRESHOLD of a door V.1.12. θʀɛʃ Nb, θʀæʃ Nb

threshboard *n* the THRESHOLD of a door V.1.12. θɹɛʃbɔːd Cu, θɹɛsbuəd We, θɹɛʃbuəd Y, fɹɛʃbuəd Y, θɹɛʃbuəˡd We

threshel *1. n* a FLAIL II.8.3. dɹɛɪʃ So, dɹɛɪʃəɫ So D, dɹɛɪʒəɫ D, θɹɛʃl Wo, θɹɛʃɫ He Wo, dɹɛʃɫ He Gl, θɹɛʃəɫ He Wo Gl, dɹɛʃəɫ So, *pl* dɹɛʃəɫz W, dɹɛɪʃəɫ D, θɹæʃl He, θɹæʃəɫ Sa, θɹæʃɫ He Wo, θɹæʃəɫ He, θɾæʃəɫ Co, dɹæɪʃɫ So, θɹaʃəɫ Sa Wo Wa, dɹaʃəɫ So Co, draˡːʃəɫ So, *pl* dɹaɪʃɫz Co, dɹaɪʃəɫ So W Co D, dɹaɪʒɫ D, dɹɒʃəɫ Gl, θɹʊʃ Wo
2. *n* the THRESHOLD of a door V.1.12. θɹɛʃʊɫ Ha, θɹɛʃl L Nf, θɹɛʃəl Nf, θɹɛʃ Nth C Sf Ess, fɹɛsɫ Ess*[old]*, θɹɛʃəɫ Nth Hu Bk Ess, fɹɛʃəɫ Bd Ess*[cement]*, θɹɛsl Nt L, θɹɛsəɫ Lei, θɹæʃl Nf, tɹæʃl Nf*[old-fashioned]*, θɹæʃəl Nf, θɹæʃɫ Nf, θɹæʃəɫ Sf, θɹaʃɫ C, θɹaɪʃ So, θɹɒʃl Nf, θɹɒʃəl Nf, θɹɒʃɫ Nf, tɹɒʃl Nf*[old x2]*, θɹɔːʃɫ Sf, dɹaʃɫ So, dɹaʃəɫ Do, dɹaːʃəɫ W, dɹaɪʃɫ So, dɹaɪʃəɫ W D Ha, dɹaɪʒəɫ D, dɹɛɪʃɫ So, dɹɛɪʃəɫ W, dɹɛʃəɫ

425

W D Do, dɹɛsəɫ Co, dɹɛɪʃəɫ D, dɹɛksəl Co, dɹɛkstəɫ Co

threshel-board *n* the THRESHOLD of a door V.1.12. θɹɛʃbɔˑəd L

threshel-door *n* the THRESHOLD of a door V.1.12. θɹɛʃdoˑə Hrt

threshel-nile *n* a FLAIL II.8.3. θɹæʃətnəɪɫ He

threshel-stone *n* the THRESHOLD of a door V.1.12. θɹɛʃlstʋən L

thresher **1.* *n* a FLAIL II.8.3. dɹaɪʃəˡ: Co

2. n the THRESHOLD of a door V.1.12. θɹɛʃə La, θɹɛɪʃə La

thresh-foot *n* the THRESHOLD of a door V.1.12. θʀɛʃfʋt Du, θɹɛʃfəd Y

threshing-frail* *n* a FLAIL II.8.3. tɪnʃɪnfɹæil Nf

threshing-stick *n* a FLAIL II.8.3. θɹɛʃɪnstɪk Ch

threshing-thrail *n* a FLAIL II.8.3. θɹaʃɪnθɹiːl Db

threshold *n* What do you call the slab of stone or piece of wood across the bottom [of a door]? V.1.12. θɹɛʃaʋld La Y[rare x1], θɹɛʃæʋɫd Hrt, θɹɛʃæʋɫ Hrt, θɹɛʃʋld La Db Nt, θɹɛʃʋd Y, θɹɛʃɔːld Cu, θɹɛʃɔʋld Wo L, θɹɛʃɔʋɫd Lei, θɹɛʃɔʋɫ Lei R MxL, θɹɛʃʌʋl Ess, θɹɛʃʌʋɫd MxL, θɹɛsʌʋɫd Bk, θɹɛsʌʋɫ Ess, θɹɛʃoːlt Sa, θɾɛʃoːɫd O, θɾɛʃoːɫ O, θɹɛʃoʋld St K, θɹɛsoʋld Wo, θɹɛʃoʋɫd Nth, θɹɛsoʋɫd So, θɹɛsoʋɫt So, θɹɛsoʋ So, θɹɛʃld La L, θɹɛʃəld Y Sa Nt, θɹɛsəld Y, θɹɛʃlt Cu La Y L, θɹɛʃəlt L, θɹɛʃəɫd He Mon Hu Bk Ess, θɹɛsəɫd Ess, θɹaʃɛʋd Db, θɾæːˡʃoʋɫ So, dɹɛʃəɫd W, dɹɛɪʃəɫd D, dɹæːʒoʋ So, dɹaʃoːɫd So Do, dɹaʃəɫd Do, dɹaʃəɫt So[old], dɹaˡ:ʃoʋɫ So, dɹaɪʃəɫt Do. ⇒ **board, cross-piece, curb, door-board, door-sill, door-step, door-threshel, door-threshwood,** *draft-stopper* ⇒ **draught-stopper, draught-board, draught-stopper, flag, flagstones, ground-sill, ground-stool, plat, saddle, sill, slab, slab-stone, sole, step, step-board, stone, thresh, thresh-board, threshel, threshel-board, threshel-door, threshel-stone, thresher, thresh-foot, threshwood, threshwood-board, trestle, weather-board**

threshwood *n* the THRESHOLD of a door V.1.12. θʀɛʃwʋd Du, θɹɛʃwʋd Du We Y, fɹɛʃwʋd Y, tɹɛʃwʋd Y, θɹɛʃʋt La, θɹɛʃəd Du Y, θɹɛʃət La Y

threshwood-board *n* the THRESHOLD of a door V.1.12. θɹɛʃətbʋəd We

thribble swell-tree *n* the main swingle-tree or EVENER of the harness of a plough pulled by three horse I.8.4. θɹɪbɫ swɛɫtɹɪ Nth

thrib-tree *n* an EVENER, the main swingle-tree of a horse-drawn plough harness I.8.4. θɹɪbtɹi: Cu, θɹɪbtɹi: We, θɹɪbtɹɹi: Cu, θɹɪbtɹɪ Cu [northern forms with *-tree* given this definition, although NBM data less specific]

thrill *n* a SHAFT-HORSE I.6.2. θɹɪɫ Ha

thrill-horse *n* a SHAFT-HORSE I.6.2. θɹɪɫɔˡ:s Ha

thrindlings *n* SHEEP-DUNG II.1.7. θɹɪndlɪnz La

thrippers *n* a CART-FRAME I.10.6. θɹɪpəz Ch, θɹɪpəɹz La, tɹɪpəz La, tɹɪpəɹz La, θɹəpəz Ch

thripples *1.* *npl* CART-LADDERS I.10.5. θɹɪplz Wo, θɹɪpɫz He Wo, θɹɪpəlz He

2. n a CART-FRAME I.10.6. θɹɪplz Sa, θɹɪpəlz He, tɹɪplz Sa St, θɹɪpɫz He Wo Gl

thriving *v-ing* **be thriving** to VOMIT, referring to a baby bringing up milk VI.13.14(b). *3prsg* ɪts θɹɑˑɪvɪn Lei

thro *prep* FROM VIII.2.11. θɹɛ La, θɹu: Y, θɹˡuː Db, θɹə Y [not an EMBM headword]

throat *1.* *n* The best way to drink nasty medicine is to pour it quickly down your .... VI.6.3. Eng. ⇒ **choke, gizzard, guggle, gullet, gulley, guzzle, neck, oozle, quilter, thropple, throttle, throttler, weasand**

2. n the NECK of a person VI.6.1. θɹɪcɪt Y, θɹɔʋct Ha, θɹʋət Y

3. vt to CHOKE somebody VI.6.4. θɹoʋt Nf

4. n the WINDPIPE VI.6.5. θɾɔːt So, dɹɔːt W D, θɹɔɪt Y, θɹɔʋt Lei R, θɹɔət Y, θɹʌʋt Ess MxL, fɹʌʋt Ess, tɹɔt Nf, θɹoːt Sa He Wo Mon, dɹɔːᵊt So, θɹoʋt St He Lei, tɹoˑʋt Nf, dɹoːʋt Gl, θɹʋt Nf, tɹʋt Nf, θɹuːt Ch, θɹʋət Y

throaty *adj* HOARSE VI.5.16. fɹʌʋtɪ Ess

throck *n* the SOLE of a horse-drawn plough I.8.9. θɹɒk He

throng *adj* BUSY VIII.4.11. θɹaŋ Cu[very commonly used x1], θʀaŋ Nb[old x2] Du, θɹaŋ Nb Cu Du We La Y, tɹaŋ Y, tʰɹɒŋ Man, θɹɒŋ La Y Nt L, θɹɒŋg Y Db, θɹɔŋ La[old x1] Y L

thropple *1.* *n* the NECK of a person VI.6.1. θɹɔpl Du

2. n a THROAT VI.6.3. θʀɒpl Nb Du[old], θɹɒpl We Y, θɹɔpl L

3. vt to CHOKE somebody VI.6.4. θʀɒpl Nb Du[old], θɹɒpl We Y, θɹɔpl La

4. n the WINDPIPE VI.6.5. θɹɒpl Du

throttle *1.* *n* a THROAT VI.6.3. θɹɑʔɫ Nth, θʀɒtl Du, θɹɒtl La Y Ch Db Sa St Wo, θɹɒʔl O, θɹɒtɫ Wa, θɹɒʔɫ O Bk, θʀɔtl Nb, θɹɔtl La Y L[old x1], θɹɔʔɫ MxL

2. vt to CHOKE somebody VI.6.4. θɹætɫ Gl, θɹɑtɫ Nth, θɹɒtl Cu, θɹɒtl Cu Du We La[old x1] Y Ch Db Sa St Wo Wa Gl Nt L Hu, θɹɒʔl O, *-ing* θɹɒʔlɪn K, tɹɒtl Y Nf, tɹɒʔl Nf, dɹɒtl Gl[old], θɹɒtɫ He Wo Wa Mon Lei R Nth Ess Brk Sr K Sx, fɹɒtɫ Nth, θɹɒʔɫ O Hu Bk Bd Ess Brk Sr, θɹɒtət Gl, θɾɒtɫ So, dɹɒtɫ W, θɹɔtl La Y Ch L, θɹɔʔl L, θɹɔʔɫ Sf Hrt, θɹʌʔɫ Sf

3. n the WINDPIPE VI.6.5. θɾɒtl Cu[uncertain], θɹɒtl Y Sa, θɹɒtt Wo, θɾɒʔl O, dɹɒdɫ D, θɹɔtl Wa

throttler *n* a THROAT VI.6.3. θɹɒtlə Ch

through *adj* EXHAUSTED, describing a tired person VI.13.8. θɹu: La

through-draught *n* a DRAUGHT of air V.3.11. θʁuːdʁaft Nb

through-fallow *n* FALLOW-LAND II.1.1. θɹuːfalə Y

through-faugh *n* FALLOW-LAND II.1.1. θɹuffɔːf Y

throw *1. vt* to OVERTURN, referring to a cart I.11.5. θɹoː Sa

2. vt to TIP a cart I.11.6. θɹa: He, θɹɔʊ Brk

3. vt to LOAD dung into a cart II.1.5. θɹɑʊ Wa

4. v to PITCH sheaves II.6.10. θʁa: Nb, *3prsg* θɹɔːz La Y, *3prsg* θɹɔʊz Y Lei, θɹʌʊ C Bk, *3prsg* fɹʌʊz Ess, θɹoː La, θɹoʊ St

5. vt **throws** SLIP*S THE CALF* III.1.11. dɹɒʊz Gl, *-ed* fɹoːd So, *3ptsg* d̠ɹoːd D; **throwed her calf before time** *ppl* d̠ɹoːd əˡː kaːv voˡː tæːm D *[Gl form taken as draws WMBM]*

6. vt to SLIP *A FOAL* III.4.6. *ptppl* θɹɑʊd Gl, *ptppl* θɹoːn Y, *ptppl* d̠ɹoːd D, *ptppl* θɹoʊd Mon, *3ptsg* d̠ɹoʊd So

7. vt to DITCH IV.2.11. d̠ɹoː So

8. vi to VOMIT, referring to a baby bringing up milk VI.13.14(b). *-ing* θɹɒʊ-ɪn Nf

throw across *vtphr* to PITCH sheaves II.6.10. θɹoʊ ... əkɹɒs Lei, θɹoʊ ... əkɹɒs Lei, *-ing* d̠ɹoːən ... kɹɔːs Do

throw back *1. vphr* to PITCH sheaves II.6.10. θɹoː bak Cu, *-ing* d̠ɹoː-ɪn bak W, *-ing* d̠ɹoːən bak Do

2. vtphr to VOMIT, referring to a baby bringing up milk VI.13.14(b). *-ing* θɹɔˑɪn ... bak Y, *pt/ptpl* θɹoːd ... baˑk Sa, *pt/ptppl* θɹoːʊd ... bæk Mon

throwing *v-ing* What would you say a boy was doing, if you saw him doing this? VIII.7.7. Eng. ⇒ **aiming, checking, chucking, clodding, clotting, cobbing, cobbling, copping, flinging, haining, hanging, heaving, hocksing, holling, hoying, hulling, jerking, pegging, pelting,** *pitch* ⇒ **pitching, pitching, scopping, shooting, shying, slewing, slinging, socking,** *squailing* ⇒ **swailing, stoning, swailing, tossing, whanging, yarking**

throwing off *vphr-ing* UNLOADING sheaves from a wagon II.6.8. d̠ɹoːɪn ɔːf So

thrown *adj* OVERTURNED, describing a sheep on its back unable to get up III.7.4. θɹoːn Db

throw out *1. vtphr* to TED hay II.9.11(a). d̠ɹoː ... æɣt Co

2.1. vphr to DITCH IV.2.11. *-ing* d̠ɹoːɪn æɣt So

2.2. vtphr to ditch. θɹæʊ ... əʊt Gl, d̠ɹoːʊ ... aʊt So

throw over *1. viphr* to OVERTURN, referring to a cart I.11.5. *-ed* θɹoːnːɪcɹ ɛʊəɹ La, θɹa: aʊə Cu We, tɹaːn aʊə Y, *-ed* θɹaːn aʊwə Y, *-ed* θɹaːn aʊəɹ Y, θɹoːɪcɹ aʊə We, *-ed* θɹoːnːɪcɹ aʊə Y, θɹa: aʊə Y, *-ed* θɹoːɪcɹ aʊə Y, θɹa: nʊə Y, θɹa:nːɪcɹ nʊwə Wa, θɹoːɪcɹ nʊwə Cu We, *3prsg* θɹoːɪcɹ ɔʊə Y, θɹoː oˑə L, θɹuː ovəˡ Man, θɹoː oːvə Mon, θɹɒʊ oːvəˡː Wo, θɹoʊʊ oʊvə St, θɹoʊ oʊvəˡ Wo, θɹæː oːʊvəˡ Gl, θɹa: ʊə La, θɹa: ʊəɹ La

2. vtphr to overturn. *3prsg* θɹɔːz ... aʊə Y, θɹɒʊ ... ʊvə Lei

throw up *1. vtphr* to TIP a cart I.11.6. θɹoː ... ʊp Cu

2. vphr to LOAD a cart with dung II.1.5. *-ing* θɹɔʊn ʌp Brk

3. vtphr to DITCH IV.2.11. d̠ɹoː ʌp Do

4.1. vphr to VOMIT, referring to an adult VI.13.14(a). *pt* θʁøːn øp Nb, θʁøː ʊp Nb, θɹa: ʊp Cu, *prppl* θʁaːn œːp Nb, θʁa: ʊp Nb Du, θʁɔː ʊp Nb, θɹɔː ʊp Cu Du La Y, θɹoː ʊp La Ch Db, *-s* θɹoʊz ʊp St, truː ɒp Man

4.2. vtphr to vomit, referring to an adult. *ptppl* θɹɔːn ... ʊp Cu

5.1. vphr to VOMIT, referring to a baby bringing up milk VI.13.14(b). θɹɒʊ ɣp Nf, tɹɒʊ ɣp Nf, *3prsg* θʁɔːz ʊp Nb, θɹɔː ʊp Wa L, *-ing* d̠ɹɔːɪn ʌp D, *-ing* θɹoʊɪn ʌp So

5.2. vtphr to vomit, referring to a baby. θɹoː ... ʊp Y, θɹoʊ ... ʊp Lei, *-ing* θɹoʊən ... ʌp Ha, d̠ɹoʊ ... ʌp Do, *?pt* θɹuː ... ʌp Ha

thuck *1. pron* THAT IX.10.1. ðʌk W

2. pron THIS IX.10.2. ðʊk Brk

3. pron THAT over there IX.10.3. ðʌk W

4. pron THOSE over there IX.10.6. ðʌk W

thucker *1. pron* THAT IX.10.1. ðʌkəˡː Co

2. pron THAT over there IX.10.3. ðʌkəˡːɹ (+V) Co

thumb *n What do you call this [indicate a thumb]?* VI.7.6. Eng. ⇒ **big finger;** ⇒ also **thumb-bond**

thumb-beans *n* ROPES used to fasten thatch on a stack II.7.7(b2). ðʌmbiːnz D

thumb-binds *1. n* straw ROPES used to fasten thatch on a stack II.7.7(b2). ðʌmbæːnz D, ðʌmbaɪnz Co

2. n ropes for binding up corn. ðʌmbæːnz D

thumb-bond *n* straw rope wrapped round the leg as a legging, ⇐ THUMB VI.7.6. θʌmbɒn Nf

thumb-bonds *n* straw ROPES used to fasten thatch on a stack II.7.7(b2). θʌmbɒndz Nf*[old]*

thumb-latch *n* the LATCH of a door V.1.9. ðʌmlɛtʃ D, θʌmlatʃ He, θʊmlatʃ Sa Lei

thumble-beams *n* straw ROPES used to fasten thatch on a stack II.7.7(b2). ðʌmbɫbiːmz D, *sg* ðʌmɫbiːm D

thumble-bean *n* a rope used to fasten thatch on a stack, ⇐ ROPES II.7.7(b2). ðʌmɫbiːn Co

thumb-ropes *n* ROPES used to fasten thatch on a stack II.7.7(b2). θɒmɹʊəps La

thumb-simes *n* ROPES used to fasten thatch on a stack II.7.7(b2). θaʊmsaɪmz La, *sg* θɒʊmsaɪm La

thumby *adj* CLUMSY, describing a person VI.7.14. θɣːmɪ Nb

thump *n* a local FESTIVAL or holiday VII.4.11. θʊmp Y

thunder *n What do you call that loud rumbling noise we often hear on very hot summer days?* VII.6.21. Eng. ⇒ **thundering**

thundering *n* THUNDER VII.6.21. θʊndəɹɪn La

thurran *n* a round stack, ⇐ STACKS II.7.1. θʊrən Man

thwart *adv* DIAGONALLY, referring to harrowing a field IX.1.8. ðɛˤːt̬ Co, θəˤːt̬ Co, θəˤːr̥t̬ Brk Sx, ðəˤːt̬ So W Co D, zəˤːt̬ D; **thwart and across** θəɾt̬ n̩ əkɾɒs O

thwart-eyed *adj* CROSS-EYED VI.3.6. ðəˤːt̬æɪd So*[old]*

thwarting it *adv* DIAGONALLY, referring to harrowing a field IX.1.8. ðəˤːt̬ɪn ... ɪt W

thwart-ways *adv* DIAGONALLY, referring to harrowing a field IX.1.8. θəˤːt̬weːz Co, ðəˤːt̬weːz Ha, θəˤːt̬wɛɪz Co, ðəˤːt̬wɛɪz D, θəˤːr̥t̬wɛɪz Sx

thyeveg *n* an EARTH-CLOSET V.1.13. θæɪˈvɛg Man, *?pl* θaɪvɛgz Man

tib *1. n* a BUMPER of a cart I.10.1(a). *pl* tɪbz Nf
2. n a TABBY-CAT, the female cat III.13.9. tɪb Y
3. n the TAG of a boot-lace VI.14.26. *pl* tɪbz Y

tibby-cat *n* a TABBY-CAT, the female cat III.13.9. tɪbɪkæt Man, tɪbɪkat Y

tib-cat *n* a TABBY-CAT, the female cat III.13.9. tɪbkat Y

tick *1. imp* the command TURN LEFT!, given to plough-horses II.3.5(a). tɪk Sa
2. imp **tick lads here** the command GO ON!, given to plough-horses II.3.5(d). 'tɪk 'lædz əˤ Sa

tickle *1.1. vt* to GROPE *FOR FISH* IV.9.10. tɪkl Sa St L Nf, *-ing* tɪklɪn He Wo Mon Gl So, tɪkɫ Wo Mon Gl Lei Nth Hrt Ess So W Sr K Do Ha Sx, *-ing* tɪkɫɪn D, tɪkʊɫ Gl Sx, *-ing* tɪglɪn Gl, tɛkɫ Sx
1.2. v to grope for fish. tɪkl La Y Ch Db Sa Wo, *-ing* tɪklɪn St Wa Gl Nt L Nf So Brk, *vbln* tɪklən Nb Cu Du, tɪkəl Y, tɪkɫ Wo Ess W Brk Sr, *vbln* tɪkɫɪn So, *-ing* tɪkɫɪn Co D Ha Sx, *-ing* tɪkɫɪn O W, *-ing* tɪkəɫɪn So, tɪkʊɫ Brk, tɪgl Wa Gl O, kɪkɫ K, *-ing* takɫɪn Ha
2. adj BRITTLE, describing cups and saucers which break easily IX.1.4. tɪkəl Y

tickle on *vphr* to GROPE *FOR FISH* IV.9.10. *vbln* tɪklɪn ɒn Y

tickle up *vtphr* to GROPE *FOR FISH* IV.9.10. tɪklɪn ... ʌp So

ticks *1. npl What do you call similar insects (to human lice) on sheep?* IV.8.3. tiːks Nf Sf Ess, tɹiːgz Sx, tɪks Nb Cu Du We La Y Ch Db*[different from lice x1]* Sa St He Wo Wa Mon Gl O Nt L Lei R Nth Hu C Bk Bd Hrt Ess So W Brk Sr K Co D Do Ha Sx*[larger than maggots x1]*, tɪgz Man Ess, tɛks Man Ess; **sheep-ticks** ʃiːptɪks Y Wo Nt L Ha Sx, *sg* ʃˡiptɪks K, *no -s* ʃiːptɪk St K*[smaller than bottle-ticks]*, ʃɪptɪks Sa St He Wo Wa Gl O Lei Nth Bk, ʃɪˈəptɪks L, ʃeːptaks Ha, ʃɛɪptɪks Db. ⇒ **bots, bottle-ticks, bugs, cades, fags, grubs, lice, maggots, quicks,**

sheep-bugs, sheep-cades, sheep-cags, sheep-dicks, sheep-fags, sheep-fly, sheep-lice, sheep's-lice, sheep-tegs, *sheep*-ticks, tegs, tits
2. npl NITS IV.8.2. tɪks Y

tick-tatting *v-ing* GOSSIPING VIII.3.5(a). tɪktæt̬ʔɪn Nf

tiddle *1. vt* to GROPE *FOR FISH* IV.9.10. *-ing* tɪdlɪn O
2. v -ing tɪdlɪn Wa, *vbln* tɪdlən Nb
[not a WMBM headword]

tiddle-brats *npl* MINNOWS IV.9.9. tɪdɫbɹɛts K

tiddler *n* a PET-LAMB III.7.3. tɪdɫə Mon, tɪdɫə Mon, tɪdləɹ He, tɪdləˤ Sa He Wo Gl, tɪdɫəˤ He Mon Gl, tɪdɫəˤː W

tiddlers *1. npl* TADPOLES IV.9.5. tɪdɫəz Ess, tɪdɫəz Ess
2. npl MINNOWS IV.9.9. tɪdləz Y Ch Db St Nt L Nth Hu C Nf Hrt Ess, tɪdɫəz MxL, tɪdɫəz Ess MxL, *sg* tɪdɫ̩ L, tɪdləɹz He, tɪdləᴶz L, tɪdləᴶz La, tɪdɫəᴶz Sr K, tɪdɫəᴶz K, tɪdɫəˤz̩ Sa Bk*[half an inch long x1]* Bd K, tɪdɫəˤɾz̩ Sx, tɪdɫəˤz̩ Gl Sr, tɪdɫəˤz̩ O Sr, tɪdɫəˤɾz̩ Ha Sx, tɪdɫəˤːz̩ Co Ha

tiddles *npl* MINNOWS IV.9.9. tɪdlz Y

tiddling *1. n* a PET-LAMB III.7.3. tɪdlɪn Sa He Wo O, tɪdlɪn He, tɪdəlɪn Sa, tɪdɫɪn He Gl
2. n a WEAKLING piglet III.8.4. tɪdlɪn Wo

tiddly-wag *n* the GRASS-NAIL of a scythe II.9.9. tɪdɫiwag Ha

tiddlywink *n* a NEWT IV.9.8. *pl* tɪdɫiwɪnks Ess

tiddy-bump *n* a SEESAW VIII.7.2 tɪdɪbʌmp Hrt

tidy *1. n* a decorative APRON V.11.2(b). taɪdi So
2. adj WELL, describing a healthy person VI.13.1(a). tɔɪdi Sf
3. adv VERY VIII.3.2. taɪdi Sr, tɔɪdi Sf
4. vt-3sg she [i.e. a tidy girl] will COLLECT her toys VIII.8.15. taɪdi Du We, taɪdi Db, *3prsg* təɪdɪz Sx

tidy away *vtphr-3sg* she [i.e. a tidy girl] will COLLECT her toys VIII.8.15. tɛɪdi ... əweː Nb

tidy off *vtphr-3sg* she [i.e. a tidy girl] will COLLECT her toys VIII.8.15. taɪd ɒf Ch

tidy up *vtphr-3sg* she [i.e. a tidy girl] will COLLECT her toys VIII.8.15. tædi ... ʌp So, taɪdi ... ʌp D, taɪdi ʊp St, taɪdi ... ʊp Cu La, taɪdi ʌp Bd, taɪdi ... ʌp Bk Hrt, taɪdi ... ʊp Db, tɒɪdi ... ʌp So Ha, tɔɪdi ʌp Sf Bk, tɔɪdi ... ʌp Hrt, tɔɪd ... ʌp Ess, tɔɪt ... ʌp Ess, tɔɪdi ... ʊp Bk, *3prsg* tʌɪdɪz ʌp Sr, tʌɪdɪ ... ʌp Nf, təɪdi ʌp Brk Sx, təɪdi ... ʌp W
[forms with no stated obj marked u.r. SBM]

tie *1. n* a TETHER for a cow I.3.4. tɒɪ Ha
2. n a rope tether. tʌɪ Nf
3. n a chain tether. tʌɪ Nf
4. n a tether made of rope or chain. tiː Y
5. n a TETHERING-ROPE used to tie up a horse I.4.2. tɒɪ Wo, tɔɪ C, tʌɪ Nf, təɪ He O
6. vt to BIND corn into a sheaf II.6.2. tiː La Db,

tɛɪ Ch Sa, taɪ Nb Cu Du Y Ch Sa St He L, taɪ Db L Lei R Nth C Bk Bd Hrt Ess, -*ing* tɑɪ-ɪn Sr, tɑːᴵ Hu C, tɒɪ Sa Wo Nf So Ha, tɒːɪ St, tɔɪ Wa O Nth Bk Ess K Ha, -*ing* tɔɪ-ɪn Sx, tʌɪ Nf Brk, -*ing* tʌɪ-ɪn Sr, təɪ He Wo Mon Gl Do Sx

tie-chain 1. *n* a TETHER for a cow I.3.4. tɔˑɪtʃɛɪn Lei, təɪtʃæɪn He

2. *n* a chain used to tie up a horse, ⇐ TETHERING-ROPE I.4.2. təɪtʃɛɪən Gl

tie-cord *n* a TETHERING-ROPE used to tie up a horse I.4.2. təɪkɑᵗːd̩ Wo

tied up *adj* MARRIED VIII.1.17. tɛɪd ʊp St[*presumably facetious*]

tie-iron *n* a TETHERING-STAKE in a cow-house I.3.3. *pl* tɑˑɪ-ɑˑɪənz Lei

tie-log *n* the CLOG on a horse's tether I.4.3. təɪlɒg Mon

tiens *n* a TETHERING-STAKE in a cow-house I.3.3. tɒɪənz So

tie-pole *n* a TETHERING-STAKE in a cow-house I.3.3. taɪpoːɬ So, təɪpæʊɬ He, təɪpɒʊɬ He, təɪpɒʊəl Gl, təɪpoːɬ Mon

tie-post *n* a TETHERING-STAKE in a cow-house I.3.3. təɪpoːst Mon, tɑɪpoːʊst Mon Gl

tier *n* a TETHERING-STAKE in a cow-house I.3.3. taɪəᵗː Do, tɑɪə Nf, təɪəᵗː Do

tie-rod *n* a TETHERING-STAKE in a cow-house I.3.3. tɑɪɹɒd Sr

tie-rope *n* a TETHERING-ROPE used to tie up a horse I.4.2. tɑɪɹʌʊp Sr, təɪɹoːp Mon, təɪɹoːʊp Mon Gl

tie round *vtphr* to BIND corn into a sheaf II.6.2. taɪ ... ɹaʊnd Y

tiers *npl* pieces of STRING used to tie up grain-sacks I.7.3. tɒɪəᵗːz̩ Ha [*marked u.r. SBM*]

tie-slip *n* a TETHERING-ROPE used to tie up a horse I.4.2. tʌɪslɪp Nf

tie-stake *n* a TETHERING-STAKE in a cow-house I.3.3. tɑˑɪstɛɪk Lei R

tie-stoop *n* the SHUTTING-POST of a gate IV.3.4. tiːstuːp La

tie-up 1. *n* a TETHERING-STAKE in a cow-house I.3.3. tɔɪ-ʌp Ess

2. *n* a chain TETHER for a cow I.3.4. təɪ-œp Gl

3. *n* a tether made of rope or chain. tiː-ʊp La

4. *n* a TETHERING-ROPE used to tie up a horse I.4.2. tiː-ʊp La, tɔɪ-ʌp Ess, təɪ-œːp Gl, təɪ-ʊp Gl

tie up *vtphr* to BIND corn into a sheaf II.6.2. tiː ... ʊp La Y, tɛɪ ʊp Ch, tɛɪ ... ʊp Db, taɪ ... ʌp D Do, taɪ ... ʊp Cu Y L, taːɪ ... ʊp St, taɪ ʌp Nth Nf Hrt Ess K, -*ing* taɪ-ɪn ʌp Sx, -*ing* ətɑɪ-ɪn ʌp Bd, *pt* tɑɪd ʌp MxL, taɪ ... ʌp Bk Bd MxL Sr, tɑɪ ... ʏp Nf, taɪ ʊp Nth, taɪ ... ʊp Wa Nt L Lei R Nth C, tɒɪ ʌp So, tɒɪ ... ʌp Nf So W Do Ha, tɒɪ ... ʊp St, tɒːɪ ... ʊp St, tɔɪ ʌp O Sf Bd, -*ing* tɔɪ-ɪn ʌp Hrt Ess, tɔɪ ... ʌp Wa Sf Bk Ess Brk, tɔɪ

... ʊp Wa Bk, tʌɪ ... ʌp Gl Nf Sf, tʌɪ ... ʏp Nf, təɪ ... ʌp He Mon Gl W Do, təɪ ... ʊp Y He Wo Gl

tie-up-line *n* a TETHERING-ROPE I.4.2. tɔɪ-ʊplɔɪn Sf

tie-ups *npl* KNEE-STRAPS used to lift the legs of working trousers VI.14.17. tɔɪ-ʌps Ess

tifting 1. *v-ing* PANTING VI.8.1. tɪftɪn We[*old*] La Y, tɪftn Cu We, tɪftən Cu We Y

2. *v-ing* gasping in a death-struggle. tɪftɪn Cu

tight on *adv* ALMOST VII.7.9. tæːt ɒn D

tight one *n* a tight one a MISER VII.8.9. ə taɪʔ n̩ K, ə təɪt ən Sx

tikant *n* a SEESAW VIII.7.2. 'tiˌkæˑnt K

tile *n* got a tile loose STUPID VI.1.5. gɒt ə təɪɬ luːs Sx

tiling *v-ing* STOOKING II.6.5. tʌɪlɪn Gl

till 1. *prep* You usually can't see a first-class football match on a Tuesday; you have to wait ... Saturday. IX.2.2. Eng. ⇒ afore, fore, than, tin, to, until, while [*also one zero form W*]

2. *prep* TO *THE QUICK* of a fingernail VI.7.9. tɪl He, tl Cu

3. *prep* THAN VI.12.4. tɪl Sa, t̩l Ch

4. *n* a SHAFT of a cart I.9.4. tɪl Man

5. *n* the VULVA of a cow III.2.3. tʃɪʊ K [*queried SBM*]

tiller *n* the SHAFT of a spade I.7.7. tɪlə Sf

tills *npl* the SHAFTS of a cart I.9.4. tɪls Man

tilt 1. *vi* to OVERTURN, referring to a cart I.11.5. tɪɬt O

2. *n* on the tilt ASKEW, describing a picture that is not hanging straight IX.1.3. ɒn ðə tɪlt St Nf

3. *n* a woman's BONNET worn outdoors or indoors VI.14.1. *pl* tɪɬts W

tilt bonnet *n* a woman's BONNET VI.14.1. tɪɬt bɒnət Do

timbern* *adj* wooden, ⇐ CLOG I.4.3. tɪmbəᵗːn̩ D

timber-stub *n* a tree STUMP IV.12.4. tɪmbəᴵstʌb K

timber-toed *adj* PIGEON-TOED VI.10.4. tɪmbətyːd Ch, tɪmbətoːd Ch Db, tɪmbətoʊd St

timber-toes *adj* PIGEON-TOED VI.10.4. tɪmbətuːz St

timble-toed 1. *adj* PIGEON-TOED VI.10.4. tɪmbltuːd St

2. *adj* SPLAY-FOOTED VI.10.5. tɪmbltoːd La

time *n* STOPPING-TIME at the end of a day's work VII.5.9. tɔɪm Wa, tʌɪm Gl; **time to give out** tɔɪm tə gɪv ɛʊt Wa; **time to go home** tɑˑɪm tə gɒʊ ɒm L; **time to knock off** tɑɪm tə nɒk ɔːf Nf Ha, tɒɪm tə nɒk ɔːf Do; **time to leave off** tɑɪm tə liːv ɔːf Nf K; **time to leave work** təɪm tə lɛf wəᵗːk So

timid *adj* SHY VIII.9.2. tɪmɪd We Y Nth Nf Bk K, tʃɪmɪd Sa

tin *1. n* a metal container for carrying horse-feed, ⇐ BASKET III.5.4. tɪn D

2. prep TILL IX.2.2. tɪn Ch, tən St

tin-alley *n* a TINKER VIII.4.9. ˌtɪnˈælɪ W

tin-bin *n* a CORN-BIN I.7.4. *pl* tɪnbɪnz Ess

tin bowl *n* a SCOOP used to take water out of a boiler V.9.9. tɪn bʊɫ Nth

tindlers *n* KINDLING-*WOOD* V.4.2. tɪnləᶜːz̞ Sa

tindling-sticks *n* KINDLING-*WOOD* V.4.2. tɪnlɪnstɪks Wo

tine *1. n* a PRONG of a fork I.7.10. tæɪn He, *pl* tæɪnz Ess, *pl* taːnz Y, taɪn Y Sa He O L Lei, *pl* taɪnz St Wa, *pl* taːnz swY Lei, taɪn Ch Wa Nt L Lei R Nth Hu Nf Sf Bk Bd Hrt Ess MxL, *pl* taɪnz Db C Sr, taɪm Nf, tɒɪn St Wo Lei Nf, *pl* tɒɪnz Sa, tɔɪn Wa Nth Sf Bk Ess, *pl* tɔɪnz Wo O Hrt Sr Sx, tʌɪn He Nf Sf Bk Sr, *pl* tʌʏnz O, təɪn He Wo Mon Gl

2. vt to fill gaps in a hedge-bank or hedge with turfs, brushwood, or similar material, ⇐ to PLASH IV.2.4. taɪn Sa

3. vt to SHUT a door IX.2.8. tɪnn La, taɪn Y

tinge-bat *n* a movable horizontal rod stretching between the shafts of a cart, fixing them to the cart-body and stopping the cart from tipping, ⇐ ROD/PIN I.10.3. tɪndӡbɛt K, tɪndӡbæt K

tingey *adj* BRITTLE, describing cups and saucers which break easily IX.1.4. tɪnӡɪ Gl *[queried WMBM]*

tinker *n What do you call the man who mends, or used to mend, pots and pans?* VIII.4.9. Eng. ⇒ **diddiky,** *mender,* **pedlar, pot-and-pan man, solderer, tin-alley, tinkler, tinman, tinner, tinsmith, whitesmith**

tinkler *1. n* a RESTIVE horse III.5.6. tɪŋklə St *[marked ir.r. WMBM]*

2. n a TINKER VIII.4.9. tɪŋklə Nb*[frequent]* Cu We La Db, tɪŋklər Cu, tɪŋkləɹ La Y, tɪŋkləᴶ Db, tɪŋkləᶜ Wa

tinks *npl* dealers in second-hand goods, ⇐ GIPSIES VIII.4.12. tɪŋks Nb

tinman *n* a TINKER VIII.4.9. tɪnman Lei, tɪnmʊn Brk

tinner *1. n* a FUNNEL V.9.3. tɪnəᶜː D

2. n a TINKER VIII.4.9. tɪnə Du*[old]* Y*[makes pans x1, makes tinware x1].* tɪnɹ L

tinniger* *n* a FUNNEL V.9.3. tɪnɪgəᶜː So D

tinsmith *n* a TINKER VIII.4.9. tɪnsmɪθ Du We Y*[makes tinware x1]* Ch St W Ha

tintant *n* a SEESAW VIII.7.2. tɪntæˑnt K*[old]*

tin-tattles *npl* MINNOWS IV.9.9. tɪntætʔlz Nf *[marked u.r. and interpreted as 'stickleback' EMBM]*

tintitant *n* a SEESAW VIII.7.2. tɪntɪtæˑnt K

tip *1. v How do you empty a cart the quickest way?* I.11.6.
v tɪp Nb Cu Du We La Y Ch Db Sa St Wo Wa Mon O Nt L Lei Nth Sf Bk Hrt Ess Sr K Ha Sx
vt tɪp We Db He Wo Gl L Ess Brk Sr D Do

⇒ **cave, cave up, chuck up, coup, coup up, empt, ent,** *give it a tipup,* **keck, keck up, kelt, kick, kick up, let up, shelve, shelve out, shelve up, shoot, shoot out, shoot up, skell, skell up, skelp, slot up, spring up, throw, throw up, tip back, tipe, tipe up, tip out, tip over, tip up, trip up, untinge, upskell, uptip**

2. vi to OVERTURN, referring to a cart I.11.5. tɪp Db O, *ptppl* tɪpt Sx

3. n the T-SHAPED PLOUGH-BEAM END of a horse-drawn plough I.8.5. tɪp Sx

4. n a BUMPER of a cart I.10.1(a). *pl* tɪps Nf W

5. n the TAG of a boot-lace VI.14.26. tɪp La He Nf Bk, *pl* tɪps Sr

6. vt to REMOVE *STALKS* from currants V.7.24. tɪpɪn Do

tip and tail *adv* HEAD OVER HEELS IX.1.10. tɪp m̩ teɪɫ So, tɪp ən taɪɫ So

tip back *vtphr* to TIP a cart I.11.6. tɪp ... bak D

tip-bar *n* a movable horizontal rod stretching between the shafts of a cart, fixing them to the cart-body and stopping the cart from tipping, ⇐ ROD/PIN I.10.3. tɪpbaᴶˑ Brk, tɪpbaᶜːɾ Sx, tɪpbaːəᶜɾ Sx

tip-cart *n* a FARMCART I.9.3. tɪpkæːɾt Brk, tɪpkaːt Wa, tɪpkaᶜːt̯ O W, tɪpkaːt Sr, tɪpkaᴶːt Brk, tɪpkaᶜːəᶜt̯ Sx

tipe *1. n* a BUMPER of a cart I.10.1(a). taɪp Nth Hu

2. vi to OVERTURN, referring to a cart I.11.5. taˑɪp L

3.1. v to TIP a cart I.11.6. taɪp L, taɪp L

3.2. vt to tip. taˑɪp L

tipe-stick *n* a vertical rod in front of a cart, perforated to allow adjustments when tipping, ⇐ ROD/PIN I.10.3. taˑɪpstɪk Nt L Lei, taˑɪpθstɪk Lei, taˑɪpstɪk L Lei R, tɔɪpstɪk L *[EMBM notes 'probably' vertical; this does not coincide with interpretation of e.g.* **tip-stick** *as horizontal in WM/SBM]*

tipe up *vtphr* to TIP a cart I.11.6. taˑɪp ... ʊp Lei, taˑɪp ... ʊp L Lei

tip out *vtphr* to empty a cart by tipping it, ⇐ TIP I.11.6. *3pt* tɪpt ... ɛʊt Sx, tɪp ... ɛʊʔ Hrt

tip over *1.1. viphr* to OVERTURN, referring to a cart I.11.5. *-ed* tɪpt ɒvə L, tɪp ɒʊvə Wa, *ptppl* tɪpt ɒʊvəᴶ K, tɪp ɒʊvəᶜ Sx, *-ed* tɪpt ɒʊvə K, *3prsg* tɪps ɔˑə Y, tɪp ɔːvəᶜː So W, *-ed* tɪpt ɔːvəᶜː D, tɪp ɔʊvə Hu, *-ed* tɪpt ɔʊvə Ess, *-ed* tɪpt ɔʊvəᴶ Brk, tɪp ɔʊvəᶜ O, *3prsg* tɪps ɔʊə Y, tɪp ʌʊvə Sf Bk Hrt Ess MxL, tɪp ʌʊvəᶜ Bk, tɪp oːvə Mon Gl, *-ed* tɪpt oːvəɹ He, tɪp oːvəᶜ Sa Mon, *-ed* tɪpt oːvəᶜ O Brk, tɪp oːvəᶜː Do Ha, *ptppl* tɪpt oːvəᶜː Co, *-ed* tɪpt oːvəᶜː W Ha, tɪp oə Ch Db, tɪp ɔʊvə Wa Nth Bk, *3prsg* tɪps ɔʊvə Lei, tɪp ɔʊvəᶜ Wa Bk, *3prsg* tɪps ɔʊvəᶜ Ha, tɪp ɔʊvəᶜː So, *3prsg* tɪps ʊvə

Lei, *-ed* tɪpt ʊvə Lei

1.2. vtphr to overturn. tɪp ... oːvəᵗ Gl

2. vtphr to TIP a cart I.11.6. tɪp ... oʊvəᵗː So

tippen-totter *n* a SEESAW VIII.7.2. tɪpntɔːtə Ess, tiˑpʔntɔːᵊtʔə Nf

tippeny-totter *n* a SEESAW VIII.7.2. tɪpnɪtɔːdə Ess, tɪpənɪtɔːtə Ess, tɪpnɪtɔːtə Ess, tɪpnɪtɔːdə Ess, tɪpnɪtɔˑətə Nf, tɪpnɪtɔːətʔə Nf, tɪpʔnɪtɔːᵊtʔə Sf*[old]*, tɪpnətɔːᵊdə Nf, tɪpnətɔːʔə Nf

tipper *n* a device fixing a cart-body to the shafts, stopping it from tipping, ⇐ ROD/PIN I.10.3. tɪpə Nf, tɪppə Db, tɪpəᴶ Brk

tippers *n* BUMPERs of carts I.10.1(a). tɪpəᵗːz̗ W

tippety-totter *n* a SEESAW VIII.7.2. tɪpədɪtɔːtə Ess

tip-pin *n* a pin fixing a cart-body to the shafts, stopping it from tipping, ⇐ ROD/PIN I.10.3. tɪppɪn W Ha

tipping *vt-ing* PUTTING your tongue OUT VI.5.4. tɪpɪn Sx

tipping-bar *n* a movable horizontal rod stretching between the shafts of a cart, fixing them to the cart-body and stopping the cart from tipping, ⇐ ROD/PIN I.10.3. tɪpənbaː Nb

tipping-piece *n* a BUMPER of a cart I.10.1(a). tɪpmpiːs Ha

tipple *1. vi* to OVERTURN, referring to a cart I.11.5. *3prsg* tɪplz Y

2. v **tipple a monkey-bank**, **tipple backwards** to turn HEAD OVER HEELS IX.1.10. **tipple a monkey-bank** tɪpl ə mʊŋkɪbaŋk Y; **tipple backwards** tɪpəl bakədz Y

tipple over *1. viphr* to OVERTURN, referring to a cart I.11.5. *-ed* tɪpld aʊə Y, *3prsg* tɪpəlz ɒvə Y, tɪpl ɒvə Nt, *-ed* tɪpld ɒvə Y, tɪpl ɒʊə Nt, tɪpl ɔvə L, *-ed* tɪpld ɔʊə L, *-ed* tɪpɫd ɔʊvə Nth, *-ed* tɪpld ɔʊwə L, tɪpld ɔwə L, *-ed* tɪpld ɔwɹə L, *-ed* tɪpɫd ʌʊvə Ess, tɪpɫ ʌʊvəᵗ Bk, tɪpl oʊvə Nf, *3prsg* tɪplz oʊvəᵗ Wo, *-ed* tɪpld oə Ch

2. vphr **tipple over top-tail** to turn HEAD OVER HEELS IX.1.10. tɪpl ʊə tɒptiːl St

tipple-stail *adv* HEAD OVER HEELS IX.1.10. tɪpəlstɛɪl Y

tippy* *n* the peak of a cap, ⇐ BRIM VI.14.3. tɪpɪ Y

tip-stick *n* a movable horizontal rod stretching between the shafts of a cart, fixing them to the cart-body and stopping the cart from tipping, ⇐ ROD/PIN I.10.3. tɪpstɪk Gl So Sr D

tip-toed *adj* PIGEON-TOED VI.10.4. tɪptʊəd L, tɪptuːd So

tip-tumbler *n* a FARMCART I.9.3. tɪptʌmblə Ess

tip up *1. viphr* to OVERTURN, referring to a cart I.11.5. tɪp ʌp Mon So W Do, *-ed* tɪpt ʌp Ess, tɪp ʊp Wo Gl Lei R, *3prsg* tɪps ʊp Y St Wa, *3ptsg* tɪpt ʊp Y

2.1. vphr to TIP a cart I.11.6. tɪp ʌp Gl Nth Hu Sf Bk Bd Hrt Ess W Brk, tɪp ʊp Nb La Ch Db St Wa Lei R Nth C Bk, tɪp əp Gl

2.2. vtphr to tip. tɪp ... œːp Gl, tɪp ... ɒp Y, tɪp ... ʌp Sa He Mon Nf Ess MxL So W Brk Sr K Co D Do Ha, *-ed* tɪpt ... ʌp Sx, tɪp ... ʋp Nf, tɪp ... ʊp Cu We La Y Ch Sa St He Wo Wa Mon Gl O Nt Lei R, tɪp ... əp Gl Lei

tire *n* *[Show a picture of a farmcart.] What do you call the iron thing round it [i.e. the wheel]?* I.9.10. tæɪə Y Mon, taɪɔᴿ Nb Du, taɪə Du Y Ch L, taɪəᴿ Du, taɪəɹ nwY He, taɪəᴶ L, taɪəᵗ Sa, taɪəᵗː D, taː Nf, taːə Hu C Nf Hrt Ess, taɪə Db L Lei R Nth Hu C Nf Sf Bk Bd Hrt Ess Sr K, taɪəᴶ La K, taɪəᵗ O Bk Bd Ha, tɒɪəᴶ K, tɒɪəᵗ Sa Wo, tɒɪəᵗː Ha, tɔɪə Wa Sf Hrt Ess, tɔɪəᴶ Brk K, tɔɪəᵗ Wo Wa Gl O Nth Bk Sx, *pl* tɔtɪəᵗɹz̗ Sr, tʌɪəᴶ Brk Sr, tʌɪəᵗ Sr, tɔɪəᵗ Gl Brk Sx. ⇒ **band, bands, bend, bind, bond, bonds, bonding, cart-hoop, hoop, hooping, iron-band, iron-banding, iron-rim, iron-tire, rim, rind, shod-tire, strakes, streaks, strigs, stropes, tirl**

tired *adj* EXHAUSTED, describing a tired person VI.13.8. taɪəɹd St, taːɪd Ess, tɒɪəᵗːd̗ So W, tɔɪəd Ess; **tired to death** taɪəd tə dɪəθ Y *[marked u.r. WM/SBM, not EMBM]*

tired out *adj* EXHAUSTED, describing a tired person VI.13.8. tɛɪəd uːt Y, tæːəᵗːd̗ ævt D, taɪɔᴿd uːt Nb, taɪəd aːt Nt, taɪəd aʊt Y, taːᴶd ɛʊt Nf, taːᵊd ɛʊt Nth, taɪəd æʊt Lei, taɪəᵗd̗ ɛət K, tʌɪəᴶd ʌʊt Brk, təᵗːd̗ ᵁuːt Gl

tirl *n* the iron TIRE round a cart-wheel I.9.10. təl Y

tissicking *v-ing* COUGHING VI.8.2. tɪzɪkɪn Ess*[quiet coughing x1]* D*[weak cough]*

tissicking about *vphr-ing* COUGHING VI.8.2. tɪzɪkɪn əbɛʊt Ess

tit *1. n* a TABBY-CAT, the female cat III.13.9. tɪt Y

2. n the TEAT of a woman's breast VI.8.6. tɪt Eng exc. Sr Do, *pl* tɪts Sr *[not a N/WMBM headword]*

tits *1. npl* HORSES used for working rather than for riding I.6.5. tɪts Ch

2. npl TICKS on sheep IV.8.3. tɪts Ha

tittema-totter *n* a SEESAW VIII.7.2. tiːdəmətɔːᵊʔdə Sf

titter *n* a SEESAW VIII.7.2. tɪtə Sf

tittery *n* a SEESAW VIII.7.2. tiʔəɹə Nf

tittery-tot *n* a SEESAW VIII.7.2. tɪtɹɪtɔt MxL

titties *npl* LICE IV.8.1(a). tɪtɪz La

tittle *1. vt* to GROPE *FOR FISH* IV.9.10. tɪtl Sa L, *-ing* tɪtlɪn Ch Db Nf, tɪtəl Mon, tɪtəɫ Mon

2. v to grope for fish. tɪtl La Y Ch St Nt L

tittle-brats *npl* MINNOWS IV.9.9. tɪtlbɹats L *[marked u.r. and interpreted as 'stickleback' EMBM]*

tittlers *npl* MINNOWS IV.9.9. tɪtləz Sf, tɪtʔləz Ess

titty *1. n* a TABBY-CAT, the female cat III.13.9. tɪdɪ Brk

2. n the TEAT of a woman's breast VI.8.6. tɪtɪ Y, tɪti K, *pl* tɪtɪz Nf

tiver *1. vt* to MARK sheep with colour to indicate ownership III.7.9. tɔɪvəɹ (+V) K

2. n red or blue chalk used to mark sheep. tɑɪvəᴶ K

tizzy *n* a silver THREEPENNY-BIT VII.7.3(a). tɪzɪ Nf

to *1. prep* THAN VI.12.4. tʊ So

2. prep TILL IX.2.2. tɪ So Brk Sr K Sx, ɒ St, tʊ So, tə He O Nf W Brk K Sx, ə Nb St

toad-paddock *n* a toadstool, ⇐ TOAD IV.9.7. tʏədpadək La

toad(s) *n* What do you call the other thing like a frog, but ugly? IV.9.7.

no -s: Eng

-s: toʊdz Brk.

⇒ **paddock**; ⇒ also **paddock-stool, toad-paddock, toad-slather**

toads *npl* TADPOLES IV.9.5. *sg* tɔːəd Man

toad-slather *n* frog-spawn, ⇐ TOAD IV.9.7. tɪadslaðə Y

toar *n* a TUSSOCK of grass II.2.9. tɔəᴶ K, tɔəᶜ K

toby *n* a TOM-CAT, the male cat III.13.8. tɔːbɪ Y

tod *1. n* a CUTTING of hay II.9.15. *pl* tɒdz So

2. v to LOP a tree IV.12.5. tɒd Ess

toe *1. n* a PRONG of a fork I.7.10. toː D, *pl* toːz Co, *pl* tuːz Co D

2. n a BUMPER of a cart I.10.1(a). *pl* tɑʊz Ess, *pl* tɔʊz Ess, tʌʊ Sf Ess, toˑʊ Nf, *pl* touz Nf Sf, *pl* tuːz Nf Sf

3. n a ROOT of a tree IV.12.1. *pl* tʊəz Y

toe-board *n* the TAILBOARD of a cart I.10.2. toʊbɔːd Sf

toes-in *adj* PIGEON-TOED VI.10.4. 'tʊəz'ɪn La

toe-stick *n* a device fixing a cart-body to the shafts, stopping it from tipping, ⇐ ROD/PIN I.10.3. tʌʊstɪk Sf Ess, toʊstɪk Nf Sf

toggers *npl* the HANDLES of a scythe II.9.8. tɒgəᶜːz̩ So, tʌgəᶜːz̩ So, tʌgəᶜːdz̩ So

tom *n* a TOM-CAT, the male cat III.13.8. tɒm Y Sa O So W Co D Do Ha, tɔm Nb Y So Do

tom-cat *n* Now for the animal that goes miaow. What do you call the male? III.13.8. tœmkat Nb Du, tœːmkat Nb, tamkat Nb Sa, tɑmkæt Nf, tamkat O, tɑːmkæt He Mon Nf, tɒmkɛt Sr K Sx, tɒmkɛɑt Ess, tɒmkæt Y Man Sa He Wa Mon Gl L Hu Nf Bk Ess So Brk Sr K Co Ha Sx, tɒmkjæt He Wo Mon, tɒmkæːʔ Hrt, tɒmkat Nb Cu Du We La Y Db Sa St He Wa Mon Gl O Nt L Lei R Nth Hu Bd Hrt So W D Do Ha, tɒmkjat Wo Gl Bd, tɒmkaʔ O Bk, tɒmkət Wa, tɒmkæt C Sf Ess MxL Sr K, tɔmkat La Y Wa L C Hrt So Ha, tɒmkjat Wo, tɔːmkɛɑt Ess, tʌmkaʔ Bk, tʊmkæt Gl, tʊmkat We La Ch Db Sa St, tʊmkjat Ch.

⇒ **cat, dick-cat, heeder, ram-cat, *the* mazger, toby, tom, tommy-cat**

tom-gudgeons *npl* TADPOLES IV.9.5. tɒmgʊdʒɪnz W

tommy *1. n* BREAD V.6.9(b). tɒmi So

2. n (off her) FOOD V.8.2. tɒmi W, tɒmɪ La

3. n a SNACK VII.5.11. tɒmɪ He Mon

4. n a MEAL OUT VII.5.12. tæmɪ Gl, tɒmi Mon So W, tɒmɪ La Y Db He Wa Mon Gl Ess

tommy-aught *n* a FARM-LABOURER I.2.4. tɒmɪ-aʊt Y, tɒmɪ-ɔʊt Y

tommy-cat *n* a TOM-CAT, the male cat III.13.8. tɒmɪkat Nb

tommy-dods *n* SWEETS V.8.4. tɒmɪdɒdz C

tommy-hook *n* a HEDGING-BILL IV.2.5. tʊmɪ-ɛʊk Db *[queried WMBM]*

tommy-lie-lodgers *npl* MINNOWS IV.9.9. tɒmɪlaɪlœdʒəz Du *[marked u.r. NBM]*

tommy-loachers *npl* MINNOWS IV.9.9. tɒmɪlʊətʃəz Nb *[marked u.r. NBM]*

tommy-lodgers *npl* MINNOWS IV.9.9. tɒmɪlɒdʒəz Du *[marked u.r. NBM]*

tommy-long-legs *n* DADDY-LONG-LEGS IV.8.10. tɒmɪlaŋlɛgz Y, tɒmɪlaŋlɛgz Y, tamɪlɒŋlɛgz Nth, tɒmɪlɒŋlɛgz Y Nt, tɒmɪlɒŋlɛgz L

tommy-minnims *npl* MINNOWS IV.9.9. tɒmɪmɪnəmz Cu

tommy-plough *n* a double-breasted PLOUGH I.8.1. tɔˑmɪplɛʊ Nf

tommy-spinner *n* DADDY-LONG-LEGS IV.8.10. tɒmɪspɪnə Y

tommy-tailor(s) *n* DADDY-LONG-LEGS IV.8.10.

no -s: tɒmiteːɫəᶜː Co

-s: tɒmɪtɪlɪəz Du

tommy-toddies *npl* TADPOLES IV.9.5. tɒmitɒdɪz D

tomorn *1. n* TOMORROW MORNING VII.3.13. tɪmɔən Y; **first thing tomorn** fɒst θɪŋ tɪmɔˑən Y; **soon on tomorn** sʊɪn ɒn təmɔən Y; **tomorn afore dinner*** təmɔˑən əfʊə dɪnə Y; **tomorn at forenoon*** təmɔᴶːn t fɔənʊɪn Y; **tomorn at morn*** tɪmɔˑən ət mɔˑən Y; **tomorn at morning** təmɔːn ət mɔːnɪn Y*[old]*, təmɔːn t mɔːnɪn Y, təmɔᴶːn ət mɔːnɪn La, təmɔᴶːn ət mɔᴶːnɪn La, tɪmɔˑən ət mɔˑənɪn Y, təmɔən ət mɔənɪn La, təmɔˑən t mɔənɪn Y, təmɔən tʔ mɔənɪn Y, təmɔᴶˑəᴶɪn ət mɔᴶˑəᴶɪnɪn La, təmɔən t mɔənɪn We, təmɔːn t mɔːnən Du; **tomorn forenoon*** təmɔən fɔənɪən Nb; **tomorn in the forenoon*** təmɔᴶːɪn ɪ t fʊəᴶnᵁʊːn La; **tomorn in the morning** təmɔːn ɪ t mɔːnɪn Y, təmɔːn ɪ t mɔˑᵊnɪn Y, təmɔᴶːɪn ɪ d mɔᴶːnɪn La, təmɔᴶːɪn ə d mɔᴶːnɪn La, təmɔᴶːɪəᴶɪn ɪ t mɔəᴶɪnɪn La; **tomorn morning** tɪmœːn məːnən Du, təmɔːᵊn mɔːnɪn

We, təmɔˑˡːn mɔˡːnɪn La

2. *n* TOMORROW VII.4.1. təmɑˡːn La, təmɔɾn Y, tɪmɔːn Du Y, təmɔːn Du La Y Db*[old]*, tʊmɔˡːɪn La, təmɔˡːn We La Y Db, tɪmɔən Y, təmɔən La Y, təmɔːən Du We La, təmɔəˡn La, təmɔːəˡɪn La, təmɔən Nb, tɪmʊən Y, təmʊən Nb Y, təməːn Du

tomorrow *1. n There's yesterday, there's today, and the 24 hours after today you call ....* VII.4.1. Eng. ⇒ **morrow,** *the* **morn,** *the* **morrow, tomorn**

2. *n* TOMORROW MORNING VII.3.13. təmɒɹə K

tomorrow morning *n [You will see him again, not this morning, not this afternoon, but ....] Not tonight, but just after you have got up, so ....* VII.3.13. Eng exc. Nb We C D. ⇒ *at* **morn,** *at* **morning,** *early in the* **morning,** *first thing in* **morning,** *first thing in the* **morning,** *first thing* **tomorn,** *in the* **morn,** *in the* **morning,** *morrow* **morning,** *next* **morning,** *soon on* **tomorn,** *the* **morning,** *the* **morn** *morning, the* **morn's** **morn,** *the* **morn's** *morning, the* **morrow** **morning, tomorn, tomorn** *afore dinner,* **tomorn** *at* **forenoon, tomorn** *at* **morn, tomorn** *at* **morning, tomorn** *forenoon,* **tomorn** *in the* **forenoon, tomorn** *in the* **morning, tomorn** *morning,* **tomorrow,** *tomorrow* **forenoon,** *tomorrow* **morn**

tom-spinner *n* DADDY-LONG-LEGS IV.8.10. tɒmspɪnəˡ Y

tom-tailor-legs *n* DADDY-LONG-LEGS IV.8.10. tɒmtɛləlɛgz Y

tom-tailor(s) *n* DADDY-LONG-LEGS IV.8.10. *no* -*s*: tɒmteːɫdəᵗ Co
-*s*: tɒmteˈələz L

tom-thumbs *npl* TADPOLES IV.9.5. tɒmðʌmz D
tom-toddies *npl* TADPOLES IV.9.5. tɒmtɒdɪz Co D

ton *n* a CUTTING of hay II.9.15. tʊn St *[queried ir.r. WMBM]*

tong(s) *n [Point to or show a picture of fire-tongs.] What do you call this?* V.3.7.
-*s*: Eng; **a tongs** ə tɒŋz Mon Nf, ə tɒŋgz K; **pair (of) tongs** pɛəɹ ə tɛŋz Y, pɛəɹ ə taŋz Y, pɛˈɹ ə tɒŋz Nf, pɛəɹ ə tɒŋz Y Nf, pəᵗː tɒŋz Do; **tongses** tɒŋzəz So
no -*s*: tɒŋ Ess, tɒŋ Sf
⇒ *a* **tongs, fire-tongs,** *pair of* **tongs, prongs, tong***es*

tongue *1. n What am I doing now [indicate putting your tongue out in derision]?* VI.5.4. Eng. ⇒ **blab, lapper, loller, lolliker, lolliper, melt**
2. *n* a vertical rod in front of a cart, perforated to allow adjustments when tipping, ⇐ ROD/PIN I.10.3. tʌŋ Mon, tʊŋ He Wo

tongue-fern *n* FERN shaped like a tongue IV.10.13. *pl* tʊŋfɪəˡnz La

tongue-peg *n* a pin used with a perforated rod in front of a cart to allow adjustments when tipping, ⇐ ROD/PIN I.10.3. *pl* tɒŋpɛgz He, tʌŋpɛg He, tʊŋpɛg He

tongue-pin *n* a pin used with a perforated rod in front of a cart to allow adjustments when tipping, ⇐ ROD/PIN I.10.3. tʌŋpɪn Mon, tʊŋpɪn He

tongue-wag *n* a GOSSIP VIII.3.5(b). tʊŋwag Wo
tongue-wagging *v-ing* GOSSIPING VIII.3.5(a). tʊŋwagɪn Wa

tongue-weed *n* GOOSE-GRASS II.2.5. tʌŋwiːd Nf, tʌŋwɹid Nf

tonight *n* LAST NIGHT VII.3.9. tənaɪt D

tons *n* A LOT (of money) VII.8.7. tʌnz Nf

too *adv And why have they [i.e. bread or cakes] been burnt? Because the oven has been ...* HOT. V.6.8. Eng exc. Nb Cu Du We. ⇒ **overheated,** *over* **hot,** *too* **brisk,** *too* **fierce**

tool *1. n* the penis of a horse, ⇐ SHEATH III.4.9. tɪul Nf
2. *n* a STUPID person VI.1.5. tuːɫ K

tooth *n [What do you call these (point to your teeth)?] And one of them?* VI.5.6(b). Eng. ⇒ **tush, tusher;** ⇒ also **four-tooth, six-tooth**

toothache *n Seeing a boy sitting like this [put your hand to your jaw] might make you ask him: [Have you got] ...?* VI.5.8. Eng exc. We. ⇒ **face-ache, jaw-ache, jaws-ache, teeth-ache, teeth-wark, tooth-warch, tooth-wark**

toothful *n* a PINCH of sugar or salt VII.8.6. tɪəθfl Y

tooths *npl* TEETH VI.5.6(a). tuːθs W

tooth-warch *n* TOOTHACHE VI.5.8. tyːθwæˑːtʃ La, tyːθwaˡːtʃ Db, tyːθwɜˡːɪtʃ La, tʊɪθwaːtʃ Y, tᵁuθwæːɪtʃ La, tᵁuːθwæˡːɪtʃ La, tᵁuːθwɜˡːɪtʃ La, tuːθwaːtʃ La, tuːθwaˡːtʃ La *[not a NBM headword]*

tooth-wark *n* TOOTHACHE VI.5.8. tɪɤθwaːk Cu, tjɤθwaːk Du, tɪɤθwaᵏːk Nb, tɪʊθwaːk Du Y, tjʊθwaːk Du, tjuθwaᵏːk Du, tɪəθwaːk Nb Cu Du We Y, tɪəθwaᵏːk Nb, tʊɪθwaːk Y, tuːθwaːk Y, tuːθwaˡːk La, tᵁuːθwɜˡːk La

top *1. n* an END-BOARD of a cart I.10.4. tɒp Sr
2. *n* an EAR of a corn-plant II.5.2(b). tɒp St, tɔp Y
3. *n* the RIDGE of a stack of corn II.7.2. tʰɑpʔ Nf, tɒp We Gl Nf, tɒpʔ Nf, tɔp La
4. *n* the RIDGE of a house roof V.1.2(a). tɒp Ess, tɔp Ess; **top of the slates** *n* tɒp ə t sleːts Y
5. *n* a CUTTING of hay II.9.15. tap Co
6. *v* to TRIM hedges IV.2.3. tɒp St Nt L*[1 year's growth]* Lei Nf So W Co D, -*ing* tɒpɪn Ch*[top]* Nth K; **top and twig** -*ing* tɒpɪn ən twɪgɪn L
7.1. *v* **butt and top, root and top, tip and top, top, top and bottom, top and snout, top and trim** to TOP AND TAIL swedes II.4.3. **butt and top** bʌt n̩ tɒp Sa, bʌt n̩ tɔːp Sa; **root and top** ɹuːt ən tɒp Cu, ʁʊt n̩ tɒp Nb, ʁʊt ən tɒp Du; **tip and top** tɪp n̩ tɒp K; **top** tɒp Ess, tɔpʔ Ess, -*ing* tɒpɪn Y Wa*[whole operation]*, tɔp La C Sf; **top and**

bottom tɒp ən bɒtəm St; **top and snout** tɒp ən snaʊt La

7.2. *vt* **root and top, top, top and bottom, top and butt, top and more, more and top, top and trim, trim and top** to top and tail swedes. **root and top** ɾuːt ... ən tɒp ... So; **top** tɒp St Wa Mon*[both ends]* Gl Ess So W Co D Do Ha, *-ing* tɒpɪn Sx, tɔp L; **top and bottom** tɔp ən bɔtəm L; **top and butt** tɒp ŋ bʌt He, tɒp ən bʌt He, tɒp ŋ bʊt He; **top and more** tɒp ən mɔˤːɾ (+V) D; **more and top** mɔˤːɾ ən tɒp Co; **top and root** tɒp ən ɾʏːt Co; **top and trim** tɔp ŋ tɹɪm L; **trim and top** tɾɪm ... ən tɒp ... Co

8. *v* to LOP a tree IV.12.5. tɒp O Ess, *-ing* tɒpɪn Hu
9. *v* to cut small branches from a tree. *-ing* tɒpɪn K
10. *v* to cut large branches from a tree. *-ing* tɒpɪn K
11. *vt* to TOP-AND-TAIL gooseberries V.7.23. tɒp Do
12.1. *vt* to REMOVE *STALKS* from currants V.7.24. tɒp Nb Ha *[marked ir.r. SBM as probably implying removal of stalk and head]*
12.2. *v* to remove stalks. tɒp We

top-and-bottoms *n* HEADLANDS in a ploughed field II.3.3. tɒpmbɒtəmz So

top-and-tail 1. *v Before putting your gooseberries into the pie-dish, what must you do to them?* V.7.23. Eng exc. Cu Du We Nt R C Do. ⇒ **chig, clean, clean** *the tails,* **cob, cut** *the ends* **off, cut** *the eyes and strigs,* **end, eye-and-stalk, head-and-tail, head-and-tail** *them,* **head-and-toe, hull,** *knep* ⇒ **nep,** *knop* ⇒ **nop, lop, nap, nep, nesp, nib, nib** *them,* **nib** *them* **off, nip, nipple, nip** *them* ⇒ **nip, nop, nose-and-tail, nose** *them,* **nub, nub-and-tail, pick, pick-and-clean, pick-and-snout, pick** *the heads and tails* **off, pick** *the noses of them,* **pick** *the stems out of them,* **pip** *them,* **pluck, slough, snip, snout, snub, snuff, snuff** *and tail them,* **snuff** *them,* **snuft, snut, stalk, strig** *them,* **strip, tail** *them, take the chigs off, take the hairs off,* **top** *them,* **trim**
2.1. *vt* to REMOVE *STALKS* from currants V.7.24. tɒpəntiːl St, tɒpənteːl Y
2.2. *v* to remove stalks. tɒpəntiːl St, tɒpnteːl Sa Mon, tɒpəntɛɪl St, *-ing* tɒp ŋ tɛɪʊɬn Ha, tɒpntæɪl He, tɒpntæɪɬ Ess K, tɒpəntæɪˤɬ Sf *[probably stalk and head removed, SBM Edd. Hyphenation of headword retained as in SED questionnaire]*

top and tail *v, vt* **top and tail, tail and top** *In gathering swedes, what do you do to each after you have pulled it out of the ground?* II.4.3. Eng exc. Nb Du We R Hu C Bk Hrt MxL Do Sx. ⇒ *butt and* **top, chop, chop off, chop** *the spurns and tops* **off, chop** *the tops and tails* **off, clean, clean** *and* **top, clean off, cut, cut off, cut** *the green* **off** *and* **cut** *the root* **off, cut** *the swedes* **off, cut** *the top and bottom* **off, cut** *the top* **off, cut** *the tops and roots* **off, cut** *the tops and tails* **off, dock, dress, fash, head** *and tail,* **knock** *the top* **off** *and the tail,* **loop, lop,** *more and* **top, pull,**

pull *swedes, root and* **shaw,** *root and* **top, shaw, slash** *the muck* **off, slike, snag, sned, snip, snout, snuff, swede-clean, swede-trim,** *tail and* **head,** *tail and top, thrash* ⇒ **thresh, thresh,** *tip and* **top, top, top** *and bottom,* **top** *and butt,* **top** *and more,* **top** *and root,* **top** *and snout,* **top** *and trim,* **trim, trim** *and* **top, trim off, trim up, wrench, wring, wring** *the tops* **off** *[open, non-hyphenated headword of SED questionnaire retained]*

top arse-board *n* an END-BOARD of a cart I.10.4. tɒp aːsboˑəd Db

top back-board *n* an END-BOARD of a cart I.10.4. tɔp bækbɔˑəd Sf, tɒp bakbɔːd Lei R, tɒp bakboˑəd Wa

top-bar *n* a DIAGONAL BAR of a gate IV.3.7. tɒpbaˤː Sa Wo

top-board 1. *n* an END-BOARD of a cart I.10.4. tɒpbɔːd Wa Lei Ess, tɒpbɔˑəd St, tɒpboːd Sa, tɒpboˑəd Man Db Wa Nth, tɒpboəˤd Db, tɒpboːəˤd̥ Sa, tɒpbʊəd La St Lei, tɒpbʊəɹd La, tɒpbʊəˤd̥ Wa, tɔpbɔːd Sf Ess
2. *n* an extension board raising the side of a cart. tɒpbʊəd Y

topcoat *n* an OVERCOAT VI.14.6. tæpkoˑᵘt Man, tapkoʊt Wo Gl, tapkoʊt Wa, tapkoˑət Nth, tapkwʊt Gl, tapkʊˑəʔ Bk, tɒpkɪʏːət La Ch, tɒpkʏˑət La Db, tɒpkøːt Nb Du, tɒpkœːˤt Nb, tɒpkɒɪt La Y, tɒpkɔːt Cu, tɒpkɔɪt Y, tɒpkɔʊt L Lei Nth, tɒpkʌʊʔ Bk Bd, tɒpkoːt La Ch Db Sa St He O Nt So W Brk Do, tɒpkoˑʔ Bk, tɒpkwoːt So, tɒpkoʊt St Wo Wa Nth Ha*[old]*, tɒpkoʊʔ O, tɒpkoət Nb Cu We La Db Wa Bd, tɒpkwoət Cu, tɒpkwɒt Cu Wo, tɒpkʊat Y, tɒpkʊət Nb Cu Du We La Y*[old x1]* Ch Wa O Nt L Nth*[old]*, tɒpkʊə? O Bk, tɒpkᵂət Gl, tɒpkuːt Ch Db Sa St*[old x1]* Wo Wa, tɒpkuːət So W, tɒpkət Nb, tɔpkɔɪt Y, tɔpkɔʊt L, tɔpkɔət Y, tɔpkʌʊt Sf MxL Sr, tɔpkoːt Du, tɔpkʊət La Y Ch L, tɔpkuːt Wa

top corner *n* the RIDGE of a stack of corn II.7.2. tɒp kɔːnə Ess

top hole *adj* WELL, describing a healthy person VI.13.1(a). tɒp hoˑəl Man

top-horse *n* the LAND-HORSE of a ploughing team II.3.4(b). tɒphɔːs Ess, tɒpoˡːs La, tɔphɔs Sf

topknot *n* the FORELOCK of a horse III.4.8. tɑpnat O Nth C, tɒpnɒt La Wo Wa Bk Sx, tɒpnət Gl, tɔpnɔt Wa

top of the roof *n* the RIDGE of a stack of corn II.7.2. taˑpʔ ə ðə ɹʏf Nf, tɒp ə ð ɹˡuːf Db, tɒp ə ðə ɹuːf St

top over *vtphr* to REMOVE *STALKS* from currants V.7.24. *-ing* tɒpɪn ... ɔːvəˤː W *[probably stalk and head removed, SBM Edd]*

toppet *n* the FORELOCK of a horse III.4.8. tɒpɪt K

topping *1. n* a chock placed behind and under a wheel to prevent a cart from going backwards on a hill, ⇐ PROP/CHOCK I.11.2. tɒpɪn Y
2. n the FORELOCK of a horse III.4.8. tœːpən Nb, tɒpɪn Nb Cu Du We La Y Ch Db Sa St Wo Wa Nt L Lei R, tɒpn Nb, tɒpən Du, tɔpɪn Nb La Y L, tɔpən Nb L
3. adj WELL, describing a healthy person VI.13.1(a). tɒpɪn Sr

topple *n* the FORELOCK of a horse III.4.8. tɒpɪl Db

topple over *1. viphr* to OVERTURN, referring to a cart I.11.5. *3prsg* tɔpəlz ɔʊə Y, tɒpəł oːvəᵗ He, tɒpl oəɹ La, tɒpl ʊːə St
2. viphr to FAINT VI.13.7. tɒpl aʊə Y

topple up *vtphr* to TED hay II.9.11(a). taːpl ... ʌp Nf

toppling over *adv* HEAD OVER HEELS IX.1.10. tɒplɪn ouvə Nf

tops *1. npl* the RIDGES between furrows in a ploughed field II.3.2. tɒps Nf, tɒpʔs Nf, *sg* taːˀp Nf
2. n POTATO-HAULMS II.4.4. taps Nf Bk, tɒps La Y Sa St Wa Lei Nf Hrt Ess Co, tɒpʔs Nf, tɔps L C Sf

topsy-turvy *adv* HEAD OVER HEELS IX.1.10. tɒpsɪtəːvɪ St

top-tail *1. n* an END-BOARD of a cart I.10.4. tɔpteəl La
2. adv HEAD OVER HEELS IX.1.10. tɒptiːl St

top-tail-board *n* an END-BOARD of a cart I.10.4. tɒpteːlbʊəᴶɪd La, tɔpteːlbʊəd La, tɔp teɪlbʊəd L, tɒp tæɪlbɒəd Nf, tɒp tæɪɫbɔːd Ess, tɔp tæɪɫbɔːd Ess, tɔp tæɪʊbɔːd Ess

torret *n* a sliding RING to which a tether is attached in a cow-house I.3.5. tɒɹɪt neY, təɹɛt La

tosie *adj* PIGEON-TOED VI.10.4. toːsɪ La

toss *1. v* to PITCH sheaves II.6.10. *3prsg* tɔsəz Nb
2. vt to TED hay II.9.11(a). tɔs Wo
3. v to BUTT III.2.10. tas Nth, tɒs Nth, *-ing* tɒsɪn Bd, tɒs Sf, *-ing* tɔːsɪn Ess

toss-cutter *n* a HAY-SPADE II.9.14(b). tɒskʊtəᴶ K

tossel* *n* the FORELOCK of a horse III.4.8. tɒsl St

tossing *v-ing* THROWING a stone VIII.7.7. tɒsɪn Y

to the side *prep* **to the side of** BESIDE a door IX.2.5. tə ðə sɔɪd əv Wa

totrils *n* an EVENER on a horse-drawn plough I.8.4. tɒtɹəlz Sa

tottering *1. n* TREMORS suffered by a person who cannot keep still VI.1.4. tɒtɹɪn Ch Db
2. adj CLUMSY, describing a person VI.7.14. tɔtəɹɪn Wo

totters *n* TREMORS suffered by a person who cannot keep still VI.1.4. tɒtəz Nt Nth, tɒʔəᵗz̩ Bk

totterums *n* TREMORS suffered by a person who cannot keep still VI.1.4. tɒtəɹəmz Y

touched *1. adj* STUPID VI.1.5. tʌtʃt Ess Sr, tətʃt Sx; **touched in the head** tʌtʃt ɪn ðɪ ɪd Sr
2. adj SILLY VIII.9.3. tʌtʃt Ess K Sx; **touched in the head** tʌtʃt ɪn ð ɪd Sr

touse *vt* to BEAT a boy on the buttocks VIII.8.10. taʊs So

touser *1. n* a working APRON V.11.2(a). tæɣsəᵗː Co, tæɣzəᵗː D*[sacking, for field-work]*, təᵗːʃəᵗː Co
2. n a decorative APRON V.11.2(b). təᵗːʃəᵗː Co

touser-apron *n* a working APRON V.11.2(a). taɪʃəᵗːɹeːpəᵗː D

tousled *adj* TANGLED, describing hair VI.2.5. tɛʊzld Wa, taʊzld Y, taʊzəld Y, tɒzɫd Bk, tuːzld Nb Y, təʊzld He

tousy *adj* TANGLED, describing hair VI.2.5. tɒʊzɪ Cu

tout-bone *n* the HIP-BONE of a cow III.2.1. tʊtbʊən L

tovven *n* a round stack, ⇐ STACKS II.7.1. tʰɒvən Man

tow *1. n* the T-SHAPED PLOUGH-BEAM END of a horse-drawn plough I.8.5. toː D
2. n HAIR VI.2.1. taʊ Y, tɑʊ Y *[one Y r. in fact 'a head of hair'; this may be the case with other rr. also]*

towpy-tails *adv* HEAD OVER HEELS IX.1.10. tɒʊpɪtɛːlz Cu

towse *vt* to PULL somebody's hair VI.2.8. tɛʊz Db

towt *n* TWINE used to fasten thatch on a stack II.7.7(b1). taʊt Du

towtil *adv* HEAD OVER HEELS IX.1.10. tʊʊtl We

towy *adj* TANGLED, describing hair VI.2.5. tɑʊɪ Y

to-year *n* THIS YEAR VII.3.18. tɪjɪəɹ Y, təjɪə Nf*[old x1]*, təjɪəɹ Nf*[old]*

trace *n* a TRACE-HORSE I.6.3. tɹɛɪs Ess, tɹæɪs Ess, tɹaɪs Ess

trace-horse *n* *[Show a picture of two horses in tandem.]* What do you call this *[the front horse]*? I.6.3. tɹɪəsɒs Y, tɹɪəsɒs We, tɹɪəsɒs Y, tɹɪəsɔːs Y, tɹɪəsɔːs Y, treːshɒs Cu, treːsɔᴶːs La, tʀeːshɔᴮːs Du, tɹeːsɑːs Mon, tɹeːsaᵗːʂ Gl, tɹeːsɑᵗːʂ Wo, tɹeːsɒs La Y Mon Gl, tɹeːsɒs Du, tɹeːsɔːs Mon Bk, tɹeːsɔəᴶs La, tɹɾeːsaᵗːʂ W Ha, tɾeːsɒs W Ha, tɾeːsɔɾs O, tɾeːsɔᵗːʂ W Do Ha, tʰreɪshɒs Man, tɹeɪshɒs Nf, tɹeɪshɔˑs Nf, tɹeɪsɔːs Wa Bk, tɹeɪsɔᵗːʂ O, tɾeɪshaᵗːʂ So, tɹeɪsaᵗːʂ So, tɹeɪʃaᵗːʂ Do, tɾeɪsɒᵗʂ Ha, tɾeɪshɔᵗːʂ So, tɾeɪsɔᵗːʂ So, tɹeːˡsaᵗːʂ Gl, tɹeːɪsaᵗːʂ He, tʀeəshɔᴮːs Nb, tɹeəsɒs Du Y, tɹeəsɒs Y, tɹeəsɔᴶːs La, tɹeˑəsɔᵗːʂ Bk, tɹeˑəˀsɔˑəˀs We, tɹeˑˀəsɔᵗːʂ Wo, tɹeˑˀəsəs Du, treˑsɔːs Cu, tɹeˑsɒs We Y, tɹeˑsɔs L, tɹeɪshɑːs Nf, tɹeɪsaᵗːʂ Wa, tɹeɪshɒs Nf Ess, tɹeɪshɔs Nf Sf, tɹeɪsɒsᶴ Sr, tɹeɪsɒᵗʂᶴ Sr, tɹeɪshɔːs Ess, tɹeɪsɔːs Wa Sf Ess K Sx, tɹeɪsɔᵗːəs Brk, tɹeɪsɔːɒᵗʂ Sr Sx, θɹeɪsɑᴶːs Brk, tɹeəsɒs Y, tɹeəsɔs Y, tɹæɪshɒˑs Nf, tɹæɪshɔːs Sf, tɹæɪshɔːs Ess, tɹæɪsɔːs Ess K, tɹaɪʃɔːs Ess, t̮ɹaɪsaᵗːʂ Do, t̮ɹaɪsɒs Ha. ⇒ **body-horse**, **chainer**, **chain-horse**, **chain-tit**, **crippin-horse**, **first-horse**, **fore-horse**, **foremost**, **foremost-horse**, **fore one**, **forrest**, **forrest-horse**, **front-horse**, **front one**, **gear-horse**, **gears-horse**, **harness-horse**, **leader**, **lead-horse**, **leading-horse**, **pin-horse**, **sling- gear-horse**, **sling-tit**, **string-horse**, **tandem-horse**, **trace**, **tracer**

trace-pole *n* a TETHERING-STAKE in a cow-house I.3.3. t̮ɹeɪspoːɫ D

tracer *n* a TRACE-HORSE I.6.3. tʁeːsɔᴿ Nb, tʁeːsɔᴿ Du, t̮ɹeːɪsəᵗː So

trace-stick *n* the STRETCHER between the traces of a cart-horse I.5.11. t̮ɹeɪstɪk C Hrt Ess, t̮ɹaɪsstɪk Ess

track *n* a track made by a horse, ⇐ HOOF-MARKS IV.3.10. t̮ɹæˑk Brk

track(s) *1. n* a PATH through a field IV.3.11.
no -s: t̮ɹɛk Gl K, træk Man, t̮ɹæk He Mon Gl Nf Ess Sr, *pl* t̮ɹæks Sx, t̮ɹæk So, t̮ɹak Y*[for humans and cows x1, for humans x1]* Ch St Wo Wa Mon
-s: t̮ɹɛks Sr
2. n a path made by cattle and sheep. t̮ɹæk K, t̮ɹak Y
3. n a path made by cattle. t̮ɹæk MxL, t̮ɹak Y St, t̮ɹak Ha
4. n a path made by animals. t̮ɹɛk K, t̮ɹæk Nf, t̮ɹak Ch Nth Bk, *pl* t̮ɹaks L

tracks *1. npl* RUTS made by cartwheels IV.3.9. t̮ɹæks Ess, t̮ɹæːks Brk, tʁaks Nb, t̮ɹaks Ch Wa*[newly-made x2]* Nth, t̮ɹaks Co *[last marked ir.r. by fw]*
2. npl the HOOF-MARKS of a horse IV.3.10. t̮ɹɛks Sx, t̮ɹæks Sa, t̮ɹaks Ch St Gl, t̮ɹaks W Co D Do

track-way *n* a PATH through a field IV.3.11. t̮ɹækwɒɪ So

trail *n* a PATH through a field IV.3.11. *pl* t̮ɹɒɪɫz Nf

trail-cart *n* a SLEDGE used to carry loads in winter I.9.1. t̮ɹeəlkaːɪt Y

trained *vt-3ptsg* he/she TAUGHT it III.13.17. tʁɪənd Nb, t̮ɹɪənd Y L, t̮ɹeːɪnt Db, tʁeːɪnd Nb, t̮ɹeːɪnd Ch Db O Nt, t̮ɹeɪnd He Bk, treˑənd Y, tʁeˑənd Nb, t̮ɹeənd La Y, t̮ɹeɪnd Wa L Ess Sr K Sx, t̮ɹeənd Y L, t̮ɹæɪnd Nf Ess Sr, t̮ɹæɪn Nf, t̮ɹaɪnd Ha

trained up *vtphr-3ptsg* he/she TAUGHT it III.13.17. t̮ɹɛɪn ... ʌp Nf

trammel *n* a CRANE on which a kettle is hung over a domestic fire V.3.4. t̮ɹæmɫ Sf, t̮ɹæmbɫ Ess

trammel-hook *n* the HOOK or *CROOK* of a crane over a domestic fire V.3.5(c). t̮ɹæmbɫhʊk Ess

tramp *1. v* to WALK VIII.7.10. t̮ɹamp Db
2. vt **tramp it** to walk. t̮ɹamp ɪt L

trap *1. n* a device consisting of a bar and a pin fixing a cart-body to the shafts, stopping it from tipping, ⇐ ROD/PIN I.10.3. t̮ɹæp Nf
*2. *n* a LITTER of piglets III.8.3. t̮ɹap Ha

trap-iron *n* a movable horizontal rod stretching between the shafts of a cart, fixing them to the

cart-body and stopping the cart from tipping, ⇐ ROD/PIN I.10.3. t̮ɹapaɪəᵗː Co

trapping-iron *n* a movable horizontal rod stretching between the shafts of a cart, fixing them to the cart-body and stopping the cart from tipping, ⇐ ROD/PIN I.10.3. t̮ɹæpɪnɑɪən K

trapping(s) *n* the BREECH-BAND of the harness of a cart-horse I.5.10.
no -s: t̮ɹapɪn Du, t̮ɹapɪn Nb, t̮ɹapən Du, t̮ɹapən Du
-s: t̮ɹapɪnz Y

trap-stick *1. n* the STRETCHER between the traces of a cart-horse I.5.11. t̮ɹæpstɪk K
2. n a movable horizontal rod stretching between the shafts of a cart, fixing them to the cart-body and stopping the cart from tipping, ⇐ ROD/PIN I.10.3. t̮ɹɛpstɪk Ess, t̮ɹæpstɪk Nf Ess K
3. n a STICK used to support the shaft of a cart I.11.1. t̮ɹæpstɪk K

trash *n* a DRAG used to slow a wagon I.11.3. t̮ɹaʃ Ch

travellers *npl* GIPSIES VIII.4.12. t̮ɹævələz Nf, t̮ɹaˑvɫəᴵz Brk, t̮ɹɑˑvɫəᴵz Brk

traverse *n* an EVENER, the main swingle-tree of a horse-drawn plough harness I.8.4. t̮ɹavɪs L

tray *n* a PASTE-BOARD V.6.5. t̮ɹæɪ Sf *[marked u.r. EMBM]*

trays *npl* HURDLES used to pen sheep in part of a field III.7.11. t̮ɹeːz Nt*[wooden]*, t̮ɹeɪz L*[wooden x1]*, t̮ɹeˑəz L*[small pens x1, lambing pens x1]*

treacle-bar *n* **piece of treacle-bar** a PIECE *OF BREAD AND BUTTER AND JAM/SUGAR* V.6.11(b). piːs ə t̮ɹɪkɫbɑː Co *[presumably with treacle, not jam: marked u.r. SBM]*

treacle-buck *n* a PIECE *OF BREAD AND BUTTER AND JAM/SUGAR* V.6.11(b). t̮ɹiːklbʊk Ch, treːklbʊk Ch *[marked u.r. WMBM]*

treacle-butty *n* a PIECE *OF BREAD AND BUTTER AND JAM/SUGAR* V.6.11(b). t̮ɹeːklbʊtɪ La, θɹeːklbʊtɪ La, tθɹeːklbʊtɪ La *[marked u.r. NBM]*

treacle-shag *n* a PIECE *OF BREAD AND BUTTER AND JAM/SUGAR* V.6.11(b). ə t̮ɹɪəklʃag We *[marked u.r. NBM]*

tread *1. vt What does the cock do to the hen?* IV.6.8. Eng exc. R. ⇒ **treaden**
2. n a RUNG of a ladder I.7.15. *pl* t̮ɹɪdz Sx
3. n a track made by a horse, ⇐ HOOF-MARKS IV.3.10. t̮ɹɪd Sx
4. vt **tread (the load)** to LOAD sheaves onto a wagon II.6.7(a). *prppl* t̮ɹɛdɪn So, *3prsg* t̮ɹɛɪdz D

treaden *v* to TREAD a hen IV.6.8. t̮ɹɛdn Nf *[queried and interpreted as probably infinitive EMBM]*

treader *n* the LOADER of sheaves onto a wagon II.6.7(c). t̮ɹɛɪdəᵗː D

treading(s) *n* TREAD inside a fertile egg IV.6.9.
no -s: tɹɛdɪn Y Ch Db Nt Bd, tɹɛɪdɪn La
sg: tɹɛɪdɪnz La
-s: tɹɛdnz Nf

tread-mark *n* TREAD in a fertile egg IV.6.9.
tɹɛdmɑ·k Nf

tread(s) *n It's no use a broody hen sitting on eggs unless they have, what inside?* IV.6.9.
no -s: Eng
pl: tɹɪədz Y
-s: tɹɪdz L
⇒ **been trodden on**, **cock's treading**, *fertile*, **germ**, **seed**, **spot**, **treading(s)**, **tread-mark**

tread-stick *n* the STRETCHER between the traces of a cart-horse I.5.11. tɹɛdstɪk Lei Nth

treddles *n* SHEEP-DUNG II.1.7. tɹɛdʊɫz K; **sheep's-treddles** ʃiːpstɹɛdɫz K

tree *n* the SHAFT of a spade I.7.7. tɹiː Sa, tɾiː So, tɹɛɪ Ch

tree-butt *n* a tree STUMP IV.12.4. tɹiːbʊt St

tree-dog *n* a tree STUMP IV.12.4. tɹᵊiːdɒg Hrt

tree-grains *npl* BOUGHS of a tree IV.12.2. tɹiːgɹɛənz Y

tree-rat *n* a grey SQUIRREL IV.5.8. tɾiːɾat O

tree-stool *n* a tree STUMP IV.12.4. tɾiːstaʊəl So, tɾiːstuːɫ Ha*[sawn off]*

tremble(s) *n* TREMORS suffered by a person who cannot keep still VI.1.4.
no -s: tɾɛmbɫ So
-s: tɹɛmblz St, tɹɛmbʊɫz Brk, tɾɛmbɫz W; **the trembles** ðə tɹɛmbɫz Mon

tremming-tree *n* the bush ELDER IV.10.6. tɾɛməntɹiː Man

tremors *n Old people often can't keep their heads still; what would you say the trouble was?* VI.1.4. tɾɛməᵗːz So. ⇒ **ague**, **dawzles**, *dither and plop* ⇒ **dithers**, **dithers**, **ditherums**, **ditters**, **dodders**, **dother(s)**, **dotherums**, **dotherum-shakums**, **fifer's dance**, **jangles**, **jitters**, **nerve(s)**, **noddering**, **nodding**, **palsy**, **quivers**, **saint fifer's dance**, **saint viper's dance**, **saint vitus' dance**, **shakers**, **shakes**, **shakiness**, **shaking(s)**, **shatter-dadders**, **shivers**, *the* **ague**, *the* **agues**, *the* **dither and pop** ⇒ **dithers**, *the* **dithers**, *the* **ditherums**, *the* **fidgets**, *the* **fifer's dance**, *the* **jaggers**, *the* **jitters**, *the* **nerves**, *the* **noddlings**, *the* **palsy**, *the* **shakes**, *the* **shaking palsy**, *the* **shiggles**, *the* **shithers**, *the* **shivers**, *the* **shudders**, *the* **trembles**, *the* **waggles**, **thithers**, **tottering**, **totters**, **totterums**, **tremble(s)**, **wackers** *[also range of adjectival and phrasal rr. recorded as u.rr. in BM]*

trench *1. n* a DRAIN in a cow-house I.3.8. tɹɛntʃ Nf Bk
2. n a CLAMP in which potatoes are stored out of doors II.4.6. tɾɛnʃ D
3. n a RIVULET IV.1.1. tʰɾɛnʃ Man *[apparently artificially widened]*

trendle *n* a SALTING-TROUGH III.12.5. tɹɛndəɫ Gl, tɾɛndɫ Co D, tɾɛnɫ So D

trest *n* a BENCH on which slaughtered pigs are dressed III.12.1. tɾɛst La

trestle *1. n* a SAWING-HORSE I.7.16. tɹiːzl St, tʰɾɛsl Man, tɾɛsl La, tɹɛsl Y L, tɹɛsɫ K, tɹʌsəɫ Mon, tɾʊsl Cu, tɹʊsl Nb Y, tɹʊsɫ Wo
2. n a SHEARING-TABLE III.7.8. tɹɛsl Y St, tɹɛsəl Y, tɹɛsɫ Ess
3. n a BENCH on which slaughtered pigs are dressed III.12.1. tɹɛsl Du La Y Ch Db, tʀɛsl Du, tθɾɛsl La, tɹɛsʊ K, pɪgtɾɛsl La
4. n the THRESHOLD of a door V.1.12. tɹɛsl Db

trestle-bottom *n* the BASE of a stack, made of wooden stakes II.7.4. θɹɛsəlbɒtəm Y

trestles *n* CART-LADDERS I.10.5. tɹəslz Y

trevice *n* the PARTITION between stalls in a cow-house I.3.2. tʀɛvɪdʒ Nb, tʀɛbɪdʒ Nb, tʀəbɪdʒ Nb

trickles *n* **sheep-trickles** SHEEP-DUNG II.1.7. ʃɪptɹɪkɫz He

tricklings *n* **sheep-tricklings** SHEEP-DUNG II.1.7. ʃɪptɹɪklɪnz Sa

tricky *adj* SLIPPERY VII.6.14. tɹɪkɪ Y*[most dialectal word x1]* Sa

triddles *n* **sheep-triddles** SHEEP-DUNG II.1.7. ʃɪptɹɪdɫz C

triddlings *npl* RABBIT-DROPPINGS III.13.15. tɹɪdlɪnz La, tɾədlɪnz Y, tɹədlɪnz Y

tridlings *n* SHEEP-DUNG II.1.7. tɹɪdlɪnz La, tɹədlɪnz Y; **sheep-tridlings** ʃiːptɹɪdlɪnz La Y, ʃiːptɹɪdlɪnz La, ʃiːptɹɪdəlɪnz Y, ʃəɪptɹɪdlɪnz Y

tried *vi-3ptsg That boy didn't manage to win a prize at the sports, but I will say, to his credit, he at least....* VIII.8.4. Eng. ⇒ **framed**, **ossed**, **tewed** *[also various idioms]*

trig *n* a chock placed behind and under a wheel to prevent a cart from going backwards on a hill, ⇐ PROP/CHOCK I.11.2. tɹɪg O, tɾɪg So Co D Do

trig-stick *n* a STICK used to support the shaft of a cart I.11.1. tɹɪgstɪk Ha, *pl* tɹɪgstɪks Brk

trigger *1. n* a STICK used to support the shaft of a cart I.11.1. tɾɪgəᵗː W
2. n a chock, sometimes specially shaped, placed behind and under a wheel to prevent a cart from going backwards on a hill, ⇐ PROP/CHOCK I.11.2. tɹɪgəᵗɾ Ha, tɾɪgəᵗː W D

trigger-bar *n* a movable horizontal rod stretching between the shafts of a cart, fixing them to the cart-body and stopping the cart from tipping, ⇐ ROD/PIN I.10.3. tɹɪgəbɑ· K

trigger-bat *n* a movable horizontal rod stretching between the shafts of a cart, fixing them to the cart-body and stopping the cart from tipping, ⇐ ROD/PIN I.10.3. tɹɪgəᵈbæt K

trigger-stick *n* a movable horizontal rod stretching between the shafts of a cart, fixing them to the cart-body and stopping the cart from tipping, ⇐ ROD/PIN I.10.3. tɹɪgəˈstɪk Sx

trig up* *vtphr* to chock a wheel to prevent a cart from going backwards on a hill, ⇐ PROP/CHOCK I.11.2. tɹɪg ʌp D Do, tɹɪg ... ʌp Co Do

trim *1. v When you take the rough growth off your hedges, what do you say you do to them?* IV.2.3.

v -ing tɹɪmɪn Man, tɹɪm La Y Db Sa He Wo Wa Gl O L Nth*[sides x1]* C Nf Sf Bk Bd Hrt Ess Sr, *prppl* tɹɪmɪn Brk, *-ing* tɹɪmɪn MxL Brk K Ha Sx, tɹɪm So W D Do Ha, *-ing* tɹɪmɪn Co, tɹɛm Man, *-ing* tɹɛmən Co; **hedge-trim** *-ing* ɛːdʒtɹɪmɪn Hrt, *-ing* ɛˈdʒtɹɪmɪn Hu

vt -ing tɹɪmɪn Nf Ess

⇒ **barge, barge down, barge out, brow, browse, browse down, browse off, browse out, brush, brush up, buck, buck-head, bush-hedge, clean, clip, crop, cut, cut back, cut down, cut out** *and chuck back*, **dike, drash, drash down, dress, dub, face in, flash,** *fore-bush* ⇒ **furbish, furbish, hedge, hedge-brush, hedge-crop, hedge-cut, hedge-top,** *hedge-trim* ⇒ **trim, hone, lob, lop, nip, pare, rid back, scotch, shave down, shear, shred, side, slanch, slash, slash down, snag, snaze, splash, splash up, split, split up, stag, swap, switch, top, top** *and twig*, **trim back, trim up, trounce,** *trouse* ⇒ **trounce, twig;** ⇒ also **browsing**

2.1. v to WHITTLE a stick I.7.19. *-ing* tʰrɪmən Man, tɹɪm Gl Sf Bk, *-ing* tɹɪmɪn Nf Ess, *-ing* tɹɪmɪn So

2.2. vt to whittle. *-ing* tɹɪmɪn W

3.1. v to TOP AND TAIL swedes II.4.3. tɹɪm Ch Gl Bk, *-ing* tɹɪmɪn Sx

3.2. vt to top and tail swedes. tɹɪm Wo L Sx, *-ing* tɹɪmɪn Brk Sr, tɹɪm So Co Ha

4. v to CLEAR grass at the edges of a field II.9.5. tɹɪm Sa He C, *prppl* tɹɪmən So

5.1. vt to LOP a tree IV.12.5. *-ing* tɹɪmɪn Nf, tɹɪm Co

5.2. v to lop. tɹɪm Du, tɹɪm Du Sa O Nt L Nf*[old x1]* Ess*[old x1]*

6. v to cut small branches from a tree. tɹɪm Wa L Nf, *-ing* tɹɪmɪn Y Ess Sr

7.1. vt to TOP-AND-TAIL gooseberries V.7.23. tɹɪm L

7.2. v to top-and-tail gooseberries. tɹɪm Sa

8. v to REMOVE *STALKS* from currants V.7.24. tɹɪm L

9. v **trim and flash** to cut the growth away from a DITCH IV.2.11. tɹɪm n̩ flæʃ Nf

trim back *vtphr* to TRIM hedges IV.2.3. tɹɪm ... bak W

trim-hide *n* the PELT of a sheep III.11.8(b). tɹɪmɑɪd Hu

trimlings *1. n* **sheep-trimlings**   SHEEP-DUNG II.1.7. ʃiːptɹɪmlənz Du, ʃiːptɹəmlɪnz Y

*2. npl RABBIT-DROPPINGS   III.13.15. tɹəmlɪnz Y

trimming-hook *n* a HEDGING-BILL IV.2.5. tɹɪmɪnʌk Hrt, tɹɪmɪnʊk Hu Sr, tɹɪmənɣk Co, tɹɪmənʊk Ha

trim off *vtphr* to TOP AND TAIL swedes II.4.3. tɹɪm ... ɔːf So Ha

trim out *1. vtphr* to WHITTLE a stick I.7.19. *-ing* tɹəmɪn əʊt Do

2.1. vtphr to CLEAR grass at the edges of a field II.9.5. tɹɪm ... ɛʊt Ha, tɹɪm ... œvt D, tɹɪm ... æʊt W Ha, tɹɪm ... əʊt Do*[with scythe x1]*

2.2. vphr to clear grass. tɹɪm æʊt Ha

3. vtphr to LOP a tree IV.12.5. tɹɪm ... ɛʊt Nf

4. vphr to cut small branches from a tree. *-ing* tɹɪmɪn aːt Y

trim round *vphr* to CLEAR grass at the edges of a field II.9.5. tɹɪm ɹɛwn Sf, tɹɪm ɹʌʊn He

trim-up *n* a haircut, ⇐ *GET YOUR* HAIR *CUT* VI.2.2. tɹɪm ʌp Ess Sr, tɹɪm ʌp Co, tɹɪmʊp St

trim up *1.1. vphr* to WHITTLE a stick I.7.19. tɹɪm ʌp C Bk, *prppl* tɹɪmɪn ʌp W

1.2. vtphr to whittle. *-ing* tɹɪmɪn ... ʌp Nf, *-ing* tɹɪmɪn ... ɣp Nf

2.1. vphr to TOP AND TAIL swedes II.4.3. tɹɪm ʌp Nth

2.2. vtphr to top and tail swedes. tɹɪm ... ʌp Brk

3.1. vtphr to CLEAR grass at the edges of a field II.9.5. tɹɪm ... ʊp Gl

3.2. vphr to clear grass. tɹɪm ʌp Sa Ess, tɹɪm ɣp Nf

4.1. vtphr to TRIM a hedge IV.2.3. *-ing* tɹɪmɪn ʌp Ess

4.2. vtphr to trim. tɹɪm ... ʌp Nf, *-ing* tɹɪmɪn ... ʊp Gl

5.1. vtphr to LOP a tree IV.12.5. *-ing* tɹɪmɪn ... ʌp Nf, tɹɪmn̩ ... ʌp Nf

5.2. vphr to lop. tɹɪm ʌp Sf, *-ing* tɹɪmɪn ʌp Mon

6.1. vtphr to cut small branches from a tree. *-ing* tɹɪmɪn ... ʊp O

6.2. vphr to cut small branches from a tree. *-ing* tɹɪmɪn ʌp K, *-ing* tɹɪmɪn ʊp Y

trindle *n* a SALTING-TROUGH III.12.5. tɹɪndɬ D, tɹɪnɬ So D

trindlings* *npl* RABBIT-DROPPINGS III.13.15. tɹɪndlɪnz La, tɹɪnlɪnz Du

trinlings *n* SHEEP-DUNG II.1.7. tɹɪnlənz Du, tɹɪnəlɪnz Y*[small]*, tɹənlɪnz We, tɹənlɪnz La; **sheep-trinlings** ʃiːptɹɪnlɪnz La*[new]*, ʃiːptɹənlɪnz Y

trinnions *n* **sheep-trinnions**   SHEEP-DUNG II.1.7. ʃɛɪptɹɪnɪənz Y

trip *1. n* a LITTER of piglets III.8.3. tɹɪp W Do Ha

2. n a BROOD of chickens IV.6.12. tɹɪp W

tripod *1. n* a CRANE on which a kettle is hung over a domestic fire V.3.4. tɹɪpɒd Wa

2. n the *HORIZONTAL* BAR of a crane over a domestic fire V.3.5(a). tɹɪpɒd Wa

tripolis* *npl* young onions sown in the autumn for early salads, ⇐ SPRING ONIONS V.7.16. tɹɪpḷoʊz He

trippers *1. npl* CART-LADDERS I.10.5. tɹɪpəz We

2. npl cart-ladders on a wagon. tɹɪpəᴶz Db

trippet *n* a GRIDIRON V.7.4(a). t̞ɹɪpɪt W

tripples *npl* SPRING ONIONS V.7.16. t̞ɹɪpɫz D

trip-stick *n* a movable horizontal rod stretching between the shafts of a cart, fixing them to the cart-body and stopping the cart from tipping, ⇐ ROD/PIN I.10.3. t̞ɹɪpstɪk Co D

trip up *vtphr* to TIP a cart I.11.6. t̞ɹɪp ... ʌp D

trivet *1. n* a CRANE on which a kettle is hung over a domestic fire V.3.4. tɹɪvɪt Ess, tɹɪvət MxL *[marked ir.r. MxL]*

2. n a GRIDIRON V.7.4(a). tɹɪvɪt Ess, tɹɪvət O*[with bars]*, t̞ɹɪvət O, t̞ɹɪvət W

trod *n* a PATH through a field IV.3.11. tɹɒd Cu, tɹɒd Cu We La, tɹɒd Du We Y*[old x1, made by trespasser x1, for people x1]*, tɹɔd We, tɹɔd Y L, tɹʊd Y*[for people]*

troddles *n* **sheep-troddles** SHEEP-DUNG II.1.7. ʃiːptɹɔdlz L

trod-marks *npl* the HOOF-MARKS of a horse IV.3.10. tʁɒdmaʁːks Nb

trolley *1. n* a WAGON I.9.2. tɹɒlɪ St K, t̞ɹɒɫɪ W Ha, tɹɔlɪ L

2. n a wagon with sides. tɹɒlɪ Lei

3. n a wagon with detachable sides. tɹɒlɪ Nth, tɹɒɫɪ Sx, t̞ɹɒɫɪ W

4. n a wagon without sides. tɹɒlɪ L Lei K, tɹɒɫɪ Mon Gl, *pl* tɹɒɫɪz Sr, t̞ɹɒli W, t̞ɹɒɫɪ Ha, tɹɔlɪ Ess, tɹʌɫɪ Mon Gl

5. n a FARMCART I.9.3. tɹʌlɪ Sa

6. n a BIER VIII.5.9(b). tʁɒlɪ Nb Du

troll-footed *adj* PIGEON-TOED VI.10.4. t̞ɹɔːɫfʊtɪd Co, t̞ɹɔːɫfʊtəd Co, t̞ɹɔːɫvʊtəd Co

troop* *n* a LITTER of piglets III.8.3. t̞ɹʊp So

trotlings *n* SHEEP-DUNG II.1.7. tɹɒtlɪnz Nb

trotter *n* the HOOF of a cow III.2.8(a). tɹɒtə Ess, t̞ɹɒtəᵗː So

trotters *n* **sheep-trotters** SHEEP-DUNG II.1.7. ʃəɪptɹɔtəz Y *[marked u.r. and queried error for -troddles NBM]*

trottles *1. n* SHEEP-DUNG II.1.7. tɹɒtlz Nt, tɹɔtlz L, tɹɔʔlz L; **sheep-trottles** ʃiːptɹɒtlz Nt, ʃiːptɹɔtlz L, ʃiːptɹɔʔlz L

2. npl RABBIT-DROPPINGS III.13.15. tɹɒtlz Nt, tɹɔtlz L, tɹɔʔlz L

troublesome *adj* *ON* HEAT, describing a cow III.1.6. t̞ɹʌbɫzʌm Co, t̞ɹʊbɫsəm Co

trough *1. n* *[Show a picture of an old-fashioned cow-house.] What do you call this?* I.3.6. tɹæʊt Wo, tɹɒf Y, tʰɹɒx Man, tɹɒf Cu La, tɹɒf We*[later than* **cow-tub***]* La Y Ch Db St Wo Mon Ess Brk Sr K Sx, tɹɒft Ch, tɹɔf Cu We, tʰɹɔːf Man, tʁɒf Nb, tɹɒf La Y Ch L, tɹɔːf Ess Brk Sr, *pl* tɹɔːvz Bk, t̞ɹɔːf Co, tɹɔːθ Ess, tɹʌʊf Bd, tɹɒʊf Hu, tɹʊf La Sa St L, θɹɛʊf La, tɹɛʊ Sx, tɹaʊ Du, tʁaʊ Nb, tɹaʊ Du, tɹɑʊ Nb, tʁɒʊ Du, tɹɒʊ Nf Sx, tɹɔː Sr, t̞ɹɔː D, tʁɒʊ Nb, tɹɒʊ Sx, tɹʌʊ Bk, t̞ɹɔː So Co D, t̞ɹoʊ So, *pl* tɹɒʊz Ha, tɹɒʊ Mon, tɹəʊ K; ⇒ **bing, bodge, boose, boosing, boosy, boother, boskin, box, cattle-trough, cooler, cow-crib, cow-crub, cow-kit, cow-trough, cow-tub, crib, feeding-pan, feeding-trough, fore-bay, gutter, lick-trough, manger, neat-tree, pat, piggin, provin-bucket, provin-trough, provin-tub, stock, tub, tumbler, water-stock, water-trough, yusen;** ⇒ also **tumbril**

2. n a trough for outside use. *pl* tɹɒʊz K

3. n a trough for pigs or sheep. tɹɔːf Ess

4. n a trough for pigs and hens. tɹʊf Wa

5. n a trough for drinking water only. tɹɔːf Ess

6. n What does a pig feed out of? III.9.3. Eng. ⇒ **pig-pat, pig('s)-stock,** *pig's-trough,* **pig-trough, troughs**

7. n a SOWING-BASKET II.3.6. tɹæu K

8. n a SALTING-TROUGH III.12.5. tɹɒf*[lead-lined]*, tɹɔːf Sf*[round]*, tɹɒʊf C

9. n the GUTTER of a roof V.1.6. tɹɛʊxf La, tɹɒf La, tɹɒʊ Db Nf, tɹɔːf Nf Sf Ess, tɹɔː Mon

10. n a container used as a PASTE-BOARD V.6.5. tɹæʊ K, tɹɒʊ Sx, tɹɔːft Sf, tɹɔːᵊf Sf Ess, t̞ɹɔː So, t̞ɹoʊ So

troughing *1. v-ing* FEEDING horses in the stable III.5.1. tɹʊfɪn St

2. n the GUTTER of a roof V.1.6. tɹɒfɪn La He Nf, tɹɒˑθɪn Nf, tɹɔːfɪn Nf, tɹɔːfɪn Hrt Ess, tɹɔːfɪn Nf Ess, tɹɔːfən Sf, tɹʌfɪn Sa He, tɹʌʊfɪn Nf, tɹʌʊɪn He, tɹɔːˑɪn Mon, tɹɒʊ-ɪn He, tɹʊfɪn Sa*[old x1]*

troughs *n* a TROUGH for pigs III.9.3. tɹɛʊz Sx

trough-top *n* the top of a container used as a PASTE-BOARD V.6.5. t̞ɹɔːtɒp So

trounce *1. v* to TRIM hedges IV.2.3. tɹɛʊnts Nf*[sides]*, tɹɛʊns Wa

2. vt to BEAT a boy on the buttocks VIII.8.10. t̞ɹæʊns Ha; **trounce his arse** t̞ɹæʊns ɪz æːs Ha

trouncing-hook *n* a HEDGING-BILL IV.2.5. tɹɛʊnsɪnʊk Wa

trousers *n What do you call this I'm wearing [indicate trousers]?* VI.14.13(a). Eng; **a trousers** ə tɹʌʊzəᵗz Mon. ⇒ *a trousers,* **breeches,** *long trousers,* **pants**

trout *v* to GROPE *FOR FISH* IV.9.10. *vbln* tɹᵊuʔn Man *[presumably referring to trout]*

trow-footed *adj* PIGEON-TOED VI.10.4. tɹɔːvʏtɪd Co, tɹɔːvʏtɪd Co

truck *1. n* a WAGON I.9.2. *pl* tɹʌks Hrt
2. n a FARMCART I.9.3. tɹʌk Sa
3. n a BIER VIII.5.9(b). tɹʊk Brk

truckles *1. n* SHEEP-DUNG II.1.7. tɹʌklz Gl, tɹʌkłz So, tɹʊkłz Gl; **sheep-truckles** ʃɪptɹʌkłz Gl
2. npl RABBIT-DROPPINGS III.13.15. tɹʌkłz Gl, tɹʌkłz So, tɹəklz Gl

truddles* *n* SHEEP-DUNG II.1.7. tɹʊdułz Sx

trudge *v* to WALK VIII.7.10. tɹɛdʒ Ess

trudgers *npl* TURNIPS II.4.1(b). tɹʊdʒəz Y

true *adj* **out of true** ASKEW, describing a picture that is not hanging straight IX.1.3. aːt ə tɹuː MxL

trug *1. n* a chock, sometimes specially shaped, placed behind and under a wheel to prevent a cart from going backwards on a hill, ⇐ PROP/CHOCK I.11.2. tɹʌg Ha, tɹʊg So
2. n a SOWING-BASKET II.3.6. tɹʊg K
3. n a BASKET III.5.4. tɹʌg Sx*[boat-shaped, handle in middle]*, tɹʊg Sx*[not defined]*
4. n a wooden, egg-shaped container for carrying horse-feed. tɹʌg K

truggan *n* a BRIDGE IV.1.2. tʰrugən Man

trug up* *vtphr* to chock a wheel to prevent a cart from going backwards on a hill, ⇐ PROP/CHOCK I.11.2. tɹʊg ... ʌp So

trump *vi* to BREAK *WIND* VI.13.16. -*ing* tɹʌmpɪn Ess, tɹʊmp Y*[polite x1]*, -*ing* tɹʊmpɪn Ch*[polite]* Brk

trumpet *vi* to BREAK *WIND* VI.13.16. tɹʌmpɪt Sr*[polite]*

trundle *n* a SALTING-TROUGH III.12.5. tɹʌndł Co D

trundlets *n* SHEEP-DUNG II.1.7. tɹʊndləts La

trunk *n* a NOSE VI.4.6. tɹʌŋk Sa

trunlets *npl* RABBIT-DROPPINGS III.13.15. tɹʊnləts La

trunlings *1. n* SHEEP-DUNG II.1.7. tɹʊnlɪnz Cu, tɹʊnlɪnz We La
*2. npl RABBIT-DROPPINGS III.13.15. tɹʊnlɪnz La Y, tɹʊnlənz Y, tɹənlɪnz We La

truss *1. n* a CUTTING of hay II.9.15. tɹʌs Sa O*[tied x1]* Nth Nf Sf Bk Hrt Ess MxL Brk Sr K Ha Sx, tɹʌs So W Do Ha, tɹʏs Nf, tɹʏst Nf, tʀʊs Nb, *pl* tʀʊsəz Du, tɹʊs La Y Ch Db St He Wo Wa Nt L Lei Nth Brk, tɹʊst La, tɹʊs Ha
2. n an amount of hay ready for carting or sale. tɹʌs Bk Bd Hrt Ess MxL, tɹʊs Y, tɹʊs Y

truss-stick *n* the STRETCHER between the traces of a cart-horse I.5.11. tɹʌstɪk Bd

trut *v* to CLEAR grass at the edges of a field by running the mower in the opposite direction from that for first cutting II.9.5. -*ing* tɹʊtn Nf *[queried EMBM]*

try *vt* to WHITTLE a stick I.7.19. -*ing* tɹɒɪ-ɪn St *[marked u.r. WMBM]*

try down *vtphr* to RENDER fat into lard III.12.9. tɹɑɪ ... dɛʊn Ess, tɹɔɪ (...) dɛʊn Sf Ess

try up *vtphr* to RENDER fat into lard III.12.9. tɹɑɪ ... ʌp Nf

t-shaped plough-beam end *n* *[Show a picture of a (horse-drawn) plough.]* *What do you call this?* I.8.5. ⇒ **adjuster, bar, beam, beam-end, beam-head, bolster-end, bridle, bridle-head, buck, butt-end, caption, cat's-head, clevis, clog-iron, cock, collar, cops, copsil, cosp, crook, cross-head, drail, draught, draught-beam, draw-bar,** *end of the beam* ⇒ **beam-end, gauge, hackle, hake(s), head, head-gear, head-rail, head-tow, head-wang, hitch, hitchings, lanes, loose-head, nicks, nose-gay, notch(es), notching-bar, plough-beam, plough-bridle, plough-buck, plough-cock, plough-head, pratt, rack, regulating bar, set-screw, shackle(s), skee-head, snotches, sway-head, swivel, tip, tow, wang, weigh-iron, wing** *[there is an overlap between rr. at I.8.4 evener and I.8.5]*

tub *1. n* a movable TROUGH in a cow-house I.3.6. tʊb We La*[wooden]*
2. n a round trough. *pl* tʌbz Ess *[marked u.r. EMBM]*
3. n a CORN-BIN I.7.4. *pl* tʌbz Mon
4. n a lidless corn-bin. tʊb So
5.1. vt to FEED cattle with cake or similar food in a tub or trough III.3.1. tʊb Y Du We
5.2. v to feed cattle. tʊb We
6. n a SALTING-TROUGH III.12.5. tʌb Nb Nf Hrt, tʊb Nb La L
7. n the BELLY VI.8.7. tʌb Nth
8. n a BARREL VI.13.12. tʌb Bk

tubs *npl* shearing-tables made of table-tops laid across logs, ⇐ SHEARING-TABLE III.7.8. tʊbz Db

tuck *n* a molar, ⇐ MOLARS VI.5.7. tʌk D

tuck-apron *n* a working APRON V.11.2(a). tʌkeɪpəᶬːɹɳ Sx

tuck in *imp* HELP YOURSELVES!, said to invite visitors to eat V.8.130. tʌk ɪn So

tuffet *1. n* a TUSSOCK of grass II.2.9. tʌfɪt W Sr K Ha Sx, tʌfɪt ə gɹæːs Ha, tʌfɪt ə gɹaːs W Ha, tʌfət Mon Gl O Ha Sx, tʊfət Mon Gl; **tuffet of grass** tʌfɪt ə gɹɑːs Sr
2. n a BEARD VI.2.7. tʌfɪt Sr

tuffock *n* a TUSSOCK of grass II.2.9. tʌfək Mon Brk, tʊfʊk Gl, tʊfək Ch Db St L

tuft *n* a TUSSOCK of grass II.2.9. tɪəf Cu, tɒf K, tɒft La, tʌf Sa Mon Sf Bd Ess So W K D Do, *pl* tʌfs MxL Co, tʌft Nb Sa Bk Ess MxL Brk Co D, tʏft Nb, tʊf Du La Y Man Ch Db Mon O, tʊf ə gɹɑːs K, tʊft Cu Du We La Y St Nt L Lei, *pl* tʊfts Nth, təːf Ch, *pl* təːfs Ess, təft Y, təːft Nf; **tuft of coarse grass** tʌf ə kʏːs gɹaːs D; **tuft of grass** tʌf ə gɹæːs So, tʌf ə gɹaːs W, *pl* tʌfs ə gɹaːs D, tʌft ə gɹaːs D *[[əː] form taken as **turf** WMBM]*

tug *1. n* a small WAGON with sides I.9.2. tʌg K
2. *vt* to PULL somebody's hair VI.2.8. *-ing* tʊgən Nb
3. *n* the TAG of a boot-lace VI.14.26. tʌg Sa, tʊg Y

tugging *vt-ing* PULLING his ear VI.4.4. tʌgɪn So

tugging at *vtphr-ing* PULLING his ear VI.4.4. tʌgɪn ət So

tug-hames *n* the HAMES of the harness of a cart-horse I.5.4. tʊgeːəmzəz D

tugs *1. n* the HAMES of the harness of a cart-horse I.5.4. tʌgz O*[for shaft-horse only]*, tʊgz K Do Ha
2. *npl* the HANDLES of a scythe II.9.8. tɒgz So, tʌgz Do, tʊgz So D Do

tumble *v* **tumble neck and heels, tumble the wild-cat** to turn HEAD OVER HEELS IX.1.10. **tumble neck and heels** *pt* tʊmlt nɛk ən hiːlz We; **tumble the wild-cat** tʊml ðə wɛɪlɪkat Nb

tumble over *1. viphr* to OVERTURN, referring to a cart I.11.5. *3prsg* tʊmlz aʊə Y, *3prsg* tʊmlz aʊəˡ Y, *-ed* tʌmbʊd ɒʊəˡ Sr, tʌmbl oʊvə Nf, tʊmbɫ oʊvəᶜ Wo, *-ed* tʊmbld ʊˈə St
2. *viphr* to FAINT VI.13.7. *pt* tʊməld aʊə Y

tumbler *1. n* a TROUGH in a cow-house I.3.6. tʊmblə L
2. *n* a FARMCART I.9.3. tʌmblə Nf, tʌmələ Nf, tʌmlə Nf, tʌmblɫ Nf

tumble-racks *npl* CART-LADDERS I.10.5. tʌmbɫɹæks Ess

tumbler-ladders *npl* CART-LADDERS I.10.5. *sg* tʌmləlæðə Nf

tumbril *1. n* a movable square feeding-trough used in a farmyard, ⇐ TROUGH I.3.6. tʊmbɹɪl Nt
2. *n* a FARMCART I.9.3. tʌmbɹɪl Nf, tʌmbɹəl Nf, tʌmbɹət Sf Ess, tʌmbɹɫ Nf, tʌmbɟɫ Nf, tʌmbɹʊ Ess, tʌmbɫ Ess, tʌmbət Sf Ess, tʌmbʊ Ess, tʊmbɹɪl Ch

tumbril-board *n* the TAILBOARD of a cart I.10.2. tʌmbɹətbɔːd Sf

tumbril-cart *n* a FARMCART I.9.3. tʌmbɹətkaːt Hu, tʌmbɹɪlkəᶜːʈ Sa, tʌmbɫkaːt Ess, tʊmbɹətkaːt Hu

tumbril-shed *n* a CART-SHED I.11.7. tʌmbɹɪlʃɛd Nf, tʌmbətʃɛd Sf

tumbril-stick *n* a rod keeping a cart-body fixed to the shafts, stopping it from tipping, ⇐ ROD/PIN I.10.3. tʌmbɫstɪk Ess

tummy *n* the BELLY VI.8.7. tɒmɪ K, tʏmɪ Nf, tʊmɪ L

tump *1. n* **tump of cow-shit** a CLOT OF COW-DUNG II.1.6. tʌmp ə kæʊʃɪt He
2. *n* a TUSSOCK of grass II.2.9. tʌmp W, tʊmp Wo
3. *n* a CLAMP in which potatoes are stored out of doors II.4.6. tʌmp Sa He Mon Gl, tʊmp Ch Sa Mon
4. *n* an ASH-MIDDEN V.1.14. tʌmp Sa, tʊmp Ch

tun *1. n* a CORN-BIN I.7.4. tʌn Nb, tʏn Nb, tʊn Nb
2. *n* a cattle-food container in a field. tʏn Nb
3. *n* a CHIMNEY V.1.3. toːn W

tun-dish *n* a FUNNEL V.9.3. tʌndɪʃ Sa He Mon Gl O So, tʊndɪʃ La Ch Db Sa St He Wo Wa Mon Gl Nt Lei, təndɪʃ St Gl

tune *vi* to SCREAM VIII.8.11. tʏːn D

tun-mill *n* a FUNNEL V.9.3. tʊnmɪl Cu

tunnel *n* a FUNNEL V.9.3. tʌnl Nf, tʌnəl Nf, tʌnɫ C Sf W Do Ha, tʌnət O Ess So W, tʌnʊ Ess, tʊnɪl Y Db Nt L, tʊnl Cu We La Y L, tʊnəl Y Nt L

tunniger *n* a FUNNEL V.9.3. tʌnɪgəᶜ So Do

tunning-dish *n* a FUNNEL V.9.3. tʊnɪndɪʃ Ch Sa Wa

tun-pail* *n* a FUNNEL V.9.3. tʌnpeːl Sa*[big]* He, tʊnpeːɫ He, tənpeɪᵊɫ Gl*[wooden]*, tənpæɪᵊɫ Gl*[wooden]*

tup *1.1. vt* to BUTT III.2.10. prppl tʊpɪn Y
1.2. *v* to butt. tʊp Db, prppl tʊpɪn Y
2. *n* a RAM III.6.7. tiːpʰ Nb, tɪp Cu We La, tɪʏp Nb, tjʏp Du, tɪʊp Du Y, tœp Gl, tʌp Sa He Mon Nth Hu C Nf Sf Bk Bd Hrt Ess MxL, tʰʏp Nf, tʊp Nb Cu Du We La Y Man Ch Db Sa St He Wo Wa Mon Gl O Nt L Lei R Nth C Bk
3. *n* a young RAM. tʊp K
4. *n* a WETHER III.6.8. tʌp Sr *[queried SBM on grounds of age and castration]*

tup-hog *n* a RAM III.6.7. tʊpɒg L

tup-lamb *n* a MALE LAMB III.6.2. tiːplam Nb, tɪplam Cu We La, tɪʏplam Nb, tjʏplam Du, tɪuplam Du Y, tɪəplæˑm Nb, tɪəplam Nb Cu Du We Y, tœplæːm Gl, tʌplæm Sa He Mon Hu Nf Sf Ess MxL, tʌplam Sa He Nth C Bk Bd Hrt, tʌplaːm He Mon, tʌpɫaːm Mon, tʊplæm He Wo Mon, tʊplæːm Wo Gl, tʊplam Nb Cu Du We La Y Ch Db St Wo Wa Gl O Nt L Lei R Nth C Bk, tʊplaːm Sa He, tʊplɑm Ch, tʊplɒm Gl, tʊplɔm Ch, təplæˑᵊm Man

turd *1. n* a CLOT OF COW-DUNG II.1.6. təˈd Nf, *pl* təːdz St K, *pl* təˡːdz St, təᶜːd̩ So K Sx; **cow's-turd** kɛʊz tʌd Nf Sf, kaʊztəᶜːd̩ So
2. *n* dried cow-dung. təᶜd̩ K
3. *n* **sheep's-turd, sheep-turd** SHEEP-DUNG II.1.7. **sheep's-turd** ʃiːpstəᶜːd̩ D, ʃɪpstəᶜːd̩ D; **sheep-turd** ʃiːptəːd L, ʃɪptəᶜːd̩ Wa*[old]*

turd(s) *n* RABBIT-DROPPINGS III.13.15.
npl: tɪuədz Y, tɒdz Y Lei R, tədz Y Db, tʌdz Nf Sf, tʌɾd̩z So, tədz Du Nf, təːdz Ch Lei Ess, təˡːdz Db, təᶜːd̩z̩ Wo Wa O Ess Co Sx
n-mass: təᶜːd̩ So

turds *n* SHEEP-DUNG II.1.7. tɔdz Y; **lamb-turds** ɫamtəᶜːd̩z̩ W; **lamb's-turds** ɫamztəᶜːd̩z̩ W; **sheep-turds** ʃiːptɪədz Y, ʃɛɪptɪuədz Y, ʃiːptɒdz Y, ʃiːptɒɹdz Y, ʃiːptɔdz Y, ʃiːptʌdz Nf, ʃɪptʌdz Hrt, ʃiːptədz Y L, ʃiːptəːdz Ch St, ʃɪptəːdz St Hrt, ʃɛɪptəːdz Db, ʃiːptəˡdẕ O*['rough dialect']* K, ʃiːptəˡːdẕ Wa Do Ha, ʃɪptəˡːdẕ Wa; **sheep's turds** ʃiːps tɔdz L, ʃɪps tʌdz Sf, ʃips tədz Nf, ʃiːps təːdz MxL, ʃiːpstəˡːdẕ Co D Do

turd-stool *n* a CLOT OF COW-DUNG II.1.6. təˡːdˌstuˑəl Gl

turf *1. n* PASTURE on a hillside II.1.3. təˡːf Wa
2. vi to CUT peat IV.4.4. *-ing* təˡːfɪn Y

turf-cutting *vbln* cutting peat, ⇐ to CUT peat IV.4.4. tɛfkʌʔɪn Nf

turf-dole *n* a place for cutting PEAT, held by a cottager from a landlord IV.4.3. təˡːfdeəl La

turf(s) *n* PEAT IV.4.3.
no -s: tɛf Nf, taːf Nf, tɒɹf Y*[top layer x1]*, tɔːf Man, tɔᴮːf Du, tɔːɹf La, təˡːf La*[when dried x1]* Y, tɔˡːɹf La, tɜːɹf Man, təˡːf La, təˡːɹf La, təf Y, təɹf Y L C, təˡf L, təɾf Nf*[shaped block x1]*, təːf Ch Db L Hu Nf, təˑɹf Nth Hu, təːɹf C, təˡːf L, təˡːf Sa Wo So Co D
-s: tʊfs Lei, təˡːfs Co

turkey-toed *adj* PIGEON-TOED VI.10.4. təːkɪtʊːd Ch

turmets* *npl* TURNIPS II.4.1(b). tɒɹməts La, tɔˡːɹmʊts La, tɔᴮːməts Nb Du, tɔˡːməts La, tʌməts Ess, təɹmɪts Cu, təːmɪts Ch Db St Wa Nth, təˡːmɪts La Ch, *sg* təˡːmɪt Db, təˡːmɪts Sa Wo D Ha, təˡːmʌts Bd So W Co D Do, təːmʊts Wa, təˡːmʊts Gl Sx, *sg* təˡːmʊt O, təːməts Cu Wa, təˡːməts La Ch O, təˡːməts Sa Bk So Ha Sx

turn *1. vt When the grass has been mown for haymaking, what do you do next?* II.9.11(b). Eng exc. MxL. ⇒ **hack, hackle, hack over, *hay-turn*, rake over, swarth-turn, swath-turn, ted, turn about, turn over**
2. vt to TED hay II.9.11(a). tɔᴮːn Nb
3.1. vt to PITCH sheaves II.6.10. təːn Gl Ess, *3prsg* təːnz Db, təˡːn̩ W, *3prsg* təˡːn̩ẕ So D Ha, *-ing* təˡːn̩ɪn So D, *-ing* təˡːn̩ən D
3.2. v to pitch. *3prsg* təɹnz He, təːn Ch Db, *3prsg* təːnz Y
4. vt to DIG in the garden with a spade I.7.8. təˡːn̩ So Co D
5. v to WEAN a calf III.1.4. təˡːn̩ D
6. vi to CHIP, referring to an egg that is about to hatch IV.6.10. təˡːn̩ Wo
7. imp **turn off** the command TURN LEFT!, given to plough-horses II.3.5(a). təːn ɔːf Hrt
8. imp **turn fromward, turn toward** the command TURN RIGHT!, given to plough-horses II.3.5(b). **turn fromward** təˡːɾn̩ vɹæməˡɾd̩ Brk; **turn toward** təːn tɔːd Hrt
9.1. vt to CURDLE milk V.5.7. tɛən Lei, tœːn Mon, tɒn Y, tɒn Y L, tɔᴮːn Nb, tɔˡːn La, tʌn Ess, tɜˡːn La, tən Y, təːn Y Ch Db St Wa Bk Bd, *3prsg* təːnz Ess, təˡːn Ch K, təˡːn̩ Sa He Mon Gl Nth So W Co D Do Ha Sx, tɛˑn Nf; **help turn it** ɛɬp təˡːn̩ ɪt W

9.2. v to curdle. təːn Du K, təˡːn Ch, təˡːn̩ He K D, *3prsg* təˡːn̩ẕ Sr
10. vi to CURDLE, referring to milk V.5.9. tɔəˡn La, tʌn Ess, təːn C Nf MxL K, *-s* təːnz Ess, təːɹn St, təˡːn Ch*[old]* K, *3prsg* təˡːn̩ẕ Ha, təˡːn̩ Sa Mon So Sr Co; **turn into curd** *-s* tʌnz ɪntə kʌdz Ess
11. vi to SPOIL, referring to meat or fish V.7.10. taːn Nf, tən Y, təːn Y, təˡːn̩ Mon So

turn about *vtphr* to TURN hay II.9.11(b). təˡːn̩ ... əbæɤt D

turn bigger *viphr* to WAX, referring to the moon VII.6.5(a). *-ing* tɔᴮnən bɪgə Nb

turn-burrel* *n* the MOULD-BOARD of a horse-drawn plough I.8.8. təˡn̩bəɾəl Ha

turned *1. v-ed* HAS NOT HELD, referring to a cow that has not conceived III.1.7. tœːnd Mon Gl, təɹnd He, təːnd Wa Nth Bk Bd, təˡːnd Brk Sr, təˡːn̩t He Bk, təˡːn̩d Sa He Wa Wo Mon Gl O Nth Bk So W Sr D Do Ha Sx; **a-turned again** ətəˡːn̩d̩ əgen Ha; **turned again** təˡːn̩d̩ əgɪən So, ʃiːz təˡːn̩d̩ əgeːn Co, əˡːẕ təˡːn̩d̩ əgeːən Co, təˡːn̩d̩ əgen Wo
2. vt-ed sprained, ⇐ to SPRAIN an ankle VI.10.8. təˡːn̩d̩ Co Do, *prppl* təˡːn̩ɪn Ha

turned over *vtphr-ed* sprained, ⇐ to SPRAIN an ankle VI.10.8. təˡːn̩d̩ ... ɔːvəˡ D Do, təˡːn̩d̩ ... ɔːvəˡː So Do

turnel *1. n* a ROPE-TWISTER II.7.8. tʊnɪl Db, tʊnəɬ Lei, tənəl Db
2. n a BENCH on which slaughtered pigs are dressed III.12.1. təːnɪl Ch St, təːnəɬ Ch
3. n a SALTING-TROUGH III.12.5. təːnɪl Ch*[wooden x1]* St*[leaden]*, təːnəɬ Ch*[wooden]*

turner *1. n* the MOULD-BOARD of a horse-drawn plough I.8.8. təːnə Hu Bd, təˑɹnə Hu, təˡːnə Bd
2. n a ROPE-TWISTER II.7.8. tɪˑənə L, tɔˡːnəɹ La

turner-up *n* a ROPE-TWISTER II.7.8. tɛˑnəɹʌp Nf

turn-furrow *1. n* the SHARE of a horse-drawn plough I.8.7. təˡːnvɒɹɒʊ Brk
2. n the MOULD-BOARD of a horse-drawn plough I.8.8. taːnfʌɹə MxL, tʌnfʌɹə MxL, təɾn̩fəɾə O, təːnfʌɹə Bk Sr, təˡːnfʌɹɔʊ Brk, təˡːn̩fɔɹə O, təˡːn̩fɒɾə O, təˡːn̩fʌɾə O, təˡːn̩vʌɾə So W Ha*[iron]*, təˡːn̩fʊɹə Gl, təˡːɾn̩vʊɹəˡ Brk, təˡːn̩vəɾɒʊ So, təˡːn̩vəɹə Gl, təˡːn̩vəɾə Gl So W, təˡːɾn̩fəɹəˡ Ha, təˡːn̩fɒˡː Sr, təˡːn̩vuːɾ D, təˡːn̩vəˡː Do, təˡːɾn̩vɔˡːɾ Sx, təˡːn̩fəˡːɾ Sx, təˡːɾn̩fəˡːɾ Sr, təˡn̩bəɾəl Ha

turnips *npl What root-crops do you grow?* II.4.1(b). tɪənəps L, tɛənəps Y L, tœːnɪps Mon Gl, taːnəps Sf Ess, tɒnɪps Y Db, tɒɹnɪps Y, tɒnəps eY, tɒɹnəps Y, tɔnɪps Y, tɔˡːnɪps Y, tɔnəps Y Nt

L Ess, tɔᵍːnəps Nb Du, tɔˑ⅃ːnəps La, tʌnɪps Nf Ess, tʌnəps C Sf Hrt Ess, toənəps Nb, tʊɹnɪps Y, tʊrnʊps Cu, tʊnəps Du, tʊrnəps Cu, tʊɹnəps nwY, tʊənəps Du, tənɪps Db Lei R Nf, *sg* tənɪp Y, təːnɪps Y Ch Db St Wa Lei Nf Hrt Ess, təˑ⅃ːnɪps Y Ch St He Sr, təᵗːɳɪps Sa He Wo Mon Gl O Nf Bk Ess Sr K Sx, *sg* təᵗːɳɪp D, *no -s* təᵗːɳɪp W, tjəᵗːɳɪps He, təːnʌps Bd Hrt, təᵗːɳʌps O So Co D Do Ha, təːnʊps Nth, təˑ⅃ːnʊps La Brk, təᵗːɳʊps Wa Gl Sr, tˡəᵗːɳʊps Wo, tənəps Cu Du We Y L Lei R Nth, *sg* təˑ⅃nəp Y, təːnəps Cu Du Y Man St Wa Nt Lei Nth Hu Bk Bd Hrt Ess MxL, *no -s* təːnəp Nf K, təˑ⅃ːnəps We L Nth Hu C Sf Brk K, *sg* tɜˑ⅃ːɹnəp La, təᵗːɳəps Sa He Mon Gl O Bk So W Brk Sr K Co Ha Sx, *no -s* təᵗːmʌp W. ⇒ **bagies, chonnocks, snedgers, trudgers, white turnips** *[there are notes in N/EM/SBM (though not in WMBM) concerning the possible collective-noun import of 'singular' forms. In N/WMBM all non-s forms are given as singular; in EM/SBM the distinction is made between singular forms and those without -s which are 'probably' collectives. Apparently singular forms, i.e. those lacking final -s, are sometimes used in the dialects to refer to turnips collectively]*

turn left! *imp When you want your (plough-)horses to move this way [indicate left], what do you say?* (*before April 1954: When you want your horses to go left....*) II.3.5(a). *back* come *here*, come *again*, come *back*, come *by the way*, come *half* ⇒ come *hauve*, come *here*, come *here back*, come *here hauve*, come *here hauve a bit*, come *here hey*, come *here hoy*, come *here round*, come *here way*, come *here wee*, come *here wo* ⇒ come *here woa*, come *here woa*, come *here woot*, come *hither*, come-*hither ho*, come-*hither round*, come-*hither wee*, come *hither weet*, come *hither whup*, come *hither woy*, come-*hither-wut*, come *huggin*, come *nearer*, come *on*, come *over there*, come *ree*, come *round*, come *round here*, come *to*, come *to us*, come *toward*, come *way*, come *wo* ⇒ come *woa*, come *woa*, come *ye here*, come *ye hither*, coop, coop *harley*, coop *here*, coop *here harley*, coop *here holt*, coop *here wee*, coop *toward*, coop *wee*, gay, gee, gee *back*, gee *up*, get-hither *there*, go *off*, hait, hait *up*, hauve, hauve *again*, hauve *back*, hauve *come again*, hauve *come here*, hauve *left*, hauve *up a bit*, hauve *way*, hauve *woot*, haw *up*, heck, heck *in*, hie, hie *way*, hie *wee*, hike, hither, hop *in*, lither *wee*, nigh, thow *wee*, tick, turn *off*, walk *way*, walve, way, way *come here*, whup *back*, whup *maller*, wo ⇒ woa, woa, woa *back*, wo *back* ⇒ woa *back*, woa come *back*, wo *come back* ⇒ woa come *back*, woa come *heller*, wo *come heller* ⇒ woa come *heller*, woa come *here*, wo *come here* ⇒ woa come *here*, woaf come *here*, woa come *hither*, wo *come hither* ⇒ woa come *hither*, woa hait, wo *hait* ⇒ woa hait, woa *hie*, woa *ree*, wo *ree* ⇒ woa *ree*, wo *up back* ⇒ whup *back*

turn over *1. vtphr* to DIG in the garden with a spade I.7.8. tɑˑn ... ouvə Nf, tʌn ... ouvə Nf, tən ... ouvə Nf, *prppl* təːnɪn ... ɔːvə Ch, təᵗːɳ ... ɔːvəᵗː So D, təᵗːɳ ... oːvəᵗː Co

2. vtphr to TURN hay II.9.11(b). tɒn aʊə Y, tɒn ɒvə Y, təᵗːɳ ... oːvəᵗː He, təᵗːɳ ... oːvəᵗː Co Do, tɑˑn ... ouvə Nf, təːn ... ouvə St, tʌn ... oˑuvə Nf, teˑn ... ouvə Nf, təɽn ... ouvəᵗ Nf

3.1. viphr to OVERTURN, referring to a cart I.11.5. tɒn ɒvə Nt, -*ed* təᵗːnd̩ ɒuvəᵗ Sr Sx, -*ed* tənd ɒuə Y, -*ed* təᵗːnd̩ ɔːvəᵗː So D, -*ed* təɹnd ɔuvə Hu, təᵗːɳ ɔuvəᵗ O, tʌn ʌuvə Ess, -*ed* tənd ʌuvə Sf, *3prsg* təːnz ʌuvə Sr Ess, təᵗːnd̩ ʌuvə Ess, -*ed* təːnd oˑə Y, tɑːn ouvə Nf, tʌn ouvə Sf, *3ptsg* tʌˑn ouvə Nf, təːn ouvə Bd, -*ed* təːnd ouvə St, -*ed* teˑnd ouvə Nf, təᵗːɳ ouvəᵗ Wo

3.2. vtphr to overturn. -*ed* tənd ... ɔvə L, təːn ... ʊvə Lei

turnpike-road-sailors *npl* GIPSIES VIII.4.12. tˡəᵗːɳpɪkɹoːdsaɪləᵗz Wo

turnpike-sailors *npl* GIPSIES VIII.4.12. tˡəᵗːɳpəɪksaɪləᵗz Wo

turn-reest-plough *n* a one-way PLOUGH with a movable mould-board I.8.1. təᵗːɽɳɹɪstpleʊ Sx

turnrice *n* a PLOUGH I.8.1. təᵗːɳɽəɪs Sx

turn right! *imp When you want your (plough-)horses to move this way [indicate right], what do you say?* (*before April 1954: When you want your horses to go right....*) II.3.5(b). **turn right** tən ˈɒɪt R. ⇒ come *here*, come *here back*, come *hither*, come-*hither-whup*, come *hither woy*, come *out*, gee, gee *about*, gee *again*, gee *back*, gee *back gee again*, gee *gee again*, gee *ho*, gee *hoot*, gee *ho round*, gee *off*, gee *over*, gee *up*, gee *whup*, gee *woa gee*, gee *wo gee* ⇒ gee *woa gee*, gee *woot*, gee *wo up* ⇒ gee *whup*, gee *wug*, get *hither*, get *off back*, get *over*, go *fromward*, go *hither*, go *off*, go *over*, hait, hait *again*, hait *up*, har, hauve, hauve *right*, hauve *way*, hauve *wee*, hauve *woa*, *heet* ⇒ hait, hike, ho, hold *off*, hoot, hoot *off*, hop, hop *back*, hop *over*, jig, jig *again*, jiggin, jiggin *off*, right, see, see *back*, see *off*, see *off a bit*, turn *fromward*, turn *toward*, walve, weesh, whup *back gee*, why, wo ⇒ woa, woa, woa *back*, wo *back* ⇒ woa *back*, woa gee, wo *gee* ⇒ woa *gee*, woa *hait*, wo *hait* ⇒ woa hait, woosh, woot, wootch, woot *gee*, woot *off*, woa *up*, wo *up* ⇒ woa *up*, wub *off*, wug, wug *around*, wug *back*, wugd, wugd *off*, wug *off*, wug *out*, wug *round*, wug *there*, wurt, wurt *off*; ⇒ also **fromward**

turns after *vphr-3prsg* he RESEMBLES VIII.1.9. də təᵗːɳ eːdəᵗː Do, təᵗːɳz̩ æftəᵗːɽ (+V) Co, *inf* təᵗːɳ æːftəᵗː Co, *pt* təᵗːnd̩ æːftəᵗː Co, də təᵗːɳ æːftəᵗː Co, təᵗːɳz̩ æːdəᵗːɽ (+V) Ha, təᵗːɳ aːftəˡ: Co, təˡːŋz̩ aˡːdəˡ: So, təˡːŋz̩ aˡːdəˡːɾ (+V) Co

turns out *viphr-3prsg* school FINISHES VIII.6.2(b). tɔnz aːt La, təˡːŋz̩ ɒut W

turn-toed *1. adj* PIGEON-TOED VI.10.4. təˡːɾn̩tɒud Sr

2. adj SPLAY-FOOTED VI.10.5. təˡːŋtoːd D

turn up *vtphr* to DIG in the garden with a spade I.7.8. təˡːŋ (...) ʌp So Co D

turtle-doves *npl* DOVES IV.7.4. taːʔldɤvz Nf, *sg* taːʔldɤv Nf, tʌtɫdʌvz Sf, təʔldʌvz Nf, təɹtldʌvz He, *sg* təᴶtldʊv L, təːʔldʌvz Ess, təːʔldɤvz Nf, təːtldʊvz L

turves *n* PEAT IV.4.3. təɹvz Y, təˡːvz So, təˡːbz Sr

tush *n* a TOOTH VI.5.6(b). tʌʃ Ess, tʊʃ St

tusher* *n* a TOOTH VI.5.6(b). tʊʃə Y

tushers* *npl* TEETH VI.5.6(a). tʊʃəz Y

tushes *npl* TEETH VI.5.6(a). tʌʃiz Ess*[older than teeth]*, tʊʃiz St*[children's word x1]*, tʊʃəz St

tushy-megs *npl* TEETH VI.5.6(a). tʊʃimɛgz St

tussock *1. n What do you call a patch [tuft] of coarse grass in a field?* II.2.9. tʌsɪk Hu C Ess, tʌsk Sf, tʌsək Sa He O Hrt Ess Sr K, *pl* tʌsəks Sf Bk Brk, tʌsəˡk He, tʊsɪk L, tʊsʊk Wo Wa Gl, tʊsək La Db Sa St He Wo Wa Gl Nt L Lei, tʊsəˡk He, tʊzzəkʰ Db, təsək O. ⇒ **bennet, bob-grass, bob of grass, bog, buffet, bull-face, bull-forehead, bull-front, bull-lump, bull-nose, bull-pate, bull-poll, bull-scalp, bull-snout, bull-topping, cleaver, clump, cluster, cow-grass, feg, fog, hassock, hillock, hut, lump, mock, mock** *of grass,* **mop, mop** *of grass,* **mould of grass,** *old* **fog, patch,** *piece of* **rough grass, rank place, ritch, roughet, rough grass, rough patch, rowet, ruck, share-grass, toar, tuffet,** *tuffet of grass,* **tuffock, tuft, tuft** *of coarse grass,* **tuft** *of grass,* **tump,** *turf* ⇒ **tuft**

2. n the FORELOCK of a horse III.4.8. tʊsʊk Wo

twang-toed *adj* PIGEON-TOED VI.10.4. twaŋtʊəd Y

twangy *adj* RANCID, describing bacon V.7.9. twæːŋi Hrt

twank *vt* to BEAT a boy on the buttocks VIII.8.10. twaŋk Nb Y*[old]*

twat *n* the VULVA of a cow III.2.3. twat Y Nth

tweaks *vt-3prsg* pulls, ⇐ PULLING his ear VI.4.4. twɪks Sr

tweedle *n* a SEESAW VIII.7.2. twiːdl Db St

tween *prep* BETWEEN IX.2.11. twiːn Nb La Y He Wa Gl O L Nth Hu C Nf Ess MxL So W Brk Sr K Co D Ha Sx, twɪn Nb Y Nf Ess, twɛɪn Co D, twəɪn Y

tween-stick *n* the STRETCHER between the traces of a cart-horse I.5.11. twiːnstɪk Sx

tweezers *n* a ROPE-TWISTER II.7.8. twɪzəˡz̩ Wo

tweezle *n* a SEESAW VIII.7.2. twiːzl St

twelvemonth(s) *1. n* A YEAR VII.3.4. *no -s:* twɛlvmʌnθ K, twɛlmʌnθ Nf, twɛɫmʌn Sx,

twɛʊmʌnθ Ess, twɛlv mʊnθ La Y, twɛlˈmn̩θ Nf, twɛlmənθ Nf

-s: twɛlv mʌnθs Nf, twɛlv mʊnθs Y Ch, twɛl mʊnθs Y

2. n **a twelvemonth(s)** a year.

no -s: ə twɛʊmɒnθ K, ə twɛʊmɒn K, ə twɛlvmʌnθ Nf K Ha, ə twɛɫvmʌnθ Ess So Brk Sr, ə twɛlmʌnθ Bk W Brk, ə twɛʊvmʌnθ Sx, ə twɛʊmʌnθ Sx, ə twɛlvmʊnθ Nb Y, ə twɛlmʊnθ La, ə twɛlvmʊnθ K

-s: ə twɛlvmʊnθs Y

twicks *n* COUCH-GRASS II.2.3. twɪks Nf

twiddler *n* a ROPE-TWISTER II.7.8. twɪdɫə Ess

twig *v* to TRIM hedges of one year's growth IV.2.3. twɪg Nt

twig-brush *n* a BESOM I.3.15. twɪgbɹʊʃ Wa

twigs *1. n* small branches of a tree, ⇐ BRANCH IV.12.3. twɪgz Sr

2. n KINDLING-*WOOD* V.4.2. twɪgz Y So

twill-toed *adj* PIGEON-TOED VI.10.4. twɪltʊəd L

twilly-toed *adj* PIGEON-TOED VI.10.4. twɪlitoːd Nt, twɪlɪtʊəd Y, twɪlɪtᵁuːd Db

twine *1. n [Show a picture of some stacks. What do you call this (i.e. thatch)?] What do you fasten it down with? [Material tied over thatch.]* II.7.7(b1). twɛɪn Du, twæɪn Man, twaɪn La Y Ch, twɑɪn La Ch Nt L Bd, twɔɪn Gl Nf Bk Ess Brk, twʌɪn Nf Brk Sr, twəɪn W Brk. ⇒ **band, billy-band, bind, binder-band, binder-string, binder-twine, binding-cord, binding-twine, cocoa-string, coconut-band, coconut-string, cord, corn-yarn, hop-string, manilla, pitch-band, ropekin, spunyarn, stack-twine, string, tar-band, tar-cord, tar-line, tar-marl, tar-marl-band, tar-marl-string, tarred band, tarred-line, tarred twine, tarry-band, tar-string, tar-twine, thack-cord, thacking-band,** *thacking-cord* ⇒ **thatching-cord, thatching-string, thatch-band, thatch-cord, thatching-cord, thatching-line, thatching-string, theaking-band,** *thick rough* **string, towt, walching, wattles** *[separation of* **twine** *and* **ropes** *terms is problematical: see also* **ropes***]*

2. n STRING used to tie up a grain-sack I.7.3. twiːn Do, twɛɪn Nb Du, twaɪn Cu Sa, twɒɪn St So, twɔɪn O Ess Brk, twʌɪn Nf Brk, twəɪn Mon

3. vt to WRING the neck of a chicken when killing it IV.6.20. twaɪn Cu*[old]* We

twined *vt-ed* sprained, ⇐ to SPRAIN an ankle VI.10.8. twaɪnt We *[marked u.r. NBM as seeming to refer to 'going over on the ankle']*

twined over *vtphr-ed* sprained, ⇐ to SPRAIN an ankle VI.10.8. twaɪnd aʊə Y *[see note at* **twined***]*

twiner *n* a ROPE-TWISTER II.7.8. twɛɪnɔ^ʁ Nb, twɛɪnə^ʁ Du, twaɪnə Cu Du We, twaɪnəɹ Y, twaɪndə Du, twɑɪnə Db, twɑɪndə Y

twinges *npl* EARWIGS IV.8.11. twɪndʒəz Y

twining on *vphr-ing* SHRIEKING, describing the shrill noise made by a baby VI.5.15. twaɪnən ɒn Du

twinny-toed *adj* PIGEON-TOED VI.10.4. twɪnɪtoːd Db

twinter 1. *n* a HEIFER approximately 2 years old III.1.5. twɪntəɹ La
2. *n* a sheep from its first to its second shearing, ⇐ GIMMER III.6.5. twɪntə Cu We

twintered *adj* wrinkled, describing the skin of very old people, ⇐ WRINKLED VI.11.2. twɪntə·ɹt La

twist 1. *vt* to WRING the neck of a chicken when killing it IV.6.20. twɪst Nb Cu Du Y St Wo So W Brk Co D, twɪs So Brk Co D
2. *vt* to pull, ⇐ PULLING his ear VI.4.4. twɪst Sr
3. *vt* to SPRAIN an ankle VI.10.8. twɪst So W Co D, twɪs So, -*ed* twɪstɪd Y L Sr Ha *[see note at **twined** for NBM]*
4. *vi* to WARP, referring to wood IX.2.9. twɪst Db He MxL, *3prsg* twɪsɪs Gl

twisted 1. *adj* TANGLED, describing hair VI.2.5. twɪstɪd So
2. *adj* ASKEW, describing a picture that is not hanging straight IX.1.3. twɪstɪd Db; **on a twist** ɒn ə twɪst Y

twister(s) *n* a ROPE-TWISTER II.7.8.
no -s: twɪstə Y Man Ch Db Wa Gl Nt L Nth Hu Bd Hrt Ess MxL, twɪstəɹ La He, twɪstə^ɪ O Nf Brk, twɪstə^ʕ Wa*[hay-bands, not straw-bands x1]* Gl O Bk*[hay-bonds x1]*, twɪstə^ʕː So W D
-s: twɪstə^ɪz Brk*[sg]*, twɪstə^ʕz̩ O*[sg]*, twɪstə^ʕːz̩ W; **pair of twisters** pɛəɹ ə twɪstəz Wa, pɛ^ʕːɾ ə twɪstə^ʕːz̩ W

twisting *v-ing* SHRIEKING, describing the shrill noise made by a baby VI.5.15. twɪstn Du*[old]*

twisting-wire *n* a ROPE-TWISTER II.7.8. twɪstɪnwaɪə Y

twist round *vtphr* to WRING the neck of a chicken when killing it IV.6.20. twɪst ... ɹuːnd Y

twitch 1. *n* a WHIP used for driving horses I.5.12. twɪtʃ Sr
2. *n* COUCH-GRASS II.2.3. twɪtʃ Cu We La Y Db St O Nt L Lei R Nth Hu C Nf Sf Bd Hrt Ess W K, twiːtʃ Sf Hrt

twitch-bells *npl* EARWIGS IV.8.11. twɪtʃbɛlz Du We Y, *sg* twɪtʃbɛl Nb Cu, *sg* twɪdʒbɛl Nb, *sg* twʊtʃbɛl Du

twitch-grass 1. *n* COUCH-GRASS II.2.3. twɪtʃgɹɛs Y L, twɪtʃgɹas Ch L, twɪtʃgɹɑs Nth, twɪtʃgɹɑːs So, twɪtʃgɹɑ·s Nf
2. *n* **lump of twitch-grass** a TUSSOCK of grass II.2.9. lʌmp ə twɪtʃgɹɑ·s Nf *[probably a type of grass]*

twitchy-bells *npl* EARWIGS IV.8.11. *sg* twɪtʃɪbɛl Nb, *sg* twʊtʃɪbɛl Nb

twitten *n* a LANE IV.3.13. twɪʔn Sx

twitterum *n* the VULVA of a cow III.2.3. twɪtəɹəm L

twixt *prep* BETWEEN IX.2.11. twɪkst St Gl*[old]* C Nf Ess Brk*[old]*, twɪks Bd

twizzler *n* a ROPE-TWISTER II.7.8. twɪzlə Nf Ess

two *pron* **two or three** A FEW VII.8.21. twɪ· ə θɹəɪ Y, tʊ ə θɹɪ Y, tuː ə θɹiː Cu Nt

two-grain *n* a HAY-FORK I.7.11. tuːgɹaɪn W

two-grained-fork *n* a HAY-FORK I.7.11. tuːgɹeɪnd fa^ʕɾk Brk, tuːgɹeəndfɔːk Y

two-grain-fork *n* a HAY-FORK I.7.11. tuːgɹaɪnfa^ʕk W

two-grain-prong *n* a HAY-FORK I.7.11. tuːgɹeːnpɾɒŋ Ha, tuːgɹɛɪnpɾɒŋ W, tuːgɹaɪnpɾɒŋ W Do

two-horse baulk *n* the main swingle-tree or EVENER of the harness of a plough pulled by two horses I.8.4. tuː-ɔs bɔːk Nt L

two-horse bit *n* the main swingle-tree or EVENER of the harness of a plough pulled by two horses I.8.4. tuː-ɒs bɪt Ess, tuːhɔːs bɪt Ess

two-horse horse-tree *n* the main swingle-tree or EVENER of the harness of a plough pulled by two horses I.8.4. t^ɪuː-ɑːs ɑstɹɪi C

two-horse tree *n* the main swingle-tree or EVENER of the harness of a plough pulled by two horses I.8.4. tuː-ɒs tɹɪi L

two-horse weigh-tree *n* the main swingle-tree or EVENER of the harness of a plough pulled by two horses I.8.4. tɪʊ-ɔːs wæɪʔtɹɪ Ess

two-horse whipple-tree *n* the main swingle-tree or EVENER of the harness of a plough pulled by two horses I.8.4. tɹuː-ɒs wɪpʔtɹɪ^əi Sf, tuːhɔːs wɪpɫɹɪi Ess, tuː-ɔːs wɪpɫɹɪ Ess

two-or-three *pron* a **two-or-three** A FEW VII.8.21. ə tʊəθɹɪi La Y, ə tʊəθɹɪi Y, ə tuːəθɹɪi La

two or three *adj* a **two or three**, **two or three** A FEW VII.1.19. **a two or three** ə tʊ ə θɹɪ Y L, ə tʊə ə θɹɪ Y, ə tuː ə θɹɪ Ch Wo*[old]*; **two or three** tɹuː ə θɹɪ Ess, twiː ə θɹɛɪ Cu, tu ə^ʕ θɹɪ K, tʊ ɾ θɹɪːɪ Sx, tʊ ə θɹɪ Y K, tʊ ə fɹɪ Sr, tʊ ə θɹɪ We La Y, tuː ə θɹɪ Y Wa O Hu Bd K, tuː ə θɹɪ La

two-quart-can *n* a SCOOP used to take water out of a boiler V.9.9. tʏːkwæ^ɹːtkan La, tʏːkwɜːɹtkan La

two-shear *n* a sheep from its first to its second shearing, ⇐ GIMMER III.6.5. tuːʃɪə Y, tuʃɪə^ɪ Man, tuːʃ^ɪiə^ɪ Man, tuːʃɪəʕ Sx, tuːʃəʕː O, tɐʃɪ Nf *[taken by WMBM Edd to refer to sheep after second shearing, and hence 'perhaps' u.r.]*

two-shear ewe *n* a GIMMER III.6.5. tuːʃɪ·ə juː Ess

two-shear gimmer *n* a GIMMER III.6.5. tuːʃɪˈə gɪmɹ L

two-spean-prong *n* a HAY-FORK with a short shaft I.7.11. tuspɹiːnpɹɒŋ Sx

two-spean-spud *n* a fork with short prongs and a short shaft, used for dock-lifting, ⇐ HAY-FORK I.7.11. tuːspɹiːnspʌd Sx

two-sprong-peek* *n* a HAY-FORK I.7.11. tuːspɾɒŋpiːk So

two-teeth *1. n* a sheep before its first shearing, ⇐ EWE-HOG III.6.4. tɤːdiːθ D *[taken in SBM to refer to sheep after first shearing, ⇒ gimmer III.6.5]*

2. n a sheep from its first to its second shearing, ⇐ GIMMER III.6.5. tɤːtiːθ So, *pl* tɤːtiːθs D, *pl* tuːtiːθs W

two-teeth ewe *n* a GIMMER III.6.5. tɤːtiːθ jɔː D, tuːtiːθ juː Ha

two–three *1. adj* a two–three, two–three A FEW VII.1.19. **a two–three** ə tɪʊθɹɪ St, ə tɛʊθɹɪ Ch Db St, ə tʌθɹɪ Sa, ə tʊθɹɪ La Y Ch Sa, ə tuːθɹɪ Ch Sa St; **two–three** tˡuːθɹɪ Db, tɛʊθɹɪ Db St, twɛɪθɹɛɪ Y, toːθɹɪ Db, tʊθɹɪ Sa St Wa, tuːθɹiː Mon, tuːθɹɪ Y Ch Sa St Wo

2. pron A FEW VII.8.21. **a two–three** ə tɪʊθɹɪ St, ə tɛʊθɹɪ St, ə toːθɹɪ Db, ə tʊθɹɪ Y Sa, ə tuːθɹiː St*[old x1]*, ə tuːθɹɪ Ch Db, ə tuːθɹɛɪ St; **two-three** tɛʊθɹɪ Db

two-tined fork *1. n* a MUCK-FORK I.3.13. tʊuːtɔɪnd fɔːk Ess

2. n a HAY-FORK I.7.11. tuːtɑɪndfɔːk Ess

two-tine-fork *1. n* a HAY-FORK I.7.11. tɹuːtɑɪnfɔːk C, tˡʉtɒɪnfɔˑk Nf, tuːtɑɪnfɔːk Hu,

tuːtɔɪnfɔːk Sf Ess, tuːtʌɪnfɔːk Sf, tuːtɔɪnfɔˤːk Wa

2. n a hay-fork with a long shaft. tˡuːtʌɪnfɔːk Nf, tutʌɪnfɔːk Nf

3. n a hay-fork with a short shaft. tɹuːtɔɪnfɔːk Sf, tuːtɑɪn fɔːk Wa, tuːtɑɪnfɔːˀk Hrt, tuːtʌɪnfɔˤːk O, tʉˑtɑɪnfɔˑk Nf

4. n a hay-fork with a long or short shaft. tˡʉtɒɪnfɔːk Nf, tutɑɪnfɔːk Nf, tuːtɑɪmfɔːk Ess, tuːtɔɪnfɔːk Ess

two-tine-short-fork *n* a HAY-FORK with a short shaft I.7.11. tˡuːtʌɪnʃɔːtfɔːk Nf

two-tooth *1. n* a sheep before its first shearing, ⇐ EWE-HOG III.6.4. tɤːtɤθ D, tɤːtɤːθ D, tuːtuːθ Sx

2. n a sheep from its first to its second shearing, ⇐ GIMMER III.6.5. tɤːtɤθ Co, tɤːtɤːθ D, tɤːtʌθ Co, tuːtʌθ W, tuːtʊθ W Brk Do Ha*[2 years old x1]*, tuːtuːθ W Sr Co Do Ha Sx

two-tooth ewe *n* a GIMMER III.6.5. tuːtʊθ joː Brk Ha, tuːtuːθ joː Co

two weeks *n* a FORTNIGHT VII.3.2. tɛʊ wɪks St

two-year-old *n* a sheep from its first to its second shearing, ⇐ GIMMER III.6.5. *pl* tɤːjəˤːɹoːɫz So, tˤʊuːjəɹoːld Sa, tˤʊuː-ɹəˤɽɒʊɫ Gl, tˤʊuːjəˤɽɒʊɫd Mon, tuːjœɹoːɫ Mon

tyal-chain *n* a TETHERING-ROPE used to tie up a horse I.4.2. tɑɪəltʃeːn Nt

tying-stoop *n* the SHUTTING-POST of a gate IV.3.4. tiːˀɪntˤʊuːp La, taɪ-ɪnstuːp La

type over *viphr* to FAINT VI.13.7. tɑːp oəɹ La, tɑɪp oəɹ La

U

udder *n* *[Show a picture of a cow.]* *What do you call this?* III.2.5. ɒdəˈl Man K, ʌðɔ^ʁ Nb, ʌdə Mon Nf Sf Ess MxL Sr K, ʌdəˈl Brk Sr K Ha, ʌdəˈ Brk Sr K Ha Sx, ʌdəˈːǀ So W Co D Do Ha, ʌðə Ess, ʊdɔ^ʁ Nb, ʊdə Cu Y St Wa L, ʊdər Y, ʊdɹ L, ʊdəɹ He, ʊdəˈl Man Ch, ʊdəˈ O Nth, ʊðər Y, ʊðəɹ Y, ʊðəˈl La, ədəˈ Gl Sx. ⇒ **bag, cow-bag, cow-ewer, dug, elder, ellerd, ewer, ither, milk-bag, uddern**

uddern *n* the UDDER of a cow III.2.5. ʌdəˈːn̩ Co D *[SBM note that this is to be taken as sg]*

udders *npl* the TEATS of a cow III.2.6. ʌdəz Ess

ulcer *n* a STYE in the eye VI.3.10. ʌɫsə Ess, ʌʊsə Ess

uncle *n* *[Show a picture of a family.]* *If this man [i.e. the children's father] had a brother, he'd be their [i.e. the children's] ....* VIII.1.12(a). Eng. ⇒ **nuncle, nunk,** *unc* ⇒ **unk, unk**

uncommon *adv* VERY VIII.3.2. ʌnkɒmən Sa

uncouth 1. *adj* STUPID VI.1.5. ʌnkuːθ Bk
2. *adj* unfamiliar, describing a stranger, ⇐ STRANGERS VIII.2.11. ʊŋkəθ La

under-arm *n* an ARMPIT VI.6.7. ʊndəɹaːm Lei R

under-bearers *npl* BEARERS who carry a coffin VIII.5.10. ʌndəbɪɔʁɔ^ʁz Nb, ʌndəbɛːɹəˈːz̩ W, ʌndəbɛˈːɹəz W, ʊndəbɪɔʁəz Nb, ʊndəbɪəʁə^ʁz Nb, ʊndɔ^ʁbɪɔ^ʁʁəz Nb, ʊndəbɛəɹəz Nb, ʊndəbɛəʁə^ʁz Du

under-carriage *n* a CART-FRAME I.10.6. ʌndəˈːkaɹɪdʒ So *[marked 'sic' SBM]*

undercreepers *npl* STRANGERS VIII.2.10. ʌndəˈkɹeˈəpəˈz̩ Ha

under-drain 1. *vt* to DRAIN wet land IV.1.9. ɒndədɹæɪn Nf, ʌndədɹæɪn Nf, ʊndédɹɪˈən L
2. *v* to drain land. ʌndədɹeɪˈn C, ʌndədɹeɪn Nf, ʊndédɹɪˈən L

under-grate *n* the place in which the ashes are collected beneath a domestic fire, ⇐ ASH-HOLE V.3.3. ʌndəˈːɡɹeɪət So

under-halter *n* a TETHERING-ROPE used to tie up a horse I.4.2. ʌndəˈːɾoːɫtəˈː W

underhanded-prong *n* a HAY-FORK with a short shaft I.7.11. ʊndə^lhændɪdpɹɒˈŋ Ha

underling *n* a WEAKLING piglet III.8.4. ʊndəˈlɪn Wo, ʊndəˈɫɪn Gl

under-math *n* AFTERMATH, a second crop of grass II.9.17. ʊndəˈmaːt Gl

undersark *n* a VEST VI.14.9. ʊndəsaːk Nb, ʊndɔ^ʁsaʁ:k Nb

undershirt 1. *n* a CHEMISE V.11.1. ˈʊndəʃɛət Lei
2. *n* a VEST VI.14.9. ɒndəʃɛˈt Nf, ɒndəʃɑˈt Nf, ɒndəʃət Nf, ɒndəʃəɾt̩ Nf, ɒndəʃəːt Nf, ʌndəʃʌt Sf Hrt Ess, ʌndəʃət Nf Sf, ʌndəɹʃəɹt He, ʌndəʃəːt Nth Hu Bd Hrt MxL *[worn by men]*, ʌndəʃəːʔ Bd Hrt, ʌndəʃəːɹt Hu, ʌndəʃəˈːt̩ He Gl O, ʌndəʃəˈːʔ Bk, ʌndəˈʃəˈt Brk *[old]*, ʌndəˈlʃəˈːt̩ K, ʌndəˈʃəˈːt̩ Sa, ʌndəˈʃəˈːʔ O, ʌndəˈʒəˈːɾt̩ Sx, ʌndəˈːʃəˈːt̩ So D Do *[old]* Ha, ʊndəʃɛt Y *[old-fashioned x1]*, ʊndəʃɛːt Nt, ʊndəʃət Nt L, ʊndəʃəˈlt Db *[old]*, ʊndəʃəːt Ch *[old x1]* Db St Wo Wa L Nth, ʊndəʃəːɹt St Nth, ʊndəʃəˈːt̩ Wa Nth, ʊndəʃəˈːʔ O *[rare]* Bk

under-strap *n* the GIRTH of the harness of a cart-horse I.5.8. ʌndəˈːʂtɾap So

undervest 1. *n* a CHEMISE V.11.1. ʌndəvɛˈst K
2. *n* a VEST VI.14.9. ɒndəvɛst Nf, ʌndəvɛst Ess, ʌndəˈvɛst Brk, ʌndəˈːvɛst W, ʊndəvɛst Ch St Db O Nth, ʊndəɾvɛst O

undone *adj* AJAR IX.2.7. ʊndʊn Ch

uneasy *adj* ACTIVE, describing a child VIII.9.1. ʊniːzɪ Nb Cu We, ʊnɪəzɪ Y Ch, ʊnɛːzɪ La; **never easy** nɪvəɹ ɪˈəzɪ L *[phrase marked u.r. EMBM]*

unedge *vt* to CLEAR grass at the edges of a field II.9.5. ʌnɛdʒ Ess, ʌnhɛdʒ Ess *[second form taken as hypercorrection, EMBM]*

unempt *v* to PITCH sheaves II.6.10. ʌnɛmt O

unempter *n* the FORKER on a wagon who unloads sheaves in a stackyard II.6.9. ɒnɛmtə Wa, ˌʌnˈɛmtəˈ W, ʌnˈɛmptəˈ Brk, ʌnɛmʔtəˈ Bk

unemptier *n* the FORKER on a wagon who unloads sheaves in a stackyard II.6.9. ʌnɛmptɪə Hrt

unempting *v-ing* UNLOADING sheaves from a wagon II.6.8. *3prsg* ɒnɛmts Wa, ʌnɛmptɪn Nth, ʌnɛmtɪn O Nth Bk W Brk, ˌʌnˈɛmpʔn W, *no -ing* ʌmɛmp O *[old]*

unemptying *v-ing* UNLOADING sheaves from a wagon II.6.8. ʌnɛmptɪ-ɪn C, ʌnɛmtɪ-ɪn Bd, *no -ing* ʌnɛmtɪ Hrt

unfit *adj* ILL, describing a person who is unwell VI.13.1(b). ʌnfɪt Ess, ənˈfɪt St

ungain *adj* CLUMSY, describing a person VI.7.14. ʊnˈɡiːn St

unhealthy *adj* ILL, describing a person who is unwell VI.13.1(b). ɒnhɛlθɪ Nf

unheppem *adj* CLUMSY, describing a person VI.7.14. ʊnɛpm Y L

unk *n* an UNCLE VIII.1.12(a). ʌŋk So, ʊŋk O

unladening *v-ing* UNLOADING sheaves from a wagon II.6.8. ʊnlɪˈədnɪn Y

unlader *n* the FORKER on a wagon who unloads sheaves in a stackyard II.6.9. ʊnlɪədə Nb

unlading *v-ing* UNLOADING sheaves from a wagon II.6.8. ʊnlɪədn Nb, ʊnlɪədən Cu, *no -ing* ʊnlead We, ʊnleˈədn Du, *no -ing* ʊnleˈəd We, ʊnlɛədɪn Y

unlatched *adj* AJAR IX.2.7. ʊnlatʃt Y

unlevel *adj* ASKEW, describing a picture that is not hanging straight IX.1.3. ʌnˈlɛvəl Sa

unloadener *n* the FORKER on a wagon who unloads sheaves in a stackyard II.6.9. ʊnlʊədnə Y, ʊnlʊədn̩ə Y, ʊnlʊədnəɹ Y

unloadening *v-ing* UNLOADING sheaves from a wagon II.6.8. ʊnlʊədnɪn Y L, ʊnlʊədn̩ɪn Y

unloader *n* the FORKER on a wagon who unloads sheaves in a stackyard II.6.9. ʊnlɪʏːdə Ch, ʊnlɪuːdə Ch, ʊnlɪədə Nb, ʊnlʏˈədə Db, ʌnlæʊdə Hrt, ʌnˈlɒʊdəˑ K, ʌnlɒʊdəˤ Sx, ʊnlɒtʊdə Nth, ʌnlɔʊdə Ess, ʌnlɔʊdəˑ Brk, ʌnlɔʊdəˤ O Sx, ʌlɔːʊdəˤ O, ʊnlɔʊdə Wa L Lei, ʌnlʌʊdə Sf Bk Bd Hrt Ess MxL K, ɒnlɔːdə Gl, ʌnlɔːdə Mon O, ʌnlɔːdəˤ Sa He Brk, ˌɒnˈlɔːdəˤː W, ʌnlɔːdəˤ Mon, ʌnlɔːdəˤː Sa So, ʌnlɔːdəˤː So W D Do Ha, ˈʌnlɔːdəˤː Do, ʊnlɔːdə Ch, ʊnlɔːdəˤ Sa He Wo, ʊlɔːdəˤ Sa, ʊnlɔːdəˤ Mon O, anlʊʊdə Bk, ɒnlʊʊdə Nf, ɒnlʊʊdəˤ Wa, ʌnlʊʊdə C Sf Bd, ʌnlʊʊdəɹ He, ʌnlʊʊdəˤ Bk Ha, ʌnˈlʊʊdəˤː So, ʌnlɔːʊdəˤ Mon, ʊnlʊʊdə Db St Wa, ʊnlʊʊdəɹ St, ʊnlʊʊdəˤ Wo Wa, ʊnlɔːʊdəˤ Gl, ʊnlɔːʊdəˤ Gl, ˌʌnˈlʊːdəˤː Co D, ʊnlʊədə La Db, ʊnlʊədəˤ La, ʊnlʏːdə Db St Lei

unloading *v-ing* [*Show a picture of three men unloading a wagon of sheaves in a stackyard.*] *What is your word for taking the sheaves out of the wagon?* II.6.8. Eng exc. We Nt R. ⇒ **chucking off, chucking on** out, **clod off, empting, emptying, forking, forking off, heaving off, off-loading, picking off, pitching, pitching off, teeming, throwing off, unempting, unemptying, unladening, unlading, unloadening, unpitching**

unloading-fork *1. n* a HAY-FORK with a long shaft I.7.11. ʌnlʌʊdɪnfɔːᵊk Bk, ʌnlʌʊdɪnfɔˤːək Bk, ɒnlʊʊdɪnfɔːk Wa, ʊnlɔːᵁdɪnfɔːk Nth

2. n a hay-fork with a short shaft. ʊnlɔˈʊdɪnfɔːk Db

unpitcher *n* the FORKER on a wagon who unloads sheaves in a stackyard II.6.9. ɒnpɪtʃə Nf, ʌnpɪtʃə Nf Sf Ess, ʌnˈpɪtʃəˑ Ha, ˌʌnˈpɪtʃəˤː Ha

unpitching *v-ing* UNLOADING sheaves from a wagon II.6.8. ɒnpɪtʃɪn Nf, ʌnpɪtʃɪn Nf Ess Ha, ʌnpɪtʃən Sf

unpowered *adj* OVERTURNED, describing a sheep on its back unable to get up III.7.4. ɒnpʊʊˤːd̩ D

unstring *vt* to REMOVE *STALKS* from currants V.7.24. *-ing* ʊnstɹɪŋɪn Y

unt *n* a MOLE IV.5.4. ʌnt Sa, ʊnt Sa He Wo Wa Mon Gl, hʊnt Sa, *pl* uːnt W, uːnts O[*old*] [*not a SBM headword*]

unteemer *n* the FORKER on a wagon who unloads sheaves in a stackyard II.6.9. ʊntiːmə Lei R

until *prep* TILL IX.2.2. ʌntɪl Mon, ʌntɪɫ Brk, ˈʌntɫ K

untinge *vt* to TIP a cart I.11.6. ʌnˈtɪndʒ K

unwell *adj* ILL, describing a person who is unwell VI.13.1.(b). ɒnwɛɫ Nf

up *adj* IN FLOOD, describing a river IV.1.4. ʊp La Y St L Lei; **well up** wɛɫ ʌp Co, wɛl ʊp Sa; **up high** ʌp hɔɪ Ess

up above *adv* UPSTAIRS V.2.5. ʊp əbɪən We, ʊp əbʊv Ch L [*marked u.r. N/WM/EMBM*]

up again *prep* BESIDE a door IX.2.5. ʊp əgɪən Y

up-aloft *adv* UPSTAIRS V.2.5. ʌpəlɒft Brk

upchurchers *npl* KNEE-STRAPS used to lift the legs of working trousers VI.14.17. ʌptʃʌtʃəz Sf [*queried EMBM*]

uphold *vt* to AGREE *WITH* somebody VIII.8.12. ʌpɔːɫd So, ʌpɔːɫ D

upland *1. n* a MEADOW II.9.2. *pl* ʌplandz Bd, ʊpland Ch

2. n grazing land above a marsh. ʌplænd Nf

upland field *n* PASTURE II.1.3. *pl* ʌplən fᵊiːldz Sf

upland hay *n* a MEADOW II.9.2. ʌplən hæi Nf

upland-pasture *n* PASTURE II.1.3. ʌpləndpɑːstjə K

up-over *adv* UPSTAIRS V.2.5. ʌpɔːvəˤː So[*old x3*] W Co D Do, ʌpoːvəˤː So[*old*], ʌpoʊvəˤː So[*old x1*]; **up-over stairs** ʌpɔːvəˤː steɪəˤːz̩ Do

upper *n* the VULVA of a cow III.2.3. ʌpə Ess

upright *1. n* a TETHERING-STAKE in a cow-house I.3.3. ʌpɹɪit He, ʌpɽɒɪt So

2. n a STICK used to support the shaft of a cart I.11.1. ʌpɽəɪt So

3. adj STEEP, describing a hill IV.1.11. pɽɒɪt Ha

4. n a DIAGONAL BAR of a gate IV.3.7. *pl* ʊpɹˡiːts We[*informant insisted*]

uprights *1. npl* GATE-POSTS IV.3.2. ʊpɹaɪts Y

2. npl the JAMBS of a door V.1.11. ʌpɹʌyts O

upset *vi* to OVERTURN, referring to a cart I.11.5. ʌpsɛt He So Co Do, ʌpzɛt Co D Ha, ʌpzɒt D, ʌpzɒd D

upside-down *adv* overturned, referring to a cart, ⇐ to OVERTURN I.11.5. ʏpsɒɪddɛʊn Nf

upskell *vt* to TIP a cart I.11.6. ʊpskɛl Y

upstairs *adv* *Where is your bedroom?* V.2.5. Eng exc. Do. ⇒ **over the scullery, up above, *up a height*, up-aloft, up-over, *up over the other rooms*, up-over *stairs*, *up the stairs*, up-top**

upstairs room *n* a BEDROOM V.2.3. *pl* ʌpstɛˑəz ɹʊmz Nf

upstrigolous *adj* ACTIVE, describing a child VIII.9.1. ʌpstɽɪgələs So

uptip *1. vi* to OVERTURN, referring to a cart I.11.5. ʌptɪp He Mon

2. vt to TIP a cart I.11.6. 'ʊp'tɪp Wo, ʊp'tɪp Gl

up to much *adj* **not up to much** ILL, describing a person who is unwell VI.13.1(b). nɔt ʌp tə mʌtʃ Sf

up-top *adv* UPSTAIRS V.2.5. ʌptɒp Sx, ʌp tɒp Nf, up tɔp L *[marked u.r. EMBM]*

urchin *n* a HEDGEHOG IV.5.5. ɒɹtʃənt Y, ɔtʃən Y, ɔᵏːtʃənt Nb, ɔˡˑtʃn La, ɔˡːɹtʃən La, ɔˡːɹtʃət La, ʊtʃɪn Cu, ʊtʃən We Y, ʊrtʃɪnt Cu, ʊɹtʃənt Y, ətʃɪn Y, əːtʃɪn Cu We Y Ch St Wa, əːtʃən Cu Du, əːtʃənt We, əᵏːtʃən Cu, əːɹtʃɪn St*[young]*, əˡːtʃɪn Y, əˤːtʃɪn Sa He Wo Wa Gl

urine *1. n [Show a picture of an old-fashioned cow-house.] What do you call the liquid that runs down the drain?* I.3.10. jʊɹɑɪn Ess, jʊɹɔɪn Ess, juɹɔɪn O, juɹʌɪn O, juːɹaɪn St, ʊɹɪn Wo; ⇒ **cow-dross, cow-juice, cow-liquor, cow-maid, cow-piddle, cow-piss, cow-slush, cow-sock, cows'-piss, cow-sump, cows' water, cows'-wash, cow-wash, cow-water, fleet, juice, lant, liquid manure, liquor, maid's-water, mig, muck, muck-juice, muck-water, piss, runnings, saur, sewer, sig, sink, sipings, slurry, slush, soak, sock, sockage, spruce, stale(s), stank, suction, sump, tank, tanking, tank-water, waste water, water, yeddle;** ⇒ also **piss-hole**

2. n In the olden days, the water that human beings made was used in cleaning blankets. What was it called? VI.8.8. ɛɹiːn He*[fertilizer or insecticide]*, ɛɹɪən Sa*[for pickling grain before sowing, to prevent rooks eating it]*, ʊɹɪn He*[fertilizer or insecticide]* Wo*[not for cleaning blankets x1, medicine for horses x1]* Mon*[fertilizer or insecticide]*, jʊɹɑɪn Ess, jʊɹɔɪn Ess*[not for cleaning blankets]*, uːɹɪn He*[for dressing wheat]*, juːɹɒɪn St, juːɹəɪn Wo*[for dressing wheat]*, uːɹəɪn Mon*[fertilizer or insecticide]*; **urine-water** ɛːɹɪnwɔːtə St. ⇒ **bedroom slops, bleach, chamberlye, chamberlyne, chamber-water, hatchel, lant, netting,** *old* **lant,** *old* **piss,** *old* **swill,** *old* **wash,** *old* **wetting, pee, piddle, piddling, piss, pissle, scour, sig, slops,** *stale* **piss,** *stale* **water,** *tainted* **water, urine-***water***, wetting**

urks *npl* PIGS III.8.1. əˤːks Gl

urn *n* a BREAD-BIN V.9.2. əˤːn̩ Do

urrins *npl* EARWIGS IV.8.11. ʊɹɪnz K *[queried BM]*

use *1. n* **in use** ON HEAT, describing a cow III.1.6. ɪn juːs K Sx

2. n **at use, on at use, in use** ON HEAT, describing a sow III.8.9. **at use** əʔ juːs O; **on at use** ɒn ət juːs Brk; **in use** ɪn juːs L Lei Nth Nf K

used *v-ed* **used up** FINISHED, referring to a store of potatoes V.7.21. juːzd ʌp Sr

useless *1. adj* STUPID VI.1.5. jusləs Nb

2. adj EXHAUSTED, describing a tired person VI.13.8. juːslɪs K *[queried u.r. SBM]*

uterus *n [Show a picture of a cow.] What do you call the place where the young animal lies inside [the cow]?* (before April 1954: *What does it [i.e. the vulva] lead to inside?]*) III.2.4. ɪutəɹʌs Mon. ⇒ **bag, barren, barren-bag, bed, bedding, body, breeding, breeding-bag, breeding-bed, breeding-gut, calf-bag, calf-bed, calf-poke, cow-bed, reed, womb, wound**

V

vairy *1. n* a WEASEL IV.5.6. veːɽi So, veːɽi So, vɛəˡːɽi D

2. *n* a POLE-CAT IV.5.7. vɛəˡːɽi D

vake *n* a DRAG used to slow a wagon I.11.3. vɛɪk Sx *[queried SBM]*

valley *1. n* a DRAIN in a cow-house I.3.8. vɛlɪ Sx

2. *n* a LITTER of piglets III.8.3. væɫɪ Mon

3. *vi* to FARROW, describing a pig giving birth to piglets III.8.10. væɫɪ Mon

vantage-whippens *n* an EVENER, the main swingle-tree of a horse-drawn plough harness I.8.4. vɑːntɪdʒwɪpɪnz Sr

vat *n* a SALTING-TROUGH III.12.5. væt Sx, vat St

vatch *n* a BROOD of chickens IV.6.12. vætʃ Sx

vault *1. n* an artificial brick-lined CESS-POOL on a farm I.3.11. vɔːɫt W

2. *n* the box of an EARTH-CLOSET V.1.13. vɔːɫt W, vɔːt W

3. *n* an ASH-MIDDEN where cinders and other rubbish are thrown away V.1.14. vɔlt L

veer *1. adj* DRY, describing a cow with no milk III.1.9. vɪəˡː Co

2. *n* a dry cow. vɪəˡːɽ (+V) Co

veerings *npl* the RIDGES between furrows in a ploughed field II.3.2. *sg* vɪəɽɪn O, vɛˡːɽʊnz W

vellop *vi* to RETCH VI.13.15. *-ing* veləpɪn O*[old]*

vent *n* the VULVA of a cow III.2.3. vɛnt Nb Cu La Db O Nth Sf Ess Sx

verge **1. n* a BUMPER of a cart I.10.1(a). *pl* vəˡːdʒəs So

2. *n* the BRIM of a hat VI.14.3. vəːdʒ Sf, wəːdʒ Nf

verger *n* a SEXTON VIII.5.4. vɛᵝʁdʒɔᵝ Nb, vɛˑədʒɔᵝ Nb, vɔᵝːdʒə Du, vədʒə Cu, vəˡdʒəˡ Ha, vəːdʒə Cu Y St Wa L Nf Hrt Ess, vəːdʒəˡ Y*[old]*, vəˡːdʒə L, vəˡːdʒəˡ Sr K, vəˡːdʒɹ L, vəˡːdʒə Wa Ess, vəˡːdʒən Ess, vəˡːdʒəˡ Wa Gl O Bk, vəˡːɽdʒəˡ Sr, vəˡːɽdʒəˡ Brk Sx

verging *n* a BUMPER of a cart I.10.1(a). vəˡːdʒɪn So, *pl* bəˡːdʒɪnz So

vermin *1. npl* LICE IV.8.1(a). veɽmɪn Nf

2. *n* PUS VI.11.9. vaːmɪnt Y

very *1. adv [If you know a berry will kill you if you eat it, you say it is ....] If it is extremely so, you say it is ... POISONOUS.* IV.11.5. vɛɹɪ Man, vɛɹɪ Mon, vɛɹɪ Y Sa Wa Lei R Hu Hrt Ess, weɹɪ Nf, veɽɪ Ha, vaɹɪ Y, vaɽɪ W, vəɹɪ La L Brk Sr K Sx, vəɹ L, vəɽɪ So Co Do, vəɽɪ So Do. ⇒ *deadly,* **deadly** *poison,* **deadly** *poisonous,* **dead** *poison,* **deathly** *poison,* **deathly** *poisonous, ever so poisonous,* **gallows** *poisonous,*

mainly *poisonous,* **main** *poison,* **main** *poisonous, poisonous,* **rank** *poison,* **right** *poisonous,* strange *poisonous,* strong *poisonous,* **terrible** *poison,* **very** deadly *poison*

2. *adv And if the caller [at the door] was a rare visitor, though a good old friend of yours, you'd say: I'm ... [glad to see you]. [If he answers without an intensifier, then ask him:] And if you felt it more strongly, you'd say: I'm ... glad to see you.* VIII.3.2. Eng exc. C. ⇒ **awful, bonny, bonny and, canny, clear, damn, damned, darned, desperate, downright, ever so, extra, fair, fairly, frightful, funny, gay, gayly, good tidy, gradely, infernal, jolly, main, master, mighty, miserable, monstrous, more than, pretty, proper, pure, rare, real, really, right, rum, some, something, suffering, terrible, terribly, tidy, uncommon, well, wholly, wonderful** *[IM forms included]*

very cold *adj [What's a room like on a winter's day without a fire? And if you were in that room for just a short time, you would be ....] And if you had been in for four or five hours, you would be ....* VI.13.19. veɪɪ kæʊl Man, vəɹ kæʊd L, vaɹɪ kaːld Y, vəɹɪ kʊʊld K, vəɹɪ kʊʊɫd K, vəᴶ kʊʊld K, vaɹɪ kɔʊd L, vəɹɪ kɔʊd L, vɛɹɪ kʌʊɫd Ess, vɛɹɪ kʌʊd Ess, vəɹɪ koˑɫd Brk, vəɽ koːɫd O, vɛɹɪ kʊʊld St, veɽɪ kʊʊɫd So, vəɽɪ kʊʊɫd So, vəˡːɽɪ kʊʊɫd So, vɛɹɪ koˑəl Man, vaɹɪ koˑəl Man; **very cold indeed** vɛɹɪ kaʊld ɪndiːd Nf. ⇒ *a-freezing* **cold, chilled, chilled** *most to death,* **cold** *as ice,* **colder** *still, damn* **nigh** scrammed, **dithery, foundered** *to death,* **freezed, freezed** *stiff,* **freezed** *to death,* **freezed up, freezing, frez, frez** *to death,* **frizzled, frizzled up, frosted up, frowened** *with cold,* **frowen** *with cold,* **froze, frozed, frozen, frozen** *stiff, frozen to dead* ⇒ **froze** *to dead,* **frozen** *to death,* **frozen** *to the death, frozen up* ⇒ **froze up, frozen** *with cold,* **froze** *stiff,* **froze** *to dead,* **froze** *to death,* **froze** *up,* **froze** *with cold, middling* **cold,** *most* **freezed,** *nearly* **cotted,** *nearly* **froze, nithered, numbed, perished, perished** *to dead,* **perished** *to death,* **perished** *to the bone,* **perished** *with cold,* **perishing, perishing** *with cold,* **pinched up, risen-on,** *rotten* **cold, scrammed, scrammed** *to death,* **scrammed up, scrammed** *with the cold,* **scrimmed** *right* **up, shivered, shrammed, shrammed** *to death,* **shrammed** *with the cold,* **shrimped, shrimped** *right* **up, shrimped up, shrimped up** *with the cold,* shrinked *right* up, shrivelled up *with the cold*, shuddered *with the cold*, shuddering, starved, starved out, starved *stiff*, starved through, starved *to dead*, starved *to death*, starved *to death with cold*, starved *to the bone*, starved *to the death*, starved up, starven *to death*, starving, starving *cold*, starving *to death*, steeved, steeved *with the cold*, stone cold, *terrible* cold, very cold *indeed*, *very nigh* froze, *very nigh* shrammed

vessel *n* a BARREL VI.13.12. vɛsɫ Ess

vest *1. n What do you call the thing [i.e. item of clothing] next to the skin?* VI.14.9. vɛst Y Sa St He*[wool x1]* Wo Mon Gl O Lei R Nf Sf Ess MxL*[worn by woman]* So W Brk Sr K Co D Do Ha Sx, wɛst Nf*[old-fashioned x1]*, vɛs Man Wo O Ess So W Sr K Co D Do Ha Sx, *pl* vɛsɪz Ch*[modern]*. ⇒ *body-flannel* ⇒ **body-flannen, body-flannen, body-jacket, body-sark, body-shirt, flannel, flannel-sark, flannel-shirt, flannel-singlet, flannel-undershirt, flannen, flannen-shirt, gansey, semmit, singler, singlet, undersark, undershirt, undervest**

2. n a WAISTCOAT VI.14.11. vɛst Y Wo Ess

victual(s) *1. n* FOOD V.8.2.
no -s: fɪtɫ He Wo, vɪtɫ He
-s: vɪtɫz Gl Nth Ess, wɪtɫz Bk, vɪtʊɫz Brk Sx, wɪtʊɫz Ess
[forms at Mon, Ess, K, and Ha not included, as these were not recorded in phrasal context]
2. n MEAL OUT VII.5.12.
no -s: fɪtɫ Wo
-s: vɪtɫz Ess, vɪtəɫz Do, wɪtɫz Ess, wɪʔɫz Ess

vim *n* full of **vim** ACTIVE, describing a child VIII.9.1. fʊɫ əv vɪm MxL

vine *n* BINDWEED II.2.4. vaɪn C, *pl* vaɪnz Hu

vinegar *n What do you call that sour liquid you pickle red cabbage, or onions in?* (before April 1955:', *or onions'* not included) V.7.19. Eng. ⇒ **alegar, sour**

vines *n* POTATO-HAULMS II.4.4. vəɪnz Brk

viper *n* an ADDER IV.9.4. væɪpə Y, vaɪpə Y Nt, vaɪpə Nth K, vaɪpəˡ Sr, vɒɪpə Nf, vɒɪpəˡ K, wɒɪpəˡ K*[large]*, vɒɪpəˡː So, vɔɪpə Gl Sf Ess, vɔɪpəˡ Brk, vɔɪpəˡ Gl O Bk K, vʌɪpə Nf, wʌɪpə Nf, *pl* wʌɪpəˡz Brk, vʌɪpəˡ Gl, vəɪpəˡ Brk, *pl* vəɪpəˡz̩ Sx, vəɪpəˡːɾ(+V) So

voider *n* a CLOTHES-BASKET V.9.7. vɔɪdə Y, vɔɪdəˡ Y

vomit *1. vi When you've eaten something that has disagreed with you and then are actually sick, what do you say you do?* VI.13.14(a). *-ing* vɑmɪʔn Nf, vɒmɪt Ch Db St Nf Ess Sr, *-ing* vɒmɪtɪn Y Hrt, vɒmət Man, vɒmənt Mon, vɔmɪt Wa*[modern]*, *-ing* vɔmɪtɪn Ch, *-ing* vɔmətɪn Ha. ⇒ *be* **sick, boke, boken, bring** *it* **up, bring up, chuck up, fetch** *it* **up, fetch up, get** *it* **up, puke, put up, retch, rift, sick,** *sick (adj),* **sicky, spew, spew** *it* **up, spew up, throw up, yocket, yack,** *yoke* ⇒ **yack**

2. vi And when a baby brings up its mother's milk, what do you say the baby does? VI.13.14(b). vɑˈmɪt? Nf, vɒmɪt We Y Ch Mon O Nt Nth Nf W Brk Sr K Sx, *-s* vɒmɪts St, vɒmɪʔ O Hrt, vɒmət Cu O Hrt, *3prsg* vɒməts Ha, *prppl* vɒmətɪn Brk, *-ing* vɒmətɪn So Sr D, vɒmənt Mon, vɔmɪt Nb Y L, *-ing* vɔmɪtɪn MxL Sx, vɔmət Nb L*[polite x1]*, *-ing* vɔmətɪn MxL, *-ing* vɔnəpɪn La, vʌmət Nb. ⇒ *be* **cruddy, belch, belge,** *be* **sick,** *be* **thriving, bring** *it* **back, bring** *it* **up, bring** *the* **milk back, bring up, come back, curdle, fetch up, frithe, gulch, heave,** *he's* **sick,** *it's* **sick, kiddle, posset, puke, put** *it* **up, retch, retch up, sick, sick** *it* **up, sick up, spew, spew** *it* **back** *again,* **spew up** *the milk,* **spill** *his* **milk back, throw, throw** *her* **milk back, throw** *his* **food up, throw** *it* **back, throw** *its* **milk back, throw** *it* **up, throw up, vomp**

vomp *1. vi* to VOMIT, referring to a baby bringing up milk VI.13.14(b). *-ing* vɒmpɪn K
2. vi to RETCH VI.13.15. *-ing* vompɪn K

vope *vi* to RETCH VI.13.15. *-ing* voʊpɪn K

vorging up *vtphr-ing* **vorging up wind** BELCHING VI.13.13. vɔːgɪn ʌp wɪnd K

voryer *n* HEADLANDS in a ploughed field II.3.3. vɔˡːjəˡː Co D

vult *n* a CUTTING of hay II.9.15. vɔːɫt So, vʌɫt So, vʊɫt So, vəɫt So

vulva *n [Show a picture of a cow.] What do you call this, outside [indicate the vulva]?* III.2.3. ⇒ **barren, body, calf-bed-neck, crimmet, crimmock, cunny, cunt, farm, flue, issue, passage, pisser, place, reed, shape, sheaf, sheath, shop, till, twat, twitterum, upper, vent, wound**

W

wackers *n* TREMORS suffered by a person who cannot keep still VI.1.4. wakəz Ch

wad *1. n* SHEEP-DUNG II.1.7. wɒd Ess

2. n a CUTTING of hay II.9.15. wæd Mon, wad Db Sa St, wɒd Sa

3. n CURDS V.5.8(a). wæd Nf

waddle(s) *n* the WATTLES of a hen IV.6.19. *no -s*: wɒdᵁɫ W

-s: wadlz La Ch Db, wɒdls Man, wɒdlz Sa St, wɒdɫz So W K Co D Do Ha, wɒdʊz Ess Sx, wɔdɫz So

wade in *imp* HELP YOURSELVES!, said to invite visitors to eat V.8.13. weːd ɪn Y

wadlets *n* the WATTLES of a hen IV.6.19. wadləts La

waffing *v-ing* PANTING VI.8.1. wafɪn Y

waffles* *n* the WATTLES of a turkey IV.6.19. wɒfɫz So *[queried SBM]*

waffly *1. adj* INSIPID, describing food lacking in salt V.7.8. waflɪ Nt

2. adj WEAK, describing a person who has been ill VI.13.2. waflɪ Cu

waffy *1. adj* INSIPID, describing food lacking in salt V.7.8. wafɪ Y L

2. adj WEAK, describing a person who has been ill VI.13.2. wafɪ Nb Du Y

wag *n* a CARTMAN on a farm I.2.2. wag Y

wagging *vt-ing* PUTTING your tongue OUT VI.5.4. wagɪn Wa

waggles *n* the waggles TREMORS suffered by a person who cannot keep still VI.1.4. ðə wɛgʊz Sr

wagon *n* What do you call a 4-wheeled [horse-drawn] vehicle with a low flat top? Has the [wagon] got sides? I.9.2.

1. provision of sides not given. wɛgɪn Db K Sx, *pl* wɛgɪnz D, wɛgn Ess Sx, wɛgən Ess D Sx, wɛəgn Ess, wægɪn He Mon Lei So Brk Sr K, *pl* wægɪnz Wo, wægʌn So, wægn Man Nf Sf Hrt Ess Brk Sx, wægən Man Wa O C Nf Sf Bk Ess Brk, *pl* wægənz Sr, *pl* wæːgənz MxL, wagɪn Cu La Y Db Sa St He Wa Mon O Nt L Lei R Nth Bk Bd Co D Do, wagʊn Nth Bk, wagn Y L Ha, wagən Du La Y St Wa O Nt L Nth Hu Bk Bd Hrt So Co Do, *pl* wagənz Ha, wagənəᵗ Sa

2. with sides. wɛgɪn Sr K D Sx, wɛgn Ess Sr K Sx, wægɪn He Wo Mon Gl So Brk D Sx, wægʊn Wo, wægn Nf Ess K Ha, wægən Sa St He Wo Mon Gl Nf Ess Sr, *pl* wægənz Hu, wagɪn Y Ch Db Sa St Wo Wa Gl O Nt L Lei Nth Bk Hrt So Co Do Ha, wagʊn Wa Gl, wagn L, wagən Nb Du Sa Mon Gl Nt L Nth C W Do Ha

3. with detachable sides. wɛgn Sr, wagɪn La Ch Db W, wagən Nb So

4. without sides. wɛgɪn D, wægɪn So Co D, wægn Ess, wægən Ess Co, wagɪn Y Lei W D, wagn La Y, wagən Y W Co Do, waˑgən Wo

⇒ **bolt-wagon, box-wagon, broad-wheel, curry, curry-cart, dray, drug, gambo, gurry- wagon, hay-bogey, lorry, reaper-rulley, rulley, trolley, truck, tug, wagons, wain**

wagoner *1. n* the FORKER of sheaves onto a wagon II.6.7(d). wagɪnəᵗ Wa

2. n the FORKER on a wagon who unloads sheaves in a stackyard II.6.9. wagɪnəᵗː Co

3. n the driver of a wagon, ⇐ CARTMAN I.2.2. wagɪnə Y, *pl* wagənəz We

wagoner(s) *n* a CARTMAN on a farm I.2.2. *no -s*: wɛgɪnəᴶ K, wɛgɪnəᵗː D, wɛgənəᵗ Sa, *pl* wɛgn,əz Ess, wɛgŋəᴶ K, wɛgnəᴶ K, wæginæ Mon, wæginəᵗ He Wo Gl, wægənə Nf Ess, wægŋə K, wægnə Sf, wægnəᵗ Sa He Mon, wægnəᵗ Wo, wagɪnə La Y Ch Db St Nt Lei R, wagɪnəᴶ Ch, wagɪnəᵗ Sa Wa O, wagɪnəᵗː W Co, wagŋə L, wagənə Du Y Ch Sa St Wa Nt L Nth, wagŋə L, wagŋəɹ L, wagənəᴶ La, wagənəɹ Y He L, wagnɹ L, wagənəᵗ Sa Wo Wa, wagənəᵗː Sa, wɑgənəᵗ Sa; **head wagoner** ɛdwagənəɹ He, jɛdwaːgɪnəᵗ Sa

-s: *sg* wæːɪgnəᴶz Brk

wagon-grease *n* CART-GREASE, used to lubricate the wheels of a cart I.11.4. wægɪngɹiːs So

wagon-house *n* a CART-SHED I.11.7. wægɪnæʊs So Do, wægɪnaʊs So, wægənaʊs So, wægœnəʊs Gl, wægɪnəʊːᵊs Gl, wagɪnæyz Co, wagɪnaʊs So, wagənɒʊs W, wagɪnᵁuːs Gl, wagənəʊs W

wagon-hovel *n* a CART-SHED I.11.7. wægənɒvɫ Hu, wagɪnɒvl L, wagɪnɒvɫ Wa Lei R Nth, wagŋɒvl Nt, wagənɒvl Wa Gl Nt, wagənɒvɫ Wa Nth Bk, wagənɔvl L, wagɪnʊvl Ch

wagon-linhay *n* a CART-SHED I.11.7. wægɪnɫəni D, wægənɫəni D

wagon-lodge *n* a CART-SHED I.11.7. wɛgɪnlɒdʒ K Sx, wɛgnlɒdʒ Ess, wægnlɒdʒ K

wagon-row *n* a row or SWATH of mown grass cut for haymaking, dried, and ready for carting II.9.4. *pl* wɛgɪnɹɒtʊz Sr

wagons *nsg* a WAGON I.9.2. wægʊnz Brk

wagon-shed *n* a CART-SHED I.11.7. wɛgɪnʃɛd Sx, wægɪnʃɛd K, wægnʃɛd Nf, wægənʃɛd Sf, wagɪnʃɛd Y Mon Nt, wagnʃɛd Y L, wagənʃɛd Y St L, wagɪnʃɛəd Y

wagon-shoe *n* a DRAG used to slow a wagon I.11.3. wægnʃuː Ess, wagɪnʃuː Y

wagon-shud *n* a CART-SHED I.11.7. wægnʃɤd Nf, wægənʃɤd Nf

wagon-skeeling *n* a CART-SHED I.11.7. wægɪnskɪłɪn Brk

wagon-slod *n* a DRAG used to slow a wagon I.11.3. wægnslɔd Sf

wagon-wheel *n* a HALO round the moon VII.6.4. wægənwiːl Nf

wain *1. n* a sideless cart with a body longer than that of a WAGON I.9.2. weːn D

2. n a long farm-cart. weːn Co

wain-cocks *npl* COCKS of hay II.9.12. wæɪnkɒks Mon

wain-house *n* a CART-SHED I.11.7. weːnaʊs Sa, weːnʌʊs Mon, weːnəʊs Mon, weːnəs Sa, weɪnaʊs He, weːɪnəʊːs Wo, weənəs Y, weɪᵊnæʊs He, wɛənəs Y, wɛːᵊnəs Wo, wæɪnæʊs He, wæɪnʌʊs He Mon, wæɪnəʊs He

wainwright *n* a WRIGHT VIII.4.4. weːnɹeɪt Db

wairish *adj* INSIPID, describing food lacking in salt V.7.8. wɛəɹɪʃ O

wairsh *adj* INSIPID, describing food lacking in salt V.7.8. weᵂʃ Nb, weəʃ Nb, weˈəᵂʃ Nb, wɛᵂʃ Nb, wɛəʃ Nb Du, wɛəᵂʃ Nb Du, waːʃ Du

waistcoat *n What do you call this [indicate a waistcoat]?* VI.14.11. Eng. ⇒ **singlet, vest**

wait *v* **wait on the stacker** to PITCH sheaves II.6.10. wæɪt ɒn ðə stækə Ess

wake *n* a row or SWATH of mown grass cut for hay-making II.9.4. weːk O W

waken *adj* ACTIVE, describing a child VIII.9.1. wakən Y

wake(s) *n* a local FESTIVAL or holiday VII.4.11.
no -s: weːk Wo Wa Gl, weːᵊk Wa Gl, weɪk Wo Wa*[small festival]*, wɛːk St, wɛɪk Wa Lei
-s: wiːks Ch St R, weːks La Ch Db St, weːɪks Db*[very old x1]*, wɛɪks St Wa Lei

walching *n* TWINE used to fasten thatch on a stack II.7.7(b1). wɛltʃɪn Db, wɛldʒɪn St

waled *vt-1ptsg* **waled his arse for him** I BEAT a boy's buttocks VIII.8.10. weːlt ɪz aːs fɒɹ ɪm Db

walk *1. v Suppose you missed the last bus or train back to here, then you'd have to set off and ....* VIII.7.10.
v Eng
vt **walk her, walk it** to walk. **walk her** wɔːk ə Db; **walk it** waːk ɪt Cu, waːk ɪʔ L, wɒłk ɪt Co, wɔːk ɪt We La Y Ch Db St He Wa O Bd So K Ha, wɔːk ət So, wɔːg ət D
⇒ **foot** *it*, **frog** *it*, **go on shanks' pony, hike** *it*, **hoof**

en, **hoof** *it*, **pad** *the hoof*, **shank** *it*, **shanks'-mare** *it*, **tramp, tramp** *it*, **trudge, walk** *her*, **walk** *it*, *walk it on* **shanks' pony,** *walk on* **shanks' pony**
2. n the GANGWAY in a cow-house I.3.7. wałk Co, wɔːk Y Man O Nf Ess So W D, wɔːłk D
3. n the gangway of a cow-house, used to store hay, ⇐ HAY-LOFT I.3.18. wɔːk O
4. imp **walk way** the command TURN LEFT!, given to plough-horses II.3.5(a). wɒk weːə Ess
5. n a PATH through a field IV.3.11. wɔːk Y
6. n a local FESTIVAL or holiday VII.4.11. wɔːk Ch; **club walk** kłʌb waːk Mon, kłʌb wɔːk He So, kłʌb wɔːk So, kłʊb wɔːk Wa, *-s* kłʊb wɔːks St

walking *adj* HEAVING *(WITH MAGGOTS)* IV.8.6. wɔːkɪn Y Ch Db Sa Wa Nt Ess, wɔːkən Cu Ha

walking-path *n* the GANGWAY in a cow-house I.3.7. wɔːłkɪnpaːθ D

wall *n What do you separate two fields by?* IV.2.1(b).
1. separating fields: *pl* wæːz Nb, *pl* walz Nb, *pl* waːlz Nb Du, waː Nb, waːl Y, waːł Gl D, wɔːl La Y Man Db St L Nf So K, *pl* wɔːlz Gl, wɔːł L Lei Nth Hu Sf Bk So W Brk Co D Do, *pl* wɔːłz O R K, wɔːʊł Brk, wɔːʊ Brk K Sx, wɔː Cu We La Y Db Bk, wɔːᵊl Nf, wɔːᵊł Sf Bk, *pl* wɔʊłz Brk, *pl* wɔːlz Db, woːᵁ Db, wʊəl Nf
2. also recorded, not separating fields: wɔːl Ch Wo Hu, *pl* wɔːlz He O, wɔːł Wa O C Bd Ess, *pl* wɔːłz MxL, wɔː Ess, *pl* wɔːz Sr, wɔːᵊł Hrt, woˈəl Nf
3. also recorded, not defined: wɔːl He, wɔːł MxL, wɔːᵁ MxL, wɔː Sr, *pl* wɔəłz Brk, *pl* woːz Db, woʊ St
⇒ **dike, dry-stone-wall, dry-wall, sod-and-stone-dike, stone-dike, stone-fence, stone-hedge, stone-wall**
[WMBM marks undefined forms, so that some IM forms, unmarked, are presumed to refer to field-walls; other BM volumes do not, and in localities/areas where walls not usually found these presumably do not refer to field-walls. Entries are as follows: unambiguous forms in 1.; other phonological forms not in 1. placed in 2. or 3. as appropriate; duplications avoided. Bank and fence/fencing omitted.]

waller *n* WILLOW IV.10.7. wɒləˡ Sa

wall-eyed* *adj* having eyes each of a different colour, ⇐ CROSS-EYED VI.3.6. wɔːləɪd So

wallies *npl* KNEE-STRAPS used to lift the legs of working trousers VI.14.17. wɒlɪz Ess *[queried EMBM]*

wallop *vt* to BEAT a boy on the buttocks VIII.8.10. waləp Du La, wɒləp Lei R, wɒłəp Sr, wɔləp MxL

wallow *1. adj* INSIPID, describing food lacking in salt V.7.8. walɪ Y L, walʊ La, walə Cu We La Y Nt L Lei, walɪ L

2. *adj* HUNGRY VI.13.9. walə Cu

wallowish *adj* ILL, describing a person who is unwell VI.13.1(b). walʃ D

walls *n* the BASE of a stack II.7.4. wɔːɫz Ess

wally *n* a row or SWATH of mown grass cut for hay-making II.9.4. wæɫɪ Gl, wɒɫɪ Gl, *pl* wɔlɪz Wo

walsh* *adj* INSIPID, describing food lacking in salt V.7.8. walʃ Du Y*[old x1]*, wɒlʃ Y, wɒɫʃ D, wɒlɪʃ O

walshy *adj* INSIPID, describing food lacking in salt V.7.8. walʃɪ Nt

walt *vi* to OVERTURN, referring to a cart I.11.5. waːt Ch, *-ed* wɔltəd Y, wɔːt La Ch Db, *3prsg* wɔːts St, *prppl* wɔːtɪn St, *3ptsg* wɔːtɪd St, *-ed* wɔːtɪd St, *3prsg* wɔəᴶts La

walted *1. vt-ed* sprained, ⇐ to SPRAIN an ankle VI.10.8. wɒltɪd Y, wɒltəd Y *[see note at twined]*

2. *adj* ASKEW, describing a picture that is not hanging straight IX.1.3. wɔltəd Y

walt over *1. viphr* to OVERTURN, referring to a cart I.11.5. *-ed* wɒltɪd ɔˑə Y

2. *viphr* to FAINT VI.13.7. wɔːt oːəɪ La, wɔːt ʊəᴶ La, wɔᴶːt ʊəᴶ La

walve *1. imp* the command TURN LEFT!, given to plough-horses II.3.5(a). waːv Y

2. *imp* the command TURN RIGHT!, given to plough-horses II.3.5(b). wɔːv Y

wammocky *adj* WEAK, describing a person who has been ill VI.13.2. waməkɪ Ch

wammy *adj* WEAK, describing a person who has been ill VI.13.2. wæmɪ Y

wamps *npl* WASPS IV.8.7. wamps Cu We*[old x1]* La

wander *n* on the wander ACTIVE, describing a child VIII.9.1. ɒn t wandə Y

wandering-willy *n* BINDWEED II.2.4. wandɹɪnwɪlɪ Y

wane *vi* *The moon is always changing its size. How do you speak of that?* VII.6.5(b). Eng exc. We Ch Mon Gl C W Co. ⇒ **abate**, *begin to go*, *be on the wane*, **come down, decline, decrease, die, die down, die out, dies away, drop back, dwindle away, fade, fade away, fades, fall, get less, get liler, get smaller, go, go away, go back, go down, go less, go off, go small, grow less,** *he begins to wane, he's waning away* ⇒ **wane away,** *he wastes away* ⇒ **waste away,** *it's on the wane, it's past its* **full, lie back, lose, lose** *size,* **on her** back, *on the* **fall,** *on the wane, on the* **waste,** *on the* **wear, pass away, set, shrink, sink, wane away, wane off, waste, waste away, wear**

wane away *viphr* to WANE, referring to the moon VII.6.5(b). weːn əwæɪ Gl, *-ing* weɪˈnɪn əweɪ Wo, *-ing* əweɪnɪn əweɪ W, *3prsg* wæɪnz əweɪ Ess

wane off *viphr* to WANE, referring to the moon VII.6.5(b). *-ing* wɪˈənɪn ɔf L

wang *1. n* an EVENER on the plough-beam end of a horse-drawn plough I.8.4. wɛŋ So

2. *n* the T-SHAPED PLOUGH-BEAM END of a horse-drawn plough I.8.5. wæŋ So D, waŋ D

wangled *adj* TANGLED, describing hair VI.2.5. wæŋɫd He

wankle *adj* WEAK, describing a person who has been ill VI.13.2. waŋkl La

wankly *adj* WEAK, describing a person who has been ill VI.13.2. waŋklɪ Y

wanky *adj* WEAK, describing a person who has been ill VI.13.2. waŋkɪ Cu Y Ch St

want *n* a MOLE IV.5.4. want So*[old x1]* Co, wɒnt So*[old x1]* W Co D Do, wɔːnt So W Do Ha, wʊnt Wa Mon W

wanty *n* the BELLY-BAND of the harness of a cart-horse I.5.7. wantɪ Hu, wantʔɪ C, wanʔɪ C, wɒntɪ Wa O Bd Ess, wɒnʔɪ Bk, wɒntʔɪ Ess, wɔːntɪ Hrt Ess MxL Brk Ha, wɔːnʔɪ Bk, wɔːntɑɪ Ess, wʌntɪ Ess

wappers *npl* WASPS IV.8.7. wɒpəz Wa, wɒpəᵗz̩ Wa Gl, wɔpəz Wa

wappies *npl* WASPS IV.8.7. wapɪz Nb*[old]* Du Db St, wabɪz Y, wɒpɪz Wa Gl *[not a WMBM headword]*

wappings *npl* COCKS of hay II.9.12. *sg* wapɪn Y

wappy *adj* SILLY VIII.9.3. wapɪ Lei

waps *1. npl* COCKS of hay II.9.12. waps Y

2. n WASPS IV.8.7.

sg: waps L, *sg* wɒps Lei Sr K Do

?sg/?pl: wɒps Gl O So*[old x2]* W Brk*[old x1]* K Do Ha, wɔps O *[phonetic forms make precise identification of sg or pl difficult]*

wapsies* *npl* WASPS IV.8.7. wæpsɪz So, wapsiːz So, wapsɪz So Co D, wɒpsiːz So*[old x1]* W D Do Ha, wɒpsɪz Y St Gl O*[old x1]* Bk Bd*[old x1]* Ess So W Brk Sr*[old x2]* K Co D Do Ha Sx*[old x1]*, wɒpsəz W, wɒpsəᵗz̩ Nth, wɔpsɪz Ess MxL*[child's word]*

warby *n* STRING used to tie up a grain-sack I.7.3. waːbɪ Ch

warch *vi* to ACHE, referring to a stomach VI.13.3(b). *3prsg* wæːtʃɪz La, wæᴶːtʃ La, *prppl* waːtʃɪn La, waᴶːtʃ Db, *3prsg* waᴶːtʃɪz La, wɜᴶːɪtʃ La *[not a NBM headword]*

warday clothes *n* ORDINARY CLOTHES VI.14.20. waːdɪ klɪəz Y, waːdɪ klɪəz Y, waːdə tlɪəz Nb Cu, waːrde kleˑaz Cu, waːdə kleaz Cu, waːdə tleaz We, waːdeː kleˑəz Du, waːdə kleəz Du, wɜːdɪ klous Man, watɪ klʊəz Y, waᴶtɪ klʊəz Y, waᴶːdə klʊəz La, waːdə tlʊəz Y, waːtɪ klʊəz Y, waːtɪ tlʊəz Y, wɜᴶːɪtə tlʊəz La*[old]*

wardays *npl* WORKDAYS VII.4.6. waːdeəz Du, waːdeəz Y, waˌtɪz Y, waˌdɪz Y, waːdɪz Y, waːdəs

Nb, waːdəz Cu*[old x1]* We Y, waˑ¹ːdeːz La, *sg* waːˑ¹tə Y, waːˌɹdeːz Y, waɪdəz Y, *sg* wɒˌɪtə La, *sg* wɔ?ldə L

warday suit *n* ORDINARY CLOTHES VI.14.20. waːtə sɪut Y

warden *n* a SEXTON VIII.5.4. wɔːdn Ess *[marked ir.r. EMBM]*

ward-pin *n* a metal LINCH-PIN holding a wheel on a cart I.9.12. wæˑ¹ːpɪn La, wɜˑ¹ːɹpɪn La

wares *npl* big potatoes, ⇐ BIG ONES II.4.5. wɛɪəz St; **ware potatoes** wɛə teːˡtəz Db

wark *vi* to ACHE, referring to a stomach VI.13.3.(b). wæːk Du*[old]*, wak Y, *3prsg* waˌɪks Y, waːk Nb*[old x1]* Cu Du*[old x1]* We Y, waʁːk Nb Du, waˑ¹ːk La Y

warm 1. *adj* **get warm** to HEAT, referring to a haystack II.9.16. *3prsg* gɛts waːm Y
2. *vt* to BEAT a boy on the buttocks VIII.8.10. wæːm Du, waːm Nb Y; **warm his backside** wɔᵗːm ɪz bakzæɪd So

warm away *viphr* to FAINT VI.13.7. waːm əweː Y

warm down *viphr* **warm down for calving** show signs of calving, ⇐ SHOWS SIGNS OF CALVING III.1.12. *3prprogsg* waːmɪn dᵊuːn fə kɔːvɪn Y

warp 1.1. *v* to slip a calf, ⇐ SLIPS *THE CALF* III.1.11. *ppl* əwaᵗːpt W, *3ptsg* wɔᵗːpt Gl
1.2. *vt* to slip a calf. *-ed* wɔᵗɹpt Brk, *-ed* wɔᵗːpt So
2.1. *v* to SLIP *A FOAL* III.4.6. waᵗːp W, wɔːp Gl
2.2. *vt* to slip a foal. *-ed* waᵗːpt W, wɔᵗːp So, *-ed* wɔᵗːpt Brk
3. *n* LOW-LYING LAND IV.1.7. waːp L
4. *vi* If a door has been made of unseasoned wood, before long it will be sure to .... IX.2.9. Eng. ⇒ **balk, buckle, cave, cave in, crine, draw, geal,** *get warped,* *get wrung* ⇒ **wring, gizzen, go skellered, kessen, leave chauns in it, pine, plim,** *rift and* **run up, run up, sag, sap** *and* **crack, shevel up, shrink, sink, skeller, skeller up, skellet, skew, swell, twist, wring, wry;** ⇒ also **gizzened**

warp-land *n* LOW-LYING LAND IV.1.7. waːpland Y L

warpy-land *n* LOW-LYING LAND IV.1.7. wɔːpɪland L

wart *n* a CALLOSITY VI.11.4. *pl* wɔəts Nf, *pl* wɤəts Nf, *pl* wʊət Nf

warterdays *npl* WORKDAYS VII.4.6. *sg* wɒˌɪtədə La

wart-spring *n* a LOOSE *PIECE OF* SKIN at the bottom of a finger-nail VI.7.11. *-s* waʁːtspʁɪŋz Du, *pl* wɔʁːtspʁɪŋz Nb

wartywell 1. *n* the QUICK of a fingernail VI.7.9. wɔːʔɪwɛl O
2. *n* a LOOSE *PIECE OF* SKIN at the bottom of a finger-nail VI.7.11. waːtɪwɛɫ Wo, wəᵗːʈɪwɛl Gl

warwicks* *npl* KNEE-STRAPS used to lift the legs of working trousers VI.14.17. wɔʁɪks Nb

wash 1. *v, vt* To get your dirty pots and pans clean, what do you do? V.9.5. Eng. ⇒ **scour, scour dishes,** *scour them, scour the pans out,* **wash** *them* **out, wash** *them* **up, wash** *the pans* **out, wash up**
2. *n* a FORD IV.1.3. wɒʃ St Ess*[tidal]*
3. *n* LOW-LYING LAND IV.1.7. wɔʃ L
4. *n* a SHEEP-HOLE in a wall IV.2.8. wɔᵗːʃ So
5. *n* old **wash** stale URINE used for cleaning blankets VI.8.8. aːld wɛʃ La*[old]* Y, aːd wɛʃ La, ɒud wɛʃ La Y Db, ɔːd wɛʃ Y, ɔuld wɛʃ Y

wash-basket *n* a CLOTHES-BASKET V.9.7. wɛʃbæːskɪt Wo, wɒʃbaˑskɪt Nf, wɔːʃbaːskət Sf

washing-basket *n* a CLOTHES-BASKET V.9.7. wɒʃɪnbaːskɪt Wa Mon Ess, wɔːʃɪnbaːskɪt Sa

washing-up-cloth *n* a DISHCLOTH V.9.6. wɒʃɪnʌpklɔːθ Ess

wash out *vtphr* to WASH pots and pans V.9.5. waɪʃ ... aʊt So, wɒʃ ... ɛʊt Nf Ess K, wɔːʃ ... aʊt Do, wɔᵗːʃ ... æʏt So, wɔᵗːʃ ... æʊt W

wash-tank *n* an artificial CESS-POOL on a farm I.3.11. wɛʃtaŋk Db

wash up 1. *vtphr* to WASH pots and pans V.9.5. wɛʃ ... ʊp We Y Nt, wɛɪʃ ... ʊp La Db, waɪʃ ... ʌp D, waʃ ... ʏp Nf, wɒʃ ... ʌp He Nf Bk Ess Brk Sx, wɒʃ ... ʏp Nf, wɒʃ ... ʊp Wa Nf Bk, wɒɪʃ ... ʌp W, wɔʃ ... ʌp Ess Sr, wɔːʃ ... ʌp Sf Sx, wɔᵗːʃ ... ʌp So
2. *vphr* to wash pots and pans. wɛʃ ʊp Y, wɒʃ ʌp Nf Hrt Brk Ha, wɔʃ ʌp MxL

wash-way *n* a FORD IV.1.3. wɒʃwæɪ Ess

wasp(s) *n* What do you call those yellow insects that get into the jam-pot; they sting you? IV.8.7.
?sg/?pl: wæsp He K, wasp L Ha*[sg and pl]*, waːsp Wo O, wɒsp So K, wɔːsp Ess
pl: wæsps Man He Wo Mon Gl Sr, *sg* wæsp So K, wasps Nb Cu Du We La Y Ch Db Sa St He Wo Wa Mon Nt L Lei R Nth So Co Do, was Ch, waːsps Sa Wo L Nf, *sg* waːsp O, wɑːsps Wo Nf, wʌsps Nf, wɒsps St He Wa Mon Lei Nth Hu Nf Bk Bd Hrt Ess So Sr Co D Sx, wɒsː Ess, wɒspɪz Hrt, wɔsps O Nf Sf Hrt Ess MxL Sr K, wɔːsps Nth C Nf Sf
[phonetic forms make precise identification of sg or pl difficult]
⇒ **apple-bees, apple-dranes, apple-drones, wamps, wappers, wappies, waps, wapsies**

waste 1. *n* RUBBISH V.1.15. wɛɪst Ess
2. *n* ASHES from a cold fire V.4.5. weˈɪst Nf *[marked u.r. EMBM]*
3. *vi* to WANE, referring to the moon VII.6.5.(b). weːst Gl Nf, *-ing* weːstɪn W, *-ing* weːstən W Ha, *-ing* weɪstɪn Hu, *-ing* weɪstn̩ Nf, *-ing* əweɪstn Nf, weɪs C, weːɪst Mon Gl, *-ing* weːᵊstn Nf, wɛɪst C Nf Sf Ess, *3prsg* wɛɪstɪz Brk, *-ing* wɛɪstɪn Brk Sr K Sx, *-ing* waɪstɪn W, *-ing* waɪstən Ha, *-ing* waɪsn Ha; **on the waste** ɒn ðə weɪst Nf

waste away *viphr* to WANE, referring to the moon VII.6.5.(b). weːs əwæɪ Gl, *3prsg* weːɪsɪz əweːɪ Wo, -ing weɪstɪn əweɪ Bk, -ing wɛɪstɪn əweɪ Sx[old], prppl waɪstɪn əwaɪ W

waste-dump n an ASH-MIDDEN V.1.14. wɛɪsdʌmp Sx

waste-heap n an ASH-MIDDEN V.1.14. wɛɪshiːp Ess

waster 1. n a BLIND TEAT III.2.7. wɛɪstə L
2. n a WEAKLING piglet III.8.4. wɛːᴵstə Nf

waste stuff n RUBBISH V.1.15. wɛɪəst stʌf Brk

waste water n URINE in a cow-house I.3.10. wɛɪs woˑtə Nf

wasting v-ing THAWING, referring to snow VII.6.15. wɛɪstɪn Sr

watch vt LOOK AFTER VIII.1.23. watʃ Nb[old] Y, prppl watʃn Nb, wɒtʃ Lei; **watch over** watʃ oˑə Db

watch-curb n a watch-CHAIN VI.14.12. watʃkəːb Y

watch-guard n a watch-CHAIN VI.14.12. wɒtʃgɑːᴵd Sr

water 1. n URINE in a cow-house I.3.10. watə Cu Y, wɔːtə Lei Ess Sx, wɔːᵊdə Sf, wɔːtəᴵ Sr K, wɔːtəᵗ He Brk Sr Sx, wɔːtˤə Nf, wɔːʔə O Nf, wɔːɪɐ K
2. n **stale water, tainted water** stale URINE used for cleaning blankets VI.8.8. **stale water** stɛɪʊ wɔːtəᵗ Brk; **tainted water** tɛɪntɪd wɔːtəᵗ Brk
3. n WHEY V.5.8(b). wɔʔə Nf [marked ir.r. EMBM, but compare **milk-water**]

water-ask n a NEWT IV.9.8. watərask We, watɹask Cu

water-cress(es) n CRESS V.7.17(b).
no -es: wiːtəgɹɛs Ch, weːtəkɹɛs La Ch, weˑtəkɹɛs St, weɪtəkɹɛs St, wæˑtərkreˑs Man, wætəᵗːkɹɛs So, watəkɹɪɪs Y, watəkɹɪˑəs L, watɹkɹɪˑs L, watəkɹɛs Y Ch L, watəkɹɛʃ Y, watəkɹæʃ Y, watəkɹaʃ Y, wɒtəᴵkɹɛˑs Brk, wɔːtəkɹɪɪs Ess, wɔːʔəkɹɪɪs Nf Sf Bd, wɔːʔətˤːkɹɪɪs W, wɔːᵊdəkɹɪɪs C, wɔːdətˤːkɹɪɪs So Ha, wɔːtətˤkɹɪɪs Sx, wɔːdəkɹeˤːs So, wɔːtəkɹɛs St Mon Nth Ess K, wɔːtəᴵkɹɛs K, wɔːtətˤkɹɛs Sx, wɔːtətˤkɹɛs Ha, wɔˑʔəkɹɛs Nf, wɔːdətˤkɹɛs So, wɔːdətˤːkɹɛːs So, wʊətəkɹɛs L
-es: wɔːtəkɹɪːsɪz Sr

water-drain n a DRAIN in a cow-house I.3.8. wɔˑʔəᴵdɹɛɪn Brk

water-dubs npl PUDDLES IV.1.6. watədʊbz Y

water-evet n a NEWT IV.9.8. wɔːdətˤːɹɛvət D

water-frost 1. n HOAR-FROST VII.6.6. wɔːʔəfɹɔɪst Nf
2. n DEW VII.6.7. watəfɹɒst Cu, wɔʔəfɹɔːst Nf[heavy dew x1], wɔʔəfɹɔːs Nf[heavy dew x2], wɔːtʔəfɹɔːs Nf, wɔːʔəfɹɔːst Nf

water-furrow n a DITCH IV.2.1(c). wɔːtəᴵfəɹʊɹ K, pl wɔːtəᴵfətˤːɹz̩ Sr

water-hole 1. n a POOL on a farm III.3.9. wɛːtəɹʊʊl St, watəhøːl Du, watəɹɔɪl Y, watɹuːl Ch, wɔːtɔɹʊʊl St
2. n a small pool. watəɹɒɪl Y, watəɹɔɪl Y

water-holes npl PUDDLES IV.1.6. watəɹɒɪlz La

watering-hole n a POOL on a farm III.3.9. watɹɪnwɒl We, watɹɪnwɒl We, wɔːtəᵗɹɪnɒːɫ Sx

watering-place n a POOL on a farm III.3.9. wetɔʁɪnpleːs Nb

watering-spot n a POOL on a farm III.3.9. watəɹɪnspɒt Y

water-lizard n a NEWT IV.9.8. wɔːtəlɪzəd K

water-logged adj BOGGY IV.1.8. watəlɒgd Y, watəlɒgd L, wɒtəlɒgd Hrt, wɔːtəlɒgd St Mon Ess, wɔːtəᴵlɒgɪd K, wɔːʔəᴵlægd Ha, wɔˑʔəlɒg Nf, wɔːdəlɒgd Ess

waterloo-rubber n a WHETSTONE made of stone II.9.10. wɔːʔəluːɹʌbəᴵ K

waterloo-stone n grey sandstone, ⇐ WHETSTONE II.9.10. wɒːʔluːstoˑn Nf, wɔʔəluston Nf

water-meadow(s) n LOW-LYING LAND IV.1.7.
no -s: wɔːtəmɛdə Gl, wɔːtətˤːmɛdoː W, wɔːdətˤːmɛdoː W Do, wɔːdətˤːmɛdə W Ha, wɔːdətˤːmɛdətˤː Do
-s: weːtətˤmɛdoːz He, wɒdətˤːmɛdətˤːz̩ Do, wɔːtəmɛdəz Lei R, wɔːtᵗmɛdəz O, wɔːdətˤːmɛdəz W D Ha, wɔːdətˤːmɛdətˤːz̩ Ha, wɔtˤːʔətˤmɛdəz Bk

water-mead(s) n LOW-LYING LAND IV.1.7.
no -s: wɒʔətˤːmiːᵊd W, wɔːdətˤːmeːd Ha
-s: wɔːdətˤːmeːdz Ha

water-pit n a POND IV.1.5. weɪtəpɪt St

water-place n a drinking-pool in a stream, ⇐ POOL III.3.9. watəpleˑəs La

water rime n HOAR-FROST VII.6.6. watɹɹaˑɪm L

water-sallow n WILLOW IV.10.7. wɔtʔəsæɫə Nf

water-slog* adj BOGGY IV.1.8. wɔʔəslɒg Nf

water-soaked adj BOGGY IV.1.8. wɔːdətˤːz̩oːkt D

water-splash n a FORD IV.1.3. wɔːtəsplæʃ Sf Bk, weːᴵtəsplaʃ Db, watəsplaʃ Y, waːtəsplaʃ Y, wɔːʔəsplaʃ Bk

water-spout n the GUTTER of a roof V.1.6. watəspaʊt La, watəspᵊuːt We, wɔːtətˤspəʊt Brk

water-stock n a TROUGH in a cow-house I.3.6. wɔːtəᴵstɒk K

water-swift n a NEWT IV.9.8. wɔːtəswɪft Sf, wɔːᵊtʔəswɪft Sf

water-table* n a shallow roadside gutter, ⇐ DITCH IV.2.1(c). wɔːdətˤːteːbɫz D

water-trough 1. n a TROUGH in a cow-house I.3.6. wɔˑʔətɹɒft Nf, wɔːtətˤtɹɒːf Ha
2. n the GUTTER of a roof V.1.6. wɔʔətɹɒʊ Nf, wɔːtətɹɒ Ess, wɔːtətɹɔːf Ess, wɔːᵊtətɹɔˑʔf Sf, pl wɔːʔːtɹɒuz Nf

water-wash n a FORD IV.1.3. watəweʃ Y

water-way n a FORD IV.1.3. wɒtˤːtˤətˤweː Mon

watery *adj* INSIPID, describing food lacking in salt V.7.8. watəɹɪ Y *[marked u.r. NBM]*

watery-meadows *n* LOW-LYING LAND IV.1.7. wɔːtɹɪmɛdəz St

wath *n* a FORD IV.1.3. waθ Cu We Y, waːθ Cu, wɔθ Y

wath-stead *n* a FORD IV.1.3. waθstɪəd Y

wat-man *n* a LEFT-HANDED person VI.7.13(a). wɒtmʊn Gl

watted *adj* LEFT-HANDED VI.7.13(a). wɒtɪd Gl

wattle *1. n* coarse fibre STRING used to tie up a grain-sack I.7.3. wɒtl Wo
2. v to PEN or FOLD sheep in part of a field to be ready for dipping III.7.10. wɒtl Db

wattle-gates *npl* HURDLES used to pen sheep in part of a field III.7.11. wætlgeɪts K, *sg* wɒdɫgeɪt K*[old]*

wattle-hurdles *npl* HURDLES used to pen sheep in part of a field III.7.11. watⳑəːdlz Ch, wɒtⳑəːdlz St, wɒdɫəᵗːdɫz Co, wɒʔthəᵗːdɫz W, wɔtɫəᵗdɫz Ha, *sg* wɔʔɫəᵗdɫ K

wattle(s) *n What do you call this part [gesticulate] hanging down underneath the beak [of a hen]?* IV.6.19.

no -s: watl Y Sa*[old]* L, watuɫ Lei, wɒtl Sa, wɒtɫ Wo Mon, wɒtuɫ Sx, wɒʔɫ K, wɔtl Y, wɔtɫ Sr
-s: wætlz Db, wætɫz He Wo Mon, watlz Cu Du We La Y Ch Db Sa St Nt L, waʔlz Ch L, watɫz Lei, waklz Y, wɒtlz La Db Sa St Wa Gl Nth, wɒtʔlz Nf, wɒʔlz Ch O Nth Nf, wɒtɫz St He Wo Wa Mon Gl Lei R Nth W Sr K Ha Sx, wɒtuɫz Lei Brk, wɒtʔlz Ess, wɒʔlz R Hu Bk Ess So Brk Ha, wɒʔətɫz Bk, wɒʔuɫz Lei, wɒplz Sa, wɔtlz Y O L, wɔtⳑz W K, wɔtʔlz MxL, wɔʔlz Ess
⇒ **beard, bells, buffs**, *chawls* ⇒ **chowls, chillicks, chole, choller(s), cholly, chonks, chowls, chuckle(s), cob, comb, crest, crop, ears, giblets, giblicks, gill(s), glot, gobble(s), gobbler**, *gobblets* ⇒ **goblet(s), goblet(s), goggle, grop, gullet, jib, joblets, jowl(s), lobe(s), lobs, lops, lugs, pocket-handkerchief, reds, tassels, waddles, wadlets, wattlings, wellits**; ⇒ also **waffles**

wattles *1. n* TWINE used to fasten thatch on a stack II.7.7(b1). watlz Wo*[coarse string]*
2. npl HURDLES used to pen sheep in part of a field III.7.11. watlz Y*[basket-work]*, wadɫz Dₑ, wɒtlz Db, wɒdɫz Sx, *sg* wɒdɫ K, wɒʔɫz Sx*[old x1]*, wɒtuɫz Sr, wɒduz Sr Sx, wɔtɫz Sr, wɔdɫz Sr

wattlings *1. n* the WATTLES of a hen IV.6.19. watlɪnz Lei
2. n the wattles of a young turkey. wɒʔlɪnz Nth

watty *adj* LEFT-HANDED VI.7.13(a). watɪ Wo

watty-handed *adj* LEFT-HANDED VI.7.13(a). wætɪ-ændɪd He, wætɪ-ɒndɪd Wo Gl, watɪ-andɪd Wo Gl, wɒtɪ-andɪd Gl, wɒʔɪ-andɪd O

waugh *adj* INSIPID, describing food lacking in salt V.7.8. wɔːf La Y

waughy *adj* INSIPID, describing food lacking in salt V.7.8. wɔːfɪ Y

wave-wind* *n* BINDWEED II.2.4. weːvwɔɪn Gl O, weɪvwɔɪn Wo *[WMBM headword **weave-wind**]*

wax *1. vi The moon is always changing its size. How do you speak of that?* VII.6.5(a). *-ing* wæksən Man, *-ing* wæksɪn Hrt Brk, waks Nb Du Y St Bk, *-ing* waksɪn Wo; **wax full** wæːks fʊɫ Hrt.
⇒ **come, come forward, come full, come** *into* **full, come on, come***s* **afresh, come** *to be* **full, come** *to the* **full, come** *to the* **full** *moon*, **come up, come up** *to the full*, **expand, fill, fill up, full, full up, gain, gather, get big, get big***ger*, **get** *for* **full, get full, get full***er*, **get full** *moon*, **get larger, get older, get** *on the* **full, get***s* **bigger, get** *to the* **full, get up, get up** *for the* **full, get up full, get up** *to the* **full, go bigger**, *go for the* **full, go up, grow, grow big, grow fuller**, *he'll soon be full, he's fulling, he's making himself* ⇒ **make**, *he's on the grow* ⇒ **grow, increase**, *in his growing* ⇒ **grow, it's getting to the** full, *it's on its first quarter*, **make**, *on the* **full**, *on the* **make**, *on the* **rise, rise, rise up, swell**, *the moon's in the first quarter*, **turn bigger, wax** *full*
2. n COW-DUNG I.3.12. wɛks K

way *1. n* **in this way, that way, thick way, thicker way, thicky way, this way** *If I asked how you fold your arms, you'd probably show me and say: Well, I just do it ....* IX.10.7. **in this way** ə ðɪs wɪə Nb, ə ðɪs weː We, ə ðɪs weə Y*[old]*, ə ðɪs weə Y; **that way** ðæt weɪ Brk, ðæt wæɪ Sf Ess, ðæʔ wæɪ Nf, ðat wɪə Nb, ðat weː Nb Y, ðat wɛɪ Wa Co, ðat waɪ W; **thick way** ðɪk weː Ha, ðɪk weɪ So, ðɪk waɪ Do; **thicker way** ðɪkə weɪ Brk; **thicky way** ðɪkɪ weɪ D; **this way** ðiːz weɪ D, ðɪs wiː St, ðɪs wɪə Du Y, ðɪs weː Nb La Y Db Sa Mon O Nt D, ðɪs weɪ Man Bd So Ha, dɪs weɪ Man, ðɪs weə Nb Du, ðɪs weː Cu We, ðɪs wɛɪ St Bk Ess W Co Ha, ðɪs wɛə Y L, ðɪs wæɪ Gl Lei Hrt MxL K, dɪs wæɪ Sx, ðɪəz waːɪ So. ⇒ **athisen(s)**, *athisn* ⇒ **athisen(s)**, *in that* **road**, *in this* **how**, *in this* **road, like so, like that, like thick, like this, like this** *here*, **so**, *that* **road**, *that* **way**, *thick* **way**, *thicker* **way**, *thicky* **lot**, *thicky* **way**, *this* **how**, *this* **road**, *this* **way**
2. imp the command stop! or WOA!, given to plough-horses II.3.5(c). weː La sw Y Ch Db Sa He Wo Gl So W Co D Do Ha, weɪ Du La Y Sa He Wo Wa Mon So W Do Ha, wɛɪ Cu We La Y Db Sa St O Nt L W Brk Sr D Sx, wœːɪ Mon, wɔɪ L, wʊɪ Nt, wəɪ Cu Du We La Y Ch Db Gl L So W D Do
3. imp the command TURN LEFT!, given to plough-horses II.3.5(a). wɛɪ K, wæɪ K
4. imp **way with you** GO AWAY! VIII.7.9(a). weː wɪ ðɪ Y, wɛˑə wɪ ðə Y

way-bind *n* BINDWEED II.2.4. wɛɪbɔɪnd Wa

way-wind *n* BINDWEED II.2.4. weːwɔɪnd O,
weɪwɔɪn O, wɛɪwɔɪn Wa O, wɛɪwɔˑɪnd Wa,
wɛəˡwɒɪnd Wo

way woa *imp* the command stop! or WOA!, given to
plough-horses II.3.5(c). 'wɛː wʊː Lei, 'wɛɪ 'wɔʊ Lei

weak *1. adj When you get up after being ill in bed for
a long time, you are sure to feel very ....* VI.13.2. Eng.
⇒ crocky, dicky, fainty, feeble, femmer, groggy,
moal, shaky, shoddy, waffly, waffy, wammocky,
wammy, wankle, wankly, wanky, weakly, wobbly,
wonkly, wonky

2. *adj* a bit weak INSIPID, describing food lacking
in salt V.7.8. ə bɪt wɪək Y

weakling *n What do you call the smallest and weakest
pig of the litter?* III.8.4. wiːklɪn La, wiːklən Man,
wɪəklɪn Y, weəklɪn Y. ⇒ anthony, cad, caddy,
crink, crit, crut, dack, dall, dall-pig, daniel,
darling, darrel, dawl, dawling, dawl-pig, degs,
diddling, dilling, *doll* ⇒ dall, dolly, dolly-pig,
dorrel, dwindler, harry, harry-hog, harry-pig,
jack, joey, *little* dawling, *little* harry, *little* jo, nestle,
nestle-bird, nestle-draf, nestle-dredge, *nestle-dris*
⇒ nestle-drish, nestle-drish, nestle-tripe, nisgal,
niskral, niskwal, nuzzle-tripe, pepman, petman,
piggy-whidden, pipman, pitman, rack, rackling,
ratling, recklien, reckling, retling, rick, rickling,
ridling, *rinklin* ⇐ rinkling, rinkling, rinnick, rit,
ritling, runt, runtling, rut, rutling, squabble,
squeaker, tiddling, underling, waster, weanel,
weaning, weedling, whidden, winkling

weakly *adj* WEAK, describing a sheep that is not
thriving VI.13.2. wɪˈəklɪ L

weals *npl* BLISTERS VI.11.5. wɪˈəlz L *[queried u.r.
BM]*

wean *v/vt When you take a calf away from its
mother's milk, what do you say you do?* III.1.4. Eng
exc. Cu Du We. ⇒ buss, hob, spane, spone, suckle,
take off, turn, weand, wean off

weand *v* to WEAN a calf III.1.4. -*ing* wiːndɪn Y,
wɛˈənd L *[not a NBM headword]*

weanel *n* a WEAKLING piglet III.8.4. wiɪnəł Ess

weaning *n* a WEAKLING piglet III.8.4. wiːnɪn Db

wean off *vtphr* to WEAN a calf III.1.4. -*ing* wiːnɪn ...
ɑːf Mon

wear *vi* to WANE, referring to the moon VII.6.5(b).
wɛəˡ He; on the wear ɒn ðə wɛəˡ Mon

weared out *adj* EXHAUSTED, describing a tired
person VI.13.8. wɛəd ɛʊt Wa, wəˡːd̩ æʏt D

wearing clothes *n* ORDINARY   CLOTHES
VI.14.20. weˀrɪn klous Man

weasand *1. n* a THROAT VI.6.3. wɔzɪn Wa

2. *n* the WINDPIPE VI.6.5. wɪzn Nb, wɛzɪn Cu,
wɛzn We Y, wɛɪzn Nb

weasel *n What do you call that small animal, reddish
brown, white throat, short legs and tail, about half as
big as a ferret; it kills rabbits?* IV.5.6. Eng. ⇒
jack-weasel, kine, mouse-hunter, puttice,
rezzle, stoat, vairy, white-neck, white- throat,
whitret, whitrick

weasums* *n* POTATO-HAULMS   II.4.4.
wiːzʊmz Ch, wiːzəmz Ch, wɛɪzʊmz Ch*[old]*

weather *n* a HALO round the moon VII.6.4.
wɛðə Ch

weather-board *n* the THRESHOLD of a door
V.1.12. wɛðəbɔəd Cu, wɛðəbɔːd Db, wɛðəbɔəd
Mon, wɛðəbɔəɹd La Db *[queried ir.r. N/WMBM]*

weather-sign *n* a HALO round the moon VII.6.4.
wɛðəsɑɪn Y

web-footed *1. adj* PIGEON-TOED   VI.10.4.
wɛbfʊtɪd Du

2. *adj* SPLAY-FOOTED VI.10.5. wɛbfʊtɪd Du

wed *adj* MARRIED VIII.1.17. wɛd Cu Du*[old
x1]* La Y Db Sa*[old x1]* Wo Gl L

wedded *adj* MARRIED VIII.1.17. wɛdɪt Cu We,
wɛdt We La, wɛdɪd Nb Cu Du We Ess, wɛdd La

wednesday-and-thursday *adj*   SPLAY-
FOOTED VI.10.5. wɛnzdɪənθɑːzdɪ Nf

wee *imp* the command stop! or WOA!, given to
plough-horses II.3.5(c). wiː Cu Y Ch St He Nf

weed *n* WEEDS, unwanted plants that grow in a
garden II.2.1. wiːd Du Y Sa St O Ess Brk K Co D,
wɪd Sx, wɛɪd Y Db, wəɪd Y

weedling *n* a WEAKLING piglet III.8.4. wiːdlɪn
Cu

weeds *n What do you call the things that grow in
your garden and shouldn't be there?* II.2.1. wiːds
Man, wiːdz Eng, wɪdz Sa Wa Mon Gl So, weːdz
Sa Ha, wɛɪdz Ch Db St He Lei, wəɪdz Y Hrt. ⇒
filth, kelter, ket, mullock, rammel, rubbish,
weed

week-a-day clothes *n* ORDINARY CLOTHES
VI.14.20. wiiːkədɪ klɒʊðz Sx, wiiːkədɛɪ klɒʊðz
Sx, wiːkədɛɪ klɒʊðz K, wiːkəde: klʊəz Y *[not a
NBM headword]*

week-a-day-days *npl* WORKDAYS   VII.4.6.
wiːkədɪdɛɪz Sf

week-a-days *1. n* ORDINARY   CLOTHES
VI.14.20. *sg* wˀiːkədɛɪ Ess, wiːkədeɪz Bk

2. *npl* WORKDAYS VII.4.6. wiːkədeɪz Bd,
wiiːkədɛɪz Sx

week-a-days clobber *n* ORDINARY CLOTHES
VI.14.20. wɪkədɛɪz klɒbə Ess

week-a-days clothes *n* ORDINARY CLOTHES
VI.14.20. wɪkədɛɪz klʌʊz Ess

weekday clothes *n* ORDINARY   CLOTHES
VI.14.20. wiːkdɪ tlɒɪz La, wiːkdɪ klɒʊðz K,
wiiːkdɛɪ klɒʊðz Sx, wɪkdɛɪ klɒʊz Wo, wɪkdeɪ
kłɔːz W, wiiːkdɛɪ klɔʊðz Brk, wiːkdɪ klɔʊz Lei,
wiːkdɛɪ klɔʊz Lei, wˀiːkdɪ klʌʊz Hrt, wiːkdɛɪ
klʌʊz Ess, wiːkdɛɪ klʌʊz Ess, wɪkdæɪ klʌʊz Ess,
wiiːkdɛɪ klo:ðz Brk, wiːkdɪ klo:z Sa, wiːkde:

kloːz Sa, wɪkdeɪ kloːz So, wɪkdæɪ kloːz He, wiːkdɪ tloːz Ch, wɪkdeː kɫoːz W, wɪikdeɪ kloˈʊðəz Brk, wᵊiːkdeɪ klouz Bd, wiːkdæi klouz Nf, wɪˈkdeɪ tlouz Nf, wɪikdæɪ tlouz Nf, wɪkdaɪ kloːʊz Gl, wiːkdɪ kluəz O, wɪkdeɪ kluəz Bk, wiːkdeˑə kluəz L, wiːkdɪ tluəz La, wiːkdeː tluəz Nt, wɪkdiː tlᵁuːz Db

weekdays *1. n* ORDINARY CLOTHES VI.14.20. wiːkdeɪz Sf

2. npl WORKDAYS VII.4.6. wiːkdɪz Lei, wiːkdeːz Y Sa Mon O, wiːkdeɪs Man, wiːkdeɪz C Bk So, wiːkdeəz Y, wiːkdɛɪz Y St Wa Lei R Nf Bk Ess MxL Brk Sr K Co, wiːkdæɪz Nf Hrt So K, wɪkdiːz St, wɪkdɪz Sa, wɪkdeːz La Y Ch Wo So W D Do, wɪkdeɪz Wo So W, wɪkdɛːz W, wɪkdɛɪz St Wo Bk Co Ha Sx, wɪkdæɪz He Mon Gl, wɪkdaɪz Ha, wɪəkdeːz Y

weekday suit *n* ORDINARY CLOTHES VI.14.20. wɪikdeɪ suːt Nf

weekday things *n* ORDINARY   CLOTHES VI.14.20. wiːkdeɪ θɪŋz Ess

weekday togs *n* ORDINARY CLOTHES VI.14.20. wɪkdeɪ tɒgz Nth

weekenday clothes *n* ORDINARY   CLOTHES VI.14.20. wikndeɪ kloːz So

weeken-days *npl* WORKDAYS VII.4.6. wiːkŋdeːz D, wiːkŋdeɪz D

week's-days *npl* WORKDAYS VII.4.6. wiːksdeɪz K

weeping-willow *n* WILLOW IV.10.7. wiːpnwɪlə Nf

weesh *imp* the command TURN RIGHT!, given to plough-horses II.3.5(b). wiˑʃ Nf, wɪʃ Nf Sf

weeting* *vt-ing* PULLING his ear VI.4.4. wiːtən Co

wee-wub *adj* ASKEW, describing a picture that is not hanging straight IX.1.3. wiːwʌb So

weigh *1. vt* If you want to know how heavy a thing is, what do you do? I.7.1. Eng. ⇒ **heft, scale, weigh off, weight**

2. n an EVENER on the plough-beam end of a horse-drawn plough I.8.4. weː Do

weigh-bar *n* an EVENER on the plough-beam end of a horse-drawn plough I.8.4. weɪbaˤː So, waɪbaˤː Do

weigh-beam *n* an EVENER on the plough-beam end of a horse-drawn plough I.8.4. weːbiːm W, wɛɪbiːm W, waɪbiːm So W Ha

weigh-iron *n* the T-SHAPED PLOUGH-BEAM END of a horse-drawn plough I.8.5. wɛɪ-ɑːᵊn Ess

weigh off *vtphr* to WEIGH something I.7.1. wɛɪ ... ɒf Brk, -*ing* wɛɪ-ɪn ... ɔːf Sx

weigh(s) *n* a SWINGLE-TREE of a horse-drawn plough harness I.8.3.

sg: wɛɪ Bk

-*s*: wɛɪz Bk

weight *1. n* the CLOG on a horse's tether I.4.3. wɛɪt Y Wo Sr, wæɪt Ch He Ess, waɪt Do

2. vt to WEIGH something I.7.1. weɪt Ha

weigh-tree *n* an EVENER, the main swingle-tree of a horse-drawn plough I.8.4. weɪtɹiː Hrt, wɛɪtɹiː Hrt Ess, wæɪtɹiː Ess

well *1. adj* If you are in good health, you must be feeling very .... VI.13.1(a). Eng. ⇒ **all right, brave, bravish, canny, fine, first rate, fit, fit** *and* **well, fitty, gay, good, grand, healthy, knicky, litty, middling, pert,** *pretty* **brave,** *pretty* **fit, proper, spruce, tidy, top hole, topping,** *up to the* **mark, well** *and fit*; ⇒ also *in the* **fettle**

2. adj **none so well, not so well, not too well, not very well** ILL, describing a person who is unwell VI.13.1(b). **none so well** nʊən sə wiːl Y, nʊən sə wɛl Y; **not so well** næt sə wiːl Y, nʊt sɪ wəɪl Y; **not too well** nɔt tuː wɛʊ Sr; **not very well** nɒt vɛɹɪ wiːl Y, nʊt vaɹɪ wiːl Y, ɪznt vaɹɪ wiːl Y, ɑːnt wɛɹɪ wɛl Nf

3. adj **none so well, not so well, not very well, not well** SICK, describing an animal that is unwell VI.13.1(c). **none so well** nʊən sə wiːl Y, nʊən sə wɛl Y; **not so well** nɔt sə wiːl Y; **not very well** nʊt vaɹɪ wiːl Y, nʊt vaɹə weɪl Y, ɪznt vaɹɪ wiːl; **not well** nɒʔ wɛʊ Ess, eɪnt wɛɫ Nf, ɛːnt wɛl Nf, ɛnt wɛʊ Sx

4. adv **pretty well** ALMOST VII.7.9. pɹɪtɪ wɛɫ C, pəˤː wɛɫ D

5. adv VERY VIII.3.2. wiːl Y

6. n a deep CESS-POOL on a farm I.3.11. wɛɫ Ess

7. n the ASH-HOLE or other place in which the ashes are collected beneath a domestic fire V.3.3. wɛl Y, wɛɫ Ha

well-dressing *n* a local FESTIVAL or holiday VII.4.11. wɛldɹesɪn Db

well-grate *n* the place in which the ashes are collected beneath a domestic fire, ⇐ ASH-HOLE V.3.3. wɛɫgɹæɪt MxL

wellits *n* the WATTLES of a hen IV.6.19. wɛlɪts L *[queried EMBM]*

welly *adv* ALMOST VII.7.9. wɛlɪ La St; ⇒ also **near**

welsh* *adj* INSIPID, describing food lacking in salt V.7.8. wɛlʃ Cu We Y

wemble *vt* to SPRAIN an ankle VI.10.8. wɛmbl L

wem-footed *adj* SPLAY-FOOTED   VI.10.5. wɛˈmpfʊˤɪd Nf *[queried EMBM]*

wench *n* a DAUGHTER VIII.1.4(b). wɛntʃ Ch Db, wɛnʃ La Ch Wa Gl*[old]* So

wenches *1. npl* GIRLS VIII.1.3(b). wɛntʃɪz La Ch St, wɛntʃəz Db, *sg* wɛntʃ O, wɛnʃɪz La*[very rare x1]* Y Ch Sa*[old x1]* St*[old x1]* He*[old x3]* Wo Wa Mon*[old x1]* Gl O Brk, wɛnʃəz Sa Gl So W, *sg* wɛnʃ Nb*[obsolete]* Cu Db L Lei Nf*[old x1, rather disrespectful x1]* Bk*[old]*

2. npl WOMEN VIII.1.10. wɛntʃɪz Y

wengs *npl* BOILS VI.11.6. *sg* wɛŋ Y

wented *adj* **go wented** to CURDLE, referring to milk V.5.9. ga wɛntɪt Cu, gaːn wɛntɪd Du*[sour and fluid]*

west *n* a STYE in the eye VI.3.10. wɛst Gl C*[rare]*
Bk Bd Hrt Ha

wet *1. adj* And if something is left out in the rain, it's
bound to get .... VII.6.24. Eng. ⇒ **soaked, soaking,
soaking wet, sogged, sopping wet, wet through,
wetty**

2. adj BOGGY IV.1.8. wɛt Ch*[good, needing
draining x1]* Hrt Ess

3.1. vt to BREW tea V.8.9. *-ing* wɪtɪn K, wɛt He
Mon O So W Sr*[old x1]* K D Do Ha Sx*[old x1]*, wɛd
(+V) D, *-ing* wɛtɪn Brk, *-ing* wɛʔən Man, wat Ha

3.2. v to brew tea. wɛt Mon Gl Sf MxL

4. adj SILLY VIII.9.3. wɛt Nf

wet-eff *n* a NEWT IV.9.8. wɛtɛf Hrt

wet-evet *n* a NEWT IV.9.8. wɛtɛfɪt K

wether *1. n* *[What do you call the animals that give
us wool? When the male lamb grows up, you call it a
....] And if it has been castrated?* III.6.8. ⇒
**fat-hogget, fat-sheep, heeder, heeder-hog, hog,
hogget, pur, shear-hog, *sheep*, tag, teg, tup,
wether-hog, wether-hogget, wether-sheep, wether-
teg**

2. n a EWE-HOG III.6.4. wɛðə Lei *[queried ir.r.
EMBM]*

3. n a GIMMER III.6.5. wɛðə Lei

wether-hog *n* a WETHER III.6.8. wɪðəᶜːɽɒːg So,
wɛðəᵍhœːgˑ Nb, *pl* wɛdəɹɒgz Y, wɛðəᶜːɽʌg So D
[queried SBM on grounds of age and castration]

wether-hogget *n* a WETHER III.6.8. wɛðəhɔˑgət Sf,
wʌðəhɒˑgət Nf

wether-lamb *n* a MALE LAMB III.6.2. wɛðəlæm
Nf, wɛðəlam Db

wether-sheep *n* a WETHER III.6.8. wʌðəʃⁱiːp Nf

wether-teg *n* a WETHER III.6.8. wɛðəˡtɛg Brk,
wɛðəᶜtɛg Sx *[queried SBM on grounds of age and
castration]*

wet land *n* LOW-LYING LAND IV.1.7. wɛt land Nt
[noted as 'probably merely descriptive' EMBM]

wet-pot *n* GRUEL V.7.2. wɪtpɒt So*[weak]* Co

wet through *adj* WET VII.6.24. wɛt tɹɛʊ Nf

wetting *n* stale URINE used for cleaning blankets
VI.8.8. wiːtɪn Y; **old wetting** ɔʊd wiːtɪn Y

wetty *adj* WET VII.6.24. wɛdi Co

whack *vt* to BEAT a boy on the buttocks VIII.8.10.
wæk Ess, wak Ha; **whack his arse** wak ɪz aːs L Do

whacked *adj* EXHAUSTED, describing a tired
person VI.13.8. wɛkt Ess, wækt Brk, wakt Wa Bd D;
fair whacked fɛə wæˑkt Hrt

whacking *vbln* a beating given to a boy on his
buttocks, ⇐ to BEAT VIII.8.10. hwakən Nb; **give
him a good whacking** gɪv ɪm ə gʊd wakɪn Ha; **whack
his arse** wak ɪz aːs L Do

whalebone *n* a MUCK-BRUSH I.3.14. weˑəlbɪan Cu

whalebone-broom *n* a BROOM used for sweeping
outdoors V.9.10. weɪᵊɬbʊnbɹuːm Bd

whalebone-brush *1. n* a MUCK-BRUSH I.3.14.
weɪɬbʊnbɹʌʃ Bd, weːlboːnbɹʊʃ La, kʰweɪlboːn
bruʃ Man

2. n a BROOM used for sweeping outdoors
V.9.10. wɪəlbɪanbɹʊʃ Cu, weːlbeanbɹʊʃ Cu,
hwɛːlbeanbɹʊʃ We, wɛˑəlbʊənbɹʊʃ L

whangers *npl* KNEE-STRAPS used to lift the
legs of working trousers VI.14.17. wæŋəz Ess
[queried EMBM]

whanging *v-ing* THROWING a stone VIII.7.7.
waŋɪn Y

whangs *1. npl* BOOT-LACES VI.14.25. hwɪəŋz
Nb*[leather]*, hweːŋz Nb*[leather x3, leather or
fibre x1, old x1]*, weəŋz Du, wɛŋz La*[leather]*
Y*[old x1, leather x1]*, hwɛŋz Nb*[leather]*,
wæːᵊŋz Nb*[leather]*, waŋz Cu*[leather]*
Du*[leather]* We*[leather]* La*[leather]* Y*[leather
x2]*, hwaŋz Nb*[leather, old]*

2. npl strips of leather. *sg* wɛŋ Y

whankie *n* a ROPE-TWISTER II.7.8. hwaŋkɪ Nb

what *pron* **what one** WHICH (ONE) VII.8.18.
wɒt wʌn Do, wɒt ən W

whauping *v-ing* SHRIEKING, describing the
shrill noise made by a baby VI.5.15. waːpɪn Y

wheat *n* *[What do you mean by corn here in these
parts?] What other kinds of cereals do you know?*
II.5.1. Eng. ⇒ **rivet-wheat, wheats**

wheat-bind *n* BINDWEED II.2.4. wəɪʔbɔɪn Hrt

wheat-cart *vbln* CARTING wheat from the field
II.6.6. weːtkaᶜːt W

wheat-flour *n* FLOUR V.6.1(a). wɹiːtflɛʊəᶜ Sr,
wiːtflæʊə Wa Sr, wiːtflaʊəɹ He

wheat-meal *n* MEAL V.6.1(b). wiˑtmɪɪl Nf,
ʌiːtʰmiːl Mon, wiˑtmiˑɬ Nf, wɹiːtʔmiːᵊl Ess,
hwˡiːtmˡiːl We, wɪətmɛɪl Y, weːtmɛːl Nf,
weɪtmɛɪl Y, wəɪtməɪl Y

wheats *n* WHEAT II.5.1. wiːts Wa Sr Ha

wheat-vine *n* BINDWEED II.2.4. wiːtvɑɪn Bd
Hrt

wheel *n* a HALO round the moon VII.6.4. wiːɬ So
Ha, wiːᵊɬ W Do, wiːᵁɬ W, wɪʊɬ Brk

wheel-block *1. n* the HUB of a cart-wheel I.9.7.
wiːlblɔk L

2. n a chock placed behind and under a wheel to
prevent a cart from going backwards on a hill, ⇐
PROP/CHOCK I.11.2. *pl* wɪˑlblɒks Nf

wheel-box *1. n* the HUB of a cart-wheel I.9.7.
wiːɬbɒks So K

2. n the metal BUSH at the centre of a cart-wheel
I.9.8. wiːɬbɒks Co, wɪʊbɔks Sr

wheel-drug *n* a DRAG used to slow a wagon
I.11.3. wiːɬdɹʌg D

wheel-grease *n* CART-GREASE, used to
lubricate the wheels of a cart I.11.4. wiːɬgɹiːs Do

wheelings *npl* RUTS made by cartwheels IV.3.9.
wiːlɪnz L Hu

wheel-lowses *npl* RUTS made by cartwheels IV.3.9. wɪʊlɒusɪz Sr

wheel-marks *npl* RUTS made by cartwheels IV.3.9. wiːlmaːks Ch, wiːɫməˡːks Wo Do, wiːᵊɫmaːks Ess, *sg* wɪlmaˡːk O, wɪlməˡks Sa*[newly made]*, wɛɪɫmaˡːks D

wheel-pin *n* a LINCH-PIN holding a wheel on a cart I.9.12. wəɪlpɪn Y

wheel-plough *n* a large PLOUGH I.8.1. wiːɫplɛu K

wheel-rakes *npl* RUTS made by cartwheels IV.3.9. wiːlɹɪks La

wheel-ruts *npl* RUTS made by cartwheels IV.3.9. wiːɫɾævts So, *sg* wiːɫɾævt D, wiːᵊɫɾæuts W, wiːɫɾʌts Co, wɪɫɹeuːts Wo, wɪʊɹʌts Sx, wɪiːlɹæuts Sa, wɪːᵊɫɹuts Gl

wheel-shoe *n* a DRAG used to slow a wagon I.11.3. wiˑlʃˡʉ Nf

wheel-spokes *npl* the SPOKES of a cart-wheel I.9.6. wiːlspɔːks Y

wheel-spurlings *npl* RUTS made by cartwheels IV.3.9. *sg* hwiːlspɔːlən Nb

wheel-spurns *npl* RUTS made by cartwheels IV.3.9. hwiːlspɔᴳːnz Nb

wheel-stock *n* the HUB of a cart-wheel I.9.7. wiːᵊɫstɒk Do, *pl* wiːɫstɒks So

wheel-tracks *npl* RUTS made by cartwheels IV.3.9. wiːɫtɾæks Co, wiːɫtɾaks So Co, wᵊiːɫtɹæks Ess, wɪʊtɹæks K

wheel-treads *npl* RUTS made by cartwheels IV.3.9. wɪʊtɹedz Sx

wheelwright *n* a WRIGHT VIII.4.4. Eng

wheezy *adj* HOARSE VI.5.16. wiːzɪ So

whelp *1. vi* When she [i.e. a bitch] is going to have young ones, you say she is going (to).... III.13.3. wɛlp Nb Cu Du We La Y*[old x2]* Ch Db*[old x1]* Sa St Wo Nt*[rare x1]* L Lei Ess K, hwɛlp Nb Du, wɛɫp He Wo Wa Mon Gl O Lei Hu C Sf Bk Bd Ess MxL So W Ha, *-ing* wɛɫpɪn K, wɛʊp Sr K Sx, wælp Ch, woup So, wəɫp So Co D Do. ⇒ *going to have a litter, going to have a litter of pups, going to have her yelps, going to have her young, going to have pups, going to have some pups, going to whelp, have a litter, have her pups, have pup, have puppies, have pups, have some pups, have whelps, have young ones, in* kindle, *in* pup, *in* whelp, *in* young, *is going to have a trip, is going to have her litter, is going to have pups, is going to* pup down, *is going to* whelp, *is going to* whelp down, *is having pups, is in* pup, *is in* whelp, *is in* yelp, *is with* pups, kindle, litter, pup, pup down, *she's in* pup, *she's in* whelp, *to have a litter, to have pups, to have some pups, to have young, to* pup, *to* pup down, *to* whelp, *to* whelp down, *to* yelp, whelp down, yelp

2. **in whelp** pregnant, describing a bitch. ɪn wɛlp Ch Db Wa L, ɪ wɛlp Ch, ɪn wɛɫp Wo Nth Ess So W K Co Do Ha, ɪn wɛʊɫp Brk, ɪn wɛʊp K

whelp down *1. viphr* to WHELP III.13.3. wɛɫp dɛun Sf, wɛɫp dæun Ha, wɛʊp dæun Sr
2. vtphr to give birth to pups. *3prsg* wəɫps ... dæun So

whelps *npl* PUPS or young dogs III.13.4. wɛlps Nb Cu Du We La Y Man Ch Db Sa St Wo Mon Nt L Lei K, hwɛlps Nb Cu Du, wɛɫps Y He Wo Wa Mon Gl O Lei Ess So, wɛʊps Ess Sx, *sg* wɛʊp Sr K, wəlps Y, wəɫps So

where *adv* Your friend says: Look at that cuckoo there. You can't see the bird, and so you ask: ... is it? IX.9.7. Eng. ⇒ **whereabouts, whereabouts to, where to**

whereabouts *adv* WHERE IX.9.7. wɪəɹəbaɪts Ch, wɛəᴶbɛuts K, wɜːɹəbɛːts La *[marked as u.r. NBM]*

whereabouts to *adv* WHERE IX.9.7. wəˡːbæɾts tɤː So

where to *adv* WHERE IX.9.7. wɪə ... tuː Co, wɛˡ ... ʈuː D, weˑtʰuː Mon, wəˡː ... tɤː So Co D, wəˡː ... tuː So W Co Do

whet *v* to WHITTLE a stick I.7.19. hwɛt Du, *-ing* hwɛtn Nb, wɛt Cu We, *-ing* wɛtɪn O *[marked u.r. WMBM]*

whether *pron* WHICH (ONE) VII.8.18. wɪðə Du*[old]*

whetstone *n* When your scythe gets blunt as you are using it, what instrument do you use on it? II.9.10. wɪtstoːn Co, wɛtstɒun Co Sx, wɛtstɔun Lei Nth Ess Brk Ha, wɛtstʌun Bk Ess K, wɛtston Nf, wɛtstoːn Ch Db Sa O So W Co Do, wɛtstoun St Wa Lei Brk, wɛtʔstoun So, wɛtstoːən So Co Do, wɛtstʊn Sf, wɛtstʊən La Nt L So W, wɛtswʊn Wa Gl, wɛtstuːn St D, wɛtstuːən W D Do Ha, wɛtstn Du We Sa Bd, wɛtstən Y Ch Db St Wa Lei Nth Bd Ess So Sr K, hwɛtstən Du, wʁtsn K, wɛdstən Ch Sa, wɛpsən Ess. ⇒

Stone: **balker, bat, bull, bull-stone, burr, carbor, carborundum, carborundum-stone, cotswold-rubbers, daker, dark rubber, emery-stone, flint-stone, free-stone, grinding-stone, grindle-stone, grindstone, grindstone-rub, hard-stone, lea-stone, noither, rough-stone, rub, rubber, rub-stone, sand-stone, scythe-rubber, scythe-stone, sharpening-stone, sharping- stone, soft-rub, stone, straik, sugg, waterloo- rubber, waterloo-stone, whetting-stone, whettle- stone, white rubber, white-stone**

Wood, greased and sanded: **rap-stick,** *riffle* ⇒ **rifle, rifle, rubber, scythe-stick, scythe-strick, straik, strick, strickle, striker**

Metal: **file**

Unspecified: **burr, rub, rubber**
⇒ also **budget**

whetting-stone *n* a WHETSTONE made of stone II.9.10. wɛtɪnstʊən La, wɛttɪnstʊən La

whettle-stone *n* a WHETSTONE II.9.10. wɛtlstʊən St

whey-lead *n* a SALTING-TROUGH III.12.5. weːɫɪd W

whey-milk *n* BEESTINGS V.5.10. waɪmɪɫk W

whey(s) *n And when the milk does that [i.e. curdles], what do you call the stuff you get? [curds and ...]* V.5.8(b).

no -s: Eng

-s: weːz Do, wɛɪz Ess

⇒ **buttermilk, curdle-milk, drainings, milk-water, skimdick, water**

which *pron* **which (one)** *If you offered a boy the choice of six apples, you'd ask him: ... will you have?* VII.8.18. Eng. ⇒ **what** *one,* **whether, whichy, whichy** *one*

whichy *pron* WHICH (ONE) VII.8.18. wɪtʃi Co D; **whichy one** wɪtʃi wʌn Co

whicker *1. vi-3prpl* they WHINNY, describing the noise horses make during feeding time in the stable III.10.3(a). wɪkəᵗ: So W D Do Ha, wɪkəᵗz̩ Gl

2. vi-3prpl they NEIGH, describing the noise horses make in the fields III.10.3(b). wɪkəᵗ Gl, wɪkəᵗ: So*[old x1]* W D Do Ha

whidden *n* a WEAKLING piglet III.8.4. wɪdn Co

while *prep* TILL IX.2.2. wɛl Nb Y L Bd, wɛɫ Sf Bd, waːl Y, waɪl La Y Ch Db Nt L, wal Y, waɪl Y Nt L Nth C Bd Hrt, waɪɫ Lei R Nth Hu C Bd Hrt, wɒl La Y, wɒˈɪɫ Lei, wɔl La Y, wɔɪɫ C Ess, wʌɪl Brk, wəɫ Sx

whim-wham *n* a ROPE-TWISTER II.7.8. wɪmwam D, wɪmwɒm Sr K Sx

whin *n* GORSE IV.10.11. wɪn Du*[old x1]* La Y Nf Sf, *pl* wɪnz Cu We, hwɪn Nb Du, *pl* wɪŋz Y, wʊn Cu, hwʊn Nb*[old]*

whin-bush *n* GORSE IV.10.11. wɪnbʊʃ Cu We La Y*[old x1]* Nf, wɪnbʊs Cu*[old]*, hwɪnbʊs Nb

whine *vi-3prpl* they WHINNY, describing the noise horses make during feeding time in the stable III.10.3(a). wɔɪn Hrt, *3prpl* wəɪnz He Wo Mon

whinge *vi* to SCREAM VIII.8.11. wɪndʒ Cu, wɪnʒ Cu*[= cry]* Du, hwɪnʒ Nb

whinging *v-ing* SHRIEKING, describing the shrill noise made by a baby VI.5.15. *no -ing* wɪndʒ Cu, hwɪnʒən Nb

whinnocking *v-ing* SHRIEKING, describing the shrill noise made by a baby VI.5.15. wɪnɪkən Sf

whinny *1. vi-3prpl [Now tell me your words for the usual cries animals make.] Horses, during feeding-time in the stable, ...* III.10.3(a). Eng exc. Man Sf Bk Hrt W Brk K Co. ⇒ **blore, blow, bray, frinny, holler, hum, hummer, laugh, moan, murr, mutter, mutter out, neigh, nicker, nucker, nutter, snicker, snort, snuffle, stortle, whicker, whine, whinny out, whistle, winker**

2. vi-3prpl (they) NEIGH, describing the noise horses make in the fields III.10.3(b). wɪnɪ Nb Du We La Y Ch Db St O Nt L Lei Nf Ess MxL, wɪnɪz Cu Sr*[mostly mares]*, hwɪnɪ Du, wɪnoʊ St, wɪnə Cu Ch Db St Lei R Nth Hu C, wɪnəz We

whinny out *viphr-3prpl* they WHINNY, describing the noise horses make during feeding time in the stable III.10.3(a). *-ing* wɪnɪ-ɪn aːt Y

whip *1. n What do some farmers lash a horse with?* I.5.12. Eng. ⇒ **cosh, horse-whip, thond,** *thong* ⇒ **thond, twitch**

2. vt to BEAT a boy on the buttocks VIII.8.10. wɪp Lei; **whip his backside** wɪp ɪz bæksaɪd Nf

3. n a SWINGLE-TREE of a horse-drawn plough harness I.8.3. wɪp Co, wɛp Co, wʌp Co

whippen(s)/whippence(s) *n* a SWINGLE-TREE of a horse-drawn plough harness I.8.3.

sg: wɪpɪn Sx, wɪpɔn Sr, wɪpən Co

-s/-ce: wɪpɪnz Brk Sr K Ha Sx, wɪpənz W Sr Ha, wɪpəns Ha, wɛpnz Sr

-ses/-ces: wɪpɪnzɪz Sr Ha, wɪpɪnɪz Sr, wɪpənsɪz Ha, wɪpənsəz W Ha, wɪpənzəz W Ha

*[SBM note indicates that plural of **whippence** or double plural of **whippen** cannot be distinguished]*

whippen-tree(s) *n* a SWINGLE-TREE of a horse-drawn plough harness I.8.3.

sg: wɪpmtɹi D, wɪpmtɹiːz Co

-s: wɪpɪntɹiːz D, wɪpɪntɹiːs D, wɪpmtɹiː Co, wɪpəntɹɪz Sr

whipper *n* the STRETCHER between the traces of a cart-horse I.5.11. wɪpəᵗ O

whipper(s) *n* a SWINGLE-TREE of a horse-drawn plough harness I.8.3.

sg: wɪpəᵗ O

-s: wɪpəᴶz Brk, wɪpəᵗz̩ O Bk D

-ses: wɪpəsɪz W

whippin-lines *npl* the REINS of a plough-horse I.5.5. wɪpɪnlaɪnz Y

whippin-strings *npl* the REINS of a plough-horse I.5.5. wɪpɪnstɹɪŋz Y

whipple *n* a ROPE-TWISTER II.7.8. wɪpɫ K

whipples-tree *n* a SWINGLE-TREE of a horse-drawn plough harness I.8.3. wɪplztɹɪ Nf

whipple-tree *n* an EVENER, the main swingle-tree of a horse-drawn plough I.8.4. wɪpɫtɹɪ Du Db Nf*[3 horses]*, wɪpɫtɹɪ: Bk Ess, wɪpɫtɹɛɪ St *[northern forms with* **-tree** *given this definition, although NBM data less specific]*

whipple-tree(s) *n* a SWINGLE-TREE of a horse-drawn plough harness I.8.3.

sg: wɪpɫtɹɪ: Y, wɪpəltɹɪ: Y, wɪpɫtɹɪ: Bk Hrt Ess MxL Brk, wɪpltɹɪ Nf, wɪpɫtɹɪ Ess K, wɪpʔɫtɹɪ Ess, wɪbɫtɹɪ: Bk

-s: wɪpəltɹɪːz Y, wɪpɫtɹɪːz O Hrt Ess, wɪpɫtɹɪːz D, wɪpʊɫtɹɪɪːz Ess Brk, wɪpʊtɹɪɪːz Ess Sr, wɪpltɹɪɪz

Nf, wɪpɫɹɪz Gl, wɪpɫɹɪs Ess, wɪbɫɹiːz Bd, wɪbɫʔɹɪz Bk

whirl-bone *n* the human HIP-BONE VI.9.1. wəᶜːɫbɔːn Co

whirlers *npl* KNEE-STRAPS used to lift the legs of working trousers VI.14.17. wəᶜːɫətz̩ Sr, wəᶜːɹɫətɹz̩ Sx

whirligigs *npl* MINNOWS IV.9.9. wɔlɪgɪgz Y

whirly *adj* GIDDY IX.1.11. wəᶜːɹɫɪ Sr

whiskers *1. n If you didn't shave here at all [point to the sides of the cheeks], you'd grow....* V.2.6. Eng exc. Man Hu C. ⇒ *beard*, **bonnet-strings, boots, granny's bonnet-strings,** *mutton-chop-whiskers,* **side-beard(s), side-bits, side-blinders, side-blinds, side-board, side-boards, side-braids, side-chats, side-lights, side-lines, side-locks, side-props, side-rails, siders, side-walls,** *side-whiskers*
2. n a BEARD VI.2.7. wɪskəs Db, wɪskəz Y Db, hwɪskəz Nb, *no -s* hwɪskə Man, kwɪskəs Man, wɪskəɹz La
3. n barley AWNS II.5.3. wɪskəz La Y Ch Db St Hrt, hwɪskəz Man*[uncommon]*, wɪskəᴶz La Ch*[childish]*, wɪskəᶜːz̩ So, wɛskəz Db

whistle *1. vi-3prpl* they WHINNY, describing the noise horses make during feeding time in the stable III.10.3(a). wɪsɫ Co, *3prpl* wɪsɫz Mon
2. vi-3prpl they NEIGH, describing the noise horses make in the fields III.10.3(b). wɪsɫ Co
3. n the WINDPIPE VI.6.5. wɪsl L

white *v* to WHITTLE a stick I.7.19. *-ing* wɪtɪn St, hwɛɪt Nb Cu, hwaɪt Du, waɪt Cu We La Y, *-ing* waɪtn Du, waɪt La

white-apron *n* a decorative APRON V.11.2(b). wɔɪtɛɪpəᴶˑn Brk, wʌɪtæɪpɹən Nf

white ash(es) *n* ASH in a burning fire V.4.4.
no -es: waɪt aʃ Y Ch, wɔɪt aʃ Wa
-es: wɔɪt aʃɪz Wo
[marked u.r. NBM]

white-belly-mouse *n* a SHREW-MOUSE IV.5.2. wʌɪtbɛlɪmɛʊs Sr

white-birch *n* a BIRCH tree IV.10.1. wʌɪtbɛk Nf, wʌɪtbəˑtʃ Nf

white bird *n* a GULL IV.7.5. wɔɪt bʊd L

white cheese *n* CHEESE V.5.4(b). wʌɪt tʃiːz Nf

white crow *n* a GULL IV.7.5. *pl* wʌɪt kɹɒuz Nf, wɔɪt kɹʌu Sf

white-flour *n* FLOUR V.6.1(a). wɛɪtfluˑə Cu, waɪtflæʊə Y, waɪtflaʊə Y, waɪtfluə Y, wɔɪtflæʊə Ess, wʌɪtflaːᵊ Nf, wʌɪtflaʊə Nf

white-frost *n* HOAR-FROST VII.6.6. hwɛɪt frɒs Man, hwɛɪ frɒs Man, wɛɪtfɹɒst Ch, wɛɪt fɹɒst Y, wɛɪtfɹɔːst Ch, wæɪt fɹɒst Y, waɪt fɹɔːst La, waɪtvɹæːst So, waɪtfɹɒst Nt, waɪt fɹɒst La Y, fɹɒst Y, waɪt fɹɔːst Y, wɑːt fɹɒst La Y, wɑːt fɹɒst Y, wɑɪtfɹɒst Ch Db Nth, wɑɪt fɹɒst La Y, wɑɪtfɹɔst Ch, wɑɪt fɹɒst La, waɪtfɹɔːst Nth Hrt MxL Sr K, wɑɪt

fɹɔːst La*[old]*, wɑɪʔfɹɔːst Bk Bd, wɑɪᵗfɹɔːs K, wɑɪʔfɹɔːs Bd, wɒɪtfɹɒst St K, wɔɪtfɹɒst Ess Brk, wɔɪtfɹɒːst Ha, wɔɪtfɹɔːst Wa Gl O Nth Sf Ess Sr, wɔɪtfɹɔːs Wa, wɔɪʔfɹɔːst O Bk, wɔɪʔfɹɔːᵊs Bk, wʌɪtfɹɒst Brk Sr, wʌɪtfɹɔːst Wa Nf Sf, wʌɪtfɹɔːs Nf Sr, wʌɪtvɹɔːst Gl, wʌʏtfɹɔːst O, wəɪtfɹɒst Brk Sx

white-hime *n* HOAR-FROST VII.6.6. waɪtaɪm Nt

white hind *n* HOAR-FROST VII.6.6. waɪt haɪnd Y

white-hoar-frost *n* HOAR-FROST VII.6.6. wɔɪtɔᶜːfɹɔːst Wa

white-neck *n* a WEASEL IV.5.6. wɪtnɪk Co, wɪdnɪk Co

white rag *n* HOAR-FROST VII.6.6. waɪt ɹag Y

white-rime *n* HOAR-FROST VII.6.6. wɑɪtɹaɪm L Nth, wɔɪtɹʌʏm O

white rind *n* HOAR-FROST VII.6.6. waɪt ɹaɪn Du

white rubber *n* a WHETSTONE made of stone II.9.10. wʌʏt ɹʌbəᶜ O

white-runners *n* BINDWEED II.2.4. hwɛɪtʁʊnəz Nb

white slugs *npl* SLUGS IV.9.2. wɛɪt slʊgz Ch

whitesmith *n* a TINKER VIII.4.9. waɪtsmɪθ Y

white snails *npl* SLUGS IV.9.2. *sg* waɪt sneːl Db, wɔɪʔ sneɪəɫz Bk

white-stone *n* a WHETSTONE II.9.10. waɪtstoʊn Nth, wɒˑɪtstuːᵊn Lei

white-throat *n* a WEASEL IV.5.6. wɪt̬d̬ɹɒt D, wɪt̬d̬ɹoːt D, hwɛɪtθʁœːt Nb, hwaɪtθʁœːt Nb

white turnips *npl* TURNIPS II.4.1(b). wɒɪt tʌnɪps Nf, *no -s* wʌɪt tæːnɪp Nf, wʌɪt tʌnɪps Nf, wʌɪt tʌnəps Nf, wʌɪt tənɪps Nf, *no -s* wʌɪt təːnɪp Nf, wʌɪʔ tɐˑnɪps Nf

white yolk *n* the white of an egg, ⇐ YOLK IV.6.5. waɪt juˑk Ch

whitlow *n What do you call that painful, festering swelling you get in the fleshy part at the finger end?* VI.7.12. Eng. ⇒ *blast*, **breeder, bustion, felon, fester, festerlow,** *fistula* ⇒ **festerlow,** *gathered finger*, **gathering,** *gathering finger*, **milk-gathering, milk-rising,** *milk-risings* ⇒ **milk-rising, nail-wart,** *nail-warts* ⇒ **nail-wart, nimpingang, plook, quick-flaw, quicklaw, rising, teat,** *whitelaw*, **whittle**

whitret *n* a WEASEL IV.5.6. wɪtɹət Sa

whitrick *n* a WEASEL IV.5.6. wɪtɹɪk Nt*[old]* L, wɪtɹɪk L, wɪtəɹɪk L

whittle *1. v What do you say a boy does when he tries out his new knife on a stick?* I.7.19.
v hwɪtl Nb, wɪtl Cu La Y Ch Db Sa St Wa O Nt L Nf, *-ing* wɪtlɪn Du Lei Nth, *-ing* wɪtlən Nb, wɪkl Du, wɪʔl L, *prppl* wɪʔlɪn Ess Brk, *-ing* wɪʔlɪn Nf, wɪtɫ Wa Lei R Nth Hu Bd Ess, *3prsg* wɪtɫz MxL,

-ing wɪtɬɪn O Brk Sr K Ha, wɪtʔɬ Ess, wɪʔɬ O Nth Bk Bd Ess, wɪtʊɬ Sr K, *3prsg* wɪʔʊz Sr, wɛtl St, waɪtl We *vt* wɪtl Db, *-ing* wɪtʔɬɪn Sr, wɪtʊɬ Ha

⇒ **bark, carve, chip, chip off, chop, circle, cut, cut out, fetch off, hew,** *make shavings,* **notch, pare, pare up, peel, peel off, point, rind, shape, sharp, sharpen, sharpen out, sharp out, shave, shave up, shirp out, shive, shrip, skiddle, skin, skob,** *spar-cutting about,* **speel, squittle, swipe, swite,** *take the peeling off,* **trim, trim out, trim up, try, whet, white, whittle off, yark**

[Some terms refer to the stick, some to the knife, some unclear. Ch r. **whittling at a stick** *assumed to be verb +prep phrase, and therefore subsumed under* **whittle]**

2. *n* a DIAPER V.11.3. wɪʔɬ So, waɪtɬ Co, waɪdɬ Co

3. *n* a WHITLOW VI.7.12. wɪtl Db

whittle off *vtphr* **whittle a bit off** to WHITTLE a stick I.7.19. *-ing* wɪtlɪn ... ɒf St

whole-horse *n* a STALLION III.4.4. hʌlhɔːs Nf, hʌʊhɔːs Ess, hʊɬhɒs Ess, hʊlhɔˑs Nf, hʊɬhɔːs Sf

wholemeal *n* MEAL V.6.1(b). həːlmiːl Nb, wɒlmiːl Db Sa, hɒʊɬmɪʊɬ Sr, hɒʊmɪʊɬ Sr, hɒʊmɪʊ Sr, ɒʊmɪʊ Sr, wɔlmiːl We, ɔʊlmɪˑəl L, ɔʊɬmɪʊɬ Sx, hɔʊmiːʊ Ess, hʌʊɬmiːᵊɬ Ess, hʌʊɬmɪːʊ Ess, hʌʊɬmɪʊ MxL, hʌʊmɪʊ MxL, oːlmiːl Ch Sa, ʍoːlmiːl Mon, hoːɬmiːᵊɬ Mon, hoːɬmɛːʊɬ So, hoʊlmiːl Nf, oʊlmiːl St, hoʊlmeˑl Nf, oʊɬmiːl Mon, oʊɬmiːᵊɬ Wa, hoʊɬmiːʊɬ Ess, oːʊmɪʊ Brk, hʊɬmiːɬ Sf, ʊːlmiːl St, uːɬmiːɬ Lei D Ha, ʊəlmɪəl Y Nt

wholemeal-flour *n* MEAL V.6.1(b). ʌʊɬmɪəɬflɛʊə Bd, oʊɬmiːᵊɬflɛʊəˤ Bk, hʊɬmiːɬflɛˑʊə Sf

whole-pluck *n* the PLUCK of a slaughtered animal III.11.6. holplʌk Nf

wholly *adv* VERY VIII.3.2. hʌlɪ Sf Ess, hʊlɪ Sf

whooking-cough *n* WHOOPING-COUGH VI.8.3. hʊkɪnkɔːf Ess, hʊkənkɔːf Nf

whooping-cough *n* *What do you call that infectious cough that children suffer from [indicate coughing]?* VI.8.3. Eng. ⇒ *chin-cough* ⇒ **chink-cough, croup, kink-cough, whooking-cough, whooping-hoast**

whooping-hoast *n* WHOOPING-COUGH VI.8.3. uːpɪnʊəst Y

whorled up *adj* TANGLED, describing hair VI.2.5. ɒɾəɬd ʌp Ha; **all whorled up** ɔːɬ ɒɾəɬd ʌp Ha *[queried SBM]*

whorls *n* **all in whorls** TANGLED, describing hair VI.2.5. ɔːɬ ɪn ɒɾəɬz Ha *[queried SBM]*

whortle-berries *npl* BILBERRIES IV.11.3. *sg* wɒtɬbəɾɪ Sr, wɔːɾtɬbəɾɪz Sr, wɔːʔɬbɛɾɪz Nf, *sg* wɔːʔɬbəɾɪ K, wəˤːtɬbɛɾɪz D, wəˤːtɬbəɾəz Co, wəˤːtɬbəɾiːz So, wəˤːtɬbəɾɪz Co, wəˤːtɬbɾiːz So, wəˤːdɬbəɾiːz So, wəˤːdɬbəɾɪz Co D

whorts *npl* BILBERRIES IV.11.3. waˤːtʂ Ha, wəˤːtʂ So*[old x1]* Co D*[old x1]* Do, wəˤːɾəts D Do, wəˤːʔs O

---

whup 1. *imp* **whup back, whup maller** the command TURN LEFT!, given to plough-horses II.3.5(a). **whup back** wʊp bak Ch; **whup maller** wʊp mælə Ess

2. *imp* **whup back gee** the command TURN RIGHT!, given to plough-horses II.3.5(b). 'wʊp bak 'dʒiː Co

3. *imp* the command stop! or WOA!, given to plough-horses II.3.5(c). wʊp Du Ha

why *imp* the command TURN RIGHT!, given to plough-horses II.3.5(b). wʌɪ Ha *[queried SBM]*

why aye *adv* YES VIII.8.13(a). wɛɪ ɛɪ Nb, wæɪ aɪ Du Y, waɪ aɪ Nb Y

why no *adv* NO VIII.8.13(b). wɛɪ nøː Nb

wick 1. *n* the QUICK of a fingernail VI.7.9. wɪk Nb Cu Du We La Y Ch Db St O Nt L Hrt So Co, hwɪk Nb

2. *adj* ACTIVE, describing a child VIII.9.1. wɪk Du*[old x1]* La Y L, hwɪk Du

wicken-grass *n* COUCH-GRASS II.2.3. wɪkəngʁas Du

wicken(s) *n* COUCH-GRASS II.2.3.
no -s: hwɪkɪn Nb, wɪkn Y, hwɪkən Nb
-s: wɪkɪnz Y, hwɪkɪnz Nb, wɪknz Y, wɪkənz Du Y, hwɪkənz Nb

wicker-basket *n* a CLOTHES-BASKET V.9.7. wɪkəbaːskɪt Hrt

wicker-hole *n* an EAR-HOLE VI.4.3. wɪkəˤjoːl Gl

wicker-hurdles *npl* HURDLES used to pen sheep in part of a field III.7.11. wɪkəhəːdlz Nf*[hazel or willow]*

wickers *npl* EARS VI.4.1. *sg* wiːkəˤɪ K, *sg* wiːkəˤ Gl*[old, facetious]*, wɪkəˤz̩ Gl*[old]*

wicker-skep *n* a wicker BASKET for carrying horse-feed III.5.4. wɪkəskɛp Lei

wick-grass *n* COUCH-GRASS II.2.3. wɪkgʁɛs Y, wɪkgʁas Y

wick(s) *n* COUCH-GRASS II.2.3.
no -s: wɪk La Y
-s: wɪks La Y L

wicks *npl* MOUTH CORNERS VI.5.2. wɪks Nb Y, weːks La; **wicks of it*/thy* mouth** wɪks əv ɪt maʊθ La, wɪks ə t muːθ Y, wɪəks ə ðɪ muːθ Y, weːks ə ðɪ maʊθ La

widdy *n* a sliding RING to which a tether is attached in a cow-house I.3.5. wɪdɪ Y

widdy-wind *n* BINDWEED II.2.4. wɪdɪwæɪn So

wide *adv* ASTRIDE VI.9.8. waɪd La Sa, wɑɪd Hu

wide-feet *adj* SPLAY-FOOTED VI.10.5. wəɪdfiit Brk

wide-foot *adj* SPLAY-FOOTED VI.10.5. wɑɪdfʊt K

wide-footed *adj* SPLAY-FOOTED VI.10.5. wæːdvɤtəd D, wʌɪdfʊʔɪd Nf

wide-legged *adv* ASTRIDE VI.9.8. wæːdɬɛgɪd D

wid-ring *n* a sliding RING to which a tether is attached in a cow-house I.3.5. wɪdɹɪŋ Y

wids *npl* DUCKS IV.6.14. wɪdz Ch

wid-wind *n* BINDWEED II.2.4. wɪdwɒɪn So

wife *n If you asked Mr. Smith, the farmer, at the door if he could let you have a dozen eggs, he'd probably say: It's nothing to do with me, you'll ... [have to ask [my wife]].* VIII.1.24. **wife** wæɪf Y, waɪf L, wɔɪf Ess; **my wife** mɪ weɪf Man, maː weɪf Y, mɪ wæɪf Ess, maɪ wæɪf Y, mɪ waɪf Cu Y L, maː waɪf Y, maɪ waɪf Y, miː waɪf K, maɪ waɪf La K, mɪ wɒɪf Wo, mɒɪ wɒɪf K, mɪ wɔɪf L Ess K, mɔɪ wɔɪf Hrt, mɪ wʌɪf Sr, mʌɪ wʌɪf Nf Brk, məɪ wəɪf Mon W Sx; **the wife** ðə wɛɪf Nb Cu Du Man Sa, ðə wæɪf Man, t wæɪf Y, ʔ waːf La, ðə waɪf Du Sa St L, t waɪf Cu Du We Y, ʔ waɪf La, d waɪf Nt, t waːf Y, tʔ waːf Y, ʔ waːf la, ðə waɪf L Bd K, t waɪf La, ʔ waɪf La, ðə wɒɪf St So W K, ðə wɔɪf Wa O L Bk Ess Sr K Ha Sx, ðə wʌɪf Nf Sr, ðɪ wəɪf Sx, ðə wəɪf He Mon Brk Sx. ⇒ **missis, mistress, old dutch, old girl, old lady, old woman, woman** *[possessive pronouns and articles included as integral to response]*

wiggle *n* a PIGLET III.8.2. *pl* wɪgʊɫz̩ Ess, *pl* wɪgʊz Ess

wiggy-arsed *adj* ACTIVE, describing a child VIII.9.1. wɪgi-aːst W

wild *adj* **gone wild, wild** *ON* HEAT, describing a cow III.1.6. **gone wild** gɒn waɪld Y; **wild** waɪld Y

wild convolvulus *n* BINDWEED II.2.4. waːɫd kənvɔɫvəs K

wild ducks *n* an EVENER on a horse-drawn plough I.8.4. wəɪɫ dʊks Brk *[queried SBM]*

wild-kale *n* CHARLOCK II.2.6. waɪldkeal Cu

wild woodbine *n* BINDWEED II.2.4. wɒɪld wʊdbɒɪn St

wilful *adv* *ON* PURPOSE IX.1.5. wɪlfʊɫ Mon

wilfully *adv* *ON* PURPOSE IX.1.5. wɪlfʊlɪ St, wɪʊfʊlɪ K

wilk *n* a STYE in the eye VI.3.10. wɪɫk Co

wilks *n* COUCH-GRASS II.2.3. wɪlks La

will-do *n* a RIDGEL III.4.7. wɪɫduː Ha

will-jill *n* a RIDGEL III.4.7. wɪldʒɪl Ch St, wɪᵊɫdʒɪᵊɫ O

willow *n What do you call that bush or tree growing near water; it sends out slender stems that easily bend?* IV.10.7. wɪlɪ Cu Du*[old]* Sa Wa, wɪle Nf, *pl* wɪlæʊz Hrt, wɪlɒʊ Brk K Sx, wɪɫɒʊ Sr*[weeping x1]* Sx, wɪlɔᴿ Nb, wɪɫɔʊ Ess Sx*[weeping]*, wɪlʌʊ MxL, wɪɫʌʊ MxL, wɪlo La, wɪloː He, wɪɫoː Ha, wɪloʊ Man St Nth Brk K, wɪɫoʊ So Ha, wɪlʊ Gl, wɪluː Sa, wɪlə Nb Cu Du We La Y Ch Db St Wa O Nt L Lei R Nth Hu C Nf Sf Bk Bd Hrt Ess K, wɪlɹ L, wɪləᵗ O Nth Bk Bd, wɪɫə O Lei Ess Brk, wɪɫəᵗ Sx, wɛlə Db, wʊlɪ Nb; **willow-tree** wɪlʌʊtɹɪ: MxL, wɪlətɹɪ: Y, *pl* wɪlətɹɪ:z R, wɪɫətɹɪ: MxL. ⇒ **osier, ozier** ⇒ **osier, sallow, sallow-tree, sallow-willow,** *sally* ⇒ **sallow, saugh,**

seal, waller, water-sallow, weeping-willow, willow-dolard, willow-*tree*, willow-wander, withe, withen, withy, withy- tree; ⇒ also **osier carr**

willow-broom *n* a BESOM made of willow I.3.15. wɪləbɹuːm Nth

willow-dolard *n* WILLOW IV.10.7. *pl* wɪlədɒləz Lei *[marked u.r. EMBM]*

willow-wander *n* WILLOW IV.10.7. wʊlɪwandɔᴿ Nb*[old]*

willy-biter *nsg* a DADDY-LONG-LEGS IV.8.10. wɪlɪbaˑɪtɹ L

willy-wind* *n* BINDWEED II.2.4. wɪlɪwɔɪn Bd *[EMBM headword willow-wind]*

willy with the wisp *n* a BOGEY VIII.8.1. wɪlɪ wɪ t wɪsp Cu

wilt *n* a STYE in the eye VI.3.10. wɪɫt Co

wim *v* to WINNOW II.8.4. wɪm Do Ha, *prppl* wɪmɪn Sx, *vbln* wɪmɪn So, *-ing* wɪmɪn So W D Sx, *-ing* wəmɪn So Do

wimb *v* to WINNOW II.8.4. *vbln* wɪmbɪn D, *-ing* wɪmbɪn D

wimberries *npl* BILBERRIES IV.11.3. wɪmbəɾiːz So, wɪmbɾiːz So, wɪmbɛɹɪz La Sa Mon, wɪmbəɹɪz Sa He Mon, *sg* wɪmbəɹɪ La, wɪmbɹɪz La Ch Db Sa He Mon

wimble *1. n* a ROPE-TWISTER II.7.8. wɪmbəɫ Bk, wɪmbɫ Bk W K Co D Do Ha, wɪmbʊl K, wɪmbʊɫ K, wɪmbʊ Sr K Ha Sx, wɪməl Y, wɪmɫ D, wɪmvəɫ Do, wɪnvəɫ Do, wɪnməɫ W, waməɫ So, wəməɫ So
2. n a FLAIL II.8.3. wɪmbɫ Bk

wimble-berries *npl* BILBERRIES IV.11.3. wɪmbɫbɛɹɪz La

wimple-berries *npl* BILBERRIES IV.11.3. wɪmpɫbɛɹɪz Gl

win *v* to WINNOW II.8.4. wɪn He Wa, *-ing* wɪnɪn La O W Brk D Sx, *-ing* wɪnən Man D

winberries *npl* BILBERRIES IV.11.3. wɪnbɛɹɪz Sa, wɪnbəɹɪz La Ch Sa Mon, wɪnbɹɪz Sa He Mon Gl, *sg* wɪnbəɾɪ La *[not a WMBM headword]*

winch *n* a ROPE-TWISTER II.7.8. wɪntʃ Ess, wɪns Ess

wind *v* to WINNOW II.8.4. *-ing* wɪndɪn La So Co D Ha, *-ing* wɪndən Co, *-ing* wɪnvɪn W, *3ptpl* wɪnvɪd Brk

windbag *n* a GOSSIP VIII.3.5.(b). wɪnbag He

wind-cocks *npl* COCKS of hay II.9.12. wɪnkɒks Gl

winder *1. n* a ROPE-TWISTER II.7.8. waɪndə Nt, wɔɪndəᴵ Ha
2. v to WINNOW II.8.4. *-ing* wɪndɪ-ɪn Y, wɪndə Nb Du La Y Db Nt L, wɪndəɹ (+V) Lei, wɪndəɹ Du La, wɪndəᵗ Bk, *-ing* wɪndɹɪn Y, *-ing* wʊndəʁɪn Nb

wind-hurdles *npl* HURDLES used to pen sheep in part of a field III.7.11. *no -s* wɛnhəˑdl Nf[*braided sticks*] [*queried EMBM*]

winding *vbln* **give him a good winding** to BEAT a boy on the buttocks VIII.8.10. gɪv ɪm ə gʊd wɛɪndɪn St

windlass *n* a ROPE-TWISTER II.7.8. wɪndləs St, wɪnləs St Bk

windpipe *n You will very likely choke, if you get a crumb stuck in your ....* VI.6.5. Eng exc. R Co. ⇒ **breathing-tube, clunker, craw, digger, gills, gizzard, gob, guggle, gullet,** *gullet-hole* ⇒ **gully-hole, gullock, gully, gully-hole, guzzle, hollows, kecker, neck-hole, oozle, quilter, throat,** *throat wrong road,* **thropple, throttle, weasand, whistle, wozzle,** *wrong throat*

windrow *1. v* to WINNOW II.8.4. wɪndʁə Nb, wɪndɹə Y

2. n a row or SWATH of mown grass cut for hay-making II.9.4. wɪnʁa Nb, wɪndʁaː Nb, wɪnɹɒʊ L

3. n a swath of grass cut for hay-making, dried, and ready for carting. wɪndɹɒʊ Sr, *pl* wɪndɹʌʊz Ess [*not a SBM headword*]

windy *adj* RANCID, describing bacon V.7.9. wɪndɪ Y

windy teat *n* a BLIND TEAT III.2.7. wɪndɪ tɪt Cu

wing *1. n* an EVENER on a horse-drawn plough I.8.4. hwɪŋg Man

2. n the T-SHAPED PLOUGH-BEAM END of a horse-drawn plough I.8.5. wɪŋ So Co Do

3. n the MOULD-BOARD of a horse-drawn plough I.8.8. wɪŋ Sx, *pl* wɪŋz K[*on Kent plough*]

wing-bonnet *n* a woman's cotton BONNET with a sun-flap at the back of the neck, worn at work in the fields VI.14.1. wɪŋbɒnɪt Nt

wing-feathered *adj* FLEDGED IV.7.2. wɪŋfɛðəˡɹd̥ Sx

wing-plate *n* the SOLE of a horse-drawn plough I.8.9. wɪŋplɛɪt K

wing-swell-tree *n* an EVENER on a plough pulled by three horses I.8.4. wɪŋswɛɫɹɪ Hu

wink *n* a ROPE-TWISTER II.7.8. wɪŋk So Co D

winker *1. vi-3prpl* they WHINNY, describing the noise horses make during feeding time in the stable III.10.3(a). wɪŋkəˡ Do Ha

2. vi-3prpl they NEIGH, describing the noise horses make in the fields III.10.3(b). wɪŋkəˡ Do Ha

winkers *npl* BLINKERS covering the eyes of a cart-horse I.5.2. wɪŋkəz Y St Wa Hu C MxL K, wɪŋkəs Man Nf, wɪŋkʔəz C Sf, wɪŋkʔəs Nf, wɪŋkəˡz La K, wɪŋkəˡz̥ Wo Bk Bd, wɪŋkəˡːz̥ Sa Wo W Co

winkles *npl* BLINKERS covering the eyes of a cart-horse I.5.2. wɪŋkɫz Hrt Ess, wɪŋkʔɫz Sf

winkling *n* a WEAKLING piglet III.8.4. wɪŋklɪn Cu

winkly-eyed *adj* SQUINTING VI.3.5. wɪŋkɫɪ-əɪd Sx

winnow *v What was their [farmworkers using flails] word for separating the grain from the husks?* II.8.4. *-ing* wɪni-ɪn W, wɪnɪ Y Ch Db Gl, wɪnʊ Brk, *-ing* wɪnʊɪn Man Sx, wɪnoː Sa He Mon Gl O W Co, wɪnoʊ Wo Wa O, *-ing* wɪnoʊɪn St So Brk Co Ha, *vbln* wɪnoʊwɪn Ha, wɪnə La Ch Db Sa St Wo Wa Mon Gl Nt L Lei R Nth Nf Bk Bd Ess MxL Sr, *-ing* wɪnəwɪn Y K, *-ing* wɪnəɹɪn Y Brk, *-ing* wɪnəʁən Du, wɪnəɹ Y, wɪnəˡ Wo Wa Mon Gl O Bk, *-ing* wɪnəˡːɾɪn W. ⇒ **blow, blow out, cave, clean, corn-clean, dight, dress, fay, riddle, screen, sieve out, sift, thrashing, wim, wimb, win, wind, winder,** *window* ⇒ **winder, windrow, winrow, wither**

winrow *v* to WINNOW II.8.4. wɪnɹɔ Y, wɪnɹʌʊ Ess

wippet *n* a FLAIL II.8.3. wɪpɪt St

wire-hook *n* the GRASS-NAIL of a scythe II.9.9. wɔɪɾʊk Ha

wire in *imp* HELP YOURSELVES!, said to invite visitors to eat V.8.13. waɪəɹ ɪn Y

wiry *adj* ACTIVE, describing a child VIII.9.1. wɛːɹɪ St, wɒɪɹɪ St, wɒɪəɾ̥ɪ So, wɒɪəˡːɾ̥ɪ Ha [*marked u.r. WM/SBM*]

wisdom-bone *n* a WISH-BONE IV.6.22. wɪzdəmbɔʊn Brk

wises *n* POTATO-HAULMS II.4.4. wɑːzəz Y, wɑɪzɪz La

wish-bone *n What do you call that forked bone [point to the breast] of a roast fowl?* IV.6.22. Eng exc. Man W. ⇒ **breast-bone, chair, drawing-bone, lucky-bone, marrying-bone, merry-bone, merry-thought,** *pull-bone* ⇒ **pully-bone, pulling-bone, pully- bone, skip-jack, wisdom-bone, wishing-bone**

wishing-bone *n* a WISH-BONE IV.6.22. wɪʃɪnbɪan Y, wɪʃɪnbɪən Y, wɪʃnbɪən Nb, wɪʃɪnbean We, wɪʃɪnbæʊn Hrt, wɪʃɪnbɒʊn Brk, wɪʃɪnbɔʊn O, wɪʃɪnbʌʊn Bk, wɪʃnbʌʊn Ess, wɪʃɪnbɔːn La Y Ch Db W Ha, wɪʃɪnbɒʊn St Wo So Ha, wɪʃɪnbɔːən So W Do, wɪʃənbɔːən Man Do, wɪʃɪnbʊən La Y O Nt L, wɪʃɪnbuːn Db D Ha, wɪʃɪnbuːən So W D

wisht *1. adj* ILL, describing a person who is unwell VI.13.1(b). wɪʃt Co

2. adj SICK, describing an animal that is unwell VI.13.1(c). wɪʃt Co

wisk *1. n* a BESOM made of hazel I.3.15. wɪsk Y

2. n an oval wicker BASKET for carrying horse-feed III.5.4. wɪsk Mon

3. n a STYE in the eye VI.3.10. wɪsk W

wisk-broom *n* a BESOM I.3.15. wɪskbɹuːm Y

wisket *1. n* a SOWING-BASKET II.3.6. wɪskɪt Ch Db

2. n a BASKET for carrying horse-feed III.5.4. wɪskɪt Ch Db[*basket-work oval x2; wicker, oval x1; basket-work x1]* Sa*[wooden, round x1; basket-work, round x1; wicker, with handles x1; wicker x1]* St*[wooden x1]* He*[wicker, round x1; wicker, round, with handles x1; wicker x1]* Wo*[wicker, round]*

3. n a container for carrying root-crops to cattle. wɪskɪt He

4. n a CLOTHES-BASKET V.9.7. wɪskɪt Sa Wo, wɪskət Sa

wisp *n* a STYE in the eye VI.3.10. wɪsp Mon Gl O*[old]* So*[old x1]* W Brk

wiss *n* a STYE in the eye VI.3.10. wɪs So W Ha

wist* *n* a STYE in the eye VI.3.10. wɪst Bk*[old]*

witch-grease *n* a 'special type' (?trade name) of CART-GREASE, used to lubricate the wheels of a cart I.11.4. wɪtʃɡɹⁱis K

withe *n* WILLOW IV.10.7. waɪð Cu

withen *n* WILLOW IV.10.7. wɪðɪn La*[bigger than a willow x1]* Y

wither *1. v* to WINNOW II.8.4. wɪðə Ch
2. vi to WRINKLE, referring to the skin of very old people VI.11.2. wɪðə La Y, *3prsg* wɪðəz Ess, wɪddə We, wɪddəɹ La, wɪvəᵗ He

withered *adj* wrinkled, describing the skin of very old people, ⇐ WRINKLE VI.11.2. wɪðəd Ess, wɛðət Ch; **get withered** *-ing* gɪʔn wɪðəᵗɽd Sx

withered-teat *n* a BLIND TEAT III.2.7. wɪðəᵗːdtɪʔ So

withered up *adj* wrinkled, describing the skin of very old people, ⇐ WRINKLE VI.11.2. wɪðəd ʊp Y

wither up *viphr* to WRINKLE, referring to the skin of very old people VI.11.2. wɪddəɹ ʊp We

without *adv Some people drink their tea with sugar; but some drink it ....* V.8.10(a). Eng. ⇒ **about, be-out, bidout, bout, out**

with-wind *n* BINDWEED II.2.4. wɪθwaɪn Bk, wɪθwɒɪn W, wɪðwɒɪn W, wɪfwɒɪn So, wɪθwəɪn W, wɪðwəɪn Mon Gl, wɪðwəɪnd Gl

withy *n* a WILLOW IV.10.7. wɪði So W Co D Do Ha, wɪdi Co, wɪði Ch Sa St He Wo Wa Mon Gl O So Brk*[old x1]* Sr*[not weeping x1, old x1]* Do Ha Sx*[not weeping]*, wɪðiː Wo, wɛði Ha

withy-tree *n* a WILLOW IV.10.7. wɪðɪtɹiː MxL

withy-wind *n* BINDWEED II.2.4. wɪðiwɪn D, wɪðiwɪnd So, wɪdɪwiːnd Do, wɪðiwæɪn So, wɪðiwaːn D, wɪðiwaɪn So, wɪðiwɒɪn So W, wɪðiwɔɪn O, wɪðəwɔɪn O, wɪðɪwʌɪnd Brk, wɪðəᵗwʌɪnd Brk, wɪðɪwəɪn Do, wɪðəᵗwəɪnd Brk, wɛðəwɔɪn Bk

wizen *vi* to WRINKLE, referring to the skin of very old people VI.11.2. wɪzn Nb Du*[infrequent]* We La*[old x1]* L *[marked u.r. EMBM]*

wizened *adj* wrinkled, describing the skin of very old people, ⇐ WRINKLE VI.11.2. wɪznd Y; **go wizened** *3prsg* ɡʊəz wɪznd L

wizened up *adj* wrinkled, describing the skin of very old people, ⇐ WRINKLE VI.11.2. wɪzənd ʊp Y

woa *1. imp [When you want your (plough-)horses to go left, what do you say? And right?] And stop?* II.3.5.(c). wøː Nb Du, wɛʊ Lei, wœː Nb, wæʊ Hrt, wɒʊ Nb St Sr K Sx, wɔː Y, wɔʊ sY St O L Hu Ess Brk K Sx, wʌʊ Sf Bk Bd Hrt Ess Sr, wʌʊʔ Ess, woː Nb Cu La Y Wa Mon Nt Nf Bk MxL Brk K Co D Ha, woʊ Nb La Man Ch Db St He Wo Wa Gl O Nt L Lei R Nth C Nf Sf Bk Bd Hrt Ess So W Brk Sr K Co D Ha Sx, woʊʔ Ess, woʊə Lei R, wuː St L Nth Ess, wʊə Nb La. ⇒ **gee back, halt, hiss, ho, hold tight,** *see back* ⇒ **gee back,** *ss* ⇒ **hiss, way, way woa, wee, whup,** *wo* ⇒ **woa, woa back, woag, woa ho, woat, woa there,** *woop* ⇒ **whup,** *woot* ⇒ **woat,** *wug* ⇒ **woag, yea**

2. imp **woa, woa back, woa ree** the command TURN LEFT!, given to plough-horses II.3.5(a). **woa** wɔː Nth*[old]*; **woa back** 'woʊ bæk So; **woa ree** wɔː ɹiː Ess

3. imp **woa, woa back, woa gee, woa up** the command TURN RIGHT!, given to plough-horses II.3.5(b). **woa** wɔː Wo, woʊ St; **woa back** wɔː 'bæk Brk, wɔʊ bak O; **woa gee** wɔː dʒiː Ess, wɔː diː Sf Ess, 'wɔːd ˌʔiː Ess, wɔːɹ diː Sf, wɔʊ dʒiː Ess, wʊ tʃiː Ess, ˌwʊ 'dʒiːʔ Ess, wʊᵊd ʔiː Ess, wʊːd ʔiːʔ Ess, wəː diː Sf; **woa up** wa wʊp O

woa back *imp* the command stop! or WOA!, given to plough-horses II.3.5(c). wʌʊ bæk Ess

woag *imp* the command stop! or WOA!, given to plough-horses II.3.5(c). wɒʊg Sx *[SBM headword wug]*

woa ho *imp* the command stop! or WOA!, given to plough-horses II.3.5(c). wə 'huː Lei

woat* *imp* the command stop! or WOA!, given to plough-horses II.3.5(c). woʊt W *[SBM headword woot]*

woa there *imp* the command stop! or WOA!, given to plough-horses II.3.5(c). wᵁuː ðɛə Y

wobbly *adj* WEAK, describing a person who has been ill VI.13.2. wɒblɪ Brk, wɔːblɪ So

woblet *n* the CLOG on a horse's harness I.4.3. wɒblət So

wolf *vt* to GOBBLE food VI.5.13(b). *-ing* wʊɫfɪn K

wolf down *vtphr* to GOBBLE food VI.5.13(b). *-ing* wʊɫfɪn ... dæʊn Sr, *-ing* wʊfɪn ... dæʊn Sr

wolpy *1. vi* to CURDLE, referring to milk V.5.9. wəɫpi So
2. adj curdled. *ptppl* ɡɔːn wəɫpi So

woman *n* my WIFE VIII.1.24. **the woman** ðə wʊmən Co, ðə ʊmən Sa

womb *n* the UTERUS of a cow III.2.4. wɔm L, woʊm Man, wʊm Db Nf Sf Ess, wuːm Cu He Nf

Bk Bd Hrt Ess So Sr K Co Do Ha, wuːmb Brk K, uːm Co D, wɵːm Lei

women *npl [Show a picture of a family.] You wouldn't call these two [point to two women] men, would you? They are ....* VIII.1.10. Eng. ⇒ **wenches**

wonderful *adv* VERY VIII.3.2. wʌndəˡːfʊɫ So

wonkly* *adj* WEAK, describing a person who has been ill VI.13.2. wɒŋklɪ Y

wonky **1. adj* STUPID VI.1.5. wɔːŋkɪ Sx

*2. adj WEAK, describing a person who has been ill VI.13.2. wɒŋkɪ Nth

3. adj GIDDY IX.1.11. wɒŋkɪ Db

wood *n* KINDLING-*WOOD* V.4.2. ʏd So, ʌd Bk, wʊd O Nth Bk Hrt MxL So W, ʊd O So Ha; **dried wood** dɹaɪd ʊd So; **top wood off the hedges** tɒp wʊd ɒf t ɛdʒɪz Y; **wood for morning** ʊd fə maˡːn̩ɪn Gl

wood-ash(es) *n* ASH in a burning fire V.4.4.

no -es: ʊdaɪʃ Ha

-es: uːdaɪʃəz Do

wood-ashes *n* ASHES from a cold fire V.4.5. ʊdaˡʃɪz So

woodbine *n* BINDWEED II.2.4. wʊdbɒɪn Wo

wood-chuck *n* a chock placed behind and under a wheel to prevent a cart from going backwards on a hill, ⇐ PROP/CHOCK I.11.2. wʊdtʃʊk Y

wood-dust *n* SAW-DUST I.7.17. ʊddʌst W, ʊddʌs W, wʊddʌst Nf Ha, wʊddʌs Nf Sx, wʊddəs Hrt

wooden *1. adj* RESTIVE, describing a horse III.5.6. wʊdn Nf

2. adj STUPID VI.1.5. wʊdn L

3. adj CLUMSY, describing a person VI.7.14. wʊdn L, ʊdn So*[old]*

4. adj GIDDY IX.1.11. ʊdn So*[old]*

wooden bar *n* the *HORIZONTAL* BAR of a crane over a domestic fire V.3.5(a). wʊdn baː Sr

wooden dick *n* an old, presumably wooden, PLOUGH I.8.1. wʊdn dɪk O

wooden-fork *n* a PORRIDGE-STICK V.9.1. wʊdnfɔːk L

wooden-headed *adj* STUPID VI.1.5. wʊdnhɛdɪd Ess

wooden-horse *n* a SAWING-HORSE I.7.16. wʌdn̩ˌɒˡːʂ Sa, wʊdn̩ɒs Du L, ʊdn̩ɒs Gl, wʊdn̩ɔːs La, ʊdn̩ɔːs He

wooden hurdles *npl* HURDLES used to pen sheep in part of a field III.7.11. wʊdn hʌdlz Nf

wooden-ladle *n* a PORRIDGE-STICK V.9.1. wʊdnleˈədɫ Sf, wʊdnlæɪdl Nf, wʊdnladl La

wooden latch *n* the LATCH of a door V.1.9. wʊdən latʃ Lei

wooden-porridge-spoon *n* a PORRIDGE- STICK V.9.1. wʊdnpɒdɪʃspuːn La

wooden-post *n* a TETHERING-STAKE in a cow-house I.3.3. wʊdnpʌʊst Ess, wʊdn pʊʊst Wo*[p]*

wooden slab *n* a PASTE-BOARD V.6.5. ʊdn slæb So

wooden-spoon *n* a PORRIDGE-STICK V.9.1. ʏdnspʏːn So D, wʏdnspʏːn So Co, wʊdnspɪʏn Du, wʊdnspjʏn Du, wʊdnspɪʊn Y, wʊdnspɪuːn Du Y Sa, wʊdnspɪɵːn Nf, wʊdnspɪən Cu Y, wʊdnspʏːn La Ch, wʊdnspɛʊn Ch Db St, ʊdnspʌn He, wʊdnspʌʊn Brk, wʊdnspoun La, wʊdnspʊn Sa Wo C Nf Sf Ess, ʊdnspʊn Sa He Wo Mon Gl, wʊdnspʊɪn Y, wʊdɪnspuːn Db Sa, wʊdnspuːn Nb Du La Y Ch Sa St He Wo Wa Mon O Nt L Lei R Nth Hu C Nf Sf Bk Bd Ess MxL Brk Sr K Co Ha Sx, wʊdənspuːn O Ha, ʊdnspuːn Wo Mon Gl O Bk So W Co Do Ha, wʊdnspəuːn Nf Hrt K Ha

wood-hive *n* a HIVE IV.8.8(a). *pl* wʊdaɪvz La

wood-hook *n* a BILLHOOK IV.2.6. wʊdhuːk So, ʊdʊk W, uːdhʊk So, ˈuːdʊk Ha

wood-horse *n* a SAWING-HORSE I.7.16. ʏdɒs D, wʏdɔˡːʂ So, wʊdɒs Co, wʊdɔːs St

wood hurdles *npl* HURDLES used to pen sheep in part of a field III.7.11. wʊd hɛdlz Nf

wood-nut *n* HAZEL IV.10.8. wʊdnʊt Nth

wood-nut-bush *n* HAZEL IV.10.8. wʊdnʌʔbʊʃ Bd

wood-nut-tree *n* HAZEL IV.10.8. wʊdnʌttɹiː Nth Hu C

wood-roller *n* a device chained to a cart used to prevent it from going backwards on a hill, ⇐ PROP/CHOCK I.11.2. *pl* wʊdɹɔʊləz Y

wood-spoon *n* a PORRIDGE-STICK V.9.1. wʊdspjʏn Du, wʊdspʊɪn Y, wʊdspuːn Nb Co

wood-stack carpenter *n* a CARPENTER or JOINER who does heavy, less skilled work VIII.4.3. wʊdstæk kɑːpndə Nf

wood-stock *n* a SAWING-HORSE I.7.16. wʊdstɒk La

wool *n What do you call the hair of the sheep?* III.7.5. Eng; **sheep's-wool** ʃiːpsɔɫ O, ʃɪpsʊɫ Gl. ⇒ **hair**, *sheep's*-**wool**

wool skin *n* a SHEEPSKIN III.11.8(a). wʊl skɪn He

woosh *imp* the command TURN RIGHT!, given to plough-horses II.3.5(b). wʊʃ Nf

woot *imp* **woot, woot gee, woot off** the command TURN RIGHT!, given to plough-horses II.3.5(b). **woot** wʊʊt W, wʊtt Gl, wuːt K; **woot gee** wʊt dʒiː Ess; **woot off** ˈwʊʊt ˈɔːf W, wəˡːt ɔːf So

wootch* *imp* the command TURN RIGHT!, given to plough-horses II.3.5(b). wʊtʃ C *[taken as* **woot gee** *EMBM]*

wore out* *adj* EXHAUSTED, describing a tired person VI.13.8. woˈəˡɹ ɛʊʔ Bk

work *1. n All those people are busy on weekdays, but on Sunday they usually rest and don't do any ....* VIII.4.8(a). Eng. ⇒ **graft**

2. vt to DIG in the garden with a spade I.7.8. wəˡːk D

3. v to KNEAD dough V.6.4. woᴿːk Nb, wərk

Cu, wəːk Du, wəˡːk Wa

4. vi **start it working** to CURDLE milk V.5.7. staːt
ıt wəkın Y

5. vt to PULL somebody's hair VI.2.8. wəˡːk So

workaday clothes *n* ORDINARY　　　CLOTHES
VI.14.20. wəˡːkədeı klɒʊðz Sx, wʌkədı klʌʊᵊz Sf,
wəːkədı klʌʊz Ess, wəˡːkıdeː kloːz Gl, wɔkədı tloːz
Nt, wəkədı klɒʊðz K, wə{kədeı klɒʊz Nf, wəˡːkədeı
tlɒʊz Nth, wɔkədeˑə klʊəz L, wəˡːkıdeı klʊəz Wa

work-a-day-days *npl* WORKDAYS　　　VII.4.6.
wʌkədıdeız Sf

work-a-days *npl* WORKDAYS VII.4.6. wɒɹkədɛəz
Y, wɔkədeˑəz L, wʌkədız Hrt, wʊkədeız L,
wəɹkədæız Hu, wəˡkıdeːz O*[old]*, wəːkədiːz Db, *sg*
wəːkədı Sf, wəːkıdeːz Mon, wəːkədeːz Nt,
wəᴶːkədeız O

work back *imp* **work**　　**it**　　**back**　HELP
YOURSELVES!, said to invite visitors to eat V.8.13.
wəˡːk ıt bæk So

work clothes *n* ORDINARY CLOTHES VI.14.20.
waːk tlıaz Y, wɔᴿːk klıəz Nb, wæːk tlıəz Du, waᴶːk
kleaz La, wɜɹːk tleˑaz La, waᴿːk kleːᵊz Nb, wəˡːk
klɒʊðz Sx, waːk klɔʊðz Ess, wəˡːk kłoːz W, wəːk
klɒʊz St, wəːɹk klɒʊz St, waᴶːk klʊəz La, wəˑɹk kluːz
Sf

workday clobber *n* ORDINARY　　　CLOTHES
VI.14.20. wəˡːkdeı klɔbə Ess

workday clothes *n* ORDINARY　　　CLOTHES
VI.14.20. wəˡːkde: kłoːz Do

workdays *npl What is your word for all the days of
the week together except Sunday?* VII.4.6. wɛəkdız
Lei, wæᴶːɹkdəz La, waɹkdeːᵊz Du, waːkdeːz Du Y,
waːkdeːəz Nb Cu*[old]*, waːkdeːz We, waːkdeᵊz Y,
waːkdəz Nb, waᴿːkdeəz Nb, waᴶːkdeᵊz La Y,
waᴶːkdeːz La, wɑːkdeız Ess, wɒkdiːz St, wɔkdeːz Nt,
wɔkdeız L, wɔkdeˑəz L, wɔᴿːkdıəz Nb Du, wʌkdız
Ess, wʌkdeız Sf, wʌkdæız Ess, wʊrkdeˑəz Cu, *sg*
wɜᴶːɹkdı La, wɜᴶːɹkdeːz La, wəkdeəz Y, wəɹkdeːz
Db, wəɹkdeəz Y, wəɹᵊkdeːz Y, wəɹkdeız Sf,
wəɹkdeəz Y L, wəˡkdæız K, wəːkdiːz Db, wəːkdeːz
Db, wəːkdeız Bd, wəːkdeːz Cu, wəːkdeız St Wa Lei
R Ess, wəːkdeˑəz L, wəːkdæız MxL, wəᴶːkdiːz Ch,
wəᴶːkdeːz Y, wəᴶːkdeız Brk Sr, wəˡːkdeız So,
wəˡːkdeːız Wo, wəˡːkdeız Wa, wəɽːkdeız Wa,
wəˡːɽkdeız Sx. ⇒ **six-days,** *warday* ⇒ **wardays,
wardays, warterdays,** *warties* ⇒ **wardays,
weekdays, week-a-day-days, week-a-days,
weeken-days, week's-days, work-a-day-days,
work-a-days, working-days,** *worky-days* ⇒
work-a-days

worker *n* **general worker** a FARM- LABOURER
I.2.4. dʒɛnʁəl wɔᴿːkə Nb

work for *vtphr* **work for** EARNED VIII.1.26. *3prsg*
wɒɹks fɒ Y, wɜᴶːɹkt fəᴶːɹ La, *inf* wəːk fɒɹ (+V) Y,
wəːkt fəɹ (+V) Man, wəːks fɔɹ (+V) Ch; *3prsg* **works
hard for** wəːks ɑːd fɔɹ (+V) Wo

working *adj* HEAVING　*(WITH　MAGGOTS)*
IV.8.6. waᴶːkın La, wəːkın Y Ch, wɜᴶːkən La,
wəᴶːkın Ch, wəˡːkın O

working clobber *n* ORDINARY　　　CLOTHES
VI.14.20. wək?n klɒbə Ess, wəːkın tlɒbə Y,
wəˑɹkın klɒbə Y, wəˡːkın klɒbəˡ Sr

working clothes *n* ORDINARY　　　CLOTHES
VI.14.20. Eng exc. Du Man Sf

working-day clothes *n* ORDINARY CLOTHES
VI.14.20. wək?ndı tlɔʊz Nf

working-days *npl* WORKDAYS VII.4.6. Eng
exc. We Man R Bd MxL

working-hood *n* a woman's cotton BONNET
with a sun-flap at the back of the neck VI.14.1.
wəːkınʊd L

working suit *n* ORDINARY　　　　CLOTHES
VI.14.20. wəˡːkın syːʔ O, weˑkn sʉ̆ˑt Nf

working tack *n* ORDINARY　　　CLOTHES
VI.14.20. wəˡːkın tak Wa

working tackle *n* ORDINARY　　CLOTHES
VI.14.20. wɜᴶːɹkın takl La, wəːkın takl Wa,
wəˡːkən takł Ha

working things *n* ORDINARY　　　CLOTHES
VI.14.20. wɔkın θıŋz L

working togs *n* ORDINARY　　　CLOTHES
VI.14.20. wəkın tɒgz Y, wəːkın tɒgz St, wəᴶːkın
tɒgz K, wəˡːkın tɒgz W Co, wəˡːkən tɒgz Co,
wəˡkın tɒgz K, wəːɹkn tɒgz Sf*[old]*, wəˡːkın
tɔːgz So

workman *n* a　　FARM-LABOURER　　I.2.4.
wəːkmən Ch, wəˡːkmɒn Wo, wəˡːkmn Sa,
wəˡːkmən Sa He Ess; **general workman** dʒɛnɹəł
wəˡːkmɒn Wo, dʒɛnɹəł wəˡːkmən Mon

work-mates *npl* MATES VIII.4.1. wœːkmeːts
Mon, waːkmeːts Y*[old]*, waːkmeıts Sf,
waːkmeˑəts L, wɒɹkmeəts Y, wɔkmeːts Y Nt,
wɔkmeˑəts L, wɔᴿːkmeəts Du, wɔᴶːkmeːts Y,
wʊkmeıts L, wɜːkmeıts Man, wɜᴶːkmeˑəts La,
wəkmeıts Nf, wəkmeːts Y, wəkmeəts Y,
wəɹkmeıts He, wəɹkmeəts Y, wəᴶkmeˑəts L,
wəːkmeːts Y Ch, wəːkmeːts Cu, wəːkmeıts Lei
R　Hu Nf, wəːkmeəts Y, wəːkmæıts MxL,
wəːkmaıts MxL, *sg* wəᴶːkmeıt St, wəᴶːkmɛˑəts
L, wəᴶːkmæıts K, wəˡːkmeːts Gl, wəˡːɽkmeːts W
Brk, wəᴶːkmeıts Brk Sr, wəˡːkmeıts Wa Ess Sr,
wəˡːɽkmeıts Brk Ha Sx, wəˡːkmæıts K

work-pals *npl* MATES VIII.4.1. wəkpalz Y

work up *vtphr* to KNEAD dough V.6.4. wɔːᵊk ...
ʊp Nb, wɔᴿːk ... ʊp Nb*[old x1]*, wəɹk ... ʊp Y,
wəːk ... ʌp C, wəːk ... ʊp Cu Y

worky clothes *n* ORDINARY　　　CLOTHES
VI.14.20. wəˡːkı tlɒʊz Wa *[queried WMBM]*

worm *n* the GRASS-NAIL of a scythe II.9.9.
wəːm Ch

worms(es) *npl [What creatures live in and on the
soil in your garden?] What do you call those long*

red creatures that you turn up with your soil; hens like them? IV.9.1.

no -es: Eng

-es: wʌmzɪz Ess*[old]*

⇒ **angle-dogs, angle-twitches, earth-worms, easses, grubs, joe-worms**; ⇒ also **palmer-worms**

worn out *adj* EXHAUSTED, describing a tired person VI.13.8. wɔːn ɛʊt Sf, wɔˡːʈn ɛʊt Sx, wɔːəˡn ɛʊt Sr, wʊəˡn aʊt L

worrish *adj* INSIPID, describing food lacking in salt V.7.8. wɒɹɪʃ Y

worry *vi* to KINDLE, describing a rabbit doe giving birth to young III.13.14. *pt* wəɹɪd

worse *adjcomp Mumps are bad, but diphtheria is much* .... VI.12.3. Eng. ⇒ **worsener, worser, worserer**

worsener *adjcomp* WORSE VI.12.3. wəsnə Y

worser *adjcomp* WORSE VI.12.3. wʌsə Sf Hrt Ess MxL, wʊsəɹ (+V) R, wʊsəˡʈ W, wɜːsə Man*[old, rare]*, wəsə Nf Sf, wəsəˡ Brk, wəːsə MxL, wəˑɹsə Nth, wəˡːsəˡ Brk K, wəˡːsəˡ K, wəˡːʂəˡ K, wəˡːʈʂəˡʈ Brk, wəˡːʂəˡː So, uːsəˡ Do

worserer *adjcomp* WORSE VI.12.3. wʌsəɹə Bd

worsest *adjsup* WORST VI.12.5. wɪsɪs D, wəˡːsɪst K

worst *adjsup Mumps are bad, diphtheria is worse, but smallpox is easily the* .... VI.12.5. Eng. ⇒ **most bad, worsest, worstest**

worstest *adjsup* WORST VI.12.5. wʌstɪst Bd, wəˡːstɪst Brk, wəˡːʂtɪst K, wəˡːʈʂtɪst Sx

wottle *n* a POKER V.3.6. wɒtl Y

wound *1. n* the AFTERBIRTH that comes from a cow's uterus after a calf is born III.1.13. wuːn Ess

2. n the VULVA of a cow III.2.3. wɤːn D, wɔˀn Man, wʊnd L, wuːnd Cu Wa Gl O Ess Brk K Sx, wuːn Man So K

3. n the UTERUS of a cow III.2.4. wuːnd O Nth, wuːn Wa Ess

wow *vi-3prpl* they MEW, referring to cats III.10.6. wæʊ L, *-ing* wæʊɪn Ess, waʊ Nb Du Y Nt L, waʊz Du Nt L

wozzle *n* the WINDPIPE VI.6.5. wɒzl Nth

wrack *n* COUCH-GRASS II.2.3. ʁak Nb

wrap *1. vt By the way, if you want to send something by parcel post, you would first have to [indicate wrapping]* ... *it up.* VII.2.9. ɹɛp Sx, ræp Ma, ɹæp Gl Hu Nf Sf Ess Brk Sr Sx, ɾæp So, rap Cu, ʁap Nb, ɹap La Y Db Sa St Wo Gl O Nt L Lei Nth Hu C Bk Bd Hrt Ess, ɾap So D Ha, ɹɒp Bk*[old]* K, ɹɔp C. ⇒ *bundle up, do up,* fold up, lap, lap *it* round, lap *it* up, lap round, lap up, lap *your string* round, *make a parcel, pack, pack it up, pack up, parcel it up, parcel up,* roll *it* up, *string up,* tie, tie up, wrap *it* up, wrap *the parcel* up, wrap up *[given the form of the q asked, it is unclear whether some or all of above forms are* wrap *or vtphr* wrap up*]*

2. n a NECKERCHIEF VI.14.4. ɹɛp K Sx, ɹæp Ess Sr*[silk]* Sx, ɹap Bk, ɾap Ha

wrapper *1. n* a working APRON V.11.2(a). ɹʌpəˡ Brk

2. n a NECKERCHIEF VI.14.4. ɹɛpɐ Ess, ɹæpə Nf Sf Ess, ɹæpʔə Nf Sf, ɹapəˡ Ha, ɾapəˡː W Do, hɾapəˡː So, ɹɑˑpə Nf*[old]*, ɹɒpəˡ O Bk

wrapper-brat *n* a working APRON V.11.2(a). ɹapəbɹat Cu, ɹapəˡbɹat La

wrap up *vtphr* to WRAP a parcel VII.2.9. ɹɛp ... ʌp Ess Sr, ræp ... ʊp Man, ɹæp ... ʌp Mon Gl Nf Hrt Ess MxL Brk Sr K Sx, ɹæp ... ʏp Nf, ɹæp ... ʊp He Wo Gl, ɾæp ... ʌp So Co, hɾæp ... ʌp So, ʁap ... œːp Nb, ɹap ... ʌp Sa He Bk Bd Ha, ɾap ʌp Ha, ɾap ... ʌp So W Co D Do Ha, ɾab ... ʌp Co, ɹap ... ʊp Y Sa St Gl O L Lei R, ɹap ... əp Gl, ɾɒp ... ʌp W Do*[old x1]*, ɹɒp ... ʊp K

wreath down *vtphr* to PLASH a hedge IV.2.4. ɹiːð ... dɛʊn Nf

wrench *1. v* to pull the tops of swedes, ⇐ TOP AND TAIL II.4.3. ɹɛnʃ MxL *[marked u.r. EMBM]*

2. vt to WRING the neck of a chicken when killing it IV.6.20. ɾɪnʃ W

3. vt to SPRAIN an ankle VI.10.8. ɹɪnʃ Gl, *-ed* ɹɪnʃt Sf, *-ing* ɹɪtʃɪn K, *-ed* ɾɪnʃt So, *-ed* ɹɪnʃt D, *-ed* ʁɛnʃt Nb, ɹɛntʃt La, *-ed* ɹɛntʃt Ess, *-ed* ɹɛnʃt Y *[-ing form at K taken as error for* [ɹɪntʃɪn] *SBM]*

wriggle *n* **on the wriggle** ACTIVE, describing a child VIII.9.1. ɒn ðə ɹɪgəl Bd *[marked u.r. EMBM]*

wright *n What do you mean by* **wright**? VIII.4.4. ɹiːt Y*[joiner or wheelwright x1]*, ɹɛɪt St, ræɪt Man*[wheel- or cartwright]*, ɹɑɪt Db K*[wheelwright x1, wainwright x1]*, ɹɒɪt K*[wheelwright]*, ɹɒːɪt St, ɹɔɪt Ess, ɹɔɪʔ O, ɹʌʏt O*[not used]*. ⇒ **boatwright, cartwright, carwright, engine-wright, millwright, shipwright, wainwright, wheelwright**

wring *1. vt If you want to kill a chicken, what do you say you do? [To* ... *its neck].* IV.6.20. Eng exc. We Ch Wo C Sf Sr Sx. ⇒ **break, break** *her neck*, **break** *his neck*, **break** *it*, **break** *its*, **break** *its neck*, **break** *their neck*, **break** *the neck*, **chop** *its head off*, **crack** *its neck*, **cut** *him in his neck*, **cut** *him in the neck*, **cut** *his throat*, **cut** *the throat*, **cut** *the throat of en*, **cut** *the throat of him*, **get** *it necked*, **neck** *him*, **neck** *it*, **neck** *them*, **pull** *his*, **pull** *his neck*, **pull** *his neck out*, **pull** *it neck*, **pull** *it neck* out, **pull** *its*, **pull** *its neck*, **pull** *its neck out*, **pull out** *his neck*, **pull** *their neck*, **pull** *their necks*, **pull** *their necks* out, **pull** *the neck*, **pull** *the neck* out, **put** *the neck* out, **rive** *his neck* out, **rive** *its neck* out, **screw** *and tug*, **screw** *his neck*, **screw** *his neck* out, **screw** *his neck* round, **screw** *it neck* round, **screw** *its*, **screw** *its neck*, **screw** *its neck* *around*, screw *its neck* out, screw *its neck* round, snobble *them*, *stick him*, *stick him his neck*, *stick him in his neck*, *stick him in his throat*, *stick it*, stretch *his*, stretch *his neck*, twine *its*, twist, twist *her neck*, twist *his*, twist *his neck*, twist *his neck* round, twist *its*, twist *its neck*, twist *their neck*, twist *the neck of him*, wrench *his neck*, wring *his*, wring *his neck*, wring *his neck* out, wring *it neck*, wring *its*, wring *its neck*, wring *their neck*, wring *them*, wring *the neck*

2. *vt* to TOP AND TAIL swedes II.4.3. ɹɪŋ Ess*[leaves x1]*, *-ing* ɹɪŋɪn K *[marked u.r. in one locality Ess]*

3. *vt* to SPRAIN an ankle VI.10.8. *-ed* ɹɪŋkt Ess, *-ed* ɹæŋ Nf, *-ed* ɹʌŋ Nf Ess

4. *vi* to WARP, referring to wood IX.2.9. ɹɪŋ Ess; **get wrung** gɛʔ ɹʌŋ Nf

wringing* *vt-ing* PULLING his ear VI.4.4. *-s* rɪŋs Man, ɹɪŋɪn Nf Ess K Ha, ɹɪŋən Sf, *no -ing* ɹɪŋ Sx

wring off *1. vtphr* to remove the tops of swedes, ⇐ TOP AND TAIL II.4.3. ɹɪŋ … ɔf Sr *[marked u.r. SBM]*
2. *vtphr* to top and tail wurzels. ɹɪŋ … ɔːf K

wring out *vtphr* to WRING the neck of a chicken when killing it IV.6.20. ɹɪŋg … aɪt St

wring over *vtphr* to SPRAIN an ankle VI.10.8. ɹɪŋ … oʊvə Nf

wrinkle *vi What happens to the skin of very old people?* VI.11.2. Eng. ⇒ creases, crease up, crimple, crinkle, crinkle up, frizzle up, furrow, *get dwindled*, *get shively*, *get withered*, *get wrinkled*, *get wrinkly*, go dry-wizened, go dry-wizzened ⇒ dry-wizened, *go wizened*, go wizzened ⇒ wizened, *go wrinkly*, nither, pith, rivel, rivelled, rivelly, rivel up, ruck, shrink, shrivel, shrivelled, shrivel up, sweal up, twintered, wither, withered, withered up, wither up, wizen, wizened, wizened up, *wizzen* ⇒ wizen, *wrinkled*, *wrinkled up*, *wrinkles*, *wrinkle up*, *wrinkly*, wrizzle

wrist *1. n What do you call this [indicate the wrist]?* VI.6.9. Eng. ⇒ arm-wrist, hand-wrist, shackle
2. *n* an ANKLE VI.10.7. ɹʊst Y; **wrist of your foot** ɹʊst ə jə fʊɪt Y
3. *n* **wrist of my foot*** the front part of the ankle. ɹʊst ə maː fʊɪt Y

wrizzle *vi* to WRINKLE, referring to the skin of very old people VI.11.2. *3prsg* ɽɛzłz So

wrong *1. adj* describing a cow's teat that is dry, or a cow with a BLIND TEAT III.2.7. ɹaŋ La*[she's wrong of one pap]*, ɹɒŋ Nf*[that quarter has gone wrong]*
2. *adj* **go wrong** to SPOIL, referring to meat or fish V.7.10. gʊː ɹaŋ Y, gʊə ɹɒŋ L, goʊ ɹɒŋ Nf, *3prsg* gʊz ɹɒŋ Sx, gɥː ɹɒŋ Lei, gə ɹɒŋ Lei, gʊ ɹɔːŋ Ess, gʊː ɹɔːŋ Ess
3. *adj* SICK, describing an animal that is unwell VI.13.1(c). ɹaŋ La, ɹɒŋ La

wrong quarter *n* a BLIND TEAT III.2.7. ʁaŋ kwaᵍtə Nb

wrought for *vtphr-3sgperf* EARNED VIII.1.26. ɹaʊt fɒ Cu

wry *1. n* **on the wry** ASKEW, describing a picture that is not hanging straight IX.1.3. ɒn ðə ɹʌi Nf
2. *vi* to WARP, referring to wood IX.2.9. ɹʌiˑ Nf

wub *imp* **wub off** the command TURN RIGHT!, given to plough-horses II.3.5(b). ˈwʊb ˈɔːf Do

wug *imp* **wug, wug around, wug back, wug off, wug out, wug round, wug there** the command TURN RIGHT!, given to plough-horses II.3.5(b). **wug** woʊg Brk, wʊg W D Ha; **wug around** ˈwʊg əˈɽœʏn D; **wug back** wʊg bak Co D; **wug off** wʊg ɔːf So W D Do Ha; **wug out** ˈwʊg ˈæʏt D; **wug round** wʊg ɽaʊn So; **wug there** ˈwʊg ðɛˤː Ha

wugd *imp* **wugd, wugd off** the command TURN RIGHT!, given to plough-horses II.3.5(b). **wugd** wɒʊgd Brk, wʊgd W; **wugd off** ˈwʊgd ˈɔːf W

wurt *imp* **wurt, wurt off** the command TURN RIGHT!, given to plough-horses II.3.5(b). **wurt** wʊɽt Gl; **wurt off** wəˤːt ɔːf So

wych *n* a BIRCH tree IV.10.1. waɪtʃ Sa

wykes* *npl* MOUTH CORNERS VI.5.2. waɪks Du; **wykes of thy mouth** waɪks ə ðɪ muːθ Y

wykings *1. npl* MOUTH CORNERS VI.5.2. waˈɪkɪnz L, wɑˈɪkɪnz L
2. *n* (WIPE YOUR) MOUTH VI.5.3. waˈɪkɪnz L

wyzles *n* POTATO-HAULMS II.4.4. wɛɪzlz Ch, waɪzlz Ch Db Sa, wəˤːz̩l̩z̩ Sa

Y, Z

yack* *vi* to VOMIT, referring to an adult VI.13.14(a). jæk So

yaddering *v-ing* GOSSIPING VIII.3.5(a). jadðəɹən We

yafful *1. n* a CUTTING of hay II.9.15. jafəł Co
2. n an ARMFUL of hay VII.8.10(c). jafəł D

yakker *n* an ACORN IV.10.3. *pl* jɛkəᵌːz̩ Ha

yampy *adj* STUPID VI.1.5. jampɪ We

yanks *npl* LEGGINGS VI.14.18. jaŋks L

yap *1. n* the human MOUTH VI.5.1. jæp Gl
2. adj HUNGRY VI.13.9. jɪap Nb

yapper *n* a GOSSIP VIII.3.5(b). jæpə Ess

yapping *v-ing* GOSSIPING VIII.3.5(a). jɛːəpn Ess, jæˑpɪn Hrt, jæpən Ess

yard *1. n* a FARMYARD I.1.3. jɛɔᴮd Nb, jæːd La, jaːd Nb Cu Y Db St Wa Mon Nt Lei Hu Nf Ess, jaᴶːd Y, jaᵂːd̩ Wo Wa Mon O So W Co D Do Ha, jɑːd Nf Ess, jaᵂːd̩ He Sr D Sx
2. n the STRAW-YARD of a farm I.1.9. jaːd Ess, jaᵂːd̩ Wa So D Ha, jaːd Hrt, jaᴶːd K, jaᵂːɽd̩ Sx, jaᵂːəd Sr, jaᵂːəᵂd̩ Brk, jaᵂːəᵂɽd̩ Sx
3. n a straw-yard in which cattle are fattened. jaːd Wa
4. n a FASTING-CHAMBER III.11.3. jaːd Nf *[marked u.r. EMBM]*

yard bridge-end *n* the CROSS-BEAM END of a cart I.10.1. jaːd bɹɪdʒɛnd L

yard-broom *1. n* a MUCK-BRUSH I.3.14. jaːdbɹʊm Sr, jaːdbɹuːm Ess K, jaːdbɹʊm Ess, jəᵂːd̩bɹuːm Sa
2. n a BROOM used for sweeping outdoors V.9.10. jaːdbɹʊm Ess, jaːdbɹuːm Y Nf Bd, jaːdbɹʊm Nf

yard-brush *1. n* a MUCK-BRUSH I.3.14. jaːdbɹʊʃ Y Ch Nt, jaᴶːdbɹʊʃ La
2. n a BROOM used for sweeping outdoors V.9.10. jæːdbɹʊʃ La, jaːdbɹʌʃ Nth Hu Bd, jaːdbɹʊʃ Cu Y Ch Nt L Lei R, jaᴶːdbɹʊʃ La

yardman *1. n* a CARTMAN on a farm I.2.2. jaːdmən Bd, jaːdman St
2. n a COWMAN on a farm I.2.3. jaːdmən Hu, jaːdmən Nf
3. n a man who looks after beef cattle on a farm. jaːdmən Nf
4. n a general helper with animals on a farm. jaːdmn̩ Nf

yard-run *n* the STRAW-YARD of a farm I.1.9. jaᴶːdɹʌn K

yards *n* the yards a FARMYARD I.1.3. ðə jaˑəɽdz̩ Brk

yark *1. vt* to WHITTLE a stick I.7.19. *-ing* jaˑɹkɪn He
2. vt to BEAT a boy on the buttocks VIII.8.10. jaᴮːk Nb

yarking *1. vt-ing* PULLING his ear VI.4.4. jaːkɪn Y
2. v-ing SHRIEKING, describing the shrill noise made by a baby VI.5.15. jaːkɪn Ch, jaʊkɪn St
3. v-ing THROWING a stone VIII.7.7. jɛkɪn Lei, jakɪn Lei

yarming *v-ing* SHRIEKING, describing the shrill noise made by a baby VI.5.15. jaːmɪn Y

yarn *1. n* STRING used to tie up a grain-sack I.7.3. jɑːn K
2. n CHAT VIII.3.4. jaːn Y L, jaᵂːn So Co Do Ha, jaːn Man K, jaᴶːn K, jaᵂːn̩ D Ha, jaᵂːɽn̩ Ha Sx; **good old yarn** gʊd woʊł jaᵂːn̩ So; **right good yarn** ɹɛɪt gʊd jaːn L

yarning *v-ing* GOSSIPING VIII.3.5(a). jaᵂːn̩ɪn So Ha, jaᵂːn̩ən Do

yaums *vi-3prsg* he GAPES VI.3.7. prppl jɔːmɪn Y

yaups *vi-3prsg* he GAPES VI.3.7. jɑːps Gl

yawl *vi-3prpl* they MEW, referring to cats III.10.6. jaːł D

yawling *v-ing* SHRIEKING, describing the shrill noise made by a baby VI.5.15. jaːłɪn He

yawning *1. v-ing* *What am I doing now [indicate yawning audibly]?* VI.13.4. Eng exc. We Hu C MxL. ⇒ **ganting, gaping, gawping, sighing, yauping** ⇒ **yawping, yawning;** ⇒ also **gapes**
2. v-ing SHRIEKING, describing the shrill noise made by a baby VI.5.15. jaːnɪn Ch

yawning about* *viphr-ing* gaping, ⇐ GAPES VI.3.7. jɔːnɪn əbɛʊt Bk

yawping *v-ing* YAWNING VI.13.4. jaːpɪn L, jɔːpɪn O L

yaye *adv* YES VIII.8.13(a). jaɪ La Y, jɑɪ La

yea *1. imp* the command stop! or WOA!, given to plough-horses II.3.5(c). jeː Sa
2. adv YES VIII.8.13(a). jeː La, jeˑə Bd, jɛ Sf, jɛɔ K, jæː C, jaː La, jɑː K*[old]*; **oh yea** oʊ jeːᵌ MxL

year *1. n* **a year** *If [something happened] twelve months back from now [you'd say: It happened] ... ago.* VII.3.4. Eng. ⇒ **a twelvemonth(s), twelvemonth(s),** *year(s)*
2. n **this year** *There's last year, there's next year, and then what do you call the one we're in now?*

472

(before Christmas 1957: ... *and what do you call the one in between?)* VII.3.18. Eng; **the present year** ðə pɹɛsənt jɪə Nf; **the year** ðɪ jɪə Hrt Ess; **thick year** ðɪk jəːʈ W, ðɪk jəʈːʈ W. ⇒ *the present* year, *the* year, *thick* year, to-year

year-grass *n* AFTERMATH, a second crop of grass II.9.17. hiːgɹaːs So Do, iːgɹaːs Do, jəʈːgɹæːs So, jəʈːgɹaːs So

yearling *1. n* a HEIFER 1 year old III.1.5. jɪəlɪn St, jaʈːɬɪn So, jəʈːɬɪn W, jəʈːɬɪn W *['1 year old' not stated SBM]*
2. n a sheep before its first shearing, ⇐ EWE-HOG III.6.4. jɪəlɪn Nf Ess MxL, jɪəᴊlɪŋ Man, jœːɬɪn Mon Gl, jəlɪn Y, jəᴊːlɪn Y, jəʈːlɪn Gl, jəʈːɬɪn He Mon Gl
3. n a sheep from its first to its second shearing, ⇐ GIMMER III.6.5. jɪəlɪn Ess MxL, -s jɪəʈɹlɪnz Brk, jœːɬɪn Mon Gl, jəʈːlɪn Gl, jəʈːɬɪn He Mon Gl *[apparently regarded as female term WMBM]*

yearling-ewe *1. n* a EWE-HOG III.6.4. jəʈːɬɪnjuː Wo
2. n a GIMMER III.6.5. jəɹlɪn juː He*[15 months old]*, jəʈːlɪn juː Wo

yearling heifer *n* a HEIFER 1 year old III.1.5. jəɹlɪn ɛfəɹ He

yearling-lamb *n* a EWE-HOG III.6.4. jɛəlɪnlam Lei

yeast *1. n Now to make bread, you put flour and water into a dish, and what else, to make it rise?* V.6.2. Eng exc. Db
2. n dry, hard, crumbly yeast. jiːst Nt Nth*[modern x1]* Hu, iːst Bk, jɪəst Nt, jɛst Nt
⇒ **barm, brewer's yeast, dry yeast, dutch yeast, german yeast, lees, slop barm**

yeddle *n* URINE in a cow-house I.3.10. jɛdl Nb Du, jadl Du

yeddle-hole *1. n* a CESS-POOL on a farm I.3.11. jɛdlhoəl Nb
2. n an artificial cess-pool. jɛtlhøəl Du

yeddle-tank *n* an artificial CESS-POOL on a farm I.3.11. jɛdltaŋk Nb

yelks *npl* KNEE-STRAPS used to lift the legs of working trousers VI.14.17. jɛɬks Bk

yell *1. vi-3prpl* they MEW, referring to cats III.10.6. jɛl Nf
2. vi to SCREAM VIII.8.11. jɛl Nb Cu La Y Db, jɛɬ Wa Lei Bk W Sr, jɛʊ Ess Sr Ha, *3prsg* jɛəɬz K, jaɬ Ha

yelland *n* LOW-LYING LAND IV.1.7. jɛlənd Y

yeller *vi* to SCREAM VIII.8.11. jɛɬə W

yelling *v-ing* SHRIEKING, describing the shrill noise made by a baby VI.5.15. jɛlɪn La Y Db St He Wa L Lei Nf Ess So, əjɛlɪn Wa, jɛlən Nb Sf, jɛɬɪn Wo O Lei Sr D, jɛɬən Ess Ha Sx, *no -ing* jɛɬ Hrt, jɛɹlɪn Y

yelling out *vphr-ing* SHRIEKING, describing the shrill noise made by a baby VI.5.15. jɛlɪn aʊt Y

yell out *viphr* to SCREAM VIII.8.11. *-ing* jɛlɪn uːt Y

yellow-arse *n* a wasp, ⇐ ARSE VI.9.2. jɛləɹæs Nf

yellow-belly *n* a NEWT IV.9.8. jɛləbɛlɪ Ess

yellow-flower *n* CHARLOCK II.2.6. jɛləflaʊə Ch, *pl* jaləflaʊəz St

yellow-runch *n* CHARLOCK II.2.6. jaləɹʊnʃ Y

yellow(s) *n* CHARLOCK II.2.6.
no -s: pl jaləz Db St
-s: jaləs Nb, jaləz Nb Du

yellow-top *n* CHARLOCK II.2.6. jalətœːp Nb

yellow-weed *n* CHARLOCK II.2.6. jɛləwiːd St, jaləwiːd Ch Db, jaləwɛɪd Ch, jɒləwiːd St

yelp *1. vi* to WHELP III.13.3. jɛɬp So, jəɬp So
2. n **in yelp** pregnant, describing a bitch. ɪn jɛɬp Ha

yelping *v-ing* SHRIEKING, describing the shrill noise made by a baby VI.5.15. jɛlpɪn Y

yelp out *viphr* to SCREAM VIII.8.11. jəɬp ɛʊt O

yelps *1. npl* PUPS or young dogs III.13.4. jɛlps Nb, jɛɬps Co
2. n very young dogs, younger than pups. jɛɬps So

yelt *n* a YOUNG SOW III.8.5. jɛɬt Ess, jɛʊɬt Hrt, jɛʊt Ess

yelve *n* a MUCK-FORK I.3.13. jɪlv Ch, jɪɬv Ch

yenky *adj* RANCID, describing bacon V.7.9. jɛŋkɪ Brk *[queried SBM]*

yes *adv If I asked you: Have you met that man, you could say: ... [, No].* VIII.8.13(a). iːs So W Co D Do, jɪs Cu Du Y*[modern x1]* Ch Wa L Lei R Hu C Nf Ess So Sr K, eːs Co D Do, jeɪs Sr, je'əs Sf, jɛs Nb Sa St Wa O Lei Nth Hu Nf Hrt Ess MxL So W Brk Sr K Do Ha Sx, ɛɪs D, jɛːəs Man Ess Brk K, jʊs Y, jəs Du Y MxL K. ⇒ **ah, aw, aye,** *oh* **ah,** *oh* **ah** *yes,* **oh yea,** *oh yes,* **why aye, yaye, yea**

yester *n* YESTERDAY VII.3.8. jɛstə Y, jəstə Y

yesterday *n [If you wanted to tell me that something happened seven days back from now, you'd say: It happened ....] If not today, but twenty-four hours ago?* VII.3.8. Eng. ⇒ **yester, yesterday-day**

yesterday afternoon *n* LAST NIGHT VII.3.9. ɪstəʈːdɪ ætəʈːnuːn So*[night 'when we do go to bed']*

yesterday-day *n* YESTERDAY VII.3.8. jɪstədədɛə Y

yesterday night *n* LAST NIGHT VII.3.9. jɪstədə niːt Cu Y, jʊstdɪ niːt Y, jɪstədə nɛɪt Y, jestədə nɛɪt Nb, jəstədə nᵊiːt We, jɛstədɪ naɪʔ MxL

yester night *n* LAST NIGHT VII.3.9. jɪstə niːt Y, jɪsdə niːt Y, jʊstə niːt Y

yetling-hook *n* a CRANE on which a kettle is hung over a domestic fire V.3.4. jɛtlɪnhuːk Nb

yewcums *n* hiccups, ⇐ HICCUPING VI.8.4. ʏːkʌmz D

yewking *v-ing* HICCUPING VI.8.4. ʏːkɪn D

yield *1. n [In looking after your cows, in the old-fashioned way, tell me what do you do?] What is your word for the amount of milk that you get at one time? Does that word apply to the whole herd or just to one cow?* III.3.5.

1. n the yield of milk from a cow. jiːld Ch St Wo Nf, jɪil Man*[rare]*, iːld Sa, jiːɬd Wo Sf So K D, iːɬd He Mon, jiːəl Man, jiːᵊɬd Gl So, jiːᵊɬ He, iːᵊɬ Mon, jiːʊɬd Ess Ha Sx, jɪɬd Wa Sr, jɪəɬd Sr K, jɪʊɬd Brk Sr*[annual yield x1]* K Ha Sx, jɪʊɬ Brk, *pl* ɪʊɬdz Brk, jɪʊd Ess Sr Sx

2. n the yield of milk from a herd of cows. jiːld St Wo, iːld Sa, jiːɬd Wo Nth Ess Ha, iːɬd He Mon, jiːəɬd Gl Ess W, jiːᵊɬ He, iːᵊɬd W, iːᵊɬ Mon, jɪil Man*[rare]*, jɪːɬ Lei, jɪəɬd Lei Ess Sr, jɪʊɬd K

3. n a yield of milk. jiːld Ch St Lei, jiːᵊld He, jiːɬd Lei Nth Bk So, jiːɬ Lei R, iːɬd Wa, jiːᵁɬd W, jiːᵊɬd Nth C Sf Bk Bd Ess So W, jiːᵊɬ Hu Sf Hrt, jɪld Ch, ɪəld Wo, jɪəɬd O Lei MxL, jɪəɬ O, jɪʊɬd O, jeːld Ch ⇒ **bail**, *bucketful*, **daffy**, *drop*, *drop of milk*, **feed**, *good bucketful*, *good lot*, *good pull*, **lash**, *lot*, **meal**, *milk*, **milking**, **quantity**, *record*, **sprinkle**, **sprinkling**, **yielding**

3. n HARVEST II.6.1. jɪiᵊɬd Ess

yielding *1. n* the YIELD of milk from a cow III.3.5. jiˈldɪn Nf, iːɬdɪn Mon*[old]*, jiːᵊlɪn Hrt, jᵊiːᵊɬɪn Hrt

2. n the yield of milk from a herd of cows III.3.5. iːɬdɪn Mon*[old]*

yiling *v-ing* SHRIEKING, describing the shrill noise made by a baby VI.5.15. jaɪlɪn Y

yilk *n* a YOUNG SOW III.8.5. jɪɬk Sf

yilt *1. n* a YOUNG SOW III.8.5. jɪlt O, jɪɬt Nth Hu C Hrt Ess MxL, jɪɬ? Sf Bk Bd, jʊɬt Ess

2. n a young sow until she has her second litter. jɪɬt Ess

3. n a SOW from the time of her first litter until she has her second litter III.8.6. jɪɬt Ess

yob *n* a FARM-LABOURER I.2.4. jɒb St

yocket *vi* to VOMIT, referring to an adult VI.13.14(a). *-ing* jɒkətɪn So *[queried SBM]*

yoke *1. n* a chain TETHER for a cow I.3.4. jouk Nf

2. n an iron tether. jʌʊk Sf

3. n a wooden device with two upright pieces, between which a cow's neck was held in a cow-house. jʌʊk Ess, jouk Bk

4.1. vt to GEAR a cart-horse I.5.1. jɒk Man, *-ing* joʊkɪn Sr, *prppl* joʊkɪn Brk, jouk Nf, jʊək Y

4.2. ɔ gear a horse. jɒʊk Nth, jɒk Nt, joːk La, jouk Nf, jʊᵪ La

5. n a DONKEY III.13.16. jʌʊk Ess

yoke in *1. vtphr* to GEAR a cart-horse I.5.1. jouk ... ɪn Nf

2. vphr to hitch a horse to a plough or cart. *-ing* joukn ... ɪn Nf

yoke out *1. vtphr* to GEAR a cart-horse I.5.1. jɒk ... aʊt L

2. vphr to gear a horse. jɒʊk ɛʊt Nth

yokes *n* barley AWNS II.5.3. joːʊks So

yoke up *vtphr* to GEAR a cart-horse I.5.1. jouk? ... ʌp Nf

yolk *n What do you call the inside of an egg?* IV.6.5. Eng. ⇒ **red**, **red yolk**; ⇒ also **white yolk**

yolt *n* a NEWT IV.9.8. jɒʊɬt Gl

yon *1. pron* THAT IX.10.1. jɒn Nb L, jɒn L

2. pron THAT over there IX.10.3. jɒn Nb Cu Du We La Y Db Nt L Lei, jɒn Nb La Y L

3. adv **over yon** that *OVER* THERE IX.10.3. ɒʊə jɒn Y, oˈəɹ jɒn La

4. pron THOSE IX.10.4. jɒn Y

5. pron THOSE over there IX.10.6. jœˑn Nb, jɒn Nb Cu Du We La Y Db Nt L, jɒn Nb La Y L

6. adv **over yon** those *OVER* THERE IX.10.6. oˈəɹ jɒn La

yond *1. pron* THAT over there IX.10.3. jɒnd La Y Db

2. pron THOSE over there IX.10.6. jɒnd La Y Db

yonder *1. pron* THAT over there IX.10.3. jandəᵗː D

2. adv that *OVER* THERE IX.10.3. jændəᵗ He, jandəᴵ O, jɒndə Wo Mon, jɒndəᴵ O, jɒndəᵗ Sa Mon O, jɒndə MxL; **over yonder** ʌʊvəᴵɹ ɛndəᵗ Bk, ɑʊə jɒndə Y, ɒʊə jɒndə We, ɔə jɒndə Y, ɔʊə jɒndə Y, ouvəᵗ jɒndəᵗ O, aʊə jɒndə Y, ɔvə jɒndə Y, ɔʊvə jɒndə Wa, ɔʊə jɒndə Y, ʌʊvə jɒndə Sr, oʊvə jɒndə Wo, ʌʊvə jɒndəᵗ Sr

3. pron THOSE over there IX.10.6. jɒndə Db

4. adv those *OVER* THERE IX.10.6. ɛndəᵗ Bk, jændəᵗ He, jandəᴵ O, jɒndə Y Wo Mon, jɒndəᵗ Sa He Mon O, jɒndə MxL; **over yonder** ouvə jɪndə Nf, ɑʊə jɒndə Y, ɔˑəˑɔ jɒndə Y, ɔʊə jɒndə Y, oːvəɹ jɒndəɹ He, ouvəᵗ jɒndəᵗ O, aʊə jɒndə Y, ɔvə jɒndə Y, ɔʊvə jɒndə Wa, ɔʊə jɒndə Y, ɔvəᴵ jɒndəᴵ Y, oʊvə jɒndə Wo, ʌʊvə jɒndə Sr, ʌʊvə jɒndəᵗ Sr

yons *1. pron* THAT over there IX.10.3. jɒnz Db

2. pron THOSE over there IX.10.6. jɒns Db

yorkers *npl* KNEE-STRAPS used to lift the legs of working trousers VI.14.17. jaᵗːkəᵗːz̧ Co, joːkɔᵏz Du*[old]*, jɔᴵːkəᴵz K, jɔᵗːkəᵗz̧ O*[old]*

yorkies *npl* KNEE-STRAPS used to lift the legs of working trousers VI.14.17. jɒɹkʊz Y, jɔɽkʊz O, joːkʊz Hu Nf, jɔːkʔiz Nf, jɔᴵːkʊz Y

yorks *npl* KNEE-STRAPS used to lift the legs of working trousers VI.14.17. jaːks W, jaᵗːks Wo Gl So W Co Do Ha, jɑːks Mon, jɑᵗːks He Wo Mon Gl Brk, jɒks Y*[straps x1]*, jɒɹks Y He, jɒʊks Ch, jɔɹks Y, jɔːks Nb Cu Du We Y*[string x2]* Ch Db Sa St Wa Mon Nt L Lei Nth Nf Ess So Brk Sr K D, jɔᵏːks Nb, jɔᴵːks We La Y, jɔᴵːɹks La, jɔᵗːks

Sa He Wa Gl O Nth Bk So Co D Ha, jɔəks Y O L, jɔəᴸks La, jɔəᵗks O*[old]*, jɔːəᴸks Sr, jɔːəᵗks Sx, joːks Wo, juəks Du L, jəːks Du St, jəᴸːks L, jəᵗːks Wo Do

yot *n* an earthenware SALTING-TROUGH III.12.5. jɒt Nf *[queried EMBM]*

young *1. n* **in young** pregnant, describing a bitch, ⇐ to WHELP III.13.3. ɪn jʌŋ K

2. vi to KINDLE, describing a rabbit doe giving birth to young III.13.14. jʌŋ Nf

3. n **in young** pregnant, describing a doe rabbit. ɪn jɒŋ K, ɪn jʌŋ So K D Sx

4. n a NESTLING IV.7.1. jʌŋ So W Do Ha

young bird *n* a NESTLING IV.7.1. jʌŋ bɛd Nf, juŋ baːd Sf, juŋ bɒd Db, *pl* juŋ bɒdz Y, *pl* juŋ bɒɹdz Y, juŋ bəd Nt L, *pl* jɒŋ boᴮ:dz Nb, juŋ boᴮ:d Du, *pl* juŋ boᴮ:dz Nb, *pl* jʌŋ bʌdz Sf Hrt, juŋ buəd Du, juŋ bəᴸːɪd La, jʌŋ bəd Nf, *pl* jʌŋ bədz Sf, juŋ bəd Y, *pl* jʌŋ bəɹdz He, juŋ bəɪd Y, jʌŋ bəːd Nf Ess, *pl* jʌŋ bəːdz Bd, juŋ bəːd We Db, *pl* juŋ bəːdz Cu Ch Wa, *pl* jʌŋ bəːɹdz C Sf, *pl* jɒŋ bəᴸːdz Brk, juŋ bəᴸːd La, *pl* juŋ bəᴸːdz Y Ch, jɒŋ bəᵗːɽd Sx, jʌŋ bəᵗːɖ D Ha Sx, *pl* jʌŋ bəᵗːdʐ O Bd So W Co Do, *pl* juŋ bəᵗːdʐ Wo Gl O Bk, juŋ bɹɪd La, *pl* juŋ bɹɪdz Ch, *pl* juŋg bɹɪdz St

young bitch *n* a girl, ⇐ GIRLS VIII.1.3(b). jʌŋ bɪtʃ Nf *[not disrespectful]*

young chickens *npl* CHICKENS IV.6.11. juŋ tʃɪkɪnz Y

young elk* *n* a YOUNG SOW III.8.5. jʌŋ ɛłk W Do

young entire *n* a STALLION up to 3 years old III.4.4. juŋ ɛntaɪə Ch

young ewe *1.* a EWE-HOG III.6.4. jʌŋ juː Nf, jʌŋ jᵿ: Nf

2. n a GIMMER III.6.5. jʌŋ jɔʊ O, jʌŋ ɪuː Sf

young fledging *n* a NESTLING IV.7.1. jʌŋ vłɪdʒɪn D, *pl* jʌŋ flɛdʒɪnz So

young fledglings *npl* young FLEDGED birds IV.7.2. jʌŋ flɛdʒłɪnz MxL

young frogs *npl* TADPOLES IV.9.5. jʌŋ vrɔːgz So *[marked u.r. SBM]*

young gilt *n* a YOUNG SOW III.8.5. *pl* juŋ gɪlts Y

young ilt* *n* a YOUNG SOW III.8.5. juŋ ɪlt Wo

young mare *n* a FILLY III.4.2. jɒŋ mɛəᵗ Sx, jʌŋ mɛːə Ess

young one *n* a NESTLING IV.7.1. *pl* juŋg wɒnz St, *pl* jʌŋ wʌnz Ess, jʌŋ ʌn Bd, *pl* juŋ ʊnz Gl, *pl* juŋg ʊnz La Db Wo, jʌŋ ən Ess MxL So Ha, *pl* jʌŋ ənz He Mon O Bk Hrt W, juŋ ən Du Y St Wo, *pl* juŋ ənz Cu We La Ch He Gl O, juŋg ən Db, *pl* juŋg ənz Sa St; **naked young one** nɪeːkəd jʌŋ ənz Sa *[marked u.r. WMBM]*

young onions *npl* SPRING ONIONS V.7.16. jʌŋ aɪnənz W, *sg* jʌŋ ɔɪnən O, jʌŋ ɔɪnjənz Ess, jʌŋ ʌnjənz Hu Nf W Ha, *sg* jʌŋ ʌnjən Sr, juŋ ʌɪnənz Bk, jəŋ ʌɪnənz Gl, *sg* jʌŋ ʌynən O, juŋ ʊnɪənz Cu La Wa, *sg* juŋ ʊnɪən Y, juŋ ʊnjənz St L Nth, juŋg ʊnjʊnz Wa, juŋ ʊnʊnz Gl, juŋg ʊnɪənz Ch, juŋg ʊnjənz Db St

young pig *n* a PIGLET III.8.2. jɒʊŋ pɪg Sr, jʌŋ pɪg He Mon O Do, *pl* jʌŋ pɪgz Sa Hu Sr D Ha, juŋ pɪg Nb Cu Du We La Y Man Ch Sa Wo Gl Nth, *pl* juŋ pɪgz Db Wa

young piglet *n* a PIGLET III.8.2. juŋ pɪglət Wo

young ram *n* a MALE LAMB III.6.2. jʌŋ ɹɛm Ess, juŋ ɹam Wo

young snails *npl* SLUGS IV.9.2. juŋ snɪːlz Db

young sow *1. n What do you call a female [pig] before she has a litter?* III.8.5. jɒŋ sɛʊ Sr, jɒŋg sɛʊ K, jʌŋ sɛʊ Nf Sx, jʏŋ sɛʊ Nf, jʌŋ zæʏ So, jʌŋ saʊ Sa, jʌŋ səʊ Nf. ⇒ **elk, elp, elt, geld, gilt, gilt pig, helk, hilt, ilt, she-pig, sow, sow-pig, yelt, yilk, yilt, young elk, young gilt,** *young hilt* ⇒ **young ilt, young ilt, young sow-pig,** *young yelt* ⇒ **young elk**

2. n a SOW III.8.6. jʌŋ sɛʊ Nf Ess, jʌŋ səʊ· Nf

young sow-pig *n* a YOUNG SOW III.8.5. jʌŋ zaʊpɪg So

youngster *n* a CHILD VIII.1.2(b). jʌŋstə Nf MxL

youngsters *npl* CHILDREN VIII.1.2(a). juŋstəz Y Wo, juŋstəɹz He

young suckers *npl* piglets, ⇐ PIGLET III.8.2. jʌŋ zʌkəᵗːʐ D

young tup *n* a MALE LAMB III.6.2. juŋ tʊp Y

yow *vi-3prpl* they MEW, referring to cats III.10.6. jaʊ Y, jaʊz L, *-ing* jaʊɪn L

yowl *1. vi-3prpl* they MEW, referring to cats III.10.6. jæʏł Co, jɛʊł Ess, jaʊl Y, jaʊlz We, *-ing* ja·ʊlɪn L, *-ing* jaʊlɪn Nf, *-ing* jʌʊłən Sf, jɒʊl La, *prppl* jɒʊlən Nb, juːlz Du

2. vi to SCREAM VIII.8.11. jɛʊl La, jaʊl Cu Y L, jɒʊl Cu, jᵁuːl We

yowling *v-ing* SHRIEKING, describing the shrill noise made by a baby VI.5.15. jɒʊlən Cu We, juːlɪn Y*[old]*, jᵁuːlən We

yuck *1. vi* to ACHE, referring to a stomach VI.13.3(b). jʊk Du *[NBM headword **yuck**, but glossed as **hook**]*

2. vi to RETCH VI.13.15. *-ing* jʊkɪn L

3. vt to BEAT a boy on the buttocks VIII.8.10. jʊk Y

yucks *vi-3prsg* it HURTS VI.13.3(a). jʊks Du

yule *n* a MOLE IV.5.4. juːᵊł Bk*[very old]*

yusen *n* a TROUGH in a cow-house I.3.6. jʏːzən Co D

zears *n* barley AWNS II.5.3. zɪəᵗːʐ Co

THE GRAMMAR

INTRODUCTION

The material in this Grammar consists of items of morphology and syntax recorded in the Survey of English Dialects that differ from their counterparts in Standard English, either in form or in context of occurrence. 'Morphology' and 'syntax' are taken to mean, primarily, the material elicited by the questions in the Survey that are specifically designated as of special morphological or syntactical significance. However, the whole text of the Survey has been scanned and drawn upon for the material discussed, in order to confirm or contradict, but especially to augment, that drawn from the special morphological and syntactical questions. Hence material elicited by questions of which the primary aim was to obtain information of lexical or phonological importance is frequently cited, as are items from the Incidental Material gathered by the Survey's editors alongside the Basic Material responses: the former has proved to be specially rich in forms of grammatical interest.

However, the account that follows is not meant to be comprehensive; it has not been considered useful to try to mention every attestation of every phenomenon under discussion. The proportion of cited material in fact varies from subject to subject. For instance, in citing present-participial forms of regular verbs with prefixed **a-** (§72), at least one example from as many counties as possible is given, but nothing like all the recorded examples of this widespread phenomenon have been mentioned. On the other hand, in the section dealing with zero-inflected forms of the possessive singulars of nouns qualifying other nouns (§38),

which do not often appear outside Yorkshire, a fairly large selection of these forms from the Incidental Material is included in order to supplement those found in responses to the two questions (IX.8.6–7) designed to elucidate this point of morphology. Questions aimed at eliciting forms of the definite article are comparatively numerous and richly productive, so the use of the Incidental Material here (§§4–17) is correspondingly sparse, being intended only to augment, where possible, the evidence for forms that the responses suggest are of only limited occurrence. On the other hand, the lists of past-tense and past-participial forms of verbs outside those forming the subjects of the special morphological questions (§81, §75) are as long as it has been possible to make them by combing through the Incidental Material. In short, material has been freely culled from wherever it is to be found, the number of examples cited depending on what seemed appropriate to the topic concerned and to giving as full an account of each item's geographical distribution as possible. The resulting picture certainly appears to give more precise detail than could have been obtained by confining the discussion to responses to the special morphological and syntactical questions.

In lists of forms, the Incidental Material is distinguished by the abbreviation 'IM' preceding the notion's reference number. For example, 'IM IV.5.1' indicates that the item following is included in the Incidental Material provided at article IV.5.1 in the Survey.

THE ARTICLES

THE INDEFINITE ARTICLE

1 The form **a** [ə] appears before a following vowel in VII.4.10 **a April fool/gowk/noddy** Nb Du We La Y Ch Db Sa St He Wo Mon Gl O Nt L Nth Hu C Nf Sf Bk Hrt Ess So K Do. [ə] occurs also in

VIII.6.3 **a holiday**, even though **holiday** has initial vowel rather than [h], in La Y Ch Db Sa St He Wa Mon Gl Ox Nt L Nth Hu Bk Bd Hrt Ess MxL So W Brk Sr K Ha Sx. The same phenomenon is attested in Incidental Material (VIII.6.3) for a few further counties, in **a 'edge** 'a hedge' Wo Do; **a 'ook** 'a hook' Lei R; **a 'orse** 'a horse' D; **a 'ouse** 'a house' W; **a hour** Co.

2 The indefinite article may appear:

(a) with nouns that are plural in form though singular in meaning, as in V.3.7 **a tongs** Mon Nf K; V.3.10 **a bellows** 'a pair of bellows' Y Sa Wa K.

(b) before numerals, e.g. VII.1.17 **(about) a ten** [calves] Y St He Wo Gl L Nf So W Co D Do Ha; VII.2.8 **about a ten** [o'clock] So W Co D Do. Similarly in IM VI.10.10 **a two-three foot** (i.e. 'two or three feet [long]') St; VII.1.19 **a two (or) three days** La Y Ch Db Sa St Wo L; IM VII.1.17 **a six months, a two year ago** Gl; **a one pint or two** He.

The pronominal form **a one** is recorded in VII.1.1 from Nb Cu Du We La Y D. Cf. also IM VII.1.17 **if there was a one** Wo.

3 In some dialects, the indefinite article is often lacking in contexts in which it appears in Standard English, e.g. VII.4.10 (you like to make a person) **April fool/gowk/noddy** Nb Cu Du We La Y Man Ch Db Sa St Wa Mon Gl O L Lei Nth Nf Sf Ess So W Brk Sr K Co D Do Ha Sx; VIII.6.3 (the children get) **holiday** Nb Cu Du We La Y Man Ch Db Sa St He Wo Wa Mon Gl O Nt L Lei Nth C Nf Sf Bk Ess So W Brk Sr Co D Do Ha Sx; VI.1.6 (What do you say you've got?) – **headache** Nb Cu Du La Y Man Ch Db Sa St He Wa Mon O Nt L Lei Nf Bk Hrt Ess So W Brk Sr K Co D Do Ha Sx; VIII.9.7 (I've never known) **such fool** Ch Gl L C Bd K D.

The indefinite article may be lacking also before fractions in expressions of time, e.g. VIII.5.3 **quarter to twelve** Nb Cu Du La Y Man Db Sa St He Wo Wa Mon Gl O L Lei R C Nf Sf Bk Hrt Ess MxL So W Brk Sr K Co D Do Ha Sx. Cf. also IM VIII.6.3 **a year and half** Man; **an hour and half** Nt; **for hour** 'for an hour' So W Co; IM VII.5.7 **hour and half** Sx.

A few further, miscellaneous, examples are VIII.3.3 **have sit-down** Mon; III.5.1 **give 'em bit grub** So; I.11.2 **with bit stone** Co.

THE DEFINITE ARTICLE

Forms

4 Recorded dialectal forms of the definite article are [t], [d], [θ], [ð], [ʔ], [tʔ], [ʔt], [ʔθ], [tθ], [tð], [tʔt], and [ə]. The following illustrations of these forms are taken mainly from: VI.14.14 **she wears the**

breeches/trousers; V.8.12 **lay the table**; VI.7.9 **to the quick** (in which **quick** has variously initial [k] and initial [w]); VI.4.1 **to/on/on to the ground**; VI.6.2 **by the scruff of the neck**; IX.2.3 **till/while/to/tin the sun goes down**; VI.13.6 **the heat** (in which **heat** has variously initial [h] and initial vowel); IX.8.8 **the other**; V.6.6 **in the oven** (in which **oven** has variously initial vowel and initial [j]).

5 [t], the only non-Standard English form of the definite article recorded in all the responses listed in §4, occurs before **breeches** Cu Du We La Y Ch Db; **trousers** Y; **table** Y L; **quick** with initial [k] Db; **quick** with initial [w] Cu Du We La Y Ch Db Nt L; **ground** Cu Du We La Y Ch Db Nt; **scruff** Cu Du We La Y Db; **neck** Cu Du We La Y Ch Db St Nt L; **oven** with initial [j] Cu Du We Y; **heat** with initial [h] Cu We Y; **heat** with initial vowel Cu Du We La Y Db; **other** Nb Cu Du We La Y Ch Db St He Wo Wa Mon Gl O Nt L Lei R Nth Hu Nf Bk Ess So W Brk Sr K Co D Do Ha Sx; **oven** with initial vowel We La Y Db Nt; **sun** Cu Du We La Y Db.

6 [d] appears before **neck** La; **quick** with initial [w] La Y; **sun** Nt; **oven** with initial vowel Y. The Incidental Material includes [d] before **calf** (III.1.10) Cu and devoiced [d] before **water** (III.3.2) Du.

7 [θ] appears before **ground** La Db St; **neck** Db; **quick** with initial [k] Db St; **quick** with initial [w] St; **scruff** La St; **sun** La St; **table** La Db St L; **trousers** St; and before the initial vowels in **heat** La Y Db; **other** Y Ch; **oven** La Db St. IM III.3.7 includes [θ] before **light** Ch Db St.

8 [ð] appears before **breeches** Db Nt L; **ground** La Ch L; **neck** Ch Db Nt; **quick** with initial [k] Db Nt L; **quick** with initial [w] Ch; **scruff** Ch Db L; **sun** Ch Db L; **table** Ch; and before the initial vowels in **heat** La Y Ch Db St Wo Wa Mon O Nt L Lei R Nth Sf So W Brk Sr K Co D Do Ha; **other** Nb Du Y Man Ch St He Wo Wa O Nt L Lei R Nth C Nf Sf Ess W Brk Sr K Co D Ha; **oven** Nb Cu La Y Ch Db St Wo Wa Gl O Nt L Lei R Nth Hu C Nf Bk Ess So W Brk Sr Co D Do Ha. The responses to III.2.11 include [ð] before **cud** St.

9 [ʔ] appears before **breeches** Cu Du We La Y Ch Db; **ground** La; **quick** with initial [w] La Y Ch Db; **scruff** La; **sun** La Y; **table** Cu Du We La Y Ch Nt; **trousers** La Ch Db Nt; and before the initial vowels in **heat** Du; **other** Y; **oven** Y.

10 [t?] appears before **ground** Y; **quick** with initial [k] La Y; **scruff** Y; **sun** La Y Ch; **table** Cu Du La Y; **trousers** Y; **other** La Y.

11 [?t] appears only in Y, before **breeches** and the initial vowel in **oven**.

12 [?θ] appears before the initial vowel in **oven** La Ch Db.

13 [tθ] appears before the initial vowel in **oven** La Y.

14 [tð] appears before the initial vowel in **oven** La.

15 [t?t] appears before the initial vowel in **oven** Y.

16 [ə] appears before **ground** Ess.

17 The form [ðə] is also widely attested, but it is often used in contexts in which RP uses [ðiː] or [ðɪ]. For instance, [ðə] appears in VI.13.6 **the heat** (with initial vowel) Y Sa He Wo Wa Mon Gl O Nt L Lei Nth Hu C Bk Bd Hrt W Co Do Ha; V.6.6 **the oven** (with initial vowel) Nb Du Man Ch Sa He Wo Wa Mon Gl O Nt L Lei Nth C Nf Sf Bk Ess Ha; IX.8.8 **the other** Nb Y Ch Sa He Wo Mon L Nth Sf Bk Brk K.

Syntactical distribution

18 The [ðə] appears in IX.8.8 **the tother (one)** 'the other (one)', thus making what is, historically, a double definite article Nb Sa St He Wo Wa Gl O L Lei Nth C Sf Bk Bd Hrt Ess MxL So Sr D; so also in **the** [θ] in **the tother** St. Further forms of 'the other' are **tothermy, totherum** So.

The appears before the names of common ailments, as in VI.1.6 **the headache** Nb Cu Du We La Y Ch Db Sa St He Wo Wa Mon Gl O Nt L Nth Hu C Nf Sf Bk Hrt Ess MxL So W Brk K Co D Do Ha; VI.5.8 **the toothache** Eng except Lei R. Cf. also IM IX.2.3 **the gout** St; **the measles** Mon; IM VI.1.4 **the palsy** L.

VIII.1.24 'My wife' is expressed by **the wife** Nb Cu Du We La Y Man Sa St He Wa Mon O Nt L Nf Bk Bd Ess So W Brk Sr K Ha Sx.

The appears in VII.2.11 **the both** Ch Mon So D Ha; **the both of them/it** So D Do Ha; VIII.5.1 **they go to/til the church** 'they go to church' Nb Cu We La Y L; VIII.6.1 (children ... have to) **go to the school** Cu We La Y.

19 The appears also in VII.8.4 **(How much) the pound?** Nb and VII.3.12 **the night** 'tonight' Nb Cu Du La So; VII.4.1 **the morrow** 'tomorrow' Cu Du; **the morn** 'tomorrow' Nb Du. Cf. also IM VII.3.1 **the day** 'today' Nb and IM VII.2.7 **at the once** 'at once' Sa.

20 On the other hand, the definite article is sometimes lacking in the dialects in contexts in which it appears in Standard English. Examples include VI.14.14 **she wears breeches/trousers** (said of a domineering wife) Cu Du We La Y Ch Db; V.8.12 **lay table** Y Db L Lei; VI.7.9 (right down) **to quick** (of the finger-nail) Y; VI.6.2 **by scruff of neck** Y; **by scruff of the neck** Y Ess W; IX.2.3 **till sun goes down** Y St L Brk D; IX.8.8 **other (one)** Brk Sr K D Sx; V.6.6 **in oven** Y Do; III.1.11 **pick(ed)/cast/slip(ped) calf** Nb Cu Du We La Y Ch St Wa Nt L Lei R Nth Hu C Sf Bk Bd Hrt Ess So W Co D Do; VII.5.1 **What's time?** K D Do Sx. The Incidental Material includes IX.2.3 **at weekend** Ch; II.3.3 **you've got plough ditch** 'you've got to plough the headlands' Co; III.10.7 **up top the hill** D; V.2.1 **just same as a living-room** Y; III.3.8 **send them to lea** La; V.2.14 **take besom, sweep causeway** Y.

NOUNS

FORMATION OF THE PLURAL

Plural in [-s]

21 Plurals formed by suffixing [-s] to stems ending in voiceless consonants (other than [s, ʃ, tʃ]) include III.1.2 **calfs** (the animals) Nb Cu La Y Sa L Ess Brk; VI.10.1 **foots** O L; III.4.10 **hoofs** Nb Cu Du We La Y Ch Db Sa St He Wo Wa Mon Gl O Nt L Lei Nth Hu C Nf Sf Bk Bd Hrt Ess MxL So W Brk Sr K Co Do Ha Sx; I.9.4 **shaffs** 'shafts'

(singular **shaff**) Y Man Sa St He Wa Mon Lei Nth Bd Hrt Ess So Sr K Co; **sharps** 'shafts' Bk Bd Hrt Ess So Co D Ha Sx; **sharts** 'shafts' Ess; II.6.3 **sheafs** Nb Cu La Y Ch Sa St He Wo Mon Gl L Sf Bd Hrt Ess Sr Sx; III.6.1 **sheeps** Cu Y L Brk; VI.5.6 **tooths** W; IM V.6.9 **loafs** He Wa.

22 From Man, and from a few other localities noted below, are recorded plural forms with [s] suffixed to stems ending in voiced sounds, e.g. VII.6.2 **clouds**; III.1.1 **cows** (also Nb Y); VI.3.1 **eyes**;

IV.8.4 **fleas** (also Nb Y W); V.7.13 **peas** (also Nb); III.8.1 **pigs**; VI.14.22 **shoes** (also Nb); IV.9.2 **slugs** (also Nb); VII.6.3 **stars**; VII.3.5 **years**. From Nb only [-s] is recorded in II.3.6 **cradles**; II.5.3 **awns**; from Nb and Du in II.9.8 **handles**.

Plural in [-z]

23 The following plurals are formed by suffixing [-z] to stems ending in voiced sounds: III.1.2 **calves** (singular **calve**) La Y Sa He Wo Mon Gl L Lei Nf Sf Ess So Co D Do Sx; VIII.1.2 **childs** Gl D; III.4.10 **hooves** (singular **hoove**) Ch D; I.9.4 **shafts** [ʃævz~ʃavz~ʃɑːvz] He Wo Gl L Lei Nth Ess So Brk D Do Ha; I.6.3 **sheaves** (singular **sheave**) Y Sa Wo Gl O L Ess So Brk K Co D.

Plural in [-ɪz~-əz]

24 The following plurals are formed by suffixing [-ɪz] or [-əz] to stems ending in [s]: IV.6.15 **gooses** Sa; V.1.1 **houses** Nb Cu Y Man St Nf Ha; IV.5.1 **mouses** Y L Brk; IV.8.7 **wopses** 'wasps' Y St Gl O Nth Bk Bd Ess MxL So W Brk Sr K Co D Do Ha Sx.

[-ɪz] is suffixed to a stem ending in [z] in IV.5.1 **mouse**, giving **mouses** Co D; and [-ɪz] or [-əz] are suffixed to a stem ending in [t] in IV.3.2 **(gate-)posts** Gl O Bd Ess So W Brk Co D Do Ha Sx.

Plural in [-ɪs~-əs]

25 V.1.1 **house** with stem ending in [s] makes plural **houses** with suffixed [-ɪs] Man. Other forms with [-ɪs] or [-əs] suffixed to an unchanged stem include II.3.2 **ridges** Nb Man; I.6.5 **horses** Nf.

Plural with mutation of stem-vowel and voicing of final stem-consonant

26 IV.6.15 **goose** with final [s] has plural **geese** with final [z] Sa.

Plural in [-n]

27 The following are plurals formed by suffixing [-n] to the stem: III.1.1 [kaɪ] **cow** giving [kaɪn] **kine** Cu Y; VI.3.1 **eyen** ([iːn~əɪn~ɛɪn]) 'eyes' Du

La Y Db St Wo; VI.14.22 **shoon** 'shoes' Nb Cu Du La Y Ch Db St; VII.6.3 **starn** 'stars' Nb Cu O.

Plural with voicing of final stem-consonant plus suffix

28

(a) The following plurals are formed by voicing final [f] of the stem to [v] and suffixing [z]: III.4.10 **hooves** Nb Cu We La Y Ch Db St Wa L Lei R Nth Ess So W K Co D Do Sx; I.9.4 **sharves** [ʃævz~ʃavz~ʃɑːvz] 'shafts' (singular with final [f]) Man He Wo Wa Gl O L Lei R Nth Hu C Nf Sf Bk Bd Hrt Ess So W Sr Co D Do Ha Sx. Similar, but with suffixed [s], are III.1.2 **calves** Man, II.6.3 **sheaves** Man.

(b) The following plurals are formed by voicing final [s] of the stem to [z] and adding a suffix. V.1.1 **houses** has suffixed [-ɪs] Nb Man Sa Wo L. V.1.1 **housen** has suffixed [-(ə)n~-ɪn] Sa He Wo Wa Gl O Lei C Nf Sf Bk Bd Ess Brk. IV.5.1 **mouses** has suffixed [-iːz] So. I.1.6 **horses** has suffix [-əs] in [hɒzəs] Man.

Plural with other changes to final stem-consonant plus suffix

29 II.6.3 SHEAF/SHEAVES take a few forms in which the plural shows other changes to the final stem-consonants than those mentioned above, namely singular [ʃiːθ] giving plural [ʃiːvz] Ess; [ʃiːf] giving [ʃiːθs] Y; [ʃiːf] giving [ʃiːðz] Brk.

Plural with mutation of stem-vowel

30 Plurals formed by simple mutation of the stem-vowel include III.1.1 **cow** [kuː] giving plural **kye** [kaɪ] Nb Cu Du We Y Ch St; III.1.2 **calf** [kɔːf] giving [kaʊf] 'calves' St.

Plural with mutation of stem-vowel plus suffixed [-n]

31 Examples of plurals formed by mutation of the stem-vowel with suffixed [-n] include VI.3.1 **eye** giving **eyen**, as follows: [aɪ~ɑɪ] giving [iːn] Nb Cu Du We Y Db; [ɪi] giving [iːn] Y; [iː] giving [əɪn] Y; [ɑɪ] giving [iːn] Y; [ɑɪ~ɒɪ] giving [ɛɪn] Ch St. Also VI.4.22 **shoe** giving **shoon** in the following forms: [ʃuː] giving [ʃun] Nb Cu Du La Y Ch Db St; [ʃuː] giving [ʃʊɪn] Y. A plural form that may also belong here (though the singular form is unattested) is IV.8.4 **flen** [flɛn] 'fleas' Sa He Wo.

Plural with mutation of stem-vowel, voicing of final stem-consonant, plus suffix

32 IV.8.1 **lice** [laɪs] the singular form of 'louse', undergoes mutation of the stem-vowel, voicing of [s] to [z], and suffixing of [-əz] to make plural [laʊːzəz] 'lice' Sa. Forms with final [f] of the stem voiced to [v] with suffixed [-z] include III.1.2 [kɑːf] 'calf', giving plural [kɔːvz] Y; II.6.3 [ʃoˈf~ʃʊf] 'sheaf' giving plural [ʃiːvz~ʃuːvz] Nf Sf Ess.

Plural in [-ə]

33 VIII.1.2 **child** has the plural **childer**, with mutation of a stem-vowel generally of an [iː] or [aɪ] type to an [ɪ] type, plus suffixed [-ə] La Y Man Ch Db St Nt So K.

Zero plurals

34 In the following cases, the plural has zero ending (i.e. it has the same form as the singular): III.1.2 **calve** Do; IV.6.11 **chicken** La He Wa Mon Gl O MxL So W Brk K Co D Do Ha Sx; VI.3.1 **eyen** [iːn] 'eye(s)' Nb Cu La Y; VI.10.1 **foot** (of the body) giving [fɪət] singular and plural Y; IV.6.15 **goose** [gɪəs] Y; V.7.13 **pease** 'pea(s)' Du We La Y Nt; III.8.1 **pig** L; VI.14.22 **shoe** Mon; **shoon** 'shoe(s)' Y; VI.5.6 **teeth** singular and plural We; VIII.1.10 **woman** Nb Cu Du Db So.

Plural forms that have zero ending when the noun is immediately preceded by a cardinal number are exemplified in VI.10.10 **five foot** (tall) Eng (although attested only in Incidental Material as regards Lei R Brk Sx), and VII.3.5 **two year ago** Eng exc. Man (although attested only in IM as regards Lei).

The Incidental Material includes III.1.13 **two beast** Y; VI.10.10 **three bucketful** He; **four bushel** K; **twenty calf** D; **two hundred duck** O; III.3.5 **four gallon** Y; VI.10.10 **eleven gallon** Ch; **three gelding** St; IV.9.11 **two or three fresh herring** Y; VI.10.10 **[two] load** He Nf; **[nine] mile** Sa He Wa Gl O L Lei Nf Ess MxL So Sr K Sx; **six pound** Wo; VII.1.15 **six hundred pound** La; VII.7.8 **[two hundred] pound** (money) Nb Du La Y Nt L Lei R Brk Sr K Co Ha; VI.10.10 **five rod** (land measure) Ha; **thirty rung high** (of a ladder) So; **four stone** (weight) Nf; VII.1.19 **two or three week** La; **a few year since** 'a few years ago' Y.

Double plurals

35 Double plurals (forms containing two plural morphemes, both of which may be suffixes, or one a mutation of a stem-vowel and one a suffix) are recorded as follows: V.3.10 **bellowses** 'a pair of bellows' Nb Cu Du La Y L R Sf So W Brk D; VIII.1.2 **childers** 'children' Ess; **chil(d)(er)n** Sa He Wo Wa Mon Gl O L Lei R Nth C Nf Sf Bk Bd So W Brk K Co D Do Ha Sx; IV.8.4 **flens** 'fleas' Sa He Wo (but if the stem-vowel is in fact a mutation of the stem-vowel of the unattested singular, this is actually a treble plural, see §36); I.6.5 **hameses** He Gl So W Co D Do; V.1.1 **housens** St He; IV.8.1 **lices** Ess; IV.5.1 **mices** Y R Ess Co; VI.5.6 **teeths** Brk.

Further examples are: VIII.2.12 **folks** Nb Du We La Y Ch Db Sa St He Wo Wa Mon Gl O Nt L Lei R Nth Nf Bk Bd Hrt Ess So Brk Sr Co D Ha Sx; IV.11.6 **hawses** 'haws' Gl O Nf Sf Bk Ess; IV.11.7 **hipsen** 'hips' (berries) O, also **hipses** Bk; V.3.7 **tongses** So.

Treble plurals

36 VIII.1.2 **chilerns** 'children', recorded from Sr, evidently contains three plural morphemes; so also IV.11.6 **hawsens** 'haws' Gl; IV.11.7 **hipsens** 'hips' (berries) Brk. **Flens** 'fleas' may also belong here (see §35).

Miscellaneous plural forms

37 Other, miscellaneous, plural forms include IM IV.6.1 [bɪɪdnɛst] 'bird-nest' giving plural [bɪɪdniːzɪz] La; IV.8.4 **flieth** 'fleas' (singular unattested) La; also various forms, in I.9.4, of 'shaft/shafts', namely **shaft** giving **shaffs** Cu We La Y Ch Db Sa St He Wa O Nt L Lei R Nf Sf Ess K; **shaff** giving **shafts** Y Ess; **shaft** giving **sharves** Y Db Sa St He Wo Wa Mon O Nt L Lei R Nth C Nf Ess MxL So W Sr Do Ha Sx; **shaft** giving **shaff** Sa; **shaff** giving **sharps** O; **sharp** giving **sharves** Bk; **sha** giving **sharves** Brk. Note also shoe [ʃʊf] giving **shoon** [ʃʊn] La. IV.3.2 includes [pɒsː] 'posts' Y; IV.8.7 includes [was] 'wasps' Ch; and VI.5.6 includes **tooth** [tʏːð] giving **teeth** [tiːθ] D.

FORMATION OF THE POSSESSIVE SINGULAR

38 Mainly in the northern dialects, the possessive singular often takes a zero ending when one noun qualifies another, as in IX.8.6 **my father boots** We La Y; IX.8.7 **this cow legs** La Y Sr. The Incidental Material furnishes many more examples, including: IM IX.8.6 **my sister husband** Y; **mother mother** 'mother's mother' Y; **our Jack wife** Y; **our Jack Mary** (i.e. 'our Jack's [wife who is called] Mary) Y; **farmer lad** 'farmer's lad' Y; **a ratton tail** 'a little rat's tail' Y; IM I.7.2 **the poke mun** 'the bag's mouth' Y.

The following words too, in the Incidental Material, are all possessive singular in their respective contexts: IM IX.8.6–7 **bairn** Y; **beast** Y; **brother** Y; **butcher** Y; **cat** Y; **calf** Y; **chap** Y; **child** Y; **cow** Cu Y; **daughter** Y; **doctor** Y; **dog** Y; **donkey** Y; **hen** Du Y; IM I.6.5 **horse** Cu We Y; **Jack** La; **man** Y; IM IX.8.6–7 **mother** We Y; **neighbour** Y; **nobody** Y; **pig** La Y; **son** Y; **tup** 'ram' (sheep) Y; **wife** Y. Also, perhaps, to be included here is IM VII.3.2 **at the fortnight end** Y.

Non-northern examples are few, but include **this cow legs** Sr (see above) and IM IX.8.6 **granny** Wa, **brother** Brk.

FORMATION OF THE POSSESSIVE PLURAL

39 From Y are recorded a very few examples of the possessive plural with zero ending, as in IM IX.8.6 **women** 'women's' and IM IX.8.7 **four day work** 'four days' work'; IM VIII.2.12 **folkses** 'folk's'.

SOME FURTHER GRAMMATICAL POINTS

40

(a) Collective singular forms include: IV.9.11 **herring** Nb Cu Du We La Y Ch Db Sa Wo Gl Nth Hu C Nf Sf Bk Hrt Ess So W Brk Sr D Do Ha Sx; I.6.5 **horse** L Nf; IV.7.8 **partridge** Nb Cu Du We La Y Man Ch Db Sa St He Wo Wa Mon Gl O Nt L Lei Hu C Bk Ess So W Brk Sr K Co D Ha Sx; IV.7.8 **pheasant** Nb Du Y Man Ch Sa St He Wo O L Lei Bk Ess So W Sr K Co Ha; III.8.1 **pig** L; III.1.3 **beast** 'cattle' Nb CU Du We La Y Ch Db Sa St Wo Wa Nt L Lei R Nth Hu C Bd So W K Do Ha, and the same at IM III.3.7 St; IV.6.11 **chicken** MxL; III.1.1 **cow** K; IV.6.2 **fowl** Ha; III.3.7 and IV.8.5 **fly** 'flies' Du Sx; II.2.1 **weed** Du Y Man.

(b) V.7.20 **broth** is treated as a plural in the response (before bringing you the broth, your wife is sure to have ...) **tasted them** Nb Cu Du We Db. Compare also IM V.7.20 **I've known my mother make them** (i.e. broth) Cu; **a few broth** Y. Similarly treated as a plural is V.7.3 **porridge** in the response (You can burn your mouth eating porridge if ...) **they are too hot** Nb Cu We La Y Ch. Compare also IM V.7.1 **we didn't make many porridge** Cu; **I don't make them** (i.e. porridge) Y. The form **a specie** in IM VI.12.4 suggests interpretation of **species** as plural (only) in Y.

(c) Possessive plural forms appear in I.1.5 **pigs' cote/-house/-pound** He Wo Mon Gl Nf Ess Co D; I.1.6 **fowls'-/hens'-house** Gl Nf So W Co D Do; I.1.8 **cows' house** Co.

NUMERALS

CARDINAL

41 In cardinal numbers above twenty, the lower digit may precede the higher, as in VII.1.12 **one-and-twenty** Nb Du Y Ch He L So. IM VII.1.3/12 includes **two-and-twenty** Y Lei; **three-and-twenty** Y; **four-and-twenty** We Y K; **five-and-twenty** Gl; **seven-and-twenty** Nf; **eight-and-twenty** O.

In expressions of age, VII.1.12 **one-and-twenty** (years) is recorded from Nb Cu Du We La Y Ch Db Sa He Wo Wa Mon Gl Nt L Nth C Nf Sf Bk Bd Hrt Ess So K; IM VII.1.12 includes **three-and-twenty** (used only in reference to age) Wa. At VII.5.5, the expression of time **five-and-twenty** (minutes) **to three** is recorded from Du We La Y Ch Db Sa St He Wo Wa Mon Gl O Nt Lei R Nth Hu Nf Sf Bk Bd Hrt Ess MxL So W Brk Sr K Co D Do Ha Sx.

VII.1.12 TWENTY-ONE is expressed by **a score and one** St.

IM VIII.1.8 shows the names of years expressed thus: **nineteen and thirty** '1930' Nb; **nineteen and fifty-three** '1953' Du.

ORDINAL

42 VII.2.5 **fifth** [fɪft~vɪft] Nb Cu Du We La Y Ch Db Sa St He Mon Gl O Nt L Lei R Sf Bk MxL W. IM VII.1.4–6/9–10 includes other ordinals ending in [t], namely **fourt** La; **sixt** Y; **sevent** Cu We Y; **elevent** Y; **twelft** Y; IM VII.2.6 **eightht** 'eighth' Du.

Sometimes, ordinals are identical in form with cardinals, as in VII.2.6 **eight** 'eighth' Nb Du We La Y Ch Wo Wa O L Nf MxL Sr Co D Ha. IM

VII.1.5–6 includes **six** 'sixth' He; **seven** 'seventh' Wo.

ADJECTIVES

POSITIVE FORMS

43 Occasionally adjectives are found in southwestern dialects that are formed from a noun plus the suffix **-en**, meaning 'made of' or 'proper to' that which is denoted by the noun. Examples include V.8.5 **a papern bag** So D Do; IM III.7.8 **a boarden floor** Do; IM I.4.3 **timberen** 'made of timber' D; IM IV.2.1 **a thornen hedge** W; VI.14.20 **weeken-day clothes** So.

VI.13.1 **badly** functions as an adjective meaning 'ill' Nb Cu Du We La Y Ch Db; and IV.11.4 **poison** as an adjective meaning 'poisonous' Nb Cu Du We La Y Ch Db Sa St He Wo Wa Gl O Nt L Nth Hu C Nf Sf Bk Bd Hrt Ess MxL So W Brk Sr K Co D Do Ha Sx. VI.13.11 **drunkard** is an attributive adjective meaning 'drunken' Y, as also are **drucken** Nb Cu Du We La Y Gl; **drunk** La; **druffen** La Y. IM V.2.11 **patchworks** functions as an adjective Mon and VI.13.12 **weakly** as 'weak' La.

III.8.4a ENOUGH appears in the form **enow** before or after the plural nouns **teats** or **paps** La Y Ch Wo Nt L R Nth Hu C Nf Sf Bd Brk.

COMPARATIVE AND SUPERLATIVE FORMS

44 Recorded forms of the comparative and superlative of adjectives include: VIII.1.21 **elder** (than their wives) Cu We La; IX.2.1 **farrer** 'further' Cu La Y; **furthers** Brk; V.1.17 **usefuller** Y Man Brk; IM VII.4.10 **foolisher** Y; IM VI.12.4 **liker** 'more like' Nb Cu; IM VII.8.20 **littler** He; IM IX.2.10 **nigh** 'nearer' Y; **nigher** Gl; IM I.7.12, IM VI.12.4 [laŋə] 'longer' Cu, [lɒŋəɹ] Y.

45 Double comparatives include VI.12.3–4 **worser** Man R Nth Nf Sf Hrt Ess MxL So W Brk K Co Do; **worsener** Y; V.1.17 **more usefuller** Y Do; IM IV.1.15 **more better** Mon; IM V.1.17 **more bolder** Do; **more commoner** St; **more fleeter** 'more shallow' Nf; IM IV.1.15 **more milder** He; IM V.1.17 **more safer** Sa K; IM IV.1.15 **more sweeter** Mon.

At VI.12.3, the triple comparative **worserer** is recorded from Bd.

46 Recorded forms of the superlative of adjectives include VI.12.5 **most bad** MxL; **worsest** K D; **worstest** Bd Brk K Sx; IM IX.2.10 **nighest** Sa Wo; IM V.1.16 **usefullest** Y; VIII.8.4 **wellest** in **did his wellest** La; IM VII.1.19 **likest** 'most likely' Nb.

DEMONSTRATIVE ADJECTIVES

47 THIS, demonstrative adjective, is expressed by **thick** [ðɪk] in IX.10.1 **thick one** He Wo; IM I.5.9 **thick hood** So; IM II.2.9 **thick field** Co; by **thicker** in IM II.6.6 **thicker field** Co; by **thicky** in IM IV.2.4 **thicky hedge** D; by **thick here** in IM IV.1.4 **thick here river** W; by **this here** in IM III.3.7 **this here iron** K.

THAT is expressed by **that there** in IM IV.12.5 **that there tree** Nf; by **thick** in IX.10.1 **thick one** Gl; by **yon** in IM IV.3.8 **yon gate-stead** Y and IM IV.2.11 **yon gutter** Co.

THESE is expressed by **these here** in IM I.3.8 **these here small whippletrees** Y.

THOSE is expressed by **yon** in IM II.4.2 **yon turnips** Y; by **they** in V.7.14 **they peas** W D Ha Sx; IM V.7.23 **they gooseberries** Ha; IM I.7.4 **they bins** D; IM V.10.4 **they buttons** Ess; IM II.4.2 **they turnips** So W; IM III.3.4 **they cows** Sx; by **they there** in II.4.2 **they there turnips** D; by **them** in IX.10.4 **them ones** Gl O; IM I.3.7 **in them days** Nb; II.9.5 **them baulks** Y; IM II.4.2, IM III.7.10 **them turnips** Du So W; V.7.14 **them peas** W; by **them there** in II.4.2 **them there turnips** W; by **thick** in V.7.14 **thick peas** So; IX.10.4 **thick ones** Gl.

See also Demonstrative Pronouns, §62.

PRONOUNS

PERSONAL

First person

48 NOMINATIVE SINGULAR: Unstressed forms of **I** following the interrogative forms of verbs in IX.7.1 AM I *right*?, IX.7.5 AREN'T I?, IX.7.6 WASN'T I? include [ɪ] La Ch Db St Wo Gl L, [æ] K, [æː] D, [a] Nb Cu Du We La Y Ch Db Sa St Wa Nt L Nth C Sf, [aː] La Db St Co, [ɑ] Nt C, [ɑː] Co D; [ɒ] Y, [ɔ] Y Ess, [ə] La Y Ch Sa St Mon Nt L Lei R C Nf Sf Hrt Ess, [tə] Y, [ɐ] Lei R Nf.

OBJECTIVE SINGULAR: VII.5.8, IX.8.2/4, and IM VIII.2.3 show stressed objective singular **I** recorded from He Gl O Ess So W Brk D Do Ha Sx. But VIII.2.2, IX.8.2/4, IX.8.4, and IM V.8.8 show 'me' expressed by **us** in all counties except R Brk.

NOMINATIVE PLURAL: VII.8.8, VIII.9.5, and IX.7.8–9 show unstressed nominative plural **us** recorded from Wa O Brk Co D. Stressed forms appear in IX.8.1 **it's us** Wa O Brk Co D; **it's only we** Ch Sa St He Wo Mon Gl Nf Sf Ess So W Brk Co D Do Ha Sx; **it's only us** Eng exc. Wo Gl. Us in this stressed position takes the following phonetic forms: [hʌz] Nb, [hØːz] Nb, [hʊs] Nb Du We, [hʊz] Nb Cu Du, [ʊs] Nb Cu Du We La Y Man Ch Sa St Wa O L R Nth C Bk K Do, [ʊz] Cu Du We La Y Ch Db St Nt L Lei, [ɤs] Nf, [ɤz] Nb, [ʌz] Hrt So W D Do Ha, [əz] So W Brk Co D Ha.

VII.2.14 WE TWO is expressed by **us both** Ch; **us pair** L; **us two** Nb Cu Du We La Y Ch Db Sa St Wa Mon Gl O Nt L Lei R Nth Hu C Nf Sf Bk Bd Hrt Ess So W Brk Sr K Co D Ha Sx.

Second person

49 NOMINATIVE SINGULAR: Stressed forms in IX.7.7 include **thou** Nb Cu Du We La Y Ch Db Sa St Nt L Brk; **thee** Ch Sa He Wo Mon Gl So W Brk Co D Do Ha; **ye** Nb.

These stressed forms of **thou** and **thee** include the following phonetic forms: **thou** [ðæː] La Nt, [θæʊ] Y, [ðɛː] La Db, [ða] La Y Ch Db, [ðaː] La Y, [ðaɪ] Ch Db, [daʊ] La, [θaʊ] Sa, [ðaʊ] Cu La Y St, [ðʌʊ] Y W, [ðʊu] Y, [ðuː] Nb Cu Du We Y L, [ð] Y St; **thee** [θiː] Sa, [ðiː] Ch Sa He Wo Mon Gl O So W Co D Do Ha, [ðɪ] Wo, [ðɪi] W Brk, [ðɛɪ] Ch St. Stressed forms of **ye** include [iː] Nb, [jiː] Nb.

Third person

50 Unstressed forms of **thou, thee**, and **ye** are recorded following interrogative forms of verbs in VII.5.1 **can you tell me the time?**, VIII.2.8 **how are you?**, VIII.3.7 **do you remember?**, VIII.8.6 **why did you do that?**, IX.7.2 **are you married?**, IX.7.3 **aren't you married?**, IX.7.5 **aren't you?**, and IX.7.6 **weren't you?** The phonetic forms of unstressed **thou, thee**, and **ye** are as follows: **thou** [ðɛʊ] Brk, [ða] Cu(IM III.13.8) La Y, [ta] Y, [ðʌʊ] Y Brk, [ðʊ] Nb Wo, [tʊ] La, [ʊ] La, [ðuː] Nb Cu Du, [ðəʊ] Gl, [θə] Y, [ðə] Nb Du La Y Ch Db Sa Wo O L, [tə] Nb Cu Du We La Y Db Nt L Co, [t] Ch Db St, [ʔ] La (following **dost**), [ə] Cu La Y Ch He Wo Co; **thee** [θiː] Sa He, [ðiː] Sa St He Wo Mon Gl O So W Co D Do Ha, [ðɪi] W Brk, [ðɪ] Y(IM VI.4.2) Ch Db St Sa He Wo Wa Mon Gl O W Brk D, [ðɛɪ] Ch Db St; **ye** [iː] Sa O So W Co D Do Ha, [ɪ] Ch Sa Gl.

Unstressed **you** appears in the forms [jɪ] Nb L Ess K Sx, [jo(ː)] Sa C, [joʊ] St, [jə] Nb Cu Du We La Y Man Ch Db Sa St He Wo Wa Mon Gl O Nt L Lei R Nth Hu C Nf Sf Bk Bd Hrt Ess MxL W Brk Sr K Ha Sx.

See also §89 for **thee, thou,** and **ye** in expressions for 'How are you?'.

51 OBJECTIVE SINGULAR: Unstressed forms in VIII.3.2 include **thou** W; **thee** Nb Cu Du We La Y Ch Db Sa St He Wo Gl O L So W Brk D Do Ha; **ye** Co D Do. **Thou** has the phonetic form [ðʊu] W. **Thee** has phonetic forms [ðiː] So W D Do Ha, [ðɪ] La Y Ch Db Sa St He Wo So Brk, [ðe] Y, [ðʊ] Wo, [θə] He Gl O, [ðə] Nb Cu Db We La Y Gl L W, [tə] Y. **Ye** has phonetic forms [iː] Gl So Co D Do, [ɪ] O D.

Third person

52 NOMINATIVE SINGULAR MASCULINE: **He** is used in the Incidental Material with reference to a cow in III.1.11 So D, and to such inanimate objects as a part of a plough, a drug-shoe, a cart (I.4.3, I.8.5, I.11.3/6) D Do Ha; also to porridge in V.7.3 Brk Co D. IM IX.11.2 shows nominative **him** So.

OBJECTIVE SINGULAR MASCULINE (unstressed) in the Incidental Material (I.2.1, I.7.1/19, I.8.5, III.10.7) and in IX.2.4 takes the form **he** Ess So W Co D Do Ha; IX.2.4 **'en** [ən] Gl So W Co D Ha, [n] So W Brk Co Do Ha Sx, [ŋ] Co Ha Sx, IM V.7.7 [ɪn] So W.

In IM I.7.1 **he** is used in reference to something to be weighed So.

Him is used with reference to such objects as a door, a ball, a cart, a drug-shoe, a knife, a parcel, something to be weighed, also to land and to gravy (responses and IM at I.7.1, I.11.6, IV.1.9, V.7.7, VII.2.9, IX.2.5–6, IX.3.1, IX.8.2) Y Ch Db Sa St He Wo Mon Gl O So W Co D Do Ha.

In I.5.1, **'en** is used with reference to a horse So W Co D Do Ha; also with reference to broth, a ball, gravy, something to be weighed, and to toothache in I.7.1, V.7.7/20, VI.5.9, and IX.8.2 Gl So W Brk Co D Do Ha.

53 NOMINATIVE SINGULAR FEMININE forms include the following that occur both stressed and unstressed at IX.7.2–3/6–7 as follows: **her** [hɛəᵗ:] So; [əː] La Ch Db St Wa; [əᵗ] Sa He Wo Mon Gl; [əᵗ:] Sa Wo Wa Gl Bk So W Co D Do Ha; [əːɾ] W; **hoo** [ɛʊ] Ch, [aʊ] St, [uː] La Y Db, [ɤː] La Ch Db; **she** [ʃɛɪ] Y, [ʃəɪ] Y; **shoo** [ʃuː] Y.

The following occur only in stressed position, at IX.7.7: **her** [əᵗ:] St He O Brk, [əːɾ] Brk; **hoo** [ɛʊ] Db.

The following occur only in unstressed position, at IX.7.2–3/6: **her** [ɛː] Db, [hɛᵗ:] So, [ə] Ch Db St He Wo Wa Mon Gl O Bk, [əɹ] He, [əː] Wo, [əːɹ] St, [həᵗ:] W Do, [əːɾ] Sr, [əᵗ:ɾ] W Brk Ha; **hoo** [oʊ] La, [ʊ] La Y, [uː] Ch; **she** [ʃe] Y, [ʃə] Nb Cu Du We La Y Db O L Lei Hu; **shoo** [ʃʊ] La Y; **he** [ɪ] Wo.

OBJECTIVE SINGULAR FEMININE unstressed is **she** in VIII.1.1 **brought she up** W; IM III.3.6 **we'd better stock she up** (referring to a cow) Ha.

Her, objective, is used to refer to such inanimate objects as a cart, a wheel, a load, broth, and gravy at V.7.7/20 and IM I.11.2/6 Y Ch Db St Nt L Lei Do.

54 NOMINATIVE SINGULAR NEUTER unstressed has the forms [t] in V.7.3 **'t is too hot** Gl So W Brk Co D Do Ha, in IM III.10.4 Y, in VII.5.1 **what time is 't?** Nb Cu Du We La Y Db St, and in IX.9.2 **whose 't is** Cu We Y Ch O Nf So W Sr Co D Do Ha Sx. Other forms are [ɪd] in IX.9.2 La, [ət] in VII.5.1 Man and in IX.9.2 Nb Sf.

V.7.3 '(You can burn your mouth in eating porridge if) it's too hot' is expressed by **that's too hot** Nf Sf Ess Brk. So too IX.9.2 '(you wonder) whose dog it is' is expressed by **... that is** Gl W Brk Sr Ha.

Otiose **it** appears in III.4.5 **the old mare, it's getten gutswark** ('got stomach-ache') Y.

55 OBJECTIVE SINGULAR NEUTER unstressed forms include the following:

Forms occurring after preceding vowel or consonant, I.7.1, V.2.8, V.7.7, VI.5.9, VII.2.12, IX.2.5–6/15, IX.8.2: [ɪd] La, [ət] Nb Cu Du La Y Man C Sf Ess So W D Do Ha, [t] Nb Cu Du We Y Ch Db St Gl So D Do Ha, [d~d̥] Nb Du So D Do.

Forms occurring only after preceding vowel, I.7.1, VII.2.12, IX.2.5–6/15, IX.8.2: [ɪd] Y, [ət] Ch, [t] La Man Sa Wa C Nf Sf Bk Ess W, [d~d̥] Cu We.

Forms occurring only after preceding consonant: IV.7.7, VI.5.9, VII.2.12, IX.2.5–5/15, IX.8.2: [ət] We, [t] Mon Bk Sr K Co, [d~d̥] Y.

56 In expressions for GIVE IT TO ME, IX.8.2, the indirect object precedes the direct object in **give me/us it/en** Nb Cu Du We La Y Man Sa St He Wo Wa Mon Gl O Nt L Lei Nth Hu C Nf Sf Bk Bd Hrt Ess MxL Sr K Ha Sx.

In localities where the order is direct object followed by indirect (**give it (to) me**), we find TO used as a marker of the indirect first singular pronoun Y St Wo Gl O L Nf Sf Ess MxL So W D Co Do Ha K. But TO is absent in **give it me** La Ch Db Sa St Wa Wo He Mon Gl O Nt L R Nth Bk Ess MxL W D Brk Sr Sx K.

See also TO, §§146–7.

57 NOMINATIVE PLURAL **them** occurs in stressed position in IX.7.7 **them is** Du. **Them** occurs also in unstressed position in the following forms that are recorded following interrogative forms of verbs at IX.7.2–3/5–6: [ðɛm] Ch Sa Brk Sr, [ʌm] Co D Ha, [ʊm] Ch St He Wo Wa Gl O, [ðəm] Brk, [əm] La Y Ch He Wo Wa Mon Gl O Bk So W Sr Co D Do Ha Sx, [ən] D.

The forms **mun** [mʌn], [mən] and **men** [mɛn] are recorded in the same unstressed contexts from Co.

Unstressed forms of **they** in the same contexts include [ðiː] Ch Db St Wo, [ðɪ] Nb Cu Du We La Y Man Ch Db Sa St He Wo Wa Mon Gl O Nt L Hu C Nf Sf Bk Bd Ess K, [ðɪə] St, [ðɛ] L Hu Nf, [ðɛː] W, [ðɛə] L, [ðə] Nb Cu Du We La Y Db Sa St Wa Nt L Lei R Nth Hu Nf Sf Bk Bd Ess, [də] Y, [ðəː] La, [ðɛ] Ess, [ə] Wo, [ð] before a following vowel in IM III.8.1 **they often ...** Y.

They is used in reference to **porridge** treated as a plural noun in V.7.3 (you can burn your mouth in eating porridge if) **they are too hot** Nb Cu We La Y Ch. Compare also §40(b).

OBJECTIVE PLURAL, unstressed is **them, mun** II.4.2, III.3.1, V.9.5, VI.5.12, in the following forms: **them** [ʌm] D, [ʊm] La Ch Db Sa St He Wo Wa Gl Nth Ha Sx, [əm] Eng, [m] Lei R Co D; **mun** [mʌn] Co.

Them is used in reference to **broth** treated as a plural noun in V.7.20 (Before bringing the broth to the table your wife is sure to have) **tasted them** Nb Cu Du We Db. Compare also §40(b).

POSSESSIVE

Conjunctive

58 SECOND PERSON SINGULAR: **thy** [ðɪ~ðə] addressed to a child in VI.5.3 **thy mouth** is recorded from Nb Cu Du We La Y Ch Db St Wo Gl L So W Co D Do Ha.

Thy addressed to an adult appears in VI.5.4 **putting thy tongue out** Cu Du La Y Ch Db St Wo Gl So W Co D Do Ha, and in VI.5.17 **I knew thy voice** Nb Cu Du We La Y Ch Db Sa Wo Gl L So W K Co D Do Ha.

THIRD PERSON SINGULAR MASCULINE 'his' is apparently expressed by **him** in I.5.1 **get him gearing on** Y. Note also the use of **his** in the Incidental Material VI.4.4: **he's pulling that chap his leg** Y.

His refers to a river at IV.1.4 Gl.

The phonetic form [hɪs] appears at VI.5.17 Man.

THIRD PERSON SINGULAR NEUTER possessive **it** appears in VI.1.7 **it forehead** (referring to a child) Cu We La Y Ch Db St Lei; compare also IM VI.1.7 **it mother** L. So too in IV.6.20 **wring it neck** (referring to a fowl) We La Y Ch Db St L. Compare also IV.6.20 **wring he's neck** Sx, and **wring the neck of him** Co D.

FIRST PERSON PLURAL **our** in VI.3.3 **with our eyes** takes the phonetic forms [wəʁ~wər~wəɹ] Nb Du We La Y L Nth Bk Bd, as also in VIII.8.8 **our own** Nb Cu Du La Y L Nth Bd. VI.3.3 also includes **with we eyes** St Sf, and **with us eyes** Y Ch Db St. VIII.8.8 also includes **one of us own** Y Ch Db St Lei, and **one of we own** Nth.

Disjunctive

59 Disjunctive forms of the possessive pronouns recorded at IX.8.5 include:

SECOND PERSON SINGULAR: **thine** Nb Cu Du We La Y Ch Db Sa St He Wo Mon Gl O So W Brk Co D Do Ha; **yourn** Sa St He Wo Wa Mon Gl(IM VIII.9.4) O Nt L Lei R Nth Hu C Bk Bd Hrt Ess MxL So W Brk Sr K D Ha.

THIRD PERSON SINGULAR MASCULINE: **he's** Gl L Nf MxL So Sr Co D Do Ha; **hisn** Db Sa St He Wo Wa Mon Gl O Nt L Lei Nth Hu C Sf Bk Bd Hrt Ess MxL So W Brk Sr Ha.

THIRD PERSON SINGULAR FEMININE: **hern** Db Sa St He Wo Wa Mon Gl O L Lei Nth Hu C Bk Bd Hrt Ess So W Brk Sr K Do Ha Sx; **hersn** St.

FIRST PERSON PLURAL: **ourn** Db Sa St He Wo Wa Mon Gl O L Lei R Nth Hu C Bk Bd Hrt Ess So W Brk Sr K D Do Ha Sx; **ourns** Wo; **oursn** St.

SECOND PERSON PLURAL: **yourn** Db Sa St He Wo Wa Mon Gl O L Lei R Nth Hu C Bk Bd Hrt Ess MxL So W Brk Sr K Do Ha Sx.

THIRD PERSON PLURAL: **theirn** Db Sa St He Wo Wa Mon Gl O L Lei Nth Hu C Bk Bd Hrt Ess MxL So W Brk Sr K D Do Ha Sx.

REFLEXIVE

60 The following are among recorded forms of reflexive pronouns:

FIRST PERSON SINGULAR: IX.11.1 **wash me** La Y Ch Db St Wo Wa W Brk Sr; **wash mysel** Nb Cu Du We La Y Man Ch Db Sa St W Sr K Co D Ha Sx; **wash mysen** Y Db St.

SECOND PERSON SINGULAR: VIII.3.3 **sit thee down** We La Y Ch Db Sa St Gl So W; **sit thysel down** Nb Cu Du La Y; **sit thyself down** Y Wo So Ha Sx; **sit thysen down** Y Ch L; **sit you down** Y Ch Sa St He L Lei Bd; **sit yoursel down** Nb We La.

THIRD PERSON SINGULAR MASCULINE: IX.11.2 **he killed he** Brk; **he killed himsell** Ch Hrt Sr; **he killed himsen** St Lei; **he killed hisself** Ch Sa St He Wo Wa Mon Gl O L Lei Nth Hu C Nf Sf Bk Bd Hrt Ess MxL So W Brk Sr K Co D Do Ha Sx; **he killed hisse(l)n** Y Ch Db St Nt L Lei R Ess; **he killed hisell** Nb Cu Du We La Y Sa Db St Wa W Brk Sr K Co D Ha Sx; **he killed self** So Co; VIII.3.6 **laid him down** Ch Db.

THIRD PERSON SINGULAR FEMININE: IX.11.2 **she killed hersell** Nb Cu Du We La Y Ch Db Sa St Hrt Ess W Brk Sr K Co D Sx; **she killed herseln** Y; **she killed hersen** La Y Db St Nt L Lei R; VIII.3.6 **laid her down** 'lay down' St.

THIRD PERSON SINGULAR NEUTER: IM IV.1.4 **it ownsel** 'itself' (unstressed) La; IM I.11.6 includes **self** 'itself' referring to a cart D.

SECOND PERSON PLURAL: V.8.13 **help thyself** Co; **help thyselves** W; **help thysens** St; **help yoursel** K Ha; **help yourself** Ess Brk Sr Sx; **help yoursen** L; **help yoursels** Nb Cu Du La Y Ch Db St; **help yoursens** Y Ch Db St Nt L.

THIRD PERSON PLURAL **them** appears in VIII.6.4 **they play(en) them** 'they play themselves', i.e. 'they disport themselves' La Db; **theirsens** appears in IM III.10.4 Y. Compare §70.

EMPHATIC

61 Emphatic pronouns recorded at IX.11.3–4 (including Incidental Material) include:

FIRST PERSON SINGULAR: **mysel** Nb Cu Du We La Y; **myseln** Y; **mysen** La Y.

SECOND PERSON SINGULAR: **thysel** Nb Cu Du La Y; **thyseln** Y, **thysen** Y; **yoursel** La; **yoursen** Y.

THIRD PERSON SINGULAR MASCULINE: **himsel** Man Ch Sa; **himsen** St Lei; **hissel** Nb Cu Du We La Y Ch Db St So W Brk Sr K Co D; **hisself** Y Sa St He Wo Wa Mon Gl O L Lei Nth Hu C Nf Sf Bk Bd Hrt Ess MxL So W Brk Sr K Co D Do Ha Sx; **hisse(l)n** Y Db St Nt L Lei R; **his own self** Nf Sf.

THIRD PERSON SINGULAR FEMININE: **hersen** Y.

THIRD PERSON SINGULAR NEUTER: **itsel** La.

FIRST PERSON PLURAL: **oursels** Nb Y; **ussels** Y.

THIRD PERSON PLURAL: **'eirself** O; **'emselves** Wo Mon; **their own selves** Nf; **theirself** Sa He Wo Gl O L C Nf Sf Bk Bd Hrt Ess So W Brk Sr K Co D Ha Sx; **theirsel** La Y Ch Db St So W K Co D; **theirseln** Y; **theirsels** Nb Cu Du We La Y Ch Db So W Brk Sr K Co Ha Sx; **theirsen** Y St; **theirsens** La Y Db St Nt L; **theirselves** Y Ch Sa St He Wo Wa Mon Gl O L Nth Hu C Nf Sf Bk Bd Hrt Ess MxL So W Sr K Do Ha; **themsels** Man; **themsens** St Lei; **themself** Y; **theyselves** K.

DEMONSTRATIVE

62 SINGULAR demonstrative pronouns include the following:

IX.10.2 THIS is expressed by **thir** Du; **this here** We Y So Brk; **this here one** Ess; **this here one here**

MxL; **thick** [ðɪk] So W Brk D Ha; **thicky** So Co D; **thick there** D Do; **thuck** [ðʊk] Brk.

IX.10.1 THAT is expressed by **tat** Y; **that there** Sr; **thick** He So W; **thick here** Do; **thick there** W Do; **thicker** Co; **thicky** So D Do; **thicky there** D; **yon** Nb L.

IX.10.3 THAT OVER THERE is expressed by **that there** La Ch; **thick other one** Ha; **thick over there** So W Do; **thicker over there** Co; **thon** Nb Du; **yon(d)** Nb Cu We La Y Db Nt L; **yons** Db. In IM VI.12.2 **yond** refers to a person Y.

PLURAL demonstrative pronouns include the following:

IX.10.4 THESE is expressed by **these here** Y Bk K D; **thesen** Sa; **theasum** W; **they** So Brk K D Do Ha; **theys** Ess; **thick** Gl; **thir** Y; **tho** Nb Du.

IX.10.5 objective THOSE is expressed by **they** Gl Bk Ess So W Brk Sr Co Do; **they over there** D Do; **thick** W Ha; **thicky** D; **thore** Y; **thosen** Sa.

IX.10.6 THOSE OVER THERE is expressed by **they over there** Gl Sf So W Brk Sr Do Ha Sx; **thick (over) there** Gl So W; **tho here** La; **thosen yonder** Sa; **yon(d)** Nb Cu Du We La Y Db Nt L; **yons** Db.

See also Demonstrative Adjectives, §47.

RELATIVE

63 Relative 'that', nominative with masculine antecedent in III.3.7 *the man* THAT *looks after the cows*, and also in IM III.3.7, is expressed by **as** La Y Ch Db Sa St He Wo Wa Mon Gl O Nt L Lei R Nth Hu C Nf Bk Bd Hrt Ess W Brk Co D Do Ha; **at** Nb Cu Du We La Y Man Ch Db Wo L Nth Sf Ess MxL So K; **'t** [t] Nb Cu Y; **what** Y Ch Db St Wa Gl O L Lei R Nth Hu C Nf Sf Bd Hrt Ess MxL So W Brk Sr K D Ha Sx; ZERO (**the man looks after the cows**) Nf Sf Ess So W K D Do Ha.

In IX.9.5 *I know a man* WHO *will do it for you*, the relative pronoun is **as** Cu La Y; **at** Nb Cu Du We Y Ess; **that** Nb Cu Du We Y St L MxL; **what** La Y; ZERO (**I know a man will do it for you**) Nb Cu Du La Y Ch Db St He Mon O L Hu C Nf Sf Hrt Ess Bk So K Sx.

IM III.3.7 includes **my brother, which ...** K, and objective 'whom' expressed by **what** Sf.

64 Relative 'whose', possessive with masculine antecedent in IX.9.6 *That's the chap* WHOSE *uncle died*, is expressed by **as his** Nb La Y Ch Db St Wa Gl O Nt L Lei Nth Hu C Sf Bk Bd Hrt Ess

So; **at his** Nb Cu We Y; **his** Y; **that his** Man D; **that's** Cu La Y Ess; **what** Ess; **what his** Db L Ess; **what's** Db Ess So; **who his** Bd.

INTERROGATIVE

65 NOMINATIVE: VII.8.18 WHICH ONE? referring to apples is expressed by **what one?** W Do; **whether?** Du; **whichy?** Co D; **whichy one?** Co. IM VII.1.1 includes **whatten a one?** 'which one?' Du.

VII.8.16 WHAT KIND OF (knife)? is expressed by **whatten?** Nb, **whatten a knife?** Du.

OBJECTIVE: IX.9.3 'to whom' in *I wonder* TO WHOM *I shall give it* is expressed by **which ... to** Sa; **who** Sa He Wo Mon Gl L Nf Sf Ess So W Brk Sr K Co D Do Ha Sx; **who ... till** Cu We; **who ... to** Eng.

POSSESSIVE: IX.9.2 WHOSE? is expressed by **whosen** St Wo Gl O Hu C Bd; **whose's** St.

66. IX.9.2 'whose it is' in *You wonder* WHOSE *it is* (referring to a dog) is expressed by **whose is it/he** Y Mon Nt Hu Sr; **whose it be** Wo Mon Gl; **who it belongs** Db.

RECIPROCAL

67 OBJECTIVE: III.13.6 'each other' in FIGHT EACH OTHER is expressed by **one another** Nb Cu Du We La Y Ch Db Sa St He Wo Wa Mon Gl O Nt L Nth Hu C Nf Sf Bk Bd Hrt Ess MxL So W Sr K Co D Do Ha; **one t'other** Co D; **theirself** Sa; **theirselves** Y Wo Gl Nf; **themselves** St.

68 POSSESSIVE: VI.2.8 'each other's' in PULL EACH OTHER'S *hair* is expressed by **one another's** Eng exc. Lei R; **one another** Y; **each other** Y; **one t'other's** So Co D Do.

VERBS: REGULAR CONJUGATION

INFINITIVE

69 In a few cases in Mon and southern Eng, the infinitive ends in [-i], e.g. II.9.11 and IM I.7.1 **teddy** 'to ted' Mon K; III.8.10 **piggy** 'to give birth to piglets' Co; IM III.3.7 **vatchy** 'to thatch' So; VIII.7.2 **linchy-lunchy** 'to seesaw' (formed on the noun **linchy-lunch**) So; IM IX.9.5 **sheary** 'to shear' D.

The old infinitive suffix **-(e)n** appears in VIII.6.4 **playen** [pliːn] Db; III.3.8 **laiten** 'to seek' We; III.7.6 **shearen** La; IX.3.3 **putten** La Y He L.

V.2.8 **nasty** and **mucky** are infinitives meaning 'to make dirty' La, **mucky** having this same function in Db Sa St.

70 The verbs **play** and **oss** 'to try' are evidently reflexive in VIII.6.4 **playing themselves** La (also III.2.10 Db); **play them** 'disport themselves' La Db; VIII.8.4 **oss thysen** 'try' Y.

71 Lake 'to play' is followed by **at** in IM VIII.6.4 **laking at football** Y.

PRESENT PARTICIPLE

72 Forms of the present participle with prefixed **a-** [ə] include: III.1.6 **a-beasting** 'on heat' (of a cow) He Wo L; **a-bulling** Nb Cu Du We La Y Man Ch Db Sa St Wo Wa Gl O Nt L Lei Nth Hu Bk W Brk Ha Sx; III.8.9 **a-brimming** 'on heat' (of a sow) Nb Cu Du We La Y Man Ch Db Sa St He Wo Wa Nt; VII.6.26 and VIII.8.5 **a-blowing** St He Wo Wa Mon Gl O Nf Sf Ess MxL W Brk; III.1.2 **a-dropping** Nf Bd Brk; VIII.6.1 and IX.4.1 **a-going** Wo Wa R Nth Nf Bd K; VIII.6.4 **a-laking** 'playing, not at work' Y; III.12.2 **a-picking** So; IM III.3.7 **a-poaching** Sr; IM I.2.1 **a-shepherding** R; III.1.12 **a-springing** Wa Gl L Bk Hrt W; IM III.3.7 **a-thacking** 'thatching' Nf.

Apparently the only counties for which present participles with prefixed **a-** are not recorded are D Co and Do.

On precedes the present participle in III.8.9 **on hogging** 'on heat' (of sows) Sf Bk Bd Hrt So W Brk Ha; **on a-brimming** Wo; and III.1.6 **on a-bulling** 'on heat' (of cows) Wo Wa Gl; **on a-beasting** Wo.

73 In Y, the present participle may appear in contexts in which the standard dialect has the past participle, as in IM VI.2.3 **thou wants thy tow** (i.e. hair) **cutting**.

PAST PARTICIPLE

74 Past participial forms elicited in responses include the following:

BREAK IX.3.5: **a-broke** So W Co D Ha; **a-broked** D; **a-broken** So; **brack** Du; **bracken** La; **broke** Y Man Ch Db Sa St He Wo Wa Mon Gl O Nt L Lei R Nth Hu C Nf Sf Bk Bd Hrt Ess MxL So W Brk Sr K Co D Do Ha Sx; **broked** Do.

CATCH IX.3.8: **catch** Y Mon Ess Sx; **catched** Nb Cu Du We La Y Ch Db Sa St He Wo Wa Mon Gl O Nt L Lei R Nth Hu C Nf Sf Bk Bd Hrt Ess MxL So W Brk Sr K Co D Do Ha Sx.

CREEP IX.1.9: **creeped** Cu We La Y Sa St Wo Mon L Nf Ess So W Brk K Co D Do Ha Sx; **crope** Do Ha; **croppen** La.

DRINK VI.3.11: **a-drank** Brk; **a-drink** D Do; **a-drinked** So W Co D Do; **a-drunk** So D Ha; **a-drunked** W; **drank** Sa St He O L Lei Nth Nf Bk Ess MxL So W Brk K Ha Sx; **drinked** O Sf So W K Co Do Ha; **drucken** Nb Cu Du Y; **druffen** Y; **drunked** W Do; **drunken** Y Ch.

EAT VI.5.11: **ate** Nb Cu La Man Ch Sa St He Wo Wa Mon Nt L Lei Nth C Nf Sf Bk Bd Hrt Ess MxL So W Brk Sr K Co D Do Ha Sx; **aten** Cu Du La Y Ch Db St He Wa O Nt L Lei R Nth Hu Bd Ess So W Brk Do; **atened** K; **eat** Db Sa He Wo Mon Gl O Nt L Nf Sf Bk Ess So W Brk Sr K Co Do Ha.

FIND IX.3.2: **founded** W Brk.

GIVE IX.8.3: **a-gi** D; **a-gived** Co D Ha; **gave** He Mon L R Nth Nf; **gi** So; **give** Man St He Wo Wa Mon Gl O L Nth Hu C Nf Sf Bk Bd Hrt Ess So W Brk Sr K Co Ha Sx; **gived** [gɪ(v)d] Sa St He Mon Gl So W Brk D Do Ha; **given** [gɪn~giːn~gɛn] Nb Cu Du We La Y Ch Db Sa St Wo Wa Gl O Nt L Lei R Nth Bk Bd Hrt Ess Brk Ha Sx; **gov** Co.

MAKE IX.3.6: **a-made** So Brk D Ha.

PUT IX.3.3: **a-put** He Brk D; **putten** Nb Cu Du We La Y Nt L Co.

REACH VI.7.15: **a-reached** Nb Nf; **reach** La Wa Lei Nf; **reched** Hu C; **roached** Nth; **rocken** (infinitive **reak**) Y.

SPEAK VI.5.5: **spacken** Y; **spake** Sr D; **speaked** Sa; **spoke** Nb Cu We La Y Man Ch Db Sa St He Wo Wa Mon Gl O Nt L Lei Nth Hu C Nf Sf Bk Bd Hrt Ess MxL So W Brk Sr K Co D Do Ha Sx.

STEAL VIII.7.5: **a-stealed** D; **a-stole** D Ha; **a-stoled** So D; **stealed** Y St So W Co D Do Ha; **stole** Cu La Y Man Ch Db Sa St He Wo Wa Mon Gl O Nt L Nth Hu C Sf Bk Bd Ess So W Brk K Co D Do Ha Sx; **stoled** Sf So W Co D Do Ha.

TAKE IX.3.7: **a-took** Brk D Ha; **a-tooked** D; **ta'en** Nb Cu Du We L Y Ch Db St L; **took** Nb We La Y Ch Db Sa St He Wo Wa Mon Gl O Nt L Lei R Nth Hu C Nf Sf Bk Bd Hrt Ess MxL So W Brk Sr K Co D Do Ha Sx; **tooked** D Do; **tooken** Cu We La St He L Lei Nf; **toon** Nb Du; also IM V.6.1 **take** Y.

75 Other forms of the past participle, from responses other than those cited in §74 and from the Incidental Material, include: III.3.7 **a-boiled** Co; III.1.2 **a-calved** Wo; III.1.3 **a-clamed** 'having discharged the afterbirth' (of a cow) W; III.2.11 **a-chewed** D; VII.3.16 **a-comed** Y; III.3.1 **a-foaled** D; III.4.6 **a-folded** 'foaled' Do; III.3.7 **a-got** Brk D; VII.2.12 **a-heard** So; I.8.1 **a-ploughed** Brk Co; V.7.7 **a-seed** So W D Do Ha; VII.2.5 **a-seen** Ess Brk Co D; III.4.6 **a-slip** D; VII.6.15 **a-thawed** Mon; III.1.7 **a-turned** W Ha; I.11.5 **a-walted** 'overturned' La; III.1.11 **a-warped** 'thrown, slipped' W; III.3.7 **beared** 'borne' Do; IX.4.4 **bet** 'beaten' Y; VI.5.9 **bore** 'borne' Wa; **borned** 'borne' Co; III.3/7 and IV.8.6 **blowed** Sa St Wo Ess D; VIII.1.12 **brung** He; IV.1.4 **brussen** 'burst' Y; III.7.4 **cassen** 'cast, overturned' Cu La; III.4.6 and III.7.4 **casted** St He C Nf Sf Bk Bd Hrt Ess; VIII.3.2 **comed** Y; I.11.5 **couped** [koupɪt] 'overturned' Nb; III.1.15 and III.8.1 **cutten** 'castrated' Y Nt L; I.7.8 **digged** D; III.1.11 **drawed** D; IX.9.6 **drownded** Nb Du We Y Nt L Lei R Nf Bk Ess So Brk Sr K Do Sx; III.5.1 **feeded** D; III.1.12 **fell** 'fallen' Gl; V.7.7 **fellen** 'felled' Wa; IV.1.4 **floodit** Nb Cu Ch He; III.4.1 **folded** 'foaled' W; VI.13.9 **freezed** So Co D; VIII.8.2 **frit** (past-participial adjective) 'frightened' Db Sa St Wo Wa O; VI.13.9 **fro'en** 'frozen' Sf Ess; **fro'ened** Sf; **froze** St Mon Gl O L Nth C Nf Sf Bk Bd Ess MxL So W Brk Sr Ha Sx; **frozed** St Do; III.4.5 and VI.5.8 **getten** Y Ch; V.7.7, VI.5.8 and IX.5.6 **gotten** Y Wo Nt L; III.3.7 and III.10.7 **growed** Sa Wa; VIII.2.6 **hearded** La; II.9.6 **het** 'heated' C; III.1.17 **holded** L; IV.3.3 **hungen** 'hung' Y; V.7.7 and VI.13.13 **hurted** Mon So Brk Co; IV.6.2 **keeped** Co D; V.6.4 **kneadened** Y; III.3.7 **knowed** Lei; VI.13.20 **naked** (past-participial adjective with final [kt]) Nb Cu Du We La Y Ch Db Nt L; III.7.4 **overthrowed** Db; III.3.7 **rid** (past participle of RIDE) Lei; IV.1.4 and V.6.12 **rose** Ess So Co; IV.1.4 **runned** Sf; V.7.7 and VIII.2.5 **saw** 'seen' MxL; **see** 'seen' Nth Hu Sf Bk Bd Brk; **seed** 'seen' Lei R Bd So W Co D Do Ha; IV.8.6 **strucken** L; III.1.13 and IV.1.4 **swelled** Gl Nf; III.13.7 **teached** Y; III.3.7 and VIII.5.1 **telled** Y O; III.1.11, III.3.7, III.4.6 and VIII.7.7 **throwed** St He Wo Wa Mon Gl O So Brk D; IV.6.8 **trudden** 'trodden' Cu; VI.14.14 **weared** Co; **wore** Ha Sx; IX.11.1 **weshen** 'washed' Du; VIII.6.6 **writ** 'written' MxL.

IMPERATIVE

76 Recorded forms of the second person singular imperative include: VIII.3.3 **sit thee/thyself/ thysen/you/yourself down** Nb Cu Du We La Y Ch Db Sa St He Wo Gl L Lei Bk Bd So W Ha; **do 'ee sit down** So; **sittest down** Co; IM IX.3.4 **comest** Co; VIII.3.1 **come you in** Nf; **come thou in** Gl; VIII.7.9 **off thee dost go** So W D Do Ha; **off thou goes** Ch Db Gl; **off thee goest** Ch Db Sa St; **off you gon** Db St; **off you goes** He Wo Mon Gl; IM III.13.8 **looks thou** and **look you** Y; VI.3.2 **sithee** Y.

For other forms of GO see §§113–116.

VERBAL NOUN

77 'Laughing' in IX.2.14 *couldn't help laughing* is expressed by **a-laughing** He Wo Mon Brk. So too in VIII.8.7 (*What am I doing now? ...*) **a-laughing** Bd. However, the expression **couldn't help but laugh** emerged at Nb Cu Du We La Y Db St Gl Nt L Nth.

The Incidental Material includes: III.8.10 **she's done farrow** 'she's finished farrowing' Man; II.1.4 **a-muck-spreading** Y; IV.5.3 **a-ratting** Wo; IV.2.11 **a-ditching** Bk.

PRESENT TENSE INDICATIVE

Inflected forms

78 Recorded inflected forms of the present tense indicative include:

FIRST PERSON SINGULAR: VI.5.11 **I eats** He Wo Bk Brk Sr Ha.

SECOND PERSON SINGULAR: IV.8.4 **thou sees** Y; IM III.3.7 **you uses** Brk; **you makes** He; VI.5.11 **you eats** Y; IM IV.2.4 **you lays** Gl; VI.14.2 **thou seems** Nb; **thou looks** Cu; **thou suits** La; IM I.11.4 **thou greases it** Y; IM II.6.2 **thou ties it up** Y.

THIRD PERSON SINGULAR: IX.3.6 (**a man who**) **make suits** Ch Db Wa Mon Gl Nt L Nth Nf Sf Bk Bd Ess So W Sr Co Do Ha Sx; VI.14.14 **she wear the breeches/trousers** (said of a domineering woman) Nf Sf Ess So W Co Do; IX.3.7 (**every chance she gets she**) **take** Nf Sf Ess So Sr K Co D; VI.5.5 (**he**) **never speak** Ch Db St He Wo Wa Mon Gl O L Nf Sf Bk Hrt Ess So W Brk Sr K Co D Do Sx; III.3.7 (**the man**

who/what/ZERO) **look after the cows** Nf Sf So W D; IM III.3.7 **live** Ess; VI.14.14 **her weareth the trousers** Co; III.1.12b **she falls** with final [s] Man; IM III.3.7 [kasɪz] 'casts' Ch; IM V.7.7 [kɔsɪz] 'costs' Wo.

FIRST PERSON PLURAL: IM III.10.7 **we calls them** He; IM II.1.4 **we hauls** Do; VI.5.11 **we eats** Ess; V.2.12 **we puts the light on** He Wo Mon Gl. Old **-(e)n** forms are attested in V.2.12 **we putten the light on** Db; IM V.7.7 **we callen** [kɔːn] Ch; IM IX.3.3 present tense plural **putten** Ch Db; IM IX.3.6 **maken** Ch.

THIRD PERSON PLURAL: IV.6.2 **they keeps chickens/hens** Du Sa He Wo Mon Gl O Brk Ha Sx; VIII.5.2 **they stops/bides/stays at home** Y Db He Wo Gl O W Brk Ha Sx; III.10.2/7 **bulls belders/bellocks/bellows/blores/roars** Nb Cu Du We La Y Ch Db Sa He Wo Wa Mon Gl O Nt L Bk So W Brk Sr K D Ha Sx (also IM III.10.2 Ess); III.10.4 **cows moos** St; VIII.7.5 **burglars steals them** Cu Du We La Y Db Sa He Wo Mon Gl O Nt L Bk So W Brk Ha Sx. IM III.3.7 includes: **good thackers** (i.e. thatchers) **as thacks these houses** Lei; **thorns as grows round it** Nth. Old **-(e)n** forms are attested in IV.6.2 **they keepen chickens** Y Db; VIII.7.5 **burglars stealen them** Ch; **burglars thieven them** St; III.10.7 **bulls belderen** (i.e. bellow) Ch; **sheep baaen** Db; VIII.5.2 **they stoppen at home** Ch Db. The Incidental Material includes III.3.7 **comen** Ch; IV.4.4 **cutten** Ch; **eaten** Db; VIII.5.1 **callen** [kɔːn] La Sa; **gin** 'give' La; **parken** (cars) La; **sayen** La; **shearen** La; **wanten** La; **looken** Y; **washen** Y; VIII.4.6 **playen** La.

Other examples include: III.12.6 and IV.6.13 **some calls it** Nb Y; IM III.10.7 **people shoots them** Nb; IM V.5.1 **some puts** Y; III.1.12 **the bones goes** He; IM VIII.5.1 **they opens** Ch; **they draws** Sa; **they gets** Wo Wa; **they calls** Wo O; **they fits** Mon; **they roostses** O; **they asks** [aːsɪz] MxL.

Periphrastic forms

79 Periphrastic forms of the present tense indicative, with unstressed DO (i.e. [də]) followed by the stem, are recorded as follows:

FIRST PERSON SINGULAR: IM III.3.7 **the only thing as I do know** He Gl.

SECOND PERSON SINGULAR: IV.3.3 **post you do hang a gate on** Mon.

THIRD PERSON SINGULAR: IX.3.6 (**a man who**) **do make suits** Mon So W Co Do Ha;

VI.14.14 **she do wear the trousers** Mon So W Co Do; IX.3.7 **(every chance she gets she) do take** So W Co Do Ha; VI.5.5 **(he) do never speak** Mon; III.3.7 **(the man) as do buy the cattle** Mon; **(the man) as do look after the cows** Gl; VIII.6.2 **school do finish** Mon; **school do shut** Gl; IM I.3.11 **that's where it do empt** (i.e. empty) Do.

FIRST PERSON PLURAL: IM IV.1.1/3 **we do call them** He Co.

THIRD PERSON PLURAL: IV.6.2 **they do keep chickens** Mon So W Co Do; VIII.7.5 **burglars do steal them** Mon Gl So W Co Do; III.10.7 **bulls do bellow/roar** So W Co Do. See also §115.

PAST TENSE INDICATIVE

Inflected forms

80 Inflected forms of the past tense indicative elicited in responses include the following, which are third person singular except where otherwise stated:

BEGIN VII.6.23: **beginned** Man D; **begun** Nb Cu Du We La Y Ch Db Sa St He Wo Wa Mon Gl O Nt L Nth Hu C Nf Sf Bk Bd Hrt Ess MxL So W Brk Sr D Do Ha Sx.

BREAK IX.3.5: **brack** Nb Cu Du We La Y Ch; **brake** with [eː] replacing stem-vowel [ɛi] Y; **breaked** Ess; **broked** D Do.

BRING VIII.1.11: **breng** K; **bring** Brk.

CATCH IX.3.8: **catch** Y Lei Nf Sf K; **catched** Eng exc. Man.

COME IX.3.4: **cam** Nb Y; **cem** Y Mon L; **co** [kɔ~kʊ] Cu We Y; **come** Eng; **comed** Du La Y So W Do; **coome** Y. IM IX.3.4 includes third person plural **comen** Ch.

CREEP IX.1.7: first person singular **creeped** Cu We La Y Sa St Wo Mon L Nf Ess So W Brk Sr K Co D Do Ha Sx; **crope** La Do Ha.

EAT VI.5.11: first person singular **eat** Nb Cu Du We La Y Db Sa He Wa Gl O Nt L Lei Hu Nf Sf Bk Ess So W Brk Sr K Co D Do Ha Sx; **eaten** Lei R; **aten** Lei.

GROW IX.3.9: third person plural **growed** Nb Cu La Y Ch Db Sa St He Wo Wa Mon Gl O L Lei R Nth Hu C Nf Bk Bd Hrt Ess So W Brk Sr K Co D Do Ha Sx.

HEAR VII.2.6: first person singular **heard** with an apparently weak conjugation: [-d] suffixed to an unmutated stem La Y Db He Wo Mon Gl O Nt L

Lei R Nth Hu Sf Bk Bd Hrt Ess So W Brk Sr Co D Do Ha Sx; **hearded** La.

LIE 'recline' VIII.3.6: **layed** Cu Du We La Y Man Db Sa He Wa Mon Gl Nt L R Nth Hu C Nf Sf Bk Bd Ess MxL So W Brk Sr K D Do Ha Sx; **lied** (infinitive **lig**) La Y L.

MAKE IX.3.6: **make** Gl Nt L Lei Nth Nf Sf Bk Bd Ess W.

PUT IX.3.3: first person singular **pat** Nb Y; **putten** L.

REACH VI.7.15: first person singular **reach** Y Wa Lei Nf; **riched** Ess; **roach** Nth.

RIDE IX.3.10: first person singular **rid** Nb Cu Du We La Y Ch Db Sa St O Nt L Lei R Nth C Nf Sf Bk Bd Hrt Ess Brk K Sx.

SEE VIII.2.5: first person singular **sawed** Sa; **seed** Nb Cu Du La Y Ch Db Sa St He Wo Wa Gl (also III.3.7 O) Nt L Lei Bd So W Brk K Co D Do Ha Sx; **see** La Y O L Nth Hu C Nf Sf Bk Bd Ess MxL Brk St K Sx; **seen** Nb Cu Du Y Man Db St He Wo Wa Mon Gl O Nt L Lei R Nth C Nf Sf Bk Bd Ess MxL So W Brk K Co D Ha Sx; **a-seed** So W Do Ha; **a-seen** He Brk Co D.

SPEAK VI.5.5: **spack** Nb Cu Du We La Y; **spake** We La Y Gl So D; **spaked** W; **speaked** Y Sa L; **spoked** Sr.

STEAL VIII.7.5: third person plural **stealed** Y St So W K Co D Do Ha; **stoled** Nth Nf So W Brk Co D Do Ha.

TAKE IX.3.7: **taed** Y Db St; **taen** L; **take** Nb; **taken** Nf; **tooked** D Do.

81 Other inflected past tense forms, recorded either in responses other than those cited in §80 or from the Incidental Material, include: IM V.7.7 **blowed** He; I.7.8 **digged** Y; IM V.7.7 **drawed** He; **feeled** D; IX.9.5 **get** 'got' La; IM V.7.7 **gen** 'gave' Ch; IM III.3.7 **gin** 'gave' Wo; IM V.7.7 and IX.8.3 **give** 'gave' Man Brk; **gived** D; IV.2.7 **grun** 'ground' St; IM III.3.7 **hanged** 'hung' Gl; IM V.7.7 **hurted** Mon; IM IV.6.2 **keeped** Co; VI.5.17 and IM III.3.7 **knowed** Nb La Y Db Sa St He Wo Wa Mon Gl O Nt L Lei R Nth Hu C Nf Sf Bk Hrt Ess MxL So W Brk Sr K Co D Do Ha Sx; **knewed** Y; IM III.3.7 **run** 'ran' Lei K (also IX.9.5 Y); IM III.1.7 **runned** Nf Sf; V.7.7 **a-said** So; VIII.3.3 **set** 'sat' Ess; **sot** 'sat' So; III.3.7 **swinged** 'swung' Gl; III.13.17 **teached** Du La Brk D Do Sx; VI.5.17 **telled** Y Ch L Gl; III.3.7, III.4.6, V.7.7, and VIII.7.7 **throwed** Sa St Wo Gl MxL So Sr D; VIII.6.6 **writ** 'wrote' L.

Periphrastic forms

82 IM III.3.7 furnishes examples from W of periphrastic past tense forms with unstressed DID followed by the stem: **a pigeon-house what did go right round; a thing as they did wear a lot.**

83 IM IX.4.15 shows 'used not to' (i.e. was/were not accustomed to) expressed by **didn't used to** Y L Nf Sf Ess; **hadn't use(d) to** Sa Wo Gl Lei Hu Bd; **hadna used to** St. Compare also **Never used to say it, had they?** Wa. See also §133.

VERBS: ANOMALOUS CONJUGATIONS
BE

PRESENT TENSE INDICATIVE

Positive: unstressed

84 Unstressed forms of BE present in responses to VIII.9.5 I AM *thirsty* etc. include the following:

FIRST PERSON SINGULAR: **I are** Sr K; **I be** Wo Wa Mon Gl O Bk So W Brk Sr Co D Do Ha Sx; **I bin** St; **I's** Nb Cu Du We La Y He. Compare also IM VIII.9.5 **I's just a-thinking** Gl.

SECOND PERSON SINGULAR: IM III.3.7 **you be** Wo O; IM I.9.1 **you'm** Co; IM I.7.19 **thou's** [ðuːz] Cu.

THIRD PERSON SINGULAR: **her be** He Gl Bk W Brk; **she be** Wa Mon O Bk So Brk Do Ha Sx; IM III.1.12 [ʃɪs] 'she' Man.

FIRST PERSON PLURAL: **us be** Co D; **we be** Wo Mon Gl O Bk So W Brk Do Ha Sx; **we'm** Sa Wo Wa Mon So Sr Co D Do Ha; **we'n** Ch Sa; **we bin** St; **we's** Ess.

THIRD PERSON PLURAL: **they be** Sa He Wo Wa Mon Gl O Bk So W Brk Sr Co D Do Ha; **they bin** Sa; **they'm** Sa St He Wo Wa So W Sr Co D; **they'n** Sa St; **they'm be** Sa; **they's** He Ess. Compare also the following, from the Incidental Material: III.1.12 **the bones be gone** Nth; III.10.7 **pigs is fond of them** Nb; **my hands is all hacked** Cu; **my lugs is cold** Du; **the horses is baiting** La; **his hands is cold** Y; **the ropes is going** Man; III.3.7 **the people as is baking** Mon; **people as is a bit suspicious** L; **people that's respectable** MxL; IV.5.7 **ferrets is called 'fitchies'** D. Responses to V.7.21 include **these is the last of the old 'taties** Cu We La Y; **the old 'taties is gone** Sa Gl; **the old 'taties be gone/done** He Mon Gl; **these am the lot** Wo; and responses to III.1.12 include **her bones is dropped** Sa; **her bones be dropped/apart/open** Gl O Nth Bk.

85 The following are unstressed forms of BE present tense indicative without predicate, recorded (unless otherwise stated) in responses to

IX.7.7 I AM etc., in which the pronoun is stressed, the verb unstressed:

FIRST PERSON SINGULAR: **I are** Wo Wa Bk Bd Hrt Sr K; **I be** St He Wo Wa Mon Gl O Bk So K Co D Do Ha Sx; **I bin** Ch Sa St; **I is** Nb Cu Du We La Y.

SECOND PERSON SINGULAR: **thee art** So Co D Do; **thou art** La Y; **thee be** He D; **you be** St He Wa Mon O Bk So Brk D Ha Sx; **thee bist** Ch Sa He Wo Mon Gl O So W Brk Ha; **thou bist** Sa; **you am** Sa Wo; **you bin** Ch Sa St; **thou is** Nb Cu Du We La Y L.

THIRD PERSON SINGULAR FEMININE: **her be** St Wa Gl Bk W Brk D; **her bin** Ch Sa Wo; **her bist** Wo; **she be** Mon O So Brk Ha Sx.

THIRD PERSON PLURAL: **they am** Sa St Wo Sr K; **they aren** Db; **they be** St He Wo Wa Mon Gl O Nth Bk So W Brk Co D Do Ha Sx; **they bin** Ch Sa St Wo; **they bist** Wo; **they is** Y.

Positive: stressed

86 The following are stressed contradictory forms of BE present tense, recorded at IX.7.9: *If I say: You people aren't English, you can contradict and say: Oh yes WE ARE* etc:

FIRST PERSON SINGULAR: **I are** St Wa Bk Bd Hrt Sr K; **I be** He Wo Wa Mon Gl O Bk So W Brk K Co D Do Ha Sx; **I bin** Ch Sa St; **I is** Nb Cu Du We La Y.

SECOND PERSON SINGULAR: **thee art** So Co D Do; **thee be** Wo So D Do Ha; **thee bist** Sa Wo Mon Gl O W Brk Ha; **thou art** La Y Ch Db St; **thou be** Brk; **thou is** Nb Cu Du La Y; **you am** Sa Wo Wa; **you be** St He Wo Wa Mon O Bk So Brk D Ha Sx; **you bin** Ch Sa St.

THIRD PERSON SINGULAR FEMININE: **he is** K; **her am** Sa; **her be** He Wo Gl So W Brk D; **she be** Mon O So W Brk Do Ha Sx; **her bin** Ch Sa; **her bist** Wo.

FIRST PERSON PLURAL: **us be** O Brk Co D; **we be** He Wo Wa Mon Gl O Bk So W Brk Co D; **we am** Ch Sa Wo Sr K; **we are 'm** Brk; **we aren** Ch; **we bin** Sa St.

Negative: stressed

87 The following are forms of BE present tense negative, stressed, recorded at IX.7.10 *If I said to you: You're drunk, you would answer: Oh no,* I'M NOT *etc:*

FIRST PERSON SINGULAR: **I ain't** Y Db St He Wo Wa Mon O Nt L Lei R Nth Hu C Nf Sf Bk Bd Hrt Ess MxL So W Brk Sr K Ha Sx; **I amma** Sa; **I amment** Nb; **I ammet** La Y; **I amna** Db St; **I anna** Ch St; **I aren't** Y L Nf Sf Ess MxL Co; **I bain't** Sa St He Wo Wa Mon Gl O Bk Ess So W Brk Co D Do Ha Sx; **I binna** Ch Sa He Wo; **I bisn't** Wo; **I in't** Sf; **I isn't** Cu Du We La Y; **I'm none** Y Db St; **I're not** K; **I's none** Y; **I's not** Nb Cu Du We La Y.

THIRD PERSON SINGULAR FEMININE: **he ain't** Brk; **her ain't** Sa St He Wo Wa Mon Gl Bk W Brk D; **she ain't** Y St He Mon Gl O L Lei R Nth Hu C Nf Sf Bk Bd Hrt Ess MxL So W Brk K Ha Sx; **her bain't** W Brk; **she bain't** O Ess So W Do Sx; **her binna** Sa; **her inna** Ch Db Sa St He; **she in't** Nt; **hoo inna** Ch; **her's not** La; **hoo isna** Db St; **hoo's not** La; **she's none** Y; **she inna** Sa; **shoo ain't** Y.

THIRD PERSON PLURAL: **they ain't** Y St He Wo Wa Mon Gl O L Lei R Nth Hu C Nf Sf Bk Bd Hrt Ess MxL So W Brk Sr K Co D Ha Sx; **they amma** Ch; **they anna** Ch Db Sa St; **they bain't** St He Wo Wa Mon Gl O Bk Ess So W Brk Co D Do Ha Sx; **they binna** Ch Sa He Wo; **they inna** Db; **they in't** Sf; **they'm not** Wo; **they're none** Y.

Interrogative: unstressed

88 The following are unstressed forms of BE present tense interrogative recorded at IX.7.1 *To find out whether you're right, you ask quite simply:* AM I *right?*, and IX.7.2 *To find out whether I had a wife, you'd ask me:* ARE YOU *married? etc.:*

FIRST PERSON SINGULAR: **are I?** Wo Wa Bk Bd Hrt Sr K; **be I?** Sa He Wo Wa Mon Gl O Bk So W Brk Sr Co D Do Ha Sx; **bin I?** Ch Sa St Wo Gl Sx; **is I?** Nb Cu Du We La Y.

SECOND PERSON SINGULAR: **are thou?** Ch Db; **aren you?** Sa; **art?** La Db St So Co; **are thee/thou?** La Y Ch Db Nt So W Co D Do; **be?** So; **be ye?** Co D; **be you?** St He Wo Wa Mon O

Bk So W Brk Sr D Do Ha Sx; **bin ye?** Sa; **bin you?** Ch Sa St; **bist?** Sa Gl So W Do; **bist thee/thou?** Sa He Wo Mon Gl O So W Brk D Do Ha; **is thee/thou?** Nb Cu Du We La Y Ch L; **ist thou?** Y. Compare also IM VI.13.1 **art thou?** Y.

THIRD PERSON SINGULAR FEMININE: **be her?** Bk W Brk; **be she?** Mon O Sx; **bin her?** Ch Sa; **is he?** Wo Brk K; **is her?** La Db Sa St He Wo Wa Mon Gl So W Brk Sr Co D Do Ha; **is hoo?** La Y Ch Db St; **is shoo?** Y. Compare also IM I.7.1 **what time be it?** Gl; VII.6.26 **which road be the wind?** Sa.

THIRD PERSON PLURAL: **am they?** Sa St; **art they?** Ch So W; **be mun?** Co; **be them?** Sa Wo Gl O So W Brk Co D Do; **be they?** Sa St He Wo Wa Mon Gl O Bk So W Brk Co D Do Ha Sx; **bin them?** Ch; **bin they?** Sa St; **is them?** Y. Compare also, in IM IV.5.7: **is them vitchy** (i.e. dark-coloured) **or white?** So; **is they?** So.

Interrogative: stressed and unstressed

89 Interrogative forms of BE, stressed and unstressed, appear as follows in expressions for HOW ARE YOU? VIII.2.8: **how am you?** Sa; **how am you getting on?** Wo; **how are thou** [tə]? La Ch; **how are thou keeping?** (where **thou** is [tə] La, [ta] Y); **how art?** Db So Co; **how art thee?** So; **how art thou?** Db; **how art getting/going on (you) now?** Db St So Co D; **how be?** Mon Gl O So Brk; **how be thee?** Ha; **how be ye?** Co D Sx; **how be you (now)?** He Wo Mon Nth Bk So W Brk Sr Do Sx; **how be getting/going on/along?** Sa O Bk So W Co D Do; **how be you getting/going on?** Wo Mon Bk Ha; **how beest?** Sa Mon Gl So W Brk; **how beest now you?** W; **how beest thee?** Sa He Mon Gl So Do; **how beest thou?** Brk; **how beest feeling/getting on (you)/going on?** Sa He Gl W D Do Ha; **how beest thee keeping/getting on/going on?** Wo W D; **how bin thee?** Sa Wo; **how bin you?** Ch; **how bin thee getting on?** Sa; **how is thou** [tə]? Nb Cu We La Y (with, also, **thou** as [θə] Y); **how's thou getting/going on?** Cu Du We Y L; **how ye getting on?** Co.

Interrogative negative: stressed

90 The following are stressed interrogative negative forms of BE copula, present tense, recorded at IX.7.4 AREN'T I *lucky?* and IX.7.3 AREN'T YOU/ISN'T SHE/AREN'T THEY *married?*:

FIRST PERSON SINGULAR: **ain't I?** Db St Sa He Wo Wa Mon Gl O L Lei R Nth Hu C Nf Sf Bk Bd

Hrt Ess MxL So Brk Sr K D Ha Sx; **ammad I?** Sa; **amment I?** Nb Man; **ammet I?** Nb La Y Db Sa; **anna I?** Ch Db St; **arem'd I?** La; **arem't I?** La; **bain't I?** St He Wo Gl O Bk So W Brk Co D Do Ha Sx; **bin I?** Gl; **binna I?** Ch Sa; **is I not?** Du; **isn't I?** Nb Cu Du We La Y St.

SECOND PERSON SINGULAR: **ain't thee?** So; **ain't you?** Db St He Wa Mon O L Lei R Nth Hu C Nf Sf Bk Bd Hrt Ess MxL So Brk Sr K Ha Sx; **ain't ye?** Ha; **amma you?** Sa; **anna thee?** Ch; **anna you?** Db Sa St; **are you not?** Nb We; **aren't thee/thou?** La Y St W Co; **aren't ye?** Co; **art not?** La Ch Db St; **art not thou?** Db; **artn't thee/thou?** Y Ch Db So D Do; **bain't thee?** He; **bain't ye?** O So W Co D Do; **bain't you?** He Wo O Bk Ess So Brk Sr Ha; **binna you?** Ch Sa; **bistn't?** Gl W; **bistn't thee?** Sa He Wo Mon Gl; **is thou not?** Nb Cu Du We; **isn't thou?** Nb Cu Du We La Y.

THIRD PERSON SINGULAR FEMININE: **ain't he?** Wo Brk; **ain't her?** St He Wo Wa Mon Gl So W Sr Ha; **ain't she?** Wa Mon Gl O L Lei R Nth Hu C Nf Sf Bk Bd Hrt Ess MxL So W Sr K Do Ha Sx; **aren't her?** Wa; **aren't she?** La L; **bain't her?** He Wo Gl Bk W Brk D; **bain't she?** O Ess Brk Sr K Sx; **binna her?** Sa; **bistn't her?** Brk; **inna her?** Ch Db Sa St He Wo; **inna hoo?** Ch; **inna she?** Ch; **innad her?** Sa; **is hoo not?** La; **is she not?** Nb Cu Du We; **isna her?** Db; **isna hoo?** Db; **isn't hoo?** La Y Ch Db; **isn't her?** Sa St Wo Wa Gl So W Co D Do Ha; **isn't shoo?** La Y.

THIRD PERSON PLURAL: **ain't they?** La Y St He Wo Wa Mon O L Lei R Nth Hu C Nf Sf Bk Bd Hrt Ess MxL W Brk Sr K Ha Sx; **ain't them?** He Wa So; **are they not?** Nb Cu Du We La; **amma they?** Sa; **anna they?** Ch Db St; **aren't them?** Y; **artna they?** Db Sa; **are no' they?** So; **bain't mun?** Co; **bain't them?** Gl So W Brk Co D Do Ha; **binna they?** Ch Sa Wo; **bain't they?** St He Wo Mon Gl O Bk Ess So W Brk Co D Ha Sx; **inna them?** Ch; **inna they?** St; **isn't them?** So Co.

91 The following are stressed interrogative forms of BE present tense without predicative, recorded at IX.7.5 *He's all right there* ISN'T HE? etc.:

FIRST PERSON SINGULAR: **ain't I?** La Db St He Wo Wa Mon Gl O L Lei R Nth Hu C Nf Sf Bk Bd Hrt Ess MxL So W Brk Sr K Co D Ha Sx; **ammad I?** Sa; **amment I?** Nb; **ammet I?** Nb Y Ch Db St; **anna I?** Ch Db Sa St; **arem't I?** La Y; **bain't I?** St Wo Gl O Bk So W Brk Co D Do Ha Sx; **bin I?** Bk; **binna I?** Ch Sa; **inna I?** Sa; **in't I?** Y; **isn't I?** Nb Cu Du We La Y.

SECOND PERSON SINGULAR: **adn't thou?** Y; **ain't thee/thou?** Y Wo Brk Co; **ain't you?** St He Wo Wa Mon O L Lei R Nth Hu C Nf Sf Bk Bd Hrt Ess MxL So W Brk Sr K Ha Sx; **ain't ye?** So K D; **amma you?** Sa; **anna you?** Sa; **aren't thou?** La Y Ch Db St Nt; **aren't ye?** Co; **art not?** Ch Db St; **artn't?** So D Do; **artn't thou?** Co; **bain't ye?** O So W Co D Do Ha Sx; **binna thee?** Ch Sa; **binna you?** Ch Sa; **bistna?** Sa; **bistn't?** Gl O So W Ha; **bistn't thee/thou?** He Wo Mon Gl W Brk Ha; **inna thee?** Sa; **isn't thou?** Nb Cu Du We La Y; **isn't ye?** K.

THIRD PERSON SINGULAR MASCULINE: **ain't en?** W; **ain't he/a?** Sa St He Wo Wa Mon Gl O L Lei R Nth Hu C Nf Sf Bk Bd Hrt Ess MxL So Brk Sr K Ha Sx; **ain't her?** So W; **bain't he/a?** O W Brk D Ha Sx; **inna he?** Ch Db Sa St; **innad he?** Sa; **innot he/a?** Sa; **in't he?** Y Man Ch Db St Nt L; **isn't a?** Co D; **isn't her?** So W D Do Ha; **isn't him?** So; **yun't a?** Gl. Note also third person singular neuter in IM V.7.7: **aren't it?** Wo.

THIRD PERSON PLURAL: **adn't they?** We Y; **ain't them?** He Wo Gl Bk So W D; **ain't they?** Nb La Y Db St He Wo Wa Mon Nt L Lei R Nth Hu C Nf Sf Bk Bd Hrt Ess MxL So Brk Sr K Ha Sx; **amma they?** Sa; **anna they?** Ch Db Sa St; **are not they?** Du Db; **aren't them?** La Co; **bain't mun?** Co; **bain't them/'em?** St He Wo Gl So W Co D Do Ha Sx; **bain't they?** St He Mon So Brk Sx; **bin 'em?** Gl; **bin they?** Ch; **binna them?** Ch; **binna they?** Sa; **bin't they?** Sa; **inna they?** Sa; **isn't them?** La Y Ch.

PAST TENSE INDICATIVE

Positive: unstressed

92 Unstressed forms of BE past tense recorded at VIII.9.5 I WAS *thirsty* etc. include the following:

FIRST PERSON SINGULAR: **I were** Nb La Y Ch Db Sa St He Wo Wa Mon Gl Nt L Lei R Nth C Sf Bk Ess So W Brk Sr Do Ha Sx; **I weren** Sa.

THIRD PERSON SINGULAR FEMININE: **her was** Ch Sa St He Wo Wa Gl O So W Brk Co D Do Ha; **her were** La Ch Db Sa St He Wo Wa Mon Gl Bk So W Brk; **hoo was** La Ch; **hoo were** La Y Ch Db; **she were** La Y Db Mon Nt L Lei R Nth Hu C Nf Sf Bk Ess So W Do Ha Sx; **shoo were** Y.

FIRST PERSON PLURAL: **us was** Co D; **we was** Du La Y Ch Sa St He Wo Wa Mon Gl O Nt L Lei Nf Sf Bk Bd Hrt Ess So W Brk Sr K Co Do Ha Sx; **we weren** Ch Sa St.

THIRD PERSON PLURAL: **they was** La Y Ch St He Wo Wa Mon Gl O Nt L Lei Nf Sf Bk Bd Hrt Ess MxL So W Brk Sr K Co D Do Ha Sx; **they weren** Ch Sa St. Compare also IM III.10.7 **the mountains was all free** Man.

Confirmatory interrogative: stressed

93 The following are stressed forms of the confirmatory interrogative of BE past tense recorded at IX.7.6 *I was late* WASN'T I? etc.:

FIRST PERSON SINGULAR: **wadn't I?** Y L Nth; **wanna I?** Ch Db Sa; **wart I?** St; **werenad I?** Sa; **weredn't I?** Wa W Do; **weren't I?** La Y Db Wa Lei Nth Bk MxL So W Brk D Ha Sx.

SECOND PERSON SINGULAR: **wanna thee?** Ch Db Sa; **wanna you?** Ch Sa; **wasna?** Db Sa; **wast not?** Db; **wasn'tst?** Wa Gl O; **wasn't ye?** So K Co D Do Sx; **wasn't thee/thou?** Nb Cu Du We La Y Ch St He Wa Mon Nt L So Brk; **wasn't you?** Y Man Sa St He Wo Wa Mon Gl O Nt L Lei R Nth Hu C Nf Sf Bk Bd Hrt Ess So W Brk Sr K Co D Do Ha Sx; **wasn't** [ɪ] Ch; **weren't thee/thou?** La Y Db He Wo Do Ha; **weren't ye?** O So W Co Sx; **wanna thee?** Ch Db Sa; **wanna you?** Ch Sa; **wertn't not?** Db; **wast not?** Db; **wertst na?** St; **weredn't?** So; **weredestn't?** So; **weredn't ye?** So D Do; **wertstnot?** W Co; **wertstn't thee?** W.

THIRD PERSON PLURAL: **wadn't they?** We Y; **wanna 'em?** Ch; **wanna they?** Ch Db Sa St; **wasna' they?** Ch; **war 'em?** St; **wasn't mun?** Co; **wasn't they?** La Y Db Sa St He Wa Mon Nt L Lei R Nth Hu C Nf Sf Bk Bd Hrt Ess W Brk Sr K Co Ha Sx; **wasn't them?** La He Wo Wa Gl O So Brk Co D Do Ha; **were not they?** Du; **weren't them?** La Y Wa O Bk So W Sr D Ha Sx; **wereno' they?** Db Lei; **weredn't them?** So W Do.

PRESENT TENSE SUBJUNCTIVE

94 The following are unstressed forms of BE present tense subjunctive recorded at IX.7.8 ... *if we* WERE *rich* etc.:

FIRST PERSON SINGULAR: **I was** Nb Cu Du We La Y Man Ch Sa St He Wo Wa Mon Gl O Nf L Lei R Nth C Nf Sf Bk Bd Hrt Ess MxL So W Brk Sr K Co D Do Ha Sx; **I weren** Sa; **I wor** Y.

THIRD PERSON SINGULAR FEMININE: **her was** Ch St He Wo Mon Gl So W Brk Co D Do Ha; **her weren** Sa; **hoo was** La Ch; **she was** Nb Cu Du We La Y Man Ch Sa St Wa Mon Gl O Nt L Lei R C Nf Sf Bk Bd Hrt Ess MxL So W Brk Sr K Co Do Ha Sx.

FIRST PERSON PLURAL: **us was** O Co D; **we was** Nb Cu La Y Ch St He Wo Wa Mon Gl O Nt L Lei R Nth C Nf Sf Bk Bd Hrt Ess So W Brk Sr K Co D Do Ha Sx; **we wor** Nb; **we weren** Ch Sa.

DO

PARTICIPLES

95 The present-participial form **a-doing** is recorded in IX.5.3 from St He Wo Wa Mon Gl O Nf Sf Ess So W Brk Sr Do Ha.

Past-participial forms of DO in IX.5.6 include **a-did** So; **a-doed** So D; **a-done** Gl So W Brk Sr Co D Do Ha; **did** Man Brk. IM V.7.7 includes **doed** So.

PRESENT TENSE

Positive: stressed

96 The following are stressed forms of DO present tense recorded at IX.5.1 *You don't care for things like that, but I* DO etc.:

FIRST PERSON SINGULAR: **I div** Nb Cu; **I does** Wo Gl O W Brk Sr Ha Sx; **I does** [duːz~dɣːz] W Brk Ha.

THIRD PERSON SINGULAR MASCULINE: **he do** Db Sa He Wo Wa Mon Gl O C Nf Sf Bk Bd Ess MxL So W Brk Sr K Co D Do Ha Sx; **he don** Sa; **he does** [dʊuz~duːz~dɣːz] He Ess W Brk Sr D Ha Sx; **he doth** [dɣːθ] D. Compare also IM III.3.7 **that's all as a stoat do** Wo; **th'only one as does** [duːz] **any good** W.

FIRST PERSON PLURAL: **we div** Cu; **we don** La Y Ch Db Sa St Wo; **we does** [dʌz~dʊz~dəz] Wo W Brk Sr K Ha Sx.

THIRD PERSON PLURAL: The Incidental Material includes III.10.7 **some folks does** Nb La; **colliers does** Mon; III.3.7 **there ain't many as does that** He; VIII.5.7 **they does** [duːz] He Sr Ha.

97 Unstressed forms of the second person singular include [s] in IM VI.8.1 **how thee dost** [ðiːs] **blow** So; VI.14.12 **thee dost** [ðiːs] **look well** So.

Negative: stressed

98 The following are stressed forms of DO present tense negative recorded at IX.5.2 *I do care for it, but he DOESN'T etc.*:

THIRD PERSON SINGULAR: **he dinna** Ch; **he disno'** Nb Cu; **he disn't** Nb Cu Du We Y; **he doesno'** La; **he doona** Ch Db Sa St He Wo; **he don't** La Man St He Wo Wa Mon Gl O L Lei R Nth Hu C Nf Sf Bk Bd Hrt Ess MxL So W Brk Sr K Co D Do Ha Sx; **he dudn't** L; **he dunt** La Lei R C Ess.

THIRD PERSON PLURAL: **they dinna** Cu; **they dinnot** Nb Du; **they dint** Y; **they divvent** Nb Cu Du; **they doona** Ch Db Sa He Lei; **they dunnot** Du.

99 The following are unstressed forms of DO present tense negative as an auxiliary verb, first person singular, in VII.5.2 I DON'T KNOW: **dinna** Nb Cu Du; **dinnot** Du; **divva** Nb Du; **divvent** Nb Cu Du; **doona** Nb Ch Db Sa St He, also Wo in IX.4.10 *I* DON'T CARE; **doonat** Du; **junt** He. IM V.6.3 includes **we dinna call it** Cu.

Interrogative: unstressed

100 The following are unstressed forms of DO present tense interrogative as an auxiliary verb, in IX.5.4 *How much rent* DO YOU *pay? etc.*:

SECOND PERSON SINGULAR: **do thee** D Do; **do ye** Gl O So W Brk Co D Do Ha; **does thou** Nb Cu Du We La Y; **does you** He Wo Wa; **don thee** Ch Db St; **don ye** Sa; **don you** Ch Db Sa St; **dost** Ch Db Sa St He Wo Gl Lei So W D Do Ha; **dost thee/thou** Nb La Y Ch Db Sa St He Wo Wa Mon Gl O L So W Brk Co D Do Ha.

THIRD PERSON SINGULAR MASCULINE: **do a** Gl So W; **do he** Sa He Wo Wa Mon Gl O Nf Sf Ess MxL So W Brk Sr Co D Ha Sx; **do him** Gl; **don he** Sa; **does a** L Nth; **dost he** Wo.

101 Auxiliary DO, second person singular, present tense interrogative in VIII.3.7 DO YOU *remember?*, includes the forms **do ye** Gl So Co D; **does thee/thou** Nb Cu Du We La Y Ch Db Sa He Wo Mon Gl O L So W Co D Do Ha; **don you** St; **dost** Ch Db Sa St Gl O So W Brk D; **dost thou** La Y Sa. Compare also VII.5.1 **Dost know the time of day?** Wo; VIII.2.8 **How dost feel?** So Ha; **How dost get on?** So.

102 Interrogative auxiliary DO + stem is sometimes used where the standard dialect has BE + present participle, as in VII.6.26 **which way do/does the wind blow?** Wo Ess; **where do the wind blow?** He; **which way do the wind lie?** Sf.

PAST TENSE

Negative: unstressed

103 Expressions for IX.5.5 I DID NOT DO IT include **I didna** Sa St; **I didna do it** Nb Cu La Ch Db Sa St He Wo Lei; **I never did it** Ch St; **I never done it** Mon Gl O Lei Nf Sf Bk Ess So W K Do Ha; **I never done 't** Y; **I never doed it** Ch.

Interrogative: unstressed

104 The following are unstressed forms of DO second person singular past tense interrogative as an auxiliary verb in IX.5.4 *How much rent* DID YOU *pay?*: **did** Db; **did thee/thou** Cu Du We La Y Ch Db St He L Ha; **did ye** Sa Gl O Nth So Co D Do; **didst** Ch Db Sa St Wa Gl Do; **didst thee/thou** Sa St He Wo Mon Gl So W Co D Do Ha.

CONDITIONAL

105 Conditional **do** meaning 'if you/we do' appears in IM IX.5.1: **We mustn't let the fire go out. Do, we should get wrong** (i.e. get into trouble) Nf; **You mustn't play with the fire. Do, you'll wet the bed** Sf. In the following, however, **do** seems to mean 'if he didn't': **The fellow had to stand up. Do, his backside was in the mud** Ess.

HAVE

PRESENT TENSE

Positive: stressed

106 The following are stressed forms of HAVE present tense recorded in IX.6.1 *Have you got a match? Yes, I* HAVE etc:

FIRST PERSON SINGULAR: **I am** Nth C; **I ha** Nb Y St C W; **I han** Sa; **I has** Brk K; **I haves** Brk Ha.

THIRD PERSON SINGULAR MASCULINE: **he ha** St C Sf; **he han** Sa; **he have** Man Ch Sa He Wo Wa Mon Gl O L Nth C Nf Sf Bk Ess So W Brk Sr Co D Do Ha Sx; **he haves** W Brk.

107 Forms of the third person plural recorded in the Incidental Material include **has** III.10.7 Nb We Y; III.8.1 We; III.3.7 Ch Wo L; **han** III.13.17 Db St. IV.6.2 includes the response **they has hens** O; IM VIII.5.1 includes **they haves** He.

Negative: stressed

108 The following are stressed forms of HAVE present tense negative in IX.6.2 *I have a match but he* HASN'T etc.:

FIRST PERSON SINGULAR: **I ain't** La Y Sa Wa Gl O Nt L Lei R Nth Hu C Nf Sf Bk Bd Hrt Ess So W Brk Sr K Co D Do Ha Sx; **I hanna** Nb Cu Ch Db Sa St He; **I hannot** Nb; **I han't** Y He Wo Gl O So W Co D Do Ha Sx; **I hasn't** Brk; **I've not** La.

THIRD PERSON SINGULAR MASCULINE: **he ain't** Db St Wo Wa Mon O L Lei R Nth Hu C Nf Bk Bd Hrt Ess So W Brk Sr K Co D Do Ha Sx; **he hanna** Ch Sa St He; **he han't** He Wo Wa Gl O Lei So W Co D Do Ha; **he hasno'** Cu Db St; **he haven't** He Wo Mon Gl O Nf Sf So W Brk Sr Co D Ha Sx; **he's not** La.

FIRST PERSON PLURAL: **we ain't** Db Wa Mon Gl O Nt L Lei R Nth Hu C Nf Sf Bk Bd Hrt Ess So W Brk Sr K Co D Do Ha Sx; **we han't** Y Bk So W Co D Do Ha Sx; **we hain't** Y; **we hanna** Cu Ch Db Sa St He; **we hannot** La Y; **we hasn't** Ha; **we hent** Nf Sf; **we've not** La.

Unstressed auxiliary

109 The following are unstressed negative forms of HAVE present tense as an auxiliary verb in IX.6.3 *I* HAVEN'T *seen it* etc.:

FIRST PERSON SINGULAR: **I ain't** Wa Gl O Nt L Lei R Nth Hu C Nf Sf Bk Bd Hrt Ess MxL So W Brk Sr K Co D Do Ha Sx; **I ha** St; **I hain't** La Y; **I ham't** St So; **I han't** Y He Wo Mon Gl O C Bd So W Co D Do Ha Sx; **I hanna** Nb Cu Ch Db Sa St He Wo; **I havena** Db; **I hent** La Y.

THIRD PERSON SINGULAR MASCULINE: **he ain't** He Wo Wa O Nt L Lei R Nth Hu C Nf Sf Bk Bd Hrt Ess So W Brk Sr K Co D Do Ha Sx; **he am't** So; **he ha** St; **he hanna** Ch Db Sa St He Wo O; **he han't** He Wo Mon Gl O Lei Bk Bd So W Brk Co D Do Ha Sx; **he hasna** Cu Db St Wa; **he haven't** He Mon Gl Nf; **he hent** La Y. III.1.7 includes (the cow) **hanna held/stood** Sa St He Gl.

110 The Incidental Material includes: III.1.7 third person singular **hath** in the form [θ] in **her'th returned** Co; III.3.7 second person singular **hast** in the form [s] in **what's never heard tell of** 'what thou hast never heard tell of' So; V.7.21 first person plural **han** in the form [n] in **we'n used ...** Ch; III.10.7 third person plural **has** in **the bairns has played** Y; IV.7.2 third person plural **han** in the form [n] in **they'n flushed** 'they've fledged' La.

Interrogative: unstressed

111 Unstressed forms of auxiliary HAVE, second person singular interrogative, recorded in the Incidental Material (III.3.4, III.4.1, III.5.2) and in responses at VII.5.1 include **hast thee/thou?** Ch Db Sa St So W D Do; **have ye?** D; **hast thou?** Du.

See also §112.

'Have got'

112 Expressions for IX.6.4 *we* HAVE GOT *one* and VI.5.8 HAVE YOU GOT TOOTHACHE? include:

(a) those in which 'have got' is expressed by HAVE only, e.g. **we han one** La Y Ch Db Sa St; **we have one** Nb Cu Du We La Y Db He Mon Nt L Ess MxL; **have you (the) toothache?** Nb Du We La Y Man. Compare also IM VI.14.9 **hast thou a flannel on under thy shirt?** Y.

(b) those in which 'have got' is expressed by GET only, e.g. **we getten one** Y; **we got one** Nb Man Sa St He Wo Wa Mon Gl O L Nth Nf Sf Bk Bd Hrt Ess So W Brk Sr K Co D Do Ha Sx; **we gotten one** L.

(c) those in which 'have got' is expressed by HAVE + GET, e.g. **we han get one** Db St; **we han getten one** La Y; **we han got one** Db Sa St Lei; **we han gotten one** Ch St; **we have a-got one** So; **we have getten one** Db; **we have gotten one** Y L; **has thou** got (the) toothache? Ch Db; **hast getten (the) toothache?** Ch; **han you got (the) toothache?** Ch Db; **hast got (the) toothache?** Db Sa St Wo Gl; **hast thee got (the) toothache?** Sa He Wo Gl.

GO

IMPERATIVE

113 Forms of the second person singular imperative of GO in VIII.7.9 *Off* YOU GO! include: **thou gans** Nb Cu Du Y; **thou gangs** La Y; **thou goes** We La Y Gl L; **thou goest** Ch Db Sa St; **thee/thou go** La W Brk Co; **thee goes** Co; **thee dost go** So W D Do Ha; **you gon** Db St; **you goes** He Wo Mon Gl W Brk Sx. IM IX.7.5 includes second person singular imperative **goest** Co.

GO AND SEE IX.5.8 is expressed by **away and see** Cu. See also §148.

PARTICIPLES

114 The Incidental Material (III.1.12, VII.5.1, VIII.6.1, and IX.4.1) includes the following forms of the present participle of GO: **a-going** Ch St He Wo Wa Gl O Lei Nth C R Hu Nf Sf Bd Ess K; **gan** Nb Cu Du We La Y; **ganning** Nb Du Y; **ga-ing** Cu La Y.

Past participles recorded at IX.5.7 include **a-gone** Brk; **went** Nb Du Man He Wo Wa Mon O; **gan** Nb We.

PRESENT TENSE

115 The Incidental Material (III.1.6, VIII.6.1) includes third person singular present tense **go** Sf; **gans** Nb Cu Du Y.

Third person plural forms expressing habitual action in VIII.5.1 THEY GO TO CHURCH include **ga** Nb Cu Du We La Y; **gan** Nb Cu Du Y; **gang** La; **goes** La Y He Wo (also IM VIII.5.1 Mon) Gl O Bk So (also IM VIII.6.1 W) Brk Sr K D Ha Sx; **gon** Y Ch St. Also recorded at VIII.5.1 is the periphrastic form with unstressed DO [də] + stem **they do go** Mon So W Co Do.

PAST TENSE

116 Third person singular past tense forms recorded at VIII.5.3 include **goed** He L Nf; **gone** Sa.

DARE

PRESENT TENSE NEGATIVE

117 IX.4.17 includes the following forms of the third person singular present tense negative, (he) DARE NOT: **daredna** Cu; **daredn't** Cu Du We La Y Lei Nth Hu Bk; **darena** Nb Du Ch Db Sa St He; **daresn't** He Lei R Nf Ess MxL So Co D Sx; **darstn't** Nb Du La Y Nf; **durdn't** Cu; **durn't** Y; **durstn't** Cu La Y Ch Db Sa St Wa Mon Gl O Nt L Lei Nf Sf Hrt Ess MxL So Sr.

PAST TENSE NEGATIVE

118 IX.4.18 includes the following forms of the third person singular past tense (he) DURST NOT: **daredna** Sa He; **daredn't** Nb Cu Y He Wa Mon Gl Lei Nth; **darena** Ch Db Sa St; **daren't** Du La Y Wa Mon Gl Nth Hu C Nf Sf Bk Bd Hrt Ess MxL So W Sr K Co D Do Ha; **daresna** Db; **daresn't** Nf Ess MxL So K Co D Do Sx; **durstn't** Cu La Man; **durrn't** Cu; **durstna** Ch Db St Lei.

MUST

119 IX.4.11 MUST in *You really* MUST *do it* is expressed by **mun** Nb Cu Du We La Y Ch Db Sa St L.

120 Forms of the second person singular present tense negative in IX.4.12 *You* MUSTN'T *play with the fire* include **maun('t)** La Y Db Wa Nt L Lei Bk Bd Hrt Ess MxL Brk D Ha Sx; **mun't** Cu We La Y Gl; **munna** Nb Cu Ch Db Sa St He Wa Lei;

munnot Du La; **mustna** Ch St He. But 'you mustn't' is expressed by **you are not to** Cu; **you haven't to** Du; and **you're none boun to** Y.

SHALL

121 The first person singular present tense of auxiliary SHALL in IX.4.1 *Tomorrow I SHALL walk to X* takes the forms [s] We La Y; [sl] Y Ch Db Wa Nt L Nth Nf Ess MxL; [səl] Y; [sə] Y; [st] La Y; [z] La Y.

Zero (i.e. **tomorrow I walk to X**) is recorded from Nf Brk; and **will** is recorded from Ess. Perhaps also to be recorded as attestations of WILL are the forms [l~ɬ~əl~əɬ] Eng exc. Man Hu.

SHALL in IX.4.3 I SHALL *beat you* takes the forms [s] Y; [sl] Y Nt L; [səl] Y; [sə] Y; [sal] Y. Zero (i.e. **I beat you**) is recorded from Nf and **will** from Ess. Perhaps also to be regarded as attestations of **will** are the forms [l~ɬ] that are recorded throughout Eng. Note also in IM IX.4.1 **we (shalle)n** Ch St; **we sh(all)en** Ch; **we s'** Db; **they (shalle)n** Sa.

122 First person singular present tense negative of auxiliary SHALL in IX.4.4 I SHAN'T *want it* takes the forms **I shall none** Y; **I s' not** La; **I shanna** Ch Db Sa St He Wo; **I'll no** Nb Cu; **I'll not** Nb Du La. Other responses include **I don't want it** Nb Cu Du We La Y L Nf Bk Brk; **I doona want it** Cu; **I woona want it** Nb.

123 SHALL in stressed position in IX.4.2 *I've always done it that way and I think I always SHALL* is expressed by **will** Nb Cu Du We La Y Man Ch St Gl L Lei R C Nf Bk Ess MxL So W Brk Sr K Co D Do Ha Sx.

124 SHOULDN'T in stressed position in IX.4.8 *Some children do what they should. And others do what they* SHOULDN'T takes the forms **shouldna** Nb Cu Ch Db Sa St He Wo; **s'ouldn't** Cu La Y. It is expressed by **shouldn't ought to do** L D.

125 Second person singular negative SHOULDN'T HAVE *done* in IX.4.9 takes the forms **shouldsn't have** W; **shouldsn't have done** W Ha; **shouldn't done** W; **shouldn't have did/doed** Man D; **shouldn't ought to** Wa; **shouldn't ought to have** Y.

126 Third person plural OUGHT TO HAVE *helped* in IX.4.7 is expressed by **should helped** Brk.

WILL

127 First person singular negative *I* WON'T, stressed, in IX.4.5 *No, I* WON'T *do it* is expressed by **I'll no** Nb Cu; **I'll not** Nb Du La; **I will not** Nb Du Y; **I winna** Nb La Ch Db; **I winnot** Du Y; **I woona** Nb Cu Ch Db Sa St He Wo; **I wod'n** La; **I woonot** Nb Du; **I 'oona** Sa He. In another set of responses, SHALL is used: **I shanna** St; **I s(h)an't** Y; **I s' not** La.

128 Second person singular interrogative **wilt** appears in VII.5.1 **Tell us time, wilt?** (i.e. 'Tell me the time, wilt thou?') So; VII.8.18 **Which one wilt have?** Gl.

MAY

129 First person singular interrogative MAY? in IX.4.13 MAY *I have one?* is expressed by: **can** Eng exc. Man; **could** Man Db O Nf Ess K.

CAN

130 Second person singular interrogative forms of CAN in VII.5.1 and VIII.3.7 include **canst thee/thou** Nb Cu Du We La Y Db St Wo Gl So W Co D Do Ha.

131 First person singular negative in IX.4.16 takes the form **canna** Nb Cu Du La Ch Db Sa St He Wo Lei; **cannot** Nb Du La Y Man. The Incidental Material includes V.7.1 **we canna call them** Cu; IX.4.16 second person singular present tense negative **ca'stn't** Gl.

OUGHT

132 The following are expressions for SHOULDN'T HAVE in IX.4.9 *I expect you as a boy often did what you* SHOULDN'T HAVE *done*, forms that employ OUGHT rather than SHOULD:

Sometimes OUGHT is conjugated with auxiliary DO, as in **didn't ought to have (done)** Ch O L Nf Bk Hrt Ess Brk K D; **didn't ought to have did** So; **didn't ought to have been doing** La. In other cases OUGHT is conjugated with auxiliary HAVE as in **hadn't ought** Gl L; **hadna/hadn't ought to do** St Wa Nf Bd; **hadn't ought to have done** Wo Wa O Lei Bd R Nth K Sx. Sometimes, too, SHOULD is used: **shouldn't ought to** Wa L; **shouldn't ought to have** Y.

USE 'be accustomed'

133 USE 'be accustomed' may in West Midland dialects form its past tense with auxiliary BE, DO, or HAVE, as illustrated in responses to IX.4.15 *Is there much butter made round here now? No, not now, but there* USED TO *be*. These expressions include **there was used to** Sa Wo; **there did used to** Sa; **there had used to** Sa St He Wo Wa Gl.

See also §83.

VERB-REITERATION

134 In northern England, BE is often reiterated within the sentence. It first appears (or is implied) in the combination Pronoun Subject + BE, then appears again in the combination BE + Noun Subject. The subject, whether expressed by a noun or pronoun, has the same reference in both parts of the sentence. Thus in IM III.8.1 **They're rum things, is the pigs** Y; **Hoo is a nice woman, is the parson's wife** La; IM III.9.1 **It's all snout and lug, is a pig's head** Du. Compare also, with ellipsis of the elements Pronoun Subject and BE: **Funniest things, are pigs** Y.

CAN is reiterated in IM VI.7.12 **It can come anywhere on the finger, can a whitlow** Y.

Sometimes the verb in the first part of the sentence is reiterated by dummy-auxiliary DO, as in IM I.7.14 **They vary, do stee-steps** Y; IM I.9.10 **She wants hopping, do that cart** Y.

ADVERBS

135 Here are listed some dialectal expressions for various adverbs:

NOT may be expressed by **no, none** as in IX.7.11 **I'm no drunk** Nb; **I'm none drunk** Nb Cu Du We La Y Db St L.

SO is expressed by **as** in VIII.1.22 **not as old as his wife** Nb Cu Du We La Y Ch Db Sa St He Wo Wa Mon Gl O Nt L Lei R Nth Nf Sf Ess So K D Ha.

TOMORROW in VII.4.1 is expressed by **the morn** Nb Du; **the morrow** Cu Du.

TONIGHT in VII.3.12 is expressed by **the night** Nb Cu Du So.

UNDERNEATH in IM I.11.2 is expressed by **in under** Do.

UPSTAIRS in V.2.5 is expressed by **up the stairs** Y He Wo.

WHERE? in IX.9.7 is expressed by **where to?** in **where to is it?** Mon; **where is it/her to?** So W Co D Do.

WHY? in VIII.8.6 is expressed by **for why?** La Y.

136 In V.2.12 WE PUT THE LIGHT ON, the whole phrasal verb PUT ON precedes the direct object in the response **we put on the light** Y Sa L MxL So W Co D Do Ha K.

PREPOSITIONS

BETWEEN

137 BETWEEN (them) IX.2.11 is expressed by **in atween, in between, in tween** Nb Du We Y Ch He Wo Wa O Lei R Nth Nf Ess So W Brk K Co Ha Sx; **in betwixt** W.

OF

138 OF may be omitted in contexts where it would appear in the standard dialect, as in VII.2.10 **a bit string ~ a piece string** Nb Cu Du Mon Ess Co; III.13.12 **a drink milk ~ a saucer milk ~ a sup milk** Nb Cu Du So D Ha; VII.8.16 **What sort knife?** So Co. Other examples (from the Incidental Material or from responses to questions not specifically designed to elicit OF) include V.7.2 **a basin oatmeal** Co; IX.2.3 **one side the fence** St; I.3.16 **catch hold the handle** So; III.10.7 **up top the hill** D; IV.4.1 **out the ground** K; VII.8.7 **plenty brass/money** Nb Cu La Y Ch Sa Wo Mon C Sf Hrt Ess; **a good bit money** Du; III.5.1 **give 'em bit grub** So; VII.2.10 **a piece thread/string** La Ess Co; VII.2.10 **a bit time** He; I.11.2 **bit stone** Co; VII.2.10 **a bit flour** So; **a bit iron** Co; III.8.4(a) **plenty teats/paps** Nb Cu.

139 On the other hand, OF may appear in contexts in which it would be otiose in the standard dialect, as in IX.5.3 **What's that child (a-)doing of?** Bd Ess So K Co D; IX.2.3 **fell off of his horse** Y O Nt L Lei Hu Nf Ess MxL So W Brk Sr K Ha. Other examples, from the Incidental Material and from responses to questions not specifically designed to elicit OF, include III.1.4 **weaning of it** Ess; III.3.4 **you're stripping of them** Y; III.1.12(b) **she's slipping of her strings** We; III.3.6 **penning of 'em** W Do; I.17.19 **sharpening of en** 'sharpening it' D; II.9.11 **tedding of it** W Brk; III.3.6 **bagging of her up** Brk and **galing of them up** Co, both of which are expressions for bagging cows' udders. OF appears also in VIII.3.7 **do you mind of?** Nb and **dost thou mind of?** Cu, both meaning 'Do you remember?'. Compare also III.8.4(a) **enough of teats** Nb Y Sa He Mon; VII.1.19 **a few of days** L.

140 OF expresses: 'with' in VII.6.23 **poured of rain** St Wo; 'to' in IM III.10.1 **whistle of a dog** Nb; and 'in' in IM IV.8.4 **of his head** Y.

141 'What kind of a knife?' at VII.8.16 is expressed by **whatten knife?** Nb Du.

ON

142 ON corresponds to Standard English OF in IX.2.15 **out on it** (i.e. 'out of the army') Nb Cu Du We La Y Ch Db Sa St He Wo Wa Mon Gl O Nt L Lei Nth Hu C Nf Sf Bk Bd Hrt Ess So W Ha; VII.2.12 **the whole on it** Nb Cu Du We La Y Man Ch Db Sa St He Wo Wa Mon Gl O Nt L Nth Hu Nf Sf(**the lot on it**) Bk Bd Hrt Ess So W Sr D Ha Sx; VII.8.16 **What sort on (a) knife?** Y Sa He Wo Mon Gl. Other examples, from the Incidental Material or from questions other than those designed primarily to elicit syntactical material, include VII.1.12 **twenty or thirty on them** Y; VII.4.10 **make a fool on them** Y; VII.2.12 **I'm tired on it** Lei; **there ain't so much on it** R; **some on it** Brk; **never heard nothing on it** K; **think on it** Co; III.3.7 **as I do know on** Gl; IX.2.4 **in front on it** Nb Cu Du We La Y Ch Db Sa St He Wo Wa Mon Gl O Nt L Nth Hu C Nf Sf Bk Bd Hrt Ess So W Co Ha Sx; VII.2.12 **I've heard on it** Lei; **I'm sure on it** R; III.3.7 **talking on** 'talking of' St; **think on** St.

143 ON often appears in contexts in which it would be otiose in the standard dialect, e.g. IX.2.3 **fell off on his horse** Y St He L Nf Bd Sr; IX.5.3 **What's that child (a-)doing on?** Nf W. So too in the Incidental Material and in responses to questions not designated as of special syntactical significance, e.g. III.3.6 **stocking on her up** (i.e. bagging a cow's udders) Ha; II.6.6 **carting on it** Nf Ess; II.7.5 **clearing on it** Sf; II.9.12 **cocking on it up** Ess; III.3.1 **foddering on them** L; I.5.1 **yoking on him** Brk; V.7.7 **thrashing on it** 'threshing it' So; **raking on it over** W; **throwing on it on** D; **he were doing on it** Ha; I.7.19 **he's wetting on it** Cu We; V.6.4 **knead on it** We; III.1.4 **weaning on it/them** L C Nf Bk.

144 ON FRIDAY WEEK at VII.4.7 is expressed by **a week come (next) Friday** Nb Cu Du We La Y Db Sa He Wa Gl Sf MxL; **a week for Friday** Man. In IM VIII.6.4 'on Sunday' is expressed by **at Sunday** Y.

TILL

145 TILL in IX.2.2 TILL *Saturday* is expressed by **than** Ch; **tin** Ch St; **to** Gl; **while** Nb La Y Ch Db Nt L Lei R Nth Hu C Sf Bd Hrt Ess Brk.

TO

146 TO may be omitted in contexts in which it would appear in the standard dialect, e.g. VIII.5.1 **they go(n) church** Ch Db St Sf So K Co D Do; VIII.6.1 **go school** Ch St So Co D Sx; VII.5.5 **twenty-five three** 'twenty-five minutes to three' Ha; VII.5.3 **(a) quarter twelve** Db Sa St Wo So K Co D Ha Sx; IX.5.9 (I went) **see the doctor** Db St He Nt Ess So W Brk Sr K Co D Ha Sx; IX.4.15 **there use(d) be** La Ess So W Brk Sr K Co D Do Ha Sx. Further examples, from the Incidental Material or from responses other than those cited above, include III.3.7 **things as they used have on** L; **they used call he 'Old Shep'** W; I.3.7 **we had walk down side** Sx; I.11.2 **you've got trig en up** 'you've got to wedge it' Co; **you'd have put** 'you'd have to put' **a stone behind** D; II.3.3 **when you come finish** Co; II.6.6 **going start harvest-cart** (i.e. harvest-carting) **today** W; III.1.11 **her's going slip** D; III.3.2 **turn them out water** Sx; III.8.10 **going farrow** So Co D Ha; III.13.13–14 **going have** So W Sr K Co D Do Sx; III.3.10 **going kitten down** Ha; III.3.7 **a mare at's** (i.e. that's) **going foal** Ch; V.2.12 **it's time light up the lamp** D; VIII.3.7 **pleased see thee/you** Ch Db St; IX.9.2 **I wonder who it belongs** Db.

OUGHT TO in IX.4.6 is expressed by **ought** Nt L Ess W Ha Sx; and OUGHT TO HAVE *helped* in IX.4.7 by **ought have helped** Sa He Wo Mon Gl O; **ought helped** Db. SHOULDN'T HAVE *done* in IX.4.9 is expressed by **oughtn't have done** So.

147 TO in expressions of time may be expressed by other prepositions, as shown in VII.5.3/5 **(a) quarter before twelve** Y; **twenty-five before three** Y; **(a) quarter fore twelve** D; **(a) quarter till twelve** Cu; **twenty-five till three** Cu; **twenty-five up to three** Bk. Compare also VII.5.6 **five till eight** Cu Ess; **five at eight** Man. AT appears also in VIII.5.1 **they go at church** Ha.

TO SEE in IX.5.9 TO *see the doctor* is expressed by **at see** La; **for see** Ch Db St Nth W Co D Ha Sx; **for to see** Nb Du We La Y Man Ch Db St L So W Sr K D Do Ha Sx. Compare also in the Incidental Material VII.6.23 **it begun for to rain** Db; I.3.5 **that's a ring for go up and down** Do; I.3.11 **for carry it away** D; I.7.1 **for see it** D; II.4.2 **going up hoe turnips** Co.

TO is expressed by **with** in IM IX.4.15 **used with him** 'used to him' Nb Cu.

THIS YEAR in VII.3.18 is expressed by **to-year** Y.

TO expresses 'of' in IM III.3.7 **there inna many as I know to** He; and 'with' in IM V.7.3 **I always have porridge to my breakfast** Y.

TO in IV.4.1 TO THE GROUND is expressed by **on to** Nb Cu Du We La Y Db Sa St He Wo Wa Gl L Nth Nf Sf Bk Ess Sr; **upon** Co; **down on to** Ch; **on** Eng exc. Man R; **down to** Y.

CONJUNCTIONS

AND

148 AND is sometimes omitted from contexts in which it would appear in the standard dialect, e.g. IX.5.8 **go see** Y Ch St Mon L D. Compare also VIII.3.3 **come sit thee down** Y; VIII.5.8 **go have a spell** Co.

THAN

149 THAN is expressed by **nor** in VIII.1.21 **older nor their wives** Nb Cu We La Y Db Wa Gl O Nt L Lei Nth C Bk Bd; VI.12.4 **worse nor mumps**

Nb Cu We La Y Ch Db Wo Wa Gl O Nt L Lei Nth Bk Ess.

Other expressions for THAN are illustrated in VIII.1.21 **older tin their wives** La Ch; **older till their wives** Ch; VI.12.4 **worse till mumps** Ch Sa; **worse as mumps** Y; **worse to mumps** So.

TILL

150 TILL in IX.2.3 TILL *THE SUN goes down* is expressed by **than** Ch; **to** O; **while** La Y Db Nt L Lei R Nth Hu C Bk Bd.

INDEX TO THE GRAMMAR